Tolley's Value Added Tax

Tolley's Value Added Tax 2018–19

Second Edition

by

Louise Hemmingsley
CTA

and

David Rudling
CTA

Tolley®

Members of the LexisNexis Group worldwide

United Kingdom	RELX (UK) Limited trading as LexisNexis, 1–3 Strand, London WC2N 5JR
Australia	Reed International Books Australia Pty Ltd trading as LexisNexis, Chatswood, New South Wales
Austria	LexisNexis Verlag ARD Orac GmbH & Co KG, Vienna
Benelux	LexisNexis Benelux, Amsterdam
Canada	LexisNexis Canada, Markham, Ontario
China	LexisNexis China, Beijing and Shanghai
France	LexisNexis SA, Paris
Germany	LexisNexis GmbH, Dusseldorf
Hong Kong	LexisNexis Hong Kong, Hong Kong
India	LexisNexis India, New Delhi
Italy	Giuffrè Editore, Milan
Japan	LexisNexis Japan, Tokyo
Malaysia	Malayan Law Journal Sdn Bhd, Kuala Lumpur
New Zealand	LexisNexis NZ Ltd, Wellington
Singapore	LexisNexis Singapore, Singapore
South Africa	LexisNexis Butterworths, Durban
USA	LexisNexis, Dayton, Ohio

Published by LexisNexis
This is a Tolley title

A CIP Catalogue record for this book is available from the British Library.

ISBN for this volume: 9780754555063

Printed in the UK by CPI Group (UK) Ltd, Croydon, CR0 4YY

Visit LexisNexis at www.lexisnexis.co.uk

About This Book

Value added tax commenced in the United Kingdom on 1 April 1973. Since that date a mass of legislation, Orders, Regulations, law cases and VAT notices support a system which has become increasingly complex. Tolley's Value Added Tax seeks to aid practitioners and traders by being their first point of reference on this tax.

This edition includes the current law and practice of value added tax up to 1 April 2018. Relevant statutory instruments, tribunal and court cases, VAT Notices, Information Sheets, and HMRC Briefs are also covered and other relevant sources of information including the provisions of *Finance Act 2018*.

Chapters in this service are in alphabetical order for ease of reference to a particular subject. Cross-references, an index and a table of statutes provide further ways of quickly finding the matter required.

We relaunched the Tolley Tax Annuals in 2010, aiming to make them more practical and easier to use. We hope that the new style continues to meet your requirement for greater accessibility to the changing VAT legislation and the ever increasing demands on you as a practitioner. We would be pleased to receive your feedback on the new style and any suggestions for further improvements. You can do this by e-mailing the Editor, Elaine Pugh at elaine.pugh@lexisnexis.co.uk. Technical queries will be dealt with by the author.

Contributors

Louise Hemmingsley

Louise Hemmingsley has been practising VAT for the last 22 years and currently works for LexisNexis as a VAT writer. Louise has worked for the top 4 firms of accountants and in industry for companies such as Siemens and Nortel Networks as their in-house VAT manager.

Contents

Abbreviations and References

All ER	All England Law Reports, (LexisNexis, Lexis House, 30 Farringdon Street, London EC4A 4HH).
Art	Article
C & E	Customs and Excise
CA	Court of Appeal
CCAB	Consultative Committee of Accountancy Bodies
CEMA	Customs and Excise Management Act 1979
Ch D	Chancery Division
CIR	Commissioners of Inland Revenue
Commrs	Commissioners
CS	Court of Session (Scotland)
ECJ	European Court of Justice
EU	European Union
EEC	European Economic Community
ESC	Extra-statutory concession
FA	Finance Act
F(No 2)A	Finance (No 2) Act
HC	High Court
HL	House of Lords
HMRC	Her Majesty's Revenue and Customs
ICTA	Income and Corporation Taxes Act
IMA 1979	Isle of Man Act 1979
ITEPA 2003	Income Tax (Earnings and Pensions) Act 2003
ITTOIA 2005	Income Tax (Trading and Other Income) Act 2005
NI	Northern Ireland
p	Page
QB	Queen's Bench Division
Reg	Regulation

s	Section
Sch	Schedule
Sec	Section
SI	Statutory Instrument
STC	Simon's Tax Cases, (LexisNexis, as above).
STI	Simon's Tax Intelligence (LexisNexis, as above).
t/a	Trading as
TC	Tax Chamber
TVC	Tolley's VAT Cases
UT	Upper Tribunal
VATA 1994	Value Added Tax Act 1994
VTD	VAT Tribunal decision

Court cases. Citation where appropriate is of Simon's Tax Cases and is preceded by the Court and year of the decision (if different from the citation).

Tribunal cases. Citation is by reference to the number assigned to the decision by the VAT Tribunals Headquarters (e.g. *(VTD 18775)*). In all tribunal cases only the appellant or applicant is named.

Tolley's VAT cases. All case citations include a reference to any summary of that case in *Tolley's VAT Cases 2018* (e.g. (TVC 39.52)). References ending with a letter (e.g. (TVC 39.52A)) are to cases subsequent to the publication of *Tolley's VAT Cases 2018* in a bound book format and are only available in the electronic version of that book.

1

Introduction and General Principles

De Voil Indirect Tax Service. See V1.101.

Introduction to VAT

European Union legislation

[1.1] The overriding law on VAT throughout the European Union (EU) is in the EU *Directives*, notably *Directive 2006/112/EC* (the *Principal VAT Directive*, formerly the *6th VAT Directive*). The form and method of compliance is left to individual EU member states but, where any of the provisions are mandatory, EU law takes precedence if there are any inconsistencies with national law. See **19 EUROPEAN UNION LEGISLATION** for further details.

UK legislation

[1.2] Value added tax (VAT) was introduced in the UK on 1 April 1973.

VAT was initially introduced into UK legislation by the *Finance Act 1972*. Subsequent amendments to the UK legislation were first consolidated in the *Value Added Tax Act 1983* (*VATA 1983*) and subsequently in the *Value Added Tax Act 1994* (*VATA 1994*). Changes to *VATA 1994* are made by successive *Finance Acts*.

Although *VATA 1994* provides the main framework of the tax, much of the detail is to be found in statutory instruments (SIs), either in the form of *Orders* made by the Treasury or *Regulations* made by HM Revenue and Customs (previously Customs and Excise). SIs both create law in their own right and amend existing law (both SIs and, occasionally, statutes). The principal *Regulations* made by HMRC are the VAT Regulations (*SI 1995/2518*).

Interpretation of the law by HMRC

[1.3] HMRC currently publish in excess of 130 Notices and Leaflets affecting VAT. With certain exceptions (as indicated in the text), these are not part of the law but explain how HMRC interpret the law. They also publish VAT Information Sheets, VAT Notes and Revenue & Customs Briefs.

The fact that HMRC publications largely only interpret the law should be borne in mind where this book indicates a Notice, etc. as source material.

Court and tribunal decisions

[1.4] If a business disagrees with HMRC's interpretation of the law, it has a right of appeal, in certain cases, to the First-tier Tax Tribunal. Either party can then appeal from that decision to the Upper Tribunal and, with leave, on to the Court of Appeal (in England, Wales and Northern Ireland) and the Supreme Court (formerly the House of Lords). In Scotland, appeals from the Upper Tribunal go to the Court of Session and, with leave, directly to the Supreme Court. A tribunal or Court may also refer a question to the Court of Justice of the European Union (CJEU).

Tribunals and even Court decisions relating to VAT do not create law but merely interpret it. They may, however, cause HMRC to change the way that they interpret the law and may lead to amendments being made to the legislation by statute or statutory instrument.

See **5 APPEALS** generally.

General principles of VAT

[1.5] VAT is a tax on consumer expenditure and is collected on business transactions and imports.

The basic principle is to charge VAT at each stage in the supply of goods and services (output tax). If the customer is registered for VAT and uses the supplies for business purposes, he will receive credit for this VAT (input tax). The broad effect is that businesses are not affected and VAT is actually borne by the final consumer.

Scope of VAT

[1.6] A transaction is within the scope of UK VAT if all the following conditions are met.

- *It is a supply of goods or services.* The term 'supply' is not defined in the legislation but is broadly interpreted. See **65.2** SUPPLY: GENERAL for the meaning of supply and **65.3** and **65.4** SUPPLY: GENERAL for supplies of goods and services respectively. Certain transactions, although supplies, are regarded as supplies of neither goods nor services and are outside the scope of UK VAT. See **65.5** SUPPLY: GENERAL.
- *It takes place in the UK.*
- *It is made by a taxable person.* A taxable person is an individual, firm or company, etc. which is registered for VAT or which is required to register for VAT but has failed to do so. See **1.14** below.
- *It is made in the course or furtherance of any business carried on by that person.* See **9.1** to **9.3** BUSINESS for the interpretation of 'business'.

A transaction which does not meet all of the above conditions is outside the scope of UK VAT.

HMRC guidance 'Register for and use the VAT Mini One Stop Shop' includes the concept of a transaction which meets all of the above conditions but is nevertheless not subject to VAT providing

- it is made by a taxable person that is registered for VAT as a result of the VAT registration arrangements referred to in HMRC guidance 'Register for and use the VAT Mini One Stop Shop' (see **60.5** REGISTRATION), and
- that person's taxable turnover is below the UK VAT registration threshold.

Place of supply

[1.7] To be within the charge to UK VAT, a supply must be made in the UK. Supplies made outside the UK are outside the scope of UK VAT (although they may be liable to VAT in another country).

Separate rules apply for determining the place of supply of goods and services. See **66.2** and **66.12** SUPPLY: PLACE OF SUPPLY for the place of supply of goods and services respectively.

> *Example*
>
> John trades as a computer consultant and is not VAT-registered, even though his annual taxable sales exceed the compulsory VAT registration limit.
>
> John is still classed as a 'taxable person' because he is legally required to be VAT-registered.

Time of supply (tax point)

[1.8] The time at which a supply of goods is treated as taking place is called the tax point. VAT must normally be accounted for in the VAT period (see **1.19** below) in which the tax point occurs and at the rate of VAT (see **1.12** below) in force at that time. Small businesses can, however, account for VAT on the basis of cash paid and received (see **1.23** below).

Basic tax point

The basic tax point for a supply of goods is the date the goods are removed (i.e. sent to, or taken by, the customer). If the goods are not removed, it is the date they are made available for his use.

The basic tax point for a supply of services is the date the services are performed. It is normally the date when all the work except invoicing is completed.

Actual tax points

In the case of both goods and services, where a VAT invoice is raised or payment is made *before* the basic tax point, there is an earlier actual tax point at the time the invoice is issued or payment received, whichever occurs first.

There is also generally an actual tax point where a VAT invoice is issued within 14 days *after* the basic tax point. This overrides the basic tax point but not the actual tax point created by the issue of an invoice or payment before the basic tax point.

There are also special provisions for particular supplies of goods and services.

For further details see **67.1–67.26 SUPPLY: TIME OF SUPPLY**.

Value of supply

[1.9] The value of a supply is the value on which VAT is due. The amount of VAT is then the value multiplied by the VAT rate (see **1.12** below).

The value of a supply normally depends upon what is given in exchange for the supply (i.e. the consideration). If this is wholly in money, the value will be based on that amount. If not, the value is the monetary equivalent of the consideration.

There are special rules relating to discounts offered, transactions between connected persons and values expressed in foreign currencies. Imports (see **1.15** below) and acquisitions from other EU member states (see **1.17** below) also have their own valuation rules.

See **71 VALUATION** for further details.

> *Example*
>
> John is VAT-registered and has sold his business van for £5,000 cash and also received another van from the buyer as part of the deal, which is worth £2,000. The value of John's sale for VAT purposes is £7,000, less the VAT.

Output tax

[1.10] Output tax is the VAT due on taxable supplies and is normally the liability of the person making the supply. In addition to straightforward business transactions, output tax may also be due on business gifts and private use of own goods and services.

A particular supply may be complicated by being a mixed supply where a single inclusive price is charged for a number of separate supplies. Where these supplies are taxable at different rates, a fair and justifiable apportionment of the total price must be made.

See **48 OUTPUT TAX** for further details.

Special schemes for retailers

Traders registered for VAT normally issue an invoice for each sale made in order to have the necessary records to calculate output tax. As this may be difficult or impossible where goods are sold directly to the public, special schemes are available for use by retailers only. See **61 RETAIL SCHEMES** for further details.

Second-hand goods

There are special provisions for second-hand goods. Subject to certain conditions being satisfied, under the margin scheme VAT is only chargeable on the amount by which the selling price of a particular item exceeds the price paid when it was obtained. The scheme extends to almost the full range of second-hand goods. There is also a Global Accounting Scheme which is a simplified scheme for VAT on low value, bulk volume second-hand goods. Under this scheme, VAT is accounted for on the difference between the total purchases and sales of eligible goods in each VAT period rather than on an item by item basis. See **62 SECOND-HAND GOODS** for further details.

Flat-rate scheme for small businesses

Small businesses with taxable turnover and total turnover below specified annual limits can opt to join a flat-rate scheme under which they calculate net VAT due by applying a flat-rate percentage to tax-inclusive turnover. The flat-rate percentage varies with the trade sector into which a business falls. See **64.15 SPECIAL SCHEMES.**

Flat-rate scheme for farmers

Farmers who are certified under the scheme do not have to account for VAT on sales of goods and services within designated activities but are not able to recover input tax incurred on purchases. To compensate for this, farmers in the scheme may charge (and retain) a fixed flat-rate addition of 4% on top of the sale price. The customer can recover the addition as if it were VAT. See **64.25** to **64.30 SPECIAL SCHEMES** for further details.

Input tax

[1.11] A taxable person is entitled to reclaim input tax suffered on goods and services supplied to him, imports from outside the EU (see **1.15** below) and acquisition of goods from other EU member states (see **1.16** below) provided that the input tax relates to

- taxable business supplies made by him; or
- supplies made by him which are outside the scope of UK VAT but which would have been taxable if made in the UK; or
- certain supplies by him of exempt insurance and financial services to persons belonging outside the EU.

Taxable supplies are those chargeable at the standard, reduced or zero rate.

VAT cannot be recovered on goods and services which are not used for business purposes (e.g. for private use). Where goods are used partly for business and partly for non-business purposes, the VAT incurred is normally apportioned.

VAT incurred on a number of items is non-deductible. These include motor cars (with certain exceptions), business entertainment, goods sold under one of the second-hand margin schemes and certain articles installed in buildings by builders.

Where input tax has been claimed but the consideration for the supply is not paid within six months, the input tax must be repaid to HMRC.

Special rules also apply to VAT incurred before registration for VAT and after deregistration and (in the case of a corporate body) before incorporation. This is not input tax as defined by law but may be recovered in certain circumstances.

See **35 INPUT TAX** for further details.

VAT rates

[1.12] There are currently three main rates of VAT, a standard rate of 20%, a reduced rate of 5% and a zero rate. See **59 REDUCED RATE SUPPLIES** and **75 ZERO-RATED SUPPLIES** (and supporting chapters) for goods and services which are currently zero-rated.

The effect of a supply being zero-rated is as follows.

- The amount of VAT on the supply is nil but it is still a taxable supply.
- As a taxable supply, it must be taken into account in determining whether registration is required (see **1.14** below).
- Input tax may be reclaimed subject to the same rules as for standard-rated supplies.
- Where a supply could be either zero-rated or exempt (see **1.13** below), zero-rating takes priority.

Exempt supplies

[1.13] Certain supplies are exempt from VAT. See **21 EXEMPT SUPPLIES** and supporting chapters. This means that no VAT is chargeable but, unlike zero-rated supplies, related input tax is not recoverable.

Where a person makes both taxable supplies and exempt supplies, he is partially exempt and may or may not be able to recover all his input tax. All input tax directly attributable to taxable supplies can be reclaimed but none of the input tax directly attributable to exempt supplies (subject to a *de minimis* limit). Special rules then apply to work out how much input tax can be reclaimed on general overheads, etc. See **50 PARTIAL EXEMPTION**.

Registration

[1.14] Where a person is in business and making taxable supplies, the value of these supplies is his taxable turnover. If:

- at the end of any month, taxable turnover in the year then ended has exceeded a specified limit; or
- at any time, there are reasonable grounds for believing that the value of taxable supplies in the next 30 days will exceed a specified limit,

that person normally becomes a taxable person and must notify HMRC of his liability to register for VAT. There are financial penalties for failing to do so. Where, however, only zero-rated supplies are made, HMRC have a discretion to exempt a person from registration.

Even if taxable turnover is below the specified limit, a person who makes or intends to make taxable business supplies can request voluntary registration.

A person who is registered for VAT ceases to be liable to be registered and can apply to be deregistered if the VAT-exclusive value of supplies in the next twelve months will not exceed a specified limit.

See **60.1** to **60.10 REGISTRATION** for further details including how to apply for registration and deregistration.

See also

- **9.5 BUSINESS** for anti-avoidance measures to combat business splitting and the conditions for the separation of a previously single business into independent parts for registration purposes;
- **28.1** to **28.5 GROUPS OF COMPANIES** for group registration;
- **49.1** to **49.4 OVERSEAS TRADERS** for registration by overseas traders; and
- **60.43 REGISTRATION** for divisional registration by companies.

Even where there is no liability to register for VAT in respect of UK supplies of goods or services, a liability may arise in respect of

- 'distance selling' to non-taxable persons in the UK by suppliers in other EU member states (see **60.11** to **60.17 REGISTRATION**); or
- acquisitions of goods in the UK from other EU member states (see **60.18** to **60.25 REGISTRATION**).

Imports

[1.15] Unless special relief applies, VAT is charged and payable on the importation of goods into the UK from outside the EU. The rate of VAT is the same as if the goods had been supplied in the UK.

Unless the goods are placed under customs or excise warehousing or certain customs arrangements (e.g. inward processing relief or Union Transit arrangements) any VAT due must normally either be paid at the time of importation or deferred with any duty if the importer or his agent are approved for deferment. VAT paid on the importation of goods can be claimed as input tax, subject to the normal rules.

See **34 IMPORTS** for further details.

Exports

[1.16] Provided various conditions are met, goods exported outside the EU are zero-rated. See **22 EXPORTS** for further details.

Transactions with other EU member states

[1.17] The concepts of 'imports' and 'exports' of goods apply only to transactions with countries outside the EU. For intra-EU movements of goods, the terms 'acquisitions' and 'despatches' are used. It is not necessary to make an import declaration on an acquisition of goods in the UK from another EU member state or to pay VAT at the frontier.

Supplies of goods to a customer registered for VAT in another EU member state can be zero-rated provided certain conditions are met. These include obtaining the customer's VAT registration number and showing it on the VAT invoice. The customer then accounts for VAT at the appropriate rate on the goods in the EU member state of destination. If the conditions cannot be met, VAT must be charged in the country of origin at the rate applicable to the goods in that country.

VAT must also be charged on supplies of goods to non-registered customers in other EU member states. Where, however, the supplier is also responsible for the delivery of the goods, once the value of such 'distance' sales to any particular EU member state exceeds an annual threshold set by that country, the supplier is automatically liable to register for VAT in that other country. VAT on any further sales is then due in the EU member state of destination.

Special rules apply to transfers of own goods between EU member states, goods installed or assembled at the customer's premises, new means of transport and goods subject to excise duty purchased by non-taxable persons. There are also special rules for 'triangulation' (i.e. where a chain of supplies of goods involves three parties and, instead of goods physically passing from one party to the next, they are delivered from the first party to the last party in the chain).

See **20 EUROPEAN UNION: SINGLE MARKET** for further details.

Invoices

[1.18] A registered taxable person must issue a VAT invoice where he makes a standard or reduced-rated supply to another taxable person in the UK or a standard, reduced or zero-rated supply to a person in another EU member state. Some other EU member states require invoices to be issued for exempt supplies as well.

See **40 INVOICES** for further details including the particulars required to be shown on the invoice and special invoices which may be issued by retailers and cash and carry wholesalers.

Returns and payment of VAT

[1.19] Every taxable person must keep a VAT account summarising the output tax and input tax for each VAT period. See **57.12 RECORDS**. A VAT period is normally three months but a one-month period is also allowed, particularly where input tax is likely to exceed output tax on a regular basis.

The information in the VAT account, plus certain statistical information, must then be shown on a VAT return for that period. The great majority of traders are required to file their returns electronically and make their payments by electronic transfer. For these traders, the return must be sent to HMRC, and any VAT due to HMRC paid, no later than seven calendar days after the end of the month following the end of the return period. Traders filing on paper must file no later than the end of the month following the return period. Certain large VAT payers must make monthly payments on account.

The current VAT return and payment procedure is being replaced by the Making Tax Digital (MTD) programme with effect from 1 April 2019. See **2.3 ACCOUNTING PERIODS AND RECORDS** for more information on the changes.

See **2 ACCOUNTING PERIODS AND RETURNS** and **52.1** to **52.5 PAYMENT OF VAT** for further details.

Annual accounting

[1.20] Smaller businesses with turnover below an annual limit may apply to join the annual accounting scheme. This allows them to complete one VAT return each year. Monthly, or with the agreement of HMRC, quarterly interim payments on account are required based on an estimate of the amount of VAT due. The annual VAT return must be completed and sent to HMRC, with any balancing payment, within two months of the end of the annual VAT accounting period. See **64.9** to **64.14 SPECIAL SCHEMES** for further details.

Records

[1.21] Every taxable person must keep such records as HMRC require. Specifically, these include business and accounting records, the VAT account (see **1.19** above), copies of all VAT invoices and credit notes issued and received, and documentation relating to imports, exports, acquisitions of goods from other EU member states and goods dispatched to other EU member states. All such records must be kept for six years unless HMRC agree to a shorter period.

See **57 RECORDS** for further details.

Bad debts

[1.22] VAT is normally due by reference to the tax point (see **1.8** above). The supplier must therefore account to HMRC for the VAT even if the debt, including the VAT, is not paid. By way of relief, VAT can be reclaimed where a debt has been written off and six months has elapsed from the date of supply and the date payment is due. See **7 BAD DEBT RELIEF**.

The problem of VAT on bad debts can also be removed by using the cash accounting system (see **1.23** below).

> *Example*
>
> A sales invoice raised by a business on 31 January 2017 is due for payment on 31 March 2017. The earliest date that bad debt relief can be claimed in the event of non-payment is 30 September 2017, i.e. after the invoice is at least six months overdue for payment.

Cash accounting

[1.23] Provided turnover is below an annual limit, a taxable person may, subject to conditions, account for and pay VAT on the basis of cash or other consideration paid and received. The main advantages of the scheme are automatic bad debt relief and the deferral of the time for payment of VAT where extended credit is given. See **64.2** to **64.8 SPECIAL SCHEMES** for further details.

Assessments

[1.24] HMRC are given powers to raise an assessment where VAT returns have not been made or it appears to them that returns are incomplete or incorrect. The assessment must normally be made within two years from the end of the return period in question or, if later, within one year of the facts on which the assessment is based coming to their knowledge. An assessment cannot be raised more than four years after the end of the return period except in cases of fraud when the period is extended to 20 years. Where the taxable person has died, an assessment cannot be made more than four years after death or relate to a period more than three years before death.

See **6 ASSESSMENTS** for further details.

Interest and penalties

[1.25] Interest is chargeable in certain circumstances where VAT has been underdeclared or overclaimed. See **52.16 PAYMENT OF VAT**. On the other hand, repayment supplement is due where HMRC do not make a repayment on time and interest can be paid to the taxpayer where VAT has been overpaid or underclaimed as a result of error by HMRC. See **52.18** and **52.19 PAYMENT OF VAT**.

There is an extensive range of criminal and civil penalties including the following.

Offence	*Maximum penalty*
Criminal Fraudulent evasion of VAT Producing false documents	 Unlimited fine or 7 years imprisonment Unlimited fine or 7 years imprisonment
Inaccuracy in a return: deliberate and concealed	Up to 100% of the potential lost revenue
Inaccuracy in a return: deliberate but not concealed	Up to 70% of the potential lost revenue
Inaccuracy in a return: careless	Up to 30% of the potential lost revenue
Failure to retain required statutory records	£500
Late payment of VAT shown on a return	Default surcharge: rising scale from 2% to 15%

See **53 PENALTIES** for further details of these and other penalties. Liability for certain civil penalties can be avoided where there is reasonable excuse for conduct and penalties can be mitigated by HMRC or a First-tier Tax Tribunal.

Brexit

[1.26] Following the referendum vote on 23 June 2016, there is considerable uncertainty about many things, including the future development of VAT in the UK. Changes to VAT are probably a low priority for the Government for the time being; certainly the tax will be retained, because it generates a great deal of revenue. It remains to be seen whether leaving the EU will be taken as an opportunity to make changes to the details or to the overall scheme of the tax that was introduced as a condition of joining the EU.

Key points

[1.27] Points to consider are as follows.

- Be aware that in relation to VAT issues, EU law will currently almost invariably take priority over UK VAT law. This situation has been the key factor behind a range of VAT court cases, whereby UK taxpayers have challenged the compatibility of UK and EU VAT law in certain areas. This will continue for the time being, although in the long term EU law may become less significant. HMRC has to apply UK law even where it is out of step with EU VAT law, if this is to the advantage of the taxpayer.
- A 'taxable person' is a VAT-registered person, or a person who is legally required to be registered for VAT. HMRC has the power to backdate a taxpayer's date of VAT registration to the date when their turnover exceeded the VAT registration limit. It is very important that a business carefully monitors its levels of taxable sales to ensure it registers for VAT at the correct time. (Note that there is a separate EU meaning of 'taxable person' under *Art 9* of *Directive 2006/112/EC*, which has considerably wider scope.)

- A business can exclude the value of any 'exempt' or 'outside the scope' sources of income in its calculations to determine whether it needs to be VAT-registered. Many sales of services to overseas customers (particularly business customers) are outside the scope of UK VAT because the sale is deemed to be taking place in the country where the customer belongs under the place of supply rules, i.e. the sale is not deemed to be taking place in the UK.
- As a general principle, input tax can only be reclaimed on costs relevant to taxable activities. However, there are two important exceptions to this general rule: a business making supplies to overseas customers that are outside the scope of VAT under the place of supply rules can still claim input tax as long as the service in question would be taxable if supplied to a UK customer (e.g. accountancy services); a business making certain exempt supplies of insurance and financial services can reclaim input tax on related costs as long as the customer receiving the service is based outside the EU.
- Taxable sales are those that are subject to VAT at either the zero-rate, reduced rate or standard rate of VAT. The zero-rate is still classed as a rate of tax, albeit at 0%. A VAT-registered business making only zero-rated sales will be in a VAT repayment position because it can still claim input tax on all of its costs (subject to normal rules).

2

Accounting Periods and Returns

Cross-references. See **52 PAYMENT OF VAT**; **53 PENALTIES**; **57 RECORDS**; **64.9 SPECIAL SCHEMES** for annual VAT returns.

De Voil Indirect Tax Service. See V5.101–108.

Introduction to accounting periods and returns

[2.1] A taxable person must account for and pay VAT by reference to VAT periods. For this purpose, subject to any additional time which HMRC may allow, he must make a return to HMRC, showing the amount of VAT payable by or to him and containing full information in respect of other matters specified in the return. [*VATA 1994, s 25(1); SI 1995/2518, Reg 25(1)*].

Currently HMRC normally allow one calendar month and seven days from the end of the VAT period to submit an online VAT return. The great majority of traders are required to make online returns. HMRC can also allow additional time to make a paper return if the VAT due is paid electronically. [*SI 1995/2518, Reg 25A(20)*].

An exception to the above is where the taxable person is using the annual accounting scheme. A taxable person using the annual accounting scheme must make a return to HMRC not later than the last working day of the second month following the end of the accounting year to which the return relates (see **64.13 SPECIAL SCHEMES**). [*SI 1995/2518, Reg 50(2)(b)*].

Electronic filing

[2.2] Since 1 April 2012 virtually all VAT-registered businesses are required to submit VAT returns and pay any VAT due electronically. [*SI 1995/2518, Regs 25A(3), 40(2A)*].

From 1 July 2014 HMRC can approve telephone filing as a form of electronic filing for use by specified categories of persons and from that date there are three categories of exemption from electronic filing:

(1) exemption for persons who HMRC are satisfied are practising members of a religious society or order whose beliefs are incompatible with the use of electronic communications;
(2) exemption for businesses which are subject to insolvency procedures;
(3) exemption for persons who HMRC are satisfied that it is not reasonably practicable to make a return using an electronic return system for reasons of disability, age, remoteness of location or any other reason.

[*SI 1995/2518, Reg 25A(6); SI 2014/1497*].

Before 1 July 2014 exemption for electronic filing was only available for the first two of the above three categories. The third category was introduced as a result of a consultation process following the Tribunal decision in *L H Bishop Electric Company Limited* [2013] UKFTT 522 (TC) (TC02910) (TVC 59.24), which held that the failure of the *VAT Regulations 1995* to take account of a person's ability to file online on account of age, disability, computer illiteracy, or remoteness of location was a breach of the European Convention on Human Rights. See *Brian Harvey t/a Sun Ice Air Conditioning Services* [2016] UKFTT 266 (TC) (TC05041) for an examination of these rules by the First-tier Tax Tribunal, which rejected the taxpayer's argument that HMRC were not competent to judge whether he had a valid religious objection to online filing: he did not fall within the category defined in the legislation, and HMRC's decision could not be faulted.

Access

In order to get access to the service, a business must:

- *Sign up*. Go to the HMRC website (online.hmrc.gov.uk/registration/organisation) and enter personal details (including setting a password). A User ID will then be displayed for future use.
- *Enrol*. Login with the User ID and password and select 'Enrol for eVAT services'. Then supply the information requested which is available from the certificate of registration and the last VAT return.
- *Activate*. An activation PIN will be sent, normally within seven days. To activate the service, go to the Government Gateway at

www.gateway.gov.uk
and Login, select the 'Activate' link and enter the activation PIN.

A business can then Login to the HMRC website (www.tax.service.gov.uk/gg/sign-in?continue=https%3A%2F%2Fonline.hmrc.gov.uk%2Fhome) to access its VAT return. Once a business has enrolled for online VAT services, HMRC expect it to continue to use the service and not use paper returns unless it has problems using the site.

Authorisation

When the online application has been successfully completed, the business is authorised to use the service although HMRC reserve the right to deny access to the service where they consider it necessary for the protection of the revenue. Unless permission to use the service has been granted (and not revoked), any return made using the service is treated as not having been made. A person is not treated as being authorised to use the service only because of

- being registered under *SI 1995/2518, Reg 6* in substitution for another person who has been so authorised on the transfer of a business as a going concern (see **60.42 REGISTRATION**); or
- acting in a representative capacity and being required by HMRC under *SI 1995/2518, Reg 30* to comply with the VAT requirements relating to accounting, payment and records (see **16.1** and **16.2 DEATH AND INCAPACITY** and **36.1 INSOLVENCY**).

Sending returns

If transmission of an eVAT return is successful, the business will receive an electronic acknowledgement from HMRC. This is evidence that the business has met its legal responsibility to submit a return. It is therefore recommended that a copy of the acknowledgement is printed and retained in the records. The acknowledgement also shows a unique reference for each return sent which should be quoted in any queries about the return. If an electronic acknowledgement is not received, the business should presume that the return has not been received.

[*SI 1995/2518, Regs 25(4A)–(4M), 25A*].

Payment of VAT

A condition of using the eVAT service is that any VAT due on the return is also paid by an approved electronic payment method. [*SI 1995/2518, Reg 40(2A)*]. See **52.2 PAYMENT OF VAT** for methods of paying electronically.

Making Tax Digital

[2.3] HMRC have announced a revised timetable for the introduction of the changes to the filing requirements under the Making Tax Digital (MTD) programme. A statement issued on 13 July 2017 announced the following with regards to VAT.

- Only businesses with a turnover above the current VAT threshold will have to keep digital records and only for VAT purposes.
- Digital records will need to be kept from April 2019. From that date, businesses above the VAT threshold have to provide their VAT information to HMRC through Making Tax Digital software.
- Businesses will not be asked to keep digital records, or to update HMRC quarterly, for other taxes until at least 2020.

Making Tax Digital will be available on a voluntary basis for the smallest businesses, and for other taxes.

This means that businesses and landlords with a turnover below the VAT threshold will be able to choose when to move to the new digital system.

As VAT already requires quarterly returns, no business will need to provide information to HMRC more regularly during this initial phase than they do now.

HMRC will start to pilot MTD for VAT by the end of this year, starting with small scale, private testing, followed by a wider, live pilot starting in Spring 2018. This will allow for well over a year of testing before any businesses are mandated to use the system.

Details of these new provisions are contained in *Finance (No 2) Act 2017, s 62*.

Regulations have been published setting out the following requirements for VAT-registered businesses:

- keeping an electronic account of all information specified in the regulations;
- obligation to use an approved form of software to prepare and submit VAT returns;
- record retention requirements.

Details of any exemptions from submitting electronic returns and other information, etc. are also provided in the new regulations. HMRC are also requesting that businesses voluntarily submit additional information that could enable them to check the accuracy of the return information submitted to reduce the numbers of queries raised.

HMRC have also produced an explanatory memorandum (see www.legislation.gov.uk/uksi/2018/261/pdfs/uksiem_20180261_en.pdf).

[*SI 2018/261*].

Accounting periods

[2.4] Subject to the exceptions below, returns must be completed for three-monthly periods ending on the dates notified in the certificate of registration (or otherwise). [*SI 1995/2518, Reg 25(1)*].

In order to spread the flow of returns over the year, taxable persons are allocated to one of the three groups of VAT periods ('VAT staggers') as follows.

- Three-month periods ending on 30 June, 30 September, 31 December and 31 March.
- Three-month periods ending on 31 July, 31 October, 31 January and 30 April.
- Three-month periods ending on 31 August, 30 November, 28 February and 31 May.

(VAT Notice 700, para 20.5).

A taxable person who was, or is, required to be registered (but has not done so) will, unless HMRC otherwise allow, be allocated to the first group.

Exceptions

[2.5] The following are exceptions to the above VAT period rules.

Annual returns

See **64.9 SPECIAL SCHEMES.**

Monthly returns

HMRC may allow or direct a person to complete returns for periods of one month and to submit these within one month of the period to which they relate. [*SI 1995/2518, Reg 25(1)(a)*]. If repayments are expected to be received (e.g. because most of the outputs are zero-rated) this method of accounting is advantageous. Where monthly VAT returns are prepared and the business changes from receiving repayments to making payment of VAT, it may have to change to three-monthly VAT periods. (VAT Notice 700, para 20.5).

First return period

The first return period commences on the effective date on which the taxable person was, or should have been, registered. [*SI 1995/2518, Reg 25(1)(b)*].

HMRC variation

HMRC may vary the length of any period or the date on which any return is to be submitted. This applies whether or not the varied period has ended. [*SI 1995/2518, Reg 25(1)(c)*]. There is no appeal against their decision to the First-tier Tax Tribunal under *VATA 1994, s 83(a)* (*Punchwell Ltd* (VTD 1085) (TVC 59.2); *Selected Growers Ltd* (VTD 10) (TVC 59.1)).

In particular:

- Written application may be made (quoting registration number and dates) to have VAT periods corresponding with the financial year of the business.
- Where there is a new registration either because of a transfer of a going concern or a change in circumstances of a registered business (see **60.42** and **60.7 REGISTRATION** respectively) application can be made to retain the VAT periods of the previous registration.
- Special consideration will also be given, where accounting systems are not based on calendar months, to arrangements for VAT periods to fit in with the particular system. For example, quarterly VAT periods

ending within 14 days of the end of the standard period *or* monthly VAT periods ending within seven days of the end of the calendar month (14 days for a four-weekly accounting cycle) are acceptable.
- Any other arrangement will be specially considered on request.

(VAT Notice 700, para 20.5).

Bankruptcy, etc.

Where control of the assets of any registered person passes to a trustee in bankruptcy, administrative receiver, liquidator or person otherwise acting in a representative capacity, the current VAT period in which the date of the receiving order, appointment of administrative receiver or provisional liquidator or winding up order, etc. (the '*relevant date*') occurs is divided into two periods. The first period ends on the day prior to the relevant date and the appropriate return must be submitted by the last day of the following month. The second period commences on the relevant date and ends (and all subsequent periods end) on the normal last day for the VAT periods. [*SI 1995/2518, Reg 25(3)*].

Final return

Any person who

- ceases to be liable to be registered, or
- ceases to be entitled to be registered under *VATA 1994, Sch 1 paras 9, 10, Sch 2 para 4* or *Sch 3 para 4* (see **60.2 REGISTRATION**)

must submit a final return *unless* the registration is allocated to the purchaser on the transfer of a business as a going concern (see **60.42 REGISTRATION**). Unless HMRC allow otherwise, the return must contain full information of the matters specified in the form and a declaration, signed by the taxpayer, that the return is true and complete. The return must be furnished by a person who was or is registered within one month of the effective date for cancellation of registration and by any other person within one month of the date on which he ceases to be liable to be registered. [*SI 1995/2518, Reg 25(4)*].

Estimated returns

[2.6] Where HMRC are satisfied that a person is not able to account for the exact amount of output tax chargeable or claim the exact amount of input tax to be deducted in any VAT period, that person may estimate a part of his output tax or input tax for that period provided

- the estimate is adjusted and exactly accounted for in the next VAT period; or
- if the exact amount is still not known and HMRC are satisfied that it could not with due diligence be ascertained, the estimate is adjusted in the next but one VAT period.

[*SI 1995/2518, Regs 28, 29(3)*].

Permission for estimated returns must be obtained in advance. If the estimated return is submitted, and the VAT shown paid, by the due date, the taxpayer will not be in default for the purposes of the default surcharge provisions (see **53.23 PENALTIES**). Permission will still be considered after the due date has passed, but it will not affect any default which has already been recorded. (VAT Notice 700, para 21.2).

See **44.10 LOCAL AUTHORITIES AND PUBLIC BODIES** for special estimation schemes for local authorities.

De Voil Indirect Tax Service. See V3.505.

Completion of return

[2.7] The completion of a return requires information to be included in the boxes shown below. [*SI 1995/2518, Reg 39.*] (VAT Notice 700/12/18, paras 3.2–3.10.)

- *Box 1* — VAT due in the period on sales and other outputs.
- *Box 2* — VAT due in the period on acquisitions from other EU member states.
- *Box 3* — Total VAT due.
- *Box 4* — VAT reclaimed in the period on purchases and other inputs (including acquisitions from the EU).
- *Box 5* — Net VAT to be paid to HMRC or reclaimed.
- *Box 6* — Total value of sales and all other outputs excluding any VAT.
- *Box 7* — Total value of purchases and all other inputs excluding any VAT.
- *Box 8* — Total value of all supplies of goods and related costs, excluding any VAT, to other EU member states.
- *Box 9* — Total value of all acquisitions of goods and related costs, excluding any VAT, from other EU member states.

Nil returns

If the business has not traded in the period and has no input tax to recover or output tax to declare, a VAT return must still be submitted with boxes 1 to 5 completed as '0.00' and boxes 6 to 9 as '0' ('None' if the return is sent on paper).

A nil return must also be submitted if the business

- has a UK taxable turnover below the UK VAT registration threshold, and
- is registered for VAT under the simplified VAT registration arrangements referred to in HMRC guidance 'Register for and use the VAT Mini One Stop Shop', and
- does not want to reclaim VAT on costs relating to sales to customers in other EU member states.

Assessments

When sending in a return after paying an assessment, the VAT return should be completed as usual without adjusting any of the figures to offset what has already been paid by assessment. If the value of Box 5 is more than the assessment, just the extra should be paid. If it is less than the assessment, no payment should be made and HMRC will pay or credit the business with the difference.

(VAT Notice 700/12/18, para 6.5.)

Declaration

The return must contain full information in respect of the matters specified in the return and a declaration, signed by the taxpayer, that the return is true and complete. [*SI 1995/2518, Reg 25(1)*]. This declaration must be unqualified (*DK Wright and Associates Ltd* (VTD 203) (TVC 59.25)).

Disagreeing with HMRC decision

[2.8] Where HMRC have given a decision or ruling concerning a business's VAT liabilities they will normally reject any claim from the business that challenges the decision or ruling. If the claim is formally rejected the business will be invited to apply for a review of the decision. The business has 30 days in which to accept this offer. If the business does not want a review, or if it does not agree with the result of the review, it can appeal to the First-tier Tribunal to decide the matter. If the business appeals, it will preserve its entitlement to a refund, but only if it has made a valid claim, should the HMRC decision be overruled. If however the business decides not to appeal to the Tribunal then any future claims will be considered to be new claims, whether made on the same basis or not, and will be subject to the normal time limits.

(VAT Notice 700/45/17, para 8.1).

Incorrect and incomplete returns or failure to make a return

[2.9] Any error in accounting for VAT or in the return generally must be corrected as required by HMRC. [*SI 1995/2518, Reg 35*]. See **57.11 RECORDS**.

The consequences of an incorrect return or failure to make a return are as follows.

- HMRC may assess the amount of VAT due to the best of their judgement (see **6.1 ASSESSMENTS**). HMRC have indicated that incomplete or incorrect returns will be returned for correction. Traders classified as 'payment traders' will be assessed and the notice of assessment will accompany the rejected return with an error-return notice. For traders classified as 'repayment traders' the period will remain open until an acceptable return is received. Repayments will not be made until the error has been corrected.

- A First-tier Tribunal cannot normally entertain an appeal unless the appellant has paid the VAT due (see **5.4 APPEALS**).
- Criminal or civil penalties may be incurred for failure to comply with the necessary requirements. See **53 PENALTIES** and particularly **53.14** for penalties for misdeclaration or neglect resulting from understatements or overclaims and **53.23** for default surcharge for failure to submit returns on time and/or pay the VAT due.

Returns by persons selling under a power of sale

[2.10] Where a business is carried on by a taxable person and goods forming part of the business are sold by another person under any power exercisable by him in satisfaction of a debt owed by the taxable person, the goods are deemed to be supplied by the taxable person in the course or furtherance of his business.

The grant, assignment or surrender of a major interest in land forming part of the assets of the business is a supply of goods. The auctioneer (on a sale by auction) or the person selling the goods must, *whether or not registered*, within 21 days of the sale, complete Form VAT 833 online and send it to the address on the form, showing:

- his name, address and registration number (if registered);
- the name, address and registration number of the taxable person;
- the date of sale;
- the description and quantity of goods sold at each rate of VAT; and
- the sales proceeds and the VAT charged at each rate.

The VAT due must be paid electronically in accordance with the instructions accompanying Form VAT 833 on the www.gov.uk website.

The auctioneer or person selling the goods must also send a copy of the statement to the taxable person within the same time limit. Both parties must then exclude the VAT chargeable from their normal returns, if any. [*VATA 1994, Sch 4 paras 7, 9, Sch 11 para 2(12); SI 1995/2518, Reg 27*].

The auctioneer, etc. must also issue a VAT invoice but giving the name, address and VAT registration number of the supplier. He need not be registered to issue it and should not ask the supplier for a VAT invoice.

This procedure does not normally apply to liquidators, administrative receivers or trustees in bankruptcy (see **36.1 INSOLVENCY**), who continue to account for VAT in the normal way.

(VAT Notice 700, para 18.4).

De Voil Indirect Tax Service. See V5.142.

EC sales lists

[2.11] Under powers given to them in *VATA 1994, Sch 11 para 2(3)*, HMRC require a business registered for VAT in the UK which

- makes supplies of goods to traders registered for VAT in other EU member states;
- transfers its own goods from the UK to another EU member state;
- is the intermediary in triangular transactions between VAT-registered traders in other EU member states; or
- makes supplies of services subject to the reverse charge in its customer's EU member state

to submit statements containing particulars of the transactions involved. Other EU member states have similar requirements. In the UK, these statements are known as EC Sales Lists (ESLs) but in other EU member states the forms are referred to as 'recapitulative statements' or 'summary statements'. The information provided is used to ensure that VAT has been correctly accounted for. A business does not need to complete an ESL if it is involved in triangulation and the goods are exported to a final customer outside the EU.

(VAT Notice 725, paras 17.1–17.3).

Supplies of services subject to reverse charge [*Directive 2008/117/EC*]

EC Sales Lists are also required for taxable supplies of services to business customers in other EU member states where the customer is required to account for VAT under the reverse charge procedure. [*VATA 1994, Sch 11 para 2(3ZA)*]. ESLs in respect of services are not required for

- supplies which are exempt from VAT according to the rules in the EU member state where the supply takes place;
- business-to-business supplies where the recipient is not VAT registered; and
- business-to-consumer supplies. (HMRC Brief 53/08).

Penalties

See **53.27** and **53.28 PENALTIES** respectively for inaccuracies in, and failure to submit, ESLs.

De Voil Indirect Tax Service. See V5.271B.

Obtaining forms

[2.12] A business will automatically be sent an ESL (Form VAT 101 or Welsh version VAT 101(W)) by HMRC if at any time it has completed Box 8 of its VAT return (total value of supplies of goods to other EU member states). The form is sent separately from the VAT return.

The form can also be obtained from the VAT Helpline (tel: 0300 200 3700) or can be downloaded from the HMRC section of the GOV.UK website at:

www.gov.uk/government/publications/vat-ec-sales-list-vat101.

The following can also be obtained from either of these sources.

- EU Sales List Continuation Sheet (Form 101A or Welsh version Form 101A(W)).

- EU Sales Correction Sheet (Form 101B or Welsh version Form 101B(W)).
- Helpful Hints VAT 101/VAT 101A for the completion of the ESL and Continuation Sheet.
- Helpful Hints VAT 101B for the completion of the ESL Correction Sheet.

(VAT Notice 725, paras 17.5, 17.6).

Return periods and submission dates

[2.13] An ESL may be submitted electronically via the VAT online service or via the paper form VAT 101. Frequency of submission depends on whether goods or services are supplied and the quarterly value (excluding VAT) of any goods supplied. However there is no requirement to submit nil ESLs.

If a business	*The business will*
makes supplies of services only,	be required to submit an ESL for each calendar quarter ending 31 March, 30 June, 30 September and 31 December but may choose to submit monthly if preferred.
makes supplies of goods and the value of those supplies has not exceeded £35,000 (excl. VAT) in the current, or four previous quarters	be required to submit an ESL for each calendar quarter ending 31 March, 30 June, 30 September, and 31 December but may choose to submit monthly if preferred.
makes supplies of goods and the value of those supplies has exceeded £35,000 (excl. VAT) in the current, or four previous quarters	be required to submit ESLs calendar monthly. (If separate ESLs are submitted for branches within the business and the total value of goods supplied from all branches is more than £35,000, each branch will have to submit a monthly ESL.)
makes supplies of goods and services and because the value of the supplies of goods is above the quarterly threshold, the business is required to submit monthly ESLs for goods,	have the choice to either: report both goods and services in each month, (using indicator 3 to identify supplies of services), or report only goods in months 1 and 2, and in month 3 report goods for the month and services for the whole quarter (using indicator 3 to identify supplies of services).

If a business	*The business will*
supplies goods or services, makes annual VAT returns and total annual taxable turnover does not exceed £145,000; and annual value of supplies to other member states is not more than £11,000; and the supplies do not include new means of transport (boats, aircraft and motorised land vehicles),	be able to apply to the VAT Helpline for approval to submit an ESL once a year and agree the due date for sending in the annual ESL.
supply goods only (including triangular transactions), have a low level of EU Sales and total taxable turnover does not exceed the VAT registration threshold plus £25,500; annual value of supplies to other member states is not more than £11,000; the supplies do not include new means of transport (boats, aircraft and motorized land vehicles),	be able to apply to the VAT Helpline for approval to submit a simplified annual ESL and agree the due date for sending in the annual ESL. If approved, the business will be allowed to complete a less detailed ESL, showing only the VAT registration numbers of EU customers. Actual values are not required but a nominal value of £1 for each entry must be entered on the ESL form.

The deadlines for submitting an ESL to HMRC, for all frequencies of submissions and for goods and services are: for paper ESLs, within 14 days of the end of the reporting period; and for electronic (online) ESLs, within 21 days of the end of the reporting period.

ESL periods cannot be aligned with non-standard VAT periods except where HMRC has, under *SI 1995/2518, Reg 25*, permitted the person to submit a VAT return for a period longer than three months and all of the following conditions are met.

- The person has not during the period made a supply of a new means of transport.
- HMRC is satisfied that at the end of any month, the value of the person's taxable supplies in the period of one year then ending is less than £145,000 or at any time there are reasonable grounds for believing that the value of the person's taxable supplies in the period of one year beginning at that or any later time will not exceed £145,000.
- HMRC is satisfied that at the end of any month, the value of the person's supplies to persons registered for VAT in other EU member states in the period of one year then ending is less than £11,000 or at any time there are reasonable grounds for believing that the value of the person's supplies to persons registered for VAT in other EU member states in the period of one year beginning at that or any later time will not exceed £11,000.

[*SI 1995/2518, Regs 21, 22A, 22B*]. (VAT Notice 725, paras 17.4, 17.7–17.9).

Information to be disclosed

[2.14] The ESL must contain the following information.

Information	*Description*
Country code	The two letter prefix which identifies the customer's country code (see below).
Customer's VAT registration number	The VAT registration number of the customer in the other member state.
Total value of supplies in £'s sterling	The total value for the appropriate period of: goods and related services supplied to each customer, leaving the indicator column blank (related services are services which form part of the price of the goods such as freight charges and insurance); triangular transactions where the business is the intermediary, entered on a separate line for each customer and using code '2' in the indicator column, and supplies of services subject to the reverse charge in the customer's member state, entered on a separate line for each customer and using code '3' in the indicator For simplified annual ESL £1 must be inserted in the value column for each entry.

Austria	AT
Belgium	BE
Bulgaria	BG
Croatia	HR
Cyprus	CY
Czech Republic	CZ
Denmark	DK
Estonia	EE
Finland	FI
France	FR
Germany	DE
Greece	EL
Hungary	HU
Ireland	IE
Italy	IT
Latvia	LV
Lithuania	LT

Luxembourg	LU
Malta	MT
Netherlands	NL
Poland	PL
Portugal	PT
Romania	RO
Slovakia	SK
Slovenia	SI
Spain	ES
Sweden	SE

[*SI 1995/2518, Reg 21, Reg 22(3)(5)*]. (VAT Notice 725, para 17.11; Form VAT 101 Notes on Completion).

Method of sending

Electronically

[2.15] An ESL may be submitted electronically using:

- an online form;
- an upload facility for large data (CSV or XML) files;
- UN-EDIFACT (to use this method send an e-mail to: ecu@hmrc.gsi.gov.uk to register); or
- visit the Electronic Data Capture Services section of the HMRC website for the Trade Specification.

The service is free with registration and enrolment via the HMRC website or Government Gateway using PIN and password.

Paper format

ESLs can also be submitted via the paper form VAT 101. (See **2.12** above for obtaining forms.) If a business has a low level of EU sales it may be eligible to complete a simplified ESL annually.

(VAT Notice 725, paras 17.4, 17.5).

Correction of errors

Errors discovered by the business

[2.16] HMRC must be informed of errors or omissions on an ESL where

- errors exceed £100;
- an incorrect VAT registration number has been quoted; or
- a business has used the wrong transaction type indicator when completing the ESL.

Errors must be disclosed by completion of a Form VAT 101B which can be downloaded from the HMRC website using the following link:

www.gov.uk/government/publications/vat-ec-sales-list-correction-sheet-va t101b

Help on the correction of errors is available from the VAT Helpline or by e-mailing:ESL.helpdesk@hmrc.gsi.gov.uk.

Errors discovered by HMRC

Where paper ESLs are submitted, HMRC will notify a business of any errors that they identify on Form VAT 104 (EU Sales List Error Report). The form will show the error lines and the reasons for the errors. The errors must be corrected in the spaces provided and the form returned within 21 days of receipt to the address shown.

If an ESL is submitted online using the ECSL service, any errors are highlighted on screen as the form is completed, allowing the business to correct them online prior to submission or up to 21 days after the date of submission.

(VAT Notice 725, paras 17.14, 17.16).

Branch and group registration

[2.17] Separate ESLs may be submitted on paper or online where there are

- individual branches of a business,
- individual companies within a group registration, or
- self-accounting branches within a group registration.

The business should contact HMRC to arrange to do this. It will be given a three-digit code for each branch or company in the business, which must be used as an identifier when the separate ESLs are completed. If the business wishes to submit data online for individual branches it must register each one separately with HMRC's online services.

If the total value of goods supplied from all the branches of the business is more than £35,000 (excluding VAT) in the current or previous four quarters, each branch will have to submit a monthly ESL.

(VAT Notice 725, para 17.17).

Other points

[2.18] *Agents.* An agent may be used to act on the business's behalf, but legal responsibility for the accurate and timely completion and submission of an ESL remains with the business. Any agent can submit an online ESL on behalf of a client but the agent must be registered for VAT and appointed online by the client to act on their behalf.

Triangular transactions. An ESL must be completed even if the only EU supplies are triangular transactions.

Services. If a business's only EU supplies are services subject to the reverse charge in the customer's member state, it is still required to submit an ESL.

Zero-rated if supplied within the UK. An ESL must be completed if a business makes supplies of goods to a trader registered for VAT in another member state, including the transfer of its own goods and goods that would be zero-rated if supplied within the UK.

Deemed supplies. Where a business supplies goods free of charge to a customer in another EU member state, it is making a deemed supply of goods and must include it on its ESL. The value to be shown is the cost to the business of the goods. Samples or gifts may be excluded provided they meet certain conditions.

Distance selling. If a business makes supplies of goods to customers who are not VAT-registered in other EU member states and it is responsible for delivery of the goods (distance selling) it should not enter these supplies on the ESL.

Temporary movements. A business should not include temporary movements of its own goods to another member state unless the conditions relating to the transfer change.

Credit notes. The value of the credit note should be deducted from the value of the supplies made to the customer. If the value of credit notes exceeds the value of supplies, the resulting negative figure should be shown using a minus sign.

(VAT Notice 725, paras 17.18–17.25).

Intrastat

[2.19] Intrastat is the name given to the system for collecting statistics on the trade in goods between EU member states. Businesses which are not registered for VAT, and private individuals who move goods within the EU, have no obligations under the Intrastat system.

The statistics are collected from the following two sources.

The VAT return

All VAT-registered businesses must complete Boxes 8 and 9 on the VAT return showing total values of goods supplied to ('dispatches') and acquired from ('arrivals') other EU member states.

Supplementary declarations (SDs)

If the annual value of intra-EU trade of a business is below the threshold in the table below, it can be treated as exempt from providing Intrastat information and is not required to prepare SDs. The thresholds apply on a calendar year basis and apply separately to

- dispatches of goods to other EU member states; and
- arrivals of goods from other EU member states.

Where the level of its dispatches or arrivals (or both) is above the threshold, the business must prepare SDs.

[*SI 1992/2790, Reg 3; SI 2013/3043*].

Calendar year	*Dispatches*	*Arrivals*
2010–2013	£250,000	£600,000
2014	£250,000	£1,200,000
2015	£250,000	£1,500,000
2016	£250,000	£1,500,000
2017	£250,000	£1,500,000

Additionally, if a business is not required to provide SDs from the start of a calendar year but the cumulative total of dispatches or arrivals from 1 January in the current calendar year exceeds the threshold for the current year, SDs must be submitted for the rest of the calendar year, commencing with the month in which the threshold is reached. Under these circumstances, the business should contact Intrastat Enquiries Team using the email – intrastatenquiries@hmrc.gsi.gov.uk stating the month the threshold for dispatches or arrivals (or both) was exceeded. HMRC will confirm the start date and advise the business of any special arrangements.

For full details about the preparation of SDs, see HMRC Notice 60.

The data provided on Intrastat declarations is provided for both Intrastat and VAT purposes. [*SI 1995/2518, Regs 23E, 23F*]. This does not require any further action on the part of the business concerned but means that the data can be also used, for example, to counter Missing Trader Intra-Community fraud.

Key points: accounting periods and returns

[2.20] Points to consider are as follows.

- It is compulsory for most VAT-registered businesses to submit VAT returns and pay tax by electronic means.
- A business that expects to receive regular repayments of VAT (e.g. a business with wholly or mainly zero-rated sales, such as a farmer or grocer) can benefit from submitting monthly VAT returns. This will improve the cash flow of the business.
- It is sensible for a business to request that its VAT quarters coincide with the end of its financial year. A request can be made to HMRC to change the periods so that they coincide with the financial year. This means that, if HMRC agree to the request, for one period only, a VAT return of one or two months will need to be submitted to bring the periods into line with the requested date.
- A useful concession is that a business can make an advance request to submit its VAT returns based on special accounting periods. For example, some businesses have an accounting period (for management accounts purposes) that ends on the final Friday

of the month, which may not be the end of the calendar month for VAT return purposes. However, care is needed to ensure VAT returns are submitted and paid by the due dates that will apply for the special accounting date. If the business fails to meet the deadline a default surcharge penalty or default surcharge liability notice could be issued by HMRC.

- If a business deregisters for VAT purposes, it will need to complete a final VAT return covering the period from its last VAT return up to the date of deregistration. It is important to remember that the final return will need to ensure output tax is properly accounted for on assets and stock held by the business when it deregisters.
- A business that is unable to submit an accurate VAT return by the due date (e.g. due to the loss of accounting records in a fire or because of computer problems) can request approval from HMRC to submit an estimated return based on its best judgment. Any under or overpayment of tax compared to the actual amount due can then be included on the VAT return for the next period. The method of making the estimate is at the discretion of the business, perhaps based on figures for the same period in the previous year, adjusting for known factors, e.g. in relation to capital expenditure or a change in the mixture of standard and zero-rated sales.
- The completion of the various boxes on VAT returns requires care and attention to ensure correct procedures are adopted. A common error is to include reverse charge transactions (accounting for the suppliers' output tax in the case of most services received from abroad and some mobile phone and computer chip purchases from a UK business) in Box 2 rather than Box 1. The Box 2 entry is only relevant to goods purchased from a VAT registered business based in an EU member state outside of the UK, known as 'acquisition tax'.
- The reverse charge entries (Box 1 and Box 4) or acquisition tax entries (Box 2 and Box 4) are not contra entries for the same amount in all cases. If an expense (goods or services) relates to exempt, private or non-business activities, then in most cases the business will not be able to recover (or will not be able to recover in full) the amount of output tax accounted for in Box 1 or 2 as input tax in Box 4.
- A business will sometimes transfer its own goods to a branch based in another EU member state. The branch is often VAT-registered in that country. The value of such transfers should be included in both Box 6 (outputs) and Box 8 (sales of goods to VAT-registered customers in other EU member states) of the return. The transaction also needs to be included on an ESL and Intrastat return where applicable.
- Box 8 and Box 9 of the VAT return (sales of goods to and purchases of goods from VAT-registered businesses in other EU member states) only relate to the sale of goods. There should be

no inclusion for the value of services bought from or sold to EU customers, e.g. accountancy services, consultancy fees, legal services.

- The ESL has been in place for many years to record the details of goods sold to a VAT-registered business in another EU member state. The requirement now includes sales of services where no VAT charge is made by a UK business under the place of supply rules.
- A business selling goods to VAT-registered customers in other EU member states will automatically be sent an ESL because of the positive entry it would make (if done correctly) in Box 8 of its VAT return. A business selling services where no VAT is charged to an EU customer will not make an entry in Box 8 so is responsible for obtaining an ESL form from HMRC (or completing it online) by the due dates.
- If there are no relevant transactions in an ESL period, no return needs to be completed by the business. There is no requirement to complete a nil return.
- A business selling goods to other EU customers (VAT-registered), with a quarterly value exceeding £35,000 (either in the current quarter or any of the four previous quarters), will need to submit a monthly EU Sales List.
- A business will need to complete Intrastat returns (giving details of its trading in goods with other VAT-registered businesses in the EU) if the value of its acquisitions or dispatches exceeds certain limits on a calendar year basis.

3

Agents

Cross-references. See **12.9 CATERING** for contract catering.

De Voil Indirect Tax Service. See V3.221.

Introduction to agents

[3.1] There is no definition of 'agent' in the legislation. An agent is someone who acts for, or represents, someone else (the principal) in arranging supplies of goods and services. Supplies arranged by an agent are made by or to the principal represented. The principal cannot avoid any liability to account for VAT on supplies, or to pay VAT on purchases, by using an agent. However, whether or not a person is an agent for another person depends upon the actual arrangement between them and not simply upon the trading titles adopted. For example, 'motor agents and distributors' usually trade as principals and travel agents and employment agencies are not usually agents in all their activities. Solicitors and architects are normally principals but may occasionally arrange supplies as agents for their clients.

An agent/principal relationship exists if both parties agree that it does *and* the agent has agreed with the principal *to act on his behalf* in relation to the particular transaction concerned. The agreement may be written, oral or merely inferred from their general relationship and the way their business is conducted. Whatever form this relationship takes, the following conditions must be satisfied.

- It must always be clearly established between the agent and principal, and acceptable to HMRC, that the agent is arranging transactions for the principal, rather than trading on his own account.
- The agent must never be the owner of the goods or use any of the services bought or sold for the principal.
- The agent must not alter the nature or value of any of the supplies made between the principal and third parties.

(VAT Notice 700, para 22.2).

In *C & E Commrs v Johnson*, QB [1980] STC 624 (TVC 1.1) Woolf J took agency as the 'relationship which exists between two persons, one of whom expressly or impliedly consents that the other should represent him or act on his behalf and the other of whom similarly consents to represent the former or so to act'.

In *Mobile Sourcing Ltd v HMRC* [2016] UKUT 274 (TCC), the Upper Tribunal confirmed that the knowledge of an agent has to be attributed to the principal. It was no defence in a case involving carousel fraud that only the agent 'knew or had the means of knowing' that the transactions were connected with fraud: the principal was deemed to know what the agent knew. The company was therefore not entitled to recover input tax on the purchases concerned.

Whether acting as agent or principal — case law

For decisions in specific cases as to whether a person was acting as agent or principal see *Tolley's VAT Cases*.

Agents and VAT

[3.2] An agent will usually be involved in at least two separate supplies at any one time.

- The supply of own services to the principal for which the agent charges a fee or commission.
- The supply made between the principal and the third party.

The VAT liability on the supply of agent's services will not necessarily be the same as the liability of the supply between the principal and the third party.

(VAT Notice 700, paras 22.3, 22.4).

Registration

In determining whether an agent is liable to be registered for VAT, turnover includes the value of services to the principal and the value of any supplies which the agent is treated as making through acting in his own name (see under **3.4** below). (VAT Notice 700, para 22.7).

Agents acting in the name of their principals

[3.3] An agent may only take a minor role in a transaction and simply introduce the principal to potential clients or suppliers. Alternatively, the agent may be more closely involved and receive/deliver goods, make/receive payment and possibly hold stocks of goods on behalf of the principal. However, provided that the invoicing for the supply is between the principal and the customer, the only VAT supply made by the agent is the provision of services to the principal. (VAT Notice 700, para 22.5).

Agents acting in their own name (undisclosed agents)

[3.4] An agent may be empowered by a principal to enter into contracts with a third party on behalf of the principal. In such cases, particularly where the principal wishes to remain unnamed or undisclosed, the agent may receive and issue invoices in his own name for the supplies concerned. In such circumstances, although in commercial terms the transaction remains between the principal and third party, for VAT purposes special rules apply as set out below. (VAT Notice 700, para 22.6).

Goods

Where an agent acts in his own name in relation to a supply and either

- goods are imported from outside the EU by a taxable person who supplies them as agent for a non-taxable person, or
- goods are acquired from another EU member state by a non-taxable person and a taxable person acts as agent in relation to the acquisition, and then supplies the goods as agent for that non-taxable person, or
- where neither of the above applies in relation to a supply, goods are supplied through an agent

then the goods *must* be treated, as the case may be, as imported and supplied by the agent, acquired and supplied by the agent or supplied to and by the agent as principal. As a result the agent is responsible for accounting for any VAT due on acquisition and onward sale of the goods. For these purposes, a person who is not resident in the UK and whose place (or principal place) of business is outside the UK may be treated as being a non-taxable person if as a result he will not be required to be registered under *VATA 1994*.

[*VATA 1994, s 47(1)(2)(2A)*].

Non-EU and intra-EU supplies

In order to put the VAT treatment of UK undisclosed agents on the same footing as that for commissionaires elsewhere in the EU, an undisclosed agent who is involved in non-EU or intra-EU supplies is seen as taking a full part in the underlying supply of any goods. There is no separate supply of the agent's own services to his principal and the commission retained is seen as subsumed in the value of the onward underlying supply. This treatment is for VAT purposes only and has no impact on the legal status of agents or the way in which they are treated for the purposes of other taxes or legislation.

> *Example*
>
> A UK undisclosed agent sells goods to final customer for £100. He retains £20 as commission and pays £80 back to his overseas principal. All figures are net of VAT.
>
> If the goods are imported, the VAT value at importation is arrived at in the normal way. If the goods are acquired from a principal in another EU member state, the VAT value at acquisition is £80 based on the value of the invoice raised by the principal to the agent. The agent must account for VAT on the acquisition.
>
> The agent can recover import/acquisition VAT, subject to the normal rules. He then makes an onward supply in his own name to the customer for £100, and accounts for output tax. The commission of £20 is treated as subsumed in the value of the onward supply of the goods and is not treated as a separate supply of own services to the non-UK principal.
>
> Cost incurred in the UK (e.g. warehousing and handling) can be treated as supplied to the agent who can recover the input tax on them (subject to the normal rules).

Domestic supplies

Subject to below, there is an underlying supply between the principal and customer and a separate supply of agent's services to the principal. The agent reclaims input tax and must account for output tax on the supply of the goods but as the nature or value of the supply is unchanged the amount of input and output tax is normally the same. The deemed supplies to and by the agent are simultaneous and he cannot reclaim the input tax on the supply to him in one period but defer the time when he is required to account for output tax to a later period in which he invoices the supply made by him (*Metropolitan Borough of Wirral v C & E Commrs*, QB [1995] STC 597 (TVC 1.81). The VAT liability of the supply of agent's services is not necessarily the same as the liability of the supply of goods.

However, if he wishes, an undisclosed agent may also adopt the VAT treatment set out above for non-EU and intra-EU supplies for his domestic transactions.

Second-hand goods

Where any supplies by an agent acting in his own name are eligible goods under one of the second-hand goods margin schemes, the agent may be able to include the value of services to the principal (i.e. commission, etc.) in calculating the VAT due. All the conditions of the scheme must be satisfied. See **62 SECOND-HAND GOODS** for full details.

Services

From 1 January 2015, where services, other than electronically supplied services and telecommunication services, are supplied through an agent who acts in his own name, HMRC may, if they think fit, treat the supply both as a supply to the agent and as a supply by the agent. From that date, where electronically supplied services or telecommunication services are supplied through an agent, the supply must be treated both as a supply to the agent and as a supply by the agent. [*VATA 1994, s 47(3); FA 2014, s 106*].

Before 1 January 2015, where an agent who acts in his own name arranges a supply of taxable services and both the agent and supplier are registered for VAT, HMRC *may*, if they think fit, treat the supply both as a supply to the agent and by the agent. [*VATA 1994, s 47(3)*]. (VAT Notice 700, para 22.6).

International supplies

In order to put the VAT treatment of UK undisclosed agents on the same footing as that for commissionaires elsewhere in the EU, where an agent is involved in international services the services are treated as supplied to the UK agent as though he was a principal and supplied on by him. The agent's commission is seen as subsumed in the value of the onward supply and he is not regarded as making a separate supply of his own services to the principal. This applies to services being supplied both to and from the UK.

Where the international services are treated as supplied where the supplier belongs, as a UK undisclosed agent is treated as the supplier, the supply takes place in the UK and will be subject to UK VAT. For international services supplied to a relevant business person [*VATA 1994, s 7A(2)(a)*] or to a non-business customer [*VATA 1994, Sch 4A para 16*] which are treated as supplied where the customer belongs (see **66.16 SUPPLY: PLACE OF SUPPLY**), a UK undisclosed agent is treated as receiving the supplies and must therefore account for VAT under the reverse charge. The agent then makes an onward supply in the UK and accounts for output tax in the normal way.

Domestic supplies

The rules for domestic supplies in relation to services are the same as for goods, as described above.

Supplies for travellers

The above arrangements cannot be used for supplies which are for the benefit of travellers (e.g. supplies of accommodation or passenger transport).

(VAT Notice 700, paras 22.6, 24.1, 24.2; Business Brief 9/2000; VAT Information Sheet 3/00).

De Voil Indirect Tax Service. See V3.221, V3.423.

Invoices for supplies made through a selling agent not using a margin scheme

Where an agent is registered for VAT and is acting in his own name

[3.5] The procedure outlined in **3.4** above may be used. Otherwise, if the principal is registered for VAT either the principal must issue a VAT invoice to the agent or the agent can use the self-billing procedure (see **40.6 INVOICES**). The agent must account for output tax on his onward supply to his customer and, if the customer is registered, issue a VAT invoice to him.

Where an agent is acting in the name of his principal

The procedures depend upon whether or not the principal is registered for VAT.

- If the principal is registered for VAT, the principal must issue the invoice made out to the customer. This can be issued direct to the customer or can be passed to the agent for onward transmission. If the agent is VAT registered, he need only account for VAT on services to the principal.
- If the principal is not registered for VAT, no VAT is due on the supply arranged by the agent.

A registered agent must account for output tax on his supply of services to the principal. The agent must also have evidence that he is arranging the supply on behalf of the principal and the supply should be readily distinguishable in his records from supplies on which VAT is charged. The evidence may be a standing agreement between agent and principal or a signed declaration from the principal giving his name and address and confirming that he is not a registered person making a supply in the course of business.

(VAT Notice 700, para 23.1).

Invoices for supplies obtained through a buying agent not using a margin scheme

Where an agent is registered for VAT and is acting in his own name

[3.6] The procedure outlined in **3.4** above may be used. Otherwise, if the supplier is registered for VAT, the supplier must issue a VAT invoice to the agent who may reclaim the VAT as input tax. The agent must account for output tax on his onward supply to the buyer and, if the buyer is registered, issue a VAT invoice to him. The principal (the buyer) should be able to know the price paid by his agent in obtaining the supply.

Where an agent is acting in the name of his principal

The procedures depend upon whether or not the supplier is registered for VAT.

- If the supplier is registered, the supplier should issue the VAT invoice made out to the principal. This can be issued direct to the principal or can be passed to the agent for onward transmission. If the agent is VAT-registered, he need only account for VAT on services to the principal.
- If the supplier is not registered for VAT, no VAT is due on the supply arranged by the agent. A registered agent must account for output tax on his supply of services to the principal.

(VAT Notice 700, para 23.2).

Disbursements

[3.7] Where a supplier incurs incidental costs (e.g. travelling expenses, postage, telephone) in the course of making the supply and charges these items separately on the invoice to the client, such costs must be included in the value when VAT is calculated. See *Rowe & Maw v C & E Commrs*, QB [1975] STC 340 (TVC 62.52) (travelling expenses billed by solicitors to client), *Shuttle-*

worth & Co (VTD 12805) (TVC 62.351) (bank transfer fees re-charged to client) and *National Transit Insurance Co Ltd v C & E Commrs*, QB 1974, [1975] STC 35 (TVC 1.93) (fee for handling insurance claim). However, where amounts are paid to third parties as agent of a client, such payments may be treated as disbursements if all the following conditions are satisfied.

- The agent acted for his client when paying the third party.
- The client actually received and used the goods or services provided by the third party. This condition usually prevents the agent's own travelling expenses, telephone bills, postage, etc. being treated as disbursements for VAT purposes.
- The client was responsible for paying the third party.
- The client authorised the agent to make the payment on his behalf.
- The client knew that the goods or services would be provided by a third party.
- The agent's outlay must be separately itemised when invoicing the client.
- The agent must recover only the exact amount he paid to the third party.
- The goods or services paid for must be clearly additional to the supplies made to the client.

If a payment qualifies as a disbursement, it can be treated in either of the following ways.

- The disbursement can be passed on to the client as a VAT-inclusive amount (if taxable) and excluded when calculating any VAT due on the main supply to the client. The agent cannot reclaim VAT on the supply (since no goods or services have been supplied to him). Unless the VAT invoice for the disbursement is addressed directly to the client, the client is also prevented from reclaiming input tax as he does not hold a valid invoice. Generally, therefore, it is only advantageous to treat a disbursement in this way if no VAT is chargeable on the supply by the third party or the client is not entitled to reclaim the VAT.
  If an agent does treat a payment as a disbursement in this way, he must keep evidence to enable him to show that he was entitled to exclude the payment from the value of his supply to his client. He must also be able to show that he did not reclaim input tax on the supply by the third party.
- The goods or services can be treated as supplied to and by the agent under **3.4** above. The agent can then reclaim the related input tax (subject to the normal rules) and charge VAT on the onward supply if appropriate.

(VAT Notice 700, para 25.1).

A recent decision (*Brabners LLP* [2017] UKFTT 666 (TC), TC06093) may impact the current treatment of certain types of disbursements. Brabners operate as a law firm, offering conveyancing services. As part of their services, Brabners obtain local authority and local land searches that cover planning, environmental and building control. Where requested, Brabners will also prepare a report for clients advising on the content of the searches undertaken.

Brabners can obtain the searches via the post, in person or electronically using Searchflow. Brabners treated the recharge of these costs to the client as a disbursement and no VAT was charged. HMRC disagreed with this treatment, concluding that the information contained in the searches was used by Brabners to provide advice to its clients and therefore the costs formed part of the overall value of the taxable supply made to the clients. Brabners appealed against this decision. The tribunal ruled in favour of HMRC, stating that in order for the costs to be treated as a disbursement, it would be necessary for Brabners to be taking on the role of the client's authorised representative in making payment for the services supplied. When Brabners obtains the searches and produces a report outlining what is contained in those searches these cannot be treated as disbursements and VAT should be charged as they are a cost component of the overall supply of services provided to the client. However the tribunal also arrived at the same conclusion for electronic searches obtained where Brabners did not prepare a report for the client.

It will be interesting to see whether HMRC issues any revised guidance on the VAT treatment of searches in general as a result of this decision. Also, any businesses that currently treat electronic searches as disbursements may wish to consider the impact of this decision.

Disbursements in particular cases

- *Counsel's fees.* A concessionary treatment has been agreed with HMRC for counsel's fees. The agent (usually a solicitor or accountant) may treat the counsel's advice as supplied directly to the client and the settlement of the fees as a disbursement. Counsel's VAT invoice may be amended by adding the name and address of the client to it and inserting 'per' before the agent's own name and address. The fee note from counsel will then be recognised as a valid VAT invoice in the hands of the client. Where the agent considers that the services of counsel, if supplied directly to the client, would be outside the scope of UK VAT, he may certify the counsel's fee note to this effect and pay the counsel only the net of VAT fee. (Tax Faculty of the ICAEW Guidance Notes 15/94, paras 23–26).
- *Debt collectors.* See **3.17** below.
- *MOT tests.* See **48.7**(13) OUTPUT TAX
- *Postal charges.* See **48.7**(19) OUTPUT TAX.
- *Search agencies.* See **3.18** below.

VAT representatives and agents for overseas principals

Direction to appoint by HMRC

[3.8] HMRC may direct a person to appoint a VAT representative (with effect from 15 September 2016, the representative must be UK-established) to act on his behalf for VAT purposes in the UK where that person

(a) is a taxable person or, without being a taxable person, makes taxable supplies or acquires goods in the UK from one or more other EU member states;

(b) is not established, and does not have a 'fixed establishment', in the UK;
(c) is established in a country or territory
- which is neither an EU member state nor part of such a country; and
- with which it appears to HMRC that there is no provision for mutual assistance similar in scope to the assistance provided between the UK and other EU member states under *FA 2011, s 87, Sch 25* (recovery of VAT due in other EU member states, see **32.2 HMRC: POWERS**), *FA 2006, s 173* (international tax enforcement arrangements, see **30.7 HMRC: ADMINISTRATION**) and *Council Regulation (EU)904/2010* (on administrative co-operation and combating fraud in the field of VAT); and

(d) in the case of an individual, does not have his 'usual place of residence' in the UK.

From 7 November 2016, HMRC have the power to either refuse to register a person as a tax representative or to cancel a person's VAT representative registration if they are satisfied that the person is not a 'fit and proper person' to act in that capacity. HMRC consider that a person meeting any of the following criteria will not be considered to be a fit and proper person if the person:

- has been disqualified as a director under Company law;
- has been involved in crime and/or have relevant criminal convictions;
- has had previous requests to act as a tax presentative revoked or refused;
- has personally received a penalty for deliberate wrongdoing;
- has any kind of connection with the business that they intend to represent, or with any personnel within that organisation, or with any fraudulent or non-compliant businesses.

HMRC will also only allow a business to appoint a tax representative who has sufficient funds to meet the principal's debt and will therefore normally expect the VAT representative to have taken out some form of financial protection.

[*SI 2016/989.*]

See **66.13 SUPPLY: PLACE OF SUPPLY** for a consideration of where a business is established, 'fixed establishment' and 'usual place of residence'.

A person is treated as having been directed to appoint a VAT representative if HMRC have served notice of the direction on him or have taken all such other steps as appear to them to be reasonable to bring the direction to his attention.

Voluntary appointment

A person who has not been directed by HMRC to appoint a VAT representative to act on his behalf under the above provisions, but who satisfies the conditions in (*a*), (*b*) and (*d*) above, may with the agreement of HMRC appoint a VAT representative to act on his behalf.

[*VATA 1994, s 48(1)(1ZA)(1A)(1B)(2)(2A)(8)*].

Effect of appointment

[3.9] Subject to below, any person appointed as a VAT representative

- is entitled to act on his principal's behalf for all purposes relating to VAT;
- must ensure (if necessary by acting on his behalf) that his principal complies with, and discharges, all his obligations and liabilities relating to VAT; and
- is jointly and severally liable with his principal for complying with UK VAT law.

A VAT representative is not, by virtue of the above, guilty of any offence committed by his principal unless he has consented to it or connived in its commission, its commission is attributable to any neglect on his part, or the offence is a contravention by the VAT representative of an obligation which, under those provisions, is imposed on both him and his principal.

[*VATA 1994, s 48(3)(5)*].

Failure to appoint a VAT representative

[3.10] Where a person fails to appoint a VAT representative when directed to do so, HMRC may require him to provide such security, or further security, as they think appropriate for the payment of any VAT which is or may become due from him. A person is treated as having been required to provide security if HMRC have served notice of the requirement on him or have taken all such other steps as appear to them to be reasonable for bringing the requirement to his attention. Where any such security has been required and is not lodged, it can be recovered by taking control of goods/distraint on goods (in Scotland through diligence) as if it were VAT due. See **32.4 HMRC: POWERS**. There may also be a liability to a criminal penalty under **53.7 PENALTIES**. [*VATA 1994, s 48(7)(7A)(8), Sch 11 para 5(10); FA 1997, s 53(6); Tribunals, Courts and Enforcement Act 2007, Sch 13 para 118*].

New rules for UK fulfilment houses

[3.11] In the March 2016 Budget, HMRC announced measures to combat evasion of VAT and customs duty by non-EU traders shipping goods to the UK for storage in local 'fulfilment houses' prior to sale via online marketplaces. HMRC calculate that evasion linked to this particular type of business accounts for £1bn–£1.5bn of the VAT gap.

HMRC carried out a consultation until 30 June 2016 on 'fit and proper' standards for the introduction of a registration scheme from 1 April 2018 for fulfilment houses that store and handle goods imported from outside the EU. Secondary legislation is also to be introduced requiring the registered fulfilment house to keep certain records and to carry out due diligence checks on their overseas customers.

Businesses will need to be registered if goods are stored and all of the following conditions apply:

- imported from a non-EU country;
- owned by, or stored on behalf of, a person who is established outside of the EU;

- offered for sale and have not been sold before in the UK.

However, businesses that own the goods stored in the warehouse or whose main business activity is transporting goods that need temporary storage, as part of the provision of the transportation services, are not required to register under this scheme.

Existing fulfilment houses can apply online from 1 April 2018 and the application to register for the scheme must be submitted by 30 June 2018.

If the fulfilment house starts trading on or after 1 April 2018 it will need to apply on or before 30 September 2018.

If the fulfilment house is late submitting its application then HMRC will levy a penalty of £500. This penalty can be increased by £500 for each month that the application is late up to a maximum of £3,000.

If the business is required to register under this scheme then it must be registered by 1 April 2019. If the business fails to register by 1 April 2019, then it will not be allowed to operate as a fulfilment business.

HMRC can impose a £10,000 civil penalty on, or take criminal proceedings against, any business that trades as a fulfilment house without approval after this date.

HMRC will undertake the following checks before granting approval:

- verify the application against information held by HMRC;
- undertake checks to ensure that the partners, directors and other key personnel within the organisation:
  - (i) have not been involved in or connected to significant revenue fraud or non-compliance;
  - (ii) that any relevant criminal convictions are spent;
  - (iii) that they are compliant with HMRC requirements.

Once approved, the business will be placed on the register and be required to ensure that it complies with the record-keeping and verification requirements specified by HMRC (see below).

With effect from 1 April 2019, businesses that are registered under the scheme are required to keep a record of:

- the overseas customer's name and contact details;
- the overseas customer's VAT registration number(s);
- the type and quantities of goods that are stored in the warehouse managed by the fulfilment house;
- the import entry numbers;
- the delivery addresses;
- notices that the business needs to provide to its overseas customer, which explain their tax duty and obligations in the UK.

These records must be held for six years. HMRC can levy a penalty of £500 if the required records are not maintained.

Registered fulfilment houses are also expected to verify the overseas customer's VAT registration numbers and if the fulfilment house has reason to suspect that the overseas customer is not complying with its UK VAT or customs obligations then the fulfilment house needs to:

- work with the overseas customer to help them to become compliant;
- notify HMRC that the customer is not compliant;
- stop working with the overseas customer if HMRC issue a Notice.

HMRC can levy a penalty of between £500–£3,000 if the registered fulfilment house fails to undertake these checks.

These measures are coupled with legislation in *Finance Act 2016* to strengthen the existing rules in *VATA 1994, s 48* that enable HMRC to direct overseas businesses selling goods in the UK to appoint a VAT representative with joint and several liability and/or provide security for the VAT that becomes due. The new measures allow HMRC to inform an online marketplace about non-compliant overseas sellers. If the marketplace takes no action to prevent the fraud, and evasion continues, the marketplace will become jointly and severally liable for the VAT that an overseas business selling goods via the online marketplace fails to account for.

The *Fulfilment Business Regulations 2018* have been published setting out the detailed rules for the operation of the new scheme. Note that these regulations replaced and revoked the *Fulfilment Businesses (Approval Scheme) Regulations 2018* which contained errors.

FA 1994, s 13A(2)(gc) was inserted by *F(No 2)A 2017, s 56(1), (2)* with effect from 1 April 2018. It contains the provisions for reviews and appeals in respect of the civil penalties described above. HMRC have also published Notice FH1 that provides details on how to apply for the scheme.

[*F(No 2)A 2017, ss 48–59, Sch 13*; *SI 2018/326*; *SI 2018/298*].

Notification of appointment and changes

[3.12] Any person appointed a VAT representative of another must notify his appointment to HMRC in the form specified in a notice published by HMRC within 30 days of the appointment first becoming effective and notification must contain the particulars (including the declaration) set out in that notice. Evidence of the appointment must also be sent. The principal being represented must complete the normal VAT registration notifications and both the principal and tax representative must complete a Form VAT 1TR (or Welsh version Form VAT 1TR(W)) authorising HMRC to accept that the representative is acting on the principal's behalf. Providing HMRC are satisfied that the representative is a fit and proper person, they must then register the name of the VAT representative against that of his principal in the register kept for the purposes of *VATA 1994*.

Once appointed, the VAT representative must, within 30 days, notify HMRC in writing of any changes in the name, constitution or ownership of his business or of his ceasing to act as his principal's VAT representative or of any other event which would require a change in the register.

The date of cessation is the earliest of the times when

- HMRC receive notification from the principal of the cessation of the existing tax representative or the appointment of a different tax representative,

- HMRC receive notification of the appointment of a different tax representative or the cessation of the existing tax representative under the above provisions, or
- a tax representative dies, becomes insolvent or becomes incapacitated (which, in the case of a company, includes going into liquidation or receivership or administration)

although if HMRC has received no notification but another person has actually been appointed as VAT representative, HMRC may treat the date of cessation of the existing tax representative as being the date of appointment of that other person.

[*SI 1995/2518, Reg 10*].

Records to be kept

[3.13] Although his principal is established abroad, a VAT representative must keep all the **57 RECORDS** required to be kept under UK law as the principal is making taxable supplies in the UK. The VAT representative must set up and maintain a separate VAT account for each principal represented and keep documents such as VAT invoices to show how the VAT account is built up.

Staff bureaux

[3.14] The bureau will act in one of the following ways.

As a principal

Supplying its own staff to the client. Workers may be employed by the bureau under a contract of service or engaged by the bureau under a contract for services. In either case, they supply their services to the bureau which makes an onward supply as principal to the client. See, for example, *MG Parkinson* (VTD 6017) (TVC 33.3).

The bureau makes one supply of staff which is normally standard-rated. Output tax is due on the full charge made to the client. Where the client asks the bureau to act on its behalf in paying the travelling and subsistence expenses of candidates attending interviews, the bureau may treat these payments as disbursements for VAT purposes under **3.7** above.

The *Conduct of Employment Agencies and Employment Business Regulations 2003* set out rules governing the conduct of employment businesses and the rights of workers using them. Under normal circumstances *any* temporary workers supplied by an employment bureau will have a contractual relationship with the bureau supplying them (either being an employee of the bureau under a contract of service or self-employed and engaged by the agency under a contract for services) and not the client hiring them. In either case, the bureau will be acting as a principal for VAT purposes and VAT will be due on the full amount received from the client, including salary and associated costs in relation to the temporary worker.

As agent for the client

Finding workers who enter into a direct contract with the client. This is an introductory service and not a supply of staff. The bureau must account for VAT on the commission charged to the client. Any payments of a worker's wages by the bureau are made on behalf of the client and may be treated as disbursements by the bureau under **3.7** above.

There have been several Tribunal cases regarding the VAT treatment of staff provided by employment agencies.

In *Reed Employment Ltd* (LON/2004/0130), the First-tier Tribunal held that Reed was providing introductory services and therefore was only required to account for VAT on the commission received.

In *Hays Personnel Services Ltd* (LON/95/2610) (VTD 14882), the First-tier Tribunal held that Hays was acting as a principal and VAT was therefore due on the total consideration received.

In *Adecco UK Ltd* [2017] UKUT 113 (TCC) (TVC 1.19) the Upper Tribunal held that Adecco made a supply of the provision of the temps to the clients in return for the total fees paid by the clients. VAT was therefore due on the total consideration received.

(HMRC Brief 32/11).

De Voil Indirect Tax Service. See V3.221.

As agent for both the client and the worker

Supplying its agency service to both parties. Once it has brought the parties together, it usually withdraws and the continuing contractual relationship is directly between worker and employer. VAT must be accounted for on the bureau's charges made to both parties, although, where this situation occurs, the bureau normally only charges commission to the employer and the supply to the worker is made for no consideration, since it is generally illegal for a bureau to make a charge to the worker.

(VAT Notice 700/34/12, para 5).

Travel agencies

[3.15] How a travel agency accounts for VAT depends upon its relationship with its customers and will normally be demonstrated by commercial documentary evidence (e.g. agreements or contracts). It may

(a) *act as a principal*, i.e. supply travel packages (including transport or accommodation), part of which is bought in from other businesses although part of which may be supplied in-house from own resources;
(b) *act as an undisclosed agent*, i.e. where the ultimate provider of the goods or services (e.g. the travel or accommodation provider) remains undisclosed to the customer; or
(c) act as an intermediary (disclosed agent).

Where (*a*) or (*b*) applies, the travel agency must account for VAT using the tour operators' margin scheme (68). The position where (*c*) applies is considered in the rest of this paragraph.

A travel agency is acting as an intermediary (disclosed agent) if:

- both the travel agency and its principal have agreed that it will act as their intermediary;
- it routinely fully discloses the name of the principal it is acting for (e.g. on all tickets it issues or in its booking terms and conditions); and
- it is not taking any significant commercial risk in relation to the services it is arranging.

The issue regarding whether an agency agreement exists was the subject of the case *HMRC v Secret Hotels2 Ltd* [2014] UKSC 16. In this case, a company (S) operated a website through which it marketed hotel accommodation outside the UK. About 94% of its sales were to travel agents and 6% to holidaymakers. S did not account for VAT on its supplies on the basis that it acted as an agent for the hoteliers. HMRC issued assessments on the basis that S was a travel agent dealing with customers in its own name within the meaning of *Directive 2006/112/EC, Art 306.1(a)*, therefore the supplies were liable to UK VAT. The First-tier Tribunal dismissed S's appeal, holding that it was acting as an independent principal supplying the holiday and therefore S was required to account for VAT under the tour operators' margin scheme. The Upper Tribunal reversed that decision but the Court of Appeal restored it. The Supreme Court allowed S's appeal, holding that it was acting as a disclosed intermediary rather than in its own name and so fell within *Art 306.1(b)*.

See also *Hotels4U.com Ltd v HMRC* [2016] UKFTT 718 (TC), TC05447 (TVC 1.77), where the First-tier Tribunal allowed the appeal in respect of the majority of contracts that had been entered into on the basis that Hotels4U was acting as a disclosed agent and the customer purchased the services directly from the supplier and they were aware that the supplier was providing the services. As a result the supplies were not liable to UK VAT under TOMS.

HMRC are currently trying to obtain a referral to the CJEU on the correct interpretation of 'acting solely as an intermediary' within *Directive 2006/112/EC, Art 306* so it will take some time for this issue to be fully resolved. There are also a number of other ongoing appeals.

(1) Value of supplies

The value of supplies upon which any VAT may be due is the amount of commission due from the principal(s) and fees charged to clients, excluding any VAT itself. It is the travel agency's responsibility to issue invoices for its supplies, although it is common practice in the travel industry for tour operators to use a self-billing system (see **40.6 INVOICES**).

See also (7) and (8) below for supplies by a travel agency to corporate clients.

(2) Place of supply of services

For a detailed consideration of the place of supply of services generally, see **66.12–66.28** supply: place of supply. If the place of supply of the services is outside the UK, the services are outside the scope of UK VAT, although if the place of supply is in another EU member state:

- the travel agency may be liable to register and account for VAT in that country; or
- if the principal is registered for VAT in a different EU member state to the travel agency, the principal may be responsible for accounting for the VAT under the 'reverse charge' procedure. See **39.4 INTERNATIONAL SERVICES.**

(3) Insurance and financial services

If a travel agency makes arrangements for the supply of insurance or makes a charge for exchanging currency or travellers' cheques, the place of supply of services is

- where the customer belongs if the customer belongs outside the EU; or in another EU member state and receives the supply of services for business purposes; and
- where the travel agency belongs in all other cases.

Where the place of supply is in the UK,

- any charges for exchanging currency are exempt under *VATA 1994, Sch 9 Group 5 Item 1* (see **24.8 FINANCIAL SERVICES**); and
- the supply of arranging travel insurance is exempt if supplied
  (a) in isolation of any travel;
  (b) in relation to a supply of travel on which no UK VAT is payable; or
  (c) in relation to a sale of travel services which bears UK VAT provided that the travel agent notifies the traveller, in writing, of the price of the insurance as due under the contract of insurance and any fee related to that insurance charged over and above the premium.

See **37.17 INSURANCE.**

(4) Liability of commission relating to passenger transport services

If a travel agency acts as the *initial* intermediary in arranging zero-rated passenger transport, such as

- scheduled flights,
- journeys from a place within to a place outside the UK and vice versa, and
- most UK transport in vehicles with a carrying capacity of not less than ten people

then its services of arranging the transport are also zero-rated. See below for sub-agents.

See **71.14** to **71.24 TRANSPORT AND FREIGHT** for a more detailed consideration of passenger transport and **71.32 TRANSPORT AND FREIGHT** for services of agents in providing transport generally.

(5) Designated travel services

If a travel agency is acting as an intermediary for a tour operator who is established (or has a fixed establishment) in the UK, then its services are standard-rated.

(6) Sub-agents

If a sub-agent is involved in the making of arrangements for travel services, the place of supply of the services follows the normal rules for supplies by intermediaries. The VAT liability on the supplies for which the sub-agent receives commission follows that of the underlying supply. Where the sub-agent is involved in the provision of zero-rated passenger transport, its commission for those transactions will also be zero-rated. Where it is involved in the provision of a package supplied by a UK tour operator under the tour operators' margin scheme, its commission is standard-rated.

(7) Individual supplies of services to business clients

Where a travel agency

- does not have an agreement or contract with a corporate client to arrange travel services, or
- it sets out what its charges and terms of business will be if the client chooses to use its services,

it will be making individual supplies of services as opposed to a continuous supply of services.

The value of any individual supply to a corporate client is the amount of the fee charged. Where any of the commission received from the travel provider is offset in calculating the fee, the value of the supply is the net fee charged. VAT must be account for on commission received under the normal rules.

'*Bundled fees*'. Where a travel agent arranges more than one service but only charges one inclusive fee (a 'bundled fee') and the services arranged have different VAT liabilities (e.g. standard-rated hotel accommodation and zero-rated flights), the fee must be apportioned according to the values of the underlying supplies.

> *Example 1*
>
> A VAT-exclusive fee of £15 is charged to a client for arranging zero-rated air travel of £412.50 and standard-rated EU hotel accommodation of £137.50 (i.e. 75% and 25% of the total cost of £550.00 respectively).
>
> VAT on the bundled fee is £0.75 (£15 x 25% x 20%).

(8) Continuous supplies of services to business clients

Where a travel agency has a contract or agreement with a corporate client to supply travel services over a period of time and the contract requires the customer to pay from time to time, it is likely that continuous supplies of services are being made. Indicators of a continuous supply are where the travel agency

- carries out periodic reconciliations of fees against services provided (see below);
- is required to have a presence in the client's premises;
- must provide periodic management information to the client under the terms of the contract; or

- is available, and is required to provide a set level of service, during business hours and may have to provide a limited service at other times.

Value and liability of supplies

The value of the travel agent's supplies will depend upon whether the commission received from the travel providers is 'ceded' or 'non-ceded'.

Commission is 'ceded' if, under the terms of the contract with a business client, the legal right to the commission is specifically passed to the client. The definition of ceded commission is not changed if, in practice, the travel agency offsets the amount of the commission against the value of its fees in determining the amount of money to be paid to or by its client.

VAT must be accounted for on commission received under the normal rules. No VAT is due from the business client on the commission passed over. VAT, where appropriate, is due the full value of fees, regardless of whether the travel agency nets it off for cash flow purposes against the commission passed to the client.

Commission is 'non-ceded' if the legal right to it is not passed to the business client by contract. A travel agency may take account of non-ceded commission (e.g. to offset commission received against costs incurred) within a calculation to determine the net amount to be paid by/to the client. This net amount is the value for VAT purposes.

VAT must be accounted for on the commission received under the normal rules. No VAT is due from the business client if the net amount is payable by the travel agency to them. VAT (where appropriate) is due from the travel agency on any net amount of fees charged to the client following the offset of commission.

The travel agency must apportion its fees based on the value of the underlying supplies arranged. (Where foreign exchange is arranged and the travel agency does not know the value of the underlying supply by the financial institution, it can calculate the value as 1% of the total amount exchanged.) It should calculate the percentages of the amount paid by the client according to the different types of underlying supply (excluding any ancillary elements, see (9) below), and apply those percentages to the whole amount charged to the client. Note that the liability of the supply of intermediary services may not be the same as the liability of the underlying supply (e.g. where the client is VAT-registered in the UK, EU hotel accommodation should be allocated as standard-rated, because the travel agency's supply is standard-rated in the UK, even though the accommodation itself is outside the scope of UK VAT).

Example 2

A travel agent has a contract with a corporate client to provide all its travel needs for a quarterly fee of 5% of the total value of supplies arranged. In the quarter to 31 March 2017, it arranges £50,000 of supplies (excluding ancillary services) which it analyses as £25,000 on zero-rated passenger transport, £15,000 on hotel stays in the UK and the EU, £9,500 on hotel stays outside the EU, and £500 on insurance.

Therefore
50% of its supplies are zero-rated
30% are standard-rated
19% are outside the scope of UK VAT
1% is exempt from VAT
The fee due for the quarter is £2,500 (£50,000 × 5%).
VAT due on the fees is
£2,500 × 30% × 20% = £150.00

The above method has been agreed with relevant trade bodies and is recommended for use by travel agencies. Another method can be used but the VAT Helpline (0300 200 3700) should be consulted for HMRC's agreement.

Accounting for VAT

Under the terms of the contract, periodic reconciliations will be made of services against fees. In what follows, '*contract accounting period*' means the time between such reconciliations (generally at least quarterly).

Where interim payments are received, the normal rules for continuous supplies apply, i.e. VAT must be accounted for on the earlier of when a VAT invoice is issued or a payment is received. Therefore, where payments are received within a contract accounting period, the travel agency must account for VAT at the time they are received. The way this is done depends on the type of interim payment received.

- If a payment is received from the customer for every transaction arranged, VAT should be declared on the amount received according to the liability of that individual transaction (e.g. if hotel accommodation within the EU is arranged, VAT should be declared on the full value of the fee).
  At the end of the contract accounting period, the amount of fees payable for the entire period must be totalled (including any final payment due following the reconciliation) and the apportionment calculation carried out as in *Example 2* above. The difference between the total VAT due and that already declared on the individual transaction must be paid to, or reclaimed from, HMRC on the VAT return covering the end of the contract accounting period (or the date the adjustment is finalised, if later (see below). A final VAT invoice or credit note must be issued to the client as appropriate.
  Where a payment in respect of ancillary services (see (9) below) is received during the contract accounting period, an estimate should be made of the VAT due on the payment.

Example 3

Using the figures in *Example 2*, interim fees in the contract accounting period were £1,000 zero-rated (nil VAT), £500 standard-rated (£100.00 VAT) and £25 exempt (nil VAT).

The final payment due is £975 (£2,500 – £1,000 – £500 – £25). VAT due for the period is £150.00 (as in *Example 2*) of which £100.00 has already been accounted for. This leaves a further balance of £50.00 due to HMRC. The invoice for final payment (assuming individual VAT invoices have already been issued for individual transactions) will show net fees of £975, VAT of £50.00 and gross due of £1,025.00.

- Where periodic interim payments are received, VAT should be declared on the amounts received by estimating the amount of the payment that is standard-rated. This can be done by any fair and reasonable method (e.g. estimating the amount of standard-rated sales for the current contract accounting period or using the figures calculated for the last period).
  At the end of the contract accounting period, the same procedure is followed as above.

Example 4

Using the figures in *Example 2*, interim fees in the contract accounting period were £1,700, the VATable proportion of which is estimated at 33%.

The final payment due is £800 (£2,500 – £1,700). VAT due for the period is £150.00 (as in *Example 2*) of which £112.20 (£1,700 x 33% x 20%) has already been accounted for. This leaves a further balance of £37.80 due to HMRC. The invoice for final payment (assuming individual VAT invoices have already been issued for interim payments) will show net fees of £800, VAT of £37.80 and gross due of £837.80.

Where the contract accounting period spans more than one VAT period, it may be necessary to account for VAT on interim payments in an earlier return to that in which the contract period ends. For example, where a contract accounting period is two-monthly (including, say, the two months from 1 June to 31 July) but VAT returns are prepared for calendar quarters, any interim payments received in June must be included on the return to 30 June but the reconciliation carried out at the end of that contract period will be made on the return to 30 September.

The apportionment for a contract accounting period must be carried out within two months of the end of that period. The adjustment must be accounted for on the VAT return during which the apportionment is finalised.

Auctioneers

Agent or principal

[3.16] The main activity of an auctioneer is to act as agent for the vendor of the goods and arrange for a sale to be made to the highest bidder. However, an auctioneer occasionally acts as principal and buys and sells goods in his own right. The key to distinguishing agent and principal activities is that only when title to the goods has passed to the auctioneer does the auctioneer become a principal.

Accounting for VAT

The rules in **3.2–3.7** above apply to auctioneers if they offer goods for sale as agents of the seller. If an auctioneer issues an invoice for goods in his own name, the goods are treated as supplied to the auctioneer by the vendor and by the auctioneer to the buyer. The auctioneer is liable to account for VAT on the supply of the goods (regardless of the VAT status of the vendor) as well as on the commission charged to the seller and, if applicable, on any fee charged to the buyer (the 'buyer's premium'). However, where an auctioneer arranges supplies of second-hand goods, works of art or collectors' items, he may be able to use the special accounting scheme for auctioneers. This scheme allows auctioneers to calculate their VAT on a margin basis. See **62.53 SECOND-HAND GOODS** for further details.

(VAT Notice 700, para 25.2).

See **2.10 ACCOUNTING PERIODS AND RETURNS** where an auctioneer arranges sales of goods in satisfaction of a debt (e.g. under a court order) of a registered person and the goods sold are part of the debtor's business assets. The procedures outlined above for agents must not be followed.

Debt collection agencies

[3.17] The following VAT treatment applies to debt collectors who act as agents.

Court fees

Amounts paid by collectors to solicitors in respect of court fees may be treated as disbursements on behalf of the creditor. Any amount recovered from debtors in respect of such fees and retained by collectors may then be regarded as reimbursement of the amount disbursed and outside the scope of VAT.

Legal fees

Two options are open to collectors in respect of VAT charged by solicitors for their services.

- Collectors may choose not to recover the VAT as input tax and treat the charges as disbursements under **3.7** above. If so, where the agreement with the creditor provides that the collector bears the cost of solicitors'

services but may retain, as reimbursement of his costs, any amounts recovered from the debtor in respect of solicitors' scale charges awarded by the court, such amounts may be treated as outside the scope of VAT.
- Collectors may choose to recover the VAT as input tax, subject to the normal rules, but recharge the legal fees, plus VAT, to the creditor under *VATA 1994, s 47(3)* (see **3.4** above). The scale charges retained represent payment of the fees recharged.

If a debt collector considers that he is acting as a principal, any VAT charged to him by a solicitor is recoverable as input tax, subject to the normal rules. However, any amounts recovered by the collector from the debtor in respect of court fees and/or solicitors' scale charges and retained represents consideration for the collector's supply of services to the creditor. Output tax must be accounted for on all such amounts in the normal way. This treatment does not apply if the collector has received an equitable or legal assignment of the debts, whether in whole or in part. Such an assignment is an exempt supply of services to the collector and the collection of the debts is outside the scope of VAT.

(VAT Notice 700, para 25.6).

Search agencies

[3.18] HMRC regard the fiche or document obtained from a source such as Companies House as a piece of information rather than a tangible object. The recharge of a search fee to the customer for the provision of a fiche or document may be treated as a disbursement under **3.7** above provided

- the information is passed on without analysis or comment; or
- the agency carries out a process on the fiche or document (e.g. conversion of a fiche to hard copy or provision of typewritten extracts) but does not use the data to inform an opinion or report.

Where the agency analyses, comments on, or produces a report on a fiche or document, or otherwise uses the information obtained on a search to make a report, the search fee is not a disbursement but a component part of the cost of providing the service to the customer, and is taxable at the standard rate.

(VAT Notice 700, para 25.5).

'Party plan' and 'direct' selling

[3.19] See **72.23 VALUATION** for supplies of goods made to non-taxable persons for retail sale.

See also *Churchway Crafts Ltd (No 1)* (VTD 782) (TVC 1.102) and *(No 2)* (VTD 1186) (TVC 67.43); *C & E Commrs v Pippa-Dee Parties Ltd*, QB [1981] STC 495 (TVC 67.41) and *Younger* (VTD 1173) (TVC 1.103). For a discussion of the nature of the distributor/dealer relationship, see *P & R Potter v C & E Commrs*, CA 1984, [1985] STC 45 (TVC 1.101) where the relationship was found to be that of principal to principal and VAT payable on the recommended retail price. See also *Betterware Products Ltd v C & E Commrs*, QB [1985] STC 648 (TVC 1.106).

For the VAT position of any incentive gifts to encourage individuals to act as agents for mail order concerns, see **48.5 OUTPUT TAX** and *GUS Merchandise Corporation Ltd v C & E Commrs*, CA [1981] STC 569 (TVC 58.1).

Key points: agents

[3.20] Points to consider are as follows.

- The VAT liability of services provided by an agent can be different to the VAT liability of the goods or services being traded. For example, the services of an estate agent selling new residential properties (zero-rated) for a housebuilder will be standard rated.
- Always review correspondence between an agent and a principal to be clear that a genuine agency arrangement is in place. The main condition is normally that the agent will never take ownership of the goods or services being provided and will receive his fee on a commission basis from the principal. There have been many cases over the years where a business has deemed itself to be acting as an agent arranging supplies for another party but the reality is that it is acting as the principal. The customer perception of what is happening in an arrangement can also be a significant factor.
- Be aware of the special rules that exist for transactions involving undisclosed agents – but remember that output tax and input tax on the goods or services in question must be accounted for in the same VAT period. The principle of an undisclosed agency arrangement does not change the underlying nature of a supply, i.e. the agent is not acting as the principal.
- Remember that zero-rated costs cannot be charged as a separate supply to a principal (e.g. as in the case of an estate agent paying a printer to produce colour brochures to help the sale of a property). The charge to the customer is part of the fee for his services as an agent.
- It is possible that agents will pay out costs on behalf of their clients – these costs can avoid a VAT charge if they are genuine disbursements and follow strict rules laid down by HMRC. One of the important rules is that a profit must not be made on the disbursement being recharged to the client.
- HMRC have introduced more stringent anti-avoidance measures regarding overseas traders who sell goods in the UK via online market places and use UK-based fulfilment houses. Overseas businesses will be required to appoint a 'fit and proper' UK resident tax representative to deal with their UK VAT affairs. The

representative will have joint and several liability for any UK VAT due.

4

Anti-Avoidance

De Voil Indirect Tax Service. See V3.233, V5.213

Introduction to anti-avoidance

[4.1] VAT planning does not, in the main, involve complicated schemes designed solely for the purpose of making a VAT liability disappear. Such schemes may give rise to one-off gains (although a significant number have been found by the courts to be ineffective) but in the longer term may simply complicate the administration and collection of the tax. Indeed, it is the creation and aggressive marketing of artificial schemes for avoiding VAT (in a similar way to what happened in the middle 1970s when artificial schemes to avoid direct tax were in vogue) which is leading to increasingly complex anti-avoidance provisions.

Historically, HMRC have sought, largely unsuccessfully, to apply the direct tax principles of *Furniss v Dawson*, *Ramsay*, *Westmoreland* and *McGuckian* to VAT. Instead, the arguments in the tribunals and courts have revolved mainly around the technical implementation of planning arrangements.

Relevant case law

Redefinition of transactions

However, in *Halifax plc v C & E Commrs (and related appeals), ECJ Case C–255/02*, [2006] STC 919 (TVC 22.61) HMRC chose not to argue the technical points, but instead argued that the transactions involved in the planning arrangements should be disregarded on the grounds that they had been entered into solely for a VAT avoidance motive (which the taxpayer accepted as being the case). The Advocate-General expressed the opinion that a person who relies upon the literal meaning of an EU law provision to claim a right that runs counter to its purposes does not deserve to have that right upheld. In such circumstances, the legal provision at issue must be interpreted, contrary to its literal meaning, as actually not conferring the right. Tax law should not become a sort of legal 'wild-west' in which virtually every sort of opportunistic behaviour has to be tolerated so long as it conforms with a strict formalistic interpretation of the relevant tax provisions. The CJEU held that the application of EU law cannot be extended to cover transactions carried out not in the context of normal commercial operations, but solely for the purpose of wrongfully obtaining advantages provided for by EU law. It was for the national court to determine whether action constituting such an abusive practice had taken place. Any transactions involved in an abusive practice must be redefined so as to re-establish the situation that would have prevailed in the absence of the transactions constituting that abusive practice. This is known as the doctrine of 'abuse of rights' or 'abuse of law'.

In *HMRC v The Atrium Club Ltd*, Ch D [2010] 1493 (TVC 22.76) it was held that the redefinition of transactions under the *Halifax* principles was not designed to create a situation that could be sustained in practice. It was a purely notional device, for the purpose of assessment to tax, that might inevitably involve ignoring the terms of existing contracts.

Prepayment scheme

BUPA Hospitals Ltd v C & E Commrs; Goldsborough Developments Ltd v C & E Commrs, ECJ Case C–419/02, [2006] STC 967 (TVC 22.252) involved a prepayment scheme intended to crystallise an entitlement to input tax before the abolition of zero-rating for drugs and prostheses supplied to hospital in-patients with effect from 1 January 1998. The Advocate-General expressed the opinion that what is now *Directive 2006/112/EC, Art 65* (previously *EC Sixth Directive, Art 10(2)*) referred to situations where a payment was to be made on account before the goods were delivered or the services performed. Properly construed, this required that those goods or services must be specifically identified when the payment on account took place. A payment on account for goods referred to in general terms in a list, from which the buyer could choose in the future one or more items (or none at all) on the basis of an agreement from which the buyer was able to unilaterally resile at any time and recover the unused balance of the prepayment made, did not constitute a payment on account within the meaning of what is now *Directive 2006/112/EC, Art 65* (previously *EC Sixth Directive, Art 10(2)*). The CJEU agreed.

Carousel missing trader fraud

In *Optigen Ltd (and related appeals), ECJ Case C–354/03,* [2006] STC 419 (TVC 22.124) HMRC rejected claims for input tax on the basis that purchases formed part of a 'carousel missing trader fraud', designed to obtain a substantial repayment of sums which had never been paid as output tax. The tribunal dismissed the companies' appeals, observing that 'a circular series of transactions comprising the carousel fraud where the goods enter and leave the UK at the same price certainly does not look like an economic transaction'. On appeal, the Ch D directed that the case should be referred to the CJEU for a ruling on the interpretation of an 'economic activity' in what is now *Directive 2006/112/EC, Art 9* (previously *EC Sixth Directive, Art 4*). The Advocate-General observed that, where an activity falls within the scope of the *Directive*, that does not mean that a country loses its power to take action against it. In fact, what is now *Directive 2006/112/EC, Art 205* (previously *EC Sixth Directive, Art 21*) expressly gives countries the opportunity to introduce joint and several fiscal liability (which the UK has done). But the fact that transactions form part of a circular supply chain in which a trader misappropriates amounts paid to it as VAT, instead of accounting for them to the VAT authorities, does not mean that the transactions cease to constitute an economic activity under what is now *Directive 2006/112/EC, Art 9(1)* (previously *EC Sixth Directive, Art 4(2)*). The CJEU agreed. The principle of fiscal neutrality prevents there being any general distinction between lawful and unlawful transactions. Consequently, the mere fact that conduct amounts to an offence is not sufficient to justify exemption from VAT. Transactions such as those at issue, which are not themselves vitiated by VAT fraud, constitute supplies of goods or services effected by a taxable person acting as such. They are economic activities (if otherwise meeting the criteria), regardless of the intention of another trader involved in the same chain of supply and/or the possible fraudulent nature of another transaction in the chain, of which that taxable person had no knowledge and no means of knowledge. The right of the taxable person to deduct input VAT is not affected.

The CJEU reconfirmed the right of recovery of input tax in such a situation in *Kittel v Belgian State, ECJ Case C–439/04,* [2008] STC 1537 (TVC 22.475). It held that where a recipient of a supply of goods was a taxable person who did not and could not have known that the transaction concerned was connected with a fraud committed by the seller, the right to deduct input tax under what is now *Directive 2006/112/EC* precludes a rule of national law under which the fact that the contract of sale is void (by reason of a civil law provision which renders that contract incurably void as contrary to public policy for unlawful basis of the contract attributable to the seller) means that the taxable person loses the right to deduct the VAT he has paid. It is irrelevant in this respect whether the fact that the contract is void is due to fraudulent evasion of value added tax or to other fraud. By contrast, where it is ascertained, having regard to objective factors, that the supply is to a taxable person who knew or should have known that, by his purchase, he was participating in a transaction connected with fraudulent evasion of VAT, it is open to the national court to refuse that taxable person entitlement to the right to deduct.

In *Mobilx Ltd, Calltell Telecom Ltd and Blue Sphere Global Ltd*, CA [2010] STC 1436 (TVC 36.136, 36.122 and 36.97) the Court of Appeal held that in deciding whether a trader ought to have known that he was participating in transactions connected with fraudulent evasion of VAT, the ultimate question was not whether the trader exercised due diligence, but rather whether he should have known that the only reasonable explanation for the circumstances in which his transaction took place was that it was connected to fraudulent evasion of VAT.

Abuse of rights

In *Blackqueen Ltd* (VTD 17680) (TVC 22.68), a scheme was devised (which would no longer be effective following the insertion of *VATA 1994, Sch 3A* by *FA 2000, s 136*) to make use of the provisions of the *EC Eighth Directive* for the refund of UK VAT to taxable persons established elsewhere in the EU. The tribunal held that the relevant transactions did not constitute 'supplies' for the purposes of VAT, since 'the series of transactions entered into by the group was wholly alien to the provisions of what is now Directive 2006/112/EC'. Furthermore, the applications had been an 'abuse of rights', applying the decision in *Emsland-Stärke GmbH v Hauptzollamt Hamburg-Jonas, ECJ Case C–110/99*, [2001] All ER (D) 34 (Jan) (TVC 22.60).

The tribunal allowed the companies' appeals in *RBS Property Developments; Royal Bank of Scotland Group plc (No 5)* (VTD 17789) (TVC 22.71). HMRC rejected a claim for input tax by two associated companies (which were not in the same VAT group) on the basis that the transactions were carried out for tax avoidance purposes and, applying *Halifax*, did not constitute supplies for VAT purposes. The tribunal held that although the series of transactions had a substantial element of tax mitigation, they were not *solely* directed to tax avoidance. As there were real and understandable business purposes for structuring the transactions, it could not be said that they were artificial. A taxpayer was entitled to so construct his activities as to obtain favourable tax consequences. The transactions were not an 'abuse of rights' as there was nothing improper, illegal or artificial about the transactions in question so the principles in *Emsland-Stärke GmbH v Hauptzollamt Hamburg-Jonas* above did not apply.

In *HMRC v Weald Leasing Ltd, ECJ Case C–103/09*, [2011] STC 596 (TVC 22.62), W purchased some assets, which it leased to another company (S), which in turn leased them to two companies (CM and CA) which were associated with W but were part of a separate VAT group making exempt supplies of insurance. W reclaimed input tax on the purchase of the assets. HMRC formed the opinion that the transactions were an 'abuse' but the tribunal held that a trader was not precluded from leasing an asset to be used for exempt activities, thus spreading the burden of irrecoverable input tax. The Ch D upheld the tribunal decision. The CA referred the case to the CJEU. The CJEU ruled that a tax advantage accruing from an undertaking's recourse to asset leasing transactions, such as those at issue in the main proceedings, instead of the outright purchase of those assets did not contravene EU law, provided that the contractual terms of those transactions, particularly those concerned with setting the level of rentals, corresponded to arm's length terms; and the involvement of an intermediate third party company in those transactions did not preclude the application of those provisions, which was a matter for the national court to determine. The fact that the undertaking did not engage in leasing transactions in the context of its normal commercial operations was irrelevant in that regard.

See also *Ministero dell'Economia e delle Finanze v Part Service Srl, ECJ Case C–425/06*, [2008] STC 3132 (TVC 22.63) which also concerned leasing transactions. In that case, the CJEU held that there *can* be a finding of an abusive practice when the accrual of a tax advantage constitutes the principal aim of the transaction at issue and that, when a transaction involves the supply of a number of services, the question arises whether it should be considered to be a single transaction or several individual and independent supplies requiring separate assessment. It was for the national court to decide whether the evidence put before it disclosed the characteristics of a single transaction.

In *Newey (t/a Ocean Finance)* (TC00487), a financial adviser (N), who was registered for VAT, was the controlling shareholder of a Jersey company (AC), which provided loan broking services in the UK. HMRC assessed N on the basis that he should be treated as supplying the loan broking services, and was liable to a reverse charge on advertising services supplied by another Jersey company (W). The tribunal found that N had established the loan broking operation in Jersey rather than the UK in order to avoid the irrecoverable VAT on advertising costs. However this finding did not entitle HMRC to treat N, rather than AC, as the supplier of the loan broking services or as the recipient of the advertising services. The transactions did not constitute an abuse. It was not permissible simply to compare the current structure with what could have been done or what had been done in the past, and to conclude that, if the current structure is more favourable it is therefore contrary to the purposes of the VAT legislation. The contractual terms could be disregarded if it became apparent that they did not reflect economic and commercial reality, but constituted a wholly artificial arrangement that was set up with the sole aim of obtaining a tax advantage (a question for the national court to decide) (*ECJ Case C–653/11, 20 June 2013 unreported*) (TVC 22.80). Following the CJEU ruling the Upper Tribunal upheld the First-tier Tribunal decision that the transactions did not constitute an abuse ([2015] UKUT 300 (TCC) (TVC 22.80)). HMRC have been granted permission to appeal to the Court of Appeal.

In *RBS Deutschland Holdings GmbH (No 4), ECJ Case C–277/09; 22 December 2010 unreported* (TVC 22.482), a Scottish bank had a German subsidiary company (D), which was registered for UK VAT as a 'non-established taxable person'. D purchased cars in the UK, reclaimed input tax on them, and leased them to UK customers. Although the cars were situated in the UK, D treated their supply under UK VAT law as being a supply of services which took place in Germany, where D had its business establishment. The German authorities did not charge VAT on the basis that the lease of the cars was a supply of goods made in the UK. Consequently D did not account for output tax in either Germany or the UK. In 2003 Customs issued a ruling that D was not entitled to reclaim input tax on its purchase of the cars, on the basis that the fact that no tax was levied takes the rentals out of the VAT system. The tribunal allowed D's appeal, but the CS referred the case to the CJEU. The CJEU ruled that the principle of prohibiting abusive practices did not preclude the right to deduct VAT where a company established in one EU member state elected to have its subsidiary, established in another EU member state, carry out transactions for the leasing of goods to a third company established in the first EU member state, in order to avoid VAT payable on those transactions, the transactions having been categorised in the first EU member state as supplies of rental services carried out in the second country, and in that second country as supplies of goods carried out in the first country.

In *HMRC v Pendragon plc and Ors* [2015] UKSC 37 (TVC 22.75) the Supreme Court decided that a scheme used by members of a group of companies involved in the sale of cars was an abuse of law. The object of the scheme was to enable the Pendragon Group to recover input tax paid on the price of new cars acquired as demonstrators from manufacturers, while avoiding the payment of output tax on the price at which the cars were ultimately sold to consumers. The effect of the scheme was to enable the Pendragon Group to sell ex-demonstrator cars as if they were second-hand cars under the margin scheme. See **62.4 SECOND-HAND GOODS**. The result was that no net charge to VAT was ever suffered, except on the small or non-existent profits realised on the resale. The Supreme Court decided that the scheme was contrary to EU policy underlying the margin scheme. The economic substance of the scheme was that it was a sale and leaseback but it had two special features, neither of which, the Supreme Court decided, had any commercial rationale other than the achievement of a tax advantage. The Supreme Court decided that the transactions should be redefined for VAT purposes so the taxpayer was required to account for output tax on the full amount of the resale price of cars to consumers.

Tackling avoidance schemes

There have been a number of results of the proliferation of avoidance schemes, including:

- HMRC have set up special units to monitor tax avoidance and have indicated that they intend to take a much more robust line in dealing with such artificial arrangements.
- The use of certain avoidance schemes and arrangements has to be notified to HMRC (see **4.2** *et seq* below).
- The introduction of specific anti-avoidance rules (see **4.14** below).

Yacht chartering or leasing activities

Following the decisions in *Halifax* and *Part Service Srl* above, HMRC have listed the following features as possibly indicating an abusive structure where pleasure craft are chartered or leased.

- the main user of a pleasure craft is the ultimate owner of the chartering or leasing entity;
- the main user of a pleasure craft funded the purchase of the vessel (directly or indirectly);
- the person who funded the purchase of a pleasure craft (directly or indirectly) uses the vessel for prolonged periods in the peak chartering season;

- the chartering of a pleasure craft to third parties would not, alone, be of sufficient continuity and substance to comprise an economic activity;
- the chartering or leasing entity shows significant ongoing losses in its financial statements;
- charter fees or lease instalments due from the main user of a pleasure craft are paper transactions only (e.g. being offset against loans);
- charter fees or lease instalments are below open market value; or
- the terms of a lease differ significantly from normal commercial practice (e.g. the duration of the lease is unusually long). (HMRC Brief 56/09).

Disclosure of VAT avoidance schemes

[4.2] Taxpayers who are party to certain VAT avoidance schemes must disclose their use to HMRC. The measures are designed to provide information to HMRC about the take-up of avoidance schemes of which they are already aware and early notice of new, potentially damaging, schemes.

Rulings

HMRC are normally prepared to give a ruling on how transactions should be treated for VAT. See **30.5 HMRC: ADMINISTRATION**. However, they will not approve tax planning arrangements and will refuse to give rulings where they suspect that the transactions are part of a tax avoidance scheme.

New rules effective from 1 January 2018

HMRC announced in Autumn Statement 2016, following their consultation, that legislation was to be introduced in *Finance Bill 2017*, intended to strengthen the disclosure regime in respect of indirect taxes. The provisions make promoters primarily responsible for disclosing schemes to HMRC.

The disclosure regime has been extended to cover all indirect taxes, as only VAT was included in the previous disclosure regime (see below). The revised scheme came into effect from 1 January 2018 and affects anyone who promotes/uses an indirect tax avoidance scheme from this date.

The anti-avoidance regulations are not intended to capture arrangements that were already in place before 1 January 2018 or are already well known. The following have been excluded from disclosure under the new rules:

- arrangements where a promoter has made the proposal for those arrangements available to another person before 1 January 2018;
- arrangements where a promoter made the proposal available for implementation by another person before 1 January 2018; and
- arrangements where a promoter becomes aware of any transactions which are part of those arrangements before 1 January 2018.

The new anti-avoidance provisions are called the Disclosure of tax avoidance schemes for VAT and other indirect taxes (DASVOIT). DASVOIT applies to notifiable arrangements or notifiable proposals in respect of all indirect taxes. DASVOIT covers both arrangements that have been implemented and those that have been proposed but not yet implemented.

Any arrangements or proposals for arrangements are notifiable and must be disclosed to HMRC under these provisions where:

- the arrangement enables, or might be expected to enable, any person to obtain an indirect tax advantage;
- the indirect tax advantage is, or might be expected to be, the main benefit or one of the main benefits of using the arrangement;
- the arrangement falls within the description of any 'hallmarks' prescribed in the *Notifiable Arrangements Regulations* (see 'Notifiable arrangements' below).

A person will be treated as a promoter in relation to a *notifiable proposal* where in the course of a relevant business (i.e. a tax services business or a bank/securities house), the person:

- is, to any extent, responsible for the design of the proposed arrangement;
- makes a firm approach to another person with a view to make proposed arrangements available for implementation by that person or others;
- makes proposed arrangements available for implementation by others.

A person will be treated as a promoter in respect of a *notifiable arrangement*, if in the course of a relevant business, he:

- is a promoter in relation to a notifiable proposal which is implemented;
- is, to any extent, responsible for the design, organisation or management of the arrangements.

UK and non-UK businesses are required to comply with the DASVOIT disclosure requirements. Employees of a promoter are not generally deemed to be promoters for the purposes of DASVOIT unless the promoter is non-resident and the UK employee will be treated as the promoter.

These terms are explained below.

(1) Designing the arrangement

The scheme designer will be treated as the promoter of the arrangement unless that person does not make the arrangement available for implementation by the user or organises/manages the scheme (see (5) below) and one of the following tests are satisfied:

- *The benign test* – this applies where a person providing indirect tax advice is not responsible for the design or any element of the proposal/arrangement including the way it is structured. The benign advice provided must not include any advice which is intended to highlight opportunities to exploit the relevant provisions.
- *Non-adviser test* – this test applies where a person involved in the design of the notifiable arrangement/proposal does not provide any tax advice. This test does not apply to banks/securities houses. HMRC have provided the following examples:
  - (a) A promoter consults a firm of lawyers for advice relating to the scheme. The lawyers are not promoters as they do not provide tax advice in respect of that arrangement.

(b) A promoter requests that a solicitor draws up a contract to support transactions used in the arrangement. The solicitor is not a promoter providing no tax advice is given during the course of carrying out his duties.

- *Ignorance test* – this test applies where the person could not have reasonably been expected to have either:
  (a) sufficient information that would enable him to know whether the arrangement/proposal was notifiable;
  (b) sufficient information that would enable him to notify HMRC of the arrangement/proposal.

This test will be applied where the person has insufficient knowledge of the overall arrangement and therefore does not know if the benign or non-adviser tests above are applicable.

(VAT Notice 799, para 3.4).

(2) Making the scheme available

It is necessary to identify who makes the notifiable proposal or arrangement available for implementation by others, as this person is treated as the promoter. HMRC state that the person makes a proposal or arrangement available for implementation where:

- the arrangement has been fully designed;
- the arrangement is capable of being implemented in practice;
- the person communicates information about the proposal or arrangement to others suggesting that they enter into transactions that form part of the arrangements.

Normally, HMRC will not consider that an intermediary between the promoter and the potential user of the scheme is a promoter. However, this person could be viewed as an 'introducer' (see below).

(VAT Notice 799, para 3.5).

(3) The person who makes a firm approach to another person with a view to making proposed arrangements for implementation by that person or others

HMRC have devised three tests that need to be used to determine whether the person meets this part of the definition of a promoter.

Test 1 – the person (P) makes marketing contact with the potential client (C)

P will be treated as making marketing contact with C where:

- P communicates information about the proposed arrangements to C;
- the communication is made with a view to C or any other person entering into transactions forming part of the proposed arrangements;
- the information communicated includes an explanation of the tax advantage that might be expected to be obtained from the proposed arrangements.

For this test to be met, it will be necessary for P to communicate information to C that includes an explanation regarding how the arrangement will operate. If the person only provides an introduction, then they are not likely to be regarded as a promoter but as an introducer (see (4) below).

Test 2 – the proposed arrangements are substantially designed

The notifiable arrangement will be deemed to be substantially designed providing the nature of the transactions that will form part of the arrangement have been sufficiently developed and that C would be able to enter into the transaction that has been developed without any substantial changes needing to be made to the design.

Test 3 – does P make, or intend to make the proposed arrangements available for implementation by a client or another person

This test would be satisfied, if the person who makes the marketing contact does so with a view to C purchasing the notifiable arrangement.

(VAT Notice 799, para 3.6).

(4) Introducer

HMRC consider that an introducer is a person who assists with marketing the notifiable proposal/arrangement on behalf of the promoter, but the person's role does not extend to that of a promoter. *F(No 2)A 2017, Sch 17, para 9* describes an introducer as a person 'who makes marketing contract'.

(5) Organisers and managers

If a person organises or manages a notifiable arrangement in the course of a relevant business, he will be treated as a promoter, regardless of whether the person designed or made the arrangements available for implementation. This will still be the case, even if the person was not connected to the person who designed or marketed the arrangements or similar arrangements that are available.

(VAT Notice 799, para 3.7).

(6) Corporate groups

If a group company provides tax services to other group companies within the same group, it will not be regarded as a promoter. Group companies that use notifiable arrangements will need to use the in-house disclosure policy outlined below.

(VAT Notice 799, para 3.8).

Notifiable arrangements

HMRC have devised five tests that must be used to determine whether the proposal or arrangement must be notified.

Test 1 – are there arrangements that enable an indirect tax advantage to be obtained?

HMRC describe a tax advantage for VAT as:

> 'A person (P) obtains a tax advantage for VAT if:
>
> (a) in any prescribed accounting period, the amount by which the output tax accounted for by P exceeds the input tax deducted by P and is less than it would otherwise be,

(b) P obtains a VAT credit when P would otherwise not do so, or obtains a larger credit or obtains a credit earlier than would otherwise be the case,
(c) in a case where P recovers input tax as a recipient of a supply before the supplier accounts for the output tax, the period between the time when the input tax is recovered and the time when the output tax is accounted for is greater than would otherwise be the case,
(d) in any prescribed accounting period, the amount of P's non-deductible VAT is less than it would otherwise be,
(e) P avoids an obligation to account for VAT, or
(f) P is not a taxable person and P's non-refundable VAT is less than it would otherwise be'.

(VAT Notice 799, para 5.1).

A tax advantage for other indirect taxes is described as:

(a) relief or increased relief from tax,
(b) repayment or increased repayment of tax,
(c) avoidance or reduction of a charge to tax, an assessment of tax or a liability to pay tax,
(d) avoidance of a possible assessment to tax or liability to pay tax,
(e) deferral of a payment of tax or advancement of a repayment of tax, or
(f) avoidance of an obligation to deduct or account for tax.

(Notice 799, para 6.1).

Test 2 – is the tax advantage the main benefit of the arrangement(s)?

Obtaining a tax advantage must be one of the main benefits of using the arrangement. It must be a significant or important element of the overall benefit obtained by the user of the arrangement. HMRC guidance states that the following general points can be made regarding whether a tax advantage is a main benefit:

- those who plan arrangements fully understand the tax advantage such arrangements are intended to achieve; therefore, it will be obvious (with or without a detailed explanation) to any potential client the relationship between the tax advantage and any other financial benefits of the product they may be involved in;
- the test is objective and considers the arrangements, or its features, in terms of the value of the expected tax advantage compared to the value of any other benefits likely to be enjoyed;
- avoidance can involve overlaying on, or inserting into, an underlying genuine commercial transaction with certain commercially unnecessary features whose aims are primarily that of acquiring a tax advantage – those features need to be assessed individually as to whether a tax advantage is a main benefit.

HMRC guidance does not provide any significant detail on how this test will work, however, it does state that the question that needs to be asked is 'does the outcome appear to provide a significant tax advantage which is not simply either an incidental or minor benefit from a commercial arrangement which happens to provide a better tax outcome for the business?'.

Test 3 – is there a promoter of the arrangements?

This test is used to identify which arrangements involve a promoter and which arrangements are designed in-house for use by the business devising the arrangement. HMRC consider that an arrangement has been promoted if the UK user is required to disclose the arrangement because the promoter is either resident outside of the UK or a UK lawyer is prevented from disclosing the arrangement under legal professional privilege.

Test 4 – the hallmarks for VAT and other indirect taxes where there is a promoter

If tests 1 and 2 above are met together with one of the relevant hallmarks (see below), then it will be a notifiable proposal/arrangement.

Test 5 – the hallmarks for in-house arrangements

If tests 1 and 2 above are met together with one of the hallmarks for in-house VAT arrangements, then it will be a notifiable proposal/arrangement.

(VAT Notice 799, paras 4 and 5).

Hallmarks

The following table summarises which hallmarks are applicable depending on the tax involved and whether there is a promoter involved. Further information on each hallmark is provided below.

VAT arrangements where there is a promoter	*In-house VAT arrangements*	*Other indirect tax arrangements where there is a promoter*	*Other in-house indirect tax arrangements*
Hallmark 1(a) Hallmark 1(b) Hallmark 3 Hallmark 4 Hallmark 5 Hallmark 6 Hallmark 7 Hallmark 8	Hallmark 2 Hallmark 3 Hallmark 5 Hallmark 6 Hallmark 7 Hallmark 8	Hallmark 1(a) Hallmark 1(b) Hallmark 3 Hallmark 4	Hallmark 2

Hallmark 1(a) – confidentiality from other promoters

According to HMRC, this test requires the person with the prima facie duty to disclose (see below) the arrangement to HMRC to ask the following hypothetical question:

> 'might it reasonably be expected that any promoter of the arrangements would wish the way in which any element of those arrangements (including the way in which they are structured) gives rise to and secures, or might secure, the expected tax advantage to be kept confidential from any other promoter at any time following the material date?'

[*SI 2017/1216, Reg 9*]. (VAT Notice 799, para 7.2.1).

Hallmark 1(b) – confidentiality from HMRC

The test that needs to be met is whether the promoter would prefer to keep the arrangement or elements of that arrangement confidential from HMRC. According to HMRC, the person with the prima facie obligation to disclose will need to ask themselves the following hypothetical question:

> 'Might it reasonably be expected that the promoter of the arrangements would wish the way in which any element of those arrangements (including the way in which they are structured) gives rise to and secures, or might secure, the expected tax advantage to be kept confidential from HMRC at any time following the material date?'
>
> 'Is a reason for doing so to facilitate the repeated or continued use of that element, or substantially the same element, in the future?'

HMRC state that in answering these questions, the promoter is only expected to use the knowledge and information that he currently holds.

HMRC also state that this hallmark is satisfied if the promoter does not provide or discourages the user from retaining any promotional material, written professional advice, data that the user would normally expect to retain when receiving professional advice.

If a promoter is involved but the user has the duty to disclose (see below) then the user must ask themselves the following hypothetical question:

> 'Do I wish to keep confidential from HMRC the way any element of the arrangements (including the way they are structured) gives rise to and secures, or might secure, the expected tax advantage, at any time following the material date?'

HMRC stress that it is not necessary for there to be an explicit confidentiality agreement between the parties for this test to be met.

[*SI 2017/1216, Reg* 9]. (VAT Notice 799, para 7.2.2).

Hallmark 2 – confidentiality from HMRC

This hallmark relates to in-house arrangements and covers all indirect taxes. It only affects a person who is a small or medium-sized enterprise (SME). A business is regarded as an SME if its turnover is less than £50m and it has less than 250 employees during the relevant period (i.e. the accounting period covering the indirect taxes that are subject to the arrangement or 12-month period ending on the day before the arrangement was implemented, where there is no accounting period). The turnover and employees of any associated business or any corporate body that could form a VAT group with the SME in question must also be included to determine whether the business has exceeded the threshold outlined above.

The test for this hallmark requires the person to consider whether a user or hypothetical user would reasonably be expected to keep the arrangements confidential from HMRC. If the in-house user would want to keep any element of the arrangement confidential then this test has been met. If the in-house user has no desire to keep it confidential from HMRC then the person is expected to ascertain whether another hypothetical user would want it kept confidential from HMRC and if so, then this test is met.

HMRC state that the test for a person using an in-house arrangement, having entered into a transaction forming part of the arrangement, is to ask the following questions at any point after the material date:

- Do I wish to keep this confidential from HMRC?
- Would another user wish to keep this confidential from HMRC?
- Do I or would another user wish to keep any elements of the arrangements (including the way they are structured) that give rise to and secure the expected tax advantage confidential from HMRC?
- Is the reason for wanting to keep it confidential from HRMC to facilitate the repeated or continued use of that element going forward?
- Reduce the risk that HMRC might start to investigate the person's tax affairs?
- Prevent HMRC from denying a tax claim, etc?

HMRC will apply the same criteria as hallmark 1(b) to determine whether this hallmark has been met.

[*SI 2017/1216, Reg 11*]. (VAT Notice 799, para 7.3.2).

Hallmark 3 – premium fee

This test applies to all indirect taxes. It applies to both promoter and in-house arrangements. It is not necessary for the premium fee to have been paid for this test to be met. The term fee includes amounts that are paid either directly or indirectly to the promoter.

This test considers whether in the absence of DASVOIT, a premium fee would be payable by the user to the promoter or another person related to the implementation of the arrangement.

HMRC state that a premium fee is a fee that is:

- reasonably expected to be obtained from a person experienced in receiving services of the type provided by the promoter or another person;
- significantly attributable to the tax advantage obtained, or which may be obtained, by any part of the arrangement; and
- to some extent contingent on the tax advantage obtained.

When applying this test, the person will need to consider whether the fee would, to a significant extent, be attributable to or contingent upon the expected tax advantage that would be obtained by the user of the arrangements. The premium fee must also, to a certain extent, be contingent upon the tax advantage being obtained because the tax analysis that underpinned the arrangement was correct.

[*SI 2017/1216, Reg 12*]. (VAT Notice 799, paras 7.4.2, 7.4.3).

Hallmark 4 – standardised tax products

This test applies to all indirect taxes.

The fundamental characteristic of a tax avoidance arrangement is normally the fact that it can easily be replicated for use by several different users of the arrangement. The user will purchase a prepared tax product that requires little or no modification to meet that business's requirements. Adopting the scheme should not require the provision of any significant professional advice.

This hallmark is met when all the tests outlined below are satisfied. Note that tests 2 and 3 must be considered with reference to how they might be applied by a hypothetical 'informed observer'. These tests require the person with the duty to disclose to consider whether an independent informed observer, who has reviewed all the arrangements and taken all relevant facts into consideration, could reasonably be expected to conclude that all the hallmark 4 tests are met.

- *Are the arrangements made generally available?* – the types of arrangements that could be included within the scope of this hallmark can vary. The promoter could engage in a proactive marketing campaign or aggressive marketing strategy or they could simply react to an enquiry made by a client. The test is not based on why or how the arrangement was promoted but on how the arrangement is made available to the users. The person will need to determine whether it is a standardised tax product or a bespoke arrangement.
- *Are the arrangements standardised?* – the arrangement must be standardised or substantially standardised using documentation that the client can use to implement the arrangement. The substance of the documentation should not require any substantial tailoring for the user to implement the arrangement. There must be standardised agreements, written understandings and contracts at the minimum. Documentation that requires a minimal amount of amendment will be viewed as a standardised product.
- *Are the arrangements a tax product?* – the following two tests should be used to determine whether the arrangement is a tax product.
  - (a) The main purpose of the arrangements is to enable the person to obtain a tax advantage.
  - (b) It is unlikely that a person should enter into the arrangements if they were not going to obtain a tax advantage.

[*SI 2017/1216, Reg 13*]. (VAT Notice 799, para 7.5).

Hallmark 5 – retail supplies – value shifting

This hallmark applies to all indirect taxes. The tests for this hallmark are designed to identify arrangements that split a supply made to a retail customer, to enable the supplier to benefit from differing VAT treatments for each supply. Under the arrangement, the supplier agrees to supply goods/services to a retail customer (supply 1) and the same business or an associated business agrees to supply other goods/services to the same customer.

If condition 1 or 2 below is met in addition to condition 3 then this is a notifiable arrangement as this hallmark is met.

- **Condition 1.** This deals with arrangements where a supply that would normally be treated as a single taxable supply that is liable to VAT at the standard or reduced rate is treated as two separate supplies to enable one of the supplies to be taxed at either the reduced rate (for standard-rated supplies), zero-rate or exempt from VAT.
  HMRC state that this condition is deemed to be satisfied where:

- if supply 1 and supply 2 were part of a single supply to the retail customer, that supply would be liable to VAT at the standard or reduced rate; and
- supply 1 or 2, or both are:
  (a) taxed at the reduced rate of VAT;
  (b) a zero-rated supply;
  (c) an exempt supply (except supplies liable to the higher rate of IPT).

  (VAT Notice 799, para 7.6.4).
- **Condition 2.** This condition deals with arrangements where a supply that would normally be treated as a single exempt supply is split into two separate supplies to enable one of the supplies to be treated as a taxable supply in order for some input tax to be recoverable.
  HMRC consider that this test is satisfied where:
  (a) were supply 1 and supply 2 made as a single supply (or part of a single supply) to the retail customer, that single supply would be exempt from VAT; and
  (b) supply 1 or 2, or both, are:
    (i) taxable at the standard or reduced rate;
    (ii) a zero-rated supply.

  (VAT Notice 799, para 7.6.5).
- **Condition 3.** HMRC consider that this test is met where it would be 'reasonable to conclude' that at least two of the following are applicable. When considering the term 'reasonable to conclude', HMRC expect the person to consider whether it would expect an independent informed observer who has reviewed the arrangements and documentation to conclude that at least two of the statements below are applicable.
  If A is responsible for supply 1 to retail customer and either A or another supplier, B, makes the supply 2 to the retail customer and:
  (a) C would not agree to receive supply 1 without also receiving supply 2;
  (b) if supply 2 is made by B to C and B makes the supply under an agreement with A;
  (c) supply 1 and supply 2 would be made as a single supply or part of a single supply to C if the parties were not attempting to obtain a tax advantage by making these supplies separately to C;
  (d) the business model of A or B assumes that:
    (i) only A will make supply 1 to C;
    (ii) only A or B will make supply 2 to C;
    (iii) the agreements to make supply 1 and supply 2 will be entered into with C at or about the same time;
  (e) supply 1 and supply 2 are dependent upon each other;
  (f) if supply 1 and supply 2 were made as a single supply or part of a single supply to C, that supply would be made at or approximately the same price as the price of both supply 1 and supply 2 is made to C under the split arrangements;
  (g) a higher profit is generated from whichever of supply 1 and supply 2 is the supply that obtains the greatest VAT advantage.

[*SI 2017/1216, Reg 4*]. (VAT Notice 799, para 7.6.6).

Hallmark 6 – offshore supplies insurance and finance

This is only applicable to VAT. This test applies to 'offshore loops' involving supplies of finance/insurance services that would be exempt from VAT had they been supplied by a UK resident business to customers located within the EU. The offshore loop involves supplies made by at least one business that is resident outside of the EU.

The UK resident business will supply the finance/insurance services to the non-EU business who will then supply the services onto the EU resident customers. As the services are supplied to a non-EU customer, input tax will be recoverable as these are treated as 'specified supplies' for the purposes of the *VAT (Input Tax) (Specified Supplies) Order 1999 (SI 1999/3121)*. HMRC state that there are three tests that need to be satisfied before this hallmark is met:

- **Test 1** – UK business makes a supply to a non-EU person and the supply is exempt from VAT or would be exempt from VAT if it had been made in the UK by virtue of *VATA 1994, Sch 9, Groups 2, 5, Items 1–6* and *8*.
- **Test 2** – the non-EU person makes a supply of services to the end customer who belongs in the EU, and the supply would be exempt from VAT had it been made by an EU-resident supplier.
- **Test 3** – the supply made by the UK business to the non-EU person is used to make the supply to the end customer.
  This test will still be met if the supply is either incorporated into a supply made by another person, split into separate supplies or the supply forms part of a chain of supplies made via several intermediaries.

[*SI 2017/1216, Reg 5*]. (VAT Notice 799, para 7.7).

Hallmark 7 – relevant business person

This only applies to VAT. This hallmark deals with arrangements where services are routed outside of the UK to prevent an UK/EU resident person incurring irrecoverable input tax on the services received. The arrangement includes a non-EU business in a supply chain who is treated as a relevant business person under *VATA 1994, s 7A(2)(a)*. The UK supplier is not required to charge VAT on the supply to the relevant business person located outside of the EU.

HMRC state that the following tests apply together to determine whether this hallmark has been met:

- A UK business makes supplies of services to a non-EU business.
- That supply would be taxable at the standard or reduced rate of VAT had it been made in the UK.
- The non-EU relevant business person receives the supply and then makes a supply to another person who is resident in the EU and either:
  (a) the supply would be exempt if it had been made in the UK;
  (b) the place of supply is outside the EU.

- The supply made by the UK business to the non-EU relevant person is used by that person to make the supply to the end customer located in the EU.

This test will still be met if the supply is either incorporated into a supply made by another person, split into separate supplies or the supply forms part of a chain of supplies made via several intermediaries.

[*SI 2017/1216, Reg* 6]. (VAT Notice 799, para 7.8).

Hallmark 8 – disapplication of the option to tax

This only applies to VAT. This hallmark deals with arrangements where the person intends to prematurely end the option to tax on a property.

HMRC consider that this hallmark is met when:

- a person (or a relevant associate of a body corporate) has opted to tax a property that is a capital item and that option has not been revoked;
- fewer than 20 years have expired since that option took effect;
- that person, or a relevant associate, makes a supply of the opted property, such that the supply is not a taxable supply as it is a supply of exempt land by the developer [*VATA 1994, Sch 10, para 12(1)*].

[*SI 2017/1216, Reg* 7]. (VAT Notice 799, para 7.9).

Duty to disclose

The duty to disclose normally resides with the promoter of the arrangement. There are however special rules, and these are explained below.

Notifiable arrangements marketed by a non-resident promoter

If a non-UK promoter is involved, then the UK user of the arrangement will be required to make the relevant disclosure under the DASVOIT provisions, if the promoter has not made the disclosure and provided the user with the reference number.

The user is required to make the disclosure within *six working days* starting on the date that the user entered into the first relevant transaction forming part of the arrangements (see below).

HMRC will not expect the user to make the disclosure where:

- the non-UK promoter has UK-based employees and they are undertaking any of the promoter's activities;
- there is at least one person in the UK who comes within the meaning of promoter, such as a financial adviser who is responsible to any extent for the organisation/management of the arrangement.

If the non-resident promoter has made the relevant disclosure to HMRC, he must provide the user(s) with the eight-digit scheme reference number issued by HMRC.

(VAT Notice 799, para 8.4.1).

Notifiable arrangements promoted by a lawyer

If a lawyer is acting as a promoter and legal professional privilege prevents the lawyer from making a full disclosure, responsibility for making this disclosure is transferred to the user of the arrangement, where no other promoter is involved. The user must make the disclosure within *five working days* starting on the date that the first transaction was entered into that forms part of the arrangements.

However, if the client waives any right to legal professional privilege then the lawyer will be required to make the relevant disclosure.

Any client waiver must be made sufficiently early to enable the lawyer to make the relevant disclosure within *30 days* of the relevant date (see below). Otherwise, the client must make the disclosure within *five working days* from the date of the first transaction that forms part of the notifiable arrangements.

If the lawyer was responsible for marketing the arrangements, then he cannot use legal professional privilege to avoid making the disclosure to HMRC.

(VAT Notice 799, para 8.4.2).

No promoter involved

If no promoter is involved in respect of the notifiable arrangement, the user of the arrangement is required to make the relevant disclosure when he enters into the first transaction that forms part of the arrangements. The disclosure rules apply to partnerships, companies, trusts and individuals.

It is important to note that only arrangements that have been implemented need to be disclosed by the user. The user of the arrangement must make the relevant disclosure to HMRC within 30 working days from the date that the user entered into the first transaction forming part of the arrangements.

(VAT Notice 799, para 8.4.3).

First transaction forming part of the arrangements

A transaction that forms part of the arrangements will be a transaction that will, either in isolation or in conjunction with other transactions, deliver the tax advantage that is expected by the user of the arrangement. It should be noted that the concept of a transaction is not limited to the performance of a contract or making a payment under a contract – entering into a contract is also deemed to be part of the transaction.

With regard to engagement letters, if the promoter or a body controlled by the promoter is a counterparty to a transaction under the arrangements and the engagement letter constitutes a contract to enter into the arrangement, the engagement letter will be viewed as a transaction forming part of the arrangements.

(VAT Notice 799, para 8.5).

Exemptions from making a disclosure

If the person has entered into at least two notifiable arrangements which are substantially the same as the first arrangement that has been notified to HMRC, where the promoter is outside of the UK or there is no promoter, the user is not required to make a further disclosure to HMRC in respect of the later arrangements.

If a promoter is involved in relation to at least two notifiable arrangements/proposals which are substantially the same, they are required to only make one disclosure even if more than one client has used the arrangement. HMRC state that arrangements will not be substantially the same if they have been revised because of legislative changes that impact the current tax/accounting treatment.

If there are two promoters involved in respect of the same, or substantially the same, arrangement, it may be possible for a single disclosure to be made rather than each promoter making a separate disclosure.

HMRC state the two rules need to be met before a single disclosure can be made:

(1) The duty of a promoter (P2) in making a disclosure will be discharged when all the following apply:
   (a) another promoter (P1) discloses the information about the arrangement;
   (b) P2 holds that information;
   (c) P1 provided the identity and address of P2 to HMRC before P2's duty to disclose has arisen.
(2) The duty of a promoter (P2) in making a disclosure is discharged when both of the following apply:
   (a) another promoter (P1) has made the relevant disclosure to HMRC and has been given a scheme reference number;
   (b) P2 holds the information and the scheme reference number.

(1) above applies where there is a co-promoter at the time of the disclosure and (2) applies where a person has become a co-promoter at a later stage.

(VAT Notice 799, paras 8.2.2, 8.2.3, 8.4.4).

Making the disclosure

HMRC specify that the relevant form shown below is used to provide the relevant disclosure.

Type of notification	*Relevant form*
Arrangement promoter makes the notification	DASVOIT1
Promoter outside of the UK – user provides the notification	DASVOIT2
There is no promoter, or the promoter is a lawyer – user makes the notification	DASVOIT3
Notification of an arrangement reference number to the user	DASVOIT4

Type of notification	*Relevant form*
Notification of an arrangement reference number to the promoter's client	DASVOIT5

[F(No 2)A 2017, Sch 17, paras 11(1)(2), 17(1), 18(2), 26(1)(3), (a), (b) and 23(2), 24(3)].

The disclosure must be made using the relevant form listed above. Failure to use the correct form could result in the imposition of a penalty (see **4.3** below).

An online disclosure can be made using the GOV.UK website and a PDF form can be printed off the website. A paper version of the form can be obtained from HMRC by contacting the Written Enquiries team.

The forms must be submitted in writing to HMRC at the following address:

HM Revenue and Customs
DASVOIT Disclosures SO483
Newcastle
NE98 1ZZ

The form needs to be completed providing all relevant information and details of the relevant indirect taxes involved and the relevant hallmark. If more than one hallmark is being used, then details of the main hallmark need to be provided.

The declarant will also need to provide the following information in addition to the form:

- The name and address of the person who has the duty to disclose.
- The user's name and address and the promoter's name if he is non-resident.
- Details of each provision in the *Notifiable Arrangements Regulations* that cover the arrangement being proposed or used.
- A summary of the arrangements used and the name of the arrangements by which it/they are referred to.
- Explanation regarding the elements of the arrangement and how the expected tax advantage will be obtained. The information provided must enable HMRC to understand what the expected tax advantage will be. Any explanations must not be overly complicated and must identify the steps involved and the relevant legislation. For complex arrangements, diagrams should be provided to HMRC.
- The statutory provisions which form the basis of the tax advantage.

(VAT Notice 799, para 9.3.1).

If a co-promoter is involved, then the promoter can provide details of the co-promoter to HMRC, however there is no legal requirement for the promoter to do so. If the co-promoter's information is provided to HMRC, then this party will not be required to provide a separate disclosure in respect of any arrangements that are the same or substantially the same.

(VAT Notice 799, para 9.4).

Arrangements that provide a tax advantage for more than one indirect tax

If the arrangement/proposal provides the user with a tax advantage for more than one indirect tax, each advantage is subject to its own disclosure considerations. The arrangements should be disclosed at the same time and only one form needs to be completed. The description provided must make it clear that there is an advantage in respect of more than one tax and provide details of how these advantages arise.

(VAT Notice 799, para 9.5).

After the disclosure is made

HMRC will issue the declarant with an eight-digit scheme reference number that is used to identify the scheme users of disclosed arrangements and to enable HMRC to check the status of the user's returns.

Promoters are required to provide details of any relevant changes in writing to HMRC within 30 days of the change occurring using the address shown above.

The person disclosing the scheme will be required to give the reference number to any users of the arrangement. Scheme users are then required to notify HMRC of the reference number using form DASVOIT4.

The relevant procedure below needs to be used to notify the user of the arrangement reference number.

Promoters – providing the number to user

The promoter and co-promoter (where applicable) will be issued with a reference number and the promoter is required to provide the reference number and other related information to the relevant client using form DASVOIT5. The DASVOIT5 must be issued within 30 days of the later of being provided with the reference number or becoming aware of a transaction that forms part of the arrangements.

HMRC state that it is acceptable for the promoter to provide the reference number to the client (using a DASVOIT5) when the arrangement is made available rather than when it is implemented if this is preferable.

The client must be included on the client list (see below) due for that reporting period.

The client should also receive the following information:

- The name and address of the promoter.
- A summary of the notifiable proposal/arrangement and any name by which it is referred to.
- The date that each reference number is issued to the client.
- Any additional information provided by HMRC which relates to avoidance schemes in general.

Users – providing the arrangement reference number to other parties to the arrangement

Upon receipt of the number, the user will be required to provide the reference number to any other person who might reasonably be expected to be a party to, or might reasonably be expected to obtain a tax advantage from the arrangements within 30 days of the later of being provided with the reference number by the promoter or becoming aware of a transaction that forms part of the arrangements. The user must notify the other person using a DASVOIT5. The user must also ensure that it provides any other information given by HMRC to the other relevant parties.

User – notifying HMRC of the scheme reference number

If a person has received a reference number from a promoter, they must provide this number to HMRC using a DASVOIT4 ensuring that all the information listed below is provided:

- Name and address of the person providing the information.
- Scheme reference number(s).
- Accounting period or date on which the person expects to obtain the tax advantage (not required for customs duties).
- Tax identifier number provided to the declarant.
- Declaration confirming that the information provided is accurate and complete and confirming whether the person is a client, another party to a notifiable arrangement or an introducer or promoter.

The DASVOIT4 must be provided to HMRC within 31 days starting on the date that the user first entered into a transaction forming part of the arrangements. A DASVOIT4 must be submitted every year until the person ceases to obtain the tax advantage covered by the disclosed arrangement. The ongoing forms must be submitted within 31 days of the anniversary of the date the user first entered into the first transaction.

If the user obtains a tax advantage in respect of more than one indirect tax, only one DASVOIT4 needs to be completed. The description must provide a clear explanation regarding the tax advantage(s) obtained in respect of all indirect taxes.

(VAT Notice 799, para 11).

Removal of reporting duties

HMRC can use discretion to remove the reporting duties by giving notice that from a specific date, the reference number need no longer be reported by the promoter/clients to HMRC.

Client lists

Promoters have a legal requirement to provide client details to HMRC where a promoter has or is providing services to a user in respect of a notifiable arrangement/proposal and the DASVOIT provisions require an arrangement reference number to be provided to the user.

The duty to disclose also includes any person in the supply chain who is responsible to any extent for the organisation/management of the arrangement.

Quarterly lists must be provided to HMRC providing details of any clients who have received the reference number during that reporting period. The lists apply to arrangements/proposals that were disclosed at any time and not just those disclosed in that period. Failure to provide a client list could result in a penalty.

The requirement to provide the client list is created when the promoter is obliged to give the client the reference number. HMRC state that the obligation is created on the **later** of the following events occurring:

- The promoter is provided with an arrangement reference number.
- The promoter becomes aware of any transaction that forms part of the arrangements.

The following must be provided on the client list:

- The full name and address of the promoter.
- The arrangement reference number issued by HMRC.
- The full name and address of each client.
- The tax identifier number for each client.
- The end date of the calendar quarter for which the information is being provided.

The client is required to provide details of his tax ID number within 11 working days beginning with the later of the date the client receives the reference number or the date the client enters into the first transaction that forms part of the arrangements.

The information must be provided to HMRC no later than 30 days after the end of the calendar quarter.

If it transpires towards the end of the prescribed period that the client has not provided his tax identifier number then it may be possible to extend the deadline upon request, providing the promoter within the normal 30-day prescribed period notifies HMRC that one of the following scenarios applies.

- The client has not provided the promoter with his tax identifier number.
- The client has not provided a written statement to the promoter that he does not have a tax identifier number.
- On the 16th day after the relevant period, the client has not complied but the time limit for the client to provide his tax identifier number has not expired.

If the conditions outlined above are satisfied, then the deadline can be extended to 60 days. If the conditions outlined above are not satisfied, then the client list submission date cannot be extended, and the promoter must advise HMRC accordingly about the missing tax ID number using one of the three reasons outlined above.

There is no specified format for providing the client list information and any format can be used providing it contains all the relevant information. HMRC recommend splitting the information into two sections, one providing the promoter's information and the other section providing the client information.

The list must be submitted to the address shown above (see 'Making the disclosure').

(VAT Notice 799, para 10).

Information powers and penalties

Information powers

[4.3] *Finance Act (No 2) 2017, Sch 17, paras 28–34* empower HMRC to:

- require a promoter to provide information about a party to an arrangement who is not a client;
- enquire regarding the reasons why a promoter/introducer has not disclosed a proposal or arrangement and require the production of information and documentation to support that claim;
- require an introducer to identify the person who provided him with information relating to the proposed arrangements and any other person with whom he has made marketing contact in relation to the proposed arrangements.

The purpose of the information powers is to enable HMRC to identify notifiable proposals/arrangements that have not been disclosed and to identify the users of such arrangements, so their indirect tax affairs can be investigated further.

If HMRC identify that a proposal/arrangement has not been disclosed, they will write to the persons demanding that an explanation be provided regarding why there is no requirement to notify HMRC of the proposal/arrangement.

If HMRC are not satisfied with the explanation provided, they can apply to the tribunal for an order requiring the person to provide specific information/documentation that is required to support this contention.

The person will be required to provide the information within 15 days beginning on the date of the order or longer if so directed by HMRC.

If HMRC understand that a person is acting as an introducer in respect of an undisclosed arrangement/proposal, a written notice can be issued requiring the person to provide the name and address of each person providing information to the introducer regarding the notifiable proposal/arrangement. The introducer will have 11 working days beginning from the date of the tribunal order to produce the required information.

HMRC can also apply to the tribunal for an order 'confirming' or 'deeming' that the arrangement/proposal should be notified under the DASVOIT rules. The tribunal will issue the order if it is satisfied that the proposal/arrangement is notifiable. The person will be required to make the necessary disclosure within 11 working days of the date of the order.

HMRC also have powers in respect of incomplete disclosures. HMRC can demand the production of specified information or documentation regarding a notifiable proposal/arrangement in addition to other prescribed information that has already been disclosed, if they consider that not all the prescribed information has been provided by the promoter or user of the arrangement. The person must provide this information within ten working days from the date that HMRC imposed the requirement unless a longer time period has been directed by HMRC.

HMRC can issue a written notice requiring a promoter to provide further information where it has reason to believe that a client that has been included on the client list is not actually a user of the arrangement. HMRC would normally request this information if they believe the person on the list is an intermediary rather than a user. The promoter must provide the information to HMRC within 11 days of receiving the notice from HMRC or any other period as directed by HMRC.

Failure to adhere to the deadlines for making the relevant disclosure could result in the imposition of a penalty (see (2) below).

(VAT Notice 799, para 12).

Penalties

There are three categories of penalties.

(1) Disclosure penalties

These penalties apply when a person fails to make the relevant disclosure and involves an initial penalty and a further penalty where the person continues to remain non-compliant. The initial penalty is set by the tribunal.

If the tribunal did not issue a disclosure order, the penalty will be levied where the person:

- failed to make the disclosure within the specified time period;
- failed to provide the required information specified by HMRC in a written information notice;
- the tribunal has issued an order regarding an incomplete disclosure.

The initial penalty will cover the period from the date the failure occurred until the current date. Further penalties can be levied by HMRC for further non-compliance.

The tribunal can levy a penalty of up to £1 million if necessary and the amount of penalty imposed will take into consideration the specific facts that are relevant including the aim of deterring that person or other persons from failing to comply in a similar manner. In certain circumstances, the tribunal can issue a penalty of more than £1 million. HMRC can issue further penalties after the initial penalty of up to £600 per day for each day that the failure continues.

HMRC state that the penalty can be imposed as a result of:

- the promoter failing to notify HMRC of the proposal or arrangement;
- scheme user failing to notify its user of the arrangement;
- promoter failing to comply with a tribunal order regarding an incomplete disclosure;
- promoter or scheme user failing to comply with an information notice issued by HMRC.

HMRC can also issue a penalty where a tribunal has issued an order stating that a proposal or arrangement is disclosable. HMRC refer to this as a '*paragraph 4 order*'. The issue of the order confirms that the proposal or arrangement was always disclosable, and the disclosure should have been made within the specified time limit. The legislation states that the promoter cannot rely on doubt regarding whether there is an obligation to disclose and the disclosure must be made within the specified time frame. For *paragraph 4* orders, the tribunal will set the rate of the initial penalty. In addition to the £600 daily penalty, HMRC can also levy a higher penalty of £5,000 for each day that the person remains non-compliant.

If the tribunal has issued an order requiring the person to provide more information in respect of which a *paragraph 4* order has been made by the tribunal, the maximum penalty for failure to comply is £5,000 per day.

If the tribunal has issued an order stating that the proposal or arrangement is deemed to be disclosable (*paragraph 5* order) then it must be disclosed within 11 working days from the date of the order. The issue of a *paragraph 5* order will not automatically result in the imposition of a penalty if the person has failed to make the relevant disclosure before the tribunal issued the order. The initial penalty will be set by the tribunal and will be imposed if the person fails to make the relevant disclosure 12 days after the issue of the order.

If the tribunal subsequently issues a *paragraph 4* order or the person agrees that the proposal/arrangement should have been disclosed and the disclosure should have been made before the issue of the paragraph 5 penalty, HMRC can apply to the tribunal to set a further penalty.

If a *paragraph 5* order has been issued and the tribunal subsequently issues an order requiring the person to provide additional information/documentation regarding the notifiable proposal/arrangement, the maximum penalty for failure to comply is £5,000.

(VAT Notice 799, para 13.5).

(2) Information penalty

HMRC can also levy an information penalty that applies to all failures to comply except those covered by the user penalty. An initial penalty will be imposed by the tribunal and further penalties for continued failure to comply will be set by HMRC.

An information penalty will be levied in the following circumstances:

- A promoter does not respond to a disclosure enquiry when required to do so.
- An introducer does not provide details of the indemnity of the person who supplied him with information regarding notifiable proposals/arrangements with whom the introducer has made marketing contracts.
- A promoter does not provide his client(s) with the reference number provided by HMRC when the scheme is disclosed.
- The client fails to provide the reference number, or other information required by HMRC to other persons who the person reasonably expects to be a party to the arrangements or is expected to obtain a tax advantage.
- A promoter fails to advise HMRC of client's details to whom he is obliged to issue the reference number.
- A promoter fails to provide information on parties to the arrangements when required to do so by a written notice.
- A client does not provide the promoter with details of his tax ID number or incorrectly advises the promoter that he is not in possession of such a number.
- A promoter who fails to provide updated information about themselves or the arrangements.

Information penalties also include situations where the information is provided after the end of the prescribed period stated in the DASVOIT regulations for the provision of information or where the information has been provided using an incorrect format that is not specified in the regulations.

The initial penalty is set by the tribunal for each failure to a maximum of £5,000. HMRC can assess further daily penalties of up to £600 for each failure if the person remains non-compliant.

(VAT Notice 799, para 13.6).

(3) User penalties

If the user of the arrangement fails to comply with the obligation to report the scheme number and other related information, then the following penalties can be imposed:

First failure	£5,000 for each set of arrangements
Second failure	£7,500 for each set of arrangements
Third and subsequent failures	£10,000 for each set of arrangements

The above penalties will also be imposed if the user fails to report the information to HMRC using the prescribed format. These penalties are assessed by HMRC and not by a tribunal.

(VAT Notice 799, para 13.7).

Publishing information

HMRC have the power to publish information regarding arrangements that have been disclosed under these provisions. Where a reference number has been allocated, HMRC can also publish the following information regarding a promoter:

- promoter's name and address;
- any of the information prescribed for the purposes of making the disclosure;
- summary of the proposal or arrangements and any names that they are known by;
- the statutory provisions upon which the tax advantage is based;
- any court or tribunal ruling relating to the arrangements or proposed arrangements or the promoter;
- any other information that HMRC deem to be appropriate in order to identify the proposal or arrangements or the promoter of these arrangements.

HMRC are not allowed to publish information about the person who entered into the arrangements (user).

HMRC are required to notify the promoter that they are intending to publish information about that person to enable that person to provide evidence/arguments regarding why their name should not be published.

(VAT Notice 799, para 14).

Reasonable excuse

No penalty will be imposed where the person has satisfied either HMRC or the tribunal that they had a reasonable excuse for the failure. There is no statutory definition of what constitutes a reasonable excuse and HMRC consider that each case needs to be considered on its own merits. HMRC state that it usually considers a reasonable excuse to be something that prevents the person from being able to meet their tax obligations despite having taken reasonable care to meet those obligations.

Finance (No 2) Act 2017, Sch 17, para 50 also contains restrictions on the use of reasonable excuse as a defence in respect of advice given or obtained by a monitored promoter under the Promoters of Tax Avoidance rules.

Paragraph 50 states:

(1) Where a person fails to comply with–

- (a) paragraph 17(2) and the promoter for the purposes of paragraph 17 is a monitored promoter; or
- (b) paragraph 18(2) and the arrangements for the purposes of paragraph 18 are arrangements of a monitored promoter,

then for the purposes of paragraph 48 legal advice which the person took into account is to be disregarded in determining whether the person had a reasonable excuse, if the advice was given or procured by that monitored promoter.

(2) In determining for the purpose of paragraph 48 whether or not a person who is a monitored promoter had a reasonable excuse for a failure to do something, reliance on legal advice is to be taken automatically not to constitute a reasonable excuse if either—

- (a) the advice was not based on a full and accurate description of the facts, or
- (b) the conclusions in the advice that the person relied on were unreasonable.

Appeals

A person has the right to appeal against any penalty imposed under these provisions.

[*SI 2017/1215; SI 2017/1216; F(No 2)A 2017, s 66, Sch 17*]. (VAT Notice 799).

Rules effective until 31 December 2017

There are two categories of schemes that must be notified.

- *Listed schemes*. Certain schemes are 'designated' schemes for these purposes and are named and described in the legislation (by statutory instrument). A business whose annual turnover exceeds £600,000 must notify HMRC if it makes a VAT return or claim (such as a voluntary declaration) which is affected by its use of a listed scheme. See **4.3–4.6** below for the detailed provisions. Failure to notify incurs a penalty of 15% of the VAT avoided. See **53 PENALTIES**.
- *Hallmarked schemes*. Certain features that are regularly associated with avoidance schemes are designated in the law (by statutory instrument). They can relate to the adoption of schemes or be components of them. Hallmarked schemes are those schemes that include at least one of the designated provisions. A business whose annual turnover exceeds £10 million must notify HMRC if it has entered into

a scheme for the purposes of securing a tax advantage, the scheme contains one or more of the hallmarks of avoidance, and it makes a return or claim which is affected by the use of the hallmarked scheme. There is also a voluntary facility for anyone, including those who devise and market avoidance schemes, to register hallmarked schemes.
See **4.8–4.12** below for the detailed provisions. Failure to notify incurs a flat-rate penalty of £5,000. See **53.31 PENALTIES**.

[*VATA 1994, s 58A, Sch 11A*].

Listed schemes: general

[4.4] The Treasury can designate a scheme for the purposes of these provisions if it appears to them that

- a scheme of a particular description has been, or might be, entered into for the purpose of enabling any person to 'obtain a tax advantage', and
- it is unlikely that persons would enter into a scheme of that description unless the main purpose, or one of the main purposes, of doing so was the obtaining by any person of a tax advantage.

A scheme may be designated even though the Treasury are of the opinion that no scheme of that description could, as a matter of law, result in the obtaining by any person of a tax advantage (i.e. they consider it to be legally ineffective).

Each listed scheme must be allocated a reference number.

[*VATA 1994, Sch 11A para 3*].

Obtaining a tax advantage

A *taxable person* obtains a tax advantage if

- in any VAT period, the excess of output tax accounted for by him over input tax deducted by him is less than it otherwise would be;
- he obtains a VAT credit when he would not otherwise do so, or obtains a larger or earlier VAT credit than would otherwise be the case;
- in a case where he recovers input tax as a recipient of a supply before the supplier accounts for the output tax, the period between the time when the input tax is recovered and the time when the output tax is accounted for is greater than would otherwise be the case; or
- the amount of his non-deductible tax is less than it would otherwise be. Non-deductible tax means input tax for which he is not entitled to credit under *VATA 1994, s 25*, and VAT on any supply of goods or services to him, or on the acquisition or importation of goods by him, which is not input tax and in respect of which he is entitled to a refund from HMRC under any provision of *VATA 1994*.

A *non-taxable person* obtains a tax advantage if his 'non-refundable tax' is less than it would otherwise be. '*Non-refundable tax*' means the VAT on any supply of goods or services to him, or on the acquisition or importation of goods by him, other than VAT in respect of which he is entitled to a refund from HMRC under any provision of *VATA 1994*.

[*VATA 1994, Sch 11A paras 2, 2A*].

Liability to notify listed schemes

[4.5] A *taxable person* must notify HMRC of the use of a listed scheme when all of the following conditions are met. This applies even if HMRC already know that he is using the scheme.

Condition 1

The total value of his VAT-exclusive taxable supplies and exempt supplies exceeded:

- £600,000 in the year immediately prior to the 'affected VAT return period'; or any of the VAT return periods that are the subject of an 'affected claim'; or
- the 'appropriate proportion' of £600,000 in the VAT return period immediately prior to the affected VAT return period; or any of the VAT return periods that are the subject of an affected claim.

The '*appropriate proportion*' means the proportion which the length of that VAT period bears to twelve months (e.g. one-quarter where quarterly VAT returns are prepared and one-twelfth where monthly VAT returns are prepared).

See Condition 3 below for 'affected VAT return period' and 'affected claim'.

See also **4.13** below for powers given to HMRC to prevent any artificial separation of business activities in an attempt to reduce turnover below the above limits.

Group undertakings

If the taxable person is a 'group undertaking', the conditions must be met by the taxable person *plus* every other group undertaking (i.e. the criteria apply to the whole group). For these purposes, the definitions in *Companies Act 2006, s 1161* apply (so that 'group' does not necessarily mean 'VAT group'). The group will comprise the undertaking in question, together with any undertaking which is

- a parent undertaking or a subsidiary undertaking of that undertaking; or
- a subsidiary undertaking of any parent undertaking of that undertaking.

For the purpose of calculating turnover, intra-corporate group transactions are included but intra-VAT group transactions are ignored. (VAT Notice 700/8/18, para 4.3.)

Condition 2

The taxable person is a party to a listed scheme under **4.7** below.

A person is a party to a scheme if he knowingly takes part in it but not if he

- is unwittingly involved in any of the steps of the scheme (i.e. has no knowledge of either the existence of the scheme or the role he plays in it); or
- acts purely in an advisory capacity.

(VAT Notice 700/8/18, para 3.3.1).

Condition 3

One of the following relevant events occurs.

- In a return for a VAT period (the '*affected VAT return period*'), the amount of VAT shown as payable by/to the taxable person is less than/greater than it would be but for the use of a listed scheme to which he is party.
- The taxable person makes a claim (the '*affected claim*') for the repayment of output tax or an increase in credit for input tax for any VAT period in respect of which he has previously delivered a return and the amount claimed is greater than it would be but for a listed scheme.
- In a return for a VAT period (the '*affected VAT return period*'), the amount of the taxable person's 'non-deductible tax' is less than it would be but for a listed scheme.

'Non-deductible tax' means

- input tax for which he is not entitled to credit under *VATA 1994, s 25*; and
- VAT on any supply of goods or services to him, or on the acquisition or importation of goods by him, which is not input tax and in respect of which he is entitled to a refund from HMRC under any provision of *VATA 1994*.

Condition 4

The taxable person has not on a previous occasion

- notified HMRC as required under these provisions that he is using the scheme; or
- provided HMRC with prescribed information in relation to the scheme under **4.9** below when it was a hallmarked scheme and before it became a listed scheme.

Where a scheme is designed to give an ongoing VAT benefit over time (so that more than one relevant event under Condition 3 above may occur), a taxable person is only required to notify the scheme once. However, a listed scheme may be used more than once (e.g. listed scheme 1 may be used to remove the VAT cost of refurbishing more than one property). Where this happens, each adoption of the scheme must be notified.

Where a new scheme becomes listed, if a taxable person has previously notified use of the scheme under the rules for hallmarked schemes, he is not required to make a new notification when the scheme becomes listed. But if the scheme is used again, he must notify the new arrangements as above.

(VAT Notice 700/8/18, para 4.4.) [*VATA 1994, Sch 11A paras 6, 7*].

Schemes involving several parties

If a listed scheme involves more than one party, all the parties to that scheme are obliged to notify HMRC if they meet the conditions set out above. However, the parties concerned can make a joint notification. The notification should make it clear that it is a joint notification and who all the parties are that are making the notification. (VAT Notice 700/8/18, para 3.3.4).

Notifying listed schemes to HMRC

Time limit for notification

[4.6] Where a taxable person must notify HMRC of the use of a listed scheme under **4.5** above, he must do so within 30 days from the end of

- the last day for submission of the return for the 'affected VAT return period';
- the date the 'affected claim' is made; or
- where HMRC make a direction under **4.13** below (artificial splitting of business), the last day for submission of the first VAT return made to HMRC following the direction.

See **4.5** above for '*affected VAT return period*' and '*affected claim*'.

[*VATA 1994, Sch 11A para 6; SI 2005/2009*].

The normal latest date for submitting the return is now seven calendar days from the end of the month following the return period, and the notification deadline is 30 days after this 'extended' filing deadline where it applies. (VAT Notice 700/8/18, para 5.1.3).

HMRC will accept early notifications (e.g. before the relevant event has taken place) provided the scheme has been implemented. (VAT Notice 700/8/18, para 5.1.1).

Method of notification

The following provisions relating to notification as set out in VAT Notice 700/8 have the force of law.

HMRC must be notified of the use of a listed scheme either

- by e-mail to: vat.avoidance.disclosures.bst@hmrc.gsi.gov.uk or
- in writing to:

  Anti-Avoidance Group (Intelligence)
  VAT Avoidance Disclosures Unit
  HM Revenue & Customs
  CTIAA Intelligence S0528
  PO Box 194
  Bootle L69 9AA

Notification sent to any other address (e.g. another office or the VAT Written Enquiries Team) is not proper notification and may give rise to a penalty.

The notification should be prominently headed

Disclosure of use of listed scheme – Notification under paragraph 6(2) of Schedule 11A to the VAT Act 1994

and give details of

- business name (where notification is by the representative member of a VAT group notifying as a result of a group member being involved in a notifiable scheme, also the name of the member);
- address; and
- VAT registration number.

Otherwise, the only information that is required is the number of the listed scheme (see **4.7** below). [*SI 2004/1929*].

If a taxable person is using more than one scheme at the same time, HMRC must be informed about all of the schemes of each type that are being used and have not been previously reported.

HMRC will acknowledge receipt of notifications received at the above addresses. They will consider what action, if any, to take in respect of the notification and the taxable person will be contacted as necessary.

(VAT Notice 700/8/18, paras 5.2–5.6).

The listed schemes

[4.7] The Treasury have designated the schemes detailed below as listed schemes. The interpretation and examples within boxes are not part of the legislation but taken from VAT Notice 700/8.

A feature of a scheme is regarded as being present where

- it is present as a matter of fact; or
- a taxable person treats it as being present for the purpose of making a VAT return or error correction notification (formerly voluntary disclosure), even if it is not actually present (whether as a matter of law or for any other reason). [*SI 2004/1933, Art 2*].

HMRC give the example of where a feature of a scheme relies on a transaction being a supply for VAT purposes. If, for the purposes of making a return, a taxable person treats the transaction as being such a supply, the feature is regarded as being present (for the purposes of deciding whether disclosure is required), even if the court subsequently decides that there has been no supply as a matter of law. (VAT Notice 700/8/18, para 6.1.1).

(1) First grant of a major interest in a building

Any scheme comprising or including the first grant of a major interest in any building of a description falling within *VATA 1994, Sch 8 Group 5 item 1*(*a*) (see **43.1 LAND AND BUILDINGS: ZERO AND REDUCED RATE SUPPLIES AND DIY HOUSEBUILDERS**) where

- the grant is made to a person 'connected with' the grantor; and
- the grantor, or any body corporate treated as a member of a VAT group (see **28 GROUPS OF COMPANIES**) of which the grantor is a member, attributes to that grant input tax incurred by him

(a) in respect of a service charge relating to the building; or
(b) in connection with any extension, enlargement, repair, maintenance or refurbishment of the building, other than for remedying defects in the original construction.

A person is '*connected with*' another for the above purposes where

- one of them is an 'undertaking' in relation to which the other is a 'group undertaking', or
- both of them are connected to the same trust

and a person is connected to a trust where

- he is the settlor of the trust, a trustee or beneficiary of it; or
- he holds any shares in a company in accordance with the terms of the trust, or is a person on whose behalf such shares are held.

See **4.5** above for the meaning of '*undertaking*' and '*group undertaking*'.

[*SI 2004/1933, Reg 2, Sch 1*].

This scheme aims to remove the VAT cost of extending, enlarging, repairing, refurbishing or servicing buildings that are zero-rated when sold by developers. Examples of the buildings concerned are houses, student halls of residence and buildings used by charities for non-business activities.

> *Examples*
>
> A housing landlord may seek to use this scheme to recover input tax on the major refurbishment of houses which he had constructed several years earlier. The landlord leases or sells them to a subsidiary in such a way that he attributes to that zero-rated disposal the VAT on the refurbishment (which may be undertaken either before or after the grant). The subsidiary may then simply lease the houses back to the landlord so that he can then let them on again to tenants.
>
> The builder of new halls of residence may try to recover future input tax on repairs and maintenance on the buildings, even though his income from the property at that time will be exempt, by building into the initial zero-rated lease or sale a payment for, and agreement to provide, repairs and maintenance in the future.

(VAT Notice 700/8/18, para 6.2).

(2) Payment handling service

Any scheme comprising or including a retail supply of goods or services together with a 'linked supply' to the same customer, where the total consideration for the retail supply and the linked supply is no different, or not significantly different, from what would be payable for the retail sale alone.

'*Linked supply*' means a supply by the retailer or any other person that

- relates to the means of payment used for the retail supply; and
- is a supply of a description falling within *VATA 1994, Sch 9 Group 5* (see **24 FINANCIAL SERVICES**).

[*SI 2004/1933, Sch 1*].

This scheme aims to reduce the VAT due on the advertised price of retail goods or services by transforming an element of the price into an exempt payment handling service (e.g. credit/debit card or cash handling).

> *Example*
>
> When a customer presents his goods at the till and decides to pay by credit or debit card, he may be informed that an element of the price is being paid to a separate company and is in consideration for processing or accepting his card as the means of payment. Agreements signed or agreed by the customer at the point of sale may be alleged to support this. There is no comparable reduction in the value for the goods if he chooses to pay by cash.

(VAT Notice 700/8/18, para 6.3).

(3) Value shifting

Any scheme comprising or including a 'retail supply' of goods or services together with a linked supply to the same customer where

- the 'linked supply' is a separate supply under the terms of any agreement made by the customer;
- part of the total consideration for the retail supply and the linked supply is attributed to the linked supply by the terms of any such agreement; and
- the total consideration for the retail supply and the linked supply is no different, or not significantly different, from what it would be for the retail supply alone.

'*Retail supply*' means a supply by retail upon which VAT is charged at standard rate.

'*Linked supply*' means a supply of goods or services made by the retailer or any other person which is zero-rated or exempt.

[*SI 2004/1933, Sch 1*].

This scheme aims to transfer value from standard-rated retail supplies into linked zero-rated or exempt supplies. Note that a version of the scheme was found by the Court of Appeal to be ineffective in law in *Debenhams Retail plc v HMRC*, CA [2005] STC 1155 (TVC 27.17). Use of the scheme was widespread when the disclosure rules were introduced, but following this decision (and the introduction of *Regulation (EU) No 282/2011, Art 42*) it has virtually disappeared.

> *Example*
>
> *Notification required.* A retail customer making a purchase is offered, at the point of sale, an insurance product with the goods. Rather than paying an additional amount for this cover, the customer is informed that the ticket price has now been apportioned to cover both the goods and the insurance. If the customer then declines the insurance, there is no reduction of the ticket price to reflect this. The overall price paid by the customer remains the same whether he takes the insurance or not.

Notification is not required. Notification is not required under this scheme where the linked goods/services are supplied 'free', with no part of the price being attributed to that supply. Notification will also not be required for normal business promotion arrangements. For example, a retailer offers a 'meal deal' where customers can buy a sandwich, a soft drink and packet of crisps for a single price that is lower than the normal combined price of the three items. When apportioning the cost between the zero-rated and standard-rated items the retailer spreads the discount across all the goods supplied. These arrangements are unlikely to be notifiable as each linked supply would not normally be subject to a separate agreement with the customer and the total amount payable is likely to be significantly different from what it would be for the standard-rated element alone.

(VAT Notice 700/8/18, para 6.4).

(4) Leaseback agreement

Any scheme comprising or including the supply of goods, or the leasing or letting on hire of goods ('the relevant supply') by a taxable person to a connected relevant person where

- the taxable person or another taxable person connected with him, including the relevant person, is entitled to credit for all the input tax arising on the purchase of the goods;
- the relevant person uses the goods in the course or furtherance of a business carried on by him, and for the purpose of that business, otherwise than for the purpose of selling or leasing or letting on hire the goods; and
- the relevant person or a person connected with him has directly or indirectly provided funds for meeting more than 90% of the cost of the goods.

'Relevant person' means any person who, in respect of the relevant supply, is not entitled to credit for all the input tax wholly attributable to the supplies he makes.

The provision of funds includes

- the making of a loan of funds; and
- the provision of any consideration for the issue of any shares or other securities issued wholly or partly for raising the funds.

The grant, assignment or surrender of a major interest in land is not a supply of goods for the purposes of this scheme.

See (1) above for the meaning of '*connected persons*'.

[*SI 2004/1933, Sch 1*].

This scheme aims to defer or reduce the VAT cost of acquiring goods by a business that could recover all of the input tax charged to it on those goods if it were directly to buy them itself.

Note that a version of this scheme was held not to constitute an abuse of rights in *HMRC v Weald Leasing Ltd, ECJ Case C–103/09*, [2011] STC 596 (TVC 22.62) (see **4.1** above).

Examples

Notification required. A partly-exempt bank requires new computer equipment. The bank's corporate group purchases the equipment outright but, in order to reduce or remove the VAT effect of the irrecoverable input tax, the group acquires the computers in a subsidiary, which then leases them to the bank. Depending on the values and length of the lease, the intention is to spread the irrecoverable VAT cost, or to avoid a proportion of it altogether.

Notification not required. Notification is not required for leasing arrangements between unconnected parties. For example, an insurance company (A) requires a new computerised telephone system for its call centres. Rather than buy the equipment outright it decides to lease it and contracts with an unconnected commercial leasing business (B) to lease the equipment for a five-year period. As B has no expertise in sourcing the equipment required, it is agreed that A will purchase the equipment from its usual supplier. A then sells the equipment to B who leases it back to A.

(VAT Notice 700/8/18, para 6.5).

(5) Extended approval period

Any scheme comprising or including a retail supply of goods whereby

- the goods are sent or taken on approval or sale or return or similar terms;
- payment for the supply is required in full by the retailer before the expiry of any approval, return or similar period; and
- for the purposes of accounting for VAT, the retailer treats the goods as supplied on a date after the date on which payment is received in full.

[*SI 2004/1933, Sch 1*].

This scheme aims to defer accounting for output tax on retail (including mail order) supplies of goods.

Example

A customer orders goods from an internet retailer. The retailer is paid on-line when the order is placed by the customer and delivery follows shortly thereafter. The retailer, either due to various guarantees or specific terms and conditions, seeks to account for VAT on the transaction at a later date, claiming the supply was on 'approval' or 'sale or return', despite the fact that payment has been received, delivery taken place and, in some cases, the goods have been consumed or used by the customer before the retailer regards the goods as having been adopted.

(VAT Notice 700/8/18, para 6.6).

(6) Groups: third party suppliers

Any scheme comprising or including supplies made to one or more group members by a 'specified body' in relation to which the 'benefits condition' is not satisfied. See **28.2 GROUPS OF COMPANIES** for whether a body is a '*specified body*' and whether the '*benefits condition*' is satisfied in relation to it.

[*SI 2004/1933, Sch 1*].

This scheme aims to reduce or remove the VAT incurred on bought in taxable services (including outsourced services) by a user that cannot recover all of the input tax charged to it for those services.

> *Example*
>
> A partly exempt insurance company (A) wishes to buy in computer services from a third party company (B) but wants to reduce the irrecoverable VAT cost of doing this. A and B establish another company (C). A controls C by owning 51% of its shares and includes C in its VAT group. B owns the remaining shares, but these shares confer rights to 99% of the dividends declared by C and 99% of the assets on winding up. C holds the contract to provide the computer services required by A from B and employs the staff to provide the service. Besides the dividends, B also receives benefits from C in the form of a management charge for managing C's activity of providing computer services. As a result almost all of the benefits of C's activity accrue to B. Thus, B has access to the profits and benefits of the computing activity, and A hopes to avoid a large VAT cost as there will be no VAT charged within the VAT group.

(VAT Notice 700/8/18, para 6.7).

(7) Exempt education or vocational training by a non-profit making body

Any scheme comprising or including the conduct of a 'relevant business' by a 'non-profit making body' where

- it receives a 'relevant supply' from a connected taxable person who is not an 'eligible body'; and
- in any one prescribed accounting period the value of all such relevant supplies is equal to or more than 20% of the cost of making the supplies comprising the relevant business.

'Relevant business' means a business whose activities consist wholly or mainly of the supply of education or vocational training to persons who are not taxable persons.

'Non-profit making body' means a body within *VATA 1994, Sch 9 Group 6 Note 1(e)* (see **17.3**(*e*) **EDUCATION**) which is not otherwise within **17.3**(*a*)–(*f*) **EDUCATION**.

'Relevant supply' means the supply, including the leasing or letting on hire, for use in a relevant business of

- a capital item used in the course or furtherance of the relevant business, and for the purpose of that business, otherwise than solely for the purpose of selling the item;
- staff;
- management services;
- administration services; or
- accountancy services.

'Eligible body' has the meaning in *VATA 1994, Sch 9 Group 6 Note (1)* (see **17.3 EDUCATION**).

'Vocational training' has the meaning in *VATA 1994, Sch 9 Group 6 Note (3)* (see **17.7 EDUCATION**) but does not include vocational training of a description falling within

- *VATA 1994, Sch 9 Group 6 Item 5* (vocational training where the consideration is ultimately a charge to funds provided under *Employment and Training Act 1973, s 2, Employment and Training Act (NI) 1950, s 1A* or *Enterprises and New Towns (Scotland) Act 1990, s 2*); or
- *VATA 1994, Sch 9 Group 6 Item 5A* (vocational training where the consideration is ultimately a charge to funds provided by the Learning and Skills Council for England or the National Council for Education and Training for Wales under *Learning and Skills Act 2000, Parts I* or *II*).

See Scheme 1 above for 'connected persons'.

[*SI 2004/1933, Sch 1*].

This scheme aims to allow a business providing education or training to avoid charging VAT on supplies to customers by arranging for those supplies to be made through a non-profit making body.

> *Example*
>
> A training company which normally trains private individuals and accounts for VAT out of its income, sets up a non-profit making body to provide the training in future, exempt from VAT. However, if the new body really is a non-profit making body, it will not be able to distribute its profits and the shareholders of the existing business will lose out. Various agreements are put in place to act as a mechanism to return those profits to the original training company. For example, the business premises may be leased, the rent for which is set at a rate directly related to the turnover or profit of the non-profit making body.

(VAT Notice 700/8/18, para 6.8).

(8) Taxable education or vocational training by a non-eligible body

Any scheme comprising or including the conduct of a 'relevant business' by a non-eligible body connected to an 'eligible body' where

- the non-eligible body benefits or intends to benefit the eligible body by way of gift, dividend or otherwise; or
- the eligible body makes any supply to the non-eligible body which is a relevant supply and, in any one prescribed accounting period, the value of all such relevant supplies is equal to or more than 20% of the cost of making the supplies comprising the relevant business.

'Eligible body' has the meaning in *VATA 1994, Sch 9 Group 6 Note (1)* (see **17.3 EDUCATION**).

'Relevant business' means a business whose activities consist wholly or mainly of the taxable supply of education or vocational training.

'Vocational training' has the meaning in *VATA 1994, Sch 9 Group 6 Note (3)* (see **17.7 EDUCATION**).

'Relevant supply' means the supply, or leasing or letting on hire, for use in a relevant business of

- a capital item used in the course or furtherance of the relevant business, and for the purpose of that business, otherwise than solely for the purpose of selling the item;
- staff;
- management services;
- administration services; or
- accounting services.

See Scheme 1 above for 'connected persons'.

[*SI 2004/1933, Sch 1*].

This scheme aims to enable eligible bodies, that would otherwise make exempt supplies, to make taxable supplies and so avoid incurring irrecoverable input VAT. The typical customers involved would be bodies such as NHS Trusts and Local Authorities, but can also include normal commercial bodies.

> *Example*
>
> A university has a contract to provide training to employees of a NHS Trust. Normally, the training would be exempt from VAT and thus the VAT on costs involved in providing it would not be recoverable. To provide this training, the university needs to build a new facility but wishes to reduce the cost of the irrecoverable VAT on the building. The university establishes a subsidiary which is expressly allowed to distribute its profits, thereby denying exemption for its training supplies as it is not an 'eligible body'. The subsidiary may have little or no resources and will need to be provided with those resources by the university under various contracts and agreements. The university may also want to access any profits from this activity and may choose to do this by having the subsidiary gift those profits to it under the Gift Aid relief. As a result, the university hopes to transform the training into a fully taxable activity and recover the input tax on the new facility in the subsidiary, together with other taxable costs.

(VAT Notice 700/8/18, para 6.9).

(9) Cross-border face value vouchers

Any scheme comprising or including the supply of a 'relevant service' (general rule reverse charge service) by a person belonging in the UK (the UK supplier) to a person belonging in an EU member state other than the UK (the non-UK recipient) where

- the service is used, or intended to be used, in whole or in part, by the non-UK recipient or any other person belonging in another EU member state for the purposes of supplying a relevant service to a person belonging in the UK (the retail supply);
- the recipient of the retail supply uses a 'face-value voucher' issued by a person belonging in a country other than the UK to obtain that supply;
- the person making the retail supply does not account for VAT on that supply in the UK or any other EU member state; and
- the UK supplier and the person making the retail supply are connected persons.

'Face value voucher' means tokens, stamps or vouchers of a description falling within *VATA 1994, Sch 10A para 1(1)* (see **70.10 TRADE PROMOTION SCHEMES**).

See **66.14 SUPPLY: PLACE OF SUPPLY** for more information on general rule services.

References in this scheme to the retail supply do not include any supply of a relevant service made to a taxable person.

[*SI 2004/1933, Sch 1*].

This scheme aims to avoid paying VAT anywhere in the EU on 'relevant services' originating from UK suppliers and provided to UK residents who use face-value vouchers (such as phone cards) to pay for them.

> *Example*
>
> A UK company (C) contracts to supply telecommunication services to a related company (R) in another EU member state (say France). A second related French company (I) issues phone cards and sells them to UK retailers. The retailers sell the cards to UK customers who use them to obtain telecommunication services from R. The cards say that, when they are used, R will provide the telecommunication services. R does this by buying in the services under its contract with C. R and I argue that no VAT is due in France or the UK. (Note that only taxable persons in the UK who are party to the scheme, such as U, are required to notify. UK retailers who are not party to the scheme (because they have no knowledge of their involvement in it) and parties who are not taxable persons in the UK are not required to notify.)

(VAT Notice 700/8/18, para 6.10).

(10) Surrender of relevant lease

Any scheme comprising or including the 'surrender' by an occupier of a building of a 'relevant lease, tenancy or licence to occupy' where

- the occupier or any person connected to him is a 'relevant person';
- the building is a capital item for the purposes of the capital goods scheme (see **11.2 CAPITAL GOODS SCHEME**);
- before the surrender, the occupier paid 'relevant VAT' and was not entitled to full credit for, or refund of, that VAT under any provision of *VATA 1994* or *Regulations*;
- following the surrender, the occupier continues to occupy at least 80% of the area previously occupied; and
- following the surrender, the occupier pays no relevant VAT or pays less than 50% of the relevant VAT paid before the surrender.

'Surrender' includes any termination by the occupier of the relevant lease, tenancy or licence to occupy where he has entered into any agreement, arrangement or understanding (whether legally binding or not) with the lessor regarding that termination.

'Relevant lease, tenancy or licence to occupy' means any lease of, tenancy of or licence to occupy the building granted or assigned to the occupier where the option to tax has been exercised (and not revoked) in relation to the building.

'Relevant person' means any person who

- is a lessor of the building;
- is an owner of the building for the purposes of the capital goods scheme; and
- has opted to tax the building.

'Relevant VAT' means VAT on rent paid or payable by the occupier in relation to the building.

'Building' includes any part of that building.

[*SI 2004/1933, Sch 1*].

This scheme aims to allow a person to escape, or substantially reduce, the VAT incurred on opted lease rentals whilst remaining in occupation of the building.

> *Example*
>
> Included are arrangements where
>
> - The occupier surrenders or terminates a taxable lease early and, despite the existence of an option to tax, the connected landlord makes a grant of a new lease, or sells the building to the occupier, exempt from VAT by reason of the option to tax disapplication rules.
> - The occupier, who is also a landlord further back in a chain of leases, arranges for all of the leases to be surrendered, leaving the occupier with the building (possibly paying a small amount of taxable ground rent to the ultimate freeholder).

(VAT Notice 700/8/18, para 6.11).

Hallmarked schemes: general

[4.8] In addition to the listed schemes falling within the provisions in **4.4–4.7** above, the Treasury can designate certain provisions (including any agreements, transactions, acts or courses of conduct) that it appears to them are, or are likely to be, included in (or associated with) schemes entered into for the purpose of enabling any person to obtain a tax advantage. See **4.4** above for the meaning of '*obtaining a tax advantage*'.

The Treasury can designate a provision even though it considers that the provision is likely to be a feature of schemes that are not tax avoidance schemes.

[*VATA 1994, Sch 11A paras 2, 4, 5*].

'**Scheme**' includes any arrangement, transaction or series of transactions. [*VATA 1994, Sch 11A para 1*].

It is not a scheme *in itself* to

- engage someone to ensure that all the input tax entitlement is claimed,
- utilise an extra-statutory concession or trade facilitation method open to all,

- use the grouping provisions, or
- negotiate a new partial exemption method

even if it involves a hallmark of avoidance. But these features may form part of a scheme.

(VAT Notice 700/8/18, para 7.3).

Liability to notify hallmarked schemes

[4.9] A *taxable person* must notify HMRC of the use of a hallmarked scheme when all of the following conditions are met.

Condition 1

The total value of his VAT-exclusive taxable supplies and exempt supplies exceeded:

- £10 million in the year immediately prior to the 'affected VAT return period', or any of the VAT return periods that are the subject of an 'affected claim'; or
- the 'appropriate proportion' of £10 million in the VAT return period immediately prior to the affected VAT return period, or any of the VAT return periods that are the subject of an affected claim.

The '*appropriate proportion*' means the proportion which the length of that VAT period bears to twelve months (i.e. one-quarter where quarterly VAT returns are prepared and one-twelfth where monthly VAT returns are prepared).

See Condition 4 below for '*affected VAT return period*' and '*affected claim*'.

See also **4.13** below for powers given to HMRC to prevent any artificial separation of business activities in an attempt to reduce turnover below the above limits.

Group undertakings

If the taxable person is a 'group undertaking', the conditions must be met by the taxable person *plus* every other group undertaking (i.e. the criteria apply to the whole group). For these purposes, the definitions in *Companies Act 2006, s 1161* apply (so that 'group' does not necessarily mean 'VAT group'). The group will comprise the undertaking in question, together with any undertaking which is

- a parent undertaking or a subsidiary undertaking of that undertaking; or
- a subsidiary undertaking of any parent undertaking of that undertaking.

For the purpose of calculating turnover, intra-corporate group transactions are included but intra-VAT group transactions are ignored. (VAT Notice 700/8/18, para 7.6.)

Condition 2

The taxable person is a party to a scheme that is not a listed scheme (see **4.4–4.7** above).

A person is a party to a scheme if he knowingly takes part in it but not if he

- is unwittingly involved in any of the steps of the scheme (i.e. has no knowledge of either the existence of the scheme or the role he plays in it); or
- acts purely in an advisory capacity.

(VAT Notice 700/8/18, para 3.3.1).

Condition 3

The main purpose, or one of the main purposes, of the scheme is to obtain a tax advantage (for any person). See **4.4** above for the meaning of 'obtaining a tax advantage'.

There is no one factor that determines whether the obtaining of a tax advantage is the main, or one of the main, purposes of a scheme. HMRC's view is that all circumstances need to be taken into consideration including

- the overall objectives of the arrangements and transactions (including the objectives of any wider corporate or VAT group to which the parties to the scheme belong and the objectives of any persons or businesses who control the parties); and
- whether the introduction of any unnecessary, complex or costly steps would have taken place were it not for the tax advantage that can be obtained.

In general, it is likely that the main purpose test would be met where, were it not for any VAT advantage arising, either the arrangements would not have been implemented or would have been implemented in a different manner. Similarly, where there are two or more ways of carrying out a genuine commercial objective and the choice is determined on grounds other than the potential VAT saving, it is unlikely the main purpose test would be met, even though a VAT advantage arises when compared to adopting one or more of the alternatives.

(VAT Notice 700/8/18, para 7.4.4).

Condition 4

One of the following relevant events occurs.

- In the return for the '*affected VAT return period*', the amount of VAT shown as payable by/to the taxable person is less than/greater than it would be but for the use of a hallmarked scheme to which he is party.
- The taxable person makes a claim (the '*affected claim*') for the repayment of output tax or an increase in credit for input tax in respect of which he has previously delivered a return and the amount claimed is greater than it would be but for a hallmarked scheme.
- In the return for a VAT period (the '*affected VAT return period*'), the amount of the taxable person's 'non-deductible tax' is less than it would be but for a hallmarked scheme.

'*Non-deductible tax*' means

(i) input tax for which he is not entitled to credit under *VATA 1994, s 25*; and

(ii) VAT on any supply of goods or services to him, or on the acquisition or importation of goods by him, which is not input tax and in respect of which he is entitled to a refund from HMRC under any provision of *VATA 1994*.

Condition 5

The scheme contains one or more of the hallmarks of avoidance. See **4.12** below.

Condition 6

The taxable person has not on a previous occasion provided HMRC with prescribed information under these provisions.

A scheme need only be notified once. If a taxable person starts a new scheme that is 'structured in the same way' as a previously notified scheme, he need not notify this new scheme. By 'structured in the same way', HMRC mean that the details of the scheme required to be notified under **4.10** below are the same as a previously notified scheme, even though the parties to the scheme and the hallmarks may be different.

However, if a taxable person starts a new scheme that is structured in a materially different way to a previously notified scheme, he must, subject to the necessary conditions being met, notify use of that scheme, irrespective of whether the hallmarks are the same.

(VAT Notice 700/8/18, para 7.7).

Condition 7

The taxable person has not been provided with a scheme number by someone who has registered the scheme with HMRC.

If someone has already registered the hallmarked scheme being used under the voluntary registration scheme (see **4.11** below) and has advised the taxable person of the scheme reference number allocated to it by HMRC (prefixed by the letters VRS), the taxable person is not required to notify HMRC. (VAT Notice 700/8/18, para 7.8).

[*VATA 1994, Sch 11A paras 6, 7*].

Schemes involving several parties

If a listed scheme involves more than one party, all the parties to that scheme are obliged to notify HMRC if they meet the conditions set out above. However, the parties concerned can make a joint notification. The notification should make it clear that it is a joint notification and who all the parties are that are making the notification. (VAT Notice 700/8/18, para 3.3.4).

Protective notifications

If a taxable person is unsure whether all of the relevant tests for notification are met, he may make a protective notification, explaining which test or tests is causing difficulty and why. (VAT Notice 700/8/18, para 7.2).

Notifying use of hallmarked schemes to HMRC

Time limit for notification

[4.10] Where a taxable person must notify HMRC of the use of a hallmarked scheme under **4.9** above, he must do so within 30 days from the end of

- the last day for submission of the return for the 'affected VAT return period';
- the date the 'affected claim' is made; or
- where HMRC make a direction under **4.13** below (artificial splitting of business), the last day for submission of the first VAT return made to HMRC following the direction.

See **4.9** above for '*affected VAT return period*' and '*affected claim*'.

[*VATA 1994, Sch 11A para 6*].

HMRC will accept early notifications (e.g. before the relevant event has taken place) provided the scheme has been implemented. (VAT Notice 700/8/118, para 8.1.1).

Method of notification

The following provisions relating to notification as set out in VAT Notice 700/8 have the force of law.

HMRC must be notified of the use of a hallmarked scheme either by e-mail to: vat.avoidance.disclosures.bst@hmrc.gsi.gov.uk or in writing to:

Anti-Avoidance Group (Intelligence)
VAT Avoidance Disclosures Unit
HM Revenue & Customs
CTIAA Intelligence S0528
PO Box 194
Bootle L69 9AA

Notification sent to any other address (e.g. another office or the VAT Written Enquiries Team) is not proper notification and may give rise to a penalty.

The notification should be prominently headed

Disclosure of use of hallmarked scheme – Notification under paragraph 6(3) of Schedule 11A to the VAT Act 1994

and give details of

- business name (where notification is by the representative member of a VAT group notifying as a result of a group member being involved in a notifiable scheme, also the name of the member);
- address; and
- VAT registration number.

Information to be notified

All of the following information must be provided to the extent that it is known. Explanations should be given of why any information cannot be provided.

- A statement as to which hallmark or hallmarks listed in **4.12** below are included in or associated with the scheme being notified.
  This need not be a standalone part of the notification and can be included as part of the general explanation of the working of the scheme. If unsure whether a feature is a hallmark, this should be stated. (VAT Notice 700/8/18, para 8.5).
- How the scheme gives rise to a 'tax advantage', including, to the extent that it is material to the tax advantage:
  (a) A description of each arrangement, transaction or series of transactions.
  Sufficient information must be provided to allow HMRC to understand how the tax advantage is obtained. The degree of information to be provided will vary from scheme to scheme but often the inclusion of a summary of the aims of the scheme and a diagrammatic representation of its structure, showing the participants, transaction flows, etc. will be of assistance. Only generic information need be provided, not detail that is specific to the particular circumstances (e.g. a step of the scheme could be described as 'building is leased to Company A' rather than '1 High Street is leased to Bank plc'). Copies of contracts and other documents do not need to be submitted. However, if it is easier to explain the scheme by referring to the specific detail, this may be done and supplementary documentation may be submitted if preferred. (VAT Notice 700/8/18, para 8.4.1).
  (b) The sequence of those arrangements, etc.
  The precise sequence should be made clear. HMRC recommend listing these as 'Step 1', 'Step 2', etc. (VAT Notice 700/8/18, para 8.4.2).
  (c) The timing, or the intervals between, those arrangements, etc.
  Explanation should be given, for example, if transactions are
  (i) due to take place within a short period of time of each other to take advantage of a VAT rule;
  (ii) due to take place over a long period to cause a VAT 'drip feed' effect; or
  (iii) timed to miss or bridge accounting periods.
  (VAT Notice 700/8/18, para 8.4.3).
  (d) The goods or services involved.
- How the involvement of any party to the scheme contributes to the obtaining of the tax advantage.
- Any provision having the force of law in the UK or elsewhere relied upon as giving rise to the tax advantage.

There is no obligation to quantify the amount or expected amount of the tax advantage. (VAT Notice 700/8/18, para 8.4).

See **4.4** above for the meaning of obtaining a '*tax advantage*'. For these purposes, a tax advantage is considered to be obtained (and any arrangement, transaction or series of transactions is considered to take place) provided a taxable person treats it as having been obtained or taken place for the purposes of a VAT return or a claim for repayment of output tax or an increase in credit for input tax.

[*SI 2004/1929*].

Acknowledgement by HMRC

HMRC will acknowledge notifications received at the above addresses. If all the required information is not received, the taxable person will be asked to provide it. If this information is not supplied within the time limit for making a notification (see above), the taxable person will be liable to a penalty. See **53.30 PENALTIES**. (VAT Notice 700/8/18, para 8.9).

Voluntary registration of hallmarked schemes

[4.11] Any person may, at any time, make a voluntary notification to HMRC of the details of a hallmarked scheme (e.g. a business that devises or markets a scheme may wish to do this to relieve its clients of the obligation of having to notify HMRC of the use of the scheme). To do so, the person should notify HMRC, and provide them with the information, as set out in **4.10** above. The notification should make clear that it is a voluntary notification.

HMRC will acknowledge the notification within ten working days of its receipt and normally state the reference number they have allocated to the scheme.

[*VATA 1994, Sch 11A para 9; SI 2004/1929*].

The hallmarks

[4.12] The Treasury have designated the following as provisions associated with ((1) to (3) below) or included ((4) to (8) below) in schemes.

A provision is treated as fitting a description listed even if it, or any feature of it, is not actually present (whether as a matter of law or for any other reason), provided a taxable person has treated that feature as being present for the purpose of making a VAT return or a claim for the repayment of output tax or an increase in credit for input tax. [*SI 2004/1933, Art 2*].

(1) Confidentiality condition

An agreement preventing or limiting the disclosure of how a scheme gives rise to a tax advantage. [*SI 2004/1933, Sch 2*].

This hallmark is aimed at confidentiality conditions that are intended to protect the competitive advantage of a promoter or creator of the scheme over other promoters and applies where

- a specific condition of confidentiality is imposed; or
- a client specifically undertakes (either in writing or verbally) not to reveal details of how a particular scheme gives rise to a tax advantage.

It is standard practice for advisers to include a 'general confidentiality condition' within their terms of engagement, prohibiting the client from passing on advice to third parties. HMRC do not regard such a clause as being a confidentiality condition if it is simply imposed in relation to all advice, not merely the scheme in question. But HMRC do consider it a hallmark if

- it is introduced specifically to prevent or limit a person from revealing details of how a particular scheme gives rise to a tax advantage; or
- it is specifically drawn to a client's attention by an adviser when introducing a scheme to the client in order to prohibit or limit the client from revealing details of how that particular scheme gives rise to a tax advantage.

(VAT Notice 700/8/18, para 10.2).

(2) The sharing of the tax advantage with another party to the scheme or with the promoter

An agreement that the tax advantage to a person accruing from the operation of the scheme be shared to any extent with another party to it or another person promoting it.

A person is a '*promoter of a scheme*' if, in the course of a trade, profession or business which involves the provision to other persons of services relating to taxation

- he is to any extent responsible for the design of the proposed arrangements; or
- he invites persons to enter into contracts for the implementation of the proposed arrangements.

[*SI 2004/1933, Sch 2*].

(3) Fee payable to a promoter which is in whole or in part contingent on tax savings from the scheme

An agreement that payment to a promoter of the scheme be contingent in whole or in part on the tax advantage accruing from the operation of the scheme.

See (2) above for the meaning of '*promoter of a scheme*'.

[*SI 2004/1933, Sch 2*].

(4) Prepayment between connected parties

A payment for a supply of goods or services between connected persons

(a) before the basic tax point for the supply (see **67.8 SUPPLY: TIME OF SUPPLY** for supplies of goods and **67.18 SUPPLY: TIME OF SUPPLY** for supplies of services) or, where applicable, the special tax point that applies to goods supplied on sale or return (see **67.12 SUPPLY: TIME OF SUPPLY**); or

(b) where the supply is a 'continuous supply' and the payment is before the goods or services are provided.

A supply is a '*continuous supply*' if it is a supply to which any of the following applies:

- *SI 1995/2518, Reg 85* (leases treated as supplies of goods, see **67.13 SUPPLY: TIME OF SUPPLY**).

- *SI 1985/2518, Reg 86* (supplies of water, gas or any form of power, heat, refrigeration or other cooling, or ventilation, see **67.15 SUPPLY: TIME OF SUPPLY**).
- *SI 1985/2518, Reg 90* (continuous supply of services, see **67.19 SUPPLY: TIME OF SUPPLY**).
- *SI 1985/2518, Reg 91* (royalties and similar payments, see **67.20 SUPPLY: TIME OF SUPPLY**).
- *SI 1985/2518, Reg 93* (supplies in the construction industry, see **43.19 LAND AND BUILDINGS: ZERO AND REDUCED RATE SUPPLIES AND DIY HOUSEBUILDERS**).

For the purposes of (*b*) above goods or services are provided at the time when, and to the extent that, the recipient receives the benefit of them.

A person is '*connected with*' another for the above purposes where

- one of them is an 'undertaking' in relation to which the other is a 'group undertaking', or
- both of them are connected to the same trust

and a person is connected to a trust where

- he is the settlor of the trust, a trustee or beneficiary of it; or
- he holds any shares in a company in accordance with the terms of the trust, or is a person on whose behalf such shares are held.

See **4.5** above for the meaning of 'undertaking' and 'group undertaking'.

[*SI 2004/1933, Art 2, Sch 2*].

(5) Funding by loan, share subscription or subscription in securities

The funding (in whole or in part) of a supply of goods or services between connected persons by means of a loan between connected persons or the subscription for shares in, or securities issued by, a connected person.

See (1) above for the meaning of '*connected persons*'.

[*SI 2004/1933, Art 2, Sch 2*].

(6) Off-shore loops

A supply of 'relevant services' which is used or intended to be used, in whole or in part, directly or indirectly, in making to a person belonging in the UK, a supply which is zero-rated, exempt or treated as made in another country (and not in the UK) by virtue of *VATA 1994, s 7(10)* (place of supply of services, see **66.14 SUPPLY: PLACE OF SUPPLY**).

'*Relevant services*' are either

- services which are exempt insurance services or exempt financial services (other than the management of an authorised unit trust scheme or an open-ended investment company) and which are
  - (a) supplied to a person who belongs outside the EU; or
  - (b) directly linked to the export of goods to a place outside the EU, insofar as they are supplies falling within *VATA 1994, Sch 9 Group 5 item 2* (the making of any advance or any credit, see **24.11 FINANCIAL SERVICES**); or

(c) consist of the provision of intermediary insurance services within *VATA 1994, Sch 9 Group 2 item 4* (see **37.13 INSURANCE**) or intermediary financial services within *VATA 1994, Sch 9 Group 5 item 5* (see **24.25 FINANCIAL SERVICES**) in relation to any transaction within (a) or (b) above; or

- a supply falling within *VATA 1994, Sch 5, paras 1–8. Schedule 5* was revoked with effect from 1 January 2010; the equivalent provision (with certain amendments) is now contained in *VATA 1994, Sch 4A, para 16* where the recipient of that supply belongs in a country, other than the Isle of Man, which is not an EU member state.

[*SI 2004/1933, Sch 2*].

(7) Property transactions between connected persons

A 'relevant grant' where

- the grantor or grantee of the interest or right is a person who is not entitled to credit for all the input tax wholly attributable to the supplies he makes;
- any work of construction, alteration, demolition, repair, maintenance or civil engineering has been or is to be carried out on the land; and
- the grant is made to a person connected with the grantor.

'*Relevant grant*' means the grant of any interest in or right over land or of any licence to occupy land or, in relation to land in Scotland, any personal right to call for or be granted any such interest or right, other than a grant of a description falling within *VATA 1994, Sch 8 Group 5 Item 1* (first grant of a major interest by a person constructing a building designed for dwelling, or intended for use solely for residential or charitable purposes; or by a person converting a non-residential building to residential use, see **43.1 LAND AND BUILDINGS: ZERO AND REDUCED RATE SUPPLIES AND DIY HOUSEBUILDERS**) or *VATA 1994, Sch 8 Group 6 Item 1* (first grant of a major interest in a protected building by a person reconstructing it, see **43.3 LAND AND BUILDINGS: ZERO AND REDUCED RATE SUPPLIES AND DIY HOUSEBUILDERS**).

'*Grant*' includes an assignment or surrender and the supply made by the person to whom an interest is surrendered when there is a reverse surrender.

See (1) above for '*connected persons*'.

[*SI 2004/1933, Art 2, Sch 2*].

(8) Issue of face value vouchers

The issue of 'face-value vouchers' for consideration except where

- the issuer expects, on reasonable grounds, that at least 75% of the face value of the vouchers will be redeemed within three years of the date on which the vouchers were issued; and
- whatever the redemption rate, the vouchers were issued to a connected person outside of any VAT group to which the issuer is a member.

'*Face value vouchers*' means tokens, stamps or vouchers of a description falling within *VATA 1994, Sch 10A para 1(1)* (see **70.10 TRADE PROMOTION SCHEMES**).

[*SI 2004/1933, Sch 2; SI 2005/1724; SI 2005/2009*].

The expected redemption rate is measured by reference to the face value of the vouchers taken together. HMRC give the following examples.

- A business issues £1m worth of vouchers and expects £900,000 worth of those vouchers to be redeemed. That is a 90% expected redemption rate (irrespective of whether the expectation is actually met).
- A business issues vouchers that can be partly redeemed and expects 100% of them to be redeemed but on average only 30% of the value to be redeemed. That would be a 30% expected redemption rate (irrespective of whether the expectation is actually met).

(VAT Notice 700/8/18, para 10.9.1).

Power of HMRC to exclude exemption from duty to notify

[4.13] Under normal circumstances, a taxable person does not have to disclose the use of a listed or hallmarked scheme where turnover is below certain limits (see 'Condition 1' in **4.5** and **4.9** above respectively).

The following provisions are, however, designed to prevent the maintenance or creation of any 'artificial' separation of business activities carried on by two or more persons from resulting in any avoidance of the obligations to notify schemes. In determining whether any separation of business activities is '*artificial*', consideration must be given to the extent to which the different persons carrying on those activities are closely bound to one another by financial, economic and organisational links.

HMRC may make a direction under which the persons specified therein become treated as a single taxable person carrying on the activities of a business described in the direction with effect from the date of the direction or such later date as is specified. Where this is done, if that single taxable person would not be excluded from notifying a scheme, then the persons named in the direction cannot be excluded.

The direction must be served on each person named in it and remains in force until it is revoked or replaced by a further direction.

Before making a direction naming any person, HMRC must be satisfied that

- he is making or has made taxable or exempt supplies;
- the activities in the course of which he makes those supplies form only part of certain activities, the other activities being carried on concurrently or previously (or both) by one or more other persons; and
- if all the taxable and exempt supplies of the business described in the direction were taken into account, the turnover would exceed the minimum turnover limits.

[*VATA 1994, Sch 11A para 8*].

Serial tax avoidance

Legislation was introduced on 15 September 2016 that is intended to deter the use of tax avoidance schemes and the serial tax avoidance legislation also covers a scheme that is disclosable, or should have been disclosed, under the old disclosure regime and the current DASVOIT regime (see **4.2** above). The serial tax avoidance regime (STAR) covers all indirect taxes.

If HMRC have successfully defeated a tax avoidance scheme that has been used by a business, they will issue a warning notice to that business. The warning notice will remain in force for the five-year warning period. Businesses will be required to provide HMRC with detailed information annually regarding any avoidance schemes used during the warning period. If HMRC successfully defeat any avoidance schemes during that period, they can levy sanctions including penalties that are based on the counteracted tax advantage and extend the existing warning period by another five years.

The following penalties will be applied:

First defeat	20% penalty will be charged in respect of the first defeat during the warning period
Second defeat	40% penalty will be charged on the second defeat of a new avoidance arrangement during the warning period
Third and subsequent defeats	60% penalty will be charged on the third and successive defeats of a new avoidance arrangement during the warning period.

HMRC must assess the penalty within 12 months of the relevant defeat. The penalty must be paid within 30 days of the date of issue of the assessment.

No penalties will be imposed if the person has provided satisfactory evidence to either HMRC or a tribunal that they had a reasonable excuse.

HMRC can also publish details of the serial tax avoider if both of the following apply:

- The person suffers a relevant defeat in relation to new avoidance arrangement(s) which the person has used during the warning period.
- The person has received at least two warning notices in respect of other defeated arrangements which were used during the same warning period. Providing all the arrangements were used during the same period then it is not relevant whether they have been defeated.

HMRC will give the person advanced warning that their details are to be published to enable that person to give arguments/evidence regarding why it is not appropriate to publish their details.

HMRC have produced detailed guidance on the Gov.UK website: https://assets.publishing.service.gov.uk/government/uploads/system/uploads/attachment_data/file/671694/Serial_Tax_Avoidance_Regime__STAR__guidance.pdf.

(HMRC CC/FS38); [*FA 2016, s 159, Sch 18*].

Specific anti-avoidance provisions

[4.14] Anti-avoidance legislation is intended to counteract transactions designed to avoid taxation, but *bona fide* transactions may sometimes be caught also. The main provisions relating to VAT are listed below.

Provisions in *VATA 1994*

- Group supplies using an overseas member. [*VATA 1994, s 43(2A)–(2E)*]. See **28.6 GROUPS OF COMPANIES**.
- Groups of companies – eligibility rules. [*VATA 1994, s 43D*]. See **28.2 GROUPS OF COMPANIES**.
- Acquisition of a business as a going concern by a partly-exempt group. [*VATA 1994, s 44*]. See **28.7 GROUPS OF COMPANIES**.
- Missing trader intra-Community fraud. [*VATA 1994, s 55A*]. See 4.**15** below.
- Joint and several liability for unpaid VAT. [*VATA 1994, s 77A*]. See **32.3 HMRC: POWERS**.
- Disaggregation of business activities (business splitting). [*VATA 1994, Sch 1 para 1A*]. See **9.5 BUSINESS**.
- Registration by overseas traders in respect of disposals of assets for which a VAT repayment is claimed. [*VATA 1994, Sch 3A*]. See **60.26 REGISTRATION**.
- Transactions between connected persons. [*VATA 1994, Sch 6 para 1*]. See **72.19 VALUATION**.
- Demonstration cars. [*VATA 1994, Sch 6 para 1A*]. See **46.7 MOTOR CARS**.
- Direct (party plan) selling. [*VATA 1994, Sch 6 para 2*]. See **72.23 VALUATION**.
- Heated water. [*VATA 1994, Sch 8 Group 2 Item 2(c)*]. See **75.2 ZERO-RATED SUPPLIES**.
- Denial of zero-rating for printed matter sold in connection with another supply that is not itself zero-rated. [*VATA 1994, Sch 8 Group 3 Note 2*]. See **55.2 PRINTED MATTER**.
- Groups of companies – registration. [*VATA 1994, Sch 9A*]. See **28.5 GROUPS OF COMPANIES**.
- Option to tax land and buildings. [*VATA 1994, Sch 10*]. See **42.27** and **42.32 LAND AND BUILDINGS: EXEMPT SUPPLIES AND OPTION TO TAX**.
- Face value vouchers. [*VATA 1994, Sch 10A*]. See **70.10 TRADE PROMOTION SCHEMES**.
- Power to require security. [*VATA 1994, Sch 11 para 4*]. See **32.1 HMRC: POWERS**.
- Duty to notify certain avoidance schemes. [*VATA 1994, Sch 11A*]. See **4.4** above.

Provisions in the *VAT Regulations 1995*

- Construction industry stage payments. [*SI 1995/2518, Reg 93*]. See **43.19 LAND AND BUILDINGS: ZERO AND REDUCED RATE SUPPLIES AND DIY HOUSEBUILDERS**.
- Assignment of debts. [*SI 1995/2518, Reg 94A*]. See **67.6 SUPPLY: TIME OF SUPPLY**.
- Continuous supplies of services – time of supply. [*SI 1995/2518, Reg 94B*]. See **67.19 SUPPLY: TIME OF SUPPLY**.
- Grants of land – time of supply. [*SI 1995/2518, Reg 94B*]. See **67.13 SUPPLY: TIME OF SUPPLY**.

- Long leases and tenancies – time of supply. [*SI 1995/2518, Reg 94B*]. See **67.13 SUPPLY: TIME OF SUPPLY.**
- Power, heat, water and gas – time of supply. [*SI 1994/2518, Reg 94B*]. See **67.15 SUPPLY: TIME OF SUPPLY.**
- Partial exemption – special method over-ride. [*SI 1995/2518, Regs 102A–102C*]. See **50.10 PARTIAL EXEMPTION.**
- Partial exemption – standard method over-ride. [*SI 1995/2518, Regs 107A–107C*]. See **50.9 PARTIAL EXEMPTION.**
- Attribution of input tax – financial services. [*SI 1995/2518, Reg 103(B)*]. See **50.12 PARTIAL EXEMPTION.**
- Capital goods scheme generally and specifically disposals of capital items during the period of adjustment. [*SI 1995/2518, Regs 112–116*]. See **11 CAPITAL GOODS SCHEME** and specifically **11.7 CAPITAL GOODS SCHEME.**
- Warehoused goods. [*SI 1995/2518, Reg 145K*]. See **73.5 WAREHOUSED GOODS AND FREE ZONES.**
- Bad debt relief – repayment of refund on assigned debts. [*SI 1995/2518, Reg 171*]. See **7.12 BAD DEBT RELIEF.**

Other provisions

- Margin scheme supplies acquired as part of a TOGC. [*SI 1992/3122, Art 8*]. See **62.4 SECOND-HAND GOODS.**
- Leased cars. [*SI 1992/3222, Art 7*]. See **46.11 MOTOR CARS.**
- Private use of services following a TOGC. [*SI 1993/1507*]. See **48.6 OUTPUT TAX.**
- Land, buildings and civil engineering works used for private purposes – self-supply charge for recovery of input tax. [*SI 1993/1507*]. See **35.7 INPUT TAX** and **48.6 OUTPUT TAX.**
- Margin scheme supplies acquired as part of a TOGC – motor cars. [*SI 1995/1268, Art 12*]. See **62.4 SECOND-HAND GOODS.**

Reverse charge: missing trader intra-community fraud

[4.15] As a general rule, the taxable person who makes a taxable supply is the person liable to pay the VAT on that supply to the tax authorities. However, to counter missing trader intra-community fraud ('MTIC'), the UK was granted a derogation from *Directive 2006/112/EC, Art 193* allowing it to introduce legislation to make the customer the person liable to register for VAT (if not already registered) and account for and pay the VAT on the supply of specified goods which are commonly used to perpetrate the fraud. A more general power to introduce such measures was extended to all EU member states and to a number of different types of potentially fraudulent activity by the insertion of *Directive 2006/112/EC, Art 193* with effect from 9 April 2010. It is intended to operate to December 2018 and is subject to review by the Commission in June 2017.

This 'reverse charge' procedure is governed by *VATA 1994, s 55A* and applies, with some exclusions, to supplies of mobile phones and computer chips which are made by one VAT-registered business to another and valued at £5,000 and over. VAT-registered businesses which sell such goods will need to consider whether the reverse charge applies to their transactions. Businesses which purchase such goods must consider whether they need to register for VAT (if not already registered) and must account for VAT on those purchases to HMRC.

Full details are given in **4.16–4.25** below.

Emissions allowances

VATA 1994, s 55A extends the scope of the reverse charge to emissions allowances supplied in the UK.

A transfer of:

- an allowance within *Art 3* of *Directive 2003/87/EC* (which established the scheme for greenhouse gas emission allowance trading within the European Union);
- an emission reduction unit that can be used by an operator for compliance with that scheme; or
- a certified emission reduction that can be used by an operator for compliance with that scheme.

Only those compliance market credits that can be used to meet obligations under the EU Emissions Trading Scheme (EUETS) are subject to the reverse charge mechanism. These currently comprise EU allowances, some certified emission reductions (CER) and some emission reduction units (ERU), as defined in *Directive 2003/87/EC.*

[*FA 2010, s 50; SI 2010/2239, Art 6*]. (VAT Notice 735, para 3.5).

Specified goods or services

[4.16] Subject to the excepted goods in **4.17** below, goods or services on which customers must account for VAT under the reverse charge are as follows.

Mobile telephones

Mobile telephones, whether or not they have any function in addition to the transmitting and receiving of spoken messages. [*SI 2010/2239, Art 5(a)*].

The definition of a mobile phone takes its everyday meaning in the UK and includes the following.

- Any handsets which have a mobile phone function (i.e. the transmitting and receiving of spoken messages), whether or not they have any other function. It therefore includes other communication devices, such as Blackberrys.
- Mobile phones supplied with accessories (such as a charger, battery, cover or handsfree kit) as a single package.
- Pre-pay (or 'pay as you go') mobile phones, whether or not the selling price includes an element attributable to the cost of future use of the phones.

- Mobile phones locked to a network but not supplied with a contract for airtime.

With the introduction of smart phones and mobile phone/tablet hybrid devices ('phablets') HMRC regard a device as being a mobile phone if:

- it has a mobile phone function (see above); and
- it has a screen size of 5 inches or less, measured diagonally from a top corner to a bottom corner, excluding the bezel; or
- it falls within 8517 11 00 or 8517 12 00 of *Annex I* to *Council Regulation 2658/87* on the tariff and statistical nomenclature and on the Common Customs Tariff (as amended).

But the reverse charge does not apply to the following.

- Mobile phones which are supplied with a contract for airtime (see **4.17** below).
- Mobile phone accessories which are supplied separately from a mobile phone.
- Walkie-talkies.
- WiFi phones unless also intended for use with mobile phone networks.
- Phones where the base unit is connected to a landline but the handset is not tethered to that base unit.
- Tablet devices that do not fall within the description provided above of devices which HMRC regard as being mobile phones.
- 3G data cards and WiFi cards.

(VAT Notice 735, para 3.2).

Integrated circuit devices

Integrated circuit devices, such as central processing units and microprocessor units, in a state prior to integration into end-user products. [*SI 2010/2239, Art 5(b)*].

The terminology surrounding computer chips can be confusing. As a guide, all computer chips covered by the reverse charge fall within the tariff commodity code 8542 3190 00. Included are

- small integrated circuits (i.e. Central Processing Units or CPUs);
- discrete integrated circuit devices (i.e. Microprocessors or Microprocessor Units (MPUs) and Microcontrollers or Microcontroller Units (MCUs)); and
- chipsets – the dedicated cluster of integrated circuits which support MPUs.

The reverse charge applies to such items when they are in a state prior to integration into end-user products, or where they are sold separately and not as part of an assembled item (e.g. a motherboard).

Items such as computer servers, laptops or desktop units are excluded from the scope of the reverse charge.

(VAT Notice 735, para 3.3).

Wholesale supplies of gas and electricity

Subject to certain exceptions, from 1 July 2014 a reverse charge applies to wholesale supplies of electricity and gas between counterparties established in the UK. This typically means wholesale supplies between UK counterparties under trading contracts (for example, European Federation of Energy Traders contracts, Grid Master Agreements, and National Balancing Point contracts) and over-the-counter or spot contracts of electricity or gas, where the gas is supplied through a natural gas system situated within the territory of an EU member state or any network connected to such a system. Businesses are not required to submit a reverse charge sales list (see **4.21**(5) below) in relation to wholesale supplies of gas and electricity. Examples of specific supplies or charges covered by the reverse charge are:

- balancing mechanism imbalance settlement charges, and other gas balancing or gas reconciliation charges;
- services supplied under a wholesale/trading contract that are ancillary to the supply of gas or electricity;
- gas loaded onto road trucks and delivered at a flange linked to Liquid Natural Gas storage facilities i.e. the gas is still within the natural gas system or a network connected to it; and
- shipper to shipper metering correction charges where the consumer has changed supplier.

Supplies to power stations and Combined Heating and Power plants will only be included in the reverse charge where they are made by way of trading rather than for consumption only.

Electricity supplied under a Power Purchase Agreement (PPA) or similar agreement may or may not be subject to the reverse charge depending on their wholesale features. Electricity sold under such an agreement will not be regarded as wholesale and therefore will not be subject to the reverse charge where:

- the seller of the electricity is a generator who is exempted from holding a generating licence, and
- the generation capacity by asset is 100MW or less; and
- the generated volume is not allocated to the generator's production account with Elexon or the generator account with the Single Electricity Market Operator (SEMO) in Northern Ireland.

Similarly, if generated power is sold under a PPA or similar agreement to the NFPA, NFPA Scotland Ltd or NFPA Services Ltd and the generated power is not allocated to a production account with Elexon or generation account with SEMO, that power is excluded from the reverse charge. The sale of the power by the NFPA by auction is also excluded from the reverse charge.

Supplies that are incidental to a reverse charge supply are also subject to the reverse charge.

The reverse charge does not apply to supplies of gas and electricity made under supply licence or metered arrangements to domestic and business premises (supplies for consumption). VAT-registered businesses that do not resell or trade the gas or electricity will not be affected by the reverse charge.

Unless the supply is incidental to a reverse charge supply, the reverse charge will not apply to:

- supplies of Liquified Natural Gas delivered 'ship-to-ship';
- supplies of natural gas liquids (ethane, propane butane and condensate) sold separate to the sale of gas;
- supplies made by an accredited feed in installation;
- supplies currently zero-rated e.g. trades on terminal markets;
- supplies to third party intermediaries and directed utilities for consumption by the directed utility or onward supply by the directed utility to an end user for consumption;
- supplies that are contracted for separately from wholesale supplies of gas and electricity, for example transportation services; and
- supplies to businesses not registered and not liable to be registered for VAT.

Further examples of specific supplies or charges not covered by the reverse charge include:

- distribution use of system charges;
- transmission network use of system charges;
- metering rental charges;
- data collection charges;
- balancing system use of system charges;
- interconnector capacity charges;
- gas storage charges;
- gas network system charges;
- payments made in respect of constraint contracts with National Grid;
- balancing and settlement code charges (Elexon market operator charges);
- Levy Exemption Certificates and/or Renewable Obligation Certificates traded separately from the underlying electricity;
- fees for exchange related settlement for example N2EX fees; and
- option premiums.

The above list is not exhaustive.

[*SI 2014/1458; SI 2014/1497*]. (HMRC Briefs 23/14 and 28/14). (VAT Notice 735, para 3.4).

Wholesale supplies of telecommunications services

Subject to certain exceptions, from 1 February 2016 a domestic reverse charge applies to wholesale supplies of telecommunications services between counterparties established in the UK.

In the context of the reverse charge the term 'wholesale supplies' means business to business supplies where the intention is to sell on the supply with no or negligible consumption of the supply by the businesses concerned. In the context of telecommunications services the term 'wholesale supplies' means supplies between carriers of these services (in the UK), or supplies of these services to network operators for onward supply to the consumer or user of the underlying service.

The reverse charge covers wholesale supplies of telecommunications services which enable speech communication instantly or with only a negligible delay between the transmission and the receipt of signal and the transmission of writing, images and sounds or information of any nature when provided in connection with these services.

Examples of services covered by the reverse charge for wholesale supplies of telecommunications services include:

- wholesale switched voice services, including switched voice over internet protocol services;
- wholesale SMS and multimedia messaging service (MMS) services (e.g. push messages);
- wholesale 'Over The Top' telecommunications messages;
- SMS hubbing; and
- SMS and voice aggregator services.

The domestic reverse charge for wholesale supplies of telecommunications services does not apply to:

- non-wholesale supplies;
- transport/capacity and related access services (i.e. wholesale line rental, lease lines);
- indefeasible right of use charges;
- broadband and other data transmission only services;
- supplies for final consumption;
- supplies to a member of a corporate group for onward supply within that corporate group where one or more corporate group members consume that supply;
- the return of unused minutes that were not originally subject to the reverse charge;
- supplies which are subject to the reverse charge on services received from abroad (see **39.4 INTERNATIONAL SERVICES**);
- supplies of face value vouchers where *VATA 1994, Sch 10A* applies (see **70.9 TRADE PROMOTION SCHEMES**); and
- businesses not registered or liable to be registered for VAT.

If supplies contain a mixture of reverse charge and non-reverse charge supplies, and it is impossible or impractical to separate out the element that is subject to the reverse charge, it is acceptable to apply the reverse charge to the whole supply.

Wholesale supplies of telecommunications services are not required to be included in a reverse charge sales list.

[*SI 2016/12*]. (HMRC Brief 1/16).

Excepted supplies

[4.17] A supply of any of the following is an excepted supply and the reverse charge does not apply.

- A supply of mobile telephones and/or computer chips where the VAT-exclusive value of the supply is less than £5,000. This figure is calculated on an invoice basis so where the total value of all the specified goods shown on a particular invoice is £5,000 or more, the reverse charge applies to the total value of the specified goods on that invoice. There is no *de minimis* rule in respect of supplies of emissions allowances, wholesale supplies of gas, electricity and telecommunication services. In many business to business transactions several separate invoices may be issued in relation to a single purchase order, for example, a separate invoice for each delivery, which, when totalled, satisfies the single purchase order. Where the single purchase order value for mobile telephones and/or computer chips is larger than the individual invoice value, it will be acceptable to apply the reverse charge to all invoices relating to the single purchase order, providing the purchase order value exceeds the £5,000 threshold and both parties agree

- A supply of specified goods within **4.16** above where the goods are also eligible goods under the margin scheme of **62 SECOND-HAND GOODS** and, in accordance with that scheme, the supplier opts to account for the VAT chargeable on the supply on the profit margin instead of by reference to its value. In such a case, the VAT payable is calculated under the margin scheme rules.
- A supply of a mobile telephone where, at the time a person enters into the agreement to purchase the telephone, he enters into an agreement (including the renewal or extension of an existing agreement) with a provider of a '*public electronic communications service*' (as defined in *Communications Act 2003, s 151*) for the supply, in relation to that telephone, of such a service; and that agreement is not one that requires periodical pre-payments in order to use the service ('Pay as You Go').
- A transfer or disposal of specified goods within **4.16** above which a business gives away for no consideration and that is treated as a supply of goods by virtue of *VATA 1994, Sch 4 para 5(1)* (business gifts). See **48.5 OUTPUT TAX.**

[*SI 2010/2239, Arts 3, 7, 8*]. (HMRC Brief 35/10).

Provision of labour in the construction sector

[4.18] Following a consultation into possible options that could be used to tackle fraud in construction industry supply chains, the Government has announced that it will be introducing a domestic reverse charge to prevent VAT losses continuing to occur.

Once the changes have been introduced the customer, rather than the supplier, will be responsible for accounting for any VAT due along the supply chain to prevent the opportunity for the supplier to under declare the VAT due. The changes are expected to come into effect from 1 October 2019. The long lead time is intended to provide adequate time for businesses to implement the changes.

Liability to register for VAT

[4.19] Where:

- a taxable (but not a zero-rated) supply of goods or services ('*the relevant supply*') is made to a person ('*the recipient*');

- the relevant supply is of specified goods or services falling within **4.16** above but is not an excepted supply within **4.17** above; and
- the total value of the relevant supply (excluding VAT), and of any other supplies to which these provisions apply (excluding VAT) made to the recipient in the month in which the relevant supply is made, exceeds £1,000,

the relevant supply and those other supplies (both excluding VAT) are to be treated for VAT registration purposes as:

(a) taxable supplies of the recipient (as well as taxable supplies of the supplier); and

(b) in so far as the recipient is supplied in connection with the carrying on by him of any business, supplies made by him in the course or furtherance of that business,

but only in so far as their total value exceeds £1,000.

Nothing in (*b*) above requires any supply to be disregarded for the purposes of VAT registration on the grounds that it is a supply of capital assets of the recipient's business.

[*VATA 1994, s 55A(1)–(5)*].

The effect of this is that a non-registered business must consider whether the purchase of goods or services, to which the reverse charge would apply if it were registered for VAT, makes it liable to be registered for VAT. This is because such purchases must be included when considering whether the value of its taxable supplies has exceeded the VAT registration threshold. The first £1,000 of such purchases per month is disregarded but any excess does count, along with the other taxable supplies of the business, towards its liability to register for VAT. That value must be included in calculating both the value of taxable supplies in the previous 12 months or less, and in the expected value of taxable supplies in the next 30 days alone, for the purpose of applying these tests for liability to register for VAT.

Reverse charge accounting for VAT

[4.20] If

- a taxable person makes a supply of goods or services to a person ('the recipient') at any time,
- the supply is of specified goods or services within **4.16** above and is not an excepted supply within **4.17** above, and
- the recipient is a taxable person at that time and is supplied in connection with the carrying on by him of any business,

it is for the recipient, on the supplier's behalf, to account for and pay VAT on the supply and not for the supplier.

Any provision of *VATA 1994*, any other *Act* and any subordinate legislation that has effect for the purposes of, or in connection with the enforcement of, any obligation to account for and pay VAT applies in relation to any person required under these provisions to account for and pay any VAT as if that VAT were VAT on a supply made by him.

[*VATA 1994, s 55(6)–(8)*].

The reverse charge applies only to supplies of specified goods or services within the UK made by one VAT-registered business to another. The rules and procedures for sales to non-business customers, dispatches of goods or services to persons in another EU member state and exports outside the EU are unaffected by the introduction of the reverse charge.

What the supplier must do

[4.21] The supplier must be aware of the following.

(1) Checking that reverse charge applies

Before applying the reverse charge, a supplier must be happy that all the necessary conditions are met. He will have first-hand knowledge as to whether the goods or services being supplied are specified goods or services and if mobile telephones and/or computer chips are being sold in quantities above the £5,000 threshold. But the goods or services must also be sold to a taxable person for a business purpose, and the supplier must obtain the customers' VAT registration number and carry out reasonable checks to establish the customer's VAT status. If he does not, he may be held liable for incorrect application of the reverse charge (see **4.24** below).

What is reasonable in any case will depend on the business sector involved and the type of relationship the supplier has with the customer. HMRC give the following as indicators in deciding how far a supplier should go before accepting a customer's representations. The list is not exhaustive or definitive.

- Do commercial checks on creditworthiness and customer status suggest any reason to doubt the customer's *bona fides*?
- Is the VAT registration number genuine and does it belong to the person who is quoting it? Suppliers may use the checking facility provided by the HMRC advice service/helpline. Large businesses may contact their Client Relationship Manager for advice.
- Is the customer a new customer or a well-established business known to the supplier? In general, there is no need for the supplier to carry out special verification of VAT registration numbers of existing customers with whom they have an established trading relationship.
- Is there any indication in the pattern of orders that the customer is attempting to disaggregate his purchases of mobile telephones and/or computer chips in order to circumvent the £5,000 *de minimis*?
- Has the supplier any grounds to doubt the *bona fides* of the customer?
- Are there features or circumstances that are out of the ordinary in respect of the transaction? If so, the supplier should establish the reasons are credible.

There is further advice at **32.3 HMRC: POWERS** relating to the integrity of a supplier and this applies equally to that of a customer under these provisions.

The supplier should keep evidence of the checks that it has performed, so it can be produced to HMRC if subsequently required.

If he cannot satisfy himself of the *bona fides* of his customer or his VAT registration status, the supplier should consider whether to proceed with the transaction. If he does proceed with a reverse charge transaction where there are doubts that the reverse charge applies, the supplier may wish to consider asking the customer for a deposit equivalent to the output tax for which he will become liable if the reverse charge is applied in error. This may be especially helpful if the customer has applied for, but not yet received, a VAT registration number. Any deposit taken in these circumstances can be refunded when evidence of the VAT registration is received.

(VAT Notice 735, paras 9.1–9.3).

(2) Notifying HMRC

On the first occasion on which a business makes a reverse charge supply of mobile telephones or computer chips under these provisions, it must notify HMRC of that fact within 30 days of the day on which the supply is made. It must also give HMRC details of the name and telephone number of a contact.

The notification must be made on-line by using a portal provided by HMRC (although if this is unavailable for any reason, HMRC may allow the notification to be made by e-mail). See under (5) below for further details of the method of notification which is also used for the RCSL system.

HMRC must also be advised of the date on which the business ceases to make reverse charge supplies and, if it subsequently again makes reverse charge supplies, it must notify HMRC of the date and again provide contact details. In each case, notification must be within 30 days of the event.

[*SI 1995/2518, Regs 23A, 23B, 23D*]. (VAT Notice 735, paras 7.7 and 11.2).

(3) Invoices

When a supplier makes a sale to which reverse charge accounting applies, he must show all the information normally required to be shown on a VAT invoice but must also annotate the invoice to make it clear that the reverse charge applies and that the customer is required to account for the VAT. Unless otherwise agreed with HMRC the amount of VAT due under the reverse charge rules must be clearly stated on the invoice but should *not* be included in the amount shown as total VAT charged.

With effect from 1 January 2013, invoices for reverse charge supplies, when the customer is liable for the VAT, must include the reference 'reverse charge'. The precise wording is not prescribed but a suggested form of wording is

- Reverse charge: *VATA 1994, s 55A* applies
- Reverse charge: Customer to pay the VAT to HMRC

If the seller produces invoices using an IT system, and that system cannot show the amount of VAT to be accounted for under the reverse charge mechanism, then the wording should state that VAT is to be accounted for by the purchaser at 20% of the VAT-exclusive selling price for reverse charge goods or services. The customer must be able to identify the reverse charge goods or services, and a legend such as the following may be helpful.

Customer to account to HMRC for the reverse charge output tax on the VAT-exclusive price of items marked reverse charge.

Electronic invoicing

HMRC will allow the use of electronic invoices that use a coded representation rather than textual form provided that the content can be demonstrated to an HMRC auditor by both parties to the electronic invoicing exchange. This is subject to the agreement of both parties.

(VAT Notice 735, para 7.5).

(4) Completion of the VAT return

A supplier who has made a reverse charge supply must include the VAT-exclusive value of the supply in the total value of sales figure in Box 6 of the VAT return. There is no output tax to include in Box 1 because that is the responsibility of the customer. (VAT Notice 735, para 7.6).

(5) Completion of a Reverse Charge Sales List (RCSL)

A business which starts to make reverse charge supplies within these provisions must notify HMRC (see (2) above). It must then, for any VAT period in which it has made a reverse charge supply of mobile telephones and/or computer chips (but not emissions allowances or wholesale supplies of gas, electricity and telecommunication services), submit an RCSL for that VAT period to HMRC no later than the day by which it is required to make the VAT return. RCSLs may therefore be due monthly, quarterly or annually depending on the length of the VAT return period.

The RCSL must contain the following particulars.

(a) The VAT registration number of the business.

(b) The UK nine-digit VAT registration number of each customer to whom it has made a reverse charge supply. Any 'GB' suffix, branch identifier or EORI number should not be included. If, exceptionally, a business does not know its customer's VAT number at the time it submits a RCSL, it should either
- enter a 'dummy' VAT registration number (e.g. 111 1111 11 or, 222 2222 22), submit with RCSL with value data and subsequently, on receipt of the customer's VAT number, amend the entry (HMRC's preferred option); or
- submit the RCSL excluding that customer and subsequently add the appropriate sales information when the customer's VAT registration number is received.

(c) For each month falling within the VAT period, the total value of the reverse charge supplies made to each customer within (*b*) above. If there are no reverse charge supplies to a customer for one or more months in the VAT period (but not every month), then '0' value for the month(s) must be inserted. Figures should be declared in whole pounds (by either rounding to the nearest pound or truncating the pence). If the total net value is negative the information should be submitted with a leading negative sign.

The RCSL system (including any notifications) is web-based and accessed through the HMRC section of the GOV.UK website at:

https://www.gov.uk/government/organisations/hm-revenue-customs

Businesses that do not already use an HRMC on-line service will need to register. Guidance on how to register is available at

www.gateway.gov.uk

The RCSL system is menu driven and provides help for each option. All aspects require completion electronically. The information can be entered directly on-line or a comma separated values (csv) file can be uploaded.

Declaration

A RCSL must contain a declaration made by the business that it is true and complete.

Nil returns

If, in any VAT period, no reverse charge supplies are made, a nil declaration is required (unless the business has notified HMRC that it has ceased making reverse charge supplies without intending subsequently to make such supplies). This is done by selecting the 'nil declaration' option on the RCSL home page. There is no facility to submit a nil CSV file.

Correcting errors

If an RCSL has been submitted and a mistake is subsequently discovered, the correct information must be supplied to HMRC by amending the original submission. If the RCSL was submitted by completing the on-line list, it is possible to add, delete or change lines on-line. But if the RSCL was submitted by uploading a csv file, the complete list must be resubmitted with the necessary additions, deletions or changes (i.e. including all the lines that were correct in the original submission).

If HMRC discovers a material inaccuracy within a submitted RCSL then they may levy a £100 penalty.

[*SI 1995/2518, Regs 23A, 23C*]. (VAT Notice 735, para 11).

Failure to submit an RCSL

If a business fails to submit a RCSL then it will be charged a daily penalty up to a maximum of 100 days. The daily penalty will increase with each further default at the following rates:

- 1st default – £5.00 per day;
- 2nd default – £210 per day;
- 3rd and subsequent default – £15 per day.

What the customer must do

[4.22] The customer must be aware of the following.

(1) Accounting for the VAT on a reverse charge supply

VAT-registered customers who are not charged VAT because the reverse charge applies must account for the VAT due on the supply. The amount of VAT should be shown on the VAT invoice issued by the supplier (see **4.20**(3) above) and should be accounted for on the VAT return for the period in which the supply is received. The normal tax point rules apply.

The customer can reclaim this VAT as input tax on the same return as it is accounted for, subject to the normal rules, including any partial exemption restriction that may apply.

(VAT Notice 735, para 8.1).

(2) Completion of VAT return

The customer must enter the output tax payable on purchases under the reverse charge in Box 1 but the value of the purchases must not be entered in Box 6. Input tax can be reclaimed, subject to the normal rules, by including it in the total shown in Box 4. The value of the purchases should be entered in Box 7 in the normal way. (VAT Notice 735, para 8.5).

(3) Onward sales of goods or services purchased under the reverse charge system

If the purchaser of reverse charge goods or services sells them on to another VAT-registered business in the UK and that sale also meets the conditions for treatment as a reverse charge supply, then the reverse charge applies to the onward sale. Otherwise, if the goods or services are sold in any other circumstances, then the appropriate normal VAT accounting rules for the transaction in question must be followed. (VAT Notice 735, para 8.2).

Adjustments and corrections

Adjustments in the course of business

[4.23] Adjustments may be required to reverse charge supplies (e.g. because of changes in price after the invoice has been issued or because of returned goods or services).

Where a supplier offers a credit or contingent discount, provided both parties agree, no VAT adjustment need be made by either party (although adjustment will still be required to the RCSL in relation to sales of mobile telephones and computer chips (see **4.21**(5) above). HMRC regard this as the easiest option because of the complexities involved in making adjustments but the following methods are also possible.

- *Return not yet made.* If the supplier or customer identifies a change in the value of reverse charge goods or services before its VAT accounting period is closed, it can simply adjust its primary records of the sale/purchase and make sure the corrected figure feeds through to the VAT account.

- *Return already made and price adjustment removes the supply out of the reverse charge.* If both parties agree, the original VAT treatment need not be reversed although an adjustment to the RCSL will still be required in relation to sales of mobile telephones and computer chips (see **4.21**(5) above). If they do not agree, the supplier will need to bring output tax to account and collect the VAT from his customer. The customer will need to reverse the output tax he has entered and correct the input tax entry to reflect the corrected value. In that case, HMRC recommend the whole supply is credited and then re-invoiced with the new VAT treatment.

Suggested forms of words for credit notes where the reverse charge applied are

- Reverse charge: Customer to account for the output tax adjustment of -£X to HMRC
- Reverse charge: UK customer to account for the output tax adjustment of -£X to HMRC
- Customer to account to HMRC for the adjustment to reverse charge output tax on the VAT-exclusive price of items marked reverse charge.

Where the output tax liability reverts to the supplier as a result of a decrease in consideration, HMRC recommend the whole supply is credited and then re-invoiced with the new tax treatment. However, if using credit notes is preferred the following would also be acceptable.

- Reverse charge: Customer to account for output tax adjustment of -£X to HMRC, supplier now accounts for £Y output tax to HMRC.

Mistakes

Mistakes made under the reverse charge procedure should be dealt with in a similar manner to other errors involving VAT. See **57.10** and **57.11 RECORDS**.

However it should be noted that the CJEU in *Tibor Farkas v Nemzeti Adó- és Vámhivatal Dél-alföldi Regionális Adó Foigazgatósága, CJEU Case C-564/15* (TVC 22.478) held that input tax cannot be recovered by the customer if the supplier has incorrectly accounted for VAT on a transaction that should have been covered by the reverse charge. This was a Hungarian referral to the CJEU, however, it does serve as a reminder that customers involved in transactions that are covered by the reverse charge should ensure that the supplier does not charge VAT, as they may not be able to recover this amount as input tax.

[*SI 1995/2518, Regs 38, 38A*]. (VAT Notice 735, paras 10.1–10.4, 10.10).

Failure to comply with the reverse charge provisions

Customers

[4.24] Failure to apply the reverse charge may arise as an oversight or where the customer has been unable to provide the supplier with a VAT registration number because a number is still awaited from HMRC. Where a customer does not account for the reverse charge when they should, HMRC may assess for the supplier's output tax, which should have been entered on the customer's VAT return.

But failure to notify a supplier that the reverse charge ought to apply will be viewed by HMRC as suspicious. If a customer takes no action where the reverse charge should apply, he may put himself in a position where he could be held to be jointly and severally liable for the VAT or unable to recover the input tax on the supply.

(VAT Notice 735, para 8.6).

Treatment in particular cases

[4.25] The treatment in particular cases is as follows.

(1) Other goods or services shown on same invoice as reverse charge goods or services

If supplies of any other goods or services are shown on the same invoice as reverse charge goods or services, the reverse charge does not apply to the other supplies. (VAT Notice 735, para 6.2).

(2) Single supplies including reverse charge goods

Where an itemised invoice relates to a single supply (e.g. a computer) which is not subject to the reverse charge, VAT should be charged as normal on the supply, even if certain of the itemised components are reverse charge goods. (VAT Notice 735, para 6.2).

(3) Multiple invoices for a single order

Where a business issues several separate invoices in relation to a single order (e.g. a separate invoice for each delivery), and the order value is larger than the invoice value, it is acceptable to apply the reverse charge to all invoices relating to the order provided the order value exceeds the £5,000 threshold (in the case of mobile telephones and/or computer chips) and both parties agree. (VAT Notice 735, para 6.3).

(4) Discounts

Where VAT is due on a value reduced by an unconditional discount (e.g. a prompt payment discount), the discounted value should be used to establish the value in applying the £5,000 *de minimis* rule in **4.17** above. But where there are contingent discounts or delayed reductions in price, the full value shown on the invoice must be used. (VAT Notice 735, para 6.4).

(5) Payments on account (POA)

The Payment on Account (POA) regime requires businesses with a total VAT liability of at least £2.3 million in a period of 12 months or less, and tax periods exceeding one month, to make monthly payments on account. See **52.5 PAYMENT OF VAT** for full details.

Because some businesses may be required to account for output tax on their purchases of reverse charge goods or services as well as on the onward sale to non-business customers, the reverse charge could have the effect of increasing their net VAT liability (and bringing them within the scope of the POA regime) or increasing their monthly payments if they are already within the regime.

A business which could be affected by this may apply to HMRC to exclude the output tax due under the reverse charge from the calculation to establish whether it is subject to POA or, if already in the regime, the monthly payments it has to make.

Applications for exclusion should be made to: The POA Team, 4th Floor Regian House, James Street, Liverpool, L75 1AD.

Some businesses may find that their net liability will decrease with the introduction of the reverse charge. If that is the case, then the normal rules for application to reduce POAs outlined in **52.5 PAYMENT OF VAT** apply.

[*SI 1993/2001, Art 2A*]. (VAT Notice 735, para 10.5).

(6) Bad debts

7 BAD DEBT RELIEF does not apply with reverse charge supplies as it is the customer who accounts for the VAT. (VAT Notice 735, para 10.6).

(7) Adjustment of output tax where change in entitlement to input tax after six months

Under *VATA 1994, s 26A*, where the customer has claimed input tax deduction on a supply but has not paid the whole or any part of the consideration for that supply within six months, he must generally repay the appropriate proportion of the input tax originally claimed. See **35.4 INPUT TAX** for full details.

If, as a result of *VATA 1994, s 26A*

- the customer is taken not to have been entitled to any credit for input tax in respect of a supply, and
- the supply is a reverse charge supply,

the customer is entitled to make an adjustment to the amount of VAT which he is required to account for and pay under the reverse charge procedure. The amount of the adjustment is equal to the amount of the credit for the input tax to which the person is taken not to be entitled.

The customer must make a negative entry in the VAT payable portion of his VAT account for the same VAT period as that in which he is required to make an entry in the VAT allowable portion of his VAT return. See **35.4 INPUT TAX.**

[*VATA 1994, s 26AB; SI 1995/2518, Regs 172K, 172L*].

Readjustment of output tax

Where a customer

- has made a negative entry in his VAT account in accordance with the above provisions, and
- in relation to the same supply, he subsequently makes an entry in his VAT account due to the restoration of the entitlement to credit for input tax (see **35.4 INPUT TAX**),

he must make a positive entry in the VAT payable portion of his VAT account for the same VAT period in which he makes that subsequent entry. The amount of the positive entry must be equal to the amount of credit for input tax restored.

The above provisions are not to be regarded as giving rise to any application of error correction notification (formerly voluntary disclosure) requirements (see **57.11 RECORDS**).

[*SI 1995/2518, Regs 172K–172N*].

(8) **Self-billing**

If the reverse charge applies, the customer will be the person issuing the self-billing invoice and accounting for the VAT. He should not charge VAT to the supplier and should indicate on the invoice that he will be accounting for the VAT himself. Suggested forms of words are as follows

- Reverse charge: We will account for and pay output tax of £X to HMRC
- Reverse charge: As the UK customer we will pay output tax of £X to HMRC.

Alternatively, any of the following would also be acceptable, provided that the amount of VAT is shown elsewhere on the invoice (but not in the box for total output tax charged):

- Reverse charge: *VATA 1994, s 55A* applies
- Reverse charge: We will account for the VAT to HMRC
- Reverse charge: We will pay the VAT to HMRC

A supplier of mobile telephones and/or computer chips (but not emissions allowances or wholesale supplies of gas or electricity or telecommunications services) will be required to complete the RCSL (see **4.21**(5) above).

(VAT Notice 735, para 10.7).

(9) **Accounting schemes**

- *Flat-rate scheme*. Reverse charge supplies must be excluded from the flat-rate scheme. Any such supplies received and made should be accounted for under the reverse charge provisions. See **64.16 SPECIAL SCHEMES**.
- *Cash accounting scheme*. Reverse charge sales and purchases should be excluded from the scheme and accounted for under the reverse charge provisions. But if a business purchases goods or services to which the reverse charge applies and sells them on so that it does not (e.g. under the £5,000 *de minimis* limit for mobile telephones and computer chips, or because the sale is to a non-business customer), then the onward sale should be dealt with under the cash accounting scheme.
- *Annual accounting scheme*. Use of this scheme is unaffected by the reverse charge and can be used in the normal way with reverse charge supplies being accounted for within the scheme.
- *Margin scheme for second-hand goods, works of art, antiques and collectors' items*. The margin scheme is one which businesses can elect to use for the sale of eligible goods. If it is used for eligible second-hand mobile telephones and/or computer chips the reverse charge does not apply and the VAT payable is calculated under the margin scheme rules.

(VAT Notice 735, para 10.8).

(10) Charities and local authorities

If a charity or local authority purchases goods or services subject to the reverse charge and the goods or services are to be used partly for business purposes and partly for non-business purposes, it should account for output tax under the reverse charge procedure and apply the appropriate restriction to the deduction of the resulting input VAT. (VAT Notice 735, para 10.9).

(11) National Health Service and government departments

If a reverse charge supply is made to the NHS or a government department for any element of business purpose, the reverse charge applies as normal. The customer should account for the VAT and restrict the recovery of the input tax as appropriate. (VAT Notice 735, para 10.9).

Key points: anti-avoidance

[4.26] Points to consider are as follows.

- The CJEU has supported the principle that VAT gains cannot be achieved by a business through what are commonly known as 'abusive practices' or 'abuse of rights'. Even though a taxpayer has the right to structure his tax affairs in the most tax efficient manner, any artificial structure intended to produce a tax saving can be disregarded by the courts and the tax outcome is based on what would have been the result if normal practices had been adopted. The courts have emphasised that the conditions of the *Halifax* decision must be met, and an arrangement is not considered 'abusive' merely because it results in less tax being payable than a possible alternative that might have been considered. There must be an 'artificial arrangement' whose 'sole or main purpose, objectively assessed' is to obtain the tax advantage, and that tax advantage must be contrary to the purpose of the *Principal VAT Directive*, as interpreted by the court.
- With effect from 1 January 2018, HMRC have introduced the Disclosure of tax avoidance schemes for VAT and other indirect taxes (DASVOIT) regime. Businesses that promote disclosable arrangements with effect from this date will be required to notify HMRC. In certain cases, the user rather than the promoter will be required to make the relevant disclosure. Penalties will be imposed by HMRC on businesses who fail to provide the necessary notification. DASVOIT covers all VAT and indirect taxes.
- Under the disclosure regime operating prior to 1 January 2018, a taxpayer was required to disclose certain avoidance schemes to HMRC, known as either 'hallmarked' or 'listed' schemes. See **4.3** above. The key feature of such schemes is that they are intended to produce a VAT saving that is not intended by the legislation.

- HMRC have also introduced the serial tax avoiders regime (STAR) which affects businesses who enter into tax avoidance arrangements that are defeated by HMRC. Businesses affected by this regime will be required to provide annual information notices to HMRC and could face penalties and having their name published by HMRC.
- The key challenge in deciding whether a hallmarked or listed scheme needs to be notified to HMRC is to consider whether it produces a lower VAT bill than would apply if the scheme was not in place. A lower VAT bill either means an increase in input tax or reduction in output tax compared to normal VAT accounting.
- Legitimate VAT planning still has an important part to play in helping to reduce the VAT bills of a business. For example, the creation of a VAT group to avoid VAT being charged on supplies between group members is an established principle of VAT planning, and a natural outcome of a group registration. VAT savings that can be made by making an option to tax election (input tax recovery) or adopting a VAT scheme (flat-rate scheme or margin scheme) do not create a problem. The key feature of avoidance schemes is that an artificial arrangement is created, solely intended to avoid VAT or tax rather than being inspired by any commercial motive.
- In an attempt to combat carousel fraud, trading in mobile phones and computer chips (value of sales invoice at least £5,000), emissions allowances, wholesale supplies of gas, electricity and telecommunication services between VAT-registered businesses in the UK requires the customer to account for output tax in many cases rather than the supplier. The customer fulfils this requirement by making a reverse charge calculation on his own VAT return based on the value of the relevant goods or services bought during the period (output tax accounted for in Box 1 and input tax claimed in Box 4).
- The reverse charge strategy for mobile phones and computer chips avoids the risk of a supplier charging output tax (usually on goods or services acquired VAT free from a supplier in another EU member state), being paid this output tax by his customer – but then disappearing before the output tax is declared on a VAT return to HMRC.
- A sales invoice raised by a supplier where the customer needs to carry out the reverse charge must be clearly noted as such (i.e. along the lines of 'reverse charge supply – customer to pay the VAT to HMRC'). It is useful to specify the actual amount of VAT subject to the reverse charge, particularly if an invoice includes both specified and non-specified goods or services, i.e. where some output tax is charged by the supplier but some needs to be accounted for by the customer.
- A supplier making a sale where the reverse charge applies will only record the value of this sale in Box 6 (outputs) on his VAT return. The Box 1 and Box 4 entries (actual VAT amounts) will be

recorded by the customer. The customer will also make an entry in Box 7 (inputs) to reflect the value of the goods or services he is buying (excluding VAT).

- A RCSL must be submitted to HMRC by the supplier of mobile telephones and/or computer chips to record the value of sales covered by the reverse charge rules. The return period coincides with the VAT periods of the supplier (i.e. usually the return will be completed quarterly). The return is always submitted online rather than in a paper format.
- In periods where no reverse charge supplies are made, a nil return still needs to be completed. A return must be completed every period unless the trader confirms to HMRC that he has ceased to trade in specified goods or services (i.e. no qualifying supplies will arise in the future).

5

Appeals

Cross-references. See **6.8** ASSESSMENTS for correction of assessments on appeal by Tribunals; **9.8** BUSINESS for appeals regarding registration of two or more persons as one taxable person; **28.5** GROUPS OF COMPANIES; **35.12** INPUT TAX for appeals in respect of input tax; **53.32** PENALTIES for mitigation of penalties by a Tribunal on appeal.

De Voil Indirect Tax Service. See V5.4.

Introduction to appeals

[5.1] The *Tribunals, Courts and Enforcement Act 2007 (TCEA 2007)* is the establishing law for the Tribunals to which VAT appeals are made in the first instance: the First-tier Tribunal and the Upper Tribunal, each of which are organised into a number of 'chambers'.

The First-tier Tribunal chambers include: Social Entitlement; Health, Education and Social Care; General Regulatory; Taxation; and Property.

The Upper Tribunal chambers are: Administrative Appeals; Immigration and Asylum; Tax and Chancery; and Lands.

VAT appeals are almost always made in the first instance to the Tax Chamber of the First-tier Tribunal. There is a right of appeal against decisions of the First-tier Tax Chamber to the Tax and Chancery Chamber of the Upper Tribunal. The First-tier Tribunal deals with the majority of appeals, apart from a small number of the most complex appeals that transfer to the Upper Tribunal at first instance. The Upper Tribunal mainly deals with appeals against decisions of the First-tier Tribunal. The Upper Tribunal has limited powers of judicial review. Some appeals are dealt with on paper without the need for HMRC or taxpayers to attend a hearing. In most cases, an appeal can be made against an Upper Tribunal decision to the Court of Appeal.

Constitution

There is a Senior President presiding over the Tribunals. Each Tribunal consists of its judges and members. Each chamber has a Chamber President. The Tribunals work under the supervision of the Administrative Justice and Tribunals Council.

Appeals lodged before 1 April 2009

Appeals decided before 1 April 2009 were heard by the VAT and Duties Tribunal. Decisions of that Tribunal are still cited as persuasive in appeals before the current Tribunals. References to VAT and Duties Tribunal decisions are in the form (VTD 16892) and to First-tier Tribunal decisions are in the form (TC03125).

Henceforth, the term 'Tribunal' refers to the First-tier Tribunal unless otherwise stated.

[*TCEA 2007, ss 3–22, 44; SI 2009/56, Sch 3 para 7; SI 2010/2655*].

Public funding

[5.2] Public funding (formerly legal aid) is not generally available for appeals to Tribunals. However, funding may be available for legal advice prior to the Tribunal and legal representation at the Tribunal where

- the proceedings concern penalties which the courts have declared to be criminal within the terms specified by the European Convention on Human Rights or where an applicant seeks to argue that issue; and
- it is in the interests of justice for an applicant to be legally represented.

In practice, funding is most likely to be available where a penalty, which is substantial either in terms of its amount or its impact, is being contested and where the amount imposed is beyond the assessed liability. The applicant must be financially eligible for funding. Applicants on Income Support and income-based Jobseekers' Allowance are automatically financially eligible. Each application is considered on an individual basis and is subject to the statutory tests of the applicant's means and the merits of the case.

Applications for funding should be made to the Legal Services Commission, 62–68 Hills Road, Cambridge, CB2 1LA via a solicitor or another authorised organisation. Information is provided on the government website at www.justice.gov.uk/legal-aid. Solicitors who carry out public-funded work can be found in the Community Legal Service Directory (available in most local libraries).

In the case of proceedings before the Upper Tribunal, a party which is granted funding of legal services at any time must as soon as practicable: (a) send a copy of the funding notice, or legal aid certificate as appropriate, to the Upper Tribunal, and (b) notify every other party in writing that funding has been granted. [*SI 2008/2698, Rule 18*].

Appealable matters

[5.3] An appeal to a Tribunal against a decision of HMRC may only be made on the following matters.

(1) The registration or cancellation of registration of any person.

(2) The VAT chargeable on the supply of any goods or services, on the acquisition of goods from another EU member state or, subject to (ii) below, on the importation of goods from a place outside the EU. A Tribunal has no jurisdiction in relation to future supplies (*Allied Windows (S Wales) Ltd v C & E Commrs*, QB April 1973 (unreported) (TVC 2.1); *Odhams Leisure Group Ltd v C & E Commrs, QB* [1992] STC 332 (TVC 2.2, 5.85)).

(3) The amount of any input tax which may be credited to a person.

(4) Any claim for a refund by virtue of regulations made under *VATA 1994, s 13(5)* (acquisitions of goods from another EU member state where VAT has also been paid in that other country).

(5) A decision by HMRC under *VATA 1994, s 18A* on the approval of a person as a fiscal warehousekeeper or the withdrawal of such approval or the fiscal warehouse status from any premises. See **73.13 WAREHOUSED GOODS**.

(6) The proportion of input tax allowable under *VATA 1994, s 26*.

(7) A claim by a taxable person under *VATA 1994, s 27* (goods imported for another person for private purposes, see **35.8 INPUT TAX**).

(8) A decision of HMRC refusing or withdrawing authorisation (i) to use the flat-rate scheme for small businesses or (ii) as to the appropriate percentage(s) to be used under the scheme, see **64.15 SPECIAL SCHEMES**.

(9) A decision by HMRC that an election under *SI 1993/2001, Art 12A* (right to elect under the payments on account provisions to pay actual liability for the preceding month rather than the predetermined amount) shall cease to have effect. See **52.5 PAYMENT OF VAT**.

(10) The amount of any refunds under *VATA 1994, s 35* (construction of certain buildings otherwise than in the course of a business by 'do-it-yourself' builders, see **43.24 LAND AND BUILDINGS: ZERO AND REDUCED RATE SUPPLIES AND DIY HOUSEBUILDERS**).

(11) A claim for a refund under *VATA 1994, s 36* or earlier provisions (see **7 BAD DEBT RELIEF**).

(12) A refusal of a repayment under *VATA 1994, s 39* (see **46.12 OVERSEAS TRADERS**).

(13) The amount of any refunds under *VATA 1994, s 40* (supplies of new means of transport to other EU member states by non-taxable persons, see **20.36 EUROPEAN UNION: SINGLE MARKET**).

(14) Any refusal of an application under *VATA 1994, s 43B* (applications re group treatment, see **28.3 GROUPS OF COMPANIES**).

(15) Notice by HMRC under *VATA 1994, s 43C* terminating group membership (see **28.3 GROUPS OF COMPANIES**).
(16) The requirement of any security under *VATA 1994, s 48(7)* or *VATA 1994, Sch 11 para 4(1A)(2)* (for the payment of VAT due or which may become due, see **32.1 HMRC: POWERS**).
(17) Any refusal or cancellation of certification under *VATA 1994, s 54* or any refusal to cancel such certification (flat-rate scheme for farmers, see **64.25 SPECIAL SCHEMES**).
(18) Any liability to a penalty or surcharge under *VATA 1994, ss 59–69B* (see **53.12–53.23** and **53.27–53.30 PENALTIES**). See also **53.33 PENALTIES** for mitigation by the Tribunal.
(19) A decision of HMRC under *VATA 1994, s 61* (liability of a director where the conduct of a company gives rise to a penalty for VAT evasion, see **53.11 PENALTIES**).
(20) The making or amount of an assessment under *VATA 1994, s 73(1)(2)* for any period for which the appellant has made a return or under *VATA 1994, s 73(7)(7A)(7B)* or *VATA 1994, s 75* (see **6.1**(*b*)–(*g*) **ASSESSMENTS**).
(21) The amount of any penalty, interest or surcharge specified in an assessment under *VATA 1994, s 76* (see **6.3 ASSESSMENTS**). But without prejudice to the Tribunal's powers of mitigation (see **53.33 PENALTIES**), the Tribunal may only vary the amount assessed insofar as it is necessary to reduce it to the amount which is appropriate under the relevant penalty, etc provision.
(22) The making of an assessment, on the basis set out in *VATA 1994, s 77(4)*, outside the normal time limit where it is believed that VAT may have been lost through fraud, conduct involving dishonesty, failure to notify liability to be registered or unauthorised issue of VAT invoices. See **6.4 ASSESSMENTS.**
(23) Any liability arising under *VATA 1994, s 77A* (joint and several liability for unpaid VAT, see **32.3 HMRC: POWERS**).
(24) Any liability of HMRC to pay interest under *VATA 1994, s 78* or the amount of the interest payable (see **52.18 PAYMENT OF VAT**).
(25) An assessment under *VATA 1994, s 78A* (interest overpayments) or the amount of such an assessment (see **6.5 ASSESSMENTS**).
(26) A claim for the crediting or repayment of overstated or overpaid VAT under *VATA 1994, s 80* (see **52.9 PAYMENT OF VAT**), an assessment under *VATA 1994, s 80(4A)* (repayment to HMRC of overpaid refund, see **6.5 ASSESSMENTS**) or the amount of such an assessment.
(27) An assessment under *VATA 1994, s 80B(1)* or *(1B)* (recovery by HMRC under the unjust enrichment provisions of credits or repayments made to a taxpayer) or the amount of such an assessment (see **6.5 ASSESSMENTS**).
(28) Any direction or supplementary direction under *VATA 1994, Sch 1 para 2* (registration of two or more persons as one taxable person, see **9.5 BUSINESS**).
(29) Any direction under *VATA 1994, Sch 6 para 1, para 1A, para 2* or *8A* under *VATA 1983, Sch 4 para 2* (VAT on transactions between connected persons, supplies of goods to non-taxable persons for retail

sale, use of stock in trade cars for less than market value and group supplies using an overseas member, see **72.19**, **72.23**, **72.30**, and **72.31 VALUATION** respectively).

(30) Any direction under *VATA 1994, Sch 7 para 1* (VAT on acquisitions of goods between connected persons to be charged on the open market value, see **72.12 VALUATION**).

(31) Any direction or assessment under *VATA 1994, Sch 9A* (anti-avoidance provisions for groups, see **28.5 GROUPS OF COMPANIES**).

(32) Any refusal to grant any permission under, or otherwise to exercise in favour of a particular person any power conferred by, any provision in *VATA 1994, Sch 10 Pt I* (option to tax, see **42.23 LAND AND BUILDINGS: EXEMPT SUPPLIES AND OPTION TO TAX**).

(33) Any refusal to permit the value of supplies to be determined by a method described in a VAT Notice published under *VATA 1994, Sch 11 para 2(6)* (see **61.1 RETAIL SCHEMES**).

(34) Any refusal of authorisation or termination of authorisation in connection with the scheme under *VATA 1994, Sch 11 para 2(7)* (cash accounting scheme, see **64.2 SPECIAL SCHEMES**).

(35) Any requirement imposed by HMRC in a particular case under *VATA 1994, Sch 11 para 2B(2)(c)* (self-billed invoices, see **40.6 INVOICES**) or *para 3(1)* (production of VAT invoices by computer, see **40.9 INVOICES**).

(36) A direction under *VATA 1994, Sch 11 para 6A* (direction to keep certain records, see **57.1 RECORDS**).

(37) A direction under *VATA 1994, Sch 11A para 8* (power of HMRC to exclude exemption from duty to notify a VAT avoidance scheme in cases of business splitting, see **4.13 ANTI-AVOIDANCE**).

(38) Any liability to a penalty under *VATA 1994, Sch 11A para 10(1)* (penalty for failure to notify use of a notifiable avoidance scheme, see **53.31 PENALTIES**), any assessment of such a penalty under *VATA 1994, Sch 11A para 12(1)* (see **6.3 ASSESSMENTS**) or the amount of such an assessment. But without prejudice to the Tribunal's powers of mitigation (see **53.33 PENALTIES**), the Tribunal may only vary the amount assessed insofar as it is necessary to reduce it to the amount as correctly calculated under the provisions.

(39) A decision of HMRC about the application of regulations under *FA 2002, s 135* concerning the mandatory electronic filing of returns (see **2.1 ACCOUNTING PERIODS AND RETURNS**). The Tribunal may only vary the amount assessed insofar as it is necessary to reduce it to the amount appropriate under the regulations.

(40) A decision of HMRC on a review under *SI 2003/3075, Reg 21* (money laundering regulations).

(41) An information notice under *FA 2008, Sch 36 paras 1, 2* (power of HMRC to obtain information and documents from taxpayer or third party, see **32.6 HMRC: POWERS**).

(42) A penalty imposed under *FA 2008, Sch 36 paras 39–40A* (standard and daily penalties for failure to comply with information notice or deliberate obstruction of HMRC officer in course of an inspection authorised by the Tribunal and penalties for inaccurate information and documents, see **53.20 PENALTIES**).

(43) A penalty imposed under *FA 2009, Sch 46 paras 4–9* (failure to comply with duties of senior accounting officers, see **53.32 PENALTIES**).
(44) A notice under *FA 2009, Sch 49 paras 1–3* (power to obtain contact details for debtors, see **32.7 HMRC: POWERS**) or a penalty imposed under *FA 2009, Sch 49 para 5* for failure to comply with such a notice (see **53.21 PENALTIES**).
(45) A data-holder notice (introduced from 1 April 2012) under *FA 2011, Sch 23* (data-gathering powers, see **32.9 HMRC: POWERS**) or a penalty imposed under *FA 2011, Sch 23 paras 30–32* for failure to comply with such a notice or inaccurate data (see **53.22 PENALTIES**).
(46) In relation to tax agents, a file access notice (see **32.17 HMRC: POWERS**); a conduct notice; a penalty for dishonest conduct; a penalty for failure to comply with a file access notice (see **53.40 PENALTIES**).

[*VATA 1994, ss 83, 84(6)(6A)(6B)*].

No appeal lies to a Tribunal on

(i) any matter which is outside (1) to (44) above (subject to below); or
(ii) any decision which HMRC can be required to review under *FA 1994, s 14* (decisions relating to customs duty or the Community Customs Code or made under *CEMA 1979*) unless no request for a review has been made or the decision relates only to whether or not zero-rating applies to the importation of the goods in question and/or the rate of VAT charged on the goods.

[*VATA 1994, s 84(9)*].

Where an appeal is against a decision of HMRC which depended upon a prior decision taken by them in relation to the appellant, the fact that the prior decision was not within (1) to (44) above (e.g. the exercise of a discretion by HMRC) does not prevent the Tribunal from allowing the appeal on the grounds that it would have allowed an appeal against the prior decision. [*VATA 1994, s 84(10)*]. This follows the decision in *C & E Commrs v JH Corbitt (Numismatists) Ltd, HL* [1980] STC 231 (TVC 60.1).

Tribunal's jurisdiction over HMRC actions and decisions

In the case of *Oxfam v HMRC* (Ch) [2010] STC 686 (TVC 11.54), HMRC had decided to amend the terms of an approved method for the apportionment of VAT incurred between business and non-business use. Oxfam sought judicial review of the decision, under the principle of legitimate expectation, as it was unsure as to whether the Tribunal had jurisdiction over the matter. The High Court held that a claim based on public law principles and the doctrine of legitimate expectation could properly be raised in an appeal to the Tribunal, where that was necessary for it to determine the outcome of an appeal against an HMRC decision whose subject matter fell within one of the headings in *VATA 1994, s 83*.

In *CGI Group (Europe) Ltd* (TC00525) (TVC 2.300), a subsequent Tribunal drew the following conclusions from the *Oxfam* decision.

- The nature of the Tribunal's jurisdiction is dependent upon the words of the relevant paragraph of *VATA 1994, s 83* and any underlying statute.

- While none of the provisions of *s 83* confers a general supervisory jurisdiction, some confer a form of supervisory review jurisdiction.
- Public law (i.e. judicial review) principles may be relevant to a particular form of appeal, and depending upon the nature of the appeal, the Tribunal may have jurisdiction to apply those principles. In particular an appeal in relation to any HMRC decision may well be one in which the Tribunal's jurisdiction may be one of supervisory review and in which it may be appropriate to consider whether, by reason of representations made or otherwise, that decision was unreasonable.
- Public law remedies will be relevant only if they are encompassed by the nature of the specific appeal in the relevant subparagraph of *s 83*. There is thus no general power to direct HMRC's actions although there are specific powers to set aside its decisions.

Conditions for hearing an appeal

[5.4] No appeal will be entertained unless the following conditions are satisfied.

- In the case of an appeal on matters under **5.3**(2), (17), (19), (20), (22), (24) or (37) above,
  - (a) the amount which HMRC have determined to be payable as VAT (or, in the case of **5.3**(24) have notified by assessment) has been paid or deposited with them; or
  - (b) on being satisfied that the appellant would otherwise suffer hardship, HMRC agree, or the Tribunal decides, that the appeal be entertained notwithstanding non-payment (see **5.10** below). Note that if the hardship application is granted but, subsequently, the appeal is lost, default interest on the amount of the disputed VAT may be payable. Conversely, if the hardship application is lost but, subsequently, the appeal is won, HMRC are liable to pay interest on any amount of disputed VAT paid or deposited with them which is repayable (see **52.18 PAYMENT OF VAT**).

  The Tribunal in *PW Coleman* (VTD 15906, VTD 16178) held that the condition in (a) above was acceptable and did not conflict with what is now *Directive 2006/112/EC* because of the hardship provision under (b) above and because HMRC's decision on that is reviewable by the Tribunal. This was also confirmed in by the Court of Appeal in *Totel Ltd* [2016] EWCA Civ 1310 (TVC 2.123) which concerned the requirement to pay, on account, VAT subject to appeal under a 'prepayment rule' which the taxpayer considered was contrary to the EU principal of equivalence, as the rule does not extend to other taxes. The Court of Appeal dismissed the appeal on the basis that the equivalence principal does not have the effect that VAT must be compared to other taxes as VAT is a very different tax. EU member states are not required to extend their most favourable tax procedural rules to VAT providing EU-derived claims are not selected for the least favourable tax treatment.

[*VATA 1994, s 84(3)(3A)*].

- The appellant has a sufficient interest in maintaining the appeal. (See *Williams and Glyn's Bank Ltd* (VTD 118) (TVC 27.1)). The appellant is not required to be the supplier (*Canterbury Hockey Club; Canterbury Ladies Hockey Club* (VTD 19086) (TVC 2.52)) or a taxable person accountable for the VAT in dispute (e.g. he may be an unregistered recipient of taxable supplies) but where he is the recipient of a supply, he should wherever possible seek the consent of the supplier to the appeal being brought jointly (*Processed Vegetable Growers Association Ltd* (VTD 25) (TVC 2.49) (TVC 62.42)). For other cases where a Tribunal allowed an appeal by the recipient of a supply, see *Dr Cameron* (VTD 41) (TVC 33.56); *Gilbourne* [1974] Lexis Citation 2 (TVC 2.50); and *Beckley (JR)* [1974] Lexis Citation 27.
- In appeals involving group registrations (see **28 GROUPS OF COMPANIES**), only the representative member may appeal.
- Where HMRC have obtained a final judgment against the appellant for VAT on an assessment, the Tribunal has no jurisdiction to entertain an appeal unless the applicant first procures the High Court judgment against him to be set aside (*Digwa* (TS) (VTD 612) (TVC 2.190)).

When an appeal is about a penalty, surcharge or an amount of interest, the appellant does not have to pay it before the appeal can be heard.

Categories of appeal

[5.5] There are three different categories of appeal to the Tribunal and procedure differs with each.

Default paper cases

These cases are normally disposed of without a hearing.

Basic cases

These cases are normally disposed of after a hearing, with a minimal exchange of documents before the hearing. Most VAT penalty surcharge cases and mitigation appeals are categorised as basic.

Standard cases

These are subject to more detailed case management and are disposed of after a hearing.

Complex cases

A case is allocated or reallocated as a complex case if the Tribunal considers that: it will require lengthy or complex evidence or a lengthy hearing; it involves a complex or important principle or issue; or it involves a large financial sum. Complex cases may, with the consent of the parties and the concurrence of the President of the Tax and Chancery Chamber of the Upper Tribunal, be transferred to and determined by the Upper Tribunal.

[*SI 2009/273, Rules 23, 28*].

Time limit for appealing

[5.6] Where HMRC are not required or requested to undertake a review, an appeal must be within 30 days of the date of the decision or, where the appellant is not the person to whom the decision was notified, within 30 days of the date when the appellant became aware of the decision. Where the time limit for requesting or requiring a review is extended, the time limit for appeal is similarly extended. From 1 June 2014, if HMRC decide not to undertake a review out of time, an appeal can only be brought if the Tribunal gives permission to do so. Where HMRC are required to undertake a review, an appeal may not be made until the conclusion date (i.e. the date of the document notifying the conclusions of the review), but must be made within 30 days of the conclusion date. Where HMRC do not notify their conclusions within the 45-day time limit, an appeal may be made from the end of that time limit until 30 days after the conclusion date. Where HMRC are requested to carry out a review which is out of time, an appeal may not be made unless HMRC have decided whether or not to undertake a review, and if they decide to undertake a review, not until the conclusion date. An appeal must be made within 30 days of the conclusion date or the date on which HMRC decide not to undertake a review, as applicable.

The Tribunal may allow an appeal to be made outside the stipulated time limits. An extension has been allowed where the appellant was mistakenly under the impression that the matter was being handled by his accountants (*Hallam* (WR) (VTD 683) (TVC 2.164)) and where the appeal was delayed through the illness of a partner (*Hornby (WW & JH)* [1975] Lexis Citation 27 (TVC 2.187)). Application was refused, although within the discretion of the Tribunal, where to admit it would be to enable the applicant to recover VAT paid voluntarily under a mistake of law (*Kyffin (R)* (VTD 617) (TVC 2.186)). In *WJ Price* (VTD 559) (TVC 2.177) an extension was allowed where, although no real excuse for delay existed, there was evidence that the taxpayer intended to appeal, but this decision was not followed in *Wan & Wan* (VTD 14829) (TVC 2.178) on the grounds that the earlier Tribunal's reasoning was inconsistent with subsequent decisions of the Court of Appeal including that in *Norwich & Peterborough Building Society v Steed*, CA [1991] 1 WLR 449; [1991] 2 All ER 880 (TVC 2.178).

The Upper Tribunal set out the principles to be considered when deciding whether to allow an extension of time in *Data Select Ltd v HMRC*, UT [2012] UKUT 187 (TCC); [2012] STC 2195 (TVC 2.183), a decision that is now regularly cited in disputes about late appeals in the First-tier Tribunal. Morgan J stated, 'Applications for extensions of time limits of various kinds are common place and the approach to be adopted is well established. As a general rule, when a court or Tribunal is asked to extend a relevant time limit, the court or Tribunal asks itself the following questions: What is the purpose of the time limit? How long was the delay? Is there a good explanation for the delay?

What will be the consequences for the parties of an extension of time? What will be the consequences for the parties if a refusal to extend the time? The court or Tribunal then makes it decision in the light of the answers to those questions.'

However, the recent decision of the Court of Appeal in *BPP Holdings v HMRC* [2016] EWCA Civ 121 (TVC 2.248) may now result in a change of approach. In *BPP* the Court held that the First-tier Tribunal must follow a stricter approach to enforcing compliance with time limits imposed by the Tribunal rules or Tribunal directions. The Court specifically did not discuss the *Data Select* case. It is nevertheless very possible that the Tribunal may conclude that the same stricter approach should apply to compliance with statutory time limits for making appeals to the Tribunal. The Tribunal may regard a delay of more than three months as 'serious and significant'. It is important to note that permission might not be granted, and that the possibility of the Tribunal refusing an application may increase as a result of *BPP*.

[*VATA 1994, s 83G; SI 2009/273, Rule 20; SI 2014/1264*].

Making an appeal

[5.7] An appeal to the Tribunal is brought by sending or delivering a notice of appeal to the Tribunal (unless it is an appeal under *FA 2008, Sch 36*, in which case the notice of appeal must be given to HMRC), with 'Tribunal' here meaning a processing centre established in Birmingham.

A notice of appeal can be made online via the GOV.UK website (www.gov.uk/tax-tribunal/appeal-to-tribunal) or using form T240, which may be downloaded from the HMRC website. The paper notice must

- state the name and address of the appellant;
- state the name and address of any representative of the appellant;
- state an address where documents may be sent or delivered to the appellant;
- state details of the disputed decision, the result being sought and the grounds of appeal; and
- have attached a document containing the disputed decision and any statement of reasons for that decision that the appellant has or can reasonably obtain; and
- have attached any request for an extension of time and the reason why the notice of appeal was not provided in time.

The online application was introduced in May 2017 and the online appeal form includes step-by-step guidance on completing an appeal, and gives a reference number when an appeal has been submitted successfully. The applicant must scan and attach a copy of the original notice or review conclusion letter and provide reasons for their appeal against the decision reached by HMRC.

When the Tribunal receives the notice of appeal it must give notice of the proceedings to the respondent.

[*VATA 1994, s 83G; SI 2009/273, Rule 20*].

Setting aside a decision

[5.8] The Tribunal may set aside a decision which disposes of proceedings and re-make the decision if it considers that it is in the interests of justice to do so and at least one of the following conditions is satisfied—

- a document relating to the proceedings was not sent to, or was not received at an appropriate time by, a party or a party's representative;
- a document relating to the proceedings was not sent to the Tribunal at an appropriate time;
- there has been some other procedural irregularity in the proceedings; or
- a party, or a party's representative, was not present at a hearing related to the proceedings.

[*SI 2009/273, Rule 38*].

Striking out an appeal

[5.9] Proceedings may or must be struck out as follows—

- where the appellant has failed to comply with a direction that stated that failure to comply would lead to striking out, the proceedings will automatically be struck out;
- where the Tribunal does not have jurisdiction in relation to the proceedings and it does not exercise its power under *SI 2009/2763, Rule 5(3)(k)(i)* to transfer the proceedings to another court or Tribunal, it must strike out the proceedings;
- where the appellant has failed to comply with a direction that stated that failure to comply could lead to striking out, the Tribunal may strike out the proceedings;
- where the appellant has failed to co-operate with the Tribunal to such an extent that the Tribunal cannot deal with the proceedings fairly and justly, the Tribunal may strike out the proceedings;
- where the Tribunal considers there is no reasonable prospect of the appellant's case succeeding, it may strike out the proceedings.

The above applies equally to the respondent (i.e. HMRC), except that a reference to the striking out of the proceedings must be read as a reference to the barring of the respondent from taking further part in the proceedings. For a recent case in which the First-tier Tribunal decided to bar HMRC for non-compliance with directions, and the Court of Appeal upheld that decision, see *BPP Holdings v HMRC*, CA [2016] EWCA Civ 121 (TVC 2.248).

[*SI 2009/273, Rule 8*].

Making an application for a direction

[5.10] An application for a direction may be made orally during the course of a Tribunal hearing, or by sending or delivering a written application to the Tribunal. An application can be made for any of the following purposes —

- the reconsideration by a judge of a decision made by a member of staff delegated to make such a decision under *SI 2009/273, Rule 4(1)*;
- the reinstatement of proceedings struck out under *SI 2009/273, Rule 8(1) or (3)(a)* (failure to comply with a direction stating that such failure could or would lead to striking out);
- a party to be added to the proceedings;
- an order for costs;
- the summoning of a person to attend as witness;
- the reinstatement of a withdrawn case;
- a case to be heard without payment of the amount in dispute (hardship application);
- the reallocation of a case to a different category;
- full written findings and reasons for decision;
- the setting aside of a decision;
- permission to appeal;
- to treat an application as a different type of application.

[*SI 2009/273, Rule 6*].

Withdrawal of an appeal

[5.11] A party to an appeal may withdraw an appeal by giving notice to the Tribunal, either orally at a hearing or by notice in writing before the hearing. [*SI 2009/273, Rule 17*].

If an appellant notifies HMRC, whether orally or in writing, that he does not wish to proceed with the appeal, then unless HMRC object in writing to the withdrawal of the appeal within 30 days of notification, the provisions relating to settling appeals by agreement (see **5.13** below) are treated as having effect as if, at the date of the appellant's notification, the appellant and HMRC had come to an agreement, orally or in writing as the case may be, that the decision under appeal should be upheld without variation. [*VATA 1994, s 85(4)*].

Review of decision by HMRC

[5.12] Taxpayers are entitled to request an internal review of appealable VAT decisions. Reviews are optional and are done by a trained review officer, who has not previously been involved with that decision. HMRC must complete reviews within 45 days (unless another period is agreed with the taxpayer). If taxpayers do not want a review, or they do not agree with the result of the review, they can appeal to the Tribunal for a decision.

[*VATA 1994, ss 83A–83G*].

Settling an appeal by agreement

[5.13] Where a person has given notice of appeal and, before the appeal is determined by a Tribunal, HMRC and the appellant come to an agreement under which the decision under appeal is to be treated as

- upheld without variation,
- varied in a particular manner, or
- discharged or cancelled,

the agreement is binding as if a Tribunal had determined the appeal in accordance with the terms of the agreement (including any terms as to costs).

The appellant may, however, within 30 days of the agreement, give written notice to HMRC that he desires to repudiate or resile from the agreement.

The agreement need not be in writing but, if it is not, the fact that an agreement was reached and the terms of that agreement must be confirmed in writing by HMRC to the appellant (or *vice versa*). The time of the agreement is then treated as the date of giving that notice of confirmation.

A person may act through an agent in all matters relating to settling appeals by agreement.

[*VATA 1994, s 85(1)–(3)(5)*].

Compounding agreement

Where HMRC and the taxpayer reach a compounding agreement, the dispute between the parties is resolved and any assessments raised effectively treated as discharged. Any outstanding appeal must be treated as having been settled by agreement (*Cummings (C)* (VTD 14870) (TVC 2.203)).

Preparation for the hearing of an appeal

Basic cases

[5.14] There is no requirement for HMRC to send a statement of case to the Tribunal. Subject to any direction given by the Tribunal, the case proceeds directly to a hearing. However, if HMRC intend to raise new grounds which have not been previously communicated to the appellant, they must notify the appellant of such grounds as soon as reasonably practicable, and in sufficient detail to enable the appellant to respond to such grounds at the hearing.

Most penalty appeals (other than those classified as default paper cases) are treated as basic cases. The following are also dealt with as basic cases:

- appeals against information notices and penalties for non-compliance with such notices;
- hardship applications in indirect tax cases;
- applications for permission to make a late appeal;
- applications for a closure notice;
- applications for postponement of tax.

Default paper cases

A 'paper' case means that there is no hearing; instead the papers are given to a judge who decides the outcome and writes the decision. Default paper cases are so called because they are automatically classified as paper cases without the parties requesting it. They include most appeals against fixed penalties amounting to no more than £2,000.

HMRC must send or deliver a statement of case to the Tribunal and the appellant so that it is received within 42 days after the Tribunal sent the notice of the appeal. The statement of case must: state the legislative provision under which the decision under appeal was made; and set out HMRC's position in relation to the case. The statement may also contain a request that the case be dealt with at a hearing or without a hearing. If the statement is made later than the prescribed time limit (or any extension thereto), it must contain a request for an extension of time and the reason why it was not provided on time. The appellant may send or deliver a written reply (with a copy to HMRC) to the Tribunal so that it is received within 30 days after the date on which HMRC sent the statement of case to the appellant. Such a reply may: set out the appellant's response to the statement of case; provide any further relevant information; request that the case be dealt with at a hearing. Where the reply is made after the 30-day period referred to above (or such longer period as the Tribunal may allow), it must include a request for an extension of time and the reason why the reply was not provided in time. Following receipt of the appellant's reply (or the expiry of time for its receipt), the Tribunal must proceed to determine the case without a hearing, unless it has otherwise directed or a party to the appeal has otherwise requested in writing.

Standard or complex cases

Cases that do not fall within the above two categories are regarded as standard or complex cases. Only a limited number of cases will be regarded as complex and the Tribunal must consider that one of the following applies before it will be regarded as complex:

- requires lengthy or complex evidence or a lengthy hearing;
- involves a complex or important principle or issue;
- involves a large financial sum.

The main difference between a standard and a complex case is that in complex cases the losing party pays the costs of the winning party. However, it is possible to 'opt out' of the costs regime as long as this is done within 28 days of the Notice stating that the case has been allocated as a complex case.

HMRC must send or deliver a statement of case to the Tribunal and the appellant so that it is received within 60 days after the Tribunal sent the notice of the appeal. Within 42 days of the date on which the statement of case was sent, each party to the appeal must send to the Tribunal and each other a list of documents of which the party providing the list has possession, the right to possession, or the right to take copies, and which the party providing the list intends to rely upon or produce in the proceedings. The party providing a list of documents must allow the other party to inspect or take copies of the listed documents (except for any which are privileged). The statement of case must state the legislative provision under which the decision under appeal was made; and set out HMRC's position in relation to the case. The statement may also contain a request that the case be dealt with at a hearing or without a hearing. If the statement is made later than the prescribed time limit (or any extension thereto), it must contain a request for an extension of time and the reason why it was not provided on time.

[*SI 2009/273, Rules 24–27*].

Witnesses

[5.15] On the application of a party to an appeal, or on its own initiative, the Tribunal may issue a summons to any person to attend as a witness at a hearing; or order any person to answer any question or produce any documents in that person's possession or control which relate to any issue in the proceedings. No person may be compelled to give any evidence or produce any document which he could not be compelled to give or produce on a trial of an action in a court of law in the part of the UK where the proceedings are due to be determined. The person must be given at least 14 days' notice of the hearing, or such shorter period as the Tribunal may direct. Provision must be made for payment of relevant expenses. The person may apply to the Tribunal for the requirement to be varied or set aside if he did not have an opportunity to object to it before it was made or issued. Such an application must be made as soon as reasonably practicable.

[*SI 2009/273, Rule 16*].

Notice and location of hearing

[5.16] The Tribunal must provide each party with reasonable notice of the time and place of any hearing (including any adjourned or postponed hearing) and any changes thereto. In relation to a hearing to consider the disposal of proceedings, at least 14 days' notice must be given unless the parties agree otherwise, or there are urgent and exceptional circumstances.

[*SI 2009/273, Rule 31*].

Postponement

A Tribunal is reluctant to postpone a hearing but if it is essential to do so, the appellant or applicant (or his representative) should contact the Tribunal giving reasons for asking for the postponement. An engagement elsewhere is not normally sufficient reason for a postponement and the appellant should be ready to explain why another engagement takes priority. In any event, it should not be assumed that a hearing will be cancelled because a postponement has been requested. The hearing will stand unless the Tribunal states otherwise.

Procedure at the hearing

Public or private

[5.17] An appeal is heard in public unless a Tribunal directs otherwise. If the hearing is to take place in private the Tribunal may determine who is permitted to attend. [*SI 2009/273, Rule 32*].

Representatives

A party may appoint a representative, legal or otherwise, to represent that party in the proceedings. The party must notify the Tribunal and the other party of the name and address of its representative (in the case of a legal representative, the representative may carry out the notification). A representative may do anything permitted or required by a party under *SI 2009/273*, a direction or a practice direction, except signing a witness statement. A party may be accompanied by another person at a hearing. With the permission of the Tribunal, that person may act as a representative or otherwise assist the party. [*SI 2009/273, Rule 11*].

Failure to appear at a hearing

If a party fails to attend the hearing, the Tribunal may proceed to consider the appeal or application in his absence, provided that it is satisfied that that party has been informed of the hearing, or that reasonable steps have been taken to inform him, and that to proceed with the hearing is in the interests of justice. [*SI 2009/273, Rule 33*].

Decision of the tribunal

[5.18] The Tribunal may give a decision orally at a hearing. It must, within 28 days or as soon as practicable thereafter, provide each party with a decision notice which states the Tribunal's decision and notifies the party of any right of appeal against the decision and the time within which, and the manner in which, the right of appeal may be exercised. Unless each party agrees that it is unnecessary, the decision notice must include a summary of the findings of fact and reasons for the decision; or be accompanied by full written findings of fact and reasons for the decision. If the Tribunal provides no such findings and reasons, or summary findings and reasons only, a party to the proceedings may apply in writing for full written findings and reasons, and must do so before making an application for permission to appeal. Such an application must be sent to the Tribunal so that it is received within 28 days after the date that the Tribunal sent the decision notice. The Tribunal must send a full written statement of findings and reasons to each party within 28 days, or a soon as practicable thereafter, of receiving the application. [*SI 2009/273, Rule 35*].

Correction of errors

The Tribunal may at any time correct any clerical mistake or other accidental slip or omission in a decision, by: sending notification of the amended decision or direction, or a copy of the amended document, to all parties; and making any necessary amendment to any information published in relation to the decision, direction or document. [*SI 2009/273, Rule 37*].

Review of decision

The First-Tier Tribunal may, on its own initiative or on application by a person who has the right to appeal to the Upper Tribunal, review its decision. It may then: correct accidental errors; amend the reasons given for the decision; or set aside the decision, in which case it must re-decide the matter concerned, or refer the matter to the Upper Tribunal for re-decision. [*TCEA 2007, s 9*].

Costs

[5.19] The costs of and incidental to all proceedings in the First-tier Tribunal, and all proceedings in the Upper Tribunal are at the discretion of the relevant Tribunal, which has full power to determine by whom and to what extent the costs are to be paid. However, the First-tier Tribunal may only make an order in respect of costs if: it considers that a party or its representative has acted unreasonably in bringing, defending or conducting the proceedings; or the proceedings have been allocated as a complex case, and the taxpayer has not requested the Tribunal in writing, within 28 days of receiving notice that the case had been allocated as complex, to exclude the proceedings from potential liability for costs. The First-tier Tribunal may not make an order for costs against a person without giving that person an opportunity to make representations and, if the person is an individual, considering his financial means. The Upper Tribunal is not so restricted, but it is required to: give a person an opportunity to make representations; and, in judicial review cases, or where the case has been transferred from the First-tier Tribunal, or where a party has acted unreasonably, to consider an individual's financial means.

Application for costs

A person making an application for costs must: send or deliver a written application to the Tribunal and to the person against whom it is proposed that the order be made; and send or deliver with the application a schedule of the costs claimed in sufficient detail to allow the Tribunal to undertake a summary assessment of such costs. The application may be made at any time during the proceedings but may not be made later than 28 days (in the case of the Upper Tribunal, one month) after the date on which the Tribunal sends: a decision notice recording the decision which finally disposes of all issues in the proceedings; or notice of a withdrawal which ends the proceedings.

Award of costs

The amount of costs paid under an order may be ascertained by: summary assessment by the Tribunal; agreement of a specified sum between the paying person and the receiving person; or assessment of the whole or a specified part of the costs incurred by the receiving person, if not agreed.

[*TCEA 2007 s 29; SI 2009/273, Rule 10*].

Ministry of Justice proposals to charge fees

In August 2015 the Ministry of Justice issued a consultation document which included proposals to charge fees for appeals to the First-tier Tribunal (Tax Chamber) and the Upper Tribunal (Tax and Chancery). Although there have been considerable protests from professional bodies about restricting access to justice and judicial procedure, the Government appears determined to introduce fees of this nature in the near future, with a further report published by the Parliamentary Justice Committee on 14 June 2016. However the secondary legislation has not been published and the date from which the new fee structure will be effective has yet to be announced.

First-tier Tribunal (Tax Chamber) – proposed fees

Issue fee for paper and basic cases	£50
Issue fee for standard and complex cases	£200

Full hearing for basic cases	£200
Full hearing for standard cases	£500
Full hearing for complex cases	£1,000

(Ministry of Justice consultation document issued in August 2015, para 130). It was subsequently announced, however, that the fee for an appeal in relation to a fixed penalty not exceeding £100 will be £20.

Upper Tribunal (Tax and Chancery) – proposed fees

Fee to seek permission to appeal	£100
Permission hearing	£200
Substantive appeal hearing	£2,000

(Ministry of Justice consultation document issued in August 2015, para 132).

Enforcement of decisions

[5.20] Except in relation to awards made by the Upper Tribunal under its judicial review jurisdiction, a sum payable in pursuance of a decision of the First-tier Tribunal or Upper Tribunal made—

- in England and Wales is recoverable as if it were payable under an order of a county court or the High Court in England and Wales;
- in Scotland may be enforced as if it were an extract registered decree arbitral bearing a warrant for execution issued by the sheriff court of any sheriffdom in Scotland; and
- in Northern Ireland is recoverable as if it were payable under an order of a county court or the High Court in Northern Ireland.

[*TCEA 2007 s 27*].

Further appeal

Appeals from First-tier Tribunal to Upper Tribunal

[5.21] If any party is dissatisfied on a *point of law* with a decision of the First-tier Tribunal, he may appeal to the Upper Tribunal. The decision of the Tribunal on a *question of fact* is final, unless exceptionally a higher court is satisfied that the Tribunal was not entitled to come to its decision on the basis of the evidence before it. The leading case on the question of the distinction between fact and law is *Edwards v Bairstow & Harrison*, HL 1955, 36 TC 207 (TVC 3.6). The right to appeal does not apply to 'excluded decisions', i.e. a decision by the First-tier Tribunal on review; a decision of the First-tier Tribunal which is set aside on review; or any decision of the First-tier Tribunal which is of a description specified in an order made by the Lord Chancellor.

An appeal may be made only with the permission of the First-tier Tribunal or, if that has been refused or not admitted, permission of the Upper Tribunal. An application to the First-Tier Tribunal must be made in writing and received within 56 days of the latest of the date on which the Tribunal sends to the applicant: full written reasons for the decision; notification of amended reasons for, or correction of, the decision following a review; notification that an application for the decision to be set aside has been unsuccessful. If the First-tier Tribunal grants permission to appeal, the appellant must provide a notice of appeal to the Upper Tribunal so that it is received within one month of the date on which the First-tier Tribunal sent notice of such permission to the appellant. An application to appeal to the Upper Tribunal must be made no later than one month after the date on which the First-tier Tribunal refused the application to appeal.

The Upper Tribunal may set aside the decision of the First-tier Tribunal. If it does so, it must either remit the case to the First-tier Tribunal with directions for its reconsideration, or re-make the decision. Proceedings on appeal to the Upper Tribunal are subject to the *Tribunal Procedure (Upper Tribunal) Rules, SI 2008/2698*, which to a large extent mirror the rules applicable in the First-tier Tribunal.

The Upper Tribunal may, on its own initiative or on application by a person who has the right to appeal to the Upper Tribunal, review a decision made by it. The Upper Tribunal may then: correct accidental errors; amend the reasons given for the decision; or set aside the decision, in which case it must re-decide the matter concerned.

[*TCEA 2007 ss 10–12; SI 2008/2698, Rule 21; SI 2009/273, Rule 39*].

Appeals from a Tribunal to the Court of Appeal

There is a right to appeal to the Court of Appeal (Court of Session in Scotland) on any point of law arising from a decision made by the Upper Tribunal. That right may be exercised only with permission given by the Upper Tribunal, or (if the Upper Tribunal has refused permission) by the Court of Appeal. In England, Wales and Northern Ireland, applications for appeal are limited to cases where the Upper Tribunal (or Court of Appeal, as appropriate) considers that the proposed appeal would raise some important point of principle or practice, or there is some other compelling reason for the Court to hear the appeal. The right of appeal does not extend to an 'excluded decision', i.e. a decision of the Upper Tribunal on review; a decision of the Upper Tribunal which is set aside on review; or any decision of the Upper Tribunal which is of a description specified in an order made by the Lord Chancellor. In determining an appeal, the Court of Appeal may set aside the decision of the Upper Tribunal. If it does so, it must either remit the case to the Upper Tribunal or the First-tier Tribunal with directions for its reconsideration, or re-make the decision.

An appeal can be made from the Court of Appeal to the Supreme Court (formerly the House of Lords), with the leave of the Court of Appeal or the Supreme Court.

[*TCEA 2007 ss 13, 14; SI 2008/2834*].

References to the Court of Justice of the European Union (CJEU)

[5.22] A Tribunal or higher court may refer a question to the CJEU if a decision on that matter is necessary to enable it to give judgment. [*EU Treaty, Art 267*]. Whether or not to refer a question is a matter within the discretion of the Tribunal or court and it cannot be compelled to do so. It is not a matter for the parties to the case, although their views are no doubt taken into account. If one of the parties is dissatisfied with a refusal to refer a point to the CJEU, it must appeal under national law and has no right of access to the CJEU direct.

The national court has three options.

- It may decide that a referral on the question is unnecessary and that the case may, for example, be decided on the basis of national law which makes the question of EU law irrelevant.
- It may decide the question of EU law itself. This may be done, for example, where the point has been settled in previous CJEU decisions (sometimes described as 'acte clair') or where the circumstances of the case make a reference inconvenient.
- It may make a reference to the CJEU.

The courts have applied the following guidelines in exercising their discretion whether or not to make a reference.

- The point must be conclusive since the purpose of a ruling is to enable judgment to be given.
- There must have been no previous ruling which decides or substantially decides the point.
- If the point is reasonably clear and free from doubt it may not be necessary to interpret but simply apply the EU law.
- It is necessary to decide the facts first.
- The question to be referred is a matter of some importance.

The CJEU cannot interpret national law or apply its interpretation of EU law to the facts of the case. Its sole function is to decide what the EU law is, and leave the national courts to implement its ruling.

Barring HMRC from taking part in the proceedings

[5.23] In *BPP Holdings Ltd v HMRC* [2016] EWCA Civ 121 (TVC 2.248), HMRC failed to comply with a number of directions of the First-tier Tax Tribunal in relation to the submission of their statement of case and providing details requested by the appellant. The First-tier Tax Tribunal issued an 'unless' order, threatening to debar HMRC from further participation in the proceedings (allowing the appellant to present its case unopposed) if the failures were not rectified within a set period. HMRC again failed to comply, and the Tribunal judge duly debarred HMRC. HMRC appealed, and the Upper Tribunal decided that the extreme measure of debarring HMRC was not justified; however, the Court of Appeal restored the First-tier Tribunal's decision, holding that there should be no special treatment for HMRC, and no reason for a relaxed approach to compliance with Tribunal directions. [*SI 2008/2698, Reg 8*].

Key points: appeals

[5.24] Points to consider are as follows.

- Most VAT appeals are heard at first instance by the First-tier Tribunal, with more complex cases (or appeals against decisions made in the First-tier Tribunal) being heard in the Upper Tribunal.
- As a general principle, any VAT assessment that is being appealed by a taxpayer should be paid before the appeal is heard. However, there is an appeal facility if the payment would cause financial hardship to the business. In reality, HMRC tend to be quite flexible in granting such requests, especially if large amounts of tax are involved. If a taxpayer pays the disputed amount in advance, and is successful with his appeal, then he will be entitled to receive interest on the period between when he paid the tax and when he received his subsequent rebate.
- In relation to appeals against interest, penalties or default surcharges, there is no requirement for the amount to be paid in advance of the appeal hearing.
- Before making an appeal to a Tribunal, a taxpayer has the right to request an internal review by a trained review officer in HMRC. The officer is required to carry out and complete his review within 45 days. If a taxpayer does not agree with the outcome of the review (e.g. if a VAT assessment is upheld) then he still has the right to appeal to the First-tier Tribunal. Equally, a taxpayer has the right to immediately appeal to the Tribunal if he does not feel there is any benefit in going through the HMRC internal review process.
- The opportunity to be awarded costs is limited. As a general principle, the First-tier Tribunal court will only award costs where it considers that one of the parties (obviously the unsuccessful party) has acted unreasonably in bringing a particular issue to appeal.
- An appeal against a First-tier Tribunal decision can only be made to the Upper Tribunal on a point of law, and not on a question of fact. The next stage of the appeal process after the Upper Tribunal will be the Court of Appeal (Court of Session in Scotland). In some cases, an appeal can then be made to the Supreme Court. At various points in the appeal process, a reference can be made to the CJEU (Court of Justice of the European Union) to answer an important matter of uncertainty about the application of EU law that affects the case and needs to be clarified.

6

Assessments

Cross-references. See **5 APPEALS; 28.5 GROUPS OF COMPANIES; 52 PAYMENT OF VAT.**

De Voil Indirect Tax Service. See V5.131–140.

Introduction to assessments

[6.1] VAT is normally paid (without any assessment being made) on the submission of a return for a VAT period.

However, subject to the time limits in **6.2** below, HMRC are given power to raise assessments where the following circumstances apply.

(a) *Returns have not been made.* Assessments will generally be based on centrally stored data concerning the trader's business and VAT history and will normally be withdrawn if an acceptable return is made and the VAT declared on it paid. From 1 January 2015 this also applies to returns that have not been made to the tax authorities in other EU member states in relation to supplies of broadcasting, telecommunication and electronic services to consumers in the UK – see **64.40** and **64.45 SPECIAL SCHEMES.** [*VATA 1994, s 73; FA 2014, Sch 22*].

(b) *Documents have not been kept* and facilities have not been afforded to verify returns.

(c) *It appears to HMRC* that the returns are incomplete or incorrect. This will most frequently happen following assurance visits by HMRC officers.

(d) *Incorrect VAT credits*, i.e. where for any VAT period an amount has been paid or credited to any person as either a repayment or refund of VAT or as being due as a VAT credit and the amount ought not to have been paid or credited. This is further extended to cover an amount which would not have been so paid or credited had the facts been known or been as they later turn out to be (e.g. where bad debt relief has been claimed and subsequently the debt, or part, has been repaid without the VAT element being paid to HMRC). Following conflicting court judgments about the period for which such an assessment should be issued, which is important in determining the application of time limits for issuing the assessment, the law was amended to specify that the assessment is to be made for the prescribed accounting period during which the repayment or refund of VAT, or the VAT credit, was paid or credited [*VATA 1994, s 73(6A)*].

(e) *Failure to account for goods*, i.e. where goods have, in the course or furtherance of a business, been supplied to a taxable person, acquired or obtained by him from another EU member state or imported by him from a place outside the EU and he is unable to prove to HMRC that the goods
- have been, or are available to be, supplied by him;
- have been exported or otherwise removed from the UK without being exported or so removed by way of supply; or
- have been lost or destroyed.

(f) *A fiscal warehousekeeper has failed to pay VAT* required under *VATA 1994, s 18E* on any missing or deficient goods or it appears to HMRC that goods have been removed from a warehouse or fiscal warehouse without payment of the VAT required under *VATA 1994, s 18(4)* or *s 18D*.

(g) *Goods subject to excise duty or new means of transport* have been acquired in the UK from another EU member state by a person who at that time was not a taxable person and
  (i) no notification of that acquisition has been given to HMRC by the person required to give it;
  (ii) HMRC are not satisfied that the particulars in a notification are accurate or complete; or
  (iii) there has been a failure to supply HMRC with the information necessary to verify the particulars contained in the notification.

  See **20.9** and **20.37 EUROPEAN UNION: SINGLE MARKET** for general provisions relating to such acquisition of dutiable goods and new means of transport respectively.

  Any amount assessed and notified under these provisions is deemed to be an amount of VAT due and, if the person fails to pay, enforcement action can be taken to recover the debt.

(h) *Inaccuracies in a return leading to a potential loss of VAT within FA 2007, Sch 24* (see **53.12 PENALTIES**), or registration irregularities or unauthorised issue of VAT invoices under *FA 2008, Sch 41* (see **53.16 PENALTIES**).

An amount assessed and notified to a person under any of the above provisions is, subject to appeal, deemed to be an amount of VAT due and is recoverable unless the assessment is subsequently withdrawn or reduced.

Where a person is assessed under either of (*a*) to (*c*) *and* (*d*) above for the same VAT period, assessments may be combined and notified to the person in one assessment.

[*VATA 1994, s 73(1)–(4)(7)(7A)(7B)(9), s 75(1)(3)*].

HMRC may raise a single or 'global' assessment covering more than one accounting period (*SJ Grange Ltd v C & E Commrs*, CA 1978 [1979] STC 183 (TVC 3.120)). This power may be necessary where it is impossible or impracticable to identify the specific accounting periods for which the VAT claimed is due but is not restricted to such cases. It is a question of fact (important for time limit purposes) whether there is one global assessment or a number of separate assessments notified together. In *Razaq and Bashir (t/a/ Streamline Taxis)* (VTD 17537) (TVC 47.16) HMRC incorrectly issued the registration certificate in the names of Razaq and Shabir and subsequently issued a global assessment covering the period 1 November 1994 to 1 November 1998. The tribunal held that the certificate was invalid. The effect of *SI 1995/2518, Reg 25(1)* was that the partnership was required to be registered and make quarterly returns from 1 November 1984 but since there was no valid certificate of registration, the effect of *VATA 1994, s 73* was that HMRC had to assess accounting period by accounting period and could not make a valid global assessment for the overall period.

The Form on which HMRC notify assessments is clearly intended to be used for either a single or a number of assessments and the fact therefore that demands for multiple accounting periods are included on the same form does not necessarily constitute a single global assessment (*C & E Commrs v Le Rififi Ltd*, CA 1994 [1995] STC 103 (TVC 3.91) not following the earlier decision in *Don Pasquale (a firm) v C & E Commrs*, CA [1990] STC 556 (TVC 2.128)).

The assessment, to be valid, must show the period covered not just the end of that period (*RE Bell* (VTD 761) (TVC 3.144)) although the information need not necessarily be on the assessment itself. See *House (PJ) (t/a P & J Autos) v C & E Commrs*, CA 1995, [1996] STC 154 (TVC 3.133) where the dates covered by the assessment were left blank but the period assessed was indicated by accompanying schedules. A notice of assessment issued 'without prejudice' is not invalid (*McCafferty* (VTD 483) (TVC 3.47)).

Where an assessment has been made as a result of a person's failure to submit a return for a VAT period and, although the VAT assessed has been paid, no proper return has been made for that period, if HMRC find it necessary to raise assessments for later periods due to the failure to submit returns by that person or a representative of his (see **6.9** below) then HMRC may raise the later assessments for amounts greater than that which they would otherwise consider to be appropriate. [*VATA 1994, s 73(8)*].

Subject to the foregoing, assessments under (*a*) to (*c*) and (*e*) to (*g*) above must be made to the best of HMRC's judgement. [*VATA 1994, s 73(1)(7)(7A)(7B), s 75(1)*]. HMRC must exercise their powers honestly and bona fide and there must be material before them on which to make their judgement. Although their decisions must be reasonable and not arbitrary, they are under no obligation to do the work of a taxpayer by carrying out exhaustive investigations but if they do make investigations, they must take into account material disclosed by them (*Van Boeckel v C & E Commrs*, QB 1980, [1981] STC 290 (TVC 3.1)). The function of the tribunal is supervisory. An assessment should only be held to fail the 'best judgement' test if made dishonestly, vindictively or capriciously, where it is a spurious estimate or guess in which all the elements of judgement are missing, or where it is wholly unreasonable. Short of such a finding there is no justification for setting aside an assessment. In the normal case, the important issue is the amount of the assessment (*MH Rahman (t/a Khayam Restaurant) v C & E Commrs*, QB [1998] STC 826 (TVC 3.8) and see also *C & E Commrs v Pegasus Birds Ltd*, CA [2004] STC 1509 (TVC 3.20)) and once the tribunal has accepted that HMRC were entitled to make that assessment, the amount is for the tribunal to decide (*Murat v C & E Commrs*, QB [1998] STC 923 (TVC 3.172)). The function of the tribunal is to decide what information HMRC relied upon to make the assessment and then make a value judgement as to how they arrived at the assessment. It is not a function of the tribunal to engage in a process that looks afresh at all the evidence before it (*Georgiou and another (t/a Mario's Chippery) v C & E Commrs*, CA [1996] STC 463 (TVC 3.6)). See also *Seto v C & E Commrs*, CS 1980, [1981] STC 698 (TVC 3.2). An assessment must be considered as a whole and if it is not made to the best of HMRC's judgement, then it is wholly invalid and void and cannot be corrected by any subsequent amendment to it or treated as partly valid. See *Barber (JH)* (VTD 7727) (TVC 3.37) where an assessment partly covered a period for which a previous assessment had already been raised.

Where an earlier assessment has been held to be defective because it was not made to the best of HMRC's judgement, HMRC are not estopped from issuing a replacement assessment by the principle of '*res judicata*', i.e. that an issue which a court has decided in an action between the parties cannot be questioned in a later action between the same parties (*Bennett v C & E Commrs (No 2)*, Ch D [2001] STC 137 (TVC 2.115) (TVC 34.14)).

Time limits

[6.2] The time limits for assessments under **6.1** above apply as follows.

(a) Under **6.1**(*a*)–(*d*), subject to the provisions relating to death below, an assessment for any VAT period cannot be made after the later of
   - (i) two years after the end of the VAT period; or
   - (ii) one year after evidence of fact, sufficient in the opinion of HMRC to justify the making of an assessment, comes to their knowledge

   but in any case not more than four years after the end of the VAT period.

   In the case of an assessment under **6.1**(*d*) above, the VAT period referred to in (i) above is that in which the repayment or refund of VAT, or the VAT credit, was paid or credited.

   See **6.6** below for further assessments.

(b) Under **6.1**(*e*)(*f*), subject to the provisions relating to death below, an assessment cannot be made more than four years after the end of the VAT period or importation or acquisition concerned.

(c) Under **6.1**(*g*), subject to the provisions relating to death below, an assessment cannot be made after the later of
   - (i) two years after the time of notification to HMRC of the acquisition of the goods in question; or

(ii) one year after evidence of fact, sufficient in the opinion of HMRC to justify the making of an assessment, comes to their knowledge

but in any case not more than four years after the end of the VAT period. See **6.6** below for further assessments.

(d) In the case of an assessment of a person ('P'), or of an amount payable by P,

(i) involving a loss of VAT brought about deliberately by P (or by another person acting on P's behalf),

(ii) in which P has participated in a transaction knowing that it was part of arrangements of any kind (whether or not legally enforceable) intended to bring about a loss of VAT,

(iii) involving a loss of VAT attributable to a failure by P to comply with a 'notification obligation', or

(iv) involving a loss of VAT attributable to a scheme in respect of which P has failed to comply with an obligation under *VATA 1994, Sch 11A para 6* (see **4 ANTI-AVOIDANCE**)

subject to the provisions relating to death below, the assessment may be made at any time not more than 20 years after the end of the VAT period or the importation, acquisition or event giving rise to the penalty, as appropriate.

A loss of VAT brought about deliberately by P or another person includes a loss that arises as a result of a deliberate inaccuracy in a document given to HMRC by that person.

'*Notification obligation*' means an obligation in connection with registration under *VATA 1994, Sch 1* (registration generally), *VATA 1994, Sch 2* (registration in respect of supplies from other EU member states), *VATA 1994, Sch 3* (registration in respect of acquisitions from other EU member states), *VATA 1994, Sch 3A* (registration in respect of disposals of assets for which a VAT repayment is claimed) and regulations under *VATA 1994, Sch 11 para 2(4)* (certain taxable acquisitions of goods which are subject to excise duty or are new means of transport and are acquired in the UK from another EU member state by a non-taxable person).

Death

Where the taxable person has died, any assessment cannot be made more than four years after death.

[*VATA 1994, s 73(6)(6A), s 75(2), s 77(1)(4)(4A)–(4C)(5)*].

Where a single global assessment is made because it is not possible to identify a specific period for which VAT is due, the two-year time limit runs from the end of the *first* VAT period it covers (*International Language Centres Ltd v C & E Commrs*, QB, [1983] STC 394 (TVC 3.41)). Where a global assessment is raised out of time on this basis, it is a nullity *ab initio* even if the taxpayer failed to lodge an appeal against it in due time with a VAT Tribunal (*Lord Advocate v Shanks (t/a Shanks & Co)*, CS [1992] STC 928 (TVC 2.192)). See, however, **6.1** above for the different interpretation of what constitutes a global assessment following the decision in *C & E Commrs v Le Rififi Ltd*, CA 1994, [1995] STC 103 (TVC 3.91).

A tribunal considering the possible application of (*a*)(ii) must decide what were the facts which, in the opinion of the officer making the assessment on behalf of HMRC, justified the making of the assessment and then decide when the last of these facts came to the knowledge of the officer. The period of one year then runs from that date (*Heyfordian Travel Ltd* [1979] VATTR 139 (TVC 3.121)). Similarly, in *Pegasus Birds Ltd v C & E Commrs*, CA [2000] STC 91 (TVC 3.57) the court observed that provided HMRC acquired the last piece of evidence of sufficient weight to justify an assessment within the one-year time limit, the test in (*a*)(ii) is satisfied. 'Evidence of facts' means what it says; the words do not encompass constructive knowledge (*Spillane v C & E Commrs*, QB 1989, [1990] STC 212 (TVC 3.4)). This was confirmed in *C & E Commrs v Post Office*, QB [1995] STC 749 (TVC 3.55) where it was held that the relevant date was not when any error should have been discovered but when evidence of facts actually came to the knowledge of HMRC. Nothing in the statutory provisions encompasses constructive knowledge. There is no obligation on HMRC to be alert to discover a mistake (*FC Milnes (Bradford) Ltd* (VTD 478) (TVC 3.122)). Following the rule in *C & E Commrs v J H Corbitt (Numismatists) Ltd*, HL [1980] STC 231 (TVC 60.1), the Court is prevented from substituting its opinion for that of HMRC and therefore it can only interfere if there is material to show that an officer's failure to make an earlier assessment was perverse (*Cumbrae Properties (1963) Ltd v C & E Commrs*, QB [1981] STC 799 (TVC 62.24)).

Where returns which are clearly incorrect are in the hands of HMRC, assessments are out of date if made outside the two-year period and no evidence of new facts have come to HMRC's attention to bring the case within (*a*)(ii) above (*Lord (t/a Lords Electrical and Fancy Goods)* (VTD 320) (TVC 3.73)).

The legislation specifies time limits for the 'making' of an assessment rather than the 'notification' of that assessment to the taxpayer. For a consideration of when an assessment is made (as distinct from notified) see *Cheeseman (t/a Well in Tune) v C & E Commrs*, Ch D [2000] STC 1119 (TVC 3.87). However, to avoid any uncertainty, for all assessments issued on or after 1 March 2001, HMRC will apply the time limit rule to the 'notified' date rather than the earlier 'made' date. See **6.7** below.

De Voil Indirect Tax Service. See V5.136–136B.

Assessments of penalties, interest and surcharges

[6.3] HMRC may assess and notify any amount due by way of

(a) default surcharge under *VATA 1994, ss 59, 59A* (see **53.23** and **53.24 PENALTIES**),
(b) penalty under *VATA 1994, ss 60–69B* (see **53.12** to **53.19** and **53.27** to **53.30 PENALTIES**),
(c) interest under *VATA 1994, s 74* (see **52.16 PAYMENT OF VAT**),
(d) penalty under *VATA 1994, Sch 11A* (see **4.2 ANTI-AVOIDANCE**),
(e) penalty in connection with the mandatory electronic filing of VAT returns (see **2.1 ACCOUNTING PERIODS AND RETURNS**), or

(f) penalty under *FA 2008, Sch 36 paras 39–40A* (see **53.20 PENALTIES**)
(g) default surcharge under *VATA 1994, Sch 3B, Sch 3BA* (see **53.25 PENALTIES**)

except that a penalty under **53.19**(*b*)(vi)–(x) **PENALTIES** can only be assessed if, within the two years preceding the date of the assessment, HMRC have issued a written warning of the consequences of a continuing failure to comply with the relevant requirement.

Unless the assessment is withdrawn or reduced, the amount is recoverable as if it were VAT due (except a penalty under (*f*) which may be enforced as if it were assessed and payable as income tax). The fact that the conduct giving rise to any penalty under (*b*), (*d*) or (*e*) above may have ceased before an assessment is made does not affect the powers of HMRC to make an assessment.

Combining assessments

Where for a particular accounting period a person is assessed for VAT due under **6.1**(*a*)–(*g*) as well as surcharge, penalty or interest under these provisions, HMRC may combine the assessments but the amount of the penalty, interest or surcharge should be shown separately.

Allocation of VAT between periods

Where any penalty, etc. must be calculated by reference to VAT which was paid late or avoided and that VAT cannot be readily attributed to one or more VAT periods, HMRC are empowered to allocate the VAT due to such period or periods as they determine to the best of their judgement.

Penalties, interest accruing on daily basis

Where a penalty or interest accrues on a daily basis, the assessment must specify a date (not later than the date of the notice) to which the penalty or interest is calculated. If the penalty or interest continues to accrue after that date, a further assessment or assessments may be made in respect of amounts so accruing. HMRC, however, may notify the person liable of a period during which he may remedy the failure or default which caused the penalty or pay the amount on which interest was charged. If the person meets this requirement, no further penalty or interest accrues after the date specified in the assessment.

Penalties for tax avoidance

Where HMRC notify a person of a penalty under (*d*) above the assessment must specify the amount of the penalty, the reasons for the imposition of the penalty, how the penalty has been calculated, and any mitigation of the penalty under *VATA 1994, s 70* (see **53.33 PENALTIES**).

[*VATA 1994, s 76, Sch 11A para 12; FA 2008, Sch 36 paras 46, 49; FA 2009, Sch 47 para 20*].

Time limits

[6.4] An assessment for any relevant period under **6.3** above cannot be made after the following times or, where there is an alternative, the *earlier* of such times.

The following time limits apply.

(a) In the case of an assessment of a person ('P'), or of an amount payable by P,
   (i) involving a loss of VAT brought about deliberately by P (or by another person acting on P's behalf),
   (ii) in which P has participated in a transaction knowing that it was part of arrangements of any kind (whether or not legally enforceable) intended to bring about a loss of VAT,
   (iii) involving a loss of VAT attributable to a failure by P to comply with a 'notification obligation', or
   (iv) involving a loss of VAT attributable to a scheme in respect of which P has failed to comply with an obligation *VATA 1994, Sch 11A para 6* (see **4 ANTI-AVOIDANCE**)

   subject to the provisions relating to death below, the assessment may be made at any time not more than 20 years after the end of the VAT period or the importation, acquisition or event giving rise to the penalty, as appropriate.

   A loss of VAT brought about deliberately by P or another person includes a loss that arises as a result of a deliberate inaccuracy in a document given to HMRC by that person.

   '*Notification obligation*' means an obligation in connection with registration under *VATA 1994, Sch 1* (registration generally), *VATA 1994, Sch 2* (registration in respect of supplies from other EU member states), *VATA 1994, Sch 3* (registration in respect of acquisitions from other EU member states), *VATA 1994, Sch 3A* (registration in respect of disposals of assets for which a VAT repayment is claimed) and regulations under *VATA 1994, Sch 11 2(4)* para (certain taxable acquisitions of goods which are subject to excise duty or are new means of transport and are acquired in the UK from another EU member state by a non-taxable person).

(b) For assessments under *VATA 1994, s 59* (default surcharge, see **53.23 PENALTIES**), *VATA 1994, s 63* (misdeclaration, see **53.13 PENALTIES**) or *VATA 1994, s 74* (interest on VAT, see **52.16 PAYMENT OF VAT**)
   - four years after the end of the relevant period; or
   - two years after the VAT due for the relevant period has finally been determined.

(c) For assessments under *VATA 1994, s 62* (incorrect certificates of zero-rating, see **53.26 PENALTIES**), *VATA 1994, s 64* (repeated misdeclaration, see **53.14 PENALTIES**), *VATA 1994, s 68* (breaches of walking possession agreements, see **53.18 PENALTIES**) or *VATA 1994, s 69* (breaches of regulatory provisions, see **53.19 PENALTIES**) four years after the event giving rise to the penalty.

(d) For assessments under *VATA 1994, s 65* (inaccuracies in EU sales statements, see **53.27 PENALTIES**) or *VATA 1994, s 66* (failure to submit EU sales statements, see **53.28 PENALTIES**)
   - four years after the event giving rise to the penalty; or

- two years after the time when sufficient facts came to the knowledge of HMRC to indicate that, as the case may be, the statement had a material inaccuracy or there had been a default in the submission of a sales statement.

(e) For assessments under *VATA 1994, s 69A* (breach of record-keeping requirements in relation to transactions in gold, see **53.29 PENALTIES**)
- four years after the transaction giving rise to the penalty; or
- two years after HMRC have evidence of facts '*sufficient in their opinion to justify the making of the assessment*' i.e. facts sufficient both to indicate that there has been a failure to comply with the provisions and to determine the value of the transaction concerned.

(f) For assessments under *VATA 1994, Sch 11A para 12* (failure to notify certain VAT avoidance schemes, see **4.2 ANTI-AVOIDANCE**) two years after the time when sufficient facts come to the knowledge of HMRC to indicate that there has been a failure to comply with those provisions in relation to a notifiable scheme.

Death

Where the taxable person has died, any assessment under (*a*)–(*d*) above cannot be made more than four years after death.

[*VATA 1994, ss 69A(4)(5), 77(1)–(5), Sch 11A para 12(4)*].

The legislation specifies time limits for the 'making' of an assessment rather than the 'notification' of that assessment to the taxpayer. For a consideration of when an assessment is made (as distinct from notified) see *Cheeseman (t/a Well in Tune) v C & E Commrs*, Ch D [2000] STC 1119 (TVC 3.87). However, to avoid any uncertainty, HMRC will apply the time limit rule to the 'notified' date rather than the earlier 'made' date. See **6.7** below.

Assessments for overpaid interest and repayments

[6.5] HMRC may raise recovery assessments to the best of their judgement in the following circumstances and notify the person accordingly.

(a) Where they have paid interest under *VATA 1994, s 78* (see **52.18 PAYMENT OF VAT**) to any person who was not entitled to it, they may assess the amount paid.

(b) Where they have credited a person with an amount under *VATA 1994, s 80(1)* or *(1A)* (see **52.9**(*a*) and (*b*) **PAYMENT OF VAT**) in excess of the amount for which they were liable at that time, they may assess the excess credited.

(c) Where any person is liable under *Regulations* made under *VATA 1994, s 80A* to pay to HMRC any VAT previously repaid by HMRC to them on the understanding that it would be reimbursed to customers (see **52.10 PAYMENT OF VAT**), they may assess the amount due.

(d) Where
   (i) they have credited a person with an amount ('the gross credit') under *VATA 1994, s 80(1)* or *(1A)* (see **52.10**(*a*) and (*b*) **PAYMENT OF VAT**),

(ii) any sums were set against that amount by HMRC, and
(iii) the amount reimbursed to customers was less than the gross credit,

they may assess so much of the gross credit as exceeds the amount reimbursed to customers. No liability can arise on the same amount under both (*c*) above and this provision.

Unless the assessment is withdrawn or reduced, the amount is recoverable as if it were VAT due.

Time limits

The time limits for making an assessment under the above provisions are as follows.

- Under (*a*), (*c*) or (*d*) above, an assessment cannot be made more than two years after evidence of facts, sufficient in the opinion of HMRC to justify the making of an assessment, comes to their knowledge.
- Under (*b*) above, an assessment cannot be made more than two years after the later of
  (i) the end of the VAT period in which the amount was credited to the person; and
  (ii) the time when evidence of facts, sufficient in the opinion of HMRC to justify the making of the assessment, comes to their knowledge.

'Evidence of facts' does not include court judgments and their effects. See *C & E Commrs v DFS Furniture Co plc*, CA [2004] STC 559 (TVC 3.117) where an HMRC assessment raised in 2001 to recover VAT relating to periods from April 1993 to June 1996 was held to be invalid even though it was within two years of the decision by the CJEU in *C & E Commrs v Primback Ltd, ECJ Case C-34/99*, [2001] STC 803 (TVC 22.265) (which overruled the 1996 decision by the CA in that case on the basis of which a repayment had been made to *DFS Furniture*).

Interest

The provisions of *VATA 1994, s 74* (interest payable on VAT, see **52.15 PAYMENT OF VAT**) apply to such an assessment except that in the calculation of the period of interest, interest runs from the date the assessment is notified until the date of payment.

HMRC may assess and notify any amount due by way of interest on a recovery assessment but (without prejudice to the power to make assessments for interest for later periods) the assessment is restricted to interest for a period of no more than two years ending with the time when the assessment to interest is made. The assessment must specify a date (not later than the date of the notice) to which the interest is calculated. If the interest continues to accrue after that date, a further assessment or assessments may be made in respect of the amounts so accruing. HMRC, however, may notify the person liable of a period during which he may pay the underlying assessment and, if the person meets this requirement, no further interest accrues after the date specified in the assessment.

Further assessments

See **6.6**(*b*) below.

Personal representatives

Notification of an assessment to a personal representative, trustee in bankruptcy, interim or permanent trustee, receiver, liquidator or person otherwise acting in a representative capacity is treated as notification to the person on whose behalf he acts.

[*VATA 1994, s 78A, s 80(4A)(4AA)(4C), s 80B*].

Further assessments

[6.6] HMRC may make further assessments in the following circumstances.

(a) Where, after an assessment has been made under **6.1**(*a*)–(*d*) or (*g*) above, further 'evidence of facts', sufficient in the opinion of HMRC to justify the making of an assessment, comes to their knowledge. [*VATA 1994, s 73(6), s 75(2)*]. The further assessment must also be within the time limit (see **6.2** above). Contents of nil returns submitted by a taxpayer do not amount to 'evidence of facts' justifying a further assessment (*Parekh & another v C & E Commrs*, QB [1984] STC 284 (TVC 3.77)). In that case, Woolf J also observed that, where the two-year time limit for an assessment has elapsed. HMRC should only be allowed to make a further assessment in relation to the VAT due based on the evidence which has come to their knowledge since the earlier assessment. Where, however, the two-year period has not elapsed, HMRC are not prevented from withdrawing the earlier assessment and replacing it by another.

(b) If, otherwise than in circumstances falling within (*a*) above, it appears to HMRC that the amount which ought to have been assessed under any of the provisions of **6.1**, **6.3** or **6.5** above exceeds the amount which was so assessed, then a supplementary assessment of the amount of the excess may be made and notified to the person concerned under the same provisions and within the same time limits as the original assessment. [*VATA 1994, s 77(6), s 78A(6); FA 1997, s 45(1)*]. Note that there is no requirement for further evidence as in (*a*) above.

De Voil Indirect Tax Service. See V5.134.

The assessment process

[6.7] Unless there is a danger of losing VAT because of the imminence of a time limit or unless the nature of the irregularity is agreed and already clear, HMRC will normally write to the taxpayer in advance of making an assessment for underdeclared or overclaimed VAT, setting out why they believe an assessment to be necessary and detailing the calculation of arrears. This letter does not constitute the 'making' of an assessment but gives the taxpayer the chance to bring further information to the attention of HMRC and help resolve any misunderstanding or disagreement before the assessment is made. Normally, HMRC give the taxpayer three weeks to reply.

The assessment process itself is made up of three stages.

(a) *The decision to assess.*

(b) *The making of the assessment.* This process includes deciding in principle to assess, the quantification of arrears and any necessary checking of arrears calculations. It ends when the HMRC officer has taken all steps necessary to establish to the best of his judgement that the taxpayer owes a quantified sum for a given reason. That officer, and any checking officer, will sign and date any schedules of calculation. HMRC will normally provide copies of these schedules to the taxpayer to help explain the basis of the assessment.

(c) *The notification of that amount.* HMRC must formally notify the taxpayer by way of assessment of the amount of VAT due [*VATA 1994, s 73(1)*] but there is no express provision as to the manner in which this is to be done. In practice, the taxpayer will be notified in one of two ways.

- Normally, an internal Form VAT 641 is completed, signed and dated. This form is the means of inputting an assessment on to HMRC's computer system which then generates Form VAT 655, the notice of assessment to be issued to the taxpayer. The Form VAT 655 is sent from the central computer centre to the local VAT office where it is checked and then dated and sent to the taxpayer.
- In certain circumstances, for example, where there is some risk of an assessment which has been made in time not being notified to the taxpayer until after the time limit has expired, the assessing officer will send a dated notification of assessment by letter to the taxpayer. The computer generated Form VAT 655 will then normally be issued in due course.

The legislation specifies time limits for the making of an assessment under (*b*) above (see **6.2** and **6.4** above) but there are no time limits rules for notifications under (*c*) above. The date an assessment is made is not normally communicated to the taxpayer. To avoid any uncertainty, where, for example, an assessment is 'made' in time but not notified until after the time limit for assessing has expired, HMRC will always apply the time limit rules to the 'notified date' rather than the earlier 'made date'. The 'notified date' for this purpose is the date on which the assessment is sent by HMRC to the taxpayer. The date will be shown on the letter or other formal notification of the assessment.

(HMRC Manual VAEC6080).

Any notice for VAT purposes can be served on a person by sending it by post in a letter addressed to him or his VAT representative (see **3.8 AGENTS**) at the last or usual residence or place of business of that person or representative. [*VATA 1994, s 98*]. See **51.5 PARTNERSHIPS** for the special provisions for serving notice on partners and **6.9** below for service on representatives.

An assessment which is incorrectly notified (e.g. by being sent to the taxpayer's solicitors without authority) is not invalid but simply unenforceable until properly notified to the taxpayer (*Grunwick Processing Laboratories Ltd v C & E Commrs*, CA [1987] STC 357 (TVC 3.62)).

De Voil Indirect Tax Service. See V5.137–V5.139.

Corrections of assessments by tribunals

[6.8] Where on an appeal against a decision within **6.1**(*b*)–(*e*) above it is found that the amount specified in the assessment is less than it ought to have been, the tribunal may give a direction specifying the correct amount. The appellant is deemed to have been notified of the revised amount. [*VATA 1994, s 84(5)*]. A tribunal may exercise its power to increase an assessment in order to correct arithmetical errors or where HMRC have argued at the hearing that the assessment should be increased. A tribunal does not have a free-standing power to increase an assessment entirely of its own initiative. Furthermore, if a tribunal was contemplating increasing an assessment, the appellant should be given a fair opportunity (by adjournment, if necessary) to consider the position (*Elias Gale Racing v C & E Commrs*, QB 1998, [1999] STC 66 (TVC 3.176)).

A tribunal may reduce or discharge an assessment on appeal. See **5 APPEALS**.

Assessments on, and notification to, representatives

[6.9] Where a person required to make a return as a personal representative, trustee in bankruptcy, receiver, liquidator or otherwise in a representative capacity fails to make that return or makes a return which appears to HMRC to be incomplete or incorrect, assessments (including assessments of penalties, interest or surcharges) may be made by HMRC on that person in his representative position and a notification to him is treated as also notifying the person for whom he acts. [*VATA 1994, s 73(5)(10), s 76(10)*].

Similar provisions apply to assessments on, and notifications to, such persons in respect of acquisitions of goods subject to excise duty or new means of transport under **6.1**(*g*) above. [*VATA 1994, s 75(4)*].

Key points: assessments

[6.10] Points to consider are as follows.

- If an HMRC officer considers VAT returns to be incomplete or inaccurate, then he has the power to assess tax he considers to be due using his 'best judgement'. A best judgement assessment does not require an analysis of all available records to be made, only those that enable the officer to accurately assess the VAT that he considers to be due from a taxpayer. Decisions of the First-tier Tribunals in recent years have shown how difficult it is to challenge an officer's conclusions without good evidence to displace them.

- The time limit for adjusting VAT errors is generally four years from the end of the relevant return period.
- Be aware that the four-year assessment period is extended to 20 years if a taxpayer has deliberately understated his VAT liability.

7

Bad Debt Relief

Cross-references. See **60.42 REGISTRATION** for effect of transfer of registration with a business as a going concern; **61.21 RETAIL SCHEMES** for bad debt relief for mail order businesses.

De Voil Indirect Tax Service. See V5.156.

Introduction to bad debt relief

[7.1] Where a business has made supplies of goods or services to customers and has not been paid, it can claim bad debt relief in respect of the unpaid VAT provided certain conditions are met. In particular, relief depends upon the supply being written off as a bad debt in the books of the claimant and a period of six months having elapsed since the date payment became due. See **7.2** below for full details. If, following a claim, the bad debt is paid, any refund received from HMRC must be repaid to them. See **7.12** below. There are also implications for a customer if he does not pay the supplier within six months. See **7.13** below.

Use of credit notes

A business cannot issue a credit note to a customer for unpaid VAT (instead of claiming bad debt relief) simply because he has not paid for a supply. A credit note can only be issued where there is a genuine mistake or overcharge or an agreed reduction in the value of the supply. (VAT Notice 700/18/13, para 5.6). See also *Peter Cripwell & Associates* [1978] Lexis Citation 36 (TVC 40.92) and *Temple Gothard & Co* (VTD 702). For a contrasting view, see *Barlin*

Associates Ltd (TC04070) (TVC 40.119), in which Judge Mosedale considered that the issue of a credit note can constitute an adjustment of consideration within *SI 1995/2518, Reg 38*, even if it is to recognise the fact that the debtor will not pay the debt.

Appeals

Where a claim to bad debt relief is refused, an appeal may be made to the First-tier Tax Tribunal. [*VATA 1994, s 83(h)*]. See **5.3**(11) **APPEALS**.

Conditions for relief

[7.2] A business is entitled, on making a claim, to a refund of VAT where the following conditions are satisfied.

(a) It has supplied goods or services and has 'accounted for and paid' the VAT on the supply.
Relief can be claimed whether the payment due is in money or in goods or services to be provided under a barter arrangement.
For a consideration of the meaning of '*accounted for and paid*' see *Times Right Marketing Ltd (in liquidation)* (VTD 20611) (TVC 4.33). Following that tribunal decision, HMRC now accept that payment is to be taken as made to the extent that output tax is covered by deductible input tax (HMRC Brief 18/09).
Normally, only the actual supplier can claim. There are two exceptions to this rule.
   - *Transfer of VAT registration number*. Where a business or part of a business has been transferred and the transferee takes over the VAT registration of the seller, the transferee acquires the seller's entitlement to any bad debt relief on supplies made by the seller. (VAT Notice 700/18/13, para 5.1).
   - *Gas and electricity suppliers*. By concession, a supplier of gas and/or electricity can obtain relief from VAT on debts owed by a domestic customer where the supplier has accepted the transfer of that customer and his debts from another supply company. See **26.8**(9) **FUEL AND POWER** for full details.

(b) The whole or part of the consideration for the supply has been written off in the accounts as a bad debt. This involves writing the debt off in the day-to-day VAT accounts and transferring it to a separate 'refunds for bad debts account' which must be kept (see **7.4** below). The debt is only regarded as written off for VAT purposes when at least six months have elapsed from the time when the consideration became due and payable to (or to the order of) the supplier.
The claimant does not have to give up chasing the debt, or even to regard it as irrecoverable.

(c) The debt must be over six months old, i.e. six months must have elapsed from the date of supply.

(d) The value of the supply must not exceed its open market value. HMRC interpret this as meaning that the value of the supply must not be more than the customary selling price.

(e) The debt must not have been paid, sold or factored under a valid legal assignment (see **7.11**(2) below).

The normal provisions as to the time of supply of goods or services apply for determining when a supply is treated as taking place for the above purposes. See **67.1** *et seq.* **SUPPLY: TIME OF SUPPLY**.

[*VATA 1994, s 36(1)(2)(4)(8); SI 1995/2518, Regs 6(3), 166A, 172(1)(1A)(2)*]. (VAT Notice 700/18/13, para 2.2).

When to claim relief

[7.3] A claim in respect of a relevant supply cannot be made until six months has elapsed from the later of

- the date on which the consideration (or part) which has been written off as a bad debt became due and payable to, or to the order of, the person who made the relevant supply; and
- the date of supply

but must be made within four years and six months from the later of those dates.

A business entitled to a refund which has not made a claim by the end of that period is regarded as having ceased to be so entitled.

In *Hurndalls v HMRC* (TC03533) [2014] UKFTT 404 (TC) (TVC 4.27) the tribunal considered the effect of the above in a situation where invoices were issued on a contingent basis at a time when the taxpayer was using the cash accounting scheme, the taxpayer paid the VAT due on deregistration (see **64.8 SPECIAL SCHEMES**) but by the time the debt was written off and bad debt relief claimed the invoices issued on a contingent basis had not become due and payable. The result was that bad debt relief was not available. The tribunal agreed with the taxpayer that the result was unfair but could not see any way of interpreting the legislation to achieve a more sensible result.

[*VATA 1994, s 36(1); SI 1995/2518, Regs 165A, 172(1A)*].

Records required

Evidence required

[7.4] Unless HMRC allow otherwise, before submitting a claim the claimant must hold the following in respect of every relevant supply.

- A copy of any VAT invoice provided or, where there was no obligation to provide a VAT invoice, a document showing the time and nature of the supply, purchaser and consideration.
- Records, or any other document, showing that VAT has been accounted for and paid on the supply and that the consideration has been written off in his accounts as a bad debt.

[*SI 1995/2518, Reg 167*].

Records required

Any business making a claim for bad debt relief must keep a record of that claim and, unless HMRC allow otherwise, that record must consist of the following information in respect of each claim made.

- In respect of each relevant supply for that claim
  - (a) the amount of the VAT chargeable;
  - (b) the VAT period in which the VAT chargeable was accounted for and paid to HMRC;
  - (c) the date and number of any invoice issued or, where there is no such invoice, such information as is necessary to identify the time, nature and purchaser; and
  - (d) any payment received for the supply (including any payment received by the claimant or by a person to whom a right to receive it has been assigned and any payment made by any person by way of consideration for the supply regardless of whether such payment extinguishes the purchaser's debt to the claimant or not).
- The 'outstanding amount' to which the claim relates (see **7.6** below).
- The amount of the claim.
- The VAT period in which the claim was made.
- A copy of any notice to the customer required under **7.2**(*e*) above.

Any records created under these provisions must be kept in a single account to be known as the '*refunds for bad debts account*'.

[*FA 1999, s 15(4); SI 1995/2518, Regs 165, 168*].

Preservation of evidence and documents

Unless HMRC allow otherwise, the claimant must preserve the evidence and records required above for a period of four years from the date of making the claim. He must also produce them, on demand, for inspection by an authorised person and permit that person to remove them at a reasonable time and for a reasonable period. [*SI 1995/2518, Reg 169*]. This requirement does not alter the standard requirement to retain records for six years (see **57.3 RECORDS**).

How to make the claim

[7.5] If all the conditions in **7.2** above are satisfied, a claim may be made for refund of the VAT on the bad debt. The claim is made by including the correct amount of the refund in Box 4 on the VAT return for the VAT period in which entitlement to the claim arises or, subject to **7.3** above, any later return.

Claimants no longer registered

If at the time the claimant becomes entitled to a refund he is no longer required to make returns, he should notify HMRC giving details of

- former VAT registration number;
- name and address of the debtor(s);
- amount of refund claimed;
- copies of supporting evidence (e.g. invoices);
- proof that the debt has remained unpaid for six months from the date payment became due and payable or, if later, the time of supply; and
- proof that he possesses a separate bad debt ledger.

[*SI 1995/2518, Reg 166*]. (VAT Notice 700/18/13, para 5.3).

Annual returns

By concession, where a business accounts for VAT using annual returns, it can claim bad debt relief on debts over six months old on the same return as that on which VAT on the debt is accounted for. (VAT Notice 700/18/13, para 5.5).

Amount of the claim

[7.6] A business is entitled, on making a claim, to a refund of VAT by reference to 'the outstanding amount'. '*The outstanding amount*' means the consideration for the supply written off in the accounts as a bad debt *less* any part of that consideration 'received' before the time of the claim. '*Received*' means received by the claimant or by a person to whom a right to receive the whole or any part of the consideration written off has been assigned.

Where the whole or any part of the consideration for the supply does not consist of money, the amount in money that is taken to represent any non-monetary part of the consideration is so much of the amount made up of

- the value of the supply, and
- the VAT charged on the supply

as is attributable to the non-monetary consideration in question.
[*VATA 1994, s 36(2)(3)(3A)*].

Where, under a voluntary arrangement, creditors receive shares in full satisfaction of outstanding debts, there is no longer an '*outstanding amount*' and bad debt relief cannot be claimed (*AEG (UK) Ltd* (VTD 11428) (TVC 4.10)).

The effect of the above is that

- where no payment has been received in respect of a supply or supplies, the claim will be for the amount of VAT accounted for and paid to HMRC; and
- where a part payment has been received in respect of a supply or supplies, a refund can be claimed relating to the amount of VAT that is still outstanding.

Special rules apply to determine the amount of the claim where

- part payments are received relating to more than one supply (see **7.7** below);

- payments are received under hire purchase or conditional or credit sale agreements (see **7.8**(1) below); and
- supplies are made under the margin scheme for second-hand goods or the tour operators' margin scheme (see **7.9** below).

Attributing part payments

[7.7] Subject to **7.8**(1) below, where

- the claimant has made more than one supply (whether taxable or not) to the purchaser, and
- a 'payment' is received in relation to those supplies,

then, unless the purchaser has specified that the payment is for a particular supply and pays for that supply in full, in calculating any VAT due on the outstanding debt the payment is attributed to earliest supplies first. Supplies made on the same day are aggregated and treated as one, the payment being rateably apportioned. [*SI 1995/2518, Reg 170*].

'*Payment*' means any payment or part payment which is made by any person to any person by way of consideration for a supply, regardless of whether such payment extinguishes the purchaser's debt to the claimant or not. [*FA 1999, s 15(4); SI 1995/2518, Reg 165*]. This definition is widely drawn and includes payment in the form of

- any non-monetary payments (e.g. goods or services provided in exchange);
- third party payments received;
- the proceeds from the sale of repossessed goods under finance agreements (see **7.8**(2) below);
- payments received from a guarantor of the customer (see **7.10**(1) below);
- payments made by the *customer's* insurers (but not by the *claimant's* insurers where it has taken out bad debts insurance) (see **7.10**(2) below);
- mutual debts (see **7.10**(3) below); and
- the value of any enforceable security (see **7.10**(5) below).

Example 1

A claimant has made the following supplies to the purchaser.

Date of supply	Supply	VAT-exclusive	VAT	VAT-inclusive
		£	£	£
30.6.16	1	1,000	Zero-rated	1,000
28.7.16	2	1,000	200	1,200
25.8.16	3	2,000	400	2,400
29.9.16	4	350	Exempt	350
27.10.16	5	800	160	960
24.11.16	6	3,000	600	3,600
		£8,150	£1,360	£9,510

A payment of only £3,500 is received. As the payment has not been allocated by the customer, it is allocated to the earliest supplies and treated as relating to supplies 1, 2 and part of 3 as follows.

Supply	**VAT-inclusive**
	£
1	1,000
2	1,200
3 (part)	1,300
Amount of payment	£3,500

The VAT-inclusive debt outstanding on supply 3 is therefore £1,100 (£2,400 – £1,300) and the VAT outstanding on the supply is £183.33 (£1,100 × 1/6).

The outstanding amount of £6,010 (£9,510 – £3,500) and the bad debt relief that can be claimed is as follows.

Supply	**VAT-inclusive**	**VAT**
	£	**£**
3 (part)	1,100	183.33
4	350	Exempt
5	960	160.00
6	3,600	600.00
	6,010	£943.33

Example 2

The figures are as in *Example 1* above except that supplies 1, 2 and 3 were all made on the same day and are therefore treated as a single supply.

The debt outstanding on supplies 1, 2 and 3 is £1,100 (£4,600 – £3,500) and the proportion of VAT included is

$$\frac{\text{VAT in supplies 1, 2 and 3}}{\text{Total VAT - inclusive value of supplies 1, 2 and 3}} \times \text{debt outstanding}$$

= 600/4,600 × £1,100 = £143.48

The outstanding amount of £6,010 (£9,510 – £3,500) and the bad debt relief that can be claimed is as follows.

Supply	VAT-inclusive £	VAT £
1–3 (part)	1,100	143.48
4	350	Exempt
5	960	160.00
6	3,600	600.00
	£6,010	£903.48

(VAT Notice 700/18/13, paras 3.3, 3.4).

Goods supplied with associated finance

[7.8] When goods are supplied with associated finance the following applies.

(1) Attribution of payments to goods or finance

Bad debt relief is available on supplies of goods made by way of hire purchase or conditional or credit sale agreements where the customer has defaulted. Such supplies have two components, a taxable supply of goods and an exempt supply of associated financial services. The time of supply for goods is typically when they are made available to the customer [*VATA 1994, s 6*] and the time of supply of the financial services is when payment is made. [*SI 1995/2518, Reg 9*]. Therefore, unless the supplier seeks an agreement with HMRC to treat the supply of finance as occurring at the same time as the supply of goods, in applying the part payment rules in **7.6** above, strictly, the supplier should allocate any payments received from their customer first to the supply of the goods and only then to the supply of financial services after the goods element has been 'paid in full'. The provisions detailed below have been implemented in order to avoid this.

In order to avoid this, the following provisions apply where

- the claimant made a supply of goods and, in connection with that supply, a supply of credit,
- those supplies were made under a hire purchase, conditional sale or credit sale agreement, and
- a payment is received in relation to those supplies (other than a payment of an amount upon which interest is not charged, e.g. a deposit).

The payment is attributed in respect of payments made on or before termination of the agreement,

- as to the supply of credit, by multiplying the payment by the fraction A÷B where
  A= is the total of the interest on the credit provided under the agreement, less any rebate of interest granted, less any interest attributable to any unpaid instalments prior to the termination; and

B= is the total amount payable under the agreement being the total of A plus the 'total for the goods'; and

- as to the balance, to the supply of goods,

'*Total for the goods*' means the amount due for the goods under the agreement, less any reduction as a consequence of termination, less any amount upon which interest is not charged, less any part of the total due for the goods which is unpaid at the time of termination.

The payment is attributed in respect of payments made after termination of the agreement, between the supply of goods and the supply of credit according to the proportion of the balances due at the time the payment is made.

Where an agreement provides for variation of the rate of interest after the date of the making of the agreement then, for the purposes of the above calculation, it is assumed that the rate is not varied.

[*SI 1995/2518, Reg 170A*]. (VAT Notice 700/18/13, para 3.5).

(2) **Repossessed goods**

When goods are supplied with finance the seller may have the right to repossess the goods if the customer does not make the payments required by the agreement at the right time. The net proceeds from the sale of goods in this situation should be taken into account, and any relief should be based upon the remaining amount unpaid. Generally the sale of repossessed goods is not treated as a supply. However, there are exceptions, and in the following cases VAT will be due on the sale.

- Where the condition of the goods has been changed after repossession and before resale.
- Where the goods have been repossessed from a customer who was entitled to reclaim input tax on the original supply to him (such as a customer who used a car for private hire or driving instruction).
- Where the goods were delivered to the customer under the finance agreement on or after 1 September 2006, and on termination of the agreement the supplier has adjusted the VAT accounted for to reflect the payments not made by the customer.

If any of these exceptions apply and VAT has been accounted for on the sale of repossessed goods, the proceeds of sale do not need to be taken into account when calculating bad debt relief.

(VAT Notice 700/18/13, para 3.6).

Second-hand goods and tour operators' margin scheme

[7.9] Bad debt relief may be claimed in respect of supplies made under the margin schemes for **62 SECOND-HAND GOODS** or the **69 TOUR OPERATORS' MARGIN SCHEME** as follows.

- If the debt is equal to or less than the profit margin, bad debt relief may be claimed on the VAT fraction of the debt.

- If the debt is greater than the profit margin, bad debt relief is limited to the VAT fraction of the profit margin (i.e. the amount of VAT which the supplier has paid to HMRC).

Debt for the above purposes means full consideration for the relevant supply *less* any payment received in respect of it. Payment means any payment which is made by any person to any person by way of consideration for a supply, regardless of whether such payment extinguishes the purchaser's debt to the claimant or not. [*FA 1999, s 15(4); SI 1995/2518, Reg 165*].

Example

Second-hand goods purchased for £400 are sold for £500 (i.e. the profit margin is £100). The customer only pays (a) £450 and (b) £350. Bad debt relief is calculated as follows.

(a) The debt is £50 which is less than the profit margin of £100. Bad debt relief can be claimed on
1/6 × £50 = £8.33

(b) The debt is £150 which is greater than the profit margin. Bad debt relief can be claimed on
1/6 × £100 = £16.67

[*SI 1995/2518, Regs 172A, 172B*]. (VAT Notice 700/18/13, paras 5.7, 5.8).

Amount of claim — miscellaneous matters

[7.10] Other matters affecting the amount of the claim are as follows.

(1) Guarantors, etc. of debts

Where a supplier receives payment, in full or in part, from a guarantor or other person (e.g. a director of the debtor company), entitlement to relief is reduced by the amount paid. If full payment is made by the guarantor or third party there is no entitlement to bad debt relief.

(VAT Notice 700/18/13, para 3.10).

(2) Insured debts

Where the claimant has insured its debts, any payment by the insurers does not affect entitlement to relief.

Where the debtor is insured for the costs of the supply (e.g. when a garage repairs a damaged vehicle), for convenience the insurer may pay the supplier direct. If the insured is VAT-registered, the VAT-exclusive amount is usually paid, leaving the customer to pay the VAT element. The supplier can only claim relief on the actual balance written off.

(VAT Notice 700/18/13, paras 3.9, 3.11).

(3) Mutual debts

Where the claimant owes an amount of money to the purchaser which can be set off, the consideration written off in the accounts must be reduced by the amount so owed.

> *Example*
>
> A bad debt arose in respect of a supply for which the claimant charged £720 (£600 + VAT). The claimant also owes £115 to the debtor.
>
> The amount of the debt for relief purposes is £720 – £115 = £605
>
> The amount of the bad debt relief is £605 x 1/6 = £100.83

[*SI 1995/2518, Reg 172(3)*]. (VAT Notice 700/18/13, para 3.7).

(4) Non-payment of VAT only

If

- a customer refuses to pay the VAT charged on an invoice, or
- the claimant did not charge VAT on a supply but issues a supplementary invoice to recover the VAT and this is not paid,

the claim to relief is limited to the VAT element of the total debt. For example, where a customer was originally charged £100 (which the customer paid) and the claimant then unsuccessfully attempts to recover the £20 VAT charge originally omitted, the claimant is only entitled to claim the VAT fraction of £20 as bad debt relief.

(VAT Notice 700/18/13, para 3.13).

In *Enderby Transport Ltd* (VTD 1607) (TVC 4.1) the customer paid the full price for the goods (£10,200) but not the VAT (£816). The tribunal held that as the amount of the debt outstanding was £816, the VAT element of this was £106.43 (3/23rds when the standard rate of VAT was 15%) and bad debt relief should be restricted to this amount. In *Palmer (t/a R & K Engineering)* (VTD 11739) (TVC 4.4) the tribunal allowed full bad debt relief where, following registration with retrospective effect, an invoice was raised charging VAT on supplies originally invoiced (and paid) without VAT and the customer went into receivership without paying the VAT. The tribunal did, however, comment that HMRC had been dilatory in dealing with registration and the position might be different where late registration is due to the trader's own default.

In *Simpson & Marwick*, CS [2013] CSIH 29 (TVC 4.9), net amounts had been charged by a firm of solicitors in respect of legal services to (and paid by) an insurance company. Only the VAT amount, charged separately to the VAT registered policyholders, remained unpaid. HMRC issued an assessment on the basis that relief was only available for the VAT fraction of the debt, as in *AW Mawer & Co* (VTD 2100) (TVC 4.8), i.e. 7/47th of the amount unpaid by the policyholders. The CS unanimously upheld the assessment. The refund to which the taxpayer was entitled was stipulated in *VATA 1994, s 36(2)* as the 'amount of VAT chargeable by reference to the outstanding amount'. The words outstanding amount were defined in *VATA 1994, s 36(3)* by reference to the amount of the 'consideration', or the extent to which the 'consideration' had been written off. But as *VATA 1994, s 19* made plain, the 'consideration' was an amount inclusive of VAT. The CS also observed that the solicitors had provided a taxable service for which they received partial payment of the consideration. There was no reason why they should not be responsible, in the normal way, for the proportionate amount of VAT on the part consideration which they received.

(5) Security for debts

Where the claimant holds an enforceable security against the purchaser, the consideration written off must be reduced by the value of the security. [*SI 1995/2518, Reg 172(4)*]. If the claimant holds a security which cannot be enforced, he can write off the full amount of the debt and base his claim to relief on that amount. (VAT Notice 700/18/13, para 3.8).

Treatment of bad debt relief in particular cases

[7.11] The treatment of this relief in particular cases is outlined below.

(1) Cash accounting scheme

Subject to conditions, including an annual turnover limit, a business may account for and pay VAT by reference to the time when the consideration for the supply is received. See **64.2 SPECIAL SCHEMES**. The adoption of such a scheme removes the problem of VAT on bad debts from the supplier.

(2) Factored debts

Where a business factors its debts, bad debt relief is not available where the assignment of the debt is absolute (i.e. where there is no provision for the reassignment of the debt in the contract).

Where there is provision for reassignment, bad debt relief is available, subject to the normal conditions, once the debt has been reassigned to the business. No bad debt relief is available during the period in which the debt remains assigned to the factor.

Any payment from the factor to the business for the purchase of the debts is consideration for an exempt supply of finance and is disregarded for the purposes of bad debt relief.

(VAT Notice 700/18/13, para 3.12).

(3) Group registration

In the case of a group registration (see **28 GROUPS OF COMPANIES**) each member must keep its own separate bad debts record for debts written off. The representative member of the group claims any refund on behalf of each member while they are in the VAT group. Where a member leaves a group, any VAT bad debt relief on supplies made by that company when it was a group member, but which cannot be claimed until after it has left the group, is due to that company (and not the representative member of the group). (VAT Notice 700/18/13, para 5.4). See also *Triad Timber Components Ltd* [1993] Lexis Citation 3297 (TVC 4.19) and *Proto Glazing Ltd* (VTD 13410) (TVC 4.20).

(4) Retail schemes

Where a bad debt relief claim is made, any refund must be accounted for outside the retail scheme. If, after claiming a refund, payment is received for the supplies, any repayment of relief to HMRC must also be dealt with outside the scheme.

(5) Reservation of title agreements

Some agreements for the sale of goods include a clause reserving title until the goods have been paid for (known as a *Romalpa* clause). There is no requirement that title to the goods must have passed before a claim for bad debt relief can be made. It is therefore possible to make a claim for supplies of goods on hire purchase and other reservation of title agreements without the requirement formally to give up the rights to title under the agreement.

(VAT Notice 700/18/13, para 5.2).

(6) Sale of property under a power of sale — recovery of VAT on costs incurred by mortgage lenders

Where a property is repossessed by the lender, although the sale of the property is a supply by the borrower, HMRC accept that the lender may be treated as agent of the borrower in relation to certain costs of sale. This applies whether or not the mortgage deed specifies such a relationship. As an agent, the lender may treat these costs incurred as supplies made to him and by him under *VATA 1994, s 47(3)*. Where the proceeds of sale are insufficient to cover all or part of the costs of sale, the lender can therefore recover any unpaid VAT under the bad debt provisions. For these purposes, the order of attribution of the sale proceeds follows the normal rules under the bad debt relief regulations (i.e. allocate to the earliest supply, the mortgage, first) rather than those under *Law of Property Act 1925, s 105* (which requires proceeds to be first allocated to the selling costs). The arrangements apply to VAT on the following costs.

(a) Costs relating directly to the sale of the property which would ordinarily have been incurred by the borrower had he arranged the sale himself (e.g. legal and estate agency fees for professional services connected with the sale).

(b) *Law of Property Act* (LPA) receiver's charges relating specifically to the sale of the property and any costs incurred by the receiver in respect of the sale, but only where the proceeds of sale received by the lender have been reduced by the VAT element of the charges (and not where the LPA receiver recovers the VAT incurred on behalf of a VAT-registered borrower and this is reflected in the proceeds passed to the lender).

(c) Build-out costs (i.e. expenses incurred on completion of a partly-completed building or major refurbishment of the property before sale) but only where
   - the sale of the building by the borrower is the subject of a taxable supply or the transfer of a going concern for VAT purposes; or
   - the property is the subject of a taxable let and output tax on the rents has been accounted for to HMRC.

The arrangement does not apply if the proceeds of sale or rent received by lenders reflect any input tax on build-out costs recovered by the borrower.

(d) Repair and maintenance expenses.

(e) A lender's own in-house estate agency or solicitor's services to the borrower provided output tax has been accounted for on the supply under normal rules.

The arrangement does not cover any costs incurred in relation to letting (other than those within (*c*) above). Nor does it cover costs incurred on services provided to, and used by, the lender as principal even if charged to the borrower under the mortgage deed (e.g. legal fees associated with taking possession; locksmith's fees for securing the property; and costs incurred in pursuing claims against a valuer for negligence).

(Business Brief 24/94).

(7) **Union and non-Union VAT MOSS scheme returns**

Where a person not registered for VAT in the UK has submitted a Union or non-Union VAT MOSS scheme return (see **64.40** to **64.45 SPECIAL SCHEMES**) to the tax authorities in another EU member state and amends the return to take account of the writing-off as a bad debt of the whole or part of the consideration for a supply of broadcasting, telecommunication or electronic services to consumers in the UK the amending of the return may be treated as the making of a claim to HMRC for bad debt relief.

[*VATA 1994, Sch 3B and Sch 3BA; FA 2014, Sch 22; SI 2014/2430, Regs 4–7*].

Repayment of refund

[7.12] Repayment of any VAT refunded by HMRC under a bad debt claim is required where

(a) a payment for the relevant supply is subsequently received;

(b) a payment is, under **7.7** or **7.8**(1) above, treated as attributed to the relevant supply;

(c) the consideration for any relevant supply (upon which the claim to refund is based) is reduced after the claim is made; or

(d) the claimant fails to comply with the requirements of **7.4**, **7.7** or **7.8**(1) above.

Under (*a*) and (*b*) above the amount of the repayment is

$$\frac{\text{Amount of payment received or attributed}}{\text{Amount of outstanding consideration}} \times \text{Amount of refund}$$

Under (*c*) above, the amount of the repayment is equal to the negative entry made in the VAT allowable portion of the VAT account as provided for in *SI 1995/2518, Reg 38* (see **40.14 INVOICES**).

Under (*d*) above repayment must be made of the full amount of the refund obtained from HMRC by the claim to which the failure to comply relates.

> *Example*
>
> A business sells goods for £120.00 (£100 plus £20.00 VAT). It receives no payment by the relevant date and claims bad debt relief of £20.00. It subsequently receives £75.00 from the customer for the goods.
>
> The business must repay to HMRC the VAT element of the £75 received, calculated as follows.
>
> £75.00 ÷ £120.00 × £20 = £12.50

The repayment is made by including the appropriate amount in Box 1 on the VAT return for the VAT period in which the payment is received under (*a*) or (*b*) or as designated by HMRC under (*c*). If, at that time, the claimant is no longer required to make returns, the repayment must still be made and the supplier should contact HMRC.

For these purposes, payment does not include a payment received by a person to whom a right to receive it has been assigned. Claimants are not therefore required to repay bad debt relief in respect of payments received by assignees after a refund has been claimed. However, as an anti-avoidance measure, this does not apply (and repayment of the VAT refund is still required) where the person to whom the right to receive a payment has been assigned (whether by the claimant or any other person) is connected to the claimant. See **72.19 VALUATION** for connected persons.

[*SI 1995/2518, Reg 171*]. (VAT Notice 700/18/13, paras 3.14, 3.15).

Repayment of input tax by purchaser

[7.13] There are general provisions requiring input tax to be repaid where a customer has not paid the supplier within six months of the date of supply or, if later, the date payment is due. These provisions apply whether or not the supplier makes a claim for bad debt relief. See **35.4 INPUT TAX**.

Key points: bad debt relief

[7.14] Points to consider are as follows.

- The two main conditions for a supplier to reclaim bad debt relief are that the debt in question must be at least six months overdue for payment, and also be written off for bad debt relief purposes in the business accounts, i.e. by making an entry in the 'refunds for bad accounts' as required by the VAT Regulations 1995. Note – if an invoice is on 60 day payment terms, the earliest point at which bad debt relief can be claimed will be eight months after the invoice date, i.e. when it is six months overdue for payment. There is no requirement for the debt to be written off so that the debtor is no longer pursued for the outstanding amount.

- A bad debt cannot be dealt with by issuing a credit note to cancel the original sales invoice. This is because a credit note can only be issued when either goods have been returned or the original value of the sale has been reduced by, for example, an agreed price reduction for the customer.
- Bad debt relief claimed on a VAT return is included in the Box 4 (input tax) figure. However, any subsequent payment made by the customer after the debt has been written off (which will create an output tax liability if the goods are standard-rated or reduced-rated) will be included in Box 1 (output tax) on the return.
- A business that uses the cash accounting scheme will automatically benefit from bad debt relief. This is because output tax is not included on a VAT return until payment has been received from a customer.
- A customer not using the cash accounting scheme will need to adjust any input tax he has claimed on a purchase invoice that is more than six months overdue for payment. The input tax must be credited on the VAT return that is covered by the date when the six-month expiry date takes place. If payment is subsequently made to settle the invoice, then input tax can be reclaimed on the VAT return covered by the payment date.
- It is possible that a debt will be written off for bad debt relief purposes in a VAT period when the standard rate of VAT is a different percentage to that which applied when the original sales invoice was raised. The key issue as far as bad debt relief is concerned is the output tax charged on the original sales invoice and the rate of VAT that applied at that time.
- In cases where a customer refuses to pay the VAT element of a charge (either on an original invoice or VAT only invoice subsequently raised), then bad debt relief is restricted to the VAT element of the VAT amount. So if an invoice was raised for £100 plus £20.00 VAT, and the customer only paid £100, then bad debt relief would be restricted to £3.33, i.e. £20.00 x 1/6.

8

Betting and Gaming

Introduction to betting and gaming

[8.1] Most supplies of recreation and sport services are standard rated if supplied within the UK. The principal exceptions are—

- betting and gaming, where some but not all activities are exempt (see **8.2** below);
- lotteries, where the granting of a right to take part in a lottery is exempt (see **8.5** below); and
- cultural and sporting activities for which there is a specific exemption when carried on by certain bodies (see **58.1–58.9 RECREATION AND SPORT**).

Betting and gaming

[8.2] For EU legislation, see **19.25**(*i*) **EUROPEAN UNION LEGISLATION**.

Under UK legislation, the provisions of any facilities for

- the placing of bets, or
- the playing of any games of chance for a prize

is exempt. '*Prize*' does not include the opportunity to play the game again.

There are, however, four important exceptions which are standard-rated.

(1) Admission to any premises where betting and gaming takes place.
(2) Participation fees for playing bingo and other games of chance for a prize are exempt.
(3) Club subscriptions (including those to gaming, bingo and bridge clubs, etc.)
(4) Until 1 February 2013 the provision of anything which is a gaming machine for the purposes of *VATA 1994, s 23* (see **8.4** below).

(5) Takings from pinball machines are standard-rated, as only games of chance played for a prize qualify for exemption.

[*VATA 1994, Sch 9 Group 4 Item 1 and Notes (1)–(11)*].

Game of chance

'*Game of chance*' includes a game that

- involves both an element of chance and an element of skill;
- involves an element of chance that can be eliminated by superlative skill; and
- is presented as involving an element of chance;

but does not include a sport.

A person plays a game of chance if he participates in a game of chance whether or not

- there are other participants in the game; and
- a computer generates images or data taken to represent the actions of other participants in the game.

[*VATA 1994, Sch 9 Group 4 Notes (2)(3)*].

The meaning of 'game' and 'game of chance' has been considered by the Court of Appeal in *IFX Investment Co Ltd v HMRC* [2016] EWCA Civ 436 in the context of a repayment claim by companies that ran 'spot the ball' competitions and treated the takings as taxable. The Court accepted that the way the competitions were run made them games of chance, and the traders were entitled to a repayment of output tax wrongly accounted for.

Value of the exempt supply

The value of the exempt output is the full amount of stakes or takings less only any money paid out as winnings or, if prizes are goods, their cost (including VAT) to the supplier. Betting or gaming duty is not deductible. (VAT Notice 701/29/17, para 2.3).

Stake money

Stake money (i.e. the amount paid by each player which they risk in the game and is returned in winning to the winning player) is outside the scope of VAT. (VAT Notice 701/29/17, para 3.2).

Composite charges

Composite charges covering admission charges, stake money and payments for the provision of facilities for placing bets must be apportioned.

Casino card room games

In addition to their conventional games of chance against the house, casinos may hold competitions or tournaments in card room games, such as backgammon or poker. The whole of the participation fee which may be described as 'table money', 'session charge' or 'competition fee' is often put towards the prizes and sometimes the casino puts in an extra sum to make the prizes more attractive. If a business holds such competitions, the entry fee is exempt from VAT even though they may make no contribution to the business's profits.

Entry stakes to card room competitions which are conducted strictly in accordance with guidelines agreed between the British Casino Association and HMRC are outside the scope of VAT. (VAT Notice 701/29/17, para 2.4.)

Agent's services

Services of pools agents, concessionaires and collectors are covered by the exemption for betting and gaming and therefore no VAT is payable on their commission charges. The services of bookmakers' agents are exempt, and so are the services of bookmakers themselves when they act as agents in accepting bets for other bookmakers or for the Tote. (VAT Notice 701/29/17, para 2.5).

Use of call centres for telephone betting

In *United Utilities plc v C & E Commrs, ECJ Case C–89/05;* [2006] STC 1423 (TVC 22.423) the court held that supplies by a company providing call centre services relating to the receipt of telephone bets on behalf of Littlewoods did not qualify for exemption as the provision of betting.

Prizes

The following treatment applies.

- Prizes of cash are outside the scope of VAT.
- Prizes of goods in free lotteries and in sports competitions should be treated as business gifts and VAT is only due if the tax exclusive cost of the prize is over £50. Input tax will then be deductible in the normal manner. However if a business purchases a car to be given away as a prize, it may only reclaim the input tax if it does not make the car available for private use before it is given away. If the business does reclaim the VAT on the purchase it must declare output tax on the tax exclusive cost of the car when it is given away. Any input tax claimed will still be subject to the partial exemption rules.
- Prizes awarded from a machine itself (e.g. a crane grab machine) may be treated as business gifts for VAT purposes.
- Prizes of goods and services in exempt betting and gaming should be treated as part of the exempt supply and no output tax is due on such prizes. Any VAT incurred in purchasing the prizes is exempt input tax which is not deductible, subject to the partial exemption rules.
- Where prizes of goods or services are given in taxable competitions, no further tax is due.
- Prizes of services awarded in free lotteries or as bonus prizes in sports competitions, are outside the scope of VAT. However, where the prize is of a holiday or tickets to sporting or other events, input tax is not deductible by virtue of the business entertainment rules. Should a business provide any other services as prizes, input tax may not be deductible.

- If a business supplies prize goods in exchange for machine tokens with a recognised cash value, it must account for VAT on the goods as if it had supplied them by normal retail sale. The value of the supply is the normal retail selling price of the goods or, if the business does not sell such goods to the general public, the equivalent cash value of the tokens it has accepted in exchange for them. The business can reclaim as input tax the VAT incurred on the purchase of the prize goods in the normal way.

(VAT Notice 701/29/17, para 13).

De Voil Indirect Tax Service. See V4.131.

Bingo

[8.3] Participation and session charges are made for the right to take part in a game or series of games of bingo. All bingo participation fees and session charges became exempt from VAT.

A bingo machine is designed or adapted to provide an electronic or video version of a game of bingo. The takings from the machine for the games are exempt.

[*FA 2009, s 113*.] (VAT Notice 701/29/17, para 8).

Machine games

[8.4] On 1 February 2013 machine games duty (MGD), where payable, replaced amusement machine licence duty and VAT. Supplies relating to the playing of dutiable machine games are exempt from VAT.

The amount a person pays to play a relevant machine game is treated as the consideration for a supply of services. The value of such supplies is the takings received, less the amount of the winnings paid out, excluding any winnings paid to the supplier or a person acting on their behalf.

Games played solely for prizes consisting of the opportunity to play the game again are not relevant machine games. However a token that enables the machine to be played again may be one of a number of prizes offered by a relevant machine game. In that case, the value of the token is deducted in calculating the value of the relevant supply.

If it is not reasonably practicable for takings and winnings to be attributed to relevant machine games, or apportioned between relevant machine games and other games, the attribution or apportionment is to be carried out on a just and reasonable basis.

A 'relevant machine game' is a game played on a machine for a prize, unless it is liable to, or is excluded from, specified gambling duties. Relevant machine games may be games of skill, games of chance, or games that involve elements of both skill and chance. A 'prize' does not include the opportunity to play the game again.

The provision of facilities for playing dutiable machine games are exempt from VAT, but only insofar as the takings and payouts from those games are taken into account in determining the charge to MGD. The amendments to *VATA*

1994, Sch 9 Group 4 mean that the provision of facilities for playing games of chance which are not relevant machine games will be exempt from VAT under *Item 1*. The provision of facilities for playing dutiable machine games will be exempt from VAT under *Item 1A*, insofar as the takings and payouts from those games are taken into account in determining the charge to MGD. Other machine games will not be exempt from VAT under *Group 4*.

[*FA 2012, Sch 24 para 64; VATA 1994, ss 23, 23A, Sch 9 Group 4*].

Meaning of machine games

A machine game is a game whether of skill or chance, or both, played on a machine for a prize. A machine may be termed as a gaming machine or amusement machine. A relevant machine game is a game of skill or chance or both that is played on a machine for a prize and which is not subject to any duty. Examples are

- non-cash prize games, like, a teddy bear in a crane grab machine;
- redemption ticket games which pay out tickets which the player can redeem for a non-cash prize (these machines are often located at family entertainment centres).

Mixed machine games offer players the opportunity to win cash and non-cash prizes.

(VAT Notice 701/29/17, para 9).

Place of supply

Supplies of services consisting of enabling the public to use machine games in amusement arcades are regarded as entertainment or similar activities within what is now *Directive 2006/112/EC, Art 52(a)*, so that the place of supply is where the services are physically carried out (*RAL (Channel Islands) Ltd v C & E Commrs (and related appeals), ECJ Case C–452/03*, [2005] STC 1025 (TVC 22.226)). The equivalent UK provisions are in SI *1992/3121, Art 15* (see **66.17 SUPPLY: PLACE OF SUPPLY**).

VAT liability of supplies

There are a number of different supplies involved in dealings connected with machine games. These are the supply of

- a machine game to a player;
- the hire of the machine, when an owner rents a machine out, either for a fixed rental charge, or perhaps for a share of the profits; and
- a licence to trade, when the owner of the premises allows a machine to be sited on those premises.

The VAT liability of the supplies is as follows

- VAT is due at the standard rate on relevant machine game takings;
- no VAT is due on dutiable machine game takings as these are exempt from VAT;
- hire charges for the machines are always subject to VAT at the standard-rate; and

- charges for siting machines are always subject to VAT at the standard-rate.

(VAT Notice 701/29/17, para 10).

Accounting for VAT on machine takings

In most cases the supply of the use of a machine to play machine games will be exempt from VAT (dutiable machine games). However, where taxable supplies are made (relevant machine games), the person who supplies the use of the machine to the public must account for VAT on the takings. There can only be one person who does this and it will usually be the person who exercises day-to-day control over the machine and is entitled to the takings.

(a) *Gaming machines*. The person who supplies the use of the gaming machine to the public is usually the occupier of the premises on which the machine is situated. In the case of
   - commercial gaming premises licensed under the *Gambling Act 2005, ss 65, 150* (e.g. casinos, bingo halls, adult gaming and family entertainment centres), it will be the holder of the licences or that person's employee;
   - clubs or miners' institutes possessing a club machine permit under *Gambling Act 2005, s 273*, it will be any officer or member of the club or any person employed by them;
   - travelling pleasure fairs, it will be the showman who owns and operates the fair;
   - public houses, it will be the person named on the licensed premises gaming machine permit under *Gambling Act 2005, s 283*;
   - unlicensed gaming machines, it will normally be the person who controls its operation, but the supply position will depend on the particular arrangements in each case. Although the machines are unlicensed, the takings from them are nevertheless liable to VAT.

(b) *Amusement machines*. The person who supplies the use of an amusement machine to the public will be either
   - the site occupier, if the machine is purchased, hired or rented by the occupier of the premises on which it is sited; or
   - the owner of the machine, where the owner of the machine pays rent to the occupier of the premises on which the machine is sited. If the machine is operated on a profit-share basis the supplier of its use to the public will be the person who controls its operation.

The amount due should be worked out as follows.

- The takings from relevant machine games will be subject to VAT at the standard rate.
- Where MGD is chargeable on the net takings from playing dutiable machine games, no VAT will be due as the supplies are exempt. The net takings constitute the value of the exempt supplies.
- Where a machine offers taxable 'relevant machine games' and other games or activities that are not taxable, the payments received should be directly attributed to each activity.

- Where it is not feasible to attribute or apportion takings and winnings between relevant machine games and other games or activities then any attribution or apportionment should be done on a just and reasonable basis.

Taxable takings are regarded as VAT inclusive. No other deductions should be made from the takings before the VAT fraction is applied. The following should not be deducted from the takings.

- Hire or rental charges paid to the company which owns the machine.
- Any share of the profits or other charge due to another person (e.g. a brewer sharing the proceeds of the machine with a tenant).
- Payments made out of the takings, such as those under maintenance contracts, or to fund an additional prize.
- VAT on any of the above charges or payments.

Site-wide operation (amusement arcades only)

In principle, the taxable receipts should be calculated for each individual machine. However, if amusement arcades with large numbers of machines are operated, it may be possible to calculate receipts upon a site-wide basis. The business should obtain approval for this procedure from HMRC's VAT Helpline.

Tax point

The tax point for supplies made from coin-operated machines is the date the machine is used although, as an accounting convenience, operators may delay accounting for VAT until each time that the takings are removed from the machine.

Tokens

When a business works out the takings it must treat a replayable token (one which can be used to play a machine) as having its recognised cash value, e.g. if a machine can be played with either a 10p coin or a token, the value of the token must be taken as 10p. Any tokens previously returned to the machine through the 'no play' token return slot by the site occupier or gaming machine owner are outside the scope of VAT. These tokens have not been used to play the machine and therefore are not part of the takings.

Non-replayable tokens cannot be used to play a machine. Their treatment in the takings depends on whether they have a recognised cash value. Where they have a recognised cash value, and are therefore exchangeable for cash or goods the business also sells, they should be treated in the same way as replayable tokens. Where they have no recognised cash value and are exchangeable for goods the business does not also sell, the full amount of cash removed from the machine should be recorded after any necessary adjustments to the cash float; no deduction should be made for tokens won or put into the float, or for prizes given in exchange for these tokens.

Foreign or fake coins

When takings removed from machines are found to contain foreign coins, fakes or facsimiles that players have inserted to obtain plays, these may be disregarded. They do not form part of the takings but equally the takings must not be reduced because of them.

Retail schemes

If a business uses one of the retail schemes, it should deal with its taxable relevant machine game takings as follows.

- The point of sale scheme—the taxable machine takings should be added to the standard-rated daily gross takings (DGT) for the day on which the cash and/or tokens are removed from the machine.
- An apportionment scheme—taxable machine takings should be excluded from the retail scheme calculations.
- A direct calculation scheme and minority goods are zero-rated (and reduced-rated where applicable)—the taxable machine takings should be added to DGT on the day which the cash and/or tokens are removed from the machine.

Where the business's minority goods are standard-rated (and reduced-rated where applicable), it should exclude the takings from its scheme calculations and keep a separate record.

Where dutiable machine game operator uses one of the retail schemes to account for VAT, the exempt outputs must not be included in the scheme calculations. Therefore the takings from playing these dutiable machine games should be excluded as this is not part of the retailer's taxable turnover.

If the value of exempt dutiable machine game takings is included in the DGT, then, when calculating the DGT for the retail scheme calculation, the retailer should reduce the DGT by the value of the exempt dutiable machine game takings.

Stolen takings

The business must account for VAT on stolen takings. The tax point for supplies made from coin-operated machines is the date the machine is used although, as an accounting convenience, operators may delay accounting for VAT until the takings are removed from the machine. For all other purposes however, the normal tax point rules apply. Therefore in the event of a theft of takings from a machine VAT must still be accounted for in full on any supplies that have been made from the machine.
(VAT Notice 701/29/17, para 11).

Supplies between machine owners and site occupiers

Examples of supplies between machine owners and site occupiers	
	Supply/accounting for VAT
Gaming/amusement machine supplied to a brewery with a managed pub.	Machine owner makes a standard-rated supply of hire of the machine to the brewery and accounts for VAT on the hire charge.

	Brewery makes a standard-rated and/or exempt supply of use of the machine to the public (depending on whether the machine offers taxable relevant machine games and/or exempt dutiable games) and accounts for VAT on the machine takings.
Gaming/amusement machine is supplied to the tenant of a brewery-owned pub.	Machine owner makes a standard-rated supply of hire of the machine to the tenant and accounts for VAT on the hire charge. Tenant makes a standard-rated and/or exempt supply of use of the machine to the public and accounts for VAT on the machine takings. Brewery makes a standard-rated supply of a licence to trade to the tenant to site the machine on its premises and accounts for VAT on the charge for siting the machine.
Owner of a gaming/amusement machine pays rent (e.g. a fixed sum or share of the profits) to a brewery with a managed or tenanted pub.	The brewery makes a standard-rated supply of a licence to trade to the machine owner in allowing the machine to be sited on its premises and accounts for VAT on the charge for siting the machine. The machine owner makes a standard-rated and/or exempt supply of the use of the machine to the public and accounts for VAT on the machine takings.

(VAT Notice 701/29/17, para 12).

Gaming and amusement machines prior to 1 February 2013

The provision of a 'gaming machine' is specifically excluded from the general exemption from VAT applying to betting and the playing of games of chance (see **8.2** above). The takings from gaming machines (and 'amusement machines' generally) are therefore standard-rated. Note that the provisions of *VATA 1994, s 23* do not apply to the Isle of Man. [*IMA 1979, s 1(d)*]. Where gaming machine takings would also qualify for exemption by satisfying the requirements for being a lottery under **8.5** below, it has been held that to exempt the supply would defeat the legislative intent (*McCann (t/a Ulster Video Amusements)* (VTD 2401) (TVC 24.20)).

In *Rank Group plc* Ch D [2009] All ER (D) 65 (Jun) (TVC 24.21) the tribunal decided that Rank's takings from gaming machines should be treated as exempt before 6 December 2005, when UK law was changed to make all gaming machine takings taxable. It said that *VATA 1994, Sch 9, Group 4, Note 3* (as originally enacted) and HMRC practice infringed the principal of fiscal neutrality as there were comparator machines which, before 6 December 2005, were exempt as a matter of law and there were comparators which

HMRC treated as exempt in practice. The Ch D upheld that decision, holding that there was no discernible justification for the differing tax treatment. The CJEU ruled that similar supplies from the point of view of the consumer should be taxed in the same way and it was not necessary to consider whether the supplies were in competition with each other ('competition test'). When determining whether there had been a breach of fiscal neutrality the actual tax treatment should be based on the legal position rather than any practice that may have been followed (*Case C–259/10, C–260/10;* [2012] STC 23 (TVC 22.424)).

HMRC considered that the CJEU decision did not provide a final determination of the domestic litigation with regard to gaming machines. The Court of Appeal reheard the case and unanimously allowed HMRC's appeal. The company appealed further to the Supreme Court, where Carnwath LJ held that the element of chance in the game was provided by means of the machine: wherever the random number generator was situated, the 'chance' arose from a player pressing a button on the terminal. The takings from the disputed machines failed to qualify for exemption, and the appeal was dismissed (*HMRC v The Rank Group plc (No 2)* [2015] UKSC 48 (TVC 22.425)). Following the decision of the Court of Appeal in HMRC's favour, HMRC announced that they would write to all affected businesses that previously received repayments of VAT on gaming machine takings detailing how the amount previously repaid to the business should now be repaid to HMRC. (HMRC Brief 1/14).

Definition of gaming machine

'Gaming machine' means a machine which is 'designed or adapted' for use by individuals to 'gamble' (whether or not it can also be used for other purposes). But a machine is not a gaming machine to the extent that it is designed or adapted

- for use to bet on future real events (see *Gambling Act 2005, s 353(1)* for the definition of '*real*');
- for the playing of any version of the game of bingo (irrespective of by what name it is described) if bingo duty is charged under *Betting and Gaming Duties Act 1981, s 17* on the playing of that bingo (or would be charged but for *Betting and Gaming Duties Act 1981, Sch 3 paras 1–5*), or
- for the playing of a real (see above) 'game of chance' if the playing of the game is dutiable gaming for the purposes of *FA 1997, s 10* (or would be dutiable gaming but for *FA 1997, s 10(3)(4)*).

For these purposes, a machine is any apparatus which uses or applies mechanical power or electrical power (or both) and a reference to a machine being

- '*designed or adapted*' for a purpose includes a reference to a machine to which anything has been done as a result of which it can reasonably be expected to be used for that purpose, and
- '*adapted*' includes a reference to computer software being installed on it.

'*Gambling*' means playing a 'game of chance' for a 'prize' and betting. '*Game of chance*' includes a game that

- involves both an element of chance and an element of skill;
- involves an element of chance that can be eliminated by superlative skill; and
- is presented as involving an element of chance,

but does not include a sport. A person plays a game of chance if he participates in a game of chance whether or not

- there are other participants in the game; and
- a computer generates images or data taken to represent the actions of other participants in the game.

'*Prize*', in relation to a machine, does not include the opportunity to play the machine again.

HMRC Brief 70/09 states that 'electronic lottery terminals' are (taxable) gaming machines for the purposes of VAT, rather than (exempt) lottery ticket dispensers or vending machines.

In *Oasis Technologies (UK) Ltd* (TC00581) (TVC 24.25), the tribunal held that the Oasis electronic lottery ticket vending machine (ELTVM) was a gaming machine. However, it also granted the right to participate in a lottery and the takings from the machine were exempt from VAT (see **8.5** below).

[*VATA 1994, s 23(4)–(6)*].

Meaning of amusement machine

An '*amusement machine*' can be either of the following.

- A machine on which there is no prize in any circumstances.
- A 'skill with prizes' machine, i.e. a machine where the prize depends on the skill or knowledge of the player and is not dependent on chance (e.g. a general knowledge quiz).

Other examples of amusement machines are pinball machines, video games (but not games that involve gambling, such as video poker machines) and juke boxes.

Lotteries

[8.5] For EU legislation, See **19.25**(*i*) **EUROPEAN UNION LEGISLATION**.

Under UK legislation, the granting of a right to take part in a lottery is exempt. [*VATA 1994, Sch 9 Group 4 Item 2*]. Exemption essentially covers the sale of the lottery tickets to the public as these acknowledge that a right to participate has been granted to the participants. If the lottery is free to enter, there is no exempt supply (but see below for prizes given in free lotteries).

The value of the exempt supply is the gross proceeds from ticket sales *less* the cash prizes given or the cost (inclusive of VAT) of the goods given as prizes.

There is no statutory definition of 'lottery'. In *Readers Digest Association Ltd v Williams*, [1976] 1 WLR 1109 it was defined as 'the distribution of prizes by chance where the persons taking part in the operation, or a substantial number of them, make a payment or consideration in return for obtaining their chance of a prize'. This includes the playing of on-line interactive lottery games. If any merit or skill plays a part in determining the outcome, the event is not a lottery but a competition.

(VAT Notice 701/29/17, paras 4.1–4.3).

Types of lawful lotteries

The promotion of lotteries is only lawful in the specified circumstances set out in the *Gambling Act 2005*. In addition to the National Lottery, there are other kinds of public lottery which fall under the regulatory powers of the Gambling Commission and local authorities, as follows.

- Large society lotteries defined by the *Gambling Act 2005*.
- Local authority lotteries operated by local authorities to support any purpose for which they have power to incur expenditure.
- Small society lotteries which are exempt from holding an operating licence, but must be registered with their local authority.

These lotteries can only be run in support of good causes, such as charity fundraising and cannot be run for commercial purposes. However, there are also three other categories of lottery permitted under the *Gambling Act*, which do not require operating licences or registration with any statutory body, and do not need to be in support of a good cause. These are

- incidental non-commercial lotteries, held at non-commercial events, where all money raised at the event goes entirely to purposes that are not for private or commercial gain;
- private society, work or residents' lotteries, where tickets can only be sold to society members, workers at or residents of a premises;
- customer lotteries, run by occupiers of business premises selling tickets only to customers on the premises itself.

If the society sets up a separate development association or other organisation to promote its lottery, it will be that association or organisation which is making the exempt supply. The net proceeds of the lottery paid by the development association to the society are outside the scope of VAT and any expense relating to the lottery, where these are deductible, cannot be reclaimed by the society as its input tax.

The National Lottery is regulated by the National Lottery Commission and is the only lottery of its kind that may legally be run in the UK.

Local authorities are allowed to promote lotteries under the *Gambling Act*. When a local authority promotes or organises a lottery this is treated the same way as those run by societies. However, an authority should contact HMRC to discuss the recovery of input tax.

(VAT Notice 701/29/17, paras 4.4–4.7).

Lottery duty

Most lotteries that are promoted lawfully (i.e. in the circumstances specifically described in the *Gambling Act 2005*) do not have to pay lottery duty. See Customs Notice 458 *Lottery duty* for further information.

(VAT Notice 701/29/17, para 4.8).

Lottery management companies

An external lottery manager (ELM) is a person or body who makes arrangements for a lottery on behalf of a society or local authority. These arrangements may include such things as arranging for tickets to be printed, organising publicity, arranging for the sale of tickets by agents and the paying out of prizes. An ELM will not be a member, officer or employee of the society or authority, and will normally be required to obtain a lottery manager's operating licence from the Gambling Commission in order to carry on lottery management activities.

The supply of lottery management services is standard-rated and VAT must be accounted for on

- any fee or commission paid by the lottery promoter, *plus*
- any additional amounts retained from gross ticket sales to cover the cost of running the lottery, *plus*
- any commission received and retained by selling agents used by the lottery management company

less the amount paid out in cash prizes by the management company (or the VAT-inclusive cost of goods given as prizes).

However, if a lottery management company also sells tickets itself using its own outlets and employees (rather than merely arranging for their sale by independent sellers), it can exempt this direct selling service like any other ticket seller (see below). If the company does not specify a separate charge for its own selling service, it must apportion its global charge to the promoter between exempt and standard-rated supplies. The exempt element must be shown separately on the VAT invoice. See **48.3 OUTPUT TAX** for apportionment of consideration.

(VAT Notice 701/29/17, paras 5.1–5.2).

Lottery ticket sales

The service of selling lottery tickets is an exempt supply. Where a retailer sells lottery tickets as an agent (for either a lottery management company or promoter) the commission received is a consideration for the exempt service of selling lottery tickets to the public.

The principal must account for the value of ticket sales to the public. This is usually the lottery promoter but where tickets are sold to a retailer who sells them on to the public at a higher price, the retailer becomes the principal. The purchase of the tickets by the retailer from the promoter is exempt, as is the money retained from sales of the tickets by the retailer.

Use of a retail scheme

Where a retailer selling lottery tickets uses one of the retail schemes to account for VAT, the proceeds from the exempt sale of tickets should be excluded from the scheme calculations. If the proceeds are included in the DGT, the retailer should reduce the DGT by the value of the tickets sold when calculating the DGT for the retail scheme calculation.

(VAT Notice 701/29/17, paras 6.1–6.4).

Electronic lottery ticket vending machines

In *Oasis Technologies (UK) Ltd* (TC00581) (TVC 24.25), the tribunal held that the Oasis electronic lottery ticket vending machine (ELTVM) was a gaming machine within *VATA 1994, Sch 9, Group 4, Note 1(d)* (see **8.4** above). However, the machine also granted the right to participate in a lottery and the takings from the machine were exempt from VAT. Following that decision, HMRC stated that VAT exemption applies to such an ELTVM where

- the machine provides a game of chance;
- the tickets are randomly distributed;
- the player, operator or manufacturer cannot influence the order in which a ticket is revealed;
- the lottery result cannot be determined or influenced by means of the machine; and
- where groups of tickets have been pre-loaded into a machine, the machine may randomly select a new group when the current one is completed.

(HMRC Brief 1/11).

De Voil Indirect Tax Service. See V4.131.

Key points: betting and gaming

[8.6] Points to consider are as follows.

- Supplies relating to the playing of dutiable machine games (games liable to MGD) are exempt from VAT. Supplies relating to the playing of relevant machine games are taxable at the standard rate.
- The tax point for supplies made from coin-operated machines is the date the machine is used although, as an accounting convenience, operators may delay accounting for VAT until each time that the takings are removed from the machine.

9

Business

Cross-reference. See **74.6 WORKS OF ART, ETC.** for sales of antiques, etc. from stately homes.

De Voil Indirect Tax Service. See V2.2.

Introduction to business

EU legislation

[9.1] *Directive 2006/112/EC* adopts the term 'economic activity' rather than business. See **19.7 EUROPEAN UNION LEGISLATION.** Unless a decision of the CJEU provides otherwise, the meaning of economic activity is not materially different from the meaning of 'business' in the UK legislation.

UK legislation

The proper identification of an activity as a 'business' activity is fundamental to the operation of VAT. Output tax must be charged on any taxable supply of goods or services made in the UK by a taxable person *in the course or furtherance of any business* carried on by him. [*VATA 1994, s 4(1)*]. Similarly, input tax must relate to supplies of goods and services to a taxable person (and, where relevant, acquisitions and importations of goods by him) used or to be used *for the purpose of any business* carried on or to be carried on by him. [*VATA 1994, s 24(1)*].

Despite the importance of the meaning of '*business*', it is not comprehensively defined in UK (or EU) legislation. *VATA 1994, s 94* (as amended) gives the following guidance as to what the term encompasses and excludes. If a particular activity is not covered, then it is necessary to apply the 'business test' developed by the Courts (see **9.2** below).

(a) It includes any trade, profession or vocation.
(b) The following (without prejudice to the generality of anything else in *VATA 1994*) are deemed to be the carrying on of a business.
  - The provision by a club, association or organisation (for a subscription or other consideration) of the facilities or advantages available to its members (but see (*c*) below). See also **15.1 CLUBS AND ASSOCIATIONS.**
  - The admission, for a consideration, of persons to any premises (see *The Eric Taylor Testimonial Match Committee* (VTD 139) (TVC 7.91)).

(c) Where a person accepts any office in the course or furtherance of a trade, profession or vocation, services supplied by him as holder of that office are treated as supplied in the course or furtherance of that trade, profession or vocation. See **9.4** below, **45.8 MANAGEMENT SERVICES AND SUPPLIES OF STAFF** and **51.6 PARTNERSHIPS.**
(d) Anything done in connection with the termination or intended termination of a business is treated as being done in the course or furtherance of that business.
(e) The disposition of a business or part of a business as a going concern, or of the assets or liabilities of the business or part of the business (whether or not in connection with its reorganisation or winding up) is a supply made in the course or furtherance of the business (but see **9.9** below).

The business test

[9.2] When considering whether an activity is to be treated as a business, if it is not one of the deemed businesses under **9.1** above then the 'business test' must be applied. This test is derived from decisions of the tribunals and Courts.

The following principles, as summarised in *C & E Commrs v Lord Fisher*, QB [1981] STC 238 (TVC 7.6) are a guide as to whether an activity is a business although the absence of one common attribute of ordinary businesses (e.g. the pursuit of profit) does not necessarily mean that the activity is not a business and the criteria are not therefore conclusive in every case.

- By providing in *VATA 1994, s 94* (see **9.1** above) that business *includes* any trade, profession or vocation, it is clear that a wide meaning of 'business' is intended.
- In determining whether any particular activity constitutes a business it is necessary to consider the whole of that activity.
- A business activity can generally be identified from the answers to the following criteria (as laid down in *C & E Commrs v Morrison's Academy Boarding Houses Association*, CS 1977, [1978] STC 1 (TVC 7.1)).
  (a) Is the activity a 'serious undertaking earnestly pursued' or a 'serious occupation not necessarily confined to commercial or profit making undertakings'?
  (b) Is the activity an occupation or function actively pursued with reasonable or recognisable continuity?

A one-off supply or a series of infrequent, unconnected supplies is not normally a business activity in its own right although it is important to consider the nature of the activity. For example, occasional sales by small speculative builders and property developers are business activities.

(c) Does the activity have a certain measure of substance as measured by the quarterly or annual value of taxable supplies made?

(d) Is the activity conducted in a regular manner and on sound and recognised business principles?

(e) Is the activity predominantly concerned with the making of taxable supplies to consumers for a consideration?

This is perhaps the most important point to establish, bearing in mind that 'consideration' need not necessarily be monetary. If a trader is carrying on an activity which does not involve the making of any supplies for a consideration and there is no intention in the future of doing so, then the activity is unlikely to be regarded as business even if all the other criteria are met.

In *C & E Commrs v The Apple and Pear Development Council*, HL [1988] STC 221 (TVC 22.85) the Council's principal activity was to advertise English apples and pears, which activity was financed by a statutory levy on growers. The CJEU ruled that the levy was not consideration because there was no direct link between the payments and the benefits of individual growers on which basis the House of Lords concluded that the activity was not 'business' in the VAT sense. Similarly, a charity raising funds in a 'business-like' manner from its activities was held not to be running a business unless taxable supplies, made for a consideration, formed the basis of the fund raising (*C & E Commrs v Royal Exchange Theatre Trust*, QB [1979] STC 278 (TVC 7.5)).

Where an activity is just beginning and no supplies are being made at the time but there is a clear intention to do so at some time in the future, then the activity may qualify as a business. See *Rompelman v Minister van Financien, ECJ Case 268/83*, [1985] 3 CMLR 202; [1985] ECR 655 (TVC 22.111) and *Merseyside Cablevision Ltd* [1987] VATTR 134 (TVC 36.603).

(f) Are the taxable supplies of a kind which are commonly made by those who seek to profit by them?

(g) If a person is carrying on an activity and it is not clear whether it amounts to a business, it is more likely to be regarded as such if others are carrying on the same type of activity and are clearly doing so on a commercial basis. See *Church of Scientology of California (No 1) v C & E Commrs*, CA 1980, [1981] STC 65 (TVC 7.4) where courses in the study of its beliefs provided by the Church, some of which competed with those offered by trained psychologists and psychiatrists, were found to be business activities.

- Whether the activity is pursued for profit or some other private purpose or motive is not decisive in determining whether the activity is a business.

- If all or a sufficient number of the above criteria are satisfied in sufficient measure to override any contra-indications which might be seen in the facts, then as a matter of law the activity must be held to be a business.

The carrying on, by a regulatory authority, of a statutory licensing activity to protect the public interest is not a business activity even though carried on for a consideration. See *Institute of Chartered Accountants in England and Wales v C & E Commrs*, HL [1999] STC 398 (TVC 62.163) in respect of the Institute's authorisation to issue licences to auditors, insolvency practitioners and persons carrying on investment business.

See the chapter *Business* in *Tolley's VAT Cases* for tribunal and court decisions involving the general meaning of 'business'.

See also **13 CHARITIES**, in particular the Court of Appeal's decision in *Longridge on the Thames v HMRC* [2016] EWCA Civ 930; [2016] STC 2362 (TVC 15.138), for comments on the approach of the UK courts and tribunals to the application of the above principles.

Business and non-business activities

Businesses with more than one activity

[9.3] Where a taxable person undertakes distinct and separate activities, some of these may be business and others non-business. A non-business activity may be a private activity (e.g. a hobby, see below) or, particularly in the grant-funded and voluntary sectors, it might be an activity which forms part of the overall objectives but be non-business for VAT purposes (see, for example, **13.5 CHARITIES** for business and non-business activities of charities). In either case, the business test must be applied to each activity. For cases where the tribunals have been concerned with multiple activities, see *Rainheath Ltd* (VTD 1249) (TVC 7.35) (yacht purchased by a farming business); *DA Walker* (VTD 240) (TVC 7.17) (accountant with furnished letting income); and *RW & AAW Williamson* (VTD 555) (TVC 7.23) (retail partnership also renting out lock-up garages).

Hobbies

Activities of pleasure and social enjoyment, though organised in a business-like way, do not amount to a 'business' if no taxable supplies are made for a consideration (*C & E Commrs v Lord Fisher*, QB [1981] STC 238 (TVC 7.6)).

Traders may sometimes have hobbies that involve the making of taxable supplies (e.g. repairing cars or selling stamps). These supplies are not automatically made in the course or furtherance of business and the business test must be applied. Hobbies which involve a registered trader making minimal supplies are unlikely to be seen as business. However, in some cases, a hobby can involve a trader making substantial supplies and may grow to become a business activity. See, for example, *Haydon-Baillie* (VTD 2072) (TVC 36.609).

Disposal of private assets

This is normally a non-business activity. Where, however, the assets are disposed of through the trader's own business the disposal may occasionally be treated as business. See, for example, *Mittu* (VTD 1275) (TVC 62.76) where a jeweller sold items of jewellery belonging to his wife through the business and paid the proceeds into the business account.

The independent disposal of private assets merely to raise funds for a business is non-business and outside the scope of VAT. See *RWK Stirling* (VTD 1963) (TVC 62.77).

Apportionment of input tax

Where a business incurs VAT on goods and services which it intends to use for both business activities and non-business activities, it is unlikely that it will be able to treat all the VAT as input tax and some form of apportionment will be required. See **35.7 INPUT TAX.**

Particular problem areas

[9.4] Particular problem areas are as follows:

- **Charities.** See **13.4 CHARITIES.**
- **Clubs and associations.** See **15.1 CLUBS AND ASSOCIATIONS.**
- **Education.** See **17.2 EDUCATION.**
- **Local authorities.** See **44.3** and **44.4 LOCAL AUTHORITIES AND PUBLIC BODIES** and for government departments and health authorities see **44.11 LOCAL AUTHORITIES AND PUBLIC BODIES.**
- **Museums and galleries.** Although the main activity of most museums and galleries is the public display of a collection, many have a number of other activities and it is necessary to identify all activities and consider the business/non-business nature of each.
  Admission charges. Where a museum, etc. makes a general admission charge for the public to enter its premises, this constitutes a 'deemed' business activity under *VATA 1994, s 94* (see **9.1**(*b*) above). In general, the full amount of any admission charge is standard-rated. However, admission charges to museums and galleries by certain eligible bodies are exempt and voluntary donations in lieu of admission charges are outside the scope of VAT. See **58.2 RECREATION AND SPORT.**
  A museum or gallery which admits the public free of charge is not carrying on a business activity. Consequently, under the normal rules any VAT it incurs in relation to the provision of free rights of admission cannot be recovered. See, however, **35.13**(21) **INPUT TAX** for a special scheme allowing certain non-charging national museums and galleries to recover related input tax.
- **Office holders.** Under *VATA 1994, s 94(4)* where a person in the course or furtherance of a trade, profession or vocation accepts any office, services supplied by him as the holder of that office are treated as supplied in the course or furtherance of the trade, profession or vocation. See also **45.8 MANAGEMENT SERVICES AND SUPPLIES OF STAFF** for directors or employees or a company, sole traders and partners as office holders.

- **Shooting rights.** See **58.12 RECREATION AND SPORT.**
- **Works of art – disposals from stately homes.** See **74.6 WORKS OF ART, ETC.**

Disaggregation of business activities

[9.5] For EU legislation, see **19.7 EUROPEAN UNION LEGISLATION.**

The following provisions are designed to prevent the avoidance of tax by the maintenance or creation of any 'artificial' separation of business activities carried on by two or more persons. In determining whether any separation of business activities is '*artificial*', consideration must be given to the extent to which the different persons carrying on those activities are closely bound to one another by financial, economic and organisational links.

Example

Mr B provides accountancy services from his office in the High Street. Mr C trades from the same premises, offering a service to complete tax returns. Neither of the two businesses is VAT-registered, as they each have sales of £45,000 per annum. The following facts apply to their respective organisations:

- Mr B and Mr C use the same computers to carry out their work – they sit together in an open plan office in the same room;
- they have many common clients, with Mr B doing the accounts work and Mr C the tax returns for these clients;
- Mr B employs a receptionist who also spends a lot of her time working for Mr C;
- Mr C employs a secretary who also spends a lot of her time doing work for Mr B;
- they have a joint advert in the local newspaper – promoting a combined service of 'preparing accounts and completing tax returns'.

This particular arrangement is one where HMRC are likely to decide that there is only one business evident in practice. There are clear financial, economic and organisational links between the two businesses. Equally important, any customer dealing with the business might perceive that there was, in reality, only one business.

HMRC may make a direction under which the persons specified therein become treated as a single taxable person carrying on the activities of a business described in the direction. That taxable person is then liable to be registered under *VATA 1994, Sch 1* with effect from the date of the direction or such later day as is specified. The direction must be served on each person named in it.

If, immediately before the direction (or any supplementary direction below) any person named therein is already registered in respect of taxable supplies made by him, he ceases to be liable to be registered from the date of the direction or, if later, the date with effect from which the single taxable person concerned became liable to be registered.

Supplementary directions

HMRC may subsequently make and serve a supplementary direction adding a further person's name to those detailed in the earlier direction where that person appears to HMRC to be making taxable supplies in the course of the activities of the business previously specified. The name is added from the date on which he began making those taxable supplies or, if later, the date with effect from which the single taxable person referred to in the earlier direction became liable to be registered under *VATA 1994, Sch 1*.

[*VATA 1994, Sch 1 para 1A, para 2(1)(3)–(5)*].

De Voil Indirect Tax Service. See V2.190C.

Preconditions for making a direction

[9.6] Before making a direction naming any person HMRC must be satisfied that

- he is making or has made taxable supplies;
- the activities in the course of which he makes or made those supplies form only part of certain activities, the other activities being carried on concurrently or previously (or both) by one or more other persons; and
- if all the taxable supplies of the business described in the direction were taken into account, a person carrying on that business would at the time of the direction be liable to be registered under the normal registration rules.

[*VATA 1994, Sch 1 para 2(2)*].

Effect of a direction

[9.7] The effects of a direction on the '*constituent members*' (i.e. all those named in the direction and any supplementary direction) are as follows.

(a) The taxable person carrying on the specified business is registrable in such name as the persons named in the direction jointly nominate in writing within 14 days of the direction. Otherwise the taxable person is registrable in such name as may be specified in the direction.

(b) Any supply of goods or services by or to one of the constituent members in the course of the specified business is treated as a supply by or to the taxable person.

(c) Any acquisition of goods from another EU member state by one of the constituent members in the course of the specified business is treated as an acquisition by the taxable person.

(d) Each of the constituent members is jointly and severally liable for any VAT due from the taxable person.

(e) Without prejudice to (*d*) above, any failure by a taxable person to comply with any VAT requirement is treated as a failure by each of the constituent members severally.

(f) Subject to (*a*)–(*e*) above, the constituent members are treated as a partnership carrying on the specified business and any question as to the scope of that business at any time is determined accordingly.

HMRC may subsequently give notice that one of the constituent members is no longer to be regarded as such for the purposes of (*d*) or (*e*) above. He then ceases to have any liability for those purposes after a date specified in the notice and, from the same date, ceases to be regarded as a member of the partnership referred to in (*f*) above.

[*VATA 1994, Sch 1 para 2(6)–(8)*].

Appeals

[9.8] An appeal may be made against a direction or supplementary direction but the tribunal cannot allow the appeal unless it considers that HMRC could not reasonably have been satisfied that there were grounds for making that direction or supplementary direction. [*VATA 1994, s 84(7)*].

Cases where HMRC's direction was upheld

See *Chamberlain v C & E Commrs*, QB [1989] STC 505 (TVC 57.36) (associated companies operating launderettes); *Osman v C & E Commrs*, QB [1989] STC 596 (TVC 57.40) (husband and wife acting as tax consultants from the same office); *TSD & Mrs M E Williams* (VTD 2445) (TVC 57.42) (married couple carrying on business as a café and bread shop from the same premises); *MJ & P Summers* (VTD 3498) (TVC 57.46) (health studio operated by married couple and son); *P & RJ Jervis* (VTD 3920) (TVC 57.49) (catering at a public house); *West End Health and Fitness Club* (VTD 4070) (TVC 57.48) (company operating a fitness club and a director and his wife operating a beauty salon in partnership from the same premises); *Old Farm Service Station Ltd & L Williams* (VTD 4261) (TVC 57.53) (company operating a service station and a director's son running a video club at the same premises); *Allerton Motors* (VTD 9427) (TVC 57.59) (car sales and car washing at same premises); *EM, PG & CP Evans* (VTD 10532) (TVC 57.60) (fairground amusement operators); and *A & S Essex (t/a Essex Associates)* (VTD 15072) (TVC 57.61) (married couple providing computer programming services via a partnership and supplying computer hardware via a limited company).

Cases where the appellants were successful

See *D & Mrs LM Horsman* (VTD 5401) (TVC 57.75) (farming and pony trekking carried on by married couple); *P, C & J Allen* (VTD 12209) (TVC 57.78) (where, to avoid inheritance tax, a husband, who ran a bookselling business and three launderettes, took his wife into partnership in the bookselling business, transferred one of the launderettes to her and took his son into partnership in another of the launderettes); *I Reayner, J Colegate & A Reayner* (VTD 15396) (TVC 57.79) (dry-cleaning businesses operated from separate premises by a mother, her son and his common law wife); and *Trippitt (S & AJ)* (VTD 17340) (TVC 57.69) (wife of publican providing bed and breakfast facilities and paying 35% of income to husband).

Transfer of a business as a going concern

[9.9] For EU legislation, see **19.8 EUROPEAN UNION LEGISLATION.**

Normally the sale of the assets of a VAT-registered business are subject to VAT at the appropriate rate. However, where certain conditions are met (see **9.10** below), the transfer of a business as a going concern ('TOGC') involving the sale of a business including assets *must* be treated as 'neither a supply of goods nor a supply of services' and is therefore outside the scope of VAT. VAT must not be charged on the assets transferred (except, in certain circumstances as indicated in **9.11** below, on the land and buildings used in the business).

Typical cases which may be covered by the provisions are where

- the assets of a business are bought by another person and the existing business ceases to trade;
- an existing owner of a business dies or retires and the business assets are taken over by another person;
- part of an existing business is sold to another person; and
- the assets of a business are transferred to a new legal entity (e.g. a sole proprietor may take on a partner, or form a limited company).

There is no TOGC simply because of a change in the constitution of a partnership or the transfer of shares in a limited company from one person to another.

The TOGC rules are compulsory and so it is important to establish from the outset whether a sale is a TOGC or not. If VAT is charged when it should not have been:

- The seller must cancel any VAT invoice issued and provide the new owner with a refund of the VAT charged (normally by issue of a credit note or document giving similar effect).
- If any VAT is incorrectly shown on a VAT invoice which is not cancelled, it is recoverable by HMRC from the seller, see **32.2 HMRC: POWERS.**
- The purchaser will not be able to reclaim this amount as input tax (even if he has paid it to the vendor in good faith) because there was no taxable supply. But it is understood that where HMRC are wholly satisfied that the amount of 'VAT' has been both declared and paid to them by the seller, they may allow the purchaser to recover it as if it were input tax.

(VAT Notice 700/9/12, paras 1.2–1.5, 2.2).

De Voil Indirect Tax Service. See V2.226.

Conditions for transfer not to be a taxable supply

[9.10] Subject to **9.11** below, the supply by a person of the assets of his business to a person to whom he transfers that business (or part thereof) as a going concern is neither a supply of goods nor a supply of services provided all the following conditions are satisfied.

Condition 1

The assets are to be used by the purchaser in carrying on the same kind of business, whether or not as part of an existing business, as that carried on by the seller in relation to the whole or part transferred. [*SI 1995/1268, Art 5(1)*]. If the purchaser is to use the assets to carry on a different kind of business, VAT must be charged in the normal way.

The purchaser does not need to have been pursuing the same type of business as the seller before the assets are transferred to him (*Zita Modes Sàrl v Administration de l'enregistrement et des domaines, ECJ Case C–497/01*, [2005] STC 1059 (TVC 22.182)).

Common areas of difficulty include companies which have more than one trading activity. For example, a brewery is in business selling beers, wines and spirits to the public via their managed house outlets. It is also in business renting properties to tenants (where the tenants are selling to the public). If a brewery was leasing a pub to tenants, and then sold the business to someone who was to run the pub himself, there would not be a TOGC. The brewery had a business of renting the property, the new owner has a business of running a pub.

HMRC accept that there is the same type of business where

- a restaurant or bar is sold but the purchaser is to immediately alter the style of the business (e.g. where a public house is subsequently aimed at different clientele and sells different beer (see *G Draper (Marlow) Ltd* [1986] Lexis Citation 1661 (TVC 65.3)) and where an Indian restaurant becomes an Italian restaurant (see *Tahmassebi (t/a Sale Pepe)* (VTD 13177) (TVC 65.99)); or
- a business is sold to someone who intends to restructure it so that it will not be the same type of business but who continues with the existing business, even if for a very short period of time

but there are different types of business where

- the seller grants franchises to operate trading sites (as opposed to operating the actual trading activity of the business); or
- the purchaser will only use the seller's product to support his existing business and will not be making any supplies of the seller's product to any third parties.

(VAT Notice 700/9/12, paras 7.1–7.3).

There is not necessarily a different kind of business because the seller made supplies to wholesalers and the purchaser sells to retail customers. See, for example, *Village Collection Interiors Ltd* [1991] Lexis Citation 1505 (TVC 65.23).

It is implied that the seller had to have been carrying on the business, or part of the business, transferred. See Condition 6 below.

Condition 2

In a case in which the seller is a taxable person (i.e. registered or liable to be registered for VAT), the purchaser must already be a taxable person or immediately become, as a result of the transfer, a taxable person (or Isle of Man equivalent). [*SI 1995/1268, Art 5(1)*]. In determining whether the purchaser is a taxable person, the turnover of the seller must also be taken into account. See **60.3 REGISTRATION**.

This condition is not met if the purchaser is not registered or required to be registered for VAT, for example, because

- at the date the transfer takes place, the purchaser does not expect the value of his taxable supplies in the next twelve months to be above the deregistration limit (e.g. because he intends to reduce trading by introducing shorter working hours); or
- the seller was registered voluntarily at the date of the transfer so that the purchaser is not required to register because the value of his taxable supplies in the twelve-month period then ended is not above the registration limit.

In such circumstances, unless the purchaser has been accepted for voluntary registration, the TOGC conditions are not met and the sale takes its normal liability. Where only part of the business is being transferred, the purchaser must consider the turnover of that part to determine whether he must be registered.

There can be no TOGC where a VAT-registered farmer transfers his business to a farmer who is certified under the agricultural flat rate scheme as the purchaser is not registered or registerable for VAT.

(VAT Notice 700/9/12, paras 1.3, 2.3.4).

Condition 3

In relation to a part transfer, that part must be capable of separate operation. [*SI 1995/1268, Art 5(1)*]. HMRC take the view that an 'in-house' function is not a business for TOGC condition purposes when it only operates internally and the assets of the part transferred must have been used to make supplies (and not merely used for the overheads of the business). However, it does not matter whether the part will, in fact, be operated separately from any other business the purchaser carries on.

(VAT Notice 700/9/12, para 2.3.7).

Condition 4

The effect of the transfer must be to put the purchaser in possession of a business which can be operated as such. A sale of capital assets is not in itself a TOGC but if the effect is to put the purchaser in possession of a business, then it is a TOGC even if the assets are transferred on different dates. (VAT Notice 700/9/12, para 2.3.1).

Condition 5

The business, or part, transferred must be a 'going concern' at the time of transfer. But it can still be a going concern even though it is unprofitable or is trading under the control of a liquidator, administrative receiver or trustee in bankruptcy. (VAT Notice 700/9/12, para 2.3.1).

See *Baltic Leasing Ltd* (VTD 2088) (TVC 65.17) and *C & E Commrs v Dearwood Ltd*, QB [1986] STC 327 (TVC 65.12).

In *JMA Spijkers v Gevroeders Benedik Abattoir CV, ECJ Case C-24/85*, [1986] 2 CMLR 296 (TVC 22.181) it was held that there could be a TOGC even if there had been a cessation of trading before the date on which the transfer took place provided the wherewithal to carry on the business, such as plant, building and employees, were available and were transferred.

Condition 6

There must not be a series of immediately consecutive transfers of the business. Where A sells its assets to B who immediately sells those assets to C, B has not carried on the business. As a result, B can neither receive nor make an onward supply of the assets under the special provisions. See *Kwik Save Group plc* (VTD 12749) (TVC 65.84) where a holding company carrying on the business of food retailers purchased food stores and then transferred them to a subsidiary which carried on a similar business but without itself (i.e. the holding company) in the meantime having traded at those food stores (the holding company's transfer to the subsidiary was a taxable supply).

Condition 7

There must be no significant break in the normal trading pattern before or immediately after the transfer. The 'break in trade' should be considered in the context of the type of business concerned. For example, HMRC do not consider that where a seasonal business has closed for the 'off-season' as normal at the time of sale, that there has necessarily been a break in trade. In addition, a short period of closure that does not significantly disrupt the existing trading pattern (e.g. for redecoration) will not prevent the business from being transferred as a going concern. (VAT Notice 700/9/12, para 2.3.6).

Deciding whether transaction amounts to TOGC

In deciding whether a transaction amounts to a TOGC, regard must be had to its substance rather than its form, and consideration must be given to the whole of the circumstances, weighing the factors which point in one direction against those which point in another. In the end, the vital consideration is whether the effect of the transaction was to put the purchaser in possession of a going concern, the activities of which he could carry on without interruption. Many factors may be relevant to this decision, though few will be conclusive in themselves. Thus, if the purchaser carries on the business in the same manner as before, this will point to the existence of a TOGC, but the converse is not necessarily true, because the transfer may be complete even though the purchaser does not choose to avail himself of all the rights which he acquires thereunder. Similarly, an express assignment of goodwill is strong evidence of a transfer of a business, but the absence of such an assignment is not conclusive the other way. The absence of the assignment of premises, stock or outstanding contracts will likewise not be conclusive, if the particular circumstances of the purchaser enable him to carry on substantially the same business as before. (*Kenmir Ltd v Frizzell*, QB [1968] 1 All ER 414) (TVC 65.10).

Relevant cases

For cases held to fall within the special provisions (so that VAT charged was not recoverable by the purchaser) see *E & E Phillips* (VTD 1130) (TVC 65.1), *Advanced Business Technology Ltd* (VTD 1488) (TVC 65.8), and *C & E Commrs v Dearwood Ltd*, QB [1986] STC 327 (TVC 65.12). For cases held not to fall within the special provisions (so that VAT was chargeable by the vendor and recoverable by the purchaser), see *Eric Ladbroke (Holbeach) Ltd* (VTD 1557) (TVC 65.56), *Computech Development Ltd* (VTD 9798) (TVC 65.46) and *E J Caunt (t/a Edward James Confectionery)* (VTD 1561) (TVC 65.41).

Example

Mike owns a computer store in a local town centre, and has decided he wants to retire and live in Spain. He holds a big closing down sale to sell his stock; he then sells the fixtures and fittings to another computer shop in the next street; a property developer buys the freehold of the shop because he wants to convert the property into luxury flats.

There is no transfer of a going concern and the VAT liability of each separate sale must be considered. However, if Mike had sold the business as a whole and the buyer was continuing to trade as a computer shop, this would have been the sale of a going concern, and no VAT would have been charged if the relevant rules had been met.

Land and buildings

[9.11] A TOGC often involves the transfer of land and buildings. In such cases, there are extra rules to determine whether VAT should be charged on the transfer of the land and buildings, even if the rest of the transfer does qualify for TOGC treatment.

A supply of assets as part of the supply of a business is not treated as a TOGC under the rules in **9.10** above to the extent that it consists of

- a grant of land or buildings, the supply of which would be exempt under *VATA 1994, Sch 9 Group 1* but for an option to tax which the *transferor* has made (see **42.23 LAND AND BUILDINGS: EXEMPT SUPPLIES AND OPTION TO TAX**), or
- a grant of the fee simple in new and uncompleted buildings liable to VAT at the standard rate under **42.18**(*a*) **LAND AND BUILDINGS: EXEMPT SUPPLIES AND OPTION TO TAX**

unless the following conditions have been met no later than the '*relevant date*', i.e. the date upon which the grant would have been treated as having been made or, if there is more than one such date, on the earliest of them.

In *Clark Hill Ltd* [2018] UKFTT 111 (TC), the taxpayer sold four tenanted freehold properties and for two of the properties a deposit was paid by the purchaser before the seller had opted to tax the property. As a result, the transfer could not be treated as a TOGC as the option to tax was not in place before the relevant date. For one property, the purchase was novated after the deposit was paid and the First-tier Tribunal considered that the relevant date was the date that the contract was novated and not the date that the original deposit was received.

Condition 1

The *transferee* must have opted to tax the land or buildings concerned and must have given written notification of the option to HMRC.

HMRC take this to mean that, for the TOGC provisions to apply, the option must be notified to HMRC in writing no later than the time of the supply. This is normally the date of the transfer but also includes receipt of a deposit which may otherwise have created a tax point. A tax point is not created by the receipt of a deposit by a third party acting as an independent stakeholder (as opposed to an agent of the vendor) until the money is released to the vendor.

Following the decision in *Chalegrove Properties Ltd* (VTD 17151) (TVC 65.93) HMRC accept that, where the written notification of the election is sent to HMRC by mail, the notification must be properly addressed, pre-paid and posted on or before the time of supply. The transferee is advised to retain evidence of posting.

(VAT Notice 700/9/12, para 2.4.1).

See also *Higher Education Statistics Agency Ltd v C & E Commrs*, QB [2000] STC 332 (TVC 65.92).

Condition 2

The transferee must have notified the transferor that his option to tax the land or buildings concerned will not be disapplied. To do this, the transferee must be satisfied that the following scenario does *not* apply to him, namely that:

- the land transferred to him would, in relation to him, become a capital item within the **11 CAPITAL GOODS SCHEME** (whether the transfer to him were to be treated as neither a supply of goods nor a supply of services under a TOGC, or otherwise); and
- his supplies of that land will, or would fall, to be exempt supplies by virtue of the disapplication of the option to tax under the anti-avoidance rules in *VATA 1994, Sch 10 para 12* (see **42.27 LAND AND BUILDINGS: EXEMPT SUPPLIES AND OPTION TO TAX**).

[*VATA 1994, s 5(3); SI 1995/1268, Art 5(2)(2A)(2B)(3)*].

If the seller is transferring land or buildings on which there is no option tax and the supply would not be otherwise standard-rated (i.e. if the supply is zero-rated or exempt) then the purchaser is not required to opt to tax. In these circumstances the transfer of the land or buildings can be included in the TOGC.

The seller is responsible for applying the correct VAT treatment and HMRC may require him to support his decision. If the transaction is to be treated as a TOGC, it is advisable for the seller to

- ask the purchaser for evidence that his option to tax is in place by the relevant date (e.g. a copy of the notification letter); and
- ask for written confirmation the transferee's option to tax will not be disapplied.

(VAT Notice 700/9/12, para 2.4).

Where the above conditions are not met, the transfer of the land and buildings is a supply subject to VAT. However, the supply of other assets may still qualify to be treated as a TOGC.

Example

Mr Smith is selling his restaurant business as a going concern to Mr Jones, and the sale includes fixtures and fittings, goodwill and a freehold property on which an option to tax election has been made.

Before the deal is completed, Mr Jones must opt to tax the property, notify HMRC and provide evidence of this action to Mr Smith. He must confirm in writing to Mr Smith that the option to tax election will not be disapplied. The whole deal will then qualify as outside the scope of VAT, assuming the other TOGC conditions are met.

However, if Mr Jones fails to make the election, or decides it is not in his best interests to make the election (e.g. he expects to make a big profit on selling the property in a few years time to a buyer that may not be able to recover VAT), then Mr Smith will have to charge VAT on the value of the property only. The fixtures, fittings and goodwill will still be outside the scope of the tax.

Transfer of a property rental business

[9.12] HMRC give the following examples of circumstances concerning the transfer of land and buildings where there may (or may not) be a transfer of a business of property rental as a going concern. In those cases where there has been such a transfer, provided the conditions in **9.11** above relating to land and buildings and the general conditions in **9.10** above are satisfied, the supply of the assets can then be ignored for VAT purposes.

Examples where a property business can be transferred as a going concern

The seller:

- Owns freehold property which is let to a tenant and is sold with the benefit of the existing lease (or where a leasehold interest is owned and assigned with the benefit of a sub-lease), even if the property is only partly tenanted.
- Owns a building where there is a contract to pay rent in the future but where the tenants are enjoying an initial rent-free period, even if the property is sold during the rent-free period.
- Granted a lease in respect of a building but the tenants are not yet in occupation.

- Owns a property and tenants have been found although no lease agreement has been entered into, and the freehold property is transferred to a third party with the benefit of a contractual agreement for a lease but before the lease has been signed.
- Is a property developer selling a site as a package (to a single buyer) which is a mixture of let and unlet, finished or unfinished properties, and the sale of the site would otherwise have been standard-rated, provided the purchaser opts to tax the *whole* site.
- Owns a number of let freehold properties, and sells one of them, the sale of this single let or partly-let property.
- Has a partially-let building, providing that the letting constitutes economic activity.

The purchaser:

- acquires the freehold and leasehold of a property from separate sellers without the interests merging, the lease has not been extinguished and the purchaser continues to exploit the asset by receiving rent from the tenant.

There is not a transfer of a going concern in the following circumstances

The seller:

- Is a property developer and has built a building which
  (a) he has allowed someone to occupy temporarily (without any right to occupy after the proposed sale); or
  (b) he is 'actively marketing' in search of a tenant.
- Sells a property where a lease previously granted is surrendered immediately before the sale (because the property rental business ceases when the lease is surrendered).
- Sells a property freehold to an existing tenant who leases the whole premises from the seller (because the tenant cannot carry on the same business of property rental).

The purchaser:

- of a property rental business has arranged for its own existing sub-tenants to sign agreements for lease with the vendor, so that the 'business' has effectively been transferred by the purchaser to the vendor in order to be transferred back again (see *HMRC v Royal College of Paediatrics and another* [2015] UKUT 38 (TCC) (TVC 65.36)).

(VAT Notice 700/9/12, paras 4.3, 6.2, 6.3).

Prior to 16 November 2012, HMRC used to hold the view that where a person owned the freehold of a property and granted a lease (even a 999-year lease) or owned a headlease and granted a sub-lease there was no TOGC because there was no transfer of a business, just the creation of a new asset (the lease). However, following the decision in *Robinson Family Ltd* (TC02046) (TVC 65.37) HMRC have accepted that the fact that the transferor of a property rental business retains a small reversionary interest in the property transferred does not prevent the transaction from being treated as a TOGC for VAT purposes. Provided the interest retained is small enough not to disturb the substance of the transaction, the transaction will be a TOGC if the usual conditions are satisfied. HMRC's change in policy is retrospective, and claims for overpaid VAT in relation to the sale of buildings which should have been regarded as TOGCs may be submitted. This is subject to the condition that the parties can provide evidence that the requirement to notify HMRC that an option to tax would not be rendered ineffective could have been given at the time of the transaction.

(HMRC Brief 30/12).

Following the case of *Intelligent Managed Services v HMRC* [2015] UKUT 341 (TCC) (TVC 65.78), HMRC have changed their policy where a business is transferred into or out of a VAT group registration. Before that case, HMRC considered that the disregarding of transactions within a VAT group meant that the following did not qualify as a TOGC:

- sale of a business into a VAT group, where the purchasing company only used the assets to make supplies within the group (business disregarded after the transfer and therefore deemed to cease);
- sale of a business out of a VAT group, where the selling company only used the assets to make supplies within the group (business not deemed to exist before the transfer);
- sale of a rental property by a landlord outside a VAT group to a landlord inside the VAT group, where the tenant or tenants were all members of the VAT group (rental activity deemed to cease);
- sale of a rental property by a landlord within a VAT group to a landlord outside the VAT group, where the tenant or tenants were all members of the VAT group (rental activity deemed not to exist before the transfer).

HMRC will now accept that all these situations are capable of being a TOGC, provided that the assets are used to make the same kind of supplies within the group to other companies that make supplies outside the group. Where a trader believes that Stamp Duty Land Tax may have been overpaid because VAT was added to consideration, HMRC will consider a claim for repayment.

(HMRC Brief 11/16).

Nominee purchaser

[9.13] Strictly, a transfer of a going concern cannot occur where the transferee is a nominee for a beneficial owner because the beneficial owner will be the person carrying on the business, not the nominee. However, where the legal title in land is to be held by a nominee for a *named* beneficial owner, that beneficial owner (and not the nominee) may optionally, for the purposes of establishing the transfer of a property letting business as a going concern, be considered to be the transferee. The transferor, nominee and beneficial owner must agree to this optional treatment in writing. Examples of where a nominee might hold property for a beneficial owner are where the legal title is held on trust for a partnership, unincorporated association or pension fund.

(VAT Notice 700/9/12, paras 8.1–8.3). Para 8.3 contains an example format that the parties can use to record their agreement.

The option does not need to apply to transactions where the nominee is the transferor of the legal title. In these cases, *VATA 1994, Sch 10 para 40* deems the beneficial owner to be the transferor. See **42.20 LAND AND BUILDINGS: EXEMPT SUPPLIES AND OPTION TO TAX.**

Miscellaneous aspects

Registration by purchaser

[9.14] See **60.3 REGISTRATION** for circumstances where the purchaser is liable to be registered at the time the business is transferred.

HMRC have pointed out that this can be a particular problem if the purchaser is a 'non-established person'. (HMRC Brief 11/16).

Transfer of registration number

See **60.42 REGISTRATION** for an application to transfer the registration number of the seller to the purchaser following a TOGC.

Deregistration by seller

If the seller is not continuing to trade, he must cancel his VAT registration. See **60.10 REGISTRATION.** If when doing so he has any goods on which input tax has been claimed and which are not transferred with the business, he must normally account for VAT on these assets. See **60.39 REGISTRATION.** If any of the assets not transferred are capital items covered by the capital goods scheme and still within its adjustment period, the seller will need to make a final adjustment. See **11.7 CAPITAL GOODS SCHEME.**

Reclaiming input tax incurred before the TOGC

One of the consequences of transferring the registration number of the seller to the purchaser is that any right of the seller to credit for, or repayment of, input tax becomes the right of the purchaser. However, even where the registration number is not transferred, there is nothing to prevent the seller from assigning to the purchaser the benefit of any claim for repayment under *VATA 1994, s 80*. See *HMRC v Midlands Co-Operative Society Ltd (No 2)*, CA [2008] STC 1803 (TVC 65.127) where a co-operative society transferred its business to another society.

For all transfers of rights to make a claim for overpaid tax that take place from 25 June 2008, the current creditor is put in the shoes of the original creditor. The current creditor does not receive any more from HMRC than if the original creditor had made the claim. The amount due from HMRC on a claim on a transferred right is determined by first setting off the amount of the outstanding liabilities of the original creditor and then any liabilities of the current creditor. Also, HMRC can refuse to pay a current creditor's claim where they can establish that payment of the claim to the original creditor would have unjustly enriched that original creditor [*FA 2008 s 133*] (HMRC Brief 31/08).

Flat-rate scheme for small businesses

See **64.23 SPECIAL SCHEMES** for the consequences of a business that is using the flat-rate scheme transferring its business as a going concern.

Deduction of related input tax

Although a transfer of a going concern is not a supply for VAT purposes, this does not prevent the deduction of input tax on related expenses (subject to the normal rules). There is, however, a distinction between the extent to which the seller and the purchaser can deduct that input tax.

For the position of the purchaser following the decision in *C & E Commrs v UBAF Bank Ltd*, see **50.12**(5) **PARTIAL EXEMPTION**.

In the case of the seller, since the sale of the business as a going concern is not a supply, the input tax incurred on the costs of selling the business cannot be attributed to a supply by the seller. In *Abbey National plc v C & E Commrs, ECJ Case C–408/98*, [2001] STC 297 (TVC 22.483) the CJEU confirmed that, in such circumstances, the seller's costs form part of his overheads and thus, in principle, have a direct and immediate link with the whole of his economic activity so that he can deduct a proportion of the input tax attributable to taxable supplies under his partial exemption method.

The CJEU also indicated that if the seller's costs have a direct and immediate link with a *clearly defined part* of his economic activities, so that the costs form part of the overheads of that part of the business, and all the transactions relating to that part of the business are subject to VAT, he may deduct all the VAT charged on his costs of acquiring those services.

Following the *Abbey National* decision, HMRC take the view that

- VAT incurred on services that have a direct and immediate link with the transferred part of a business should be treated as an overhead of that part of the business;
- where that part of the business makes only taxable supplies, then the VAT incurred is deductible;
- where that part of the business makes only exempt supplies, then the VAT incurred is not deductible; and
- in instances where both taxable and exempt supplies are made by that part of the business, the VAT incurred is partly deductible by reference to the partial exemption method in place. If the partial exemption method fails to achieve a fair and reasonable result, HMRC may be prepared to approve an alternative method.

(VAT Notice 700/9/12, para 2.6.2).

Retention of records

Business records generally have to be kept for up to six years. Where a business (or part of a business) is transferred as a going concern,

- in all but a few specified cases where the purchaser retains the seller's VAT number, the seller must keep any of its business records which are required to be kept after the transfer under the six-year rule. But, so far as is necessary for the purposes of complying with the purchaser's duties under *VATA 1994*, the purchaser (P) may require the seller to

(a) give P within such time and form as P may reasonably require, such information contained in the records and such copies of documents forming part of the records, as P may reasonably specify; and
(b) make the records available for inspection by P at such time and place as P may reasonably require (and permit P to take copies of, or make extracts from them); and

- HMRC may disclose to the purchaser information relating to the business when it was carried out by the seller to enable the purchaser to comply with its duties under *VATA 1994*.

[*VATA 1994, s 49(4)–(6)*].

Supplies to partly-exempt VAT groups

On certain transfers of businesses to partly-exempt VAT groups, the chargeable assets transferred are treated as being supplied to and by the representative member of the group at the open market value. See **28.7 GROUPS OF COMPANIES**. HMRC have commented that this is more likely to apply following the change of policy on TOGCs into groups after *Intelligent Managed Services*. (HMRC Brief 11/16).

Capital goods scheme

Where a business is sold as a going concern and the assets transferred include land or buildings or a civil engineering work worth £250,000 or more and/or computer equipment, ships, boats and aircraft worth £50,000 or more, the purchaser takes over responsibility for applying the capital goods scheme. See **11.12**(4) **CAPITAL GOODS SCHEME**.

Anti-avoidance — subsequent free supply

Where goods or services are transferred as part of a TOGC and the seller (or any previous owner) has deducted input tax on those goods or services, output tax is chargeable on any subsequent free supply of those goods or services by the purchaser. See **48.5** and **48.6 OUTPUT TAX**.

Surrender of a property lease

In a surrender of a property lease the buyer is the landlord and the lease will normally merge with the landlord's existing interest in the property so that the lease ceases to exist. HMRC traditionally took the view that transactions involving the surrender of a property lease could not be a TOGC because the landlord would not use the same asset, the lease, in carrying on the business. In July 2014 HMRC announced that they have changed their policy and now consider that there is in principle no obstacle to the surrender of a lease being a TOGC, subject to all the normal conditions for TOGC treatment being met. For example, where a tenant subletting premises by way of a business surrenders its interest in the property together with the benefit of the subtenants or where a retailer sells its retailing business to its landlord.

The above applies equally were the landlord's interest is held via one or more nominees so that the transaction involves a transfer to the nominee(s) for the landlord's benefit. See **9.13** above.

HMRC accept that there will be cases, prior to July 2014, when businesses did not regard transactions involving the surrender of a property lease as qualifying for TOGC treatment because of HMRC's policy at the time. VAT may have been charged where it need not have been or input tax may have been restricted because the surrender was treated as exempt rather than outside the scope of VAT. Subject to the normal time limits, HMRC accept that it may be possible for the businesses to treat the transactions as qualifying for TOGC treatment and to make the appropriate VAT adjustments. A potential difficulty is that the landlord would not normally have provided the vendor with the notification that the option to tax would not be disapplied (see **9.11** 'Condition 2'). HMRC have confirmed that, providing the parties can satisfactorily evidence that the notification could have been given, it will accept that the legal requirement to give the notification has been complied with.

(HMRC Brief 27/14).

Key points: business

[9.15] Points to consider are as follows.

(a) Business or non-business

- In most cases, it will be clear whether an activity carried out by an individual or other entity is classed as a 'business' (or 'economic activity' to use the phrase adopted in EU VAT law). As a general rule, an intention to make a profit from an activity that is carried out on a regular basis will be classed as a business. As a general principle, the exploitation of land (rental arrangement etc.) is always deemed to be business.
- It is important to be clear about the date when a business actually starts to trade as this can have an impact on a person's date of VAT registration, which is usually based on the value of past taxable sales. If early sales can be legitimately considered to be a 'hobby' rather than a 'business', then this could produce a useful extension to the date when a business needs to first register for VAT on a compulsory basis. The 'business test' guidelines (see **9.2** above) confirm that occasional sales made on an infrequent basis are unlikely to be classed as business related.
- Although an important indicator of 'business', the profit motive is not always the crucial factor. Many business activities are intended to just cover costs and, in some cases, serve as a loss leader for other commercial motives. But an intention to make a profit is usually a key indicator of a business arrangement being in place.
- For a VAT-registered business, it is important to identify which of its activities are classed as business and those (if any) that are deemed to be non-business. Input tax cannot be claimed on costs relevant to non-business activities, and a sensible apportionment method is needed if an expense has both business and non-business use. This issue is particularly important for charities.

(b) Separation of business activities

- The separation of business activities into different legal entities (disaggregation) can be blocked by HMRC if they issue a notice of direction that treats the different entities as a single taxable person. However, they can only issue a direction if they consider that the different entities are closely linked by 'financial, economic and organisational' factors. Note the significance of the word 'and' in the legislation. This means that HMRC must prove all three links (financial, economic and organisational) before a direction can be issued.
- A direction can only be issued by HMRC from a current or future date. However, as a warning, if HMRC can prove that the different entities were never actually separated (no separate accounting records, confusion with banking and invoicing arrangements, no proper system of recharging shared overheads etc.), they may seek to assess tax on a retrospective basis (i.e. on the basis that there has only ever been one business).
- As a general observation, it is harder for two businesses to be separated if family members are involved in both entities. This is because the motives for ensuring overheads are properly recharged are reduced when profits are relevant to a single family. Most VAT tribunal cases lost by taxpayers on this issue involve family members (e.g. husband trading as a publican and VAT registered but wife carrying out catering activity on the same premises and trading below the VAT registration limit).

(c) Transfer of a going concern

- When acting for the buyer of a business, ensure that VAT is not incorrectly charged by the vendor – if a transfer of a going concern arrangement is evident, then HMRC has the power to disallow any input tax claimed by the buyer, even if he holds a proper tax invoice and has paid the VAT to the seller in good faith. The only exception to this approach is if HMRC are wholly satisfied the seller has fully declared and paid output tax on its own VAT return.
- Don't forget that the transfer of a going concern rules are compulsory. There is no possibility of choosing to 'opt out' by, for example, playing safe and charging VAT. The various conditions need to be fully considered to see if a transfer of a business is taking place that is outside the scope of VAT.
- It is also important for buyers to avoid paying VAT if possible because of the cash flow problems of paying the VAT to the seller and then waiting up to three months to reclaim it on a VAT return. It is likely to take longer than three months to recover such VAT as HMRC may choose to carry out a pre-payment credibility check.
- If acting for the VAT-registered seller, remember that the buyer must be VAT-registered or liable to be VAT-registered as a result of the sale – otherwise the transfer of a going concern rules are not

met. The buyer must take into account the taxable sales of the previous owner as far as the VAT-registration limits are concerned. This usually produces a requirement for the buyer to become VAT-registered from his first day of trading.

- In most cases, it will be clear if a business is being sold as a going concern, or whether individual assets are being sold. Advisers need to be aware of the key rules to consider in cases that are not clear-cut.
- Be aware that even though the proceeds from a transfer of a going concern sale are outside the scope of VAT, the related input tax on selling costs can still be reclaimed as long as the business has activities that are wholly taxable. If part of the business income is exempt, then a restriction on the input tax claimed will be evident using the normal partial exemption method adopted by the business.
- There are important issues to consider if the sale of a going concern includes a property where the option to tax election has been made by the seller – as explained at **9.11**. The main requirement is that if the seller has made an election, then the buyer must also make an election before the transfer takes place, and have notified this election to HMRC. The decision to opt to tax a property is very important for any business, because once made, it is in place for at least 20 years.
- If a seller has no option to tax election in place on a property, then there is no requirement for the buyer to make an election. This is an important point to avoid an unnecessary election being made by the buyer, which could create future problems if he wants to either rent out or sell the property to a business that cannot fully reclaim input tax (e.g. an exempt or partly exempt business such as an insurance broker).
- A common error relating to a transfer of a going concern arises where a landlord rents property to a tenant (and the tenant trades in goods or services) and the premises are then sold to the tenant. This is not a transfer of a going concern situation because the activity of the seller (property rental) is not the same as the buyer (selling goods or services).
- A transfer of a going concern can also occur if only part of a business is sold, as long as this part is capable of independently carrying on trading in its own right. An example might be a firm of accountants selling its tax department and maintaining its audit and accountancy sections.
- It is possible, where the buyer has no current VAT registration, for the buyer of a business to retain the seller's VAT registration number. This course of action is risky because the buyer will then be taking over the liability of any potential underpayments of VAT in the last four years. There are very few advantages in retaining the seller's VAT registration number – possibly only a saving of stationery (showing the VAT number) might be the only benefit.

- It is important that the buyer is aware of any potential issues that apply with the capital goods scheme. The buyer will take over any remaining intervals of the seller, i.e. to produce a ten-year input tax adjustment in the case of relevant buildings and five years in the case of relevant computer, ship, boat and aircraft purchases.

10

Business Entertainment

De Voil Indirect Tax Service. See V3.446.

Introduction to business entertainment

[10.1] VAT charged on any goods or services supplied to a taxable person, or on any goods acquired or imported by him, is excluded from any credit where the goods or services in question are used or to be used for the purpose of 'business entertainment' unless the entertainment is provided for an overseas customer and is of a reasonable kind and on a reasonable scale (see below). [*SI 1992/3222, Art 5(1)*].

'*Business entertainment*' means entertainment (including hospitality of any kind) provided by a taxable person in connection with a business carried on by him, but does not include the provision of any such entertainment for either or both

- employees of the taxable person; or
- if the taxable person is a company, its directors or persons engaged in the management of the company

unless the provision of entertainment for such persons is incidental to its provision for others. [*SI 1992/3222, Art 5(3)*].

General scope

[10.2] Following on from the definition in **10.1** above, HMRC regard business entertainment as including

- provision of food and drink;
- provision of accommodation (hotels, etc.);
- provision of theatre and concert tickets;
- entry to sporting events and facilities;

- entry to clubs, nightclubs, etc.; and
- use of capital goods such as yachts and aircraft for the purpose of entertaining.

(VAT Notice 700/65/12, para 2.2).

See *C & E Commrs v Shaklee International and Another*, CA [1981] STC 776 (TVC 8.3) for the provision of food and accommodation for self-employed agents undergoing training; *BMW (GB) Ltd v C & E Commrs*, QB [1997] STC 824 (TVC 8.33) for hospitality provided to dealers and potential customers at 'track days' where vehicles could be test driven; *Medicare Research Ltd* (VTD 1045) (TVC 8.6) for refreshments and hospitality provided at business discussion meetings in the course of making taxable supplies; *Webster Communications International Ltd* (VTD 14753) (TVC 8.38) for meals and refreshments provided at sponsored conferences to delegates nominated by the sponsor and attending free of charge; *Wilsons Transport Ltd* (VTD 1468) (TVC 8.10) for launching parties; *Polash Tandoori Restaurant* [1993] Lexis Citation 3334 (TVC 8.21) for free drinks supplied to customers; and *William Matthew Mechanical Services Ltd* [1982] VATTR 63 (TVC 8.8) for subscription for theatre seats used to extend hospitality and entertainment to clients. However, if the entertainment is not given gratuitously but is provided under a contractual obligation, it does not fall within the scope of the provision. See *Celtic Football and Athletic Club Ltd v C & E Commrs*, CS [1983] STC 470 (TVC 8.35) and *C & E Commrs v Kilroy Television Company Ltd*, QB [1997] STC 901 (TVC 8.47).

Employees

[10.3] For business entertainment purposes, HMRC regard '*employee*' as including

- directors or anyone engaged in the management of the business (including partners);
- self-employed persons (subsistence expenses only) treated by the employer in the same way for subsistence purposes as an employee; and
- helpers, stewards and other people essential to the running of sporting or similar events

but not as including pensioners and former employees, job applicants and interviewees, and shareholders (who are not also employees).

(VAT Notice 700/65/12, paras 2.3, 2.4).

Staff entertainment

Following the decision in *Ernst & Young* (VTD 15100) (TVC 8.43) HMRC accept that where an employer provides entertainment for the benefit of its employees (e.g. to reward them for good work or to maintain and improve staff morale), it does so wholly for business purposes. Thus, the VAT incurred on entertainment of employees (e.g. staff parties, team building exercises, staff outings and similar events) is input tax and is not blocked from recovery under the business entertainment rules. There are two exceptions to this general rule.

- Where entertainment is provided only for directors, partners or sole proprietors of a business, the VAT incurred is not input tax as the goods or services are not used for a business purpose. But where directors, etc. attend staff parties together with other employees, HMRC accept that the VAT incurred is input tax and is not blocked from recovery.
- Where employees act as hosts to non-employees, the costs are incurred solely for the purpose of entertaining the non-employees and the input tax is blocked under the business entertainment rules.

(VAT Notice 700/65/12, paras 3.1–3.3).

Subsistence expenses

Where meals etc. are provided away from the place of work on a business trip, the VAT incurred on the employee's meal can be claimed as input tax under the subsistence rules (see **35.13**(26) **INPUT TAX**). (VAT Notice 700/65/12, para 2.5).

A useful concession is that input tax can also be claimed on subsistence expenses for self-employed workers (subcontractors etc.), even though they are not employees. However, a condition of the rules is that they must only be entitled to the same subsistence arrangements as employees.

Staff parties with guests, etc.

Where a business entertains both employees and non-employees, it can only recover as input tax the VAT it incurs on entertaining its employees. The portion of the input tax incurred in entertaining others is blocked under the business entertainment rules. (VAT Notice 700/65/12, para 3.4). In *KPMG (No 2)* (VTD 14962) (TVC 8.34) an accountancy firm organised dinner dances for its employees, each of whom was entitled to bring one guest. It was held that the related input tax should be apportioned on the basis that the proportion of the expenditure attributable to the guests constituted business entertainment. The entertainment of the non-employees could not be treated as incidental to the entertainment of the employees (in contrast to the specific provision made in the converse situation, see **10.1** above). This decision came after the decision in *Thorn EMI plc v C & E Commrs*, CA [1995] STC 674 (TVC 8.30) (see **10.4** below) that input tax relating to business entertainment can be apportioned. The decision in *KPMG (No 2)* was distinguished in *Ernst & Young* (VTD 15100) (TVC 8.43) where a charge of £15 per head was made for guests. The tribunal held that the crucial characteristic of 'entertainment' in the phrase 'business entertainment' was that it was provided free of charge. Although the £15 charge was considerably less than the cost of the party, it was not so small as to say the meal was provided free of charge.

Apportionment between business entertainment and other use

[10.4] In *Thorn EMI plc v C & E Commrs*, CA [1995] STC 674 (TVC 8.30), HMRC sought to exclude credit for all input tax on hospitality chalets constructed to receive customers at shows although accepting that the chalets were used partly for business purposes. It was held, upholding the decision in the High Court and reversing the decision in *C & E Commrs v Plant Repair*

& Services (South Wales) Ltd, QB [1994] STC 232 (TVC 8.30), that HMRC's approach was unreasonable. Applying the general principle in *Directive 2006/112/EC* (previously *EC 6th Directive, Art 17*), apportionment should be allowed. HMRC now accept this. (VAT Notice 700/65/12, para 2.7).

Consumable goods

Some goods may be used for a variety of purposes, e.g. food and drink may be used for trading stock or subsistence meals for employees (VAT fully recoverable) or business entertainment (VAT not recoverable). Where possible, stocks to be used for entertaining should be kept separately. If, however, it has not been decided how the goods will be used at the time of purchase, a record should be kept of goods used for entertainment so the input tax recoverable can be calculated at the end of each VAT period. This record forms part of the VAT records and should be available for inspection by visiting VAT officers.

Capital goods

Where a capital asset, such as a yacht or private aircraft, is used solely for business entertainment, the VAT incurred is not recoverable. If it is used for both business entertainment and other business purposes, the input tax must be apportioned.

Exceptions

[10.5] Details of exceptions from the business entertainment rules are shown in the table below.

Who is affected	*Scenario*	*Business entertainment position*
Recognised sporting body.	The 'body' provides through necessity free accommodation and meals to amateur sports persons and officials who attend an event.	Recovery of input tax allowed. This is not business entertainment.
Airlines.	The airlines provide catering and accommodation expenses for passengers who have been delayed.	Recovery of input tax allowed. This is not business entertainment. See *British Airways plc (No 3)*, (VTD 16446) (TVC 36.160).

(VAT Notice 700/65/12, para 2.8).

'Free' meals for coach drivers at motorway service stations

These are considered to be supplies made for consideration (the consideration being the coach driver's action in bringing passengers to the service station) on which output tax may be due. See **48.5 OUTPUT TAX** and *C & E Commrs v Westmorland Motorway Services Ltd*, CA [1998] STC 431 (TVC 67.152).

Amateur sports persons

[10.6] Amateur players are, by definition, not employees and input tax on business entertainment provided for them is therefore blocked. Where the entertainment is provided by a club out of players' subscriptions to it, input tax may be reclaimed under the provisions above for entertainment of members of clubs. Where, however, certain bodies choose, from affiliated clubs, individual amateur sports persons to represent their country or county, the persons selected are not full subscribing members of the representative body and therefore the provisions applying to clubs above cannot apply. By concession HMRC have agreed that input tax necessarily incurred on the provision of accommodation and meals for team members selected by such representative bodies, and committee members of that body, may be deductible as input tax. The concession does not cover alcoholic drinks and tobacco. (VAT Notice 48, ESC 3.10).

Supplies by a taxable person

[10.7] Special provisions as below apply where, as a result of **10.1** above, no input tax on goods or services used for business entertaining has been claimed and the taxable person subsequently supplies the goods or services in question.

Supplies of goods

Following the decision in *EC Commission v Italian Republic, ECJ Case C–45/95*, [1997] STC 1062 (TVC 22.392), where, as a result of **10.1** above, no input tax has been claimed by a taxable person on a supply, acquisition or importation of any *goods*, the disposal of those goods is an exempt supply under *VATA 1994, Sch 9 Group 14*, regardless of whether they are sold at a profit or loss. See **21.4 EXEMPT SUPPLIES.**

It should be noted that the provisions only apply where *no* input tax has been claimed (e.g. where a yacht or private aircraft is used solely for entertaining). Where, however, the asset was used for both entertaining and business purposes, on resale VAT must be accounted for on the full selling price. (VAT Notice 700/65/12, para 2.9).

Supplies of services

The *Italian Republic* decision is regarded by HMRC as only applicable to goods, so *VATA 1994, Sch 9 Group 14* does not exempt supplies of services in similar circumstances. Where, as a result of **10.1** above, a taxable person has claimed no input tax on a supply of any services to him, VAT must be charged on a supply by him of those services as if made for a consideration equal to the excess of

(a) the consideration for which the services are supplied by him, over
(b) the consideration for which they were supplied to him.

Where (*b*) is greater than (*a*), the supply is treated as outside the scope of VAT. [*SI 1992/3222, Art 5(2)*].

Overseas customers

[10.8] In the light of the CJEU judgment in *Danfoss A/S v Skatteministeriet (and related appeal), ECJ Case C-371/07*, [2009] STC 701 (TVC 22.206), HMRC concluded that the UK's block on the recovery of input tax on the business entertainment of overseas clients, introduced in 1988 after the *6th VAT Directive* took effect in the UK, was inconsistent with EU law. Consequently the legislation was amended to permit input tax recovery in relation to the entertainment of 'overseas customers' if it is of a reasonable kind and on a reasonable scale (see below). [*SI 1992/3222, Art 5(1)*]. An overseas customer, in relation to a taxable person, is

(a) any person who is not ordinarily resident nor carrying on a business in the United Kingdom or the Isle of Man and avails himself or herself, or may be expected to avail himself or herself, in the course of a business carried on by that person outside the United Kingdom and the Isle of Man, of any goods or services the supply of which forms part of the taxable person's business; and

(b) any person who is not ordinarily resident in the United Kingdom or the Isle of Man and is acting, in relation to such goods or services, on behalf of an overseas customer as defined in paragraph (*a*) above or on behalf of any government or public authority outside the United Kingdom and the Isle of Man.

Private use charge

Two cases, *Julius Fillibeck Sohne GmbH & Co KG, ECJ Case C-258/95*, [1998] STC 513 (TVC 22.204) and *Danfoss A/S, ECJ Case C-371/07*, [2009] STC 701 (TVC 22.206), introduce separate tests that should be applied when considering private use of the business expenditure.

In the *Fillibeck Sohne* case an employer provided transport to his staff to get them from their homes to a construction site. As commuting expenditure is private, the CJEU was asked to consider whether having recovered tax on the cost of the transport it was appropriate to apply a charge to reflect the private use by the employees. The CJEU's starting point was that a charge applied in principle, but on the particular facts of the case it was practically impossible for the employees to get to the site on their own, and therefore a private use charge should not be applied. Following that decision, HMRC have stated that the 'necessity test' is whether it is necessary for the taxable person to provide goods or services that are enjoyed privately in order for him to make his taxable supplies.

The *Danfoss* case involved the provision of free meals to both employees and business contacts. In the context of the business having recovered VAT on the meals, the CJEU was asked to consider whether it was appropriate to apply a private use charge. The CJEU concluded that where the meals were provided for a strict business purpose no such charge should arise. In reaching this conclusion they carefully considered the circumstances of the free meals, in particular the lack of choice by the recipient of what, when and where to eat, the relatively basic nature of the fare and crucially the fact that the meals were provided to ensure the smooth running of business meetings. This, according to HMRC, is the 'strict business purpose test'.

Example 1

For a meeting, if normal basic food and refreshments such as sandwiches and soft drinks are provided in the office to enable the meeting to proceed without interruption, then a private use charge will not apply. If there is no other alternative than to hold a meeting outside the office, only similar basic provisions would be allowable. Hospitality provided following a meeting will not meet the strict business purpose test and neither will hospitality involving the provision of alcohol. Taking a customer to a restaurant is very likely to lead to a private use charge.

Example 2

At corporate hospitality events, many businesses offer their customers or potential customers general entertainment and hospitality. Examples include: golf days; track days; trips to sporting events; evening meals; or trips to nightclubs. Where the related expenditure is incurred for the purpose of the business, and recovered, an output tax charge will be due. This is because such events are unlikely to have a strict business purpose or be necessary for the business to make its supplies.

(VAT Notice 700/65/12, para 2.6).

Key points: business entertainment

[10.9] Points to consider are as follows.

- Input tax can be reclaimed on the costs of entertaining staff, unless the role of staff members is to act as host at an event for non-employees. This provision is intended to recognise that the entertaining of staff can be a key component of rewarding good work or loyalty, i.e. as a motivational tool. Input tax can therefore be claimed on the costs of office Christmas parties, staff outings and other social events provided to employees.
- Input tax cannot be reclaimed on the costs of entertaining if they are relevant to either a director of a company or business owner (sole trader, partner). The exception to this rule is if the director or owner is attending an event that is open to all staff (annual Christmas party etc.), in which case input tax can be claimed.
- Entertaining is only applicable if it is provided without charge. If a charge is made to attend an event, e.g. a charge for the spouses of employees to attend the firm's Christmas party, then input tax

can be reclaimed on the costs and output tax will then be due on the payments received from the individuals in question. This is a useful planning opportunity – the charge to the non-employees does not need to cover the full cost of attending the event, i.e. input tax claimed can exceed output tax declared on the payments received.

- If entertaining is provided as part of a contractual obligation, then the input tax block does not apply. So if an overseas football team needs to be provided with food and accommodation by its UK opponents as a condition of a competition rule, then this is not business entertainment in the traditional sense (the entertainer has no choice) and input tax can therefore be claimed on these expenses.
- Input tax can be claimed on the costs of food and drink provided at 'business meetings' where some of the delegates are overseas customers – see **10.8** above. HMRC have issued guidance on these points.

11

Capital Goods Scheme

Cross-references. See **38.1 INTERACTION WITH OTHER TAXES** for the effect on capital allowances where adjustments are made to input tax deduction under the capital goods scheme.

De Voil Indirect Tax Service. See V3.470.

Introduction to the capital goods scheme

[11.1] The capital goods scheme (CGS) applies to certain items of capital expenditure on computer equipment, land and buildings, civil engineering works and refurbishments and fitting-out works which are acquired or brought into use and which are not used wholly for making taxable supplies. It also applies to certain ships and aircraft obtained on or after 1 January 2011. The scheme recognises that such items of capital expenditure can be used by a business over a number of years and that there may be variation over those years in the extent to which the items are used to make taxable supplies. It provides a mechanism whereby the initial input tax claimed can be adjusted over a period of up to ten years. Because adjustments are required over such a long period, it is necessary to bear in mind the possibility that different rules applied to the purchase of an item that is under consideration in the current period. There were significant changes to the CGS in 2011; land and buildings acquired before that date may still be subject to adjustment under the previous version of the rules.

When a capital item within the scheme (see **11.2** below) is acquired, the normal rules for claiming input tax apply, i.e.

- if it is used wholly in making taxable supplies, input tax is recoverable in full;

- if it is used wholly in making exempt supplies, none of the input tax is recoverable; and
- if it is used for making taxable and exempt supplies, a proportion of the input tax may be claimed under the partial exemption rules.

Where, subsequently, in the adjustment period for that item (see **11.3** below) there is a change in the extent of taxable use, an input tax adjustment has to be made to take account of this. If taxable use increases, a further amount of input tax can be claimed and, if it decreases, some of the input tax already claimed must be repaid.

With effect from 1 January 2011, the CGS also takes into account fluctuations in the extent to which a capital item within the scheme is used for business/non-business purposes. This effectively replaces, for such items, the 'Lennartz' method of adjustment described in **35.7**.

Capital items within the scheme

[11.2] Capital items to which the CGS applies are any items within (*a*)-(*f*) and (i)-(vii) below which the owner (or person who holds an interest) uses in the course or furtherance of a business carried on by him, and for the purpose of that business. The scheme does not apply to assets acquired or expenditure on assets held solely for resale (e.g. stock-in-trade). However, if an asset is used in the business before it is sold, it is no longer treated as an asset held solely for resale and the CGS will apply; conversely if a capital item is acquired for use in the business but is sold before being used, it is no longer treated as a capital item.

All values are VAT-exclusive. Where, prior to 1 January 2011, any capital item is only partly used for business purposes, if all the VAT incurred is treated as input tax and output tax is accounted for on the non-business use (the 'Lennartz approach', see **35.7 INPUT TAX**), the value of the capital item is the full tax-exclusive value of the item. Otherwise, if VAT incurred is apportioned between business and non-business use, the value of the capital item is the VAT-exclusive value of the part attributed to business activities. In respect of capital assets obtained on or after 1 January 2011, non-business use is accounted for under the scheme and hence the value in question is the full tax-exclusive value.

From 1 January 2011

(a) Land, where the owner incurs VAT bearing capital expenditure on its acquisition, the value of which is at least £250,000.

(b) A building or part of a building, where the owner incurs VAT bearing capital expenditure on its acquisition, construction, refurbishment, fitting out, alteration or extension, the value of which is at least £250,000.

(c) Civil engineering work or part of a civil engineering work, where the owner incurs VAT bearing capital expenditure on its acquisition, construction, refurbishment, fitting out, alteration or extension, the value of which is at least £250,000.

(d) A computer or item of computer equipment, where the owner incurs VAT bearing capital expenditure on its acquisition, the value of which is at least £50,000.

(e) An aircraft, where the owner incurs VAT bearing capital expenditure on its acquisition, construction, refurbishment, fitting out, alteration or extension, the value of which is at least £50,000.

(f) A ship, boat or other vessel, where the owner incurs VAT bearing capital expenditure on its acquisition, construction, refurbishment, fitting out, alteration or extension, the value of which is at least £50,000.

From 1 October 2012 where

- the owner of land, a building (or part of), or a civil engineering work (or part of) (or a person to whom he has granted an interest in that item) uses that item to make a grant that falls within *VATA 1994, Sch 9, Group 1, item 1(ka)* (self-storage facilities excluded from exemption);
- the owner has, no later than 31 March 2013, decided to treat the item (which would not otherwise be a capital item) as a capital item; and
- has made a written record of that decision specifying the date it was made,

then £250,000 is substituted by £1. No adjustment of deductions of input tax should be made for any intervals ending before 1 October 2012 that fall within the period of adjustment for the capital item.

This is to enable businesses affected by the change in the liability of the grant of self-storage facilities with effect from 1 October 2012 (see **42.18**(*l*) **LAND AND BUILDINGS: EXEMPT SUPPLIES AND OPTION TO TAX**) to recover the input tax on buildings that are not otherwise capital items, and which are used to provide self-storage facilities. Without this provision, input tax on such buildings incurred before the change in liability would be irrecoverable as exempt input tax. [*SI 1995/2518, Reg 113A; SI 2012/1899, Reg 17*].

Prior to 1 January 2011

(i) A computer, or an item of computer equipment, worth £50,000 or more supplied to, or acquired or imported by, the owner.
Any delivery or installation costs should be included unless invoiced separately. If imported, the value for VAT at importation (including import duty) should be taken.
The scheme applies only to individual computers and items of computer equipment, not to complete networks. *Excluded* are
  - computerised equipment, e.g. a computerised telephone exchange or computer-controlled blast furnace; and
  - computer software.

> *Example*
> A VAT-registered business buys 60 computers on one purchase invoice costing £1,000 each plus VAT. This expenditure is not relevant to the CGS because each computer is considered as a capital item in its own right, i.e. the relevant figure is £1,000 not £60,000.

(ii) Land, a building or part of a building or a civil engineering work or part of a civil engineering work where the value of the interest supplied to the owner, by a taxable supply other than a zero-rated supply, is £250,000 or more. When determining whether the value of the supply is £250,000 or more
- any part of that value consisting of rent (including charges reserved as rent) is excluded provided that it is neither payable nor paid more than twelve months in advance nor invoiced for a period in excess of twelve months; and
- any associated costs (e.g. legal or estate agency fees) should be excluded.

(iii) A building or part of a building where the owner's interest in, right over or licence to occupy it is treated as self-supplied to him under the provisions in **43.1 LAND AND BUILDINGS: ZERO AND REDUCED RATE SUPPLIES AND DIY HOUSEBUILDERS** (change of use of residential or charitable buildings).
The value of the supply, as determined under the respective provisions, must be £250,000 or more. See also *C & E Commrs v Trustees for R & R Pension Fund* QB, [1996] STC 889 (TVC 6.52).

(iv) A building or part of a building where the owner's interest in, right over or licence to occupy was, on or before 1 March 1997, treated as supplied to him under the developer's self-supply charge and the value of that supply was £250,000 or more.

(v) A building not falling, or capable of falling, within (iii) or (iv) above constructed by the owner where the aggregate of
- the value of taxable grants relating to the land on which the building is constructed made to the owner after that date, and
- the value of all the taxable supplies of goods and services, other than any that are zero-rated, made or to be made to him for, or in connection with, the construction of the building after that date

is £250,000 or more.

(vi) A building which the owner alters, or an extension or an annexe which he constructs, where additional floor area is created in the altered building, extension or annexe, of 10% or more of the original floor area before the work was carried out. The value of all taxable supplies of goods and services, other than any that are zero-rated, made or to be made to the owner for, or in connection with, the alteration, etc. must be £250,000 or more.

(vii) A civil engineering work constructed by the owner where the aggregate of

- the value of taxable grants relating to the land on which the civil engineering work is constructed made to the owner, and
- the value of all the taxable supplies of goods and services, other than any that are zero-rated, made or to be made to him for, or in connection with, the construction of the civil engineering work

is £250,000 or more.

Civil engineering work should be given its everyday meaning and includes such items as roads, bridges, golf courses, running tracks and installation of pipes for connection to mains services.

(viii) A building which the owner refurbishes or fits out where the value of capital expenditure on the taxable supplies of services and of 'goods affixed' to the building, other than any that are zero-rated, made or to be made to the owner for, or in connection with, the refurbishment or fitting out in question is £250,000 or more.

'*Goods affixed*' should be given its everyday meaning. Usually, this includes items of fixtures and fittings and interior decoration that are not easily portable or easily removed. In general terms, these are items that would be sold with the property. Common inclusions (although the deciding factor will be whether the item becomes part of the fabric of the building) are

- materials to build internal and external walls, roofs and ceilings and floors and hard flooring;
- permanent partitioning;
- windows;
- lifts;
- 'built-in' storage such as cupboards or shelving;
- air conditioning;
- lighting; and
- decorative features.

It excludes items secured to the floor for safety or security reasons. Common exclusions are

- office furniture;
- storage unless 'built in';
- carpets;
- computers and computer equipment; and
- factory and office machinery.

Where it is difficult or costly to identify the value of goods affixed from the value of other goods which do not become affixed to the property, by concession, businesses may include any additional amount of capital expenditure (over and above that incurred on items affixed to the building) incurred in connection with the refurbishment, etc. in the total value of capital expenditure for the purposes of the CGS. The concessionary value must then be used in calculating adjustments to the claimed input tax for the whole of the adjustment period. This applies even if those items not affixed have been disposed of (unless they are disposed of as part of the disposal of the whole interest in the building when a final adjustment must be made in the normal way). Businesses must keep a record of the concessionary value of the capital expenditure, including full details of the supplies on which the value was determined. HMRC may withdraw the concession or restrict its use if it considers that it is being used to avoid VAT.

Phased refurbishments/developments are those undertaken in stages. Whether, for the purposes of the CGS, a phased refurbishment/development should be treated as a whole or as more than one refurbishment/development will usually be a matter of fact. Indicators that there is more than one refurbishment might be

- separate contracts for each phase of the work or a contract where each phase is a separate option which can be selected; and
- each phase is completed before work on the next phase starts.

If the refurbishment is of one building only and is only 'phased' because the contractors have to do one floor at a time since the building remains occupied throughout, this would usually indicate there is only one refurbishment.

The issue of whether a phased development came within the scope of the CGS was the subject of *Water Property Ltd* [2016] UKFTT 721 (TC) (TC05450) (TVC 6.14). In this case, the WPL acquired land and buildings and the cost of acquiring the building and each stage of the phased development works to create a children's nursery and two flats did not exceed £250,000. However, the total aggregated cost did exceed the CGS threshold. HMRC considered that it was a capital item. The tribunal ruled in favour of the taxpayer, stating that in this case the development costs for each phase were financed using different means, there were separate contracts in place for each phase and there was no overlap in time between phases. Therefore, the property was not a capital item for the purposes of the CGS.

> ***Example***
>
> A company is to undertake a big office refurbishment project costing £300,000 excluding VAT, analysed as follows.
>
> - new windows and air conditioning system £170,000;
> - new office furniture £130,000.
>
> The project is outside the CGS because the value of the building related supplies (windows and air-conditioning system) is less than £250,000.

What is capital expenditure?

'Capital expenditure' is normally expenditure capitalised for accounting purposes. HMRC will not normally challenge a business's capitalisation policy for the purposes of the CGS, except in cases of avoidance or abuse. In some cases charities may incur expenditure of a capital nature on land and property which is not capitalised in their accounts (e.g. certain heritage buildings, churches etc.). This is generally because the charity does not have unfettered freedom to exploit or dispose of the land or property concerned. This will not prevent expenditure that is essentially capital in nature from being adjusted under the CGS.

Value of capital item

The value of a capital item is the VAT-exclusive value of the item. Only the value of standard or reduced-rated taxable supplies is considered. Before 1 January 2011, the value of a capital item was determined by reference to the business-related expenditure. With effect from 1 January 2011, the value is determined by reference to total expenditure on an asset. This includes both business and non-business expenditure on an asset.

> *Example*
>
> A business purchases a building for £1 million and incurs £200,000 VAT. The building is to be used for 60% business purposes and 40% non-business purposes (e.g. charitable use). Before 1 January 2011, £600,000 (60% of £1 million) determined the value for CGS purposes. Under the new rules that took effect from 1 January 2011, all of the expenditure on the building (£1 million) is the value for CGS purposes. As the CGS threshold for buildings remains at £250,000, the building is a capital item in both scenarios.

Expenditure incurred before and after 1 January 2011

Where expenditure was incurred on a particular capital item both before and after 1 January 2011, it is necessary to determine the amount of business-related expenditure incurred on the asset up to 31 December 2010 and the total amount of expenditure (business and non-business) incurred on or after 1 January 2011. If the sum of these amounts exceeds the relevant CGS threshold, the asset falls within the CGS.

Adjustable amount of VAT

Prior to 1 January 2011, only VAT on the business-related expenditure on an asset (i.e. input tax) fell within the CGS. With effect from 1 January 2011, all of the VAT on an asset (in this instance input tax and non-business VAT) falls within the CGS.

> *Example*
>
> Following on from the above example; prior to 1 January 2011, input tax of £105,000 (17.5% of £600,000) fell within the CGS. With effect from 1 January 2011, VAT of £175,000 (17.5% of £1 million), or £200,000 (20% of £1 million, if the expenditure was incurred after the VAT rate increase on 4 January 2011) falls within the CGS.

If expenditure is incurred both before and after 1 January 2011, the VAT on the business-related expenditure incurred up to 31 December 2010 and the total VAT incurred on the asset on or after 1 January 2011 fall within the CGS.

Estimated values

If a business does not know whether a project exceeds the value threshold for the CGS until all invoices have been received it will need to estimate the value of the supplies it has received. This may happen with construction projects and refurbishments where VAT is incurred over a period of time and also with contracts that include a retention clause. A retention clause involves a proportion of the contract price being held back and only paid when the work has been satisfactorily completed. If, when a business starts the CGS, it estimates that the value of relevant supplies will exceed the value threshold, the item will become a capital item. Even if it finds later on that the value does not reach the threshold, the item remains in the scheme and it should continue to make adjustments as necessary. If a business does estimate the value of a capital item it will need to keep all the documents it based its estimation on, such as a contract, as HMRC may ask to see it.

Value of land or buildings acquired

A business should only include the value of the interest in the land and/or building supplied to it, if the supply was taxable and not zero-rated. It should not include any associated costs such as legal or estate agency fees. In calculating the value of the interest, it does not need to include the value of any rent or service charges unless

- it has been paid or is payable more than 12 months in advance; or
- it is invoiced by the supplier for a period of more than 12 months. In that case, it should include the value of rent/service charges when calculating the value of the capital item.

Value of constructed building or civil engineering work

The business should include the total VAT-exclusive cost of any of the following supplies made to it.

- The interest in the land, if the supply to it was taxable (other than zero-rated).
- Taxable (other than zero-rated) goods and services supplied for, or in connection with, the construction of the building or civil engineering work.

All the costs involved in making the building ready should be included, such as

- professional and managerial services including architects, surveyors and site management;
- demolition and site clearance;
- building and civil engineering contractors' services;
- materials used in the construction;
- security;
- equipment hire;
- haulage;
- landscaping; and
- fitting out, including the value of any fixtures.

Alteration, extension or annex

Where the value of the goods and services received is £250,000 or more, the total value of all taxable (other than zero-rated) goods or services supplied to the business for, or in connection with, the alteration, extension or annex should be included in the value of the alteration, extension or annex. All the costs involved in making the building or civil engineering work ready should be included.

Refurbishment or fit out

If a capital item is refurbished or fitted out, the value should only include the value of capital expenditure on the taxable (other than zero-rated) supply of services and of goods affixed to the building or civil engineering work supplied for or in connection with the refurbishment or fit out.

What are 'goods affixed' to building?

These are goods which become part of the fabric of the building. Generally these are items that are sold with the property and are not portable or easily removed. 'Goods affixed' does not include items secured for safety or security reasons or computers or computer equipment. These may be subject to the CGS in their own right. The deciding factor is usually whether the item becomes part of the fabric of the building. Common inclusions are

- materials to build;
- internal and external walls;
- roofs and ceilings;
- floors and hard flooring;
- permanent partitioning;
- windows;
- lifts;
- 'built in' storage such as cupboards or shelving;
- air conditioning;
- lighting; and
- decorative features.

Common exclusions are

- office furniture;
- storage unless it is 'built in';
- carpets;
- computers and computer equipment; and
- factory and office machinery.

For capital items where the capital costs are incurred on or after 1 January 2011 there is no longer a requirement for goods used for a refurbishment to be affixed to a building. For capital items where the capital costs were incurred before 1 January 2011, this treatment is already allowed in relation to the 'goods affixed' condition by concession (ESC 3.22) and is adopted by most businesses.

Refurbishment in phases

If the refurbishment is in phases, the business will need to decide whether the work should be treated as a whole for CGS purposes or whether there is more than one refurbishment. If it thinks that each phase is really a separate refurbishment then they should be treated separately for CGS purposes. Normally there is more than one refurbishment when

- there are separate contracts for each phase of the work; or
- there is a contract where each phase is a separate option which can be selected; and
- each phase of work is completed before work on the next phase starts.

A refurbishment which is only undertaken in phases because the building is occupied and where the contractors work on one floor at a time is normally considered to be only one refurbishment.

Regular refurbishments

Regular refurbishments are sometimes referred to as 'rolling refurbishments'. Problems may occur if successive refurbishments begin before each adjustment period has expired. If this happens the business should either

- treat the original refurbishment as destroyed if there is nothing left of the earlier refurbishment or this earlier work is stripped out or replaced. The effect of this is that no further adjustments would be required to the input tax on the previous refurbishment; or
- continue to make adjustments for the remainder of the adjustment period if elements of the earlier refurbishment are retained.

Value of computers

The value of computers should include any delivery and installation costs, unless these are supplied separately. If a business imports a computer it should use the value for VAT at importation. This will include any import duty payable.

[*SI 1995/2518, Regs 112, 113.*] (VAT Notice 706/2/18, paras 3.1–4.14).

The adjustment period

From 1 January 2011

[11.3] The adjustment period is normally

- ten successive intervals in the case of: land, a (or part of a) building or a (or part of a) civil engineering work;
- five successive intervals in the case of: a computer or item of computer equipment, an aircraft, or a ship, boat or other vessel.

Adjustment period exceeding period of owner's interest

If, at the time of the owner's first use, the number of intervals exceeds the number of complete years that the owner's interest in the capital item has to run by more than one, the number of intervals should be reduced to one more than the number of complete years that the owner's interest has to run, calculated from the date of the owner's first use (but not to less than three intervals). In such a case, the denominator in the fraction for the method of adjustment (see **11.6** below) should be adjusted accordingly.

Ownership before VAT registration

Where a person who registers for VAT already owns the capital item, for the purposes of calculating the period of adjustment

- one complete interval should be deducted for each complete year that has elapsed since the date of that person's first use of the capital item prior to the date of registration; and
- the first interval applicable to the capital item that ends after the date of registration should be treated as a subsequent interval (see **11.5** below).

[*SI 1995/2518, Reg 114*].

Prior to 1 January 2011

The adjustment period is the period of time in which the business must review the extent to which a capital item is used in making taxable supplies. It consists of

- five successive intervals for
  - (i) computers, etc. under **11.2**(i) above, and
  - (ii) land, buildings and civil engineering works under **11.2**(ii) above where the interest has less than ten years to run at the time it is supplied to the owner (e.g. an eight-year lease); and
- ten successive intervals for all other land and buildings not within (ii) above.

[*SI 1995/2518, Reg 114(3)*].

First interval

From 1 January 2011

[11.4] Subject to the special case below, the rules relating to the transfer of a business as a going concern (see **11.12**(4) below), and the rules relating to the groups of companies (see **11.12**(5) below), the first interval commences on the day on which the owner first uses the capital item and ends on the day before the start of his next tax year, whether or not this is his first tax year.

[*SI 1995/2518, Reg 114(4).*] (VAT Notice 706/2/18, para 6.4).

Prior to 1 January 2011

Subject to the special case below, the rules relating to the transfer of a business as a going concern (see **11.12**(4) below) and the rules relating the groups of companies (see **11.12**(5) below), the first interval commences, as the case may be,

- where the owner is a registered person when he imports, acquires or is supplied with the item as a capital item (or when he appropriates an item to use as a capital item), the date of importation, acquisition, supply or appropriation,
- where the capital item falls within **11.2**(iii) above, on the date of the self-supply under those provisions,
- where the capital item falls within **11.2**(iv) above, on the day the owner first used the building (or part of the building),
- where the capital item falls within **11.2**(v)–(viii) above, on the date that the owner first uses the building, altered building, extension, annexe, civil engineering work or building which has been refurbished or fitted out

and ends on the day before the start of the owner's tax year following that date, i.e. it normally runs to the following 31 March, 30 April or 31 May depending upon his VAT periods, see **50.13 PARTIAL EXEMPTION.**

'*Use*' includes any use in the business. For buildings, it usually consists of the granting of a lease or physical occupation. 'First use' will be the time that any part of the constructed, altered, extended, refurbished or fitted out building is used.

Where the owner is not registered when he first uses an item as a capital item

- if he subsequently becomes a registered person, the first interval commences on his effective date of registration and ends on the following 31 March, 30 April or 31 May depending upon the VAT period allocated to him; and
- if he is subsequently treated as a member of a group for VAT purposes (see **28 GROUPS OF COMPANIES**), the first interval corresponds with, or is that part still remaining of, the then current tax year of the group.

[*SI 1995/2518, Reg 114(4)*.] (VAT Notice 706/2/18, para 6.4).

Special case — extended first interval

Where

- the extent to which a capital item is used in making taxable supplies does not change between what would otherwise have been the first interval and the first subsequent interval under **11.5** below, and
- the length of the two intervals taken together does not exceed twelve months

the first interval applicable to the capital item ends on what otherwise would have been the end of the first subsequent interval, i.e. the two periods are combined to become the first interval.

[*SI 1995/2518, Reg 114(5B)*].

Subsequent intervals

[11.5] Subject to the rules relating to the transfer of a business as a going concern (see **11.12**(4) below) and the rules relating the groups of companies (see **11.12**(5) below), each subsequent interval after the first interval corresponds with a longer period applicable to the owner or, if no longer period applies, a tax year. In either case this will normally run to the following 31 March, 30 April or 31 May depending upon the owner's VAT periods, but see **50.13 PARTIAL EXEMPTION** for exceptions. [*SI 1995/2518, Reg 114(5)*].

Method of adjustment

[11.6] Where the extent to which a capital item is used in making taxable supplies in a subsequent interval increases or decreases from the extent to which it was so used (or to be used) at the time the original entitlement to deduction of the input tax was determined under the partial exemption rules, an adjustment is required. This is calculated by the formula

$$\frac{\text{Total input tax on the capital item}}{A} \times \text{the adjustment \%}$$

where

A = usually 5 or 10 depending on the number of intervals in the period of adjustment (see **11.3** above)

From 1 January 2011, '*total input tax on the capital item*' means

- in relation to any capital item, all VAT incurred by the owner on the capital expenditure on that item, including any non-business VAT; and
- where a person is treated as making a supply to himself under *VATA 1994, Sch 10, para 37(1)*, the VAT charged on that supply.

Prior to 1 January 2011, '*total input tax on the capital item*' means

- for a capital item within **11.2**(i) or (ii) above, VAT charged on the supply, acquisition or importation. Any VAT charged on rent (including charges reserved as rent) is excluded unless it is payable or paid more than twelve months in advance or invoiced for a period in excess of twelve months;
- for a capital item within **11.2**(iii) or **11.2**(iv) above, the VAT charged on the supply which the owner is treated as making to himself; and
- for a capital item under **11.2**(v)–(viii) above, the aggregate of the VAT charged on the supplies described, other than VAT charged on rent (if any)

and includes any VAT treated as input tax under the rules relating to pre-registration or pre-incorporation input tax (see **35.10 INPUT TAX**).

'*The adjustment %*' is the difference (if any), expressed as a percentage, between the extent to which the whole or part of the capital item

- was used or to be used for making taxable supplies at the time the original entitlement to deduction of the input tax was determined under the partial exemption rules; and
- is so used, or treated as used as the result of a disposal under **11.7** below, in the subsequent interval in question.

Where the owner of a building within these provisions grants or assigns a tenancy or lease in the whole or part of the building and the premium (or if no premium is payable the first payment of rent) is zero-rated, any subsequent exempt supply arising from the grant (e.g. rent) is disregarded in determining the extent to which the building is used in making taxable supplies.

The percentage is

- 100% where the item is used wholly for making taxable supplies;
- 0% where it is used wholly for making exempt supplies; and
- where it is used for making both taxable and exempt supplies, normally the claimable percentage of residual input tax following the partial exemption annual adjustment for the respective year (see **50.13 PARTIAL**

EXEMPTION) (although HMRC may allow, or direct, the use of another method). Where the standard method is used (see **50.4 PARTIAL EXEMPTION**) the same percentage applies to the whole of the residual input tax. If a special method is used (see **50.10 PARTIAL EXEMPTION**) involving different calculations for different parts of the business, the percentage to be used is that which applies to the part of the business in which the capital item is used.

Where different percentages are used for different parts of the business, the percentage to be used is that for the part of the business in which the item is used.

[*SI 1995/2518, Reg 115(1)(2)(5), Reg 116*]. (VAT Notice 706/2/18, para 7.4).

Disposals of capital items during the adjustment period

[11.7] From 1 January 2011, the provisions below also apply to the part disposal of a capital item. Therefore references in this paragraph to the supply of a capital item cover the supply of whole or part of a capital item. [*SI 1995/2518, Reg 115(3)*].

If a capital item is sold without ever having been used, HMRC do not regard it as a capital item for the purposes of the CGS. Otherwise, where, during an interval other than the last interval, the owner of a capital item either

- supplies it, or
- is deemed to supply it on ceasing to be a taxable person (see **60.40 REGISTRATION**), or
- would have been deemed to supply it on ceasing to be a taxable person but for the fact that VAT on the deemed supply would not have been more than the amount specified in **60.40**(*c*) **REGISTRATION** (whether by virtue of its value or because it is zero-rated or exempt),

then

(a) if that supply is a taxable supply, the owner is treated as having used the capital item for each of the remaining *complete* intervals wholly in the making of taxable supplies; and

(b) if that supply is an exempt supply, he is treated as not using the capital item for each of the remaining *complete* intervals in making any taxable supplies.

The effect of this is as follows.

For the interval in which the capital item is sold, the adjustment is calculated (or, if it is the first interval, input tax is reclaimed) in the normal way under **11.6** above *as if the capital item had been in use for the whole of that interval.*

For any remaining complete intervals in the adjustment period, the recovery percentage will be 100% where (*a*) above applies or 0% where (*b*) above applies, but subject to the following proviso.

Proviso

Unless HMRC allow otherwise (see below), a 'disposal test' applies. Where the total amount of input tax deducted or deductible by the owner of a capital item as a result of

- the input tax initially recovered on the capital item;
- any adjustments already made under the CGS; and
- any final adjustment that is required as a result of the sale of the item

would exceed the output tax chargeable on the supply of the capital item, then the owner must pay to HMRC, or as the case may be may deduct, such an amount as results in the total input tax deducted or deductible being equal to the output tax chargeable on the supply of the whole or part of the capital item.

The 'disposal test' is an anti-avoidance measure to ensure that partly exempt businesses such as banks, insurance companies, educational establishments, sports clubs and providers of private healthcare do not obtain an unjustified tax advantage, for example, by making a substantial exempt supply of a long lease of a property followed immediately by the taxable disposal of the freehold for low consideration. HMRC do not intend that the disposal test should be applied to *bona fide* commercial transactions. Given the policy objective, the disposal test will not be applied

- to sales of computer equipment;
- where the owner disposes of an item at a loss due to the market conditions (such as a general downturn in property prices);
- where the value of the capital item has depreciated (as is normally the case with computers);
- where the value of the capital item is reduced for other legitimate reasons (such as accepting a low price for a quick sale);
- where the amount of output tax on disposal is less than the total input tax only because of a reduction in the VAT rate; and
- where the item is used only for taxable (including zero-rated) purposes throughout the adjustment period (which includes the final disposal).

Where there is no unjustified tax advantage, a business need not apply these provisions and it is not necessary to apply to HMRC for a specific ruling. Where there is an unjustified tax advantage, a business must calculate the net tax advantage (i.e. the overall benefit derived from the avoidance device, normally the amount of input tax that would still be subject to adjustment under the scheme were it not for the sale of the capital item less any output tax due on the sale) and then work out how much of the net tax advantage is unjustified. Normally this could be achieved by using the ratio that the value of the final taxable sale bears to the value of both the exempt supply and the final taxable sale.

Example 1

A partly-exempt business purchases a computer for £100,000 (plus £20,000 VAT at 20%). For the first three periods it is used for making taxable and exempt supplies. In the fourth period it is sold for £10,000 plus VAT. The percentages of taxable use are as follows.

Interval 1	48%
Interval 2	51%
Interval 3	43%

Interval 4 (until sale) 45%

Interval 1

Initial input tax claim

£20,000 × 48% = £9,600

Interval 2

Additional input tax claimed

£20,000 ÷ 5 × (51 – 48)% = £120

Interval 3

Input tax repayable

£20,000 ÷ 5 × (48 – 43)% = £200

Interval 4

Input tax repayable

£20,000 ÷ 5 × (48 – 45)% = £120

Interval 5

Additional input tax claimed

£20,000 ÷ 5 × (100 – 48)% = £2,080

but restricted under proviso (1) above to £10,000 × 20%* = £2,000

A final adjustment of £1,880 (£2,000 – £120) should be made in respect of interval 4.

Example 2

A developer, whose tax year ends on 31 March, completes a commercial development on 1 June 2013 at a cost of £25 million plus VAT of £5,000,000. The developer opts to tax the property and leases it for two years to a third party tenant at market value plus VAT. On 1 June 2015 the developer grants a 99 year lease at a premium of £24 million and a peppercorn rent to its wholly-owned subsidiary which is wholly exempt. On 1 May 2016 the developer sells the freehold, subject to the 99 year lease, for £250,000 plus VAT of £50,000 to the wholly owned subsidiary.

Interval 1 (to 31 March 2014). The developer can initially deduct all the VAT incurred on the development because of the option to tax.

Interval 2 (to 31 March 2015). No adjustment is required for interval 2 as the building continues to be let under a taxable lease.

Interval 3 (to 31 March 2016). On the grant of the lease, *VATA 1994, Sch 10 para 2(3AA)* operates so as to disapply the developer's option to tax and the premium is not subject to VAT. An adjustment in respect of 1/10th (£500,000) of the initial input tax incurred is required at the end of interval 3. On the basis of that during that interval the property was used for taxable purposes for two months and exempt purposes of ten months, VAT of £416,667 (305/366 × £500,000) must be paid back to HMRC.

Interval 4 (to 31 March 2017). The sale of the property on 1 May 2016 is compulsorily standard-rated under *VATA 1994, Sch 9 Group 1 Item 1(a)* as it is less than three years old (see **42.18**(*a*) LAND AND BUILDINGS: EXEMPT SUPPLIES AND OPTION TO TAX). Output tax is therefore due of £50,000 (£250,000 × 20%).

Since the building is only used for exempt purposes up to the sale, an adjustment in respect of the full 1/10th (£500,000) of the initial input tax incurred is required.

Intervals 5–10. Since the output tax on the sale of the freehold is less than the input tax claimed in the adjustment period, the disposal test applies. In this instance there is an unjustified tax advantage because the high value exempt grant in interval 3 enables a low value taxable sale of the freehold. At the same time the taxable sale enables full recovery of input tax in respect of the six remaining intervals 5–10. In principle £4,033,333 would be due as follows

Interval	Input tax claim	Output tax declared	Cumulative difference
	£	£	£
1	5,000,000	–	5,000,000
2	–	–	5,000,000
3	(416,667)		4,583,333
4	(500,000)	(50,000)	4,033,333
5–10			4,033,333

However, the net tax advantage is that the developer is able to secure the amount of input tax that would still be subject to adjustment under the scheme for intervals 5–10 were it not for the sale of the property (6/10ths of £5,000,000 = £3,000,000) by making a taxable supply giving rise to output tax of £50,000. The net tax advantage is therefore £2,950,000.

Some form of fair and reasonable apportionment needs to be applied to work out how much of the net tax advantage is unjustified. This could be achieved by using the ratio that the value of the exempt supply bears to the value of both the exempt supply and the final taxable sale, i.e.

24,000,000 ÷ 24,250,000 × £2,919,588

Thus, in practice the disposal test would be applied, but the amount due to HMRC would be the value of the unjustified tax advantage, i.e. £2,919,588.

[*SI 1995/2518, Reg 115(3)–(3B)*]. (VAT Notice 706/2/18, paras 9.1–9.7, 11.1–11.3; Business Brief 30/97).

Lost, stolen, destroyed or expired assets

[11.8] If, during the adjustment period, a capital item is irretrievably lost or stolen or is totally destroyed, no further adjustment must be made in respect of the remaining *complete* intervals applicable to it. [*SI 1995/2518, Reg 115(4)*].

The normal scheme adjustment is made for the interval of loss, etc. as if the capital item had been used for the whole interval.

Where a capital item is lost, stolen or destroyed, any evidence of the loss (e.g. an insurance claim) should be kept for possible inspection by a visiting VAT officer.

See also **11.12**(3) below for 'rolling reburbishments' where the original refurbishments are stripped out and replaced before the end of the adjustment period.

(VAT Notice 706/2/18, para 9.8.)

Capital items temporarily not used

[11.9] Once the CGS has started, if a capital item is not used for a period of time (e.g. a computer is overhauled) it is treated as still being used during that period for the same purpose as it was previously used. But if a capital item is never used in the business, HMRC do not regard it as an asset for the purposes of the CGS. (VAT Notice 706/2/18, paras 7.12, 9.7).

VAT returns

[11.10] Where an adjustment is required under **11.6** to **11.9** above, it should be included in the return for the second VAT period following the interval to which the adjustment relates or in which the supply as a result of sale, or deemed supply as a result of deregistration, takes place. This is the period after the one in which the partial exemption annual adjustment is made for the year. The adjustment should be included in Box 4 of the VAT return.

HMRC may allow any adjustment to be made in a later return but only if it is a return for a VAT period commencing within four years of the end of the period when the adjustment should have been made.

If VAT registration has been cancelled, the adjustment should be entered on the final VAT return for the period ending with the effective date of deregistration.

[*SI 1995/2518, Reg 115(6)–(8)*]. (VAT Notice 706/2/18, para 8.1).

Example

Company A is partly exempt and uses the standard method. It also has an annual adjustment calculation to make under the CGS. The company completes VAT returns on a calendar quarter basis.

The company will make annual adjustment calculations up to 31 March year for both partial exemption purposes and for the CGS. It has the choice of including the partial exemption adjustment on its March or June VAT return. However, the CGS adjustment must be declared on the September VAT return each year, i.e. the second return after the end of the tax year.

Records

[11.11] See **57 RECORDS** for general requirements for records. In respect of each capital item, the records kept must enable a business to work out the CGS adjustment for each subsequent interval in the adjustment period and should therefore include

- a description of the capital item;
- its value;
- the amount of input tax incurred on it;
- the amount of input tax reclaimed on it;

- the start and end date of each interval, including the first;
- when adjustments are due; and
- the date and value of disposal if the item is sold before the end of the adjustment period.

Although, by law, records only have to be kept for six years, businesses are advised to keep records of *all* capital items for longer in case a CGS adjustment becomes necessary. It is also important to keep detailed records because if

- the capital item is sold as part of the transfer of a business as a going concern (see **11.12**(4) below), or
- the owner moves in or out of a VAT group (see **11.12**(5) below),

the new owner is responsible for any adjustments for the remainder of the adjustment period.

(VAT Notice 706/2/18, paras 2.1, 2.2).

Treatment in particular cases

[11.12] The treatment in particular cases is outlined below.

(1) Input tax incurred before the first interval

Where a business incurs input tax before the first interval, it must work out the overall initial claimable percentage against which it can measure the percentage of taxable use in subsequent periods. This could be done, for example, by expressing the total input tax recovered as a percentage of the input tax incurred on the capital item.

> *Example*
>
> A partly exempt business constructs a new headquarters building. It incurs £600,000 of input tax on the building in the tax year ending 31 March 2015. Its partial exemption reclaimable percentage for the year as a whole is 75% so it reclaims £450,000. In the following tax year, the year ending 31 March 2016, it incurs another £400,000 of input tax on the building and reclaims £320,000 because its partial exemption reclaimable percentage for the year is 80%. It occupies the building for use in its partly exempt business on 1 September 2015 so the first interval runs from 1 September 2015 to 31 March 2016 (the day before the start of the next tax year, which is 1 April 2016).
>
> The business has therefore incurred some VAT before the first interval and will need to work out an overall average reclaimable percentage to measure against for future subsequent intervals:
>
> Total input tax reclaimed × 100% = Average reclaimable percentage
>
> Total VAT incurred = £770,000
>
> £1,000,000 × 100% = 77%
>
> Therefore, 77% is the "baseline" against which future adjustments are measured.

(VAT Notice 706/2/18, para 7.6).

(2) Input tax incurred after the first interval

Some projects, for example, construction projects and refurbishments where the work is carried out over a period of time, may result in additional input tax being incurred after the first interval. This may also occur where a contract includes a retention clause. Input tax incurred in the second interval does not form part of the CGS adjustment in the second interval but should be adjusted where necessary from the third interval onwards.

(VAT Notice 706/2/18, para 7.7. See para 7.8 for examples of how to calculate the adjustments due using the 'combined adjustments' and 'parallel adjustments' methods.)

(3) Rolling refurbishments

Rolling refurbishments occur where a property is refurbished on a regular basis and some or all of the original refurbishments are replaced. If a second refurbishment is undertaken before the original adjustment period has ended

- where the original refurbishment is completely stripped out or replaced, it should be treated as destroyed (see **11.8** above) and no further adjustments made to the input tax on that refurbishment; or
- where elements of the original refurbishment are retained, adjustments to the original input tax must still be made for the remainder of the adjustment period of that refurbishment.

(VAT Notice 706/2/18, para 4.13).

(4) Transfer of a business as a going concern

Where a business or part of a business is transferred as a going concern (see **9.9 BUSINESS**), any capital items included as part of the transfer are not 'sold' for the purposes of the CGS and therefore **11.7** above does not apply. The responsibility for applying the CGS to any capital item transferred passes to the new owner for any remaining intervals. The timing of intervals depends upon whether the new owner takes over the original owner's VAT registration number.

If the new owner takes over the seller's VAT registration number

The interval during which the business is transferred does not end at the time of the transfer and continues without a break. The seller does not need to make any adjustments for that interval. The interval ends on the last day of the new owner's longer period ending immediately after the transfer (or if no longer period then applies, on the last day of his tax year following the day of transfer). The new owner must make any adjustment for that interval and any remaining intervals in the normal way. Longer periods and tax years both normally run to the following 31 March, 30 April or 31 May depending upon the owner's VAT periods, but see **50.13 PARTIAL EXEMPTION** for exceptions.

If the new owner does not take over the seller's VAT registration number

The interval applying to the capital item ends on the day before the transfer takes place. The seller should make any adjustment for that interval on his VAT return for the second period after the end of his tax year in the normal way or, if he is cancelling his registration, he can make any adjustment on his final return. The new owner is responsible for the next interval which runs from the date of transfer to the anniversary date and any other remaining intervals which run for twelve months from each anniversary date. Subsequent intervals applicable to the transferred item may or may not coincide with the new owner's partial exemption tax year. If they do not, the new owner will need to agree a way of calculating subsequent intervals with HMRC.

As the new owner takes over responsibility for applying the CGS, for each relevant capital item the original owner must supply

- a description of the capital item;
- the date of acquisition and number of remaining intervals in the period of adjustment;
- the total input tax incurred; and
- the percentage of that input tax which was claimed on the item in the first interval.

[*SI 1995/2518, Reg 114(5A)(7).*] (VAT Notice 706/2/18, paras 9.2–9.5).

(5) VAT groups

On the first occasion during an adjustment period applicable to a capital item that the owner of the item

- being VAT-registered subsequently becomes a member of a group of companies for VAT purposes (see **28 GROUPS OF COMPANIES**), or
- being a member of a group for VAT purposes ceases to be a member of that group (whether or not it immediately becomes a member of another such group)

the interval then applying ends on the day before the owner becomes a member of the group or the day the owner ceases to be a member of the group (as the case may be). The original owner of the capital item must make any adjustment for this interval. The new owner becomes responsible for subsequent intervals (if any) applicable to the capital item which end on the successive anniversaries of that day (irrespective of whether there are any further movements into or out of VAT groups since this provision only applies on the *first* occasion of joining or leaving a group). The new owner will need to agree a way of calculating adjustments for any such intervals with HMRC in the likely event that these intervals do not coincide with its longer periods.

As the new owner takes over responsibility for applying the CGS, for each relevant capital item the original owner must supply

- a description of the capital item;
- the date of acquisition and number of remaining intervals in the period of adjustment;
- the total input tax incurred; and
- the percentage of that input tax which was claimed on the item in the first interval.

[*SI 1995/2518, Reg 114(5A)*]. (VAT Notice 706/2/18, paras 12.1–12.3).

(6) Disposal of property by grant of lease followed by sale of freehold reversion

See *Centralan Property Ltd v C & E Commrs, CJEC Case C–63/04*; [2006] STC 1542 (TVC 22.532).

(7) Residential property – sale by developer of long leasehold interest separately from the freehold interest

The first grant of a major interest (freehold sale or lease exceeding 21 years) in residential property by its developer is zero-rated but all subsequent grants in the property are exempt. When a developer makes a first grant of a major interest in a property he has constructed or converted from non-residential property, any input tax incurred is recoverable in full as being wholly attributed to that taxable first grant.

However, if a developer's first grant of a major interest in the building is a long lease, he is using the building for a business purpose other than solely for the purpose of selling the building and, as a result, the building will be treated as a capital item under the CGS. The input tax incurred on the construction or conversion and wholly attributed to the zero-rated long lease will have to be adjusted through the CGS should a subsequent exempt grant be made of the building. (Where the developer's first grant of a major interest is the sale of the freehold, he is using the building solely for the purpose of selling the building and will not have to treat the building as a capital item.)

HMRC identify three ways a developer might grant all the leases and the reversionary interest in the freehold of a residential property (typically a block of flats).

(a) *All flats sold followed by the freehold*. The sale of each individual flat is zero-rated as first grant of a major interest. Although the developer will hold a capital item, HMRC consider that, when the freehold is sold, this is only exempt to the extent that it relates to those areas of the building that were previously the subject of the zero-rated grants of individual flats. Most of the sale of the freehold is zero-rated as it relates to the common parts that have not been subject to any previous supply. Any CGS adjustment would be negligible and, in this situation, HMRC do not require any adjustment to be made.

(b) *Freehold sold before any flats are sold*. The sale of the freehold is zero-rated and since no leases had been granted, is not a capital item. All input tax incurred on the construction costs is fully deductible.
As the new freeholder, the purchaser normally makes any exempt grants of leases to buyers of flats. Even where the consideration for such sales accrues to the developer (so that VAT law treats the developer as the person supplying the flats), this does not impact on the initial deduction of input tax by the developer. It may, however, have implications for any input tax incurred on selling costs.

(c) *Freehold sold after some flats have been sold*. The flats sold before the freehold has been supplied are each a zero-rated first grant of a major interest. Although the developer holds a capital item, HMRC consider that, when the freehold is sold, this is only exempt to the extent that it relates to those areas of the building that were previously the subject of the zero-rated grants of individual flats. Most of the supply of the freehold is zero-rated relating to the common parts and unsold flats that have not been subject to any previous supply. As in (*a*) above, no CGS adjustments are required.

If, under the agreement for sale, the developer has retained the right to receive the monies from the sale of the remaining unsold flats, the considerations set out in (*b*) above apply.

(Business Brief 23/06).

Key points: CGS

[11.13] Points to consider are the following.

- The CGS applies when a building is purchased (plus VAT) costing more than £250,000 (excluding VAT) or if it is refurbished or altered with the cost of the project again exceeding £250,000. However, note that any zero-rated costs are excluded from this figure. The scheme also applies when a building is extended, with additional floor space of 10% or more of the original area being created, again subject to the £250,000 limit. Any expenditure on fixtures and fittings is excluded from the scheme (e.g. carpets and machinery).
- The scheme can apply to property that is used for the provision of storage facilities. This change came into effect on 1 October 2012 to provide businesses that had been making exempt supplies up to that point an opportunity to recover some of the input tax they may have incurred in acquiring the premises. The value in this case is only £1. The property owner had to have elected to do this by 31 March 2013.
- The scheme also applies in relation to computer equipment costing at least £50,000 (excluding VAT). However, it should be noted that this is a per-item basis rather than an amount shown on an invoice from a supplier. So 55 laptops costing £1,000 each, bought at the same time, would be excluded from the scheme because each laptop is a purchase in its own right. The scheme only applies to expenditure relating to computer hardware and equipment rather than software.
- From 1 January 2011 the scheme applies to ships and aircraft costing at least £50,000.
- In the case of scheme adjustments for land and building-related costs, the relevant period is ten years. A period of five years is relevant to computer equipment. The first interval runs from when the item is purchased until the end of the taxpayer's partial exemption year, i.e. 31 March, 30 April or 31 May, depending on when VAT periods end.
- Be aware that adjustments under the scheme will always be nil if an item was initially bought and wholly related to taxable supplies (full input tax recovery) and this situation continued

throughout the five or ten-year interval period. The same outcome would result if the item was wholly relevant to exempt supplies (no input tax recovery) when first purchased, and this situation continued throughout the five or ten-year period.

- Adjustments will only affect the amount of tax due if either a change of use occurs within the five or ten-year period (e.g. an asset used for exempt activities becomes used for taxable purposes) or if the item is used for both exempt and taxable purposes where the percentage of input tax recovery changes each year according to the percentage of taxable income for the business as a whole.
- Any adjustments made under the scheme are always made on the second VAT return after the end of the partial exemption year, i.e. the VAT period that includes 30 September. Adjustments (both payments and repayments) are declared in the Box 4 (input tax) figure of the VAT return. The adjustment is a normal accounting adjustment carried out in accordance with the scheme – it is not classed as a VAT error. The timing of the annual adjustment is different to the partial exemption year-end adjustment, which is either declared on the return at the end of the tax year (31 March, 30 April or 31 May) or in the first VAT quarter of the new tax year (i.e. the return which includes 30 June).
- It is important that tax advisers do not see the CGS as a threat, e.g. by recommending to clients that they deliberately try to keep projected capital expenditure below the £50,000 and £250,000 limits. In the case of a partly-exempt business that expects to increase its level of taxable activities in the future, any expenditure on assets relevant to taxable and exempt supplies will actually produce a tax advantage by being within the scheme because the adjustments each year will result in additional input tax claims.
- Remember, the key point of the CGS is 'fairness' – so if the final calculations indicate that a business with 90% exempt income has managed to reclaim 50% of the input tax on a capital item, there is likely to be an error in the computations.
- Although a business is only obliged to keep accounting records for six years, it is important to ensure that records relating to a CGS item are kept for the full ten-year period (if the item relates to property).
- Be aware of the 'disposal test' to ensure there is no unfair input tax recovery on assets that are sold by a partly-exempt business before the end of the adjustment period.
- Remember that the new owner must take over the responsibility for any remaining scheme calculations of the seller in the event of a business sale (transfer of a going concern). It is important that the buyer is given adequate records from the seller to ensure accurate calculations can be carried out.
- If a business deregisters, and there is a deemed or actual supply of a scheme asset at the time of deregistration, then the VAT liability of the final sale will determine the recovery percentage for the

remaining intervals. So if an asset is a deemed exempt supply at the date of deregistration, and there are four interval adjustments remaining with the CGS, then the final VAT return will treat all these final intervals as exempt and pay any tax due or repayable on this return.

12

Catering

De Voil Indirect Tax Service. See V4.220.

Introduction to catering

[12.1] A supply of food and drink in the course of catering is standard-rated. [*VATA 1994, Sch 8 Group 1(a)*].

To decide whether any supply is in the course of catering, the following three questions should be considered in turn.

- Is it within the ordinary meaning of catering? See **12.2** and **12.3** below.
- Is it for 'on premises' consumption? See **12.4** below.
- Is it hot take-away food? See **12.5** below.

If the answer to any of these questions is 'yes', the supply is a standard-rated supply of catering (but see **12.3** below for special treatment in certain cases).

(VAT Notice 709/1/13, para 1.3).

In joined German cases *Bog and others, Cases C–497/09, C–499/09, C–501/09 and C–502/09* ([2011] STC 1221 (TVC 22.167)), the CJEU held that

- the supply of food or meals freshly prepared for immediate consumption from snack stalls or mobile snack bars or in cinema foyers is a supply of goods within *Directive 77/388/EEC, Art 5* (now *Directive 2006/112/EC, Art 14*), if a qualitative examination of the entire transaction shows that the elements of supply of services preceding and accompanying the supply of the food are not predominant;
- this is unlike the activities of a party catering service which are supplies of services within *Directive 77/388/EEC, Art 6* (now *Directive 2006/112/EC, Art 24*) except where a party catering service does no more than deliver standard meals without any additional elements of supply of services;

- the term 'foodstuffs' in *Directive 77/388/EEC, Annex H, category 1* (now *Directive 2006/112/EC, Annex III, category 1*) must be interpreted as also covering food and meals which have been prepared for immediate consumption by boiling, roasting, baking or other means.

HMRC consider that the CJEU judgment has no implications for the UK treatment of supplies of hot food and businesses should continue to treat their supplies in accordance with published guidance (HMRC Brief 19/11).

Ordinary meaning of catering

[12.2] Where a supply can be identified as catering in its everyday meaning, it is *per se* standard-rated and it is not necessary to consider the problems relating to premises and hot take-away food in **12.4** and **12.5** below. This point was clarified in *C & E Commrs v Cope, QB* [1981] STC 532 (TVC 29.45).

The word 'catering' is not defined in the legislation but in its ordinary meaning includes the supply of prepared food and drink. It is characterised by a supply involving a significant element of service. Examples of supplies in the course of catering include

- supplies made in restaurants, cafés, canteens and similar establishments (except supplies of cold take-away food);
- third party supplies of catering for events and functions (e.g. wedding receptions, parties or conferences);
- a supply of cooking and/or preparation of food provided to a customer at the customer's home (e.g. for a dinner party); and
- delivery of cooked ready-to-eat food or meals (with or without crockery or cutlery).

Examples of supplies that are *not* in the course of catering include

- retail supplies of cold take-away food;
- retail supplies of groceries; and
- supplies of food that require significant further preparation by the customer (see below).

(VAT Notice 709/1/13, para 2.1).

Catering contracts

Any supply of food and/or drink as part of a contract for catering is standard-rated. (A contract that merely entitles a food retailer to occupy a set of premises from which they make their supplies does not automatically determine that a supply is one of catering; in such cases it is necessary to consider all of the activities being carried out.)

- *Food for customer preparation.* The supply of food which customers must prepare themselves before it can be consumed is not a supply in the course of catering. This applies whether the food is delivered to, or collected by, the customers. For these purposes, 'preparation' includes thawing frozen food, cooking food, reheating food and arranging food on serving plates. See **48.7**(19) OUTPUT TAX for the treatment of any delivery charge.

- *Delivered sandwiches and groceries*. Where sandwiches, or other items of food and drink, are taken to buildings in order to sell them, if the supplier
  (a) has no contract or agreement to do so, this is not a supply in the course of catering and any item can be zero-rated if eligible (see **25.3–25.13 FOOD**); and
  (b) is supplying the food under a contract to do so (e.g. to cater for an event), this is a supply in the course of catering and all supplies are standard-rated.

  See **48.7**(19) **OUTPUT TAX** for the treatment of any delivery charge. See also *Zeldaline Ltd* (VTD 4388) (TVC 29.28).
- *Grocery items sold from a catering outlet*. Provided these items are in the same form as when sold by a grocer or supermarket, and are clearly not intended for on-premises consumption, they need not be treated as being made in the course of catering. Examples of items that are clearly not intended for on-premises consumption include: packets of tea; packaged coffee granules, powder, beans etc.; sugar; loaves of bread; and cartons of factory-sealed milk.
- *Packed lunches*. Where packed meals are provided as an incidental to an event or a function (e.g. coach parties or race meetings), HMRC consider the meals are supplied in the course of catering and should be standard-rated.

  Where a hotel or similar establishment supplies a packed meal for which a separate charge is made, then provided the supply is for consumption off the premises, the supply can be zero-rated unless comprising items which are always standard-rated (see **25.3–25.13 FOOD**). (Where the supply by a hotel, etc. consists of accommodation and board, including packed meals, at an inclusive price, this should be treated as a single standard-rated supply.)

(VAT Notice 709/1/13, para 2.2).

Cold take-away buffets

A problem often arises in deciding whether a supply of cold buffet platters, etc. is a standard-rated supply of catering or simply a supply of zero-rated food items. There have been a number of tribunal decisions. In *Out to Lunch (a firm)* (VTD 13031) (TVC 29.7) and *Happy Place Ltd (t/a The Munch Box)* (VTD 17654) (TVC 29.6) it was held that the supply of sandwich platters comprising sandwiches, fruit, cakes, etc. available for take-away or delivery from the shop was not in the course of catering even though described as 'for meetings'. But in *Wendy's Kitchen* (VTD 15531) (TVC 29.12) and *PJ & LJ Lawson (t/a Country Fayre)* (VTD 14903) (TVC 29.9) on the evidence, including advertising material, 'finger buffets' supplied to local offices were held to be supplies in the course of catering. See also *C & E Commrs v Safeway Stores plc, QB 1996,* [1997] STC 163 (TVC 29.5) for 'party trays' of food sold from delicatessen counters.

Vending machines

Vending machine supplies follow the same general principles as food and drink supplied from catering outlets.

- Items that are standard-rated under **25.3–25.13 FOOD** are also standard-rated when supplied from vending machines (e.g. sales of beverages or confectionery).
- Supplies of food and drink from vending machines in canteens and restaurant-type areas are standard-rated as supplies to be consumed on the premises where they have been supplied. HMRC will only allow an apportionment to be made if the food seller can produce evidence to show that a proportion of the items of cold food (that would be eligible for zero-rating) are taken-away from the canteen/restaurant premises (see **12.4** below).
- Supplies from machines sited in thoroughfares and areas not designated for the consumption of food follow the liability of the product sold.

See **12.10** below if the machine is on a university campus and is run by the students' union.

(VAT Notice 709/1/13, para 2.4).

As a planning point, items sold from a vending machine could qualify for zero-rating if the vendor can show that some or all of the items are consumed away from the site of the machine. So if a vending machine is located in a café, and it is clear that all items will be eaten in the café, then all sales will be standard-rated. However, an apportionment can be made if it can be shown that a percentage of the purchases are consumed away from the site where the machine is located. This assumes that the items in question are zero-rated as a matter of course (e.g. a sandwich rather than a packet of crisps).

See also **48.7**(34) **OUTPUT TAX** for hiring of vending machines.

Special cases

[12.3] Special treatment is required in certain cases as listed below.

(1) Catering on aircraft, ships, etc.

Where the catering is an adjunct to the supply of the transport and no separate charge is made for it, the consideration for the ticket should not be apportioned. The catering is treated as part of the supply of the passenger transport (*British Airways plc v C & E Commrs, CA* [1990] STC 643 (TVC 66.13)).

Care is needed when catering is supplied in conjunction with zero-rated transport. The key factor is to determine whether the catering is an aim in its own right (separate supply that is standard-rated) or is merely intended to enhance the customer's enjoyment of the journey. In the latter case, the entire payment made by the customer will be classed as a supply of zero-rated transport, with no output tax liability on the catering element. A practical example is that a cup of tea and biscuit supplied on a flight would not be considered a supply of catering. But a three-course meal and wine on the Orient Express would definitely be classed as a 'mixed' supply. In this situation, the customer expects to receive and enjoy both the zero-rated train journey and the standard-rated catering provided during the trip.

(2) **Schools, universities, colleges, etc.**

Certain supplies of education, training and research are exempt from VAT. Where an educational institution provides exempt education to its own pupils and students, then the supply of catering they make can also be exempt. See **17.9 EDUCATION**. If the supply of education is non-business, as in the case of a local authority school, the supply of catering will also be non-business, provided it is made at, or below, cost.

Whichever treatment is appropriate, it applies to anything provided by way of catering. This includes food supplied at mealtimes and break times from the refectory, canteen or other similar outlet but not items purchased from a university campus shop, as they are not provided by way of catering.

Food and drink supplied at or below cost from a tuck shop run by the school itself takes on the same liability as the education.

VAT must be accounted for on supplies of catering to staff and visitors (except visiting students). In the case of *HMRC v Brockenhurst College* [2015] EWCA Civ 1196 (TVC 21.35), the First-tier and Upper Tribunals both held that exemption could extend to supplies of meals to visitors where providing the meals was an essential part of the education of students on catering courses. As consideration was paid by the people who consumed the food, HMRC ruled that the supply was not made 'to the student' and could not be exempt. The Court of Appeal has referred questions to the CJEU to determine the matter. The CJEU delivered the opinion of the Advocate-General on 21 December 2016. The AG's opinion was that supplies 'closely related to education' do not include the supply of restaurant and entertainment services by an educational establishment to paying members of the public who are not recipients of the education. However, the decision of the Full Court was in accordance with that of the First-tier and Upper Tribunals; the catering was ancillary to a supply of education and complied with the conditions for exemption within *Directive 2006/112/EC*.

See **12.10** below for catering provided by a student union on behalf, and with the agreement, of the parent institution.

(VAT Notice 709/1/13, para 2.6).

(3) **Catering in hospitals, clinics, nursing homes, etc.**

Care provided in a hospital or other statutorily-registered institution is exempt from VAT (see **29.10 HEALTH AND WELFARE**). This exemption includes the supply by such institutions of prepared food and drink directly to their patients in the course of care.

Supplies of catering to other persons such as staff and visitors are not exempt and the hospital, etc. must account for VAT on such sales.

(VAT Notice 709/1/13, para 2.7).

Premises

[12.4] A supply in the course of catering is standard-rated. Specifically included is a supply of

- anything for consumption on the premises in which it is supplied; and
- hot food for consumption off those premises (see **12.5** below).

[*VATA 1994, Sch 8 Group 1 Note 3(a)*].

The wording ensures that all food and drink supplied in premises such as restaurants, cafés and canteens is excluded from zero-rating. But 'premises' can be more than just the outlet where food or drink is sold and problems can arise where a catering outlet is within a larger site, e.g. a shopping centre, stadium or office block. In addition, and with effect from 1 October 2012, the term 'premises' includes any area set aside for the consumption of food by the supplier's customers, whether or not the area may also be used by the customers of other suppliers.

[*VATA 1994, Sch 8 Group 1 Note 3A*].

For the purposes of *VATA 1994, Sch 8 Group 1*, 'premises' are the areas occupied by the retailer and/or, any area set aside for the consumption of food by the food retailers' customers, whether or not the area may also be used by the customers of other food retailers. See *HMRC v Compass Contract Services UK Ltd, CA* [2006] STC 1999 (TVC 29.31).

HMRC give the following as examples of premises.

Outlet	*Extent of premises*
Restaurant (or similar café or canteen-type business)	The whole restaurant area, plus any chairs/tables on the pavement, concourse or similar area adjacent to the main premises
Retail outlet in a shopping centre	The outlet itself and any areas with chairs and tables in designated areas belonging to that outlet or provided for the exclusive use of that outlet and areas with tables and chairs in food courts shared with other food retailers.
Retail outlet in a high street	The outlet itself plus any areas containing chairs and tables outside the establishment provided for use of customers.
Retail outlet within an office building	The outlet, plus any facilities provided adjacent to the outlet for the use of customers
Supermarket	Any seating areas within the shop, plus any areas of chairs and tables outside the shop for use of customers
Stall in a sports stadium, amusement park, exhibition, gallery or similar pay-entry venue	The stall itself, plus any facilities provided adjacent to the stall for the use of customers

The definition of premises does not include areas with tables and chairs provided for general use by members of the public who are not customers of one or more food retailer. Examples include

- benches in shopping centres designed as general seating for customers to rest or wait;

- tables and chairs in a public picnic area, e.g. picnic benches by a motorway service station where people can eat sandwiches that they have prepared themselves (as well as ones that have been purchased from the service station), and where the area is not regularly cleaned and cleared by the retailer or landlord; and
- seating areas in airport lounges and railway stations where customers wait for their planes and trains.

Packed lunches provided by hotels

A useful concession allows a hotel or similar establishment to zero-rate the sale of packed lunches, as long as the items in question are cold food items that qualify for zero-rating. The intention must be for the lunch to be consumed away from the hotel premises, e.g. a guest at a seaside hotel buying a packed lunch to take to the beach with him.

(VAT Notice 709/1/13, para 2.2).

Evidence and apportionment

As a result of the above, subject to considering whether there is a supply of catering *per se* (see **12.2** above), the supply of cold food for consumption away from the premises is zero-rated. Where a retailer makes sales of cold food to be taken away from the premises but also has on-site facilities where such food can be consumed, it will need to apportion sales of cold food between those consumed on the premises (standard-rated) and those taken-away (zero-rated). If the retailer is unable to ascertain the correct liability at the point of sale, it must retain satisfactory evidence to support a fair and reasonable apportionment.

(VAT Notice 709/1/13, paras 3.1–3.3).

Hot take-away food

[12.5] Any supply of 'hot food' for consumption off the premises ('*hot take-away food*') on which it is supplied is standard-rated. See **12.4** above for the meaning of 'premises'. (Cold take-away food and drink is zero-rated, provided it is not of a type that is always standard-rated.)

From 1 October 2012, 'hot food' means food which, or any part of which, is hot at the time it is provided to the customer ('the precondition') and

- has been heated for the purposes of enabling it to be consumed hot;
- has been heated to order;
- has been kept hot after being heated;
- is provided to a customer in packaging that retains heat (whether or not the packaging was primarily designed for that purpose) or in any other packaging that is specifically designed for hot food; or
- is advertised or marketed in a way that indicates that it is supplied hot.

Something is 'hot' if it is at a temperature above the ambient air temperature, and something is 'kept hot after being heated' if the supplier stores it in an environment which provides, applies or retains heat, or takes other steps to ensure it remains hot or to slow down the natural cooling process.

References to food being heated include references to it being cooked or reheated.

[*VATA 1994, Sch 8 Group 1 Notes 3–3D*].

Prior to 1 October 2012, '*hot food*' meant food which, or any part of which,

- had been heated for the purposes of enabling it to be consumed at a temperature above the ambient air temperature; and
- was above that temperature at the time it was provided to the customer.

[*VATA 1994, Sch 8 Group 1 Note 3(b)*].

Meaning of 'hot'

Under the precondition (see above), only food that is hot at the time it is provided to the customer is standard rated. Something is hot if it is at a temperature above 'the ambient air temperature'. Generally speaking, businesses do not need to specifically check whether the precondition is satisfied as it is clear whether or not the food is hot at the time they provide it to the customer.

Test 1: The food has been heated for the purposes of enabling it to be consumed hot

Taking into account all the relevant facts and circumstances, it is the purpose of the supplier (and not the customer) in heating the food that is the determining factor. This means that the sale of products that have been cooked specifically to enable consumption whilst still hot (as a result of being freshly prepared, baked, cooked, reheated or kept warm) are standard rated. This is in contrast to products that are not intended to be eaten while hot and are sold warm simply because they happen to be freshly baked and are in the process of cooling down. Examples of standard-rated products under this test include

- chips, fish and chips, and similar items;
- Chinese, Indian take-away meals, pizzas, kebabs etc.;
- baked potatoes with a hot or cold filling;
- hot dogs and hamburgers;
- pies, rolls, sausage rolls, pasties and similar items (unless the products do not meet any of the tests and are sold warm simply because they happen to be freshly baked and are in the process of cooling down);
- tea, coffee, chocolate and other hot drinks;
- hot soup.

Test 2: The food has been heated to order

This test confirms that the sale of food that has been heated to the customer's order is standard rated. Examples of standard-rated products under this test include

- toasted bread, sandwiches, panini, teacakes and similar items;
- garlic bread;
- pizzas;
- hamburgers;
- kebabs.

Test 3: The food has been kept hot after being heated

This test confirms that food that is kept hot after being cooked, heated or reheated is standard-rated. This includes instances where a supplier of hot take-away food stores the food in an environment which provides, applies or retains heat, or takes other steps to ensure that it remains hot or to slow down the natural cooling process after it has been heated. In practice, this will mainly affect products that are kept warm in heated cabinets (for example under heat lamps), on spits, in hot water or on hot shelves or trays. It will also include any products kept warm in cooling down ovens or other appliances that slow down the rate of cooling. Examples of standard-rated products under this test include

- freshly baked croissants, pretzels and similar items that are kept hot in a heated cabinet;
- hot dogs kept hot in water or on a tray;
- hamburgers kept hot on a hot shelf;
- doner kebabs kept hot on a spit;
- cooked chickens kept in a heated cabinet or on a hot tray;
- meat pies kept in cabinets during a controlled cooling process.

Test 4: The food is provided to a customer in heat retentive packaging

This test confirms that food that is provided to a customer in packaging that retains heat (whether or not the packaging was primarily designed for that purpose) or in any other packaging that is specifically designed for hot food is standard rated. In practice, this will mainly affect products that are sold in specialised packaging, such as foil lined bags and insulated containers including specially designed cardboard boxes. It will not affect products that are sold in ordinary paper bags or similar packaging. Examples of standard-rated products under this test include

- naan bread and garlic bread sold in a foil lined bag;
- Chinese and Indian takeaway meals sold in foil lined containers;
- pizza sold in specially designed cardboard boxes;
- cooked chickens that are sold in heat retentive packaging or packaging designed to prevent leakage of hot fluids or grease.

Test 5: The food is advertised or marketed in a way that indicates that it is supplied hot

This test confirms that take-away food that is advertised or marketed in a way that indicates that it is supplied hot is standard-rated. This will be established by examining the nature of the advertising or marketing campaign and whether this indicates that the take-away food in question is sold hot. This could include pictures of the products showing steam rising from them. 'Advertised or marketed in a way that indicates that it is supplied hot' does not include advertised or marketed as 'freshly baked'. Examples of products that are standard rated under this test include

- rotisserie chickens;
- roasted chestnuts; or
- soup

which, in each case, are advertised or marketed as 'hot'.

What types of hot food remain zero-rated?

The above tests ensure that the vast majority of hot take-away food is standard-rated. The exception is food that is either not hot at the time it is provided to the customer or which is hot at the time it is provided to the customer but does not satisfy any of the above tests. For example, freshly baked bread or bakery products that are incidentally hot at the time that they are sold but which are frequently eaten cold (i.e. when they have cooled down to ambient air temperature). Businesses selling food that is hot at the time it is provided to the customer will need to work through each test to confirm that none apply before zero-rating their products. This is illustrated in the following examples.

Example 1

A retailer sells a Cornish pasty that has been baked and left to cool naturally but is still hot at the time that it is provided to a customer (and so the precondition is satisfied). However, the retailer does not intend that the pasty will be consumed hot by the customer (Test 1 is not met); it has not been cooked to order (Test 2 is not met); it has not been kept hot after being cooked (Test 3 is not met); it has been provided to the customer in a standard paper bag (Test 4 is not met) and it is advertised as 'freshly baked' (Test 5 is not met). As none of the tests are satisfied, the sale of the pasty is zero-rated.

Example 2

The retailer in Example 1 decides to keep its pasties under heat lamps to slow the cooling process. In this example, Test 3 is met as the pasties are being kept hot after they have been cooked and the sale of the pasties is standard rated.

Example 3

The retailer in Example 1 decides to advertise its pasties as 'hot' rather than 'freshly baked'. In this example, Test 5 is met and so the sale of the pasties is standard rated.

Example 4

A retailer bakes batches of fruit pies, tarts, cakes, buns and bread for sale throughout the day. None of these products are baked with the intention of being eaten hot, baked to order, kept hot after being baked (they have been allowed to cool naturally), provided in heat retentive packaging or advertised as 'hot'. The sales of all of these products are zero-rated as, even where they are hot at the time they are provided to the customer, none of the five additional tests are satisfied.

Example 5

A retailer sells hot freshly cooked chickens that have not been heated for the purposes of enabling them to be consumed hot, have not been cooked to order, have not been kept hot after cooking (they have been allowed to cool naturally), are provided to customers in specially designed (foil lined) bags designed to prevent leakage of fluids and grease from the chicken, and are not advertised as 'hot'. The sale of these hot chickens is standard rated as Test 4 is met as the chicken is provided to customers in packaging that is specially designed for hot chickens.

Example 6

A retailer sells joints of beef that are kept hot in a cabinet after roasting. The sale of these joints at this point is therefore standard rated as Test 3 is met. At the end of the day, the retailer removes the joints that have not been sold from the heated cabinet. These are sold cold the next day or are used to make cold take-away sandwiches. As they are no longer hot at the time that they are provided to the customer the precondition ceases to be met and so this sale is zero-rated for VAT purposes.

Relevant case law

In *John Pimblett & Sons Ltd v C & E Commrs, CA 1987,* [1988] STC 358 (TVC 29.56) the court held that for supplies of freshly baked pies to be taxed as hot take-away food, it had to be shown that the predominant subjective purpose of the seller in heating the food was to enable it to be consumed while still hot. If the seller's predominant purpose was to assure customers that it had been freshly baked, the food was not standard-rated, even though some customers consumed the food while still hot.

However, in *Sub One Ltd (t/a Subway) (No 2)* [2012] UKUT 34 (TCC) (TVC 29.84), the Upper Tribunal held that European law required an objective test rather than a subjective test. The company's sales of toasted sandwiches and 'meatball marinara' were standard-rated as they had been heated for the purposes of enabling them to be consumed at a temperature above the ambient air temperature. The company's appeal against the Upper Tribunal decision was dismissed by the Court of Appeal ([2014] EWCA Civ 733).

In *The Lewis's Group Ltd* (VTD 4931) (TVC 29.65) it was held that the supply of hot freshly roasted chickens from the food department was not a supply in the course of catering because it was not the supplier's predominant purpose, in heating the chicken, to enable customers to eat it at any particular temperature.

In *Pret A Manger (Europe) Ltd* (VTD 16246) (TVC 29.80) the tribunal rejected the argument that filled croissants were heated to keep them fresh and to prevent them from hardening. On the evidence, it found that the company's predominant purpose in cooking the savoury croissants and presenting them for sale hot was so that they could be consumed at a temperature above the ambient air temperature. However, in *The Great American Bagel Factory Ltd* (VTD 17018) (TVC 29.60) the tribunal accepted that the purpose of toasting bagels was to create a crunchy interior and promote freshness rather than enable them to be consumed hot.

In *Deliverance Ltd v HMRC* [2011] UKUT 58 (TC) (TVC 29.69), D delivered a wide range of foods including crispy duck pancakes, spring rolls, samosas, falafels, sesame prawn toasts and onion bhajis. The First-tier Tribunal upheld HMRC's ruling that these items failed to qualify for zero-rating. However the Upper Tribunal allowed D's appeal, holding that D's purpose in heating the food had been to comply with food hygiene regulations, rather than to enable the food to be consumed at a temperature above the ambient air temperature. Accordingly, the supplies qualified for zero-rating.

Microwave ovens provided for use of customers

If food is sold to be taken away for consumption elsewhere but a microwave oven is made available for customers to heat up the food (either before or after the till point) the supply is one of hot food and must be standard-rated (whether or not a charge is made for the use of the oven).

Hot and cold ingredients supplied as a single item

If an item of hot food, together with an ingredient which is cold, is sold as a single item, the whole supply is standard-rated (see *Marshall (t/a Harry Ramsbottom's)* (VTD 13766) (TVC 29.76)). This includes anything in a bun, bap, baguette or other speciality bread with any hot filling such as a sausage, reheated cheese and ham, pastrami, etc. Examples include hot dogs, hamburgers, bacon sandwiches, chip butties, baked potatoes with a cold filling, hot steak sandwiches and kebabs.

Hot and cold food sold at the same time

Where a mixture of standard-rated and zero-rated items is sold for an inclusive price for consumption off the premises, the VAT value of each item must be worked out in order to calculate how much VAT is due on the standard rated item. This can be done on the basis of cost or market values (see **48.3 OUTPUT TAX**). Examples of mixed supplies include

- burger, chips and a milkshake;
- a cup of tea with a non-chocolate coated biscuit; or
- a meal consisting of hot and cold items or dishes supplied in separate containers.

A supply is normally considered to be a mixed supply if each of the items in the inclusively-priced package can be purchased separately from the menu. This is not the same as a single item of food that happens to have hot and cold ingredients for which one charge is made (see above).

Condiments, etc.

Any minor items for which no charge is made (e.g. salt, pepper, vinegar or mustard) should be ignored. This applies whether or not the customer uses the condiments on the food.

(VAT Notice 709/1/13, paras 4.3–4.8).

Service charges and tips

[12.6] Service charges are standard-rated. Any tips given freely are outside the scope of VAT, because they are not regarded as consideration charged for the supply by the taxable person. Simply stating on a bill that a service charge is 'optional' is enough to make it non-VATable. (VAT Notice 700, para 8.14; VAT Notice 709/1/13, para 2.3).

Accounting for VAT

Catering provided by the owner of the catering facilities

[12.7] The owner of catering facilities is acting as principal and must account for VAT on any supplies of catering or hot take-away food. He can reclaim any VAT charged as input tax, subject to the normal rules. (VAT Notice 709/1/13, para 5.1).

Normal method of accounting

If each sale can be recorded as it takes place, the normal method of accounting can be used. This applies whether sales are only standard-rated or a mixture of standard-rated and zero-rated.

Retail scheme calculations

If each sale cannot be recorded as it takes place, then the Point of Sale scheme must normally be used (see **61.14 RETAIL SCHEMES**) unless the catering adaptation described below can be used. (It is not normally possible to use the Apportionment or Direct Calculation schemes. These assume that goods bought at one rate of VAT will be sold at the same rate and food bought at the zero rate often becomes standard-rated when supplied in the course of catering.)

A business that sells both zero-rated and standard-rated items will usually need to adopt a Point of Sale retail scheme to enable it to calculate output tax due on its standard-rated sales, because of the difficulties in applying apportionment or mark-up schemes to supplies of catering. An important check carried out by HMRC on VAT visits will be to ensure that the caterer does not misdescribe some of his standard-rated sales as being zero-rated. It is therefore very important that the business retain subsidiary records, such as till rolls and other workings, to support the declared split of sales. It is also important that a business owner ensures that staff are properly trained in the issues of VAT liability, again to confirm that proper VAT systems are in place.

Catering adaptation

A caterer may use a special catering adaptation to account for VAT provided

- he can satisfy HMRC that it is impracticable to keep records to operate the Point of Sale scheme;
- he has reasonable grounds for believing that the VAT-exclusive value of standard-rated and zero-rated catering supplies will not exceed £1 million in the next twelve months; and

- the use of the catering adaptation produces a fair and reasonable result in any period.

If the conditions (which have the force of law) are met, he must notify HMRC that he intends to operate the catering adaptation and may then begin to operate it as soon as acknowledgement of the letter is received.

To calculate output tax for each VAT period

Step 1	Add up daily gross takings	A
Step 2	Calculate the percentage of total supplies of catering made at the standard rate (see below)	B%
Step 3	Apply the percentage at Step 2 to the daily gross takings in Step 1	
Step 4	To calculate output tax, multiply the total at Step 3 by the VAT fraction	

In algebraic form, output tax is

$A \times (B \div 100) \times V$

See **61.8** and **61.9 RETAIL SCHEMES** for general rules applying to the calculation of daily gross takings. Service charges (but not tips) and the value of any meals or drinks given in exchange for an identifiable benefit to the business (see **12.8** below) should be included. It is not necessary to include the cost of food or drink used for free meals for family and staff but the full cost of any standard-rated items of food taken out of business stock for own or family use should be included (see **12.8** below).

The percentage of total supplies of catering made at the standard rate must be based on a sample of actual sales for a representative period. The period depends on the nature of the business but HMRC must be satisfied that it takes account of hourly, daily and seasonal fluctuations. Details of the sample, including dates and times, must be retained and a new calculation must be carried out in each VAT period.

If the conditions of the adaptation are not complied with, HMRC may assess for any undeclared VAT and/or refuse use of the adaptation for future periods.

(VAT Notice 727, paras 8.3–8.8 which have the force of law).

Example

A fish bar sells both fried fish and chips and wet fish and seafoods. It also has a small restaurant. It is impractical for the owner to keep a record of each sale as it takes place. He can, however, note his zero-rated supplies over the representative period, which are

	£
Receipts from wet fish rounds	724
Shop sales of wet fish and seafoods	285
Sundries (cold leftovers)	28
Total	1,037
Overall gross takings	7,580

At the end of a given quarterly tax period, gross takings total £24,016,28.
Standard-rated percentage is
(7,580 – 1,037) ÷ 7,580 × = 86%
Output tax for the VAT period is
£24,016.28 × 86% × 1/6 = £3,442.33

Other retail supplies

Where other retail non-catering supplies are made, it may be possible to run separate retail schemes for each part of the business provided separate books are kept. See **61.4 RETAIL SCHEMES**.

Free supplies of catering

Catering for employees

[12.8] Where employees are provided with food or drink free of charge (including supplies from vending machines), the consideration for the supply is taken to be nil (and no VAT is chargeable) (VAT Notice 709/1/13, para 5.8).

The value of catering supplied by an employer to its employees is to be taken to be nil unless made for a consideration wholly or partly in money in which case the value is determined without regard to any consideration other than money. [*VATA 1994, Sch 6 para 10*].

If employees are supplied with food and drink in the employer's establishment and they pay for it, the payments are treated as including VAT which the employer must account for on its VAT return. Where employees pay for meals and so on from their pay, including under a salary sacrifice arrangement, employers must account for VAT on such supplies unless they are zero-rated. (VAT Notice 709/3/13, para 4.2).

In *Goodfellow* (VTD 2107) (TVC 62.13) it was decided that where employees were paid a minimum wage under a *Wages Order* for an industry and that *Order* allowed for appropriate reductions to be made for catering and accommodation, those calculations were steps in arriving at the amount of the weekly wage to be paid and were not monetary consideration on which the employer was liable to VAT.

Catering for self and family

Where the proprietor of a restaurant, café or other catering establishment provides meals for himself or his family, these are not regarded as catering and VAT need not be accounted for on them. But VAT must be accounted for on the full cost of any standard-rated items which are taken out of business stock for own or family use. See **25.3–25.13 FOOD** for standard-rated items of food. (VAT Notice 709/1/13, para 5.8).

Catering for customers and friends

Free meals or drink provided for customers or friends are regarded as business entertainment and any input tax incurred in the provision of the meal or the purchase of the drink is non-deductible. See also **10 BUSINESS ENTERTAINMENT.** Free sweets or drinks provided as part of a meal which a customer pays for (e.g. mints or liqueurs with the bill) can be treated as attributable to the taxable supply of the meal and any input tax recovered.

Where meals or drinks are given in exchange for an identifiable benefit to the business (e.g. coach drivers or group organisers in return for bringing a party to the establishment) any VAT incurred can be deducted but output tax must also be accounted for. Output tax should be calculated on the cost of the goods purchased or, if this cannot be established, on the cost of producing the goods. However, if the value of the supply has been implicitly agreed between the parties (e.g. by setting a value of meal to which the coach driver is entitled in return for bringing in the customers), the agreed value is used instead of cost (*C & E Commrs v Westmorland Motorway Services Ltd*, CA [1998] STC 431 (TVC 67.152)).

(VAT Notice 709/1/13, para 5.7).

Contract catering

[12.9] The following rules apply to contract catering.

(1) Catering provided by a catering contractor acting as principal

A catering contractor running catering facilities on someone else's premises as a principal must account for VAT at the standard rate on the following.

- Any supplies of catering or hot take-away food under the rules explained in **12.1** to **12.5** above. VAT charged on supplies is deductible under the normal rules.
- Sales of other standard-rated food items.
- Any fee to the owner of the catering facility.
- Any subsidy received from the owner of the catering facilities. This subsidy should include payments received to balance a profit and loss account for the catering given to the principal.

VAT must be charged on these supplies even if the owner of the facilities makes exempt supplies (as in **12.3**(2) and (3) above).

(2) Catering provided by a catering contractor acting as agent

Although such a person runs the canteen etc., the food and drink is supplied by the owner of the catering facilities (the principal). The owner must account for VAT on the supplies of catering or hot take-away food (unless they make exempt supplies as in **12.3**(2) and (3) above).

The catering contractor should act as follows.

- *Invoices made out to the principal.* If the contractor buys goods or services for his principal and they are invoiced to the principal, the supplier should send the invoices direct to the principal who can reclaim the VAT subject to the normal rules. The contractor should show a VAT-inclusive amount against the purchase of the item in any profit and loss account for the catering given to the principal (see below).
- *Invoices made out to the contractor.* If the contractor buys goods or services for his principal and they are invoiced to the contractor, the contractor should re-invoice them to his principal and account for VAT on them. If the contractor buys goods or services from unregistered suppliers, the principal must be aware that the contractor will have to charge VAT where appropriate. The contractor can reclaim the VAT on the invoice subject to the normal rules.
  Provided the contractor issues a separate VAT invoice for these goods or services when charging them on to the principal, the contractor should merely record the VAT-inclusive amount in any profit and loss account for the catering given to the principal (see below). However, if it is the contractor's normal practice to issue a single document to serve as both the VAT invoice and the profit and loss account, he must clearly show the dual purpose of the document and keep the VAT invoice details separate from the other information.
- *Contractor's fee for services to his principal.* The contractor must account for VAT on the fee charged for running the catering facilities. The canteen owner can reclaim the VAT charged subject to the normal rules.
- *Profit and loss account.* If the contractor provides the canteen owner with a profit and loss account, he must show the VAT-inclusive amounts spent on food and received from supplies of meals. If there is a profit that the agent pays to the canteen owner or a loss reimbursed by the canteen owner to the contractor, these amounts are outside the scope of VAT.

(3) Catering provided by a catering contractor acting as both principal and agent

If a catering contractor supplies food and drink to the owner of the catering facilities and then prepares and serves it to the users of the canteen, etc. on the owner's behalf, the contractor is acting both as a principal in his own right and as an agent of the owner. The contractor must account for VAT on both

- his supplies of prepared food and drink to the owner (reclaiming any VAT invoiced to him subject to the normal rules); and
- his fee for services to the owner of the catering facilities for running the canteen.

Although under these arrangements the contractor runs the canteen, he is supplying the food and drink to the canteen owner and the owner supplies the food and drink to the users of the canteen. The owner must therefore account for VAT on standard-rated supplies of catering and hot take-away food under the rules in **12.1** to **12.5** above, unless the owner makes exempt supplies as in **12.3**(2) and (3) above.

(VAT Notice 709/1/13, paras 5.2–5.4).

Catering provided by student unions

[12.10] Where a student union supplies catering or hot take-away food to students both on behalf, and with the agreement, of the parent institution, as a concession it can treat its supplies in the same way as the parent institution itself. This means that a student union can treat its supplies as exempt when made at universities and other institutions supplying exempt education and outside the scope of VAT when supplied at further education and sixth form colleges.

As a result, most supplies of food and drink made by a student union, where the food is sold for consumption in the course of catering, is exempt. This covers food and drink sold from canteens, refectories and other catering outlets, plus food and drink sold from vending machines situated in canteens and similar areas.

The concession does not cover food and drink sold from campus shops, bars, tuck shops or other similar outlets because they are not considered supplies that are made in the course of catering. In addition, the concession does not cover any other goods or services supplied by the student unions.

(VAT Notice 709/1/13, para 5.5).

Key points: catering

[12.11] Points to consider are as follows.

- A supply of food that requires a significant element of service to prepare it will usually be classed as a supply of catering and therefore be standard-rated. This outcome would include buffets and food provided for wedding receptions, office functions etc. A supply of catering also extends to any supply of hot take-away food or any food that is intended for consumption on the same premises as it is sold. This means that a sandwich served to a customer in a café will be standard-rated but the same item sold to a customer in a carrier bag for him to take away from the premises will be zero-rated.
- If a supply of take-away food requires further preparation to be carried out by the customer, then it will not represent a supply of catering and could be zero-rated if it relates to cold food. For these purposes, 'preparation' includes thawing frozen food, cook-

ing food, reheating food and arranging food on serving plates. In the case of food delivered to a customer's premises (e.g. in a delivery van), the sale will be classed as supply of catering if it is to cater for a specific event or a supply of cold zero-rated food if a delivery is for a specific order of items (e.g. ten cheese sandwiches).

- The scope for zero-rating of cold food for take away purposes was extended when HMRC accepted the principles decided in the case of *HMRC v Compass Contract Services UK Ltd*, CA [2006] STC 1999 (TVC 29.31). Following this case, HMRC changed its view that premises consisted of an entire area of a building or arena to the specific area that was under the control of the caterer. So a caterer selling food at a sports stadium would only need to class any seating area linked to his outlet as 'premises' as opposed to the entire stadium.
- There is no output tax liability on tips paid by a customer to a restaurant or similar outlet. However, the payment of the tip must be at the total discretion of the customer. A service charge added to a bill is not classed as a tip if the customer is obliged to make the payment and is therefore standard-rated.
- There is no output tax liability (or input tax disallowance) on free food or drink provided to an employee. However, in the case of own consumption (food or drink enjoyed by the business owner), output tax needs to be accounted for on the cost of any standard-rated items that have been consumed.
- Free food or drink supplied to customers and friends is classed as business entertainment and an input tax block will apply on the items in question.

13

Charities

Cross-references. See **26 FUEL AND POWER** for reduced rate on supplies to charities for non-business use.

De Voil Indirect Tax Service. See V4.146, V4.171, V4.261, V4.262, V4.266, V4.406, V4.409, V4.419.

Introduction to charities

[13.1] From 1 April 2012 a separate definition of 'charity' was introduced for VAT purposes. A charity means a body of persons or trust that is established for charitable purposes only and

- falls under the jurisdiction of the High Court, Court of Session, High Court of Northern Ireland (or the corresponding jurisdiction in another EU member state);
- complies with any requirement to be registered under *Charities Act 2011, s 29* (or corresponding provisions in other territories);
- is managed by 'fit and proper persons'.

[*FA 2010, Sch 6 paras 1–4*].

With reference to the first of the above three bullet points, *FA 2016* has amended *FA 2010, Sch 6 para 2(2)* to put it beyond doubt that charities subject to the jurisdiction of the High Court of the Isle of Man are capable of qualifying for UK VAT reliefs for charities.

[*FA 2016, s 125*].

A 'charitable purpose' is a purpose which is for the public benefit and falls within the following descriptions.

- The prevention or relief of poverty.
- The advancement of education.
- The advancement of religion.
- The advancement of health or the saving of lives.
- The advancement of citizenship or community development
- The advancement of the arts, culture, heritage or science.
- The advancement of amateur sport.
- The advancement of human rights, conflict resolution or reconciliation or the promotion of religious or racial harmony or equality and diversity.
- The advancement of environmental protection or improvement.
- The relief of those in need by reason of youth, age, ill-health, disability, financial hardship or other disadvantage.
- The advancement of animal welfare.
- The promotion of the efficiency of the armed forces of the Crown or of the efficiency of the police, fire and rescue services or ambulance services.
- Other recognised charitable purposes, or purposes analogous to or within the spirit of the above purposes.

[*Charities Act 2011, ss 2, 3(1)*].

There is no distinction for VAT purposes between those charities registered with one of the charity regulators and those that are not. However, unregistered charities claiming VAT relief may need to demonstrate that they have 'charitable status'. This may be achieved from their written 'objects' or by the recognition of their charitable status by HMRC. (VAT Notice 701/1/14, para 2.2).

Charities and VAT

[13.2] Since the introduction of VAT, the law has provided a range of special reliefs which cover many supplies to and by charities. Zero-rating applies to some supplies to charities and there are some exemptions, zero-rating and other concessions for business supplies by charities. However, there is no general relief from VAT for goods supplied to charities and in general the normal VAT rules apply to business supplies made by charities.

Under charity law, charities can carry out '*primary purpose trading*', i.e. trading activities in the course of carrying out their primary purpose (e.g. the holding of an art exhibition by a charitable art gallery or museum in return for admission charges).

But charities may also wish to carry out '*non-primary purpose trading*' as a way of raising money (e.g. a charity whose primary purpose is providing education may sell Christmas cards and gifts through a catalogue). Charity law does not permit charities to carry out non-primary purpose trading in their own right on a substantial basis. In order to carry out non-primary purpose trading on a significant scale, charities have to establish 'subsidiary trading companies'. These are trading companies controlled by one or more charities but are not themselves charities. Although profits of these subsidiaries can be passed to the charity free of corporation tax, they are not charities and most of the VAT reliefs available to charities are not available to subsidiary trading companies.

Where a charity and its trading subsidiaries are both bodies corporate it may be possible, under certain conditions, for them to register as a VAT group. See **28 GROUPS OF COMPANIES.**

(VAT Notice 701/1/14, para 2.3).

Business activities
It is important not to confuse the term 'trading' as frequently used by a charity to describe its non-charitable commercial fund-raising activities (usually carried out by a trading subsidiary) with 'business' as used for VAT purposes. Although trading activities will invariably be business activities, 'business' for VAT purposes can have a much wider application and include some or all of the charity's primary or charitable activities. See **13.4** and **13.5** below for further consideration of business and non-business activities.

Registration and basic principles

Registration

[13.3] Any business (including a charity or its trading subsidiary) that makes taxable supplies in excess of the VAT registration threshold (see **60.3 REGISTRATION**) must register for VAT. Taxable supplies are business transactions that are liable to VAT at the standard rate, reduced rate or zero rate. See **13.4** below for a consideration of what are business activities generally and **13.5** below for common business and non-business activities of charities.

If a charity's income from taxable supplies is below the VAT registration threshold it can voluntarily register for VAT (see **60.2 REGISTRATION**) but a charity that makes no taxable supplies (either because it has no business activities or because its supplies or income are exempt from VAT) cannot register.

Example
A charity has three sources of income – the annual amounts are as follows:

Mediation services	£50,000
Local authority grant towards costs of child helpline service	£20,000
Donations from members	£15,000

The value of taxable supplies made by the charity is £50,000 in relation to the mediation services. The income from the local authority and members' donations is outside the scope of VAT. The taxable income is therefore below the VAT registration threshold and the charity does not need to register on a compulsory basis.

The next question to consider is whether it may be worthwhile for the charity to register for VAT on a voluntary basis. The answer is probably no, because this will create an output tax liability on the mediation services, which will either create an extra VAT charge to the users of this facility – or reduce the net income of the charity if fees are kept at the same rate. The input tax benefits are unlikely to outweigh the output tax charges.

Charging VAT

Where a VAT-registered charity makes supplies of goods and services in the course of its business activities, the VAT liability of those supplies is, in general, determined in the normal way as for any other business. See, however, **13.6** below for certain supplies by charities which are zero-rated and **13.10** below for certain exempt supplies by charities. Even if VAT-registered, a charity should not charge VAT on any non-business supplies or income.

Reclaiming VAT

Except where the provisions relating to certain charities from 1 April 2015 (see **13.16** below) apply, the first stage in determining the amount of VAT which a VAT-registered charity can reclaim is to eliminate all the VAT incurred that relates to its non-business activities. It cannot reclaim any VAT it is charged on purchases that *directly* relate to non-business activities. It will also not be able to reclaim a proportion of the VAT on its general expenses (e.g. telephone and electricity) that relate to those non-business activities. See **35.7 INPUT TAX** for various methods which can be used to calculate this proportion.

Once this has been done, the remaining VAT relating to the charity's business activities is input tax.

- It can reclaim all the input tax it has been charged on purchases which *directly* relate to standard-rated, reduced-rated or zero-rated goods or services it supplies.
- It cannot reclaim any of the input tax it has been charged on purchases that relate *directly* to exempt supplies.

It also cannot claim a proportion of input tax on general expenses (after adjustment for non-business activities) that relates to exempt activities unless this amount, together with the input tax relating directly to exempt supplies, is below a *de minimis* limit. See **50.3** to **50.11 PARTIAL EXEMPTION**.

Example

A charity that provides support for homeless people buys some new kitchen equipment that includes VAT. The charity provides free meals to homeless people but is VAT-registered because it also sells meals and snacks as a business activity from the kitchen.

In this situation, a proportion of the input tax must be initially disallowed to reflect the non-business use of the equipment, i.e. to provide free meals to homeless people. This calculation can be based on any method that is fair and reasonable, e.g. time basis, number of meals served, number of business customers compared to non-business customers.

Business and non-business activities

[13.4] An organisation such as a charity that is run on a non-profit-making basis may still be regarded as carrying on a business activity for VAT purposes. This is unaffected by the fact that the activity is performed for the benefit of the community. It is therefore important for a charity to determine whether any particular activity is a 'business' or a 'non-business' activity. This applies both when considering registration (if there is no business activity a charity cannot be registered and therefore cannot recover any input tax) and after registration.

If registered, a charity must account for VAT on taxable supplies it makes by way of business. Income from any non-business activities is not subject to VAT and affects the amount of VAT reclaimable as input tax (see **13.3** above).

'*Business*' has a wide meaning for VAT purposes based upon *Directive 2006/112/EC* (which uses the term 'economic activity' rather than 'business'), UK VAT legislation and decisions by the Courts and tribunals. See **9.1** to **9.3** **BUSINESS** for a fuller consideration of the meaning of 'business' and in particular the business test in **9.2 BUSINESS**.

An activity may still be business if the amount charged does no more than cover the cost to the charity of making the supply or where the charge made is less than cost (but see non-business supplies of welfare services in **13.5** below). If the charity makes no charge at all the activity is unlikely to be considered business.

An area of particular difficulty for charities when considering whether their activities are in the course of business is receipt of grant funding (see **13.5** below).

(VAT Notice 701/1/14, para 4.1).

A series of UK tribunal and court decisions has held that charities have been engaged in 'non-business activity' rather than 'exempt business activity' where the charity is 'not predominantly concerned with making supplies for consideration'. This has enabled charities to enjoy relief on the purchase of buildings and construction services, which can be zero-rated if purchased for a non-business purpose but which must be charged to VAT in the same way as commercial buildings if used for an exempt business purpose. Examples of these cases include *Yarburgh Children's Trust*, Ch D 2001, [2002] STC 207 (TVC 15.120) and *St Paul's Community Project*, Ch D 2004, [2005] STC 95 (TVC 15.121) (see **13.5**(17) below).

These decisions were criticised by the Court of Appeal in *Longridge on the Thames v HMRC* [2016] EWCA Civ 930; [2016] STC 2362 (TVC 15.134). The judges ruled that the UK courts had departed from the European line of case law, in which 'economic activity' is an objective concept based on making supplies for consideration. The UK courts had placed too much emphasis on the charity's motivation for its activities, which may be relevant but cannot predominate. Where there was a direct link between the service which the recipient received and the payment which was made to the service provider, an economic activity was established. As a result, the charity in the case would have to pay an additional £135,000 of VAT on the building, none of which would be recoverable (because it was either used for non-business activities or for exempt business activities, neither of which would give rise to a right of recovery).

Common income/activities of charities

[13.5] This paragraph considers the VAT treatment of some of the more common income-producing activities of charities.

(1) Admission to premises

Where a charity admits visitors to places of interest, gardens, exhibitions, entertainment, functions, etc. for a charge, this is a business activity.

Fixed admission charges

A VAT-registered charity must account for VAT on this income at the standard rate unless

- the income is for admittance to a qualifying fund-raising event, in which case it is exempt from VAT (see **13.10** below); or
- the income is covered by the exemption for admission to museums, galleries, art exhibitions, zoos and theatrical, musical or choreographic performances (see **58.2**(3) **RECREATION AND SPORT**).

Donations in lieu of admission

True donations are outside the scope of VAT. If admission to the premises is not dependent on a payment then the monies received are donations but if admission is conditional upon payment, VAT must be accounted for at the standard rate.

A charity which 'suggests' an amount that visitors may wish to contribute, but does not insist on payment of that amount before allowing admission, can treat the amounts received as donations. An admission fee of £20 plus a 'minimum voluntary contribution' of £30 has been held to fail this test, implying that the £30 donation was compulsory (*Glasgow's Miles Better Mid Summer 5th Anniversary Ball* (VTD 4460) (TVC 67.141)).

No charge for admission. If no charge is made for admission, there is no business activity and any monies received can be treated as donations and outside the scope of VAT.

(VAT Notice 701/1/14, para 5.1).

(2) Advertising in brochures, programmes, annual reports, etc.

The sale of such advertising space is a business activity and is normally standard-rated with the following exceptions.

(a) By concession, provided 50% or more of the total number of advertisements in a publication are clearly placed by private individuals, the charity can treat *all* sums received from advertisers as non-business and outside the scope of VAT. A private advertisement must make no reference to a business. An example of a private advertisement is one that says 'Good wishes from John and Susan Smith'; but not one taken out by 'John and Susan Smith, Grocers, 49 High Street'.

(b) The supply of advertising to another charity can be zero-rated (see **13.7**(*f*) below).

(c) The sale of advertising space in brochures or programmes for a fund-raising event is exempt (see **13.10** below) unless overridden by zero-rating under (*b*) above.

(VAT Notice 701/1/14, para 5.2).

(3) Affinity credit cards

A charity may receive payments from a bank, building society or other financial institution in return for the charity endorsing that institution's credit card and recommending its use to the charity's members or supporters. This is a business activity and the payments would normally be treated as standard-rated marketing services provided to the financial institution. However, HMRC recognise that a large element of such payments could be charitable and not payment for services rendered. Provided the charity is not acting as an intermediary between the card provider and the applicant (see below), HMRC allow charities to treat part of these payments as standard-rated and the remainder as outside the scope of VAT. Note that this treatment only applies to income from affinity credit cards and does not extend to any other financial products.

Typically, a card provider will pay a fixed amount to the charity (or its trading subsidiary) on the issue of each new card and a percentage of the turnover (value of purchases) on the card.

To benefit from this treatment there must be two separate agreements.

- One agreement, between the charity (or its trading subsidiary) and the card provider should provide for the supply by the charity (or its trading subsidiary) of the necessary marketing and publicity services, access to membership lists and other promotional activity for the card (marketing services). These supplies are taxable at the standard rate.
- A second and separate agreement between the charity and the card provider should provide for contributions to be made by the card provider in respect of the use only of the charity's name and/or logo. Contributions made under this agreement can be treated as outside the scope.

Part (at least 20%) of the initial payment is then treated as the consideration for the standard-rated business supplies by the charity. The remaining 80% (or less) of the initial payment and all subsequent payments based on turnover are outside the scope of VAT.

Intermediary services

A charity acts as an intermediary in arranging a contract between its members and a credit card provider where it

- stands between the parties to a contract in the performance of a distinct act of negotiation, without having any interest of its own in the terms of the contract;
- brings the two parties to the contract together; and
- undertakes preparatory work, such as completing or assisting with completion of application forms, forwarding forms to the credit card company, and making representations on behalf of either party.

If a charity is providing intermediary services the payment they receive from the credit card provider is exempt from VAT. HMRC do not see clerical tasks (e.g. providing a list of names or access to a database) as intermediary services.

See also *BAA plc v C & E Commrs,* CA 2002, [2003] STC 35 (TVC 27.27); *Institute of Directors v C & E Commrs,* CA 2002, [2003] STC 35 (TVC 27.29). Following these cases, charities should consider whether supplies involving affinity credit cards are exempt although HMRC have confirmed that, if they wish, charities can continue to treat their income as before. (Business Brief 18/03).

(VAT Notice 701/1/14, paras 5.3, 8.1, 8.2).

(4) Charity shops and sales of goods

The sale of donated and bought-in goods by charities and their trading subsidiaries is a business activity.

Donated goods

The sale, hire or export of donated goods by a charity and, in most instances, its trading subsidiary is zero-rated. See **13.6**(*a*) and (*b*) below. This also applies where the goods are sold at a qualifying fund-raising event (see **13.10** below).

Bought-in goods

If a charity buys in goods for resale, it must account for VAT at the standard rate on the sale unless the goods are zero-rated or reduced-rated under the general provisions (e.g. children's clothes, books, etc.). Bought-in goods sold at qualifying fund-raising events are exempt (see **13.10** below).

(VAT Notice 701/1/14, para 5.5).

(5) Catering

Catering is normally a business activity liable to VAT at the standard rate. See **12 CATERING**. But some catering can be exempt from VAT when carried out by a charity, e.g.

- catering supplied as part of welfare services (see (21) below), such as meals for residents of care homes, and supplies of food and drink (but not alcohol) from trolleys, canteens and shops to patients in hospitals or inmates in prisons; and

- catering provided as part of a qualifying fund-raising event (see **13.10** below).

Catering may also be non-business when it forms part of a non-business supply of welfare (see (21) below).

(VAT Notice 701/1/14, para 5.6).

(6) Donations

A donation which

- is freely given; and
- does not entitle the donor to any further benefit

is not consideration for a supply and is outside the scope of VAT. The giving of a low value token as an acknowledgement of the donation is not treated as a supply for a consideration, provided no minimum payment is specified.

(VAT Notice 701/1/14, para 5.9.1).

> *Example*
> A commercial company agrees to give a donation of £1,000 to a VAT-registered charity, in return for which it will be allowed to display its products and circulate leaflets at the AGM of the charity, to be attended by 200 members/supporters.
>
> This payment is not a donation because the company is obtaining a marketing benefit from the arrangement. The charity is providing a service to the company by giving it the right to promote its products. The income is therefore standard-rated.

(7) Dividends and interest

Dividends received on shares, and interest received from banks, building societies and other financial institutions, are outside the scope of VAT and regarded as part of the charity's non-business income.

(8) Education, research and training

See **17 EDUCATION**.

(9) Free export of goods

The export of *any* goods by a charity (i.e. including goods exported free of charge, usually in the form of relief-aid) to a place outside the EU is treated as a business activity. See **13.6**(*b*) below.

(10) Free supplies

A free supply of services is a non-business activity and outside the scope of VAT. This may cover many of the services typically provided by a charity (e.g. first aid at public functions, rescue at sea). If the recipient makes a financial contribution towards the work of the charity this does not turn the activity into a business activity, provided it is freely given.

A free supply of goods is also usually a non-business activity (but see (9) above for the free export of goods).

(11) Fund-raising

Fund-raising covers a wide range of activities which must be judged to be business or non-business under normal rules. Some of the most common methods are:

Donations

These are outside the scope of VAT if freely given. See (6) above.

Qualifying fund-raising events

Subject to conditions and exclusions, the supply of certain goods and services in connection with a qualifying event whose primary purpose is the raising of money is exempt from VAT. See **13.10** below.

Sponsored events in the UK

Many charities organise walks, runs, swims and other similar sponsored events or arrange for teams of representatives to participate in these events in order to raise funds.

If a charity is organising and promoting the event it may be able to take advantage of the fund-raising exemption. See **13.10** below.

Sometimes a charity may organise an exempt fund-raising event in association with a different event which may or may not be an exempt fund-raising event in its own right (e.g. a charity may have a marquee and hold an auction of sporting memorabilia at a national sporting event). The charity can use the fund-raising exemption provided the event it is organising meets the conditions set out in **13.10** below.

There are, however, many events that individuals take part in to raise funds for charity that do not fall within the fund-raising exemption (e.g. a commercially organised sports event such as a marathon). Charities may pay for places within such events and then offer those places to individuals.

Where a charity allows individuals to take part in the event regardless of the amount they raise, and the individuals do not receive any benefits in return, the monies they raise can be treated as a donation and outside the scope of VAT. HMRC do not consider the following to be benefits.

- Provision of free training and health advice.
- A free t-shirt, running vest or similar which clearly portrays the charity that the individual is representing.
- Free massages and support for physical well-being during the event.
- Free pre-event meeting, which may include free professional advice or support, a simple meal, energy drinks and encouragement from the charity and other participants.
- Free post-event meeting, which may include medical treatment or advice, changing facilities, light refreshments and gives the charity the opportunity to thank participants.

If the charity provides free travel or accommodation and other benefits or gifts (e.g. bicycles or watches) the amount raised by the participant is taxable at the standard rate.

If a charity requires individuals to pay a registration fee or insists that they raise a minimum amount of sponsorship before they can take part in the event, this is effectively an entry fee and is taxable at the standard rate. Any payment in excess of the minimum amount can be treated as a donation and outside the scope of VAT.

If a charity asks individuals to 'pledge' or 'commit' to raise a certain amount of sponsorship, but does not insist on any payment before allowing the individual to take part in the event, the total amounts raised can be treated as donations and outside the scope of VAT. A charity can encourage individuals to pass on sponsorship money as they receive it, but cannot insist on receiving a certain amount before allowing the individual to take part.

Some charities offer prizes to top fund-raisers. These are not benefits for VAT purposes and do not affect the VAT treatment of income from participants.

Charity challenge events

Charities (or their trading subsidiaries) frequently organise treks, bike rides and other sponsored events in order to raise funds. These are usually arranged to include travel and accommodation and are often known as 'charity challenge events'.

Fund-raising events that include a package of both travel and accommodation; or bought-in accommodation; or more than two nights' accommodation from a charity's own resources do not qualify for the fund-raising VAT exemption. Charities involved with challenge events need to consider the following issues—

- Is the charity making a supply? If the charity insists that the participant makes a payment before allowing them to take part in the challenge event the charity will be making a supply for VAT purposes. The payment might consist of a registration fee; a deposit; and/or payment of a proportion of the target figure that the participant is aiming to raise through sponsorship. However the amount is calculated, if the charity insist on payment before allowing the participant to take part then the charity is making a supply. That supply may be of a package to the participant (if the charity acted as a principal or undisclosed agent) or of agency services in selling the package/holiday for a specialist company who has put the event together (if the charity acted as an agent).
- Is the charity acting as a disclosed agent, undisclosed agent, or principal? Most charities use the services of a specialist company to organise challenge events, in which case they will normally have a contract setting out exactly who is responsible for what. A charity will be acting as a disclosed agent if both the charity and the specialist company have agreed that the charity will act as the company's agent; and the charity discloses the name of the principal (the specialist company), e.g. in the event terms and conditions and on all tickets

issued; and the charity is not taking any significant commercial risk in relation to the event (e.g. the charity does not have any financial liability should something go wrong). If these agency disclosure conditions are not met (in which case the charity is acting as an undisclosed agent), or the charity acts as a principal, buying and selling the entire event or putting together the challenge event itself – buying travel, accommodation, itinerary, professional guides, etc. direct – then the charity must account for VAT using the **69 TOUR OPERATORS' MARGIN SCHEME** (TOMS).

- What is the correct VAT treatment? If the charity is acting as a disclosed agent, the participant contracts with the specialist company and the charity receives a commission. VAT will be due on the commission that the charity charges as an agent. If the charity is acting as principal or undisclosed agent, under TOMS VAT will be due on the margin between what it has cost (excluding overheads) the charity to provide a place on the event and what the charity insists on receiving as payment before allowing the participant to take part. If the charity is providing up to two nights accommodation from its own resources, and is not providing a package of travel and accommodation, the income from the event will be exempt under the fund-raising exemption.

Sponsorship of a charity

Many charities receive money, goods or services from sponsors.

- If the charity is obliged to provide the sponsor with a significant benefit in return the sponsorship (e.g. free tickets, free advertising space in a charity event programme), this is a business activity and is taxable at the standard rate.
- If the sponsor receives no significant benefits in return for its contribution, the charity may be able to treat the income as non-business. HMRC accept that giving a flag or sticker to a donor, or naming a donor in a list of supporters is insignificant.

See **58.4 RECREATION AND SPORT** for further details.

(VAT Notice 701/1/14, para 5.9).

Professional fund-raising

Charities frequently engage the services of professional fund-raisers to collect donations from the public. Following the decision in *Church of England Children's Society v R & C Commrs*, Ch D [2005] STC 1644 (TVC 11.48) HMRC accept that such fund-raising activities are 'general overheads' and thus 'cost components' of the charity's economic activities.

- Where funds are raised solely for a restricted charitable purposes involving wholly non-business activities, the VAT incurred on raising those funds is not input tax and not recoverable.
- Where, on the other hand, the funds raised are wholly to support the making of business supplies, all of the VAT incurred can be treated as input tax. It will be recoverable in full (subject to the normal rules) where the business supplies are taxable but not recoverable where they are exempt (subject to the *de minimis* rules).

- Where funds raised support both business and non-business activities, VAT incurred can only be recovered to the extent that it supports taxable business supplies. In practice, this means that the VAT incurred is first subject to a business/non-business apportionment to determine how much of the VAT is input tax and then, if the charity has exempt activities, this input tax is subject to the rules of partial exemption.

(Business Brief 19/05).

(12) Grant funding

Charities often receive funding to support their charitable activities. If funding is freely given, with nothing supplied in return, then no VAT is due. The funding is not consideration for any supply and is therefore outside the scope of VAT. But if funding is given in return for goods or services supplied by the charity, such funding is consideration for a supply and VAT may be due on the income if the goods and/or services supplied by the charity in return are taxable at either the standard or reduced rate.

To decide whether funding is consideration for a supply, a charity should consider the following questions.

- Does the donor receive anything in return for the funding? (Certain 'benefits' to the donor, such as copies of reports, are seen as necessary safeguards to ensure the money is spent correctly and that the end product is put to proper use; they can be ignored where they are incidental to the primary purpose of the project and are minimal in relation to the amount of funding.)
- If the donor does not benefit, does a third party benefit instead? And if so, is there a direct link between the money paid by the funder and the supply received by the third party?
- Are any conditions attached to the funding, which go beyond the requirement to account for the funds (commonly referred to as 'good housekeeping')?

If the answer to any of the above questions is 'yes', this is an indication that the funding *may* not be freely given and may be consideration for a supply.

Where a charity is supported by outside the scope funding, this does not determine the nature of any supplies it makes (i.e. it does not follow that outside the scope income means that the charity will only have non-business activities).

(VAT Notice 701/1/14, para 5.10).

Example

A charity is responsible for promoting a music festival on behalf of the local council. It will receive a grant from the council for its efforts. The intention is to encourage more people to attend the event and to co-ordinate ticket sales and other support services. In this situation, the grant is standard-rated, as a supply of services is being performed by the charity that benefits the council. If the supply is standard-rated, this means the charity can claim input tax on its related costs. The local authority is not concerned about the VAT charge because it gets special treatment that allows it to reclaim input tax on its non-business expenditure.

Note – the above circumstances applied in the case of *Bath Festivals Trust Ltd* (VTD 20840) (TVC 42.20).

(13) Hiring out buildings, including village halls

The hiring out of a building for a fee is normally a business activity. The fees received are exempt from VAT unless the charity has opted to tax the building. If so, the fees received are standard-rated except where the option to tax cannot be applied because the hirer is intending to use it

- as a dwelling (e.g. a residential flat above a charity shop);
- for a relevant charitable purpose (e.g. as a village hall or similarly, or for a non-business purpose); or
- for a relevant residential purpose (e.g. a residential home for children or disabled people, or a hospice),

in which case the fees remain exempt.

See **42.17** LAND AND BUILDINGS: EXEMPT SUPPLIES AND OPTION TO TAX for exempt supplies of land and **42.23** *et seq* LAND AND BUILDINGS: EXEMPT SUPPLIES AND OPTION TO TAX for the option to tax.

Where the hire of the building (or part of a building) is incidental to the provision of facilities (e.g. the hiring of facilities for playing sport), the supply is normally standard-rated. However, where rooms are hired as facilities for playing sport for a period exceeding 24 hours or for a series of ten or more sessions, the supply may be exempt. See **58.2** *et seq* RECREATION AND SPORT.

(14) Bequeathed property

HMRC take the view that land and buildings are not goods which have been donated for sale (see **13.6** below). Additionally, the property in most cases would not have been a business asset of the deceased or the charity.

Any supply of property flowing from a bequest is normally therefore outside the scope of VAT and the charity cannot recover input tax on the expenses of sale. (Business Brief 12/92).

(15) Museums and galleries

Where a charity running a museum or gallery makes a charge for admission, the normal rules in (1) above apply.

Admission to a museum or gallery for no charge is a non-business activity. Normally, this means that no input tax can be reclaimed. See, however, **35.13**(21) INPUT TAX for a special scheme allowing certain non-charging national museums and galleries to recover related input tax.

Other activities (e.g. catering and the sale of books and postcards) must be considered separately.

(16) Membership subscriptions

The provision of membership benefits to members is a business activity and the VAT liability of a membership subscription depends on the benefits being supplied. Normally, this means that the provider must decide whether it is making a single or multiple supply and tax the subscription accordingly. However, as a concession, a charity may, if it wishes, treat a single supply of membership benefits as a multiple supply. The VAT treatment of each benefit can then be considered separately and the subscription charge apportioned so that, for example, the supply of magazines or handbooks to members can be zero-rated. See **15.2 CLUBS AND ASSOCIATIONS** for further details.

(17) Nursery and crèche facilities

In *C & E Commrs v Yarburgh Children's Trust,* Ch D 2001, [2002] STC 207 (TVC 15.120) the charity undertook to provide nursery and crèche facilities for pre-school age children as part of its charitable objectives. It charged fees for its services but these were set at a level designed to ensure that it merely covered its costs. The Court decided that the charity was not making supplies by way of business. Despite that decision, HMRC's position remained that the provision of nursery and crèche facilities in such circumstances was a business activity for VAT purposes. However, in the subsequent case of *C & E Commrs v St Paul's Community Project Ltd,* Ch D 2004, [2005] STC 95 (TVC 15.121) in similar circumstances the Court again decided in favour of the charity. It found that the intrinsic nature of the enterprise was not the carrying on of a business, identifying the distinguishing features as the social concern for the welfare of disadvantaged children, lack of commerciality in setting fees and the overall intention simply to cover costs.

Although HMRC do not agree that these features point to the activities being non-business, considering that the charities are making supplies of services for consideration in much the same way as a commercial nursery, they decided not to appeal further and now accept that the provision of nursery and crèche facilities by charities, along the same lines as those in the *Yarburgh* and *St Paul's* cases, is not a business activity for VAT purposes. In cases that are not broadly in line with the *Yarburgh* or *St Paul's* cases, HMRC will continue to apply the business test, in order to determine whether the supplies concerned are being made by way of business.

(Business Brief 2/05).

(18) Patron and supporter schemes

Many charities operate patron or supporter schemes offering benefits (e.g. free admission to special exhibitions, the right to receive regular publications, discounts on shop purchases, etc.) in return for a minimum payment. The minimum payment is business income and is standard-rated, although if one of the benefits to patrons or supporters is the right to receive publications, it may be possible to treat part of the payment as zero-rated.

If a patron or supporter pays more than the minimum amount, the excess can be treated as a donation and outside the scope of VAT provided the patron or supporter is aware that scheme benefits are available for a given amount, and that anything in excess of that amount is a voluntary donation. This should be explicit in the patron or supporter scheme literature.

(VAT Notice 701/1/14, para 5.14).

In *The Serpentine Trust Ltd v HMRC* (TC03992) (TVC 62.128) it was held that certain payments made by supporters of a charity that ran an art gallery were in return for a package of standard-rated benefits, such as free invitations to events.

(19) Secondment of staff to other charities

Income received for the supply of staff is a business activity and is normally taxable at the standard rate. However if staff are jointly employed there is no supply of staff for VAT purposes. See **45.6 MANAGEMENT SERVICES AND SUPPLIES OF STAFF**. By concession, where staff are seconded from one charity or non-profit-making 'voluntary organisation' to another, the income from the hire or loan can be treated as non-business and outside the scope of VAT provided

- the employee seconded has been engaged only in the non-business activities of the lending charity/organisation and is being seconded to assist in such activities of the borrowing organisation; and
- the payment for the supply of the employee's services does not exceed 'normal remuneration' (calculated *pro rata* for part-time secondments). '*Normal remuneration*' means the total cost incurred by the lending charity/organisation including salary, NIC, pension costs, etc.

A '*voluntary organisation*' is a body that operates otherwise than for profit, but does not include any public or local authority.

(VAT Notice 701/1/14, para 5.17).

(20) Share dealing

The acquisition or disposal of shares and other securities by a charity is not a business activity. Any VAT incurred in connection with such acquisition or disposal, or the management of the investments, cannot be treated as input tax. See *National Society for the Prevention of Cruelty to Children* (VTD 9325) (TVC 11.52) where the tribunal held that the charity's investment activities, although having a turnover in excess of £7 million, did not amount to a business as the charity was not predominantly concerned with those supplies. See also *The Wellcome Trust Ltd v C & E Commrs, ECJ Case C-155/94*, [1996] STC 945 (TVC 22.120) where the court confirmed that the concept of an economic activity is to be interpreted as not including the purchase and sale of shares and other securities by a trustee in the course of the management of the assets of a charitable trust.

(21) Welfare

The supply of welfare services by a charity are normally business and exempt from VAT. Similar provisions apply to such supplies made by public bodies and state-regulated private welfare institutions. Please note that supplies of welfare advice and information may be liable to VAT at the reduced rate. See **29.12 HEALTH AND WELFARE.**

Non-business welfare services

By concession, charities that provide welfare services at significantly below cost, to 'distressed' persons for the relief of their distress, *may* treat these supplies as non-business and outside the scope of VAT. To qualify:

- The subsidy must be at least 15%.
- The subsidy must be available to all distressed persons, i.e. both to those who can and cannot afford to pay the full rate.
- The services must be provided to the distressed individual (and not, for example, to a local authority).

See **29.12 HEALTH AND WELFARE** for the definition of '*welfare services*'.

'*Distressed*' means suffering pain, grief, anguish, severe poverty, etc.

(VAT Notice 701/1/14, para 5.18).

Zero-rated supplies by charities

[13.6] Certain supplies by charities are zero-rated not because of the charitable status of the supplier but because they are covered by general application. See **75.1 ZERO-RATED SUPPLIES**. In addition, the following zero-rating provisions apply specifically to charities.

(a) Sale of donated goods

Subject to below, zero-rating applies to the sale or letting on hire of any 'goods' donated to

- a charity, or
- a taxable person who is a 'profits-to-charity' person in respect of the goods

where the goods are donated for sale, letting or any combination of these two and export.

'*Goods*' means goods in the normal sense of the word. It does not, in particular, include anything that is not goods, even though *VATA 1994* or any other enactment provides that the supply of it is, or is treated as, a supply of goods. Land, for example, is therefore excluded from zero-rating under these provisions.

Goods are donated for letting only if they are donated for letting, re-letting after the end of any first or subsequent letting *and* sale, export or disposal as waste if not, or when no longer, used for letting.

'*Profits-to-charity*' person. A taxable person is a profits-to-charity person in respect of any goods if

- he has agreed in writing (whether or not by deed) to transfer to a charity his profits from supplies and lettings of the goods; or
- his profits from supplies and lettings of the goods are otherwise payable to a charity.

Zero-rating does not apply

(i) unless the sale or letting takes place as a result of the goods having been made available for purchase or hire (whether in a shop or elsewhere such as a charity auction) to

- the general public; or
- two or more persons who are chronically sick or disabled and/or entitled to receive one or more means-tested benefits (income support, housing benefit, council tax benefit, income-based jobseeker's allowance, any element of child tax credit other than the family element, working tax credit or universal credit under the *Welfare Reform Act 2012*);

(ii) if the sale or letting takes place as a result of any arrangements (whether legally binding or not) relating to the goods and entered into, before the goods were made available as under (i) above, by
- each of the parties to the sale or letting; or
- the donor of the goods and either or both of those parties; or

(iii) to any sale or letting of particular donated goods if the goods, at any time after they are donated but before they are sold, exported or disposed of as waste, are whilst unlet used for any purpose other than being available for purchase, hire or export.

[*VATA 1994, Sch 8 Group 15 Items 1, 1A; Tax Credits Act 2002, Sch 3 para 49*].

By concession, zero-rating also applies where the goods, although of a kind made available for purchase by the general public under (i) above, are by reason of their poor quality not fit to be so made available. This concession will benefit many charities, particularly those selling scrap clothing to rag merchants or those who are prevented under safety legislation from selling certain goods to the public (e.g. second-hand electrical goods and toys). (VAT Notice 48, ESC 3.21; Business Brief 13/97).

Where a rescue charity takes steps to return genuinely lost animals to their owners so that those offered for re-homing have been deliberately abandoned, the animals given to the charity by the local authority, police and members of the public have been donated (as well as those directly donated by the original owners) and therefore can be zero-rated when sold by the charity (*Gables Farm Dogs and Cats Home* (VTD 20519) (TVC 11.2)). HMRC have accepted this decision. (HMRC Brief 14/08).

(b) Export of goods

Export of any goods by a charity is zero-rated. [*VATA 1994, Sch 8 Group 15 Item 3*]. Proof of export is required. See **22.24 EXPORTS**.

The export is treated as a supply made by the charity in the UK and in the course or furtherance of a business carried on by the charity. [*VATA 1994, s 30(5)*]. This enables a charity to reclaim any VAT paid on the purchase of the goods and any overheads of exporting them (or to register for VAT in order to do so) where the VAT would not otherwise be deductible (e.g. where the goods are given away overseas as part of a non-business activity such as relief aid).

Zero-rated supplies to or for charities

[13.7] The following supplies to charities are zero-rated.

(a) Talking books for the blind and disabled

The supply to the Royal National Institute for the Blind, the National Listening Library or other similar charity of

- (i) magnetic tape specially adapted for the recording and reproduction of speech for the blind or severely disabled;
- (ii) apparatus designed or specially adapted for the making on magnetic tape, by way of transfer of recorded speech from another magnetic tape, of a recording as in (vi) below;
- (iii) apparatus designed or specially adapted for transfer to magnetic tapes of a recording made by apparatus within (ii) above;
- (iv) apparatus for rewinding magnetic tape described in (vi) below;
- (v) apparatus designed or specially adapted for the reproduction from recorded magnetic tape of speech for the blind or severely disabled which is not available for use otherwise than by them;
- (vi) magnetic tape on which has been recorded speech for the blind or severely disabled, such recording being suitable for reproduction only in the apparatus mentioned in (v) above;
- (vii) apparatus solely for the making on a magnetic tape of a sound recording which is for use by the blind or severely disabled;
- (viii) parts and accessories (other than a magnetic tape for use with apparatus in (vii) above) for goods comprised in (i) to (vii) above; and
- (ix) the supply of a service of repair or maintenance of any goods within (i) to (viii) above.

Included is the letting on hire of eligible goods under (i) to (vii) above. [*VATA 1994, Sch 8 Group 4 Item 1*].

(b) Wireless sets for the blind

Wireless receiving sets or apparatus solely for the making and reproduction of sound recording on a magnetic tape permanently contained on a cassette. In each case, the goods must be solely for gratuitous loan to the blind. Included is the letting on hire of eligible goods. [*VATA 1994, Sch 8 Group 4 Item 2*].

(c) Aids for disabled persons

Certain goods to be made available to persons with disabilities and services of adapting, repairing and installing goods for such persons. See **29.14** to **29.34** **HEALTH AND WELFARE.**

(d) Donations of goods

The donation of any 'goods' for sale, export or letting by

- a charity; or
- a taxable person who is a 'profits-to-charity' person in respect of the goods.

'*Goods*' means goods in the normal sense of the word. It does not, in particular, include anything that is not goods, even though *VATA 1994* or any other enactment provides that the supply of it is, or is treated as, a supply of goods. Land, for example, is therefore excluded from zero-rating under these provisions.

Goods are donated for letting only if they are donated for letting, re-letting after the end of any first or subsequent letting *and* sale, export or disposal as waste if not, or when no longer, used for letting.

A taxable person is a '*profits-to-charity*' person in respect of any goods if

- he has agreed in writing (whether or not by deed) to transfer to a charity his profits from supplies and lettings of the goods; or
- his profits from supplies and lettings of the goods are otherwise payable to a charity.

[*VATA 1994, Sch 8 Group 15 Item 2*].

(e) Lifeboats

Lifeboats, including repairs and maintenance, spares and accessories, and fuel for use in a lifeboat supplied to a charity providing rescue and assistance at sea. See **71.14 TRANSPORT AND FREIGHT.**

(f) Advertising

Subject to the exclusions below, the supply to a charity of

(i) a right to make known an advertisement by means of any medium of communication with the 'public';

(ii) making known an advertisement by means of such a medium;

(iii) services of design or production of an advertisement that is, or was intended to be, made known by means of such a medium (e.g. the design of a poster or the filming or recording of an advertisement to be broadcast); and

(iv) goods closely related to a supply within (iii) above. This would include
  - a finished article like a film or recorded cassette;
  - an element to be incorporated in the advertisement such as a photograph, picture or a sound track; or
  - all alternative versions of an advertisement produced, to see which works best, even if it is the intention that only one version will be used.

(VAT Notice 701/58/16, para 4.2).

Exclusions

Zero-rating does not apply in the following cases.

- Neither (i) or (ii) above includes a supply where any of the members of the public (whether individuals or other persons) who are reached though the medium are 'selected' by or on behalf of the charity. '*Selected*' includes selection by address (whether postal address or telephone number, e-mail address or other address for electronic communications purposes) or at random.
- Selected people could be individually named people, all those at the same address (e.g. family groups) or everyone in a particular building. Advertisements targeted at general groups (e.g. readers of a trade or religious magazine) are not considered to be selected. Neither are groups in particular parts of the country who are, for example, targeted for a general poster campaign in their area. (VAT Notice 701/58/16, paras 3.2, 3.3).

- Direct mail (by post, fax and e-mail) and telesales are both excluded from zero-rating because they are not a supply of advertising time or space but are marketing and advertising addressed to selected individuals or groups. (Individual elements of a postal package may qualify for zero-rating as **55 PRINTED MATTER, ETC.** or under the class concession for goods used by charities in connection with collecting monetary donations (see (*g*) below).) (VAT Notice 701/58/16, para 3.4).
- None of (i)–(iv) above include any supply used to create, or contribute to, a website that is the charity's own. For this purpose, a website is the charity's own even though hosted by another person. Zero-rating does not therefore apply to advertising in, on or through a charity's own website whether or not the website is owned, rented or loaned to the charity. (VAT Notice 701/58/16, para 3.7).
- Neither of (iii) or (iv) above include a supply to a charity that is used directly by the charity to design or produce an advertisement.
- Where the supply is not directly to a charity but to one of its trading companies, e.g. a wholly-owned subsidiary.
- Any method of advertising which is not a supply of someone else's advertising time and space or is in the form of general marketing and promotion, including direct mail and telesales (see above); anything on the charity's own website (see above); advertisements where there is no supply of time and space to the charity (e.g. advertisements on a charity's own greetings cards); exhibition stands and space; services of distribution; and commemorative items whether or not they bear the charity's logo (e.g. pens and adult clothing). (VAT Notice 701/58/16, para 3.8).

[*VATA 1994, Sch 8 Group 15 Items 8–8C*].

The relief covers all types of advertisement on any subject, including staff recruitment. There is no requirement that they mention the name of the charity or show its logo to obtain relief. The wide relief is allowed in the expectation that charities will only place advertisements which comply with their charitable objects. The relief does not override charity law or the need to comply with the British Codes of Advertising or any other relevant regulations.

Zero-rating applies to advertisements placed in any medium which communicates with the public, including conventional advertising media such as television, cinema, billboards, sides of vehicles, newspapers and printed publications. The important factor is whether the advertisement is placed in someone else's time or space. If space is sold to a charity for advertising on other items, such as beer mats, calendars, till rolls, etc. this will be covered by the zero rate although the sale of the items themselves is not zero-rated (unless qualifying in their own right, e.g. advertising on books or children's clothing).

(VAT Notice 701/58/16, paras 2.3, 3.1).

Services involving advertising agencies

If a charity uses an advertising agency instead of contacting the suppliers of advertising or printing direct, the VAT liability depends on whether the agency is acting as a principal or an agent and normal VAT rules for agent/principal agreements apply. See **3 AGENTS** generally but broadly

- where an advertising agency is the principal, the advertising agency's supply of qualifying advertising time or space (e.g. television broadcasting time) and associated production costs to the charity are zero-rated but supplies to the agency are standard-rated; and
- where an advertising agency acts solely as an agent, the agency fees, charged to the charity, are standard-rated. The supply of the advertising time or space is direct to the charity and eligible for zero-rating under this relief in the normal way.

(VAT Notice 701/58/16, para 4.4).

Pay-per-click advertisements

Pay-per-click (PPC) charity advertising is used by organisations on search engines such as Google to encourage searchers to click on the organisation's link. The organisation pays the search engine provider an agreed amount each time their website is accessed through the sponsored link. HMRC previously took the view that a PPC-sponsored link was not an advertisement itself but simply a means of access to the charity's website. As such, HMRC considered the costs of providing PPC were excluded from zero-rating by *VATA 1994, Sch 8, Group 15, Note 10B*, which excludes zero-rating on the costs of providing a charity's website. Following representations from charities, HMRC have revised their VAT treatment and now accept that PPC-sponsored links appearing on search engine websites are advertisements for the purpose of *Items 8 and 8A*, and qualify for zero-rating when supplied to a charity. It follows that the supply of copyright and design services associated with such sponsored links fall within the zero-rating. However, HMRC still maintain that services supplied by copywriters and designers for the purpose of search engine optimisation (structuring a website so that it contains as many keywords as possible) do not qualify for relief; and nor does the listing of a charity in the results of a search engine ('natural hits').

(HMRC Brief 25/10).

Claiming relief

A supplier is responsible for determining the liability of the supplies he makes and must be sure that all the relevant conditions for relief are met. He must take reasonable steps to check with the charity any condition which he cannot verify for himself. For this reason, it is recommended that a charity gives its supplier a declaration that the specific conditions for the claimed relief are fulfilled. See VAT Notice 701/58/16, Part 10 for a suggested form of declaration. Other types of declaration (whether in paper form, faxed or electronic) that contain sufficient verifiable information to accurately identify the customer are acceptable to HMRC. Declarations are not always required, e.g. when a charity requests repeat orders and the information contained in a declaration for the first order has not changed. If a supplier has taken reasonable steps to check the validity of a declaration but fails to identify an inaccuracy and in good faith makes the supplies concerned at the zero rate, HMRC will not seek to recover the VAT due from the supplier. See HMRC ESC 3.11. (VAT Notice 701/58/16, paras 10.1–10.5).

(g) Goods used by charities in connection with collecting monetary donations

By concession, supplies of the following goods to a charity may be treated as if they were zero-rated.

(i) Lapel stickers or attachments designed to be worn on the lapel, which are of no intrinsic value, low cost to the charity and are given as a token in acknowledgement of a donation.
Included are paper stickers, ribbons, artificial flowers (if used as a symbol of the charity) and metal pins and badges. Large items for decorating buildings, vehicles, monuments, etc. are not eligible for relief even if bigger versions of a lapel badge.
Emblems or badges given in return for any non-specified donation or a suggested donation of up to £1 are considered to be of no intrinsic value or low cost. Lapel attachments which are offered for a fixed price, even if this is less than £1, do not qualify for relief because they are not given away freely. Relief will apply if a charity suggests a donation of £1.
If a charity makes its own lapel attachments, equipment for manufacturing badges is not covered by the concession but where it buys identifiable constituent parts which it will assemble into badges in-house, these come within the concession.

(ii) Component parts of items described in (i) above when supplied for self-assembly.

(iii) Any form of receptacle which
- is manufactured specifically for the purpose of collecting donated money;
- is used solely for collecting money for charity;
- is, or will be, clearly marked as collecting for a named charity; and
- can be secured by lock or tamper evident seal.

Examples of receptacles which might be made to comply with the above requirements are pre-printed card collecting boxes, moulded plastic collecting boxes, and models in any material including hollow plaster, wood, base metal or glass. Boxes may be of types that are hand held, floor standing, wall mounted or for placing on a table-top or shop counter. Boxes of greater value, such as those made of precious metal, are not zero-rated. Boxes where a simple balance mechanism moves money from one level to another or the weight of the coin causes it to roll helter-skelter fashion into the box are included; but more elaborate boxes which have additional purposes (e.g. gaming or quiz machines) or have some form of mechanical entertainment are not covered by the concession.
All boxes must bear the name of the charity, for example, by indelible printing or embossing or having raised letters, or allow for the charity name to be added later.

(iv) Bucket lids, designed to fit buckets and provide a secure seal, for use solely in connection with collecting money for charity.

(v) Pre-printed letters the primary purpose of which is to appeal for money for the charity (not necessarily including the addressees' particulars).

(vi) Envelopes used in conjunction with letters in (v) above for forwarding donations, provided that they are over-printed with an appeal request related to that contained in the letter.

(vii) Outer envelopes used in conjunction with letters in (v) above provided that they are over-printed with an appeal request related to that contained in the letter.

(viii) Pre-printed collecting envelopes appealing for money (of the type used by the welfare charities and which are usually hand delivered to domestic premises).

(ix) Stewardship envelopes used for planned giving which, as a minimum requirement, are pre-printed with the name of the relevant place of worship or other charity.
Plain envelopes bearing only a symbol such as a cross printed on them, and available from retailers as general stationery, do not qualify.

The Commissioners may withdraw or restrict the application of this concession if they have reasonable cause to believe that it is being abused.

(VAT Notice 48, ESC 3.3).

There is a separate concession (the 'package test') for determining the liability of a mixed supply of printed items (e.g. items for a mailshot). That concession has been extended to some of the charity stationery zero-rated under the concession for charities above. See **55.16 PRINTED MATTER, ETC.**

(VAT Notice 701/58/16, paras 6.2, 6.4, 7.1–7.3, 7.5, 8.1, 8.3, 8.4, Part 12).

Claiming relief

A supplier is responsible for determining the liability of the supplies he makes and must be sure that all the relevant conditions for relief are met. He must take reasonable steps to check with the charity any condition which he cannot verify for himself. For this reason, it is recommended that a charity gives its supplier a declaration that the specific conditions for the claimed relief are fulfilled. See VAT Notice 701/58/16, Part 10 for a suggested form of declaration. Other types of declaration (whether in paper form, faxed or electronic) that contain sufficient verifiable information to accurately identify the customer are acceptable to HMRC. Declarations are not always required, e.g. when a charity requests repeat orders and the information contained in a declaration for the first order has not changed. If a supplier has taken reasonable steps to check the validity of a declaration but fails to identify an inaccuracy and in good faith makes the supplies concerned at the zero rate, HMRC will not seek to recover the VAT due from the supplier. See HMRC ESC 3.11. (VAT Notice 701/58/16, paras 10.1–10.5).

(h) Medicinal products

The supply to a charity

- providing care or medical or surgical treatment for human beings or animals; or
- engaging in medical or veterinary research

of a 'medicinal product' or 'veterinary medicinal product' where the supply is solely for use by the charity in such care, treatment or research.

'*Medicinal product*' means any 'substance' or article (not being an instrument, apparatus or appliance) which is for use wholly or mainly in either or both of the following ways, viz. by being 'administered' to one or more human beings for 'medicinal purposes' or as an 'ingredient' in the preparation of a substance or article to be so administered.

'*Veterinary medicinal product*' means any substance (or combination of substances) (i) presented as having properties for treating or preventing disease in animals; or (ii) that may be used in, or administered to, animals with a view *either* to restoring, correcting or modifying physiological functions by exerting a pharmacological, immunological or metabolic action *or* to making a medical diagnosis.

'*Substance*' means any natural or artificial substance, whether in solid or liquid form or in the form of a vapour or gas.

'*Administer*' means administering whether orally, by injection or by introduction into the body in any other way, or by external application, whether by direct contact with the body or not and includes both administering a substance in its existing state or after it has been dissolved, diluted or mixed with some other substance used as a vehicle. See also *Pasante Healthcare Ltd* (VTD 19724) (TVC 11.32) where the tribunal held that condoms given by a charity to its clients were being 'administered for medicinal purposes' and therefore the supply to the charity could be zero-rated. HMRC have accepted this decision. (Business Brief 16/06).

Use for '*medicinal purpose*' includes use for treating or preventing of disease; diagnosing disease or ascertaining physiological condition; contraception; inducing anaesthesia; or otherwise bringing about some alteration in the physical or physiological state of the patient or animal.

'*Ingredient*', in relation to the manufacture or preparation of a substance, includes anything which is the sole active ingredient of that substance as manufactured or prepared.

[*VATA 1994, Sch 8 Group 15 Item 9; Medicines Act 1968, s 130(2)(9), s 132*].

(i) Substances for medical or veterinary research

The supply to a charity of a 'substance' directly used for synthesis or testing in the course of medical or veterinary research. See (*h*) above for '*substance*'. [*VATA 1994, Sch 8 Group 15 Item 10*].

(j) Major interests in land and buildings

The grant by a person constructing a building of a major interest in it provided the building is intended solely for use for a relevant residential purpose or use for a relevant charitable purpose. See **43.1 LAND AND BUILDINGS: ZERO AND REDUCED RATE SUPPLIES AND DIY HOUSEBUILDERS.**

(k) Construction services

Supplies to a charity of services in the course of construction of a new building intended solely for use for a relevant residential purpose or use for a relevant charitable purpose. See **43.7 LAND AND BUILDINGS: ZERO AND REDUCED RATE SUPPLIES AND DIY HOUSEBUILDERS.**

Proof of zero-rating

Zero-rating of items under (*a*), (*b*), (*e*), (*h*) and (*j*) above may depend on the *use* rather than the nature of the item. The charity must, therefore, give the supplier a certified declaration that the goods are to be used for the specified purpose. Declaration forms are not supplied by HMRC but examples can be found in VAT Notice 701/6 Supplement. These can be reproduced in any convenient way, e.g. by incorporating them in any order form. It is the supplier's responsibility to take reasonable steps to satisfy himself that the charity is entitled to zero-rating and the declaration is correct. Where, however, despite taking all reasonable steps, nonetheless the supplier fails to identify the inaccuracy and in good faith makes the supplies concerned at the zero rate, HMRC will not seek to recover the VAT due from the supplier. (VAT Notice 48, ESC 3.11).

Importation

Imports by charities of any goods within (*a*), (*b*), (*e*), (*h*) and (*j*) above can be zero-rated under the same conditions as supplies made to them in the UK. The appropriate declaration (see under *Proof of zero-rating* above) must be presented with the customs entry form.

Charity-funded equipment for medical, veterinary uses, etc.

[13.8] The following supplies are zero-rated.

(a) Relevant goods (see (1) below) supplied *for donation* to a nominated eligible body (see (2) below). To qualify for relief
- the funds for the purchase (or the letting or hire) must be provided by a charity or from voluntary contributions (see (3) below); and
- where the *donee* of the goods is not a charity, it must not have contributed, wholly or in part, to the purchase (or hiring) of the goods.

[*VATA 1994, Sch 8 Group 15, Item 4 and Notes (5A), (6) and (9)*].
This *Item* zero-rates qualifying goods and services when they are supplied to any person, body or organisation for donation to an eligible body. (VAT Notice 701/6/14, para 6.1).

(b) Relevant goods (see (1) below) supplied to an eligible body (see (2) below). To qualify for relief
- the eligible body must pay for the relevant goods (or hire them) with funds provided by a charity or from voluntary contributions (see (3) below); and
- where the eligible body is not a charity, it must not have contributed, wholly or in part, to the purchase (or hiring) of the goods.

[*VATA 1994, Sch 8 Group 15, Item 5 and Notes (7) and (9)*].

(c) Relevant goods (see (1) below) supplied (or hired) to an eligible body which is a charitable institution providing care or medical or surgical treatment (see (4) below) for disabled persons (see (5) below). [*VATA 1994, Sch 8 Group 15, Item 5* and *Note (9)*].

(d) The repair and maintenance of relevant goods (see (1) below) owned by an eligible body (see (2) below), and any goods supplied in connection with the repair and maintenance, provided
- the supply is paid for with funds which have been provided by a charity or from voluntary contributions (see (3) below); and
- where the owner (or hirer) of the goods repaired or maintained is not a charity, it must not have contributed, wholly or in part, to those funds.

[*VATA 1994, Sch 8 Group 15, Items 6, 7 and Note (8)*].

(e) By concession, relevant goods (see (1) below) supplied to a charity
- whose sole purpose and function is to provide a range of care services to meet the personal needs of disabled people (see (5) below) (e.g. a charity established to: provide care or welfare services to disabled people; lobby on behalf of disabled people; or fund medical research into the causes, prevention or cure of disablement); or
- which provides transport services predominantly to disabled people.

Zero-rating also applies to the repair and maintenance of those goods and the supply of any further goods in connection with that repair and maintenance.

In theory, any relevant goods can be supplied at the zero rate under this concession. In practice, the type of relevant goods which are most likely to be purchased by these charities are motor vehicles adapted for use by disabled passengers (with space for at least one wheelchair user) or a motor vehicle to transport mainly blind, deaf, mentally impaired or terminally sick persons. Boats that are designed or permanently adapted for use by disabled people are also eligible for zero-rating.

It is the responsibility of the purchasing charity to prove that it is entitled to buy the relevant goods at the zero rate. To avoid charities having to keep detailed records simply to prove eligibility, HMRC will use records and documentation already kept by the charity for non-VAT purposes, for example,
- its charitable aims and objectives;
- its publicity and advertising material;
- any documents issued for the purpose of obtaining funds from a third party such as a local authority;
- evidence of its day-to-day operations; and
- any other relevant evidence.

When a charity claims zero-rating on an adapted motor vehicle (or any other relevant goods), it must issue a certificate to the supplier claiming eligibility for zero-rating and, where required, it must attach documentary evidence (as outlined above) to support the claim. (Some documents, particularly funding documents or aims and objectives, are lengthy. A charity need not provide the whole document, but it should provide the parts which will enable it to make the declaration for relief.)

The charity should make up two sets of the documents listed above, one set for itself and one to present to *each* supplier. This means the charity in reality has to search for and collate the information only once. It can

then be retained by the charity for any future supplies. A charity need only provide the supporting evidence once to each supplier unless there have been relevant changes to its operation.
(VAT Notice 48, ESC 3.19; VAT Information Sheet 8/98, paras 3.3–3.5; VAT Notice 701/6/14, para 3.4.1). See Annexes B to E of the VAT Information Sheet for examples of documents which might be produced by charities intending to purchase an adapted motor vehicle.

(1) Relevant goods

These comprise the following.

(a) Medical, scientific, computer, video, sterilising, laboratory or refrigeration equipment

For use in

- medical or veterinary research (i.e. original research into disease and injury of human beings or animals);
- medical or veterinary training (i.e. training doctors, nurses, surgeons (including dental and veterinary surgeons) and other professionals involved in medical or veterinary diagnosis or treatment. The overall programme of training must include the physical application by the students of theoretical knowledge so that the teaching of subjects such as biology and zoology, where the trainee has no practical medical or veterinary involvement with patients, is not regarded as training for these purposes); or
- medical or veterinary diagnosis or treatment (i.e. the diagnosis and treatment of a physical or mental abnormality by a medical or paramedical practitioner or a veterinary surgeon).

Included are parts and accessories for use with any such equipment.

[*VATA 1994, Sch 8 Group 15, Note (3)(a)(c)*]. (VAT Notice 701/6/14, para 4.3).

'*Equipment*' means articles designed for a specific purpose. It will usually be durable but certain disposable items (e.g. syringes which are designed to be used once only) may still be equipment. *Not included* are

- bulk materials (e.g. liquids, powders, sheets, pellets, and granules);
- clothing (other than specialist medical equipment such as surgical masks, gowns and gloves); and
- consumables (e.g. chemical reagents, fuel, ink, medicines, oil, paper, and cleaning and sterilising fluids).

(VAT Notice 701/6/14, para 4.2.1).

The equipment only qualifies for relief if purchased 'for use in' medical or veterinary research, etc. Where equipment is to be used partly for a qualifying use and partly for other use, it is only eligible for relief where its main use is a qualifying use. In this context, 'main' means real, substantial and continuing. (VAT Notice 701/6/14, para 4.3).

Medical equipment is equipment that has features or characteristics that identify it as having been designed for a medical (including dental) purpose or function, such as the diagnosis or treatment of patients.

Eligible are anaesthetic apparatus; aprons (lead lined for X-ray protection); bandages; bedpans; highly specialised beds (e.g. net suspension beds, medical water beds); catheters; medical clamps; dental chairs, drills, mirrors and spittoons; drip poles; endoscopes; electro-cardiographs; eye test charts; adjustable examination couches; first aid kits (supplied as pre-packaged units); forceps; surgical gloves; heart pacemakers; hypodermic needles; identification bracelets for patients; kidney bowls; mattresses specially designed for the relief/prevention of pressure sores; medicine measures (graduated); operating lights; patient trolleys and stretchers; specialised physiotherapy equipment (other than gymnasium equipment); orthopaedic pillows specially designed and used for neck or spinal injuries; radiography equipment; renal dialysis units; resuscitation equipment; scalpels; sphygmomanometers; splints; stethoscopes; surgical gloves, gowns and masks; suture needles; swabs; clinical thermometers; tongue depressors; wound dressings; X-ray films and plates; medical X-ray machines and X-ray viewers.

Not eligible are alarm bracelets; aprons (not lead lined); blankets; cotton wool; disinfectants; drugs trolleys; gloves (other than surgical); gymnasium equipment; hearing aids; nurse call systems; occupational therapy materials; overbed tables; pagers; pillows (other than specially designed orthopaedic pillows as above); screens; towels; and uniforms. (VAT Notice 701/6/14, paras 4.2.2, 4.11).

Dental simulation equipment and artificial heads for use in training dentists have both been held to be medical equipment. See *The Anglodent Company* (VTD 16891) (TVC 11.6) and *Medical & Dental Staff Training Ltd* (VTD 17031) (TVC 11.7).

Scientific equipment is equipment designed to perform a scientific function. It includes precision measuring equipment and analytical equipment. Equipment that is not designed to perform a scientific function, but merely works on a scientific principle, is not scientific equipment. *Eligible* are barometers; centrifuges; microscopes; non-clinical thermometers; spectrometers; weighing machines; and non-medical X-ray machines. (VAT Notice 701/6/14, paras 4.2.3, 4.11).

Computer equipment includes computer hardware. Machinery or other equipment, that is either operated by computer or has computerised components, is not computer equipment. *Eligible* are computer keyboards; computer disks, tapes, mouses, printers, screens, and screen filters (as accessories to computer equipment); and computer servers. *Not eligible* is computer stationery. (VAT Notice 701/6/14, paras 4.2.4, 4.11). See (*g*) below for certain computer software.

Video equipment includes video recording and playback equipment. *Eligible* are video cameras, tapes, players and monitors. (VAT Notice 701/6/14, paras 4.2.6, 4.11).

Sterilising equipment includes specialised equipment using steam or other high temperature processes. *Eligible* are autoclaves and bedpan washers with sterilising steam cycles. *Not eligible* are microwave ovens and other cooking appliances even if they can be used to sterilise; and sterilising solutions. (VAT Notice 701/6/14, paras 4.2.7, 4.11).

Laboratory equipment includes equipment designed for use in a laboratory. *Eligible* are Bunsen burners; centrifuges; cryostats; fume cupboards; laboratory benches and glassware; microscopes; microtomes; pipettes; specialised sinks and catchpots; and test tubes. *Not eligible* are ordinary cupboards, lockers, seats and other furniture even if used to equip a laboratory; bulk materials such as liquids, powders, sheets, pellets, granules; general purpose items used to equip a laboratory; consumables such as chemical reagents, medicines, and cleaning and sterilising fluids; and laboratory animals. (VAT Notice 701/6/14, paras 4.2.8, 4.11).

In *Research Establishment* (VTD 19095) (TVC 11.11) a ventilation system was held to qualify as laboratory equipment as it had been specifically designed to control not only temperature and humidity but also pressure, allowing experiments to take place under laboratory conditions controlled to the highest practicable level.

Following the decision in *Supplier Ltd* (VTD 18247) (TVC 11.15) HMRC accept that cage and tray liners and research grade litter, bedding and nesting materials are accessories (see below) when designed for use in or with specialised laboratory caging. (Business Brief 21/03).

Refrigeration equipment includes all cooling and freezing equipment, whether designed for industrial, domestic or any other purpose. *Eligible* are deep freezer and ice-making machines. (VAT Notice 701/6/14, paras 4.2.9, 4.11).

Parts means integral components without which the equipment is incomplete. (VAT Notice 701/6/14, para 4.5.2).

Accessories means optional extras that are not necessary for the equipment to operate in its normal course, but which are used to

- improve the operation of the equipment; or
- enable it to be used, or be used to better effect, in particular circumstances.

This would include, for example, a printer for use with a computer; a specially designed camera for use with a microscope; or a rack for holding test tubes.

Not included are items which have independent uses (e.g. televisions); accessories to accessories; and generic bulk substances (e.g. liquids, powders, sheets, pellets and granules).

(VAT Notice 701/6/14, para 4.5.2).

Whether an item is an accessory is to be judged subjectively and the fact that the item can also be used otherwise than with relevant goods does not necessarily mean that it fails to qualify as an accessory. See *Royal Midland Counties Home for Disabled People v C & E Commrs,* Ch D 2001, [2002] STC 395 (TVC 11.14) where a stand-by generator, bought as a precaution against power failure, was held to be an accessory where most of the patients were dependant on electrically-powered medical equipment, even though the generator would also power lights, televisions, etc in the event of a power failure.

Ineligible equipment is equipment purchased or hired for any other use than medical or veterinary research, training, diagnosis or treatment and is not eligible for zero-rating under this provision. This includes equipment for

- general biological studies;
- environmental research;
- research into animal husbandry or food production;
- general administration; or
- domestic or leisure purposes.

Examples of ineligible equipment include air conditioners; security and smoke alarms; still cameras; catering equipment; cleaning equipment; closed circuit television systems; curtains; fuel; lockers; overhead projecting units; stationery; tape recorders; television sets; waste disposal bags, boxes, jars and sacks; and waste disposal machinery.

(VAT Notice 701/6/14, paras 4.3, 4.11).

(b) Ambulances (including parts and accessories) [VATA 1994, Sch 8 Group 15, Note (3)(b)(c)].

An '*ambulance*' is an emergency vehicle used for transporting sick and injured people or animals. It includes specially equipped air ambulances or watercraft. The vehicle must have

- the front and both sides permanently fitted with signs indicating that the vehicle is an ambulance;
- in the case of an ambulance for transporting human patients, adequate door space for the loading of a patient on a stretcher;
- seating at the rear of the driver or pilot for at least one attendant; and
- at least one stretcher that, with handles extended, measures at least 1.95 metres, together with permanent fittings to hold it in position. (This size specification applies only to ambulances that transport human patients. For ambulances that transport animals, any reasonable lifting or carrying equipment is acceptable.)

'*Parts*' are integral components without which the ambulance is incomplete. '*Accessories*' means optional extras that are not necessary for the ambulance to operate but are used to improve the operation or enable the ambulance to be used, or be used to better effect, in particular circumstances.

(VAT Notice 701/6/14, para 4.4).

(c) Goods used by people with disabilities of a kind described in VATA 1994, Sch 8 Group 12 Item 2 [VATA 1994, Sch 8 Group 15, Note (3)(d)].

This covers medical and surgical appliances; certain electrically or mechanically adjustable beds, sanitary devices, chair or stair lifts, hoists and lifters; motor vehicles capable of carrying up to 12 people designed, or substantially and permanently adapted, for the carriage of a person in a wheelchair or on a stretcher; boats designed, or substantially and permanently adapted, for use by a disabled person; and other equipment and appliances designed solely for use by a chronically sick or disabled person. See **29.15–29.24 HEALTH AND WELFARE** for full details.

(d) Motor vehicles adapted for wheelchairs

Motor vehicles (other than vehicles with more than 50 seats) designed or substantially and permanently adapted for the safe carriage of a disabled person (see (5) below) in a wheelchair provided that

- vehicles with 17 to 26 seats have provision for at least two such persons;
- vehicles with 27 to 36 seats have provision for at least three such persons;
- vehicles with 37 to 46 seats have provision for at least four such persons; and
- vehicles with 47 to 50 seats have provision for at least five such persons.

The vehicle must have either a fitted electrically or hydraulically operated lift or, in the case of a vehicle with less than 17 seats, a fitted ramp to provide access for a passenger in a wheelchair.

[*VATA 1994, Sch 8 Group 15, Note (3)(e)*].

(e) Motor vehicles for the disabled or terminally sick

Motor vehicles with 7 to 50 seats for use by an eligible body (see (2) below) providing care for blind, deaf, mentally disabled or terminally sick persons mainly to transport such persons. [*VATA 1994, Sch 8 Group 15, Note (3)(f)*].

(f) Telecommunication, aural, visual, light enhancing or heat detecting equipment

Telecommunication, aural, visual, light enhancing or heat detecting equipment (not being equipment ordinarily supplied for private or recreational use) solely for use for the purpose of rescue or first aid services undertaken by a charitable institution providing such services. [*VATA 1994, Sch 8 Group 15, Note (3)(g)*].

Eligible are image intensifiers, heat seekers and similar specialist equipment used to locate casualties; flares used to illuminate large areas for search purposes; and two-way radios that are pre-calibrated to the emergency frequency. *Not eligible* are general items such as mobile phones and pagers, binoculars, torches, searchlights and loudhailers. (VAT Notice 701/6/14, para 4.8).

Early warning sirens were held to be aural equipment in *Severnside Siren Trust Ltd* (VTD 16640) (TVC 11.16).

(g) Computer software

Computer software when purchased by an eligible body (see (2) below) solely for use in medical research, diagnosis or treatment. [*VATA 1994, Sch 8 Group 15, Note (10)*].

Zero-rating does not apply to computer software or programs that are purchased

- for a purpose other than medical research, diagnosis or treatment; or
- by a person, body or organisation other than an eligible body (even if purchased for *donation* to a nominated eligible body).

(h) Resuscitation training models

By concession, human resuscitation training models (i.e. models which include a head and torso) acquired for use in first-aid training in either 'cardiopulmonary resuscitation' or defibrillation techniques or both, together with parts and accessories for training models used for such purposes. '*Cardiopulmonary resuscitation*' means a combination of expired air ventilation and chest compression. (VAT Notice 48, ESC 3.25). Other resuscitation dummies, including intravenous cannulation models, blood transfusion models and static anatomical models are not within the scope of the concession and therefore not eligible for relief. (Business Brief 10/99).

Installation

If the normal selling price of the relevant goods includes an amount for fixing or connecting to mains services and/or testing the equipment on site, the whole selling price can be included in the relief. Any building work (e.g. removal of walls or reinforcing floors) necessary in order to install large items of equipment is standard-rated even if carried out by the supplier of the equipment. (VAT Notice 701/6/14, para 4.10).

(2) **Eligible body**

Eligible body means any of the following.

- A Strategic Health Authority (previously Health Authority) or Special Health Authority in England.
- A Health Authority, Special Health Authority or Local Health Authority in Wales.
- A Health Board in Scotland.
- A Health and Social Services Board in Northern Ireland.
- A hospital or research institution whose activities are 'not carried on for profit'.
  '*Not carried on for profit*' means that the hospital or research establishment
  (a) cannot, and does not, distribute any profit achieved; and
  (b) applies any surplus that arises from supplies of hospital or research services to the furtherance of its objectives.
- A charitable institution providing care or medical or surgical treatment (see (4) below) for disabled persons which satisfies one of the following conditions.
  (a) It provides the care or medical or surgical treatment in a relevant establishment (see (6) below), the relevant goods are used in that establishment, and the majority of persons who receive the care or treatment there are disabled (see (5) below).
  HMRC accept that a charitable institution may still be an eligible body if, for a temporary period, disabled people form less than 50% of the recipients of care or treatment services provided that, over an extended period, the majority of recipients are disabled.
  (b) It provides medical care (see (7) below) to disabled persons (see (5) below) in their own homes, the relevant goods are medical equipment falling within (1)(*a*) above or are parts or accessories for use in or with such equipment, and the goods are used in, or in connection with, the provision of that care.

- The Common Services Agency for the Scottish Health Service, the Northern Ireland Central Services Agency for Health and Social Services, or the Isle of Man Health Services Board.
- A charitable institution providing rescue or first-aid services. Rescue services do not include the operation of a website to help practitioners involved in paediatric medicine to diagnose potential complications (*Isabel Medical Charity* (VTD 18209) (TVC 11.22)).
- A NHS trust established under *National Health Service and Community Care Act 1990, Part I* or *National Health Service (Scotland) Act 1978*.
- A Primary Care Trust established under *National Health Service Act 1977, s 16A*.

Non-eligible bodies under these provisions include day centres, residential care homes or providers of home care services

- that are not charities; or
- where over an extended period the majority of the recipients of care provided are not chronically sick or disabled people (see (5) below).

Animal charities qualify as eligible bodies if

- they are animal *hospitals* providing 'in-patient' facilities; or
- they provide rescue or first-aid services to animals.

Animal clinics or surgeries are not eligible bodies unless they are part of an animal hospital or are run by a charity that also provides rescue or first-aid services.

[*VATA 1994, Sch 8 Group 15 Items 4, 4A, 5A, 5B*]. (VAT Notice 701/6/14, paras 3.3, 3.4.1, 3.5, 3.6).

(3) Voluntary contributions

Where a person, group or organisation contributes funds to an eligible body, and does not receive anything in return, this is a voluntary contribution or donation. Lottery funding is also regarded as a voluntary contribution for the purposes of this relief. (VAT Notice 701/6/14, para 5.1).

(4) Care or medical or surgical treatment

This includes protection, treatment, supervision, control or guidance that is provided to meet medical, physical, personal or domestic needs of an individual. Care or treatment will usually involve some personal contact between the provider and recipient. Examples include

- helping a person with daily personal needs (e.g. bathing, dressing, feeding or toileting);
- medical or surgical treatment;
- nursing sick or injured patients in a hospital, hospice or nursing home; and
- looking after or supervising vulnerable people.

Not included are catering, laundry and other services that do not require direct contact with the recipient.

(VAT Notice 701/6/14, para 3.4.2).

(5) Disabled

The term disabled also includes a person who is chronically sick. [*VATA 1994, Sch 8 Group 15, Note (5)*].

Chronic sickness is a condition regarded as such by the medical profession. Disability is a physical or mental impairment that has a substantial and long-term adverse effect on a person's ability to carry out day-to-day activities. Frail elderly people who are not disabled, or people whose mobility is temporarily impaired by short-term illness or injury are not chronically sick or disabled for the purposes of this VAT relief. (VAT Notice 701/6/14, para 3.4.3).

(6) Relevant establishment

Relevant establishment means either of the following.

- A day centre other than one that exists primarily as a place for activities that are social or recreational or both.
  Examples of day centres which would qualify include charitable physiotherapy centres for disabled children and charitable centres that run daily rehabilitation or training classes for disabled adults.
- An institution which is approved, licensed or registered under the relevant social legislation or which is exempt from any such requirement by that legislation.

Examples include charitable hospices and residential care homes.

[*VATA 1994, Sch 8 Group 15, Note (4B)*]. (VAT Notice 701/6/14, para 3.4.1).

(7) Medical care

Medical care includes medical treatment and the sort of care that a nurse might carry out or supervise (e.g. washing or feeding a patient, helping a patient out of bed, and administering drugs). It does not include assistance with general domestic tasks such as cooking, cleaning or shopping.

(VAT Notice 701/6/14, para 3.4.4).

Evidence of eligibility

The supplier is responsible for ensuring that all the conditions for zero-rating are met. As this may not always be evident at the time of supply, HMRC recommend that suppliers obtain a written declaration of eligibility from each customer who claims entitlement to VAT relief. The declaration should

- contain sufficient information to demonstrate that the conditions for the relief are satisfied; and
- be separate, or clearly distinguishable from, any order form or invoice against which the goods or services are supplied (i.e. a customer signing an order should not automatically be signing a declaration of eligibility for VAT relief).

There is a link to suggested template declaration form in paragraph 3.6 of VAT Notice 701/7/14. Any other declaration form used must require the purchaser to provide the same information.

In addition to a written declaration, suppliers may require evidence that the purchaser is an eligible body. This may include in the case of

- a charitable body, evidence that it is a charity;
- domiciliary care agencies, day centres or other establishments, evidence that care or treatment services are provided mainly to chronically sick or disabled people;
- charitable transport providers, evidence that transport services are provided mainly to disabled people;
- other charities, evidence that its sole purpose is the provision of services for, or on behalf of, chronically sick or disabled people.

Suppliers must retain evidence that any supply was eligible for relief.

The receipt of a declaration and/or other evidence from a customer does not authorise the zero-rating of a supply. A supplier must take reasonable steps to check any apparent inconsistencies and to confirm that any information given by the customer is correct. However, the purchaser has a responsibility to make truthful statements and to provide appropriate documentation to support this. HMRC will not, therefore, seek to recover VAT due from a supplier who has taken reasonable steps to check the validity of a declaration, but has failed to identify an inaccuracy, and, in good faith, has zero-rated a supply.

(VAT Notice 48, ESC 3.11; VAT Notice 701/6/14, paras 8.1–8.4).

Imports

Goods that meet all the conditions for zero-rating when purchased in the UK can be zero-rated on importation. Importers should lodge the relevant declaration of eligibility (see above) with HMRC at the point of importation. Special provisions apply to the importation of computer software. (VAT Notice 701/6/14, para 7.1).

Acquisitions from other EU member states

Where a VAT-registered eligible body acquires goods from another EU member state, the normal rules for acquisitions apply. If the supply meets all the conditions for relief, no VAT is due. Eligibility declarations do not need to be provided to the overseas supplier but evidence that the supply is correctly zero-rated should be retained.

Where an eligible body is not VAT-registered, any goods acquired from another EU member state are subject to VAT at the rate in force in that country. The UK relief for charity-funded equipment does not apply.

(VAT Notice 701/6/14, para 7.2).

Supplies to eligible bodies outside the UK

Apart from the specific UK Health Boards, etc., there is no requirement in the legislation that an eligible body must be within the UK. Therefore

- where a supply is made to an eligible body (i.e. a qualifying hospital, research institution or charitable institution) based in another EU member state and that body is not VAT-registered there, this relief can be used to zero-rate the supply provided all the conditions are met; and
- if the customer is VAT-registered in another EU member state or is outside the EU, the supply of goods can be zero-rated under the normal rules.

(VAT Notice 701/6/14, para 7.3).

Exempt supplies by charities

[13.9] Certain supplies by charities are exempt from VAT not because of the charitable status of the supplier but because they are covered by general application. See **21 EXEMPT SUPPLIES**. In addition, the exemptions in **13.10** and **13.11** below apply specifically to charities and certain other qualifying bodies.

Fund-raising events by charities and other qualifying bodies

[13.10] Subject to the exclusions below, the supply of goods and services in connection with an 'event' whose primary purpose is the raising of money and which is promoted as such is exempt from VAT where

- the supply of goods and services is by a 'charity' and the event is organised for charitable purposes by one or more charities;
- the supply of goods and services is by a 'qualifying body' and the event is organised exclusively for the body's own benefit; or
- the supply of goods and services is by a charity or a qualifying body and the event is organised, jointly by one or more charities and the qualifying body, exclusively for charitable purposes or that body's own benefit or a combination of those purposes.

[*VATA 1994, Sch 9 Group 12 Items 1 and 2; SI 2000/802*].

'*Event*' includes an event accessed (wholly or partly) by means of electronic communications including an electronic communications network (such as the internet). [*VATA 1994, Sch 9 Group 12 Note 1; Communications Act 2003, Sch 17 para 129*].

'*Charity*' includes a body corporate which is wholly-owned by the charity if

- the body has agreed in writing (whether or not by deed) to transfer its profits from whatever source to a charity; or
- the body's profits from whatever source are otherwise payable to a charity.

[*VATA 1994, Sch 9 Group 12 Note 2*].

A '*qualifying body*' is

- a non-profit making body within **15.7**(*a*)–(*f*) **CLUBS AND ASSOCIATIONS**;
- any eligible body as defined in **58.5 RECREATION AND SPORT** whose principal purpose is the provision of facilities for persons to take part in sport and physical recreation; or

- any body which is an eligible body for the purposes of *VATA 1994, Sch 9 Group 13 Item 2* (exempt admission charges to entertainment, cultural activities, etc.) as defined in **58.2 RECREATION AND SPORT**.

[*VATA 1994, Sch 9 Group 12 Note 3*].

For further information see HMRC helpsheet 'Fund-raising events: exemption for charities and other qualifying bodies' at www.hmrc.gov.uk/charities/fund-raising-events.htm.

Exclusions

The following events are excluded from exemption.

(a) *Multiple events of the same kind at the same location*. Exemption does not apply to *any* event where in its financial year a charity or qualifying body organises (whether alone or in association with another charity or qualifying body) more than 15 events of the same kind in the same 'location' (i.e. if a charity or body organises 16 similar events in the same location in its financial year, none of those events are exempt). In determining whether the limit of 15 events has been exceeded, there can be disregarded any event of that kind at that location in a week during which the aggregate gross takings from events involving the charity or body of that kind in that location do not exceed £1,000.
Where a charity's or body's financial year is longer or shorter than a year, the maximum number of events qualifying for exemption is
(15 × number of days in financial year ÷ 365)
expressed to the nearest whole number.
[*VATA 1994, Sch 9 Group 12 Notes 4–7*].

(b) *Events where accommodation also provided*. An event does not qualify for exemption where accommodation in connection with the event is provided, directly or indirectly, by
- any of the charities or the qualifying body organising the event, or
- any charity connected with any charity organising the event

unless the accommodation so provided does not exceed two nights in total (whether or not consecutive) *and* the supply of accommodation does not fall within the **69 TOUR OPERATORS' MARGIN SCHEME**.
[*VATA 1994, Sch 9 Group 12 Notes 8, 9*].

(c) *Distortion of competition*. An event does not qualify for exemption if it is likely to cause distortion of competition and place a commercial enterprise carried on by a taxable person at a disadvantage.
[*VATA 1994, Sch 9 Group 12 Note 11*].

Non-qualifying events

Supplies made by a charity or qualifying body at a fund-raising event which does not qualify for exemption are subject to VAT in the normal way. See **13.5**(1) above.

Welfare services

[13.11] The supply by a charity of welfare services, and of goods supplied in connection with those services, is exempt. [*VATA 1994, Sch 9 Group 7, Item 9*]. Identical provisions apply to such supplies made by public bodies, state-regulated private welfare institutions and state-regulated private welfare agencies. See **29.12 HEALTH AND WELFARE** for full details.

See **13.5**(21) above for welfare services supplied consistently below cost.

Reduced rate supplies by charities

[13.12] Supplies of welfare advice or information by a charity (or a state-regulated private welfare institution or agency) are subject to a reduced rate of VAT. See **29.35 HEALTH AND WELFARE** for details.

Reduced rate supplies to charities

[13.13] Supplies to charities can be subject to the reduced rate as follows.

(a) **Fuel and power.** Supplies of fuel and power can be subject to the reduced rate in certain circumstances. These include
- use in a dwelling or a building used for a relevant residential purpose; and
- use by a charity otherwise than in the course or furtherance of a business.

See **26 FUEL AND POWER.**

(b) **Energy-saving materials.** Before 1 August 2013 the installation of certain energy saving materials in a building used solely for a relevant charitable purpose was liable to VAT at the reduced rate. See **59.2 REDUCED RATE SUPPLIES.**

Relief for importations

[13.14] No VAT is payable on the importation of certain goods by or for charities and other philanthropic organisations. See **34.15**(6) **IMPORTS**.

New building projects on a self-build or self-help basis

[13.15] Refunds of VAT may be available to a charity involved in a self-build project of a building intended solely for use for a relevant charitable purpose. See **43.23 LAND AND BUILDINGS: ZERO AND REDUCED RATE SUPPLIES AND DIY HOUSEBUILDERS.**

Refunds of VAT to certain charities from 1 April 2015

[13.16] Certain charities can claim a refund of the VAT incurred on goods and services used for their non-business activities (but not for private purposes) in relation to purchases, acquisitions and importations taking place after 31 March 2015. Those charities are:

- palliative care charities;
- air ambulance charities;
- search and rescue charities; and
- medical courier charities.

A palliative care charity is a charity the main purpose of which is the provision of palliative care to persons who are in need of such care as a result of having a terminal illness, where the care is provided at the direction of, or under the supervision of, a registered medical practitioner or a registered nurse. A terminal illness is a progressive disease which will result in a person's death. Palliative care charities often operate adult and children's hospices.

An air ambulance charity is a charity the main purpose of which is to provide emergency air ambulance services in pursuance of arrangements made by, or at the request of, a National Health Service (NHS) body that delivers an NHS ambulance service. The following are NHS bodies for this purpose:

- an NHS foundation trust in England;
- an NHS trust in Wales;
- a Special Health Board constituted under the *National Health Service (Scotland) Act 1978, s 2*; and
- a Health and Social Care trust established under the *Health and Personal Social Services (Northern Ireland) Order 1991*.

A search and rescue charity is a charity that meets condition A or condition B below.

Condition A is that the main purpose of the charity is to carry out the activities of searching for and rescuing persons who are, or may be, at risk of death or serious injury in the UK or the UK marine area, where the activities are co-ordinated by at least one of the following relevant authorities.

- The Secretary of State.
- The Scottish Fire and Rescue Service.
- A police force within the meaning of the *Police Act 1996*.
- The Police Service of Scotland.
- The Police Service of Northern Ireland.
- The Police Service of Northern Ireland Reserve.
- The British Transport Police Force.
- The Civil Nuclear Constabulary.
- The Ministry of Defence Police.
- Any other person or body specified by an order made by the Treasury for the purposes of *VATA 1994, s 33D(6)*.

Condition B is that the main purpose of the charity is to support, develop and promote the activities of a charity which meets condition A above.

A medical courier charity is a charity that meets condition A or condition B below.

Condition A is that the main purpose of the charity is to provide services for the transportation of items or substances intended for use for medical purposes, including in particular, blood, medicines and other medical supplies, and items relating to people who are undergoing medical treatment.

Condition B is that the main purpose of the charity is to support, develop and promote the activities of a charity which meets condition A above.

A charity whose main purpose is to support, develop and promote other search and rescue charities or medical courier charities will undertake at least one of the following activities:

- co-ordinate and provide support to such charities;
- support and help with the establishment of such charities;
- promote good practice for charitable search and rescue or medical courier activities – examples may include training, knowledge and information sharing;
- arrange supplies of goods and services to such charities which are required for charitable search and rescue or medical courier activities; and
- represent such charities regionally and/or nationally.

The main purpose of a charity is its primary function. This should be evident from documents such as the charity's memorandum and articles of association, constitution, trust deed or declaration of trust and its annual report.

If a charity makes no charge for providing a service the provision of the service is likely to be a non-business activity (see **13.4** for the distinction between business and non-business activities). A hospice charity that receives grant funding from the NHS, Clinical Commissioning Group and/or local authority to support its provision of palliative care can treat the funding as non-business income for VAT purposes. A hospice charity that receives funding under a standard NHS service level contract from the NHS, Clinical Commissioning Group and/or local authority to support its provision of palliative care can treat the funding as non-business income for VAT purposes providing there is no direct link between the palliative care provided and the funding received.

Charities that provide welfare services to individuals at significantly below cost may be able to treat the income as non-business for VAT purposes (see **13.5** above).

Charities that have a mixture of business and non-business activities need to apportion any VAT incurred on overhead costs relating to both activities.

A charity that qualifies for refunds of VAT on its non-business activities can, subject to HMRC approval, be included in a VAT group with its trading subsidiaries, but the facility to recover VAT incurred on non-business activities does not extend to the VAT group as a whole.

VAT on goods and services used by a qualifying charity for its non-business purposes can be recovered if the charity places the order, receives the supply and a VAT invoice addressed to it, and pays the invoice from its own funds, which can include funds awarded to it. VAT can only be recovered where the supply takes place after 31 March 2015. The method of claiming the VAT and the time limits for claiming it vary depending on whether the charity is registered for VAT or not.

A charity that is registered for VAT should claim the VAT refund in box 4 of its VAT return for the period the VAT was incurred, and include the net value of its claim in box 7. If a claim is not included on the VAT return for the relevant period the charity can submit a claim in writing to HMRC stating the amount it is claiming, the VAT period(s) covered and the basis of the calculation of the claim. The charity must hold evidence to support the claim. A four-year time limit applies to late claims, subject to the condition that only VAT incurred after 31 March 2015 can be recovered.

A charity that is not registered for VAT should claim the VAT refund by completing a Form VAT 126 (can be downloaded from the HMRC website) and sending it to the following address:

HM Revenue and Customs
DMB Banking 2
7th Floor
Regian House
James Street
Liverpool
L75 1AD

Claims made using a Form VAT 126 should relate to a period of at least one calendar month, or at least 12 months if the claim is for less than £100. The period of the claim should end on the last day of a calendar month and should be made within four years of the end of the month the VAT was incurred, subject to the condition that only VAT incurred after 31 March 2015 can be recovered. Invoices and other records to support the claim should be retained for six years, unless HMRC have confirmed in writing that they can be kept for a shorter period.

Claims made using a Form VAT 126 will normally be refunded by HMRC using BACS or a payable order. After the first claim using a Form VAT 126 HMRC should provide the claimant with a unique number to quote on future claims. This does not mean that HMRC have registered the claimant for VAT.

The facility to recover VAT incurred on non-business activities does not extend to non-deductible input tax, for example VAT on motor cars (see **35.8 INPUT TAX**).

From time to time HMRC will select claims for verification.

[*VATA 1994, ss 33C, 33D; FA 2015, s 66*]. (VAT Notice 1001).

Key points: charities

[13.17] Points to consider are as follows.

- It will be clear in most cases whether an organisation is a charity and able to benefit from VAT concessions available to charities. In other cases, it will be necessary to consider the aims and objectives of the organisation and put forward a strong argument to HMRC that charitable status is appropriate. Any requirement to be registered under the *Charities Act 2011* must be complied with.

- In some cases, it may be worthwhile for a charity to register for VAT on a voluntary basis. This would be particularly useful if the charity has a high proportion of zero-rated sales, e.g. sales of donated goods.
- In considering whether a charity has to register for VAT on a compulsory basis, remember that it is only the value of taxable supplies that need to be taken into account as far as the registration limit is concerned. Exempt supplies and outside the scope income are excluded from the calculations.
- An important challenge for many charities as far as VAT is concerned is to ensure that input tax is only reclaimed to the extent that it relates to the charity's taxable supplies. Effective procedures need to be in place to ensure that input tax is not reclaimed on non-business expenditure or expenditure relating to exempt supplies. This includes an apportionment of input tax on general overheads where appropriate. Qualifying palliative care charities, air ambulance charities, search and rescue charities and medical courier charities can recover VAT incurred after 31 March 2015 on goods and services used for their non-business activities.
- A charity can use any method to apportion input tax between business and non-business activities on general overhead items as long as the method gives a fair and reasonable result. Remember that an income-based apportionment may not be the most suitable method if the expenditure in question is not directly linked to income.
- Be aware that many sources of income for a charity can be zero-rated or exempt from VAT. For example, income from a fundraising event will be exempt in most cases – although obviously any input tax relevant to the event will not be reclaimable as it relates to an exempt supply. The rules concerning exemption for fundraising events basically require the event to be publicised as such, either on promotional literature or in committee meeting minutes. There are restrictions on the number of similar events that can be held at the same location in the same financial year (15) but these will not be relevant in most cases. The exemption for fundraising also extends to non-profit making bodies (e.g. members of sporting clubs).
- A donation can be treated as outside the scope of VAT as long as the donor does not receive any benefits for his payment. It is important to ensure that donations are freely given by the donor, for example, the request for a 'minimum donation of £x' in connection with the supply of goods or services would not be classed as a freely given donation.
- Do not assume that all grant income received by a charity is outside the scope of VAT. If grant income is linked to the performance of services by a charity, then it will be standard-rated in most cases, although could be exempt if it relates to welfare services.

- There is a range of concessions available to charities as far as VAT on their expenditure is concerned. For example, a charity placing an advert in a local newspaper for a new member of staff should not pay VAT because the supply is zero-rated as advertising for a charity. The reduced rate of VAT (currently 5%) applies to supplies of fuel and power to a charity for its non-business activities.
- The 2016 Court of Appeal decision in *Longridge on the Thames* marks a significant victory for HMRC and a change in the way that the UK courts will regard the difference between a charity that is not in business at all, and a charity that is carrying on an exempt business activity. The full implications of the decision may take some time to become clear.

14

Clothing and Footwear

De Voil Indirect Tax Service. See V4.287

Introduction to clothing and footwear

[14.1] Zero-rating applies to

- articles of clothing or footwear designed for young children and not suitable for older children (see **14.2** to **14.7** below); and
- certain supplies of protective boots and helmets (see **14.8** below).

Other supplies of clothing and footwear are standard-rated.

Young children's clothing and footwear

[14.2] Articles designed as clothing (including hats and other headgear) or footwear for young children and not suitable for older persons are zero-rated. [*VATA 1994, Sch 8 Group 16 Item 1 and Note 1*]. Special provisions apply to clothing made wholly or partly of fur (see **14.4** below).

In order to qualify for zero-rating, an article must therefore satisfying all of the following conditions.

- It must be an article of clothing or footwear. See **14.3** below.
- It must not be made of fur (with minor exceptions). See **14.4** below.
- It must be designed for young children. See **14.5** below.
- It must only be suitable for young children. See **14.6** below.

(VAT Notice 714, para 1.4).

What qualifies as clothing and footwear

[14.3] The word 'clothing' must be given its ordinary meaning and whether an item is clothing or not is a question of fact. To have a function as clothing, an item should provide cover for the body (either for decency or protection from the elements). But the purpose for which an item was intended to be used is not conclusive and a garment designed primarily for another purposes (see, for example, safety aids below), but also fulfilling a clothing function, can still qualify for zero-rating (*British Vita Co Ltd* (VTD 322) (TVC 12.4)).

For a consideration of the phrase 'articles designed as clothing' see *C & E Commrs v Ali Baba Tex Ltd,* QB [1992] STC 590 (TVC 12.4).

If an item is not an article of clothing or footwear it is standard-rated.

(1) Clothing in general

As well as all the obvious garments, clothing includes items such as hats, caps, braces, belts, garters and scarves.

Not included are clothing accessories and items of haberdashery sold separately, such as

- items of Guide and Scout uniform comprising belt pouches, pins, woggles and sash pins (see *BG Supplies (Birmingham) Ltd* (VTD 11663) (TVC 12.7));
- fastenings such as buckles, buttons and zips;
- badges, collars, cuffs, patches and other sew-on or iron-on items;
- hand muffs and ear muffs; and
- wristbands for sport, etc. (see *Vidhani Brothers Ltd* (VTD 18997) (TVC 12.6)).

(2) Baby wear

Most items of baby wear (e.g. bonnets, bootees and matinee jackets) can be clearly recognised as clothing, but the following less obvious items are also considered to be articles of clothing.

- Bibs, including plastic bibs with a curved tray at the base.
- Hooded rain covers for pushchairs, provided they are suitable for the baby to wear as a rain cape when out of the pushchair.
- Nappies (and nappy liners), both disposable and re-usable, provided they are held out for sale appropriately.
- Babies' shawls, provided they are designed and held out as such.
- Padded sleeping garments, similar in construction to sleeping bags, but shaped at the neck and armholes or having sleeves and/or legs.
- Towelling bathrobes designed with a hood or sleeves enabling the baby to be wrapped in them as a garment.

See also *Snugglebundl Ltd* [2014] UKFTT 1121 (TC) (TC04209) (TVC 12.10).

The following are *not* considered to be baby clothing and are standard-rated.

- Pram and pushchair covers not designed to serve as rain capes outside the pram or chair.
- Disposable nappy material sold in a continuous role from which individual nappies are cut.
- 'Mother-and-baby' shawls intended to wrap around both mother and child.

- Sleeping bags not designed with neck and arm holes or sleeves and/or legs.

See also *Mothercare Ltd* (VTD 323) (TVC 12.1) and *Little Rock Ltd* (VTD 424) (TVC 12.2).

(3) Footwear

Articles of footwear include

- boots, shoes, sandals and slippers, even if they are designed for special purposes (such as ballet shoes or studded football boots); and
- ice-skating or roller-skating boots, with or without skating blades or rollers attached;

but do not include

- blades or rollers sold on their own, or platform type roller skates for attaching to normal shoes; and
- shoelaces, insoles, heel protectors and stick-on soles sold as separate items.

(4) Headgear

Some articles worn on the head cannot be zero-rated even though they are for young children because they are accessories rather than clothing. HMRC regard this as including all articles that do not cover the whole head, e.g.

- alice bands (see *Cassidy (t/a Balou)* (VTD 5760) (TVC 12.5));
- hair ribbons and slides;
- scrunchies;
- sports and other headbands; and
- sun visors and ear muffs.

Novelty hats, party hats and play hats made out of materials such as paper or plastic are toys rather than clothing and are standard-rated.

(5) Safety aids

Clothing includes items that, although primarily designed as safety aids, have the form and function of clothing (e.g. cyclists' tabards and sailors' lifejackets). Other safety aids which have no clothing functions (e.g. reflective armbands and buoyancy aids) are always standard-rated.

(6) Incomplete articles

An unfinished article may be considered to be clothing if it has been processed to such an extent that it could not reasonably be used for any other purpose (e.g. cut-out parts of a garment or pleated skirt lengths). See *Ali Baba Tex Ltd* above.

(VAT Notice 714, paras 2.1–2.3).

Items made of fur

[14.4] Clothing does not included any articles made wholly or partly of 'fur skin' apart from

- headgear,
- gloves,
- buttons, belts and buckles; and
- any garment merely trimmed with fur skin unless the trimming has an area greater than one-fifth of the area of the outside material or, in the case of a new garment, represents a cost to the manufacturer greater than the cost of the other components.

'*Fur skin*' means any skin with fur, hair or wool attached except

- rabbit skin;
- woolled sheep or lamb skin; and
- the skin, if neither tanned nor dressed, of bovine cattle (including buffalo), equine animals, goats or kids (other than Yemen, Mongolian and Tibetan goats or kids), swine (including peccary), chamois, gazelles, deer or dogs.

[*VATA 1994, Sch 8 Group 16 Notes 2 and 3*].

These provisions are designed to exclude zero-rating for children's clothing made from luxury furs. Subject to satisfying the other tests in **14.2** above, zero-rating can be applied to

- articles made using artificial fur; and
- fur lined boots.

(VAT Notice 714, paras 3.1, 4.4).

Items designed for young children

[14.5] Although sizes and measurements are not referred to in the legislation, it has been agreed with the industry working party that they represent a fair reflection of the interpretation of the law.

(1) Clothing

HMRC in general accept that garments are designed for young children provided they are up to the tabled measurements below. These measurements are based on those for children up to the eve of their 14th birthday (as set out in the r"elevant British Standard). The garments should be measured on a flat surface, with creases smoothed out, buttons (or equivalent) fastened and any intended overlap in place. Chest measurements should normally be taken 2.5 cms below the base of the armhole and multiplied by two. Similarly, waist measurements should be taken from one side of the fastened waistband to the other and multiplied by two.

Maximum garment sizes	*Boys*				*Girls*			
	Chest	**Waist**	**Chest**	**Waist**	**Chest**	**Waist**	**Chest**	**Waist**
Shirts	104cm	—	41"		105cm	—	41.5"	
Knitwear	104cm	—	41"		105cm	—	41.5"	
Jackets/waistcoats	109cm	—	43"		110cm	—	43.5"	

Maximum garment sizes	*Boys*				*Girls*			
	Chest	**Waist**	**Chest**	**Waist**	**Chest**	**Waist**	**Chest**	**Waist**
Top coats/outerwear	114cm	—	44.5"		115cm	—	45"	
Dresses	—	—			98cm	—	39.5"	
Skirts*	—	—			—	71cm		28"
Trousers/shorts*	—	72cm		28.5"	—	71cm		28"
Underwear/ swimwear	88cm	72cm	34.5"	28.5"	89cm	71cm	35"	28"
Nightwear	105cm	73cm	41.5"	29"	106cm	72cm	42"	28.5"

* Garments with elasticated waistbands should be measured at their full stretch. Those that have no fastening may be zero-rated up to a maximum stretched waist of 85 cms for boys and 90 cms for girls.

Some products are normally judged by different criteria or measurements. The following garments are also accepted as being designed for young children.

Maximum garment sizes — other garments
Lifejackets — Max body weight 52kg
Leotards/body stockings/swimsuits — Shoulder to crotch 70cm/27.5"
Saris — 442cm × 104cm/166"x41.5"
Lungis — 156cm × 94cm/61.5x37"
Socks (by shoe size) — Boys 6.5; Girls/unisex 5.5
Tights — Waist-crotch-waist measurement 51cm/20" for lightweight and 56cm/22" for heavyweight
Teen bras — Size 34B

Style considerations

In a minority of cases, it may be necessary to consider factors inherent in the garment as making it suitable for older persons. If this applies, a garment within the maximum measurements above could still fail the 'design' test and be standard-rated. See, for example, *Walter Stewart Ltd* [1974] Lexis Citation 11 (TVC 12.12) where a leather coat which did not exceed the maximum measurements failed the test because it was a relatively high-cost fashion garment more likely to appeal to adults and because a three-inch bust dart had been inserted.

Larger sizes

If the above measurements are exceeded, HMRC will still accept that garments are designed for young children if *either* of the following conditions can be satisfied. If they're:

- designed to fit a body not larger than those outlined in the table below; and
- restricted by some other design feature to those under 14 years of age.

HMRC must be satisfied that the body sizes used are appropriate to the under 14s and the garments produced are only suitable for that age group. They must be given the specifications and reasoning and must have given written agreement before zero-rating can be applied in such cases.

Body size	*Boys*		*Girls*	
Height	163cms	64"	161cms	63"
Chest	84cms	33"	85cms	33.5"
Waist	70cms	27.5"	69cms	27"
Hips	85cms	33.5"	90cms	35.5"
Arm (shoulder to wrist)	59cms	23"	57cms	22.5"
Inside leg	77cms	30"	76cms	30"

(VAT Notice 714, para 4.2.1)

One-size and stretch garments

Zero-rating cannot be applied to articles of clothing which are sold in one size only and that are suitable for both children and adults. Articles that stretch to fit, such as some sportswear, can be zero-rated provided the garment is designed to fit a body size in accordance with the second table above or at its maximum stretch does not exceed the measurements for maximum garment sizes in the first table above. See also *Jeffrey Green & Co Ltd* [1974] Lexis Citation 8 (TVC 12.11).

(2) **Footwear**

HMRC accept that footwear is designed for young children up to the following measurements.

- Boys' shoes — up to and including UK size 6.5 or American size 7 (unless 7.5 is marked as equal to UK 6.5) or Continental size 40
- Girls' court shoes (i.e. low cut shoes without straps or other fastenings) — up to and including UK size 3 or American size 4.5 or Continental size 35.5 (or 35 if no half sizes)
- Other girls' shoes — as for court shoes but where the heel height does not exceed the sole depth by more than 4 cms, up to UK size 5.5 or American size 7 or Continental size 38.5 (38 if no half sizes)

See also *Brays of Glastonbury Ltd* (VTD 650) (TVC 12.14) and *Gura (t/a Vincent Footwear)* (VTD 18416) (TVC 12.15).

Larger sizes

It may still be possible to zero-rate larger sizes if HMRC are satisfied that

- the product has been designed exclusively for children under 14; and
- it is held out for sale to this age group (see **14.6** below),

but HMRC must be given the specifications and reasoning and must have given written agreement before zero-rating can be applied in such cases.

Unisex footwear

Most lines of footwear are designed for one sex or the other and should be zero-rated according to the rules relating to girls' or boys' footwear as appropriate. True 'unisex' footwear can only be zero-rated up to and including size 5.5 (the maximum size for girls' footwear).

Feet of differing sizes

Where a child has one foot significantly larger than the other, or requires an unusually high heel for one foot, the pair of shoes can be zero-rated if the smaller shoe qualifies for the relief.

(3) Hats and other headgear

Many children's hats fit adults. It is still possible to zero-rate hats (including caps and other items of headgear) which are suitable by design only for young children (e.g. babies' bonnets, school hats) or which are clearly held out for sale for young children.

In *Benrose Ltd (t/a Multi-Stock Ltd)* (VTD 15783) (TVC 12.25) which concerned knitted acrylic hats bearing logos of famous football teams, the tribunal held that, although it was physically possible for an adult to wear the hats, they were too close-fitting for comfortable wear over an extended period. Also, as they were intended as cheap imitations of official football club hats, supporters over 14 would want the official hats. This decision stresses the point that size is not always the crucial test and that design or style must be considered.

HMRC have accepted the following items as falling within the relief.

- Protective helmets (such as those for skateboarding or ice hockey) up to a maximum size of 59 cms as long as they are designed and marketed exclusively for children (**14.6** below).
- Riding hats up to and including size 6.75 (jockey skulls up to size 1) even if they are not held out for sale for children. Sales of larger riding hats specifically for young children can be zero-rated as long as they are fitted, adapted or otherwise appropriate only for young children (e.g. by being less sophisticated in terms of design and appearance) but HMRC's written approval must be received before zero-rating larger sizes.

All cycle helmets are zero-rated irrespective of size or how they are held out for sale (see **14.9** below).

(4) Belts, braces and other items

HMRC accept belts, braces, neckties, gloves, garters, scarves, ruffs, collars and shirt frills as traditional items of clothing and they may be zero-rated irrespective of size as long as they are held out for sale for the under 14s only (see **14.6** below).

(VAT Notice 714, paras 4.1–4.5).

Items suitable only for young children

[14.6] The final test that must be satisfied if an item is to be zero-rated (see **14.2** above) is that it must only be suitable for young children, i.e. not suitable for older persons. This can be met by ensuring that it is 'held out for sale' for young children.

'*Held out for sale*' means the way in which an article is labelled, packaged, displayed, invoiced or advertised. It includes any promotional items and the heading under which an article is listed in a catalogue, web page or price list.

Articles cannot necessarily be zero-rated on sale simply because they were zero-rated when purchased. How they are held out for sale affects their VAT liability. Goods, which may qualify at the design stage, fail the suitability test if they are labeled

- to fit sizes larger than those in **14.5** above;
- as suitable for age '13/14' and above; or
- by the ladies sizing system (8, 10, 12, and so on).

In particular:

- *Manufacturers* must be able to show that items qualify for zero-rating from product specification or other documentation and must identify them appropriately on any labelling and packaging, and in any promotional material and on invoices.
- *Wholesalers and distributors* must clearly identify the article as being only suitable for children on invoices and price lists. If the goods are on display they must clearly be identified and segregated. Any catalogue should identify the articles as being for young children, preferably in a separate children's section and the identical product must not appear in both adults' and children's sections.
- *Retailers* can zero-rate clothing for young children only if it is clear from labels, signs, packaging, advertising, etc. that it is intended for young children and they either
  (i) sell it from a shop, a separate department in a shop, or a separate section of a catalogue which caters exclusively for children; or
  (ii) keep it apart from adult garments by selling it from separate shelves, racks, etc. which are clearly marked up as 'boys', 'girls' or 'children's'.

  The extent to which this is possible will vary depending upon the size and type of retail outlet but any retailer should be able to show that it has as good a system as is practical in the circumstances. The potential purchaser should not be left in any doubt that the retailer is selling items for young children.
- *Mail order and internet suppliers* must clearly identify the goods as being for young children in any price list, page, catalogue or other promotional material, preferably using a discrete children's section. The potential purchaser should be in no doubt that the goods they are looking at are for young children and the identical goods must not appear in both adults' and children's sections.

(VAT Notice 714, paras 5.1–5.6).

Treatment in particular cases

[14.7] Children's clothing and footwear can be zero-rated in particular cases as outlined below.

(1) School uniforms

There is no specific relief for items of school uniform which are subject to the normal rules for children's clothes. But, by concession, if garments are supplied under a specific agreement with a school catering exclusively for pupils under 14 years of age, it is possible to apply the zero rate beyond the garment measurements in **14.5** above provided the garments are

- unique to that school by design, such as a prominent badge or piping in school colours, and
- held out for sale as being for that school only.

Where a school also caters for pupils of 14 and over, the normal rules apply and obtaining a declaration that the relevant garment is intended for a pupil under the age of 14 is not sufficient for zero-rating to apply (*Smart Alec Ltd* (VTD 17832) (TVC 12.21)).

(VAT Notice 714, para 6.1).

(2) Youth organisations

By concession, garments worn only as uniform by members of groups or organisations which cater exclusively for under-14 year olds (e.g. Beavers and Brownies) qualify for zero-rating, irrespective of size, provided they are

- designed exclusively for the organisation;
- worn only by under 14s; and
- clearly identifiable to the organisation.

Zero-rating does not apply to items that may also be worn by older groups such as Scouts.

(VAT Notice 714, para 6.1).

(3) Cloth kits

Packaged kits for making children's clothes can be zero-rated provided

- the clothes themselves would be zero-rated;
- the material is already cut to the pattern or the pattern is indelibly printed on the material; and
- it is clear from the labelling or other promotional material that the made-up garment is only suitable for young children.
  (VAT Notice 714, para 7.1).

(4) Multiple supplies

Where an article consists of both zero-rated clothing and *incidental* standard-rated items at an inclusive price (e.g. a cowboy suit with a toy gun or a policeman's uniform with toy handcuffs), HMRC consider this a single supply of children's clothing and the whole price can be zero-rated.

Where the standard-rated element is not incidental (e.g. a baby's gift set comprising of a bib and feeding cup) there is a multiple supply which must be apportioned between the zero-rated and standard-rated elements. See **48.3 OUTPUT TAX.**

(VAT Notice 714, para 8.1).

(5) Hire or loan of children's clothing and footwear

The hire or loan of any item of children's clothing or footwear is zero-rated if the item would itself be zero-rated. [*VATA 1994, Sch 8 Group 16 Note 5*]. This covers, for example, hire of bridesmaids' and page boys' outfits, fancy dress costumes, and nappy hire services where the nappies are collected for laundering and replaced with fresh ones.

The separate supply of ice-skates, roller skates, ten-pin bowling shoes, etc. is also eligible for zero-rating in accordance with the size criteria for footwear in **14.5** above. However, if a single price is charged for admission that also includes the loan of footwear, it is necessary to consider whether the supply should be treated as single or multiple supplies.

In *The Ice Rink Co and PI (Milton Keynes) Ltd v HMRC* [2017] UKFTT 698 (TC) (TVC 62.596), the Tribunal held that supplies of admission to an ice skating rink and the hire of children's ice skates should be treated as two separate supplies even though they had been supplied as a single package. The Tribunal concluded that the taxpayer was entitled to zero-rate the supply of the children's ice skates and VAT was only due on the admission fee levied to use the ice rink. See **48.3 OUTPUT TAX.**

(6) Supplies of services

Cut, make and trim

Making up young children's clothing from cloth owned by someone else can be zero-rated. Other processes may also be eligible for zero-rating if, after the work is finished, the processed article clearly becomes a child's garment which itself is normally zero-rated or the processed goods can only be incorporated in such an item. This is because such work is treated as a supply of services and zero-rated under *VATA 1994, s 30(2A)* as the application of a process to another person's goods which produces goods which are themselves zero-rated.

Alteration, repair, embroidery and similar services

These services do not qualify for zero-rating as they are applied to goods that maintain their essential nature. For example, a blazer that has its sleeve length altered, its collar repaired, or a school badge embroidered on its pocket, is not sufficiently changed by that process to produce a new item. However, if the blazer were changed into a waistcoat by the process, the service would have produced a new item and, if this waistcoat meets the criteria for zero-rating, the process would also be zero-rated.

(VAT Notice 714, paras 9.1–9.3).

Protective boots and helmets for industrial use

[14.8] The supply to a person for use otherwise than by employees of his of protective boots and helmets for industrial use is zero-rated. [*VATA 1994, Sch 8 Group 16 Item 2*]. In addition to outright sales, zero-rating also applies to a supply of services where the articles are hired or loaned or where they are put to private use provided that, in each case, the articles are for use otherwise than by the employees of the person to whom the services are supplied. [*VATA 1994, Sch 8 Group 16 Note 5; SI 2000/1517*].

The following conditions apply.

Condition 1

The articles must be protective boots or helmets. The British Standards Institution (BSI) defines a boot as having a minimum leg height of 90mm measured vertically from the insole at the back. The European Standard gives the minimum height of the upper (measured vertically from the insole at the back) of 103mm for a size 36 (UK 3) and below, through to a minimum height of the upper of 121mm for a size 45 (UK 11) and above. (The British Standard specifications will eventually be withdrawn and the definition of a boot will then be based on the European specification. In the meantime, HMRC accept both Standard measurements.)

Protective shoes that fall outside these specifications are not eligible for zero-rating, even if they meet the remaining requirements.

(VAT Notice 701/23/11, para 2.2).

Condition 2

The articles must be for industrial use. HMRC apply the normal day-to-day meaning to the words 'industrial use'. They do not see the phrase as covering, for example, motorcycle boots. (VAT Notice 701/23/11, para 2.6).

Condition 3

The articles concerned must

- be manufactured to standards approved by the British Standards Institution and bear a mark indicating conformity with those standards; or
- be manufactured to standards which satisfy requirements imposed (whether under UK law or that of another EU member state) to give effect to *EU Council Directive 89/686/EEC as amended* and bear any mark of conformity required to that effect.

[*VATA 1994, Sch 8 Group 16 Note 4; SI 2000/1517; SI 2001/732*].

Approved markings include the appropriate European Standard (EN) or British Standard (BS) numbers and the EU 'CE' mark (indicating conformity with the EU Directive) and/or the British Standard 'kitemark'. The EN for boots and helmets sourced in other EU member states may be prefixed by another country code such as 'NF' for a French manufactured product or 'DS' for one of Danish manufacture.

VATA 1994, Sch 8 Group 16 lists the current standards to which boots and helmets must conform to qualify for zero-rating. It also indicates that the scope of the zero rate will depend on any future amendments to those standards.

In some instances, particular boots and helmets may have been manufactured to a different specification to those laid down in the harmonised European Standards. These alternative specifications must satisfy the requirements of the Directive and be approved by a 'notified body', which in turn has been approved and appointed by the authorities of an EU member state. These boots and helmets will still carry the 'CE' mark, but also the notified body number.

(VAT Notice 701/23/11, paras 2.3–2.5).

Condition 4

The articles must not be supplied to a person for use by his employees. Supplies from a manufacturer to a wholesaler who in turn supplies them to a retailer, and supplies from an employer to an employee, can be zero-rated subject to the above conditions. But otherwise, before zero-rating a supply, the supplier should establish that the customer is not an employer purchasing the boots or helmets for use by employees by asking himself does

- the customer's trading style suggest the customer is an employer;
- the quantity ordered suggest a bulk purchase by an employer for use of employees; and
- the nature of the contract indicate a trade order, e.g. a number of pairs of boots paid for by one customer for delivery to individuals.

(VAT Notice 701/23/11, para 2.7).

Zero-rating covers accessories (e.g. visors and ear protectors) fitted as an integral part of a qualifying helmet but not accessories supplied on their own. (VAT Notice 701/23/11, para 2.8).

Protective helmets

[14.9] The supply of protective helmets for wear by a person driving or riding a motor bicycle or riding a pedal cycle is zero-rated provided the helmets are

- of a type that on 30 June 2000 was prescribed by regulations made under *Road Traffic Act 1988, s 17* (types of helmet recommended as affording protection to persons on or in motor cycles from injury in the event of accident), see the *Motor Cycles (Protective Helmets) Regulations 1988* (*SI 1988/1807*); or
- manufactured to a standard which satisfies requirements imposed (whether under UK law or the law of another EU member state) to give effect to *EU Council Directive 89/686/EEC as amended* and bear any mark of conformity required to that effect.

In addition to outright sales, zero-rating also applies to a supply of services where the articles are hired or loaned or where they are put to private use.

[*VATA 1994, Sch 8 Group 16 Item 3, Notes 4A, 5; SI 2000/1517; SI 2001/732*].

Motor cycle helmets

To qualify for zero-rating, motor cycle helmets must comply with the appropriate British Standard (in which case it will be marked with a British Standard 'kitemark') or European Standard (in which case it will be marked with a UN 'E' mark).

Zero-rating covers accessories (e.g. visors, ear protectors or communication systems) fitted as an integral part of a qualifying helmet but not accessories supplied on their own.

(VAT Notice 701/23/11, paras 3.1–3.3).

Pedal cycle helmets

Approved markings include the appropriate European Standard (EN) number and the EU 'CE' mark (indicating conformity with the EU Directive). The EN for helmets sourced in other EU member states may be prefixed by another country code such as 'NF' for a French manufactured product or 'DS' for one of Danish manufacture.

Some cycle helmets may have been manufactured to a different specification to those laid down in the harmonised European Standards. These alternative specifications must satisfy the requirements of the Directive and be approved by a 'notified body', which in turn has been approved and appointed by the authorities of an EU member state. These helmets will still carry the 'CE' mark, but also the notified body number.

Zero-rating covers accessories (e.g. visors or ear protectors) fitted as an integral part of a qualifying helmet but not accessories supplied on their own.

(VAT Notice 701/23/11, paras 4.1–4.5).

Key points: clothing and footwear

[14.10] Points to consider are as follows.

- It is important that garments are designed and held out for sale as being suitable for children in order to be eligible for zero-rating. The general aim of the legislation is that zero-rating can apply to clothes worn by children up to the eve of their 14th birthday. If they are 14 or older, then the clothes they wear become standard-rated. To assist this process, HMRC have produced a list of garment sizes, with separate lists obviously in place for boys and girls. If these sizes are exceeded, then the item becomes standard-rated unless there is some other feature of the garment in place that clearly makes it unsuitable for wear by older children. In such cases, the garment must be within another range of sizes published by HMRC or have some restrictive design feature or size measurement that means it is only suitable for young children. There have been a number of VAT cases lost by taxpayers where garments have been within the stipulated size ranges published by HMRC but have a design feature that makes them only suitable for wear by older children or adults.

- Clothing includes items such as hats, caps, braces, belts, garters and scarves but there is an exclusion for items such as badges, wristbands for sport, ear muffs and zips. In the latter cases, the items are not classed as clothing in the traditional meaning of the word and are therefore standard-rated.
- Many businesses that sell children's clothes will also sell adult clothing, and will often be a retailer as well. This means the business must operate a retail scheme that enables it to accurately calculate the output tax payable on its VAT returns. The ideal scheme will be based on a point of sale till reading because this is the most accurate method. But a scheme based on marking up either the zero-rated or standard-rated purchases, or even based on the proportion of standard-rated purchases and applying this to the total sales made by a business, should also produce a sensible result. However, it is important to be aware of the conditions of the various retail schemes, e.g. the scheme based on the proportion of standard-rated purchases can only be adopted by a business with annual sales of £1m or less.
- The increased use of websites to generate sales of goods and services means that extra care is needed in relation to children's clothing and zero-rating. The website or other medium must make it clear that the item being sold is only suitable for young children and not for older children or adults. A separate section on the website for children's clothing will almost certainly achieve this aim. The prospective buyer must be clear that they are buying children's clothing and the same garment sizes should not therefore appear in the adult section of the website.
- The hire of children's clothing qualifies for zero-rating, even though this is a service rather than goods arrangement. This could be particularly useful for a business that specialises in wedding outfits (e.g. bridesmaid dresses or page boy outfits). See paragraph 9.3 of VAT Notice 714 for more information.
- Be aware that the zero-rating for protective boots only applies if the items are intended for industrial use. This would exclude, for example, motor bike boots. Another important condition is that zero-rating would not apply if the items are being bought by an employer for his employees. It is up to the supplier to make a reasonable assessment as to whether this might be the case (e.g. a bulk order might suggest an employer is buying the items for his workers).
- The zero-rating for protective helmets is more generous. As well as zero-rating for industrial use (again with the exception concerning employers buying helmets for employees), zero-rating also applies to the sale of motor bike and pedal cycle helmets. The

items must meet certain British or European Standard conditions.

15

Clubs and Associations

Cross-references. See **10.6 BUSINESS ENTERTAINMENT** for free entertainment of members; and **17.17 EDUCATION** for the provision of youth club facilities.

De Voil Indirect Tax Service. See V2.112, V4.156.

Introduction to clubs and associations

[15.1] Under *Directive 2006/112/EC*, countries must exempt certain activities in the public interest. Those relating to clubs and associations are covered by *Art 132(1)(l)* (see **19.24**(*l*) **EUROPEAN UNION LEGISLATION**). The provisions have been incorporated into UK legislation in two ways.

First, under *VATA 1994, Sch 9* Group 9, if the organisation is a non-profit making trade union, professional or representative body, supplies to members referable to its aims and available without payment other than a membership subscription are exempt. Exemption also applies to such supplies made by a non-profit making body with objects which are in the public domain and are of a political, religious, patriotic, philosophical or philanthropic nature. [*VATA 1994, s 94(3)*]. See **15.7** below.

Secondly, subject to the above, if a 'club, association or organisation' provides facilities or advantages to its members in return for a 'subscription or other consideration', it is deemed to be carrying on a business activity. [*VATA 1994, s 94(2)(a)*]. Such a body must therefore register for VAT (subject to the registration limit) and account for VAT on its subscription income (but see **15.2** below for apportionment of subscriptions).

Particular types of clubs and associations

The provisions of *VATA 1994, s 94(2)(a)* have been held to be applicable in *C & E Commrs v British Field Sports Society*, CA [1998] STC 315 (TVC 13.10) (campaigning on behalf of stag and deer hunting), *Eastbourne Town Radio*

Cars Association v C & E Commrs, HL [2001] STC 606 (TVC 62.32) (association of taxi-drivers) and *Manor Forstal Residents Society Ltd* (VTD 245) (TVC 13.1) (association of local residents); and not applicable in *New Ash Green Village Association* (VTD 245) (TVC 13.12) (village development association), *Nottingham Fire Service Messing Club* (VTD 348) (TVC 13.13) (canteen at fire station) and *Friends of the Ironbridge Gorge Museum* (VTD 5639) (TVC 13.15) (fund-raising association for a museum).

Subscriptions

Single and multiple supplies

[15.2] The same person may be supplied, at the same time, with a number of different goods or services or both. If the individual components are all liable to VAT at the same rate, VAT can be calculated in the normal way but if they are not, it is necessary to decide whether a single or multiple supply is being made.

- In a single supply where one component of the supply is the principal component to which all the other components are ancillary, integral or incidental, the whole transaction is treated as having the VAT liability of the principal component. See below, however, for a concession in the case of non-profit making bodies.
- In a multiple supply, each component is distinct and independent and takes its own VAT liability.

See **65.6 SUPPLY: GENERAL** for more detailed coverage of single and multiple supplies.

(VAT Notice 701/5/13, paras 4.2–4.5).

Treatment of subscriptions for VAT purposes

Single supplies

Where members pay a subscription to obtain or gain entitlement to any 'substantive' benefits of membership, VAT due is calculated on the total amount of the subscription. The VAT liability of subscriptions depends on the liability of the membership benefits supplied in return. In most cases clubs supply a package of benefits so the supply will have more than one component. However, just because membership may offer a package of benefits does not necessarily mean that multiple supplies are being made. In fact in most cases there is one principal benefit or reason for joining. For example, being a member of a professional body or trade union allows the member to enjoy the rights that membership may bring. In addition, other benefits, such as the provision of a hand book or newsletters are an integral or incidental part of the main supply. In these circumstances, the subscription is consideration for a single supply and its liability is determined by the liability of the main benefit. No apportionment may be made.

However, there is an exception for non-profit making bodies making a single supply which comprises a mixture of benefits with different VAT liabilities. These bodies may apportion their subscriptions to reflect the value and VAT liability of each individual benefit. It is up to the organisation whether to take advantage of the concession, but it cannot apply the concession retrospectively. If it wishes to apportion, e.g. subscriptions to cover separate benefits such as zero-rated printed matter, it must apportion all types and elements of subscriptions, it cannot 'pick and choose'. The concession does not work in reverse, i.e. non-profit making bodies may not treat their multiple supplies as single supplies. (VAT Notice 48, ESC 3.35).

Multiple supplies

In some cases certain elements of the package of membership benefits received are clearly not related at all to the main purpose of joining the membership body or club, meaning that multiple supplies are being made. If the subscription is consideration for multiple supplies and the separate elements have different VAT liabilities, the subscription must be apportioned between those different elements. Examples of benefits which may need to be apportioned include

- priority booking rights;
- guaranteed seats;
- discounts on admission charges; and
- items with a resale value.

These benefits are considered to be substantive regardless of whether there is any cost to the organisation in supplying them and what that cost might be.

Subscriptions which are voluntary payments or donations

If the whole of the subscription is an entirely voluntary payment and secures nothing or only nominal benefits in return, it is all a donation and must be treated as being outside the scope of VAT.

Subscriptions which may include a voluntary payment or donation

It is only possible to treat part of a subscription as a voluntary payment or donation if the organisation is a charity or a body which has objects that are both in the public domain and of a philanthropic nature (see **15.7**(*e*) below) and either

- all the substantive benefits (i.e. ignoring any nominal benefits) provided are available to non-members at no charge or more cheaply than the subscription; or
- some or all of the substantive benefits are exclusive to members and the organisation can demonstrate that the amount paid is higher than the amount that the subscriber would normally have to pay for similar goods or services.

If these requirements are met, see below for how to apportion the subscription.

A charity or organisation having objects in the public domain (e.g. philanthropic body), may receive a subscription which includes a donational element.

Exempt subscriptions

The supply of benefits to members by trade unions and political, religious, patriotic, philosophical, philanthropic or civic bodies may qualify for exemption. See **15.8** below. See also **58.5 RECREATION AND SPORT** for certain membership subscriptions of non-profit making bodies providing sport and physical education services.

Additional joining fees

Any additional joining fee of a *general* nature should be treated in the same way as a subscription, applying the same apportionment, if any. Where an additional fee is charged for obtaining a *particular* facility, VAT must be accounted for based on the liability of the particular service or goods provided.

Life membership fees

These must be treated in the same way as annual subscriptions, unless life members are supplied with additional benefits not available to ordinary members.

Charges for being placed on a waiting list for membership

Such a fee is exempt if it is

- deducted from the new member's first subscription or entrance fee and the subscription or fee itself will qualify for exemption; and
- refundable in the event that the candidate fails to become a member for any reason, including voluntary withdrawal.

In all other circumstances, the fee is consideration for the right to be on the waiting list and is standard-rated.

Payment by instalments

Where an organisation allows a member to pay a subscription by instalments over the subscription period and the total instalments exceed the single payment subscription, the liability of the additional amount is the same as that of the subscription.

Deferred payments

Where an organisation offers annual membership and allows members to defer subscription payment for an additional charge over and above the subscription, the charge is consideration for the exempt grant of credit.

VAT Notice 701/5/13, para 5.8 states:

> 'Where you allow a member to pay a subscription by instalments over the subscription period and the total instalments exceed a single payment subscription, the liability of the additional amount is the same as that of the subscription.'

Paragraph 5.9, by contrast, states:

> 'Where an organisation offers annual membership and allows members to defer subscription payment for an additional charge over and above the subscription, the charge is consideration for the exempt grant of credit.'

It would therefore appear that exemption only applies where it is clear to the customer that an additional fee (rather than simply a higher price) is being charged for being able to defer payment. HMRC guidance VATFIN3170 expands on this:

> 'The supplier of the goods or services may openly disclose any additional charges in the documents put before the customer. However, in some cases, e.g. with leisure facilities, the disclosure may not be so apparent, but that isn't to say that the additional charge hasn't been disclosed. So long as there is a reasonable expectation that the customer would be aware that by deferring payment he is paying a greater amount than if he had not deferred payment, then this is enough to ensure the disclosure provisions have been met.'

The guidance also states that 'Where the customer is not provided with an option to defer payment (e.g. he can only pay in instalments over a period of time) there is no grant of credit and any additional charge is treated as being further consideration for the main supply'; however, it is difficult to see why there should be an 'additional charge' in such circumstances, or what it would be 'additional' to.

In *Sports and Leisure Group Ltd* [2016] UKFTT 27 (TC) (TC04836) (TVC 27.20), the First-tier Tribunal had to consider a situation in which subscribers to a gym were offered a choice between paying their first year's subscription by a lump sum or by a monthly direct debit. The lump sum was equal to 11 monthly payments. HMRC accepted that the monthly payments included a charge for credit (1/12 of the extra amount in each month). However, where a customer continued to pay the direct debits into a second year of membership, there was no new lump sum alternative. Although the monthly direct debits were exactly the same amount as for the first year, in the second year they were entirely standard-rated.

How to apportion subscriptions

There are no specific rules for making an apportionment. See **48.3 OUTPUT TAX** for general guidance on apportionment. HMRC generally accept apportionment of the total subscription income to reflect the relative cost of providing the different supplies to members. The calculations for the current financial year can be based on the accounts for the previous financial year, provided this method is adopted consistently. Calculations must be kept for inspection by HMRC.

Where a subscription includes a donation (see above), if the organisation calculates the value of any standard-rated, zero-rated and exempt supplies, it can treat the balance of the subscription as a donation and outside the scope of VAT. It should calculate the value of the substantive benefits (i.e. ignoring nominal benefits), using the price at which they are available to non-members or the amount the subscriber would normally have to pay for similar goods or services. The difference between the amount of the subscription and the total value of the benefits is the donation.

Subscriptions from overseas members

Overseas subscriptions normally follow the same VAT liability as subscriptions paid by UK members but are treated differently where overseas members

- receive different benefits from UK members in return for their subscription to a UK club; or
- receive the same benefits as UK members, but the VAT rules require a different treatment.

In these circumstances, the apportionment of the overseas subscription must be carried out separately.

The different treatment of benefits for overseas members is as follows.

- *Services.* In certain situations, some supplies of services are treated as made where the customer belongs, and therefore fall outside the scope of UK VAT.
- *Goods sent to members outside the EU* are zero-rated as exports.
- *Goods sent to VAT-registered members in other EU member states for use in their business* are zero-rated subject to certain conditions.
- *Goods sent to non VAT-registered members in other EU member states.* VAT is due on the goods in the UK until the value of such supplies exceeds a threshold set by the EU member state to which the goods are sent. Once this threshold is exceeded, VAT is due in that EU member state and the organisation may need to register for VAT there to fulfil its obligations. See **20.10 EUROPEAN UNION: SINGLE MARKET.**

(VAT Notice 701/5/13, paras 4.6, 5.1–5.13).

Registration

[15.3] Any club or association with business activities and a turnover from standard-rated, reduced-rated and zero-rated supplies (including subscriptions) above the current registration limits must register for VAT and account for VAT on its taxable supplies. Business activities include

- providing benefits to members in return for membership subscriptions (for members' racing clubs where subscriptions finance the purchase of racehorses, see **64.33 SPECIAL SCHEMES**);
- providing benefits to members in return for a separate charge;
- making supplies to non-members for a charge;
- admission to any premises for a charge; and
- providing catering, social and other facilities to non-members in return for a charge.

(VAT Notice 701/5/13, paras 2.1, 2.2).

For the requirements relating to registration see **60 REGISTRATION.** Even if a club, etc. is not required to register under the general requirements based on taxable supplies in the UK, it may be liable to register for VAT where it makes certain acquisitions of goods from other EU member states, in excess of an annual threshold. See **60.18 REGISTRATION**.

A club, etc. may be registered in the name of that club and in determining whether goods and services are supplied to or by it, or whether goods are acquired by it from another EU member state, no account is taken of any change in its members. HMRC are empowered to make provisions to determine what persons are responsible for carrying out the requirements of the VAT legislation where a club, etc. is managed by its members or a committee. Under these powers HMRC have regulated that the necessary requirements are the joint and several responsibility of

- every member holding office as president, chairman, treasurer, secretary or any similar office; or in default of any thereof,
- every member holding office as a member of a committee; or in default of any thereof,
- every member.

[*VATA 1994, s 46(2)(3); SI 1995/2518, Reg 8*].

Clubs in sections and multi-tiered bodies

[15.4] There are no set rules for determining whether a section or branch has its own separate legal status, independent of its parent organisation, or whether that section or branch should register separately for VAT purposes. Unless the section or branch concerned can demonstrate that it has both constitutional and financial independence from its parent organisation, its supplies should be included with those of the parent organisation when accounting for VAT.

(VAT Notice 701/5/13, para 2.4).

Common transactions other than subscriptions

[15.5] The following is a list of some of the more common transactions made by clubs and associations.

(1) Admission charges

Admission charges are standard-rated in most cases but admission charges to

- museums, galleries, art exhibitions and zoos; and
- theatrical, musical and choreographic performances of a cultural nature

supplied by public authorities and by certain other eligible bodies may qualify for exemption.

See **58.2 RECREATION AND SPORT**.

(2) Bar sales, catering and teas

Food and drink is always standard-rated if it is supplied in the course of catering. This includes hot take-away food and food and drink supplied for consumption on the premises. See **12 CATERING**. The argument that there is no 'supply' because, in law, drinks obtained by members are not sold to them has been dismissed. (*Carlton Lodge Club v C & E Commrs*, QB [1974] STC 507 (TVC 13.30)).

(3) Bingo

The fees for participation in bingo are exempt from VAT. See **8.3 BETTING AND GAMING.** Admission charges are standard-rated with an exception for certain one-off fund-raising events (see below).

(4) Competition entry fees

Competition entry fees are normally standard-rated but may be exempt in the case of certain competitions in sport or physical recreation (see **58.1 RECREATION AND SPORT**).

(5) Culture

Admission charges to: museums, galleries, art exhibitions and zoos; and theatrical, musical and choreographic performances of a cultural nature, supplied by public authorities and by certain other eligible bodies may qualify for exemption (see **58.2 RECREATION AND SPORT**).

(6) Discos, dances, socials and similar events

Admission charges are standard-rated (but see below for certain one-off fund-raising events).

VAT must be accounted for on the gross amount of taxable supplies (e.g. admission, catering, etc.) and not on the net amounts after band, floor shows, etc. expenses are paid.

(7) Fixture cards

Fixture cards are standard-rated if any portion for completion occupies more than 25% of total area, otherwise they are generally zero-rated. See also **55.5 PRINTED MATTER, ETC.**

(8) Fund-raising events

Admission charges to qualifying events held by charities for charitable purposes and by non-profit making qualifying bodies exclusively for their own benefit may be exempt. See **13.10 CHARITIES.**

(9) Machine games

Most receipts from playing machine games are VAT exempt. See **8.4 BETTING AND GAMING.**

(10) Gaming club subscriptions

Subscriptions to gaming, bingo, bridge, etc. clubs, in return for which members have the right to place bets or play games of chance for no further payment, are standard-rated. See **8.2 BETTING AND GAMING.**

(11) Hire of rooms, halls and facilities

The hire of a room or a hall, including the provision of lighting and furniture, is generally exempt from VAT provided that

- the person to whom the room or hall is hired has exclusive occupation of it during the period of hire; and
- the organisation has not opted to tax the building in which the room or hall is situated.

(12) Insurance supplied with goods or other services

Depending on the circumstances, where a charge is made for insurance, that charge could be exempt where it is the member's own risk which is insured (rather than the club's risk). See **37.17 INSURANCE**.

(13) Jumble sales

Unless they qualify as fund-raising events (see above)

- any charge for admission is standard-rated; and
- the goods sold are liable to VAT at the rate applicable to such goods.

(14) Levies

These are normally demanded from existing members when a body requires additional funds. Where a levy is raised and members' benefits remain unaltered, the levy is liable to VAT as if it was an additional subscription. However, if the levy entitles the member to different benefits, VAT must be accounted for, where appropriate, based on the liability of those benefits.

(15) Lotteries

Income from lotteries (including raffles, totes, instant bingo tickets, etc.) is exempt (see **8.5 BETTING AND GAMING**).

(16) Loans from members

Clubs often raise capital to finance the renewal or development of facilities by means of loans from members.

Compulsory interest-free loans

VAT must be accounted for on the notional interest on the loans. This is determined by establishing the amount of interest free loans and calculating the notional interest using the London Clearing Bank's Base Lending Rate in force either on the first day of the month in which the subscriptions are due to be paid or the first day of the club's financial year if more convenient. VAT liability is calculated by applying the same VAT liability to the notional interest as the subscription and using the appropriate VAT fraction to calculate the VAT due.

Obtaining loans at a significantly lower interest rate than from the bank

If the interest rate charged to members is significantly lower than the bank would have charged, VAT liability is determined by

- calculating the notional interest as for compulsory interest-free loans above;

- deducting the amount of interest actually paid, including any on returned loans, from the notional interest; and
- applying the same VAT liability to the remainder as applies to the subscriptions and using the appropriate VAT fraction to calculate the VAT due.

Additional loan repayments to members who are leaving

Members are often required to lend a specified sum which is only repaid on cessation of membership. It is often also a requirement that the member will find a new member to take over the loan or to make an equivalent loan. On cessation the ex-member receives a sum, frequently based on the rate of inflation. VAT liability is determined by

- calculating the notional interest as for compulsory interest-free loans above;
- deducting the amount of interest actually paid (if any);
- deducting the additional payment; and
- applying the same VAT liability to the remainder as applies to the subscriptions and using the appropriate VAT fraction to calculate the VAT due.

Reducing or waiving a member's subscription in return for an interest-free loan or purchase of a share or debenture

Where this is done, VAT must be accounted for, at the time the subscriptions are due, on the amount of subscription payable by a member who has not made any such payment.

Compulsory loans where members decide unconditionally to waive entitlement to repayment

The loan can be regarded as having been converted into an outside the scope donation and the club will no longer be required to account for VAT from the date of waiver on the notional interest.

See also *Exeter Golf and Country Club Ltd v C & E Commrs*, CA [1981] STC 211 (TVC 13.33) and *Dyrham Park Country Club Ltd* [1978] VATTR 244 (TVC 13.32).

(17) Payphone charges

See **48.7**(17) **OUTPUT TAX**.

(18) Prizes

Special rules apply to prizes in betting, gaming and lotteries. See **8.1–8.5 BETTING AND GAMING**. Otherwise prizes awarded to competitors in sports and games competitions are always treated in the same way, regardless of whether the entry fees for the competition are exempt or taxable.

- Where the prize is goods, VAT must be accounted for based on the cost of the goods unless the cost of the individual prize to the organisation was £50 or less (excluding VAT).

- Where the prize is in the form of services (e.g. a holiday), if input tax has been claimed on the purchase of services given away as prizes, an equal sum of output tax is due at the time the prize is awarded. If no input tax is incurred no output tax is due.
- Cash prizes are outside the scope of VAT. However, it is important to distinguish between prize money and payments made by sponsors to event organisers which are called prize money but are, in fact, payments for taxable supplies.
- A trophy which remains the property of the competition organiser is outside the scope of VAT, because there is no supply.

For prize money from horseracing see **64.31** SPECIAL SCHEMES.

(19) Shares and debentures

These are used by clubs to raise extra finance from members or prospective members. It is necessary to consider:

- Whether or not there is a single supply (and, if so, whether it is of an exempt security or standard-rated subscriptions).
- If there is a mixed supply, can either component be disregarded on minimal grounds.
- Whether the standard-rated benefits are only being granted as an inducement to persuade people to acquire the exempt supply. See *Hinckley Golf Club Ltd* (VTD 9527) (TVC 13.16) where the tribunal held that the offer of free membership to certain shareholders was simply an inducement to invest and the only supply to those shareholders was an exempt supply of shares in consideration for the purchase price of those shares. See also *Rugby Football Union* (VTD 18075) (TVC 27.65) where the whole of the amount paid by the purchasers of 75-year non-interest-bearing debentures was held to relate to the exempt supply of the debentures and no part to the right given to them to purchase tickets for rugby matches at Twickenham for ten years.

Where any part of the consideration for a share or debenture is to be treated as an additional payment for the advantages of membership, it should be treated as a levy or, for non-monetary consideration, as an interest-free loan (see above).

(20) Sponsorship rights

Output tax is due not only on the money received from the sponsor but also on any payments made by the sponsor to third parties. This includes expenses of staging a competition or event and the value of any prizes given under the terms of the sponsorship agreement. See **58.14** RECREATION AND SPORT.

(21) Sport and physical recreation facilities

Use of such facilities (including billiards, pool and snooker, tennis courts, bowling greens, etc.) are normally exempt when made by an eligible body and standard-rated in other cases. Where a grant of facilities for playing any sport or participation in any physical recreation amounts to a grant of land or property, it may qualify for exemption under the '24 hour' rule or the 'series of lets' provisions. See **58.3–58.9** RECREATION AND SPORT.

When payments are linked to the operation of lighting e.g. squash courts or snooker tables, the full amount payable by players is standard-rated as the charge is for the right to use the facilities and does not relate to the supply of electricity. See *St Anne's-on-Sea Lawn Tennis Club Ltd* (VTD 434) (TVC 30.4).

(22) Swipe cards, vouchers and other types of payment credits

If an organisation arranges for its members to maintain credit balances in order to make payment for goods and services (e.g. when using the bar facilities), it must consider the following points to determine when it must account for VAT.

- Where a member makes a payment that creates or contributes to a credit balance, (whether as a compulsory or voluntary levy) on either
  - (a) the issue, renewal or topping up of a card; or
  - (b) the purchase of vouchers

  the organisation need not account for VAT until the credit is used to make taxable purchases, even if the payment is not refundable. The payment must not be treated as part of the subscription for VAT purposes.
- Where an unused credit balance is repayable to the member, the credit and refund have no VAT consequences.
- Where unused balances or unredeemed vouchers revert to the organisation, it does not need to account for VAT on the balances or vouchers as there is no consideration for a supply at the time of reversion.

(23) Tours organised by clubs, etc.

Where a club buys hotel accommodation and travel, for example, from a third party, and sells them on as principal, the club must use the **69 TOUR OPERATORS' MARGIN SCHEME.**

(VAT Notice 701/5/13, paras 6.1–6.7, 7.1, 8, 9.1–9.4, 10.1–10.3).

Non-business activities

[15.6] A club or association may have non-business activities. These are mainly activities for which no payment is required or, where there is a payment, no benefit is provided in return. Examples include

- free admission to premises for non-members;
- spreading political beliefs or lobbying for a public or charitable good cause (but not lobbying on behalf of members which is a business activity);
- providing free literature to non-members; and
- the receipt of freely given donations, where no benefit is supplied in return (see **15.2** above for more information on subscriptions and donations).

See **9 BUSINESS** generally for what constitutes a business for VAT purposes.

Any VAT incurred on goods or services used wholly for the purpose of a non-business activity is not input tax and cannot be reclaimed.

If goods or services are purchased partly for business and partly for non-business purposes, the VAT incurred must be apportioned to reflect the amount attributable to business activities. Only this amount can be reclaimed. Alternatively, in the case of goods (but not services) purchased partly for business and partly for non-business purposes, the full amount of tax can be reclaimed as input tax provided output tax is accounted for on the non-business use in each VAT period. See **35.7 INPUT TAX** for fuller details.

(VAT Notice 701/5/13, paras 2.3, 3.2).

Trade unions, professional and other public interest bodies

[15.7] The provision of facilities and advantages to members of clubs, associations and other organisations is normally standard-rated (see **15.1** above) but their provision by certain professional, learned or representational associations can be exempt. See **19.24**(*l*) and (*o*) **EUROPEAN UNION LEGISLATION** for the provisions of *Directive 2006/112/EC*.

The eligible organisations are those 'non-profit making' bodies falling into one of the following categories.

(a) Trade unions and other organisations

Trade unions and other organisations whose main objectives are to negotiate the terms and conditions of employment of their members.

'*Trade union*' is an organisation (whether permanent or temporary) which consists wholly or mainly of

- workers of one or more descriptions; or
- constituent or affiliated organisations; or
- representatives of such constituent or affiliated organisations. The principal purposes of the organisation must include the regulation of relations between workers and employers or employers' associations.

[*VATA 1994, Sch 9 Group 9 Item 1(a); Trade Union and Labour (Consolidation) Act 1992, s 1*].

Directive 2006/112/EC, Art 132(1)(l) refers to 'organisations with aims of a . . . trade-union . . . nature'. The CJEU has held this to mean 'an organisation whose main aim is to defend the collective interests of its members—whether they are workers, employers, independent professionals or traders carrying on a particular economic activity—and to represent them vis-à-vis the appropriate third parties, including the public authorities' provided those objects were put into practice. (*Institute of the Motor Industry v C & E Commrs, ECJ Case C–149/97*, [1998] STC 1219 (TVC 22.346)).

(b) Professional associations

Professional associations, membership of which are 'wholly or mainly' restricted to individuals who have or are seeking a qualification appropriate to the practice of the profession concerned. [*VATA 1994, Sch 9 Group 9 Item 1(b)*].

Membership of the association should be obligatory, or at least customary, for those pursuing a career in that profession.

'*Wholly or mainly*' is regarded as 75% or more.

The qualifications held or sought must relate to what is a recognised profession. They should be obligatory or customary to enable the profession to be undertaken and should be awarded by the association of which the holder is a member.

'Profession' is not defined but HMRC regard it as restricted to those occupations which would be generally understood to be professions. Indications which point towards this are

- the status of the occupation and those engaged in it;
- whether or not persons within the occupation require a qualification;
- whether the persons within the occupation are governed by a code of conduct;
- a distinctive and broad base of knowledge from which a person may subsequently diversify into more specialised areas;
- the association's aims and objectives; and
- the actual activities carried out by it.

However, these are not fixed criteria and some occupations which are not currently regarded as professions may acquire that status in the future.

(VAT Notice 701/5/13, paras 11.6, 11.8).

Bookmaking (*The Bookmakers' Protection Association (Southern Area) Ltd* (VTD 849) (TVC 64.14)), driving a taxi-cab (*City Cabs (Edinburgh) Ltd* (VTD 928) (TVC 64.15)), the practice of reflexology (*The Association of Reflexologists* (VTD 13078) (TVC 64.28)) and careers advice (*Association of Graduate Careers Advisory Services* [2016] UKFTT 560 (TC) (TC05309)) have been held not to be professions but the teaching of dance has been so held (*Allied Dancing Association Ltd* [1993] Lexis Citation 3401 (TVC 64.1)). See also *Institute of Leisure and Amenity Management v C & E Commrs*, QB [1988] STC 602 (TVC 64.19). For a fuller list of associations which have been held to fall within or, as the case may be, outside these provisions, see the chapter *Trade Unions, Professional and Public Interest Bodies* in *Tolley's VAT Cases*.

(c) Learned societies

Learned societies, i.e. any association, the 'primary purpose' of which is the advancement of a particular 'branch of knowledge' or the fostering of professional expertise, connected with the past or present professions or employments of its members. Membership must be restricted 'wholly or mainly' to individuals whose present or previous professions or employments are directly connected with the purposes of the association. [*VATA 1994, Sch 9 Group 9 Item 1(c)*].

An association can have only one primary purpose (although it does not have to be the sole purpose) which should be clear from

- the objects and objectives set out in the memorandum and articles of association or constitution;

- the powers and actual activities of the association;
- what the association itself and the members consider its primary purpose to be.

The *'branch of knowledge'* must be a recognised branch of science or the arts and should therefore be more academic than practical in content. Normally it would be included in a degree course or equivalent. Knowledge relating to the confined area of a specific job does not constitute a branch of knowledge.

See (*b*) above for a consideration of 'profession'. Professional expertise is construed accordingly.

'*Wholly or mainly*' is regarded as 75% or more.

(VAT Notice 701/5/13, paras 11.11–11.14).

See *Royal Photographic Society* (VTD 647) (TVC 64.13) (where lack of the restriction on membership disqualified the Society from exemption) and *Institute of Leisure and Amenity Management v C & E Commrs*, QB [1988] STC 602 (TVC 64.19).

(d) Representational trade associations

Representational trade associations, i.e. any association, the 'primary purpose' of which is to make representations to the Government on legislation and other public matters which affect the business or professional interests of its members. Membership must be restricted 'wholly or mainly' to individuals or corporate bodies whose business or professional interests are directly connected with its aims. [*VATA 1994, Sch 9 Group 9 Item 1(d)*].

See (*c*) above for the primary purpose test. The representations should be to the UK government.

'*Wholly or mainly*' is regarded as 75% or more.

(VAT Notice 701/5/13, para 11.15).

In *European Tour Operators Association*, an association of tour operators accounted for VAT on its membership subscriptions, but submitted a repayment claim on the basis that it should have treated these subscriptions as exempt under *VATA 1994, Sch 9, Group 9, Item 1(d)*. HMRC rejected the claim and the association appealed. The tribunal held that, for the purpose of *Item 1(d)*, the reference to 'the Government' should not be construed as being restricted to the UK Government; exemption should include representations to EU institutions in relation to matters that will have effect in the UK. The tribunal allowed the appeal in principle (TC00965). The Upper Tribunal remitted the case for rehearing, holding that the First-tier Tribunal had erred in law, as the primary purpose of the association was not what its directors and members considered to be the most important matter it was seeking to achieve or doing in return for membership subscriptions. The relevant enquiry was an objective one, to be answered primarily by an examination of the stated objects and the actual activities of the body in question ([2012] UKUT 377 (TCC)). On reconsideration of the case on that basis, the First-tier Tribunal decided that the association's predominant primary purpose was to provide a political lobbying body representing tour operators based in Europe. It satisfied the requirement in *Item 1(d)* 'to make representations to the Government on legislation and other public matters which affect the business or professional interests of its members'. The association's appeal was allowed. (*European Tour Operators Association* [2014] UKFTT 213 (TC) (TC03353) (TVC 64.8).)

(e) Bodies of a political, religious, patriotic, philosophical, philanthropic or civic nature

Bodies of a political, religious, patriotic, philosophical, philanthropic or civic nature which have objects in the public domain. [*VATA 1994, Sch 9 Group 9 Item 1(e); FA 1999, s 20; SI 1999/2834*]. These bodies have objects which are directed outside the particular organisation and beyond the members themselves to the general community. Bodies which are not registered charities may qualify. Major political or religious bodies will also often satisfy this requirement because the public will have a general interest in their activities.

There are no legal definitions of the various bodies included but HMRC suggest that the following describes their everyday meaning.

- A political body is one that campaigns for or against legislative and constitutional changes or campaigns in local and central government elections.
- A religious body includes all denominations, creeds, old and new, that command a following.
- A patriotic body does good work for the benefit of a nation state or for those who have served their country and their dependants.
- A philosophical body is one whose primary purpose is the advancement of a particular way of thinking but which is not of a political or religious nature. It is very similar to a learned society as described in (*c*) above in that they are both of an academic nature.
- A philanthropic body does good work for the direct benefit of the general community or a particular section of the community or is designed to promote the wellbeing of mankind.
- A civic body is one which has objects which promote rights and duties of citizens in matters of public interest and public affairs, and whose objects do not solely or mainly benefit its members.

(VAT Notice 701/5/13, paras 12.1, 12.2).

See the *English-Speaking Union of the Commonwealth* (VTD 1023) (TVC 13.5). In *Hallé Concerts Society* [2016] UKFTT 294 (TC) (TC05067) (TVC 64.12), the First-tier Tax Tribunal considered that subscriptions to a company limited by guarantee were not for the rights of corporate membership, but were rather for the advantages (rights to priority booking) that were conferred by membership; however, the Society was 'the epitome of a philanthropic body', so the subscriptions were exempt. The judge commented that 'philanthropy' was a wider concept than 'charity'.

(f) Constituent or affiliated associations

An organisation or association, the membership of which consists wholly or mainly of constituent or affiliated associations which as individual associations would be within (*a*) to (*d*) above. [*VATA 1994, Sch 9 Group 9 Note (3)*].

'Non-profit making'

HMRC consider, when judging whether an organisation is non-profit making, the objects for which an organisation has been established, as distinct from the financial policy being pursued. Although the organisation may generate income surpluses from various activities, they will not refuse recognition as a non-profit making organisation simply because these surpluses subsidise other activities. If a body has a constitution or articles of association that bars it from distributing surpluses of income over expenditure to its members, shareholders or any other party, other than in the event of a liquidation or cessation of activities, HMRC normally accept it as non-profit making for the purposes of this exemption. However, the existence of any provision barring distribution will not necessarily be the sole factor in determining whether an organisation is non-profit making. (VAT Notice 701/5/13, para 11.3).

Fund-raising events

The supply of goods and services by a non-profit making body within (*a*)–(*f*) above in connection with an event whose primary purpose is the raising of money and which is promoted as such is exempt from VAT where

- the event is organised exclusively for its own benefit; or
- the event is organised, jointly by one or more charities and the non-profit making body, exclusively for charitable purposes or that body's own benefit or a combination of those purposes.

See **13.10 CHARITIES** for full details.

Exempt supplies

[15.8] Supplies of services, and related goods, by a non profit-making body within **15.7**(*a*)–(*f*) above to its members are exempt provided

- they are made available without payment (other than a membership subscription); and
- they are referable only to the aims of the organisation.

[*VATA 1994, Sch 9 Group 9 Item 1*].

Exemption does not apply to

(a) supplies that do not relate to the body's aims as set out in its rules, articles of association, constitution, etc. (although see **15.9** below for provision of hospitality to members);

(b) the supply of any right of admission to any premises, event or performance (e.g. for a conference) for which non-members have to pay [*VATA 1994, Sch 9 Group 9 Note (1)*];

(c) any supplies which are not provided automatically as part of the membership benefits and for which an additional sum is charged; and
(d) supplies to non-members.

Supplies within (*a*)–(*d*) above are taxable unless exempt under any other provision. These might include training under *VATA 1994, Sch 9 Group 6* (see **17.7 EDUCATION**), fund-raising events organised by charities and non-profit making bodies under *VATA 1994, 9 Sch Group 12* (see **13.10 CHARITIES**) and sporting events under *VATA 1994, Sch 9 Group 10* (see **58.5 RECREATION AND SPORT**).

Subscriptions with a taxable component

Where a subscription includes a component which is not exempt, the rules in **15.2** above on apportionment of subscriptions should be considered.

Subscriptions which include a right of admission

The right of admission to any premises, event or performance is specifically excluded from the exemption. This means that

- any payments for admission in addition to the subscription are always standard-rated; and
- if an event is subsidised by subscriptions, a component of that subscription is standard-rated and an apportionment may be necessary.

The table below sets out examples of possible methods of charging and the VAT consequences. In each case, it is assumed that the organisation is a qualifying organisation that has satisfied all the other criteria for exemption and the event is referable to the organisation's aims.

Method of charging for admission	*Is the standard-rated right of admission included in the subscription?*
Free admission to members only or member and guest	No
Free admission to members: charge to non-members	Yes
Members only for a charge: event self-financing	No
Members only for a charge: event subsidised by subscriptions	Yes
Members and non-members admitted for a charge but members pay less: event self-financing	No

(VAT Notice 701/5/13, paras 13.1–13.3).

Other supplies

Registration fees

[15.9] In certain professions, persons cannot practice unless they are registered with a statutory body and have paid fees which are prescribed by law. Such registration fees are normally outside the scope of VAT because, in carrying out these statutory functions, the organisation is not supplying a service in the course of its business. Where, however, there is no such statutory requirement, the liability is as follows.

- *Registration in return for a subscription payment.* Where no additional fee is charged and the member is automatically registered on payment of the subscription, the service of registration is standard-rated unless referable to the aims of the association in which case it qualifies for exemption under **15.8** above.
- *Registration for a separate fee.* As the registration is in return for a payment 'other than a membership subscription' it cannot qualify for exemption under **15.8** above and is standard-rated.

If the registration is accompanied by other clearly identifiable supplies of goods or services, the fee must be apportioned accordingly.

Collection charges for union subscriptions

Charges raised by employers for deducting union subscriptions from employees' pay are exempt under *VATA 1994, Sch 9 Group 5*. See **24.9**(3) **FINANCIAL SERVICES.**

Provision of hospitality

Where meals, hotel accommodation, etc. are provided to members without charge, then unless directly connected with the organisation's aims (e.g. at the annual conference), the supply is standard-rated and the subscription must be apportioned. Such hospitality is not business entertainment (because the membership in general is paying for it in the subscription) and input tax incurred can therefore be deducted, subject to the normal rules. The business entertaining provisions do apply to free hospitality to non-members and input tax cannot be deducted.

The provision of hospitality for a charge to members or non-members is standard-rated.

(VAT Notice 701/5/13, paras 13.5–13.7).

Key points: clubs and associations

[15.10] Points to consider are as follows.

- A club or association that provides benefits to its members in return for a subscription payment will generally have income that is both taxable and exempt. If it receives donations and grants, it will also have income that is outside the scope of VAT. In deciding whether the club needs to be VAT-registered on a compulsory basis, it is important to only consider taxable sources of income. If the total of these income sources has exceeded the VAT registration limit in the past twelve months, or is expected to exceed the limit in the next 30 days, then it will need to be VAT-registered.

- Many clubs and associations have non-business activities. It is important that input tax is initially blocked on any expenditure relating to non-business activities. If an expense is partly for business and partly for non-business purposes, then an apportionment must be made using any method that is fair and reasonable.
- The fact that many clubs and associations have both taxable and exempt income means they are partly exempt as far as VAT is concerned. It is therefore important that input tax is claimed on any expenditure directly relevant to taxable activities, e.g. bar stock for resale but not on any expenditure relevant to exempt activities. In terms of apportioning input tax on general overhead items (known as residual input tax in partial exemption terms), it might be worthwhile considering the benefits of a special method of calculation. A special method must be approved by HMRC and can relate to any method of calculation apart from the standard method based on income.
- Many smaller clubs and associations might be able to achieve full input tax recovery on costs relevant to their exempt activities if they are classed as *de minimis* as far as partial exemption is concerned. See **50.11** PARTIAL EXEMPTION.
- A useful concession for non-profit making bodies is that subscription income can be apportioned according to the different VAT rates that apply to specific membership benefits, even if there is one main supply that would normally determine the rate at which VAT is charged on the entire subscription. This concession could be useful to produce zero-rating on the value of any newsletter provided as part of a membership scheme. However, zero-rating of printed matter does not apply to a newsletter sent by electronic means (e.g. by email).
- A donation is only relevant if the person making the donation receives no benefits in return for his donation, i.e. no goods or services are supplied by the club or association receiving the donation. A simple acknowledgement of thanks, for example, in an event programme is not classed as a benefit. However, a marketing opportunity or benefit, such as an advertisement on the association website, would be classed as a benefit.
- The supply of benefits to members by trade unions, professional associations, learned societies, representational trade associations and bodies of a political, religious, patriotic, philosophical or philanthropic nature may qualify for VAT exemption. The same principle applies to membership subscriptions relevant to non-profit making bodies providing sport and physical education services (e.g. a members' golf club).
- A challenge for clubs and associations can sometimes occur when it is necessary to decide whether a branch or section of the main association is classed as being independent as far as VAT is concerned (i.e. no output tax due on its income unless it is separately VAT-registered in its own right), or whether it is part of

the association and therefore within the scope of the main VAT registration. The key factor will be the constitution of the branch or section, and establishing whether it has its own financial independence.

- It is sometimes thought (incorrectly) that VAT exemption in relation to fundraising events only applies if the event is being organised by a charity. This is incorrect. The exemption also applies to events organised by non-profit making bodies (e.g. the annual fundraising dinner for a members' rugby club).
- The VAT liability of room hire income earned by a club or association can sometimes cause a problem. As a general principle, such income is exempt from VAT if the hirer has exclusive use of the room in question, and assuming there is no option to tax election in place on the building where rental income is being generated. However, room hire income can become standard rated (or a mixed supply situation) if the hirer is mainly paying for other benefits (e.g. catering).

16

Death and Incapacity

Introduction to death and incapacity

Assets passing to personal representatives

[16.1] Where the control of a deceased person's assets passes to a personal representative or person otherwise acting in a representative capacity, that person must comply with the VAT requirements relating to accounting, payment and records. However, any requirement to pay VAT is limited to the assets over which he has control in his capacity as personal representative. [*SI 1995/2518, Reg 30*]. HMRC may therefore require the personal representative to account for any outstanding returns or VAT which was due on the date of death.

Carrying on a business

Where a taxable person dies, HMRC may, from the date of death until some other person is registered in respect of the taxable supplies made (or intended to be made) by a business, treat any person carrying on the business as a taxable person. The person carrying on the business must, within 21 days of commencing to do so, inform HMRC in writing of the date of death and the fact that the business is being continued. [*VATA 1994, s 46(4); SI 1995/2518, Reg 9*]. The person carrying on the business is responsible for ensuring that all the VAT obligations are complied with and must account for any VAT due on supplies made by the business whilst he controls the business as if he were the taxable person.

Death of a partner

Under *Partnership Act 1890, s 33(1)*, subject to any agreement between the partners, every partnership is dissolved as regards all the partners by the death of any partner. Until the death is notified to HMRC in writing, the registration and VAT liability of the partnership continues unchanged. See **51.3 PARTNERSHIPS**.

The death of a partner should be notified to the VAT Registration Service within 30 days. If two or more partners remain, and they intend to continue in business, they should notify the VAT Registration Service accordingly and HMRC will amend their details in the HMRC records. If there is a single surviving partner and that partner intends to recruit a replacement partner, the VAT Registration Service should be informed of the details of the new partner within 30 days of the new partner's appointment. If there is a single surviving partner and that partner decides to continue the business as a sole proprietor, the VAT Registration Service should be notified within 30 days of the change taking place.

If a partner dies, and two or more partners continue to run the business after his death, there is no need for the partnership to deregister. An amendment to form VAT2 (list of partners) can be made instead. If only one partner survives, then he has the choice of either retaining the same VAT registration number by completing form VAT68 to register as a sole trader, or the partnership can deregister and he can reregister as a sole trader from a current date with a new VAT number.

In some cases, it is possible that the death of a partner will mean that taxable sales of the business in the next 12 months could be less than the deregistration threshold. In such cases, the opportunity to deregister might be a worthwhile planning opportunity. However, it is important to be aware of the need to account for output tax on most stock and assets held at the time of deregistration.

(VAT Notice 700, para 26.8).

VAT consequences of incapacity

Assets passing to another person

[16.2] Where a person becomes 'incapacitated' and control of his assets passes to another person, that person must comply with the VAT requirements relating to accounting, payment and records. However, any requirement to pay VAT is limited to the assets of the incapacitated person over which he has control. [*SI 1995/2518, Reg 30*]. HMRC may therefore require that person to account for any outstanding returns or VAT which was due when incapacity commenced.

Carrying on a business

Where a taxable person becomes incapacitated, HMRC may, from the date of incapacitation until some other person is registered in respect of the taxable supplies made (or intended to be made) by a business, treat any person carrying on the business as a taxable person. The person carrying on the business must, within 21 days of commencing to do so, inform HMRC in writing of the date of incapacity and the fact that the business is being continued. [*VATA 1994, s 46(4); SI 1995/2518, Reg 9*]. The person carrying on the business is responsible for ensuring that all the VAT obligations are complied with and must account for any VAT due on supplies made by the business whilst he controls the business as if he were the taxable person.

Relief for importations of goods acquired by inheritance

[16.3] Certain persons who have become entitled as legatees to property situated outside the EU may import that property without payment of VAT (and duty). See **34.15**(13) **IMPORTS**.

Relief for importations re war graves, funerals

[16.4] Certain goods can be imported without payment of VAT (and duty). These comprise goods for the upkeep of war graves, memorials, etc.; coffins and urns containing human remains; and flowers, wreaths, etc. with no commercial intent. See **34.15**(12) **IMPORTS**.

American war graves

[16.5] In order to place inland purchases on the same footing as imported goods, VAT is remitted on the supply of goods and services to the American Battle Monuments Commission for the maintenance of the American Military Cemetery and Memorial at Madingley, Cambridge and Brookwood, Surrey. (VAT Notice 48, ESC 2.5).

Burial and cremation

[16.6] *Directive 2006/112/EC, Art 371* allows EU member states to continue to exempt certain services listed in *Annex X*. These include services supplied by undertakers and cremation services, together with goods related thereto. Under this provision, UK law exempts

- the disposal of the remains of the dead, and
- the making of arrangements for, or in connection with, the disposal of the remains of the dead.

[*VATA 1994, Sch 9 Group 8*].

Certain other services, such as the right to a grave space and the right to place an urn in a niche, are exempt under *VATA 1994, Sch 9 Group 1* (see **16.7** below).

HMRC has always regarded the EU and UK law in *Group 8* as applying only to the *essential* goods and services that an undertaker or crematorium has to supply in order to dispose of the remains of the dead. This follows the opinion of the tribunal in *UFD Ltd* [1981] VATTR 199 (TVC 24.27) which considered that the normal meaning of the words 'disposal of the remains of the dead' were to be construed to mean, and to be confined to, the services supplied by undertakers *as such* and cremation services. This allows undertakers and crematoria to exempt their services of burial (including burial at sea) and cremation, and the arrangements that have to be made to provide those services.

Funerals for pets are standard-rated.

(1) Supplies by undertakers and funeral directors

The table below indicates HMRC's view of the liability of supplies provided by undertakers and funeral directors.

Supply	*VAT liability*
The following goods and services when provided as part of a funeral package that includes the disposal of the remains of the dead • Supply of a coffin • The cover and fittings for a coffin • The casket or urn • Embalming • The digging, preparation and refilling of graves • The transport of the deceased to the burial ground or crematorium • A shroud or robe • Use of a chapel of rest • Provision of bearers • Transport of mourners in own limousines • Bell tolling and music at the funeral service	Exempt
The following services provided the dead body has been released from the mortuary to the bereaved family to arrange the funeral (regardless of whether the service is provided direct to the bereaved or to a third party, such as another undertaker or funeral director) • Embalming • Use of a chapel of rest • Digging, preparation and the refilling of graves • Burial or cremation • The interment of ashes	Exempt
Selling coffins, urns, shrouds or embalming fluid	Standard-rated (unless provided by an undertaker as part of a funeral package – see above)
Flowers, wreaths, announcement cards and other commemorative items	Standard-rated
Newspaper announcements	Standard-rated
Hire of hearse with driver by an undertaker or funeral carriage master	Exempt
Hire of limousine with driver from one undertaker to another for the transport of mourners as part of the funeral	Exempt
Hire of vehicle with driver in other circumstances	Standard-rated
Hire of a hearse or limousine without a driver	Standard-rated
Catering	Standard-rated

Supply	*VAT liability*
Fees payable to Registrars for certified copies of death certificates	Outside the scope of VAT
Fees payable to churches for ministers' services	Outside the scope of VAT
Orders of service for use in funeral commemorative services	Zero-rated as printed matter
Agency services	Standard-rated
Services aimed at checking customer satisfaction	Standard-rated

Packages of mixed supplies

Where exempt supplies and standard-rated supplies are provided as a single price package, a suitable apportionment must be made for VAT purposes. There is no special method of apportionment but the result must be fair and justifiable. See **48.3 OUTPUT TAX** for various methods of apportionment.

Disbursements

Funeral packages frequently contain 'bought in' supplies (e.g. an undertaker may pay a hotel, caterer, newspaper publisher, etc. for goods and services as the agents of his client and recharge the client the exact amount paid out. If the payments meet the relevant conditions set out in **3.7 AGENTS**, they may be treated as disbursements and can be excluded when calculating any VAT due on the main supply.

(VAT Notice 701/32/12, para 3).

(2) Supplies by cemeteries and crematoria

The following supplies are exempt from VAT.

- Burial (including reburial) and cremation
- Interment of ashes
- Digging, preparation and refilling of a grave
- Supplying an urn or casket in connection with a particular funeral
- Brick, block or concrete lining of a grave when constructed as a requirement of the cemetery management (or in the case of a churchyard, the church authorities) where, for example, the soil is unstable
- Any interest in, right over or licence to occupy land within *VATA 1994, Sch 9 Group 1* (see **42.17 LAND AND BUILDINGS: EXEMPT SUPPLIES AND OPTION TO TAX**) including the right to a grave space and the right to place an urn in a niche
- The exhumation of a body that is reburied elsewhere at the behest of the bereaved
- The supply of a cremation certificate (form B, C or F) by a doctor
- The removal of a pacemaker from the deceased prior to cremation

The following supplies are not exempt from VAT and are standard-rated.

- Charges for erecting, working on, or repairing monuments within a cemetery or crematorium, except where the removing or refixing of memorial headstones is necessary to allow further burial

- Any interest in, right over or licence or to occupy land that the business has opted to tax, including the right to any grave space or the right to place an urn in a niche
- Goods and services in connection with the commemoration of dead people
- Exhumation services not connected with reburial to another site

See also **16.7** below.

(VAT Notice 701/32/12, para 5).

Local authorities

In *Rhondda Cynon Taff County Borough Council* (VTD 16496) (TVC 22.154) the tribunal held that the provision and maintenance of *cemeteries* by a local authority was not a business activity for VAT purposes as the activities had been carried out under a special legal regime applicable to public authorities. The tribunal also concluded that, as there are so few privately-owned cemeteries, the non-business ruling would not distort competition. Following this decision, HMRC take the view that:

- The decision only applies to the provision and maintenance of local authority cemeteries. Non-business activities include the grant of a right to an exclusive burial, the right to place and maintain a tombstone, the keeping and storage of the plans and records of burials, general maintenance, and any actions intended to remove dangerous obstructions, e.g. collapsed vaults or broken headstones. Other services offered for which a charge is made (e.g. the provision of books of remembrance and the erection of headstones) remain business activities as the provision of these services is not covered by the special legal regime applicable to cemeteries.
- Although crematoria are governed by special legal provisions similar to those which apply to cemeteries, the higher incidence of privately-owned crematoria means that a distortion of competition would result if local authorities were allowed to treat these activities as non-business.
- Where local authorities operate sites which contain both cemeteries and crematoria and they have exceeded the partial exemption *de minimis* limits, a business/non-business apportionment must be made between the activities.

(3) Memorials and commemoration of the dead

Supplies of goods or services which are concerned with the commemoration, as opposed to the burial or cremation, of the dead are normally standard-rated. These include

- The supply of memorial headstones
- Erecting, repairing or maintaining memorial headstones
- Inscribing services for headstones, plaques or other commemorative items
- Flowers and wreaths
- Planting trees or rosebushes
- Memorial vases and seats

- Plaques including services of fixing them
- Placing 'In Memoriam' announcements in newspapers
- Recording entries in books of remembrance.

The removal, refixing and incidental cleaning of a memorial headstone, when a grave is disturbed to allow for a further burial, is exempt as it forms part of the arrangements made in connection with that burial. But VAT must be charged for adding another inscription to the memorial.

(VAT Notice 701/32/12, para 6).

(4) Transportation of the dead

Within the UK

Where an undertaker or a funeral carriage master transports a dead person	*Tax treatment*
to a burial ground or crematorium as part of a funeral (whether this service is supplied to the bereaved family or to another undertaker)	Exempt
to an undertaker or funeral director who will provide the funeral	Exempt
from a school, university or research institution to a burial ground or crematorium	Exempt
to a public mortuary	Standard-rated

Repatriation packages supplied by undertakers

Where an undertaker or business specialises in repatriation and supplies a repatriation package consisting of goods and services that are normally provided by undertakers, the supply will be exempt from VAT to the extent that it consists of the supply of:

- goods and services such as coffin, embalming, use of chapel of rest (see those exempt in **16.6**(1) above);
- services of obtaining documents and permits necessary to repatriate the deceased; and
- transportation of the deceased to burial ground, crematorium or to another undertaker.

The place of supply is where the customer (that is, the person with whom they contract) belongs if the customer is 'in business' (e.g. an insurance company or undertaker) and receives the services otherwise than wholly for private purposes.

If the customer is a private individual, such as a member of the deceased's family, the place of supply is where the undertaker belongs.

International transportation supplied by airlines and other carriers

If an airline or other general purpose carrier transports a body between the UK and another country, they should apply the same VAT rules as those for transporting goods. A summary is below.

If a body is transported for an insurer, undertaker or other business customer, the place of supply is where the customer belongs for the purposes of receiving the supply. It does not matter where the dead body is being transported to or from.

A dead person is transported for a business customer, and the customer belongs	*then, the place of supply of services is*	*Tax treatment*
In the UK	UK	supply is zero rated if the dead person is transported from a place within to a place outside the EU (or vice versa). Otherwise, it is standard-rated.
In another EU member state	EU member state in which the customer belongs	the customer should account for VAT (if applicable) in their EU member state under the 'reverse charge'
	outside the EU	the supply is outside the scope of EU VAT

If the transport services are supplied to a non-business/private individual, such as a relative of the deceased, the place of supply is as follows.

A dead person is transported for a private individual	*Tax treatment*
The transportation is from the EU to a third country (or vice versa)	the place of supply is where the transportation is performed in proportion to the distances covered. The supply is zero rated to the extent that it takes place in the UK. The supplier may have to register for VAT in the other EU member state.
The transportation begins and ends in the EU	the place of supply is wholly where the transportation begins. If the transportation begins in the UK, the supplier must account for standard-rated VAT in the UK (unless the movement is from, to or between the islands of the Azores or Madeira, in which case it is zero-rated). If the transportation begins in another EU member state, the supplier may have to register for VAT there.

If the place of supply is outside the UK then the supply is outside the scope of UK VAT and there is no VAT liability within the UK. However, the supplier will be able to recover any input tax incurred in making the supply, subject to the normal rules. The supplier may have a liability to VAT register in other EU member states where the supplies are made.

When human remains are brought to the UK from overseas, there is no import VAT or acquisition tax due when a coffin containing a dead body or an urn containing ashes is brought into the UK from overseas. The same rules apply to flowers and wreaths accompanying the coffin or urn.

(VAT Notice 701/32/12, para 7).

(5) Prepayments and funeral plans

Many individuals wish to pay for their funeral in advance. As funeral directors cannot legally accept advance payments for a funeral, this can be done by either of the following methods.

A trust-based plan

The individual pays a plan provider, by lump sum or instalments, for an agreed funeral package. On the death of the plan holder, the provider pays the nominated funeral director for the funeral as specified in the plan.

The nature of the supplies by the plan provider depends upon whether it is acting as principal or agent.

- If the plan provider acts as principal (i.e. is contractually responsible for delivering the funeral to the plan holder's estate), the full amount paid by the plan holder into the plan is consideration for the provider's supply of a funeral package. The provider must apportion the payment between exempt and standard-rated elements of the package.
- If the plan provider acts as agent (i.e. the contract for the delivery of the funeral is between the funeral director and the plan holder and the plan provider's role is to facilitate this arrangement), any administration or other fee charged by the plan provider is standard-rated.

The payments which the funeral director receives for providing the funeral are exempt to the extent that the plan covers exempt supplies. If the plan covers any standard-rated supplies, an apportionment must be made.

Any commissions or marketing fees received by funeral directors (or others) for selling trust-based prepayment plans are standard rated.

A whole life insurance policy

The following table covers the VAT liability of payments and supplies made in connection with each.

Supply	*VAT liability*	
	Trust-based plan	*Life insurance plan*
Payment from plan provider to nominated funeral director on death of customer for burial or cremation	Exempt	Exempt

Supply	*VAT liability* *Trust-based plan*	*Life insurance plan*
Payment from plan provider to nominated funeral director on death of customer for a funeral package of different liabilities	The funeral director must apportion the payment between the exempt and standard-rated supplies	The funeral director must apportion the payment between the exempt and standard-rated supplies
Deposit or advance payment made by plan provider to nominated funeral director for a funeral package of different liabilities	Generally to be apportioned on same basis as whole package	Generally to be apportioned on same basis as whole package
Payments made by individual to a plan provider	If plan provider is acting as agent — outside the scope of VAT If plan provider is acting as principal — apportioned between the exempt and standard-rated elements of the funeral package	Exempt
Management fee charged by plan provider	If plan provider is acting as agent — standard-rated If plan provider is acting as principal — apportioned between the exempt and standard-rated elements of the funeral package	N/A
Agent's fee for selling a plan (but see *Funeral Planning Services Ltd*) (VTD 19975) (TVC 16.5)	Standard-rated	Exempt
Payment by deceased's estate to nominated funeral director to cover shortfall	Exempt to the extent that it relates to exempt elements of the package	Exempt to the extent that it relates to exempt elements of the package
Charges for cancelling or amending plan	Standard-rated	N/A

(VAT Notice 701/32/12, para 4).

De Voil Indirect Tax Service. See V4.151.

Grants re land

[16.7] The grant or an interest in, right over or licence to occupy land is exempt under *VATA 1994, Sch 9 Group 1*. See **42.17 LAND AND BUILDINGS: EXEMPT SUPPLIES AND OPTION TO TAX.** Services which are exempt under this *Group* do not have to rely on a connection with a particular funeral. Examples include the right to

- a grave space; and

- place an urn in a niche.

(VAT Notice 701/32/12, para 5.1).

The grantor, however, has the option to tax any such supply at the standard rate (see **42.23 LAND AND BUILDINGS: EXEMPT SUPPLIES AND OPTION TO TAX**).

Key points: death and incapacity

[16.8] Points to consider are as follows.

- In the event of the death of a sole trader, the person carrying on the business after his death will be treated as a taxable person by HMRC in terms of expecting all VAT responsibilities to be met and tax to be correctly accounted for and declared on VAT returns. The situation is not the same if a member of a partnership dies because continuity will be given by the surviving partners.
- The services of funeral directors and undertakers are mainly exempt from VAT if they relate to arrangements for the disposal of the dead. However, some services are not exempt because they do not directly relate to the disposal procedures. For example, services linked to arranging flowers, catering and newspaper announcements are all standard-rated.
- In certain situations, an undertaker or funeral director will arrange for costs to be paid on behalf of his client, which he will include on his final sales invoice. If he is merely acting as an agent in arranging and paying for these supplies, then they could qualify as a disbursement and be outside the scope of VAT. However, it is important that the rules relating to disbursements are correctly applied to avoid the potential risk that HMRC could deem them to be standard-rated.
- Be aware that the supply of goods or services intended to recognise or commemorate the dead, as opposed to being linked to their burial or cremation, are standard-rated rather than exempt from VAT. An example is the cost of supplying and erecting a memorial headstone.

17

Education

Cross-references. See **19.23 EUROPEAN UNION LEGISLATION** for the provisions of *Directive 2006/112/EC*; **26.8 FUEL AND POWER** for supplies of fuel and power to charitable schools; **29.12 HEALTH AND WELFARE** for supplies by registered nurseries and playgroups.

De Voil Indirect Tax Service. See V4.141.

Introduction to education

[17.1] VAT exemption for education and training is largely dependent on

- whether the body is in business for VAT purposes (see **17.2** below); and
- if so, whether it is an eligible body (see **17.3** below).

Having established that the activities are business

(a) supplies of education and vocational training by an eligible body are exempt (see **17.4** and **17.7** below respectively); and

(b) supplies of certain goods and services related to exempt supplies within (*a*) and (*b*) above are also exempt (see **17.10** below).

Supplies of research by an eligible body to another eligible body were exempt prior to 1 August 2013 (see **17.6** below).

Where the business is not an eligible body, exemption may also apply, subject to conditions, to

- private tuition (see **17.11** below);
- examination services (see **17.12** below); and
- government approved training schemes (see **17.16** below).

Business

[17.2] For VAT purposes, business has a wide meaning and includes any continuing activity which is mainly concerned with making supplies to other persons for any form of payment or consideration. For a general consideration of the meaning of business, see **9.1** to **9.3 BUSINESS**.

A supply of education takes place for VAT purposes where it is provided by way of business and in return for a consideration. If there is no payment, the education is not a supply and is a non-business activity outside the scope of VAT.

Education is normally funded in one of three ways.

(1) By making a charge

In such cases, there is a business activity whoever pays the charges (e.g. a student, an employer or a local authority) and whether charges raised are sufficient to meet full costs or are subsidised (e.g. by central government grant, bursaries or scholarships).

Establishments which normally provide education in return for fees and are therefore in business include

- independent fee paying schools, including non-maintained special schools;
- universities; and
- institutions teaching English as a foreign language.

(2) By direct funding from local or central government

Education funded in this way is not a business activity and the supply is outside the scope of VAT. This normally applies to

- community schools;
- foundation schools;
- voluntary aided schools, including former special agreement schools;
- voluntary controlled schools;
- community special schools;
- foundation special schools;
- grant maintained (integrated) schools (Northern Ireland);
- self-governing schools (Scotland);
- city technology colleges; and
- free schools; and
- academies.

Where such schools charge for additional tuition (e.g. music or sport instruction), this is a business activity.

(3) By a combination of government grants and charges

In such cases, there is a supply for VAT purposes. The government funding is an outside the scope contribution to a business activity. Institutions which *may* require payment include

- sixth form colleges;
- tertiary colleges; and
- colleges of further education.

These institutions normally provide education for no charge to students who are 19 or under (18 or under in Scotland) at the start of their courses (non-business) but charge for older students and foreign nationals (business). The important factor is always whether they require payment, not the age or identity of the student.

(VAT Notice 701/30/17, paras 2.1–2.5, 3.1–3.2).

Eligible bodies

[17.3] An '*eligible body*' for the purposes of providing exempt education comprises any of the following.

(a) Schools

A school within the meaning of *Education Act 1996*, *Education (Scotland) Act 1980*, *Education and Libraries (Northern Ireland) Order 1986 (SI 1986/594)* or *Education Reform (Northern Ireland) Order 1989 (SI 1989/2406)* which is

(i) provisionally or finally registered (or deemed to be registered) as a school within the meaning of that legislation in a register of independent schools;

(ii) a school in respect of which grants are made by the Secretary of State to the proprietor or managers;

(iii) a community, foundation or voluntary school within the meaning of the *School Standards and Framework Act 1998*, a special school within the meaning of *Education Act 1996, s 337* or a maintained school within the meaning of *Education and Libraries (Northern Ireland) Order 1986*;

(iv) (before 31 December 2004) a public school within the meaning of *Education (Scotland) Act 1980, s 135(1)*; or

(v) a grant-maintained integrated school within the meaning of *Education Reform (Northern Ireland) Order 1989, Art 65*.

This covers all of the schools listed in **17.2** above. Many of these schools (notably community, foundation and voluntary schools and their counterparts in Scotland and NI) do not generally make a charge for the education they provide and this education is, for the most part, non-business and outside the scope of VAT (see **17.2** above). However, under limited circumstances, they can make a charge (e.g. music or sport tuition or mature students filling sixth form places) and, because they are eligible bodies, such charges are exempt.

Schools not covered by (i)–(vi) above may be covered by the eligible body criteria in (e) below.

(b) Universities

A UK university, and any college, institution, school or hall of such a university. Not included are subsidiary companies that universities and colleges set up to pursue commercial business.

Previously, HMRC treated companies owned or controlled by universities as eligible bodies only where they had been formally approved by the parent university as a college, institution, school or hall of the university. Following the cases of *C & E Commrs v School of Finance and Management (London) Ltd*, Ch D [2001] STC 1690 (TVC 21.11) and *HIBT Ltd* (VTD 19978) (TVC 21.17), HMRC have revised their policy with regard to education supplied by university trading companies. A university owned/controlled company is regarded as an eligible body where it provides university level education leading to a qualification awarded by a university or nationally recognised body; and it has close academic links with the parent university, e.g. students on the company's courses are registered/enrolled with the parent university, subject to its rules and regulations and awarded qualifications by it. (VAT Information Sheet 3/10).

A number of cases have concerned claims by commercial companies to be 'a college of a university' on the basis of the factors in the *School of Finance and Management* case (the 'SFM factors'). In *Finance & Business Training Ltd v HMRC* [2016] EWCA Civ 7 (TVC 21.23), the Court of Appeal ruled that a commercial college could not justify eligible body status on the EU legal principle of fiscal neutrality: the Directive provided that certain bodies were exempt and others were not, and this college was not sufficiently integrated with a university. Similarly in *HMRC v SAE Education Ltd* [2016] UKUT 193 (TCC) (TVC 21.24), the Upper Tribunal held that the First-tier Tax Tribunal had placed too much weight on certain of the SFM factors and not enough on others, and had come to an unjustified decision. The Upper Tribunal allowed HMRC's appeal, holding that the company was not sufficiently integrated to be a college of the university.

A Students Union was held not to be an integral part of the University and therefore not part of an eligible body in *C & E Commrs v University of Leicester Students Union*, CA 2001, [2002] STC 147 (TVC 21.25).

The UK campus of a foreign university is not covered but it is likely to be an eligible body under (e) below.

(c) Further and higher education

An institution

- falling within *Further and Higher Education Act 1992, s 91(3)(a) or (b) or s 91(5)(b) or (c)*;
- which is a designated institution as defined in *Further and Higher Education (Scotland) Act 1992, s 44(2)*;
- managed by a board of management as defined in *Further and Higher Education (Scotland) Act 1992, s 36(1)*; or
- to which grants are paid by the Department of Education for Northern Ireland under *Education and Libraries (Northern Ireland) Order 1986, Art 66(2)*.

This includes all further education colleges or organisations defined or designated as such under the various *Education Acts* (including the Workers' Educational Association (WEA)), together with higher educational institutions defined in the *Education Acts* but not covered by (b) above.

(d) Public bodies

A government department or local authority (or a body which acts for public purposes and not for its own profit and performs functions similar to those of a government department or local authority). Included are executive agencies and Health Authorities.

(e) Charities, etc.

A body which

(i) is precluded from distributing and does not distribute any profit it makes; and
(ii) applies any profits made from exempt supplies of education, research or vocational training to the continuance or improvement of such supplies.

(f) Teaching English as a foreign language

A body not falling within *(a)*–*(e)* above which provides the teaching of English as a foreign language (see **17.13** below).

[*VATA 1994, Sch 9 Group 6 Note 1*].

Eligible bodies do not include bodies such as tutorial colleges, computer training organisations, secretarial schools and correspondence colleges which operate with a view to making and distributing a profit.

(VAT Notice 701/30/17, paras 4.1–4.6).

Education

[17.4] The provision of 'education' is exempt

- when provided by an '*eligible body*' (see **17.3** above); or
- to the extent that the consideration payable is ultimately a charge to funds provided by the Learning and Skills Council for England or the National Assembly for Wales under *Learning and Skills Act 2000, Parts I or II*. *Included* is the supply of any goods or services essential to the education provided directly to the person receiving the education by the person providing the education. See, for example, *Creating Careers* (VTD 19509) (TVC 21.31).

[*VATA 1994, Sch 9 Group 6 Items 1(a), 5A; Learning and Skills Act 2000, Sch 9 para 47*].

'*Education*' is not defined in the legislation. HMRC regard education as meaning a course, class or lesson of instruction or study in any subject, regardless of where and when it takes place. Education includes lectures, educational seminars, conferences and symposia, together with sporting and recreational courses. It also includes distance learning (see **17.5** below) and associated materials. Any separate charge for registration is part of the supply of education.

In the sports sector, education includes classes that are led and directed rather than merely supervised. For example

- in a gymnasium, the supply of instruction in the use of equipment and warming-up techniques and the assessment of a person when he or she first enrols is the supply of education; but a charge to use the gym in a separate session where no instruction takes place is a charge for admission; and
- in a swimming pool, if the staff are on hand primarily to coach, any charge is the supply of education; but if staff are on hand primarily to satisfy health and safety and insurance requirements, any charge is for admission.

(VAT Notice 701/30/17, paras 5.1, 5.2.)

See **17.13** below for the teaching of English as a foreign language.

Distance learning

[17.5] Distance learning covers home study or correspondence courses from suppliers that range from commercial businesses to colleges of further education and universities and in subjects that range from leisure pursuits to those leading to full academic qualifications.

The VAT liability of the supply depends upon the exact nature of what is being supplied. This may be

- an exempt supply of education by an eligible body;
- a standard-rated supply of education by a business which is not an eligible body;
- a single supply of zero-rated printed matter; or
- a multiple supply of printed matter and education, in which case an apportionment is necessary.

In *The College of Estate Management v C & E Commrs*, HL [2005] STC 1597 (TVC 5.38) the tribunal held that there was single exempt supply of education and the House of Lords upheld this decision stating that it was inappropriate to analyse the transaction in terms of what was a principal and ancillary supply.

See also *The Rapid Results College Ltd* (VTD 48) (TVC 5.2) where fees for correspondence courses were held to be apportionable between the supply of books and tuition but compare *International News Syndicate Ltd* (VTD 14425) (TVC 5.3) where the small element of external tuition was held to be incidental and the whole supply treated as zero-rated. However, these decisions pre-dated the decision in *Card Protection Plan* and must be read in the light of the criteria set out in that case.

In the more recent case of *Metropolitan International Schools* [2015] UKFTT 517 (TC) (TC04675) (TVC 5.40), the First-tier Tribunal accepted the company's argument that its distance learning supplies were entirely zero-rated as printed matter with incidental tutorial help. HMRC had agreed for many years that the supplies were split between 75% printed matter and 25% taxable education; when HMRC changed this view and ruled that the courses should be entirely standard-rated going forward, the taxpayer argued the reverse and won.

See **17.12** below for supplies of online education/examination services.

Research

VAT treatment from 1 August 2013

[17.6] HMRC accept that research includes

- original investigation undertaken in order to gain, advance or expand knowledge and understanding;
- devising a specialised software programme as part of a research project before carrying out the main tasks.

HMRC do not accept that research includes

- merely confirming existing knowledge or understanding;
- consultancy;
- business efficiency advice;
- collecting and recording statistics without also collating, analysing, or interpreting them;
- market research;
- opinion polling;
- writing computer programmes;
- routine testing and analysis of materials, components and processes.

The fact that a project may have a specific commercial application does not necessarily mean that it cannot be research. For example, much research funded by the Department for Business, Innovation & Skills and by Research Councils is aimed at developing improved equipment or techniques for use in industry.

(VAT Notice 701/30/17, para 5.6).

The UK received notification from the European Commission that its exemption for business supplies of research between eligible bodies did not comply with European legislation. The UK accepted that that was the case and withdrew the exemption from 1 August 2013. As a transitional arrangement, for supplies of business research where the written contract was entered into before 1 August 2013, whether or not work has already commenced, the exemption continues to apply to services within the scope of the contract.

Supplies under the contract will be a continuous supply of services. Each liability of each supply is individually determined. If the supply made is for a supply wholly under the contract as it was on 31 July 2013, that supply will be exempt from VAT. If a supply is wholly for an extended part of the contract, that supply will be standard-rated. If a supply relates in part for the contract as it stood as at 31 July 2013 and in part from extended parts of the contract, then the whole supply is taxable at the standard rate. In order to benefit from the exemption all supplies that are within the scope of the contract as at 31 July 2013 should be invoiced separately from any work relating to extended supplies.

Supplies can generally only be exempt if they fall wholly within the scope of the contract as at 31 July 2013. However, HMRC accept that some minor variations will not affect the liability of the original contract, for example:

- changing the supplier of a sub-contracted service;

- changing the order the contract is performed in;
- changes of less than three months to the delivery time of the contract providing there is no additional consideration.

If a substantial variation is made to a written contract as it stood at 31 July 2013, supplies that relate to the changes will be subject to VAT and supplies that remain within the scope of the contract as it stood at 31 July 2013 will be exempt. HMRC regard the following as examples of substantial variations.

- Increases in the length of the contract of over three months.
- Payment of additional consideration.
- Requirement for new or additional tests to be performed.
- Changes to the product or topic on which research is to be carried out.

(HMRC Brief 21/13; VAT Notice 701/30/17, para 5.7).

HMRC have provided the following guidance on the distinction between

- supplies of research that are outside the scope of VAT; and
- those that are exempt business supplies which will be affected by the withdrawal.

Collaborative research

Collaborative research is where several bodies (typically universities or other eligible bodies) get together to apply for grant funding to undertake a research project. It is not uncommon for one of the applicants to be shown as the head or lead body which deals primarily with the funding body including receiving funding which is passed to other applicant bodies for their contribution to the project. For ease, contracts are often concluded only in the name of the funding body and the lead research body even though this is a collaborative project. HMRC accept that in such cases of collaborative research, all research services provided by each of the bodies involved in the project are outside the scope of VAT, even if the funding may be passed on by the lead research body to others, and only the lead research body is party to the contract with the funding body.

Further guidance

For there to be a supply of services for VAT purposes, there must be a direct and immediate link between consideration paid and a service provided. HMRC do not consider this to happen in the case of research which is funded, either by the public sector or by the charitable sector, for the wider public benefit.

Where a subsidy is granted by the donor to the recipient to enable a third party to obtain a specific service (or to obtain it more cheaply) this would, as a general rule, be a taxable transaction.

The main question to answer is whether the funding is the consideration or part of the consideration for any specific supply. If not, then it is outside the scope of VAT.

Situations where the funding will be outside the scope of VAT include the following.

- Research which is funded for the 'general public good' and there is no direct benefit for the funding body.
- Research which is funded for the general public good and is either not expected to generate any intellectual property (IP), or if it does then any reports or findings will be freely available to others.
- Where there is a collaborative agreement between different research institutions where all parties to the grant are named on the application.
- Where the funding flows through one named party—and they act purely as a conduit passing on the funds to others involved in the research project—the funding remains outside the scope of VAT.

Where funding is provided to a named party for research that will either generate IP to be exploited by the funder and/or is not for the public good and they subsequently decide to sub-contract some of the research to an eligible body (for example a university), the initial funding to the named party (assuming an eligible body) will be taxable consideration for a supply.

[*SI 2013/1897*]. (HMRC Brief 10/13).

VAT treatment prior to 1 August 2013

Note. In *EC Commission v Federal Republic of Germany, ECJ Case C–287/00*, [2002] STC 982 (TVC 22.338) the CJEU held that remunerated research activities of State universities were not closely related to university education and did not fall within the scope of the exemption. While such projects might be of assistance to university education, they were not essential to the objective of teaching students to enable them to carry out a profession and many universities achieved that aim without carrying out research projects for consideration. The exemption of research under UK law was revised from 1 August 2013 to take account of the decision, and the following summarises the position before those changes.

The provision of research supplied *by* an 'eligible body' *to* an eligible body was exempt. [*VATA 1994, Sch 9 Group 6 Item 1(b)*]. See **17.3** above for '*eligible body*'.

'*Research*' is not defined in the legislation. HMRC regard research as meaning 'original investigation undertaken in order to gain knowledge and understanding'. It is the intention at the beginning of a project that determines whether a supply qualifies as research. If the intention is to advance knowledge and understanding, the supply is one of research. By contrast, merely confirming existing knowledge and understanding is not research. The fact that a project may have a specific commercial application does not necessarily mean that it cannot also be research.

The following are examples of work which HMRC do not regard as being research.

- Consultancy and business efficiency advice.
- Collection and recording statistics, without also collating, analysing or interpreting of them.
- Market research and opinion polling.
- Writing computer programs.

- Routine testing and analysis of materials, components and processes.

But some of these activities do qualify if supplied as an integral part of a research project (e.g. where a specialised software program must be devised before the provider can embark upon the main body of the project).

(VAT Notice 701/30/11, para 5.6 – cancelled).

If either of the parties to a supply of research is not an eligible body (e.g. a commercial organisation) the supply will normally be standard-rated (but see below for supplies to overseas bodies). Note, however, that the recipient of the supply does not have to be involved in the field of education, research or vocational training. If the recipient is a non-profit making body satisfying the criteria in **17.3**(*e*)(i) above, but making no supplies of education, etc., the criteria of **17.3**(*e*)(ii) above have no relevance and it is an eligible body. Supplies of research to that body are exempt. The supplier must determine the status of the customer and, if not satisfied that the customer is an eligible body, must standard-rate the supply.

European Commission Framework 6 and 7 research programmes

If a research provider carried out research under the Framework 6 programme, payments received are consideration for a supply. VAT should not be charged to the Commission as it is recognised as an international organisation by its host country, Belgium, and the supply is therefore exempt under *Directive 2006/112/EC, Art 151(1)(b)*, see **19.30**(*b*) **EUROPEAN UNION LEGISLATION**. The provider can recover input tax directly attributable to the exempt supply under *Directive 2006/112/EC, Art 169(b)*.

However, funding under the Framework 7 programme is grant income. As such, where VAT is incurred on goods and services purchased purely to support non-business research activities, it is not input tax and cannot be recovered.

(VAT Notice 701/30/17, para 5.8).

Government grant-funded research

Grants provided by central government to fund research (as opposed to research commissioned by the government) are generally paid by the granting body to fulfil the body's statutory and public duties to fund research, not to secure a benefit for it or any third parties. The majority of public-funded research is generally for the public good and the body funding it does not receive any supply of goods or services in return for the funding. In those cases, the grant does not constitute consideration for a supply and is thus outside the scope of VAT.

(VAT Information Sheet 4/08).

Vocational training

[17.7] The provision of 'vocational training' by an 'eligible body' is exempt. [*VATA 1994, Sch 9 Group 6 Item 1(c)*]. See **17.3** above for '*eligible body*'.

'*Vocational training*' means training, re-training or the provision of work experience for

- any trade, profession or employment; or
- any voluntary work connected with education, health, safety or welfare or with the carrying out of activities of a charitable nature.

[*VATA 1994, Sch 9 Group 6 Note 3*].

Vocational training includes courses, conferences, lectures, workshops and seminars designed to prepare those attending for future employment or to add to their knowledge in order to improve their performance in their current work. *Not included* are services such as counselling, business advice and consultancy, which are designed to improve the working practices and efficiency of an organisation as a whole.

Supplies by persons other than eligible bodies

Although falling outside the above provisions, such supplies may be exempt if

- the business contracts or subcontracts to provide vocational training under one of the government's approved vocational training schemes and its services 'are ultimately a charge to funds provided by the Secretary of State' for Education, see **17.16** below; or
- provided by a sole proprietor or partnership and also qualifying as private tuition within **17.11** below.

(VAT Notice 701/30/17, paras 5.5, 6.1–6.2.)

Advanced learner loans

[17.8] HMRC have published HMRC Brief 2/18 which explains HMRC's view of the current tax treatment of advanced learner loans paid by Student Finance England via educational bodies. Student Finance England is part of the Student Loan Company and acts as an agent of the Department for Education.

The Brief does not apply to educational bodies that are eligible bodies.

A summary of the Brief has been provided below.

Advanced learner loans are provided under a contract between the student and the Secretary of State for Education and are administered by Student Finance England. The student is required to repay the loan in accordance with the regulations in force at the time the repayment becomes due. HMRC consider that the loan is ultimately funded by the student, who is required to repay it plus interest, and not by the Secretary of State.

As a result, the receipt of the advanced learner loan by the education provider is not exempt from VAT under *VATA 1994, Sch 9, Group 6, Items 5–5c*. VAT is due at the standard rate on the education provider's full charge for the education that is provided to the student. The only exception is where the provider meets the criteria for being an eligible body for the purposes of the education exemption. These bodies can exempt all of their supplies of education and closely related services regardless of how the funding is received.

HMRC have stated that as this Brief is only intended to provide clarification of its existing policy, it has immediate effect. HMRC will be contacting all businesses that have received an incorrect ruling from HMRC to issue a revised ruling that will be effective from a current or future date, depending on the individual circumstances of the education provider in question.

(HMRC Brief 2/18).

Apprenticeship training

[17.9] HMRC have produced guidance in Notice 701/30/17 regarding the VAT treatment of funds taken from the new apprenticeship service account to pay external providers with effect from 1 May 2017.

Apprenticeship training is covered by the VAT exemption to the extent that it is funded by levy contributions. However, if the trainee or employer pays part of the cost of the training from their own funds, that part of the supply will not be exempt from VAT.

If the training is provided by a non-eligible body then the supplies of training will be exempt from VAT, if someone is contracted or subcontracted to provide the education or vocational training under one of the governments approved training schemes and the services are ultimately funded by funds taken from the new apprenticeship service account to pay external providers for apprenticeship training as outlined in the Department of Education 'Apprenticeship funding: how it will work' guidance note.

The VAT exemption also covers vocational training schemes that are approved by a relevant body and will include apprenticeships funded from the new apprenticeship service account with effect from 1 May 2017 as detailed in the 'Apprenticeship funding: how it will work' guidance.

(HMRC Notice 701/30/17, paras 5.5, 13.1–13.7).

Related goods and services

[17.10] Exemption also applies to the supply of any goods or services (other than examination services within **17.12** below) which are 'closely related' to an exempt supply within **17.4** to **17.7** above (the 'principal supply') provided

- the supply is made *by* or *to* the 'eligible body' making the principal exempt supply;
- the goods or services are for the direct use of the pupil, student or trainee (as the case may be) receiving the principal supply; and
- where the supply is *to* the eligible body making the principal supply, it is made by another eligible body.

[*VATA 1994, Sch 9 Group 6 Item 4*].

See **17.3** above for '*eligible body*'.

Meaning of closely related

'*Closely related*' limits the provisions to goods and services that are necessary for delivering the education to the pupil, student or trainee. An eligible body may treat as closely related any accommodation, catering, transport, school trips and field trips it provides (subject to the rules below for selling goods to pupils).

HMRC give the following examples of goods and services that are not closely related to supplies of education and are taxable, in principle, unless relief is available elsewhere. (This is subject to the overriding principle that supplies of catering by an eligible body to its pupils, students or trainees may be treated as closely related.)

- Supplies to staff (including tutors on summer schools) and to other non-students.
- Sales of goods from school shops, campus shops and student bars.
- Sales from vending machines.
- Sales of goods that are not needed for regular use in class.
- Separately charged laundry and other personal services.
- Sales of school uniforms and sports clothing.
- Admission charges (other than for taking part in sports activities), e.g. admissions to plays, concerts, dances, sporting venues, exhibitions, museums, zoos.
- Administration and management services.
- Commission for allowing sales by outside organisations at an educational establishment.
- Sales by a sole proprietor or partnership in connection with private tuition.

Where closely related supplies are eligible for exemption and zero-rating (e.g. books and other printed matter and transport) either liability may be applied. Supplies of goods and services which are not closely related to education are taxable unless relief is available elsewhere.

In *HMRC v Brockenhurst College* [2014] UKUT 46 (TCC) (TVC 21.35) the Upper Tribunal decided that the First-tier Tribunal was correct to conclude that restaurant and entertainment services supplied by the college to members of the public in order to provide its students with the opportunity to learn skills in a practical context are exempt as supplies of goods and services closely related to the provision of education by the college. HMRC appealed the Upper Tribunal decision to the Court of Appeal and confirmed that their policy that such supplies are not exempt will only be reviewed after the Court of Appeal releases its judgment. (HMRC Brief 39/14). The Court of Appeal has referred questions to the CJEU. The CJEU delivered the opinion of the Advocate-General on 21 December 2016. The AG's opinion was that supplies 'closely related to education' do not include the supply of restaurant and entertainment services by an educational establishment to paying members of the public who are not recipients of the education. However, the decision of the Full Court was in accordance with that of the First-tier and Upper Tribunals; the catering and entertainment services were ancillary to a supply of education and complied with the conditions for exemption within *Directive 2006/112/EC*.

HMRC have published amended guidance in VATEDU5340 as a result of the CJEU decision (*CJEU Case C-699/15*, [2017] STC 1112) and it has confirmed that it will treat the supplies concerned as exempt from VAT providing the following conditions are satisfied:

- the education in question must be provided by way of business. Most further education is fully grant funded and is therefore regarded as a non-business activity. If a further education college has claims that relate to both grant funded and exempt education (fee paying), then HMRC will require the proportion of students whose education is a business activity in each case;
- the activity in question must be student led and essential to their education; and
- the activity must not have the purpose of generating additional income for the body in direct competition with commercial enterprises. Claimants must be able to provide satisfactory evidence to HMRC that is not run in order to generate further income.

HMRC also state that it will apply the guidance on a case-by-case basis in order to decide if the supplies are exempt from VAT as closely related to exempt supplies of education or standard-rated. It will also apply the judgment to cases where it is clear that the supplies are not being provided in competition with commercial enterprises. They state that this will be the case if the supplies are not advertised and the cost of providing the supplies to the general public clearly exceeds any income generated.

Closely related goods and services sold to pupils by an eligible body providing education, etc.

The provisions relating to closely related supplies only apply where the principal supply is an *exempt* supply. They do not apply where the principal supply is outside the scope of VAT as a non-business supply. As a result where education, research or vocational training is supplied by an eligible body

- in the course or furtherance of business (an exempt supply), closely related goods or services sold to pupils are also exempt; and
- for no charge (outside the scope of VAT), closely related goods or services sold to pupils are non-business and outside the scope of VAT provided they are sold at or below cost (otherwise they assume their normal VAT liability).

If the goods and services sold to pupils are not closely related to the education, etc. provided, they are standard-rated unless relief is available elsewhere.

(VAT Notice 701/30/17, paras 8.1–8.7).

Private tuition

[17.11] The supply of private tuition is an exempt supply provided it is

(a) in a subject ordinarily taught in a school or university; and
(b) given by an individual teacher acting independently of an employer.

[*VATA 1994, Sch 9 Group 6 Item* 2].

A reasonable test for 'ordinarily' is whether the subject is taught in a number of schools and/or universities on a regular basis.

Following the tribunal decision in *C & E Clarke; A & H Clarke* (VTD 15201) (TVC 21.51) HMRC accept that private tuition is exempt when supplied by a sole proprietor, a partnership or any member of a partnership. However, because of the wording in (*b*) above, exemption does not extend to instruction delivered by anyone employed (even if the teacher concerned is the sole shareholder of a company) and is restricted to tuition provided by a teacher acting in an individual or personal capacity (see *HMRC v Empowerment Enterprises Ltd*, CS [2006] CSIH 46 (TVC 22.342)); see also *Marcus Webb Golf Professional* [2012] UKUT 378 (TCC) (TVC 21.52). Where a sole proprietor or partnership also employs teachers, supplies can be apportioned between exempt and taxable elements using and fair and reasonable method. If this is impractical, all supplies of tuition can be treated as standard-rated regardless of who actually delivers them. Employing someone in a non-teaching capacity has no effect on the VAT liability of tuition supplied.

Supplies of any goods and services in connection with the supply of tuition

Even if such supplies are closely linked, they are standard-rated unless relief is available elsewhere (e.g. books may be zero-rated).

(VAT Notice 701/30/17, paras 6.1–6.2).

Examination services

[17.12] The provision of 'examination services'

(a) by or to an 'eligible body', or

(b) to a person receiving education or vocational training which is
- exempt under **17.4, 17.7** or **17.11** above or **17.16** below, or
- provided otherwise than in the course or furtherance of a business

is an exempt supply.

'*Examination services*' include

- the setting and marking of examinations;
- the setting of educational or training standards;
- the making of assessments; and
- other services provided with a view to ensuring educational and training standards are maintained.

[*VATA 1994, Sch 9 Group 6 Item 3* and *Note 4; Learning and Skills Act 2000, Sch 9 para 47*].

See **17.3** above for '*eligible body*'.

Examples of activities treated as examination services are services connected with GCSE examinations, etc., National Vocational Qualification (NVQ) assessments, course accreditation services, validation, certification, assessment and registration of candidates. *Not included* are

- services of printers, graphic designers, and typesetters; and
- non-specialist secretarial, advertising or promotional services (unless provided as part of a broader package of predominantly examination services by the same person who provides those services).

Supplies direct to pupils

Included under (*b*) above is the supply of examination services *directly* to

- pupils of independent fee paying schools;

- pupils of community, foundation or voluntary schools;
- students of further education colleges;
- trainees of government approved training schemes; and
- employees receiving in-house training from their employers.

Examination boards normally provide GCSE examinations direct to school pupils. Schools can usually treat as disbursements the payments they receive from and on behalf of pupils for these examinations. See **3.7 AGENTS** for the treatment of disbursements.

Provision of online education/examination services

Supplies of education, training, or a similar service delivered by a person over the Internet or an electronic network (such as a webinar) are not treated as an electronically supplied service from a VAT perspective. The place of supply is the place where the service is physically performed. However, unlike webinars or distance learning, automated learning does not involve any human involvement and is considered to be an e-service, and with effect from 1 January 2015, the place of supply of business to consumer (B2C) services changed from the supplier's place of establishment to the customer's place of establishment.

The place of supply for examination services will depend on whether or not the service requires or involves any human intervention. If a student is required to complete and submit an online examination paper, and this is automatically checked and scored by computer, then this is an e-service. From 1 January 2015, any B2C supplies will be taxed in the customer's place of establishment. However, if the service involves the completed examination paper being marked or assessed by an assessor, for B2C supplies the place of supply will remain the place where the service is physically performed.

Organisations that provide automated examination and educational services that do not involve human intervention will need to consider whether they need to be VAT registered in other EU member states in respect of any B2C services provided to students located in another EU member state. More information can be found in **66 SUPPLY: PLACE OF SUPPLY**.

School inspections

School inspections are in principle within the scope of exemption for examination services and are therefore exempt if provided by or to an 'eligible body' (see (*a*) above).

(VAT Notice 701/30/17, paras 7.1–7.4).

English as a foreign language (EFL)

[17.13] Exemption applies to tuition in EFL by *any* body (see **17.3**(*f*) above). Where, however, the body does not also qualify as an eligible body under another category within **17.3**(*a*)–(*e*) above, exemption does not extend to any other supplies which the body makes apart from the 'teaching of English as a foreign language'. [*VATA 1994, Sch 9 Group 6 Note 2*].

HMRC interpret this as meaning that exemption does not extend to other education, research or vocational training (e.g. tuition in a language other than English or training in the teaching of EFL) supplied by a commercial provider of EFL who is not within **17.3**(*a*)–(*e*) above.

Following the decision in *Pilgrims Languages Courses Ltd v C & E Commrs*, CA [1999] STC 874 (TVC 21.25) HMRC accept that all elements integral to the supply of any course in the teaching of EFL by a commercial provider are covered by the exemption (e.g. sports, recreational, sightseeing or social activities aimed at promoting fluency in the use of the English language). In addition, any separate supplies of closely related goods and services are also exempt provided they meet the conditions set out in **17.10** above.

Where courses are supplied in modular form, comprising some tuition in EFL plus broader coverage of other subjects, the supply can be apportioned to reflect the exempt element using any fair and reasonable method. If this is inconvenient or impractical, the whole supply can be standard-rated.

(VAT Notice 701/30/17, paras 9.1–9.3).

Education supplied by local authorities

[17.14] Any education or vocational training provided by local authorities for no charge, or which they provide acting as a public authority, is a non-business activity. Local authorities are, however, eligible bodies (see **17.3**(*d*) above) and all other educational or vocational training courses that they provide for any form of charge or payment are generally exempt business supplies, irrespective of any subsidy they may receive. See *City of London Corporation* (VTD 17892) (TVC 22.156) where the tribunal held that, on the facts, the Corporation was not carrying on a business activity in respect of three schools, even though it charged fees to most of the parents. The schools had been established under special legal provisions and the Corporation was required to maintain them.

Most schools in the state sector belong to one of three categories of 'maintained school', namely community, foundation or voluntary. All such schools are maintained by a local authority (LA) and receive funding from it. The governing body of each school acts as agent of the LA for goods and services it pays for either out of the school's delegated budget from the LA or from amounts given to the school from LA central funds for specific purposes. Where the local authority has a statutory duty to defray all expenses of maintaining a school, e.g. community schools, then it can recover VAT incurred on such purchases under *VATA 1994, s 33* (see **44.7 LOCAL AUTHORITIES AND PUBLIC BODIES**). However, in the case of voluntary aided schools the governing body retains statutory responsibility for certain capital expenditure, including when made from the school's delegated budget. HMRC previously accepted that local authorities could recover the VAT incurred on expenditure which is the responsibility of the governing bodies but which the authority funds. They are now of the opinion that *VATA 1994, s 33* is confined to VAT incurred by local authorities etc. on the goods and services that they purchase, not on the goods and services that another legal entity purchases. Therefore VAT may not be recovered by local authorities in these circumstances, as the supplies are not made to them (whether or not paid for from the delegated budget). A local authority may, however, recover VAT on expenditure at a voluntary aided school for which the local authority is statutorily responsible, or where the local authority, rather than the governing body, procures a supply of works and pays for that supply from its own funds.

Private funds of LA schools

LA maintained schools can also generate income independently (e.g. through vending machines or charges for the use of the premises outside normal hours). Such 'private fund' income is generally kept in a separate bank account and is not part of the local authority for VAT purposes but a separate entity. The private fund might be held in the name of the governing body, the head teacher (acting as agent of the governing body) or some other entity (e.g. a Parent Teacher Association). Subject to the normal threshold, a school (in the guise of its private fund) must register for VAT separately if it makes taxable supplies that generate income which does not belong to the LA and which it uses purely to augment its own funds.

Input tax recovery on purchases using private funds

If the private fund is separately registered for VAT, it can recover input tax subject to the normal rules and the local authority cannot recover the VAT incurred on any private fund purchases.

Alternatively, where a private fund has obtained income other than via the local authority, it can opt to donate the money to the local authority for them to buy goods and services on the private fund's behalf. The local authority can then recover the VAT incurred provided it

- makes the purchase itself (i.e. places the order, receives the supply and a VAT invoice addressed to it, and makes the payment);
- retains ownership of the purchase and uses it for its own non-business activities; and
- keeps sufficient records of the purchase and the purpose for which it is made.

This donational route is not, however, available in respect of

- certain direct grants from the Department for Education and Skills (DfES) to the governing bodies of foundation schools; and
- income, including direct grants from the DfES, used to fund works which are the responsibility of the governors of a voluntary aided school.

Where the school keeps the income it obtains from letting its premises, the income can be treated in the same way as budget share funds when the school uses it to buy goods and services (i.e. the school is deemed to be acting as agent of the LA in spending the money and the LA is entitled to recover VAT incurred on the purchases).

Sales of 'closely related' supplies made by a local authority to its own pupils and students

Local authorities are 'eligible bodies' so that any education they provide for a charge (e.g. adult education classes) is an exempt business activity. Any closely related goods and services they supply in connection with this education are also exempt (see **17.10** above). However, most of the education that local authorities provide is not for a charge and is therefore a non-business activity and outside the scope of VAT. Because LA maintained schools do not supply education in the course or furtherance of business, it follows that any goods and services they provide to their pupils for a charge in connection with this education are not exempt, even though they might be closely related. As a concession, LA maintained schools can treat the closely related goods and services they supply to pupils as non-business, provided it complies with the following rules which have been agreed with CIPFA.

- The goods and services must be closely linked to the education provided (i.e. for the direct use of the student and necessary for delivering the education to the student).
- The pupil must receive education from the LA in either an LA maintained school or in connection with some other LA run educational activity (e.g. an orchestra).
- The goods and services required must be purchased from the LA.
- Payment for the goods must be made either to the LA or to the school (and, if the latter, it must be paid into official funds).
- Some evidence (e.g. an order form) must be kept to show that the recipient of the goods and services has been receiving education from the LA, and that what has been supplied was essential to that education.
- The price of the goods and services supplied must be at or below cost. 'Cost' means the overhead-inclusive price of supplying the goods or services to the pupil.

Where any goods are leased, the same conditions apply as for sales.

In practice, regardless of the precise nature of the activity, any school trips that a school organises for the benefit of its pupils can be treated as part of its non-business provision of education.

Supplies of food and drink in LA schools

Sales of food and drink by an LA in its maintained schools to its pupils are non-business and therefore outside the scope of VAT if made at or below cost (see above). The 'at or below cost' criterion can be determined in one of two ways.

- A school can look at all the LA catering outlets on its premises (e.g. canteen, refectory, tuck shop, kiosk, trolley, vending machine. etc.). Provided the total sales are at or below cost, the school can treat all its sales of food as non-business. HMRC, exceptionally, allow a school to apply the 'at or below cost' criterion for each catering outlet. Output tax would then only be due in relation to the outlets where cost is exceeded.
- An LA can analyse all its school catering outlets together. This will produce a single set of figures, from which the LA can determine whether catering is provided at or below cost across its whole school portfolio.

This treatment applies only to sales of food and drink by a local authority school to its pupils and from outlets operated by either the local authority itself or the governing body. If the supply of food and drink is by a catering contractor, see **12.9 CATERING**.

If staff and visitors are free to use any of the catering outlets provided by the school, an apportionment by any fair and reasonable means must be applied to determine the level of taxable business sales.

Closely related supplies made by a local authority other than to its own pupils and students

By concession, LA maintained schools may treat as non-business any closely related goods and services they supply direct to the *pupils* of other schools and to the students or trainees of eligible bodies (e.g. FE colleges and universities). They cannot exempt any closely related goods and services they supply to *other eligible bodies* unless they also supply the education or training itself.

Grant assistance for students on training courses

Where a local authority provides a grant to a student attending further education establishments (e.g. to cover tuition, board, and other necessary expenses), regardless of whether the grant is paid to the training establishment or the student, it does not represent payment for any supplies made to the local authority. As the supplies are made to the student and not the local authority, there is no entitlement to input tax recovery by the local authority. This remains the case even where the local authority is billed direct for any of the supplies made.

Community education

Local authorities must ensure that certain forms of community education are available in their area although they are not obliged to supply it themselves. If they choose to do so, they compete with a broad range of education providers offering similar services in different parts of the country. This is a business activity.

School photographs

See **17.17** below.

Fuel and power

See **26.8**(1) **FUEL AND POWER.**

(VAT Notice 701/30/17, paras 10.1–10.9; VAT Notice 749, para 5.8; Business Brief 14/95; HMRC Brief 53/09).

Education Action Zones ('EAZs')

[17.15] EAZs consist of local clusters of maintained schools working in partnership with the local authorities ('LAs'), local parents, businesses, Training and Enterprise Councils and others. A major aim of the EAZ initiative is to raise education standards in certain deprived areas. Under the scheme, the governing bodies of participating schools can delegate their powers to the Education Action Forum which runs the EAZ. Membership of the Forum is drawn from the above groups. EAZs receive Government funding each year and are expected to raise further funding from the private sector. They are not, however, part of the local authority and are not entitled to make use of the refunds scheme for non-business activities under *VATA 1994, s 33* (see **44.7 LOCAL AUTHORITIES AND PUBLIC BODIES**).

Recovery of VAT by an EAZ

If a statutory EAZ buys goods and services

- using funds delegated to it by an LA via the governors of participating schools, the LA can recover any VAT incurred (as the EAZ is acting as agent to the LA in the purchase);
- using funds that it has obtained from other sources, the LA cannot recover any VAT incurred (as the EAZ is not acting as its agent);
- via the governors of participating schools using funds it has obtained from non-LA sources, the LA cannot recover any VAT incurred (as the governors are not acting as its agent);
- and incurs VAT that the LA cannot recover, the VAT sticks with the EAZ as a real cost (as the EAZ makes no taxable supplies of its own and so is not registrable for VAT); and
- from an LA using funding channelled to it by the LA via the governors of participating schools, the transaction is outside the scope of VAT (as the EAZ is acting as agent of the LA and no supply takes place).

If an LA supplies teaching staff to an EAZ for purposes of instruction, the LA should not charge VAT (as both the LA and the EAZ are eligible bodies and the supply is exempt).

If an EAZ is non-statutory (i.e. one not established under the *School Standards and Framework Act 1998*), then the LA can recover VAT on goods and services supplied to the EAZ (as the EAZ is acting as agent of the LA in the purchase).

(VAT Notice 701/30/17, paras 11.1–11.3).

Government approved vocational training schemes

[17.16] The provision of 'vocational training' is exempt to the extent that the consideration payable is ultimately a charge to funds provided

- pursuant to arrangements made under *Employment and Training Act 1973, s 2*, *Employment and Training Act (Northern Ireland) 1950, s 1A* or *Enterprises and New Towns (Scotland) Act 1990, s 2*; or
- by the Learning and Skills Council for England or the National Council for Education and training for Wales under *Learning and Skills Act 2000, Parts I or II*.

Included is the supply of any goods or services essential to the vocational training provided directly to the trainee by the person providing the training. [*VATA 1994, Sch 9 Group 6 Item 5 and Note 5; Learning and Skills Act 2000, Sch 9 para 47*].

The provisions exempt the supply of vocational training under government approved vocational training schemes by suppliers who are not 'eligible bodies' within **17.3** above. Supplies of vocation training by eligible bodies are exempt under the wider provisions in **17.7** above, which see for a general consideration of 'vocational training'.

This exemption covers supplies of

- vocational training, including work experience, and
- any goods and services supplied directly to trainees that are essential to the training

to the extent that they are ultimately funded by schemes approved by the Department for Education, the Department for Work and Pensions (through Job Centre Plus), and devolved administrations in Wales, Scotland and Northern Ireland. The schemes are administered and funded by the Young People's Learning Association (YPLA), the Skill Funding Agency (SFA), local authorities in England (working together with the YPLA), the Welsh Assembly, Skills Development Scotland, and the Training and Employment Agency in Northern Ireland. Approved schemes also include schemes that are paid for using funds derived from the European Social Fund, training administered by further education colleges and funded by any of the bodies listed above, training of workplace assessors in connection with NVQs, and training aimed at providing additional skills for use in the workplace.

Exemption does not cover

- counselling and careers guidance services (unless a compulsory part of a vocational training package); or
- accreditation or assessment services (although these might qualify for exemption as examination services (see **17.12** above).

Supplies by training providers

Where a training provider contracts to supply vocational training under one of the government's approved schemes, its supply is exempt to the extent that the consideration payable is ultimately a charge to funds from one of the approved schemes. But the following should be taken into account.

- If the contract allows for a separate supply of management services, these are not covered by the exemption and must be standard-rated.
- If the trainee or an employer pays part of the cost of the training from their own resources, that part of the supply is not covered by the special exemption. The training provider should apportion between the exempt and standard-rated elements (unless it is an eligible body, see **17.3** above).
- Where the training provider's contract is with a further education college, it must find out what proportion of the payment by the college derives from approved funds within these provisions as, similarly, only this proportion qualifies automatically for exemption (unless the training provider is an eligible body). In determining the proportion, the college may opt to apply a global formula rather than perform a separate calculation each time it buys in a supply of vocational training,

i.e. it may express its annual funding allocation as a percentage of its total income for the year and apply this percentage to each purchase of vocational training made in the subsequent year in order to arrive at the proportion that qualifies for exemption.

Where a training provider is given a training credit voucher by a trainee to redeem with the local office of the YPLA or SFA, the income received from the voucher is part of the consideration for the exempt supply.

Supplies by subcontractors

Exemption also extends to a subcontractor's supplies to the extent that the training provider pays for the supplies using government funding obtained within these provisions. It may be difficult to establish the extent to which exemption applies. The subcontractor should ask the training provider for, and keep, evidence that all or part of the supplies are ultimately funded under the scheme. The subcontractor can then exempt supplies to the extent of the funding. If not fully funded, HMRC should accept any apportionment which seems reasonable on the available information. Otherwise, unless the subcontractor is an eligible body within **17.3** above, it should account for VAT on its supplies if the training provider does not confirm that the supplies are ultimately funded under an approved scheme.

Any funding received which must be passed on to trainees or students (e.g. statutory living allowances, travel costs and lodging expenses) is outside the scope of VAT and does not form part of the supply of vocational training.

Work placement providers

Where a work placement provider supplies work experience to a trainee who is its own employee, any payments made to the trainee as wages or allowances are outside the scope of VAT. Where it supplies work experience to

- a trainee or employee of another business, or
- a college student under one of the government's approved vocational training schemes,

any charge for the services of the employee by the business, or the trainee by the college, are standard-rated. This is separate from the supply of exempt vocational training by the work provider to the trainee or student.

Unemployed trainees qualify for a statutory living allowance and, in some cases, expenses. If the work provider funds any such allowances or expenses from its own resources, the amount paid is consideration for a standard-rated supply of the trainee's services by the training provider or college. This applies even if no actual payment is made to the training provider or college.

(VAT Notice 701/30/17, paras 13.1–13.5; Business Brief 13/96).

School photographers

[17.17] The photographer may supply the photographs

- direct to the pupils, in which case the school or LA makes a separate supply of the use of premises, facilities and other services to the photographer in return for the commission or discount they receive; or
- to the school or local authority (LA), in which case the school or LA sells the photos on to the pupils.

Sales of photographs by the photographer directly to pupils

The photographer must account for VAT on the final selling price of the photographs to the pupils.

The position of the school depends upon whether it is independent or LA maintained and, if the latter, also upon whether it acts for the LA or for the governing body in supplying the use of its facilities to the photographer, the type of school and whether it is VAT-registered.

In order to decide the correct VAT treatment of the commission or discount, each time a contract is entered into, the photographer must first establish whether the head teacher is acting for the LA or the governors.

In the following examples, the head teacher is employed by the governors of the school and acts as such on their behalf.

- Foundation and voluntary aided schools in England.
- Self-governing schools in Scotland.
- Voluntary maintained, voluntary grammar and grant maintained integrated schools in Northern Ireland.

In these cases the school will have to charge VAT on the supply of the premises and use of facilities to the photographer, if either

- the taxable turnover from the school, including the income that the school receives from the photographer, exceeds the VAT registration threshold; or
- the school has registered voluntarily for VAT.

The consideration for this supply is the commission or the discount that the photographer pays to the school.

Sales of photographs by the photographer to LAs or schools

Where the contractual arrangements provide that the supply of photographs is to the LA, school or other body,

- *if the LA, etc. is registered for VAT*, the photographer must account for VAT on the price actually charged. The LA, etc. can recover the VAT as input tax subject to the normal rules and must account for output tax on the full value of the supply to the pupils.
- *if the LA, etc. is not registered for VAT*, the photographer should contact HMRC and, pending their advice, account for VAT on the amount actually charged to the LA, etc. HMRC may subsequently issue a Notice of Direction under *VATA 1994, Sch 6 para 2* requiring the photographer to account for VAT on the final selling price charged by the unregistered school to the pupils.

(VAT Notice 701/30/17, paras 12.1–12.3).

Youth clubs

[17.18] The provision of 'facilities' is exempt if supplied by

- a 'youth club' or an 'association of youth clubs' to its members; or
- an association of youth clubs to members of a youth club which is a member of that association.

Youth club

A club is a '*youth club*' if

(a) it is established to promote the social, physical, educational or spiritual development of its members;
(b) its members are mainly under 21 years of age;
(c) it is precluded from distributing and does not distribute any profit it makes; and
(d) it applies any profits made from exempt supplies to the continuance or improvement of such supplies (i.e. it must not use any of its income to subsidise any outside activity).

[*VATA 1994, Sch 9 Group 6 Item 6 and Note 6*].

An '*association of youth clubs*' is an organisation, the members of which are youth clubs.

In addition to (*a*)–(*d*) above, HMRC expect a club to meet the following conditions in order to qualify as a youth club.

- It should provide a range of activities. A single activity club (e.g. a swimming club) is not regarded as a youth club even if its members are mainly under 21 years of age.
- It should have its own constitution. HMRC do not regard youth sections of organisations such as sports clubs, cultural societies and environmental groups as youth clubs unless separately constituted. See also *Haggs Castle Golf Club* (VTD 13653) (TVC 21.65).
- It should be able to produce its own accounts.

Exemption

Exemption covers

- in the case of a youth club, any facilities which the club supplies to members in return for their subscriptions or, provided the facilities are directly related to the club's ordinary activities, for an additional payment; and
- in the case of an association of youth clubs, any facilities which the association supplies to
  (i) youth clubs that are members of the association in return for subscriptions, affiliation fees or similar payment; and
  (ii) members of an individual youth club that is part of the association of youth clubs where the facilities are of a type that would be exempt if provided by a youth club.

Not exempt

Not exempt under these provisions are

- supplies to non-members; and
- supplies not commonly provided by a youth club to its members, e.g.
  - — sales of foods and drink;
  - — overnight accommodation similar to the type provided by a hotel;
  - — purely recreational holidays; and
  - — fund-raising events where tickets are sold to the public (although certain fund-raising events may be exempt under *VATA 1994, Sch 9 Group 12*, see **13.10 CHARITIES**).

Facilities

HMRC takes '*facilities*' to mean the provision of an amenity or service that enables an activity to be carried out. Facilities therefore include

- a shop (but not selling items from the shop);
- a fitness centre (but not aerobics classes);
- an internet café (but not surfing the web);
- a library (but not the hire of videos and DVDs or use of photocopier); and
- access to student union bar through payments of union subscriptions (but not the purchase of alcohol and food from the bar).

(VAT Notice 701/35/11).

Key points: education

[17.19] Points to consider are as follows.

- As a general principle, supplies of education are standard-rated if provided by a commercial business (excluding private schools). Exceptions to this statement include private tuition provided by a sole trader or member of a partnership, courses that are funded by the Young Persons Learning Agency (YPLA) or the Skills Funding Agency (SFA) (or similar bodies in Wales, Scotland and Northern Ireland), examination services and courses where English is taught as a foreign language.
- Education provided by schools, colleges and universities is exempt from VAT as these institutions are classed as eligible bodies. However, it is likely that these bodies will have other sources of taxable income so they may need to be VAT-registered. This means they will be partly exempt as an entity (with input tax restrictions) so will need to consider whether a special method might be worthwhile for partial exemption purposes. A special method requires HMRC approval, and is appropriate when the standard method based on income does not produce a fair and reasonable result in terms of input tax recovery.

- A training course provided by a charity or non-profit making body is only exempt if any profit that may be made from the course is reinvested into future courses. This is an important condition of the legislation that is often overlooked.
- Be aware that exemption in relation to training courses and education does not apply if a course or event is provided by a trading subsidiary of a charity. The trading subsidiary company is not a charity in its own right (but a private limited company in most cases) and courses are therefore standard-rated, even though the company probably pays any surplus back to the main charity.
- Any business that teaches English as a foreign language can benefit from VAT exemption on these courses. This exemption is usefully extended to other activities that are intended to improve the English skills of the students, e.g. sightseeing trips, recreational or sporting activities. However, the exemption would not extend to other courses provided to the students, e.g. computer training for foreign students. The only exception would be if the training business was an eligible body (charity/non-profit making body etc.) able to benefit from VAT exemption through a different section of the legislation.
- The exemption for educational services extends to the supply of goods and services that are closely related to the education in question. For example, exemption also extends to accommodation and catering charges if the nature of a course is residential. However, for such supplies to be exempt, the main supply of the education must be exempt as a starting point.
- A common arrangement in relation to a course that is ultimately funded by the YPLA, SFA or similar body is for part of the course fee to be directly paid by the students or their employees. In such cases, this income is not exempt from VAT unless the training provider is an eligible body. In the situation where a training provider (e.g. commercial company) provides training services to a course provider that receives part funding from the YPLA or SFA or similar body, then an apportionment of the training provider charges must be made between standard-rated and exempt supplies. Only the proportion of the training funded by the government approved body can benefit from exemption.
- If a course or training event is provided without charge, then it is classed as a non-business activity and is therefore outside the scope of VAT. There is no scope for input tax recovery on costs related to non-business activities. This would mean, for example, that if a charity used premises partly for business courses (a charge being made to customers) and partly for non-business courses, then an initial amount of input tax should be blocked to recognise the principle of non-business use. Any method can be used that is fair and reasonable, although a time-based apportionment will probably give the fairest result.
- The rules concerning exemption for private tuition are very strict. If a course is provided by an employee of a sole trader or partnership business, then the exemption does not apply. It does

not apply to any education provided by a limited company. This is because a director of a limited company is classed as an employee of the business and is therefore not creating a private tuition arrangement.

- The scope of subjects that can benefit from the private tuition exemption is very wide. It generally covers subjects normally taught in a school or university but HMRC accepts that this extends to subjects of a sporting or recreational nature. So piano lessons would be included as an example. The exemption is not affected by whether lessons are given on an individual or group basis by the tutor concerned.
- Distance learning courses will be subject to VAT in most cases if provided by a commercial business. There may be an opportunity to separately sell course material, which will be zero-rated in most cases as a supply of printed material. However, recent tribunal cases have highlighted that it is very difficult to split an inclusive course fee so that some of the fee relates to the course books and is therefore zero-rated. The outcome in most of these tribunal cases has been that the business is providing a single supply of education, standard-rated in most cases.

18

European Union: General

Introduction to general matters regarding the EU

[18.1] The European Union was set up by *The First Treaty of Rome* ('*EC Treaty*') with effect from 1 January 1958 and was entered into initially by Belgium, Federal Republic of Germany, France, Italy, Luxembourg and The Netherlands (who were also the initial members of European Coal and Steel Community and European Atomic Energy Community). By *The Treaty of Accession*, the UK, Ireland and Denmark entered with effect from 1 January 1973. The relevant UK legislation is *European Communities Act 1972*. Greece joined with effect from 1 January 1981, Spain and Portugal with effect from 1 January 1986 and Austria, Finland and Sweden with effect from 1 January 1995. Cyprus, Czech Republic, Estonia, Hungary, Latvia, Lithuania, Malta, Poland, Slovak Republic and Slovenia joined with effect from 1 May 2004. Bulgaria and Romania joined with effect from 1 January 2007, and Croatia joined with effect from 1 July 2013, raising the total number of EU member states to 28.

The current treaty, *Treaty on the Functioning of the European Union ('EU Treaty')*, is widely drafted and there is an emphasis on provisions for the free movement of persons, goods, services and capital as well as powers for the implementation of common policies in many areas of economic and social life. It provides for a *Council of Ministers* which is composed of representatives of the governments of the member countries and effectively has the power to make decisions.

Following the referendum vote on 23 June 2016, the United Kingdom is beginning the process of leaving the EU. This is governed by *Article 50* of the *Treaty on European Union*. Once the UK has given notice to the Council under that article, the EU treaties will cease to apply to it not later than two years afterwards, unless that period is extended by the unanimous agreement of all EU member states. The consequences are still uncertain, and will develop through negotiation over the coming years. In the meantime, the UK remains a member of the EU, and is subject to its treaties. In particular, all the rules on VAT continue to apply.

The *European Commission* is the executive of the EU and also formulates the policy acted upon by the Council.

The *European Parliament* has, primarily, only supervisory and consultative powers in relation to taxation.

The *Court of Justice of the European Union* (CJEU) is empowered to ensure that in the interpretation and application of the *EU Treaty* the law is observed. In this connection it is the ultimate court of appeal.

The *European Council*, consisting of Heads of State of the member countries, provides the Union with the necessary impetus for its development, and defines the general political directions and priorities thereof.

Territories of the EU

VAT territory

[18.2] The VAT territory of the EU consists of

- Austria
- Belgium
- Bulgaria
- Croatia
- Cyprus (including the British Sovereign Base Areas of Akrotiri and Dhekelia but excluding the UN buffer zone and the part of Cyprus to the north of the buffer zone where the Republic of Cyprus does not exercise effective control)
- Czech Republic
- Denmark (excluding the Faroe Islands and Greenland)
- Estonia
- Finland (excluding the Aland Islands)
- France (including Monaco but excluding Martinique, French Guiana, Guadeloupe, Reunion, Mayotte and Saint-Martin (French Republic))
- Germany (excluding Büsingen and the Isle of Heligoland)
- Greece (excluding Mount Athos (also known as Agion Oros))
- Hungary
- Ireland
- Italy (excluding Campione d'Italia, the Italian waters of Lake Lugano and Livigno)
- Latvia
- Lithuania
- Luxembourg
- Malta

- Netherlands (excluding the Antilles)
- Poland
- Portugal (including the Azores and Madeira)
- Romania
- Slovakia
- Slovenia
- Spain (including the Balearic Islands but excluding the Canary Islands, Ceuta or Melilla)
- Sweden
- United Kingdom (including the Isle of Man but excluding the Channel Islands and Gibraltar)

[*VATA 1994, s 93; SI 1995/2518, Regs 136, 137, 139; SI 2013/3211*].

Other areas *not* within the VAT territory include Leichtenstein, the Vatican City, Andorra and San Marino.

De Voil Indirect Tax Service. See V1.213–218.

Customs territory

[18.3] The customs territory of the EU consists of the VAT territory plus

- Andorra (only Tariff Chapters 25 onwards)
- The Aland Islands
- Channel Islands
- The Canary Islands
- The overseas departments of the French Republic (Guadeloupe, Martinique, Reunion and French Guiana)
- Mount Athos (Agion Poros)

Excise territory

[18.4] The excise territory of the EU consists of the VAT territory plus

- San Marino

Trade statistics territory

[18.5] EU member states and their associated or dependent territories for Intrastat purposes are as follows.

Austria

Belgium

Bulgaria

Croatia

Cyprus (including the British Sovereign Base Areas but excluding Northern Cyprus (see note below)

Czech Republic

Denmark (excluding the Faroe Islands)

Estonia

Finland (including the Aland Islands)

France (including Monaco but excluding all French Overseas Departments and territories (see note below))

Germany (including Heligoland but excluding Busingen)

Greece (including Mount Athos)

Hungary

Ireland

Italy (excluding Campione d'Italia, San Marino, the Italian Waters of Lake Lugano, The Vatican, and Livigno (see note below))

Latvia

Lithuania

Luxembourg

Malta

Netherlands

Poland

Portugal (including the Azores and Madeira)

Romania

Slovakia

Slovenia

Spain (including the Balearic Islands but excluding Ceuta, Melilla, and the Canary Islands (see note below))

Sweden

United Kingdom (including the Channel Islands and the Isle of Man but excluding Gibraltar)

Notes. The French territories of French Guiana, Guadeloupe, Martinique and Reunion are part of the statistical territories of France, and Canary Islands are part of the statistical territory of Spain, and Livigno is part of the statistical territory of Italy. However, as customs documentation (the SAD) is still required for trade with these territories HMRC continue to collect trade statistics from the SAD.

The EU *acquis* (the body of European law) is currently only applicable in the Government Controlled Area of the Republic of Cyprus.

Andorra and Liechtenstein are both outside the customs territory, and therefore the statistical territory, of the EU.

(HMRC Notice 60, para 2.5).

Trade with territories with which the EU has special relations

[18.6] The following rules apply.

- For trade with such territories outside the VAT, customs, excise *and* trade statistics territories, the same procedures apply as for any other non-EU country.
- For trade with the Azores, the Balearic Islands, Madeira and Monaco (which are within the VAT, customs, excise *and* trade statistics territories), the same procedures apply as for trade with other EU member states. This also applies to trade between the Isle of Man and EU member states other than the UK.
- Where goods are imported into the EU from any of the additional territories within the customs territory, there is no liability to customs duty but VAT may be payable. (There are special schemes for goods such as cut flowers which enter the UK from the Channel Islands.) Excise duty may also be payable but not on goods imported from San Marino (which is inside the Excise territory).

Refunds of VAT for EU businesses: overview

[18.7] The electronic cross-border refund system enables a business that incurs VAT on expenditure in an EU member state where it is not established and makes no supplies, to recover that VAT directly from that EU member state (the member state of refund). Requests for refunds are dealt with by the member state of refund. The amount refundable is determined under the deduction rules of the member state of refund and the relevant repayment will be made directly by that EU member state to the business. The system is an electronic one, with specified timescales and interest payable if these are not met. Any references below to the UK are taken to include the Isle of Man.

General rules

Electronic claims must be completed and submitted via the competent authorities in the EU member state in which the claimant is established.

Applicants

The applicant must be a taxable person established in other than the member state of refund, or their authorised agent. The applicant must meet the following conditions

- they must not be registered, liable or eligible to be registered in the EU member state from which they are claiming the refund;
- they must have no fixed establishment, seat of economic activity, place of business or other residence there; and

- during the refund period they must not have supplied any goods or services in the member state of refund with the exception of: transport services and services ancillary thereto; supplies of goods or services where VAT is payable by the person to whom the supply is made (reverse charge services); and services where the VAT is accounted for via the EU VAT Mini One Stop Shop (MOSS).

Checks

Basic registration checks will be carried out by the EU member state of establishment before the application is forwarded electronically to the EU member state from which the refund is being claimed. The EU member state of establishment will not forward the application to the member state of refund where during the period of refund the applicant

- is not a taxable person for VAT purposes;
- makes only exempt supplies;
- is covered by the exemption for small enterprises; or
- is operating the flat-rate scheme for farmers.

If the EU member state of establishment decides not to forward the application it must notify the applicant of this decision.

Applications

A separate application must be completed for each EU member state. Applications can be commenced and stored in an incomplete state on the system and may be recalled and finalised to be submitted at a later date.

The refund period must not be more than one calendar year or less than three calendar months unless the period covered represents the remainder of a calendar year (e.g. where interim applications have already been submitted earlier in the year, or if the applicant has recently become VAT registered).

If the refund application relates to a period of less than a calendar year, but not less than three months the minimum amount claimable is €400 or the equivalent in national currency. If the refund application relates to a period of a calendar year or the remainder of a calendar year the minimum amount claimable is €50 or the equivalent in national currency.

Properly completed applications must be submitted to the EU member state of establishment at the latest on 30 September of the calendar year following the refund year. If the applicant deregisters for VAT during the refund year they should submit their application as soon as possible following deregistration.

Scope of the application

A claim can be made for supplies of goods or services received with a tax point during the period of the refund application; and goods imported into the EU member state of refund during the period of the refund application. In addition, the application may include supplies or imports not included in a previous application as long as they relate to the same calendar year. The application may not include: amounts of VAT that have been incorrectly invoiced; or amounts of VAT that have been invoiced in respect of goods despatched to other EU member states or exported outside the EU.

Standard fields

The use of the following standard fields of information and expense codes will aid completion and are mandatory:

- Applicant's name and full address.
- An address for contact by electronic means (email address).
- A description of the applicant's business activity for which the goods and services are acquired.
- Period dates to which the refund application relates.
- The applicant's VAT identification number or tax reference number.
- Bank account details including IBAN and BIC codes.

Standard fields for invoices or importations included in the refund application:

- Name and address of the supplier.
- Except in cases of importation the VAT identification number or tax reference number of the supplier.
- Except in the case of importation, the prefix of the member state of refund.
- Date and number of the invoice or importation document.
- Taxable amount and amount of VAT expressed in the currency of the member state of refund.
- The amount of deductible VAT expressed in the currency of the member state of refund. This is the amount of VAT recoverable taking account of any partial exemption restriction, and any restriction on the recovery of input tax applying in the member state of refund.
- Where applicable the deductible proportion calculated in accordance with the rules applying in the EU member state of establishment.
- Nature of the goods and services acquired, described according to the following expenditure codes.

Expenditure codes:

(1) Fuel.
(2) Hiring of means of transport.
(3) Expenditure relating to means of transport.
(4) Road tolls and road user charge.
(5) Travel expenses, such as taxi fares, public transport fares.
(6) Accommodation.
(7) Food, drink and restaurant services.
(8) Admissions to fairs and exhibitions.
(9) Expenditure on luxuries, amusements and entertainment.
(10) Other.

Members States may require further sub codes to be used in respect of each of the above. If code 10 is used without a sub code, a narrative description of the goods and services must be provided.

Method of payment

The payment will be made in the member state of refund or, at the applicant's request, in any other EU member state. In the latter case, any bank charges for the transfer will be deducted by the member state of refund from the amount to be paid to the applicant.

Time limits for processing applications

The member state of refund must notify the applicant of the decision to approve or refuse the application within four months of the date they first received the application. If the member state of refund requires additional information in order to process the application, it can request this from the applicant, the applicant's tax authority, or a third party before the expiry of the four-month period. The additional information must be provided by the person to whom the request is made within one month of receiving the request. Once the member state of refund has received the additional information it has two further months in which to notify its decision. If further additional information is requested by the member state of refund the final deadline for making a decision can be extended up to a maximum of eight months from the date they received the application. Payment must be made within ten working days following expiry of the appropriate decision deadline.

Incorrect application/payment errors

If an applicant discovers that it has made an error on an application, a corrected application can be submitted. The correction procedures allows existing lines on the application to be amended or deleted (by reducing to 'nil'), but does not allow new lines to be added. The correction procedure can also be used to amend incorrect bank details, email addresses etc. If an application is found to be incorrect any overpayment will be recovered, normally by deducting it from any refund due. All EU member states take a very serious view of incorrect applications. Refunds obtained on the basis of any incorrect application can be recovered, penalties and interest may be imposed and further refund applications suspended.

Refused applications

If the member state of refund refuses an application fully or partly they must also notify the applicant of the reasons for refusal. If this happens the applicant can appeal against the decision using the appeals procedure of that EU member state. This means that the normal VAT appeals rules of that EU member state on time limits, form of appeal etc., will apply. If the member state of refund has not notified its decision within the appropriate decision deadline the applicant should consider that the application has been rejected unless any alternative procedures apply in that EU member state. The applicant's own VAT authority cannot intervene on its behalf. Section 8 of the online version of Notice 723A includes a link to contact details for the tax authorities in other EU member states.

Interest

Interest may be payable by the member state of refund to the applicant if payment is made after the final payment deadline set out above. If applicable it will be paid from the day following that deadline up to the date the refund is actually paid. Interest rates must be the same as those applied to refunds of VAT to taxable persons established in the member state of refund under the national law of that EU member state. If no interest is payable under national law in respect of refunds to established taxable persons, the interest payable will be equal to the interest or equivalent charge which is applied by that EU member state in respect of late payments of VAT by taxable persons.

[*SI 1995/2518, Regs 173–173X; SI 2014/2430, Reg 8*]. (VAT Notice 723A, paras 2.1–2.21).

Refunds for UK and Isle of Man businesses claiming from other EU member states

[18.8] All applications must be submitted using the electronic online system. In order to be able to make an electronic application for refund of VAT the applicant first needs to register for VAT Online Services, using details on their VAT 4 Certificate of Registration and last VAT return. An activation PIN number will be mailed to the business address registered with HMRC within set time limits (currently seven to ten days). Once this is received the applicant will have 28 days from the date of the letter to activate the service.

Agents

Agents can register to enable them to make refund applications on behalf of their clients and additional security procedures have been built in to their online application process.

Eligibility

An applicant must be a taxable person registered for VAT in the UK or in the Isle of Man, and must meet the following conditions:

- must not be registered, liable or eligible to be registered in the member state of refund;
- must not have any fixed establishment, seat of economic activity, place of business or other residence in the member state of refund;
- during the refund period they must not have supplied any goods or services in the member state of refund with the exception of: transport services and services ancillary thereto; and any goods or services where VAT is payable by the person to whom the supply is made and services where the VAT is accounted for via the EU VAT Mini One Stop Shop (MOSS).

If the applicant is registered as a VAT group, and the group has member companies in the member state of refund, they may only use the refund scheme to claim VAT incurred by companies who are not established in, and do not make supplies in, the member state of refund.

Proof of taxable person status

Applications will be subjected to automated registration verifications by HMRC before being forwarded electronically to the EU member state from which the refund is being claimed. Certificates of Status (VAT 66) are therefore no longer required for refund applications from other EU member states. Applications will only be forwarded to the member state of refund if these checks are satisfactory. If the checks are not satisfactory the application will be rejected by the electronic portal and they will receive an appropriate error message. Deregistered applicants must submit their applications as soon as possible, and not later than three months from their date of deregistration.

Claims

A separate online application is required for each EU member state from which the applicant wishes to claim. In order to start an application they must access the relevant online services section using their unique PID and password and enter their standard data into the required fields, along with invoice or importation details for expenditure they wish to reclaim. Applications can be commenced and saved if incomplete and can be recalled for completion and submission at a later date.

Refund period

The refund period must not be more than one calendar year or less than three calendar months (unless the period covered represents the remainder of a calendar year, for example, where interim applications have already been submitted earlier in the year covering more than nine months, or if they have recently become VAT registered). Generally refund periods do not have to cover strict calendar quarters. For example, they may submit two applications covering five months each, and a final one covering two months. However, some EU member states have their own requirements, and details of these can be obtained from the relevant tax authority. Generally refund periods may not overlap. For example, they may not submit an application covering 1 January to 31 March and another for 1 March to 31 May. However they may submit a further application covering the whole refund year after the year end. This enables them to claim for any purchases which they have missed in earlier periods.

Minimum claim

If the refund application relates to a period of less than a calendar year, but not less than three months the minimum amount claimable is €400 or the equivalent in national currency. If the refund application relates to a period of a calendar year or the remainder of a calendar year the minimum amount claimable is €50 or the equivalent in national currency.

Invoices

The following can be included on the application: invoices relating to supplies of goods or services with a tax point during the period of the refund application; and invoices relating to an importation of goods into the member state of refund during the period of the refund application. Also, invoices or imports not included in a previous application can be claimed as long as they relate to the same calendar year. The application may not include amounts of VAT that have been: incorrectly invoiced; invoiced in respect of goods despatched to another EU member state or exported outside the EU; or incurred in respect of non-business activities.

EU member states may require invoices with values of €1,000 or more (€250 or more in the case of fuel), or the equivalent in national currency, to be scanned and submitted electronically with the application. All other invoices should be retained as they may be requested at a later date by the member state of refund. If there are imported goods, the applicant must have the VAT copy of the import entry or other Customs document showing the amount of VAT paid.

Partial exemption

The applicant must apply the appropriate recovery rate for the goods or services purchased against each invoice or importation on their application, and show the amount of VAT recoverable in the appropriate box. The recovery rate to be applied is the last percentage appropriate to the refund period covering the invoice date. For example, if the claimable percentage for the March 2016 period is 5% and the application is submitted in April before the annual adjustment is calculated the claim should be restricted to 5%. However if they only make one application at the year end and have already calculated that the annual adjustment covering the March 2016 quarter is 3% then they may only claim 3%. Following the annual adjustment, they will not be required to amend refund applications already submitted. The invoices can only be entered once and the percentage to be used is that covering the invoice date.

Non-business expenses

Expenditure incurred in another EU member state that relates to non-business activities is not claimable under the refund scheme.

[*SI 1995/2518, Regs 173–173X*]. (VAT Notice 723A, paras 3.1–3.22).

Refunds in the UK for EU businesses

[18.9] The applicant must be a taxable person established in an EU member state other than the UK and must meet the following conditions:

- must not be registered, liable or eligible to be registered in the UK;
- must not have any place of business in the UK or in the Isle of Man; and
- must not make any supplies in the UK other than transport services related to the international carriage of goods, or goods and services where VAT is payable by the person to whom the supply is made (reverse charge services); and services where the VAT is accounted for via the EU VAT Mini One Stop Shop (MOSS).

Agents

If the applicant uses an agent to submit the application and/or receive payment of refunds on their behalf, they must submit a letter of authority, in hard copy, to the UK Overseas Repayment Unit (ORU).

Refund period

The refund period must not be more than one calendar year or less than three calendar months (unless it covers the remainder of a calendar year, for example, where applications have already been submitted covering more than nine months). Refund periods do not have to cover strict calendar quarters. For example, they may submit two applications covering five months each, and a final one covering two months. Generally, refund periods may not overlap. For example, they may not submit an application covering 1 January to 31 March, and another for 1 March to 31 May. However, they may submit a further application covering the whole of the refund year after the year end. This enables them to claim for any purchases or imports which they have missed in earlier periods.

Submission

The applicant must submit the application through the electronic facility provided by the tax authority in their EU member state, at the latest by 30 September of the year following that in which the VAT was incurred.

Claim limits

There is no maximum limit, but there are minimum limits below which an application cannot be submitted. These are: £295 where the application covers less than a calendar year but not less than three calendar months, and £35 where the application covers a calendar year or the remainder of a calendar year.

Claimable VAT

The applicant can claim VAT on goods and services purchased during the refund period, and VAT on goods imported into the UK during the refund period. They may not claim:

- amounts of VAT that have been incorrectly invoiced, or where VAT has been charged on the despatch of goods to another EU member state, or the export of goods outside the EU (they must take this up with the supplier);
- VAT on the purchase of a motor car;
- VAT on goods and services used for business entertainment; or
- VAT on goods and services used for non-business activities.

In addition, where VAT is incurred on charges for hiring or leasing a motor car, only 50% of the total VAT charged may be claimed.

Taxable and exempt supplies

The applicant must apply the appropriate restriction to the VAT reclaimed, following the rules that apply in their own EU member state, with any pro-rata adjustments submitted through their tax authority's electronic facility.

Scanned invoices

Scanned copies of all invoices and import documents must be attached where the taxable amount exceeds: £200 in the case of fuel; and £750 in the case of all other goods and services.

[*SI 1995/2518, Regs 173–173X*]. (VAT Notice 723A, paras 4.1–4.14).

Key points: EU general matters

[18.10] Points to consider are as follows.

- Be aware that the Isle of Man is part of the UK as far as VAT is concerned whilst the Channel Islands (Jersey and Guernsey) and Gibraltar are outside the UK and EU for VAT purposes. The Channel Islands are within the EU for customs purposes.
- New rules on invoicing were introduced on 1 January 2013. The aim was to make cross-border transactions easier. HMRC considered that these EU rules would have little impact on the UK's rules.

19

European Union Legislation

De Voil Indirect Tax Service. See V1.220–233.

Introduction to EU legislation

[19.1] Statements of the European Council and European Commission are graded under the *EU Treaty* as follows.

- **Regulations** are binding in their entirety and have general effect to all EU member states. They are directly applicable in the legal systems of EU member states.

- **Directives** are binding as to result and their general effect is specific to named EU member states. The form and methods of compliance are left to the addressees.
- **Decisions** are binding in their entirety and are specific to an EU member state, commercial enterprise or private individual.
- **Recommendations and Opinions** are not binding and are directed to specific subjects on which the Council's or Commission's advice has been sought.

EU legislation as part of UK legislation

[19.2] EU law is made effective for UK legislation. [*European Communities Act 1972, s 2*]. The effects of EU law as regards UK VAT legislation can be summarised as follows.

Direct effect

Although *EU Treaty, art 288* does not specifically allow for direct effect in an EU member state, the Court of Justice of the European Union (CJEU) has held 'wherever the provisions of a directive appear . . . to be unconditional and sufficiently precise, those provisions may . . . be relied upon as against any national provision which is incompatible with the directive insofar as the provisions define rights which individuals are able to assert against the state' (*Becker v Finanzamt Münster-Innenstadt, ECJ Case 8/81*, [1982] ECR 53, [1982] 1 CMLR 499 (TVC 22.395)). See also *Staatssecretaris van Financien v Cooperatieve Vereniging Cooperatieve Aardappelenbewaarplaats GA, ECJ Case 154/80*, [1981] ECR 445, [1981] 3 CMLR 337 (TVC 22.83) which case was considered in *UFD Ltd* [1981] VATTR 199 (TVC 24.28) in which it was said 'in all appeals involving issues of liability, the tribunal should consider the relevant provisions of the Council directives to ensure that the provisions of the UK legislation are consistent therewith'. See also *Yoga for Health Foundation v C & E Commrs, QB* [1984] STC 630 (TVC 22.315) where exemption from VAT was allowed for certain welfare services although there was no corresponding provision in the UK legislation.

Primacy of EU Directives over national legislation

A national court which is called upon, within the limits of its jurisdiction, to apply provisions of EU law, is under a duty to give full effect to those provisions, if necessary refusing of its own motion to apply any conflicting provision of national legislation, even if adopted subsequently, and it is not necessary for the court to request or await the prior setting aside of such provisions by legislative or other constitutional means (*Amministrazione delle Finanze dello Stato v Simmenthal SpA, ECJ Case C–106/77*, [1978] ECR 629, [1978] 3 CMLR 263 (TVC 22.23)).

In *EC Commission v United Kingdom, ECJ Case C–416/85*, [1988] STC 456 (TVC 22.580) the CJEU ruled that the UK had contravened the provisions of what is now *Directive 2006/112/EC* by zero-rating certain supplies of sewerage and water, news services, supplies of fuel and power and the construction of commercial buildings. In the earlier decision *EC Commission v United Kingdom, ECJ Case–353/85*, [1988] STC 251 (TVC 22.301) the CJEU had similarly ruled in relation to the exempting of supplies of spectacles, contact lenses and hearing aids. As a result of each decision, the UK law was amended.

In *Direct Cosmetics v C & E Commrs, ECJ Case C-5/84*, [1985] STC 479 (TVC 22.571) it was held that an amendment to UK legislation, which had been previously enacted under the derogation powers in what is now *Directive 2006/112/EC, Art 395* (previously *EC 6th Directive, Art 27*) (see **19.30** below), was itself a 'special measure' requiring derogation to be authorised by the European Commission. As this had not been obtained, the whole provisions failed and could not be relied on against the taxpayer.

Interpretation of UK law

If the domestic VAT legislation of the UK is unclear or ambiguous, tribunals are 'entitled to have regard to the provisions of the [*Directive 2006/112/EC*] in order to assist in resolving any ambiguity in the construction of the provisions under consideration' (*English-Speaking Union of the Commonwealth* (VTD 1023) (TVC 13.5)).This was confirmed by the European Court in *Marleasing SA v La Comercial Internacional de Alimentacion SA, ECJ Case C-106/89*, [1990] 1 ECR 4135 (TVC 22.16); if the national court finds that the national legislation is capable of different interpretations, it is required to follow an interpretation which is consistent with a Directive rather than one that is not consistent. This has become known as 'the Marleasing principle'. If EU law appears unclear it may be interpreted by referring to the legislative history ('*travaux preparatoires*') but such evidence has been held to be admissible only by reference to tests in *Fothergill v Monarch Airlines Ltd*, [1981] AC 251 (*The Open University* [2013] UKFTT 326 (TC) (TVC 21.3)). This decision is open to doubt. See, for example, *EC Commission v The Kingdom of Belgium, ECJ Case 324/82*, [1984] ECR 1861 [1985] 1 CMLR 364 (TVC 22.573) where the Belgium government used minutes of a Council meeting held prior to the adoption of the *EC Sixth VAT Directive* in evidence.

State liability to pay damages for failure to implement Directive

In an Italian case, the CJEU held that the Italian government was liable to pay compensation to employees of an insolvent company, who had suffered financial loss through Italy's failure to implement a directive guaranteeing such employees their arrears of wages (*Francovich v Italian State, ECJ Case C–6/90*, [1991] 1 ECR 5357; [1993] 2 CMLR 66 (TVC 22.31)). The principles laid down in *Francovich* were applied in two subsequent cases in which national legislation was held to be contrary to EU law. The CJEU ruled that 'the principle that member states are obliged to make good damage caused to individuals by breaches of EU law attributable to the state is applicable where the national legislature was responsible for the breach in question' (*Brasserie du Pêcheur SA v Federal Republic of Germany*; *R v Secretary of State for Transport (ex p. Factortame Ltd & Others) (No 3), ECJ Cases C–46/93, C–48/93*, [1996] 1 ECR 1029, [1996] 1 CMLR 889; [1996] 2 WLR 506;

[1996] AEECR 301 (TVC 22.31)) See also *R v Secretary of State for Employment (ex p. Equal Opportunities Commission), HL* [1994] 1 All ER 910 (TVC 22.37) where Lord Keith of Kinkel observed that 'if there is any individual who believes that he or she has a good claim to compensation under the *Francovich* principle, it is the Attorney-General who would be defendant in any proceedings directed to enforcing it'.

Judgments in the CJEU also have supremacy over domestic decisions even if the proceedings commenced in another EU member state.

De Voil Indirect Tax Service. See V1.235.

VAT harmonisation directives

[19.3] A directive must be read as a whole. The preamble, which sets out the purpose of the legislation, is an essential part of it. Moreover, as distinct from UK law, it is acceptable when determining the purpose of the legislation to consider the discussions, decisions, etc. ('*travaux preparatoires*') which led to the legislation being drafted in its final form.

The principal directives issued by the EU Council on the harmonisation of legislation of EU member states concerning turnover taxes, and which are relevant in the UK, are as follows.

- *1st Directive*. [*67/227/EEC*]. This provided for a common VAT system to be operated by EU member states. It is now incorporated in *Directive 2006/112/EC*.
- *6th Directive*. [*77/388/EEC*]. This was the so-called 'harmonisation directive' and clarified many of the definitions of basic terms used in the legislation of individual EU member states. It is now incorporated in *Directive 2006/112/EC*.
- *7th Directive*. [*94/5/EEC*]. This provided for special arrangements applicable to second-hand goods, works of art, collectors' items and antiques. See **62 SECOND-HAND GOODS**.
- *8th Directive*. [*79/1072/EEC*]. This provided for the refund of VAT suffered by EU traders in those EU member states where they do not have a business establishment. It was replaced from 1 January 2010 by *Directive 2008/9/EC*. See **19.43** below.
- *10th Directive*. [*84/386/EEC*]. This amended and clarified the provisions of the *6th Directive* in connection with the hiring out of movable tangible property.
- *13th Directive*. [*86/560/EEC*]. This provided for refund of VAT to taxable persons not established in the EU. See **19.44** below.
- *18th Directive*. [*89/465/EEC*]. This abolished a number of derogations provided for in what is now *Directive 2006/112/EC*.
- *Directive 2006/112/EC*. This recast the provisions of the *1st Directive* and *6th Directive* as amended. See **19.4** *et seq* below.
- *Directive 2008/8/EC*. This amended the place of supply of services rules in *Directive 2006/112/EC*. See **19.14** below.
- *Directive 2008/9/EC*. This repealed and replaced the *8th Directive*. It introduced an electronic procedure for the claiming of VAT incurred in other EU member states. See **19.43** below.

- *Directive 2008/117/EC*. This amended *Directive 2006/112/EC* with regard to the submission of EU sales lists (ESLs) (see **19.40**(8) below) and the time of supply of services subject to the reverse charge (see **19.16**(1) below).
- *Directive 2009/162/EU*. This amended *Directive 2006/112/EC* with regard to supplies of gas, electricity, heat or cooling energy (see **19.8**(iv), **19.12**(4) below), and with regard to immovable property used both for business and non-business purposes (see **19.33** below).
- *Directive 2010/45/EU*. This amended *Directive 2006/112/EC* with regard to the rules on invoicing (see **19.40** below). EU member states were required to bring into force the necessary implementing laws with effect from 1 January 2013.

A number of subsidiary directives have also been issued.

Directive 2006/112/EC (Principal VAT Directive)

[19.4] Many of the Articles of *Directive 2006/112/EC* are similar to the provisions of the *VATA 1994* because the UK legislation represents the implementation of the Directive in domestic law. Where they differ, and the words of the Directive are unconditional and precise (e.g. as evidenced by the use of the word 'must' in the text below) the Directive wording takes precedence over that in the *VATA 1994*. Where *Articles* are discretionary (e.g. as evidenced by the use of the words 'countries may' in the text below) the UK may apply the provisions or not as it wishes. However, where they are applied, the provisions once adopted must be applied precisely.

Council Regulation (EU)282/2011 lays down implementing measures for *Directive 2006/112/EC*, in particular giving guidance on determining the status of the customer, whether he acquires services for business use and where he is located. This 'Implementing Regulation' is an important guide to the interpretation and application of many of the rules in the *Principal VAT Directive*.

Definitive arrangements

The arrangements provided for in **19.5** to **19.42** below for the taxation of trade between EU member states are transitional and due to be replaced by definitive arrangements based in principle on the taxation in the EU member state of origin of the supply of goods or services. [*Directive 2006/112/EC, Art 402*]. The possibility of this happening is becoming increasingly unlikely as time passes and the members of the EU increase.

Introduction

[19.5] This Directive establishes the common system of VAT throughout the EU. This entails the application to goods and services of a general tax on consumption, exactly proportional to the price of the goods and services, however many transactions take place in the production and distribution process before the stage at which the tax is charged.

On each transaction, VAT, calculated on the price of the goods or services at the rate applicable to such goods or services, must be chargeable after deduction of the amount of VAT borne directly by the various cost components.

VAT must be applied up to and including the retail trade stage.

[*Directive 2006/112/EC, Art 1*].

Scope

[19.6] Subject to the derogation and exceptions below, the following transactions must be subject to VAT.

(a) The supply of goods for consideration within the territory of an EU member state by a taxable person acting as such.

(b) The intra-EU acquisition of goods for consideration within the territory of an EU member state by the following persons.

   (i) A taxable person acting as such, or a non-taxable legal person, where the vendor is a taxable person acting as such who is not eligible for the exemption for small enterprises provided for in **19.41**(2) below and who is not covered by *Art 33* or *Art 36* (see **19.12**(*b*) below).

   (ii) In the case of new means of transport (as defined), a taxable person, or a non-taxable legal person, whose other acquisitions are not subject to VAT pursuant to *Art 3* below, or any other non-taxable person.

   (iii) In the case of products subject to excise duty (as defined), where the excise duty on the intra-EU acquisition is chargeable within the territory of the EU member state, a taxable person, or a non-taxable legal person, whose other acquisitions are not subject to VAT pursuant to *Art 3* below.

(c) The supply of services for consideration within the territory of an EU member state by a taxable person acting as such.

(d) The importation of goods.

[*Directive 2006/112/EC, Art 2*].

Derogation

By way of derogation from (*b*)(i) above, the following transactions must not be subject to VAT.

(i) The intra-EU acquisition of goods by a taxable person or a non-taxable legal person, where the supply of such goods within the territory of the EU member state of acquisition would be exempt pursuant to **19.29** below and *Art 151* (see **19.30** below).

(ii) The intra-EU acquisition of goods other than

- those referred to in (i) above,
- the *Exceptions* below, and
- new means of transport or products subject to excise duty,
- by a taxable person

- for the purposes of his agricultural, forestry or fisheries business subject to the common flat-rate scheme for farmers, or
- who carries out only supplies of goods or services in respect of which VAT is not deductible,

or by a non-taxable legal person.

But this only applies if during the previous calendar year and during the current calendar year, the total value of intra-EU acquisitions of goods does not exceed a threshold to be determined by each EU member state (which may not be less than €10,000 or the equivalent in national currency).

Taxable persons and non-taxable legal persons must be granted the right to opt out of this derogation and to apply the general scheme provided for in (*b*)(i) above.

[*Directive 2006/112/EC, Art 3*].

Exceptions

In addition to the transactions referred to in *Art 3* above, the following transactions must not be subject to VAT.

- The intra-EU acquisition of second-hand goods, works of art, collectors' items or antiques where the vendor is a taxable dealer acting as such and VAT has been applied to the goods in the EU member state in which their dispatch or transport began, in accordance with the margin scheme provided for in **19.41**(5) below.
- The intra-EU acquisition of second-hand means of transport where the vendor is a taxable dealer acting as such and VAT has been applied to the means of transport in the EU member state in which their dispatch or transport began, in accordance with the transitional arrangements for second-hand means of transport.
- The intra-EU acquisition of second-hand goods, works of art, collectors' items or antiques where the vendor is an organiser of sales by public auction, acting as such, and VAT has been applied to the goods in the EU member state in which their dispatch or transport began, in accordance with the special arrangements for sales by public auction.

[*Directive 2006/112/EC, Art 4*].

For consideration

It follows from the above that there is no supply for VAT purposes where there is no consideration. See *Staatssecretaris van Financiën v Cooperatieve Vereniging 'Cooperatieve Aardappelenbewaarplaats GA', ECJ Case 154/80*, [1981] ECR 445, [1981] 3 CMLR 337 (TVC 22.83). Similarly, in *Staatssecretaris van Financiën v Hong Kong Trade Development Council, ECJ Case 89/81*, [1982] ECR 1277, [1983] 1 CMLR 73 (TVC 22.84) the CJEU held that the provision of services for no consideration could not be subject to VAT and, where no other activity was involved, the provider of the services could not be regarded as a taxable person.

In *Apple & Pear Development Council v C & E Commrs, ECJ Case 102/86*, [1988] STC 221 (TVC 22.85) the CJEU held that, for a supply of services to be for consideration within the above provisions, there must be a direct link between the service provided and the consideration received. On the evidence in that case, there was no relationship between the level of the benefits which individual fruit growers obtained from the Council's services and the amount of the mandatory charges which they were obliged to pay. Accordingly, the compulsory annual charges did not constitute 'consideration' and the Council was not making supplies of services for consideration.

In *Tolsma v Inspecteur der Omzetbelasting Leeuwarden, ECJ Case C–16/93*, [1994] STC 509 (TVC 22.89) an individual who played a barrel organ on the public highway and invited donations from the public was held not to be supplying services for a consideration. There was no agreement between the parties and also 'no necessary link between the musical service and the payment to which it gave rise'.

Lawful and unlawful transactions

The principle of fiscal neutrality precludes a generalised differentiation between lawful and unlawful transactions except where, because of the special characteristics of certain products, all competition between a lawful economic sector and an unlawful sector is precluded. Thus the illegal sale of drugs is not a supply for VAT purposes (*Mol v Inspecteur der InVoerrechten Accijinzen, ECJ Case C–269/86*, [1988] ECR 3627, [1989] BVC 205 (TVC 22.86)) but the supply of counterfeit perfume is. See *R v Goodwin and Unstead, ECJ Case C–3/97*, [1998] STC 699 (TVC 22.87). The prohibition on such products stems from the fact that they infringe intellectual property rights and is conditional not absolute (as in the case of drugs and counterfeit money). There is scope for competition between counterfeit perfumes and perfumes which are traded lawfully and although supply of the former is unlawful, such perfume is not liable to seizure in the hands of the final customer. The unlawful operation of a form of roulette was similarly held to be a supply for VAT purposes in *Fischer v Finanzamt Donaueschingen, ECJ Case C–283/95*, [1998] STC 708 (TVC 22.405). However, although the unlawful playing of a game of chance is a supply, it is not taxable where the corresponding activity is exempt when carried on lawfully by a licensed casino.

Taxable person acting as such

In *Finanzamt Ülzen v Armbrecht, ECJ Case C–291/92*, [1995] STC 997 (TVC 22.99), a hotelier sold a guesthouse, part of which had been used for private rather than business purposes. The CJEU ruled that where a taxable person sold property, part of which he had chosen to reserve for private use, the sale of that part was outside the scope of the above provisions. This should be compared to the decision in *Bakcsi v Finanzamt Fürstenfeldbruck, ECJ Case C–415/98*, [2002] STC 802 (TVC 22.100) where a trader purchased a car and used it mainly for business purposes but partly for private purposes. The CJEU held that where a taxable person used a capital item for both business and private purposes, and had incorporated that item wholly into his business assets, the sale of that item was wholly subject to VAT. The CJEU also observed that a taxable person who acquired a capital item for mixed purposes 'may retain it wholly within his private assets and thereby exclude it entirely' from the VAT system.

Taxable persons

[19.7] '*Taxable person*' means any person who independently carries out in any place any economic activity whatever the purpose or result of that activity.

Any activity of producers, traders and persons supplying services, including mining and agricultural activities and activities of professions, must be regarded as an economic activity. Included is the exploitation of tangible and intangible property for the purposes of obtaining income on a continuing basis.

In addition to the persons referred to above, any person who, on an occasional basis, supplies a new means of transport, which is dispatched or transported to the customer by the vendor or the customer, or on behalf of the vendor or the customer, to a destination outside the territory of an EU member state but within the territory of the EU, must be regarded as a taxable person.

Economic activity

In *Rompelman v Minister van Financien, ECJ Case 268/83*, [1985] 3 CMLR 202; [1985] ECR 655 (TVC 22.111) the acquisition of a future right of joint ownership in property under construction with a view to letting that property in due course was held to be an economic activity although objective evidence (e.g. proposed contracts, planning permission) that arrangements have been made to begin making taxable supplies should be produced. The first investment expenditure incurred for the purpose of a business can be regarded as an economic activity even if it does not give rise to any taxable transactions. See *Intercommunale voor Zeewaterontzilting (in liquidation) v Belgian State, ECJ Case C–110/94*, [1996] STC 569 (TVC 22.119) where VAT was held to be deductible on a profitability study although, as a result of the study, the company did not move to the operational phase. See also *WM van Tiem v Staatssecretaris van Financien, ECJ Case C–186/89*, [1993] STC 91 (TVC 22.118) and *Finanzamt Goslar v Breitsohl, ECJ Case C–400/98*, [2001] STC 355 (TVC 22.132). In the latter case it was held that the right to deduct the VAT paid on transactions carried out with the view to a realisation of a planned economic activity still existed even where the tax authorities were aware, from the time of the first tax assessment, that the economic activity envisaged, which was to give rise to taxable transactions, would not be taken up (although, in such cases, the input tax recovery might be subject to later adjustment).

The holding of shares does not amount to an economic activity if the shareholder is not involved in the management of the companies whose shares it holds. Neither is it the exploitation of assets for the purposes of obtaining income because any dividend received arises from the ownership of the shares, not from an economic activity (*Polysar Investments Netherlands BV v Inspecteur der Invoerrechten en Accijnzen, Arnhem, ECJ Case C–60/90*, [1993] STC 222 (TVC 22.114)). See also *Harnas & Helm CV v Staatssecretaris van Financien, ECJ Case C–80/95*, [1997] STC 364 (TVC 22.121). The purchase and sale of shares by trustees in the course of the management of a charitable trust does not amount to an economic activity (*The Wellcome Trust Ltd v C & E Commrs, ECJ Case C–155/94*, [1996] STC 945 (TVC 22.120)).

See **9.1 BUSINESS** for the meaning of 'business' under UK legislation.

Independently

The hiring out of intangible property with a view to obtaining income therefrom on a continuing basis is an economic activity even where a person's sole economic activity consists in the letting of such an item to a company or partnership of which he is a member (*Staatssecretaris van Financiën v Heerma*, *ECJ Case C–23/98*, [2001] STC 1437 (TVC 22.116)).

The use of the word 'independently' excludes employed and other persons from VAT in so far as they are bound to an employer by a contract of employment or by any other legal ties creating the relationship of employer and employee as regards working conditions, remuneration and employer's liability.

Occasional transactions

Countries may also treat as taxable persons anyone who carries out, on an occasional basis, a transaction relating to an economic activity and in particular

- the supply before first occupation of buildings (or part) and the land on which they stand. Countries may apply criteria other than first occupation, e.g. the period elapsing between the date of completion of the building and the date of first supply (not exceeding five years) or the period elapsing between the date of first occupation and the date of subsequent supply (not exceeding two years); and
- the supply of building land.

Single taxable person

Each country may treat different persons established in their territory as a single taxable person where those persons, although legally independent, are closely bound to one another by financial, economic and organisational links. See **9.5 BUSINESS** for UK provisions.

Local authorities, etc.

States, regional and local government authorities and other bodies governed by public law must not be regarded as taxable persons in respect of the activities or transactions in which they engage as public authorities, even where they collect dues, fees, contributions or payments in connection with those activities or transactions. But when they engage in such activities or transactions, they must be regarded as taxable persons in respect of those activities or transactions where their treatment as non-taxable persons would lead to significant distortions of competition.

In any event, bodies governed by public law must be regarded as taxable persons in relation to certain activities, provided they are not carried out on such a small scale as to be negligible. Those activities are telecommunications; the supply of water, gas, electricity and thermal energy; the transport of goods; port and airport services; passenger transport; the supply of new goods manufactured for sale; transactions in respect of agricultural products carried out by agricultural intervention agencies; the organisation of trade fairs and exhibitions; warehousing; the activities of commercial publicity bodies and travel agents; the running of staff shops, cooperatives and industrial canteens and similar institutions; and activities carried out by radio and television bodies of a commercial nature. For a general consideration of these provisions see *Ufficio Distrettuale delle Imposte Dirette di Fiorenzuola d'Arda v Comune di Carpaneto Piacentino* and *Ufficio Provinciale Imposta sul Valore Aggiunto di Piacenza v Comune di Rivergaro and Others, ECJ Case 231/87*, [1991] STC 205 (TVC 22.139).

Countries may also treat certain exempt activities of these bodies as activities they engage in as public authorities. This applies even if the body acted in a similar manner to a private trader (*Finanzamt Augsburg-Stadt v Marktgemeinde Welden, ECJ Case C–247/95*, [1997] STC 531 (TVC 22.143)).

See **44.1** for the recent cases of *Gemeente Borsele v Staatssecretaris van Financiën, ECJ Case C-520/14* and *Gemeente Woerden v Staatssecretaris van Financiën, ECJ Case C-267/15*.

[*Directive 2006/112/EC, Arts 9–13*].

See **44 LOCAL AUTHORITIES AND PUBLIC BODIES** for EU and UK provisions.

Supply of goods

[19.8] Supply of goods means the transfer of the right to dispose of 'tangible property' as owner.

'*Tangible property*' includes electricity, gas, heat, or cooling energy and the like. Countries may consider it to include certain interests in immovable property; rights *in rem* giving the holder a right of user over immovable property (see *WM van Tiem v Staatssecretaris van Financien, ECJ Case C–186/89*, [1993] STC 91 (TVC 22.118)); and shares, etc. giving the holder *de jure* or *de facto* rights of ownership or possession over immovable property.

The following must be treated as supplies of goods.

(a) The transfer, by order made by or in the name of a public authority or in pursuance of the law, of the ownership of property against payment of compensation.
(b) The actual handing over of goods under a contract for the hire of goods for a certain period, or for the sale of goods on deferred terms, where the contract provides that in the normal course of events ownership is to pass at the latest upon payment of the final instalment.
(c) The transfer of goods pursuant to a contract under which commission is payable on purchase or sale.
(d) The application by a taxable person of goods forming part of his business assets for his private use or for that of his staff, or their disposal free of charge or, more generally, their application for purposes other than those of his business, where the VAT on those goods or the component parts thereof was wholly or partly deductible. But the application of goods for business use as samples or as gifts of small value must not be treated as a supply of goods for consideration.

(e) The transfer by a taxable person of goods forming part of his business assets to another EU member state. But the dispatch or transport of goods for the purposes of any of the following transactions must not be regarded as a transfer to another EU member state.

  (i) The supply of the goods by the taxable person within the territory of the EU member state in which the dispatch or transport ends, in accordance with the conditions laid down in *Art 33* (see **19.12**(2) below).

  (ii) The supply of the goods, for installation or assembly by or on behalf of the supplier, by the taxable person within the territory of the EU member state in which dispatch or transport of the goods ends, in accordance with the conditions laid down in *Art 36* (see **19.12**(2) below).

  (iii) The supply of the goods by the taxable person on board a ship, an aircraft or a train in the course of a passenger transport operation, in accordance with the conditions laid down in *Art 37* (see **19.12**(3) below).

  (iv) The supply of gas through a natural gas system situated within the EU or any network connected to such a system, or the supply of electricity, or the supply of heat or cooling energy through heating or cooling networks, in accordance with the conditions laid down in *Arts 38* and *39* (see **19.12**(4) below).

  (v) The supply of the goods by the taxable person within the territory of the EU member state, in accordance with the conditions laid down in *Arts 138* (see **19.26**(1) below), *146* or *147* (see **19.28** below), *148* (see **19.29** below), or *151* or *152* (see **19.30** below).

  (vi) The supply of a service performed for the taxable person and consisting in valuations of, or work on the goods in question physically carried out within the territory of the EU member state in which dispatch or transport of the goods ends, provided that the goods, after being valued or worked upon, are returned to that taxable person in the EU member state from which they were initially dispatched or transported.

  (vii) The temporary use of the goods within the territory of the EU member state in which dispatch or transport of the goods ends, for the purposes of the supply of services by the taxable person established within the EU member state in which dispatch or transport of the goods began.

  (viii) The temporary use of the goods, for a period not exceeding 24 months, within the territory of another EU member state, in which the importation of the same goods from a country outside the EU with a view to their temporary use would be covered by the arrangements for temporary importation with full exemption from import duties.

If one of the conditions governing eligibility under any of the above situations is no longer met, the goods must be regarded as having been transferred to another EU member state at the time when that condition ceases to be met.

The following may be treated as supplies of goods.

(i) The handing over of certain works of construction.
(ii) The application by a taxable person for the purposes of his business of goods produced, constructed, extracted, processed, purchased or imported in the course of the business, where the VAT on the goods, had they been acquired from another taxable person would not be wholly deductible.
(iii) The application of goods by a taxable person for the purposes of a non-taxable area of activity, where the VAT on such goods became wholly or partly deductible upon their acquisition or upon their application in accordance with (ii) above.
(iv) With the exception of business transfers below, the retention of goods by a taxable person, or by his successors, when he ceases to carry out a taxable economic activity, where the VAT on such goods became wholly or partly deductible upon their acquisition or upon their application in accordance with (ii) above.

[*Directive 2006/112/EC, Arts 14–18*].

Transfers of businesses, etc.

In the event of a transfer (whether for consideration or not or as a contribution to a company) of a totality of assets or part thereof, an EU member state may consider that no supply of goods has taken place and that the person to whom the goods are transferred is to be treated as the successor to the transferor. See **9.9 BUSINESS** for UK provisions. [*Directive 2006/112/EC, Art 19*].

See **65.3 SUPPLY: GENERAL** for the UK provisions.

Intra-EU acquisition of goods

[19.9] '*Intra-EU acquisition of goods*' means the acquisition of the right to dispose as owner of movable tangible property dispatched or transported to the person acquiring the goods, by or on behalf of the vendor or the person acquiring the goods, in an EU member state other than that in which dispatch or transport of the goods began.

Non-taxable legal persons

Where goods acquired by a non-taxable legal person are dispatched or transported from a country outside the EU and imported by that non-taxable legal person into an EU member state other than the EU member state in which dispatch or transport of the goods ends, the goods must be regarded as having been dispatched or transported from the EU member state of importation. That EU member state must grant the importer liable for payment of VAT a refund of the VAT paid in respect of the importation of the goods, provided that the importer establishes that VAT has been applied to his acquisition in the EU member state in which dispatch or transport of the goods ends. [*Directive 2006/112/EC, Art 20*].

Taxable persons

The application by a taxable person, for the purposes of his business, of goods dispatched or transported by or on behalf of that taxable person from another EU member state

- within which the goods were produced, extracted, processed, purchased or acquired, or
- into which they were imported by that taxable person for the purposes of his business,

must be treated as an intra-EU acquisition of goods for consideration.

[*Directive 2006/112/EC, Art 21*].

Armed forces

The application by the armed forces of a State party to the North Atlantic Treaty, for their use or for the use of the civilian staff accompanying them, of goods which they have not purchased subject to the general rules governing taxation on the domestic market of an EU member state must be treated as an intra-EU acquisition of goods for consideration, where the importation of those goods would not be eligible for the exemption provided for in **19.27**(*i*) below). [*Directive 2006/112/EC, Art 22*].

Treatment of transactions

EU member states must take the measures necessary to ensure that a transaction which would have been classed as a supply of goods if it had been carried out within their territory by a taxable person acting as such is classed as an intra-EU acquisition of goods. [*Directive 2006/112/EC, Art 23*].

Supply of services

[19.10] '*Supply of services*' means any transaction which does not constitute a supply of goods. This may include

- the assignment of intangible property;
- an obligation to refrain from an act or to tolerate an act or situation; and
- the performance of services in pursuance of an order made by or in the name of a public authority or in pursuance of the law.

The following transactions must be treated as a supply of services for consideration.

(i) The use of goods forming part of the assets of a business for the private use of a taxable person or of his staff or, more generally, for purposes other than those of his business, where the VAT on such goods was wholly or partly deductible.

(ii) The supply of services carried out free of charge by a taxable person for his private use or for that of his staff or, more generally, for purposes other than those of his business.

Countries may derogate from the provisions of (i) and (ii) above provided that this does not lead to distortion of competition. However, this power to derogate from the obligation to charge tax on private use of business assets does not allow them to impose tax where VAT on the original purchase was not wholly or partly deductible (*Kühne v Finanzamt München III*, *ECJ Case 50/88*, [1990] STC 749 (TVC 22.196)).

Where a taxable person acting in his own name but on behalf of another person takes part in the supply of services, he must be deemed to have received and supplied the services himself.

Self-supply of services

To prevent distortion of competition, countries may treat as a supply of services for consideration the supply by a taxable person of a service for the purposes of his business, where the VAT on such a service, were it supplied by another taxable person, would not be wholly deductible.

Transfers of businesses, etc.

Art 19 (see **19.8** above) applies in like manner to the supply of services.

[*Directive 2006/112/EC, Arts 24–29*].

See **65.4 SUPPLY: GENERAL** for the UK provisions.

Importation of goods

[19.11] '*Importation of goods*' means the entry into the EU of goods which are not in free circulation.

In addition, the entry into the EU of goods which are in free circulation, coming from outside the VAT territory of the EU but from a territory forming part of the customs territory of the EU, must be regarded as importation of goods.
[*Directive 2006/112/EC, Art 30*].

Place of supply of goods

[19.12] See *Council Regulation (EU)282/2011, Chapter V section 2* for implementing measures for *Directive 2006/112/EC, Arts 31–39* on place of supply of goods.

The place of supply of goods is deemed to be as follows.

(1) Supply of goods without transport

Where goods are not dispatched or transported, the place of supply is deemed to be the place where the goods are located at the time when the supply takes place. [*Directive 2006/112/EC, Art 31*].

(2) Supply of goods with transport

Where goods are dispatched or transported by the supplier, the customer or a third person, the place of supply is deemed to be the place where the goods are located at the time when dispatch or transport of the goods to the customer begins. But if dispatch or transport of the goods begins outside the VAT territory of the EU, both the place of supply by the importer liable for payment of VAT and the place of any subsequent supply is deemed to be in the EU member state of importation of the goods. [*Directive 2006/112/EC, Art 32*].

Derogation

By way of derogation from *Art 32* (but subject to *Art 34* below), the place of supply of goods dispatched or transported by or on behalf of the supplier from an EU member state other than that in which dispatch or transport of the goods ends is to be deemed to be the place where the goods are located at the time when dispatch or transport of the goods to the customer ends, where the following conditions are met.

- The supply of goods is carried out for a taxable person, or a non-taxable legal person, whose intra-EU acquisitions of goods are not subject to VAT pursuant to *Art 3* (see **19.6** above) or for any other non-taxable person.
- The goods supplied are neither new means of transport nor goods supplied after assembly or installation, with or without a trial run, by or on behalf of the supplier.

Where the goods supplied are dispatched or transported from outside the VAT territory of the EU and imported by the supplier into an EU member state other than that in which dispatch or transport of the goods to the customer ends, they are regarded as having been dispatched or transported from the EU member state of importation.

[*Directive 2006/112/EC, Art 33*].

Exception to derogation

Provided the following conditions are met, *Art 33* above does not apply to supplies of goods, all of which are dispatched or transported to the same EU member state, where that country is the country in which dispatch or transport of the goods ends.

- The goods supplied are not products subject to excise duty.
- The total value, exclusive of VAT, of such supplies effected under the conditions laid down in *Art 33* within that EU member state does not in any one calendar year exceed €100,000 (or the equivalent in national currency).
- The total value, exclusive of VAT, of the supplies of goods, other than products subject to excise duty, effected under the conditions laid down in *Art 33* within that EU member state did not in the previous calendar year exceed €100,000 (or the equivalent in national currency).

EU member states may substitute €35,000 for €100,000 if the higher threshold might cause serious distortion of competition.

But EU member states within the territory of which the goods are located at the time when their dispatch or transport begins must grant those taxable persons who carry out supplies of goods eligible under this exception the right to opt for the place of supply to be determined in accordance with the derogation under *Art 33*.

[*Directive 2006/112/EC, Art 34*].

Second-hand goods, etc.

Arts 33 and *34* above do not apply to supplies of second-hand goods, works of art, collectors' items or antiques, nor to supplies of second-hand means of transport, subject to VAT in accordance with the relevant special arrangements. [*Directive 2006/112/EC, Art 35*].

Installed or assembled goods

Where goods dispatched or transported by the supplier, by the customer or by a third person are installed or assembled, with or without a trial run, by or on behalf of the supplier, the place of supply is deemed to be the place where the goods are installed or assembled. Where the installation or assembly is carried out in an EU member state other than that of the supplier, the EU member state within the territory of which the installation or assembly is carried out must take the measures necessary to ensure that there is no double taxation in that country. [*Directive 2006/112/EC, Art 36*].

(3) Supply of goods on board ships, aircraft or trains

Where goods are supplied on board ships, aircraft or trains during the 'section of a passenger transport operation effected within the EU', the place of supply is deemed to be at the point of departure of the passenger transport operation.

'*Section of a passenger transport operation effected within the EU*' means the section of the operation effected, without a stopover outside the EU, between the 'point of departure' and the 'point of arrival' of the passenger transport operation.

'*Point of departure*' of a passenger transport operation means the first scheduled point of passenger embarkation within the EU, where applicable after a stopover outside the EU.

'*Point of arrival*' of a passenger transport operation means the last scheduled point of disembarkation within the EU of passengers who embarked in the EU, where applicable before a stopover outside the EU.

In the case of a return trip, the return leg is regarded as a separate transport operation.

Pending adoption of the proposals of a report to the Council, EU member states may exempt or continue to exempt, with deductibility of the VAT paid at the preceding stage, the supply of goods for consumption on board in respect of which the place of taxation is determined in accordance with the above.

[*Directive 2006/112/EC, Art 37*].

(4) Supply of goods through distribution systems

Supplies to taxable dealers

In the case of the supply of gas through a natural gas system situated within the EU or any network connected to such a system, or of electricity, or of heat or cooling energy through heating or cooling networks to a 'taxable dealer', the place of supply is deemed to be the place where that taxable dealer has established his business or has a fixed establishment for which the goods are supplied (or, in the absence of such a place of business or fixed establishment, the place where he has his permanent address or usually resides).

'*Taxable dealer*' means a taxable person whose principal activity in respect of purchases of gas or electricity, heat or cooling energy is reselling those products and whose own consumption of those products is negligible.

[*Directive 2006/112/EC, Art 38*].

Other supplies

In the case of the supply of gas through a natural gas system situated within the EU or any network connected to such a system, or of electricity, or supply of heat or cooling energy through heating or cooling networks, not covered by *Art 38*, the place of supply is deemed to be the place where the customer effectively uses and consumes the goods.

Where all or part of the gas, electricity or heat or cooling energy is not effectively consumed by the customer, those non-consumed goods are deemed to have been used and consumed at the place where the customer has established his business or has a fixed establishment for which the goods are supplied. In the absence of such a place of business or fixed establishment, the customer is deemed to have used and consumed the goods at the place where he has his permanent address or usually resides.

[*Directive 2006/112/EC, Art 39*].

Place of an intra-EU acquisition of goods

[19.13] See *Council Regulation (EU)282/2011, Chapter V section 3* for implementing measures for *Directive 2006/112/EC, Arts 40–42* on place of intra-EU acquisitions of goods.

Subject to below, the place of the intra-EU acquisition of goods is deemed to be the place where dispatch or transport of the goods to the person acquiring them ends. [*Directive 2006/112/EC, Art 40*].

Without prejudice *Art 40* but subject to *Art 42* below, the place of an intra-EU acquisition of goods referred to in **19.6**(*b*)(i) above is deemed to be within the EU member state which issued the VAT identification number under which the person acquiring the goods made the acquisition (unless the person acquiring the goods establishes that VAT has been applied to that acquisition in accordance with *Art 40*).

If VAT is so applied to the acquisition and subsequently applied, under *Art 40*, to the acquisition in the EU member state in which dispatch or transport of the goods ends, the taxable amount must be reduced accordingly in the EU member state which issued the VAT identification number under which the person acquiring the goods made the acquisition.

[*Directive 2006/112/EC, Art 41*].

The first paragraph of *Art 41* above must not apply (and VAT is deemed to have been applied to the intra-EU acquisition of goods in accordance with *Art 40*) where the following conditions are met.

- The person acquiring the goods establishes that he has made the intra-EU acquisition for the purposes of a subsequent supply, within the territory of the EU member state identified in accordance with *Art 40*, for which the person to whom the supply is made has been designated in accordance with *Art 197* (see **19.38**(*e*) below) as liable for payment of VAT.
- The person acquiring the goods has satisfied the obligations laid down in *Art 265* (see **19.40**(8) below) relating to submission of the recapitulative statement.

[*Directive 2006/112/EC, Art 42*].

Place of supply of services

Taxable person

[19.14] See *Council Regulation (EU)282/2011, Chapter V section 4* for implementing measures for *Directive 2006/112/EC, Arts 43–59* on place of supply of services.

For the purpose of applying the rules concerning the place of supply of services

- a taxable person who also carries out activities or transactions that are not considered to be taxable supplies of goods or services in accordance with *Art 2(1)* shall be regarded as a taxable person in respect of all services rendered to him;
- a non-taxable legal person who is identified for VAT purposes shall be regarded as a taxable person.

[*Directive 2006/112/EC, Art 43*].

General rules

The place of supply of services to a taxable person acting as such shall be the place where that person has established his business. However, if those services are provided to a fixed establishment of the taxable person located in a place other than the place where he has established his business, the place of supply of those services shall be the place where that fixed establishment is located. In the absence of such place of establishment or fixed establishment, the place of supply of services shall be the place where the taxable person who receives such services has his permanent address or usually resides.

The place of supply of services to a non-taxable person shall be the place where the supplier has established his business. However, if those services are provided from a fixed establishment of the supplier located in a place other than the place where he has established his business, the place of supply of those services shall be the place where that fixed establishment is located. In the absence of such place of establishment or fixed establishment, the place of supply of services shall be the place where the supplier has his permanent address or usually resides.

[*Directive 2006/112/EC, Arts 44, 45*].

Supply of services by intermediaries

The place of supply of services rendered to a non-taxable person by an intermediary acting in the name and on behalf of another person shall be the place where the underlying transaction is supplied in accordance with this *Directive*.

[*Directive 2006/112/EC, Art 46*].

Supply of services connected with immovable property

The place of supply of services connected with immovable property, including the services of experts and estate agents, the provision of accommodation in the hotel sector or in sectors with a similar function, such as holiday camps or sites developed for use as camping sites, the granting of rights to use immovable property and services for the preparation and coordination of construction work, such as the services of architects and of firms providing on-site supervision, shall be the place where the immovable property is located.

[*Directive 2006/112/EC, Art 47*].

Supply of transport

The place of supply of passenger transport shall be the place where the transport takes place, proportionate to the distances covered.

The place of supply of the transport of goods, other than the intra-EU transport of goods, to non-taxable persons shall be the place where the transport takes place, proportionate to the distances covered.

The place of supply of the intra-EU transport of goods to non-taxable persons shall be the place of departure.

'Intra-EU transport of goods' shall mean any transport of goods in respect of which the place of departure and the place of arrival are situated within the territories of two different EU member states. 'Place of departure' shall mean the place where transport of the goods actually begins, irrespective of distances covered in order to reach the place where the goods are located and 'place of arrival' shall mean the place where transport of the goods actually ends.

Member states need not apply VAT to that part of the intra-EU transport of goods to non-taxable persons taking place over waters which do not form part of the territory of the EU.

[*Directive 2006/112/EC, Arts 48–52*].

Supply of cultural, artistic, sporting, scientific, educational, entertainment and similar services, ancillary transport services and valuations of and work on movable property

The place of supply of services in respect of admission to cultural, artistic, sporting, scientific, educational, entertainment or similar events, such as fairs and exhibitions, and of ancillary services related to the admission, supplied to a taxable person, shall be the place where those events actually take place.

The place of supply of services and ancillary services, relating to cultural, artistic, sporting, scientific, educational, entertainment or similar activities, such as fairs and exhibitions, including the supply of services of the organisers of such activities, supplied to a non-taxable person shall be the place where those activities actually take place.

The place of supply of the following services to a non-taxable person shall be the place where the services are physically carried out: (a) ancillary transport activities such as loading, unloading, handling and similar activities; (b) valuations of and work on movable tangible property.

[*Directive 2006/112/EC, Arts 53, 54*].

Supply of restaurant and catering services

The place of supply of restaurant and catering services other than those physically carried out on board ships, aircraft or trains during the section of a passenger transport operation effected within the EU, shall be the place where the services are physically carried out.

[*Directive 2006/112/EC, Art 55*].

Hiring of means of transport

The place of short-term hiring of a means of transport shall be the place where the means of transport is actually put at the disposal of the customer. For these purposes, 'short-term' shall mean the continuous possession or use of the means of transport throughout a period of not more than 30 days and, in the case of vessels, not more than 90 days.

The place of supply of the long-term hire of means of transport to a relevant business customer in another EU member state is where the customer belongs. If the customer is a non-taxable person then the place of supply is the EU member state where the customer belongs, subject to any use and enjoyment provisions that may apply.

However, the place of hiring a pleasure boat to a non-taxable person, other than short-term hiring, shall be the place where the pleasure boat is actually put at the disposal of the customer, where this service is actually provided by the supplier from his place of business or a fixed establishment situated in that place.

[*Directive 2006/112/EC, Art 56*].

Supply of restaurant and catering services for consumption on board ships, aircraft or trains

The place of supply of restaurant and catering services which are physically carried out on board ships, aircraft or trains during the section of a passenger transport operation effected within the EU, shall be at the point of departure of the passenger transport operation. For these purposes, 'section of a passenger transport operation effected within the EU' shall mean the section of the operation effected, without a stopover outside the EU, between the point of departure and the point of arrival of the passenger transport operation.

'Point of departure of a passenger transport operation' shall mean the first scheduled point of passenger embarkation within the EU, where applicable after a stopover outside the EU. 'Point of arrival of a passenger transport operation' shall mean the last scheduled point of disembarkation within the EU of passengers who embarked in the EU, where applicable before a stopover outside the EU. In the case of a return trip, the return leg shall be regarded as a separate transport operation.
[*Directive 2006/112/EC, Art 57*].

Supply of electronic services to non-taxable persons

Before 1 January 2015

The place of supply of electronically supplied services, in particular those referred to in *Annex II* (i.e. website supply, web-hosting, distance maintenance of programmes and equipment; supply of software and updating thereof; supply of images, text and information and making available of databases; supply of music, films and games, including games of chance and gambling games, and of political, cultural, artistic, sporting, scientific and entertainment broadcasts and events; supply of distance teaching), when supplied to non-taxable persons who are established in an EU member state, or who have their permanent address or usually reside in an EU member state, by a taxable person who has established his business outside the EU or has a fixed establishment there from which the service is supplied, or who, in the absence of such a place of business or fixed establishment, has his permanent address or usually resides outside the EU, shall be the place where the non-taxable person is established, or where he has his permanent address or usually resides. Where the supplier of a service and the customer communicate via electronic mail, that shall not of itself mean that the service supplied is an electronically supplied service. (These provisions to be substituted by *Directive 2008/8/EC, Art 5(1)* with effect from 1 January 2015.)

[*Directive 2006/112/EC, Art 58*].

From 1 January 2015

These provisions were substituted by *Directive 2008/8/EC, Art 5(1)* with effect from 1 January 2015. The place of supply of digital services (broadcasting, telecommunication and e-services) to consumers in other EU member states is now the place where the customer belongs. The supplier must therefore register and account for output tax in the customer's country. See **64.40** for details of the Mini One Stop Shop (MOSS) system that enables businesses to make only one return covering supplies liable to output tax in potentially 27 other countries.

Supply of services to non-taxable persons outside the EU

The place of supply of the following services to a non-taxable person who is established or has his permanent address or usually resides outside the EU, shall be the place where that person is established, has his permanent address or usually resides—

(a) transfers and assignments of copyrights, patents, licences, trade marks and similar rights;

(b) advertising services;
(c) the services of consultants, engineers, consultancy firms, lawyers, accountants and other similar services, as well as data processing and the provision of information;
(d) obligations to refrain from pursuing or exercising, in whole or in part, a business activity or a right referred to in this *Article*;
(e) banking, financial and insurance transactions including reinsurance, with the exception of the hire of safes;
(f) the supply of staff;
(g) the hiring out of movable tangible property, with the exception of all means of transport;
(h) the provision of access to, and of transport or transmission through, natural gas and electricity distribution systems and the provision of other services directly linked thereto;
(i) telecommunications services (before 1 January 2015);
(j) radio and television broadcasting services (before 1 January 2015);
(k) electronically supplied services, in particular those referred to in *Annex II* (i.e. website supply, web-hosting, distance maintenance of programmes and equipment; supply of software and updating thereof; supply of images, text and information and making available of databases; supply of music, films and games, including games of chance and gambling games, and of political, cultural, artistic, sporting, scientific and entertainment broadcasts and events; supply of distance teaching) (before 1 January 2015).

Where the supplier of a service and the customer communicate via electronic mail, that shall not of itself mean that the service supplied is an electronically supplied service.

Points (*i*), (*j*), (*k*) were substituted by *Directive 2008/8/EC, Art 5(2)* with effect from 1 January 2015. There is no change to the effect, because the place of supply to a person belonging outside the EU remains 'where the customer belongs'; however, that has now become the rule within the EU as well for supplies to consumers.

[*Directive 2006/112/EC, Art 59*].

Prevention of double taxation or non-taxation

In order to prevent double taxation, non-taxation or distortion of competition, EU member states may, with regard to services the place of supply of which is governed by *Arts 44, 45, 56 and 59*

(a) consider the place of supply of any or all of those services, if situated within their territory, as being situated outside the EU if the effective use and enjoyment of the services takes place outside the EU;
(b) consider the place of supply of any or all of those services, if situated outside the EU, as being situated within their territory if the effective use and enjoyment of the services takes place within their territory.

However, before 1 January 2015, this provision did not apply to the electronically supplied services where those services were rendered to non-taxable persons not established within the EU. This provision was substituted by *Directive 2008/8/EC, Art 5(3)* with effect from 1 January 2015.

Before 1 January 2015, EU member states were required to apply (*b*) above to telecommunications services and radio and television broadcasting services, as referred to in point (j) of *Art 59* above, supplied to non-taxable persons who are established in an EU member state, or who have their permanent address or usually reside in an EU member state, by a taxable person who has established his business outside the EU or has a fixed establishment there from which the services are supplied, or who, in the absence of such a place of business or fixed establishment, has his permanent address or usually resides outside the EU. (This provision was repealed by *Directive 2008/8/EC, Art 5(3)* with effect from 1 January 2015.)

[*Directive 2006/112/EC, Arts 59a, 59b*].

See **66.12 SUPPLY: PLACE OF SUPPLY** for the UK provisions.

Place of importation of goods

[19.15] The place of importation of goods is the EU member state within whose territory the goods are located when they enter the EU. [*Directive 2006/112/EC, Art 60*].

By way of derogation from *Art 60*, where, on entry into the EU, goods which are not in free circulation are placed under

- one of the arrangements or situations referred to in *Art 156* (see **19.32**(*a*) below),
- temporary importation arrangements with total exemption from import duty, or
- external transit arrangements,

the place of importation of such goods is the EU member state within whose territory the goods cease to be covered by those arrangements or situations. [*Directive 2006/112/EC, Art 61*].

Chargeable event and chargeability of VAT

[19.16] The provisions relating to a chargeable event and the chargeability of VAT are outlined below.

(1) Supply of goods or services

A chargeable event occurs and VAT becomes chargeable when the goods or the services are supplied. [*Directive 2006/112/EC, Art 63*].

Where it gives rise to successive statements of account or successive payments, the supply of goods (other than that consisting in the hire of goods for a certain period or the sale of goods on deferred terms) or the supply of services is regarded as being completed on expiry of the periods to which such statements of account or payments relate. Continuous supplies of goods over a period of more than one calendar month which are dispatched or transported to an EU member state other than that in which the dispatch or transport of those goods begins and which are supplied VAT-exempt or which are transferred VAT-exempt to another EU member state by a taxable person for the purposes of his business, in accordance with the conditions laid down in *Art 138* (see **19.26**(1) below), shall be regarded as being completed on expiry of each calendar month until such time as the supply comes to an end. Supplies of services for which VAT is payable by the customer pursuant to *Art 196* (see **19.38**(e) below), which are supplied continuously over a period of more than one year and which do not give rise to statements of account or payments during that period shall be regarded as being completed on expiry of each calendar year until such time as the supply of services comes to an end. But EU member states may provide that, in certain other cases, the continuous supply of goods or services over a period of time is to be regarded as being completed at least at intervals of one year. [*Directive 2006/112/EC, Art 64*].

Where a payment is to be made on account before the goods or services are supplied, VAT becomes chargeable on receipt of the payment and on the amount received. [*Directive 2006/112/EC, Art 65*].

Derogation

By way of derogation from *Arts 63–65* above, countries may provide that VAT is to become chargeable, in respect of certain transactions or certain categories of taxable person, either

- no later than the time the invoice is issued;
- no later than the time the payment is received; or
- where an invoice is not issued, or is issued late, within a specified time no later than on expiry of the time limit for issue of invoices imposed by EU member states pursuant to the second paragraph of *Art 222* (see **19.40**(2) below) or where no such time limit has been imposed, within a specified period from the date of the chargeable event.

The derogation shall not, however, apply to supplies of services in respect of which VAT is payable by the customer pursuant to *Art 196* (see **19.38**(*e*) below) and to supplies or transfers of goods referred to in *Art 67* (see below).

[*Directive 2006/112/EC, Art 66*].

Where, in accordance with the conditions laid down in *Art 138* (see **19.26**(1) below),

- goods dispatched or transported to an EU member state other than that in which dispatch or transport of the goods begins are supplied VAT-exempt, or
- goods are transferred VAT-exempt to another EU member state by a taxable person for the purposes of his business,

VAT becomes chargeable on issue of the invoice, or on expiry of the time limit referred to in the first paragraph of *Art 222* (see **19.40**(2) below) if no invoice has been issued by that time. *Article 64*(1), the third paragraph of *Art 64(2)* and *Art 65* (see above) do not apply to such supplies and transfers of goods.

[*Directive 2006/112/EC, Art 67*].

See **67.1 SUPPLY: TIME OF SUPPLY** for the UK provisions.

(2) Intra-EU acquisition of goods

The chargeable event occurs when the intra-EU acquisition of goods is made, i.e. when the supply of similar goods is regarded as being effected within the territory of the relevant EU member state. [*Directive 2006/112/EC, Art 68*].

VAT becomes chargeable on issue of the invoice, or on expiry of the time limit referred to in the first paragraph of *Art 222* (see **19.40**(2) below) if no invoice has been issued by that time. [*Directive 2006/112/EC, Art 69*].

See **20.7 EUROPEAN UNION: SINGLE MARKET** for the UK provisions.

(3) Importation of goods

The chargeable event occurs and VAT becomes chargeable when the goods are imported. [*Directive 2006/112/EC, Art 70*].

Where, on entry into the EU, goods are placed under one of the arrangements or situations referred to in

- *Art 156* (see **19.32**(*a*) below),
- under temporary importation arrangements with total exemption from import duty, or
- under external transit arrangements,

the chargeable event occurs and VAT becomes chargeable only when the goods cease to be covered by those arrangements or situations.

However, where imported goods are subject to customs duties, to agricultural levies or to charges having equivalent effect established under a common policy, the chargeable event occurs and VAT becomes chargeable when the chargeable event in respect of those duties occurs and those duties become chargeable.

Where imported goods are not subject to any duties referred to above, countries must, as regards the chargeable event and the moment when VAT becomes chargeable, apply the provisions in force governing customs duties.

[*Directive 2006/112/EC, Art 71*].

See **34.2 IMPORTS** for the UK provisions.

Taxable amount: open market value

[19.17] For the purposes of this *Directive, 'open market value'* means the full amount that, in order to obtain the goods or services in question at that time, a customer at the same marketing stage at which the supply of goods or services takes place, would have to pay, under conditions of fair competition, to a supplier at arm's length within the territory of the EU member state in which the supply is subject to VAT.

Where no comparable supply of goods or services can be ascertained, '*open market value*' means

- in respect of goods, an amount that is not less than the purchase price of the goods or of similar goods or, in the absence of a purchase price, the cost price, determined at the time of supply; and

- in respect of services, an amount that is not less than the full cost to the taxable person of providing the service.

[*Directive 2006/112/EC, Art 72*].

Taxable amount: supply of goods and services

[19.18] Apart from (*a*)–(*d*) below, the taxable amount in respect of the supply of goods or services includes everything which constitutes consideration obtained (or to be obtained) by the supplier in return for the supply from the customer or a third party, including 'subsidies directly linked to the price' of the supply. [*Directive 2006/112/EC, Art 73*].

'*Subsidies directly linked to the price*' must be interpreted as covering only subsidies which constitute the whole or part of the consideration for a supply of goods or services and which are paid by a third party to the seller or supplier (*Office des Produits Wallons ASBL v Belgium, ECJ Case C–184/00*, [2003] STC 1100 (TVC 22.271)).

But

(a) where a taxable person applies or disposes of goods forming part of his business assets, or where goods are retained by a taxable person, or by his successors, when his taxable economic activity ceases, the taxable amount is the purchase price of the goods or of similar goods or, in the absence of a purchase price, the cost price, determined at the time when the application, disposal or retention takes place [*Directive 2006/112/EC, Art 74*];

(b) in respect of the supply of services where goods forming part of the assets of a business are used for private purposes or services are carried out free of charge, the taxable amount is the full cost to the taxable person of providing the services [*Directive 2006/112/EC, Art 75*];

(c) in respect of the supply of goods consisting in transfer to another EU member state, the taxable amount is the purchase price of the goods or of similar goods or, in the absence of a purchase price, the cost price, determined at the time the transfer takes place [*Directive 2006/112/EC, Art 76*]; and

(d) in respect of the self-supply by a taxable person of a service for the purposes of his business, the taxable amount is the open market value of the service supplied [*Directive 2006/112/EC, Art 77*].

The taxable amount includes

- taxes, duties, levies and charges, excluding the VAT itself; and
- incidental expenses, such as commission, packing, transport and insurance costs, charged by the supplier to the customer,

but does not include

(i) price reductions by way of discount for early payment;

(ii) price discounts and rebates granted to the customer and obtained by him at the time of the supply; and

(iii) amounts received by a taxable person from the customer, as repayment of expenditure incurred in the name and on behalf of the customer, and entered in his books in a suspense account. The taxable person must furnish proof of the actual amount of such expenditure and cannot deduct any VAT which may have been charged.

[*Directive 2006/112/EC, Arts 78, 79*].

In order to prevent tax evasion or avoidance, where the consideration

- is lower than the open market value and the recipient of the supply does not have a full right of deduction,
- is lower than the open market value and the supplier does not have a full right of deduction and the supply is subject to an exemption, or
- is higher than the open market value and the supplier does not have a full right of deduction

countries may take measures to ensure that, in respect of the supply of goods or services involving family or other close personal ties, management, ownership, membership, financial or legal ties as defined by the country, the taxable amount is to be the open market value.

[*Directive 2006/112/EC, Art 80*].

Works of art, etc.

Countries which, at 1 January 1993, were not applying a reduced rate may, if they opt under *Art 89* (see **19.20** below) to treat the taxable amount on importation to be equal to a fraction (at least 5%) of the otherwise taxable amount, provide that the taxable amount is also reduced to a fraction (at least 5%) on the supply of works of art. [*Directive 2006/112/EC, Art 81*].

Exempt investment gold

Countries may provide that, in respect of the supply of goods and services, the taxable amount is to include the value of exempt investment gold which has been provided by the customer to be used as a basis for working and which as a result, loses its VAT-exempt investment gold status when such goods and services are supplied. The value to be used is the open market value of the investment gold at the time that those goods and services are supplied. [*Directive 2006/112/EC, Art 82*].

See **72 VALUATION** for the UK provisions.

Taxable amount: intra-EU acquisition of goods

[19.19] In respect of the intra-EU acquisition of goods, the taxable amount is established on the basis of the same factors as are used in **19.17** above to determine the taxable amount for the supply of the same goods within the territory of the EU member state concerned. In the case of the transactions to be treated as intra-EU acquisitions of goods referred to in *Arts 21* and *22* (see **19.9** above), the taxable amount is the purchase price of the goods or of similar goods or, in the absence of a purchase price, the cost price, determined at the time of the supply. [*Directive 2006/112/EC, Art 83*].

Countries must take the measures necessary to ensure that the excise duty due from or paid by the person making the intra-EU acquisition of a product subject to excise duty is included in the taxable amount. Where, after the intra-EU acquisition of goods has been made, the person acquiring the goods obtains a refund of the excise duty paid in the EU member state in which dispatch or transport of the goods began, the taxable amount must be reduced accordingly in the EU member state in the territory of which the acquisition was made. [*Directive 2006/112/EC, Art 84*].

Taxable amount: importation of goods

[19.20] In respect of the importation of goods, the taxable amount is the value for customs purposes, determined in accordance with the EU provisions in force. [*Directive 2006/112/EC, Art 85*].

The taxable amount includes, in so far as they are not already included,

- taxes, duties, levies and other charges due outside the EU member state of importation, and those due by reason of importation, excluding the VAT to be levied; and
- incidental expenses, such as commission, packing, transport and insurance costs, incurred up to the 'first place of destination' within the territory of the EU member state of importation, as well as those resulting from transport to another place of destination within the EU, if that other place is known when the chargeable event occurs.

'*First place of destination*' means the place mentioned on the consignment note, etc. or, if no such mention is made, the first place of destination is deemed to be the place of the first transfer of cargo in the EU member state of importation.

[*Directive 2006/112/EC, Art 86*].

The taxable amount does not include

- price reductions by way of discount for early payment; or
- price discounts and rebates granted to the customer and obtained by him at the time of importation.

[*Directive 2006/112/EC, Art 87*].

Where goods temporarily exported from the EU are reimported after having undergone, outside the EU, repair, processing, adaptation, making up or re-working, countries must take steps to ensure that the tax treatment of the goods for VAT purposes is the same as that which would have been applied had the repair, processing, adaptation, making up or re-working been carried out within their territory. [*Directive 2006/112/EC, Art 88*].

Works of art, etc.

Countries which, at 1 January 1993, were not applying a reduced rate may provide that in respect of the importation of works of art, collectors' items and antiques the taxable amount is to be equal to a fraction (at least 5%) of the otherwise taxable amount. [*Directive 2006/112/EC, Art 89*].

See **72.15 VALUATION** for UK the provisions.

Taxable amount: miscellaneous provisions

[19.21] Miscellaneous provisions are outlined below.

(a) In case of *cancellation, refusal or total or partial non-payment*, or where the price is reduced after the supply takes place, the taxable amount must be reduced accordingly under conditions determined by each EU member state although, in the case of total or partial non-payment, countries may derogate from this rule.

(b) Where information for determining the taxable amount is expressed in *foreign currency*,
- for importations, the exchange rate must be determined in accordance with EU provisions governing the calculation of the value for customs purposes; and
- the exchange rate applicable for transactions other than importations is the latest selling rate recorded, at the time the VAT becomes chargeable, on the most representative exchange market or markets of the EU member state concerned.

EU member states shall accept instead the use of the latest exchange rate published by the European Central Bank at the time the tax becomes chargeable. Conversion between currencies other than the euro shall be made by using the euro exchange rate of each currency. EU member states may require that they be notified of the exercise of this option by the taxable person.

For certain transactions, countries can use the exchange rate determined in accordance with the EU provisions in force governing the calculation of the value for Customs purposes.

See **72.18 VALUATION** for the UK provisions.

(c) As regards *returnable packing costs*, countries may either
- exclude them from the taxable amount and take the necessary measures to see that this amount is adjusted if the packing is not returned; or
- include them in the taxable amount and take the necessary measures to see that this amount is adjusted where the packaging is returned.

[*Directive 2006/112/EC, Arts 90–92*].

Rates

[19.22] The rate applicable to taxable transactions is that in force at the time of the chargeable event. However, in the following situations, the rate applicable is that in force when VAT becomes chargeable.

- In the cases referred to in *Arts 65* and *66* (see **19.16** above).
- Intra-EU acquisitions of goods.
- In the cases, concerning the importation of goods, referred to in *Art 71* (see **19.16** above).

[*Directive 2006/112/EC, Art 93*].

Intra-EU acquisitions and imports

The rate applicable to the intra-EU acquisition of goods is that applied to the supply of like goods within the territory of the EU member state. Subject to the option under *Art 103* of applying a reduced rate to the importation of works of art, etc. (see below) the rate applicable to the importation of goods is that applied to the supply of like goods within the territory of the EU member state. [*Directive 2006/112/EC, Art 94*].

Standard rate

Each EU member state must fix a standard rate which must be the same for goods and services. [*Directive 2006/112/EC, Art 96*]. The standard rate may not be less than 15% (this provision has recently been extended to 31 December 2017, even though no EU member state currently has a standard rate lower than 17%). [*Directive 2006/112/EC, Art 97*].

Reduced rates

Countries may apply either one or two reduced rates (which cannot be less than 5%). They can only apply to selected categories of goods and services comprising

- foodstuffs;
- supply of water;
- pharmaceutical products, medical equipment and aids for the disabled;
- children's car seats;
- transport of passengers and their accompanying luggage;
- supply of books and other printed matter;
- admission to shows, theatres, circuses, fairs, amusement parks, concerts, museums, zoos, cinemas, exhibitions and similar cultural events and facilities;
- reception of radio and television broadcasting services;
- supply of services by writers, composers and performing artists, or of the royalties due to them;
- housing supplies as part of a social policy;
- renovation and repairing of private dwellings, excluding materials which account for a significant part of the value of the service supplied;
- window cleaning and cleaning in private households;
- supply normally intended for use in agricultural production (excluding capital goods);
- accommodation in hotels and similar establishments, including holiday accommodation and the letting of places on camping or caravan sites;
- admission to sporting events and use of sporting facilities;
- restaurant and catering facilities, if it is possible to exclude the supply of beverages;
- supply of goods and services by organisations recognised as being devoted to social well-being;
- supply by undertakers and cremation services;
- medical and dental care;
- street cleaning, refuse collection and waste treatment;
- minor repairing of bicycles, shoes and leather goods, clothing and household linen;

- domestic care services such as home help and care of young, elderly, sick or disabled;
- hairdressing;
- supplies of natural gas, electricity or district heating (after consultation of the VAT Committee);
- the importation of works of art, collectors' items and antiques and, provided the reduced rate is applied to such imports, the supply of works of art, etc.
  - (i) by their creator or his successors in title; and
  - (ii) on an occasional basis, by a taxable person other than a taxable dealer, where the works of art have been imported by the taxable person himself, or where they have been supplied to him by their creator or his successors in title, or where they have entitled him to full deduction of VAT.

[*Directive 2006/112/EC, Arts 98, 102, 103, Annex III*].

Transitional provisions

During a transitional period until a definite VAT system is decided upon, exemptions with refund of VAT paid at the preceding stage (i.e. zero-rating in the UK) may be maintained provided they were in force on 1 January 1991 and were in accordance with EU law. [*Directive 2006/112/EC, Art 110*].

Exemptions

[19.23] EU member states must exempt certain activities under conditions that they lay down for the purpose of ensuring the correct and straightforward application of those exemptions and of preventing any possible evasion, avoidance or abuse. [*Directive 2006/112/EC, Art 131*]. These are divided into

- exemptions for certain activities in the public interest (see **19.24** below);
- exemption for other activities (see **19.25** below);
- exemptions for intra-EU transactions (see **19.26** below);
- exemptions on importation (see **19.27** below);
- exemptions on exportation (see **19.28** below);
- exemptions related to international transport (see **19.29** below);
- exemptions relating to certain transactions treated as exports (see **19.30** below);
- exemptions for the supply of services by intermediaries (see **19.31** below); and
- exemption for transactions related to international trade (see **19.32** below).

Exemptions for certain activities in the public interest

[19.24] The following activities should be exempt.

(a) The supply by the public postal service of services other than passenger transport and telecommunications services, and the supply of goods incidental thereto. In *R (oao TNT Post UK Ltd) v HMRC, ECJ Case C–357/07* [2009] STC 1438 (TVC 22.302), the CJEU held that 'public postal services' must be interpreted as including operators, whether they are public or private, who undertake to provide, in an EU member state, all or part of the universal postal service. The exemption only applies to the services that Royal Mail supplies in its capacity as universal service provider (i.e. its services available to the public at the standardised rates). It does not extend to services that the Royal Mail supplies under contracts individually negotiated with customers to meet their specific needs.

(b) Hospital and medical care and closely related activities undertaken by bodies governed by public law or, under social conditions comparable to those applicable to bodies governed by public law, by hospitals, centres for medical treatment or diagnosis and other duly recognised establishments of a similar nature. See *Future Health Technologies Ltd v HMRC, ECJ Case C–86/09* [2010] STC 1836 (TVC 20.105) for the CJEU's interpretation of 'hospital and medical care' and 'closely related activities'.

(c) The provision of medical care in the exercise of the medical or paramedical professions as defined by the country concerned. See *Future Health Technologies Ltd v HMRC, ECJ Case C–86/09* [2010] STC 1836 (TVC 20.105) for the CJEU's interpretation of 'provision of medical care'.

(d) Supplies of human organs, blood and milk. See CJEU decision in *TMD Gesellschaft für transfusionsmedizinische Dienste mbH v Finanzamt Kassel II – Hofgeismar, ECJ Case C-412/15* (TVC 20.110), where the Court held that the exemption could not extend to supplies of blood plasma that was used to manufacture medicinal products as it was not used directly for any therapeutic or healthcare purpose.

(e) Services supplied by dental technicians in their professional capacity and dental prostheses supplied by dentists and dental technicians.

(f) Services supplied by independent groups of persons whose activities are exempt from or not subject to VAT, for the purpose of rendering their members the services directly necessary for the exercise of their activity, where these groups merely claim from their members exact reimbursement of their share of joint expenses, provided that such exemption is not likely to produce distortion of competition. This covers services supplied by independent groups to their members even if those services were supplied to only one or several of those members (*Stichting Centraal Begeleidingsorgaan voor de Intercollegiale Toetsing v Staatssecretaris van Financien, ECJ Case C–407/07*, [2009] STC 869 (TVC 22.325)).

(g) The supply of services and of goods closely linked to welfare and social security work, including those supplied by old people's homes, by bodies governed by public law or by other organisations recognised as being devoted to social well-being. The expression 'social welfare' means the well-being (whether in the physical, mental or material sense) of individuals as members of society. The provision of benefits which tends directly to improve the health or conditions of life of individuals comes *prima facie* within the expression 'social welfare' (*Yoga for*

Health Foundation v C & E Commrs, QB [1984] STC 630 (TVC 22.326)). 'Spiritual welfare' is also included (*International Bible Students' Association v C & E Commrs*, QB 1987, [1988] STC 412 (TVC 22.327)).

In *Bulthuis-Griffioen v Inspector der Omzetbelasting, ECJ Case C–453/93*, [1995] STC 954 (TVC 22.330) the CJEU held that this exemption was only available to 'bodies governed by public law or other organisations' and did not apply to sole proprietors. This decision was not followed in *J & M Gregg v C & E Commrs, ECJ Case C–216/97*, [1999] STC 934 (TVC 22.331) where the CJEU held that the provisions were sufficiently broad to include natural persons as well.

(h) The supply of services and of goods closely linked to the protection of children and young persons by bodies governed by public law or by other organisations recognised as being devoted to social well-being.

(i) Children's or young people's education, school or university education, vocational training or retraining, including the supply of services and of goods closely related thereto, provided by bodies governed by public law having such as their aim or by other organisations defined by the country concerned as having similar objects. Exemption does not extend to the undertaking by State universities of research projects for consideration as this cannot be regarded as an activity closely related to university education (*EC Commission v Federal Republic of Germany, ECJ Case C–287/00*, [2002] STC 982 (TVC 22.338)).

(j) Tuition given privately by teachers and covering school or university education.

(k) Certain supplies of staff by religious or philosophical institutions for the purposes of (*b*), (*g*), (*h*) or (*i*) above and with a view to spiritual welfare.

(l) The supply of services and goods closely linked thereto for the benefit of their members in return for a subscription fixed in accordance with their rules by non-profit-making organisations with aims of a political, trade union, religious, patriotic, philosophical, philanthropic or civic nature, provided that this exemption is not likely to cause distortion of competition.

(m) Certain services closely linked to sport or physical education supplied by non-profit-making organisations to persons taking part in sport or physical education.

(n) Certain cultural services and goods closely linked thereto supplied by bodies governed by public law or by other cultural bodies recognised by the country concerned. The expression 'other cultural bodies' does not exclude soloists performing individually (*Hoffmann, ECJ Case C–144/00*, [2004] STC 740 (TVC 22.354)).

(o) The supply of services and goods by organisations whose activities are exempt under (*b*), (*g*), (*h*), (*i*), (*l*), (*m*) and (*n*) above in connection with fund-raising events organised exclusively for their own benefit provided that exemption is not likely to cause distortion of competition. Countries may introduce any necessary restrictions in particular as regards the number of events or the amount of receipts which give entitlement to exemption.

(p) The supply of transport services for sick or injured persons in vehicles specially designed for the purpose by duly authorised bodies.

(q) Activities of public radio and television bodies other than those of a commercial nature.

The supply of goods and services under (*b*), (*g*), (*h*), (*i*), (*l*), (*m*) and (*n*) above is not exempt if

- it is not essential to the transaction exempted; or
- its basic purpose is to obtain additional income for the organisation by carrying out transactions which are in direct competition with those of commercial enterprises liable for VAT.

Countries may make the granting to bodies other than those governed by public law of exemption under (*b*), (*g*), (*h*), (*i*), (*l*), (*m*) and (*n*) above subject to one or more of the following conditions.

(i) They do not systematically aim to make profit. Any surplus arising must not be distributed but assigned to the continuance or improvement of the services supplied.

(ii) They must be managed and administered on an essentially voluntary basis by persons who have no direct or indirect interest in the results of the activities concerned. See *C & E Commrs v Zoological Society of London*, *ECJ Case C–267/00*, [2002] STC 521 (TVC 22.359).

(iii) They charge prices approved by the public authorities or which do not exceed such approved prices or, in respect of those services not subject to approval, prices lower than those charged for similar services by commercial enterprises subject to VAT.

(iv) Exemption of the service concerned must not be likely to create distortions of competition such as to place at a disadvantage commercial enterprises liable to VAT.

[*Directive 2006/112/EC, Arts 132–134*].

Exemption of other activities

[19.25] Countries must exempt the following transactions.

(a) Insurance and reinsurance transactions, including related services performed by insurance brokers and agents.

(b) The granting and the negotiation of credit and the management of credit by the person granting it.

(c) The negotiation of, or any dealings in, credit guarantees or any other security for money and the management of credit guarantees by the person who is granting the credit.

(d) Transactions, including negotiations, concerning deposit and current accounts, payments, transfers, debts, cheques and other negotiable instruments, but excluding debt collecting and factoring.

(e) Transactions, including negotiations, concerning currency, bank notes and coins used as legal tender, with the exception of collectors' items.

(f) Transactions, including negotiations but excluding management and safekeeping, in shares, interests in companies or associations, debentures and other securities, excluding documents establishing title to goods.

(g) Management of special investment funds as defined by countries.

(h) The supply at face value of postage stamps valid for use for postal services within the territory of the country, fiscal stamps and similar stamps.

(i) Betting, lottery and other forms of gambling, subject to conditions and limitations laid down by each country.

(j) The supply of buildings or parts thereof, and of land on which they stand, other than the supply before first occupation.

(k) The supply of land which has not been built on other than building land as defined by each country.

(l) The leasing or letting of immovable property other than

- the provision of accommodation in the hotel or similar sectors, including holiday camps and camping sites;
- the letting of premises and sites for parking vehicles;
- letting of permanently installed equipment and machinery; and
- hire of safes.

The letting of a building constructed from prefabricated components fixed to or in the ground in such a way that they cannot be either dismantled or easily moved constitutes a letting of immovable property, even if the building was to be removed at the end of the lease and reused on another site (*Maierhofer v Finanzamt Augsburg-Land, ECJ Case C–315/00*, [2003] STC 564 (TVC 22.376)).

The letting of a football stadium under a contract reserving certain rights and prerogatives to the stadium owner and providing for the supply, by the owner, of various services, including services of maintenance, cleaning, repair and upgrading, representing 80% of the charge which is agreed in the contract to be payable, does not constitute, as a general rule, letting of immovable property for VAT purposes (*Régie Communale Autonome du Stade Luc Varenne v État Belge, ECJ Case C-55/14, 22 January 2015 unreported* (TVC 22.390)).

(m) Supplies of goods

- used wholly for an activity exempted by **19.24**(*a*)–(*q*) above, (*a*)–(*l*) above or by an EU member state under a derogation if these goods have not given rise to deductibility; or
- on the acquisition or application of which VAT was not deductible.

For a consideration of the scope of (*d*) and (*e*) above see *Sparekassernes Datacenter (SDC) v Skatteministeriet, ECJ Case C–2/95*, [1997] STC 932 (TVC 22.400). See also *Paymex Ltd* (TC01210) (TVC 20.137) with regard to the inclusion of insolvency practitioners' services within (*d*). Electronic messaging services do not fall within (*d*) and (*f*) above (see *Nordea Pankki Suomi Oyj v Finland, ECJ Case C–350/10*, [2011] STC 1956 (TVC 22.408)). See also *Bookit Ltd v HMRC, ECJ Case C-607/14*, [2016] All ER (D) 78 (Jun) and *HMRC v National Exhibition Centre Ltd, ECJ Case C-130/15*, [2016] All ER (D) 69 (Jun) for further consideration of the scope of 'transactions concerning payments' (see **24.28 FINANCIAL SERVICES**).

Countries may allow taxable persons a right of option to tax in cases of

- the financial transactions in (*b*)–(*g*) above;

- the supply of a building or of parts thereof, and of the land on which the building stands, other than the supply before first occupation;
- the supply of land which has not been built on other than the supply of building land; and
- the leasing or letting of immovable property.

[*Directive 2006/112/EC, Arts 135–137*].

Exemption for intra-EU transactions

[19.26] Exemptions for intra-EU transactions are listed below.

(1) Exemptions related to the supply of goods

Countries must exempt the following transactions.

(a) Supplies of goods dispatched or transported to a destination outside their own territory but within the EU, by or on behalf of the vendor or the person acquiring the goods, for another taxable person or a non-taxable legal person acting as such in an EU member state other than that in which dispatch or transport of the goods began. This exemption does not apply to
   - supplies of goods carried out by taxable persons who are covered for the exemption for small enterprises provided for in *Arts 282–292* (see **19.41**(2) below);
   - supplies of goods to taxable persons or non-taxable legal persons whose intra-EU acquisitions of goods are not subject to VAT under *Art 3* (see **19.6** above);
   - the supply of goods subject to VAT in accordance with the margin scheme provided for in *Arts 312–325* (see **19.41**(5) below) or the special arrangements for sales by public auction; or
   - the supply of second-hand means of transport, subject to VAT in accordance with the transitional arrangements for second-hand means of transport.

(b) Supplies of new means of transport, dispatched or transported to the customer at a destination outside their own territory but within the EU, by or on behalf of the vendor or the customer, for taxable persons or non-taxable legal persons whose intra-EU acquisitions of goods are not subject to VAT under *Art 3* (see **19.6** above), or for any other non-taxable person.

(c) Supplies of products subject to excise duty, dispatched or transported to a destination outside their own territory but within the EU, to the customer, by or on behalf of the vendor or the customer, for taxable persons or non-taxable legal persons whose intra-EU acquisitions of goods other than products subject to excise duty are not subject to VAT under *Art 3* (see **19.6** above). This does not, however, apply to
   - the supply of products subject to excise duty by taxable persons who are covered by the exemption for small enterprises provided for in *Arts 282–292* (see **19.41**(2) below); or
   - the supply of goods subject to VAT in accordance with the margin scheme provided for in *Arts 312–325* (see **19.41**(5) below) or the special arrangements for sales by public auction.

(d) The supply of goods, consisting in a transfer to another EU member state, which would have been entitled to exemption under (*a*) to (*c*) above if it had been made on behalf of another taxable person. This does not, however, apply to
   - the supply of goods subject to VAT in accordance with the margin scheme provided for in *Arts 312–325* (see **19.41**(5) below) or the special arrangements for sales by public auction; or
   - the supply of second-hand means of transport, subject to VAT in accordance with the transitional arrangements for second-hand means of transport.

[*Directive 2006/112/EC, Arts 138, 139*].

(2) Exemptions for intra-EU acquisitions of goods

Countries must exempt the following transactions.

- The intra-EU acquisition of goods the supply of which by taxable persons would in all circumstances be exempt within their respective territory.
- The intra-EU acquisition of goods the importation of which would in all circumstances be exempt under **19.27**(*a*), (*b*), (*c*) or (*e*) to (*m*) below.
- The intra-EU acquisition of goods where, pursuant to *Arts 170 and 171* (see **19.33** below) the person acquiring the goods would in all circumstances be entitled to full reimbursement of the VAT due under **19.6**(*b*) above.

[*Directive 2006/112/EC, Art 140*].

Each EU member state must also take specific measures to ensure that VAT is not charged on the intra-EU acquisition of goods within its territory where the following conditions are met.

(a) The acquisition of goods is made by a taxable person (A) who is not established in the EU member state concerned but is identified for VAT purposes in another EU member state.
(b) The acquisition of goods is made for the purposes of the subsequent supply of those goods, in the EU member state concerned, by A.
(c) The goods thus acquired by A are directly dispatched or transported, from an EU member state other than that in which he is identified for VAT purposes, to the person for whom he is to carry out the subsequent supply (B).
(d) B is another taxable person, or a non-taxable legal person, who is identified for VAT purposes in the EU member state concerned.
(e) B has been designated in accordance with *Art 197* (see **19.38** below) as liable for payment of the VAT due on the supply carried out by A.

[*Directive 2006/112/EC, Art 141*].

(3) Exemptions for certain transport services

Countries must exempt the supply of intra-EU transport of goods to and from the islands making up the autonomous regions of the Azores and Madeira, as well as the supply of transport of goods between those islands.

[*Directive 2006/112/EC, Art 142*].

Exemptions on importation

[19.27] Countries must exempt the following transactions.

(a) The final importation of goods of which the supply by a taxable person would in all circumstances be exempt within their own territory.

(b) The final importation of goods governed by *Council Directives 69/169/EEC*, *83/181/EEC* and *2006/79/EC*.

(c) The final importation of goods, in free circulation from third territory forming part of the EU customs territory, which would be entitled to exemption under (*b*) above if they had been imported within the meaning of the first paragraph of *Art 30* (see **19.11** above).

(d) The importation of goods dispatched or transported from a third territory or a third country into an EU member state other than that in which the dispatch or transport of the goods ends, where the supply of such goods by the importer designated or recognised as liable for payment of VAT is exempt under *Art 138* (see **19.26**(1) above).

(e) The reimportation, by the person who exported them, of goods in the state in which they were exported, where those goods are exempt from customs duties.

(f) The importation, under diplomatic and consular arrangements, of goods which are exempt from customs duties.

(g) The importation of goods by the European Community, European Atomic Energy Community, the European Central Bank or the European Investment Bank, or by the bodies set up by the Communities to which the Protocol of 8 April 1965 on the privileges and immunities of the European Communities applies, within the limits and under the conditions of that Protocol and the agreements for its implementation or the headquarters agreements, in so far as it does not lead to distortion of competition.

(h) The importation of goods by international bodies (other than those referred to in (*g*)) recognised as such by the public authorities of the host EU member state, or by members of such bodies, within the limits and under the conditions laid down by the international conventions establishing the bodies or by headquarters agreements.

(i) The importation of goods, into EU member states party to the North Atlantic Treaty, by the armed forces of other EU member states party to that Treaty for the use of those forces or the civilian staff accompanying them or for supplying their messes or canteens where such forces take part in the common defence effort.

(j) The importation of goods by the armed forces of the UK stationed in the island of Cyprus pursuant to the *Treaty of Establishment concerning the Republic of Cyprus*, dated 16 August 1960, which are for the use of those forces or the civilian staff accompanying them or for supplying their messes or canteens.

(k) The importation into ports, by sea fishing undertakings, of their catches, unprocessed or after undergoing preservation for marketing but before being supplied.

(l) The importation of gold by central banks.

(m) The importation of gas through a natural gas system or any network connected to such a system or fed in from a vessel transporting gas into a natural gas system or any upstream pipeline network, of electricity or of heat or cooling energy through heating or cooling networks.

(n) The supply of services relating to the importation of goods where the value of such services is included in the taxable amount.

[*Directive 2006/112/EC, Arts 143, 144*].

Exemptions on exportation

[19.28] Countries must exempt the following.

(a) The supply of goods dispatched or transported to a destination outside the EU
- by or on behalf of the vendor, or
- by or on behalf of a customer not established in the country (except for goods transported by the customer himself for equipping, fuelling, etc. pleasure boats and private aircraft or any other means of transport for private use). In the case of a supply of goods to be carried in the personal luggage of travellers, this exemption applies on condition that the traveller is not established within the EU; the goods are transported to a destination outside the EU before the end of the third month following that in which the supply takes place; and the total value of the supply (including VAT) is more than the equivalent of 175 euro in national currency (countries may exempt supplies with lower values).

(b) Goods supplied to approved bodies which export them from the EU as part of their humanitarian, charitable or teaching activities outside the EU.

(c) The supply of services consisting of work on movable property acquired or imported for the purpose of undergoing such work in the EU and dispatched or transported out of the EU by the supplier, by the customer if established outside the country or on behalf of either of them.

(d) The supply of services including transport and ancillary transactions (but excluding the supply of services exempted under **19.24** and **19.25** above) where these are directly linked with the export of goods or the import of goods covered by *Art 61* (see **19.15** above) or *Art 157(1)(a)* (importation of goods intended to be placed under warehousing arrangements other than customs warehousing).

[*Directive 2006/112/EC, Arts 146, 147*].

Exemptions related to international transport

[19.29] Countries must exempt the following transactions.

(a) The supply of goods for the fuelling and provisioning of
- vessels used for navigation at sea and carrying passengers for reward or used for the purposes of commercial, industrial or fishing activities;

- vessels used for rescue or assistance at sea;
- vessels used for inshore fishing (but not ship's provisions); or
- vessels of war leaving the country and bound for foreign ports or anchorages.

(b) The supply, modification, repair, maintenance, chartering and hiring of vessels within (*a*) above or aircraft used by airlines operating for reward chiefly on international routes and the supply, hiring, repair and maintenance of equipment (including fishing equipment) incorporated or used therein.

(c) The supply of goods for the fuelling and provisioning of aircraft within (*b*) above.

(d) The supply of services other than those referred to in (*b*) above to meet the direct needs of sea-going vessels or aircraft referred to in (*b*) above or of their cargoes.

[*Directive 2006/112/EC, Art 148*].

Exemptions relating to certain transactions treated as exports

[19.30] Countries must exempt the following transactions.

(a) The supply of goods or services under diplomatic and consular arrangements.

(b) The supply of goods or services to the European Community, European Atomic Energy Community, the European Central Bank or the European Investment Bank, or by the bodies set up by the Communities to which the Protocol of 8 April 1965 on the privileges and immunities of the European Communities applies, within the limits and under the conditions of that Protocol and the agreements for its implementation or the headquarters agreements, in so far as it does not lead to distortion of competition.

(c) The supply of goods or services to international bodies (other than those referred to in (*b*)) recognised as such by the public authorities of the host EU member state, and to members of such bodies, within the limits and under the conditions laid down by the international conventions establishing the bodies or by headquarters agreements.

(d) The supply of goods or services within an EU member state which is a party to the North Atlantic Treaty, intended either for the armed forces of other countries party to that Treaty for the use of those forces, or of the civilian staff accompanying them, or for supplying their messes or canteens when such forces take part in the common defence effort. See *HMRC v Able UK Ltd, ECJ Case C–225/11*, [2013] STC 1550 (TVC 20.171).

(e) The supply of goods or services to another EU member state, intended for the armed forces of any State which is a party to the North Atlantic Treaty, other than the EU member state of destination itself, for the use of those forces, or of the civilian staff accompanying them, or for supplying their messes or canteens when such forces take part in the common defence effort.

(f) The supply of goods or services to the armed forces of the UK stationed in Cyprus pursuant to the *Treaty of Establishment concerning the Republic of Cyprus*, dated 16 August 1960, which are for the use of those forces, or of the civilian staff accompanying them, or for supplying their messes or canteens.

Under (*a*)–(*f*) above, where the goods are not dispatched or transported out of the EU member state in which the supply takes place, and in the case of services, the exemption may be granted by means of a refund of the VAT.

Countries must also exempt the supply of gold to central banks.

[*Directive 2006/112/EC, Arts 151, 152*].

Exemptions for the supply of services by intermediaries

[19.31] Countries must exempt the supply of services by intermediaries, acting in the name and on behalf of another person, where they take part in the transactions referred to in **19.28–19.30** above or transactions carried out outside the EU. This exemption does not apply to travel agents who, in the name and on behalf of travellers, supply services which are carried out in other EU member states. [*Directive 2006/112/EC, Art 153*].

Exemptions for transactions relating to international trade

[19.32] Countries may take special measures designed to exempt all or some of the following transactions, provided that those measures are not aimed at final use or consumption and that the amount of VAT due on cessation of the arrangements or situations corresponds to the amount of tax which would have been due had each of those transactions been taxed within their territory. [*Directive 2006/112/EC, Art 155*].

(a) The supply of goods which are intended to be
  (i) presented to customs and, where applicable, placed in temporary storage;
  (ii) placed in a free zone or in a free warehouse;
  (iii) placed under customs warehousing arrangements or inward processing arrangements;
  (iv) admitted into territorial waters in order to be incorporated into drilling or production platforms, for purposes of the construction, repair, maintenance, alteration or fitting-out of such platforms, or to link such drilling or production platforms to the mainland; or
  (v) admitted into territorial waters for the fuelling and provisioning of drilling or production platforms.

(b) The importation of goods which are intended to be placed under warehousing arrangements other than customs warehousing.

(c) The supply of goods which are intended to be placed under warehousing arrangements other than customs warehousing. But countries may not apply exemption in such a way for goods which are not subject to excise duty where those goods are intended to be supplied at the retail stage unless, by derogation, the goods are intended for

- (i) tax-free shops, for the purposes of the supply of goods to be carried in the personal luggage of travellers taking flights or sea crossings outside the VAT territory of the EU where that supply is exempt under **19.28**(*a*) above;
- (ii) taxable persons, for the purposes of carrying out supplies to travellers on board an aircraft or a ship in the course of a flight or sea crossing where the place of arrival is situated outside the EU; or
- (iii) taxable persons, for the purposes of carrying out supplies which are exempt from VAT under **19.30**(*a*)–(*f*) above.

(d) The supply of services relating to the supply of goods under (*a*) or (*c*) above.

(e) The supply of goods or services carried out in the locations referred to in (*a*) or (*c*) above where one of the situations specified therein still applies within their territory.

(f) The supply of goods (and related services) while they remain covered by arrangements for temporary importation with total exemption from import duty or by external transit arrangements.

(g) The supply of goods imported from a territory within **18.2 EUROPEAN UNION: GENERAL** while they remain covered by the internal Union transit procedure.

Where countries exercise the option to exempt under the above provisions, they must take the measures necessary to ensure that the intra-EU acquisition of goods intended to be placed under one of the arrangements or in one of the situations under (*a*) or (*c*) above is covered by the same provisions as the supply of goods carried out within their country under the same conditions.

If the goods cease to be covered by the arrangements or situations referred to above (thus giving rise to an importation for the purposes of **19.15** above), the EU member state of importation must take the measures necessary to prevent double taxation.

[*Directive 2006/112/EC, Arts 156–163*].

Re-exportations

Countries may exempt the following transactions carried out by, or intended for, a taxable person up to an amount equal to the value of the exports carried out by that person during the preceding twelve months.

- Intra-EU acquisitions of goods made by the taxable person, and imports for and supplies of goods to the taxable person, with a view to their exportation from the EU as they are or after processing.
- Supplies of services linked with the export business of the taxable person.

Where countries exercise this option of exemption, they must apply that exemption also to transactions relating to supplies carried out by the taxable person, in accordance with the conditions under **19.26**(1) above, up to an amount equal to the value of the supplies carried out by that person, in accordance with the same conditions, during the preceding twelve months.

[*Directive 2006/112/EC, Art 164*].

Deductions

[19.33] The right of deduction arises at the time the deductible VAT becomes chargeable. [*Directive 2006/112/EC, Art 167*].

EU member states may provide within an optional scheme that the right of deduction of a taxable person whose VAT solely becomes chargeable in accordance with *Art 66(b)* (see **19.16**(1) above) be postponed until the VAT on the goods or services supplied to him has been paid to his supplier. EU member states that apply the optional scheme shall set a threshold for taxable persons using the scheme within their territory, based on the annual turnover of the taxable person calculated in accordance with *Art 288* (see **19.41**(2) below). That threshold may not be higher than €500,000 or the equivalent in national currency. EU member states may increase that threshold up to €2,000,000 or the equivalent in national currency after consulting with the VAT Committee. However, because the UK had a cash accounting threshold of £1,350,000 at 31 December 2012, no such consultation was necessary. [*Directive 2006/112/EC, Art 167a*].

To the extent that goods and services are used for the purposes of the taxed transactions of a taxable person, the taxable person is entitled, in the EU member state in which he carries out these transactions, to deduct the following from the VAT which he is liable to pay.

(a) VAT due or paid in that EU member state in respect of supplies to him of goods or services, carried out or to be carried out by another taxable person.
(b) VAT due in respect of transactions treated as supplies of goods or services under the self-supply rules.
(c) VAT due in respect of intra-EU acquisitions of goods.
(d) VAT due on transactions treated as intra-EU acquisitions in accordance with *Arts 21* and *22* (see **19.9** above).
(e) VAT due or paid in respect of the importation of goods into that EU member state.

[*Directive 2006/112/EC, Art 168*].

In the case of immovable property forming part of the business assets of a taxable person and used both for the purposes of the business and for his private use or that of his staff, or, more generally, for purposes other than those of his business, VAT on expenditure related to this property shall be deductible in accordance with the principles set out in *Arts 167, 168, 169* and *173* only up to the proportion of the property's use for business purposes.

By way of derogation from *Art 26* (see **19.10** above), changes in the proportion of use of immovable property are to be taken into account in accordance with the principles provided for in A*rts 184–192* as applied the respective EU member state (see **19.37** below).

EU member states may also apply this provision in relation to VAT on expenditure related to other goods forming part of the business assets as they specify.

[*Directive 2006/112/EC, Art 168a*].

The taxable person is also entitled to deduct the VAT referred to in so far as the goods and services are used for the following purposes following.

- Transactions relating to economic activities carried out outside the EU member state in which that VAT is due or paid, in respect of which VAT would be deductible if the transactions had been carried out within that EU member state.
- Transactions which are exempt under **19.26**(1)(3), **19.27**(*n*), **19.28–19.31**, **19.32** (other than **19.32**(*b*)) above.
- Transactions which are exempt under **19.5**(*a*)–(*f*) above where the customer is established outside the EU or where those transactions relate directly to goods to be exported from the EU.

[*Directive 2006/112/EC, Art 169*].

See **35.1–35.3 INPUT TAX** for the UK provisions.

All taxable persons who are not established in the EU member state in which they purchase goods and services or import goods subject to VAT are entitled to obtain a refund of that VAT in so far as the goods and services are used for the purposes of transactions

- within *Art 169* above; or
- for which the VAT is solely payable by the customer in accordance with *Arts 194–197* or *Art 199* (see **19.38** below).

Where the taxable person is established in another EU member state, the VAT is refunded under Directive 2008/9/EC (see **19.43** below) and where the taxable person is not established in the EU, the VAT is refunded under the *13th Directive* (see **19.44** below).

[*Directive 2006/112/EC, Arts 170, 171*].

New means of transport

Any person who is regarded as a taxable person by reason of the fact that he supplies, on an occasional basis, a new means of transport is, in the EU member state in which the supply takes place, entitled to deduct the VAT included in the purchase price or paid in respect of the importation or the intra-EU acquisition of this means of transport, up to an amount not exceeding the amount of VAT for which he would be liable if the supply were not exempt. A right of deduction arises and may be exercised only at the time of supply of the new means of transport. [*Directive 2006/112/EC, Art 172*].

Proportional deduction

[19.34] Where goods or services are used by a taxable person both for transactions in respect of which VAT is deductible under **19.33** above and for transactions in respect of which VAT is not deductible, only such proportion of the VAT as is attributable to the former transactions is deductible. This is determined by the formula

$$A \div B$$

where

A = the total amount, exclusive of VAT, of turnover per year attributable to transactions in respect of which VAT is deductible; and

B = the total amount, exclusive of VAT, of turnover per year attributable to transactions within A and transactions in respect of which VAT is not deductible.

The proportions must be determined on an annual basis, fixed as a percentage and rounded up to a figure not exceeding the next whole number. The provisional proportion for a year is to be calculated on the basis of the preceding year's transactions. In the absence of any such transactions or where they were insignificant, the deductible proportion is to be estimated provisionally, under the supervision of the tax authorities, by the taxable person on the basis of his own forecasts. Deductions made on the basis of such provisional proportions must be adjusted when the final proportion is fixed during the following year.

By derogation, countries may exclude from the calculation supplies of capital goods, incidental real estate and financial transactions and incidental transactions within **19.25**(*b*)–(*g*) above.

Countries may, however, authorise or compel the taxable person to determine a proportion for each sector of his business and keep separate accounts for each sector or to make deductions on the basis of the use of the goods and services. Countries may also provide that where non-deductible VAT is insignificant it is treated as nil.

[*Directive 2006/112/EC, Arts 173–175*].

See **50 PARTIAL EXEMPTION** for the UK provisions.

Restrictions on the right of deduction

[19.35] The Council must determine the expenditure in respect of which VAT is not deductible. VAT must in no circumstances be deductible in respect of expenditure which is not strictly business expenditure, such as that on luxuries, amusements or entertainment.

Pending the entry into force of these provisions, countries may retain all the exclusions provided for under their national laws at 1 January 1979 (or, in the case of the countries which acceded to the EU after that date, on the date of their accession).

[*Directive 2006/112/EC, Art 176*].

Exercising of the right of deduction

[19.36] In order to exercise the right of deduction, a taxable person must for the purposes of deductions under

(a) **19.33**(*a*) hold a proper invoice;
(b) **19.33**(*b*) comply with the formalities as laid down by each EU member state;
(c) **19.33**(*c*) set out in the VAT return all the information needed for the amount of the VAT due on his intra-EU acquisitions of goods to be calculated and hold a proper invoice;
(d) **19.33**(*d*), complete the formalities as laid down by each EU member state; and
(e) **19.33**(*e*), hold an import document specifying him as consignee or importer, and stating the amount of VAT due or enabling that amount to be calculated.

When required to pay VAT as a customer where *Arts 194–197* or *Art 199* apply (see **19.38** below), he must comply with the formalities as laid down by each EU member state.

[*Directive 2006/112/EC, Art 178*].

The taxable person makes the deduction by subtracting from the total amount of VAT due for a given tax period the total amount of VAT in respect of which, during the same period, the right of deduction has arisen.

Countries may require that taxable persons who carry out occasional transactions exercise their right of deduction only at the time of supply.

[*Directive 2006/112/EC, Art 179*].

Where, for a given tax period, the amount of deductions exceeds the amount of VAT due, countries may, in accordance with conditions which they determine, either make a refund or carry the excess forward to the following period. [*Directive 2006/112/EC, Art 183*].

Adjustment of deductions

[19.37] The initial deduction must be adjusted where it is higher or lower than that to which the taxable person was entitled. [*Directive 2006/112/EC, Art 184*]. Adjustment must, in particular, be made where, after the VAT return is made, some change occurs in the factors used to determine the amount to be deducted (e.g. where purchases are cancelled or price reductions are obtained). [*Directive 2006/112/EC, Art 185*].

Capital goods

In the case of capital goods, adjustments must be spread over five years including that in which the goods were acquired or manufactured. By derogation the period may commence from the time the goods are first used. The annual adjustment must be made only in respect of one-fifth of the VAT charged on the goods and must be made on the basis of the variations in the deduction entitlement in subsequent years in relation to that for the year in which the goods were acquired or manufactured (or, where applicable, used for the first time).

In the case of immovable property, the adjustment period may be extended to up to 20 years.

Where capital goods are supplied during the period of adjustment, they are treated as if they had still been applied to an economic use of the taxable person until the expiry of the period of adjustment. Such economic activity is presumed to be fully taxed in cases where the supply of the goods is taxed and fully exempt where the supply is exempt. The adjustment is made only once for the whole period of adjustment still to be covered.

[*Directive 2006/112/EC, Arts 187, 188*].

See **11 CAPITAL GOODS SCHEME** for the UK provisions.

Persons liable for payment of VAT

[19.38] The person liable to pay the VAT is as follows.

(a) Any taxable person carrying out a taxable supply of goods or services, except where the VAT is payable by another person in the cases referred to in (*b*)–(*g*) and (*j*) below. [*Directive 2006/112/EC, Art 193*].

(b) Where the taxable supply of goods or services is carried out by a taxable person not established in the EU member state in which the VAT is due, that country may provide that the person liable for payment of the VAT is the person for whom the goods or services are supplied. [*Directive 2006/112/EC, Art 194*].

(c) VAT is payable by any person who is identified for VAT purposes in the EU member state in which the tax is due and to whom goods are supplied in the circumstances under **19.12**(4) above, if the supplies are carried out by a taxable person not established within that country. [*Directive 2006/112/EC, Art 195*].

(d) VAT is payable by

- any taxable person to whom the services referred to in *Art 56* are supplied, or
- any person identified for VAT purposes in the EU member state in which the tax is due to whom the services referred to in *Arts 44, 47, 50, 53, 54* and *55* are supplied,

if the services are supplied by a taxable person not established in that EU member state.

In *Kollektivavtalsstiftelsen TRR Trygghetsrådet v Skatteverket, ECJ Case C–291/07*, [2008] All ER (D) 71 (Nov) (TVC 20.57), the CJEU ruled that *Art 56(1)(c)* must be interpreted as meaning that where consultancy services are supplied to the customer by a taxable person established in another EU member state, and the customer carries out both an economic activity and an activity which falls outside the scope of the directive, that customer is to be regarded as a taxable person even where the supply is used solely for the purposes of the latter activity.

(e) VAT shall be payable by any taxable person, or non-taxable legal person identified for VAT purposes, to whom the services referred to in *Art 44* (see **19.14** above) are supplied, if the services are supplied by a taxable person not established within the territory of the EU member state.

[*Directive 2006/112/EC, Art 196*].

(f) The person to whom the goods are supplied where

- the taxable transaction is a supply of goods carried out in accordance with the conditions in *Art 141* (see **19.26**(2) above);
- the person to whom the goods are supplied is another taxable person, or a non-taxable legal person, identified for VAT purposes in the EU member state in which the supply is carried out; and
- the invoice issued by the taxable person not established in the EU member state in question conforms to the requirements in *Arts 219a–237* (see **19.40**(2)–(4) below).

A country may, however, provide for a derogation from this obligation where the non-established taxable person has appointed a tax representative in that country as the person liable for the tax.
[*Directive 2006/112/EC, Art 197*].

(g) Where specific transactions relating to investment gold between a taxable person who is a member of a regulated gold bullion market and another taxable person who is not a member of that market are taxed under *Art 352* (see **19.41**(6) below), countries must designate the customer as the person liable for payment of VAT.
If the customer is a taxable person required to be identified for VAT purposes in the EU member state in which the tax is due solely in respect of the transactions under *Art 352*, the vendor must fulfil the tax obligations on behalf of the customer, in accordance with the law of that country.
Where gold material or semi-manufactured products of a purity of 325 thousandths or greater or investment gold is supplied by a taxable person exercising one of the options under *Arts 348–350* (see **19.41**(6) below), countries may designate the customer as the person liable for payment of VAT.
[*Directive 2006/112/EC, Art 198*].

(h) Countries may provide that the person liable for payment of VAT is the taxable person to whom any of the following supplies are made.
 (i) The supply of construction work, including repair, cleaning, maintenance, alteration and demolition services in relation to immovable property, as well as the handing over of construction works regarded as a supply of goods.
 (ii) The supply of staff engaged in activities covered by (i) above.
 (iii) The supply of immovable property, as referred to in **19.25**(*j*) and (*k*) above, where the supplier has opted for taxation of the supply.
 (iv) The supply of used material, used material which cannot be re-used in the same state, scrap, industrial and non-industrial waste, recyclable waste, part processed waste and certain goods and services, as listed in *Directive 2006/112/EC, Annex VI*.
 (v) The supply of goods provided as security by one taxable person to another in execution of that security.
 (vi) The supply of goods following the cession of a reservation of ownership to an assignee and the exercising of this right by the assignee.
 (vii) The supply of immovable property sold by a judgment debtor in a compulsory sale procedure.

[*Directive 2006/112/EC, Art 199*].

(i) As a fraud prevention measure, countries may, until 31 December 2018 and for a minimum period of two years, provide that the person liable for payment of VAT is the taxable person to whom any of the following supplies are made.
   (i) The transfer of greenhouse gas emission allowances.
   (ii) The supply of mobile telephones.
   (iii) The supply of integrated circuit devices such as microprocessors.
   (iv) The supply of gas and electricity to a taxable dealer, and supplies of gas and electricity certificates.
   (v) The supply of telecommunications services as defined in *Art 24(2)*.
   (vi) The supply of game consoles, tablet PCs and laptops.
   (vii) The supply of cereals and industrial crops.
   (viii) The supply of raw and semi-finished metals.

   [*Directive 2006/112/EC, Art 199a*].

(j) VAT is payable by any person making a taxable intra-EU acquisition of goods. [*Directive 2006/112/EC, Art 200*].

(k) On importation, VAT is payable by any person or persons designated or recognised as liable by the EU member state of importation. [*Directive 2006/112/EC, Art 201*].

(l) VAT is payable by any person who causes goods to cease to be covered by the arrangements or situations listed in **19.32** above. [*Directive 2006/112/EC, Art 202*].

(m) VAT is payable by any person who enters the VAT on an invoice. [*Directive 2006/112/EC, Art 203*].

(n) Where, under (*a*)–(*e*), (*g*) and (*h*) above, the person liable for payment of VAT is a taxable person who is not established in the EU member state in which the VAT is due, countries may allow that person to appoint a tax representative as the person liable for payment of the VAT.

   Furthermore, where the taxable transaction is carried out by a taxable person who is not established in the EU member state in which the VAT is due and no legal instrument exists with the country in which that taxable person is established or has his seat, relating to mutual assistance similar in scope to that provided for in *Directive 2010/24/EU* (mutual assistance recovery directive, which replaces *Directive 2008/55/EC* with effect from 1 January 2012) and *Council Regulation (EU)904/2010* (on administrative co-operation and combating fraud in the field of VAT, which recasts and repeals *Council Regulation (EC)1798/2003* with effect from 1 January 2012), countries may take measures to provide that the person liable for payment of VAT is to be a tax representative appointed by the non-established taxable person. But countries may not apply this option to a non-established taxable person who has opted for the special scheme for electronically supplied services.

   [*Directive 2006/112/EC, Art 204*].

(o) In the situations referred to in (*a*)–(*h*) and (*j*)–(*l*) above, countries may provide that a person other than the person liable for payment of VAT is to be held jointly and severally liable for payment of VAT. [*Directive 2006/112/EC, Art 205*].

Payment arrangements

[19.39] Any taxable person liable for payment of VAT must pay the net amount of the VAT when submitting the VAT return. Countries may, however, set a different date for payment of that amount or may require interim payments to be made. [*Directive 2006/112/EC, Art 206*].

Obligations of taxable persons

[19.40] Taxable persons should be aware of the following obligations.

(1) Identification

Every taxable person must state when his activity as a taxable person commences, changes or ceases. Countries must allow, and may require, the statement to be made by electronic means, in accordance with conditions which they lay down.

Without prejudice to the above, every taxable person or non-taxable legal person who makes intra-EU acquisitions of goods which are not subject to VAT under **19.6**(i) and (ii) above must state that he makes such acquisitions if the conditions, laid down in that provision, for not making such transactions subject to VAT cease to be fulfilled.

[*Directive 2006/112/EC, Art 213*].

(2) Issue of invoices

Invoicing is subject to the rules applying in the EU member state in which the supply of goods or services is deemed to be made. By way of derogation, invoicing shall be subject to the rules applying in the EU member state in which the supplier has established his business or has a fixed establishment from which the supply is made or, in the absence of such place of establishment or fixed establishment, the EU member state where the supplier has his permanent address or usually resides, where

(a) the supplier is not established in the EU member state in which the supply of goods or services is deemed to be made, or his establishment in that country does not intervene in the supply within the meaning of *Art 192a*, and the person liable for the payment of the VAT is the person to whom the goods or services are supplied. However where the customer issues the invoice (self-billing), invoicing is subject to the rules applying in the EU member state in which the supply of goods or services is deemed to be made;

(b) the supply of goods or services is deemed not to be made within the Community.

[*Directive 2006/112/EC, Art 219a*].

Every taxable person must ensure that, in respect of the following, an invoice is issued, either by himself or by his customer or, in his name and on his behalf, by a third party.

(i) Supplies of goods or services which he has made to another taxable person or to a non-taxable legal person.
(ii) Supplies of goods as referred to in *Art 33* (see **19.12**(2) above).
(iii) Supplies of goods carried out in accordance with the conditions specified in **19.26**(1) above.
(iv) Any payment on account made to him before one of the supplies of goods referred to in (i)–(ii) above was carried out.
(v) Any payment on account made to him by another taxable person or non-taxable legal person before the provision of services was completed.

By way of derogation, the issue of an invoice shall not be required in respect of supplies of services exempted under *Art 135(1)(a)–(g)* (see **19.25** above).

[*Directive 2006/112/EC, Art 220*].

EU member states shall allow taxable persons to issue a simplified invoice where

(a) the amount of the invoice is not higher than €100 or the equivalent in national currency;
(b) the invoice issued is a document or message treated as an invoice pursuant to *Art 219*.

EU member states shall not allow taxable persons to issue a simplified invoice where invoices are required to be issued pursuant to points (2) and (3) of *Art 220(1)* or where the taxable supply of goods or services is carried out by a taxable person who is not established in the EU member state in which the VAT is due, or whose establishment in that country does not intervene in the supply within the meaning of *Art 192a*, and the person liable for the payment of VAT is the person to whom the goods or services are supplied.

[*Directive 2006/112/EC, Art 220a*].

EU member states may

- impose on taxable persons an obligation to issue an invoice in respect of supplies of goods or services, other than those referred to in *Art 220(1)*;
- impose on taxable persons who have established their business in the territory or who have a fixed establishment in their territory from which the supply is made, an obligation to issue an invoice in respect of supplies of services exempted under *Art 135(1)(a)–(g)* which those taxable persons have made in their territory or outside the Community;
- release taxable persons from the obligation to issue an invoice in certain cases in respect of supplies of goods or services which they have made in their territory and which are exempt.

For supplies of goods carried out in accordance with the conditions specified in *Art 138* or for supplies of services for which VAT is payable by the customer pursuant to *Art 196*, an invoice shall be issued no later than on the fifteenth day of the month following that in which the chargeable event occurs. For other supplies of goods or services EU member states may impose time limits on taxable persons for the issue of invoices.

[*Directive 2006/112/EC, Arts 221, 222*].

Self-billing

Invoices may be drawn up by the customer in respect of the supply to him, by a taxable person, of goods or services, if there is a prior agreement between the two parties and provided that a procedure exists for the acceptance of each invoice by the taxable person supplying the goods or services. EU member states may require that such invoices be issued in the name and on behalf of the taxable person. [*Directive 2006/112/EC, Art 224*].

See **40.6 INVOICES** for the UK provisions.

(3) Content of invoices

Without prejudice to the particular provisions laid down in the *Directive*, only the following details are required for VAT purposes on invoices.

- (1) The date of issue.
- (2) A sequential number, based on one or more series, which uniquely identifies the invoice.
- (3) The VAT identification number under which the taxable person supplied the goods or services.
- (4) The customer's VAT identification number referred to in *Art 214*, under which the customer received a supply of goods or services in respect of which he is liable for payment of VAT, or received a supply of goods as referred to in *Art 138* [see **19.26**(1) above].
- (5) The full name and address of the taxable person and of the customer.
- (6) The quantity and nature of the goods supplied or the extent and nature of the services rendered.
- (7) The date on which the supply of goods or services was made or completed or the date on which the payment on account referred to in points (4) and (5) of *Art 220* was made, in so far as that date can be determined and differs from the date of issue of the invoice.
- (7a) Where the VAT becomes chargeable at the time when the payment is received in accordance with *Art 66(b)* and the right of deduction arises at the time the deductible tax becomes chargeable, the mention 'cash accounting'.
- (8) The taxable amount per rate or exemption, the unit price exclusive of VAT and any discounts or rebates if they are not included in the unit price.
- (9) The VAT rate applied.
- (10) The VAT amount payable, except where a special arrangement is applied under which, in accordance with the *Directive*, such a detail is excluded.
- (10a) Where the customer receiving a supply issues the invoice instead of the supplier, the mention 'self-billing'.
- (11) In the case of an exemption, reference to the applicable provision of this Directive, or to the corresponding national provision, or any other reference indicating that the supply of goods or services is exempt.
- (11a) Where the customer is liable for the payment of the VAT, the mention 'reverse charge'.
- (12) In the case of the supply of a new means of transport, its identifying characteristics.
- (13) Where the margin scheme for travel agents is applied, the mention 'margin scheme—travel agents'.

(14) Where one of the special arrangements applicable to second-hand goods, works of art, collectors' items and antiques is applied, the mention 'margin scheme—second-hand goods'; 'margin scheme—works of art' or 'margin scheme—collector's items and antiques' respectively.

(15) Where the person liable for payment of VAT is a tax representative for the purposes of *Art 204*, the VAT identification number of that tax representative, together with his full name and address.

[*Directive 2006/112/EC, Art 226*].

See **40.3 INVOICES** for the UK provisions.

In *Barlis 06 – Investimentos Imobiliários e Turísticos SA v Autoridade Tributária e Aduaneira, ECJ Case C-516/14* (TVC 20.217), the CJEU held that an invoice for continuous services should specify the period over which the services were supplied; it should include both the start and the end of that period. This might render a vague invoice insufficient to justify an input tax deduction for the purchaser. However, asserting the fundamental right of a business to deduct input tax on supplies received by it, the court ruled that the tax authorities must take into account alternative evidence provided by the purchaser to support the deduction. If the substantive conditions for the claim can be shown to have existed, a defect in the paperwork (the 'formal conditions for deduction') should not cancel the trader's rights.

Where the invoice is issued by a taxable person, who is not established in the EU member state where the tax is due or whose establishment in that country does not intervene in the supply within the meaning of *Art 192a*, and who is making a supply of goods or services to a customer who is liable for payment of VAT, the taxable person may omit the details referred to in *Art 226(8)*, *(9)* and *(10)* above and instead indicate, by reference to the quantity or extent of the goods or services supplied and their nature, the taxable amount of those goods or services.

[*Directive 2006/112/EC, Art 226a*].

As regards simplified invoices issued pursuant to *Art 220a* and *Art 221(1)* and *(2)*, EU member states shall require at least the following details.

(a) The date of issue.
(b) Identification of the taxable person supplying the goods or services.
(c) Identification of the type of goods or services supplied.
(d) The VAT amount payable or the information needed to calculate it.
(e) Where the invoice issued is a document or message treated as an invoice pursuant to *Art 219*, specific and unambiguous reference to that initial invoice and the specific details which are being amended.

They may not require details on invoices other than those referred to in *Arts 226, 227* and *230*.

[*Directive 2006/112/EC, Art 226b*].

Tax authorities may also require the customer's VAT identification (see (1) above) to be indicated in other cases [*Directive 2006/112/EC, Art 227*]. They cannot require invoices to be signed [*Directive 2006/112/EC, Art 229*].

The amounts which appear on the invoice may be expressed in any currency, provided that the amount of VAT payable or to be adjusted is expressed in the national currency of the EU member state, using the conversion mechanism laid down in **19.21**(*b*) above. [*Directive 2006/112/EC, Art 230*].

(4) Sending invoices by electronic means

The use of an electronic invoice shall be subject to acceptance by the recipient. [*Directive 2006/112/EC, Art 232*].

The authenticity of the origin, the integrity of the content and the legibility of an invoice, whether on paper or in electronic form, shall be ensured from the point in time of issue until the end of the period for storage of the invoice. Each taxable person shall determine the way to ensure the authenticity of the origin, the integrity of the content and the legibility of the invoice. This may be achieved by any business controls which create a reliable audit trail between an invoice and a supply of goods or services. Other than by way of such business controls, examples of technologies that ensure the authenticity of the origin and the integrity of the content of an electronic invoice are

- an advanced electronic signature; or
- electronic data interchange (EDI) if the agreement relating to the exchange provides for the use of procedures guaranteeing the authenticity of the origin and integrity of the data.

[*Directive 2006/112/EC, Art 233*].

(5) Simplification of invoices

EU member states may, in accordance with conditions which they may lay down, provide that in the following cases only the information required pursuant to *Art 226b* shall be entered on invoices in respect of supplies of goods or services.

(a) Where the amount of the invoice is higher than €100 but not higher than €400, or the equivalent in national currency.

(b) Where commercial or administrative practice in the business sector concerned or the technical conditions under which the invoices are issued make it particularly difficult to comply with all the obligations referred to in *Art 226* or *Art 230*.

These simplified arrangements shall not be applied where invoices are required to be issued pursuant to points (2) and (3) of *Art 220(1)* or where the taxable supply of goods or services is carried out by a taxable person who is not established in the country in which the VAT is due or whose establishment in that country does not intervene in the supply within the meaning of *Art 192a* and the person liable for the payment of VAT is the person to whom the goods or services are supplied.

[*Directive 2006/112/EC, Art 238*].

(6) **Accounting**

Every taxable person must

- keep accounts in sufficient detail for VAT to be applied and its application checked by the tax authorities;
- keep a register of the goods dispatched or transported, by that person or on his behalf, to a destination outside the EU member state of departure but within the EU for the purposes of transactions consisting in valuations of those goods or work on those goods or their temporary use as referred to in **19.8**(*e*)(vi)–(viii) above;
- keep accounts in sufficient detail to enable the identification of goods dispatched to him from another EU member state, by or on behalf of a taxable person identified for VAT purposes in that other country, and used for services consisting in valuations of those goods or work on those goods;
- ensure that copies of the invoices issued by himself, or by his customer or, in his name and on his behalf, by a third party, and all the invoices which he has received, are stored and made available to the competent authorities without undue delay whenever they so request.

[*Directive 2006/112/EC, Arts 242–245*].

(7) **Returns**

Every taxable person must submit a return within an interval after the end of the VAT period (not more than two months) to be determined by each EU member state. The tax authorities must allow, and may require, the taxable person to make such returns by electronic means. The return must set out

(i) all the information needed to calculate the VAT that has become chargeable and the deduction to be made;

(ii) where appropriate, the total value of transactions relative to the VAT and deductions within (i) above and the value of any exempt transactions;

(iii) the total value, exclusive of VAT, of supplies of goods within **19.26**(1) above on which VAT has become chargeable in the period;

(iv) the total value, exclusive of VAT, of the supplies of goods referred to in *Arts 33* and *36* (see **19.12**(2) above) carried out within the territory of another EU member state in respect of which VAT has become chargeable in the return period, where the place where dispatch or transport of the goods began is situated in the EU member state in which the return must be submitted;

(v) the total value, exclusive of VAT, of intra-EU acquisitions of goods, or transactions treated as such, made in the EU member state in which the return must be submitted and in respect of which VAT has become chargeable during the tax period;

(vi) the total value, exclusive of VAT, of supplies as in (iv) above carried out in the EU member state in which the return must be submitted and in respect of which VAT has become chargeable during this tax period, where the place where dispatch or transport of the goods began is situated within the territory of another EU member state; and

(vii) the total value, exclusive of VAT, of the supplies of goods carried out in the EU member state in which the return must be submitted and in respect of which the taxable person has been designated as liable for payment of VAT and in respect of which VAT has become chargeable during this tax period.

[*Directive 2006/112/EC, Arts 251–253*].

(8) Recapitulative statements

Every taxable person identified for VAT purposes shall submit a recapitulative statement of

- the acquirers identified for VAT purposes to whom he has supplied goods in accordance with the conditions specified in **19.26**(1)(*a*) and (*d*) above; and
- the persons identified for VAT purposes to whom he has supplied goods which were supplied to him by way of intra-EU acquisitions referred to in *Art 42* (see **19.13** above).

The recapitulative statement must be drawn up for each calendar month within a period not exceeding one month. However, countries may allow taxable persons to submit it for each calendar quarter within a time limit not exceeding one month from the end of the quarter, where the total quarterly amount, excluding VAT, of the supplies of goods as referred to in *Art 264(1)(d)* and *Art 265(1)(c)* does not exceed either in respect of the quarter concerned or in respect of any of the previous four quarters the sum of €50,000 or its equivalent in national currency. Until 31 December 2011, countries may set the sum at €100,000 or its equivalent in national currency. In the case of supplies of services as referred to in *Art 264(1)(d)*, countries may allow taxable persons to submit the recapitulative statement for each calendar quarter within a time limit not exceeding one month from the end of the quarter. Countries must allow (and may require) statements to be submitted by electronic means. With approval from the Council, countries may allow

- taxable persons to submit simplified annual statements where their supplies do not exceed specified limits; and
- taxable persons who already prepare annual VAT returns to prepare the recapitulation statements for the same periods where their supplies do not exceed (higher) specified limits.

The statement must set out details of the VAT registration numbers of the taxable person and his customers in other EU member states and the aggregate value of supplies to each of those customers.

[*Directive 2006/112/EC, Arts 262–265, 270, 271*].

See **2.11 ACCOUNTING PERIODS AND RETURNS** for the UK provisions.

Special schemes

[19.41] The provisions relating to special schemes are outlined below.

(1) Simplified procedures for charging and collection

Countries which might encounter difficulties in applying the normal VAT arrangements to small enterprises, by reason of the activities or structure of such enterprises, may, subject to such conditions and limits as they may set, apply simplified procedures for charging and collecting VAT provided that they do not lead to a reduction in the VAT. [*Directive 2006/112/EC, Art 281*].

(2) Exemptions and graduated relief

Countries may provide exemption (and graduated tax relief) for the supply of goods and services by small enterprises. [*Directive 2006/112/EC, Art 282*]. Countries which, at 17 May 1977 (when the *EC Sixth Directive* came into force), exempted taxable persons whose annual turnover was equal to or higher than the equivalent in national currency of €5,000 at the conversion rate on that date, may raise that ceiling in order to maintain the value of the exemption in real terms. [*Directive 2006/112/EC, Art 286*].

Turnover for these purposes consists of (exclusive of VAT)

- the value of taxable supplies of goods and services; and
- the value of real estate transactions, financial transactions within **19.25**(*b*)–(*g*) above and insurance services, unless those transactions are ancillary transactions

but disposals of the tangible or intangible capital assets of an enterprise are not to be taken into account for the purposes of calculating turnover.

[*Directive 2006/112/EC, Art 288*].

Taxable persons exempt from VAT must not be entitled to deduct VAT in accordance with **19.33** to **19.35** above and may not show the VAT on their invoices. [*Directive 2006/112/EC, Art 289*].

Taxable persons who are entitled to exemption from VAT may opt either for the normal VAT arrangements or for the simplified procedures provided for in *Art 281* above. [*Directive 2006/112/EC, Art 290*].

See **60.2** and **60.3 REGISTRATION** for the UK provisions.

(3) Common flat-rate scheme for farmers

Countries may apply such a scheme to farmers where the application of the normal VAT scheme, or the simplified rules for small undertakings above, would give rise to difficulties. [*Directive 2006/112/EC, Art 296*].

See **64.25 SPECIAL SCHEMES** for UK provisions.

(4) Special scheme for travel agents

Where a travel agent (including a tour operator) deals with customers in his own name and uses supplies of goods and services provided by other taxable persons in the provision of travel services, transactions made in respect of a journey are treated as a single service supplied by him to the traveller. The single service is taxable in the EU member state in which the travel agent has established his business or has a fixed establishment from which he has carried out the supply of services. The taxable amount and the price exclusive of VAT in respect of the single service provided is the travel agent's margin, i.e. the difference between the total amount (exclusive of VAT) to be paid by the traveller and the actual cost to the travel agent of supplies of goods and services provided by other taxable persons where these transactions are for the direct benefit of the traveller.

The above provisions do not apply to travel agents where they act solely as intermediaries and to whom **19.18**(iii) above applies for the purposes of calculating the taxable amount.

[*Directive 2006/112/EC, Arts 306–308*].

See *Independent Coach Travel (Wholesaling) Ltd* (VTD 11037) (TVC 63.3) where the tribunal held that 'customers' should be construed as a reference to 'travellers' and that these provisions only apply to travel agents dealing with travellers and not those who act as wholesalers making supplies to retailers.

If transactions entrusted by the travel agent to other taxable persons are performed by such persons outside the EU, the supply of services carried out by the travel agent is treated as an intermediary activity exempt under **19.31** above. If the transactions are performed both inside and outside the EU, only that part of the travel agent's service relating to transactions outside the EU may be exempted. [*Directive 2006/112/EC, Art 309*].

VAT charged to the travel agent by other taxable persons on the transactions which are referred to in *Art 307* above and which are for the direct benefit of the traveller is not eligible for deduction or refund in the EU. [*Directive 2006/112/EC, Art 310*].

The fact that the travel agent provides accommodation only, and not transport, does not exclude such a service from the ambit of these provisions (*Beheersmaatschappij Van Ginkel Waddinxveen BV and Others v Inspecteur der Omzetbelasting, Utrecht, ECJ Case C–163/91*, [1996] STC 825 (TVC 22.560)).

See **69 TOUR OPERATORS' MARGIN SCHEME** for the UK provisions.

(5) Second-hand goods, works of art, collectors' items and antiques

In respect of the supply of second-hand goods, works of art, collectors' items or antiques (all as defined) carried out by taxable dealers, countries must apply a special scheme for taxing the profit margin made by the taxable dealer where those goods have been supplied to him within the EU by

- a non-taxable person;
- another taxable person, in so far as the supply of goods by that other taxable person is exempt under **19.25**(*m*) above;
- another taxable person, in so far as the supply of goods by that other taxable person is covered by the exemption for small enterprises under (2) above and involves capital goods; and
- another taxable dealer, in so far as VAT has been applied to the supply of goods by that other taxable dealer in accordance with this margin scheme.

The taxable amount is the profit margin (i.e. the difference between the selling price and the buying price) made by the taxable dealer less the amount of VAT relating to the profit margin.

[*Directive 2006/112/EC, Arts 313–315*].

Countries must allow taxable dealers the right to opt to use the scheme for supplies of works of art, collectors' items and antiques which they have imported and works of art supplied to the taxable dealer by their creators (or their successors in title). [*Directive 2006/112/EC, Art 316*].

To simplify the procedure for collecting VAT, countries may provide that, for certain transactions or certain categories of taxable dealer, the taxable amount of supplies of goods subject to the scheme is to be determined for each VAT period as a whole (rather than for each individual transaction). The definitions of 'taxable amount' and 'profit margin' are suitably adjusted. [*Directive 2006/112/EC, Art 318*].

A taxable dealer may apply the normal VAT arrangements to any supply covered by the margin scheme. [*Directive 2006/112/EC, Art 319*].

Where supplies are made under the scheme, any input tax incurred on the purchase of the goods cannot be deducted.

In so far as goods are used for the purpose of supplies carried out by him and subject to the margin scheme, the taxable dealer may not deduct the following from the VAT for which he is liable.

- The VAT due or paid in respect of works of art, collectors' items or antiques which he has imported himself.
- The VAT due or paid in respect of works of art which have been, or are to be, supplied to him by their creator or by the creator's successors in title.
- The VAT due or paid in respect of works of art which have been, or are to be, supplied to him by a taxable person other than a taxable dealer.

[*Directive 2006/112/EC, Art 322*].

The taxable dealer must not enter separately on the invoices which he issues the VAT relating to supplies of goods to which he applies the margin scheme. [*Directive 2006/112/EC, Art 325*].

Sales by public auction. Countries may make special arrangements for taxation of the profit margin made by an organiser of a sale by public auction (an 'auctioneer') in respect of the supply of second-hand goods, works of art, collectors' items or antiques by that auctioneer, acting in his own name and on behalf of the persons referred to below, pursuant to a contract under which commission is payable on the sale of those goods by public auction. [*Directive 2006/112/EC, Art 333*].

Where such special arrangements are adopted, they apply to supplies carried out by an auctioneer, acting in his own name, on behalf of

- a non-taxable person;
- another taxable person, in so far as the supply of goods, carried out by that taxable person in accordance with a contract under which commission is payable on a sale, is exempt under **19.25**(*m*) above;

- another taxable person, in so far as the supply of goods, carried out by that taxable person in accordance with a contract under which commission is payable on a sale, is covered by the exemption for small enterprises provided for in (2) above and involves capital goods; and
- a taxable dealer, in so far as the supply of goods, carried out by that taxable dealer in accordance with a contract under which commission is payable on a sale, is subject to VAT in accordance with the margin scheme.

The supply of goods to a taxable person who is an auctioneer is to be regarded as taking place when the sale of those goods by public auction takes place.

The taxable amount in respect of each supply of goods within these provisions is the total amount invoiced as below to the purchaser by the auctioneer less

- the net amount paid or to be paid by the auctioneer to his principal (i.e. the difference between the auction price of the goods and the amount of the commission obtained or to be obtained by the auctioneer from his principal pursuant to the contract under which commission is payable on the sale); and
- the amount of the VAT payable by the auctioneer in respect of his supply.

An auctioneer using the scheme must indicate in his accounts, in suspense accounts, both the amounts obtained or to be obtained from the purchaser of the goods and the amounts reimbursed or to be reimbursed to the vendor of the goods.

An auctioneer must

- issue to the purchaser an invoice itemising
  - (i) the auction price of the goods;
  - (ii) taxes, duties, levies and charges; and
  - (iii) incidental expenses, such as commission, packing, transport and insurance costs, charged by the organiser to the purchaser of the goods;

  but not indicating any VAT separately; and
- issue a statement to his principal specifying separately the amount of the transaction (i.e. the auction price of the goods less the amount of the commission obtained or to be obtained from the principal). This statement serves as the invoice which the principal, where he is a taxable person, must issue to the auctioneer.

[*Directive 2006/112/EC, Arts 334–340*].

See **62 SECOND-HAND GOODS** for UK provisions.

(6) Special scheme for investment gold

All countries must exempt the supply, intra-EU acquisition and importation of investment gold (as defined), including investment gold represented by certificates for allocated or unallocated gold or traded on gold accounts and including, in particular, gold loans and swaps, involving a right of ownership or claim in respect of investment gold, as well as transactions concerning investment gold involving futures and forward contracts leading to a transfer of right of ownership or claim in respect of investment gold. Countries must also exempt services of agents who act in the name of and on behalf of another person, when they take part in the supply of investment gold for their principal. [*Directive 2006/112/EC, Arts 336, 347*].

Option to tax

Countries must allow taxable persons who produce investment gold, or transform any gold into investment gold, the right to opt for the taxation of supplies of investment gold to another taxable person who would otherwise be exempt under the above provisions. They may also allow taxable persons who, in the course of their economic activity, normally supply gold for industrial purposes, the right to opt for the taxation of supplies of gold bars or wafers to another taxable person. [*Directive 2006/112/EC, Arts 348, 349*].

Where the supplier has exercised a right to opt for taxation, any agent acting for that supplier must be allowed to opt to tax his services. [*Directive 2006/112/EC, Art 350*].

Transactions on the regulated gold bullion market

An EU member state may apply VAT to specific transactions relating to investment gold which take place in that country (other than intra-EU supplies or exports)

- between taxable persons who are members of a regulated bullion market; or
- between a member of a regulated bullion market and another taxable person who is not such a member.

[*Directive 2006/112/EC, Art 352*].

Input tax

Where a taxable person's subsequent supply of investment gold is exempt under the above provisions, he is entitled to deduct the VAT due or paid in respect of

- investment gold supplied to him by a person who has exercised the right of option to tax as above or under the procedure for regulated bullion markets as above;
- the supply to him, or intra-EU acquisition or importation by him, of gold other than investment gold which is subsequently transformed by him (or on his behalf) into investment gold; and
- services supplied to him consisting of change of form, weight or purity of gold including investment gold.

Taxable persons who produce investment gold, or transform any gold into investment gold, are entitled to deduct VAT due or paid in respect of supplies, intra-EU acquisitions, importations or services linked to the production or transformation of that gold as if their subsequent supply of the gold exempted under these provisions were taxable.

[*Directive 2006/112/EC, Arts 354, 355*].

See **27 GOLD AND PRECIOUS METALS** for the UK provisions.

(7) Special scheme for non-established taxable persons supplying electronic services to non-taxable persons

EU member states must permit a 'non-established taxable person' (NETP) supplying 'electronic services' to a non-taxable person who is established or has his permanent address or usually resides in an EU member state to use a special scheme in accordance with the following provisions. The special scheme must apply to all those supplies within the EU. A '*non-established taxable person*' means a taxable person who has not established his business in the EU, who has no fixed establishment within the EU and who is not otherwise required to be identified for VAT purposes in the EU. 'Electronic services' mean those referred to in **19.15** above. [*Directive 2006/112/EC, Arts 358, 359*].

The NETP must state to the '*EU member state of identification*' (i.e. the EU member state which he chooses to contact to state when his activity as a taxable person within the EU commences in accordance with these provisions) when his activity as a taxable person commences, ceases or changes to the extent that he no longer qualifies for the special scheme. Such a statement must be made electronically. [*Directive 2006/112/EC, Art 360*].

The information from the NETP to the EU member state of identification when his taxable activities commence must contain details of name; postal address; electronic addresses, including websites; national tax number, if any; and a statement that the person is not identified for VAT purposes within the EU. The NETP must notify the EU member state of identification of any changes in the information provided. The EU member state of identification must allocate to the NETP an individual VAT number and must notify him of the number allocated by electronic means. Based on the information used for this identification, the *EU member state of consumption* (i.e. the EU member state in which the supply of the electronic services is deemed to take place under *Art 57*, see **19.15** above) may keep its own identification systems. [*Directive 2006/112/EC, Arts 361, 362*].

The EU member state of identification must strike the NETP from the identification register if

- he notifies it that he no longer supplies electronic services;
- it otherwise can be assumed that his taxable activities have ended;
- he no longer meets the conditions necessary to use the special scheme; or
- he persistently fails to comply with the rules concerning the special scheme.

[*Directive 2006/112/EC, Art 363*].

The NETP must submit a VAT return by electronic means, whether or not electronic services have been supplied, to the EU member state of identification for each VAT return period within 20 days following the end of the period. The VAT return must set out the identification number and, for each EU member state of consumption where VAT is due, the total value, less VAT, of supplies of electronic services for the VAT period and total amount of the corresponding VAT. The applicable VAT rates and the total VAT due must also be indicated. The VAT return must be made in euro. EU member states which have not adopted the euro may require the VAT return to be made in their national currencies. If the supplies have been made in other currencies, they must be converted using the exchange rates published by the European Central Bank for the last date of the reporting period or, if there is no publication on that day, on the next day of publication. [*Directive 2006/112/EC, Arts 364–366*].

The NETP must

- pay the VAT when submitting the return to a bank account designated by the EU member state of identification [*Directive 2006/112/EC, Art 367*];
- instead of making deductions for input tax under **19.33** above, be granted a refund under the *EC 13th Directive* (see **19.44** below) [*Directive 2006/112/EC, Art 368*]; and
- keep records of the transactions covered by the special scheme in sufficient detail to enable the tax authorities of the EU member state of consumption to verify that the VAT return is correct. These records should be made available electronically on request to the EU member states of identification and consumption. They must be maintained for a period of ten years from the end of the year when the transaction was carried out. [*Directive 2006/112/EC, Art 369*].

Derogations

[19.42] The Council may authorise any EU member state to introduce special measures for derogation from the provisions of this *Directive* in order to simplify the procedure for collecting VAT (without affecting the overall amount of VAT due at the final consumption stage except to a negligible extent) or to prevent certain types of tax evasion or avoidance. In addition, countries are allowed to retain special measures which were in force on 1 January 1977 provided that they notified the Commission of them before 1 January 1978 (when the *6th Directive* was implemented). [*Directive 2006/112/EC, Arts 394, 395*].

Countries which, at 1 January 1978, taxed the transactions listed in *Directive 2006/112/EC Annex X, Part A* may continue to tax those transactions. Similarly, countries which exempted the transactions listed in *Directive 2006/112/EC Annex X, Part B*, may continue to exempt those transactions in accordance with the conditions applying in the EU member state concerned on that date. [*Directive 2006/112/EC, Arts 370, 371*].

The derogations granted to the UK government include the following.

- Special **61 RETAIL SCHEMES**.
- Exemption from registration where, although taxable supplies exceed the registration limit, all supplies are, or would be, zero-rated if the taxable person was registered. See **60.6 REGISTRATION**.

- Valuation for VAT purposes where certain companies, for example, in the field of cosmetics, sell products to individuals who are outside the tax net for resale to the final customer. See **19.2** above and **72.23 VALUATION.**
- Operation of UK **68 TERMINAL MARKETS.**
- Long stays in hotels. See **33.2 HOTELS AND HOLIDAY ACCOMMODATION.**
- Treatment of goods in warehouse.
- Voluntary accounting scheme for transactions in **27 GOLD AND PRECIOUS METALS.**
- Fuel expenditure for company cars. See **46.16 MOTOR CARS.**
- Cash accounting scheme. See **64.2 SPECIAL SCHEMES.**
- Transfer of assets to a partly exempt group. See **28.7 GROUPS OF COMPANIES.**
- Direction to use open market value for exempt supplies to connected persons (see **72.19 VALUATION**) and acquisitions of goods from connected persons (see **72.12 VALUATION**).
- Taxation of self-supplies of land and buildings to be based on open market value. This derogation has not been introduced.
- Preparation of annual EU sales lists by persons with low turnover and by persons who prepare annual VAT returns. See **2.13 ACCOUNTING PERIODS AND RETURNS.**
- Transport services directly linked to an intra-EU transport of goods. See **71.27 TRANSPORT AND FREIGHT.**
- Restricting to 50% the right of the hirer or lessee to deduct input tax on car hire or leasing transactions where the car is used for private purposes and waiving VAT payable on the private use of the car in question. See **46.11 MOTOR CARS.**
- The place of supply of telecommunications services. See **66.19 SUPPLY: PLACE OF SUPPLY.**

Refunds of VAT to persons established in other EU member states

[19.43] The salient features of *Directive 2008/9/EC* are as follows.

A claim for VAT incurred in one EU member state (the member state of refund) may be submitted by a person established in another member state, provided:

- that person is not established, and does not have an establishment, or its domicile or normal place of business, in the member state of refund;
- that person has not made any supplies of goods or services in the member state of refund, other than certain zero-rated services relating to transport, goods or services where the reverse charge applies, and businesses registered under MOSS;
- the VAT claimed meets the normal conditions for its recovery as input tax; and
- the activities of the person give rise to a right to input tax credit in the EU member state where it is established. In the case of a partly exempt person, the extent of the claim must be in accordance with the rules applying in the EU member state of establishment.

The claimant must submit an electronic refund application to the EU member state of refund via an electronic portal set up by the EU member state in which it is established. The application is then forwarded to the member state of refund. The application must contain information about the claimant, with codes identifying the type of expenditure. The submission of invoices is not required unless the EU member state of refund specifically requests and the invoice value exceeds the equivalent of €1000 (€250 for fuel), in which case an electronic copy of the invoice must be submitted.

A claim must be submitted within nine months of the end of calendar year. Any claim must be for a period of at least three months (and must be for at least the equivalent of €400), unless it is a claim for the remainder of the year (in which case the minimum is the equivalent of €50).

The member state of refund must notify the claimant that the claim has been received. It must notify its decision to approve or refuse the refund within four months of the date of receipt, although this may be extended to a maximum of eight months if the member state of refund requests further information. If approved, the refund must be made within four months and ten days of the date the claim is received (extended to a maximum of eight months and ten days if the member state of refund has requested additional information). If refunds are made late, the claimant is entitled to interest.

If a false claim is made, penalties and interest applicable in the member state of refund may be imposed.

See **18.7–18.9 EUROPEAN UNION: GENERAL** for more details.

Refunds of VAT to persons established outside the EU

[19.44] The *13th Directive* (*Directive 86/560/EEC*) requires each EU member state to introduce a scheme to enable a taxable person established outside the EU to recover VAT suffered in that EU member state provided he is not already registered there.

The taxable person must not make supplies of goods or services in the particular EU member state other than

- supplies of transport (and related) services carried out in connection with the international carriage of goods; or
- services where the VAT on the supply is accounted for solely by the person to whom they are supplied.

Countries may make the refunds conditional upon the granting of comparable advantages regarding turnover tax by the territory where the taxable person is established. [*13th Directive, Arts 1, 2*].

Administrative arrangements and conditions for submitting applications, time limits and periods covered, minimum amounts claimable and methods of repayment are left to the individual countries. Refunds cannot be granted on terms more favourable than those applied to EU taxable persons. Countries may provide for the exclusion of certain expenditure. [*13th Directive, Arts 3, 4*].

See **49.5 OVERSEAS TRADERS** below for the scheme introduced in the UK.

Key points: EU legislation

[19.45] Points to consider are as follows.

- In situations where UK VAT law contradicts the provisions of EU law, the latter must take priority. This outcome has led to many revisions to UK VAT law over the years, to ensure it is compatible with the provisions of EU law.
- The standard rate of VAT adopted by an EU member state must be at least 15%. The highest rate is charged by Hungary (27%), with no other rate above 25%. The UK rate is very close to the average EU rate.
- Be aware that the definition of 'taxable person' has a different meaning in UK and EU VAT law. In the case of UK law, a 'taxable person' is someone who is either registered for VAT or should be so registered. In the case of EU law, a 'taxable person' is someone who carries out an 'economic activity' (the EU phrase for 'business') anywhere in the world.
- An important outcome of the phrase 'economic activity' is that any income earned on a continuing basis from the exploitation of land and property is within the VAT system. So a sole trader registered for VAT as a car mechanic, for example, cannot disregard the VAT implications of any property income he earns through the same legal entity. As a practical example, this is a relevant factor in relation to the flat-rate scheme (a scheme available to a small business with taxable sales of less than £150,000 per annum excluding VAT) which means that scheme users must include all exempt business income in the tax calculations, i.e. including buy-to-let income from a residential property.
- The UK has acquired a number of derogations from the EU that enable the burden of VAT to be eased in many practical situations. An example of a useful derogation is where a business that has exceeded the relevant VAT registration limits can avoid being VAT-registered if it would submit repayment returns on a regular basis, i.e. because all or most sales are zero-rated. In such cases, the business can agree with HMRC that it does not need to register for VAT.
- A business registered for VAT in one EU member state has always had the right, in most cases, to claim VAT paid on expenses incurred in other EU member states (subject to normal rules). This VAT is repaid through a separate claims system, rather than by an inclusion as input tax on the VAT returns of the business in question. The electronic claims system has deadlines for claims to be submitted and repaid (a claim must be submitted within nine months of the end of a calendar year), with an interest penalty

payable by countries who did not meet the relevant repayment deadline.

20

European Union: Single Market

Cross-references. See **2.11** ACCOUNTING PERIODS AND RETURNS for EU sales statements; **2.19** ACCOUNTING PERIODS AND RETURNS for Intrastat; **18.2** EUROPEAN UNION: GENERAL for the VAT territory of the EU; **40.5** INVOICES for particulars required on VAT invoices issued to persons in other EU member states and **40.12** INVOICES for the time limit for issuing invoices; **57** RECORDS generally; **60.11** *et seq* REGISTRATION for the liability to register in the UK in respect of distance sales from another EU member state; **60.18** *et seq* REGISTRATION for the liability to register in the UK in respect of acquisitions from other EU member states; **66.2** SUPPLY: PLACE OF SUPPLY for the place of supply of goods; **71.26** and **71.31** TRANSPORT AND FREIGHT for special provisions applying to intra-EU freight transport and handling and storage; **72.11–72.14** VALUATION for the valuation rules applying to acquisitions from other EU member states; **73** WAREHOUSED GOODS for movement of goods in warehouse and free zones to and from EU member states.

Introduction to the EU: Single Market

[20.1] The concepts of 'imports' and 'exports' of goods applies only to transactions with countries outside the EU. For intra-EU movements of goods, goods coming into the UK from other EU member states are referred to as 'acquisitions' and goods leaving the UK to go to other EU member states are referred to as 'despatches' or 'removals'.

The rules are complex and were only intended to be transitional until a definitive system for the taxation of trade between EU member states was introduced, based on the principle of taxing goods and services in the EU member states of origin. However, there seems little possibility that such a system will be introduced in the near future.

See **18.2** EUROPEAN UNION: GENERAL for a list of the territories which make up the VAT territories of the EU.

De Voil Indirect Tax Service. See V1.210, V3.361–V3.398, V4.341–V4.361.

Movement of goods between EU member states: general provisions

Transfers of goods to be treated as supplies

[20.2] Unless specifically overridden by other provisions, where goods forming part of the assets of a business are

- removed from any EU member state, by or under the directions of the person carrying on the business, and
- so removed in the course or furtherance of the business for the purpose of being taken to another EU member state

then whether or not the removal is, or is in connection with, a transaction for a consideration, there is a supply of goods by that person. [*VATA 1994, Sch 4 para 6(1)*]. Specifically excluded is the removal of gas through a natural gas system situated within the territory of an EU member state or any network connected to such a system; electricity; or heat or cooling supplied through a network [*SI 2010/2925*]. The supply is treated as taking place in the EU member state from which the goods are removed. [*VATA 1994, s 7(7)*].

There is no supply under these provisions where

- the goods are removed from an EU member state in the course of their removal from one part of that country to another part of the same country (e.g. goods removed from England to Northern Ireland via Ireland); or
- the goods have been removed from a place outside the EU for entry into the territory of the EU and are removed from an EU member state before the time when any EU customs duty on their entry into the EU would be incurred. See **34.18 IMPORTS**.

[*VATA 1994, Sch 4 para 6(2)*].

The effect of these provisions is that, in addition to normal commercial transactions, certain transfers by a business of its own goods to another EU member state are also treated as supplies of goods (see **20.25** below).

Charging and accounting for VAT

Subject to special rules in the cases listed below:

- *For transactions between VAT-registered traders*, a supplier in one EU member state need not charge VAT on dispatch of goods to a customer in another EU member state. Any VAT due is payable on acquisition of the goods by the customer who must account for it on their normal VAT return at the rate in force in the country of destination of the goods.
- *Where the customer in another EU member state is a private individual or is not registered for VAT*, VAT is normally charged and accounted for by the supplier in the EU member state from which the goods are dispatched.

See **20.3** *et seq* below for acquisitions of goods in the UK from other EU member states and **20.11** *et seq* below for supplies from the UK to other EU member states.

Special rules

Special rules apply to the following.

- The supply of goods subject to excise duty purchased by non-taxable persons. See **20.9** below for acquisitions in the UK and **20.17** below for supplies to other EU member states.
- Distance sales (i.e. sales to non-taxable persons in other EU member states where the supplier is responsible for delivery) above certain limits. See **20.10** below for distance selling to the UK and **20.18** for distance selling from the UK.

- Goods lost or stolen in transit. See **20.19** below.
- Supplies to diplomats, international organisations, NATO forces and other entitled persons and bodies in other EU member states which may in certain circumstances be relieved from VAT. See **20.21**(1) below.
- Freight containers. See **20.21**(2) below.
- Samples. See **20.21**(3) below).
- Triangulation. See **20.22** below.
- Certain transfers of own goods between EU member states, including goods sold on sale or return. See **20.25** and **20.26** below.
- Certain temporary movements of goods. See **20.27** below.
- Goods sent for valuation, repair, etc. see **20.28** and **20.29** below.
- The supply of goods to be installed or assembled at a customer's premises in another EU member state. See **20.31** below.
- Call-off stock. See **20.32** below
- New means of transport. See **20.33** *et seq* below.
- Acquisitions by non-VAT-registered businesses and non-taxable organisations in excess of an annual threshold. See **60.18 REGISTRATION** for the liability to register for VAT in the UK in respect of acquisitions where there is no liability to be registered in respect of UK supplies.

Returns

In addition to the appropriate entries on the VAT return, a business trading with other EU member states may also have to complete

- an EC Sales List (a list of supplies made to VAT-registered traders in other EU member states, see **2.11–2.18 ACCOUNTING PERIODS AND RETURNS**); and
- an Intrastat supplementary declaration (for use, together with VAT returns, in the compilation of statistics on the trade in goods between EU member states, see **2.19 ACCOUNTING PERIODS AND RETURNS**).

De Voil Indirect Tax Service. See V3.213.

Acquisitions of goods in the UK from other EU member states

[20.3] There is an acquisition in the UK for VAT purposes where

- there is an intra-EU movement of goods to the UK;
- the goods are received in the UK by a VAT-registered trader; and
- the supplier is registered for VAT in the EU member state of departure.

Under these circumstances, it is not necessary to make an import declaration (with certain exceptions) or pay VAT at the frontier. Instead, the UK VAT-registered trader is required to account for VAT on the goods acquired in the UK. [*VATA 1994, s 1(1)*]. The rate of VAT due is that applicable to the supply of identical goods in the UK. No VAT will therefore be due on the acquisition of goods which are currently zero-rated in the UK. Any VAT due must be accounted for on the VAT return for the period in which the tax point occurs and, subject to the normal rules, may be treated as input tax on the same VAT return.

(VAT Notice 725, paras 7.1, 7.2, 7.4).

These provisions are considered in more detail in **20.4** to **20.10** below.

De Voil Indirect Tax Service. See V3.361–V3.398.

Meaning of 'acquisition of goods from another EU member state'

[20.4] An '*acquisition of goods from another EU member state*' is any acquisition of goods under a transaction where both of the following conditions are satisfied.

- The transaction is, or is treated for the purposes of *VATA 1994* as, a supply of goods.
- The transaction involves the movement of goods from another EU member state.

For these purposes, it is immaterial whether the removal of the goods is undertaken by or on behalf of the supplier, the customer or some other person.

Where the person with the property in the goods does not change in consequence of anything treated as a supply under *VATA 1994*, that supply is to be treated as a transaction under which there is an acquisition of goods by the person making it. (The transfer of a business's own goods to another EU member state therefore leads to an acquisition of goods by it in that country. See **20.25** below.)

The Treasury may provide by Order that, in relation to any type of transaction, the acquisition of goods under such a transaction is not to be treated as an acquisition of goods from another EU member state. See, for example,

- **27.7 GOLD AND PRECIOUS METALS** for gold supplied to a Central Bank by a supplier in another EU member state; and
- **62.7 SECOND-HAND GOODS** for goods bought from a registered business in another EU member state where VAT on the supply is accounted for in that EU member state by reference to the profit margin.

[*VATA 1994, s 11*].

De Voil Indirect Tax Service. See V3.363.

Scope of VAT on acquisitions

[20.5] Subject to the provisions under *Zero-rating* and *VAT relief* below, VAT is charged in the UK on any acquisition from another EU member state where the following conditions are satisfied.

(a) The acquisition is a 'taxable acquisition' and takes place in the UK. See **20.6** below for the place of acquisition.
An acquisition from another EU member state is a '*taxable acquisition*' if the goods are
   - acquired by
     (i) a person in the course or furtherance of a business carried on by him, or

(ii) by a body corporate, club, association, organisation or other unincorporated body in the course or furtherance of any activities carried on by it otherwise than by way of business,

and the supplier is taxable in another EU member state at the time of the relevant transaction and is acting in the course or furtherance of a business carried on by him, or

- a new means of transport (see **20.33** below)

but provided that, in either case, the acquisition is not an '*exempt acquisition*' i.e. an acquisition where the goods are acquired in pursuance of an exempt supply falling within *VATA 1994, Sch 9* (see **21 EXEMPT SUPPLIES**).

(b) The acquisition is not in pursuance of a taxable supply in the UK. See, for example, **20.30** below for installed and assembled goods.

(c) Either

(i) the person making the acquisition is a '*taxable person*' (i.e. a person who is, or is required to be, registered);

(ii) the goods are subject to excise duty (see **20.9** below); or

(iii) the goods are a new means of transport (see **20.33** below).

[*VATA 1994, ss 10, 31(1)*].

See **60.18 REGISTRATION** for the requirement to register by persons within (*a*)(ii) above who make acquisitions above an annual threshold and who would not otherwise be liable for registration in respect of supplies made.

Liability for VAT

The VAT on any acquisition is a liability of the person who acquires the goods and, subject to provisions about accounting and payment, becomes due at the time of acquisition (see **20.7** below). [*VATA 1994, s 1(3)*].

Zero-rating

Where the goods acquired fall within *VATA 1994, Sch 8*, no VAT is chargeable on their acquisition, except as otherwise provided in that *Schedule*. [*VATA 1994, s 30(3)*].

VAT relief

Certain goods imported into the UK from outside the EU are subject to relief from import VAT under *SI 1984/746*. These goods are also subject to relief when coming into the UK from other EU member states

- if supplied by a taxable person in another EU member state to a taxable person in the UK; or
- where there is a deemed supply on the transfer of a taxable person's own goods from another EU member state to the UK (see **20.25** below).

See **34.15**(1)–(12) **IMPORTS** for details of the qualifying goods.

Samples. See **20.21**(3) below.

[*VATA 1994, s 36A; SI 2002/1935*].

ERICs

From 1 January 2013, VAT is not chargeable on the importation or acquisition of goods by a European Research Infrastructure Consortium ('ERIC'), subject to the following conditions.

- The statutory seat of the ERIC referred to in *Council Regulation (EC) 723/2009, Art 8(1)* on the Community legal framework for a European Research Infrastructure Consortium is located in an EU member state.
- The goods are for the official use of the ERIC.
- Relief is not precluded by the limitations and conditions laid down in the agreement between the members of the ERIC referred to in *Council Regulation (EC)723/2009, Art 5(1)(d)*.
- A certificate has been provided confirming that the ERIC is entitled to receive a zero-rated supply. The supplier should retain the certificate as evidence they have made a zero-rated supply.

[*SI 2012/2907, Art 2*].

Under *para 8* of the preamble to *Council Regulation (EC)723/2009* an ERIC should have as its principal task the establishment and operation of a research infrastructure on a non-economic basis and should devote most of its resources to this principal task. In order to promote innovation and knowledge and technology transfer, the ERIC should be allowed to carry out some limited economic activities if they are closely related to its principal task and they do not jeopardise its achievement.

For the zero-rating of supplies to ERICs, see **75.15 ZERO-RATED SUPPLIES**.

De Voil Indirect Tax Service. See V3.361–V3.398.

Place of acquisition

[20.6] VAT on an acquisition is due in the country where the acquisition is deemed to take place. Subject to below, the following provisions apply for determining whether goods acquired from another EU member state are acquired in the UK.

(a) Goods are treated as acquired in the UK if the transaction involves their removal to the UK and does not involve their removal from the UK (i.e. the transport of the goods ends in the UK). The goods are otherwise, subject to the following provisions, to be treated as acquired outside the UK.

(b) Goods are treated as acquired in the UK where a business uses a UK VAT registration number in order to acquire the goods (whether or not the goods are to be transported to the UK) unless it can establish to HMRC that VAT fell to be paid (and has been paid) in another EU member state on the acquisition of those goods there under provisions corresponding to the UK provisions in (*a*) above.

The above is subject to the special provisions applying to

- warehoused goods (see **73.6 WAREHOUSED GOODS**);
- triangulation where three parties are involved in the transaction (see **20.22** below); and
- installed or assembled goods (see **20.30** below).

[*VATA 1994, s 13*].

In most cases, VAT on an acquisition will only be due under (*a*) above in the country where the goods are received and (*b*) above is a 'fallback' provision that applies where the VAT registration number quoted to the supplier to secure zero-rating has been issued in a different EU member state to that in which the goods are received.

Following the CJEU decision in the joined cases of *X, ECJ Case C–536/08* and *Facet Trading BV, CJEU Case C–539/08*, [2010] STC 1701 (TVC 22.467), HMRC have clarified that there is no right to recover the acquisition VAT as input tax where it fell due under the fallback provision. The only basis on which the UK VAT may be adjusted is where it can be demonstrated that acquisition VAT has been accounted for in the EU member state of arrival. (HMRC Brief 20/11).

Example

A UK business acquires goods from a supplier in Germany for delivery to the UK and quotes its VAT registration number.

The place of supply is the UK under both (*a*) and (*b*) above.

But if a UK business quotes its UK VAT registration number to a supplier in Germany and the goods are delivered to France, there is an acquisition in France (under French rules similar to (*a*) above) and an acquisition in the UK under (*b*) above. In such circumstances

- the business is liable to account for acquisition VAT in the UK unless it can demonstrate that VAT has already been paid in the EU member state to which the goods were sent (France); and
- if it has accounted for acquisition VAT in the UK and is later required to pay VAT on the acquisition in France, it can obtain a refund of the VAT paid in the UK but only where it has not claimed, or not been able to claim, full input tax credit in respect of the acquisition (see **20.8** below).

(VAT Notice 725, paras 7.7–7.9).

De Voil Indirect Tax Service. See V3.368–V3.372.

Time of acquisition

[20.7] Any VAT on an acquisition becomes due in the VAT period in which the tax point (time of acquisition) occurs. Subject to below, the time of acquisition of goods from another EU member state (which is the same time as the corresponding supply of goods in the EU member state of dispatch, see **20.16** below) is the earlier of

(a) the 15th day of the month following that in which the *first* removal of the goods involved in the transaction forming the basis of the acquisition occurred; and

(b) the date of issue of an invoice in respect of the transaction containing such details as HMRC require. For this purpose, the invoice is one which is issued by the supplier or the customer under the provisions of the law of the EU member state from which the goods were despatched and which correspond to the provisions in *SI 1995/2518, Regs 13, 13A, 14* relating to invoices for supplies in the UK. See **40 INVOICES**.

Note that, unlike the rules for supplies in the UK, part or full payment for an intra-EU supply of goods does not create a tax point for the acquisition. However, the receipt of a payment on account does make the supplier liable to raise an invoice which will in turn trigger a tax point under (*b*) above.

HMRC may make Regulations relating to the time at which an acquisition is treated as taking place where the whole or part of any consideration is determined or payable periodically, or from time to time, or at the end of a period.

See also **73.6 WAREHOUSED GOODS** for special rules for warehoused goods.

[*VATA 1994, s 12; SI 1995/2518, Reg 83*]. (VAT Notice 725, paras 7.3, 7.5, 7.6).

De Voil Indirect Tax Service. See V3.388.

Recording and accounting for VAT due on acquisitions

[20.8] In addition to the normal VAT records, a UK-registered business which acquires goods from businesses registered for VAT in other EU member states must

(a) keep VAT invoices issued to it and any other documents relating to the goods it acquires from other EU member states;
(b) calculate the VAT due on the acquisition of these goods and enter it on the 'VAT payable' side of its VAT account; and
(c) subject to the normal rules for allowable input tax, deduct the VAT due on the acquisition as input tax on the 'VAT allowable' side of the VAT account.

Where the time of acquisition of any goods from another EU member state is determined under **20.7**(*b*) above by reference to the issue of an invoice, VAT must be accounted for and paid in respect of the acquisition only on so much of its value as is shown on the invoice. [*SI 1995/2518, Reg 26*].

The amount of VAT due on an acquisition is the tax value multiplied by the VAT rate. See **72.11–72.14 VALUATION** for the valuation rules applying to acquisitions from other EU member states.

VAT return

VAT due under (*b*) above should be entered in Box 2 of the VAT return for the VAT period in which the time of acquisition occurs (see **20.7** above) and the input tax under (*c*) above in Box 4 on the same return. The value of the acquisition must be included in Boxes 7 and 9.

Supplementary declarations

Details of an acquisition may have to be disclosed on a supplementary declaration as an arrival. See **2.19 ACCOUNTING PERIODS AND RETURNS**.

(VAT Notice 725, paras 7.11, 16.4, 16.6).

Acquisition of goods subject to excise duty

[20.9] All taxable acquisitions (i.e. acquisitions for business purposes and acquisitions for non-business purposes by clubs, associations, etc. from registered businesses in other EU member states, see **20.5** above) of exciseable goods are taxed in the EU member state of destination.

Acquisitions by VAT-registered businesses

Where the business that acquires the exciseable goods from a supplier in another EU member state is UK VAT-registered, it must account for VAT in the same way as for any other acquisition.

Acquisitions of goods liable to excise duty by non-registered persons

Where the person making the taxable acquisition is not registered for UK VAT (because turnover is under the registration limit or because activities are not business activities), VAT cannot be accounted for by means of a VAT return. In order to avoid the need to register all persons making acquisitions of goods liable to excise duty, HMRC are empowered to introduce a special mechanism to collect the VAT due.

Under these provisions, where

(a) a taxable acquisition of goods subject to excise duty takes place in the UK,
(b) the acquisition is not in pursuance of a taxable supply (see below), and
(c) the person acquiring the goods is not a taxable person at the time of the acquisition,

the person acquiring such goods must notify HMRC of the acquisition at the time of the acquisition or the arrival of the goods in the UK, whichever is the later. The notification must be in writing in English and contain the following particulars.

- The name and current address of the person acquiring the goods.
- The time of acquisition.
- The date when the goods arrived in the UK.
- The value of the goods including any excise duty payable.
- The VAT due on the acquisition.

The notification must include a signed declaration that all the information given is true and complete.

The VAT due is payable at the time of notification and, in any event, not later than the last date on which the person is required to make such notification as above. Where the person required to make the notification dies or becomes incapacitated, the liability to notify passes to the personal representative, trustee in bankruptcy, liquidator, etc., as does the liability to pay the VAT (although only to the extent of assets passing to that person).

Note

The effect of (*b*) above is that the provisions are only necessary where the person acquiring the goods arranges for their delivery. If the supplier arranges delivery, the distance selling provisions in **20.10** below apply and the supplier must register for VAT in the UK, whatever his level of sales in this country.

[*VATA 1994, Sch 11 para 2(4)(5); SI 1995/2518, Regs 31(3), 36*].

De Voil Indirect Tax Service. See V5.126.

Distance selling to the UK from other EU member states

[20.10] Distance selling occurs when a taxable supplier in one EU member state supplies and delivers goods to a customer in another EU member state who is not registered or liable to be registered for VAT. Such customers are known as 'non-taxable persons' and include not only private individuals but public bodies, charities and businesses too small to register for VAT or with activities that are entirely exempt. The most common examples of distance sales are goods supplied by mail order and goods ordered over the internet.

Such distance sales to non-taxable persons in the UK from another EU member state are normally subject to VAT in that other country. But once the value of such distance sales to the UK exceeds the UK annual threshold of £70,000

- the supplier is automatically liable to register for VAT in the UK (see **60.11 REGISTRATION**);
- the UK becomes the place of supply (see **66.5 SUPPLY: PLACE OF SUPPLY**); and
- VAT on any further sales is taxed in the UK.

The supplier may, if he wishes, opt to make the UK the place of supply before reaching the annual threshold. See **60.14 REGISTRATION**.

Note that each EU member state has the option of applying a distance selling threshold of €35,000 or €100,000 per calendar year (or its own currency equivalent). The UK has adopted a threshold of €100,000, set at £70,000.

Goods subject to excise duty

Distance sales of goods subject to excise duty are not subject to the threshold. An EU supplier must register for VAT immediately it makes any supplies of such goods.

Reporting requirements

The following table summarises the reporting requirements for distance sales to the UK.

Type of supply	*VAT return*	*EC Sales List*
Distance sales to UK below UK distance selling threshold	No	No
Distance sales to UK above UK distance selling threshold (or where the seller has voluntarily registered in the UK)	Enter the output tax in Box 1 and the value of the supply in Box 6	No

(VAT Notice 725, paras 6.4, 6.16, 6.17).

Supplies of goods from the UK to other EU member states

[20.11] Supplies of goods to other EU member states can be zero-rated provided the following conditions are satisfied.

(a) The supply involves the removal of the goods from the UK to another EU member state.

(b) The goods are acquired by a customer who is registered for VAT in another EU member state (not necessarily the same one).

(c) The supplier obtains his customer's VAT registration number and shows this (including the 2-letter country code prefix) on his VAT invoice. See **20.12** below for checking a customer's VAT registration number and **40.1** and **40.5 INVOICES** for the obligation to provide a VAT invoice and the particulars to be included thereon.

(d) The supplier obtains and keeps valid commercial documentary evidence that the goods have been removed from the UK
- within three months of the time of supply (see **20.16** below) for direct and indirect removals and goods involved in groupage or consolidation prior to removal; and
- within six months of the time of supply for goods involved in processing or incorporation prior to removal.

See **20.13–20.15** below for evidence of removal.

(e) The goods must not be second-hand goods or works of art, etc. which the supplier has opted to tax on the profit margin. See **62.12 SECOND-HAND GOODS.**

[*VATA 1994, s 30(8); SI 1995/2518, Reg 134*]. (VAT Notice 725, paras 4.3, 4.4 which have the force of law; VAT Information Sheet 2/00).

If all of the above conditions cannot be met, the UK supplier must charge VAT at the same rate applicable to a supply of the goods in the UK. The standard UK time of supply rules will then apply (see **67.8 SUPPLY: TIME OF SUPPLY**). A sale must not be zero-rated, even if the goods are subsequently removed to another EU member state, where

- the goods are supplied to a UK VAT-registered customer (unless that customer is also registered for VAT in another EU member state in which case the customer must provide his EU VAT registration number and the goods must be removed to another EU member state);

- the supplier delivers to, or allows the goods to be collected by, a UK customer at a UK address; or
- the supplier allows the goods to be used in the UK in the period between supply and removal (except where specifically authorised to do so).

(VAT Notice 725, para 4.3).

Supplies of goods

See **65.3 SUPPLY: GENERAL** for a general consideration of what is a supply of goods (as opposed to a supply of services).

Reporting requirements

The following table summarises the reporting requirements for supplies of goods to customers in other EU member states.

Type of supply	*VAT return*	*EC Sales List*
Supplies of goods to VAT-registered customers in other EU member states where the zero-rating conditions above are satisfied	Enter the value of the supply in Boxes 6 and 8	Enter the customer's VAT number and the value of the supply
Supplies of goods to customers in other EU member states where the zero-rating conditions above are not satisfied	Enter the VAT due in Box 1 and the value of the supply in Box 6	No

(VAT Notice 725, para 3.7).

Invoicing requirements

See **40.5 INVOICES**.

Failure to receive evidence of removal

Where a supply is initially zero-rated on the assumption that the necessary evidence of removal will be received within the time limit but this is not the case, the supplier must account for VAT on the supply at the standard rate (unless the goods are zero-rated in their own right). VAT records must be amended and VAT accounted for on the taxable proportion of the invoiced amount or consideration received, i.e. 1/6th of the total for a VAT rate of 20%. This amount must be entered on the VAT payable side of the VAT account and included in Box 1 of the VAT return for the period in which the time limit expires. If the supplier subsequently receives the evidence of removal of the goods, he can then zero-rate the supply and adjust the VAT account for the period in which the evidence is obtained (provided the goods have not been used in the UK before removal).

(VAT Notice 725, paras 16.10, 16.11).

Effect of failure to comply with conditions

Where the supply of any goods has been zero-rated under the above provisions and either any of the above conditions is not complied with or the goods are found in the UK after the date of alleged removal, the goods are liable to *forfeiture*. Any VAT which would have been due but for zero-rating is payable forthwith by the person to whom the goods were supplied or by any other person in whose possession the goods are found in the UK. HMRC may waive payment of the VAT in whole or in part. [*VATA 1994, s 30(10)*].

See, however, the decision in *Teleos plc & Others v C & E Commrs, ECJ Case C–409/04*, [2008] STC 706 (TVC 22.589). The court confirmed that goods must physically leave the territory of the EU member state of supply to qualify for zero-rating. But if the supplier, acting in good faith, has done everything in his power to ensure the proper application of the VAT provisions and presents objective proofs that the goods supplied by him have left that country, the tax authorities cannot hold the supplier to account for the VAT on the goods if it turns out that the proofs relied upon contained false information and the supplier neither knew nor could have known anything of it. Thus the supplier must not be involved in tax evasion and must take every reasonable step to ensure that the transaction did not lead to his participation in VAT evasion.

De Voil Indirect Tax Service. See V4.341–V4.361.

Checking VAT registration numbers

[20.12] A business should carry out normal commercial checks such as bank and trade credit worthiness references before it starts making supplies to an EU customer. As part of these checks it should ask its customer to supply its EU VAT registration number. HMRC strongly recommend that the business obtains confirmation of the registration number in writing. It should retain the letter or advice received from the customer for future reference.

When writing to the customer, the business should ask them to provide it with the number which has been allocated to them for intra-EU trade. In certain countries e.g. Spain and Italy, businesses are required to register their VAT number for intra-EU use and if they don't do this, the number will show as invalid on the Europa website. If they do not supply the VAT number then the business is obliged to charge UK VAT on any supplies of goods. If it is supplying services and the customer cannot supply a VAT number then the business must make sure it has sufficient evidence to show that the supply is to a business in order to zero-rate the supply. However, see the CJEU decision in *Euro Tyre, ECJ Case C–21/16* which concerned the supply of tyres by the Portuguese branch of Euro Tyre (ET) to a Spanish customer who was VAT-registered in Spain but had not registered for intra-EU trade. ET treated the supply as a zero-rated intra-EU dispatch but the Portuguese tax authority disagreed stating that the relevant conditions had not been satisfied. The CJEU held the EU legal definition of a taxable person includes a person who independently carries out an economic activity at any place regardless of the results of that activity. It does not specify that the person is required to have an intra-EU transaction VAT registration number or that the person is registered on VIES. Therefore this requirement is not a substantive requirement for the purposes of applying the exemption to these types of transactions. These are merely formal requirements which cannot be used to prevent a supplier's entitlement to exempt a transaction from VAT where all of the substantive conditions have been met. The CJEU also stated that the principal of fiscal neutrality requires that the transaction be exempt from VAT if the substantive conditions have been met, even where the supplier has failed to comply with all of the formal requirements. However the CJEU did also state that the failure to meet the formal requirements may result in a loss of entitlement, where the taxpayer intentionally participated in tax evasion or where non-compliance with a formal requirement effectively prevents the supplier from complying with the substantive requirements. In this case the supplier was not involved in tax evasion and they had satisfied the substantive conditions and as a result the tax authority could not refuse to allow the transaction to be exempt from Portuguese VAT.

The business should check the validity of the number it has been given by making sure it follows the correct format. Further checks should be made using the Europa website. It must also regularly check the customer's VAT registration number to make sure that the details are still valid and that the number has not been recently deregistered. Alternatively it can contact the VAT Helpline on 0300 200 3700 to validate the customer's registration number and to verify that the name and address is correct.

A business will not be liable to account for VAT where a supply is zero-rated and a customer's VAT number subsequently proves to be invalid but only if

- it has genuinely done everything it can to check the validity of the VAT number;
- can demonstrate it has done so;
- has taken heed of any indications that something might be wrong; and
- has no other reason to suspect the VAT number is invalid.

HMRC do not regard reasonable steps as having been taken if a VAT number is used

- which does not conform to the published format for the customer's country;
- that the business has not regularly checked using the Europa website or with HMRC;
- that the business has already been informed is invalid; or
- which is known not to belong to the customer.

(VAT Notice 725, paras 4.7–4.11).

Evidence of removal of goods

[20.13] A combination of the documents shown below must be used to provide clear evidence that a sale has taken place and that the goods have been removed from the UK.

- Customer's order (including customer's name, VAT number and delivery address for the goods).
- Inter-company correspondence.
- Copy sales invoice (including a description of the goods, an invoice number and customer's EU VAT number etc.).
- Advice note.
- Packing list.

- Commercial transport document(s) from the carrier responsible for removing the goods from the UK.
- Details of insurance or freight charges.
- Bank statements as evidence of payment.
- Receipted copy of the consignment note as evidence of receipt of goods abroad.
- Any other documents relevant to the removal of the goods in question which would normally be obtained in the course of intra-EU business.

Photocopy certificates of shipment or other transport documents are not normally acceptable as evidence of removal unless authenticated with an original stamp and dated by an authorised official of the issuing office.

Documents used as proof of removal must clearly identify the following. (These requirements have the force of law.)

- The supplier.
- The consignor (where different from the supplier).
- The customer.
- The goods.
- An accurate value.
- The mode of transport and route of movement of the goods.
- The EU destination.

Vague descriptions of goods, quantities or values are not acceptable (e.g. 'various electrical goods' must not be used when the correct description is '2000 mobile phones Make ABC and Model Number XYZ2000').

Goods delivered by the supplier

In addition to the examples of acceptable documentary evidence listed above, travel tickets can also be used to demonstrate that an intra-EU journey took place for the purpose of removing the goods from the UK.

(VAT Notice 725, paras 5.1, 5.2, 5.4).

Goods collected in the UK by the customer

[20.14] If a VAT-registered EU customer collects the goods, or arranges for their collection and removal from the UK, it can be difficult for the supplier to obtain adequate proof of removal as the carrier is contracted to the customer. As a result, for this type of transaction the standard of evidence required to substantiate VAT zero-rating is high. The supplier should seek confirmation of how the goods are to be removed from the UK and what evidence of removal will be provided. He should also consider taking a deposit from the customer equal to the amount of VAT, in case satisfactory evidence of removal is not received.

Evidence must show that the goods supplied have left the UK. Copies of transport documents alone are not sufficient and information held must identify the date and route of the movement of goods and the method of transport involved. It should include the following.

- A written order from the customer which shows their name, address and EU VAT number, and the address where the goods are to be delivered.

- Copy sales invoice showing customer's name, EU VAT number, a description of the goods and an invoice number.
- Date of departure of goods from the supplier's premises and from the UK.
- Name and address of the haulier collecting the goods.
- Registration number of the vehicle collecting the goods and the name and signature of the driver.
- Where the goods are to be taken out of the UK by a different haulier or vehicle, the name and address of that haulier, signature for the goods and registration number of the vehicle.
- Route (e.g. Channel Tunnel, port of exit).
- Copy of travel tickets.
- Name of ferry or shipping company and date of sailing or airway number and airport.

The information held should also include (where applicable):

- Trailer number.
- Full container number.
- Name and address for consolidation, groupage, or processing.

(VAT Notice 725, para 5.5).

See *K J Services Ltd* [2016] UKFTT 140 (TC) (TC04925) for a situation in which the trader failed to qualify for zero-rating of a despatch. The UK trader sold a piece of machinery in the UK to a Belgian company which provided a VAT registration number. However, the goods did not leave the UK before the Belgian company sold them to another UK company, which in turn sold them to an Australian customer and exported them. Although the goods had eventually left the UK, the appellant's transaction did not qualify for zero-rating: it was not itself an export, and the conditions for despatch required that the goods left the UK as part of that supply. The Belgian company had presumably also broken registration rules by making the sale in the UK, but the appellant had to account for output tax.

Other forms of evidence in particular cases

[20.15] See also VAT Notice 725 for acceptable forms of evidence in the following cases.

Removal of goods to the Republic of Ireland across the Irish Land Boundary	Para 5.3
Groupage or consolidation transactions	Para 5.8
Goods sent by post	Para 5.9
Couriers and fast parcel services	Para 5.10

Time of supply

Zero-rated supplies to taxable persons in another EU member state

[20.16] Where any supply of goods involves both

- the removal of the goods from the UK, and

- their acquisition in another EU member state by a person who is liable for VAT on the acquisition under the provisions of that country corresponding to those in **20.3** above,

the time of supply (tax point) is the earlier of

- the 15th day of the month following that in which the goods are removed (i.e. sent to the customer or, as the case may be, taken away by the customer); and
- the day of the issue of a VAT invoice or other prescribed invoice in respect of the supply.

Unlike a UK domestic supply, the receipt of payment before the issue of an invoice does not create a tax point. However, it does make the supplier liable to issue an invoice for the amount paid (see **40.1 INVOICES**) which in turn will create a tax point in respect of the amount invoiced.

Where a series of invoices are issued relating to the same supply of goods, the three-month time limit for obtaining valid evidence of removal (see **20.11**(*d*) above) begins from the date of the final invoice.

The tax point should be used as the reference date for including these supplies on the VAT return and EC Sales List.

Supplies to non-taxable persons in another EU member state

These are taxable in the UK and the tax point is determined under the normal rules. See **67.1** *et seq* **SUPPLY: TIME OF SUPPLY**.

[*VATA 1994, s 6(7)(8)*]. (VAT Notice 725, paras 3.4–3.6, 6.2).

Supplies of exciseable goods to other EU member states

Accompanying documents

[20.17] All exciseable goods must travel with an accompanying document which will be either an Administrative Accompanying Document (AAD) or a Simplified Administrative Accompanying Document (SAAD).

- If the goods are moving between warehouses and they are moving under authorised duty suspension arrangements (e.g. from an excise warehouse), the consignor must complete an AAD. There must be a financial guarantee to cover all excise duty liabilities during the movement. The consignee must complete a certificate of receipt for the goods on the reverse of Copy 3 of the AAD and return it to the consignor.
- If the goods are moving between warehouses and UK excise duty has already been paid, they should travel with a SAAD. The customer must also provide evidence that the excise duty has been paid in the EU member state of destination or secured to the satisfaction of the VAT authorities there, *before* the supplier despatches the goods.

Excise goods supplied to a VAT-registered customer

Excise goods sold to a VAT-registered customer in another EU member state are treated in the same way as any other type of goods.

Excise goods supplied to persons not VAT-registered but not for private purposes

There are special arrangements for supplies of exciseable goods to non-registered persons in other EU member states when the purchases are made for *non-private* purposes. This applies to purchases by businesses which are below the registration threshold in their country or by non-registered legal persons (associations and unincorporated bodies, etc.) whose activities are not business activities for VAT purposes. Such supplies can be zero-rated provided the following conditions are met.

(1) The goods are removed from the UK to a destination in another EU member state.

(2) The supply is to a person who is non-taxable in another EU member state but the place of supply is not treated as outside the UK under the place of supply rules in **66.6 SUPPLY: PLACE OF SUPPLY**. (This effectively means that the goods must be removed by or on behalf of the customer as if the supplier arranges for delivery of excise goods to a non VAT-registered person in another EU member state he is liable to register in that country under the distance selling arrangements whatever the level of sales.)

(3) Within 15 days of the end of the month in which they are moved, the supplier must obtain (and keep) a receipted copy 3 of the AAD. This must be certified by the consignee or VAT authority in the EU member state of destination. The movement of goods must be completed as soon as possible and the certificate of receipt for the goods must be issued within four months of the time of supply.

(4) The goods are not second-hand goods or works of art, etc. which the supplier has opted to tax on the profit margin. See **62.12 SECOND-HAND GOODS**.

If these conditions are met, the customer is liable for the excise duty and VAT. If duty suspended goods go missing in transit, the person who supplied the movement guarantee is liable for the duty, along with any person who may be jointly and severally liable.

Excise goods supplied for private purposes

Excise goods supplied for private purposes where the supplier arranges delivery to a customer in another EU member state. are covered by the special VAT arrangements for distance selling (see **20.18** below). The vendor must pay the duty in the EU member state of destination at the time the goods are delivered and may therefore have to register for excise purposes with the VAT authorities in that country. In the UK, people receiving goods under distance selling arrangements, must appoint a duty representative to account for UK excise duty, before the goods are dispatched.

[*SI 1995/2518, Reg 135*]. (VAT Notice 725, para 15.4).

De Voil Indirect Tax Service. See V4.352.

Distance selling from the UK to other EU member states

[20.18] Distance selling occurs when a taxable supplier in one EU member state supplies and delivers goods to a customer in another EU member state who is not registered or liable to be registered for VAT. Such customers are known as 'non-taxable persons' and include not only private individuals but public bodies, charities and businesses too small to register for VAT or with activities that are entirely exempt. The most common examples of distance sales are goods supplied by mail order and goods ordered over the internet.

Distance sales by a UK business to customers in another EU member state are subject to UK VAT until

- the value of supplies to any particular EU member state exceeds an annual threshold set by that country for distance selling; or
- the UK business exercises the option below.

Then

- the supplier is automatically liable to register for VAT in that country;
- that country becomes the place of supply (see **66.6 SUPPLY: PLACE OF SUPPLY**); and
- VAT on any further sales is taxed in the EU member state of destination of the goods.

A UK business that is required to register for VAT in another EU member state must notify the tax authority in that country, allowing sufficient time to become registered by the appropriate date in accordance with the rules of that country.

Each EU member state sets its own distance selling threshold and has the option of applying a threshold of €35,000 or €100,000 per calendar year (or its own currency equivalent). The thresholds published by the EU on 1 April 2017 are as follows (see Annex I at ec.europa.eu/taxation_customs/sites/taxation/files/resources/documents/taxation/vat/traders/vat_community/vat_in_ec_annexi.pdf).

Country	
Austria	€35,000
Belgium	€35,000
Bulgaria	70,000 BGN
Croatia	270,000 HRK
Cyprus	€35,000
Czech Republic	1,140,000 CZK
Denmark	280,000 DKK
Estonia	€35,000
Finland	€35,000
France	€35,000
Germany	€100,000
Greece	€35,000
Hungary	€35,000

Country	
Ireland	€35,000
Italy	€35,000
Latvia	€35,000
Lithuania	€35,000
Luxembourg	€100,000
Malta	€35,000
Netherlands	€100,000
Poland	160,000 PLN
Portugal	€35,000
Romania	118,000 RON
Slovakia	€35,000
Slovenia	€35,000
Spain	€35,000
Sweden	320,000 SEK
UK	£70,000

Goods subject to excise duty

Distance sales of excise goods to another EU member state are always taxed (for excise duty and VAT purposes) in the country of destination *whatever the level of sales* and a UK supplier must register in that country.

New means of transport

See **20.32** below.

Records

A UK business must keep a separate record of its distance sales to each EU member state to allow it to determine whether a liability to register for VAT in that country arises.

Tax representatives

If a UK business has to register in another EU member state, it may be obliged to appoint someone to act on its behalf there and should contact the relevant VAT authority. Alternatively it may be able to register personally and deal with its VAT obligations itself.

Option to account for VAT in another EU member state

A UK business may, if it wishes, opt to make the EU member state of destination the place of supply of goods *before* reaching the distance selling threshold as above. If it does so, it must

- notify HMRC (by writing to the written enquiries team or phoning the VAT Helpline, see **30.4 HMRC: ADMINISTRATION**) not less than 30 days before the date of the first supply to which the option relates, informing HMRC of the name of the country/countries involved;

- notify the EU member state/countries involved, at least 30 days before making the first supply, of its exercise of the option, providing written evidence that it has informed the UK authorities;
- register for VAT in country/countries concerned from the date of the first supply and comply with the VAT rules there; and
- within 30 days of the first supply after the option, provide HMRC with documentary evidence that it has notified the tax authority in the other EU member state/countries.

Where a business has exercised such an option, it can be withdrawn (and the place of supply moved back to the UK) by further written notice to HMRC but not earlier than

- 1 January which is, or next follows, the second anniversary of the date of the first supply following the option (i.e. until at least two full *calendar* years have elapsed); and
- 30 days after the receipt by HMRC of notification of withdrawal;

and not later than 30 days before the date of the first supply the business intends to make after the withdrawal.

[*SI 1995/2518, Reg 98*].

VAT groups

UK VAT groups are not recognised outside the UK and each individual group member must monitor the value of its own distance sales to each EU member state to determine whether it is liable to register for VAT in that country in its own right. A group member can exercise the option to account for VAT on its distance sales before it reaches an EU member state's threshold.

Reporting requirements

The following table summarises the reporting requirements for supplies of goods to customers in other EU member states.

Type of supply	*VAT return*	*EC Sales List*
Distance sales from the UK below the distance selling threshold in the EU member state of arrival of the goods	Enter the VAT due in Box 1 and the value of the supply in Box 6	No
Distance sales from the UK on or over the distance selling threshold in the EU member state of arrival (or where the business has opted to register there before reaching the threshold)	Enter the value of the supply in Boxes 6 and 8	No

If the business is required to submit an Intrastat declaration then any distance sales from the UK need to be included on the Intrastat declaration using the VAT exclusive amount.

(VAT Notice 725, paras 6.4–6.17).

Example

Marie sells handbags to wealthy individuals through her internet site and she is VAT-registered in the UK where she lives. Her sales to Ireland are as follows:

Trading month	Sales
October 2016 (first month of trading)	€10,000
November 2016	€10,000
December 2016	€10,000
January 2017	€10,000
February 2017	€10,000
March 2017	€20,000

The distance selling limits are based on calendar years. Marie did not exceed the Irish limit of €35,000 in 2016 (total sales in 2016 were €30,000) so the point at which she has exceeded the limit on a calendar year basis is at the end of March 2017. She will now need to register for VAT in Ireland and charge Irish VAT (rather than UK VAT) on all future sales to non-registered customers in that country. She will then complete an Irish VAT return each quarter and pay VAT to the Irish tax authorities.

Goods lost, destroyed or stolen in transit

[20.19] Whether or not there is a liability to account for VAT on goods lost, destroyed or stolen in transit depends on the circumstances.

- **If lost, etc. before supplied** (e.g. whilst in storage awaiting delivery) no VAT is due.
- **If lost, etc. while being transported in the UK** (by either the supplier or the customer), VAT is due unless the supplier holds evidence of loss, destruction or theft (e.g. an insurance claim or police investigation).
- **If lost, etc. while being transported outside the UK** (by either the supplier or the customer), the goods may continue to be zero-rated provided the supplier has valid proof of removal of the goods from the UK and the VAT registration number of the customer. The customer may still be liable to account for acquisition tax. It should also be noted that there may be additional VAT liabilities if the loss, etc. occurs *en route* through an EU member state.

(VAT Notice 725, para 3.8).

Sales at ports/airports and on ships/aircraft

[20.20] There are no VAT and duty-free sales to travellers on 'intra-EU journeys'.

'*Intra-EU journeys*' are those commencing in one EU member state and ending in another EU member state without calling at any country or territory outside the EU. It is irrelevant whether or not the journey passes through international seas or airspace.

As a result, subject to those transitional arrangements

(a) *sales from a shop at a port or airport situated in the UK* to persons travelling on intra-EU journeys are subject to UK VAT (and duties) at rates applicable to other retail sales in the UK; and

(b) *sales on board a ship or aircraft on an intra-EU journey* are subject to VAT at the rate applicable in the EU member state of departure (i.e. the first passenger point of embarkation in the EU) provided
- the goods are to be taken away at the end of the journey (see below for 'onboard consumption'); and
- the sales take place either on a wholly intra-EU journey or a leg of a journey from the first point of passenger embarkation of the ship or aircraft in the EU until the final point of passenger disembarkation in the EU.

Examples

(1) Goods sold on a Dover to Calais ferry are subject to UK VAT. On the return Calais-Dover leg they are subject to French VAT.

(2) Goods sold on an aircraft flying from London to Paris and then on to Rome are subject to UK VAT throughout the journey.

(3) Goods sold on a flight from London to New York are outside the scope of UK/EU VAT.

(4) A flight from London to New York makes a stop-over in Paris. If passengers disembark at Paris, the London to Paris leg is an intra-EU journey and UK VAT is due on goods sold during the leg; the Paris to New York leg is an international journey and sales of goods are outside the scope of UK/EU VAT. If passengers do not disembark at Paris, the whole flight is an international journey and sales of goods on board are outside the scope of UK/EU VAT.

(5) A flight from New York to Frankfurt makes a stop-over at London. If passengers embark at London, the London to Frankfurt leg is an intra-EU journey and any goods sold are subject to UK VAT. If there is no passenger embarkation in London, the sale of goods throughout the journey is outside the scope of UK/EU VAT.

(6) A flight from New York to Vienna makes stop-overs at London and Frankfurt with passengers embarking in London. The New York to London leg is an international journey outside the scope of UK/EU VAT. The first place of passenger embarkation in the EU is at London and therefore UK VAT is due on goods sold on board during the entire journey from London to Frankfurt to Vienna. The Frankfurt to Vienna journey is not a separate leg for VAT purposes.

As VAT is due in the EU member state of departure, airline and ferry operators may be liable to register for VAT in more than one EU member state.

On board consumption

Goods (e.g. foods, drink and tobacco) sold for consumption on

- ships and aircraft are free of VAT and excise duty; and
- trains are free of VAT (but not excise duty).

All sales of these commodities from an on-board bar or restaurant are treated as being for immediate consumption although sales of alcohol and tobacco are subject to certain conditions and restrictions. For example, alcohol must be sold by the glass or, in the case of wine, from opened bottles and there are set maximum quantities for tobacco products on ferries. (As smoking is not permitted in aircraft, no sales of tobacco qualify for consumption on board.)

For VAT purposes, food, confectionery and soft drinks sold anywhere on board a ship or aircraft are treated as goods consumed on board and relieved of VAT, provided it is self-evident that these products are of a type that are more suitable for on-board consumption than gift purchase or home use. Products that, by virtue of their packaging, are clearly not suitable to be treated as consumed on board (e.g. boxes of chocolates or tins of biscuits) are subject to VAT in the normal way, even if actually consumed on board the ship or the aircraft.

Cruises

HMRC accept that food, drink, tobacco and most toiletries sold on an intra-EU cruise ship are normally consumed on board. Sales of these goods continue to be relieved from VAT provided the quantities sold indicate that the passengers are unlikely to take them away at the end of the cruise. Such goods bought with the intention of taking them away at the final port of disembarkation are subject to VAT at the rate applicable in the country of departure (see (*b*) above). Where a cruise which starts and ends in the UK calls at a non-EU member state (e.g. Egypt) or a place outside the EU fiscal territory (e.g. the Channel Islands) VAT-free sales to passengers for take-away are allowed provided the passengers have the opportunity to disembark and make purchases in that country or territory. See also *Köhler v Finanzamt Düsseldorf-Nord, ECJ Case C-58/04*, [2006] STC 469 (TVC 22.215) where the court held that stops made by a ship in the port of a country outside the EU during which passengers could leave the ship, even for a short period, were stops within a third territory. As a result, any sales made from a shop on board whilst the ship had stopped at that territory were not taxable in the EU but fell within the tax jurisdiction of that territory.

(VAT Information Sheet: Excise duty and VAT arrangements following the withdrawal of duty free sales of goods to intra-Community travellers; Business Brief 17/04).

Miscellaneous

[20.21] Miscellaneous matters relating to supplies of goods to other EU member states are outlined below.

(1) Arrangements for diplomatic missions, consulates, 'international organisations' and 'NATO visiting forces' in other EU member states

Under international agreements, certain people and bodies hosted by other EU member states may make purchases free of VAT. The host government determines who qualifies and it may impose limitations. If the customer has any doubts regarding these arrangements, it should contact its host VAT authority for advice.

These arrangements apply only to supplies that would otherwise be subject to UK VAT at a positive rate. They do not apply to new means of transport (which may be zero-rated but under the different rules in **20.34** below).

For these purposes:

- '*International organisation*' means an organisation established by a treaty between sovereign governments. An organisation formed by agreement between non-governmental bodies (e.g. limited companies or charities) is not an international organisation for these purposes; nor is a body set up by a single state or government (e.g. a government department). Well-known international organisations include the institutions of the European Union, the United Nations and its various subsidiary organisations, and the North Atlantic Treaty Organisation (NATO).
- '*NATO visiting force*' means an armed force contingent that belongs to a NATO Member State, is stationed in an EU member state, and does not belong to the country in which it is stationed.

Zero-rating supplies of goods

A supply qualifies for zero-rating if it satisfies the following conditions:

- The supplier receives a certificate of entitlement (see below).
- The goods must be for
  - (a) the 'official use' of an embassy, high commission, consulate, international organisation, NATO visiting force or British armed force contingent based in Cyprus; or
  - (b) the personal use of a member of staff of one of these bodies.

  '*Official use*' includes goods the body receives for distribution (including sale) to its members and their accompanying dependants.

  '*Personal use*' includes distributing goods to their accompanying dependants for no reward.
- The supplier, or a forwarder acting on its behalf, must remove the goods to an official address of the embassy, etc. It may consign goods to the post or to a courier or fast parcel service, including the British Forces Post Office (BFPO). If the customer is a British embassy or high commission in another EU member state, the supplier may consign goods to the Foreign and Commonwealth Office for delivery through diplomatic channels.
- The supplier must obtain and keep proof of the removal of the goods from the UK to the customer's address in the host country. Proof of posting is sufficient.
- If the supply is for a contingent of British forces in Cyprus or its staff, or for a NATO visiting force in Germany or its staff, the order must be placed by an Official Procurement Agency for the force, such as the NAAFI or a regimental purchasing officer.

Zero-rating supplies of services

A supply of services qualifies for zero rating if it satisfies the following conditions:

- The supplier receives a certificate of entitlement (see below).

- The supply of services must be made to an international organisation, a NATO visiting force, or a British force in Cyprus, for the official use of the force or organisation.
- The person placing the order must be based in an office of the force or international organisation in an EU member state other than the UK.
- A supply of services to British forces must in addition satisfy the following conditions:
  - (a) The service must consist of training, software development, a supply of staff, or goods forwarding.
  - (b) For training, the trainees must all be members of a British contingent based in an EU member state other than the UK, or members of British forces Cyprus.
  - (c) For software development, the software must be for the use of the force, and not for use in the UK.
  - (d) For a supply of staff, the staff must work exclusively for the force in the visiting force's host country or in a Sovereign Base Area in Cyprus.
  - (e) If the service is goods forwarding, the goods must all be forwarded to or from the force's premises in the other EU member state or in a Sovereign Base Area in Cyprus.

Certificate of entitlement

The supplier must obtain and keep documentation uniquely identifying the supply and claiming entitlement under *Directive 2006/112/EC, Art 151*. This must be either

- a certificate bearing the original signature of the head or acting head of the embassy, etc. with evidence of the qualifying status of the signatory; or
- any other form of certificate specified by their host government.

Exceptionally, in the case of a supply for the British force in Cyprus or its members, or for a visiting force in Germany or its members, the supplier must obtain and keep a certificate from the person placing the order uniquely identifying the supply for which relief is claimed, and claiming entitlement

- for British forces in Cyprus – under *Directive 2006/112/EC, Art 143(i)*; or
- for a visiting force in Germany – under *Directive 2006/112/EC, Art 151*.

EC Sales Lists

Entries on EC Sales Lists are not required for these supplies.

Distance sales

In general, transactions zero-rated under these provisions are not regarded as distance sales and do not count towards distance selling thresholds. Exceptionally supplies to Germany, do count towards the distance selling threshold in that country.

(VAT Notice 725, paras 14.1–14.7, 14.9; VAT Notice 48, ESC 2.6).

(2) Freight containers

The removal of a container to another EU member state can be zero-rated provided

- the supplier obtains the customer's VAT registration number (with a two digit country code prefix) and shows this on the VAT invoice;
- the container is sent from the UK to a destination in another EU member state; and
- within three months of the date of supply, the supplier obtains and keeps valid commercial evidence that the container has been removed from the UK.

See **22.8 EXPORTS** for the definition of a 'container'.

Where the customer collects or arranges collection of the container and its removal from the UK, the supplier should confirm with the customer how the container is to be removed and what evidence of this will be available.

If the customer is not registered for VAT in another EU member state, or all the above conditions are not met, the supply is standard-rated.
(VAT Notice 703/1/10, para 4 which has the force of law).

Leasing or hiring of containers

Where a container is leased/hired to a customer in business in another EU member state, the supply is treated as made in that other country. No UK VAT is due and the customer will normally have to account for VAT there under the reverse charge procedure. If the customer is a private individual then the place of supply is where the supplier belongs, and the supplier must charge UK VAT.

Incidental charges which under the terms of the lease agreement are charged to the lessee are regarded as part of the consideration for the leasing of the container and have the same VAT liability. Included are repair, delivery, regulator and handling charges, extra rental and any charge for the option to terminate the lease at an earlier date.
(VAT Notice 703/1/10, paras 5.3, 5.5).

Temporary movements of containers

The temporary movement of a container from the UK to another EU member state (whether involved in transporting goods or where the container is on lease/hire) is not treated as a removal from the UK with acquisition in the destination country. See **20.27** below. Details of the movement must be entered in a register of temporary movements. See **20.30** below. (VAT Notice 703/1/10, para 6).

(3) Samples

Movements of goods that qualify as samples are disregarded for intra-EU supply and acquisition purposes provided the conditions in **48.7**(26) **OUTPUT TAX** are met.

Reporting requirements

Where qualifying samples are sent to, or received from, another EU member state, no entry is required on the VAT return or EC Sales List.

(VAT Notice 725, para 15.7).

(4) Goods sent for testing

Goods sent to another EU member state for testing are disregarded provided

- ownership remains unchanged; and
- the goods are either returned to the country of departure or destroyed.

No entry is required on a VAT return or an EC Sales List.

(VAT Notice 725, para 15.8).

(5) Goods removed to customers in other EU member states after processing or incorporation

The following provisions have the force of law.

When a business makes a supply of goods to a VAT-registered customer in another EU member state but has to deliver them to a third person in the UK who is also making a taxable supply of goods or services to that customer, the business can zero-rate the supply provided

- it obtains and shows the customer's EU VAT registration number, including the two-letter country prefix code, on its VAT sales invoice;
- the goods are only being delivered and not supplied to the third person in the UK;
- no use is made of the goods other than for processing or incorporation into other goods for removal;
- it obtains and keep valid commercial evidence that the goods have been removed from the UK within the time limits in **20.11** above; and
- its records show
  - (a) the name, address and VAT number of the customer in the EU;
  - (b) the invoice number and date;
  - (c) the description, quantity and value of the goods;
  - (d) the name and address of the third person in the UK to whom the goods were delivered;
  - (e) the date by which the goods must be removed; and
  - (f) proof of removal obtained from the person responsible for transporting the goods out of the UK; and
  - (g) the date the goods were actually removed from the UK.

The records must also be able to show that the goods supplied have been processed or incorporated into the goods removed from the UK.

In cases where the third person is not in the UK but in another EU member state, the same conditions generally apply to allow a business to zero-rate its supply.
(VAT Notice 725, para 4.5).

(6) Tools for the manufacture of goods for export

Machine tools are goods used in the manufacture of other goods (e.g. jigs, patterns, templates, dies, moulds, punches and similar tools). The supply of machine tools, that remain in the UK, are normally standard-rated. However, the supply of a tool can be zero-rated if

- the customer specifically asks the supplier to make it, or buy it, for him;
- the supplier uses the machine tool to manufacture goods for the same customer and makes a specific charge to him for the supply of the tool;
- the tool is an integral part of the contract, or series of contracts, to supply goods to a VAT-registered customer in another EU member state and title to the tool passes to the customer;
- the supplier obtains and shows the customer's VAT registration number (with its two digit country code prefix) on the VAT sales invoice;
- the manufactured goods are sent or transported out of the UK to a destination in another EU member state; and
- the supplier holds commercial documentary evidence that the goods have been removed from the UK.

(VAT Notice 701/22/17, paras 1.2–1.4, 3.1).

Triangulation

[20.22] Triangulation is the term used to describe a chain of intra-EU supplies of goods involving three parties. Instead of the goods physically passing from one party to the other as in a normal two-party transaction, they are delivered directly from the first party to the last party in the chain.

> *Example*
>
> A (the '*intermediary supplier*') receives an order from a customer (C) in another EU member state. To fulfil the order, A orders the goods from another supplier (B) (the '*original supplier*') in a third EU member state who delivers the goods directly to C. The original supplier B invoices the intermediate supplier A who in turn invoices the customer C.

Normal procedure

Unless the simplified procedure below is adopted, such supplies are treated for VAT purposes as follows.

- The supply by B to A involves the removal of goods from one EU member state to another (even though this is not to the country where A is established). B can therefore zero-rate the supply of goods to A, subject to meeting the normal conditions in **20.11** above.
- The supply by A to C does not involve the movement of goods from the country where A belongs. As a result, A is treated as making an acquisition of the goods in the EU member state to which the goods are delivered (see **20.6**(*a*) above) and an onward supply of the goods there. A should therefore register for VAT in that country and account for VAT there on its acquisition and onward supply.
- C need do nothing as it is receiving a domestic supply.

A is therefore required to register for VAT in the EU member state to which the goods are delivered.

(VAT Notice 725, paras 13.1–13.4).

Simplified procedure

To avoid imposing this burden of registration on A, all EU member states have agreed to a simplified procedure. As a result, businesses registered for VAT in one EU member state may no longer be required to register for VAT in another EU member state purely because of such triangular transactions. Instead, based on the above example, provided A is not registered or otherwise required to be registered in the country to which the goods are sent, and C is registered there, A can opt to have C account for the VAT due in the country of destination on his behalf. If A does so opt, C *must* account for the VAT on the supply of goods made to him (i.e. the simplification procedure is compulsory if A so opts) and the acquisition of the goods by A is disregarded both in the country where he belongs and the country of destination. B still treats his transaction in the same way as any other intra-EU supply, i.e. he may zero-rate the supply subject to the usual conditions in **20.11** above and should record the supply on an EC Sales List in the normal way. (VAT Notice 725, paras 13.5, 13.6).

> *Example*
>
> Jeff is VAT-registered in the UK and has received an order to supply goods to a Spanish customer. However, the Spanish customer is reselling the goods in question to a French customer, and has asked for the goods to be shipped direct to France rather than via Spain. The Spanish and French customers are both registered for VAT in their own countries.
>
> As long as Jeff obtains proof of export that the goods have left the UK, and the VAT number of his Spanish customer, he can zero-rate the supply of goods on his invoice to the Spanish customer.

UK provisions

UK provisions specifically cover the two positions where either the customer C is registered in the UK (see **20.23** below) or the intermediary supplier A is registered in the UK (see **20.24** below).

De Voil Indirect Tax Service. See V3.369.

Simplified procedure: customers registered in UK

[20.23] Where

- the original supplier A (in France) makes a supply of goods to an intermediary supplier B who 'belongs in another EU member state' (Germany),
- that supply involves the removal of the goods from another EU member state (France) and their removal to the UK but does not involve the removal of goods from the UK,
- both the supply by A, and the removal of the goods to the UK, are for the purposes of making a supply by B to a customer C who is UK VAT-registered,
- neither of those supplies involves the removal of the goods from an EU member state in which B is taxable at the time of the removal without also involving the previous removal of the goods to that country, and

- there would be a taxable acquisition by C in the UK if the supply to him involved the removal of goods from another EU member state to the UK,

then, provided B complies with requirements laid down by HMRC, the supply by A to B is disregarded for the purposes of *VATA 1994*, and the supply by B to C is treated, other than for the purposes of *VATA 1994, Sch 3* (registration in respect of acquisitions from another EU member state), as a taxable acquisition. The taxable acquisition is treated as taking place on the date of the issue of the invoice for the transaction.

A person 'belongs in another EU member state' if

- he has no business establishment or other fixed establishment in the UK and does not have his usual place of residence in the UK;
- he is neither registered nor required to be registered under *VATA 1994* (ignoring supplies disregarded under these provisions);
- he does not have, and is not for the time being required to appoint, a VAT representative; and
- he is taxable in another EU member state.

[*VATA 1994, s 14(1)(3)(4)(5)*].

Notification

Where an intermediate supplier B wishes to take advantage of the simplified procedure, he must notify HMRC and the customer C in writing of his intention to do so. The notification must include

- his name and address;
- his VAT registration number (including alphabetical code, see **40.5 INVOICES**) used, or to be used, for the purposes of obtaining zero-rating of the supply to him by the original supplier A;
- the date upon which the goods were first delivered (or are intended to be delivered) to the customer; and
- the name, address and VAT registration number of the UK customer to whom the goods are supplied (and who will account for the VAT).

Notification to HMRC must be direct to the Non-Established Taxable Persons Unit (NETPU), HMRC, Ruby House, 8 Ruby Place, Aberdeen AB10 1ZP.

The notification must be made no later than the provision of the first invoice in relation to the supply (see below).

A separate notification must be made for each customer to whom supplies are made under these provisions but, once made in relation to the first supply to any particular customer a notification is deemed to apply to all subsequent supplies to that customer as long as the intermediary supplier B continues to belong in another EU member state.

[*SI 1995/2518, Reg 11*]. (VAT Notice 725, Section 14).

Invoices

The intermediary supplier B must issue an invoice to the UK customer which must comply with the requirements of the EU member state in which he is VAT-registered. The invoice must be issued no later than 15 days after, and must relate to a supply of at least the same extent as would have been required under, the normal time of supply rules if these provisions had not applied. Such an invoice is then treated as if it were an invoice for the purposes of **20.7**(*b*) above. [*SI 1995/2518, Reg 18; SI 2007/2085, Reg 9*].

Recording and accounting for VAT

On receipt of a copy of the supplier's notification to HMRC (see above), the UK customer C must account for the VAT on the goods supplied to him under the simplified procedure as an acquisition. See **20.8** above.

(VAT Notice 725, paras 13.9–13.11).

Simplified procedure: intermediate suppliers registered in UK

[20.24] If the simplified procedure is used in a triangular transaction where the intermediate supplier B in the example above is registered in the UK and the goods are removed to another EU member state of destination, the supply of those goods by the original supplier A to B and the supply of those goods by B to the customer C are both disregarded for the purposes of *VATA 1994* but without prejudice to the power of HMRC to require production of records and accounts and furnishing of information. [*VATA 1994, s 14(6)*]. In order to use the simplified procedure, the intermediate supplier B must

- use his UK VAT registration number to allow the original supplier A to zero-rate the supply of the goods in the EU member state from which the goods were dispatched;
- issue his customer C with a VAT invoice which must contain all the details normally required for intra-EU supplies (see **40.5 INVOICES**). [*SI 1995/2518, Reg 17; SI 2007/2085, Reg 8*];
- not enter details of triangular transactions on his VAT return; and
- on his EC Sales Lists
  - (a) include the supply, quoting the VAT number of the customer C in the country of destination of the goods;
  - (b) enter the total value of the triangular transactions to each EU customer on a single line separately from the total of other intra-EU supplies to that customer; and
  - (c) identify triangular transactions by inserting the figure '2' in the indicator box.

If an intermediate supplier's intra-EU supplies only involve triangular transactions, he should contact the VAT Helpline who will arrange for EC Sales Lists to be sent to him automatically.

(VAT Notice 725, paras 13.7, 13.8).

Transfer of own goods to another EU member state

[20.25] Subject to the exceptions below, and unless specifically overridden by other provisions, the transfer of goods within the same legal entity from one EU member state to another (e.g. between branches of the same company) is deemed to be a supply of goods for VAT purposes under the general provisions of *VATA 1994, Sch 4 para 6* (see **20.2** above) and is liable to VAT under the normal arrangements for intra-EU supplies. Specifically excluded is the removal of gas through a natural gas system situated within the territory of an EU member state or any network connected to such a system; electricity; or heat or cooling supplied through a network [*SI 2010/2925*].

As a result, where a UK business transfers its own goods from the UK to another EU member state in the course of its business (e.g. to sell them on from that country or to use them there), it must register for VAT in that country in order to

- support zero-rating of the deemed supply when the goods leave the UK (subject to the conditions in **20.11** above); and
- account for acquisition VAT in that country and account for output VAT if there is a subsequent supply of the goods there.

If the UK business does not register in the EU member state to which its own goods are transferred, the deemed supply must be treated as a domestic supply. It must account for VAT in the UK on the goods (and cannot recover this as input tax in the other EU member state). In *Cudworth* (TC01173) (TVC 23.24), C was a clothing retailer. He sometimes travelled to Germany, where he made sales from trade stands at agricultural shows. He was VAT registered in the UK but not in Germany. The tribunal held that when C travelled with his goods to Germany, there was a deemed supply on the removal of the goods from the UK. He should have accounted for VAT on the cost price when he removed the goods from the UK, not on the sale price when he sold them to German customers.

Similarly, where a business transfers its own goods from another EU member state to the UK in the course of its business, if not already registered here it may need to do so in order to account for VAT on the acquisition of the goods in the UK. But see **20.5** above for VAT relief on certain transfers.

Exceptions

The rules relating to transfers of own goods do not apply to

- temporary movements of goods within **20.27** below;
- movements of goods for repair, etc. under **20.28** below; and
- installed and assembled goods under **20.30** below.

Reporting requirements

The following table summarises the reporting requirements for transfers of own goods to other EU member state.

Type of supply	*VAT return*	*EC Sales List*
Transfers of own goods from the UK to other EU member states	Enter the value of the goods based on cost in Boxes 6 and 8	Enter value based on cost of the goods

Type of supply	*VAT return*	*EC Sales List*
Transfers of own goods from another EU member state to the UK	Enter acquisition VAT (for positive-rated goods) in Box 2 and input tax (subject to the normal rules) in Box 4. Enter the value of the goods based on cost in Boxes 7 and 9	No

The movement of the goods will also need to be included on an Intrastat declaration where a business is required to file and the amount should be based on the cost value of the goods.

(VAT Notice 725, paras 9.1–9.9).

Consignment stock

Consignment stocks are goods that a business transfers between EU member states in order to meet future supplies to be made by the business, or on its behalf, in the country of arrival. The important feature is that the movement of the goods occurs *before* a customer has been found for them. It can include goods not meeting the all conditions necessary for treatment as call-off stocks (see **20.32** below).

Consignment stocks are treated as a transfer of own goods for VAT accounting and reporting purposes.

(VAT Notice 725, para 15.3).

Goods sent on sale or return, approval or similar terms

[20.26] Goods sent on sale or return, approval or similar terms are not supplied until

- the customer indicates that he is going to keep them; or
- a time when it is agreed between the parties that the goods are to be automatically treated as accepted (if earlier).

Consequently, when such goods are sent to another EU member state, they should be treated as a transfer of own goods.

(a) When a UK business sends goods on such terms to a customer in another EU member state
   - it initially makes an acquisition of the goods in that country; and
   - it makes a supply of the goods there if, and when, the goods are eventually adopted by the customer.

   The business may need to register there to account for any VAT due on the acquisition and supply of the goods.

(b) When a business in another EU member state sends goods on such terms to a UK customer
   - it initially makes an acquisition of the goods in the UK;
   - it makes a supply of goods in the UK on the earlier of
     (i) the date when the goods are eventually adopted by the customer;

(ii) twelve months after their time of removal to the UK; or
(iii) the time of issue a VAT invoice in respect of the goods under the normal UK rules for sale or return goods in the UK (see **67.12 SUPPLY: TIME OF SUPPLY**).

The business will be liable to register for VAT in the UK to account for any VAT due on the acquisition and supply of the goods.

Reporting requirements

The following table summarises the UK reporting requirements for goods sold on sale or return, approval or similar terms.

Type of supply	*VAT return*	*EC Sales List*
Goods sent from UK to another EU member state	Enter the value based on the cost of the goods in Boxes 6 and 8	Enter value based on cost of the goods
Goods sent to the UK from another EU member state	Enter acquisition VAT (for positive-rated goods) in Box 2 and input tax (subject to the normal rules) in Box 4. Enter the value based on the cost of the goods in Boxes 7 and 9	No

(VAT Notice 725, para 15.6).

Temporary movements of goods

[20.27] The following temporary movements of own goods between EU member states are not treated as deemed supplies of goods for VAT purposes under **20.25**. No acquisition VAT is due in the country to which the goods are transferred.

Where

(i) the owner is established in the EU member state of dispatch but not that of arrival;
(ii) the goods are removed for the sole purpose of being used by the owner in the course of a supply of services to be made by him;
(iii) at the time of their removal, there is a legally binding obligation to make that supply of services (i.e. a specific contract to fulfil); and
(iv) the owner intends to remove the goods back to the EU member state of dispatch upon ceasing to use them in making the supply (and does in fact do so).

This could apply, for example, to tools and equipment taken to another EU member state for use there to repair machinery. It also applies to goods that are loaned or leased to someone there.

The removal back to the EU member state of dispatch under (iv) is also not treated as a supply for VAT purposes.

Where goods are removed to another EU member state for temporary use there and

(i) temporary importation relief would have been given if the goods had been imported from outside the EU; and
(ii) the owner intends to export the goods outside the EU or remove them to an EU member state other than the country to which the goods have been removed, in either case not later than two years after the day upon which the goods were removed (and he does in fact do so).

See **34.27 IMPORTS** for goods eligible for temporary import relief.

The export or removal under (ii) is also not treated as a supply for VAT purposes.

If the circumstances of the transfer outlined above change and the movement no longer qualifies for treatment under these temporary movement provisions (e.g. the goods are sold or are to remain in the other EU member state for more than two years), the original movement should be treated, belatedly, as a deemed supply and acquisition under **20.25** above. The owner must account for VAT in the VAT period in which the condition is not complied with.

[*SI 1992/3111, Arts 4(f)(g)(h), 5; SI 1995/2518, Reg 42*]. (VAT Notice 725, paras 10.1–10.6).

Although the above transfers are not treated as supplies for VAT purposes, commercial documentary evidence should be held to prove that the goods have left the UK and have later returned. (VAT Notice 725, para 10.7).

Register of temporary movements of goods

See **20.30** below for the requirement to keep such a register.

Reporting requirements

No entries are required on the VAT return or EC Sales List when goods are sent from the UK and the conditions above are satisfied.

If the goods are sent from the UK in order to make a supply of services in another EU member state and the goods remain outside of the UK for more than two years, the transaction must be included on a Dispatches Intrastat return (where required) and the value should be based on the cost of the goods. (VAT Notice 725, para 10.8).

Goods sent for valuation or carrying out work

[20.28] A supply of goods is not treated as taking place when goods are removed from one EU member state to another in the following circumstances.

Where

(i) the goods have been removed to another EU member state for the purpose of delivering them to a person (other than the owner) who is to value or to carry out any work on the goods in that country; and

(ii) the owner intends that the goods will be returned to him by their removal to the country of dispatch upon completion of the valuation or work.

The return of the goods to the original EU member state is also not treated as a supply of goods.

Where the intention of the owner under (ii) above is not fulfilled, the original movement of goods must be belatedly treated as a deemed intra-EU supply and acquisition and the owner must account for VAT in the VAT period in which the condition is not complied with.

[*SI 1992/3111, Art 4(e)(h), Art 5; SI 1995/2518, Reg 42*].

See **20.30** below for the requirement to keep a register of movement of the goods.

Accounting for VAT on the movements of goods for valuation, repair, etc.

[20.29] Special place of supply rules apply to the *services* of work carried out on goods and the valuation of goods where the goods are moved between EU member states. See **66.18 SUPPLY: PLACE OF SUPPLY** for full details.

The VAT treatment of goods that are moved between EU member states in circumstances where some form of service (e.g. repair and valuation) is to be applied to those goods is as follows.

(1) Goods sent from the UK for work to be carried out in another EU member state

Provided the conditions in **20.28** above are satisfied, there is no deemed supply of own goods when a UK business sends goods from the UK for work to be carried out in another EU member state. The UK owner must

- record the movement of the goods in his register of temporary movements of goods (see **20.30** below);
- hold commercial documentary evidence that the goods have been removed from the UK; and
- account for VAT on each of the supplies of services he has received as a reverse charge.

The movement of goods is not required to be shown on EC Sales Lists or Intrastat declarations.

Where the conditions are not met (e.g. the goods are not returned to the UK), the normal rules for transfer of own goods to another EU member state in **20.25** apply. The UK owner may be liable to register for VAT in the other EU member state.

(2) Goods sent to the UK for work to be carried out

Provided the conditions in **20.28** above are satisfied, no entry is required on the VAT return of the UK supplier of services in relation to the goods either when they are received in the UK from the EU customer or subsequently returned to him. But he must

- record the movement of the goods in his register of temporary movements of goods (see **20.30** below); and
- hold commercial documentary evidence that the goods have been removed from the UK.

The movement of goods is not required to be shown on EC Sales Lists or Intrastat declarations.

Where the conditions are not met (e.g. the goods are not returned to abroad), the normal rules for transfer of own goods to another EU member state in **20.30** apply. The owner may be liable to register for VAT in the UK.

(3) Work performed on goods in another EU member state before removal to the UK

A UK business may buy goods in another EU member state and have work performed on them before they are removed to the UK. In these circumstances, the provisions in **20.28** above do not apply (because the goods are not physically sent to another EU member state for processing as they are already there). The UK customer must

- account for acquisition VAT on the supply of the goods in the normal way; and
- account for VAT on the supplies of the services of work performed on the goods under the reverse charge procedure.

(4) Work performed on goods in the UK before removal to another EU member state

A customer in another EU member state may buy goods from a UK business but have work performed on the goods by another UK business before removing the goods from the UK. The UK business can still zero-rate the supply under **20.11** above provided it meets all the relevant conditions. In particular, it must ensure that the customer provides evidence of removal of the goods from the UK once the work has been completed.

(VAT Notice 725, paras 12.1–12.7).

Register of temporary movement of goods

[20.30] Every taxable person must keep and maintain a register of goods moved to, and goods received from, other EU member states on a temporary basis. The register need not be kept in any particular format but it must be readily available for all goods temporarily moved to and from the UK.

The register *must* include the following information for all goods moved between the UK and other EU member states if they are to be returned within a period of two years after their first removal or receipt. (It would be advisable also to include any goods where the date of return is not certain.)

- The date of removal of goods to another EU member state and the date of receipt of those goods when they are returned from that or another EU member state.

- The date of receipt of goods from another EU member state and the date of removal of those goods when they are returned to that or another EU member state.
- A description of the goods sufficient to identify them.
- A description of any process, work or other operation carried out on the goods either in the UK or in another EU member state.
- The consideration for the supply of the goods.
- The consideration for the supply of any processing, work or other operation carried out on the goods either in the UK or another EU member state.

[*SI 1995/2518, Reg 33*]. (VAT Notice 725, paras 16.7–16.9).

De Voil Indirect Tax Service. See V5.212.

Installed and assembled goods

[20.31] A supply of installed or assembled goods occurs where the supplier of the goods has a contractual obligation to install or assemble them (e.g. a supplier of studio recording equipment could have a contractual obligation to supply the equipment and install it in the customer's studio). (VAT Notice 725, para 11.1).

General rule

Where the supply of goods involves their installation or assembly, they are treated as supplied in the country where they are installed or assembled. [*VATA 1994, s 7(3)*].

Reporting requirements

Unless the simplification procedure below is applied, the reporting requirements for installed or assembled goods are as follows.

- Where a UK business supplies goods which it is to install or assemble in another EU member state, its supply takes place in that country and it is liable for any VAT there. The business may need to register there in order to account for the VAT due. For UK VAT purposes, the value of the supply should be included in Box 6 on the VAT return and the value based on the cost of the goods at the time of dispatch should be entered in Box 8. No entries are required on an EC Sales List. The transaction should be included on a Dispatches Intrastat declaration (where required) using the cost of the goods where known or the open market value of the goods.
- Where a business supplies goods from outside the UK to be installed or assembled here (the goods may be sourced from another EU member state or from a third country), the supply is liable to UK VAT and the business may have to register for VAT in the UK. If the business registers, it must include output tax in Box 1 of its VAT return and the value of the supply in Box 6. No entries are required on an EC Sales List. The transaction needs to be included on a UK Arrivals Intrastat (where required) and the cost value of the goods should be used where known, otherwise the open market value should be used.

(VAT Notice 725, paras 11.6, 11.11).

Simplification procedure

To avoid imposing the burden of registration in another EU member state on the supplier of installed or assembled goods, *some* EU member states have adopted a simplified procedure under which the supplier can opt to have his customer account for the VAT due in the country of installation or assembly. Where the simplification procedure is available, it can be used provided

- the customer is registered for VAT in the EU member state of installation or assembly;
- the supplier is not required to be registered in that country for any other reason;
- the supplier is registered for VAT in another EU member state; and
- the necessary procedures required by the VAT authorities in the country of installation or assembly are complied with.

If the supplier so opts, the customer *must* account for the VAT (i.e. the simplification procedure is compulsory if the supplier opts).

The operation of this simplified procedure is a matter for each EU member state. A business should contact the VAT authority in the EU member state where it is proposing to make a supply to find out if they are operating a simplified procedure. In the absence of simplification arrangements, the general rules above apply.

Installation or assembly in the UK

The UK has adopted the simplification procedure. Under those provisions, where

(a) a 'person belonging in another EU member state' makes a supply of goods to a UK VAT-registered person and the supply involves their installation or assembly at a place in the UK to which they are removed; and

(b) there would be a taxable acquisition by the UK-registered person if, instead of treating that supply as a taxable supply in the UK (under the general rule above), it was treated as involving the removal of the goods from another EU member state to the UK,

then, provided the supplier complies with the requirements laid down by HMRC, the supply is treated, other than for the purposes of *VATA 1994, Sch 3* (registration in respect of acquisitions from another EU member state), as a taxable acquisition. The taxable acquisition is treated as taking place on the date of the issue of the invoice for the transaction.

For these purposes, a person is treated as '*belonging in another EU member state*' if

- he has no business establishment or other fixed establishment in the UK and does not have his usual place of residence in the UK;
- he is neither registered nor required to be registered under *VATA 1994* (ignoring supplies disregarded under these provisions);

- he does not have, and is not for the time being required to appoint, a VAT representative; and
- he is taxable in another EU member state.

[*VATA 1994, s 14(2)–(5)*].

Notification

If the EU supplier wishes to take advantage of the simplification provisions and avoid registering for VAT in the UK, he must notify HMRC of his intention to do so. The notification must include

- his name and address,
- his VAT registration number (including alphabetical code, see **40.5 INVOICES**) by which he is identified for VAT in the EU member state in which he belongs,
- the date upon which the installation or assembly of the goods began or will begin, and
- the name, address and VAT registration number of the UK VAT-registered customer

and be sent in writing to the Non-Established Taxable Persons Unit (NETPU), HMRC, Ruby House, 8 Ruby Place, Aberdeen AB10 1ZP.

The notification must be made no later than the provision of the first invoice in relation to the supply (see below). A separate notification must be made for each customer to whom it is intended to make supplies under the simplification procedure but, once made in relation to the first supply to any registered person, is deemed to apply to all subsequent supplies to that registered person as long as the person making the supply continues to belong in another EU member state.

A copy of the notification must be sent to the UK customer to advise him that the simplified arrangements are to be applied and that he will be required to account for the VAT. The copy must be sent no later than the date of issue the first invoice.

[*SI 1995/2518, Reg 12*]. (VAT Notice 725, para 11.8).

Invoices

The EU supplier must issue an invoice to the UK VAT-registered customer which must comply with the requirements of that EU member state. The invoice must

- be issued no later than 15 days after what would have been the normal time of supply in the UK, and
- relate to a supply of at least the same extent as would have been required under the normal time of supply rules

if these provisions had not applied. The invoice is then treated as if it were an invoice for the purposes of **20.7**(*b*) above. [*SI 1995/2518, Reg 19*].

Reporting requirements

The following table summarises the UK reporting requirements for installed or assembled goods when they arrive in the UK or are dispatched from the UK. However this table does not deal with any onward sale of the goods in the UK for a supplier who is VAT registered in the UK.

Type of supply	*VAT return*	*EC Sales List*
Goods received in the UK from VAT-registered suppliers in other EU member states and the simplification is used	UK customer – enter acquisition VAT (for positive-rated goods) in Box 2 and input tax (subject to the normal rules) in Box 4. Enter the value based on the cost of goods in Boxes 7 and 9	No
Goods sent from the UK for installation/assembly in another EU member state	UK supplier – enter the value of the supply in Box 6 and Box 8	No
Goods received in the UK and the overseas supplier is VAT registered in the UK (simplification not used)	Overseas supplier – Box 2 – acquisition tax based on the cost value of the goods Box 4 – input tax Net value based on the cost of goods in Boxes 7 and 9	No

The transaction should be included on a UK Arrivals Intrastat declaration (where required) using the cost value of the goods where known, otherwise the open market value of the goods should be used.

(VAT Notice 725, para 11.11).

De Voil Indirect Tax Service. See V3.370.

'Call-off' stocks

[20.32] Call-off stocks are goods transferred by the supplier between EU member states to be held for an individual customer in the country of arrival pending 'call-off' for use by the customer as needed. Until call-off, title and ownership of the goods remains with the supplier. To be treated as call-off stock, the goods must be transferred for a single identified customer either

- for consumption within its business (e.g. as part of a manufacturing process); or
- to make onward supplies to their own customers.

Goods that are transferred to maintain the suppliers own stocks in another EU member state, or are available for call-off by more than one customer, must be dealt with as consignment stocks (see **20.25** above).

The goods should normally be stored by the supplier at the customer's premises. But goods delivered to storage facilities operated by the supplier can still be treated as call-off goods provided the above conditions are met and the customer is aware of the details of deliveries into storage. If not, the goods should be treated as consignment stocks (see **20.25** above).

The VAT treatment of call-off stock is as follows.

(a) If a UK business sends goods to another EU member state to be held as call-off stock, the normal intra-EU rules apply. The supply is treated as taking place in the UK and can be zero-rated when sent from the UK subject to the normal requirements in **20.11** above.

(b) If a UK business receives call-off stocks in the UK from a supplier in another EU member state, the normal intra-EU rules apply and it should account for acquisition VAT in the normal way.

Reporting requirements

The following table summarises the UK reporting requirements for call-off stocks.

Type of supply	*VAT return*	*EC Sales List*
Goods supplied to VAT-registered customers in other EU member states	Enter the value based on the cost of the goods in Boxes 6 and 8	Enter value based on cost of the goods
Goods received in the UK from VAT-registered suppliers in other EU member state	Enter acquisition VAT (for positive-rated goods) in Box 2 and input tax (subject to the normal rules) in Box 4. Enter the value based on the cost of goods in Boxes 7 and 9	No

The movement should also be recorded on an Intrastat declaration, where required, and using the cost of the goods.

(VAT Notice 725, para 15.2).

New means of transport

[20.33] The following are regarded as new means of transport (NMT) for the purposes of **20.34–20.38** below, provided that, in each case, it is intended for the transport of persons or goods.

(a) Any ship, including a hovercraft, exceeding 7.5 metres in length (overall) provided that three months or less have elapsed since its first entry into service or, since that time, it has travelled under its own power for 100 hours or less. A ship is treated as having first entered into service
   - when it is delivered from its manufacturer to its first purchaser or owner or is first made available to that person (whichever is the earlier); or
   - if applicable, when its manufacturer first takes it into use for demonstration purposes.

(b) Any aircraft, the take-off weight of which exceeds 1,550 kilograms, provided that three months or less have elapsed since its first entry into service or, since that time, it has travelled under its own power for 40 hours or less. An aircraft is treated as having first entered into service

- when it is delivered from its manufacturer to its first purchaser or owner or is first made available to that person (whichever is the earlier); or
- if applicable, when its manufacturer first takes it into use for demonstration purposes.

(c) Any motorised land vehicle which
- has an engine with a displacement or a cylinder capacity exceeding 48 cc; or
- is constructed or adapted to be electrically propelled using more than 7.2 kilowatts

provided that six months or less have elapsed since its first entry into service or, since that time, it has travelled under its own power for 6,000 kilometres or less. A motorised land vehicle is treated as having first entered into service

(i) on its first registration for road use in the EU member state of its manufacturer or when a liability to register for road use is first incurred there (whichever is the earlier); or

(ii) where (i) does not apply, its removal by its first purchaser or owner, its first delivery or its being made available to its first purchaser (whichever is the earlier); or

(iii) if applicable, when its manufacturer first takes it into use for demonstration purposes.

Where the time of first entry into use under *(a)*–*(c)* above cannot be established to the satisfaction of HMRC, a means of transport is to be treated as having first entered into service on the issue of an invoice relating to its first supply.

[*VATA 1994, s 95; SI 1995/2518, Reg 147*].

De Voil Indirect Tax Service. See V1.294.

Supplies by persons registered in the UK to non-registered persons in other EU member states

[20.34] A non-registered person who buys an NMT in the UK to take to another EU member state must pay any taxes due on it in the EU member state of destination under the laws of that country. To avoid double taxation, a UK-registered supplier can zero-rate the supply of an NMT to such a person provided the following conditions are met (which have the force of law).

(a) The means of transport qualifies as 'new' under **20.33** above.

(b) The purchaser (or his authorised chauffeur, pilot or skipper) personally takes delivery of the NMT and removes it from the UK to the EU member state of destination within two months of the date of supply.

(c) The supplier and the customer make a joint declaration on Form VAT 411.

The CJEU recently confirmed in *Santogal M-Comercio e Reparaco de Automoveis Lda v Autoridade Tributaria e Aduabeira, CJEU Case C-26/16* that the exemption of an intra-community supply of a new means of transport is not subject to the condition that the purchaser resides in the member state of destination.

Form VAT 411 is a declaration by the customer that he will take the NMT to another EU member state within two months and pay the VAT there. It is also a declaration by the supplier that he has supplied an NMT to the customer for removal from the UK.

Copies of Form VAT 411 are obtainable from the VAT Helpline (tel: 0300 200 3700). It comprises an original (or top sheet) and three copies. When the form has been fully completed, the supplier must send the original to HMRC, Personal Transport Unit, Priory Court, St Johns Road, Dover, Kent CT17 9SH within six weeks of the end of the calendar quarter in which the supply is made.

The first copy of Form VAT 411 should be given to the customer. The second copy is retained by the supplier and, where the NMT is a vehicle, the third copy is used to register it for road use if it is to be driven out of the UK (see below).

Sales subject to a finance agreement

Where a non-registered person funds the purchase of the NMT using a hire purchase or similar agreement, the dealer makes a standard-rated supply to the finance house and the finance house makes a zero-rated supply of the NMT to the non-registered person. The dealer should ensure that the VAT 411 clearly shows that it is the finance house supplying the vehicle and must send the second copy of the Form VAT 411 to the finance house to support the zero-rating of the supply. The other copies of the form should be distributed in the normal manner.

Using a new vehicle on UK roads

Any new vehicle cannot be used on UK roads before its removal to another EU member state unless it is licensed, registered and properly insured against third party liability. If the vehicle is not already licensed at the time of purchase, the supplier will obtain the registration number (a special 'VAT-free' series which allows the vehicle to be identified as tax free whilst it remains in the UK prior to removal) by presenting the third copy of the completed Form VAT 411, attached to the application for registration, to one of the DVLA local offices. An updated list of UK DVLA offices can be found at http://www.dft.gov.uk/dvla/contactus/localoffices/findnear.aspx and for DVA Northern Ireland at http://www.dvani.gov.uk.

Failure to remove the NMT from the UK within the time allowed

If, in exceptional circumstances, the customer is unable to remove the NMT from the UK, he must inform HMRC immediately in writing at HM Revenue and Customs, Personal Transport Unit, Priory Court, St Johns Road, Dover, Kent CT17 9SH. HMRC will then calculate the VAT due and issue a demand for immediate payment. If the NMT is not removed from the UK within the time allowed and HMRC have not been informed, the vehicle may be liable to forfeiture.

Type approval

'*Type approval*' is the official recognition that the vehicle has satisfied certain international safety standards. A vehicle cannot be licensed and registered in the UK unless it is type approved or otherwise exempt. For type approval purposes a motor vehicle is

- a passenger vehicle with four or more wheels, or three wheels if it has a maximum gross weight of more than 1,000 kilograms, intended to carry no more than eight passengers, excluding the driver; or
- a three-wheeled passenger vehicle with a maximum gross weight of under 1,000 kilograms, if it has either a maximum speed of more than 50 kilometres per hour or an engine capacity of more than 50 cubic centimetres; or
- a goods vehicle.

Further information on type approval can be found from The Vehicle Certification Agency, 1 The Eastgate Office Centre, Eastgate Road, Bristol BS5 6XX (Tel: 01272 524125).

NMT vehicles supplied in the UK are exempted from UK-type approval requirements for as long as they are relieved from VAT whilst awaiting removal from the UK. If the vehicle is not removed, and as a consequence becomes liable to UK VAT, the exemption from type approval is withdrawn. The absence of type approval may affect the customer's ability to register the vehicle in the UK for permanent use on UK roads.

[*SI 1995/2518, Regs 22C, 155*]. (VAT Notice 728, paras 6.1–6.7, 9.2, 9.5, 9.6, 10.2, 10.5, 10.7, 10.9, 10.10, 11).

De Voil Indirect Tax Service. See V4.356, V5.272.

Supplies by persons registered in the UK to persons registered in other EU member states

[20.35] A supplier who is registered for VAT in the UK should zero-rate the supply of an NMT to a VAT-registered person from another EU member state provided

(a) the means of transport qualifies as 'new' under **20.33** above;
(b) the customer's VAT registration number (with two digit code prefix) is shown on the invoice;
(c) the NMT is dispatched or transported from the UK to another EU member state within two months of the date of issue of the invoice for the supply; and
(d) the supplier holds valid commercial documentary evidence that the NMT has been removed from the UK (see **20.13** above).

The customer must account for any VAT due on the acquisition in the EU member state of destination under the laws of that country.

Using a new vehicle on UK roads

If any new unregistered vehicle is to be used in the UK before its removal to another EU member state, it must be licensed, registered and insured against third-party liabilities before delivery. The supplier and the customer must complete and sign a declaration on Form VAT 411A obtainable from the VAT Helpline (tel: 0300 200 3700). This form must be sent or produced to one of the DVLA local offices who will allocate a registration mark in the tax-free series.

If the customer's plans change and he decides to keep the vehicle in the UK permanently, he cannot retain the tax-free registration mark and should contact HMRC at HM Revenue and Customs, Personal Transport Unit, Priory Court, St Johns Road, Dover, Kent CT17 9SH.

Failure to remove the NMT from the UK within the time allowed

If the customer does not remove the NMT from the UK in the time allowed, he will be liable to pay UK VAT.

Type approval

See **20.34** above.

EC Sales Lists

An entry is required in any EC Sales List. See **2.11** *et seq* **ACCOUNTING PERIODS AND RETURNS.**

(VAT Notice 728, paras 9.2, 9.4, 9.8, 10.3–10.5).

Supplies by non-registered persons: recovery of VAT

[20.36] Where a non-taxable person supplies an NMT which involves its removal to another EU member state, HMRC must, on a claim, refund to him the VAT which he paid on the supply to him (or acquisition or importation by him, as the case may be) but not exceeding the amount of VAT which would have been payable on the supply by him involving removal if it had been a taxable supply by a taxable person and had not been zero-rated. [*VATA 1994, s 40*].

The claim must be in writing and be made no earlier than one month, and no later than 14 days, before the making of the supply by virtue of which the claim arises. It must include a signed declaration that all the information entered in, or accompanying it, is true and complete and must be sent to HM Revenue and Customs, Personal Transport Unit, Priory Court, St Johns Road, Dover, Kent CT17 9SH. It must contain the following information. (A form for the purpose is reproduced in VAT Notice 728, section 12.)

- The name, current address and telephone number of the claimant.
- The place where the NMT is kept and the times when it may be inspected. (HMRC may need to inspect the NMT before it is sold to confirm its eligibility for refund.)
- The name and address of the person who supplied the NMT to the claimant.
- The price paid by the claimant for the supply of the NMT to him, excluding VAT.
- The amount of any VAT on that supply.

- The amount of any VAT paid by the claimant on the acquisition or importation of the NMT by him.
- The name and address of the proposed purchaser, the EU member state to which the NMT is to be removed and the date of the proposed purchase.
- The price to be paid by the proposed purchaser.
- A full description of the NMT (make, model, colour, registration number, engine number and chassis/hull/airframe number) including, in the case of a motorised land vehicle, its mileage since first entry into service and, in the case of a ship or aircraft, its hours of use since that time. See **20.33** above for the time of first entry into service.
- Details (as the case may be) of
  - (i) the ship's length in metres
  - (ii) the aircraft's take-off weight in kilograms; or
  - (iii) the motorised land vehicle's displacement or cylinder capacity in cubic centimetres (if powered by a combustion engine) or maximum power output in kilowatts (if an electrically propelled vehicle).
- The amount of the refund being claimed.

HMRC will advise the claimant if they wish to examine the NMT before it is sold to confirm its eligibility for refund.

Before any refund is received, HMRC will also need to see

- proof of original purchase (normally the invoice or import entry);
- evidence that the VAT has been paid on the original purchase;
- proof of sale (normally the bill of sale and evidence that payment has been received); and
- evidence that the NMT has been removed to another EU member state.

[*SI 1995/2518, Regs 146, 149–154*]. (VAT Notice 728, paras 7.1–7.5).

Acquisitions of new ships or aircraft from other EU member states by non-registered persons

[20.37] Where a taxable acquisition of a new ship or new aircraft takes place in the UK,

- the acquisition is not in pursuance of a taxable supply; and
- the person acquiring the goods is not a taxable person at the time of the acquisition,

the person acquiring the goods should notify HMRC of the acquisition within 14 days of the time of the acquisition or the arrival of the goods in the UK, whichever is the later. The notification should be in writing in English and should contain the following particulars.

- The name and current address of the person acquiring the new ship or new aircraft.
- The time of the acquisition.
- The date when the new ship or new aircraft arrived in the UK.
- A full description of the new ship or new aircraft which should include any hull or airframe identification number and engine number.

- The consideration for the transaction in pursuance of which the new ship or new aircraft was acquired.
- The name and address of the supplier in the EU member state from which the new ship or new aircraft was acquired.
- The place where the new ship or new aircraft can be inspected.
- The date of notification.

The notification should include a declaration, signed by the person who is required to make the notification or a person authorised in that behalf in writing, that all the information entered in it is true and complete. The notification should be made at, or sent to, any office designated by HMRC for the receipt of such notifications. Any person required to notify HMRC of an acquisition of a new ship or new aircraft must pay the VAT due upon the acquisition at the time of notification or within 30 days of HMRC issuing a written demand to him detailing the VAT due and requesting payment.

[*SI 1995/2518, Reg 148*].

Acquisitions from other EU member states by persons registered in the UK

[20.38] Where a VAT-registered person in the UK acquires an NMT free of VAT from a registered person in another EU member state, he should

- provide the supplier or vendor with his UK VAT registration number to enable them to zero-rate the supply of the vehicle;
- account for the VAT due on his normal VAT return for the period in which he acquires the NMT.

If the NMT is a land vehicle, it must be licensed and registered before it is used on public roads. HMRC must first have been notified about the vehicle's arrival through the NOVA system (see **20.39** below).

Onward supply

Where a VAT-registered person acquires and makes an onward supply of an NMT, he must still account for acquisition VAT on the vehicle. If it forms part of his stock in trade, he can recover input tax equal to the amount of acquisition VAT declared. Output tax must be charged on the onward supply.

(VAT Notice 728, paras 8.1–8.4).

Acquisitions of motorised land vehicles (NOVA)

[20.39] From 15 April 2013, any person (other than an excepted relevant person) bringing a motorised land vehicle into the UK, for permanent use on the road must notify (or arrange for an authorised third party to notify) HMRC of the arrival of the vehicle within 14 days, prior to the vehicle being registered with the DVLA. If a non-registered business or private individual brings a car into the UK from an EU supplier, payment of the VAT due is required at the same time as the notification is made. Any vehicle that has not had the appropriate VAT charges paid will not be able to be registered with the DVLA. For VAT-registered businesses, the VAT charge due on the vehicle is to be accounted for on the VAT return, as with other goods acquired from the EU. The notification may be made either in paper form or electronically. It must contain

- the name and current address of the person bringing the land vehicle into the UK;
- the date when the land vehicle arrived in the UK;
- a full description of the land vehicle which shall include any vehicle registration mark allocated to it by any competent authority in another EU member state prior to its arrival and chassis identification number;
- where applicable, the registration number of the person bringing the land vehicle into the UK;
- the date of the notification;
- in the case of an acquisition arising from a deemed supply under *VATA 1994, Sch 4 para 6*
  - the value of the transaction determined in accordance with *VATA 1994, Sch 7 para 3*;
  - details of any relief claimed or to be claimed in relation to the acquisition under *VATA 1994, Sch 8 Group 12 Item 2(f)* (zero rating: drugs, medicines, aids for the handicapped etc.);
- in the case of any other acquisition
  - the consideration for the transaction in pursuance of which the land vehicle was acquired;
  - the name and address of the supplier in the EU member state from which the land vehicle was acquired;
  - details of any relief claimed or to be claimed in relation to the acquisition under *VATA 1994 Sch 8, Group 12 Item 2(f)*; and
- any other particulars specified in a notice published by HMRC.

The notification must be made in English, and must include a declaration that the information provided is true and complete.

From 1 April 2014, where there is a relevant decision regarding a vehicle after the vehicle has entered the UK the date of the relevant decision is treated as the date of arrival in the UK. A relevant decision is a decision that affects the notification process, e.g., a decision that a vehicle is not required to be registered for road use in the UK. (HMRC Brief 12/14).

[*VATA 1994, Sch 11 para 2(5D); SI 1995/2518, Reg 148A; SI 2014/548, Reg 5*].

Sales and purchases of second-hand goods

[20.40] The liability of sales and purchase of second-hand goods within the EU is as follows.

Sale by UK-registered person to a person registered in another EU member state

Such a sale under the second-hand margin scheme is taxable in the UK with no further liability to pay VAT on acquisition in another EU member state. If the sale is excluded from the margin scheme, it may be zero-rated subject to the normal conditions but the customer must account for VAT on the acquisition and will not be able to include the goods in a margin scheme in his own country.

Sale by UK-registered person to a private individual in another EU member state

Such a sale is taxable in the UK. VAT is calculated on the margin for eligible goods sold under one of the margin schemes for **62 SECOND-HAND GOODS**.

Acquisition by UK-registered person from a person registered in another EU member state

Such an acquisition from a seller who deals with the goods under a margin scheme is subject to VAT in the other EU member state with no liability to acquisition VAT on entry into the UK. Eligible goods may be sold under one of the schemes for **62 SECOND-HAND GOODS** as the invoice will not show VAT as a separate item. If the sale is not dealt with under a margin scheme in the other EU member state, it will be zero-rated subject to the normal conditions and the UK buyer must account for any VAT due on the acquisition. The UK buyer cannot deal with the goods under the second-hand margin scheme.

Acquisition by UK-registered person from a private individual in another EU member state

No VAT is due when the goods are brought into the UK and the goods can therefore be sold under one of the special margin schemes for **62 SECOND-HAND GOODS**.

Acquisition by a private individual in the UK from a registered person in another EU member state

Such an acquisition is subject to VAT in the other EU member state.

The CJEU recently held in *'Litdana' UAB v Valstybine mokesciu inspekcija prie Lietuvos Respublikos finansu ministerijos, CJEU Case C-624/15* (TVC 60.22) that the purchaser can still use the margin scheme even if the supplier located in another EU member state has failed to meet their obligations under the scheme. However, the taxable person must take all reasonable steps to check and confirm that the transactions they are involved with will not result in tax evasion.

Goods obtained in the EU by travellers returning to the UK via a non-EU member state

[20.41] Where travellers return to the UK through non-EU member states (including the Channel Islands) carrying goods, purchased for their personal use, duty and VAT paid in another EU member state, no further duty will be payable in the UK on production, if requested, of evidence of payment of that duty and VAT (e.g. an invoice).

Key points — EU: Single Market

[20.42] Points to consider are as follows.

- An important principle of the EU VAT system is that no VAT is charged on the sale of goods to a VAT-registered business in a different EU member state. In such cases, the customer accounts for any tax that is due on its own VAT returns (known as acquisition tax). A business making sales of goods to non-VAT registered customers will charge domestic VAT based on the same rate that would apply if it was supplying goods to a customer in its own country. However, it is important to remember that if the value of such sales exceeds certain limits (known as 'distance selling' limits), then it will need to become VAT-registered in the country where the customer is resident.
- Each EU member state has a choice of adopting either a €35,000 or €100,000 annual limit for distance selling (calendar year basis). As a general observation, countries with higher rates of VAT favour the lower level of €35,000, i.e. to minimise the VAT disadvantage to businesses that are based in their own countries.
- A business in another EU member state outside the UK that is selling goods to non-VAT registered customers in the UK will exceed the distance selling limits if sales exceed £70,000 in a calendar year. The exception is if the goods in question are subject to excise duty, in which case a nil threshold applies.
- An important clause in VAT law (and often forgotten) is that if a UK business that is not VAT-registered acquires goods from other EU member states that has exceeded the VAT registration limit on a calendar year basis (or will exceed the VAT registration limit in the next 30 days), then it will need to register for VAT in the UK under what are known as the 'acquisition' rules. This situation means that a business could be VAT-registered on a compulsory basis, even though it makes no taxable supplies in the UK. The aim of the rules is to ensure a business unable to reclaim input tax cannot gain a VAT advantage by buying goods from EU member states where the standard-rate of VAT is lower than in its own country.
- It is often forgotten that an acquisition of goods still takes place if a business transfers its own goods from one EU member state to another (e.g. a branch it has in another EU member state). In this situation, it is classed as making an acquisition in the country where the goods are received.
- A UK VAT-registered business acquiring goods from another EU member state will account for acquisition tax in Box 2 of its relevant VAT return, based on the value of the goods and the UK's rate of VAT, providing that the goods are not zero-rated in

the UK. In most cases, the business will reclaim the same amount of VAT as input tax in Box 4 of the same VAT return. However, such a claim would not be correct if the goods in question either suffered an input tax block, or related to exempt, non-business or private activities. The net value of the acquisition will also be recorded in both Box 7 and Box 9 of the same VAT return.

- If a UK business sells goods to a VAT-registered customer in another EU member state then in order to zero-rate the sale, it must obtain the customer's VAT registration number and show this on its sales invoices. It must also obtain and retain satisfactory evidence that the goods have left the UK. This evidence will be needed in the event of a visit by an HMRC officer to review the records.
- The proof that the goods have left the UK must be obtained within three months of the supply taking place. If this deadline is not met, then output tax should be declared on the supply in question, as if it had taken place in the UK. However, the output tax paid can be subsequently adjusted if evidence is eventually obtained in the future.
- If a supplier obtains proof of goods leaving the UK they will not usually be penalised by HMRC if the documentation is subsequently found to be false. However, the supplier must have acted in good faith and received documentation that appears to provide satisfactory evidence that the goods have left the UK.
- A business selling goods to VAT-registered customers in other EU member states must also take reasonable steps to ensure the customer has provided a genuine VAT registration number. There are a number of ways of checking the validity of a number but the most important check is that a supplier should always be satisfied that he is dealing with a bona fide customer.
- A higher risk situation is where a customer collects the goods from a supplier and is responsible himself for shipping the goods out of the UK, and acquiring the relevant transport documents. In such cases, a sensible strategy would be for the supplier to take a refundable deposit from the customer, equivalent to the amount of VAT on the transaction, on condition that the deposit will be refunded once the supplier has provided adequate proof to confirm the goods have left the UK.
- Triangulation will avoid the need for a business having to register for VAT in a country where goods are delivered from its supplier (based in another EU member state other than its own) directly to the country of the customer in a third EU member state. For example, a UK business buying goods from a French supplier, for sale to its customer in Germany, and where the goods are delivered directly from France to Germany, would avoid the need to register for VAT in Germany if the triangulation simplification procedure is adopted. The end result is that the final German

customer will account for acquisition tax on his own VAT return.

customer will be unable to claim input tax on his own VAT return.

21

Exempt Supplies

Introduction to exempt supplies

[21.1] A supply of goods or services is an exempt supply if it is of a description for the time being specified as such under various Group headings in *VATA 1994, Sch 9*. [*VATA 1994, s 31(1)*]. A person who makes exempt supplies but no taxable supplies is not a taxable person and cannot be registered. [*VATA 1994, s 3(1), s 4(2)*]. Output tax is not chargeable on exempt supplies or recoverable on related input tax. Where both exempt and taxable supplies are made, the rules as to **50 PARTIAL EXEMPTION** are applied and only part of the input tax may be reclaimable.

The general categories of exemption are

Group 1	Land (see **42.17 LAND AND BUILDINGS: EXEMPT SUPPLIES AND OPTION TO TAX**)
Group 2	Insurance (see **37 INSURANCE**)
Group 3	Postal services (see **21.2** below)
Group 4	Betting, gaming and lotteries (see **8.2–8.5 BETTING AND GAMING**)
Group 5	Finance (see **24 FINANCIAL SERVICES**)
Group 6	Education (see **17 EDUCATION**)
Group 7	Health and welfare (see **29.1 HEALTH AND WELFARE; 13.11 CHARITIES; 44.12 LOCAL AUTHORITIES AND PUBLIC BODIES** and **21.3** below)
Group 8	Burial and cremation (see **16.6 DEATH AND INCAPACITY**)
Group 9	Subscriptions to trade unions, professional and other public interest bodies (see **15.7 CLUBS AND ASSOCIATIONS**)
Group 10	Sport, sports competitions and physical education (see **58.1** and **58.5 RECREATION AND SPORT**)
Group 11	Works of art, etc. — certain disposals exempted from capital taxes (see **74.1 WORKS OF ART, ETC.**)
Group 12	Fund-raising events by charities and other qualifying bodies (see **13.10 CHARITIES**)
Group 13	Cultural services, etc. — admission to museums, exhibitions, zoos and performances of a cultural nature supplied by public bodies and eligible bodies (see **58.2 RECREATION AND SPORT**)

Group 14	Supplies of goods where input tax cannot be recovered (see **21.4** below)
Group 15	Investment gold (see **27.2 GOLD AND PRECIOUS METALS**)
Group 16	Cost sharing (see **21.5** below)

[*VATA 1994, Sch 9*].

The descriptions of the Groups above are for ease of reference only and do not affect the interpretation or the description of items within them. [*VATA 1994, s 96(10)*]. The Treasury may vary the Groups (and notes contained therein which form an integral part) by adding, deleting or amending any description of supply for the time being specified. The *Schedule* may also be varied so as to describe a supply of goods by reference to the use which has been made of them or to other matters unrelated to the characteristics of the goods themselves. [*VATA 1994, s 31(2), s 96(9)*].

Where a supply of goods falls within one of the above Groups but is also covered by the provisions relating to **75 ZERO-RATED SUPPLIES**, the latter take priority. [*VATA 1994, s 30(1)*].

De Voil Indirect Tax Service. See V4.101–V4.103.

Postal services

[21.2] For EU legislation see **19.24**(*a*) and **19.25**(*h*) **EUROPEAN UNION LEGISLATION.**

From 1 January 2011

Following the CJEU decision in *R (oao TNT Post UK Ltd) v HMRC, ECJ Case C–357/07*, [2009] STC 1438 (TVC 22.302) (see **19.24 EUROPEAN UNION LEGISLATION**), under UK legislation, the following are exempt from VAT.

- The supply of public postal services by a universal service provider.
- The supply of goods by a universal service provider which is incidental to the supply of public postal services by that provider.

A '*universal service provider*' (USP) is a person providing a (or part of a) universal postal service in the UK.

'*Public postal services*' are any postal services that a USP is required to provide in the discharge of a specified condition. These include postal services allowing a person access to the USP's postal network and which are required to be provided by a specified condition.

However, services are not public postal services if

- the price is not controlled by or under a condition; or
- if any of the other terms on which the services are provided are freely negotiated,

unless a specified condition requires the USP to make the services available to persons generally at the same price or on such terms.

(Note that under EU law, the term 'public postal services' appears to be a reference to the provider of the service, rather than the service itself; see, for example, *Directive 2006/112/EC, Art 132(1)(a)*.)

A 'specified condition' means a designated USP condition, a USP access condition or a transitory condition under the *Postal Services Act 2011, Sch 9 para 5*.

[*VATA 1994, Sch 9 Group 3; SI 1995/2518, Reg 2(1)*].

The cost of postage charged by a supplier in addition to the cost of goods is not within the exemption, see **48.7**(19) **OUTPUT TAX.**

Stamps

Unused current or valid UK and Isle of Man postage stamps are not chargeable with VAT if supplied at or below face value. *First day covers* are taxable at the standard rate on their full value whether supplied by the Post Office Philatelic Bureau or stamp dealers. For stamps generally, see **58.15 RECREATION AND SPORT.**

De Voil Indirect Tax Service. See V4.126.

Religious communities

[21.3] The supply, 'otherwise than for a profit', of goods and services incidental to the provision of 'spiritual welfare' by a religious community (e.g. a nunnery or monastery) is exempt when supplied to a resident member of that community in return for a subscription or other consideration paid as a condition of membership. [*VATA 1994, Sch 9 Group 7 Item 10*].

Otherwise than for a profit

Following the decision in *C & E Commrs v Bell Concord Educational Trust Ltd*, CA 1988, [1989] STC 264 (TVC 21.9), HMRC accept that supplies are made '*otherwise than for a profit*' if they are made by charities in circumstances where any surpluses are applied solely to the furtherance of the activity which generated the surplus. Where, however, a charity pursues more than one activity, the welfare services will not be supplied otherwise than for a profit if surpluses from welfare services are applied to the maintenance or furtherance of the other activities, even though charitable.

Spiritual welfare

'*Spiritual welfare*' can include

- spiritual counselling to an individual;
- guided exploration of spiritual needs and development; and
- discussion, meditation and prayer or worship sessions

but does not include

- conferences or retreats when the predominant purpose is not spiritual welfare;

- educational courses in theology, or similar subjects, where the predominant purpose is to expand knowledge of spiritual matters rather than to provide spiritual welfare services; or
- meetings to discuss theology or aspects of Church doctrine.

(VAT Notice 701/2/11, para 2.3).

Supplies of goods where input tax cannot be recovered

[21.4] A supply of goods is an exempt supply where each of the following conditions is satisfied.

(a) The person making the supply (the '*relevant supplier*'), or any 'predecessor' of his, has incurred (or will incur) input tax on obtaining
- the goods supplied; or
- any other goods used in the process of producing the goods supplied so as to be incorporated in them.

For this purpose, input tax is deemed to include VAT incurred by the person concerned when he was not a taxable person (i.e. when he was not registered or liable to be registered).

In the particular case where the supply is the grant of a 'major interest' in land (see **42.10 LAND AND BUILDINGS: EXEMPT SUPPLIES AND OPTION TO TAX**), other than one excluded under (*c*) below, the input tax must be incurred on either
- acquiring a major interest in the land concerned; or
- goods used in the construction of a building or civil engineering work so as to become part of the land.

(b) All of the input tax referred to in (*a*) above is 'non-deductible input tax'. '*Non-deductible input tax*', subject to below, comprises the following.
- Input tax on goods used to make exempt supplies. No part of the input tax may be deductible as attributable to supplies giving a right to input tax deduction, whether the right to deduction arises before or after the supply of goods under consideration. However, an input tax entitlement arising only from the operation of the partial exemption *de minimis* rules (see **50.11 PARTIAL EXEMPTION**) is ignored.
- Input tax which is solely excluded from credit under the provisions relating to
  - **10 BUSINESS ENTERTAINMENT**;
  - non-building materials incorporated in a building or its site (see **43.4 LAND AND BUILDINGS: ZERO AND REDUCED RATE SUPPLIES AND DIY HOUSEBUILDERS**); or
  - motor cars (see **46.3 MOTOR CARS**).
- VAT incurred by the person concerned when he was not a taxable person (i.e. when he was not registered or liable to be registered).

Specifically excluded from non-deductible input tax is any VAT which has been, or will be, recovered under *VATA 1994, s 33* (see **44.7 LOCAL AUTHORITIES AND PUBLIC BODIES**), *VATA 1994, s 33A* (museums and galleries, see **35.13**(22) **INPUT TAX**), *VATA 1994, s 33B* (academies, see

35.13(30) **INPUT TAX**), *VATA 1994, s 39* (repayments of VAT to overseas traders, see **49.5 OVERSEAS TRADERS**) or *VATA 1994, s 41* (refunds to government departments, see **44.11 LOCAL AUTHORITIES AND PUBLIC BODIES**). This ensures that exemption under these provisions cannot apply in such cases.

(c) The supply made by the relevant supplier is not a supply which would be exempt under *VATA 1994, Sch 9 Group 1 Item 1* (see **42.17 LAND AND BUILDINGS: EXEMPT SUPPLIES AND OPTION TO TAX**) but for the option to tax having been exercised (see **42.23 LAND AND BUILDINGS: EXEMPT SUPPLIES AND OPTION TO TAX**).

Self-supplies

Input tax arising on any supply, acquisition or importation of goods is disregarded for the purposes of (*a*) and (*b*) above if, after that supply, etc. and before the supply by the relevant supplier, the relevant supplier or any predecessor of his is treated as having self-supplied the goods to himself under any provision of *VATA 1994*. This ensures that, in cases of self-supplies (e.g. the self-supply of a motor car, on which input tax was initially recovered, following a change of use) exemption under these provisions can still apply.

A person (A) is the '*predecessor*' of another (B) if the goods (or anything comprised in the goods)

- are transferred from A to B as part of a transfer of a going concern which was treated as neither a supply of goods nor a supply of services (see **9.9** *et seq.* **BUSINESS**); or
- formed part of the assets of A when it became a member of a VAT group of which B was the representative member;
- formed part of the assets of A, or any other company which was a member of the same VAT group as A, when the representative member of the VAT group changed from A to B; or
- formed part of the assets of B when it ceased to be a member of a VAT group of which A was the representative member.

A person's predecessors include the predecessors of his predecessor through any number of transactions.

[*VATA 1994, Sch 9 Group 14*].

Examples where the above provisions apply

- Business cars (see **46.3 MOTOR CARS**).
- Goods used for business entertainment (see **10.7 BUSINESS ENTERTAINMENT**).
- Fixtures and fittings incorporated by developers in new homes (see **43.4 LAND AND BUILDINGS: ZERO AND REDUCED RATE SUPPLIES AND DIY HOUSEBUILDERS**).
- Goods used by charities for exempt and non-business activities, provided VAT has been incurred on the goods and has not been recovered.

Examples where the above provisions do not apply

- Goods on which any part of the input tax has been or will be recovered, either on purchase or later as a result of partial exemption or capital goods scheme adjustments.
- Goods eligible for the second-hand margin scheme.
- Goods on which no VAT is incurred.

The resale of services of any type (e.g. copyrights).

Cost sharing

Background

[21.5] The cost sharing exemption applies when two or more organisations (whether businesses or otherwise) with exempt and/or non-business activities join together on a cooperative basis to form a separate, independent entity, a cost sharing group (CSG), to supply themselves with certain services at cost and exempt from VAT. As a result a 'cooperative self-supply' arrangement is created. The CSG is a separate taxable person from that of its members. It is therefore able to make supplies for VAT purposes to its members. These supplies will be exempt if the relevant conditions are met. This type of arrangement enables the creation of the same economies of scale for smaller businesses and organisations as larger businesses and organisations naturally enjoy. Thus the more members of a CSG there are the greater the potential savings and lower the costs per member of operating the relevant CSG.

A member of a CSG is a business or organisation that

- is capable of jointly owning and controlling a CSG
- receives qualifying supplies from the CSG.

As the exemption is mandatory all supplies that meet the relevant conditions will be subject to the exemption.

There are five conditions attached to the exemption.

- There must be an 'independent group of persons' (a CSG) supplying services to persons who are its 'members'.
- All the members must carry on an activity that is exempt from VAT or one which is not a business activity for VAT purposes.
- The services supplied by the CSG, to which the exemption applies, must be 'directly necessary' for a member's exempt and/or non-business activity.
- The CSG only recovers, from its members, the members' individual share of the expenses incurred by the CSG in making the exempt supplies to its members.
- The application of the exemption to the supplies made by the CSG to its members is not likely to cause a distortion of competition.

All these conditions must be satisfied for a supply to be exempt. If any of the conditions are not met the supplies will be taxable.

The exemption only applies to the recharges, at cost, of services supplied by a CSG to its group members. The exemption does not apply to commercial outsourced services or arrangements that amount to the provision of commercial outsourced services. Such services are generally made by specialist providers to unconnected third parties on a commercial for-profit basis and would not, therefore, meet the conditions of the exemption. They are not 'cooperative self-supply' arrangements.

A CSG can make supplies to non-members, but such supplies, unless covered by another exemption, will be taxable. If such supplies are cross border the normal place of supply and reverse charge rules apply.

Scope of the cost sharing exemption to 31 May 2018

Any business or organisation that is capable of meeting the relevant criteria/conditions has the opportunity to use the exemption to their benefit. The types of businesses and organisations that might benefit are

- charities
- banks
- education institutions
- insurance businesses
- social housing organisations
- betting and gaming organizations
- health and welfare businesses and organizations
- financial services businesses
- local authorities, government departments and NDPBs.

[*VATA 1994, Sch 9 Group 16*]. (VAT Information Sheet 7/12).

HMRC do not allow members and CSGs located outside of the EU to take advantage of the UK CSE (cost sharing exemption). However, CSGs and members located in other EU member states can take advantage of the UK CSE.

Relevant case law affecting scope of the CSE

A number of recent CJEU decisions have significantly reduced the potential scope of the cost sharing exemption. A brief update of the latest position can be found below.

In *Aviva, CJEU Case C-605/15* and *DNB Banka, CJEU Case C-326/15*, the AG's Opinion that the cost sharing exemption only applies to supplies to members with activities covered by the public interest exemption (*Directive 2006/112/EC, Art 132(1)*) and does not cover supplies made in the financial services sector which came as a bit of a surprise because neither the European Commission nor a number of member states, including the UK, held that view. The AG was also of the opinion that the cost sharing exemption does not cover cross-border supplies and the exemption cannot apply if the costs have been marked up for transfer pricing purposes. It will be interesting to see whether the CJEU follows the AG Opinion because if it does, the scope of the cost sharing exemption could be significantly narrowed in other EU member states. In the UK, the cost sharing exemption has not been as widely used as exempt organisations have tended to use the UK VAT grouping rules.

The CJEU judgment in the combined cases of *Aviva, CJEU Case C-605/15*; *DNB Banka, CJEU Case C-326/15* and *European Commission v Germany, CJEU Case C-616/15* (TVC 20.114) was released on 21 September 2017 and the Court has held that the cost sharing exemption can only be used by organisations which provide VAT exempt services that are stated in the law as being in the 'public interest'. As a result of this decision, businesses in the financial services, insurance, betting and gaming and real estate are not eligible to use the cost sharing exemption. However, the CJEU also went onto state that tax authorities who have extended to scope of the exemption to include other types of businesses cannot take action against these businesses in light of this judgment.

The CJEU has released its decision in *EC Commission v Luxembourg, CJEU Case C-274/15* (TVC 20.113) regarding the approach taken by Luxembourg when it implemented the CSE. The CJEU agreed with the Commission that Luxembourg had failed to comply with EU law when it implemented its cost sharing exemption laws and practices. The Court indicated that it considered that Luxembourg's implementation was incompatible with the Directive in that:

- Only the services rendered by a cost sharing group (CSG) which are 'directly necessary' for the exercise of the exempt activities of its members can come within the scope of the CSE. By allowing exemption to apply to persons with up to 30% of taxable activities by annual turnover, Luxembourg has incorrectly transposed *Directive 2006/112/EC.*
- A CSG is a separate independent taxable person which provides services independently to its members. As the CSG and its members are separate, members should not be allowed to recover VAT incurred by the CSG.
- Similarly, because of the CSG's independence from its members, any transaction between the CSG and one of its members must be regarded as a transaction between two taxable persons and thus as falling within the scope of VAT. Luxembourg has failed properly to transpose *Directive 2006/112/EC* by enabling transactions carried out by a member in his name but on behalf of the group to come within the scope of the CSE.

Scope of the cost sharing exemption from 1 June 2018

HMRC have published HMRC Brief 3/18 which provides details of the updated guidance on the scope of the cost sharing exemption that will be applicable from 1 June 2018. The scope has been severely limited because of the CJEU decisions outlined above. HMRC have introduced a limited transition period that runs until 1 June 2018 to enable effected businesses to make the necessary changes. The transition rules are outlined below.

The changes will impact businesses that are in the finance, insurance and other business sectors that do not provide goods and services that are in the 'public interest'. The CSE will be limited to the following sectors:

- Cultural services
- Education
- Fundraising
- Health and welfare

- Postal services
- Sport
- Subscriptions to trade unions and professional bodies

The CSG and its members must all be resident in the UK as it is no longer possible to have cross-border CSGs. The limitation on cross-border CSGs is because the AG considered that having cross-border groups could result in a distortion of competition due to the fact that cross-border groups could take advantage of any differing tax treatments between member states which could result in further tax benefits being achieved.

The CSG cannot uplift costs and all costs must be recharged at cost. No allowances can be made for any transfer pricing adjustments that are required.

The CJEU judgments do not impact any non-business activities carried on by the group and therefore these activities are not impacted by the changes.

HMRC are aware that the CJEU decision may impact housing associations and it intends to publish further guidance at a later stage once it has had the opportunity to fully consider the impact. Housing associations are therefore entitled to use the old rules until HMRC publish their guidance.

HMRC also announced that the current rules for 'directly necessary' (see above) continue to apply whilst the CJEU decision in *EC Commission v Luxembourg, CJEU Case C-274/15* (TVC 20.113) is considered further. HMRC state that it will produce further information at a later stage.

Transitional period

HMRC have published Information Sheet 2/18 which outlines the impact of the CJEU judgments on the current treatment of a CSG and the CSE.

The pre-1 June 2018 treatment can continue to apply until that date where the CSG has correctly implemented the CSE rules as outlined by HMRC in the VAT Cost Sharing Exemption manual. However, the transitional arrangements cannot be relied upon or applied in cases where the members have been involved in tax avoidance. Also, they cannot be used if they will cause a distortion of competition based on exploiting any differences between the tax treatment between member states for cross-border CSGs.

If any services are paid or invoiced before 1 June 2018, the CSG is only entitled to take advantage of the transitional arrangements to the extent that the services were performed before that date and the basic tax point was created before the end of the transitional period. Any pre-payments or invoices that cover the period after the transitional period ends must be apportioned on a fair and reasonable basis.

HMRC have stated that if a CSG is going to experience difficulties transitioning to the new rules then it should contact them to discuss this further to see what HMRC can to do to assist.

Cross-border CSGs may be allowed to use the transitional arrangements providing they meet all the following conditions:

- The CSG is in another EU member state.

- The CSG has correctly implemented the CSE in accordance with HMRC's previous guidance (if this is different to the member state where it is established).
- The CSG can provide satisfactory evidence to HMRC that there is no distortion of competition resulting from any differences in the tax treatment between member states.

Any CSG located in other EU member states who wishes to take advantage of the transitional period must write to HMRC before 1 May 2018 providing details of its cross-border arrangements.

Key points: exempt supplies

[21.6] Points to consider are as follows.

- Exempt supplies of goods or services are not classed as taxable and therefore input tax cannot be reclaimed on related costs. Also the value of exempt sales is ignored when deciding whether a business has exceeded the VAT registration limit and needs to register for VAT on a compulsory basis.
- It is an advantage for sales to either the general public or other exempt businesses to be exempt from VAT because there is no output tax charge to customers that they are unable to recover. In most cases, this situation will outweigh the disadvantages of the input tax relevant to the supply not being reclaimable.
- There are occasions when a standard-rated supply being incorrectly treated as exempt could prove costly for a business. For example, a VAT charge to another registered business would not be a problem if the business could reclaim the charge as input tax. The supplier can then recover related input tax on its own expenses because it has made a taxable supply. It is important to get the VAT liability right on all sources of business income.
- Output tax is not charged on the sale of goods where the original input tax was not reclaimed because it was either non-deductible or relevant to an exempt supply. The sales in these cases are exempt from VAT. A motor car available for private use is an example of an input tax block that means the subsequent sale of the vehicle by the business will be exempt from VAT.

22

Exports

De Voil Indirect Tax Service. See V4.301–339.

Introduction to exports

[22.1] Some general notes are as follows:

Trade with other EU member states

The provisions of this chapter only apply to goods which are exported outside the EU. See **18.2 EUROPEAN UNION: GENERAL** for the VAT territory of the EU. For the provisions relating to supplies of goods from the UK to other EU member states, see **20.11 EUROPEAN UNION: SINGLE MARKET**.

Cyprus

The European Commission has advised that the application of *Directive 2006/112/EC* is to be suspended in those areas of Cyprus in which the Government of the Republic of Cyprus does not exercise control. Goods sent to these destinations continue to be eligible for treatment as exports.

The Isle of Man

Although the Isle of Man has its own VAT authority, sales to the Isle of Man are treated as any other sale within the UK and cannot be treated as exports. (VAT Notice 703, para 2.7).

The Channel Islands

The Channel Islands are part of the EU for customs purposes but *outside* the EU for VAT purposes. Supplies of goods sent to the Channel Islands are therefore regarded as exports. (VAT Notice 703, para 2.7).

Gibraltar

Gibraltar is treated as being outside of the EU for VAT and customs purposes. Therefore supplies of goods sent to Gibraltar are regarded as exports. (VAT Notice 703, para 2.9).

Conditions for zero-rating

[22.2] To zero-rate supplies for export, an 'exporter' must comply with all the following conditions (which have the force of law). If all the conditions cannot be met, the supply cannot be zero-rated as an export and VAT must be accounted for at the appropriate UK rate.

(a) The exporter must ensure that the goods are exported from the UK within a specified time limit. For 'direct exports' and 'indirect exports' the time limit is three months from the time of supply.
In most cases, the time of supply is the earlier of
- the date on which the goods are sent to the customer or the customer takes them away, and
- the date full payment is received for the goods.

Any deposit or progress payment received is an advance part payment towards the total cost of the supply and has the same VAT liability as the final supply. If the final supply is to be zero-rated as an export, these payments can also be zero-rated. But if the goods are not eventually exported (or the supplier fails to obtain valid evidence of export), he must account for VAT on the total value of the supply, including any deposit or progress payments.
'*Direct exports*' are where the supplier sends the goods to a destination outside the EU and is responsible either for arranging the transport himself or appointing an agent (see below). The goods may be exported in own baggage or transport, by rail, by post or courier service, by a shipping line or airline, or by an agent employed by the supplier (but not by the customer).

'*Indirect exports*' are where the *overseas* customer (see definition of overseas person below) or his agent collects, or arranges for the collection of, the goods from the supplier in the UK and then takes them outside the EU.

(b) The exporter must obtain and keep valid commercial evidence or official evidence of export. See **22.25** *et seq* below for acceptable proof of export. The time limit for obtaining this evidence is, for direct exports and indirect exports, three months from the time of supply.

(c) In the case of direct exports, the supplier must not
- deliver or post the goods to a customer's address in the EU (including the UK); or
- allow the goods to be collected by or on behalf of the customer even if it is claimed that they are for subsequent export. See **22.10** below for details of deliveries made to another UK trader for consolidation, processing or incorporation prior to export.

(d) In the case of indirect exports, the supplier must not supply goods to
- a private individual who is resident in the UK;
- an overseas business that has a place of business in the UK from which taxable supplies are made (see **22.9** below).

Since 1 October 2013 the indirect export can still be zero-rated even if the overseas business has a UK VAT registration number providing all of the other conditions are satisfied.

(e) The exporter must keep satisfactory evidence of the export transaction (see **22.25** *et seq* below).

(f) The exporter must comply with the conditions specified in the legislation and in VAT Notice 703 which for this purpose has the force of law. As to whether the conditions laid down by HMRC are reasonable or complied with, see *Henry Moss of London Ltd and Another v C & E Commrs*, CA 1980, [1981] STC 139 (TVC 25.1).

If the overseas customer collects the goods from a UK supplier, it may be prudent to collect a refundable deposit from the customer that is equal to the amount of VAT due on the supply. The deposit can then be refunded to the customer once satisfactory export evidence has been provided confirming that the goods have left the EU.

An '*exporter*' is the person who, for VAT purposes,

- supplies or owns goods and exports or arranges for them to be exported to a destination outside the EU; or
- supplies goods to an 'overseas person', who arranges for the goods to be exported to a destination outside the EU. An '*overseas person*' is either
  - (i) a person or company that is not resident in the UK;
  - (ii) a person or company that has no business establishment in the UK from which taxable supplies are made; or
  - (iii) an overseas authority.

(VAT Notice 703, paras 2.3, 2.4, 2.10, 2.11, 2.13, 3.3, 3.4, 11.5).

Effect of failure to comply with conditions

Where the supply of any goods has been zero-rated as an export and either

- any of the above conditions (or any other specific conditions relating to a particular type of export) is not complied with, or
- the goods are found in the UK after the date of alleged exportation,

the goods are liable to *forfeiture*. Any VAT which would have been due but for zero-rating is payable forthwith by the person to whom the goods were supplied or by any other person in whose possession the goods are found in the UK. HMRC may waive payment of the VAT in whole or part. [*VATA 1994, s 30(10)*].

Appointment of an agent

A supplier (or for indirect exports a customer) can appoint a freight forwarder, shipping company, airline or other person to handle the export transactions and produce the necessary declarations to customs on their behalf. The agent must then

- take reasonable steps to ensure that the goods are as described by the exporter;
- ensure the customs formalities are complied with;
- ensure the goods exported within the time limits;
- keep records of each export transaction; and
- obtain and provide valid evidence of export and send it to the exporter once the goods have been exported.

(VAT Notice 703, paras 2.5, 2.6).

Categories of zero-rated exports

[22.3] Subject to meeting the general conditions in **22.2** above and any specific conditions in the appropriate paragraph of this chapter, the following categories of exports are zero-rated.

- **Direct exports.** [*VATA 1994, s 30(6)*]. See **22.2**(*a*) above.
- **Stores for ships, aircraft, etc.** [*VATA 1984, s 30(6)*]. See **22.4** below.
- **Certain supplies in connection with the management of defence projects.** [*VATA 1994, Sch 8 Group 13 Item* 2]. See **22.5** below.
- **Tools for the manufacture of goods for export.** [*VATA 1994, Sch 8 Group 13 Item 3*]. See **22.6** below.
- **Goods exported by a charity** (whatever the nature of the goods). [*VATA 1994, Sch 8 Group 15 Item* 3]. See **13.6 CHARITIES.**
- **Exports of freight containers.** [*SI 1995/2518, Reg 128*]. See **22.8** below.
- **Supplies to overseas persons.** [*SI 1995/2518, Reg 129*]. See **22.9** and **22.10** below.
- **Supplies to persons departing from the EU – retail export scheme.** [*SI 1995/2518, Regs 130, 131*]. See **22.12** to **22.16** below.
- **Exports of motor vehicles.** [*SI 1995/2518, Regs 132, 133*]. See **22.17** to **22.19** below.
- **Sailaway boats supplied for export.** See **22.20** below.
- **Supplies to the FCO and other government departments.** See **22.21** below.

- **Supplies to regimental shops.** See **22.22** below.
- **Supplies intended for continental shelf installations.** See **22.23** below.
- **Supplies at tax-free shops.** Where goods which are liable to VAT are supplied to persons leaving on flights to destinations outside the EU at tax-free shops approved by HMRC, the supplier may be regarded as the exporter and zero-rate the supply of those goods which are exported. See VAT Notice 48, ESC 9.1.

Stores for use in ships, aircraft or hovercraft

[22.4] Stores are goods for use in a ship, aircraft or hovercraft and include

- fuel;
- goods for running repairs or maintenance (e.g. lubricants, spare and replacement parts);
- goods for general use on board by the crew; and
- goods for sale by retail to persons carried on voyages or flights who intend to use the stores on board only.

A supplier can zero-rate supplies of stores for the fuelling and provisioning of vessels and aircraft provided

- they are for use on a voyage or flight with a non-private purpose and with an eventual destination outside the UK (see below for an extra-statutory concession covering supplies of marine fuel to vessels for voyages in home waters);
- they are shipped from the UK within three months of supply; and
- the conditions outlined in (*b*) below are met.

A VAT-registered shipping line or airline operator can choose either of the following options for supplies made to it.

(a) It can have all supplies, including those intended for stores, delivered to its premises and charged to VAT at the appropriate rate. If so, input tax can be deducted (subject to the normal rules) and the subsequent transfer of the goods from the premises to the ship or aircraft is a non-supply.

(b) It can have supplies of eligible stores made direct to the foreign-going craft. Such supplies can then be zero-rated provided the following conditions are met.
  - (i) The person to whom the goods are supplied is the end user (e.g. the master of the vessel).
  - (ii) The goods are for use as stores on a voyage or flight which is to be made for a non-private purpose and the person to whom the goods are to be supplied declares this in writing.
  - (iii) The stores are to be shipped from the UK within three months of supply.
  - (iv) The supplier obtains and keeps a written order or confirmation given by the master or duly authorised agent. This must contain a declaration that the goods are solely for use as stores on a named ship or aircraft that is entitled to duty-free stores for the voyage or flight in question i.e. to an eventual destination

outside the UK. Aircraft making through international flights are eligible to receive VAT-free stores even if the aircraft makes one or more stops in the UK in the course of such a flight.

(v) The goods must be sent either direct to the ship or aircraft or through freight forwarders for consolidation and delivery direct to the ship or aircraft or addressed and delivered to the master c/o the shipping company or agent.

(vi) The supplier must obtain and keep a receipt confirming delivery of the goods on board the ship or aircraft signed by the master, commander or other responsible officer of the ship or aircraft. The supplier can accept such a receipt signed by a responsible official of the airline concerned but airlines using this facility must obtain prior written agreement from HMRC. The airline must confirm that the signatory is in a position to provide the receipt based on personal knowledge of flight details and that the airline will maintain documentation enabling HMRC staff to verify entitlement to relief.

(vii) Where supplies are made direct from a warehouse not operated or owned by the supplier to an eligible vessel or aircraft, the supplier must hold a signed and dated certificate of export from the warehousekeeper. The advice note issued by the warehouse-keeper normally serves this purpose.

Where goods are supplied to a shore-side storage tank, the supplier may not zero-rate the supply unless he holds the necessary evidence that his customer is the exporter of the goods.

Goods for sale

These provisions also apply to goods supplied for sale in ships' shops and on board aircraft even though there may be no taxable supply at the time of shipment (e.g. transfer of own goods, supply on sale or return terms). Where goods have been shipped on a foreign-going ship or aircraft, any later sale of the goods is a supply outside the UK and there is no further liability to VAT unless they are re-landed (see below). VAT is charged on goods sold on board a vessel on a coastwise journey or aircraft on an internal flight.

Relanded stores

Stores supplied under the above provisions and re-landed are treated as **34 IMPORTS**.

Marine fuel

By concession, vessels engaged on commercial voyages within UK territorial waters (or within the limits of a port) may receive certain types of fuel VAT-free. The supplier can zero-rate the supply provided

- a written declaration is obtained from the person to whom the marine fuel is supplied that the goods are for use as stores on a non-private voyage;
- a written order or confirmation is obtained from the master, owner or duly authorised agent of the vessel declaring that the fuel is solely for use on a named ship;

- the fuel is sent direct to the ship or addressed and delivered to the master of a named vessel c/o the shipping agent or line; and
- a receipt confirming delivery of the fuel on board, signed by the master or other responsible officer, is held.

The concession extends only to those supplies of fuel which were zero-rated before 1 July 1990. It does not cover petrol, ultra low sulphur diesel (ULSD) or lubricating oil.

Mess and canteen stores

Goods can be zero-rated where supplied for use as mess and canteen stores on HM ships about to leave for a foreign port or a voyage outside UK territorial waters of more than 15 days' duration. The goods must be ordered for the general use on board by the ship's company. Orders must be certified by the Commanding Officer and goods delivered direct to the ship. A receipt must be obtained and kept.

Duty-free goods supplied on sale or return to messes in HM ships cannot be zero-rated when sent out to the ship. The taxable supply occurs only when the goods are adopted, i.e.

- when the customer pays for the goods or otherwise indicates his wish to keep them; or
- at the end of twelve months or any shorter period agreed for the goods to be bought or returned.

The supplier is responsible for ensuring that the messes inform him promptly of when the adoption of the goods took place. If adoption occurs when the vessel is in UK territorial waters, the supply is taxable; if outside, there is no supply for VAT purposes. Commanders of HM ships will provide suppliers with this information.

[*VATA 1994, s 30(6)*]. (VAT Notice 703, paras 8.2, 10.1–10.7; VAT Notice 48, ESC 9.2).

International collaboration defence arrangements (ICDAs)

[22.5] The supply to, or by, an 'overseas authority', 'overseas body' or 'overseas trader', charged with the management of any defence project which is the subject of an 'international collaboration arrangement' (or under direct contract with any government or government-sponsored international body participating in defence projects under such an arrangement) of goods or services made for the purpose of fulfilling contracts is zero-rated. The zero-rating only applies to a limited number of projects and traders who are concerned with them are notified individually by HMRC.

'*Overseas authority*' means any country other than the UK or any part of, or place in, such a country or the government of such a country, part or place.

'*Overseas body*' means a body established outside the UK.

'*Overseas trader*' means a person who carries on a business and has a principal place of business outside the UK.

An '*international collaboration arrangement*' is any arrangement made between the UK government and the government of one or more other countries (or any government-sponsored international body, e.g. NATO) for collaboration in a joint project of research, development or production. The arrangement must specifically provide for participating governments to relieve the cost of the project from taxation.
[*VATA 1994, Sch 8 Group 13 Item* 2].

Tools for the manufacture of goods for export

[22.6] The supply to an 'overseas authority', 'overseas body' or 'overseas trader' (see **22.5** above) of jigs, patterns, templates, dies, moulds, punches and similar machine tools used in the UK solely for the manufacture of goods for export is zero-rated. The overseas authority, etc must not be

- a taxable person,
- another EU member state,
- any part of or place in another EU member state,
- the government of any such country, part or place,
- a body established in another EU member state, or
- a person who carries on business, or has a place of business, in another EU member state,

otherwise the supply is taxable in the normal way.

[*VATA 1994, Sch 8 Group 13 Item 3*].

A machine tool is supplied for these purposes where the customer specifically asks the supplier to make it, or buy it, for him and the supplier

- uses the machine tool to manufacture goods for the same customer; and
- makes a specific charge to the customer for the supply of the tool.

In addition to holding normal commercial proof of export, the supplier must obtain a signed statement (or other similar definite evidence) from the customer that they are neither registered nor required to be registered in the UK and are not an authority, body or trader in another EU member state.

(VAT Notice 701/22/17, paras 1.4, 2.1).

Export houses

[22.7] An 'export house' is any person registered for VAT in the UK who, in the course of business in the UK, arranges or finances the export of goods from the UK to a place outside the EU.

Supplies by export houses

Export houses can zero-rate supplies to overseas customers as exports subject to the normal conditions.

Supplies to export houses

Supplies to export houses are treated in the same way as any other supplies made to UK customers.

Freight containers supplied for export

[22.8] Subject to such conditions as HMRC impose, the supply of a 'container' is zero-rated where HMRC are satisfied that it is to be exported.

For these purposes, a '*container*' is defined as an article of transport equipment (lift-van, movable tank or similar structure)

- fully or partially enclosed to constitute a compartment for goods;
- of a permanent character strong enough for repeated use;
- designed to facilitate the carriage of goods, by one or more modes of transport, without intermediate reloading;
- designed for ready handling and to be easy to fill and empty; and
- having an internal volume of one cubic metre or more.

It includes accessories and equipment as appropriate but excludes vehicles, spares for vehicles and packaging.

[*SI 1995/2518, Regs 117(2), 128*].

Although not strictly within the definition, 'flats' or 'Lancashire flats' (i.e. bases with or without head and tail boards which are designed to carry goods and have the floor area of a 20 ft or 40 ft container) are included, as are air transport containers whatever their internal volume. Pallets, road vehicles and trailers including tanks on wheels are not included. (VAT Notice 703/1/10, para 2.2).

Direct export

The supply of a container for direct export may be zero-rated provided the container is actually exported and the normal conditions for export are complied with. (VAT Notice 703/1/10, para 3.1).

Indirect export

The supply of a freight container for indirect export may be zero-rated provided the supplier obtains a written undertaking from the customer that

(a) the container will be exported from the EU;

(b) the container will not be used in the EU except for
   - (i) a single domestic journey before export (on which inland freight may be carried) on a reasonably direct route between the point of supply and the place where the container is to be loaded with the export cargo or exported; and
   - (ii) international movement of goods (which may include a journey within the UK for the purpose of loading or unloading the goods);

(c) the customer will keep records sufficient to satisfy HMRC that
   - (i) the container has not been used in the EU (except as allowed under (*b*) above); and
   - (ii) the container has either been exported or has been sold/leased to someone else who has given a similar written undertaking.

(VAT Notice 703/1/10, paras 3.2, 3.3 which have the force of law).

Lease or hire of containers

Where the supplier and the customer both belong in the UK, the supply is treated as made in the UK and VAT must be charged on the supply. However, if the customer is to export the container from the EU, the leasing/hiring may be zero-rated provided the supplier obtains a written undertaking from the customer as for indirect exports above.

Where the supplier belongs in the UK but the customer belongs outside the EU, the supply is treated as being made in the customer's country and no UK VAT is due.

Where the customer belongs in another EU member state and is in business in another EU member state, the supply is treated as being made in the customer's country, and so the supplier does not charge UK VAT. The customer will normally have to account for VAT under the reverse charge procedure. If the customer is a private individual then the place of supply is where the supplier belongs, and the supplier must charge UK VAT.

Incidental charges which under the terms of the lease agreement are charged to the lessee are regarded as part of the consideration for the leasing of the container and have the same VAT liability. Included are repair, delivery, regulator and handling charges, extra rental and any charge for the option to terminate the lease at an earlier date.

(VAT Notice 703/1/10, paras 5.1–5.5).

Supplies to overseas persons

[22.9] Where HMRC are satisfied that goods intended for export have been supplied to an 'overseas person', the supply is zero-rated.

For export of motor vehicles generally, see **22.17** to **22.19** below.

'*Overseas person*' is

- a person not resident in the UK;
- a trader who has no business establishment in the UK from which taxable supplies are made; or
- an overseas authority (i.e. any country other than the UK or any part or place in such a country or the government of any such country, part or place). This includes goods ordered through embassies, High Commissions and purchasing agents of foreign governments in the UK.

[*SI 1995/2518, Regs 117(7), 129; SI 2013/2241*].

Supplies to overseas persons generally are indirect exports and must meet the normal conditions for zero-rating of such supplies (see **22.2** above). In addition, in the case of supplies to overseas authorities which are ordered through their embassies, High Commissions or purchasing agents in the UK, HMRC require the following conditions to be satisfied before the supply can be zero-rated.

- The supplier must keep a separate record of each transaction, including evidence that the supply has been to an overseas authority (e.g. the order for the goods, sales invoice made out to the overseas authority, evidence of payment from the overseas authority, etc.).

- The goods must not be used between the time of leaving the supplier's premises and export, either for their normal purpose or for display, exhibition or copying.

(VAT Notice 703, paras 3.4, 4.12).

Supplies to overseas persons for export after consolidation, processing or incorporation

[22.10] Goods supplied for export to an overseas person but delivered to a third person in the UK who is also making a taxable supply to that overseas person are zero-rated provided

(a) the goods are only being delivered and not supplied to the third person in the UK;
(b) no use is made of the goods other than for processing or incorporation into other goods for export;
(c) the goods are exported from the EU within six months of the time of supply and proof of export is obtained within the same time limit;
(d) the supplier's records show the
- name and address of the overseas person,
- invoice number and date,
- description, quantity and value of goods,
- name and address of the third person in the UK to whom the goods were delivered,
- date by which the goods must be exported and proof of export obtained, and
- date of actual exportation.

The records must be able to show that the goods supplied have been processed or incorporated into the goods exported.

In cases where the third party is not the UK but in another EU member state, the same conditions will generally apply to allow the supply to be zero-rated.

(VAT Notice 703, paras 3.5, 3.6).

Racehorses

Where a racehorse is supplied to an overseas person but is to remain in the UK for breaking, conditioning, training or covering before export, under an agreement between HMRC, the British Horseracing Board and the Thoroughbred Breeders Association the vendor can ask HMRC to extend the time limit in (*c*) above from six months to twelve months from the date of purchase. The extension is subject to the conditions that

- the horse must not be raced in the UK before export; and
- the relief cannot be transferred to another overseas person.

(VAT Notice 700/57/14).

Multiple transactions leading to a single movement of goods

[22.11] Where a single movement of goods is supported by two or more transactions, only the final transaction can be zero-rated.

(VAT Notice 703, para 4.1).

> *Example*
>
> A (outside the EU) orders goods from B (in the UK). B purchases the goods from C (also in the UK) but instead of taking delivery of the goods, agrees with C that it will send the goods directly to A.
>
> The supply of goods from C to B is a UK supply and VAT must be charged at the appropriate rate. The supply of goods by B to A is zero-rated as an export if the necessary conditions are met.

Retail export scheme

[22.12] The VAT retail export scheme allows

- overseas visitors (see **22.13** Condition 1 below) to receive a refund of VAT paid on goods exported to destinations outside the EU subject to the conditions in **22.13** below being met; and
- retailers to zero-rate goods sold to overseas visitors when they have the necessary evidence of export and have refunded the VAT to the customer.

See **18.2 EUROPEAN UNION: GENERAL** for the VAT territory of the EU.

It is a voluntary scheme and retailers do not have to operate it. Where it is operated, retailers

- need not operate it for all lines of goods; and
- can set a minimum sales value below which they will not operate the scheme.

A simplified Notice aimed specifically at travellers, VAT Notice 704/1/16 *Tax free shopping in the UK*, highlights the main aspects of the scheme. It is available, in various languages, from the VAT Helpline (tel: 0300 200 3700). Copies can be usefully given to customers using the scheme.

In Autumn Statement 2016, the Government announced that it intends to provide funding that will be used to fully digitise the Retail Export Scheme in order to reduce the administrative burden currently faced by travellers making a refund claim.

(VAT Notice 704, paras 1.5, 2.1, 2.2, 2.7).

Conditions for using the scheme

[22.13] Retailers and refund companies can only operate the scheme when the following conditions (which have the force of law) are met.

Condition 1

The customer must be an 'overseas visitor'. For these purposes, an '*overseas visitor*' is one of the following.

(a) A traveller (including a member of the crew of a ship or aircraft) who is not established in the EU. This means a person

- whose domicile or habitual residence is not situated within the EU. For this purpose, a person's domicile or habitual residence is the place entered as such on their valid passport, identity card or other acceptable document such as a driving licence (which must be produced to the retailer to prove eligibility);
- who intends to leave the UK for a final destination outside the EU, with the goods, by the last day of the third month following that in which the goods were purchased; and
- who exports the goods having produced them, their receipts and the VAT refund document to an HMRC officer at the point of departure from the EU.

Student or migrant workers entering the UK from outside the EU are classed as overseas visitors but to avoid abuse of the system (by reclaiming VAT under the scheme prior to returning home and then bringing the goods back to the UK within a short period of time), such persons additionally

- are only entitled to purchase goods under the scheme during the last four months of their stay in the UK; and
- having left the EU must remain outside the EU for a minimum period of twelve months.

Such a visitor will have been issued with a pre-entry visa and, in the case of work periods of six months or more, a separate work permit document by the UK authorities. The visa is contained in the passport and shows the start and end date for the study or work period authorised. Retailers should ask to see the visa or work permit before selling goods under the scheme.

(b) For the purposes of this scheme only, a traveller established in the EU who

- intends to leave the UK with the goods by the last day of the third month following that in which the goods were purchased for an immediate destination outside the EU;
- remains outside the EU for a period of at least twelve months (which must be proved to the retailer typically by evidence such as an overseas work permit, approved visa application or residency permit); and
- exports the goods having produced them, their receipts and the VAT refund document to an HMRC officer at the point of departure from the EU.

Condition 2

The goods must be eligible to be purchased under the scheme. Any standard-rated and lower-rated goods can be sold under the scheme except for the following.

- New and second-hand motor vehicles for personal export (see **22.17** below).
- Sailaway boats (see **22.20** below).
- Goods over £600 in value (excluding VAT) exported for the customer's business purposes.
- Goods that will be exported as freight or unaccompanied baggage.

- Goods requiring an export licence (apart from antiques). Antiques may be exported only on production of a valid export licence to HMRC at the point of departure from the UK. Further advice can be obtained from
  The Department of Culture, Media and Sport
  2–4 Cockspur Street
  London SW1Y 5DH
  A retailer selling goods treated as antiques should explain this to customers as they will probably need assistance to obtain an export licence.
- Unmounted gemstones.
- Bullion (over 125g, 2.75 troy ounces or 10 Tolas).
- Goods for consumption in the EU. (No certification of export will be given for used consumable items (e.g. perfumes) which are wholly or partly consumed in the EU.)
- Goods purchased by mail order including those purchased over the internet. However, a mail order company or an internet retailer with a retail outlet can use the scheme for goods sold from that outlet provided all the conditions of the scheme are complied with.

The scheme cannot be used for

- zero-rated goods (e.g. books and children's clothing); or
- supplies of services (e.g. hotel accommodation, meals and car hire). This applies even where services are sold with the goods (e.g. labour costs for fitting spare parts to a motor vehicle). Where a vehicle brought into the UK for the use of the overseas visitor requires repairs, the sale of the spare parts only and not the cost of fitting can be included in the scheme. Extended warranty work cannot be zero-rated under the retail export scheme.

Condition 3

The customer must make the purchase in person and complete the form in full at the retailer's premises at the time of sale (although a third party may pay for the goods). It is not possible for a representative to attend in place of the customer at the time of sale.

Condition 4

The goods must be exported from the EU by the last day of the third month following that in which the goods are purchased (e.g. goods bought on 3 February must be exported by 31 May). This time limit cannot be extended. Goods exported after the time limit must not be zero-rated even if the VAT refund document has been stamped in error by a UK or other EU Customs officer.

Condition 5

The customer must send the retailer or refund company evidence of export stamped by HMRC on an official version of Form VAT 407, an approved version of Form VAT 407 or an officially approved invoice. See **22.14** below.

Condition 6

The retailer or refund company must not zero-rate the supply until the VAT has been refunded to the customer (see **22.16** below).

[*SI 1995/2518, Regs 117(7A)–(7D)*]. (VAT Notice 704, paras 2.3, 2.4, 2.6, 2.8, 2.9, 3.1, 6.5).

Procedure

[22.14] *At the time of sale*, a retailer should:

- Check that the customer is entitled to use the scheme (see **22.13** Condition 1 above).
- Check that the goods are eligible for the scheme (see **22.13** Condition 2 above).
- Check the eligible customer is present to buy the goods (see **22.13** Condition 3 above).
- Check that the customer intends to leave the EU with the goods for a final destination outside the EU by the last day of the third month following that in which the goods were purchased.
- Fill in a VAT refund document (see below). A responsible member of staff should ensure all sections are fully completed, unused lines are ruled through and the customer and retailer declarations are signed at the time of the sale.

  By concession, HMRC allow completion of the refund form on production of receipts for past purchases provided the retailer can satisfy HMRC that it has adequate security procedures in place to prevent abuse of the scheme. This includes
  - stamping till receipts to show that the goods have been purchased under the retail export scheme (e.g. 'VAT Export');
  - a till system allowing the retailer to check that the receipts produced are genuine and can only appear once on a VAT 407 refund document; and
  - a system allowing the retailer to check whether a refund for returned goods has already been made for a receipt produced or a VAT 407 refund document has been issued for goods where a refund for returned goods is sought.
  - Where a retailer cannot show that it has adequate security procedures in place, it must only complete VAT refund documents at the time of the sale.

  Where a retailer does have adequate safeguards in place and a customer asks for a refund document to cover a series of purchases over a period of time, the retailer must include only those goods that will be exported by the last day of the third month following that in which the goods were purchased. The purchase date entered on the refund document must be the date of the earliest purchase.
- Give the customer a copy of VAT Notice 704/1 *Tax free shopping in the UK*.
- Agree with the customer how the refund will be made.
- Explain any administrative or handling fees to be deducted from the VAT refund to avoid any subsequent misunderstanding.

- Mark the customer's sales receipt to indicate that the goods have been included on a VAT refund document (e.g. 'VAT Export').
- Explain that no refund will be made on items (e.g. perfume) wholly or partly consumed in the EU.
- Advise the customer that any items not exported from the UK should be clearly deleted from the refund document before it is presented to a UK or EU Customs officer for stamping and that it is an offence to make a false declaration.
- Advise the customer that he must produce the refund document (together with the goods and receipts, if required) to the Customs officer for stamping at the point of departure from the EU and explain that failure to do so will mean that a VAT refund will not be made.
- Advise the customer to allow plenty of time in which to produce the goods and refund form prior to departure. (This is particularly important if they are exporting goods in hold baggage as they may need to allow up to two hours in addition to the advised check in time.)
- Advise the customer to carry items of high value (e.g. jewellery, furs, cameras, watches, silverware, lap top computers and small antiques) in hand baggage.

VAT refund document

The VAT refund document can be either of the following.

(a) Form VAT 407, in which case it can be either
- Form VAT 407 issued by HMRC and available free of charge from the National Advice Service; or
- the retailer's or refund company's own version of Form VAT 407 containing the same information as HMRC's version and approved beforehand by HMRC.

Part A of the form must be completed in full by the customer at the time of sale.

Part B, which is for completion by the retailer, must include a full and accurate description of the goods quoting identification numbers, serial numbers or other identifying marks (e.g. hallmarks) together with the quantity (and weight in the case of jewellery) of goods sold. Descriptions such as stock numbers, 'See invoice attached', 'Jewellery' or 'Designer goods' are not acceptable. The description must be clear enough to allow the UK or EU Customs officer to readily identify the goods. Any unused lines on the form should be crossed through. Each of the following must be shown.
- The total amount payable (including VAT) in both words and figures.
- The VAT included in the price.
- The amount of any administration fee that will be deducted from the refund.
- The amount of refund to be paid to the customer.

Part C is the retailer's declaration. It must show
- the retailer's full business name, address and VAT number; and
- the date the goods were sold to the customer;

and must be signed by a responsible person.

Part D is for official use and will be stamped by the Customs officer at the point of departure from the EU to validate the export. (Whilst desirable, it is not essential the Customs officer signs the form.) Customs officers may refuse to stamp refund forms completed incorrectly or not completed in full. For example, forms showing inadequate descriptions of goods may be rejected.

(b) A sales invoice approved beforehand by HMRC. It must closely follow the design of Form VAT 407.

It must include the data protection statement shown on the face of the form and the information shown on the reverse side of the HMRC version of Form VAT 407. This includes

- the heading 'Retail Export Scheme';
- providing spaces for the retailer's and the customer's declarations as stipulated on the Form VAT 407, including details of the customer's passport/identity number and country of issue, date of arrival in the EU, intended date of departure from the EU; and
- a separate box not less than 5cm by 3.5cm for official stamping by a Customs officer at the customer's point of departure from the EU.

The total amount payable must be shown in words as well as figures. The invoice must also show the amount of any administrative charge and the net refund due to the customer.

(c) In addition, any officially approved invoice must also meet the requirements of invoicing legislation generally. See **40.7 INVOICES** for requirements of a retailer's less detailed invoice where the consideration does not exceed £250 and, where the customer agrees, a modified invoice. Otherwise the invoice must comply with the full requirements of an invoice under **40.4 INVOICES.**

Whilst a single refund document is acceptable, it is recommended that retailers issue separate VAT refund documents (but make only one administrative charge) for customers intending to carry some goods in hand baggage and other goods in hold baggage. This is particularly important for customers leaving on a through (transit) flight via another EU airport because the goods in hold baggage must be declared before check in, whilst the goods in hand baggage must be declared at the final point of departure from the EU.

On completion of the refund document, the customer should be given

- the refund document;
- a reply-paid envelope addressed to the retailer or, as the case may be, the refund company administering the refund (alternatively, the retailer should make it clear that it is the customer's responsibility to provide the envelope and pay the correct postage); and
- a copy of VAT Notice 704/1

and advised to produce the refund document (together with the goods and receipts if required) to the Customs officer at the point of departure from the EU.

Control of blank or partly completed VAT refund documents

Whichever form of refund document is used, retailers must keep stocks of the blank documents secure and not issue blank or partly completed forms to any person outside the business.

Goods returned for refund or exchange

If a customer wishes to return goods that have been sold under the scheme (either for a full refund or for exchange) he must take the receipt and the VAT refund document back to the retailer. The retailer should delete the entry for the returned goods (or cancel the VAT refund document and issue a new one) as appropriate.

Action required by the customer on leaving the UK

If the customer decides to leave any goods bought under the scheme in the EU, he must clearly delete those items from the VAT refund document before presenting it, and the remaining goods, to HMRC for examination and stamping.

Action required for goods which are taken outside the EU depends upon how the customer is leaving the EU.

- If leaving for an immediate destination outside the EU, the VAT refund document must be presented to HMRC at the port/airport of departure from the UK. The goods and receipts must be available for inspection if required. (If leaving by air, goods too large or too heavy to be carried on board an aircraft can be packed in hold baggage but, in this case, the VAT refund document should be presented to HMRC before checking in. But high value items including jewellery, furs, cameras, expensive watches, silverware, laptop computers and small antiques, should be carried in hand baggage.)
- If leaving the EU via another EU member state, the goods and the refund form must be presented to the Customs authorities of that country.
- If leaving the EU on a through (transit) flight via another EU airport,
  (i) goods carried as hand baggage must be produced, with the refund form, to Customs in the last EU airport before leaving the EU; and
  (ii) goods carried as hold baggage must be produced, with the refund form, to HMRC before checking in baggage.

Where a HMRC officer cannot be located to stamp the refund document (e.g. because there is no 24-hour HMRC presence) there will either be a telephone to speak to HMRC or a clearly marked post box to deposit the refund document and a reply-paid envelope.

There is no facility to have a refund document stamped in the country of destination outside the EU.

If satisfied, HMRC will certify the VAT refund document and return it to the customer. The customer must then (depending on whichever method was agreed with the retailer)

- post the refund document back to the retailer to arrange payment of the refund;
- post the refund document to a VAT refund company to arrange payment of the refund; or
- hand the refund document to a cash refund booth operated by the refund company at the airport of departure from the UK which will arrange immediate payment. (Not all airports or refund companies offer this facility.)

Receipt of evidence by the retailer

On receipt of a refund document stamped by UK or other EU Customs, the retailer or refund company must check that all goods have been exported from the EU by the last day of the third month following that in which the goods were purchased and, if so, make the refund to the customer by the method agreed at the time of sale. If a refund document is sent back unstamped, the retailer cannot zero-rate the supply because export of the goods from the EU has not been certified as required by the scheme.

Loss of VAT refund documents

If a customer loses the refund document *before* leaving the EU, the retailer may provide a duplicate clearly marked as such. When issuing the document, the retailer should

- make sure the original document has not been received and already processed;
- be satisfied that a sale took place by the production of till receipts or other information; and
- advise the customer that, if he subsequently finds the original refund document, it is to be cancelled.

If the customer loses the refund document *after* certification by HMRC, a duplicate may only be issued where a photocopy of the stamped original is produced. The duplicate and photocopy must then be sent to the HMRC officer who stamped the original document for certification of the duplicate. Only then should the refund be made.

(VAT Notice 704, paras 3.1–3.7, 4.1–4.4, 4.7, 4.8, 4.10, 4.11, 6.1, 6.4, 7.5–7.7).

Special arrangements for intra-EU cruises

[22.15] Non-EU passengers on wholly intra-EU cruises may not have access to their luggage and to any purchases made under the retail export scheme from disembarkation until they arrive at their final non-EU destination. They cannot, therefore, produce the goods and VAT refund document to the Customs officer for stamping at their point of final departure from the EU. The special arrangements outlined below apply to wholly intra-EU cruises

- which start in the UK; and
- where the final port of disembarkation is also within the UK.

(a) Individual purchases below £1,000

Cruise operators may produce an omnibus bulk refund document for all eligible goods below £1,000 per item purchased on board by entitled individual passengers. This document must accompany the passengers' luggage to the airport of departure. If satisfied, the Customs officer will stamp the bulk refund form and return it to the cruise operator. On receipt of the certified form, the cruise operator must account for the sales in their VAT records as under **22.16** below.

The format of the bulk refund document must be approved beforehand by HMRC. It must be clearly headed 'Retail Export Scheme' and must only include those goods that

- were sold on board the vessel;
- are supplied to entitled customers (see **22.13** Condition 1 above); and
- are eligible to be supplied under the retail export scheme (see **22.13** Condition 2 above).

It must also give the following details.

- Cruise operator's name, address and VAT registration number.
- Customers' name and usual address.
- Customers' passport number and country of issue.
- A description which clearly identifies the goods and the quantity involved.
- The amount payable per item. (Where this includes VAT, the amount payable inclusive of VAT and the amount of VAT included in the total price should be shown.)

In addition, the refund document must include a retailer declaration as stipulated on Form VAT 407 which must be signed by a responsible ship's officer, and a separate box (at least 5 cm by 3.5 cm) for official certification by Customs.

The cruise operator must account for VAT on any goods on the bulk refund form that are not exported from the EU within the prescribed limits.

(b) Individual purchases over £1,000

The normal VAT 407 form or equivalent (see **22.14** above) must be completed for individual purchases over £1,000 per item. The customer must produce the goods and the form for certification to the Customs officer at the point of final departure from the EU.

(VAT Notice 704, paras 8.1, 8.2).

Accounting for VAT

[22.16] At the point of sale, any standard-rated and lower-rated goods sold under the scheme must be treated as liable to VAT. It is therefore in the interest of the retailer to initially charge VAT to the customer. A sale can only be zero-rated when

- the stamped refund document has been received; and

- the refund of VAT has been made to the customer by the agreed method.

The stamped refund document must be retained together with evidence of the refund made to the customer to support zero-rating.

If the certified VAT refund document is received after VAT has been accounted for, the VAT can be refunded and the sale can be zero-rated by reducing output tax by the relevant amount in Box 1 of the VAT return for the period in which the evidence is received and the refund is made.

Suppliers also using a special retail scheme

See **61.9 RETAIL SCHEMES**.

Retailers not using a retail scheme

Such retailers must keep a record of all sales including VAT under the retail export scheme. When a stamped VAT refund document is received and the VAT has been refunded, the sale can be zero-rated in the records.

Refund companies

Where a retailer contracts with a refund company to administer the refund on its behalf, the refund company normally provides an officially approved VAT refund document of its own design for use by the retailer. In such circumstances, the retailer must still account for the VAT as explained above and must retain the certified VAT refund documents and evidence that the VAT has been refunded in its records to support any zero-rating claimed.

Concession shops

Where a larger store operates concessions for other retailers within its own store:

- If the sale is rung through the main store tills, it is acceptable for the VAT refund document to be issued by the host store (typically at the main customer service desk). The host store is then responsible for complying with the conditions of the scheme and accounting for the VAT.
- If the concession operates its own tills and issues receipts showing its own name and VAT number, any VAT refund documents must be issued by the concession and not the host store. The concession is then responsible for complying with the conditions of the scheme and accounting for the VAT.

Direct reclaim system

This involves two distinct transactions: a retailer sells goods to a refund company who immediately sells them on to an eligible traveller. The accounting procedure is as follows.

- The retailer must invoice the sale to the refund company as this is a business-to-business supply (not a retail sale) and must account for VAT on the supply. It may, however, include the sale in its daily gross takings for retail scheme purposes if it wishes.

- The refund company may use the retailer's invoice to reclaim input tax on the purchase. It must also account for VAT on the sale to the traveller. It may subsequently zero-rate the supply but only where all the conditions of the scheme are met.

Sales under the margin scheme for second-hand goods

The margin scheme for second-hand goods and the retail export scheme can both be used for the same transaction but as the amount of VAT charged cannot be shown separately on a valid invoice under the margin scheme, the VAT refund document should be adapted as follows.

- Head the document 'Second-hand goods – this document is adapted in accordance with Notice 704, para 5.8'.
- Leave the line 'Amount of VAT included in the price' blank.
- Complete the refund due box.

Sales by auctioneers

If an auctioneer sells goods on behalf of a retailer to a person entitled to use the retail export scheme and a VAT refund document is completed, the retailer can zero-rate the sale when the stamped refund document is returned and the refund has been made to the customer. Note, however, that the scheme cannot be used for goods exported as freight.

If the auctioneers are registered for VAT and sell goods in their own name to someone who is entitled to use the scheme then, for VAT purposes, they may be treated as both receiving and making a supply of goods. They can zero-rate the sale provided they hold a certified VAT refund document and have refunded the VAT to the customer.

Administration or handling fees

If an amount is deducted from the VAT refund due to cover administrative or handling expenses, the amount deducted is consideration for the supply of services to the customer in connection with the export of goods to a destination outside the EU, and is zero-rated under *VATA 1994, Sch 8 Group 7 Item 2(a)*.

(VAT Notice 704, paras 5.1–5.10).

Motor vehicles

Direct exports

[22.17] Any motor vehicle, new or second-hand, supplied for direct export may be zero-rated provided it is exported from the EU and the conditions in **22.2**(*a*) above are satisfied. Evidence of exportation must be obtained and retained.

Indirect exports

The supply of a new or second-hand motor vehicle can be zero-rated under the conditions in **22.18** below. A motor vehicle can also be zero-rated under the Personal Export Scheme in **22.19** below.

Vehicles delivered in the UK for subsequent export by or on behalf of the purchaser

[22.18] The supply to an overseas person (see **22.9** above) of any motor vehicle (new or second-hand) can be zero-rated provided

- the supplier keeps supplementary evidence of the export (see **22.26** below);
- the vehicle is exported within three months of the supply; and
- the supplier obtains proof of export within three months of the time of supply.

Vehicles delivered in the UK for temporary use and subsequent export by the purchaser (the 'Personal Export Scheme')

[22.19] The Personal Export Scheme allows new and used motor vehicles (including motor cycles and motor caravans but not pedal cycles and trailer caravans) to be purchased free of VAT provided certain conditions (which have the force of law) are met. It should be noted that

- it is not possible to get a refund of VAT on a motor vehicle purchased VAT-paid even if it is later exported and would have qualified under the scheme; and
- it can be very difficult to import motor vehicles into some countries and it is advisable to check with the relevant Embassy or High Commission in the UK before ordering a vehicle under the scheme.

The conditions are as follows.

(a) The vehicle must be purchased from a VAT-registered business which operates the Personal Export Scheme.

(b) Only the purchaser who applies to use the scheme may take delivery of the vehicle in the UK without the written authority of the Personal Transport Unit (see below for contact details).

(c) The purchaser must intend to leave the EU within
  - 15 months or less if an 'overseas visitor'; or
  - nine months or less in any other case.

  See **18.2 EUROPEAN UNION: GENERAL** for the VAT territory of the EU.

(d) An '*overseas visitor*' for these purposes is a person who has not been in the EU for more than either 365 days in the two years immediately before the date of application or 1,095 days in the six years immediately before that date.

(e) The purchaser must export the vehicle within
  - twelve months of the date of delivery if an overseas visitor (see (*c*) above); or
  - six months of the date of delivery in any other case.

  For new vehicles, the final date for exportation is shown in the registration document. *For second-hand vehicles*, the final date of export is shown on the Form VAT 410 (see below).

(f) The purchaser (whether or not an overseas visitor) must intend to leave and remain outside the EU with the vehicle for a period of at least six months.

(g) The vehicle may be driven in the UK in the period before exportation but only by
- the purchaser or their spouse;
- a chauffeur; or
- provided the purchaser is still in the UK, any other person who has his permission to use it and who intends to leave the EU.

(h) The purchaser must not attempt to dispose of the vehicle in the UK (or elsewhere in the EU) by hire, pledge as security, sale, gift or any other means.

If any of the above conditions are broken, the vehicle is liable to forfeiture and may be seized. VAT is then payable on the value of the vehicle when purchased. Even if the vehicle cannot be exported for unavoidable reasons (e.g. theft or accident write-off) the VAT must still be paid.

(1) Procedure at time of sale

If the supplier is satisfied that the applicant is entitled to use the scheme, he should

- give the applicant a copy of Notice 707 *VAT Personal Export Scheme* and an application form VAT 410 (both obtainable from the VAT Helpline on 0300 200 3700);
- explain the conditions of the scheme; and
- advise the applicant that it is an offence to give incorrect information on the form and that, if they do so, they may be liable to prosecution.

The applicant must complete the form and sign the declaration. In doing so, the applicant declares that they have received, read and understood Notice 707 and will comply with all the conditions of the scheme.

The form VAT 410 is carbonated and incorporates 4 copies:

Part 1 (blue) – HMRC copy

Part 2 (green) – Purchaser's copy

Part 3 (pink) – Supplier's copy

Part 4 (yellow) – DVLA/DVA copy.

Completed application forms must be serially numbered by the supplier in the top right hand corner. (Each separate franchise at the same location requires a separate series of numbers.) Part 1 must be submitted, at least two weeks before date of delivery of the vehicle, to

HM Revenue and Customs
Personal Transport Unit
Priory Court
St Johns Road
Dover
Kent CT17 9SH
Tel: 01304 664171
Fax: 01304 664179

An incomplete or incorrect application form will be returned to the supplier for correction and this may delay the delivery of the vehicle.

(2) Cancellation of order before delivery

If, after the application is approved, the order for the vehicle is cancelled by the applicant before delivery, the supplier must immediately notify the PTU at the above address, quoting

- name of applicant,
- make/model of vehicle;
- serial number of the application; and
- in the case of second-hand vehicles, the vehicle registration number.

(3) Invoicing

The supplier must supply and invoice a VAT-free vehicle direct to the applicant. Factory fitted extras can only be supplied VAT-free if they are included on the initial invoice for the supply of the vehicle at the time of purchase.

(4) Registration and licensing with the Driver and Licensing Agency (DVLA)

New vehicles. To register a new vehicle, the supplier must complete an application form V55 headed prominently in block letters 'PERSONAL EXPORT (VAT FREE) VEHICLE', attach it to the DVLA copy (Part 4) of form VAT 410, and send it to a DVLA local office.

Second-hand vehicles. As a second-hand vehicle will already have been registered, the supplier must notify the DVLA local office of the change of keeper and apply for a special tax disc. This is done by submitting

- the completed V5 Registration Document,
- form V10 (vehicle licence application form),
- the DVLA copy (Part 4) of form VAT 410, and
- form VX304 if the purchaser is entitled to claim exemption from payment of vehicle excise duty

to a DVLA local office.

A second-hand vehicle must not be supplied with any pre-existing tax disc. If a disc is already in force, it should be surrendered separately to the DVLA local office for a refund.

(5) Insuring the vehicle

The purchaser should insure the vehicle for its full VAT-inclusive value because

- it must be insured before it is used; and
- if the purchaser is unable to export the vehicle (e.g. because it has been stolen or involved in an accident and written-off), the VAT amount not paid at the time of purchase becomes due.

(6) Delivering the vehicle

Before delivering a new vehicle, the supplier must complete the details required on pages 5 and 8 of the pink registration book, showing the amount of VAT remitted, the date of delivery, and the final date for export (see (*c*) above).

The vehicle must be delivered to the applicant in the UK (see (*b*) above). On delivery, the supplier must obtain a dated certificate of receipt for the vehicle signed by the applicant. This must be kept with the other records.

(7) Urgent delivery procedure

Where an overseas visitor intends to leave the UK within one month of their application to use the scheme, the supplier must complete a Certificate for Urgent Delivery authorised by a sole proprietor, partner, director, company secretary or a duly authorised person at a responsible level. At least three working days before the date of delivery of the vehicle to the applicant, the supplier must then fax to the Personal Transport Unit

- a copy of the Certificate for Urgent Delivery;
- a copy of the VAT 410 form; and
- for new vehicles, the V55 Form.

The original papers should then be posted to the Personal Transport Unit.

This procedure must not be used if the initial application by the customer has been rejected or returned for amendment.

(8) Supplier's records

For a new vehicle, in addition to the normal VAT records and his copy of the form VAT 410, the supplier must keep a separate record of each vehicle supplied under the scheme showing

- date of delivery;
- applicant's name and UK address;
- particulars of the vehicle including type, chassis number and registration number;
- amount of VAT remitted on the delivery price (including any accessories or extras and any delivery charges, less any discount allowed); and
- a certificate of receipt of the vehicle, detailing chassis number and registration number, which must be signed and dated by the applicant.

For a second-hand vehicle, the supplier should already have a record of it in his second-hand stock book under the margin scheme for second-hand goods. When he sells a second-hand vehicle under the Personal Export Scheme, he must close this stock book entry and include a cross-reference to the serial number of the form VAT 410, inserting 'zero-rate' in the VAT rate column of his stock book and 'Nil' in the VAT due column. He must then record the sale separately and include the same details as required for sales of new vehicles above. He can, if he wishes, include his second-hand sales with his records of new vehicle sales (if any).

(9) Use of vehicle before exportation from the EU

The vehicle can be used in the UK before exportation provided it is insured, exported by the final due date (see (*d*) above) and only used by an approved person (see (*f*) above).

It may also be used to make a temporary visit to another EU member state. If so, it can be brought back to the UK without any Customs formalities provided it is returned to the UK before the final due date for exportation (see (*d*) above) and the customer still intends to export and depart with the vehicle from the EU by that date. The purchaser is advised to check with the relevant VAT authority of the other EU member state to establish whether, because the vehicle has been supplied free of VAT, it is necessary to comply with any Customs requirements on entry into that country.

It is not normally advisable to make a temporary visit to a non-EU member state prior to the final date for export (see (*d*) above). When the vehicle is re-imported into either the UK or another EU member state, the VAT amount not paid at the time of purchase will become due (unless qualifying for relief under the re-importation rules (see below).

(10) Change of plans by purchaser before exportation from EU

If the purchaser changes his plans before the vehicle is removed from the UK and can no longer comply with the conditions in (*c*) or (*d*) above, he must notify the Personal Transport Unit immediately and pay the full amount of VAT not paid when the vehicle was bought. If the vehicle is in another EU member state, the purchaser should contact the fiscal authorities of that country (and pay VAT and any other local taxes due).

(11) Procedure on exportation

For new vehicles, the final date for exportation is shown on the pink registration document. The tear-off section of the document must be completed and returned to the DVLA local office as shown on the document.

For second-hand vehicles, the final date of exportation is shown on the customer's copy (Part 1) of form VAT 410. The customer must complete the relevant section of the V5 registration document and send the entire document to the DVLA local office as shown on the document. The DVLA will issue an export certificate to enable the vehicle to be re-registered in the country of destination. If the purchaser intends to leave the UK within 14 days of acquiring the vehicle, he should tell the dealer before purchase so that the dealer can arrange for the DVLA to issue an export certificate straightaway.

Shipping arrangements must be made in good time to ensure that the vehicle is exported by the final date.

(12) Reimportation

If the vehicle is brought back into the UK after the date shown for export, taxes must be paid on importation unless the person is eligible for relief from VAT and duty (see Customs Notice 3 Bringing your belongings and private motor vehicle to the UK from outside the European Community) in which case no VAT will be charged. Where the purchaser is not eligible for relief,

- if the vehicle is re-imported six months or more after the date for export (or the owner can show that he and the vehicle have remained outside the EU for at least six consecutive months), the VAT payable will be based on the value of the vehicle at the time of re-importation; and
- in all other cases, the VAT payable will be that which was not charged on purchase.

The vehicle must also be registered and licensed on return to the UK unless it is not to be used or kept on the public roads. The owner should contact the nearest DVLA local office and produce proof of payment of, or exemption from, VAT in order to re-license or re-register the vehicle.

If the vehicle is re-imported into another EU member state after it was exported from the EU, the owner should contact the VAT authority in that country and pay the VAT (and any other local taxes) due.

[*SI 1995/2518, Regs 117(8), 132, 133*]. (VAT Notice 707, para 7).

Sailaway boats supplied for export

[22.20] Under the conditions outlined below (which have the force of law) it is possible to zero-rate the supply of a '*sailaway boat*', i.e. a boat to be

- delivered to the purchaser or their authorised skipper within the EU; and
- to be exported under its own power to a destination outside the VAT territory of the EU (see **18.2 EUROPEAN UNION: GENERAL**).

As the supply can only be zero-rated after receipt of evidence that the boat has been exported in the time limit allowed, it is advisable to treat any sale under the scheme as liable to VAT until this evidence is received. It is recommended, therefore, that a deposit is taken equal to the amount of VAT, to be refunded when the required evidence of export is received.

Who is entitled to use the scheme

The scheme can only be used for the private purchase of a boat by an overseas visitor who intends to export the boat under its own power to a destination outside the EU within six months of the 'date of delivery'.

The scheme must not be used for commercial purchases.

'*Date of delivery*' is normally the date the boat leaves the manufacturer's or supplier's premises.

The scheme cannot be used

- where the supplier arranges delivery of the boat (either on a trailer or by using a skipper employed by the supplier) to a destination outside the EU (see **22.2**(*a*) above for the conditions for zero-rating direct exports);
- for a boat supplied for private use for removal from the UK to another EU member state (see **20.34 EUROPEAN UNION: SINGLE MARKET** for the conditions for zero-rating such a sale); or
- for parts or accessories (which may be supplied under the retail export scheme (see **22.12** above)).

Forms

The supplier needs to prove that the boat has been removed from the EU before zero-rating the sale in his records. The forms needed for this purpose are

- **Form VAT 436** – Notification of VAT-free purchase of a sailaway boat, and customers declaration. This form is in four parts.

Copy 1	copy for certification
Copy 2	Customs copy
Copy 3	customer's copy
Copy 4	supplier's copy

- **Form C88** (Single Administrative Document). This form is in three parts.

Copy 1	Community transit copy where applicable
Copy 2	UK Customs copy
Copy 3	For certification when the boat finally leaves the EU

- **Form C1331** – to advise departure from the UK.

Action required by the supplier

The supplier must

- check that the customer is entitled to use the scheme (see above);
- ensure that the customer intends to export the boat from the EU under its own power within the permitted time limit;
- give the customer a copy of VAT Notice 703/2/11 and an application form VAT 436;
- ensure that the customer knows that he must not dispose, or attempt to dispose, of the boat in the EU by hire, pledge as security (other than as part of the financing arrangement for the purchase of the boat itself), sale, gift or any other means;
- agree how any refund of deposited VAT will be paid;
- ensure that Form VAT 436 is fully completed and, at least two weeks before due delivery of the boat, that Part 2 is submitted to: HMRC, Personal Transport Unit (PTU), Priory Court, St John's Road, Dover, CT17 9SH (Tel: 01304 664171; Fax: 01304 664179). Forms which are incorrect or incomplete will be returned for correction and this may delay the delivery of the boat. If, after the form is processed, the order for the boat is cancelled by the customer before delivery, the supplier must immediately notify the PTU of the customer's name, details of the boat, and the reference number of the form; and
- keep a separate record for the sale.

Export procedure

If the customer is leaving the UK directly for a destination outside the EU, the customer must

- ensure that the boat is exported within time limits;
- complete Form C1331 Notice of Intended Departure;
- make the boat available for inspection by Customs at exportation (where possible this should be arranged in advance);

- take completed Form VAT 436 and Form C1331 to the UK Customs nearest the place of departure. Customs will retain Form C1331, sign and stamp Form VAT 436 to show that the boat has been declared for exportation, and return the Form VAT 436 to the customer; and
- return the certified Form VAT 436 to the supplier.

If the customer is calling into another EU member state before finally exporting the boat from the EU, the customer must

- ensure that the boat is exported within time limits;
- take the completed Form C88 (copies 2 and 3) and Form VAT 436 to the UK Customs office nearest the place of departure from the UK. Customs will keep copy 2 of Form C88 and return copy 3 with Form VAT 436 to the customer;
- take copy 3 of Form C88 and VAT 436 to the Customs office at the place of final departure from the EU for certification; and
- return the certified Form C88 and VAT 436 to the supplier.

Accounting arrangements

A separate record must be kept of all boats sold under the scheme. The sales invoice must clearly show that the supply of the boat was made under the sailaway boat scheme.

If evidence of export within time limits is not obtained and held, VAT must be accounted for. Any deposit taken of the VAT due should be brought to account. Where no deposit has been taken, the VAT records must be amended and VAT accounted for on the taxable proportion of the invoiced amount or consideration received (i.e. where the rate of VAT is 20%, the VAT element is 1/6). The amendment should be made in the VAT account and VAT return for the period in which the time limit expires.

If evidence of export within the permitted time limit is subsequently received, the supply can be zero-rated and any deposit refunded. The VAT account can be adjusted for the period in which evidence is received.

Re-importation of VAT-free boats

If a boat that was supplied VAT free at purchase is brought back to the EU, it must be declared to Customs in the EU member state of importation. The supplier should ensure that the customer is fully aware of the need to make an import declaration. VAT will be payable unless some other relief is available.

The Channel Islands

The Channel Islands are outside the EU VAT area and therefore qualify as a final destination for boats supplied under the sailaway boat scheme. EU residents who register VAT-free boats in the Channel Islands cannot claim VAT-free temporary importation of such boats into an EU member state. VAT is payable on these importations. Private persons resident in the Channel Islands may be entitled to import their own boats temporarily into the VAT territory of the EU for their own personal use for up to 18 months, without payment of import VAT.

(VAT Notice 703/2/11).

Supplies to the FCO and other government departments

Foreign and Commonwealth Office (FCO)

[22.21] Goods ordered by British Embassies, High Commissions and diplomats abroad which are delivered to FCO for export via diplomatic channels can be zero-rated provided a certificate of receipt for the goods is obtained from the FCO within three months of the time of supply of the goods. See VAT Notice 703, para 12.1 for an example of the certificate. The certificate may be on a copy of the sales invoice or itemised list and must be retained. To show that the supply was to an overseas person, the supplier must also retain documents (e.g. the order) to identify the destination of the goods. The supply of goods ordered by and delivered to the FCO for general distribution cannot be zero-rated.

Ministry of Defence (MOD)

The MOD is registered for VAT in the UK and all supplies to them or to any military establishment in the UK on their behalf should include VAT at the appropriate rate. Direct exports to overseas military and similar installations may be zero-rated provided the supplier holds valid proof of export.

Other government departments

The supply of goods to other government departments can only be zero-rated if supplied by direct export to a destination outside the EU. Goods for export delivered to government departments in the UK must not be zero-rated even if the goods are ordered for or by an overseas establishment.

(VAT Notice 703, paras 4.9, 4.11 7.11).

Supplies to regimental shops

[22.22] Supplies to regimental shops are normally taxable. However, where the regiment (or equivalent military unit) is about to be posted to a location outside the EU, supplies of goods (except new and second-hand motor vehicles) to a regimental shop can be zero-rated provided the following conditions are satisfied.

- Each written order received from the President of the Regimental Institute (PRI) states that the regiment is about to take up an overseas posting and that the goods ordered will be exported from the EU.
- The goods are delivered to the PRI ready packed for shipment no more than 48 hours before the regiment is due to depart for the overseas posting.
- The goods are exported outside the EU.
- The supplier retains a certificate of receipt signed by the PRI which clearly identifies the goods, gives full shipment details and states the date on which they were exported from the EU.

The PRI will keep a full record of such transactions for reference purposes for a period of not less than six years.

(VAT Notice 703, para 4.10).

Supplies intended for continental shelf installations

[22.23] The following provisions apply to the export of goods to structures such as oil rigs, dwelling units, accommodation platforms and similar oil or gas exploration/exploitation structures. It also applies to mobile floating structures such as drill ships, tankers, jack-up rigs, semi-submersible rigs and Floating Production Storage and Offloading (FPSO) vessels which are often stationed at fixed locations.

Exports to installations outside EU territorial waters

- *Goods supplied and exported by a supplier to an installation which he does not own.* Such supplies are zero-rated as direct exports provided proof of export is obtained within three months of the supply.
- *Goods sent to an installation owned by the supplier or goods sent to replenish own stocks on an installation not owned by the supplier.* This is a transfer of own goods and not a taxable supply (see **22.24** below). Valid proof of export must still be held to demonstrate how the goods have been disposed of.

Goods supplied for sale on installations situated outside UK territorial waters

Such supplies can be zero-rated provided

- a written order for the goods is obtained from a responsible person on the installation to which the goods are to be sent;
- the goods are supplied either direct to the installation or through an agent for consolidation followed by direct delivery to the installation; and
- a receipt for the goods, signed by a responsible person on the installation, is obtained within three months of the time of supply.

(VAT Notice 703, paras 4.7, 4.8).

Goods supplied and delivered within the UK (including territorial waters)

If such goods are

- supplied to an overseas person (see **22.9** above) for export by that person as an indirect export and the necessary conditions in **22.2** above are met, or
- supplied to an overseas person but delivered to a third person in the UK for processing, etc. and subsequent export and the conditions in **22.10** above are met,

the supply can be zero-rated.

Otherwise, VAT must be charged at the appropriate rate.

Exports where there is no taxable supply

[22.24] There is no need to account for VAT in the following circumstances.

- The supply and export of goods which the supplier is to install outside the EU for his customer (as the supply takes place in the country where the goods are installed).
- The temporary export of goods for exhibition or processing.
- The export of goods on sale or return where the goods remain the property of the supplier until they are sold.
- The transfer of own goods to a place outside the EU by a UK business. Any related input tax can be deducted (subject to the normal rules) but the value of any transferred goods should not be included in Box 6 of the VAT return.

The supplier must still hold valid proof of export to demonstrate to HMRC how the goods were disposed of. He must also declare any goods returned to the UK.

(VAT Notice 703, paras 2.14, 2.15).

Proof of export

[22.25] A supplier must ensure that he has proof of export readily available for HMRC. This must be obtained within the appropriate time limit (see **22.2**(*a*) above) and retained for six years.

Proof of export consists of:

- *Official evidence* — this is produced by HMRC (e.g. Goods Departed Messages (GDM) generated by the New Export System (NES)). Alternatively it may be in the form of a Single Administrative Document (SAD) endorsed by HMRC at the point of exit from the EU or confirmation of the electronic discharge of an NCTS movement.
- *Commercial evidence* — e.g. authenticated sea-waybills or air-waybills; PIM/PIEX International consignment notes; master air-waybills or bills of lading; certificates of shipment containing the full details of the consignment and how it left the EU; or International Consignment Note/Lettre de Voiture International (CMR) fully completed by the consignor, the haulier and the receiving consignee, or Freight Transport Association (FTA) own account transport documents fully completed and signed by the receiving customer.

Equal weight is put on official and commercial evidence but both must be supported by supplementary evidence.

Supplementary evidence

A supplier must hold sufficient evidence to prove that a transaction has taken place and that the transaction relates to the goods physically exported. Accounting records are likely to include the following (although it will probably not be necessary to hold all the items listed).

- Customer's order.
- Sales contract.
- Inter-company correspondence.
- Copy of export sales invoice.
- Advice note.
- Consignment note.
- Packing list.
- Insurance and freight charges documentation.
- Evidence of payment.
- Evidence of the receipt of the goods abroad.

Evidence of export

The evidence obtained as proof of export, whether official or commercial, or supporting must clearly identify the following. (These requirements have the force of law.)

- The supplier.
- The consignor (where different from the supplier).
- The customer.
- The goods.
- An accurate value.
- The export destination.
- The mode of transport and route of the export movement.

Vague descriptions of goods, quantities or values are not acceptable (e.g. 'various electrical goods' must not be used when the correct description is '2000 mobile phones make ABC and model number XYZ2000').

Lost or mislaid export evidence

If an exporter has lost or mislaid the official or commercial evidence of export supplied by the ship owner or carrier, duplicate evidence of export may be obtained. The replacement evidence of export must be clearly marked 'DUPLICATE EVIDENCE OF EXPORT' and be authenticated and dated by an official of the issuing company.

Photocopies

Photocopy certificates of shipment are not normally acceptable as evidence of export, nor are photocopy bills of lading, sea waybills or air waybills (unless authenticated by the shipping or airline).

(VAT Notice 703, paras 6.1–6.5, 6.10).

Evidence where the supplier does not arrange shipment

[22.26] If the overseas customer collects or arranges the collection of the goods and their removal from the UK, it can be difficult for the supplier to obtain adequate proof of export as the carrier is contracted to the customer. As a result, for this type of transaction the standard of evidence required to substantiate VAT zero-rating is high. The supplier should seek confirmation of what evidence of export will be provided. He should also consider taking a deposit from the customer equal to the amount of VAT, in case satisfactory evidence of export is not received.

Evidence must show that the goods supplied have left the EU. Copies of transport documents alone are not sufficient and information held must identify the date and route of the movement of goods and the method of transport involved. It should include the following.

- A written order from the customer which shows their name, address and the address where the goods are to be delivered.
- Copy sales invoice showing invoice number, customer's name, and a description of the goods.
- Delivery address for the goods.
- Date of departure of goods from the supplier's premises and from the EU.
- Name and address of the haulier collecting the goods, registration number of the vehicle collecting the goods and the name and signature of the driver.
- Where the goods are to be taken out of the EU by an alternative haulier or vehicle, the name and address of that haulier, the registration number of the vehicle and a signature for the goods.
- Route (e.g. Channel Tunnel, port of exit).
- Copy of travel tickets.
- Name of ferry or shipping company and date of sailing or airway number and airport.

The information held should also include (where applicable):

- Trailer number.
- Full container number.
- Name and address for consolidation, groupage, or processing.

(VAT Notice 703, para 6.6).

Evidence in specific circumstances

[22.27] See VAT Notice 703 as indicated below for specific evidence of export that must be obtained according to the method of export used. In all cases the official or commercial transport evidence obtained must be supported by the supplementary evidence in **22.25** above to show that the transaction has taken place.

Air and sea freight	Para 7.1
Road freight	Para 7.2
Merchandise in Baggage (MIB)	Para 7.3
Groupage or consolidation transactions	Para 7.4
Postal exports	Para 7.5
Exports by courier and fast parcel services	Para 7.6
Exports by rail	Para 7.7
Exports through packers	Para 7.8
Exports from Customs, Excise and/or fiscal warehouses	Para 7.10

Exports through auctioneers

Auctioneers not acting in their own name

[22.28] A supplier who sells goods through auctioneers who

- are not acting in their own name; and
- export the goods

may zero-rate the supply provided a certificate of export is obtained from the auctioneers within three months of the time of supply (see VAT Notice 703, paras 12.2 and 12.3 for the format of the certificates). The auctioneer must hold valid evidence of export for the goods.

Auctioneers acting in their own name

If a supplier sells goods through auctioneers who act in their own name, the goods are treated as being supplied to the auctioneer and must not be zero-rated by the supplier as an export. The auctioneer will be able to zero-rate the onward supply subject to the normal rules.

(VAT Notice 703, para 7.9).

Exports to the Channel Islands

[22.29] Evidence of export for goods sent to the Channel Islands is one of the following (as appropriate).

- Official proof of export produced by NES.
- For goods shipped by air — an authenticated master air-waybill or house air-waybill.
- For goods carried as Merchandise in Baggage — a Customs' certified copy 3 of the SAD (Form C88).
- For goods shipped through a freight forwarder — a certificate of shipment issued by the freight forwarder or an authenticated copy of the Consignment Note and Customs Declarations (CNCD).
- For goods shipped through a fast parcel or courier service — evidence as per VAT Notice 703, para 7.6.
- For goods shipped directly by the south coast ferry companies — an authenticated copy of the CNCD.

(VAT Notice 703, para 7.12).

Exports via EU member states

[22.30] Where goods are exported outside the EU but via other EU member states, official or commercial documentary evidence is required that the goods have left the EU.

(VAT Notice 703, para 7.13).

Records and returns

[22.31] Where goods are exported (or supplied as ships' stores), the normal rules for record keeping still apply (see **57 RECORDS**). In addition, evidence of export must be retained as set out in **22.25** to **22.27** above.

Exports can be zero-rated in the records at the time of supply to the customer. But if the supplier does not ensure the goods have been exported and obtain and hold the required evidence of export within the relevant time limit for the supply, he must account for VAT at the appropriate rate on a supply of the goods in the UK.

VAT must be accounted for on the taxable proportion of the invoiced amount or consideration received (i.e. for a VAT rate of 20% the VAT element is calculated at 1/6). This VAT must be included in Box 1 of the VAT return for the period in which the relevant time limit expires.

If the goods are subsequently exported and/or evidence of export is obtained, the supply can then be zero-rated and the VAT account adjusted for the period in which the evidence is obtained.

Retail schemes

See **61.9** RETAIL SCHEMES for treatment of exports where a retail scheme is used.

Goods returned damaged

Where export goods are damaged after shipment and relanded in the UK, they must be declared to HMRC. If the supplier, or a member of a salvage association, subsequently sell the goods, the seller must account for VAT at the appropriate UK rate on the sale price.

(VAT Notice 703, paras 11.1–11.4).

Goods accidentally lost, destroyed or stolen before export

[22.32] VAT must be accounted for on goods destined for export outside the EU which have been accidentally lost, destroyed or stolen in the UK as follows.

- Where lost, etc. before being supplied, no VAT is due.
- Where lost, etc. after being supplied for direct export, no VAT is due provided that evidence of loss, destruction or theft is held (e.g. an insurance claim, police investigation etc.).
- Where lost, etc. after being supplied for indirect export, VAT is due at the appropriate rate if the goods have been delivered to or collected by the overseas person, or their agent, in the UK.

(VAT Notice 703, para 2.16).

Key points: exports

[22.33] Points to consider are as follows.

- There can only ever be one exporter in a supply of goods arrangement. So if UK business 'A' takes an order from UK business 'B' to supply goods, then this cannot be an export arrangement, even if business 'A' directly ships the goods to a customer outside the EU. It is only business 'B' that can be classed as the exporter, as it is effectively making the sale to the final customer based outside the EU. The sale from business 'A' to 'B' is standard-rated, although business 'B' can reclaim input tax subject to the normal rules.

- The importance of obtaining proper export evidence to support zero-rating cannot be emphasised enough. If HMRC is not satisfied with the export evidence provided, it can treat the goods as being supplied in the UK from a VAT point of view. This could create an output tax charge if the goods in question are standard-rated. Export evidence must be obtained within three months of the export taking place.
- If export evidence is not acquired within three months of the supply, then the exporter must treat the sale as taking place in the UK, i.e. as a standard-rated sale if the goods in question would be standard-rated if sold in the UK. If evidence is subsequently acquired at a future date, then the output tax adjustment can be credited on the VAT return when the evidence was acquired, i.e. so that zero-rating again applies to the sale.
- The retail export scheme can offer commercial benefits to some retailers by giving certain overseas customers the chance to buy goods on a VAT-free basis. The conditions of the scheme must be fully met in order to secure zero-rating. One of the conditions is that the customer buying the goods must take them to a destination outside of the EU before the last day of the third month following his purchase (e.g. goods bought on 3 February must be exported before 31 May).

23

Extra-Statutory Concessions

Extra-statutory concessions

[23.1] HMRC have the power to give statutory effect to concessions by Treasury Order [*FA 2008, s 160*]. The following is a summary of all VAT concessions in force as published by HMRC in Notice 48 (12 September 2017).

International field

2.1 **VAT, excise and customs duties: goods and services.** VAT (and duty including all import and excise duties) are remitted or refunded in accordance with agreements with the authorities concerned on VAT, excise and customs duties:

- (a) goods and services imported by or supplied to visiting forces and their instrumentalities, for the official use of the force, or their instrumentalities;
- (b) goods and services imported by or supplied to NATO military headquarters, organisations or agencies, for their official use;
- (c) US and Canadian government expenditure on mutual defence or mutual aid contracts; and
- (d) temporary importations of equipment required by contractors for fulfilling NATO infrastructure contracts or in connection with the provision and maintenance of US forces defence facilities in the UK.

2.3 **VAT, excise and customs duties: United States Air Force.** Relief from VAT and/or excise duty is allowed, in accordance with certain conditions agreed with the US Air Force, on:

- (a) charges for admission to air shows and open days; and
- (b) goods sold by US forces organisations during air shows and open days to persons not entitled to receive/consume them unless customs charges have been paid.

2.4 **VAT and customs duty: Gifts.** VAT and duty are remitted on gifts (whether imported or purchased in the UK) from US forces to charitable organisations.

2.5 **American war graves.** See **16.5 DEATH AND INCAPACITY**.

2.6 **VAT: supplies to diplomatic missions, international organisations, NATO forces etc. in other European Community (EC) countries.** See **20.21 EUROPEAN UNION: SINGLE MARKET**.

2.7 **VAT and customs duty: certain aircraft ground and security equipment.** See **34.22 IMPORTS**.

Concessions designed to remove inequities or anomalies in administration

3.3 **VAT: zero-rating of supplies of certain goods used in connection with collection of monetary donations.** The supply to a charity of certain goods may be treated as if it were a zero-rated supply. See **13.7 CHARITIES.**

3.6 **VAT: coin-operated machines.** As an accounting convenience, operators may delay accounting for VAT until the takings are removed from the machine. See **8.4 BETTING AND GAMING** and **67.25 SUPPLY: TIME OF SUPPLY.**

3.7 **VAT on minor promotional items supplied in linked supplies schemes.** These are schemes in which a minor article is linked with a main article and sold at a single price. Provided the cost of the minor article is within certain limits, it can be treated as taxable at the same rate as the main article. See **70.5 TRADE PROMOTION SCHEMES.**

3.9 **VAT: recoveries under *VATA 1994, Sch 11 para 5* (VAT charged by unregistered persons).** Where an amount is shown or represented as VAT on an invoice issued by a person who is neither registered nor required to be registered for VAT at the time the invoice is issued, HMRC may require that person to pay an equivalent amount to them. By concession, the person may be permitted to deduct any VAT incurred on supplies to him that were directly attributable to the invoiced supplies. Also by concession, if the recipient of the supplies is a taxable person HMRC may allow the recipient to treat the amount shown or represented as VAT as input tax. See **32.2 HMRC: POWERS.**

3.10 **VAT on necessary meals and accommodation provided by recognised representative sporting bodies to amateur sports persons chosen to represent that body in a competition.** In such circumstances, the input tax incurred may be deductible as input tax and not treated as business entertainment. See **10.6 BUSINESS ENTERTAINMENT.**

3.11 **VAT: incorrect customer declaration.** Where a customer provides an incorrect declaration claiming eligibility for zero-rating under *VATA 1994* or eligibility for reduced rate under *Group 1, Sch 7A* (fuel and power) and the supplier, despite having taken all reasonable steps to check the validity of the declaration, fails to identify the inaccuracy and, in good faith, zero-rates the supply, HMRC will not seek to recover the VAT due from the supplier. See **13.7 CHARITIES, 26.2 FUEL AND POWER, 29.33 HEALTH AND WELFARE, 43.22 LAND AND BUILDINGS: ZERO AND REDUCED RATE SUPPLIES AND DIY HOUSEBUILDERS, 48.1 OUTPUT TAX, 71.14 TRANSPORT AND FREIGHT** and **75.2 ZERO-RATED SUPPLIES.**

3.13 **VAT: repayment of import VAT to shipping agents and freight forwarders.** Under certain conditions, import VAT may be repaid directly to shipping agents and freight forwarders where importers go into insolvency or receivership leaving the agents unable to recover VAT paid on their behalf. See **34.8 IMPORTS.**

3.14 **VAT: zero-rating of certain supplies of free zone goods.** From 1 August 1991, the supply of goods subject to import VAT which are free zone goods in the UK may be zero-rated on condition that there's an agreement between the supplier and the customer that the customer will clear the goods for removal from the zone and will take responsibility for payment of the import VAT.

3.15 **VAT: printed matter published in instalments.** Individual component parts of loose-leaf books may be zero-rated. See **55.3 PRINTED MATTER, ETC.**

3.17 **VAT: zero-rating of supplies of training for foreign governments.** Zero-rating applies to training services supplied to a foreign government in furtherance of its sovereign activities. See **39.6 INTERNATIONAL SERVICES.**

3.18 **VAT: exemption of all domestic service charges.** All mandatory service charges paid by occupants of residential property towards the upkeep of the property and the provision of caretakers are exempt. See **42.19** LAND AND BUILDINGS: EXEMPT SUPPLIES AND OPTION TO TAX.

3.19 **VAT: supplies of 'relevant goods' to charities.** Zero-rating may be applied to supplies of 'relevant goods' to a charity either whose sole or main purpose is to provide a range of care services to meet the personal needs of handicapped people or which provides transport services predominantly for handicapped people. See **13.8** CHARITIES.

3.21 **VAT: sales of poor quality donated goods.** The supply by a charity of goods which have been donated to it for sale can be zero-rated where the goods, although of a kind normally zero-rated by being made available to the general public for purchase, are by reason of their poor quality not fit to be so made available. See **13.6** CHARITIES.

3.24 **VAT: charities providing care in an institution and also supplying goods to disabled persons resident in their own and other institutions.** Where conditions are met, zero-rating can be applied to supplies by a charity at or below cost of certain goods designed solely for use by a visually handicapped person even though the recipient of the supply is a resident, or is attending the premises of, the charity's own institution. See **29.15** HEALTH AND WELFARE.

3.25 **VAT: resuscitation training models supplied to charities and other eligible bodies for use in first aid training.** These can be treated as relevant goods for the purposes of *VATA 1994, Sch 8 Group 15 Note (3)* and their supply zero-rated in certain cases. See **13.8** CHARITIES.

3.26 **VAT: works of art, antiques and collectors' items.** Where certain works of art, collector's items and antiques are imported for exhibition with a view to possible sale, any sale of those items by auction when still subject to temporary importation arrangements is treated as neither a supply of goods nor a supply of services. See **74.4** WORKS OF ART, ETC.

3.27 **VAT: use of the auctioneers' scheme for sales of goods at auction on behalf of non-taxable persons.** An auctioneer selling, on behalf of a third party vendor who is a non-taxable person, goods which have been grown, made or produced (including bloodstock or livestock reared from birth) by that person, may enter the goods into the auctioneers' scheme provided he holds an appropriate certificate from the vendor. See **62.54** SECOND-HAND GOODS.

3.30 **VAT: retail pharmacists.** In applying a retail scheme, certain goods which are standard-rated when dispensed to individuals for personal use whilst an inpatient or resident of, or attending, a hospital or nursing home may be treated as zero-rated. See **61.19** RETAIL SCHEMES.

3.34 **VAT reclaimed by museums and galleries covered by *VATA 1994, s 33A*.** Museums and galleries specified in an *Order* made under *VATA 1994, s 33A(9)* are not required to repay input tax, properly recovered at the time, on goods and services used in connection with taxable supplies of admitting the public for payment, solely on account of the move to free admission. See **35.13**(21) INPUT TAX.

3.35 **VAT: apportionment of certain membership subscriptions to non-profit making bodies.** Bodies that are non-profit making and supply a mixture of zero-rated, exempt and/or standard-rated benefits to their members in return for their subscriptions may apportion such subscriptions to reflect the value and VAT liability of those individual benefits, without regard to whether there is one principal benefit. See **15.2** CLUBS AND ASSOCIATIONS.

> *Example*
> An annual subscription to a charity includes a monthly newsletter being sent in the post to subscribers, giving details about the charity's activities and events. The value of the newsletter within the subscription can be treated as zero-rated, producing either an output tax saving on the subscription if it is standard-rated or increased input tax recovery if it is exempt from VAT.

Non-commercial transactions

9.1 **VAT on goods supplied at duty-free and tax-free shops.** Where goods liable to VAT are supplied to intending passengers at duty-free and tax-free shops approved by HMRC, the supplier may be regarded as the exporter and zero-rate the supply of those goods which are exported. See **22.3 EXPORTS**.

9.2 **VAT: marine fuel.** Certain supplies of marine fuel may be received free of VAT. See **22.4 EXPORTS**.

9.3 **VAT and excise duties: personal reliefs for goods permanently imported from third countries.** Property purchased by diplomats, members of certain international organisations and NATO forces which otherwise qualifies for relief on the transfer of normal residence from outside the EU will not be refused relief solely because HMRC cannot satisfy themselves that the goods have borne all duties and taxes normally applicable in their country of origin. See **34.15**(13) **IMPORTS**.

9.4 **VAT and excise duties: personal reliefs for goods permanently imported from third countries.** Property purchased outside the EU by UK forces which otherwise qualifies for relief on the transfer of normal residence from outside the EU will not be refused relief solely because HMRC cannot satisfy themselves that the goods have borne all duties and taxes normally applicable in their country of origin. See **34.15**(13) **IMPORTS**.

9.5 **VAT and excise duties: personal reliefs for goods permanently imported from third countries.** Property purchased under a UK export scheme by members of the UK diplomatic service, members of UK forces and members of International Organisations and which otherwise qualifies for relief on the transfer of normal residence from outside the EU will not be refused relief solely because HMRC cannot satisfy themselves that the goods have borne all duties and taxes normally applicable in their country of origin. See **34.15**(13) **IMPORTS**.

9.6 **VAT and excise duties: personal reliefs for goods permanently imported from third countries.** Personal belongings otherwise qualifying for relief on the transfer of normal residence from outside the EU may still be granted relief from VAT on importation if failing to qualify only because they have not been possessed and used for the specified period. See **34.15**(13) **IMPORTS**.

9.7 **VAT and excise duties: personal reliefs for goods permanently imported from third countries.** Personal belongings otherwise qualifying for relief on the transfer of normal residence from outside the EU may still be granted relief from VAT on importation if failing to qualify only because the property is declared for relief outside the specific periods. See **34.15**(13) **IMPORTS**.'

De Voil Indirect Tax Service. See V1.239.

Agreements with trade bodies

[23.2] HMRC have entered into a number of agreements with trade bodies which permit their members to use procedures to meet their obligation under VAT law and which take into account their individual circumstances.

The agreements apply only to areas where HMRC can exercise discretion and they convey no direct financial advantage or relief from the legal requirements. Some of the agreements might usefully be applied to other businesses but note that any special method based on these arrangements can only be adopted with the approval of HMRC.

Agreements entered into at the time of publication are as follows. For full details, see VAT Notice 700/57/14.

- London Bullion Market Association (supplies of bullion).
- Brewers' Society (deduction of input tax in respect of brewers' tenanted estate).
- Association of British Factors and Discounters (partial exemption).
- Finance Houses Association Ltd (partial exemption).
- Association of British Insurers (recovery of input tax incurred in the UK in connection with supplies by branches outside the EC).
- Association of Investment Trust Companies (partial exemption).
- British Printing Industries Federation (apportionment of subsidy publishing supplies).
- Marine, aviation and transport insurance underwriters who are members of an (unnamed) trade organisation (claims-related input tax and associated imported services).
- Association of British Insurers, Lloyd's of London, the Institute of London Underwriters and the British Insurance and Investment Association (coding supplies of marine, aviation and transport insurance services).
- National Caravan Council Limited and the British Holiday and Home Park Association Limited (method of valuing removable contents sold with zero-rated caravans).
- Association of Unit Trust and Investment Managers (VAT liability of charges made in connection with personal equity plans).
- British Bankers' Association (VAT liability of electronic banking/cash management services).
- British Vehicle Rental and Leasing Association (car leasing and repairs and maintenance services).
- Society of Motor Manufacturers and Traders (output tax on the self-supply of a motor vehicle).
- Gaming Board for Great Britain and the British Casino Association (competitions in card rooms).
- British Phonographic Industry (VAT liability of promotional items given free of charge).
- Thoroughbred Breeders Association (arrangements under which racehorse owners may register for VAT).
- British Horseracing Board (revised arrangements under which racehorse owners may register for VAT).

- British Horseracing Board and Thoroughbred Breeders Association (racehorses applied permanently to personal or other non-business use).
- British Horseracing Board and Thoroughbred Breeders Association (keeping of stallions at stud).
- British Horseracing Board and Thoroughbred Breeders Association (racehorses and time limits for exportation).
- Agriculture and Horticulture Development Board (VAT treatment of levies collected (invoiced) by the Board from operators of slaughter-houses and exporters of live animals).
- Society of Motor Manufacturers and Traders Ltd (how the one tonne payload test will be applied in practice to double cab pick-ups).
- Society of Motor Manufacturers and Traders Ltd (simplified method by which motor manufacturers, importers and wholesale distributors may calculate the VAT due on the private use of stock in trade cars provided to directors and employees free of charge).
- Retail Motor Industry Federation (simplified method by which retail motor dealers may calculate the VAT due on the private use of demonstrator cars provided to directors and employees free of charge).
- British Vehicle Rental and Leasing Association (simplified method which daily rental companies may use to calculate the VAT due on the incidental private use of their hire fleets).

Key points: ESCs

[23.3] Points to consider are as follows.

- A useful concession for charities and non-profit making bodies in relation to their subscription income is that the usual mixed supply rules can be overridden so that each element of the supply (benefits to members) can be considered in isolation. So if a minor part of the subscription fee gives zero-rated benefits (e.g. a newsletter or book), this part of the supply can be treated as zero-rated, even if it would usually be incidental to the main supply and therefore ignored.
- HMRC have agreed a number of special VAT concessions with various trade bodies and associations in the UK. It is always worth suggesting to clients that they check with their trade association (if applicable) whether any such agreements are in place as they may save time and administration costs in relation to VAT accounting.
- Remember, these are concessions and HMRC are entitled to withdraw them at any time and can do this on a case by case basis.
- HMRC are gradually replacing these concessions with legislation where it is possible to do so. Unfortunately some concessions are being withdrawn.

24

Financial Services

Cross-reference. See **19.25 EUROPEAN UNION LEGISLATION** for the provisions of *Directive 2006/112/EC*.

De Voil Indirect Tax Service. See V4.136, V4.136A–V4.136J.

Introduction to financial services

[24.1] Before considering the question of the VAT liability of financial services, there are other relevant related areas of VAT law which affect financial services and which need to be taken into account.

Place of supply of financial services

[24.2] The supply of financial services falls within the general rule for the place of supply of services:

- if they are supplied to a relevant business person, they are supplied where the customer belongs;
- if they are supplied to a recipient who is not a 'relevant business person', they are supplied where the supplier belongs (see **66.14** supply: place of supply), unless the customer belongs in a country which is not an EU member state (other than the Isle of Man). In such a case, the place of supply is where the recipient belongs.

[*VATA 1994, Sch 4A para 16*].

Special 'easement' rule for sales of securities

If a business belonging in the UK sells securities and cannot identify the customer or their place of belonging, it may either

- treat the supply as being in the UK and exempt;
- use the place of belonging of a nominee account for the purchaser to determine the place of supply; or
- use a special rule known as the 'easement' which determines the place of supply by using the following tests in sequential order.
  - (1) Where the place of transaction (i.e. the relevant security exchange) is known, a sale transacted
    - (i) in the UK is treated as made to a person belonging in the UK and exempt;
    - (ii) in any other EU member state is treated as made to a taxable person belonging in that country, and is outside the scope of UK VAT; and
    - (iii) outside the EU is treated as made to a person belonging outside the EU and is outside the scope of UK VAT.
  - (2) Where the place of the transaction is not known, then the place of supply is deemed to be a place where the security is listed.
  - (3) Where the place of transaction is not known and the security is not listed or is listed on both an EU and non-EU exchange, then the place of supply is deemed to be the place where the last known broker in the transaction belongs.

(VAT Notice 701/49/17, para 6.16).

Input tax recovery

[24.3] Subject to the normal rules, input tax may be recovered which relates to

- taxable supplies of financial services (i.e. supplies with a place of supply in the UK other than exempt supplies);
- supplies of financial services with a place of supply outside the UK but which would be taxable supplies if made in the UK;
- supplies of financial services which
  - (i) are supplied to a person who belongs outside the EU; or
  - (ii) are directly linked to the export of goods to a place outside the EU; or
  - (iii) consist of the provision of intermediary services (see **24.25** below) in relation to any transaction within (i) or (ii) above

provided the supply is exempt or would have been exempt if made in the UK.

[*VATA 1994, s 26(1)(2); SI 1999/3121*].

Reverse charge on financial services from abroad

[24.4] A supply of financial services is treated as made by the recipient if:

- the services are treated as supplied in the UK and (if the services fall within *VATA 1994, Sch 4A Parts 1 and 2*) the recipient is registered for VAT in the UK (see **66.12** *et seq.* **SUPPLY: PLACE OF SUPPLY**);
- the recipient belongs in the UK;
- the recipient is a relevant business person (see **66.14 SUPPLY: PLACE OF SUPPLY**); and
- the services are supplied by a person who belongs in a country other than the UK.

[*VATA 1994, s 8(1), (2)*].

He must account for output tax, calculated on the full value of the supply received, in Box 1 of its VAT return and, subject to the normal rules, can include the VAT as input tax in Box 4 on the same return.

This 'reverse charge' procedure does not apply to services provided by an overseas head office or branch which is the same legal entity as the business (unless it simply pays for such a service received by the UK business). But it does apply to certain services received within a VAT group, which are bought in by an overseas group member and supplied on either in their own right or as a component in a larger supply, to the UK members of the group. See **28.6 GROUPS OF COMPANIES**.

Outsourcing

[24.5] Financial institutions often buy-in or sub-contract services that once would have been provided in-house. This is sometimes known as 'outsourcing'. It can include such services as data processing, telephone helplines and general administration. Outsourcing is a contentious area because financial institutions seek exemption wherever possible in order to keep overheads down.

The key decision on outsourcing is *Sparekassernes Datacenter (SDC) v Skatteministeriet, ECJ Case C-2/95*, [1997] STC 932 (TVC 22.400). A company (SDC) carried out a variety of operations on behalf of Danish savings banks which each bank would have otherwise had to carry out for itself. These included the execution of transfers of funds by electronic means between the various banks and between those banks and their clients, the provisions of advice on and trade in securities, and the management of deposits, purchase contracts and loans. The CJEU held that exemption is not restricted to transactions effected by financial institutions or any particular type of legal person. Nor does it matter that the supply is carried out wholly or partly by electronic means or manually. It is not necessary for the services to be provided by an institution which has a legal relationship with the end customer and the fact that the services are provided by a third party does not prevent those services from falling within the exemption. Transactions concerning transfers and payments, and services consisting of the management of deposits, purchase contracts and loans included operations carried out by a data-handling centre if those operations were distinct in character and were specific to, and essential for, the exempt transactions. However, services which merely consisted of making information available to banks and other users did not qualify for exemption.

The liability of a supply of outsourced services to a supplier of exempt financial services depends, therefore, on the nature of the services performed, not whether it is supplied to someone who is making exempt supplies. The exact nature of the supply must be determined and, to be exempt, the outsourced service must, when viewed broadly, form a distinct whole fulfilling the essential functions of a supply which itself falls within the exemption for financial services.

If the business providing the outsourced services is acting as an intermediary, see **24.25** below. If it is providing outsourced services to a loan provider, see **24.11** below.

(VAT Notice 701/49/17, para 1.8).

In *CSC Financial Services Ltd v C & E Commrs, ECJ Case C–235/00,* [2002] STC 57 (TVC 22.403) a company supplied services to a group of companies which issued personal equity plans. It dealt with telephone enquiries and with replies to advertisements placed by the group and sent application forms to potential customers and checked completed application forms. The CJEU held that exemption under *Directive 2006/112/EC, Art 135(1)(f)* for 'transactions including negotiation' did not extend to services limited to providing information about a financial product and, as the case may be, receiving and processing applications for subscriptions, without issuing them.

Single or multiple supply

[24.6] Certain financial services (e.g. intermediary services and outsourcing) can constitute a number of component services which, if supplied separately, may have different VAT liabilities. In order to establish the correct liability of such packaged services, certain tests must be applied to determine the overall VAT liability. See **65.6 SUPPLY: GENERAL**. (VAT Notice 701/49/17, para 1.7).

Overview of the law on the liability of financial services

EU legislation

[24.7] Certain financial services are exempt from VAT under *Directive 2006/112/EC, Art 135(1)(b)–(g)*. See **19.26**(*b*)–(*g*) **EUROPEAN UNION LEGISLATION.**

UK law

The equivalent UK provisions are in *VATA 1994, Sch 9 Group 5*. This lists a number of *Items* which provide for exemption for the following categories (subject to qualifications and definitions which are dealt with in the appropriate part of the chapter).

(1) The issue, transfer or receipt of, or any dealing with, money, any security for money or any note or order for the payment of money. See **24.8** below.

(2) The making of any advance or the granting of any credit. See **24.11** below.

(3) The management of credit by the person granting it. See **24.11** below.

(4) The provision of the facility of instalment credit finance in a hire purchase, conditional sale or credit sale agreement for which facility a separate charge is made and disclosed to the recipient of the supply of goods. See **24.11** below.

(5) The provision of administrative arrangements and documentation and the transfer of title to the goods in connection with the supply described in Item (3) if the total consideration therefore is specified in the agreement and does not exceed £10. See **24.11** below.

(6) The provision of intermediary services in relation to any transaction comprised in Items (1), (2), (3), (4) or (6) (whether or not any such transaction is finally concluded) by a person acting in an intermediary capacity. See **24.25** below.

(7) The underwriting of an issue within Item (1) or any transaction within Item (6). See **24.23** below.

(8) The issue, transfer or receipt of, or any dealing with, any security or secondary security. See **24.17** below.

(9) (Deleted).

(10) The operation of any current, deposit or savings account. See **24.24** below.

(11) The management of authorised open-ended investment companies, authorised unit trust schemes or certain collective investment schemes. See **24.20** below.

(12) The management of closed-ended collective investment undertakings. See **24.21** below.

Many services which are associated with finance are not covered by the exemption. In addition to services covered in the text generally when dealing with exemptions, see **24.29** below for a list of some of the more common finance-rated supplies which are standard-rated.

Dealings with money and securities for money

[24.8] Exemption applies to the issue, transfer or receipt of, and any dealings with

- money,
- any security for money; or
- any note or order for the payment of money

but excludes the following.

- All services falling within **24.17** below (which are exempt under those provisions).
- Preparatory services carried out separately, before an exempt transaction concerning money (e.g. the preparation and delivery of data such as a wages roll, which is then put into effect by someone else). Preparatory services carried out by an intermediary as part of their overall exempt supply are exempt (see **24.25** below).
- The supply of coins or banknotes (whether legal tender or not) as collectors' pieces, investment articles or items of numismatic interest. Such a supply is normally taxable on the full selling price, whether or not they are sold for more than their face value. Examples include bank notes, proof coins, Maundy money and precious or base metal coins. See, however, **62.3 SECOND-HAND GOODS** for the use of the second-hand scheme for supplies of collectors' pieces. Sales of some gold coins are exempt as investment gold. See **27 GOLD AND PRECIOUS METALS.**

[*VATA 1994, Sch 9 Group 5 Item 1 and Notes 1, 1A, 2*]. (VAT Notice 701/49/17, paras 2.4, 2.6).

Issue

The issue of *money* can only be by a bank or similar financial institution. A coin or banknote can only be issued once (the first time) and this can only be done by a bank with a statutory entitlement to do so (e.g. the Bank of England). The above exemption is normally superseded by *VATA 1994, Sch 8 Group 11 Item 1* which zero-rates the issue by a bank of a note payable to the bearer on demand (see **75.4 ZERO-RATED SUPPLIES**). But see *Royal Bank of Scotland Group plc v C & E Commrs,* CS [2002] STC 575 (TVC 27.4) where the bank was authorised to issue its own bank notes, which it did from automated cash machines. The court held that the 'reciprocity fees' which the bank received from other banks whose customers had used its machines to withdraw cash were not consideration for a zero-rated supply of bank notes but for an exempt supply of the provision of the facilities to obtain money.

Transfer

For the purposes of *Directive 2006/112/EC, Art 135(1)(d)* a 'transfer' has been defined as a 'transaction consisting of the execution of an order for the transfer of a sum of money from one bank account to another. It is characterized in particular by the fact that it involves a change in the legal and financial situation existing between the person giving the order and the recipient and between those parties and their respective banks.' (*Sparekassernes Datacenter v Skatteministeriet, ECJ Case C–2/95* [1997] STC 932 (TVC 22.400)).

In *HMRC v Axa UK plc, ECJ Case C–175/09*, [2010] STC 2825 (TVC 22.405) the CJEU ruled that the exemption provided by *Art 13B(d)(3)* did not cover A's services, which consisted in collecting fees from dental patients by monthly direct debit instalments and passing the fees (less A's remuneration) on to the dentists, sending the dentists statements, contacting patients with regard to non-payment, and other services such as registration and use of a website. Such services fell within the exclusion for 'debt collection and factoring'. Following the CJEU decision, the CA unanimously allowed HMRC's appeal ([2011] EWCA Civ 1607 (TVC 22.405)).

Following the CJEU decision in *Axa*, HMRC stated that 'debt collection' does not apply solely to the service of chasing and recovering overdue payments on behalf of the creditor. All services principally concerned with collecting payments from the person owing them for the benefit of the entity to which those payments are owed (regardless of whether those payments are received before, on or after their due date) fall within the exclusion to the exemption. (HMRC Brief 54/10).

A competitor of the business considered in the *Axa* case set up arrangements to attempt to avoid the effect of the decision and the change in HMRC's policy that followed it. It began to make charges to the patients for processing their payments, rather than charging the dentist for collecting them. The First-tier Tribunal and Upper Tribunal agreed with the taxpayer that a service was being provided to the patient, and that this could not constitute 'debt collection' because that is something supplied to and paid for by a creditor. The tribunals also rejected HMRC's contentions that this was an artificial arrangement or an abuse of rights. However, following the CJEU's decision in *Bookit Ltd* (see **24.28** below), the Upper Tribunal has decided to refer questions to the CJEU on whether processing direct debits for patients is an exempt financial service or a taxable administrative one (*HMRC v DPAS Ltd* [2016] UKUT 373 (TCC) (TVC 27.11)).

Money

'*Money*' includes currencies other than sterling [*VATA 1994, s 96(1)*] and comprises currency, coins or banknotes, in sterling or any other currency, when supplied as legal tender in a financial transaction. With effect from 1 July 2006, it does not include platinum nobles. (VAT Notice 701/49/17, para 2).

For VAT purposes decentralised digital currencies (cryptocurrencies) such as bitcoin are treated as follows.

- When bitcoin is exchanged for sterling or foreign currencies such as euros or dollars no VAT is due on the value of the bitcoin.
- Charges made over and above the value of the bitcoin for arranging or carrying out any transactions in bitcoin are exempt from VAT under *Directive 2006/112/EC, Art 135(1)(d)*.
- The value of a supply of goods or services on which VAT is due is the sterling value of the cryptocurrency at the point the transaction takes place. See **72.18 VALUATION**.
- New bitcoin is produced by solving a complex cryptographic algorithm and income from this activity is generally outside the scope of VAT on the basis that there is an insufficient link between any services provided and any consideration received.
- Income received by producers of bitcoin for other activities, such as for the provision of services in connection with the verification of specific transactions for which specific charges are made, is exempt from VAT under *Directive 2006/112/EC, Art 135(1)(d)*.

(HMRC Brief 9/14).

The CJEU decided in *Skatteverket v David Hedqvist, ECJ Case C-264/14* (TVC 20.140) that:

- *Article 2(1)(c)* of *Council Directive 2006/112/EC* must be interpreted as meaning that transactions which consist of the exchange of traditional currency for units of the bitcoin virtual currency and vice versa, in return for payment of a sum equal to the difference between, on the one hand, the price paid by the operator to purchase the currency and, on the other hand, the price at which he sells that currency to his clients, constitute the supply of services for consideration within the meaning of that article.
- *Article 135(1)(e)* of *Council Directive 2006/112/EC* must be interpreted as meaning that the supply of services which consist of the exchange of traditional currency for units of the bitcoin virtual currency and vice versa, in return for payment of a sum equal to the difference between, on the one hand, the price paid by the operator to purchase the currency and, on the other hand, the price at which he sells that currency to his clients, are transactions exempt from VAT, within the meaning of that provision and that *Art 2(1)(d)* and *(f)* of *Council Directive 2006/112/EC* must be interpreted as meaning that such a supply of services does not fall within the scope of application of those provisions.

Security for money

A 'security for money' has been defined as a document under seal or under hand at a consideration containing a covenant, promise or undertaking to pay a sum of money (*Dyrham Park Country Club Ltd* (VTD 700) (TVC 13.32)). Examples include bills of exchange, financial guarantees and promissory notes.

For the purposes of *Item 1* above, securities do not include stocks, shares, bonds and other similar securities for which exemption is covered by *VATA 1994, Sch 9 Group 5 Item 6* (see **24.17** below).

(VAT Notice 701/49/17, para 3.1).

The Court of Appeal recently released its decision in *Wilton Park Ltd* [2016] EWCA Civ 1294 (TVC 27.12) regarding the VAT treatment of vouchers issued to customers in a lap/table dancing club who had run out of cash so they could remain in the club. The club argued that the vouchers were exempt from VAT as securities for money. HMRC argued that the vouchers formed part of the taxable consideration paid for the provision of the clubs facilities. The First-tier Tribunal and Upper Tribunal held that although the vouchers issued by the club did constitute a security for money that could potentially be exempt from VAT, the services of redeeming those vouchers formed part of a composite taxable supply of performance facilitation services and the purpose of the vouchers was to keep customers in the club. The Court of Appeal dismissed the taxpayer's appeal agreeing with the Upper Tribunal that when the vouchers were redeemed they formed part of the taxable consideration for the provision of the club's facilities.

This case serves as a reminder that the issue of a voucher that may constitute security in money may not necessarily be exempt if the voucher has been issued in these types of situations.

Dealing with money

A supply of services involving dealing with money is exempt provided a financial transaction is carried out.

The more obvious dealings with money are the routine financial transactions carried out by banks, building societies, bureaux de change and similar institutions, e.g.

- the acceptance of deposits of money on current account or otherwise;
- money transfer services; and
- exchange of legal tender.

(VAT Notice 701/49/17, para 2.1).

Related transactions

[24.9] Listed below are examples of common transactions connected with supplies within **24.8** above and their VAT liability.

(1) Automatic teller machines (ATMs)

The supply of

- an ATM or the software required to run it (whether or not the consideration is based on the ATM's use), and
- services provided in connection with the routine operation of an ATM (e.g. filling with cash, maintenance and repair)

are taxable supplies.

ATM providers sometimes make charges described as convenience fees, interchange fees or reciprocity fees. These are charges to banks by other banks when those other bank's customers use their ATM facilities. Where the charge is for

- the facility to obtain money,
- the provision of money,
- transaction processing, or
- the operation of accounts

the supply is exempt.

The granting of a right to permanently attach an ATM to the ground, or for its incorporation into the fabric of a building, is an exempt supply unless the grantor has elected to waive exemption.

(VAT Notice 701/49/17, para 2.9).

See also *Royal Bank of Scotland Group plc v C & E Commrs*, CS [2002] STC 575 (TVC 27.4).

In *Concept Direct Ltd* (VTD 19721) (TVC 27.3) a company found suitable sites for ATMs on behalf of a bank and received commission for each site plus a 'swipe fee' of 15p on each occasion the machine was used. The swipe fee (as well as the commission) was held to be standard-rated as the company took no part in the operation of the machine or the issue of money.

(2) Clearing and settlement services

A service supplied by a clearing-house for settling indebtedness between members is an exempt supply. (VAT Notice 701/49/17, para 2.8).

(3) Deductions from pay

Charges made by an employer for deductions from pay of employees for items such as insurance premiums, mortgage repayments or union subscriptions are exempt.

Any charges made for deductions from the pay in compliance with an attachment of earnings order are seen as reimbursement for expenses incurred in carrying out a statutory duty and are outside the scope of VAT.

(VAT Notice 701/49/17, para 2.13).

(4) Derivatives

Derivatives are financial instruments. They are known as 'derivatives' because their price is directly dependant upon the value of the underlying commodity, financial instrument or currency. To establish the VAT liability of the derivative, it is necessary to know what the 'underlying' product is.

(a) Commodity futures, options and other derivatives

A commodity is a raw material such as grain, coffee, metal or oil and is traded on a commodity market. This can be based in the country of the commodity's origin or on a 'terminal market' (a commodity market in a trading centre, such as London). As commodity prices fluctuate widely, commodity exchanges assist in enabling producers and users of the commodity to hedge the price risk with outside speculators and investors.

See **70 TERMINAL MARKETS** for the zero-rating of transactions traded on certain terminal markets by or with a member of that market or by a person acting as an agent or broker between a member of the market and another person.

For transactions not traded on one of those terminal markets:

- Commodity futures and actuals follow the liability of the underlying commodity.
- The premium paid for a commodity option is separate from the price of underlying commodity and is payable whether or not the buyer exercises the option. The payment for the right to buy a commodity, rather than a contract to buy it, is a standard-rated supply of services. If the option is exercised, there will be a separate supply of the commodity itself.

(b) Futures contracts

Financial futures are exempt from VAT and for VAT purposes are divided into two categories, cash settled contracts and non-cash settled contracts. Although both are exempt, which category the supply falls into is important because it may affect whether the supply by an agent or intermediary arranging the transaction is exempt or taxable. See **24.28** below.

(i) *Cash settled contracts* (*Item 1* contracts) are contracts where there are no underlying deliverable securities or contracts. These include short-term interest rate futures, FT-SE 100 futures, other stock index futures and weather derivatives.
The supply of cash settled contracts for a consideration is exempt from VAT. Where a futures contract runs to maturity, there is no further supply for VAT purposes. Cash settlements under these contracts are not consideration for a supply and must be excluded from partial exemption calculations and VAT returns.

(ii) *Non-cash settled contracts* (*Item 6* contracts) i.e. contracts where there are underlying deliverable securities. These include gilts, T-bonds and other securities (not being securities for money).
The supply of a non-cash settled contract is exempt. If a contract runs to maturity there is a separate exempt supply of the underlying security. Transactions on exchanges are treated as being made between either the member and the client or the member and the relevant clearing house. The value of the supply of the securities is the price that was agreed when the contract was made.

(c) Financial futures – exchange trading

- *Fees charged by members*. Members of certain exchanges deal as principals and the 'turn' (or commission) charged by the member to a client for transacting a financial futures contract represents the value of the member's supply. A member may charge for each leg, or for a 'round trip' in a closed-out transaction. The full value of each charge is the measure of the supply for VAT purposes. The 'turn' (or commission) is consideration for an exempt supply of financial futures.
Where a member acts for another member in executing a transaction, he is a principal and the 'turn' (or commission) charged is exempt. The value of the supply is the amount charged to the member. Clearing fees charged by a clearing member to a non-clearing member are also consideration for an exempt supply.
- *Client-to-member transactions*. There is no supply by a client to a member in a closed-out financial futures transaction.
- *Margin payments*. Margin payments (whether initial or variation) fall outside the scope of VAT.

(d) Financial options

Financial options are exempt from VAT. The sale of an option as a financial instrument is a supply of services separate from the underlying transaction to which the option relates.

There are three main types of financial options contracts.

- *Options based on financial futures contracts*. Options on short-term interest rate futures, index-based futures and cash settled futures are exempt from VAT. (These are options on cash settled contracts under (*b*)(i) above.) There is no further supply when an option is exercised to obtain or supply the underlying futures contracts.
- *Equity options*. These options have equities, rather than financial futures contracts, as the underlying instrument and are exempt from VAT. (These are options on non-cash settled contracts under (*b*)(ii) above.)
- *Index-based options*. Unlike equity options, index-based options do not provide for delivery but are cash settled. This type of option is exempt (as an option on a cash settled contract under (*b*)(i) above).

When a financial option is sold for a premium, a right has been granted. The value of the supply is the premium charged and the supply is exempt.

*(e) **Trade by locals***

Locals are traders registered to members of exchanges who act in an independent capacity to some degree, but in the embodiment of the member to whom the local is registered. Locals can be employees, self-employed or engaged in a joint venture or partnership with a member. The VAT treatment depends on the status of the local.

- Employee locals may manage or trade on an account for their member and will be on the member's payroll. The payments from the member to the local are outside the scope of VAT.
- Self-employed locals may trade on their own account. When the local makes a trade, the member is the principal to the contract. However, when the trade is completed there is another contract between the member and the local, now in the same position for VAT purposes as a third party client, in which both parties are also principals (i.e. there is a back-to-back arrangement). The supply made by the member to the client is an exempt supply of a financial futures contract or, as the case may be, a taxable supply of a commodities contract.
  A self-employed local may also act as the embodiment of the member with which the local is registered. For VAT purposes the local is acting as an agent.
- Where the local and the member are engaged in a joint venture or partnership, every trade executed by the local is a trade of the member to whom the local is registered and the rules regarding transactions by members (see above) apply to this initial transaction.
  The VAT liability of the remuneration received by the local under the joint venture or partnership arrangements depends on the nature of the agreement between the parties.

*(f) **Trading Over-The-Counter (OTC)***

Financial futures and options can be traded OTC. These are non-standard contracts traded off-exchange. Both are exempt from VAT. See **24.28** below acting as an intermediary.

Commodity futures and options can similarly be traded OTC. Both are taxable.

(g) Trading on non-UK exchanges

The value and liability of the supplies made for VAT purposes depends on whether the supplier is a principal or an agent in respect of transactions in commodities contracts or financial futures and options contracts traded on non-UK exchanges. The rules of the overseas exchange and the local legislation could also have a significant effect on how the transaction should be viewed for UK VAT purposes. Each transaction must be examined and the VAT liability determined on its own merits.

(h) Interest rate swaps

For VAT purposes, during the term of the swap, there is a continuous supply of services and, to the extent that any money changes hands, there is an exempt supply under the *VATA, Sch 9 Group 5, item 1*.

(i) Currency swaps

Currency swaps provide both a currency and interest hedge. For VAT purposes no supply takes place in relation to the exchange of principal amounts of underlying loans in currency swaps.

(j) Financial Spread Bets (FSBs)

This involves speculating by placing a bet on an index, eg commodity prices or the FT-SE100 index. In the same way as sports betting, financial spread betting is liable to general betting duty and is exempt from VAT under the *VATA 1994, Sch 9 Group 4*. Duty is calculated by the bookmaker based on the total amount due from customers less any winnings paid out.

(k) Contracts for Differences (CFDs)

Contracts offer speculators the opportunity to buy or sell the performance of a share, equity, etc. without the need to own the underlying asset. A CFD provided for a consideration (turn/commission) is an exempt supply of financial services. The CFD is treated as a cash settled contract for the purposes of defining the VAT liability of an intermediary's supply (see **24.28** below).

(VAT Notice 701/9/11, paras 2.1, 2.2; VAT Notice 701/49/17, paras 8.1–8.11).

(5) Dishonoured cheques or direct debit payments

A bank or a supplier of goods or services may charge a customer because

- it has failed to honour its cheques or direct debit payments; or
- in the case of a supplier, the supplier has borne the cost of bank charges.

Where a bank makes such a charge to its customer, the charge will be a part of the overall service for running the customer's account and exempt from VAT.

Where a supplier makes such a charge to its customer, the charge will be outside the scope of VAT.

(VAT Notice 701/49/17, para 2.11).

(6) Face value vouchers

Face value vouchers that give a right to goods or services are not seen as securities for money. However, at the point the voucher can be exchanged for money, it is a security for money and any consideration for it is exempt. For example, where the voucher is presented to a retailer as payment for goods or services it is not a security for money, but when the retailer presents the voucher to a third party to be exchanged for money, it becomes a security for money at that point. See **72 TRADE PROMOTION SCHEMES**. (VAT Notice 701/49/17, para 3.2).

(7) Foreign exchange transactions

Foreign exchange transactions are normally exempt supplies. Where a person acts as principal, the consideration is any fees or commission charged. Following the decision in *C & E Commrs v First National Bank of Chicago, ECJ Case C–172/96,* [1998] STC 850 (TVC 22.94) HMRC accept that where no specific commission or fee is charged on particular transactions (e.g. where services are paid for by the spread between the bid and offer rates), those transactions are nevertheless supplies for VAT purposes, the consideration being 'the net result of the transactions of the supplier of the service over a given period of time', i.e. the net profit on the transactions. In most cases it will be appropriate to isolate the input tax incurred on foreign exchange transactions and deal with VAT separately within the partial exemption method used.

However, in *Willis Pension Trustees Ltd* (VTD 19183) (TVC 62.202) a company which acted as trustee of the pension fund entered into a number of foreign currency transactions with a number of banks in order to hedge or minimise the pension scheme's exposure to adverse exchange rate fluctuations. The tribunal decided that any 'profit' retained by Willis from the foreign exchange transactions was not consideration for a supply. HMRC accept this decision which will apply to a business entering a foreign exchange transaction in the specific set of circumstances in *Willis*. In such cases, VAT paid on associated costs of foreign exchange transactions relates to the business as a whole. It can be treated as residual input tax under a partial exemption method. HMRC are considering whether the decision has any wider application.

Despite the decision in *Willis*, the CJEU judgment in *First National Bank of Chicago* remains the leading authority on the VAT treatment of forex transactions. In general, forex transactions are supplies for VAT purposes if a spread position is adopted over a period of time when buying and selling currency. This applies whether this is being carried out by a business on its own account (in support of other areas of its business) or to reduce any exposure position in forex that it holds. Such forex transactions include both 'spot' and 'forward' transactions.

HMRC have indicated that in their opinion

- a business simply exchanging one currency for another to realise foreign earnings into sterling, for example, or to acquire currency to settle liabilities incurred outside the UK, or
- a business entering into forward forex deals in order to limit its exposure to forex fluctuations in respect of future obligations

is unlikely to be seen as making supplies for VAT purposes provided such transactions are not part of a wider economic activity being carried out for an identifiable consideration.

But a business with a corporate treasury operation that typically runs a 'forex desk' in a similar manner to any other financial institution or market maker is likely to be taking a spread position and making supplies. HMRC take the view that all their forex transactions (whether spot or forward and whether proprietary or in support of other activities or areas of the business) should be treated as forex supplies.

(VAT Notice 701/49/17, para 2.7; Business Briefs 16/98, 21/05; HMRC Brief 5/07).

(8) Guarantees and surety bonds

The VAT liability of these types of products depends on the precise nature of the arrangements. To qualify for exemption, they must be financial instruments which are securities for money. This means that an exempt guarantee or surety involves a third party providing a guarantee or security for payments to be made under a contract. Exemption does not extend to

- performance guarantees whereby a third party performs a service or makes payment if a contractual party fails to fulfil their obligations (to perform a service or supply/repair goods) under the contract; or
- the supply of warranties or contracts for the supply, repair or maintenance of goods even though they are sometimes referred to as guarantees.

(VAT Notice 701/49/17, para 3.3).

(9) Household bills

Any charge for the acceptance of over-the-counter payments for household bills is an exempt supply. (VAT Notice 701/49/17, para 2.5).

(10) Sorting and counting money

Services of carriage of cash, re-stocking cash machines, sorting and counting money are, when supplied on their own, taxable. This is because the services being applied to the money are the same as that which could be applied to any type of goods. For the exemption to apply the service must deal with money as money and not purely as goods. See *Williams & Glyn's Bank Ltd* (VTD 118) (TVC 27.1) and *Nationwide Anglia Building Society* (VTD 11826) (TVC 27.2). A service provided by a machine that accepts loose coins, counts them and returns a voucher for 90.1% of the value was held to be exempt in *Coinstar Ltd* [2016] UKFTT 610 (TC) (TC05346) (TVC 27.14); the customer was paying for a service of exchanging one form of currency into another that was more convenient to spend, and this was more than merely sorting and counting.

Services that include an element of making payments or transfers between bank accounts are exempt. Where a supply has a mixture of taxable and exempt elements, its overall character will determine the liability.

(VAT Notice 701/49/17, para 2.2).

(11) Travellers' cheques

The issue or encashment of travellers' cheques is exempt. Unissued or unsigned travellers' cheques are neither securities for money nor notes for the payment of money, and their supply to, or importation by, the issuing bank is taxable on their value as stationery.

(VAT Notice 701/49/17, para 3.4).

Debts and related services

[24.10] Debts and related services are treated as follows:

(1) Sale of debts

Instead of waiting for payment of a debt and carrying the risk of late settlement or default, a business may sell the debt to someone else. The unencumbered sale of a debt for a consideration is exempt under *VATA 1994, Sch 9 Group 5 Item 1* (see **24.8** above). The value of the supply is the gross amount that the purchaser pays for the debt. (VAT Notice 701/49/17, para 5.1).

(2) Factoring and invoice discounting

A client assigns his debts to the factor. The factor opens a client account to which he credits the face value of the debts and debits his charges. These charges may be consideration for a number of standard-rated administrative, clerical and accounting services. The balance, less an agreed retention, is available for the client to draw upon. Depending on the extent to which he does so, the factor debits a further charge, often described as 'discount'.

The factor may operate on a recourse or non-recourse basis.

- In a recourse agreement the factor puts the responsibility for bearing any loss on the client. If the debtor defaults, the factor re-assigns the debt to the client.
- In a non-recourse agreement the factor accepts the risk of default.

The VAT treatment of the various services supplied by a factor to his client are as follows.

Supply	*VAT liability*
Assignment or re-assignment of debt	Not treated as a supply for VAT purposes
Discount or interest charge	Exempt
Administration or service charge (this may cover the provision of a full sales ledger management service, credit advice, debt collection service and the provision of management information)	Standard-rated
Guarantee of payment	Standard-rated

Supply	*VAT liability*
Electronic transfer of funds (if charged for separately)	Exempt supply

Bad debt relief

A factor cannot claim bad debt relief for debts assigned to him by his client. The client cannot claim bad debt relief for a debt assigned to a factor but can do so if the factor re-assigns the debt to him. See **7.1 BAD DEBT RELIEF**.

Cash accounting scheme

See **64.6 SPECIAL SCHEMES** for accounting for VAT where the cash accounting scheme is used.

(VAT Notice 701/49/17, paras 5.2–5.8).

(3) Debt negotiation

In *Debt Management Associates Ltd* (VTD 17880) (TVC 27.38) the tribunal held that a creditor who granted his debtor some indulgence in repayments was granting him credit (even if it was additional credit) and that a company providing the 'debt negotiation services' was providing exempt intermediary services.

Following this tribunal decision, HMRC accept that debt negotiation services involving bringing together the credit provider with the debtor and acting between them in an attempt to mediate a change to the payment terms is an exempt supply. But see (4) and (5) below. (VAT Notice 701/49/17, para 5.9).

'*Debt negotiation services*' may include

- taking details of income and expenditure, along with details of the creditor(s) and the amounts outstanding, and preparing and presenting a payment plan to the creditor;
- agreeing to act on behalf of such a debtor with the creditor in negotiating the payment plan; and
- agreeing to receive payments from the debtor and passing these payments on to the creditors (with or without first taking a fee or commission for doing so).

'*Negotiation*' is taken to refer to the activity of an intermediary providing a distinct act of mediation in order for two parties to enter into a contract, but without the person who is acting as the intermediary having any interest of his own in the terms of the contract. If that person is merely providing a service typically undertaken by a company as part of its contract this is not 'negotiation of debts' and falls within (4) below.

(Business Brief 30/03).

(4) Debt collection

The supplies made by a debt collection agency, or by a business involved in debt collection, are taxable.

Although debt collection services undertaken on behalf of a creditor company may involve some negotiation of the repayment of a debt by the debtor to the creditor this is not an exempt debt negotiation service. For example, if a business

- issues letters to the debtor on behalf of the creditor demanding payment,
- chases the debt in some other form (e.g. contacting the debtor by telephone etc.),
- attempts to locate a debtor on behalf of the creditor, or
- provides accounting services to the creditor (i.e. monitors the debtor's payment account and notifies the creditor of any defaulted payments)

these services are taxable. Any debt negotiation services are ancillary to the principal service of debt collection.

(VAT Notice 701/49/17, para 5.10).

(5) Insolvency practitioner services

Supplies made by insolvency practitioners are normally taxable. Where an insolvency practitioner acts as both nominee and supervisor in any type of formal voluntary arrangement then the supplies by the insolvency practitioner are exempt. (VAT Notice 701/49/17, para 5.11).

Provision of credit

[24.11] The following supplies of financial services in the UK are exempt from VAT.

(a) The making of any advance or the granting of any credit. *Included* is the supply of credit by a person, in connection with the supply of goods or services by him, for which a separate charge is made and disclosed to the recipient of the supply of goods or services. [*VATA 1994, Sch 9 Group 5 Item 2 and Note 3*].
Item 2 covers most of the normal types of credit transactions, e.g. loans, overdrafts and other forms of advances. The value of the exempt supply is the gross interest or other sum received.
Interest paid on deposits with a bank or building society is also consideration for the making of an advance – the advance being made by the customer.
(VAT Notice 701/49/17, para 4.1).

(b) The management of credit by the person granting it. [*VATA 1994, Sch 9 Group 5 Item 2A*]. But the provision of credit management by a person who does not grant the credit is taxable.
A supply of third party taxable credit management could typically include the following transactions:
(i) Credit checking (includes debt profiling, assessing credit worthiness, electoral roll checks and obtaining references).
(ii) Valuation of assets such as property, land, vehicles.

(iii) Authorisation services (including those that go beyond just checking the applicant's signature or agreeing credit or payment limits set by the person providing the credit).
(iv) Taking decisions on credit applications on behalf of the credit provider.
(v) Creating and maintaining records on behalf of the credit provider in order to enable them to fulfil legal obligations.
(vi) Monitoring a creditor's payment record or dealing with overdue payments.

(VAT Notice 701/49/17, para 4.10).

(c) The provision of the facility of instalment credit in a hire purchase, conditional sale or credit sale agreement for which a separate charge is made and disclosed to the recipient of the goods. [*VATA 1994, Sch 9 Group 5 Item 3 and Note 3*]. The value of the exempt supply is the interest paid with each repayment. See **24.12** to **24.15** below for hire purchase, conditional sale and credit sale agreements generally.

(d) The provision of administrative arrangements and documentation and the transfer of title to the goods in connection with the supply within (*c*) above if the total consideration is specified in the agreement and does not exceed £10. [*VATA 1994, Sch 9 Group 5 Item 4*]. The value of the exempt supply is the fee for the administrative arrangements, etc.

See, however, *Wagon Finance Ltd* (VTD 16288) (TVC 27.24) where the tribunal held that administrative fees in connection with credit transactions were exempt from VAT irrespective of the £10 limit as the company had provided customers with the facility of instalment credit within (*c*) above. HMRC decided not to appeal against this decision and accept that exemption applies to any connected credit ancillary charge unless the contract explicitly states that the charge relates, wholly or partially, to the supply of goods. Such exempt charges are likely to be shown as administration, documentation or acceptance fees. Fees related to the goods (e.g. option fees or fees for transfer of title) are taxable unless within the £10 limit. (Business Brief 27/99).

Hire purchase, etc.

[24.12] If the possession of goods is transferred under agreements which expressly contemplate that the property also will pass at some time in the future (determined by, or ascertainable from, the agreements but in any case not later than when the goods are fully paid for) a supply of goods takes place. [*VATA 1994, Sch 4 para 1(2)(b)*].

The most common methods of supplying goods with credit are:

(a) **Hire purchase agreements.** Legally, under such agreements goods are hired for periodic payments and the hirer has the option to purchase. However, the VAT supply position is the same as for conditional sale (see below) because it is intended that ownership is to be transferred.

(b) **Conditional sale agreements.** These are agreements for the sale of goods where the price is payable by instalments and the goods remain the property of the seller until the full price is paid or another condition is met by the customer. The full amount of VAT on the goods is normally payable with the first instalment.

(c) **Credit sale agreements.** These are agreements for the sale of goods which immediately become the property of the customer but where the price is payable by instalments.

Supplies not involving finance companies

If an agreement is made to supply goods under (*a*)–(*c*) above without involving a finance company (self-financed credit), any charge for credit disclosed as a separate charge to the customer is exempt. The consideration for the taxable supply of goods is the cash price stated in the agreement, before any deposit is paid.

If the goods are supplied on interest-free credit, allowing the customer to pay for the goods over a set period without charging interest, the supply of the goods is taxed according to their liability. As there is no charge for credit, there is no exempt supply for VAT purposes.

Any connected credit ancillary charges are exempt unless the contract explicitly states that the charge relates, wholly or partially, to the supply of goods. If the supply relates to the credit, normally shown as administration, documentation or acceptance fees, it is exempt. Fees that relate to the goods (e.g. option fees or fees for transfer of title) are not exempt unless the charge for them is £10 or less (see **24.11**(*d*) above).

Finance companies

If the finance company becomes the owner of goods (e.g. when a purchase is financed by a hire-purchase agreement) the supply of goods is by the supplier to the finance company, not the customer, and is taxable. The finance company in turn, makes a supply of goods and a supply of credit. The supply of credit is exempt if the credit charge is disclosed to the customer in writing.

If the finance company does not become owner of the goods (e.g. when a purchase is financed by a loan agreement) the supply of goods is to the customer, not the finance company, even though that company may make the payment direct to the supplier. The supply is taxable and VAT is due on the selling price to the customer even if a lesser amount is received from the finance company. See *C & E Commrs v Primback Ltd, ECJ Case C–34/99*, [2001] STC 803 (TVC 22.265). The finance company, in a separate transaction, makes a supply of credit facilities to the customer.

(VAT Notice 700, para 8.4).

Time of supply

VAT is due on the full value of the *goods* at the time of supply (see **67.1 SUPPLY: TIME OF SUPPLY**). The tax point for the exempt supply of the *services* is treated as taking place each time a payment is received unless HMRC has approved a written application for an earlier date to be used. (VAT Notice 700, para 15.11). For administrative reasons, application is often made to treat the supply of goods and exempt services as taking place together.

Transfers of agreements

[24.13] Transfers of agreements are treated as follows:

(a) **By the owner.** If the owner of the goods assigns his rights, interests and ownership under a hire-purchase or conditional sale agreement to

- *a bank or finance company* (for example, under a block discounting arrangement) the transfer is outside the scope of VAT. [*SI 1995/1268, Art 5(4)*]; or
- *a dealer* (for example, under a recourse agreement) the transfer is a single supply of goods and is taxable in the normal way.

(b) **By the customer.** If a customer buys goods under a hire purchase or conditional sale agreement and subsequently transfers his rights and obligations to another customer, he is making a standard-rated supply of services to the new customer. There is no supply for VAT purposes from the owner to the new customer. VAT must be accounted for on the open market value of the supply, i.e. the total amount payable by the new customer to the owner to complete the agreement plus any amount he pays to the original customer to secure the transfer. See also *Phillip Drakard Trading Ltd v C & E Commrs,* QB [1992] STC 568 (TVC 62.108).

Repossession of goods

[24.14] Repossession of goods is treated as follows:

- *Hire purchase and conditional sale agreements.* Where goods are supplied under such agreements (including a reservation of title (Romalpa) agreement) title does not pass in the goods until all payments under the agreement have been made. But all VAT due under the agreement on the goods is payable at the outset (see **24.12** above). Where the goods are subsequently repossessed or returned and the agreement ends early, if the agreement includes terms that result in the customer becoming liable to pay nothing more or a lesser amount than the remaining instalments, an adjustment can be made to the VAT accounted for at the outset of the agreement. (There may be circumstances where no VAT was accounted for on the sale of the goods, such as the sale of second-hand goods where no margin is achieved. In such a case there is no VAT adjustment to make.) Where the reduction in price contains elements of capital and interest, any reasonable method for apportioning the value of the reduction may be used. The method of allocation should be consistent and reflect the accounting methods used within the business.

  If the customer is VAT-registered, he must be sent a document effecting the adjustment to ensure that he makes a corresponding adjustment to any input tax he may have claimed.
- *Conditional sale agreements.* Under these agreements, title passes at the outset of the agreement and the return of the goods is treated as a supply from the customer to the finance company. The value of the original sale is not affected by the return.

Where goods are repossessed (following default by a customer), the supplier may be entitled to claim bad debt relief on any amount outstanding following the adjustment. See **7.8 BAD DEBT RELIEF.**

(VAT Notice 701/49/17, para 4.3).

Sale of repossessed assets

[24.15] As a result of (*d*) below, sales of most repossessed goods under hire purchase and conditional sale agreements will be supplies for VAT purposes and VAT must be accounted for in the normal way. However, the disposal of

(i) works of art, antiques and collectors' items (see **74.3 WORKS OF ART, ETC.**), and second-hand goods by a person who has repossessed them under the terms of a finance agreement, or
(ii) boats and aircraft by a mortgagee after he has taken possession of them under the terms of a marine or aircraft mortgage,

remain outside the scope of VAT if the following conditions are met.

(a) The goods so disposed are in the same condition at the time of disposal as when they were repossessed or taken into possession. The condition of goods has been changed if any improvements, repairs, replacement parts or the generally making good of any damage has been carried out. The cleaning of goods generally does not affect the condition nor does the inclusion of instruction manuals if they are otherwise missing. (Business Brief 19/01).
(b) For goods other than motor cars,
  - if the goods had been supplied in the UK by the person from whom they were obtained, that supply would not have been chargeable with VAT or would have been chargeable on less than full value (e.g. because the defaulting customer had not acquired the goods for business purposes or they were margin scheme supplies);
  - if the goods have been imported into the UK, they must have borne VAT which has neither been reclaimed nor refunded; and
  - the goods must not have been reimported having previously been exported from the UK free of VAT by reason of zero-rating.
(c) In the case of motor cars, the VAT on any previous supply, acquisition or importation must have been wholly excluded from credit.
(d) In relation to all goods, where (i) above applies no adjustment must have taken place, or may later take place, of VAT on the initial supply under the finance agreement as a result of repossession.

[*SI 1992/3122, Arts 2, 4; SI 1995/1268, Arts 2, 4*].

See **37.11 INSURANCE** for insurers taking possession of goods in settlement of claims under insurance policies.

Where the above conditions are not satisfied, VAT is normally chargeable on the full amount realised on the sale (not the original cost of the asset, see *Darlington Finance Ltd* (VTD 1337) (TVC 44.81)). Where, however, the goods in question were second-hand at the time when a finance agreement was entered into, the repossessed goods can be sold under the margin scheme. The purchase price for the purpose of calculating the margin is then the original price paid by the finance company to the dealer.

Following the decision in *C & E Commrs v General Motors Acceptance Corporation (UK) plc*, Ch D [2004] STC 577 (TVC 44.52) HMRC accept that, in the case of a finance company, 'repossessed goods' can mean goods

- voluntarily returned under an HP agreement;
- repossessed under the terms of a finance agreement; or
- returned by a customer under the *Consumer Credit Act* once they have made 50% of the total payments due.

(VAT Notice 718, para 13.8).

De Voil Indirect Tax Service. See V3.117.

Transactions related to the provision of credit

[24.16] Transactions related to the provision of credit are treated as follows:

(1) Credit, debit and charge cards

Any supply by a person carrying on a credit card, charge card or similar card operation is exempt when made in connection with that operation to a person who accepts the card used in the operation when presented to him in payment for goods or services. [*VATA 1994, Sch 9 Group 5 Note (4)*]. The consideration for these supplies usually takes the form of a discount on the amount reimbursed to the retailer, etc. See *C & E Commrs v Diners Club Ltd and Another*, CA [1989] STC 407 (TVC 27.73).

Credit, debit and charge cards include MasterCard, Visa, American Express, Diner's Club, Connect and Switch. Banks and financial services institutions issue these cards under the umbrella of these organisations. In addition, certain companies provide in-house card schemes for retailers or retail outlets.

Accounting for VAT on retail credit, debit and charge card sales

Retailers must account for VAT at the time of supply on the full price charged to the customer for the goods/services supplied. If the retailer charges for accepting payment by one of the above cards, the charge is further consideration for the supply of goods/services. VAT is chargeable at the same rate as the goods or services supplied.

Liability of various associated services

Cardholders can either pay their outstanding balance on the receipt of their statement or pay on an instalment basis, interest being charged on the outstanding amount. The following list of charges are normally consideration for exempt supplies:

- Interest charged on the outstanding balance on a card account.
- Annual membership, joining and subscription charges or charges made by card companies to the cardholder for the issue of the card.
- The charge made to merchants (retailers) by credit card companies. This charge usually takes the form of discounts from the amounts the card companies reimburse the merchant.
- Joining fees charged to merchants by card companies.
- Interchange fees.
- Imprinter/terminal rental charges when provided as an ancillary part of other exempt card services.

The following charges are consideration for taxable supplies:

- Imprinter/terminal rental charges when an optional or additional service by card company to retailer.
- The consideration for a sale of goods (e.g. imprinters/terminals in connection with any card scheme).

(VAT Notice 701/49/17, paras 4.6–4.8).

(2) Deferred payment

The expression 'the granting of credit' in **24.11**(*a*) above is wide enough to encompass credit provided by a supplier of goods in the form of deferment of payment for the goods. The wording does not require exemption to be confined to credit granted by banks and financial institutions (*Muys en De Winters's Bouw-en Aannemingsbedriff BV v Staatssecretaris van Financiën, ECJ Case C–281/91,* [1997] STC 665 (TVC 22.385)).

Where customers are allowed to defer payment but for an extra charge, if the charge relates to

- periods before and up to the time of the supply, it is not a charge for credit but further consideration for the supply of the goods or services; and
- periods beyond the time of supply, such a charge is consideration for an exempt supply of credit.

(VAT Notice 701/49/17, para 4.5).

(3) Discount for prompt payment

VAT treatment of prompt payment discounts from 1 April 2015

Where goods or services are supplied for a consideration which is a price in money, and the terms on which those goods or services are supplied allow a discount for prompt payment of that price, and payment of that price is not made by instalments, and the payment of that price is made in accordance with those terms so that the discount is applied in relation to the payment, the consideration is the discounted price paid. See **72.24 VALUATION** for detailed guidance.

Note – the above treatment took effect on the earlier date of 1 May 2014 for supplies of broadcasting and telecommunication services where there was no obligation to provide a VAT invoice.

[*VATA 1994, Sch 6 para 4 as amended by FA 2014*].

VAT treatment of prompt payment discounts before 1 April 2015

Where goods are supplied for a consideration in money and on terms allowing a discount for prompt payment, the consideration is to be taken as reduced 'by the discount', whether or not payment in made in accordance with those terms. [*VATA 1994, Sch 6 para 4*].

In *Saga Holidays Ltd* (VTD 18591) (VTD 67.94) S sold holidays and offered customers discounts for prompt payment. It failed to take account of such discounts and submitted a repayment claim. HMRC agreed to refund the amounts which S had overpaid where customers actually received discounts but rejected the claim where discount had been offered but the customers had not actually taken advantage of it. The tribunal agreed with this treatment, observing that the legislation provided that the consideration should be taken as reduced 'by the discount' and holding that these words could more readily be interpreted as a reference to a discount that has actually come into existence than to one that was available but may never come into existence. Therefore, *Sch 6 para 4(1)* should be construed as meaning that the consideration is only reduced where the discount is achieved.

(4) Fuel card schemes

See **46.14 MOTOR CARS**.

(5) Late payment penalties

It is common for hire-purchase companies, credit card companies and similar institutions to impose a penalty for late payment. Where a customer is not explicitly allowed to defer payment and a late payment penalty is imposed because payment is not made by the due date, the penalty is not consideration for a supply and is outside the scope of VAT. (VAT Notice 701/49/17, para 4.4).

(6) Loan arrangements and execution services

In *C & E Commrs v Electronic Data Systems Ltd*, CA [2003] STC 688 (TVC 22.404) a bank (L) arranged for a company (EDS) to operate a call centre on its behalf. EDS received and processed loan applications, gathered and verified information about applicants, signed loan agreements on behalf of L, and released L's funds to borrowers. The Court of Appeal held that the supplies qualified for exemption under what is now *Directive 2006/112/EC, Art 135(1)(b)*. Following that decision, HMRC accept that where a business provides a package of outsourced service to a loan provider, the supply is exempt if

- it consists of services prior to and after the granting of a loan; and
- the business provides, as a central part of the supply, the services of
  - (i) the operation of bank accounts on behalf of the credit provider;
  - (ii) arranging the transfers of funds to the borrower; and
  - (iii) the processing of loan repayments (and any additional charges or fees) by direct debit or cheque.

(VAT Notice 701/49/17, para 4.11).

(7) Pawnbrokers

Redeemed pledges. There is no supply for VAT purposes if a person redeems a pledge within the agreed redemption period.

Unredeemed pledges. The following rules apply. The relevant law is in *Consumer Credit Act 1974, ss 120, 121*.

(a) Loans not exceeding £75 with a six month redemption period

Ownership of the pledge passes to the pawnbroker if the goods are not redeemed within the six months statutory redemption period. A disposal of the goods to a third party after that time is a taxable supply.

Where, however, the goods are restored by the pawnbroker to their original owner within three months following the end of the redemption period, the transaction is treated as a redeemed pledge and there is no supply for VAT purposes. [*SI 1986/896*]. The pawnbroker must record the redemption in his pledge stock records and stamp the 'Credit Agreement and Pawn Receipt' with the date of redemption and keep it for inspection by HMRC. If the pawnbroker and pledgor have agreed to extend the original agreement by one or more further six month periods, the three month 'grace period' starts when the extension expires.

The restoration of an unredeemed pledge more than three months after the redemption period is a taxable supply.

(b) Other loans

For loans over £75 or where the redemption period has been agreed for a period other than six months, ownership of the pledge does not pass to the pawnbroker at the end of the redemption period. The onward supply to a third party is not, therefore, a taxable supply by the pawnbroker. It is, however, a taxable supply by the pledgor if he is a taxable person and the pledge is something he has acquired in the course of his business. The pawnbroker (or auctioneer if the goods are sold by auction) must follow the procedure in **2.10 ACCOUNTING PERIODS AND RETURNS.**

Other charges.

- *Interest payments* received under credit agreements are exempt from VAT.
- *Valuation fees* relating to the pledged goods are regarded as part of the charge for the loan and are exempt.
- *Charges for selling unredeemed pledges*, provision for which is made in the loan contract, are exempt as a further charge for the granting of credit. Included is an element for cleaning and repairing the goods before they are put on display.

Second-hand goods scheme. Pawnbrokers may use the scheme for **SECOND-HAND GOODS (61)** for sales of unredeemed pawns within (*a*) above provided they have taken title to the goods and the normal scheme conditions are met. The purchase price is the amount of the loan plus the initial six months interest payable, less any payment received. The interest relating to the three month period of grace and other items such as cleaning, repair charges, storage and overhead expenses must not be added to the purchase price.

Pawnbrokers may, if they wish, use the credit agreement and pawn receipt as the purchase invoice provided

- the contract number is entered in the stock record and is cross-referred to the agreement; and
- a copy of the interest calculations and total purchase value for margin scheme purposes is attached to the document if it differs from the amount shown.

(VAT Notice 718, paras 18.1–18.4).

Pawnbrokers selling at auction. A pawnbroker may use the auctioneers' scheme for the sale of eligible second-hand goods (see **62.61 SECOND-HAND GOODS**) provided the pawn value is greater than £75 and the pledgor is not VAT-registered. If the pledgor is VAT-registered, VAT must be accounted for on the full selling price. (VAT Notice 718, para 7.10).

Securities

[24.17] The issue, transfer or receipt of, or any dealing with, any security or secondary security in the UK is exempt from VAT. For these purposes, a security or secondary security comprises

- shares, stock, bonds, notes (other than promissory notes), debentures, debenture stock or shares in an oil royalty;
- any document relating to money, in any currency, which has been deposited with the issuer or some other person, being a document which recognises an obligation to pay a stated amount to bearer or to order, with or without interest, and being a document by the delivery of which, with or without endorsement, the right to receive that stated amount, with or without interest, is transferable;
- any bill, note or other obligation of the Treasury or of a Government in any part of the world, being a document by the delivery of which, with or without endorsement, title is transferable, and not being an obligation which is or has been legal tender in any part of the world;
- any letter of allotment or rights, any warrant conferring an option to acquire a security included in these provisions, any renounceable or scrip certificates, rights coupons, coupons representing dividends or interest on such a security, bond mandates or other documents conferring or containing evidence of title to or rights in respect of such a security;
- units or other documents conferring rights under any trust established for the purpose, or having the effect of providing, for persons having funds available for investment, facilities for the participation by them as beneficiaries under the trust, in any profits or income arising from the acquisition, holding, management or disposal of any property whatsoever.

[*VATA 1994, Sch 9 Group 5 Item 6*].

Securities transactions

Despite the wording of the legislation, following the decision of the CJEU in *Kretztechnik AG v Finanzamt Lenz, ECJ Case C–465/03,* [2005] STC 1118 (TVC 22.96) the first issue of securities such as shares, bonds, loan notes, debentures, etc by a company is not a supply for VAT purposes. For further details, including the input tax recovery position, see **50.8**(3) **PARTIAL EXEMPTION.**

Transactions in shares which are already in existence are exempt where they are sold or transferred in the ordinary course of business and the normal partial exemption rules apply.

(VAT Notice 701/49/17, para 6.1).

International transactions

See **24.2** above for the place of supply of services within these provisions, including the special rule for the place of supply of securities sold where the identity of the purchaser is not known. The place of supply affects both the VAT liability of a financial service and whether the supplier can reclaim related input tax. See **24.3** above.

Stock lending

[24.18] Stock lending describes a situation where one person (the 'lender') transfers to a second person (the 'borrower') the legal title, along with all dividends and rights, to securities. The borrower agrees to return to the lender an equivalent number of the same securities at a later date.

For VAT purposes, there is an exempt supply under **24.17** above by the lender to the borrower, the consideration being the fee charged to the borrower. The borrower should not account for the value of securities returned to the lender. Any dividends which the borrower receives whilst the stocks are loaned are not consideration for a supply.

(VAT Notice 701/49/17, para 6.3).

Transactions related to securities

[24.19] Transactions related to securities are treated as follows:

(1) Custody services

Safe custody services are standard-rated. This includes the provision of the purely physical service of safekeeping (safe deposit facilities). Supplies by a UK-established business to a customer other than a relevant business person are chargeable in the UK irrespective of where the recipient belongs. This is because such services are expressly excluded from services within *VATA 1994, Sch 4A para 16* and therefore the place of supply is, under the general rule, where the supplier belongs.

Where a specific site is hired to a client (rather than the service of secure storage within the supplier's own premises), the supply is in the UK if the site is in the UK, but outside the scope of UK VAT if the site is overseas, because it constitutes a supply of land rather than a supply of a financial service. There may, however, be a liability to account for VAT in another EU member state if the place of supply is elsewhere in the EU.

Global custody services involve a package of services that may include safe custody, collection of dividends/interest on securities held, dealing with scrip/rights issues, and payment against the delivery or receipt of stock. In such a case, the supply of the whole service, including the safe custody element, is exempt.

(VAT Notice 701/49/17, para 6.6).

(2) Dealing systems and data services

The operation of a dealing system which allows

- a user to insert bid and offer quotes for securities,
- another user to insert acceptance, and
- for the system to match buy and sell deals,

is exempt.

Electronic data services which simply provide subscribers with a message facility or an information service (e.g. on share price movements or financial news) are taxable.
(VAT Notice 701/49/17, paras 6.12, 6.13).

(3) Management of special investment funds

EC Directive 2006/112/EC, Art 135(1)(g) exempts 'the management of special investment funds as defined by each EU member state. UK law (*VATA 1994, Sch 9 Group 5 Items 9 and 10*) originally restricted the exemption to the management of authorised unit trust schemes (AUTS) and open-ended investment companies (OEIC). Following a CJEU ruling (*JP Morgan Claverhouse, ECJ Case C–363/05*, [2008] STC 1180 (TVC 22.414)) the exemption was extended so that there is a level VAT playing field for all similar collective investment undertakings which compete in the UK retail market (that is, for investment by the general public) under comparable conditions. This includes closed or open-ended collective investment undertakings (UCITS, or 'undertakings for collective investment in transferable securities', which are the subject of EU Directives on investment regulation) which meet the revised definitions regardless of where they are established. UCITS are in the business of collective investment, that is they pool and invest capital raised from the public and do so for a fee or 'management charge'. It is this management charge that is the subject of the VAT exemption. UCITS may be constituted in various legal forms, but common to all of these is that investors hold shares or units in the UCITS. See **24.20** and **24.21** below.

(VAT Notice 701/49/17, paras 7.1, 7.2).

(4) Listing fees charged by regulatory bodies

Fees charged by regulatory bodies, such as the Financial Services Authority, for listing companies that wish to float on an exchange are outside the scope of VAT. (VAT Notice 701/49/17, para 6.8).

(5) Nominee services

The services of acting as nominal holder of securities on behalf of the beneficial owner are exempt. (VAT Notice 701/49/17, para 6.5).

(6) Share registration services

Share registration services may include some or all of the following (the list is not exhaustive).

- All aspects of operating company share registers.
- Administration of scrip schemes, share option schemes, profit-sharing schemes and dividend reinvestment plans.
- Arrangements for advertising the closure of a share offer.
- Attending shareholders' meetings and organising polls at such meetings.
- Arranging 'break out' for bulk nominee accounts.
- Capital gains enquiries and other correspondence and enquiries.
- Conversion of loan stock.
- Preparation, designation and despatch of certificates, correction of errors on certificates, and issuing of duplicated documents.
- Administrative services in relation to mergers, placings, rights issues, reorganisations and acquisitions.
- Processing forms of proxy.
- Registration of grants of probate.
- Regular reports on share movements.
- Administrative services in relation to savings plan schemes.

These services are treated as supplied where the business customer belongs under the general rule for the supply of services (see **66.14 SUPPLY: PLACE OF SUPPLY**). They are standard-rated if supplied in the UK unless provided as one element of a single composite supply featuring other services with a different VAT liability, in which case the liability may change. See **65.6 SUPPLY: GENERAL** for single and multiple supplies.

See **24.20** and **24.21** below where share registration services are supplied for an authorised unit trust or an open-ended investment company.

(VAT Notice 701/49/17, para 6.7).

(7) Specialist services

In most cases, the exemption for intermediary services (see **24.25** below) does not cover

- the professional services of accountants and lawyers; and
- services of advice in general (e.g. to investors deciding whether to accept or reject a take-over bid).

Services supplied in connection with share issues, acquisitions or disposals that do not bring together the buyer and seller are also taxable. This includes

- valuation of assets;
- assessing the direct tax liabilities of a holding;
- investment analysis;
- market sector research;
- share consultancy;
- general financial or investment advice;
- accountancy services;
- tax and legal advice; and
- supplying a draft prospectus.

One or more of these services may qualify for exemption if they are provided as part of a complete service and are ancillary to an exempt financial service.

See **24.20** and **24.21** below where such services are provided to either an authorised unit trust or open-ended investment company.

(VAT Notice 701/49/17, para 6.14).

(8) Fees charged by stock exchanges

Basic admission or membership charges are taxable at the standard rate, with the place of supply being where the supplier belongs.

The liability of other charges (e.g. market maker charges, transaction charges and exchange charges) depends on exactly what is being done by the exchange for the charge. If the service is not an intermediary service then the fee will be taxable at the standard rate.

(VAT Notice 701/49/17, para 6.9).

Investment funds

[24.20] Following the decision of the CJEU in *Kretztechnik AG v Finanzamt Lenz, ECJ Case C–465/03,* [2005] STC 1118 (TVC 22.96) the issue of units in an authorised unit trust are not supplies for VAT purposes. (Business Brief 21/05).

A unit trust itself will hold and carry out transactions in securities within **24.17** above. The sale of these underlying securities is an exempt supply by the trust.

Investment management services are normally taxable (see **24.19**(3) above). However, under *EC Directive 2006/112/EC, Art 135(1)(g)* (previously *EC Sixth Directive, Art 13B(d)(6)*) 'the management of special investment funds as defined by an EU member state' is exempt. The UK has applied this exemption to the management of

- an authorised open-ended investment company;
- (from 28 June 2013) an authorised contractual scheme;
- an authorised unit trust scheme;
- a Gibraltar collective investment scheme that is not an umbrella scheme, or a sub-fund of any other Gibraltar collective investment scheme;
- an individually recognised overseas scheme that is not an umbrella scheme, or a sub-fund of any other individually recognised overseas scheme;
- a recognised collective investment scheme authorised in a designated country or territory that is not an umbrella scheme, or a sub-fund of any other recognised collective investment scheme authorised in a designated country or territory; or
- a recognised collective investment scheme constituted in another EEA state that is not an umbrella scheme, or a sub-fund of any other recognised collective investment scheme constituted in another EEA state.

'Authorised open-ended investment company', *'authorised contractual scheme'* and *'authorised unit trust scheme'* have the meaning given in the *Financial Services and Markets Act 2000, s 237(3).*

'*Collective investment scheme*' has the meaning given in *FSMA 2000, s 235*.

'*Gibraltar collective investment scheme*' means a collective investment scheme to which *FSMA 2000, s 264* applies pursuant to an order made under *FSMA 2000, s 409(1)(d)*; or a collective investment scheme to which *FSMA 2000* applies pursuant to an order made under *FSMA 2000, s 409(1)(f)*.

'*Individually recognised overseas scheme*' means a collective investment scheme declared by the Financial Services Authority to be a recognised scheme pursuant to *FSMA 2000, s 272*.

'*Recognised collective investment scheme authorised in a designated country or territory*' means a collective investment scheme recognised pursuant to *FSMA 2000, s 270*.

'*Recognised collective investment scheme constituted in another EEA state*' means a collective investment scheme which is recognised pursuant to *FSMA 2000, s 264*.

'*Sub-fund*' means a separate part of the property of an umbrella scheme that is pooled separately.

'*Umbrella scheme*' means a collective investment scheme under which the contributions of the participants in the scheme and the profits or income out of which the payments are to be made to them are pooled separately in relation to separate parts of the scheme property.

'*Trust based scheme*' means a scheme the purpose or effect of which is to enable persons taking part in the scheme, by becoming beneficiaries under a trust, to participate in or receive profits or income arising from the acquisition, holding, management or disposal of property of a kind described in *Financial Services and Markets Act 2000, s 239(3)(a)* or sums paid out of such profits or income.

The above provisions do not cover a collective investment scheme, or sub-fund, that is not for the time being marketed in the UK if it has never been marketed in the UK or less than 5% of its shares or units are held by, or on behalf of, investors who are in the UK.

[*VATA 1994, Sch 9 Group 5 Item 9 and Notes 6, 6A; SI 2013/1402*]. (HMRC Brief 35/08 and HMRC Brief 48/08).

Meaning of 'management': the VAT exemption concerns the management charge or fee which is normally deducted from the assets in the CIU periodically. For UK open-ended funds, the manager is required by regulation to be a separate entity. The term 'management' also includes certain activities of administering the CIU as well as investment management of the assets. If a third party is delegated to carry out a package of administrative services which overall has the distinct characteristic of a single supply of fund management services, this too will be exempt. Trustee and depositary services in relation to funds are always taxable.

(VAT Notice 701/49/17, para 7.5).

Management of an unauthorised unit trust is liable to VAT at the standard rate.

Occupational pension schemes

In *Wheels Common Investment Fund Trustees Ltd v HMRC (and related appeals), ECJ Case C-424/11; 7 March 2013 unreported*, a company (C) provided fund management services to several companies which administered defined-benefit occupational pension schemes. The recipient companies contended that C's supplies qualified for exemption as 'special investment funds' within *EC Directive 2006/112//EC, Art 135(1)(g)*. The First-tier Tribunal referred the case to the CJEU for a ruling on whether the term 'special investment funds' was capable of including an occupational pension scheme established by an employer that is intended to provide pension benefits to employees and/or a common investment fund in which the assets of several such pension schemes are pooled for investment purposes. The CJEU held that *Art 135(1)(g)* must be interpreted as meaning that an investment fund pooling the assets of a retirement pension scheme is not a special investment fund where the members of the scheme do not bear the risk arising from the management of the fund and the contributions which the employer pays into the scheme are a means by which he complies with his legal obligations towards his employees. However, in *ATP Pension Services A/S v Skatteministeriet, ECJ Case C-464/12; 12 December 2013* (TVC 22.417) the CJEU held that defined contribution pension funds were special investment funds.

The clear distinction between *Wheels Common Investment Fund Trustees Ltd* and *ATP Pension Services A/S* is that the former related to defined benefit schemes, whereas the latter related to defined contribution schemes. In contrast to defined benefit schemes, the beneficiaries of defined contribution schemes bear the investment risk.

Closed collective investment undertakings

[24.21] *EC Directive 2006/112/EC, Art 135(1)(g)* (previously *EC Sixth Directive, Art 13B(d)(6)*) exempts the management of 'special investment funds' as defined by individual EU member states. In *JP Morgan Fleming Claverhouse Investment Trust plc v HMRC (and related appeal), ECJ Case C-363/05*, [2008] STC 1180 (TVC 22.414) the CJEU held that the phrase 'special investment funds' was capable of including closed investment funds such as investment trust companies (ITCs). Although the EU provisions gave EU member states discretion to determine the special investment funds whose management is exempt from VAT, in exercising that power, countries must have regard to the objectives of the provision and to the principle of fiscal neutrality.

Following the decision in *Morgan Fleming Claverhouse*, the management of 'closed collective investment undertakings' is exempt. 'Closed collective investment undertaking' means an undertaking in relation to which the following conditions are satisfied

- its sole object is the investment of capital, raised from the public, wholly or mainly in securities;
- it manages its assets on the principle of spreading investment risk;

- all of its ordinary shares (of each class if there is more than one) or equivalent units are included in the official list maintained by the Financial Services Authority pursuant to the *Financial Services and Markets Act 2000, s 74(1)*; and
- all of its ordinary shares (of each class if there is more than one) or equivalent units are admitted to trading on a regulated market situated or operating in the UK.

[*VATA 1994, Sch 9 Group 5 Item 10 and Note 6*]. (HMRC Brief 35/08; VAT Notice 701/49/17, para 7.4).

Wrapper products, administrative agreement and wrap accounts

Wrapper products

[24.22] Wrapper products hold investments in a tax-efficient wrapper making them free of income and capital gains tax, and are aimed at trying to stimulate the general public into saving and investing money. Examples of these products (current and historical) include Individual Savings Accounts (ISAs), Child Trust Funds (CTFs), Personal Equity Plans (PEPs) and Self-Invested Person Pensions (SIPPs). See the VAT Finance Manual for more information on these products and the VAT treatment of the associated charges.

Administrative agreement

An agreement was entered into on 1 April 1994 between HMRC and the Investment Management Association (formerly the Association of Unit Trusts and Investment Funds or 'AUTIF') concerning the VAT treatment of PEP managers' charges. This was used in subsequent years as a basis to determine the treatment of charges in respect of other tax-efficient wrapper products. Following discussions with industry representatives, the AUTIF Agreement has now been withdrawn and replaced with the tax treatments outlined in the VAT Finance Manual.

Wrap accounts

A wrap account is an arrangement that holds a range of investments, providing a single point of contact and management for investors and their agents. A wrap manager is usually a separate legal entity within a financial services or insurance group that offers to hold, manage and administer the whole or part of an individual's portfolio. The wrap account itself might typically be an interest-bearing bank account, with a set of sub-accounts, allowing payments to be made and received within broad product silos. The wrap manager nominates a third-party discretionary investment manager and an execution-only broker. The discretionary investment manager generally offers, or is required by the wrap manager to offer, nominee account services. It may also offer custody services, or these may be provided by another entity. The typical charging structures for wrap products are based on transaction charges, calculated by reference to the value of investments within the wrap account (taken as a strong indicator of activity going through the account), including dividends, interest, and principal amounts. Because the nature of the supplies made in connection with a 'wrap' account vary from one product to another, the VAT liability of wrap-related services depends upon whether the supplies in question fall within the VAT exemptions for either principal or intermediary financial services. For further information on wrap accounts and their VAT treatment see the VAT Finance Manual.

(VAT Notice 701/49/17, paras 7.7–7.9).

Underwriting

[24.23] The underwriting of an issue within *VATA 1994, Sch 9 Group 5 Item 1* (see **24.8** above) or any transaction within *VATA 1994, Sch 9 Group 5 Item 6* (see **24.17** above) is exempt. [*VATA 1994, Sch 9 Group 5 Item 5A*].

A share underwriter guarantees to buy a proportion of any unsold shares when a new issue is offered to the general public, and usually receives either commission or charges a fee. A share underwriter may also underwrite an issue by agreeing to guarantee that buyers will be found. In either case the supply is exempt.

The sale of the securities by the issuer to the underwriter is not a supply for VAT purposes but there is a subsequent exempt supply by the underwriter when those securities are sold.

Where an underwriter's charge for services is adjusted to reflect the entitlement to purchase his allotted securities at a special price, the value of the discount must be regarded as part of the consideration for his exempt supply of underwriting services. However, where an underwriter is obliged to buy further securities which remain unsold and the underwriting agreement allows him to buy these unsold securities at a price lower than the offer price, this reduction is not regarded as consideration for the underwriting service and is outside the scope of VAT.

Sub-underwriters

Exemption also applies to the supply made by a sub-underwriter who agrees to underwrite a proportion of the issue or sale, whether the sub-underwriter's services are supplied to the underwriter or to the issuer.

(VAT Notice 701/49/17, para 6.4).

Banks and building societies

[24.24] The operation of any current, deposit or savings account is exempt. [*VATA 1994, Sch 9 Group 5 Item 8*].

Many of the charges made by banks, building societies or similar organisations are covered by this exemption including

- the issue of certain types of financial certificate (e.g. audit and balance certificates supplied to third parties); and

- the extra cost of special printing or overprinting of cheque books and paying-in books.

(VAT Notice 701/49/17, para 2.10).

Electronic banking and cash management services

Electronic banking services (including account management) are supplied by banks to business and individual customers as an addition, or alternative, to conventional banking services. In the case of business customers, the business uses computer equipment (sometimes leased or purchased from the bank) to obtain

- services which would otherwise have been provided by the bank in the course of its operation of the business's account (e.g. statements of the business's current balance or transfers of funds between accounts); and
- general finance related services (e.g. information about share prices or foreign exchange rates).

To determine the liability of an electronic banking service, it is first necessary to determine whether it is provided as a supply in its own right or as part of a package of services. In principle, services which would have been treated as exempt under *VATA 1994, Sch 9 Group 5* if they had been provided by the bank by conventional means should be treated as exempt when provided within the framework of electronic banking services. Other finance-related services which are not so covered should be treated as standard-rated.

HMRC have indicated the following VAT liabilities.

Supply	*Liability*
Provision of information on share prices, foreign exchange rates, balances on accounts with other financial institutions	Standard-rated
Provision of information on the state of the client's accounts by the bank providing the electronic banking services, bank statements, the transfer of funds and the debiting and crediting of accounts	Exempt
Hire of equipment and related charges, such as training	
(a) if supplied and shown as a separate item on the invoice	Standard-rated
(b) if not shown as a separate item on the invoice	Dependent on predominant or intended use when absorbed with other charges
Hire of equipment which can be used for other purposes (e.g. where the link gives access to Bloomburg, etc.)	Standard-rated
Sale of equipment	Standard-rated
Service charges/overall service charges	Dependent on predominant use

(VAT Notice 701/49/17, para 2.12).

Intermediary services

[24.25] *Directive 2006/112/EC* exempts the 'negotiation' of many financial services. See **19.25**(*b*)–(*f*) **EUROPEAN UNION LEGISLATION**.

Under UK legislation, the provision of 'intermediary services' in relation to a transaction within

(a) *VATA 1994, Sch 9 Group 5 Item 1* (the issue, transfer or receipt of, and any dealings with money or securities for money, see **24.8** above),
(b) *VATA 1994, Sch 9 Group 5 Item 2* (the making or an advance or the granting of credit, see **24.11**(*a*) above),
(c) *VATA 1994, Sch 9 Group 5 Item 3* (the provision of instalment credit finance by hire purchases, etc, see **24.11**(*c*) above),
(d) *VATA 1994, Sch 9 Group 5 Item 4* (the provision of administrative arrangements, etc. in connection with a supply under *Item 3* where the consideration does not exceed £10, see **24.11**(*d*) above), or
(e) *VATA 1994, Sch 9 Group 5 Item 6* (the issue, transfer or receipt of, or dealings with certain securities and secondary securities, see **24.17** above)

by a person 'acting in an intermediary capacity' is exempt. This applies whether or not any such transaction is finally concluded so that where qualifying intermediary services are performed but the deal falls through and there is no financial transaction, the intermediary service is still exempt.

'*Intermediary services*' for these purposes consist of

- 'bringing together' persons who are or may be seeking to receive financial services and persons providing such services, with a view to the provision of such services; *together with*
- in the case of financial services falling within (*a*)–(*d*) above (but *not* (*e*) above) the performance of 'work preparatory to the conclusion of contracts' for the provision of those financial services

but do not include the supply of any market research, product design, advertising, promotional or similar services or the collection, collation and provision of information in connection with such activities.

A person is '*acting in an intermediary capacity*' where he is acting as an intermediary (or one of the intermediaries) between

- a person providing financial services; and
- a person who is or may be seeking to receive such services.

[*VATA 1994, Sch 9 Group 5 Item 5 and Notes 5, 5A, 5B*].

'*Bringing together*'. An intermediary should be independent of the parties entering into a financial services contract and not carrying out sub-contracted services for one of the parties. In *CSC Financial Services Ltd v C & E Commrs, ECJ Case C–235/00,* [2002] STC 57 (TVC 22.403), CSC supplied services to Sun Alliance, which issued personal equity plans. It dealt with telephone enquiries, sent application forms to potential customers and checked completed application forms. But the customers had already been approached by Sun Alliance and the parties were not brought together by CSC, who acted not in an intermediary capacity but as a sub-contractor for Sun Alliance in processing applications. The CJEU confirmed that CSC was not an intermediary because it was standing in the shoes of Sun Alliance while taking calls and receiving forms, and also because CSC's activities were clerical activities which would normally have been done by Sun Alliance.

'*Work preparatory to the conclusion of contracts*' refers to work done of a specialised nature. This could include helping to set the terms of the contract or making representations on behalf of a client, but would not include work done of a general nature such as administrative or clerical formalities. (VAT Notice 701/49/17, para 9.3). Note that the legislation provides that, in relation to a transaction falling within (*e*) above, preparatory work is not necessary and exemption can apply to the mere introduction of a person seeking to buy or sell securities to a person effecting transactions in securities.

Intermediary services may contain more than one component. Services which include market research, product design or similar services excluded above may still be exempt provided that this is a minor and ancillary part of the overall intermediary service. (VAT Notice 701/49/17, para 9.13). See also **24.28** below for where financial advisers provide mixed supplies of advice and intermediary services.

International transactions

The VAT liability of transactions with an international element are affected by the place of belonging of the recipient of the services. In addition, where the underlying supply is made to a person belonging outside the EU, this may affect the entitlement to input tax deduction. The following table summarises the liability of intermediary services in the most common transactions.

Underlying supplier belonging in		*Sells to*	*Underlying recipient belonging in*	
	VAT on commission charged to supplier			*VAT on commission charged to recipient*
UK or other EU (private)	E		UK or other EU (private)	E
UK or other EU (private)	E		Other EU (business)	OS
UK or other EU (private)	E(R)		Non-EU	OS(R)
Other EU (business)	OS		UK or other EU (private)	E
Other EU (business)	OS		Other EU (business)	OS
Other EU (business)	OS(R)		Non-EU	OS(R)
Non-EU	OS(R)		UK or other EU (private)	E
Non-EU	OS(R)		Other EU (business)	OS

Underlying supplier belonging in		*Sells to*	*Underlying recipient belonging in*	
	VAT on commission charged to supplier			*VAT on commission charged to recipient*
Non-EU	OS(R)		Non-EU	OS(R)
Key E = Exempt E(R) = Exempt but with refund of related input tax OS = Outside the scope of UK VAT with no refund of related input tax OS(R) = Outside the scope of UK VAT with refund of related input tax				

> *Example*
>
> An intermediary arranges for the sale of shares from a UK customer to a Japanese counterparty. The intermediary's supply is exempt and because the place of supply of the underlying supply is outside the EU, he is entitled to deduct related input tax.

It should be noted that the above table only applies where there is an underlying supply. There is no entitlement to deduct input tax in relation to underlying transactions, such as issues of securities, which are not supplies for VAT purposes. (VAT Notice 701/49/17, para 9.12).

Securities broking services

[24.26] The introductory service of bringing together a person who wishes to buy securities to a person selling securities is exempt if made in the UK, even if the intended securities transaction later falls through (see **24.25**(*e*) above). The exemption covers

- any stock or share broking services (see below); and
- arranging issues or placements of securities whether as offers for sale, rights issues, cash offers, vendor placings or bids with underwritten cash alternatives, including the service of co-ordinating an issue when a number of participants are involved in the share or other placing. But see **24.27** below which covers corporate finance services.

Broking services

Where a broker acts as an 'execution only' broker, buying or selling securities on client's instructions, but does not offer advice on securities, his supply is exempt. Where a broker provides advice and this is incidental to transactions in securities, the supply is exempt.

Where a broker arranging a securities transaction splits the contract note to show as separate items the basic charge for execution services and any compliance or regulatory charges made to cover the cost of meeting regulatory requirements, the additional charges are still part of the consideration for his exempt broking service. This does not, however, apply to any statutory levies (e.g. stamp duty) which are a liability of the client. These are outside the scope of VAT.

(VAT Notice 701/49/17, paras 6.10, 6.11).

Corporate finance services

[24.27] The provision of advisory services (e.g. on raising capital or defending take-over bids) is taxable. Where advice leads to, or is associated with, a transaction in securities by the client, the services may themselves be exempt as a provision of intermediary services for a transaction in securities, but only if the criteria set out in **24.25** above are met.

These principles may be applied to contracts that are aborted, but in some circumstances it may be necessary to apportion the liability of the supplies between taxable advice and exempt intermediary services.

(VAT Notice 701/49/17, para 9.7).

Other intermediary services

[24.28] Other intermediary services are treated as follows:

(1) Affinity credit card schemes

These schemes typically involve a charity or interest group endorsing a credit card and recommending its use to their members, supporters or customers. The charity or interest group receive a commission or similar income, usually linked to the taking out and subsequent usage of the card.

Charities have been granted a special concession which recognises a 'donational' element in the affinity card scheme. See **13.5**(3) **CHARITIES**.

Non-charity organisations operating affinity credit card schemes are subject to the normal VAT rules. In *BAA plc v C & E Commrs,* CA 2002, [2003] STC 35 (TVC 27.27) a company, in return for a commission, provided a bank with information concerning potential credit card customers. It targeted suitable applicants, issued applications, assisted in the completion of the forms and screened and processed them on return. In *Institute of Directors v C & E Commrs, CA 2002,* [2003] STC 35 (TVC 27.29), which case was heard in the Court of Appeal with *BAA plc*, the IoD similarly provided a list of suitable members, encouraged members to apply, and assisted them with their applications and validated completed forms. The Court of Appeal held that, in both cases, the activities carried out were within the definition of 'negotiation of credit' for the purposes of what is now *Directive 2006/112/EC, Art 135(1)(b)* and exempt from VAT in the UK as intermediary services.

As a result of these judgments, HMRC take the view that a body that introduces its members, supporters or customers to a credit card provider and brings the two parties together, carrying out independent negotiation services as a distinct act of mediation, is providing exempt intermediary services.

HMRC view marketing and promotional services supplied in isolation, and the performing of clerical functions (e.g. providing a list of names or access to a database) as standard-rated.

(VAT Notice 701/49/17, para 4.9).

(2) Credit and debit card handling services

In *Bookit Ltd v R & C Commrs,* CA [2006] STC 1367 (TVC 27.30) the company arranged advance bookings for cinema seats by telephone or the internet. It checked seat availability and took details of the customer's card details. It charged an administration fee of 50p per ticket. The Court held that it was making exempt supplies because its services involved transmitting the card information with the necessary security information and the card issuers' authorisation codes to Girobank (i.e. it had the effect that funds were transferred to its account with Girobank).

Following this decision, HMRC accepted that if an agent, acting for the supplier of the goods or services, makes a charge to the customer over and above the price of the actual goods or services, for a separately identifiable service of handling payment by credit or debit card, *and that service includes the transfer of funds to its account*, the additional charge is exempt. (Business Brief 18/06).

However, HMRC ruled again that what Bookit Ltd was doing was not exempt. They raised several arguments:

- the claimed card handling service was in reality simply part of the sale of the taxable tickets, or was incidental to it;
- the arrangement was an abuse of rights;
- even if it was genuine and separate, the service carried out by Bookit was not an exempt financial service.

The First-tier Tax Tribunal [2014] UKFTT 856 (TC) (TC03972) and Upper Tribunal (2015) rejected the first two arguments, which were also raised in a similar dispute with *National Exhibition Centre Ltd* [2015] UKUT 23 (TCC). Questions were referred to the CJEU, asking whether the services fell within the exemption following the principles of the *Sparekassernes Datacenter* case (see **24.5** and **24.8** above), or whether they fell outside the exemption in line with the more recent case of *Nordea Pankki Suomi Oyj v Finland, ECJ Case C-350/10*. In that case, the CJEU had held that an electronic messaging service that led to international banking transfers was not sufficiently involved in the transfer of ownership of funds to qualify for exemption.

The CJEU ruled that the card handling services supplied by Bookit Ltd (*ECJ Case C-607/14*, [2016] All ER (D) 78 (Jun)) and National Exhibition Centre Ltd (*ECJ Case C-130/15*, [2016] All ER (D) 69 (Jun)), 'played no specific and essential part in achieving the changes in the legal and financial situation that are the result of a transfer of ownership of the funds concerned'. They did no more than 'provide technical and administrative assistance for the obtaining of information and the communication of that information to its merchant acquirer, and to receive, by the same means, the communication of information that enables it to effect a sale and to receive the corresponding funds'. That was not an exempt financial service.

It is likely that HMRC will issue a Brief in due course explaining their approach to other traders who have used this arrangement and have regarded the income as exempt, possibly relying on Business Brief 18/06.

(3) Derivatives

Services of a person acting as an agent, broker or other intermediary for supplies of *financial* derivatives may be exempt from VAT. The rules are different depending on the type of financial service which is provided.

- Cash settled contracts (see **24.9**(4) above). The supply is exempt if the intermediary
  - acts between a person selling and a person buying a cash settled financial derivative;
  - brings those parties together; and
  - carries out some form of preparatory work to the conclusion of contracts.
- Non-cash settled contracts (see **24.9**(4) above). The supply is exempt if the intermediary
  - acts between a person selling and a person buying non-cash settled financial derivatives; and
  - brings those parties together.

(VAT Notice 701/49/17, para 8.12).

(4) Financial investigations

Financial investigation includes activities such as checking the validity of documents, normally on behalf of a financial institution. These services are taxable. (VAT Notice 701/49/17, para 9.6).

(5) Independent financial advisors (IFAs)

An IFA may

(a) provide advice only (a taxable supply);
(b) act between his customer and the provider of a financial product, in which case his supply is exempt if he meets the criteria in **24.25** above; or
(c) provide a mixture of (*a*) and (*b*).

Where (*c*) above applies, it is necessary to establish which of the two elements of the service predominates.

(a) Where the advice directly results in the customer taking out a financial product and all the criteria for intermediary services in **24.25** above are met, the whole of the service (including the advice element) is exempt. The advice is seen as ancillary to an exempt intermediary service. If any commission is received from the finance product provider, it is consideration for a separate exempt supply by the IFA of intermediary services.
(b) Where the advice far outweighs the work done to arrange a contract (e.g. because a customer has received a general financial review, with advice covering a range of financial issues, but then only buys a minor product requiring minimal intermediary services), those intermediary services are ancillary to the advice, and VAT is due on the whole supply.

(VAT Notice 701/49/17, para 9.9).

IFA networks

IFA firms frequently operate as networks through agreements with persons known as appointed representatives (ARs) for whom the authorised IFA firm takes regulatory responsibility. The arrangements enable the AR to carry out regulated activities without the need to be authorised directly by the Financial Services Authority (FSA).

These network arrangements are permitted under UK legislation and are subject to strict regulatory rules. In particular, the following should apply.

- The network appoints the ARs and trains them to operate in accordance with FSA requirements.
- In all dealings with the client, the ARs make it clear, both orally and on any paperwork, that they are acting on behalf of the network.
- The network has the contractual relationship with the financial product providers and at all times the AR acts on the network's behalf.
- The network maintains a high level of control over the ARs, carrying out regular checks and audits and imposing sanctions where appropriate.
- The network accepts responsibility for the actions of the ARs and handles all customer complaints made against the AR.
- The network holds liability insurance to cover any claims resulting from the activities of the ARs and is legally liable for any sanctions imposed under the *FSMA 2000*.
- All fees or commissions for regulated activities are paid by the clients or product providers to the network and these form part of the income of the network for accounting and direct tax purposes.
- The network pays the ARs for their services and these payments can be adjusted at the discretion of the network should, for example, the AR be found to have failed to conduct the business in accordance with the regulatory requirements.

When networks operate in this way, a 'sub-agency' or 'sub-contract' arrangement in effect exists between the network and the ARs. The network acts as principal, making supplies of financial intermediary services to the financial product providers and supplies of advice and/or financial intermediary services to the clients. The networks effectively sub-contract their functions to the ARs who interact directly with the client and the product providers in the provision of individual supplies on behalf of the network.

The VAT treatment of such arrangements is as follows.

- All payments (whether by fee or commission) received from the product providers or clients for the supplies of financial *intermediary services* provided via the ARs is the network's VAT exempt income and the onward payments made to the ARs is consideration for the AR's VAT exempt intermediary services supplied to the network.
- Fees either paid directly to the network or via the ARs, in respect of *advice only* services supplied via the ARs (which fall outside the exemption for financial intermediary services) is the network's standard

rated income. Any onward payments made to the ARs is consideration for the provision of those services by the ARs to the network on which VAT is due if the AR's taxable income is above the VAT registration threshold.

- Any optional services supplied by the network to their ARs for additional consideration (e.g. specific compliance or IT services) are separate supplies and the relevant VAT liability applies.
- Any non-regulated services provided by ARs fall outside the network arrangements altogether and are made directly by the ARs to the client/product provider.

A different VAT treatment applies to supplies made by networks that do not operate in the way outlined above (e.g. firms which on first appearance look like networks but are not authorised entities and are set up to provide marketing and/or compliance support services to directly authorised IFA firms). In the event of any doubt, businesses are advised to contact HMRC.

(VAT Notice 701/49/17, para 9.10).

(6) Soft commissions

Soft commissions are an arrangement by which an intermediary can use his income from the provider to fund (either directly or indirectly) some of his client's costs, in recognition of the amount of business the client will (or has) put his way. Such commissions are outside the scope of VAT as they do not represent consideration for any supply. (VAT Notice 701/49/17, para 9.8).

(7) Individual voluntary arrangements

In *Paymex Ltd* (TC01210) (TVC 20.137) a company provided insolvency practitioners (IPs) to run and maintain individual voluntary arrangements (IVAs) for consumers who had fallen into financial difficulties. The tribunal found that the company was making supplies of financial services concerned with debts, which qualified for exemption under *Directive 2006/112/EC, Art 135(1)(d)*. It held that the services were related to a financial transaction which has as its purpose both a change in the legal and financial situation of the debtor and creditors, and the alteration and/or extinguishment of their respective rights and obligations in relation to those debts.

Following that decision, HMRC have stated that:

- Although the tribunal decision itself applied purely to consumer IVAs, HMRC considers that the terms of the tribunal decision read across to all IVAs. The important point for IPs to consider here is not the specific type of IVA, but rather whether the nature of the services they provide are covered by the terms of the *Paymex Limited* ruling.
- Although HMRC did not consider the terms of the tribunal decision to be restricted to a particular type of IVA, they initially stated that the tribunal decision did not deal with company voluntary arrangements (CVAs) or partnership voluntary arrangements (PVAs). However, they have subsequently revised their opinion and now consider that the VAT exemption arising from *Paymex Limited* applies to CVAs, PVAs and protected trust deeds (applicable only in Scotland).

Refund claims are subject to the rules on input tax adjustments, the four-year cap and unjust enrichment.

(HMRC Brief 35/11; HMRC Brief 3/12).

For the services of an IP to be covered by the *Paymex* ruling, those services must constitute a single supply for VAT purposes including both the nominee and supervisory stages. While there is no dispute that the nominee element of the supply is exempt for VAT purposes, HMRC does not accept that the supervisory stage, when provided alone, can always be deemed as exempt. It is HMRC's view that where an IP firm provides the services of a supervisor in a voluntary arrangement and no-one from that firm has previously acted as nominee in that particular voluntary arrangement then the supplies made by the supervisor remain taxable at the standard rate.

(HMRC Brief 17/13).

Standard-rated supplies

[24.29] There are various services which, although associated with finance, are not covered by the exemption. These include:

- Bookkeeping services
- Debt collection (see **24.10** above) and credit control
- Depository and trustee services
- Equipment leasing
- Executor and trustee services and the administration of estates
- Investment, finance and taxation advice
- Management consultancy
- Merger and take-over advice
- Portfolio management (see **24.19**(4) above)
- Registrar services (see **24.19**(7) above)
- Safe custody services (see **24.19**(1) above) and safe transportation services
- Service companies' activities, e.g. administration, payment of salaries and wages

(VAT Notice 701/49/17, para 1.6).

Islamic products

[24.30] According to Sharia'a principles the following are prohibited.

- The charging or receipt of interest ('riba').
- Uncertainty or deception (e.g. an ambiguity or lack of clarity in the terms of a contract that can give rise to speculation ('gharar')).
- Gambling or speculation (e.g. any transaction undertaken for purely speculative purposes ('maisir')).
- Unethical investments (e.g. dealing in activities or commodities that include pork, pornography, arms or munitions, conventional financial services, cinema, tobacco, gambling or alcohol).

Because of this, many Muslims have been unable or unwilling to obtain conventional credit finance in order to purchase goods and/or services because those products are prohibited in their faith. In order to be able to provide Sharia'a compliant products, financial institutions and boards of Sharia'a scholars have worked together to create certain products which operate via a trade or rental arrangement as these are allowed under Sharia'a.

See VAT Information Sheet 11/06 for details of the schemes and their VAT treatment.

Key points: financial services

[24.31] Points to consider are as follows.

- Many financial services supplied by a business are exempt from VAT. This means that input tax recovery is not possible on related costs under the rules of partial exemption. However, if the exempt financial service is provided to a customer who belongs outside the EU then input tax recovery is allowed (subject to the normal rules).
- A key challenge for any business making supplies of financial services, or related support services, is to be very clear about the exact nature of the service being performed. In the past, many tribunal decisions have confirmed that services being provided are of an 'administrative' nature (and therefore standard-rated) rather than being directly relevant to arranging financial services that are exempt.
- A hire purchase transaction involves a supply of goods because the intention is that the hirer will take ownership of the goods at the end of the agreement. This means that the hirer can claim input tax on the full value of the goods (subject to the normal rules, e.g. not in relation to motor cars available for private use where an input tax block applies) at the time he first acquires the goods in accordance with the agreement. The finance company will account for output tax.
- It is common practice for many retail outlets to charge an additional fee for goods and services, where the customer pays for the goods by credit card, rather than by cheque or cash. In such cases, this is an additional charge for the goods or services in question. It is not relevant to an exempt supply of financial services. The CJEU decision in *Bookit Ltd* has shown that one arrangement to exempt such a charge, using a subsidiary that levies a separate charge for 'card handling', does not achieve its objective.
- The activities of independent financial advisers (IFAs) can be both exempt and standard-rated. Advisory services for a client are standard-rated, but services of arranging a financial product for the client (with a commission earned from either the client or

financial institution in question) is exempt from VAT because the IFA is acting as a financial intermediary.

25

Food

Cross-references. See also **12 CATERING** for supplies in the course of catering and take-away food; **48.7**(16) **OUTPUT TAX** for packaging of food products.

De Voil Indirect Tax Service. See V4.217–V4.225.

Introduction to food

[25.1] The supply of food (including drink) comprised in the following *General items*, is zero-rated.

(a) Food of a kind used for human consumption (see **25.2** to **25.14** below).
(b) Animal feeding stuffs (see **25.15** and **25.19** below).
(c) Seeds or other means of propagation of plants within (*a*) or (*b*) above (see **25.20** below).
(d) Live animals of a kind generally used as, or yielding or producing, food for human consumption (see **25.21** to **25.23** below).

There are, however, a number of *Excepted items* (which are standard-rated) and *Overriding items* (which are zero-rated because they override the *Excepted items*).

Catering

Specifically excluded from zero-rating is any supply in the course of catering which includes

- any supply of food for consumption on the premises where it is supplied; and
- any supply of hot food for consumption off those premises.

See **12 CATERING** for full details.

[*VATA 1994, Sch 8 Group 1 General Items 1–4*].

Food for human consumption

[25.2] The supply of food of a kind used for human consumption is zero-rated. Food includes drink. [*VATA 1994, Sch 8 Group 1 General Item 1*].

Meaning of '*food*'

The law does not include a definition of 'food' and the word should therefore be given its ordinary and everyday meaning (applying *Brutus v Cozens*, [1972] 2 All ER 1297).

A product is considered to be 'food' if the average person would consider it so. HMRC regard the term as including products eaten as part of a meal or snack. However, many products are sold in a form in which they are not fit to be consumed without some preparation by the user and the words 'of a kind used for' are included to reflect this fact (*C & E Commrs v Macphie & Co (Glenbervie) Ltd*, CS [1992] STC 886 (TVC 29.93)). Products, therefore, like flour which, although not eaten by themselves, are generally recognised as food ingredients are included. 'Food' would not normally include

- medicines and medicated preparations (but see **29.13 HEALTH AND WELFARE** for zero-rating of certain medicines),
- dietary supplements (see **25.11** below), or
- food additives and similar products (see **25.12** below)

which, although edible, are not generally regarded as 'food'.

Palatability and other matters may be taken into account (*Marfleet Refining Co Ltd* [1974] Lexis Citation 5 (TVC 29.102)) and also nutritive value (*Soni* (VTD 897) (TVC 29.87)).

Waste and contaminated food products (including used cooking oil) are not allowed zero-rating because, although they could be described as 'food', they are not 'of a kind used for human consumption'. (They may, however, qualify for zero-rating as animal feeding stuffs, see **25.15** below.)

(VAT Notice 701/14/15, para 2.3).

Exceptions

Food of a kind used for human consumption is generally zero-rated under *General Item 1* above. There are, however, a number of categories of *Excepted items* (including ice cream and similar products, confectionery, alcoholic and other beverages, crisps, roasted and salted nuts) which are standard-rated and *Overriding items* (including tea and coffee) which override the *Excepted items* and remain zero-rated.

For a consideration of food for human consumption generally, see **25.3** to **25.14** below.

Catering

For food supplied in the course of catering and take-away food generally, see **CATERING (11)**.

Basic foodstuffs

[25.3] All supplies of unprocessed foodstuffs such as raw meat and fish, vegetables and fruit, nuts and pulses and fresh culinary herbs are zero-rated provided they are of a quality fit for human consumption. This applies whether the produce is supplied direct to the public or for use as ingredients in the manufacture of processed foods. (If not fit for human consumption, it may still be eligible for zero-rating as animal feeding stuffs, see **25.15** below.)

Meat and poultry

Zero-rating applies whether sold as a complete carcass or butchered and extends to more exotic meats such as ostrich, crocodile, kangaroo, horsemeat, etc. (The rules are different for sale of live animals where zero-rating only applies if the animal is of a species generally used for consumption in the UK so that, for example, the sale of a live horse is standard-rated, see **25.21** below.)

Fish

The same rules apply as for meat above. Provided the species is one generally used for human consumption in the UK, it is zero-rated whether supplied live, whole or filleted.

Vegetables, fruit and culinary herbs

These are zero-rated when sold unprocessed provided they are fit for human consumption (e.g. ornamental cabbages are standard-rated). See **25.20** below for supplies of growing plants and seeds. Zero-rating only applies to culinary herbs not medicinal ones (unless in the form of herbal teas). See **25.12** below for a list of herbs accepted by HMRC as culinary.

Fruit and vegetable pulps are zero-rated but pulps that are to be made into beverages and most juices and juice concentrates are standard-rated as beverages (see **25.8** below).

Cereals

Cereals (wheat, barley, maize, etc.) of a kind fit for human consumption are zero-rated whether supplied as a growing crop, in bulk, or cleaned and packaged for retail sale. (Cereals unfit for human consumption may be eligible for zero-rating as animal feeding stuffs, see **25.15** below.)

See **25.14** below for processing other people's cereal crop.

Nuts and pulses

Raw and unprocessed nuts and pulses fit for human consumption are zero-rated, as are nuts roasted or salted in their shells. This applies whether they are sold in bulk or in small retail packs. Nuts which are shelled and either roasted or salted are standard-rated (see **25.9** below).

Bakery products

Bread and bread products (e.g. rolls, baps, pitta bread) are zero-rated unless supplied as part of a hot take-away meal (e.g. a bun containing a hot hamburger). For hot take-away food, see **12 CATERING**. *Cakes* and *biscuits* (other than chocolate covered biscuits) are normally zero-rated (see **25.6** below) but other confectionery is normally standard-rated (see **25.5** below).

Freshly baked products

Many bakery products (e.g. pies, pasties and other savouries) are baked on the premises and sold while hot. See **12.2 CATERING** for the distinction between freshly baked food (zero-rated) and hot take-away food (standard-rated).

Processed food

Canned and *frozen foods* take the liability of the equivalent unprocessed product. Ice creams, etc. are standard-rated (see **25.4** below).

Ready meals: sales of convenience foods and prepared meals which require further preparation (e.g. reheating) at home are zero-rated; but where premises and/or facilities for eating the food are provided or hot take-away food is supplied, there could be a supply of standard-rated catering. See **12 CATERING**.

Cold sandwiches are zero-rated as prepared food unless they are a supply made in the course of catering. See **12 CATERING**.

(VAT Notice 701/14/15, paras 3.1, 3.3, 3.4).

Ice cream, etc.

[25.4] The supply of ice cream, ice lollies, frozen yoghurt, water ices and similar frozen products, and prepared mixes and powders for making such products, are standard-rated. [*VATA 1994, Sch 8 Group 1 Excepted Item 1*]. Yoghurt unsuitable for immediate consumption when frozen is zero-rated. [*VATA 1994, Sch 8 Group 1 Overriding Item 1*]. The use of the expression 'similar frozen products' assumes that the adjective 'frozen' applies to any of the former, specifically enumerated items. What those items have in common is that they are supplied for consumption at a temperature below the freezing point of water. They do not have in common any particular degree of viscosity or solidity. See *Meschia's Frozen Foods v C & E Commrs*, Ch D 2000, [2001] STC 1 (TVC 29.135) where the court held that frozen yoghurt in the context of *Excepted Item 1* meant yoghurt reduced to a temperature below the freezing point of water.

Standard-rated items include

- sorbets and granitas
- ice cream gateaux and cakes, including arctic rolls
- fruit syrups sold in plastic tubes for home freezing as ice lollies

Zero-rated items include

- products which are supplied frozen but which have to be cooked (e.g. baked alaska) or thawed completely (cream gateaux, mousse) before eating
- desserts which can be eaten either straight from the freezer or left to thaw (unless primarily designed for eating while frozen and made substantially of ice cream or any of the other excepted items)
- toppings, sauces and syrups for serving with ice cream (unless sold on the ice cream)

Wafers, cones, etc. sold complete with ice cream are standard-rated as part of that ice cream. If sold separately, they are treated as biscuits (i.e. zero-rated unless wholly or partly covered in chocolate or a similar product) (see **25.6** below).

(VAT Notice 701/14/15, para 3.5).

Confectionery

[25.5] 'Confectionery' is standard-rated. '*Confectionery*' includes chocolates; sweets; biscuits wholly or partly covered with chocolate or with some product similar in taste and appearance; drained, glacé or crystallised fruits (but not drained cherries or candied peel which are zero-rated); and any item of sweetened prepared food which is normally eaten with the fingers. [*VATA 1994, Sch 8 Group 1 Excepted Item 2; Overriding Items 2 and 3* and *Note (5)*].

In *Popcorn House Ltd*, [1968] 4 All ER 782 (TVC 29.155) (a purchase tax case) 'confectionery' was described as any form of food normally eaten with the fingers and made by a cooking process, other than baking, which contains a substantial amount of sweetening matter.

In *C & E Commrs v Ferrero UK Ltd*, CA [1997] STC 881 (TVC 29.146), the Court confirmed the following principles adopted by the tribunal as the correct approach to take when deciding whether a product is confectionery or a cake or biscuit.

- The words in the law must be given their ordinary meaning.
- What is relevant is the view of the ordinary man in the street.
- VAT treatment of other products is not relevant.
- If a product has characteristics of two categories, it can be placed in the category in which it has sufficient characteristics to qualify.
- Factors that should also taken into account include appearance, size and ingredients, manufacturing process, taste and texture, time and place of eating, and packaging. Marketing may also be of varying degrees of relevance.

Items of sweetened prepared food do not need to have added sweetening if they are inherently sweet, e.g. certain fruit and cereal bar products. Standard-rating applies to products falling within the general definition of confectionery even if intended to meet special nutritional needs (e.g. chocolate for diabetics and slimmers' meal replacements in biscuit form with a chocolate or similar coating).

Standard-rated items include

- chocolates, chocolate bars (including those containing nuts, fruit, toffee, biscuit or any other ingredient), liqueur chocolates
- boiled sweets, lollipops and candyfloss
- fruit pastilles and gums and similar jelly sweets
- turkish delight
- sherbet
- marshmallows, fondants and similar confectionery
- chewing and bubble gum
- nuts or fruit with a coating, e.g. of chocolate, yoghurt or sugar
- crystallised or sugared ginger (but ginger preserved in syrup, drained ginger or dusted ginger can be zero-rated as long as not held out for sale as confectionery)
- compressed fruit bars and other items or prepared dried fruit confectionary that are sweet to the taste
- bars consisting mainly of sesame seeds and sugar or other sweetening matter (but halva is zero-rated unless coated with chocolate or chocolate substitute or held out for sale as confectionery)
- marrons glacé
- sweetened popcorn (*C & E Commrs v Clark's Cereal Products Ltd*, QB 1965, [1968] 3 All ER 778 (TVC 29.154) – a purchase tax case)
- sweetened dried fruit, e.g. banana chips, pineapple and papaya (unless sold as suitable for confectionery/snacking *and* home cooking (see **25.12** below) when zero-rated irrespective of bag size)
- cereal bars, whether or not coated with chocolate (except for bars qualifying as cakes)
- florentines
- coconut ice

Zero-rated items include

- Angelica, 'glacé' cherries, and cocktail or maraschino cherries
- cakes (see **25.6** below)
- biscuits not covered with chocolate or a similar product (see **25.6** below)
- chocolate spread
- liquid chocolate icing
- toffee apples (*Candy Maid Confections Ltd & Others v C & E Commrs*, Ch D [1968] 3 All ER 773 (TVC 29.137) – a purchase tax case) and other apples on a stick covered with chocolate, nuts, etc.
- traditional Indian and Pakistani delicacies, e.g. barfis, halvas, jelabi, laddoos (but not petha which is crystallised fruit)
- traditional Japanese delicacies
- chocolate cups

See **25.6** below for edible and inedible cake decorations and **25.13** below for mixtures and assortments.

(VAT Notice 701/14/15, paras 3.4, 3.6).

Cakes and biscuits

[25.6] Cakes and biscuits (other than biscuits wholly or partly covered with chocolate or some product similar in taste and appearance) are zero-rated. [*VATA 1994, Sch 8 Group 1 Excepted Item 2*].

Cakes

Cakes include (whether or not they are covered with chocolate)

- sponges and fruitcakes
- meringues
- slab gingerbread (gingerbread men are treated as biscuits)
- flapjacks (but not flapjack-type products containing cereals other than oats, which are confectionery, see **25.5** above. See also *Asda Stores Ltd* (TC00211) (TVC 29.171) in which it was held that, apart from oats, the 'flapjack bars' did not contain the typical ingredients of a flapjack)
- marshmallow teacakes (despite the fact that they comprise a combination of chocolate coated biscuit and marshmallow, both of which are regarded as standard-rated confectionery)
- 'crunch cakes' consisting of corn flakes or other breakfast cereal products coated in chocolate or carob and pressed into flat cakes (see *Doves Farm Foods Ltd* (VTD 17805))
- caramel or 'millionaire's' shortcake (*Marks & Spencer plc* (VTD 4510) (TVC 29.143))
- lebkuchen
- jaffa cakes (see *United Biscuits (UK) Ltd* (VTD 6344) (TVC 29.144))
- Scottish snowballs (see *Lees of Scotland Ltd & Thomas Tunnock Ltd* (TC03754) (TVC 29.150)).

In *Lees of Scotland Ltd & Thomas Tunnock Ltd* (TC03754) (TVC 29.150) the Tribunal considered that the following factors should be taken into account when deciding whether a product is a cake:

- ingredients
- process and manufacture
- unpackaged appearance
- taste and texture
- circumstances of consumption
- packaging
- marketing
- shelf life
- name and description
- how the product behaves when it is removed from packaging.

In keeping with previous classification exercises the Tribunal acknowledged that there are no objective tests that can be imposed to determine whether a particular item of confectionary is or is not a cake, and that each case must turn on its own particular facts.

The type of snowball considered in *Lees of Scotland Ltd & Thomas Tunnock Ltd* (TC03754) (TVC 29.150) was a dome of marshmallow coated in a combination of the following:

- chocolate
- sugar strands
- carob
- cocoa
- coconut

which may or may not include a jam filling.

Products which are not the same as the products in *Lees of Scotland Ltd & Thomas Tunnock Ltd* (TC03754) (TVC 29.150) may not be zero-rated simply by referring to them as snowballs.

HMRC consider that the borderline between confectionary and cakes causes few problems, but with the ever changing selection of confectionary available there will always be some products whose status as cakes is not necessarily self-evident.
(HMRC Brief 36/14).

HMRC have explained in Notice 701/14 that Scottish snowballs are a dome of marshmallow coated with chocolate or coconut, aerated and boiled (not baked), having a short shelf life (they harden rapidly when removed from the packet). Other types of snowballs such as Swedish snowballs with a longer shelf life are standard-rated.

Cakes provided as part of a supply of catering are standard-rated as part of that supply. See **12 CATERING**. However, if a commemorative cake is provided to a caterer or individual, the supply can be zero-rated provided the supplier

- takes no further part in the provision of catering; and
- does not take the cake to the premises to set it up/supervise its disposal.

Cake decorations

Inedible cake decorations are standard-rated where sold on their own. If supplied as part of a cake, an inedible decoration can be zero-rated unless it is clearly a separate item in its own right (e.g. a toy with a child's birthday cake intended to be used after the cake is eaten although, even then, if the linked goods concession can be applied, the supply can be treated as a single supply, see **25.13** below).

Edible cake decorations are zero-rated when sold as part of a cake. They are also zero-rated when sold separately unless standard-rated as confectionery (see **25.5** above) or roasted nuts (see **25.9** below).

Zero-rated cake decorations include

- chocolate couverture
- chocolate chips
- hundreds and thousands, vermicelli and sugar strands
- chocolate leaves, scrolls, etc., jelly shapes, and sugar flowers, leaves, etc. (provided designed specifically for cake decorations)

- royal icing
- toasted coconut and toasted almonds held out specifically for baking use
- cherries used in baking ('glacé')

Standard-rated cake decorations include

- chocolate buttons except packets of mini-chocolate buttons sold for use in baking
- chocolate flakes (except where supplied within the bakery and ice cream industries when they may be zero-rated if sold in packs of 144 or more and clearly labelled 'for use as cake decorations only: not for retail sale')
- any other items sold in the same form as confectionery

Biscuits

Biscuits covered or partly covered in chocolate (or some other product similar in taste and appearance) are standard-rated. Other biscuits are zero-rated.

Standard-rated biscuits include

- chocolate shortbread
- gingerbread men decorated with chocolate (unless only dots for eyes)
- ice cream wafers partly covered in chocolate, e.g. chocolate oysters (but see *Marcantonio Foods Ltd* (VTD 15486) (TVC 29.140) for waffle cones)

Zero-rated biscuits include

- chocolate chip biscuits where the chips are either included in the dough or pressed into the surface before cooking
- bourbon and other biscuits whether the chocolate or similar product only forms a sandwich layer
- biscuits coated with caramel or some other product that does not resemble chocolate in taste and appearance

See also *C & E Commrs v Ferrero UK Ltd*, CA [1997] STC 881 (TVC 29.146).

Mixtures and assortments

See **25.13** below.

(VAT Notice 701/14/15, para 3.4).

Alcoholic drinks

[25.7] Beverages chargeable with any excise duty specifically charged on spirits, beer, wine or made-wine and preparations thereof are standard-rated. [*VATA 1994, Sch 8 Group 1 Excepted Item 3*].

All supplies of drinks containing alcohol are standard-rated, whether sold for consumption on or off the premises. This includes

- beer, cider and perry (including black beer and shandy)
- wine (including made-wine and fermented communion wine)

- spirits and liqueurs

Food products, other than beverages, containing alcohol follow the normal liability rules, e.g. fruit preserved in alcohol is zero-rated as any other preserved fruit and rum babas are zero-rated as cakes. Liqueur chocolates are standard-rated.

(VAT Notice 701/14/15, para 3.7).

Non-alcoholic drinks

[25.8] Supplies of 'beverages' not within **25.7** above (including fruit juices and bottled waters) and syrups, concentrates, essences, powders, crystals or other products for the preparation of beverages are standard-rated, subject to the following overriding exceptions which are zero-rated.

(a) Tea, maté, herbal teas and similar products, and preparations and extractions thereof.
(b) Cocoa, coffee and chicory and other roasted coffee substitutes, and preparations and extractions thereof.
(c) Milk and preparations and extracts thereof.
(d) Preparations and extracts of meat, yeast or eggs.

[*VATA 1994, Sch 8 Group 1 Excepted Item 4, Overriding Items 4–7; FA 1999, s 14*].

In *Dr X Hua* (VTD 13811) (TVC 29.89) the tribunal held that herbal teas sold at a homeopathic clinic were substantially the same as herbal teas sold commercially and can be zero-rated. In *Thorncroft Ltd* (TC01536) (TVC 29.187) it was held that iced tea concentrates were zero-rated as tea was the principal ingredient.

All hot beverages and any drinks, including zero-rated drinks, sold for consumption on the premises, are standard-rated. Cold drinks that are zero-rated in their own right, e.g. milk, and are supplied for off-premises consumption are zero-rated.

'*Beverage*' must be given its ordinary meaning and covers drinks and liquids that are commonly consumed. Liquids that are commonly consumed are those that are characteristically taken to increase bodily liquid levels, to slake thirst and to fortify or give pleasure (*Bioconcepts Ltd* (VTD 11287) (TVC 29.176)). HMRC have accepted this definition.

Following the tribunal decision in *McCormick (UK) plc* (VTD 15202) (TVC 29.184) HMRC accept that mulling spices, whiskey todd mixtures, spiced cider mixtures, etc. are not 'products for the preparation of beverages' and are zero-rated.

Standard-rated beverages include

- carbonated drinks such as lemonade, cola and mixers such as tonic and soda
- fruit cordials and squashes
- mineral, table and spa waters held out for sale as beverages

- alcohol-free beer and wines
- fruit and vegetable juices (but lemon juice for culinary use is not a beverage)
- ginger, glucose, honey, peppermint and barley water drinks
- flavourings for milk shakes (except preparations and extracts of cocoa or coffee, which are zero-rated)
- purgative and laxative 'teas', such as senna, and similar medicinal teas
- soft drinks containing tea as only one of several ingredients, e.g. fruit flavoured 'iced tea', see *Snapple Beverage Corporation* (VTD 13690) (TVC 29.186).

Khat (or Chat) is standard-rated as HMRC do not regard it as a food product. (Business Brief 25/97).

Drinks which are not beverages

Some drinks do not fall within the definition of 'beverage'. Such drinks, and mixes, etc. for making them, can therefore be zero-rated. These include

- plain soya or rice milk (unflavoured and unsweetened)
- coconut milk
- meal replacement drinks for slimmers or invalids
- unfermented fruit juice specifically for sacramental purposes (see **25.11** below)
- angostura bitters

Milk based drinks

In *Rivella (UK) Ltd* (VTD 16382) (TVC 29.189) a canned sparkling drink included 35% lactoserum but on a dry analysis of the ingredients (i.e. excluding water) the lactoserum was over 50% of the contents. The tribunal noted that the relative weight of the four factors considered in the *Snapple* case above (i.e. ingredients, manufacturing process, appearance and taste, and marketing and packaging) would vary on a case by case basis but, in this case, it found that the first two were predominant and decisive, supported by the marketing process which has been successful in linking in the minds of the potential consumers the principal source of the products as extracts of milk. The appearance and taste test had little or no value because the lactoserum did not possess the 'milkiness' of milk or preparations of milk. The tribunal concluded that Rivella was zero-rated.

Fruit-flavoured soya milk was held not to be a beverage and zero-rated in *Alpro Ltd* (VTD 19911) (TVC 29.191).

In *Nestlé UK Ltd v HMRC* [2016] UKFTT 158 (TC) (TC04944) (TVC 29.111), the First-tier Tax Tribunal considered the liability of fruit-flavoured Nesquik, a powder that was generally mixed with milk. Chocolate-flavoured Nesquik was accepted as zero-rated under the heading 'Cocoa ... and preparations and extractions thereof', but fruit-flavoured Nesquik did not qualify for any relief. The powder was not itself a milk-based drink, even though it might be used to make one; it was a powder for the preparation of beverages, and was excluded from zero-rating. Nestlé appealed against the decision and the Upper Tribunal dismissed the latest appeal stating that whilst there was clearly an indication to zero-rate milk and milk preparations, there was no wider intention to extend the scope of the zero-rating provisions to a separate supply of powders that could be added to milk. (*Nestlé UK Ltd v HMRC* [2018] UKUT 29 (TCC) (TVC 29.111).)

Sports drinks

Sports drinks that are advertised or marketed as products designed to enhance physical performance, accelerate recovery after exercise or build bulk, and other similar drinks, including (in either case) syrups, concentrates, essences, powders, crystals or other products for the preparation of such drinks are standard-rated.

[*VATA 1994, Sch 8, Group 1, Excepted Item 4A*]. (VAT Notice 701/14/15, para 3.7).

Savoury snacks

[25.9] The following are standard-rated.

(a) Potato crisps, sticks or puffs and similar products made from potato, potato flour or potato starch when packaged for human consumption without further preparation.

(b) Savoury food products made by swelling cereals or cereal products when packaged for human consumption without further preparation.

(c) Salted or roasted nuts other than nuts in shell.

[*VATA 1994, Sch 8 Group 1 Excepted Item 5*].

Standard-rated products include

- potato crisps, potato sticks, potato puffs, and similar products including those made from a combination of potato starch or flour and cereal flour
- savoury popcorn (but not corn for popping, e.g. 'microwave' popcorn)
- prawn crackers made from cereals (but not unpackaged prawn crackers, e.g. those supplied in unsealed bags as part of a takeaway meal)
- rice cakes (but not unflavoured rice cakes intended for consumption with cheese or other toppings)
- all roasted or salted nuts not zero-rated below

Zero-rated products include

- savoury snacks consisting of sliced and dried or roasted vegetables other than potatoes, e.g. beetroot, carrot etc.
- tortilla chips, corn chips, bagel chips, cocktail cheese savouries and Twiglets
- prawn crackers made from tapioca
- roasted pulses and legumes, e.g. chick peas and lentils
- roasted or salted nuts supplied while still in their shells (such as 'monkey nuts' and pistachios), toasted coconut, toasted almonds and other toasted chopped nuts held out for sale in retail packs specifically for home baking

(VAT Notice 701/14/15, para 3.8).

In *Procter & Gamble UK*, CA [2009] All ER (D) 177 (May) (TVC 29.196) a partnership manufactured a product known as 'Pringles', which contained potato flour, corn flour, wheat starch and rice flour. About 42% of the product consisted of potato, and about 33% was fat. HMRC issued a ruling that they were excluded from zero-rating by *VATA 1994, Sch 8, Group 1, Excepted Item No 5*. The partnership appealed, contending that the products were not 'potato crisps' or 'similar products'. The Court of Appeal rejected this contention, holding that the Pringles were similar to the potato crisp and made from the potato, and there was no requirement that the products should be made wholly (or substantially wholly) from the potato or potato derivative.

In *United Biscuits (UK) Ltd (No 8)* (TC01515) (TVC 29.197), the tribunal held that the defining essential ingredient of savoury snacks ('Discos' and 'New recipe frisps') made from a blend of wheat and potato was wheat, and therefore the products were not excluded from zero-rating as potato crisps or similar products.

See **25.13** below for mixtures containing standard and zero-rated items (e.g. Bombay mix).

Ingredients for domestic beer and wine making

[25.10] Goods otherwise qualifying as food for human consumption, animal feeding stuffs (see **25.15** below) or seeds (see **25.20** below) but which are canned, bottled, packaged or prepared for use in domestic

- brewing of beer,
- making of cider or perry, or
- production of wine or made-wine

are standard-rated. [*VATA 1994, Sch 8 Group 1 Excepted Item 7*].

Included are

- kits for home-brewing, wine-making, etc.
- retail packs of hopped malt extract, malted barley, roasted barley and hops
- special wine and brewer's yeast
- grape concentrates
- retail packs of foods which are specialised to home wine-making, e.g. dried elderberries or sloes

Any general food product that is held out for sale specifically for home wine making or brewing must also be standard-rated. In this context, goods are held out for sale for home brewing and wine making if

(a) sold in a retail outlet (or department or section of a general outlet) specialising in home brewing and wine making;
(b) labelled, advertised or otherwise displayed as materials for home brewing or wine making; or
(c) provided or packaged with any brewing or wine making recipes or instructions for using them in the making of beer or wine.

(VAT Notice 701/14/15, para 3.7).

Specialised products

[25.11] The liability of such products depends upon whether they fall within the normal meaning of 'food' (see **25.2** above). If they do, then they are treated under the normal rules and are zero-rated unless falling within one of the *Excepted items*.

(a) Food supplements

Dietary supplements of a kind not normally purchased and used as food are standard-rated. This includes

- vitamin and mineral supplements of all kinds
- royal jelly products but not regular products such as honey which have royal jelly added (see *Grosvenor Commodities Ltd* (VTD 7221) (TVC 29.103))
- tablets, pills and capsules containing, for example, wheatgerm, iron, calcium, fibre, yeast, garlic, pollen, propolis, seaweed, evening primrose, guarana or other similar herbal preparations, and powders of these other than garlic and yeast. See *Nature's Balance Ltd* (VTD 12295) (TVC 29.105) and *Hunter Ridgeley Ltd* (VTD 13662) (TVC 29.106) for algae tablets and *National Safety Associates of America (UK) Ltd* (VTD 14241) (TVC 29.107) for fruit and vegetable tablets. See *Durwin Banks (No 1)* (VTD 18904) (TVC 29.103) and *Durwin Banks (No 2)* (VTD 20695) (TVC 29.98) for linseed oil. A high protein powder marketed as a dietary supplement and intended to be mixed with water and drunk was held to qualify as food in *Arthro Vite Ltd* (VTD 14836) (TVC 29.95)
- charcoal biscuits
- cod liver oil and other fish oils held out for sale as dietary supplements (see *Marfleet Refining Co Ltd* (VTD 129) (TVC 29.102))
- elixirs and tonics, including mixtures of cider vinegar and honey sold as a dietary supplement
- malt extract with cod liver oil (but the supply of plain malt extract, with or without added vitamins, is zero-rated unless held out for sale for home brewing, etc.)

(b) Invalid foods

These products, including parenteral products given intravenously, can be zero-rated (subject to the normal rules) provided they are designed to meet the nutritional needs of the consumer and not to provide treatment for any medical condition. See *Ridal* (C149) (TVC 29.97) (a customs duty case) where the tribunal held that NuTriVeneD powder, an anti-oxidant specially formulated for Down's Syndrome sufferers and taken mixed with a fruit puree at each meal, was exempt from customs duty and VAT on importation from the USA as being within the definition of food. Foods intended to build patients up which are sold in liquid form are zero-rated as food since they fall outside the definition of a beverage (see **25.8** above).

(c) Diabetic and hypoallergenic products

Specialised foods designed for diabetics or allergy sufferers are zero-rated (e.g. sugar-free preserves or gluten-free flour and cakes) unless falling within any of the *Excepted items* (e.g. sugar-free confectionery or gluten-free chocolate biscuits) in which case they are standard-rated.

(d) Slimmers' foods

Low calorie foods for slimmers are treated in the same way as their mainstream food equivalent. Slimmers' meal replacement products (including drinks) are zero-rated unless in the form of confectionery (see **25.5** above).

Appetite suppressants in whatever form are not food and must be standard-rated. Genuine slimmers' food products containing appetite suppressants (e.g. soups containing cellulose) can be zero-rated provided the product is obviously food and is meant to take the place of a 'normal' food equivalent in the slimmers' daily food intake.

(e) Sports products

HMRC express the following opinion on the VAT liability of sports products.

- *Sports/energy drinks*. Sports drinks that are advertised or marketed as products designed to enhance physical performance, accelerate recovery after exercise or build bulk, and other similar drinks, including (in either case) syrups, concentrates, essences, powders, crystals or other products for the preparation of such drinks are standard-rated.
- *Tablets* are standard-rated with the exception of glucose, dextrose and Horlicks tablets which are zero-rated.
- *Creatine*. With the exception of sports/energy drinks (see above), items made up wholly or mainly of creatine are standard-rated. Where it is clear that the main benefit of the product is not the creatine but carbohydrate, protein or fat, then it is treated as a food, and is zero-rated unless falling within one of the excepted items.
- *Cereal/fruit bars*. Standard-rating applies to any product falling within the general definition of confectionery even when that product is intended to meet the special nutritional needs of athletes. See **25.5** above.

In *GlaxoSmithKline Services Unlimited*, UT November 2011, FTC/06/2011 (TVC 29.184) the tribunal held that 'Lucozade Sport', containing carbohydrates and electrolytes, was a beverage and thus excluded from zero-rating, as it was drunk by a significant number of consumers when not engaging in sport or any exercise and was not mainly purchased or consumed on account of its nutritional ingredients.

(f) Food and drink for religious and sacramental use

Religious laws requiring certain foods to be prepared in particular ways (e.g. kosher or halal) does not affect the liability of the final product. However, by concession, zero-rating has been agreed for the following food products which have exclusive sacramental use.

- Communion wafers used in the celebration of the Christian Communion, Mass or Eucharist
- Unfermented communion wine (fermented wine is standard-rated)
- Unfermented grape juice for use at the Jewish seder or kaddish provided it is marked prominently in English 'for sacramental use only'

(VAT Notice 701/14/15, paras 4.1–4.7).

Ingredients and additives

Home cooking

[25.12] Most ingredients used in home cooking and baking (e.g. flour and sugar) are clearly foodstuffs in their own right. As a general principle, products sold for use as an ingredient in home cooking or baking can be zero-rated if

- it has some measurable nutritional content;
- it is used solely or predominantly, in the particular form in which it is supplied, in the manufacture of food; and
- it does not fall within any *Excepted item*.

Pre-mixes: prepared cake, soup, sauce and other mixes sold for making up in the home kitchen are zero-rated except for mixes for ice creams and similar frozen products within **25.4** above.

Cooking oils: maize (corn) oil, rapeseed oil, groundnut (arachis) oil, olive oil (including olive oil BP), almond oil (but not bitter almond oil), sesame seed oil, sunflower seed oil, palm kernel oil, walnut oil, soya oil and blends of any of these oils can be zero-rated provided

- they are of a type suitable for culinary use; and
- they do not contain any substance, such as perfume, that would make them unsuitable for culinary use.

If they meet these conditions, such oils may be zero-rated even if held out for sale for other purposes (e.g. massage or cosmetic oils).

Essential oils are always standard-rated. Waste and used oils for recycling are ineligible for relief as 'food for human consumption' but may be eligible for relief as animal feeding stuffs (see **25.15** below).

Starch and gelatine are zero-rated if edible but standard-rated if inedible or unsuitable for human consumption (e.g. starch for stiffening collars and 'photographic' gelatine).

Salt for culinary use is zero-rated. This includes fine salt (undried vacuum and pure dried vacuum), dendritic salt, and rock and sea salt in retail packs for culinary use (12.5 kilo packs or less). Non-culinary salt is standard-rated. This includes compacted, granular and soiled salt, and salt of any type specifically held out for use in dishwashers or for other non-food use.

Sweeteners: natural products used as sweeteners (e.g. sugar and honey) are food products in their own right and zero-rated. Artificial sweeteners (e.g. saccharin, aspartame and sorbitol) can also be zero-rated.

Sweetened dried fruit sold as suitable for home baking *and* snacking can be zero-rated irrespective of the bag size. If sold purely as confectionery, it is standard-rated under **25.5** above. (Business Brief 18/98).

Herbs: see **25.20** below.

Other flavourings and flavour enhancers: zero-rating applies to

- natural flavouring essences (e.g. vanilla, peppermint and culinary rosewater)
- synthetic flavourings if designed specifically for food use
- flavouring mixes (e.g. dusting powders or blended seasonings) whether made or natural or synthetic components
- mixes for marinating meat, fish or poultry before cooking
- mulling spices, whiskey todd mixtures, spiced cider mixtures, etc. (see *McCormick (UK) plc* (VTD 15202) (TVC 29.180))

Unflavoured brining mixes (wet or dry) and flavour enhancers (e.g. monosodium glutamate) which do not contribute flavour themselves are standard-rated.

Other additives: by concession, zero-rating applies to baking powder, cream of tartar and rennet. Pectin is zero-rated if supplied in retail packs for culinary use.

HMRC consider that bicarbonate of soda is always standard-rated (however see *Phoenix Foods Ltd* below), as are saltpetre and other single chemicals that may be sold for use in the brining or other processing of meats or fish.

(VAT Notice 701/14/15, para 3.2).

Phoenix Foods Ltd (PFL) supplied dried powdered and granular products to retailers. PFL purchased bicarbonate of soda in bulk which it repackaged for resale to certain retailers. The product packaging for Tesco's own brand described the product as 'a versatile raising agent for soda bread, cookies and gingerbread'. The packaging for Lidl described the product as 'a gentle raising agent for use in sticky toffee pudding, cookies, gingerbread, soda bread and a wide range of recipes'. The packaging also referred to the fact that the product could also be used around the house for cleaning, deodorising and as a mild abrasive. PFL zero-rated the bicarbonate of soda supplied to Tesco and Lidl as they considered it to be a food of the kind used for human consumption. HMRC however considered that the product was standard-rated as it was a generic product with a wide variety of uses and the question of whether it should be treated as food fit for human consumption should be determined by the nature of the product and not by how it is marketed.

The First-tier Tribunal considered that the product was intended to be used as a baking ingredient primarily and, even though the product supplied to Lidl did indicate that it could be used for other purposes, the packaging was consistent with it being primarily intended to be used as a culinary ingredient. In this case, the bicarbonate of soda was supplied in a form that was intended to be primarily used as a baking ingredient and therefore comes within the scope of *VATA 1994, Sch 8, Group 1, Item 1*. Appeal allowed. (*Phoenix Foods Ltd v HMRC* [2018] UKFTT 18 (TC), (TC06296) (TVC 29.98A)).

Commercial food manufacture

Many substances are used in the preparation of commercially produced foodstuffs which would not be used in the domestic kitchen. The distinction between standard and zero-rated products is largely the distinction between zero-rated ingredients (which are included for their nutritional content and are food products in their own right) and standard-rated additives (which are included for other than strictly nutritional reasons and are not themselves food).

Ingredients

Most ingredients in commercial food production are the same as those used in home cooking and baking and clearly foodstuffs in their own right. As a general principle, any edible product supplied for incorporation as ingredients in foodstuffs be zero-rated if

(a) it has some measurable nutritional content;
(b) it is used solely or predominantly, in the particular form in which it is supplied, in the manufacture of food; and
(c) it is not one of the *excepted items*.

Products which do not meet these criteria are standard-rated as food additives with the exception of flavourings (natural and synthetic) which may be zero-rated provided they meet the criteria in (*b*) and (*c*) above. This includes sausage skins (see *Devro Ltd* (VTD 7570) (TVC 29.94)).

Additives

Products supplied for incorporation in foodstuffs which do not meet the requirements in (*a*)–(*c*) above are treated as additives and standard-rated. They are generally included for commercial reasons (e.g. to prolong shelf life) and do not fall within the everyday meaning of the word 'food' (see **25.2** above). This includes

- preservatives including unflavoured wet and dry brine mixes and cures for curing or salting meats
- anti-oxidants including vitamins A and E
- vitamin supplements (including those required by law to fortify flour before it can be put on the market)
- stabilisers and thickening agents (e.g. agar, carageenan, guar gum, gum arabic, gum tragacanth and xanthan gum, but not corn starch)
- fillers and bulking agents other than flour and starch
- colourants other than naturally-derived colourings which are also culinary spices in their own right (e.g. caramel, cocoa, saffron, turmeric and cochineal)
- flavour enhancers (e.g. monosodium glutamate), ribonucleotides and hydrolysed vegetable protein
- flour improvers and bleaching agents

Some commercial additives are accepted for VAT purposes as food in their own right. These are

- food grade, naturally derived emulsifiers and stabilisers (e.g. lecithin) specifically tailored and mixed for food purposes which are essential to the production of that food and cannot be used for any other purpose
- artificial sweeteners and artificial flavourings

(VAT Notice 701/14/15, paras 5.1–5.3).

Mixed supplies and assortments

[25.13] There is a mixed supply if standard and zero-rated food items, or zero-rated food items and standard-rated non-food items) are supplied together for a single price. Examples of mixed supplies containing foodstuffs include

- food hampers
- special gift or presentation packs containing linked items (e.g. coffee supplied with a mug, tea with a pack of chocolate biscuits)
- linked goods promotions
- food supplied in or with re-usable storage containers

Normally, the total price must be apportioned in order to arrive at the output tax due. See **48.3 OUTPUT TAX** for the general rules on the treatment of mixed supplies and various methods of apportionment.

Linked goods concession

Where, however, a *minor* standard-rated item is supplied with a main zero-rated item, the supply can be treated as a single supply of the main zero-rated item provided the standard-rated item

- is not charged at a separate price;
- costs no more than 20% of the total cost of the supply; and
- costs no more than £1 (excluding VAT).

Once these conditions have been met, the linked goods are treated as a single zero-rated supply throughout the distribution chain. A wholesaler or retailer receiving goods already linked, and who is unsure whether the conditions have been met, should refer to the supplier's supporting documentation and, if still in doubt, check with the supplier.

In *Supercook UK LLP* (TC00332) (TVC 29.92), S sold kits for making 'chocolate-flavoured lollies'. The kits comprised a plastic tray of moulds, lolly sticks, edible icing and chocolate-flavoured edible buttons. HMRC contended that the principal element of each supply was the tray and the sticks, so that the supplies were standard-rated. The tribunal found that since the buttons contained no cocoa they were not 'chocolate'; the lollies were not 'ice lollies'; and the buttons and icing were not 'confectionery'. Accordingly none of the edible components of the supply were excluded from zero-rating. They represented more than 81% of the total cost, whereas the mould and the sticks represented less than 19%. The principal element of each supply was of 'food', and the mould and sticks were ancillary, so that the whole of the consideration qualified for zero-rating.

Mixtures and assortments

Some food contains mixtures which are both zero-rated and standard-rated when supplied separately. Generally, the tax value of each part must be ascertained to calculate VAT due. See **48.3** OUTPUT TAX. However, the following products, containing only small quantities of standard-rated items, may, by concession, be treated as a single zero-rated supply.

- Assortments of biscuits where the weight of standard-rated chocolate biscuits (see **25.6** above) does not exceed 15% of total net weight.
- Fruit and nut mixes (including Bombay and similar savoury mixes) where the weight of standard-rated items (e.g. sweetened fruit, chocolate pieces or roasted nuts) does not exceed 25% of total net weight.
- Petits fours where the net weight of chocolate biscuits and sweets does not exceed 15% of total net weight (25% where sweets only are included).

The concession only applies to mixtures and assortments supplied in a single pack, not to 'variety' selections of individual packs.

If any of the above assortments fail to meet the conditions, they can still be treated as a single zero-rated supply if they satisfy the linked goods concession above.

(VAT Notice 701/14/15, paras 6.1, 6.2; VAT Notice 48, ESC 3.7).

For mixtures involving food packaging (e.g. containers, storage jars), see **48.7**(16) OUTPUT TAX.

Food processing

[25.14] Any work done on another person's goods is a supply of services. The supply of a treatment or process to another person's goods can be zero-rated, if by doing so, zero-rated goods are produced. [*VATA 1994, s 30(2A)*]. Processing which results in the production of a new zero-rated food product may therefore be zero-rated. Processing which does not result in the production of a new food product, or which results in the production of a standard-rated food product, is a standard-rated supply.

New goods are produced when a process alters the essential characteristics of the goods. This may include size and shape, appearance, composition, use and, specifically for food items, readiness to use or eat. For example, the process of smoking salmon is zero-rated because the new product, the smoked salmon, is a new zero-rated food item. The smoked salmon is immediately edible and thus distinct and different following the process of smoking. The process of smoking cod, on the other hand, is standard-rated as it does not produce a new zero-rated food item (because the smoked cod is not immediately edible) and the essential characteristics have not changed following the smoking.

Zero-rated processes

Meat and fish processing

- butchering carcasses including boning and jointing meat

- brining or curing pork into ham
- processing meat into sausages
- smoking trout and salmon

Fruit and vegetable processing

- drying, cleaning and coating seeds or grain to make it marketable as seed for sowing
- milling grain into flour, meal or semolina
- cooking, canning or otherwise preserving fruit and vegetables
- drying fruit
- roasting and/or grinding coffee beans
- grinding granulated sugar into caster or icing sugar

Other services

- refining crude oil into edible oil
- processing used or contaminated oil into edible oil
- processing of liquid milk into dried milk
- kneading blocks of frozen butter, adding salt and water and packing

Standard-rated processes

Meat and fish processing

- slaughtering animals without further process (see **25.24** below)
- smoking herring to make kippers
- smoking cod and haddock
- shelling shrimps, prawns or other shellfish
- skinning fish

Fruit and vegetable processing

- cleaning and conditioning grain
- drying grain
- harvesting crops
- malting barley
- blending tea
- roasting or salting peanuts or other nuts

Other services

- sorting, grading or packaging any product
- maturing cheese or any other product (effectively a process of storage during which a natural change occurs)
- pasteurisation or sterilisation
- supervision of foodstuffs to ensure that manufactured and prepared foods meet religious dietary regulations

(VAT Notice 701/40/11, paras 1.1–1.4, 2.1, 2.2).

Animal feeding stuffs

[25.15] The supply of 'animal' feeding stuffs is zero-rated. '*Animal*' includes bird, fish, crustacean and mollusc. [*VATA 1994, Sch 8 Group 1 General Item* 2].

Most commodities recognised as animal feeds are zero-rated unless

- sold for non-food purposes (e.g. bedding, packaging, thatching, fertiliser); or
- 'held out for sale' (see **25.1** above) as pet food or food for wild birds (see **25.19** below).

Zero-rated items

Zero-rated items (subject to the above) include the following.

- Cereal and cereal by-products including bran, sharps and similar residues
- Compound feeds consisting of a number of different ingredients (including major minerals, trace elements, vitamins and other additives), mixed and blended in appropriate proportions to provide properly balanced diets for all types of livestock at every stage of growth and development
- Feed blocks
- Fish meal and fish residue meal
- Forage crops
- Ground oyster shell
- Hay and straw unless held out for sale for non-feed purposes (e.g. bedding). In the case of straw holding out for sale for non-food use includes supplies to customers known to be market gardeners or other horticultural concerns and industrial packers or other non-agricultural businesses
- Molasses
- Oils and fats (including tallow) suitable for use in animal feeding stuffs unless *either* they require further processing before becoming suitable for inclusion in animal feeds *or* are held out for sale for non-feed purposes. Waste oil from fish and chip shops, etc. normally requires processing and is therefore standard-rated (a need for sieving, decanting or heating does not disqualify the oil from zero-rating)
- Oilseed residue (except castor oil)
- Peanuts
- Protein concentrates
- Rabbit food
- Specialised diets formulated for laboratory animals
- Specialised diets formulated for racing greyhounds (other than biscuit or meal)
- Straights
- Supplements. Nutritional supplements are zero-rated (whether intended to be added to normal feed or given separately, e.g. in pill or capsule form). Included are grit (soluble and insoluble) for poultry and game; and mineral blocks, mixes and licks. Supplements designed for pet species, and held out for sale for pets, are standard-rated

Standard-rated items

Standard-rated items include the following.

- Additives

- Bait (e.g. lugworms, maggots) except for fish of a kind and quality suitable for human consumption which may be zero-rated. See also *Fluff Ltd (t/a Mag-It) v C & E Commrs*, QB 2000, [2001] STC 674 (TVC 29.115)
- Castor oil seed residue
- Single chemicals and minerals, other than salt (even when fed direct to animals)
- Thatching material (e.g. Norfolk reed, wheat reed or straw reed)
- Urea (unless specifically held out for sale for animal feeding purposes)

(VAT Notice 701/15/11, paras 5.1, 5.3, 5.4, 9.3, 9.5, 9.7, 9.8).

Keep of animals and grazing rights, etc.

Keep of animals

[25.16] The supply of the keep of animals is standard-rated. Even if animal feed is supplied as part of the service of keeping animals, the full consideration for the service provided is standard-rated, i.e. the feed cannot be treated as a separate zero-rated supply.

Grazing rights

The granting of grazing rights (i.e. the right to allow someone else's animal(s) to graze on your land, also known as grass keep letting) is zero-rated as a supply of animal feeding stuffs (i.e. grass). However, if an element of 'care' for the animal(s) is included, then the supply becomes that of the keep of animals and the whole consideration is standard-rated as above. In this context 'care' includes turning the animals out to graze, feeding, mucking out, spreading straw or other bedding, exercising, and taking on behalf of the owner any responsibility for the welfare of the animal(s) beyond a minimal 'seen daily' or 'twice daily' arrangement.

Stabling services

Where a business rents stabling to a horse owner then, provided the owner is allowed exclusive use of the stabling (i.e. is allocated all or an identifiable part of the stabling for the sole use of their horse), there is a supply of a right over land. This is an exempt supply unless the business has exercised the option to tax (see **42.23** LAND AND BUILDINGS: EXEMPT SUPPLIES AND OPTION TO TAX). Where the business does not make a supply of a right over land, the supply is standard-rated.

Where, in conjunction with a supply of stabling, the owner is also supplied with feed (either as general animal feed or in the form of grazing rights) this can be treated as a separate zero-rated supply of animal feeding stuffs *provided* that there is no element of care. If any elements of care are present, then there is a single supply of the keep of animals, and the whole supply is standard-rated (see above).

Livery services

Livery services are services provided for horses in a stable that go beyond the right to occupy the stable. They may include feeding or turning the animal out to graze; mucking out, spreading straw or other bedding; worming and clipping; grooming and plaiting; or taking on any responsibility for the welfare of the animal, including arranging for veterinary treatment (but not clearly identifiable separate supplies such as vets' services).

The supply of livery services must be standard-rated, including any food provided, unless the stabling is an exempt right over land that the business has not opted to tax.

If the supply of stabling is a right over land and the business has not opted to tax it, the whole livery package is exempt unless it is provided by a special purpose stable. Livery packages provided by special purpose stables (such as race horse trainers, stud farms and stables involved in schooling horses or breaking them in) are standard-rated. (See *Window* [2001] Lexis Citation 693 (TVC 41.16)).

D-I-Y livery is a supply of stabling only (see above).

(VAT Notice 701/15/11, paras 10.1–10.3; Business Brief 21/01).

Products which may be used both as animal feed and for other purposes

[25.17] Many products sold as animal feed ingredients have other uses. In deciding the VAT liability of these products, it is necessary to determine whether the trader is supplying the product as zero-rated animal feed or some other standard-rated supply.

The borderline between feed and medicine

[25.18] Purely medicinal products are not covered by the zero rate even where they are administered in an animal's feed. The VAT liability of feeding stuffs incorporating medicines is determined by the basic nature of the product. A product is zero-rated only if the addition of medicinal substances does not alter the essential nature of the product as a feeding stuff. As a general guideline, a product is standard-rated if it is the subject of a product licence or marketing authorisation issued by the Department for Environment, Food and Rural Affairs.

Probiotics, which act on the digestive system but have no nutritional value in themselves, are always standard-rated.

(VAT Notice 701/15/11, paras 5.2, 9.4).

Pet food

[25.19] The following items are standard-rated.

(a) Pet food which is canned, 'packaged' or 'prepared'. [*VATA 1994, Sch 8 Group 1 Excepted Item 6*]

Meaning of 'pet': there is no definition of 'pet' in *VATA 1994*. In *Popes Lane Pet Food Supplies* (VTD 2186) (TVC 29.199) the tribunal suggested that a pet was 'an animal (tamed if it was originally wild) which is kept primarily as an object of affection [including] an animal kept primarily for ornament.' On this basis, HMRC regard the following animal species as 'pet species' in that the great majority of that species are kept and reared as objects of affection.

- Cage birds.
- Cats.
- Dogs (but see below for working dogs and racing greyhounds).
- Ferrets.
- Goldfish, aquarium fish and pond fish.
- Guinea pigs.
- Hamsters, gerbils, rats and mice (except rats and mice bred specifically for the laboratory).

Other species (including most farm animals) can be as clearly identified as 'non-pets'.

Between these extremes are animals that are not pet species but which may be kept as pets (e.g. chickens, horses and ponies, rabbits, reptiles and sheep). Their food can be zero-rated unless it is packaged or held out for sale in a way that shows it is intended for a pet. Tribunals have also treated dogs as within this category, distinguishing between pet dogs and working dogs (e.g. sheep dogs, police dogs, guard dogs, gun dogs and packs of hounds). See *Popes Lane Pet Food Supplies* above, *LJ & H Norgate (t/a Dog's Dinner)* (VTD 5241) (TVC 29.202) and *Peters & Riddles (t/a Mill Lane Farm Shop)* (VTD 12937) (TVC 29.203). In *Supreme Petfoods Ltd* (TC00896) (TVC 29.206) the tribunal held that ferrets could be classified generally as a pet species, notwithstanding that a minority were kept as working ferrets.

'*Packaged*' means pre-packed for retail sale in a sealed bag, carton or other container of 12.5 kilograms or less. Putting a loose product in a plain paper or polythene bags at the point of sale (whether after purchase by the customer or in anticipation of sales) is not considered packaging. See *B Beresford* (VTD 9673) (TVC 29.206).

'*Prepared*' means having undergone any of the following (or similar) processes.

(1) Products, other than food for working dogs (see below) and food for human consumption, which have undergone any of the following processes are pet food and are standard-rated however they are held out for sale.
  - The addition of colouring, flavouring, preservative or gelling agents (e.g. sodium metabisulphite).
  - The mixing or blending of ingredients to meet specific nutritional requirements of a pet species (e.g. blending a mix of cereal products specifically for hamsters).
  - The cooking of meats or meat products.
  - The mixing or blending of four or more meats, fish or fish and meat products.

(2) Products which have undergone any of the following processes are animal food but are standard-rated only if they are packaged or held out for sale as pet food
  - Mixing or blending of different ingredients (other than those described in (1) above).

- Washing or polishing.
- Cooking (except meat or meat products, see (1) above).
- Mincing, dicing and similar processes (except meat for dogs, see below).
- Inclusion of additives.

Food for working dogs: food claimed as suitable for all breeds is standard-rated. But food which is specially formulated and held out for sale exclusively for

- working sheep dogs of any breed,
- dogs trained and used as gun dogs, or
- racing greyhounds

can be zero-rated unless it is biscuit or meal (see (*c*) below).

Dead animals: dead mice, rats and day old chicks sold for feeding to 'exotic' pets (e.g. reptiles) may be zero-rated unless they are specifically prepared or canned or otherwise packaged as pet food. See **25.21** below for sales of live animals.

(b) Bird food

Packaged foods (not being pet food) for birds other than poultry (see **25.22** below) and game is standard-rated. [*VATA 1994, Sch 8 Group 1 Excepted Item 6*].

Cage birds

Cage birds (e.g. budgerigars, finches, parrots, etc.) are treated as a 'pet species' (see (*a*) above). Food for such birds is therefore treated as pet food. Prepared foods include mixes specifically designed for cage bird species and seeds compressed into blocks, millet sprays or seeds and sunflower seed. Packaged foods include packaged seeds.

Wild bird food

Any food which is both packaged and held out for sale for feeding to wild birds (other than poultry or game) is standard-rated. As well as ordinary retail packages (see above), special packs (e.g. 'bird nets' of food designed for hanging from a tree or bird table) are standard-rated.

Special mixes of foods for wild birds are zero-rated provided they are not packaged for retail sale.

Other birds

Zero-rating can be applied to

- food for game birds;
- pigeon food (unless containing ingredients similar to food for caged birds when standard-rated); and
- pigeon grit.

(c) **Biscuits and meal for cats and dogs.** [*VATA 1994, Sch 8 Group 1 Excepted Item 6*]

Biscuits and meal for cats and dogs is standard-rated whether or not for pet animals and whether or not sold packaged or loose. HMRC regard the terms 'biscuit' and 'meal' as meaning dry products either

- coarsely ground basic commodities; or
- baked products consisting predominantly of cereal and fat and not providing all the nutrients required by the animal.

(VAT Notice 701/15/11, paras 6.1–6.5, 7.2–7.5, 8.1–8.5, 9.2).

Seeds and plants

[25.20] Plants grown as food for human consumption or animal feeding stuffs are zero-rated under *VATA 1994, Sch 8 Group 1 General Items 1 and 2*. See **25.2** *et seq* and **25.15** *et seq* above. Any crop that generally produces items that are not fed to humans or animals (i.e. for 'industrial' purposes) is always standard-rated.

Seeds or other means of propagation of plants used for human consumption or animal feeding stuffs are also zero-rated. [*VATA 1994, Sch 8 Group 1 General Item 3*].

Examples of zero-rated plants and seeds

- Seeds, seedlings, crowns, spores, tubers and bulbs of edible vegetables and fruit.
- Mushroom spawn.
- Cucumber and tomato 'rootstock'.

Examples of standard-rated plants and seeds

- Plants that are primarily grown for their ornamental effect (e.g. ornamental nursery stock including trees, shrubs, herbaceous plants, alpines and pot plants).
- Seeds, tubers, bulbs, corms, crowns, rhizomes, cuttings, etc. of flowers (but see (5) below for seeds producing edible flowers).
- Cut flowers which are bought for their ornamental effect.
- Plants, seeds and fruit of a kind used for the production of perfumes, pharmaceutical products, insecticides, fungicides and other non-food uses (e.g. evening primrose which is grown for the extraction of its oils and Norfolk reed which is grown for thatching material).
- Any produce which is 'held out for sale' as pet food or packaged as food for birds other than poultry or game (see **25.19** above).
- Any produce which is 'held out for sale' for non-food purposes.
- Rootstock (plants, usually the common thorn, used in the horticultural industry for grafting purposes) irrespective of whether they are used in the growing of zero-rated or standard-rated plants and trees (but not cucumber and tomato rootstocks which are zero-rated).

'*Held out for sale*' means the way a product is labelled, packaged, displayed, invoiced, advertised or promoted and the heading under which the product is listed in any catalogue, web page or price list.

In addition to the general provisions above, HMRC give the following information.

(VAT Notice 701/38/11, paras 2, 3.1, 3.2).

(1) Trees and fruit bearing shrubs

Plants, bushes and trees normally used in this country for the production of edible fruit (including nuts) are zero-rated.

HMRC regard the following as the *definitive* list of fruit-producing plants which may be zero-rated.

Almond (not 'flowering almond')	Apple	Apricot
Blackberry	Blackcurrant	Blueberry
Boysenberry	Bullace	Cherry (not 'flowering cherry')
Citrus trees (not ornamental varieties)	Cobnut	Common quince (not chaenomeles)
Cowberry	Crab (only fruiting varieties)	Cranberry
Damson	Fig	Filbert
Gages	Gooseberry	Grapevines
Hazel	Huckleberry	Loganberry
Medlar	Mulberry	Nectarine
Peach	Pear	Raspberry plum (not 'flowering plum')
Redcurrant	Strawberry	Sweet chestnut
Tayberry	Walnut	Whitecurrant
Wineberry	Worcesterberry	

(VAT Notice 701/38/11, para 3.5).

(2) Oilseed rape

Some varieties of oilseed rape are not suitable for human consumption. The liability of those that are not suitable will depend on the purpose for which they are supplied.

(a) *'OO' type*. Most oilseed rape is of this type and the oilseed yields oil fit for human consumption as well as meal for animals. These 'OO' varieties of oilseed rape, including the actual seeds and edible meal by-products, are zero-rated.

(b) *'HEAR' varieties*. These varieties of oilseed rape give a high erucic acid content in the oil and this is regarded as nutritionally undesirable in food for human consumption. The pressed oil is primarily used as an anti-corrosion agent and lubricant in mineral oil extraction and is standard-rated. The residual meal can be used to feed ruminant livestock and it is zero-rated when supplied for feeding purposes. The actual seeds of the HEAR varieties are used to plant for subsequent crops and as an animal feed and are zero-rated.

(VAT Notice 701/38/11, para 3.3).

(3) Linseed and flax

Varieties of the crop are grown for its seeds and subsequent oil and residual meal, or for its flax fibre. As the predominant use of linseed oil is for industrial purposes (e.g. paint, varnish, linoleum), it is standard-rated. The residual meal is largely used for incorporating into animal feed and can be zero-rated. Zero-rating also applies to the actual seed when used as animal feed or for sowing.

Where flax varieties are grown for the resulting fibre, both the stems (processed into linen) and the left over woody portion (used for making paper) are standard-rated. The small yield of seeds are zero-rated when used as animal feed.

(VAT Notice 701/38/11, para 3.4).

(4) Herbs

Culinary herbs

Plants of species which are generally accepted as reared primarily for culinary use are zero-rated irrespective of how they are held out for sale. These comprise the following.

Angelica	Anise	Anise hyssop
Basil	Borage	Caraway
Cardamom	Cardoon	Celery wild
Celery wild alpine	Chervil	Chicory
Chives	Coriander	Cumin
Curry leaf	Dandelion	Dill
Fennel	Fenugreek	Garlic
Ginger	Good King Henry	Horseradish
Lemon grass	Liquorice	Lovage
Marjoram	Mint	Onion
Orache	Oregano	Parsley
Pennyroyal	Rocket	Rosemary
Saffron	Sage	Salad burnet
Savory	Skirret	Sorrel
Tarragon	Thyme	Watercress

Ornamental herbs sometimes used for culinary purposes. Plants which, although not species supplied predominantly as culinary herbs, do have recognised culinary uses, may be zero-rated provided

- they have been raised according to the conditions required by *Food and Environment Protection Act 1985* (evidence of which may be required);
- they have been held out for sale (see above) as culinary herbs and, where appropriate, displayed apart from ornamentals with other culinary herbs;

- they are supplied in individual pots (not bedding strips) of a size less than two litres; and
- in the case of bay plants, they do not exceed 50cm in height and have not been clipped, shaped or topiarized in such a way as to specialise them as ornamentals.

Provided the above conditions are satisfied, the following herbs can also be zero-rated.

Alecost	Alexanders	Allspice
Asafoetida	Bay	Bergamot
Bistort	Catmint	Chamomile
Comfrey	Clove pink	Clover
Cowslip	Curry plant	Elder
Feverfew	Hop	Hyssop
Juniper	Landcress	Lavender
Lemon balm	Lemon verbena	Marigold, pot
Melilot	Nasturtium, salad	Pelarqonium (scented)
Purslane	Rue	Sweet Cecily
Tansy	Violet (sweet)	Woodruff

Medicinal herbs

Herbs supplied for medical rather than culinary use are not eligible for zero-rating as 'food' and are standard-rated, even if they have been raised under the same conditions as culinary herbs. This includes plants used in the preparation of food supplements (e.g. evening primrose and ginseng).

(VAT Notice 701/38/11, para 4).

(5) Seeds

All seeds that produce food of a kind for human consumption or animal feeding stuffs can be zero-rated. Included are

- vegetable seeds;
- seeds for producing culinary herbs; and
- wheat, barley and other agricultural seeds grown to produce food for human or animal consumption.

But any seed that generally produces items that are not fed to humans or animals is always standard-rated. This applies to

- seeds or bulbs for growing flowers (but see edible flowers below);
- plants and trees mainly for ornamental effect; and
- agricultural crops for industrial/non-feed use.

Seeds producing edible flowers

The seed varieties listed below are zero-rated where it can be demonstrated that they are held out for sale as food of a kind used for human consumption. For these purposes, seeds would be so held out for sale if

- the variety is indicated as edible in a catalogue (or, where no catalogue is produced, in information at the point of display);
- further details of food usage can be supplied on a customer's request; and
- food-based information is available on seed packets (e.g. recipe ideas).

Bergamot Nasturtium Poppy Violets	Clove pink Pelargonium Pot Marigold	Lavender Pink Sunflower

Grass seed

Most grass seed is zero-rated because of the extensive use of grass as animal feed. This includes supplies to and by garden centres, local authorities and grass seed to be grown on set aside land. Pre-germinated grass seed and turf are not used for the propagation of animal feed and are therefore standard-rated. See **25.15** above for supplies of hay and straw and **25.16** above for grazing rights.

Seeds that undergo a treatment or process. See **25.14** above.

Seeds sold with a book. See (6) below.

(VAT Notice 701/38/11, para 5).

(6) Plant-growing kits

Plant-growing kits typically include seeds, growing medium, fertilizer, a container, and an instruction leaflet. Such kits are generally standard-rated but may be zero-rated if the seeds are zero-rated and either

- the standard-rated element (e.g. growing medium, fertiliser and pot) accounts for less than 10% of the total cost; or
- the planting medium, which is impregnated with edible vegetable or fruit seeds, is no more than a means of simplifying the planting of the seeds (e.g. peat cubes of less than 125cc impregnated with seeds, or thin layers of tissue incorporating seeds).

(VAT Notice 701/38/11, para 6.1).

Mushroom growing kits

VAT treatment depends upon the container. If the kit is supplied in a non-reusable container, HMRC take the view that the whole supply can be zero-rated as the container is seen as normal and necessary packaging.

If the kit is supplied in a plastic bucket or similar reusable container, there may be a mixed supply, the spawn and growing medium being zero-rated and the container standard-rated. Each case needs to be judged on its own merits after consideration of general principles in *Card Protection Plan* (see **65.6 SUPPLY: GENERAL**). See also the decisions in *Kimberley-Clark Ltd v C & E Commrs*, Ch

D [2004] STC 473 (TVC 12.26) (which related to nappies sold in a plastic reusable box) and *Cheshire Mushroom Farm* [1974] Lexis Citation 9 (TVC 29.126) (although the latter case preceded the judgment in *Card Protection Plan*).

(VAT Notice 701/38/11, para 6.2).

Live animals

[25.21] The 'supply' of 'animals' of a kind generally used as, or yielding or producing, food for human consumption is zero-rated. '*Supply*' includes sale, hire or loan and supply of a part interest (a share) as '*animals*' include birds, fish, crustacea and molluscs. [*VATA 1994, Sch 8 Group 1 General Item 4*].

Examples of zero-rated animals are

- meat animals;
- dairy animals;
- poultry (see **25.22** below) including those for egg production;
- honey bees; and
- fish (except ornamental breeds and coarse fish), including those for production of edible roes (see **25.23** below).

Examples of standard-rated animals are

- bumble bees;
- ornamental birds and fish;
- racing pigeons; and
- horses.

The test is whether the animal is of a kind generally used as, or yielding or producing, food for human consumption. Subject to this, the actual use does not matter. For example:

- Kangaroo steak may be sold as food in shops but kangaroos are not animals of a kind generally reared for food in the UK so that live kangaroos are standard-rated.
- Rabbits, other than ornamental breeds, are animals of a kind that is normally used for human food production and are therefore always zero-rated even if kept as pets.
- Sheep kept mainly for their wool, or bulls used for breeding, are zero-rated because they are animals of a kind normally producing food for human consumption.

Animals which are removed from the human food chain because they are no longer fit for human consumption (e.g. because of disease) are standard-rated.

Embryos, eggs and semen for breeding

Embryos of species which are normally used for human food may be zero-rated if they are to be used for breeding. Anything below the embryo stage is standard-rated. Eggs and fish roes which are normally used for food for human consumption and are fit for such use are always zero-rated.

(VAT Notice 701/15/11, paras 2.1–2.8).

Birds

[25.22] Most breeds of chicken are zero-rated, as are game birds and ostriches. Ornamental breeds of birds are standard-rated.

The following breeds of ducks, geese and turkeys are zero-rated.

- Ducks (Aylesbury, Campbell (Khaki Campbell), Indian Runner, Muscovy, Pekin and derivatives and crossbreeds of these).
- Geese (Brecon Buff, Chinese Commercial, Embdem, Roman, Toulouse and derivatives and crossbreeds of these).
- Turkeys (Beltsville White, British White, Broadbreasted White, Bronze (Broadbreasted Bronze), Norfolk Black and derivatives and crossbreeds of these).

(VAT Notice 701/15/11, para 3.1).

Fish

[25.23] The VAT liability of fish is as follows.

- *Freshwater fish*. Eels, salmon and trout and others recognised as food for human consumption are zero-rated. Bream, perch, pike, carp and tench are standard-rated.
- *Shellfish*. Oysters, mussels, whelks, etc. are zero-rated but non-food species are standard-rated.
- *Fish for aquaria* are standard-rated.
- *Fish used as* bait. Fish of a kind used for, and fit for, human consumption are zero-rated. All other supplies are standard-rated.
- *Ornamental fish* are standard-rated. See *JR Chalmers* (VTD 1433) (TVC 29.126) for koi carp.

(VAT Notice 701/15/11, para 3.2).

Abattoirs

Processing generally

[25.24] Any work done on another person's goods is a supply of services. The supply of a treatment or process to another person's goods can be zero-rated, if by doing so, zero-rated goods are produced. [*VATA 1994, s 30(2A)*]. Processing which results in the production of a new zero-rated food product may therefore be zero-rated. Processing which does not result in the production of a new food product, or which results in the production of a standard-rated food product, is a standard-rated supply. New goods are produced when a process alters the essential characteristics of the goods. This may include size and shape, appearance, composition, use and, specifically for food items, readiness to use or eat.

Slaughtering and dressing

The service of slaughtering animals without applying further processes is standard-rated (see *Darlington Borough Council* (VTD 961) (TVC 29.101)). If other processes are applied at the same time to produce new zero-rated goods, for example, dressing the carcass, then the whole supply is zero-rated. Not all services of slaughtering and dressing produce new zero-rated goods. The liability of some of the goods produced by abattoirs is considered below.

Standard-rated goods

Goods produced in abattoirs are standard-rated if

- held out for sale for a non-feeding purpose, e.g. blood for fertiliser (normally recognisable by declaration of nitrogen/phosphoric acid content);
- used for a non-feeding purpose, e.g. hair, hides, horns, hoofs, manure, pelts, skins and wool;
- held out for sale without further process as canned, packaged or prepared pet food (see **25.19** above);
- they have undergone some further preparation beyond mincing and dicing, which would specialise the products to the pet food market (see **25.19** above); or
- used exclusively in the preparation of pharmaceutical products, e.g. gall bags, glands, ovaries, placenta.

Greaves supplied in pieces of a size suitable for feeding to pets are also standard-rated.

Zero-rated goods

Goods produced in abattoirs are zero-rated if

- they are fit for human consumption; or
- they are animal materials, used in the manufacture of food for animals or pets, and
  - (a) the *Animal By Products Order 1992* permits the use of the materials, and
  - (b) the animal materials are used in premises approved by that *Order*.

Examples of zero-rated goods from cattle, sheep, goats and pigs are

- *Organs* including bladders, hearts, kidneys, livers, lungs or lites, manifolds, pancreas glands, rede, stomach, and sweetbreads (pancreas only in cattle);
- *Body parts* including bones, feet, paddywacks, runners (except cattle), tails, udders and weasand; and
- *Fluids and tissue* including blood, dripping, fat (provided it is not attached to specific risk material), and meat.

Other zero-rated parts commonly produced from cattle include melts (from calves under six months), tripe and vells.

Incidental supplies

Where the services of slaughtering and then processing the carcass produce new standard-rated and zero-rated goods (e.g. standard-rated skins and zero-rated foodstuffs)

- if the standard-rated goods are incidental to the main zero-rated supply back to the owner of the animal, the whole supply is zero-rated; and
- if the new standard-rated goods are the main element of the supply to the owner of the animal, and the zero-rated goods are incidental, then the whole supply is standard-rated.

Ancillary services supplied by abattoirs

Supplies of separate ancillary services are normally standard-rated, for example

- cold storage;
- pennage;
- carriage; and
- porterage.

If specific stalls or pens are allocated for the exclusive use of a customer, the supply is exempt from VAT (subject to the option to tax being exercised, see **42.23 LAND AND BUILDINGS: EXEMPT SUPPLIES AND OPTION TO TAX**).

Agriculture and Horticulture Development Board (AHDB)

There is a levy in two parts: on slaughterers and livestock exporters; and on livestock producers. The levy is absorbed and paid to AHDB by the slaughterers/exporters, of which 50% is to be reclaimed statutorily from the producer. The levy is payment for a range of benefits received from AHDB and includes VAT.

A *slaughterer* is charged the whole amount of levy by the AHDB, and then must recharge the producers 50% of the levy. AHDB provides one invoice to the slaughterer confirming the amount of levy and the output and input tax due. The slaughterer can recover the VAT charged on his 50% of the general levy as input tax, subject to the normal rules. As he acts as agent for AHDB in recharging their part of the levy to the producers, he must account for the VAT as follows.

- The input tax he incurred on the rechargeable elements of the levy may be recovered in full.
- He must charge, and account for in the same period, a corresponding amount of output tax to the producers.

A producer can recover the VAT charged to him by the slaughterer as input tax, subject to the normal rules.

An exporter of live animals must follow the above procedures to account for VAT on levies incurred and recharged.

(VAT Notice 700/57/14; VAT Notice 701/40/11; VAT Notice 701/15/11, para 9.1).

Key points: food

[25.25] Points to consider are as follows.

- A fundamental principle of the rules concerning VAT and food is that a supply of any food intended for consumption on the premises where it is sold is standard-rated. The same outcome applies if food is served hot and is for take-away consumption. There have been a number of tribunal cases over the years that have challenged both the meanings of 'hot' and 'premises' as far as the legislation is concerned.
- A key conclusion in recent years has been that 'premises' only includes an immediate area surrounding an outlet, not the wider area such as entire sports stadium. This outcome gives more scope for zero-rating of cold take away food sold by a business in such cases.
- There are a number of specific items that are excluded from the zero-rating provisions in relation to food. These exceptions include confectionery items, alcoholic drinks, and snacks such as crisps. It is important that any business selling food items is very clear about the items that qualify for zero-rating and, equally importantly, those that are exceptions to the zero-rating provisions and are therefore standard-rated.
- A retail business selling both standard-rated and zero-rated items must have proper accounting procedures in place to ensure the mix of takings is properly identified at the point of sale. The relevant split will need to be accurately recorded in the books and records of the business on a daily basis and output tax must be correctly declared on a VAT return.
- HMRC visiting officers will be keen to ensure that zero-rated sales are not being overstated by, for example, the wrong till button being entered at the point of sale. They are likely to apply an overall mark-up calculation to zero-rated and standard-rated purchases to check that the declared output tax figures are credible.
- HMRC officers will also be keen to ensure that staff involved in selling goods where more than one rate of tax is applicable (e.g. cashiers in a supermarket) are properly trained in till management procedures. This would be particularly relevant if goods do not have a pre-coded bar reader that will automatically determine the rate of VAT at the point of sale.
- Some retail schemes base output tax payments on the ratio of standard-rated and zero-rated purchases made by a business, or by applying a mark-up to either zero-rated or standard-rated purchases. In the case of many businesses selling food, these schemes will not be suitable because of the hot food or consumption on premises provisions. For example, a meat pie would be zero-rated when purchased from a wholesaler but standard-rated if supplied as either a hot product (take away or on the premises

where sold) or a cold product on the premises where it is sold.

26

Fuel and Power

Cross-reference. See **22.4 EXPORTS** for stores for use in ships, aircraft and hovercraft; **67.15 SUPPLY: TIME OF SUPPLY** for the time of supply rules; **75.2 ZERO-RATED SUPPLIES** for supplies of hot water and steam.

De Voil Indirect Tax Service. See V4.406.

Introduction to fuel and power

[26.1] The supply of any form of power, heat, refrigeration or other cooling, or ventilation is a supply of goods (and not a supply of services). [*VATA 1994, Sch 4 para 33*].

The rates of VAT on supplies of fuel and power are as follows.

4.1.11 onwards	5% for 'qualifying use' 20% for all other supplies

The reduced rates also apply to acquisitions from other EU member states and importations from outside the EU.

[*VATA 1994, ss 2(1A)–(1C), 29A(1)(2)*].

Qualifying use

[26.2] '*Qualifying use*' means domestic use or use by a charity otherwise than in the course or furtherance of a business.

The following *de minimis* supplies are always supplies for domestic use, even when supplied to a business.

(a) A supply of not more than one tonne of coal or coke held out for sale as domestic fuel. The weight limit of one tonne applies to the total delivered weight of all types of such coal or coke supplied at any one time, not to the weight of supplies of individual products (e.g. lignite, anthracite, etc.).

(b) A supply of wood, peat or charcoal not intended for sale by the recipient (regardless of the amount supplied).

(c) A supply to a person at any premises of '*piped gas*' (i.e. gas within **26.4** below, or petroleum gas in a gaseous state, provided through pipes) where the gas (together with any other piped gas provided to him at the premises by the same supplier) was not provided at a rate exceeding 150 therms a month or, if the supplier charges for gas by reference to the number of kilowatt hours supplied, 4397 kilowatt hours a month. (This limit applies whether the bill is based on a meter reading or on an estimate.)

(d) A supply of petroleum gas in a liquid state where the gas is supplied in cylinders the net weight of each of which is less than 50 kilogrammes and either the number of cylinders supplied is 20 or fewer or the gas is not intended for sale by the recipient.

(e) A supply of petroleum gas in a liquid state, otherwise than in cylinders, to a person at any premises at which he is not able to store more than two tonnes of such gas.

(f) A supply of not more than 2,300 litres of fuel oil, gas oil or kerosene. HMRC regard a supply for this purpose as comprising all deliveries to the same customer at the same site on the same day. This is the case even if separate delivery notes or invoices are issued. Deliveries that take place on different days or to different sites are regarded as separate supplies, even if a single invoice is raised for more than one delivery. Supplies of different products (e.g. fuel oil and gas oil) are always regarded as separate supplies. But supplies of different types of the same product (e.g. different grades of kerosene) must not be broken down into each type when considering whether the *de minimis* limit has been exceeded.

(g) A supply of electricity to a person at any premises where the electricity (together with any other electricity provided to him at the premises by the same supplier) was not provided at a rate exceeding 1,000 kilowatt hours a month. (This limit applies whether the bill is based on a meter reading or on an estimate.)

Supplies not within (*a*)–(*g*) above are supplies for domestic use if, and only if, the goods supplied are supplied for use in

(i) a building, or part of a building, which consists of a dwelling or number of dwellings or which is used for a 'relevant residential purpose';

(ii) self-catering holiday accommodation (including any accommodation advertised or held out as such);

(iii) a caravan; or

(iv) a 'houseboat' i.e. a boat or other floating decked structure designed or adapted for use solely as a place of permanent habitation and not having means of, or capable of being readily adapted for, self-propulsion.

Use for a *'relevant residential purpose'* means use as a home or other institution providing residential accommodation either for children or with personal care for persons in need of such care by reason of old age, disablement, past or present dependence on alcohol or drugs or past or present mental disorder; a hospice; residential accommodation for students or school pupils or members of any of the armed forces; a monastery, nunnery or similar establishment; or an institution which is the sole or main residence of at least 90% of its residents. *Excluded* is use as a hospital, a prison or similar institution or an hotel or inn or similar establishment.

[*VATA 1994, Sch 7A Group 1, Notes 3, 5, 6, 7*]. (VAT Notice 701/19/16, paras 6.1, 7.1).

The following are treated as a part of the same residential unit.

- Buildings such as garages used with houses.
- Subsidiary buildings situated a short distance away (e.g. a garage in a block located away from the house).
- Corridors, lifts, hallways and stairways in a residential unit.

(VAT Notice 701/19/16, para 3.2).

Part qualifying use

Where a supply of fuel or power is partly for qualifying use and partly not, then provided at least 60% is supplied for qualifying use, the whole supply is to be treated as a supply for qualifying use. In any other case, an apportionment must be made. [*VATA 1994, Sch 7A Group 1, Note 4*].

Certificates

If in doubt about the liability of the supply under (i)–(iv) above, the supplier should get a certificate from the customer declaring what percentage of the fuel or power supplied for use at each premises is for qualifying use. A certificate is not required if the supply falls within (*a*)–(*g*) above. The following information should be shown on the certificate.

- Supplier's name and address.
- Customer's name, address and, if applicable, VAT registration number.
- Address of the premises to which the supply relates.
- Amount of qualifying use expressed as a percentage of the total use. A precise percentage should always be given. Do not say 'over 60%' or use any similar form of words.
- A declaration given by a responsible officer or official of the customer as to the truth and accuracy of the facts given. This should include
  - (i) the signature, name, and position of the person giving the declaration;
  - (ii) the date on which it is made; and
  - (iii) an endorsement that the customer has read and understood the guidance, and that they know they must notify the supplier if there is a change in the qualifying use.

If any supply is incorrectly charged at the reduced rate, the supplier may have to pay any VAT undercharged unless he holds a valid certificate *and* has good reason to believe that the fuel or power supplied to the customer is for qualifying use. It is the supplier's responsibility to take reasonable steps to satisfy himself that the customer is entitled to be charged at the reduced rate and the declaration is correct. Where, however, despite taking all reasonable steps, the supplier fails to identify the inaccuracy and in good faith makes the supplies concerned at the reduced rate, HMRC will not seek to recover the VAT due from the supplier. (VAT Notice 48, ESC 3.11).

(VAT Notice 701/19/16, para 3.5).

See **53.26 PENALTIES** for the penalty for giving an incorrect certificate.

Solid fuels

[26.3] Supplies of coal, coke and other solid substances are taxable at the reduced rate provided they are held out for sale solely as fuel and are supplied for qualifying use (see **26.2** above). Included are combustible materials put up for sale for kindling fires but not matches. [*VATA 1994, Sch 7A Group 1 Item 1(a) and Note 1*]. All other supplies of solid fuels are standard-rated.

To be taxable at the reduced rate, the fuel must be offered in a form and at a price that is compatible with it being sold as fuel.

'*Held out for sale*' as fuel means that the supplier advertises and otherwise describes the product at its point of sale as fuel or firewood, and that this is consistent with the packaging and wrapping in which it is supplied.

Reduced-rate supplies

Provided the conditions for qualifying use are met, the reduced rate can be applied to the following solid fuels.

- Coal (including anthracite and lignite)
- Coal dust
- Coal briquettes
- Coke (e.g. Coalite, Thermabrite, Coalite Nuts, Beacon Beans, Sunbrite small nuts, Blazeglow)
- Pulverised coal
- Smokeless fuel
- Wood logs
- Other firewood (including offcuts, chips, shavings, scrap or damaged wood and compresses or agglutinated sawdust)
- Barbecue fuels
- Briquettes of straw and recycled waste or other combustible materials
- Charcoal
- Firelighters
- Peat blocks, sods or briquettes
- Solid methaldehyde (solid meths)

Standard-rated supplies

The following items are always standard-rated.

- Any product not consumed in the lighting process (e.g. pumice blocks, pottery, etc soaked in paraffin, gas pokers, electric hot-air igniters)
- Artists' charcoal
- Binding agents used to convert coal dust or sawdust in blocks
- Coke for use in manufacturing
- 'DIY' offcuts and remnants
- Filtration charcoal or coke
- Forestry thinnings for fencing or staking
- Laboratory charcoal blocks
- Matches
- Peat for use in horticulture or as cattle litter
- Sawdust, chips or shavings for pet litter
- Standing trees
- Wood for pulping

(VAT Notice 701/19/16, para 7.1).

Barbecue food flavour enhancers (e.g. hickory chips) which are absorbed into the food by burning are not fuel (or food for human consumption) and are standard-rated. (VAT Notes 1992 No 1).

Gases

[26.4] Coal gas, water gas, producer gas and similar gases and petroleum gases, and other gaseous hydrocarbons, whether in a gaseous or liquid state, are taxable at the reduced rate provided they are supplied for qualifying use (see **26.2** above). Excluded is any road fuel gas (within the meaning of the *Hydrocarbon Oil Duties Act 1979*) on which excise duty has been or is chargeable. [*VATA 1994, Sch 7A Group 1 Items 1(b)(c) and Note 1*].

Reduced rate supplies

Provided the conditions for qualifying use are met, the reduced rate can be applied to liquefied petroleum gas (e.g. propane or butane), acetylene, coal gas, butylene, methane, natural gas, propylene, producer gas and water gas. Minor impurities in a hydrocarbon gas can be ignored but otherwise any such gas that does not consist entirely of carbon and hydrogen is standard-rated.

Standard-rated supplies

Supplies of all other gases (e.g. carbon dioxide, hydrogen, oxygen, ammonia, chlorine, nitrogen and refrigeration and aerosol gases) are standard-rated although certain gases for medical care (e.g. anaesthetics and oxygen) may be zero-rated under *VATA 1994, Sch 8 Group 12* or exempt under *VATA 1994, Sch 9 Group 7*.
(VAT Notice 701/19/16, paras 4.1, 4.3).

Standing charges

Gas bills include a variable consumption charge and a fixed standing charge. The standing charge represents the upkeep of the pipes required to deliver gas. For VAT purposes it is regarded as part of the charge for a supply of gas even though shown separately on bills. If the supply of gas is for qualifying use (see **26.2** above) the whole bill, including the standing charge, is taxable at the reduced rate.

Where standing charges for gas are made by a third party (e.g. a local authority) rather than the fuel supplier, they do not form part of the supply of gas and are standard-rated, regardless of the customer.

(VAT Notice 701/19/16, para 10.10).

Charges made by fuel and power suppliers

See **26.7** below.

VAT treatment in particular cases

See **26.8** below.

Special rules for place of supply and supplies by persons outside the UK

See **26.9** below.

Gas sold in cylinders and similar containers

Disposable cartridges

When gas is supplied in disposable cartridges at an inclusive price covering both gas and cartridge, the supply is standard-rated throughout the supply chain until the point of final sale. A supply of disposable cartridges at the point of final sale is taxable at the reduced rate.

Charged refillable cylinders

On the first sale of a refillable cylinder containing gas taxable at the reduced rate, the price must be apportioned and VAT accounted for on the standard-rated cylinder which becomes the property of the buyer. (The price of the cylinder should be taken as the difference between the VAT-exclusive price of the filled cylinder and the charge for refilling a customer's own cylinder.)

When a filled container is exchanged for an empty one of the same size owned by the customer, the refill charge is treated as being wholly for the supply of gas and any nominal charge for inspection and maintenance can be ignored.

Rented cylinders

On the first supply of gas in a rented cylinder, VAT must be accounted for at the standard rate on the hire charge. When an empty cylinder is exchanged for a full one of the same size, any refill charge, including any nominal charge for inspection or maintenance, can be taxed at the reduced rate (subject to qualifying use of the gas). Any charge made for a lost or damaged cylinder (such as the loss of a deposit) is outside the scope of VAT. But if a separate charge is made for the retention of a cylinder this is standard-rated.

Bulk storage tanks

Bulk storage tanks installed on customers' premises normally remain the property of the supplier. Charges for gas consumed are at the reduced rate (subject to qualifying use) but any charge specifically for repair, maintenance etc of equipment is standard-rated.

(VAT Notice 701/19/16, paras 4.5–4.8). See *Calor Gas Ltd* (VTD 47) (TVC 30.1).

Gases used as road fuel

Supplies of gases for use as road fuel are standard-rated. VAT is due on the total value including the excise duty chargeable. (VAT Notice 701/19/16, para 4.4).

Oils

[26.5] 'Fuel oil', 'gas oil' and 'kerosene' are taxable at the reduced rate provided they are supplied for qualifying use (see **26.2** above). Excluded is hydrocarbon oil on which a duty of excise has been or is to be charged without relief from, or rebate of, such duty by virtue of the provisions of the *Hydrocarbon Oil Duties Act 1979*. The exclusion does not apply to oil that is kerosene or oil for which a relevant declaration has been made under the *Hydrocarbon Oil Duties Act 1979, s 13AC(3)* (use of rebated kerosene for private pleasure flying) or *s 14E(3)* (use of rebated heavy oil for private pleasure craft). All other supplies of oil are standard-rated.

'*Fuel oil*' means heavy oil containing in solution an amount of asphaltenes of not less than 0.5 per cent or which contains less than 0.5 per cent but not less than 0.1 per cent of asphaltenes and has a closed flash point not exceeding 150°C.

'*Gas oil*' means 'heavy oil' of which not more than 50 per cent by volume distils at a temperature not exceeding 240°C and of which more than 50 per cent by volume distils at a temperature not exceeding 340°C.

'*Kerosene*' means heavy oil of which more than 50 per cent by volume distils at a temperature not exceeding 240°C.

'*Heavy oil*' has the same meaning as in the *Hydrocarbon Oil Duties Act 1979*.

Fuel oil, gas oil and kerosene chargeable with excise duty at a full (unrebated) rate, together with other heavy hydrocarbon oils, light hydrocarbon oils, lubricating oils and lubricants, are standard-rated.

[*VATA 1994, Sch 7A Group 1 Item 1(d) and Notes 1, 2*].

The effect of the above is that fuel oil, gas oil or kerosene (which includes paraffin) within the above definitions are taxed at the reduced rate provided they are supplied for qualifying use, are not supplied as road fuel and (except fuel for propelling private pleasure craft and for private pleasure flying) are either chargeable with excise duty at a rebated rate or are relieved from excise duty.

Standard-rated supplies

Standard-rated supplies include any heavy oil for use as road fuel; aviation spirit; avgas; creosote; crude oil; derv; kerosene, paint thinners or white spirit; liquid lighter fuel; waste oil; bitumen; black varnish; coal tar; lubricating oils and greases; methylated spirit; white diesel; other articles which contain hydrocarbon oil but are not themselves wholly hydrocarbon oil; petrol substitutes; and petrol and other light oils (e.g. benzene, toluene and naphtha).

(VAT Notice 701/19/16, paras 6.1, 6.2).

Marine fuel

Supplies of fuel to foreign-going vessels is zero-rated provided certain conditions are met. By concession, commercial vehicles engaged on voyages within UK territorial waters may also receive certain types of fuel VAT-free. See **22.4 EXPORTS**.

Lifeboats

Fuel supplied to a charity providing rescue at sea is zero-rated where the fuel is for use in a lifeboat. See **71.14 TRANSPORT AND FREIGHT**.

Electricity, heat and air conditioning

[26.6] Supplies of electricity, heat and air conditioning are taxable at the reduced rate provided they are supplied for qualifying use (see **26.2** above). [*VATA 1994, Sch 7A Group 1 Item 1(e)*]. All other supplies of electricity, etc. are standard-rated.

Electricity supplied by mobile generator

Where electricity is supplied through the use of a mobile generator, the liability of the supply depends upon whether the supplier is supplying the electricity or hiring out the machine.

- If the supplier operates the equipment and charges for power supplied for a qualifying use, the total charge is at the reduced rate.
- If the supplier charges for the hire of the generator to the customer, the supply is standard-rated.
- The supply of the installation of stand-by equipment is standard-rated.

Batteries

Supplies of batteries on hire, recharging of batteries or exchanging charged batteries for discharged ones are standard-rated.

Standing charges

Electricity bills include a variable consumption charge and a fixed standing charge. The standing charge represents the upkeep of the wires required to deliver electricity. For VAT purposes it is regarded as part of the charge for a supply of electricity even though shown separately on bills. If the supply of electricity is for qualifying use (see **26.2** above) the whole bill, including the standing charge, is taxable at the reduced rate.

Where standing charges for electricity are made by a third party (e.g. a local authority) rather than the fuel supplier, they do not form part of the supply of electricity and are standard-rated, regardless of the customer.

(VAT Notice 701/19/16, para 10.10).

Charges made by fuel and power suppliers

See **26.7** below.

VAT treatment in particular cases

See **26.8** below.

Special rules for place of supply and supplies by persons outside the UK

See **26.9** below.

Use of system, transmission and other charges

Where a price includes a charge for electricity and standing and/or other charges, the whole supply is taxed at the reduced rate (even if the supplier has incurred costs in making that supply that were taxed at the standard rate).

If a supplier makes a charge to allow the use of transmission or distribution lines, transformers, meters, or makes other similar supplies of services, without any supply of electricity, such supplies are always standard-rated.

Wholesale electricity trading arrangements

Generators, suppliers, and non-physical traders negotiate bilateral and multilateral contracts 'over-the-counter'. These contracts are for wholesale supplies of electricity and are standard-rated. The arrangements provide a mechanism for the settlement of imbalances between physical and contractual positions. The following elements arising from the balancing mechanism are standard-rated.

- Balancing mechanism unit cash flow
- Non-delivery charges
- Energy imbalance cash flow
- Residual element cash flow

The information imbalance charges are outside the scope of VAT.

(VAT Notice 701/19/16, paras 5.4–5.7).

Steam and heated water

Supplies of steam and heated water are not eligible for the zero-rating applicable to water (see **75.2 ZERO-RATED SUPPLIES**). Instead they are, for VAT purposes, a form of heat.

Supplies of steam and heated water for qualifying use (see **26.2** above) are taxed at the reduced rate. For these purposes

- water that has been heated as part of a treatment process but is supplied at the temperature at which it was before it was heated (i.e. after it has cooled down) is not heated water;
- water that is hot because it is drawn from a hot spring is not treated as heated water; and

- water that has been deliberately heated by geo-thermal, solar or other natural heat or energy sources is treated as heated.

(VAT Notice 701/19/16, para 8.1).

Ventilation, air-conditioning and refrigeration

Supplies of air-conditioning, refrigeration and quick-freezing for a qualifying use (see **30.2** above) are taxed at the reduced rate. Supplies of ventilation, air-conditioning or refrigeration provided from a central plant are taxable at the reduced rate when supplied for a qualifying use.

Where premises are in multiple occupation, any charges to tenants in addition to the rent which are made in respect of the common parts or areas, are treated as further payment for the right to occupy and have the same liability as the main supply. See **42.19**(6) **LAND AND BUILDINGS: EXEMPT SUPPLIES AND OPTION TO TAX.**

(VAT Notice 701/19/16, para 9).

Charges made by fuel and power suppliers

Reduced rate supplies

[26.7] Any of the charges listed below are treated as part of the payment for a reduced rate supply of fuel and power provided the charges are

(a) made by a person who supplies the fuel and power to the consumer (up to and including the meter),
(b) charged to that consumer, and
(c) inseparable from a supply of fuel or power to that consumer

and the supply of fuel and power is for a qualifying purpose;

- Disconnection and re-connection of the supply and special meter readings at the instigation of the supplier
- Installation by a supplier of liquefied petroleum gas of a bulk gas tank regarded as essential to the supply of liquefied petroleum gas
- Installation of check meters
- Installation or replacement of lines and switchgear belonging to the electricity supplier
- Installation tests and re-tests where required by the supplier to protect their equipment
- Maximum demand and minimum guarantee charges
- Removal of damaged coins from meters
- Rental charges for meters, including secondary meters used by landlords to apportion charges between their tenants
- Rental of a bulk gas tank in conjunction with the supply of liquid petroleum gas to that tank
- Repair, maintenance or replacement of equipment and gas pipes or electric cables belonging to the supplier up to and including the consumer's meter. (Where the supplier's conduits are within the fabric

of a building, reduced rate supplies by the supplier are limited to work essential for getting at the conduits, and making good. All consequential work is standard-rated. Contractors' supplies to the supplier are standard-rated.)

- Replacing a credit meter with a pre-payment meter under the supplier's Code of Practice, or replacing or re-siting by a supplier of their meter at their instigation
- Replacement of mains fuses and provisions of earthing terminals
- Standing charges (see also **26.4** and **26.6** above).

Any of the above supplies are standard-rated when supplied

- by a contractor other than the supplier of fuel and power (even if a fuel and power supplier instructs a contractor to send a bill direct to a consumer for work that would have been at the reduced rate if invoiced by the supplier); and
- by a subcontractor to a fuel and power supplier.

(VAT Notice 701/19/16, para 2.2).

Standard-rated supplies

The following supplies are always standard-rated.

- Wholesale supplies of fuel and power
- Matches
- Any road fuel gas or hydrocarbon oil on which excise duty is chargeable (with certain hydrocarbon oil exceptions)
- Hire of mobile generators for operation by the customer
- Repairs, maintenance and replacement of pipes not belonging to the fuel or power supplier (normally those on the consumer's side of the meter)
- Servicing contracts (other than supplies of insurance)
- Sale of meters to commercial, industrial and domestic consumers for their own use
- Altering coin mechanisms of secondary meters
- Services in connection with tests carried out, for example, at the request of estate agents or prospective purchasers of premises
- Replacement of meters not under the supplier's Code of Practice and re-siting meters at the request of the consumer
- Diverting mains to meet local authority requirements (these supplies are zero-rated when work is carried out in the course of construction of new dwellings)
- Raising or lowering of overhead power lines in connection with the movement of abnormal loads, including escorting the loads (these supplies are zero-rated when work is carried out in the course of construction of new dwellings)
- Supply, repair and maintenance of public lighting circuits to local authorities
- Temporary floodlighting, emergency or decorative lighting

- Charges for playing games such as squash, tennis, billiards and snooker collected by means of a coin-operated lighting meter (i.e. a time switch controlling the availability of light for a fixed period of time (may be exempt in certain circumstances, see **58.5 RECREATION AND SPORT**)
- Blast freezing

(VAT Notice 701/19/16, para 2.3).

Outside the scope supplies

The following charges are outside the scope of VAT.

- Replacement by the gas or electricity supplier of dangerous, obsolete or inefficient appliances or parts, after the meter, under statutory contractual obligation. (This covers only the limited circumstances of work undertaken by gas and electricity utilities to comply with their statutory contractual obligations to supply fuel and power. It does not cover modification works to gas water heater flues in caravans.)
- Charges by a gas or electricity supplier for repairs to its own property following damage.

(VAT Notice 701/19/16, para 2.4).

Connecting dwellings to mains power

Supplies of civil engineering services in the course of construction, alteration or conversion of a building may be zero-rated in certain circumstances. See **43.7** to **43.10 LAND AND BUILDINGS: ZERO RATING AND REDUCED RATE SUPPLIES AND DIY HOUSEBUILDERS.** This includes the first time provision of gas and electricity from the building up to the nearest existing supply.

The treatment of one-off charges for the first time connection to electricity or gas is as follows.

- If the supply of the connection and provision of the utility is made by the same person (or by members of the same VAT group), the connection charge will follow the treatment of the utility and be reduced-rated.
- If the supplies are not made by the same person or if at the time of connection the suppler of the utility has not been determined, the connection charge will continue to be standard-rated (irrespective of who eventually provides the utility).
- The first time connection of a new dwelling or relevant residential or relevant charitable building to the gas or electricity mains supply is zero-rated under *VATA 1994, Sch 8 Group 5* if the connection is made as part of the construction of the building.
- Works in connection with the means of providing fuel and power as part of the renovation or alteration of empty residential premises, or of the conversion of premises to a different residential use may be reduced-rated under *VATA 1994, Sch 7A Groups 6 and 7* if performed on the immediate site of the premises.
- Grant-funded connection or reconnection to a mains gas supply relating to a qualifying person's sole or main residence is reduced-rated under *VATA 1994, Sch 7A Group 3 Item 4.*

All other connections are standard-rated.

(VAT Notice 701/19/16, para 2.6).

VAT treatment in particular cases

[26.8] In particular cases, VAT is treated as follows:

(1) Supplies to schools and other educational institutions

Supplies of fuel and power to educational institutions are taxed at the reduced rate in the following circumstances.

(a) *The institution has charitable status and is receiving the supply for non-business use.* If the charity does not make a charge, its activities are generally non-business. Independent and other schools which are charities but which do charge fees are in business for VAT purposes and supplies of fuel and power to them are generally standard-rated (but see (*b*) below).

(b) *The fuel and power is supplied to separate residential premises for the accommodation of pupils and students.* Where the residential quarters form part of the main building, the supply partly qualifies for the reduced rate and must be apportioned (subject to the 60% rule, see **26.2** above) unless the school, etc. also qualifies under (*a*) above.

(VAT Notice 701/19/16, para 10.1).

(2) Supplies by wholesalers to retailers

Supplies of fuel and power by wholesalers to retailers are standard-rated unless supplied in small *de minimis* amounts (see **26.2** above). This applies even if it is known that the goods will eventually be supplied for qualifying use. (VAT Notice 701/19/16, para 10.2).

(3) Supplies by shops and other retailers

There are no special rules for supplies by retailers. In practice, most supplies of fuel and power by retail (e.g. coal supplied in bags) will be taxed at the reduced rate because the amount supplied will be below the *de minimis* limits for that fuel (see **26.2** above). (VAT Notice 701/19/16, para 10.3).

(4) Supplies to landlords, managing agents, caravan park owners and residents' associations

Such supplies are taxable at the reduced rate provided the fuel or power is used for qualifying purposes. The charge should be apportioned if only part of the premises to which the supply relates is used for qualifying purposes (e.g. on-site accommodation for employees or proprietors). In all other cases supplies of fuel and power to landlords, etc. are standard-rated. (VAT Notice 701/19/16 para 10.4).

(5) Supplies by landlords (other than local authorities)

(a) Heated, air-conditioned or refrigerated accommodation

Where a landlord supplies fuel and power to tenants in the form of heated, air-conditioned or refrigerated accommodation, this will usually be a single supply of accommodation. This accommodation can be used for any purpose (domestic, charitable or business). In practice, heated and air-conditioned accommodation is usually used for residential or office purposes and cold stores are used for storing perishable goods. Storage with no specific right over land is normally standard-rated. If the landlord grants the user of a cold store a right over land, then the supply is exempt (subject to the option to tax, see **42.23 LAND AND BUILDINGS: EXEMPT SUPPLIES AND OPTION TO TAX**).

- Where a landlord and tenant contract for a single supply of heated, air-conditioned or cooled accommodation, it is a single supply of accommodation and is taxed as such. If the landlord makes a fixed charge for supplies of gas or electricity or includes an amount in the rent to cover them, the payment is normally treated as part of the rent and liable to VAT at the same rate as the supply of accommodation.
- Where a landlord and tenant contract for two separate supplies, one of heat, air-conditioning or cooling, and the other of accommodation, each supply is dealt with separately. If tenants have coin-operated gas or electricity meters, the money placed in the coin box is payment for a supply of gas or electricity and is taxed at the reduced rate when made for qualifying use. This applies whether the gas or electricity is supplied at cost or with a mark-up. If the landlord rents or owns a secondary credit meter, supplies of gas or electricity are liable to VAT at the reduced rate when made for a qualifying use.

In *HMRC v Colaingrove Ltd* [2015] UKUT 80 (TCC) (TVC 30.14), the Upper Tribunal decided that there was a single standard-rated supply of serviced accommodation in circumstances where a separate but compulsory charge was made for power supplied to static caravans and chalets where the charge was based on the length of the holiday rather than the amount of power used.

(b) Service charges for common areas

Mandatory charges for fuel and power used in common areas (e.g. corridors and stairwells in blocks of flats) that are included in the service charge made to owners of flats and/or freehold property, form part of the payment for the overall supply. See **42.19**(6) **LAND AND BUILDINGS: EXEMPT SUPPLIES AND OPTION TO TAX.**

(VAT Notice 701/19/16, paras 10.6, 10.7).

(6) Supplies by local authorities

(a) Domestic tenants – single supplies of heated accommodation

The supply of accommodation by a local authority is a non-business activity for VAT purposes. The VAT liability of any supplies of fuel and power made by local authorities to their domestic tenants as part of the single supply of heated accommodation follows that of the main supply which is one of accommodation. The fuel and power element of the supply is therefore outside the scope of VAT.

(b) Separate supplies of fuel and power

Separate supplies for domestic use is liable to VAT at the reduced rate. Where a local authority continues to supply fuel and power to accommodation it previously owned, it is a business activity and the supply is taxed at the reduced rate if it is for a qualifying use (see **26.2** above).

(c) Mandatory service charges

Mandatory service charges raised by a local authority to leasehold owners are non-business and outside the scope of VAT.

(VAT Notice 701/19/16, paras 10.5, 10.7).

(7) Heating contracts

If a contractor, under a heating contract, supplies both the fuel and the staff required to operate and maintain a customer's heating system, the whole supply is taxable at the reduced rate (subject to qualifying use of the heat). But maintenance or repairs or replacement of the plant alone can only be taxable at the reduced rate if

- covered by an overall contract for the supply of heat; and
- directly related to and essential for maintaining that supply of heat.

Where a contract is for labour only for the operation and routine maintenance of a customer's boiler and distribution system, and the customer obtains fuel from another source, the supply is always standard-rated.

(VAT Notice 701/19/16, para 10.8).

(8) Facilities requiring fuel and power

The use of washing machines, hot showers and all other facilities (including those for playing sport) which depend on temporary power or light and which are charged for by meter, are *not* supplies of fuel and power. They are supplies of the particular facility concerned and liable to VAT at the appropriate rate. (VAT Notice 701/19/16, para 10.9). See *Mander Laundries Ltd* (VTD 31) (TVC 69.1) and *St Anne's-on-Sea Lawn Tennis Club Ltd* (VTD 434) (TVC 30.4).

See also *Showtry Ltd* (VTD 10028) (TVC 30.10) where the supply of fuel for use in hired agricultural machinery was held to be part of a composite standard-rated supply under the hire contract.

(9) Gas and electricity suppliers: bad debt relief on transferred debts

Subject to meeting certain conditions, a business can recover some or all of the VAT it has paid to HMRC on supplies made where a customer has failed to pay. See **7 BAD DEBT RELIEF**. One of the conditions is that the person who makes the supply is the only person entitled to claim relief.

By concession, a supplier of gas and/or electricity can obtain relief from VAT on debts owed by a domestic customer where the supplier has accepted the transfer of that customer and his debt from another supply company. The detailed provisions of the concession are as follows.

Where a contract for the supply of 'gas' or electricity is substituted by a new contract ('novation') as a result of a 'domestic consumer' transferring from one supplier to another, then, by concession, the new supplier may claim bad debt relief on a supply of gas or electricity made by the former supplier to that consumer, provided that

- the whole or any part of the consideration for the supply is outstanding at the time of the novation;
- the whole of the debt is transferred to the new supplier;
- at the time of the novation, the former supplier (if he has not already done so) accounts for VAT on the supply at the appropriate rate or, if he has already received a refund upon a claim for bad debt relief in relation to that supply, repays to HMRC the amount of that refund;
- the claim is not made until six months after payment for the novation and takes account of any payments made by the customer after the date of the novation;
- both the former supplier and the new supplier have evidence of
  - (i) the value of the debt (including the VAT amount) that has been transferred, and
  - (ii) the date of payment for the novation; and
- the new supplier has a copy of the document issued by him to the consumer to recover the debt (not required if a pre-payment meter is in use).

'*Gas*' means gas that is conveyed through pipes to premises by a person authorised to do so under *Gas Act 1986, s 7*.

'*Domestic consumer*' means a person to whom fuel or power is supplied for domestic use (see **26.2** above).

This concession does not apply in circumstances where its application would give rise to tax avoidance.

(Business Brief 20/04).

Special rules for gas, electricity, and heat or cooling supplies

[26.9] There are special rules for supplies of '*relevant goods*', which means

- gas supplied through a natural gas system situated within the territory of an EU member state or any network connected to such a system;
- electricity; and
- heat or cooling supplied through a network.

[*VATA 1994, s 9A*].

Place of supply

The place of supply of relevant goods is determined as follows.

(a) Relevant goods supplied to a 'dealer' are treated as supplied at

- the place where that dealer has established his business or has a fixed establishment to which the relevant goods are supplied, or
- in the absence of such a place of business or fixed establishment, the place where he has his permanent address or usually resides.

'*Dealer*' means a person whose principal activity in respect of receiving supplies of relevant goods is the re-selling of those goods and whose own consumption of those goods is negligible. Re-selling does not include

- re-sale as part of a single composite supply of other goods or services, or
- re-sale as a supply that falls to be disregarded as a supply to another member of the same VAT group where relevant goods are to be effectively used and consumed by a member of the VAT group.

(b) Supplies of relevant goods not falling within (*a*) above are treated as supplied at

(i) the place where the recipient of the supply has effective use and consumption of the goods or

(ii) in relation to any part of the goods not consumed,

- the place where the recipient of the supply has established his business or has a fixed establishment to which the goods are supplied, or
- in the absence of such place of business or fixed establishment, the place where he has his permanent address or usually resides.

For the purposes of (i) above effective use and consumption includes a supply of the goods

- by the recipient as part of a single composite supply of other goods or services; and
- to a member of a VAT group, where the goods are effectively used and consumed by a member of that group.

[*SI 2004/3148, Arts 9–13*].

Reverse charge on supplies by persons outside the UK

The reverse charge procedure applies where a person who is outside the UK supplies 'relevant goods' to a person who is registered under *VATA 1994* for the purposes of any business carried on by the recipient. The recipient is treated as if he had himself supplied the relevant goods in the course or furtherance of his business and as if that supply were a taxable supply. He must therefore account for output tax on the full value of the supply received. He can, however, subject to the normal rules, include the VAT as input tax on the same VAT return. Supplies which are treated as made by the recipient under these rules are not taken into account when calculating any entitlement to input tax under the **50 PARTIAL EXEMPTION** rules.

[*VATA 1994, s 9A*].

For these purposes a person is outside the UK if

- he has established his business or has a fixed establishment outside the UK; or

- in the absence of such a place of business or fixed establishment, the place where he has his permanent address or usually resides is outside the UK.

[*SI 2004/3148, Art 14*].

Time of supply

Goods which are treated as supplied by a person under *VATA 1994, s 9A* above are treated as being supplied when the goods are paid for or, if the consideration is not in money, on the last day of the VAT accounting period in which the goods are removed or made available. [*SI 1995/2518, Reg 82A*].

Valuation of supply

Where any goods are treated as made by a UK VAT-registered recipient under *VATA 1994, s 9A* above, the value of the supply is taken to be

- where the consideration for the supply was in money, the amount of that consideration; and
- where the consideration did not consist, or not wholly consist, of money, such amount in money as is the equivalent to that consideration.

[*VATA 1994, Sch 6 para 8*].

Anti-avoidance – reverse charge on wholesale supplies of gas and electricity

With effect from 1 July 2014, the scope of the anti-avoidance reverse charge provisions were extended to include wholesale supplies of gas and electricity. See **4.16 ANTI-AVOIDANCE.**

Key points: fuel and power

[26.10] Points to consider are as follows.

- The reduced rate of VAT applies to domestic supplies of fuel and power and also supplies to a charity for a building it uses for its non-business purposes. The latter is an example of a useful concession that is available to a charity to save VAT on its costs. In cases where a charity has incorrectly paid standard rate VAT over the last four years, there will be scope to approach the utility supplier and obtain a credit note for overpaid VAT. Any VAT incorrectly paid before this date is out of date under the error correction rules.
- The onus is on the supplier to get the VAT treatment right. This gives some protection to the customer if the reduced rate of VAT has been incorrectly charged on fuel and power supplied to a building.
- A useful concession is that any non-qualifying use of a building is ignored, e.g. a charitable building partly used for business purposes, as long as the qualifying use is at least 60% of total use. If

the qualifying use is less than 60%, then an apportionment must be made so that the reduced rate of VAT is only charged on the percentage of qualifying use.

27

Gold and Precious Metals

Cross-reference. See **68 TERMINAL MARKETS** for zero-rating of certain transactions in gold on the London Gold Market.

De Voil Indirect Tax Service. See V4.186, V4.277, V5.143.

Introduction to gold and precious metals

[27.1] A special scheme applies for investment gold. It puts investment in gold on a similar footing with other financial investments, e.g. shares, by making it exempt from VAT (see **27.2** below). Businesses are generally unable to reclaim input tax directly attributable to an exempt supply. Unlike shares, however, gold may be purchased from a variety of taxable sources before being transformed into investment gold. If the normal rules applied, the input tax incurred on these costs would not be reclaimable and the seller would either have to absorb the VAT cost or pass it on to the investor (which would make investing in the gold less attractive). The scheme for investment gold therefore has three special features.

- Certain persons may opt to tax specified transactions, so enabling them to reclaim all of their input tax (subject to the normal rules). See **27.3** below.
- Taxable persons can reclaim the input tax incurred on purchases of gold and on the costs of transforming any gold into investment gold. See **27.4** below.
- Taxable persons who are producers and transformers of investment gold can reclaim the input tax they incur on certain costs linked to the production or transformation process. See **27.4** below.

The special scheme for investment gold also allows special procedures for transactions on the London Bullion Market. See **68.3 TERMINAL MARKETS**.

Exempt supplies of investment gold

[27.2] The following supplies are exempt.

(a) The supply of 'investment gold'.

(b) The grant, assignment or surrender of any right, interest, or claim in, over or to investment gold if the right, interest or claim is or confers a right to the transfer of possession of investment gold. *Not included* is
- the grant of an option; or
- the assignment or surrender of a right under an option at a time before the option is exercised.

A supply of this description includes supplies of unallocated investment gold (i.e. gold which is an unidentifiable part of a larger stock held by the supplier), loans, swaps, and forward and future contracts concerning investment gold. (VAT Notice 701/21/13, para 2.2).

(c) The supply, by a person acting as an agent for a disclosed principal, of services consisting of
- effecting a supply within (*a*) or (*b*) above that is made by or to his principal; or
- attempting to effect such a supply which is not in fact made.

The effect of this is that if an agent (including an auctioneer) sells and invoices the goods in the name of their principal, the supply of investment gold is made by the principal (and exempt under (*a*) or (*b*) above). The agent supplies only his services which are exempt under this provision. The agent may opt to tax the services if the principal also opts to tax his onward supply (see **27.3**(*c*) below).

Where an agent acts in his own name (i.e. for an undisclosed principal), the goods are treated for VAT purposes as supplies both to and by the agent. See **3.4 AGENTS**. The special scheme for investment gold applies to the agent in the same way as it would apply to a principal and the agent's supply is exempt unless he can opt to tax under **27.3** below. However, when an agent or auctioneer is acting in their own name their supply of services to either the buyer or the seller is taxable.
(VAT Notice 701/21/13, para 7.3 which has the force of law).

Excluded is a supply
- between members of the London Bullion Market Association; or
- by a member of that association to a taxable person who is not a member; or
- by a taxable person who is not a member to a member of that association.

'*Investment gold*' means any of the following.

(i) Gold of a purity not less than 995 thousandths in the form of a bar or wafer of a weight accepted by the bullion markets. See VAT Notice 701/21/13, para 15 for list of the weights in which bars and wafers are commonly traded.

(ii) A gold coin minted after 1800 that
- is of a purity of not less than 900 thousandths;
- is, or has been, legal tender in its country of origin; and

- is of a 'type' that is 'normally sold' at a price that does not exceed 180% of the open market value of the gold contained in the coin.

(iii) A gold coin of a 'description' laid down in VAT Notice 701/21A/12, Section 3 which for these purposes has the force of law. The list, comprising over 500 gold coins from around the world, is produced by the EU Commission and is updated annually. It applies in all EU member states.

All gold coins falling within (ii) or (iii) above that have the same denomination (face value), size and gold fineness constitute a single 'type' or 'description' for the purposes of these provisions. Thus a gold coin type may be a single issue for one year or may have been produced for many years (e.g. a British sovereign). (VAT Notice 701/21A/12, para 2.2).

HMRC regard the price at which a coin is 'normally sold' as the price that can most usually be demanded for that particular type of coin. It does not matter that an individual coin is of special interest to collectors; if the usual value of the coin type does not exceed 180% of the value of the gold contained therein, all coins of that type are exempt. Similarly, if a coin type is usually valued at more than 180% of the gold value (because of interest to collectors), any coin of that type is taxable even if a particular coin is in such poor condition that it is worth less than 180% of its gold value. The normal selling price of coins is affected by the finish. Investment gold coins fall into two broad classes. First, relatively older issues made to circulate as currency and normally worn from circulation. Secondly, generally more recent issues primarily produced as a store of wealth. The second type may have been issued in a number of finishes (e.g. 'brilliant uncirculated' or 'proof') and if the majority of a type of coin are, for example, of brilliant uncirculated quality, then the brilliant uncirculated value normally reflects the normal selling price. If a trader is uncertain whether the normal selling value falls within the 180% criterion, he should contact HMRC. (VAT Notice 701/21A/12, paras 2.4, 2.5).

[*VATA 1994, Sch 9 Group 15*].

Option to tax investment gold

[27.3] The special scheme for investment gold allows some businesses to opt to tax certain otherwise exempt transactions provided they meet conditions laid down by HMRC (which have the force of law).

(a) **Producers and transformers of gold.** Where a taxable person supplies investment gold which he has produced or transformed *to another taxable person* and the supply would otherwise fall within **27.2**(*a*) or (*b*) above, the supplier can elect to waive exemption and opt to tax the supply. The business must notify HMRC if it intends to make use of this provision who will send an acknowledgement. If this is not received within 28 days, it is the responsibility of the business to check that HMRC have received the notification.

(b) **Other taxable persons.** HMRC may permit a taxable person, who in the normal course of his business makes supplies of gold for industrial purposes, to opt to tax the supply of investment gold described in

27.2(i) above if made to another taxable person. Prior permission must be obtained by writing to HMRC, giving the VAT registration number and confirming that the business normally trades in gold for industrial purposes. If permission is given, HMRC will send a letter of approval within 28 days setting out the conditions of permission. Once authorisation is received, the business may opt to tax supplies of investment gold bars or wafers made to other taxable persons. It cannot opt to tax supplies of investment gold coins or sales to non-taxable persons. HMRC may withdraw authorisation for the protection of the revenue. In such a case, the election ceases to have effect from the date specified in the notification.

(c) **Agents.** Where an agent acts on behalf of a named principal and that principal has made an election under (*a*) or (*b*) above as supplier, then the agent may also opt to tax any supply of services which would otherwise fall to be exempt under **27.2**(*c*) above and which is directly linked to the relevant supply. The agent must notify HMRC that he intends to opt to tax his services. HMRC will send an acknowledgement. If this is not received within 28 days, it is the agent's responsibility to check that HMRC have received the notification.

Any such election made by the supplier or his agent is subject to any conditions laid down by HMRC and

- applies in respect of an individual supply;
- has effect on or after the day from which the election is made;
- is irrevocable.

How to opt

Once the conditions outlined above have been fulfilled, to opt to tax a particular transaction it is simply necessary to include the following statement on the sales invoice.

'We have opted to tax this transaction.'

Special accounting arrangements for opted transactions

By opting to tax a transaction in investment gold, the transaction becomes subject to the special accounting scheme under which the responsibility to account for and pay the output tax falls to the purchaser. See **27.9** below.

Invoicing requirements

A taxable person selling investment gold which he has opted to tax must comply with all the normal invoicing requirements for taxable transactions (see **40 INVOICES**) and the requirements of the special accounting scheme for gold (see **27.9** below).

[*SI 1999/3116, Reg 3*]. (VAT Notice 701/21/13, paras 4.3–4.7 which have the force of law).

Deduction of input tax

[27.4] Where a business opts to tax a particular supply of investment gold (see **27.3** above) it can reclaim all the related input tax as it is making a taxable supply of investment gold. To reclaim all input tax, it must be able to show that none of its input tax relates to any exempt supplies of investment gold.

As a general rule, input tax incurred on goods or services which are used to make exempt supplies cannot be reclaimed. Exceptionally, where a taxable person makes exempt supplies of investment gold within **27.2**(*a*) or (*b*) above

- input tax incurred in any VAT period in respect of such supplies is allowable as being attributable to those supplies to the extent that it is incurred on
  - (i) the purchase of investment gold which would have fallen to be exempt within **27.2**(*a*) or (*b*) above but for
    - an option to tax having been exercised under **27.3** above; or
    - the supply having been excluded from exemption because it was between a member of the London Bullion Market Association and a taxable person who was not a member;
  - (ii) the acquisition of investment gold from another EU member state;
  - (iii) a supply to him, or an acquisition or importation by him, of gold other than investment gold which is to be transformed by him (or on his behalf) into investment gold; and
  - (iv) services supplied to him comprising a change of form, weight or purity of gold; and
- if he produces investment gold or transforms any gold into investment gold, he is also entitled to credit for input tax incurred on any goods or services supplied to him, or goods acquired or imported by him, to the extent that they are linked to the production or transformation of that gold into investment gold. This includes, for example, in addition to the gold itself
  - tools, tooling and equipment;
  - machinery, plant and fittings;
  - fuel and power;
  - crucibles and furnace linings;
  - buildings and maintenance of buildings;
  - laboratory instruments and equipment; and
  - fume abatement and effluent treatment

  but not, for example, a computer used to record exempt sales because the input tax is not directly linked to the production or transformation process.

  If a building is to be used for the production of investment gold which will be sold exempt from VAT and an area of the building is set aside for the sale of that investment gold, the input tax on the building must be apportioned to reflect the fact that only a part of it is linked to the *production* of the investment gold.

Input tax partly attributable to exempt supplies of investment gold

Where input tax has been incurred on goods or services which are used or to be used in making supplies of investment gold within **27.2**(*a*) or (*b*) above and other supplies, the proportion attributable to the investment gold must first be established (by being expressed as a proportion of the whole use or intended use) and the rules in (*a*) and (*b*) above must then be applied to the proportion attributable to the investment gold.

Examples

(1) A business makes exempt supplies of investment gold but is not a producer or transformer of gold and does not buy in transformation services. It receives a mixed supply, part of which is investment gold that it intends to supply partly as exempt investment gold and partly as other goods or services.

The business can only deduct VAT incurred on the investment gold itself. It must first work out the extent to which the input tax on the mixed supply received is attributable to the various supplies to be made. For the element attributable to the exempt supply of investment gold, it must then work out how much of that input tax relates to the gold itself. It cannot, for example, deduct any input tax incurred on a separate delivery service of that gold.

(2) A business makes exempt supplies of investment gold and is not a producer or transformer of gold. However, it does buy in transformation services.

The business can deduct VAT incurred on the investment gold itself (or other gold) and the VAT incurred on any out-sourced transformation services. If it incurs any input tax which is partly attributable to supplies of exempt investment gold and party attributable to other supplies, it must first work out the extent to which the input tax incurred is attributable to its various supplies. Then, for the element attributable to the exempt supply of investment gold, it must work out the extent to which it relates to the gold itself and to the transformation services.

(3) A business makes exempt supplies of investment gold and is also a producer and/or transformer of gold.

The business can deduct the VAT incurred on any related gold and also any VAT incurred on production and/or transformation costs. If it incurs any input tax which is partly attributable to its supplies of exempt investment gold and partly attributable to other supplies, it must first work out the extent to which that input tax is attributable to its various supplies and then, for the element attributable to the exempt supply of investment gold, it must work out the extent to which it relates only to the gold and production/transformation.

[*SI 1995/2518, Reg 103A*]. (VAT Notice 701/21/13, paras 5.1–5.4).

Accounting and record keeping requirements

[27.5] There are special accounting and record keeping requirements for persons who trade in exempt investment gold. The requirements apply to exempt sales of investment gold where the gold is delivered, or otherwise made available, to the customer. The requirements apply whether or not the supplier is registered or liable to be registered for VAT. [*SI 1995/2518, Regs 31A, 31B*]. (VAT Notice 701/21/13, para 6.1). See **53.29 PENALTIES** for penalties for failure to comply with the record-keeping requirements.

Notification

On the first occasion that a person makes an exempt supply of investment gold which exceeds £5,000 in value, or when the value of his supplies of investment gold to any one customer exceeds £10,000 in any twelve-month period, he must notify HMRC at the following address.

HM Revenue and Customs
Written Enquiries Section
Alexander House
Victoria Avenue
Southend
Essex SS99 1BD

If, at the time of notification, the person is not VAT-registered, he must also provide the following information.

- Name of company, partnership or sole proprietor.
- Company number or details of partners.
- Address(es).
- Telephone number.
- Contact name.
- Accountant name, address and telephone.
- Any associated VAT registration numbers.

HMRC will send an acknowledgement. If this is not received within 28 days, it is the person's responsibility to check that HMRC have received the notification.

It is not necessary to notify HMRC of subsequent supplies.

(VAT Notice 701/21/13, para 3.1 which has the force of law). See VAT Notice 701/21/13, para 3.2 for a standard letter which may be used.

Invoicing requirements

Where an invoice is issued for the sale of exempt investment gold which is over £5,000 or the total value of sales of exempt investment gold to that customer have exceeded £10,000 in the last year, the invoice must contain the following details if appropriate.

(i) A unique identifying number.
(ii) Name and address of seller and name and address of person raising invoice (if different to the seller, e.g. an agent).
(iii) Name and address of the purchaser, delivery address (if different) and unique customer reference (see under *Customer record* below).
(iv) Date of invoice and delivery date.
(v) Type of supply (for example, sale).
(vi) If the seller, agent or the customer is registered for VAT, the VAT registration number of the seller and agent.
(vii) A description of the gold supplied.
(viii) For bars and wafers: the form, weight and purity and any other identifying feature (including any proprietary mark, hallmark and serial number where applicable).
(ix) For investment gold coins: the coin type, country of origin and whether or not the coin is included on the list of gold coins reproduced in VAT Notice 701/21A/12, Section 3.
(x) The number of items.
(xi) The total amount payable.

Where a business sells investment gold on which it has charged VAT (e.g. because it has opted to tax), the invoice must comply with the normal invoicing requirements (see **40 INVOICES**) and the requirements for the special accounting scheme for gold (see **27.9** below).

(VAT Notice 701/21/13, paras 6.2, 6.4 which have the force of law).

Where taxable items (including gold) and exempt investment gold are supplied together, all the items may be included on the same invoice, provided the invoice contains all the appropriate details.

(VAT Notice 701/21/13, para 6.6).

Purchasing investment gold from persons not trading in investment gold

Where a person purchases exempt investment gold from a person who does not trade in investment gold and

- the value of the purchase is more than £5,000, or
- if more than one purchase has been made from the same customer, the total value of purchases from that customer has exceeded £10,000 in the last year,

the purchaser must issue an invoice on behalf of the seller containing all the relevant details specified in (i)–(xi) above.

In addition, the invoice must bear the following declaration which must be signed by the seller.

'I declare that to the best of my knowledge the details shown on this invoice are correct.' (signature and name).

The purchaser must keep and maintain a copy of the invoices so issued with his purchase records.

(VAT Notice 701/21/13, para 6.3 which has the force of law).

Special records

Subject to below, any person (whether or not registered for VAT) who sells exempt investment gold which is delivered or available to be taken away by the customer must keep and maintain a record showing the following information as part of the business records.

(A) Accounting records

Accounting records showing

- invoice number;
- invoice date;
- customer reference number;
- customer's VAT registration number (if applicable);
- description of the gold (form, quantity and purity);
- name and address of the agent (if applicable);
- name and address of the purchaser; and
- transaction value.

(B) Customer record

Customer record identifying customers who purchase exempt investment gold. This record must have a unique reference number and contain details of the purchaser's

- name;
- date of birth;
- current address; and
- telephone number if available.

The seller must take reasonable steps to ensure that the customer has given correct information. In order to do this, the seller must ask for and examine at least one document from each of the following lists.

List 1
Passport
Full driving licence
National Insurance card
Birth certificate
National identity card

List 2
Telephone bill
Other utility bill
Deeds
Tenancy lease
Council tax bill
Hotel key card (for non-UK residents only)

Alternative satisfactory evidence may be agreed with HMRC.

If possible, copies should be kept of the documents seen. The seller should write on each copy 'certified as original document' and must sign and date this declaration. If it is not possible to keep a copy of any document seen, the seller must record, as part of your customer record, sufficient details to enable HMRC to obtain a copy if they so require. As a minimum the seller should record

- the name of the document;
- the reference number; and
- the name and address of the issuing authority.

The seller must insist that the customer produces the original document.

Internet and mail order sales

If investment gold is sold over the internet or by mail order, the seller may as an alternative to the customer record under (B) above keep and maintain the following record.

- If the supply is paid for by credit card and the delivery address is also the card holder's address, a record of the customer's name, the credit card issuer and the card number.
- If the supply is paid for by cheque, a record of the customer's name, the name of the bank and the customer's account number.

Whether payment is by credit card or cheque, the seller must also keep proof of despatch of the investment gold to the customer's address.

Sales to other VAT-registered businesses

If investment gold is sold to another VAT-registered business, the seller may, as an alternative to the customer record under (B) above, ask the customer for their VAT registration number. The seller must, however, check with HMRC that the VAT registration number provided is authentic.

Banks and other financial service businesses

If the seller is a bank or other financial service business which, for the purposes of the *Money Laundering Regulations 1993* (*SI 1993/1933*) is a 'relevant financial business' it may, as an alternative to the customer record set out in (B) above, keep and maintain the records specified in those *Regulations*. Relevant financial businesses to whom this applies must conduct the appropriate identification procedures and keep the required records in the case of all transactions in investment gold where

- the value of a one-off transaction exceeds 15,000 euro, or
- two or more one-off transactions appear linked and their value together exceeds 15,000 euro.

For these purposes, the exchange rate between the euro and the UK £ is the rate published in the Official Journal of the Communities.

(VAT Notice 701/21/13, paras 7.1, 7.2, 7.4, 7.6 which have the force of law).

Additional special record for taxable persons

If the seller is registered for VAT and is

- authorised to opt to tax supplies of investment gold (see **27.3** above), or
- a producer or transformer of investment gold,

he must keep and maintain with his VAT account, in addition to the records set out above, a record of any supply of investment gold made to another taxable person where the seller has delivered or otherwise made the gold available to that person, and on which the seller has *not* opted to tax.

(VAT Notice 701/21/13, para 7.5 which has the force of law).

Records of exports and dispatches

A seller is not required to keep any of the records described above for supplies of investment gold physically exported outside the EU or despatched to a business in another EU member state. (VAT Notice 701/21/13, para 7.1). See **27.8** below.

Retention of records

The seller must retain all the documents and records specified above for a minimum of six years from the date of the transaction. In the case of regular customers, he must keep the customer record under (B) above for six years following the most recent supply of investment gold.

Any person who purchases investment gold must keep the purchase invoice for a minimum of six years from the date of the transaction.

(VAT Notice 701/21/13, para 7.7 which has the force of law).

Supplies of gold other than investment gold

Zero-rated supplies of gold involving Central Banks

[27.6] The supply of gold (including gold coins) held in the UK by

- a Central Bank to either another Central Bank or a member of the London Bullion Market, or
- a member of the London Bullion Market to a Central Bank

is zero-rated. Included is the granting of a right to acquire gold and the supply of a part interest in gold. [*VATA 1994, Sch 8 Group 10*].

Other supplies

The VAT liability of a supply of gold which is not

- zero-rated under the above provisions,
- investment gold within the meaning in **27.2** above, or
- eligible for relief under the provisions relating to **68 TERMINAL MARKETS**

generally falls into one of the following categories.

(a) **'Allocated gold'**. The supply of allocated gold held
  (i) outside the UK is outside the scope of UK VAT; and
  (ii) in the UK is standard-rated (unless zero-rated because the gold is physically exported under the normal rules for the export of goods).

  '*Allocated gold*' is gold set apart and designated as belonging to or reserved for specific persons or purposes. If gold, etc. is delivered, it is of necessity allocated.

(b) **'Unallocated gold' supplied by UK traders**. The supply is
  (i) standard-rated if the customer belongs in the UK;
  (ii) outside the scope of UK VAT (but with input tax credit) if made to a customer who belongs outside the EU;
  (iii) outside the scope of UK VAT (but with input tax credit) if the customer is a business in another EU member state; and
  (iv) standard-rated if made to a customer in another EU member state not fulfilling the conditions in (iii).

  '*Unallocated gold*' is gold or gold coins forming an unidentifiable part of a large stock held by a supplier. The supply of unallocated gold or gold coins is a supply of a service for VAT purposes. Under (iii) above, it is therefore outside the scope of UK VAT as it is made where the customer belongs in accordance with the general rule for the supply of services. It is a financial service for the purposes of *VATA 1994, Sch 4A para 16*, so under (ii) above it is also treated as made where the customer belongs. Under (i) and (iv) the supply is made in the UK and chargeable to output tax under the general rules for place of supply. As a result, under (ii) and (iii) above, the place of supply of services is treated as made where the recipient belongs under *SI 1992/3121, Art 16* but under (i) and (iv) is made where the supplier belongs under the general rule for place of supply of services.

(c) **Unallocated gold—supplies received in the UK from suppliers belonging abroad.** Such a supply of 'unallocated gold' (see (*b*) above) is
- standard-rated as the importation of a financial service if received by a taxable person, the UK customer accounting for the VAT under the reverse charge procedure (see **39.4 INTERNATIONAL SERVICES**); and
- outside the scope of UK VAT if received by a private or non-taxable person.

See **18.2 EUROPEAN UNION: GENERAL** for the VAT territory of the EU.

(VAT Notice 701/21/13, paras 10.2, 16).

Importations and acquisitions of gold

Importations

[27.7] VAT is not chargeable on

- the importation of gold (including gold coin) from outside the EU by a Central Bank [*SI 1992/3124*]; or
- the importation of investment gold (see **27.2** above) from outside the EU [*SI 1999/3115*]. The investment gold must be entered to Customs Procedure Code (CPC) 40 00 73 in order to gain the exemption.

Other importations of gold are chargeable to VAT at the standard rate. But see **74.3 WORKS OF ART, ETC.** for special valuation provisions applying to the importation of gold coins which are collectors' pieces.

Acquisitions

Acquisitions of gold in the UK from another EU member state are subject to the normal rules, i.e. the rate of VAT is the same as would be applicable if the gold in question was the subject of a supply in the UK (see **20.3 EUROPEAN UNION: SINGLE MARKET**). The effect of this is that the acquisition of investment gold is exempt from VAT but the acquisition of other gold is standard-rated.

Central banks

Where gold is supplied to a Central Bank by a supplier in another EU member state and the transaction involves the removal of the gold from that or some other EU member state to the UK, the taking possession of the gold by the Central Bank concerned is not treated as an acquisition of goods from another EU member state. [*SI 1992/3132*]. Consequently, VAT does not become chargeable on the receipt of such gold by the Central Bank concerned.

(VAT Notice 701/21/13, paras 8.1, 10.7).

Exports and removals

[27.8] Exports and removals of gold are treated as follows:

- **Investment gold.** The supply of investment gold which is physically exported to a place outside the EU or despatched to a business in another EU member state does not attract UK VAT. It is not necessary to keep the special records in **27.5** above but the normal evidence of the export or despatch is required. See **22.25 EXPORTS** and **20.13 EUROPEAN UNION: SINGLE MARKET.**
  EU sales lists/intrastat. There is no need to complete ESLs for exempt sales of investment gold to businesses in other EU member states but any required intratstat declaration must be completed.
  (VAT Notice 701/21/13, paras 8.2, 8.3).
- **Other gold.** The supply of gold, other than investment gold which is physically exported to a place outside the EU or despatched to another business in another EU member state is zero-rated with input tax recovery (subject to the normal rules).
  (VAT Notice 701/21/13, para 10.8).

For the liability of sales to overseas customers where the gold is not physically removed from the UK, see **27.6** above.

Special accounting scheme for gold transactions

[27.9] A special accounting scheme for gold must be used for certain transactions between VAT-registered traders. Where it applies, it transfers the responsibility for paying the VAT due to HMRC from the seller to the buyer. The detailed provisions are set out below.

The scheme must be applied in relation to 'supplies of gold', where

(a) the seller and buyer are both registered for VAT or liable to be registered as a consequence of the transaction (see below),
(b) the supply by the seller is by way of business, and
(c) the buyer is making the purchase in connection with any business carried on by him.

In determining liability for registration under (*a*) above for the purposes of *VATA 1994*, *Sch 1* and *Sch 1A*, a standard-rated supply of gold (but not a zero-rated supply) is treated as a taxable supply by the buyer in the course or furtherance of his business (as well as a taxable supply by the seller). The supply by the purchaser cannot be disregarded for the purposes of *Sch 1* on the grounds that it is a supply of capital assets for his business. In such a case, if the purchaser is not entitled to register or is exempted from registration, he must account for output tax on the purchase directly to HMRC.

'*Supplies of gold*' within the scheme are as follows.

(i) Supplies of fine gold of a purity of 995 parts per thousand or greater. *Excluded* are supplies of dental gold, gold slugs and gold targets.
(ii) Supplies of gold grain of any purity.

(iii) Supplies of gold coins of any purity. Gold coins, if they are collectors' items of numismatic interest, may be accounted for under the margin scheme for **SECOND-HAND GOODS (61)**. However, gold coins may not be sold under the margin scheme if they are investment gold coins or if they were purchased under the special accounting scheme.

(iv) Supplies of goods containing gold where the amount paid or payable for the supply (apart from the VAT) does not exceed, or exceeds by no more than a negligible amount, the 'open market value' of the gold contained in the goods. This includes supplies of scrap (including live scrap, i.e. scrapped jewellery, broken jewellery, watch cases, cigarette cases, etc.) and sweepings. The '*open market value*' of the gold is the 'fix price' of the gold at the time of supply. This is the price set twice a day in London by members of the London Bullion Market Association.

(v) The supply of the services of treating or processing goods to make fine gold, gold grain or gold coins.

(vi) The supply of investment gold which would otherwise fall to be exempt under **27.2**(*a*) or (*b*) above but which is standard-rated because the seller has exercised the option to tax under **27.3** above. [*SI 1999/3116, Reg 4*].

(vii) A supply of investment gold by

- a member of the London Bullion Market Association (LBMA) to a taxable person who is not a LBMA member, or
- a taxable person who is not a LBMA member to a LBMA member.

Such a transaction is not zero-rated, is specifically excluded from the exemption applying under **27.2** above and as a result is standard-rated. The special accounting scheme applies to these transactions regardless of whether the supply is classed as a supply of goods or a supply of services.

However, where the non-member who makes or receives the supply is only liable to be registered for VAT under *VATA 1994, Sch 1* or *Sch 3* solely by virtue of that supply or acquisition, the non-member is not required to notify liability for registration and the LBMA member must, on the non-member's behalf, keep a record of the transaction and pay the VAT due to HMRC.

[*SI 1973/173, Arts 5–7*].

Operation of the scheme

If a VAT-registered person supplies goods within (i)–(vii) above, the goods must be sold to another VAT-registered person in order for the scheme to apply. The seller may therefore wish to ask his customer to provide a purchase order detailing the name, address and VAT registration number appropriate to the business.

Under the special scheme, the purchaser of the gold pays the seller the VAT-exclusive price of the gold and must declare the VAT due to HMRC on his VAT return. At the same time the purchaser can deduct, as input VAT, the amount of VAT shown on the seller's invoice (subject to normal rules).

If a VAT-registered person purchases manufactured goods containing gold which are held out for sale as such, and pays over VAT to the seller, the purchaser may be required to prove that the purchase did not fall within the provisions of the special accounting scheme for gold. If he cannot prove this, he may be treated as if he purchased gold and will be required to account for the output tax due under the special accounting scheme.

Issue of VAT invoices

For supplies under the special scheme, the seller must issue a VAT invoice to the buyer showing all the information normally required on a VAT invoice (see **40.4 INVOICES**) and, for investment gold, the information required under **27.5** above. The time of supply is ordinarily the date of delivery of the gold or when the gold is made available for removal by the purchaser. The description of the goods must include the weight and purity of the gold; the number of individual items where possible; and the fix price of the gold on the day of delivery.

The invoice must also include a form of words to the effect that the output tax shown on the invoice is payable to HMRC by the purchaser of the gold. The suggested form of words is:

'£. . . . . output tax on this supply of gold to be accounted for to HM Revenue and Customs by the buyer.'

Completion of the VAT return

Box 1

Include VAT due on any purchases of gold under the special scheme in the period covered by the return. VAT on any sales of gold under the scheme should *not* be shown in this box.

Box 2

Include acquisition VAT on gold acquired from other EU member states.

Box 4

Include the VAT due on purchases of gold under the special scheme (subject to the normal rules).

Box 6

Include the VAT-exclusive value of sales under the special scheme and purchases under the scheme (which are treated as deemed supplies).

Box 7

Include the value of gold purchased under the special scheme.

Sales of gold to non-registered persons

Where gold that falls within the scheme is sold to a person who is not registered or liable to be registered for VAT, the seller should charge and account for VAT in the normal way. The purchaser should pay the full amount due including VAT.

Antique items

Antique items containing gold may fall outside the scheme (because the value of the goods substantially exceeds the open market value of the gold in them or because VAT due on the supply of the item may be treated under the second-hand scheme). However, antique gold coins cannot be sold under the second-hand scheme if they are investment gold or if they were purchased under the special accounting and payment scheme.

Smuggled gold

All smuggled gold is liable to forfeiture even if the gold is found in the hands of an innocent purchaser. It is therefore important that a purchaser of gold looks at the evidence of origin of the gold before agreeing to buy it. See VAT Notice 701/21/13, para 14.1 for guidance for dealers who may be invited to purchase gold so that they can satisfy themselves as to the origin of the gold on offer.

[*VATA 1994, s 55*]. (VAT Notice 701/21/13, paras 11.1–11.6, 12.14).

De Voil Indirect Tax Service. See V5.143.

Manufactured gold jewellery

[27.10] For a consideration of the basis of the valuation of a supply for VAT purposes where gold jewellery is made for customers wholly or partly by refashioning gold supplied by the customer, see *C & E Commrs v SAI Jewellers*, QB [1996] STC 269 (TVC 67.64).

Other precious metals

[27.11] The provisions in **27.6**(*b*) and (*c*) above relating to supplies of unallocated gold also apply to supplies of unallocated silver, platinum, palladium, rhodium, ruthenium, osmium and iridium. (Business Brief 20/94).

Key points: gold and precious metals

[27.12] Points to consider are as follows.

- The special VAT scheme for investment gold means that an option to tax can be applied in certain situations, i.e. to ensure input tax recovery on related costs. If a business decides to use this facility, it must notify HMRC within 28 days of the decision being made and note sales invoices with the narrative 'We have opted to tax this transaction.'
- In certain situations, a business that buys gold and converts it into investment gold can also claim input tax on the conversion and buying costs, even though the final sale of the investment gold is exempt from VAT. This is intended to create parity with share investments, because the latter investments do not have associated costs that include VAT.

- In situations where an option to tax applies, the output tax will be accounted for by the buyer of the gold rather than the seller. The buyer will pay the seller the VAT-exclusive value of the gold, and include output tax in Box 1 of his return, usually claiming the same amount as input tax in Box 4.

28

Groups of Companies

Cross-references. See **7.11 BAD DEBT RELIEF; 20.18 EUROPEAN UNION: SINGLE MARKET** for distance selling from the UK by VAT groups; **42.23 LAND AND BUILDINGS: EXEMPT SUPPLIES AND THE OPTION TO TAX** for the option to tax.

De Voil Indirect Tax Service. See V2.114, V2.190, V2.190B.

Introduction to groups of companies

EU legislation

[28.1] EU legislation allows countries to treat independent legal persons as a single taxable person provided such legal persons are closely bound to one another by financial, economic and organisational links and are established within the confines of the particular country. [*Directive 2006/112/EC, Art 11*].

UK legislation

UK legislation applicable to the registration of groups of companies is considered in **28.2** to **28.4** below. It should be noted that the term 'group' in this context is used for VAT purposes only.

VAT group registration reduces the burden on businesses by allowing two or more associated companies to account for VAT as a single taxable person. It may be administratively convenient where a group accounting function is centralised. Also, because supplies between group members are normally disregarded for VAT purposes, VAT invoices need not be issued for such supplies. On the other hand, because a single VAT return is submitted for the whole group, there may be practical problems in gathering together the information necessary to complete the return on time.

Eligibility for group treatment

[28.2] Two or more 'bodies corporate' (see (1) below) are eligible to be treated as members of a group if

- each of the bodies is 'established' (see (3) below) or has a 'fixed establishment' (see (4) below) in the UK;
- they satisfy the control test, i.e.
  - (a) one of them 'controls' (see (2) below) each of the others,
  - (b) one person (whether a body corporate or an individual) controls all of them, or
  - (c) two or more individuals carrying on a business in partnership control all of them; and
- where applicable, they satisfy the anti-avoidance provisions below.

But a body corporate cannot be treated as a member of more than one group at a time and a body which is a member of one group is not eligible by virtue of the above provisions to be treated as a member of another group.

[*VATA 1994, ss 43A(1), 43D(1)(2)*].

HMRC have no discretion to accept group registration where these requirements are not met (*E Du Vergier & Co Ltd* (VTD 4) (TVC 32.1)).

In *European Commission v UK, ECJ Case C–86/11,* [2013] STC 2076 (TVC 20.21), the CJEU dismissed the application by the European Commission for a declaration that, by permitting non-taxable persons to be members of a group of persons regarded as a single taxable person for purposes of VAT, the UK had failed to fulfil its obligations under *Directive 2006/112/EC, Art 9* and *Art 11*. The CJEU decided that the Commission had not established that the objectives of *Art 11* militated in favour of an interpretation according to which non-taxable persons could not be included in a tax group.

In the joined cases of *Beteiligungsgesellschaft Larentia + Minerva mbH & Co. KG v Finanzamt Nordenham, ECJ Case C–108/14* and *Finanzamt Hamburg-Mitte v Marenave Schiffahrts AG, ECJ Case C–109/14* the CJEU decided that EU member states are precluded from making the formation of a VAT group subject to the following two conditions:

(a) that all members of the group must have legal personality; and
(b) be linked to the controlling company of the VAT group in a relationship of subordination

unless the above two conditions are justified by the prevention of abusive practices or of tax evasion or avoidance. The decision was made in the context of German law in which partnerships, in particular limited partnerships, have no legal personality.

On 14 January 2016 HMRC published HMRC Brief 3/16 which indicated that changes may be made to UK law and VAT grouping provisions. The changes are likely to include:

- extending VAT grouping to non-corporate bodies; and
- identifying new rules to determine close economic, financial and organisational links for corporate and non-corporate bodies, replacing the current control test based on a company law definition of a subsidiary.

(HMRC Brief 3/16).

The Government announced at Autumn Statement 2016 that a consultation on VAT grouping will run from 5 December 2016 to 27 February 2017. The consultation is intended to assist with forming UK policy in light of the two significant CJEU decisions in the joined cases of *Beteiligungsgesellschaft Larentia + Minerva mbH & Co. KG v Finanzamt Nordenham, ECJ Case C–108/14* and *Finanzamt Hamburg-Mitte Marenave Schiffahrts AG, ECJ Case C–109/14* and *Skandia America Corp (USA), ECJ Case C–7/13*. These cases were regarding eligibility for VAT grouping and the VAT treatment of cross-border transactions. The consultation invites views from UK businesses on what UK legal changes may be required following these cases and the international response.

Anti-avoidance provisions

Special provisions apply in order to stop abusive arrangements whereby a jointly-owned entity would otherwise be able to join a VAT group, even though it was run by and for the benefit of an external third party which exercised control over it in practice. Additional conditions prevent certain suppliers from being in the same VAT group as their customers where third parties control the suppliers or receive most of the benefits of their activities.

Specifically, a body corporate that is a 'specified body' (see (5) below) is only eligible to be treated as a member of a group if

- it satisfies the control test above; *and*
- it satisfies both the 'benefits condition' (see (6) below) and the 'consolidated accounts condition' (see (7) below).

[*SI 2004/1931, Art 2*].

A specified body which was a member of a VAT group at 1 August 2004 but failed either the benefits condition or consolidated accounts provision at that date was no longer eligible to be a member of a VAT group. It was required to leave the group from a date agreed with, or determined by, HMRC. (VAT Notice 700/2/14, para 3.3).

Definitions for the above purposes

(1) Body corporate

A body corporate is a form of corporation where a number of persons are united and consolidated together so as to be considered as one person in law. There are several ways in which a body might be incorporated.

- *Companies Act 2006* provides five ways in which a body may be incorporated (public limited companies limited by shares or by guarantee with a share capital; private companies limited by shares; private companies limited by guarantee with a share capital; private companies limited by guarantee; and unlimited companies).
- Bodies may also be incorporated by Act of Parliament, Royal Charter or company law of another country.

(VAT Notice 700/2/14, paras 9.1–9.3).

(2) Control

A body corporate is taken to control another body corporate in two sets of circumstances.

- If it is 'empowered by statute' to control the company's activities. 'Empowered by statute' means empowered by a provision contained in an Act of Parliament (*British Airways Board* [1983] VATTR 191 (TVC 32.3)).
- If it is the company's 'holding company' within the meaning of *Companies Act 2006, s 1159 and Sch 6*.

An individual or individuals shall be taken to control a body corporate if he or they, were he or they a company, would be that body's holding company.

[*VATA 1994, s 43A(2)(3)*].

A company is a subsidiary of another company, its 'holding company', if

- that other company holds a majority of the voting rights in it;
- that other company is a member of it and has the right to appoint or remove a majority of its board of directors;
- that other company is a member of it and controls alone, pursuant to an agreement with other shareholders or members, a majority of the voting rights in it; or
- it is a subsidiary of a company which is itself a subsidiary of that other company.

[*CA 2006, s 1159 and Sch 6*].

> *Example*
>
> Holding Co Ltd owns 75% of the shares in Sub Ltd. The latter company owns 100% of the shares in Second Sub Ltd. Holding Co Ltd also has a joint venture arrangement whereby it owns 50% of the shares in Joint Ltd.
>
> To date, each of the companies has been registered for VAT in its own right – but the group finance director now wishes to apply for a group registration to bring all four companies under one VAT umbrella.
>
> There is no problem with Sub Ltd being part of the group registration as it is controlled by Holding Co Ltd because of share capital ownership. Equally, Second Sub Ltd is effectively owned by Holding Co Ltd as well through its relationship with Sub Ltd. However, Joint Ltd cannot be part of the group because it is not controlled by Holding Co Ltd. A separate company has the same level of control over the company (the joint owner) so the control test is not met.

(3) Established

A company is established in the UK if it has its principal place of business or registered office in the UK, which means if

- the central management and control of the company are carried on in the UK; or
- its headquarters or head office are in the UK.

A company will normally be established in only one country.

(VAT Notice 700/2/14, para 9.4).

(4) Fixed establishment

A company has a fixed establishment in the UK for VAT group purposes if it has a real and permanent trading presence in the UK. This would apply, for example, if it has

- a permanent place of business with the necessary human and technical resources to carry on its business activities; or
- a branch or office in the UK with its own staff and equipment.

For VAT group purposes, a company does not have a fixed establishment in the UK purely by virtue of the fact that

- it is incorporated and has its registered office in the UK;
- it has a simple brass plate presence in the UK; or
- it has a UK-based branch.

(VAT Notice 700/2/14, para 9.4).

(5) Specified body

A body corporate or limited liability partnership which is in, or applying to join, a VAT group is a specified body if all of the following conditions are satisfied.

(a) It carries on a relevant business activity (see (6) below). A dormant company cannot therefore be a specified body.

(b) The value of the group's supplies in the year then ending has exceeded £10 million or there are reasonable grounds for believing that it will exceed £10 million in the year then beginning.
Turnover is the value of all supplies made by the VAT group to persons outside the group whether (i.e. it excludes intra-group supplies) whether or not the place of supply is in the UK. This is the same as the definition for Box 6 of the VAT return. The expected turnover for the coming year should be determined on the assumption that the specified body applying to join the group is included in the group. If the body corporate is the sole general partner of a limited partnership, then the limited partnership's turnover is included. (VAT Notice 700/2/14, para 3.2).

(c) At any time when the relevant business activity is being carried on the body corporate concerned is
    - not a 'wholly-owned subsidiary' of a person who controls all of the other members of the group (or, where the body corporate is or will be a member of the group, all of the other members apart from himself);
    - managed, directly or indirectly, in respect of the business activity concerned, by a third party (see (9) below) in the course or furtherance of a business carried on by him; or
    - the sole general partner of a limited partnership.

A body corporate is a 'wholly-owned subsidiary' of a person if it has no members except that other person and that other person's wholly-owned subsidiaries or persons acting on behalf of that other person or his wholly-owned subsidiaries. In determining whether a body corporate is a wholly-owned subsidiary of a person, the membership of

- any employee or director of the body, or
- where the body is a limited liability partnership, any member of the body

is disregarded.

(d) The body corporate is not

- a body corporate that controls all of the members of the VAT group (or, where it is a member of the group, all of the members apart from itself);
- a body corporate whose activities another body corporate is empowered by statute to control;
- a body corporate whose only activity is acting as the trustee of an occupational pension scheme (as defined by *Pension Schemes Act 1993, s 1*) established under a trust; or
- a charity.

[*SI 2004/1931, Arts 3, 7(3)*].

(6) Relevant business activity

A relevant business activity is one where

(a) the business activity involves making one or more supplies of goods or services to one or more members of the VAT group;
(b) those supplies are not 'incidental' to the business activity;
(c) at least one of those supplies is chargeable to VAT at a rate other than the zero rate (or would be if the body corporate was not in the VAT group); and
(d) the representative member is not entitled to credit for the whole of the VAT on supplies falling within (*c*) above as input tax (or would not be able to do so if the body corporate was not in the VAT group).

When applying this criteria to a body corporate which is already a member of the VAT group, it is deemed not to be a member.

[*SI 2004/1931, Art 4*].

'*Incidental*' has its normal meaning. In general, intra-group supplies are incidental to a business activity if:

- they are occasional or minor supplies made in connection with the activity;
- they do not employ a substantial proportion of the resources devoted to the activity; and
- they are not sufficiently separate from the main business activity to constitute a business activity in their own right.

HMRC give the example of occasional intra-group supplies made by a retailer whose business is mainly selling to the public.

(VAT Notice 700/2/14, para 3.10).

(7) Benefits condition

The benefits condition is satisfied unless 50% of the benefits of the relevant business activity (see (6) above) 'accrue', directly or indirectly, to one or more third parties (see (9) below).

The following are benefits of a business activity for these purposes.

(a) Profits (whether or not distributed).

(b) Charges for managing the business activity (including charges for providing staff to manage it).

(c) The amounts, if any, by which any other charges made to the body exceed the open market value of the goods or services concerned.

If there are no such benefits, any business activity is deemed to generate profits of £100.

Benefits that accrue to a person in his capacity as a member of a body corporate which controls all of the other members of the group (or, where the body is or will be a member of the group, all of the other members apart from itself) are not to be regarded as accruing to a third party.

If the specified body is the sole general partner of a limited partnership, then the benefits concerned are those arising from the limited partnership's business activity.

[*SI 2004/1931, Arts 5, 7(1)*].

Benefits do not include

- cost savings made by being a customer of the body corporate (e.g. price reductions, discounts or rebates); and
- under (*b*) above remuneration or bonuses paid to directors or employees of the body.

As regards (*c*) above, HMRC do not expect traders in normal commercial relationships to undertake extra work to verify that transactions are at open market value.

'*Accrue*'. Technically the benefits condition applies at a given time but profits, etc. are normally determined for a period (usually a year). They can be taken to accrue evenly over that period. Profits accrue to the persons who are expected to get the benefit in practice (e.g. side agreements between shareholders or expectations that profits are to be gifted to a particular person should be taken into account). If ownership of a company changes during the year, profits up to the point of change will normally accrue to the former owner (whether or not distributed to him).

(VAT Notice 700/2/14, para 3.11).

(8) Consolidated accounts condition

The consolidated accounts condition is satisfied if

(a) consolidated accounts prepared for the person who controls all of the other members of the group (or, where the person is or will be a member of the group, all of the other members apart from himself) would be required by 'generally accepted accounting practice' to include accounts for the specified body as his subsidiary; and

(b) consolidated accounts prepared for a third party (see (9) below) would not be required by generally accepted accounting practice to include accounts for the specified body as his subsidiary.

Where the specific body is the general partner of a limited liability partnership, then the consolidation condition applies to the limited partnership (e.g. the limited partnership must be consolidated as a subsidiary in the consolidated group accounts).

In applying this test at any particular time

- the reference to consolidated accounts is a reference to consolidated accounts for a period including that time and insofar as they relate to that time;
- any principle of generally accepted accounting practice that permits accounts of a subsidiary undertaking to be excluded from a consolidation as being immaterial are disregarded; and
- the reference to consolidated accounts prepared for a person is a reference to consolidated accounts of a kind that could be prepared for him in accordance with generally accepted accounting practice; and for this purpose it does not matter
  - (i) whether accounts are actually prepared for him (whether for a particular period or at all), or
  - (ii) in particular, whether he is required to prepare accounts.

  This covers the rare situations where a person controlling a VAT group with a turnover of over £10 million does not have to prepare consolidated accounts (e.g. where the only person controlling the VAT group is an individual or partnership).

'*Generally accepted accounting practice*' means the same as it does for corporation tax purposes. It is normal accounting practice in the UK. Before 1 January 2015, the accounts should comply with UK Financial Reporting Standards (FRSs), in particular UK FRS 2 (Subsidiary undertakings), FRS 5 (Reporting the substance of transactions) and FRS 9 (Associates and joint ventures); GAAP also included consolidated accounts prepared to International Accounting Standards (IASs), e.g. IAS 27 (Consolidated and separate financial statements), IAS 28 (Investment in associates) and IAS 31 (Investment in joint ventures). New UK GAAP apply for accounting periods commencing on or after 1 January 2015, based on FRS 100–102 issued by the Financial Reporting Council. It is likely that the application of the anti-avoidance rules will not change significantly.

If more than one person controls the VAT group (e.g. there is a series of holding companies), condition (a) above only has to be satisfied by one of them.

The consolidated accounts provision has to be applied at a current date for which consolidated accounts will not yet have been prepared. In most cases, whether the condition is satisfied will be obvious from the most recent consolidated accounts unless there has been some significant change in the specified body since then. Where the position is not clear, HMRC will normally accept a professional accountant or auditor's statement that the specified body will be consolidated as a subsidiary in the accounts for the current period.

[*SI 2004/1931, Art 6*]. (VAT Notice 700/2/14, para 3.12).

(9) Third party

For the purposes of (5), (7) and (8) above, a third party is any person or partnership except

(a) anyone who controls the body corporate and all of the other members of the group (i.e. the direct holding company and indirect holding companies up to the ultimate holding company);
(b) anyone controlled by a person in (a) above (which therefore includes all fellow subsidiaries);
(c) an individual who is an employee or director of the body corporate; and
(d) where the body corporate is a limited liability partnership, any individual who is a partner in the partnership.

Broadly speaking, therefore, any person outside the corporate group that includes the VAT group is a third party, except individuals working for the body corporate itself.

[*SI 2004/1931, Art 7(3)*]. (VAT Notice 700/2/14, para 3.5).

Divisional registration

Group treatment and divisional registration under **60.43 REGISTRATION** are mutually exclusive. A corporate body which is registered for VAT in the names of its divisions cannot have one of its divisions included in a VAT group. Similarly, a company that is a member of a VAT group will not be allowed to register one of its divisions separately outside the group. (VAT Notice 700/2/14, para 1.4).

Applications re group treatment and termination of membership

Applications

[28.3] An application can be made to HMRC for

(a) two or more eligible bodies corporate (see **28.2** above) to be treated as members of a group;
(b) another eligible body corporate to be treated as a member of an existing group;
(c) a body corporate to cease to be treated as a member of an existing group;
(d) a member to be substituted as the group's representative member (see **28.4** below); or
(e) the bodies corporate forming an existing group no longer to be treated as members of a group.

An application is taken to be granted with effect from the day on which the application is received by HMRC or such earlier or later time as HMRC allow. In practice, a grouping application is given immediate provisional effect from the date it is received (although HMRC then have 90 days in which to make enquiries and refuse it, see below). HMRC aim to respond within 10 working days of receipt to confirm the application has been approved and give the new VAT registration number or advise that further enquiries need to be made. HMRC should be contacted immediately if a new VAT registration number has not been received within 15 working days.

[*VATA 1994, s 43B(1)–(4)*]. (VAT Notice 700/2/14, paras 2.14, 2.15, 2.20).

Making the application. The application must be made using the following forms.

Under (*a*) above	Form VAT 1 signed by the representative member Form VAT 50 (signed by either the applicant company or the person controlling the group) Form VAT 51 for each company applying to join the group (signed by the same person as the Form VAT 50)
Under (*b*) and (*c*) above	Form VAT 50 and a Form VAT 51 for each company joining or leaving the group
Under (*d*) above	Form VAT 56 (and Forms VAT 50 and VAT 51 if the new representative member is not already a member of the group)
Under (*e*) above	Form VAT 50 and a Form VAT 51 for each member of the group to be excluded
Agent	If an agent is going to register or make changes to a VAT group on its behalf then a VAT53 needs to be completed to give authorisation.

The completed application form should be sent to HM Revenue and Customs, Imperial House, 77 Victoria Street, Grimsby DN31 1DB.

Existing VAT registration numbers already held are cancelled in respect of new members forming a group. The group itself is allocated a new registration number (in the name of the representative member) which identifies the group as a taxable person. This number remains unchanged even if the membership is varied or the representative member changes. On the termination of the group treatment, the group registration number is cancelled. Any member still liable to be registered, or wishing to register voluntarily, is allocated a new number.

(VAT Notice 700/2/14, paras 2.5, 2.11, 2.12, 6.3, 6.4).

Retrospective effect

The wording of the legislation permits retrospective group registration but only within the discretion of HMRC and not a tribunal (*C & E Commrs v Save and Prosper Group Ltd,* QB 1978, [1979] STC 205 (TVC 32.4)). HMRC may give retrospective effect to an application to form a new group or amend an existing one by up to 30 days before the date on which the application is received by HMRC or, if later

- the beginning of the current VAT period of an existing group; or
- the beginning of the current VAT period of any of the companies applying to form, join or leave the VAT group.

Applications for retrospective group registration for periods longer than 30 days will only be allowed if

- HMRC lose an application and the applicant can supply details of its original application and attempts to follow it up; or
- if the delay was caused by lack of action on HMRC's part.

(VAT Notice 700/2/14, paras 2.21, 2.22).

In *Copthorn Holdings Ltd* [2015] UKFTT 405 (TC) (TC04582) (TVC 32.8), the First-tier Tribunal criticised HMRC's inflexible policy in refusing retrospective grouping to a fully taxable company that would be left with a £2 million irrecoverable VAT cost because of an administrative oversight, when Parliament had given HMRC the power to make such a consequence 'disappear with the stroke of a pen'. The judge cannot force HMRC to decide to allow retrospective grouping, but the decision was remitted to the Commissioners for reconsideration (twice, after an earlier First-tier Tribunal decision came to the same conclusion). HMRC have appealed the decision to the Upper Tribunal.

Companies already members of another VAT group

Where

- an application is made under (*a*) above and at the time of the application one or more of bodies corporate is already a member of another VAT group, the application has effect but with the exclusion of that body or those bodies;
- an application is made under (*b*) above and the applicant body is already a member of another VAT group, the application has no effect; and
- a body is subject to two applications under (*a*) or (*b*) above that have not been granted or refused, the applications have no effect.

[*VATA 1994, s 43D(3)*].

Refusal of application

HMRC may refuse an application within 90 days of receipt

- under (*a*) above if the bodies corporate are not eligible to be treated as members of a group under the criteria in **28.2** above;
- under (*b*) above if the proposed additional member is not eligible to be treated as a member of the group under the criteria in **28.2** above; or
- under any of (*a*)–(*e*) above if necessary for the protection of the revenue.

[*VATA 1994, s 43B(5)(6)*].

HMRC have given the following as broad examples of where an application for group treatment may be refused, but the list should not be taken as exhaustive.

- The proposed group members have poor compliance records which might pose a threat to HMRC's ability to collect VAT.
- HMRC have reason to believe that the applicants intend to use the grouping facilities to operate a VAT avoidance scheme.

- Group treatment would create a distortion in the VAT liability of the group's supplies (e.g. where exempt supplies would become taxable with consequent increase in input tax recovery or where entitlement to recover previously irrecoverable input tax is increased).

(Business Brief 31/97).

Where application is refused, it will be treated as if it had never been made in the first place. As a result:

- If any of the proposed members were registered for VAT before applying for group treatment, the previous registration will be reinstated with effect from the date on which it was cancelled.
- If, during the period that a company was provisionally treated as a member of a VAT group, it would have been required to notify its liability to register for VAT, it will have 30 days after the date of the letter of refusal to register.
- If a company was not liable to register at the time it applied for grouping and it would not have become liable during the period when it was provisionally treated as a member of a VAT group, it can apply for voluntary registration after group membership has been annulled.
- If, while the application to join a VAT group was being considered, the group submitted a VAT return which included supplies made and received by any 'group' company, the representative member must correct the error by adjusting the return following HMRC's decision (if below an upper limit) or by submitting an error correction notification (formerly voluntary disclosure).

(VAT Notice 700/2/14, para 2.18).

'Protection of the revenue'

The protection in question may be against any loss of revenue which is not *de minimis* whether or not it follows from the normal operations of grouping. It certainly covers an artificial avoidance scheme but it also covers a straightforward case which would not be characterised as avoidance or abusive. The phrase must be considered in its totality and involves a balancing exercise in which HMRC must weigh the effect of refusal on the applicant (e.g. higher administrative costs) against the loss of revenue likely to result from grouping (*National Westminster Bank plc* (VTD 15514)). HMRC will not normally use their protective powers when they consider that the revenue loss follows from the normal operating of the group, i.e. because VAT is eliminated on supplies between group members. This includes any loss arising from supplies between group members being disregarded where the recipient would not normally be able to deduct that VAT because it makes exempt supplies.

If HMRC have concerns that the revenue loss goes beyond the accepted consequences of VAT grouping, they will ask for

- relevant information about the administrative savings that grouping brings in the particular circumstances, and
- an estimate of the revenue impact of grouping.

They will also normally ask for comment on the impact on the business of any refusal to allow grouping or removal of a company from the VAT group.

HMRC will make a judgement based on the information provided, and any other information that they have. If a business fails to provide the information requested, although HMRC will endeavour to come to a balanced decision based on the information that they have, some factors may not be taken into account and this may affect the outcome of their considerations. Consistent failure to provide information or records reasonably requested in the course of enquiries may be treated as sufficient grounds for exercising the revenue protection powers.

(VAT Notice 700/2/14, paras 4.1–4.4).

Appeals against HMRC's refusal

An appeal may be made against HMRC's refusal of an application under (*a*)–(*e*) above. See **5.3**(13) **APPEALS**. Where the refusal of the application is on the grounds of protection of the revenue, the tribunal's jurisdiction is supervisory in that it cannot allow the appeal unless it considers that HMRC could not reasonably have been satisfied that there were grounds for refusing the application. Any refusal has effect pending the determination of the appeal but, if the appeal is allowed, the refusal is deemed not to have occurred. [*VATA 1994, s 84(4A)*].

Ceasing to satisfy eligibility criteria

If any member of a VAT group ceases to satisfy the criteria for group treatment under **28.2** above (e.g. by ceasing to be a subsidiary or ceasing to be established, or have a fixed establishment, in the UK) HMRC must be notified within 30 days of the change in circumstances. [*SI 1995/2518, Reg 5(2)*]. This is effectively done in the application to HMRC for the company in question to cease to be a member of the VAT group. The application is taken to be granted with effect from the day on which it is received by HMRC or such earlier or later time as HMRC allow (see above). This means that, if the application is made *after* the company leaves the group, HMRC are not obliged to exclude the company as soon as it ceases to be a member. This was confirmed in *C & E Commrs v Barclays Bank plc*, CA [2001] STC 1558 (TVC 32.17) where HMRC were able to prevent the company leaving the VAT group before the introduction of the anti-avoidance provisions in **28.5** below. HMRC have confirmed that, as this could cause commercial difficulties, in practice their policy will be to agree the date requested by the selling group. They will set a later date only if VAT avoidance is involved or is otherwise likely to arise. (Business Brief 30/02).

Termination of membership by HMRC

Where a body corporate is treated as a member of a group and it appears to HMRC that the body is not, or is no longer, eligible to be so treated under the criteria in **28.2** above, they must give notice to that body terminating its treatment as a member of the group from a date specified in the notice. [*VATA 1994, s 43C(3)*]. The date specified can be earlier than the date the notice is given but cannot be *earlier* than the date on which, in HMRC's opinion, the body became ineligible to be treated as a member of the group. [*VATA 1994, s 43C(4)*].

HMRC may also give notice to a body terminating its treatment as a member of a group from a specified date if it appears necessary for the 'protection of the revenue' (see above). The date specified can be the date the notice is given or any later date. [*VATA 1994, s 43C(1)(2)*].

Appeals

An appeal may be made against any notice by HMRC terminating membership of a group. See **5.3**(14) **APPEALS**. Where the appeal is against

- notice of termination of membership due to ineligibility and the grounds for the appeal relate (wholly or partly) to the date specified in the notice, or
- notice of termination of membership on the grounds of protection of the revenue,

the tribunal's jurisdiction is supervisory in that it cannot allow the appeal unless it considers that HMRC could not reasonably have been satisfied that date was appropriate or, as the case may be, there were grounds for giving the notice.

In either case, the notice has effect pending the determination of the appeal but, if the appeal is allowed, the notice is deemed never to have had effect.

[*VATA 1994, s 84(4B)–(4D)*].

Consequences of group treatment

[28.4] Group registration is a facilitation method which allows two or more corporate bodies to be treated as a single taxable person. One of the companies applying for group treatment is nominated as the representative member (see **28.3** above) and the registration is then made in the name of that member (VAT Notice 700/2/14, paras 1.2.1, 2.1).

The consequences of group treatment include the following.

(a) Any business carried on by a member of the group is treated as though carried on by the representative member.
(b) Subject to the anti-avoidance provisions in **28.5** below and the provisions relating to group supplies using an overseas member in **28.6** below, any supply of goods or services by a member of the group to another member of the group is disregarded for VAT purposes. This means that VAT need not be accounted for on these supplies and no VAT invoices must be issued in respect of them.
(c) Any supply not disregarded under (*b*) above which is a supply of goods (including a **63 SELF-SUPPLY**) or services (including deemed supply) by or to a group member is treated as a supply by or to the representative member.
(d) Any VAT paid or payable by a group member on the acquisition of goods from an EU member state or on the importation of goods from outside the EU is treated as paid or payable by the representative member and the goods are treated as having been acquired or imported by the representative member.

(e) Input tax recovery is determined in accordance with the use of the VAT group as a whole of the goods and services received by each individual member.

> *Example*
>
> Group member A buys in computer equipment and leases it to group member B, who uses the equipment to make exempt supplies to third parties outside the group.
>
> The input tax is attributable to exempt supplies and restricted (subject to the normal *de minimis* limits).

Input tax incurred by all the group members can be deducted to the extent that it is attributable to supplies made to persons outside the group which carry the right to deduct input tax.

(f) All members of the group are jointly and severally liable for any VAT due from the representative member. If the representative member is unable to meet a debt of the group, each member will be held liable for the amount of the debt until it is discharged. A former member is also liable for VAT due during its period of membership.
For liability of members when the representative member goes into liquidation, see **36.13 INSOLVENCY**, and where a corporate pension trustee is a member, see **54.4 PENSION SCHEMES**.

(g) Assessments can be validly raised on the representative member where relating to earlier periods when it was not the representative member and even if it was not a member of the group at that time (*Thorn plc* (VTD 15283) (TVC 32.24)). Also, under the anti-avoidance provisions in **28.5** below, current members of a VAT group may be held liable for assessments relating to periods when they were not members of the group.

(h) Most of the **50 PARTIAL EXEMPTION** rules apply to a VAT group in the same way as they would to a stand-alone business. Therefore
- the *de minimis* limits apply to the group as a whole and not the members individually; and
- any change in the group members may have a significant effect on an agreed special method which may need revising.

Special care should be taken over a prospective member which makes any exempt supplies to ensure that the group as a whole does not suffer the loss of input tax through the partial exemption rules.
See also **28.7** below for special provisions where a partly exempt group acquires a business as a going concern.

(i) The limit for error correction notifications (formerly voluntary disclosures) applies to the group as a whole. See **57.11 RECORDS**. The representative member must be informed of any misdeclarations made by any other members of the group since joining it, and either
- enter the amount to the group's VAT account; or
- if necessary, make a single error correction notification (formerly voluntary disclosure) on behalf of the whole group.

(j) The cash accounting limits apply to the group as a whole and not to the members individually. See **64.2** and **64.7 SPECIAL SCHEMES.**

(k) The payment on account limits (see **52.5 PAYMENT OF VAT**) apply to the group as a whole and not to the members individually.

(l) Special provisions also apply under the capital goods scheme when a VAT group is formed or disbanded or there is a change in membership. See **11 CAPITAL GOODS.**

(m) In *J & W Waste Management Ltd; J & W Plant & Tool Hire Ltd* (VTD 18069) (TVC 32.11) the tribunal held that VAT group membership does not imply abandonment of any right to appeal against demands for VAT. It specifically disapproved of the earlier decision in *Davis Advertising Service Ltd* (VTD 5) (TVC 2.71) that only the representative member has *locus standi* to bring an appeal.

The representative member is therefore responsible for

- accounting for any VAT due on supplies made by the group to third parties outside the group;
- completing a single VAT return and paying/reclaiming VAT on behalf of the whole group.

This is particularly helpful if accounting is centralised but group members will need to make sure that the representative member has all the necessary information to submit a VAT return for the group by the due date.

No taxable supplies outside the VAT group

The fact that no taxable supplies are made outside the VAT group does not prevent a group being formed provided one of the members is making taxable supplies which would make it liable or eligible for registration in its own right. However, as taxable supplies between group members are ignored, a group will not be able to recover any input tax unless it makes

- UK taxable supplies outside the group;
- supplies outside the UK that would be taxable supplies if made in the UK; or
- exempt financial/insurance supplies to customers outside the EU.

See **35.3 INPUT TAX** for fuller details.

> *Example*
>
> Good Causes Ltd is a registered charity that owns a trading subsidiary called Good Causes Trading Ltd. Neither company is registered for VAT because their supplies are either outside the scope of VAT or exempt from VAT. However, Good Causes Ltd incurs costs on behalf of Good Causes Trading Ltd, and wants to make a management charge of £100,000 per annum for these services.
>
> The problem with the above situation is that Good Causes Ltd will need to charge output tax on the management services once it has exceeded the VAT registration limit but Good Causes Trading Ltd will not be able to reclaim this VAT as input tax because it is not making any taxable supplies.

> However, the two companies could register for VAT as a group registration (the control conditions are met without any problem), which means that supplies of goods and services between group members are made without charging VAT.

'Special status' companies

The VAT liability of certain supplies, acquisitions and importations is dependent on the status of the person by or to whom the supply, etc. is made (e.g. education, water and certain supplies involving charities). In such cases, the VAT liability is decided by looking at the status of the person actually making/receiving the supply, even though for other VAT purposes the representative member is treated as making/receiving the supply.

[*VATA 1994, s 43(1)(1AA)(1AB)*]. (VAT Notice 700/2/14, paras 2.2–2.4, 5.1, 5.3, 5.5–5.7, 5.10).

Anti-avoidance provisions

[28.5] HMRC may direct that

- separately registered companies eligible to be treated as members of a VAT group are to be treated as grouped from a specified date;
- a company within a group is removed from that group from a specified date; or
- a supply within a VAT group initially treated as a disregarded supply is to be subjected to VAT.

The provisions are designed for use only against certain categories of avoidance scheme which rely on the existence of the group registration provisions in *VATA 1994, ss 43–43C*. Features common to such avoidance schemes are that input tax deduction is taken against standard-rated supplies, but output tax does not fall on the full value of those supplies because they are treated to some extent as being made between members of the same VAT group and so are disregarded for VAT. The simplest means of bringing the disregard into play is by moving a company into or out of a VAT group at a critical moment. But a similar result could be secured by entering into some other transaction, such as the transfer of assets or the assignment of an agreement to or from a group member.

The detailed provisions are outlined below. HMRC issued a Statement of Practice (SP) dated June 1996 setting out how they will seek to apply the provisions. Extracts are included in the text where appropriate.

The operation of these provisions (*VATA 1994, Sch 9A*) has never been tested in a tax case; it is possible that they have never been used in the 20 years since they were introduced.

Power to give directions

HMRC may give a direction if certain conditions are met. [*VATA 1994, Sch 9A para 1(1)*]. Taken together, the conditions require that a relevant event causes a situation where standard-rated supplies, which have given rise to an input tax credit by any person, are not taxed on their full value, so leading to a tax advantage. The conditions are as follows.

(a) A '*relevant event*' has occurred, ie a company has either
   (i) joined or ceased to be a member of a group, or
   (ii) entered into any 'transaction'

   after that date. [*VATA 1994, Sch 9A para 1(2), para 4(2)*].

   The word '*transaction*' is capable of a very wide meaning but, in the context of this provision, the key to its interpretation is that a relevant event occurs when a taxpayer *enters into* a transaction. Generally, HMRC will take this to mean when the taxpayer enters into a contract or other disposition, such as a gift. For example, HMRC will regard entering into a lease or the assignment, variation or surrender of a lease as a transaction which might potentially bring a company within the provisions. The performance of obligations under the lease (e.g. carrying out repairs or paying rent) would not normally be caught unless, exceptionally, such obligation constituted the entering into of a separate contract. (SP, para 3.5).

(b) There has been (or will or may be) a taxable supply on which VAT has been (or will or may be) charged otherwise than by reference to its full value due to the supply in question being disregarded under **28.4**(*b*) above. [*VATA 1994, Sch 9A para 1(3)(a)(9)*]. Supplies which, although not disregarded under **28.4**(*b*) above, are less than full value for other reasons are not covered. HMRC could not, for example, compulsorily group the parties to a lease and leaseback agreement under arrangements that had nothing to do with the operation of an intra-group disregard. (SP, para 3.6).

(c) At least part of the supply in (*b*) above is not (or would not be) zero-rated. [*VATA 1994, Sch 9A para 1(3)(b)*].

(d) The charging of VAT on the supply in (*b*) above otherwise than by reference to full value gives rise (or would give rise) to a tax advantage because a person has become entitled to
   (i) credit for input tax as attributable to that supply (or part of it); or
   (ii) a repayment of VAT under the provisions in **18.9 EUROPEAN UNION: GENERAL** or **49.5 OVERSEAS TRADERS** (refunds of VAT to persons in business abroad).

   [*VATA 1994, Sch 9A para 1(3)(c)(4)(5)*].

   It is not essential that the right to credit or repayment should be that of the supplier of the undercharged supply. The legislation specifically provides that the condition is also fulfilled where the supplier acquires the goods and/or services VAT free under the provisions relating to the transfer of a business as a going concern, and the transferor (or some previous owner) of the business has been entitled to an input tax credit. [*VATA 1994, Sch 9A para 1(6)(7)*].

(e) The requirements in (*b*)–(*d*) above would not be fulfilled apart from the occurrence of the relevant event.

(f) Where the relevant event is a transaction within (*a*)(ii) above, the supply on which VAT is undercharged must not be the only supply by reference to which the case falls within (*a*)–(*e*) above.

To pre-empt avoidance of the provisions, in determining whether the input tax credit is used to make an undercharged supply, separate rights to goods or services (including options or priorities in connection with goods or services), and the goods or services themselves are treated as a single supply. [*VATA 1994, Sch 9A para 1(8)(10)*].

HMRC must not give a direction if satisfied that the main purpose, or each of the main purposes, of the relevant event was a genuine commercial purpose unconnected with the consequences in (*b*)–(*d*) above. This does not apply where the relevant event is the termination of a body corporate's treatment as a member of a group by HMRC under *VATA 1994, s 43C* (see **28.3** above). [*VATA 1994, Sch 9A para 2*]. This recognises the fact that, in the vast majority of cases, businesses are moved into and out of groups for reasons which have no avoidance motive whatsoever. However, it is important to realise that where, in addition to acceptable commercial purpose, HMRC also identify other main purposes indicating VAT avoidance, they will seek to use their powers to nullify that advantage. (SP, paras 3.11–3.13, Annexes 1–3).

Form of directions

A direction may take the following forms.

(i) That a supply of goods or services, in whole or part, from one company to another does not fall within **28.4**(*b*) above (where it otherwise would).

(ii) That for such periods as may be described in the directions a company is not to be treated as a member of a group (where it otherwise would). To the extent that the direction applies to VAT periods after the direction is issued, *all* supplies between that company and other group members are treated as taxable supplies. For events prior to the issue of the direction, see under the heading *Assessments* below.

(iii) That for such periods as may be described in the directions, a company is to be treated as a member of a group (where it otherwise would not). Such a direction may also identify the company which is assumed to be the representative member of the group for those periods.

Subject to the time limits below, the periods under (ii) or (iii) above may comprise times before the giving of the direction or times afterwards or both.

Where a direction requires any assumptions to be made, *VATA 1994* has effect from the date of the direction in accordance with those assumptions. (For periods before the date of the direction, the assumptions are given effect by HMRC raising an assessment for unpaid VAT, see below.)

The fact that HMRC have accepted or refused an application for a company to join a group does not prejudice their powers to make a direction to the opposite effect.

[*VATA 1994, Sch 9A para 3(1)–(6)(8)*].

Withdrawal of direction

HMRC may withdraw a direction at any time by notice in writing to the person to whom it was given.[*VATA 1994, Sch 9A para 3(7)*].

Time limits

A direction cannot be given more than six years after the later of

- the occurrence of the relevant event; and
- the time when the entitlement to input tax under (*d*)(i) or (*d*)(ii) above arose.

However, where a direction is appropriate, it can require assumptions to be made about transactions made before either of those times without any limit. [*VATA 1994, Sch 9A para 4(1)(3); FA 1996, Sch 1*].

HMRC will not, however, seek application of any direction from a date earlier than that required to nullify the tax advantage derived from the relevant event. Usually, this will be the first day of the VAT period in which the scheme commences or the relevant event occurs (whichever is earlier). (SP, para 3.18).

Method of giving directions

A direction relating to a supply under (i) above may be given to the person who made the supply and a direction relating to a company under (ii) or (iii) above may be given to that company. In either case, the direction may also be given to the representative member of the group. Any direction must be in writing and must specify the relevant event by reference to which it is given. [*VATA 1994, Sch 9A para 5; FA 1996, Sch 1*].

Assessments

Where a direction is given and there is an amount of unpaid VAT for which a 'relevant person' would have been liable based on the assumptions specified in the direction, HMRC may, to the best of their judgement, assess the amount of unpaid VAT as VAT due from a relevant person and notify their assessment to that person. The assessment may be incorporated in the direction. See **6.1 ASSESSMENTS** for interpretation of 'to the best of HMRC's judgement'. Where, however, HMRC are satisfied that the actual revenue loss is less than the unpaid VAT the amount assessed must not exceed the revenue loss (calculated to the best of their judgement). [*VATA 1994, Sch 9A para 6(1)–(5)*].

'*Relevant person*' means the person to whom the direction is given, the representative member of the group to which that person was treated as being a member, or any company which, under the direction, is treated as being the representative member of such a group. [*VATA 1994, Sch 9A para 6(11); FA 1996, Sch 1*].

Calculation of VAT charge

- Where a direction is made under (i) above, VAT will become payable according to its value (adjusted as appropriate to take account of any direction issued under *VATA 1994, Sch 6 para 1* — supplies between connected persons, see **72.19 VALUATION**). A credit will be allowed for that part of the VAT which would have been deductible according to the partial exemption method of the VAT group registration.
- Where a direction is made under (ii) above, in relation to events prior to the issue of the direction, only those transactions relevant to the tax advantage will be affected. Input tax that would have been deductible

on the basis of the assumptions in the direction can be taken into account in appropriate cases. All other supplies made by the parties involved will be unaffected so there will be no need for any retrospective VAT accounting adjustment in their regard.

- Where a direction is made under (iii) above, the purpose of the direction will normally be to enable HMRC to recoup any excess claim to input tax. In such cases, the amount of VAT to be charged will be the amount of input tax recovered less the amount which would otherwise have been recoverable in accordance with the partial exemption method of the appropriate VAT group registration. A credit will also be allowed in connection with any output tax charged between the parties which would not have been due according to the assumptions specified in the directive.

(SP, paras 3.18, 5.1–5.3).

The amount assessed and notified to a person is, subject to appeal, deemed to be an amount of VAT due and is recoverable, from that person or the representative member of the group, unless the assessment is subsequently withdrawn or reduced. To the extent that more than one person is liable for the same unpaid VAT under any assessment, they are each jointly and severally liable for the full amount. [*VATA 1994, Sch 9A para 6(7)(8)*].

Time limit

An assessment under these provisions cannot be made more than one year after the date of the direction or in the case of any direction which has been withdrawn. [*VATA 1994, Sch 9A para 6(6)*].

Supplementary assessments

Where it appears to HMRC that the amount which ought to have been assessed exceeds the amount actually assessed, a supplementary assessment of the amount of the excess may be made and notified under the same provisions and within the same time limit as the original assessment. [*VATA 1994, Sch 9A para 6(9)*].

Interest payable

The provisions of *VATA 1994, s 74* on interest (see **52.16** PAYMENT OF VAT) also apply to assessments under the above provisions, except that interest runs from the date on which the assessment is notified rather than the reckonable date. The period for interest is confined to the two years ending with the time when the assessment to interest is made. [*VATA 1994, Sch 9A para 6(9)(10)*].

Appeals against directions by HMRC

An appeal may be made against a direction by HMRC under the above provisions. See **5.3**(30) APPEALS. The tribunal must allow the appeal if satisfied that

- the conditions for making the direction were not fulfilled; or
- the main purpose, or each of the main purposes, of the relevant event was a genuine commercial purpose unconnected with the consequences in (*b*) above.

[*VATA 1994, s 84(7A)*].

Following correction of a tax advantage

Following correction of a tax advantage to the satisfaction of HMRC, they will consider any subsequent application to join or leave a group subject to their normal powers of discretion. (SP, para 3.20).

De Voil Indirect Tax Service. See V2.190B.

Group supplies using an overseas member

[28.6] A supply between a member of a VAT group ('*the supplier*') and another member of the group ('*the UK member*') is not disregarded under **28.4**(*b*) above if the following conditions are satisfied.

(a) If there were no group, the supply would be a supply of services to which *VATA 1994, s 7A(2)(a)* applies, to a person belonging in the UK.
(b) Those services are not within any of the descriptions specified in *VATA 1994, Sch 9* (exempt supplies).
(c) The supplier has been supplied (whether or not by a person belonging in the UK) with any services where *VATA 1994 s 7A(2)(a)* applies to the supply (see **66.14 SUPPLY: PLACE OF SUPPLY**), which are not within any of the descriptions specified in *VATA 1994, Sch 9* (exempt supplies).
(d) The supplier belonged outside the UK when it was supplied with the services in (*c*) above.
(e) Those services have been used by the supplier for making the onward supply to the UK member.
The provisions apply even if the bought-in supply only forms a cost component of the onward supply to the UK group member but generally HMRC will treat bought-in supplies as *de minimis* if their value is less than 5% of the value of the onward supply. However, HMRC will not apply this rule rigidly (e.g. where they suspect that supplies or values have been manipulated to meet the 5% test or where, despite the fact that the 5% test is not met, the charge would be insignificant). The extent to which VAT on the charge could be recovered under the group's partial exemption method, along with the amount of the charge in the context of the group's size, will also be considered when deciding whether a potential charge is *de minimis*. (Business Brief 11/97).

Where the conditions are met, the following consequences apply.

(1) The supply is treated as a taxable supply in the UK by the representative member to itself.
(2) Except as allowed by HMRC, the deemed supply by the representative member cannot be taken into account when determining its allowable input tax.
(3) The deemed supply is treated as a supply between connected persons for the purposes of any direction by HMRC as to open market value under *VATA 1994, Sch 6 para 1* (see **72.20 VALUATION**).

(4) Subject to (3) above, the deemed supply has the normal value rules for supplies subject to the reverse charge (see **39.4 INTERNATIONAL SERVICES**), i.e. it is calculated on the value of the supply by the overseas member to the UK member. However, the value may be reduced to the value of the services *purchased* by the overseas group member where
(i) evidence of this valuation can be produced in the UK; and
(ii) those services have not been undervalued.
(*VATA 1994, Sch 6, para 8A*).
Under (1) above, where a service is bought in by an overseas group member for the exclusive use of a UK group member, copies of invoices from the external supplier are acceptable evidence of value. Alternatively, businesses may be able to agree with their VAT office that different evidence is adequate (e.g. evidence that the overseas group member buys in services and applies a fixed mark-up would normally be satisfactory evidence that the value of the bought-in service was equal to the value of the onward supply less the mark-up). Where services are not bought in for exclusive use or mark-ups vary, a fair and reasonable value must be calculated. HMRC have indicated that, in most cases, the evidence required to support the reduced value consists of a summary statement of the overseas member's costs; an outline of the basis on which the overseas member calculates its charge; and a record of the method for reducing the charge to an amount based on the bought-in supplies. (Business Briefs 11/97, 16/11).

In *Skandia America Corp (USA) v Skatterverket, ECJ Case C-7/13* (TVC 20.5) Skandia America Corp (USA) purchased IT services and sold them to its branch in Sweden, Skandia Sverige, which was registered as a member of a VAT group. Skandia Sverige processed the IT services and sold them to various companies in the Skandia group, both within and outside the VAT group. The case concerned the interaction of VAT grouping rules on transactions between establishments of a business established both outside and inside Sweden. The Swedish Court referred two questions to the CJEU:

- whether supplies of services from a main establishment outside the EU to its branch in an EU member state constitute taxable transactions when that branch belongs to a VAT group in the EU member state in which the branch is established, and if so;
- whether the person liable to pay the VAT is the supplier of the services (the main establishment outside the EU) or the recipient of the services (the VAT group in the EU member state).

The CJEU noted that under the Swedish grouping provisions, the supplier and the recipient were separate taxable persons and accordingly found that the supplies in question constituted taxable transactions and that the recipient of the services is liable for the VAT under the reverse charge procedures.

HMRC published HMRC Brief 37/14 on 13 October 2014 indicating that it will need to consider what impact, if any, the CJEU decision has on the UK rules and whether any changes in the UK legislation are required. HMRC noted that the UK VAT grouping rules differ from the Swedish VAT grouping rules and that the judgment did not consider what the position under the UK rules should be or whether the Swedish rules were the only permissible VAT grouping rules.

(HMRC Brief 37/14).

Further to HMRC Brief 37/14, HMRC published HMRC Brief 2/15 on 10 February 2015. HMRC Brief 2/15 explains that HMRC do not consider that any changes to the UK grouping provisions are required but sets out what HMRC regard as the implication of the judgment in *Skandia America Corp (USA) v Skatterverket, ECJ Case C-7/13* (TVC 20.6) and a change to UK VAT accounting.

The implication of the judgment in *Skandia America Corp (USA) v Skatterverket, ECJ Case C-7/13* (TVC 20.6) is that an overseas establishment of a UK-established entity is part of a separate taxable person if the overseas establishment is VAT-grouped in an EU member state that operates similar 'establishment only' grouping provisions to Sweden. This will be the case whether or not the entity in the UK is part of a UK VAT group.

(HMRC Brief 2/15).

UK VAT accounting from 1 January 2016

As a result of the judgment in *Skandia America Corp (USA) v Skatterverket, ECJ Case C-7/13* (TVC 20.6), from 1 January 2016 businesses must treat intra-entity services provided to or by overseas establishments VAT-grouped in any EU member states that operate similar 'establishment only' grouping provisions to Sweden as supplied to or by a separate taxable person and account for VAT accordingly. Services provided by the overseas VAT-grouped establishment to the UK establishment will normally be treated as supplies made in the UK under the place of supply rules and subject to the reverse charge if taxable. Services provided by the UK establishment to the overseas VAT-grouped establishment will normally be treated as made outside the UK under the place of supply rules and will need to be taken into account for ascertaining input tax credit for the UK establishment. If the supplies are reverse charge services they should be reported on the EC Sales List.

If the UK entity is part of a UK VAT group the above method of VAT accounting applies to supplies between the overseas establishment and other UK VAT group members in the UK. Under these circumstances the anti-avoidance legislation in *VATA 1994, s 43(2A)–(2E)* does not apply as the overseas establishment is not seen as part of the UK VAT group.

The above method of VAT accounting applies to intra-entity services supplied to or from a UK entity and its overseas establishment if the overseas establishment is VAT-grouped in an EU member state that operates establishment only grouping provisions which create intra-establishment supplies.

HMRC Brief 18/15, updated by Brief 23/15, includes the following information outlining how HMRC expects EU member states to operate VAT grouping in the light of the decision in *Skandia America Corp (USA) v Skatterverket, ECJ Case C-7/13* (TVC 20.6):

EU member state	*Position as at 11 December 2015*
Cyprus, Finland, Germany, Spain (advanced method)	The intention of these EU member states is uncertain.
Austria, Ireland, the Netherlands, UK	HMRC does not expect these EU member states to apply establishment only VAT grouping to create intra-establishment supplies when the establishment in the EU member state is VAT grouped.
Italy, Romania, Spain (basic method)	Italian, Romanian and basic Spanish VAT grouping is purely administrative, treating each member as a separate taxable person and just amalgamating their VAT figures on a single return.
Belgium, the Czech Republic, Denmark, Estonia, Hungary, Latvia, Slovakia, Sweden	HMRC expects these EU member states to apply establishment only VAT grouping to create intra-establishment supplies when the establishment in the EU member state is VAT grouped.
Bulgaria, Croatia, France, Greece, Lithuania, Luxembourg, Malta, Poland, Portugal, Slovenia	HMRC understands these EU member states do not have VAT grouping.

HMRC confirmed in HMRC Brief 23/15 that the above information regarding how it expects EU member states to operate VAT grouping should be regarded as a guide only and it is the responsibility of individual businesses to check the position regarding their own circumstances with the tax authorities of the relevant EU member states.

(HMRC Briefs 18/15 and 23/15).

Transfers of going concerns

Where a business or part of a business is transferred as a going concern and is treated as neither a supply of goods nor services under **9.9 BUSINESS** (or would be so treated if made in the UK), if the transferor satisfied conditions (*c*) and (*d*) above before the transfer and the services in question are used by the transferee to make the supply within (*e*) above, the services are deemed to have been supplied to the transferee at a time when the transferee belonged outside the UK (so that the above conditions are deemed to have been met). The conditions are also deemed to be met in cases involving successive business transfers.

[*VATA 1994, s 43(2A)–(2E), Sch 6 para 8A*].

Interim payments

Where interim payments are made in respect of supplies subject to these provisions, VAT must be accounted for on each payment. If the group cannot calculate the reduced value of the charge by the time it has to account for VAT, it should account for VAT from month to month on a best estimate, making an appropriate adjustment at the end of the year.

Misdeclaration penalties

Failure to comply with the provisions may incur a misdeclaration penalty, subject to normal rules. See **53.14 PENALTIES**.

(Business Brief 11/97).

De Voil Indirect Tax Service. See V3.267.

Acquisition of a business as a going concern by a partly exempt VAT group

[28.7] Where a business, or part of a business, carried on by a taxable person is transferred as a going concern to any member of a VAT group and the transfer of any 'chargeable assets' involved is treated as neither a supply of goods nor a supply of services (see **9.9 BUSINESS**), then, subject to below, the chargeable assets are treated (at the time of the transfer) as being supplied to the representative member of the group for the purpose of its business and supplied by that member in the course or furtherance of its business. The supply is at the 'open market value' of the chargeable assets.

Assets are '*chargeable assets*' if their supply in the UK by a taxable person in the course or furtherance of his business would be a taxable supply (and not a zero-rated supply).

'*Open market value*' is the price that would be paid on a sale (on which no VAT was payable) between a buyer and seller who are not in such a relationship as to affect the price.

The above provisions do not apply if

(a) the representative member is entitled to credit for the whole of the input tax on supplies to it and acquisitions and importations by it during the VAT period in which the assets are transferred *and* any longer accounting period over which input tax is attributed under the partial exemption provisions;
(b) HMRC are satisfied that the assets were assets of the taxable person transferring them more than three years before the day on which they are transferred; or
(c) the chargeable assets consist of certain computers, computer equipment, land or buildings covered by the capital goods scheme (see **11.2 CAPITAL GOODS**).

A supply treated as made by the representative member under these provisions is not taken into account when determining the allowance of input tax for the group under the partial exemption provisions.

[*VATA 1994, s 44*].

HMRC may reduce the VAT chargeable under these provisions if they are satisfied that the previous owner did not receive credit for the full amount of input tax arising on the supply to him, or acquisition or importation by him, of the chargeable assets (e.g. because he was partly exempt or the input tax was blocked on the purchase of a car).

If the previous owner is unconnected with the VAT group, the open market value will normally be accepted as the consideration paid for the assets on which VAT is due. If VAT is not due on some of the assets, the consideration must be apportioned fairly between the standard-rated and other assets.

In a case where the seller's partial exemption recovery rate (during the partial exemption tax year in which the assets were purchased) is equal to or less than the purchaser's recovery rate (during the partial exemption tax year in which the assets were acquired), the VAT charge will be reduced to nil, although no VAT will be refunded.

(VAT Notice 700/9/12, paras 5.2–5.4).

De Voil Indirect Tax Service. See V3.246.

Until the decision of the Upper Tribunal in *Intelligent Managed Services Ltd v HMRC* [2015] UKUT 341 (TCC), HMRC's policy was that the disregarding of intra-group supplies meant that a trade would cease if it was transferred to a VAT group member and only used to make supplies to other group members. In the case, a company had acquired assets and developed know-how in relation to banking processing; instead of carrying on its intended business as an internet bank, it sold the assets and undertaking to a subsidiary within the Virgin Money group, which used the assets to make supplies of processing services to other group members. HMRC issued assessments on the basis that the transferor had made a taxable supply, because the business ceased once all its supplies were disregarded. The Upper Tribunal held that this was not correct: the fiction of the VAT group did not extend to disregarding the continued use of these assets in the same kind of economic activity.

HMRC have accepted this decision and changed their policy, noting that the same principle would apply where a business, which had previously involved only intra-group supplies, is transferred out of a VAT group. One situation in which this is likely to arise is where a rented property with a group member as a tenant is either transferred to another group company by an outside landlord, or transferred by a group property company to an outside landlord. HMRC comment that where SDLT has been charged on VAT-inclusive consideration in a situation where the new policy would treat the transfer of a building as part of a VAT-free TOGC, the taxpayer should contact HMRC to request a repayment.

The possible application of *VATA 1994, s 44* to the TOGC into the group was not considered in the *Intelligent Managed Services Ltd* case, possibly because HMRC were convinced that the liability fell on the transferor. The Brief accepting the decision also points out that *s 44* will apply when a TOGC is made into an exempt or partially exempt group.

(HMRC Brief 11/16).

Surrender of corporation tax losses

[28.8] Under *CTA 2010, Part 5*, companies within a *corporation tax* group may surrender the benefit of corporation tax losses from one to another under certain circumstances. The company receiving the benefit usually makes a payment for the use of the losses. See *Tolley's Corporation Tax*. Where the two companies involved are also within the same VAT group the surrender has no VAT effect following **28.4** above. Where the two companies are not in the same VAT group HMRC have stated that group relief payments in themselves do not usually give rise to taxable supplies (CCAB Statement TR 344 June 1979). See, however, **45.3 MANAGEMENT SERVICES AND SUPPLIES OF STAFF.**

Holding companies

[28.9] The basic functions of a holding company are to acquire and hold shares in subsidiaries from which it may receive dividends; defend itself and its subsidiaries from takeovers; and make disposals. From time to time it may invest, deposit or lend money, and issue or sell shares. Some of these activities are outside the scope of VAT while others are exempt. A holding company which has no other activities is not eligible to register for VAT and is not able to recover any VAT on its purchases.

Registration

Holding companies are liable to register for VAT where they have taxable trading activities, supply management services to subsidiaries or are included in a VAT group with trading subsidiaries.

In *Cibo Participations SA v Directeur régional des impôts du Nord-Pas-de-Calais, ECJ Case C–16/00,* [2002] STC 460 (TVC 22.122) the CJEU held that the management of subsidiary companies could qualify as an economic activity if it was accompanied by activities such as the performance of administrative, financial, commercial or technical services. See also *Polysar Investments Netherlands BV v Inspecteur der Invoerrechten en Accijnzen, ECJ Case C–60/90,* [1993] STC 222 (TVC 22.114) and *Newmir plc* (VTD 10102) (TVC 7.122).

Input tax deduction

Subject to below, deduction of input tax for holding companies is calculated on the following basis.

- Input tax on supplies to the holding company must be attributed to taxable, exempt or other non-taxable outputs to the greatest possible extent, and the normal rules applied.
- Any residual input tax which cannot be directly attributed will be accepted as a general overhead of the taxable person.
- The amount of the residual input tax which can be recovered will be determined in accordance with the partial exemption rules.

Most costs related to acquisitions and defence against takeovers fall into the 'overhead' category.

However if a holding company is not providing genuine management services to its subsidiaries then it will not be able to recover input tax on costs incurred in acquiring another company, disposing of a subsidiary, restructuring the group or any subsidiary, or holding investments. This is because HMRC do not regard such costs as relating to any taxable supply (see below).

In *Empresa de Desenvolvimento Mineiro SGPS v Fazenda Publica, ECJ Case C–77/01,* [2005] STC 65 (TVC 22.518) the CJEU held that the simple sale of securities (e.g. holdings in investment funds) did not constitute economic activities and that placement in investment funds did not constitute supplies of services effected for a consideration. As a result, turnover relating to such transactions should be excluded from any partial exemption calculation. However, the annual granting by a holding company of interest-bearing loans to companies in which it had shareholdings and placements by that holding company in bank deposits or in securities (e.g. Treasury notes or certificate of deposit) constituted economic activities carried out by a taxable person acting as such (and were exempt from VAT under what is now *Directive 2006/112/EC, Art 135(1)*). In any partial exemption calculation, such transactions were to be regarded as 'incidental transactions' insofar as they involved 'only very limited use of assets or services subject to VAT' and it was for the national court to establish whether this was the case.

See also *BLP Group plc v C & E Commrs, ECJ Case C–4/94,* [1995] STC 424 (TVC 22.453) where input tax on professional fees incurred in connection with the disposal of shares in a subsidiary company to pay debts was held as being not recoverable as relating to the exempt sale of shares (rather than recoverable as relating to the payment of debts derived from taxable transactions effected by the company).

In the joined cases of *Beteiligungsgesellschaft Larentia + Minerva mbH & Co. KG v Finanzamt Nordenham, ECJ Case C–108/14* (TVC 22.471) and *Finanzamt Hamburg-Mitte v Marenave Schiffahrts AG, ECJ Case C–109/14* (TVC 22.471) the CJEU decided that expenditure connected with the acquisition of shareholdings in subsidiaries by a holding company which involves itself in the management of those subsidiaries must be regarded as belonging to the holding company's general expenditure and the VAT paid on the expenditure must, in principle, be deducted in full, subject to the normal rules.

In *Norseman Gold plc v HMRC* [2016] UKUT 69 (TCC) (TVC 20.16), the appellant (N) considered that it was entitled to recover input tax incurred on various costs as it intended to make taxable supplies of management services to its subsidiaries at some point in the future. The First-tier Tribunal accepted that N had an active role in the management of the subsidiaries; however there was no firm agreement between N and its subsidiaries regarding how much the charge would be and exactly when the management charges would be levied. The subsidiaries were involved in prospecting for gold in Australia and were loss making so N decided not levy the charge as it would need to fund the subsidiaries in order for them to pay that charge. The First-tier Tribunal held that the services provided by N to its subsidiaries were capable of being regarded as taxable supplies, however in this case no supply had been made because there was no consideration. The tribunal considered that the concept of consideration relies on the reciprocal performance of obligations. The First-tier Tribunal held that the lack of a reciprocal obligation was fatal to N's case and dismissed its appeal. N appealed and during the appeal argued that there was an intention at some point in the future for the subsidiaries to pay for the services provided and therefore they should be treated as taxable supplies. The Upper Tribunal did not agree and dismissed the appeal. N has appealed against this decision and the Court of Appeal is scheduled to hear the appeal on 10 May 2017.

In *Magyar Villamos Művek Zrt. (MVM) v Nemzeti Adó- és Vámhivatal Fellebviteli Igazgatósága, ECJ Case C-28/16* (TVC 22.472), the CJEU issued an Order dated 12 January 2017, in respect of the Hungarian referral which confirms that the holding company that is engaged in the management of its subsidiaries must levy a charge for the management services provided. If the holding company does not levy a charge then the management services provided will not be regarded as an economic activity and it cannot deduct VAT on costs connected with those management activities unless there is a link to the taxable business activities as a whole. The fact that the holding company may be engaged in other economic activities in its own right will not automatically give rise to a deduction on costs associated with managing the subsidiaries.

HMRC guidance on holding companies and their right to deduct input tax

HMRC have issued updated guidance in respect of holding companies and their right to deduct input tax.

In VIT40100 HMRC discussed the VAT status of holding companies states the following which may prove helpful in determining the 'VAT status' of a holding company:

> "In order to determine the extent to which a holding company is engaged in an economic activity and can recover VAT, an important consideration is whether the holding company is holding and managing its investments in subsidiaries for the purpose of receiving dividends in a fashion that is no different from that of a private investor whose activities do not amount to a business (i.e. an economic activity), as in *Polysar* (see VIT64050).
>
> Alternatively, the holding company may provide management services to its subsidiaries and in these circumstances the cost of acquiring the shares in those subsidiaries may have a direct and immediate link with the holding company's general economic activity and form part of their general overheads, as in *Cibo* (see VIT64050).
>
> The CJEU released its decision in the German cases of *Larentia + Minerva & others* (C-108/14 and C-109/14) In July 2015. The CJEU found that VAT incurred on raising capital for acquisition of shareholdings in subsidiaries, to which the holding company also intends to provide management services, must be regarded as belonging to the holding company's general expenditure and is deductible (subject to any partial exemption restriction in place). This decision is relevant in determining the extent to which UK holding companies, which make or intend to make management supplies to subsidiaries, can recover the VAT incurred on the cost of acquiring those shares."

In VIT40600 HMRC have confirmed that VAT can be recovered on shareholding where it is used as part of an economic activity. Simply holding shares in order to receive dividends and potentially sell them as a capital gain is an investment activity and VAT cannot be recovered. HMRC have reviewed its policy following the CJEU decision in the joined cases *Beteiligungsgesellschaft*

Larentia + Minerva mbH & Co. KG v Finanzamt Nordenham, ECJ Case C–108/14 (TVC 22.471) and *Finanzamt Hamburg-Mitte v Marenave Schiffahrts AG, ECJ Case C–109/14* (TVC 22.471). HMRC state the following:

> "In *L+M* the CJEU held that VAT incurred by a holding company on the costs of acquiring shareholdings in subsidiaries, to which it also intends to provide taxable management services, must be regarded as belonging to the Holding company's general expenditure and is deductible subject to any Partial Exemption restriction in place.
>
> In order to be able to deduct VAT incurred on costs of acquiring shareholdings in subsidiaries the following conditions must be satisfied:
>
> - the holding company making the claim must be the recipient of the supply
> - the holding company must be undertaking economic activity for VAT purposes
> - that economic activity must involve the making of taxable supplies.
>
> If the holding company is VAT grouped with its subsidiaries, it makes taxable supplies or loans for which it earns interest and the loans support the making of taxable supplies by the VAT group.
>
> If the holding company is not the recipient of the supply, or is not undertaking economic activity, it will not be able to recover VAT."

The holding company must be the recipient of the supply and HMRC consider that the recipient will have entered into the contract for the supply or had that contract novated to him, made use of the supply and been invoiced for that supply.

Dividends and interest

Dividends received by a holding company from subsidiaries where there is no involvement in the management are to be excluded from total income in making partial exemption calculations (*Satam SA v Minister Responsible for the Budget, ECJ Case C-333/91*, [1997] STC 226 (TVC 22.511)). This was confirmed in *Floridienne SA v Belgian State; Berginvest SA v Belgian State, ECJ Case C-142/99*, [2000] STC 1044 (TVC 22.517) where the court also held that interest paid on loans to subsidiaries should be similarly excluded where the relevant loans did not constitute an economic activity of the holding company within what is now *Directive 2006/112/EC, Art 9(1)*. Whether the loans were within the charge to VAT was for the national courts to decide.

Key points: groups of companies

[28.10] Points to consider are as follows.

- A worthwhile advantage of group registration is that no VAT is charged on supplies of goods or services made between group members. This reduces the risk that supplies between connected companies could forget to take VAT into account where the entities are separately VAT-registered. A common error is for such recharges to be forgotten about when they are made by journal through inter-company accounts, or as a year-end adjustment by accountants. A group arrangement avoids this risk.

- For a group registration to be accepted by HMRC, the control test needs to be fully met. This means that joint venture arrangements (50:50 control between separate parties) are ineligible for group registration.
- HMRC have the power to allow group registration on a retrospective basis but only in limited circumstances and where the backdating is 30 days or less. It is therefore important that a business identifies the benefits of a group registration in advance, e.g. to avoid a potential VAT liability on charges from a business to a connected party that is input tax blocked because of partial exemption.
- A holding company making management charges to its trading subsidiaries will have to charge VAT on these supplies if it is registered for VAT. This could lead to a source of non-claimable VAT if the recipient makes some exempt supplies. A group registration avoids this problem because no VAT is charged on supplies between entities within the same group.
- However, be aware of the need to consider input tax for the group as a whole and its relationship to supplies made to external customers. If input tax incurred by one group company relates to exempt supplies made by another group company, then the input tax will be classed as relevant to an exempt supply, i.e. partial exemption implications.
- It is important that a holding company registered for VAT is making genuine taxable supplies to its trading subsidiaries, e.g. for management services, consultancy fees, etc. If no taxable supplies are being made, the holding company should not be registered for VAT. The case of *Norseman Gold plc* shows that it is also important that consideration should be linked to the provision of those genuine services.
- There is scope for a group registration to be formed even if the only taxable supplies relate to management services between group members. This strategy will avoid output tax being charged on such supplies and therefore prevent non-reclaimable input tax being incurred by the recipient, e.g. in relation to exempt or non-business activities.
- Although HMRC tend to approve a request for group registration within 15 days, it is common practice for them to inform the applicant in writing about their power to make further checks of the application within 90 days of it being approved. In most cases, this statement will not cause a problem as long as the fundamental rules concerning group registration have been properly met and there are no anti-avoidance issues that cause a problem.

29

Health and Welfare

Cross-references. See **13.8 CHARITIES** for charity funded equipment for medical and veterinary use; **19.24**(*b*)–(*e*), (*g*), (*h*), (*o*) and (*p*) **EUROPEAN UNION LEGISLATION**; **34.15**(5) **IMPORTS** for relief from VAT on the importation of various health-related goods.

De Voil Indirect Tax Service. See V4.146.

Introduction to health and welfare

[29.1] The UK's approach to exemption for health supplies is to link it to statutory registration of the relevant 'health professional'. By '*health professional*', HMRC mean the following professionals when they are enrolled or registered on the appropriate statutory register.

- Medical practitioners (see **29.3** below).
- Optometrists and dispensing opticians (see **29.4** below).
- Professionals registered under the *Health Professions Order 2001* (see **29.5** below).
- Osteopaths (see **29.5** below).
- Chiropractors (see **29.5** below).
- Nurses, midwives and health visitors (see **29.6** below).
- Dentists, dental hygienists, dental therapists, dental nurses, clinical dental technicians, dental technicians, orthodontic therapists (see **29.7** below).
- Pharmacists (see **29.9** below).

This means that therapists such as acupuncturists, psychologists, hypnotherapists and others who do not have statutory registers cannot currently exempt their services. (Psychiatrists are qualified medical practitioners and are exempt under **29.3** above.)

(VAT Notice 701/57/14, paras 2.1, 2.2).

Qualifying services

Historically, the UK's position was that where registered health professionals provided services using their professional training and knowledge, those services (with certain limited and specified exceptions) were exempt from VAT. This was taken to be the correct implementation of what is now *EC Directive 2006/112/EC, Art 132(1)(c)* which provides for the exemption of 'the provision of medical care in the exercise of the medical and paramedical professions as defined by the Member State concerned'. However, in *d'Ambrumenil v C & E Commrs; Dispute Resolution Services Ltd v C & E Commrs, ECJ Case C–307/01,* [2005] STC 650 (TVC 22.314) the CJEU defined the term 'medical care' for the purposes of the *Directive* as services having a therapeutic nature and examinations or other medical interventions of a preventative nature for persons not suffering from any disease or heath disorder. The effect of this is that exemption is limited to those services intended principally to protect (including maintain and restore) the health of individuals. Services not intended principally to do this should be taxable. Liability is therefore dependent on the principal purpose for which the supply is made.

In accordance with this decision, services provided by registered health professionals can only qualify for exemption when consisting of medical care. General advice on registration, VAT liability and VAT recovery is available in VAT Information Sheet 5/07.

The concepts of 'hospital and medical care' in *EC Directive 2006/112/EC, Art 132(1)(b)* and 'the provision of medical care' in *Art 132(1)(c)* are both intended to cover services that have as their purpose the diagnosis, treatment and, in so far as possible, cure of diseases or health disorders. See *Future Health Technologies Ltd v HMRC, ECJ Case C–86/09* [2010] STC 1836 (TVC 20.105).

Exemption for services

[29.2] Following the decision in *d'Ambrumenil* (see **29.1** above) HMRC regards services of a health professional as exempt when

(a) the services are within the profession in which he is registered to practise; and
(b) the primary purpose of the services is the protection, maintenance or restoration of the health of the person concerned.

Goods supplied with exempt services

HMRC also regard the exemption as extending to any charge made for bandages, drugs, medicines or prostheses, administered or applied to a patient in the course of exempt medical treatment. Any items that are separable from the treatment (e.g. privately dispensed drugs supplied for self-administration by a patient) are not exempt from VAT, and will normally be standard-rated. The supply of drugs, medicines and other items to patients by a pharmacist or doctor is zero-rated in certain circumstances (see **29.13** below).

Examples of exempt services

Health services provided under General Medical Services, Primary Medical Services, Alternative Provider Medical Services, Primary Care Trust Medical Services, General Dental Services and Personal Dental Services contracts

Sight testing and prescribing by opticians (only in England, Wales and Northern Ireland)

Primary eye examinations and secondary eye examinations (only in Scotland)

Enhanced eye health services

Laser eye surgery

Hearing tests

Treatment provided by osteopaths and chiropractors

Nursing care provided in a patient's own home

Pharmaceutical advice

Certain insurance or education-related services may be exempt regardless of purpose because they qualify under other exemptions (see below).

Examples of standard-rated services

Health services not performed by an appropriately qualified and registered health professional (except when either directly supervised by such a person (see **29.8** below) or provided within a hospital or similar institution (see **29.10** below)

Services not aimed at the prevention, diagnosis, treatment or cure of a disease or health disorder, such as paternity testing and the writing of articles for journals

Services directly supervised by a pharmacist

General administrative services such as countersigning passport applications and providing character references

Supplies of health professional staff, except where they are treated as being exempt from VAT under the nursing agencies' concession

(VAT Notice 701/57/14, paras 2.3, 2.5, 3.1).

Services that can be taxable or exempt

Some services may be taxable or exempt, depending on whether or not the primary purpose falls within (*b*) above. Some of the more common services are considered below. The services will normally be provided by doctors although some may be carried out by other registered health professionals. To avoid duplication, 'doctor' should be taken as including other health professionals where appropriate.

(1) Clinical trials

The supply is only exempt if it involves patient care, e.g. where the doctor is required to monitor a patient involved in the trial for adverse reactions which may be detrimental to his health. If involvement with the patient is restricted to monitoring side-effects for analytical purposes, or if the doctor is providing analytical testing services with no patient contact, the service is standard-rated.

(2) Access to medical records

In certain circumstances individual patients or their representatives are entitled to access to, or copies of, health records (including hand-written clinical notes, copies of letters to and from other health professionals, laboratory reports, X-rays and other imaging records, and printouts from monitoring equipment) or medical reports written about them.

- Under the *Data Protection Act 1998*, where the holder of the records receives a subject access request (SAR), it must provide the information requested but may make a charge for so doing. The maximum amount of the fee is a nominal sum to cover the expense of complying.
- Under the *Access to Medical Reports Act 1988*, a patient is entitled to ask for a copy of any medical reports made by his GP for insurance or employment purposes. Where such a request is made, the GP can charge a reasonable fee to cover costs incurred.
- Under the *Access to Health Records Act 1990* and the *Access to Health Records (Northern Ireland) Order 1993*, any individual's personal representatives, and anyone with a claim arising out of the death, may have access to the health records of the deceased. The record holder may charge a fee.

Where a doctor provides a copy of all or part of a medical record or report under these statutory requirements, that activity is outside the scope of VAT. But where a copy of a health record is provided in other circumstances, there is a standard-rated supply of services.

(3) Certificates and reports

Most supplies of certificates and reports are standard-rated because they enable a third party to make a decision and contain no element of therapeutic care (e.g. they may enable claims to compensation, benefits or registration as a blind or disabled person). But where the principal purpose of a certificate or report is to protect, maintain or restore the health of the individual (e.g. sick notes and certain reports required as part of adoption procedures) then the supply is exempt.

Fitness certificates were one of the supplies considered by the CJEU in the *d'Ambrumenil* case (see **29.1** above). It was held that exemption applied

- where the certificate was intended principally to protect the health of the individual such as the certification
  (i) of fitness to travel; or
  (ii) provided to an employer so that the employer recognises that the individual's health places limitations on certain activities (e.g. heavy lifting due to a severe back problem),

but that standard-rating applied

- to giving certificates as to a person's medical condition for purposes such as entitlement to war pension (see also *Unterpertinger v Pensionversicherungsanstalt der Arbeiter, ECJ Case C–212/01*, [2005] STC 678 (TVC 22.313) where the services of a doctor in making an expert report on a person's health in order to support a claim for disability pension was held to be subject to VAT);
- to the preparation of medical reports following examinations concerning
  (i) issues of liability and the quantification of damages for individuals contemplating personal injury litigation; or
  (ii) professional medical negligence for individuals contemplating litigation

  or the preparation of reports for these purposes based on medical notes without conducting a medical examination; or
- where certificates are provided as a condition of a person taking up a particular profession or sporting activity.

See also under Occupational health at (12) below.

(4) Psychologists' services

Practitioner psychologists are regulated by the Health Professionals Council, meaning that any supplies of medical care they make are exempt from VAT. Practitioner psychologists come under seven domains: clinical, counselling, educational, forensic, health, occupational, and sport/exercise. Psychologists who work purely in academic research and experimental psychology and who do not offer services to the general public are excluded from regulation, meaning that there is no change in the VAT treatment of their services.

'Medical care' means any service relating to the protection, maintenance or restoration of the mental health of the person concerned. Medical care includes services such as counselling, working with children with emotional problems, dealing with criminals' behavioural problems or running stress management courses. It does not include supplies of time management services, which are not related to the mental health of the client.

(5) Cosmetic services

HMRC will generally accept that cosmetic services are exempt where they are undertaken as an element of a health care treatment programme. But where services are undertaken purely for cosmetic reasons, they are standard rated.

(6) Education services

Doctors carry out a wide variety of education-related activities. Before considering whether there is an exempt supply of healthcare, consideration should be given as to whether the services qualify as an exempt supply of education. For example, lectures given as part of a medical training course or as continuing professional development and training sessions to first aiders are exempt as a supply of private tuition where provided by a doctor in either a sole proprietor or partnership capacity. See **17 EDUCATION** generally.

Presentations aimed at promoting health are exempt but presentations given to a non-medical audience on, for example, the latest medical developments are considered to be standard-rated.

(7) Family planning

HMRC accept that services such as counselling, contraception and sterilisation (and reversals) are exempt.

(8) Forensic physicians

Where crime levels do not justify the appointment of a full-time forensic physician employed by the Home Office, and this work is undertaken as and when required by local doctors on a fees basis, HMRC accept that the principal purpose is to provide medical services to those requiring it and that there is a single supply of exempt healthcare. If a statement or report is required at a later stage, this is a separate supply which is standard-rated.

(9) Insurance services

Medicals and reports are requested by insurance companies for a broad range of insurance purposes. Some services, whilst forming a mandatory condition of the policy once accepted, have a therapeutic purpose and HMRC accept that the following medical services commissioned by insurance companies in principle qualify as exempt supplies of health.

- Health screening under private medical insurance policies.
- Medical services where the policy holder under an income/credit protection insurance has fallen ill (as opposed to losing his job) and which are aimed at assisting the individual in returning to a normal life.
- Medicals services provided under a motor insurance policy to assist in enabling an injured motorist to return to full health and/or work. (This does not include medicals undertaken for DVLA purposes to ensure initial or continued fitness to drive which are standard-rated).

- Any other medical service provided in connection with an insurance policy where the principal aim is to assist in restoring the health of the individual.

Where medicals and reports are provided in connection with the bringing together of parties to a contract of insurance, the administration of policies or the handling of insurance claims under such contracts, these services are exempt as insurance-related services. See **37 INSURANCE**.

Medicals and reports provided purely for the purposes of valuing policies for tax reasons (e.g. in relation to inheritance tax) are standard-rated.

(10) Medico-legal work

This includes such work as medicals, reports and expert witness testimony for the judicial system and is considered to be standard-rated, even where the ultimate decision arrived at by the court may concern the well-being of an individual. Medical evidence services that are outsourced administrative services, such as arranging the provision of expert witnesses and obtaining medical reports, are also liable to VAT at the standard rate.

(11) Mental health tribunals

These are panels of registered health professionals who determine whether a person should commence or continue being detained under the *Mental Health Act*. HMRC accept that services provided by way of the preliminary examination, observations and the tribunal sitting are exempt.

(12) Occupational health

Occupational health services are provided by individual doctors and a wide range of organisations with varying legal status. Broadly speaking, services provided in this field fall into the following categories with liability as indicated.

- Pre-employment medicals. These are taxable supplies as they are primarily for the purpose of enabling a prospective employer to take a decision on recruitment. This includes medicals (and reports) for the purpose of determining whether a person is medically fit enough to join a professional register. However, in most cases medicals now only take place once an applicant has been offered a job and a job offer is made conditional on the results of the medical. Again these medicals are taxable because they are primarily done so that the employer can make a decision on recruitment. Sometimes medicals are performed on successful job applicants to help determine the most suitable location for them to work within an organisation. As the medical is done primarily with the health interests of the successful applicants in mind, the employers having already decided to recruit them, such supplies are exempt.
- Post-employment medicals. Where these are to
  - (i) ensure a person is medically well enough to undertake proposed work activities,
  - (ii) assess whether proposed work could adversely affect a person's health and to make recommendations to minimise any risk accordingly, or

(iii) to determine whether early retirement on ill-health grounds is appropriate,

then the supply is exempt. But where the medical is undertaken to determine whether a person can join a pension scheme, the supply is taxable.

- In-service health screening.
- Risk assessments including advice on ergonomic layouts. These identify, quantify and advise on risk in the workplace. Whilst many are undertaken as a result of statutory health and safety requirements, they are generally not undertaken by health professionals in the exercise of their professions. As such, HMRC consider them to be standard-rated whether undertaken by a registered or non-registered health professional.
- Training and advice. This may qualify as an exempt supply of education (see (6) above), but otherwise essentially represents the occupational health provider's role in promoting and advising on health issues for the purposes of maintaining the good health of the company's employees. It is therefore considered to qualify for exemption as medical care.

(13) Rehabilitation services

These services are exempt if their principal purpose is to improve both the physical and psychological health of the individual. Reports commissioned for the purpose of determining what is required to assist rehabilitation and recovery are also exempt. Reports commissioned for the purpose of quantifying the additional costs of disability and hence, the value of any claims for compensation are liable to VAT at the standard rate.

(14) Statutory services

Doctors supply various services under various statutes. Where no fee is charged, there is no consideration and therefore no supply. Where a fee is charged, but the doctor is compelled by statute to provide the service, it will be outside the scope of VAT. In all other circumstances, the doctor will be making a supply by way of business, which may be taxable or exempt depending on the principal purpose of the supply. Examples of the type of services covered by statute include

- Registration of deaths. The medical practitioner attending a person during their last illness prior to death must issue a death certificate. No fee is chargeable.
- Public health legislation. A medical practitioner who becomes aware that a patient is suffering from a notifiable disease or food poisoning must issue a certificate to the local authority. The practitioner is entitled to make a charge for this but the supply is outside the scope of VAT.
- Legislation relating to coroners' services. Coroners can appoint a pathologist to carry out a post mortem if necessary. As the pathologist is compelled to accept this appointment, the charge made for this supply is outside the scope of VAT.

- *Supreme Court Act 1981*. A High Court may call in the aid of a specialist to give evidence of facts. As the specialist is required to attend where called, the charge made for attending (including any re-imbursement of allowances) is outside the scope of VAT.
- *Blood Test (Evidence of Paternity) Regulations*. Doctors are not obliged by statute to provide these services (although fees charged are set by statute). Fees charged are therefore consideration for a supply and are standard-rated.

(15) Witness testimony and allowances

Services of providing

- professional witness evidence (giving evidence of facts acquired as a result of a professional position and not covered by the *Supreme Court Act 1981* under (13) above), and
- expert witness evidence (giving an expert opinion)

for the courts are standard-rated. Allowances paid to doctors to cover their costs whilst appearing in court as professional or expert witnesses (including travelling and accommodation costs and reimbursement of a locum's charges) are regarded as part of the overall payment for the witness's services and are also standard-rated.

Allowances paid to doctors where they are called as an ordinary witness are considered to be outside the scope of VAT as they are called as a member of the public and not in their professional capacity.

(VAT Notice 701/57/14, paras 2.4, 2.6, 4.1–4.14).

(16) Laboratory pathology services

Services supplied by a pathology laboratory or other similar state-registered institutions are exempt if they are

- made in respect of an individual; and
- medical services, that is, they are connected with the protection, maintenance or restoration of the health of an individual. These include, but are not necessarily limited to
  - tests performed as part of a routine check-up to confirm whether or not an individual has been exposed to a particular virus or is suffering from a certain medical condition;
  - diagnostic services or services helping another health professional or health institution to make a diagnosis;
  - tests to establish the overall health of patients to ensure that they are fit enough to have an operation; or
  - other tests provided as part of the medical treatment of a patient.

(HMRC Brief 16/13).

Supplies of staff

Generally speaking, apart from the nursing agencies' concession mentioned below, all supplies of health professional staff are taxable for VAT purposes. An agent's commission, fee or any other charge made for arranging and administering the supply is standard-rated. Whether a supplier is acting as an agent or principal is determined by reference to the contractual and other arrangements.

Supplies of registered health professionals (other than nurses) by employment businesses acting as a principal

The *Employment Agencies Act 1973* defines an 'employment business' as a 'business (whether or not carried on with a view to profit and whether or not carried on in conjunction with any other business) of supplying persons in the employment of the person carrying on the business, to act for, and under the control of, other persons in any capacity'. Staff supplied by an employment business may be either employees of that business, or self-employed and engaged by that business. In both cases the workers' services are provided to the employment business, which in turn makes a supply of that worker to the client. If the worker comes under the direction and control of the client, this is a supply of staff. The employment business in these circumstances is acting as the 'principal'. When an employment business supplies registered health professionals (other than staff subject to the nursing agencies' concession below) as a principal to a third party, where the health professional is working under the control and guidance of the third party, it is making a taxable supply of staff to that third party – not an exempt supply of healthcare. It is the third party which is responsible for providing healthcare to the final patient, rather than the business supplying the staff which has no such responsibility. A taxable supply of staff is made even where the employment business is responsible for ensuring that the workers it provides are properly trained and qualified when they work under the control of the third party. However, if the employment business maintains the direction and control of its health professional staff to make a supply of medical care directly to a final consumer, then the employment business is providing medical services rather than merely a supply of staff. In these circumstances, the business is making an exempt supply of health services.

Supplies of self-employed locum GPs

When self-employed locum GPs supply their services to an employment business which makes an onward supply to a third party who is legally responsible for providing health care to the final patient, both the supplies to and from the employment business are taxable. The fact that the locum GPs may be supplied to a prison or other institution where they may not be supervised by any medical staff does not mean that the employment business supplying the locum doctor to the third party is legally responsible for providing healthcare to the final patient.

Supplies of nurses, nursing auxiliaries and care assistants by state-regulated agencies (the nursing agencies' concession)

By an informal extra-statutory concession, nursing agencies (or employment businesses that provide nurses and midwives, as well as other health professionals) may exempt the supply of nursing staff and nursing auxiliaries supplied as a principal to a third party, if the supply is of

- a person registered in the register of qualified nurses and midwives maintained under the *Nursing and Midwifery Order 2001, Art 5* providing medical care to the final patient;
- an unregistered nursing auxiliary who is 'directly supervised' by one of the above; or
- an unregistered nursing auxiliary, whose services are supplied to a hospital (NHS or private), hospice, care home with nursing under *VATA 1994, Sch 9 Group 9 item 4* and form part of the care made to the patient.

A nursing auxiliary (also known as a healthcare assistant) is an individual who is not enrolled on any register of medical or health professionals but whose duties must include the provision of medical, as well as personal, care to patients. The institution to which staff are supplied may be operated by a local authority, NHS body, charity or other organisation operating in the public or private sector. To qualify for the concession, the employment business must be registered with one of the following organisations.

- Scottish Commission for the Regulation of Care
- Care Standards Inspectorate for Wales
- Northern Ireland Health and Personal Social Services Regulation and Improvement Authority
- Care Quality Commission (if the requirement to register with the CQC changed as a result of the *Health and Social Care Act 2008*, the concession applies to employment business that would have been required to be registered with the Care Quality Commission before 1 October 2010)

For the supply of nursing auxiliaries or care assistants to benefit from the concession, they must undertake some direct form of medical care, such as administering drugs or taking blood pressures, for the final patient. The concession does not apply to supplies of general care assistants who are

- only involved in providing personal care such as catering, washing or dressing the patients;
- working in care homes without nursing where they do not require supervision by health professionals to provide their services.

However, where a state-regulated domiciliary care agency supplies the services of its care assistants directly to the final patient, HMRC would see the agency as making an exempt supply of welfare services.

Wording of terms and conditions of agreements

Some employment businesses state in their contract terms that their staff are still working under their control and direction rather than the third party to which their staff are being supplied. If that is the case, the business is not acting as an 'employment business' within the definition of the *Employment Agencies Act 1973*. The VAT liability of a supply is not determined conclusively by the terms of any contract or other documentation alone. If the wording of a contract does not reflect any changes in the way that the business actually operates in practice, the VAT liability of a taxable supply of staff will not change.

Supplies of contracted-out health services

As is clear from the above, employment businesses in the health sector make a taxable supply of staff to third parties, such as hospitals or hospices, if the third party is legally responsible for the onward supply of providing care to the final recipient. This is subject to the nursing agencies' concession. The mere fact that an employment business is state-regulated does not mean that its supplies of staff are exempt if they are not covered by the nursing agencies' concession. However, when state-regulated health providers provide health services to the final consumer, these services remain exempt even if they are contracted out and paid for by a hospital or other third party.

(VAT Notice 701/57/14, para 6).

Doctors

[29.3] The supply of services consisting in the provision of medical care by a person registered or enrolled on the register of medical practitioners is exempt. [*VATA 1994, Sch 9 Group 7 Item 1(a)*].

See **29.1** and **29.2** above for an overview of the conditions for exemption and the liability of various services supplied by health professionals and, in particular, doctors.

NHS work

GP practices receive a monthly Statement of Fees of NHS payments due to the practice. All of these payments (other than accounting or timing adjustments) are consideration for the practice's supplies of medical services.

Payments are liable to VAT depending on their principal purpose and according to the principles and guidance outlined in **29.1** and **29.2** above. Thus, payments relating to activities where the principal purpose is the protection, maintenance or restoration of the health of the patient are payments for exempt supplies. Examples include payments relating to anti-coagulant monitoring, childhood immunisations, flu and pneumococcal vaccinations. However, payments in relation to services such as the completion of forms to enable persons to obtain blue/orange disability badges are liable to VAT at the standard rate.

'General' payments and reimbursements of practice costs (e.g. General Medical Services global sum, Minimum Practice Income Guarantee correction factor, computer costs, notional rent) are also payments directly related to exempt services unless the practice has dispensing activity, in which case they cover taxable and exempt supplies.

(VAT Notice 701/57/14, para 7.1).

Payments for dispensing

GPs can, in certain cases, be authorised to dispense drugs to particular patients. Payments received from the NHS for items dispensed to those patients are zero-rated under *VATA 1994, Sch 8 Group 12 Item 1* (see **29.13** below).

Fees for private dispensing are always standard-rated.

(VAT Notice 701/57/14, para 7.4).

Payments for personally administering drugs

All GPs can administer drugs at the time of treatment (whether or not they are also NHS dispensing GPs). HMRC have always taken the view that drugs and other items (e.g. vaccines, anaesthetics, injections, diagnostic reagents, intra-uterine, contraceptive caps and diaphragms, and pessaries) personally administered ('immediately administered' in Scotland) to the patient by the doctor at the time of treatment are an inseparable part of the exemption for medical care under *VATA 1994, Sch 9 Group 7 Item 1(a)* above. This was confirmed in *C & E Commrs v Dr Beynon & Partners*, HL 2004, [2005] STC 55 (TVC 19.10) (reversing the earlier tribunal decision in *Drs Woodings, Rees, Crossthwaite & Jones* (VTD 16175) (TVC 19.9)). Applying the principles laid down in *Card Protection Plan Ltd v C & E Commrs, ECJ Case C–349/96*, [1999] STC 270 (TVC 22.362), the court held that, where drugs are administered at the time of treatment, there is a single supply of exempt services, the transaction being the patient's visit to the doctors which should not be split into smaller units.

Deputising services to doctors

The provision of a deputy for a person registered in the register of medical practitioners is exempt. [*VATA 1994, Sch 9 Group 7 Item 5; SI 2006/1914*].

Visiting EEA practitioners

If a national of any European Economic Area (EEA) State is lawfully established in medical practice in an EEA State other than the UK, and is visiting the UK to provide medical services temporarily, he is required to register in the register of medical practitioners as a visiting EEA practitioner before he can exempt his supplies.

In an urgent case a medical practitioner from an EEA State may not be in a position to register in the register for medical practitioners prior to visiting the UK and providing services, e.g. where a visitor to the UK is taken ill and wishes to be treated by his own doctor. The practitioner can exempt his supply in such circumstances provided he seeks registration as a visiting practitioner, usually no longer than 15 days after the service has been performed.

(VAT Notice 701/57/14, para 9.1).

Opticians

Overview

[29.4] The supply of services by a qualified optician is exempt (see below). Exemption can also extend to the services of unqualified staff if they are directly supervised by a qualified optician (see **29.8** below). But the supply of spectacles and contact lenses is standard-rated (see below). As the charge for spectacles or contact lenses normally includes an element for services, an apportionment is required.

Supplies of services

The supply of services consisting in the provision of medical care by persons registered in

- either of the registers of ophthalmic opticians or the register of dispensing opticians kept under the *Opticians Act 1989*, or
- either of the lists under *section 9* of that *Act* of bodies corporate carrying on business as ophthalmic opticians or as dispensing opticians

is exempt. [*VATA 1994, Sch 9 Group 7 Item 1(b)*].

See **33.1** to **33.3** above for an overview of the conditions for exemption and the liability of various services supplied by health professionals in general.

Supplies of spectacles

Supplies of spectacles are standard-rated unless the goods are certain specialised appliances designed solely for use by the disabled (e.g. artificial eyes and certain low vision aids), in which case they are zero-rated (see **29.21** below). Supplies of ancillary goods (e.g. cases, cleaning solution) are also standard-rated.

In *C & E Commrs v Leightons Ltd*, QB [1995] STC 458 (TVC 33.8), the court held that the price paid for spectacles includes two separate supplies – a standard-rated supply of goods (the spectacles) and an exempt supply of opticians' services. Although this decision pre-dated the criteria for single/multiple supplies set out by the CJEU in *Card Protection Plan Ltd v C & E Commrs, ECJ Case C–349/96*, [1999] STC 270 (TVC 22.362) (see **65.6 SUPPLY: GENERAL**) a tribunal has subsequently accepted that the decision in *Leightons* was correct in law and that payments should be apportioned (*Leightons (No 2); Eye-Tech Opticians (No 3)* (VTD 17498) (TVC 33.9)).

In *Prescription Eyewear Ltd v HMRC* (TC02759) (TVC 20.108), a company (P) began selling prescription spectacles via the internet. It claimed that part of the consideration should be attributed to supplies of medical care which were exempt from VAT. HMRC rejected the claim as the spectacles had not been personally dispensed by an optician in a shop. The First-tier Tribunal allowed P's appeal on the basis that P's sales were effected under the supervision of a registered optician or medical practitioner.

There are no set methods of apportionment of spectacle sales between exempt and standard-rated elements. If practicable, opticians should calculate VAT by separating the standard-rated and exempt elements at the point of sale. If this is not possible, an individual method must be agreed with HMRC which gives a fair and reasonable valuation of VAT payable without placing an undue burden on the optician.

The following is the suggested method of apportionment based on full cost apportionment.

*(1) **Establish the cost of goods***

This is made up of the following.

- Cost of purchase of bought-in frames.
- Cost of purchase of bought-in lenses. (Where, rather than buying in lenses cut to individual patients' prescriptions, a business purchases blank lenses and glazes them in-house, establish the cost of glazing and the directly attributable expenses incurred on consumables. Indirect costs such as depreciation of equipment should not be included.)
- Cost of delivery if the business has frames/lenses delivered from a central point of distribution to a chain of outlets. (The cost must be apportioned where the delivery charge also relates to other goods such as cases, chains, contact lens fluids, etc.)

These costs should include any VAT.

*(2) **Establish the cost of services***

This is made up of the following.

- 'Direct costs' of any ophthalmic optician (OO) relating to spectacle sales. An OO is allowed to carry out sight tests as well as dispense spectacles. Eye tests have always been exempt and opticians need to determine what proportion of the cost of an OO is attributable to the exempt eye test and what proportion is to be attributed to the exempt dispensing service element of spectacle sales. In some practices, the OO may also perform various administrative activities. If the actual costs attributable to each activity are not identifiable, the total costs will need to be apportioned, possibly using the formula

$$\frac{\text{Income from spectacles}}{\text{Income from spectacles} + \text{contact lenses} + \text{sight tests}} \times \text{direct cost of OO}$$

  This formula may not be appropriate for all opticians and alternatives may be agreed with HMRC. For example, if an OO spends half his time providing eye examinations and the other half dispensing, it would be more appropriate simply to use half the costs for the purposes of the apportionment calculation. An optician who considers that factors other than time should be taken into account in the apportionment should identify those factors and submit an appropriate apportionment method for HMRC's approval.

In general, HMRC are prepared to accept that an element of an OO's time is spent on dispensing activity. The actual level of dispensing activity should be demonstrated and agreed with HMRC.

- 'Direct costs' of any dispensing optician (DO). The direct labour costs to the practice of the time that any DO spends in the dispensing of spectacles must be calculated.
- 'Direct costs' of directly supervised persons. A proportion of the direct labour costs of those unqualified employees providing a dispensing service, and who either work as part of a qualifying body corporate or who are directly supervised by a registered optician (see **29.8** below) may also be included in the calculation. The actual percentage of these costs relating to dispensing duties must be agreed between the trader and HMRC.

'*Direct costs*' should be calculated using conventional accounting procedures. In calculating the direct cost of OOs, DOs and directly supervised persons, the following principal costs should be included (although this is not necessarily an exhaustive list).

- Salary
- Employers' national insurance contributions
- Pension contributions by employer
- Cost of provision of vehicle to OOs and DOs involved in dispensing of spectacles
- Optical training of opticians and supervised persons
- Professional body subscriptions incurred by the practice (only in respect of services received, not goods)
- Professional indemnity costs incurred by the practice
- Recruitment costs

These costs should include any VAT.

(3) Calculation of percentage of income from spectacle sales attributable to taxable supplies

Once the above costs of goods and services have been calculated, it is necessary to establish the average cost of each supply. This is achieved by dividing the costs of the goods and services by the number of spectacles (new and re-glazed) dispensed in the period.

The taxable element of the sale is then calculated using the formula

$$\text{VAT due on sale} = \frac{\text{Cost of goods}}{\text{Cost of goods and services}} \times \text{spectacles income} \times \frac{1}{6}$$

Having established the percentage applicable to taxable sales, this percentage should be used as the basis of the optician's VAT return. As businesses change over time, the percentage should be recalculated whenever a major change takes place in the optician's business, and in any case at three-yearly intervals. HMRC consider a 'major change' as constituting anything which significantly alters the costs of the supplies including

- opening an additional branch or closing an existing one;

- increasing or decreasing the number of OOs, DOs or supervised staff employed;
- restructuring the practice (e.g. where an OO who has previously performed both eye examinations and dispensing services exclusively performs eye examinations); and
- changing from buying in lenses to glazing in-house (or vice versa).

New business

When a new practice opens, it is not possible to immediately perform an accurate apportionment of the charges made for spectacles and dispensing, particularly if the apportionment method is based on costs. New practices should therefore agree a provisional basis of apportionment with HMRC and revise the apportionment in the light of actual costs at the end of the first year's trading.

(VAT Information Sheet 8/99).

Supplementary professions, osteopaths and chiropractors

EU law

[29.5] Under *Directive 2006/112/EC, Art 132(1)(c)*, EU member states must exempt the provision of medical care in the exercise of the paramedical professions as defined by the EU member state concerned. See *Solleveld v Staatssecretaris van Financiën, ECJ Cases C–443/04 and C–444/04*, [2001] STC 71 (TVC 22.316) for a consideration of how countries must apply their discretion in applying exemption.

UK law

The supply of services consisting in the provisions of medical care by persons on the following registers is exempt. See **29.1** and **29.2** above for an overview of the conditions for exemption and the liability of various services supplied by health professionals in general.

- Any register kept under the *Health Professions Order 2001* (*SI 2002/254*). [*VATA 1994, Sch 9 Group 7 Items 1(c)*]. These professionals are
  arts therapists;
  biomedical scientists;
  chiropodists/podiatrists;
  clinical scientists;
  dieticians;
  hearing aid dispensers;
  occupational therapists;
  operating department practitioners;
  orthoptists;
  paramedics;
  physiotherapists;
  practitioner psychologists;
  prosthetists and orthotists;

radiographers; and
speech and language therapists.
(VAT Notice 701/57/14, para 2.1).

Any drugs, appliances etc. which are administered by the above practitioners at the time of treatment are considered a minor and inseparable part of their professional service and also exempt.

Standard-rating applies to

- supplies of goods which are not minor and inseparable; and
- supplies by practitioners who are not registered under the *Health Professions Order 2001* (e.g. acupuncturists, psychologists, psychotherapists and psychoanalysts). (Psychiatrists are qualified medical practitioners and are exempt under **29.3** above.)

- The register of osteopaths maintained in accordance with the provisions of the *Osteopaths Act 1993*. [*VATA 1994, Sch 9 Group 7 Items 1(ca)*].
- The register of chiropractors maintained in accordance with the provisions of the *Chiropractors Act 1994*. [*VATA 1994, Sch 9 Group 7 Items 1(cb)*].

Nurses, midwives and health visitors

[29.6] The supply of services consisting in the provision of medical care by a person registered in the register of qualified nurses, midwives and health visitors kept under *Nurses, Midwives and Health Visitors Act 1997, s 7* is exempt. [*VATA 1994, Sch 9 Group 7 Item 1(d); Nurses, Midwives and Health Visitors Act 1997, Sch 4*].

See **29.1** and **29.2** above for an overview of the conditions for exemption and the liability of various services supplied by health professionals in general.

Exemption only applies to the professional services for which the nurse, etc. has been trained. HMRC do not accept that, for example, a nurse can exempt supplies of acupuncture or osteopathy under this provision.

Dentists, etc.

[29.7] The supply of

(a) any services consisting in the provision of medical care or dental prostheses by
- a person registered in the dentists' register, or
- a person registered in the dental care professions register established under *Dentists Act 1984, s 36B*, or

(b) any services or dental prostheses by a dental technician

is exempt. [*VATA 1994, Sch 9 Group 7 Items 2, 2A*].

Exemption covers drugs or appliances provided in the course of dental care and treatment but items, other than prostheses, that are separable from dental treatment provided to a patient are normally standard-rated (e.g. toothbrushes, toothpaste and dental floss).

Dental prostheses

These include dentures, artificial teeth, crowns, bridges, palates and other orthodontic appliances.

Advisory services

Services such as advising on clinical governance, poor performance and standards supplied on a *self-employed basis* by dentists to Primary Care Trusts are standard rated. Where such services are provided on an *employee* basis, any income received is outside the scope of VAT.

Cosmetic dentistry services

These must be considered on a case-by-case basis and are exempt only where supplied as an element of oral health treatment by a registered health professional.

(VAT Notice 701/57/14, para 10.1).

Supplies between dentists in the same practice

Where there is more than one dentist within a practice operating from the same premises, there may be payments between the dentists in respect of shared facilities, equipment, prostheses and staff. Such charges are exempt if relating to services or facilities that are predominantly medical in nature and are necessary to allow the recipient to perform dentistry. This exemption does not apply to

- any supplies made by a dentist who has ceased to practise, or by a landlord who is not a dentist;
- supplies of goods (other than dental prostheses) that are held out for sale to patients (e.g. toothpaste and toothbrushes); or
- any sales of dental equipment by a practice owner.

(VAT Notice 701/57/14, para 10.2).

Services performed by persons not registered, etc.

[29.8] Health and nursing care services performed by a person not enrolled on a statutory medical register can be exempt in some circumstances but only when provided

- under the direct supervision of certain health professionals (see below); or
- in a hospital or nursing home (see **29.10** below).

(VAT Notice 701/57/14, para 5.2).

Supervised services

Supplies of services made by a person who is not registered or enrolled in any of the registers or rolls specified in **29.3** to **29.6** or **29.7**(*a*) above are exempt where the services are 'wholly performed' or 'directly supervised' by a person who is so registered or enrolled. [*VATA 1994, Sch 9 Group 7 Note 2*].

See **29.1** and **29.2** above for limitations on the services which are exempt.

'Wholly performed'

This covers, for example, the situation where a company (which is not a 'person registered or enrolled') makes the supply but uses the services of its medically qualified staff (e.g. a company employing registered chiropodists).

'Directly supervised'

HMRC require all the following conditions to be satisfied.

(1) The services are supervised by one of the registered health professionals listed in **29.1** above (other than a hearing aid dispenser or pharmacist), and the supervisor is professionally qualified to perform and supervise the service.

(2) The service requires supervision by a registered health professional, and is provided predominantly to meet the medical needs of a client.

(3) The supervisor has a direct relationship with the staff performing the service, and is contractually responsible for supervising their services.

(4) A qualified supervisor is available for the whole time that the care service is provided.

(5) No more than 2000 hours per week of staff time are supervised by a single health professional.

(6) A supervisor has a say in the level of care to be provided to the client, and will usually see the client prior to the commencement of the care service.

(7) The supervisor must be able to demonstrate that he monitors the work of the unregistered staff.

Where the above conditions are not met, the services are standard-rated, even when performed to meet the medical or health care needs of a client.

(VAT Notice 701/57/14, para 5.3).

The above guidelines were considered in detail in *Land (t/a Crown Optical Centre)* (VTD 15547) (TVC 33.6) where the tribunal held that an unqualified dispenser of spectacles, and his unqualified staff, were directly supervised by an ophthalmic medical practitioner who performed eye tests in the shop on five half-days a fortnight. On the evidence, the tribunal held that the supplies were supervised even though there was no explicit contract requiring the supervisor to undertake this task (as required by HMRC, see condition (3)). The tribunal observed that, although a contract may be valuable evidence of responsibility, its absence did not prove that there was no responsibility. On the evidence, supervision was an implicit term of the relationship.

See also *A & S Services* (VTD 16025) (TVC 33.25).

Supervision does not necessarily require the supervisor continually to observe the unqualified person or necessarily be on the same premises provided there is a check as often as the circumstances require and a system for that person to contact the supervisor. Supervision is 'direct' if carried out on a one-to-one basis without an intermediary. (*Elder Home Care Ltd* (VTD 11185) (TVC 33.4)). See also *M G Parkinson* (VTD 6017) (TVC 33.3).

VATA 1994, Sch 9 Group 7 Note 2 above does not exempt services of complementary practitioners, who do not appear on any statutory register, to whom patients are referred by consultants or medical practitioners. Neither the act of referral nor the relationship between the two parties (who are invariably from two distinct areas of medicine/treatment and thus, have different skills) constitute any degree of supervision. This was confirmed in *Pittam* (VTD 13268) (TVC 33.26) which related to patients referred to a chiropractor. (Note that the services of a registered chiropractor are now exempt (see **29.5** above) but the principle involved still applies.)

Pharmacists

[29.9] The supply of any services (but not the letting on hire of goods) by

- a person registered in the register of pharmacists maintained under the *Pharmacy Order 2010, Art 19 (SI 2010/231)* or in the register of pharmaceutical chemists kept under the *Pharmacy (Northern Ireland) Order 1976*, or
- by a person who is not so registered (e.g. a company or partnership) but where the services are performed by a person who is so registered

is exempt. [*VATA 1994, Sch 9 Group 7 Item 3 and Notes 2A and 3*].

See **29.1** and **29.2** above for limitations on the services which are exempt.

Item 3 above exempts professional services for which a pharmacist has been trained and is required to exercise professional judgement.

Community pharmacies

Under a revised contractual framework for community pharmacy services in England and Wales, community pharmacies are obliged to provide patients with certain essential services; they may also provide advanced and enhanced services depending on the terms of their contract. These services have varying VAT liabilities.

Essential services

These comprise:

(a) Dispensing. Supplies of qualifying goods prescribed by appropriate practitioners and dispensed by a pharmacist are zero-rated under *VATA 1994, Sch 8 Group 12, Item 1* (see **29.13** below).

(b) Disposal of unwanted medicines, i.e. taking in unwanted medicines, sorting and storing them until the Primary Care Trust (in Wales, the local Health Board) arranges for them to be collected and destroyed. This supply is standard-rated.

(c) Signposting, i.e. providing patients with information about other, non-pharmaceutical services which might be beneficial to them. The service does not need to be performed by a registered pharmacist and is standard-rated.

(d) Promotion of healthy lifestyles. This comprises
   - the provision of information by means of leaflets and poster displays; and

- individually tailored advice given by the pharmacist to patients in certain identified at-risk groups.

As the latter element is the predominant one and is aimed at the maintenance of a person's health, this service is exempt.

(e) Support for self-care, i.e. providing patients with pharmaceutical advice about medicines and other products available over-the-counter. The pharmacist's provision of advice is exempt but any medicines sold over-the-counter are a separate, standard-rated supply.

(f) Support for people with disabilities. This activity is a further aspect of dispensing prescribed medicines and is zero-rated when the medicines themselves are zero-rated. See **29.12** below.

Clinical governance

This is funding to support the professional delivery of NHS pharmacy services and is outside the scope of VAT.

Essential service payments (from 1 December 2016)

Since 1 December 2016, according to the Pharmaceutical Services Negotiating Committee (PSNC) website, pharmacies will receive a Single Activity Fee for every item that it dispenses including medicines and appliances. The fee is currently set at £1.25 per item (was £1.13 per item from December 2016 to March 2017).

Pharmacies can also claim a range of additional fees which are set out in Part IIIA of the Drug Tariff including fees for items such as dispensing unlicensed specials or imports, measuring and fitting hosiery and trusses as well as the dispensing controlled drugs.

Pharmacies will also receive an expensive prescription fee that is equivalent to 2% of the net ingredient cost of items that are dispensed costing over £100.

Pharmacies can also claim monthly Establishment Payments and the levels are set out in Part VIA of the Drug Tariff. Top-up payments can also be claimed from the pharmacy's local NHS England Team where appropriate.

It is important to note that currently, HMRC has not reached any agreement with PSNC regarding the VAT treatment of the payments received from 1 December 2016. As a result, no updated guidance has been produced by HMRC with regard to the revised payment structure. However, once agreement has been reached, according to the PSNC website, it will have retrospective effect from the date of implementation and pharmacies will be expected to recalculate the amount of VAT due and correct any returns previously submitted.

More information can be found on the PSNC website (psnc.org.uk/funding-and-statistics/funding-distribution/vat/).

Practice payment (until 30 November 2016)

All supplies within (*b*) to (*f*) above and clinical governance were covered by the 'practice payment' until 1 December 2016. The practice payment was therefore made up of six elements (two standard-rated, two exempt, one zero-rated and one outside the scope) and should have been apportioned to reflect the different liabilities. Information on the percentage weighting to be applied to each element is available from the PSNC. See http://psnc.org.uk/funding-and-statistics/funding-distribution/vat/ for more information.

Advanced services

The 'Medicines Use Review' and 'Appliance Use Review' are advance services. These involve reviewing a patient's needs for and use of medicines, including whether the patient is experiencing any side effects or other problems. These are exempt services.

Locally commissioned (enhanced) services

Primary Care Trusts and local Health Boards can also contract with pharmacies to deliver local enhanced services. HMRC advice on the most commonly encountered services is set out below but as enhanced services are tailored to meet local needs and actual contractual terms can be subject to variation, the correct VAT liability will depend upon the particular arrangements, the single/multiple supply rules and the status of the person performing the services.

- Needle and syringe exchange. This service may involve making clean needles and syringes available free of charge to drug users and diabetics; disposing of used needles safely; and providing health education advice and information to service users.
  The free issue of sterile needles and other materials is not subject to VAT.
  Where a registered pharmacist
  (a) assesses the condition of service users and, where appropriate, provides one-to-one health advice or treatment,
  (b) provides one-to-one advice to service users about safe injecting techniques, or
  (c) provides one-to-one advice on dealing with injecting or drug-related infections and illnesses
  the service is an exempt supply. The pharmacist does not need to provide these services to every service user for exemption to apply but HMRC expect the contract to require these services to be provided to service users on request or where considered appropriate by the pharmacist.
  The service will be standard rated where
  (a) the pharmacist is merely issuing new needles and overseeing the surrender of old ones and has no role in assessing the health condition of the service user;
  (b) the service does not require the skills and experience of a pharmacist, and is such that it could be, or is, carried out by a pharmacy assistant or any other member of staff who is not a registered pharmacist; or
  (c) the pharmacist's provision of health education or information goes no further than issuing standard leaflets to service users.

- Minor ailment service. Under this service, pharmacies provide support to eligible patients presenting with a minor ailment (e.g. conjunctivitis or diarrhoea). Following assessment, the pharmacist might give advice, supply appropriate over-the-counter medicines or dressings to treat the ailment and/or refer the patient to another health professional. In providing the service the pharmacy works to guidelines set out in a local protocol.
  Where assessment of the patient's condition and the provision of advice and support in managing the ailment are carried out by a pharmacist, this is an exempt service. But any medicines or dressings issued are standard-rated where they constitute separate supplies of goods. Payment for the goods is made by the NHS rather than the patient.
- Patient group directions (PGDs). These directions are drawn up locally and permit pharmacists to issue defined drugs to a class of patients presenting with particular conditions. PGDs do not amount to 'prescriptions' because they are not written in respect of an identified, individual patient. The supply of goods is standard-rated.

The Electronic Prescription Service (EPS)

This enables prescriptions to be sent and received electronically rather than by paper prescriptions. Fees for implementing and operating the system are not consideration for supplies made and are outside the scope of VAT.

Exit payments

During the first year of the framework, any pharmacy dispensing less than 2000 items per month, and which decides to close, receives a one-off payment. This payment is outside the scope of VAT.

(VAT Notice 701/57/14, para 11).

Hospitals and health institutions

[29.10] Exemption applies to the provision of

- care or medical or surgical treatment, and
- in connection with it, the supply of any goods,

in any hospital or other institution approved, licensed or registered (or exempted from registration) by any Minister or other authority pursuant to a provision of a public general Act of Parliament or the Scottish Parliament (or equivalent NI legislation) other than a provision that is capable of being brought into effect at different times in relation to different local authority areas. [*VATA 1994, Sch 9 Group 7 Item 4 and Note 8*].

Qualifying institutions

Exemption under this provision covers

- hospitals
- hospices and nursing homes which are approved, licensed or registered under the relevant social legislation (or exempted from obtaining such an approval or registration by the relevant legislation).

- any other state-regulated institution providing medical care.

An institution may be qualifying regardless of whether its activities are carried out on a charitable or commercial basis.

(VAT Notice 701/31/14, paras 2.1, 2.2).

A pathology laboratory which is state-regulated qualifies for the purposes of the exemption, irrespective of the location from which it provides its services. It makes no difference whether it occupies premises with or within a hospital or in a separate location.

(HMRC Brief 16/13).

Care and treatment

Examples of medical care or treatment supplied by a qualifying institution include

- performing medical or surgical procedures with the aim of protecting, maintaining or restoring the health of an individual;
- nursing of sick or injured patients in a hospital, hospice or nursing home;
- other state-regulated institutions providing diagnostic services or services helping to enable another health professional or health institution to make a diagnosis, for example, pathology laboratories or scanning units; and
- meals and accommodation provided to in-patients, residents or other care beneficiaries;

(VAT Notice 701/31/14, para 2.3).

Services supplied by qualifying institutions which are not exempt

Supplies which are not exempt under these provisions include the following.

- Any service that is not provided under the terms of an approval, license, registration or exemption from registration, granted under the appropriate social legislation.
- Any service provided to a person other than an in-patient, resident or other beneficiary of care or treatment. This includes any supply made to visitors. Special rules apply to the supply of meals and accommodation to parents staying with a sick child in hospital (see below).
- Any goods or services that are separable from care or treatment provided within the institution (e.g. charges made for the use of public telephones).

Class 3B and 4 lasers and Intense pulse light source (IPL) machine

Use of such machines is exempt when supplied as part of a treatment programme drawn up by a registered health professional following the diagnosis of a medical condition. But where treatment is carried out for a purely cosmetic reason, this service is standard-rated.

(VAT Notice 701/31/14, paras 2.4, 2.6).

Drugs and other items supplied to patients in a hospital or nursing home

Drugs, medicines, bandages, plasters or ointments provided by a qualifying institution in the course of care or treatment are exempt when provided to

(a) an in-patient;
(b) any person attending the premises of the qualifying institution for care or treatment; or
(c) any other person or establishment where the item is for use by, or in connection with, either of the above.

Supplies of drugs or medicines to any of the above people other than by a qualifying institution are usually standard-rated (even when the items are dispensed on the prescription of a medical practitioner). However, by concession, HMRC allow pharmacists (including in-house or independent pharmacists operating from hospital premises) to zero-rate drugs, medicines and other qualifying goods that are supplied to any person within (*a*) or (*b*) above if all of the following conditions are met.

- The items dispensed are goods designed or adapted for use in connection with medical or surgical treatment.
- The items are dispensed by a pharmacist in the normal way on the prescription of a medical practitioner who is providing primary health care services.
- The items are intended for self-administration by the person named on the prescription.
- The items are supplied separately from, and do not form any part of, any medical services, treatment or care provided in the hospital or nursing home.
- In the case of NHS prescriptions, the pharmacist is acting under the appropriate NHS Pharmaceutical regulations, and is reimbursed for the dispensed items by one of the NHS bodies that pay for community pharmacy services.

The application of this concession must not give rise to any abuse of the VAT system and HMRC may withdraw or restrict the application of the concession if they have reasonable cause to believe that it is being used for VAT avoidance purposes.

(VAT Notice 701/31/14, para 2.9).

Goods supplied as part of a package of care and treatment in a qualifying institution

Most goods supplied by a qualifying institution as part of a package of care or treatment are exempt. Examples include

- incontinence products; drugs and medicines; bandages; plasters and ointments supplied to hospital patients;
- meals and refreshments provided to in-patients, residents or other beneficiaries of care or treatment; and

- accommodation and meals provided to relatives staying with a sick child in hospital (see *Nuffield Nursing Homes Trust* (VTD 3327) (TVC 33.43) where the provision of accommodation and catering to a parent of a child patient was held to be a supply of care to the patient). No other supplies to visitors, relatives or carers qualify for exemption;
- transport provided that forms an integral part of an exempt supply of care or treatment (see also **29.11** below); and
- toiletry products provided to in-patients, residents or other beneficiaries of care or treatment for which no additional charge is made.

Items that are separable from the care and treatment provided by the qualifying institution are not exempt. Examples include cigarettes, use of bedside phones and televisions, toiletries provided to in-patients for an additional charge, newspapers, merchandise such as commemorative T-shirts, and goods provided to any person other than the beneficiary of the medical care or surgical treatment (but see above for accommodation and meals provided to relatives staying with a sick child in hospital). The liability of such goods should be determined in accordance with the normal liability rules.

(VAT Notice 701/31/14, paras 2.7, 2.8, 2.12).

Goods and services supplied on the premises of a qualifying institution

Some qualifying institutions allow outside businesses or practitioners to operate from their premises.

For a supply made by such a business to qualify for exemption, all of the following conditions must be met.

- The goods or services supplied must form part of the medical care or treatment provided within the qualifying institution.
- The goods or services supplied must be of a type commonly provided to beneficiaries of such services.
- The supply must not consist of drugs, medicines, incontinence products, bandages, plasters, ointments or any other items that are integral to the care or treatment provided in the qualifying institution.
- The supply must involve direct contact between the provider and the beneficiary, and must contribute directly to the welfare of the beneficiary.
- The supply must not take place in a qualifying institution for reasons of geographical convenience only. This means that the supply must not be of a type that might equally be provided at a location other than the premises of a qualifying institution.

There are very few supplies made by outside businesses from the premises of a qualifying institution that meet all of the above conditions but examples include

- care supplied by unregistered nursing staff and other carers; and
- treatment supplied by outside contractors providing renal dialysis services in hospitals.

(VAT Notice 701/31/14, para 3.1; VAT Notice 701/57/14, para 5.4).

Other exempt supplies

[29.11] Other exempt supplies are as follows:

(1) Human blood, organs and tissue

The supply of

- human blood,
- products for therapeutic purposes derived from human blood, and
- human (including foetal) organs or tissue for diagnostic or therapeutic purposes or medical research

is exempt. [*VATA 1994, Sch 9 Group 7 Items 6–8*].

The importation of these items is also exempt from VAT. See **34.15**(5) **IMPORTS**.

The CJEU held in *TMD Gesellschaft für transfusionsmedizinische Dienste GmbH v Finanzamt Kassel II - Hofgeismar, ECJ Case C-412/15* (TVC 20.110) that the term blood for the purposes of the exemption, does not include the supply of blood plasma that will not be used directly for healthcare or therapeutic activities that are in the public interest. Industrial plasma that will be used in the manufacture of medicinal products will not be exempt from VAT.

Recombinant factor VIII (as opposed to plasma-derived human factor VIII) is outside the exemption as it is not derived from human blood. (HC Written Answer, Vol 267 col 837, 30 November 1995; *Baxter Healthcare Ltd* (VTD 14670) (TVC 33.67)).

(2) Transport of sick and injured

The supply of transport services for sick or injured persons in vehicles specially designed for that purpose is exempt. [*VATA 1994, Sch 9 Group 7 Item 11*].

(3) Hire of equipment

The letting on hire of goods in connection with a supply of other services within *VATA 1994, Sch 9 Group 7 Item 1* (see **29.3** to **29.6** above) is exempt. [*VATA 1994, Sch 9 Group 7 Note 1*].

Increasingly, companies are purchasing specialised equipment and offering the use of it to NHS and private hospitals. The effect of *Note 1* above is that

- if goods are let on hire without attendant staff, or the attendant staff are not qualified under *Item 1*, the supply is taxable; and
- if the equipment is supplied as part of a package,
  - (a) where the principal supply is the hire of equipment and the provision of *Item 1* services is subsidiary to that supply, the whole supply is standard-rated; and
  - (b) where the principal supply is the provision of *Item 1* services and the hire of the equipment is subsidiary to that supply, the whole supply is exempt under *Item 1*.

  See *Aslan Imaging Ltd* (VTD 3286) (TVC 33.18) where the tribunal held that the principal supply was the standard-rated hiring of a radiological scanner and the services supplied by the radiographer who accompanied it were subsidiary and *Cleary & Cleary (t/a Mobile X-rays)* (VTD 7305) (TVC 33.1) where the tribunal held that the principal supply was an exempt mobile chest X-ray service and the equipment hiring was secondary.

Welfare services

[29.12] *Directive 2006/112/EC, Art 132(1)(g)* directs countries to exempt 'the supply of services and of goods closely linked to welfare and social security works'. In *Yoga for Health Foundation v C & E Commrs*, QB [1984] STC 630 (TVC 22.326), it was held that the word 'welfare' was not confined to services connected with the relief of poverty or provision of purely material benefits.

Under UK legislation, the supply by a

(a) charity,
(b) 'public body',
(c) 'state-regulated' private welfare institution (e.g. a residential care home), or
(d) 'state-regulated private welfare agency'

of 'welfare services', and of goods supplied in connection with those welfare services, is exempt.

The supply of accommodation or catering is excluded unless ancillary to the provision of care, treatment or instruction. The supply of catering to elderly people in sheltered housing accommodation was held to be ancillary in *Viewpoint Housing Association Ltd* (VTD 13148) (TVC 33.69) and the supply of hotel accommodation and catering to cancer patients and their families was held to be ancillary in *Trustees for the Macmillan Cancer Trust* (VTD 15603) (TVC 33.76).

See **13.1 CHARITIES** for bodies qualifying as charities. It should be noted that not all welfare services provided by charities are business. If such services are provided consistently below cost to distressed people for the relief of their distress, they are non-business supplies. See **13.5**(21) **CHARITIES**.

'*Public body*' means

- a government department,
- a local authority, or
- any other body which acts under any enactment or instrument for public purposes and not for its own profit and which performs functions similar to those of a government department or local authority (e.g. most NHS trusts).

'*State-regulated*' means approved, licensed, registered or exempted from registration by any Minister or other authority pursuant to a provision of a public general Act of Parliament or the Scottish Parliament (or equivalent NI legislation) other than a provision that is capable of being brought into effect at different times in relation to different local authority areas.

[*VATA 1994, Sch 9 Group 7 Item 9 and Notes 5, 7 and 8*].

Supplies by intermediaries

In *Staatssecretaris van Financiën v Stichting Kinderopvang Enschede, ECJ Case C-415/04* [2007] STC 294 (TVC 22.335) the CJEU held exemption could apply under these provisions to services provided by a qualifying body where it was acting as an intermediary between persons seeking, and persons offering, a qualifying welfare service. For exemption to apply

- the qualifying welfare service must be of a nature or quality that recipients cannot be assured of obtaining a service of the same value without the assistance of such an intermediary service; and
- the basic purpose of the intermediary services must not be to obtain additional income for the service provider by carrying out transactions which are in direct competition with those of commercial enterprises liable for VAT.

State-regulated private welfare institution or agency

A state-regulated private welfare institution or agency means an institution or agency that is registered with and/or regulated by

- Care Quality Commission;
- Scottish Commission for the Regulation of Care;
- Care Standards Inspectorate for Wales;
- Northern Ireland Health and Personal Social Services Regulation and Improvement Authority;
- Office for Standards in Education (OFSTED); or
- any other similar regulatory body.

It can include a domiciliary care agency, an independent fostering agency, a voluntary adoption agency, and a nursing agency.

(VAT Notice 701/2/11, para 3.3).

Welfare services

Welfare services mean services directly connected with (1)–(3) below. In the case of services supplied by a state-regulated private welfare institution under (*c*) above, it only includes those services in respect of which the institution is so regulated.

(1) Provision of care, treatment or instruction designed to promote physical or mental welfare of elderly, sick, distressed or disabled. [VATA 1994, Sch 9 Group 7 Note 6(a); SI 2002/762]

In *Watford & District Old People's Housing Association Ltd (t/a Watford Help In The Home Service)* (VTD 15660) (TVC 33.70) the tribunal held that domestic help services such as cleaning, cooking and shopping could constitute 'care' when supplied to people for whom there is either current or imminent substantial risk to the health and welfare of the person, and who are unable to provide even basic self care or who have major difficulty in safely carrying out some key daily living tasks. The tribunal stressed the significance of the high level of recipients' needs which, in that case, had been identified by Social Services assessments.

Following that case, HMRC reviewed their interpretation of 'care'. They regard care or treatment as including 'the protection, control or guidance of an individual, when this is provided to meet medical, physical, personal or domestic needs'. The following are examples of care that is a welfare service when: provided to an elderly, sick, disabled or distressed person; the care is part of a specific individual care plan and the service relates to it; and an assessment of the recipient's health condition and medical needs has been carried out by an appropriately trained person.

- Personal or nursing care (including assistance with bathing, dressing, toileting and other personal hygiene).
- General assistance and support with everyday tasks such as form-filling, letter reading/writing, bill-paying.
- Certain routine domestic tasks (such as housework, simple odd jobs, shopping and collecting a prescription or pension) provided all of the following conditions are met.
  - (a) An assessment of the recipients' health condition, medical needs and ability to perform each task has been carried out by an appropriately trained person (e.g. a medical or health professional or any person with relevant training or experience in social work or social care).
  - (b) This assessment has shown that the recipient is unable to carry out the tasks safely (because performance involves a likelihood of physical harm or injury) or properly or effectively (e.g. an elderly or disabled person who has mobility problems may be unable to shop regularly enough to meet their nutritional needs) or without 'significant' pain or discomfort and that this inability presents a risk to their health or welfare. 'Significant' is used to distinguish between low levels of pain or discomfort (experienced by many people in carrying out routine domestic tasks) and a significant level of pain or discomfort (that restricts ability to carry out such tasks).
  - (c) A record of each assessment is maintained by the supplier of the service.
  - (d) The service provided is a routine domestic task that the majority of the population would expect to carry out for themselves and which is required to keep a household going. This would exclude specialist services (e.g. non-essential gardening, decorating and other house maintenance including re-roofing, plumbing and electrical services).
- Counselling.
- Looking after or supervising vulnerable people.
- Support or instruction designed to develop or sustain a person's capacity to live independently in the community.
- Protection, control, guidance or companionship that is required to meet an individual's personal or domestic needs.
- Residential care, including accommodation, board and other services provided to residents as part of a care package.

(VAT Notice 701/2/11, para 2.1).

(2) The care or protection of children and young persons. [VATA 1994, Sch 9 Group 7 Note 6(b)]

HMRC regard this as applying to services directly connected with the care and protection of specific children, rather than children in general. Examples include

- care provided in a children's home;
- day care services such as those provided by a nursery, playgroup or after school club (but not activity-based clubs such as dance classes, etc.);
- the placement of children with foster carers by fostering agencies;
- the assessment of families to be included on the risk register;
- the care, support and protection of looked-after children; and
- training and assessment of prospective adopters by an adoption agency.

After school clubs and other providers of *non-residential* care for children, including after-school clubs, are only required to register under the appropriate social legislation if they provide a designated number of hours of care to children under the age of eight. A qualifying institution that

- provides care on a commercial basis to children who are under the age of eight as well as to older children,
- operates identical hours of opening for all age groups, and
- provides activities for over-eights that are comparable with those provided for younger children,

may, if it wishes, treat the care provided to over-eights as VAT exempt (in addition to the care provided to younger children).

Some welfare providers, such as independent fostering agencies, receive fees for services that, although concerned with the overall welfare of one or more child, are not primarily and directly connected with the care or protection of a specific child. HMRC do not usually regard these services as exempt unless they are provided as part of an exempt composite supply of care and protection. Examples include fees received for

- training of carers, or potential carers, where this is not linked to the needs of a specific child;
- assessment of potential foster carers suitability to look after children, where this is not linked to the needs of a specific child;
- play centres and activity-based clubs that provide services such as football and dancing lessons, indoor soft play areas and children's entertainment;
- consultancy or research services; and
- education of children.

See, however, **17 EDUCATION** for exemption for certain education and training services provided by eligible bodies.

(VAT Notice 701/2/11, para 2.2).

(3) Provision of spiritual welfare by religious institution as part of course of instruction or retreat, not being course or retreat designed primarily to provide recreation or a holiday. [VATA 1994, Sch 9 Group 7 Note 6(c)]

Examples include

- spiritual counselling to an individual;
- guided exploration of spiritual needs and development; and
- discussion, meditation and prayer or worship sessions

but does not include

- conferences or retreats when the predominant purpose is not spiritual welfare;
- educational courses in theology, or similar subjects, where the predominant purpose is to expand knowledge of spiritual matters rather than to provide spiritual welfare services; and
- meetings to discuss theology or aspects of Church doctrine.

(VAT Notice 701/2/11, para 2.3).

Goods provided in connection with welfare services

Goods provided as part of, or in connection with, an exempt supply of welfare services are also exempt. Examples include

- meals and refreshments provided to beneficiaries of welfare services in the course of care or spiritual welfare services for which no additional charge is made;
- bandages, plasters or ointments supplied in the course of a supply of care and treatment in the recipient's home; and
- items provided to children by playgroups or nurseries (e.g. picture books, crayons and toys) when provided in connection with the care.

Any goods that are separable from an exempt welfare service, or are not provided in connection with such a service, are not exempt.

(VAT Notice 701/2/11, para 3.4).

De Voil Indirect Tax Service. See V4.146.

Zero-rated dispensing of drugs, etc.

[29.13] The supply of goods can be zero-rated in the following circumstances.

(1) Pharmacists

The supply (including the letting on hire) of any 'qualifying goods' dispensed to an individual for his 'personal use' where the dispensing is by a registered pharmacist (as defined) on the 'prescription' (NHS or private) of an appropriate practitioner, i.e.

- a registered medical practitioner;
- a person registered in the dentists' register under the *Dentists Act 1984*;
- a community practitioner nurse prescriber;
- a nurse independent prescriber;
- an optometrist independent prescriber;
- a pharmacist independent prescriber;

- a physiotherapist independent prescriber;
- a podiatrist independent prescriber; or
- a supplementary prescriber.

Note – a physiotherapist independent prescriber and a podiatrist independent prescriber were added to the above list of appropriate practitioners and included in *VATA 1994, Sch 8 Group 12 Note 2B* with effect from 21 May 2014. [*SI 2014/1111*].

For these purposes, a person who is not registered in the visiting EU practitioners lists in the register of medical practitioners at the time he performs services in an urgent case (as mentioned in *Medical Act 1983, s 18(3)*) is treated as being so registered where he is entitled to be registered under that section.

[*VATA 1994, Sch 8 Group 12 Item 1 and Notes 2B, 5*].

'*Qualifying goods*' means any goods designed or adapted for use in connection with any medical or surgical treatment except hearing aids, dentures, spectacles and contact lenses [*VATA 1994, Sch 8 Group 12 Note 2A*].

'*Personal use*' is not defined but see **29.15** below for a general consideration of the term. Specifically, however, it does not include use by an individual while being provided with medical or surgical treatment, or any form of care, as an in-patient or resident of, or whilst attending, a hospital, nursing home or other institution which is approved, licensed or registered (or exempted by legislation from any requirement to be so approved, etc.). [*VATA 1994, Sch 8 Group 12 Notes 5A, 5I*].

Acquisitions and imports

Goods prescribed as above which are acquired in the UK from another EU member state or imported from a place outside the EU are not zero-rated on acquisition or importation. [*VATA 1994, Sch 8 Group 12 Note 1*].

There are a number of NHS payments which relate to the dispensing activity, all of which are zero-rated where the conditions for zero-rating are met. These are

- item fee;
- establishment payment;
- protected payment;
- repeat dispensing annual payment;
- transitional payment; and
- special fees for dispensing controlled or expensive drugs and for measuring and fitting appliances that the pharmacy also customises.

Support for people with disabilities

Pharmacists are required to give support to patients, in response to their assessed need, in order to facilitate their safe self-administration of medicines. This can comprise

- special labelling of containers for use by visually disabled patients;
- removing drugs from blister packs and repackaging them in replacement containers such as multi-compartment boxes; and

- reminder charts.

This activity is an adjunct to the dispensing of prescribed medicines and is zero-rated where the medicines themselves are zero-rated.

(VAT Notice 701/57/14, para 11.4.6).

Drugs administered by nurse at home of patient

In *Healthcare at Home Ltd* (VTD 20379) (TVC 19.8) a company, which had its own pharmacists and whose supply of drugs alone to patients was accepted as being zero-rated, also arranged for nurses to visit patients and administer drugs that had been prescribed for them. HMRC ruled that, the effect of the decisions in *Dr Beynon & Partners* (see **29.3** above) was that the company was making a single exempt supply of medical services. The tribunal, however, held that the supply was zero-rated since, in the present case, the determining characteristic was the requirement for the drug and not the necessity for a nurse (whereas in *Beynon* it was the supply of the doctor's services and not the drugs administered to the patients).

(2) Dispensing doctors

The supply (including the letting on hire) of any 'qualifying goods' where dispensing is in accordance with a requirement or authorisation under NHS regulations, on the 'prescription' (NHS or private) of an appropriate practitioner, i.e.

- a registered medical practitioner;
- a person registered in the dentists' register under the *Dentists Act 1984*;
- a community practitioner nurse prescriber;
- a nurse independent prescriber;
- an optometrist independent prescriber;
- a pharmacist independent prescriber;
- a physiotherapist independent prescriber;
- a podiatrist independent prescriber; or
- a supplementary prescriber.

Note – a physiotherapist independent prescriber and a podiatrist independent prescriber were added to the above list of appropriate practitioners and included in *VATA 1994, Sch 8 Group 12 Note 2B* with effect from 21 May 2014. [*SI 2014/1111*].

[*VATA 1994, Sch 8 Group 12 Item 1 and Note 5*].

Under such regulations dispensing doctors can be required or authorised by the NHS to provide pharmacy services to particular patients. The usual qualification is that the patient lives more than one mile from the nearest pharmacy (although there are others). Dispensing doctors cannot dispense drugs to their other patients and other doctors are not authorised to dispense drugs to any of their patients.

See under (1) above for '*qualifying goods*'.

Acquisitions and imports

Goods dispensed as above which are acquired in the UK from another EU member state or imported from a place outside the EU are not zero-rated on acquisition or importation. [*VATA 1994, Sch 8 Group 12 Note 1*].

Registration

Dispensing doctors who wish to recover VAT incurred on the drugs they dispense must register for VAT. General advice for doctors seeking to register is available in VAT Information Sheet 3/06 *Dispensing doctors and VAT registration: how and when to register; taxable or exempt supplies; VAT recovery and what records need to be kept* and VAT Information Sheet 12/06 *Further information for dispensing doctors.*

Administration of drugs at the time of treatment

This must be distinguished from the dispensing of drugs and is an exempt supply. See **29.3** above. As a result, zero-rating under *VATA 1994, Sch 8 Group 12 Item 1A* above only applies to dispensing of 'take-away' goods which the patient will self-administer.

Private prescriptions

The dispensing of goods on private prescription (e.g. drugs, vitamin supplements and homeopathic preparations) by a doctor is always standard-rated.

De Voil Indirect Tax Service. See V4.281.

Zero-rated supplies to disabled persons and charities

[29.14] The legislation zero-rates certain supplies of specialised goods and services when needed by '*handicapped*' persons. As the term 'handicapped' is not now in general usage in the following paragraphs the term 'disabled' is used instead.

Meaning of 'disabled'

'*Handicapped*' in the context of zero-rating is defined as 'chronically sick or disabled' [*VATA 1994, Sch 8 Group 12 Note 3*] but there is no further definition of 'chronically sick' and 'disabled' in the legislation.

The Shorter Oxford English dictionary defines 'chronic' as 'lasting a long time, lingering, inveterate' or 'constant, also bad'. The opposite of chronic is 'acute' which is defined as 'coming sharply to a crisis, not chronic'.

HMRC regard a person as 'chronically sick or disabled' if he/she

- has a physical or mental impairment which has a long-term (as opposed to acute or short-term) and substantial adverse effect upon his/her ability to carry out everyday activities,
- has a condition which the medical profession treats as a chronic sickness (e.g. diabetes), or

- is terminally ill

but do *not* regard the term as extending to

- a frail elderly person who is otherwise able-bodied (see also *C & E Commrs v Help the Aged*, QB [1997] STC 406 (TVC 11.18)); or
- any person who is only temporarily disabled or incapacitated (e.g. where suffering from a broken limb).

Tribunals have similarly held that a person is not chronically sick or disabled where suffering from a slipped disc (*Aquakraft Ltd* [1986] Lexis Citation 1050 (TVC 19.12)) or neck and back pain *Posturite (UK) Ltd* (VTD 7848) (TVC 19.58)).

See *Tempur Pedic (UK) Ltd* (VTD 13744) (TVC 19.34) for a consideration of the meaning of the words 'chronically sick'.

Despite the tribunal decisions in *The Dyslexia Institute Ltd* (VTD 12654) (TVC 11.24) and *GD Searle & Co Ltd* (VTD 13439) (TVC 19.66), HMRC accept that equipment designed for people suffering from asthma, psoriasis and dyslexia qualifies for zero-rating if they can be regarded as disabled sufferers of the condition.

(VAT Notice 701/7/14, paras 3.2, 4.5.2).

Parents, spouses, etc.

If a parent, spouse or guardian acts on behalf of a disabled person, the supply is treated as being made to that disabled person. (VAT Notice 701/7/14, para 3.2).

Conditions for zero-rating

For zero-rating to apply, it is essential that both

- the goods or services qualify; and
- the recipient qualifies.

The relief is not intended to cover all supplies of goods and services to disabled persons (or charities providing facilities for the disabled), nor does it mean that eligible goods and services can be zero-rated when supplied to people who are not disabled. For example, supplies to a nursing home would not be zero-rated under these provisions even if all the residents were disabled. See *Conroy* (VTD 1916) (TVC 19.104).

The supplier is responsible for correctly accounting for VAT and ensuring that all the conditions for zero-rating are met. Therefore where relief depends on the designer's intention and the supplier has not designed or manufactured the goods himself (e.g. a retailer), he should seek written confirmation from the manufacturer (or importer) that the goods are eligible for VAT relief (see below and also **29.21** below). HMRC will not normally provide binding VAT rulings to a retailer or distributor on the eligibility of specific items for VAT relief. They also recommend that suppliers obtain written declarations from each customer claiming entitlement to VAT relief. See **29.33** below.

(VAT Notice 701/7/14, para 2.1).

De Voil Indirect Tax Service. See V4.281.

Supplies of goods

[29.15] Subject to the exclusions below, zero-rating applies to the supply (including the letting on hire) to

- a disabled person for 'domestic or personal use', or
- a charity for making available, by sale or otherwise, to disabled persons for domestic or personal use

of any of the goods within **29.16** to **29.23** below. [*VATA 1994, Sch 8 Group 12, Item 2* and *Note 5*].

See **29.14** above for the interpretation of 'disabled'.

Domestic or personal use

This phrase is not defined in the legislation (apart from the specific exclusion below). See *Attorney General v Milliwatt Ltd*, KB [1948] All ER 331 (TVC 19.12) where Cassels J stated that domestic in the context of that case (which concerned electric pads and blankets) meant the house or the home.

In *Aquakraft Ltd* [1986] Lexis Citation 1050 (TVC 19.13) the tribunal held that 'personal use' meant 'private or exclusive' use. HMRC therefore take the view that the goods must be used specifically by an eligible individual (or series of eligible individuals) so that zero-rating will not apply under these provisions to

- goods and services used for business purposes; or
- supplies made widely available for a whole group of people to use as they wish, even if all such users are disabled (see *Portland College* (VTD 9815) (TVC 19.64)). For example, a stair lift in a charity building for the use or convenience of all disabled persons who might use the building would not qualify for relief. This is because the charity is making the lift available for the general use of all those people who might require it, rather than for the personal use of specified individuals.

(VAT Notice 701/7/14, para 3.4).

Exclusions

Subject to the extra-statutory concession below, zero-rating is restricted in the following circumstances.

(1) '*Domestic or personal use*' does not include any use by the disabled person in question while being provided (whether or not by the person making the supply) with medical or surgical treatment or any form of care
   - as an in-patient or resident of a 'relevant institution', or
   - whilst attending at the premises of a relevant institution

   in respect of
   (a) supplies to a disabled person by

(i) a Strategic Health Authority or Special Health Authority in England; a Health Authority, Special Health Authority or Local Health Authority in Wales; a Health Board or Special Health Board in Scotland; a Health and Social Services Board in Northern Ireland; the Common Services Agency for the Scottish Health Service, the Northern Ireland Central Services Agency for Health and Social Services and the Isle of Man Health Services Board; a National Health Service trust established under the *National Health Service Act 2006*, the *National Health Service (Wales) Act 2006* or the *National Health Service (Scotland) Act 1978*; an NHS Foundation Trust; a Primary Care Trust established under the *National Health Service Act 2006, s 18*; or a Health and Social Services trust established under the *Health and Personal Social Services (Northern Ireland) Order 1991, Art 10*, or

(ii) any person not falling within (i) above who is engaged in the carrying on of any activity in respect of which a relevant institution is required to be approved, licensed or registered or as the case may be, would be so required if not exempt

other than the supply of a wheelchair or invalid carriage or any parts or accessories designed solely for use therein; and

(b) supplies to a disabled person by any other person not within (*a*) above of

- medical or surgical appliances within **29.16** below and parts and accessories designed solely for use with such goods; and
- incontinence products and wound dressings.

Supplies to charities are not affected by this restriction.

(2) Zero-rating does not apply to

(a) a supply made in accordance with an agreement, arrangement or understanding to which any of the persons mentioned in (1)(*a*)(i) or (ii) above is or has been a party otherwise than as the supplier, or

(b) a supply where all or any part of the consideration has been provided (directly or indirectly) by any such person

but in the case of a supply of an invalid wheelchair or invalid carriage to a disabled person only if *either* a person within (1)(*a*)(ii) is involved *or* the *whole* of the consideration has been provided by a person within (1)(*a*)(i) above.

For the purposes of (1) and (2) above, references to an invalid wheelchair and invalid carriage do not include references to any mechanically propelled vehicle intended or adapted for use on roads.

A '*relevant institution*' is any institution (whether a hospital, nursing home or other institution) which provides care or medical or surgical treatment and is *either* approved, licensed or registered *or* specifically exempt from any such requirement.

By concession, the above exclusions do not apply (and a supply of goods can be treated as if it were zero-rated) where

- the goods fall within **29.21** below and are supplied by a charity at or below cost;
- the goods are goods other than spectacles or contact lenses, and are designed solely for use by a visually disabled person;
- the recipient of the supply is a resident, or is attending the premises of, a relevant institution; and
- the charity is not actively engaged in supplying such goods solely to disabled persons who are resident in or attending the premises of a relevant institution operated, managed or controlled by the charity.

(VAT Notice 48, ESC 3.24).

[*VATA 1994, Sch 8 Group 12 Notes 5B–5I; Health and Social Carer (Community Health and Standards) Act 2003, Sch 4 para 96; National Health Service (Consequential Provisions) Act 2006, Sch 1 paras 173, 174*].

The effect of the above exclusions is that it prevents institutions such as private hospitals, nursing homes and residential homes from recovering VAT charged on the purchase of supplies for disabled persons which are used in their supply to in-patients and residents. It also prevents them, and the NHS, from making arrangements for third parties to make VAT-free supplies (e.g. incontinence products and wound dressings) on the institution's behalf to patients who live in their own homes and for which the institution pays. Instead, such supplies are supplied by the institution as part of its exempt care. Supplies of incontinence products, etc direct to the disabled person by independent suppliers and for which the disabled person pays are not affected. (VAT Information Sheet 6/97).

Medical and surgical appliances

[29.16] Provided the conditions in **29.15** above are met, zero-rating applies to medical or surgical 'appliances' designed solely for the relief of a 'severe abnormality' or 'severe injury'.

Excluded are hearing aids (unless designed for auditory training of deaf children, see **29.21** below); dentures (but these are usually exempt under **29.7** above); and spectacles and contact lenses (but see **29.21** below for certain low vision aids).

Included are

- clothing (e.g. mastectomy bras and swimwear), footwear and wigs (which are often supplied during illness to mask hair loss); and
- renal haemodialysis units, oxygen concentrators, artificial respirators and other similar apparatus.

[*VATA 1994, Sch 8 Group 12, Item 2(a) and Note 4*].

An '*appliance*' is a device or piece of equipment with a specific function. It can be designed for use outside or inside the body.

The words 'severe abnormality' and 'severe injury' are not defined but among the disabilities falling within this category are amputation, rheumatoid or severe osteo-arthritis, severe disfigurement, congenital deformities, organic nervous diseases, learning disabilities and blindness.

Examples of zero-rated appliances, in addition to those specified in the legislation above, include

- artificial joints;
- artificial limbs;
- heart pacemakers;
- leg braces; and
- neck collars.

Examples of appliances that are not zero-rated, in addition to those specified in the legislation above, include

- plates or pins for use in repairing broken bones, bandages, plasters or other wound dressings as they are not appliances; and
- medical or surgical appliances that are not designed solely for the relief of a severe abnormality or severe injury, particularly those used in cosmetic surgery, such as breast implants.

(VAT Notice 701/7/14, para 4.2).

Adjustable beds

[29.17] Provided the conditions in **29.15** above are met, zero-rating applies to electrically or mechanically adjustable beds designed for invalids. [*VATA 1994, Sch 8 Group 12, Item 2(b)*].

A distinction must be made between a bed and a mattress (*Back In Health Ltd* (VTD 10003) (TVC 19.61)). The same tribunal also considered what makes a bed 'electrically or mechanically adjustable' and held that the key factor was whether it was adjustable for height, drop and angle, so as to enable a person to slide from a wheelchair to a bed at a lower level.

Beds must clearly stand out as being something specialised for the use of invalids. As well as being electrically or mechanically adjustable, they should additionally have specific design features which distinguish them from a standard bed. (VAT Notice 701/7/14, para 4.3).

See also *Niagara Holdings Ltd* (VTD 11400) (TVC 19.17) and *Hulsta Furniture (UK) Ltd* (VTD 16289) (TVC 19.18).

Sanitary devices

[29.18] Provided the conditions in **29.15** above are met, zero-rating applies to

- commode chairs and stools,
- devices incorporating a bidet jet and warm air drier, and
- frames or other devices for sitting over or rising from sanitary appliances.

[*VATA 1994, Sch 8 Group 12, Item 2(c)*].

Chair lifts and stair lifts

[29.19] Provided the conditions in **29.15** above are met, zero-rating applies to chair lifts and stair lifts designed for use in connection with invalid wheelchairs. [*VATA 1994, Sch 8 Group 12, Item 2(d*].

Although the lift must be capable of conveying a wheelchair-bound disabled person up and down stairs or from one level to another, the legislation does not require the disabled person to be seated in the wheelchair when using the lift. (VAT Notice 701/7/14, para 4.3).

See also **29.29** below for zero-rating of ordinary vertical lifts for disabled people who are not wheelchair-bound.

Hoists and lifters

[29.20] Provided the conditions in **29.15** above are met, zero-rating applies to hoists and lifters designed for use by invalids. [*VATA 1994, Sch 8 Group 12, Item 2(e)*].

Equipment designed solely for the disabled

[29.21] Provided the conditions in **29.15** above are met, zero-rating applies to equipment and appliances not falling within **29.16** to **29.20** above but which is 'designed solely for use by a disabled person'. *Specifically included* are invalid wheelchairs and carriages (other than mechanically propelled vehicles intended or adapted for use on roads) and hearing aids designed for the auditory training of deaf children. *Excluded* are other types of hearing aids, dentures (but these are usually exempt under **29.7** above); and spectacles and contact lenses (but see below for certain low vision aids). [*VATA 1994, Sch 8 Group 12, Item 2(g)* and *Notes 4, 5G*].

It is not sufficient that the equipment or appliance is merely intended for use by a disabled person, or is mainly purchased by disabled persons. General purpose equipment (e.g. ordinary or orthopaedic beds, orthopaedic or reclining chairs, etc.) may benefit disabled people but is designed for general use or for use by disabled and able-bodied people alike. Such products are not, therefore, eligible for relief. On the other hand, equipment designed solely for use by disabled people will remain eligible for relief when supplied to a disabled person or charity, even though available to be purchased by able-bodied people. (VAT Notice 701/7/14, para 4.5.1).

'Designed solely for use by a disabled person'

In the opinion of HMRC, this means that the original intention of the designer was to produce equipment or an appliance designed solely to meet the needs of persons with one or more disabilities (see also, for example, *Tempur Pedic (UK) Ltd* (VTD 13744) (TVC 19.34)). The design must succeed in that the product does, in fact, meet the needs of disabled persons. There are a number of conditions which may, but do not invariably, result in disability (e.g. asthma, psoriasis and dyslexia). Equipment which meets the needs of people with such conditions only qualifies for zero-rating if designed solely for the purpose of meeting the needs of *disabled* sufferers of the condition. (VAT Notice 701/7/14, para 4.5.2).

In *The British Disabled Flying Association*, UT [2013] UKUT 162 (TCC) (TVC 19.40), the British Disabled Flying Association (BDFA) contended that its purchases of two light aircraft and its subsequent expenditure on adapting, repairing and maintaining the aircraft, qualified for zero-rating under *VATA 1994, Sch 8, Group 12, Item 2(g)*. The Upper Tribunal held that the question of whether an item has the physical characteristics to qualify as designed solely for use by a disabled person must be decided by reference to the item's physical characteristics at the time of supply. One of the aircraft qualified for zero-rating, since it had been adapted for use by disabled persons prior to its sale to the BDFA. However, the other aircraft did not qualify, as it had not been adapted for use by disabled persons at the time the BDFA purchased it.

In *Iansyst Ltd* (TC05126) [2016] UKFTT 372 (TC) (TVC 19.41), the First-tier Tax Tribunal accepted that the relief applied to mobile phones and tablets with software installed to enable their use by visually impaired and dyslexic people. At the time of supply, the software constituted an 'adaptation' of the equipment. Although it was capable of use by non-disabled people, the Tribunal accepted that such people would not pay extra for something that was of little use to them. The fact that the software on its own would be standard-rated was irrelevant. The case concerned the supply of the goods, and the trader's appeal was allowed.

Determination of zero-rating

Only the designer or manufacturer can determine whether the goods qualify for zero-rating. The designer, manufacturer or importer of the goods must retain evidence which demonstrates that the goods in question fulfil the conditions for relief including

- the disability needs to be addressed;
- the product specification for meeting those needs;
- results of tests demonstrating that the product meets the design intention; or
- patents or patent applications.

If necessary, the manufacturer or importer should seek liability rulings from HMRC.

Any other person, who thinks that the equipment or appliances he is selling have been designed solely for use by a disabled person, should seek confirmation from the manufacturer or importer. (Their advertising literature may contain a statement to this effect.) Local Business Advice Centres have been asked to refuse requests for liability rulings from retailers.

(VAT Notice 701/7/14, para 4.5.3).

VAT liability of specific equipment and appliances

The following is a list of equipment and appliances which have been considered (either by HMRC, a tribunal or the courts) for inclusion within *VATA 1994, Sch 8 Group 12, Item 2(g)*.

Air conditioning, etc.

Air-conditioning and similar general purpose equipment does not qualify for relief.

See also *Simmons* (VTD 6622) (TVC 19.57) where two air-conditioning units, purchased by a person suffering from multiple sclerosis, and which helped considerably in coping with the condition, were held to have been designed for general purpose use and not for use by a disabled person. The fact that the design would have been the same whether the equipment was to be used by a disabled person or for the general purposes did not bring the equipment within the scope of Item 2(g). Air-conditioning units could also not be regarded as 'similar apparatus' (see above) and therefore fall within **29.16** above.

An air filtration system installed in the house of a person suffering from multiple allergies was held to qualify for zero-rating in *Symons* (VTD 19174) (TVC 19.36).

Asthma, hay fever and allergy products

Supplies of all vacuum cleaners, air purification products and similar allergy relief products are standard-rated irrespective of to whom they are supplied. (Business Briefs 16/96, 17/96, and 20/97).

See also *GD Searle & Co Ltd* (VTD 13439) (TVC 19.66) which concerned aerosol pesticide sprays, designed to kill dust mites and supplied to pharmacists for sale to asthmatics or sufferers from eczema. The tribunal held that, as not all sufferers from asthma could be described as 'chronically sick or disabled', the sprays were not 'designed solely for use by a disabled person', and thus failed to qualify for zero-rating.

Carpets

In *The David Lewis Centre*, QB [1995] STC 485 (TVC 19.42) woollen carpets, purchased to protect patients from scorching when falling as a result of an epileptic seizure, were held not to qualify for zero-rating since the carpets were not specifically designed for the use of the disabled.

Similarly, in *Vassall Centre Trust* (VTD 17891) (TVC 19.46) carpets, adapted by having a light coloured strip along both edges up to the doorway or access point to assist the partially sighted in moving about the building, were held not to be designed solely for use by disabled persons.

Computer equipment

Computer systems are increasingly being used to aid disabled people. Most are general use products which may be useful for disabled people but are designed to be used by disabled and non-disabled people. Examples include laptops and tablets. Such products are generally not eligible to be supplied at the zero rate of VAT, even if they are sold with certain applications that may assist disabled people such as voice recognition. This is because the equipment has not been designed solely for use by disabled people. Only those products which have been designed solely for use by a disabled person are eligible to be supplied at the zero rate of VAT.

(VAT Notice 701/7/14, para 4.6).

Although not reflected in the 2014 version of VAT Notice 701/7, it is understood at the time of writing that HMRC currently allows the following concessions in relation to computer equipment that is generally made up of both standard-rated, general use items of hardware and software, together with other items designed solely for use by a disabled person and which are therefore eligible for zero-rating. To simplify the application of VAT for such computer systems sold as a complete package, suppliers may use either or both of the following concessions provided

- the computer system is a tool to aid the disabled person to overcome communication problems; and
- the computer system is for the personal or domestic use of a disabled person.

The arrangements apply only to complete packages. Replacement units or upgrading items are subject to VAT at the standard rate unless they are designed solely for use by disabled people.

(a) *Concession 1 – zero-rating of central processor.* A central processor may be zero-rated if
   - it is sold as part of a computer system; and
   - it has software installed which enables a disabled person to use the computer system or other software effectively, or to carry out tasks effectively when otherwise they could not.

   No other general purpose hardware may be zero-rated under this or any other concession.

(b) *Concession 2 – composite rate of VAT for computer systems.* Traders supplying disabled people with complete computer systems that contain significant specialist items for use by disabled customers may use a composite VAT rate for such supplies. This rate is based on supplies of such packages made by that supplier over a recent representative period. In addition to the items of equipment designed solely for the use of a disabled person, the suppliers may include the values of the following elements of the package in the zero-rated portion.
   - The central processor described in (a) above; and
   - costs charged to the customer for the installation of the equipment and for the training in its use.

Example

Z Ltd supplies five different qualifying packages of computer equipment in a representative period of three months. In package A, the zero-rated element (central processor, speech synthesiser, Braille embosser, specialist software, installation and training) is £1,500 at sales value and the standard-rated element (printer, keyboard, VDU and standard software) is £500 plus £100.00 VAT. The total cost of the package is £2,100.00 of which £100.00 is VAT. The composite rate is the rate which needs to be applied to the total VAT-exclusive sale value (£2,000) to ensure the correct VAT is declared, i.e.

100 ÷ 2,000 × 100 = 5% (usually rounded to one decimal place)

The composite rates and value of sales for each of the five packages offered in the representative period are as follows.

Package	Composite rate	Sales value £	VAT £
A	5%	50,000	2,500
B	6%	20,000	1,200
C	3%	10,000	300
D	3.8%	10,000	380
E	4.1%	10,000	410
		£100,000	£4,790

The overall composite rate is

4,790 ÷ 100,000 × 100 = 4.79% (rounded to 4.8%)

Z Ltd can apply a composite rate of 4.8% to all sales of qualifying packages. The overall composite rate should be recalculated every twelve months.

Golf buggies

In *Foxer Industries* (VTD 13817) (TVC 19.67) single-seat golf buggies, marketed for sale to elderly golfers, were held not to have been designed solely for the use of disabled persons. (In a subsequent appeal (*Foxer Industries* (VTD 14469) (TVC 19.83)) the partnership claimed that work done in adapting a number of buggies for specific customers should be treated as qualifying for zero-rating. The tribunal held that, in one case, the modifications to the basic design were so fundamental that the entire buggy should be treated as zero-rated under *Item 2(g)*. In the other eight cases, an appropriate proportion of the price was treated as zero-rated under **29.25** below.)

See also *C F Leisure Mobility Ltd* (VTD 16790) (TVC 19.68).

Hearing aids and induction loop systems

Most hearing aids are specifically excluded from zero-rating (see above). But certain specialist equipment designed for people with severely defective hearing as the term is generally used, may be zero-rated. These include the following.

- Hearing aids designed for the auditory training of deaf children. [*VATA 1994, Sch 8 Group 12 Note 4*].
- Tinnitus maskers (an earpiece which generates a constant noise to mask the effect of ringing in the ears).
- Induction loop equipment.

(VAT Notice 701/7/14, para 4.7).

Hydrotherapy pools

Following the decisions in *The David Lewis Centre* (VTD 10860) (TVC 19.42) and *Boys' and Girls' Welfare Society* (VTD 15274) (TVC 19.43), although it remains their general policy that swimming pools are not equipment that has been designed solely for the use of disabled persons, HMRC now accept that a hydrotherapy pool qualifies for zero-rating in certain conditions.

Incontinence products

HMRC have always accepted that incontinence products are goods of a kind which qualifying for zero-rating but their supply can only be zero-rated in certain circumstances.

- *Retail sales*. People who are incontinent and live in their own homes are entitled to buy incontinence products at the zero rate. Eligible incontinence products can be zero-rated on the shelf without a written declaration under **29.33** below to the retailer by the customer.
- *Internet and mail order sales* also qualify for zero-rating provided they are made to individuals and not institutions.

Zero-rating does not apply to incontinence products supplied to a disabled person (whether by a Health Authority, hospital or any other person) whilst that person is an in-patient or receiving residential care (see under **29.16** below).

Bulk sales: HMRC will expect retailers, internet and mail order suppliers to have a signed declaration, or other supporting evidence that the supply is to an incontinent individual (and not to an institution such as a nursing home) for customers who buy more than

- 200 disposable pads;
- 50 washable pads;
- 5 collecting devices; or
- 10 pairs of waterproof or leak-proof underwear.

(VAT Notice 701/7/14, para 4.5.4).

Kitchens

Kitchen furniture fitted into a kitchen during the construction of a new dwelling may be zero-rated under *VATA 1994, Sch 8 Group 5 Item 4* (see **43.16 LAND AND BUILDINGS: ZERO AND REDUCED RATE SUPPLIES AND DIY HOUSEBUILDERS**).

For existing kitchens, equipment designed solely for use by a disabled person, together with the services of installation (see **29.27** below) and the services of adapting goods to suit the condition of a disabled person (see **29.25** below) can also be zero-rated.

See also *Softley Ltd (t/a Softley Kitchens)* (VTD 15034) (TVC 19.33) where it was held that certain items of kitchen equipment could be zero-rated when made to the individual specifications of a disabled person.

Low vision aids and other aids for the blind

Although spectacles and contact lenses are specifically excluded (see above), zero-rating can be applied to other types of low vision aids. This equipment tends to fall into two categories.

- Spectacle-mounted low vision aids which are custom made to the prescription of a qualified optician where the prescription identifies the appliance as a low vision aid.

- Other low vision aids, including technical aids for reading and writing, which are designed exclusively for visually impaired people (e.g. closed circuit video magnification equipment capable of magnifying text and images).

HMRC also list the following as examples of equipment qualifying for relief.

- Braille embossers.
- Whistling cups for blind people.
- White canes for blind people.

(VAT Notice 701/7/14, para 4.8).

Over bed tables

This type of equipment is designed for use by hospital patients in general and not just those who are chronically sick or disabled. They therefore cannot be said to be 'designed solely for use by a disabled person' and do not qualify for relief. See *Princess Louise Scottish Hospital* [1983] VATTR 191 (TVC 19.47).

Pain relief equipment

Following the tribunal decision in *Neen Design Ltd* (VTD 11782) (TVC 19.13) TENS (Transcutaneous Electrical Nerve Stimulators) machines are taken as designed solely for use by disabled persons (i.e. sufferers of chronic pain) even though frequently used by sufferers of acute (short-term) pain (e.g. sports injuries and labour pains). Neither the latter, nor the fact that the product was subsequently marketed for use by sufferers of chronic *and* acute pain, outweighed the original design intention. As a result, TENS machines can be zero-rated when meeting the conditions in **29.17** above. TENS machines supplied for use by people suffering short-term pain are taxable at the standard rate.

Radiators

In *The David Lewis Centre* (VTD 10860) (TVC 19.42) low surface temperature radiators, designed so that their surface would not burn the skin of a disabled person who fell against them, were held to be zero-rated because the heating system in its entirety had been designed specifically for the charity. HMRC regard this decision as one made on the facts of the case.

In *Boys' and Girls' Welfare Society* (VTD 15274) (TVC 19.98) the tribunal held that low surface temperature radiators did not qualify for zero-rating under *Item 2(g)* since they were not 'designed solely for use by a disabled person', but that they qualified for zero-rating under **29.28** below where they were installed in bathrooms, washrooms or lavatories.

In *Joulesave EMES Ltd* (VTD 17115) (TVC 19.37) the tribunal held that radiator and pipe covers had been designed solely for use by disabled people and were eligible for zero-rating when meeting the conditions in **29.17** above.

Soft games rooms and observation windows

The design, supply and equipping of soft games rooms, and observation windows, used by disabled persons were held to be standard-rated supplies of construction services in *C & E Commrs v The David Lewis Centre*, QB [1995] STC 485 (TVC 11.9).

Spa baths

In *Aquakraft Ltd* [1986] Lexis Citation 1050 (TVC 19.13) the tribunal held that a spa bath supplied to hospitals and nursing homes, even though it had special features such as handrails, provision for the fitting of a hoist and recessed taps for safety, was not subject to relief under *Item 2(g)* because all kinds of hospital patients could be expected to use it.

A spa bath might be eligible for zero-rating under **29.28** below (as a supply of goods in connection with extending or adapting a bathroom in a disabled person's private residence).

Walkways

Walkways do not incorporate any special features that render them 'designed solely for use by a disabled person' and so are not eligible for zero-rating under *Item 2(g)*. See *Portland College* (VTD 9815) (TVC 19.60).

Wheelchairs

Invalid wheelchairs and carriages (other than mechanically propelled vehicles intended or adapted for use on the roads) are specifically included in *VATA 1994, Sch 8 Group 12 Item 2* by *Notes 4(b)* and *5G*.

An '*invalid carriage*' is defined by *The Chronically Sick and Disabled Persons Act 1970, s 20* as a vehicle, whether mechanically propelled or not, constructed or adapted for the carriage of one person, being a person suffering from some physical defect or disability.

Writing boards

Zero-rating does not apply to a general purpose item that is marketed for use by disabled people, even if some changes are made to the design to make it useful for them. An objective test must be applied to see if the item has been designed solely for use by a disabled person. The design intention must be met for zero-rating to be achieved. See *Posturite (UK) Ltd* (VTD 7848) (TVC 19.59).

Parts and accessories

[29.22] Provided the conditions in **29.15** above are met, zero-rating applies to 'parts' and 'accessories' designed solely for use in or with goods described in **29.16** to **29.21** above and **29.24**(*a*) below. [*VATA 1994, Sch 8 Group 12, Item 2(h)*].

'*Parts*' means integral components without which the equipment is incomplete.

'*Accessories*' means optional extras which can be used to improve the operation of the equipment, or enable it to be used, or to be used to better effect, in particular circumstances.

Zero-rating does not apply to general use items even if purchased to be used with a zero-rated item. See *Poole Shopmobility* (VTD 16290) (TVC 19.81) (standard batteries) and *Mills* (VTD 1893) (TVC 19.79) (portable generator). If, however, batteries were designed solely to operate within a zero-rated item, they would be eligible for zero-rating. (VAT Notice 701/7/14, para 4.9). See also *The Princess Louise Scottish Hospital* [1983] VATTR 191 (TVC 19.47) where overbeds were held not to qualify as accessories to a zero-rated bed within **29.17** above, even though designed by the same designer, as they could be used on other beds.

Boats

[29.23] Provided the conditions in **29.17** above are met, zero-rating applies to boats designed, or substantially and permanently adapted, for use by disabled persons. [*VATA 1994, Sch 8 Group 12, Item 2(i)*].

To qualify for relief, the boat should include all or most of the following features.

- A ramp for wheelchairs.
- Lifts and level non-cambered surfaces to accommodate wheelchair movements.
- Specialised washing and lavatory facilities accessible to disabled people.
- Specially equipped galley and sleeping areas and steering facilities designed for use by disabled people.
- Handrails.
- Wheelchair clamps.
- Steering or other controls adapted for use by disabled people.

(VAT Notice 701/7/14, para 4.4).

Zero-rating does not apply to the supply of parts and accessories designed solely for use in or with boats designed or adapted for use by disabled persons. However, zero-rating does apply to parts and accessories used in connection with repairs or maintenance to qualifying boats; and parts and accessories that are included as part of the single supply of qualifying boats. (HMRC Brief 42/11).

Motor vehicles

[29.24] Zero-rating applies to the supply of a motor vehicle in the following circumstances.

(a) The supply (including the letting on hire) to
   - a disabled person for 'domestic or personal use', or
   - a charity for making available, by sale or otherwise, to disabled persons for domestic or personal use

   of a motor vehicle designed or substantially and permanently adapted for the carriage of a disabled person in a wheelchair or on a stretcher and of no more than eleven other persons.

   See **29.15** above for the interpretation of '*domestic and personal use*'. [*VATA 1994, Sch 8 Group 12, Item 2(f)*].

(b) The supply (including the letting on hire) of a 'qualifying motor vehicle' to

- a disabled person, who usually uses a wheelchair or is usually carried on a stretcher, for domestic or his personal use; or
- a charity for making available to such a disabled person, by sale or otherwise, for domestic or his personal use.

A '*qualifying motor vehicle*' is a motor vehicle (other than one capable of carrying 12 or more persons including the driver) that

- is designed or substantially and permanently adapted to enable a disabled person, who usually uses a wheelchair or who is usually carried on a stretcher, to enter, and drive or otherwise be carried in, the motor vehicle; or
- by reason of its design, or being substantially or permanently adapted, includes features whose design is such that their sole purpose is to a allow a wheelchair used by a disabled person to be carried in or on the motor vehicle.

[*VATA 1994, Sch 8 Group 12 Item 2A and Notes 5, 5L*].

Zero-rating does not apply to a motor vehicle if the vehicle was adapted shortly *after* it was supplied to the disabled person. However, zero-rating does apply on motor vehicles that are adapted *before* the supply. (HMRC Brief 41/11).

HMRC issued a consultation document on 30 June 2014 in relation to changing the way zero-rating applies to the supply of motor vehicles that have been substantially and permanently adapted for the use of disabled wheelchair users. The aim is to reduce fraud, better target the relief, and make the legislation clearer, including clarifying that users of lower limb prosthetics can benefit from the relief.

(Budget 2014, para 2.180).

In December 2014, it was announced that legislative changes would be taken forward in *Finance Bill 2016* to limit VAT relief to one substantially and permanently adapted motor vehicle purchased for the personal use of a disabled wheelchair user in any three-year period. Provision is to be made to allow more than one vehicle in exceptional circumstances. The words 'substantially' and 'permanently' are to be defined in the legislation and motor vehicle suppliers are to be required to submit details of zero-rated sales to HMRC. However, no such provisions were included in the Finance Bill issued in March 2016.

(VAT relief on substantially and permanently adapted motor vehicles for disabled wheelchair users – Summary of Responses – December 2014).

The Government subsequently announced in Autumn Statement 2016 that legislation would be introduced in *Finance Bill 2017* in order to tackle abuse of the zero-rating provisions in respect of cars adapted for wheelchair users, while ensuring that the person who is entitled to benefit from the relief can continue to do so. HMRC established during a review of this zero-rating provision that some people are targeting and abusing the relief. These people are obtaining a VAT zero-rate relief on vehicles with minor adaptions and later reversing the changes in order to sell the vehicle on for profit.

The revised legislation:

- limits the number of vehicles that can benefit from the relief in a given period. An eligible individual may purchase one vehicle every three years. There are some instances when this limit can be exceeded (see below);
- make submission of customer eligibility declarations using form VAT1615A to HMRC mandatory. The declaration must be submitted no later than 12 months after the relevant supply to a customer;
- motor dealers are required to send information regarding these zero-rated sales to HMRC using form VAT1617A no later than 12 months after each individual sale (the form can be submitted earlier if preferable);
- the *VATA 1994, s 62* penalty will apply to a person who gives an incorrect customer eligibility declaration to the supplier of a vehicle. The relevant penalty is equivalent to the amount of VAT chargeable on a standard-rated supply of the vehicle.

HMRC have published VAT Notice 1002 which contains information regarding the changes that came into effect from 1 April 2017.

HMRC have stated in Notice 1002 that if a disabled wheelchair or stretcher user (hereafter referred to as disabled wheelchair user) nominates another individual to purchase the motor vehicle on his behalf, they expect the nominated person to have a close personal relationship with the disabled wheelchair user and for them to live reasonably close. Suppliers will be required to check and confirm that the disabled wheelchair user will obtain the most benefit from the use of the vehicle before the supply can be zero-rated.

HMRC have placed additional burdens on suppliers who will be required to undertake reasonable due diligence checks to confirm that the disabled wheelchair user, or their representative, meet the eligibility requirements, before they zero-rate the sale.

(Notice 1002, paras 3.4, 6.3, 13.4).

HMRC have also provided guidance on situations where a vehicle can be purchased before the three-year time period since the date of the last relevant supply has expired. In summary, HMRC will accept the following exceptions to the three-year rule:

(1) the vehicle has been stolen;
(2) the vehicle has been destroyed or damaged beyond repair in circumstances beyond the control of the disabled person;
(3) the disabled wheelchair user's condition changes and because of this the vehicle is no longer suitable for use by that person.

If (1) or (2) above applies, the disabled wheelchair user, or their representative, will be expected to provide satisfactory evidence to the supplier to support their entitlement to acquire another eligible vehicle. Under (3) above, the disabled wheelchair user, or their representative, will need to contact HMRC to explain the situation and if HMRC agrees that their circumstances make them eligible for a new vehicle they will issue a letter to this effect. This letter must be provided to the supplier. The supplier can only supply a new vehicle under the zero-rating provisions where they are satisfied that the disabled wheelchair user, or their representative, has satisfied all of the conditions laid down in the relevant legislation and Notice 1002.

(Notice 1002, paras 6.2, 13.3).

Please note that the three-year rule does not affect the short-term lease or hire of a motor vehicle.

[*FA 2017, Sch 7*].

Motability scheme

See also **29.31** below for zero-rating of motor vehicles under this scheme.

Adaptation of goods

[29.25] Zero-rating applies to the supply

- to a disabled person of services of adapting general purpose goods to suit his or her condition, and
- to a charity of services of adapting general purpose goods to suit the condition of a disabled person to whom the goods are to be made available, by sale or otherwise, by the charity,

and to any goods necessarily supplied in connection with the services of adaptation.

Zero-rating applies only to the adaptation services (and incidental goods). It does not apply to the goods themselves being adapted. Therefore, where the supplier of the services also supplies the goods, and has adapted them prior to the supply of adaptation services, he must apportion the value of the supply between the unadapted standard-rated goods and the zero-rated service of adaptation.

[*VATA 1994, Sch 8 Group 12 Items 3, 4, 6 and Note 8*].

Separate rules apply to the sale of substantially and permanently adapted motor vehicles. See **29.24** above.

Buildings

Apart from the first grant of a major interest in a building which is deemed to be a supply of goods by virtue of the *VATA 1994, Sch 4 para 4*, buildings are not 'goods' and therefore the adaptation of a building to suit the condition of a disabled person does not fall within the above provisions. See *Arthritis Care* (VTD 13974) (TVC 19.71). The only reliefs which apply to adaptations of buildings are those in **29.28** and **29.29** below.

Apportionment

See **48.4 OUTPUT TAX** for various methods of apportionment. It may not be valid to look merely at the price difference between the adapted model and a standard factory model. Any initial research and development costs related to the adaptation should be costed as zero-rated in addition to the basic extra cost passed on to the customer (see *Foxer Industries* (VTD 14469) (TVC 19.83)).

Repair and maintenance

[29.26] Zero-rating applies to the supply to a disabled person or charity of a service of repair or maintenance of

- any goods which were zero-rated on supply under **29.15** to **29.24** above,
- any goods supplied in connection with adaptation services under **29.25** above or repair and maintenance services under these provisions,
- any goods supplied in connection with the installation of a lift under **29.29** below, and
- any alarm call system zero-rated under **29.30** below

together with a supply of any goods in connection with those repair and maintenance services.

[*VATA 1994, Sch 8 Group 12 Items 5 and 6*].

See also **29.28** below under the heading *Goods supplied in connection with construction services.*

Installation of goods

[29.27] Zero-rating applies to the supply to a disabled person or to a charity of services necessarily performed in the installation of equipment or appliances (including parts and accessories for them) which are zero-rated under **29.15** to **29.23** above. [*VATA 1994, Sch 8 Group 12 Item 7*].

Examples of services of installation which can be zero-rated under these provisions are

- plumbing in a sanitary appliance;
- wiring up an electrically adjustable bed; and
- installing a chair lift.

(VAT Notice 701/7/14, para 5.1).

Where parts and accessories are used, these are eligible for zero-rating under this provision provided they are part of the single supply of installation services. Parts and accessories supplied separately are eligible for relief under **29.22** above.

Building alterations

[29.28] Zero-rating applies to the following supplies.

(a) The supply to a disabled person of a service of constructing ramps or widening doorways or passages (but not constructing new doorways or passages) for the purposes of facilitating his entry to, or movement within, his private residence. [*VATA 1994, Sch 8 Group 12 Item 8*]. Construction of a ramp includes
  - the raising of a floor level to match that of another existing floor level so as to remove a step or steps;
  - the reduction of the angle of an incline; or
  - the creation of a slope.

A passage can be outdoors as well as indoors. Widening a passage includes

- the widening of a room through which a disabled person passes to gain access to another room, e.g. a bedroom which has an en suite facility (see *Cannings-Knight* (VTD 11291) (TVC 19.90)); or
- the widening of an existing path across a disabled person's garden (but not the construction of a new path).

(VAT Notice 701/7/14, para 6.2).

(b) The supply to a charity of services within (*a*) above for the purpose of facilitating a disabled person's entry to, or movement within, *any* building (not just a private residence). [*VATA 1994, Sch 8 Group 12 Item 9*].

(c) The supply to a disabled person of a service of providing, extending or adapting a bathroom, 'washroom' or lavatory in that person's private residence where such provision, extension or adaptation is necessary by reason of his condition. [*VATA 1994, Sch 8 Group 12 Item 10*].

(d) The supply to a charity of a service of providing, extending or adapting a bathroom, 'washroom' or lavatory for use by disabled persons

- in a residential home or self-contained living accommodation, in either case provided as a residence (whether on a permanent or temporary basis or both) for disabled persons (but not including an inn, hotel, boarding house or similar establishment or accommodation in any such type of establishment), or
- in a day-centre where at least 20% of the individuals using the centre are disabled persons

where such provision, extension or adaptation is necessary by reason of the condition of the disabled persons.
[*VATA 1994, Sch 8 Group 12 Item 11 and Note 5J*].
Zero-rating applies even if the residential home, etc. is not managed or used by the charity to which the supply is made. Care, however, should be taken when supplies are made to residential homes as many such homes are not operated by charities, in which case supplies to them do not qualify for zero-rating under these provisions. (VAT Notice 701/7/14, para 6.3).

(e) The supply to a charity of a service of providing, extending or adapting a 'washroom' or lavatory for use by disabled persons in a building (or part of a building) used principally by a charity for charitable purposes (e.g. a church hall, day centre or village hall) where such provision, etc. is necessary to facilitate the use of the washroom or lavatory by disabled persons. [*VATA 1994, Sch 8 Group 12 Item 12*].

(f) The supply of goods in connection with the supply of services within (*a*)–(*e*) above. [*VATA 1994, Sch 8 Group 12 Item 13*].
Building materials and other goods can be zero-rated under this provision when supplied by

- the building contractor in connection with the zero-rated services (see above), or
- a builders merchant, etc. to the disabled person or charity themselves for use by their building contractor (see *Flather* (VTD 11960) (TVC 19.91)) provided the builders merchant is

happy that the actual building work will qualify for zero-rating and can demonstrate this subsequently to any visiting HMRC officer

but not when the materials are bought by a disabled person or charity in connection with building works which will be performed free of charge by a friend or relative, or in a do-it-yourself capacity by the disabled person or charity themselves (because there is no subsequent supply of zero-rated construction services to which these materials can be connected).

(VAT Notice 701/7/14, para 6.8).

For the purposes of (*c*)–(*e*) above

- '*washroom*' means a room that contains a lavatory or washbasin (or both) but does not contain a bath or a shower or cooking, sleeping or laundry facilities [*VATA 1994, Sch 8 Group 12 Notes 5K*];
- bathroom includes a shower room (VAT Notice 701/7/14, para 6.3); and
- lavatory is a room containing a toilet and possibly, but not always, a washbasin (VAT Notice 701/7/14, para 6.3).

Preparatory work

Preparatory work and necessary restoration work can also be zero-rated provided the supply is made to the disabled person or charity concerned, as the case may be. This would include, e.g.

- when widening a doorway, the removal of bricks and mortar and restoration of the immediate décor; and
- when providing a bathroom, the preparation of footings, including ground levelling, work for the provision of water, gas, electricity and drainage as necessary, and restoration of the immediate décor.

Professional services

Services of an architect, surveyor or any person acting as a consultant or in a supervisory capacity, even when supplied in connection with a supply of qualifying building services, are standard-rated in all circumstances.

Additional construction work in the course of a zero-rated supply

Where economy and feasibility dictate that a bathroom, washroom or lavatory has to be constructed in, or extended into, a space occupied by an existing room (e.g. a bedroom or kitchen), the restoration of that room to its original size can be regarded as part of the work essential to the provision of the bathroom, etc. and can be zero-rated provided the supply is also made to the disabled person. Where, on the other hand, a builder constructs, extends or adapts a bathroom, washroom or lavatory and at the same time constructs additional accommodation (e.g. an adjoining new bedroom/day room), the supply must be apportioned between the zero-rated and standard-rated parts.

(VAT Notice 701/7/14, para 6.6).

Lift installation

[29.29] The following supplies are zero-rated.

(a) The supply to a disabled person of services necessarily performed in the installation of a lift for the purpose of facilitating his or her movement between floors within that person's own private residence. [*VATA 1994, Sch 8 Group 12 Item 16*].

This provision overlaps with **29.19** above (zero-rating of chair and stair lifts) but extends relief to lifts which, although not specially designed for use by disabled people, help them to move between floors within their home.

(b) The supply to a charity providing a permanent or temporary residence or day centre for disabled persons of services necessarily performed in the installation of a lift for the purpose of facilitating movement of disabled persons between floors in that building. [*VATA 1994, Sch 8 Group 12 Item 17*].

To qualify as a day centre, the building need not have been set up principally or exclusively for disabled persons but it must be capable of being regarded as a day centre in the ordinary sense of the term. This probably means that the disabled persons receive some form of care. See *Union of Students of the University of Warwick* (VTD 13821) (TVC 19.106) and *Aspex Visual Arts Trust* (VTD 16419) (TVC 19.107) where a lift in a students union building and an art gallery respectively failed to qualify for zero-rating.

Educational institutions. As a consequence of comments made by the High Court in *C & E Commrs v Help the Aged*, QB [1997] STC 406 (TVC 11.19) HMRC initially formed the view that charitable educational institutions (e.g. grant-maintained schools and universities) could be regarded as day centres providing care for disabled people and therefore the installation of lifts in their *non-residential* buildings could be zero-rated under the above provisions (providing all other conditions were met). They subsequently decided that this view was incorrect. Where the installation of a lift was zero-rated before this change of view, subsequent supplies of repair and maintenance of that lift can also be zero-rated. Where a contract for the installation of a lift in a non-residential building is entered into after that date, the supply of installation services (and any subsequent supplies of repair and maintenance) is standard-rated. This does not apply to lift installations in those buildings where an educational institution provides permanent or temporary residence, which remains zero-rated, provided all other conditions are met. (Business Brief 3/05).

(c) The supply of goods in connection with the supply of services within (*a*) or (*b*) above. [*VATA 1994, Sch 8 Group 12 Item 18*].

Building materials and other goods can be zero-rated under this provision when supplied

- by the building contractor in connection with the zero-rated services (see above), or
- by a builders merchant, etc. to the disabled person or charity themselves for use by their building contractor (see *Flather* (VTD 11960) (TVC 19.89)) provided the builders merchant is happy that the actual building work will qualify for zero-rating and can demonstrate this subsequently to any visiting HMRC officer

but not when the materials are bought by a disabled person or charity in connection with building works which will be performed free of charge by a friend or relative, or in a do-it-yourself capacity by the disabled person or charity themselves (because there is no subsequent supply of zero-rated construction services to which these materials can be connected).
(VAT Notice 701/7/14, para 6.5).

Preparatory work

Preparatory work and necessary restoration work can also be zero-rated provided the supply is made to the disabled person or charity concerned, as the case may be.

Professional services

HMRC take the view that services of an architect, surveyor or any person acting as a consultant or in a supervisory capacity, even when supplied in connection with a supply of qualifying building services, are standard-rated in all circumstances. See, however, the decision in *Friends of the Elderly* (VTD 20597) (TVC 19.108). The lift manufacturer required the appellant to approve technical designs and insure the installer of the structural capability of the building, etc. which required professional advice. Since the installation of a lift is complicated and potentially dangerous, the tribunal held that there was no reason to suppose that Parliament impliedly intended to exclude architect's services from being zero-rated as 'necessarily performed in the installation of a lift'.

(VAT Notice 701/7/14, para 6.7).

Repair and maintenance of any qualifying goods is zero-rated under **29.26** above.

Alarm call systems

[29.30] The following supplies are zero-rated.

(a) The supply to
- a disabled person for his 'domestic or personal use', or
- a charity for making available to disabled persons, by sale or otherwise, for domestic or their personal use

of an alarm system designed to be capable of operation by a disabled person, and to enable him to alert directly a 'specified person or a control centre'.

(b) The supply of services necessarily performed by a control centre in receiving and responding to calls from an alarm system within (*a*) above.

A '*specified person or control centre*' is a person or centre who or which is appointed to receive directly calls activated by the alarm system; and who or which retains information about the disabled person to assist that person in the event of illness, injury or similar emergency.

[*VATA 1994, Sch 8 Group 12 Items 19, 20* and *Note 9*].

See **29.15** above for HMRC's interpretation of '*domestic or personal use*'.

Not included is the installation of ordinary telephone lines or the supply of ordinary telephones, internal communication systems, and intruder alarm systems which activate bells, lights or sirens.

(VAT Notice 701/7/14, para 7.1).

Repair and maintenance of any qualifying item is zero-rated under **29.26** above.

Motability scheme

[29.31] Zero-rating applies to the letting on hire of *any* motor vehicle (i.e. whether or not specially designed/adapted for a disabled person) to a disabled person in receipt of a disability living allowance by virtue of entitlement to the mobility component, of a personal independence payment by virtue of entitlement to the mobility component, of an armed forces independence payment or of mobility supplement (as defined) provided

- the lessor's business consists predominantly of the provision of motor vehicles to such persons;
- the vehicle is unused at the commencement of the period of letting;
- the letting is for a period of not less than three years; and
- the consideration for the letting consists wholly or partly of sums paid to the lessor, directly by the Department for Works and Pensions or the Ministry of Defence on behalf of the lessee, in respect of mobility allowance or mobility supplement to which the lessee is entitled.

[*VATA 1994, Sch 8 Group 12 Item 14; SI 2013/601, para 3*].

In practice, only vehicles leased under the Motability scheme meet the above conditions. Further information on the scheme is available from Motability Operations, City Gate House, 22 Southwark Bridge Road, London SE1 9HB (Tel: 0845 456 4566) or from their website at www.motability.co.uk.

Sale of ex-lease vehicles

The sale of the motor vehicle which has been let on hire under the above conditions is also zero-rated provided the sale constitutes the first supply after the period of letting. [*VATA 1994, Sch 8 Group 12 Item 15*]. In practice, Motability only sells the vehicle back to the car dealer from whom it was originally purchased. Following the tribunal decisions in *Peugeot Motor Co plc* (VTD 15314) (TVC 44.68), HMRC accept that the subsequent sale by the dealer of these motor vehicles is within the margin scheme.

See also **29.24** above for letting on hire of other vehicles.

Imports, acquisitions, exports and removals

Imports into the UK

[29.32] Where goods within **29.15** to **29.31** above are imported from outside the EU by

- a disabled person for domestic or his personal use, or
- a charity for making available to disabled persons (by sale or otherwise),

they can be relieved of the VAT due on importation under the same conditions as for zero-rating the supply of such goods in the UK. [*VATA 1994, Sch 8 Group 12 Note 1*].

The disabled person or charity (as the case may be) must make a declaration in the appropriate form (see **29.33** below) and lodge it with the import entry declaration made to HMRC at the port, airport or postal depot of importation.

A supplier importing goods does not qualify for relief in this way. He must pay any VAT due on importation but can reclaim it as input tax, subject to the normal rules.

(VAT Notice 701/7/14, para 8.1).

Acquisitions from other EU member states

VAT-registered traders acquiring goods from other EU member states are not normally required to pay VAT at the place of importation but must account for any VAT due (and, subject to the normal rules, claim it back as input tax) on their next VAT return. A *VAT-registered* charity which acquires qualifying goods within **29.15** to **29.31** above from another EU member state for disabled persons can account for VAT at the zero rate on its acquisition of such goods.

Persons who are not registered for VAT (including disabled persons and non-registered charities) do not have this facility.

- If they buy goods in another EU member state, they may be required to pay tax on those goods in that EU member state at the prevailing rate there. Any tax payable cannot be refunded in the UK by HMRC. Each EU member state has its own rules about the extent of VAT relief on goods for disabled persons and the reliefs set out in **29.15** to **29.31** above do not apply to supplies made in other EU member states.
- If they buy goods in another EU member state but the supplier arranges delivery, special 'distance selling' rules apply (see **20.10 EUROPEAN UNION: SINGLE MARKET**) and the VAT treatment will depend upon whether the supply is treated as taking place in that other EU member state or the UK.

(VAT Notice 701/7/14, para 8.2).

Exports and removals of goods from the UK

Goods or services supplied to disabled people from other countries, who are visiting the UK, can be zero-rated under the conditions set out in **29.15** to **29.31** above. If the goods do not qualify for this VAT relief, it may still be possible to zero-rate the supply, subject to certain conditions, under the retail export scheme (see **22.11 EXPORTS**) which applies to persons resident outside the EU who are exporting the goods to a place outside the EU. VAT must be charged on all other retail sales of standard-rated goods. (VAT Notice 701/7/14, para 8.3).

The eligibility declaration regime (see **29.33** below) applies to these exports and removals in exactly the same way as it does to internal UK sales.

Where the value of a UK supplier's sales to citizens (whether disabled or not) of any single EU member state exceeds that country's threshold for distance selling, then

- the other country becomes the place of supply; and
- VAT on any sales to that country becomes due there at the rate applicable in that country.

See **20.18 EUROPEAN UNION: SINGLE MARKET** for further details.

Eligibility declarations by disabled persons and charities

[29.33] HMRC recommend that a supplier obtains a written declaration from each customer claiming entitlement to VAT relief for goods and services under **29.15** to **29.31** above. Such a declaration should contain sufficient information to demonstrate that a customer fulfils all the criteria for eligibility. It should be separate, or clearly distinguishable from, any order form or invoice against which the goods or services are supplied. A customer signing an order should not automatically be signing a declaration of eligibility for VAT relief.

A link to a suggested form of declaration is included in VAT Notice 701/7. The supplier should keep this declaration for production to any VAT officer.

Electronic declarations (e.g. received over the internet or by fax) are acceptable. Not all electronic declarations will have the means to incorporate a signature. In these circumstances, it is important that the supplier retains evidence of the origin of the document, such as the e-mail message incorporating the sender's address. As with paper declarations, electronic ones should be distinguishable from an order form or invoice.

Where a disabled person is unable to sign a declaration, the signature of a parent, guardian, doctor or another responsible person is acceptable.

A declaration only confirms the customer's status as a person eligible to receive zero-rated goods and services and the use to which he will put them. It does not mean that the goods and services themselves fulfil all the conditions for zero-rating. It is still the supplier's responsibility to take reasonable steps to satisfy himself that the goods or services being supplied qualify for zero-rating, the customer is entitled to zero-rating and the declaration is correct. If he believes an eligibility declaration to be inaccurate or untrue, he must not zero-rate the supply. The supplier should also take care that procedures, forms and literature do not encourage or lead customers to make such a declaration. HMRC will not, however, seek to recover VAT due from a supplier where a customer provided an incorrect declaration and the supplier, having taken all reasonable steps to check the validity of the declaration, fails to identify the inaccuracy and, in good faith, makes the supply at the zero rate. (VAT Notice 48, ESC 3.11).

(VAT Notice 701/7/14, paras 3.6–3.9).

Zero-rated 'talking books' for the blind

[29.34] 'Talking books' for the blind and severely disabled are zero-rated when supplied to the Royal National Institute for the Blind, the National Listening Library and other similar charities. Included is certain apparatus and tapes designed or specially adapted for such use and non-specialist sound recording equipment. Also zero-rated are wireless receiving sets and non-specialist sound recording equipment supplied to a charity for free loan to the blind. See **13.7**(*a*) and (*b*) **CHARITIES** for full details.

Reduced rate supplies of welfare advice or information

[29.35] Supplies of 'welfare advice or information' by

- a charity, or
- a 'state-regulated' private welfare institution or agency

are subject to a reduced rate of VAT of 5%.

'*Welfare advice or information*' means advice or information which directly relates to the following.

(a) The physical or mental welfare of elderly, sick, distressed or disabled persons.
Examples include advice on
  - caring for people with Alzheimer's disease;
  - dealing with domestic violence; and
  - home safety for the elderly.

(b) The care or protection of children and young persons.
Examples include advice on
  - contraception and sexual health for young people;
  - caring for children with special needs or disabilities;
  - stranger awareness for children and young people; and
  - strategies for dealing with bullying.

'*State-regulated*' has the same meaning as in **29.12** above.

The reduced rate does *not* apply to the following.

- Supplies that would be exempt by virtue of *VATA 1994, Sch 9 Group 6* (education) if they were made by an eligible body within the meaning of that *Group* (see **17 EDUCATION** generally and **17.3** for eligible bodies).
- Supplies of goods, unless the goods are supplied 'wholly or almost wholly' for the purpose of conveying the advice or information.
  HMRC treat '*wholly or almost wholly*' as meaning that at least 90% of the purpose of any goods used must be the conveying of the welfare advice. Subject to this, the inclusion of incidental information (e.g. an appeal for donations or information on the charity's objects) does not affect the reduced rate.
  The reduced rate can, therefore, apply not only to advice given in person but also by means of DVD, audio cassette or CD Rom. Where supplied in the form of a book, leaflet, pamphlet or similar item then the supply is zero-rated if certain conditions are met. See **55 PRINTED MATTER, ETC.**

Goods that have an independent use and also carry incidental welfare advice (e.g. mugs and T-shirts bearing a slogan) are not covered by the reduced rate.

- Supplies of advice or information provided solely for the benefit of a particular individual or according to his personal circumstances. (This is a supply of welfare services and exempt under **29.12** above.)

Free supplies of welfare advice or information are a non-business activity for VAT purposes.

[*VATA 1994, Sch 7A Group 9*]. (VAT Notice 701/2/11, paras 6.1, 6.3–6.5).

Reduced rate supplies of mobility aids for elderly

[29.36] A reduced rate of VAT of 5% applies to

- the supply of services of installing 'mobility aids', and
- the supply of mobility aids by a person installing them

for use in 'domestic accommodation' by a person who, at the time of the supply, is aged 60 or over.

'*Mobility aids*' for these purposes means

- grab rails;
- ramps;
- stair lifts;
- bath lifts;
- built-in shower seats or showers containing built-in shower seats; and
- walk-in baths fitted with sealable doors.

'*Domestic accommodation*' means a building, or part of a building, that consists of a dwelling or a number of dwellings.

[*VATA 1995, Sch 7A Group 10*].

Key points: health and welfare

[29.37] Points to consider are as follows.

- VAT exemption generally applies to medical services provided by a registered health professional, as long as the services are intended to protect, maintain or restore the health of individuals.
- In certain cases, a supply can be partly exempt and partly taxable – for example, an optician supplying a pair of spectacles is providing standard-rated goods but exempt medical services in making the spectacles suitable for the patient, i.e. dispensing services. A cost-based apportionment method will normally determine how much output tax is payable on a mixed sale.
- Exemption can also apply in relation to services provided by non-registered health professionals, as long as they are being directly supervised by a registered health professional. HMRC impose very strict conditions concerning the supervisory arrangements in order for exemption to apply.

- Welfare services provided by relevant bodies and institutions are also exempt from VAT if intended to help people in need (e.g. elderly, disabled, sick people). The scope of the exemption is very wide and includes, for example, assistance with form filling and general every day needs.
- Zero-rating applies to a wide range of goods and services that are specifically intended for disabled people. The zero-rating does not include everyday items that might make life easier for a disabled person, only those that are specifically designed for their use. Various conditions need to be met by suppliers in order to secure zero-rating.
- The reduced rate of VAT (5%) applies to welfare advice provided by a charity or a state-regulated private welfare institution or agency. The advice must be for the benefit of elderly, sick, distressed or disabled persons, or relevant to the care or protection of children and young persons.
- HMRC have tightened up the zero-rating provisions relating to the purchase of a motor car for use by a disabled wheelchair or stretcher user and a three-year rule has been introduced, together with additional reporting and due diligence requirements that suppliers must adhere to. A penalty has also been introduced for customers who provide an incorrect customer eligibility declaration that is equivalent to the VAT due on the supply of the vehicle.

30

HMRC: Administration

De Voil Indirect Tax Service. See V1.262–V1.287A.

Introduction to HMRC: administration

[30.1] The collection and management of VAT is the responsibility of the Commissioners for Her Majesty's Revenue and Customs ('HMRC'). [*VATA 1994, s 96(1), Sch 11 para 1; CRCA 2005, Sch 4 para 56*].

Most VAT returns are now filed online, and the associated payments and repayments are made electronically. HMRC have a number of dedicated VAT offices around the country responsible for such matters as written enquiries, accounting, debt management, registration and non-established taxable persons. Contact details for the appropriate office are given in VAT Notices, or can be obtained by contacting the VAT Helpline (0300 200 3700).

HMRC Charter

[30.2] On 12 November 2009, HMRC launched a 'Charter', setting out what individuals, businesses and other groups dealing with HMRC can expect from the department, as well as what it expects from them. An updated version has been issued in January 2016 and can be viewed in full at: www.gov.uk/government/publications/your-charter/your-charter.

The main headings are:

Your rights – what you can expect from us:

Respect you and treat you as honest

Provide a helpful, efficient and effective service

Be professional and act with integrity

Protect your information and respect your privacy

Accept that someone can represent you

Deal with complaints quickly and fairly

Tackle those who bend or break the rules

Your obligations – what we expect from you:

Be honest and respect our staff

Work with us to get things right

Find out what you need to do and keep us informed

Keep accurate records and protect your information

Know what your representative does on your behalf

Respond in good time

Take reasonable care to avoid mistakes

Publications and interpretation of law

[30.3] HMRC issue

- **Notices** and (formerly) **leaflets**, which are numbered booklets explaining various aspects of VAT. See **31.1 HMRC NOTICES, INFORMATION SHEETS AND FORMS** for those currently in issue. Most of the notices and leaflets are available from the VAT Helpline (tel: 0300 200 3700). When requesting a new or revised Notice or an update, it is advisable to quote the issue date or update number to check that the correct copy is received (and not an out-of-date one). It is also advisable to make a note of the date of the request.
- **VAT Notes** to bring to the notice of all registered persons details of information available from VAT offices. They are sent out with VAT return forms.
- **News releases** and **briefs** are issued as informative news items. They are numbered and dated.
- **VAT information sheets** on items of particular interest.

Changes in interpretation of the law

When HMRC advise on the correct interpretation of the law, taxpayers will usually only be required to apply the new interpretation from a current or future date announced by HMRC. If, following HMRC's announcement of its new interpretation of the law, a business nevertheless chooses to correct historical errors, HMRC will accept the corrections providing all of the following conditions are met.

- all past errors are corrected;
- the neutrality of the tax is respected; and
- the business is no better off and the Exchequer no worse off than they would have been if the mistaken interpretation had not been made.

(HMRC Brief 14/11).

Contacting HMRC

VAT Helpline

[30.4] The VAT Helpline deals with all general telephone enquiries from both businesses and the public on 0300 200 3700. A textphone service, for customers with hearing difficulties, is available on 0300 200 3719 and a Welsh speaking service is available on 0300 200 3705. All services are available from 8.00am to 8.00pm on Mondays to Fridays.

The service is for all general enquiries about HMRC's taxes and duties, including VAT, Excise, Customs, Insurance Premium Tax, Landfill Tax, Aggregates Tax, Air Passenger Duty, Climate Change Levy and Mineral Oils. The service should be used in particular for

- queries on HMRC rules and procedures;
- rates of VAT chargeable on particular goods;
- requests for publications (e.g. forms and notices); and
- requests for duplicate VAT returns.

Where a question cannot be answered, it will be re-routed to the appropriate office or the caller will be given the phone number of the office required.

General written enquiries

The single postal address for VAT general enquiries is HM Revenue & Customs, Written Enquiries Section, 4th Floor, Alexander House, Victoria Avenue, Southend-On-Sea, Essex SS99 1BD apart from supplies by or to charities which should be sent to HMRC Charities, St Johns House, Merton Road, Bootle, Merseyside L69 9BB.

E-mail enquiries

The e-mail address for all enquiries relating to VAT is:

Enquiries.estn@hmrc.gsi.gov.uk

Personal visits

The VAT Helpline can make appointments for one-to-one consultations on any VAT matter at a mutually convenient venue.

VAT registration, change in registration details and deregistration

General applications for registration that are not made online should be made directly to HM Revenue & Customs, VAT Registration Service, Crown House, Birch Street, Wolverhampton, WV1 4JX. Changes and applications for deregistration should be notified to HM Revenue & Customs, Imperial House, 77 Victoria Street, Grimsby DN31 1DB.

All VAT 68 (request to retain VAT registration number of previous owner of business), VAT group applications, annual accounting requests and agricultural flat-rate scheme applications should be made to HM Revenue & Customs, Imperial House, 77 Victoria Street, Grimsby DN31 1DB.

VAT registration of overseas traders with no UK establishment, tax representative or agent

Contact should be made directly with:

VAT Registration Service, Crown House, Birch Street, Wolverhampton, WV1 4JX.

Payment problems

Where a business has problems in clearing an existing VAT debt, it should contact the VAT Helpline (0300 200 3700) and will be put in touch with the appropriate Regional Debt Management Unit.

National Insolvency Helpdesk

Telephone 03000 540 808.

Tax advisers

Tax advisers should address written queries about specific client's affairs to the client's VAT office. Factual queries which are not specific to a particular client should be by telephone to the VAT Helpline (see above) or in writing to the tax adviser's own VAT office. Approach should only be made to HMRC Headquarters if enquiries are being made on behalf of an entire industry or if lobbying or otherwise acting as a member of a representative or consultative body concerned with the effect of present or proposed legislation.

HMRC rulings

[30.5] The non-statutory clearance service offered by HMRC to all taxpayers and their advisers is described at https://www.gov.uk/non-statutory-clearance-service-guidance. Rulings are not given in relation to hypothetical transactions, perceived tax planning or avoidance, or where the point is covered by notices or other published guidance.

Making complaints about HMRC

[30.6] The following remedies are available to a person who has a complaint against HMRC.

(a) Complaints to HMRC

If a person is unhappy with HMRC's services (e.g. because of unreasonable delays, mistakes or how he has been treated by staff) then he should first try to resolve the problem with the officer/office with whom he has been dealing, or phone one of HMRC's helplines. If the officer/office or helpline have been unable to resolve the concerns, they will pass the complaint to a complaints handler. If the person would prefer not to discuss the matter with the officer/office directly, he may ask for the complaint to be passed to a complaints handler straight away. A complaint may be made by phone or in writing, using the address on any papers HMRC have sent to him or the relevant HMRC office address from the Contact HMRC section at https://www.gov.uk/contact-hmrc. The letter should be clearly marked as a complaint so it can be directed to a complaints handler quickly and should include as much information as possible to help HMRC understand and investigate the complaint. For example

- what went wrong;
- when it happened;
- who the person dealt with;
- what effect HMRC's actions had on him;
- how he would like HMRC to put things right;
- his full name and address; and
- any relevant numbers (e.g. National Insurance number, tax reference, VAT registration number, employer reference) so that HMRC can identify his records quickly.

(Complaints factsheet at https://www.gov.uk/government/publications/putting-things-right-how-to-complain-factsheet-cfs).

(b) Complaint to the independent Adjudicator

The Adjudicator for the Inland Revenue also deals with unresolved complaints about HMRC. The Adjudicator will consider (amongst other things) complaints about delay, rudeness, mistakes, harassment during a VAT investigation, application of extra-statutory concessions, requests for time to pay and refusal of information under the Open Government provisions. The Adjudicator will not examine cases which are appealable to a VAT tribunal nor intervene once a matter is before the criminal courts.

The address of the Adjudicator is

The Adjudicator's Office
8th Floor
Euston Tower
286 Euston Road
London NW1 3US
Tel: 020 7667 1832
Fax: 020 7667 1830

(c) Complaint to a Member of Parliament

A person can complain to his local MP. If appropriate, the MP can deal with the complaint

- personally (e.g. by direct correspondence with HMRC or by asking a Parliamentary question); or
- with the person's consent, by forwarding the complaint to the Parliamentary Commissioner for Administration (PCA) normally known as the 'Ombudsman'.

The PCA can only act on written complaints forwarded by an MP alleging maladministration and has no power to enforce a remedy.

The postal address for MPs is (Name of MP), House of Commons, London SW1A 1AA or, as the case may be, The Scottish Parliament, Edinburgh EH99 1SP, The National Assembly for Wales/Cynulliad Cenedlaethol Cymru, Cathays Park, Cardiff CF10 3NQ, or The Northern Ireland Assembly, Parliament Buildings, Belfast BT4 3XX.

(d) Appeal to the First-tier Tribunal

An appeal to a tribunal can be made against a decision of HMRC falling, for the most part, within one of the categories in *VATA 1994, s 83* (see **5.3 APPEALS**). Although some of these categories relate to administrative decisions, in general a tribunal does not have supervisory jurisdiction over administrative decisions taken by HMRC. Tribunals do have jurisdiction to hear appeals against decisions which, although not falling within *VATA 1994, s 83*, result in a decision (e.g. an assessment) which does. [*VATA 1994, s 84(10)*]. Tribunals also have jurisdiction to hear appeals against certain other decisions, primarily in relation to penalties under *FA 2007, Sch 24 and FA 2008, Sch 41*.

(e) Judicial review

Where a tribunal does not have power to review an administrative decision, a taxpayer can apply to the High Court for a judicial review. Applications are heard by the Administrative Court. The Upper Tribunal also has some judicial review functions, as seen in the case of *R (oao Telefonica Europe plc) v HMRC* [2016] UKUT 173 (TCC) (TVC 2.356). In judicial review proceedings, the court or tribunal will consider whether the decision was properly made in accordance with correct procedures and not unreasonable, unlawful or oppressive.

Disclosure of information by HMRC officials

[30.7] Subject to **30.8** below, 'Revenue and Customs officials' may not disclose information which is held by HMRC in connection with a function of it. '*Revenue and Customs officials*' is a reference to any person who is or was

- a Commissioner of HMRC;
- an HMRC officer;
- a person acting on behalf of the Commissioners or an officer; or
- a member of a committee established by the Commissioners.

[*CRCA 2005, s 18(1)(4)*].

Authorised disclosure

[30.8] The general provisions in **30.7** above do not apply, and disclosure of information is allowed, in the following circumstances. But it should be noted that this does not authorise the making of a disclosure which

- contravenes the *Data Protection Act 1998*; or
- is prohibited by *Regulation of Investigatory Powers Act 2000, Part 1*.

[*CRCA 2005, s 22*].

Circumstances where disclosure is permitted

(a) Functions of HMRC

Disclosure of information is permitted where it is made for the purposes of a function of HMRC and does not contravene any restriction imposed by the Commissioners. [*CRCA 2005, s 18(2)(a)*].

(b) Public interest disclosure

Public interest disclosure is permitted where

- it is of a kind listed below or as specified in regulations made by the Treasury, and
- it is made on the instructions of the Commissioners (which may be general or specific) and the Commissioners are satisfied that it is in the public interest.

The listed categories are as follows.

(i) Disclosure made to a person exercising public functions (whether or not within the UK) for the purposes of the prevention or detection of crime, and in order to comply with an obligation of the UK government under an agreement relating to the movement of persons, goods or services.

(ii) Disclosure to a body which has responsibility for the regulation of a profession and which relates to misconduct on the part of a member of the profession relating to a function of HMRC.

(iii) Disclosure to a constable where either the constable is exercising functions which relate to the movement of persons or goods into or out of the UK or the disclosure is made for the purposes of the prevention or detection of crime.

(iv) Disclosure to the National Criminal Intelligence Service for a purpose connected with its functions under *Police Act 1997, s 2(2)* (criminal intelligence).

(v) Disclosure to a person exercising public functions in relation to public safety or public health and for the purposes of those functions.

(vi) Disclosure to the National Policing Improvement Agency for the purpose of enabling information to be entered in a computerised database, and which relates to a person suspected of or arrested for an offence, the results of an investigation, or anything seized.

[*CRCA 2005, ss 18(2)(b), 20*].

(c) Disclosure to a 'prosecuting authority'

Disclosure to a prosecuting authority is permitted if made for the purpose of enabling the authority

- to consider whether to institute criminal proceedings in respect of a matter considered in the course of an investigation conducted by or on behalf of HMRC;

- to give advice in connection with a criminal investigation or criminal proceedings; or
- in the case of the Director of Revenue and Customs Prosecutions, to exercise his function under *Proceeds of Crime Act 2002, Pt 5* or *8*.

'*Prosecuting authority*' means the Director of Revenue and Customs Prosecutions, in Scotland, the Lord Advocate or a procurator fiscal and, in Northern Ireland, the Director of Public Prosecutions for Northern Ireland.

It is an offence to disclose further any information disclosed to a prosecuting authority under these provisions except for a purpose connected with the exercise of the prosecuting authority's functions or with the consent of the Commissioners (which may be general or specific).

[*CRCA 2005, ss 18(2)(b), 21; Proceeds of Crime Act 2002, Sch 8 para 164*].

(d) Civil and criminal proceedings, etc.

Disclosure of information is permitted if made for the purposes of civil proceedings, criminal investigation or criminal proceedings (in each case whether or not within the UK) relating to a matter in respect of which HMRC have functions. [*CRCA 2005, s 18(2)(c)(d)*].

(e) Court orders

Disclosure of information is permitted if made in pursuance of an order of a court. [*CRCA 2005, s 18(2)(e)*].

(f) Her Majesty's Inspectors of Constabulary, etc.

Disclosure of information is permitted if made to Her Majesty's Inspectors of Constabulary, the Scottish inspectors or the Northern Ireland inspectors for the purpose of an inspection by virtue of *CRCA 2005, s 27*. [*CRCA 2005, s 18(2)(f)*].

(g) Independent Police Complaints Commission

Disclosure of information is permitted if made to the Independent Police Complaints Commission, or a person acting on its behalf, for the purpose of the exercise of a function by virtue of *CRCA 2005, s 28*. [*CRCA 2005, s 18(2)(g)*].

(h) With agreement of parties

Disclosure of information is permitted if made with the consent of each person to whom the information relates. [*CRCA 2005, s 18(2)(h)*].

(i) Other parts of HM Revenue and Customs (e.g. in relation to income tax)

Following the formation of HMRC, information acquired by HMRC in connection with a function may be used by them in connection with any other function (subject to any provision which restricts or prohibits the use of information and which is contained in any *Act* (other than of the Scottish Parliament or NI Assembly) or international or other agreement of which the UK is a party). [*CRCA 2005, s 17(1)(2)*].

(j) Department of Works and Pensions

HMRC may disclose information to the Department for the purposes of preventing, detecting, investigating and prosecuting offences relating to social security and for maintaining and improving the accuracy of social security information. [*Social Security Administration (Fraud) Act 1997, s 1; SI 1997/1577*].

(k) Charity Commission

HMRC may disclose to the Charity Commission the name and address of any institution which they have treated as established for charitable purposes; information on the purposes of an institution (and the trusts under which it is established or regulated) in order to determine whether that institution should be treated as established for charitable purposes; and information about an institution which has been so treated but which HMRC believe has carried on activities which are not charitable or has applied funds for non-charitable purposes. [*Charities Act 1993, s 10*].

(l) Statistics Board or the Department for Business, Enterprise and Regulatory Reform

For statistical purposes, HMRC are authorised to disclose the following to the Statistics Board or the Department for Business, Enterprise and Regulatory Reform: VAT registration numbers allocated to persons and reference numbers for members of a group; the names, trading styles and addresses of persons so registered or of members of groups and status and trade classifications of businesses; and actual or estimated value of supplies. The information disclosed may be further disclosed only to another government department for similar purposes. Otherwise it may only be disclosed with the consent of the registered person or in such a form that individual particulars cannot be identified. [*VATA 1994, s 91; Statistics and Registration Service Act 2007, Sch 2 para 6*].

Further, HMRC may disclose to the Statistics Board information relating to the estimated or actual value of business purchases, excluding VAT, contained in a return, and the date on which the return was received. [*SI 2011/2878*].

(m) Isle of Man Customs

Isle of Man Customs may be given information for the purpose of facilitating the proper administration of common duties and the enforcement of prohibitions or restrictions on imports or exports between the IOM and the UK. [*IMA 1979, s 10*].

(n) Tax authorities of other EU member states

No obligation as to secrecy (imposed by statute or otherwise) precludes HMRC from disclosing to the competent authority of another EU member state any information required to be so disclosed under *Council Regulation (EU)904/2010* (on administrative co-operation and combating fraud in the field of VAT, which recasts and repeals *Council Regulation (EC)1798/2003* with effect from 1 January 2012). Before disclosing any information, they must be satisfied that the competent authority is bound by, or has undertaken to observe, rules of confidentiality not less strict than in the UK and that it will use the information for tax purposes or to facilitate legal proceedings for failure to observe the tax laws of the receiving country. [*FA 2003, s 197*].

Council Regulation (EU)904/2010 lays down the rules and procedures to enable the competent authorities of EU member states to cooperate and exchange with each other any information that may help to effect a correct assessment of VAT, monitor the correct application of VAT, particularly on intra-Community transactions, and combat VAT fraud. In particular, they lay down rules and procedures for EU member states to collect and exchange such information by electronic means. Under the Regulation, information may be exchanged

- on the request of an EU country (which must have exhausted its own usual sources of information); or
- without prior request where
  - taxation is deemed to take place in the EU member state of destination and the information provided by the EU member state of origin is necessary for the effectiveness of the control system of the country of destination;
  - the EU member state has grounds to believe that a breach of VAT legislation has been committed or is likely to have been committed in the other EU member state;
  - there is a risk of tax loss in the other EU member state

  either by
  - automatic exchange (i.e. the systematic communication of predefined information); or
  - spontaneous exchange, where information has not been forwarded under the automatic exchange of which the country is aware, and which it considers may be useful to the other EU member states.

(o) Proceeds of crime

Information may be disclosed to the Criminal Assets Bureau in Ireland (the 'CAB') and any other specified body (in the UK or elsewhere) to enable it to exercise any of its functions in connection with the identification of proceeds of crime, the bringing of civil proceedings for enforcement purposes in relation to proceeds of crime or the taking of other action in relation to proceeds of crime. Information so disclosed must not be further disclosed unless relating to the exercise of any of the functions of the CAB or specified public authority in connection with such matters and, even then, only with the consent of the HMRC. [*Serious Crime Act 2007, s 85*].

Compounded settlements

Although not specifically covered in legislation, HMRC have powers under *CEMA 1979 s 152* to compound any offence (whether or not proceedings have been instituted in respect of it) and compound proceedings, i.e. offer an alleged offender the option of paying a penalty out of court rather than be prosecuted. See **53.2 PENALTIES**. HMRC will disclose details of any settlement reached to

- other Government Departments whose statutory responsibilities are directly affected;
- the courts for sentencing purposes after conviction, in cases where there has been an earlier compounded settlement for a similar matter within the five-year time limit specified for offences by the *Rehabilitation of Offenders Act*;
- employers when it is apparent that
  - (i) the nature of the employment has facilitated the offence; or
  - (ii) where drugs offences or indications of serious alcohol abuse are involved, the nature of the employment or duties requires a high degree of unimpaired judgment or faculties; and
- in response to enquiries from Parliament or the media about cases which have excited public attention, if disclosure is considered to be in the public interest.

In all cases, persons considering an offer to compound for an alleged offence will be warned when the offer is made that details of the settlement may be disclosed in the above circumstances.

(Hansard Vol 151, cols 562, 563, 26 April 1989).

Wrongful disclosure

[30.9] A person commits an offence if he contravenes the provisions of **30.7** above by disclosing 'revenue and customs information relating to a person' whose identity is specified in the disclosure or can be deduced from it.

'*Revenue and customs information relating to a person*' means information about, acquired as a result of, or held in connection with, the exercise of a function of HMRC in respect of the person; but it does not include information about internal administrative arrangements of HMRC (whether relating to Commissioners, officers or others).

It is a defence for a person charged with an offence under these provisions to prove that he reasonably believed that

- the disclosure was lawful, or
- the information had already and lawfully been made available to the public.

A person guilty of an offence under these provisions is liable, on conviction on indictment, to imprisonment for a term not exceeding two years or to a fine or to both and, on summary conviction, to imprisonment for a term not exceeding twelve months (six months in Scotland and NI) or to a fine not exceeding the 'statutory maximum' or to both. The '*statutory maximum*' is currently £5,000.

[*CRCA 2005, s 19*].

Before the merger of the Inland Revenue and Customs, the offence for wrongful disclosure was contained in *FA 1989, s 182*. The provisions, which also apply to VAT tribunals (and the General and Special Commissioners), have not been repealed and therefore continue to apply to Revenue and

Customs officers. Under those provisions, a person who discloses any information which he holds or has held in the exercise of 'tax functions' is guilty of an offence if it is information about any matters relevant, for the purposes of those functions, to VAT in the case of any 'identifiable person'.

'*Tax functions*' means, *inter alia*, functions relating to VAT of HMRC and its officers and persons carrying out the administration work of any VAT tribunal, together with any other person providing, or employed in the provision of, services to any such officer or person.

'*Identifiable person*' means a person whose identity is specified in the disclosure or can be deduced from it.

The provisions do not apply to any disclosure of information with 'lawful authority'; with the consent of any person in whose case the information is about a matter relevant to VAT; or which has been lawfully made available to the public before the disclosure is made. A disclosure of information is made with '*lawful authority*' if, and only if, it is made

- by a Crown servant in accordance with his official duty,
- by any other person for the purposes of the function in the exercise of which he holds the information and without contravening any restriction duly imposed by the '*person responsible*' i.e. the Commissioners,
- to, or in accordance with an authorisation duly given by, the person responsible,
- in pursuance of any enactment or of any order of a court, or
- in connection with the institution of, or otherwise for the purposes of, any proceedings relating to any matter within the general responsibility of HMRC.

It is a defence for a person charged under these provisions to prove that, at the time of the alleged offence, he believed that he had lawful authority to make the disclosure and had no reasonable cause to believe otherwise *or* he believed that the information had previously been lawfully made available to the public and had no reasonable cause to believe otherwise.

A person guilty of an offence under these provisions is liable, on conviction on indictment, to imprisonment for a term not exceeding two years or a fine or both, and on summary conviction, to imprisonment for a term not exceeding six months or a fine not exceeding the statutory maximum or both.

[*FA 1989, s 182; CRCA 2005, Sch 4 para 39*].

Disclosure of information to HMRC

[30.10] The following are authorised to disclose information to HMRC.

Department of Works and Pensions

The Department are authorised to pass information to the Commissioners (or any person by whom services are being provided to the Commissioners) for use in the prevention, detection, investigation or prosecution of offences which it is the function of HMRC to prevent, etc. The information may also be used in connection with the assessment or determination of non-criminal penalties and to check the accuracy of information held by HMRC. [*FA 1997, s 110; Tax Credits Act 2002, Sch 5 para 13; SI 1997/1603*].

Charity Commission

The Charity Commission may disclose to HMRC any information received by them, under or for the purposes of any Act or statutory instrument, where the disclosure is made for any purpose connected with the discharge of their functions and to enable or assist HMRC to discharge any of its functions. Where any information has been disclosed to the Charity Commission under *Charities Act 1993, s 10* (which also applies to other government departments, etc.) subject to any express restriction on the disclosure of the information by the Charity Commission, their power of disclosure to HMRC (and other government departments, etc.) under these provisions is exercisable subject to any such restriction. [*Charities Act 1993, s 10*].

Other parts of HM Revenue and Customs (e.g. in relation to income tax)

Following the formation of HMRC, information acquired by HMRC in connection with a function may be used by them in connection with any other function (subject to any provision which restricts or prohibits the use of information and which is contained in any Act (other than of the Scottish Parliament or NI Assembly) or international or other agreement of which the UK is a party). [*CRCA 2005, s 17(1)(2)*].

Information about tax advice for a client

[30.11] A notice requiring information or documents (see **32.6**) does not require a tax adviser to provide information or documents about tax advice given for a client and does not require a person appointed as an auditor to provide certain information or documents related to that function. This exclusion does not cover explanatory material provided to a client by an accountant in connection with information or documents provided to HMRC. [*FA 2008, Sch 36 paras 24–26*].

Direct correspondence between HMRC and tax advisers

[30.12] HMRC cannot reveal confidential information it holds on individual taxpayers unless statutory provisions allow (see **30.8** above).

As many taxpayers instruct their tax advisers to assist in their VAT affairs, HMRC have produced the following standard wording so that they can disclose confidential information to them. The signed letter should be sent to the appropriate written enquiry office (see **30.4** above).

Example letter from a taxpayer to HMRC authorising disclosure of confidential information to a third party

[Date]

I [name and VAT registration number] authorise HM Revenue and Customs to disclose VAT information held about my business affairs to [name and address of nominee], who is acting on my behalf. This authorisation covers all VAT matters within the responsibility of HM Revenue and Customs and includes approaches which may be made to obtain information from all sections of the department, such as the National Advice Service, Debt Management Units, National Registration Service and Complaints Units. This authority will remain in force until I give you written notice to the contrary.

I do not wish the following information to be disclosed*

I undertake to inform HM Revenue and Customs of any change to the above authorisation.

(Signed)

*To be included if applicable.

Key points — HMRC: administration

[30.13] Points to consider are as follows.

- The HMRC charter was published in November 2009 and updated in January 2016, and explains what service and behaviour a taxpayer can expect to receive from HMRC and its officers. It also explains what the department expects from a taxpayer in terms of behaviour. The status of the charter is untested: it could be a useful reference point in the event of a dispute with HMRC or where concerns are evident about the standard of service being given in relation to a particular issue, but there is as yet no precedent for HMRC being held to account for the standards contained in it.
- As a general principle, a taxpayer who makes every effort to correctly calculate and pay his tax should not have any concerns about his relationship with HMRC. Even in situations where honest errors have been made, the approach of HMRC should be to support rather than penalise a taxpayer. This strategy is consistent with the behaviour-based penalty regime that has been in force since April 2009.
- Be aware of the 'What's New' facility on the HMRC website, which highlights all relevant changes that have been announced or introduced by HMRC. For example, the facility will alert a user to new Business Briefs that have been issued and when relevant HMRC public notices have been reissued.
- A telephone enquiry to the VAT Helpline can be worthwhile in many situations, e.g. to clarify a minor point or to obtain VAT forms or contact telephone numbers. However, it is important to recognise that a telephone ruling does not give protection to a

VAT-registered business in the same way as a written ruling. If an issue has important outcomes, e.g. whether a major product being sold by a business is exempt or standard-rated, then a written ruling is essential.

When contacting the VAT Helpline remember to ask for the call reference number.

- In the case of written requests to HMRC for a ruling on a particular VAT issue, it is important that full, accurate and complete information is given about the transaction in question. If a key piece of information is omitted or reported incorrectly, then it could invalidate the subsequent ruling given by HMRC.

31

HMRC Notices, Information Sheets, Briefs and Forms

HMRC Notices

[31.1] The following notices relating to VAT have been issued and not withdrawn or superseded as at 1 April 2018.

48	Extra-statutory concessions
60	Intrastat—general guide
101	Deferring duty, VAT and other charges
117	Authorised Economic Operator
143	A guide for international post users
160	Compliance checks into indirect tax matters
179	Motor and heating fuels – general information and accounting for excise duty and VAT
252	Valuation of imported goods for customs purposes, VAT and trade statistics
317	Imports by charities free of duty and VAT
340	Importing scientific instruments free of duty and VAT
341	Importing donated medical equipment free of duty and VAT
342	Importing miscellaneous documents and other related articles free of duty and VAT
343	Importing capital items free of duty and VAT
361	Importing museum and gallery exhibits fee of duty and VAT
364	Importing decorations and awards free of duty and VAT
365	Animals for scientific research free of duty and VAT
366	Importing biological and chemical substances for research free of duty and VAT
368	Importing inherited goods free of duty and VAT
369	Importing blood grouping, tissue typing and certain therapeutic substances free of duty and VAT
371	Importing goods for disabled people free of duty and VAT

372	Importing commercial samples free of duty and VAT
373	Importing visual and auditory materials free of duty and VAT
374	Importing goods for test free of duty and VAT
431	Visiting forces
700	The VAT guide
700/1/18	Should I be registered for VAT? Plus Supplement to Notices 700/1 and 700/11
700/2/14	Group and divisional registration
700/7/12	Business promotions
700/8/18	Disclosure of VAT avoidance schemes
700/9/12	Transfer of business as a going concern
700/11/18	Cancelling your registration
700/12/18	How to fill in and submit your VAT return
700/14/17	Video cassette films: rental and part-exchange
700/17/12	Funded pension schemes
700/18/13	Relief from VAT on bad debts
700/21/16	Keeping VAT records
700/24/15	Postage, delivery charges and direct marketing
700/25/16	Taxis and private hire cars
700/34/12	Staff
700/41/12	Late registration penalty
700/42/12	Misdeclaration penalty and repeated misdeclaration
700/43/10	Default interest
700/44/15	Barristers and advocates
700/45/17	How to correct VAT errors and make adjustments or claims
700/46/12	Agricultural flat rate scheme
700/50/17	Default surcharge
700/56/18	Insolvency
700/57/14	Administrative agreements entered into with trade bodies
700/58/17	Treatment of VAT repayment returns and supplements
700/60/17	Payments on account
700/62/17	Self-billing
700/63/15	Electronic invoicing
700/64/14	Motoring expenses
700/65/12	Business entertainment
700/67/17	Registration scheme for racehorse owners
701/1/14	Charities
701/2/11	Welfare
701/5/13	Clubs and associations
701/6/14	Charity-funded equipment for medical, veterinary, etc. uses
701/7/14	VAT reliefs for disabled and older people
701/8/17	Postage stamps and philatelic supplies
701/9/11	Commodities and terminal markets
701/10/16	Zero-rating of books and other forms of printed matter
701/12/11	Disposal of antiques, works of art etc from historic houses

701/14/15	Food
701/15/11	Animals and animal food
701/18/11	Women's sanitary protection products
701/19/16	Fuel and power
701/20/13	Caravans and houseboats
701/21/13	Gold
701/21A/12	Investment gold coins
701/22/17	Tools for the manufacture of goods for export
701/23/11	Protective equipment
701/29/17	Betting, gaming and lotteries
701/30/17	Education and vocational training
701/31/14	Health institutions
701/32/12	Burial, cremation and the commemoration of the dead
701/35/11	Youth clubs
701/36/13	Insurance
701/38/11	Seeds and plants
701/40/11	Food processing services
701/41/02	Sponsorship
701/45/16	Sport
701/47/11	Culture
701/48/14	Corporate purchasing cards
701/49/17	Finance
701/57/14	Health professionals and pharmaceutical products
701/58/16	Charity advertising and goods connected with collecting donations
702	Imports
702/7/17	Import VAT relief for goods supplied onward to another country in the EC
702/8/12	Fiscal warehousing
702/10/12	VAT: Tax warehousing
703	Exports of goods from the UK
703/1/10	Supply of freight containers for export or removal from the UK
703/2/11	Sailaway boats supplied for export outside the EU
704	VAT Retail exports
704/1/16	Tax free shopping in the UK
706	Partial exemption
706/2/18	Capital goods scheme
707	VAT personal export scheme
708	Buildings and construction
708/6/14	Energy-saving materials
709/1/13	Catering and take-away food
709/3/13	Hotels and holiday accommodation
709/5/16	Tour operators margin scheme
709/6/17	Travel agents and tour operators
714	Zero-rating young children's clothing and footwear
718	Margin scheme and global accounting

718/1/16	Margin scheme on second-hand cars and other vehicles
718/2/17	The auctioneers' scheme
723A	Refunds of VAT in the European Community for EC and non-EC businesses
725	The single market
726	Joint and several liability for unpaid VAT
727	Retail schemes
727/2/11	Bespoke retail schemes
727/3/13	Retail schemes: how to work the point of sale scheme
727/4/13	Retail schemes: how to work the apportionment schemes
727/5/13	Retail schemes: how to work the direct calculation schemes
728	New means of transport
730	Civil Penalty investigations – statement of practice
731	Cash accounting
732	Annual accounting
733	Flat rate scheme for small businesses
735	VAT domestic reverse charge on specified goods and services
741	Place of supply of services before 1 January 2010
741A	Place of supply of services
742	Land and property
742A	Opting to tax land and buildings
742/3/11	Scottish land law terms
744A	Passenger transport
744B	Freight transport and associated services
744C	Ships, aircraft and associated services
747	VAT notices having the force of law
749	Local authorities and similar bodies
799	Disclosure of tax avoidance schemes for VAT and other indirect taxes
998	VAT refund scheme for national museums and galleries
999	Catalogue of publications
1001	VAT refund scheme for certain charities
1002	Adapted motor vehicles for disabled people and charities
3001	Customs special procedures for the Union Customs Code
SIVA 1	Simplified Import VAT Accounting
FH1	Apply for the Fulfilment House Due Diligence Scheme

VAT information sheets

[31.2] The following information sheets relating to VAT had been issued and not withdrawn or superseded as at 1 April 2018.

3/96	Tour operators' margin scheme: practical implementation of the 'airline charter option' following the changes which came into effect on 1 January 1996

4/96	Tour operators' margin scheme: practical implementation of the 'agency option' following the changes which came into effect on 1 January 1996
1/97	Tour operators' margin scheme: practical implementation of the 'trader to trader (wholesale) option' following the changes which came into effect on 1 January 1996
3/98	Local authorities and NHS joint stores depots
5/98	Local authorities: supplies to new unitary authorities under local government reorganisation (transitional arrangements)
6/98	Local authority pension funds: VAT treatment and administrative concessions
8/98	Charities: supply, repair and maintenance of relevant goods (including adapted motor vehicles) (with correction)
2/99	Local authorities: agreement of section 33 recovery methods
6/99	Charities: liability of routine domestic tasks
8/99	Opticians: apportionment of charges for supplies of spectacles and dispensing
2/00	Exports and removals: conditions for zero-rating
3/00	Supplies through undisclosed agents: revised VAT treatment
2/01	Single or multiple supplies — how to decide
4/02	Budget 2002: VAT: partial exemption – standard method over-ride
1/03	Electronically supplied services and broadcasting services: new EU place of supply rules
3/03	Modernisation of face value vouchers
4/03	Electronically supplied services: a guide to interpretation
5/03	Electronically supplied services: evidence of customer location and status
6/03	Tribunal decision on VAT treatment of repossessed and voluntarily returned cars
7/03	Electronically supplied services: special scheme for non-EU businesses
10/03	Electronically supplied services: supplementary information on the special scheme for non-EU businesses
11/03	Electronic point of sale (EPOS) systems
12/03	Face value vouchers
14/03	New time of supply rules for on-going supplies
3/04	Electronically supplied services: EU enlargement
5/04	Claims made in the light of GMAC High Court decision: VAT treatment of returned cars and other goods
7/04	Eligibility rules for VAT grouping
6/05	British travel agents
8/05	Recovery of VAT by businesses on road fuel purchased by their employees on their behalf
3/06	Dispensing doctors and VAT registration: how and when to register; taxable or exempt supplies; VAT recovery and what records need to be kept
5/06	Supplies of goods under finance agreements
11/06	Guidance on the VAT treatment of certain Islamic products

12/06	Further information for dispensing doctors
5/07	Further information for health professionals affected by the changes to exemption for medical services announced in HMRC Brief 6/07
6/07	Reverse charge for purchases and sales of mobile phones and computer chips
8/07	Reverse charge for purchases and sales of mobile phones and computer chips
11/07	Accounting for VAT on standard-rated prescription products
12/07	TOGCs: changes to VAT record-keeping requirements
14/07	HMRC guidance: assets used partly for non-business purposes
15/07	Supply of parts and equipment for qualifying ships and aircraft
4/08	Supplies of government grant funded research
6/08	Electronically supplied services: special scheme for non-EU businesses – changes
7/08	Partial exemption – VAT adjustments when house builders let their dwellings before selling them
3/09	Withdrawal of the VAT staff hire concession on 1 April 2009
4/09	Partial exemption – changes to the standard method
7/09	Private use charge for motor manufacturer's company cars, dealer demonstrators and daily rental cars
8/09	Changes to the zero-rate for buildings used for a relevant charitable use
14/09	Changes to the operation of the option to tax on supplies of land and buildings
3/10	VAT status of university trading companies – new guidelines
4/10	Partial exemption – changes to the de minimis rules
13/10	Calculating qualifying use for a charitable or a communal residential building
21/10	Place of supply of natural gas and electricity (also heat and cooling)
4/11	Change in use provisions
5/11	Dispensing doctors (Scotland) and VAT registration
6/11	Implementing the VAT technical directive and changes to the partial exemption and capital goods scheme rules
8/11	Motor manufacturer's company cars, dealer demonstrators, daily rental cars
9/11	VAT refund scheme for academies
7/12	Guidance on the cost sharing exemption – from 17 July 2012
9/12	Anti-forestalling for approved alterations to listed buildings
10/12	Approved alterations to listed buildings
11/12	Taxing holiday caravans
12/12	Hot food and premises
13/12	Hairdressers' chair rental
14/12	Self storage
15/12	Sports nutrition drinks
18/12	New Form VAT 411
1/13	Special scheme for non-EU businesses – exchange rates for period ending December 2012

2/13	Electronically supplied services – special scheme for non-EU businesses – Cyprus
4/13	Taxing holiday caravans
5/13	Special scheme for non-EU businesses – exchange rate for period ending March 2013
6/13	Notification of vehicles arrivals (NOVA) – revised June 2014
9/13	Special scheme for non-EU businesses – exchange rates for period ending June 2013
10/13	Provision of storage facilities
11/13	Supplies of research between eligible bodies
13/13	Special scheme for non-EU businesses – exchange rates for period ending September 2013
15/13	Special scheme for non-EU businesses – exchange rates for period ending September 2013
16/13	Special scheme for non-EU businesses – exchange rates for period ending December 2013
2/14	VAT on buildings that are dwellings and used for a relevant residential purpose
3/14	VAT treatment of refunds made by manufacturers
4/14	Special scheme for non-EU businesses – exchange rates for period ending March 2014
5/14	Electronically supplied services – special scheme for non-EU businesses – France
6/14	Cross Border VAT Refunds – Republic of Serbia
7/14	Special scheme for non-EU businesses – exchange rates for period ending June 2014
8/14	VAT place of supply of services – mini one stop shop
9/14	Special scheme for non-EU businesses – exchange rates for period ending September 2014
10/14	Special scheme for non-EU businesses – exchange rates for period ending December 2014
1/15	Claims by non-profit making members' sports clubs for overpaid VAT on supplies of sporting services made to non-members
2/15	VAT Mini One Stop Shop – exchange rates for period ending March 2015
3/15	VAT Mini One Stop Shop – exchange rates for period ending June 2015
4/15	VAT Mini One Stop Shop – exchange rates for period ending September 2015
1/16	VAT Mini One Stop Shop – exchange rates for period ending December 2015
2/16	VAT Mini One Stop Shop – exchange rates for period ending March 2016
3/16	Changes to the VAT rate for Greece 1 June 2016
4/16	VAT Mini One Stop Shop – exchange rates for period ending June 2016
5/16	VAT Mini One Stop Shop – exchange rates for period ending September 2016

1/17	VAT Mini One Stop Shop – exchange rates for period ending December 2016
2/17	VAT Mini One Stop Shop – changes in the VAT rate for Romania
3/17	Changes to the VAT rate for Hungary
4/17	VAT MOSS – exchange rates for the period ending March 2017
5/17	VAT MOSS – exchange rates for the period ending June 2017
6/17	VAT MOSS – exchange rates for the period ending September 2017
8/17	Claims by local authorities for overpaid VAT on supplies of sporting services
9/17	Changes to the VAT rate for Hungary
1/18	VAT MOSS – exchange rates for period ending December 2017
2/18	Impact on existing cost share groups following changes to HMRC's policy

HMRC Briefs

[31.3] The following list provides details of the HMRC Briefs issued since January 2013. Please see the National Archives (webarchive.nationalarchives.gov.uk/20130102175236/http://hmrc.gov.uk/thelibrary/briefs.htm) for details of any issued before this date.

2/13	Rooms provided in hotels of similar establishments with catering
7/13	Levy on 'single use' carrier bags in Northern Ireland
9/13	Treatment of 'consultancy charges' for services supplied to employers
10/13	Withdrawal of the VAT exemption for supplies of research
11/13	Modified treatment for certain portfolio management fees
15/13	Judgement in the High Court in *Investment Trust Companies*
16/13	Laboratory pathology services
17/13	Tribunal decision in *Paymex Ltd v HMRC*
21/13	Withdrawal of the VAT exemption for supplies of research between eligible bodies
23/13	Guidance on the provision of storage facilities
25/13	VAT treatment of supervisors fees in light of the *Paymex* judgement
28/13	Avoidance cases – what happens to the repayments
33/13	Withdrawal of the partial exemption concession in relation to Road Fuel Scale Charges
36/13	VAT reverse charge for mobile phones, computer chips and emissions allowances
38/13	Intrastat – changes from January 2014
1/14	VAT – fiscal neutrality and gaming
3/14	Construction works to buildings used 'for a relevant residential purpose'
4/14	VAT information sheet 2 (2014)
5/14	Tour Operators Margin Scheme
6/14	Deduction of VAT on pension fund management costs

8/14	Sports leagues
9/14	Bitcoin and other cryptocurrencies
13/14	VAT deregistration of insolvent businesses
14/14	Withdrawal of concessions for student accommodation and dining halls
18/14	VAT exemption for education
19/14	VAT First-tier Tribunal decision on the UK's 'party plan' derogation
20/14	High Court judgement on interest payments for *Littlewoods Retail Ltd*
21/14	Zero-rating of the dispensing of prescribed drugs
22/14	Judgement on the deduction of VAT on pension fund management costs
23/14	VAT – introduction of domestic reverse charge for businesses wholesale trading in gas and electricity
26/14	Sharing of non-financial VAT registration data and exporter data
27/14	Transfer of a business as a going concern
28/14	Domestic reverse charge for businesses wholesale trading in gas and electricity
32/14	VAT – policy on holding companies
35/14	*Lok'nStore Group Plc* decision on calculating deductible VAT
36/14	VAT – liability of snowballs
37/14	VAT grouping rules
38/14	VAT – compulsory charge on single use carrier bags in Scotland
39/14	VAT – liability catering and other services linked to education
43/14	VAT on pension fund management costs
44/14	VAT treatment of pension fund management services
47/14	Changes to the Intrastat arrival threshold from 1 January 2015
49/14	VAT – Prompt Payment Discounts
2/15	VAT grouping rules and *Skandia*
8/15	Deduction of VAT on pension fund management costs
9/15	HMRC position following the Court of Appeal decision in *Littlewoods Retail and others*
10/15	VAT – direct marketing services using printed matter
12/15	VAT liability of verandahs sold with caravans
13/15	Reduced rate of VAT for the installation of energy saving materials
14/15	VAT – compulsory charge on single use carrier bags in England
17/15	Deduction of VAT on pension fund management costs
18/15	VAT grouping rules and the *Skandia* judgement
21/15	VAT zero-rating – liability of residential caravans
22/15	Changes to VAT regulations following judgement in the case of *Le Credit Lyonnais* (C-388/1)
23/15	VAT grouping rules and the *Skandia* judgement
3/16	Review of VAT grouping provisions following the *Larentia + Minerva and Marenave* (C-108/14 and C-109/14) and *Skandia* (C-713) judgements
4/16	VAT MOSS – simplifications for businesses trading below the registration threshold

7/16	Reminder of the withdrawal of the VAT Misdirection Extra Statutory Concession 3.5 in cases of a VAT liability change
8/16	Release by HMRC of exporter information
9/16	VAT treatment of conversions of non-residential buildings into dwellings under permitted development rights
10/16	VAT – unjust enrichment: non-profit making sports clubs
11/16	VAT and the transfer of a going concern
12/16	Senior Accounting Officer guidance
13/16	VAT: the liability treatment of a dwelling formed from more than one building
14/16	VAT: deduction of VAT on pension fund management costs following the Court of Justice of the European Union decision in *PPG*
15/16	VAT: use and enjoyment of insurance repair services
16/16	Treatment of VAT incurred on assets that are used by the business prior to VAT registration
17/16	VAT – treatment of colouring and dot-to-dot books
1/17	VAT – historical bad debt relief claims
2/17	VAT – care homes and hospitals
3/17	VAT – treatment of pension fund management services
4/17	Judgment of the Supreme Court in *Investment Trust Companies*
5/17	Final judgment in *Littlewoods*
6/17	VAT – treatment of sports facilities by local councils
1/18	VAT – treatment of affiliation fees for sports clubs
2/18	VAT – treatment of Advanced Learner Loans
3/18	Changes to the VAT exemption for cost sharing groups

HMRC Standard Forms

[31.4] The following is a list of the more common forms issued by HMRC for VAT use and which can be downloaded from the GOV.UK website (apart from Form VAT 100) at

www.gov.uk/government/organisations/hm-revenue-customs

SIVA 1	Application for simplified VAT accounting (SIVA)
SIVA 2	Deferment schedule — SIVA reduced security
VAT 1	VAT — application for registration (see **60.5 REGISTRATION**)
VAT 1A	Application for registration — distance selling (see **60.13 REGISTRATION**)
VAT 1B	Application for registration — acquisitions (see **60.20 REGISTRATION**)
VAT 1C	VAT registration notification (see **60.28 REGISTRATION**)
VAT 1TR	Appointment of tax representative (see **3.12 AGENTS**)
VAT 2	VAT — partnership details (see **60.5 REGISTRATION**)
VAT 5L	Registration — land and property
VAT 7	Application to cancel your VAT registration (see **60.32 REGISTRATION**)

VAT 50	Application for VAT group treatment (see **28.3 GROUPS OF COMPANIES**)
VAT 51	Application for VAT group treatment — company details (see **28.3 GROUPS OF COMPANIES**)
VAT 53	Authority for an agent to form or amend a VAT group
VAT 56	Application to change the representative member of a VAT group (see **28.3 GROUPS OF COMPANIES**)
VAT 65A	Application for VAT refund by a business person not established in the Community (see **49.5 OVERSEAS TRADERS**)
VAT 66A	VAT — certificate of status of business person
VAT 68	Request for transfer of a registration number (see **60.42 REGISTRATION**)
VAT 69	Notification of insolvency details
VAT 98	Agricultural flat rate scheme — application for certification (see **64.27 SPECIAL SCHEMES**)
VAT 101	EC sales lists (see **2.12–2.15 ACCOUNTING PERIODS AND RETURNS**)
VAT 101A	EC sales list continuation sheet
VAT 101B	VAT — EC sales list correction sheet (see **2.12 ACCOUNTING PERIODS AND RETURNS**)
VAT 126	Claim for refund of VAT by certain bodies (see **44.9 LOCAL AUTHORITIES AND PUBLIC BODIES**)
VAT 407	VAT — tax free shopping — retailer's checklist (see **22.13 EXPORTS**)
VAT 411	New means of transport — removal from the UK to another member state of the EU (see **20.34 EUROPEAN UNION: SINGLE MARKET**)
VAT 411A	New motorised land vehicle purchase by EC VAT registered enterprises only (see **20.35 EUROPEAN UNION: SINGLE MARKET**)
VAT 415	New means of transport (ships and aircraft) — notification of acquisition (see **20.37 EUROPEAN UNION: SINGLE MARKET**)
VAT 426	Insolvent traders claim for input tax after deregistration (see **36.12 INSOLVENCY**)
VAT 427	Reclaim or claim VAT relief on cancelling of registration (see **35.11 INPUT TAX**)
VAT 431C	VAT refunds for DIY housebuilders — claim form and notes for conversions (see **43.24 LAND AND BUILDINGS: ZERO AND REDUCED RATE SUPPLIES AND DIY HOUSEBUILDERS**)
VAT 431NB	VAT refunds for DIY housebuilders — claim form for new houses (see **43.24 LAND AND BUILDINGS: ZERO AND REDUCED RATE AND DIY HOUSEBUILDERS**)
VAT 484	Changes to registration details
VAT 600 AA	Application to join the annual accounting scheme (see **64.10 SPECIAL SCHEMES**)
VAT 600 AA/FRS	Application to join the annual accounting and the flat rate scheme (see **64.10 SPECIAL SCHEMES**)
VAT 600 FRS	Application to join the flat rate scheme (see **64.18 SPECIAL SCHEMES**)
VAT 622	Pay by BACS or standing order
VAT 623	Annual accounting scheme — direct debit form
VAT 652	Notification of errors in VAT returns (see **57.11 RECORDS**)

VAT 769	VAT — notification of insolvency details (see **36.2 INSOLVENCY**)
VAT 833	Statement of VAT on goods sold in satisfaction of debt (see **36.12 INSOLVENCY**)
VAT 908	Mineral oils — deferment advice for VAT due on removal from warehouse
VAT 1614A	Notification of an option to tax land and/or buildings
VAT 1614B	Ceasing to be a relevant associate in relation to an option to tax
VAT 1614C	Revoking an option to tax within 6–month 'cooling off' period
VAT 1614D	Certificate to disapply the option to tax for conversions into dwelling, etc
VAT 1614E	Notification of a real estate election
VAT 1614F	New buildings — exclusion from an option to tax
VAT 1614G	Certificate to disapply the option to tax to land sold to housing associations
VAT 1614H	Application for permission to opt
VAT 1614J	Revoking an option to tax after 20 years
VAT 1615A	Customer declaration for zero-rated VAT supply of an adapted motor vehicle
VAT 1617A	Supplier information about zero-rated VAT supply of an adapted motor vehicle
VAT 1617B	Survey of purchases of adapted boats
WT2	VAT — late submission of online VAT return — reasonable excuse

Key points

[31.5] Points to consider are as follows.

- A useful tip if a public notice is being viewed on the GOV.UK website is to use the facility at the top of the screen that says 'See more information about this Notice'. This section should state which version of the Notice the current version replaces and where to find details of the changes made. As a general principle, it is also important to recognise that information in a public notice is only totally correct at the time that it is published. Subsequent changes may be announced in VAT Information Sheets or HMRC Briefs.
- It is possible to view updates to HMRC information relating to VAT on the GOV.UK website by searching for the HMRC home page, clicking on VAT, then clicking on 'See latest changes to this content'.
- A lot of useful information is often provided by HMRC in VAT information sheets and HMRC Briefs.

32

HMRC: Powers

Cross-references. See **6.1 ASSESSMENTS** for powers of HMRC to raise assessments and to assess an over-repayment and **6.3 ASSESSMENTS** for assessments of penalties, interest and surcharges; **9.5 BUSINESS** for powers to make a direction treating two or more persons as one taxable person; **30.7 HMRC: ADMINISTRATION** for the power to disclose or exchange information with other authorities and government departments; **28.5 GROUPS OF COMPANIES** for powers re groups; **52.6 PAYMENT OF VAT** for power to withhold a repayment of VAT due where returns are outstanding; **53.2–53.5 PENALTIES** for powers of arrest; **53.33 PENALTIES** for power of mitigation; **57.1 RECORDS** for the power to require records to be kept; and **60.10 REGISTRATION** for powers to enforce compulsory deregistration.

Introduction to HMRC: powers

[32.1] HMRC have the following powers relating to the production of evidence and the requirement for security.

(a) HMRC can, as a condition of allowing or repaying any input tax to any person, require the production of such evidence relating to VAT as they may specify. [*VATA 1994, Sch 11 para 4(1)*].

(b) If they think it necessary for the protection of the revenue, HMRC can require, as a condition of making any VAT credit, the giving of such security for the amount of the payment as appears appropriate to them. [*VATA 1994, Sch 11 para 4(1A)*].

(c) If they think it necessary for the protection of the revenue, HMRC may require a taxable person, as a condition of his supplying or being supplied with goods and services under a taxable supply, to give security (or further security) for the payment of any VAT that is or may become due from the taxable person. The security can be of such amount, and must be given in such a manner, as HMRC determine. [*VATA 1994, s 48(7), Sch 11 para 4(2)(4)(5)*].

(d) If they think it necessary for the protection of the revenue, HMRC may require a taxable person, as a condition of his supplying or being supplied with goods and services under a taxable supply, to give security (or further security) for the payment of any VAT that is or may become due from any person by or to whom goods or services supplied by or to the taxable person are supplied. The security can be of such amount, and must be given in such a manner, as HMRC determine. [*VATA 1994, s 48(7), Sch 11 para 4(2)–(5)*].

(e) Where a person fails to appoint a VAT representative when required to do so (see **3.8 AGENTS**), HMRC may require him to provide security, or further security, as they think appropriate for the payment of any VAT which is or may become due from him. [*VATA 1994, s 48(7)*].

(f) *Schedule 8* of *Finance (No 2) Act 2015* provides an administrative measure that allows HMRC to recover debts directly from taxpayers' bank and building society accounts without the need to apply to a court. Taxpayers with debts of £1,000 or more, which could consist of two or more debts across a range of taxes, e.g. a £400 debt relating to income tax and a £600 debt relating to VAT, may be subject to the measure. [*F(No 2)A 2015, Sch 8*].

Reconsiderations and appeals

Where a business has been issued with a Notice of Requirement under (*b*)–(*e*) above, they can ask HMRC to review the requirement or appeal against the decision to a tribunal (see **5.3**(15) **APPEALS**).

Where an appeal is brought against a requirement for security under (*d*) above, the tribunal must allow the appeal unless HMRC satisfy the tribunal that

- there has been an evasion of, or an attempt to evade, VAT in relation to goods or services supplied to or by that person, or
- it is likely, or without the requirement for security it is likely, that VAT in relation to such goods or services will be evaded

and for these purposes evading VAT includes obtaining a VAT credit that is not due or a VAT credit in excess of what is due.

[*VATA 1994, s 84(4E)(4F)*].

Subject to this, when considering HMRC's requirement for security, the tribunal's jurisdiction is appellate rather than merely supervisory. The tribunal should consider whether HMRC acted reasonably and took account of all relevant material, but has no power to substitute its own decision for one reached on an incorrect basis (except that it can dismiss an appeal where it is shown that, even if additional material had been taken into account, the decision would *inevitably* have been the same). The tribunal should consider whether HMRC acted in a way in which no reasonable panel of Commissioners could have acted or whether they took into account some irrelevant matter or disregarded something to which they should have given weight. However, the tribunal cannot exercise a fresh discretion since the protection of the revenue is not a responsibility of the tribunal or of a court (*C & E Commrs v John Dee Ltd*, CA [1995] STC 941 (TVC 14.31)). In that case, the tribunal found that HMRC had failed to enquire into the company's financial status and that, if it had done, the result would not have inevitably been the same.

In *C & E Commrs v Peachtree Enterprises Ltd*, QB [1994] STC 747 (TVC 14.60) Dyson J observed that the tribunal must limit itself to considering facts and matter which existed at the time the challenge to the decision was taken and should not, for example, take into account the fact that the person concerned had subsequently made all returns and paid the VAT due on time.

In *Half Penny Accountants Ltd* [2016] UKFTT 45 (TC) (TC04845), an accountancy practice was seriously in arrears with VAT payments, and an officer issued a notice of requirement to deposit security. The trader asked for a statutory review, providing further information about a proposed sale of some or all of the business that would generate enough cash to settle all the debts. The reviewing officer rejected this as a reason to cancel the security demand, stating that to allow it would give the taxpayer an unfair advantage over other traders. The Tribunal decided that this was an unreasonable decision based on an irrelevant matter, and also that the trader could appeal against the review decision as well as the original decision (which had been reasonably made on the basis of the information available at the time). It was not inevitable that the reviewing officer would have come to the same decision if he had approached the task in the correct way, so the appeal was allowed.

De Voil Indirect Tax Service. See V5.186, V5.225.

Recovery of VAT

[32.2] Where an invoice shows a supply of goods or services with VAT chargeable on it, the person issuing the invoice is liable for the amount of VAT shown (or the amount of VAT included if not shown separately) whether or not

(a) the invoice has been correctly prepared as required by the legislation (see **40 INVOICES**);
(b) the supply actually takes, or has taken, place;
(c) the amount shown as VAT, or any amount of VAT, is or was chargeable on the supply; or
(d) the person issuing the invoice is a taxable person.

[*VATA 1994, Sch 11 para 5(1)–(3)*].

If any of the conditions in (*b*)–(*d*) above are not met, the sum recoverable is not VAT due under *VATA 1994* but is a debt due to the Crown. The practical effect of this is that normal assessment procedures cannot be used. The recovery of the incorrectly shown VAT is effected by means of a formal demand letter.

Penalties for unauthorised issue of invoices (see **53.16 PENALTIES**) and interest on late paid VAT (see **52.16 PAYMENT OF VAT**) may also be due.

Concessionary reliefs

Where HMRC requires payment under the above provisions because of (*d*) above, the person issuing the invoice has no legal entitlement to treat the VAT incurred on his own related purchases as input tax. Equally, the person receiving the invoice has no legal entitlement to claim the VAT shown on the invoice as representing VAT. However, by concession, HMRC may

- allow the person making such a payment to HMRC to deduct from it the amount of VAT incurred on supplies to him of goods and services directly attributable to any invoiced supply in respect of which payment is required; and
- take no action against a taxable person who has received the supply and, in good faith, treated the amount shown as representing VAT as his input tax.

(VAT Notice 48, ESC 3.9).

Partnerships

See also **51.4 PARTNERSHIPS** for recovery of VAT from individual partners.

VAT due to other EU member states

Where recovery of a debt in any EU member state proves unsuccessful, that country can request another EU member state to attempt recovery where it appears that the debtor now resides, or has assets, there. The provisions of the Mutual Assistance Recovery Directive (*Directive 2010/24/EU*) are enacted in the UK as *FA 2011, s 87, Sch 25* (and supporting regulations) in relation to the recovery in the UK of amounts in respect of which a request for enforcement has been made by the tax authorities of another EU member state. Such proceedings may be taken by, or on behalf of, HMRC to enforce the foreign claim (by way of legal proceedings, distress, diligence or otherwise) as might be taken to enforce a corresponding UK claim.

Unless otherwise permitted, no proceedings can be taken against any person if he shows that proceedings relevant to his liability on the foreign claim are pending, or about to be instituted, in the other EU member state concerned but proceedings may be taken in the UK if the proceedings in that other country are not prosecuted or instituted with reasonable expedition. If the person shows that a final decision on the foreign claim has been given in his favour in the other EU member state, no proceedings can be taken in the UK under these provisions.

De Voil Indirect Tax Service. See V1.271; V5.171, V5.175.

Direct recovery of VAT debts

HMRC can recover cash directly from the bank and building society accounts, and funds held in cash Individual Savings Accounts, of debtors who owe £1,000 or more. The measure is known as Direct Recovery of Debts (DRD) and three conditions must be satisfied in order for it to apply.

Condition 1 is that the amount due must amount to £1,000 or more. This could consist of more than one debt across a range of taxes, including tax credit debts. For example, condition 1 would be met if a person owed a £400 debt relating to income tax and a £600 debt relating to VAT.

Condition 2 is that the amount due must be an established debt or a debt due under the accelerated payments legislation in *FA 2014*. An established debt is a debt against which there is no right of appeal or, where there is a right of appeal, the appeal period has either expired or the appeal has been settled or withdrawn. The accelerated payment legislation in *FA 2014* is relevant to non-VAT debts.

Condition 3 is that HMRC is satisfied that the debtor is aware that the sum is due and payable to HMRC.

A sum that is due and payable to HMRC is an established debt if there is no possibility that the sum, or any part of it, will cease to be due and payable to HMRC on appeal.

The DRD legislation includes a requirement for HMRC to consider whether a person may be at a particular disadvantage in dealing with their taxes before making a decision to proceed with DRD action against the person.

[*F(No 2)A 2015, Sch 8*].

Joint and several liability for unpaid VAT

[32.3] Where

- a taxable person receives a taxable supply of 'relevant goods and services',
- at the time of the supply he knew, or had 'reasonable grounds to suspect', that some or all of the 'VAT payable' on that supply, or on any previous or subsequent supply of those goods or services, would go unpaid to HMRC, and
- HMRC have served on him a notice of liability under these provisions

that person, and the person otherwise liable for the amount specified in the notice, are jointly and severally liable to HMRC for the 'net VAT unpaid' on those goods or services.

> *Example*
>
> A business buys 100 mobile phones from a supplier who bought them as part of an order for 1000 mobile phones.
>
> It may be held liable, under joint and several liability, for any unpaid VAT on the 100 phones it has bought (but not the remaining 900 phones which its supplier has bought).

Relevant goods and services

The provisions apply to '*relevant goods and services*' which fall within any one or more of the following descriptions.

- Any equipment made or adapted for use as a telephone and any 'other equipment' made or adapted for use in connection with telephones or telecommunication.
- Any equipment made or adapted for use as a computer and any 'other equipment' made or adapted for use in connection with computers or computer systems (including, in particular, positional determination devices for use with satellite navigation systems).
- Any other electronic equipment made or adapted for use by individuals for the purposes of leisure, amusement or entertainment and any 'other equipment' made or adapted for use in connection with any such electronic equipment.

'*Other equipment*' includes parts, accessories and software.

[*VATA 1994, s 77A(1)–(3)*].

Parts and accessories include computer chips, telephone chargers, memory cards and games cards but not parts such as screws and wires used in the manufacture of general items when sold separately. (VAT Notice 726, para 1.4).

Reasonable grounds to suspect

Without prejudice to any other way of establishing reasonable grounds for suspicion, a person is presumed to have reasonable grounds for suspecting some or all of any VAT payable has not been paid if the price payable by him for the goods or services in question was less than the

- lowest price that might reasonably be expected to be payable for them on the open market, or
- price payable on any previous supply of those goods.

This presumption is, however, rebuttable on proof that the low price payable for the goods was due to circumstances unconnected with failure to pay VAT.

[*VATA 1994, s 77A(6)–(8)*].

Businesses trading within a market should have a reasonable idea of the market prices for the goods an any given day. If goods are offered for what appears to be bargain prices, a business should find out the reason for the low cost. (VAT Notice 726, para 3.2).

VAT payable

The amount of VAT that is payable in respect of a supply is the lesser of

- the amount chargeable on the supply, and
- the amount shown as due on the supplier's return for the VAT period in question (if he has made one), together with any amount assessed as due from him for that period (subject to any appeal by him). The latter includes any amount assessed by HMRC even where it is not notified to the supplier because it is impracticable to do so.

[*VATA 1994, s 77A(4)(5)*].

Net VAT unpaid

'*Net VAT unpaid*' means the VAT charged on the goods or services in question less any input tax incurred on their purchase by the person who has not paid the VAT. For goods acquired from another EU member state, the net VAT unpaid on the first UK supply is the amount of the output tax (acquisition VAT – input tax + output tax). (VAT Notice 726, para 2.2). An amount of VAT counts as unpaid only to the extent that it exceeds the amount of any refund due. [*VATA 1994, s 77A(1)*].

Exceptions

HMRC will not apply these provisions on the supply of specified goods and services where

- VAT goes unpaid as a result of genuine bad debts or genuine business failure;
- goods are bought by a business for its own use, rather than onward sale;
- a business can demonstrate that the low purchase price paid for the goods was due to circumstances unconnected with the failure to pay VAT; or
- a business has genuinely done everything it can to check the integrity of the supply chain and its suppliers and customers, can demonstrate it has done so, has addressed concerns raised through its checks and has no other reason to suspect VAT would go unpaid.

HMRC will use this measure to combat MTIC fraud. As this fraud generally involves the wholesale of the relevant goods and their dispatch from the UK, it is highly unlikely that manufacturers or retail suppliers of the relevant goods will be affected by these provisions.
(VAT Notice 726, paras 2.4, 4.9).

HMRC's application of the provisions

HMRC will send a notification letter to a business if

- the business has bought and/or sold relevant goods or services;
- the transaction took place within a supply chain where VAT was unpaid by another supplier in the chain; and
- they believe they can show that the business knew, or had reasonable grounds to suspect, that VAT would go unpaid.

Before the issue of a notification letter, each case will be independently reviewed and authorised by a central team within HMRC to ensure that the case is an appropriate one for the joint and several liability provisions and that there is sufficient evidence, on balance of probabilities, to show the requisite knowledge or reasonable grounds for suspicion.

A notification letter will be sent to each known business in the chain of supply that HMRC considers may be jointly and severally liable for the unpaid VAT. Each business will have 21 days to demonstrate that it did not know, or have reasonable grounds to suspect, that VAT would go unpaid and, where applicable, that there was a legitimate reason for the low purchase price of the goods. Any factors a business wishes to bring to HMRC's attention will be considered by the officer who issued the letter and then independently reviewed.

If, after a period of 21 days, a business has not responded or HMRC do not accept that the evidence or explanation provided is satisfactory, HMRC will issue the business with a notice of liability for the net tax unpaid. This will demand payment of the amount of VAT for which HMRC consider it is jointly and severally liable.

(VAT Notice 726, paras 4.1–4.3).

Reasonable checks

HMRC advise that it is good commercial practice for a business to carry out checks to establish the credibility and legitimacy of its customers, suppliers and supplies in order to avoid being involved in a supply chain where VAT would go unpaid. They do not expect a business to go beyond what is reasonable but they do expect a business to make a judgement on the integrity of its supply chain and the suppliers, customers and goods within it. Factors which a business may wish to take into account include the nature of the supply, payment arrangements and conditions and details of the movement of goods. (VAT Notice 726, para 4.5).

See VAT Notice 726, para 6.1 for examples of indicators that could alert a business to the risk that VAT might go unpaid and VAT Notice 726, para 6.2 for examples of specific checks which could be made (although the list is not exhaustive).

HMRC also recommend that any paperwork received in addition to invoices (e.g. purchase orders, pro-forma invoices, delivery notes, CMRs (Convention Merchandises Routiers) or airway bills, allocation notifications, and inspection reports, etc.) should be kept as evidence of a transaction's legitimacy. (VAT Notice 726, para 6.2).

If the checks carried out by a business indicate that there may be a fraud, it should consider whether it wishes to continue with the transaction and may also wish to inform HMRC Confidential on 0800 595 000. (VAT Notice 726, para 4.7).

Online marketplaces

The Government introduced legislation in *Finance Act 2016* that holds an online marketplace joint and severally liable for any unpaid VAT due by an overseas business that sells goods in the UK via an online marketplace's website and who has failed to meet its UK obligation. [*FA 2016, ss 123–124 inserting VATA 1994, ss 77B–77D.*]

The Government announced additional measures in Autumn Budget 2017 that extended the scope of the joint and several liability regime. Three measures were introduced:

- The existing joint and several liability provisions for online marketplaces have been extended to cover all businesses that should be registered for VAT in the UK (including UK businesses). This will address non-compliance by UK businesses and encourage them to register for VAT when they need to and pay the VAT due on their sales.

- The joint and several liability for online marketplaces in relation to overseas businesses, where the online marketplace allows an unregistered overseas business to sell goods through its marketplace, has been extended to include situations when the online marketplace, knew or should have known, that the overseas business was required to be VAT registered.
- Online marketplaces are required to confirm that the VAT registration number provided by the seller is valid and that the valid VAT number is displayed on the website for all sales of goods made by that seller within ten days of receipt.

HMRC have issued Extending joint and several liability for online marketplaces and displaying VAT numbers online – guidance note (www.gov.uk/government/publications/vat-extending-joint-and-several-liability-for-online-marketplaces-and-displaying-vat-numbers-online-guidance-note) which provides further information on the changes.

The new legislation is contained in *Finance Act 2018, s 38* and came into effect from 15 March 2018.

Taking control of goods for unpaid VAT

[32.4] There are special provisions to allow HMRC to enforce the recovery of VAT due but not paid. Different rules and procedures apply in England and Wales, Scotland and Northern Ireland.

England and Wales

With effect from 6 April 2014, if a person does not pay a sum that is payable by that person to HMRC

- under or by virtue of an enactment, or
- under a '*contract settlement*', i.e. an agreement made in connection with any person's liability to make a payment to HMRC under or by virtue of any enactment

HMRC may use the procedure in *Tribunals, Courts and Enforcement Act 2007, Sch 12* (taking control of goods) to recover that sum.

[*FA 2008, ss 127, 139; SI 2014/768*].

See *Tribunals, Courts and Enforcement Act 2007, Sch 12* and supporting Regulations for full details.

Before 6 April 2014, the same provisions apply as in Northern Ireland. [*FA 1997, s 51; Tribunals, Courts and Enforcement Act 2007, Sch 13 para 126*].

Northern Ireland

Where, following a written demand, a person neglects or refuses to pay any VAT due (or any amount recoverable as if it were VAT) an HMRC officer may levy distress on that person's goods and chattels. He may also direct, by warrant, any authorised person to levy such distress in which case distress must be levied by or under the direction of, and in the presence of, that authorised person. [*FA 1997, s 51; SI 1997/1431*].

Scotland

If a person does not pay a sum that is payable by that person to HMRC

- under or by virtue of an enactment, or
- under a '*contract settlement*', i.e. an agreement made in connection with any person's liability to make a payment to HMRC under or by virtue of any enactment

an HMRC officer may apply to the sheriff for a summary warrant. The application must be accompanied by a signed certificate which

- states that
  - (a) none of the persons specified in the application has paid the sum payable by that person;
  - (b) the officer has demanded payment from each such person of the sum payable by that person; and
- specifies the sum payable by each person specified in the application.

When granted, a summary warrant authorises the recovery of the sum payable by attachment, money attachment, earnings arrestment, or arrestment and action of forthcoming or sale.

[*FA 2008, ss 128, 139*].

De Voil Indirect Tax Service. See V5.173, V5.174.

Investigations under Police and Criminal Evidence Act 1984

[32.5] Certain provisions of the *Police and Criminal Evidence Act (PACE) 1984* (as modified in some cases) apply, in England and Wales, to relevant criminal investigations conducted by officers of Revenue and Customs. This does not confer on such officers any power to charge a person with an offence, release a person on bail or detain a person for an offence after he has been charged with it.

Where *PACE 1984* gives a constable power to seize and retain any thing found upon a lawful search of person or premises, an officer of Revenue and Customs has the same power, despite the fact that the thing found is not evidence of an offence which relates to a matter in relation to which HMRC have functions.

The provisions of *PACE 1984* which apply to officers of Revenue and Customs are as follows.

- *s 8* (power of justice of the peace to authorise entry and search of premises)
- *s 9 and Sch 1* (special provisions as to access and special procedure)
- *s 14A* (exception re excluded material and special procedure material)

- *s 14B* (restriction on other powers to apply for production of documents)
- *s 15* (search warrants – safeguards)
- *s 16* (execution of warrants)
- *s 17(1)(b)(2)(4)* (entry for purpose of arrest, etc.)
- *s 18* (entry and search after arrest) (as modified by *SI 2007/3175, Art 8*)
- *s 19* (general power of seizure etc.)
- *s 20* (extension of powers of seizure to computerised information)
- *s 21* (access and copying) (as modified by *SI 2007/3175, Art 5*)
- *s 22(1)–(4)* (retention)
- *s 24(2)* (arrest without warrant: constables) (as modified by *SI 2007/3175, Art 17*)
- *s 28* (information to be given on arrest)
- *s 29* (voluntary attendance at police station, etc.)
- *s 30(1)–(4)(a), (5)–(11)* (arrest elsewhere than at police station)
- *s 31* (arrest for further offence)
- *s 32(1)–(9)* (search upon arrest) (as modified by *SI 2007/3175, Art 5*)
- *s 34(1)–(5)* (limitations on police detention)
- *s 35(1)(2)(3)(4)* (designated police stations) (as modified by *SI 2007/3175, Art 9*)
- *s 36(1)(2)(3)(4)(5)(6)(7)(8)(9)(10)* (custody officers at police stations) (as modified by *SI 2007/3175, Art 10*)
- *s 37* (duties of custody officer before charge)
- *s 39* (responsibilities in relation to persons detained)
- *s 40* (review of police detention)
- *s 41(1)(2)(4)(6)–(9)* (limits on period of detention without charge) (as modified by *SI 2007/3175, Art 11*)
- *s 42(1)(2)(4)–(11)* (authorisation of continued detention)
- *s 43(1)–(12)(14)–(19)* (warrants of further detention)
- *s 44* (extension of warrants of further detention)
- *s 50* (records of detention) (as modified by *SI 2007/3175, Art 12*)
- *s 51(d)* (savings)
- *s 54* (searches of detained persons)
- *s 55* (intimate searches) (as modified by *SI 2007/3175, Arts 5, 13*)
- *s 56(1)–(9)* (right to have someone informed when arrested)
- *s 57* (additional rights of children and young persons)
- *s 58(1)–(11)* (access to legal advice)
- *s 62* (intimate samples)
- *s 63* (other samples)
- *s 64* (except (6B)) (destruction of fingerprints and samples) (as modified by *SI 2007/3175, Art 14*)
- *s 66* (codes of practice)
- *s 67* (codes of practice-supplementary)
- s 77 (confessions by mentally handicapped persons) (as modified by *SI 2007/3175, Art 15*)
- *s 107* (police officers performing duties of higher rank)

Search of persons

Where an officer searches premises under a warrant obtained under *PACE 1984, s 8* or *Sch 1*, he may search any person found on the premises where he has reasonable cause to believe that person to be in possession of material which is likely to be of substantial value to the investigation of the offence. But no person should be searched except by a person of the same sex.

[*FA 2007, ss 82, 84; SI 2007/3175*].

Furnishing of information and production of documents

Notice requiring information or documents

[32.6] An HMRC officer may serve a notice on a taxpayer or a third party requiring the production of information or documents that are reasonably required to check the taxpayer's tax position. The requirement for a notice does not preclude oral requests, but such requests are not enforceable until formalised in a written notice. A third party notice must name the taxpayer to whom it relates unless the tribunal has approved the notice and disapplied this requirement. A third party notice may not be given without the consent of the taxpayer or the tribunal, unless the notice refers only to information or documents that form part of a person's statutory records and relate to the supply of services or supply, acquisition or importation of goods. The HMRC officer must give the relevant taxpayer a copy of the third party notice unless the tribunal disapplies this requirement. If the tribunal has approved the giving of an information notice then the notice must say so, as this affects whether the rules on penalties (see **53.19 PENALTIES**) or the rules on offences (see **53.3 PENALTIES**) apply. Applications to the tribunal for approval of notices are heard without the taxpayer being present.

With the tribunal's approval, an authorised HMRC officer may require a person to provide information or produce a document by a written notice that is reasonably required to check the tax position of a person or class of persons whose identities are not known.

An information notice may specify or describe the information or documents to be produced or provided. The option to 'describe' means that HMRC are not restricted to asking for documents that they can specifically identify.

Where a person is required to provide information or documents it must be done within the period and time and in the means and format specified in the notice. The notice does not need to specify means or form, but it may be necessary, for example where an original is required. A copy of the requested document may be produced unless the notice specified the original document or an HMRC officer subsequently makes a written request for the original document. Where a notice requires production of a document it must be produced at either a mutually agreed place or a place specified by an HMRC officer, but the officer must not specify a place used solely as a dwelling (i.e. a home).

An officer may take copies of, or make extracts from, documents produced. He may remove and retain documents produced where it appears to him to be necessary, but he must provide a receipt or copy where requested.

An information notice only requires a person to produce documents in his possession or power. It does not require the production of information relating to the conduct of a pending tax appeal; journalistic material; personal records, except where they omit personal information; documents that are more than six years old, except with the agreement of an authorised officer. An information notice does not require a person to provide or produce legally privileged information or documents. A dispute as to whether information or a document is subject to legal professional privilege can be referred to the tribunal.

Where a third party notice is given to check the tax position of a group's parent undertaking and any subsidiary undertaking, the notice need only state this and name the parent, not every subsidiary. Only the parent undertaking needs to be sent a copy of the notice. Where a business is carried on in partnership and a third party notice is given for the purpose of checking the tax position of more than one partner, the notice need only state this and give the partnership's registered name, not each partner's name. A copy of the notice need only be given to one of the partners.

[*FA 2008, Sch 36 paras 1–9, 15–23, 34, 35, 37; FA 2009, Sch 47 para 3*].

Appeals against information notices

There is no right of appeal against a decision of the tribunal to approve an information notice. Where an information notice was not approved by the tribunal, the taxpayer may appeal to the tribunal against the notice or any requirement therein, except a requirement to provide information or documents forming part of his statutory records. A right of appeal also exists for third party notices and notices requiring information and documents about persons whose identities are not known, but only where it would be unduly onerous to comply with the notice or requirement. Notice of an appeal must be given in writing before the end of the period of 30 days from the date on which the information notice is given. On appeal, the tribunal may confirm, vary or set aside the notice or a requirement therein, and the tribunal's decision is final.

[*FA 2008, Sch 36 paras 29–33; FA 2009, Sch 47 para 4*].

De Voil Indirect Tax Service. See V5.234.

Power to obtain contact details for debtors

[32.7] Where:

- a sum is payable by a person ('the debtor') to HMRC under or by virtue of an enactment or under a contract settlement;
- an HMRC officer reasonably requires contact details for the debtor for the purpose of collecting that sum;
- the officer has reasonable grounds to believe that a person ('the third party') has any such details; and
- the third party is a company, a local authority or a local authority association, or the officer has reasonable grounds to believe that the third party obtained the details in the course of carrying on a business

an HMRC officer may by notice in writing require the third party to provide the details. The notice must name the debtor. These provisions do not apply if the third party is a charity and obtained the details in the course of providing services free of charge, or the third party is not a charity but obtained the details in the course of providing services on behalf of a charity that are free of charge to the recipient of the service.

The third party must provide the details within such period, and at such time, by such means and in such form (if any), as is reasonably specified or described in the notice. The third party may appeal against the notice or any requirement in the notice on the grounds that it would be unduly onerous to comply with the notice or requirement. Notice of an appeal must be given in writing before the end of the period of 30 days from the date on which the notice is given. On appeal, the tribunal may confirm, vary or set aside the notice or a requirement therein, and the tribunal's decision is final.

If the third party fails to comply with the notice, he is liable to a penalty (see **53.21 PENALTIES**).

[*FA 2008, Sch 36, para 32; FA 2009, Sch 49 paras 1–5*].

De Voil Indirect Tax Service. See V5.234.

Data-gathering powers

[32.8] HMRC have information powers for collecting data from certain third parties for use in HMRC's compliance activities. HMRC may by notice in writing require a relevant data-holder to provide relevant data, i.e. data of a kind specified in regulations made by the Treasury. The data may be general or relating to particular persons and matters, and may include personal data.

The powers are additional to and not limited by other HMRC powers to obtain data, but may not be used in place of the power to obtain information under a taxpayer notice (see **32.6** above) to obtain data required to check the relevant data-holder's own tax position, except for the purpose of obtaining data relating to the beneficial ownership of certain payments.

The data-holder notice must specify the data to be provided, which HMRC must have reason to believe could have a bearing on chargeable or other periods ending on or after the first day of the period of four years ending with the day on which the notice is given.

HMRC may ask for the approval of the tribunal before giving a data-holder notice. The decision of the tribunal is final. The tribunal may not approve the giving of the notice unless

- the application for approval is made by, or with the agreement of, an authorised officer;
- the tribunal is satisfied that, in the circumstances, the officer giving the notice is justified in doing so;
- the data-holder has been told that the data are to be required and has been given a reasonable opportunity to make representations to HMRC, unless the tribunal is satisfied that this might prejudice any purpose for which the data are required; and

- the tribunal has been given a summary of any representations made by the data-holder, unless the tribunal is satisfied that this might prejudice any purpose for which the data are required.

An HMRC officer may take copies of, or make extracts from, any document provided pursuant to a data-holder notice.

If an HMRC officer thinks it reasonable to do so, HMRC may retain documents provided pursuant to a data-holder notice for a reasonable period. The retention does not break any lien on the document. The data-holder may request a copy of the document if it is reasonably required. If a document is lost or damaged, HMRC are liable to compensate its owner for replacement or repair costs.

[*FA 2011, Sch 23, paras 1–7*].

Relevant data-holders

The term 'relevant data-holder' includes many categories of persons involved in the following

- salaries, fees or commission;
- interest paid or credited;
- income or assets belonging to others;
- payment card transactions (merchant acquirers);
- payments derived from securities;
- grants and subsidies out of public funds;
- licences or approvals;
- rent and other payments arising from land;
- dealing in securities;
- dealing in other property;
- Lloyd's;
- investment plans;
- petroleum activities;
- insurance activities;
- environmental activities;
- settlements; and
- charities.

[*FA 2011, Sch 23, paras 8–27; FA 2013, s 228*].

The Government announced in Autumn Statement 2016, that legislation will be introduced to extend HMRC's data gathering powers to Money Service Businesses (MSB) which provide cheque cashing, currency exchange services and money transfers. Banks providing these services are not included in the scope of the revised legislation. Details have been included in *Finance (No 2) Act 2017, s 69*. The provision will apply to relevant data with a bearing on any period (i.e. before or after the date the legislation is passed).

The 'relevant data' for data-holders of the types listed above have been specified in regulations. [*SI 2012/847*].

Appeals

If the tribunal approved the giving of the notice, there is no right of appeal. Otherwise, the data-holder may appeal against a notice, or any requirement in such a notice, on the following grounds

- it its unduly onerous to comply with (unless the data form part of his statutory records);
- he is not a relevant data-holder; or
- the specified data are not relevant data.

Notice of appeal must be given in writing to the HMRC officer who gave the data-holder notice, within 30 days from the date on which the notice was given. The tribunal may confirm, vary or set aside the notice or a requirement in it. The tribunal's decision is final.

[*FA 2011, Sch 23, paras 28–29*].

De Voil Indirect Tax Service. See V5.234, V5.404.

Power to take samples

[32.9] A person acting under the authority of HMRC may at any time, if he deems necessary on the grounds of fraud or mistake, take samples from the goods in the possession of

- any person who supplies goods or acquires them from another EU member state, or
- a fiscal warehousekeeper

in order to determine how the goods, or the materials of which they are made, should be treated for VAT purposes. Any sample may be disposed of and accounted for as HMRC may direct but where it is not returned in a reasonable time (not defined) and in good condition, HMRC must pay compensation of the cost of the sample or any greater amount as they determine. [*VATA 1994, Sch 11 para 8*].

De Voil Indirect Tax Service. See V5.240.

Opening of machines on which relevant machine games are played

[32.10] A person acting under the authority of HMRC may at any reasonable time require a person supplying services by means of a relevant machine game (see **8.3 BETTING AND GAMING**) (or any person acting on his behalf) to open any machine on which relevant machine games are capable of being played and to carry out any other operation which may be necessary in order to ascertain the value of taxable supplies.

[*VATA 1994, Sch 11, para 9*].

De Voil Indirect Tax Service. See V5.238.

Inspection of premises

[32.11] An HMRC officer may enter a person's business premises and inspect the premises, business assets and business documents if the inspection is reasonably required for the purpose of checking that person's tax position. An

HMRC officer may also enter premises and inspect the premises, any goods and related documents where he has reason to believe that the premises are used in connection with the supply/acquisition of goods under taxable supplies/acquisitions and the goods or related documents are on the premises, or the premises are used as or in connection with a fiscal warehouse. These powers do not include the power to enter or inspect any part of the premises that is used solely as a dwelling. An inspection may be carried out at a time agreed to by the occupier or, if the occupier has been given at least seven days' notice or the inspection is carried out by or agreed to by an authorised HMRC officer, at any reasonable time. In the latter case, the inspecting officer must provide a notice in writing to the occupier or other person who appears to be in charge, or it must be left in a prominent place on the premises. The notice must state the possible consequences of obstructing the officer (see **53.19 PENALTIES**).

An officer may ask a tribunal to approve an inspection. If the giving of the notice has been approved by the tribunal then the notice must say so, as this is relevant to the rules on offences (see **53.3 PENALTIES**). Applications to the tribunal to approve an inspection of a business are heard without the taxpayer being present. There is no right of appeal against a decision of the tribunal to approve an inspection.

An officer may take copies of, or make extracts from, inspected documents. He may remove and retain inspected documents where it appears to him to be necessary, but he must provide a receipt or copy where requested. An officer may mark business assets to indicate that they have been inspected, and may obtain and record information relating to inspected premises, property, goods, assets and documents. An HMRC officer can only inspect a business document if an information notice at the time of inspection could have required production of the document or part of it.

[*FA 2008, Sch 36 paras 10–17, 28*].

The Government announced at Autumn Statement 2016 that it was extending HMRC's power to enter premises and inspect goods and force entry to a locked vehicle where they believe that no duty has been paid on the goods locked inside. The following provisions were included in Autumn Budget 2017.

The Government announced that it will amend *CEMA 1979* in order to clarify the powers that allow HMRC officers to use force to gain access to a locked vehicle, when stopping it or searching it, when they suspect it contains goods that are liable to forfeiture. Legislation was included in *FA 2018* and has effect on or after 15 March 2018.

The Government also included legislation in *FA 2018* that extends HMRC's powers under *FA 1994, s 24* so that officers can examine and take account of goods thoroughly, post clearance, inland, where a customs offence is suspected. These powers will enable an officer to move, open, or unpack goods or containers, or require them to be opened or unpacked, and to search the containers and anything in them, as well as mark them as necessary.

[*FA 2018, ss 46, 47*].

De Voil Indirect Tax Service. See V5.231–233.

Order for access to recorded information

[32.12] Subject to below, on application, a justice of the peace (justice in Scotland) may make an order permitting a person acting under the authority of HMRC (an '*authorised person*') to have access to, copy or make extracts from, or remove recorded information reasonably required. Where the recorded information consists of data stored in electronic form, the information must be produced in a visible and legible form (or from which it can be produced in a visible and legible form) and, if required, in a form which can be removed. The justice must be satisfied that there are reasonable grounds for believing that a VAT offence has, is being, or is about to be committed and that the information in the possession of the person named in the order may be required as evidence. The order must be acted upon within seven days of issue (or such longer period as the order specifies). [*VATA 1994, Sch 11 para 11; Criminal Procedure (Consequential Provisions) (Scotland) Act 1995, Sch 4 para 91; Criminal Justice and Police Act 2001, Sch 2 para 13*].

For the conditions for making an order, see *R v Epsom Justices (ex p Bell and Another)*, QB 1988 [1989] STC 169 (TVC 14.100) and *R v City of London Magistrates (ex p Asif and Others)*, QB [1996] STC 611 (TVC 14.101).

Restrictions on use of the above powers

An authorised person can only make an application under the above provisions if he thinks that the material required does not consist of or include 'special procedure material'. If he does, then he must instead make an application under *PACE 1984, Sch 1*. See **32.5** above.

'*Special procedure material*' broadly means either of the following.

- Materials in the possession of a person who
  (a) acquired or created it in the course of any trade, business, profession or other occupation or for the purpose of any paid or unpaid office; and
  (b) holds it subject to *either* an express or implied undertaking to hold it in confidence *or* a restriction on disclosure or an obligation of secrecy contained in any enactment

  other than
  - items subject to legal privilege;
  - personal records acquired or created as in (a) above and held in confidence; and
  - human tissue or tissue fluid which has been taken for the purposes of diagnosis or medical treatment and which a person holds in confidence.
- Journalistic material other than such material which a person holds in confidence.

[*SI 2007/3175, Art 7*].

Procedure where documents are removed

Where an authorised person removes any documents under **32.11** above or recorded information under the above provisions, he must, on request and within a reasonable time, provide a record of what has been removed. The officer in overall charge of the investigation (i.e. the person whose name is endorsed on the order) must, on request, allow access to such documents etc. and allow them to be copied or photographed unless he has reasonable grounds for believing that to do so would prejudice any investigation or criminal proceedings. Where a person acting on behalf of HMRC has failed to comply with these requirements, an application may be made to a magistrate's court (sheriff in Scotland and court of summary jurisdiction in Northern Ireland) which may order that person to comply.

[*VATA 1994, Sch 11 paras 12, 13*].

De Voil Indirect Tax Service. See V5.236.

Computer records, etc.

[32.13] A person authorised by HMRC may, at any reasonable time, obtain access to, and inspect and check the operation of, any computer (and any associated apparatus or material) used in connection with a document that a person has been, or may be, required to

(i) produce, furnish or deliver (or cause to be produced, etc.) to HMRC; or
(ii) permit HMRC to inspect, to make or take copies of or extracts from, or to remove.

An authorised person may also require the person by whom, or on whose behalf, the computer is used, or any person concerned with the operation of the computer, apparatus or material, to provide the authorised person with such reasonable assistance as may be required for those purposes.

Any enactment which requires a person to comply with (i) or (ii) above has effect as if

- any reference to a document were a reference to anything in which information of any description is recorded; and
- any reference to a copy of a document were a reference to anything onto which information recorded in the document has been copied, by whatever means and whether directly or indirectly.

Any person who obstructs the exercise of a power conferred by the above provisions or who fails to assist an authorised person within a reasonable time is liable to a penalty of £300. *FA 2008, Sch 36 paras 45–49A, 52; SI 2009/404* (assessment of and appeals against penalties) (see **53.20 PENALTIES**) apply to the penalty here as they apply to a penalty under *FA 2008 Sch 36 para 39*.

[*FA 2008, s 114*].

Note that these provisions allow computer records to be copied and removed but the computer itself may not be removed.

De Voil Indirect Tax Service. See V5.237.

Visits by HMRC officers

[32.14] From time to time a business will be visited at its principal place of business by an officer from its VAT office. The officer will examine the business records, methods and premises and give the business guidance.

Timing of visits depends on the size and complexity of the business and its past compliance with legislation. Businesses which send in late or incorrect declarations and payments are visited more often. Before a visit HMRC will agree a mutually convenient appointment date and time. On occasion HMRC will call without an appointment. One reason for this may be to see the day-to-day operation of the business.

For a small business, a visit may only take a few hours. For a large or complex business it can last two or more days.

During the visit the officer will

- discuss the various aspects of the business;
- give an indication of the length of the visit;
- examine the records of the business; and
- advise the business of overpayments as well as underpayments.

At the end of the visit the officer will

- review the work performed;
- discuss any concerns arising; and
- agree what is to be done in the future.

When an error is found, the officer will

- describe how the adjustment will be made;
- agree the adjustment whenever possible; and
- tell the business that it has the right to a review of their decision by an officer not previously involved in the matter or to appeal to an independent tribunal. If the business opts for a review it can still appeal to the tribunal after the review has finished if it is unhappy with the outcome.

There are a number of things that the business can do to help the visit go smoothly. These include

- advising HMRC early of the reasons for any significant changes in the tax or duties declared. This should be done by writing to the VAT Written Enquiries Team;
- keeping records and payments up to date;
- providing HMRC with the information and explanations requested;
- asking HMRC if unsure of any matter connected with the tax;
- helping HMRC to understand the business and records;
- replying to enquiries within the specified time; and
- quoting the VAT number when contacting HMRC.

(VAT Notice 700, para 2.2).

De Voil Indirect Tax Service. See V5.221–224.

Estoppel

[32.15] Where, following a visit or otherwise, a Revenue and HMRC officer makes representations which are later shown to be incorrect, a taxpayer may seek to claim that the doctrine of estoppel should be applied. This doctrine prevents a person from acting inconsistently with a representation which he has made to another party, in reliance upon which that other party has acted to his detriment. The representation may be by words, conduct or silence, but it must be a representation of existing fact and not a representation of law or of intention.

In *Société Internationale de Télécommunications Aeronatiques (No 2)* (VTD 17991) (TVC 2.113) a Belgian company (S) operated a telecommunications network for aircraft. In 1973, HMRC issued a ruling that its supplies should be standard-rated but a tribunal allowed an appeal by S that its supplies should be treated as zero-rated (VTD 19) (TVC 66.45). In 1997 HMRC issued a further ruling that the supplies were standard-rated. S appealed contending, amongst other things, that HMRC were bound by the earlier tribunal decision. The tribunal rejected this and held that the 1973 decision did not give rise to any estoppel, observing that the public policy behind the general application of issue estoppel is to ensure the finality of litigation. In taxation cases, however, that aspect of public policy has been overridden by a different element of public policy. Where recurring business transactions, which fall to be assessed period by period, are involved (as is the case of supplies of a VAT-registered trader), administrative flexibility is needed to enable the even-handed management of the revenue. To impose on a trader the unalterable privilege or disadvantage of a particular tax treatment of his supplies as the result of a decision of a tribunal or court might lead to inequity as between him and other traders making similar supplies the liability of which had been determined at a later date. The principle of public policy that applies in that situation is that of ensuring that the tax operates uniformly.

It has been held that there is no question of estoppel against HMRC (*Cupboard Love Ltd* (VTD 267) (TVC 2.99)), the Crown (*T Wood* (VTD 6992) (TVC 2.104)) or the mandatory provisions of a taxing statute (*Medlam* (VTD 545) (TVC 2.101)). More specifically, there is no claim if the element of detriment or prejudice is lacking e.g. where on advice VAT has been incorrectly calculated but the taxpayer has had the benefit of the cash he should have accounted for at the time and there is no evidence that he has charged lower prices because of the advice (*Ribbans* (VTD 346) (TVC 2.100)). It has also been held that an inspection of a trader's records and a general assurance that they are in order is insufficient to form the basis of an estoppel (*GUS Merchandise Corporation Ltd* (VTD 553) (TVC 2.119)).

Scotland

In Scotland, the equivalent of estoppel is a plea of personal bar. It has been held that such a plea, at all events in matters of taxation, does not operate against the Crown, following *Lord Advocate v Meiklam*, (1860) 22 D 1427 (TVC 2.109) and other authorities (*Milne and Mackintosh (t/a Jack and Jill)* (VTD 1063) (TVC 2.109, 2.110)).

HMRC's practice where taxpayer misled by an officer

The HMRC online guidance "When you can rely on advice provided by HMRC" states that where HMRC provide information or advice that is incorrect in law, they are bound by such advice provided that it is clear, unequivocal and explicit and the taxpayer can demonstrate that: he reasonably relied on the advice; where appropriate, he made full disclosure of all the relevant facts; and the application of the statute would result in his financial detriment. Where this is the case, to apply the statute may be so unfair that it could amount to an abuse of power. But, where HMRC have given incorrect information or advice, their primary duty always remains to collect the correct amount of tax as required by the law. Therefore there will be some circumstances where they will not be bound by the advice they have given. Where HMRC provide erroneous advice that is binding on them and subsequently notify the taxpayer that it is incorrect, the established legal position is that the taxpayer will only be required to start accounting for tax on the correct basis from the date of notification. (HMRC Brief 15/09).

De Voil Indirect Tax Service. See V1.286; V1.287.

Evidence by certificate, etc.

[32.16] A certificate of HMRC of any of the following is sufficient evidence of that fact until proved to the contrary.

- A person was, or was not, at any date, registered.
- Any return required has not been made or had not been made at any date.
- Any EU sales list (see **2.11 ACCOUNTING PERIODS AND RETURNS**) has not been submitted or had not been submitted by any given date.
- Notification of liability on an acquisition of exciseable goods or a new means of transport (see **20.9** and **20.37 EUROPEAN UNION: SINGLE MARKET**) has not been given or had not been given by any date.
- A person was or was not, at any date, taxable in another EU member state.
- Any VAT payable under the law of another EU member state has or has not been paid.

A photograph of any document furnished to HMRC, certified by them, is admissible in any civil or criminal proceeding to the same extent as the document itself.

Any document purporting to be a certificate under the above provisions is deemed to be such a certificate until the contrary is proved.

[*VATA 1994, s 92(5), Sch 11 para 14*].

Subject to any provision treating a certificate as *conclusive* evidence, a certificate of an HMRC officer that, to the best of that officer's knowledge and belief, any VAT has not been paid is *sufficient* evidence that the sum mentioned in the certificate is unpaid. Any document purporting to be such a certificate is treated as if it were such a certificate until the contrary is proved.

[*CRCA 2005, s 25A*].

Tax agents

[32.17] From 1 April 2013 HMRC have been given powers to obtain documents from tax agents who engage in dishonest conduct, impose penalties on them (see **53.40 PENALTIES**) and publish their details. For criminal offences in relation to tax agents see **53.39 PENALTIES**.

HMRC may, by notice (a 'file access notice'), require the production of 'relevant documents' by

- a tax agent (i.e. an individual who, in the course of business, assists other persons with their tax affairs); or
- any other person who HMRC believe may hold such documents.

The person to whom a file access notice is given is referred to as 'the document-holder'. A file access notice may only be given where the tribunal's approval has been given, and

- (Case A) where a conduct notice (see **53.40 PENALTIES**) has been given to an individual (the tax agent) and either
  - (i) the time allowed for giving notice of appeal against the determination has expired without any such notice being given; or
  - (ii) notice of appeal against the determination was given within that time, but the appeal has been withdrawn or the determination confirmed; or
- (Case B) where
  - (i) an individual (the tax agent) has been convicted of an offence relating to tax that involves fraud or dishonesty;
  - (ii) the offence was committed after the individual became a tax agent (whether or not the individual was still a tax agent when it was committed and regardless of the capacity in which it was committed);
  - (iii) either the time allowed for appealing against the conviction has expired without any such appeal being brought, or an appeal against the conviction was brought within that time, but the appeal has been withdrawn or the conviction upheld; and
  - (iv) no more than twelve months have elapsed since the date on which (iii) was satisfied.

A determination or conviction which is appealed is not considered to have been confirmed or upheld until the time for bringing any further appeal has expired, or if a further appeal is brought, that further appeal has been withdrawn or determined.

File access notice

A file access notice may require the production of specified relevant documents, or all relevant documents in the document-holder's possession or power. It does not need to identify the clients of the tax agent, but if it is addressed to someone other than the tax agent, it must name the tax agent. The notice may require documents to be provided within such period, by such means and in such form, and to such persons and at such place, as is reasonably specified in the notice or document referred to therein. Copies of the documents specified will suffice unless a contrary indication is given.

HMRC may take copies or extracts of documents provided pursuant to a file access notice. They may also retain such documents if they consider it necessary, but must provide the document-holder with copies free of charge on request, and compensate the document-holder if they lose any documents.

Exclusions

A document-holder cannot be required to provide

- a document which is not within his possession or power;
- parts of a document that contain information relating to the conduct of a pending appeal relating to tax;
- journalistic material (as defined in the *Police and Criminal Evidence Act 1984, s 13*);
- personal records (as defined in the *Police and Criminal Evidence Act 1984, s 12*), although he may be required to produce such documents omitting such information whose inclusion makes the documents personal records;
- a relevant document if the whole of the document originated before the first day of the period of 20 years ending with the day on which the file access notice is given, and no part of it has a bearing on tax periods ending on or after that day;
- any part of a document that is privileged.

Relevant documents

'Relevant documents' means the tax agent's working papers (whenever acting as a tax agent) and any other documents received, created, prepared or used by the tax agent for the purposes of or in the course of assisting clients with their tax affairs. It does not matter who owns the papers or other documents.

[*FA 2012, Sch 38 paras 2, 7–19; SI 2013/279*].

Key points — HMRC: powers

[32.18] Points to consider are as follows.

- HMRC has the power to request security from a taxpayer when it considers there is a potential risk to the revenue that VAT charged to customers may not be paid and declared when returns are submitted. This decision is usually made when a business is managed or owned by a person or persons who have previously been involved with a business that has failed with a major debt owing to the crown. The HMRC approach is justified by the need to 'protect the revenue'. Experience shows that a VAT tribunal rarely supports a taxpayer who challenges an HMRC request for security. The tribunal's power is limited to deciding whether HMRC has acted reasonably in requesting security from a taxpayer – the tribunal cannot substitute its own decision, even if it feels an alternative measure was more appropriate in the circumstances.

- It is very important that a business checks that its suppliers are correctly charging VAT. A basic principle of VAT law is that a business can only reclaim correctly charged VAT as input tax. This requires the business to ensure that the supplier is registered for VAT (showing VAT registration number on tax invoices etc.) and that the goods or services in question are standard-rated rather than zero-rated or exempt. Although HMRC will not generally hold a customer responsible for any fraudulent actions of the supplier (assuming he was not aware of such intentions), it is important that a business receiving goods or services carries out reasonable checks to ensure a charge of VAT has been correctly made by a bona-fide business.
- It is important that advisers know how MTIC (Missing Trader Intra-Community Fraud) works and the main goods used by the fraudsters. This is not only to ensure they do not act for fraudulent companies but also to advise innocent traders of the potential risks of receiving illegal goods in a supply chain.
- Recent court cases have supported HMRC's strategy of disallowing input tax on the purchase of any fraudulent goods (assuming they are 'relevant goods' as defined in the legislation, i.e. mobile phones etc.) if it can prove that the trader had reason to suspect that the goods were part of an illegal supply chain where output tax was unlikely to be declared by the supplier. The onus is on HMRC to prove that the trader knew or ought to have known that he was dealing in goods where the intention was to fraudulently evade VAT.
- It is important that all traders in 'relevant' high-risk goods take adequate measures to 'ensure the integrity of their supply chain'. HMRC does not provide an exhaustive list of the measures that need to be taken – but it gives very clear guidelines as to the issues that should be considered.
- HMRC officers have the power to demand the production of documents to check a taxpayer's tax position, as long as the demand is given in writing to the taxpayer. Other powers include the right to open machines on which relevant machine games are played and the right to take away samples to check the VAT position of the goods in question. An officer also has the right to inspect premises where goods or services are supplied by a

business but not in relation to the private dwelling of a taxpayer. Separate provisions also give an officer the power to copy computer records but not to physically remove the computer itself.

- VAT visits are now carried out by HMRC officers largely on the basis of 'risk' factors. A business that is partly exempt, or has transactions where the VAT liability is complex, may expect to receive more regular visits than say a small business using the flat rate scheme. Equally, a business that has submitted a lot of error notifications for large amounts may also receive a visit if it is suspected that accounting controls in the business are not particularly strong. The aim of any VAT-registered business should be to ensure checks and procedures are in place to confirm that figures declared on VAT returns are accurate and complete. This is particularly important now that past errors (underpayments as well as overpayments) can be corrected going back four years rather than three and heavy penalties could be charged if 'careless behaviour' has caused underpayments of VAT.
- A taxpayer can acquire protection regarding the VAT treatment of a transaction if he has received a written ruling from HMRC confirming the procedure to adopt. However, this ruling will only give protection if the taxpayer has fully disclosed all relevant facts and information about the transaction at the time of requesting a decision. The information provided must also be complete and accurate. If a key piece of information is subsequently found to be missing, then HMRC could overrule their written guidance and seek to collect VAT on a retrospective basis. This could apply if, for example, a product has been incorrectly treated as zero-rated on the basis of incorrect data provided by the taxpayer to HMRC.

33

Hotels and Holiday Accommodation

Cross-reference. See **69 TOUR OPERATORS' MARGIN SCHEME.**
De Voil Indirect Tax Service. See V4.113.

Introduction to hotels and holiday accommodation

Supplies of accommodation

[33.1] The provision in a hotel, inn, boarding house or 'similar establishment' of

(a) sleeping accommodation;
(b) accommodation in rooms which are provided in conjunction therewith (e.g. private bathrooms and sitting-rooms in suites); and
(c) accommodation for the purpose of a supply of catering

is standard-rated.

'*Similar establishment*' includes premises in which there is provided furnished sleeping accommodation (with or without board or facilities for the preparation of food) and which are used by or held out as being suitable for use by visitors or travellers.

[*VATA 1994, Sch 9 Group 1 Item 1(d)*].

Accommodation in motels, guest houses, bed and breakfast establishments, private residential clubs, hostels and serviced flats (other than those for permanent residential use) is included. In most cases such establishments will provide one or more meals, possibly at an inclusive price, but board, or the facilities for the preparation of food, is *not* necessary for an establishment to be regarded as a hotel, etc. (VAT Notice 709/3/13, para 2.1).

See also *International Student House* (VTD 14420) (TVC 41.103) where buildings were not held to be 'similar establishments' and fees for accommodation were held to be exempt because the charity was providing the accommodation to help overseas students and improve international relations. But compare *Acorn Management Services Ltd* (VTD 17338) (VTD 41.103) where accommodation for US students was held to be standard-rated.

In *Namecourt Ltd* (VTD 1560) (TVC 41.106) the tribunal held that *Item 1(d)* above was directed at the sort of establishment which provided accommodation for a transient or floating class of resident. It could be long-term (see also *McGrath v C & E Commrs*, QB [1992] STC 371 (TVC 41.113)) or short-term but it was accommodation which a person would go to with a view to moving on from in due course.

A lodge used to provide supervised residential accommodation for people with mental health problems was held not to be a 'similar establishment' in *Dinaro Ltd (t/a Fairway Lodge)* (VTD 17148) (TVC 41.108).

Accommodation used for catering

Where accommodation is supplied in a hotel, etc. for the purpose of a supply of catering, the supply is standard-rated under (*c*) above whatever the length of the let. Thus, wedding receptions, private parties and other functions held in hotels, etc. are fully taxed. See *Willerby Manor Hotels Ltd* (VTD 16673) (TVC 41.120) where the tribunal held that, following the decision in *Card Protection Plan Ltd v C & E Commrs, ECJ Case C–349/96*, [1999] STC 270 (TVC 22.362), the hire of a function room for an evening reception was a supply ancillary to those of wedding reception facilities and the company had made a composite supply of standard-rated wedding reception facilities, the main ingredient of which was a supply of catering.

(VAT Notice 709/3/13, para 4.1).

Hotel conference/function facilities

Hotels and similar establishments often provide rooms for meetings, conferences and similar functions organised by third parties, making inclusive charges per delegate. Unless the primary purpose for the use of the room is a supply of catering (in which case the supply is always standard-rated) the VAT liability depends on the requirements of individual delegates.

- *Delegates requiring use of the conference room only*. The supply by the hotel is exempt from VAT (unless an option to tax has been made).
- *Delegates requiring use of conference room plus meal(s) ('8 hour conference delegate rate')*. Each element is treated as a separate supply. The conference room element is exempt from VAT (unless an option to tax has been made) but the part of the consideration relating to the provision of food is standard-rated (unless the provision of refreshments is minimal, such as tea and biscuits).
- *Delegates requiring use of conference room plus meals plus overnight sleeping accommodation ('24 hour conference delegate rate')*. HMRC accept that supplies under the 24 hour delegate rate, even where made in return for an inclusive charge, should be treated as separate supplies. These are taxable supplies, with the exception of the conference/function room hire, which is an exempt supply, unless the

hotel has opted to tax its supplies. In cases where a single consideration is paid for supplies having different liabilities, a fair and reasonable apportionment of the consideration must be made.

Where hotels organise and run conferences or similar events themselves and charge for entry to delegates, their supplies are always taxable supplies.

As a result of the above rules, some hotels will make exempt supplies and the input tax that they incur may be subject to restriction under the partial exemption rules. If hotels prefer, they can continue to treat their supplies as taxable (and be entitled to continue claiming their input tax in full) by opting to tax.

(Business Brief 1/06).

Any goods or services provided such as restaurants, car parking, use of equipment, licensed bars, commissions from taxi firms, or goods or services charged for separately, are standard-rated.

Stays over four weeks

[33.2] For the first four weeks of any stay VAT is due on the full amount payable in the normal way.

Where accommodation within **33.1** above is *provided to an individual* for a period exceeding four weeks, from the 29th day of the stay (or letting) VAT is only due on

(a) meals, drinks and service charges; and
(b) facilities provided apart from the right to occupy the accommodation (i.e. the value of the accommodation is excluded from the VAT calculation).

The value of the facilities subject to VAT under (*b*) above must not be less than 20% of the total amount due for those facilities and the accommodation.

Throughout the period the accommodation must be provided *for the use of the individual* either alone or with one or more other persons who occupy the accommodation with him but not either directly or indirectly at their own expense.

[*VATA 1994, Sch 6 para 9*].

The rule does not apply to bookings by companies where the accommodation is used by a succession of short-term occupants, and each stay is less than 29 days at a time (e.g. it does no apply where airlines make block bookings of hotel accommodation for crew stopovers). However, where the supply is made to someone other than the individual who will be using the accommodation, but the stay by the individual is for more than 28 days, then the rule does apply. This often occurs where the supply of accommodation for homeless people is made to a local authority. In such cases the reduced value applies from the 29th day of each individual's stay. See also *Afro-Caribbean Housing Association Ltd* (VTD 19450) (TVC 67.94).

(VAT Notice 709/3/13, para 3.3).

Example

Weekly terms for accommodation, facilities and meals are £720 (£600 plus £120 VAT) of which £288 (£240 + £48 VAT) represents the charge for meals. For the first 4 weeks, the VAT charge is the full £120 but thereafter a reduced VAT value may be calculated in one of the following ways. The proportion for meals has been taken to be 40% but this will not always be so.

(a) *If charges are expressed in VAT-exclusive terms*

	£	£
Total VAT-exclusive weekly charge	600.00	
VAT-exclusive charge for meals	240.00	48.00
	£360.00	
VAT-exclusive value of facilities (20% minimum)	72.00	14.40
VAT due		£62.40

Weekly terms are therefore £600.00 + £62.40 VAT.

(b) *If charges are expressed in VAT-inclusive terms and the total amount charged to the guest is reduced to take account of the reduced element of VAT*

VAT is as under (*a*) above but the calculation is

	£	£
Total VAT-inclusive charge	720.00	
VAT-inclusive charge for meals	288.00	48.00
VAT-inclusive charge for facilities and accommodation	432.00	
VAT included 1/6 × £423	72.00	
Balance (exclusive of VAT)	£360.00	
VAT-exclusive value of facilities (20% minimum)	72.00	14.40
VAT due		£62.40

The weekly terms are £600 + £62.40 VAT.

(c) *If charges are expressed in VAT-inclusive terms but the total amount charged to the guest is not reduced to take account of the reduced element of VAT*

	£	£
Total VAT inclusive charge	720.00	
VAT-inclusive charge for meals	288.00	48.00
VAT-inclusive charge for facilities and accommodation	432.00	
VAT included 1/26 × £423	16.62	16.62
VAT-exclusive charge for facilities and accommodation	£415.38	
Total VAT		£64.62

The weekly terms are not reduced (i.e. £720 including £64.62 VAT).

* = (20 × facilities element %) ÷ (100 + [20 × facilities element %])

= 1/26 where the facilities element is 20%

Although VAT is only due on the reduced amount, the full VAT-exclusive amount (£600.00 in (*a*) and (*b*) and £655.38 in (*c*)) must be included in Box 6 of the VAT return. This is because the accommodation element of the total charge continues to be the consideration for a standard-rated supply even though the value for the purposes of calculating the VAT becomes nil after the first four weeks.

Breaks in stays

Normally, the reduced value rules above cannot be used unless the guest stays for a continuous period of more than four weeks. For example, stays of three weeks in every month are subject to VAT in full. Similarly, if a guest stays for five weeks, is away for a week and then returns for five weeks, each stay is treated separately and the reduced value basis can only be used for the fifth week of each stay. There are exceptions to this. Before 1 April 2015, a guest's departure is not treated as ending a stay if the guest

- is a long-term resident and leaves for an occasional weekend or holiday; or
- is a student who leaves during the vacation but returns to the same accommodation for the next term; or
- pays a retaining fee.

In such cases, the stay is treated as continuous and VAT need only be charged in full for the first four weeks of the overall stay. A guest need not necessarily occupy the same room for his stay to be treated as continuous.

If a retaining fee is paid for a period of absence during the first four weeks of a stay, VAT is due on it at the standard rate. If paid for a period of absence after that period, then the reduced value rules above apply. Provided the fee is no more than the amount treated as payment for accommodation, no VAT is due. Otherwise the fee must be treated as payment for both accommodation and facilities using the rules outlined above.

(VAT Notice 709/3/13, paras 3.3, 7.4).

From 1 April 2015 the departure of a long-term resident for an occasional weekend or holiday and the departure of a student during the vacation is treated as ending their stay, and their return is treated as starting a new period of occupation, unless they have a continuing right to occupy the room, or a similar room in the same establishment, throughout the period when they are absent.

(HMRC technical note issued on 31 January 2014).

Breaks in stays from 1 April 2015

On 31 January 2014 HMRC published a technical note advising that with effect from 1 April 2015 hotels, inns, boarding houses and similar establishments must treat all breaks in the guest's stay as starting a new period for the purposes of the 28-day rule, unless the guest can return at any time and continue their occupancy of the room, or a similar room, as if they had never vacated it.

Accommodation and catering supplied by employers to employees

[33.3] The value of catering or accommodation in a hotel, etc. supplied by an employer to its employees is to be taken to be nil unless made for a consideration wholly or partly in money in which case the value is determined without regard to any consideration other than money. [*VATA 1994, Sch 6 para 10*].

If employees are supplied with accommodation or food and drink in the employer's establishment and they pay for it, the payments are treated as including VAT which the employer must account for on its VAT return.

Where employees pay for meals and so on from their pay, including under a salary sacrifice arrangement, employers must account for VAT on such supplies unless they are zero-rated. The reduced value provisions in **33.2** above may apply to accommodation. (VAT Notice 709/3/13, para 4.2).

In *Goodfellow* (VTD 2107) (TVC 62.13) it was decided that where employees were paid a minimum wage under a *Wages Order* for an industry and that *Order* allowed for appropriate reductions to be made for catering and accommodation, those calculations were steps in arriving at the amount of the weekly wage to be paid and were *not* monetary consideration on which the employer was liable to VAT.

Deposits, cancellation charges, booking fees and retention fees

[33.4] Most deposits are advance payments on which VAT must be accounted for in the return period in which they are received. If a deposit has to be refunded, any VAT accounted for can be reclaimed.

HMRC state that if a cancellation charge is made when a customer cancels a booking, no VAT is due on the charge (because it is not a payment in respect of a supply). They also indicate that, if the customer has to forfeit a deposit, any VAT accounted for on the deposit can be reclaimed. See also *Société Thermale d'Eugénie-les-Bains v Ministère de l'Économie, des Finances et de l'Industrie, ECJ Case C–277/05* (unreported) (TVC 22.91) where the court held that a deposit in relation to standard-rated hotel services must be regarded, where the purchaser uses a cancellation option available and the deposit is retained by the hotelier, as a fixed cancellation charge paid as compensation for the loss suffered as a result of the client default and which has no direct connection with the supply of any service for a consideration. As such, it is not subject to VAT. The earlier decision in *C & E Commrs v Bass plc*, QB 1992, [1993] STC 42 (TVC 62.93) (where the court held that charges levied on customers who book hotel accommodation but do not take up that accommodation are subject to VAT as making the room available is a supply for VAT purposes) must now be read in the light of the CJEU decision.

If a business arranges or provides a guarantee or insurance against a customer having to pay a cancellation charge, the charge may be exempt if the business has a block insurance policy. See **37.6 INSURANCE**. Also, if the business arranges for insurance to be provided to the customer along with the goods or services supplied and, under the policy, it is the individual customer's risk which is insured, the supply by the business of arranging the insurance may be exempt providing certain disclosure requirements are met. See **37.17 INSURANCE**.

Booking fees charged by a person supplying accommodation are treated as deposits above. Booking fees charged by agents who arrange a supply on behalf of someone else are the consideration for a taxable supply and VAT is due whether or not the accommodation is taken up.

Retention fees paid to reserve accommodation for future use are standard-rated (but see **33.2** above for retention fees paid for a period of absence after the first 28 days).

(VAT Notice 700, para 8.13; VAT Notice 709/3/13, paras 7.1–7.4).

Holiday accommodation, etc. in the UK

[33.5] The grant of any interest in or right over or licence to occupy 'holiday accommodation' is standard-rated. *Included* is

- the grant of an interest in, or in any part of, a building designed as a dwelling or number of dwellings or the site of such a building if
  - (a) the interest granted is such that the grantee is not entitled to reside in the building, or part, throughout the year; or
  - (b) residence there throughout the year, or the use of the building or part as the grantee's principal private residence, is prevented by the terms of a covenant, statutory planning consent or similar permission; and
- any supply made pursuant to a tenancy, lease or licence under which the grantee is or has been permitted to erect and occupy holiday accommodation.

Excluded (and therefore exempt) is the grant of the fee simple, or a tenancy, lease or licence to the extent it is granted for consideration in the form of a premium, in a building or part which is not a 'new building'. A '*new building*' is one completed less than three years before the grant.

'*Holiday accommodation*' includes any accommodation in a building, hut (including a beach hut or chalet), caravan, houseboat or tent which is advertised or held out as holiday accommodation or as suitable for holiday or leisure use, but excludes any accommodation within **33.1** above. Residential accommodation that happens to be situated in a holiday resort is not necessarily holiday accommodation.

See **42.8 LAND AND BUILDINGS: EXEMPT SUPPLIES AND OPTION TO TAX** for the meaning of '*interest in or right over*' and **42.9 LAND AND BUILDINGS: EXEMPT SUPPLIES AND OPTION TO TAX** '*licence to occupy*'.

[*VATA 1994, Sch 9 Group 1 Item 1(e), Notes 11–13*].

The effect of the above is that the sale or lease of a house, flat or other accommodation is generally standard-rated as holiday accommodation if the property is new and the purchaser cannot reside there throughout the year or use it as his principal private residence. VAT must be accounted for on the initial charge and on any periodic charges such as ground rent and service or other charges. If the accommodation is no longer new, any payment for the freehold or premium under the lease is exempt but any periodic charges, including rent and service charges, are standard-rated. However, following the tribunal decision in *Ashworth (Mrs B)* (VTD 12924) (TVC 41.138), the sale or lease of a flat or house which can be used as a person's principal private residence but which cannot be occupied throughout the year due to a time-related restriction on occupancy (in *Ashworth* the lessees were unable to occupy the property for the month of February each year) is exempt provided the development on which the property is situated is not a holiday development and is not advertised or held out as such. This also applies to any periodic charges such as rent and service charges.

The provision of a site for holiday accommodation under a tenancy, lease or licence is standard-rated even if the person to whom the site is provided is responsible for erecting the accommodation on it.

(VAT Notice 709/3/13, paras 5.1, 5.3, 5.4).

See *RW and B Sheppard* (VTD 481) (TVC 41.127) for a case concerning short letting of furnished flats treated as holiday accommodation in which the above tests were considered.

Even where a property has been 'held out' as holiday accommodation, where there is no causative nexus between the publication of the advertisement of holiday accommodation and the letting of the whole building for some different purpose, there is no provision of holiday accommodation. See *Cooper and Chapman (Builders) Ltd v C & E Commrs*, QB 1992, [1993] STC 1 (TVC 46.219).

The Upper Tribunal held that supplies of fractional ownership interests in a property that enable the purchaser to occupy the residence at the property for a maximum number of nights each year, should be treated as an exempt grant of a right to occupy a residence. The supply of the right to occupy a reserved residence should not be treated as the standard-rated supply of holiday accommodation as it was not a supply of a series of short-term stays but the supply of a long-term right to occupy a reserved residence during the relevant periods. As the Upper Tribunal overturned the decision reached by the First-tier Tribunal about whether the accommodation should be treated as holiday accommodation, HMRC may appeal against this decision. See *Forty-seven Park Street Ltd v HMRC* [2018] UKUT 41 (TCC), [2018] STC 541 (TVC 41.126).

Options to purchase interests or rights

The grant of any right to call for or to be granted an interest or right which would be standard-rated under the provisions above is also standard-rated. *Included* is an equitable right, a right under an option or right of pre-emption and, in relation to Scotland, a personal right. [*VATA 1994, Sch 9 Group 1 Item 1(n)*].

Value for VAT purposes

VAT is payable on the full amount due for the holiday accommodation, including incidental services, irrespective of the length of the stay. (See **33.2** above for long stay arrangements in hotels, etc.) (VAT Notice 709/3/13, para 5.8).

Deposits, cancellation charges and booking fees

See **33.4** above.

Off-season letting

[33.6] Holiday accommodation let during the off-season can be treated as exempt from VAT provided

- it is let to a person as residential accommodation;
- it is let for more than 28 days; and
- holiday trade in the area is clearly seasonal.

A copy of the tenancy agreement or similar evidence should be kept to show that the accommodation was occupied for residential purposes only. In such cases the whole of the let, including the first 28 days, can be treated as an exempt supply.

The holiday season normally lasts from Easter to the end of September, though some areas such as London and Edinburgh are not regarded as having a seasonal holiday trade.

(VAT Notice 709/3/13, para 5.6).

See, however, **42.23 LAND AND BUILDINGS: EXEMPT SUPPLIES AND OPTION TO TAX** for the option to tax such lettings.

Time-share and multi-ownership schemes

[33.7] A supply of holiday accommodation in a house, flat, chalet, etc. under a time-share or multi-ownership scheme is standard-rated if the supply is of 'new' accommodation. The supply of a timeshare, etc. in a property that is not new is exempt to the extent that the grant is made for a consideration in the form of a premium. A property is '*new*' if completed less than three years before the grant. Rent payments made after the initial lump sum, and any annual management fees and service charges, are standard-rated in all cases. (VAT Notice 709/3/13, para 5.7).

See *American Real Estate (Scotland) Ltd* [1980] VATTR 80 (TVC 41.129). Time-shares, etc. cannot be zero-rated as tenancies for a term certain exceeding 21 years (or Scottish equivalent) within the definition of 'major interest'.

[*VATA 1994, Sch 8 Group 5 Item 1 and Note 13; SI 1995/280*]. See also *Cottage Holiday Associates Ltd v C & E Commrs*, QB 1982, [1983] STC 278 (TVC 15.197) and *Mr & Mrs Cretney* (VTD 1503) (TVC 41.130) where an option to purchase freehold reversion was also offered.

For time-sharing of a yacht based abroad, see *Oathplan Ltd* [1983] 1 CMLR 191 (TVC 41.132).

Construction of holiday accommodation

[33.8] A builder can zero-rate the supply of services in the course of construction of a dwelling even though it will be used to supply holiday accommodation. The word 'dwelling' takes on its normal everyday meaning.

Caravans and camping

[33.9] Holiday accommodation provided in any type of caravan already sited on a pitch is standard-rated. (The provision of *other* accommodation in such a caravan is exempt.)

[*VATA 1994, Sch 8 Group 9 Item 3; Sch 9 Group 1 Item 1(e)*]. (VAT Notice 709/3/13, para 6.2).

Caravan pitches

See **42.18**(*e*) **LAND AND BUILDINGS: EXEMPT SUPPLIES AND OPTION TO TAX** for caravan pitches.

Camping

The provision of holiday accommodation in a tent is standard-rated. [*VATA 1994, Sch 9 Group 1 Item (e)*]. Any associated facilities are also standard-rated. See **42.18**(*e*) **LAND AND BUILDINGS: EXEMPT SUPPLIES AND OPTION TO TAX** for tent pitches.

Key points: hotels and holiday accommodation

[33.10] Points to consider are as follows.

- The basic principle that renting land is exempt from VAT (*VATA 1994, Sch 9, Group 1*) is overridden in cases where accommodation is provided in a hotel, inn or similar establishment. In such cases, the supply is standard-rated. It is important to recognise that the accommodation charge is still standard-rated in such cases, even if no catering is provided as part of the deal. So a 'room only' booking in a hotel will be standard-rated in exactly the same way as a 'bed and breakfast' arrangement. It is the nature of the facility that counts, i.e. furnished accommodation usually for short-term occupancy provided by an establishment similar to a hotel.
- There have been a number of VAT tribunal cases over the years regarding the definition of a 'similar establishment' to a hotel. There can be grey areas, but a key indicator has often been the

fact that the facility is provided on a furnished basis for the use (generally) of short term visitors who generally move on to alternative accommodation within a short space of time, i.e. holiday makers, tourists, visitors on short term breaks etc.

- In the case of a hotel providing an inclusive package to delegates at a conference or similar event (for example, a 24-hour delegate package to include food, overnight accommodation and the hire of a room), then the element of the charge for room hire is exempt from VAT. This assumes there is no option to tax election in place on the building, in which case this element of the charge will also be standard rated.
- The exempt element of the delegate charge above will produce an output tax saving (very useful if the customer(s) are not VAT-registered or using the venue for private or non-business purposes, e.g. a wedding function) but means that the hotel business is partly exempt. The ideal situation would then be that there is no input tax block through partial exemption rules because of the 'de minimis' limits (see **50.11**). In basic terms, if a partly-exempt business is within the *de minimis* limits, then it obtains full input tax recovery (subject to normal rules), including recovery on those costs relating to its exempt activities.
- An individual staying in a hotel or similar establishment will not be charged VAT on his accommodation charges, once he has stayed in the hotel for four weeks. However, the other services provided by the venue as part of the deal (catering, service charges etc.) are still standard-rated and this element must represent at least 20% of the payment he makes. The facility also extends to bookings made through an organisation (e.g. a charity or housing association), as long as the same person is staying in the hotel room.
- No output tax is payable on free food or accommodation provided by a hotel to its employees – the value of the supply is taken to be nil. However, output tax will be payable on any contribution made by employees towards their food or accommodation, including any deductions made from their wages.
- A deposit received from a customer to secure a hotel booking is classed as an advance payment and therefore creates a tax point for VAT purposes. However, if the customer does not arrive to take up his booking, and sacrifices the deposit, then the output tax accounted for by the hotel can be reclaimed because the payment then represents a cancellation charge. A cancellation charge is outside the scope of VAT because the customer (hotel guest) has received no supply of goods or services in return for his payment.
- Holiday accommodation is always standard-rated – the key issue is how the accommodation is held out for sale and advertised. So accommodation provided in a holiday cottage, holiday flat, caravan or tent at a camp site would always be standard-rated. In the cases of caravan lettings, there is usually an exclusion to prevent twelve-month occupation, i.e. so that the caravan cannot

be classed as a residential letting. This is not always the overriding factor in confirming whether an arrangement is classed as holiday accommodation but it is often a key factor.

- Holiday accommodation rented out as residential accommodation during the 'off season' period (usually between October and Easter) can qualify for VAT exemption if certain conditions are met. The accommodation must be intended to serve as the main residence of the tenant for the period of the agreement, and must be for at least 28 days. In such cases, the whole of the letting period can qualify for VAT exemption. There should be evidence of a residential arrangement, i.e. letting agreement, contract with terms etc.
- A useful concession is that building services provided by a builder to construct new holiday accommodation for a developer or landlord can still qualify for zero-rating as work being carried out on a new dwelling (e.g. a block of holiday flats). The zero-rating would extend to any materials provided by the builder as part of his work.

34

Imports

Cross-references. See **27.7 GOLD AND PRECIOUS METALS** for importations of gold; **39.4 INTERNATIONAL SERVICES** for imported services; **53.34–53.37 PENALTIES** for penalties for evasion of, and non-compliance with, import VAT; **72.15 VALUATION** for valuation of imports; **73 WAREHOUSED GOODS**; **74.3**, **74.4** and **74.5 WORKS OF ART, ETC.** for importations and reimportations.

De Voil Indirect Tax Service. See V3.301–358.

Introduction to imports

Trade with other EU member states

[34.1] The provisions of this chapter only apply to importations of goods from outside the EU. See **20.2 EUROPEAN UNION: GENERAL** for the VAT territory of the EU. For the provisions relating to acquisitions of goods from other EU member states, see **20.3 EUROPEAN UNION: SINGLE MARKET.**

Cyprus

The European Commission has advised that the application of *Directive 2006/112/EC* is to be suspended in those areas of Cyprus in which the Government of the Republic of Cyprus does not exercise control. Goods from these areas continue to be treated as imports.

The Isle of Man

Although not part of the UK, the Isle of Man is treated as part of the UK for VAT purposes. VAT is chargeable in the Isle of Man under Manx law which generally parallels UK legislation. Goods removed from the Isle of Man to the UK are not normally treated as imports provided any VAT has been accounted for in the Isle of Man or, if the goods were relieved of VAT in the Isle of Man, the conditions of that relief have not been broken. However, where goods are removed from the Isle of Man into the UK and were charged to VAT in the Isle of Man at a different rate to that applicable in the UK (or were relieved from VAT subject to a condition which was not subsequently complied with) the difference in the tax will be charged in the UK. [*SI 1982/1067, Art 3*]. (VAT Notice 702, para 1.7).

The Channel Islands and Gibraltar

The Channel Islands are part of the Customs territory of the EU but not part of the VAT territory. Any goods received from the Channel Islands are therefore regarded as imports.

Gibraltar is not regarded as being part of the EU for VAT or customs duty purposes. Any goods received from Gibraltar are regarded as imports.

(VAT Notice 702, section 9).

Economic Operator Registration and Identification (EORI)

All regular importers of goods from outside the EU are given an Economic Operator Registration and Identification (EORI). In the UK this number comprises the letters 'GB' followed by the importer's VAT registration number plus a three-digit suffix. Computer-generated VAT certificates (Form C79) are sent to the importer whose EORI is shown on the import entry. Since Form C79 constitutes evidence of entitlement to input tax, the use of the correct EORI is essential to ensure that the import VAT appears on the correct certificate.

(VAT Notice 702, paras 8.2, 8.7).

The charge to VAT

[34.2] VAT is charged and payable on the importation of goods into the UK (which for VAT purposes includes the territorial sea of the UK i.e. waters within twelve nautical miles of the coastline) as if it were a duty of customs. The rate of VAT is the same as if the goods had been supplied in the UK (whether or not the person importing the goods is registered for VAT). The VAT is chargeable in addition to any customs and/or excise duty or other charges due and is calculated on the value which includes such charges. See **72.15 VALUATION.**

CEMA 1979 and other UK legislation relating to customs or excise duties charged on importation into the UK and any Union legislation relating to customs duties charged on goods entering the EU, apply in modified form so as to relate to VAT on importations.

Goods are treated as imported from a place outside the EU where

- they arrive in the UK directly from outside the EU and are entered for free circulation in the UK (or customs duty otherwise becomes payable on them); or
- they have been placed, in another EU member state or in the UK, under one of the customs arrangements listed in **34.25** below and are entered for free circulation in the UK (or customs duty otherwise becomes chargeable on them).

[*VATA 1994, s 1(1)(4), s 2(1), s 15, s 16, s 96(11)*].

Example

Jean is VAT-registered in the UK and has imported 500 special plant pots at a cost of £20 each from a supplier in Hong Kong (outside the EU). The plant pots will attract Customs duty of £10 each when they arrive in the UK.

VAT is charged and payable on the importation of goods into the UK – and the VAT is charged on the value of the goods, including customs duty. The total amount of VAT charged on the importation is £3,000 (500 x £30 x 20%) and Jean can reclaim this amount in Box 4 of her next VAT return. No entry is needed in Box 9 of the return because the purchase is not an acquisition of goods from another EU member state.

Time of importation

The time of importation of any goods is

- where brought by sea, when the ship carrying them comes within the limits of a port;
- where brought by air, when the aircraft carrying them lands in the UK or when the goods are unloaded in the UK, whichever is the earlier;
- where brought by land, when the goods are brought across the boundary into Northern Ireland;
- where brought by pipeline, when the goods are brought within the limits of a port or brought across the boundary into Northern Ireland.

[*CEMA 1979, s 5(2)(6)*].

In short, the time of importation for VAT purposes is the moment when customs duty is due on the goods.

Supplies between the time of arrival in the UK and before delivery of import entry

If imported goods are supplied between the time of their arrival in the UK and the time when an import entry is delivered to Customs, the supply can be zero-rated provided, by arrangement, the purchaser is required to make the import entry. [*VATA 1994, Sch 8 Group 13 Item 1*].

Import entry procedure

[34.3] Goods are declared to Customs using the Single Administrative Document (SAD) (Form C88). Import VAT is dealt with in the same way as customs duty.

The import declaration must normally be accompanied by a declaration of value on Form C105A (for importers using Method 1), or C105B (for importers using Methods 2–6).

Unless the goods are placed under excise warehousing or one of the customs arrangements listed in **34.25** below, any VAT due must normally either be paid at the time of importation or be deferred with any duty if the importer or his agent are approved for deferment.

Amendment of declarations

Where amendment of a declaration is made after the goods have been released out of official charge and this results in less VAT being payable than was originally declared and paid, the higher amount of VAT can be reclaimed in the normal way. Alternatively, the procedure for reclaiming VAT overpaid in **34.6** below can be used. Where amendment of a declaration results in more VAT being payable, a completed Form C18 must be submitted together with the additional amount of VAT due. The additional payment will appear on the import VAT certificate as evidence for input tax deduction (see **34.11** below).

Postal imports

(1) *Consignments not exceeding £873 (€1,000) (was £2,000 before 1 May 2016) in value*. Where a VAT-registered person is importing goods in the course of his business Royal Mail/Parcelforce will normally ask him for payment of VAT when the package is delivered. He must keep the charge label which was attached to the package to support any claim to input tax. To support his claim to import tax he should keep the charge label, postal wrapper and any Customs declaration that was attached to the package. Where a VAT-registered person is authorised by HMRC to do so, he may account for the VAT due in the VAT return covering the period of importation rather than pay the VAT due at the time the package is delivered. [*SI 1995/2518, Reg 122*].

(2) *Consignments over £873 (€1,000) (was £2,000 before 1 May 2016) in value*. For these imports, a declaration on Form C88 (which will be sent to the consignee) must be made and returned to HMRC together with an invoice or other acceptable evidence of value. VAT and other charges due at importation are payable immediately unless the consignee is approved to use the deferment scheme. After payment, HMRC send the consignee a copy of the entry to support any claim to input tax.

(Notice 143).

Goods imported from outside the EU and destined for another EU member state

Where a person receives goods from outside the EU and consigns them to a destination in another EU member state, he must normally either

- put the goods in free circulation in the UK, paying any customs duty and/or import VAT due; or
- place the goods under the external Community Transit (T1) arrangements, in which case any duty and/or VAT is payable in the EU member state of destination.

See, however, **34.18** below for VAT relief for goods imported and put into free circulation in the UK in the course of a zero-rated supply of those goods to a taxable person in another EU member state.

(VAT Notice 702, paras 2.2, 4.1–4.4).

Payment of VAT

[34.4] Payment of VAT on imported goods is due at the time of importation (or removal from warehouse) unless the importer or his agent is approved for deferment. [*CEMA 1979, s 43(1), s 44(1), s 45, s 93(1)(2); VATA 1994, s 38*].

De Voil Indirect Tax Service. See V5.115–122.

Deferment of VAT

[34.5] A business, approved by HMRC and holding a Deferment Approval Number (DAN), can defer paying charges due on importation or removal of goods from a customs or an excise warehouse. An agent (including a warehousekeeper) who enters goods for an importer or owner may also use the scheme.

The charges which can be deferred are:

- *Where payable on imported goods at the time of import or on removal from Customs warehouses*: import VAT; customs duties; excise duties (including tobacco products duty); levies imposed under the Common Agricultural Policy (CAP) of the EU; positive Monetary Compensatory Amounts under the CAP; anti-dumping or countervailing duties imposed by the EU; compensatory interest on IP goods diverted to free circulation; temporary import interest on TA goods diverted to free circulation; and interest charged on Customs debts.

- *Where payable on removal from excise warehouse*: VAT and excise duty on the following home-produced or home-manufactured goods, namely spirits and liqueurs (including perfume and composite goods containing excisable spirit); wine and made-wine fortified or rendered sparkling in the warehouse; cider and perry; beer and other alcoholic beverages.
- *Where payable on hydrocarbon oils on removal from warehouse*: Excise duty and VAT.

Deposits for the above charges may also be deferred.

Period of deferment

Except for excise duties, charges deferred during a calendar month (*'the accounting period'*) must be paid as a total sum on the 15th of the next month or, if that is not a 'working day', on the next working day *after* it. For excise duty, the accounting period runs from the 15th of one month to the 14th of the next month and payment must be made on the 29th of the latter month (28th February in non-leap years) or, if that is not a working day, on the working day *before* it. '*Working day*' is any day on which the Bank of England in London is open for business.

Payment

Payment must be made by the BACS system of direct debit (although HMRC may require special arrangements if an emergency prevents them collecting that way). No other method of payment is accepted for the deferment scheme. A business wishing to pay by other means must pay each time its goods are cleared.

If a direct debit fails, the business will be expected to settle immediately. Failure to do so may result in the duty deferment facility being stopped or even withdrawn. Other customs facilities that are dependent upon duty deferment may also be affected and interest charges may also arise.

An agent (see below) acting in his own name but on behalf of an importer is jointly and severally liable for any customs debt that may arise.

It is not currently possible to make BACS direct debit payments in euro.

Guarantees

A guarantee on Form C1201 is required from an approved bank, insurance company or building society. The form is obtainable from the Central Deferment Office, (see below under *Approval*) although some guarantors hold their own supplies. The guarantor agrees to cover all amounts deferred up to an overall maximum amount in any calendar month (the '*deferment limit*') which must be enough to cover all deferrable liabilities (but see below for import VAT under SIVA).

If the guarantee level/deferment limit is exceeded in any calendar month, it is not possible to defer any more charges for the remainder of that month (and all further import charges would need to be paid immediately by another payment method until either the guarantee level/deferment limit is increased or a new calendar month begins). The guarantee can be varied by replacement with a bigger (or smaller) amount or by giving a supplementary guarantee to cover extra liabilities in peak periods.

Guarantees can be cancelled by contacting the guarantor or by advising the Central Deferment Office directly in writing. A period of notice of termination of no less than seven days must be given.

Simplified import VAT accounting (SIVA)

A trader who holds a live deferment account (or who intends to apply for one) can apply to reduce the level of financial guarantee required to operate it *for VAT purposes only*. Customs duties and excise duties must still be fully secured. Applicants must satisfy the following criteria.

- VAT-registered for at least three years or from 1 January 2015 satisfy additional financial solvency and risk credibility tests if the applicant is not VAT-registered for at least three years.
- A good VAT compliance history.
- A good payment history with HMRC.
- Sufficient financial means to meet any amount deferred under SIVA.
- A good HMRC offence record (serious offences will result in automatic expulsion).
- A twelve-month record of international trade operations.
- A good compliance record for international trade.

(Customs Information Paper (14)65).

The SIVA application form (SIVA 1) can be downloaded from the HMRC section of the GOV.UK website:

www.gov.uk/government/publications/vat-application-for-simplified-import-vat-accounting-siva1.

Application forms should be completed and returned to SIVA Approvals Team, HMRC, Ruby House, 8 Ruby Place, Aberdeen, AB10 1ZP.

If approval is granted, businesses will then have to arrange any subsequent changes to their guarantee amount with their guarantor and then with HMRC. The deferment account will have two limits.

- A deferment account limit which must be sufficient to cover all deferred charges.
- A deferment guarantee level which must be backed up by a deferment guarantee and sufficient to cover all deferred customs and excise duties.

Approval

Application forms for deferral can be downloaded from HMRC's website (see above) and are also available from HM Revenue and Customs, A&CGs Branch 6, Central Deferment Office, 10th Floor South East, Alexander House, 21 Victoria Avenue, Southend-on-Sea, Essex SS99 1AA (Tel: 01702 367425/29/31/50; Fax: 01702 366091). A set of forms comprises

Form C1200	Application for approval of deferment arrangements
Form C1201	Guarantee for payment of sums due to HMRC
Form C1202	Duty deferment – instruction to bank or building society to pay by direct debit
Form C1207N	Standing authority for agent/freight forwarder to request duty deferment of duty payment against importer's DAN (see below)

If satisfied with the application, guarantee given and payment arrangements, HMRC will issue a Certificate of Approval showing a deferment approval number (DAN). This must be quoted on each request for deferment and in any correspondence with HMRC (including correspondence from the guarantor).

Approval covers the business to the limit of its guarantee (or deferment account limit if SIVA is approved, see above) for deferment of all eligible charges and can be used at any port, airport, warehouse, etc in the UK. Companies which are members of the same group registration for VAT can apply for group approval.

The CDO must be notified immediately if the business

- changes its name, address or VAT registration number;
- ceases to trade (including where the business is carried on by another legal entity); or
- wishes to cancel its duty deferment account.

A new direct debit mandate on Form C1202 must be sent at least ten days before the next payment is due if the bank account is transferred to another bank.

Approval can be revoked at any time for reasonable cause. The direct debit mandate must not be cancelled until all deferred payments have been made.

Procedure

At importation, deferment is requested on the import entry by entering the DAN and the correct payment code in the boxes provided. Charges may be deferred against the importer's DAN or an agent's DAN (see below). Deferment cannot be requested on importations for which no entry is required (unless an entry is made for them) or on postal importations (except those with a value exceeding £2,000 and entered on Form C88A).

On removal from an approved customs and excise warehouse, deferment is requested on the entry or warrant for removal. This also applies under scheduling or other approved simplified arrangements where the entry is presented after the removal of the goods. Charges due on deficiencies in warehouse or in transit cannot be deferred.

Where, after having allowed deferment, it is found that more or less was payable on the entry, HMRC will normally adjust the deferment account accordingly. Where this is not possible, if more was payable, the balance is payable immediately and if less was payable, the amount overdeclared will be repaid on, or as soon as possible after, the direct debit day on which it is paid. However, repayments of VAT are not normally made to VAT-registered traders who are expected to recover the amount on their next VAT return.

Agents

An agent making an entry can request deferment against his principal's approval number provided he is authorised to do so. This can be done in two ways.

- On Form C1207N, at the time of seeking approval for deferment (see above) or subsequently. This is a standing authority which allows the agent to use his principal's approval number whenever or wherever entering goods on his behalf.
- On Form C1207S which is a 'one-off' authority in respect of a specific consignment or removal of goods. The form is available on the HMRC website (see above). The completed form must be given to the agent to present with the entry.
- In emergencies (e.g. when goods are diverted to another port at short notice) HMRC will accept:
  - (a) A fax on company-headed paper authorising the agent to act. It must be signed by a responsible officer and sent to the agent to present with the entry. The fax should be worded:
    To HM Revenue and Customs at (insert name of port/airport)
    - (1) I am/we are (insert name of business)
    - (2) My/our telephone number is (insert number)
    - (3) I/we hereby authorise (insert name of agent) to use my/our deferment approval number (insert number) when requesting deferment of the charges on the goods imported by me/us on the attached entry.
  - (b) A fax copy of a completed Form C1207S signed by a responsible officer. It must be sent to the agent to present with the entry.
  - (c) A fax copy of a completed Form C1207N sent to the Central Deferment Office.
  - (d) An e-mail from the importer, sent to the port of entry, giving specific authority and providing a contact name and telephone number for the importer, along with all other importer and agent's details. Customs at the port of entry should be contacted for the appropriate e-mail address.

If an agent appoints a sub-agent (e.g. because he has no office at a particular port)

- where the sub-agent is shown as declarant on the entry, he can request deferment against his own DAN or the importer's DAN if authorised under the above procedure; and
- where the main agent is shown as the declarant on the entry and the sub-agent signs the declaration as a representative of the main agent, the sub-agent can request deferment against the importer's DAN (if that importer has authorised the main agent) or against the main agent's DAN.

An agent making a bulked entry of goods consigned to several importers may use his own account to defer the charges payable but cannot defer the charges against individual importer's accounts.

Statements

HMRC send out 'periodic deferment statements' at approximately weekly intervals summarising details of deferments at each of their accounting centres and showing the total amount deferred so far in that particular month. Any queries should be taken up immediately with the accounting centre concerned. 'Nil' statements are not normally sent.

Deferment statements cannot be used as evidence for input tax deduction. See **34.11** below for evidence required.

The Duty Deferment Electronic Statements (DDES) service offers a facility to obtain copies of periodic deferment statements electronically via the internet. In order to use DDES a business must register, enrol and activate the service through a central registration process within the Government Gateway. Once registered, DDES can be accessed via the HMRC website and selecting the 'Electronic services' and 'DDES' links. More information on electronic services is provided on the Government Gateway website at

www.gateway.gov.uk

[*SI 1976/1223*]. (Customs Notice 101).

De Voil Indirect Tax Service. See V3.306, V5.117–V5.119.

The Union Customs Code (*Regulation (EU) No 952/2013*) is effective from 1 May 2016. Deferment accounts can continue to be used after 1 May 2016 without requiring reauthorisation. However, reauthorisation of deferment accounts is required for any changes to the deferment guarantee. Simplified Import VAT Accounting Scheme (SIVA) authorisations can continue to be used after 1 May 2016 until the authorisation is reassessed. From 1 May 2016 businesses requesting SIVA authorisations need to meet the same standards as those required for a guarantee waiver under the Union Customs Code, which involves applying for a comprehensive guarantee.

Under the Union Customs Code there are some circumstances where the provision of a guarantee is mandatory but businesses may continue to operate certain regimes or procedures after 1 May 2016 without providing a guarantee until they are changed to a new Union Customs Code authorisation and approval. The regimes and procedures are as follows.

- Inward processing (see **34.31**).
- Outward processing with prior importation under the Standard Exchange System.
- Temporary admissions where the Union Customs Codes does not provide for an outright guarantee exemption (see **34.26**).
- End use (see **34.35**).
- Temporary storage (see **34.25**).
- Customs warehousing (see **73.2**).

Businesses can apply for a reduction in the level of guarantee required. If eligible a 0% guarantee or waiver may be granted.

(Notice 3001).

Reclaiming VAT overpaid

[34.6] Non-VAT registered and non-fully taxable traders can claim overpaid import VAT using Form C285 'Application for repayment/remission'. VAT registered traders must claim any overpaid import VAT as input tax on their VAT return subject to the normal VAT rules.

Current month adjustments (CMA)

Where the overpayment of import VAT is made via his deferment account, the trader may (regardless of his VAT status) apply to have his deferment account adjusted to reflect the correct amount of import VAT. His request for CMA must be made on Form C285 and sent to the National Duty Repayment Centre (NDRC) at the address quoted in **34.8** below.

Current month adjustments can only be made in the month that the error occurs and therefore the trader must make his application for adjustment before the last day of the month in which the overpayment was made. He must ensure that he submits all supporting documents with his claim as there will be no time for further enquires to be made. If his application is received after the month end or without all supporting documentation it will be dealt with as a standard repayment. This means that if he is a VAT-registered trader requesting the adjustment of overpaid import VAT his claim will be refused and he will have to claim the equivalent amount as input tax on his VAT return.

Repayments to agents

If an importer fails to pay the trader the import VAT that the trader paid on the importer's behalf, the trader's only recourse is to the importer, except in the circumstances set out in **34.8** below.

(VAT Notice 702, para 2.6).

Goods lost or destroyed before release from official control

[34.7] In such an event, application can be made to HMRC at the place where the import entry was presented for repayment or remission of the VAT due using Form C285 (see above under *Reclaiming VAT overpaid*). (VAT Notice 702, para 2.10).

Repayment of import VAT to shipping and forwarding agents by HMRC if the importer fails to pay them

[34.8] If an importer fails to pay a shipping or forwarding agent any VAT paid by the agent on his behalf, in normal circumstances the agent's only recourse is to the importer. However, by concession, if an importer becomes insolvent without reimbursing the agent for VAT paid or deferred, HMRC will repay the import VAT to the agent provided all the following conditions are satisfied.

(a) Either
- the importer has gone into liquidation; or

- an administrator or administrative receiver has been appointed who certifies that in his opinion the assets of the insolvent importer are insufficient to cover payment of *any* dividend to the unsecured creditors.

(b) The interval between the date of import entry for the goods and the date of insolvency is no more than six months.

(c) The agent entered the goods in accordance with instructions from the importer.

(d) The goods have been re-exported from the UK in the same state as they were imported and, during the time they were in the UK, the goods were under the control of the agent and were not used.

(e) The agent must write to the National Duty Repayment Centre – Salford, Ralli Quays, 3 Stanley Street, Salford, M60 9HL enclosing
- evidence that the input tax has been paid to HMRC;
- a certificate from the liquidator, etc. that the VAT has not been, and will not be, reclaimed as input tax;
- confirmation from the liquidator, etc. of (*b*) above;
- a declaration that he will not recover the relevant VAT in whole or in part from the insolvency; and
- evidence to satisfy HMRC of (*c*) above.

(VAT Notice 702, para 2.5; VAT Notice 48, ESC 3.13).

De Voil Indirect Tax Service. See V5.160.

Unregistered persons

[34.9] Where goods are imported for business purposes, the same procedures apply for entry of goods on importation and payment or deferment of VAT as for registered traders except that an unregistered person does not require an import VAT certificate (C79) and is not entitled to claim import VAT and does not therefore receive a copy of the import VAT certificate. He may reclaim VAT paid on imported goods only when VAT was overpaid at importation (by using Form C285) or the goods are not what he ordered or are otherwise not in accordance with contract (see **34.20** below). See also **34.19** below for relief for re-importations by unregistered persons. (VAT Notice 702, para 6.1).

> *Example*
>
> Alan buys and sells toy cars and is not VAT-registered because he trades below the compulsory VAT-registration limits. He buys a shipment of toy cars from Holland (EU) and another one from Australia (non-EU). In the case of the purchase from the Dutch supplier, he will be charged Dutch VAT, based on the rate of VAT that applies in Holland. In the case of the purchase from the Australian supplier, he will not be charged Australian GST (Goods and Service Tax), but will be charged UK import VAT and possibly customs duty at the point the goods enter the UK.

Input tax deduction

[34.10] VAT paid on the importation of goods can be claimed as input tax subject to the normal rules.

Evidence for input tax deduction

[34.11] The normal evidence of the payment of import VAT is the Import VAT Certificate (Form C79) which is issued monthly. This certificate is received, normally around the 24th day of the following month, by the VAT-registered person whose Economic Operator Registration and Identification (EORI) is shown on the import entry. In the UK the EORI comprises the letters 'GB' followed by the importer's VAT registration number plus a three-digit suffix. The date when the VAT shown on the certificate may be treated as input tax is normally the accounting date alongside each item, not the date when the certificate is issued.

The certificate may be copied for internal purposes and a copy is allowed as an accounting document for input tax deduction provided the original is made available for inspection by the control officer on demand.

If a monthly certificate is lost, replacements can be obtained (for up to six years) from HM Revenue and Customs, VAT Central Unit, Microfilm Section, 8th Floor Alexander House, Victoria Avenue, Southend-on-Sea, SS99 1AU. Applications should be in writing, by faxing the request to fax number 03000 594271 on business headed paper, quoting VAT registration number and the month(s) for which replacement is required.

There are still, however, some types of importation which do not appear on Form C79. The following list summarises the various methods of import procedures and the acceptable evidence of payment.

Import procedure	*Evidence for input tax deduction*
Air/sea imports Single Administration Document (SAD) – manually processed	Monthly VAT certificate
SAD – trader input/computer processed	Monthly VAT certificate
SAD – Customs input/computer processed	Monthly VAT certificate
SPIC imports not exceeding £600 Form C1451	Monthly VAT certificate
Bulked entries (SAD)	Customs authenticated invoices
Registered consignees	Customs authenticated invoices
Period entry	Trader produced computer schedule
SAD (simplified)	PE 33 (not authenticated by Customs)
Period entry – Adjustment schedules only	Monthly VAT certificate
Transit Shed Register – imports not exceeding £600 (non-DTI)	Customs authenticated commercial invoice or locally produced forms certified by Customs. The concession allowing use of copies of agents' disbursement invoices in certain circumstances will continue

Import procedure	*Evidence for input tax deduction*
Postal imports	
Exceeding £873 (€1,000)	Authenticated copy 8 SAD
Not exceeding £873 (€1,000)	CN22/CN23 plus the wrapper
Post entry correction	Monthly VAT certificates
Removals from ware-house	
Customs warehouse	Monthly VAT certificates
Excise	Monthly VAT certificates
Hydrocarbon oils	Monthly VAT certificates

(VAT Notice 702, paras 8.1, 8.6, 8.7, 8.11, 8.16, 8.17).

Shipping and forwarding agents

[**34.12**] Where a shipping or forwarding agent acts for an importer and pays the VAT on his behalf (or defers it under his own deferment guarantee), this is only a commercial arrangement. The agent cannot claim the VAT as input tax as the goods are not imported for the purpose of his business. Only the importer has the legal right to reclaim the VAT paid on the imported goods as input tax, subject to the normal rules. (VAT Notice 702, para 2.4). See, however, **34.8** above for concessional repayment of import VAT to agents in certain cases where the importer fails to pay him.

It is also important to note that importers cannot use the shipping or forwarding agents invoice to recover any import VAT incurred. The importer must use the C79 or other official evidence in order to recover any import VAT incurred.

In *Hemisphere Freight Services Ltd* [2017] UKFTT 740 (TC) (TC06151) (HFS), HFS, acting as agent for A-Sure Technology Co Ltd (A-Sure), imported goods into the UK and completed the required Customs Entry. However, due to an incorrect exchange rate being used, there was an overpayment of VAT and customs duty. HFS submitted a C285 to request a refund of the duty and VAT paid at import. HMRC repaid the duty but refused to make payment of the VAT, stating that the VAT paid at import should be included as input tax on the importer's (A-Sure) VAT return using the VAT C79. HMRC also stated that any money owed to HFS should be settled through A-Sure as a normal commercial transaction. However, HMRC also requested that HFS obtain a disclaimer from A-Sure confirming that it would not recover the VAT charged via its VAT return; despite HFS obtaining this disclaimer HMRC still refused to repay the VAT charged. HFS challenged the decision, asking for an explanation regarding why the disclaimer had been requested if repayment of the VAT was going to be refused. It also raised the matter of the fact that A-Sure had ceased to trade in the UK and that there was little prospect of receiving settlement of the VAT charged and that HMRC had been unjustly enriched.

The Tribunal directed that HMRC were required to answer a number of questions regarding its practices and the legal foundation for HMRC's position with regard to issuing refunds in these situations. HMRC informed the Tribunal that it no longer intended to defend the appeal and the appeal as therefore allowed. The Tribunal went on to explain the position in law as it understood it and it held that HMRC was wrong to hold that the normal VAT accounting system applies to the charge to VAT on imports. Also it considered that HMRC has confused a repayment of VAT in error with a credit for input tax and the two things are wholly separate. HFS does have a remedy, the repayment of VAT that it wrongly paid.

This case challenges HMRC's approach to VAT recovery on imports via agents. Whilst import VAT is usually claimed through the C79 process, by the importer, this decision does provide a potential remedy if an agent/freight forwarder incurs a VAT cost through circumstances beyond their control.

Goods lost or destroyed after release from official control

[34.13] In such an event, the VAT paid can be deducted as input tax (subject to the normal rules) provided the goods were to be used for business purposes. There is no need to account for output tax unless the goods were supplied to someone else before the loss or destruction. (VAT Notice 702, para 2.10).

Reliefs from charge

[34.14] There are a number of reliefs available as a result of which import VAT is not due on specific goods.

- Aircraft ground and security equipment (see **34.22** below).
- Capital goods and equipment on transfer of activities from abroad (see **34.15**(2) below).
- Certain imports by and for charities (see **34.15**(6) below).
- Decorations and awards (see **34.15**(9) and **34.15**(13) below).
- Electricity and natural gas (see **34.23** below).
- Fuel, animal fodder and feed, and packing necessary during transportation (see **34.15**(11) below).
- Funerals, war graves, etc. (see **34.15**(12) below).
- Goods for examination, analysis or test purposes (see **34.15**(4) below).
- Goods imported for sale to another EU member state (see **34.18** below).
- Health, including animals and biological or chemical substances for research, blood and human organs, blood-grouping and tissue-typing re-agents, and equipment for medical research funded by charities and voluntary contributions (see **34.15**(5) below).
- Inherited goods (see **34.15**(13) below).
- Miscellaneous items, including consignments not exceeding £15 in value (low value consignment relief (LVCR)) (see **34.15**(8) below).
- Personal belongings (see **34.15**(13) below).
- Printed matter (see **34.15**(3) and **34.15**(7) below).
- Promotion of trade (see **34.15**(3) below).

- Reimported goods (see **34.19** below).
- Rejected goods (see **34.20** below).
- Small non-commercial consignments (see **34.16** below).
- Temporary admissions (see **34.26** below).
- Travellers' allowances (see **34.17** below).
- United Nations visual and auditory materials (see **34.15**(1) below).
- Visiting forces (see **34.21** below).
- Works of art and collectors' pieces. See **34.15**(10), **34.25** and **34.27** below and **74.3** and **74.4** **WORKS OF ART, ETC.**
- Zero-rated goods under *VATA 1994, Sch 8* (with some exceptions). See **75.1 ZERO-RATED SUPPLIES.** [*VATA 1994, s 30(3)*].

Imports relieved under EC Council Directive 83/181/EEC and equivalent UK provisions

[34.15] The following provisions describe goods that can be imported into the UK free of VAT from

- outside the customs territory of the EU (see **18.3 EUROPEAN UNION: GENERAL**); and
- the 'special territories' or countries having a customs union with the EU.

The 'special territories' are the Aland Islands, the Canary Islands, the Channel Islands, French Guiana, Guadeloupe, Martinique, Mount Athos and Reunion. These countries or areas are part of the customs territory of the EU but not part of the VAT territory. VAT is therefore due on imports from these territories unless any of the reliefs detailed below are applicable and claimed.

The customs territory of the EU has customs unions with Turkey, San Marino and Andorra. These enable most goods in free circulation to move freely between them without the need to claim duty relief, subject to the production of any necessary preference or Community Transit documentation. (In the case of Andorra, the union only covers goods in Chapters 25–97 of the Tariff.) VAT is still due on imports from Turkey, San Marino and Andorra, however, unless any of the reliefs detailed below are applicable and claimed.

General condition for relief

Where relief is available under any of the provisions listed below by reference to a use or purpose of the goods, the goods must be put to that use or purpose in the UK.

(1) United Nations visual and auditory materials

No VAT is charged on the importation of the following types of goods, produced by the United Nations or one of its specialised agencies, providing they are used for educational, scientific or cultural purposes. The goods must have been compiled, collated, published or created by the UN and any of its specialised agencies:

- Holograms for laser projection.
- Multi-media kits.

- Materials for programmed instructions, including materials in kit form, with the corresponding printed materials.
- Films and film strips.
- Newsreels/video tapes (with or without soundtrack) depicting events of current news value (limited to two copies of each for copying) and archival film material (with or without soundtrack) for use with newsreel/video tapes.
- Discs, microcards or other information storage media required in computerised information and documentation services.
- Recordings.
- Wall charts, patterns, mock-ups and models designed solely for demonstration and education purposes.

See Customs Notice 373 for more information on the import procedure and claiming relief.

[*SI 1984/746, Art 4, Sch 1; EC Council Directive 2009/132/EC, Art 81, Annex*].

(2) Capital goods and equipment on transfer of activities from abroad

No VAT is charged on 'capital goods and equipment' imported by a person for the purposes of a business which:

- he has completely ceased to carry on *either* outside the customs territory of the EU *or* in the 'special territories' *or* in countries having a customs union with the EU (see above);
- will be moving to the UK to carry on a similar activity there or to merge with an existing UK business which will then produce or provide new products or services;
- which is concerned exclusively with making taxable supplies; and
- either have or expect to have a taxable turnover that exceeds the UK VAT registration threshold.

The goods must:

(a) have been used continuously by the business for at least twelve months before the activities were transferred to the UK;
(b) be used for an identical purpose in the UK;
(c) be appropriate both to the nature and size of the business to be carried on in the UK;
(d) be imported from their previous location within twelve months of the date the business' overseas activities ceased.

HMRC can waive the conditions under (*a*) and (*d*) above in special circumstances (e.g. if political upheaval in the country where the business was located prevented twelve months use or the import within twelve months of cessation). (Customs Notice 343, para 2.4).

Relief can be obtained on the following types of *'Capital goods and equipment'*:

- computer and other technical equipment needed to run the business;
- livestock belonging to an agricultural business;

- means of transport that are used for the purposes of production or for providing services;
- office and shop equipment/machinery and other tools of trade.

(Customs Notice 343, para 2.2).

The following goods are not eligible for relief:

- fuel and stocks of raw materials or finished/semi-finished products that include horticultural products for resale, such as plants shrubs and seeds;
- means of transport that are not used for production or for providing a service;
- livestock that belongs to a dealer;
- supplies of any kind that are intended for human consumption or animal feed.

The goods must not be lent, hired out, transferred or given away as security for twelve months from the date of importation unless HMRC is notified an any import VAT and customs duty paid.

See Customs Notice 343 for more information on the import procedure and claiming relief.

[*SI 1984/746, Sch 2 Group 1; EC Council Directive 2009/132/EC, Arts 25–29*].

(3) Promotion of trade

No VAT is charged on the following imports.

(a) Articles of no intrinsic commercial value sent free of charge by suppliers of goods and services for the sole purpose of advertising.

(b) Samples of negligible value of a kind and in quantities capable of being used solely for soliciting orders for goods of the same kind. Where HMRC require, the goods must be rendered permanently unusable, except as samples, by being torn, perforated, clearly and indelibly marked, or by any other process.
Relief is not available for goods not presented as samples at import but subsequently to be made into samples (e.g. unaltered rolls of fabric imported to be cut up and made into swatch books). (Notice 372, para 2.6).

(c) Printed advertising matter, including catalogues, price lists, directions for use or brochures, which relates to goods for sale or hire by a person established outside the EU or to transport, commercial insurance or banking services offered by a person established outside the EU. The material must clearly display the name of the person established outside the EU by whom the goods or services are offered. Subject to below, relief does not apply to consignments containing two or more copies of different documents or to consignments containing two or more copies of the same document (unless the total gross weight of the consignment does not exceed one kilogram). Any goods which are the subject of grouped consignments from the same consignor to the same consignee are also excluded. These restrictions on relief do not apply in the case of imported printed matter intended for free distribution and relating to either goods for sale or hire.

(d) Goods to be distributed free of charge at an 'event' as small 'representative samples' for use or consumption by the public (excluding fuels, alcoholic beverages and tobacco products).

(e) Goods imported solely for the purpose of being demonstrated at, or used in the demonstration of any machine or apparatus displayed at, an 'event' (excluding fuels, alcoholic beverages and tobacco products).

(f) Paints, varnishes, wallpaper and other low value materials to be used in the fitting out or decoration of a temporary stand at an 'event'.

(g) Catalogues, prospectuses, price lists, advertising posters, calendars, unframed photographs and other printed matter or articles advertising goods displayed at an 'event', supplied without charge for distribution free of charge to the public at such event.

'*Event*' comprises

- any trade, industrial, agricultural or craft exhibition, fair or similar show or display which is not being organised for private purposes in a shop or on business premises with a view to the sale of the goods displayed;
- any exhibition or meeting primarily organised for charitable purposes or to promote *either* friendship between peoples *or* religious knowledge or worship *or* any branch of learning, art, craft, sport or scientific, technical, educational, cultural or trade union activity or tourism;
- any meeting of representatives of international organisations and ceremonies of an official or commemorative character; and
- any representative meeting or ceremony of an official or commemorative character.

'*Representative samples*' means goods which are

- imported free of charge or obtained at such event from goods imported in bulk;
- identifiable as advertising samples of low value;
- not easily marketable and, where appropriate, packaged in quantities which are less than the lowest quantity of the same goods as marketed; and
- intended to be consumed at such event, where the goods comprise foodstuffs or beverages not so packaged.

Relief under (*d*)–(*g*) above only applies where the aggregate value and quantity of the goods is appropriate to the nature of the event, number of visitors and extent of the exhibitor's participation. Where relief is available under (*e*) or (*f*) above in respect of goods for demonstration or use, the goods must be consumed, destroyed or rendered incapable of being used again for the same purpose either in the course of, or as a result of, such demonstration or use.

See Customs Notice 372 for more information on the import procedure and claiming relief.

[*SI 1984/746, Art 6(2), Sch 2 Group 3, item 2 (as amended); EC Council Directive 2009/132/EC, Arts 63–71*].

(4) Goods for examination, analysis or test purposes, etc.

No VAT is charged on goods imported for examination, analysis or testing (hereafter referred to as testing):

- to determine their composition, quality or their technical characteristics;
- to provide information; or
- for industrial or commercial research.

To qualify for relief:

- the quantities imported must not exceed the amounts necessary for their purpose;
- the examination, etc. itself must not constitute a sales promotion or publicity exercise;
- the goods must normally be used up or destroyed in the course of the testing. See below for more information on the treatment of goods remaining after testing is complete.

[*SI 1984/746, Art 6(3), Sch 2 Group 4; EC Council Directive 2009/132/EC, Arts 72–78*].

Businesses wishing to import goods for testing, etc. must provide the National Import Reliefs Unit (NIRU) at the address below with at least 48 hours' notice in writing providing the following details:

- full description and quantity of the goods;
- address where the testing, etc. will take place;
- date of the testing, etc.

The NIRU will provide the importer with an approval note that must be presented with the import declaration where they are satisfied the goods can be imported under this relief.

Testing must normally be completed by the date stated on the SAD or postal form. If this is not possible, a letter of explanation with a request for an extension of time should be sent, before the stated time is reached, to

National Import Reliefs Unit
HM Revenue and Customs
Dorchester House
52–58 Great Victoria Street
Belfast
Northern Ireland
BT2 7WF
Tel: 03000 513310
Email: niru@hmrc.gsi.gov.uk

If the goods are transferred, at least 48 hours prior notice must be given to NIRU stating to whom and where the goods are to be transferred.

When testing is completed, NIRU must be informed in writing of

- place of importation or postal depot;
- number and date of the customs entry or postal docket;
- quantity, value and description of the goods and date of receipt;
- details of the tests, including the address(es) where the testing took place and where records are available for inspection;
- the date on which testing was completed; and
- details of any materials remaining and proposals for their disposal.

Any materials remaining (including goods not used, or not completely used up in the test and goods resulting from the test, including waste and scrap) may

- have VAT (and duty) paid on them at the rates applicable on the date of completion of the test; or
- with HMRC's permission, be destroyed, free of duty and VAT; or
- with HMRC's permission, be converted into waste or scrap pay any VAT (and duty) which may be due on the residue.

NIRU will consider applications to export goods remaining after the testing is over on satisfactory explanation of why the goods cannot be destroyed or converted into waste or scrap and have to be exported. (Customs Notice 374, paras 4.2–4.5).

See Customs Notice 374 for more information on the import procedure and claiming relief.

(5) Health

Certain goods can be zero-rated on supply in the UK to disabled persons or to charities for making available to disabled persons. Such goods can also be relieved of any VAT payable on importation. See **29.14** to **29.33** **HEALTH AND WELFARE**.

In addition, the following importations are free of VAT.

(a) Animals specially prepared for laboratory use and sent free of charge to a 'relevant establishment'.
'Relevant establishment' means
   - a public establishment, or a department of such, principally engaged in education or scientific research (e.g. a university, NHS or teaching hospital, mobile health laboratory, research laboratory of a government department, or laboratory of a research council); or
   - a private establishment so engaged, which is approved by the Home Office.

   A private establishment must apply for a letter from the Home Office confirming that it is a designated establishment under the terms of the *Animals (Scientific Procedures) Act 1986*. (Customs Notice 365, para 2.1). Also see Customs Notice 365 for import prohibitions and restrictions and animal welfare provisions.
   [*SI 1984/746, Sch 2 Group 5 item 1; EC Council Directive 2009/132/EC, Art 36*].

(b) Approved biological or chemical substances (see Customs Notice 366, para 4) imported by on or behalf of a 'relevant establishment' (see (*a*) above) from outside the EU which will be used for non-commercial educational or scientific research.

A private establishment must apply to the National Import Reliefs Unit (at the address under (4) above) for authorisation to claim relief. The application must be made in advance of importation and detail the research project for which the imported substance will be used. If the application is successful, NIRU will issue an approval letter. (Customs Notice 366, para 3.1).

[*SI 1984/746, Sch 2 Group 5 item 3; EC Council Directive 2009/132/EC, Art 36*].

(c) Any of the following goods, namely:

- therapeutic substances of human origin, which means human blood and its derivatives (whole human blood, dried human plasma, human albumin and fixed solutions of human plasmic protein, human immunoglobulin and human fibrinogen);
- blood-grouping reagents, which means all reagents whether of human, animal, plant or other origin used for blood-type grouping and for the detection of blood incompatibilities;
- tissue-typing reagents, which means all reagents whether of human, animal, plant or other origin used for the determination of human tissue types;
- the special packaging essential for the transport of the above goods and also any solvents and accessories needed for their use which may be included in the consignments.

'Approved institutions and laboratories' include:

- a public establishment or laboratory (e.g. Regional and District Health Authorities, Health Boards in Scotland, Health and Social Service Boards in Northern Ireland, public health laboratories, research laboratories of government departments, research councils and similar bodies, all blood transfusion services, schools of pharmacy and medical schools); and
- a private establishment which has been authorised by the Department of Health (DoH) to receive such goods VAT (and duty) free.

A private establishment must apply in advance of importation to the Department of Health Public Health Group, PH6.6, Room 631B, Skipton House, 80 London Road, London SE1 6TE (tel: 020 7972 5142) indicating

- the status of the establishment;
- the nature of activities (e.g. medical research); and
- the type of goods to be imported.

If the application is successful, the DoH will issue a letter of authorisation. (Customs Notice 369, para 3.1).

[*SI 1984/746, Sch 2 Group 5 items 4–8; EC Council Directive 2009/132/EC, Arts 36–38*].

(d) Pharmaceutical products by or on behalf of persons or animals for their use while visiting the UK to participate in an international sporting event.

[*SI 1984/746, Sch 2 Group 5 item 9; EC Council Directive 2009/132/EC, Art 41*].

(e) Samples of reference substances approved by the World Health Organisation for the quality control of materials used in the manufacture of medicinal products provided the samples are addressed to consignees authorised to receive them free of VAT.
[*SI 1984/746, Sch 2 Group 5 item 10; EC Council Directive 2009/132/EC, Art 40*].

(6) Charities, etc.

Certain goods which can be zero-rated on supply to or for charities in the UK can also be relieved of any VAT payable on importation. See **13.7** and **13.8 CHARITIES**.

In addition, no VAT is payable on the importation of the following goods.

(a) Basic necessities for the needy (i.e. food, medicines, clothing, blankets, orthopaedic equipment and crutches, required to meet a person's immediate needs) obtained without charge for distribution free of charge to the needy by a 'relevant organisation'. *Excluded* are alcoholic beverages, tobacco products, coffee, tea and motor vehicles other than ambulances.
(b) Goods donated by a person established outside the EU to a 'relevant organisation' for use to raise funds at occasional charity events for the benefit of the needy. There must be no commercial intent on the part of the donor. *Excluded* are alcoholic beverages, etc. as in (*a*) above. HMRC treat an occasional charity event as one held not more than four times a year by any one organisation.
(c) Equipment and office material, including machines, tools and equipment of the service industry, fixtures and fittings which are donated by a person established outside the EU to a 'relevant organisation'. There must be no commercial intent on the part of the donor. The equipment must be used solely to help run the organisation and carry out its charitable and philanthropic aims for the benefit of the needy. *Excluded* are alcoholic beverages, etc. as in (*a*) above.
(d) Goods imported by a 'relevant organisation' for distribution or loan, free of charge, to victims of, or for meeting its operating needs in the relief of, a disaster affecting the territory of one or more EU member states. This relief only applies where the EU Commission has made a decision authorising the importation of the goods. However, relief is not available for materials and equipment intended for rebuilding disaster areas.
(e) Articles donated to and imported by an approved organisation principally engaged in the education of, or the provision of assistance to, blind or other physically or mentally handicapped persons for loan, hiring out or transfer other than on a profit-making basis (and whether for consideration or free of charge) to such persons and specially designed for their education, employment or social advancement. There must be no commercial intent on the part of the donor.

(f) Spare parts, components or accessories for any article within (*e*) above, including tools for its maintenance, checking, calibration or repair. The goods must be imported with an article within (*e*) above to which they relate or, if imported subsequently, must be identifiable as being intended for such an article.

The above reliefs are conditional on

- any guarantee, declaration, undertaking, document or other details being given to HMRC as required;
- the goods being put to the use or purpose specified; and
- unless specifically allowed above, the goods not being lent, hired out or transferred unless to an organisation which would itself be entitled to the relief if importing the goods on that date. In the latter case, prior notification in writing must be received from HMRC and the goods must be used solely in accordance with the relieving provisions.

Where any condition ceases to be satisfied and written notice of this fact is given to HMRC, VAT becomes payable as if the goods had been imported on that date and VAT is calculated accordingly. The VAT must not, however, exceed the VAT relieved in the first place.

'*Relevant organisation*' means a State organisation or other approved charitable or philanthropic organisation. HMRC have given general approval to the following charitable and philanthropic organisations.

- Organisations registered with the Charity Commissioners or the Office of the Scottish Charities Regulator.
- State organisations which are devoted to welfare.
- Any of the following organisations provided they are non-profit making and their objective is the welfare of the needy, *viz* hospitals; youth organisations; clubs, homes and hostels for the aged; orphanages and children's homes; organisations set up for the relief of distress caused by particular disasters in the EU; and organisations concerned with the relief of distress generally (such as the British Red Cross and the Salvation Army).

See Customs Notice 317 for detail on the importation procedure and claiming relief.

[*SI 1984/746, Art 6(1), Art 7, Art 8, Sch 2 Group 6; EC Council Directive 2009/132/EC, Arts 43–57*]. (Customs Notice 317, para 2.1).

(7) ***Printed matter, etc.***

The following printed matter may be imported free of VAT from a country outside the EU.

- Documents sent free of charge to public services in the UK.
- Publications of foreign governments or official international organisations for free distribution.
- Ballot papers for elections organised by bodies outside the EU.
- Specimen signatures and circulars concerning signatures forming part of exchanges of information between banks and public services.

- Official printed matter sent to a Central Bank in the UK.
- Documents from a company incorporated outside the EU to holders of its issued securities.
- Files and other documents for use at international meetings, etc and reports of such gatherings.
- Plans, drawings, traced designs and other documents sent by any person for participating in a competition in the UK or to obtain or fulfil an order executed outside the EU.
- Documents to be used in examinations held in the UK on behalf of institutions established outside the EU.
- Printed forms to be used as official documents in the international movement of vehicles or goods pursuant to international conventions.
- Printed forms, labels, tickets and similar documents sent to travel agents (including airlines, national railway undertakings, ferry operators and similar organisations) in the UK by transport and tourist undertakings outside the EU.
- Used commercial documents.
- Official printed forms from national or international authorities.
- Printed matter conforming to international standards for distribution by an association in the UK and sent by a corresponding association outside the EU.
- Documents (leaflets, brochures, books, magazines, guidebooks, posters (whether or not framed), unframed photographs and photographic enlargements, maps (whether or not illustrated) window transparencies, and illustrated calendars for free distribution to encourage persons to visit foreign countries, in particular to attend cultural, tourist, sporting, religious, trade or professional meetings or events (provided the goods do not contain more than 25% of private commercial advertising)).
- Free distribution copies of hotel lists and yearbooks published by or on behalf of official tourist agencies and timetables for foreign transport services (provided the goods do not contain more than 25% of private commercial advertising).
- Yearbooks, lists of telephone and telex numbers, hotel lists, catalogues for fairs, specimens of craft goods of negligible value and literature on museums, universities, spas or similar establishments, supplied as reference material to accredited representatives or correspondents appointed by official national tourist agencies and not intended for distribution.
- Official publications issued under the authority of the country of exportation, international institutions, regional or local authorities and bodies governed by public law established in the country of exportation (provided VAT or any other tax has been paid on the publication or printed matter in the third country from which it has been exported and the publication, etc. has not benefited from any relief from payment by virtue of exportation).
- Printed matter distributed by officially recognised political organisations, established outside the EU on the occasion of European Parliament or national elections in the country in which the printed matter originates (provided VAT or any other tax has been paid on the

publication or printed matter in the third country from which it has been exported and the publication, etc. has not benefited from any relief from payment by virtue of exportation).

See Customs Notice 342 for more information on the import procedure and claiming relief.

[*SI 1984/746, Art 2(5), Sch 2 Group 7; EC Council Directive 2009/132/EC, Art 81*].

(8) Articles sent for miscellaneous purposes

No VAT is charged on the following imports.

- Materials relating to trademarks, patterns or designs and supporting documents and applications for patents imported for submission to competent bodies to deal with protection of copyright or industrial or commercial patent rights.
- Objects imported for submission as evidence, or for a like purpose, to a court or other official body in the EU.
- Photographs, slides and stereotype mats for photographs sent to press agencies and publishers of newspapers or magazines.
- Recorded media, including punched cards, sound recordings and microfilm, sent free of charge for the transmission of information.
- Goods (other than alcoholic beverages or tobacco products) sent on an occasional basis as a gift of friendship or goodwill between bodies, public authorities or groups carrying on an activity in the public interest. The goods must not be of a commercial character.
- Any consignment of goods (other than alcoholic beverages, tobacco products, perfumes or toilet waters) not exceeding £15 in value (decreased from £18 from 1 November 2011). This relief is called low value consignment relief (LVCR). From 1 April 2012 to 25 September 2014 LVCR does not apply to goods sent to the UK from the Channel Islands under a distance selling arrangement. A distance selling arrangement in relation to any goods means any transaction, or series of transactions, under which the person to whom the goods are sent receives them from a supplier without the simultaneous physical presence of the person and the supplier at any time during the transaction or series of transactions. From 26 September 2014 LVCR does not apply to goods imported on mail order from the Channel Islands. Mail order in relation to any goods means any transaction or series of transactions under which a seller sends goods in fulfilment of an order placed remotely.

[*SI 1984/746, Sch 2 Group 8 Items 1–4, 7, 8; SI 2014/2364; EC Council Directive 2009/132/EC, Arts 59–63, 79, 80*].

(9) Decorations and awards

No VAT is charged on the following imports.

- Any honorary decoration conferred by a government or Head of State outside the EU on a person resident in the UK and imported on his behalf.

- Any cup, medal or similar article of an essentially symbolic nature, intended as a tribute to activities in the arts, sciences, sport or public service, or in recognition of merit at a particular event. It must be donated by an authority or person established outside the EU for the purpose of being presented in the UK or awarded outside the EU to a person resident in the UK and imported on his behalf.
- Awards, trophies and souvenirs of a symbolic nature and of limited value intended for free distribution at business conferences or similar international events to persons normally resident in a country other than the UK.

The awards, etc must not be of a commercial character.

[*SI 1984/746, Sch 2 Group 8 Items 5, 6, 9; EC Council Directive 2009/132/EC, Art 58*].

A person is resident where he spends at least 185 days in a period of twelve months because of personal ties and occupational ties (if any) but if personal ties are in one country and occupational ties in another, HMRC treat a person as resident in the country of his personal ties if

- his stay in the country of his occupational ties is in order to carry out a task of definite duration; or
- he returns regularly to the country of his personal ties.

Not eligible for relief are

- watches, cameras, cars;
- long service awards made to employees by employers or colleagues;
- prizes won in unimportant competitions such as deck games and card games;
- articles purchased with prize money;
- gifts or prizes given in lieu of payment;
- gifts where the donor appears to be motivated largely by commercial considerations;
- any consumables, e.g. alcoholic drinks, tobacco products, foods; and
- souvenirs distributed which are not in keeping with the nature of the event.

VAT relief may be claimed by the recipient or the person who is to present the award, etc. As proof that relief is due, HMRC will normally be satisfied with any certificate or press publicity material relating to the decoration or award, or a letter or statement from the donor or organiser of the event.

(Customs Notice 364, paras 2.1, 2.3–2.5).

Please see Customs Notice 364 for more information on the import procedure and claiming relief.

(10) Works of art and collectors' pieces for exhibition

Works of art and collectors' pieces imported by approved museums, galleries or other institutions for a purpose other than sale can be imported free of VAT provided the following conditions are met.

- The institution must be approved by the National Import Reliefs Unit. It should apply for approval in writing to NIRU as far in advance of the first anticipated importation as possible. If successful, NIRU will issue a letter of approval against which HMRC will allow relief.
- The exhibits must be of an educational, scientific or cultural character and not for resale.
- The exhibit must be dispatched directly to the approved establishment and must be used exclusively as exhibits or specimens under its control.
- Records of the imported exhibits must be kept.
- The exhibits must be imported either free of charge, or, if for a consideration, must not be supplied to the importer in the course or furtherance of any business.

The exhibits may be lent, hired out or transferred to other institutions which are approved under this procedure provided the NIRU has received prior notification.

Please see Customs Notice 361 for more information on claiming relief.

[*SI 1984/746, Sch 2 Group 9; EC Council Directive 2009/132/EC, Art 81*].

(Customs Notice 361, paras 2.1, 3.1).

See also **74.3** and **74.4 WORKS OF ART, ETC.** for an effective reduced rate of VAT of 5% on the importation of works of art including any antique more than 100 years old.

(11) Fuel, animal fodder and feeding stuffs, and packing for use during transportation

No VAT is charged on the following imports.

- Fuel contained in the standard tanks (as defined) of a motor road vehicle or of a 'special container', for use exclusively by such vehicle or such special container. '*Special container*' means any container fitted with specially designed apparatus for refrigeration, oxygenation, thermal insulation and other systems.
- Fuel, not exceeding ten litres for each vehicle, contained in portable tanks carried by a motor road vehicle, for use exclusively by such vehicle. This does not apply to a special purpose vehicle or one which, by its construction and equipment, is designed for and capable of transporting goods or more than nine persons including the driver.
- Lubricants contained in a motor road vehicle, for use exclusively by such vehicle and necessary for its normal operation during the journey.
- Litter, fodder and feeding stuffs contained in any means of transport carrying animals, for the use of such animals during their journey.
- Disposable packings for the stowage and protection (including heat protection) of goods during their transportation to the UK and where the cost is included in the consideration for the goods transported.

[*SI 1984/746, Sch 2 Group 10; EC Council Directive 2009/132/EC, Arts 82–83*].

(12) Funerals, war graves, etc.

The following goods are relieved from VAT on importation from a country outside the EU.

- Goods imported by an approved organisation for use in the construction, upkeep or ornamentation of cemeteries, tombs and memorials in the UK which commemorate war victims of other countries.
- Coffins containing human remains and urns containing human ashes, together with accompanying flowers, wreaths or other ornamental objects.
- Flowers, wreaths or other ornamental objects imported without commercial intent by a person resident outside the EU for use at a funeral or to decorate a grave.

[*SI 1984/746, Art 2, Sch 2 Group 11; EC Council Directive 2009/132/EC, Arts 89, 90*].

(13) Personal belongings, etc.

Personal property can be imported without VAT liability in the circumstances set out in (*a*)–(*e*) below. See also **34.19**(1) below for belongings returned to the UK after previously being exported.

In addition to any specific conditions, relief is only due if the following general conditions are met.

- The goods are declared for relief to the proper officer on importation. Where any goods are declared before the date on which a person becomes normally resident in the UK or, if he intends to become so resident on the occasion of his marriage, before such marriage has taken place, relief is subject to such security as HMRC require being furnished.
- Where relief is given otherwise than under (*c*) or (*d*) below, the goods must not, unless indicated otherwise below, be lent, hired-out, given as security or transferred in the UK without authorisation from HMRC within a period of twelve months from the relief being given. Where HMRC do give authorisation, they may discharge the relief and require payment of the VAT at the rate then in force (or, if lower, the rate at the time of importation).
- Any conditions for receiving relief (including the intention of becoming normally resident and the use to which the goods are put) must be complied with. If not, the VAT becomes payable forthwith (unless HMRC see fit to waive payment or part) and the goods are liable to forfeiture.

[*SI 1992/3193, Arts 6–10*].

(a) Relief for persons transferring their normal residence from outside the EU

A person entering the UK is not required to pay VAT (or duty) chargeable on 'property' imported into the UK provided

- he has been 'normally resident' outside the EU for a continuous period of at least twelve months;

- he intends to become normally resident in the UK;
- the property has been in his possession and used by him in the country where he has been normally resident for at least six months before its importation;
- the property is intended for his personal or household use in the UK;
- the property is declared for relief not earlier than six months before the date of becoming normally resident in the UK (or earlier where HMRC are satisfied that a person has given up normal residence outside the EU but is prevented by occupational ties from becoming normally resident in the UK) and not later than twelve months after that date; and
- HMRC are satisfied that the property has borne (and not been exempted from, or had refunded, because of exportation) all duties and taxes normally applicable in its country of origin or exportation.

'*Property*' means any personal property intended for personal use or meeting household needs, including household effects, provisions and pets; riding animals, cycles, motor vehicles, caravans, pleasure boats and private aircraft; but excluding any goods which, by their nature or quantity, indicate they are being imported for a commercial purpose. Specifically excluded are

- alcoholic beverages and tobacco products;
- any motor vehicle designed for or capable of transporting more than nine persons including the driver, or goods;
- any special purpose vehicle or mobile workshop; and
- any articles for use in a trade or profession, other than portable instruments of the applied or liberal arts.

'*Normally resident*'. A person is treated as normally resident in a country where he usually lives

(i) for a period, or aggregate of periods, of at least 185 days in a period of twelve months; and
(ii) because of his 'occupational ties'; and
(iii) because of his 'personal ties'.

Where a person has no occupational ties, he is treated as normally resident in a country on the basis of (i) and (iii) above only, provided his personal ties show close links with that country.

Where a person has occupational ties and personal ties in different countries, he is treated as normally resident in the country where he has personal ties provided

- the stay in the country where he has occupational ties is to carry out a task of a definite duration; or
- he returns regularly to the country with personal ties.

However, a UK citizen with personal ties in the UK but with occupational ties outside the EU may be treated as normally resident in the country of his occupational ties provided that he satisfies the condition in (i) above in the country with occupational ties.

'*Occupational ties*' do not include attendance by a pupil or student at a school, college or university.

'*Personal ties*' mean family or social ties to which a person devotes most of his time not devoted to occupational ties.

[*SI 1992/3193, Arts 2, 3, 11, 12; EC Council Directive 2009/132/EC, Arts 3–11*].

See also *Rigsadvokaten v N C Ryborg*, ECJ [1993] STC 680.

By concession, relief may still be granted where personal belongings fail to qualify only because they have not been possessed and used for the specified period or have been declared for relief outside the specified time limit. In addition, property (including motor vehicles) purchased

- by diplomats, members of certain international organisations and NATO forces,
- by UK forces (or civilian staff accompanying them) outside the EU, and
- under a UK export scheme by members of the UK diplomatic service, members of UK forces and members of certain international organisations

which otherwise qualifies for relief will not be refused relief solely because HMRC cannot satisfy themselves that the goods have borne all duties and taxes normally applicable in their country of origin.

(VAT Notice 48, ESCs 9.3–9.7).

(b) Relief on marriage

A person entering the UK is not required to pay VAT (or duty) on 'property' imported into the UK provided

- he has been 'normally resident' outside the EU for a continuous period of at least 12 months;
- he intends to become normally resident in the UK on the occasion of his marriage; and
- declared for relief not earlier than two months before the date fixed for the marriage (in which case security for the VAT and duty will be required which will be discharged on subsequent submission of the marriage certificate to HMRC) and not later than four months after the marriage.

'*Property*' for these purposes is limited to household effects and trousseaux, other than tobacco products and alcoholic beverages (i.e. it does not extend to motor vehicles and their trailers, caravans, mobile homes, pleasure boats and aircraft although some of these may alternatively qualify for relief under (*a*) above).

In addition, such a person is not required to pay VAT (or duty) on any wedding gift (meaning any property, other than tobacco products or alcoholic beverages, customarily given on the occasion of a marriage) not exceeding £800 in value imported into the UK by him or on his behalf provided the gift is

- given or intended to be given to him on the occasion of his marriage by a person normally resident outside the EU; and

- declared for relief not earlier than two months before the date fixed for the marriage (in which case security for the VAT and duty will be required which will be discharged on subsequent submission of the marriage certificate to HMRC) and not later than four months after the marriage.

See (*a*) above for the definition of '*normally resident*'.

[*SI 1992/3193, Arts 13–15; EC Council Directive 2009/132/EC, Arts 12–16*].

(c) Pupils and students

A person is not required to pay VAT (or duty) in respect of 'scholastic equipment' imported in to the UK provided

- he is a pupil or student normally resident outside the EU who has been accepted to attend a full-time course at a school, college or university in the UK; and
- the equipment belongs to him and is intended for his personal use during the period of his studies.

'*Scholastic equipment*' means household effects representing the normal furnishings for the room of the pupil or student, clothing, uniforms, and articles or instruments normally used by pupils or students for their studies, including calculators and typewriters.

[*SI 1992/3193, Art 16; EC Council Directive 2009/132/EC, Arts 21, 22*].

(d) Honorary decorations, awards and goodwill gifts

No VAT (or duty) is chargeable on the importation into the UK

- by a person normally resident in the UK of any honorary decoration confirmed on him by a government outside the EU or any cup, medal or similar article of an essentially symbolic nature awarded to him outside the EU as a tribute to his activities in the arts, sciences, sport or public service or in recognition of merit at a particular event;
- by a person normally resident in the UK, returning from an official visit outside the EU, of goods not intended for a commercial purpose given to him on his visit by the host authorities; or
- by a person normally resident outside the EU paying an official visit to the UK of goods not intended for a commercial purpose which are in the nature of an occasional gift he intends to offer to the host authorities during his visit.

Imports of tobacco products and alcoholic beverages are excluded.

See Customs Notice 364 for information on the import procedure and claiming relief.

[*SI 1992/3193, Arts 17–20; EC Council Directive 2009/132/EC, Art 58*].

(e) Personal property acquired by inheritance

A person who is either

- 'normally resident' in the UK or Isle of Man,

- a '*secondary resident*' who is not normally resident outside the EU, or
- a body incorporated in the UK or Isle of Man solely concerned with carrying on a non-profit making activity

and who has become entitled as legatee to 'property' situated outside the EU is not liable to pay any VAT (or duty) on importation of the property into the UK provided

- the property is imported not later than two years after the date of entitlement as legatee is finally determined (unless HMRC allow otherwise); and
- the person produces the property to the proper officer for examination and furnishes proof of his entitlement as legatee.

'*Property*' means any personal property intended for personal use or meeting household needs, including household effects, provisions and pets; riding animals, cycles, motor vehicles, caravans, pleasure boats and private aircraft; but excluding any goods which, by their nature or quantity, indicate they are being imported for a commercial purpose. Specifically excluded are

- alcoholic beverages and tobacco products;
- any motor vehicle designed for or capable of transporting more than nine persons, including the driver, or goods;
- any special purpose vehicle or mobile workshop;
- articles (other than portable instruments of the applied or liberal arts) used in the exercise of a trade or profession before his death by the person from whom the legatee has acquired them;
- stocks of raw materials and finished or semi-finished products; and
- livestock and agricultural products exceeding the quantities for normal family requirements.

See (*a*) above for the meaning of '*normally resident*'.

A '*secondary resident*' is a person who, without being normally resident in the UK or Isle of Man, has a home there which he owns or is renting for at least twelve months.

[*Customs and Excise Duties (General Reliefs) Act 1979, s 7; SI 1992/3193, Art 21; EC Council Directive 2009/132/EC, Arts 17–20*].

The following must be provided as proof of inheritance.

- A copy of the will (or other legal documents if the deceased died intestate) proving entitlement to the relief and identifying the goods, certified by the executors of the estate or other persons responsible for winding up the deceased's estate.
- If the goods are not precisely specified in the will, etc. (e.g. where they formed part of the residue) a list of the goods and their approximate value prepared by the executors, etc and confirmation from them that title to the goods passed to the legatee.
- A signed declaration on Form C1421 (claim for relief) which can be downloaded from the GOV.UK website.

(Customs Notice 368, paras 3.1, 4 – see also for more information on making a claim and declaring the goods).

Small non-commercial consignments

[34.16] No VAT is charged on the importation of a small non-commercial consignment, not forming part of a larger consignment, provided

- the consignment is of an occasional nature;
- the value for customs purposes does not exceed £39 (£34 before 1 January 2017, £36 before 1 January 2016, £40 before 1 January 2013) (€45) [*SI 2015/2015*];
- it is consigned by one private individual to another;
- it is not imported for any consideration in money or money's worth; and
- it is intended solely for personal use of the consignee, or of his family, and not for any commercial purpose.

Any of the following goods included in the consignment must be below the permitted quantities shown. Otherwise no relief is given for any goods of that description in the consignment.

Tobacco	50 cigarettes *or* 25 cigarillos *or* 10 cigars *or* 50g of smoking tobacco
Alcoholic beverages	1 litre of spirits, etc. with an alcoholic strength exceeding 22% by volume *or* 1 litre of spirits, aperitifs, etc. with an alcoholic strength of no more than 22% by volume, fortified wines and sparkling wines *or* 2 litres of still wines
Perfume and toilet water	50g of perfume *or* 250cc/ml of toilet water

This relief does not apply to goods contained in the baggage of, or carried with, a person entering the UK (for which see **34.17** below).

[*SI 1986/939*].

Travellers' allowances

[34.17] A person who has travelled from a country outside the VAT territory of the EU (see **18.2 EUROPEAN UNION: GENERAL**) is relieved from payment of VAT on goods of up to the values listed below which he has obtained outside the VAT territory of the EU (or in a duty free shop in the EU on an outward journey) and which are contained in his personal luggage. The goods must not be imported or used for commercial purposes otherwise they are liable to forfeiture.

Tobacco	200 cigarettes *or* 100 cigarillos *or* 50 cigars *or* 250g of smoking tobacco
Alcoholic beverages	1 litre with an alcoholic strength of more than 22% by volume *or* 2 litres with an alcoholic strength of no more than 22%; 4 litres of still wines; 16 litres of beer
Other goods	£390 if travel by air or sea; £270 if travel not by air or sea

No one under the age of 17 is entitled to relief for tobacco or alcoholic beverages. Private pleasure-flying or private pleasure-sea-navigation do not constitute travel by air or sea.

[*SI 1994/955*].

Goods imported for sale to another EU member state

[34.18] Subject to such conditions as HMRC impose, the VAT charged on the importation of goods from outside the EU is not payable where

- a taxable person imports goods in the course of an onward zero-rated supply of those goods by him to a taxable person in another EU member state; and
- HMRC are satisfied that he intends to remove the goods to another EU member state and he does in fact so remove the goods within one month of the date of importation (i.e. the date the goods enter free circulation). HMRC may approve a longer period.

HMRC may require the deposit of security up to the amount of the VAT chargeable on the importation.

[*SI 1995/2518, Reg 123*].

In the above circumstances, no import VAT is due in the UK or the EU member state of destination but VAT on the supply/acquisition is accounted for by the purchaser in the EU member state of destination.

Relief under these provisions cannot be claimed for goods imported for process and supply to a customer in another EU member state.

To claim the relief the person must be making a zero-rated supply of the imported goods, not merely acting as freight forwarder/shipper, to a taxable person in another EU member state.

Records

As the onward supply is to a consignee in another EU member state who will account for tax on the acquisition, the normal procedures must be adopted. In particular a VAT invoice must be issued and details recorded on an EC Sales List and, where appropriate, an Intrastat Declaration.

(VAT Notice 702/7/17).

Reimported goods

[34.19] Goods which have previously been exported can be reimported without payment of VAT in the following circumstances.

(1) Returned goods relief

Returned goods relief renders the payment of VAT unnecessary on the importation of goods into the UK that are in the same state as when they were previously exported from the EU by the importer.

The rules for such import VAT relief are aligned with those for returned goods relief from import duty.

Goods which, having been exported from the EU, are reimported and released for free circulation within a period of three years (or such longer period as may be allowed in special circumstances) may be granted relief from VAT provided:

- The goods are reimported by the same person who originally exported them.
- The goods are reimported in the state in which they were exported. This does not apply where they only received
  - (i) treatment necessary to maintain them in good condition or handling which altered their appearance only; or
  - (ii) treatment or handling not falling within (i) above but which proved to be defective or unsuitable for their intended use and *either* the treatment or handling was applied to the goods solely with a view to repairing them or restoring them to good condition *or* their unsuitability for their intended use became apparent only after such treatment or handling had commenced.
- The goods were not exported under the outward processing procedure (unless those goods remain in the state in which they were exported).

Relief is not available if

- the reimporter
  - (i) supplies the goods whilst under the inward processing procedure or in the course of, or after, the relevant exportation;
  - (ii) the place of that supply is outside the UK; and
  - (iii) the goods may be stored or physically used in the UK by or under the direction of that reimporter or the recipient; or
- the goods in question were supplied at any time to any person under *SI 1995/2518, Regs 131–133* (persons departing from the EU, see **22.13** and **22.19 EXPORTS**).

But where, prior to their exportation, the returned goods had been released for free circulation at the reduced or zero-rate of VAT because of their use for a particular purpose, exemption from VAT can be granted only if they are to be reimported for the same purpose. Where the purpose for which the goods in question are to be imported is no longer the same, the amount of VAT chargeable on them is reduced by any amount charged on the goods when they were first released for free circulation. Should this amount exceed that charged on the entry for free circulation of the returned goods, no refund will be granted.

The amount of the relief due is reduced by any '*unpaid VAT*', i.e. any part of the VAT charged and due on

- a supply or acquisition of the goods in another EU member state before the reimportation, or
- an importation of the goods from outside the EU before the reimportation,

but repaid, remitted or otherwise not paid. Paid does not mean deducted as input tax.

Returned goods are exempt from VAT even where they represent only a proportion of the goods previously exported from the EU. The same applies where the goods consist of parts or accessories belonging to machines, instruments, apparatus or other products previously exported from EU.

[*SI 1995/2518, Reg 121D; Regulation (EU) 952/2013, Art 203; Regulation (EU) 2015/2447, Arts 253–257*].

(2) Reimportation after exportation for treatment or process

Subject to any conditions that HMRC may impose, VAT chargeable on the importation of goods which have been temporarily exported outside the EU and are reimported

- after repair, process or adaptation outside the EU, or
- after having been made up or reworked outside the EU

is payable as if such treatment or process had been carried out in the UK, provided HMRC are satisfied that

- at the time of exportation the goods were intended to be reimported after completion of the treatment or process; and
- the ownership in the goods was not transferred to any other person at exportation or at any time the goods were abroad.

[*SI 1995/2518, Reg 126*].

See also Customs Notice 3001, Annex D 'Inward and Outward Processing Relief'.

Repayment or remission of VAT on rejected goods

[34.20] Repayment or remission of VAT on rejected goods is treated as follows:

(1) Goods not in accordance with contract

Repayment or remission of VAT can be claimed on goods imported if the goods

- are rejected because, at the time of declaring them to Customs, they
  - (i) are defective;
  - (ii) do not comply with the terms of the contract under which they were imported; or
  - (iii) were damaged before being cleared by Customs;
- are those declared to Customs;
- have not been used more than was necessary to establish that they were defective or did not comply with contract;
- have not been sold after they have been found to be defective or not to comply with the contract; and
- are disposed of by
  - (i) exportation;
  - (ii) destruction at the expense of the importer;

(iii) destruction by order of a public authority; or
(iv) placing in a customs warehouse.

HMRC must be notified on Form 1179, which can be downloaded from the GOV.UK website, at least 48 hours before the intended disposal and disposal must take place under Customs control. Any waste or scrap resulting from authorised destruction of the goods is liable to VAT (and duty) unless exported from the EU.

Claims must be made within 12 months of the date Customs charges became due and for an amount exceeding €10.

A fully taxable VAT-registered person importing goods for business purposes should normally be able to deduct the VAT due on importation on his next VAT return. However, a direct repayment can be claimed under the above provisions. If so, he must surrender the import VAT certificate relating to the goods and make a signed declaration that he will not make a corresponding claim for input tax deduction on a VAT return.

A partly exempt person whose method of apportionment does not allow him to recover all the relevant input tax, a non-registered person or a taxable person importing goods for non-business purposes should submit a claim for direct repayment.

See Customs Notice 266 for details of how to make the claim.

(2) Goods in special situations

Repayment or remission of VAT can be claimed on imported goods in a number of special situations provided the goods have not been used or sold after import and the claim (which must be for an amount exceeding 10 euros) is made within twelve months of the date Customs charges became due. Each case will be decided on its merits but examples include where the goods are

- in a means of transport which it is impossible to open on arrival at its destination after the goods have been released for free circulation (provided the goods are immediately re-exported);
- forbidden to be marketed by a judicial body and are re-exported from the EU or destroyed under customs supervision (provided the goods have not been used in the UK);
- entered by a declarant empowered to do so on their own initiative and which, through no fault of the declarant, cannot be delivered to the consignee;
- addressed to the consignee in error, e.g. wrongly labelled, not ordered by the consignee, or received in excess of the quantity ordered (provided the goods are re-exported to the original supplier or to an address specified by them and, in the case of excess goods, the consignee refused the goods immediately the excess was discovered);
- found to be unsuitable because of an obvious error in the consignee's order (e.g. wrong goods received due to quoting an incorrect reference number);
- found not to have complied, at the time of entry into free circulation, with the rules in force concerning their use or marketing and cannot therefore be used as the consignee intended;

- unable to be used because of official measures taken after the date of entry for free circulation (e.g. new safety or hygiene laws);
- delivered to a consignee after a fixed delivery date (e.g. because of shipping delays); and
- found to be unsaleable in the EU and are to be donated to charity, in which case the goods must either be
  - (i) exported and given free of charge to a charity operating outside the EU, provided that the charity is also represented in the EU; or
  - (ii) delivered free of charge to a charity operating in the EU, provided the charity is eligible to import similar goods free of VAT and duty under **34.15**(6) above, **13.7, 13.8 CHARITIES** or **29.32 HEALTH AND WELFARE.**

(Customs Notice 266, paras 3.1, 3.2).

Visiting forces

[34.21] No VAT is required where

- an 'entitled person' imports any goods, or
- a gift of goods, other than tobacco products or alcoholic beverages, is made to an entitled person by dispatching them to him from outside the EU

subject to the following conditions.

(a) The goods must not be lent, hired-out, given as security or transferred in the UK without the prior authorisation in writing by HMRC. Where HMRC do authorise such disposal, the entitled person must then pay the VAT relieved at the lower of the rate in force at the time of relief and the rate at the time of disposal.

(b) The goods must be used exclusively by the entitled person or a member of his family forming part of his household.

(c) In the case of a motor vehicle,
- no relief is available if the entitled person has previously been afforded relief in respect of any other motor vehicle unless he has disposed of all such vehicles (or all but one if his spouse or civil partner is present in the UK) and paid any duty or tax required by HMRC as under (*a*) above; and
- the entitled person must deliver, or cause to be delivered, four copies of a completed Form C941, each signed by the entitled person and his commanding officer. One copy is to be delivered to the visiting forces, and three copies to the proper officer.

An '*entitled person*' means a person who is

- a serving member of a visiting force, other than the UK, which is a member of NATO or a person recognised by the Secretary of State as a member of the civilian component of such a force; or
- a person who is a military or civilian member of NATO International Military Headquarters

who is neither a UK national nor a permanent resident of the UK.

Where any conditions are not complied with, the VAT becomes payable forthwith (unless HMRC sanction non-compliance in writing) and the goods are liable to forfeiture. Any VAT due is the liability of the entitled person or any person in possession of the goods at that time.

[*SI 1992/3156*].

Aircraft ground and security equipment

[34.22] By concession, no VAT or duty is chargeable on the importation of the following ground and security equipment for aircraft by an airline of another contracting state of the Convention on International Civil Aviation (Chicago Convention).

- All repair, maintenance and servicing equipment; material for airframes, engines and instruments; specialised aircraft repair kits; starter batteries and carts; maintenance platforms and steps; test equipment for aircraft, aircraft engines and aircraft instruments; aircraft engine heaters and coolers; ground radio equipment.
- Passenger-handling equipment: passenger-loading steps; specialised passenger-weighing devices; specialised catering equipment.
- Cargo-loading equipment: vehicles for moving or loading baggage, cargo, equipment and supplies; specialised cargo-loading devices; specialised cargo-weighing devices.
- Component parts for incorporation into ground equipment including the items listed above.
- Security equipment: weapon-detecting devices; explosives-detecting devices; intrusion detecting devices.
- Component parts for incorporation into security equipment.

Claims for relief under this concession should be addressed to the Customs Entry Processing Unit where the goods are to be cleared.

(Customs Notice 48, ESC 2.7).

Gas, electricity, heat and cooling

[34.23] VAT is not payable on the importation of

- gas through a natural gas system or any network connected to such a system, or fed in from a vessel transporting gas into a natural gas system or any upstream pipeline network;
- electricity; or
- heat or cooling supplied through a network.

[*SI 2010/2924*].

ERICs

[34.24] From 1 January 2013, VAT is not chargeable on the importation or acquisition of goods by a European Research Infrastructure Consortium ('ERIC'), subject to the following conditions.

- The statutory seat of the ERIC referred to in *Art 8(1)* of *Council Regulation (EC) No 723/2009* on the Community legal framework for a European Research Infrastructure Consortium is located in an EU member state.
- The goods are for the official use of the ERIC.
- Relief is not precluded by the limitations and conditions laid down in the agreement between the members of the ERIC referred to in *Art 5(1)(d)* of *Council Regulation (EC) No 723/2009*.
- A certificate in writing has been given to the Commissioners on behalf of the ERIC that the above three requirements are met in relation to the importation or acquisition.

[*SI 2012/2907, Art* 2].

Under *para 8* of the preamble to *Council Regulation (EC) No 723/2009*, an ERIC should have as its principal task the establishment and operation of a research infrastructure on a non-economic basis and should devote most of its resources to this principal task. In order to promote innovation and knowledge and technology transfer, the ERIC should be allowed to carry out some limited economic activities if they are closely related to its principal task and they do not jeopardise its achievement.

For the zero-rating of supplies to ERICs, see **75.15 ZERO-RATED SUPPLIES.**

[*SI 2012/2907, Art* 2].

De Voil Indirect Tax Service. See V3.357B.

Goods imported under customs special procedures

[34.25] For import VAT purposes, goods are normally treated as imported when they arrive in the UK and are entered to free circulation (whether by direct import from a place outside the customs territory of the EU or by indirect import on removal to the UK via another EU member state).

But for any goods placed under one of the following customs special procedures, import VAT (and duty) only become due when the goods are removed to free circulation in the UK.

The special procedures are:

- Temporary admission with total relief from customs duties (see **34.26–34.30** below).
- IP suspension (see **34.31–34.33** below).
- Processing under customs control. Please note that this customs procedure ceased to exist with the introduction of the Union Customs Code and has been combined with inward processing.
- External transit (T1) arrangements or internal transit (T2) arrangements. (Although internal transit is not a customs suspensive procedure it is included here as import VAT may become due if the goods are subsequently removed to free circulation.) See **34.34** below.
- Customs warehousing (see **73.2 WAREHOUSED GOODS**).

- Temporary storage. (Although such goods are not strictly under customs arrangements, goods arriving from outside the EU have the status of temporary storage until they are entered and cleared to free circulation or another procedure.)

Suspension of import VAT does *not* apply to goods entered to:

- Temporary admission with partial relief from customs duty.
- End-use relief (other than goods for the continental shelf). See **34.35** below.
- Outward processing relief.

Transfers of goods under special customs procedures

Goods can be moved from one suspensive regime to another without payment of import VAT.

Acquisitions of goods held under special customs procedures

VAT-registered traders who acquire goods held in one of the customs procedures listed above from a taxable person in another EU member state must normally account for VAT on the acquisition in accordance with the normal rules, even though the import VAT remains suspended.

Valuation

The valuation rules for imports (see **72.15 VALUATION**) also apply to any of the reliefs mentioned in this notice with the exception of certain goods entered to temporary admission relief (see **34.27** below).

Onward supply relief

Any goods imported under IP, temporary admission, or Customs warehousing arrangements which are imported in the course of an onward supply to a taxable person in another EU member state may be put into free circulation in the UK without the payment of import VAT. VAT is accounted for on the supply/acquisition by the purchaser in the EU member state of destination.

Any goods imported for processing and supply to a customer in another EU member state under IP may claim onward supply relief once the imported goods are entered to free circulation in the UK and dispatched to that EU member state.

Supplies of goods under special customs procedures

Supplies of goods held under customs procedures are chargeable with VAT in the normal way. This is subject to the following special rules.

- *Goods in temporary storage*. Where there is a supply of imported goods between the time of their arrival in the UK and the time when a customs entry is made and the purchaser is required to make the import entry, then the supplier may zero-rate the supply.
- *Goods under temporary import arrangements supplied to persons established outside the EU*. Where goods held under temporary import arrangements are supplied, that supply is treated as neither a supply of goods nor a supply of services provided that

(i) the goods remain eligible for temporary admission arrangements; and
(ii) the supply is to a person established outside the EU.
[*SI 1992/3130*].

- *Second-hand goods and works of art under temporary import arrangements.* Subject to below, where
(a) second-hand goods are imported with a view to their sale by auction, or
(b) 'works of art' are imported for exhibition with a view to possible sale,

any sale of the second-hand goods (provided it is by auction) or the works of art at a time when the goods are still subject to temporary admission arrangements with total exemption from import duty is treated as neither a supply of goods nor a supply of services and can be disregarded for VAT purposes.
The provision of any services relating to such supplies (e.g. auctioneers' charges) may similarly be disregarded (but must be included in the value for VAT at importation).
'*Works of art*' mean any such items falling within the definition in *VATA 1994, s 21* (see **74.3**(*a*) **WORKS OF ART, ETC.**).
The above treatment does not apply where
  - any goods falling within **74.3**(*a*)–(*c*) **WORKS OF ART, ETC.** are sold by auction at a time when they are subject to the temporary admission arrangements; and
  - following the sale by auction, arrangements are made by or on behalf of the purchaser which result in the importation of the goods from a place outside the EU.
  Such transactions are treated as supplies of goods in the ordinary way.
  [*SI 1995/958*].

Relief for temporary admissions (TA relief)

[34.26] Persons who temporarily import goods may either

- take advantage of the TA relief provisions, pay no VAT (or duty) at the time of importation but comply with the authorisation requirements for operating TA, which include obtaining guarantees for an amount of the VAT (and duty) which would become due if the conditions for temporary admission are not met; or
- if they are taxable persons importing the goods for business purposes, pay the VAT at the time of temporary admission (or defer it under the provisions relating to deferment of VAT, see **34.5** above) and reclaim the VAT paid as input tax subject to the normal rules. If this is done, there is no limit on the length of time that the goods may be held in the UK before re-exportation (although the relevant controls and time limits for any duty remain).

Subject to meeting certain conditions, it is possible to obtain total relief from import duties and VAT on a range of goods imported from outside the EU if they are intended for re-export within a specified time (usually a maximum of two years). See **34.27** below for eligible goods. In most cases, application for authorisation to use TA relief can be made at the time of importation. There are, however, other types of authorisations available. See Customs Notice 3001 for the various types of authorisation and how to apply for them, and the documentary evidence which must be presented to HMRC to use the relief.

For most importations, it is necessary to provide security by mandatory bank guarantee equal to the full amount of duty and import VAT potentially due. This may be reclaimed when the goods have been re-exported and satisfactory documentary evidence can be provided. See **34.28** below.

Goods eligible for TA relief

[34.27] The various TA reliefs that provide for total relief from duties and VAT on importation are as listed below. The following general conditions apply.

- Unless otherwise stated, goods imported under TA provisions may remain in the EU for a maximum of two years. Application can be made in writing, before expiry of the original TA period, for a longer period. If TA goods are transferred to another Customs suspensive arrangement (e.g. IP or customs warehousing) only the remaining balance of the TA period will be available to those goods if they are re-entered to TA at a later date.
- Goods must remain in the same state. Repairs and maintenance, including overhaul and adjustments or measures to preserve the goods or to ensure their compliance with the technical requirements for their use under the arrangements are admissible.

(Notice 3001, Annex C, paras 1.1, 1.2).

(1) Pallets

Total relief from import duty shall be granted for pallets that are temporary imported for re-export. Pallets not imported for re-export should be declared to free circulation.

(Notice 3001, Annex C, para 2.2).

(2) Containers

Total relief from import duties shall be granted for containers which have been durably marked in an appropriate and clearly visible place with the following information.

- The identity of the owner or operator shown by either full name or an established identification (symbols such as emblems or flags being excluded).
- (With certain exceptions), the identification marks and numbers of the container, given by the owner or operator; its tare weight, including all its permanently fixed equipment.
- Apart from containers used for transport by air, the country to which the container belongs.

(Notice 3001, Annex C, para 2.4).

(3) Means of transport

Means of road, rail, air, sea and inland waterway transport may be relieved from VAT under the TA provisions where

- they are registered outside the EU in the name of a person established outside the EU (or, if the means of transport are not registered, they are owned by a person established outside the EU);
- they are used by a person established outside the EU.

Detailed rules are given in Notice 3001, Annex C, section 2. Without prejudice to other special provisions, the periods for discharge are as follows.

- For means of rail transport: twelve months.
- For commercially used means of transport other than rail transport: the time required for carrying out the transport operations.
- For means of road transport privately used by students: the period the student stays in the EU for the sole purpose of pursuing their studies.
- For means of road transport privately used by persons fulfilling assignments of a specified duration: the period this person stays in the EU for the sole purpose of fulfilling their assignment.
- For means of road transport privately used in other cases, including saddle or draught animals and the vehicles drawn by them: six months.
- For privately used means of air transport: six months.
- For privately used means of sea and inland waterway transport: 18 months.

(Notice 3001, Annex C, para 2.11).

(4) Personal effects and goods for sports purposes

For personal effects and goods for sports purposes imported by a traveller from outside the EU see Notice 3001, Annex C, para 3.1.

(5) Welfare materials for seafarers

Where they are

- used on a vessel engaged in international maritime traffic;
- unloaded from such a vessel and temporarily used ashore by the crew; or
- used by the crew of such a vessel in cultural or social establishments managed by non-profit-making organisations or in places of worship where services for seafarers are regularly held.

(Notice 3001, Annex C, para 3.2).

(6) Disaster relief material

Where it is used in connection with measures taken to counter the effects of disasters or similar situations within the EU and intended for state bodies or bodies approved by the competent authorities. (Notice 3001, Annex C, para 3.3).

(7) Medical, surgical and laboratory equipment

Where it is dispatched on loan at the request of a hospital or other medical institution which has urgent need of such equipment to make up for the inadequacy of its own facilities and where it is intended for diagnostic or therapeutic purposes. (Notice 3001, Annex C, para 3.4).

(8) Animals owned by a person established outside the EU

(Notice 3001, Annex C, para 3.5).

(9) Goods for use in frontier zones

Goods for use in frontier zones, i.e.

- equipment owned by a person established in the frontier zone adjacent to the frontier zone of temporary admission and used by a person established in that adjacent frontier zone, and
- goods used for the building, repair or maintenance of infrastructure in such a frontier zone under the responsibility of public authorities.

(Notice 3001, Annex C, para 3.6).

(10) Sound, image or data carrying media

For processing information for the purpose of presentation prior to commercialisation, or free of charge, or for provision with a sound track, dubbing or copying. (Notice 3001, Annex C, para 3.7).

(11) Publicity material

Included are

- display material in show-cases, stands and similar articles, including electrical and mechanical equipment required for operating such display;
- documentary films, records, tape recordings and other sound recordings intended for use in performances at which no charge is made, but excluding those whose subjects lend themselves to commercial advertising and those which are on general sale in the EU member state of temporary importation;
- reasonable number of flags;
- dioramas, scale models, lantern-slides, printing blocks, photographic negatives;
- specimens, in reasonable numbers, of articles of national handicrafts, local costumes and similar articles of folklore.

(Notice 3001, Annex C, para 3.7).

(12) Professional equipment

- owned by a person established outside the EU;
- imported either by a person established outside the EU or by an employee of the owner (the employee may be established in the EU); and

- used by the importer, or under their supervision, except in cases of audiovisual co-productions.

Relief does not apply to equipment to be used for the industrial manufacture or packaging of goods or, except in the case of hand tools, for the exploitation of natural resources, for the construction, repair or maintenance of buildings or for earth moving and like projects.

Included are

- Equipment for the press.
- Sound broadcasting, television broadcasting and cinematographic equipment and vehicles designed or specially adapted for use with such equipment.
- Other equipment for erection, testing, commissioning, checking, control, maintenance or repair of machinery, plant, means of transport, etc.
- Equipment necessary for: business persons, business efficiency consultants, productivity experts, accountants and members of similar professions; experts undertaking topographical surveys or geophysical prospecting work; experts combating pollution; doctors, surgeons, veterinary surgeons, midwives and members of similar professions; archaeologists, palaeontologists, geographers, zoologists and other scientists; entertainers, theatre companies and orchestras; lecturers to illustrate their lectures; photography trips; and vehicles designed or specially adapted for these purposes (e.g. mobile inspection units, travelling workshops and travelling laboratories).

(Notice 3001, Annex C, para 3.8).

(13) Pedagogic material and scientific equipment

- owned by a person established outside the EU;
- imported by public or private scientific, teaching or vocational training establishments which are essentially non-profit making and exclusively used in teaching, vocational training or scientific research under their responsibility;
- imported in reasonable numbers, having regard to the purpose of the importation; and
- not used for purely commercial purposes.

The time required to use the goods is subject to a maximum of 24 months.

Included are

- sound or image recorders or reproducers;
- sound and image media;
- specialised material (e.g. bibliographic equipment and audio-visual material for libraries, mobile libraries, language laboratories, simultaneous interpretation equipment, programmed teaching machines, mechanical or electronic, material specially designed for the educational or vocational training of handicapped persons);
- other material (e.g. wall charts, models, graphs, maps, plans, photographs and drawings, instruments, apparatus and models designed for demonstration purposes, collections of items with visual or audio

educational information, prepared for the teaching of a subject, instruments, apparatus, tools and machine-tools for learning a trade or craft equipment, including specially adapted or designed vehicles for use in relief operations, which is imported for the training of persons involved in relief operations); and

- other goods imported in connection with educational, scientific or cultural activities (e.g. costumes and scenery items sent on loan free of charge to dramatic societies or theatres, music scores sent on loan free of charge to music theatres or orchestras).

(Notice 3001, Annex C, para 3.9).

(14) Packings

Where

- if imported filled, packing are intended for re-exportation whether empty or filled; and
- if imported empty, are intended for re-exportation filled.

Packings are not to be used in internal traffic, except with a view to the export of goods. In the case of packings imported filled, this condition only applies from the time that they are emptied of their contents.

(Notice 3001, Annex C, para 3.10).

(15) Moulds, dies, etc.

Moulds, dies, blocks, drawings, sketches, measuring, checking and testing instruments and other similar articles

- owned by a person established outside the EU, and
- used in manufacturing by a person established in the EU

provided at least 50% of the production resulting from their use is exported. (Notice 3001, Annex C, para 3.11).

(16) Special tools

Special tools and instruments where the goods are

- owned by a person established outside the EU, and
- they are made available to a person established in the customs territory of the Union for the manufacture of goods and more than 50% of the production resulting from their manufacturing is exported.

Note: Evidence of ownership of the special tools and instruments should be provided. If the user does not export 50% of the goods produced, customs charges relieved under TA will be due even if the special tools and instruments are re-exported. The time required to carry out the operation subject to a maximum of six months.

(Notice 3001, Annex C, para 3.12).

(17) Goods for testing, etc.

Relief applies to

(a) goods subjected to tests, experiments or demonstrations;

(b) goods subject to satisfactory acceptance tests that are imported in connection with a sales contract containing the provisions of the satisfactory acceptance tests and subjected to those tests; and
(c) goods used to carry out tests, experiments or demonstrations without financial gain.

The period for re-export of goods under (b) or (c) above is six months. For (a) it is 24 months.

(Notice 3001, Annex C, para 3.13).

(18) Samples

Imported in reasonable quantities and solely used for being shown or demonstrated in the EU. (Notice 3001, Annex C, para 3.14).

(19) Replacement means of production

Temporarily made available to a customer by a supplier or repairer, pending the delivery or repair of similar goods. The period for re-export is six months. (Notice 3001, Annex C, para 3.15).

(20) Goods to be exhibited or used at a public event

Not purely organised for the commercial sale of the goods, or obtained at such events from goods placed under TA arrangements. (Notice 3001, Annex C, para 3.16).

(21) Goods for approval

Where they cannot be imported as samples and the consignor wishes to sell the goods and the consignee may decide to purchase them after inspection. The period for re-export is six months. (Notice 3001, Annex C, para 3.16).

(22) Works of art, collectors' items and antiques

Imported for the purposes of exhibition, with a view to possible sale. The maximum period is 24 months. (Notice 3001, Annex C, para 3.16).

(23) Second-hand goods

Imported with a view to their sale by auction, also subject to a limit of 24 months. (Notice 3001, Annex C, para 3.16).

(24) Spare parts, accessories and equipment

Used for repair and maintenance, including overhaul, adjustments and preservation of goods entered for the arrangements. (Notice 3001, Annex C, para 3.18).

(25) Miscellaneous goods

Goods

- not falling within other than those listed in (1)–(24) above, or

- falling within (1)–(24) above but not complying with the relevant conditions

which are imported

- occasionally and for a period not exceeding three months; or
- in particular situations having no economic effect.

(Notice 3001, Annex C, para 3.19).

Security and guarantees

[34.28] Security is required on some temporary admissions to cover the full amount of charges (including VAT and duty) that could become due if the goods are not ultimately re-exported.

(Notice 3001, Annex C, para 3.22).

Customs checks and records

[34.29] While goods remain in the EU they are subject to Customs supervision. A record must be kept of

- the declaration entering the goods to TA;
- when, where and how the goods are used;
- how the goods are identified (e.g. manufacturers marks, serial numbers, technical descriptions or illustrations); and
- evidence of disposal.

These records must be kept for four years after disposal of the goods. For the reliefs in **34.27**(5) and (16) above, it is also necessary to keep records of products manufactured using TA goods and evidence that the manufactured products are exported outside the EU.

(Notice 3001, Annex C, section 4).

Discharging TA arrangements

[34.30] Details of the discharge periods and procedures for different types of goods are given in Notice 3001, Annex C, section 2.

Inward processing relief (IP)

[34.31] IP provides relief to promote exports from the EU and assist Community processors to compete on an equal footing in the world market. Duty is relieved on imports of non-EU goods which are processed in the Community and re-exported providing the trade does not harm the essential interests of Community producers of similar goods. Under IP drawback the import VAT must be paid at the time of entry. However under IP suspension, the payment of import VAT is suspended and only becomes due if the goods are subsequently diverted to free circulation.

(Notice 3001, Annex D, section 2).

Calculation of import VAT

[34.32] Import VAT is payable at diversion to free circulation. It is based on the value of the diverted goods, inclusive of duty, at first entry to IP in the EU and the rate to be applied is that of the EU member state of diversion at the date of diversion.

(Notice 3001, Annex D, section 1).

Onward supply relief

[34.33] If goods are imported for processing and supplied to another EU member state onward supply relief may be claimed if the goods originally intended for process and re-export are diverted to free circulation in the UK with payment of customs duty and compensatory interest using CPC 42 51 000. If the business is a taxable person in the UK and its goods are held under IP suspension it may claim onward supply relief providing the goods are

- eligible for zero-rating under *VATA 1994, s 30(8)*;
- the goods so imported are subject to that supply under *SI 1995/2518, Reg 123*; and
- the goods are removed to another EU member state within one month of the date of importation.

The effect of this is that import VAT is not paid anywhere, but VAT on the supply/acquisition is accounted for by the purchaser in the EU member state of destination.

External and internal transit

[34.34] Community transit (CT) is a customs procedure which enables goods to be moved within the customs territory of the EU without the payment of import duties and other charges until they reach their final destination.

The external transit (T1) procedure allows the movement of mainly 'non-Union goods' within the customs territory of the EU without their being subject to import duties and other charges. The external procedure ends (and the obligations of the holder are met) when the goods placed under the procedure and the required documents are produced at the office of destination in accordance with the provisions of the relevant customs procedure.

The internal transit procedure (T2) allows the movement of 'Union goods' from one point to another within the customs territory of the EU to pass through the territory of a country outside the customs territory without any change in their customs status.

'*Non-Union goods*' are goods which are not of EU origin or imported goods which have not been released into free circulation.

'*Union goods*' are goods which are

(a) entirely obtained or produced in the Customs territory of the EU, without the addition of goods from third countries or territories that are not part of the Customs territory of the EU;

(b) imported from countries or territories not forming part of the Customs territory of the EU which have been released for free circulation in an EU member state; or

(c) obtained or produced in the Customs territory of the EU either wholly from those under (*b*) or partly from (*a*) and (*b*).

Treatment for import VAT

Any goods placed under external transit have the import VAT (and customs duty) suspended. Import VAT (and customs duty) only become due if the goods are subsequently removed to free circulation in the UK.

Goods placed under internal transit may have the import VAT suspended in particular circumstances (e.g. the 'T2F' procedure for movements to/from 'special territories', i.e. territories which are within the EU for customs purposes but outside it for VAT purposes, see **18.3 EUROPEAN UNION: GENERAL**).

End-use relief

[34.35] End-use relief is a trade facilitation regime to assist certain industries and trades within the EU by allowing reduced or nil rates of customs duty on certain goods imported from non-EU member states, provided the goods are put to a prescribed use.

End-use relief does not generally affect liability to import VAT, which must be paid or accounted for in the normal way, unless one of the reliefs under **34.14** above applies. End-use relief is described in Notice 3001, Annex C, sections 4–11.

Importing computer software

[34.36] Imported computer software may be classified as goods and/or services.

Goods

Goods are the tangible carrier medium on which the software resides.

- If the tangible carrier medium is magnetic tape, disk, diskette compact disk (CD) and read only CD videos, the VAT treatment depends on whether, at the time of importation, the items are 'normalised' (off the shelf) or 'specific' (custom made) products as explained below.
- If the information resides on semiconductors, integrated circuits or similar devices or articles incorporating such circuits or devices, VAT must be paid on the whole value of the medium/device, including information residing on it.

Services

Services may comprise the data, program and/or instructions (but not sound, cinematographic or video recordings). The VAT treatment of services received from outside the EU depends on whether they are 'normalised' (off the shelf) or 'specific' (custom made) software as explained below.

The transmission and provision of information by satellite, telephone, telex, facsimile, etc. is treated as a service. See **39.9 INTERNATIONAL SERVICES.**

Normalised

'*Normalised*' comprises mass-produced items which are freely available to all customers and usable by them independently, after installation and limited training, in a standard form to carry out the same applications or functions. They are made up of a coherent set of programs and support material and often include the service of installation, training and maintenance. *Included are* personal and home computer software, game packages, etc. and standard packages adapted at the supplier's instigation to include security or similar devices.

Importations of normalised items are regarded as importations of both goods (made up of the carrier medium, see above) and services (the data and/or the instructions).

- Where the goods and services are not identified separately, the whole importation is treated as an importation of goods.
- Where the goods and services are identified separately, a UK taxable person may pay VAT on importation only on the cost or value of the carrier medium. Normal valuation rules apply (see **72.15 VALUATION**). The supply of services falls within *VATA 1994, Sch 5 para 3* and VAT on these must be accounted for under the 'reverse charge' procedure (see **39.4 INTERNATIONAL SERVICES**).

Specific software

'*Specific*' software products are

- items made to customers' special requirements (either as unique programs or adaptations from standard programs);
- inter-company information data and accounts;
- enhancements and updates of existing specific programs; and
- enhancements and updates of existing normalised programs supplied under contractual obligation to customers who have bought the original program.

The importation of a specific item of software is made up of an importation of goods (the carrier medium, see above) and a supply of services (the data and/or the instructions) but to simplify import procedures, the carrier medium is treated as a supply of services. No import VAT is charged on the carrier medium at importation.

The supply of services falls within *VATA 1994, Sch 5 para 3* and a UK business must account for VAT on the supply under the 'reverse charge' procedure. See **39.4 INTERNATIONAL SERVICES.** No VAT is payable for specific items imported free of charge.

(VAT Notice 702, paras 7.1–7.13).

Importing motorised land vehicles

[34.37] From 15 April 2013, any person (other than an excepted relevant person) bringing a motorised land vehicle into the UK, for permanent use on the road must notify (or arrange for an authorised third party to notify) HMRC of the arrival of the vehicle within 14 days, prior to the vehicle being registered with the DVLA. If a non-registered business or private individual brings a car into the UK from an EU supplier, payment of the VAT due is required at the same time as the notification is made. Any vehicle that has not had the appropriate VAT charges paid will not be able to be registered with the DVLA. For VAT-registered businesses, the VAT charge due on the vehicle is to be accounted for on the VAT return, as with other goods acquired from the EU. The notification may be made either in paper form or electronically. It must contain

- the name and current address of the person bringing the land vehicle into the UK;
- the date when the land vehicle arrived in the UK;
- a full description of the land vehicle which shall include any vehicle registration mark allocated to it by any competent authority in another Member State prior to its arrival and any chassis identification number;
- where applicable, the registration number of the person bringing the land vehicle into the UK;
- the date of the notification;
- the price actually paid or payable for the land vehicle including any deposit, commission and fees;
- the entry number of the Customs declaration as defined in (with effect from 1 May 2016) *Regulation (EU) 952/2013, Art 5 para 12*;
- the relevant commodity code entered on the Customs declaration; and
- any other particulars specified in a notice published by HMRC.

The notification must be made in English, and must include a declaration that the information provided is true and complete.

From 1 April 2014, where there is a relevant decision regarding a vehicle after the vehicle has entered the UK the date of the relevant decision is treated as the date of arrival in the UK. A relevant decision is a decision that affects the notification process, e.g. a decision that a vehicle is not required to be registered for road use in the UK. (HMRC Brief 12/14).

[*VATA 1994, Sch 11 para 2(5D); SI 1995/2518, Reg 148A; SI 2014/548, Reg 5*].

Key points: imports

[34.38] Points to consider are as follows.

- It is important to recognise that different VAT rules apply depending on whether goods being acquired from overseas are imports (i.e. from a non-EU member state) or acquisitions (i.e.

from another EU member state). Advisers need to ensure that relevant clients have procedures in place to deal with the two different situations.

- It should be noted that no VAT is due on imported goods if the item in question would be zero-rated if supplied in the UK. Examples include books, children's clothing and many food items.
- Ensure that all importers obtain an Economic Operator Registration and Identification (EORI) number so that evidence will be sent by HMRC to support input tax claims (C79 certificate).
- Be aware one of the main benefits of holding a deferment account with HMRC is to delay paying VAT on imports until the 15th day of the following month. However, it is important to note that periodic deferment statements are unacceptable as evidence for input tax purposes – the C79 certificate is the evidence required to support any input tax claim. The payment method on the 15th day is always through a direct debit arrangement.
- It is worthwhile for importers with (or applying for) a deferment account to utilise the SIVA arrangements. This scheme reduces the level of a bank guarantee required for VAT on imports via a deferment account.
- If a business is not registered for VAT, it is important to monitor the value of its EU acquisitions to ensure it knows when they exceed the VAT registration limits during a calendar year on a cumulative basis. If the limits are exceeded the business will have to register for VAT.
- Some import transactions will be processed through the deferment account of the import agent. However, this is a commercial arrangement only and there is no entitlement for the import agent to reclaim input tax as he is not buying the goods himself. Only the importer can claim input tax, supported by a C79 document as evidence.

35

Input Tax

Cross-references. See **10 BUSINESS ENTERTAINMENT** for disallowed input tax; **11 CAPITAL GOODS SCHEME; 18.7 EUROPEAN UNION: GENERAL** for recovery of input tax suffered in another EU member state; **28.9 GROUPS OF COMPANIES** for recovery of input tax by holding companies; **34 IMPORTS; 43.23 LAND AND BUILDINGS: ZERO AND REDUCED RATE SUPPLIES AND DIY HOUSEBUILDERS** for refund of VAT to do-it-yourself housebuilders; **44.7 LOCAL AUTHORITIES AND PUBLIC BODIES** for refund of input tax for non-business purposes; **46 MOTOR CARS** for disallowed input tax on cars, accessories and petrol, etc.; **50 PARTIAL EXEMPTION** for restriction on recovery of input tax where exempt supplies are made; **54.2** and **54.3 PENSION SCHEMES.**

Introduction to input tax

EU legislation

[35.1] See **19.33 EUROPEAN UNION LEGISLATION** for the provisions of *Directive 2006/112/EC.*

UK legislation

Input tax, in relation to a taxable person, comprises VAT

- on goods and services supplied to him;
- on the acquisition of any goods by him from another EU member state; and
- paid or payable by him on the importation of goods from outside the EU

provided the goods or services are used, or to be used, for the purpose of business carried on, or to be carried on, by him.

[*VATA 1994, s 24(1)*].

VAT paid does not, however, become input tax simply because it has been incurred. It becomes input tax when it satisfies various criteria in **35.2** below arising out of the above definition and other legal requirements.

Criteria for VAT incurred to be treated as deductible input tax

[35.2] Before any VAT paid can be deducted as input tax, the following criteria must be met.

(a) The recipient of the supply, or the person acquiring or importing the goods, must be a taxable person (i.e. registered or required to be registered under *VATA 1994*) at the time the VAT was incurred. See, however, **35.10** and **35.11** below for pre-registration and post-deregistration VAT.

(b) The VAT must relate to an actual supply, acquisition or importation. Where payments are made in advance but the goods are never physically supplied, input tax cannot be reclaimed as no supply has taken place. See *Weldons (West One) Ltd* [1980] Lexis Citation 1349 (TVC 36.672), *Theotrue Holdings Ltd* [1983] VATTR 88 (TVC 36.674) and *C & E Commrs v Pennystar Ltd*, QB 1995, [1996] STC 163 (TVC 36.669). However, in *David Peters Ltd* (TC01819) (TVC 36.682) the tribunal decided that the company was entitled to reclaim input tax on the purchase of goods that were never delivered. The tribunal distinguished the case from *Pennystar* and *Icon Construction* (VTD 16416) in that there was no invoice made to the purchaser in *Pennystar* and the goods which were being purchased did not exist in *Icon Construction*. In *David Peters Ltd* the goods existed and there was a valid invoice made out to the purchaser.

(c) The amount to be claimed is the VAT properly chargeable and not the VAT actually charged where this is different. See *Podium Investments Ltd* (VTD 314) (TVC 36.717) and *Genius Holding BV v Staatssecretaris van Financien, ECJ Case 342/87*, [1991] STC 239 (TVC 22.473). This gives rise to a number of problems.

    (i) If the supplier is not a taxable person but shows VAT on the invoice, the VAT is not input tax and there is no automatic right of deduction. However, by concession, HMRC may allow a claim in these circumstances where they are satisfied that

    - the recipient of the supply is neither involved in nor has close knowledge of the supplier's business;
    - it was reasonable for the recipient to consider that he had been lawfully charged VAT; and
    - the claim is made in respect of goods and services genuinely supplied at the stated value.

    (ii) If the supplier is a taxable person but is not registered for VAT.

In *Ellen Garage (Oldham) Ltd* (VTD 12407) (TVC 40.12), a supplier had failed to register for VAT. The tribunal held that any VAT charged was recoverable as input tax (subject to meeting the other conditions for recovery) even though there could be no valid VAT invoice because, *inter alia*, the supplier has no registration number.

In *Ahmed (t/a New Touch)*, LON/04/1840 (VTD 20119) (TVC 40.42) a supplier had previously been registered for VAT but had subsequently been deregistered by HMRC. The tribunal held that VAT was not recoverable on invoices issued after deregistration and the fact that the supplier had remained a 'taxable person' was not conclusive. Disapproving of the decision in *Ellen Garage* above, the tribunal held that HMRC were entitled to require some corroborative documents or other similar evidence of the specific transactions entered into.

The decision in *Ellen Garage* above was also disapproved of in *Hargreaves (UK) plc* (VTD 20382) (TVC 36.716) where a haulage company reclaimed VAT on substantial quantities of 'laundered' rebated fuel which it was illegal to use in road vehicles and where the VAT numbers shown on the invoices belonged to deregistered companies. The tribunal held that a taxable person who knew (or should have known) that by making a purchase he was taking part in a transaction connected with the fraudulent evasion of VAT must be regarded as a participant in that fraud. As a result, it lost the right to deduct the VAT it paid.

(iii) VAT wrongly charged on a supply, etc. which is outside the scope of VAT, exempt or zero-rated is not input tax. See *Da Conti International Ltd* (VTD 6215) (TVC 36.725).

(d) The goods or services on which the VAT was charged must have been supplied to, or acquired or imported by, the person seeking to claim the input tax. See **35.5** below.

(e) The supplies must have been incurred for the purpose of the business. See **35.6** below.

(f) The supplies received must not be subject to input tax restriction either in the form of a Treasury 'blocking order' or otherwise. See **35.8** below.

(g) The supplies must normally be received in the accounting period in which the claim is to be made. See **35.9** below.

(h) The person seeking to claim input tax must hold a valid invoice or other satisfactory documentation. See **57.7 RECORDS**.

See, however, *Croydon Hotel & Leisure Co Ltd* (VTD 14920) (TVC 36.694) where it was held that a person is entitled to reclaim input tax even where a VAT invoice has not been issued, the right to deduct not being limited to cases were output tax has been paid but extending to cases where it is payable. In that case, the tribunal held that a payment of £2 million by the company was VAT-inclusive even though an earlier tribunal (*Holiday Inns (UK) Ltd* (VTD 10609) (TVC 62.146)) had (incorrectly in the second tribunal's opinion) held that in the hands of the recipient the payment did not represent consideration for a taxable supply.

(VAT Notice 48, ESC 3.9).

De Voil Indirect Tax Service. See V3.402.

> *Example*
> John is VAT-registered and buys a book that is relevant to his business. He pays £50 plus VAT to the book seller. In this situation, John cannot reclaim input tax on the cost of the book, even if he obtains a VAT invoice from the seller, because it is a zero-rated supply (printed matter). The VAT has been incorrectly charged by the book seller. John should obtain a VAT credit note from the book dealer to correct the position.

Amount of allowable input tax

[35.3] The amount of allowable input tax is so much of the input tax on supplies, acquisitions and importations in the period as is allowable as being attributable to the following supplies made, or to be made, by the taxable person in the course or furtherance of his business.

(a) '*Taxable supplies*', i.e. supplies of goods or services made in the UK other than exempt supplies.

(b) Supplies outside the UK which would be taxable supplies if made in the UK.

(c) Supplies of services which
   (i) are supplied to a person who belongs outside the EU, or
   (ii) are directly linked to the export of goods to a place outside the EU, or
   (iii) consist of the provision of intermediary services in relation to any transaction within (i) or (ii) above

   provided that the supply is exempt (or would have been exempt if made in the UK) by virtue of *VATA 1994, Sch 9 Group 2* (insurance) or *VATA 1994, Sch 9 Group 5 Items 1–8* (finance).

(d) Supplies made either in or outside the UK which fall, or would fall, within *VATA 1994, Sch 9 Group 15 item 1* or 2 (investment gold, see **27.2 GOLD AND PRECIOUS METALS**).

HMRC must make regulations for securing a fair and reasonable attribution of input tax to the supplies within (*a*) to (*c*) above.

[*VATA 1994, ss 4(2), 26; SI 1992/3123; SI 1999/3121*].

See **19.33 EUROPEAN UNION LEGISLATION** for the provisions of *Directive 2006/112/EC*.

The effect of the above is that VAT cannot be reclaimed on goods and services which are not used for business purposes (see **35.6** below) and, where exempt supplies are made, it may not be possible to recover all input tax incurred. See **50 PARTIAL EXEMPTION.**

If input tax can be reclaimed in full, the amount to reclaim is normally that shown on the VAT invoice received from the supplier (but see **35.2**(*c*) above where VAT is incorrectly charged). In the case of a less detailed tax invoice (see **40.7 INVOICES**) which does not show VAT separately, input tax is found by applying the VAT fraction (see **48.2 OUTPUT TAX**) to the total amount charged.

No taxable supplies

Where a person has made no taxable supplies in the period concerned or any previous period, any refunds of input tax are subject to such conditions as HMRC think fit to impose, including conditions as to repayment in specified circumstances. [*VATA 1994, s 25(6)*]. This could arise, for example, where a person has recently registered and is incurring expenditure but has yet to make any supplies. See, however, *D A Rompelman v Minister van Financien, ECJ Case 268/83*, [1985] 3 CMLR 202 (TVC 22.110) for when input tax credit becomes deductible.

De Voil Indirect Tax Service. See V3.418.

> *Example*
>
> ABC Accountants is VAT-registered in the UK. The firm has just completed some accounts for a business in Belgium. The fee from this work is outside the scope of VAT under the place of supply rules (place of supply is Belgium where the customer is based because this is a business to business sale). However, ABC Accountants can still get full input tax recovery on related costs (subject to normal rules) because the service provided would be subject to VAT if supplied to a UK customer.

Repayment of input tax where consideration not paid

[35.4] Where a person has

- claimed deduction of the whole or part of the VAT on the supply as input tax, and
- not paid the whole or any part of the consideration for that supply by the '*relevant date*' i.e. within six months of
  - (i) the date of the supply, or
  - (ii) if later, the date on which the consideration for the supply, or (as the case may be) the unpaid part of it, became payable

then, subject to below, he must make a negative entry in the VAT allowable portion of his VAT account for the VAT period in which the end of the relevant six-month period falls. The amount of this negative entry is calculated by formula

$$I \times \frac{U}{C}$$

where

I = the input tax claimed on the supply

U = consideration unpaid at the end of the relevant six-month period; and

C = the total consideration for the supply.

The above provisions

- do not apply where the cash accounting scheme is used and the operative date for the recovery of input tax is the date of payment (see **64.6 SPECIAL SCHEMES**); and
- are not to be regarded as giving rise to any application of the error correction notification (formerly voluntary disclosure) requirements (see **57.11 RECORDS**).

> *Example 1*
>
> B purchases goods for £1,200 (£1,000.00 plus £200.00 VAT) and reclaims the full amount of VAT. By the relevant date, it has only paid £500.00 (leaving £700 unpaid).
>
> It must make a repayment of input tax to HMRC of
>
> 200 × (700 ÷ 1,200) = £116.67

For the purposes of (ii) above, HMRC will accept the date of invoice as the due date for payment. This means that, normally, the date on which input tax becomes repayable is six months after the date of invoice (unless the supplier allows time to pay, for example, 30 or 60 days, in which case repayment of input tax is not required until six months from this later date). The only exception is, on the rare occasions, where the invoice is not issued within 14 days of the date of supply and where the due date for payment falls before the date on which the invoice is issued. In such a case, the input tax will become repayable six months after the date of supply or, if later, the date when the payment was due. (VAT Notice 700/18/13, para 4.3).

Where a customer is in dispute with the supplier, and the supplier agrees to extend the due date for payment of the amount in dispute, repayment is not required until six months after the agreed extended date for payment. (VAT Notice 700/18/13, para 4.4).

Insolvency

By concession, an insolvency practitioner need not repay input tax under the above provisions where the supply was made prior to the insolvency procedure commencing but the requirement to repay input tax occurs after that date provided

- HMRC have been properly notified of the insolvency (see **36.2 INSOLVENCY**); and
- the application of the concession does not give rise to tax avoidance.

The concession applies whether or not the business of the insolvent person is carried on.

The '*insolvency procedures*' to which the concession applies are bankruptcies, compulsory liquidations, creditors' and members' voluntary liquidations, administrative receiverships, administration orders, individual and company voluntary arrangements, Scottish trust deeds, deeds of arrangement, partnership voluntary arrangements and liquidations, partnership administration orders, sequestrations, county court administration orders, schemes of arrangement, and deceased persons' administration orders.

The effective date for the application of the concession is the date of HMRC's claim in the insolvency (i.e. the relevant date of the insolvency and the date of the insolvency meeting if applicable or, in the case of an administration order, the date of that order). The concession only applies to a provisional liquidation if it is followed by a permanent liquidation although, in such a case, the concession takes effect from the date of the provisional liquidation.

If an insolvency arrangement fails, the requirement to account for clawback is reinstated.

ESC 3.20 was designed to ensure insolvency practitioners do not become liable for clawback of input tax on bad debts where the supply took place prior to the insolvency of the business for which they act. On 4 November 2015 HMRC issued a technical consultation on draft legislation intended to put on a statutory basis the existing concessionary treatment. This ESC was replaced with legislation in *SI 2017/495* with effect from the 6 April 2017.

(VAT Notice 48, ESC 3.20; VAT Notice 700/18/13, para 4.9).

Restoration of an entitlement to credit for input tax

Where a person

- has made an entry in his VAT account in accordance with the above provisions ('*the input tax repayment*'),
- has made the return for the VAT period concerned, and has paid any VAT payable by him in respect of that period, and
- after the end of the relevant period, has paid the whole or part of the consideration for the supply in relation to which the input tax repayment was made,

then, subject to below, he may make a positive entry in the VAT allowable portion of his VAT account for the VAT period in which payment of the whole or part of the consideration is made. The amount of this positive entry is calculated by the formula

R x P ÷ C

where

R = the amount of the input tax repayment;

P = the whole or part of the consideration for the supply in relation to which the input tax repayment was made and which is subsequently paid; and

C = the consideration for the supply which was not paid before the end of the relevant period.

> *Example 2*
>
> The facts are the same as in *Example 1* above. After making the repayment of £116.67 to HMRC, B subsequently makes a further payment of £300.
>
> B can now reclaim VAT from HMRC of
>
> 116.67 × (300 ÷ 700) = £50.00

The above provisions are not to be regarded as giving rise to any application of the error correction notification (formerly voluntary disclosure) requirements (see **57.11 RECORDS**).

Attribution of payments

The rules on the attribution of payments in **7.6** under Method A and in **7.8**(1) **BAD DEBT RELIEF** apply for determining whether anything paid is to be taken as paid by way of consideration for a particular supply.

[*VATA 1994, s 26A; FA 2002, s 22; SI 1995/2518, Regs 172F–172J; SI 2002/3027, Reg 8; SI 2002/3028; SI 2003/532*].

Who can claim input tax

[35.5] Subject to below, for an input tax claim to be valid, the claim must be made by the person to whom the supply was made.

Where a third party pays for goods or services which are supplied to another person, the third party does not have the right to deduct input tax. This applies whether the payment was made due to a legal requirement or is simply a normal commercial practice. Examples of where this is likely to occur include

- payment of legal costs awarded against the unsuccessful party in litigation (see **35.13** below);
- payment of a landlord's costs by a tenant for the drawing up of a lease (see **42.4 LAND AND BUILDINGS: EXEMPT SUPPLIES AND OPTION TO TAX**); and
- payment by a business of the costs of a viability study undertaken by a bank in respect of the business's activities (see **36.10 INSOLVENCY**).

For a consideration of whether a supply has been made to a taxable person, even though it is physically delivered to a third party (e.g. in a tripartite arrangement) see *Leesportfeuille 'Intiem' CV v Staatssecretaris van Financien, ECJ Case 165/86*, [1989] 2 CMLR 856 (TVC 22.457) (petrol supplied to employees) and *C & E Commrs v Redrow Group plc*, HL 1998, [1999] STC 161 (TVC 36.159) (estate agents' fees for sales of existing homes paid for by builder on purchase of one of its new houses). See also the Input Tax chapter in *Tolley's VAT Cases* under the heading *Whether supplies made to the appellant*.

In *WHA Ltd v HMRC*, SC [2013] UKSC 24 (TVC 36.199), a group of companies instituted a scheme which was intended to allow the recovery of input tax charged on repair services made under insurance policies relating to vehicle breakdown. The scheme involved the use of two Gibraltar insurance companies, one of which (V) appointed a UK company (W) to handle claims and pay the repair bills. HMRC rejected the repayment claims, considering that the garages were making their supplies to the insured customers, rather than to W. W and V appealed, contending that the garages were supplying their services to W, which in turn was making onward supplies to V. The VAT Tribunal rejected this contention and dismissed the appeals, finding that there was no evidence showing that the benefit of the garage's supply of labour and parts was used for the purposes of W's business. There was no supply by W to V of the benefit of the supplies of labour and parts. The Supreme Court unanimously dismissed the companies' appeals. The garages had not made any supplies of repair services to W. The payments which W had made to the garages simply fulfilled the obligations which one of the insurance companies had undertaken to its customers. W was simply acting as a paymaster.

In *HMRC v Aimia Coalition Loyalty UK Ltd (aka Loyalty Management UK Ltd)*, L operated a points scheme in which a customer, purchasing goods or services from a participating retailer, received points which could be redeemed for 'rewards' from certain suppliers ('redeemers'). L paid the redeemers for these rewards and reclaimed input tax. HMRC rejected the claim on the basis that the rewards were supplied to the customers, not L. The Court of Appeal held that the redeemer made a supply of rewards to the customer. But the redeemer also made a supply of redemption services to L, in respect of which L was entitled to input tax credit ([2008] STC 59). The House of Lords referred the case to the CJEU, which ruled that L's payment to the redeemer was third party consideration for a supply by the redeemer to the customer, although payment might also include consideration for a separate supply of services (a question for the national court to decide) [2010] STC 2651 (TVC 22.162). The Supreme Court upheld the Court of Appeal decision in favour of L. The Supreme Court held that VAT should be chargeable on L's taxable supplies only after deduction of the VAT borne by L's necessary costs. This included the cost of securing that goods and services were provided to collectors in exchange for their points, i.e. the payments made by L to the redeemers. Therefore L should be authorised to deduct from the VAT for which it is accountable the VAT charged by the redeemers, so that it accounted for VAT only on the added value for which it was responsible ([2013] STC 784 (TVC 22.163)).

In *HMRC v Airtours Holiday Transport Ltd* [2016] UKSC 21 (TVC 36.201), a large holiday company suffered financial difficulties. It agreed that a major accountancy firm (P) should liaise on its behalf with its banks, bondholders and other creditors, and prepare a detailed report on its financial status. The holiday company reclaimed input tax in respect of P's supplies. HMRC issued assessments to recover the tax, on the basis that the supplies had actually been made to the holiday company's creditors, rather than to the company itself. The Upper Tribunal upheld the assessments, finding that the company's creditors had first approached P, and contracted for the work and therefore authorised it. The Court of Appeal confirmed this decision by a 2-1 majority, and the Supreme Court has also dismissed the company's appeal by a majority of 3-2. The majority of the judges considered that the commercial and economic reality was that no services were supplied to Airtours: the only reason it was a party to the engagement letter was its commitment to pay for the services. The principles established by the House of Lords in the *Redrow* case could not convert this into a supply that was made to Airtours. The dissenting judges considered that the company obtained rights under the contract (to sue the accountants if the services were not provided), and this was enough to show that something was received for the purpose of the business. This decision is an important victory for HMRC, who have long regarded professional fees in connection with lending activities to be something on which the borrower should not be entitled to claim input tax, because the services are in reality being supplied for the purposes of the financial institution's exempt lending transaction.

In *U-Drive Ltd v HMRC* [2017] UKUT 112 (TCC) (TVC 36.200), U-Drive Ltd (U) operated self-drive car and van hire and customers hiring a vehicle were provided with U's fleet insurance. U was effectively self-insuring using a captive insurance company so U had a vested interest in trying to keep the cost of repairing any vehicles involved in a collision to a minimum. If a hired vehicle was involved in an accident and it was likely that a third party would claim against U, then U sought to reduce the amount claimed via its captive insurance company. All customers involved in a collision were requested to give the third party a 'bump card' which encouraged that party to contact U rather than their own insurance company. U then tried to persuade the third party to use its accident and repair handling team who would negotiate with the third party and the vehicle repair shop to keep costs down. If the third party agreed then U would use one of its repair shops to undertake the work and give the third party a courtesy car. The repair shop invoiced U for the cost of the work undertaken. U sought to recover the VAT incurred on these costs. HMRC refused to pay the input tax claimed on the basis that the services were not provided to U. U appealed against this decision. The First-tier Tribunal dismissed the appeal and U appealed to the Upper Tribunal, who held that there was a two-tier process to determine the recipient of a supply. Firstly the contractual position must be determined and secondly whether the contractual position actually represented the reality of the situation. The VAT treatment must be based on the reality of the situation rather than the contractual situation where they differ. In this case the repair services were provided to the third party and not U and as a result U could not recover the VAT incurred on the repairs.

Supplies to employees

HMRC accept that, in certain circumstances, a supply which is *prima facie* to an employee, can be treated as made to the employer provided the employer meets the full cost and the supply is legitimately financed by the employer for the purposes of the business. Examples include

- road fuel (see **46.15 MOTOR CARS**);
- subsistence costs (see **35.13**(21) below); and
- removal expenses arising from company relocations or transfer of staff (see **35.13**(18) below).

See also *Stormseal (UPVC) Window Co Ltd* (VTD 4538) (TVC 62.252) where the tribunal held that the company was also entitled to recover input tax on hotel accommodation in respect of *self-employed* representatives whom the company required to work outside their normal area as the accommodation was made available to them in their capacity as persons engaged on company business.

> *Example*
>
> A business is borrowing some money from a bank to develop its trading activities. A condition of the loan, which is secured against its property, is that the business must pay for a survey fee on the property to ensure adequate security is in place for the bank.
>
> In this situation, the business cannot claim input tax on the survey fee, despite the fact that it has paid the cost, including VAT. The surveyor is working for the bank, not the borrower, so a key condition for input tax recovery is not being met.

Use for business purposes

[35.6] There is no definition of whether goods or services have been supplied for the 'purposes of the business'. Where the connection between the expenditure and the business is not clear, the following tests can be applied.

(a) Determine the intention of the person at the time of incurring the expenditure. This is a subjective test and where there is no obvious association between the business and the expenditure concerned, the court should approach any assertion that it is for the business with circumspection and care (*Ian Flockton Developments Ltd v C & E Commrs*, QB [1987] STC 394 (TVC 36.379)).

(b) Establish whether or not there is a clear connection between the actual or intended use of the goods or services and the activities business. This is an objective test of the use to which the goods or services are put.

Expenditure, even if for the benefit of the business, is not necessarily for the purpose of the business. See, for example, *C & E Commrs v Rosner (t/a London School of International Business)*, QB 1993, [1994] STC 228 (TVC 36.271) and *Wallman Foods Ltd* (VTD 1411) (TVC 36.275) where VAT on legal costs incurred in defending a sole trader/director against criminal charges was held to be non-deductible under this principle. Compare, however, *P & O European Ferries (Dover) Ltd* (VTD 7846) (TVC 36.269) where VAT on legal costs in defending the company and certain of its employees charged with manslaughter following the sinking of a ferry was held to be deductible as it had clearly been incurred for the purpose of the business even though it also had the effect of benefiting individual employees.

The recent case of *Praesto Consulting UK Ltd* [2017] UKUT 395 (TCC) (TVC 36.247) has been appealed successfully by HMRC. This was a case where a company paid legal fees charged to a director in a dispute with the director's former employers over breach of restrictive covenants. The Tribunal had accepted the VAT claim on the basis that the company had no business without winning the case, and the distinction between the director and the company was essentially illusory in practical terms. But the Upper Tribunal has decided that this is the wrong analysis as it simply ignores the contracts, and the issue as to which party was the subject of the legal proceedings. The Upper Tribunal held that there was no direct and immediate link between the supply of legal services and Praesto's taxable supplies or Praesto's taxable activity as a whole. On this basis, the Upper Tribunal held that VAT was not recoverable on the legal costs of defending the director.

Where goods or services supplied are not used for business purposes, any VAT suffered is not input tax and cannot be reclaimed. This includes

- expenditure related to domestic accommodation (see **35.13**(7) below);
- pursuit of personal interests such as sporting and leisure activities (see also **35.13**(20) below);
- expenditure for the benefit of company directors, proprietors, etc.;
- supplies used in connection with a non-business activity (see **35.7** below for apportionment where used for both a business and non-business activity);
- supplies for another person's business; and
- supplies to another person, even if the taxable person pays for them (see **35.5** above).

Tribunal and court decisions

There have been a large number of court and tribunal cases concerned with whether supplies are used for the purpose of the business, in particular in relation to legal costs, premises costs of sole traders and partnerships, sporting activities (horse racing, show jumping, powerboat racing, motor racing and rallying, yachting, etc.) and personalised number plates. See the chapter Input Tax in *Tolley's VAT Cases* under the heading *Whether supplies used for the purposes of the business.*

De Voil Indirect Tax Service. See V3.405A–V3.410.

Goods and services only partly used for business purposes

[35.7] Where a taxable person incurs VAT on goods and services (whether by way of supply to him or, in the case of goods, acquisition or importation by him) that are intended for both business and private/non-business purposes, he has a choice as to how to treat the goods and services for VAT purposes.

- He may treat them as wholly non-business or private. In this case, the VAT incurred is not deductible. But if an asset treated in this way is later sold, no VAT is payable.
- He may treat them as part business, part non-business, in which case the VAT incurred is only deductible to the extent that it relates to the taxable business activities. [*VATA 1994, s 24(5)*]. See (1) below for apportionment for private use and (2) below for apportionment for non-business use.

  If an asset treated in this way is later sold, VAT is due on the 'portion' of the asset which was originally treated as a business asset.

A taxable person may use a partial exemption special method to apportion input tax incurred on goods or services which are used/to be used partly for business purposes and partly for other purposes (see **50.10 PARTIAL EXEMPTION**).

- In some cases, he may treat the goods or services as wholly business, under the 'Lennartz' approach (see (3) below), in which case the VAT incurred is treated as input tax and is deductible in full (subject to any partial exemption restriction). But
  (i) VAT must be accounted for if the goods are used for private or non-business purposes; and
  (ii) if an asset treated in this way is later sold, VAT is due on the full selling price as it was originally treated as wholly business.

(1) Apportionment for private use

Common examples of goods and services which are part business/part private are telephone, light and heat, repairs and maintenance, etc. where a business is conducted from home or the taxpayer lives above a shop.

Example
VAT of £100 is paid on an item and one quarter of its use is for business purposes.
Input tax is £100 × ¼ = £25

(2) Apportionment for non-business use

Where both business and non-business activities are undertaken (e.g. by a charity) it is unlikely that all the VAT incurred can be treated as input tax. The following procedure should be adopted.

- Identify as far as possible VAT which relates to goods or services obtained solely for the purposes of the business activity. This is input tax and can be recovered subject to the normal rules.
- Identify as far as possible VAT which relates solely to the non-business activity. This is not input tax and cannot be recovered.
- VAT which relates to both business and non-business activities (e.g. VAT incurred on overhead costs) should be apportioned in order to identify the proportion which is input tax.

Methods of apportionment

The VAT legislation does not specify any particular method of apportionment. Any method used must be fair and reasonable taking into account the various activities and the purposes for which the expenditure is incurred. It may be that a single apportionment of all overhead VAT does not achieve a 'fair and reasonable' result and that a range of apportionments for different items of overhead expenditure is required. The following are example methods of how VAT could be apportioned.

(a) *Fixed percentage*. The simplest method is to adopt a fixed percentage figure and apply this to the total non-attributable VAT incurred. This can be an acceptable approach where the balance between business and non-business activities does not fluctuate.

(b) *Income methods*. These are probably the most common methods of apportionment. The apportionment is calculated each quarter by dividing the total of business income by total income.

> *Example*
>
> A taxable person pays £1,000 VAT on purchases which are used for both business and non-business purposes. Income from business activities (taxable and exempt supplies) amounts to £20,000 in the VAT period. Total income from all sources, including business activities, grants and donations, amounts to £50,000. Input tax is calculated as follows.
>
> Proportion of income which is business income =
>
> £20,000 ÷ £50,000 = 40%
>
> VAT to be provisionally treated as input tax = £1,000 × 40% = £400

Income methods, although simple, will not give a fair and reasonable result where

- the balance of business/non-business activities does not reflect the balance of funding (e.g. where the majority of time and resources is devoted to non-business activities but the majority of income arises from business supplies); or
- commercial activities are partially subsidised by the receipt of grants (e.g. where a heavily subsidised transport operator also runs free community projects).

It may be possible to adapt income methods so that distortive income is removed from the calculation or alternatively the calculation is weighted in some way.

(c) *Expenditure-based methods*. These are similar in calculation to the income-based methods except that the ratio of business/non-business expenditure is applied to the unattributable VAT. Such methods are only appropriate if

- the majority of expenditure can be attributed to distinct business/non-business categories; and
- this ratio is a fair reflection of business/non-business activities (e.g. an expenditure-based method would not be appropriate where a charity with overwhelmingly non-business expenditure purchased a computer system principally to make taxable business supplies).

(d) *Time-based methods*. Where detailed records are kept of the amount of time that staff spend on business and non-business activities, these can provide the basis for a method of apportionment if the business/non-business ratio of staff time reflects the extent of business use of non-attributable expenditure. Such methods would not be appropriate where non-business activities are staff intensive but business activities are goods and services intensive.

A time-based method can also be applied by keeping records of the use made of an object (e.g. a yacht or aircraft).

(e) *Transaction-based methods*. A method can be based upon a record of transactions (e.g. paid admissions to a museum or books loaned out for a charge by a library). A common difficulty with such a method is that non-business activities often do not involve recordable transactions. HMRC officers are advised not to automatically dismiss transaction-based methods but to take extra care to ensure that they are founded on a valid indicator of business and non-business activity.

(f) *Area-based methods*. These, for example, involve calculating within a building the extent to which the floor areas are used for business and non-business purposes.

Whatever method of apportionment is used, provisional input tax is reclaimed at the end of each VAT period, subject to the normal rules. At the end of each VAT year, an adjustment is made by applying the same calculation to total figures for the year. Where quarterly returns are made, the VAT year ends on 31 March, 30 April or 31 May depending on the VAT periods allocated. Where monthly returns are made, the VAT year ends on 31 March.

Waiver of apportionment

Where the non-business element is regarded as insignificant, HMRC officers may use their discretion to allow a waiver of apportionment, in which case the business will be advised that the concession applies only for as long as the existing rate of non-business activity prevails.

Change in method of apportionment

If any method used is considered no longer suitable, details of a proposed new method should be submitted to HMRC. A retrospective change will only be agreed if the business can show that

- the former method did not produce a fair and reasonable result; and
- the proposed method does achieve this objective.

See *Victoria & Albert Museum Trustees v C & E Commrs*, QB [1996] STC 1016 (TVC 11.56). Although the income-based method of apportionment outlined in (*b*) above previously used by the Museum was criticised in *Whitechapel Art Gallery v C & E Commrs*, QB [1986] STC 156 (TVC 11.48) on the grounds that grants and donations received should not be included in the calculation, that method was still held to be a fair and reasonable method of apportionment and its adoption, even if disadvantageous, did not constitute an 'error' which could be subsequently corrected.

(3) The Lennartz mechanism

In *Lennartz v Finanzamt Munchen III, ECJ Case C–97/90*, [1995] STC 514 (TVC 22.529), the court ruled that a person who had a genuine intention to use a car partly for business and partly for private purposes had a right to a full and immediate input tax deduction in respect of VAT incurred on the purchase of the car. (Note that, unlike the UK, Germany did not have a specific restriction preventing deduction of VAT in respect of cars purchased for business use. The UK restriction prevents use of Lennartz VAT accounting in respect of cars intended to be used for business and private or non-business purposes, see below.) The Court also ruled that where goods are acquired *solely* for a private or non-business purpose, VAT incurred is not recoverable, even if the goods in question are later put to a deductible business use. This is because the right to deduct VAT arises, and is exercisable, at the time when the VAT is incurred.

It should be noted that:

- The choice to use the 'Lennartz' mechanism must be made at that time the input tax is incurred (i.e. in sufficient time for the VAT to be deducted in the return period in which the VAT was charged). The input tax claim cannot be re-visited at a future date even if business use of the asset subsequently increases. If the choice is not made, the apportionment route must be followed if and when the taxable person seeks to deduct any of the VAT. The taxable person should therefore retain contemporaneous evidence of a decision to treat the goods as wholly a business asset, to support the resulting input tax claim.
- The 'Lennartz' mechanism can be used even if the use to which the goods will be put will be overwhelmingly private, providing there is some genuine business use intended.
- A taxable person cannot use the 'Lennartz' mechanism where the only business use of the asset is exempt.
- Where the 'Lennartz' mechanism is applied, the taxable person is then obliged to account for output tax in respect of any private or non-business use over the economic life of the goods. See **48.6 OUTPUT TAX**. Records must be kept showing how the relevant asset has been used.

VNLTO case

The case of *Vereniging Noordenlijke Land en Tuinbouw Organisatie (VNLTO) v Staatssecretaris van Financien, ECJ Case C–515/07*, [2009] STC 935 (TVC 22.207), concerned an association, VNLTO, that promotes the interests of the agricultural sector. Its members, who are traders in that sector, pay a membership subscription to it, the greater part of which goes towards activities designed to promote their general interests. In addition to promoting those interests, VNLTO provides a number of individual services to its members for which it charges a fee. Even though the activities of promoting members' interests are not subject to VAT, the CJEU held that this did not mean they were non-business activities. The CJEU stated that 'business' in the context of 'Lennartz' accounting extends beyond economic activities giving rise to supplies within the scope of VAT. It also includes use for any activity that forms part of the wider purpose of the taxable person's undertaking or enterprise, even those activities that are not economic activities (such as those outside the scope of VAT), and that are not normally regarded as 'business' for UK VAT purposes.

As a result of that decision, HMRC stated that 'Lennartz' accounting is only available where:

- the goods are used in part for making supplies in the course of an economic activity that give a right to input VAT deduction (broadly, taxable supplies, supplies that would be taxable if made in the UK, or certain financial and insurance supplies to non-EU customers); and
- they are also used in part for the private purposes of the trader or his staff, or, exceptionally, for other uses which are wholly outside the purposes of the taxpayer's enterprise or undertaking.

Where 'Lennartz' accounting is not available, and goods are used (or to be used) for both economic activities and non-economic business activities, subject to the transitional provisions, the VAT incurred must be apportioned between these different activities on the basis of use (or intended use). The VAT attributed to the economic activities is input tax and is recoverable to the extent that the economic activities give rise to supplies with a right to input VAT deduction. The VAT attributed to the non-economic business activities is not input tax and cannot be recovered. (HMRC Brief 2/10).

'Lennartz' applied before 1 January 2011

It is possible that a trader may have claimed the whole of the input tax on an item of expenditure before the current rules were introduced, and is still accounting for output tax on private use each quarter because the expenditure had a very long useful life. Such circumstances will be rare, and the trader will be required to continue to adopt the treatment that it has done since the expenditure was incurred. For detailed information, see *Tolley's Value Added Tax 2015–16, Second Edition.*

From 1 January 2011

For VAT incurred on or after 1 January 2011, 'Lennartz' accounting cannot be used for any of the following:

- interest in land;
- building or part of a building;
- civil engineering work or part of such a work;
- goods incorporated or to be incorporated in a building or civil engineering work (whether by being installed as fixtures or fittings or otherwise);
- ship, boat or other vessel; or
- aircraft.

It is replaced by the ability of a taxpayer to adjust for subsequent changes in private use under the capital goods scheme. See **11.1 CAPITAL GOODS SCHEME.**

[*VATA 1994, s 24(5A), Sch 4 para 5(4A)*].

Partial exemption

Taxpayers who use, or intend to use, goods or services to make exempt supplies as well as taxable supplies must also consider the impact of their partial exemption method on any claim:

- Where initial apportionment is used, the apportionment of VAT incurred between business and private/non-business use must be made first. Only then should any apportionment of input tax be made because of the partial exemption rules.

- Where the 'Lennartz' mechanism is used, if the current partial exemption method does not facilitate the 'Lennartz' mechanism, HMRC will consider proposals for a revised partial exemption method. The revised method must result in a fair and reasonable attribution of input tax to taxable supplies for all the trading activities within the VAT registration. Methods that give a good result for the 'Lennartz' sector but do not achieve a fair and reasonable result overall will not be approved.

(VAT Notice 700, paras 33.1–33.7; Business Brief 15/05; VAT Information Sheet 14/07, paras 2.1–2.8).

De Voil Indirect Tax Service. See V3.408; V3.409.

Non-deductible input tax

[35.8] Input tax cannot usually be reclaimed on the following.

- Goods to be sold under one of the margin schemes for **62 SECOND-HAND GOODS.**
- Goods or services to be used for the purpose of **10 BUSINESS ENTERTAINMENT.**
- Motor cars other than taxis unless purchased for one of the qualifying uses (see **46.3 MOTOR CARS**).
- Certain accessories installed in motor cars (see **46.13 MOTOR CARS**).
- Purchases which fall within the **69 TOUR OPERATORS' MARGIN SCHEME.**
- Certain articles to be installed in new dwellings (see **43.4 LAND AND BUILDINGS: ZERO AND REDUCED RATE SUPPLIES AND DIY HOUSEBUILDERS**).
- Assets acquired under the transfer of a business as a going concern (see **9.9 BUSINESS**).
- Domestic accommodation for its directors or proprietors (see **35.13**(7) below).
- Goods imported by a taxable person where
  - (i) at the time of importation the goods belong wholly or partly to another person, and
  - (ii) the purposes for which they are to be used include private purposes either of himself or of the other person.

  In such a case, the VAT due on import is not available for deduction as input tax, but a separate claim for repayment may be made to HMRC if a double charge to VAT would arise. The repayment of VAT to the taxable person will be made only to the extent necessary to avoid a double charge and HMRC will have regard to the circumstances of the importation and, as far as appears relevant, things done with, or occurring in relation to, the goods at any subsequent time.
  [*VATA 1994, s 27*].

De Voil Indirect Tax Service. See V3.416.

When to claim input tax

[35.9] A '*taxable person*' (i.e. a person who is, or is required to be, registered under *VATA 1994*) is entitled, at the end of each VAT period, to credit for so much of his input tax as is allowable. [*VATA 1994, s 3(1), s 25(2)*].

Input tax should be claimed on the VAT return for the period in which the VAT became chargeable, i.e. the period covering

- for supplies of goods and services, the supplier's tax point;
- for goods acquired from another EU member state, the date of acquisition;
- for imported goods, the date of the importation; and
- for goods removed from a customs and/or excise warehouse, the date of removal.

However, the taxpayer cannot make a claim until he holds the evidence that is required to substantiate that claim.

[*SI 1995/2518, Reg 29(1)*].

Late claims for input tax

The time limit described below for deducting input tax starts to run from the due date for the return that the business is liable to make after it has both incurred the input tax and received the associated VAT invoice. In practice, most traders will deduct any input tax they are entitled to on the next VAT return after they have received the invoice from their supplier.

If the business had the necessary evidence to enable it to claim the input tax in the VAT accounting period in which it became chargeable, but did not record it in its VAT account, this is an error. It cannot claim it on a later return. It may be required to make a return adjustment or an error correction notification.

(VAT Notice 700/45/17, paras 6.1–6.2).

Time limit for late claims

Input tax cannot be claimed more than four years after the date by which the return for the first period in which input tax could be claimed is required to be made. [*SI 1995/2518, Reg 29(1A)*]. The validity of this time limit was confirmed in *Local Authorities Mutual Investment Trust v C & E Commrs*, Ch D 2003, [2004] STC 246.

An extended opportunity to claim input tax from before the introduction of the cap in 1996/97 was allowed up to 31 March 2009, following legal challenges to the legality of the way in which the cap was introduced. The consequences of these 'Fleming' claims continue to be disputed in the courts, but no new claims can be made. For details of the rules relating to 'Fleming' claims and the background to the extended window for making claims, see *Tolley's Value Added Tax 2015–16, Second Edition*.

Cash accounting

Certain small businesses are allowed to account for VAT on the basis of cash paid and received. See **64.2 SPECIAL SCHEMES**. Where the cash accounting scheme is used, a taxable person must not reclaim input tax until the necessary evidence is received and the supply has been paid for.

Pre-registration VAT

[35.10] Although VAT incurred before registration is not input tax, it can be treated as such subject to certain conditions. The VAT should be claimed on the first VAT return required to be made following registration. HMRC may allow the claim to be made on a later return but cannot allow a claim to be made more than four years after the date the first return was required. Any claim must be supported by invoices and such other evidence as HMRC require.

This provision does not apply to items falling within the Capital Goods Scheme, since the VAT in question may from that date be adjusted under the scheme.

VAT on goods

HMRC may allow a taxable person to treat as input tax any VAT on goods supplied to him before the date on which he was (or was required to be) registered or paid by him on the acquisition or importation of goods before that date provided the following conditions are satisfied.

- The goods are for the purpose of a business which either was carried on or was to be carried on by him at the time of the supply or payment.
- The goods have not been supplied by or (unless HMRC otherwise allow) consumed by the taxable person before the date with effect from which he was (or was required to be) registered (see *Schemepanel Trading Co Ltd v C & E Commrs*, QB [1996] STC 871 (TVC 36.660)). HMRC deem this condition to be satisfied if the goods have been used to make other goods which are still held at that date. (VAT Notice 700, para 11.2).
- The goods must not have been supplied to, or imported or acquired by, the taxable person more than four years before the date with effect from which he was (or was required to be) registered.
- All the normal rules allow the input tax to be reclaimed.
- A stock account is compiled (and preserved for such a period as HMRC require) showing separately quantities purchased, quantities used in the making of other goods, date of purchase and date and manner of subsequent disposals of both such quantities.

HMRC changed their policy regarding the amount of input tax that could be recovered if a business had used an asset before it registered for VAT. HMRC had previously expected the business to apportion the amount of recoverable VAT to take into consideration the fact that the asset had depreciated during the time it was used prior to the business registering for VAT.

The correctness of this policy was questioned, as many practitioners believed that HMRC's long-standing policy was to allow the whole of the pre-registration VAT incurred in this situation, rather than requiring some form of 'depreciation'. The position has now been clarified by HMRC Brief 16/16, which appears to endorse the views of such practitioners. It states:

> 'HMRC policy hasn't changed and is as set out below. This brief has been issued because VAT on assets held prior to EDR hasn't always been treated consistently.
>
> Subject to the normal rules on VAT deduction:
>
> - VAT on services received within 6 months of EDR and used in the business at EDR is recoverable in full
> - VAT on stock is deductible to the extent that the goods are still on hand at EDR (for example apportionment may be required)

- VAT on fixed assets purchased within 4 years of EDR is recoverable in full, providing the assets are still in use by the business at EDR . . .

HMRC will accept corrections for overpayment of VAT in the following circumstances:

- the business has reduced the VAT it deducted on fixed assets, to account for pre-EDR use
- HMRC has raised an assessment of tax to account for pre-EDR use of fixed assets
- HMRC has reduced a repayment claim to account for pre-EDR use of fixed assets

HMRC will consider claims for repayment of penalties and interest charged as a result of assessments.'

VAT on services

HMRC may allow a taxable person to treat as input tax any VAT on services supplied to him before the date on which he was (or was required to be) registered provided the following conditions are satisfied.

- The services are for the purpose of a business which either was carried on or was to be carried on by him at the time of such supply.
- The services have not been supplied *by* the taxable person before the date with effect from which he was (or was required to be) registered.
- The services have not been performed on
  - (i) goods which have been supplied *by* or (unless HMRC otherwise allow) consumed by the taxable person before the date with effect from which he was (or was required to be) registered (e.g. repairs to a machine sold before registration); or
  - (ii) goods which have been supplied to, or imported or acquired by, the taxable person more than four years before that date.
- The services have not been supplied to the taxable person more than six months before the date with effect from which he was, or was required to be, registered. There is no discretion to allow VAT recovery on services received more than six months before registration. The only way that this can be done is by backdating the registration.
- All the normal rules allow the input tax to be reclaimed.
- A list showing the description, date of purchase and date of disposal (if any) of the services is compiled and preserved for such period as HMRC require.

Example

Steve trades as a car mechanic, repairing vehicles for a wide range of customers. He became VAT-registered on 1 June.

Steve uses the services of a sub-contractor to repair a lot of the cars, who is also VAT-registered. However, Steve cannot reclaim input tax on the fees charged by the subcontractor in the six months before he became VAT-registered if the work on the vehicles in question was completed (and therefore an invoice raised by Steve to his customer) before Steve became VAT-registered.

VAT on supplies before incorporation

HMRC may allow a body corporate (including a company, charity or association) to treat as input tax any VAT on goods obtained for it before its incorporation, or on the supply of services before that time for its benefit or in connection with its incorporation, provided the following conditions are satisfied.

- The person to whom the supply was made or who paid VAT on the importation or acquisition
  - (i) became a member, officer or employee of the body and was reimbursed (or has received an undertaking to be reimbursed) by the body for the whole amount of the price paid for the goods or services;
  - (ii) was not at the time of supply, acquisition or importation a taxable person; and
  - (iii) imported, acquired or was supplied with the goods or received the services for the purpose of a business to be carried on by the body and has not used them for any purpose other than such business.
- The conditions for recovery of input tax on goods or, as the case may be, services as detailed above are satisfied. In the case of pre-incorporation supplies, the references in those conditions to supplies, etc. of goods and services to and by the taxable person before registration are to be taken as references to such supplies to and by the person who obtained the supplies for the company before registration.

This provision does not apply to items falling within the Capital Goods Scheme, since the VAT in question may from that date be adjusted under the scheme.

[*SI 1995/2518, Reg 111(1)–(4)*].

Partial exemption

The provisions in *Reg 111* above do not specify how pre-registration VAT of a partly exempt business should be treated. HMRC take the view that it is only allowable to the extent that, at the time the VAT was incurred, the relevant goods and services were used, or to be used, to make taxable supplies, i.e. they apply direct attribution. This approach was upheld by the tribunal in *T Douros (t/a Olympic Financial Services)* (VTD 12454) (TVC 46.235) and *GN Byrd (t/a GN Byrd and Co)* (VTD 12675) (TVC 46.237).

De Voil Indirect Tax Service. See V3.431; V3.432.

Post-deregistration VAT

[35.11] As a general rule, input tax cannot be claimed on supplies received after the date of deregistration. However, on a claim, HMRC may refund to a person any VAT on *services* supplied to him after the date from which he ceased to be (or to be required to be) registered and which relate to taxable supplies of the business carried on by him before deregistration. No such claim can be made more than four years after the date on which the supply of services was made. [*SI 1995/2518, Reg 111(5)–(7)*].

This covers, for example, solicitors' and accountants' services which cannot be claimed on the final returns as the invoices are not received in time. Claims should be made as soon as possible after cancellation of registration on Form VAT 427. The relevant invoices must be submitted. (VAT Notice 700/11/18, paras 9.2, 9.5.)

See also *I/S Fini H v Skatteministeriet, ECJ Case C–32/03*, [2005] STC 903 (TVC 22.113) where the court held that a person who has ceased an economic activity but who continued to pay the rent and charges on premises previously used for that activity was entitled to deduct the VAT on the amounts thus paid. There had to be a direct and immediate link between the payments made and the commercial activity and an absence of any fraudulent or abusive intent.

Insolvencies

For the procedure for claiming post-deregistration input tax in insolvencies, see **36.12 INSOLVENCY**.

The provisions of *Reg 111* above do not specify how post-deregistration VAT of a partly-exempt business should be treated. It is suggested that direct attribution should be used and with regard to non-attributable input tax, the recoverable proportion applicable immediately prior to deregistration should be used.

Dissolved and struck-off companies

If a company is dissolved or struck-off the register at Companies House, it ceases to exist. Immediately upon dissolution, all assets of the company are deemed bona *vacantia* and become the property of the Crown. It is therefore very important to ensure that the affairs of the company are settled prior to dissolution as HMRC are unable to repay any VAT to a company if it has been dissolved. (VAT Notice 700/11/18 para 9.6.)

De Voil Indirect Tax Service. See V3.431A; V5.165.

Appeals in respect of input tax

[35.12] An appeal may be made to a VAT tribunal in connection with the amount of input tax that may be credited and the proportion of input tax allowable under *VATA 1994, s 26*. See **5.3**(3)(6) **APPEALS**.

Luxuries, amusements and entertainment

In any appeal relating to input tax where

(a) the appeal relates, in whole or in part, to a determination by HMRC
    (i) as to the purposes for which any goods or services were, or were to be, used by any person, or

(ii) as to whether and to what extent input tax was attributable to matters other than the making of supplies within **35.3**(*a*)–(*c*) above, and

(b) the input tax for which, following the determination, there is no entitlement to credit relates to a supply, acquisition or importation or something in the nature of a luxury, amusement or entertainment,

the tribunal cannot allow the appeal so far as it relates to that determination unless it considers that it was unreasonable to make that determination. In reaching this conclusion, the tribunal may take into consideration information brought to their attention which could not have been made available to HMRC at the time.

[*VATA 1994, s 84(4)(11)*].

The effect of the above provisions is that in cases involving expenditure on luxuries, amusements and entertainment, a tribunal cannot apply a decision of its own to the case but is restricted to considering whether HMRC's decision was reasonable. Even though it might not have arrived at the same decision, the tribunal must uphold HMRC's decision unless it considers that they acted unreasonably.

Treatment of input tax in particular cases

[35.13] In particular cases, input tax is treated as follows:

(1) Accountancy fees

A sole trader's or a partnership's accountancy costs generally relate to a number of services provided to the taxpayer by the accountant. These may include

- general accountancy advice;
- VAT advice;
- income tax advice.

It is arguable that income tax is the responsibility of the sole trader or partner as an individual and is not strictly a business matter. In order to avoid disputes over small amounts of tax HMRC's policy is that VAT on a sole trader's or a partnership's accountancy fees should usually be claimed in full subject to the normal rules. The only exception to this is where the accountant's fees clearly relate to taxation matters that do not relate to the VAT-registered business. An individual might for example be charged significant costs relating to inheritance tax. This would not normally be related to the VAT registration and input tax should not be claimed. Usually, however, a sole trader's or a partner's tax advice can be treated as entirely business related.

The position is similar in the case of companies. Companies pay corporation tax, which is clearly a business matter. However, a company might want to reclaim input tax on advice relating, for example, to a director's inheritance tax. This should be dealt with in the same way as any other director's private expense that is paid for by a company. The supply of advice is not to the company and is not used by the company. As a result there is no entitlement to input tax.

Businesses will also sometimes agree to pay for UK tax advice needed by employees who have come to work in this country. HMRC accept this is a business expense.

(HMRC Manual VIT13700).

(2) Unpaid consideration

See **35.4** for repayment of input tax by the purchaser on supplies not paid for within six months of the later of the due date or time of supply.

(3) Barristers in chambers

Barristers may share chambers, office equipment and services, etc. and apportion costs between them on an agreed basis. Invoices for the supply of common goods or services may be made out to the head of chambers, a nominated member or the barristers' clerk (if the clerk is not a registered person). The appropriate payment is then made by each member of the chambers for their share of the expenses.

Three special accounting methods have been agreed. The choice of method is up to the barristers, but whichever method is chosen the conditions relating to it must be complied with.

Method 1

The nominated member to whom invoices are addressed treats the full amount of VAT as input tax. Output tax is accounted for on the shares charged to all the other members of chambers. VAT-registered members are entitled to deduct the VAT charged to them as input tax. By concession, VAT invoices need not be issued by the nominated member. Each member's record must be cross-referenced to

- output tax charged by the nominated member;
- the input tax deducted by other members; and
- the original VAT invoice.

This will help to ensure that no more than the total VAT stated on the invoice is deducted.

The records of all members of chambers must be available during a visit to any one of them.

Method 2

The nominated member to whom invoices are addressed does not charge output tax on the member's contributions. The input tax is apportioned so that registered members may deduct it on the basis of their own contributions. Records must be kept of the apportionment of input tax between the members of chambers. Each member's records should cross-reference the input tax deducted to the VAT invoice to ensure that no more than the total VAT stated on the invoice has been deducted. The records of all members of chambers must be available during a visit to any one of them.

Method 3

The nominated member to whom invoices are addressed deducts the whole amount of input tax but also pays an equal amount into the common fund. This method may only be used when all members of chambers are registered for VAT.

Special rules must be followed by chambers using Method 3 if any of the barristers use the flat-rate scheme. See **64.22**(7) **SPECIAL SCHEMES**.

(VAT Notice 700/44/15, paras 6.3, 6.4).

(4) Capital goods

See **11 CAPITAL GOODS SCHEME** for possible adjustment in subsequent years to the initial input tax recovery on certain items of computer equipment, land and buildings and civil engineering works used for non-taxable purposes.

(5) Churches and cathedrals, etc.

Cathedrals and churches exist primarily for non-business purposes but frequently derive significant income from their status as tourist attractions. Informal agreement has been reached between HMRC and The Churches Main Committee on the recovery of input tax which is not directly attributable to a business or non-business activity, notably repairs and maintenance, etc. to the cathedral or church itself and all associated buildings within its curtilage except domestic accommodation. A *cathedral* is allocated to one of the following bands for rate of recovery of input tax.

- Band A (90%) — to apply where there are significant admission charges to all main areas (e.g. St Paul's Cathedral, Ely Cathedral).
- Band B (65%) — to apply where there is no admission charge into the Cathedral, but there are high numbers of visitors and significant taxable income (e.g. from admission charges to other areas such as crypt, museum, tower, etc.; lettings for concerts, etc.).
- Band C (45%) — to apply where is no admission charge into the Cathedral, insignificant taxable income from admission charges for other areas, but a reasonable number of visitors generating income from other sources (e.g. the book/souvenir shop).
- Band D (25%) — to apply where there are no admission charges or only a few small charges and small numbers of visitors and little taxable income.

Where any exempt supplies are made, a separate partial exemption calculation must be made based on the total of input tax attributable to business activities and the proportion of residual input tax as calculated above.

Churches such as Bath Abbey, Beverley Minster, etc. are considerable tourist attractions and make significant taxable supplies. Where a church is in this position it can be allowed to use the 'Cathedral' banding system above. The vast majority of churches, however, have only minimal business activities, i.e. the sale of books, magazines, postcards, etc. (often on an 'honesty' basis from a table near the church door) and in these cases the normal apportionment provisions should apply.

Domestic accommodation is outside the banding system. HMRC consider input tax recovery to be dependent upon the occupants' terms of employment and duties and whether they are engaged on business or non-business activities. For persons engaged by the Church for religious purposes HMRC consider none of the tax is input tax. For lay persons engaged on some business activities an apportionment of VAT may be agreed. See *The Dean and Chapter of Hereford Cathedral* (VTD 11737) (TVC 36.337), concerning VAT incurred on renovation work to accommodation lived in by vergers. On the facts, the tribunal allowed 50% of the VAT to be treated as input tax although each case will need to be decided on its own merits. (Only 25% of the VAT on refurbishing houses occupied by the Dean and three Canons was allowed in *Dean and Chapter of Bristol Cathedral* [1993] Lexis Citation 1337 (TVC 36.600).)

(HMRC Manuals VIT45600, VIT45700).

The decision reached by the First-tier Tribunal in *Durham Cathedral* (TC05477) [2016] UKFTT 750 (TC) may enable further input tax to be recovered if the organisation can establish a direct and immediate link to taxable supplies made by the organisation. In this case, the cathedral incurred input tax on the maintenance of a bridge that allowed visitors to access the cathedral site. The cathedral attempted to recover the input tax incurred on the basis that it had a nexus to the taxable supplies made by the cathedral but HMRC disagreed and the cathedral appealed.

HMRC had originally directed that the expenditure on the bridge had no 'direct and immediate link' with the cathedral's taxable supplies, and as a result no input tax could be recovered. HMRC continued to reject the cathedral's claim following the CJEU decision in *'Sveda', ECJ Case C-126/14* on the basis that the bridge was too far away from the cathedral. The tribunal held that the principles in *Sveda* should be applied to this case and that VAT recovery was permitted. Since Durham cathedral is within Band B of the Cathedral banding scheme, 35% of the cathedral's general use is regarded as being non-business and 65% as being for business. The cathedral's claim was only for the 65% (minus an element to reflect exempt supplies), and the tribunal upheld that claim and rejected HMRC's arguments.

Repairs to listed places of worship: a special grant scheme (the 'Listed Place of Worship Grant Scheme') has been introduced for all works of repair and maintenance to listed buildings throughout the UK that are principally used as places of worship. See **43.10 LAND AND BUILDINGS: ZERO AND REDUCED RATE SUPPLIES AND DIY HOUSEBUILDERS.**

(6) Clothing

Subject to the special cases below, the provision of clothing is normally a personal responsibility. VAT on clothing purchased 'to cultivate a professional image' in order to attract business was disallowed in *BJ Brown* (VTD 6552) (TVC 36.224) as was VAT on suits worn while working in *JK Hill and SJ Mansell (t/a JK Hill & Co)*, [1988] STC 424 (TVC 36.225). VAT on a fur coat purchased by an author was held to be partly input tax in *RA Sisson* (VTD 1056) (TVC 36.223) although an appeal in such a case would now be restricted under **35.12** above. The following special cases are recognised.

(a) *Uniforms and protective clothing*. VAT incurred by a business person on uniforms or protective clothing worn by the proprietors or their employees in the performance of their duties is input tax.

(b) *Employees*. Perks are an accepted business expense therefore if employers decide to provide their employees with clothing (not falling within (*a*) above) the VAT incurred is input tax. However, a supply of goods has also taken place and the normal business gifts rules apply. See **48.5 OUTPUT TAX.**

(c) *Barristers*. The wig, gown and bands that a barrister is required to wear in court are considered to be a uniform and the VAT incurred is input tax. It is also a court requirement that barristers wear dark clothing. For example, male barristers may wear striped trousers, a black jacket and a waistcoat with a white wing-collar, and for a female barrister a dark (black, navy or grey) suit and a white blouse. If barristers claim that this clothing would not have been purchased if they did not have to attend court, the VAT may be deducted as input tax. See also *EM Alexander* (VTD 251) (TVC 36.222).

(d) *Entertainers*. The VAT on clothing used solely as stage costumes is input tax. Ordinary clothing worn by an entertainer or TV personality will usually be worn privately as well, in which case HMRC regard the provisions of **35.7** above for part business/private use as applying. See, however, *J Pearce* (VTD 7860) (TVC 36.228) where the tribunal allowed full input tax recovery on clothing such as dress suits worn by a actor where it had not been worn privately. See also *JM Collie* (VTD 6144) (TVC 36.230) where input tax was allowed in full on a wig purchased by a professional musician to maintain his image.

(HMRC Manual VIT43800).

(7) Debt enforcement services provided by Under Sheriffs and Sheriffs' Officers

HMRC are prepared to treat debt enforcement services provided by Under Sheriffs and Sheriffs' Officers in enforcing High Court judgment debts, and those of the County Court transferred to the High Court for enforcement, as supplies by Under Sheriffs to creditors. As a result, where such creditors are registered for VAT, they can recover VAT charged on the services, subject to the normal rules. Where Under Sheriffs and Sheriffs' Officers collect fees for their enforcement services from debtors, they must only issue VAT invoices to creditors. Any documents issued to debtors must make it clear that they are not VAT invoices.

(Business Brief 6/00).

(8) Domestic accommodation

As a general principle, the provision of domestic accommodation is regarded as a personal rather than a business responsibility and in most cases the VAT incurred is not input tax. However, the fact that a business is operated from home does not prevent VAT that is genuinely incurred for business purposes being deducted as input tax.

(a) Sole proprietors and partners. If a sole proprietor or partner carries on a business from home and uses a particular room or area specifically for business (e.g. an office or workshop), VAT incurred on costs which can be identified specifically to that area can be treated wholly as input tax. This would apply mainly to fixtures and fittings and decorating costs. VAT on any items used purely for domestic purposes (e.g. a bedroom suite) is not deductible. Where expenditure relates to both domestic and business use (e.g. fuel and power, security systems and general maintenance), the procedure in **35.7** above should be followed. (HMRC Manual VIT41600). See also under (c) below for farmhouses.

(b) Employees. Where a business has to provide domestic accommodation to its employees in order to facilitate the running of the business, the expenditure is regarded as having been incurred wholly for a business purpose. The most frequent instances of employers providing accommodation for staff are in the farming and hotel industries where it is essential to have staff available at all times of the day and where there is very little or no suitable accommodation available within reasonable distance of the business premises.

If an employer pays for

- goods which become the property of its employees
- the domestic fuel and power of its employees, or
- the private telephone calls of employees

the VAT incurred is treated as the employer's input tax, but the business must account for output tax as a supply of goods or services as appropriate (see **48.6 OUTPUT TAX**).
(HMRC Manual VIT41700).

(c) Repairs, renovations, etc. to farmhouses. The following guidelines have been agreed with the National Farmers Union as regards input tax claims by sole proprietors and partnerships. Where the occupant of the farmhouse is a director of a limited company, or a person connected with the director of the company, the provisions under (*a*) above apply. The guidelines do not give an automatic entitlement to recover VAT and businesses should continue to consider their own particular circumstances, and use the guidelines to assess the proportion of input tax that is claimable.

- Where VAT is incurred on repairs, maintenance and renovations, 70% of that VAT may be recovered as input tax provided the farm is a normal working farm and the VAT-registered person is actively engaged full-time in running it. Where farming is not a full-time occupation and business for the VAT-registered person (i.e. income is received from either full-time employment or other sources) input tax claimable is likely to be between 10%–30% on the grounds that the dominant purpose is a personal one.
- Where the building work is more associated with an alteration (e.g. building an extension) the amount that may be recovered will depend on the purpose for the construction. If the dominant purpose is a business one then 70% can be claimed. If the

dominant purpose is a personal one HMRC would expect the claim to be 40% or less, and in some cases, depending on the facts, none of the VAT incurred would be recoverable.

(Business Brief 18/96).

De Voil Indirect Tax Service. See V3.410.

(9) Employee benefits and perks

(a) General. Businesses commonly provide their employees with certain benefits and rewards. These may take the form of either goods or services. Such benefits are a legitimate business expense and are provided for the purposes of the business (mainly to reward or motivate staff). The VAT incurred on their provision is consequently all input tax and no apportionment under **35.7** above is necessary although a charge to output tax may be necessary under **48.6 OUTPUT TAX**. Even if a charge to output tax is due, HMRC do not generally apply such a charge to benefits or facilities which are provided to all employees. However, 'perks' which are provided to specific individuals within a business should generally be subject to an output tax charge.

(b) Retraining prior to redundancy. VAT incurred on the provision of such programmes is incurred for the purposes of the employer's business and is input tax. It is not HMRC's policy to apply a charge to output tax on the free supply of services to the employees. (HMRC Manual VIT43910).

(c) Relocation expenses. See (23) below.

(d) Home computers made available by employers. A business is only able to claim full VAT recovery (subject to partial exemption restrictions) without any requirement to account for VAT on private use where the provision of a computer is necessary for the employee to carry out the duties of employment. In such circumstances, HMRC's view is that it is unlikely that any private use will be significant when compared with the business need.

Where a business cannot show that a home computer is necessary in order to carry out the duties of employment, only a proportion of the VAT incurred is recoverable as input tax. HMRC will accept any method of apportioning the VAT incurred as long as the result fairly and reasonably reflects the extent of business use. It may be possible to agree a set percentage with HMRC based on a representative period.

(e) Mobile telephones. See (18) below.

(f) Domestic accommodation. See (8) above.

(g) Sports, canteen and recreational facilities available to staff in general. Where such facilities are provided by a business and are available to all employees, whether or not for a charge, the VAT incurred in the provision of these facilities can be treated as input tax. It is not HMRC's policy to apply a charge to output tax on the free supply of services to the employees.

If a business is unable to provide suitable facilities within its own organisation and chooses to provide membership for their employees at external establishments, input tax can be recovered (and no output tax

charge applies) as long as all employees are provided with the facilities. Where such facilities (e.g. membership of a golf or health club, etc.) are provided as a 'perk' to specific employees, there is an onward supply of services under **48.6 OUTPUT TAX.**
(HMRC Manual VIT43700).

(10) Entertainment

See **10.1–10.6 BUSINESS ENTERTAINMENT.**

(11) Financial services

See **24.3 FINANCIAL SERVICES** for input tax recovery in respect of financial services.

(12) Holding companies

See **28.9 GROUPS OF COMPANIES.**

(13) Imports

See **34.10–34.13 IMPORTS.**

(14) Insurance

See **37.3 INSURANCE** for input tax recovery in respect of insurance services and **37.10 INSURANCE** for input tax re insurance claims.

(15) Land and buildings

See **43.4 LAND AND BUILDINGS: ZERO AND REDUCED RATE SUPPLIES AND DIY HOUSEBUILDERS** for deduction of input tax by developers; and **43.23 LAND AND BUILDINGS: ZERO AND REDUCED RATE SUPPLIES AND DIY HOUSEBUILDERS** for deduction of input tax by do-it-yourself housebuilders.

(16) Legal costs

For VAT on legal costs to be recoverable as input tax, the legal services should be supplied for the purpose of the business rather than for the trader, directors or employees in a personal capacity.

Criminal cases

VAT on legal costs has been disallowed in *Wallman Foods Ltd* (VTD 1411) (TVC 36.277) (handling stolen property); *Britwood Toys Ltd* (VTD 2263) (TVC 36.278) (successfully defending a charge of corruption in relation to acquisition of stock); *LHA Ltd* (VTD 11911) (TVC 36.280) (personal assault); *C & E Commrs v Rosner (t/a London School of International Business)*, QB 1993, [1994] STC 228 (TVC 36.271) (conspiracy to defraud); and *RN Scott* (VTD 2302) (TVC 36.274) (motoring offences). VAT has been held to be deductible in *P & O European Ferries (Dover) Ltd* (VTD 7846) (TVC 36.269) (employees charged with manslaughter). In *SR Brooks* (VTD 12754) (TVC 36.270) VAT on legal costs of successfully defending charges in connection with evasion of Customs duties on gold transactions was held to be allowable although the tribunal indicated that this might not have been the case if the defendant had been charged with a smuggling offence.

Civil cases

VAT on legal costs has been disallowed in *JG & MV Potton* (VTD 2882) (TVC 36.49) (freeholder's costs paid by lessees in a breach of covenant case); *Ingram (t/a Ingram & Co)* (VTD 4605) (TVC 36.60), *C Mills* (VTD 4864) (TVC 36.243), *B Stone* (VTD 12442) (TVC 36.63) and *K Lister* (VTD 13044) (TVC 36.244) (partnership disputes); *G A Swinbank* (VTD 18192) (TVC 36.256) (defending claim by former wife over assets including business assets); *Brucegate Ltd* (VTD 4903) (TVC 36.57) and *Ash Fibre Processors Ltd* (VTD 12201) (TVC 36.248) (transfer of share capital); *Morgan Automation Ltd* (VTD 5539) (TVC 36.257) (director's dispute with previous company); and *HD Marks* (VTD 11381) (TVC 36.260) and *P Oldfield* (VTD 12233) (TVC 36.261) (action against former employer).

Payment of another party's legal costs

See the note published in the Law Society's Gazette (July 1983).

Debt collection agencies

See **3.16 AGENTS.**

(17) Local authorities

See **44.6 LOCAL AUTHORITIES AND PUBLIC BODIES.**

(18) Mobile phones provided to employees

HMRC have agreed the following treatment where a business provides its employees with mobile phones.

(a) *Purchase and connection.* If the phones are provided for business use, the business can treat as input tax all VAT incurred on purchasing the phone and on standing charges for keeping it connected to the network (whether or not it allows private use of the phone). See, however, (*e*) below.

(b) *Calls where business use only.* If the business does not allow employees to make private calls, all VAT incurred on calls is input tax. HMRC will accept that this is the case where a business has imposed clear rules prohibiting private use and enforces them. Under such circumstances, a small amount of private use will be treated as insignificant and will not prevent all VAT incurred being treated as input tax.

(c) *Charges by business for private use.* If a business charges its employees for any private calls, it may treat all VAT incurred on calls as input tax but must account for output tax on the amount it charges.

(d) *Free private calls.* If a business allows its employees to make private calls without charge, it must apportion the VAT incurred on the call charges by a method which produces a fair and reasonable result. For example, it could analyse a sample of bills taken over a reasonable period of time and use the ratio for future VAT recovery.

(e) *Fixed monthly charges*. Where the phone package allows the business to make a certain quantity of calls for a fixed monthly payment and there is no separate standing charge, it must apportion the VAT on the total charge for the package. Similarly, where the contract is for the purchase of the phone and the advance purchase of a set amount of call time for a single charge, apportionment applies to the whole charge.

(VAT Notice 700, paras 12A.1–12A.3).

(19) Motor cars and motoring expenses

See in particular **46.3 MOTOR CARS** for purchases of cars, **46.7 MOTOR CARS** for car dealers, **46.11 MOTOR CARS** for leasing or hiring motor cars, **46.12 MOTOR CARS** for repairs and maintenance, **46.13 MOTOR CARS** for accessories and **46.14** and **46.15 MOTOR CARS** for motor fuel.

(20) Museums and galleries

Museums and galleries that offer free admission to the public are not regarded as being engaged in any business in relation to this activity. Ordinarily, it is not possible to recover the VAT incurred on goods and services purchased to support non-business activities and VAT incurred in connection with the free admission of the public would be irrecoverable. However, the Government reimburses this otherwise irrecoverable VAT to certain national museums and galleries under a special VAT refund scheme. The detailed provisions are set out below. (VAT Notice 998, paras 1.1, 1.5).

Where

- VAT is chargeable on the supply of goods or services to, or the acquisition or importation of goods by, a specified 'body',
- the supply, acquisition or importation is attributable to the provision by the body of free rights of admission to a 'relevant museum or gallery', and
- the VAT is not excluded from credit under *VATA 1994, s 25(7)* (see, for example, **10 BUSINESS ENTERTAINMENT** and **46.3 MOTOR CARS**),

HMRC must, on a claim being made in the appropriate form, refund to the body the amount of VAT so chargeable. The claim must be made within the period of four years beginning with the day on which the supply is made or the acquisition or importation takes place (or such shorter period as HMRC determine). [*FA 2008, Sch 39 para 33*].

Where the goods or services in question cannot conveniently be distinguished from goods or services supplied to, or acquired or imported by, the body that are not attributable to free admissions, the refund is the amount remaining after deducting from the whole of the VAT to which the claim relates such proportion as HMRC consider to be attributable otherwise than to free admissions.

'Bodies' and their 'relevant museums and galleries'

Please see VAT Notice 998 for a list of all of the entities that are currently treated as *VATA 1994, s 33A* bodies for the purposes of these provisions.

[*VATA 1994, s 33A; SI 2014/2858*] (VAT Notice 998, Annex).

Input tax refundable under the scheme

Refunds of VAT can be claimed on most goods and services purchased in order to grant free rights of admission to the principal collections in the museum or gallery. The museum must place the order, receive the supply, receive a VAT invoice addressed to it, and pay from its own funds (including funds awarded to it, e.g. lottery funds). Provided these conditions are met, VAT incurred can be reclaimed on

- items and collections on display provided they have borne VAT (e.g. buying, acquiring or importing the items and collections);
- goods and services necessary for their upkeep (e.g. storing, cleaning and restoring the displayed items);
- upkeep of the part of the building (including common areas) in which the items are housed (e.g. making secure, cleaning, repairs and maintenance);
- provision of free information in relation to the items on display (e.g. advertising and other promotional material; 'virtual' access to, and information about items, including virtual museum tours via a free website provided it is not a business activity; free lectures);
- building a new wing to house items; and
- costs related to those areas, such as office space, that are not themselves open to the public but which are used for administration purposes in connection with free admissions.

Provided the public has free access to the principal collections on display, it does not matter that the public are occasionally charged to see special exhibitions, etc. However, any VAT incurred in relation to such a special exhibition is subject to the normal rules of input tax deduction.

VAT cannot be reclaimed under the scheme on

- non-business activities other than providing free admission to the public (e.g. grant-funded research); or
- any business activities (e.g. shops, catering outlets, commercial sponsorship (including commercially sponsored websites), or educational courses provided for consideration).

(VAT Notice 998, paras 2.4, 2.6–2.9).

Recovering the VAT

- *VAT-registered museums* should claim a refund in Box 4 of the VAT return (in addition to any input tax incurred in making taxable business supplies). The net value of total purchases should be included in Box 7.
- *Non-VAT-registered museums* must make a claim in writing to HMRC, Banking/GABS, 6th Floor SW, Alexander House, 21 Victoria Avenue, Southend-on-Sea SS99 1AU. Any claim must relate to a period of at least one calendar month or, if it is for less than £100, at least twelve months. The period chosen must end on the last day of a calendar month.

There is no special form to apply for the repayment and a declaration can be made along the following lines

> I am claiming a refund of £ for the period to cover VAT charged on goods and services bought for (name of body) in connection with the provision of free admission to the public.
>
> Signed
>
> For (name of body)
>
> Address
>
> Contact name
>
> Contact telephone number

The basis of calculation should be explained and the museum should keep invoices and other records to support its claims for six years unless HMRC agrees in writing to a shorter period.

(VAT Notice 998, paras 3.2, 3.5, 4.3–4.5).

VAT groups

Bodies within these provisions can group for VAT purposes if they meet the requirements for VAT group treatment in **28.2 GROUPS OF COMPANIES**. (VAT Notice 998, para 1.9).

Extra-statutory concession

A qualifying museum or gallery can recover the VAT attributable to the free right of admission from the date specified in the above list. The scheme is not retrospective and does not, therefore, extend to goods or services acquired before the admission date (and used in connection with the taxable business activity of charging admissions) but subsequently used in connection with the non-business activity of admitting the public free of charge.

By concession, HMRC will apply the following provisions (unless used for VAT avoidance) to ensure that a museum or gallery is not required to repay input tax, properly recovered at the time, solely on account of the move to free admission. The concession takes effect from 1 April 2001 (or such later date specified for the qualifying museum or gallery in the above table), whether or not that date was before the date of publication of the concession.

- A qualifying museum or gallery need not account for output tax on goods and services which, after purchase, are subsequently put to a non-business use. Such transactions, which would otherwise be taxable (see **48.6 OUTPUT TAX**), are treated as neither a supply of goods nor a supply of services, provided the change in use of the goods and services arose solely as a direct result of the body using them for the purpose of offering free rights of admission to their relevant museum or gallery.

- A qualifying museum or gallery need not make adjustments in the case of goods within the **11 CAPITAL GOODS SCHEME** where input tax has been recovered, insofar as a change in use of a capital item relates to free admission with related refunds under the scheme. Where this applies, the museum, etc. should, in each subsequent interval, adjust the total input tax on the capital item and the extent of its taxable use as follows.
  - (i) The total input tax on the capital item is deemed to be the proportion that would have been input tax if admissions, which have subsequently become free, had been free at the time the VAT was incurred.
  - (ii) The extent of taxable use of the capital item, at the time the original entitlement to deduction was determined, is deemed to be the extent of taxable use at that time if admissions which have subsequently become free had been free at that time.

(VAT Notice 48, ESC 3.34; VAT Notice 998, para 2.11).

(21) Pension schemes

See **54.2** and **54.3 PENSION SCHEMES** for input tax deductible by employers.

(22) Removal/relocation expenses

Employers may provide assistance to employees or future employees in relocating nearer their new job. Assistance may take many forms, including

- the payment of estate agent's fees,
- payment for a removal firm when moving house,
- the provision of maintenance/gardening for an employee's former property awaiting sale, and
- short-term accommodation in a hotel, etc.

Providing such expenditure is linked to the actual relocation, it can be treated as being the employer's input tax. It is not HMRC's policy to apply a charge to output tax on the free supply of services to the employees.

If, however, the expenditure is not linked specifically to the relocation, but forms part of the ongoing living expenses at the new property, then it is not input tax. For example, the provision of new, bespoke curtains or carpets for a new house is acceptable as it is a normal expense of moving house; but the provision of a new stereo system would not be acceptable as it is an expenditure unrelated to the relocation.

(HMRC Manuals VIT42100, VIT43920).

(23) Second-hand goods

See **62.2 SECOND-HAND GOODS** for disallowance of input tax on goods sold under the scheme.

(24) Sporting, recreational and sponsorship activities

There can be considerable difficulties in establishing to what extent, if any, there is entitlement to deduct input tax in respect of sporting, recreational and sponsorship activities. HMRC's policy in this area is to ensure that the legitimate costs of a taxable person in promoting his business or providing facilities to his staff are allowed, whilst not providing, in effect, a tax subsidy to persons who control businesses in respect of their own favoured sporting or recreational activities.

(a) Provisions for staff

Where sports and recreational facilities are available to all employees, whether or not for a charge, any VAT incurred can be treated as input tax. This equally applies where smaller businesses are unable to provide suitable facilities within their own organisation and provide membership for their employees at external establishments.

Where such facilities (e.g. membership of a golf or health club, etc.) are provided as a 'perk' to specific employees, the provisions relating to private use of services in **48.6 OUTPUT TAX** may apply.

(b) Provisions for sole proprietors, partners and company directors

Where the sporting or recreational facilities provided (e.g. membership of a golf or country club) are available only to the proprietor, partners, or directors of a company (and the relatives and friends of these persons), it is unlikely that this expenditure can be treated as being for the purpose of the business and the VAT incurred does not therefore qualify as input tax. Even if membership does result in business contacts, following the decision in *C & E Commrs v Rosner (t/a London School of International Business)*, QB 1993, [1994] STC 228 (TVC 36.267), the expenditure is probably not sufficiently connected to the purpose of the business.

(c) Sponsorship, advertising and business promotion

In certain cases, there is undoubtedly widespread exposure gained by the sponsoring business (e.g. 'Dunhill' golf masters, FA Barclays Premiership, etc.) so that no difficulty arises in allowing input tax deduction. In the case of sponsorship of sporting events by smaller businesses, there is, however, more likelihood that the 'sponsorship' is actually conducted for a private purpose (e.g. a trader may 'sponsor' a local amateur football club because of a personal connection with the team).

Similarly, participation in various sporting or recreational events may be claimed to be for business purposes in the form of advertising or promotion.

HMRC approach such cases by applying the 'business purpose' test in **35.6** above. If, at the time the VAT is incurred, the business purpose tests are met, the VAT is input tax. It is irrelevant whether the business's intentions are misconceived or that the envisaged benefits do not materialise, and the fact that the participant enjoys the activity is not sufficient reason in itself to deny input tax.

(HMRC Manual VIT44000).

(25) Subsistence expenses

Where an employee is paid a flat rate for subsistence expenses, no VAT can be claimed as input tax. If the business pays the actual cost of the supplies, input tax incurred can be reclaimed as below. If the business pays a proportion of the actual costs, it can reclaim as input tax the VAT fraction (see **48.2 OUTPUT TAX**) of the amount it pays.

Meals

If the business provides canteen facilities, all input tax incurred in providing these facilities can be recovered subject to the normal rules (even on meals for a sole proprietor, partner or director). Any VAT incurred on meals for employees can be treated as input tax. In the case of a sole proprietor, partner or director, the VAT must be incurred on meals taken away from the normal place of work on a business trip.

Hotel accommodation

All VAT incurred on accommodation for employers and employees when away from the normal place of work on business trips can be treated as input tax. See, however, *Co-operative Insurance Society Ltd* (VTD 14862) (TVC 36.19) where input tax was disallowed on hotel accommodation reserved by employees and only deductible if reserved by the company.

(VAT Notice 700, para 12.1).

See also *British Broadcasting Corporation* (VTD 73) and *Ledamaster Ltd* (VTD 344). See **10 BUSINESS ENTERTAINMENT** where accommodation, meals etc. are provided for persons other than employees.

(26) Tour operators' margin scheme

See **69.14 TOUR OPERATORS' MARGIN SCHEME** for disallowance of input tax on goods or services acquired for re-supply as margin scheme supplies.

(27) Transfers of going concerns

See **9.14 BUSINESS** for deduction of related input tax.

(28) Viability studies by accountants

See **36.10 INSOLVENCY**.

(29) Academies

Proprietors of academies may recover the VAT incurred on supplies received, and acquisitions and importations, in relation to non-business activities, primarily the provision of free education. Academies are schools in England that enter into academy arrangements with the Secretary of State under the *Academies Act 2010, s 1* or have entered into an agreement with the Secretary of State under the *Education Act 1996, s 482*. Any refund claim must be made before the end of the four-year period beginning on the day the supply is made or the acquisition or importation takes place (or such shorter period as HMRC determine). Where the goods or services cannot be conveniently distinguished from goods or services supplied, acquired or imported for business purposes, the refund is the amount remaining after deducting from the whole of the VAT chargeable such proportion as HMRC consider to be attributable to the carrying on of the business.

[*VATA 1994, s 33B*].

Paragraph 1.171 of the Spending Review and Autumn Statement 2015 document explained that, as part of the Government's one-off restructuring of post-16 education and training, sixth form colleges in England will be given the opportunity to become academies, allowing them to recover VAT on their non-business costs.

(Spending Review and Autumn Statement 2015).

Key points: input tax

[35.14] Points to consider are as follows.

- A number of important conditions must be met before input tax can be claimed on a VAT return. The expense must be relevant to both the business that is registered for VAT and its taxable supplies. So input tax cannot be claimed on a non-business or private expense, or an expense that is attributable to exempt activities.
- It is important that a business does not pay incorrectly charged VAT on the basis that it is VAT-registered and able to reclaim input tax. The regulations are clear that only properly charged VAT can be claimed, so if a supplier incorrectly charges VAT on a zero-rated item (e.g. a book) then the correct route is to get a VAT credit note from the supplier rather than make an incorrect input tax claim. An HMRC officer has the power to disallow any input tax claimed where it is incorrectly charged VAT.
- A useful concession is that input tax can still be claimed on expenses relevant to supplies of services to non-UK customers that are outside the scope of VAT under the place of supply rules. The requirement here is that the service in question must be taxable (not exempt) if it had been supplied to a UK customer.
- Input tax is usually claimed according to the date of a purchase invoice. An exception to this situation is where a business uses the cash accounting scheme (see **64.1**) where the payment date become the relevant date as far as a claim is concerned. If an invoice (or any part of the invoice) becomes more than six months overdue for payment, then any input tax claimed by the customer must be credited in its VAT account until it is actually paid.
- A general requirement is that input tax can only be claimed by a business if it is receiving a supply and also acquires a purchase invoice/receipt that is addressed to the business. An important exception to this rule is where expenses are incurred by employees

of a business in relation to, for example, road fuel and hotel bills. Input tax can be claimed in such cases as long as the expense is business related and paid for by the employer. There is not a problem if the employee pays for the expense himself and is then subsequently reimbursed by his employer.

- A key challenge is to consider whether an expense is for the 'benefit' of the business or 'purpose' of the business in deciding whether input tax can be claimed. There are many cases where an expense can be shown to 'benefit' a business, e.g. a sole trader could probably show that membership of his local golf club produces benefits as a source of potential customers. However, it is the 'purpose' of the expense that is relevant and must be linked to the business.
- There is an assumption (incorrect) that if an expense is partly relevant to business and partly relevant to non-business purposes, and the input tax claimed therefore needs to be apportioned, the amount of input tax claimed as business related must be made using an income-based apportionment method. The legislation allows any method to be used as long as it produces a 'fair and reasonable' result. There are many situations where an apportionment based on the ratio of business to total income does not produce a fair result because the expense in question is not determined by income.
- For a business that has both non-business and exempt supplies, it is important to adopt the correct order in dealing with VAT incurred on expenditure. The first challenge is to eliminate any VAT relevant to private or non-business activities (this VAT is not input tax) and the remaining VAT will then need to take into account the principles of partial exemption. This means that a further VAT loss will be evident if the expense in question is partly or wholly used for exempt purposes.
- The main input tax blocks in the UK (known as non-deductible input tax) apply to business entertainment and motor cars available for private use. However, it should be noted that the input tax block on entertaining does not apply to staff entertaining, and there are certain businesses that can reclaim input tax on motor cars if they are a tool of the trade, i.e. driving school business, taxi or car hire firm.
- A newly VAT-registered business can claim input tax on its first return on stock or assets bought within the four years before it became registered as long as certain conditions are met. The stock and assets in question must still be held by the business at the time of VAT registration and be used for taxable business purposes. There is also scope to claim input tax on certain services bought in the six-month period before VAT registration.
- There is also an opportunity to claim input tax on certain services invoiced to a business after it has deregistered. The VAT that can be claimed will mainly relate to professional services and can be claimed by completing form VAT427. There is no scope to reclaim VAT on goods acquired by a business after it has deregistered.

- Input tax can be claimed on costs incurred by a sole trader or partner who uses part of his house for business purposes and incurs costs, e.g. decorating his office, a proportion of light and heat bills. Input tax can also be claimed on the cost of providing domestic accommodation to employees (but not directors) as long as this is done for business purposes, e.g. the need for a farm or hotel to have an employee living on the premises.

36

Insolvency

Cross-references. See **5.7 APPEALS** by persons becoming insolvent; **6.9 ASSESSMENTS** for assessments on persons representing insolvent persons.

Introduction to insolvency

[36.1] Insolvency occurs when businesses do not have sufficient assets to cover their debts, or are unable to pay their debts when they become due. HMRC refer to the official receiver, or to the insolvency practitioner appointed over an insolvent business's affairs, as the 'office holder'. Office holders are liable to account for VAT in the normal way following their appointment (see below).

It is important to note that if a business is struggling to pay its VAT on time but it has not entered into any type of insolvency procedure, it might be possible to negotiate a time to pay agreement with HMRC see **52 PAYMENT OF VAT** for more information.

Types of insolvency

There are various types of insolvency procedure into which a VAT-registered business may enter. HMRC group them into formal insolvencies and business rescue procedures. There are also certain receiverships which HMRC do not treat procedurally as insolvencies.

Formal insolvencies

- *Administrative receivership*. An administrative receiver may be appointed to manage the affairs of a company by a secured creditor who holds a debenture agreement containing floating, or fixed and floating, charges over the whole, or substantially the whole, of a company's assets. Upon the appointment of the administrative receiver, the floating charges crystallise. The administrative receiver must treat the business assets covered by the charges in such a way as to recover the money due to the secured creditor. If the administrative receiver deems it to be in the best interests of the secured creditor, the business may continue to trade.
- *Bankruptcy*. A bankrupt is an individual against whom a bankruptcy order has been made by the court. The court can declare a person bankrupt on petition from the individual, one or more creditors, or the supervisor of an individual voluntary arrangement. The order indicates that the person is unable to pay his debts and, subject to certain exceptions, deprives him of his property, which can then be sold in order to pay creditors.
  The bankruptcy process of an individual or partnership (firm) in Scotland is known as sequestration.
- *Creditors' voluntary liquidation*. A creditors' voluntary liquidation usually relates to an insolvent company and is commenced by a resolution of the shareholders. A creditors' meeting is called so that the creditors of the company may, if they wish, appoint another insolvency practitioner in place of the shareholders' appointee.
- *Members' voluntary liquidation*. The directors of a company, or the majority of its directors, make a Declaration of Solvency stating that, in their opinion, the company will be able to settle its debts in full (plus interest) within the period of twelve months from the date of liquidation. The declaration must be made within the five weeks immediately preceding the date of the passing of the resolution for winding up. Liquidation takes place when the resolution is passed.
- *Compulsory winding up*. A compulsory winding up is ordered by the court as the result of the presentation of a petition by the company, its creditors, its directors, one or more of its shareholders, or the Secretary of State.
- *Partnership winding up*. A compulsory winding up is ordered by the court as a result of the presentation of a petition by the members of the partnership or by a creditor.
- *Provisional liquidation*. A provisional liquidator may be appointed by the court after the presentation of a petition for a winding up in order to protect the assets of a company before a winding up order is made. Where a provisional liquidator has been appointed, HMRC do not treat the case as an insolvency until a winding up order is made and a 'permanent' liquidator appointed.

Business rescue procedures

- *Administration.* An administrator may be appointed by a court order following an application by either the company, its directors or one or more of its creditors. In addition, an administrator may be appointed out of court by the company or its directors or the holders of a qualifying floating charge. The administrator's main function is to rescue the company. If this is not possible, the second objective is to achieve a better result for the company's creditors as a whole than would be achieved on a winding up. If that is not possible, the third objective is to do the best for the secured and preferential creditors without unnecessarily harming the interests of the creditors as a whole.
- *Partnership administration.* An administrator is appointed by a court order following an application by the members of the partnership or by a creditor, which is intended to allow
  - (a) the partnership, or part of it, to survive in a restructured form;
  - (b) the approval of a partnership voluntary arrangement; and
  - (c) a better realisation of the partnership's assets than would be obtained from winding up the partnership.
- *County court administration.* The court makes an order for regular payments to be made over a period of time in settlement of debts. The court administers the scheme. The scheme is only available to individuals.
- *Administration of a deceased person's estate.*
- *Deed of arrangement.* This is a method by which an individual can arrange terms with creditors.
- *Scheme of arrangement.* This term is normally used to describe a compromise or arrangement between a company and its creditors or members (or any class of them) which may involve a scheme for the reconstruction of the company.
- *Scottish trust deeds.* A debtor grants a deed in favour of the trustee which transfers their assets to the trustee for the benefit of creditors.
- *Voluntary arrangements.* A voluntary arrangement provides an alternative to bankruptcy or liquidation. The debtor makes proposals through a licensed insolvency practitioner which are presented at a meeting of creditors. Creditors must be given 14 clear days' notice of such a meeting. The proposals usually entail delayed and/or reduced payment of debts, and can be advantageous to both the debtor and the creditors. A supervisor is appointed to monitor the scheme for its duration, although the business usually continues to be responsible for its own business activities.
- *Partnership and company voluntary arrangements.* These are similar to *Voluntary arrangements* above but have no moratorium.

Procedures not treated as insolvencies by HMRC

- *Agricultural charge receivership.* A secured creditor can appoint a receiver under the *Agricultural Credits Act 1928* over the assets of a farm estate.

- *Fixed charge receivership*. A receiver, or receiver and manager, is appointed by a secured creditor who holds a fixed charge over specific assets which belong to a business. The assets are used for the benefit of the secured creditor.
- *Law of Property Act receivership*. A lender, such as a bank, can appoint a receiver over a mortgaged property under the *Law of Property Act 1925* to recover money advanced. The receiver usually tries to arrange for the property to be sold or is responsible for collecting rents for the mortgagee. The business may continue to trade independently of the receiver's appointment.
- *Court appointed receivership*. The court is able to appoint a receiver to collect property over which he is appointed. No property is invested in such a receiver, but his appointment acts as an injunction restraining other parties from realising assets, which the receiver has been appointed to receive.

(VAT Notice 700/56/18, paras 2.1–2.5).

Person carrying on the business

If a taxable person becomes 'bankrupt or incapacitated', HMRC may treat any person carrying on the business as a taxable person from the date of the bankruptcy or incapacity until either some other person is registered in respect of the taxable supplies made (or intended to be made) by that taxable person or the incapacity ceases. Any person carrying on the business must notify HMRC in writing within 21 days of

- the nature of any incapacity and the date on which it began; and
- the date of any bankruptcy order.

The VAT provisions apply to any person treated as carrying on the business as though he were a registered person.

[*VATA 1994, s 46(4); SI 1995/2518, Reg 9*].

See **36.2** and **36.3** below.

Where any person becomes bankrupt or incapacitated and control of his assets passes to another person, that other person must, if HMRC require and so long as he has control, comply with the general accounting, record and payment requirements of VAT. However, any requirement to pay VAT only applies to the extent of the assets of the incapacitated person over which he has control so that he is treated to that extent as if he were the incapacitated person himself. [*SI 1995/2518, Reg 30*].

If no person carries on the business

If no person carries on the business (i.e. taxable supplies cease to be made) the normal procedures for cancellation of registration apply (see **60.39 REGISTRATION**).

Companies in receivership and liquidation

In relation to a company which is a taxable person, the references above to a taxable person becoming 'bankrupt or incapacitated' are to be construed as references to its going into liquidation or receivership or to administration. [*SI 1995/2518, Reg 9*].

Notification of insolvency

[36.2] Subject to below, a person appointed as

- trustee in the bankruptcy/sequestration of a VAT-registered individual;
- liquidator of a VAT-registered company;
- receiver in the administrative receivership of a VAT-registered company; and
- administrator in the administration of a VAT-registered company

must notify HMRC within 21 days of appointment (or, in the case only of an office holder appointed after an official receiver and who has difficulty in obtaining the necessary information, within 21 days of becoming aware of the required information). This must be done on Form VAT 769, which should be downloaded from the HMRC section of the GOV.UK website.

For new appointments in bankruptcies/sequestrations, administrative receiverships and liquidations (excluding members voluntary liquidations) the completed Form VAT 769 should be sent to HM Revenue & Customs, Insolvency Claims Handling Unit, Benton Park View, Longbenton, Newcastle, NE98 1ZZ. Email: insolvencyhelpdesk@hmrc.gsi.gov.uk.

For new appointments in company administrations the completed Form VAT 769 should be sent to HM Revenue & Customs, Enforcement and Insolvency Service, Durrington Bridge House, Barrington Road, Worthing, BN12 4SE. Email: insolvencyhelpdesk@hmrc.gsi.gov.uk.

For new appointments for members voluntary liquidations the completed Form VAT 769 should be sent to HM Revenue and Customs, Enforcement and Insolvency Service, MVL Team, Elgin House, 20 Haymarket Yards, Edinburgh, EH12 5WN. Email: eisw.mvl.team@hmrc.gsi.gov.uk. Telephone: 0300 322 7815.

For new appointments in voluntary arrangements, the completed Form VAT 769 should be sent to HM Revenue & Customs, Voluntary Arrangement Service, Durrington Bridge House, Barrington Road, Worthing, BN12 4SE. Email: vas@hmrc.gsi.gov.uk

For new appointments for trust deeds (Scotland) the completed VAT 769 needs to be send to HM Revenue and Customs, Enforcement and Insolvency Service (EIS), Elgin House, 20 Haymarket Yards, Edinburgh, EH12 5WT. Telephone: 03000 520738.

Requests for VAT deregistration should be sent to HM Revenue & Customs, Grimsby Deregistration Unit, Imperial House, 77 Victoria Street, Grimsby, DN31 1NH.

Form VAT 769 should not be used in the following circumstances and notification should simply be made in writing to the VAT Business Advice Centre which controls the area of the principal place of business of the insolvent business.

- Notification of a proposed creditors meeting for either voluntary arrangements or creditors' voluntary liquidations.
- The appointment of a receiver under *Law of Property Act.*
- The appointment of a receiver or manager under a fixed charge only.
- The appointment of a receiver under the *Agricultural Credits Act 1928* over assets of a farm estate.
- The appointment of a provisional liquidator (as such a person has no status with regard to the trader's VAT registration).
- Notification to appoint a liquidator under *IA 1986, s 98.*

Where a liquidator is appointed after the appointment of an administrative receiver

It is not necessary to complete a second Form VAT 769. HMRC will, however, need extra information (e.g. who is in control of the assets and who will be responsible for completing VAT returns). This information, together with the trader's VAT registration number, the name, address and date of appointment of the liquidator, should be sent to HMRC, Insolvency Claims Handling Unit, Benton Park View, Longbenton, Newcastle, NE98 1ZZ.

(VAT Notice 700/56/18, paras 3.1, 3.2, 3.6).

Claims by HMRC

[36.3] On notification of an insolvency, HMRC will calculate its claim based on the amount outstanding at the 'relevant date'. A more detailed breakdown of the claim is available on request.

'*Relevant date*' is

- in relation to a company which is being wound up
  (i) where the company is being wound up by a court and the winding-up order was made immediately upon the discharge of an administration order, the date of the making of the administration order;
  (ii) in a case not within (i) above where the company is being wound up by the court and had not commenced to be wound up voluntarily before the date of the making of the winding-up order, the date of appointment (or first appointment) of a provisional liquidator or, if no such appointment has been made, the date of the making of the winding-up order; and
  (iii) in any other case not within (i) or (ii) above, the date of the passing of the resolution for the winding up of the company;
- in relation to a company in receivership, the date of appointment of the receiver; and
- in relation to a bankrupt

- (i) where at the time the bankruptcy order was made there was an interim receiver of the debtor's estate appointed under *Insolvency Act 1986, s 286*, the date on which the interim receiver was first appointed after the presentation of the bankruptcy petition; and
- (ii) in any other case, the date of making the bankruptcy order.

[*Insolvency Act 1986, Sch 6*]. (VAT Notice 700/56/18, paras 2.3, 2.4).

Where the business continues to trade, the office holder has responsibility for the VAT affairs of the business from the relevant date onwards with the exception of bankrupts continuing to trade, voluntary arrangements, deeds and schemes of arrangement, and county court administration orders (see **36.1** above for these terms).

(VAT Notice 700/56/18, paras 4.1, 4.2).

De Voil Indirect Tax Service. See V5.187.

Amount of claim

[36.4] HMRC's claim comprises the following.

- The amount of outstanding VAT at the relevant date.
- The amount of any penalty, default surcharge or default or penalty interest assessed in respect of any period before the relevant date. This is because the penalty, etc. is recoverable 'as if it were' VAT and is not VAT as such.

(VAT Notice 700/56/18, paras 4.1, 4.5).

Assessments

[36.5] Where a return has not been submitted for any VAT period prior to the relevant date, HMRC will raise an assessment and initially base their claim upon the amount so assessed. Where the office holder submits an acceptable VAT return for the period in question, the assessment will be withdrawn.

(VAT Notice 700/56/18, para 4.4).

Set-off of credits

[36.6] As a general rule, under *VATA 1994, s 81(3)(3A)* any amount due from HMRC to any person ('the credit') must be set against any sum due from that person by way of VAT, penalty, interest or surcharge ('the debit') and to the extent of the set-off, the obligations of both HMRC and that person are discharged. See **52.7 PAYMENT OF VAT** for full details.

However, this general rule does not apply where

- an 'insolvency procedure' has been applied to the person entitled to the credit;
- the credit became due after that procedure was so applied; and

- the liability to pay the debit either
  - (a) arose before that procedure was so applied; or
  - (b) (having arisen afterwards) relates to, or to matters occurring in the course of, the carrying on of any business at times before the procedure was so applied.

For these purposes, the time when an '*insolvency procedure*' is to be taken to be applied to any person is when

- a bankruptcy order, winding up order or an award of sequestration is made or an administrator is appointed in relation to that person;
- that person is put into administrative receivership;
- that person, being a corporation, passes a resolution for voluntary winding up;
- any approved voluntary arrangement comes into force in relation to that person;
- a registered deed of arrangement takes effect in relation to that person; or
- that person's estate becomes vested in any other person as that person's trustee under a trust deed.

But references to the application of an insolvency procedure to a person do not include

- the application of an insolvency procedure to a person at a time when another insolvency procedure applies to the person; or
- the application of an insolvency procedure to a person immediately upon another insolvency procedure ceasing to have effect.

[*VATA 1994, s 81(4A)–(4D)(5)*].

De Voil Indirect Tax Service. See V5.172.

Crown set-off

[36.7] HMRC can offer credits arising from insolvent traders' VAT repayment claims accruing before the relevant date to other government departments. [*IA 1986, s 323; SI 1986/1925, Rule 4.90*]. See also *Re Cushla v C & E Commrs*, Ch D [1979] STC 615 (TVC 37.17) and *Re DH Curtis (Builders) Ltd* [1978] 2 All ER 183 (TVC 37.18).

In the case of VAT repayment claims for pre-appointment periods, HMRC will conduct set-off enquiries to establish whether there are any pre-appointment debts owed by the insolvent taxpayer to the Crown against which the VAT repayment claim may be set-off. The time taken to conduct these enquiries will not be counted in determining the trader's entitlement to repayment supplement.

HMRC are entitled to set-off any pre-insolvency credits against pre-insolvency debt owed by the debtor in respect of other duties administered by HMRC. HMRC can offer any remaining credits arising from an insolvent trader's VAT repayment claims accruing before the relevant date to other government departments. This will allow other government departments to reduce or satisfy their claims against the same insolvent trader.

The credits may arise from VAT repayment claims, credits for Insurance Premium Tax, Landfill Tax or Air Passenger Duty. HMRC will undertake such set-off wherever it is cost-effective for it to do so and this usually means that credits below £250 will not be set-off. The balance of any credit remaining following such set-off should be repaid automatically to the insolvent estate care of the office holder or to the trader if the business is in a voluntary arrangement, deed or scheme of arrangement or county court administration order. Crown set-off will take place after all pre-relevant date returns have been received and/or assessments raised and set-off.

Crown set-off will not apply if the credit is secured by a valid fixed charge on book or other debts. See also **36.10**(3) below.

(VAT Notice 700/56/18, paras 5.8 and 13.1).

Dividends

[36.8] If the office holder declares a dividend from an insolvent estate, cheques should be made payable to HM Revenue and Customs and sent to HMRC, VAT 833 Team, St Mungo's Road, Cumbernauld, G70 5TR. The VAT registration number of the business concerned should be included on the back of the cheque.

Dividends for businesses subject to

- any form of administration orders, should be sent to HMRC, Enforcement and Insolvency Service (EIS), Durrington Bridge House, Barrington Road, Worthing, BN12 4SE;
- Scottish trust deeds and deeds or schemes of arrangement, should be sent to HMRC, Portcullis House, 21 India Street, Glasgow, Strathclyde, G24 PHY; and
- voluntary arrangements should be sent to HMRC, Voluntary Arrangement Service, Durrington Bridge House, Barrington Road, Worthing, West Sussex BN12 4SE.

(VAT Notice 700/56/18, paras 8.1, 8.2).

Returns

[36.9] Businesses subject to an insolvency procedure are not subject to the requirement to file electronic VAT returns. Returns are issued automatically to the officeholder. All returns completed by the office holder for pre- and post-insolvency periods must be sent to HMRC, VAT Controller, VAT Central Unit BX5 5AT. See **36.16** below for bankrupts continuing to trade.

Pre-insolvency returns

The insolvent business is responsible for submitting pre-insolvency returns. However, the office holder may submit a return for any pre-relevant date period for which the business has not rendered a return. Such a return should be unsigned but carry the legend, 'completed from the books and records of the company/trader'.

The final pre-insolvency return covering the period up to the relevant date is issued automatically to the office holder and is not subject to default surcharge.

Split period returns

Where the relevant date (see **36.3** above) falls within a VAT period, that period is divided into two periods. The first period ends on the day prior to the relevant date. The return for that period is issued directly to the person in charge of the insolvency and must be submitted by the last day of the following month. Default surcharge is not applicable to this return. The second period begins on the relevant date and ends (and all subsequent periods end) on the normal last day for the VAT periods of the insolvent trader. [*SI 1995/2518, Reg 25(3)*].

Post-insolvency returns

Post-insolvency returns are the legal responsibility of the office holder (except for voluntary arrangements, deeds and schemes of arrangement, and county court administration orders, see **36.1** above for these terms). Returns are issued automatically to the office holder. The returns must be submitted, and any VAT paid, by the normal due date (see **52.1 PAYMENT OF VAT**).

Repayments

Repayments due are, subject to below, repaid in the name of the insolvent business, c/o the office holder. The repayment should be made by HMRC within 30 days of receipt of the return but may be delayed by any inaccuracies on the Form VAT 769 or failure to notify HMRC of the appointment of the officeholder.

Repayments for businesses in voluntary arrangements, deeds and schemes of arrangement or county court administration orders (see **36.1** above for these terms) are sent to the address of the registered business unless the trader has given written permission for the payment to be sent to the officeholder.

Repayment supplement is added if the normal conditions are satisfied (see **52.17 PAYMENT OF VAT**).

In the case of VAT repayment claims for pre-appointment periods, HMRC will conduct set-off enquiries to establish whether there are any pre-appointment debts owed by the insolvent taxpayer to the Crown against which the VAT repayment claim may be set-off.

Penalties, etc.

Penalties, default surcharge and default interest are not normally applied to post-insolvency VAT returns. They are, however, applied in the case of administration orders, partnership administration orders, deceased persons' administration orders, deeds and schemes of arrangement, Scottish trust deeds, county court administration orders; and voluntary arrangements (see **36.1** above for these terms). Inaccuracy penalties due under *FA 2007, Sch 24* (see **53.15 PENALTIES**) are applied to both pre- and post-insolvency VAT returns and relevant documents in all cases.

Compliance

HMRC have the right to check the accuracy of all returns submitted and to require that the books and records of the business are made available for inspection. In certain circumstances, where it can be shown that an office holder has consistently not complied with regulations, a report may be made to the appropriate licensing authority.

(VAT Notice 700/56/18, paras 5.1–5.9).

Miscellaneous VAT procedures

[36.10] Some miscellaneous VAT procedures are as follows:

(1) Bad debt relief

Bad debt relief (see **7 BAD DEBT RELIEF**) can be claimed in insolvencies subject to the normal rules. Claims can be made on the normal VAT return where the VAT registration remains open and on Form VAT 426 where registration has been cancelled. A letter scheduling the claim, together with copies of the relevant invoices, must be submitted to HMRC for approval. (VAT Notice 700/56/18, paras 10.1, 10.2). See also **7.13 BAD DEBT RELIEF** for a concession concerning the repayment of input tax where an insolvency practitioner receives notice of a claim for bad debt relief on a pre-insolvency transaction.

(2) Cash accounting

The cash accounting scheme allows VAT-registered businesses to account for VAT on the basis of payments received and made rather than on VAT invoices issued and received. See **64.2 SPECIAL SCHEMES**. The office holder responsible for the business may use the scheme in the post relevant date period if the insolvent business was eligible to use the scheme pre-insolvency and continues to be eligible to do so. This may be appropriate in cases where trading has continued after the relevant date.

The office holder must also, within two months of the date of insolvency, account for VAT due on all supplies made or received up to the date of the insolvency which have not previously been accounted for. [*SI 1995/2518, Reg 62*]. The VAT due should be entered on to the VAT return for the period immediately preceding the relevant date, and is treated as a liability arising before the insolvency.

(VAT Notice 700/56/18, paras 11.1–11.3).

(3) Charges over book debts

HMRC and Redundancy Payments Service have agreed a joint approach to the question of fixed charges over book debts following the decision of the Privy Council in *Re Brumark Investments Ltd* [2000] 1 BCLC 353 casting new light on the distinction between fixed and floating charges. This will impact on the distribution of book debt proceeds in insolvent cases.

A fixed charge is a form of mortgage debenture on specified property, including uncollected book debts. In insolvency cases, lenders holding a fixed charge are paid ahead of all other creditors, including preferential creditors. The decision in *Brumark* states that a charge that allows the collection and free use of the proceeds of a book debt by the company is not a fixed charge. A fixed charge requires the collected proceeds to be paid into a blocked account (i.e. an account to which the company does not have unfettered access and cannot draw on the proceeds without the specific consent of the chargeholder). It is not enough for a debenture to provide for a blocked account: such an account must actually be operated.

The ruling means that the Crown Departments will monitor the distribution of book debt proceeds in insolvency cases and reserve the right to challenge distributions made to fixed chargeholders if they believe the charge in question was actually a floating charge. In addition, pre-insolvency VAT credits will be paid to companies subject to insolvency procedures in preference to other Crown creditors only in cases where a debenture is provided showing a fixed charge over book debts that HMRC are satisfied is a valid fixed charge.

(Business Brief 5/02).

(4) Credit notes

Where a credit note evidencing a decrease in consideration is issued or received by an office holder after the date that establishes HMRC's claim in the insolvency (the relevant date) adjustments of VAT resulting from such credit notes relate to the VAT accounting period in which the original supply was made or received.

If a credit note is issued evidencing a decrease in consideration for supplies made in a pre-insolvency VAT period, the effect is to reduce the output tax due in that period and thus reduce HMRC's claim in the insolvency.

If a credit note is received evidencing a decrease in consideration for supplies made in a pre-insolvency VAT period, the effect is to reduce the input tax which can be claimed in that period and thus increase HMRC's claim in the insolvency.

For bankruptcies, company administrations, administrative receivership, compulsory windings up and voluntary windings up any adjustments of VAT are related back to the period in which the original supply took place. If the VAT return for the period in which the original supply took place has already been submitted to HMRC the credit note adjustment should be declared by letter or by means of an error correction notification to the relevant HMRC office, giving details of the VAT element and the date of the original supply. If the VAT return for the period in which the original supply took place has not been submitted to HMRC the credit note adjustment should be included on the VAT return when it is submitted.

For other insolvencies, voluntary arrangements and Scottish trust deeds any credit note adjustments should be made in the period the adjustment takes effect in the business accounts of the taxable person issuing the credit note or the customer receiving the credit note.

Note that because of the four-year time limit for VAT adjustments, a credit note adjustment cannot take effect if the credit note is issued more than four years after the end of the VAT accounting period in which the original supply took place.

(VAT Notice 700/56/18, paras 12.1–12.3).

(5) Partial exemption

The provisions relating to **50 PARTIAL EXEMPTION** apply to all VAT-registered businesses including those which are insolvent. The person in charge must comply with these requirements in respect of returns completed for pre- and post-relevant date VAT periods. An insolvent business can apply to change the method of calculating entitlement to input tax recovery if there has been a substantial change in circumstances although such changes cannot be applied retrospectively.

Where a business is already partly exempt, the annual adjustment should be made at the end of the business's partial exemption year. Approval may be sought from HMRC to allow the annual adjustment to be made in the VAT period which ends with the relevant date. Such applications should be clearly marked 'VAT partial exemption query' and sent to the VAT Written Enquiries Team.

(VAT Notice 700/56/18 paras 15.1, 15.2).

(6) Capital goods scheme (CGS)

If the insolvent business had assets covered by the CGS (see **11.2 CAPITAL GOODS SCHEME**) then those assets pass to the office holder on insolvency. If the use of the assets changes while under the office holder's control then adjustments may arise, which must be declared on returns due from the office holder. The office holder will need to establish the following information

- what assets covered by the CGS are held;
- when they came into use in the business; and
- how much input tax was initially incurred and deducted on them.

Assets still used within the business

Any adjustments are likely to be modest as they will only address the time of use by the office holder and the difference between their use and that originally made by the business prior to insolvency. If the office holder brings the company out of insolvency or sells its assets as a transfer of a business as a going concern (TOGC) (see **9.9 BUSINESS**) then any CGS items will pass on to the new owners at that point.

Assets no longer used within the business but held for eventual sale

If the original use was taxable and the sale will be exempt then there may be substantial adjustments due. As the sale will be made by and under the direction of the office holder adjustments must be declared by them on returns that they submit. If the asset is a building then it may be possible to prevent the sale from being exempt by opting to tax (see **42.23 LAND AND BUILDINGS:**

EXEMPT SUPPLIES AND OPTION TO TAX), although this may restrict which buyers may be interested. If the original use of the assets was partly exempt, and if the sale is to be taxable, then adjustments in the office holder's favour may arise. If the business is deregistered without a sale of the asset taking place then an adjustment may arise at that time.

(VAT Notice 700/56/18, para 15.3).

(7) VAT on insolvency practitioners' fees

As the practitioner's services do not relate to any specific supply, fees are a general overhead of the business concerned.

Insolvent businesses which continue to trade

- Where the business remains fully taxable it can deduct input tax on the practitioner's fees.
- Where the business remains or becomes partly exempt, deduction of input tax is subject to restriction in accordance with the partial exemption method used.

Insolvent businesses which cease to trade but which remain registered

The principal activity will be the sale of assets. As anything done in connection with the termination or intended termination of a business is done in the course or furtherance of that business, input tax incurred on the practitioner's fees should be considered in the light of the taxable status of the business prior to the insolvency. Where the business was previously fully taxable, the input tax on these fees is fully deductible. Where the business was previously partially exempt, the business should continue to use the method in place in the normal way.

A change of partial exemption method should be requested from HMRC if, in the light of changing circumstances, the method in place no longer produces a fair and reasonable attribution of input tax to taxable supplies.

(VAT Notice 700/56/18, para 15.4).

(8) Taking Control of Goods/distraint/attachment

Distraint (attachment in Scotland) is a method of recovery by taking possession of a debtor's goods and selling them, usually at public auction, after which the proceeds are set against the debt and costs.

Taking Control of Goods (TCoG) replaced distraint in England and Wales from 6 April 2014 but distraint continues to be used in Northern Ireland.

TCoG is a process by which a debtor's goods are seized and sold in settlement of outstanding costs, tax and interest. The legislation relating to TCoG is in *Part 3* ('enforcement by taking control of goods') of the *Tribunals, Courts and Enforcement Act 2007* and supporting regulations, which is Ministry of Justice legislation binding on the whole bailiff industry in England and Wales.

HMRC may use TCoG (distraint in Northern Ireland) (attachment in Scotland). See **32.4** and **32.5** **HMRC: POWERS** respectively. In the case of

- a bankruptcy order (or compulsory winding up order), any incomplete action (i.e. the goods seized have not been sold) may be completed by HMRC with the authority of the trustee in bankruptcy/liquidator, or the trustee/liquidator may insist on the goods being released to him to sell subject to an undertaking provided by HMRC. If the goods have been sold within the three months immediately preceding the date of a bankruptcy order, the proceeds may be surrendered to the trustee/liquidator if the trustee/liquidator is unable to pay the preferential creditors in full from other realisations. The trustee/liquidator must satisfy HMRC that such a shortfall regarding preferential creditors exists. Where the goods have been sold more than three months before the making of the bankruptcy/winding up order HMRC are entitled to retain the sale proceeds. In Scotland, attachment will not be taken against a sequestrated trader for the duration of the sequestration; and
- a creditors' or members' voluntary winding up or an administrative receivership, if distraint has been levied (goods attached) before the appointment of a liquidator or administrative receiver, then the distraint/attachment remains valid and will be maintained and/or completed.

In the case of voluntary arrangements, TGoC/distraint action will normally be suspended once an interim order has been made, a moratorium granted or proposals for a voluntary arrangement have been received and a creditors' meeting arranged unless there are exceptional circumstances which justify not suspending, e.g. evidence of fraud or lack of probity. Where the proposals are rejected at the creditors' meeting HMRC will proceed to complete the TGoC/distraint by sale. If the proposals are approved HMRC will normally withdraw the TGoC/distraint, though in exceptional circumstances they may maintain it and include it as security in modified proposals.

In the case of administration orders, once an administrator has been appointed, TGoC/distraint may not be instituted or continued against the company or the property of the company except either with the consent of the administrator or leave of the court. HMRC will generally try to reach a financial settlement with the administrator without the need to seek court directions.

Any money received by HMRC for the sale of TGoC/distrained goods will be set against costs and then against the earliest pre-insolvency liability, with HMRC's claim amended accordingly.

Where a floating charge crystallises on the appointment of an administrative receiver or some other event specified in the debenture, the distraint will be maintained and completed if HMRC have already levied on goods which are subject to the floating charge. HMRC may choose to let the administrative receiver sell the goods, subject to an undertaking, and pass the proceeds to HMRC.

(VAT Notice 700/56/18, paras 14.1–14.4).

(9) Retention of records

The liquidator of an insolvent company may destroy the books, papers and records, including the VAT records, one year after the date of dissolution of the company. [*SI 1994/2507, Reg 16*]. By concession, official receivers may also, on request and with HMRC approval, destroy the books and records of a company after six months. Normal rules for retention of records apply to other insolvencies, i.e. records should normally be retained for six years.

(VAT Notice 700/56/18, para 19.1).

(10) Viability studies by accountants

Accountants engaged to conduct viability studies are treated as making supplies of their services to the person who has commissioned the work, instructed them and who receives the end product. The effect of this is as follows.

- Where either the company or the bank commission the work, the accountants should issue any invoices to the company or bank (as the case may be). The supply is then received for business purposes and input tax is deductible subject to the normal rules. The fact that the other party, or a third party, receives a copy of the report is not relevant.
- Where the bank receives one report and the company another, the accountant is making two separate supplies and should issue separate invoices to allow recovery of input tax subject to the normal rules.
- Where the company and bank issue joint instructions and receive copies of the same report, the accountant should issue invoices for 50% of the cost to each party.
- Where the company commissions the work but does not receive a copy of the report, the accountant's supply is to the company but is not used for business purposes. Therefore neither the company nor the bank can recover any input tax.

(Business Brief 6/95).

See also *Eagle Trust plc* (VTD 12871) (TVC 36.197).

Deregistration

[36.11] If the officer responsible for the insolvent business decides that it is appropriate to deregister, the normal procedures for deregistration are followed.

(VAT Notice 700/56/18, paras 6.1–6.5; Notice 700/11/18).

In the past HMRC allowed insolvency practitioners to cancel the VAT registration of the business they had been appointed over at an early stage and account for VAT on any subsequent supplies using Form VAT 833 (Statement of Value Added Tax on goods sold in satisfaction of a debt). However, as a deregistered business cannot issue a valid VAT invoice an early deregistration could result in VAT-registered buyers of assets from insolvent businesses being denied claims for input tax on the purchase of the assets in question. HMRC no longer allow such early deregistration of insolvent businesses.

Even if trading has ceased the business may be making taxable supplies above the VAT registration threshold, e.g. asset realisations by an insolvency practitioner. HMRC now keep VAT registrations open until all trading has ceased and all assets are realised (though an insolvent business has the same right as any other business to apply to deregister on the grounds that it is continuing to trade but below the VAT registration threshold, if that situation applies). Insolvency practitioners are required to render VAT returns and appropriate payment, if any, for each VAT period until the registration ceases. Where this requirement causes a problem, e.g., in a situation where all trading has ceased but the insolvency practitioner is experiencing difficulties in selling a property, the situation should be discussed with HMRC.

(HMRC Brief 13/14).

Post-deregistration

Output tax

[36.12] HMRC now generally keep VAT registrations open until all trading has ceased and all assets are realised. See **36.11** above. Insolvent businesses that continue to trade may deregister voluntarily if they meet the conditions for voluntary deregistration (see **60.10 REGISTRATION**).

VAT on taxable stocks and assets remaining at the date of insolvency must be accounted for on post-appointment returns including the final return, Form VAT 193.

VAT must not be charged post-deregistration, since a deregistered business cannot legally issue a VAT invoice.

Form VAT 833 can be used for deeds and schemes of arrangement, county court administration orders, Scottish trust deeds and deceased persons' administration orders (see **36.1** above for these terms). Form VAT 833 can be completed on GOV.UK and submitted to HMRC Banking, VAT 833 Team, St. Mungo's Road, Cumbernauld, G70 5TR.

See **36.15** below for how *Law of Property Act* receivers should account for output tax.

Input tax – Form VAT 426 procedure

A special scheme for claiming post-deregistration input tax on Form VAT 426 can be used by a trustee in bankruptcy, a trustee in sequestration (in Scotland), an official receiver, a liquidator or an administrative receiver. The scheme is *not* available for use by solvent deregistered traders, office holders in business rescue procedures (see **36.1** above) and other incapacitated traders. These categories include supervisors in voluntary arrangements, administrators in administration orders, a trustee appointed under a trust deed (in Scotland), a receiver appointed under the *Law of Property Act 1925*, a receiver appointed in a partnership dispute, a receiver appointed by a court, a receiver appointed under the *Agricultural Credits Act 1928*, an office holder appointed for a scheme of arrangement, an administrator appointed for a deceased persons' administration order, and a liquidator in a members' voluntary liquidation.

Subject to the normal rules, the form can be used to claim VAT on

- services supplied after deregistration but relating to business carried on before deregistration. Input tax cannot be claimed on pre-insolvency VAT return periods;
- goods and services supplied and invoiced before deregistration that has not already been claimed on a VAT return. Input tax cannot be claimed on charges made that relate to exempt supplies;
- the services of agents (e.g. solicitors, estate agents, stockbrokers) unless relating to exempt supplies:
- bad debt relief; and
- realisation fees. Input tax cannot be claimed on cost relating to a petitioning creditor.

The completed form should be sent to HMRC, Birmingham DRT Office, VAT 426 Processing only, DMB 490, BX5 5AB. Supporting invoices should be provided for amounts claimed of £20,000 or over. The claim should be processed and paid within 30 working days. HMRC select some claims for verification, in which case a VAT officer will make arrangements to visit the office holder within 30 working days of receipt of the claim. Most verification visits will be made after HMRC have authorised the repayment claim. Because of the possibility of verification, all invoices supporting the claim must be retained with the relevant books and records.

Input tax – Form VAT 427 procedure

The normal procedure for reclaiming post-deregistration VAT on Form VAT 427 (see **35.11 INPUT TAX**) should be used where a liquidator has been appointed in

- members' voluntary liquidations and all administration orders;
- Scottish trust deeds and deeds or schemes of arrangement; and
- voluntary arrangements.

The completed Form 427 should be sent to HMRC Corporate Finance, VAT 2 (VAT427 Processing), DMB 612, BX5 5AB.

(VAT Notice 700/56/18, paras 7.1–7.9).

Groups

[36.13] In a VAT group of companies, the claim for preferential debts extends to a non-representative member because under *VATA 1994, s 43(1)* such a member is jointly and severally liable for VAT due from the representative member (*Re Nadler Enterprises Ltd*, Ch D [1980] STC 457 (TVC 32.12)). See **28 GROUPS OF COMPANIES**.

Where the representative member of a group becomes insolvent, HMRC regard the group treatment as ceasing to have effect from the relevant date. All the members of the group are automatically deregistered and each solvent member which continues to trade is automatically re-registered. Any insolvent member can also apply to be re-registered provided the company continues to trade. Continuation of group treatment may be allowed on request, however, but this will require prompt action to avoid automatic deregistration.

If the representative member of a group remains solvent but another group member becomes insolvent, HMRC will not automatically exclude that member from the group.

Partnerships

[36.14] Where a partnership becomes insolvent, HMRC may pursue any of the partners for any liability due.

If all partners are insolvent

HMRC will lodge one claim with the office holder in the name of the partnership. This claim should stand in the joint estate and separate estates of all the insolvent partners. HMRC should therefore be included in any dividend declared in any of the insolvent estates.

If one or more partners remain solvent

Responsibility for rendering returns and paying VAT remains with the solvent partner(s). HMRC may lodge a claim with the office holder of the estate of the insolvent partner(s) for any debts accrued up to the date of insolvency. An office holder who has VAT to account for on the administration of the insolvent estate must not account for it on a solvent partner's return. HMRC will issue forms to the office holder on request so that the VAT can be accounted for direct to HMRC.

If a partnership is wound up but individual partners remain solvent

The office holder is treated as the taxable person with effect from the date of the winding up and will be responsible for rendering returns and paying any VAT due on returns for the period after the date of winding up. A claim will be lodged with the office holder in the name of the insolvent partnership for any liabilities due to HMRC up to the date of winding up.

Where insolvent partners have different relevant dates

HMRC will lodge individual claims in the individual estates of the partners calculated from their respective relevant dates.

(VAT Notice 700/56/18, paras 16.1–16.5).

Receivers appointed under the Law of Property Act 1925

[36.15] A receiver appointed under the *Law of Property Act* is unable to register separately for VAT. This is because the receiver is appointed under a legal charge and is deemed to be the agent of the business. The business retains responsibility for its own VAT registration and all taxable supplies made and expenditure incurred by either the business or the receiver must be accounted for on the VAT return or the business's registration. See *Sargent v C & E Commrs*, CA [1995] STC 399 (TVC 37.12) where it was held that 'incapacitated' in *SI 1995/2518, Reg 9* should be construed as 'incapable of carrying on business'. This would only result from administrative receivership, liquidation or administration and not from the partial incapacity resulting from the appointment of a receiver of specific properties.

If a *Law of Property Act* receiver makes continuing supplies such as renting or leasing, then any VAT due should be accounted for through the business's VAT account and its VAT registration number should be used on any invoices issued. If the VAT-registered person does not agree to this, the receiver may account for output tax separately on a Form VAT 833.

If assets are sold, then the VAT due must be accounted for and paid to HMRC using Form VAT 833. The business's VAT registration number should be used on sales invoices and quoted on Form VAT 833. Payment may be made electronically, with the exception of card payments via Online/Telephone Payment Services and online direct debit.

Law of Property Act receivers cannot make a separate claim for the input tax which should properly be claimed via the trader's VAT return.

(VAT Notice 700/56/18, paras 17.1, 17.3).

Bankrupt continuing to trade

[36.16] Where trading continues after bankruptcy, the bankrupt retains responsibility for the submission of VAT returns and payment of VAT covering post-bankruptcy periods. HMRC will establish the pre-bankruptcy position so that they can lodge a claim with, or make a repayment to, the office holder, or operate Crown set-off (see **36.7** above) as appropriate.

If the office holder has VAT to account for in respect of the period of office, he must not include this VAT on the business's post-bankruptcy returns. HMRC will issue forms on request so that VAT can be accounted for. Completed forms should be returned to the National Insolvency Unit.

(VAT Notice 700/56/18, paras 9.1, 9.2).

Key points: insolvency

[36.17] Points to consider are as follows:

- HMRC no longer allows an insolvency practitioner to cancel a VAT registration number early and account for any output VAT due using a Form 833. The business must normally remain registered for VAT until all of the assets have been disposed of. The VAT registration number can be cancelled if the business continues to trade under the VAT registration threshold where preferable. Care needs to be taken to ensure that the value of any assets to be disposed of will not exceed the VAT registration threshold.

- Insolvency practitioners must not issue a VAT invoice in respect of any supplies made after the VAT registration number has been cancelled as the customer is not in a position to recover any output tax incorrectly charged.
- In cases where an insolvent business has deregistered, there is a facility for input tax to be claimed after the cancellation of the registration using form VAT426. There are various conditions that need to be met for a claim to be valid, the key one being that the cost must relate to the business that was VAT-registered. The majority of input tax claims made on form VAT426 relate to professional fees.

37

Insurance

De Voil Indirect Tax Service. See V4.121–V4.124.

Introduction to insurance

Characteristics of insurance

[37.1] There is no legal definition of insurance. In *Medical Defence Union Ltd v Department of Trade* [1979] 2 All ER 421 the judge held that there must be three specific elements present in any contract of insurance.

- The contract must provide that the insured will become entitled to money or money's worth on the occurrence of some event. The reference to 'money or money's worth' means that a claim can be settled through the provision of a service or replacement goods.
- The event must be one which involves some element of uncertainty. If the element of uncertainty is absent, any 'premiums' paid would more closely resemble contributions to a savings plan. (It could be argued that there is no uncertainty involved with life insurance. However, the timing of claims is the uncertain factor.)
- The insured must have an insurable interest in the subject matter of the contract. This means that if the insured risk occurs, the person who is insured stands to suffer some loss.

Generally, HMRC regard something as insurance for VAT purposes if it is an activity that requires the provider to be authorised as an insurer under the provisions of the *Financial Services and Markets Act 2000 (FSMA)*.

In addition to this, they accept that

- certain funeral plan contracts are insurance (and therefore exempt from VAT) even though they are not regulated as such under the *FSMA* insurance regulatory provisions (see **37.6**(3) below); and
- vehicle breakdown insurance is insurance even though providers are given a specific exclusion under the *FSMA* from the requirement to be authorised (see **37.6**(11) below).

The regulation of insurance

Financial services, including insurance, are regulated in the UK by the *Financial Services and Markets Act 2000.*

The provisions of the *FSMA* make it illegal for UK businesses to effect contracts of insurance without being authorised to do so (with the exception of certain bodies specifically granted exemption from the need for authorisation). The regulation of companies and unincorporated bodies under *FSMA, s 19* is carried out by the Financial Services Authority (FSA).

(VAT Notice 701/36/13, paras 2.2, 2.3).

Place of supply of insurance services

[37.2] Although no VAT is payable on insurance wherever it is supplied, the place of supply is important for VAT purposes because it determines whether or not VAT can be recovered on any costs incurred in making that supply.

The supply of insurance services falls within the general rule for the place of supply of services (see **66.14 SUPPLY: PLACE OF SUPPLY**): they are supplied where the customer belongs if the customer is a 'relevant business person', and where the supplier belongs if the customer is not a 'relevant business person', unless the non-business customer belongs in a country which is not an EU member state (other than the Isle of Man). In such a case, the place of supply is where the recipient belongs.

[*VATA 1994, Sch 4A para 16*].

Changes have been made to the place of supply of insurance repair services with effect from 1 October 2016. See **66.20 SUPPLY: PLACE OF SUPPLY** for details.

See **66.13 SUPPLY: PLACE OF SUPPLY** for the place of belonging and **18.2 EUROPEAN UNION: GENERAL** for the countries comprising the EU.

The place of supply rules for insurance above, also apply to reinsurance. Supplies of reinsurance are made to the principal insurer and not to the parties insured under the policy. The VAT treatment of a supply of reinsurance, therefore, is determined by the place of belonging of the insurer to whom the reinsurance is supplied.

Multiple insured parties

Some policies name more than one party as being insured under the contract. The customer's place of belonging in such instances should be determined by reference to the principal insured. Where there is no one principal insured and insured parties are based both inside and outside the EU, the supply of insurance should be treated as being received where the majority of the insured parties belong or, where applicable, where the party belongs that has been most directly involved in entering into the contract and/or stands to be the main beneficiary.

(VAT Notice 701/36/13, paras 6.1, 6.3, 6.4).

Input tax recovery in respect of insurance services

[37.3] Subject to the normal rules, input tax may be recovered which relates to

(a) taxable supplies of insurance services (i.e. supplies with a place of supply in the UK other than exempt supplies);

(b) supplies of insurance services with a place of supply outside the UK which would be taxable if made in the UK; and

(c) supplies of insurance services which
   - (i) are supplied to a person who belongs outside the EU; or
   - (ii) are directly linked to the export of goods to a place outside the EU; or
   - (iii) consist of the provision of intermediary services in relation to any transaction within (i) or (ii) above

   where that supply is exempt or would have been exempt if made in the UK.

   See **66.13** SUPPLY: PLACE OF SUPPLY for the place of belonging and **18.2** EUROPEAN COMMUNITY: GENERAL for the countries comprising the EU.

Apart from the special cases in (*c*) above, input tax which relates to exempt supplies of insurance services cannot be recovered.

[*VATA 1994, s 26(1)(2); SI 1999/3121*].

HMRC regard the entitlement to input tax under (*c*)(ii) above as only applying where

- the goods are being exported by the recipient of the insurance;
- the insurance is directly linked to the specific goods being exported; and
- the insurance covers the risks of the person who owns the goods or is responsible for their export.

(VAT Notice 701/36/13, para 6.6).

Supplies of insurance and reinsurance

[37.4] For EU legislation see **19.25**(*a*) EUROPEAN UNION LEGISLATION.

Exemption applies to all insurance and reinsurance transactions [*VATA 1994, Sch 9 Group 2, Item 1*] and does not depend upon the status of the provider.

This follows the decision in *Card Protection Plan Ltd v C & E Commrs, ECJ Case C–349/96*, [1999] STC 270 (TVC 22.348) where the CJEU held that under EU law the UK could not restrict the scope of exemption for insurance transactions exclusively to supplies by insurers who were permitted by national law to pursue the activity of an insurer. The House of Lords subsequently held that, in the light of the ECJ ruling, the company was making exempt supplies of insurance (HL [2001] STC 174 (TVC 38.47)).

Although this means that insurance supplied by an unauthorised insurer is exempt from VAT, such a business could be liable to prosecution under the *Financial Services and Markets Act 2000* and HMRC may refer cases that come to their attention to the Financial Services Authority. Businesses are therefore advised to clarify their regulatory position with the Financial Services Authority (Authorisation Enquiries Department, 25 The North Colonnade, Canary Wharf, London E14 5HS: tel 020 7676 1000).

As a result of the UK legislation, the place of supply rules in **37.2** above, and the input tax recovery rules in **37.3** above, the VAT position of insurance and reinsurance in the UK can be summarised as follows.

	Insured belonging in			
	UK	***EU (non-business)***	***EU (business)***	***Non-EU***
Insurance directly related to the export of goods to a place outside the EU	E(R)	E(R)	OS(R)	OS(R)
All other classes of insurance	E	E	OS	OS(R))

Key

E = Exempt (no input tax recovery)

E(R) = Exempt but with refund of related input tax

OS = Outside the scope of UK VAT with no refund of related input tax

OS(R)= Outside the scope of UK VAT with refund of related input tax

(VAT Notice 701/36/13, para 6.6).

In *Winterthur Life UK Ltd* (VTD 14935) (TVC 38.11) the operation of personal pension schemes by a group of companies was held to be an exempt supply of insurance services. On the facts, the services were not simply trust administration but embodied insurance contracts and were 'part and parcel' of the provision of insurance.

Reinsurance

[37.5] Reinsurance contracts are those under which an original insurer is indemnified by a reinsurer for a risk undertaken by the original insurer. (VAT Notice 701/36/13, para 2.2). Unless specifically stated otherwise, references to insurance in this chapter are to be taken to include reinsurance.

Particular supplies of insurance

[37.6] Particular supplies of insurance are as follows:

(1) Block insurance policies

The key characteristics of a block policy are that

- there is a contract between the block policyholder and the insurer which allows the block policyholder to effect insurance cover subject to certain conditions;
- the block policyholder, acting in its own name, procures insurance cover for third parties from the insurer;
- there is a contractual relationship between the block policyholder and third parties under which the insurance is procured; and
- the block policyholder stands in place of the insurer in effecting the supply of insurance to the third parties.

Following the decision in *Card Protection Plan Ltd v C & E Commrs, ECJ Case C–349/96*, [1999] STC 270 (TVC 22.362) HMRC regard supplies made by block policyholders as being insurance transactions for the purposes of the VAT exemption, even though they would not be seen as insurance for regulatory purposes. This means that block policyholders are acting as principals when they are effecting insurance transactions rather than as intermediaries arranging supplies of insurance.

This type of policy is often taken out by a supplier of goods or services to cover a number of small transactions over a set period, e.g.

- a removal company may take out a block policy to provide its customers with insurance against the risk of damage to their belongings during the house move; or
- a pony club may arrange insurance under a block policy to provide its members with cover against the risk of injury or liability for another's injury whilst taking part in equestrian events.

Sometimes a block policy will cover the risks of the block policyholder as well as those of their customers (e.g. the removal company's policy may also cover its own risk of damaging its customers' property).

Block policyholders supply VAT-exempt insurance transactions as principals rather than insurance-related services as intermediaries. As a result, the whole consideration received by a block policyholder (i.e. in respect of own services and the purchase of the insurance cover for customers) is income of the business. This could have implications for the calculation of recoverable input tax under the partial exemption method used.

(VAT Notice 701/36/13, para 2.5).

(2) Supplies by Friendly Societies

Friendly Societies are organisations registered under the *Financial Services and Markets Act 2000*. Their main purpose is to provide insurance against distress in the event of accident, sickness, old age and widowhood. Their insurance capital is provided by subscriptions from members.

Where these subscriptions relate solely to the provision of insurance, they are exempt from VAT. If the subscription also covers other goods and services, the part of the subscription relating to those other supplies is not exempt as insurance but may qualify for VAT relief elsewhere (e.g. under the exemption which covers certain supplies relating to health and welfare).

(VAT Notice 701/36/13, para 3.2).

(3) Funeral plans

Some funeral plans are written under contracts of insurance, so that on death a life insurance policy pays out the cost of the funeral. These types of funeral plan are treated as insurance for VAT purposes, and therefore exempt, even though they are not regulated as such.

Where a funeral plan represents pre-payment for a funeral it will not be exempt as insurance but will probably be eligible for exemption as the provision of a funeral (see **16.6 DEATH AND INCAPACITY**).

Management charges for funeral plans which are not insurance and are not prepayments (for example, where the client's money is placed in a trust to be spent on a funeral on his death) are standard-rated.

(VAT Notice 701/36/13, para 3.5).

(4) Guarantees and warranties

Retailers often sell guarantees and warranties with certain goods, such as domestic electrical equipment and cars.

Under a '*guarantee or warranty arrangement*', the purchase price of the goods includes an amount in consideration of which the manufacturer or retailer undertakes to replace or repair defective goods within a specified period.

Under an '*extended warranty arrangement*' the provider enters into a distinct contract under which it undertakes, for a consideration, to be subject to the same (and possibly some additional) obligations as covered in the original warranty. The provider of an extended warranty could be the retailer or manufacturer of the goods (or possibly a company within the same group as either of them), or be an independent third party company completely unconnected to the original supply of the goods.

Guarantees and warranties that are written under contracts of insurance (that is, those which are recognised as insurance by the Financial Services Authority (FSA)) will, in principle, fall within the VAT exemption for insurance (but see **37.7** below for insurance supplied with other goods and services).

The supply of a non-insurance warranty by a UK business is standard-rated. Guarantees and warranties provided by the manufacturer or retailer of the goods are very unlikely to be seen as insurance by the FSA because

- when provided by the retailer, the guarantee or warranty is seen as an automatic (often statutory) consequence of the contract of sale, not the provision of insurance cover; and
- in the case of the manufacturer's warranty, the risk of product failure lies within the control of the manufacturer and contracts under which the occurrence of an uncertain event lie within the control of either the provider or the recipient are unlikely to be regarded as insurance.

Some extended warranties may not be seen as insurance by the FSA regardless of who provides them (e.g. because the provider undertakes to maintain or repair goods at least partly at the recipient's expense or because the contract contains both insurance and non-insurance elements, such as regular servicing, and on balance the provider's obligation is not seen as being one to insure).

Where a business takes out an insurance policy to protect against the risk of there being a shortfall in the fund used to pay for any repairs covered by a warranty, there is no contract of insurance between the insurer and the customer taking out the warranty. The supply of the insurance and the supply of the warranty are two separate supplies, one exempt and one taxable.

(VAT Notice 701/36/13, para 3.7).

(5) Insurance directly linked to exports of goods outside the EU

There is specific provision for input tax to be recovered if it is incurred in respect of supplies of insurance which are *directly linked* to exports of goods to a place outside the EU. See **37.3**(*c*) above.

(6) Marine Aviation and Transport (MAT) insurance

The classes of risk covered by MAT insurance are

- accident (in connection with MAT risks only);
- railway rolling stock;
- aircraft;
- ships;
- goods in transit;
- aircraft liability; and
- liability of ships

but not

- motor and land vehicles;
- oil and gas rigs permanently fixed to the sea bed;
- specific policies for ships laid-up or aircraft grounded;
- specific policies for ships and aircraft under repair; and
- port and airport owners and operators' liability and manufacturers' liability.

Due to the nature of MAT insurance, HMRC have agreed guidelines with trade representatives for determining and recording where MAT insurance is supplied for VAT purposes. The trade agreement, summarised below, only applies to supplies of MAT insurance, it does not extend to supplies of other types of insurance or to MAT reinsurance.

Coding MAT insurance

There are three codes that should be used to identify the VAT status of supplies of MAT insurance.

X	to indicate that the supply of insurance was not directly related to an export of goods from inside to outside the EU and was made to a customer belonging within the EU and therefore carries with it no entitlement to input tax recovery.
Z	to indicate that the insurance was supplied to a customer belonging outside the EU or directly related to an export of goods from inside to outside the EU and therefore carries with it an entitlement to input tax recovery.

M	only if the insurance does not directly relate to the export of goods from inside to outside the EU and the policy has no clear principal insured and at least one, but not all, of the insured parties belongs outside the EU. The M (mixed) code gives an entitlement to treat 50% of input tax incurred on related goods and services as recoverable and 50% as non-recoverable.

Determining the place of supply for MAT insurance

The following rules should be used to determine whether the X or the Z code is appropriate, based on the location of the insured party/ies.

(a) *Single insured*. The insurer's address shown on the broker's slip (or equivalent document) is to be taken as the place of belonging of the insured. If no address is shown, the address should be determined by asking the broker or other intermediary who arranged the supply.
Where the insured has more than one address, the address on the slip or equivalent document should be used unless it is clear that this is simply an administrative address for payment or other purposes.

(b) *Multiple insureds*. Certain types of insurance (e.g. hull) often have multiple insureds identified on the slip, including the owner, managers, operators, the manning or crew agents, time charterers and mortgagors. Where possible, the principal insured should be identified and their place of belonging used to decide the VAT code as with a single assured under (*a*) above. The principal insured may be the only named insured (as distinct from others shown as additional insured) or may be the first-named on the policy. Where the principal insured cannot be identified, the places of belonging of all the insureds should be ascertained (if practicable) and the business coded according to whether the insured parties are all based in the EU, or all outside the EU or some inside and some outside.

(c) *Unidentified insured(s)*. Where the place(s) of belonging of the insured(s) cannot otherwise be determined, VAT coding should be decided by reference to
- the country of origin of the business;
- the address of the originating broker/cover holder;
- the address of the overseas agent (where applicable) and
- any additional information on the slip.

In the case of conflict between indicators, best judgement should be used.
Where it is not possible to determine whether the X or Z code is appropriate using the above guidelines, then specific transactions may be coded M. The M code should only be used as a last resort where it is not possible to determine the place of belonging of the insured party or where an insurance contract provides cover for insured parties belonging both inside the EU and outside the EU and it is not possible to identify the principal insured party.
(VAT Notice 701/36/13, para 6.7; VAT Notice 700/57/14).

Also see VAT Notice 700/57/14 for details of an arrangement allowed to MAT insurance underwriters who are members of a particular trade association in respect of claims-related input tax and associated imported services.

(7) Supplies by Medical and Welfare funds

Subscriptions to such funds which, although not friendly societies, provide *specified* benefits in the event of illness, accident, etc. are exempt from VAT as insurance.

Where the benefits are *not specified* and the amounts paid out are at the discretion of persons controlling the fund, the subscriptions may qualify as donations and be outside the scope of VAT.

(VAT Notice 701/36/13, para 3.3).

(8) Protection and indemnity (P & I) clubs

A P & I club is normally a mutual association of ship owners established to insure its members and specialising mainly in third party liability cover and insurance of the balance of collision risks not covered by the company or London market. P & I clubs are non-profit making and operate on a system of payments (usually based on the previous year's costs) with supplementary payments (termed 'calls') to settle claims and rebates to balance underwriting years. The club is deemed to be making a supply of insurance, the liabilities of which are determined as in the table in **37.4** above.

(VAT Notice 701/36/13, para 3.4).

(9) Run-off business

Where an insurer has ceased to underwrite insurance (or a particular class) but a liability remains to deal with claims under contracts already underwritten, such contracts are said to be 'running-off'. Any additional premiums receivable under existing contracts follow the liability of the original supply of insurance.

An insurer will often appoint third parties to administer the run-off of contracts on their behalf. Where a third party takes over responsibility for an insurer's run-off business, (including handling and settling claims and dealing with premium adjustments), the services supplied are not exempt as insurance transactions (i.e. as supplies of insurance). This is because the third party does not have a contractual relationship with the insured party and is not taking on the risk attached to the insurance which remains with the original insurer. It is possible, however, that some or all of the run-off services supplied by the third party will qualify for exemption as insurance-related services (see **37.15** below).
(VAT Notice 701/36/13, para 3.8).

(10) Sale of part paid endowment policies

The sale of part-paid endowment policies is not exempt under the insurance exemption because the risk covered by the underlying insurance remains that of the original policyholder. There is, however, a financial transaction taking place and the consideration received is exempt as finance.

(VAT Notice 701/36/13, para 3.9).

(11) Vehicle breakdown services

Subscriptions to motoring organisations usually include an element for assistance in the event of a breakdown provided under a contract of insurance. With this kind of insurance the benefits to the insured party (the member) are given in kind rather than in monetary form (that is, roadside repairs and recovery services).

Where vehicle breakdown insurance is provided as an independent supply, the element of the subscription that is attributable to it will be exempt from VAT. See **37.7** below for information on the VAT treatment of goods and/or services supplied together.

(VAT Notice 701/36/13, para 3.6).

Insurance supplied with other goods or services

[37.7] Where exempt insurance is supplied with goods or services that are liable to VAT, it is necessary to determine the correct VAT treatment of the supplies. See **65.6 SUPPLY: GENERAL** for the tests laid down in *Card Protection Plan Ltd v C & E Commrs, ECJ Case C–349/96*, [1999] STC 270 (TVC 22.362). These involve:

(1) Identifying the essential features of a transaction to determine what the customer is actually receiving (i.e. is the customer receiving two or more supplies each distinct and independent from the other or is the customer receiving one supply made up of a number of component parts).

(2) If (1) above does not identify separate supplies, it is necessary to consider whether any of the parts can properly be regarded as a principal supply to which the other goods or services are ancillary (i.e. they do not constitute an aim in themselves but rather a means of better enjoying the principal supply).

Applying these tests to

- where there are two or more distinct supplies each independent of the other, the part of the consideration received which relates to insurance is exempt from VAT and the rest of the consideration is liable to VAT at the appropriate rate; and
- where there is one principal supply to which the other goods or services are ancillary, the whole transaction will take the VAT treatment of the principal supply. As a result,
  - (i) where the insurance is the principal supply, the whole consideration received for both the insurance and the taxable goods or services is VAT-exempt; and
  - (ii) where the insurance is ancillary to a supply of taxable goods or services, the whole consideration received is liable to VAT at the appropriate rate.

Each case has to be considered on its own merit but factors that could indicate separate rather than composite supplies include

- whether the customers can choose to have the goods or services without the insurance and (where appropriate) vice versa;
- whether both the insurance and the goods or services have their own price and this is reflected in the amount customers pay should they choose to have one without the other (i.e. the overall amount customers pay is reduced by the cost of the insurance should they decide to buy your goods or services without insurance); and
- whether customers are fully aware they are receiving more than one supply, as evidenced by the invoicing and contractual arrangements in place.

(VAT Notice 701/36/13, paras 4.1–4.3).

In *Peugeot Motor Co plc and Another v C & E Commrs*, Ch D [2003] STC 1438 (TVC 38.54), the appellants sold cars to the public (end-users) either through dealers within the same VAT group (direct sales) or through independent franchised dealers or finance houses (indirect sales). In both categories, the appellants used various promotion schemes in which the end-user received motor insurance from an insurance company for no additional payment, the insurance company being paid by the appellants. The court held that the appellants made an insurance-related supply in respect of both direct and indirect sales but that, first, this formed part of a single supply with the motor car and, secondly, the insurance element of the supply was ancillary to the supply of the car. The full price paid for the car by the end-user (in the case of direct sales) or by the independent dealer or finance house (in the case of indirect sales) was taxable at the standard rate.

See also *Ford Motor Co Ltd v HMRC*, CA [2007] EWCA Civ 1730 (TVC 38.30).

Add-on services

[37.8] Add-on services are additional services supplied as part of a package with the main supply of insurance (e.g. helplines). They may be supplied under the contract of insurance itself or under a separate contract. They may also be provided by

- companies (which may or may not be insurers) other than the insurance company or companies underwriting a particular contract of insurance; or
- one or more of the underwriting insurers themselves.

The VAT treatment of these services depends upon the contractual arrangements in place between the parties and the nature of the services being supplied.

Add-on services supplied by third party to insurers

Where the add-on service being supplied to an insurer for incorporation into an insurance contract is

- itself insurance provided by one insurer (the 'add-on insurer') to another insurer (the 'direct insurer') who has a contract with a policyholder, the premium received by the add-on insurer from the direct insurer is exempt from VAT; and

- not insurance, and the service does not fall within another exemption or zero rate, VAT is chargeable on the supply by the third party to the insurer.

Some add-on services may qualify for VAT exemption as insurance-related services.

Add-on services supplied to policyholders

Where the add-on service is insurance, the entire supply is exempt. Each insurer is treated as making an exempt supply, the value of which is the part of the premium they have underwritten.

Where the add-on service is not insurance but is supplied by the insurer under the same contract as the insurance, there may be a liability to VAT on the consideration received by the insurer in respect of the add-on service. This depends on the liability of the add-on service and the nature of the package being supplied by the insurer (see **37.7** above).

Where the add-on service is not insurance and is supplied under a separate contract from that under which the insurance is supplied, there may be a liability to VAT on the consideration received in respect of the add-on service. In this instance, the add-on service is less likely to be ancillary to the supply of insurance and more likely to be a separate supply in its own right, but consideration should still be given to the guidance on single and composite supplies in **37.7** above.

(VAT Notice 701/36/13, para 4.4).

Engineering insurance and inspection services

[37.9] Engineering insurance provides cover for large items of capital plant, machinery or structures on land such as industrial boilers, cranes and lifts. It is intended to protect the insured against the risk of the plant or equipment going wrong.

Insurers providing such insurance may also contract with customers to provide inspection services in connection with the insurance, perhaps to identify ways to reduce cover or prevent the need for a claim. Inspection services supplied on their own are subject to VAT at the standard rate. Therefore, an insurer supplying inspection services with insurance will need to determine the correct VAT treatment for its supplies under the rules in **37.7** above.

(VAT Notice 701/36/13, para 4.5).

Insurance claims

[37.10] Establishing who is receiving supplies made in connection with, or in settlement of, insurance claims is important because this will determine who could have the right to recover any VAT charged on those supplies as input tax.

Supplies made to the insured party

Where supplies of claims-related goods or services are made to the insured party and the claim relates to their VAT-registered business, any VAT incurred on those supplies may be deducted as input tax subject to normal rules. Where the insured party can recover the VAT from HMRC, the insurer need normally only pay the net amount due (less any excess payable by the insured party) under the insurance claim.

Supplies made to the insurer

Where supplies of claims-related goods and services are made to the insurer, the amount of VAT recoverable depends on the insurer's partial exemption method.

Where an insurer incurs costs in respect of an individual claim (e.g. legal costs where the insurer is in dispute with the policyholder), any VAT on those costs is directly attributable to the associated supply of insurance and the recoverability of any VAT charged will depend upon whether or not the relevant supply of insurance gives a right to input tax deduction (see **37.3** above). See also *C & E Commrs v Deutsche Ruck Reinsurance Co Ltd*, QB 1994, [1995] STC 495 (TVC 46.5).

Goods supplied to the insurer for transfer to the insured party

The insurer may choose to recover the VAT charged on the goods as input tax and account for output tax on the cost price when the goods are handed over. Alternatively, the insurer may refrain from claiming the VAT charged and, therefore, not be liable to account for output tax when the goods are transferred to the insured party.

Legal costs

Where an insurer obtains legal services in connection with, for example, policy interpretation or in relation to a dispute with a policyholder, the supply of the legal services is to the insurer. In the case of subrogated claims (i.e. claims where the insurer exercises its right to pursue or defend a claim against a third party in the name of the insured party) supplies of legal services in connection with those claims are made to the insured party and not to the insurer.

Loss adjusters, etc.

Loss adjusters are normally contracted to act on behalf of the insurer and the supply of their services is therefore made to the insurer rather than the insured party. Loss assessors, on the other hand, are normally appointed by, and act in the interest of, the insured party and the supply of their services is therefore made to the insured party rather than to the insurer.

Indemnification by way of replacement goods or services

Where settlement of a claim is made by way of replacement goods or services, the supply position depends upon the terms of the contractual arrangements between the parties concerned. The supply of these replacement goods or services by a third party supplier is normally seen as being made to the insured party, although in some instances, the facts, including the terms of the insurance contract, may mean that the supply is made to the insurer.

Financial indemnification

If an insurer settles an insurance claim by paying money by way of financial indemnification to the insured party, there is no supply for VAT purposes. The money paid by the insurer in settlement of the claim is outside the scope of VAT.

(VAT Notice 701/36/13, paras 5.1–5.5).

Surrender of goods following an insurance claim

[37.11] The disposal of

- works of art, antiques and collectors' items (see **74.3 WORKS OF ART, ETC.**), and
- second-hand goods (i.e. tangible movable property that is suitable for further use either as it is or after repair)

by an insurer who has taken possession of them in settlement of a claim under an insurance policy (e.g. salvaged goods damaged by fire or water or stolen goods recovered after a claim has been paid) is outside the scope of VAT provided the following conditions are met.

- The goods are in the same condition at the time of disposal as when they were taken into the insurer's possession. The condition of goods has been changed if any improvements, repairs, replacement parts or the generally making good of any damage has been carried out. The cleaning of goods generally does not affect the condition nor does the inclusion of instruction manuals if they are otherwise missing. (Business Brief 19/01).
- For goods other than motor cars
  - (a) if the goods had been supplied in the UK by the policyholder, that supply would not have been chargeable with VAT or would have been chargeable on less than full value;
  - (b) if the goods have been imported into the UK, they must have borne VAT which has neither been reclaimed nor refunded; and
  - (c) the goods must not have been reimported having previously been exported from the UK free of VAT by reason of zero-rating.
- In the case of motor cars, the VAT on any previous supply, acquisition or importation must have been wholly excluded from credit.

[*SI 1992/3122, Arts 2, 4; SI 1995/1268, Arts 2, 4*].

Where the above conditions are not satisfied, VAT is chargeable on the full amount realised on the sale (not the original cost of the asset, see *Darlington Finance Ltd* [1982] VATTR 233 (TVC 44.81)).

The insurer will therefore need to know the VAT status of the policyholder and be able to cross reference this information to the disposal of each item in order to decide whether VAT must be accounted for.

Motor vehicles received by an insurer as scrap metal are treated as tangible movable property rather than motor cars. Insurers are not required to account for VAT on the disposal of the scrap unless the policyholder would have charged VAT.

(VAT Notice 701/36/13, para 5.6).

Accounting for VAT on insurance transactions

Recovery of input tax

[37.12] See **37.3** above for the rules on input tax recovery. Where input tax is recoverable relating to insurance within **37.3**(*c*)(i) or (ii), HMRC will expect to see appropriate documentation in support of the claim, such as

- policy documents;
- cover notes;
- credit/debit notes;
- broker's slips; and
- any relevant correspondence.

Recovery of input tax incurred on supplies made by overseas branches

UK insurers can recover VAT incurred in the UK in connection with supplies made by overseas branches belonging outside the EU. As insurance companies may have difficulty identifying this input tax, HMRC have agreed with the Association of British Insurers (ABI) methods by which the amount of recoverable input tax can be arrived at. See VAT Notice 700/57/14.

Contact and representative offices of overseas insurers

Such offices are established for public relations purposes generally. They are not permitted to accept insurance business in the UK and do not normally make supplies in the UK.

A contact office can apply for voluntary registration in the UK if it incurs input tax in connection with supplies of insurance made outside the EU by the overseas insurer. Input tax reclaimed should be based on the proportion of supplies made by the overseas supplier as a result of contacts made by the contact office. It can only recover input tax on supplies on which VAT would have been recoverable had they been supplied in the UK.

Where the overseas insurer is unable to provide a breakdown of actual supplies made to policyholders, the notional liability of its supplies can be determined as follows.

- If the head office/branch is in the EU, it is treated as if it makes all supplies within the EU with no entitlement to recovery of related input tax.
- If the head office/branch is outside the EU, it is treated as if it makes all its supplies outside the EU with entitlement to recovery of input tax.
- If some establishments to which the contact office supplies services are inside, and some outside, the EU, the proportion of its input tax which may be reclaimed can be arrived at using the ratio of the number of non-EU establishments to the total number of establishments.

The contact office may apply for an alternative method. The agreement referred to above for recovery of input tax incurred in connection with supplies made by overseas branches also applies to overseas insurers with branches in the UK.

Tax point (time of supply)

Although, as a general rule, supplies of insurance are exempt, the time of supply may be important for partial exemption purposes, e.g. to determine the recoverable proportion of non-attributable output tax where an outputs-based method is used.

The tax points for supplies of insurance covering one-off (short-term) risks are

- basic tax point – this occurs on completion of cover (i.e. when the insurance contract is finalised and signed); and
- actual tax point — this may arise when some or all of the premium is received in advance of the basic tax point.

Renewable policies covering long-term risks will normally represent continuous supplies of services, in which case the only tax point is the date of receipt of the premium.

Value of supplies

The value of supplies of insurance is the total gross premiums due under the contract without deducting any commission due to brokers and agents.

Accounting for VAT on run-off business

Where an insurer has contracts in run-off (see **37.6**(9) above, and uses a partial exemption method based on the ratio of supplies which attract input tax recovery to total supplies, it should exclude return premiums from its calculations for run-off business only. This is to prevent the return premiums that are attributable to earlier VAT years/periods distorting the ratios of the current VAT year/period. Alternatively, to avoid complex calculations it may apply in writing to HMRC to use a method whereby a flat-rate recovery percentage is applied to its gross input tax based on the premium income for the last three years of active underwriting.

Accounting arrangements for the Lloyd's insurance market

HMRC have agreed special VAT accounting arrangements for the Lloyd's insurance market.

- *Syndicates with two or more members*. Where a syndicate has two or more members, it is the syndicate rather than the member that is registered for VAT as the taxable person for all syndicate transactions. Where there is a syndicate registration, a Lloyd's member, whether corporate or natural, can also have its own registration in relation to non-syndicate activities. Syndicate activities cannot, however, be dealt with through that registration.
- *Syndicates with only one member*. Where syndicate has only one member (which in practice only occurs with a corporate member) the syndicate cannot itself be registered. The corporate member must be

registered and all syndicate business accounted for under its registration. Where the corporate member is covered by a group VAT registration, the group registration is used.

- *Managing agents*. Managing agents administer syndicates on behalf of members but are not themselves insurers. They may be VAT registered, and their supplies are those of an insurance agent (see **37.13** below). The VAT treatment follows that of the insurance underwritten by the syndicate or syndicates that they manage.

Each Lloyd's syndicate, member or managing agent that registers for VAT and makes taxable and/or specified supplies in addition to exempt supplies, must agree a special partial exemption method with HMRC.

(VAT Notice 701/36/13, paras 7.1–7.7).

Intermediary services

[37.13] Note: In *Staatssecretaris van Financiën v Arthur Andersen & Co, ECJ Case C–472/03*, [2005] STC 508 (TVC 22.365) (a Netherlands case) the CJEU held that what is now *Directive 2006/112/EC, Art 135(1)(a)* must be interpreted as meaning that 'back office' activities, consisting in rendering services, for payment, to an insurance company do not constitute the performance of services relating to insurance transactions carried out by an insurance broker or an insurance agent within the meaning of that provision and do not qualify for exemption. The activities carried out by Andersen Consulting Management Consultants (ACMC) included the issuing, management and cancellation of policies, the management of claims and, in most cases, taking decisions that bound the insurer to enter into insurance contracts. To qualify for exemption, ACMC had to qualify as either insurance brokers or insurance agents. The CJEU held that the essential characteristic of insurance brokers was that they had complete freedom as to choice of insurer for their clients and that, although insurance agents were tied to a particular insurer, their essential characteristic was that they introduced prospective customers to that insurer. As ACMC did not qualify on either count, its services were taxable at the standard rate. The CJEU judgment is binding on the UK and the UK VAT exemption for insurance-related services is too wide and must be amended. However, as a review of the VAT treatment of financial services and insurance had been announced by the European Commission, the Government decided to delay implementation of the CJEU judgment. The Commission has in 2015 abandoned the idea of reforming the exemptions, so the government may be considering when to make the necessary changes to UK law. Businesses have been entitled to ignore the UK exemption and apply the direct effect of the EU law since the decision in 2005. (Business Brief 11/05; Business Brief 23/05).

Subject to the above and the exceptions in **37.14** below, the provision by an insurance broker or an insurance agent of any of the 'services of an insurance intermediary' is exempt from VAT where those services are

- related to an insurance transaction or a reinsurance transaction (whether or not a contract of insurance or reinsurance is finally concluded); and

- provided by the broker or agent in the course of acting in an '*intermediary capacity*' i.e. acting as an intermediary (or one of the intermediaries) between a person providing insurance or reinsurance and a person who is seeking insurance or reinsurance or is an insured person.

'*Services of an insurance intermediary*' consist of any of the following.

(a) Bringing together, with a view to the insurance or reinsurance of risks, of persons seeking and persons providing insurance and reinsurance

It is sometimes difficult to distinguish between exempt introductory services under this heading and advertising services which are excluded from exemption (see **37.14**(*a*) below). In such cases, HMRC accept that there is a single exempt supply of insurance-related introductory services where

- the intermediary is targeting its own customer base;
- the intermediary is paid per successful take-up of an insurance policy; and
- the product or the insurer is endorsed by the intermediary.

Example

A finance company is an agent for an insurer providing loan protection insurance. It recommends this insurance to all its customers. Those customers that take out a policy when taking out a loan complete a proposal form included with the loan agreement papers and returning this to the finance company. The finance company forwards it to the insurer and receives commission.

There is an argument that the finance company is providing an advertising service. However, as the finance company is targeting its own customers; is recommending the product; and is being paid per successful take up, the commission it receives is treated as consideration for an exempt supply of introductory insurance services.

(VAT Notice 701/36/13, para 8.3).

Note that in *JCM Beheer BV v Staatsseccretaris van Financiën, ECJ Case C–124/07*, [2008] STC 3360 (TVC 22.366) the CJEU concluded that the fact that an insurance broker or agent did not have a direct relationship with the parties to the insurance or reinsurance contract in the conclusion of which he had been instrumental (but merely had an indirect relationship through the intermediary of another taxable person who was in a direct relationship and to whom the insurance broker or agent was contractually bound) did not prevent his services from being exempt from VAT.

In *The Governor & Company of the Bank of Ireland* (VTD 20824) (TVC 38.26) a bank formed a subsidiary company to provide insurance products to customers of the Post Office. The bank paid commission to the Post Office for introducing potential customers. The bank was not itself an authorised insurer, and referred the customers to an unrelated company (J), which in turn arranged for a panel of insurers to quote for the customers' business. It was accepted that the services which the bank provided to J qualified for exemption as the services of an insurance intermediary. However, these arrangements did not prove profitable for either the bank or the Post Office, and the bank decided to select a specific insurance company (N) as a 'primary insurer' with the opportunity to undercut any quotes provided by other members of the panel of insurers. N paid commission to the bank. The tribunal decided that the revised arrangements continued to qualify for exemption, holding that N was paying for the continued existence of the whole intermediary structure that was the panel, albeit in a refigured form. The bank was assisting in bringing about a contract of insurance. Its supplies to N were exempt services of an insurance intermediary.

In *InsuranceWide.com Services Ltd and Trader Media Group Ltd*, CA [2010] STC 1572 (TVC 38.24), it was held that certain supplies of insurance introductory services provided via the internet were exempt from VAT. Following that decision, HMRC accepted that insurance introductory services are exempt from VAT where the provider of such services ('the introducer') is doing much more than acting as a 'mere conduit' through which a potential customer is passed to an insurance provider. This can be demonstrated by all of the following four conditions being met.

- The introducer is engaged in the business of putting insurance companies in touch with potential clients or more generally acting as intermediary between the two parties (although this may not necessarily be their principal business activity).
- The introducer provides the means (that is, by way of an internet 'click through' or some other form of introduction) by which a person seeking insurance is introduced to a provider of insurance or to another intermediary in a chain leading to an insurance provider.
- That introduction takes place at the time a customer is seeking to enter into an insurance contract (although in some instances an insurance contract may not actually go on to be finally concluded).
- The introducer also plays a proactive part in putting in place the arrangements under which that introduction is effected. (HMRC Brief 31/10).

(b) Carrying out work preparatory to the conclusion of a contract of insurance or reinsurance

(c) Assistance in the administration and performance of such contracts, including claims handling

Assistance in the administration

HMRC regard assisting in the administration and performance of contracts as covering the services that insurance intermediaries perform in connection with the day-to-day administration of policies, e.g.

- maintaining up-to-date details of policyholders; and
- dealing with requests from policyholders for changes to cover.

UK courts have found that the definition of assisting in the administration and performance of contracts of insurance goes wider than the examples above and, until 31 March 2013, included the following.

- Pension mis-selling review services (see *Century Life plc v C & E Commrs*, CA 2000, [2001] STC 38 (TVC 38.14)). As a result of that decision, HMRC accepted that mis-selling review services carried out on behalf of insurers were exempt when the supplier was required to be involved in the decision-making process (i.e. assessing whether, and how much, loss had occurred and/or the amount and appropriate form of redress) and acted as an insurance intermediary, having contact with insured persons on behalf of insurers.
  From 1 April 2013, following enquiries from the European Commission, HMRC considers all mis-selling review services to be liable to standard-rated VAT. (HMRC Brief 33/12).
- Certain kinds of stand-alone helpline services. See *C & V (Advice Line) Services Ltd* (VTD 17310) (TVC 38.18) where a company providing a telephone helpline service to an insurance company's customers was held to be acting as an insurance intermediary so that its supplies qualified for exemption.
  HMRC accepted that where telephone helplines provided assistance to insured parties on matters such as variations of contract and the making of claims, these services were directly related to the supply of insurance and, where a third party supplied them to the insurer, their supplies were exempt.
  From 1 April 2013, following enquiries from the European Commission, HMRC no longer accepts that exemption applies to such helpline services. However, if an insurance broker or agent provides helpline services to an insurer as part of a single supply which also includes the provision of exempt insurance-related services, the supply will have a single VAT liability to be determined in accordance with its principal element. (HMRC Brief 33/12).

Claims handling

The term 'claims handling' is used to describe a number of services that may be provided by an intermediary following the making of a claim by a policyholder, including

- checking that documents are correctly completed;
- ensuring that the claim falls within the terms of a policy;
- processing the claim;
- ensuring that insurers are advised of their exposure;
- agreeing the validity and/or quantum of the claim and
- arranging for settlement to be made.

The supply of claims handling may also include a number of elements of an advisory, investigative, or administrative nature that would be subject to VAT if supplied in isolation. Where these elements form a minor and ancillary part of a single composite supply of claims handling, however, the entire supply will be exempt from VAT. See also **37.16** below for the VAT treatment of claims handling services supplied by loss adjusters and other experts in connection with the assessment of a claim.

(VAT Notice 701/36/13, paras 8.4, 8.5, 10.3, 10.4).

The treatment of claims handling in the UK is uncertain following the CJEU judgment in *Minister Finansów v Aspiro SA, ECJ Case C-40/15*. Aspiro SA, a Polish company supplies services relating to the settlement of insurance claims on behalf of an insurer. The company receives insurance claims and conducts investigations. It establishes contact with the insured person, with whom it has no contractual relationship itself, and if necessary produces assessments and damage reports. After analysing the assembled documents, it adjusts losses and takes decisions on claims. The company also conducts proceedings for recovery against third parties and handles complaints in respect of claim settlements. The company performs various other administrative and technical functions in connection with these activities. The referring court was essentially seeking to ascertain whether settlement of claims which are carried out in the name and on behalf of the insurer by a third party which has no contractual relationship with the insured person are to be exempted from VAT under *Directive 2006/112/EC, Art 135(1)(a)*. The court held that the services did not meet the conditions for exemption in *Directive 2006/112/EC, Art 135(1)(a)*. To do so, they would have to be 'insurance related services of an insurance agent'; in accordance with the earlier decision in *Andersen Consulting*, an insurance agent is involved in finding customers and selling insurance, rather than in settling claims. A similar decision, based on a 'conforming construction' of the UK legislation in line with the Directive, was reached by a First-tier Tribunal judge in *Riskstop Consulting Ltd* [2015] UKFTT 469 (TC) (TC04636). This suggests that HMRC are now reviewing the extent of this exemption, having accepted for some years after the *Arthur Andersen* case that the UK exemption was wider in scope than the EU law.

(d) The collection of premiums

An insurance intermediary may collect insurance premiums as part of another supply (e.g. exempt insurance introductory or administration services) but where a separate charge is made for these services, it will be exempt under this heading.

If the premium collection services are not supplied in connection with other insurance intermediary services, they may be liable to VAT (e.g. the services of a debt-collector collecting overdue premiums for an insurer).

Where an employer, who did not arrange the original insurance, allows an insurer to use its payroll system to collect premiums from its employees by deductions from their pay, the consideration received by the employer falls within the exemption for finance rather than insurance.

(VAT Notice 701/36/13, para 8.6).

[*VATA 1994, Sch 9 Group 2 Item 4, Notes (1), (2)*].

In *Re Försäkringsaktiebolaget Skandia, ECJ Case C–240/99*, [2001] STC 754 (TVC 22.363) (a Swedish case) an insurance company (S) undertook to run the insurance business of one of its subsidiary companies including the sale of insurance and the settlement of claims. The CJEU held that the undertaking did not qualify as an 'insurance transaction' so that the supply was one of management services on which VAT was chargeable. The decision was reached on the basis that the third party service provider did not have any relationship with the insured. The Court did not examine whether the services could have been exempt 'insurance-related services', because the terms of Skandia's licence under Swedish insurance regulations prevented it from acting as an agent or broker. As a result, the decision is expected to have limited impact in the UK, where services provided to an insurer on an outsourced basis would normally fall within the 'insurance-related services' definition.

Brokers and agents

For VAT purposes, brokers and agents are defined in terms of what they do rather than what they are and, as well as insurance brokers and agents by profession, it can apply to other intermediaries making supplies of 'related services'. (VAT Notice 701/36/13, para 9.1).

Members' agents for Lloyd's underwriters

In *SOC Private Capital Ltd* (VTD 17747) (TVC 38.16) the tribunal held that supplies of insurance were made by underwriting members (rather than the syndicates) and therefore a company acting as a members' agent for Lloyds' underwriters was an insurance agent within *VATA 1994, Sch 9 Group 2 Item 4* above and its supplies qualified for exemption.

Supplies not regarded as services of an insurance intermediary

[37.14] Supplies of the following services are specifically excluded from exemption under **37.17** above.

(a) Market research, product design, advertising, promotional or similar services (or the collection, collation and provision of information for use in connection with such activities).

(b) Valuation or inspection services. See also **37.9** above for inspection services and engineering insurance.

(c) Services by loss adjusters, average adjusters, motor assessors, surveyors or other experts unless
  (i) the services consist of claims handling under a contract of insurance or reinsurance; and
  (ii) the person handling the claim is authorised to act on behalf of the insurer or reinsurer and has written authority to accept or reject the claim, and to settle any amount agreed to be paid.

  See also **37.16** below.

(d) Services supplied in pursuance of a contract of insurance or reinsurance (or any arrangements in connection with such a contract) either instead of any financial indemnity which the insurer is contractually obliged to provide or for the purpose of satisfying any claim under that contract (in whole or part). This applies, for example, where a plumber's services are supplied free of charge to the insured to mend a burst pipe and the insurer meets the plumber's fee. The fee is excluded from exemption. (VAT Notice 701/36/13, para 8.2).

[*VATA 1994, Sch 9 Group 2 Notes (7)–(10)*].

Where one of the above excluded supplies is provided as a minor and ancillary part of a single composite supply of exempt insurance-related services provided in an intermediary capacity, the entire supply is treated as exempt.

(VAT Notice 701/36/13, para 8.2). See also **24.30** **FINANCIAL SERVICES** for mixed supplies of advice and financial services by a financial adviser. These provisions equally apply to mixed supplies of advice and insurance-related intermediary services.

Particular supplies of insurance-related services

[37.15] See the Note at **37.13** above.

(1) Broker-managed funds offered by life assurance companies

Life assurance backed broker-managed funds are provided under contracts between the life company which operates the fund, the policyholder and the broker who arranges the policy (usually referred to as the 'Broker Fund Adviser'). The Broker Fund Adviser, with authorisation from the policy holder/investor, provides investment advice to the life assurance company, recommending the switching of money invested between the various funds operated by the assurance company or, where permitted, directly into other forms of investment (e.g. shares or gilts).

Commission paid to the Broker Fund Adviser for arranging the life insurance policy is exempt under **37.13** above. Any other fees for services (including investment advisory services and any 'performance fee' based on the increased value of investments) are standard-rated.

(VAT Notice 701/36/13, para 10.7).

(2) Internet services

There are any number of ways in which the internet can be used in connection with insurance and the liability of supplies of internet services to insurers (or possibly to insured or prospective insured parties) needs to be considered on the supplies' own merits using the guidance laid out in **37.13** above. Factors indicating that a supply of Internet services is exempt as a supply of insurance-related services include:

- acting between insurers and insured (or prospective insured) parties;
- requirement for some specific insurance input rather than just pure facilitation; and
- direct connection to contracts of insurance either by bringing them about initially, or administering them, or handling claims made under them.

(VAT Notice 701/36/13, para 10.5).

See also *InsuranceWide.com Services Ltd* and *Trader Media Group Ltd* CA [2010] STC 1572 (TVC 38.24), in which it was held that internet introductory services to insurers or brokers qualified as exempt intermediary services.

(3) Protection and Indemnity (P & I) Club managers and agents

See **37.6**(8) above for what is meant by a P & I Club.

In the UK, P & I Club managers are separate legal entities from the clubs they represent. Managers normally provide a complete range of insurance agency services for P & I Clubs. Their functions can be broadly divided into

- business development (i.e. acquiring new insurance business for the club);
- underwriting (including negotiating terms of insurance and reinsurance);
- policy administration; claims-handling and settlement; and
- general and financial management.

HMRC accept that P & I Club managers providing the full range of services listed above are insurance intermediaries making supplies of related services that are exempt from VAT when supplied in the UK.

Managers predominantly supplying the general management services in the fourth bullet point above will be liable to charge VAT at the standard rate.

A P & I Club agent acts for a P & I Club manager when the manager has no presence in the UK. If an agent supplies the services listed above the VAT treatment of the agent's supply will follow that outlined for P & I Club managers above. This means that if an agent supplies services to a P & I Club manager belonging in the EU that would be exempt if supplied in the UK the agent's supply will be outside the scope of VAT with no input tax recovery. If an agent supplies services to a P & I Club manager belonging in the EU that would be taxable in the UK or to a manager based outside the EU, the agent's supply will be outside the scope of VAT with input tax recovery.

If a UK-based agent (that is, a P & I Club agent or any other kind of agent) is prospecting for customers in the UK and arranging new insurance contracts on behalf of an overseas insurer they should contact HMRC with regard to the possible registration of that insurer for VAT purposes in the UK.

(VAT Notice 701/36/13, para 10.2).

(4) Run-off services

See **37.6**(9) above for run-off business generally. An insurer will often appoint a third party to administer the run-off of insurance contracts on its behalf. The sort of services supplied could include

- responsibility for accountancy and legal work in connection with the business in run-off;
- services of handling and settling claims; and
- dealing with additional or return premium adjustments.

A composite supply of such run-off services falls within the VAT exemption as insurance-related services. Separate supplies of administrative services (such as accountancy, supplies of staff and management of invested premiums) do not qualify for exemption and are liable to VAT when supplied in the UK.

(VAT Notice 701/36/13, para 10.6).

(5) Telephone sales services

In *Teletech UK Ltd* (VTD 18080) (TVC 38.17) the company acted on behalf of an insurance company, cold-selling health insurance policies by telephone using contact lists provided by the insurer. The tribunal held that the company's services were exempt on the grounds that it was selling (or trying to sell) insurance policies as agents. The decisive factor was that, where calls led to sales, the company was able to put the insurer on risk and the customer on cover. The Tribunal Chairman also observed that the manner of remuneration, i.e. whether by flat fee (as in this case) or commission, had no bearing on the VAT treatment.

As a result of this decision, HMRC now accept that supplies of telephone sales services to insurers are exempt when the call centre is able to put the insurer 'on risk' and the customer 'on cover' at the point of sale. This applies regardless of whether the call centre provider is remunerated by way of commission or flat-rate fee.

(VAT Notice 701/36/13, para 10.4.1; Business Brief 7/03).

Loss adjusters and similar 'experts'

[37.16] See the Note at **37.13** above.

Services of loss adjusters, average adjusters, motor assessors, surveyors or 'other experts' (e.g. assessing damage or investigating potential fraud) are normally standard-rated. If they also provide insurance claims handling services, however, their services will be exempt when acting as the agent of the insurer when supplying those services. But services qualify for exemption where all of the following conditions are met.

- The services consist in the handling of a claim under a contract of insurance or reinsurance;
- The person handling the claim is authorised when doing so to act on behalf of the insurer or reinsurer.
- That person holds the insurer's written authority (see below) to determine whether to accept or reject a claim.
- Where the claim is accepted in whole or in part, that person has the insurer's written authority to settle the amount to be paid on the claim.

[*VATA 1994, Sch 9 Group 2 Note (9)*].

'*Other experts*' means anybody who is contracted by insurers to assess or value insurance claims because of their expertise in a particular field and could include

- solicitors assessing loss in personal injury claims cases;
- jewellers valuing items of stolen jewellery; or
- antiques experts assessing damage to antique furniture.

The term 'other expert' does not apply to specialist claims handling organisations. Where an insurer contracts a supply of claims handling services from a business, not because of that business's expertise in a particular field, but because of its expertise in claims handling generally, the services of the business are exempt under **37.13**(c) above and the above provisions do not apply.

Note, however, the commentary in **37.13**(c) above in relation to the CJEU judgment in *Minister Finansów v Aspiro SA, ECJ Case C-40/15*.

Insurer's written authority

If an insurer gives written authority to another person (such as a broker) who in turn issues written authority to a loss adjuster, the loss adjuster's services will still be exempt provided that the original authority from the insurer gave the original recipient power to delegate the authority in this way.

The written authority must allow the loss adjuster, etc. to investigate claims, perform any service necessary for the claim to be settled and agree the amount of a claim or cost of repairs or replacement without reference to the insurer. The authority may also include avoiding or repudiating claims. In all circumstances it must bind the insurance company to pay the amount of a claim or meet the cost of repair or replacement as determined by the loss adjuster.

Claims handling supplied with valuation/assessment services

Where a loss adjuster, etc. supplies exempt claims handling services with taxable claims valuation and/or assessment services, the VAT treatment of the services depends upon whether they are provided as two separate supplies or as one composite supply with the claims handling services ancillary to the taxable services or vice versa. Where taxable valuation and/or assessment services are ancillary to a principal supply of claims handling, the whole supply is exempt from VAT.

(VAT Notice 701/36/13, para 9.3).

Insurance-related services supplied with other goods or services

[37.17] See the Note at **37.13** above.

Insurance is frequently arranged by businesses in connection with other services or goods they are supplying as their main business activity, e.g.

- mechanical breakdown insurance (MBI) with cars and domestic appliances;
- travel insurance with holidays;
- insurance with removal services;
- insurance with rented property; and
- insurance with car hire.

Where this insurance is provided under a block insurance policy with the supplier of the goods or services being the policyholder, the appropriate VAT treatment is given in **37.6**(1) above.

In other instances not involving block policies, there will be a separate supply of exempt insurance by the insurer to the customer buying the goods or services where

- the cover being supplied is genuine insurance which qualifies for exemption under **37.4** above; and
- it is the customer's own risk which is being insured and not the risk of the supplier of the goods or services.

A supplier of the goods or services who arranges cover for customers may be able to treat the insurance premiums received from the customers or onward payment to the insurer as a disbursement. See **37.19** below.

Treatment of arrangement fees and commission charged by suppliers of goods and services

Where

(i) a person supplies goods or services to a customer,
(ii) those goods or services are liable to VAT (and not zero-rated),
(iii) a transaction under which insurance is to be, or may be, arranged for the customer is entered into in connection with that supply,
(iv) insurance-related services are provided by the supplier of the goods or services (or a person 'connected' with that person (see **72.19 VALUATION**) who deals directly with the customer in connection with the insurance), and
(v) the insurance-related services are not claims handling services (which are exempt under **37.13**(c) above without considering these requirements),

any amount charged by the supplier to the customer (e.g. an arrangement fee or commission) in addition to the premium is not exempt under **37.13** above unless

- a document containing details of the amount of the premium, and also any fees charged in addition to the premium, is prepared;
- those matters are disclosed to the customer at or before the time when the insurance transaction is entered into; and
- the supplier complies with any published requirements of HMRC as to the preparation and form of the document, the manner of disclosing those matters to the customer and delivery of a copy of the document to the customer.

If these conditions are not met, there is still no VAT chargeable on the amount collected by the supplier and passed on to the insurer for the supply of insurance. But any fees or commission received by the supplier for arranging the insurance is liable to VAT at the same rate as the goods or services themselves.

HMRC have published specific requirements in the following circumstances (which have the force of law).

(1) *Transactions by telephone or electronic communication*. The disclosure conditions may create a problem in such cases as the customer and supplier are not physically together when the sale takes place. To overcome this, if the insurance-related services are to be exempt, HMRC require a supplier selling taxable goods by such means to
   - make full disclosure of the premium at the time of the transaction (e.g. a trader selling holidays over the telephone must orally inform the customer of the amount of the premium and any fee charged over and above the premium in relation to the insurance);

- have in place a system whereby the sales staff must annotate a document (even if this only involves ticking a box) at the time they make the oral or electronic disclosure to customers to indicate that they have done so;
- prepare, and issue to the customer, a document with the information required as above (albeit after the time the insurance transaction has been entered into); and
- retain a copy of these records as they would their normal VAT records.

(2) *Second-hand schemes.* Where a person supplies goods or services under one of the second-hand schemes, the disclosure must be made on the relevant VAT invoice issued by that person.

Subject to these requirements, it was held in *Smith Glaziers (Dunfermline) Ltd v C & E Commrs*, HL [2003] STC 419 (TVC 38.23) that the above provisions are concerned with identifying the information which the document must disclose rather than specifying any particular form. All that is necessary is that the allocation is unequivocally stated in the document, even if this requires some knowledge of arithmetic.

[*VATA 1994, Sch 9 Group 2 Notes (3)–(6)*]. (VAT Notice 701/36/13, paras 11.1–11.3).

Insurance-related services supplied outside the UK

[37.18] See the Note at **37.13** above.

Place of supply

Although no VAT is payable on qualifying insurance-related services regardless of where those services are supplied, the place where insurance-related services are supplied for VAT purposes is important because it helps to determine whether VAT on any costs incurred making that supply can be recovered. See **37.2** above for determining the place of supply of insurance services.

Determining who the customer is for services related to insurance and reinsurance

An insurance intermediary could be supplying insurance-related services to either the insured party (or the party seeking insurance) or to the insurer supplying the insurance. He could also be acting as a sub-agent and be supplying his services to another agent in the chain of supply of the insurance. It is, therefore, important to determine precisely who the customer is when one or more of the parties in the supply chain belongs outside the UK. This will be clear-cut in some cases (based on the contractual, financial and practical arrangements in place at the time) but in other instances, it is not so easily determined. HMRC will normally see the supply of intermediary services as being made to the insured party unless there are clear indications to the contrary. In the case of reinsurance, unless there are clear indications otherwise, services related to reinsurance are assumed to be made to the ceding insurer.

This issue was recently the subject of a successful appeal by *Unicom Insurance Services Ltd* (TC05509) [2016] UKFTT 782 (TC) which concerned whether the intermediary services provided by Unicom were to the UK consumer or to the insurance company located in Gibraltar. Unicom argued that 95% of the intermediary services provided by Unicom were supplied to Tradewise Insurance Company Limited ('TWIC') who belongs in Gibraltar and as a result Unicom was entitled to input tax recovery in costs incurred in respect of these supplies under *Art 3* of the *VAT (Input Tax) (Specified Supplies) Order 1999, SI 1999/3121*. HMRC argued that the supplies were made to the UK consumers as the documents referred to the consumers as the 'clients'. The First-tier Tribunal allowed the taxpayer's appeal on the basis of the contractual terms agreed by TWIC and Unicom and between Unicom and the consumers. The contractual terms clearly pointed to the conclusion that Unicom supplied its intermediary services to TWIC and that Unicom acted as an agent of TWIC. TWIC also had the contractual right to compel Unicom to provide intermediary services and the consumers only had a limited contract with Unicom.

Input tax recovery

See **37.3** above. The following table summarises the position in relation to supplies of intermediary services by UK businesses.

	VAT treatment where place of supply is		
	UK	***Elsewhere in EU***	***Outside EU***
Services related to insurance directly linked to the export of specific goods from the EU to outside the EU	E(R)	OS(R)	OS(R)
Other insurance-related services when insured party belongs in the UK or elsewhere in the EU	E	OS	OS(R)
Other insurance-related services when the insured party belongs outside the EU	E(R)	OS(R)	OS(R)

Key

E = Exempt (no input tax recovery)

E(R)= Exempt but with refund of related input tax

OS = Outside the scope of UK VAT with no refund of related input tax

OS(R)= Outside the scope of UK VAT with refund of related input tax

(VAT Notice 701/36/13, paras 12.1–12.3).

Claims handling services supplied to non-UK customers

The recipient of claims handling services is usually the insurer and not the insured. In order to determine the liability of claims handling services supplied outside the UK, it is necessary to establish the place of belonging of

- the insurance company;
- the claimant (the insured party); and
- the person providing the claims handling service.

The supply to an insurer of claims handling services that fall within the insurance exemption will be

- exempt if the insurer belongs in the UK;
- outside the scope of VAT with no input tax recovery if the insurer belongs in the EU; and
- outside the scope of VAT with input tax recovery if the insurer belongs outside the EU.

However, where the insurer belongs in the UK or elsewhere in the EU, there is a right of input tax recovery where the insured party belongs outside the EU.

If a supply of claims handling services does not qualify for exemption as an insurance-related service, it is liable to VAT at the standard rate when supplied in the UK and outside the scope with input tax recovery when supplied elsewhere.

(VAT Notice 701/36/13, para 12.4).

Accounting for VAT on insurance-related services

Input tax recovery

[37.19] See **37.3** above for the rules on input tax recovery.

Tax points (time of supply)

The time of supply for insurance-related services follows the normal tax point rules (see **67.18** *et seq.* **SUPPLY: TIME OF SUPPLY**). The actual tax point occurs when a debit note or (where appropriate) VAT invoice is issued to the customer to collect the premium or separate fee (if one is charged) or the date on which payment is received, whichever happens first.

Value of supplies of related services

The value of a supply of insurance-related services is the amount of consideration received in respect of gross commission, flat-rate fee and/or recharge of costs incurred, whichever payment method applies to the particular transaction. In the case of commission, no deduction should be made for any commission payable in turn to other intermediaries employed. It is the gross commission, not the net retained or earned commission, that is the value for VAT purposes.

The amount of any premium collected to be passed back to the insurer in respect of the supply of insurance itself should not be included in the value of the supplies of related services.

Mechanical breakdown insurance (MBI)

There are special rules for determining the value attributable to MBI when it is sold with a used vehicle for a single selling price. See **62.31 SECOND-HAND GOODS.**

Repairs carried out under insurance contracts

HMRC introduced revised legislation with effect from 1 October 2016 that affects the place of supply of repairs under a contract of insurance. Under the old rules, when an insurance claim was submitted for damaged goods, the insured person was normally be the recipient of the services and the insurance company just covered the cost of the repairs. However under certain arrangements the services were provided to the insurance company and if one of the parties was established outside of the EU then the place of supply was where the recipient of the service was located. HMRC considered that the old place of supply rules were being used in order to obtain a VAT advantage as the insurer would receive UK repair services free of UK VAT.

With effect from the 1 October 2016, the use and enjoyment provisions were extended to business-to-business (B2B) repairs carried out under insurance contracts. As a result of the changes if the supply of repair services is undertaken as a result of an insurance claim made to an insurer, or their agent, established outside of the EU, the supply will be covered by the new use and enjoyment provisions and if the repairs are undertaken for persons resident in the UK, the repair services will be liable to UK VAT.

[*VATA 1994, Sch 4A para 9D; SI 2016/726*]. (HMRC Brief 15/16).

Disbursements

If a business makes supplies of goods or services and arranges insurance cover for its customers in connection with those goods or services, any premium collected from the customer to be passed on to the insurer for the supply of insurance may, in certain circumstances, be treated as a disbursement and therefore outside the scope of VAT. This applies only to the amount due from the customer to the insurer. It does not cover any amount retained by the business in respect of commission for insurance-related services or costs incurred in making the supplies (e.g. travel, subsistence and overhead costs passed on).

For the premium due to an insurer to qualify as a disbursement, all of the following conditions must be met.

- The customer must have specifically requested that the insurance cover is obtained on his behalf.
- It must be the customer's own risks which are insured under the policy.
- The supplier must recover only the exact amount of net premium from the customer.
- The amount paid by the customer must be in respect of cover for the customer alone.
- The exact amount of the net premium must be separately itemised on any invoice issued by the supplier to the customer.

Accounting procedures for groups of companies

Where a holding company arranges insurance cover for the group as a whole, any amount charged to each company for arranging the insurance are exempt as insurance-related services (subject to the conditions **37.17** above if the insurance is supplied with other goods or services). Where the exact insurance premium is charged to an associated or subsidiary company, this may be treated as a disbursement if the conditions under the heading *Disbursements* above are satisfied.

If the companies are all part of the same VAT group (see **28 GROUPS OF COMPANIES**), any charges between the members are not supplies for VAT purposes.

(VAT Notice 701/36/13, paras 13.1–13.5).

VAT registration

Insurance providers and insurance intermediaries who only make exempt supplies of insurance will not be entitled to VAT register in the UK. However, an insurance-related business will also need to be aware of the other situations when VAT registration might be necessary, e.g. if the value of acquisitions from other EU member states exceeds the VAT registration threshold, or if the value of supplies which are subject to the reverse charge exceeds the threshold. These rules are intended to prevent a business that is making wholly exempt supplies (and therefore is not registered for VAT) from gaining a significant VAT advantage by buying goods or services from overseas suppliers. See **60.18 REGISTRATION**.

Key points: insurance

[37.20] Points to consider are as follows.

- As a general principle, supplies of insurance are exempt from VAT. This means that input tax is not recoverable on any costs relevant to the activity. However, it is important that a business involved in insurance still reviews all its sources of income to identify if taxable sales are being made. If the level of taxable sales exceeds the VAT registration limit then the business will still need to register for VAT.
- An important concession for insurance-related services is that if a customer receiving a supply of insurance is based outside the EU (or insurance is being arranged by a business as an intermediary for someone outside the EU), then input tax recovery is still allowed on related costs, even though the supply of insurance would be exempt if supplied to an EU customer. This is a very worthwhile concession, one of the few situations in VAT legislation where input tax recovery is allowed on costs relevant to an exempt supply.
- Care is needed in determining the VAT liability of 'extended warranties' or guarantees provided by a retailer or manufacturer of goods. In most cases, these warranties will not relate to a contract of insurance and therefore payment received from the customer will be standard-rated.
- The exemption for insurance activities also extends to the services of an insurance agent or broker in bringing together an insurer and insured for the purposes of arranging insurance, i.e. acting as an intermediary. Care is needed to ensure the intermediary is actually providing an intermediary service rather than providing, for example, standard-rated advertising or marketing services.

The key point with brokers and agents is to look at what they are actually providing as a service, rather than looking at the payment arrangements in relation to a particular deal. Recent cases have suggested that it is also crucial for the supplier to be an 'insurance agent' in accordance with the understanding of that term employed by the CJEU in the *Arthur Andersen* case: it is an essential function of insurance agents that they bring together potential insured persons and the insurer, rather than only dealing with policyholders once they have entered into a contract.

- It is important to recognise that the professional services of loss adjusters, average adjusters, motor assessors, surveyors and solicitors are usually standard-rated. If they also provide insurance claim handling services, their services will be exempt when they are acting as an agent for the insurer in supplying those services.

38

Interaction with Other Taxes

Introduction to interaction with other taxes

[38.1] Direct taxes which are likely to interact with VAT are income tax, corporation tax and capital gains tax. In general such taxes are imposed on profits or gains or some other measure of monies receivable less monies payable. VAT as an indirect tax is charged on the *supply* of goods and services in the course or furtherance of a business [*VATA 1994, s 4*], so it is immaterial for the charging of VAT whether there is any money payment and whether any profit is made on the supply. For information regarding direct taxes see *Tolley's Income Tax*, *Tolley's Corporation Tax* and *Tolley's Capital Gains Tax*.

Business profits

Taxable persons making wholly taxable supplies

[38.2] In general, a taxable person making wholly taxable supplies should treat the receipt for income tax or corporation tax purposes as being exclusive of any VAT charged. Similarly, expenditure for income tax, etc. purposes (including capital items) should be treated as being exclusive of VAT if input VAT is able to be reclaimed on the related supply. If credit for input tax is specifically denied (e.g. most supplies of motor cars and business entertainment) the expenditure inclusive of VAT should be taken into account for income tax purposes. Any allowance made for bad debts for income tax purposes is inclusive of the VAT which has been accounted for on the related supply. (VAT on bad debts may be reclaimed from HMRC in certain circumstances, see **7 BAD DEBT RELIEF**. It follows that if VAT is recoverable from HMRC it cannot be claimed for income tax purposes or alternatively a recovery of VAT should be treated as a taxable income receipt if a VAT-inclusive bad debt has previously been allowed.)

Taxable persons making both exempt and taxable supplies

A taxable person who makes both exempt and taxable supplies should treat income tax receipts as above. However, as under the partial exemption rules such a person will only be able to obtain credit for part of the input VAT applicable to expense etc. payments made, it is necessary to allocate the VAT ultimately suffered to the various expense payments made. Inspectors of taxes are prepared to consider any reasonable arrangements made to carry out this apportionment. Where credit for VAT input is specifically denied, the related expenditure is VAT-inclusive for income tax purposes as explained above.

Non-taxable persons

A person who is *not* a taxable person (e.g. making wholly exempt supplies or below the registration limit) should treat all expenses, etc. as being VAT-inclusive for income tax, etc. purposes (including capital allowances).

(Inland Revenue Statement of Practice SP B1 7 May 1973).

Stock

[38.3] Individuals, partnerships and companies, who are taxable persons for VAT should treat the cost of purchases, and hence the value of stock, as being VAT-exclusive. A taxable person who makes both taxable and exempt supplies is unable to obtain credit for input tax attributable to exempt supplies and accordingly the cost of purchases and value of trading stock should be inclusive of the VAT unable to be credited. (Inland Revenue Statement of Practice SP B2 3 December 1974).

Tax on employment income

[38.4] Returns of expenses incurred by employees, etc. and subsequently reimbursed by the employer (Forms P9D and P11D) should include any amounts of VAT suffered in connection with the expenses, whether or not the employer may subsequently obtain credit for the relevant input tax. Similar observations apply to returns of employee pecuniary liabilities met by the employer and to expenditure incurred by the employer in providing a benefit (including the use of an asset) for an employee. (Inland Revenue Statements of Practice SP A6 29 March 1973 and SP A7 17 July 1974).

Entertainers' expenses

Where agents' fees paid by actors, musicians, etc. are deductible for employment income purposes, any additional VAT payable is also deductible. [*ITEPA 2003, s 352*].

Subcontractors in the construction industry

[38.5] A subcontractor who is a taxable person for VAT should account for VAT on the total consideration which he charges for his services. Where the appropriate valid tax exemption certificate is not held or not presented, the person paying the consideration is obliged to make a deduction at a specified rate from the part of the payment representing labour and profit on materials. VAT and cost of materials are excluded. [*ICTA 1988, s 559(4)*]. (Inland Revenue Pamphlet IR 14/15).

Capital gains tax

[38.6] If VAT is payable in respect of the acquisition of an asset but is available for credit by a taxable person, then the cost of the asset for capital gains tax purposes is the cost exclusive of VAT. Where no VAT credit is available the cost is inclusive of VAT ultimately suffered.

Where an asset is disposed of, any VAT on the supply of the asset is disregarded in computing the disposal consideration for capital gains tax purposes. It appears that a taxable person making both taxable and exempt supplies should treat as part of the capital gains tax cost of an asset the input VAT that was not available for credit in respect of the acquisition (see under **38.2** above). (Inland Revenue Statement of Practice SP D7 7 June 1973).

Capital allowances

[38.7] Where the **11 CAPITAL GOODS SCHEME** applies adjustments to the original input tax reclaimed may be necessary for a period of up to ten years. Any additional VAT liability under the scheme is to be treated as extra qualifying capital expenditure incurred at the time when the VAT is paid. Similarly, any additional VAT rebate is to be taken into account in the capital allowances computation for the period in which it is repaid by HMRC. Earlier capital allowances computations are not disturbed. [*FA 1991, s 59, Sch 14*].

VAT penalties, surcharge and interest

[38.8] No deduction is allowed in computing any income, profit or loss for tax purposes in respect of

- default surcharge under *VATA 1994, s 59* (see **53.23 PENALTIES**);
- a penalty under *VATA 1994, ss 60–70* (see **53.12–53.19, 53.26–53.29 PENALTIES**); or
- interest under *VATA 1994, s 74* (see **52.16 PAYMENT OF VAT**).

Repayment supplement for VAT under *VATA 1994, s 79* is disregarded for income tax and corporation tax purposes.

As a result of the landmark case in *Littlewoods Ltd and others v HMRC* [2015] EWCA Civ 515, [2015] STC 2014 the Government introduced a special corporate tax of 45% in *Finance Act 2015*, in respect of restitution interest paid to taxpayers. Restitution interest is generally defined as any element of a restitution payment made by HMRC to a company following a Common Law claim in relation to tax paid 'under a mistake of law' where HMRC has acted unlawfully and it is intended to represent compensation for the time value of money.

[*ICTA 1988, s 827; VATA 1994, Sch 14 para 10; IT(TOI)A 2005, ss 54(1)–(3), 869(3)–(5)*].

Indirect taxes

[38.9] In valuing imported goods for VAT purposes, indirect taxes (e.g. customs duty) levied (whether abroad or in the UK) are specifically taken into account if not already included in a price in money. See **72.15 VALUATION**.

Key points: interaction with other taxes

[38.10] Points to consider are as follows.

- A business that pays VAT on an expense that it cannot reclaim as input tax should follow the accounting treatment for the VAT element as for the rest of the expense. So the VAT element on a capital asset bought by a business where the VAT cannot be reclaimed (e.g. a motor car available for private use where an input tax block applies) will be capitalised to the balance sheet rather than debited as an expense on the profit and loss account. The VAT element of the asset will then qualify for any capital allowances (for direct tax purposes) in the normal way.
- A subcontractor in the building trade who suffers a deduction of income tax at source (construction industry scheme) must still account for VAT on his gross fee where appropriate, i.e. the amount he is entitled to receive before any income tax or other deduction.
- The capital goods scheme requires input tax on certain capital items to be adjusted over a five-year period (e.g. in relation to computer hardware expenditure exceeding £50,000 excluding VAT) and ten years (e.g. in relation to certain property expenditure exceeding £250,000 excluding VAT). The extra amounts of VAT that are payable or repayable over the life of the capital goods scheme will be adjusted for capital allowance purposes in the year of the relevant VAT adjustment. This means that capital allowance calculations in the year when the asset was originally purchased are not disturbed.
- Amounts paid to HMRC in relation to either penalties, interest or default surcharges cannot be deducted against profits for direct tax purposes. However, a repayment supplement received from HMRC, for example a delay in a repayment due on a VAT return being received also avoids a charge for direct tax purposes.
- There are many occasions when VAT is due on a price that includes other indirect taxes, e.g. the VAT charge for imported goods subject to Customs duty will be based on the price including the Customs duty. In the case of certain property transactions, subject to stamp duty land tax (SDLT) or the Scottish land and buildings transaction tax (LBTT), there is an

SDLT or LBTT charge based on the VAT-inclusive cost of the property.

39

International Services

Cross-references. See **37.4** and **37.18 INSURANCE** for the supply of international insurance services; **41 ISLE OF MAN**; **71 TRANSPORT AND FREIGHT** for certain international movements of passengers and freight.

De Voil Indirect Tax Service. See V4.246.

Introduction to international services

[39.1] Certain services *received by* UK persons from outside the UK are deemed to be *supplied by* those persons who must account for VAT on them if required to be registered. See **39.4** below.

In addition, certain supplies of international services *made by* UK taxable persons are zero-rated or outside the scope of UK VAT. See **39.5** *et seq* below.

Territorial extent of UK

[39.2] The UK consists of Great Britain, Northern Ireland and the territorial sea of the UK (i.e. waters within 12 nautical miles of the coast line). [*VATA 1994, s 96(11)*].

For VAT purposes the Isle of Man is treated as part of the UK and VAT is chargeable there under Manx law which generally parallels UK legislation. See **41 ISLE OF MAN.** *References in this chapter to the UK apply also to the Isle of Man unless otherwise indicated.*

De Voil Indirect Tax Service. See V1.215.

Place of supply of services

[39.3] See **66.12** *et seq* **SUPPLY: PLACE OF SUPPLY** for a detailed consideration of the place of supply of services.

Reverse charge on services received from abroad

[39.4] Normally, the supplier of a service is the person who must account to the tax authorities for any VAT due on the supply. However, in certain situations, the position is reversed and it is the customer who must account for any VAT due. This is known as the '*reverse charge*' procedure.

The reverse charge applies to almost all business to business ('B2B') supplies of services except those of a description in *VATA 1994, Sch 9* (exemptions). It does not apply to land on which the option to tax has been exercised. Under the procedure, the customer credits their VAT account with an amount of output tax, calculated on the full value of the supply they have received, and at the same time debits their VAT account with the input tax to which they are entitled, in accordance with the normal rules. If the customer can attribute the input tax to taxable supplies, and can therefore reclaim it all, the reverse charge has no net cost to them. If they cannot, the effect is to make them pay VAT on the supply at the UK rate. This puts them in the same position as if they had received the supply from a UK supplier rather than from one outside the UK.

Valuation of supplies

The amount payable to the overseas supplier for the services excludes UK VAT. The value of the transaction on which VAT must be accounted under the reverse charge is the total amount paid together with the value of any other form of consideration. This includes any taxes levied abroad.

Time of supply

The time of supply (tax point) for these services depends on whether a single supply of services is made or continuous supplies of services. The time of supply for a single supply of services subject to the reverse charge is the date of completion of the service or, to the extent a payment for the service is made before completion, the date of payment. The time of supply for continuous supplies of services subject to the reverse charge is the end of each periodic billing or payment period (or payment where this is earlier), with a compulsory tax point on 31 December each year in cases where a billing/payment period or payment has not arisen.

UK suppliers

The reverse charge does not apply to supplies of services where both the supplier and the customer belong in the UK. It only applies where services are supplied in the UK by suppliers belonging overseas. Services which, under the place of supply rules, are supplied in another country are outside the scope of UK VAT. Such services can only be subject to tax in that country.

International companies

The reverse charge does not apply to services provided by an overseas establishment to a customer belonging in the UK within the same legal entity as the overseas establishment, since this is not a supply for VAT purposes.

UK VAT incurred by non-UK suppliers

Suppliers who belong outside the UK, and whose customers account for UK VAT by means of the reverse charge, may be able to reclaim VAT incurred in the UK (see Notice 723A *Refunds of VAT in the EC for EC and non-EC businesses*).

B2B general rule services

If the customer belongs in the UK and receives supplies of any B2B general rule services where the supplier belongs outside the UK the reverse charge applies. The reverse charge does not apply to exempt services or zero-rated services. If the customer is not already UK VAT registered and they receive supplies of B2B general rule services which meet these conditions and are treated as supplied where the recipient belongs, the value of those supplies must be added to the value of their own taxable supplies in determining whether they should be registered for UK VAT. Even if they make no taxable supplies themselves they will still be a taxable person if the value of their imported services exceeds the registration limits.

Groups

Where B2B general rule services (except services of a description in *VATA 1994, Sch 9* (exemptions) and land on which the option to tax has been exercised) are purchased by an overseas member of a UK VAT group and provided to a UK member of that VAT group, its representative member is required to account for any UK VAT due under the intra-group reverse charge.

Extension to other services supplied in the UK

The reverse charge also applies to the following services when they are made in the UK:

- services relating to land and property (except opted supplies of land);
- restaurant and catering services, admission to an event and work on goods;
- passenger transport;
- services that are treated as supplied in the UK as a result of the use and enjoyment provisions.

The extension to the reverse charge applies if the customer is UK VAT registered and receives B2B supplies of the above services which are supplied in the UK, where the supplier belongs outside the UK. The customer should give their UK VAT registration number to their supplier as evidence that the supplier is not liable to account for any UK VAT due. If the customer receives supplies for wholly private purposes the reverse charge does not apply; the customer should not give a UK VAT registration number; and the supplier is liable to account for any UK VAT due. If the customer is not UK VAT registered and receives such services supplied in the UK the reverse charge does not apply. Such supplies do not count as their taxable supplies for the purposes of determining whether they are liable to be registered as a taxable person. The supplier is liable to account for any UK VAT due. For a non-UK supplier of these services, where the customer does not give a UK VAT registration number, the supplier is responsible for accounting for any UK VAT due on the supply, and if not already registered in the UK may be liable to register.

[*VATA 1994, s 8(4); SI 1995/2518, Reg 82*]. (VAT Notice 741A, paras 5.9–5.11).

De Voil Indirect Tax Service. See V3.231.

VAT liability of international services

[39.5] The liability of a supply of international services depends on the rules for the place of supply of services. These are considered in detail in **66.12** *et seq* **SUPPLY: PLACE OF SUPPLY**. Where the place of supply is deemed to be outside the UK, the services are outside the scope of UK VAT. Where the place of supply is deemed to be in the UK, the services are subject to the normal UK provisions. Apart from the specific categories of zero-rating for international services in **39.6–39.8** below, international services deemed to be supplied in the UK are therefore standard-rated unless they can be treated as **75 ZERO-RATED SUPPLIES** or **21 EXEMPT SUPPLIES** under the general rules.

See **35.3 INPUT TAX** for the position regarding the right to deduct input tax in respect of most (but not all) international services deemed to be made outside the UK.

Training supplied to overseas Governments

[39.6] By concession, zero-rating applies to training services (other than exempt training within **17.7 EDUCATION**) supplied in the UK to overseas Governments for the purpose of their sovereign activities (and not their business activities). The supplier must retain a statement in writing from the Government concerned (or its accredited representative) certifying that the trainees are employed in the furtherance of its sovereign activities. *Included* is the training of Government officials, public servants and members of organisations such as the armed forces, police, emergency services and similar bodies answerable to the Government concerned. *Excluded* is training of personnel from Government-owned businesses or sponsored commercial organisations such as state airlines or nationalised industries. Relief does not extend to any associated services supplied *separately* (e.g. accommodation or transport). (VAT Notice 48, ESC 3.17; VAT Notice 741A, para 8.2).

Work on goods obtained, acquired or temporarily imported for that purpose and subsequent export

[39.7] For EU legislation see **19.28**(*c*) **EUROPEAN UNION LEGISLATION.**

Note: The following provisions do *not* apply where the work is carried out for a VAT-registered customer in another EU member state, the goods physically leave the EU member state where the work has been carried out, and the customer gives a valid VAT registration number. In such a case, the place of supply moves to the country where the customer belongs and the customer must account for VAT under the reverse charge procedure. See **66.18 SUPPLY: PLACE OF SUPPLY.**

The supply of services of work carried out on goods which, for that purpose, have been obtained or acquired in, or imported into, any EU member state is zero-rated provided the goods are intended to be (and are) subsequently exported to a place outside the EU. The goods must be exported by (or on behalf of) the supplier or, where the recipient of the services belongs outside the EU, by (or on behalf of) the recipient. *Excluded* are any services of a description falling within *VATA 1994, Sch 9 Group 2* (insurance) or *Group 5* (finance). [*VATA 1994, Sch 8 Group 7 Item 1*].

See **66.13 SUPPLY: PLACE OF SUPPLY** for the concept of belonging. The goods must be exported within a reasonable time after the work on them has been carried out. The goods must not be used in the UK between the time of leaving the supplier's premises and exportation. Normal rules apply for proof of export of the goods (see **22.24 EXPORTS**). If, in anticipation of export, the supply is zero-rated but, in the event, the goods are either used before export or export does not take place, it will be necessary to reconsider both the place of supply of the services and, if it is in the UK, the appropriate VAT rate.

Any goods used in conjunction with the work performed (e.g. spare parts, paint, etc.) should be treated as part of the supply of services.

Included are

- processing, manufacturing or assembling;
- repairs, cleaning or restoration;
- alterations, calibrations, insulating, lacquering, painting, polishing, resetting (jewellery), sharpening, varnishing and waterproofing; and
- nominations to stallions/covering (that is, attempting to secure the pregnancy of mares).

Not included is

- work which is not physical work carried out on the goods themselves (e.g. mere inspection or testing and analysis);
- valuation of, or work carried out on, land or property; and
- veterinary services.

(VAT Notice 741A, para 9.7).

De Voil Indirect Tax Service. See V4.246.

Services of intermediaries

[39.8] There are special place of supply rules for services of intermediaries. See **66.27 SUPPLY: PLACE OF SUPPLY**. Where the supply of an intermediary's services is within the scope of UK VAT, it is zero-rated if consisting of the making of arrangements for

- the export of any goods to a place outside the EU;
- a supply of services of the description specified in *VATA 1994, Sch 8 Group 7 Item 1* (see **39.7** above); or
- any supply of services which is made outside the EU.

Excluded are any services of a description falling within *VATA 1994, Sch 9 Group 2* (insurance) or *Group 5* (finance).

[*VATA 1994, Sch 8 Group 7 Item 2*].

The intermediary's services can be supplied to the supplier (in finding a customer) or the customer (in finding a supplier) or even to both.

(VAT Notice 741A, paras 11.1–11.5).

Telecommunication services

[39.9] There are special rules for relevant telecommunications services. See **66.19** SUPPLY: PLACE OF SUPPLY for the definition of telecommunication services.

Place of supply rules and summary of UK VAT position

See **66.20–66.24** SUPPLY: PLACE OF SUPPLY.

Reverse charge on services received from abroad

Where the reverse charge procedure on services received from abroad applies to relevant telecommunication services, the normal value and time of supply rules are applied (see **39.4** above) but only to the extent that the services are not chargeable to VAT in another EU member state.

[*SI 1997/1523, Regs 4, 7, 10*].

Continuous supplies of telecommunications services

Special time of supply rules apply to continuous supplies of any services. See **67.19** SUPPLY: TIME OF SUPPLY.

Rights to relevant telecommunications services

The place of supply of a 'right' to services is the same as the place in which the supply of services to which the right relates would be treated as made by the supplier of the right to the recipient in question. A 'right' includes any right, option or priority with respect to the supply of services and the supply of an interest deriving from any right or services.

[*SI 1992/3121, Art 21*].

Broadcasting and electronically supplied services

[39.10] The place of supply of radio and TV broadcasting services and electronically supplied services is normally in the country where the customer belongs subject, in certain circumstances, to where the services are effectively used and enjoyed. See **66.19** SUPPLY: PLACE OF SUPPLY for further details of the place of supply rules.

For special scheme for non-EU suppliers of electronically supplied services, see **64.34** SPECIAL SCHEMES.

Key points: international services

[39.11] Points to consider are as follows.

- It is important to be aware of the difference between a service for an overseas customer that is zero-rated, and one that avoids a charge of UK VAT under the place of supply rules. In the latter case, a supply will be outside the scope of UK VAT, rather than zero-rated. A supply can only be zero-rated if it is within *VATA 1994, Sch 8*.
- For the majority of business-to-business (B2B) supplies, the place of supply is where the customer is based and, for EU business customers outside the UK, this means they will account for the VAT on their own return by making a reverse charge calculation.
- In most cases, the reverse charge calculation will produce a nil payment effect because the customer will account for output tax on his return and be entitled to claim the same amount as input tax. Exceptions to this situation would apply if the service in question was used for either non-business or exempt purposes, i.e. where an input tax block is relevant.
- It should be noted that the Isle of Man is deemed to be part of the UK as far as VAT is concerned but that the Channel Islands are excluded.
- Certain services provided by a UK supplier to an overseas customer are zero-rated under *VATA 1994, Sch 8, Group 7*. In such cases, there is no VAT charge on these services, even if the place of supply is in the UK. Examples of zero-rated supplies include training services provided for an overseas government in connection with its sovereign activities, and work on goods that are intended to be exported (before use) to a country outside the EU.

40

Invoices

Cross-references. See **53.16 PENALTIES** for improper use of invoices; **57.3** and **57.10 RECORDS** for obligations to retain invoices and adjustments of errors in invoices; **64.30 SPECIAL SCHEMES** for invoices raised by flat-rate farmers; **72.24 VALUATION** for discounts on invoices.

De Voil Indirect Tax Service. See V3.511–V3.529.

Introduction to invoices

[40.1] With certain exceptions or unless HMRC allow otherwise, a registered person *must* provide the customer with an invoice showing specified particulars including VAT (a '*VAT invoice*') in the following circumstances.

(a) He makes a supply of goods or services in the UK (other than an exempt supply) to a taxable person.

(b) He makes a supply of goods or services to a person in another EU member state for the purposes of any business activity carried on by that person. But no invoice is required where the supply is an exempt supply which is made to a person in another EU member state which does not require an invoice to be issued for the supply. (Because practice varies widely across the EU, HMRC guidance is that businesses should be guided by their customers as to whether invoices are required for exempt supplies.) Also no invoice is required where the supply falls within the exemptions in *VATA 1994, Sch 9 Group 2* (insurance) or *Group 5* (finance).

(c) He receives a payment on account from a person in another EU member state in respect of a supply he has made or intends to make.

A VAT invoice is important as it is normally essential evidence to support a customer's claim for deduction of input tax. The supplier must keep the copy and the original should be retained by the recipient.

[*VATA 1994, Sch 11 para 2A; SI 1995/2518, Reg 13(1)–(1B)*].

Exceptions

The above provisions do not apply to the following supplies.

- Zero-rated supplies (other than supplies for acquisition by a person registered in another EU member state, see (*b*) above). [*SI 1995/2518, Reg 20(a)*].
- Supplies where the VAT charged is excluded from credit under *VATA 1994, s 25(7)* (e.g. business entertaining and certain motor cars) [*SI 1995/2518, Reg 20(b)*] although a VAT invoice may be issued in such cases.
- Supplies on which VAT is charged but which are not made for a consideration. [*SI 1995/2518, Reg 20(c)*]. This includes gifts and private use of goods. See, however, **40.2** below under the heading *Business gifts* for 'tax certificates' issued in connection with business gifts to support a deduction of input tax.
- Sales of second-hand goods under one of the special schemes. [*SI 1995/2518, Reg 20(d)*]. Invoices for such sales must not show any VAT. See **62.11** and **62.45 SECOND-HAND GOODS** for the special invoices required.
- Supplies that fall within the **69 TOUR OPERATORS' MARGIN SCHEME**. VAT invoices must not be issued for such supplies.
- Supplies where the customer operates a self-billing arrangement. See **40.6** below.
- Supplies by retailers unless the customer requests a VAT invoice.
- Supplies by one member to another in the same VAT group.
- Transactions between one division and another of a company registered in the names of its divisions. See **60.43 REGISTRATION**.
- Supplies where the taxable person is entitled to issue, and does issue, invoices relating to services performed in fiscal and other warehousing regimes. [*SI 1995/2518, Reg 13(1)*]. See **73.19 WAREHOUSED GOODS AND FREE ZONES**.

Continuous supplies of services

In *Europhone International Ltd v Frontier Communications Ltd*, Ch D [2001] STC 1399 (TVC 62.487) F agreed to provide E with telecommunications services. E fell into arrears with its payments. F continued to provide the relevant services but did not issue invoices (which would have obliged it to account for output tax). E went into receivership and the receivers claimed that F was obliged to issue a VAT invoice. The court held that *SI 1995/2518, Reg 13(1)* above imposed a requirement to provide a VAT invoice upon a person who made a taxable supply. The making of the taxable supply must, therefore, precede or be contemporaneous with the arising of the obligation. Under the rules for continuous supplies of services (see **67.19 SUPPLY: TIME OF SUPPLY** for full details), F only made a taxable supply to E when it received payment or it issued a VAT invoice. As there was no question of E making a payment in respect of the services supplied by F, *Reg 13* was ineffective to impose an obligation on F to issue a VAT invoice.

Documents treated as VAT invoices

[40.2] Although not strictly VAT invoices, certain documents listed in (1)–(4) below are treated as VAT invoices either under the legislation or by HMRC.

(1) Self-billing invoices

Self-billing is an arrangement between a supplier and a customer in which the customer prepares the supplier's invoice and forwards it to him, normally with the payment. See **40.6** below.

(2) Sales by auctioneer, bailiff, etc.

Where goods (including land) forming part of the assets of a business carried on by a taxable person are, under any power exercisable by another person, sold by that person in or towards satisfaction of a debt owed by the taxable person, the goods are deemed to be supplied by the taxable person in the course or furtherance of his business.

The particulars of the VAT chargeable on the supply must be provided on a sale by auction by the auctioneer and where the sale is otherwise than by auction by the person selling the goods. The document issued to the buyer is treated as a VAT invoice. [*VATA 1994, Sch 4 paras 7, 9; SI 1995/2518, Reg 13(2)*]. See **2.10 ACCOUNTING PERIODS AND RETURNS.**

(3) Authenticated receipts in the construction industry

See **43.21**(1) **LAND AND BUILDINGS: ZERO AND REDUCED RATE SUPPLIES AND DIY HOUSEBUILDERS.**

(4) Business gifts

Where a business makes a gift of goods on which VAT is due (see **48.5 OUTPUT TAX**), and the recipient uses the goods for business purposes, that person can recover the VAT as input tax (subject to the normal rules). The donor cannot issue a VAT invoice (because there is no consideration) but instead may provide the recipient with a 'tax certificate' which can be used as evidence to support a deduction of input tax. The tax certificate may be on normal invoicing documentation including with the statement:

> **Tax certificate**
>
> No payment is necessary for these goods. Output tax of £xx.xx (insert amount) has been accounted for on the supply.

(VAT Notice 700/7/12, para 2.4).

Not VAT invoices

The following are not to be regarded as VAT invoices (even if showing all the details required of a VAT invoice) provided they are clearly marked 'This is not a VAT invoice'.

- Any consignment note, delivery note or similar document (or any copy thereof) issued by the supplier before the time of supply where
  - (a) goods are removed before it is known whether a supply will take place (e.g. goods on approval or sale or return), or
  - (b) the tax point is treated as taking place at the time an invoice is issued under the 14-day rule (see **67.8 SUPPLY: TIME OF SUPPLY**).
- Any pro-forma invoice used to offer goods or services to a potential customer.

[*SI 1995/2518, Reg 14(3)*]. (VAT Notice 700, para 17.3).

Invoicing requirements and particulars

[40.3] A VAT invoice must contain certain basic information. See **40.4** below. In addition, special rules apply to

- VAT invoices issued to persons in other EU member states (see **40.5** below);
- self-billing invoices (see **40.6** below);
- retailers' invoices (see **40.7** below);
- invoices issued by cash and carry wholesalers (see **40.8** below);
- electronic invoicing (see **40.9** below);
- invoices using corporate purchasing cards (see **40.10** below); and
- simplified invoices (see **40.4** below).

VAT invoices generally

[40.4] Unless HMRC allow otherwise, a VAT invoice must show the following particulars.

(a) A sequential number based on one or more series which uniquely identifies the document.
The 'invoice number' can be numerical, or it can be a combination of numbers and letters, as long as it forms part of a unique and sequential series. Where there is a break in the series (e.g. where an invoice is cancelled or spoiled and never issued to a customer), this is still acceptable as long as the relevant invoice is retained. (VAT Information Sheet 10/07).

(b) The time of the supply, i.e. tax point.
(c) The date of issue of the document.
(d) The name, address and registration number of the supplier.
(e) The name and address of the person to whom the goods or services are supplied.
(f) A description sufficient to identify the goods or services supplied.
See **40.8** below for use of coded descriptions by cash and carry wholesalers. Coded descriptions may also be accepted in other circumstances (e.g. builders' merchants) where businesses whose trade is restricted to a large number of specialised parts or fittings issue illustrated catalogues to customers.
See *Deadoc Construction Ltd* [2015] UKFTT 433 (TC) (TC04610) for a consideration by the First-tier Tribunal of what is a 'description sufficient'. The Tribunal held that it was necessary for the descriptions to be sufficient for the purposes of HMRC to carry out their monitoring functions; it was not enough for the descriptions to be sufficient only for the trader to be satisfied that the invoice should be paid.
(g) For each description, the quantity of the goods or extent of the services, the rate of VAT and amount payable, excluding VAT, expressed in any currency.
(h) The unit price.
This applies to 'countable' goods and services. For services, the countable element might be, for example, an hourly rate or a price paid for standard services. If the supply cannot be broken down into countable elements, the total VAT-exclusive price is the unit price. Additionally, the unit price may not need to be shown at all if it is not normally provided in a particular business sector *and* is not required by the customer. (VAT Notice 700, para 16.3).
(i) The gross amount payable, excluding VAT, expressed in any currency.
(j) The rate of any cash discount offered.
(k) The total amount of VAT chargeable expressed in sterling.
(l) Where the margin scheme for **62 SECOND-HAND GOODS** or the **69 TOUR OPERATORS' MARGIN SCHEME** is applied, *either* a reference to the appropriate provision of *EC Council Directive 2006/112/EC* or the corresponding provision of *VATA 1994 or* any indication that the margin scheme has been applied.
The way in which margin scheme treatment is referenced on an invoice is a matter for the business and not HMRC but examples of acceptable indications include
- This is a second-hand margin scheme supply/This invoice is for a second-hand margin scheme supply.
- This is a Tour Operators Margin Scheme supply/This supply falls under the Value Added Tax (Tour Operators) Order 1987.

The requirement only applies to TOMS invoices in business to business transactions.
(VAT Information Sheet 10/07).

(m) Where a VAT invoice relates in whole or in part to a supply where the person supplied is liable to pay the VAT, *either* a reference to the appropriate provision of *EC Council Directive 2006/112/EC* or the corresponding provision of *VATA 1994 or* any indication that the supply is one where the customer is liable to pay the VAT.
This covers UK supplies where the customer accounts for the VAT (e.g. under the gold scheme or any reverse charge requirement under the missing trader intra-community rules). The way in which margin scheme treatment is referenced on an invoice is a matter for the business and not HMRC but examples of acceptable indications include
- Reverse charge supply.
- This supply is subject to the reverse charge.

(VAT Information Sheet 10/07).

Exempt or zero-rated supplies

Invoices do not have to be raised for exempt or zero-rated transactions when supplied in the UK. But if such supplies are included on invoices with taxable supplies, the exempt and zero-rated supplies must be totalled separately and the invoice must show clearly that there is no VAT payable on them.

Leasing of motor cars

Where an invoice relates wholly or partly to the letting on hire of a motor car other than for self-drive, the invoice must state whether the car is a qualifying vehicle (see **46.11 MOTOR CARS**).

[*VATA 1994, Sch 11 para 2A; SI 1995/2518, Reg 14(1)(4)(6)(8)*].

Prompt payment discounts

See **72.24 VALUATION** for detailed guidance on the treatment of discounts for prompt payment offered on a VATable supply, including the wording required on the VAT invoice.

Example of a VAT invoice

ABC plc
26 Green Road, South Croydon, CR2 5ZX
VAT Reg. No. 987 6543 21

Sales invoice No 15,618
AN Other Ltd
9 North Street
London N8 5QQ

	Time of supply 31/01/16			Date of Issue 3/02/16
Quantity	Description and price	Amount excluding VAT	VAT rate	VAT
		£	%	£
12	Purple kingsize quilt covers @ £15	180.00		
20	Pillows at £12.50	250.00		
50	Purple pillow cases at £8.50 per pair	212.50		
		642.50	20	128.50
	Delivery (strictly net)	12.00	20	2.40
	Terms: payment due within 30 days of invoice date	654.50		130.90
	VAT	130.90		
	Total	£785.40		

Simplified invoices

From 1 January 2013, in any case where the consideration for a supply does not exceed £250 and the supply is other than to a person in another EU member state, the VAT invoice that a registered person is required to provide need contain only the following particulars.

- The name, address and registration number of the supplier.
- The time of the supply.
- A description sufficient to identify the goods or services supplied.
- The total amount payable including VAT.
- For each rate of VAT chargeable, the gross amount payable including VAT, and the VAT rate applicable.

[*SI 1995/2518, Reg 16A*].

VAT invoices to persons in other EU member states

[40.5] Unless HMRC allow otherwise, where a registered person provides a person in another EU member state with

- a VAT invoice or,
- any document that refers to a VAT invoice and is intended to amend it (e.g. a credit note)

it must show the following particulars.

(a) A sequential number based on one or more series which uniquely identifies the document.
The 'invoice number' can be numerical, or it can be a combination of numbers and letters, as long as it forms part of a unique and sequential series. Where there is a break in the series (e.g. where an invoice is cancelled or spoiled and never issued to a customer), this is still acceptable as long as the relevant invoice is retained. (VAT Information Sheet 10/07).

(b) The time of the supply, i.e. tax point.

(c) The date of issue of the document.

(d) The name, address and registration number of the supplier. The letters 'GB' must be shown as a prefix to the registration number.

(e) The name and address of the person to whom the goods or services are supplied.

(f) The registration number, if any, of the recipient of the supply of goods or services containing the alphabetical code of the EU member state in which the recipient is registered, namely

Austria—AT
Belgium—BE
Bulgaria—BG
Croatia—HR
Cyprus—CY
Czech Republic—CZ
Denmark—DK
Estonia—EE
Finland—FI
France—FR
Germany—DE
Greece—EL
Hungary—HU
Ireland—IE
Italy—IT
Latvia—LV
Lithuania—LT
Luxembourg—LU
Malta—MT
Netherlands—NL
Poland—PL
Portugal—PT
Romania—RO
Slovak Republic—SK
Slovenia—SI
Spain—ES
Sweden—SE

Enquiry letters in a number of foreign languages to request the correct VAT registration number from an EU customer are available on the HMRC website.

(g) A description sufficient to identify the goods or services supplied. Where the supply is of a new means of transport (see **20.33 EUROPEAN UNION: SINGLE MARKET**) a description sufficient to identify it as such.

(h) For each description, the quantity of the goods or the extent of the services, and where a positive rate of VAT is chargeable, the rate of VAT and the amount payable, excluding VAT, expressed in sterling.

(i) The unit price.

This applies to 'countable' goods and services. For services, the countable element might be, for example, an hourly rate or a price paid for standard services. If the supply cannot be broken down into countable elements, the total VAT-exclusive price is the unit price.

Additionally, the unit price may not need to be shown at all if it is not normally provided in a particular business sector *and* is not required by the customer. (VAT Notice 700, para 16.3).

(j) The gross amount payable, excluding VAT.

(k) The rate of any cash discount offered.

(l) Where the supply of goods is a taxable supply, the total amount of VAT chargeable expressed in sterling.

(m) Where the margin scheme for **62 SECOND-HAND GOODS** or the **69 TOUR OPERATORS' MARGIN SCHEME** is applied, *either* a reference to the appropriate provision of *EC Council Directive 2006/112/EC* or the corresponding provision of *VATA 1994 or* any indication that the margin scheme has been applied.
The way in which margin scheme treatment is referenced on an invoice is a matter for the business and not HMRC but examples of acceptable indications include
- This is a second-hand margin scheme supply/This invoice is for a second-hand margin scheme supply.
- This is a Tour Operators Margin Scheme supply/This supply falls under the Value Added Tax (Tour Operators) Order 1987.

The requirement only applies to TOMS invoices in business to business transactions.
(VAT Information Sheet 10/07).

(n) Where a VAT invoice relates in whole or in part to a supply where the person supplied is liable to pay the VAT, *either* a reference to the appropriate provision of *EC Council Directive 2006/112/EC* or the corresponding provision of *VATA 1994 or* any indication that the supply is one where the customer is liable to pay the VAT.
The way in which margin scheme treatment is referenced on an invoice is a matter for the business and not HMRC but examples of acceptable indications include
- Reverse charge supply/This supply is subject to the reverse charge.
- Subject to reverse charge in the country of receipt/Subject to reverse charge in another member state.
- This is a UK exempt supply which may be chargeable in the country of receipt/This is a UK exempt supply which may be chargeable in another member state.

(VAT Information Sheet 10/07).

(o) Where the supply is an exempt or zero-rated supply, *either* a reference to the appropriate provision of *EC Council Directive 2006/112/EC* or the corresponding provision of *VATA 1994 or* any indication that the supply is exempt or zero-rated as appropriate.
For these purposes, an exempt supply is a supply that, if made in the UK, would be exempt under *VATA 1994, Sch 9*.
The way in which the intra-EU exempt or zero-rated treatment is referenced on an invoice is a matter for the business and not for HMRC, but examples of acceptable indications include
- Exempt supply/Exempt supply for VAT purposes/This is an exempt supply.

- Zero-rated intra-EU supply/This is an intra-Union supply/Intra-Union supply subject to VAT in the country of acquisition. (VAT Information Sheet 10/07).

[*VATA 1994, Sch 11 para 2A; SI 1995/2518, Regs 2, 14(2)*].

Note that there is no requirement for the gross amount payable (excluding VAT) to be in sterling. Where, therefore, a VAT invoice is issued in respect of a zero-rated supply for acquisition by a customer registered in another EU member state and their registration number is quoted on the invoice, the invoice may be in any currency. Where UK VAT is chargeable (e.g. on distance sales) this must always be expressed in sterling.

Example of a VAT invoice

ABC plc
26 Green Road, South Croydon, CR2 5ZX
VAT Reg. No. GB987 6543 21

Sales invoice No 15,618
Eine Andere AG
9 Nord Straße
Berlin
VAT Reg. No. DE 123456789

Time of supply 31/01/12 **Date of Issue** 3/02/12

Quantity	Description and price	Amount excluding VAT	VAT rate	VAT
		£	%	£
12	Purple kingsize quilt covers @ £15	180.00		
20	Pillows at £12.50	250.00		
50	Purple pillow cases at £8.50 per pair	212.50		
		642.50	0	0
	Delivery	35.00	0	0
Terms: Cash discount of 5% if paid within 30 days		677.50		
	VAT	0.00		
	Total	£677.50		

Self-billing

[40.6] Self-billing is an established practice under which the customer prepares a VAT invoice in the name of, and on behalf of, the supplier and then sends it to the supplier, normally with the payment.

Prior approval from HMRC is no longer required but all businesses wishing to use the scheme need to meet conditions set out in *SI 1995/2518, Reg 13* and VAT Notice 700/62. HMRC may also impose further conditions in particular cases.

The detailed provisions are as follows.

Where a registered person (the '*customer*') provides a document to himself (a '*self-billed invoice*') that purports to be a VAT invoice in respect of a supply of goods or services to him by another registered person (the '*supplier*'), that document is treated as the VAT invoice required to be provided by the supplier provided certain conditions are met.

(a) The self-billed invoice must have been provided under an agreement (a '*self-billing agreement*') entered into between the supplier and the customer.
(b) The self-billed invoice must contain the particulars required under **40.4**(*a*)–(*m*) above or, as the case may be, **40.5**(*a*)–(*o*) above.
(c) The self-billed invoice must relate to a supply or supplies made by a supplier who is a taxable person. If not, any amount claimed as input tax will be disallowed, see *MJ Gleeson plc* (VTD 13332) (TVC 40.63).
(d) The self-billed invoice must be clearly marked 'SELF BILLING' and it is advisable to include the following statement
'THE VAT SHOWN IS YOUR OUTPUT TAX DUE TO HM REVENUE & CUSTOMS'.
(e) The customer must keep the names, addresses and VAT registration numbers of all the suppliers who have agreed to self-billing, and be able to produce them for inspection by HMRC if required.
(f) The customer must raise self-billed invoices for all transactions with the supplier during the currency of the agreement.

If all the conditions are not met, any self-billed invoices issued are not proper VAT invoices. As such, they cannot be used as evidence of entitlement to input tax by the customer and the supplier will have to issue his own invoices.

The supplier still remains responsible for ensuring that VAT has been correctly accounted for on the supply made. Therefore the supplier should check that the invoice issued by the customer is accurate and that the correct rate of VAT has been applied.

Self-billing agreements

A self-billed invoice can only be issued under an agreement between the customer and supplier (see (*a*) above).

A self-billing agreement must:

- Include the supplier's agreement to the customer to producing self-billed invoices in respect of supplies made by the supplier.
- Specify that the supplier will not issue VAT invoices in respect of supplies covered by the agreement.
- Specify that the supplier will accept each self-billed invoice created by the customer in respect of supplies made to him by the supplier.
- Contain a start date and expiry date. The expiry date can however be related to the term of the contract between the supplier and the customer.

- Specify that the supplier will notify the customer if he ceases to be a taxable person, changes his registration number or transfers his business as a going concern. (A new agreement must be set up if the supplier changes his VAT registration number or if he transfers his business as a going concern and the new supplier wants to continue operating self-billing.)
- Bind both parties and it must be in writing (either on paper or in electronic form).
- Be produced to HMRC on request (by the customer or supplier).
- Make it clear if the customer intends to outsource responsibility for issuing the self-billed invoices to a third party (e.g. an accounting bureau), although it should be noted that in such a case the customer still remains responsible for ensuring that all the conditions of the scheme are met.

An example of a self-billing agreement acceptable to HMRC is reproduced below. It is not necessary to follow the exact wording provided the agreement used contains all the relevant information.

Self-Billing Agreement

This is an agreement to a self-billing procedure between

Customer name	VAT number
Supplier name	VAT number

The self-biller (the customer) agrees:

(a) To issue self-billed invoices for all supplies made to them by the self-billee (the supplier) until. . . . ./. . . . ./. . . . . (insert either an end date for the agreement or the date the contract ends).
(b) To complete self-billed invoices showing the supplier's name, address and VAT registration number, together with all the other details which constitute a full VAT invoice.
(c) To make a new self-billing agreement in the event that their VAT registration number changes.
(d) To inform the supplier if the issue of self-billed invoices will be outsourced to a third party.

The self-billee agrees:

(1) To accept invoices raised by the self-biller on their behalf until . . . ./. . . . ./. . . . . (insert either an end date for the agreement or the date the contract ends).
(2) Not to raise sales invoices for the transactions covered by the agreement.
(3) To notify the customer immediately if they

- change their VAT registration number
- cease to be VAT-registered; or
- sell their business, or part of their business.

Signed by	Signed by
On behalf of	On behalf of
Date	Date

Customers in other EU member states

Self-billing is not restricted to domestic supplies and self-billing agreements can be made with businesses in other EU member states and in countries outside the EU. Individual EU member states cannot impose additional conditions for VAT self-billing, so there are no additional conditions or procedures for self-billing in the EU member state in whose territory the goods or services are supplied. Points to bear in mind include:

If the business is a	*then it needs to*
self-biller being supplied with goods from another EU member state	be aware that the self-billed invoice may establish the time of acquisition in the same way as an invoice issued by the supplier.
self-billee supplying goods to another EU member state	be able to meet the conditions for evidence to support the zero-rating of that supply.
self-biller being supplied with goods from a country outside the EU	familiarise itself with the rules on import VAT. It may also need to check what information must be included in the invoices it raises on the supplier's behalf so that they are acceptable to the supplier's own tax authorities as evidence of export.
self-billee making supplies of goods to a country outside the EU	meet the requirements for documentary evidence of export.

For supplies of services to and from all non-UK businesses, the UK customer/supplier must be familiar with the place of supply rules (see **66.12–66.27** supply: place of supply) and agree the correct VAT treatment of the supply with the other party from the outset.

Tax points for self-billed supplies

See **67.4 SUPPLY: TIME OF SUPPLY**.

Self-billed debit notes

Where a self-billing arrangement is in operation, a customer cannot reduce the value of the supply on a subsequent self-billed invoice. He must issue a debit note showing the amount of the adjustment to the value of the supply.

[*SI 1995/2518, Reg 13(3)(3A)–(3F)*.] (VAT Notice 700/62/17 paras 3.1, 3.3, 3.4, 4.1, 4.2, 4.4, 4.6, 7.1–7.4, 8.)

Understated VAT

If the self-billed invoice understates the VAT chargeable on the supply, HMRC may, by notice served on the recipient and the supplier, elect that the amount of VAT understated by the document is VAT due from the recipient and not the supplier. [*VATA 1994, s 29*].

Retailers' invoices

[40.7] Where the registered taxable person is a retailer, he is not required to provide a VAT invoice unless a customer requests it. Where an invoice is requested, one of the following options may be available.

(a) **Less detailed VAT invoices.** Provided the consideration does not exceed £250 and provided the supply is not to a person in another EU member state, the VAT invoice need only contain particulars of
- the name, address and registration number of the retailer;
- the time of supply;
- a description sufficient to identify the goods or services supplied;
- the total amount payable including VAT; and
- for each rate of VAT chargeable, the gross amount payable including VAT, and the VAT rate applicable.

The effect of the above is that where an EU customer requests an invoice a full VAT invoice must be issued.

The invoice must not contain any reference to any exempt supply. [*SI 1995/2518, Reg 16*].

See below for VAT invoices for petrol and derv.

Where *credit cards* are accepted, the sales voucher given to the cardholder at the time of sale may be adapted to serve as a less detailed VAT invoice by including all the above information. Where an invoice is issued as well as the credit card voucher, only one of the documents must be in the form of a VAT invoice.

To calculate the amount of VAT in a VAT-inclusive price, the VAT fraction (1/6) must be applied to the total invoice amount.

(b) **Modified VAT invoices.** Provided the customer agrees, an invoice can be issued showing the *VAT-inclusive* value of each standard-rated or reduced rate supply (instead of the VAT-exclusive value — see **40.4**(*g*) above). At the foot of the invoice, there must be shown separately
- the total VAT-inclusive value of standard-rated or reduced rate supplies;
- the total VAT payable on those supplies shown in sterling;
- the total value, excluding VAT, of those supplies;
- the total value of any zero-rated supplies included on the invoice; and
- the total value of any exempt supplies included on the invoice.

In all other respects the invoice should show the details required for a full VAT invoice (see **40.4** above).

Where options (*a*) or (*b*) are not available, a full VAT invoice under **40.4** above must be supplied. (VAT Notice 700, para 16.6).

Petrol and diesel oil (derv)

Where the VAT-inclusive amount is £250 or less, a less detailed VAT invoice may be issued (see (*a*) above). Where the VAT-inclusive amount is more than £250 the particulars required on a full VAT invoice are modified so that the vehicle registration number and not the customer's name and address is shown on the VAT invoice. The type of supply and the number of gallons/litres need not be shown. (VAT Notice 700, para 17.1).

Foreign currency invoices

If a VAT invoice is issued in a foreign currency, all values required to be entered for VAT purposes under (*a*) and (*b*) above must be converted into sterling. See **72.18 VALUATION**.

Cash and carry wholesalers

[40.8] Cash and carry wholesalers may adapt their till rolls to meet the VAT invoice requirements provided all the following conditions are met. If not, HMRC may require normal VAT invoices to be issued.

- A product code is used which identifies the different classes of goods sold. The coding system should be devised by the wholesaler using a number of at least two digits and probably three or more digits where the range of products sold is wide.
- Product code lists are prepared and provided to all VAT-registered customers.
- The till roll must provide all the details required for a full VAT invoice (see **40.4** above).
- Copy till rolls and product code lists must be kept for six years or such shorter period as HMRC may allow.

(VAT Notice 700, para 17.2).

Electronic invoicing

[40.9] '*Electronic invoicing*' is the transmission and storage of invoices, without the delivery of paper documents, by electronic means. Electronic equipment employing wires, radio transmission, optical technologies or other electromagnetic means is used for the processing (including digital compression) and storage of data.

Conditions for invoices in an electronic format

Where, in respect of a supply of goods of services, a registered business provides a document that purports to be a VAT invoice in any electronic format, the document can only be treated as a VAT invoice if certain conditions are satisfied.

(a) *Contents of the invoice*. Electronic invoices must contain the same information as paper invoices. See **40.4** and, in respect of invoices to other EU member states, **40.5** above.

Batches of invoices. Where a business provides invoices in batches to the same recipient in an electronic format, details common to each invoice need only be stated once for each batch file (rather than once per invoice). For example, instead of repeating the full name and address of the customer on every invoice in the batch, a business could include the full information on the batch header and use an abridged or coded version of that information within each individual invoice message.

Credit notes. See **40.14** below for details required on credit notes raised for UK supplies. Where a business provides a person in another EU member state with a document which amends a VAT invoice (e.g. a credit note) that document must contain all the information required to be included on an invoice (see **40.5** above).

(b) *The use of the electronic invoice must be accepted by the customer.*

Supplies to other EU member states

Where a UK business issues electronic invoices for supplies to other EU member states, it must meet the UK conditions for electronic invoicing. But it should also check whether the customer's system can accept invoices in the format used before mutually agreeing to invoice electronically. The tax authorities of certain other EU member states, although accepting the use of advance electronic signature and EDI, do not accept all the electronic methods of raising invoices that are permissible in the UK.

Supplies to non-EU member states

Invoices and credit notes in an electronic format to non-EU member states are permitted provided the acceptability of this is confirmed with the tax authorities in the receiving country.

Conditions for electronic storage

A business (whether supplier or customer) must:

- Guarantee the authenticity and integrity of its invoice data during and after application processing (see (*d*) above) and throughout the storage period by electronic or procedural means, and store all the data related to its invoices.
- Store its invoices in a readable format and be able to readily recreate the invoice information as at the time of its original transmission.
- Keep history files so that it can find the appropriate details from any particular time in the past if asked to do so by an HMRC officer.
- Keep copies of all electronic invoices issued or received for six years (although if this causes serious storage problems or undue expense, HMRC may agree to a shorter period for some records).

This also applies to scanned images of paper documents used and stored as electronic records for VAT purposes.

Storage abroad

Electronic invoices can be stored in another EU member state provided they can be produced to HMRC when required in a readable form, and within a reasonable period of time, at a mutually agreed place. HMRC recommend that a business maintains on-line access to its records if it stores them outside the UK. Electronic invoices can also be stored outside the EU provided that, additionally, the country where they are stored respects European Data Protection principles regarding the storage of personal data (names, addresses, etc.).

Outsourcing electronic invoices

A business may outsource the physical responsibility for the issuing of its electronic sales invoices to a third party, although all the legal obligations relating to the contents, storage and production of the invoices raised remain with the business.

Inability to meet the e-invoicing conditions

If a business

- is unable to meet all the conditions for transmission and storage of electronic invoicing set out above, it must issue paper invoices;
- has issued and stored invoices electronically, but failed to meet the conditions, it must issue paper invoices until HMRC are satisfied that its system is acceptable; and
- persistently fails to meet the conditions, it may be liable to a penalty.

Use of paper and electronic VAT invoicing at the same time

In normal circumstances, it is only possible for a business to run a dual system (i.e. raising both electronic and paper invoices for the same supplies or with the same trading partners) when running a controlled trial of an electronic invoicing system. Once the trial is over, the business must stop running the dual system and the electronic invoice becomes the legal document for VAT purposes. However, where a business has a specific need to run a dual system, it should contact the National Advice Service who will decide whether an exception can be made.

HMRC access to electronic systems

In order to check electronic systems, HMRC may request access to

- the operations of any computer systems which produce or receive VAT invoices or documents, and to the data stored on them;
- supporting documentation including file structures etc., audit trail, controls, safe keeping, and information on how the accounting system is organised; and
- advice on interrogation facilities available on the system.

HMRC must be able to take copies of information from the system, if required. A business may be able to meet its obligations as regards production of records by giving HMRC

- physical access to systems at its premises;
- indirect access (by providing information on electronic media or possibly via remote access);

- a resident audit programme installed at the request of the visiting HMRC officer; or
- any other reasonable method agreed with HMRC.

See also **32.11 HMRC: POWERS** for powers of HMRC to inspect computers generally.

[*SI 1995/2518, Regs 13A; 14(6)*].

(VAT Notice 700/63/15; VAT Information Sheet 16/03, para 5.3).

Corporate purchasing (procurement) cards

[40.10] Such cards are designed to eliminate much of the paperwork in the purchasing process. Where a purchase is made, the supplier normally transmits the invoice information to the appropriate card company or bank (the 'transmission date'). At agreed intervals, the purchaser receives a VAT invoice report from the card company or bank. Some purchasing cards offer two levels of invoice detail, the level of detail received by the cardholder being dependent upon the capability of the supplier's accounting system. *The provisions in both (1) and (2) below have the force of law.*

(1) Line Item Detail (LID) invoices

These provide detailed, itemised information on a line-by-line basis. HMRC have agreed to waive the requirement to show the date of issue of the document under **40.4**(*c*) above. The invoice report issued to the purchaser will show the transmission date for each transaction and is acceptable as evidence for input tax recovery (subject to the normal rules) from that date.

(2) Summary VAT invoices

Where a supplier's system cannot transmit LID invoices, HMRC generally do not require a supplier to issue an invoice to the customer. Instead they accept a Summary VAT invoice report issued by the card company or bank in support of an input tax claim provided no single transaction has a value of more than £5,000 and the report contains the following information.

- Value of the supply.
- VAT amount charged.
- VAT rate.
- Time of supply.
- Description of the goods.
- Supplier's name, address and VAT registration number.
- Customer's name and address.

A supplier must issue a VAT invoice if the value of a 'single transaction' exceeds £5,000 or if specifically requested by the customer. In the latter case, the invoice must be clearly endorsed 'Paid by Purchasing Card – Supplementary VAT invoice'. A '*single transaction*' is the total value of purchases made using a card at any one time, e.g. one 'swipe' of the card.

In all cases, the supplier must continue to generate contemporaneous VAT invoices for output tax accounting purposes for all purchasing card transactions.

(VAT Notice 701/48/14, paras 4.1–4.3).

Rounding of VAT on invoices

Invoice traders

[40.11] By concession, invoice traders (as opposed to retailers) may round *down* the total VAT payable on all goods and services shown on a VAT invoice to a whole penny (i.e. they may ignore any fraction of a penny). The concession is applicable only where the VAT charged to customers and the VAT paid to HMRC is the same.

Calculations of VAT based on lines of goods or services included with other goods or services in the same invoice must either be made by

(a) rounding down to the nearest 0.1p; or
(b) rounding to the nearest 1p or 0.5p.

For example, 86.76p and 86.74p would both be rounded down to 86.7p under (*a*) but rounded up to 87p and down to 86.50p respectively under method (*b*).

Whichever method is used must be adopted consistently. The final amount of VAT payable may be rounded down to the nearest whole penny.

Calculations of VAT based on VAT per unit or per article, e.g. for price lists, must be either

- to four decimal places and then rounded down to three places (e.g. £0.0024 rounded down to £0.002 (0.2p)); or
- to the nearest 1p or 0.5p (but not to 'nil' on any unit or article, i.e. a minimum of 0.5p per article or unit).

Calculation of VAT at retailers

Retailers who do not use a retail scheme but use till technology to identify the VAT due on each transaction and issue an invoice, calculating VAT at line level or invoice level, must not round the VAT figure down. They may, however, round (up and down) each VAT calculation. Retailers using a retail scheme to account for VAT are not affected by these provisions.

(VAT Notice 700, paras 17.5, 17.6).

See also *Fiscale eenheid Koninklijke Ahold NV v Staatssecretaris van Financiën, ECJ Case C-484/06; 24 January 2008 unreported* (TVC 22.647) where the Advocate-General held that the VAT Directives do not regulate in detail the rounding up or down of amounts of VAT. This is therefore a matter for national law although this must comply with all the relevant rules and principles which flow from the Directives. Those rules and principles do not permit retailers to round down the amount of VAT in the VAT-inclusive price of each item sold, in order to determine the amount of output tax which they must declare in their regular returns. For a similar case see *JD Wetherspoon plc v HMRC, ECJ Case C-302/07* [2009] STC 1022 (TVC 22.648).

Time limits for issuing invoices

[40.12] A VAT invoice or a document treated as VAT invoice under **40.2** above must be provided within 30 days after the time when the supply is treated as taking place (see **67.1** *et seq* **SUPPLY: TIME OF SUPPLY**) or within such longer period after that time as HMRC allow in general or special directions.

[*VATA 1994, Sch 11 para 2A; SI 1995/2518, Reg 13(5)*].

Extension of this time limit is permitted *without application* where

- an extension has been allowed for tax point purposes under the 14-day rule (see **67.8** and **67.18 SUPPLY: TIME OF SUPPLY**);
- special accounting arrangements have been approved; or
- where a newly registered business has not been notified of its VAT registration number (in which case the VAT invoice must be issued within 30 days from the date of advice of that number).

In all other cases, application must be made, in writing, to HMRC for an extension of the time limit.

(VAT Notice 700, para 16.2).

In the case of a supply of goods falling within *VATA 1994, s 6(7)*, a VAT invoice (or a document treated as such) must be provided by the 15th day of the month following that in which the removal from the UK takes place.

In the case of a supply of services falling within *SI 1995/2518, reg 82* (services from outside the UK), a VAT invoice (or a document treated as such) must be provided by the 15th day of

- the month following that in which the services are treated as being performed under *reg 82(2)*;
- the month following that during which the services are treated as separately and successively made as a result of payments being made under *reg 82(4)*; or
- the January following the 31 December on which the services are treated as being supplied under *reg 82(6)*.

[*SI 1995/2518, Reg 13(6)*].

Transmission of invoices

[40.13] As an alternative to sending VAT invoices by post, they may be sent to customers by fax or e-mail. The normal rules regarding VAT invoices apply. Invoices received in either of these ways are acceptable as evidence for input tax deduction (subject to the normal rules). However, where transmission is by fax, if the customer has a thermal-paper fax machine, the invoice may not be permanent and the customer may not be able to fulfil the obligation to preserve the invoice for six years. It is suggested that the supplier warns the customer of this possibility, preferably on the VAT invoice itself.

See also **40.9** above for invoices in an electronic format, including the use of 'outsourcing' for the issue of invoices.

(VAT Notice 700, para 17.8).

Credit and debit notes

[40.14] Where credit or contingent discount (e.g. discount on condition that the customer buys more goods at a later date) is allowed to a customer who can reclaim all the VAT on the supply as input tax, there is no obligation to adjust the original VAT charge provided both parties agree not to do so (although records of outputs and inputs will still need to be adjusted). Otherwise an adjustment should be made to the original VAT charge in the appropriate period. See **57.6 RECORDS**. A credit note should be issued to the customer and a copy retained. Alternatively, if both parties agree, the customer can issue a VAT debit note. A valid debit note places the same legal obligations on both parties as a valid credit note and must fulfil the same conditions.

To be valid for VAT purposes, a credit or debit note must reflect a genuine mistake or overcharge or an agreed reduction in the value of the supply and be issued within one month of this being discovered or agreed. It must give value to the customer, i.e. represent a genuine entitlement or claim on the part of the customer for the amount overcharged to be either refunded or offset against the value of future supplies. It should be headed 'credit note' or 'debit note' as appropriate and show

(a) identifying number and date of issue;
(b) supplier's and customer's name and address;
(c) supplier's registration number;
(d) description identifying goods or services for which credit is given;
(e) quantity and amount credited for each description and reason for credit, e.g. 'returned goods';
(f) total amount credited excluding VAT;
(g) rate and amount of VAT credited;
(h) number and date of the original VAT invoice. If not possible, HMRC will need to be satisfied that VAT has been accounted for on the original supply.

Where a credit note includes credits for zero-rated or exempt supplies, each must be totalled separately and the credit note must show clearly that no credit for VAT has been given for them.

Credit notes issued without VAT adjustment should state 'This is not a credit note for VAT'. It will still be necessary to adjust records of outputs and inputs in order to complete the VAT returns.

Credit notes to persons in other EU member states

A credit note issued to a person in another EU member state must contain the same particulars as the VAT invoice(s) that it is intended to amend. See **40.5** above.

Accounting for credit or debit notes

A taxable person who makes a supply and a taxable person who receives the supply must adjust their VAT account where

- there is an increase or decrease in the consideration due on a supply;
- the increase or decrease is evidenced by a debit note, credit note or any other document having the same effect;
- the increase or decrease includes an amount of tax; and
- the increase or decrease occurs after the end of the prescribed accounting period in which the original supply took place.

The person receiving the supply must enter the relevant amount of tax as a positive amount (in the case of an increase) or a negative amount (in the case of a decrease). The entry is made in the tax allowable portion of his VAT account which relates to either

- the prescribed accounting period in which the supply was received (if he is insolvent); or
- the prescribed accounting period in which he gives effect to the increase or decrease in his business accounts (in any other case).

The three-year time limit that applied to the adjustment of VAT accounts as a result of changes in consideration was removed with effect from 1 April 2009.

Bankruptcy, insolvent liquidation and administrative receivership

The tax point for credit or debit notes issued by or on behalf of insolvent traders is the date on which the supply was originally made or received.

Reverse charge supplies

For adjustments relating to supplies where the recipient is liable to account for VAT under the reverse charge procedure for mobile phones and computer chips, see **4.23 ANTI-AVOIDANCE**.

Cancelled registrations

The tax point for any credit or debit note issued or received after the date of cancellation of registration is the date of the original supply. If this happens after the final VAT return has been submitted, HMRC should be contacted.

VAT rate

The rate of VAT to be used for a credit or debit note is the one in force at the tax point of the original supply.

Returned or replaced goods

Where such goods are replaced with similar goods, the original VAT charge may stand or be cancelled (by issuing a credit note if a VAT invoice has previously been issued) and VAT charged on the replacement. If the original VAT charge is allowed to stand, VAT need not be accounted for on the replacement goods provided they are supplied free of charge. If supplied at a *lower* price, the VAT charged may be reduced by a credit note. If supplied at a *higher* price, additional VAT must be accounted for.

[*SI 1995/2518, Reg 38*]. (VAT Notice 700, paras 18.2, 18.3).

Bad debts

Output tax paid on an invoice which proves to be a bad debt cannot subsequently be reclaimed by issuing a credit note for the unpaid amount. See **7 BAD DEBT RELIEF.**

Correction of VAT invoices following a change in the VAT rate

[40.15] Under *VATA 1994, s 88*, a trader may elect to override certain of the normal tax point rules which determine whether a particular supply is taxable at the old or new rate when there is a change in the rate of VAT or in the descriptions of exempt, zero-rated or reduced-rate supplies. The trader is allowed to account for VAT at the old rates on supplies actually 'made' before the date of change but for which the invoice and payment tax points would have occurred later. See **56.10 RATES OF VAT** for full details.

Where under the above circumstances a VAT invoice is issued before the election, the supplier must within 45 days provide the customer with a credit note headed 'Credit note – change of VAT rate' showing the information required in **40.14**(*a*)–(*d*), (*g*) and (*h*) above. [*SI 1995/2518, Reg 15*]. See **57.6** and **57.9 RECORDS** for the recording of credit notes.

Anti-forestalling invoices: self-storage and approved alterations of protected buildings

[40.16] From 1 October 2012 there are invoicing requirements in relation to the anti-forestalling charge under *FA 2012, Sch 27* applying to approved alterations to protected buildings (see **43.10 LAND AND BUILDINGS: ZERO AND REDUCED RATE SUPPLIES AND DIY HOUSEBUILDERS**) and self-storage of goods (see **42.18**(*l*) **LAND AND BUILDINGS: EXEMPT SUPPLIES AND OPTION TO TAX**). Where

- an anti-forestalling charge becomes due under *Sch 27*;
- the supplier would have been required to issue a VAT invoice had the supply been standard-rated at the time it was made; and
- the anti-forestalling charge has not been included in a related VAT invoice (if any),

the supplier must, within 45 days after the date on which the anti-forestalling charge becomes due, issue an invoice headed 'Anti-forestalling charge invoice' containing the particulars set out below.

Where the supply has not been included in a VAT invoice, the particulars are those required on a VAT invoice (see **40.4** above).

Where the supply has been included in a VAT invoice, the particulars are

- the identifying number and date of issue of the anti-forestalling charge invoice;

- the amount of the anti-forestalling charge to VAT;
- the name, address and registration number of the supplier;
- the name and address of the recipient; and
- the identifying number and date of issue of the VAT invoice in which the supply was previously included.

[*SI 1995/2518, Reg 15B; SI 2012/1899, Reg 9*].

Foreign language invoices

[40.17] Where a person in the UK receives a VAT invoice (or part of a VAT invoice) in a language other than English, HMRC may, by notice in writing, require that person to provide them with an English translation of the invoice within 30 days of the date of the notice. [*SI 1995/2518, Reg 13B*]. This will be done on an exceptional basis and any requests will be targeted at selective invoices only. (VAT Information Sheet 16/03, para 7.1).

Key points: invoices

[40.18] Points to consider are as follows.

- Sometimes there is confusion about when a business must issue a VAT invoice as a compulsory requirement. In basic terms, an invoice must be issued for any supply to a VAT-registered business in the UK that is taxable at a positive rate (i.e. excluding a zero-rated or an exempt supply). A tax invoice must be issued for any supply of goods or services to a business customer elsewhere in the EU, even though in most cases no output tax will be shown. There is an exception for exempt supplies made to customers in countries that do not require an invoice to be issued for exempt supplies (i.e. which have invoicing rules similar to the UK).
- There is no requirement to issue a VAT invoice in relation to an exempt supply or any supply where the input tax is blocked for the customer, e.g. if relevant to motor cars or business entertainment.
- It is important that a VAT invoice is issued to any VAT-registered business in the UK that requests one because this will then serve as input tax evidence for the business in question. In certain circumstances (see below) a less detailed VAT invoice can be issued which is also acceptable as input tax evidence.
- If a sale is made under a margin scheme, e.g. for second-hand car dealers, the invoice issued must not show VAT as a separate a amount. In the case of a sale under the tour operators margin scheme no VAT invoice is to be issued.
- It is possible that sales made by a retailer will be subject to an input tax claim by the buyer (e.g. in the situation where stationery or computer-related items are being bought from a retail stationery store). In such cases, the retailer is obliged to issue a VAT invoice, although a less detailed VAT invoice may again be sufficient.

- A convenient and acceptable approach in some commercial situations is for the customer to issue a self-billed invoice to a supplier. This document is a substitute for a VAT invoice, and must contain certain pieces of information as a requirement (e.g. supplier's VAT registration number and a message confirming that output tax needs to be declared by the supplier). Self-billing is particularly relevant in those situations when the price of a transaction is fixed by the customer (e.g. the valuation of measured building work in the case of construction services).
- There is no need to obtain permission from HMRC to operate self-billing, although the conditions imposed by HMRC must be fully met for the arrangement to be valid. A self-billing agreement must be in place and agreed between the customer and supplier.
- Another substitute for a VAT invoice in the construction industry is an authenticated receipt. The document will be issued by the customer but only becomes valid for VAT purposes (input tax claim) if it has been signed (authenticated) by the supplier. The authenticated receipt system can only be adopted if payments for building services are made on a continuous basis (i.e. it would not be relevant to a single supply of services) and if the customer and supplier both agree to adopt the procedure.
- Visiting officers from HMRC will check arrangements for both self-billing and authenticated receipts are being operated correctly. The onus is on the customer to get the procedures right, otherwise a claim for input tax could be invalidated.
- It is common practice in many professions (e.g. accountancy and legal profession) for VAT invoices to be issued only when payment has been made by a customer in relation to a continuous supply of services. Alternative documents raised in advance of the invoice, e.g. fee note, application for payment, pro-forma invoice or request for payment are not classed as a VAT invoice. This means that no output tax liability has been incurred by the supplier (assuming other relevant conditions are met) and no input tax can be claimed by the customer.
- As a technical point, it is suggested that alternative documents that are not VAT invoices (as listed in previous paragraph) be clearly highlighted along the lines of: 'This document is not a VAT invoice, which will be issued to you when payment has been received.'
- It is compulsory for each VAT invoice issued by a business to have a 'unique' identifying number. So a business issuing invoices from a pre-printed pad where numbers 001 to 100 are shown on each pad must take steps to ensure each pad has a unique feature to make the numbers in each series different, e.g. pre-fixed by a letter or extra number. The key point is that no two invoices issued by a business should ever have the same number.
- If a customer is responsible for paying the output tax on a sales invoice (e.g. supply to an overseas business customer in another EU member state under the reverse charge rules, or to a UK

business because of sales of mobile phones/computer chips with an invoice value exceeding £5,000), then a note needs to be included on the invoice to alert the customer to his responsibilities.

- A retailer can issue a less detailed VAT invoice, as long as the total value of the sale (including VAT) is less than £250. In such cases, the VAT does not need to be separately itemised on the invoice, and the name and address of the customer does not need to be shown. However, the invoice must still show enough detail to enable the customer to know exactly how much VAT he has been charged on the sale (e.g. by recognising any zero-rated elements of the sale) for input tax purposes.
- An EU customer (outside the UK) can request a full VAT invoice rather than a less detailed tax invoice, even if the conditions for a less detailed invoice are met, e.g. value of sale is less than £250.
- Always remember that a credit note can only be issued if there is a genuine reduction in the value of the original sale in relation to a supply of goods or services (e.g. due to a pricing error or goods being returned). A credit note cannot be issued to adjust a bad debt – there are separate accounting procedures for bad debt relief.
- If a credit note is issued, the VAT adjustment will be based on the rate of VAT that applied when the original invoice was raised.

41

Isle of Man

De Voil Indirect Tax Service. See V1.216; V1.217.

Isle of Man: introduction

[41.1] The Isle of Man (IOM) is not part of the UK and the common tax area between the two countries results from an administrative agreement between the UK and the IOM governments contained in the *Customs and Excise Agreement 1979* (as amended). In the UK, the agreement was implemented by the *Isle of Man Act 1979*. *Section 6* of that Act relates to VAT.

VAT is administered and collected in the IOM by the Manx Customs and Excise Service under the *Value Added Tax Act 1996* (of Tynwald).

The spirit of the agreement between the UK and IOM is that IOM legislation parallels UK legislation and procedures, with certain exceptions, but so that VAT is not charged twice on the same transaction. [*IMA 1979, s 6; SI 1982/1067; SI 1982/1068*]. Differences include

- legislation relating to machine games under *VATA 1994, s 23* (see **8.4 BETTING AND GAMING**) does not have an equivalent in the IOM [*IMA 1979, s 1(d)*];
- legislation relating to refund of VAT on the construction of new homes by do-it-yourself housebuilders under *VATA 1994, s 35* (see **43.23 LAND AND BUILDINGS: ZERO AND REDUCED RATE SUPPLIES AND DIY HOUSEBUILDERS**) does not have an equivalent in the IOM [*SI 1982/1067, Art 9*]; and
- the rate of VAT on accommodation in hotels and similar establishments in the IOM, including the provision of holiday accommodation and the letting of camp sites, is 5%.

Registration

[41.2] Separate VAT registers are maintained in the IOM and the UK. There are special provisions for determining, or enabling HMRC to determine, where a person is to be registered who would otherwise be liable to be registered in both places.

A person who is *liable to be registered* in the UK under *VATA 1994, Sch 1 para 1* (see **60.3 REGISTRATION**) and who

- has 'an establishment' both in the UK and the IOM, or
- does not have an establishment in either country

will be registered in the UK or IOM as HMRC determine; but unless or until they determine that he should be registered in the IOM, he is required to be registered in the UK. HMRC may, however, at any time determine that a person within (*a*) or (*b*) above

- who is registered in the UK, is instead to be registered in the IOM, in which case he ceases to be, or required to be, registered in the UK from such date as they determine (although still remaining liable for payment of VAT on business assets held on the last day of registration, see **60.40 REGISTRATION**); and
- who is registered in the IOM, is instead to be registered in the UK from such date as they determine, in which case any amount of VAT required to be paid in the IOM is deemed to have been an amount of VAT due in the UK.

Where a person is registered, or required to be registered, in the IOM, the provisions of *VATA 1994, Sch 1 para 5* (notification of liability for, and date of registration in, the UK, see **60.4 REGISTRATION**) and *VATA 1994, Sch 1 para 9* (entitlement to be registered, see **60.2 REGISTRATION**) do not apply to that person. HMRC may, however, determine that any person to whom those provisions do apply shall be registered in the IOM.

A person registered in the UK who has no establishment in the IOM, or is the representative member of a VAT group (see **28.2 GROUPS OF COMPANIES**) no member of which has an establishment there, must notify HMRC if such an establishment is subsequently acquired. Such notification may be treated as an event requiring the cancellation of the person's, or that group's, registration.

'*An establishment*' in a country is where there is a place from which a person carries on a business in that country or carries on business through a branch or agent in that country. For this purpose an agent is a person who has the authority or capacity to create legal relations between his principal and a third party. [*SI 1982/1067, Arts 11, 12*].

De Voil Indirect Tax Service. See V2.127; V2.140; V2.156.

Imports, exports and removals

[41.3] Within the common tax area of the UK and the IOM, a registered business accounts for VAT in the country in which it is registered. For example, an IOM business, making taxable supplies in the UK accounts for the VAT in the IOM. If the business imports goods into the common tax area, the import VAT can be paid (or deferred) and reclaimed as input tax in the IOM subject to the normal rules for input tax deduction.

Movements of goods from the UK to the IOM and vice versa are not normally treated as exports or imports provided that, for goods removed from the IOM to the UK

- any VAT due has been accounted for in the IOM, or
- if the goods are relieved of VAT in the IOM, the conditions of that relief have not been broken.

Key points: the Isle of Man

[41.4] Points to consider are as follows.

- By agreement, the IOM and UK adopt a common VAT system, even though the IOM is not part of the UK. This agreement is important to both avoid tax being charged twice in some cases and also to ensure the overall systems are consistent with each other. There are some minor differences in the rules between the two countries – for example, holiday accommodation in the Isle of Man is taxed at 5% rather than being standard-rated as in the UK.
- Goods that are despatched between the UK and IOM and vice versa are not normally treated as exports or imports provided that, for goods removed from the IOM to the UK, any VAT due has been accounted for in the IOM, or if the goods are relieved of VAT in the IOM, the conditions of that relief have not been broken.

42

Land and Buildings: Exempt Supplies and Option to Tax

Cross-references. See **7.11 BAD DEBT RELIEF** for sales of repossessed properties by lenders; **11 CAPITAL GOODS SCHEME** for the deduction, and adjustment of deduction, of input tax on certain land and buildings by partly exempt businesses; **60.39 REGISTRATION** for land and buildings in hand in cancellation of registration; **66.15 SUPPLY: PLACE OF SUPPLY** for the place of supply of services relating to land outside the UK and the Isle of Man; **67.13 SUPPLY: TIME OF SUPPLY** for the time of supply of land and property.

Definitions and meanings of terms

[42.1] The following general definitions and terms apply for the purposes of this chapter and chapter **43 LAND AND BUILDINGS: ZERO AND REDUCED RATE SUPPLIES ETC.**

Approved alteration

[42.2] Approved alterations to protected buildings could be the subject of a zero-rated supply in certain circumstances up to 30 September 2015. See **43.10** for details. Transitional rules operated between 1 October 2012 and 30 September 2015, but no further supplies can be zero-rated under this heading.

An approved alteration means any of the following.

(a) In the case of a '*protected building*' (see **42.13** below) which is an ecclesiastical building excluded from the planning consent requirements by *Planning (Listed Buildings and Conservation Areas) Act 1990, s 60*, any works of alteration. A building used or available for use by a minister of religion wholly or mainly as a residence from which to perform the duties of his office is not to be treated as an ecclesiastical building for these purposes. [*VATA 1994, Sch 8 Group 6, Note (6)*].
In England and Wales, the religious denominations which have been granted exclusion are the Church of England, the Church in Wales, the Roman Catholic Church, the Methodist Church, the Baptist Union of Great Britain and the Baptist Union of Wales, and the United Reformed Church.
In Scotland and Northern Ireland, all listed places of worship that are in ecclesiastical use are exempt from listed building controls, although they are still subject to planning controls.
Any alteration, which is not work of repair or maintenance (see below), to the fabric of a listed place of worship that has ecclesiastical exemption is an approved alteration.
(VAT Notice 708, para 9.5).
Alterations to ecclesiastical buildings which require planning consent fall within (*b*) below.

(b) In any other case, works of alteration which cannot be carried out unless authorised under *Planning (Listed Buildings and Conservation Areas) Act 1990, Planning (Listed Buildings and Conservation Areas) (Scotland) Act 1997, Planning (Northern Ireland) Order 1991* or *Ancient Monuments and Archaeological Areas Act 1979* and for which consent has been obtained under the appropriate legislation. [*VATA 1994, Sch 8 Group 6, Note (6)*].

'Crown' and 'Duchy' interest buildings

Listed building consent may not be needed for alterations to buildings on Crown or Duchy land even though it would be needed for similar alterations to listed buildings elsewhere. In such a case, an alteration to the fabric of the building which would otherwise have required consent and which is not work of repair or maintenance (see below) is an approved alteration. [*VATA 1994, Sch 8 Group 6, Note (6)*].

Scheduled monuments

All work affecting scheduled monuments requires scheduled monument consent from the Secretary of State. Approved alterations are those works of alteration for which consent has been obtained. It is possible for a building to be both scheduled and listed. If so, only scheduled monument procedures apply and it should be treated as a scheduled monument for VAT purposes.

Listed building consent

In most cases, an approved alteration falls within (*b*) above and is an alteration for which listed building consent is both needed and has been obtained from the appropriate planning authority (or, in some circumstances, the Secretary of State) prior to the commencement of the work. A supplier will need to find out from his customer (or their architect or surveyor) to what extent the work he is contracted to do has both required and received listed building consent. Listed building consent is not the same as planning permission. In general terms, listed building consent is needed for work on a listed building which would affect its character as a building of special architectural or historic interest. The construction of an extension, or alterations following partial demolition, would certainly require consent but it is difficult to generalise about less radical work, especially as regards internal alterations. It is an offence to carry out work to a listed building without obtaining any required listed building consent. Where this happens, the planning authority cannot issue retrospective listed building consent for the work, although they may permit the unauthorised works to be retained. Such works are *not* then approved alterations (because consent has not been granted at the time the work is carried out) and are standard-rated. Where works to a listed building are carried out without listed building consent being obtained or where work carried out does not comply with a condition in the consent, the local planning authority may issue a 'listed building enforcement notice' for the carrying out of further work. An alteration, which is not work of repair or maintenance (see below), to the fabric of the building under the terms of an enforcement notice is an approved alteration.
(VAT Notice 708, para 9.5).

Alteration or repair and maintenance?

HMRC regard a building as being altered when its fabric, such as its walls, roof, internal surfaces, floors, stairs, windows, doors, plumbing and wiring is changed in a meaningful way. Works of repair or maintenance, or any incidental alteration resulting from works of repair or maintenance, are standard-rated, even if the work has been included in the listed building consent.

See *C & E Commrs v Viva Gas Appliances*, HL [1983] STC 819 (TVC 56.17) where Lord Diplock stated that alteration of a building should be construed as any work on the fabric of the building except that which is so slight or trivial as to attract the application of the *de minimis* rule (although it should be noted that in *The Vicar and Parochial Church Council of St Petroc Minor* (VTD 16450) (TVC 55.57) the tribunal specifically declined to apply this *dicta* on the basis that the context in which 'alteration' was used in that case no longer appears in *VATA 1994*).

Works of repair or maintenance are those tasks designed to minimise, for as long as possible, the need for, and future scale and cost of, further attention to the fabric of the building. Changes to the physical features of the building are not zero-rated alterations if, in the exercise of proper repair and maintenance of the building, they are either

- trifling or insignificant, or
- dictated by the nature and use of modern building materials.

Similarly, if the amount of work or cost is significant, that does not make the work a zero-rated alteration if the inherent character of the work is repair and maintenance.

Examples

Work	*VAT treatment*
Extensions	Alteration
Opening/closing doorways	Alteration
Replacement of rotten wooden windows with UPVC double glazing	Repair or maintenance
Replacement of UPVC double glazing with copies of original wooden windows for aesthetic reasons	Alteration
Installing a window where one did not exist before	Alteration
Re-felt and batten roof	Repair or maintenance
Replacement of a flat roof with a pitched roof	Alteration
Replacement of straw thatch with reeds; and changes to the ridge detail of a thatched roof	Repair or maintenance when carried out as part of the normal renewal programme.
Damp proofing	Repair or maintenance
Making good	Follows the liability of the main work
Re-decorating	Repair or maintenance
Re-pointing	Repair or maintenance
Re-wiring	Repair or maintenance
Extending wiring and plumbing systems	Alteration
Replacing boilers with a larger capacity boiler while extending plumbing systems	Alteration
Flood lighting	Alteration when installed on the building. But neither an alteration nor repair or maintenance (and therefore standard-rated) when installed within the grounds of a building – there is no work to the fabric of the building.

(VAT Notice 708, para 9.4).

Only mains electrical wiring and lighting systems that are either on, or in, the structure of the building itself will be considered to be part of the fabric of the building. Those parts which extend beyond the structure into the grounds (e.g. wiring to floodlights) will not. Electrical appliances which are attached to, and serviced by, the mains supply are not considered to be part of the mains wiring system. (Business Brief 7/2000).

The construction of a building 'separate' from, but in the curtilage (see **42.4** below) of, a protected building does not constitute an alteration of the protected building and cannot be zero-rated as an approved alteration, even if the work has listed building consent. [*VATA 1994, Sch 8 Group 6 Item 2* and *Notes (6)–(8), (10)*]. The construction of, and the alteration to, fences, walls, railings and other curtilage structures such as patios and terraces, are therefore standard-rated. Zero-rating may, however, be available under the rules for construction of new buildings (see **43.7 LAND AND BUILDINGS: ZERO AND REDUCED RATE SUPPLIES AND DIY HOUSEBUILDERS**) (i.e. if it is (i) the construction of a completely new self-contained dwelling (including a garage built at the same time for use with it) where there are no restrictions on disposal; or (ii) a completely new self-contained building for use solely for a '*relevant residential purpose*' or a '*relevant charitable purpose*' (see **42.16** and **42.14** below respectively)). (VAT Notice 708, para 9.4).

See *C & E Commrs v Arbib*, QB [1995] STC 490 (TVC 55.42) for a consideration of the meaning of 'separate'. In that case, a swimming pool connected to a listed farmhouse by a covered walkway and a brick wall was held not to be a separate building so that the building work on it fell to be zero-rated.

Construction of a building

[42.3] There is no definition in the legislation of the '*construction of a building*' for zero-rating purposes, other than it does not include

(a) the conversion, reconstruction or alteration of an existing building;
(b) any enlargement of, or extension to, an existing building except to the extent that this creates an additional dwelling or dwellings; or
(c) the construction of an annexe to an existing building unless
   (i) the whole or a part of the annexe is intended solely for use for a '*relevant charitable purpose*' (see **42.14** below);
   (ii) it is capable of functioning independently from the existing building; and
   (iii) the only access (or main access where more than one) to the annexe is *not* via the existing building and *vice versa*.

The significance of (i) above is that, in conjunction with *VATA 1994, Sch 8 Group 5 Note 10* (which provides for apportionment between zero-rated and standard-rated supplies), zero-rating can be applied to supplies made in connection with a part of an annexe which is to be used *solely* for relevant charitable purposes. Where an annexe, or part of an annexe (including common areas such as entrance lobbies) will be used for a mixture of relevant charitable and other purposes, it (or that part) is not used solely for a relevant charitable purpose and is standard-rated. By concession, minor non-qualifying use can be ignored (see **42.14** below).

For these purposes, a building only ceases to be an existing building when

- it is demolished completely to ground level; or
- the part remaining above ground level consists of no more than a single façade (double façade where a corner site), the retention of which is a condition or requirement of statutory planning consent or similar permission.

[*VATA 1994, Sch 8 Group 5 Notes (16)–(18)*].

In *HMRC v Astral Construction Ltd* [2015] UKUT 21 (TCC), a disused church was converted into the reception and administration area of a residential care home. Two residential 'wings' were constructed adjacent to the church, both significantly larger than the original building. HMRC ruled that the combined effect of *Notes 16* and *18* was that the construction of the wings could not qualify for zero-rating, because the project involved the conversion or extension of the existing building. The Upper Tribunal allowed the company's appeal, holding that what was new construction and what was an extension was a question of fact, impression and degree, and in this case the only sensible conclusion was that the residential blocks were new construction adjacent to the existing building. They were not extensions of it, nor annexes to it.

Examples of the construction of a zero-rated building

HMRC give the following as examples of construction work that can be zero-rated.

- The building is either '*designed as a dwelling*' (see **42.5** below) or a number of dwellings, intended for use solely for a '*relevant residential purpose*' (see **42.16** below) or a '*relevant charitable purpose*' (see **42.14** below) and one of the following scenarios apply.
  - (i) It is built from scratch, and, before work starts, any pre-existing building is demolished completely to ground level (cellars, basements and the 'slab' at ground level may be retained).
  - (ii) The new building makes use of no more than a single facade (or a double facade on a corner site) of a pre-existing building, the pre-existing building is demolished completely (other than the retained facade) before work on the new building is started *and* the facade is retained as a condition or requirement of statutory planning consent or similar permission.

    In *Boxmoor Construction Ltd v HMRC* [2016] UKUT 91 (TCC) (TVC 15.262), the Upper Tribunal ruled that the retention of a facade has to be an explicit requirement of the planning consent. An 'understanding' between the architect and the planning officer that the facade would be retained, not reflected in the consent itself, was not sufficient. By contrast in *Andrew David Reeves* [2016] UKFTT 195 (TC) (TC04980) (TVC 15.264), the First-tier Tribunal commented that showing the facade as retained on the plans, with a requirement in the planning consent that the project had to be carried out in accordance with the plans, would be enough to satisfy the rule. The appeal failed because the retained wall was a gable end, which the Tribunal did not consider to be a 'facade'.

(iii) A new building is constructed against an existing building so that they share a wall but there is no internal access between them.

- An existing building is enlarged or extended and the enlargement or extension creates an additional dwelling or dwellings which is/are wholly within the enlargement or extension. So, for example, a new eligible flat built on top of an existing building can qualify for zero-rating. If the new dwelling is partly or wholly contained within the existing building, the work does not qualify for zero-rating, although it may qualify for reduced-rating as a 'changed number of dwellings conversion' under the provisions in **43.12 LAND AND BUILDINGS: ZERO AND REDUCED RATE SUPPLIES AND DIY HOUSEBUILDERS.**
- *Relevant charitable purpose annexes.* The construction of a building intended for use solely for a '*relevant charitable purpose*' (see **42.14** below) is zero-rated, with additions to an existing building normally being standard-rated. However, an addition can qualify as the construction of a building (and be zero-rated subject to the normal conditions) when all the following conditions are met.

(i) The construction is an 'annexe', rather than an extension or enlargement. There is no legal definition of '*annexe*'. It can be either a structure attached to an existing building or a structure detached from it. (If detached, it is treated as a separate building for VAT purposes and the following does not apply.) If attached to an existing building, in order to be considered an annexe, a structure must not be attached in such a way so as to be considered an enlargement or extension. An enlargement or extension would involve making the building bigger so as to provide extra space for the activities already carried out in the existing building (e.g. a classroom or a sports hall added to an existing school building or an additional function room, kitchen or toilet block added to an existing village hall). An annexe should provide extra space for activities distinct from, but associated with, the activities carried out in the existing building. The annexe and the existing building should form two separate parts of a single building that operate independently of each other (e.g. a day hospice added to an existing residential hospice, a self-contained suite of rooms added to an existing village hall, a church hall added to an existing church or a nursery added to a school building).

(ii) The whole annexe, or a part of it, is intended for use solely for a relevant charitable purpose. The annexe need not be an annexe to a building used solely for a relevant charitable purpose. What is important is that the annexe itself is intended for use solely for a relevant charitable purpose.

(iii) The whole annexe must be capable of functioning independently from the existing building, even if only part of it is used solely for a relevant charitable purpose. An annexe is capable of functioning independently when the activities in the annexe can be carried on without reliance on the existing building, ignoring the existence of building services (electricity and water supplies, etc.) that are shared with the existing building.

(iv) The annexe and the existing building each has its own independent main access. So, even if the annexe has its own entrance, the main access to the annexe must not be through the existing building and the annexe must not create the main access to the existing building.

The demolition and reconstruction of an annexe to an existing building can be zero-rated subject to the above conditions being met. But the demolition and reconstruction of part of an existing building, such as the wing of a building, or the conversion of an existing building (or part) to an annexe, cannot be the construction of an annexe.

- *Infilling*. The building of a new house within an existing terrace of houses on the site of a house that has been totally demolished ('*infilling*') apart from party walls shared with adjoining houses that are not being re-developed.

  Where neighbouring houses in a terrace are being re-developed, the party wall between those houses will also need to be demolished if the works are to qualify as 'constructing a building' for VAT purposes. A party wall need not separate a building from another building, it can also be the wall of a building on one property and a boundary or garden wall for the adjoining property.
- A garage is built, or a building is converted into a garage; and the construction or conversion takes place at the same time as, and the building is intended to be occupied with, a building 'designed as a dwelling or number of dwellings' (see **42.5** below).
- A building is built that is one of a number of buildings constructed at the same time on the same site and it is intended to be used together with those other buildings as a unit solely for a 'relevant residential purpose' (see **42.16** below).

Examples not qualifying as the construction of a zero-rated building

HMRC give the following as examples of construction work that cannot be zero-rated.

- A 'granny' annexe which cannot be used, or disposed of, separately from a main house. This is because the conditions of a building 'designed as a dwelling' (see **42.5** below) have not been met in full.
- A house that cannot be used, or disposed of, separately from a business premises. This is because the conditions of 'a building designed as a dwelling' have not been met in full.
- A house that incorporates a part or parts of an earlier building on the site, e.g. planning permission has been given to alter and extend an existing dwelling. That dwelling is substantially but not fully demolished in order to comply with the planning permission and a new dwelling constructed, incorporating the parts not demolished.

- A detached, enclosed swimming pool in the grounds of a new house. This is because the building being constructed is not a building 'designed as a dwelling' (see **42.5** below).
- A detached building in the grounds of an existing care home which extends the facilities of the home, such as an accommodation or administration block or 'extra care' units. This is because the building being constructed will not be used for a 'relevant residential purpose' (see **42.16** below) in its own right and it was not constructed at the same time as the rest of the home. See also HMRC Brief 66/07.

(VAT Notice 708, para 3.2).

Curtilage

[42.4] In VAT Notice 708 (August 1997 Edition) HMRC defined curtilage as a reasonable amount of land, surrounding the building, which may include other buildings. What constitutes a reasonable amount of land will depend on the type of building and its setting. Although this definition is not reproduced in the latest edition of VAT Notice 708, there is no reason to suppose that their interpretation of the term has changed.

Designed as a dwelling

[42.5] There is no definition in the legislation of 'dwelling' but see *Calam Vale* and *Amicus Group* considered in **42.11** below.

For the purposes of zero-rating, a building is designed as a dwelling or number of dwellings where the following conditions are satisfied in relation to each dwelling.

(a) The dwelling consists of self-contained living accommodation.
(b) There is no provision for direct internal access from the dwelling to any other dwelling or part of a dwelling.
(c) The separate use, letting or disposal of the dwelling is not prohibited by the terms of any covenant, statutory planning consent or similar provision. An occupancy restriction is not a prohibition on separate use or disposal if all it does is restrict the occupancy of a building to a certain type of person, such as persons working in agriculture or forestry, or persons over a specified age. But if the wording of the restriction prevents the building from being used separately from another building or from being sold, or otherwise disposed of, separately from another building then it is a prohibition on separate use or disposal. (VAT Notice 708, para 14.2).
(d) Statutory planning consent has been granted in respect of that dwelling and its construction or conversion has been carried out in accordance with that consent.

[*VATA 1994, Sch 8 Group 5 Note (2)*].

See *University of Bath* (VTD 14235) (TVC 15.88) (students' accommodation) and *A J White* (VTD 15388) (TVC 65.90) (living accommodation over public houses) where in each case cooking and toilet facilities were shared.

For cases where (*c*) above was in point, see *Sherwin & Green* (VTD 16396) (TVC 15.45), *P Thompson*, (VTD 15834) (TVC 15.62), *PH Wiseman* (VTD 17374) (TVC 15.68) and *JFB & FR Sharples* (VTD 20775) (TVC 15.46) and for a case where (*d*) was in point, see *AI Davison* (VTD 17130) (TVC 15.83).

In *Oldrings Development Kingsclere Ltd* (VTD 17769) (TVC 15.42) a single storey, self-contained building was constructed in the grounds of a large house. It comprised one large room, plus a small room with a WC and washbasin, and had its own central heating system, hot water and electricity supply. The tribunal held that it was 'designed as a dwelling' and qualified for zero-rating, even though it was primarily used as an artist's studio, as it was capable of being used as a studio flat.

HMRC accept that 'extra care accommodation' (i.e. accommodation sold or let with the option to purchase varying degrees of care to suit individual needs as and when they arise) is designed as a dwelling if it meets the standard conditions above. (HMRC Brief 47/11).

HMRC accept that there may be instances where a building could qualify for zero-rating as a dwelling and qualify for zero-rating as a relevant residential purpose building (see **42.16** below). In such cases a taxpayer can rely on either provision to achieve zero-rating. (HMRC VAT Information Sheet 2/14).

Bedsits do not qualify as dwellings in their own right because they do not constitute 'self-contained' living accommodation: normally they share facilities for cooking and washing. A building designed as a number of bedsits is not, therefore, 'a building designed as a number of dwellings' (as blocks of flats or semi-detached houses are). However, in *Capital Focus Ltd* [2016] UKFTT 440 (TC) (TC05193), the First-tier Tax Tribunal held that a building containing bedsits could be 'designed as a dwelling' and so could qualify for zero-rating. In the case, the appellant was involved in converting a non-residential building for sale, but the principle could equally apply to new construction.

Dwellings formed from more than one building

HMRC formerly regarded construction of more than one building as incapable of fully qualifying for zero-rating as the construction of a single dwelling. Either one would be an 'annexe' or extension of the other, or one would not be 'self-contained' because some of the essential facilities were located in the other. On 23 August 2016 HMRC published a change in policy, accepting two 2012 Tribunal decisions (*Catchpole* (TC01995) and *Fox* (TC01957)) in which it was held that more than one building could be designed to function together as a single dwelling.

HMRC will accept that zero-rating can apply, subject to a number of conditions:

- the development must meet the conditions of a 'building designed as a dwelling' and to this end 'building' can mean more than one building;
- all buildings must be constructed or converted under a single project and under a single consent;

- if a new dwelling that is made up of more than one building is constructed in stages, HMRC will view subsequent stages as annexes to the original building, which will not benefit from the zero-rate unless the buildings are on the same site and the stages are completed with no unreasonable delay between them; and
- none of the buildings are occupied until all the stages are complete (in the sense described at para 3.3.2 of VAT Notice 708).

Where work is undertaken to convert premises consisting of more than a single building into a dwelling (for example, where premises are being converted to a different residential use), HMRC now accept that it would qualify for the reduced rate (5%) of VAT.

(HMRC Brief 13/16).

Grant

[42.6] Grant includes assignment or surrender. [*VATA 1994, Sch 8 Group 5 Note 2*]. It also includes the supply made by the person to whom an interest is surrendered when there is a reverse surrender (i.e. where the person to whom the interest is surrendered is paid by the person by whom the interest is being surrendered to accept the surrender). [*VATA 1994, Sch 9 Group 1 Notes 1, 1A*].

A grant is a sale of a freehold or other interest, or a lease or letting of land. An assignment is the transfer of a lease by the existing tenant to a new tenant. A surrender is the giving up of an 'interest in or right over' land (see **42.8** below) to the grantor. (VAT Notice 742, para 2.2).

The grant of any interest frequently gives rise to a number of further supplies at later times. For example, a supply is made each time that a payment is received for rent. In such cases, the liability of each subsequent supply is determined at the time when that supply is made rather than by reference to the time of the original grant. [*VATA 1994, s 96(10A)*].

In the course of construction

[42.7] Services supplied 'in the course of the construction' comprise

(a) work on the building itself prior to its 'completion'; and
(b) any other service closely connected to the construction of the building.

For examples of services included, and not included, see **43.14 LAND AND BUILDINGS: ZERO AND REDUCED RATE SUPPLIES AND DIY HOUSEBUILDERS**.

'*Completion*' of a building takes place when an architect issues a certificate of practical completion in relation to it or it is first fully occupied, whichever happens first. [*VATA 1994, Sch 9 Group 1 Note 2*]. HMRC expand on this by saying that completion takes place at a given moment in time. That point in time is determined by weighing up the relevant factors of the project, such as

- when a Certificate of Completion is issued;
- accordance to approved plans and specifications;

- the scope of the planning consent and variations to it; and
- whether the building is habitable or fit for purpose.

Generally, once a building has been completed, any further work to the building is standard-rated. But see **43.14 LAND AND BUILDINGS: ZERO AND REDUCED RATE SUPPLIES AND DIY HOUSEBUILDERS**.

Examples

- A developer is in the process of constructing a house for sale. The buyer would like to include an attached conservatory and so contracts with a conservatory specialist to supply and install it prior to moving in. The developer refuses the conservatory supplier access to the site until after he has finished his work and the house has been conveyed to the buyer.

  In such circumstances, the supply of the conservatory is not work in the course of the construction of the house but work to an existing building and cannot be zero-rated.
- A developer constructs and sells 'shell' loft apartments for fitting out by the buyer. When the developer sells the lofts, their construction is not 'complete'.

  Future work to fit them out can be zero-rated until such time as they are habitable.
- A non-fee paying school obtains planning permission to construct a building that will be used solely for a relevant charitable purpose. Due to limited funds, the extent of the work is scaled down and a smaller building is constructed instead. Funds are later obtained to extend and enlarge the building to produce a building of the same capacity as originally planned.

  In such circumstances, the building would be 'complete' at the end of the first set of works and the later works are standard-rated.

(VAT Notice 708, para 3.3).

In *C & E Commrs v St Mary's Roman Catholic High School*, QB [1996] STC 1091 (TVC 15.240), work began on the building of a new secondary school in 1979 and the school opened to pupils in 1981, although some of its original buildings were not completed until 1983. Under the original plans, the school was to have been equipped with two playgrounds but these were not completed until 1994. The QB held that, on the evidence, the interval between the completion of the building work on the school and the construction of the playgrounds was far too long to establish the necessary temporal link. Accordingly, the building of the playgrounds failed to qualify for zero-rating.

In *Hoylake Cottage Hospital Charitable Trust* (TC00925) (TVC 15.226) the construction of a nursing home at a charity's premises was completed in 2008. In 2009 HMRC issued a ruling that VAT would be chargeable on the proposed construction of a kitchen and laundry block at the site. The charity appealed, contending that this work should be treated as having taken place in the course of construction of the nursing home. The tribunal allowed the appeal, specifically distinguishing the decision in *St Mary's Roman Catholic High School*, and holding that a period of 18 months between the developments was not an unreasonable delay in the circumstances.

A building has been held to be in the course of construction until the main structure is completed, the windows glazed and all essential services and fittings, such as plumbing and electricity, have been installed. Thereafter the building ceases to be in course of construction and the phase of fitting out and furnishing is ready to begin (*University of Hull* (VTD 180) (TVC 15.238)). See also *JM Associates* (VTD 18624) (TVC 15.232) where the supply and construction of conservatories for newly-built houses was held to be standard-rated as the work of construction only took place after the house was completed.

In *B Bowley* [2015] UKFTT 683 (TC) (TC04800) (TVC 15.164), the First-tier Tribunal allowed a DIY builder's claim in respect of a garage that was completed 20 years after a certificate of completion had been issued in respect of his house (and 32 years after obtaining planning permission for the construction of the house). He claimed that he had only just completed the garage, and it was all part of a single continuous project that had taken many years. HMRC accepted that, in principle, it was possible for a DIY project to take 30 years; a claim would still be 'in time' if submitted within three months of the final completion. The Tribunal was satisfied that the construction of the garage was a single project with the construction of the house, and the claim was therefore in time.

Interest in or right over

[42.8] An interest in land can be

- a *legal interest*, i.e. the formal ownership of an interest in or right over land such as a freehold or leasehold interest in it; or
- a *beneficial (or equitable) interest*, i.e. the right to receive the benefit of supplies of it (e.g. the sales proceeds or rental income).

A beneficial interest may be held and transferred separately from the legal interest.

Rights over land include

- *rights of entry* which allow an authorised person or authority to enter land (e.g. they might allow someone to come onto land to perform a specific task);
- *easements* which grant the owner of neighbouring land a right to make their property better or more convenient, such as a right of way or right of light;
- *wayleaves*, i.e. a right of way to transport minerals extracted from land over another's land, or to lay pipes or cables over or under another's land; and
- *profits à prendre*, i.e. rights to take produce from another's land, such as to extract minerals.

UK law currently exempts the supply of rights over land. However, these are often supplied together with freehold or leasehold interests in land and form part of a single supply. For example, a lease may be granted of a single floor in an office block with an easement over the common areas, such as reception and lifts, to allow the lessee to access his floor. In such cases the supply of the right over land (in this case the easement) will share the same tax treatment as the principal supply.

Some profits à prendre, such as the right to fell and remove timber, are standard-rated under the exceptions to exemption in UK law. In addition, the right granted to harvest and remove crops may in some cases be treated as a zero-rated supply of food or animal feed stuff.

(VAT Notice 742, paras 2.3, 2.4).

Licence to occupy

[42.9] A licence to occupy is a written or oral agreement which falls within the European concept of 'leasing or letting of immovable property' but falls short of being a formal lease for the purpose of UK land law. For a licence to occupy to exist, the agreement has to have all characteristics of a 'leasing or letting of immovable property'. This is the case if the licensee is granted right of occupation of a *defined* area of land (land includes buildings)

- for an agreed duration,
- in return for payment, and
- has the right to occupy that area as owner and to exclude others from enjoying that right.

All of these characteristics must be present. Where a licence to occupy is granted together with other goods and services as part of a single supply, the nature of the overarching supply will determine how it should be categorised for VAT purposes.

(VAT Notice 742, para 2.5).

See also *Abbotsley Golf and Squash Club Ltd* (VTD 15042) (TVC 41.172) where, applying dicta of Lord Templeman in *Street v Mountford*, HL [1985] 2 All ER 289 (TVC 41.172), the tribunal held that exclusivity of occupation was an essential condition of a tenancy but not of a licence to occupy.

Examples of licences to occupy land

- The provision of a specific area of office accommodation (e.g. a bay, room or floor together with the rights to use shared areas such as reception, lifts, restaurant, rest rooms, leisure facilities, etc.).
- The provision of a serviced office which includes use of telephones, computer system, photocopier, etc.
- Granting a concession to operate a shop within a shop where the concessionaires are granted a defined area from which to sell their goods or services.
- Granting space to erect advertising hoardings.
- Granting space to place a fixed kiosk on a specific site (e.g. newspaper kiosks, flower stands at railway stations).
- Hiring out a hall or other accommodation for meetings, parties, etc. (but not wedding or party facilities where the supplier does more than supplying accommodation, e.g. by assisting with entertainment and arranging catering) including use of a kitchen area, lighting, furniture.

- Granting a catering concession, where the caterer is granted a licence to occupy specific kitchens and restaurant areas, even if the grant includes the use of kitchen or catering equipment.
- Granting traders a pitch in a market or at a car boot sale (even if only for one day, see *Tameside Metropolitan Borough Council* (VTD 733) (TVC 41.5)).
- Granting a specific space for the installation of a 'hole in the wall' cash machine (ATM).
- Supplies of fractional ownership interests in a property may, in certain circumstances, be treated as a grant of a right to occupy a residence and therefore exempt from VAT. The Upper Tribunal has held that the supply of the right to occupy a reserved residence should not be treated as the standard-rated supply of holiday accommodation as it was not a supply of a series of short-term stays but the supply of a long-term right to occupy a reserved residence during the relevant periods. See *Forty-seven Park Street Ltd v HMRC* [2018] UKUT 41 (TCC), [2018] STC 541 (TVC 41.126).

Not included as licences to occupy land (and therefore standard-rated)

- The rental by a hairdressing salon of chair spaces to individual stylists, unless a clearly demarcated area is provided (such as a floor or whole salon) and no other services. See *Simon Harris Hair Design Ltd* (VTD 13939) (TVC 41.91).
- The hire of tables in nail bars to self-employed manicurists.
- Providing another person with access to office premises to make use of the facilities (e.g. remote sales staff away from home having access to photocopiers, etc. at another office).
- Allowing the public to tip rubbish on land.
- Storing someone else's goods in a warehouse without allocating any specified area for them.
- Granting an ambulatory concession (e.g. ice-cream vans on the sea front, hamburger vans at sporting events).
- Allowing the public admission to premises or events (see **58.2 RECREATION AND SPORT** but note that admission to certain one-off fund-raising events by charities may be exempt).
- Wedding facilities (including, e.g. use of rooms for a ceremony, wedding breakfast and evening party).
- Hiring out safes to store valuables.
- Granting someone the right to place a free-standing or wall-mounted vending or gaming machine on premises, where the location is not specified in the agreement. See *Sinclair Collis Ltd v C & E Commrs, ECJ Case C–275/01*, [2003] STC 898 (TVC 22.365).

(VAT Notice 742, paras 2.6, 2.7).

See also *Altman Blane & Co* (VTD 12381) (TVC 41.8) where payments for non-exclusive use of a room were held to be exempt; and *International Antiques and Collectors Fairs Ltd* [2015] UKFTT 354 (TC) (TC04538) where facilities for stallholders at antiques fairs were held to constitute an opportunity to sell rather than a mere licence to occupy. A trader offering a similar supply was held to be exempt by the First-tier Tribunal, but this decision was overturned; her organisation of craft fairs went beyond the passive provision of the site to stallholders, and constituted a taxable supply of the opportunity to participate in the fair (*HMRC v Kati Zombory-Moldovan t/a Craft Carnival* [2016] UKUT 433 (TCC) (TVC 41.42)).

Major interest

[42.10] *In relation to England, Wales and Northern Ireland*, a major interest in relation to land means the 'fee simple' or a tenancy for a term certain exceeding 21 years.

In relation to Scotland, following the abolition of feudal tenure, it will mean the interest of the owner or the lessee's interest under a lease for a period of not less than 20 years. Until the abolition, it is

(a) the estate or interest of the proprietor of the *dominium utile*, or
(b) in the case of land not held under feudal tenure, the estate or interest of the owner, or the lessee's interest under a lease for a period of not less than 20 years.

'Fee simple'

- in relation to England and Wales means the freehold;
- in relation to Scotland means the interest of the owner (and, until the abolition of feudal tenure, the estate or interest of the proprietor of the *dominium utile*); and
- in relation to Northern Ireland, includes the estate of a person who holds land under a fee farm grant.

[*VATA 1994, s 96(1); Abolition of Feudal Tenure etc (Scotland) Act 2000, Sch 12 para 57*].

Non-residential

[42.11] A building or part of a building is 'non-residential' if

(a) it is neither
  (i) designed nor adapted for 'use as a dwelling' or number of dwellings (see **42.5** above); nor
  (ii) designed nor adapted for use for a '*relevant residential purpose*' (see **42.16** below), or
(b) it is designed or adapted for use within (*a*)(i) or (ii) above but
  (i) where the provision in **43.1**(*c*) **LAND AND BUILDINGS: ZERO AND REDUCED RATE SUPPLIES AND DIY HOUSEBUILDERS** applies (grant of major interest by a developer), it was constructed more than ten years before the grant of the major interest and no part of it has been used as a dwelling or for a relevant residential purpose in the period of ten years immediately preceding the grant;
  (ii) where the provision in **43.9 LAND AND BUILDINGS: ZERO AND REDUCED RATE SUPPLIES AND DIY HOUSEBUILDERS** applies (conversion services supplied to housing associations), it was constructed more than ten years before the commencement of the

conversion work, no part of it has been used as a dwelling or for a relevant residential purpose in the period of ten years immediately preceding the commencement of those works, and no part of it is being so used; and

(iii) where the provision in **43.23**(*a*)(iii) **LAND AND BUILDINGS: ZERO AND REDUCED RATE SUPPLIES AND DIY HOUSEBUILDERS** applies (D-I-Y housebuilders), it was constructed more than ten years before the commencement of the conversion work and no part of it has been used as a dwelling or for a relevant residential purpose in the period of ten years immediately preceding the commencement of those works.

References to a non-residential building or a non-residential part of a building do not include a reference to a garage occupied together with a dwelling. But see the tribunal decision in *Cottam* (VTD 20036) (TVC 15.158) where the tribunal allowed a claim for a refund under *VATA 1994, s 35* in relation to a two-storey outbuilding, the lower floor of which had been used as a garage.

[*VATA 1994, Sch 8 Group 5 Notes (7)(7A)(8)*].

For a building to be have been in '*use as a dwelling*' under (*a*)(i) above, HMRC state that the living accommodation need not have been self-contained or to modern standards. Buildings, therefore, that have been in use as a dwelling include

- public houses and shops where any private living accommodation for the landlord, owner, manager or staff is not self-contained – normally because part of the living accommodation, such as the kitchen, is contained within the commercial areas rather than the private areas;
- bed-sit accommodation; and
- crofts.

As a result, where these types of property are converted into a building '*designed as a dwelling or number of dwellings*' (see **42.5** above) or intended for use solely for a '*relevant residential purpose*', (see **42.16** below) then, unless the ten-year rule applies, the sale of, or long lease in, the property cannot be zero-rated under the provision in **43.1**(*c*) **LAND AND BUILDINGS: ZERO AND REDUCED RATE SUPPLIES AND DIY HOUSEBUILDERS** and the supply of conversion services to housing associations cannot be zero-rated under the provisions in **43.9 LAND AND BUILDINGS: ZERO AND REDUCED RATE SUPPLIES AND DIY HOUSEBUILDERS**.

The case law in this area has been confusing. In *Temple House Developments Ltd* (VTD 15583) (TVC 15.146) the tribunal held that living accommodation over a public house did not satisfy the test of 'designed as a dwelling' as the cooking and toilet facilities were shared with the public house below. In particular, it read (*a*)(i) above in terms of the test for dwellings in *VATA 1994, Sch 8 Group 5, Note (2)* which requires that a dwelling consists of self-contained living accommodation (see **42.5** above). In *Look Ahead Housing Association* (VTD 16816) (TVC 15.256) the tribunal similarly held that bedsits were non-residential. Although it concluded that (*a*) above should *not* be read in terms of *Note (2)*, it followed the tribunal decision in *University of Bath* (VTD 14235) (TVC 15.88). To be a dwelling in the ordinary sense, each of the bedsits would have to have contained within it all the major activities of life, particularly sleeping, cooking and feeding, and toilet facilities. As they had shared bathroom and kitchen facilities, they were not 'dwellings' and qualified as 'non-residential'.

However, in *Calam Vale Ltd* (VTD 16869) (TVC 15.172) the tribunal, although following *Look Ahead Housing Association* in concluding that (*a*) above should *not* be read in terms of *Note (2)*, decided that living accommodation which had shared a kitchen with a downstairs public house was, in common usage of the term, a dwelling because the landlord and his family had lived there. Subsequently, in *Amicus Group Ltd* (VTD 17693) (TVC 15.274) where a housing association converted two properties from bedsits into self-contained flats, the tribunal specifically disapproved of the decision in *Look Ahead Housing Association*. Applying the *dicta* of Lord Irvine in *Uratemp Ventures Ltd v Collins*, HL, [2002] 1 All ER 46 (TVC 15.275) (a non-VAT case) a 'dwelling' should be interpreted as 'a place where one lives, regarding and treating it as a home'. It was no less a person's home because he did not cook there. Therefore, the bedsit accommodation had qualified as 'dwellings' and did not qualify as 'non-residential'. These later cases are more in line with HMRC's views. See also *Agudas Israel Housing Association Ltd* (VTD 18798) (TVC 15.44) where, again applying *Uratemp Ventures* above, the tribunal held that premises with their own front door, en suite bathing facilities and the ability to cook with a microwave cooker and a kettle were self-contained living accommodation.

See also *C & E Commrs v Lady Blom-Cooper*, CA [2003] STC 669 (TVC 15.171) where a claim for refund under the D-I-Y builders scheme was made for work on converting a former public house into a single family dwelling. HMRC rejected the claim on the basis that the first and second floors had previously been used by the publican as residential accommodation, so that it was not a 'non-residential building' as defined above and the work was therefore not a residential conversion as defined by *VATA 1994, s 35(1D)*. The CA upheld HMRC's rejection of the claim, holding that the effect of *VATA 1994, Sch 8, Group 5, Note 9* (conversion of a non-residential part of a building which already contains a residential part is not zero-rated unless the result of the conversion is to create an *additional* dwelling or dwellings) was that no refund was due. *VATA 1994, s 35(4)* plainly required that that same restricted meaning also applied for the purposes of *VATA 1994, s 35(1D)*.

In *Alexandra Countryside Investments Ltd v HMRC* [2013] UKFTT 348 (TC) (TC02751) (TVC 15.156) the tribunal considered the company's appeal against a decision by HMRC not to allow its claim for input tax on the cost of converting a public house into two semi-detached houses. HMRC had rejected the claim on the basis that parts of what had previously been the manager's flat had been incorporated into both of the semi-detached houses. Declining to follow the decision in *Calam Vale Ltd* (VTD 16869) (TVC 15.172), referred to above, the tribunal allowed the company's appeal. In *DM & DD Macpherson* [2015] UKFTT 626 (TC) (TC04756), a First-tier Tribunal judge disagreed with the *Alexandra Countryside* decision and applied HMRC's preferred treatment in line with *Calam Vale*; however, shortly afterwards a different judge came to the opposite conclusion in *Languard New*

Homes Ltd [2016] UKFTT 129 (TC) (TC04917), disagreeing with the decision in *Macpherson* and *Calam Vale* and setting out an analysis of the law to support her decision. HMRC's response is awaited; at present the correct treatment is uncertain.

Unoccupied for ten years

It is the responsibility of the developer, contractor or D-I-Y converter (as the case may be) to hold evidence that, on balance, the property has not been lived in for the relevant ten-year period under (*b*) above. Evidence can include electoral roll and council tax data, information from utilities companies, evidence from empty property officers in local authorities, or information from other reliable sources. If a developer, etc. holds a letter from an empty property officer certifying that a property has not been lived in for ten years, no other evidence is needed. If an empty property officer is unsure about when a property was last lived in, he should write with his best estimate and HMRC may then call for other supporting evidence.

When considering when a dwelling was last lived in, any

- illegal occupation by squatters;
- occupation by 'guardians' (i.e. persons installed by the owner to deter squatters and vandals); and
- use that is not residential in nature, such as storage for a business

can be ignored.

If the dwelling has been lived in on an occasional basis (e.g. because it was a second home) in the ten-year period, it does not qualify as 'non-residential'.

(VAT Notice 708, paras 5.3, 6.3).

Person constructing a building

[42.12] A person is a 'person constructing' a building if, in relation to that building, he is, or has at any point in the past

- acted as a developer (i.e. physically constructed, or commissioned another person to physically construct, the building, in whole or in part, on land that he owns or has an interest in); or
- acted as a contractor or subcontractor (i.e. provided construction services to the developer or another contractor for the construction of the building, sub-contracting work as necessary).

More than one person can enjoy 'person constructing' status but such status is not always transferred when the property is transferred. Except in transfer of going concern (TOGC) circumstances each person must meet the conditions specified above. For example, where a developer takes over and finishes a partly completed building, both the first and second developer has 'person constructing' status because they have both been involved in physically constructing the building.

HMRC traditionally took the view that 'person constructing' status did not move to a person acquiring a completed building as part of a TOGC transaction. In July 2014 HMRC announced that they now accept that a person acquiring a completed residential or charitable development as part of a TOGC inherits 'person constructing' status and is capable of making a zero-rated first major interest grant in that building or part of it as long as:

(a) a zero-rated grant has not already been made of the completed building or relevant part by a previous owner – the grant giving rise to the TOGC should be ignored for this purpose;
(b) the person acquiring the building as a TOGC would suffer an unfair VAT disadvantage if its first major interest grants were treated as exempt; and
(c) the person acquiring the building as a TOGC would not obtain an unfair VAT advantage by being in a position to make zero-rated supplies.

HMRC refer to a developer restructuring its business in such a way that it transfers as a TOGC its entire property portfolio of newly constructed residential/charitable buildings to an associated company which will make first major interest grants as an example of a person acquiring the building as a TOGC suffering an unfair VAT disadvantage under (*b*) above. If the first major interest grants made by the transferee were treated as exempt, the transferee might become liable to repay input tax recovered by the original owner on development costs under the capital goods scheme or partial exemption claw back provisions and would incur input tax restrictions on selling fees that would not be suffered by businesses in similar circumstances.

HMRC refer to a person recovering input tax on a refurbishment of an existing building as an example of a person obtaining an unfair VAT advantage under (*c*) above.

The above principles also apply in respect of 'person converting' status for buildings converted from non-residential to residential use and 'person substantially reconstructing' status for substantially reconstructed buildings.

Businesses fitting the above criteria are entitled to claim retrospective effect of the policy change announced by HMRC in July 2014, subject to the normal four-year cap.

(HMRC Brief 27/14).

VAT groups

Although for VAT purposes, any business carried on by a member of a VAT group is treated as carried on by the representative member, when determining whether a supply can be zero-rated, 'person constructing' status is only considered from the perspective of the group member who, in reality, makes the supply (which may not be the representative member).

Examples

A VAT group includes a holding company as the representative member and a development company as a member. The development company constructs and sells houses to the public.

The development company has 'person constructing' status and so the sales can be zero-rated.

A VAT group includes a development company as representative member and an investment company as a member. The development company constructs a block of flats and sells it to the investment company, which in turn leases the flats to the public on long leases.

The investment company does not have 'person constructing' status. Even though the representative member does, the leases cannot be zero-rated and are exempt.

Beneficial interests

Where the beneficial owner of a property must register for VAT instead of the legal owner (see **42.20** below), the beneficial owner must have 'person constructing' status before the sale or long lease of the property can be zero-rated.

(VAT Notice 708, para 4.5).

In *C & E Commrs v Link Housing Association Ltd*, CS [1992] STC 718 (TVC 15.1), the court held that the phrase 'a person constructing' should be read as meaning 'a person who has constructed' and the original builder is therefore entitled to zero-rate his supply of a dwelling, however long after construction that might be. (In the case of *Link* the houses had been constructed before the introduction of VAT in 1973.) It held that the phrase is purely descriptive and designed only to ensure that it was the person who was constructing or had constructed the building who was entitled to zero-rating. HMRC have taken the narrow view that the decision applies only in relation to input tax on disposal costs. (Business Brief 15/92).

Protected building

[42.13] A protected building means any building which is

- a listed building (within the meaning of *Planning (Listed Buildings and Conservation Areas) Act 1990* or *Planning (Listed Buildings and Conservation Areas) (Scotland) Act 1997* or *Planning (Northern Ireland) Order 1991*), or
- a scheduled monument (within the meaning of *Ancient Monuments and Archaeological Areas Act 1979* or *Historic Monuments and Archaeological Objects (Northern Ireland) Order 1995*)

and which satisfies one of the following conditions.

(a) It is designed to remain as or become a dwelling or number of dwellings. This condition is satisfied where, in relation to each dwelling
  - the dwelling consists of self-contained living accommodation; and
  - there is no provision for direct internal access from the dwelling to any other dwelling or part of a dwelling; and
  - the separate use or disposal of the dwelling is not prohibited by the terms of any covenant, statutory planning consent or similar provision. An occupancy restriction is not a prohibition on separate use or disposal if all it does is restrict the occupancy of a building to a certain type of person, such as persons working

in agriculture or forestry, or persons over a specified age. But if the wording of the restriction prevents the building from being used separately from another building or from being sold, or otherwise disposed of, separately from another building then it is a prohibition on separate use or disposal. (VAT Notice 708, para 14.3).

In *Lunn* [2009] UKUT 244 (TCC) (TVC 55.10) the Upper Tribunal decided that planning permission specifying that the house 'shall only be used for purposes either incidental or ancillary to the residential use' of the main house did prohibit separate use.

Included is a garage (occupied together with the dwelling) either constructed at the same time as the building or, where the building has been substantially reconstructed, at the same time as that reconstruction. Following the decision in *Grange Builders (Quainton) Ltd* (VTD 18905) (TVC 55.6) HMRC accept that, provided a garage is in use as a garage before any alteration or reconstruction takes place and continues to be used as one afterwards, it is not necessary for the garage to have been constructed as a garage. It can also have been constructed as something different (e.g. as in this instance, as a barn). (Business Brief 11/05).

(b) It is intended for use solely for a '*relevant residential purpose*' or a '*relevant charitable purpose*' (see **42.16** and **42.14** below respectively) after the reconstruction or alteration.

[*VATA 1994, Sch 8 Group 6 Notes (1)* and *(2)*].

Listed buildings

A listed building is one included in a statutory list of buildings of special architectural or historic interest compiled by the Secretary of State for National Heritage in England and by the Secretaries of State for Scotland, Wales and Northern Ireland. In England and Wales there are three categories of listed building, Grade I, Grade II*, and Grade II. In Scotland the equivalent categories are Grade A, Grade B and Grade C(S). In Northern Ireland the equivalent categories are Grade A, Grade B+ and Grade B. Unlisted buildings in conservation areas, or buildings included in a local authority's non-statutory list of buildings of local interest, which used to be known as Grade III buildings, are not 'protected' buildings for VAT purposes.

Under *Planning (Listed Buildings and Conservation Areas) Act 1990, s 1(5)*, a listed building also includes

(i) any object or structure fixed to the building; and
(ii) any object or structure within the curtilage of the building which, although not fixed to the building, forms part of the land and has done so since before l July 1948 (the date listed building control began in its present form).

For VAT purposes, any approved alteration carried out to buildings within (ii) above could only be zero-rated (up to 30 September 2015 – see **43.10 LAND AND BUILDINGS: ZERO AND REDUCED RATE SUPPLIES AND DIY HOUSEBUILDERS**) if the building being altered falls within (*a*) or (*b*) above. It must therefore either be a qualifying garage (see (*a*) above) or an outbuilding, etc. which is itself designed to remain as or become a dwelling within (*a*) above or is intended solely for relevant residential or charitable purposes under (*b*) above. This view has been upheld in *C & E Commrs v Zielinski Baker & Partners Ltd*, HL [2004] STC 456 (TVC 55.7). In that case, the owners of a protected building arranged for the conversion of an outbuilding into changing rooms and a games room. Both the protected building and the outbuilding had been built in 1830 but the outbuilding, which was accepted as being within the curtilage of the protected building, had only been used for residential purposes for about twelve months in 1945. The court held that the outbuilding was not designed to remain as or become a dwelling house. As it was only the outbuilding, not the house, that was altered and it was the house, not the outbuilding, that had been listed, the outbuilding was not within the definition of a 'protected building' and the work on it failed to qualify for zero-rating.

(VAT Notice 708, para 9.3).

Relevant charitable purpose

[42.14] This means use by a charity in either or both of the following ways.

(a) *Otherwise than in the course or furtherance of a business*. It is essential that all or part of the building is used for non-business purposes. The term 'business' is a widely drawn concept. See **9 BUSINESS**. See also *Newtownbutler Playgroup Ltd* (VTD 13741) (TVC 15.119).
Activities that do not make a profit, or activities where any profit is only used to further the aims and objectives of the charity, can still be business activities.
Examples of buildings typically seen as non-business
- places of worship;
- offices used by charities for administering non-business activity, such as the collection of donations;
- school buildings where no fee is charged for the provision of education;
- research buildings where the research is grant-funded; and
- scout and guide huts that are used purely for scouting and guiding activities.

Examples of buildings typically seen as being used for business purposes
- buildings used by membership organisations where the organisation charges a membership fee;
- school buildings where a fee is charged for the provision of education;
- offices used by charities for administering business activities, such as fund-raising events where an entrance fee is charged; and
- village halls and similar buildings (but see (*b*) below).

The construction of a garage, within the curtilage of a church building, for cars used for pastoral work has been held to be for a relevant charitable purpose, any private use being *de minimis* and disregarded (*St Dunstan's Roman Catholic Church Southborough* (VTD 15472) (TVC 15.128)).

Interpretation of 'solely' for relevant charitable purpose

In HMRC's view, the term 'solely', as used in the phrase 'solely for a relevant residential or relevant charitable purpose', can incorporate an appropriate *de minimis* margin. In order to avoid unnecessary disputes in marginal cases, HMRC accept that this statutory condition is satisfied if the relevant use of the building is 95% or more.

For the purposes of determining whether a building is eligible for the zero rate or not, any method may be used to calculate the qualifying use of the building, so long as it is fair and reasonable, and prior approval from HMRC for the method is not required. If a building is zero-rated as a result of applying this interpretation, there will be a change of use charge if it ceases to be eligible within ten years of the buildings completion.

Under their interpretation, HRMC accept that, where the customer and supplier agree, the option to tax can be excluded on supplies of a building (or part of a building) that is to be used 95% or more for a relevant purpose where

- a building (other than used as an office) will be used by a charity solely for a relevant charitable purpose;
- a grant is made in a building designed solely for a relevant residential purpose;
- a grant in a building is made to a person who intends to use it solely for a relevant residential purpose. (HMRC Brief 33/10).

Previous concessionary treatment

Until 30 June 2009, and subject to transitional arrangements for the year to 30 June 2010, HMRC operated a concession whereby a charity could disregard 10% business use of a building and receive a supply of the whole building zero-rated. A charity that has taken the benefit of this concession is potentially exposed to a charge on a change of use in the ten years following the receipt of the supply. For details of the concession as it operated in the past, see *Tolley's Value Added Tax 2015–16, Second Edition.*

If, during the ten years following zero-rating, the qualifying charitable use of a building (or part) falls below the 90% concessionary limit, the charity is potentially liable to a deemed self-supply charge under the provisions in **43.2 LAND AND BUILDINGS: ZERO AND REDUCED RATE SUPPLIES AND DIY HOUSEBUILDERS** on the change of use. HMRC will not enforce this charge where there has been change of use that was not anticipated at the time that zero-rating was obtained under the concession. But if it is apparent that, at the time zero-rating was obtained, it was intended that non-qualifying use would exceed 10% within the ten-year adjustment period, HMRC will consider that the original supply should never have been zero-rated in the first place.

In *HMRC v Wakefield College* [2016] UKUT 19 (TCC) (TVC 15.131), HMRC refused to authorise the issue of a zero-rating certificate by a charitable college. The college appealed, arguing that it did not intend to use the building for business purposes. The case has been heard twice by the First-tier Tribunal and twice by the Upper Tribunal, and is now subject to appeal to the Court of Appeal. The latest decision is that too many of the students pay fees for their education for the college to qualify as not carrying on a business. Although education provided for a block grant is non-business, and students whose level of fees is dependent on their income or ability to pay are not counted as paying consideration for the supply, there were other students who paid the published fee for the course irrespective of their means. The fact that the fees might be lower than the cost of provision, because of grant subsidies, did not prevent those fees from being consideration, or the activity from being business. The Upper Tribunal held that zero-rating could not apply.

See also **13.4 CHARITIES** for further consideration of 'relevant charitable purpose'.

(b) *As a village hall or similarly in providing social or recreational facilities for a local community*. In the opinion of HMRC, in order to qualify, the building must have the following characteristics.

- There must be a high degree of local community involvement in the building's operation and activities. See *C & E Commrs v Jubilee Hall Recreation Centre Ltd*, CA 1998, [1999] STC 381 (TVC 55.15) in which a charity used premises to run a sports and fitness centre. The charity contended that work on a substantial refurbishment should be zero-rated on the basis that the building was intended for use solely for a 'relevant charitable purpose'. The CA rejected this contention. On the evidence, the use of the building was not 'similar to the use of a village hall in providing social or recreational facilities for a local community'. The relevant conditions were only satisfied 'where a local community is the final consumer in respect of the supply of the services . . . in the sense that the local community is the user of the services (through a body of trustees or a management committee acting on its behalf) and in which the only economic activity is one in which they participate directly'. *Jubilee Hall* was heard together with *C & E Commrs v St Dunstan's Educational Foundation*, CA 1998, [1999] STC 381 (TVC 15.135) in which a charity arranged for the construction of a sports hall, which was intended to be used by an independent fee-paying school, and to be made available for community use at specified times. The Court similarly held that the building was not intended for use 'in providing . . . recreational facilities for a local community', since the community use was secondary to the use by the school. Insofar as pupils at the school benefited from that facility, they did so not as members of the local community, but as pupils on whose behalf fees were paid to the school. See also *Ormiston Charitable Trust* (VTD 13187) (TVC 15.133).
- There is a wide variety of activities carried on in the building, the majority of which are for social and/or recreational purposes (including sport).

The users of the building need not be confined to the local community but can come from further afield.

Any part of the building which cannot be used for a variety of social or recreational activities cannot be seen as being used as a village hall.

The term 'similar' refers to buildings run by communities that are not villages but who are organised in a similar way to a village hall committee. It does not include buildings that provide a range of activities associated with village halls but who are not organised on these lines.

In order to be similar to a village hall, a charity would have trustees who are drawn from representatives of local groups who intend to use the hall. The trustees would therefore be made up of individuals from groups such as the Women's Institute, the Bridge Club, or the Amateur Dramatics Society. The building would be hired out to the local community for a modest fee for use by a range of local clubs and groups, and also for wedding receptions, birthday parties, playgroups and other leisure interests. Whilst, the size, and level of provision and facilities will be decided by the local community, HMRC at the very least expect the principal feature of a village hall to be a large multi-purpose hall where members of different households can meet to undertake shared activities.

The emphasis for a village hall should be on promoting the use of the facilities for the benefit of the whole community rather than for the benefit of one particular group. An important characteristic is that the building must be available for use by all sectors of the community. It must therefore be capable of meeting the social and recreational needs of the local community at large and not be predominantly confined to a special interest group. It should also be arranged on a first come first served basis and no single group should have priority over all the others.

On the other hand, a building designed for a particular sporting activity, for example, a cricket pavilion or football clubhouse and ancillary facilities is not seen as being similar to a village hall. Whilst these types of buildings are often made available to the wider community; this would be required to fit in around the sports club's usage. In essence it would be the sports club who would determine how the building was to be used and not the wider community.

Buildings that are seen as being similar to village halls when the relevant characteristics noted above are present include

- scout or guide huts (where they are not used purely for scouting and guiding activities);
- sports pavilions;
- church halls;
- community centres; and
- community sports centres.

Buildings that are not typically seen as being similar to village halls include

- community swimming pools;
- community theatres (but see *Ledbury Amateur Dramatic Society* (VTD 16845) (TVC 15.115) where a theatre was held to be used similarly to a village hall);
- membership clubs (although community associations charging a notional membership fee can be excluded); or
- community amateur sports clubs.

The following recent cases have considered the meaning and application of the rules on village halls: *New Deer Community Association v HMRC* [2015] UKUT 604 (TVC 15.118) and *Witney Town Bowls Club* [2015] UKFTT 421 (TC) (TC04598) (TVC 15.141). In addition, the Upper Tribunal has considered the definition in *HMRC v Caithness Rugby Football Club* [2016] UKUT 354 (TCC), [2016] STC 2028 (TVC 15.112). The First-tier Tribunal had been satisfied that a building could be used for purposes similar to a village hall even though it was constructed and managed by a rugby club for use as its pavilion on Saturdays during the season. The Upper Tribunal rejected HMRC's contention that a village hall had to be controlled and managed by the local community; the legislation referred to an intention of use, not to control, and the First-tier Tribunal had been entitled to come to the conclusion that it reached.
The First-tier Tribunal has also recently issued its decision in *Greenisland Football Club v HMRC* [2018] UKFTT 43 (TC) (TC06321) (TVC 15.112A) where it held that the construction of a new clubhouse that was used by the local community extensively for a wide range of activities, could be treated as the construction of a relevant charitable purpose building.

[*VATA 1994, Sch 8 Group 5 Note 6*]. (VAT Notice 708, para 14.7; VAT Information Sheet 8/09).

Relevant housing association

[42.15] A relevant housing association is

- a private registered provider of social housing;
- in Wales, a Welsh registered social landlord within the meaning of *Housing Act 1996, Part I*;
- in Scotland, a Scottish registered social landlord within the meaning of *Housing (Scotland) Act 2001 (asp 10)*; or
- in Northern Ireland, a Northern Irish registered housing association within the meaning of *Housing (Northern Ireland) Order 1992 (SI 1992/1725), Part II*.

Until the coming into force of a provision defining 'private registered provider of social housing', it means persons listed in the register of providers of social housing maintained under the *Housing and Regeneration Act 2008, Pt 2 Ch 3* who are not local authorities within the meaning of the *Housing Associations Act 1985*.

[*VATA 1994, Sch 8 Group 5 Note (21)*].

Relevant residential purpose

[42.16] Use for a relevant residential purpose means use as

- a home or other institution providing residential accommodation for children;

- a home or other institution providing residential accommodation with personal care for persons in need of such care by reason of old age, disablement, past or present dependence on alcohol or drugs or past or present mental disorder;
- a hospice;
- residential accommodation for students or school pupils;
- residential accommodation for members of any of the armed forces;
- a monastery, nunnery or similar establishment; or
- an institution which is the sole or main residence of at least 90% of its residents.

Excluded is use as a hospital, prison or similar institution or an hotel, inn or similar establishment.

Where a number of buildings are constructed at the same time and on the same site and are intended to be used together as a unit solely for a relevant residential purpose, each of those buildings (to the extent that they would not otherwise be so regarded) are to be treated as intended for use solely for a relevant residential purpose.

[*VATA 1994, Sch 8 Group 5 Notes (4) and (5)*].

'*Home*' and '*institution*': to determine if a building (or group of buildings) is used as a home or institution, all relevant factors need to be considered including

- the use to which the building is put;
- whether the building is used in conjunction with other buildings nearby;
- whether there is common ownership, financial control, management or administration;
- how the use of the building is promoted in advertising, etc.; and
- how the use of the building is licensed by any controlling authority.

For example, a bedroom block constructed in the grounds of a registered care home cannot be zero-rated as the construction of a building intended for use solely for a relevant residential purpose because it is not, in itself, a home or institution but part of a larger home or institution.

A rehabilitation home for people who have suffered brain injuries has been held to be a 'home or other institution providing residential accommodation' rather than a 'hospital or similar institution' (*General Healthcare Group Ltd* (VTD 17129) (TVC 15.97)).

Self-contained flats constructed by a charity for occupation by elderly licensees, who were offered accommodation by the charity on the basis that they were persons who were 'in need' within the terms of its charitable objects, were held to be within the meaning of an 'institution' (*TGH (Construction) Ltd* [2014] UKFTT 1039 (TC) (TC04132) (TVC 15.102)).

'*Residential accommodation*' means lodging, sleeping or overnight accommodation and does not suggest the need for such accommodation to be for any fixed or minimum period. See *Urdd Gobaith Cymru* (VTD 14881) (TVC 15.94). For example, accommodation for students attending a residential training course is residential accommodation. A building containing living accommodation is not residential accommodation unless the building contains sleeping accommodation. For example, if the only living accommodation in a building is a dining hall then that is not residential accommodation. But a dining hall constructed at the same time as another building (or buildings) containing sleeping accommodation with the intention that they are to be used together to provide living accommodation, is residential accommodation. If a building contains both bedrooms and a dining hall then both parts are residential accommodation. The dining hall must be used exclusively by those persons using the sleeping accommodation in that building. Use by persons sleeping in other buildings prevents the dining hall from being residential accommodation unless all the buildings involved were constructed together and were intended to be used collectively as living accommodation.

HMRC accept that there may be instances where a building could qualify for zero-rating as a dwelling (see **42.5** above) and qualify for zero-rating as a relevant residential purpose building. In such cases a taxpayer can rely on either provision to achieve zero-rating. (HMRC VAT Information Sheet 2/14).

(VAT Notice 708, para 14.6).

De Voil Indirect Tax Service. See V4.232–V4.232H.

Exempt supplies

[42.17] See **19.24**(*k*) and (*l*) **EUROPEAN UNION LEGISLATION** for the provisions of *Directive 2006/112/EC.*

The 'grant' of any

- 'interest in or right over' land,
- 'licence to occupy' land, or
- in relation to Scotland, any 'personal right' to call for or be granted any such interest or right (see below)

is, subject to certain exceptions, an exempt supply. [*VATA 1994, Sch 9 Group 1*].

See **42.6** above for the meaning of '*grant*', **42.8** above for '*interest in or right over*' and **42.9** above for '*licence to occupy*'.

'*Land*' includes buildings, civil engineering works, walls, trees, plants and other structures and natural objects in, under or over it as long as they remain attached to it. (VAT Notice 742, para 2.1). Where fixtures are included with a building or land, they are not treated as supplies for VAT purposes and their liability is the same as that for the land or buildings with which they are being supplied. (VAT Notice 742, para 7.9).

A '*personal right*' in Scotland is right enforceable only against a specific person or limited class of persons, e.g. a contractual right. The disadvantage of personal rights is that, if the person against whom the right is enforceable becomes insolvent, the right is likely to be worthless in practice. (VAT Notice 742/3/11).

Under *Directive 2006/112/EC, Art 135(1)(k)* countries must exempt the supply of land which has not been built upon other than '*building land*' i.e. any unimproved or improved land defined as such by the individual country. In *Norbury Developments Ltd v C & E Commrs, ECJ Case C–136/97*, [1999] STC 511 (TVC 22.587) the tribunal held that building land should therefore be taxable rather than exempt unless the exemption was authorised by the *6th VAT Directive, Art 28(3)(b)* (which allows countries to continue to exempt certain supplies, including building land, for a transitional period). The tribunal referred the case to the CJEU which held that the UK was entitled to exempt the supply under *Art 28(3)(b)*.

Anti-avoidance provisions

Where any grant of a fee simple (freehold) is exempt under the above provisions (and not standard-rated under the provisions in **42.18** below), those standard-rating provisions do not prevent the exemption of a supply arising from the prior exempt grant. This is designed to block avoidance schemes involving the sale of vacant land and the subsequent construction of a commercial building. [*VATA 1994, s 96(10B)*].

Exceptions include

- the first grant of a major interest in a 'qualifying building' i.e.
  - (i) a dwelling or building intended for use for a relevant residential or charitable purpose,
  - (ii) a dwelling converted from a non-residential building, or
  - (iii) a substantially reconstructed protected building

  by the person constructing, converting or, as the case may be, reconstructing it (which is zero-rated, see **43.1** and **43.3 LAND AND BUILDINGS: ZERO AND REDUCED RATE SUPPLIES AND DIY HOUSEBUILDERS**);
- the sale of the freehold interest in a new or uncompleted non-qualifying building or civil engineering work (which is standard-rated, see **42.18**(*a*) below);
- supplies falling within one of the categories in **42.18**(*b*)–(*l*) below which are specifically excluded from exemption and standard-rated;
- any supply which would otherwise be exempt but in respect of which an election to waive exemption ('option to tax') has been exercised (see **42.23** below); and
- certain supplies which form part of the transfer of a business as a going concern (which are outside the scope of VAT, see **9.9 BUSINESS**).

> ***Example***
>
> In the case of a building being converted from offices into flats, the subsequent sale of the flats would be zero-rated as the grant of a major interest in a qualifying building. However, the sale of two flats that had been converted from a detached house would be exempt from VAT rather than zero-rated. This is an important distinction in terms of input tax recovery on related costs.

Options to purchase/sell or lease land

The grant of a right to purchase an interest in land or buildings within a specified time (a 'call option') is a supply of an interest in land. The liability of the supply is whatever the liability of the land or building would be if supplied at that time (see **42.18**(*k*) below).

The grant of a right to require someone to purchase an interest in land or buildings within a specified time (a 'put' option) is not a supply of an interest in land and is generally standard-rated.

(VAT Notice 742, para 7.4).

'Virtual assignments'

In *Abbey National plc v C & E Commrs (and cross-appeal) (No 4)*, CA [2006] STC 1961 (TVC 6.62) a bank outsourced its property holdings, including its lease interests, to an unconnected company (M) for a lump sum. The bank was unable legally to assign some short leases to M as the landlord's permission had not, or could not, be obtained. In the absence of such permission, the bank entered into an agreement whereby it assigned to M the 'economic benefits and burdens' of the leases. The intention was to leave M in the same economic position as though the leases had been legally assigned to it, so that it could then grant purported leases of those properties back to Abbey. The bank remained in occupation of the premises, and paid a fee to M which was similar to the rent which would have been charged under a formal leaseback. This was referred to as a 'virtual assignment'.

HMRC took the view that M was making a standard-rated supply of agency and property management services to the bank. The Court agreed with this view. As M had acquired no right of occupation (and thus could not retransfer such a right), the supply made by M to the bank under the contractual arrangements was not a supply of leasing or letting within the meaning of what is now *Directive 2006/112/EC, Art 135(1)(l)* and thus not exempt from VAT.

A secondary issue in the case (which did not go to the Court of Appeal) was the VAT treatment of those leases that the bank had virtually assigned to M and where the property was occupied by the bank's sub-tenants. The Court held that the agreement between the bank and M incorporated a clear and unambiguous declaration of trust, whereby the rents paid by the sub-tenants accrued in full for the benefit of M. There was a deemed supply under what is now *VATA 1994, Sch 10 para 40* by M to the sub-tenants as the consideration for the sub-leases granted by the bank accrued to M, despite M not having a legal interest in the property. The deemed supply was exempt unless the option to tax had been exercised.

Serviced building plots

Following the decision in *D & S Virtue (t/a Lammermuir Game Services)* (VTD 20259) (TVC 41.22), HMRC accept that the supply of a serviced building plot of land (i.e. bare land in respect of which civil engineering works have been carried out to provide access to essential services such as gas, electricity, water, drainage and sewerage) is a single exempt supply of land by the landowner. *Previously*, HMRC had treated the supply of a services building plot by the landowner as a mixed supply of exempt land and standard-rated civil engineering work. (HMRC Brief 64/07).

De Voil Indirect Tax Service. See V4.111; V4.112.

Standard-rated supplies

[42.18] The supplies of within *(a)–(l)* below are excluded from the general VAT exemption for land under **42.17** above and are standard-rated.

(a) New and uncompleted non-qualifying buildings and civil engineering works

The 'grant' or assignment of the fee simple (freehold interest) in

- a building which has not been 'completed' and which is not a '*qualifying building*' (i.e. is neither designed as a 'dwelling' or number of dwellings nor intended for use for solely a 'relevant residential purpose' or a 'relevant charitable purpose'),
- a 'new' building which is not to be used as a qualifying building after the grant,
- a civil engineering work which has not been completed, or
- a new civil engineering work

is standard-rated. (Supplies of qualifying buildings are exempt unless zero-rated under the provisions in **43.1** or **43.3** **LAND AND BUILDINGS: ZERO AND REDUCED RATE SUPPLIES AND DIY HOUSEBUILDERS.**)

A building/civil engineering work is to be taken as '*completed*' when an architect/engineer issues a certificate of practical completion in relation to it or it is fully occupied/used, whichever happens first. It is to be taken as '*new*' if it was completed less than three years before the grant.

See **42.6** above for the meaning of '*grant*', **42.16** above for '*relevant residential purpose*' and **42.14** above for '*relevant charitable purpose*'.

Issue of certificates

A grant or assignment cannot be taken as relating to a building (or part) intended for use solely for a relevant residential or charitable purpose as above unless

- it is made to a person who intends to use the building (or part) for such a purpose; and
- before it is made, that person has given the grantor a certificate stating that the grant relates to such a building.

See **43.22** **LAND AND BUILDINGS: ZERO AND REDUCED RATE SUPPLIES AND DIY HOUSEBUILDERS** for further details on the issue and form of certificates.

Part-qualifying buildings

Where part of a building is designed as a dwelling or number of dwellings or intended for relevant use as above and part is not (e.g. shop premises with a flat over them) an apportionment is necessary if the grant does not relate exclusively to one part or the other.

[*VATA 1994, Sch 9 Group 1 Item 1(a) and Notes 1 to 6*].

Anti-avoidance provisions

- Where any grant is standard-rated under these provisions, any subsequent supply arising from that grant is also standard-rated. This is designed to block avoidance schemes that deliberately made the price uncertain in order to take advantage of the provisions of *SI 1995/2518, Reg 84(2)* allowing VAT to be declared when the payment is received rather than at the date of sale. See **67.13 SUPPLY: TIME OF SUPPLY**.
- Where any grant of a fee simple (freehold) is exempt under **42.17** above (and not standard-rated under these provisions), these provisions do not prevent the exemption of a supply arising from the prior exempt grant. This is designed to block avoidance schemes involving the sale of vacant land and the subsequent construction of a commercial building.

[*VATA 1994, s 96(10B)*].

Options, etc. to purchase

See (*k*) below.

Supplies of land and civil engineering work

Where the freehold interest in bare land is sold but that land is ancillary to new or part completed civil engineering works (e.g. an airfield or oil refinery) there is a single standard-rated supply.

See **42.17** above for the sale of serviced building plots of land.

(b) Gaming and fishing rights

The 'grant' of any interest, right or licence to take game or fish is standard-rated unless, at the time of the grant, the grantor grants to the grantee the fee simple of the land over which the right to take game or fish is exercisable. Where a grant of an interest in or right over land or a licence to occupy land includes a valuable right to take game or fish, an apportionment must be made to determine the exempt and standard-rated parts. [*VATA 1994, Sch 9 Group 1 Item 1(c)* and *Note 8*]. See **58.10 RECREATION AND SPORT** for further details.

Options, etc. to purchase

See (*k*) below.

(c) Hotel accommodation

The provision in a hotel, inn, boarding house or 'similar establishment' of sleeping accommodation or of accommodation in rooms which are provided in conjunction with sleeping accommodation or for the purposes of a supply of catering is standard-rated. '*Similar establishment*' includes premises in which there is provided furnished sleeping accommodation, whether with or without the provision of board or facilities for the preparation of food, which are used by, or held out as being suitable for use by, visitors or travellers. [*VATA 1994, Sch 9 Group 1 Item 1(d)* and *Note 9*].

Where guests stay for a continuous period of four weeks or more, VAT is chargeable on a reduced value from the 29th day.

See **33.1** to **33.4** **HOTELS AND HOLIDAY ACCOMMODATION** for further details.

Options, etc. to purchase

See (*k*) below.

(d) Holiday accommodation

The grant of any interest in or right over or licence to occupy holiday accommodation (including any accommodation in a building, hut, chalet, caravan, houseboat or tent which is advertised or held out as holiday accommodation or as suitable for holiday or leisure use) is standard-rated. *Excluded* is the grant of the fee simple, or a lease, etc. for a premium, in a building which is not a 'new building'. [*VATA 1994, Sch 9 Group 1 Item 1(e)* and *Notes 12* and *13*]. See **33.5** to **33.9** **HOTELS AND HOLIDAY ACCOMMODATION** for further details.

Options, etc. to purchase

See (*k*) below.

(e) Caravan and tent pitches and camping facilities

The provision of 'seasonal pitches' for caravans, and the grant or assignment of facilities at caravan parks to persons for whom such pitches are provided, are standard-rated. The provision of pitches for tents or of camping facilities is also standard-rated.

A 'seasonal pitch' is

- a pitch on a holiday site other than an employee pitch; or
- a non-residential pitch on any other site.

'Employee pitch' means a pitch occupied by an employee of the site operator as that person's principal place of residence during the period of occupancy. 'Holiday site' means a site or part of a site which is operated as a holiday or leisure site. 'Non-residential pitch' means a pitch which is provided

- for less than a year; or
- for a year or more and is subject to an occupation restriction,

and which is not intended to be used as the occupant's principal place of residence during the period of occupancy. 'Occupation restriction' means any covenant, statutory planning consent or similar permission, the terms of which prevent the person to whom the pitch is provided from occupying it by living in a caravan at all times throughout the period for which the pitch is provided.

[*VATA 1994, Sch 9 Group 1 Items 1(f)(g)* and *Notes 14, 14A*].

In *HMRC v Tallington Lakes Ltd*, Ch D [2007] STI 2018 (TVC 41.146) licence agreements for caravans provided that, in accordance with relevant planning permission, they could not be occupied during February of each year. However, the company had ceased to enforce this restriction. The court held that the effect of the *Town and Country Planning Act 1990, s 171B(3)* was that the local authority had retained the right to enforce the original planning permission which prevented occupation during February. The fact that Tallington had allowed some owners to breach that condition did not prevent the definition of 'seasonal pitch' above from applying. Accordingly, the receipts did not qualify for exemption.

Following the tribunal decision in *Ashworth (Mrs B)* (VTD 12924) (TVC 41.139), HMRC accept that a pitch is only regarded as seasonal under (ii) above if it is on a site, or part of a site, which is advertised or held out for holiday use. (VAT Notice 701/20/13, para 4.1).

The effect of the above is that exemption applies to the provision of pitches

- on permanent residential sites where caravans can be lived in at all times throughout the year;
- on sites for travellers where the caravans are used as principal private residences;
- for restricted occupancy periods provided
  - (i) the site is not advertised or held out for holiday/leisure use; and
  - (ii) the pitch is intended to be used as the occupant's principal private residence;
- any type of site (including holiday/leisure sites) if the pitch is occupied by a warden or other employee of the site operator as his principal private residence.

(VAT Notice 701/20/13, para 4.1).

The supply of rented accommodation in any caravan or mobile home is exempt unless the accommodation is holiday accommodation which is always standard-rated under (*d*) above.

See also **43.26 LAND AND BUILDINGS: ZERO AND REDUCED RATE SUPPLIES AND DIY HOUSEBUILDERS** for caravans generally.

Options, etc. to purchase

See (*k*) below.

(f) Parking facilities

The grant or assignment of facilities for parking a vehicle is standard-rated. [*VATA 1994, Sch 9 Group 1 Item 1(h)*].

There is normally a standard-rated supply of parking facilities if a grant of the right to use facilities is made and the facilities are designed for, or provided specifically for the purpose of, parking vehicles.

Standard-rated supplies

Standard-rated supplies include the following.

- The letting or licensing of garages (even if the facilities are not used for storing a vehicle, unless the lease or licence specifically prohibits parking) or designated parking bays or spaces. See *C & E Commrs v*

Trinity Factoring Services Ltd, CS [1994] STC 504 (TVC 41.155) where the court held that the lease of a lock-up garage was standard-rated even though the lessor and lessee had agreed in advance that the garage would be used for the storage of goods. *Prima facie* facilities had been granted for parking a vehicle and the terms of the lease did not preclude such usage.

- The provision of rights to park vehicles (and accompanying trailers) in, for example, car parks and commercial garages.
- The letting or licensing of land specifically for the construction of a garage or for use solely for the parking of a vehicle.
- The letting or licensing of a purpose-built car park (e.g. to a car park operator).
- The letting of taxi ranks.
- The provision of storage for bicycles.
- The provision of storage (or parking) for touring caravans.
- The freehold sale of a 'new' or partly completed garage, car park or car parking facilities other than in conjunction with the sale of a new dwelling. A garage or car park is 'new' for three years following the date on which it was completed (see (*a*) above). (The sale of a garage or parking space together with a new dwelling by the person constructing it is normally zero-rated under the provisions in **43.1 LAND AND BUILDINGS: ZERO AND REDUCED RATE SUPPLIES AND DIY HOUSEBUILDERS** unless the dwelling is standard-rated holiday accommodation under (*d*) above.)

Exempt supplies

The following supplies are not regarded by HMRC as supplies of parking facilities and are therefore exempt under the general provisions in **42.17** above (subject to the exercise of an option to tax under **42.23** below).

(i) The letting of land or buildings (other than garages, designated parking bays or other facilities specifically designed for parking) where the conveyance or contract makes no specific reference to use for parking vehicles.

(ii) The letting of land or buildings where any reference to parking a vehicle is incidental to the main use.

(iii) The letting of land or buildings to a motor dealer for storing stock-in-trade.

(iv) The letting of land or buildings to a vehicle transportation firm, a vehicle distributor or a vehicle auctioneer for business use.

(v) The letting of land (including land used at other times as a car park) for purposes such as a market or car boot sale.

(vi) The letting of land for the exhibition of vehicles.

(vii) The letting of land to a travelling fair or circus (and the incidental parking of vehicles).

(viii) The freehold sale of garages, car parks or parking facilities which are not 'new' (more than three years have elapsed from the date they were completed (see (*a*) above)).

(VAT Notice 742, paras 4.2, 4.3).

Dwellings and commercial premises

The following list explains the correct VAT treatment where supplies of parking facilities relate to dwellings or commercial premises.

(i) If there is a zero-rated sale or long lease of a building designed as a dwelling or number of dwellings and a garage or other parking facility is supplied to the purchaser of the dwelling, this can be zero-rated if it is reasonably close to the dwelling and it is intended to be used in conjunction with the dwelling. Garages are also treated as part of a zero-rated dwelling if constructed at the same time (or converted from a non-residential building at the same time) and intended to be occupied with the dwelling. However, zero-rating can only apply to the extent that the consideration is in the form of a premium or first payment of rent for the sale or long lease of the dwelling and parking.

(ii) For parking supplied after the zero-rated sale or long lease of a new dwelling, the first sale or long lease of a garage or other parking facility is zero-rated if it is within the 'site' of the dwelling and the grant is made by the same person that constructed the dwelling, e.g. a developer sells a long lease of a flat to an individual who decides several months later to purchase a long lease in a parking space within the site of the block of flats from the same developer. In the case of a long lease, zero-rating only applies to the extent that consideration is in the form of a premium or first rental payment for the parking space.

(iii) The VAT treatment of the letting of parking facilities to owners of dwellings depends on the arrangements. However, the following general principles apply.

   (1) Where the freehold of a dwelling has been purchased and a licence or letting agreement for parking facilities is granted at a later date under a separate contract or agreement, supplies under the licence agreement are standard-rated. This is because there are no periodic supplies of domestic accommodation with which to associate the supplies of parking facilities.

   (2) Where a leasehold of a dwelling has been purchased in return for a premium and the use of parking facilities are granted at a later date under a separate contract or agreement, the supplies of the parking facilities are normally standard-rated. However, the supplies may be exempt where (3) below applies (see also above where the parking is subject to a separate major interest grant).

   (3) Where the dwelling has been purchased under an agreement which either

   - includes the provision of parking facilities (even though these are only to be made available at a later date); or
   - includes an obligation on the tenant to accept a later grant of parking facilities (where they become available),

   in return for a periodic rent or licence fee payable to the same landlord, the supplies of the parking facilities are exempt as long as

   - the garage or parking facility is reasonably close to the dwelling; and
   - it is intended to be used in conjunction with the dwelling.

The above does not apply to the provision of parking in conjunction with holiday accommodation. This is normally standard-rated.

(iv) The letting of garages or parking spaces in conjunction with the letting of dwellings for permanent residential use (under shorthold tenancy agreements or similar) is exempt providing that

- the garage or parking space is reasonably near to the dwelling; and
- the tenant takes up both the lease of the dwelling and the lease of the garage or parking space from the same landlord.

In some cases the dwelling and parking facilities can be the subject of separate letting agreements entered into at separate times. This can occur, for example, where an existing tenant agrees to rent a garage. In such circumstances the supplies of the dwelling and parking facilities can still be treated as single exempt supplies of domestic accommodation as long as

- there are periodic rental payments (supplies) being made in respect of the dwelling to which the parking supplies can be associated; and
- the two conditions in the bullet points above are met.

The position above contrasts with that applicable where leases have been purchased in return for premiums and periodic rents are not payable. It also applies to shared ownership properties as long as the purchaser continues to pay rent for the remaining share in the property. Where parking facilities are supplied in conjunction with holiday accommodation the supply is normally standard-rated.

(v) For commercial premises, the same general principles set out in paragraphs (iii) and (iv) apply. If a lease is granted in commercial premises under an agreement that includes the provision of parking facilities, this is treated as a single supply (the parking has the same VAT liability as the commercial premises) provided that

- the parking is within or on the premises, reasonably close, or within a complex (e.g. an industrial park made up of separate units with a 'communal' car park for the use of tenants of the units and their visitors); and
- it is intended to be used in conjunction with the commercial premises.

The same treatment applies where the agreement for the lease of the premises includes an obligation on the tenant to accept a later grant of parking facilities if or when they become available. This means that if the rents from the commercial premises are exempt from VAT, the parking facilities will also be exempt. In other circumstances the provision of parking facilities in conjunction with the letting of commercial property will normally be a separate standard-rated supply. Where the agreements allow the actual number of parking spaces to be varied from year to year this will not normally affect the position of the parking facilities as part of a single supply of the commercial premises.

See *Skatteministeriet v Henriksen, ECJ Case 173/88*, [1990] STC 768 (TVC 22.371) and *Civilscent Ltd* (TC00070) (TVC 41.150).

(VAT Notice 742, paras 4.4, 4.5).

Excess charges

Where a car park operator makes an offer of parking under clear terms and conditions, setting punitive fines for their breach, the fines constitute penalties for breaching the contract, rather than additional consideration for using the facilities. Consequently they are outside the scope of VAT. However, where the terms and conditions make it clear that the driver can continue to use the facilities after a set period upon payment of a further amount without being in breach of the contract then the payment is consideration for use of the facilities and subject to VAT.

(HMRC Brief 57/08).

In *Vehicle Control Services Ltd v HMRC*, CA [2013] EWCA Civ 186 (TVC 62.223) the Court of Appeal held that where a company (V) imposed an additional parking charge instead of towing away a vehicle, that charge represented damages for trespass which was outside the scope of VAT.

Local authorities

See **44.4** LOCAL AUTHORITIES AND PUBLIC BODIES.

Caravans and houseboats

See **43.26** and **43.27** LAND AND BUILDINGS: ZERO AND REDUCED RATE SUPPLIES AND DIY HOUSEBUILDERS for parking facilities for caravans and houseboats.

Options, etc. to purchase

See (*k*) below.

(g) Timber rights

The grant or assignment of any right to fell and remove standing timber is standard-rated. [*VATA 1994, Sch 9 Group 1 Item 1(j)*].

The grant must be separate and specific. If land is sold which happens to contain standing timber which the buyer will be able to fell, the whole supply is exempt with the option to tax under **42.23** below. (VAT Notice 742, para 3.1).

Options, etc. to purchase

See (*k*) below.

(h) Storage, mooring of aircraft, ships, etc.

The grant or assignment of facilities for housing, or storage of, an aircraft or for 'mooring', or storage of, a ship, boat or other vessel is standard-rated. '*Mooring*' includes anchoring or berthing. [*VATA 1994, Sch 9 Group 1 Item 1(k) and Note 15*].

Included is both the letting of water-based mooring berths for pleasure boats and land sites for storage of boats on port land. (*Fonden Marselisborg Lystbådehavn v Skatteministeriet, ECJ Case C-428/02* [2006] STC 1467 (TVC 22.363)).

Even if a person is merely granted permission to lay down his own mooring and owns the ground tackle, the grant is considered to be excluded from exemption and is standard-rated whether or not there is a formal lease or licence. (C & E Press Notice 355, 25 June 1975). See also *J W Fisher* (VTD 179) (TVC 41.155) and *Strand Ship Building Co Ltd* (VTD 1651) (TVC 41.162).

See, however, **71.9 TRANSPORT AND FREIGHT** for facilities zero-rated when supplied in ports or customs airports and **43.27 LAND AND BUILDINGS: ZERO AND REDUCED RATE SUPPLIES AND DIY HOUSEBUILDERS** for exempt mooring of qualifying houseboats.

Options, etc. to purchase

See (*k*) below.

(i) Boxes, seats, etc.

The grant or assignment of any right to occupy a box, seat or other accommodation at a sports ground, theatre, concert hall or other place of entertainment is standard-rated. [*VATA 1994, Sch 9 Group 1 Item 1(l)*]. Included is any kind of accommodation which is intended for use by individuals or groups for viewing a match, race, show or other form of entertainment, regardless of whether the entertainment is actually in progress when the accommodation is used. (VAT Notice 742, para 3.4).

Options, etc. to purchase

See (*k*) below.

(j) Sports facilities

The grant or assignment of facilities for playing any sport or participating in any physical recreation is standard-rated. [*VATA 1994, Sch 9 Group 1 Item 1(m)*].

Exemption is, however, retained where the facilities are to be used for more than 24 hours or, provided certain conditions are met, a series of at least ten shorter periods. See **58.4 RECREATION AND SPORT**. See also **58.5 RECREATION AND SPORT** for certain sporting services provided by non-profit making bodies.

(k) Options, etc. to purchase interests or rights within (*a*) to (*j*) above

The grant of any right, including

- an equitable right,
- a right under an option or right of pre-emption, or
- in relation to land in Scotland, a 'personal right',

to call for or to be granted an interest or right which would fall to be standard-rated under (*a*) to (*j*) above is also standard-rated.

A 'personal right' in Scotland is right enforceable only against a specific person or limited class of persons, e.g. a contractual right. The disadvantage of personal rights is that, if the person against whom the right is enforceable becomes insolvent, the right is likely to be worthless in practice. (VAT Notice 742/3/11).

[*VATA 1994, Sch 9 Group 1 Item 1(n)*].

(l) Self storage

From 1 October 2012 supplies of self storage (i.e. the allocation of a discrete area to the customer) no longer qualify for exemption, and are treated in line with supplies of other types of storage (such as those provided by traditional removal companies, where the customer is not provided with a discrete area and the supplier is able to move the customer's goods around within its premises).

To prevent businesses entering into avoidance arrangements, an anti-forestalling charge arose where a supply of the grant of facilities for the self storage of goods, or the grant of a right to receive such a supply was treated as taking place on or after 21 March 2012 but before 1 October 2012, and the supply was linked to the post-change period, i.e. the services were provided on or after 1 October 2012. The amount of the charge was the amount of VAT which would have been due on the supply had it been taxable at 20%. The charge was to be treated as if it were VAT, is the supplier's liability, and became due on 1 October 2012. But if the supplier ceased to be a taxable person before that date, he had to account for the charge in his final VAT return. Where the supply was not wholly linked to the post-change period, the charge was to be applied after the consideration for the supply had been apportioned on a just and reasonable basis. Where there was an anti-forestalling charge, the consideration for the supply was to be increased by the amount of the charge, unless the contract provided otherwise.

[*VATA 1994, Sch 9 Group 1 Item 1(ka)*].

(m) Hairdressing facilities

From 1 October 2012, the grant of facilities to a person who uses them wholly or mainly to supply hairdressing services is standard-rated.

[*VATA 1994, Sch 9 Group 1 Item 1(ma)*].

De Voil Indirect Tax Service. See V4.113.

Supplies between landlords and tenants

[42.19] Supplies between landlords and tenants are treated as follows:

(1) Lease payments

Inducements (reverse premiums) by landlords

Lease obligations, to which tenants are normally bound, do not constitute supplies for which inducement payments on entering leases are consideration. As a result, the majority of such inducements are likely to be outside the scope of VAT, being no more than inducements to tenants to take leases and to observe the obligations in them. There will be a taxable supply only where a payment is linked to benefits a tenant provides outside normal lease terms.

This effectively puts inducement payments on a similar VAT footing to rent free periods (see below) in being mainly outside the scope of VAT and only a taxable consideration where directly linked to a specific benefit supplied by a tenant to a landlord.

Examples of taxable benefits by tenants that may be supplied in return for such inducements are

- carrying out building works to improve the property by undertaking necessary repairs or upgrading the property (undertakings to use improved materials as part of continuous repairs under a tenant repairing lease would not constitute a taxable benefit to the landlord);
- carrying out fitting-out or refurbishment works which the landlord has responsibility for and is paying the tenant to undertake; and
- acting as anchor tenant (publicity indicating that Company X is to take a lease in a development does not, in itself, determine that the company is an anchor tenant).

(Business Brief 12/05).

Inducements (reverse premiums) from old tenant to new tenant

The provisions above do not apply in the situation where a tenant *assigns* his interest in a lease to another tenant and makes an inducement payment for him to take the assignment. In such circumstances, in accordance with the decision in *C & E Commrs v Cantor Fitzgerald International, ECJ Case C-108/99*, [2001] STC 1453 (TVC 22.373) any payment made is taxable. But where a tenant pays an inducement to another party to take a sub-lease from him, the provisions outlined in Business Brief 12/05 above will apply as the payment is effectively a landlord inducement.

Grant of a lease

The grant of a lease is, subject to certain exceptions, exempt from VAT. See **42.17** above.

Subsequent supplies under a lease

The granting of a lease usually gives rise to a number of further supplies at later times. For example, a supply is made each time that lease is surrendered or assigned. In such cases, the liability of each subsequent supply is determined at the time when that supply is made rather than by reference to the time of the original grant. [*VATA 1994, s 96(10A)*].

Variations of leases

Sometimes a lease is varied either to alter its terms (e.g. so that it can be used for different purposes), to extend the length of the tenancy or to alter the demised premises (e.g. by renting additional floor space). Under English land law, the effect of such a variation is that the old lease is deemed to be surrendered (see below) and a new lease granted in its place. Where there is no monetary consideration, no supply is seen as taking place if the variation merely extends the term and/or extends right of occupation to a larger part of the same building. (VAT Notice 742, para 10.5).

Surrender of lease

The grant of an 'interest in or right over' land or a 'licence to occupy' land includes a surrender of that interest, etc. [*VATA 1994, Sch 9 Group 1 and Note (1); SI 1995/282*].

The general provisions relating to grants in **42.17** above therefore also apply to surrenders, i.e. they are exempt subject to certain exceptions. Similarly, the assignment of any interest, etc. back to the lessor or licensor, by the lessee or licensee, is generally exempt. However, a surrender of an interest falling within the exclusions from exemption in **42.18** above remains standard-rated and where a tenant has, prior to the surrender, opted to tax the property in question under **42.23** below, the surrender is covered by the election and therefore taxable. (VAT Notice 742, para 10.3).

Reverse surrenders and assignments

Normally, when a lease is surrendered, consideration is paid by the landlord to the tenant. A '*reverse surrender*' occurs where a tenant surrenders an onerous lease to the landlord before the term of the lease has expired and pays the landlord to accept the surrender.

The grant of an interest in or right over land, or of any licence to occupy land, includes the supply made by the person to whom an interest is surrendered when there is a reverse surrender. [*VATA 1994, Sch 9 Group 1 and Notes (1) and (1A)*]. The general provisions relating to grants in **42.17** above therefore also apply to reverse surrenders, i.e. they are exempt subject to certain exceptions. Where the person making the supply (i.e. the landlord) has opted to tax the property, the supply is standard-rated. (VAT Notice 742, para 10.4).

Dilapidation payments

A lease may provide for the landlord to recover from a tenant, at or near the end of the lease, an amount to cover the cost of restoring the property to its original condition. Such dilapidation payments represent a claim for damages by the landlord against the tenant. The payment is not consideration for a supply for VAT purposes and is outside the scope of VAT. (VAT Notice 742, para 10.12).

Indemnity payments under lease agreements

In general any payment made by a prospective tenant to obtain the grant of a lease or licence, including any disbursement or indemnification of the costs incurred by the landlord, is part of the consideration for that grant.

Many leases provide that an existing tenant reimburses the landlord for legal or other advisory costs incurred by the landlord as a result of the tenant exercising rights already granted under the lease. For example, the tenant may be able to assign the lease, sublet or make alterations provided the tenant first obtains the landlord's consent. Such reimbursements by the tenant to the landlord are consideration for the principal supply of the lease.

If a tenant makes a payment to the landlord to obtain an *additional* right, it is consideration for the variation of the lease (see above).

(VAT Notice 742, para 10.8).

(2) Mesne profits

These are damages for the profits lost by a landlord by reason of wrongful occupation of his property and can only be recovered in respect of continued occupation of property after that right of occupation has expired. As such, an award of mesne profits is not consideration for a supply and is outside the scope of VAT. Where a landlord on the cash accounting system has opted to tax and, in addition to a claim for mesne profits, arrears of rent accrue, payment received following litigation should be treated firstly as relating to rent arrears and only then as relating to mesne profits to the extent that the total received exceeds the outstanding rents. (If the landlord is not on the cash accounting basis, the tax points for the periods in respect of which he is claiming rent arrears will have already been determined under the normal rules.) (Law Society's Gazette, 14 October 1992, p 16).

(3) Rental payments

Rent is the periodic payment made by a tenant to a landlord and is normally the subject of a written agreement. Rent payments can be non-monetary, and can include costs incurred by the landlord under the agreement which are recharged to the tenant. This may include items such as service charges and rates where the landlord is the rateable person.

Rental income is generally exempt from VAT although the landlord may opt to tax rents from non-domestic property (see **42.23** below).

Rent adjustments when buildings are sold or leases assigned

Rent adjustments between landlords on the sale of tenanted property and between tenants on the assignment of a lease are outside the scope of VAT. For VAT purposes the consideration for the sale of the building or the assignment of the lease is the full value of the supply before any rent adjustment is made. (VAT Notice 742, para 10.9).

Recovery of rent from a third party

There are three common ways in which a landlord can recover rent from a third party. Where such payments are received, the landlord should still address any related VAT invoice to the tenant to whom the premises have been leased or let. The supply is still to the tenant, not the third party.

(i) If a tenant sub-lets land or buildings to a third party and the tenant defaults on payment of rent to the landlord, the landlord can issue a notice under the *Law of Distress Amendment Act* and collect the rent arrears from the third party. In turn, the third party can reduce his rent payable to the tenant by the amount he has paid to the landlord. If this happens the supply chain remains the same. There is a supply of the land or building from the landlord to the tenant and from the tenant to the third party. If the landlord has opted to tax, any VAT invoice must be issued to the tenant.

(ii) A surety or guarantor is normally party to any agreement between the landlord and the tenant. If the tenant is unable to meet the agreed periodic rental payments to the landlord, the surety or guarantor will make the payments on the tenant's behalf. There is no supply by the landlord to the surety or guarantor who will not be able to recover any VAT paid.

(iii) Under common law, landlords have had the historic right to recover unpaid rent from former tenants (and their guarantors and sureties) as well as from current tenants, their guarantors and sureties. This right was regulated more tightly following the *Landlord and Tenant (Covenants) Act 1995* but the principle is the same, i.e. the supply is to the defaulting tenant and not to the former tenant or the guarantors or sureties of either. However, the *1995 Act* does permit a former tenant who settles the outstanding debt to apply for an intermediary lease.

(VAT Notice 742, para 7.5).

Rent-free periods

The grant by a landlord of a rent-free period is not a supply for VAT purposes except where the rent-free period is given in exchange for something which the tenant agrees to do (e.g. carry out works for the benefit of the landlord). (VAT Notice 742, para 10.2). See *Neville Russell* (VTD 2484) (TVC 62.131) where a rent-free period was held not to be consideration for a supply but compensation for the fact that the landlord had failed to finish the fitting out before occupation of the building by the tenant; and *Port Erin Hotels v The Isle of Man Treasury* (VTD 5045) (TVC 62.134) and *Ridgeons Bulk Ltd v C & E Commrs*, QB [1994] STC 427 (TVC 3.187) where waiver of rent was held to be consideration for building work carried out by the tenant and therefore subject to VAT.

Rent paid while premises unoccupied

In *Harper Collins Publishers Ltd* (VTD 12040) (TVC 46.56), the company, following reorganisation, moved out of two floors of its leased business premises but was unable to sublet immediately. The landlords in the meantime exercised the option to tax (see **42.23** below). The tribunal held that, although unoccupied, the two floors were still retained by the company for business purposes, the original purpose in taking the leases not having changed. Input tax suffered on the rents paid could be recovered (in this instance in part only by inclusion in the residual input tax on general overheads under the company's partial exemption computations).

(4) Restricted covenants

Restrictive covenants may be placed on land to control its use. The lifting of such a restricted covenant (e.g. to permit development which was previously forbidden) is exempt from VAT (unless the person receiving the payment has opted to tax or the supply of the land is itself excluded from exemption). (VAT Notice 742, para 10.6).

(5) Service charges, etc.

The VAT treatment of service charges and other payments relating to premises depends upon the nature of the property and the terms of the arrangements.

General services for tenants of leasehold non-domestic property provided by the landlord

Leases often stipulate that the landlord will provide, and the tenants pay for, the services required for the upkeep of the building as a whole. The lease may provide for an inclusive rental or it may require the tenants to contribute by means of an additional charge to the basic rent, generally referred to as a service or maintenance charge or additional rent. The services provided may include

- repairs and maintenance to the building;
- the management of repairs and maintenance;
- management of the lease;
- provision of concierge and warden; and
- insurance.

If a landlord or licensor is obliged under the terms of the lease to provide services similar to those above, the service charges follow the same VAT liability as the premium or rents payable under the lease or licence (normally exempt, unless they have opted to tax (see **42.23** below)). If services are provided to the occupants of holiday accommodation the supply is standard-rated (see **33.5 HOTELS AND HOLIDAY ACCOMMODATION**).

(VAT Notice 742, paras 11.1, 11.2, 11.4).

Specific services for tenants of leasehold non-domestic property provided by the landlord

A payment made by a tenant to the landlord may be

(a) further payment for the main supply of accommodation and therefore exempt or, if the option to tax has been exercised, standard-rated,
(b) for supplies other than accommodation (normally standard-rated), or
(c) disbursements and therefore outside the scope of VAT (see **3.7 AGENTS**).

The following are typical examples.

(i) *Insurance and rates.* If the landlord is the policyholder or rateable person, any payment for insurance or rates from the tenant is part payment for the main supply. If the tenants are the policyholders or rateable persons, any payments on their behalf by the landlord should be treated as disbursements. See also **37.17 INSURANCE** for insurance supplied with other goods and services.
(ii) *Telephones.* If the telephone account is in the name of the landlord, any charge to the tenants (including calls, installation and rental) is standard-rated. If the account is in the name of the tenant but the landlord pays the bill, any recovery from the tenant is a disbursement.
(iii) *Reception and switchboard.* A charge by the landlord under the terms of the lease for use of such facilities which form a common part of the premises is further consideration for the main supply.

(iv) *Office services*. A separate charge for such services (e.g. typing and photocopying) is a separate standard-rated supply. If, however, under the terms of the lease, one inclusive charge is made for office services and accommodation, and the tenant is expected to pay for the services whether used or not, the liability for the services follows that of the main supply.

(v) *Fixtures and fittings*. These are regarded as part of the overall supply of the property and any charges for them are normally included in the rent. Where a separate charge is made by the landlord, the supply is standard-rated.

(vi) *Electricity, light and heat*. If the landlord makes a separate charge for un-metered supplies of gas and electricity used by tenants, it should be treated as further payment for the main supply of accommodation. However, where a landlord operates secondary credit meters, the charges to the tenants for the gas and electricity they use are consideration for separate supplies of fuel and power. These supplies will be standard-rated. See **26.8 FUEL AND POWER** for further details. See, however, *Suffolk Heritage Housing Association Ltd* (VTD 13713) (TVC 30.15) where the tribunal held that the association's long standing practice of recovering heating costs as a separate charge from the rent should be treated as a separate supply for VAT purposes.

(vii) *Management charges*. Charges by landlords for managing a development as a whole and administering the collection of service charges is additional consideration for the main supply.

(viii) *Recreational facilities*. If the charges for the use of recreational facilities are compulsory, irrespective of whether the tenant uses the facilities, then the liability follows the main supply of accommodation.

(VAT Notice 742, para 11.7).

Services for occupants of leasehold non-domestic property provided by third parties

Where a person is responsible for providing services to occupants of property but has no interest in that property (e.g. a managing agent) the supply of services is always standard-rated as they are not part of the supply of the accommodation itself. (VAT Notice 742, para 11.5).

Services supplied to freehold occupants of non-domestic property

Where services are provided to someone who owns the freehold of a building and there are no continuing supplies of accommodation to which the service charge can be linked, the charge is always standard-rated. (VAT Notice 742, para 11.3).

Shared premises

Where the owner or tenant of premises does not grant other occupants an exempt licence to occupy, any service charge must be standard-rated. This applies even if the owner/tenant is simply passing on appropriate shares of costs (e.g. electricity, gas, telephone and staff wages). The only exception is where a bill is paid which is entirely the liability of another occupant (e.g. a telephone bill or insurance premium in the other occupant's name) which can be treated as a disbursement. (VAT Notice 742, para 11.8).

Service charges on domestic accommodation

Common areas

Service charges relating to the upkeep of common areas of an estate of dwellings, or the common areas of a multi-occupied dwelling, are exempt from VAT so long as they are required to be paid by the leaseholder or tenant to the landlord under the terms of the lease or tenancy agreement. This is because the service charge is treated as ancillary to the main supply of exempt domestic accommodation.

Services provided to freehold owners of dwellings are taxable because there is no supply of domestic accommodation to link those services to. However, by concession, all *mandatory* service charges paid by occupants of dwellings toward the

(a) upkeep of the common areas of a housing estate (e.g. such as paths, driveways and communal gardens),
(b) upkeep of the common areas of a block of flats (e.g. lift maintenance, corridors, stairwells and general lounges),
(c) general maintenance of the exterior of the block of flats or individual dwellings (e.g. painting) if the residents cannot refuse this, and
(d) provision of an estate warden, house manager or caretaker,

can be treated as exempt from VAT. (VAT Notice 48, ESC 3.18).

In *Devine* (VTD 15312) (TVC 41.57) the leaseholders were obliged to keep their properties in good repair with the landlords reserving the right to appoint a factor to ensure this was done. The landlords subsequently appointed a factor and imposed VAT on the service charge. The tribunal held that the charges did not qualify for exemption (because they were not part of the original supply of land) and noted that they did not fall within ESC 3.18 because they were not mandatory in the sense required by the concession, drawing a distinction between the obligations to maintain the property (which were mandatory) and the methods by which the proprietors chose to implement those obligations (which were not).

Electricity, light and heat

If the landlord makes a separate charge for *un-metered* supplies of gas and electricity used by occupants, it should be treated as further payment for the main supply of exempt domestic accommodation. However, if the landlord operates a secondary credit meter, the charges to the occupants for the gas and electricity they use are separate supplies of fuel and power subject to VAT at the reduced rate. See, however, *Suffolk Heritage Housing Association Ltd* (VTD 13713) (TVC 30.15) where the tribunal held that the association's long standing practice of recovering heating costs as a separate charge from the rent should be treated as a separate supply for VAT purposes.

Optional services

Optional services supplied personally to occupants (e.g. shopping, carpet cleaning or painting a private flat) are standard-rated. See *RLRE Tellmer Property sro v Finanční ředitelství v Ústí nad Labem, ECJ Case C–572/07* [2009] STC 2006 (TVC 22.386), in which the tenants were not required to obtain the cleaning of the common parts from their landlord. The court ruled that the letting of immovable property and the cleaning service of the common parts must, in circumstances such as those at issue, be regarded as independent, mutually divisible operations.

Managing agents

A managing agent acting on behalf of a landlord can treat the mandatory service charges to occupants as exempt, providing the agent invoices and collects the service charges directly from the occupants. Any management fee collected from the occupants is standard-rated because it relates to the managing agent's supply to the landlord.

Tenant-controlled management companies

Occupants of an estate may form a tenant-controlled management company which sometimes purchases the freehold of the estate and engages a service provider to maintain the common areas and provide any necessary warden or housekeepers. Providing the company is bound by the terms of the lease to maintain the common areas of the estate (or provide a warden), and the occupants are invoiced by, and pay the service charges directly to, the service provider, the service charges may still be treated as exempt. However, any management fee collected from the occupants is standard-rated (subject to the VAT registration threshold) because it relates to the service provider's supply to the tenant-controlled management company.

(VAT Notice 742, paras 12.1–12.5).

(6) Statutory compensation

Statutory compensation paid by a landlord to a tenant under the terms of the *Landlord and Tenant Act 1954* or the *Agricultural Tenancies Act 1995* is outside the scope of VAT. This applies even if, for example, an agricultural tenant has issued a 'notice to quit' having decided to retire from farming. Examples of items for which statutory compensation is given on a tenant quitting property are milk quotas left behind, manurial values and standing crops.

Where the landlord and tenant agree that the tenant will leave in return for additional payments, these payments are consideration for the tenant surrendering the lease and are exempt unless the tenant has opted to tax.

(VAT Notice 742, para 10.7).

De Voil Indirect Tax Service. See V4.111.

Joint ownership of land and beneficial interests

[42.20] Where more than one person owns land or buildings or receives the benefit of the consideration from the grant of an interest in land or buildings, (e.g. tenants in common), those persons are treated as a single person. If they are required to register for VAT purposes, they must register as if they were a partnership even if no legal partnership exists. (VAT Notice 742, para 7.2).

Beneficial interests

Where the benefit of the consideration for the grant of an interest in, right over or licence to occupy land accrues to a person (the 'beneficiary') other than the person making the grant, the beneficiary is to be treated for VAT purposes as the person making the grant. So far as any input tax of the person actually making the grant is attributable to the grant, it is to be treated for VAT purposes as input tax of the beneficiary. [*VATA 1994, Sch 10 para 40*]. For example, where property is held on bare trusts, although the trustees are the legal owners, if the benefit of the income accruing from the property passes to beneficiaries it is they who are treated as the person making the grant and who may need to register for VAT and, if so, can, subject to the normal rules, claim any input tax arising. (VAT Notice 742, para 7.1).

Benefit accruing to trustees

Where the benefit of the consideration for a grant, etc. accrues directly to trustees, it is the trustees who should, if required, register for VAT. (VAT Notice 742, para 7.1).

Commonhold

[42.21] The *Commonhold and Leasehold Reform Act 2002* recognises a third form of property ownership in addition to freehold and leasehold. This is known as commonhold and is available for residential, commercial or mixed use developments. It confers upon owners ('unit-holders') of parts of a building occupied in common, freehold interests in their respective parts (units) of the property. The freehold interest in the property's communal area and often its structure (the common parts) is owned by a commonhold association whose membership comprises the owners of the units. The commonhold association is responsible for the upkeep of the common parts and provides an estimate of annual expenditure (the commonhold assessment).

A commonhold unit is a freehold in a property that follows the normal VAT accounting rules. Some of the more common situations where a VAT liability may arise are considered below.

(1) Supplies of qualifying buildings (e.g. residential property)

Where the normal conditions for zero-rating are met (see **43.1 LAND AND BUILDINGS: ZERO AND REDUCED RATE SUPPLIES AND DIY HOUSEBUILDERS**), the developer of a '*qualifying building*' (i.e. a building designed as a dwelling or number of dwellings or intended for use solely for a relevant residential or a relevant charitable purpose) can zero-rate

- the first sale of the freehold units in a commonhold to prospective unit-holders; and
- the transfer by operation of law of the freehold of the common parts in the commonhold to the commonhold association, on the registration of the commonhold.

Any subsequent supplies of the units are exempt.

(2) Supplies of non-qualifying buildings (e.g. commercial property)

Such supplies are exempt from VAT unless the supply is either the sale of

- a commonhold unit or freehold of a new building (i.e. one that is less than three years old) or a partly-completed 'non-qualifying' building; or
- a commonhold unit or freehold of a commercial property where the option to tax has been exercised (and not disapplied), see **43.8** *et seq.* below),

in which case it is standard-rated.

(3) Setting up of a commonhold by a developer following construction of a new building

In the case of commercial property, the first supply of each unit is standard-rated provided it is made before the property is three years old or, if not, the developer has opted to tax (subject to the disapplication rules).

In the case of residential property, the supply is zero-rated.

For both residential and commercial property, the freehold interest in the common parts is vested in the commonhold association. Although there is normally no consideration attributed to this disposal, it may be a supply for VAT purposes with a requirement to charge VAT. See **42.22**(4) below.

(4) A number of freeholds are converted into a single commonhold

This may occur where freeholders apply for commonhold status because they have communal facilities (e.g. shared roadways, paths or services, etc.) and may involve some of the existing freeholders giving up title to areas of their land which are to become the common parts. It is likely that any payment made to a former freeholder will be seen as consideration for the surrender of the freehold interest with the VAT liability being

- in the case of commercial property, exempt (standard-rated where the property is less than three years old or an option to tax has been made (and not disapplied)); and
- in the case of residential property, exempt (zero-rated where a major interest has not been previously granted in the property, e.g. because the freeholder was also the person who constructed the building for his own occupation).

(5) A leasehold is converted into commonhold

On registration as commonhold, all pre-existing leases are extinguished.

Where the former leaseholder gains ownership of a commonhold unit in the same property as under the lease, the only supply is that of the freehold. The lease ceases to have legal effect and there is no supply of it for VAT purposes.

However, where the lease is extinguished and the freehold is transferred to some other person, or the freehold units have different boundaries from the previous leasehold premises, for VAT purposes there is a supply of a surrender of an interest in the property by the former leaseholder with the VAT liability being

- in the case of commercial property, exempt (standard-rated if the lessee has opted to tax the supply (subject to the disapplication rules); and
- in the case of residential property, exempt.

Where the leaseholder pays a consideration for the freehold interest in the unit he acquires, the liability for

- commercial property is exempt (unless the property is less than three years old or the option to tax has been exercised), and
- residential property is exempt (unless it is the first supply of a major interest in which case it is zero-rated).

(6) Sale of a commonhold unit by a unit holder

The disposal of a unit in a commercial property is exempt unless the property is less than three years old or an option to tax has been made (and not disapplied) in which case the supply is standard-rated.

The disposal of a unit in a residential property is exempt.

On purchase of a commonhold unit, the purchaser will also acquire membership of the commonhold association and an interest in the common parts. Normally, there will be no consideration attributed to the transfer of interest but it is a supply for VAT purposes and VAT must be charged if the conditions in **42.22**(4) below apply.

(7) The termination of a commonhold

A commonhold can be terminated in the following circumstances.

- *Voluntary winding up.* The commonhold association must specify proposals for the transfer of the commonhold land and explain how the assets of the association are to be distributed. Any payment received by either the commonhold association or by the unit-holders is consideration for a freehold interest and the liability is in accordance with the normal rules as above.
- *Winding up by court.* Where a commonhold association becomes insolvent, a successor commonhold association may be registered as the proprietor of the freehold estate in the common parts. Normally, there will be no consideration attributed to the disposal but it is a supply for VAT purposes and VAT must be charged if the conditions in **42.22**(4) below apply.

(8) Treatment of the commonhold assessment

Charges ('commonhold assessments') will normally be levied by the commonhold association to pay for the upkeep of common parts. These charges are treated in the same way as service charges to a long leaseholder or a non-commonhold freeholder. See **42.19**(5) above.

(VAT Notice 742, paras 13.1–13.8).

Other land transactions

[42.22] Other land transactions are treated as follows:

(1) Compulsory purchase

The disposal of land under a compulsory purchase order is an exempt supply unless standard-rated because it is a new building or civil engineering work within **42.18**(*a*) above, holiday accommodation less than three years old (see **42.18**(*d*) above) or the option to tax has been exercised (see **42.23** below). Payments described as 'disturbance' are treated as part of the consideration for the supply. If the full amount of compensation is not known at what would otherwise be the time of supply under the normal rules, there is a tax point each time any compensation payment is received. (*SI 1995/2518, Reg 84(1)*; VAT Notice 742, para 7.3). See, however, *L Landau* (VTD 13644) (TVC 57.105) where the tribunal chairman gave the opinion that VAT generally became chargeable on the transfer of the right to dispose of the land and the taxable amount included consideration to be obtained later. Where consideration was not quantified, there was no reason why VAT should not be accounted for on an estimated amount.

(2) Dedications of roads and sewers, transactions under planning agreements, etc.

If a developer

(a) dedicates, for no monetary consideration, a new road to a local authority (under *Highways Act 1980* or *Roads (Scotland) Act 1984*) or a new sewer or ancillary works to a sewerage undertaker (under *Water Industries Act 1991* or *Sewerage (Scotland) Act 1968*),

(b) provides goods or services free, or at a purely nominal charge, to a local or other authority (under *Town and Country Planning Acts* or other similar agreements which may loosely be described as 'planning gain agreements'), or

(c) transfers (usually for a nominal consideration) the *basic* amenities of estate roads, footpaths, communal parking and open space of a private housing or industrial estate to a management company which maintains them,

this does not constitute a taxable supply by the developer and no VAT is chargeable.

Included under (*b*) are buildings such as community centres or schools, amenity land or civil engineering works or an agreement to construct something on land already owned by a local authority or third party.

Any input tax incurred on such work is, however, attributable to the supply (or self-supply) of the main development (i.e. houses, shops, community centre, factory units, etc.) and recoverable or not depending upon whether that supply is taxable or exempt.

Any sums of money which have to be paid by the developer to the local authority, etc. (e.g. for the future maintenance of the building or land or as a contribution towards improvement of the infrastructure) are not consideration for a taxable supply to the developer by the local authority, etc.

(3) Agreements with the Highways Agency or a strategic highways company

When a development is undertaken, there may need to be road improvements. These will normally be undertaken in one of the following ways.

Works carried out by the Highways Agency or a strategic highways company

Where the Highways Agency or a strategic highways company arranges for road improvement works to be carried out the costs it recovers from a developer may include irrecoverable VAT. As there is no supply between the Highways Agency, or the strategic highways company, and the developer, merely a reimbursement of VAT-inclusive costs, the developer is not entitled to recover the VAT element as input tax.

From 1 April 2015 a strategic highways company appointed under *Infrastructure Act 2015, s 1* can recover VAT incurred on goods or services purchased for non-business purposes in so far as the Treasury directs (see **44.11 LOCAL AUTHORITIES AND PUBLIC BODIES**).

[*VATA 1994 s 41(7)(l); FA 2015, s 67*].

Works carried out by the developer

If the developer is permitted by the Highways Agency to carry out the works at his own cost, then there is no supply by the developer of the works to the Highways Agency (because the developer does not receive any consideration for the works from the Highways Agency). However, the developer may recover the input tax as attributable to his own ultimate supply of land and buildings from the development if the development is a taxable supply.

(VAT Notice 742, paras 8.1–8.6).

(4) Free supplies of land and buildings

If a business transfers or disposes of land or buildings that form part of the assets of the business free of charge it will still be making a supply. Where it has previously been eligible for input tax recovery in respect of the land or building (whether on the purchase or on the construction services when the building was built or substantially reconstructed) then its free disposal or transfer may trigger an output tax charge. The value of such charges is calculated by reference to the market value of the property at the time of the disposal or transfer.

The business must account for output tax on such supplies if

- it was charged VAT on the purchase, construction or substantial reconstruction of the land or buildings;
- it was entitled to recover all or part of the input tax; and
- the supply is standard-rated, e.g. if the business is disposing of the freehold of a new commercial building or it has opted to tax and the option is not disapplied.

Where a business intends to put a building to private or non-business use and the acquisition, construction, reconstruction or refurbishment costs have been incurred on or after 1 January 2011 it must only recover that proportion of the VAT that relates to the taxable business supplies. When considering the appropriate apportionment, the business must take into account all the intended future use over the economic life of the building (normally reckoned as ten years, in line with the capital goods scheme (CGS) (see **11.1 CAPITAL GOODS SCHEME**)). If the acquisition, construction, reconstruction or refurbishment costs incurred on or after 1 January 2011 are assets of the business and create a capital item, i.e. have a value of £250,000 or more, CGS adjustments will be carried out to reflect any changes in business and/or taxable use of the building.

(VAT Notice 742, para 7.6).

See **48.5** and **48.6 OUTPUT TAX** for full details.

(5) Mortgages

The mortgaging of a property, as security for borrowing money, is not regarded as a supply of the property for VAT purposes.

Sales of repossessed property

- *Sales under a power of sale.* Where a financial institution or any other lender sells land or buildings under a power of sale in satisfaction of a debt owed to it, there is a supply of the property by the *borrower*. If VAT is due on that supply, the *lender* or other person selling the property is responsible for accounting for that VAT using the procedure set out in **2.10 ACCOUNTING PERIODS AND RETURNS**.
- *Foreclosures.* If, instead of selling property under a power of sale, a lender obtains a Court Order and forecloses on land or buildings belonging to the borrower, there is a supply by the borrower to the lender of the land or building unless it is treated as an asset of a business transferred as a going concern (see **9.9 BUSINESS**). If the land or building is subsequently sold, this is a supply by the lender foreclosing, who may, if he wishes, opt to tax the property.

Renting out of repossessed property

If a lender

- repossesses land or buildings, or
- appoints a *Law of Property Act* receiver without foreclosing

and rents the property out to tenants, the borrower makes a supply to the tenant if the rental income received by the lender is used to reduce the debt owed or to service interest payments due in respect of that debt. If the supply is a standard-rated supply, the lender or LPA receiver should account for VAT using the procedure set out in **2.10 ACCOUNTING PERIODS AND RETURNS.**

(VAT Notice 742, paras 9.1–9.4).

See also **7.11 BAD DEBT RELIEF** for recovery of VAT on costs incurred by mortgage lenders.

(6) Transfer of a business as a going concern

See **9.9 BUSINESS.**

Option to tax

[42.23] The option to tax provisions allow for a person to tax certain supplies of land which would otherwise be exempt. The purpose of the option is to allow the recovery of input tax which would otherwise be lost. For these purposes, '*land*' includes any buildings or structures permanently affixed to it. A business does not need to own the land in order to opt to tax. (VAT Notice 742A, para 1.3).

The provisions relating to the option to tax in *VATA 1994, Sch 10* were recast and amended in relation to supplies made on or after 1 June 2008. In addition, certain provisions in VAT Notice 742A have the force of law as tertiary legislation. The current rules are considered in **42.24** to **42.36** below. An option made under the previous rules will continue in force unless disapplied or revoked, so the old rules will continue to have an effect for many years. The transitional provisions are considered below, but the detail of the old rules is now unlikely to be relevant.

Transitional provisions

(1) The re-enactment of any provision does not affect the continuity of the law (except where there is a change in the law relating to that provision). Anything done (or having effect as if done) under a superseded provision which was in force or effective immediately before the commencement of the corresponding rewritten provision has effect afterwards as if done under or for the purposes of the rewritten provisions.

(2) Any reference (express or implied) in any enactment, instrument or document to
- a rewritten provision, or
- things done or falling to be done under or for the purposes of a rewritten provision,

is to be read as including, in relation to times, circumstances or purposes in relation to which any corresponding superseded provision had effect, a reference to the superseded provision or (as the case may be) things done or falling to be done under or for the purposes of the superseded provision.

(3) Any reference (express or implied) in any enactment, instrument or document to
- a superseded provision, or
- things done or falling to be done under or for the purposes of a superseded provision,

is to be read as including, in relation to times, circumstances or purposes in relation to which any corresponding rewritten provision has effect, a reference to the rewritten provision or (as the case may be) things done or falling to be done under or for the purposes of the rewritten provision.

An election made before 1 November 1989 continues to have effect from 1 August 1989 (or any later day specified in the election).

(4) An election made before 1 March 1995 and having effect before that day continues to have effect notwithstanding that it has not been notified to HMRC.

(5) The fact that the words 'or of a description specified' in *VATA 1994, Sch 10 para 3(2)* as it stood before rewriting are not rewritten does not affect the continued operation of an option to tax any land which was made before 1 June 2008 and which specified a description of land.

Effect of the option to tax

[42.24] If

- a person exercises the option to tax any land, and
- a 'grant' is made in relation to the land at any time when the option to tax it has effect,

the grant does not fall within *VATA 1994, Sch 9 Group 1* (exemption for land) if it is made by

- the person exercising that option; or
- where that person is a body corporate, a 'relevant associate' (see **42.25**).

'*Grant*' includes an assignment or surrender and the supply made by the person to whom an interest is surrendered when there is a reverse surrender (i.e. where the person to whom the interest is surrendered is paid by the person by whom the interest is being surrendered to accept the surrender).

[*VATA 1994, Sch 10 paras 2, 33*].

Once a business has opted to tax any property, it must charge VAT on *all* future supplies it makes in relation to that property which would otherwise be exempt unless

- the anti-avoidance provisions in **42.27** below prevent the supplies from being taxable even if though the option to tax has been made; or
- the option has been revoked (see **42.31** below).

It is not possible, for example, for a business to opt to tax rents but then not tax a subsequent sale of the property. The option remains effective even if the business ceases to be registered for VAT due to a fall in turnover but subsequently has to register again (VAT Notice 742A, para 12.1).

Only supplies which the business makes are affected. Its option to tax will not affect supplies made by anyone else. For example, if a business is selling an opted building, the purchaser has the choice of whether to opt to tax or not. Similarly, if a tenant of the business is sub-letting, they too have this same choice. For this reason, it is advisable to inform any tenant of the decision to opt at the earliest opportunity so that they may safeguard their right to recover input tax by opting to tax, if they should so wish. (VAT Notice 742A, para 4.4).

Supplies arising from earlier grants

If an option to tax is exercised after the time of a grant relating to land, any supplies arising from the grant which are made after the option takes effect are treated as taxable supplies. [*VATA 1994, Sch 10 para 31*].

Effect on existing leases

Unless the lease specifically provides otherwise, the lessor or licensor has a right to add VAT to the rent agreed under the lease following an option to tax. [*VATA 1994, s 89*]. If an election has been made but, under the terms of the lease, VAT cannot be added, any rent received should be treated as VAT-inclusive and the VAT element calculated by multiplying the rent received by the appropriate VAT fraction.

Example

Company A is the landlord of a commercial building and owns the freehold of the building. It has made an option to tax election with HMRC, and will therefore charge VAT on the rent to its tenant Company B. The latter company sublets part of the premises to Company C but is not obliged to opt to tax its own interest in the building and charge VAT on the rent to Company C just because Company A has made an election. It will make a commercial decision as to whether an election is in its best interests and act accordingly.

Groups of companies

[42.25] An option to tax made by a member of a VAT group is generally binding upon other members of the same VAT group (see **42.24**). A body corporate that is bound by another body corporate's option to tax under these rules is known as a 'relevant associate' of the opter. If a body corporate is a relevant associate, it must normally charge VAT on any supplies it makes of the opted property, even after it has left the VAT group.

Relevant associate

Where a body corporate ('the opter') exercises an option to tax in relation to any building or land, another body corporate is a relevant associate of the opter if

- it was treated as a member of the same group as the opter at the time when the option first had effect;

- it has been treated as a member of the same VAT group as the opter at any later time when the opter had a 'relevant interest' in the building or land; or
- it has been treated as a member of the same VAT group as the opter, or a relevant associate of the opter, at a time when either of them had a relevant interest in the building or land.

A '*relevant interest*' in the building or land means an interest in, right over or licence to occupy the building or land (or any part of it).

Ceasing to be a relevant associate

A body corporate ceases to be a relevant associate of the opter in relation to the building or land in the following circumstances.

(a) The body corporate ceases to be a relevant associate of the opter in relation to the building or land at the time when all of the following conditions are first met.
   - The body corporate has no relevant interest in the building or land.
   - Where the body corporate has disposed of such an interest, it is not the case that a supply for the purposes of the charge to VAT in respect of the disposal is yet to take place, or would be yet to take place if one or more conditions (such as the happening of an event or the doing of an act) were to be met.
   - The body corporate or the opter is no longer a member of the group mentioned above.
   - The body corporate is not connected with any person who has a relevant interest in the building or land where that person is the opter or another relevant associate of the opter. For these purposes, whether a person is connected with another person is determined in accordance with *ICTA 1988, s 839* (see **72.19 VALUATION**). A company is not connected with another company only because both are under the control of the Crown, a Minister of the Crown, a government department, or a Northern Ireland department.

   If these conditions are met, the body corporate automatically ceases to be a relevant associate from the time that all three conditions are met. There is no need to notify HMRC or to seek permission.

(b) If the conditions in (*a*) above are not met, a body corporate also ceases to be a relevant associate of the opter in relation to the building or land at a time when it meets all of the conditions specified below *and* has notified HMRC that it does so on.

   The conditions are:

   (1) *The grouping condition*. The body corporate has ceased to be treated as a member of the VAT group by virtue of which it became a relevant associate of the opter.

   (2) *The 20-year condition*. The body corporate has
      - held any 'relevant interest' in the building or land acquired whilst a member of that VAT group for a period of at least 20 years; and

- been treated as a relevant associate of the opter for a period of at least 20 years.

(3) *The capital item condition.* Any land or building that is subject to the option is not, in relation to the body corporate, subject to input tax adjustment as a capital item under the capital goods scheme.

(4) *The valuation condition.* The body corporate, or a person connected with it, has not, within a period of ten years ending on the date that the body corporate ceases to be a relevant associate, made a supply of a relevant interest in the building or land that is subject to the option that
- was for a consideration that was less than the open market value of that supply; or
- arose from a 'relevant grant'.

(5) *The pre-payment condition.* No supply of goods or services has been made for a consideration to the body corporate (or to a person connected with it) which will be wholly or partly attributable to a supply or other use of the land or buildings made by that body (or by a person connected with it) more than twelve months later.

See above for the meaning of '*relevant interest*'. '*Relevant grant*' means a grant that the grantor intends or expects will give rise to a supply for a consideration significantly greater than any consideration for any earlier supply arising from the grant (except as a result of a rent review determined according to normal commercial practice).

Notification must be made on form VAT 1614B and must contain the information requested on that form. The form can be downloaded from https://www.gov.uk/government/organisations/hm-revenue-customs or obtained from the VAT Helpline on 0300 200 3700.

(c) If a body corporate does not meet all the conditions in (*a*) or (*b*) above, it may apply for written permission from HMRC to cease to be a relevant associate.

Permission will not be granted unless both conditions 1 and 2 under (*b*) above are met. In deciding whether or not to grant permission, HMRC will give particular consideration to whether or not the applicant or a third party has received a VAT benefit as a result of the applicant's actions.

If HMRC grants permission, the body corporate ceases to be a relevant associate of the opter from the day on which HMRC give their permission or such earlier or later day as is specified in their permission. HMRC may specify an earlier day only if

- the body corporate has previously purported to give a written notification of its ceasing to be a relevant associate of the opter;
- the conditions specified in (*b*) above are not, in the event, met in relation to the body corporate; and
- HMRC consider that the grounds on which those conditions are not so met are insignificant.

The day specified may be the day from which the body corporate would have ceased to be a relevant associate of the opter if those conditions had been so met.

HMRC may specify conditions subject to which their permission is given and, if any of those conditions are broken, they may treat the application as if it had not been made.
Application for permission must be made on form VAT 1614B (obtainable as in (*b*) above).

[*VATA 1994, Sch 10, paras 3, 4, 34*]. (VAT Notice 742A, para 6.3).

Exclusions from effect of the option to tax

[42.26] There are some supplies of land and buildings where, even if the business has opted to tax, the option will not apply and the supplies remain exempt from VAT. This may have an impact on how much input tax can be claimed.

(1) Dwellings designed or adapted, and intended for use, as dwelling, etc.

An option to tax has no effect in relation to any grant in relation to a building or part of a building if the building or part of the building is designed or adapted, and is intended, for use

- as a dwelling or number of dwellings; or
- solely for a 'relevant residential purpose' (see **42.16** above) provided the purchaser or tenant has informed the grantor of his intention to use the property for such a purpose and has given him a certificate to that effect.

See **42.5** above for when building is '*designed as a dwelling*'.

[*VATA 1994, Sch 10 paras 5, 33*].

Where a building or part of a building is used for both relevant residential purposes and business purposes, the option to tax will not apply to the part used for relevant residential purposes, provided that the different functions are carried out in clearly defined areas. In such circumstances the value of the supply should be fairly apportioned between the exempt and taxable elements. (VAT Notice 742A, para 3.3).

(2) Conversion of buildings for use as dwelling, etc.

An option to tax has no effect in relation to any grant made to a person ('*the recipient*') in relation to a building or part of a building (not designed, adapted or used as a dwelling or part of a dwelling) if the recipient certifies that the building or part of the building is intended for use

(a) as a dwelling or number of dwellings; or
(b) solely for a 'relevant residential purpose' (see **42.16** above).

The recipient must give a certificate on form VAT 1614D to the person making the grant ('*the seller*'), containing the information requested on that form. Copies of the form can be downloaded from

https://www.gov.uk/government/organisations/hm-revenue-customs

or obtained from the VAT Helpline on 0300 200 3700.

The certificate must normally be given before the price for the grant to the recipient by the seller is legally fixed (e.g. by exchange of contracts, by letters or missives, or by the signing of heads of agreement). The seller may, at his discretion, accept a certificate at a later time, but only in respect of supplies that arise after the certificate is given. For example, where a lease for periodic rental payments has been granted, the seller may only exempt the rental supplies that take place after the certificate is received. The recipient may give the certificate to the seller only if the recipient satisfies one of the following conditions.

- He intends to use the building or part of the building as mentioned in (*a*) or (*b*) above.
- He intends to convert the building or part of the building with a view to its being used as mentioned in (*a*) or (*b*) above.
- He is a '*relevant intermediary*', i.e.
  - he intends to dispose of the whole of the interest in the building or part of the building that is to be supplied to him by the seller to another person (P); and
  - P has already given the recipient a certificate stating that he (P) intends to *either* convert the building for use as in (*a*) or (*b*) above *or* dispose of the interest to another person who intends to convert the building for such use *or* dispose of the interest to another person who, in turn, intends to dispose of it to another person for such use.

For these purposes, a building or part of a building is not to be regarded as intended for use as a dwelling or number of dwellings at any time if there is intended to be a period before that time during which it will not be so used (but disregarding use for incidental or other minor purposes).

Where only part of a building is to be converted or adapted for use as in (*a*) or (*b*) above, the certificate must make it clear that this is the case and must contain a description of the qualifying part. The option to tax will apply to the part of the building that is not intended for qualifying use and the seller must fairly apportion his supply between the exempt and taxable elements.

[*VATA 1994, Sch 10 para 6*]. (VAT Notice 742A, para 3.4).

(3) Charities

An option to tax has no effect in relation to any grant made to a person in relation to a building or part of a building intended by the person for use solely for a '*relevant charitable purpose*' (see **42.14** above) but *not* as an office, provided the purchaser or tenant has informed the grantor of his intention to use the property for such a purpose and has given him a certificate to that effect.

[*VATA 1994, Sch 10 para 7*].

HMRC do not specify the form of a certificate.

Where a building or part of a building is used for relevant charitable purposes and business or general administration purposes, the option to tax will not apply to the part used for relevant charitable purposes, provided that the different functions are carried out in clearly defined areas. In such circumstances, the value of the supply should be fairly apportioned between the exempt and taxable elements. (VAT Notice 742A, para 3.5).

(4) Residential caravans

An option to tax has no effect in relation to any grant made in relation to a pitch for a residential caravan. A caravan is not a residential caravan if residence in it throughout the year is prevented by the terms of a covenant, statutory planning consent or similar permission. [*VATA 1994, Sch 10 para 8*].

(5) Residential houseboats

An option to tax has no effect in relation to any grant made in relation to facilities for the 'mooring' of a residential 'houseboat'.

'*Mooring*' includes anchoring or berthing.

'*Houseboat*' means a boat or other floating, decked structure that is designed or adapted for use solely as a place of permanent habitation and not having the means of, or capable of being readily adapted for, self-propulsion.

A houseboat is not a residential houseboat if residence in it throughout the year is prevented by the terms of a covenant, statutory planning consent or similar permission.

[*VATA 1994, Sch 10 para 9*].

(6) Relevant housing associations

An option to tax has no effect in relation to any grant made to a 'relevant housing association' in relation to any land if the association certifies that the land is to be used (after any necessary demolition work) for the 'construction of a building' or buildings intended for use

- as a dwelling or number of dwellings; or
- solely for a 'relevant residential purpose'.

A relevant housing association is

- a private registered provider of social housing;
- in Wales, a Welsh registered social landlord within the meaning of *Housing Act 1996*;
- in Scotland, a Scottish registered social landlord within the meaning of *Housing (Scotland) Act 2001*; or
- in Northern Ireland, a Northern Irish registered housing association within the meaning of *Housing (Northern Ireland) Order 1992 (SI 1992/1725)*.

Until the coming into force of provision defining 'private registered provider of social housing', it means persons listed in the register of providers of social housing maintained under the *Housing and Regeneration Act 2008, Pt 2 Ch 3* who are not local authorities within the meaning of the *Housing Associations Act 1985*.

See **42.16** above for '*relevant residential purpose*' and **42.3** above for '*construction of a building*'. The construction of a building includes the construction of a garage provided the dwelling and the garage are constructed at the same time and the garage is intended for occupation with the dwelling or one of the dwellings.

The housing association must give a certificate, on form VAT 1614G to the person making the grant ('*the seller*'), containing the information requested on the form. The form can be downloaded from

https://www.gov.uk/government/organisations/hm-revenue-customs

or obtained from the VAT Helpline on 0300 200 3700.

The certificate must normally be given before the price for the grant to the recipient by the seller is legally fixed (e.g. by exchange of contracts, by letters or missives, or by the signing of heads of agreement). The seller may, at his discretion, accept a certificate at a later time, but only in respect of supplies that arise after the certificate is given. For example, where a lease for periodic rental payments has been granted, the seller may only exempt the rental supplies that take place after the certificate is received.

[*VATA 1994, Sch 10 paras 10, 33*]. (VAT Notice 742A, para 3.6).

The certificate cannot be issued retrospectively (*Langstane Housing Association Ltd* (VTD 19111) (TVC 6.8)).

(7) Grant to individual for construction of dwelling (DIY buildings)

An option to tax has no effect in relation to any grant made to an individual if

- the land is to be used for the 'construction of a building' intended for use by the individual as a dwelling; and
- the construction is not carried out in the course or furtherance of a business carried on by the individual.

See **42.3** above for the meaning of '*construction of a building*'. The construction of a building includes the construction of a garage provided the dwelling and the garage are constructed at the same time and the garage is intended for occupation with the dwelling.

[*VATA 1994, Sch 10 paras 11, 33*].

Where a grant within (1) to (7) above gives rise to supplies at different times after the making of the grant (e.g. rent), the liability of each of those supplies is determined at the time when the supply is made rather than by reference to the time of the original grant. [*VATA 1994, s 96(10A)*].

Supplies partially affected by an option

Where a business has opted to tax a property but the option cannot have effect in relation to part of that property (e.g. a shop with a flat to be used as a dwelling over it), the consideration for any supply must be apportioned between the standard-rated element and the exempt or zero-rated part. [*VATA 1994, Sch 8 Group 5 Note 10, Sch 10 para 32*]. The business can choose the method of apportionment but it must provide a fair and reasonable result. (VAT Notice 742A, para 3.10).

Anti-avoidance provisions

[42.27] Certain businesses, which are not entitled to recover all of the input tax they incur on the purchase of land or buildings or on major construction projects, enter into arrangements designed to either increase the amount of input tax they can claim or to spread the VAT cost of the purchase or construction over a number of years. To counter this, HMRC have introduced anti-avoidance provisions which are applied each time a grant is made. If the provisions apply, the option to tax will not have effect (it will be 'disapplied') in respect of the supplies that arise from that particular grant. A business that normally receives credit for most of the input tax it incurs is unlikely to be affected by these anti-avoidance measures. (VAT Notice 742A, para 13.1).

A supply is not, as a result of an option to tax, a taxable supply if

- the 'grant' giving rise to the supply was made by a person ('*the grantor*') who was a developer of the land; and
- at the time when the grant was made (or treated for these purposes as having been made), the grantor or a 'development financier' intended or expected that the land
  - (i) would become exempt land whether immediately or eventually and whether or not as a result of the grant; or
  - (ii) would continue, for a period at least, to be exempt land.

Supply by a person other than the grantor

If a supply is made by a person other than the person who made the grant giving rise to it, for the above purposes

- the person making the supply is treated as the person who made the grant giving rise to it; and
- the grant is treated as made at the time when that person made the first supply arising from the grant.

[*VATA 1994, Sch 10 para 12*].

The following definitions apply for the above purposes.

(1) Grant

Grant refers to the act that transfers the land or building (e.g. a freehold sale of land or a building, the leasing or licensing of land or a building, or the assignment or surrender of that lease or licence). (VAT Notice 742A, para 13.3).

(2) Grantor

The grantor is the person who sells, leases or lets any of the land or buildings and can be anywhere in the chain of people who have an interest in the land or buildings concerned. For example, where a freeholder sells land to another party who constructs a new commercial building on the land and lets it to another business for occupation for its own use, there are two grantors: the seller of the land and the business which constructs and leases the new commercial building. If the occupying business sub-lets part of the building to another business, there would then be three grantors. The test should be applied to each grant made. (VAT Notice 742A, para 13.3).

(3) Grants made by a developer

A grant made by any person ('the grantor') in relation to any land is made by a developer of the land if the following conditions are met.

(a) The land either
  - (i) is a relevant capital item (i.e. the land, or the building or part of a building on the land, is a capital item under the capital goods scheme in relation to the grantor); or
  - (ii) was intended or expected to be a relevant capital item (i.e. the grantor, or a 'development financier' intended or expected that the land, or a building or part of a building on or to be constructed on, the land, would become a capital item under the capital goods scheme in relation to the grantor or any 'relevant transferee').

  A person is a *'relevant transferee'* if the person is someone to whom the land, building or part of a building was to be transferred in the course of a supply or in the course of a transfer of a business or part of a business as a going concern.

(b) The grant is made at an eligible time as respects that capital item (i.e. it is made before the end of the period provided for the making of adjustments relating to the deduction of input tax as respects the capital item under the capital goods scheme).

But if

- a person other than the grantor is treated as making the grant of the land (see above), and
- the grant is consequently treated as made at what would otherwise be an ineligible time,

the grant is treated instead as if it were not made at an ineligible time.

[*VATA 1994, Sch 10 para 13*].

(4) Development financier

A development financier in relation to the grantor of any land means a person who

- has provided finance for the grantor's development of the land, or
- has entered into any agreement, arrangement or understanding (whether or not legally enforceable) to provide finance for the grantor's development of the land,

with the intention or in the expectation that the land will become 'exempt land' or continue (for a period at least) to be exempt land.

Providing finance for the grantor's development of the land is widely defined. It covers directly or indirectly providing funds *either* for meeting the whole (or any part) of the cost of the grantor's development of the land *or* for discharging (in whole or in part) any liability that has been or may be incurred by any person for or in connection with the raising of funds to meet that cost. It also includes directly or indirectly procuring the provision of such funds by another person for either of those purposes. The ways funds can be provided include

- making a loan of funds that are, or are to be, used for that purpose;
- providing any guarantee or other security in relation to such a loan;
- providing any of the consideration for the issue of any shares or other securities issued wholly or partly for raising those funds;
- providing any consideration for the acquisition by any person of shares or other securities issued wholly or partly for raising those funds; or
- any other transfer of assets or value as a consequence of which any of those funds are made available for that purpose.

For these purposes, references to

(a) the grantor's development of the land are to the acquisition by the grantor of the asset which
  (i) consists in the land or a building or part of a building on the land; and
  (ii) is, or (as the case may be) was intended or expected to be, a relevant capital item under the capital goods scheme in relation to the grantor (within the meaning in (3) above); and
(b) the acquisition of the asset includes
  (i) its construction or reconstruction; and
  (ii) the carrying out in relation to it of any other works by reference to which it is, or was intended or expected to be, a relevant capital item under the capital goods scheme in relation to the grantor (within the meaning in (3) above).

[*VATA 1994, Sch 10 para 14*].

(5) Exempt land

Land is exempt land if, at any time before the end of the adjustment period under the capital goods scheme as respects that land

- the land is occupied by
  (i) the grantor,
  (ii) a person connected with the grantor,
  (iii) a development financier, or
  (iv) a person connected with a development financier; and
- that occupation is not wholly (i.e. 100%) or substantially wholly (i.e. at least 80%) for 'eligible purposes'.

Where a person is in occupation of the land at any time before the end of the relevant adjustment period, he is treated as not in occupation of the land at that time if

- the building occupation conditions are met at that time; or
- his occupation of the land arises solely by reference to any automatic teller machine of his.

The building occupation conditions are met if

- the grant consists of or includes the grant of a relevant interest in a building; and

- the person (or anyone connected with him if occupation is not wholly, or substantially wholly, for eligible purposes) does not, at the time in question, occupy any part of the land that is not a building, or more than the maximum allowable percentage of any relevant building.

The maximum allowable percentage means

- 2% where the person is (or is connected with) the grantor; and
- 10% where the person is (or is connected with) a development financier (but not also (or connected with) the grantor).

For these purposes, whether a person is connected with another person is determined in accordance with *ICTA 1988, s 839* (see **72.19 VALUATION**).

[*VATA 1994, Sch 10 paras 15, 15A, 34*]. (VAT Notice 742A, para 13.11).

'Eligible purposes'

Occupation for eligible purposes means one of the following.

- Occupation by a taxable person for the purposes of making supplies which
  - (i) are, or are to be, made in the course or furtherance of a business carried on by the person; and
  - (ii) are supplies of such a description that the person would be entitled to a credit for any input tax wholly attributable to those supplies.
- Occupation of land by a body within *VATA 1994, s 33* (see **44.2 LOCAL AUTHORITIES AND PUBLIC BODIES**) so far as the occupation is for purposes other than those of a business carried on by the body.
- Occupation of land by a Government department (see **44.11 LOCAL AUTHORITIES AND PUBLIC BODIES**).

In determining whether land is held for eligible purposes

- if a person occupying land
  - (i) holds the land in order to put it to use for particular purposes, and
  - (ii) does not occupy it for any other purpose,

  that person is treated, for so long as the conditions in (i) and (ii) continue to be met, as occupying the land for the purposes for which the person proposes to use it;
- if land is in the occupation of a person ('A') who
  - (i) is not a taxable person, but
  - (ii) is a person whose supplies are treated for the purposes of *VATA 1994* as made by another person ('B') who is a taxable person,

  the land is treated as if A and B were a single taxable person; and
- a person occupies land whether the person
  - (i) occupies it alone or together with one or more other persons; and
  - (ii) occupies all of the land or only part of it.

[*VATA 1994, Sch 10 para 16*].

Intentions and expectations

HMRC will consider commercial documents and other evidence such as minutes of meetings, business plans and finance requests to establish the intention and expectation of the businesses that are involved in the particular development. There does not have to be an intention to avoid VAT for a grant to be caught by the anti-avoidance provisions. (VAT Notice 742A, para 13.4).

In occupation of

In *Newnham College in the University of Cambridge* [2008] STC 1225 (TVC 6.12) the House of Lords held that a college was not in occupation of a library as it did not have the right to occupy the library as if it were the owner and to exclude any other person from enjoyment of such a right. HMRC's interpretation is that to be 'in occupation' a person must have actual possession of the land along with a degree of permanence and control. Such a right will normally result from the grant of a legal interest or licence to occupy. Occupation could also, however, be by agreement or de facto and it is therefore necessary to take account of the day-to-day arrangements, particularly where these differ from the contractual terms. An exclusive right of occupation is not a requirement, nor is it necessary for a person to be utilising all of the land for all of the time. A person whose interest in land is subject to an inferior interest, such as to prevent him from having rights of occupation for the time being, is not in occupation until the inferior interest expires. However, the test is forward looking and takes account of the intended or expected occupation of the building at any time during the Capital Goods Scheme (CGS) adjustment period. As a result, a person who has granted an inferior interest but intends during that adjustment period to occupy the land himself would intend to be in occupation and so must consider whether his intended occupation was for eligible purposes. However, a person can ignore the following types of occupation for the purposes of the test: occupation which is purely for the purpose of making his rental supplies under the grant, since those are the very supplies whose liability he is trying to determine by applying the test (e.g. occupation by the grantor between the date of the grant and the start of occupation by the tenant which is for the purpose of undertaking refurbishment or repairs, or occupation by maintenance, security or reception staff (or similar), unless it is for the purpose of providing ongoing services separate from the letting itself); and occupation at a future date, but within the CGS adjustment period, which is solely for the purpose of re-letting the property or making a fresh grant. (HMRC Brief 33/09)

Scope of the option to tax

[42.28] An option to tax has effect in relation to the particular land specified in the option.

If an option to tax is exercised in relation to

- a building or part of a building, the option has effect in relation to the whole of the building and all the land within its curtilage; and

- any land but is not exercised by reference to a building or part of a building, the option is nonetheless taken to have effect in relation to any building which is (or is to be) constructed on the land (as well as in relation to land on which no building is constructed).

For these purposes

- buildings linked internally are treated as a single building unless the internal link is created after the buildings are completed;
- buildings which are linked by a covered walkway (apart from a covered walkway to which the general public has reasonable access) are treated as a single building unless the walkway starts to be constructed after the buildings are completed;
- complexes consisting of a number of units grouped around a fully enclosed concourse are treated as a single building; and
- '*building*' includes an enlarged or extended building, an annexe to a building, and a planned building.

HMRC also make the following comments.

(a) A link does not include a car park (above or below ground), a public thoroughfare or a statutory requirement (e.g. a fire escape).

(b) *Land.*

- An option to tax covers all the land, and any buildings or civil engineering works which are part of the land.
- It covers only the discrete area of land that is specified and does not affect any adjoining land.

(c) *Buildings.*

- An option to tax covers the whole of the building, and the land under and immediately around that building (e.g. forecourts and yards). If the business's interest in the building is restricted to one floor, the option to tax will still cover the remaining floors of the building.
- If the building stands in a large area of land, how far the option to tax extends over the land depends on how far the services of the building can be utilised. For example, a racecourse grandstand may provide electricity and shelter for stalls, or other facilities, within its peripheral area. An option to tax on the grandstand would extend over the whole area of land that uses the benefits.
- If a building is demolished or destroyed, any option to tax will still apply to the land on which the building stood and to any future buildings that are constructed on the land. However, if a business opted to tax before 1 June 2008 (under the 'old rules') *and* it is clear from the notification that the option was made on the building only, then it can, if it wishes, treat the option as revoked once the building is demolished. There is no need to notify HMRC before revoking but the business should retain evidence in case it is requested in the future.

- From 1 June 2008, if a new building is constructed on land that has been opted, the building will be covered by the option to tax unless the business notifies HMRC that it wishes to exclude the building from the effect of the option (see **42.33**).
- If a business make changes to a building after it has opted to tax, it will need to consider whether the option to tax covers those changes. The most common changes are as follows.
  - (i) *Extensions*. Any option to tax a building will apply to any later extension (whether upwards, downwards or sideways).
  - (ii) *Linked buildings*. If a link is created after buildings are completed, the option to tax will not flow through with the link.
  - (iii) *Forming a complex*. Where a group of units that have been treated as separate buildings for the option to tax are subsequently enclosed, the option to tax will not spread to the un-opted units.

[*VATA 1994, Sch 10 para 18*]. (VAT Notice 742A, paras 2.3–2.6).

Day from which the option has effect

[42.29] Subject to

- the requirement to notify HMRC of the option (see **42.30**), and
- the provisions where the application for prior permission is required under **42.34** below,

an option to tax has effect from the start of the day on which it is exercised or the start of any later day specified in the option. But if, when an option to tax is exercised, the person exercising the option intends to revoke it under the cooling-off in **42.33** below, the option is treated as if it had never been exercised.

[*VATA 1994, Sch 10 para 19*].

In no circumstances can an option to tax have effect from a date before a business makes the decision to opt. (VAT Notice 742A, para 4.3).

Time of supply (tax point)

The normal tax point rules apply to all supplies of land or buildings. See **67.13** SUPPLY: TIME OF SUPPLY. In a tenanted building, a tax point might not occur until payment is received. In these circumstances, where a business opts to tax after the rent becomes due but before it is paid, it must account for output tax on the rental receipt. This is the case even if the payment covers a period before the option to tax took effect. (VAT Notice 742A, para 10.3).

Making and notifying the option

[42.30] There are two stages in opting to tax.

- Making the decision to opt which may take place at a board meeting or similar, or less formally. However reached, HMRC recommend that a written record is kept showing clear details of the land or buildings to be covered by the option and the date the decision is made. (Notice 742A, para 4.1).
- Notifying HMRC of the decision. An option to tax has effect only if
  - (i) notification of the option is given to HMRC before the end of the period of 30 days beginning with the day on which the option was exercised (or such longer period as HMRC may in any particular case allow); and
  - (ii) that notification is given together with such information as HMRC may require.

Notification of an option to tax does not need to be given under this provision where the option is treated as exercised in accordance with *VATA 1994, Sch 10 para 29(3)* (requirement for prior permission where previous exempt supply, see **42.34** below).

[*VATA 1994, Sch 10 para 20*].

Notification must be in writing and state clearly what land or buildings is covered by the option to tax and the date from which the option has effect. HMRC suggest that Notification Form VAT 1614A is used. The Form VAT 1614A is downloaded from the HMRC section of the GOV.UK website and completed online before it is printed and sent to the relevant HMRC address shown on the completed form. If a business is opting to tax discrete areas of land, HMRC suggests that it sends a map or plan clearly showing the opted land with the notification. Similarly, if opting to tax a building, the full postal address, including post code, should be included.

It is important that an appropriate person signs the notification, and any accompanying list or schedule (see further below).

Where a business becomes liable to be registered for VAT purposes as a result of the option to tax, the application to register for VAT *and* the notification of the option to tax should be submitted together to the appropriate VAT registration unit.

HMRC will normally acknowledge receipt of notification within 15 working days but this is not necessary for the option to tax to have legal effect and a business should not delay charging VAT just because it has not received acknowledgement.
(VAT Notice 742A, para 4.2).

Belated notification: clarification of HMRC policy

HMRC has discretion to accept notification later than the 30-day period allowed (although they cannot grant retrospective permission). This discretion is designed to cover situations where a business has genuinely made the decision to opt to tax, but has failed to notify it to HMRC in time. Before considering whether to exercise this discretion, HMRC would need to be satisfied that the decision was made on the date stated in the written notification. HMRC will usually accept a belated notification if a business provides evidence (e.g. the minutes of a Board or management meeting, correspondence referring to the decision, etc.). If this is not available, they would normally accept a statement from the responsible person, plus evidence that

- all the relevant facts have been given;
- output tax has been properly charged and accounted for from the date of the supposed election; and
- input tax recovery in respect of the land or building is consistent with the trader having made taxable supplies of it.

Belated notification may also be accepted in other cases depending on the individual circumstances.

On the other hand, HMRC may not accept that a decision to opt was taken, even when the above conditions are met if, for example

- there has been correspondence concerning, or investigation into, the liability of supplies of the property in question since the supposed date of the option, and no mention of the option to tax was made; or
- the business or its representative has previously put forward an alternative explanation for the charging of output tax (e.g. that the supply was not of land and buildings, or was of a sports facility).

HMRC reserves the right to refuse to accept belated notification if to do so would produce an unfair result, or if the exercise of the discretion was sought in connection with a tax avoidance scheme.

(Business Brief 13/05).

Responsibility for opting to tax

The person responsible for making the decision and notifying the option to tax depends on the type of legal entity holding (or intending to hold) the interest in the land or building, and who within that entity has the authority to make decisions concerning VAT. Following the tribunal decision in *Blythe Limited Partnership* (VTD 16011) (TVC 6.17) where written notification of an option made by solicitors acting for the partnership was held to be inaccurate and not binding, HMRC have issued guidance on notifying an option to tax.

In most cases notification will be made by the sole proprietor, one or more partners (or trustees), a director or an authorised administrator. If a business authorises a third party to notify an option on its behalf, HMRC require confirmation that the third party is authorised to do so. They would also like to be notified if the business withdraws that authority. Other more unusual situations are as follows.

- *Beneficial owners*. Where there is a beneficial owner and a legal owner of land or buildings (e.g. a bare trust), for VAT purposes it is the beneficial owner who is making the supply of the land or building and who should opt to tax. Where, however, there are numerous beneficiaries (e.g. unit trusts and pension funds) the person making the supply is the trustee who holds the legal interest and receives the immediate benefit of the consideration.

- *Joint owners* should together notify a single option to tax if they want supplies of the jointly-owned land or building to be standard-rated.
- *Limited partnerships*. The general partner(s) should opt to tax. Where title to the land or building is held jointly in the names of the general partner(s) and the limited partner(s), only the titleholders can make any supplies of that land or building together. That suggests that the limited partner(s) is/are involved in the management and running of the partnership and, as such, HMRC treat them as general partners. If the partnership decides to opt to tax, one or more of the partners should sign the notification.
- *Limited liability partnerships*. A limited liability partnership is a corporate body and is liable to register for VAT, subject to the normal registration rules. If the partnership decides to opt to tax, one or more members must sign the notification.

(VAT Notice 742A, paras 7.1–7.5).

Real estate elections

[42.31] A real estate election ('REE') is a formal decision to opt to tax all future property acquisitions. If a person makes an REE, he is treated (with certain exceptions) as having opted to tax every property in which he subsequently acquires an interest.

Under an REE, each property is treated as separately opted, with effect from the time of acquisition. This means that each option is capable of being separately revoked if the conditions for revocation are met. For example, if a person has made an REE but acquires a property that he does not want to be opted, he may be able to revoke within six months of acquisition under the cooling-off provisions (see **42.32** below) and the option is treated as though it was never made. (VAT Notice 742A, para 14.3).

The detailed provisions are considered below.

(1) Making an REE

A person (P) may make a real estate election (an 'REE') in relation to 'relevant interests' in any building or land which

- P acquires after the election is made; and
- a body corporate acquires after the election is made at a time when the body is a 'relevant group member'.

A '*relevant interest*' in relation to any building or land means any interest in, right over or licence to occupy the building or land (or any part of it) and a '*relevant group member*', in relation to any person making an REE at any time means a body corporate which is treated as a member of the same VAT group as that person at that time.

The time at which a relevant interest in any building or land is acquired is the time at which a supply is treated as taking place for the purposes of the charge to VAT in respect of the acquisition, or if there is more than one such time, the earliest of them.

[*VATA 1994, Sch 10 para 21(1)(12)(13)*].

Any member of a VAT group can make an REE although HMRC expect that normally this will be done by the VAT group representative member. (VAT Notice 742A, para 14.14).

(2) Consequences of making an REE

If P makes an REE

- P is treated as if P had exercised an option to tax in relation to the building or land in which the relevant interest is acquired;
- that option is treated as if it had been exercised on the day on which the acquisition was made and as if it had effect from the start of that day; and
- the requirement to notify an option under **42.30** above does not apply in relation to that option.

[*VATA 1994, Sch 10 para 21(2)*].

(3) Acquisitions excluded from the effects of an REE

An REE will not generate an option to tax for the following types of acquisitions.

- Any acquisition of a property in respect of which the person has already exercised an option to tax: if a person acquires an interest in a property and has (or a body corporate that was in their VAT group at the time, has) previously opted to tax the building or land, under the normal rules, with effect from a date prior to the acquisition date, the REE has no effect in relation to that property.
- Any acquisition of a property in respect of which the person already holds an interest when acquiring another different interest: if the person who acquires an interest after the REE is made already held a different interest in the property before the REE was made and continues to hold that interest when acquiring the further, different interest, the REE will not generate an option to tax. This situation can typically arise where a leasehold interest is held prior to the purchase of the freehold. Alternatively, an interest in part of a building (e.g. one floor) may be held at the time an interest in another part of the same building is acquired.
- Any acquisition of a property for which permission to opt might ordinarily be required: the REE will not generate an option to tax for an acquisition if the person has made exempt supplies of the property within the ten years prior to the date of acquisition.

[*VATA 1994, Sch 10 para 21(3)–(6)*]. (VAT Notice 742A, para 14.4).

(4) Automatic revocation where no interest held

Any options to tax exercised by the person (or by a person within their VAT group at the time) before making an REE will generally be revoked automatically when he makes an REE if he does not hold an interest in the opted land or building at that time (and no one within the VAT group holds an interest). Details are in the table below. However, there are exceptions to this rule, which are explained below the table.

If . . .	*and . . .*	*then . . .*
The person previously opted to tax a building (or part of a building)	he does not have a relevant interest in the building at the time he make an REE	his option is revoked (subject to the exceptions below)
The person previously opted to tax land (without reference to a particular building or buildings)	he does not have a relevant interest in the land at the time he makes an REE	his option is revoked (subject to the exceptions below)
The person previously opted to tax land (without reference to a particular building or buildings)	he only has an interest in part of the land at the time he makes an REE	his option is revoked in relation to the parts of land in which he does not hold a relevant interest (subject to the exceptions below)

Exceptions to automatic revocation?

Automatic revocation of an option will not occur at the time an REE is made in any of the following circumstances. All references to 'relevant time' mean the time the REE is made or, in other words, the time the option would otherwise be revoked:

(a) Where the opter has sold the property on terms that may require the purchaser to make additional payment after the 'relevant time'. Such payments are often referred to as 'overages' and can be contingent on such things as the purchaser obtaining planning permission.
The following two circumstances can only apply if the person who opted to tax ('the opter') is or has been a member of a VAT group.

(b) Where a 'relevant associate' of the opter in relation to the opted property has sold the property on terms that may require the purchaser to make additional payment after the relevant time.

(c) Where before the relevant time a relevant associate of the opter in relation to the property left the opter's VAT group and at the time of leaving any of the following applied:
- the relevant associate had an interest in or licence to occupy the property;
- the relevant associate had, prior to leaving the VAT group, disposed of an interest on terms that might have required the purchaser to make additional payment at a later date; or
- the relevant associate was connected to the opter or another relevant associate of the opter and that person had an interest in or licence to occupy the property.

[*VATA 1994, Sch 10 para 22(2)–(5)*]. (VAT Notice 742A, para 14.8).

(5) Conversion of a single option (e.g. a global option) into separate options

An option to tax ('*the original option*') exercised in relation to any land (otherwise than by reference to any building or part of a building) by

- a person (E) who makes an REE, or
- any relevant group member

before the making of the REE may, in certain circumstances, be converted by E into separate options to tax different parcels of land. This choice is only available in relation to land or buildings in which E or any relevant group member has a relevant interest at the time of making the REE. (If there is no relevant interest in the property at that time, the option is revoked, see (4) above.)

Each parcel of land that is to be treated as being separately opted must

- be identified by at least one of the following, namely its postal address, land registry title number, map or plan or other description sufficient to identify it; and
- meet the conditions relating to the scope of an option in **42.28**.

The separate options to tax are treated as if they had been exercised by E (in the case of a VAT group, irrespective of which member of the group made the original option) and as if they had effect from the time from which the original option had effect. But the cooling-off period for revocation of an option (see **42.32** below) does not apply to those separate options to tax.

[*VATA 1994, Sch 10 para 22(6)–(10)*]. (VAT Notice 742A, paras 14.8.3).

(6) Notifying a real estate election

A real estate election has effect only if

- notification of the election is given to HMRC before the end of the period of 30 days beginning with the day on which it was made (or such longer period as the HMRC may in any particular case allow);
- the notification is made on form VAT 1614E and contains the information requested on that form. The form can be downloaded from https://www.gov.uk/government/organisations/hm-revenue-customs or obtained from the VAT Helpline on 0300 200 3700.

[*VATA 1994, Sch 10 para 21(7)*]. (VAT Notice 742A, para 14.9).

If the person making the REE holds relevant interests in any property other than in dwellings or buildings designed or adapted for use as a dwelling (see **42.5** above), in addition to notifying the REE, he must also provide a list of all properties in which he holds a relevant interest at the time of notifying the REE. This list must be sent to HMRC within the time specified for notifying the REE; otherwise the REE will not be effective. This list must contain the following information in respect of each property (other than dwellings or buildings designed or adapted for use as a dwelling) in which the person holds a relevant interest.

- A description of the land or buildings, identified by reference to postal address, land registry title number, map, plan or other description.

- In the case of land or buildings in respect of which no option to tax made by the maker of a REE has effect, the date of acquisition of a relevant interest in that land or buildings.
- In the case of land or buildings in respect of which an option to tax made by the maker of a REE has effect, the date when the relevant interest in the land or building was first acquired or, if later, the date when the option first had effect.
- Where an option has effect in relation to two or more separately listed parcels of land or buildings, they must be identified as being subject to the same option.

For these purposes, if the person making an REE

- has more than one relevant interest in a parcel of land or a building that were acquired at different times, only the date of acquisition of the most recently acquired relevant interest is to be provided; and
- is required to provide the date when an option first had effect in relation to a parcel of land or a building and that date is unknown, that person should record that fact and enter an approximate date, using best judgement, and provide a written explanation of why that date is considered reasonable.

If an incomplete list, or one which contains incorrect information, is submitted, a revised and current up-dated list should be submitted (to the person's Client Relationship Manager or, if he does not have one, to the Option to Tax Unit in Glasgow) as soon as the error is identified.

(VAT Notice 742A, paras 14.9, 14.11).

(7) **Information requirements after a real estate election has been made**

HMRC may require a person who has made an REE to give them information specified in a public notice within 30 days (or such longer period as they in any particular case allow).

If a person (P) does not comply with that requirement, HMRC may revoke the election, in which case that revocation has effect in relation to relevant interests in any building or land acquired after the 'notified time' by P or a body corporate which is a relevant group member at the time of acquisition.

The '*notified time*' means the time specified in a notification given by HMRC to P (which may not be before the notification is given).

[*VATA 1994, Sch 10 para 21(8)(9)*].

Under these powers, the maker of an REE must provide to HMRC the information detailed below in relation to any land or buildings (other than buildings designed or adapted for use as a dwelling) in which that person or a relevant group member

(i) holds a relevant interest at the time of providing the required information; or
(ii) has ceased to hold a relevant interest since making an REE or, if later, since the last occasion on which the maker of the REE provided such information to HMRC.

In respect of every such property

- the description of the land or buildings identified by reference to its postal address, land registry title number, map, plan or other description;
- in the case of land or buildings in respect of which no option to tax made by the maker of a real estate election or relevant group member has effect, the date of acquisition of the relevant interest in the land or buildings;
- in the case of land or buildings in respect of which an option to tax made by the maker of a real estate election or a relevant group member has effect, the date when the relevant interest in the land or building was acquired or, if later, the date when the option first had effect; and
- where an option has effect in relation to two or more separately listed parcels of land or buildings, they must be identified as being subject to the same option.

In respect of every property in which a relevant interest has been acquired or disposed of by the maker or the REE or a relevant group member since the date of the last such list (if any)

- as appropriate, the date of the maker of the REE or a relevant group member
  - (i) acquiring a relevant interest in land or buildings in which that person has no other relevant interest;
  - (ii) ceasing to hold a relevant interest in land or buildings without retaining another relevant interest in that property;
  - (iii) opting to tax land or buildings otherwise than by virtue of an REE;
  - (iv) converting a building or buildings into a dwelling or dwellings;
  - (v) excluding a new building from the effect of an option; and
  - (vi) revoking an option to tax in relation to land or buildings;

  identifying the land or building to which each occurrence relates;
- the VAT-exclusive value of the supply of a relevant interest acquired or disposed of by the maker of an REE or relevant group member; and
- the VAT (if any) charged on the supply of a relevant interest by the maker of an REE or, where the supply occurred before its admission to the group, the relevant group member.

For these purposes,

(a) where the maker of an REE or relevant group member has more than one relevant interest in the same land or building that were acquired at different times, only the date of acquisition of the most recently acquired relevant interest is to be provided;

(b) in the case of land or a building in which an interest has been held before the date of an REE, the date of the occurrence of the making of an option to tax by the person making an REE or a relevant group member is the date when that option first has effect; and

(c) the date of the occurrence of the revocation of an option is the date from which the revocation has effect.

The requirement to provide the information set out above does not apply to the revocation of an option to tax by virtue of the 'cooling-off' period or the lapse of six years since having a relevant interest (see **42.32** below).

(VAT Notice 742A, para 14.12).

(8) Revocation of a real estate election

Once made, an REE may not be revoked except by HMRC under their powers in (7) above for failure to provide information. If an REE made by a person (P) is so revoked by HMRC, another REE may be made at any subsequent time by P or any body corporate which is a relevant group member at that subsequent time, but only with the prior written permission of HMRC. [*VATA 1994, Sch 10 para 21(10)(11)*]. In such circumstances, (5) above will not apply to the new REE. (VAT Notice 742A, para 14.15).

Revocation of the option to tax

[42.32] Once made, the option to tax can only be revoked

- by the taxpayer in a six-month cooling-off period (see (1) below);
- automatically where no interest has been held in the property for over six years (see (2) below); or
- by the taxpayer where more than 20 years has lapsed since it first had effect (see (3) below).

(1) Revocation of an option to tax during the cooling-off period

An option to tax any land exercised by any person ('*the taxpayer*') may be revoked with effect from the day on which it was exercised if all of the following conditions are satisfied.

(a) The time that has lapsed since the day on which the option had effect is less than six months.

(b) The taxpayer has not used the land since the option had effect (including own occupation). This condition was removed with effect from 1 April 2010. [*SI 2010/485, Art 7*].

(c) No VAT has become chargeable as a result of the option.

(d) Since the option had effect, no grant in relation to the land has been made which is treated as neither a supply of goods nor a supply of services because the supply is a supply of the assets of a business by
  (i) the taxpayer to a person to whom the business (or part of it) is transferred as a going concern; or
  (ii) a person to the taxpayer to whom the business (or part of it) is so transferred.

(e) Notification of the revocation is given to HMRC on form VAT 1614C and contains the information requested on that form. The form can be downloaded from https://www.gov.uk/government/organisations/hm-revenue-customs or obtained from the VAT Helpline on 0300 200 3700.

(f) Any further conditions published by HMRC in a notice are satisfied. HMRC have specified that either prior permission for the revocation must be sought from HMRC, or one of the following conditions must be met

- neither the opter nor any relevant associate has recovered extra property input tax;
- by virtue of the revocation, the opter and all relevant associates would be liable to account for all extra property input tax they have recovered; or
- extra property input tax has been recovered entirely on one capital item and amounts to less than 20% of the total input tax incurred on that item.

The 'cooling-off' period does not apply to new options to tax of a person making an REE that are created following the conversion of an existing option to tax into several separate options to tax at the time an REE is made. See **42.31**(5) above.

[*VATA 1994, Sch 10 para 23*]. (VAT Notice 742A, para 8.1).

(2) Revocation of option to tax where no interest has been held for more than six years

Subject to the anti-avoidance provisions below, an option to tax exercised by any person in relation to any building or land is treated as revoked if the person does not have a 'relevant interest in the building or land' throughout any continuous period of six years beginning at any time after the option has effect. The option to tax is then treated as revoked from the end of that period.

'*Relevant interest in the building or land*' means an interest in, right over or licence to occupy the building or land (or any part of it).

[*VATA 1994, Sch 10 para 24*].

(3) Revocation of option where more than 20 years have lapsed since option first had effect

An option to tax any land exercised by any person (the taxpayer) may be revoked if the time that has lapsed since the day on which the option had effect is more than 20 years and either of conditions (*a*) or (*b*) below are met.

(a) At the time when the option is to be revoked the conditions specified by HMRC in a public notice are met in relation to the option and notification of the revocation is given to HMRC on form VAT 1614J which contains the information requested on that form. The form can be downloaded from https://www.gov.uk/government/organisations/hm-revenue-customs or obtained from the VAT Helpline on 0300 200 3700.
    The conditions specified by HMRC are that *either* condition 1 below *or* all of conditions 2 to 5 are met.
    (1) *The relevant interest condition*. The 'taxpayer' or a relevant associate connected to the taxpayer has no 'relevant interest in the building or land' at the time when the option is revoked; and (from 1 April 2010) if either of them has disposed of such an interest, no supply is yet to take place or would be yet to take place if one or more conditions were to be met.

(2) *The 20-year condition.* The taxpayer or a relevant associate connected to the taxpayer held a relevant interest in the building or land after the time from which the option has effect and more than 20 years before the option is revoked.

(3) *The capital item condition.* Any land or building that is subject to the option at the time when it is revoked does not fall, in relation to the taxpayer or a relevant associate connected to the taxpayer, for input tax adjustment as a capital item under the capital goods scheme.

(4) *The valuation condition.* The taxpayer or a relevant associate connected to the taxpayer has made no supply of a relevant interest in the building or land subject to the option in the ten years immediately before revocation of the option that was *either* for a consideration that was less than the open market value of that supply *or* arose from a 'relevant grant'.

(5) *The pre-payment condition.* No part of a supply of goods or services made for consideration to the taxpayer or a relevant associate connected to the taxpayer before the option is revoked will be attributable to a supply or other use of the land or buildings by the taxpayer more than twelve months after the option is revoked.

'*Taxpayer*' means

(i) a person who exercised the option to tax or who is treated as making that option by virtue of a real estate election (see **42.31** above); and

(ii) in relation to an option to tax treated as exercised by virtue of a real estate election by a body corporate treated as a member of a VAT group other than the person described in (i) above, the body corporate whose relevant interest gave rise to the option to tax.

'*Relevant interest in the building or land*' means an interest in, right over or licence to occupy the building or land (or any part of it).

'*Relevant grant*' means a grant that the taxpayer intends or expects will give rise to a supply made after the option is revoked for a consideration significantly greater than any consideration for any supply arising from the grant before the revocation (except as a result of a rent review determined according to normal commercial practice).

In relation to condition (2) above, it does not matter whether, at the time the option is revoked, the taxpayer continues to hold the relevant interest in the building or land that meets the condition.

(b) If all the conditions in (*a*) above are not met, a taxpayer may still seek permission from HMRC to revoke an option, although they cannot give permission unless condition 2 (the 20-year condition) is met. Application must be made on form VAT 1614J and must contain the information requested on that form. In deciding whether or not to grant permission, HMRC will give particular consideration to whether or not the taxpayer or a third party has received a VAT benefit as a result of his actions.

Once HMRC have granted permission, the revocation will have effect from the day permission is granted, or such earlier or later day or time specified in their permission. They may specify a time by reference to the happening of a particular event or meeting of a condition, e.g. they may specify that revocation will take effect after the sale of a property has been completed. They can only specify an earlier day if the taxpayer has purported to give a notification of the revocation, and HMRC consider that the grounds on which the conditions are not met are insignificant. In granting permission HMRC may specify further conditions subject to which the permission is given. If any of these conditions are subsequently broken, they may treat the revocation as if it had not been made.
[*VATA 1994, Sch 10 para 25*]. (VAT Notice 742A, para 8.3).

Anti-avoidance provisions

The revocation provisions under (2) above (lapse of six years since having a relevant interest) do not apply if condition A, B or C is met, and the revocation provisions under **42.31**(4) (revocation of existing options to tax on property in which the taxpayer has no relevant interest at the time of making a real estate election) do not apply if condition A or B is met.

Condition A is met if at the relevant time, further supplies will or may arise (for example overages) in relation to the prior disposal of the building or land by the opter or a relevant associate of the opter.

Condition B is met if the opter was a member of a VAT group prior to the relevant time and a relevant associate of the opter in respect of the property had left the VAT group, without at the same time meeting all of the following additional conditions

- at the time the relevant associate left the VAT group they did not hold an interest in the property;
- where an interest had been held by the relevant associate but previously disposed of no further supplies will or may yet arise in relation to that disposal (for example, overages);
- the relevant associate was not connected with any person who has a relevant interest in the property where that person is the opter or another relevant associate of the opter.

Condition C is met if at the relevant time, a relevant associate of the opter is in the same VAT Group as the opter and holds or has held a relevant interest in the property at any time in the previous six years.

[*VATA 1994, Sch 10 para 26; SI 2009/1966, Art 6*]. (VAT Notice 742A, para 8.2).

Exclusion of new building from effect of an option

[42.33] With effect from 1 June 2008, the provisions make it clear that an option to tax land equally applies to a building upon it (either at the time of opting or constructed later) and vice versa. Previously, HMRC had a policy of allowing businesses to opt to tax land and buildings separately. In order to provide business with similar flexibility to earlier provisions, a new building (and the land within its curtilage) may be permanently excluded from the effects of an option to tax at certain points in time as follows.

If

- a person ('the taxpayer') has at any time opted to tax any land,
- at any subsequent time the 'construction of a building' ('the new building') on the land begins (which is taken to be the time when it progresses above the level of the building's foundations), and
- no land within the curtilage of the new building is within the curtilage of an existing building

the taxpayer may exclude the whole of the new building, and all the land within its curtilage, from the effect of the option. Notification of the exclusion must be made on form VAT 1614F and must contain the information requested on that form. The form can be downloaded from

https://www.gov.uk/government/organisations/hm-revenue-customs

or obtained from the VAT Helpline on 0300 200 3700.

The earliest time that a building can be excluded is when construction begins. Construction of a building begins when it progresses above the level of the building's foundations, which is usually the point at which the first brick is laid.

Exclusion has effect from the earliest of the following times.

- When a grant of an interest in, or in any part of, the new building is first made.
- When the new building, or any part of it, is first used.
- When the new building is completed.

An exclusion is only valid if it is notified to HMRC. Notification must be made after construction has begun and normally within 30 days of the date the exclusion has effect. A longer period may be allowed in exceptional circumstances.

'*Construction of a building*' for these purposes is to be read in accordance with *VATA 1994, Sch 8 Group 5 Notes (16)–(18)* (see **42.3** above but ignoring (*a*)(ii) and the reference to a building ceasing to be an existing building when the part remaining above ground level consists of no more than a single façade).

If a taxpayer decides to exclude a new building from an option to tax, the effect of that exclusion is permanent (although he may make a fresh option to tax in the future).

Requirement for prior permission to opt to tax where prior exempt grant

[42.34] Where

- a person wants to exercise an option to tax any land with effect from a particular day,

- an exempt supply of the land has been made in the period of ten years before that day

he cannot exercise the option to tax the land unless either of the following applies.

(a) Any of the following conditions for automatic permission specified in VAT Notice 742A, para 5.2 (which have the force of law) are met

(1) It is a mixed-use development and the only exempt supplies have been in relation to the dwellings.

(2) The person does not wish to recover any input tax in relation to the land or building incurred before the option to tax has effect; *and*

- the consideration for exempt supplies has, up to the date when the option to tax is to take effect, been solely by way of rents or service charges and excludes any premiums or payments in respect of occupation after the date on which the option takes effect. Regular rental and/or service charge payments can be ignored for the purposes of this condition. Payments are considered regular where the intervals between them are no more than a year and where each represents a commercial or genuine arms-length value; and
- the only input tax relating to the land or building that the person expects to recover after the option to tax takes effect will be on overheads, such as regular rental payments, service charges, repairs and maintenance costs. If he expects to claim input tax in relation to refurbishment or redevelopment of the building, he will not meet this condition.

In deciding whether this condition is met, a person should disregard

- any VAT refundable to a local authority or similar body under *VATA 1994, s 32(2)(b)* (see **44.8** LOCAL AUTHORITIES AND SIMILAR BODIES);
- any input tax he can otherwise recover by virtue of the partial exemption *de minimis* rules; and
- any input tax he is entitled to recover on general business overheads not specifically related to the land or building, such as audit fees.

(3) *Obsolete since 30 April 2009.*

(4) Automatic permission may be granted where Condition A and, if applicable, Condition B, are satisfied.

Condition A: The person does not intend or expect that any supply which is taxable as a result of the option will: (a) be made to a connected person, unless that person will be entitled to recover at least 80% of the VAT on that supply; or (b) arise from an agreement under which an exempt supply in respect of a right to occupy the property has been or will be made, and that right begins or continues after the effective date of the option. 'Permissible exempt supplies' may be disregarded.

Condition B (this condition only applies where the person has been, or expects to be, entitled to credit for any input tax incurred on capital expenditure on the property by virtue of the option): The person does not intend or expect to use any part of the capital expenditure for the purposes of:

- making exempt supplies which do not confer a right to credit under *VATA 1994, s 26(2)(c)*, unless: (a) all the exempt supplies fall within *VATA 1994, Sch 10 paras 5-11* (compulsory exclusions); or are permissible exempt supplies; or are incidental supplies falling within *VATA 1994, Sch 9 Group 5* (finance); or (b) exempt supplies are made but it is intended or expected that input tax on capital expenditure on the property which is attributed to those exempt supplies will not exceed £5,000; or (c) the person expects to be entitled to full credit for all input tax incurred on capital expenditure on the property under *VATA 1994, s 33(2)* (statutory bodies: insignificant exempt input tax); or
- for private or non-business purposes, other than those giving right to a refund under *VATA 1994, s 33* (statutory authorities), *s 33A* (museums and galleries) or *s 41(3)* (Government departments).

(5) The exempt supplies have been incidental to the main use of the land or building. For example, where the person has occupied a building for taxable purposes, the following would be seen as incidental to the main use and this condition would be met.

- Allowing an advertising hoarding to be displayed.
- Granting space for the erection of a radio mast.
- Receiving income from an electricity sub-station.

The letting of space to an occupying tenant, however minor, is not incidental.

If any one of the above conditions is met, the person must still notify HMRC of the option on form VAT 1614A which must contain the information requested on the form. The form can be downloaded from

https://www.gov.uk/government/organisations/hm-revenue-customs

or obtained from the VAT Helpline on 0300 200 3700.

The notification should state that, although the business has made previous exempt supplies of the land or building, it satisfies the conditions for automatic permission.

(b) The person gets the prior permission of HMRC

If a person does not meet any of the conditions for automatic permission in (*a*) above, before he can opt to tax he must obtain written permission. An application for prior permission must be made on form VAT 1614A and contain the information requested on the form. Form VAT 1614A is downloaded from the HMRC section of the GOV.UK website and completed online before it is printed and sent to the relevant HMRC address shown on the completed form.

The taxpayer must also advise HMRC of the date from which it would like the option to have effect (which can be any date on or after he makes the application).

HMRC cannot grant permission to opt to tax unless the taxpayer has provided all the specified information, and any additional information requested. They must refuse their permission if they are not satisfied that there would be a fair and reasonable attribution of relevant input tax. In deciding this, they must have regard to all the circumstances of the case, but in particular to

- the total value of any exempt supply to which any grant in relation to the land gives rise and which is made or to be made before the day from which the person wants the option to have effect;
- the expected total value of any supply to which any grant in relation to the land gives rise that would be taxable (if the option has effect); and
- the total amount of input tax incurred, or likely to be incurred, in relation to the land.

If HMRC are satisfied, permission is granted and the option takes immediate effect from the start of the day on which the application was made or the start of any later day specified in the application. There is no requirement for separate written notification after permission is granted.

HMRC cannot grant retrospective permission. Therefore

- any VAT charged in error is not output tax and, unless it is corrected, HMRC will collect it as a debt due to them; and
- any input tax claimed in error is exempt input tax and is not allowable.

Purported exercise where prior permission not obtained

If an option to tax has been notified to HMRC under **42.30** but should have been subject to their prior permission, HMRC *may* subsequently dispense with the requirement for their prior permission and allow the option to be retained. In such a case, the option is treated as having been validly made and effective from the date it was originally notified. HMRC will generally only exercise this discretion in cases of genuine error, or where tax would otherwise be at risk.

[*VATA 1994, Sch 10 paras 28–30*]. (VAT Notice 742A, paras 5.2–5.8; VAT Notice 742A, paras 5.2–5.8).

Input tax

Input tax incurred on or after the date of the option

[42.35] Once the option to tax has been exercised, a business can recover input tax on any related expenditure subject to the normal rules.

- Where taxable supplies of the land or buildings are made, any input tax relating to those supplies can be recovered.
- Where wholly exempt supplies of the land or building are made (because the supplies are not affected by the option to tax, see **42.26** above), any input tax relating to those supplies cannot be recovered.

- Where supplies that are both taxable and exempt are made (e.g. where an opted building is to be used for both commercial and residential purposes), the input tax relating to the taxable supplies can be recovered under the partial exemption rules.

Input tax incurred before the date of the option to tax

This can be recovered in the following circumstances.

- Where the supply of land or buildings is taxable in its own right (e.g. a freehold sale of a commercial building within three years of its completion is always taxable).
- Input tax prior to the making of supplies can be recoverable where there is a clear intention, at the time the costs are incurred, that the supplies of the buildings or land will be taxable. An option to tax is the best evidence of an intention to make taxable supplies for land and property transactions. But where, exceptionally, a business wishes to delay the making of the option until a future date, it may still be able to recover the input tax relating to supplies which will follow the option if it can produce unequivocal documentary evidence that, at the time it seeks to reclaim the input tax, it intends the supplies to be taxable.
  HMRC give the following as examples of the types of documents that may contain evidence of intention.
  (i) A signed agreement/contract that specifies that the vendor will opt to tax prior to the sale.
  (ii) An investment appraisal or business plan accepted by a bank that confirms that supplies will be treated as taxable.
  (iii) Marketing literature that has been distributed to the public and where the scale and type of distribution, together with the nature of the advertisement itself, makes it clear that taxable supplies will be made.
  (iv) Instructions or advice from professional advisers that specifies the VAT treatment, together with confirmation of acceptance of the advice by the business.
  (v) Any other similar document that shows that the intention is to make taxable supplies.
  The list is not intended to be exhaustive and whether a particular document provides the evidence will depend largely upon its content. It is unlikely that any single document alone will provide sufficient evidence and a business is advised to hold a number of separate documents to prove its intention. HMRC will normally consider evidence as satisfactory where it involves third parties and shows a firm commitment to the making of taxable supplies. A document that merely sets out an option or number of options will not be acceptable.
  Where input tax relating to future taxable supplies has been recovered, a business should retain any documents used as evidence of intention and make them available to HMRC on request. If there is any change in the intention to make taxable supplies, a record must be kept of the date of change (together with appropriate evidence) and HMRC must

also be informed of the change as soon as possible. Any VAT previously deducted before the intention changed may need to be adjusted and repaid to HMRC.

An option to tax must be made and notified to HMRC prior to any supplies of the land or buildings being made.

- Where, prior to supplies being made, the intention to make exempt supplies changes to an intention to make taxable supplies, a business may be able to recover previously exempt input tax under the 'payback' rule. See **50.14 PARTIAL EXEMPTION**. But where the change of intention is not accompanied by an option to tax, the business will need to retain suitable evidence of its new intention (see (i) to (v) above).
- Where a business made exempt supplies of the land or building before opting to tax and incurred exempt input tax, it may be able to recover this under the permission procedure in **42.34** above.

Pre-registration VAT

A business may become registered for VAT as a result of the option to tax. Special rules apply to all newly registered businesses under which they may be entitled to claim relief for VAT incurred on supplies they obtained before registration. See **35.10 INPUT TAX.** The amount claimable is restricted on supplies of services to those received not more than six months before registration. This restriction may lead to inequitable treatment compared with a business carrying out similar activities, but which was already VAT-registered when the tax was incurred. If a business considers that it has suffered because of this, it should write to the Option To Tax National Unit, HM Revenue and Customs, Portcullis House, 21 India Street, Glasgow, G2 4PZ and explain the circumstances.

In all cases, relief for VAT incurred before registration is restricted to VAT which can be directly attributed to a taxable activity. If a business incurred VAT before registration that was attributable both to exempt supplies before registration as well as taxable supplies after registration, the relief will be restricted proportionately.

(VAT Notice 742A, paras 9.1, 9.2, 9.4).

Appeals

[42.36] An appeal may be made against any refusal by HMRC to grant any permission under, or otherwise to exercise in favour of a particular person any power conferred by, any provision in **42.23** to **42.34** above.

Where there is an appeal against such a refusal,

- the tribunal must not allow the appeal unless it considers that HMRC could not reasonably have been satisfied that there were grounds for the refusal; and
- the refusal has effect pending the determination of the appeal.

[*VATA 1994, ss 83(wb), 84(7ZA)*].

Key points

[42.37] Points to consider are as follows.

- Zero-rating for approved alterations to listed buildings has now been phased out. For a builder to zero-rate his services on a listed building, it was important that he confirmed that the work qualified as an approved alteration, i.e. the building fell within one of the definitions in **42.2** above and listed building planning consent had been obtained. Fail to meet these conditions and the work was standard-rated regardless of the protected nature of the property.
- Work that is classed as repair or maintenance on a listed building is always standard-rated.
- It is possible for a building to still be classed as new, and benefit from zero-rated building services in some cases, even if it has not been totally demolished. The retention of a single facade, or double façade on a corner site, will still enable a building to be classed as new as long as the retention of the facade(s) is a condition of planning consent.
- A new building either designed as a dwelling, or to be used for a relevant charitable or residential purpose, can benefit from zero-rated construction services, as long as the builder holds a certificate from the building user in the case of charitable or residential buildings.
- It is important to recognise that any zero-rating of building work is only possible up to the time when the building is completed, e.g. certificate of completion issued by an architect. Any work carried out after this date tends to be standard-rated, unless it is to correct a defect or problem with the original building work.
- A relevant charitable purpose only applies to a building that is solely used by a charity for non-business purposes (e.g. a place of worship). Any business use, other than a very minor amount, would mean the building would not qualify as being for a relevant charitable purpose.
- Minor business use of a charitable building can be ignored if it is up to 5% of total use. The previous 10% concessionary treatment remains relevant because of the possibility of a charge on the charity if use changes within ten years of receiving a zero-rated supply that depended on the concession.
- There are many exceptions to the general rule that supplies involving land are exempt from VAT. For example, accommodation provided in a hotel or similar establishment is always standard-rated, as is a charge for parking a vehicle on land.
- A service charge from a landlord to a tenant to cover building repairs, window cleaning and other costs etc., will follow the same VAT liability as the main rental payment. So if an option to

tax election is in place on the building by the landlord, the service charge and rental payments will both be standard-rated – otherwise, they will both be exempt.

- An option to tax election on a building means that income generated by the building will be standard-rated rather than exempt (with important exceptions for residential parts of the building and building use by a charity for non-business purposes other than as an office). The motive for making an election with HMRC is to enable input tax to be recovered on the related costs of the building.
- There is no such thing as an 'opted building'. Each person with an interest in a property makes his own decision as to whether an election is worthwhile. So a landlord may have opted to tax a property, and will charge VAT on the rent to his tenant, but the tenant might have decided not to make an election, i.e. he will not charge VAT on the rent to a subtenant.
- If a person sells a building on which he has made an option to tax election, and the opted building includes both a residential and non-residential element, then the value of the sale should be apportioned so that only the non-residential element is standard-rated. The option to tax election does not apply to residential properties.
- A common practical problem with option to tax arrangements is where a business decides to opt to tax a property, but forgets to notify HMRC of the option. In such cases, a belated notification can be made to HMRC, as long as it can be shown that the intention was clearly made (e.g. through a board meeting, correspondence or charging of VAT on rent to a tenant).
- The decision to make an option to tax election should only be made after a great deal of consideration. This is because it cannot be revoked for 20 years (apart from an initial cooling off period in limited circumstances) so has long-term consequences.
- It is important for tenants or buyers of a building to enquire whether the option to tax election could be revoked by a landlord under the 20-year rule. This is particularly important if the buyer or tenant has an input tax restriction (partly exempt etc.) but there are often also cash flow and stamp duty land tax (SDLT) or Scottish land and buildings transaction tax (LBTT) advantages in not being charged VAT on the purchase of a building.

43

Land and Buildings: Zero and Reduced Rate Supplies and DIY Housebuilders

Property developers

Zero-rated supplies of qualifying buildings

[43.1] The following supplies are zero-rated.

(a) **New dwellings**

The first 'grant' of a 'major interest' in, or in any part of, a building, dwelling or its site by a 'person constructing a building' 'designed as a dwelling' or number of dwellings unless either

(i) the interest granted is such that the grantee is not entitled to reside in the building, or part, throughout the year (e.g. a time-share); or

(ii) residence there throughout the year or the use of the building or part as the grantee's principal private residence, is prevented by the terms of a covenant, statutory planning consent or similar permission (i.e. accommodation which cannot lawfully be occupied as a permanent residence).

[*VATA 1994, Sch 8 Group 5 Item 1(a)* and *Note (13)*].

See **42 LAND AND BUILDINGS: EXEMPT SUPPLIES AND OPTION TO TAX** at **42.6** for the definition of 'grant', **42.10** for 'major interest', **42.12** for 'person constructing a building' and **42.5** for 'designed as a dwelling'.

First sale or long lease

The above provisions only zero-rate the first sale of, or grant of a long lease in, a building but zero-rating is not affected by

- the length of time between completion of construction and sale of, or grant of a long lease in, the building;
- any sale of, or grant of a long lease in, the building made by other people (even if they also have 'person constructing' status or have made their own zero-rated supply in the building);
- any short leases that may have been made (although this is likely to affect input tax recovery); or
- any sales of, or grant of long leases in, other parts of the building that the same person may have made (e.g. the developer of a block of flats can zero-rate his first long lease in each flat).

A grantor cannot zero-rate any second or subsequent long lease in the building (or the sale of the building after leasing it on a long lease).

If the first grant is a long lease, and the developer is using the building for a business purpose, other than solely for the purpose of selling it, the building may have to be treated as a capital for the purposes of the **11 CAPITAL GOODS SCHEME**.

Where house builders are unable to sell new dwellings due to the economic climate, they may wish to make, in advance of any short term lets, the first grant of a major interest in completed dwellings to a connected person who is not a member of the builder's VAT group. The connected person would then rent out the properties until such a time as they can be sold. The rentals would be exempt and not give rise to input tax deduction on ongoing costs, including the costs of the eventual sale (e.g. estate agency and legal costs), but deduction of the VAT associated with the original construction would have been secured. HMRC have stated that such arrangements would not be seen as abusive. However, if the VAT deducted goes beyond that which would normally be deducted in relation to the supply of the new dwelling (e.g. VAT on costs such as repairs, maintenance or refurbishment, which is not normally deductible) such arrangements are likely to be challenged by HMRC as abusive.

Land included

In addition to the dwelling, zero-rating also applies to

- the land on which the building stands (the 'footprint');
- a reasonable plot of land surrounding it. This will depend on the size, nature and situation of the building and the nature of the surrounding land; and
- the right to park a vehicle, so long as the parking place is close by and is intended to be used in conjunction with the building or dwelling.

Partly-constructed buildings

Provided the other conditions above are met, zero-rating also applies to the sale of, or grant of a long lease in, land that will form the site of a building provided a building is clearly under construction.

Deposits relating to sales of land

Where development land is sold, in particular to registered social landlords (RSLs), it is common for a deposit to be released to the vendor (thus creating a tax point) at the time of exchange of contracts when construction has not commenced and the land is still bare land. HMRC's view is that where the deposit is released to the vendor and it is clear from the contract or agreement that what will be supplied at completion, or the time of the grant, will be partly completed dwellings (beyond 'golden brick'), the deposit is part payment for the grant/supply that will occur at that time. It follows that the VAT liability of the deposit is determined by the anticipated nature of the supply and that zero-rating will be appropriate if it is intended that the conditions for zero-rating will be satisfied at the time of completion. For example, there must be a clear intention that the vendor will have commenced construction of the dwellings at that time and acquired 'person constructing' status. It is possible that the state of the land at completion will differ from that which was anticipated and where this is the case it will be necessary to revisit the VAT treatment of the deposit. (HMRC Brief 36/09).

Apportionment for part-qualifying buildings

(1) *General.* Where part of a building qualifies for zero-rating under the above provisions and part does not (e.g. shop premises with a flat over them), a grant or supply relating only to the part within these provisions is to be treated as relating to a zero-rated building and, similarly, a grant or supply relating only to the part outside those provisions is not to be so treated. In the case of any other grant or supply, an apportionment must be made to determine the extent to which it is to be so treated. [*VATA 1994, Sch 8 Group 5 Note (10)*].

> ***Example***
>
> ABC Property Ltd has built a new ground floor shop and first floor flat, which is being sold to DEF Ltd for an inclusive price of £500,000 plus any VAT that is due. The proceeds of the sale need to be apportioned so that VAT is charged on the market value of the shop, which is standard-rated because it is a new commercial building that is less than three years old. The element of the sale relating to the flat is zero-rated as relevant to the first sale of a new dwelling by the person constructing it.

(2) *Live-work units.* In a live-work unit (i.e. a property that combines, within a single unit, a dwelling and commercial or industrial working space as a requirement or condition of planning permission), zero-rating is only available to the extent that the unit comprises the dwelling

(provided it meets the other conditions for zero-rating above). Dwellings that contain a home office are not live-work units and no apportionment is needed.

Units where the work area is shown as a discrete area of floor space, whether an office or workshop, must be apportioned to reflect the presence of the commercial element. Where planning permission requires that a minimum amount of the unit (e.g. 20%) must be used for commercial or industrial purposes, the remaining amount (i.e. 80%) can be treated as being the dwelling element for VAT purposes.

HMRC's Notice states that where a unit has neither

- an area that must, as a requirement or condition of planning permission, be used for commercial or industrial purposes, nor
- planning permission requiring a certain percentage of the floor space be used for commercial or industrial purposes;

it may be treated for VAT purposes as if it were entirely a dwelling and no apportionment is required.

However, there have been several cases in which HMRC have argued that the terms of the planning consent for a 'live-work unit' prevent the building from satisfying *Group 5 Note 2*, in that the 'live' part cannot be used or disposed of separately from the 'work' part. The taxpayer succeeded in *H Pearson* [2013] UKFTT 332 (TC) (TC02735) (TVC 15.59); HMRC's view was upheld in *J & Mrs S Kear* [2013] UKFTT 95 (TC) (TC02513) (TVC 15.82). The decisions in each case depended on the precise terms of the planning consent.

Apportionment for mixed sites

Where a person sells, or grants a long lease in, a qualifying dwelling at the same time as a non-qualifying building or land that does not form part of the site (see under *Land included* above), an apportionment must be made between them on a fair and reasonable basis.

Shared ownership schemes

These involve the sharing of equity in a dwelling between, typically, an occupier and a housing association. The occupier purchases a dwelling at a proportion of its value and then pays rent to cover the share in the retained equity. Occupiers have the option of increasing their share of the equity by making additional payments, acquiring a further share related to the current value of the property ('staircasing'). The rent is then reduced accordingly. The initial payment by the occupier for his share of the equity can be zero-rated but the subsequent rental payments and any additional 'staircase' payments are not zero-rated but exempt.

Holiday homes

The restrictions under (i) and (ii) above typically prevent the sale of holiday homes by a developer from qualifying for zero-rating.

(VAT Notice 708, paras 4.3, 4.4, 4.6, 4.8, 16.1–16.4; HMRC Brief 54/08).

(b) New residential and charitable buildings

The first 'grant' of a 'major interest' in, or in any part of, a building, dwelling or its site by a 'person constructing a building' intended for use solely for a 'relevant residential purpose' or a 'relevant charitable purpose'. [*VATA 1994, Sch 8 Group 5 Item 1(a)*].

See **42 LAND AND BUILDINGS: EXEMPT SUPPLIES AND OPTION TO TAX** at **42.6** for definition of 'grant', **42.10** for '*major interest*', **42.12** for '*person constructing a building*', **42.16** for '*relevant residential purpose*' and **42.14** for '*relevant charitable purpose*'.

The provisions within (*a*) above under the headings *First sale or long lease*, *Land included*, *Partly constructed buildings*, *Apportionment for part-qualifying buildings* and *Apportionment for mixed sites* also apply for these purposes.

In addition, where the supply is in connection with a building intended for use as

- residential accommodation for students or school pupils, or
- residential accommodation for members of any of the armed forces

the supply can only be zero-rated to the extent that it relates to the residential accommodation. Where the supply is in connection with a building intended for use as a home or other institution, zero-rating or reduced-rating is not restricted to the residential accommodation but can extend to other areas within the building(s) such as administration offices or leisure or educational facilities.

(VAT Notice 708, paras 4.6, 4.8, 16.5).

Care homes

HMRC have released HMRC Brief 2/17 which confirms that the construction and first grant of a major interest in a building, intended for use solely for a relevant residential purpose as a care home, is zero-rated. The purpose of the Brief is to provide clarification on the difference between a hospital and a care home, as the construction and the grant of the first major interest in a hospital cannot be zero-rated. HMRC's change in policy is the result of a recent VAT case, *Pennine Care NHS Trust* [2016] UKFTT 222 (TC) (TC04998) where the Tribunal ruled in favour of the taxpayer.

Issue of certificates

Where all, or any part of, a building is intended for use solely for a relevant residential purpose or relevant charitable purpose, the grant of a major interest cannot be zero-rated under this provision unless, before the grant is made, the grantee has given the grantor a certificate to that effect. See **43.22** below.

(c) Conversion of non-residential buildings

The first 'grant' of a 'major interest' in, or in any part of, a building, dwelling or its site by a 'person converting'

(i) a 'non-residential' building, or

(ii) a non-residential part of a building

into a building 'designed as a dwelling' or number of dwellings or a building intended for use solely for a 'relevant residential purpose' unless either

(A) the interest granted is such that the grantee is not entitled to reside in the building, or part, throughout the year (e.g. a time share); or

(B) residence there throughout the year or the use of the building or part as the grantee's principal private residence, is prevented by the terms of a covenant, statutory planning consent or similar permission (i.e. accommodation which cannot lawfully be occupied as a permanent residence).

Where (ii) applies and the building already contains a residential part, then for zero-rating to apply, the conversion must either be to a building for use for a relevant residential purpose or must create an additional dwelling or dwellings.

[*VATA 1994, Sch 8 Group 5 Item 1(b)* and *Note (9)*].

See **42 LAND AND BUILDINGS: EXEMPT SUPPLIES AND OPTION TO TAX** at **42.6** for the definition of '*grant*', **42.10** for '*major interest*', **42.11** for '*non-residential*', **42.5** above for '*designed as a dwelling*', and **42.16** for '*relevant residential purpose*'.

'*Person converting*' a building has the same meaning as 'person constructing' a building in **42.12** above substituting references to converting/conversion for constructing/construction throughout.

Examples of a non-residential conversion include the conversion of

- a commercial building (such as an office, warehouse, shop, etc.),
- an agricultural building (such as a barn), or
- a redundant school or church

into a building designed as a dwelling or number of dwellings.

The provisions within (*a*) above under the headings *First sale or long lease* and *Land included* apply in the same way for these purposes.

Garages

The conversion of a garage, occupied together with a dwelling, into a building designed as a dwelling is not a non-residential conversion. '*Garage*' not only covers buildings designed to store motor vehicles but also buildings such as barns which are used as garages. But if it can be established that the garage was never used to store motor vehicles (or has not been used as a garage for a considerable length of time prior to conversion) its conversion into a building designed as a dwelling can be a non-residential conversion.

Holiday homes

The restrictions under (A) and (B) above typically prevent the sale of holiday homes by a converter from qualifying for zero-rating.

Amalgamating non-residential parts of a building with other parts

According to HMRC's settled view, to qualify for zero-rating, the conversion must only use non-residential parts of the building. For example, if a two-storey public house containing bar areas downstairs and private living areas upstairs (and so in part being used as a dwelling) is converted into two flats, one created out of the bar areas and one out of the private living area, then in HMRC's view the onward sale or long lease of the former is zero-rated but that of the latter will be exempt. On the other hand, if the conversion uses a mixture of non-residential parts of the building and other parts, such as when the same property is converted

- into a single house, or
- by splitting it vertically into a pair of semi-detached houses, each of which use part of what was the living accommodation,

the onward sale or long lease is not zero-rated and is exempt. See the case law uncertainty on this point in **42.11 LAND AND BUILDINGS: EXEMPT SUPPLIES AND OPTION TO TAX** – different First-tier Tribunals have agreed and disagreed with HMRC's interpretation, and further developments are awaited. The logical conclusion of the most recent decision (*Languard New Homes Ltd* [2016] UKFTT 129 (TC) (TC04917)) is that:

- a conversion of a mixed use building into a single house would lead to an exempt sale; but
- any conversion of a mixed use building into a building containing more dwellings than there were before, whether split horizontally or vertically, would qualify for zero-rating on subsequent sales of all the new dwellings created.

Partly converted buildings

Subject to satisfying the other conditions, zero-rating can be applied to the sale of, or grant of a long lease in, a building where a real and meaningful start on the conversion has been made. This means that the work must have been more than securing or maintaining the existing structure.

Apportionment

(1) *Apportionment for converted parts of buildings.* It is only possible to zero-rate the sale of, or grant of a long lease in, a building (or part of a building) when the new qualifying residential accommodation is created wholly from a non-residential building or part of a building. Where a mixture of qualifying and non-qualifying conversions in a building is carried out, the charge can be apportioned and zero-rating applied to the sale of, or grant of a long lease in, the qualifying parts. For example
   - A shop is converted into a flat and existing flats above the shop, that have been lived in within the last ten years, are refurbished. Zero-rating applies to the sale of, or grant of a long lease in, the converted shop but not the refurbished flats.
   - A two-storey public house containing private living areas and bar areas is converted into a pair of flats. The living areas have been 'used as a dwelling' (although see the case law uncertainty on this point in **42.11 LAND AND BUILDINGS: EXEMPT SUPPLIES AND OPTION TO TAX**) and so the sale of, or long lease in, those

parts cannot be zero-rated. The sale of, or grant of a long lease in, the converted bar areas can be zero-rated provided that the new flat is created solely from the non-residential areas.

(2) *Apportionment for mixed sites*. Where a development site, containing a mixture of buildings that qualify for zero-rating as the conversion of a non-residential building (or part of a building) and other buildings, is sold or long-leased, the supplies must be apportioned on a fair and reasonable basis.

(VAT Notice 708, paras 5.3–5.8).

Issue of certificates

Where all, or any part of, a building is intended for use solely for a relevant residential purpose, the grant of a major interest cannot be zero-rated under these provisions unless, before the grant is made, the grantee has given the grantor a certificate to that effect. See **43.22** below.

Garages

The construction of a building under (*a*) above or the conversion of a non-residential building under (*c*) above includes the construction of, or conversion of a non-residential building to, a garage provided

- the dwelling and the garage are constructed or converted at the same time; and
- the garage is intended for occupation with the dwelling or one of the dwellings.

[*VATA 1994, Sch 8 Group 5 Note (3)*].

Tenancies and leases

Where the major interest granted under (*a*)–(*c*) above is a tenancy or lease, zero-rating only applies to the premium payable on the grant or, if no premium is payable, the first payment of rent due under the tenancy or lease. [*VATA 1994, Sch 8 Group 5 Note (14)*]. Ongoing payments, such as further rents, ground rent or service charges cannot be zero-rated.

Change of use of relevant residential or charitable buildings

Where the grant of a major interest in a building is zero-rated under these provisions because the grantee certifies that the building will be used for a relevant residential purpose or a relevant charitable purpose, the grantee will be treated as making a standard-rated supply of the property if, within ten years of its completion, he either sells, lets or uses the building for any other purpose. See **43.2** below for full details.

Groups of companies

In the rare situation when a group member makes more than one grant of a major interest in a building, the first of which is to another group member, HMRC do not consider that first grant to be the 'first grant of a major interest' in the building for the purpose of zero-rating. In effect, this means that the first grant of a major interest to a person outside the group can be zero-rated, regardless of the previous activity within the VAT group, so long as the group member making the grant is a person constructing (or converting) the building and it meets all the other criteria. (Business Brief 11/03).

Joint ownership and beneficial interests

See **42.20 LAND AND BUILDINGS: EXEMPT SUPPLIES AND OPTION TO TAX.**

De Voil Indirect Tax Service. See V4.233; V4.234.

Residential and charitable buildings: change of use

[43.2] A charge to VAT arises where the construction of, or grant of an interest in, a building has been zero-rated on the basis of its intended use (a relevant residential or charitable purpose) and that use changes after the grant has been made.

Before 1 March 2011, the charge to tax and the method of calculating it differed depending on whether or not the recipient of the zero-rated supply subsequently granted an interest to a third party. Where a change in use occurred in an unidentifiable part of the premises, the charge arose on the entire premises or part of the premises. These rules can still be relevant because the charge arises on a change of use or disposal takes place within ten years of a zero-rated grant or construction supply.

From 1 March 2011

A charge arises on each occasion that there is an increase in the use of the premises for a non-relevant purpose, where a person disposes of the entire interest in the premises (or part of), or the premises (or part of) are used for a non-relevant purpose.

Where use is made of the premises (or part of) for both a relevant and a non-relevant purpose, the proportion of use for a non-relevant purpose is to be calculated in the same proportion as if an identifiable part of the building were used for a non-relevant purpose.

Where a charity is using the relevant premises (or a part of) as a village hall or similarly in providing social or recreational facilities for a local community, the premises are (or the part is) treated as being used for a relevant charitable purpose whether or not the occupier is using them for a relevant charitable purpose.

Where the charge applies, the person's interest, right or licence in the relevant premises held immediately prior to the time when the increase occurs is treated as

- supplied to him for the purposes of a business which he carries on; and
- supplied by him in the course or furtherance of that business

immediately prior to the time of that increase.

The supply is taken to be a taxable supply which is not zero-rated, the value of which is taken to be

- in the case of the first deemed supply, the amount obtained by the formula
  R2 × Y × ((120 – Z) / 120); and
- in the case of any subsequent deemed supply, the amount obtained by the formula
  (R2 – R1) × Y × ((120 – Z) / 120)

Where

R2 is the proportion of the relevant premises disposed of or used for non-relevant purposes in the relevant period.

R1 is the proportion of the relevant premises disposed of or used for non-relevant purposes at an earlier time in the relevant period.

Y is the amount that yields the amount of VAT that would have been chargeable on the relevant supply if it had not been zero-rated (or the aggregate amount of VAT if there was more than one supply).

Z is the number of whole months since the day on which the relevant premises were completed.

'Relevant zero-rated supply' means a grant or other supply relating to a building (or part of) intended for use solely for a relevant residential or charitable purpose and which is zero-rated as a result of *VATA 1994, Sch 8, Group 5*.

'Relevant premises' means the building (or part of) in relation to which a relevant zero-rated supply has been made to the person.

'Relevant period' means ten years beginning with the day on which the relevant premises are completed.

[*VATA 1994, Sch 10, paras 35–37*].

Example

A charity constructs/acquires a new five-floored building, which it intends to use solely for a non-business purpose. The value of the zero-rated supply is £5 million. After five years, during which the building is used as intended, the charity decides that it will use the top floor for a business purpose. The VAT due on the self-supply is calculated as follows.

Proportion of building affected by change is 1/5 floors, ie 20%.

Number of months remaining in ten-year period that part of the building will not be used as intended is 60/120 months, ie 50%.

Value of self-supply is 20% × £5m × 50% = £500,000.

VAT due on self-supply is £500,000 × 20% = £100,000*.

After a further two years, the charity decides that it will use a further two floors for a business purpose. The VAT due on the self-supply is calculated as follows.

Proportion of building now being used for a non-relevant purpose is 3/5 floors, ie 60%.

Number of months remaining in ten-year period that the further part of the building will not be used as intended is 36/120 months, ie 30%.

Value of self-supply is (60 – 20)% x £5m × 30% = £600,000.

VAT due on the self-supply is £600,000 × 20% = £120,000*.

*This VAT may be recovered to the extent that it relates to a taxable activity in accordance with the normal VAT rules.

These rules were considered by the First-tier Tax Tribunal in *Balhousie Holdings Ltd* [2016] UKFTT 377 (TC) (TC05131). A company had constructed three care homes and had issued zero-rating certificates on each of them for relevant residential purpose. It then entered into a sale-and-leaseback transaction to raise finance for its operations. HMRC ruled that the disposal to a Real Estate Investment Trust triggered the self-supply charge, and raised assessments for over £800,000 plus interest and an inaccuracy penalty. The judge accepted the company's argument that it had not disposed of its whole interest in the building: the leaseback was inextricably linked to the sale. The judge considered that it was appropriate to interpret the legislation in accordance with what appeared to be its purpose. The self-supply charge appeared to be an anti-avoidance measure, whereas this was a commercial financing transaction which did not involve a change of the relevant residential use. HMRC appealed against this decision. The Upper Tribunal reversed the First-tier Tribunal's decision and held that a clawback had been triggered where the owner had done a sale and leaseback of the care home they had built. The Upper tribunal concluded that by the sale of the care home, the subsidiary had 'disposed of its entire interest' and this constituted a change of use triggering a self-supply charge. The Upper Tribunal reached the conclusion that it doesn't matter, that by a further linked transaction, it acquired under the lease a right of a similar character. That outcome does not result in an unrealistic or artificial approach and properly flows from the terms of *VATA 1994, Sch 10, para 36(2)*.

RCP building acquired before 1 March 2011

(1) Disposal, part disposal or letting

The following provisions apply if

- one or more 'relevant zero-rated supplies' relating to a building (or part of a building) have been made to a person;
- within the period of ten years beginning with the day on which the building is 'completed', the person grants an 'interest in, right over or licence to occupy'
  - (i) the building or any part of it; or
  - (ii) the building or any part of it including, consisting of or forming part of the part to which the relevant zero-rated supply or supplies related; and
- after the grant
  - (i) the whole or any part of the building or of the part to which the grant relates, or
  - (ii) the whole of the building or of the part to which the grant relates, or any part of it including, consisting of or forming part of the part to which the relevant zero-rated supply or supplies related,

is not intended for use solely for a 'relevant residential purpose' or a 'relevant charitable purpose'.

In such circumstances, so far as the grant relates to so much of the building as

- by reason of its intended use gave rise to the relevant zero-rated supply or supplies, and
- is not intended for use solely for a relevant residential purpose or a relevant charitable purpose after the grant,

it is taken to be a taxable supply in the course or furtherance of a business which is not zero-rated as a result of *VATA 1994, Sch 8 Group 5*.

A '*relevant zero-rated supply*' means a grant or other supply which relates to a building (or part of a building) intended for use solely for a 'relevant residential purpose' or a 'relevant charitable purpose' and which, as a result of *VATA 1994, Sch 8 Group 5* is zero-rated in whole or in part.

See **42 LAND AND BUILDINGS: EXEMPT SUPPLIES AND OPTION TO TAX** at **42.7** for when '*completion*' of a building takes place; **42.8, 42.9** for the meaning of '*interest in, right over or licence to occupy*'; **42.14** for '*relevant charitable purpose*' and **42.16** for '*relevant residential purpose*'.

The VAT due must be accounted for on the VAT return for the VAT period in which the supply is made.

[*VATA 1994, Sch 10 paras 35, 36, 38; SI 2008/1146, Art 2*]. (VAT Notice 708, para 19.2).

(2) Change of use without disposal

The following provisions apply if

- one or more 'relevant zero-rated supplies' (see (1) above) relating to a building (or part of a building) have been made to a person; and
- within the period of 10 years beginning with the day on which the building is completed (see (1) above), the person uses
  - (i) the building or any part of it, or
  - (ii) the building or any part of it including, consisting of or forming part of the part to which the relevant zero-rated supply or supplies related,

  for a purpose which is neither a 'relevant residential purpose' nor a 'relevant charitable purpose'.

In such circumstances, the person's 'interest in, right over or licence to occupy' so much of the building as

- by reason of its intended use gave rise to the relevant zero-rated supply or supplies, and
- is used otherwise than for a relevant residential purpose or a relevant charitable purpose,

is treated as supplied *to* the person for the purposes of a business which the person carries on and supplied *by* the person in the course or furtherance of the business when the person first uses it for a purpose which is neither a relevant residential purpose nor a relevant charitable purpose.

The supply is taken to be a taxable supply which is not zero-rated as a result of *VATA 1994, Sch 8 Group 5*. The value of the supply is calculated by the formula

$$A \times (10 - B) \div 10$$

where

A = the amount that yields an amount of VAT chargeable on it equal to the VAT which would have been chargeable on the relevant zero-rated supply (or, if there was more than one supply, the aggregate amount of the VAT which would have been chargeable on the supplies) had so much of the building not been intended for use solely for a relevant residential purpose or a relevant charitable purpose.

B = the number of whole years since the day the building was completed for which the building or part concerned has been used for a relevant residential purpose or a relevant charitable purpose.

See **42 LAND AND BUILDINGS: EXEMPT SUPPLIES AND OPTION TO TAX** at **42.8, 42.9** for the meaning of '*interest in, right over or licence to occupy*'; **42.14** for '*relevant charitable purpose*' and **42.16** for '*relevant residential purpose*'.

[*VATA 1994, Sch 10 paras 35, 37*].

Example

A charity paid £1 million for a new zero-rated building for its non-business use. After seven years and seven months it changes the use of the entire building to business use. At the time of purchase the VAT rate was 17.5%.

The VAT that would have been payable if the initial supply had been standard-rated is

£1m × 17.5% = £175,000

The amount due to HMRC is £175,000 × 30% = £52,500.

The VAT due on the deemed self-supply must be accounted for as output tax on the VAT return for the period in which the use is changed. The VAT can be deducted as input tax on the same return to the extent that it relates to any other taxable supplies made. It may be necessary to make subsequent adjustments to the amount of input tax deducted under the **11 CAPITAL GOODS SCHEME** where

- the tax charge is £250,000 or more, and
- the building is used to make exempt supplies.

(VAT Notice 708, para 19.2).

Limitation of above provisions

The effect of the above provisions only applying to zero-rating under *VATA 1994, Sch 8 Group 5* means that the rules only apply where the original grant or supply was

- zero-rated as the construction of a new building;
- zero-rated as the sale of, or long lease in, a new building;
- zero-rated as the sale of, or long lease in, a non-residential building; or
- zero-rated as the conversion of a non-residential building for a relevant housing association,

and the concession for minor non-qualifying use in buildings intended for use solely for a relevant charitable purpose has not been invoked (see **42.14 LAND AND BUILDINGS: EXEMPT SUPPLIES AND OPTION TO TAX**).

The rules do not apply to the extent that the original grant or supply was

- zero-rated as approved alterations to a protected building;
- zero-rated as the sale or long lease in a substantially reconstructed protected building;
- reduced-rated;
- an interest in a building that was exempt from VAT; or
- more than ten years ago

or where a refund was received under the D-I-Y builders scheme.

VAT registration

The charges and deemed self-supplies described above are included in taxable turnover when deciding whether VAT registration is required.

(VAT Notice 708, paras 19.1, 19.2).

De Voil Indirect Tax Service. See V3.248.

Substantial reconstructions of protected buildings

[43.3] The first 'grant' by a person 'substantially reconstructing' a 'protected building' of a 'major interest' in, or in any part of, the building or its site is zero-rated. [*VATA 1994, Sch 8 Group 6 Item 1*].

See **42 LAND AND BUILDINGS: EXEMPT SUPPLIES AND OPTION TO TAX** at **42.6** for the definition of '*grant*', **42.13** for '*protected building*' and **42.10** for '*major interest*'.

The grant of an interest in a building 'designed as a dwelling' (see **42.5 LAND AND BUILDINGS: EXEMPT SUPPLIES AND OPTION TO TAX**) or number of dwellings (or the site of such a building) is *not* zero-rated under these provisions if either

(i) the interest granted is such that the grantee is not entitled to reside in the building throughout the year (e.g. a time-share); or
(ii) residence there throughout the year, or use of the building as the grantee's principal private residence, is prevented by the terms of a covenant, statutory planning consent or similar permission (i.e. accommodation which cannot lawfully be occupied as a permanent residence).

[*VATA 1994, Sch 8 Group 5 Note (13), Group 6 Note (3); SI 1995/283*].

The restrictions under (i) and (ii) above typically prevent holiday homes from qualifying for zero-rating. (VAT Notice 708, para 10.6).

'Substantially reconstructing'

A protected building is substantially reconstructed when reconstruction takes place that is a major work to its fabric, including the replacement of much of the internal or external structure. (VAT Notice 708, para 10.4). In addition, a protected building is not to be regarded as substantially reconstructed unless when the reconstruction is completed at least one of the following two conditions for zero-rating is fulfilled.

From 1 October 2015 the second condition must be satisfied, as the first condition no longer applies from that date. Between 1 October 2012 and 30 September 2015, it was still possible to satisfy the first condition under transitional arrangements that are described below.

(1) At least 3/5ths (i.e. 60%) of the cost of the reconstruction work would, if supplied by a taxable person, qualify for zero-rating as the supply of services in the course of approved alterations under **43.10** below or building materials and other items to carry out those works under **43.16** or **43.17** below. When determining if at least 3/5ths of the work could be zero-rated as 'approved alterations', all of the work to the building should be considered, even if only part will be used for qualifying purposes. But only those alterations to the qualifying parts can count towards the zero-rated element.
Under transitional arrangements, the first grant of a substantially reconstructed protected building could be zero-rated until 30 September 2015 where
   - at least 3/5ths of the work (measured by reference to cost) would, if supplied by a taxable person, be relevant supplies under the transitional arrangements for approved alterations (see **43.10** below); or
   - at least 10% (measured by reference to cost) of the reconstruction was completed before 21 March 2012 and at least 3/5ths of the work would, if supplied by a taxable person, be relevant supplies under the transitional arrangements for approved alterations (see **43.10** below) but for the requirement for a written contract to have been entered into or relevant consent to have been applied for before 21 March 2012.

(2) The reconstructed building incorporates no more of the original building before reconstruction began than the external walls, together with other external features of architectural or historic interest.

[*VATA 1994, Sch 8 Group 6 Note (4)*].

Tenancies and leases

Where the major interest is a tenancy or lease, zero-rating only applies to the premium payable on the grant or, if no premium is payable, the first payment of rent due under the tenancy or lease. [*VATA 1994, Sch 8 Group 5 Note (14); Group 6 Note (3)*]. (The effect of this is that zero-rating only covers the sum payable when the lease is granted and subsequent payments such as ground rent or service charges cannot be zero-rated.)

Part-qualifying buildings

Where part of a protected building qualifies for zero-rating of a grant under the above provisions and part does not (e.g. shop premises with a flat over them), the same principles apply as for new buildings, as described in **43.1** above. [*VATA 1994, Sch 8 Group 6 Note (5)*].

Apportionment for mixed sites

Where a person sells, or grants a long lease in, a development site containing buildings that qualify for zero-rating as substantially reconstructed protected buildings (or parts of buildings) and other buildings, he must apportion the charge between them on a fair and reasonable basis.

Issue of certificates

Where all or any part of the substantially reconstructed building is intended for use solely for a relevant residential or charitable purpose, the grant of a major interest cannot be zero-rated under these provisions unless, before the grant is made, the grantee has given the grantor a certificate to that effect. See **43.22** below.

'Person substantially reconstructing' status

A person is a 'person substantially reconstructing' a protected building if, in relation to that building, he is, or has at any point in the past

- acted as a developer (i.e. physically substantially reconstructed, or commissioned another person to physically substantially reconstruct, the building that he owns or has an interest in); or
- acted as a contractor or subcontractor (i.e. provided reconstruction services to the developer or another contractor for the substantial reconstruction of the building, sub-contracting work as necessary).

More than one person can enjoy 'person substantially reconstructing' status but such status is not transferred when the property is transferred. Each person must meet the conditions specified above. For example, where a developer takes over and finishes a partly reconstructed building, both the first and second developer has 'person substantially reconstructing' status because they have both been involved in physically reconstructing the building.

VAT groups

Although for VAT purposes, any business carried on by a member of a VAT group is treated as carried on by the representative member, when determining whether a supply can be zero-rated, 'person substantially reconstructing' status is only considered from the perspective of the group member who, in reality, makes the supply (which may not be the representative member). For example

(1) A VAT group includes a holding company as the representative member and a development company as a member.
The development company substantially reconstructs and sells a protected building. It has 'person substantially reconstructing' status and so the sales can be zero-rated.

(2) A VAT group includes a development company as representative member and an investment company as a member. The development company substantially reconstructs a block of flats and sells it to the investment company, who in turn leases the flats to the public on long leases.
The investment company does not have 'person substantially reconstructing' status. Even though the representative member does, the leases cannot be zero-rated and are exempt.

Beneficial interests

Where the beneficial owner of a property must register for VAT instead of the legal owner (see **42.20 LAND AND BUILDINGS: EXEMPT SUPPLIES AND OPTION TO TAX**), the beneficial owner must have 'person substantially reconstructing' status before the sale or long lease of the property can be zero-rated.

First sale or long lease

The same principles apply as for new construction (see **43.1** above).

Land included

The same principles apply as for new construction (see **43.1** above).

Garages

Where a grant of a major interest in a substantially reconstructed dwelling is zero-rated under these provisions, zero-rating extends to a garage constructed, or converted from a non-residential building, provided that

- the dwelling and the garage are constructed or converted at the same time; and
- the garage is intended to be occupied with the dwelling or one of the dwellings.

Extensions

A protected building is not 'substantially reconstructed' where the only major alteration is the addition of an extension. However, as work to extend a protected building could be zero-rated as an 'approved alteration' if supplied by a builder, provided other major works are carried out to reconstruct the building, the construction of the extension can count towards the 60% substantial reconstruction calculations (see above).

Joint owners and beneficial interests

See **42.20 LAND AND BUILDINGS: EXEMPT SUPPLIES AND OPTION TO TAX.**

Exempt supplies

Other supplies of protected buildings not within the above provisions are normally exempt, e.g. where

- the building has not been substantially reconstructed;

- the interest granted is not a major interest;
- a major interest is granted by a person other than someone with 'person substantially reconstructing' status (see above);
- the building is not used as a dwelling or for a qualifying purpose.

See, however, **42.23 LAND AND BUILDINGS: EXEMPT SUPPLIES AND OPTION TO TAX** for the option to tax under certain circumstances.

(VAT Notice 708, paras 10.4, 10.7–10.10).

De Voil Indirect Tax Service. See V4.235.

Deduction of input tax

Speculative and abortive costs

[43.4] Developers must normally attribute input tax to either taxable or exempt supplies, depending on the supplies they intend to make, using the partial exemption rules. However, they may investigate many potential projects and incur costs (e.g. finders' fees in looking for sites, options to purchase lands, oil tests, general feasibility, viability and research studies, consultants and other professional fees, etc.) without knowing what, if any, supplies they will eventually make. Such '*speculative supplies*' may not be followed through, in which case they are '*abortive supplies*'.

- Where a developer has a clear intention of what supplies he intends to make, he must attribute the input tax incurred to the liability of the intended supply. So, for example, if the intention is only to build and sell new houses, input tax on speculative costs is attributable to the intended taxable (zero-rated) supplies. See also *Beaverbank Properties Ltd* (VTD 18099) (TVC 36.605).
- Where a developer has no firm intention of what supplies he will make, VAT incurred on speculative costs is input tax (because investigating potential projects is a business activity) but the input tax is 'residual' for partial exemption purposes.

If potential projects are not followed through and no supplies are actually made, where, up to the time of aborting the project, there is no firm intention regarding the liability of the supplies to be made (and as a result it is not possible to attribute the input tax to the liability of the intended supply), the related input tax should be left as residual.

If, on the other hand, the developer decides to proceed with a project, he will have a clear intention as to what supplies will be made and hence what the VAT liability of those supplies will be. (It is normally at this point that the developer decides whether to opt to tax for land and property supplies.) If the developer has not attributed the input tax previously, he should then adjust the input tax accordingly under the 'payback' and 'clawback' rules (see **50.14 PARTIAL EXEMPTION**). Input tax on the ongoing costs should be attributed to the expected taxable or exempt supplies.

Example

ABC Property Ltd has paid £20,000 plus VAT to an architect for developing plans in relation to land that the company would like to buy and build new houses on. The project is aborted because the cost of the land is excessive but the architect is still entitled to his fee.

If the company intended to sell the new houses if the project had proceeded, then the input tax on the architect fees can be fully reclaimed because they relate to an abortive taxable supply. If the intention was to rent them out, then the input tax would be blocked as relevant to an abortive exempt supply.

If the company had no fixed intention to sell or to rent out, the input tax on the abortive costs would be treated as residual expenditure.

(VAT Notice 742A, para 9.3).

Goods incorporated into the building or its site

Where a taxable person constructing a building or effecting any works to a building, in either case for the purpose of granting a major interest in the building (or any part of it) or its site, incorporates goods other than building materials in any part of the building or its site, input tax on the supply, acquisition or importation of the goods is excluded from credit. [*SI 1992/3222, Art 6; SI 1995/281*].

See **43.16** and **43.17** below for examples of zero-rated building materials and zero-rated electrical goods and **43.18** below for a list of standard-rated goods on which VAT is not recoverable under these provisions.

Input tax on related services of installing the goods can be reclaimed provided the services are separately identified and VAT is correctly charged by the person supplying them.

Goods not incorporated into the building

Input tax can be recovered on goods which are not incorporated into the building or its site (e.g. free-standing items). A separate supply takes place when these goods are sold with the building on which output tax must be accounted for at their normal rate.

Showhouses

VAT cannot be reclaimed on standard-rated goods within **43.18** below incorporated into a showhouse if they are to be included in the sale of the house. No output tax is due when these goods are sold with the house.

Removing and disposing of goods on which input tax has been blocked

Where goods to which 'blocking' applies are removed from a property and sold independently (e.g. where the customer prefers a different model appliance), the developer is blocked from deducting input tax on both the original item and any replacement. The disposal of the original item is exempt from VAT.

(VAT Notice 708, paras 12.1–12.4).

Supplies of goods on which input tax blocked

With effect from 1 March 2000, where, under the above provisions, input tax has been blocked on goods incorporated in a building, any onward supply of those goods is an exempt supply. See **21.4 EXEMPT SUPPLIES.** This includes items incorporated in showhouses where these sales are not treated as part of the supply of the building.

De Voil Indirect Tax Service. See V3.444, V3.461B.

Supplies in the construction industry

Introduction

[43.5] The construction of a new building and work to an existing building is normally standard-rated. There are, however, various exceptions to this.

- Certain supplies of construction services may qualify for zero-rating. See **43.6** below.
- Other construction services may be taxable at the reduced rate of 5%. See **43.11** below.

All work that is not specifically zero-rated or taxable at the reduced rate is standard-rated.

Rate of VAT chargeable

The lowest rate applicable to a supply should be charged. For example, where an approved alteration to an empty listed dwelling qualifies for zero-rating under **43.10** below (as an approved alteration to a protected building) and for reduced-rating under **43.13** below (as an alteration of an empty dwelling), zero-rating should be applied.

Retention payments

The same VAT rate applies to retention payments as applied to previous payments made under the contract.

Subcontractors

Subcontractors are contractors who work for other contractors. In most circumstances they can zero-rate or reduce-rate their suppliers in the same way as a main contractor. But where the work requires a certificate for VAT purposes, a subcontractor must standard-rate his supplies to the main contractor (see **43.7** below for supplies in connection with buildings for relevant residential/charitable purposes and **43.9** below for conversion services supplied to housing associations).

(VAT Notice 708, para 2.1).

> *Example*
>
> Mainwell Housing Association has commissioned a building contractor to construct a new building that will be used as a home for elderly people. This building will qualify as a new relevant residential building, so the Association can benefit from zero-rating on the building work if it issues a certificate to the contractor before the work is started.
>
> However, the services provided by subcontractors working for the main contractor are standard-rated because they will not hold a valid certificate from the Association.

De Voil Indirect Tax Service. See V4.237–V4.242.

Zero-rated supplies

[43.6] Zero-rating applies to the following.

- Services supplied in the course of construction of new qualifying dwellings and certain other residential properties and charitable buildings. See **43.7** below.
- Services supplied in the course of construction of civil engineering work for the development of a new permanent residential caravan park. See **43.8** below.
- Services supplied to housing associations in the course of converting non-residential buildings into residential buildings. See **43.9** below.
- Approved alterations to protected buildings. See **43.10** below.
- Building materials and certain electrical goods incorporated into a building by a builder who is also supplying any of the above zero-rated services. See **43.16** to **43.18** below.
- Certain goods and services supplied to disabled persons. See **29.14** *et seq* **HEALTH AND WELFARE.**
- Until 31 December 2011, the first time connection to the gas or electricity mains of dwellings and certain other residential buildings. See **26.7 FUEL AND POWER.**

Construction services

[43.7] Services supplied 'in the course of construction' of a building

(a) 'designed as a dwelling' or number of dwellings, or
(b) intended for use solely for a 'relevant residential purpose' or 'relevant charitable purpose'

and which relate to the construction, are zero-rated. Specifically excluded (and therefore standard-rated) are

- the separate supply of architectural, surveying, consultancy or supervisory services. See **43.21**(1) below for where a supply of such services takes place under different forms of building contract;
- the hire of goods on their own (e.g. plant and machinery without an operator, scaffolding without erection/dismantling, security fencing and mobile office); and

- the private use of goods.

[*VATA 1994, Sch 8 Group 5 Item 2(a)* and *Note (20)*]. (VAT Notice 708, para 3.4).

Building materials and certain electrical goods, supplied by the person providing the above services and incorporated into the building in question, are also zero-rated. See **43.16** to **43.18** below.

See **42 LAND AND BUILDINGS: EXEMPT SUPPLIES AND OPTION TO TAX** at **42.7** for the definition of '*in the course of construction*', **42.5** for '*designed as a dwelling*', **42.16** for '*relevant residential purpose*', and **42.14** for '*relevant charitable purpose*'.

With certain exceptions, '*constructing a building*' specifically excludes converting, reconstructing, altering, enlarging and extending an existing building or constructing an annexe to an existing building. See **42.3 LAND AND BUILDINGS: EXEMPT SUPPLIES AND OPTION TO TAX** for full details.

See **43.14** below for examples of services zero-rated under these provisions and other services not regarded as within these provisions and therefore standard-rated.

Garages

The construction of a building designed as a dwelling or number of dwellings includes the construction of a garage provided that

- the dwelling and the garage are constructed at the same time; and
- the garage is intended to be occupied with the dwelling or one of the dwellings.

[*VATA 1994, Sch 8 Group 5 Note (3)*].

Holiday homes

Following the decision in *Jennings* (TC00362) (TVC 15.60), HMRC have accepted that the restriction on zero-rating of holiday homes only applies to grants within *Group 5 Item 1*, not to construction services within *Item 2*. As long as a holiday home satisfies the conditions of *Note 2*, the fact that planning consent prohibits year-round occupation does not prevent a builder zero-rating construction services. If the builder constructs the building for a developer who sells the building to a customer, the benefit of the zero-rating is lost; for a planning arrangement in which the sale of new holiday homes was successfully split into building plots (standard-rated) and construction services (zero-rated) supplied by two different companies, see *Lower Mill Estate Ltd v HMRC (and related appeal)*, UT [2011] STC 636 (TVC 22.78).

An apparent attempt to secure the same favourable treatment as that enjoyed by Lower Mill Estate failed in *Fairway Lakes Ltd v HMRC* [2016] UKUT 340 (TCC) (TVC 15.347). A landowning company and a building company made separate contracts with customers for a lease over the plot of land and the construction of a holiday home on it; however, the building company's contract contained a number of provisions relating to the land itself, amounting to an undertaking to procure the grant of the lease for the customer. Because it was not a pure building contract, it could not qualify for zero-rating.

Civil engineering work on serviced plots

In accordance with the decision in *D & S Virtue (t/a Lammermuir Game Services)* (VTD 20259) (TVC 41.22) that a supply of a serviced building plot is a single exempt supply (and not a mixed supply of exempt land and standard-rated civil engineering work), HMRC accept that the supply of civil engineering works *to* a landowner in connection with the supply of a serviced plot of land *by* the landowner is zero-rated where the landowner can demonstrate that the civil engineering services have been made in the course of the construction of qualifying buildings within (*a*) or (*b*) above. For zero-rating to apply, HMRC would normally expect all the following conditions to be met to demonstrate that zero-rating is appropriate.

- The landowner holds sufficient planning consent to demonstrate that the civil engineering works were received in the course of construction of qualifying buildings.
- The civil engineering is closely connected with or facilitates the construction of buildings.
- The construction of the buildings will follow on closely after the completion of the civil engineering works.

The extent to which the above conditions have been met will be a matter of fact and degree. HMRC would need to be satisfied that, at the time the civil engineering is supplied, any potential purchaser of a serviced plot can only construct qualifying buildings on the plot. In addition, it must be clear that the landowner has a firm intention to sell the serviced plots once the civil engineering is complete and that any purchaser is ready to begin actual construction of the buildings as soon as possible.

(HMRC Brief 64/07).

Apportionment for part-qualifying buildings

(1) *General.* Where part of a building qualifies under the above provisions and part does not (e.g. shop premises with a flat over them), a supply of services relating only to the qualifying part of the building is zero-rated and, similarly, a supply of services relating only to the non-qualifying part is standard-rated. In the case of any other supply, an apportionment must be made to determine the extent to which the supply is zero-rated. [*VATA 1994, Sch 8 Group 5 Note (10)*].
Building work that relates to the fabric of the building affecting both qualifying and non-qualifying parts of the building must be apportioned, such as work to
  - roofs,
  - foundations,
  - lifts, and
  - building services that supply the whole building (e.g. wiring and plumbing).

(2) *Communal areas in blocks of flats.* Blocks of flats normally consist of individual dwellings and areas for the use of all residents (e.g. lounge, laundry, refuse area and, occasionally, gym, pool and leisure facilities). The first sale of each flat is zero-rated and the buyer also acquires a right

to use the communal areas. Where the communal areas are only used by residents and their guests, HMRC accept that the construction of the whole building is zero-rated. Where the communal areas are partly used by others, then the construction of the communal areas is standard-rated.

(3) *Live-work units*. In a live-work unit (i.e. a property that combines, within a single unit, a dwelling and commercial or industrial working space as a requirement or condition of planning permission) zero-rating is only available to the extent that the unit comprises the dwelling (provided it meets the other conditions for zero-rating above). Dwellings that contain a home office are not live-work units and no apportionment is needed.

Units where the work area is shown as a discrete area of floor space, whether an office or workshop, must be apportioned to reflect the presence of the commercial element. Where planning permission requires that a minimum amount of the unit (e.g. 20%) must be used for commercial or industrial purposes, the remaining amount (i.e. 80%) can be treated as being the dwelling element for VAT purposes.

However, where a unit has neither

- an area that must, as a requirement or condition of planning permission, be used for commercial or industrial purposes, nor
- planning permission requiring a certain percentage of the floor space be used for commercial or industrial purposes;

it may be treated for VAT purposes as if it were entirely a dwelling and no apportionment is required.

(4) *Relevant residential purpose buildings*. Where the supply is in connection with a building intended for use as

- residential accommodation for students or school pupils, or
- residential accommodation for members of any of the armed forces

the supply can only be zero-rated to the extent that it relates to the residential accommodation. Where the supply is in connection with a building intended for use as a home or other institution, zero-rating or reduced-rating is not restricted to the residential accommodation but can extend to other areas within the building(s) such as administration offices or leisure or educational facilities.

(VAT Notice 708, paras 3.5, 16.1–16.5).

Apportionment for mixed sites

Where a service falling within the above provisions is supplied in part in relation to the construction of a building and in part for other purposes (e.g. a mixed site development including new dwellings and shops), an apportionment may be made to determine the extent to which the supply is to be treated as falling within the above provisions.

[*VATA 1994, Sch 8 Group 5 Note (11)*].

Buildings for relevant residential/charitable purposes

The following additional provisions apply where all or part of a building is intended for use solely for a relevant residential or relevant charitable purpose.

- *Issue of certificates.* Where all or part of a building is intended for use solely for a relevant residential or relevant charitable purpose, a supplier of services within these provisions cannot zero-rate the supply until the customer has given him a certificate to that effect. See **43.22** below.
- *Subcontractors' supplies, etc.* No supply of services relating to a building (or part of it) can be taken for the above purposes as relating to a building intended for such use unless it is made to a person who intends to use the building (or part) for such a purpose. [*VATA 1994, Sch 8 Group 5 Note (12)*]. The main effect of this is that, although the main contractor can zero-rate the construction of such a building, a subcontractor must standard-rate all supplies to the main contractor on such building projects.

Civil engineering work for residential caravan parks

[43.8] Services supplied 'in the course of construction' of any civil engineering work necessary for the development of a permanent park for 'residential caravans', and which relate to the construction, are zero-rated. Specifically excluded (and therefore standard-rated) are

- the separate supply of architectural, surveying, consultancy or supervisory services. See **43.21**(1) below for where a supply of these services takes place under different forms of building contract;
- the hire of goods on their own (e.g. plant and machinery without an operator, scaffolding without erection/dismantling, security fencing and mobile office); and
- the private use of goods.

Building materials, supplied by the person providing the above services and incorporated into the site in question, are also zero-rated. See **43.16** below.

See **42.7** LAND AND BUILDINGS: EXEMPT SUPPLIES AND OPTION TO TAX for the meaning of '*in the course of construction*'. The construction of a civil engineering work does not include the conversion, reconstruction, alteration or enlargement of a work.

'Residential caravan'

A caravan is not a residential caravan if residence in it throughout the year is prevented by the terms of a covenant, statutory planning consent or similar permission. The development of a holiday park of fixed caravans, or parks for touring caravans, is, therefore, normally standard-rated. (VAT Notice 708, para 20.2).

[*VATA 1994, Sch 8 Group 5 Item 2(b)* and *Notes (15)*, *(19)* and *(20)*].

Examples of zero-rated civil engineering work

- Laying new roads, drives, parking bays and paths
- Laying new pitches or bases for the caravans
- Installing water, electricity and gas supplies
- Installing drainage and sewerage

Examples of civil engineering work that is unnecessary (and standard-rated)

- Construction of playgrounds
- Hard landscaping

Examples of work that is not civil engineering work (and standard-rated)

- Indoor swimming pools
- Social centres
- Shops
- Fitness clubs
- A doctor's surgery
- A manager's house (although the work may be zero-rated under **43.7** above)

Alterations to existing works

The reconstruction, alteration or improvement of an existing work (e.g. widening or upgrading an existing road) cannot be zero-rated.

Apportionment

(1) *Zero-rated and standard-rated work*. Where both zero-rated and standard-rated civil engineering work is supplied, an apportionment must be made to reflect the differing liabilities.

(2) *Mixed site developments*. Where a service is supplied in part in relation to necessary civil engineering work and in part for other purposes, an apportionment may be made to determine the extent to which the supply is treated as being zero-rated. If the supplier decides not to make an apportionment, then none of the work can be zero-rated.

(VAT Notice 708, paras 20.1, 20.3–20.5).

Conversion services supplied to housing associations

[43.9] Zero-rating applies to services supplied to a 'relevant housing association' 'in the course of conversion' of

(a) a 'non-residential' building, or
(b) a non-residential part of a building

into a building (or part of a building) which is

(i) 'designed as a dwelling' or number of dwellings, or
(ii) intended solely for use for a 'relevant residential purpose'

and where the services relate to the conversion.

Specifically excluded (and therefore standard-rated) are

- the separate supply of architectural, surveying, consultancy or supervisory services. See **43.21**(1) below for where a supply of such services takes place under different forms of building contract;
- the hire of goods on their own (e.g. plant and machinery without an operator, scaffolding without erection/dismantling, security fencing and mobile office); and

- the private use of goods.

Building materials and certain electrical goods, supplied by the person providing the above services and incorporated into the building in question, are also zero-rated. See **43.16** to **43.18** below.

Where (*b*) above applies and the building already contains a residential part, for zero-rating to apply the conversion must either be to a building for use for a relevant residential purpose or must create an additional dwelling or dwellings.

See **42 LAND AND BUILDINGS: EXEMPT SUPPLIES AND OPTION TO TAX** at **42.15** for the definition of '*relevant housing association*', **42.11** for '*non-residential*', **42.5** for '*designed as a dwelling*', and **42.16** for '*relevant residential purpose*'.

[*VATA 1994, Sch 8 Group 5 Item 3* and *Notes (9), (20)* and *(21)*].

Conversions to garages

The conversion of a non-residential building to a building designed as a dwelling or number of dwellings includes the conversion of a non-residential building to a garage, provided that

- the dwelling and the garage are converted at the same time; and
- the garage is intended to be occupied with the dwelling or one of the dwellings.

[*VATA 1994, Sch 8 Group 5 Note (3)*].

Examples of a non-residential conversion include the conversion of

- a commercial building (such as an office, warehouse, shop, etc.),
- an agricultural building (such as a barn), or
- a redundant school or church,

into a building designed as a dwelling or number of dwellings.

Conversions of garages

The conversion of a garage, occupied together with a dwelling, into a building designed as a dwelling is not a non-residential conversion. '*Garage*' not only covers buildings designed to store motor vehicles but also buildings such as barns which are used as garages. But if it can be established that the garage was never used to store motor vehicles (or has not been used as a garage for a considerable length of time prior to conversion) its conversion into a building designed as a dwelling can be a non-residential conversion.

See **43.14** below for examples of services zero-rated under these provisions and other services not regarded as within these provisions and therefore standard-rated.

Evidence and certificates

A supplier must hold evidence to show that his customer is a relevant housing association (e.g. a copy of their registration certificate). In addition, a supplier who is converting the building into a building intended for use solely for a relevant residential purpose must also hold a certificate confirming the intended use of the building. See **43.22** below.

Subcontractors

Subcontractors' services are not made directly to a relevant housing association and are, therefore, not zero-rated.

Amalgamating non-residential parts of a building with other parts

To qualify for zero-rating, the conversion must only use non-residential parts of the building. For example, a two-storey public house containing bar areas downstairs and private living areas upstairs (and so in part being used as a dwelling, although see the case law uncertainty on this point in **42.11 LAND AND BUILDINGS: EXEMPT SUPPLIES AND OPTION TO TAX**) is converted into two flats, one created out of the bar areas and one out of the private living area. The onward sale or long lease of the former is zero-rated but that of the latter will be exempt. On the other hand, if the conversion uses a mixture of non-residential parts of the building and other parts, such as when the same property is converted

- into a single house, or
- by splitting it vertically into a pair of semi-detached houses, each of which use part of what was the living accommodation,

the onward sale or long lease is not zero-rated and is exempt.

Apportionment

(1) *Part qualifying buildings*. Where part of a building qualifies under the above provisions and part does not (e.g. shop premises with a flat over them), a supply of services relating only to the qualifying part of the building is zero-rated and, similarly, a supply of services relating only to the non-qualifying part is standard-rated. In the case of any other supply, an apportionment must be made to determine the extent to which the supply is zero-rated. [*VATA 1994, Sch 8 Group 5 Note (10)*]. For example, if a shop is converted into a flat and at the same time an existing flat above the shop (that has been lived in within the last ten years) is refurbished, zero-rating applies to the work to convert the shop but not the refurbishment of the flat.

(2) *Mixed sites*. Where a service falling within the above provisions is supplied in part in relation to the conversion of a building and in part for other purposes (e.g. a mixed site development including new dwellings and shops), an apportionment may be made to determine the extent to which the supply is to be treated as falling within the above provisions. [*VATA 1994, Sch 8 Group 5 Note (11)*]. For example, a road that serves a building being converted and a neighbouring house (e.g. a barn and a farm house) is upgraded as part of the conversion. As the road serves both buildings, the work carried out relates, in part, to the conversion and, in part, for other purposes. The liability of upgrading the road may be apportioned on a fair and reasonable basis. If the supplier decides not to make an apportionment, then none of his work can be zero-rated.

(VAT Notice 708, paras 6.2, 6.3, 6.5, 6.6).

Approved alterations of protected buildings

From 1 October 2012

[43.10] *VATA 1994, Sch 8 Group 6* was amended by *Finance Act 2012* to remove *Item 2* (see below) and *Item 3* (see **43.16** below) which zero-rated construction services and related building materials in the course of an approved alteration of a protected building. Under transitional arrangements, 'relevant supplies', i.e. supplies of services (other than excluded services) and related building materials made in the course of an approved alteration of a protected building, pursuant to a contract entered into or a relevant consent applied for before 21 March 2012, could continue to be zero-rated until 30 September 2015.

To prevent businesses entering into avoidance arrangements, an anti-forestalling charge arose where a supply of services or building materials was treated as taking place on or after 21 March 2012 but before 1 October 2012, and the supply was linked to the post-change period, i.e. the services were provided, or the materials were incorporated into the building, on or after 1 October 2012. The amount of the charge was the amount of VAT which would have been due on the supply had it been taxable at 20%. The charge was to be treated as if it were VAT, is the supplier's liability, and was due on 1 October 2012. If the supplier ceased to be a taxable person before that date, he was required to account for the charge in his final VAT return. Where the supply is not wholly linked to the post-change period, the charge applied after the consideration for the supply was apportioned on a just and reasonable basis. Where there was an anti-forestalling charge, the consideration for the supply was increased by the amount of the charge, unless the contract provided otherwise.

[*FA 2012, Sch 26, paras 3(2), 7, Sch 27, paras 1–9*].

Prior to 1 October 2012

Until 1 October 2012 the supply of services in the course of an 'approved alteration' of a 'protected building' was zero-rated. Specifically excluded (and therefore standard-rated) were:

- The separate supply of architectural, surveying, consultancy or supervisory services. See **43.21**(1) below for where a supply of such services takes place under different forms of building contract.
- The hire of goods on their own (e.g. plant and machinery without an operator, scaffolding without erection/dismantling, security fencing and mobile office).
- The private use of goods.

Building materials and certain electrical goods, supplied by the person providing the above services and incorporated into the building in question, are also zero-rated. See **43.16** to **43.18** below.

See **42 LAND AND BUILDINGS: EXEMPT SUPPLIES AND OPTION TO TAX** at **42.2** for the definition of '*approved alteration*' and **42.13** for '*protected building*'.

[*VATA 1994, Sch 8 Group 6 Item 2* and *Note (11); SI 1995/283*]. (VAT Notice 708, para 9.7).

Provided the necessary conditions were satisfied, this provision could be used to zero-rate services supplied in carrying out an approved alteration to

- a protected building which was a dwelling, relevant residential building or relevant charitable building; and
- any other protected building in order to convert it into a dwelling, relevant residential building or relevant charitable building.

Services 'in the course of an approved alteration'

A business supplies services in the course of an approved alteration of a protected building when it

(a) physically carries out the approved alteration; or
(b) provides any other service closely connected to the alteration (see **43.14** below).

The effect of (*b*) above is that, even if the work did not require approval, it can still be zero-rated provided it is closely connected to an approved alteration. Examples include

- preparation work for an approved alteration; or
- the carrying out of remedial work resulting from an approved alteration.

(VAT Notice 708, para 9.6).

Issue of certificate by recipient of services

Where all or part of a protected building is intended for use solely for a relevant residential or relevant charitable purpose, a supplier of approved alterations to the building within these provisions cannot zero-rate the supply until the customer has given him a certificate to that effect. See **43.22** below.

Apportionment

(1) *Part qualifying work*. In cases where a service is supplied partly in relation to an approved alteration and partly for other purposes (e.g. repairs and maintenance), an apportionment can be made to determine the part zero-rated. [*VATA 1994, Sch 8 Group 6 Note (9)*].
(2) *Part qualifying buildings*. Where only part of a building is a protected building, zero-rating can be applied to the work to the qualifying parts. For example, if alterations are carried out to a listed building used by a charity, it may be that only part of the building will be used solely for a relevant charitable purpose. If so, only the approved alterations to that part of the building can be zero-rated.
(3) *Mixed site developments*. Where a service (e.g. carrying out civil engineering work) is supplied in part in relation to an approved alteration and in part for other purposes, a fair and reasonable apportionment may be made to determine the extent to which the supply is treated as falling within these provisions.

If the supplier decides not to make an apportionment, then none of his work can be zero-rated.

(VAT Notice 708, para 9.8).

Note – zero-rating applied to approved alterations to protected buildings.

VATA 1994, Sch 8 Group 6 was amended by *Finance Act 2012* to remove *Item 2* and *Item 3* but transitional rules applied until 30 September 2015. On 4 November 2015 HMRC issued a technical note relating to the withdrawal of the concessionary treatment described in VAT Notice 708, para 9.8, regarding the apportionment of works of approved alterations to protected buildings on the basis that the concessionary treatment is now obsolete.

Repairs to listed places of worship

Unless qualifying as part of an approved alteration under the above provisions, any repair and maintenance work is standard-rated and the UK is not permitted under current EU legislation to tax such supplies at a reduced rate.

The Department of Culture Media and Sport administers the Listed Places of Worship Grant Scheme for repairs to listed places of worship. The scheme can refund the full amount of VAT spent on eligible repairs, but this will depend on the funds available. (VAT Notice 708, para 9.4.3).

Following the Budget 2012 announcement that the zero rate of VAT for approved alterations to listed buildings would be withdrawn from 1 October 2012, the Government announced that the Listed Places of Worship Grant Scheme would also cover approved alterations.

During 2013 the Government announced further changes to the scope and operation of the Listed Places of Worship Grant Scheme. From 1 October 2013 works to pipe organs, turret clocks, bells and bell ropes are eligible for claims under the scheme. Professional services directly related to eligible building work such as architect fees are also eligible. These changes apply to works supplied from 1 October 2013. From that date, applications to make use of the scheme will be accepted from religious and charitable groups whose main purpose is to conserve, repair and maintain redundant listed places of worship which are not in private ownership.

Documentation relating to the scheme can be obtained

- via the internet at www.lpwscheme.org.uk;
- by telephoning 0845 601 5945; or
- by writing to Listed Places of Worship Grant Scheme, PO Box 609, Newport NP10 8QD.

Reduced rate supplies

[43.11] VAT is charged at the reduced rate of 5% on

(a) qualifying services supplied in the course of certain residential conversions (see **43.12** below);
(b) qualifying services supplied in the course of renovating and altering certain buildings that have been empty for two or more years (see **43.13** below);

(c) building materials and certain electrical goods incorporated into a building by a builder who is also supplying services within (*a*) or (*b*) above (see **43.16** to **43.18** below);

(d) installation of energy-saving materials and the grant-funded installation of heating equipment or security goods or connection of a gas supply. See **59.2** and **59.3 REDUCED RATE SUPPLIES**; and

(e) installation of mobility aids for the elderly for use in domestic accommodation. See **29.36 HEALTH AND WELFARE.**

On 4 June 2015 the European Court published its decision that the UK had implemented the reduced rate of VAT for the installation of energy saving materials in a way that was not in accordance with EU law. HMRC has advised that any legislative changes will not be implemented before *Finance Act 2016*.

(HMRC Brief 13/15).

Residential conversions

Overview

[43.12] The VAT liability of conversion work generally is summarised in the following table.

Before conversion	*After conversion*		
	Single household dwelling(s)	*Multiple occupancy dwelling(s)*	*Relevant residential purpose building*
Single household dwelling(s)	Normally standard-rated unless the number of dwellings changes when reduced-rated	Reduced-rated	Reduced-rated
Multiple occupancy dwelling(s)	Reduced-rated	Standard-rated	Reduced-rated
Relevant residential purpose building	Reduced-rated	Reduced-rated	Standard-rated
Any building not listed above (e.g. a building which has never been lived in)	Reduced-rated	Reduced-rated	Reduced-rated

Detailed provisions

'Qualifying services' supplied in the course of a 'qualifying conversion' and which are related to the conversion are subject to a reduced rate of VAT of 5%.

Building materials and certain electrical goods, supplied by the person providing the above services and incorporated into the building in question or its immediate site, are also subject to the reduced rate. See **43.16** to **43.18** below.

The reduced rate also applies to the acquisition from another EU member state, or the importation from outside the EU, of goods the supply of which would be subject to the reduced rate.

[*VATA 1994, s 29A(1)(2), Sch 7A Group 6 Items 1* and 2].

'Qualifying conversion'

A '*qualifying conversion*' means one of the following three types of conversion provided, in each case, any statutory planning consent needed and any statutory building control approval needed for the conversion has been granted. [*VATA 1994, Sch 7A Group 6 Note (10)*].

(1) **Conversions into 'single household dwellings'**, i.e. the conversion of premises consisting of a building or part of a building where
  - (i) after the conversion the premises being converted contain a number of single household dwellings that is different from the number (if any) that the premises contain before the conversion, and greater than, or equal to, one; and
  - (ii) there is no part of the premises being converted that is a part that, after the conversion, contains the same number of single household dwellings (whether zero, one or two or more) as before the conversion.

  [*VATA 1994, Sch 7A Group 6 Note (3)*].
  This covers the following scenarios.

Building before conversion	*Building after conversion*
One single household dwelling	Two or more single house dwellings
A number of single house dwellings	A different number of single house dwellings (more or less)
Non-residential	One or more single house dwellings
One or more houses in multiple occupation	One or more single house dwellings
Relevant residential property	One or more single house dwellings

  The provisions also cover the conversion of a building which may have been lived in but which does not qualify as a single household dwelling (such as a public house with staff accommodation) into one or more single household dwellings. (VAT Notice 708, para 7.3).

(2) **Conversions into 'multiple occupation dwellings'**, i.e. the conversion of premises consisting of a building or part of a building where the following conditions are satisfied.
  - (i) Before the conversion the premises being converted do not contain any multiple occupancy dwellings.
  - (ii) After the conversion those premises contain only a 'multiple occupancy dwelling' or two or more such dwellings.

(iii) The use to which those premises are intended to be put after the conversion is not to any extent use for a 'relevant residential purpose'.

[*VATA 1994, Sch 7A Group 6 Note (5)*].

A qualifying conversion includes the conversion into a multiple occupancy dwelling of

- a single household dwelling;
- a building used for a relevant residential purpose, such as a care home; and
- a property that has never been lived in.

It does not include, for example, the creation of additional bedrooms at a dwelling consisting of bed-sits.

(VAT Notice 708, para 7.4).

(3) **Conversions into premises for use for a 'relevant residential purpose'**, i.e. a conversion of premises consisting of one or more buildings or one or more parts of buildings (or any combination of buildings and parts of buildings) where the following conditions are satisfied.

(i) The use to which the premises being converted were last put before the conversion was not to any extent use for a relevant residential purpose and those premises are intended to be used solely for a relevant residential purpose after the conversion.

(ii) Where the relevant residential purpose for which the premises are intended to be used is an 'institutional purpose', the premises being converted must be intended to form, after the conversion, the entirety of an institution used for that purpose.

For such a conversion to be subject to the reduced rate

- it must be made to the person who intends to use the premises being converted for the relevant residential purpose; and
- before it is made, that person must give the supplier a certificate of intended use. See **43.22** below.

[*VATA 1994, Sch 7A Group 6 Notes (7)(8)*].

A qualifying conversion includes the conversion of

- a single household dwelling,
- a multiple occupancy dwelling, and
- a property that has never been lived in

into premises that will be used solely for a relevant residential purpose.

It does not include

- the remodelling of an existing relevant residential purpose building; or
- any conversion where a new qualifying residential home or institution is not created in its entirety, such as the conversion of outbuildings into additional bedrooms for an existing care home.

'Single household dwelling'

A single household dwelling means a dwelling that

- is designed for occupation by a single household either because

    (i) it was originally designed on construction for occupation for that purpose and has not been subsequently adapted for occupation of any other kind; or
    (ii) it is so designed as a result of adaptation;
- consists of self-contained living accommodation;
- has no provision for direct internal access to any other dwelling or part of a dwelling; and
- is not prohibited from separate use or separate disposal by the terms of any covenant, statutory planning consent or similar provision. An occupancy restriction is not a prohibition on separate use or disposal if all it does is restrict the occupancy of a building to a certain type of person, such as persons working in agriculture or forestry, or persons over a specified age. But if the wording of the restriction prevents the building from being used separately from another building or from being sold, or otherwise disposed of, separately from another building then it is a prohibition on separate use or disposal. (VAT Notice 708, para 14.4).

[*VATA 1994, Sch 7A Group 6 Note (4)*].

'Multiple occupancy dwelling'

A multiple occupancy dwelling means a dwelling that

- is designed for occupation by persons not forming a single household either because
    (i) it was originally designed on construction for occupation for that purpose and has not been subsequently adapted for occupation of any other kind; or
    (ii) it is so designed as a result of adaptation;
- is not to any extent used for a relevant residential purpose;
- consists of self-contained living accommodation;
- has no provision for direct internal access to any other dwelling or part of a dwelling; and
- is not prohibited from separate use or separate disposal by the terms of any covenant, statutory planning consent or similar provision. An occupancy restriction is not a prohibition on separate use or disposal if all it does is restrict the occupancy of a building to a certain type of person, such as persons working in agriculture or forestry, or persons over a specified age. But if the wording of the restriction prevents the building from being used separately from another building or from being sold, or otherwise disposed of, separately from another building then it is a prohibition on separate use or disposal. (VAT Notice 708, para 14.5).

[*VATA 1994, Sch 7A Group 6 Note (4)*].

A multiple occupancy dwelling is normally a dwelling consisting of a number of bed-sits. it does not include

- single household dwellings with accommodation for au pairs, family guests or 'live-in' lodgers; or
- hotels, guest houses, and similar establishments providing accommodation for holiday makers, travellers and similar temporary guests.

(VAT Notice 708, para 14.5).

Use for a relevant residential purpose

'*Use for a relevant residential purpose*' means use as

(a) a home or other institution providing residential accommodation for children;
(b) a home or other institution providing residential accommodation with personal care for persons in need of such care by reason of old age, disablement, past or present dependence on alcohol or drugs or past or present mental disorder;
(c) a hospice;
(d) residential accommodation for students or school pupils;
(e) residential accommodation for members of any of the armed forces;
(f) a monastery, nunnery or similar establishment; or
(g) an institution which is the sole or main residence of at least 90% of its residents.

except use as a hospital, prison or similar institution or an hotel, inn or similar establishment.

Use for an '*institutional purpose*' means a purpose under (*a*)–(*c*), (*f*) or (*g*) above.

[*VATA 1994, Sch 7A Group 6 Notes (6)(7)*].

Qualifying services

Qualifying services mean either of the following.

- Carrying out work to the fabric of the building/part of the building being converted (excluding the incorporation, or installation as fittings, in the building/part of any goods that are not building materials).
- Carrying out work within the immediate site of the building in connection with
  (i) the means of providing water, power, heat or access to the building/part,
  (ii) the means of providing drainage or security for the building/part, or
  (iii) the provision of means of waste disposal for the building/part.

[*VATA 1994, Sch 7A Group 6 Note (11)*].

This includes all works of repair, maintenance (e.g. decoration) or improvement (e.g. the construction of an extension or the installation of double glazing) to the fabric of the building where the work forms an intrinsic part of changing the number of dwellings.

> ***Example 1***
>
> A block of flats consists of four floors, each with four flats. A lift is installed and work is carried out throughout the whole building. On the ground, first and second floors the footprint of each flat is changed to take account of the new lift. This results in the internal configuration of each flat being changed. On the third floor three penthouse flats are created from the original four.

Although the overall number of dwellings in the building has changed (there has been a reduction by one unit) only the work to convert the top floor will be eligible for the reduced rate because it is only in this part of the building that the number of dwellings has changed.

Example 2

The facts are as in *Example 1* except that the reduction in the number of flats on the third floor happens by combining two of the original flats together, the other two being refurbished.

The reduced rate will only apply to the work to merge the two flats together.

Example 3

The facts are as in *Example 1* above except that, as well as the changes to the top floor, the number of flats on the ground floor is changed to five smaller units.

Although the overall number of dwellings in the building has not changed (there are 16 units both before and after the work) as the number of dwellings has changed on both the ground floor and the third floor, the reduced rate can apply to the conversion work done on these floors.

All other services are standard-rated. For example

- the installation of goods that are not building materials, such as carpets and fitted bedroom furniture;
- the hire of goods;
- landscaping; and
- the provision of professional services, such as those provided by architects, surveyors, consultants and supervisors.

(VAT Notice 708, paras 7.3, 7.6).

Part-qualifying services

Where part of a supply of services qualifies under these provisions and part does not, the supply can be apportioned to determine the extent to which the reduced rate can be applied. [*VATA 1994, Sch 7A Group 6 Note (1)*].

Garages

A qualifying conversion within (1)–(3) above includes the construction of a garage or the conversion of a 'non-residential' building (or of a non-residential part of a building) that results in a garage provided

- the garage works are carried out at the same time as the conversion; and
- the resulting garage is intended to be occupied
  - (i) where (1) above applies, with a single household dwelling that will after the conversion be contained in the building, or part of a building, being converted;
  - (ii) where (2) above applies, with a multiple occupancy dwelling that will after the conversion be contained in the building, or part of a building, being converted; or
  - (iii) where (3) above applies, with the institution or other accommodation resulting from the conversion.

'*Non-residential*' means neither designed, nor adapted, for use as a dwelling or two or more dwellings, or for a relevant residential purpose.

[*VATA 1994, Sch 7A Group 6 Note (9)*].

Provided the above conditions are satisfied, the reduced rate can be applied to the construction of a drive serving the garage. (VAT Notice 708, para 7.6).

Subcontractors

Subcontractors who carry out some or all of the qualifying renovation or conversion work can apply the reduced rate to their services *unless* the work is the conversion into a relevant residential property.

Dwellings adapted for non-residential use and subsequently converted back into a dwelling

If a property was originally a dwelling but then adapted for non-residential use, on conversion back to a dwelling the reduced rate would apply where the whole building had been used for a non-residential purpose as the conversion is of a non-residential building into a single household dwelling. It is the use of the building at the time of conversion that is relevant and not any earlier use.

Example 1

A building originally designed as a dwelling has been adapted for use as a dental surgery. No part of the building after adaptation has been used as living accommodation.

The reduced rate applies to the work of converting the building back into a dwelling as there has been a change in the number of single household dwellings from none to one.

Example 2

A building originally designed as a dwelling is adapted for use as a dental surgery on the ground floor with a self-contained flat on the first floor.

The reduced rate does not apply to the conversion of the whole building back into a single dwelling as the building is a single household dwelling before and after conversion.

Example 3

A room in a building designed as a single dwelling is used as an office. The rest of the house is used as living accommodation.

The conversion of the room used as an office back into use as part of the existing house does not qualify for the reduced rate as there is single household dwelling before and after conversion. However, if the area used as the office is converted to create a self-contained dwelling, there would be a change in the number of single household dwellings (from one to two) the work would then qualify for the reduced rate.

De Voil Indirect Tax Service. See V4.411.

Residential renovations and alterations

[43.13] VAT is charged at the reduced rate of 5% on the renovation or alteration of a single household dwelling that has not been lived in for two years or more and a building to be used solely for a relevant residential purpose (e.g. a care home) or a multiple occupancy dwelling (e.g. bed-sits), again provided the premises have not been lived in for at least two years. Included are works in connection with garages. The detailed provisions are considered below.

'Qualifying services' supplied in the course of the renovation or alteration (including extension) of 'qualifying residential premises', and which are related to the renovation or alteration, are subject to a reduced rate of VAT of 5% provided the following conditions are satisfied.

- Empty home condition (1) below is satisfied or, if the premises are a 'single household dwelling' either empty home condition (1) or (2) below is satisfied.
- Any statutory planning consent needed for the renovation or alteration has been granted.
- Any statutory building control approval needed for the renovation or alteration has been granted.
- Where the premises in question are a building, or part of a building, which, when it was last lived in, was used for a relevant residential purpose,
  - (i) the building or part must be intended to be used solely for such a purpose after the renovation or alteration, and
  - (ii) before the supply is made, the person to whom it is made must give the supplier a certificate stating that intention. See **43.22** below.

  Where a number of buildings on the same site are renovated or altered at the same time and intended to be used together as a unit solely for a relevant residential purpose, then each of those buildings, to the extent that it would not be so regarded otherwise, is to be treated as intended for use solely for a relevant residential purpose.

Building materials and certain electrical goods, supplied by the person providing the above services and incorporated into the qualifying residential premises in question or their immediate site, are also subject to the reduced rate. See **43.16** to **43.18** below.

The reduced rate also applies to the acquisition from another EU member state, or the importation from outside the EU, of goods the supply of which would be subject to the reduced rate.

[*VATA 1994, s 29A(1)(2), Sch 7A Group 7 Items 1, 2* and *Notes (3)(4)(4A)*].

'*Qualifying residential premises*' means

- a 'single household dwelling',
- a 'multiple occupancy dwelling', or
- a building, or part of a building, which, when it was last lived in, was used for a 'relevant residential purpose'. Where a building, when it was last lived in, formed part of a 'relevant residential unit' then, to the extent that it would not be so regarded otherwise, the building is to be treated as having been used for a relevant residential purpose. For these purposes, a building forms part of a relevant residential unit at any time when

- (i) it is one of a number of buildings on the same site, and
- (ii) the buildings are used together as a unit for a relevant residential purpose.

The expressions '*multiple occupancy dwelling*', '*single household dwelling*', and '*use for a relevant residential purpose*' have the same meaning as in **43.12** above.

[*VATA 1994, Sch 7A Group 7 Note (2)*].

Empty home conditions

Empty home condition (1) below must be satisfied, or if the premises are a single household dwelling either condition (1) or (2) must be satisfied.

(1) Neither
- (a) the premises concerned, nor
- (b) where those premises are a building, or part of a building, which, when it was last lived in, formed part of a 'relevant residential unit' (see above), any of the other buildings that formed part of the unit,

have been lived in during the period of two years ending with the commencement of the 'relevant works'.

(2) To cover the situation where a dwelling is occupied whilst the work is being carried on, the reduced rate can also be applied where
- (i) the dwelling was not lived in during a period of at least two years;
- (ii) the person, or one of the persons, whose beginning to live in the dwelling brought that period to an end was a person who (whether alone or jointly with another or others) acquired the dwelling at a time
  - no later than the end of that period, and
  - when the dwelling had been not lived in for at least two years;
- (iii) no works by way of renovation or alteration were carried out to the dwelling during the period of two years ending with the acquisition (although HMRC are prepared to ignore any minor works that were necessary to keep the dwelling dry and secure, see VAT Notice 708, para 8.3);
- (iv) the supply is made to a person who is
  - the person, or one of the persons, whose beginning to live in the property brought to an end the period in (i), and
  - the person, or one of the persons, who acquired the dwelling as mentioned in (ii); and
- (v) the 'relevant works' are carried out during the period of one year beginning with the day of the acquisition.

For the purposes of (1) and (2) above, the '*relevant works*' means

- where the supply is qualifying services within these provisions, the works that constitute the services supplied; and
- where the supply is building materials supplied with those services, the works by which the materials concerned are incorporated in the premises concerned or their immediate site.

References in (2) above to a person acquiring a dwelling are to that person having a major interest in the dwelling granted, or assigned, to him for a consideration.

[*VATA 1994, Sch 7A Group 7 Note (3)*].

To reduce-rate his supply, a supplier must hold evidence that, on balance, shows the premises have not been lived in during the two years immediately before his work starts. The evidence can include the electoral roll and council tax data, information from empty property officers in local authorities and other sources of reliable information. If a contractor holds a letter from an empty property officer certifying that a property has not been lived in for two years, or will have been when the work starts, no other evidence is needed. If an empty property officer is unsure about when a property was last lived in, he should write with his best estimate. HMRC may then call for other supporting evidence.

In determining whether a property has been lived in, any

- illegal occupation by squatters,
- occupation by 'guardians' (persons installed by the owner to deter squatters and vandals), and
- non-residential use, such as storage for a business

can be ignored but if the dwelling has been lived in on an occasional basis (e.g. as a second home) in the two years immediately before work starts, the supply cannot be reduced-rated.

(VAT Notice 708, para 8.3).

Qualifying services

Qualifying services means either of the following.

- Carrying out work to the fabric of the premises (excluding the incorporation, or installation as fittings, in the premises of any goods that are not building materials).
- Carrying out work within the immediate site of the premises in connection with
  - (i) the means of providing water, power, heat or access to the premises;
  - (ii) the means of providing drainage or security for the premises; or
  - (iii) the provision of means of waste disposal for the premises.

[*VATA 1994, Sch 7A Group 7 Note (5)*].

This includes any work of repair, maintenance (e.g. redecoration) or improvement (e.g. an extension or the installation of double glazing) carried out to the fabric of the premises.

All other services are standard-rated, including

- the installation of goods that are not building materials, such as carpets or fitted bedroom furniture;
- the hire of goods;

- landscaping; and
- the provision of professional services, such as those provided by architects, surveyors, consultants and supervisors.

(VAT Notice 708, para 8.4).

Part-qualifying services

Where part of a supply of services qualifies under these provisions and part does not, the supply can be apportioned to determine the extent to which the reduced rate can be applied. [*VATA 1994, Sch 7A Group 7 Note (1)*].

Related garage work

For the above purposes, a renovation or alteration of any premises includes any 'garage works' related to the renovation or alteration. '*Garage works*' means

- the construction of a garage,
- the conversion of a building, or of a part of a building, that results in a garage, or
- the renovation or alteration of a garage

and garage works are related to a renovation or alteration if

- they are carried out at the same time as the renovation or alteration of the premises concerned, and
- the garage is intended to be occupied with the premises.

[*VATA 1994, Sch 7A Group 7 Note (3A)*].

Subcontractors

Subcontractors who carry out some or all of the qualifying renovation or conversion work can apply the reduced rate to their services unless the work is the renovation of an empty single household dwelling where the owner is in residence (as only a person making supplies to the occupier can apply the reduced rate, see (2)(iv) above).

De Voil Indirect Tax Service. See V4.413.

Construction services — examples

Zero-rated services

[43.14] The services which can be zero-rated under **43.7** to **43.10** above include the following where supplied in the course of construction.

(a) *Work on the building itself* (including applying any usual decorative features) prior to 'completion' of the building (see **42.7 LAND AND BUILDINGS: EXEMPT SUPPLIES AND OPTION TO TAX**).
'*Snagging*' (or the correction of faults) is often carried out after the building has been completed. The work can be zero-rated if provided by the supplier who carried out the initial building work and the snagging

forms part of that building contract. If, however, the work is carried out as a separate supply (e.g. a builder may be contracted to correct work performed by another person) and it is performed after the building has been completed, then the work is to an existing building and cannot be zero-rated under these provisions.

(b) *Work closely connected to the construction of the building*. Subject to (*c*) below, work is closely connected to the construction of the building when it either

(i) allows the construction of the building to take place, for example

- demolishing existing buildings and structures as part of a single project to construct a new building/buildings in their place (the grant of a right to remove materials is not a supply of demolition services and is standard-rated);
- providing or improving an access point to a building site to allow deliveries to be made;
- carrying out ground works (including the levelling and drainage of land) as part of the process of constructing a new building or buildings in its place;
- providing site clearance or 'builders' clean' services; and
- securing the site; or

(ii) produces works that allow the building to be used, such as works in connection with

- the means of providing water and power to the building (this can extend to the work required to make the connection to the nearest existing supply);
- the means of providing, within the development site, access to the building (e.g. roads, footpaths, parking areas, drives and patios);
- the means of providing security (such as walls, fences and gates – but note that most electrical appliances are always standard-rated, see **43.17** below); or
- the provision of soft landscaping within the site of building (e.g. the application of top-soil, seeding with grass or laying turf); the planting of shrubs, trees and flowers to the extent that it is detailed on a landscaping scheme approved by a planning authority under the terms of a planning consent condition. It does not include work outside the plot (e.g. screening planted along roadside verges) or the replacement of trees and shrubs that die, or become damaged or diseased. See *Rialto Homes plc* (VTD 16340) (TVC 15.317).

The lists are not exhaustive.

(c) *Services carried out before or after the construction of the building*. Services closely connected to the construction of the building, and carried out either before or after the physical construction of the building takes place, may only be zero-rated if it can be shown that there is a close connection between when they are performed and when the physical construction of the building takes place. Where there is a time delay, both the reason for, and the length of, any delay must be considered.

Services described in (*b*) above may be zero-rated (subject to the normal conditions) where, for example

- civil engineering services are supplied to a landowner for the purposes of servicing a building plot and it is clear that the construction of a qualifying building by a developer will take place shortly afterwards;
- soft landscaping work is carried out after the building has been completed because the work has been delayed due to seasonal weather conditions

but are standard-rated where, for example

- site investigation or demolition work is carried out prior to the letting of a building contract;
- the services for a building (water, electricity, etc.) are installed on land which is to be sold as building land and where it is not clear that the construction of a qualifying building will take place shortly afterwards; or
- the work is delayed until after the building is complete owing to an insufficiency of funds.

(d) *Connecting utilities to existing buildings*. The connection of utilities to an existing building is normally standard-rated as work to an existing building. However, as a concession, until 31 December 2011, the first time connection of gas or electricity supplies can sometimes be zero-rated. See **26.7 FUEL AND POWER**.

(VAT Notice 708, para 3.3).

Standard-rated services

[43.15] Examples of work that cannot be zero-rated include

- the provision of on-site catering;
- the cleaning of site offices;
- landscaping, except to the extent zero-rated above;
- the provision of outdoor leisure facilities for a dwelling such as tennis courts and swimming pools (although the provision of a playground at a school would qualify as it is needed for the school to be used);
- works outside the site of the building (other than those zero-rated above), including where that work is carried out under a 'planning gain' agreement with a planning authority; and
- the granting of a right to remove materials.

(VAT Notice 708, para 3.3; Business Brief 7/2000).

Building materials and other goods

[43.16] Subject to the exceptions in **43.18** below, where a person supplies

- zero-rated construction services within **43.7** to **43.10** above, or
- reduced rate construction services within **43.12** or **43.13** above,

building materials, supplied by the person providing those services and incorporated into the building in question or its immediate site, are also zero-rated or, as the case may be, subject to the reduced rate.

'*Building materials*' in relation to a particular building, mean goods 'ordinarily' incorporated or installed as fittings by builders in a building of that description (or its site) but do not include any of the supplies within **43.18**(*a*)–(*c*) below.

[*VATA 1994, Sch 7A Group 6 Note (12), Sch 7A Group 7 Note (6), Sch 8 Group 5 Item 4* and *Notes (22)* and *(23), Sch 8 Group 6 Item 3* and *Note (3)*].

The effect of the above is that building materials can be zero-rated or reduced-rated, as the case may be, along with the supply of building services where all of the following conditions are met.

(1) The articles are 'incorporated' in the building or its site

HMRC regard an article as 'incorporated' in a building (or its site) when it is fixed in such a way that its fixing or removal would either

- require the use of tools; or
- result in either the need for remedial work to the fabric of the building (or its site), or substantial damage to the goods themselves.

Examples of articles incorporated in a building (or its site) include

- built-in and fitted furniture (although only built-in or fitted *kitchen* furniture are building materials, see **43.18**(*a*) below);
- built-in, wired-in or plumbed-in appliances such as boilers or wired-in storage heaters (although only certain gas and electrical appliances are building materials, see **43.17** below, and most are normally standard-rated, see **43.18**(*b*) below);
- flooring (although carpets are not building materials, see **43.18**(*c*) below); and
- topsoil, trees, shrubs, turf, grass seed and plants (although trees, shrubs and plants are only 'building materials' in certain circumstances, see **43.14** above).

Examples of goods that are not incorporated in a building (or its site) include

- free-standing appliances that are merely plugged in; and
- free-standing furniture such as sofas, tables and chairs, etc.

(2) The articles are 'ordinarily' incorporated by builders in that type of building

HMRC take the view that an article is '*ordinarily*' incorporated in a building or its site when, in the ordinary course of events, it would normally be incorporated in a building of that generic type, such as a dwelling, church, or school. They do not split generic types of buildings into sub-categories so no distinction is drawn between large detached houses and small terraced houses. HMRC also take the same approach when determining if the goods themselves are the 'norm' for that type of building (e.g. a tap would be regarded as being ordinarily incorporated whether it is chromium or gold-plated). The range of items considered to be ordinarily incorporated is likely to change over time in line with trends and consumer expectations. Goods which need to be installed in defined areas of the country (e.g. sound-proofing near airports) can still qualify (*British Airports Authority (No 5)* [1975] Lexis Citation 3 (TVC 15.300)).

Examples of articles ordinarily incorporated in a dwelling include

- Air conditioning
- Bathroom accessories, such as fixed towel rails, toilet roll holders, soap dishes, etc.
- Builders' hardware
- Burglar alarms
- Central controls to the extent that these relate to light, heat or ventilation
- Curtain poles and rails
- Decorating materials
- Doors
- Dust extractors and filters (including built-in vacuum cleaners)
- Fencing permanently erected around the boundary of the dwelling
- Fireplaces and surrounds
- Fire alarms and sprinkler systems
- Fitted furniture (although only kitchen furniture is building materials, see **43.18**(*a*) below)
- Flooring materials (but not carpet or carpeting materials, see **43.18**(*c*) below)
- Gas and electrical appliances when wired-in or plumbed-in (although only certain gas and electrical appliances are building materials, see **43.17** below)
- Guttering
- Heating systems (including radiators and controls, ducted warm-air systems, storage heaters and other wired in heating appliances, gas fires, underfloor heating and solar powered heating)
- Immersion heaters, boilers, hot and cold water tanks
- Kitchen sinks, work surfaces and fitted cupboards
- Letter boxes
- Lifts and hoists
- Light fittings (including chandeliers and outside lights)
- Mirrors
- Plumbing installations, including electric showers and 'in line' water softeners
- Power points (including combination shaver points)
- Sanitary ware
- Saunas
- Shower units
- Smoke detectors
- Solar panels
- Solid fuel cookers and oil-fired boilers

- Swimming pools inside the house, including water heaters and filters but not diving boards and other specialist equipment. Movable tiled floors that can be locked at varying depths are not ordinarily incorporated in a building, see *Rainbow Pools London* (VTD 20800) (TVC 15.299)
- Turf, topsoil, grass seed, plants and trees (although the trees, shrubs and plants are only 'building materials' in certain circumstances, see **43.14** above)
- TV aerials and satellite dishes
- Ventilation equipment (including cooker hoods)
- Warden call systems
- Window frames and glazing
- Wiring (including power circuits and computer, telephone and TV cabling)

Examples of articles ordinarily incorporated in buildings used for a relevant residential purpose include

- Mirrors
- Safes
- External lighting systems

Examples of articles ordinarily incorporated in buildings used for a relevant charitable purpose include

- Blinds and shutters
- External lighting systems
- Mirrors
- Safes

Examples of articles ordinarily incorporated in schools include

- Blackboards/whiteboards fixed to or forming part of the wall
- Gymnasium wall bars
- Notice and display boards
- Mirrors and barres (in ballet schools)

Examples of articles ordinarily incorporated in churches include

- Altars
- Church bells
- Fonts
- Lecterns
- Pipe organs
- Pulpits

(3) Other than kitchen furniture, the articles are not finished or prefabricated furniture, or materials for the construction of fitted furniture.

See **43.18**(*a*) below.

(4) With certain exceptions, the articles are not electrical or gas appliances

See **43.17** and **43.18**(*b*) below.

(5) The articles are not carpets or carpeting material

See **43.18**(*c*) below.

(VAT Notice 708, paras 13.2–13.4, 13.8).

Electrical and gas appliances

[43.17] Most electrical and gas appliances are not building materials for VAT purposes, even if they are required to be incorporated in a building as a requirement of *Building Regulations*. They are, therefore, standard-rated (see **43.18**(*b*) below). The following can, however, be zero-rated when supplied with zero-rated construction services within **43.7** to **43.10** above or charged at the reduced rate when supplied with reduced rate construction services within **43.12** and **43.13** above.

(a) An appliance designed to heat space or water (or both) or designed to provide ventilation, air cooling, air purification or dust extraction.
(b) A door-entry system, waste disposal unit or machine for compacting waste but only if in each case it is intended for use in a building designed as a number of dwellings (e.g. a block of flats).
(c) A burglar alarm, fire alarm or fire safety equipment designed solely for the purpose of enabling aid to be summoned in an emergency.
(d) A lift or hoist.

[*VATA 1994, Sch 7A Group 6 Note (12), Sch 7A Group 7 Note (6), Sch 8 Group 5 Note (22), Group 6 Note (3)*].

Cookers which are designed to have the dual purpose of heating the room or the building's water are included under (*a*) above but telephones or electric gates and barriers are not included under (*c*) above. Fixed amplification equipment in churches may also be zero-rated.

Appliances powered by other fuels (e.g. solid fuel or oil-fired cookers) are building materials when they are ordinarily incorporated in the building.

(VAT Notice 708, para 13.6).

In *Leisure Contracts Ltd* (VTD 19392) (TVC 15.298) it was held that electric covers for indoor swimming pools were electrical applicances and therefore standard-rated. However, in the subsequent decision in *Rainbow Pools London Ltd* (VTD 20800) (TVC 15.299) such covers were held to be zero-rated.

Standard-rated goods

[43.18] The following goods are specifically excluded from the definition of building materials and their supply is always standard-rated.

(a) Finished or prefabricated 'furniture' (other than furniture designed to be fitted in kitchens) and materials for the construction of 'fitted furniture' (other than kitchen furniture)

'*Furniture*' is not defined in law and whether an item is furniture is very much a matter of impression (see *C & E Commrs v McLean Homes Midland Ltd*, QB [1993] STC 335 (TVC 15.285)).

HMRC give the following as examples of articles which are *not* furniture and are building materials for VAT purposes. They therefore qualify for zero-rating or reduced-rating, subject to meeting the conditions in **43.16** above.

- Basic storage facilities formed by becoming part of the fabric of the building, such as airing cupboards and under-stair storage cupboards.
- Items that provide storage capacity as an incidental result of their primary function, such as shelves formed as a result of constructing simple box work over pipes, and basin supports which contain a simple cupboard beneath.
- Basic wardrobes installed on their own with *all* the following characteristics.
  - (i) The wardrobe encloses a space bordered by the walls, ceiling and floor. But units whose design includes, for example, an element to bridge over a bed or create a dressing table are furniture and are not building materials.
  - (ii) The side and back use three walls of the room (such as across the end of a wall), or two walls and a stub wall. But wardrobes installed in the corner of a room where one side is a closing end panel are furniture and are not building materials.
  - (iii) On opening the wardrobe the walls of the building can be seen. These would normally be either bare plaster or painted plaster. Wardrobes that contain internal panelling, typically as part of a modular or carcass system, are furniture and are not building materials.
  - (iv) The wardrobe should feature no more than a single shelf running the full length of the wardrobe, a rail for hanging clothes and a closing door or doors. Wardrobes with internal divisions, drawers, shoe racks or other features are furniture and are not building materials.

All other finished or prefabricated furniture, and materials for the construction of fitted furniture, are not building materials for VAT purposes and cannot be zero-rated or reduced-rated as the case may be. These include

- wardrobes (other than the basic wardrobes described above) including basic wardrobes installed as part of a larger installation of furniture in the room;
- elaborate vanity units;
- wall units, such as bathroom cabinets;
- laboratory work benches; and
- pews, choir and clergy stalls.

(b) Electrical or gas appliances

Except for those specifically covered in **43.17** above. Standard-rated items include refrigerators; cookers (including split-level cookers); washing and dish-washing machines; tumble dryers; and waste disposal units and entry phone systems (except in buildings designed as a number of dwellings, e.g. blocks of flats, see **43.17** above).

(c) Carpets or carpeting material

Carpets, carpet tiles and underlay are not building materials for VAT purposes. Other forms of flooring or floor covering, such as linoleum, ceramic tiles, parquet and wooden floor systems are building materials.

> *Example*
>
> Carpet Fitters Ltd have fitted carpets into ten new dwellings for a property developer. If a single charge is made to the developer for supplying and fitting the carpets, then the fee will be wholly standard-rated. However, if a separate charge is made for the 'fitting' element, this charge can be zero-rated as relevant to building services carried out on a new dwelling. The supply of the carpets (goods only) will then be standard-rated, and an input tax block will apply to the builder.

[*VATA 1994, Sch 7A Group 6 Note (12), Sch 7A Group 7 Note (6), Sch 8 Group 5 Note (22), Group 6 Note (3)*]. (VAT Notice 708, paras 13.5, 13.7).

The validity of input tax block on certain goods incorporated into new homes by builders was unsuccessfully challenged by *Taylor Wimpey plc* [2017] UKUT 34 (TCC) (TVC 36.743). In this case Taylor Wimpey (TW) submitted a *Fleming* claim in respect of the blocked input tax incurred on carpets and white goods installed in new homes. TW argued that the input tax block should not be applied to these items as it was unlawful under EU law. The First-tier Tribunal held that the input tax block was applicable to the items installed by TW and the blocking order was 'probably' unlawful under EU law. Therefore TW had the option of either exempting these supplies and not recovering input tax or treating them as taxable supplies and recovering input tax and then accounting for output tax on the value of the goods. However, HMRC would be able to refuse TW's claim even though it was now out of time to assess. The fact that HMRC was out of time to assess was irrelevant as TW was only entitled to claim the net amount after input tax had been off-set against any output tax due. TW's appeal was dismissed. TW appealed to the Upper Tribunal who held that the input tax blocks introduced by the UK government were not unlawful under EU law and as a result TW had no right to choose which option it wanted to implement in order to deal with the VAT treatment of these items installed in new homes. The Upper Tribunal refused to make reference to the CJEU in respect of this issue. The Upper Tribunal went on to consider what was meant by 'incorporated' and 'ordinarily incorporated by builders in a building of that description'. The Upper Tribunal provided useful guidance in this regard and concluded that the test of incorporation should not be determined by either reference to the English land law definition or by whether the item was part of a single supply of a zero-rated dwelling. The Upper Tribunal held that they did not consider that there should be a prescriptive test, but there must be a material degree of attachment of the item in order for it to be treated as installed or incorporated into a building. The installation must also be designed to make the item more than temporary, such as attachment either to a physical part of the building or to the supply of electricity, gas, drainage, water or ventilation. The Upper Tribunal decision means that most of the input tax incurred on the items claimed but TW will not be recoverable as a result of either being incorporated in the building or being specifically covered by the blocking orders. The Upper Tribunal heard another case connected with input tax recovery on certain goods installed in new homes and the second decision provides further guidance on the terminology used within the VAT legislation and it also provides further confirmation that claims for input tax incurred on these items are severely restricted ([2018] UKUT 55 (TCC), [2018] STC 689).

Time of supply

[43.19] The rules applying to the time of supply are outlined below.

(1) Single payment contracts

Single payment contracts are subject to the normal tax point rules (see **67.18 SUPPLY: TIME OF SUPPLY**) including the creation of a basic tax point when the work has been completed. (VAT Notice 708, para 23.1).

Retention payments

Building contracts frequently include retention clauses which allow customers to hold back a proportion of the contract price on completion of the work pending confirmation that the supplier has done the work properly and has rectified any immediate faults that might be found.

There are special tax point rules that apply to retention payments generally *other than those for stage or interim payment contracts under (2) below*. The tax point for the retention element of the contract is the earlier of

- the time when a payment in respect of any part of the retention is received by the supplier; or
- the date that the supplier issues a VAT invoice relating to the retention.

[*SI 1995/2518, Reg 89*]. (VAT Notice 708, para 23.1).

(2) Stage or interim payment contracts

Where services, or services together with goods, are supplied in the course of the construction, alteration, demolition, repair or maintenance of a building or of any civil engineering work under a contract which provides for payment for such supplies to be made periodically or from time to time (often referred to as 'stage' or 'interim' payment contracts), those services (or goods and services) are normally treated as separately and successively supplied at the earliest of the following times.

(a) Each time a payment is received by the supplier.
(b) Each time the supplier issues a VAT invoice.

There is, therefore, no basic tax point when the work is completed unless the contract is covered by the following special anti-avoidance rules that can apply in some cases.

(VAT Notice 708, para 23.1).

Special anti-avoidance rules

If a VAT invoice is not issued, the tax point (and therefore VAT payment) can be delayed. The special anti-avoidance rule counters the VAT effect of contracts where payment does not become due for many years after the completion of the work. The rules are complex but, briefly, do *not* apply if

- whoever will be occupying the works will be doing so wholly or mainly for eligible purposes;
- the supplier is unconnected with the proposed occupiers *and* can be sure that neither he, nor any of his subcontractors, is receiving any form of finance from the proposed occupiers, nor anyone connected with them. In this connection, finance does not include interim payments for supplies, on which VAT is accounted for.

(VAT Notice 708, para 24.2).

In more detail, where services are 'relevant services' which have not already been treated as supplied under (*a*) or (*b*) above, there is an additional tax point on the day on which the services are performed.

Services are '*relevant services*' if, at the time they are performed, either of the following conditions is satisfied.

(a) The supplier or a 'person responsible for financing the supplier's costs' intends or expects that the land on which the building or civil engineering work in question is situated will be occupied (whether immediately or eventually) or will continue to be occupied (for a period at least) by
   - the supplier,
   - a person responsible for financing the supplier's costs, or
   - a person connected with either such person under *CTA 2010, s 1122* (see **72.19 VALUATION**). A company is not connected with another for these purposes only because both are under the control of the Crown, a Minister of the Crown, a government department or a Northern Ireland department

   other than wholly or mainly (see under the heading *The 80% test* below) for 'eligible purposes'.
   Occupation for '*eligible purposes*' means
   - occupation by a taxable person for the purpose of making supplies which are in the course of furtherance of a business and are supplies of such a description that any input tax wholly attributable to those supplies would be input tax for which he would be entitled to credit, or
   - occupation by a specified body within *VATA 1994, s 33* (see **44.2 LOCAL AUTHORITIES AND PUBLIC BODIES**) to the extent that the body occupies the land for non-business purposes, or
   - occupation by a government department

   and for these purposes, where occupation is by a person who is not a taxable person but whose supplies are treated for the purposes of *VATA 1994* as made by another person who is a taxable person, those two persons are to be regarded as a single taxable person.

(b) The supplier has received (and used in making his supply) from a subcontractor any supply of services, or services together with goods, the time of supply of which was determined under these anti-avoidance provisions (or would have been but for the issue by that subcontractor of a VAT invoice other than one which has been paid in full).
Thus a main contractor is affected by the anti-avoidance rules if any of his subcontractors are affected by it. If, for example, a bank gives a loan to a subcontractor specifically to do work on one of its banks, the subcontractor would be affected by the anti-avoidance rule, and so would the contractor. However, HMRC will not be seeking to catch a contractor out on a technicality in this area, and if it does come to their attention that a contractor is inadvertently affected by the rule because of his subcontractors, they will look at his case sympathetically. (VAT Notice 708, para 24.8).

A '*person responsible for financing the supplier's costs*' is a person who has

- provided finance for the supplier's costs; or
- entered into an agreement or understanding (whether or not legally enforceable) to provide finance for the supplier's costs.

Providing funds is widely defined. It includes directly or indirectly providing funds *either* to meet the whole or part of the supplier's costs *or* to discharge the whole or part of any liability incurred in raising funds to meet those costs. It also includes directly or indirectly procuring the provision of funds by another person for either of those purposes. The funds may be provided by way of loan, guarantee or other security, consideration for a share issue used to raise the funds or any other transfer of assets or value as a consequence of which the funds are made available. Providing funds does not include making interim payments for construction work on which VAT is accounted for.

A '*supplier's costs*' are his costs of supplying the services, or services together with goods, and comprise

- amounts payable by the supplier for supplies to him of goods and services used in making his supply; and
- the supplier's staff and other internal costs of making his supply.

[*SI 1995/2518, Reg 93*].

HMRC give the following decision table to show the questions a supplier must ask himself to determine whether the anti-avoidance provisions apply to him.

(1) Do you know who will occupy the works?
If 'yes', go to step 3.
If 'no', go to step 2.

(2) Do any of your subcontractors know who will occupy the works?
If 'yes', go to step 4.
If 'no', you do not have to account for VAT when you complete your work and you can follow the normal rules for stage and interim payment contracts.

(3) Will you, or someone connected with you, occupy the works?
If 'yes', go to step 7.
If 'no', go to step 4.

(4) Will one of your subcontractors, or someone connected with one of your subcontractors, occupy the works?
If 'yes', go to step 7.
If 'no', go to step 5.

(5) Will someone who gave you finance to pay for the costs of your work, or someone connected with your financer, occupy the works?
If 'yes', go to step 7.
If 'no', go to step 6.

(6) Will someone who gave your subcontractor finance to pay the costs of his work, or someone connected with his financer, occupy the works?
If 'yes', go to step 7.
If 'no', you do not have to account for VAT when you complete your work and you can follow the normal rules for stage and interim payment contracts.

(7) Will the occupier be doing so wholly or mainly for eligible purposes?
If 'yes', you do not have to account for VAT when you complete your work and you can follow the normal rules for stage and interim payment contracts.
If 'no', you must account for VAT no later than when you complete your work.

(VAT Notice 708, para 24.3).

'Wholly or mainly' test

HMRC take the view that a building is used 'wholly or mainly' for eligible purposes if the occupier can recover 80% or more of the VAT relating to that building. It does not matter whether their overall ability to recover VAT is greater or less than 80%. Buildings that *are not* normally seen as being 'wholly or mainly for eligible purposes' include those used

- as a bank, or the headquarters of a banking group;
- as an insurance broker's office, or the office of an insurance company;
- as a school, college or university;
- as an office for a charity (but the special anti-avoidance rules do not apply if the work for a charity is zero-rated);
- as a private hospital, or the head office of a private healthcare business; or
- for any purpose if the occupier is not registered for VAT (but the special anti-avoidance rules do not apply if the work is zero-rated, such as constructing a house).

Buildings that *are* normally seen as being 'wholly or mainly for eligible purposes' include those used

- as the head office of a fully taxable business
- for any purpose where the occupier is a government department
- by a local authority for carrying on its statutory functions
- as a retail shop,
- as a wholesale outlet,
- as a factory or workshop,
- as an importer's office or warehouse, or
- as a charity shop

provided that the retailer, etc. is registered for VAT.

(VAT Notice 708, para 24.7).

When services are performed

HMRC treat services as performed when the work is completed. See **42.7 LAND AND BUILDINGS: EXEMPT SUPPLIES AND OPTION TO TAX** for a general consideration of the meaning of 'completion'. (VAT Notice 708, para 24.9).

Accounting for VAT

Where the anti-avoidance rules apply, VAT must be accounted for on the full value of the contract, less any amounts on which VAT has already become due because a payment has been received or a VAT invoice issued. The full value of the contract includes retentions and disputed amounts.

Where there is a dispute, or where it is not possible to know the exact value of the contract for any other reason, a reasonable estimate of the value must be made. In cases of dispute, a supplier need not account for VAT on the full amount he is claiming from the customer if he feels that he will most likely be forced in the end to settle for a lower amount. He should account for VAT on his best estimate of the amount that will eventually be agreed. (HMRC recommend that the supplier documents the basis of his estimate, so that he can later show that it was reasonable.) Subsequently, when the value of the contract is finalised, the supplier may need to make an adjustment to the VAT paid.

(VAT Notice 708, para 24.10).

Public/Private Partnership (formerly Private Finance Initiative)

If a PPP or PFI arrangement relates to a building that will be occupied exclusively by a government department (including an NHS hospital), the anti-avoidance rules do not apply. However, some PPP and PFI arrangements relate to buildings that will be occupied by private sector businesses as well as government departments. In such cases, the part of the building occupied by the private sector business may be caught by the special anti-avoidance rules. If so, there is no need to account for VAT on the entire building on completion, only on a proportion of the overall price that fairly reflects the part of the building that will be occupied by private companies. (VAT Notice 708, para 24.7).

(3) Self-billing

Under a self-billing arrangement, the customer makes out VAT invoices on behalf of the VAT-registered supplier (e.g. a main contractor makes out VAT invoices on behalf of its registered subcontractor) and sends a copy of the invoice to the supplier with the payment. See **40.6 INVOICES** for conditions of self-billing and **67.4 SUPPLY: TIME OF SUPPLY** for the time of supply and a notional tax point for input tax deduction purposes.

(4) Goods supplied without services

Building materials supplied without services will generally be standard-rated, unless one of the other categories of *VATA 1994, Sch 7A*, *Sch 8* or *Sch 9* applies.

(5) Materials not supplies in connection with supply of services

Where materials, etc. are not supplied in connection with the supply of services (e.g. a supply by a builders' merchant to a builder), the time of supply is that under the normal rules for supplies of goods. See **67.8 SUPPLY: TIME OF SUPPLY**.

(6) Insolvency

There are no concessions for tax points in the construction industry when a business becomes insolvent. The normal tax point rules as in (1)–(4) above apply equally to transactions before and after the appointment of an insolvency practitioner. (Business Brief 4/96).

Self-supply of construction services

[43.20] Where a person, in the course or furtherance of a business carried on by him, and for the purpose of that business and otherwise than for a consideration, performs any services in connection with

(a) the construction of a building,
(b) the extension or alteration of, or the construction of an annexe to, any building such that additional floor area of not less than 10% of the floor area of the original building is created,
(c) the construction of any civil engineering work, or
(d) the carrying out of any demolition work at the same time as, or in preparation for, any of the services in (*a*) to (*c*) above

those services are treated as both supplied to him for the purpose of that business and supplied by him in the course or furtherance of it (i.e. self-supplied) unless

- the open market value of the services performed is less than £100,000, or
- such services would, if supplied for a consideration in the course or furtherance of a business by a taxable person, be zero-rated.

VAT must be accounted for on the open market value of the services performed (subject to the *de minimis* limit of £100,000) in the VAT return for the period in which the services are performed. This output tax on the self-supply can be recovered as input tax in the same period to the extent that it is attributable to taxable supplies under the normal rules, i.e. to the extent that the building in question is used or to be used for making taxable supplies. Therefore

- where the building or work is occupied or used for a taxable business activity, or is sold or let after the exercise of an option to tax, the self-supply VAT should be fully recoverable;
- where the building or work is used wholly for exempt purposes or let without the option to tax being exercised, the self-supply VAT is not recoverable; and
- where the building or work is used partly for exempt and partly for taxable business purposes, VAT on the self-supply charge is recoverable according to the partial exemption method used.

Where the value of the self-supply exceeds £250,000, adjustments may be required in future years under the **11 CAPITAL GOODS SCHEME**.

Input tax incurred on goods and services for such building works are treated as relating to the taxable self-supply and can be deducted in full (subject to the normal rules).

In relation to **28 GROUPS OF COMPANIES**, for these purposes all companies within a VAT group are treated as one person but anything done which would fall to be treated under these provisions as services supplied to and by that person are to be treated as supplied to and by the representative member (see **28.4 GROUPS OF COMPANIES**).

Registration

Where a person not registered for VAT makes a self-supply falling within these provisions, the value of the self-supply will make him liable for registration.

[*SI 1989/472*]. (VAT Notice 708, paras 25.3, 25.4).

De Voil Indirect Tax Service. See V3.244.

Treatment in particular circumstances

[43.21] The treatment of land and buildings in particular circumstances is outlined as follows.

(1) Architects, surveyors, consultants and supervisors

The separate supply of architectural, surveying, consultancy and supervisory services is always standard-rated. However, these services can be procured in a number of ways.

Design and build

The building client engages a contractor to carry out both the design and construction elements of the project. Where it is clear in the contract that any services of architects, surveyors or others acting as a consultant or in a supervisory capacity are no more than cost components of the contractors supply and are not specifically supplied on to the customer, then the whole supply can be treated as being eligible for the zero rate.

Project management

The building client engages a project manager (usually a construction company) to plan, manage and co-ordinate the whole project, including establishing competitive bids for all elements of the work. The successful contractors are employed directly by the building client. Management fees paid by the building client to the project manager are standard-rated.

Management contracting

This system can take various forms but normally the building client first appoints a professional design team and engages a management contractor to advise them. If the project goes ahead, the management contractor acts as the main contractor for the work (engaging 'works contractors' to carry out work to him as necessary). His preliminary advisory services are then treated in the same way as his main construction services. If the project does not go ahead, his preliminary advisory services are standard-rated.

(VAT Notice 708, para 3.4).

(2) Authenticated receipts

The authenticated receipt procedure (not to be confused with self-billing, see **40.6 INVOICES**) allows a supplier to issue an authenticated receipt for payment instead of a normal VAT invoice.

The procedure works by the customer preparing a receipt for a supply received and forwarding it to the supplier with payment. The receipt is only valid for VAT purposes when the supplier has authenticated it. The time limits for the issue of an authenticated receipt is the same as for a VAT invoice (see **40.12 INVOICES**).

The procedure can only be used when all of the following conditions are satisfied.

- The customer and the supplier mutually agree to operate the procedure.
- Services, or services together with goods, are supplied in the course of the construction, alteration, demolition, repair or maintenance of a building or of any civil engineering work.
- The contract provides for payments for such services to be made periodically, or from time to time ('stage' or 'interim payment' contracts). The procedure should not therefore be used for supplies made under single payment contracts.
- The receipt contains all the particulars required on a VAT invoice (see **40.4 INVOICES**).
- No VAT invoice or similar document is issued.

An authenticated receipt is not a VAT invoice and its issue does not create a tax point. The tax point for the supply is therefore solely determined by the receipt of payment by the supplier or, where the special anti-avoidance rules described in **43.19**(2) above apply, the date the work is completed.

An authenticated receipt is, however, acceptable as evidence for input tax purposes. The customer may claim input tax in the VAT period in which the supplier receives the stage payment, without waiting for an authenticated receipt. But he must obtain and keep a copy of the authenticated receipt. Suppliers cannot authenticate a receipt and return it to the customer until they have received the payment.

If a customer experiences difficulty in obtaining an authenticated receipt from a supplier, he should contact HMRC in writing on the third successive occasion that this happens. A claim to input tax may still be allowed if satisfactory alternative evidence is available, or the customer can show that reasonable efforts were made to secure an authenticated receipt and the claim is otherwise correct.

[*SI 1995/2518, Reg 13(4)*]. (VAT Notice 708, para 23.4).

(3) CITB levy

Any agreed deduction in respect of the Construction Industry Training Board levy can be deducted from the gross amount for the purposes of calculating VAT due, and the value of the supply is treated as reduced by any such levy. (VAT Notice 708, para 22.2).

(4) Income tax deductions

Where a contractor is required to make a deduction on account of income tax from a payment to a subcontractor who is not exempt from such deduction, the value of the subcontractor's services for VAT purposes is the gross amount before income tax is deducted. (VAT Notice 708, para 22.1).

(5) Liquidated damages

Liquidated damages are agreed pre-estimated sums to be paid in the event of a breach of contract by one of the parties. The amount is either a set figure or determined by a formula.

- Liquidated damages received are not payment for a supply made and no VAT is due on the amount received.
- Where a person is due to make a payment for liquidated damages and also due to receive from the other party a payment for a supply, he cannot reduce the value of his supply (and therefore cannot reduce the amount of VAT chargeable), even if he sets the amounts off against each other.

(VAT Notice 708, para 22.3).

Certificates

Certificates for relevant residential/charitable purposes

[43.22] Where a zero-rated or reduced-rated supply is made in connection with all or part of a building which is intended for use solely for a '*relevant residential purpose*' or a '*relevant charitable purpose*' (see **42.16** and **42.14** **LAND AND BUILDINGS: EXEMPT SUPPLIES AND OPTION TO TAX** respectively), the grant or other supply cannot be taken as relating to the building (or part) intended for such use unless

(a) it is made to the person who intends to use the building (or part) for such purposes (the 'customer'); and

(b) before it is made, the customer has given to the grantor or supplier a certificate, in such form as is prescribed by HMRC, stating that the grant or other supply relates to such a building (or part).

[*VATA 1994, Sch 7A Group 6 Note (8), Group 7 Note (4A), Sch 8 Group 5 Note (12), Group 6 Note (3)*].

The effect of the above is that, before a developer or builder can zero-rate or reduce-rate certain grants and other supplies, he must obtain a certificate from the customer. A certificate must be used for any of the following supplies.

(1) The first grant of a major interest in a building (or part of a building) for use solely for a relevant residential purpose or a relevant charitable purpose (see **43.1** above).

(2) The first grant of a major interest in a building (or part of a building) for use solely for a relevant residential purpose by the person who has converted it (see **43.11** above).

(3) The first grant of a major interest by a person substantially reconstructing a protected building where the building is to be used solely for a relevant residential purpose or a relevant charitable purpose (see **43.13** above).
(4) The supply of goods and services in the course of construction of a new building intended solely for a relevant residential purpose or a relevant charitable purpose (see **43.17** above).
(5) The supply to a relevant housing association of goods and services in the course of conversion of a non-residential building (or a non-residential part of a building) into a building (or part of a building) intended for use solely for a relevant residential purpose (see **43.9** above).
(6) The supply of goods and services in the course of an approved alteration to a protected building intended solely for use for a relevant residential purpose or a relevant charitable purpose (see **43.10** above).
(7) The supply of qualifying services in the course of a qualifying conversion into premises for use for a relevant residential purpose (see **43.13** above).
(8) The supply of qualifying services in the course of the renovation or alteration of a qualifying residential property last used for a relevant residential purpose (see **43.13** above).

Possession of a valid certificate does not mean that a supplier can automatically zero-rate or reduce-rate his charge. He must still meet all of the conditions for zero-rating or reduced-rating. The supplier must also take all reasonable steps to check the validity of the certificate, including corresponding with his customer to confirm the details of the use of the building. Such correspondence should be retained within his records. Where, however, despite taking all reasonable steps to check the validity of the certificate, a supplier fails to identify the inaccuracy and, in good faith, zero-rates or reduce-rates the supply, HMRC will not seek to recover VAT due from the supplier.

Subcontractors

Subcontractors working for a main contractor should not be issued with a certificate and so should always standard-rate their supplies.

Issue of certificates

The customer issues the certificate. He can either copy the certificate from VAT Notice 708 or create his own certificate provided it contains the same information and declaration. It must be issued before the supplier makes his supply. However, as a concession, HMRC will allow a supplier to adjust his VAT charge on receipt of a belated certificate (subject to the three-year cap) provided that

- the customer can demonstrate to the supplier that, at the time of supply, he intended that the building would be used in the way being certified; and
- all other conditions for zero-rating or reduced-rating are met.

The two available certificates confirm that the customer is eligible to receive either

- zero-rated or reduced-rated building work; or
- a zero-rated sale or long lease.

Penalties for incorrect certificates

See **53.26 PENALTIES.**

Form of certificate

The two certificates prescribed by HMRC (which have the force of law) are as follows.

Certificate for zero-rated and reduced-rated building work
1. Address of the building:
2. Name and address of organisation receiving the building work: VAT Registration number (if registered): Charity registration (if registered):
3. Date of completion (or estimated date of completion) of the work: Value (or estimated value) of the supply: £ Name, address and VAT registration number of building contractor:
4. I have read the relevant parts of Notice 708 *Buildings and construction* and certify that this organisation (in conjunction with any other organisation where applicable) will use the building, or the part of the building, for which zero-rating or reduced rating is being sought solely for (tick box as appropriate): • a relevant charitable purpose, namely by a charity in either or both of the following ways: (a) otherwise than in the course or furtherance of business,☐ or (b) as a village hall or similarly in providing social or recreational facilities for a local community.☐ • a relevant residential purpose, namely as: (a) a home or other institution providing residential accommodation for children,☐ (b) a home or other institution providing residential accommodation with personal care for persons in need of personal care by reason of old age, disablement, past or present dependence on alcohol or drugs or past or present mental disorder,☐ (c) a hospice,☐ (d) residential accommodation for students or school pupils,☐ (e) residential accommodation for members of any of the armed forces,☐ (f) a monastery, nunnery or similar establishment,☐ or (g) an institution which is the sole or main residence of at least 90 per cent of its residents;☐ and will not be used as a hospital, prison or similar institution or an hotel, inn or similar establishment.

Certificate for zero-rated and reduced-rated building work

5. I certify that the information given is complete and accurate and acknowledge that if the building, or the part of the building, for which zero-rated supplies have been obtained, within a period of 10 years from the date of its completion:

- ceases to be used solely for a relevant residential purpose and/or relevant charitable purpose;
- is no longer used to the same extent for a relevant residential purpose and/or relevant charitable purpose decreases; or
- is disposed of,

a taxable supply will have been made, on which this organisation will have to account for VAT at the standard rate.

Name (print): Position held:

Signed: Date:

General warning

1. Customs reserves the right to alter the format of the certificate through the publication of a new notice. You must ensure that the certificate used is current at the time of issue.

Warnings for the issuer

2. You may be liable to a penalty if you issue a false certificate.

3. You are responsible for the information provided on the completed certificate.

Warnings for the developer

4. You must take all reasonable steps to check the validity of the declaration given to you on this certificate.

5. You must check that you meet all the conditions for zero-rating or reduced-rating your supply – see Notice 708 *Buildings and construction*.

Certificate for sales and long leases of zero-rated buildings

1. Address of the building:

2. Name and address of organisation buying, or entering into a long lease on, the building (or part of the building):

VAT Registration number (if registered):

Charity registration (if registered):

3. Date (or estimated date) of purchase or commencement of the lease:

Value (or estimated value) of the supply: £

Name, address and VAT registration number of the developer:

4. I have read the relevant parts of Notice 708 *Buildings and construction* and certify that the building, or the part of the building, for which zero-rating is being sought will be used solely for (tick box as appropriate):

- a relevant charitable purpose, namely by a charity in either or both of the following ways:
  - (a) otherwise than in the course or furtherance of business,☐ or
  - (b) as a village hall or similarly in providing social or recreational facilities for a local community.☐

Certificate for sales and long leases of zero-rated buildings	
• a relevant residential purpose, namely as: (a) a home or other institution providing residential accommodation for children,☐ (b) a home or other institution providing residential accommodation with personal care for persons in need of personal care by reason of old age, disablement, past or present dependence on alcohol or drugs or past or present mental disorder,☐ (c) a hospice,☐ (d) residential accommodation for students or school pupils,☐ (e) residential accommodation for members of any of the armed forces,☐ (f) a monastery, nunnery or similar establishment,☐ or (g) an institution which is the sole or main residence of at least 90 per cent of its residents;☐ and will not be used as a hospital, prison or similar institution or an hotel, inn or similar establishment.	
5. I certify that the information given is complete and accurate and acknowledge that if the building, or the part of the building, for which zero-rated supplies have been obtained, within a period of 10 years from the date of its completion: • ceases to be used solely for a relevant residential purpose and/or relevant charitable purpose; • is no longer used to the same extent for a relevant residential purpose and/or relevant charitable purpose decreases; or • is disposed of, a taxable supply will have been made, on which this organisation will have to account for VAT at the standard rate. Name (print): Signed:	 Position held: Date:
General warning 1. Customs reserves the right to alter the format of the certificate through the publication of a new notice. You must ensure that the certificate used is current at the time of issue. **Warnings for the issuer** 2. You may be liable to a penalty if you issue a false certificate. 3. You are responsible for the information provided on the completed certificate. **Warnings for the developer** 4. You must take all reasonable steps to check the validity of the declaration given to you on this certificate. 5. You must also check that you meet all the conditions for zero-rating your supply—see Notice 708 *Buildings and construction*.	

Student accommodation

Provided a new building is clearly intended primarily for use as student accommodation for ten years from the date of its completion, HMRC previously agreed that higher education institutions may issue a certificate for the construction or acquisition of such a building as a relevant residential building despite any letting of the accommodation for holiday use or for non-educational conferences, etc. during vacations. (Concordat between HMRC, University Vice-Chancellors and Principals, para 37a). See also *R v C & E Commrs (oao Greenwich Property Ltd)*, Ch D [2001] STC 618 (TVC 2.83). However, the concessionary arrangement which allows Higher Education Institutions (HEIs) to ignore vacation use when determining whether new student accommodation is intended to be used solely for a relevant residential purpose was withdrawn from 1 April 2015.

On 31 January 2014 HMRC issued a technical note advising that from 1 April 2015, HEIs will have to include vacation use when determining whether they can issue a certificate as evidence that the building is intended for use solely (at least 95%) for a relevant residential purpose.

The construction or acquisition of new student accommodation will continue to be zero-rated where

- it is used solely (at least 95%) as residential accommodation for students without relying on the concession, and so qualifies for zero-rating under *VATA 1994, Sch 8 Group 5 Note (4)* as a relevant residential building; or
- it is designed as a dwelling or as a number of dwellings (see below) and so qualifies for zero-rating under *VATA 1994, Sch 8 Group 5 Note (2).*

Until 1 April 2015, HEIs could choose either to use the concession or rely on the statutory position. The law requires that, in order for the construction or acquisition of a relevant residential building to be zero-rated, a certificate must be issued to the builder or vendor stating that the building in question is to be used solely for a qualifying purpose, before the supply takes place.

Certificates which rely on the concession to meet the 'solely' for a relevant residential purpose test will still be valid where

- for construction services, the first supply was made before 1 April 2015 and relates to a meaningful start to the construction of the building by that date, and the works are expected to progress to completion without interruption (demolition or site clearance works will only be accepted where construction starts immediately afterwards);
- for the first grant of a major interest in new student accommodation, either a meaningful deposit (for example, on exchange of contracts) has been paid to the vendor (or their solicitor before 1 April 2015) (options to purchase will not be accepted – irrespective of intention) or an agreement or lease (or purchase) has been signed with the vendor or landlord before 1 April 2015 and a meaningful start to the construction of the building has taken place by that date, and the works are expected to progress to completion without interruption (demolition or site clearance works will only be accepted where construction starts immediately afterwards).

With reference to the above two bullet points, for single developments of more than one block of student accommodation constructed in phases, a meaningful start to the construction of the building means a meaningful start to the construction of the first building and expected to progress to completion without interruption means expected to progress to completion of all phases without interruption.

Where a building has been zero-rated because it is intended for use solely for a relevant residential purpose, under existing rules taxpayers must review the actual use of that building for a period of ten years and account for a VAT self-supply charge under *VATA 1994, Sch 10 Part 2* when there has been a change in its use. Taxpayers with student accommodation which has been zero-rated as a result of using the concession can continue to rely on the concession when determining whether there has been a change in the use of the building for the purposes of the change of use charge.

Student accommodation – designed as a dwelling or a number of dwellings

HMRC accept that there may be circumstances where a building could qualify for zero-rating as a dwelling as well as qualifying for zero-rating as a relevant residential purpose building. This will be the case if the building meets the 'designed as a dwelling or a number of dwellings' conditions at *VATA 1994, Sch 8 Group 5 Note (2)* as well as the 'use' test at *VATA 1994, Sch 8 Group 5 Note (4)*. HMRC have advised that in such circumstances a taxpayer is free to rely on either provision to achieve zero-rating.

The 'use' test at *VATA 1994, Sch 8 Group 5 Note (4)* can only be relied on if it is intended from the outset that the building will be used at least 95% (solely) for relevant use and a change of use charge may arise if there is a change of use or ownership within ten years. A change of use charge will not apply if the building was eligible for zero-rating under *VATA 1994, Sch 8 Group 5 Note (2)*.

VATA 1994, Sch 8 Group 5 Note (2) is a design test which requires that in order to be 'designed as a dwelling or a number of dwellings' it must meet four conditions.

- *Condition 1* – the dwelling must consist of self-contained living accommodation. HMRC consider that the dwelling must have the basic elements of living accommodation and so would expect there to be a kitchen, bathroom, sleeping area and living area. HMRC expect there to be a minimum of two rooms, one room being a bathroom and the other room providing an area that has facilities for living, cooking and sleeping (for example, a studio flat).
  In the case of a studio flat the living area should include an area that can be used for the purpose of food preparation – usually including a sink, storage for cups and utensils, a worktop, space for a fridge and a means of cooking (for example, a cooker, or hob/oven). If no cooking appliance is installed, HMRC expect there to be an appropriate connection for such an appliance (for example, cooker ring, main circuit or gas pipe designed for connecting to a cooker or similar built-in appliances). A general plug socket only – perhaps intended for the use of a microwave oven, kettle or toaster is unlikely to be sufficient unless most of the other features of a kitchen referred to above are also present. Self-contained living accommodation can potentially include what are sometimes termed 'cluster flats' – single flats that have their own front door and typically contain a number of en-suite bedrooms let to individual students. Within the cluster flat there will be a kitchen and common area used by all occupants of the flat.

- *Condition 2* – there is no provision for direct internal access from the dwelling to any other dwelling or part of a dwelling. There is no direct internal access when you cannot move from one dwelling to another dwelling or part of a dwelling, without first moving across an area outside the dwelling, such as a landing or corridor. However, if there is a fire door connecting one dwelling to another, HMRC do not see this door as failing this condition, providing it is fitted with an appropriate fire door lock and secured at all times other than in the event of a fire or fire test. If the door is capable of being routinely opened to allow occupants to move freely from one dwelling to another, HMRC would regard this as a failure to meet this condition.
- *Condition 3* – the separate use or disposal of the dwelling is not prohibited by the terms of any covenant, statutory planning consent or similar provision. Separate use or disposal means that the use or disposal of the dwelling must not be tied to another building, structure or even land. If it is tied it fails this condition. Accordingly, the condition will normally exclude 'granny' annexes constructed in the grounds of a main house; and where a dwelling can't be used or sold separately from other premises, such as a caretaker's house at a school or assisted living units within the grounds of care or nursing homes. In the example of a development like student accommodation where the dwellings take the form of studio or cluster flats, HMRC would regard conditions or prohibitions under the terms of the planning consent that prevents individual flats from being sold or leased as a failure to meet condition 3. However, HMRC would regard condition 3 as being met if any prohibition on the sale of individual flats arises only as a result of a financial agreement (for example, terms of mortgage or finance of the property) or from agreements to let the accommodation to students of a particular university or other educational body.
- *Condition 4* – statutory planning consent has been granted in respect of that dwelling and its construction or conversion has been carried out in accordance with that consent. To meet condition 4, the dwelling that meets conditions 1, 2 and 3 above must have been granted planning permission and have been constructed or converted in accordance with that consent. This will be a matter of fact in each case. However, variations to the planning consent, resulting in a change in appearance, or to the composition or distribution of the accommodation, will normally be accepted. More radical departures resulting, for example, in a much larger dwelling being constructed, will fail to satisfy the condition, unless there is evidence that the planning authorities have decided not to pursue the matter.

Student accommodation – dining rooms and kitchens

The concessionary arrangement which allowed dining rooms and kitchens to be zero-rated for students and school pupils if they are used 'predominantly' by the living in students was also withdrawn from 1 April 2015. The concession allowed the construction of dining halls to be zero-rated if constructed at the same time as student accommodation and if residents in that student accommodation make up at least 50% of the users of the dining hall, providing the dining hall and/or kitchen is owned by the educational establishment and not a third party.

From 1 April 2015, HEIs and schools will only be able to issue a certificate as evidence to support zero-rating for a dining hall and kitchen if the building is constructed at the same time as student accommodation and is intended to be used solely (at least 95%) by the students in that accommodation, their guests or anyone who looks after the building for a relevant residential purpose, therefore meeting the statutory test on intended use.

Until 1 April 2015, HEIs could choose either to use the concession or rely on the statutory position. The law requires that, in order for the construction or acquisition of a relevant residential building to be zero-rated, a certificate must be issued to the builder or vendor stating that the building in question is to be used solely for a qualifying purpose, before the supply takes place.

Certificates which rely on the concession to meet the 'solely' for a relevant residential purpose test will still be valid where

- for construction services, the supply was made before 1 April 2015 and relates to a meaningful start to the construction of the building by that date, and the works are expected to progress to completion without interruption (demolition or site clearance works will only be accepted where construction starts immediately afterwards);
- for the acquisition of new student dining halls and kitchens, a meaningful deposit (for example, exchange in contracts) has been paid to the vendor before 1 April 2015 (options to purchase will not be accepted – irrespective of intention).

Under existing rules, where a building has been zero-rated because it is intended for use solely for a relevant residential purpose, taxpayers must review the actual use of that building for a period of ten years and account for a VAT self-supply charge under *VATA 1994, Sch 10 Part 2* when there has been a change in its use. Taxpayers with dining halls which have been zero-rated as a result of using the concession can continue to rely on the concession to determine whether there has been a change in the use of the building for the purposes of the change of use charge.

Student accommodation – what is a student?

The 'use' test at *VATA 1994, Sch 8 Group 5 Note (4)(d)* refers to relevant residential purpose accommodation for students or school pupils. In essence VAT relief on the construction of residential accommodation for school pupils who are boarders will be subject to the same rules that apply to residential accommodation constructed for students. However, what is meant by a student may be less obvious than what is meant by a school pupil.

In the context of *VATA 1994, Sch 8 Group 5 Note (4)(d)* a student is a person undertaking a course of educational study or instruction and who is receiving education or vocational training from a university (or a centrally funded higher education institution or a further education institution) or from any other supplier who is providing similar, or the same type of, education or vocational training to a similar, or the same, academic standard.

Examples include (but are not necessarily limited to) individuals who have left school and are undertaking higher or further education or training with a view to

(1) obtaining a generally recognised academic or professional qualification;
(2) maintaining an existing professional qualification where accreditation is received – this would include continuing professional development in cases where a professional body requires from its members the continuing recognition of a qualification or an employer requires employees to maintain or improve relevant technical skills; or
(3) undertaking a course of study which, whilst not leading to a recognised qualification, has a high level of academic content and is intended to improve the knowledge and understanding of the student in an area of academic interest.

The following are illustrative examples of the kind of educational activity which is included in (3) above.

- Summer schools in which international students and others have the opportunity to undertake a programme of study comparable with the work done by full time students.
- Residential events the purpose of which is to show aspiring university applicants what it is like to study at university – whilst the academic content is high and the participants are school pupils, the purpose of their attendance is not either part of their A-level curriculum nor is it part of a programme which leads to a qualification.
- English as a Foreign Language (EFL) courses.
- Academic conferences which offer development and ongoing learning to the academic staff of universities and colleges to ensure that academics are able to share ideas, learn from each other and embed the latest thinking into their own research and teaching.

People who attend classes, often badged as 'summer schools', which may offer a life-enhancing experience and promote greater cultural or spiritual awareness but the subject matter of which falls into the category of hobbies or leisure interests (for example pottery workshops, art or literature appreciation courses etc.) as opposed to receiving educational or vocational training to an academic standard, will not qualify as 'students'.

Whilst persons engaging in theological studies in order to become a minister of faith (such as a priest, rabbi or imam) will qualify as 'students', those attending seminaries or religious retreats which do not serve this purpose but are intended primarily to foster or reinforce faith, are not considered to be receiving educational or vocational training to an academic standard and will not qualify as 'students'.

(VAT Notice 48, ESC 3.11; VAT Notice 708, paras 17.1–17.7, 18.1, 18.2; VAT Information Sheet 2/14; HMRC Brief 3/14; HMRC Brief 14/14).

D-I-Y housebuilders

[43.23] A special VAT Refund Scheme puts D-I-Y builders and converters in a broadly similar position to a developer selling a zero-rated property, by refunding them the VAT on their main construction or conversion costs.

Under the scheme, HMRC must refund any VAT chargeable on the supply, acquisition or importation of any goods used in connection with construction or conversion work where the following conditions are satisfied.

(a) The work must comprise
 (i) the 'construction of a building' 'designed as a dwelling' or number of dwellings;
 (ii) the constructing of a building for use solely for a 'relevant residential purpose' or for a 'relevant charitable purpose'; or
 (iii) a '*residential conversion*', i.e. the conversion of a 'non-residential' building or a non-residential part of a building into *either* a building designed as a dwelling or number of dwellings *or* a building intended solely for a relevant residential purpose *or* anything which would fall into either of those categories if different parts of a building were treated as separate buildings.

(b) The work is carried out lawfully and otherwise than in the course or furtherance of any business.

(c) The goods are building materials which, in the course of the works, are incorporated in the building in question or its site. See **43.16** to **43.18** above for goods which do and do not qualify. Refunds can be claimed on the building materials which would be zero-rated when supplied with the zero-rated work but *not* on those which would be standard-rated.

(d) The claim is made within such time and in such form and manner, contains such information, and is accompanied by such documents as HMRC require. See **43.24** below.

See **42 LAND AND BUILDINGS: EXEMPT SUPPLIES AND OPTION TO TAX** at **42.3** for the definition of '*construction of a building*', **42.5** for '*designed as a dwelling*', **42.16** for '*relevant residential purpose*', **42.14** for '*relevant charitable purpose*' and **42.11** for '*non-residential*'.

Refund also covers VAT chargeable on a supply of any goods under the law of another EU member state.

Conversions using contractors, etc.

Where a person carries out a residential conversion and arranges for the work to be done by someone else ('a contractor'), then provided

(i) the person's carrying out of the residential conversion is lawful and otherwise than in the course or furtherance of any business, and

(ii) the contractor is not acting as an architect, surveyor or consultant or in a supervisory capacity,

HMRC must, on a claim, refund any VAT chargeable on any services consisting of work done by the contractor.

Garages

The construction of, or the conversion of a non-residential building to, a building designed as a dwelling or number of dwellings includes the construction of, or conversion to, a garage. The dwelling and the garage must be constructed or converted at the same time and the garage must be intended for occupation with the dwelling or one of the dwellings.

[*VATA 1994, s 35*].

Conversion of mixed use buildings

Following the decision in *C & E Commrs v Jacobs*, CA [2005] STC 1518 (TVC 15.154) (in which a former boys' school used for residential and non-residential purposes was converted into four dwellings) HMRC accept that the conversion of a building that contains both a residential part and a non-residential part comes within the scope of the Refund Scheme provided the conversion results in an additional dwelling being created. It is not necessary for the additional dwelling to be created exclusively from the non-residential part. However, VAT recovery is restricted to the conversion of the non-residential part. (Business Brief 22/05).

Holiday homes

In *Jennings* [2010] UKFTT 49 (TC) (TC00362) (TVC 15.60) the tribunal decided that *VATA 1994, Sch 8, Group 5, Note 13* (which denies relief if residence throughout the year is not permitted) only applied to cases within *Group 5, Item 1*, i.e. where a building was purchased from a developer. It did not apply to cases within *Group 5, Item 2*, i.e. where a landowner arranged for a contractor to construct a building on his land. Also it should not be treated as applying to cases within *VATA 1994, s 35*, where a landowner purchased materials for the construction of a building. The tribunal observed that if a DIY builder agrees with a contractor for the construction of the entire building, that supply is zero-rated by *Group 5, Items 2 and 4*, both of which are unaffected by *Note 13*. The materials used in the construction are effectively zero-rated.

Following the *Jennings* decision, HMRC have accepted that the DIY house-builders and converters refund scheme applies to the construction of new holiday homes and to the conversion of non-residential buildings into holiday homes. HMRC had previously never applied the scheme to holiday homes since their supply by a developer attracts VAT at the standard rate. However, they have now stated that the relevant legislation does allow the same recovery of VAT on building materials for holiday homes that have been constructed by the individual for a non-business purpose (HMRC Brief 29/10).

De Voil Indirect Tax Service. See V5.164.

Making the claim

[43.24] The following two claim packs, each consisting of a claim form and guidance notes, are available from the VAT Helpline (Tel: 0300 200 3700) or from https://www.gov.uk/government/organisations/hm-revenue-customs – VAT 431C 'Claim form for conversions' and VAT 431NB 'Claim form for new houses'.

Conversions

A person is eligible to claim back VAT on building materials and services if they

- are converting a previously non-residential property (e.g. an office, shop, agricultural building or redundant school or church) into a dwelling (not for business purposes but to be used either by them or their relatives as a principal place of residence);
- are converting a previously residential property, that has not been lived in for the last ten years or more into a principal place of residence for either them or their relatives;
- have bought a converted building as a 'shell' from a developer and are fitting it out to completion as a principal place of residence for either them or their relatives; or
- are converting a building into one that is intended solely for a relevant residential purpose so long as it is not for business purposes. A relevant residential purpose means a building that is to be used for communal residential accommodation such as a children's home, student accommodation, hospice, residential accommodation for members of the armed forces, monastery, nunnery or similar establishment.

HMRC released HMRC Brief 9/16 which provided clarification on the VAT treatment of the conversion of a non-residential building into dwellings where individual planning consent is not required because the development is covered by permitted development rights (PDR). HMRC have stated in the Brief

> 'that where the builder, developer or DIY House Builder Scheme claimant establishes that the conversion is covered by a PDR and individual SPC is not required, they must be able to evidence it by at least one of the following:
>
> (a) Written notification from the LPA advising of the grant of prior approval. Or
> (b) Written notification from the LPA advising that prior approval is not required. Or
> (c) Evidence of deemed consent (ie evidence that you have written to the LPA and your confirmation that you have not received a response from them within 56 days) and evidence that the development is a permitted development. This will include all of the following (where the documents have been created), plans of the development, evidence of the prior use of the property (eg evidenced by its classification for business rates purposes etc.), confirmation of which part of the planning legislation is relied upon for the development and a lawful development certificate where one is already held.'

The conversion can be zero-rated providing the requirements specified in HMRC Brief 9/16 are satisfied.

New builds

A person is eligible to claim back VAT on building materials if they

- are constructing a new dwelling not for business purposes but to be used either by them or their relatives as a principal place of residence;
- have bought a new building as a 'shell' from a developer and are fitting it out to completion, as a principal place of residence for either them or their relatives; or
- are constructing a new building that is intended for use solely for either a relevant charitable purpose (i.e. intended to be used for non-business purposes such as a place of worship or offices used by charities for administering non-business activity, such as the collection of

donations), or a relevant residential purpose (so long as it is not for business purposes). A relevant residential purpose means a building that is to be used for communal residential accommodation such as a children's home, student accommodation, hospice, residential accommodation for members of the armed forces, monastery, nunnery or similar establishment.

Extra work

Once the building has been completed, the following are examples of work that cannot be claimed for – a conservatory, a patio, double-glazed windows, tiling or a garage. Also, a person cannot claim for extra work that is done to a building which has been completed before they purchased it from a builder or developer.

Outbuildings

A claim cannot be made for any work that has been carried out on outbuildings, e.g. rooms above or attached to a detached garage; detached workshops or store rooms; sheds; stables; detached swimming pools; and annexes (such as 'granny' annexes) that cannot be disposed of or used separately from another dwelling because the annexe is not 'designed as a dwelling' in its own right. The only outbuilding that can count as part of the eligible building project is a garage, providing it is constructed or converted at the same time as the eligible building, and it is intended to be used at the same time as that building.

Submission of claims

As at 31 January 2016, the claim forms VAT 431NB and VAT 431C include the following telephone number to contact HMRC to obtain the up-to-date address for submitting claims – 03000 569 145.

The following documentation must be sent with the claim forms.

- The planning permission.
- Evidence that the work is completed.
- A full set of building plans.
- The original VAT invoices, bills and credit notes.

Receiving the refund

HMRC aim to acknowledge a claim within five working days, and deal with the claim within six weeks of receipt, unless they need more information. If the claim is successful they will write to the taxpayer to tell them when they can expect to receive the refund.

[*SI 1995/2518, Regs 200, 201, 201A*].

Appeals

If a claim for a refund is refused or HMRC disagree with the amount of the refund, an appeal may be made to a VAT tribunal. See **5.3**(*g*) **APPEALS**.

Caravans and houseboats

Zero and reduced rate supplies

[43.25] The term 'caravan' is not defined in the VAT legislation. In practice, HMRC follow the definition in *The Caravan Sites and Control of Development Act 1960*. A caravan 'is a structure designed or adapted for human habitation that, when assembled, is physically capable of being moved from one place to another (whether being towed, or by being transported on a motor vehicle so designed or adapted)'. In addition, it is no more than 20 metres long (exclusive of any drawbar), 6.8 metres wide, or 3.05 metres high (measured internally). This definition can include a twin unit caravan if composed of no more than two sections designed to be assembled on site by means of bolts, clamps and other devices, as long as, once assembled, it is physically capable of being moved from one place to another.

HMRC see the term 'caravan' as including mobile homes, static caravans but not motor caravans.

At present the size limits referred to below are 7 metres long and 2.55 metres wide (excluding towing bars and similar apparatus used solely for the purpose of attaching the caravan to a vehicle).

(VAT Notice 701/20/13, paras 2.1, 2.2).

Reduced rate supplies

From 6 April 2013 supplies of caravans which exceed the limits of size of a trailer for the time being permitted to be towed on roads by a motor vehicle having a maximum gross weight of 3,500 kilogrammes are reduced rate supplies (unless they meet the additional conditions for zero-rating (see below)). This extends to a supply of services within *VATA 1994 Sch 4 paras 1(1)* or *5(4)* in respect of such a caravan. Excluded are removable contents, other than incorporated building materials, and the supply of accommodation in a caravan.

[*VATA 1994, Sch 7A Group 12*].

Zero-rated supplies

Supplies of the following are zero-rated.

(a) **Caravans** (prior to 6 April 2013) exceeding the limits of size currently in force for trailers which may be towed on roads by a motor vehicle having an unladen weight of less than 2,030 kilogrammes.
Caravans (from 6 April 2013) which exceed the limits of size of a trailer for the time being permitted to be towed on roads by a motor vehicle having a maximum gross weight of 3,500 kilogrammes and which were manufactured to standard BS 3632 (or a previous version of that standard) approved by the British Standards Institution. This legislation is aimed at zero-rating static residential caravans and taxing (at the reduced rate) static holiday caravans, based on the test of whether they meet standard BS 3632.

A new version of BS 3632 was published on 30 November 2015 (BS 3632:2015) and *VATA 1994, Sch 8 Group 9* was amended from 2 December 2015 by *SI 2015/1949* to include sales of residential caravans built to standard BS 3632:2015. (HMRC Brief 21/15). *Excluded* are certain removable contents, see **43.26** below. [*VATA 1994, Sch 8 Group 9 Item 1 and Note (a); SI 2015/1949*].

(b) **Houseboats**, i.e. boats or other floating decked structures designed or adapted for use solely as places of permanent habitation and not having means of, or capable of being readily adapted for, self-propulsion. *Excluded* are certain removable contents. [*VATA 1994, Sch 8 Group 9 Item 2 and Note (a)*].
The term '*self-propulsion*' refers to any vessel that is either
- independently propelled; or
- not independently propelled but could readily be adapted to be capable of self-propulsion (e.g. by installing an engine, propeller or mast).

It is unlikely, therefore, that a vessel such as a barge or a yacht would be regarded as a houseboat.
(VAT Notice 701/20/13, para 7.2).

(c) **Caravans or houseboats** qualifying under *(a)* or *(b)* above which are let or loaned or, if business assets, are put to any private use or are used, or made available to any person for use, for non-business purposes, subject to the overriding exception for accommodation below. [*VATA 1994, Sch 8 Group 9 Item 3*].

The supply of *accommodation* is excluded. [*VATA 1994, Sch 8 Group 9 Note (b)*].

De Voil Indirect Tax Service. See V4.275.

Supplies associated with caravans

[43.26] For a general consideration of the recovery of input tax in relation to caravan parks, see *Stonecliff Caravan Park* (VTD 11097) (TVC 15.201) and *Harpcombe Ltd*, QB [1996] STC 726 (TVC 46.27).

(1) Accommodation

Holiday accommodation

The provision of accommodation in a caravan

- sited on a park advertised or held out for holiday use; and
- let to a person as holiday accommodation

is standard-rated.

Off-season letting

The provision of accommodation in a caravan during the off-season can be treated as exempt provided

- it is let to a person as residential accommodation;

- it is let for more than 28 days; and
- holiday trade in the area is clearly seasonal.

The supplier should keep a copy of his tenancy agreement or similar evidence to show that the caravan was occupied for residential purposes only. In such cases the whole of the let, including the first 28 days, should be treated as an exempt supply.

The holiday season normally lasts from Easter to the end of September although some areas (e.g. London) are not regarded as having a seasonal holiday trade.

Residential accommodation

The provision of accommodation in a caravan is exempt where it is

- on a site designated by the local authority as for permanent residential use; and
- let to a person as residential accommodation.

(VAT Notice 701/20/13, paras 5.1–5.3).

(2) Brick skirting

The provision of brick skirting is generally integral to the agreement to supply a caravan and its liability follows the liability of that supply.

The input tax that is attributable to these supplies should be determined accordingly.

(VAT Notice 701/20/13, para 3.6).

(3) Car parking/garage fees

The supply of a garage or parking space in conjunction with the supply of a permanent residential caravan pitch is exempt providing

- the supplier retains ownership of the land on which the garage or parking space is sited; and
- the garage or parking space is reasonably close to the caravan pitch.

In all other circumstances supplies of garages and parking are standard-rated.

(VAT Notice 701/20/13, para 6.1).

(4) Caravan pitches

See **42.18**(*e*) **LAND AND BUILDINGS: EXEMPT SUPPLIES AND OPTION TO TAX** for the liability of pitch fees and rents received for the granting of the right to caravan owners to keep their caravans on pitches.

Pitch agreements generally impose certain obligations upon site owners such as the construction of pitches, bases and the park infrastructure. Any one-off charge raised which is directly related to these obligations follows the liability of the supply of the pitch.

Reservation fees or premiums charged by a park owner are part of the consideration for the pitch and follow the liability of the pitch fee or rent.

(VAT Notice 701/20/13, paras 4.1, 4.7).

(5) Commission received

Park owners' commission on sales of second-hand sited caravans

The 'commission' which a park owner is entitled to receive under the *Mobile Homes Acts* and/or Code of Practice when a caravan owner sells a caravan 'on site' at his park follows the liability of the pitch fee or rent.

Any additional charge to the seller in connection with the sale (e.g. for agency services) is standard-rated.

Charges made to dealers, allowing them to place caravans which have been sold on an owner's site, are standard-rated. Where the charge is passed on to the caravan purchaser it is treated as part of the dealer's costs and forms part of the consideration for the caravan. The VAT treatment will follow the liability of the caravan.

Fees received by park owners from third parties

Any commission from a caravan manufacturer/dealer for the sale of a caravan is standard-rated.

(VAT Notice 701/20/13, paras 3.4, 3.5).

(6) Delivery, unloading and positioning charges

Such charges made by the supplier of the caravan at the same time as that supply, provided they are reasonable, follow the liability of the 'delivered' caravan. This applies whether the supply is made by the manufacturer, dealer or site owner. Any delivery service provided which is unconnected with the supply of the caravan is standard-rated.

(VAT Notice 701/20/13, para 3.3).

(7) Electricity, gas, water and sewerage charges

Connection to mains services

Charges made by caravan site owners for first time connection to electricity, gas, water and sewerage will be subject to the same VAT liability as the pitch (generally standard-rated, in the case of holiday/leisure sites; exempt, in the case of residential sites) unless the site owner identifies and charges for the actual consumption of users (i.e. through metering at the pitch), in which case the connection charge will be subject to the same VAT liability as the supply of the utility (reduced-rated for electricity and gas; zero-rated for water and sewerage).

Electricity and gas

Supplies of electricity and gas to a caravan are liable at the reduced rate provided the users actual consumption can be identified (i.e. it is metered). Otherwise, the liability of the supply follows that of the main supply of the pitch rental.

Where, for touring caravans and motor homes, an optional hook-up charge is made and the caravan owner chooses to have electricity supplied to the pitch, the supply is subject to VAT at the reduced rate. Any non-optional charge forms part of the overall pitch fee which is standard-rated.

Water and sewerage charges

Charges made by caravan site owners for water and sewerage will remain zero-rated if actual consumption can be identified (i.e. through metering at the individual pitch). In other circumstances, charges will follow the VAT liability of the caravan pitch (generally standard-rated, in the case of holiday/leisure sites; exempt, in the case of residential sites).

Where, for touring caravans and motor homes, an optional hook-up charge is made, the supply is zero-rated. Any non-optional charge forms part of the overall pitch fee which is standard-rated.

(VAT Notice 701/20/13, paras 3.2, 4.2, 4.3).

(8) Fixtures, fittings and removable contents

Where the supply of a caravan is zero-rated, then zero-rating also applies to those goods which a builder would ordinarily incorporate into a new house (e.g. sinks, baths, WCs, fixed partitions and water heaters). See **43.16** and **43.17** above for further details. Other fixtures and any removable contents supplied with the caravan (e.g. tables, chairs, mattresses, seat cushions, fridges, carpets, washing machines) are standard-rated. The fact that they form a single supply with the zero-rated caravan does not prevent the fixtures from being standard-rated under UK legislation. *Talacre Beach Caravan Sales Ltd v C & E Commrs, ECJ Case C-251/05*, [2006] STC 1671 (TVC 22.575).

If a caravan and its removable contents are advertised at separate prices and the customer is entirely free to purchase the caravan at the lower price without the removable contents, then, provided the breakdown between the two figures is not a sham, the charges for the removable contents may be treated as a separate taxable supply. Otherwise, and in all cases where there is a single consideration, an apportionment is required. Methods for arriving at the value of the removable contents in new and used caravans are described below. These methods do not have to be used but any different method must give a fair and reasonable result.

In *Talacre Beach Caravan Sales Ltd v C & E Commrs, ECJ Case C-251/05*, [2006] STC 1671 (TVC 22.582) (referred to above) the ECJ decided that the principles considered in the judgment of the ECJ in *Card Protection Plan Ltd v C & E Commrs, ECJ Case C-349/96*, [1999] STC 270 (TVC 22.362) (see **65.6 SINGLE AND MULTIPLE SUPPLIES**) did not prevent VAT at the standard rate applying to items which the legislation had excluded from the scope of a different VAT treatment. In *Colaingrove Ltd v HMRC* [2015] UKUT 0002 (TCC) (TVC 69.14) the Upper Tribunal decided that the *Card Protection Plan* principles should apply to the sale of verandas with static caravans so that the sale of a static caravan with a veranda is a single supply. The nature of such a single supply would be one comprising a principal element of a static caravan and an ancillary element of a veranda. The VAT treatment of the single supply would be that of the principal element, the static caravan, and so the single supply would, as a whole, be zero-rated. An important distinguishing feature between the *Talacre Beach Caravan Sales Ltd* case regarding caravans sold with removable contents and the *Colaingrove Ltd* case regarding static caravans sold with verandas is that removable contents are specifically excluded from the scope of zero-rating by virtue of *VATA 1994, Sch 8 Group 9 Note (a)* but there is nothing in *VATA 1994, Sch 8 Group 9* to exclude a veranda from the scope of zero-rating.

Following the decision in *Colaingrove Ltd v HMRC* [2015] UKUT 0002 (TCC) (TVC 69.14) HMRC confirmed that it accepts that the VAT liability of verandas and decking structures sold with static caravans is the same as the VAT liability of the caravan.

(HMRC Brief 12/15).

New caravans

Standard-rated removable contents included in the price of a new caravan can be calculated by reference to the costs incurred.

Example

A caravan is purchased from a manufacturer for resale. Its cost is £20,000 plus £150 VAT giving a total cost of £20,150. It is sold for £30,000 including VAT.

The VAT on sale must be the same proportion of the sale price as it was of the total cost.

VAT due = sale price × VAT on purchase ÷ total cost

= £30,000 × 150 ÷ £20,150 = £223.32

If further removable contents are added to those provided by the manufacturer (or some provided are taken out) before sale, these costs must be added/subtracted as appropriate before making the above calculations.

Used caravans

Standard-rated removable contents included in the price of used caravans can be calculated using either of the following methods. Whichever method is adopted, it must be applied consistently and a supplier must not alternate between methods when calculating the VAT due on each of his supplies.

- *Actual values*. Calculate a precise value for each of the standard-rated removable contents. Adequate documentary evidence must be produced to support each valuation if required.
- *Standard apportionment of values*. This is a standard method of apportionment that has been agreed with the National Caravan Council Ltd and the British Holiday and Home Parks Association Ltd. The value of the standard-rated removable contents is taken as 10% of the VAT-exclusive selling price of the complete caravan. If a caravan is sold at a VAT-inclusive price, the VAT element in that price is 1/6.

If the margin scheme for **62 SECOND-HAND GOODS** is used for sale of the caravan, then the 10% apportionment is applied to the margin rather than the full selling price. The margin is always be VAT-inclusive, so the VAT is calculated as follows:
Margin on the sale of caravan × 10% × 1/6.

Other charges included in the selling price

Charges made at the time of supply of the caravan for delivery, unloading and positioning (see (6) above) and for connections to mains services (see (7) above) are regarded as part of a single supply of the caravan, and form part of its price. If any of the above methods of apportionment are used, the calculation should be made on the total of all such amounts. Other charges, such as reservation fees or premiums, pitch fees or commissions should be excluded from the calculations.

(VAT Notice 701/20/13, paras 3.1, 8.1–8.6; VAT Notice 700/57/14).

(9) Insurance

Insurance premiums paid by a park owner to cover general liability or risks are exempt. If the park owner recovers this cost by making a separate charge to caravan owners, the charge is treated as part of the overall consideration for the supply of the pitch and has the same VAT liability as the pitch fee or rent.

Where a park owner is asked by a caravan owner to arrange insurance cover for the caravan owner's risks, any charge made, or any commission earned, for arranging the insurance is exempt provided the caravan owner is the recipient of the supply of insurance made by the insurer.

Any payments received in relation to the renewal of existing insurance policies follow the liability of the original supplies as above.

(VAT Notice 701/20/13, para 4.6).

(10) Local authority charges

Where a caravan is used as a person's sole or main residence, it is generally subject to council tax, for which the resident or owner of the caravan/park home is liable. Caravans on seasonal or holiday parks are not subject to council tax (unless used as a person's sole or main residence). Instead, the owner of the caravan site is liable to pay non-domestic rates for the whole site. If a site owner passes on the cost of non-domestic rates to individual caravan owners, the recharge forms part of the pitch fee or rental and is standard-rated.

(VAT Notice 701/20/13, para 4.4).

(11) Maintenance of common areas

Any costs relating to the development or maintenance of the common areas of the park (e.g. installation of street lighting, resurfacing of roads, planting of trees and erection of fences) relate exclusively to the supply of the pitches. Recovery of the input tax depends on whether the site is a residential or holiday site.

(VAT Notice 701/20/13, para 6.3).

(12) Miscellaneous charges

Other charges made to individual caravan owners by the park owner are standard-rated. These include:

- Holiday booking services
- Off-season storage and security (on-pitch or off-pitch). Storage of touring caravans is always standard-rated (whether or not a specific area of land is granted to the caravan owner and including contracts where the period of storage is in excess of one year).
- Club membership.
- Repair and maintenance of caravans.
- Drainage of water-systems.

(VAT Notice 701/20/13, paras 6.2, 6.4).

(13) Service charges

Service charges to individual caravan owners for general upkeep and maintenance of the park as a whole (its common areas) follow the liability of the pitch fee or rent. Specific services provided to particular residents are normally standard-rated.

(VAT Notice 701/20/13, para 4.5).

Houseboats

Accommodation; Delivery, unloading and positioning charges; Connection to mains services; and Fixtures, fittings and removable contents

[43.27] The same provisions apply as for caravans in **43.26** above.

Mooring rights

Mooring rights for a houseboat are exempt. See **42.18**(*h*) **LAND AND BUILDINGS: EXEMPT SUPPLIES AND OPTION TO TAX** for moorings generally.

Garages and parking spaces

The supply of a garage or parking space to the owner of a houseboat is exempt provided it is

- supplied by the person who is supplying the mooring; and
- reasonably close to the mooring.

(VAT Notice 701/20/13, paras 7.4–7.8).

Key points

[43.28] Points to consider are as follows.

- The freehold or long leasehold sale of a new dwelling by the person constructing it is zero-rated. This includes the sale of a building that has been converted from a non-residential building, e.g. a barn converted to a bungalow and sold.
- A long leasehold sale means a lease that is greater than 21 years (20 years in Scotland).
- The advantage of a property sale being zero-rated rather than exempt (as in the case of the second and subsequent sales of the dwelling) is that input tax can be reclaimed on the related costs of the project, i.e. building materials, professional fees.
- A planning point, if a builder rents out a new dwelling rather than sells it (rental income is exempt), is to sell the new building to a connected business, and the latter business then generates the rental income. This protects the input tax recovery for the first business, i.e. it has still made the zero-rated sale of a new dwelling, even though to a connected party.
- A property can only be classed as a new dwelling if the conditions of building use (usually linked to planning issues) allow the buyer to use the property as his main residence and live there throughout the year. Restrictions on use mean that zero-rating will not apply (e.g. as in the case of holiday accommodation).
- In cases where a sale includes both a new dwelling and another building, e.g. flat above a shop, then the value of the sale must be apportioned on a fair and reasonable basis so that zero-rating only applies to the new dwelling. Surveyor or estate agent valuations are usually the best methods of determining the split.
- Zero-rating also applies to the first time sale of a new building by a builder if it is to be used as either a 'relevant residential building' (e.g. an elderly persons home, student accommodation) or as a 'relevant charitable building' (e.g. a church). In both cases, the builder must obtain a certificate from the buyer to confirm the use will qualify for zero-rating.
- The services of a builder involved in the construction of a new dwelling are also zero-rated. This applies irrespective of whether the builder is acting as the main contractor or a sub-contractor working for the main contractor.
- In the case of building services carried out on a new relevant residential building or relevant charitable building, zero-rating only applies in relation to the services of the main contractor. He must hold a certificate from the building owner confirming the intended use of the building when it has been completed. The services provided by subcontractors working for the main contractor are always standard-rated.

- Professional services relating to architects, surveyors and managing agents etc. are always standard-rated, irrespective of the work being carried out.
- It is important to identify when the reduced rate of VAT can be applied by builders working on a project. This is particularly important if the landlord cannot reclaim input tax on the project as there is a big difference between the reduced rate of VAT (5%) and the standard rate of VAT.
- The main situations when the 5% rate of VAT applies to building works are as follows: conversion of a non-residential property into a residential property; work on a residential property that has been empty for two or more years; work on a residential property (or properties) where a different number of units is evident after the work has been completed compared to the beginning (e.g. converting a detached house into two flats).
- The reduced rate of VAT also applies to the services of subcontractors, unless it relates to a relevant residential building, when only the main contractor in receipt of a certificate from the building owner can benefit from charging the reduced rate.
- In the case of work carried out on a property that has been empty for two years or more, it is important that the builder obtains and retains evidence of the empty period (e.g. council tax records etc.). This evidence is important to confirm the reduced rate of VAT was correctly charged in the event of an HMRC visit.
- An input tax block applies to certain goods installed in a new dwelling, if the items are not classed as building materials. Carpets, white goods (washing machines, dishwashers etc.) and furniture items are examples of goods where an input tax block is applied. There is no problem with wood flooring or tiling.
- A useful planning point for a builder supplying standard-rated (or reduced rated) services is to raise an application for payment or request for payment in relation to ongoing contracts, rather than a tax invoice. If an invoice is then issued when payment has been received from the customer, this will become the date when VAT is payable on a return.
- Many builders could also benefit from the cash flow advantages of the cash accounting scheme. The scheme is available to any business with annual taxable sales (excluding VAT) of £1.35m or less. The disadvantage of the scheme is that input tax cannot be reclaimed on a supply until payment has been to a supplier.
- The flat-rate scheme can be used by a builder with annual taxable sales of £150,000 or less (excluding VAT). However, the scheme is unlikely to be worthwhile for a builder who has some zero-rated or reduced rated sales because the relevant scheme percentage is applied to these sales as well.
- Private individuals building their own homes (or converting a non-residential property into a new dwelling) can benefit from VAT recovery on material costs through the DIY scheme.

- It is important that any zero-rated or reduced rated building services are correctly identified because HMRC will not refund any incorrectly charged VAT through the DIY scheme.
- Alterations to listed buildings will be at the standard rate in all circumstances after 30 September 2015. The sale of a substantially reconstructed protected building can now only be zero-rated in very restricted circumstances.

44

Local Authorities and Public Bodies

Cross-references. See **9.1 BUSINESS** for the meaning of 'business'; **17.13 EDUCATION**; **52.17 PAYMENT OF VAT** for repayment supplement; **53.14 PENALTIES** for serious misdeclaration or neglect resulting in understatements or over-claims; **54 PENSION SCHEMES**.

Introduction: local authorities and public bodies

[44.1] For a transaction to be within the scope of VAT, it must, amongst other conditions, be made by a taxable person. Certain 'bodies governed by public law' are given special treatment under EU legislation. They are not treated as being taxable persons when they engage in certain transactions which, if engaged in by other persons, would result in them being considered taxable persons.

Although the term *'bodies governed by public law'* is used in *Directive 2006/112/EC*, the phrase is not used in UK law. In *EC Council Directive 93/36* it is interpreted as any body

- established for the specific purpose of meeting needs in the general interest, not having an industrial or commercial character;
- having legal personality; and
- financed, for the most part, by the State, or regional or local authorities, or other bodies governed by public law, or subject to management supervision by those bodies, or having an administrative, managerial or supervisory board, more than half of whose members are appointed by the State, regional or local authorities or by other bodies governed by public law.

Treatment as non-taxable persons

Specifically, state, regional and local government authorities and other bodies governed by public law are not considered taxable persons in respect of activities or transactions where the following conditions are met. This applies even where they collect dues, fees, contributions or payments in connection with these activities or transactions. Recent CJEU cases have considered whether the transactions of local authorities fall within the scope of VAT as constituting supplies made for consideration.

In *Gemeente Borsele v Staatssecretaris van Financiën, CJEU Case C-520/14*, the CJEU considered the activities of a local authority that bought in school bus services, incurring VAT, and charged parents of children a fixed fee to be registered for the service. The overall revenue from the fees was only 3% of the total costs incurred. The CJEU held that this was not economic activity, and the authority was not entitled to recover VAT (nor obliged to account for output tax on the fees received).

By contrast, in *Gemeente Woerden v Staatssecretaris van Financiën, CJEU Case C-267/15*, the CJEU considered the construction of two buildings by another Netherlands municipality. These were sold to a non-profit foundation that let part of the buildings rent-free to a special school. The CJEU held that the municipality's transactions were carried out as economic activity, even though the amount charged to the foundation was only 10% of the cost of the buildings. It was therefore entitled to recover VAT on the costs. The Court affirmed that economic activity does not require the making of profit.

If the local authority's activities pass the basic standard of economic activity in that it is regarded as making supplies for consideration, they may still be outside the scope of VAT if certain further conditions of the PVD are satisfied.

(a) The body is engaged in the activity or transaction 'as a public authority'

There is nothing in EU legislation specifying those activities in which bodies engage as public authorities and it does not follow that just because a body is a public authority that all activities it undertakes are non-taxable activities (or 'non-business' as such activities are more commonly referred to in the UK).

In *Comune di Carpaneto Piacentino and Others v Ufficio Provinciale Imposta sul Valore Aggiunto di Piacenza, ECJ Case C–4/89*, [1990] 3 CMLR 153 (TVC 22.140) the CJEU held that activities pursued as 'public authorities' were those engaged in by bodies governed by public law under the special legal regime applicable to them, but did not include activities pursued by them under the same legal conditions as those applying to private traders.

For example, a body would be acting as a public authority where the law gives it

- the right to make people or organisations pay for a service provided but without giving them any say in what is, or how it is provided; and
- powers to impose penalties where people do not comply.

Following the Court of Session decision in the case of *Edinburgh Telford College v HMRC* [2006] STC 1291 (TVC 22.157), HMRC accept that when considering whether activities are undertaken under a 'special legal regime', it is necessary to consider the wider legal regime governing the management and conduct of an activity, and not to focus solely on the legal regime governing the delivery of a particular service (HMRC Brief 27/08).

In *Norwich City Council* (VTD 11822) (TVC 42.12) it was accepted that the Council was a body governed by public law. The Council granted advertising facilities to commercial sponsors of various campaigns which it organised but did not account for VAT on the sponsorship payments. The tribunal held that although the Council was using the sponsorship payments in support of its statutory functions, the sponsorship deals were not in themselves part of the statutory functions of the Council and were carried out under the same legal provisions as applied to private traders.

In *Arts Council of Great Britain* (VTD 11991) (TVC 7.83) the Council's main activity was the distribution of an annual Parliamentary grant. The tribunal held that this was not an economic activity. Although the Council was not a specified body within *VATA 1994, s 33(3)* (see **44.2** below), it was 'a public body, performing a public function, whose costs were paid out of public funds'.

See also *Royal Academy of Music* (VTD 11871) (TVC 55.15) where the tribunal held that the Academy was not a public authority body and was not governed by public law so that its activities fell outside the scope of what is now *Directive 2006/112/EC, Art 13*.

Following the High Court judgment in *Riverside Housing Association Ltd v HMRC* [2006] STC 2072 (TVC 15.144), HMRC stated that the term 'body governed by public law' was narrow in application, in that a body only satisfies that criterion if it is a public body that forms a part of the UK's public administration, such as a government department, a local authority or a non-departmental public body (HMRC Brief 27/2008). HMRC's view was confirmed by the High Court in *The Chancellor, Masters & Scholars of the University of Cambridge*, Ch D [2009] STC 1288 (TVC 30.12), a decision now regularly cited as authoritative on the definition.

A trader challenged HMRC's ruling that local authorities provide trade waste collection services as non-taxable persons. It argued that the local authority's status under the *Environmental Protection Act* did not justify treating it as non-taxable. The Upper Tribunal, hearing the case as an application for judicial review, concluded that there was no general principle that could be applied; the trader would have to demonstrate in particular circumstances either that the authority was acting outside its statutory powers, or that treating it as non-taxable would lead to a significant distortion of competition (*R (oao The Durham Company Ltd (t/a Max Recycle)) v HMRC* [2016] UKUT 417 (TCC) (TVC 20.26)).

(b) Treatment as a non-taxable person does not lead to a significant distortion of competition

There is no definition in UK law to quantify the term 'significant' in relation to distortion of competition. In *Comune di Carpaneto Piacentino* above the CJEU considered the matter but did no more than decide that individual EU countries should determine whether distortion of competition was significant and that they were not required to lay down precise quantitative limits. In *HMRC v Isle of Wight Council (No 2), ECJ Case C–288/07* [2008] STC 2964 (TVC 2.167) the CJEU held that significant distortions of competition must be evaluated by reference to the activity in question, without such evaluation relating to any local market in particular. The expression 'would lead to' was to be interpreted as encompassing not only actual competition, but also potential competition, and the word 'significant' was to be understood as meaning that the actual or potential distortions of competition must be more than negligible. Applying this to the facts of the case, the First-tier Tax Tribunal decided that allowing local authorities not to charge VAT on off-street parking would deter other providers from entering the market, and would therefore represent a significant distortion of competition. This decision was upheld by the Upper Tribunal and Court of Appeal (*Isle of Wight Council v HMRC* [2015] EWCA Civ 1303 (TVC 22.158)).

HMRC take the view that significant distortion of competition occurs when non-business treatment

- places private traders at a commercial disadvantage compared to the body; or
- deters private traders from starting up businesses supplying similar goods or services in competition with the body.

Significant distortion can result if a body

- does not charge VAT on a supply, while its competitors making similar supplies have to; or
- recovers the VAT attributable to an exempt supply or a non-business activity, while the VAT incurred by its competitors in making similar supplies effectively sticks with them as a real cost.

See *Metropolitan Borough of Wirral* (VTD 14674) (TVC 22.153) where a district council operated an information service, collecting and distributing information relating to the county in which it was located, in accordance with a statutory requirement. The tribunal held that the work in question could have been undertaken by a private organisation and that to treat the council as a non-taxable person would be unfair on private organisations.

If a body has no local competitor, an activity can be treated as non-business provided no other person could carry out the activity in the same way, and in similar conditions, as the body has to carry it out, and thereby achieving the results as the body has to achieve. HMRC regard this as normally applying where

- the body's clients could not equally well obtain the goods or services from some other supplier;
- the activity is not carried on generally by suppliers outside the public authority sector, unless on such a small scale as to be negligible; and
- non-business treatment would not act as a disincentive to a private trader capable of going into business in direct local competition with the body.

The question of the extent of competition was considered in *The Lord Mayor and Citizens of the City of Westminster* (VTD 3367) (TVC 22.152). The city council managed a hostel providing accommodation to homeless men. The tribunal held that the accommodation provided was of such a type that the council was clearly not supplying services in competition with proprietors of commercial hotels, inns or boarding houses and therefore no distortion of competition arose from the supply being treated as non-business.

In most cases it should be clear whether treating a particular activity as non-business would lead to significant distortion of competition. In cases of doubt, the body should contact HMRC.

Many of the activities which local authorities have a statutory obligation to provide are now subject to contracting out and competitive tendering (e.g. domestic refuse collection). In these cases, whilst the tenderers are in competition to supply the service to the responsible local authority, there is no competition to provide the service to third parties. Such services provided under a statutory obligation to a third party using an outside body acting as agent are non-business provided there is no competition between the local authority and others to supply the services to the third party.

(c) Unless carried out on such a scale as to be negligible, the activity does not relate to

- telecommunications;
- the supply of water, gas, electricity and steam;
- the transport of goods;
- port and airport services;
- passenger transport;
- supply of new goods manufactured for sale;
- the transactions of agricultural intervention agencies in respect of agricultural products carried out pursuant to Regulations on the common organisation of the market in these products;
- the running of trade fairs and exhibitions;
- warehousing;
- the activities of commercial publicity bodies;
- the activities of travel agencies;
- the running of staff shops, co-operatives and industrial canteens and similar institutions; and
- transactions of radio and television bodies of a commercial nature.

[*Directive 2006/112/EC, Art 13(1)*]. (VAT Notice 749, paras 5.4–5.7).

Exempt activities

EU member states *may* consider activities of bodies governed by public law which are exempt under *Directive 2006/112/EC, Arts 132–137* (see **19.24** and **19.25 EUROPEAN UNION LEGISLATION**) or *Art 371* (see **19.42 EUROPEAN UNION LEGISLATION**) as activities which they engage in as public authorities. [*Directive 2006/112/EC, Art 13(2)*].

UK provisions

[44.2] UK law does not specifically refer to 'bodies governed by public law' (see **44.1** above), but see **44.11** below for 'public bodies'. UK law does provide special treatment for 'specified bodies'. The combined effect of the EU and UK provisions is as follows.

(1) All 'bodies governed by public law', which phrase includes but is not restricted to 'specified bodies', can treat certain of their activities as non-taxable activities (or 'non-business' activities as they are more commonly referred to in the UK). See **44.3** below for a consideration of business and non-business activities.
Any such body that is registered, or liable to be registered, for VAT (see **44.5** below) must charge and account for VAT on all its business activities, subject to the normal rules. This applies whether the customer is a private individual, trader, government department or another public body. It must not charge VAT on non-business activities.

(2) As a general rule, it is only possible to recover VAT incurred if registered for VAT and if the VAT can be attributed to taxable business activities. Where VAT relates to non-business or (subject to certain *de minimis* limits) exempt activities, any VAT incurred 'sticks' as a real cost. To minimise this sticking VAT, a special scheme allows 'specified bodies', whether or not registered for VAT, to
- reclaim the VAT suffered on non-business activities (see **44.7** below); and
- recover any VAT attributed to exempt business activities where HMRC consider it an insignificant proportion of the total VAT incurred (see **44.8** below).

It should be noted that 'bodies governed by public law' which are not 'specified bodies', although not benefiting from the special scheme under (2) above, are still able to treat certain otherwise taxable business supplies as non-business.

The '*specified bodies*' are as follows.

(a) A '*local authority*', i.e.
- the council of a county, county borough, district, London borough, parish or group of parishes (or, in Wales, community or group of communities),
- the Common Council of the City of London,
- the Council of the Isles of Scilly,
- any joint committee or joint board established by two or more of the foregoing, and
- in relation to Scotland, a regional, islands or district council within the meaning of the *Local Government (Scotland) Act 1973*, any combination and any joint committee or joint board established by two or more of the foregoing, and any joint board to which *section 226* of that *Act* applies.

The following are not considered to be local authorities.

- Joint boards/committees set up by bodies other than local authorities, even where they include local authorities as members or participants, e.g. boards established by order of a Minister of the Crown.
- Bodies which merely receive financial assistance from local authorities.
- Purely advisory committees which do not carry out local authority functions.
- Community Councils in England or Scotland.
- Community Associations.
- Parish meetings.
- Parochial church councils.
- Village hall management committees.
- Charities.

(b) A river purification board established under *Local Government (Scotland) Act 1973, s 135* and a water development board within the meaning of the *Water (Scotland) Act 1980, s 109*.

(c) An internal drainage board.

(d) An integrated transport authority, passenger transport authority or passenger transport executive for the purposes of *Transport Act 1968, Part II*.

(e) A port health authority within the meaning of *Public Health (Control of Disease) Act 1984*, and a port local authority and joint port local authority constituted under *Public Health (Scotland) Act 1897, Part X*.

(f) A police authority.

(g) A development corporation within the *New Towns Act 1981* or the *New Towns (Scotland) Act 1968*; a new town commission within the *New Towns Act (Northern Ireland) 1965* and the Commission for the New Towns.

(h) A general lighthouse authority within the meaning of *Merchant Shipping Act 1995, Part VIII* (except that no VAT refund is made which HMRC consider is attributable to activities other than the provision, maintenance or management of lights or other navigational aids).

(i) The British Broadcasting Corporation.

(j) The appointed news provider referred to in *Communications Act 2003, s 280* (except that no VAT refund is made which HMRC consider is attributable to activities other than the provision of news programmes for broadcasting by holders of regional Channel 3 licences within the meaning of *Broadcasting Act 1990, Part 1*).

(k) Any body specified by an order made by the Treasury. Currently, these comprise

- the Commissions for Local Administration in England, Wales, and Scotland; and the Commission for Local Authority Accounts in Scotland [*SI 1976/2028*];
- the Inner London Education Authority, the Inner London Interim Education Authority; The Northumbria Interim Police Authority; the London Fire and Civil Defence Authority; the London Residuary Body; a metropolitan county Police Authority, Fire and Civil Defence Authority, Passenger Transport Authority or Residuary Body [*SI 1985/1101*];

- a probation committee constituted by the *Powers of Criminal Courts Act 1973, s 47, Sch 3 para 2* (now replaced by local probation boards under *Criminal Justice and Courts Act 2000*); a magistrates' courts committee established under *Justice of the Peace Act 1979, s 19*; and the charter trustees constituted by *Local Government Act 1972, s 246(4)* or *(5)* [*SI 1986/336*];
- authorities established under *Local Government Act 1985, s 10* (waste regulation and disposal authorities) [*SI 1986/532*];
- National Rivers Authority [*SI 1989/1217*];
- the Environment Agency [*SI 1995/1978*];
- a National Park authority (within the meaning of *Environment Act 1995, s 63*) [*SI 1995/2999*];
- a fire authority constituted by a combination scheme made under *Fire Service Act 1947, s 6* [*SI 1995/2999*];
- charter trustees established under *Local Government Act 1992, s 17* or any other statutory instrument made under *Part II* of that Act [*SI 1997/2558*];
- the Broads Authority [*SI 1999/2076*];
- the Greater London Authority [*SI 2000/1046*];
- the London Fire and Emergency Planning Authority [*SI 2000/1515*];
- Transport for London (the body established under *Greater London Act 1999, s 154*) [*SI 2000/1672*];
- the Greater London Magistrates' Courts Authority [*SI 2001/3453*];
- the London Pensions Fund Authority [*SI 2006/1793*];
- a Transport Partnership created by an order made under *Transport (Scotland) Act 2005, s 1(1)* [*SI 2006/1793*];
- the Charter Trustees for the City of Chester, Crewe, the City of Durham, Ellesmere Port and Macclesfield [*SI 2009/1177*];
- the Wimbledon and Putney Commons Conservators [*SI 2009/1177*];
- chief constables and the Commissioner of Police of the Metropolis [*SI 2012/2393*];
- the Natural Resources Body for Wales [*SI 2013/412*].
- the Barnsley, Doncaster, Rotherham and Sheffield Combined Authority [*SI 2014/863*];
- the Durham, Gateshead, Newcastle Upon Tyne, North Tyneside, Northumberland, South Tyneside and Sunderland Combined Authority [*SI 2014/1012*];
- the Greater Manchester Combined Authority [*SI 2011/908*];
- the Halton, Knowsley, Liverpool, St Helens, Sefton and Wirral Combined Authority [*SI 2014/865*];
- the West Yorkshire Combined Authority [*SI 2014/864*]; and
- the London Legacy Development Corporation [*SI 2015/449*]; and
- Old Oak and Park Royal Development Corporation [*SI 2016/307*].

[*VATA 1994, ss 33(3)–(5), 96(4); Merchant Shipping Act 1995, Sch 13; Communications Act 2003, Sch 17 para 129*]. (VAT Notice 749, paras 2.2, 4.1, 4.2).

Business and non-business activities

[44.3] Because of the special provisions which apply to them, it is important for 'bodies governed by public law' (see **44.1** above), which include the 'specified bodies' listed in UK law (see **44.2** above), to distinguish between their business and non-business activities. The following steps should be considered in reaching a decision.

(a) Is the body making the supply a 'body governed by public law' (see **44.1** above)?
(b) If Yes, go to (*b*).
If No, the activity is business.
(c) Is the body engaged in the activity 'as a public body' (see **44.1**(*a*) above)?
If Yes, go to (*c*).
If No, the activity is business.
(d) Would non-business treatment lead to a significant distortion of competition (see **44.1**(*b*) above)?
If Yes, the activity is business.
If No, go to (*d*).
(e) Is the activity one of those specified in the list in **44.1**(*c*) above?
If Yes, go to (*e*) below.
If No, go to (*f*) below.
(f) Is the activity carried out on a negligible scale?
If Yes, go to (*f*) below.
If No, the activity is business.
(g) Is the body a Government Department or Health Authority (see **44.11** below)?
If Yes, go to (*g*) below.
If No, the activity is non-business.
(h) Is the activity subject to a Treasury direction (see **44.11** below)?
If Yes, the activity is business.
If No, the activity is non-business.

The restriction on non-business treatment for the activities under (*d*) above has little practical effect on most specified bodies as

- they do not generally engage in these activities as 'public authorities' and therefore fail the test under (*b*) above; and
- where the activities are carried out as 'public authorities', they are generally also provided by private bodies and non-business treatment would lead to a significant distortion of competition so that the test under (*c*) above would be failed.

(VAT Notice 749, para 5.1).

De Voil Indirect Tax Service. See V2.108, V2.231.

Common activities of local authorities and police authorities

[44.4] Specified bodies within **44.2** above which are registered for VAT can claim a refund of the VAT they incur on both their business and their non-business activities (see **44.7** below) and do not have to separate the VAT incurred on the two types of activity. It is, however, important to distinguish between business and non-business activities for output tax and partial exemption purposes. It is also important to distinguish between such activities when dealing with non VAT-registered bodies who may incorrectly treat business activities as non-business and consequently not register for VAT at the correct time.

This paragraph considers a number of activities in relation to specified bodies.

(1) Bailiffs

If local authorities are unsuccessful in obtaining payment of council tax from defaulters, they may contract with bailiffs to collect the arrears plus any statutory charges for the enforcement of the debt. Bailiffs supply their services to, and should therefore invoice, the local authority for their statutory charges and any agreed commission based on the amount of the arrears due or collected. VAT is chargeable on the full value of these services and not the lesser amount received from the local authority where payments from debtors are retained and netted-off against the total charge. The local authority can recover the VAT it is charged because it relates to its non-business activity of collecting the council tax. (HMRC Manual VATGPB8600).

(2) Beach huts

Under *Public Health Act 1936, s 232* local authorities may provide huts or other conveniences for bathing on any land belonging to them or under their control, and may make charges for their use. The law neither requires local authorities to provide beach huts nor states that they must do so in a particular way. Consequently, provision of beach huts by a local authority is a standard-rated business activity. See also *Shearing* (VTD 16723) (TVC 7.26) and *Poole Borough Council* (VTD 7180) (TVC 41.137). (HMRC VATGPB8625).

(3) Car parking charges

Where a public authority imposes charges (including excess parking charges) for parking at meter bays on the public highway, it does so under statutory powers that nobody other than a public authority can exercise. This activity is non-business.

In the case of *Isle of Wight Council*, four district councils had accounted for VAT on receipts from off-street car parks. They claimed repayments on the basis that they should have treated these receipts as outside the scope of VAT, by virtue of *Art 4(5)* of the *EC Sixth Directive*. The issue of EU law (whether non-taxation would lead to significant distortion of competition) is considered at **44.1** above (see *HMRC v Isle of Wight Council (No 2) (and related appeals), ECJ Case C-288/07*, [2008] STC 2964 (TVC 2.167)). The High Court remitted the case to the tribunal, which found that failing to tax the council's car parks would distort competition to a more than negligible extent. The Upper Tribunal and Court of Appeal dismissed further appeals by the councils. See *Isle of Wight Council v HMRC (No 4) (and related appeals)* (TC02320) (TVC 22.158).

HMRC have always accepted that penalty charges imposed by local authorities operating off-street parking under the *Road Traffic Act 1991* are outside the scope of VAT. In *Bristol City Council* (VTD 17665) (TVC 62.222) the tribunal decided that excess charges levied by the Council in its off-street car parks were outside the scope of VAT because they were levied under the *Road Traffic Regulation Act 1984* and were not part of the contract between the driver and the council. In HMRC's view, where a car park operator makes an offer of parking under clear terms and conditions, setting punitive fines for their breach, the fines constitute penalties for breaching the contract, rather than additional consideration for using the facilities. Consequently they are outside the scope of VAT. However, where the terms and conditions make it clear that the driver can continue to use the facilities after a set period upon payment of a further amount without being in breach of the contract then the payment is consideration for use of the facilities and subject to VAT. This applies whether the operator of the car park is a local authority or a commercial enterprise.

(VAT Notice 749, para 5.8; HMRC Brief 57/08).

(4) Care and welfare

Most local authorities are required to provide a wide range of services to people of all ages, ranging from children and young persons to the provision of accommodation and domiciliary care for elderly persons. They may be entitled to make a charge to recover all or part of the costs they incur in providing these services.

- Where an authority is acting under a special legal regime applicable to it and not under the same legal conditions as those that apply to private traders, these activities are non-business.
- Where an authority merely provides residential accommodation, for example, because someone has chosen it in preference to similar facilities available from a charity or commercial provider, if such accommodation is not provided under a statutory function the supply of accommodation by the authority is a business activity. Similarly, the supply of services such as creches and playgroups, and recreational holidays for elderly people not in statutory care is a business activity.

(VAT Notice 749, para 5.8).

(5) Cemeteries and crematoria

The provision and maintenance of cemeteries by a local authority is a non-business activity but the provision of crematoria is primarily a business activity. (VAT Notice 749, para 5.8). See also **16.6 DEATH AND INCAPACITY**.

(6) Coastal defence contributions

Local authorities which border the sea are required to obtain contributions, usually from those who derive most benefit, towards the cost of maintaining coastal defence facilities (e.g. sea walls). HMRC take the view that these contributions are not consideration for a supply of services but outside the scope of VAT. (HMRC Manual VATGPB8655).

(7) Education

See **17.13 EDUCATION.**

(8) Housing and property improvements

Local authorities have wide statutory obligations and powers in relation to housing.

(a) The provision and operation of social housing

(i) *Bed and breakfast accommodation.* Where, due to a shortage of its homes for letting, a local authority has to place homeless people in bed and breakfast accommodation, it is carrying out a non-business activity. The local authority does not have to account for output tax on any contributions it receives towards the cost of providing such accommodation (e.g. housing benefit paid directly to it by the Department of Work and Pensions).
The supply of the accommodation is to the local authority, not to the homeless, so the reduced VAT rate for long-term residents cannot be applied.

(ii) *Home improvements and tenants contributions.* Most local authorities have a rolling programme to maintain or improve the quality of their housing stock. Where a tenant has no choice in the matter, any permanently increased rent is a charge for the overall supply of the right to occupy the accommodation which is a non-business activity.
Where improvements are carried out only at the tenants request, the local authority may seek a contribution from the tenant towards the costs of the improvement work. These contributions may take the form of a lump sum payment or instalments paid with the rent. Lump sum payments, or instalments paid with the rent but over a limited period only, are generally standard-rated (but see **29.14** *et seq* **HEALTH AND WELFARE** for zero-rating of certain supplies to disabled persons). Any permanently increased rent is a charge for the overall supply of the right to occupy the accommodation which is a non-business activity.

(iii) *Third party management of local authority housing stock.* Many local authorities delegate the management and maintenance of their housing stock to a tenant management company either in the form of a Tenant Management Co-operative (TMC) or a Tenant Management Organisation (TMO).
A TMC enters into a standard agreement with the local authority under which repairs and maintenance are the delegated responsibility of the TMC. It acts as principal in purchasing materials and carrying out the work or engaging contractors to carry it out on its behalf. The TMC

receives the supplies of goods or services and receives a management and maintenance allowance from the local authority. The local authority cannot recover input tax on the supplies of goods and services. But, if the TMC is VAT-registered, as the delegated maintenance relates to the non-business activity of providing housing, the local authority can recover any VAT charged to it by the TMC under **44.7** below.

A TMO takes on varying degrees of management responsibility and receives payments from the local authority for a range of services it may undertake. It can also administer and collect rents. Most supplies received by the TMO, whose costs are reimbursed by the local authority, are supplies to an agent acting in its own name. The only supplies a TMO normally makes as principal relate to its management charges to the local authority. If the TMO is VAT-registered, this can be recovered by the local authority under **44.7** below as relating to its non-business activity.

(iv) *Local authority garage rentals*. The letting of garages is normally standard-rated but, subject to certain conditions, where it is let in conjunction with a dwelling it can take on the same liability as the dwelling. See **42.18**(*f*) **LAND AND BUILDINGS: EXEMPT SUPPLIES AND OPTION TO TAX** for further details. As the letting of houses and flats by a local authority is a non-business activity, where it lets garages/parking spaces to a housing tenant and the necessary conditions are met, the supply is non-business.

Under 'right to buy' legislation, council tenants can buy, rather than rent, their homes. Where they have continued to rent a garage, the liability of the garage rental depends on whether the main property has been sold freehold or leasehold. Following a freehold sale, the rental of the garage becomes a taxable supply because the local authority is no longer the landlord for the dwelling. But following a leasehold sale, where the tenant continues to pay ground rent to the local authority, the local authority remains the landlord (albeit only the ground landlord). In these circumstances, where a tenant pays ground rent for both the dwelling and the garage, or pays ground rent for the dwelling and rents the garage, the provision of the parking facility is a non-business activity.

(v) *Repair and maintenance of dwellings*. Any repairs to its housing stock which a local authority is responsible for and which it carries out without charge are considered to be part of the non-business activity of providing public sector housing.

Any charge made to a tenant still in residence is a standard-rated supply of services to the tenant. Any charge for repairs and making good to a tenant who has vacated premises and left them in an unfit condition are regarded as compensation and outside the scope of VAT. Similarly, charges made to third parties to recover the costs of repairing damage to council dwellings are also regarded as compensation.

Any VAT incurred in carrying out repairs to dwellings can be recovered, either as input tax or under the refund scheme in **44.7** below.

(vi) *Refugees*. The provision of housing (and lighting, heating, food, etc.) for refugees by a local authority is a non-business activity.

(b) Property improvements, including grant funding

(i) *Care and Repair scheme.* This is designed to provide help to elderly and disabled homeowners to enable them to improve their property. Any grant from a local authority or the Office of the Deputy Prime Minister is outside the scope of VAT. The scheme is administered by a limited company but is carried out by a care and repair agency which may be a charity or housing association but is usually a local authority. The agency makes all arrangements for the work to be carried out and makes all payments on behalf of the homeowner, charging a percentage of the cost of the building works as its fee.

The services of the agency are a business activity when carried out by a local authority although the supplies are exempt under *VATA 1994, Sch 9 Group 7, Item 9* (see **29.12 HEALTH AND WELFARE**).

As actual contracts for the work are between the homeowner and the building contractor, the local authority cannot recover VAT charged by the builder to the homeowner.

(ii) *Default works.* A local authority may issue an enforcement notice to a person who has failed to maintain their property in a satisfactory state of repair.

Where the recipient of the notice agrees to the work being carried out and arranges for either the local authority or some other contractor to undertake it, the contractor's service are supplies to the recipient of the notice. If the local authority arranges the contractor's supplies on behalf of the recipient, it may treat the supply as being made both to it and by it under *VATA 1994, s 47(3)* (see **3.4 AGENTS**).

Where the recipient of the notice refuses to comply, the local authority may exercise its statutory powers to have the work carried out and recover the cost from the recipient. As only a local authority can issue the default notice and exercise these statutory powers, this is a non-business activity. See also *Glasgow City Council* (VTD 15491) (TVC 42.6) where the tribunal held that works in default and the subsequent recovery of costs under *Housing (Scotland) Act 1987, ss 108, 109* were not supplies for VAT purposes.

When the supply of the work is to the local authority, it can recover the VAT charged by the contractor. If it makes an onward taxable supply of the work in the course or furtherance of business, it can recover the VAT incurred as input tax. If it does not make a taxable supply but imposes the work under its statutory powers, it can recover the VAT under the refund scheme in **44.7** below.

(iii) *Property improvement grants.* For a consideration of grants generally, see **72.9**(2) **VALUATION**. The most important points to consider are to whom is the supply made, who actually owns the grants, and what happens to any contributions made by third parties.

The most common situations are those where a local authority funds part of the cost of a householder's planned improvements work by means of a grant. There are normally two ways in which grant-funded improvements are carried out.

The first method is where the homeowner has arranged directly with a builder to carry out some works and a grant is paid by the local authority for that work to be done. The local authority payment is a third party consideration which does not entitle it to recovery under the scheme in **44.7** below. See *Doncaster Borough Council* (VTD 12458) (TVC 42.2).

The second method is where the homeowner has arranged with the local authority for it to act as his agent in organising the building work. The local authority's contributions are still third party consideration and it is not entitled to recovery under the scheme in **44.7** below. If the local authority charges for its agency services to the homeowner, then that fee is standard-rated. This follows the decision in *Ashfield District Council v C & E Commrs*, Ch D [2001] STC 1706 (TVC 42.3).

(iv) *Group repair schemes and block improvement grants*. Local authorities in England and Wales have powers under *Housing Grants, Construction and Regeneration Act 1996, s 65* to carry out improvements to the exterior of blocks and terraces of private sector housing with the permission of the properties' owners ('group repair schemes'). Normally, the local authority receives a grant from central government and a compulsory contribution from the property owner towards the costs of the work. The contribution by the property owner and any grant received direct from central government are also outside the scope of VAT. However, where the owner asks the local authority to provide additional works for a separate payment, this is a business supply.

The local authority can recover any VAT incurred in carrying out non-business activities under the provisions in **44.7** below but any VAT incurred in making business supplies must be recovered under the normal rules.

(c) Building inspection fees

(i) *Planning, building notice, inspection and reversion fees. In England and Wales*, competition exists across the whole range of building control work and such services provided by local authorities are business. *In Scotland and Northern Ireland*, the supply of building control services is the monopoly of local authorities and classed as non-business for VAT purposes.

Local authorities retain their statutory monopoly over planning applications and reversions and the fees they charge for this work is non-business.

(ii) *Regularisation fees*. Where a local authority issues a regularisation certificate because building work has been carried out without its prior approval, as approved inspectors in the private sector do not have the legal power to carry out this function, this is a non-business activity.

(d) The provision and maintenance of community projects, including village halls

(i) *Village halls owned by the local authority*. Where the local authority uses its own funds to carry out work to the hall, it is not making a supply for VAT purposes. Where it receives funds from another body (e.g. a village hall management committee) the funds are most likely to be consideration for its use of the hall. Alternatively, the funds may be a donation and outside the scope of VAT.

Whether the local authority can recover the VAT incurred on the work depends on the use to which the hall is put. If it is used for the local authority's own non-business activities, the VAT is recoverable under **44.7** below. If it is used to make a business supply (e.g. use in return for a payment), the normal VAT rules will apply. If the local authority uses donated funds to make a purchase it can recover the VAT incurred under **44.7** below provided it makes the purchase itself (i.e. places the order, receives the supply and a VAT invoice addressed to it and makes payment), retains ownership of the purchase and uses it or makes it available for its own non-business purposes, and keeps sufficient records for the purchase (and the purpose for which it is made) to be easily identified.

(ii) *Village halls not owned by the local authority.* If the local authority uses its own funds to carry out work to such a hall, and it then gives this work away to the owners (e.g. a voluntary group), this is not a supply for VAT purposes provided that it receives nothing in return. Any VAT incurred is recoverable under the scheme in **44.7** below. If it does receive something in return (including non-monetary consideration such as use the hall) it is likely to be consideration for the taxable business supply of the works.

If the hall is owned by a voluntary group and they, or a third party, pass funds to the local authority which arranges work to the hall, then these funds are likely to be the consideration for the supply of the work to the voluntary group. The local authority may act as a 'main contractor' (receiving supplies and making an onward business supply to the voluntary group, the consideration for which is the funding received) or may act as the agent of the voluntary group in arranging the work on its behalf.

(e) Shared ownership schemes

Such arrangements usually involve the sharing of equity in a dwelling between an occupier and a housing association. The occupier purchases a dwelling at a proportion of its value and then pays rent to cover the share in the equity retained by the housing association. Under these circumstances, the rent paid by the occupier is consideration for a supply in the course of business by the housing association. Where local authorities enter into similar shared ownership schemes and receive payment of rents, the activity is also business.

(f) Sales and letting of land

Where a local authority sells and lets land and property, it is in direct competition with the private sector. These are normally business transactions. However, by concession, where a local authority provides domestic accommodation to people seeking housing (normally on a list maintained by the authority) or disposes of properties under the 'right to buy' legislation, it is non-business, regardless of the circumstances and whether or not they are acting under any special legal regime applicable to them.

(g) Housing stock transfers

In order to bring their housing stock up to the Government's 'decent homes standard', many local authorities have transferred their stock to registered social landlords (RSLs) once residents have been balloted and agreed to proposals.

The transfer of housing stock is considered to be a non-business activity by the selling local authority (apart from any commercial properties, shops, garages for non-residents and residential or other properties bought for investment purposes, where the normal rules apply).

Housing stock transfers can take one of two forms with differing VAT consequences.

Under the first method, the RSL agrees to purchase the housing stock in its existing condition, and any refurbishment works that may be required is paid for by the purchasing RSL. Any VAT that the purchasing RSL incurs on the refurbishment works cannot be recovered as it is wholly attributable to the letting activities of the RSL. This was confirmed in *South Liverpool Housing Ltd* (VTD 18750) (TVC 42.22).

Under the second method, the RSL agrees to purchase the housing stock, but as a condition of purchase (normally a contractual requirement) requires the local authority to improve the properties. As sometimes thousands of properties are involved, and it would be impractical for the parties to enter into a piecemeal arrangement whereby a housing unit only passed to the RSL once the local authority had upgraded it, normally the house stock passes to the RSL before it has been upgraded, but the local authority enters into a binding obligation to ensure that the necessary works of maintenance are undertaken at its expense. The local authority can recover the VAT incurred on these works under the scheme in **44.7** below (even though most of the work actually takes place after the housing has been transferred) provided the following conditions are satisfied.

- The transfer contract must contain a clear obligation on the part of the local authority to carry out the works (or there must be a suitable addendum or other document detailing this obligation).
- The scope and quantum of the works must have been agreed prior to the transfer, and this information should form part of the contract.
- The scope of the works should only relate to local authority tenants, common areas, and the outside fabric for right-to-buy leaseholders or freeholders.
- The works in question must be supplied to the local authority (i.e. the local authority must have entered into one or more contracts for the works to be done and paid consideration for the works).
- From time to time the local authority will be expected to substantiate any VAT claims by providing a clear audit trail which links the VAT to the works required under the transfer contract.

It does not matter that the parties have agreed for the RSL to undertake the works as building contractor and charge the local authority accordingly. The local authority is not allowed to recover VAT on works that are the responsibility of the RSL after the transfer has taken place (e.g. day-to-day repairs and maintenance).

(VAT Notice 749, para 5.8; Business Brief 19/98).

(9) Local authority and NHS joint stores depots

Operation

Some joint store depots are operated by a local authority and others by NHS bodies. The organisation which operates and maintains a depot must charge VAT on the income received as payment for the services it supplies (e.g. salary costs and fuel and power). This charge is often made as a supplement to charge for stock or as a periodic charge. A local authority recipient of these services is able to reclaim this VAT (subject to the normal rules). An NHS body recipient may currently claim it as a refund under the contracted-out service regime.

Stock purchase

Only one participant in a joint stores' arrangement is responsible for accounting for an item of stock within its books. It is this participant that is to incur any VAT charged when the goods are taken into stock. When stock is ordered, arrangements should be made to ensure that the purchase invoice provided by the supplier to the operator is made out to the participant with accounting responsibility for the item in question. However, HMRC are willing to grant prior approval for an alternative to cover the few occasions where this may cause difficulty (e.g. the inability to use bulk purchase facilities). This allows the store operator

(i) to initially purchase the stock;
(ii) to sell on those items for which the other party has accounting responsibility; and
(iii) for the items referred to at (ii) to reclaim the equivalent VAT on the supplier's invoice as input tax, having invoiced the other party and charged VAT as output tax.

VAT reclaims on stock items are available only by a local authority recipient and only when it has accounting responsibility (subject to the normal rules).

Hire of stock

Where the participant with responsibility for accounting for an item of stock within its books 'lends' or hires it to the other (i.e. to cover temporary shortages) VAT should not be levied on any charge made because this is not seen to be a business activity for VAT purposes. Where items are hired in from outside contractors, VAT reclaims are available only to a local authority recipient and only when it has accounting responsibility (subject to the normal rules)

(HMRC Manual VATGPB6700).

(10) Local authority purchasing consortia

Under *Local Authorities (Goods and Services) Act 1970* a number of authorities may get together to form a joint committee which acts as a central purchasing organisation known as a Local Authority Purchasing Consortia (LAPC).

Following the decision in *Comune di Carpaneto Piacentino and Others v Ufficio Provinciale Imposta sul Valore Aggiunto di Piacenza, ECJ Case C–4/89*, [1990] 3 CMLR 153 (TVC 22.140) HMRC have concluded that LAPCs are not acting under any special legal regime and that their supplies do not fall to be treated as non-taxable under *Directive 2006/112/EC, Art 13*. They are not, therefore, entitled to use the refund scheme under **44.7** below.

(HMRC Manual VATGPB8835).

(11) Mayoral/chairman's expenses

A mayor or chairman, although elected, is treated in the same way as an employee when carrying out official duties. Any input tax incurred in the course of official duties can be recovered provided

- the local authority accepts responsibility for the actual expenses incurred and enters them in its normal accounts;
- the goods/services are ordered in the name of the authority and invoices are addressed to it, and
- adequate records are kept.

If a car is used to transport the mayor between home and civic events, the related motoring expenses can be recovered if the above conditions are met. If a car is made available for a mayor's private use, VAT recovery on its purchase is blocked.

Input tax cannot be recovered on any flat-rate allowance given in the form of money placed freely at the disposal of the mayor/chairman.

(HMRC Manual VATGPB8775).

(12) Meals on wheels

Local authorities may use the services of their own staff to provide the meals or may buy them in from outside contractors. Alternatively, they may use the services of voluntary organisations who act as their agent in preparing and/or delivering the meals. The provision of meals to the elderly for a charge is a non-business activity of the local authority if provided as a part of a package of care (see **44.12** below). Otherwise the supply is liable to VAT at the standard rate. Any charge made to the local authority by the voluntary body or other organisation for implementing the service is also taxable, regardless of whether the supply is below cost or whether it includes an incidental element of care provided to the recipient of the meal. However, the local authority can recover the VAT charged under **44.7** below.

Facilities for home cooking

Instead of making arrangements for a daily delivery of meals on wheels, some local authorities make periodic deliveries of frozen meals. To support this activity, they supply cost price mini freezers, microwaves and steamers to the recipients of the food. Equipment sold in this way to facilitate a package of non-business welfare is itself a non-business supply. Any equipment that is sold for a profit, or which does not form part of a package of care, is subject to normal VAT liabilities.

(HMRC Manual VATGPB8140).

(13) Motor mileage allowances and fuel scale charges

Where a local authority or other 'specified body' within **44.2** above pays its employees mileage allowances to reimburse them for the cost of road fuel incurred on business activities, the body can recover the input tax under the same conditions as apply to other businesses. See **46.15 MOTOR CARS**. By concession, a statutory body can recover the VAT it incurs on mileage allowances paid to all persons engaged on its official activities, including its non-business activities. The concession extends not only to employees but also to councillors, JPs and voluntary workers acting as agents of the authority (e.g. the WRVS delivering meals on wheels). It also covers mileage rates paid to police doctors and to parents taking their children to school where the local authority would otherwise be obliged to provide transport (e.g. in rural areas). HMRC require that

- the individual receiving the mileage allowance is not a taxable person;
- there is a contract (written or oral) between the body and the individual covering the activities in question;
- the individual carries out the activity on a regular basis; and
- the body is obliged to undertake the activity on which the road fuel costs are incurred (or would be if the recipient of the mileage allowance did not do so).

Alternatively, where a specified body provides an employee or other person with road fuel or reimburse them for fuel used, VAT must be accounted for using the scale charges in **46.17 MOTOR CARS** if the car is used for the *business* activities of the body and the latter funds any private motoring.

(HMRC Manual VATGPB8785).

(14) Open government

Normally, the provision of information is a standard-rated supply, unless it can be zero-rated as printed matter. But under the *Freedom of Information Act 2000* public authorities (including all local authorities, police authorities and Government departments) must provide certain information if requested. Any charge made is non-business. This non-business treatment also extends to information that they are not obliged to provide (because the cost of provision is too high) but which they choose to provide for a charge.

There is no obligation for authorities to provide information that is available from other sources, even if the enquirer cannot readily access those other sources (e.g. because they do not have internet access). Information provided in these circumstances is a business activity.

(HMRC Manual VATGPB8710).

(15) Police authorities

(i) *The escort and transportation of prisoners.* Following the increasing tendency for the majority of such services to be supplied by private security firms, this is now regarded as a business activity. In a few instances, there is still a legal requirement for police authorities, or other similar official bodies, to carry out prisoner escort duties. Such services remain non-business activities.

(ii) *Police attendance at sporting events.* Local authorities are required by the *Safety of Sports Grounds Act 1975* to issue safety certificates on such terms and conditions as they consider necessary to designated stadia in their area. Where such a certificate includes conditions which make it obligatory on the holder to request the provision of police officers prior to each event, this creates a statutory monopoly for the police authority and therefore the provision of the police is a non-business activity. If, however, the holder of the certificate is not under an obligation to request the presence of the police but can instead have the event 'policed' by a private sector security firm, there is no statutory monopoly. Provision of police in these circumstances is in competition with the private sector and is a business activity.

Policing outside a stadium is non-business as this is policing in a public place. Policing in off-street shopping centres is commonly a business supply when a charge is made because many of these sites are privately owned, and the police patrol at the request of the centre managers. The supply is standard-rated as private security firms can also provide such a service.

(iii) *Contracted out vehicle removal.* See **48.7**(14) **OUTPUT TAX.**

(HMRC Manuals VATGP5215, VATGPB5230, VATGP5270).

(16) Recycling credits

Under *Environmental Protection Act 1990, s 52(1)* waste disposal authorities must pay waste collection authorities when they divert waste from the household waste stream for recycling. Where waste is collected and sent for recycling by third parties (e.g. local scout groups or existing recycling companies) then both disposal and collection authorities have powers, under *Environmental Protection Act 1990, s 52(3)(4)* to pay credits to the third parties.

The payment of these recycling credits is not the consideration for a supply and is therefore outside of the scope of VAT. However, in some cases, although credits may be due to a third party, they may be retained by a local authority as consideration for a supply made to that third party (e.g. the granting of a licence to occupy a site for a bottle bank). In these circumstances, the credits retained by the local authority are not outside the scope of VAT but follow the liability of the supply for which they are being treated as consideration.

(HMRC Manual VATGPB8840).

(17) Returning officers' and other election expenses

Parliamentary and European elections

Council officers frequently act as returning officers in Parliamentary and European elections. However, they are not acting as an officer of the council but in a different capacity. The Office of the Deputy Prime Minister (ODPM) makes a payment to the local authority for the provision of a returning officer to compensate it for one of its staff being diverted from local authority functions. As a local authority has to provide a returning officer by law, this payment is not subject to VAT. Similarly, where a local authority is required by law to provide polling places (e.g. schools) and other services, any reimbursement by the ODPM is not subject to VAT. The transport of ballot boxes is not done under any statutory obligation and is standard-rated.

Where local authorities have to provide certain facilities by law, any VAT incurred on their provision will be recoverable under **44.7** below. But where the returning officer has bought goods or services from sources other than the local authority, any VAT incurred is not recoverable by the local authority and should be included in any reimbursement received from the ODPM.

The ODPM also provides funding for the purchase of such election requirements as polling booth screens and ballot boxes. Often these will be bought for the returning officer by the local authority. If the items will be used in a local election (see below) as well as other elections, the local authority can recover the VAT in full. If, however, they are bought exclusively for Parliamentary or European elections, the local authority can only recover VAT to the extent that it recharges it to the returning officer as his buying agent. Such VAT recharged to the returning officer should form part of his funding from the ODPM.

Local elections

The local authority is under a statutory obligation to provide the returning officer and it can recover any VAT it incurs in connection with local elections under the refunds scheme in **44.7** below.

(HMRC Manual VATGPB8680).

(18) Social services activities

See HMRC Manual VATGPB8200 for a list of the duties and VAT status of various social services activities in relation to children, the elderly, and the disabled.

(19) Sports and leisure

If a local authority charges members of the public for sporting or recreational facilities, it is not acting in its capacity as a public authority and the activity is business.

(i) *Supplies of sporting services*. Most sporting services are exempted from VAT. See **58.5 RECREATION AND SPORT**. However, local authorities are specifically excluded from the exemption and sporting services provided by them remain taxable. If the services include an element of educational training or instruction, they may qualify as exempt supplies of education. See **17.4 EDUCATION**.

(ii) *Operation of leisure centres.* Local authorities may deliver leisure services by means of a
- direct service organisation (DSO) within the local authority's own leisure services department;
- non-profit distributing organisation (NPDO) such as a trust or industrial and provident society, in which the local authority may have a degree of representation; or
- a wholly independent 'for profit' leisure management contractor.

In the case of a DSO, it is the local authority itself that makes all supplies. Otherwise, the various arrangements that flow from the contracting-out process can give rise to a number of potential supplies for VAT purposes. The precise nature of these supplies and the VAT treatment of them is set out in a Memorandum of Understanding jointly agreed by HMRC and the Chartered Institute of Public Finance and Accountancy.

Leisure service membership schemes

Many local authorities offer leisure schemes where a customer can make periodic payments, normally monthly or annually, to receive free or discounted use of the authority's leisure facilities. This scheme membership is a standard-rated charge for the right to use the facilities unless the membership is exclusively for exempt activities when the charge is exempt. If the membership is used for a variety of taxable and exempt activities the charge is not to be apportioned, but is treated as wholly standard-rated. A tax point arises every time that the member pays an instalment of the fee. If the total charge for paying by instalments is greater than that for a one-off fee, then the extra charge is for an exempt supply of finance.

(VAT Notice 749, para 5.8; HMRC HMRC Manual VATGPB8400). See HMRC Brief 28/07 for the Memorandum of Understanding referred to above.

(20) Statutory licences, etc.

Public authorities charge for various forms of licensing and approval in a broad range of public activities taking place in their area (e.g. approving premises for civil marriages, registering childminders, issuing fire certificates, and licensing and registering firearms). In doing so, they are empowered to act under special legal provisions that private traders cannot call upon. This is a non-business activity. (VAT Notice 749, para 5.8).

(21) Supplies between local authorities

(i) *Supplies of goods.* Following the decision in *Comune di Carpaneto Piacentino and Others v Ufficio Provinciale Imposta sul Valore Aggiunto di Piacenza, ECJ Case C–4/89*, [1990] 3 CMLR 153 (TVC 22.140) HMRC have concluded that supplies of goods between local authorities are not made under any special legal regime and that the supplies do not fall to be treated as non-taxable under *Directive 2006/112/EC, Art 13*. They are not, therefore, eligible for the refund scheme under **44.7** below.

(ii) *Supplies of services.* Supplies of services which include a supply of goods should be treated as business and taxable according to the normal rules. Services supplied between local authorities are non-business where they are made under a statutory obligation or where they are not in competition with the private sector. Otherwise supplies of services are business supplies.

(VAT Notice 749, para 5.2; HMRC HMRC Manual VATGPB8855; Business Brief 9/95).

(22) Supplies of staff

Following the decision in *Comune di Carpaneto Piacentino and Others v Ufficio Provinciale Imposta sul Valore Aggiunto di Piacenza, ECJ Case C–4/89*, [1990] 3 CMLR 153 (TVC 22.140), if a specified body within **44.2** above supplies the services of its staff

- under the same legal conditions as those applying to private businesses, it is not acting in its capacity as a public body and the supply is in the course or furtherance of a taxable business activity; and
- under a special legal regime applicable to it, the body is acting in its capacity as a public body. It can treat the supplies of staff it makes as non-business providing that such treatment would not lead to a significant distortion of competition with other bodies. See **44.1**(*b*) above.

Taxable business activities include secondments of staff by

- one police authority to another for purely administrative purposes;
- a police authority to outside organisations to advise, for example, about security matters;
- a local fire service to an outside organisation to advise on fire safety matters;
- a local authority Direct Labour Organisation (DLO) to boost the management team of another DLO; or
- an LEA to an examination board to advise on methods of assessment.

Non-business activities include

- a police authority providing normal policing assistance to another force (e.g. in connection with an ongoing investigation) or seconding officers to the National Crime Squad or the National Criminal Intelligence Service;
- local authority fire brigades seconding experienced serving officers to the Fire Service College to act as instructors in advanced safety and rescue techniques (as no other organisations have the necessary expertise to offer an equivalent service to the college); and
- agreements to release, rather than supply, staff (e.g. where teachers undertake GCE and GCSE exam work or where staff are seconded to other government departments or commercial companies for career development purposes). Where staff are seconded in these circumstances and have two discrete contracts, then the authority is not considered to be making a taxable supply of the services of staff. Any

reimbursement of salary is not liable to output tax. However, if the authority makes a charge for administration, this is consideration for the supply of a payroll service, and it must account for output tax on the supply.

(VAT Notice 749, para 5.8; HMRC Manual VATGPB8860).

(23) Voucher schemes

Local authorities operate a number of different voucher schemes to enable them to fulfil their statutory obligations (e.g. for clothing/school uniform, decorating materials, etc.). The schemes involve the issue of vouchers by the local authority which the holder can exchange for specific goods or services at nominated suppliers. The supplier forwards the redeemed vouchers to the local authority which then refunds the supplier up to the value of the vouchers redeemed.

There are no output tax implications for the authority when the vouchers are issued (providing it receives no consideration). It can only recover input tax on goods/services supplied under the various schemes where the supply is to the local authority which then makes an onward supply to the recipient. These conditions are met if the local authority

- holds a proper VAT invoice addressed to it from the supplier;
- has entered the purchase in its normal accounts; and
- holds the redeemed vouchers submitted to it by the supplier of the goods.

The local authority can only recover input tax on the value of the voucher or, if less, the value of the goods or services supplied.

(HMRC Manual VATGPB8870).

(24) Weighing instruments

The *evaluation* and *surveillance* of non-automatic weighing instruments, to meet EU requirements, is a service that any trader with the necessary expertise can supply commercially. If a local authority carries it out, the activity is business. On the other hand, where a local authority charges to *verify* such instruments, it does so in its capacity as a public authority, using legal powers that no private contractor is entitled to exercise. Such verification is a non-business activity. (VAT Notice 749, para 5.8).

(25) Youth centres

There are two types of youth centre.

- *A youth centre which is part of the local authority*. HMRC accept that any purchase it makes from its own funds is actually made by the local authority which can reclaim any VAT incurred (subject to the normal rules). If income from taxable activities of the youth centre accrues to the local authority, it must also account for output tax.
- *Youth centres with charitable status*. These are independent of the local authority which is not normally entitled to recover VAT on any of the costs incurred.

However, in some cases, independent youth centres may donate funds to the local authority for a specific purpose. Where this occurs, the local authority is eligible for VAT refund if it

(i) makes the purchase (i.e. places the order, etc.);
(ii) retains ownership;
(iii) uses the items purchased for its own non-business purposes; and
(iv) keeps sufficient records of the purchase and the purpose for which it was made to enable it to be easily identified.

If these conditions are not met, the normal VAT rules apply. The money given represents consideration for a supply by the local authority to the independent youth centre and the local authority must account for VAT.

VAT recovery

Common areas of expenditure incurred by youth centres include the following.

(a) *Utility costs* (e.g. gas and electricity). The VAT incurred is only recoverable by the local authority under **44.7** below if the youth centre is part of the local authority (and not if the centre is independent of the local authority but donates money to it to cover utility costs).
(b) *Repairs and maintenance to buildings*. The treatment is broadly similar to that under (*a*) above. However, if the local authority holds the freehold or lease on the premises and does not charge the independent youth centre for use of the premises, the authority is normally entitled to recover any VAT incurred.
(c) *Minibuses*. Where an individual youth centre purchases a minibus, the VAT treatment is as under (*a*) above. Where the purchase is by a local authority using donated funds, the local authority can recover the VAT if it satisfies (i)–(iv) above. Alternatively, HMRC may accept that the local authority can recover VAT on the purchase if
    - use of the minibus is pooled, i.e. it is available for use by more than one youth centre;
    - the minibus carries the local authority logo;
    - the local authority treats it as part of its assets, covering repair and maintenance costs; and
    - the local authority does not charge the centres for use of the minibus.

    Where this applies, however, the local authority must account for output tax when the vehicle is sold.

    Where an independent youth centre buys a minibus using grants provided by the local authority, the authority cannot recover the VAT.
(d) *Fixtures and fittings*. A local authority can recover VAT it incurs on fixtures and fittings, including sports equipment, at its own youth centres. If it uses donated funds to make the purchase, it can recover VAT if it satisfies (i)–(iv) above. This means that the items must become assets of the local authority and be available for use by other youth centres. A local authority may also recover the VAT it incurs on purchases made from its own funds and then freely given away to independent youth centres.

(e) *Private fund income.* Some local authority youth centres may undertake activities independently of the local authority. Any income arising as a result is 'private fund' income, normally paid to a separate account, and does not form part of local authority funds. The private fund is a separate entity for VAT purposes and the local authority cannot recover the VAT incurred on any of its purchases and need not account for output tax on supplies made by the fund.

Liability of income of local authority youth clubs

Because local authority youth centres are provided under the *Education Act 1996*, and this is a special legal regime, membership fees and subscriptions are non-business. Separately charged for activities and events will also generally be non-business.

- *Social evenings, outings and similar events.* Where such activities are arranged by the youth service for the members of the club, this income is non-business. This does not apply to events organised by other parties (e.g. where the youth service merely arranges for its members to be able to buy discounted tickets from an event organiser which remains a business supply by the event organiser to the individuals who take up the offer). Neither does it apply to events and activities attended by other people unless the numbers of such people are minimal (e.g. family outings where youth club members will not be in the significant majority are not non-business).
- *Coin operated machines.* The provision of games, amusements and entertainment machines form part of the youth service and any income derived from them is non-business.
- *Tuck shops and cafes.* Provided that sales within club premises to club members are made at or below their overhead-inclusive cost, they can be treated as non-business.

(HMRC Manual VATGPB8885).

(26) Youth offending teams (YOTs)

YOTs are set up by local authorities, in partnership with police authorities, probation committees and health authorities, to establish a local structure of teams and services to deal with young offenders. Each YOT must contain at least a social worker, probation officer, police officer, a person nominated by a health authority in the local authority area, and a person nominated by the local authority's Chief Education Officer. The local authority receives funding from the Home Office for the project and the partners (who may or may not receive Home Office funding) are responsible for their share of staff and any associated costs.

Local authorities and police authorities can recover any costs under the refund scheme in **44.7** below. The only bodies unable to benefit from the refund scheme are health authorities and probation committees, although they are able to recover VAT on certain contracted out services under *VATA 1994, s 41* (see **44.11** below).

Because of the possibility of double claims by different bodies, HMRC suggest that YOT committees should 'appoint' the local authority as the claiming body for the purposes of **44.7** below (although they have no objections to the police being appointed). Any staff provided by the members would be outside the scope of VAT (as they are not being supplied to the local authority but to the scheme) and any funds that may be given would be considered outside the scope contributions.

In certain cases, local authorities may form joint YOTs. In such cases, HMRC recommended that one authority takes the lead for refund purposes, with the other simply making outside the scope contributions.

(HMRC Manual VATGPB8890).

Registration

Public bodies other than local authorities

[44.5] The normal registration rules apply to public bodies other than local authorities, including those specified bodies listed in **44.2** above, i.e. they are required to be registered only if their taxable supplies exceed the registration limit (see **60.3 REGISTRATION**) but they may apply for voluntary registration under **60.2 REGISTRATION**. Exemption from registration can be sought in cases where the majority of supplies are zero-rated and if registered, they would normally be in a repayment situation. See **60.6 REGISTRATION**.

Local authorities

Every local authority which makes taxable supplies (including zero-rated supplies) in the course or furtherance of its business is required to be registered *whatever the value of its supplies*. [*VATA 1994, s 42*]. Despite this, if a local authority makes only infrequent or minimal taxable supplies, it may not need to register for VAT. Advice should be sought from HMRC.

Group registration

Public bodies cannot normally meet the requirements of joining a VAT group. But HMRC will normally grant a request by a local authority joint committee to account for VAT under the registration of its lead authority or any other member if satisfied that

- it does not want the arrangement merely for tax avoidance purposes; and
- it does not create distortion.

(VAT Notice 749, paras 3.1–3.3).

Acquisitions of goods from other EU member states

Even if a local authority or other statutory body is not required to register under the general requirements based on taxable supplies in the UK, it may be liable to register for VAT where it makes certain acquisitions of goods from other EU member states in excess of an annual threshold. See **60.18 REGISTRATION**.

Reclaiming VAT

[44.6] Where bodies within **44.2** above incur VAT in connection with taxable business activities, they can recover the VAT as input tax subject to the normal rules.

However, many of the activities of such bodies are non-business activities for VAT purposes and outside the scope of VAT. As a general rule, it is only possible to recover any VAT incurred if registered for VAT and if the VAT can be attributed to taxable business activities. Any VAT that relates to non-business or (subject to certain limits) exempt activities is not recoverable. To minimise this 'sticking' VAT for such bodies, a special scheme allows them to

- reclaim the VAT suffered on non-business activities (see **44.7** below); and
- recover any VAT attributed to exempt business activities where HMRC consider it an insignificant proportion of the total VAT incurred (see **44.8** below).

Refund scheme for non-business activities

[44.7] Generally, there is no entitlement to recovery of VAT incurred for the purposes of non-business activities. However, a special refund scheme permits a specified body within **44.2** above to reclaim the VAT chargeable on supplies of goods or services to it, acquisitions of goods by it from other EU member states and imports of goods by it from outside the EU if

- the supply, acquisition or importation is not for the purposes of a business activity carried on by the body concerned; and
- the VAT is not excluded from credit in relation to business activities (see under *Non-recoverable VAT* below).

[*VATA 1994, s 33(1)(6)*].

The scheme applies whether or not the body is registered for VAT or makes taxable supplies but non VAT-registered bodies, who cannot quote a VAT registration number when purchasing from other EU member states, will be charged VAT at source on such purchases. Any VAT charged by other EU member states is not recoverable under the scheme and refunds to non VAT-registered bodies are therefore restricted to VAT incurred on supplies and importations only.

The purpose of the scheme is to prevent VAT being a burden on local authority funding. A body can claim refunds on goods and services supplied, etc. to it for non-business purposes provided the following conditions are met.

- It places the order.
- It receives the supply.
- It receives a VAT invoice addressed to it.
- It makes payment from its own funds.

(VAT Notice 749, para 7.1).

The scheme extends to the following.

(a) Goods and services bought using funds given to a body for specified purposes provided
  (i) the person who gives the money does not do so on condition that the body gives something or does something in return or that other persons benefit as a direct result of the payment;
  (ii) the person who has given the money does not in fact receive anything in return;
  (iii) the body buys the goods or services itself (i.e. places the order, receives the supply and a VAT invoice addressed to it and makes payment);
  (iv) the body remains the owner of the goods or services and uses them, or makes them available, for its own non-business purposes; and
  (v) the body keeps sufficient records for HMRC to identify the goods and services bought and the reason for buying them.

  Supplies which are likely to meet these conditions are funds used by community and foundation schools received from Parent Teacher Associations and school funds but funds used for exterior maintenance and repair at a voluntary aided school received from the governors are unlikely to qualify.

(b) Purchases made from funds of a trust but only if
  - the body acts as sole managing trustee without payment;
  - the activities of the trust relate so closely to the functions of the body that they cannot be easily distinguished; and
  - the claim relates to the non-business activities of the trust.

(VAT Notice 749, paras 7.3–7.5).

Where such non-business supplies, acquisitions or importations cannot be conveniently distinguished from business supplies, etc. the refund is the amount remaining after deducting from the whole of the VAT chargeable such proportion as HMRC consider to be attributable to business purposes. [*VATA 1994, s 33(2)*].

HMRC published a policy paper on the power to provide VAT refunds to certain persons on 9 December 2015. The proposals have been enacted by inserting a new *VATA 1994, s 33E* will allows named non-departmental public bodies and similar public bodies to obtain refunds of VAT incurred under shared services arrangements used to support their non-business activities. The measure is intended to ensure that what would otherwise be irrecoverable VAT does not deter public bodies from sharing back-office services, where this would result in greater efficiencies of scale.

[*FA 2016, s 122*].

The Government announced in Autumn Budget 2017 that *VATA 1994, s 33(3)* will be extended to entitle combined authorities, fire and rescue authorities which are a function of police and crime commissioners, the London Fire Commissioner, the Scottish Fire and Rescue Service, and the Scottish Police Authority to recover the VAT incurred on purchases made to support their non-business activities.

This removes the need for individual statutory instruments on the establishment of each new combined authority and PCC Fire and Rescue authorities.

The changes will take effect on and after the date of Royal Assent to *Finance Bill 2017–18*. It is important to note that these organisations cannot recover any input VAT incurred before this date.

Non-recoverable VAT

VAT which is specifically excluded from credit by the Treasury under *VATA 1994, s 25(7)* in relation to business activities is also excluded from credit by bodies in respect of their non-business activities. See, for example, **10 BUSINESS ENTERTAINMENT** and **46.3 MOTOR CARS.**

Input tax attributable to exempt business activities

[44.8] A specified body within **44.2** above can recover input tax incurred directly attributable to its exempt business activities where HMRC consider it to be an 'insignificant' proportion of the total VAT incurred. [*VATA 1994, s 33(2)(b)*].

Where a special partial exemption method for specified bodies within *Sec 33* is used, '*insignificant*' means

- not more than £625 per month on average (i.e. not more than £7,500 p.a.); or
- less than 5% of the total VAT incurred on all goods and services purchased in a year. This total includes goods and services for business and non-business activities but excludes those on which input tax cannot be reclaimed, see **35.8 INPUT TAX.**

If the input tax attributable to exempt supplies exceeds both of the above limits, then none of it may be recovered.

Where a body chooses not to adopt a special partial exemption method for specified bodies within *Sec 33*, it can use any alternative method of partial exemption calculation (see **50 PARTIAL EXEMPTION**) but in that case the normal *de minimis* limits in **50.7 PARTIAL EXEMPTION** apply.

(VAT Notice 749, paras 8.2–8.4).

See also **54.4 PENSION SCHEMES** for concessional treatment for certain local authority pension funds.

Where any partial exemption method is used, the body must do a calculation at the end of each period, followed by an annual adjustment at the end of each financial year. This adjustment should be included in the VAT return for the next period.

Partial exemption methods

All bodies must have a partial exemption method in place that has been agreed with HMRC and continue using it until it is either withdrawn by HMRC or a new method is agreed. If a body has not agreed a special method with HMRC, it must either use the *special method for specified bodies within Sec 33* outlined below or the standard partial exemption method (see **50.4 PARTIAL EXEMPTION**) but in the latter case it must then separate business and non-business activities.

A body wishing to opt for a special partial exemption method must

- contact HMRC before the start of the financial year in order to obtain advice on using a special method;
- by the start of the financial year, agree with HMRC the broad principles of the method intended to be used;
- by three months before the end of the financial year, complete discussions with HMRC and have the final method agreed in writing; and
- by 31 October following the end of the financial year include all annual calculations on a return and submit it to HMRC.

If a special method has not been agreed before the end of a financial year, it cannot be applied to that year. Under these circumstances

- a body can only begin using a special method from the start of the next tax year; and
- in the meantime, it should use the model special partial exemption method outlined below.

(VAT Notice 749, paras 8.5–8.7).

Special partial exemption method for specified bodies within *Sec 33*

This method, which is based on the budget structure, takes a worst case scenario. It assumes that where a budget heading contains an exempt activity, than all taxable expenditure within that heading is attributable to that exempt activity. If this approach shows that a body's exempt input tax is insignificant, there is no requirement to refine the calculations.

Step 1	*Identifying exempt activities.* List, within committee, all budget headings/cost centres that contain any element of exempt activity.
Step 2	*Identifying taxable expenditure.* Within each budget heading/cost centre identified under Step 1, record all expenditure (net of VAT) for both capital and revenue that would normally carry VAT.
Step 3	*Recharges.* For recharges to budget headings/cost centres that contain any element of exempt activity, record all expenditure that would normally carry VAT.
Step 4	*Calculate the percentage of exempt-related input tax.* Add up the standard-rated expenditure identified in Steps 2 and 3 and calculate the VAT on it by multiplying by 20% (17.5% from 1 January 2010 to 3 January 2011; 15% from 1 December 2008 to 31 December 2009).

If the total at Step 4 is insignificant (see above), no further calculations are required. If it is not, a progressively detailed analysis must be made of the amount of expenditure which is put to exempt use. If, at any stage, a result is achieved showing that the VAT is insignificant, no further action is required. There is no set method of allocation or apportionment. A body may adopt a different method for each particular area or activity based on the information available (e.g. number of staff, amount of income, floor area used, number of sessions, or time, etc.) provided it can demonstrate that any method used is fair and equitable. Where, despite detailed analysis of the amount of expenditure put to exempt use, the VAT identified still exceeds the 'insignificant' limit, none of the VAT relating to exempt supplies is recoverable.

(VAT Notice 749, paras 9.1–9.5).

Capital goods scheme and change of intention

Where a specified body within **44.2** above incurs VAT which it has attributed to an intended activity under the **11 CAPITAL GOODS SCHEME** but subsequently changes its intention before undertaking that activity, it must review its original attribution and make any appropriate adjustment as follows.

(1) Identify the VAT attributable to the activity for which there has been a change of intention.

(2) If the change of intention is from a taxable or non-business activity to an exempt activity, add the VAT identified to the exempt input tax already identified for the year in which the VAT was originally incurred. If the new total cannot be treated as insignificant (see above), the VAT identified must be repaid to HMRC.

(3) If the change of intention is from an exempt activity to a taxable or non-business activity, the VAT identified should be deducted from the exempt input tax already identified for the year in which the VAT was originally incurred. If the new total can be treated as insignificant, the VAT identified can be reclaimed from HMRC (if it has not already been reclaimed).

It is not necessary to rework the calculation itself in full providing the new amount of exempt input tax can be quantified.

Error in attribution

If there has been an error in attribution, the entire calculation must be reworked for the relevant years.

Capital goods items adjustments

The appropriate adjustment to the amount of VAT reclaimed on the initial acquisition must be carried out in accordance with the normal rules of the capital goods scheme except that

- non-business use should be treated as if it were taxable use; and
- if exempt input tax is insignificant, no adjustment is required.

(VAT Notice 749, paras 10.1–10.5).

Claiming the refund

VAT-registered bodies

[44.9] VAT-registered bodies make the claim by including the amount refundable in Box 4 of the VAT return.

Unregistered bodies

The first claim for a refund made by a non-registered body must be in writing. The claim must relate to a period of at least one month and, if for under £100, must cover a period of at least twelve months. The period chosen should always end on the last day of a calendar month. The claim should be set out as follows.

> HM Revenue and CustomsMiscellaneous Charges Unit
> DMB 601
> West Yorkshire
> BX5 5AB
>
> I am claiming a refund of £ for the period to   to cover VAT charged on goods and services bought for [insert name of body] non-business activities. *The tax claimed includes VAT incurred for exempt business activities which can be reclaimed under Notice 749 *Local authorities and similar bodies*.
>
> Signed
>
> For [insert name of authority]
>
> Address
>
> Contact name
>
> Contact telephone number
>
> * Delete as appropriate

Second and subsequent claims are made on Form VAT 126 which is sent out with each repayment.

Time limits for claims

VAT refund claims under *VATA 1994, s 33* are subject to the three-year time limit.

- For VAT-registered bodies, the time limit is three years after the due date for the return for the VAT period in which the VAT became chargeable.
- For bodies which are not registered for VAT, the time limit is three years after the end of the month in which the body received the supply, acquisition or importation.

(VAT Notice 749, paras 8.8, 12.3–12.5).

Repayment supplement, interest and penalties

- *VAT-registered bodies*. Where the repayment of a claim is delayed, repayment supplement may be due. See **52.17 PAYMENT OF VAT**. Any supplement due is calculated on the full amount of the claim, including both business and non-business activities.

Where any VAT has been overpaid or underclaimed under *VATA 1994, s 78*, statutory interest may be payable. See **52.18 PAYMENT OF VAT**. Any interest or penalties due as a result of errors made on VAT returns or late submission/payment of returns is calculated on the full amount of VAT involved, including VAT attributable to both business and non-business activities.

- *Non-VAT-registered bodies.* Claims by such bodies are subject to neither repayment supplement nor interest/penalties. Statutory interest, may be due in certain circumstances.

De Voil Indirect Tax Service. See V5.162.

Estimated returns by local authorities

[44.10] A local authority, because of the wide range of its activities, is not always able to process all its purchase invoices in time to include them on the appropriate VAT return. It may therefore apply to HMRC for permission to estimate input tax and *VATA 1994, s 33* refunds due.

Public bodies and Government departments

[44.11] Under EU law, Government departments and health authorities are 'bodies governed by public law' and, as such, are covered by *Directive 2006/112/EC, Art 13* and treated as non-taxable persons when satisfying the conditions in **44.1** above.

Under UK law, *VATA 1994* applies in relation to taxable supplies made by the Crown as it applies to taxable supplies by taxable persons. [*VATA 1994, s 41(1)*].

Supplies by public bodies

From 17 July 2012, where goods or services are supplied by a body mentioned in *Directive 2006/112/EC, Art 13(1)* (see **44.1** above) in the course of activities or transactions in which it is engaged as a public authority, if the supply is in respect of an activity listed in *Directive 2006/112/EC, Annex I* (activities in respect of which public bodies are to be taxable persons), it is to be treated for the purposes of UK law as a supply in the course or furtherance of a business, unless it is on such a small scale as to be negligible. If the supply is not in respect of such an activity, it is to be treated for the purposes of UK law as a supply in the course or furtherance of a business if (and only if) not charging VAT on the supply would lead to a significant distortion of competition.

[*VATA 1994, s 41A*].

Supplies by Government departments

Prior to 17 July 2012, where a 'Government department' supplies goods or services which do not amount to the carrying on of a business but it appears to the Treasury that similar supplies are, or might be, supplied by taxable persons in the course of furtherance of any business, then the Treasury may direct that the supplies by that department are treated as supplies in the course or furtherance of a business carried on by it.

[*VATA 1994, s 41(2)*].

'*Government department*' includes the Scottish Administration, the Welsh Assembly Government, the National Assembly for Wales Commission, a NI department, a Northern Ireland health and social services body, any body of persons exercising functions on behalf of a Minister of the Crown (including a health service body, a National Health Service trust, an NHS foundation trust, a Primary Care Trust, a Local Health Board, a clinical commissioning group, the Health and Social Care Information Centre, the National Health Service Commissioning Board, the National Institute for Health and Care Excellence, Health Education England (established by the *Care Act 2014*), the Health Research Authority (established by the *Care Act 2014*), and a strategic highways company (appointed under the *Infrastructure Act 2015, s 1*)) and any part of such a department designated for these purposes by the Treasury.

[*VATA 1994, s 41(6)–(8); Government of Wales Act 1998, Sch 12 para 35; Scotland Act 1998, Sch 8 para 30; Health Act 1999, Sch 8 para 86; National Health Service Reform and Health Care Professions Act 2002, Sch 5 para 40, Health and Social Care (Community Health and Standards) Act 2003, s 33(3); FA 2013, s 191; FA 2014, s 107; FA 2015, s 67*].

The Treasury from time to time issues a direction listing, for each Government department, those supplies which are treated as supplied in the course or furtherance of a business when supplied by that department.

For supplies by government departments of welfare services otherwise than for a profit, see **29.12** HEALTH AND WELFARE.

Supplies to Government departments

Where VAT is chargeable on

- the supply of goods or services to a 'Government department' (see above),
- the acquisition of goods by a Government department from another EU member state, or
- the importation of any goods by a Government department from outside the EU

and the supply, acquisition or importation is not for the purpose of any business carried on by the department (or any supply treated as such under *VATA 1994, s 41A*) then, on a claim, the VAT may still be refunded if the Treasury so directs. The claim must be in such form and manner as HMRC determine and any refund is conditional on the department complying with requirements as to the keeping, preservation and production of records relating to the supply.

[*VATA 1994, s 41(3)(4)*].

The Treasury periodically issues a direction with a list of eligible government departments and a list of eligible goods and services on which VAT will be refunded provided the supply of those goods and services is not for the purposes of either any business carried on by the department or any supply by the department treated as a supply in the course or furtherance of a business. In practice, the only activities where such a direction is issued are those services which have been 'contracted out' to private contractors and on which the private contractor then charges VAT. See also Business Brief 18/03 for HMRC's views on the VAT position of two PFI (Private Finance Initiative) arrangements, i.e. 'Composite Trade' ('Contract Debtor') and 'NHS LIFT'.

'*Government department*' includes the Scottish Administration, the Welsh Assembly Government, the National Assembly for Wales Commission, a NI department, a Northern Ireland health and social services body, any body of persons exercising functions on behalf of a Minister of the Crown (including a health service body, a National Health Service trust, an NHS foundation trust, a Primary Care Trust, a Local Health Board, a clinical commissioning group, the Health and Social Care Information Centre, the National Health Service Commissioning Board, the National Institute for Health and Care Excellence; Health Education England (established by the *Care Act 2014*), the Health Research Authority (established by the *Care Act 2014*) and a strategic highways company (appointed under the *Infrastructure Act 2015, s 1*)) and any part of such a department designated for these purposes by the Treasury.

[*VATA 1994, s 41(6)–(8); Government of Wales Act 1998, Sch 12 para 35; Scotland Act 1998, Sch 8 para 30; Health Act 1999, Sch 8 para 86; National Health Service Reform and Health Care Professions Act 2002, Sch 5 para 40, Health and Social Care (Community Health and Standards) Act 2003, s 33(3); FA 2013, s 191; FA 2014, s 107; FA 2015, s 67*].

HMRC published a policy paper on the power to provide VAT refunds to certain persons on 9 December 2015. The proposals have been enacted by inserting a new *VATA 1994, s 33E* which allows named non-departmental public bodies and similar public bodies to obtain refunds of VAT incurred under shared services arrangements used to support their non-business activities. The measure is intended to ensure that what would otherwise be irrecoverable VAT does not deter public bodies from sharing back-office services, where this would otherwise result in greater efficiencies of scale. [*FA 2016, s 122*].

Registration

Government departments and health authorities are subject to the normal VAT registration requirements. They must notify their liability to registration once their taxable turnover exceeds the registration limits (see **60.3 REGISTRATION**). Alternatively, they may seek voluntary registration if their taxable turnover is below the registration threshold (see **60.2 REGISTRATION**).

Accounting for VAT by government departments to the Consolidated Fund

Where a government department makes taxable supplies of goods or services and its receipts include amounts paid to it in respect of those supplies, the Treasury may allow the department to deduct any or all of the output tax due to HMRC on those supplies from the gross receipts due to the Consolidated Fund. [*FA 1999, s 21*]. In practice, such procedures have generally been adopted since the introduction of VAT.

De Voil Indirect Tax Service. See V2.108, V2.213, V5.161.

Welfare services

[44.12] For EU legislation see **19.24**(*g*) **EUROPEAN UNION LEGISLATION.**

The supply by a public body of welfare services and of goods supplied in connection therewith is exempt. [*VATA 1994, Sch 9 Group 7 Item 9*].

The identical provisions apply to such supplies made by charities, state-regulated private welfare institutions and state-regulated private welfare agencies. See **29.12 HEALTH AND WELFARE** for full details.

Transport services

The supply of transport services for sick or injured persons in vehicles specially designed for that purpose is exempt. [*VATA 1994, Sch 9 Group 7 Item 11*].

Admission charges

[44.13] Subject to certain restrictions, admission charges by public bodies to

- a museum, gallery, art exhibition or zoo, or
- a theatrical, musical or choreographic performance of a cultural nature

are exempt. See **58.2 RECREATION AND SPORT** for full details.

Key points: local authorities and public bodies

[44.14] Points to consider are as follows.

- Local authorities and certain other specified bodies get special VAT treatment through being able to reclaim input tax on their non-business activities and, in some cases, their exempt activities as well. This is an exception to one of the key principles of VAT, i.e. that input tax can only be reclaimed on expenditure that relates to taxable activities.
- The fact that local authorities can reclaim input tax on non-business activities could create an opportunity for VAT to be charged by a supplier to the authority, with the VAT element not causing a problem because of input tax recovery. A common example is where a charity can justify a local authority grant being taxable (as a supply of services) rather than outside the scope of VAT, in order to claim input tax on its related expenses. An increasing number of charity grants now require a specific delivery of services to be met in order to secure the grant, i.e. creating more grants that could be standard rated rather than outside the scope of VAT.

- Other examples of 'specified bodies' that get input tax recovery on non-business activities include the police authority and BBC. So any supplier working for these bodies does not need to worry about a VAT charge reducing its competitive position.
- The rules about a local authority (or other specified body) claiming input tax on exempt business activities state that this is allowed if the activities in question form an insignificant part of the authority's overall activities. In reality, 'insignificant' means less than 5% of the total VAT incurred on all goods and services purchased in a year. This total includes goods and services for business and non-business activities but excludes those on which input tax cannot be reclaimed. If the input tax attributable to exempt supplies exceeds both of the above limits, then none of it may be recovered.

45

Management Services and Supplies of Staff

Introduction to management services and supplies of staff

[45.1] Management services commonly arise where several traders who are separately registered for VAT, but are associated in some way, decide that one of them should purchase overhead items required by the various businesses, pay all the bills, and then recover an agreed proportion of the costs from the other traders participating in the scheme. Such an arrangement is common where the same office facilities and/or staff are shared. The 'management charges' or 'service charges' normally contain elements of staff salaries, office equipment, rent, rates, heating and lighting, stationery, telephone and postage, etc. Although such arrangements are 'domestic' and may not involve any element of profit, there may nevertheless be a taxable supply for VAT purposes, as under *VATA 1994, s 5(2)(b)* anything which is not a supply of goods but is done for a consideration is a supply of services.

However, there is no taxable supply if the persons involved are part of the same legal entity or if facilities are provided between businesses covered by a single VAT registration, e.g. businesses run by the same legal partnership or business included in a VAT group registration (see **28 GROUPS OF COMPANIES**).

See *Smith & Williamson; Smith & Williamson Securities* (VTD 281) (TVC 43.14) and *C & E Commrs v Tilling Management Services Ltd* at **45.3** below. For decisions as to whether such supplies are made in the course or furtherance of a business or are domestic arrangements not in the course of any business, see *Cumbrae Properties (1963) Ltd v C & E Commrs*, QB [1981] STC 799 (TVC 62.24), *Durham Aged Mineworkers' Homes Association v C &*

E Commrs, QB [1994] STC 553 (TVC 62.45) and *Processed Vegetable Growers Association Ltd* (VTD 25) (TVC 62.42). For the position where charges are raised between companies for use of capital, see *Laurence Scott Ltd* (VTD 2004) (TVC 40.99).

Sharing of premises

[45.2] The VAT treatment of any costs recovered relating to premises shared with other persons depends upon the precise terms of the arrangements. See **42.19 LAND AND BUILDINGS: EXEMPT SUPPLIES AND OPTION TO TAX** for a general consideration of service charges and joint occupation of premises.

Management services and group relief

[45.3] HMRC have expressed the following views.

(a) If Company A incurs a tax loss and surrenders it to Company B under *CTA 2010, Chapter 5* without any payment, HMRC do not see any taxable supply of goods or services for VAT purposes.

(b) If Company A incurs a tax loss and surrenders it to Company B under *CTA 2010, Chapter 5* with a payment or credit to current account for the surrender of the tax loss, again HMRC do not see any taxable supply of goods or services.

(c) It is possible in cases (*a*) and (*b*) above, that Company A might render management services to Company B without a separate charge being made for those services. The position here depends on whether there is any arrangement linking the provision of management services to, say, the procurement or making of group relief payments. If there is, then HMRC would see a non-monetary consideration for the management services which would have to be valued to determine the amount of VAT due. If there is no such arrangement, then if the management services are provided free of charge there is no taxable supply.

(d) Again, Company A may render management services to Company B and make a charge for those services, at the same time surrendering group relief, with or without payment. In such a case there is clearly a taxable supply of management services, but what has to be determined is whether the money charge is the full consideration for the supply. If there is an arrangement linking the supply of management services to the procurement or making of group relief payments, then once again there would be a non-monetary consideration which would have to be valued. In such circumstances VAT would be due on the full consideration, i.e. on the sum of the monetary and non-monetary considerations. However, if there is no link between the management services and the group relief payments, then VAT will be due only on the charge actually made for the management services.

HMRC have also confirmed that where services are rendered between companies within the same VAT group registration then no liability to VAT arises.

(CCAB Statement TR344 June 1979).

See also *C & E v Tilling Management Services Ltd*, QB 1978, [1979] STC 365 (TVC 43.8).

Supplies of staff

Definition

[45.4] A supply of staff (which includes directors and other office holders) is made for VAT purposes if the use of an individual who is contractually employed by the supplier is provided to another person for consideration. This applies whether the terms of the individual's employment are set out in a formal contract or letter of appointment, or are on a less formal basis. The determining factor is that the staff are not contractually employed by the recipient but come under its direction. Where staff are supplied to another person but continue to operate under the direction of the supplier, this is not a supply of staff, but is a supply of those services. (The distinction is significant where the services may be zero-rated or exempt, or when determining whether or not the supply is made in the UK.)

Liability

A supply of staff is normally regarded as being made in the course or furtherance of a business and VAT must be accounted for at the standard rate. This is subject to the following exceptions.

- Certain supplies of staff are not always made in the course or furtherance of business and thus may be outside the scope of VAT. These include
  - (i) secondments between and by government departments,
  - (ii) secondments between National Health bodies, and
  - (iii) some secondments between local authorities and by local authorities where they have a statutory obligation or monopoly.
- The supply of staff to a person who belongs outside the EU or to a business belonging in another EU member state is outside the scope of UK VAT.

Where supplies of staff are received from a person who belongs outside the UK, VAT must be accounted for on those supplies at the standard rate under the 'reverse charge' procedure (see **39.4 INTERNATIONAL SERVICES**).

Value of supply

VAT must be charged on the full amount of the consideration for the supply of staff (whether full-time or part-time). As well as any fee, this includes recovery of staff costs from the recipient (e.g. salary, NICs and pension contributions). VAT is due on the full consideration, including payments by the recipient direct to the worker (e.g. NICs, PAYE and similar items). There are a limited number of exceptions and these are outlined below.

(VAT Notice 700/34/12, paras 1.1, 2.1–2.3).

(1) Concession for secondment of staff by businesses other than employment businesses

Where an employer (other than an employment business within the meaning of the *Employment Agencies Act 1973*) seconds a member of its staff (the employee) to another business which

(a) exercises exclusive control over the allocation and performance of the employee's duties during the period of secondment; and
(b) is responsible for paying the employee's remuneration directly to the employee and/or discharges the employer's obligations to pay to any third party PAYE, NICs, pension contributions and similar payments relating to the employee,

then, to the extent that any payments within (*b*) above form the consideration (or part) for the secondment of the employee to the other business, they are disregarded in determining the value of seconding the employee. For these purposes, an employer is not to be treated as seconding an employee to another business if the placing of the employee with that other business is done with a view to the employer (or any person associated with him) deriving any financial gain from

- the placing of the employee with the other business, or
- any other arrangements or understandings (whether or not contractually binding and whether or not for any consideration) between the employer (or any person associated with him) and the other business (or any person associated with it) with which the employee is placed.

(2) Concession for placement of disabled workers under the Sheltered Placement Scheme (or any similar scheme)

Where the sponsor of a disabled worker places the worker with a host company under the Sheltered Placement Scheme (or any similar scheme) and the host company

- is responsible for paying the worker's remuneration directly to the worker; and/or
- discharges the sponsor's obligations to pay to any third party PAYE, NICs, pension contributions and similar payments relating to the worker,

then, to the extent that any such payments form the consideration (or part) for the placing of the worker with the host company, they are disregarded in determining the value of placing the worker with the host company.

(VAT Notice 700/34/12, para 4; HMRC Budget 2008 technical note; VAT Information Sheet 3/09).

Employment agencies and bureaux

See **3.14 AGENTS**.

Charities

See **13.5**(19) **CHARITIES**.

Temporary suspension of an employment contract

[45.5] Where an employee takes up a temporary post with another employer, there is no supply of staff provided that

(a) the temporary post is organised on the employee's own initiative; and
(b) the second employer issues the employee with a new contract or letter of appointment.

To avoid doubt, a temporary suspension should normally be supported by evidence that

- there is an agreement with the first employer that the employee is to be transferred for a fixed or open-ended period, often with an entitlement to return;
- there are new conditions of employment with the second employer;
- the second employer has control over the terms and conditions of employment; or
- the second employer fixes the salary.

(VAT Notice 700/34/12, para 3.1).

Joint employment

[45.6] In cases of joint employment, there is no supply of staff for VAT purposes between the joint employers.

Staff are regarded as jointly employed if their contracts of employment or letters of appointment make it clear that they have more than one employer. The contract must specify who the employers are (e.g. 'Company A, Company B and Company C' or 'Company A and its subsidiaries').

Staff are not regarded as jointly employed (and the provisions of **45.4** above apply) if their contract is with a single company or person, even if it

- lays down that the employee's duties include assisting others;
- lays down that the employee will work full-time for another; or
- shows by the job title that the employee works for a group of associated companies (e.g. group accountant).

(VAT Notice 700/34/12, para 3.2).

See *Agilysis Contact Services Ltd* [2016] UKFTT 289 (TC) (TC05062) for an examination by the First-tier Tribunal of a situation in which HMRC accepted that certain employees were jointly employed by two companies, but still regarded payments from one company to the other as consideration for taxable services rather than reimbursement of salaries disbursed. The Tribunal concluded that there was a genuine joint venture between the companies, and the reimbursement of salaries was genuinely separate from the consideration for the taxable services supplied.

Paymaster services for associated companies

[45.7] Paymaster services commonly occur between associated companies in two situations.

- Where staff are jointly employed, one of the joint employers may undertake to pay all salaries, National Insurance and pension contributions which are then recovered from the other employers.
- Where a number of associated companies each employs its own staff, one company may pay all salaries, etc. on behalf of the others, each associate then paying its share of the costs to the paymaster.

In either case, the recovery of monies paid out by the paymaster is not subject to VAT and is treated as a disbursement (see **3.7 AGENTS**).

VAT must be accounted for on any charge made for paymaster services over and above the reimbursement of the costs paid out unless

- the recipient belongs outside the EU or is a business which belongs in another EU member state (in which case the supply is outside the scope of UK VAT); or
- the supply is between companies within the same VAT group registration (in which case it is disregarded).

(VAT Notice 700/34/12, para 3.3).

Appointments to directorships and other offices

[45.8] The appointments of an individual as a director or other paid office holder (e.g. secretary, treasurer) can give rise to a VAT liability as a supply of staff in the following circumstances.

(1) Sole proprietors and partnerships providing professional services

A sole proprietor providing professional services (e.g. a solicitor or accountant) or a partner in a firm providing such services who takes up a professional appointment as a director or other office holder must account for VAT on any payment received if

(i) the appointment results from the professional expertise exercised in the business or partnership business,
(ii) the duties as a director or other office holder involve, at least in part, the use of that expertise, and
(iii) in the case of a partnership, the payments received accrue to the partnership and are not retained by the partner personally.

See *Birketts* (VTD 17515) (TVC 62.171) concerning various offices held by partners in the firm. The tribunal held that the tests to be applied were 'did one or more of the solicitors accept the offices in the course of furtherance of their profession' and 'did one or more of the solicitors accept the offices in the course or furtherance of the partnership business'.

See also *Oglethorpe Sturton & Gillibrand* (VTD 17491) (TVC 62.170).

Where, however, under the terms of an appointment as an office holder, the person concerned is treated as an employee, any fees or payments made to the sole proprietor or partner personally are outside the scope of VAT.

(2) Employees and directors

(a) *Request made to a company for the supply of a director.* If a company allows an employee or director to serve as a director of a second company, following an approach from that company, it must account for VAT on any payment it receives for agreeing to the appointment.

(b) *Common directors.* An individual involved in a number of companies may be a director of each. In general, where, for convenience, his total emoluments from all the businesses are paid by one company which recovers appropriate proportions from the others, any services to which the charges relate (e.g. attending meetings or approving expenditure) can only be the director's supplies to the companies of which he is a director. As these services are supplied directly to the relevant businesses by the individual and not across from one company to another, there is no supply from one company to another and no VAT is due on the share of money recovered from each company.

(c) *Voluntary personal appointment of a director.* Where an individual director or employee personally arranges to be appointed to the directorship of a second company and receives payment from that company in return, the first company is not required to account for VAT on any payments to the appointee. The appointment must be a purely personal one and not a means for the first company to deliver its service (e.g. consultancy services).

(d) *Right of a company to appoint a director.* Where a company exercises a legal or contractual right to appoint a director to the board of another company (e.g. a company in which it is investing) and that director does not give expert advice or take an active part in the running of the company, there is no supply for VAT purposes and any remuneration is outside the scope of VAT. Normally, however, in such circumstances the director is appointed because of his specialist knowledge and to give expert advice to the other company. In such a case, any fee charged by the company appointing the director for such advice and for taking an active part in the running of the other company is a supply for which the remuneration is taxable.

(e) *Banks, etc.* Where a bank or similar institution appoints a director to the board of a UK investee company as the condition of a loan, any charges for the director's services are part of the consideration for the loan and treated as an exempt supply. (Hansard 3 February 1993, Cols 185, 186).

(VAT Notice 700/34/12, paras 3.4, 4).

Key points: management services and supplies of staff

[45.9] Points to consider are as follows.

- A problem could occur if a business makes a management charge to an associated business that cannot fully reclaim input tax on its expenses due to partial exemption rules. In such cases, a possible solution to avoid a VAT loss might be to create a group registration. With a group registration, supplies of goods or services between group members are outside the scope of VAT.
- Another possible solution to avoid VAT being added to a supply of management services is where a joint contract of employment is in place for the employees whose salaries are being recharged. In such cases, the charge from one employer to the other is outside the scope of VAT.
- It is important to be clear about whether a supply of employees relates to a supply of 'staff' or a supply of specific services. A supply of staff is usually standard-rated (if provided to a UK customer) but a supply of specific services might be exempt or zero-rated in some cases (e.g. in relation to medical services). The key issue is to identify whether the staff concerned are acting under the instruction of the customer (supply of staff) or the supplier (as an employee/employer arrangement) to perform specific tasks for the customer.
- A supply of staff to an EU business customer or any customer outside the EU (business or non-business) is outside the scope of VAT under the place of supply rules. This would apply if, for example, staff employed by a UK airline were supplied to a Spanish airline company based in Spain, working under the instruction of the Spanish management team. In this situation, the VAT on fees charged by the UK airline will be accounted for by the Spanish airline on its own VAT return using the reverse charge calculation.
- If a UK business buys in staff from an overseas business, it must account for the VAT on its own VAT return by applying the reverse charge calculation. This is because the place of supply for the service is based on the location of the customer, i.e. UK. If the supply in question relates to a UK business that is partly exempt, then the reverse charge calculation will produce an input tax restriction in Box 4 of its VAT return, unless it directly relates to the taxable activities of the business, i.e. giving full input tax recovery.

46

Motor Cars

Cross-references. See **20.36 EUROPEAN UNION: SINGLE MARKET** for the refund of VAT on the supply of a new motor car by a non-taxable person to another EU member state; **20.37 EUROPEAN UNION: SINGLE MARKET** for the acquisition of a new motor car from another EU member state by a non-taxable person; **22.17 EXPORTS** for sale of vehicles outside the EU; **34.15**(13) **IMPORTS; 62 SECOND-HAND GOODS** for the second-hand scheme for motor cars and **63 SELF-SUPPLY** for explanation of such deemed supplies.

Introduction to motor cars

[46.1] For VAT purposes a motor car is any motor vehicle of a kind normally used on public roads which has three or more wheels and either

(a) is constructed or adapted solely or mainly for the carriage of passengers; or

(b) has to the rear of the driver's seat roofed accommodation which is fitted with side windows or which is constructed or adapted for the fitting of side windows.

It does not include the following.

(i) Vehicles capable of accommodating only one person.

(ii) Vehicles capable of carrying twelve or more seated persons and which meet the requirements of *Road Vehicles (Construction of Use) Regulations 1986, Sch 6* (road safety regulations).

(iii) Vehicles of not less than three tonnes unladen weight (as defined in *Road Vehicles (Construction of Use) Regulations 1986*).

(iv) Vehicles constructed to carry a 'payload' of one tonne or more. '*Payload*' is the difference between a vehicle's kerb weight and its maximum gross weight, both terms as defined in *Road Vehicles (Construction of Use) Regulations 1986*. This change means that certain dual purpose vehicles, commonly called twin cab or double cab pick-ups, are no longer cars for VAT purposes. A few double cabs carry a payload of under one tonne. Customs Centre of Operational Expertise for the Motor Trade (COPE) maintains a schedule of double cab pick-up vehicles and their ex-works payloads. Agreement has been reached with the Society of Motor Manufacturers and Traders about the treatment of optional accessories which dealers or others may add to a double cab potentially converting it into a car (by increasing the kerb weight and decreasing the payload). (See VAT Notice 700/57/14).

(v) Caravans, ambulances and prison vans.

(vi) Vehicles constructed for a special purpose other than the carriage of persons and having no other accommodation for carrying persons than such as is incidental to that purpose.

[*SI 1992/3122, Art 2; SI 1995/1268, Art 2*].

In a case concerning provisions in *Car Tax Act 1983* similar to *SI 1992/3122, Art 2*, it was held that in (*b*) above 'accommodation' means only accommodation for passengers and, if the space is unsuitable for this purpose, the vehicle is not within the definition even if there are side windows (*R v C & E Commrs (ex p Nissan UK Ltd)* CA [1988] BTC 8003 (TVC 44.39)).

Vehicles regarded as motor cars (subject to (iv) above)

- *Imported versions of saloon cars* even where they are 'normally used on public roads' which are outside the UK (*Withers of Winsford Ltd v C & E Commrs*, QB [1988] STC 431 (TVC 44.3)).
- An *estate car* with the rear seat removed (*County Telecommunications Systems Ltd* (VTD 10224) (TVC 44.8)); used for business purposes by a builder (*Gardner* (MC) (VTD 588) (TVC 44.6)); and licensed as a goods vehicle and used by a garage and grocery store (*Howarth* [1987] Lexis Citation 188 (TVC 44.7)).
- A Chevrolet K10 Blazer (*Yarlett* (VTD 1490) (TVC 44.9)).
- A Citroen van modified by fitting windows behind the driver's seat (*Browsers Bookshop* (VTD 2837) (TVC 44.22)).
- A Daihatsu Fourtrak Estate (*Specialised Cars Ltd* (VTD 11123) (TVC 44.24)).

- A Datsun pick-up truck, modified by the addition of a detachable hard top superstructure with two side windows and a hatchback to the rear of the driver's seat but no seating accommodation (*HKS Coachworks Ltd* [1981] Lexis Citation 816) (TVC 44.39) but see *R v C & E Commrs (ex p Nissan UK Ltd)* above).
- A Ford Escort, the rear seats of which could be folded away (*RC Lucia* (VTD 5776) (TVC 44.4)).
- An Isuzu pick-up (*BC Kunz (t/a Wharfdale Finance Co)* (VTD 13514) (TVC 44.28)).
- A Land Rover converted into a 'motor car' by being fitted with a hard top body with side windows and upholstered seats (*Chartcliff Ltd* (VTD 262) (TVC 44.1)); or by being modified by the addition of a metal canopy with side windows (*Wigley* (VTD 7300) (TVC 44.2)).
- A Range Rover even though first registered, and taxed, as a heavy goods vehicle and not used for domestic purposes (*C & E Commrs v Jeynes (t/a Midland International (Hire) Caterers)*, QB 1983, [1984] STC 30 (TVC 44.17)).
- A Suzuki jeep modified by the fitting of a rear seat although it had no rear windows (*S Compton (t/a Stan Compton Electrical Engineers & Contractors)* (VTD 10259) (TVC 44.20)); and a Suzuki Vitara Sport (*W McAdam* [1995] Lexis Citation 898 (TVC 44.26)).
- A Toyota Hiace van fitted with side windows (*Knapp* (VTD 778) (TVC 44.11)); a Toyota Hilux (*Western Waste Management Ltd* (VTD 17428) (TVC 44.15)); a Toyota Previa with the middle and rear rows of seats removed for delivery purposes (*Gorringe Pine* (VTD 14036) (TVC 44.12)); and a Toyota Spacecruiser with the rear seats removed and a hanging rail for transporting clothes installed (*Mr & Mrs M Gohil (t/a Gohil Fashions)* (VTD 15435) (TVC 44.14)).
- A Volkswagen tipping truck with, in addition to the driver's cab with room for one other passenger, a second roofed cab behind the driver's cab with room for three more passengers (*Weatherproof Flat Roofing (Plymouth) Ltd* (VTD 1240) (TVC 44.5)); a Volkswagen pick-up truck with roofed accommodation fitted with side windows to the rear of the driver's seat (*Readings & Headley* (VTD 1535) (TVC 44.10)); and a Volkswagen Caravelle with removable rear seats (*Intercraft UK Romania* (VTD 13707) (TVC 44.31)).

Vehicles not regarded as motor cars

- Ice cream vans, mobile shops and offices, hearses (see also *KP Davies* (VTD 831) (TVC 44.36)) and bullion vans (which are all regarded as falling under (v) above). (VAT Notice 700/64/14, para 2).
- Vehicles that can seat fewer than 12 passengers solely because they have been adapted for wheelchair users. [*SI 1992/3222, Art 2(b)(ii)*].
- A pick-up truck with an attached, removable canopy (*K M Batty* (VTD 2199) (TVC 44.37)).
- A Daihatsu Fourtrak Commercial Hard Top with two folding rear seats (*AL Yeoman Ltd* (VTD 4470) (TVC 44.43)).

- A Ford van fitted with wooden benches but no side windows (*Chartcliff Ltd* (VTD 262) (TVC 44.35)); and a Ford Transit van adapted by inserting rear seats of heavy duty plastic but with no rear windows, handrails or seat belts (*Chichester Plant Contractors Ltd* (VTD 6575) (TVC 44.41)).
- A Land Rover with two folding seats in the rear (*Bolinge Hill Farm* (VTD 4217) (TVC 44.42)); a 12-seat Land Rover with the rear bench seats removed (*P Oddonetto* [1990] Lexis Citation 2666 (TVC 44.44)); and a Land Rover modified by a half-sized window in the nearside rear panel (*TH Sheppard* (VTD 13815) (TVC 44.45)).
- A Peugeot van modified by adding a window on each side behind the driver's seat for safety reasons (*John Beharrell Ltd* (VTD 6530) (TVC 44.46)).
- A Lamborghini Murcielago two-seater sports car, with suspension programmed solely for track use (*Sixth Gear Experience Ltd* (VTD 20890) (TVC 44.51)).

Car-derived vans

A number of manufacturers' models start life as a motor car but are subsequently altered. On the exterior, these vehicles look like a motor car but their interior has been altered to give the appearance and functionality of a van. The rear seats and seat belts along with their mountings have been completely removed and the rear area of the shell is fitted with a new floor panel to create a load area. In addition, the side windows to the rear of the driver's seat are fitted with immovable opaque panels. HMRC do not view such a car-derived vehicle as a motor car for VAT purposes if:

- The technical criteria specified in HMRC guidance are met by the manufacturer. The criteria relate to how any alterations to the vehicle have been effected.
- The adaptations give the vehicle the functionality of a commercial vehicle. (The removal of a bench seat or similar from what is essentially a two-seater car would not automatically satisfy HMRC's requirements.)
- The space that remains behind the front row of seats is highly unsuitable for carrying passengers.

HMRC have published a list of vehicles that have been notified to them by manufacturers or sole concessionaires which have or have not been modified in accordance with HMRC guidance on motoring expenses as either a car derived van, a combination van or as a passenger car. If businesses are in any doubt, they should obtain confirmation in writing from the vendor that the vehicle meets the technical criteria.

(Business Brief 16/04).

Combination vans

Whilst these vehicles have the appearance of vans, they are designed to be fitted with or include additional seats behind the front row of seats to enable the carriage of passengers. Such vehicles are motor cars for VAT purposes except in the case of:

- Larger vehicles which have a payload of more than one tonne (see (iv) above).
- Those vehicles where the dedicated load area (i.e. that load area which is completely unaffected by the additional seating) is of a sufficient size compared to the passenger area to make the carriage of goods the predominant use of the vehicle.

Where a business has bought a combination van which does not fall within the above exceptions, it is a motor car under VAT legislation. If it has recovered the VAT incurred on the purchase, it must make an adjustment to correct this overclaim.

(Business Brief 16/04).

See, however, *Vauxhall Motors Ltd* (VTD 19425) (TVC 44.47) where the tribunal held that the Vauxhall Combo Crew van was a commercial vehicle and the fact that it contained three folding rear seats did not take it within the statutory definition of a car.

De Voil Indirect Tax Service. See V1.293.

HMRC have published a list of vehicles that have been notified to them by manufacturers or sole concessionaires which have or have not been modified in accordance with HMRC guidance on motoring expenses as either a car derived van, a combination van or as a passenger car. VAT-registered businesses can use the list to determine if VAT can be reclaimed as input tax on particular makes and models of car derived vans and combination vans. Where a vehicle is classed as a passenger car input tax is not normally recoverable if the vehicle is available for private use.

The table below is based on a list published by HMRC on 20 May 2015 of vehicles that have been notified to HMRC by manufacturers or sole concessionaires which have or have not been modified in accordance with HMRC guidance on motoring expenses as either a car derived van, a combination van or as a passenger car.

Make	*Model*	*Variant*	*Car or van for input tax deduction*
BMW	Mini	Clubvan from 25 July 2012 onwards	Van
Citroen	Xsara	Enterprise	Van
Citroen	Dispatch	Window van	Car
Citroen	Dispatch	Panel van	Van
Dacia	Duster	Commercial Ambiance 4X2 Feb 2015	Van
Dacia	Duster	Commercial Ambiance 4X4 Feb 2015	Van
Dacia	Duster	Commercial Laureate 4X2 Feb 2015	Van
Dacia	Duster	Commercial Laureate 4X4 Feb 2015	Van

Make	*Model*	*Variant*	*Car or van for input tax deduction*
Diahatsu	Hijet	Blind panel van	Van
Diahatsu	Extol	Blind panel van	Van
Fiat	Scudo	Combi 2.0JTD 16v 6 seat	Car
Fiat	Punto Van	1.2MPI Petrol	Van
Fiat	Punto Van	1.3 16v multi jet	Van
Ford	Fiesta	3 door van	Van
Ford	Transit Connect Crew van	SWB 1.8 (75ps) Diesel L	Van
Ford	Transit Connect Crew van	SWB 1.8 (90ps) Diesel L	Van
Ford	Transit Connect Crew van	SWB 1.8 (90ps) Diesel LX	Van
Ford	Transit Connect Crew van	SWB 1.8 (110ps) Diesel LX	Van
Ford	Transit Connect Crew van	LWB 1.8 (90ps) Diesel L	Van
Ford	Transit Connect Crew van	LWB 1.8 (90ps) Diesel LX	Van
Ford	Transit Connect Crew van	LWB 1.8 (110ps) Diesel LX	Van
Isuzu	Trooper Commercial		Van
Jeep	Cherokee	Pioneer 2.5CRd	Van
Kia	Sorento	Variant 2.5 XE-C manual	Van
Kia	Sorento	Variant 2.5 XE-C automatic	Van
Land Rover	Freelander 1 Commercial	1.8 Petrol 2000 to 2006	Van
Land Rover	Freelander 1 Commercial	2.0 Diesel 2000 to 2006	Van
Land Rover	Freelander 2 Commercial	2.2 TD4 Diesel 2009 onwards	Van
Land Rover	Discovery 2 Commercial	2.5 Diesel 2001 to 2006	Van
Land Rover	Discovery 3 Commercial	2.7 TDV6 2007 manual/automatic	Van
Land Rover	Discovery 3 Commercial	XS 2.7 TDV6 2007 manual/automatic	Van
Land Rover	Discovery 4 Commercial	2.7 TDV6 2010 manual/automatic	Van
Land Rover	Discovery 4 Commercial	XS 2.7 TDV6 2010 manual/automatic	Van
Land Rover	Discovery 4 Commercial	3.0 TDV6 2011 manual/automatic	Van

Make	*Model*	*Variant*	*Car or van for input tax deduction*
Land Rover	Discovery 4 Commercial	3.0 TDV6 and SDV6 2012 automatic	Van
Mazda		No car derived or combination vans	
Mercedes	Vito 109CDI	Compact dualiner Long dualiner Extra long dualiner	Van
Mercedes	Vito 109CDI	Long dualiner high roof Extra long dualiner with luxury seat pack	Car
Mercedes	Vito 111CDI	Compact dualiner Long dualiner Extra long dualiner	Van
Mercedes	Vito 111CDI	Long dualiner high roof Extra long dualiner with luxury seat pack	Car
Mercedes	Vito 115CDI	Compact dualiner Long dualiner Extra long dualiner	Van
Mercedes	Vito 115CDI	Long dualiner high roof Extra long dualiner with luxury seat pack	Car
Mercedes	Vito 120CDI	Compact dualiner Long dualiner Extra long dualiner	Van
Mercedes	Vito 120CDI	Long dualiner high roof Extra long dualiner with luxury seat pack	Car
MG	Express 105	CDV 1.4	Van
MG	Express	CDV 2.0 TD	Van
MG	Express 160	CDV 1.8 VVC	Van
Mitsubishi	Outlander 4 Work	2.0 Litre DI-D Equippe December 2006 (manual)	Van
Mitsubishi	Outlander 4 Work GX1	2.2 Litre DI-D GX45s Payload 520kgs September 2010 (manual)	Van
Mitsubishi	Outlander 4 Work GX1	2.2 Litre DI-D Payload 705kgs February 2013 (manual)	Van
Mitsubishi	Shogun Pinin 4 Work	1.8 MPi 3 door	Van
Mitsubishi	Shogun Pinin 4 Work	2.0 GDi 5 door	Van
Mitsubishi	Shogun Pinin 4 Work	2.5TD Classic	Van

Make	*Model*	*Variant*	*Car or van for input tax deduction*
Mitsubishi	Shogun Pinin 4 Work	2.5TD Equippe	Van
Mitsubishi	Shogun 4 Work	3.2 DI-D SWB Classic	Van
Mitsubishi	Shogun 4 Work	3.2 DI-D SWB Equippe	Van
Mitsubishi	Shogun 4 Work	3.2 DI-D LWB Classic	Van
Mitsubishi	Shogun 4 Work	3.2 DI-D LWB Equippe	Van
Mitsubishi	ASX 4 Work	1.8 MIVEC 4WD Manual Diesel (2011)	Van
Peugeot	206	Van	Van
Renault	Twizy Emport/Cargo	Electric Van (February 2014)	Van
Rover	Commerce	CDV 1.4	Van
Rover	Commerce	CDV 2.0 TD	Van
Tata	Safari	CDV DL Turbo	Van
Vauxhall	Corsa	Corsavan	Van
Vauxhall	Astra	Astravan	Van
Vauxhall	Corsa	Combo	Van
Vauxhall		Combo crew cab	Van
Vauxhall	Combo	L1H1 Crewvan Load area 991 mm (July 2012)	Van
Vauxhall	Combo	L2H1 Crewvan Load area 1341 mm (July 2012)	Van

Transactions involving motor cars

[46.2] The Treasury may, by order, provide that VAT charged on specified supplies, acquisitions and importations is excluded from credit for input tax against output tax. [*VATA 1994, s 25(7)*]. Provisions relating to motor cars have been made under *The Value Added Tax (Cars) Order 1992* (*SI 1992/3122*) and the *Value Added Tax (Input Tax) Order 1992* (*SI 1992/3222*) as amended. With certain exceptions, a taxable person cannot reclaim input tax on the purchase of a car (see **46.3** below) and no VAT is chargeable when the car is sold unless the selling price exceeds the purchase price (see **46.4** below). Certain transactions are not treated as taxable supplies (see **46.5** below) and special rules apply to self-supplies (see **46.6** below). For the position of car dealers see **46.7** below.

The validity of the UK input tax blocking order was upheld in *Royscot Leasing Ltd and others v C & E Commrs, ECJ Case C–305/97*, [1999] STC 998 (TVC 22.492).

Fleet buyer bonuses and dealer demonstration bonuses

A fleet buyer bonus is given by a manufacturer or sole concessionaire to a customer who makes a bulk purchase of vehicles. A dealer demonstrator bonus is a payment made, or credit allowed, by a manufacturer or sole concessionaire to a dealer who agrees to adopt a car as a demonstration vehicle. HMRC accept that such bonuses are normally to be treated as discounts by the manufacturer or sole concessionaires which reduce the value of their supplies. (Business Brief 16/97).

Fleet leasing bonuses

A fleet leasing bonus is given by a car manufacturer or dealer to a business which has leased a number of vehicles previously sold by the manufacturer or dealer to intermediaries. HMRC accept that such bonuses are normally to be treated as discounts by the manufacturer or dealer which reduce the value of their supplies (rather than consideration for a supply of services by the customer). (Business Brief 1/98).

Purchase of a car

[46.3] Apart from the special cases listed below, VAT cannot be reclaimed on the purchase (including acquisition or importation) of a motor car as defined in **46.1** above. Purchase means not only outright purchase but also any purchase under a hire purchase agreement or any other agreement whereby property in the car eventually passes e.g. a lease-purchase agreement. See **46.11** below for input tax on cars leased or hired.

VAT on supplies integral with the supply of a motor car is only deductible where input tax on the motor car is deductible. This includes manufacturer's warranty (although VAT on the purchase of an extension of the period of warranty is deductible). It has been held to include manufacturer's delivery charges passed on by dealers to customers. See *Wimpey Construction UK Ltd* [1979] VATTR 174 (TVC 44.101) and *C & E Commrs v British Telecommunications plc*, HL [1999] STC 758 (TVC 44.102).

See **46.13** below for fitted optional extras and accessories.

Special cases

VAT may be reclaimed on the purchase, acquisition or importation of a motor car in the following special circumstances.

(a) Exclusive business use

The motor car is a 'qualifying' motor car (see below) supplied to, or acquired or imported by, a taxable person who intends to use the motor car exclusively for business purposes. This condition is *not* satisfied if the taxable person intends to

(i) let it on hire to any person either for no consideration or consideration less than would be payable in an arm's length commercial transaction; or

(ii) make it available, otherwise than by letting on hire, to any person (including, where the taxable person is an individual, himself or, where the taxable person is a partnership, a partner) for private use (whether or not for a consideration).

A car is used exclusively for a business purpose if it is used only for business journeys *and* it is not available for private use. A car is available for private use when there is nothing preventing the owner or employees from using the car for private use. HMRC accept that

- VAT can be recovered on the purchase of a pool car provided it is
  (1) normally kept at the principal place of business;
  (2) not allocated to an individual; and
  (3) not kept at an employee's home;
- cars bought or imported for the purpose of sale and lease back will not be treated as available for private use provided output tax is accounted for on the resale to the leasing company in the same VAT period as input tax is recovered on the purchase; and
- VAT can be recovered on cars bought for in-house leasing provided the amounts charged to the lessee are not less than those for a commercial arm's length letting.

(VAT Notice 700/64/14, paras 3.5–3.9).

In *Upton (t/a Fagomatic) v C & E Commrs*, CA [2002] STC 640 (TVC 44.113) the High Court held that the trader's evidence that he did not need to use a car privately was not conclusive. The only cars which could be held to be used exclusively for business purposes were

- those which were not physically available for private use (e.g. cars used for leasing);
- cars which it would not be realistically possible to put to a private use (e.g. marked police cars and emergency vehicles); and
- cars which were insulated from the possibility of private use through the way in which they were allocated to staff (e.g. business cars held in a pool and not allocated to any individual).

The Court of Appeal upheld this decision. The 'intention to use' is not synonymous with the 'intention to make available'. Where an individual trader acquires a car, the very fact of his deliberate acquisition of the car, whereby he makes himself the owner of the car and controller of it, means that he must intend to make it available to himself for private use, even if he never intends to use it privately.

The decision in *Upton* was approved in *C & E Commrs v Skellett (CH) (t/a Vidcom Computer Services)*, CS 2003, [2004] STC 201 (TVC 44.114). It was held that the effect of (i) and (ii) above was that where a motor vehicle is acquired by a sole trader, the vehicle will have been made available to that person for private use unless effective steps are taken to render the vehicle *incapable* of such use by that person.

However, in *C & E Commrs v Elm Milk Ltd*, CA [2006] STC 792 (TVC 44.142) a claim for input tax recovery was allowed where a company had minuted a resolution that a car was for business use only and that it would be breach of the employee's terms of employment to use it for private use. The legislation did *not* state that, in order to show that there was no intention to make a car available for private use, the taxable person had to show that it was not physically so available. There was no reason, therefore, why a car could not be made unavailable for private use by suitable effective legal constraints.

The difference between the treatment of a company (which can enter into a binding agreement with its sole director prohibiting him from using a car for private purposes) and a sole trader (who cannot make a binding contract with himself) was confirmed in *HMRC v Shaw*, Ch D 2006, [2007] STC 1525 (TVC 44.119) although Lindsay J observed that it was difficult to imagine that Parliament intended to devise a test which expressly included sole traders and yet was such that it was hard to see how a sole trader could ever pass the test.

In *Jane Borton (t/a Contract Build)* (TC05224) [2016] UKFTT 472 (TC), the First-tier Tribunal accepted that a sole trader had demonstrated an intention to make a car unavailable for her private use. According to her statement, she had had input tax disallowed in relation to the purchase of a previous car, and had been told by HMRC that it would be necessary to obtain 'business use only' insurance to justify a deduction. She claimed that she had done this with the purchase of the disputed vehicle, but that HMRC had lost the documents she sent them to prove this. The First-tier Tribunal judge decided that it would not be reasonable in the circumstances to require her to obtain duplicate evidence, and found as a fact that the car had been insured for business purposes only. This was considered sufficient to show the intention to make the car unavailable, even though in practice it would still have been possible for her to drive it.

Other recent cases include *Zone Contractors Ltd* (TC05330) [2016] UKFTT 594 (TC) (in which the *Elm Milk* conditions were held to be satisfied) and *Venda Valet Ltd* (TC05321) [2016] UKFTT 572 (TC) (in which they were held not to be satisfied).

(b) Mini-cabs, self-drive hire, driving instruction

The motor car is a 'qualifying' motor car supplied to, or acquired or imported by, a taxable person who intends to use the motor car primarily

(i) to provide it on hire with the services of a driver for the purposes of carrying passengers;
(ii) to provide it for 'self-drive hire'; or
(iii) as a vehicle in which instruction in driving of a motor car is to be given by him.

'*Self-drive hire*' means hire where the hirer is the person normally expected to drive the motor car and the period of hire to each hirer (together with the period of hire of any other motor car expected to be hired to him by the taxable person) will normally be less than both 30 consecutive days and 90 days in any twelve-month period.

(c) Motor dealers and manufacturers

The motor car forms part of the 'stock in trade' of a 'motor manufacturer' or a 'motor dealer'.

'*Stock in trade*' means new or second-hand motor cars (other than second-hand motor cars which are not qualifying motor cars as defined below) which are

- produced by a motor manufacturer for the purpose of resale and intended to be sold by that manufacturer within twelve months of their production, or
- supplied to, or acquired from another EU member state or imported by, a motor dealer for the purpose of resale and intended to be sold by that motor dealer within twelve months of their supply, acquisition or importation.

Such motor cars do not cease to be stock in trade where they are temporarily put to a use in the motor manufacturer's or motor dealer's business which involves making them available for private use. Where a car does cease to be stock in trade and no longer qualifies for input tax recovery, a self-supply arises under **46.6** below.

'*Motor manufacturer*' means a person whose business consists (in whole or part) of producing motor cars including producing a motor car by conversion of a vehicle (whether a motor car or not).

'*Motor dealer*' means a person whose business consists (in whole or in part) of obtaining supplies of, or acquiring from another EU member state or importing, new or second-hand motor cars for resale with a view to making an overall profit on the sale of them (whether or not a profit is made on each sale).

(d) Motability Scheme

The motor car is unused and is supplied to a taxable person whose only taxable supplies are concerned with the letting of motor cars on hire to another taxable person whose business consists predominantly of making supplies within *VATA 1994, Sch 8 Group 12 Item 14* (see **29.31 HEALTH AND WELFARE**).

'Qualifying' motor cars

A 'qualifying' motor car for the purposes of (*a*)–(*c*) above is generally one which has never been supplied, acquired or imported in circumstances where VAT was wholly excluded from credit as input tax. Under normal circumstances, therefore, a qualifying car will be a new car or a used car where the previous owners were able to recover VAT on their purchase in full (e.g. cars disposed of by a leasing company, which will have recovered input tax on the purchase of a new car acquired for the purpose of renting out).

[*SI 1992/3222, Art 7*].

Fleet buyer bonuses

See **46.2** above.

De Voil Indirect Tax Service. See V3.443.

Disposal of a motor vehicle used in a business

Input tax wholly excluded from credit on the purchase of a car

[46.4] Following the decision in *EC Commission v Italian Republic, ECJ Case C–45/95*, [1997] STC 1062 (TVC 22.392), the onward sale of a motor car on which input tax was blocked on purchase is an exempt supply under *VATA 1994, Sch 9 Group 14*, regardless of whether it is sold at a profit or loss. See **21.4 EXEMPT SUPPLIES.** Any directly attributable input tax incurred in making the sale (e.g. auction fees) is exempt input tax and not recoverable. (VAT Notice 700/64/14, para 7.2). In addition, the decision in *Nordania Finans A/S v Skatteministeriet, ECJ Case C–98/07*, [2008] STC 3314 (TVC 22.521) has led HMRC to require that 'Italian Republic' claims (in respect of cars on which output tax was accounted for incorrectly on the profit margin) must be revisited and adjusted to take account of the effect on the partial exemption calculation of including the value of cars in the denominator. See **50.5 PARTIAL EXEMPTION.** (HMRC Brief 43/10). HMRC's view was upheld by the First-tier Tribunal in *Cleckheaton Holdings Ltd* [2015] UKFTT 686 (TC04803) (TVC 9.11).

Input tax deductible on purchase

Where any input tax was deductible on purchase

- *in the case of a motor car*, output tax must be accounted for on the full selling price. A VAT invoice must be issued to a VAT-registered buyer who requests one. Such a car cannot be sold under the margin scheme for **62 SECOND-HAND GOODS.**
- *in the case of a commercial vehicle*, output tax must be accounted for on the full selling price (even if part of the VAT charged was not recoverable because the business was partly exempt).

(VAT Notice 700/64/14, paras 7.1, 7.4).

VAT not charged on the purchase of a vehicle

Where VAT was not charged on the purchase of a vehicle (e.g. a purchase from a private individual or from a dealer who sold it under the VAT second-hand margin scheme) VAT need not be accounted for on the full selling price. The second-hand margin scheme can be used to account for VAT only on any profit made on the sale. See **62 SECOND-HAND GOODS.** (VAT Notice 700/64/14, para 7.3).

Transactions not treated as taxable supplies

[46.5] The following transactions relating to motor cars have been designated as outside the scope of VAT so as to be neither a supply of goods nor a supply of services.

(a) The disposal of a used motor car by a person who repossessed it under the terms of a 'finance agreement' provided the following conditions are met.

- The motor car so disposed must be in the same condition at the time of disposal as when it was repossessed or taken into possession. The condition of goods has been changed if any improvements, repairs, replacement parts or the generally making good of any damage has been carried out. The cleaning of goods generally does not affect the condition nor does the inclusion of instruction manuals if they are otherwise missing. (Business Brief 19/01).
- VAT on any previous supply, acquisition or importation must have been wholly excluded from credit under **46.3** above.
- No adjustment must have taken place, or may later take place, of VAT on the initial supply under the finance agreement as a result of repossession.

'*Finance agreement*' means any agreement for the sale of goods whereby the property in those goods is not to be transferred until the whole of the price has been paid and the seller retains the right to repossess the goods.

(b) The disposal of a used motor car by an 'insurer' who has taken it in settlement of a claim under a policy of insurance where the car is disposed of in the same condition as it was when it was so acquired. This does not apply unless the VAT on any previous supply, acquisition or importation was wholly excluded from credit under **46.3** above.

(c) The disposal of a motor car for no consideration (e.g. scrap). This does not apply unless the VAT on any previous supply, acquisition or importation was wholly excluded from credit under **46.3** above.

(d) Services in connection with a supply of a used motor car provided by an agent acting in his own name to the purchaser of the motor car, the consideration for which is taken into account in calculating the price at which the agent sold the car. See **62.26 SECOND-HAND GOODS.**

(e) Services in connection with the sale of a used motor car provided by an auctioneer acting in his own name to the vendor or purchaser of the motor car, the consideration for which is taken into account in calculating the price at which the agent obtained (or, as the case may be, sold) the car. See **62.53 SECOND-HAND GOODS.**

(f) Where a taxable person has purchased or has let on hire a motor car

(i) the letting on hire of that motor car by the taxable person to any person for no consideration or consideration less than would be payable in an arm's length commercial transaction, or

(ii) the making available of that motor car (otherwise than by letting on hire) by the taxable person to any person for private use (whether or not for a consideration)

provided that VAT on any previous supply, acquisition, importation or letting on hire of the motor car was wholly excluded from credit under **46.3** above or partly excluded from credit under **46.11** below.

Where the taxable person is an individual or partnership, included under (ii) above is the making available of the motor car to the individual himself or a partner.

The effect of this is that most charges to employees for the private use of a car are not taxable. See **46.22** below.

[*VATA 1994, s 5(3); SI 1992/3122, Arts 2, 4*].

Self-supply

[46.6] Where a person has obtained input tax credit on a motor car, and has put it to a use that would not qualify for such credit, special 'self-supply' provisions require him to account for VAT on the motor car. The detailed provisions are as follows.

A motor car is treated as self-supplied where

(a) it is produced by a taxable person otherwise than by conversion of a vehicle obtained by him,

(b) it is produced by a taxable person by the conversion of another vehicle (whether a motor car or not) and VAT on the supply to, or acquisition or importation by, the taxable person of that vehicle was not wholly excluded from credit, or

(c) it is supplied to, or acquired from another EU member state or imported by, a taxable person and input tax on that supply, acquisition or importation was not wholly excluded from credit,

and that motor car has not been supplied by the taxable person in the course or furtherance of any business carried on by him but is used by him such that, had the motor car been supplied to, or acquired or imported by, him at that time, any input tax would have been wholly excluded from credit under **46.3** above.

A motor car is also treated as self-supplied where

(i) it was transferred to a taxable person under a transaction relating to the transfer of a business as a going concern (TOGC) which was treated as neither a supply of goods nor a supply of services (see **9.9** *et seq* **BUSINESS**);

(ii) in the hands of the transferor or any 'predecessor' of his the self-supply provisions applied by virtue of (*a*), (*b*) or (*c*) above; and

(iii) the motor car has not been treated as self-supplied under these provisions by the transferor or any of his predecessors.

For this purpose, a person is the '*predecessor*' of the transferor where the transferor acquired the motor car from him under a TOGC which was treated as neither a supply of goods nor a supply of services; and a transferor's predecessors include the predecessors or his predecessor through any number of transactions.

Where a group registration is in operation, self-supplies by group members are deemed to be made by the representative member.

[*VATA 1994, s 5(5), s 43(2); SI 1992/3122, Arts 5, 7*].

Value of self-supply

If the car is new, the value of the self-supply by a UK manufacturer is the full cost of manufacturing the vehicle including related production overheads. For volume manufacturers, this can be taken to be 2/3rds of the current retail list price. Non-volume manufacturers may also use this approximation with the agreement of HMRC. For non-manufacturing traders, the self-supply cost should include the purchase price plus any cost of incorporated parts of UK manufacture and delivery charge. Discounts received after the time of supply should be disregarded unless contractually agreed before that time. Where delivery charges cannot be determined, a fixed charge of £50 per vehicle may be used. (VAT Notice 700/57/14.)

If the car is used, the value of the self-supply is the current purchase price of a vehicle *identical* in every respect (including age and condition and, where appropriate, any accessories fitted) to the car concerned or, if that is not available, the price for the purchase of a *similar* car. Failing this, it is the current production cost [*VATA 1994, Sch 6 para 6*] or two thirds of the current list price approximation of a new vehicle. (VAT Notice 700/57/14).

Time of self-supply

The time of supply is treated as taking place when the motor car is appropriated to the use giving rise to the self-supply. [*VATA 1994, s 6(11)*]. The tax point can only be decided once the vehicle has been used in the business, e.g. as a demonstration model. The tax point is then the date when, by any positive and recorded action, the car is transferred from new car sales stock. (VAT Notice 700, para 15.2).

See **46.8** below if the vehicle has been converted and then applied for business use.

See also *A & B Motors (Newton-le-Willows) Ltd* (VTD 1024) (TVC 44.55).

De Voil Indirect Tax Service. See V3.242.

Motor dealers

[46.7] The position of motor dealers is outlined below.

(1) Purchase of 'stock in trade' motor cars

A motor dealer can reclaim input tax charged on used and unused cars purchased as stock in trade for resale even where there is temporary private use (see **46.3** above).

(2) Private use of stock in trade cars

Dealers must account for VAT on the private use by employees or similar persons of cars which form part of the stock in trade. They are not obliged to account for VAT on the private use of cars which they have loaned to third parties (e.g. cars loaned to potential customers) for business purposes.

As the normal rules are complex, HMRC's policy is to allow dealers to use the normal method or a simplified method.

(a) The 'normal rules'

Under *VATA 1994, Sch 4 para 5(4)* (see **48.6 OUTPUT TAX**), where a manufacturer or dealer allows a demonstration car to be made available for private use, whether or not for a consideration, this is a deemed supply of services. Where there is no consideration, the value of the deemed supply is the full cost to the manufacturer or dealer. [*VATA 1994, Sch 6 para 7*]. Where there is consideration, subject to the anti-avoidance provisions below, the value of the supply is that consideration.

Anti-avoidance provisions. Under the above rules, where a nominal consideration is charged (say £1 per year) for the use of a motor car, VAT is only due on that nominal amount rather than the full cost of providing the motor car. The following anti-avoidance rules allow HMRC to direct that VAT is accounted for on an open market valuation of supplies of such motor cars to employees.

In relation to any use, or availability of use, of a motor car on or after a date to be appointed, where

- the value of a supply made by a taxable person for a consideration is (apart from these provisions) less than its open market value,
- the taxable person is a 'motor manufacturer' or 'motor dealer',
- the person to whom the supply is made is *either* an employee of the taxable person *or* a person who, under the terms of his employment, provides services to the taxable person *or* a relative (i.e. husband, wife, brother, sister, ancestor or lineal descendant) of such a person,
- the supply is a supply of services by virtue of *VATA 1994, Sch 4 para 5(4)* (see above),
- the supply relates to a motor car (whether or not any particular motor car) that forms part of the 'stock in trade' of the taxable person, and
- the supply does not fall within the general rules for transactions between connected persons in *VATA 1994, Sch 6 para 1* (see **72.19 VALUATION**)

HMRC may direct that the value of the supply (and any further supplies satisfying these conditions) is to be taken to be its open market value. Any such direction must be given by notice in writing to the motor manufacturer or dealer but no direction may be given more than three years after the time of the supply.

See **46.1** above for the definition of '*motor car*' and **46.3**(*c*) above for the definitions of '*motor manufacturer*', '*motor dealer*' and '*stock in trade*'.

[*VATA 1994, Sch 6 para 1A*].

(b) A standard simplified method

HMRC have agreed a simplified method with both the Retail Motor Industry Federation (RMI) and the Society of Motor Manufacturers and Traders Ltd (SMMT). Dealers who choose to use a simplified method must use it for all their cars that are put to private use.

RMI agreement: for each individual who has used a stock in trade car for private journeys in a VAT period, the trader must identify the list price of the car he has typically used and identify the appropriate price band to determine the VAT payable for private use.

SMMT agreement: for each individual who has used a stock in trade car for private journeys in a VAT period, the trader must identify the list price of the car he has typically used and identify the appropriate price band to determine the VAT payable for private use.

(VAT Notice 700/57/14; VAT Information Sheet 7/09).

(3) Disposals of cars on which input tax was recovered

VAT must be charged on the full selling price. See also **46.6** above for self-supply, e.g. where an unused car on which VAT has been reclaimed is transferred from sales stock to use in the business that would not qualify for input tax recovery.

(4) 'Bumping'

A car dealer may accept a second-hand car in part-exchange and then make arrangements with a finance company for the sale of the replacement car to the customer, treating the part-exchange value as the deposit required by the finance company. As the finance company normally requires a minimum deposit, it is common practice to inflate the part-exchange value and the sales price of the replacement car by a similar amount so that the minimum deposit can be met without resort to a cash payment from the customer (a practice known as 'bumping'). In such cases, the car dealer must account for VAT on the inflated price of the car as shown on the HP agreement (*North Anderson Cars Ltd v C & E Commrs*, CS [1999] STC 902 (TVC 44.158)).

In *N & M Walkingshaw Ltd v HMRC* [2015] UKUT 123 (TCC) (TVC 44.90) it was decided that the consideration on which VAT should be accounted for is the agreed price for a car that a dealer sells regardless of whether an over-allowance is paid by the dealer for a car taken in part-exchange and that there is no scope for treating the value of the new car as having been discounted by the over-allowance paid for the car taken in part-exchange.

(5) Premium, 'nearly new' and 'personal import' cars

Franchised dealers are not permitted by the terms of their franchise to sell a new car to another dealer. Therefore, non-franchised dealers must secure regular supplies by other means, e.g. by employing an agent to purchase a car from a franchised dealer. Similarly, 'personal import' cars are sometimes acquired by VAT-registered dealers from private importers immediately following their importation.

The normal rules for supplying goods through buying agents apply (see **3.6 AGENTS**). Non-franchised dealers are only able to recover input tax on the purchase of a motor car if it is purchased

- directly from a manufacturer or another dealer;
- through an agent acting in the name of the non-franchised dealer; or
- through an 'undisclosed agent' acting in his own name if the agent is registered for VAT and has issued a proper VAT invoice. However, to be registered, such an agent must be in business for VAT purposes and, given the nature of the tests which must be applied to establish this (see

9.2 BUSINESS), it is unlikely that HMRC will regard the intention to sell a single car as constituting 'business'. Even if registered, an undisclosed agent will suffer a block on input tax recovery on the purchase of a car if it is made available for private use. This may apply if there is a gap between the purchase of the car and the supply to the non-franchised dealer.

(Business Brief 4/98).

(6) Dealer demonstration bonuses

See **46.2** above.

Conversion of a vehicle into a motor car and vice versa

Conversion of a commercial vehicle into a car

[46.8] A commercial vehicle can be converted into a car for VAT purposes. Where VAT is recovered on the purchase of the vehicle, output tax must be accounted for when the conversion is completed. The value for VAT purposes is the value of the vehicle at the time the conversion is completed, including the cost of the conversion. VAT incurred on any parts bought for the conversion are recoverable.

Examples of the conversion of a vehicle into a motor car are:

- The fitting of a side window or windows into a van to the rear of the driver's seat.
- The fitting of a rear seat or seats to a van, even without the insertion of side windows.
- The removal of seats from a twelve-seater vehicle.

(VAT Notice 700/64/14, para 2.4).

See, however, *Bolinge Hill Farm* (VTD 4217) (TVC 44.42); *P Oddonetto* [1990] Lexis Citation 2666 (TVC 44.44); *John Beharrell Ltd* (VTD 6530) (TVC 44.46) and *Chichester Plant Contractors Ltd* (VTD 6575) (TVC 44.41).

Conversion of a car into a commercial vehicle

This can be done, for example, by removing rear seats and windows or by adding additional seats so that the vehicle can legally seat twelve or more people. VAT can only be recovered on the car if it was bought specifically for this conversion and not used as a car. (VAT Notice 700/64/14, para 2.5).

Car kits

[46.9] Where a car is made from a kit or separately purchased parts, any VAT charged as input tax may be reclaimed subject to the normal rules. If the finished car is used in the business for a purpose that would not qualify for input tax recovery, VAT must be accounted for under the self-supply rules (see **46.6** above). The tax value must be based on the VAT-exclusive cost of the parts and the cost of construction. The VAT cannot be reclaimed. If the finished car is sold, VAT must be accounted for on the full selling price in the normal way. (VAT Notice 700/64/14, para 2.6).

Motor expenses

[46.10] Provided the vehicle is used in the business, VAT on leasing or hiring a vehicle, road fuel (whether bought by the business or reimbursed to employees) and repair and maintenance charges can be treated as input tax. This applies even if the vehicle is used partly for private motoring. Private usage may, however, create a liability to output tax.

The provisions are considered in more detail in **46.11** to **46.22** below. For these purposes it is important to understand the difference between 'business' and 'private' motoring.

A '*business*' journey is one made by an employer or employee for the purpose of the business.

A '*private*' journey is any journey not for the purpose of the business.

Travel between a person's home and normal workplace is private motoring. Travel from home to any other place for business purposes is a business journey.

Leasing or hiring a motor car

[46.11] The following provisions apply to motor cars that are hired or leased for business purposes. The provisions do not apply to hire purchase or lease-purchase agreements, for which see **46.3** above.

If a motor car as defined in **46.1** above is leased or hired, only 50% of the input VAT on the rental charges is available for the credit except in the following circumstances when 100% relief is available.

(a) The motor car is a 'qualifying' motor car let on hire to a taxable person who intends to use the motor car exclusively for business purposes. This condition is *not* satisfied if the taxable person intends to
- let it on hire to any person either for no consideration or consideration less than would be payable in an arm's length commercial transaction; or
- make it available, otherwise than by letting on hire, to any person (including, where the taxable person is an individual, himself or, where the taxable person is a partnership, a partner) for private use (whether or not for a consideration).

(b) The motor car is a 'qualifying' motor car let on hire to a taxable person who intends to use the motor car primarily
- to provide it on hire with the services of a driver for the purposes of carrying passengers;
- to provide it for 'self-drive hire'; or
- as a vehicle in which instruction in driving of a motor car is to be given by him.

'*Self-drive hire*' means hire where the hirer is the person normally expected to drive the motor car and the period of hire to each hirer (together with the period of hire of any other motor car expected to be hired to him by the taxable person) will normally be less than both 30 consecutive days and 90 days in any twelve-month period.

(c) The motor car is not a 'qualifying' motor car (i.e. the lessor obtained no input tax credit on its purchase or acquisition).

(d) The motor car is unused and is let on hire to a taxable person whose business consists predominantly of making supplies within *VATA 1994, Sch 8 Group 12 Item 14* (see **29.31 HEALTH AND WELFARE**) by a taxable person whose only taxable supplies are concerned with the letting on hire of motor cars to such taxable persons.

See **46.3** above for the definition of a '*qualifying*' motor car.

[*SI 1992/3222, Art 7*].

Charges subject to the 50% restriction

There are frequently two distinct elements of the rental: basic rental for the provision of the car (including depreciation, funding cost, VED and a proportion of overheads/profit) and an optional additional charge (covering repairs, maintenance and roadside assistance and a proportion of overheads/profit). The optional charges are also subject to the 50% restriction unless they are separately described in the contract hire agreement and periodic invoices and are genuinely optional, in which case they are recoverable in full subject to the normal rules. VAT on an excess mileage charge should similarly be separated into two distinct elements on a basis identical to the split of the rental. For full details, see the agreement between the British Vehicle Rental and Leasing Association and HMRC reproduced in VAT Notice 700/57/14.

Rental rebates

Where a lessor sells a car at the end of a lease and uses the proceeds to rebate the monthly rental payments made to the lessee, a lessee who incurred a 50% input tax restriction on the rental charges on the car need only adjust for 50% of the VAT on the credit note issued by the lessor for rebate of rentals.

Early lease termination

Where a lessee terminates the lease early, the leasing company may choose to either

- treat both the termination payment and any associated rebate of rental as taxable; or
- treat both as outside the scope of VAT.

If the leasing company chooses to tax, it will normally offset the termination payment against the rebate.

- Where the termination payment exceeds the rebate, any VAT is not subject to the 50% restriction.
- Where the rebate exceeds the termination payment, the leasing company must issue a VAT credit note for the balance. A lessee who incurred a 50% input tax restriction on the rental charges need only adjust for 50% of the VAT credit in the VAT account.

Self-drive hire (daily rental)

The 50% restriction applies to self-drive hire as well as leasing on a longer-term basis. If the car is hired simply to replace an off-the-road ordinary company car, the 50% block applies from the first day of hire. By concession,

HMRC accept that in other cases (e.g. where the business does not have a company car) the 50% block does not apply if a car is hired for not more than 10 days to use specifically for business purposes.

Interaction with other apportionments

Where the 50% input tax restriction applies and there are both business and non-business activities and/or exempt supplies, the order for carrying out the various apportionments is

- VAT incurred between business and non-business activities (see **35.7 INPUT TAX**)
- 50% input tax restriction on the VAT amount which relates to business activities
- any necessary **50 PARTIAL EXEMPTION** calculation.

(VAT Notice 700/64/14, paras 4.4–4.10; VAT Information Sheet 12/95; Business Brief 15/95).

VAT due by daily rental companies on incidental private use of their hire fleet

Under the normal rules, where assets are used for private purposes a supply of services takes place. Where the services are provided for no consideration, the value of those services is the cost to the employer of providing those services. The calculation of this value would involve, in each VAT period, reference to

- the depreciation of the capital cost of the car;
- the value (excluding VAT) of repairs, maintenance and other running costs (excluding road fuel) on which VAT had been recovered; and
- the actual proportion of business and private use.

As these calculations might be complex, HMRC and the British Vehicle Rental and Leasing Association have agreed that daily rental companies may choose to apply a simplified method of establishing the output tax due. Daily rental companies who choose to use the simplified method must do so for all their daily rental cars which are put to private use. Daily rental companies who choose not to adopt the simplified method must either apply the normal rules or apply to HMRC to use an individual simplified method. For each VAT period, the daily rental company must calculate output VAT on the private use of the daily rental cars as follows.

- Identify staff that use a daily rental car for private journeys in the period.
- For each person, identify the list price of car they have typically used in the period.
- For each person, identify the appropriate price band to determine the VAT payable for private use.

Fleet leasing bonuses

See **46.2** above. Receipt of such a bonus reduces the VAT recoverable by the customer (if any) on the lease payments. For example, where 50% of the VAT incurred on lease payments can be recovered, VAT due on the bonus payment is 1/6 × 50% × gross bonus payment.

(Business Brief 1/98).

Repairs and maintenance

[46.12] If a vehicle is used for business purposes, VAT on repairs and maintenance can be treated as input tax provided the work done is paid for by the business. This applies even if the vehicle is used for private motoring and even if no VAT is reclaimed on any road fuel in order to avoid use of the scale charges, see **46.16** below. VAT on repairs, etc. relating to a vehicle used solely for private motoring by a sole proprietor or partner cannot be treated as input tax. (VAT Notice 700/64/14, para 5.1).

Accessories

[46.13] Where a car is purchased on which input tax is blocked, VAT charged on accessories fitted to a car when purchased cannot be reclaimed even if optional and separately itemised on the sales invoice. See *Turmeau* (VTD 1135) (TVC 44.103).

VAT on accessories subsequently purchased can only be treated as input tax if

- the vehicle is owned by the business or used in the business but not owned by it (e.g. an employee's or director's own car); and
- the accessory has a business use.

(VAT Notice 700/64/14, paras 5.2, 5.3).

Input tax on personalised number plates has been disallowed in a considerable number of cases including *Ava Knit Ltd* (VTD 1461) (TVC 36.515) and *E N Jones* (VTD 5023) (TVC 36.525) but allowed in *MW Alexander* (VTD 7208) (TVC 36.506); *Sunner & Sons* (VTD 8857) (TVC 36.509) and *Hamlet's (Radio & TV) Ltd* (VTD 12716) (TVC 36.510). See *Tolley's VAT Cases.*

Fuel bought by the business

[46.14] Where a business pays for road fuel, if the fuel is used for business motoring only, subject to the normal rules it can claim all of the VAT because 100% is used for business purposes. Where the fuel purchased is used both for business and private motoring, the business has three options.

(a) In the case of motor cars, it can claim all VAT charged and apply the fuel scale charge (see **46.16** below).

(b) It can use detailed mileage records to separate business mileage from private mileage. This avoids using the scale charge. Records must be kept of total mileage, split between business and private mileage, and total fuel costs.

Example

Total business mileage is 4,290 of which 3,165 relates to business mileage. The total cost of fuel is £250.

The cost of the business mileage is

£250 × 3,165 ÷ 4,290 = £184.44

Input tax is £184.44 × 1/6 = £30.74

(c) It can neither claim input tax on any road fuel purchased nor apply the scale charge (see **46.16** below).

(VAT Notice 700/64/14, paras 8.1–8.5).

Non-business activities

VAT on non-business journeys (e.g. journeys in connection with charitable activities of charities) is not reclaimable. Where fuel is used for both business and non-business activities, the total cost should be apportioned.

Fuel card schemes

Fuel cards allow companies who own fleets of vehicles to purchase fuel, and other motor-related goods and services, from garages by means of a card. The schemes are designed contractually to provide that, where a card is used to buy fuel, the fuel is supplied from the garage to the card company and then by the card company to the cardholders. (With a normal credit card transaction, the garage supplies goods and services direct to the cardholders, the credit card being used simply as a means of payment.) Whether the schemes work depends upon the precise terms of the contractual arrangements between the parties.

See *Harpur Group Ltd* (VTD 12001) (TVC 27.46) where five different schemes were considered.

See also *Auto Lease Holland BV v Bundesamt fur Finanzen, CJEC Case C–185/01*, [2005] STC 598 (TVC 22.161) where a Netherlands company (H) leased a number of motor vehicles and gave the lessees the use of a credit card to purchase fuel. It contended that it should be treated as having received the fuel from the retail companies and as having made an onward supply to the lessees. The Court held that, in the circumstances of the case, the lessor of a vehicle did not make any supply of fuel to the lessee even if the vehicle was filled up in the name and at the expense of that lessor.

Fuel bought by employees

[46.15] Where

- road fuel is supplied to an employer in circumstances where it is delivered to and paid for by an employee, acting in the employer's name and on its behalf, for use by the employee either in whole or in part for the purposes of the employer's business, and
- the employer has agreed to reimburse (and does so reimburse) the employee for the cost of the road fuel so used in one of the ways specified below,

the employer can deduct input tax on the road fuel in question, quantified by reference to the amount it pays to the employee as reimbursement. The employer must hold a VAT invoice which contains the details prescribed under

(i) **40.4 INVOICES** (VAT invoices generally),
(ii) **40.5 INVOICES** (VAT invoices to persons in another EU member state), or
(iii) **40.7**(*a*) **INVOICES** (retailers' less detailed invoices)

as applicable. Where required by those provisions, the prescribed invoice must be made out to the employer as the recipient of the supply. (Note. In the vast majority of cases, the invoice will fall under (iii) where there is no requirement for the name of the recipient of the supply to appear on the invoice.)

The specified ways are

(a) *where all the road fuel is used for the purposes of the employer's business*, by payment of the actual cost of the road fuel; and
(b) *where only part of the road fuel is used for the purposes of the employer's business*, by payment of either
   (i) an amount which represents the actual cost of the road fuel so used determined by the total distances travelled by the relevant vehicle and the cylinder capacity of that vehicle; or
   (ii) the actual cost of the road fuel in circumstances where the employer accounts for output tax on any private use using the scale charge (see **46.16** and **46.17** below).

'*Use for the purposes of the employer's business*' means use for the purposes by the employer in making onward taxable supplies.

[*SI 2005/3290*].

Mileage allowances

Where employees are paid mileage allowances, input tax is calculated by multiplying the fuel element of the mileage allowance by the VAT fraction. The allowance paid to employees must be based upon mileage actually done. (VAT Notice 700/64/14, para 8.7).

Records of mileage

Where employees are paid a mileage allowance, HMRC require the business to keep a record for each employee showing

- mileage travelled;
- whether journeys are both business and private;
- the cylinder capacity of the vehicle;
- the rate of the mileage allowance; and
- the amount of input tax claimed.

(VAT Notice 700/64/14, para 8.8).

Advisory fuel rates

For income tax purposes, HMRC publish advisory fuel rates for company cars based on the engine capacity of the car and the type of fuel used. HMRC will also accept these figures for VAT purposes as the basis for reimbursing an employee for fuel bought for business purposes, although the employer must retain receipts in line with the current legislation.

www.gov.uk/government/publications/advisory-fuel-rates

The rates applying in recent periods are as follows.

1.3.18				
Engine size		*Fuel cost per mile*		
Petrol/LPG	*Diesel*	*Petrol*	*Diesel*	*LPG*
Up to 1,400cc	Up to 1,600cc	11p	9p	7p
1,401–2,000cc	1,601–2,000cc	14p	11p	8p
Over 2,000cc	Over 2,000cc	22p	13p	13p

1.12.17–28.2.18				
Engine size		*Fuel cost per mile*		
Petrol/LPG	*Diesel*	*Petrol*	*Diesel*	*LPG*
Up to 1,400cc	Up to 1,600cc	11p	9p	7p
1,401–2,000cc	1,601–2,000cc	14p	11p	9p
Over 2,000cc	Over 2,000cc	21p	13p	14p

1.9.17–30.11.17				
Engine size		*Fuel cost per mile*		
Petrol/LPG	*Diesel*	*Petrol*	*Diesel*	*LPG*
Up to 1,400cc	Up to 1,600cc	11p	9p	7p
1,401–2,000cc	1,601–2,000cc	13p	11p	8p
Over 2,000cc	Over 2,000cc	21p	12p	13p

1.6.17–31.8.17				
Engine size		*Fuel cost per mile*		
Petrol/LPG	*Diesel*	*Petrol*	*Diesel*	*LPG*
Up to 1,400cc	Up to 1,600cc	11p	9p	7p
1,401–2,000cc	1,601–2,000cc	14p	11p	9p
Over 2,000cc	Over 2,000cc	21p	13p	14p

HMRC also accept rates set by recognised motoring agencies (e.g. RAC, AA).

De Voil Indirect Tax Service. See V3.436.

Fuel for private use

[46.16] Where in any VAT period a taxable person supplies 'fuel for private use' to an individual, VAT must be accounted for using the scale charges in **46.17** below which represent the VAT-inclusive value of the fuel in respect of any one vehicle. If fuel is supplied for private motoring free or for less than the amount paid for it, the only way to avoid accounting for VAT using the scale charge is by not reclaiming input tax on *any* fuel purchased whether used for business or private motoring in cars or commercial vehicles.

'*Fuel for private use*' is fuel which is (or has previously been) supplied to, acquired from another EU member state by, imported from outside the EU by, or manufactured by, a taxable person in the course of his business and which is

(1) provided to an employee or office holder for private use in a vehicle allocated to him;
(2) provided to some other person for private use in a vehicle allocated to an employee or office holder;
(3) provided to an employee or office holder for private use in his own vehicle;
(4) provided to any partner (in the case of a partnership) for private use in his own vehicle; or
(5) appropriated by the proprietor (in the case of a sole trader) for private use in his own vehicle.

Fuel appropriated to the proprietor under (5) above is treated as being supplied to himself in his private capacity.

From 11 December 2012, fuel is not regarded as provided to any person for his private use under (1)–(4) above if it is supplied for consideration. Prior to 11 December 2012, fuel was not regarded as provided to any person for his private use under (1)–(4) above if it was supplied at a price not less than that at which it was supplied to or imported by the taxable person, or in the case of manufactured fuel, at a price not less than the aggregate of costs of raw materials and of manufacturing together with any excise duty thereon [*VATA 1994, s 56(2); FA 2013, Sch 38 para 7(2)*]. See below for the VAT treatment where fuel is charged at such a price from 17 July 2013.

'*Business travel*' is that which an individual is necessarily obliged to do in the performance of the duties of his employment, the partnership, or in the case of the taxable person himself, his business.

'*Own vehicle*' includes any vehicle of which for the time being the individual has the use (other than a vehicle 'allocated to' him).

'*Vehicle*' means any mechanically propelled road vehicle other than a motor cycle or an invalid carriage. HMRC have, however, confirmed that the scale rate charges will apply only to cars.

A vehicle is at any time '*allocated to*' an individual if at that time it is made available (without any transfer of property in it) either to the individual himself or to any other person, and is so made available by reason of the individual's employment and for private use. However, a vehicle is not regarded as allocated to an individual by reason of his employment if, in any VAT period, it is a pooled car i.e.

- it was made available to, and actually used by, more than one of the employees or one or more (of the) employers and, in the case of each of them, it was made available to him by reason of his employment but was not in the period ordinarily used by any one of them to the exclusion of the others;
- in the case of each of the employees, any private use of the vehicle made by him was merely incidental to his other use of it in that period; and

- it was not normally kept overnight on or in the vicinity of any residential premises where any of the employees was residing, except while being kept overnight on premises occupied by the person making the vehicle available to them.

The provision of fuel is treated as a supply in the course or furtherance of a business by the taxable person at the time when fuel for private use is put into the fuel tank of the individual's own vehicle or a vehicle allocated to him. An appropriation by a taxable person to his own private use is treated as a supply to himself in his private capacity. A provision of fuel by a member of a group within *VATA 1994, s 43* (see **28 GROUPS OF COMPANIES**) is treated as provision by the representative member.

Input tax

VAT on the supply, acquisition or importation of fuel for private use is to be treated as input tax subject to the normal rules notwithstanding that the fuel is not used or to be used for business purposes.

Changing vehicles

Where an individual is supplied with fuel for private use for one vehicle in respect of part of a VAT period and another vehicle for another part of the same period, then, provided that at the end of the period one of the vehicles neither belongs to him nor is allocated to him, supplies made to the individual are treated as made in respect of one vehicle only. Where each vehicle falls within the same category in the above tables, the table is applied as if fuel had been supplied for one vehicle only throughout the period. Otherwise the figures are rateably apportioned depending on the period for which fuel for private use was supplied for each vehicle.

[*VATA 1994, ss 56, 57; VATA 1994, Sch 6 para A1*].

Records

Where the scale charge is used, records must be kept showing

(1) the number of cars for which free or below cost fuel is supplied;
(2) the CO2 band for each car;
(3) the cylinder capacity of each car if the car is too old to have a CO2 emissions figure; and
(4) if a vehicle is changed, the date of the change.

(VAT Notice 700/64/14, para 9.7).

Accounting for VAT

The VAT due per the scale charge table in **46.17** below should be included in the total output tax figure on the return. The net amount (i.e. the scale charge for the fuel less the VAT due) should be included in the total value of outputs on the return.

Example

L Ltd provides its employees with cars and pays all day-to-day running expenses, including the cost of any petrol used for private motoring. Each employee submits a monthly return showing opening and closing mileage, together with fuel and servicing receipts for the period.

T, the sales director, has a car with a scale charge based on CO_2 emissions of £156 gross and puts in a monthly claim for February 2016. He supports this with petrol bills totalling £176.49 and a service invoice for £288.00 (£240.00 plus VAT £48.00). The company prepares monthly VAT returns.

The company should code the expenses claim as follows.

		£
Debit		
Servicing		240.00
Fuel £176.49 x 5/6	147.07	
Scale charge — 1/6 x £156	26.00	
		173.07
Input VAT — on service	48.00	
— on petrol £176.49 x 1/6	29.42	
		77.42
		£490.49
Credit		
Expenses reimbursed to T		
£176.49 + £288.00		464.49
Output VAT		26.00
		£490.49

From 1 February 2014 — no charge made for private fuel

For prescribed accounting periods commencing on or after 1 February 2014, the deemed supply arising where road fuel is provided for, or appropriated to, private use may be taxed

- by reference to the provisions in *VATA 1994, Sch 4* (matters to be treated as supply of goods or services); or
- on a flat-rate basis, i.e. by the application of the scale charge.

Road fuel is provided for, or appropriated to, private use where a taxable person (P)

- provides the fuel to an individual for private use in the individual's own car or a car allocated to the individual, and the fuel is provided by reason of the individual's employment;
- appropriates the fuel for private use in his own car (where P is an individual); or
- provides the fuel to individual partners for private use in the partners' own cars (where P is a partnership).

Details of the scale charge are contained in an order published by the Treasury. The order sets out a table of scale charges (to be revalorised at regular intervals), together with rules and notes setting out the application of the charges.

In accordance with the *Value Added Tax (Flat-rate Valuation of Supplies of Fuel for Private Use) Order 2013 (SI 2013/2911)* which is in force from 1 February 2014, the value of all supplies of road fuel made to any one individual in respect of any one car for a prescribed accounting period is to be determined in accordance with a valuation table having effect during the period and the notes to the valuation table. If fuel is supplied for private motoring free or for less than the amount paid for it, the only way to avoid accounting for VAT using the scale charge is by not reclaiming input tax on *any* fuel purchased whether used for business or private motoring in cars or commercial vehicles.

See **46.18** for the current table.

HMRC are required to revalorise the amounts specified in the base valuation table, with the first revalorisation taking effect from 1 May 2014. HMRC are required to carry out subsequent revalorisations, with each revalorisation taking place not more than 12 months after the previous revalorisation.

Each time HMRC revalorise the amounts they must publish an updated valuation table with a statement specifying the revalorisation start date. See **46.18** for the current table.

The following notes apply to the valuation table.

(1) For a car of a description in the first column of the valuation table, the value on the flat-rate basis of all supplies of road fuel made to any one individual in respect of that car for a prescribed accounting period is the amount specified under whichever of the second, third or fourth columns corresponds with the length of the prescribed accounting period.

(2) Where a CO_2 emissions figure is specified in relation to a car in a UK approval certificate or in a certificate of conformity issued by a manufacturer in another member state corresponding to a UK approval certificate ('corresponding certificate of conformity'), the car's CO_2 emissions figure for the purposes of the valuation table is determined as follows—

  (a) if only one figure is specified in the certificate, that figure is the car's CO_2 emissions figure for those purposes;

  (b) if more than one figure is specified in the certificate, the figure specified as the CO_2 (combined) emissions figure is the car's CO_2 emissions figure for those purposes;

  (c) if separate CO_2 emissions figures are specified for different fuels, the lowest figure specified, or, in a case within sub-paragraph (b), the lowest CO_2 (combined) emissions figure specified is the car's CO_2 emissions figure for those purposes.

(3) For the purpose of paragraph 2, if the car's CO_2 emissions figure is not a multiple of 5 it is rounded down to the nearest multiple of 5 for those purposes.

(4) Where no UK approval certificate or corresponding certificate of conformity is issued in relation to a car, or where a certificate is issued but no emissions figure is specified in it, the car's CO_2 emissions figure for the purposes of the valuation table is—

(a) 140 if its cylinder capacity is 1,400 cubic centimetres or less,
(b) 175 if its cylinder capacity exceeds 1,400 cubic centimetres but does not exceed 2,000 cubic centimetres, and
(c) 225 or more if its cylinder capacity exceeds 2,000 cubic centimetres.

(5) For the purpose of paragraph 4, the car's cylinder capacity is the capacity of its engine as calculated for the purposes of the Vehicle Excise and Registration Act 1994.

(6) In any case where—
(a) in a prescribed accounting period, there are supplies of fuel for private use to an individual in respect of one car for a part of the period and in respect of another car for another part of the period, and
(b) at the end of that period one of those cars neither belongs to, nor is allocated to, the individual, the flat-rate value of the supplies is determined as if the supplies made to the individual during those parts of the period were in respect of only one car.

(7) (1) Where paragraph 6 applies, the value of the supplies is to be determined as follows—
(a) if each of the 2 or more cars falls within the same description of car specified in the valuation table, the value specified in the valuation table for that description of car applies for the whole of the prescribed accounting period, and
(b) if one of those cars falls within a description of car specified in that table which is different from the others, the value of the supplies is the aggregate of the relevant fractions of the consideration appropriate for each description of car in the valuation table.

(2) 'The relevant fraction' in relation to any car is that which the part of the prescribed accounting period in which fuel was supplied for private use in respect of the car bears to the whole of that period.

(8) 'CO_2 emissions figure' means a CO_2 emissions figure expressed in grams per kilometre driven.

(9) 'UK approval certificate' means a certificate issued under—
(a) Section 58(1) or (4) of the Road Traffic Act 1988, or
(b) Article 31A(4) or (5) of the Road Traffic (Northern Ireland) Order 1981.

(10) 'Company car' means a car that is made available for private use (without any transfer of the property in it) by an employer to an employee, or member of an employee's family or household, by reason of the employee's employment for which fuel is provided for private use.

The flat rate basis may also be used as an alternative to accounting for VAT on the open market value where the fuel is supplied for a consideration below that value (see below).

From 1 January 2014 — withdrawal of partial exemption concession in relation to road fuel scale charges

Prior to 1 January 2014 a concession allowed partly exempt businesses to reduce the road fuel scale charges by applying the partial exemption recovery rate to the scale charges. This meant that the output tax declared on private use fuel was consistent with the input tax deduction on that fuel. From 1 January 2014 this concession has been withdrawn and partly exempt businesses must account for the full amount of the road fuel scale charges applicable to their vehicles.

Input tax will continue to be recoverable in accordance with the business's agreed partial exemption method. HMRC have suggested that the following formula will give a similar overall result to that achieved under the concession previously available.

VAT on fuel scale charges + ((VAT charged on fuel purchased in the period – VAT on fuel scale charges) × the partial exemption recovery rate)

> *Example*
>
> ABC Ltd has a partial exemption recovery rate of 40%. VAT on the scale charge for the period is £300 and VAT of £630 was incurred on fuel purchased. Applying the above formula would result in an input tax recovery of £432, calculated as follows:
>
> £300 + ((£630 – £300) × 40%)
>
> £300 + (£330 x 40%)
>
> £300 + £132 = £432

Although HMRC consider that the above formula gives a similar overall result to that achieved under the concession previously available, they have said that businesses may propose their own alternative. HMRC have also stated that until formal approval is granted businesses should not adopt the above formula or make any other change to their partial exemption calculation method. Any business that wants to change their partial exemption calculation method should contact HMRC.

(HMRC Brief 33/13).

From 17 July 2013 — charge made for private fuel

Where a charge is made for the private use of fuel, there is no deemed supply (since there is an actual supply), and VAT is normally due on the consideration for the supply. If

- a taxable person (P) makes a supply of road fuel for a consideration,
- the recipient of the supply is
  - connected with P, or
  - an employee or partner of P or a person who is connected with such an employee or partner,
- the value of the supply would (apart from these provisions) be less than its open market value, and
- the recipient of the supply is not entitled to credit for the whole of the input tax arising on the supply,

then the value of the supply is to be taken to be an amount equal to its open market value.

This is an anti-avoidance measure to prevent the situation where a nominal charge is made for the fuel. The measure came into force on 11 December 2012, and has effect in relation to supplies made on or after 17 July 2013. As an anti-forestalling measure, it also applies to supplies made in the period beginning on 11 December 2012 and ending immediately before 17 July 2013, if and to the extent that the fuel is not made available to the person to whom it is supplied before the end of that period.

P may alternatively choose to account for VAT under the flat rate basis set out above.

[*VATA 1994, Sch 6 paras A1–C1, 2A; FA 2013, Sch 38*].

De Voil Indirect Tax Service. See V3.163A, V3.266.

Fuel for private use — scale charges

[46.17] The UK is authorised, under *Council Decision 659/2006/EC*, to fix flat-rate scale charges in relation to expenditure on fuel used for private purposes based on the CO2 emissions level of the vehicle. This change aligns the basis of the VAT private use charge with that operated for direct tax purposes.

On 1 February 2014 the *Value Added Tax (Flat-rate Valuation of Supplies of Fuel for Private Use) Order 2013* came into force. The Order requires HMRC to revalorise the scale charges at intervals not exceeding 12 months from the previous revalorisation. The Order also requires HMRC to publish a table containing the revalorised figures and a statement specifying the revalorisation start date prior to that start date. [*SI 2013/2911*]

Determination of CO_2 emissions figure

(a) If a CO_2 emissions figure is specified in relation to a vehicle in an EU certificate of conformity or a UK approval certificate, the vehicle's CO_2 emissions figure for the purposes of the scale charge is determined as follows.
  - (i) If only one figure is specified in the certificate, that figure is the vehicle's CO_2 emissions figure for those purposes.
  - (ii) If more than one figure is specified in the certificate, the figure specified as the CO_2 (combined) emissions figure is the vehicle's CO_2 emissions figure for those purposes.
  - (iii) If separate CO_2 emissions figures are specified for different fuels, the lowest figure specified or, in a case within (ii) above, the lowest CO_2 emissions (combined) figure specified is the vehicle's CO_2 emissions figure for those purposes.
  - (iv) If the vehicle's CO_2 emissions figure (determined in accordance with (i)–(iii) above is not a multiple of five, it is rounded down to the nearest multiple of five for those purposes.

(b) If no EU certificate of conformity or UK approval certificate is issued in relation to a vehicle or no emissions figure is specified in relation to it in any such certificate, the vehicle's CO_2 emissions figure for the purposes of the scale charge is
  - (i) 140 if its cylinder capacity is 1,400cc or less;
  - (ii) 175 if its cylinder capacity exceeds 1,400cc but does not exceed 2,000cc; and
  - (iii) 225 (decreased from 230 from 1.5.11) or more if its cylinder capacity exceeds 2,000cc.

[*VATA 1994, s 57(3)(4A)–(4G)(9)(10); F(No 2)A 2005, s 2; SI 2007/966; SI 2011/898*].

VAT periods beginning on or after 1.5.18

[46.18]

	Annual VAT returns		Quarterly VAT returns		Monthly VAT Returns	
CO_2 emissions, g/km	Scale charge	VAT due at 20%	Scale charge	VAT due at 20%	Scale charge	VAT due at 20%*
	£	£	£	£	£	£
120 or less	562	93.66	140	23.33	46	7.67
125	842	140.33	210	35	70	11.67
130	900	150	224	37.33	74	12.33
135	954	159	238	39.67	79	13.17
140	1,013	168.83	252	42.00	84	14.00
145	1,067	177.83	266	44.33	88	14.67
150	1,125	185.70	280	46.66	93	15.50
155	1,179	196.50	295	49.17	98	16.33
160	1,238	206.33	309	51.50	102	17.00
165	1,292	215.33	323	53.83	107	17.83
170	1,350	225	336	56.00	111	18.50
175	1,404	234.00	351	58.50	116	19.33
180	1,463	243.83	365	60.83	121	20.17
185	1,517	252.83	379	63.17	125	20.83
190	1,575	262.50	393	65.50	130	21.67
195	1,630	271.66	407	67.83	135	22.50
200	1,688	281.33	421	70.17	140	23.33
205	1,742	290.33	436	72.67	145	24.17
210	1,801	300.16	449	74.83	149	24.83
215	1,855	309.17	463	77.17	154	25.67
220	1,913	318.83	477	79.50	159	26.50
225 or more	1,967	327.83	491	81.83	163	27.17

VAT periods beginning on or after 1.5.17 and before 1.5.18

[46.19]

	Annual VAT returns		Quarterly VAT returns		Monthly VAT Returns	
CO_2 emissions, g/km	Scale charge	VAT due at 20%	Scale charge	VAT due at 20%	Scale charge	VAT due at 20%*
	£	£	£	£	£	£
120 or less	563	93.83	140	23.33	46	7.67
125	842	140.33	211	35.17	70	11.67
130	901	150.17	224	37.33	74	12.33
135	955	159.17	238	39.67	79	13.17
140	1,013	168.83	252	42.00	84	14.00
145	1,068	179.00	267	44.50	88	14.67
150	1,126	187.67	281	46.83	93	15.50
155	1,180	196.67	295	49.17	98	16.33
160	1,239	206.50	309	51.50	102	17.00
165	1,293	215.50	323	53.83	107	17.83
170	1,351	225.17	337	56.17	111	18.50
175	1,405	234.17	351	58.50	116	19.33
180	1,464	244.00	365	60.83	121	20.17
185	1,518	253.00	379	63.17	125	20.83
190	1,577	262.83	393	65.50	131	21.83
195	1,631	271.83	408	68.00	136	22.67
200	1,689	281.50	422	70.33	140	23.33
205	1,743	290.50	436	72.67	145	24.17
210	1,802	300.33	449	74.83	149	24.83
215	1,856	309.33	463	77.17	154	25.67
220	1,914	319.00	478	79.67	159	26.50
225 or more	1,696	328.17	492	82.00	163	27.17

VAT periods beginning on or after 1.5.16 and before 1.5.17

[46.20]

	Annual VAT returns		Quarterly VAT returns		Monthly VAT Returns	
CO_2 emissions, g/km	Scale charge	VAT due at 20%	Scale charge	VAT due at 20%	Scale charge	VAT due at 20%*
	£	£	£	£	£	£
120 or less	467	77.83	116	19.33	38	6.33
125	699	116.50	175	29.17	58	9.67
130	747	124.50	186	31.00	61	10.17
135	792	132.00	197	32.83	65	10.83
140	841	140.17	209	34.83	69	11.50
145	886	147.67	221	36.83	73	12.17
150	934	155.67	233	38.83	77	12.83
155	979	163.17	245	40.83	81	13.50
160	1,028	171.33	256	42.67	85	14.17
165	1,073	178.83	268	44.67	89	14.83
170	1,121	186.83	279	46.50	92	15.33
175	1,166	194.33	291	48.50	96	16.00
180	1,214	202.33	303	50.50	101	16.83
185	1,259	209.83	314	52.33	104	17.33
190	1,308	218.00	326	54.33	108	18.00
195	1,353	225.50	338	56.33	112	18.67
200	1,401	233.50	350	58.33	116	19.33
205	1,446	241.00	362	60.33	120	20.00
210	1,495	295.17	373	62.17	123	20.50
215	1,540	256.67	384	64.00	128	21.33
220	1,588	264.67	396	66.00	132	22.00
225 or more	1,633	272.17	408	68.00	135	22.50

VAT periods beginning on or after 1.5.15 and before 1.5.16

[46.21]

CO_2 emissions, g/km	Annual VAT returns		Quarterly VAT returns		Monthly VAT Returns	
	Scale charge	VAT due at 20%	Scale charge	VAT due at 20%	Scale charge	VAT due at 20%*
	£	£	£	£	£	£
120 or less	536	89.33	133	22.17	44	7.33
125	802	133.67	200	33.33	66	11.00
130	857	142.83	213	35.50	70	11.67
135	909	151.50	227	37.83	75	12.50
140	965	160.83	240	40.00	80	13.33
145	1,016	169.33	254	42.33	84	14.00
150	1,072	178.67	267	44.50	88	14.67
155	1,123	187.17	281	46.83	93	15.50
160	1,179	196.50	294	49.00	97	16.17
165	1,231	205.17	308	51.33	102	17.00
170	1,286	214.33	320	53.33	106	17.67
175	1,338	223.00	334	55.67	111	18.50
180	1,393	232.17	347	57.83	115	19.17
185	1,445	240.83	361	60.17	119	19.83
190	1,501	250.17	374	62.33	124	20.67
195	1,552	258.67	388	64.67	129	21.50
200	1,608	268.00	401	66.83	133	22.17
205	1,660	276.67	415	69.17	138	23.00
210	1,715	285.83	428	71.33	142	23.67
215	1,767	294.50	441	73.50	146	24.33
220	1,822	303.67	455	75.83	151	25.17
225 or more	1,874	312.33	468	78.00	155	25.83

Private use of cars or other vehicles and charges to employees

[46.22] If a business has recovered 100% of the VAT on a car or other vehicle and then puts it to private use, it may have to account for VAT but no VAT is due if the car was

- subject to a 50% input tax block; or
- bought under the second-hand margin scheme.

If the employee pays nothing for the use of the vehicle, VAT must be accounted for on the cost of making the car available for private use. This cost will usually include depreciation, repairs and other running costs (but not any VAT the business has recovered as input tax). See **46.7** above for simplified schemes for calculating the VAT due on free private use of stock in trade cars.

If the employee pays a charge for the private use of the car or other vehicle, the business must account for VAT on these charges.

(VAT Notice 700/64/14, paras 6.1–6.6).

Salary sacrifice

Where an employer gives an employee a choice between

(a) a particular rate of wages, salary or emoluments, or
(b) in the alternative a lower rate of wages, etc. and, in addition, the right to the private use of a motor car provided by the employer,

and the employee chooses (*b*) above, then the provision to the employee of the right to use the motor car privately is not liable to VAT to the extent that the consideration is the difference between the wages, etc. available to him under (*a*) and (*b*) above. [*SI 1992/630*].

However, the case of *Astra Zeneca UK Ltd v HMRC, ECJ Case C–40/09*, [2010] STC 2298 (TVC 22.97), has had a significant impact on HMRC's future policy regarding salary sacrifice. In that case, a pharmaceutical company gave its employees face-value vouchers as part of their remuneration. HMRC ruled that this was a supply of services for consideration, which was subject to VAT. The company appealed, contending that it was not making any supply of services but that it should be allowed an input tax deduction on the costs of purchasing and providing the vouchers. The tribunal referred the case to the CJEU. The Court ruled that the provision of a retail voucher by a company, which acquired that voucher at a price including VAT, to its employees in exchange for their giving up part of their cash remuneration constituted a supply of services effected for consideration.

HMRC regard a salary sacrifice arrangement as the consideration for a supply of goods/services. Where that supply is taxable, VAT will be due. In most cases the value of the benefit for VAT purposes will be the same as the amount of salary deducted or the amount forgone. Where this is less than the true value (e.g. where employers supply the benefits at below what it cost to buy them in), the value should be based on the cost to the employer. Most businesses are prevented from recovering VAT in full on the purchase and leasing of company motor cars. The input tax block on cars means that employers do not account for output tax when cars are made available to employees [*SI 1992/3122, Art 4*]. Where VAT recovery is restricted and output VAT is not due the *Astra Zeneca* judgment has no direct impact. Where an employer suffers no input tax restriction, output tax remains due (HMRC Brief 28/11). (HMRC Brief 36/11).

Trading down

Where a business allows employees to trade down to a cheaper model with a smaller salary sacrificed, HMRC accept that no VAT is due and the above provisions can be applied.

Trading up

Where a business allows employees to trade up to a more expensive model than they are entitled to, and a charge is made for the use of the car, the charge made is consideration for a supply.

Sacrificing benefits

There is a general move in industry towards providing a package of benefits for staff as part of the remuneration package (e.g. enhanced termination arrangements, longer holidays, payment of non-pensionable allowances, and private health insurance). Rather than simply sacrificing salary, employees may also effectively sacrifice other routine benefits and entitlements. However, as long as no specific charge is made for the use of the car, HMRC do not regard the sacrificing of routine benefits rather than salary as consideration for a supply.

(Business Brief 9/92).

Second-hand scheme for motor cars

[46.23] In general, VAT is charged on the full value of any goods, including second-hand motor cars, sold by a taxable person. The Treasury may, however, by order, provide for a taxable person to opt to charge VAT on the profit margin (instead of full value). [*VATA 1994, ss 32, 50A: FA 1995, s 24*]. An order under these provisions has been made by *SI 1995/1268* which covers all second-hand goods. The effect of the provisions is that, provided all the conditions are met, the margin scheme may be used to account for VAT only on the amount by which the selling price exceeds the purchase price. The gross margin includes the VAT to be accounted for.

For full details of the margin scheme, see **62 SECOND-HAND GOODS**.

Key points: motor cars

[46.24] Points to consider are as follows.

- A basic principle of VAT law is that input tax cannot be reclaimed on the purchase of a motor car that is available for private use. There must be some physical or legal restriction in place to prevent private use, e.g. in relation to insurance. The question about a vehicle being available for private use is a different question as to whether a vehicle is used 100% of the time for business purposes.
- The input tax restriction above does not apply to a car bought for use by a taxi firm, driving school or car hire business, where the vehicle becomes a tool of trading directly linked to the business. In such cases, there is no problem with claiming input tax on the cost of the vehicle, and the same opportunity is also available to a vehicle used as a genuine pool car arrangement.
- If an input tax block applied on the purchase of a vehicle, then no output tax is due on the subsequent resale of the vehicle in the future. The sale in this situation is exempt from VAT, irrespective of whether the car might be sold at a profit (unlikely anyway because of depreciation).
- If input tax has been reclaimed on the purchase of a car, then output tax must be declared on the full value of any future resale of the vehicle by the business that has claimed input tax.

- It is common practice for many car dealers to sell a new vehicle to a customer, the sale being partly funded by the dealer taking the customer's old vehicle as a part-exchange arrangement. In such cases, there are two transactions taking place. Output tax is due on the full selling price of the new vehicle, even though the net cash payment from the customer will obviously be much lower, i.e. to reflect the part-exchange value.
- An alternative method of a business acquiring a vehicle is through a lease hire arrangement. In these situations, the intention is for the business to use the vehicle for an agreed period (often three years), in return for a monthly hire payment that includes VAT. In this situation, the hirer is able to reclaim 50% input tax on the monthly hire payment, subject to normal rules, unless the use is by a business above (taxi-firm, car hire business etc.) in which case 100% input tax recovery is allowed.
- An important concession is that HMRC allows full input tax recovery on the repair costs of a vehicle (subject to normal rules, e.g. vehicle not used for exempt activities), as long as the vehicle has some business use. It is accepted that the vehicle must be in a good state of repair in order to carry out business journeys. This opportunity to claim input tax also extends to the private vehicles of employees, as long as the repair cost is paid by the business and the vehicle has some business use.
- Input tax can be fully reclaimed on road fuel purchased for a business car, or private car used for business purposes, as long as output tax is accounted for on private use based on a scale charge system. The only alternatives to adopting the scale charge are for input tax to be apportioned on a mileage basis between business and non-business/private use or for no input tax at all to be reclaimed on road fuel.
- The opportunity to avoid a scale charge payment by not claiming input tax on road fuel bought by the business applies to all road fuel purchases, not just fuel bought in relation to motor cars. This requirement could work against a business that buys road fuel that is used for commercial vehicles, e.g. vans or lorries.
- Input tax can be claimed by a business on the fuel element of any mileage allowance paid to an employee. HMRC assist this process by producing fuel advisory rates normally four times a year, which are accurate in most cases. A condition of claiming input tax in such cases is that the employee should include tax invoices with his mileage claim, ensuring that the VAT on the invoices is equal to or greater than the VAT being claimed on the mileage rate.
- The fuel scale charges are based on CO2 emissions. The rates are usually revised by HMRC on an annual basis in May. The amounts of output tax payable will also change, as a matter of course, when there is a change in the standard rate of VAT.

47

Northern Ireland

[47.1] The provisions of the *VATA 1994* apply to Northern Ireland [*VATA 1994, s 101(3)*] but not the Republic of Ireland.

Refund of VAT to Government of Northern Ireland

HMRC must refund to the NI Government any VAT charged on

- the supply of goods or services to that Government,
- the acquisition of goods by that Government from another EU member state, or
- the importation of any goods by that Government from a place outside the EU

after deducting an amount (agreed between HMRC and the Department of Finance and Personnel for NI) attributable to supplies, acquisitions and importations for the purposes of a business carried on by that Government.

[*VATA 1994, s 99*].

See also **44.11 LOCAL AUTHORITIES AND PUBLIC BODIES** for supplies by 'government departments', including those in NI.

Key points: Northern Ireland

[47.2] Points to consider are as follows.

- The standard rate of VAT is higher in the Republic of Ireland (23%) compared to Northern Ireland (20%). This means there may be an incentive for Republic of Ireland shoppers and some businesses not able to reclaim VAT to buy goods and services in Northern Ireland.
- A potential planning point could allow a small business registered for VAT in Northern Ireland to use the flat-rate scheme to calculate its VAT payments due to HMRC each quarter, but then also benefit from VAT recovery on some expenses bought in the Republic of Ireland, i.e. VAT reclaim is made by making an overseas VAT claim to the Republic of Ireland under the electronic refund system. This approach has been adopted by some transport-related businesses registered for VAT in Northern Ireland that buy road fuel in the Republic of Ireland. A flat-rate scheme user cannot reclaim input tax on expenses paid in its own country, unless it relates to capital expenditure goods costing more than £2,000 including VAT.

48

Output Tax

Cross-references. See **2.10 ACCOUNTING PERIODS AND RETURNS** for goods sold in satisfaction of a debt by a person selling under a power of sale; **7 BAD DEBT RELIEF**; **21 EXEMPT SUPPLIES**; **24.12 FINANCIAL SERVICES** for output tax under hire purchase, conditional sale and credit sale agreements; **56.3–56.17 RATES OF VAT** for changes in the rate of tax; **60.40 REGISTRATION** for output tax on the deemed supply of business assets when a trader is deregistered; **61 RETAIL SCHEMES** for special schemes for retailers; **62 SECOND-HAND GOODS** for special schemes in operation for such goods; **63.2 SELF-SUPPLY** for output tax on stationery produced and used by partly exempt traders; **72.24 VALUATION** for calculation of output tax where discounts are allowed; **75 ZERO-RATED SUPPLIES.**

De Voil Indirect Tax Service. See V3.5.

Introduction to output tax

[48.1] Output tax in relation to a 'taxable person' means VAT on

- supplies which he makes; and
- acquisitions of goods by him from another EU member state (including VAT which is also counted as input tax under **35.1 INPUT TAX**).

A '*taxable person*' is a person who is, or is required to be, registered under *VATA 1994*.

[*VATA 1994, s 3(1), s 24(2)*].

Output tax on supplies

A taxable person must charge VAT on any taxable supply of goods or services made in the UK in the course or furtherance of any business carried on by him.

A '*taxable supply*' is a supply of goods or services made in the UK other than an exempt supply. [*VATA 1994, s 4*]. See **9.1 BUSINESS** for the meaning of 'business'. For VAT purposes the UK includes the territorial sea of the UK (i.e. waters within twelve nautical miles of the coast-line).

The output tax is normally the liability of the person making the supply. [*VATA 1994, s 1(2)*]. As a general rule, the determination of the liability of VAT is the responsibility of the supplier. In certain special cases, a supply can be zero-rated where a customer gives the supplier a declaration claiming eligibility for such treatment. Under these circumstances, if the supplier, despite having taken all reasonable steps to check the validity of the declaration, fails to identify any inaccuracy and, in good faith, makes the supply at the zero rate, HMRC will not seek to recover the VAT due from the supplier. (VAT Notice 48, ESC 3.11).

The VAT becomes due at the time of supply [*VATA 1994, s 1(2)*] but in practice is accounted for and paid by reference to tax returns completed for VAT accounting periods. See **2 ACCOUNTING PERIODS AND RETURNS** and **52 PAYMENT OF VAT**.

Certain small businesses are allowed to account for VAT on the basis of cash received and/or by means of only one VAT return a year. See **64 SPECIAL SCHEMES**.

Output tax on acquisitions

See **20.3 EUROPEAN UNION: SINGLE MARKET** for tax on acquisitions from other EU member states.

Rates of output tax

There are currently three main rates of output tax, standard rate (20%), reduced rate (5%) and zero rate (0%). See **75 ZERO-RATED SUPPLIES** for the effects of zero-rating and the categories of goods and services to which it applies. See **59 REDUCED RATE SUPPLIES** for a 5% reduced rate applying to a limited number of supplies.

VAT fraction

[48.2] Normally, VAT is calculated at the appropriate percentage of a price which has first been decided without VAT and the VAT invoice shows these separate amounts. Sometimes, however, VAT has to be calculated from a price in which it is already included (e.g. in a less detailed tax invoice). To do this, the VAT fraction is required.

$$\text{VAT fraction} = \frac{\text{rate of VAT}}{100 + \text{rate of VAT}}$$

Rate of VAT	*VAT fraction*
Standard rate 20%	1/6
Reduced rate 5%	1/21

> *Example*
>
> In June 2016 M refills his car with petrol and receives a less detailed invoice totalling £36.78.
>
> The VAT included is £36.78 × 1/6 = £6.13

Apportionment of monetary consideration

[48.3] A single monetary consideration may be the payment for two or more supplies of different liabilities. In such a situation, the business must allocate a fair proportion of the total payment to each of the supplies. [*VATA 1994, s 19(4)*]. The legislation prescribes no set method by which this is to be achieved. The commonest methods are based upon the costs incurred in making the supplies or the normal selling prices of the supplies. Various methods of apportionment are considered in **48.4** below.

Apportionment is only necessary where the price charged is the only consideration for the supplies. If the consideration is not wholly in money, VAT must be accounted for as explained in **72.5 VALUATION**.

However, before an apportionment calculation is carried out, the following questions should be considered in order to determine whether an apportionment is appropriate and, if it is, what supplies it relates to.

(a) **Is there more than one supply?** It is important to distinguish between a single (composite) supply and a multiple (mixed) supply. In a single supply (e.g. air travel and catering during the flight), there is only one overall type of supply and one VAT liability with no scope for apportionment. In a multiple supply, a single inclusive price is charged for a number of separate supplies of goods or services each with their own VAT liability. See **65.6 SUPPLY: GENERAL** for further details.

(b) **Is there a single consideration?** Apportionment can only be applied to a single consideration that is given in return for more than one supply. If each supply has its own consideration, then there is no power under the *VATA 1994* to reapportion the value between them, although it is possible that the arrangement can be challenged if it is purely a 'sham'. See, for example, *Charlesworth (t/a Centurions)* (VTD 9015) (TVC 38.39) regarding the apportionment of profits between a second-hand car and an additional charge for a warranty.

    In practice it is not always simple to distinguish between a payment that is a single consideration and a payment that is made up of several considerations that appear to be one because they are made simultaneously. There is no definitive test as to whether there are one or more considerations in any given case but it is likely that the customer has to know the charge for each particular supply before it can be accepted that there is more than one consideration. See *Thorn EMI plc; Granada plc* (VTD 9782) (TVC 38.9).

(c) **What are the liabilities of the supplies in question?** All the supplies to which a consideration relates must be identified and their respective liabilities established. Where all supplies are liable to VAT at the same rate, output tax due is calculated in the normal way and no apportionment is necessary. Otherwise the tax value of each supply must be calculated in order to arrive at the total output tax due.

Example 1

John takes a flight from London to Edinburgh (supply of zero-rated air travel). During the journey, he receives a cup of tea and a biscuit (supply of standard-rated catering).

In this case, the purpose of John's expenditure is to benefit from the air travel. The cup of tea and biscuit serves no other purpose than to make the flying experience more comfortable for him, i.e. it is incidental to the main supply. The whole of the payment made by John will be zero-rated as far as VAT is concerned.

Example 2

John and Jean have booked a day trip on the Orient Express. As well as the comfortable rail journey, their trip also includes a five-course meal with wine and champagne. The rail journey is zero-rated for VAT – catering supplies are standard-rated.

Imagine the likely response of John and Jean if they boarded the train and were suddenly told that the five-course meal was not available and they were only going to benefit from the train journey. They would almost certainly complain to the rail company and demand a refund of part of their fee. In other words, they expect to receive two very distinct benefits – the rail journey and the meal.

The five-course meal is an aim in itself, and cannot be dismissed as incidental to the rail travel. The rail company must account for output tax on the value of the catering supply – the rail travel can be zero-rated.

Example 3

Steve has decided to go and watch a football match at the ground of Hale Town. Hale Town is VAT-registered and charges Steve £10 for admission and, as a special offer just for today's match, his admission fee includes two hamburgers and a portion of chips.

In this situation, the supplies involved (admission fee to watch a football match and supply of catering when inside the ground) are both standard-rated. No VAT problem here – output tax of £1.67 is due on the full price (£10 × 1/6 – assuming a VAT rate of 20%).

Methods of apportionment

[48.4] Although *VATA 1994, s 19(4)* provides for apportionment of consideration, it does not stipulate how this has to be done, simply that the values attributed to the various supplies are 'properly attributable', i.e. on a fair and reasonable basis. There are two basic apportionment methods that, with appropriate adaptations, can be used in most circumstances. One of these uses the costs attributable to the different supplies being made, the other is based upon the normal selling prices. However, a business is not obliged to use these methods and can propose any method of apportionment. HMRC have no power to insist that any particular method must be used unless a business refuses to make an apportionment calculation or declines to change a method that produces an unfair result.

Cost-based method of apportionment where costs of all supplies can be identified

Example 1: Apportionment based on cost of both supplies: VAT-inclusive price

A VAT-inclusive price of £142 is charged for a supply of zero-rated goods that cost £23 and standard-rated goods that cost £40 (excluding VAT).

Proportion of the total cost represented by standard-rated goods =	
(40 + VAT) ÷ ([40 + VAT] + 23) = 48/71	
VAT-inclusive price of standard-rated goods = 48/71 × £140 =	£96
VAT included = £94 × VAT fraction = £96 × 1/6 =	£16
Tax value of zero-rated supply = £140 – £96 =	£46
Total price is therefore apportioned	
Value of standard-rated supply	80
VAT on standard-rated supply	16
Value of zero-rated supply	46
	£142

Example 2: Apportionment based on cost of both supplies: VAT-exclusive price

A VAT-exclusive price of £126 is charged for a supply of zero-rated goods that cost £23 and standard-rated goods that cost £40 (excluding VAT).

Proportion of the total cost represented by standard-rated goods = 40/63	
VAT-exclusive value of standard-rated goods = 40/63 × £126 =	£80
VAT on standard-rated goods = £80 × 20% =	£16
Tax value of zero-rated supplies = £126 – £80 =	£46
Total price is therefore	
Value of standard-rated supply	80
Value of zero-rated supply	46
	126
VAT on £80 at 20%	16
	£142

Costs-based method of apportionment where the costs of only one supply can be identified

Difficulties are more likely to be met where it is only possible to directly attribute costs to one of the supplies involved. This is particularly the case if the supply to which a direct attribution of costs is not possible is a significant element of the outputs. Two methods of apportionment have been approved by VAT tribunals in such cases.

In *IC Thomas* (VTD 1862) (TVC 67.125) admission to a greyhound stadium (standard-rated) included the provision of a programme (zero-rated) and it was not possible to directly attribute any costs to the supply of admission. The tribunal approved an apportionment which applied a 'mark-up' to the costs that could be directly attributed, deducted this figure from the total selling price and treated the remainder as the value of the other supply. If appropriate, the figures derived from a sampling exercise in this way can be expressed as a percentage and applied to total relevant income over a period. (Note that, following the decision in *Card Protection Plan v C & E Commrs, ECJ Case C–349/96*, [1999] STC 270 (TVC 22.375) HMRC now expect that, in the majority of cases such as this, there is a single supply of standard-rated admission, the programme being an ancillary item.)

In *BH Bright* (VTD 4577) (TVC 67.125) which was concerned with membership fees of a dating agency, the approved method of apportionment similarly applied a 'mark-up' to the costs that could be directly attributed (annual cost of zero-rated literature). It then calculated the uplifted figure as a percentage of the total costs for the year, arriving at a proportion of costs attributable to zero-rated supplies and, by deduction, the proportion attributable to standard-rated supplies. The latter proportion was then applied to subscription income for the year to arrive at the consideration for standard-rated supplies and consequently the output tax due.

Arguments that standard-rated items are supplied at cost and all profits are derived from exempt or zero-rated supplies are likely to be rejected. See *Waterhouse Coaches Ltd* (VTD 1417) (TVC 67.122) and *Tynewydd Labour Working Men's Club and Institute Ltd v C & E Commrs*, QB [1979] STC 570 (TVC 24.12).

Example 3: Apportionment based on the cost of one supply only

A VAT-inclusive price of £142 is charged for a supply of zero-rated goods that cost £26 and standard-rated services, the cost of which cannot be identified. A fair and reasonable uplift on the zero-rated goods, consistent with actual profit margins of the business, is 50%.

Value of zero-rated supplies = £26 + 50% =	£39.00
VAT-inclusive price of standard-rated goods = £142 – £39 =	£103.00
VAT on standard-rated goods = £103 × 1/6 =	£17.17
The total price is therefore apportioned	
Value of zero-rated supply	39.00
Value of standard-rated supply	85.83
	124.83
VAT on £85.83 at 20%	17.17
	£142.00

Example 4: Apportionment based on the cost of one supply only—annual calculation using the method approved in Thomas

Assume that the figures in Example 3 above are representative of similar transactions and the total VAT-inclusive income from such transactions in the year is £25,000.

Zero-rated percentage = 39/142 × 100 =	27.465%
Value of zero-rated supplies in year = £25,000 × 27.465%	£6,866
Consideration for standard-rated supplies in year =	
£25,000 – £6,866 =	£18,134
Output tax due = £18,134 × 1/6 =	£3,022.33

Example 5: Apportionment based on the cost of one supply only—annual calculation using the method approved in Bright

A VAT-inclusive subscription income of £400,000 is received in a year in respect of supplies of zero-rated literature with direct costs of £42,000 and standard-rated services, the direct cost of which cannot be identified. The total costs of the business (excluding depreciation) amount to £250,000 in the year. A fair and reasonable uplift to the direct costs of the zero-rated literature to allow for indirect costs is 100%.

Direct cost of zero-rated supplies	42,000
Uplift of 100%	42,000
Full cost of providing zero-rated supplies	£84,000
Proportion of costs attributable to zero-rated supplies =	
84,000/250,000 × 100 =	33.6%
Proportion of costs attributable to standard-rated supplies =	66.4%
Consideration for standard-rated supplies =	
£400,000 × 66.4% =	£265,600.00
Output tax = £265,600.00 × 1/6 =	£44,266.67

Apportionment based upon normal selling prices (market values)

This method is based on the prices the particular business normally charges for supplies, when made for separate considerations, and uses these amounts to apportion a single consideration given in return for comparable supplies.

Example 6: Apportionment based on normal selling-prices: VAT-inclusive price

A VAT-inclusive price of £200 is charged for a zero-rated supply (which would separately be charged at £50) and a standard-rated supply (which would separately be charged at £200 including VAT).

Proportion of the total normal price represented by standard-rated goods = 200 ÷ (200 + 50) = 4/5	
VAT-inclusive price of standard-rated goods = 4/5 × £200 =	£160.00
VAT included = £160 × VAT fraction = £160 × 1/6 =	£26.67
Tax value of zero-rated supply = £200 – £160	£40.00
The total price is therefore apportioned	
Value of standard-rated supply (£160 – £26.67)	133.33
VAT on standard-rated supply	26.67
Value of zero-rated supply	40.00
	£200.00

(VAT Notice 700, paras 8.1, 32.1, 32.2).

Business gifts

[48.5] For VAT purposes, an article is a gift where the donor is not obliged to give it and the recipient is not obliged to do or give anything in return. (VAT Notice 700, para 8.9). Business gifts cover a wide range of items including

- brochures, posters and advertising matter;
- 'executive presents';
- long service awards (see *RHM Bakeries (Northern) Ltd v C & E Commrs*, QB 1978, [1979] STC 72 (TVC 62.9));
- retirement gifts;
- goods supplied to employees under attendance or safety at work schemes;
- items distributed to trade customers;
- prizes dispensed from amusement and gaming machines (see **8.4 BETTING AND GAMING**); and
- prizes of goods in betting and gaming and free lotteries (see **8.2 BETTING AND GAMING**).

(VAT Notice 700/7/12, para 2.2).

Gifts of goods

A gift of business assets (including land) is a supply of goods [*VATA 1994, Sch 4 paras 5(1), 9; FA 2007, s 99(3)*] and is taxable as such subject to certain exceptions and special rules, including the following.

(a) There is no supply (and no VAT liability arises) unless the donor (or any of his 'predecessors') has or will become entitled to
   (i) credit for the whole or any part of the input tax on the supply, acquisition or importation of the goods or of anything comprised in them; or

(ii) a refund of VAT on the supply or importation of those goods (or anything comprised in them) under the rules for refunds of VAT to persons established in other EU member states (see **18.9 EUROPEAN UNION GENERAL**) or the *EC 13th Directive* (refunds of VAT to persons established outside the EU, see **49.5 OVERSEAS TRADERS**).

For this purpose, a person is the '*predecessor*' of the donor where the donor acquired the goods from him under a transaction relating to the transfer of a business as a going concern which was treated as neither a supply of goods nor a supply or services (see **9.9** *et seq* **BUSINESS**). The donor's predecessors include the predecessors of his predecessor through any number of transactions. The effect of this is that, for no VAT liability to arise, no entitlement to input tax on the goods must have arisen through any number of such going concern transactions. [*VATA 1994, Sch 4 para 5(5)(5A)*].

The wording in (i) above is derived from *Directive 2006/112/EC, Art 16*. This was considered in *Finanzamt Burgdorf v Fischer, ECJ Case C–322/99*, [2001] STC 1356 (TVC 22.173) where a car dealer who had not reclaimed input tax on the initial purchase of a vintage car subsequently did so on substantial repairs to it. On ceasing to trade he retained the car as a private asset. The CJEU held that the effect of *Art 16* was that VAT was payable on 'component parts' in respect of which input tax had been deducted (but not on the whole value of the car, since input tax had not been reclaimable on its initial purchase). The taxable amount for this purpose should be determined by reference to the price, at the time of the allocation, of the goods incorporated in the vehicle which constitute component parts of the goods allocated. Furthermore, where input tax had been reclaimed but there was no output tax liability under *Art 16* (e.g. on extensive bodywork repairs which did not involve the addition of component parts), the input tax deducted had to be adjusted under *Directive 2006/112/EC, Arts 184, 185* where the value of the work in question had not been entirely consumed in the context of the business activity of the taxable person before the vehicle was allocated to his private assets.

(b) There is no supply (and no VAT liability arises) on a gift of goods made in the course or furtherance of a business where 'the cost to the donor of acquiring or producing the goods', together with the cost of any other such business gifts made to the same person in 'the same year', was not more than £50. '*The same year*' means any period of twelve months that includes the day on which the gift is made.

In *EMI Group plc v HMRC, ECJ Case C–581/08* [2010] STC 2609, the Court held that what is now *Directive 2006/112/EC, Art 16* did not preclude national legislation that fixed a monetary ceiling for gifts made to the same person within a set period, but it did preclude a presumption that gifts to different individuals having the same employer were to be treated as gifts to 'the same person'.

In determining the '*cost to the donor of acquiring or producing the goods*', where the donor acquired the goods under a transaction relating to the transfer of a business as a going concern which was treated as neither a supply of goods nor a supply or services (see **9.9** *et*

seq **BUSINESS**), the donor and his 'predecessors' are treated as if they were the same person. For this purpose, a '*predecessor*' is the transferor under such a transaction and a person's predecessors include the predecessors of his predecessor through any number of transactions. The effect of this is that the cost of the goods gifted remains unchanged by the transfer of a business as a going concern through any number of such transfers.
[*VATA 1994, Sch 4 para 5(2)(2A)*].

(c) Samples (see **48.7**(28) below).

(d) No VAT is due on free meals or drinks to employees by way of catering (see **12.8 CATERING**) or the provision of accommodation for employees in a hotel, etc. (see **33.3 HOTELS AND HOLIDAY ACCOMMODATION**). [*VATA 1994, Sch 6 para 10*].

(e) No further VAT may be due where additional goods or services are offered with normal taxable supplies as part of a business promotion (see **72 TRADE PROMOTION SCHEMES**).

(f) Prizes donated for competitions in newspapers and magazines (for which special rules apply, see **58.14 RECREATION AND SPORT**).

(g) Free fuel to employees for private use (for which special rules apply, see **46.16 MOTOR CARS**).

(h) Free meals or drinks to non-employees is not normally a supply and no VAT is due (but see **10 BUSINESS ENTERTAINMENT** for non-deductible input tax).

(i) A gift of goods for sale, export or letting by a charity (or a taxable person who is a profits-to-charity person) is zero-rated. See **13.7 CHARITIES**.

(j) Where a business consists of promoting a sporting, entertainment or similar activity and
- the business does no more than organise an event at which trophies are given away,
- there is no other associated competition/event, and
- a charge is made for admission to see the presentation

no further VAT is due on the 'gift' of the trophies because part of the admission charge is regarded as being payment for the trophies and VAT will have been accounted for on that supply.
(VAT Notice 700/7/12, para 2.6).

Input tax on goods purchased for business gifts is deductible. If the recipient of the goods also uses them for business purposes, that person can recover any VAT charged on the gift as input tax (subject to the normal rules). The donor cannot issue a VAT invoice (because there is no consideration) but see **40.2 INVOICES** for the form of a VAT certificate which can be issued instead.

Value of the supply

Where a gift of goods is a taxable supply, the value of the goods on which VAT must be accounted for is the price the person would have to pay (excluding VAT), at the time of the supply, to purchase goods *identical* in every respect (including age and condition) to the goods concerned. Where that value cannot be ascertained, the price for the purchase of goods *similar* to, and of the same age and condition as, the goods concerned must be used. If that value is also not possible to ascertain, the cost of producing the goods concerned at that time is to be used. [*VATA 1994, Sch 6 para 6*].

A gift of services

Where the recipient is not required to do or give anything in return is generally not a taxable supply. See, however, **48.6** below where bought-in services are used by any person outside the business free of charge.

Inducements, etc.

Goods or services supplied on condition that a purchase is made or some action is performed of benefit are not true gifts but constitute supplies in return for non-monetary consideration. This includes articles supplied under 'self-introduction' or 'introduce-a-friend' schemes by retail mail order companies where the introducer has a contractual right to receive the chosen articles. See **72.5 VALUATION** and *GUS Merchandise Corporation Ltd v C & E Commrs*, CA [1981] STC 569 (TVC 58.1) and *Empire Stores Ltd v C & E Commrs, ECJ Case C–33/93*, [1994] STC 623 (TVC 22.256). See also *C & E Commrs v Westmorland Motorway Services Ltd*, CA [1998] STC 431 (TVC 67.152) where free meals given to coach drivers as an inducement to stop at a motorway service station were held to be valued at the normal retail price of the meals.

Private or non-business use

[48.6] Private or non-business use is treated as follows:

(1) Goods

Special rules apply to private use of road fuel and motor cars. See **46.16** and **46.22 MOTOR CARS** respectively.

Otherwise, where, by or under the direction of a person carrying on a business, goods held or used for the purpose of the business are

- put to any private use, or
- used, or made available to any person for use, for any non-business purpose

a supply of services is treated as taking place (whether or not there is any consideration for the supply). [*VATA 1994, Sch 4 para 5(4)*].

This provision does not apply to any

- interest in land;
- building or part of a building;
- civil engineering work or part of such a work;
- goods incorporated or to be incorporated in a building or civil engineering work (whether by being installed as fixtures or fittings or otherwise);

- ship, boat or other vessel, or
- aircraft.

[*VATA 1994, Sch 4 para 5(4A)*].

There is no supply (and no VAT liability arises) where

- no consideration is received; and
- the person carrying on the business (or any of his 'predecessors') has not or will not become entitled to credit for *any* of the input tax on the supply, acquisition or importation of the goods.

For this purpose, a person is a '*predecessor*' of the person carrying on the business where the later acquired the goods from the predecessor under a transaction relating to the transfer of a business as a going concern (TOGC) which was treated as neither a supply of goods nor a supply or services (see **9.9** *et seq* **BUSINESS**). A person's predecessors include the predecessors of his predecessor through any number of transactions. The effect of this is that, for no VAT liability to arise, no entitlement to input tax on the goods must have arisen through any number of such TOGCs.

[*VATA 1994, Sch 4 para 5(5)(5A), para 9*].

The provisions set out below determine the value of the supply and therefore the VAT due. They apply in cases where the 'Lennartz' mechanism has been used for the initial recovery of input tax on the purchase of the goods. See **35.7 INPUT TAX.**

Value of supply where consideration is given: the value of the supply will normally be the consideration actually given although HMRC may direct the value to be the open market value in the case of transactions between connected parties. See **72.10 VALUATION**. See also **72.5 VALUATION** where any of the consideration is non-monetary.

Value of the supply where no consideration is given: except in the cases covered by **72.27 VALUATION** (supplies of accommodation and catering by employers to employees) output tax is due on the 'full cost' of the goods to the person making the relevant supply (or any of his predecessors) who was entitled to credit for the input tax. [*VATA 1994, Sch 6 para 7; SI 1995/2518, Reg 116B*].

'*Full cost*' is determined by reference to taxable VAT-bearing costs of the goods/asset, excluding the VAT itself. If any of the costs of purchase, acquisition or construction are either exempt or zero-rated they should not be included in the 'full cost' of the goods (see *Finanzamt München III v Mohsche, ECJ Case C–193/91*, [1997] STC 195 (TVC 22.198)). All VAT-bearing costs of obtaining the asset are included, even if there are elements that do not depreciate (e.g. the value of bare land). See *J & S Wollny v Finanzamt Landshut, CJEC Case C–72/05* [2008] STC 1618 (TVC 22.276).

The cost of obtaining the goods or asset is then spread over a period called the 'economic life'. The cost attributed to a particular VAT return period is then multiplied by the percentage of private/non-business use in that period to give the 'full cost' of the deemed supplies of making the goods or asset available for private/non-business use in that VAT return period.

After the end of the economic life, the deemed supplies cease as no charge can arise if, at the time when the goods are made available, they have no economic life. [*SI 1995/1268, Art 10A*].

(VAT Information Sheet 14/07, paras 2.9.1, 2.9.2).

The provisions are considered in more detail below.

(a) Economic life of goods

Detailed rules were introduced from 1 November 2007 to regulate the use of the 'Lennartz' mechanism. Where an asset has a long economic life, it is possible that output tax is still being charged in relation to expenditure that was incurred before the current rules took effect. However, that is likely to be rare in practice. The following section describes the rules that apply to expenditure incurred under the present law.

Goods held or used for the purposes of a business have an economic life beginning on the day when they are first used for any purpose after they have been supplied to, or acquired or imported by, a person (or any of his predecessors) and lasting for a period of

- 120 months in the case of land, a building or part of a building, and
- 60 months for all other goods

unless the economic life of the interest of a person (or any of his predecessors), in land and/or buildings begins at a time when that interest has less than 120 months to run. In such a case, the economic life is limited to the number of months remaining before expiry of that interest (and the value of B in the formula in (*b*) below and D in the formula in (*d*) below are reduced accordingly). This would apply where, for example, a taxable person acquires a short lease with five years left to run.

See also (*c*) and (*d*) below.

[*SI 1995/2518, Regs 116C, 116D*]. (VAT Information Sheet 14/07, paras 2.9.2, 2.9.3).

Where a taxable person has acquired the goods from a predecessor as part of a TOGC, the 'full cost' is based on the taxable asset cost incurred by their predecessor and the economic life starts on the predecessor's first use. The taxable person will therefore need to confirm this cost and date with the predecessor if there is a possibility of private/non-business use of the asset. (VAT Information Sheet 14/07, para 2.9.4).

Before 1 November 2007 there were no statutory periods, but HMRC guidance said that the calculation for private/non-business use of land or buildings should be made over 20 years and the calculation for other goods should be made over five years.

(b) Value of the deemed supply

Subject to below and (*c*) and (*d*) below, the value of the deemed supply is the amount determined using the formula

$$(A \div B) \times (C \times U\%)$$

where

A = the number of months in the VAT period during which the deemed supply occurs and which fall within the economic life of the goods concerned;

B = the number of months of the economic life of the goods concerned or, in the case of an economic life beginning on 1 November 2007 by virtue of (*d*) below, what would have been its duration if it had been determined according to (*a*) above or (*c*) below as appropriate;

C = the full cost of the goods excluding any increase resulting from a supply of goods or services giving rise to a new economic life; and

U% = the extent, expressed as a percentage, to which the goods are put to any private/non-business use as compared with the total use made of the goods during the part of the VAT period occurring within the economic life of the goods.

If A or B is not a whole number of months, it must be computed to two decimal places. For example, the period from 8 February 2016 to 31 March 2016 is one month (March) and 22/29 of another month (February), i.e. 1.76 months to two decimal places.

There is no prescribed method for determining the non-business use percentage of the goods although the method must arrive at a fair and reasonable figure and must reflect the actual use of the goods. For example, in respect of a piece of machinery the appropriate measure may be by reference to hours of usage of the machinery while in respect of a building the appropriate measure may be by reference to the floor area occupied for private/non-business activities.

It should be noted that U% is based on use of the goods so where, for example, in a 90-day VAT return period a yacht is used 10 days for private purposes, 10 days for business purposes and is unused for 70 days, U% is 50% (10/20) and not 11.11% (10/90).

[*SI 1995/2518, Reg 116E*]. (VAT Information Sheet 14/07, para 2.10.1).

Non-use of goods in a VAT period: where a VAT period in which a deemed supply occurs immediately follows a VAT period during which the goods in question were not used (or made available for use) for *any* purpose (i.e. there was no business or non-business/private use), A in the formula above must (without prejudice to any other element of the formula) comprise the total number of months falling within the economic life concerned covered by

- the VAT period in which the deemed supply occurs; and
- all preceding VAT periods which began after the end of the VAT period during which the goods were last used (or made available for use) for any purpose before the VAT period in which the deemed supply occurs.

This situation is particularly common with yachts (which are removed from the water during winter) and buildings (which may close for refurbishment)

[*SI 1995/2518, Reg 116F*]. (VAT Information Sheet 14/07, para 2.10.2).

Example 1

A taxable person buys a yacht for £1,000,000 plus £200,000 VAT at the start of his three-month VAT return period ending 31 January 2016. He decides to make the yacht wholly a business asset and recovers all of the VAT incurred as input tax. Private usage of the yacht in the VAT period to 31 January 2016 is 50%.

The 'economic life' of a yacht is 60 months and the 'full cost' is £1,000,000. Applying the formula above, the net value of the deemed supply is

3/60 × (£1,000,000 × 50%) = £25,000

The output tax due is £25,000 × 20% × £5,000

Assuming that the private use percentage and the VAT rate do not change, the output tax due over the yacht's economic life will be

£5,000 × 20 VAT return periods = £100,000

which is 50% of the total VAT incurred on purchase.

Example 2

The facts are the same as in *Example 1*. The yacht is unused (for business or non-business/private purposes) throughout the VAT return period ended 30 April 2016 so that no output tax is due. In the VAT return period ended 31 July 2016, the yacht is again used and private usage is 50%.

The 'economic life' of a yacht is 60 months and the 'full cost' of the asset is £1,000,000 (as before). Applying the formula above, A must be taken to be 6 months (to include the previous VAT period when the yacht was unused) and the net value of the deemed supply is

6/60 × (£1,000,000 × 50%) = £50,000

The output tax due is £50,000 × 20% = £10,000

(c) Subsequent increase in 'full cost' of goods

Where

- a supply of goods or services is made to a person (or any of his predecessors) in respect of any goods held or used for the purposes of a business (whether or not the goods have an economic life in relation to that person at that time),
- VAT is chargeable on that supply which is eligible (in whole or part) for input tax credit, and
- by virtue of that supply, the 'full cost' of the goods is greater than their full cost immediately before that supply,

without prejudice to any other economic life having effect in relation to those goods, a new economic life must be treated as commencing in respect of them in accordance with (*a*) above as if they had been supplied, acquired or imported at the time when the supply of goods or services is made.

The calculation of the value of a deemed supply made during a new economic life in accordance with the formula in (*b*) above is varied so that

(i) C is the increase in the full cost of the goods resulting from the supply of the goods or services giving rise to the new economic life; and

(ii) U% is the extent, expressed as a percentage, to which the goods are put to any private/non-business use as compared with the total use made of the goods during the part of the VAT period occurring during the new economic life of the goods.

Where a deemed supply occurs in relation to goods that have two or more economic lives at the time when the private/non-business use takes place, the value of that supply is such amount as represents the total of the amounts calculated in respect of those economic lives.

[*SI 1995/2518, Regs 116G–116I*].

This situation will arise where a taxable person already has an existing asset (e.g. land or a building) which has commenced or completed its 'economic life'. The first use of a new building on the land, or an extension or annex to the building is treated as the commencement of a new 'economic life'. Although under UK law there is only one asset (the land), the asset is treated as having two economic lives (which may overlap), each with its own related costs (e.g. the cost of the land and the cost of the building where a building is constructed on previously used land). The deemed supply value calculation for a VAT return period is done separately for each economic life that is running in the period and the results added together. (VAT Information Sheet 14/07, para 2.9.5).

(d) Transitional provisions

The legislation applying with effect from 1 November 2007 contains specific provisions to assist with the transition from a pre-existing 'Lennartz' calculation. The change principally affects existing calculations for land and buildings (where the 'economic life' of an asset has now normally been set at ten years whereas a period of 20 years was used before that date) although it may apply to other goods where the taxable person has used a different 'economic life' from the five years required by the new legislation.

The transitional provisions should have no effect if the asset is not land or buildings and before 1 November 2007 the taxable person was already using a five-year basis for calculating 'Lennartz' charges. For details of the transitional rules, consult *Tolley's Value Added 2015-16, Second Edition.*

[*SI 1995/2518, Regs 116J–116M*]. (VAT Information Sheet 14/07, paras 2.9.2, 2.12).

For worked examples of the transitional provisions, see VAT Information Sheet 14/07, para 2.12.

(e) Cessation of provisions

The charging provisions cease to apply in the following circumstances.

- At the end of the asset's economic life or lives.
- On sale of the asset. On sale, the asset ceases to be an asset of the business and therefore the charging provisions cease to apply. Where appropriate, VAT is chargeable on the disposal proceeds.

- On disposal of the asset for no consideration or on taking the asset into wholly private/non-business use. As with a sale, the asset ceases to be an asset of the business and the charging provisions cease to apply. In this case, there may be a deemed supply of the asset under *VATA 1994, Sch 4 para 5(1)*. See **48.5** above.
- On deregistration. In this case there may be a deemed supply of the asset under *VATA 1994, Sch 4 para 8*. See **60.40 REGISTRATION**.

A new economic life will start upon the first use by a new owner after the purchase if he also applies the 'Lennartz' mechanism to the goods.

(VAT Information Sheet 14/07, paras 2.9.3, 2.14).

(f) Partly-exempt businesses

Partly-exempt businesses may adopt 'Lennartz' treatment for their assets in the same way as other businesses. Where an asset will be used partly for taxable purposes and partly for exempt purposes, the input tax on it will be 'residual' for partial exemption purposes and its deductibility will depend on the terms of the partial exemption method.

The private/non-business use provisions above do not affect a taxable person's existing partial exemption method. If this leads to an unfair deduction of input tax on the 'Lennartz' asset then a new partial exemption method will be needed. HMRC will agree a new method in these circumstances provided it gives a fair and reasonable result for the business overall. HMRC will not allow the 'Lennartz' asset to be separated out as a sector for more accurate deduction while the overall result remains unfair. If the existing partial exemption method gives an unfairly large recovery of VAT on the asset, then the partial exemption method override provisions may apply or HMRC may direct a new, fairer method.

(VAT Information Sheet 14/07, para 2.11 which also see for worked examples).

See **67.23 SUPPLY: TIME OF SUPPLY** for the time of supply of the private use of goods.

(2) Services

Where a person carrying on a business puts services which have been supplied to him to any private or non-business use, he is treated as having supplied those services in the course or furtherance of the business. Private use includes use outside the business by any person and own personal use where a business is carried on by an individual.

In *HMRC v Associated Newspapers Ltd* [2015] UKUT 641 (TCC), a newspaper publisher purchased retailer vouchers to give to customers who ordered its newspapers for a set period. The promotional scheme was very successful. HMRC raised assessments under *SI 1993/1507*, but the First-tier and Upper Tribunals agreed that the vouchers were not put to any non-business use – their use by the company for the purposes of a promotional scheme was not within *SI 1993/1507*, and the use by the customer to whom they were given was also irrelevant. However, VAT should not be charged on the issue of retailer vouchers, so the publisher's input tax claims were invalid. HMRC appealed to the Court of Appeal who decided in favour of the taxpayer on this point. HMRC and the taxpayer have been refused leave to appeal to the Supreme Court. The Court of Appeal's decision is now final and businesses should consider the VAT treatment of any vouchers given away free of charge to customers, where this is done for a business purpose.

Exceptions

The provisions do not apply, however,

- where the services are used, or made available for use, for a consideration;
- where no input tax has been deducted or will become deductible on the supply to him;
- where any part of the input tax on the supply to him was not counted as input tax because of an apportionment under *VATA 1994, s 24(5)*, see **35.7 INPUT TAX** (i.e. the provisions do not apply where an apportionment has been made between business and non-business use at the time of supply);
- where the services supplied consist of
  - (i) the provision in the course of catering of food or beverages to employees; or
  - (ii) the provision of accommodation for employees in a hotel, inn, boarding house or similar establishment; or
- where the services supplied consist of the letting on hire of a motor car and 50% of the input tax has already been excluded from credit (see **46.11 MOTOR CARS**).

Value of supply

The value of the supply is that part of the value of the supply of services to him as fairly and reasonably represents the cost to him of providing the services. The total VAT charged (cumulative where the services are supplied on more than one occasion) cannot exceed the amount of input tax which has been deducted or will become deductible.

Anti-avoidance re business transfers

Where the transfer of the assets of a business as a going concern is treated as neither a supply of goods nor a supply of services (see **9.9** *et seq* **BUSINESS**) the liability of the transferee to tax under these provisions is determined as if the transferor and the transferee were the same person. Where the business has been transferred VAT-free as a going concern more than once, the transferee is treated as if he and all the previous transferors were the same person.

[*SI 1993/1507*].

The above provisions relating to private use of services are concerned with major changes of use which continue over time or are permanent. Minor or occasional private or non-business use will be treated as *de minimis* and will not give rise to a liability to VAT. The type of services affected include computer software, building construction and refurbishment, particularly to domestic premises, and sporting rights.

Calculating the VAT due

There are no set rules for calculating the VAT due. If use of services permanently changes from business to non-business use, the accounting convention normally adopted for depreciating business assets may be used to calculate the VAT due, i.e. the value on which VAT is due is

$$\text{Cost of services} \times \frac{\text{Projected period of non-business use}}{\text{Period over which comparable assets are depreciated}}$$

Alternatively, any other fair and reasonable basis can be used. VAT should not be accounted for beyond the point at which

- the asset is fully depreciated, or
- the accumulated VAT accounted for equals the amount of input tax on the service which has proved to be not attributable to business use,

whichever is the earlier.

(Business Brief 17/94).

De Voil Indirect Tax Service. See V3.212; V3.216, V3.405A–V3.409.

Treatment of output tax in particular cases

[48.7] In particular cases, output tax is treated as follows:

(1) Accommodation

See **33.1–33.4 HOTELS AND HOLIDAY ACCOMMODATION** for supplies of accommodation in hotels, boarding houses, etc. and **33.5–33.9 HOTELS AND HOLIDAY ACCOMMODATION** for the provision of holiday accommodation in the UK, including time share, caravans and camping.

(2) Adoption services

Charities

Services provided by a charitable adoption agency in connection with domestic adoptions are exempt from VAT where the supply is made 'otherwise than for profit' (see **13.11 CHARITIES**). This includes the provision of pre-adoption training, advice and guidance; the assessment of prospective adopters; as well as the actual placement of a child.

Any charge made by a charitable adoption agency for a home study assessment in connection with an inter-country adoption application is also exempt from VAT, provided that the assessment is supplied on an 'otherwise than for profit' basis. Previously, these assessments had been subject to VAT at the standard rate.

Local authorities

Services provided by a local authority in connection with adoption are non-business activities. They are not subject to VAT when carried out as part of the local authority's statutory responsibility.

Other suppliers

All supplies in connection with any adoption that are not made by a charity on an 'otherwise than for profit' basis or by a local authority are standard-rated.

(Business Brief 21/01).

(3) Agricultural grant schemes

VAT is not to be applied to payments under the following grant schemes.

DEFRA

Farm Woodland Scheme
Set Aside Scheme
Agricultural Act 1986, s 18 (Environmentally Sensitive Areas)
Outgoers under the *Milk (Cessation of Production) Act 1985*

Department of the Environment

Nature Conservancy Council management agreements
Countryside Premium Scheme for Set Aside Land
Countryside Commission Community Forests Scheme

Forestry Commission

Woodland Grant Scheme
Farm Woodland Scheme

(C & E Press Release 58/89, 9 August 1989).

EU grants

Grants paid by the Intervention Board to processors of dried animal fodder are within the scope of VAT although, to the extent that supplies of animal fodder are zero-rated, no VAT is due. Processors who supply dried fodder must include the value of grants received in the total value of sales in Box 6 of the VAT return. Where the grant relates to fodder for the processors' own use, there is no VAT supply and grants should continue to be treated as outside the scope of VAT.

Other EU grants are generally outside the scope of VAT.

(Business Brief 28/99).

(4) Carrier bags

From 1 October 2011 the Welsh Assembly Government introduced a compulsory charge on single use carrier bags which retailers must charge to customers in Wales. The charge is consideration for the bag and is taxable at the standard rate of VAT. In order that customers pay the same amount regardless of the VAT status of the business, the stated minimum charge (initially 5 pence) is the minimum total to be charged by non-VAT-registered businesses. The stated minimum charge will be deemed to include VAT when charged by a VAT-registered business.

On 8 April 2013 a levy (minimum of 5 pence) was introduced on single use carrier bags in Northern Ireland. Retailers must pay the 'net proceeds' of their charges to the Department of Environment Northern Ireland (DoENI). Where a retailer charges the minimum of 5 pence, the full amount must be paid to DoENI. However, a retailer who charges more per bag must pay DoENI 5 pence less VAT (5p x 5/6 = 4.17p). Where only the 5 pence levy is charged and it is remitted in full to the DoENI, no VAT is due from the retailer in any circumstance. However, where the charge exceeds 5 pence, VAT is payable on the total amount where the bags are supplied by VAT-registered businesses. For example, if a retailer charges 12 pence for a bag then VAT of 2 pence will be due from the retailer (12p x 1/6 = 2p).

(HMRC Brief 23/11; HMRC Brief 7/13).

The compulsory minimum charge on single use carrier bags, introduced by the Scottish Parliament with effect from 20 October 2014 and relevant to retailers in Scotland, is inclusive of VAT unless the retailer is not registered for VAT and is not required to be registered for VAT.

(HMRC Brief 38/14).

The compulsory minimum charge on single use carrier bags in England, introduced by Parliament with effect from 5 October 2015, is inclusive of VAT unless the supplier is not registered for VAT and is not required to be registered for VAT. The legislation applies to suppliers with at least 250 full-time equivalent employees which provide single use carrier bags when selling goods in England or which provide such bags when selling goods for delivery in England.

(HMRC Brief 14/15).

(5) Change in rate of VAT

See **56.6** *et seq* RATES OF VAT for the effects on the calculation of output tax where there is a change in either the rate of VAT or the VAT liability of a particular supply.

(6) Compensation payments

Compensation payments for damage or loss are normally outside the scope of VAT as they are not consideration for a supply. This is because the payments are made either as a result of a Court Order or through an agreement between the two parties involved to compensate one party for suffering some inconvenience, loss or damage.

Early termination of contracts

Two conflicting tribunal decisions on exactly the same facts show the difficulties in determining the VAT position of payments arising out of early contract termination. In *Holiday Inns (UK) Ltd* (VTD 10609) (TVC 62.145) a company (C) owned a hotel which was managed by another company (H) under a management agreement. As the agreement did not allow for early termination, the parties entered into a separate termination agreement under which C paid H £2m as compensation. C wished to reduce the cost of the settlement by treating part of the payment as VAT (which it recovered as input tax) on the basis the H had made a supply of granting C the right to terminate. The tribunal held that, although drawn up years apart, the termination agreement constituted a part of the original management agreement, effectively inserting a termination clause into the latter. As this meant C already had the right to terminate, it could not have purchased the right from H and therefore there had been no supply for VAT purposes.

As a result of this decision, HMRC sought to obtain repayment of the input tax that C had claimed and C appealed (*Croydon Hotel & Leisure Company Ltd* (VTD 14920) (TVC 36.684)). The tribunal, with the same facts as the earlier hearing, held that the termination agreement and £2m payment did represent a supply for VAT purposes, following the ECJ's subsequent decision in *Lubbock Fine & Co, ECJ Case C–63/92*, [1994] STC 101 (TVC 22.359).

In *Lloyds Bank plc* (VTD 14181) (TVC 62.146) the bank decided to vacate a property it leased. The lease did not provide for early cancellation. Lloyds and its landlord therefore agreed a variation to the lease, setting out terms for early termination and the bank paid £597,220 as compensation. Because the parties effected the early termination on the same day as agreeing the variation, the tribunal held that there had been a supply by the landlord of granting and exercising an option to terminate the lease in return for a payment by Lloyds and its vacating the premises.

Liquidated damages

Agreements that allow for early termination usually include related clauses that provide a formula for payment of compensation in the event of such termination. These amounts are generally to compensate for loss of earnings and are often referred to as liquidated damages. They are not consideration for supplies and are outside the scope of VAT.

Leases for goods

Lease agreements for movable goods frequently include clauses that allow lessees to terminate early on payment of liquidated damages. Such sums are not liable to VAT. However, an agreement with the leasing industry allows lessors to treat lease terminations generally as taxable supplies if they wish (although they cannot be required to do so).

Breach of contract

Leases and other agreements may terminate early if a particular event occurs (e.g. the customer breaches the terms or the lessee calls in receivers). The contract deems that such events cancel its terms or effectively allow the lessor to terminate as though there had been a breach. Again, any moneys deemed to be due as a result are damages and outside the scope of VAT. See *Financial & General Print Ltd* (VTD 13795) (TVC 36.693).

Settlement of disputes

Where disputes involve an argument over price or poor standard of workmanship, any settlement is consideration for the goods or services previously supplied and the value of the supply is the agreed amount of settlement (either following a Court Order or an out of court agreement). If an 'interest' payment is also due under the settlement, this is not consideration for any supply and is a form of damages to compensate the supplier for being paid late.

See *Whites Metal Co* (VTD 2400) (TVC 36.690), *Cooper Chasney Ltd* (VTD 4898) (TVC 62.140) and *Hurley Robinson Partnership* (VTD 750) (TVC 62.139).

Land and property payments

See **42.19 LAND AND BUILDINGS: EXEMPT SUPPLIES AND OPTION TO TAX** for dilapidation payments and statutory compensation from landlords to tenants.

Manufacturers' and retailers' warranties

See **72.9 VALUATION.**

Surrender of firearms

Compensation payments made by the Home Office to VAT-registered firearms dealers required to surrender certain calibre handguns are taxable supplies where the surrendered firearms were business stock. The compensation payments therefore include a VAT element. Under powers contained in *SI 1995/2518, Reg 25(5)*, HMRC are prepared to allow any VAT due to be accounted for on the VAT return for the period in which the payment of compensation is received. (Business Brief 27/97). See also *Parker Hale Ltd v C & E Commrs*, QB [2000] STC 388 (TVC 62.149).

Compensation payments generally

For cases concerning whether compensation was in respect of a taxable supply or outside the scope of VAT, see *F Penny (t/a FMS Management Services)* (VTD 10398) (TVC 62.145) (compensation payment for loss of consultancy); *Galaxy Equipment (Europe) Ltd* (VTD 11415) (TVC 40.61) (compensation for faulty goods); and *Hometex Trading Ltd* (VTD 13012) (TVC 36.691) (compensation payments made by order of court). Compensation under *EC Council Regulation 1336/86* for discontinuing milk production is not subject to VAT (*Mohr v Finanzamt Bad Segeberg, ECJ Case C–215/94*, [1996] STC 328 (TVC 22.188)).

See also **72.9**(1) **VALUATION** for fines and penalty charges.

Example 1

Garage Doors Ltd supplied a customer with a garage door for £1,000 plus VAT that had a loose nut in it. As a consequence, the garage door collapsed on the customer's head when she was opening it – she had to have hospital treatment for cuts and bruises. Garage Doors Ltd pays her £500 compensation. However, the company cannot reduce its output tax figure because the payment to the injured customer is compensation for her inconvenience and suffering – it is not linked to the taxable supply of goods. The payment is outside the scope of VAT.

Example 2

Garage Doors Ltd supplies another customer with a red painted door for £1,000 plus VAT. However, after two weeks the customer notices that the paint is peeling from the door and she demands compensation for the poor quality of the product. Garage Doors Ltd pays her £500 compensation and reduces its output tax by £83.33 (i.e. £500 × 1/6 with a VAT rate of 20%).

In this case, the output tax adjustment is correct because the payment directly relates to the goods supplied. In effect, the customer is receiving a reduction in the original price because the goods are sub-standard – there is no compensation for damage or injury suffered.

(7) Energy-saving materials and grant-funded installation of heating equipment or security goods, etc.

Supplies of certain energy-saving materials and other qualifying goods and their installation are subject to VAT at the reduced rate of 5%. On 4 June 2015 the CJEU published its decision that the UK had implemented the relief in a way that was not in accordance with EU law. HMRC have not announced the date that the revised legislation will take effect. See **59.2** and **59.3 REDUCED RATE SUPPLIES**.

(HMRC Brief 13/15).

(8) Exempt supplies

Output tax is not chargeable on exempt supplies. See **21 EXEMPT SUPPLIES** for a list of the categories of exemption and cross-references to supporting chapters.

(9) Gifts

See **48.5** above.

(10) Goods obtained by fraud

Where the agreement for the supply of goods has been rescinded, no supply has taken place and the supplier can adjust the output tax he has paid provided he gets authorisation before doing so. Adjustment is specifically to the VAT account and credit notes should not be issued. In order to get authorisation, the trader must apply to HMRC enclosing evidence of fraud and a copy of the invoice. The evidence required by HMRC is

- evidence that the trader has been victim of the fraud proved in the courts or, where the person who committed the fraud goes missing, confirmation from the police that they are satisfied that a fraud has actually taken place;
- evidence that the trader has made a statement to the police for use in the prosecution; and
- a verifiable description of the goods involved.

Suitable evidence might take the form of police letters and press reports describing the injured party and the goods.

If the person who committed the fraud is convicted, any part payment made in the course of the fraud (e.g. by paying some cash and the balance by fraudulent cheque) cannot be the consideration for a supply and is outside the scope of the tax. If the person who committed the fraud is ordered to make restitution, that is compensation and outside the scope of the VAT.

If payment is made after conviction and output tax has been adjusted, there is a new contract or agreement and any supply would be considered on its own merits.

Where rescission of the supply is blocked because

- the supplier affirms the agreement by pursuing the person who committed the fraud for payment rather than the return of goods,
- the supplier unduly delays in rescinding the contract after discovering the fraud, or
- the goods have been supplied on to a third party,

by concession, the supplier is allowed to recover the VAT declared if the fraud is reported to the police and HMRC are satisfied that the business has been defrauded.

(HMRC Manual VATSC99400).

See also *Harry B Litherland & Co Ltd* (VTD 701) (TVC 62.173).

De Voil Indirect Tax Service. See V5.158.

(11) Lost, stolen or destroyed goods

HMRC may require a taxable person from time to time to account for goods supplied to, or acquired or imported by, him in the course or furtherance of his business (including any goods transferred from another EU member state). If such goods have been lost or destroyed, HMRC may assess him on the VAT which would have been chargeable in respect of the supply of the goods if he is unable to prove such loss or destruction. [*VATA 1994, s 73(7)*].

Where, therefore, a taxable person can prove that his goods have been lost, stolen or destroyed, output tax is only chargeable if the goods have been supplied. Where goods are *lost, etc. in transit* to the customer, then

- if, under the contract, the customer is responsible for any loss before delivery, output tax is due; and
- if, under the contract, the supplier is responsible for any such loss, output tax is due where a VAT invoice has been issued. If a VAT invoice has not been issued, no output tax is due because there has not been a supply.

See also **20.19 EUROPEAN UNION: SINGLE MARKET** for goods lost, etc. in transit to other EU member states.

(VAT Notice 700, para 8.10).

(12) Management services

See **45.1–45.3 MANAGEMENT SERVICES AND SUPPLIES OF STAFF.**

(13) Milk quotas

On 31 March 2015, milk quotas were abolished. The section below relates to the period when they were still in operation.

The VAT liability of the supply or transfer of a milk quota to another farmer depends upon whether it is supplied with or without land.

- Where the supply or transfer of a milk quota is linked with the supply of land under one agreement, there is a single supply and VAT liability follows that of the land. This applies whether the land is sold freehold or leasehold and even if separate identifiable sums are shown on the invoice and paid for the land and quota.

- The supply or transfer of a milk quota without land is a standard-rated supply of services.
- Where a milk quota is transferred with a grazing licence, there are two separate supplies, a zero-rated supply of animal feeding stuffs through the grazing licence and a standard-rated supply of the milk quota.

(Business Brief 17/94).

See (3) above for surrender of a milk quota in return for a DEFRA grant.

(14) Motor cars

See **46.4 MOTOR CARS** for disposal of a motor car used in a business and **46.16 MOTOR CARS** for VAT on fuel supplied for private use.

(15) Motor vehicles — statutory fees, etc.

MoT tests

The charge for an MoT test provided direct by an approved garage to its customers is outside the scope of VAT, provided it does not exceed the statutory maximum. Any discount given by an approved garage to an unapproved garage is treated as a normal trade discount and not seen as consideration for a taxable supply by the unapproved garage.

HMRC take the view that where an unapproved garage shows the exact amount charged by an approved garage separately on the invoice to its customer, and meets the other conditions for disbursements in VAT Notice 700, para 25.1 (see **3.7 AGENTS**), it may treat this element as a disbursement and also outside the scope of VAT. Any amount charged over and above the amount charged by the approved garage is consideration for its own service of arranging the test on behalf of its customer and is taxable at the standard rate. If the unapproved garage chooses not to treat the amount charged by the approved garage as a disbursement, or otherwise does not satisfy all the conditions for disbursements (e.g. by not showing the exact amount charged by the approved garage separately), HMRC take the view that it must account for VAT on the full invoiced amount. The view was followed in *Ward (t/a Acorn Garage)* (VTD 15875) (TVC 44.166) and a number of subsequent tribunal decisions but was not followed in *Duncan (t/a G Duncan Motor Services)* (VTD 20100) (TVC 44.169). In that case, the tribunal held that this approach did not pay sufficient regard to the legal monopoly of approved testing stations in relation to the conduct of MoT tests. It held that, even if not disclosed separately, the amount paid to the approved garage should not be treated as part of the overall supply of the unapproved garage. The decision in *Duncan* was approved of in *Jamieson (t/a Martin Jamieson Motor Repairs)* (VTD 20269) (TVC 44.170).

(VAT Notice 700, para 25.4; Business Brief 21/96).

Driving tests

Fees charged by the Department of Transport (and training bodies appointed by them) for Part 1 of the *motorcycle* driving test are liable to VAT at the standard rate. The Department of Transport supplies Part 2 of that test and *other motor vehicle* driving tests as part of its statutory obligation and the fees involved are outside the scope of VAT. (C & E Press Notice 909, 27 April 1984).

Removal/recovery services

Statutory fees for removal and storage of vehicles are outside the scope of VAT when levied by the police on the motorist or owner of the vehicle. If the police contract out this service, such fees collected by the contractor on behalf of the police are not consideration for any supply by the contractor to the motorist and are also outside the scope of VAT. Where, however, in such circumstances the contractor retains some or all of the amounts collected, the retained amount represents consideration for the supply of services from the contractor to the police authority and is liable to VAT at the standard rate. (Business Brief 9/99).

Vehicle clamping and towaway fees

Where landowners use parking enforcement contractors to enforce parking restrictions on their premises, fees payable to the contractor, as agent for the landowner, are outside the scope of VAT, being damages or compensation for the trespass suffered by the landowner. Where, however, under the terms of the agreement with the landowner, the contractor retains some or all of the amount collected, the retained amount represents consideration for the supply of services by the contractor to the landowner and is liable to VAT at the standard rate. VAT is also due on any management charge to the landowner. (Business Brief 7/00).

(16) Non-existent goods

A supply of goods is made only when they are passed to someone. Therefore, where goods do not exist and do not later come into existence, no supply can occur, no output tax is chargeable and no input tax is claimable. See also *P Howard* (VTD 1106) (TVC 36.683), *Theotrue Holdings Ltd* [1983] VATTR 88 (TVC 36.665) and *MS Munn* (VTD 3296) (TVC 36.674).

(17) Packaging

General. Normal and necessary packaging, including ordinary tins, bottles and jars, is treated as part of the goods which it contains so that if the goods are zero-rated, zero-rating also applies to the packaging. However,

- where the packaging is more than normal or necessary, there may be a multiple supply. The consideration must then be apportioned if the goods are not standard-rated and VAT is due on the packaging (see **48.3** above). This could apply to storage containers and other types of packaging which could be sold separately;

- where an additional charge is made with a supply of goods for their container to ensure that it is safely returned and the additional charge is to be refunded on its safe return, this additional charge is not subject to VAT; and
- where an additional charge is raised to cover the loan, hire or use of a container, then the charge is standard-rated.

(VAT Notice 700, para 8.2).

Food packaging. Where the purpose of the packaging is simply to contain, protect and promote the food it contains, HMRC consider it as part of the supply of the food inside, rather than a supply in its own right, and it takes the same liability as its contents. This is so even if the packaging is more than the minimum strictly necessary. This follows the decision in *C & E Commrs v United Biscuits (UK) Ltd t/a Simmers*, CS [1992] STC 325 (TVC 29.90) where it was held that decorative biscuit tins amounting to 55% of the total production cost (as opposed to 28% for ordinary cardboard packaging) were normal packaging for biscuits. The court held that the tin was integral to the biscuits, not merely in the sense that it was the container in which they were packaged, but further in that it prolonged their shelf-life and kept the biscuits in better condition once consumption had begun.

Where packaging is clearly designed to be 'extra' to the food, there is a multiple supply of food and packaging and normally the total price must be apportioned in order to arrive at the output tax due (see **48.3** above). Subject to the linked goods concession below, this applies to the following types of containers.

- Any container specifically advertised or held out for sale as having a value in its own right (e.g. by advertising the product as 'with a free storage tin').
- Any container with a clear and obviously intended after-use (e.g. tumblers containing coffee, honey or preserves in ceramic serving bowls).
- Storage jars obviously intended for use in storing future supplies of the product.
- Biscuit tins containing built-in hydroscopic crystals.
- Tea caddies (but not simple tins bearing the supplier's name and details of the weight and variety of tea where it is the supplier's practice to sell tea in this way).
- Ceramic pâté pots and other ceramic containers which are clearly suitable for future decorative use. See, however, *Paterson Arran Ltd* (VTD 15041) (TVC 29.91) where, following *United Biscuits Ltd* above, zero-rating was applied to the sale of quality biscuits in a ceramic jar aimed at the Christmas market, even though the jar represented 70% of the total cost.
- Hampers and picnic baskets (other than simple cardboard cartons).

Outer cases and boxes, etc. and seasonal packaging (although frequently more elaborate than supplied during the rest of the year) are not normally considered separate supplies unless falling within one of the above categories.

Linked goods concession

Where, however, standard-rated packaging is supplied with zero-rated food, the supply can be treated as a single supply of zero-rated food provided the packaging

- is not charged at a separate price;
- costs no more than 20% of the total cost of the supply; and
- costs no more than £1 (excluding VAT).

(VAT Notice 701/14/15, para 6.1).

(18) Payphones

Telephones

Where a payphone is rented from British Telecom or another supplier, the person renting the machine makes the supplies to the users and VAT is due on these supplies. Output tax is calculated by applying the VAT fraction to the money removed.

With some installations it is possible to switch from payphone mode to domestic mode and make calls without inserting money. If the domestic mode is used to make non-business calls, all VAT charged by British Telecom cannot be treated as input tax.

Phonecards

See **61.9**(3) **RETAIL SCHEMES.**

(VAT Notice 700, para 8.12).

(19) Pension consultancy charges

Employee benefit consultants (EBCs) and other pensions consultants should account for standard-rated VAT on consultancy charges and any separate fees charged to employers for services in connection with the setting up and administration of work place pension schemes.

(HMRC Brief 9/13).

(20) Personal service companies

A service company could be set up to provide the services of a single worker to a client in circumstances where, without the service company, the worker would be an employee of the client. The use of a service company in this way allows the client to make payments to the company, rather than the individual, without deducting PAYE or NICs. The worker could then take the money from the service company in the form of dividends rather than salary, again avoiding NICs. In order to counter such avoidance, under IR35 rules, HMRC can treat the payments made by the service company to the worker as chargeable to income tax on employment and subject to NICs. This 'IR35' status in respect of income ascribed to the worker does not affect the VAT position on supplies by the service company to the client. This is because the company, not the worker, contracts to provide the services to the client and it is, subject to registration requirements, liable to account for VAT on these supplies.

(21) Postage and delivery charges

A supply of goods may involve delivery to the customer. The way any delivery charge is treated for VAT purposes depends on the circumstances in which the goods are supplied.

- Where goods are delivered to a customer with no additional charge. If delivery is free, or the cost is built into the normal price, VAT is accounted for on the goods in the normal way based on the liability of the goods themselves. This applies whether or not delivery is required under the contract.
- Where delivery is required under the sales contract and a charge is made. If, under the terms of the contract, the seller has to deliver the goods to a place specified by the customer (e.g. the address of the customer, his friends or relatives or his own customers), the seller is making a single supply of delivered goods for which the VAT liability is based on the liability of the goods being delivered. The position is not affected by whether the charge made for delivery is separately itemised or invoiced to the customer. For example, any element of the price attributed to the doorstep delivery of milk and newspapers will also be zero-rated. On the other hand, any element attributed to the delivery of standard-rated mail order goods will be standard-rated.
  See also *C & E Commrs v Plantiflor Ltd*, HL [2002] STC 1132 (TVC 24.2).
- Where delivery is not required under the contract or someone else's goods are delivered. Delivery services are normally treated as a separate supply of services where
  (i) goods are supplied under a contract that does not require delivery but where, nevertheless, the seller agrees to deliver the goods and make a separate charge; or
  (ii) a business provides a service of delivering somebody else's goods (see also below for direct mailing services).
  In such cases, the liability of the delivery charge is not affected by the liability of the goods being delivered and there is a separate supply of delivery services which is normally standard-rated (although special rules apply if the delivery forms part of the movement of goods to or from a place outside the UK, see **71.25 TRANSPORT AND FREIGHT**). For example, the charge for the distribution of a publisher's zero-rated newspapers is a standard-rated supply of services. Similarly, where the seller arranges for goods to be delivered by post, the supply of delivery services is taxable even though the charges are identical to the exempt supply to him by the Post Office.

Direct mailing services. Where a supplier provides the service of posting client's mail (e.g. publicity or advertising material or promotional goods), the supplier may treat the charges by the Royal Mail (which for these purposes includes other operators licensed by Postcomm) as a disbursement for VAT purposes provided

(a) the general conditions for treatment as a disbursement are satisfied (see **3.7 AGENTS**);

(b) the client specifies who to send the mail to or has access to the mailing list before the mail is sent out;
(c) the supplier's responsibility for the mail ceases when it is accepted for safe delivery by Royal Mail; and
(d) the supplier passes on any Royal Mail discount or rebate to the client in full or, if the supplier obtains any discount or rebate from posting various clients' mail at the same time, it is apportioned fairly between them.

If conditions (*a*)–(*d*) are not met, the full amount of postal charges must be included in the value of the direct mailing service. This is normally standard-rated if the mail is sent to addresses in the UK. Special rules, however, apply if the delivery is, or forms part of, the movement of goods to or from a place outside the UK, see **71.25 TRANSPORT AND FREIGHT**.

Freepost

Freepost is an arrangement whereby the recipient (i.e. the advertiser) of a returned mailshot pays the postage costs on behalf of the sender (e.g. a member of the public). Commonly a PO box number will also be used. The supply by Royal Mail of the Freepost and PO Box licences, plus any handling service for which an additional fee is charged, is made to the licence holder. This may be the recipient (advertiser) or an agent handling the mail on the recipient's behalf. However, the supply of postage is made to the sender of the mail, although the recipient (advertiser) or the agent meets the cost. This means that where an agent is employed to handle the Freepost

- any recovery of the postage costs by the agent from the recipient (advertiser) is not liable to VAT; and
- where the licence is taken out by the agent in the name of the recipient (advertiser), the costs may be disbursed to the recipient, subject to the normal rules referred to above.

Retail schemes. For supplies of *delivered goods*,

- under the Point of Sale scheme, include the full amount charged in daily gross takings;
- under Apportionment Scheme 1, include the full amount charged in daily gross takings and do not adjust the record of purchases; and
- under Apportionment Scheme 2 and the Direct Calculation schemes, include the full amount charged in daily gross takings and also allow for the delivery charge element in the calculation of expected selling prices.

If delivery services are provided for an extra charge,

- under the Point of Sale scheme and the Apportionment schemes, account for VAT due on the delivery services outside the scheme used; and
- under the Direct Calculation schemes,
  (i) where minority goods are zero-rated, include delivery charges in daily gross takings; and

(ii) where minority goods are standard-rated, the delivery charges will not be included in the expected selling prices calculation and can be added back as part of the standard-rated sales figure. Otherwise, account for VAT due on delivery services outside the scheme.

Packing services

A separate supply of packing services will normally be standard-rated. Special rules, however, apply if the delivery forms part of the movement of goods to or from a place outside the UK, see **71.25 TRANSPORT AND FREIGHT**.

(VAT Notice 700, para 8.3; VAT Notice 700/24/15; VAT Notice 727/3/13, para 6.10; VAT Notice 727/4/13, para 7.11; VAT Notice 727/5/13, para 6.10).

(22) Postage stamps and philatelic supplies

See **58.15 RECREATION AND SPORT**.

(23) Private or non-business use of goods

See **48.6** above.

(24) Promotion schemes

See **70 TRADE PROMOTION SCHEMES**.

(25) Reduced rate supplies

VAT is chargeable on certain supplies at a reduced rate (currently 5%). See **59 REDUCED RATE SUPPLIES**.

(26) Retail consortium

Retailers may join together to form a purchasing consortium for the purposes of negotiating lower prices for the goods they purchase. Any payments made by a manufacturer or supplier to the consortium are regarded as the consideration for a taxable supply of services by the consortium of introducing the manufacturer/supplier to a larger customer base. The purchasing consortium must account for VAT at the standard rate on all such receipts. See *Landmark Cash and Carry Group Ltd* (VTD 883) (TVC 62.187). (Business Brief 12/93).

(27) Royalty and licence fees

Where a customer is recharged with payments made for royalty or licence fees incurred in making the supply to him, these charges are not disbursements for VAT purposes. The recharge is part of the consideration for the supply to the customer and VAT must be accounted for on the full value including the recharge. (VAT Notes (No 2) 1985/86).

(28) Samples

The provision to a person, otherwise than for a consideration, of a sample of goods is not a taxable supply [*VATA 1994, Sch 4 para 5(2)*], regardless of how many samples are provided to any one recipient.

In *EMI Group plc v HMRC, ECJ Case C–581/08,* [2010] STC 2609, the Court held that a 'sample' within what is now *Directive 2006/112/EC, Art 16* was a specimen of a product that was intended to promote the sales of that product, and that allowed the characteristics and qualities of the product to be assessed without resulting in final consumption (other than where final consumption was inherent). National legislation could not limit, in a general way, the term 'sample' to specimens presented in a form that was not available for sale, or to the first of a series of identical specimens given to the same recipient.

(29) School photographers

See **17.17 EDUCATION.**

(30) Second-hand goods

See **62 SECOND-HAND GOODS.**

(31) Solicitors

Oath fees

Under *Solicitors Act 1974, s 81* every solicitor holding a practising certificate may exercise the powers of a commissioner for oaths. Oath fees are regarded as deriving from the personal qualification of a solicitor, such that the solicitor who administers oaths receives the fees in a personal capacity. Whether or not VAT is due will depend upon the circumstances of the individual solicitor concerned.

(a) *Sole practitioners and partners.* Fees received in respect of oaths administered by a solicitor in sole practice or a partner in a firm of solicitors are regarded as consideration for services supplied in the course of the business. If the practice/partnership is registered for VAT, VAT is due. Fees received in a VAT period should be treated as VAT-inclusive.

(b) *Assistant solicitors.* VAT treatment depends upon whether or not the assistant solicitor accounts to the firm for oath fees received.
- Where fees are accounted for to the firm, they are part of the firm's business receipts and VAT must be accounted for as under (*a*) above.
- Where the firm allows the assistant solicitor to retain fees personally, the fees will not be subject to VAT unless the assistant solicitor is individually registered for VAT by virtue of other activities (or required to be registered taking into account the level of oath fees received).

(c) *Solicitors employed otherwise than in practice or retired solicitors.* Any fees received will not be subject to VAT unless the individual is registered for VAT by virtue of other activities (or required to be registered taking into account the level of oath fees received).

(Law Society's Gazette, 8 June 1994).

(32) Sponsorship income

See **58.14 RECREATION AND SPORT.**

(33) Sport and physical recreation facilities

See **58.3 RECREATION AND SPORT.**

(34) Supplies of staff

See **45.4–45.8 MANAGEMENT SERVICES AND SUPPLIES OF STAFF.**

(35) Toll charges

In *EC Commission v UK, ECJ Case C–359/97*, [2000] STC 777 (TVC 22.144) the court ruled that, in certain circumstances, central and local government bodies act as public authorities when they operate tolled bridges, tunnels and roads. Tolls in this category are outside the scope of VAT. This applies to

- Cleddau Bridge
- Dartford Crossing
- Erskine Bridge
- Forth Road Bridge
- Humber Bridge
- Itchen Bridge
- Mersey Tunnel
- Tamar Bridge
- Tay Bridge
- Tyne Tunnel

But the court held that, in any other circumstances, a toll charge is consideration for a standard-rated supply. As a result:

- Tolls payable to private sector operators for use of roads, road bridges and road tunnels are subject to VAT. As this becomes a business activity, toll operators affected can recover input tax on many of their costs. Arrangements have been put in place by the Department of Transport and the Scottish Executive to manage the impact of these changes.
- VAT-registered businesses can recover the VAT charged on tolls if they are entitled to do so under the normal rules. It is not necessary to obtain a VAT invoice to support a claim for input tax on a toll paid at a toll booth for a single or return journey costing up to £25. Otherwise a VAT invoice or other proof of payment must be obtained as appropriate. Businesses are advised to enquire about the VAT status of toll charges when they pay them.

(Business Brief 3/03).

(36) Vending machines

Where customers are provided with 'free' use of vending or similar machines then, provided the customer pays the same price for the products dispensed (coffee, tea, etc.) as other customers who simply buy the product, no VAT is due on the loan of the machines. If, however, a higher amount is charged, VAT must be accounted for at the standard rate on the price difference. (VAT Notice 700/7/12, para 11.8). For supplies in the course of catering, see **12.2 CATERING.**

(37) Video/DVD films and games

Rental of a video/DVD, where the customer must normally return it by a given date and the film/game remains the property of the supplier, is a supply of services. The value for VAT purposes is the amount paid for the use of the film/game over the rental period.

In a part-exchange transaction, the customer's film/game is accepted as payment (or part payment) for another film/game which then becomes the customer's property. Part-exchange is a supply of goods the value of which is the amount the customer would have had to pay for the film/game if there were no part-exchange. See *C & E Commrs v Bugeja*, CA [2001] STC 1568 (TVC 67.79). In that case, a trader (B) sold videos for, say, £20 but where a customer offered a video previously purchased from B in part-exchange, B only charged the customer £10 for the new video. The Court of Appeal held that the consideration for such a sale was £20 (rejecting both the contention of the appellant that he should only be required to account for output tax on the £10 cash payment and the High Court decision (QB 1999, [2000] STC 1) that consideration for the sale was the £10 paid in cash plus the value of the second-hand video which, on the evidence, could not be more than £2 to £3).

Output tax using one of the special **61 RETAIL SCHEMES.**

Rental: all rental payments and membership fees (see below) can be included in gross takings under

- the Point of Sale scheme; and
- Direct Calculation Schemes 1 and 2 (provided the minority goods under the scheme are zero-rated or taxable at the reduced rate).

Under any other scheme, such receipts must be excluded from gross takings and dealt with outside the scheme. The value of any videos/DVDs bought for rental must also be excluded from the scheme calculations.

Part-exchange: whichever scheme is used, the full normal retail selling price, including VAT, must be included in gross takings without deduction for the value of films/games taken in part-exchange. Where videos/DVDs taken in part-exchange are subsequently resold, it may be possible to use the margin scheme for **62 SECOND-HAND GOODS**. If not, they can be included in the retail scheme calculations.

Other charges

Membership fees are taxable on the full amount charged even if refunded when the customer gives up membership.

Deposits: a refundable deposit for the safe return of a rental film/game is not taxable even if retained because the film/game is lost or damaged.

Overdue films/games: a charge for an overdue film/game is further payment for the use of the film/game and liable to VAT.

(VAT Notice 700/14/17).

(38) Zero-rated supplies

Output tax is not chargeable on zero-rated supplies. See **75 ZERO-RATED SUPPLIES** for a list of the categories of zero-rating and cross-references to supporting chapters.

Key points: output tax

[48.8] Points to consider are as follows.

- A zero-rated supply is a taxable supply but at a rate of 0%. This is important to recognise because it means that full input tax recovery is allowed on the related costs of the activity (subject to normal rules). Input tax cannot be reclaimed on costs that are relevant to exempt activities.
- The standard rate of VAT in the UK is 20%. The VAT fraction used to work out the VAT element within an inclusive price is 1/6.
- The reduced rate of VAT is 5%. The relevant fraction used to work out the VAT element within a price that includes 5% VAT is 1/21.
- When assessing whether a single or multiple supply situation exists, it is necessary to consider whether each supply constitutes an aim in itself, or whether the secondary supply is incidental to the main supply. In the latter situation, the output tax payable will wholly depend on the liability of the main supply. Remember that an analysis of mixed supply situations is only relevant if the goods or services in question attract VAT at different rates.
- Be aware of the two different methods of apportionment in mixed supply situations (i.e. cost-based and revenue-based calculations) and identify if one of the methods gives a fairer result.
- Any errors of principle in apportioning output tax on mixed supplies can be adjusted by going back four years and correcting the error. If the amount of tax involved is less than £10,000 (or 1% of the Box 6 figure on the relevant VAT return up to a maximum of £50,000), this can be done by adjusting the next VAT return, otherwise, a separate disclosure must be made to HMRC.
- It is unlikely to be acceptable for a taxpayer to readjust his method of output tax apportionment on a historic basis, unless the method adopted was totally unfair. HMRC will be rightly suspicious about recalculations that are made just to try and get a better result in terms of output tax paid in the past.
- Recent court cases relevant to mixed supply issues have emphasised the importance of looking at the situation from the perspective of the customer rather than the supplier. In other words, consider whether the customer considers that he is only paying for one main benefit (single supply outcome) or a range of benefits subject to different rates of VAT (multiple supply).

- Output tax is not due on a business gift that costs less than £50 to the donor. This assumes that the total cost of all goods donated to the recipient in any previous twelve-month period is also less than £50. Other situations where no output tax is due include free food and drink provided to employees and also to customers (although an input tax block would need to be considered in the latter case under the business entertainment rules).
- It is important to be clear about whether any donation made by a person or business (e.g. to a charity) is a genuine donation, i.e. the donor is not entitled to receive any goods or services from the recipient as a result of making his donation. If obligations were evident (a small acknowledgement of thanks in a publication would not be classed as a benefit to the donor) then the VAT liability of the benefits provided to the donor need to be considered. If these benefits are standard-rated, e.g. sponsorship benefit, then output tax will need to be declared on the payment in question.
- When dealing with compensation payments to customers, output tax can be reduced on a payment if it relates to a specific problem with goods supplied, e.g. compensation to reflect the poor quality of a product. However, general compensation payments for injury or inconvenience to the customer will be outside the scope of VAT.
- A business should ensure that it keeps full details of any goods that have been lost, stolen or destroyed, e.g. police reference numbers, documents relating to insurance claims. This could avoid problems on HMRC visits if an officer tries to assess output tax on goods he cannot trace.

49

Overseas Traders

Cross-references. See **3.8 AGENTS** for tax representatives and agents employed by overseas traders; **39 INTERNATIONAL SERVICES** for services generally made to or by overseas traders.

Introduction to overseas traders

[49.1] An '*overseas trader*' (also referred to as a '*non-established taxable person*') is any person who

- is not normally resident in the UK;
- does not have a 'UK establishment'; and
- if a company, is not incorporated in the UK.

A UK establishment exists if

- the place where essential management decisions are made and the business's central administration is carried out is in the UK;
- the business has a permanent physical presence with the human and technical resources to make or receive taxable supplies in the UK.

If a business has a UK establishment, it is not a non-established taxable person. It will be registered for VAT in the UK at the address of its principal UK place of business. It must keep its VAT records and accounts at this address which must be available for HMRC to inspect. Someone responsible for VAT affairs should be available at the address. If that person is an employee, he must have written authority to act on behalf of the business A suggested form of words for this authority is at **49.3** below under the appointment of an agent. A separate authority will not be required if

- the name of the person concerned has been notified to the Registrar of Companies under the *Companies Act 2006, Part 34* as a UK resident authorised to accept service of process on behalf of the company; or
- for a partnership the person concerned is a partner, resident in the UK.

(VAT Notice 700/1/18, paras 9.1, 9.2, 9.4).

Registration of overseas traders

[49.2] An overseas trader *must* register for VAT in the UK if

- he makes taxable supplies of goods and services in the UK in the course of furtherance of his business (see **48.1 OUTPUT TAX**) and, prior to 1 December 2012, the total value of those supplies exceeds the VAT registration threshold (see **60.3 REGISTRATION**). From 1 December 2012 a person who makes taxable supplies in the UK but has no establishment here has to register and account for VAT on those supplies irrespective of their value (see **60.33 REGISTRATION**). If, however, a UK recipient of services accounts for the UK VAT due via the reverse charge procedure there is no requirement for the overseas supplier to register for VAT in the UK relation to those services;
- the business is registered for VAT in another EU member state, he sells and delivers goods in the UK to customers who are not VAT-registered ('distance sales') and the value of those distance sales exceeds the relevant threshold (see **60.12 REGISTRATION**);
- he acquires goods in the UK directly from a VAT-registered supplier in another EU member state (see **20.3 EUROPEAN UNION: SINGLE MARKET**) and the total value of the acquisitions exceeds the acquisitions threshold (see **60.19 REGISTRATION**); or
- he makes a claim under the electronic cross-border refund system (formerly the *EC 8th Directive*) or *EC 13th Directive* and subsequently supplies, or intends to supply, the relevant goods in the UK (see **60.27 REGISTRATION**).

For VAT purposes, the UK includes the territorial sea of the UK (i.e. waters within twelve nautical miles of the coastline).

There is no need to register if the only UK supplies are supplies of services on which the customer is liable to account for any VAT due under the 'reverse charge' procedure. See **39.4 INTERNATIONAL SERVICES.**

An overseas trader *may* also apply to be registered if

- he has started in business but is not yet making taxable supplies, provided he can show the intention of making taxable supplies in the future as part of his business; or
- his turnover is below the threshold, provided he can prove to HMRC that he is carrying on a business for VAT purposes and making taxable supplies.

See **60.2 REGISTRATION.**

Consequences of registration

An overseas trader who is registered or required to be registered for VAT in the UK must account for VAT in respect of those supplies and acquisitions taking place in the UK. He is also liable to VAT on importations of any goods into the

UK (see **34 IMPORTS**) and on the acquisition in the UK of exciseable goods or of new means of transport from another EU member state whether or not he is required to be registered (see **20.9** and **20.37 EUROPEAN UNION: SINGLE MARKET** respectively).

[*VATA 1994, ss 1, 3, 4, 10, 96(11)*]. (VAT Notice 700/1/18, para 9.3).

See **66.2 SUPPLY: PLACE OF SUPPLY** for the place of supply of goods and **66.12 SUPPLY: PLACE OF SUPPLY** for the place of supply of services.

Registration options available

[49.3] An overseas trader who is required or entitled to be registered in the UK can normally choose between three registration options.

(1) He may appoint a VAT representative who must keep his VAT records and accounts and account for UK VAT on his behalf, and who will be jointly and severally liable for any VAT debts. When the overseas trader registers online, he will be asked for information about his tax representative. See **3.8 AGENTS** for further details on VAT representatives. In some cases, HMRC can direct that a tax representative is appointed although this cannot be done where the overseas trader is based in a country where certain mutual assistance arrangements exist. The *Finance Act 2016* contains provisions to counter the risk of tax avoidance and evasion by overseas traders selling goods to UK consumers through online marketplaces. The right of HMRC to insist on the appointment of a VAT representative is strengthened, and there are new powers to put an online marketplace on notice that a particular seller is not complying with the rules. This may lead to the online marketplace becoming jointly liable for VAT on that seller's transactions. [*FA 2016, ss 123–124*].

(2) He may appoint an agent to deal with the VAT affairs. The agent cannot be held responsible to HMRC for any VAT debts and HMRC reserve the right not to deal with any particular agent. The overseas trader must still complete a VAT registration form. In addition, HMRC will need a letter of authority. A suggested letter of authority approved by HMRC is:
(Insert principal's name) of (insert principal's address) hereby appoints (insert name of UK agent or employee) of (insert address of UK agent or employee) to act as agent for the purpose of dealing with all their legal obligations in respect of VAT.
This letter authorises the above-named agent to submit VAT returns (VAT 100) and any other document needed for the purpose of enabling the agent or employee to comply with the VAT obligations of the principal.
Signed (insert principal's signature)
Date (insert date)

(3) He may deal with all the VAT obligations (including registration, returns and record-keeping) personally.

(VAT Notice 700/1/18, paras 11.1–11.6).

Alternatives to registration

Accounting for VAT through customers

[49.4] *VATA 1994, s 14* implements the VAT simplification procedures for triangular trade between EU member states and the UK. The provisions allow UK customers to be designated as liable to account for the VAT that would otherwise be due to be accounted for by intermediate suppliers in other EU member states. See **20.22 EUROPEAN UNION: SINGLE MARKET** for fuller details.

Non-UK traders and their agents

If a non-UK trader with a UK establishment

- imports goods for onward supply in the UK, and
- does not make any other supplies in the UK

he can arrange for a UK-resident agent registered for VAT to import and supply the goods on his behalf. If the trader does this, he will not need to register for VAT in the UK. He must agree with the agent that they will issue proper tax invoices for the supplies of the goods. The agent is treated as importing and supplying the goods as principal. The agent must make any necessary Customs entries as the importer, pay or defer the VAT and take delivery of the goods. He can reclaim any import VAT as input tax (subject to the normal rules), but must treat the transactions as a supply by him and charge and account for VAT on the onward sale in the normal way. See **3.4 AGENTS** for the treatment of commission.

The above also applies if a non-UK trader without a UK establishment

- imports goods for onward supply in the UK; and
- does not make any other taxable supplies in the UK.

(VAT Notice 702, paras 2.7, 2.8).

Applications to the UK for refunds of VAT by persons established in another EU member state

[49.5] The electronic cross-border refund system (formerly the *EC 8th Directive*) needs to be used by EU resident businesses to recover input tax incurred in another EU member state. See **18.7 EUROPEAN UNION: GENERAL.**

Applications to the UK for refunds of VAT by persons established outside the EU

[49.6] When a trader registered for business purposes in a country outside the EU buys goods or services in the UK, he may have to pay UK VAT. If goods are bought for export, there is usually no problem as the supply will be zero-rated. But if the goods or services bought in the UK are also used here (e.g. at a trade fair), the trader cannot treat the VAT incurred as input tax because he is not registered here.

To avoid this, the *EC 13th Directive* has set up a scheme which allows overseas traders, subject to conditions being met, to reclaim VAT charged on imports into the UK or purchases of goods and services used in the UK. See **19.44 EUROPEAN UNION LEGISLATION** for a summary of the provisions of the *EC 13th Directive*. The provisions have been implemented in the UK as set out below.

Persons to whom the provisions apply

The provisions apply to any trader carrying on a business established in a '*third country*' (i.e. a country outside the EU) provided that in the period of claim

(a) he was not registered or liable to be registered for VAT in the UK;
(b) he was not established in any EU member state;
(c) he made no supplies of goods and services in the UK other than
  (i) transport of freight outside the UK or to or from a place outside the UK (and ancillary services);
  (ii) services where the VAT on the supply is payable solely by the person to whom they are supplied under the reverse charge provisions (see **39.4 INTERNATIONAL SERVICES**); or
  (iii) goods where the VAT on the supply is payable solely by the person to whom they are supplied; and
(d) where the trader is established in a third country having a comparable system of turnover taxes, unless HMRC allow otherwise, that country provides reciprocal arrangements for refunds to be made to taxable persons established in the UK.

For these purposes a person is treated as established in a country if

- he has a business establishment there; or
- he has no business establishment (there or elsewhere) but his permanent address or usual place of residence is there. The usual place of residence of a company is where it is legally constituted.

A person carrying on business through a branch or agency in any country is treated as having a business establishment there.

Refundable/non-refundable VAT

A person to whom the provisions apply is entitled to be repaid VAT charged on

- goods imported by him into the UK in respect of which no other relief is available; and
- supplies made to him in the UK if that VAT would be input tax of his were he a taxable person in the UK.

Refunds cannot be claimed on VAT incurred on

- non-business supplies (if a supply covers both business and non-business use, VAT can be reclaimed on the business element of the supply);
- any supply or importation which the trader has used, or intends to use, for the purpose of any supply by him in the UK;

- any supply or importation which has been exported, or is intended for exportation, from the UK by or on behalf of the trader;
- a supply or importation where input tax recovery is restricted in the UK (e.g. most motor cars, business entertainment and second-hand goods for which no VAT invoice is issued, see **35.8 INPUT TAX**);
- VAT charged on a supply to a travel agent, tour operators, etc. which is for the direct benefit of a traveller other than the travel agent or his employee; and
- in relation to VAT charged after 2 December 2004, VAT on a supply used (or to be used) in making supplies of insurance and financial services within **35.3**(*c*) **INPUT TAX**.

Method of claiming

Claim forms (VAT 65A) are obtainable from the GOV.UK website.

Forms must be completed in English, using block capitals, and must be sent to the address below, together with the original copy of all invoices and, if appropriate, a certificate of status.

HM Revenue and Customs
Compliance Centres
VAT Overseas Repayment Unit
S1250
Benton Park View
Newcastle upon Tyne NE98 1YX

Proof of VAT paid

A claim form must be supported by correctly completed invoices, vouchers or receipts from suppliers showing

- supplier's name, address and VAT registration number;
- the date of supply;
- details of goods or services supplied;
- the cost of the goods or services (including VAT); and
- the rate of VAT

and additionally if the value of the supply is over £250 (including VAT)

- an identifying number;
- the claimant's name and address; and
- the amount of VAT charged.

If the goods have been imported, the VAT copy of the import entry or other Customs document showing the amount of VAT paid is also required.

Only originals of documents are acceptable. HMRC will refuse to accept any supporting documentation if it already bears an official stamp indicating that it has been furnished in support of an earlier claim.

Certificate of status

When making the first claim in the UK, a trader must also include a certificate from the official authority in his own country showing that he is registered for business purposes there. When applying for the certificate, it is important to make sure that it shows all the information that the UK authorities will need to process the claim (e.g. if the invoices are made out in a company's trading name, the certificate must show this, as well as the name under which it is registered).

The certificate must be an original (not a photocopy) and contain

- the name, address and official stamp of the authorising body;
- the claimant's name and address;
- the nature of the claimant's business; and
- the claimant's business registration number.

Form VAT 66A may be used. Each certificate is valid for twelve months from its date of issue and will cover any claims made during that year. Once the certificate has expired, the trader must send a new one with his next claim.

Time limit

The claim must be made not later than six months after the end of the 'prescribed year' in which the VAT is incurred. The '*prescribed year*' is the year ended 30 June. See *Comoretel Holdings Ltd* [2015] UKFTT 606 (TC) (TC04750) for a discussion of what must be submitted by the deadline: all the paperwork has to be provided in the proper form, and deficiencies cannot be corrected later. A *13th Directive* 'claim' has not been made, and has no standing, until all the requirements have been met.

Period of claim

Any claim must be for a period of not less than three months (unless less than three months of the prescribed year remains) and not more than one year. Items missed on earlier claims can be included as long as they related to VAT charged in the year of the claim.

Minimum claim

If the claim is for less than one year, it must be for at least £130 (unless it is for the final part of the prescribed year). No claim can be for less than £16.

Repayment

The refund will be made within six months of receiving a satisfactory claim. Payments can be made by any of the following methods.

- Directly to the claimant's own bank through SWIFT (Society for Worldwide Inter-Bank Financial Telecommunications). The claimant must provide full bank account details (bank name, address and identification code; account name and number; and currency of account) and a copy of a bank credit slip with the claim form.
- To any UK bank.
- By payable order in sterling directly to the claimant or an appointed agent.

Where any repayment is made to a claimant in the country in which he is established, HMRC may reduce the repayment by the amount of any bank charges or costs incurred.

Use of agents

An overseas trader can prepare and send in his own claim or have this done by an agent. Any agent will need either a Power of Attorney or letter of authority before HMRC will accept that he is acting for, and can receive money on behalf of, the trader.

The following is an example of the format of a letter of authority acceptable to HMRC.

I [name and address of claimant] hereby appoint [name and address of agent] to act on my behalf in connection with any application I make to the Commissioners of HMRC under the Value Added Tax Regulations 1995 as from time to time amended or replaced. Any repayment of VAT to which I am entitled pursuant to any such application made on my behalf by my above named agent shall be paid to [name and address of payee].

Date Signed [by the claimant]

Appeals

An appeal may be made to an independent VAT tribunal against a refusal by HMRC to allow all or part of a repayment. A Notice of Appeal must be served at the VAT tribunal within 30 days of the date of the letter notifying the refusal. Alternatively, the applicant may first ask HMRC to reconsider their decision and extend the time for service of a Notice of Appeal. If HMRC allow an extension but do not change their decision, the applicant then has a further 21 days from the date of the letter upholding the decision to serve a Notice of Appeal.

Isle of Man

For VAT purposes, the Isle of Man is treated as part of the UK. VAT is chargeable in the Isle of Man under Manx legislation, which is broadly similar to UK legislation. The above scheme applies equally to refunds of VAT incurred in the Isle of Man and any references above to the UK are to be taken to include the Isle of Man.

[*VATA 1994, s 39; SI 1995/2518, Regs 185–197; SI 2004/3140, Reg 15*]. (VAT Notice 723A, paras 5.2, 5.5, 5.6, 6.1–6.8).

Insurance and financial transactions

The European Commission (EC) formally requested the UK to amend its legislation relating to the *EC 13th Directive* on insurance or financial transactions. Under UK law a taxable person established outside the EU is denied the right to recover VAT paid or due in the UK on goods or services in so far as they are used for the purpose of insurance or financial transactions supplied to customers established outside the EU. By contrast, a taxable person established in the EU (in the UK or otherwise) is entitled to recover VAT in such cases.

The UK did not take any action to amend its legislation, and so the EC referred the matter to the CJEU. The Advocate General (AG) found in favour of the UK, on the ground that the UK was entitled to rely on *EC 13th Directive, Art*

2(1), which does not mention the possibility of obtaining a refund in the case of financial and insurance transactions. The Court could not read into *Art 2(1)* the provisions of *Directive 2006/112/EC, Art 169(c)* (which allows for the recovery of VAT incurred in making non-EU supplies of insurance and finance). See *EC Commission v UK (No 7), ECJ Case C–582/08* [2010] STC 2364 (TVC 22.628).

Retail export scheme

A VAT retail export scheme allows non-EU visitors a refund of VAT on certain goods that they buy in the EU. See **22.12 EXPORTS**.

Special scheme for electronically supplied services

There is a special scheme for overseas businesses which provide electronically supplied services to non-business customers in the EU. See **64.34 SPECIAL SCHEMES**. The special scheme provides only for payment of the VAT due on sales to EU customers without any deductions of EU VAT incurred on purchases. However, a business in the scheme can reclaim VAT charged on

- goods it imports into the UK; and
- supplies it makes in the UK

in connection with making qualifying supplies while it is a participant in the special scheme. The provisions outlined above apply with the omission of conditions (*c*) and (*d*) above.

[*VATA 1994, Sch 3B para 22*].

De Voil Indirect Tax Service. See V5.152.

Key points: overseas traders

[49.7] Points to consider are as follows.

- A common situation where an overseas business will need to register for VAT in the UK is when the 'distance selling' limits are exceeded. This occurs when a business based in another EU member state has sold goods into the UK exceeding £70,000 on a calendar year basis but only to customers who are not VAT-registered. If a customer is VAT-registered in the UK, then the VAT is dealt with by the customer (acquisition tax) on his own VAT return.
- If an overseas business based in another EU member state sells services into the UK, e.g. accountancy services there is no need to register for VAT in the UK. This assumes that the business in question does not have a fixed or business establishment in the UK, i.e. premises from which it trades. In the cases of B2B (business to business) sales, the customer in the UK will account for VAT by doing a reverse charge calculation.
- There are no distance selling rules for services as there are for goods. So as an example, a Dutch accountancy firm completing private tax returns for UK individuals (B2C – business to con-

sumer sale) will charge Dutch VAT on the services provided, without any need to become VAT-registered in the UK. This again assumes that the Dutch firm does not have an establishment in the UK, i.e. it trades from an office in Holland.

- Subject to HMRC's agreement an overseas business can register for VAT in the UK on either a voluntary basis (taxable sales below the compulsory VAT registration limit) or intending trader basis (intention to make taxable sales at a future date). Many businesses will favour this option to ensure VAT paid on expenditure in the UK can be easily reclaimed as input tax on a UK VAT return.
- A UK business acting for an overseas trader in relation to VAT matters (e.g. a firm of accountants based in the UK) should avoid the option of becoming the VAT representative of the business in question. In such cases, the VAT representative is jointly responsible for the VAT debts of the overseas business.
- A more sensible option to avoid any problems is for an overseas business to appoint a UK agent to deal with its UK VAT affairs. A letter of authority (signed by a director or business owner) must be given to HMRC to confirm the agent's involvement. The main advantage is that the agent cannot be held responsible for the debts of the overseas trader.
- An overseas business can handle its own VAT affairs i.e. without the involvement of a UK agent. In such cases, it will deal directly with HMRC (see **49.3**).
- It is possible for an overseas business based outside the EU that is not VAT-registered in the UK (or making supplies in the UK) to reclaim VAT paid in the UK through the EU *13th Directive* system. This system allows a business based outside the EU to reclaim UK VAT, usually as long as there is a reciprocal arrangement in place that allows a UK business to reclaim indirect taxes paid in that country. Example – a reciprocal arrangement is in place with Australia that allows a UK business to reclaim Australian GST.
- *13th Directive* claims made by a non-EU business are dealt with by HMRC's VAT Overseas Repayment Unit in Newcastle upon Tyne (see **49.6**). The claimant cannot reclaim tax on any expenses that are input tax blocked to a UK business, e.g. business entertainment costs, motor cars etc. or any expenses relevant to an exempt supply. The claim is made on form VAT65A and must be completed in English. The claimant must also provide evidence (certificate of status) to confirm his business registration in his own country.
- An overseas business making a *13th Directive* claim must comply with a very strict time deadline. Claims for the twelve-month period ending 30 June must be submitted by the following 31 December. HMRC will then pay the claim (assuming it is correct) within six months of receipt.

- From 1 December 2012 an overseas business must register in the UK even if its taxable turnover is below the current registration limit for UK businesses. This follows the ruling of the CJEU in the case of *Schmelz (C-97/09)*, [2011] STC 88 (TVC 20.225).

50

Partial Exemption

Cross-references. See **11 CAPITAL GOODS SCHEME** for deduction, and adjustment of deduction, of input tax on capital items by partly exempt businesses; **28.9 GROUPS OF COMPANIES** for input tax incurred by holding companies; **19.33, 19.34 EUROPEAN UNION LEGISLATION; 21 EXEMPT SUPPLIES.**

De Voil Indirect Tax Service. See V3.461–467.

Introduction to partial exemption

[50.1] A registered business which makes both taxable and exempt supplies cannot charge VAT on the exempt supplies and equally cannot normally reclaim the VAT incurred on the purchases used to make those supplies. Where input tax cannot be claimed because it relates to an exempt supply, it is known as *exempt input tax* and the registered business is known as *partly exempt*. See **21 EXEMPT SUPPLIES** and supporting chapters for details of goods and services the supplies of which are exempt.

A partly exempt business will normally have to use an approved partial exemption method (see **50.3–50.10** below) to work out how much of its input tax can be reclaimed. This would usually be the standard method (see **50.4–50.8** below) unless it feels that this would not give a fair or reasonable result, in which case it can apply to HMRC for a special method (see **50.10** below). All methods should provide for direct attribution and apportionment of the input tax incurred. Direct attribution involves identifying VAT on goods and services which are used exclusively to make taxable supplies or exempt supplies: the former is deductible, the latter is not. Apportionment is required for the remaining input tax (e.g. on overheads) which cannot be directly attributed.

Where a partly exempt business prepares VAT returns and deducts input tax on a quarterly or monthly basis, the input tax deduction is provisional. The business also has a longer period at the end of which it is required to review the extent of its allowable input tax and revise its deduction accordingly. In general, the longer period ends on the last day of the quarter ending March, April or May and the adjustment is known as the annual adjustment. Newly registered traders have a longer period known as a registration period. See **50.13** below.

Even if a partial exemption method has to be used, the *de minimis* limits in **50.11** below may allow all input tax to be recovered (subject to the normal rules).

Where a business has deducted VAT based on its intention to use the relevant goods and services to make taxable supplies and at any time within six years, not having made the intended supply, it changes its mind and uses, or forms the intention to use, the goods and services to make an exempt supply, it must adjust its original claim. Conversely, rules permit a claim where VAT was restricted because the business's original intention was to make exempt supplies but in the event a taxable supply is either subsequently intended or made. See **50.14** below.

Capital goods scheme

The capital goods scheme covers input tax incurred in respect of land and property or computers above certain values. Under the scheme, the owner of the capital item must review the extent to which the item is used to make taxable supplies over a period of time (five or ten years) and make an adjustment where appropriate. See **11 CAPITAL GOODS SCHEME.**

General provisions relating to allowable input tax

[50.2] The amount of allowable input tax for which a taxable person is entitled to credit at the end of any period is so much of the input tax on supplies, acquisitions and importations in the period as is allowable as being attributable to the following supplies made, or to be made, by the taxable person in the course or furtherance of his business.

(a) '*Taxable supplies*', i.e. supplies of goods and services made in the UK other than exempt supplies.

(b) Supplies outside the UK which would be taxable supplies if made in the UK.

(c) Supplies of services which
  - (i) are supplied to a person who belongs outside the EU, or
  - (ii) are directly linked to the export of goods to a place outside the EU, or
  - (iii) consist of the provision of intermediary services in relation to any transaction within (i) or (ii) above

  provided that the supply is exempt (or would have been exempt if made in the UK) by virtue of *VATA 1994, Sch 9 Group 2* (insurance) or *VATA 1994, Sch 9 Group 5 Items 1–8* (finance).

(d) Supplies made either in or outside the UK which fall, or would fall, within *VATA 1994, Sch 9 Group 15 Item 1 or 2* (investment gold, see **27.2 GOLD AND PRECIOUS METALS**).

HMRC must make regulations for securing a fair and reasonable attribution of input tax to the supplies within (*a*) to (*c*) above.

[*VATA 1994, ss 4(2), 26; SI 1999/3121*].

Regulations made are considered in **50.3** to **50.14** below. In those paragraphs:

(1) '*Exempt input tax*' means input tax incurred by a taxable person on
- goods or services supplied to, or goods imported or acquired by, him insofar as they are used by him, or a 'successor' of his, in making exempt supplies, or
- supplies outside the UK which would be exempt if made in the UK,

other than input tax which is allowable under
- *SI 1995/2518, Reg 102* (special methods, see **50.10** below);
- *SI 1995/2518, Reg 103* (attribution of input tax to foreign and specified supplies, see **50.12**(1) below);
- *SI 1995/2518, Reg 103A* (input tax attributable to exempt supplies of investment gold, see **27.4 GOLD AND PRECIOUS METALS**); or
- *SI 1995/2518, Reg 103B* (incidental financial services, see **50.12**(2) below).

See **50.9** below for the meaning of '*successor*'.

(2) Nothing is to be construed as allowing a taxable person to deduct the whole or any part of the VAT on the importation or acquisition by him of goods or the supply to him of goods or services where those goods or services are not used or to be used by him in making supplies in the course or furtherance of a business carried on by him.

[*SI 1995/2518, Regs 99(1)(a), 100*].

Calculation of reclaimable input tax

[50.3] If a business is not fully taxable, subject to the *de minimis* limit in **50.11** below, it cannot recover all its input tax. It is therefore necessary to determine how much of the input tax incurred can be reclaimed. This must be done in accordance with the following rules.

(a) Identify goods imported or acquired by, and goods or services supplied to, the business in the VAT period which are used
- *exclusively* in making taxable supplies; and
- *exclusively* in making exempt supplies.

This process is known as *direct attribution.*

(b) Input tax is reclaimable on such of those goods and services as are used, or are to be used, *exclusively* in making taxable supplies or other supplies which carry the right to deduct.

(c) No part of the input tax can be reclaimed on such of those goods or services as are used, or are to be used, in making exempt supplies or other supplies in respect of which input tax is non-deductible.

[*SI 1995/2518, Reg 101(2)*].

In most partly-exempt businesses, however, there will still be further input tax which cannot be directly attributed under (*a*)–(*c*) above because it relates to

- goods and services used, or intended to be used, for making both taxable and exempt supplies; or
- general overheads of the business (e.g. accountancy costs, telephone bills).

Input tax on these costs which cannot be directly attributed is normally referred to as 'non-attributable' or 'residual' input tax. A partial exemption method must then be used to apportion this residual input tax to determine how much of it is reclaimable. A business should normally use the standard method in **50.4–50.8** below to calculate provisionally how much residual input tax can be reclaimed but in certain circumstances it may be possible to apply a special method, subject to prior approval of HMRC. See **50.10** below.

Unless the *de minimis* limit in **50.11** below applies (in which case all input tax is recoverable subject to the normal rules), the total VAT reclaimable in the VAT period is then the directly attributable input tax under (*b*) above plus the reclaimable portion of residual input tax. The provisional amount reclaimed in the VAT period may then need to be adjusted at the end of a 'longer period', normally twelve months. See **50.13** below.

Both the provisional attribution and the annual adjustment must be made on the basis of facts as they existed at the time when the input tax was incurred, not on the changed facts as they existed at the time the claim was made. See *C & E Commrs v University of Wales College Cardiff*, QB [1995] STC 611 (TVC 46.229) where apportionment was based on income received in the relevant periods rather than subsequent use.

The standard method

[50.4] Under the standard method (use of which does not require HMRC approval), the percentage of residual input tax (see **50.3** above) which can be reclaimed is calculated on the basis of proportionate values.

De Voil Indirect Tax Service. See V3.461–V3.461C.

Values-based calculation

[50.5] This can be calculated as follows.

$$\text{Claimable \%} = \frac{\text{Value of taxable supplies in the period (excluding VAT)}}{\text{Value of all supplies in the period (excluding VAT)}} \times 100$$

If the resulting percentage is not a whole number, it should be rounded *up* to the next whole number except that, where the residual input tax to which the fraction is applied is £400,000 per month on average or greater, it should be rounded up to two decimal places.

In making the calculation, the value of all the following supplies must be excluded.

(a) Any sum receivable in respect of a supply of capital goods used for the purposes of the business. There is no statutory definition of capital goods but the term is wider than simply goods within the **11 CAPITAL GOODS SCHEME**. In *C & E Commrs v JDL Ltd*, Ch D 2001, [2002] STC 1 (TVC 46.107) motor cars were held to be capital goods as they were of substantial durability and value as compared to other articles used in the management and day-to-day running of the business. In *Nordania Finans A/S and anor v Skatteministeriet, ECJ Case C–98/07*, [2008] STC 3314 (TVC 22.521), the CJEU ruled that where goods (in this case, cars) were leased and subsequently sold on the termination of the leasing contracts, those goods were not to be regarded as capital goods. In HMRC's view, the decision in *Nordania* overturns the decision in *JDL Ltd*. Businesses which have submitted a claim for repayment of VAT as a result of the *Italian Republic* case (*Case C–45/95* – sales of cars where the input tax on purchase has been blocked are exempt) will be required to review their claims to take account of the *Nordania* decision. This means that the value of cars owned and used in the business and on which a repayment claim has been made (mainly demonstrator cars) will have to be included in the denominator of the partial exemption calculation, which will have the effect of reducing the amount of residual input tax which is recoverable. (HMRC Brief 43/10). HMRC's view was upheld by the First-tier Tribunal in *Cleckheaton Holdings Ltd* [2015] UKFTT 686 (TC) (TC04803) (TVC 9.11).

(b) Any sum receivable in respect of any of the following descriptions of supplies made where such supplies are incidental to one or more of the business activities.
- Any supply of a description falling within *VATA 1994, Sch 9 Group 5* (exempt supplies of finance).
- Any other financial transaction.
- Any '*real estate transaction*' including any grant, assignment (including any transfer, disposition or sale), surrender or reverse surrender of any interest in, right over or licence to occupy land.

In *C H Beazer (Holdings) plc* [1987] VATTR 164 (TVC 46.108) the tribunal considered incidental to mean 'occurring or liable to occur in fortuitous or subordinate conjunction with'.

(c) That part of the value of any supply of goods on which output tax is not chargeable by virtue of a Treasury order under *VATA 1994, s 25(7)* unless the business has imported, acquired or been supplied with the goods for the purpose of selling them.

(d) The value of any supply which, under or by virtue of any provision of *VATA 1994*, the business makes to itself.

(e) Supplies within *VATA 1994, Sch 9 Group 5 Items 1 or 6* (dealings with money or securities) or supplies made from an establishment outside the UK.

[*SI 1995/2518, Reg 101*].

(f) The value of transactions that are not supplies for VAT purposes, such as the transfer of a business as a going concern and the issue by a company of new shares in the company to raise capital, along with the value of EU acquisitions.

(VAT Notice 706, para 4.8).

Annual adjustments

The claimable proportion of residual input tax for a tax period as calculated is only provisional and subject to adjustment at the end of the 'longer period'. See **50.13** below.

Use-based calculation

[50.6] A business that is partly exempt for the first time (e.g. because it has just commenced its activities, but also if it changes from being wholly taxable to partly exempt) has the option of recovering input tax on the basis of use in the following situations.

- *During its registration period.* This is the period running from the date a business is first registered for VAT to the day before the start of its first tax year (normally 31 March, 30 April or 31 May depending on the periods covered by the VAT returns).
- *During its first tax year (normally the first period of twelve months commencing on 1 April, 1 May or 1 June following the end of the registration period)*, provided it did not incur input tax relating to exempt supplies during its registration period.
- *During any tax year*, provided it did not incur input tax relating to exempt supplies in its previous tax year.

A recovery on the basis of use means that input tax is attributed in accordance with the use or intended use of input tax bearing costs in making taxable supplies. A business is required to examine its main categories of expenditure and determine the extent to which they relate to taxable supplies. Most businesses that embark upon a new activity will have carefully considered how costs will be used, in accordance with cost accounting principles, when preparing its business plan. Provided this is logical, objective and transparent it will invariably form an ideal basis for a fair recovery of input tax.

Where a business calculates its recovery of input tax on the basis of use, it is also required to calculate its annual adjustment on the basis of use. Also, where a business does not recover input tax on the basis of use but would nevertheless have been entitled to do so, it may still calculate a use-based annual adjustment.

Example

A business is registered for VAT on 15 July 2016 and its first year begins on 1 April 2017. Its registration period is therefore 15 July 2016 to 31 March 2017. To secure funding it drew up a three-year business plan which projects taxable and total income as follows.

Year ending	Estimated value of taxable supplies (a)	Estimated value of total supplies (b)	Recovery percentage = (a) × 100/(b)
31 March 2017	4,000	20,000	20%
31 March 2018	70,000	100,000	70%
31 March 2019	150,000	200,000	75%
Total	224,000	320,000	70%

It incurs total residual input tax on start-up costs of £50,000 during the registration period.

The business is satisfied that overall it uses the start-up costs in proportion to the value of taxable and exempt supplies that it makes and intends to make over the three-year period. However, if it operated the normal standard method calculation using the values of supplies made during the registration period, it would only be able to recover 20% of its input tax (£10,000) which does not reflect its intended use of costs.

The new rules allow the business to recover the input tax on costs incurred in each VAT return within the registration period in accordance with the principle of use. Therefore, the business can select its own calculation for recovering the input tax provided it is fair and reasonable. In this case, as the business intends the start-up costs to be used in proportion to the values of supplies made over the three-year period, it can provisionally recover a total of 70% of the residual input tax (£35,000) in the VAT returns that fall within the registration period. It would also be required to perform its first annual adjustment on the basis of use to finalise the calculation. However, this will only affect its input tax recovery if its use or intended use of costs have changed by that time. For simplicity, if we assume that in this example there are no significant changes, the finalised amount of recoverable input tax would be £35,000 and so the annual adjustment would be nil.

For its first tax year that runs from 1 April 2017 to 31 March 2018, the business reverts to the normal values-based calculation. Change 1 means that the business can provisionally recover its input tax during its first year by reference to the recovery percentage determined for the registration period (70% in this example), although this would be finalised by way of an annual adjustment at year-end on the basis of values.

The business is therefore able to recover its input tax on the basis of use for almost two years, after which it reverts to the normal values-based calculation. It is only if the business anticipates that a values-based calculation would be unsuitable that it would need to consider applying for a special method.

[*SI 1995/2518, Reg 101*]. (VAT Information Sheet 4/09, para 4).

De Voil Indirect Tax Service. See V3.461A, V3.461B, V3.462.

Use of previous year's recovery percentage

[50.7] A business may use its previous year's recovery percentage to determine the provisional recovery of residual input tax in each VAT return, which is then finalised as normal by way of an annual adjustment. The finalised annual recovery percentage is then used as the provisional recovery percentage for the next year, and so on. A business may continue to operate the old rules and calculate separate recovery percentages for each of its VAT returns. A business must consistently apply either the new rules or the old rules in any given tax year.

Example

ABC Ltd uses the standard method and reclaimed 75% of its residual input tax in the year to 31 March 2017. It will reclaim the same percentage of residual input tax in relation to VAT returns submitted during the year ending 31 March 2018. It will then calculate its annual adjustment for the year and reclaim additional input tax if the percentage of taxable income exceeded 75%, i.e. the provisional recovery rate was too low. It will repay tax to HMRC if the percentage of taxable income was less than 75%, i.e. the provisional recovery rate was too high. The percentage of taxable income for year ended 31 March 2018 will then form the basis of quarterly calculations during year ended 31 March 2019.

[*SI 1995/2518, Reg 101*]. (VAT Information Sheet 4/09, para 2).

Scope of the standard method

[50.8] Up to the change described below, the scope of the standard method included supplies of services to customers outside the UK; certain financial supplies such as shares and bonds; and supplies made from establishments located outside the UK.

SI 2015/1978 amended *SI 1995/2518, Reg 101* in relation to any standard method longer period beginning after 31 December 2015 so that the value of supplies made by overseas establishments is excluded from the standard method. An affected business can apply to use a special method (see **50.10** below) or:

- If the business continues to use the standard method it will need to apply the UK recovery rate when recovering input tax used to make supplies from overseas establishments.
- If the business continues to use the standard method, and the difference between the result of using that method and a method which fairly reflects the use of tax bearing costs exceeds £50,000 (or £25,000 in the case of group undertakings), it will need to account for the difference because of the effect of the standard method over-ride (see **50.9** below).
- If the business continues to use the standard method and there is a material difference between the result using the standard method and the result using a method which reflects the extent input tax is used in support of overseas supplies, HMRC will expect the business to apply to use a special method, and may direct the business to use a special method, even if the standard method over-ride is not engaged. Whether a difference is material will depend on the circumstances of the business, such as the amount of VAT incurred and the difference in VAT recoverable.

Apart from this change in relation to supplies by foreign establishments, the standard method covers input tax on all supplies unless it is dealt with separately under *SI 1995/2518, Reg 103A* (investment gold).

Supplies described in *VATA 1994, Sch 9 Group 5 Items 1 and 6* (mainly supplies of financial instruments such as shares and bonds) and supplies made from overseas establishments (see above amendments to *SI 1995/2518, Regs 101, 102* and *103* intended to prevent businesses from taking into account supplies made by foreign establishments when carrying out their partial exemption calculations) are catered for by the standard method but are excluded from the values-based calculation, irrespective of their place of supply. Instead, input tax relating to these supplies is ring-fenced and recovered on the basis of use.

All remaining input tax is recovered by reference to the values-based calculation (unless a new partly exempt business opts to recover on the basis of use in accordance with *VATA 1994, s 4*).

(VAT Information Sheet 4/09, para 5). (HMRC Brief 22/15).

Example

In its tax year beginning on 1 April 2017, X Ltd makes the following supplies.

	Total (excl VAT)	Standard-rated (excl VAT)	Exempt
	£	£	£
First quarter	442,004	392,286	49,718
Second quarter	310,929	266,712	44,217
Third quarter	505,867	493,614	12,253
Fourth quarter	897,135	876,387	20,748
	£2,155,935	£2,028,999	£126,936

Input tax for the year is analysed as follows

	Attributable to taxable supplies	Attributable to exempt supplies	Remaining input tax	Total input tax
	£	£	£	£
First quarter	36,409	4,847	11,751	53,007
Second quarter	20,245	311	5,212	25,768
Third quarter	34,698	1,195	10,963	46,856
Fourth quarter	69,707	5,975	9,357	85,039
	£161,059	£12,328	£37,283	£210,670

First quarter

	£	£
Input tax attributable to taxable supplies	36,409	
Proportion of residual input tax deductible = 392,286/442,004 = 88.75%		
£11,751 × 89% =	10,458	
		46,867

Second quarter

	£	£
Input tax attributable to taxable supplies	20,245	
Proportion of residual input tax deductible = 266,712/310,929 = 85.78%		
£5,212 × 86% =	4,482	
	£24,727	
The value of exempt input tax is £1,041 (311 + [5,212 – 4,482]). As this is not more than £625 per month on average and is less than 50% of all input tax in the quarter, all input tax in the quarter is recoverable.		
Deductible input tax		25,768

Third quarter

	£	£
Input tax attributable to taxable supplies	34,698	
Proportion of residual input tax deductible = 493,614/505,867 = 97.58%		
£10,963 × 98% =	10,744	
	£45,442	
The value of exempt input tax is £1,414 (1,195 + [10,963 – 10,744]). As this is not more than £625 per month on average and is less than 50% of all input tax in the quarter, all input tax in the quarter is recoverable.		
Deductible input tax		46,856

Fourth quarter

	£	£
Input tax attributable to taxable supplies	69,707	
Proportion of residual input tax deductible = 876,387/897,135 = 97.69%		
£9,357 × 98% =	9,170	
		78,877
		£198,368

For the annual adjustment required, see Example 1 in **50.13** below.

De Voil Indirect Tax Service. See V3.461A, V3.461B, V3.462.

Standard method over-ride

[50.9] The standard method is a simple way of calculating how residual input tax can be attributed to taxable supplies and deducted. In the vast majority of cases, it provides for a fair and reasonable apportionment. But a number of larger businesses have aggressively exploited the standard method to deduct large amounts of input tax on purchases used to make exempt supplies. Also, in a few other cases not involving abuse, businesses have been able to either deduct large amounts of input tax on purchases used in making exempt supplies or unable to deduct input tax on purchases used to make taxable supplies. The over-ride provisions below were introduced to address these difficulties. They apply to VAT incurred on or after that date. Except in cases of deliberate abuse, HMRC believe that the provisions will rarely apply. In any case, the provisions do not apply to businesses using a special method.

The over-ride can apply in the two situations in (*a*) and (*b*) below. Normally, it applies, if at all, under (*b*) at the end of a tax year and any over-ride adjustment is made and accounted for in the same period as the annual adjustment (or longer period adjustment). However, where a business does not carry out an annual adjustment (because it first becomes partly exempt in the last period of a tax year) any over-ride adjustment must be accounted for under (*a*) on the next VAT return.

(a) Where
- for a VAT period, a taxable person has used the standard method to attribute a proportion of the residual input tax to taxable supplies using the formula in **50.5** above,
- that VAT period does not form part of a longer period (see **50.13** below),
- the attribution differs substantially from one which represents the extent to which the goods or services are used by him, or are to be used by him, or a 'successor' of his, in making taxable supplies, and
- residual input tax incurred in the VAT period is more than £50,000 p.a. (£25,000 p.a. for group undertakings (as defined in *Companies Act 2006, s 1161*) which are not members of the same VAT group), adjusted *pro rata* for the length of the VAT period in question,

the taxable person must calculate the difference and account for it on the return for the VAT period next following the VAT period in question (unless HMRC allow otherwise). If his registration has been cancelled at or before the end of that VAT period, he must account for any adjustment on his final return.
[*SI 1995/2518, Regs 107A, 107E*].

(b) Where
- a taxable person has determined for a longer period (see **50.13** below) the input tax attributable to that period under the standard method,
- the attribution differs substantially from one which represents the extent to which the goods or services are used by him, or are to be used by him, or a 'successor' of his, in making taxable supplies, and

- residual input tax incurred in the longer period is more than £50,000 p.a. (£25,000 p.a. for group undertakings (as defined in *Companies Act 2006, s 1161(5)*) which are not members of the same VAT group), adjusted *pro rata* for a period which is not twelve months,

the taxable person must calculate the difference and, in addition to any amount required to be included as over-deducted or under-deducted in respect of the normal annual adjustment, account for the amount so calculated on the return for the VAT period next following the longer period (unless HMRC allow otherwise). If his registration has been cancelled at or before the end of that VAT period, he must account for any adjustment on his final return.
[*SI 1995/2518, Regs 107B, 107E*].

For the above purposes, a difference is substantial if it exceeds

- £50,000; or
- 50% of the residual input tax incurred in the VAT period or longer period, as the case may be, and £25,000.

A person is the '*successor*' of another if he is a person to whom that other person has transferred assets of his business by means of a transfer as a going concern which is treated as neither a supply of goods nor a supply of services (see **9.9** *et seq* **BUSINESS**). Successor in this context includes a reference to a successor's successor through any number of transfers.

[*SI 1995/2518, Regs 107C, 107D*].

The over-ride only applies where the standard method produces a result that does not fairly reflect the extent to which purchases are used, or to be used, to make taxable supplies. The over-ride may apply when

- costs are incurred in one year that will not result in supplies until a later year;
- high value transactions are undertaken that do not consume inputs to an extent significantly greater than transactions of a lower value;
- there are different business units that make different supplies and use costs in different ways; or
- costs are incurred relating to an intended supply that never comes about.

Calculating the extent of use

The over-ride incorporates the concept of 'fair and reasonable' even though the regulations do not say so explicitly. All UK partial exemption is based on *VATA 1994, s 26*, which requires that regulations exist to provide a fair and reasonable deduction of input tax. Any calculation is acceptable if it produces a fair and reasonable attribution of input tax according to the use, or intended use, of purchases in making taxable supplies. The easiest way to prepare a fair and reasonable calculation is to consider why the standard method breaks down and to correct for it. Provided residual costs (those relating to both taxable and exempt supplies) are used in proportion to the values of taxable and exempt supplies made in the period in which they are incurred, the standard method will give a deduction that reflects use. Any costs that are not used in proportion to the values of supplies made can be dealt with separately from the standard method calculation.

The existing *de minimis* provisions (see **50.11** below) continue to apply. If, after an over-ride adjustment, the input tax attributed to exempt supplies is within the current *de minimis* limits, then all input tax for that period can be deducted.

Capital goods scheme (CGS)

If a business incurs input tax on an item subject to the CGS (see **11 CAPITAL GOODS SCHEME**) within a period covered by the over-ride, it must include that input tax when considering whether the over-ride applies and, if so, consider the use or intended use of the capital item in determining if there is a substantial difference.

CGS adjustments must not be counted as input tax when determining whether the over-ride applies. However, where the over-ride does apply to a tax year or longer period that is also a subsequent CGS interval, the CGS adjustment will be affected if the standard method is used as the basis of adjustment for the scheme.

(VAT Notice 706, paras 5.3, 5.5, 5.7, 5.8, 5.11). See also VAT Information Sheet 4/02 for examples of how HMRC see the over-ride provisions applying in practice.

De Voil Indirect Tax Service. See V3.461A.

Special methods

[50.10] HMRC may approve or direct the use of another method other than the standard method in **50.4–50.8** above. But this is subject to the following.

- In calculating the proportion of any input tax on goods or services used (or to be used) by a taxable person in making both taxable and exempt supplies which is to be treated as attributable to taxable supplies, the value of any supply of a description within **50.5**(*a*)–(*d*) above (whether made within or outside the UK) must be excluded (i.e. those supplies which must be excluded from the standard method of calculation must also be excluded from any special method). This applies despite any provision in the method approved which purports to have contrary effect.
- The requirement for a declaration by the taxable person (see below).
- *SI 1995/2518, Reg 103* (attribution of input tax to foreign and specified supplies, see **50.12**(1) below).
- *SI 1995/2518, Reg 103A* (input tax attributable to exempt supplies of investment gold, see **27.4 GOLD AND PRECIOUS METALS**).
- *SI 1995/2518, Reg 103B* (incidental financial services, see **50.12**(2) below).
- *SI 1995/2518, Reg 102*, as amended by *SI 2015/1978*, will have effect in relation to any methods approved or directed by HMRC after 31 December 2015. This means that methods that are not based on sectors cannot include the value of supplies made from overseas establishments. (HMRC Brief 22/15).

Application and approval

A taxable person may apply to HMRC to use a special method if it considers that the standard method does not provide a fair and reasonable result. HMRC require precise details of how the proposed method will work in practice and are prepared to discuss proposals before a formal application is submitted. HMRC will normally approve a special method provided it is fair and reasonable.

A method approved or directed under these provisions must be in writing and must identify the supplies in respect of which it attributes input tax by reference to the relevant categories in **50.2**(*a*)–(*d*) above.

A method may attribute input tax which would otherwise fall to be attributed under *SI 1995/2518, Reg 103* (attribution of input tax to foreign and specified supplies, see **50.12**(1) below) but where it attributes any such input tax, it must attribute it all.

Example

John has two activities – both generating equal levels of income (i.e. 50% taxable and 50% exempt). The main expenditure of the business on which input tax is incurred is linked to its property. The taxable activity is the organisation of fitness classes which takes up 80% of the premises; the exempt activity is the sale of insurance which takes up 20% of the premises.

Most of the input tax for this particular business relates to the property from which it trades – and 80% of this property is used for taxable activities. But in reality only 50% of the input tax will be recovered on property costs using the standard method of calculation based on income.

In this particular situation, the business would be best advised to submit a special method declaration to HMRC to apply for a special method of calculation based on floor area.

Declaration by the business

HMRC will not approve the use of a special method under these provisions unless the taxable person has made a declaration to the effect that, to the best of his knowledge and belief, the method fairly and reasonably represents the extent to which goods or services are used (or are to be used) by it in making taxable supplies. A declaration is required each time a new method is approved and must relate (i.e. it cannot be restricted to parts of the method or to parts of the business). The declaration must be in writing and be signed by the taxable person or by a person authorised to sign it on his behalf. It must include a statement that the person signing it has taken reasonable steps to ensure that he is in possession of all relevant information.

If HMRC think that a declaration made is incorrect in that it is not fair and reasonable and the person signing the declaration knew (or ought reasonably to have known) this at the time when the declaration was made, they may serve a notice on the taxable person to that effect. The notice must set out their reasons and state the effect of the notice. But HMRC cannot serve such a notice unless they are satisfied that the overall result of the application of the method is an over-deduction of input tax by the taxable person.

Where such a notice is served by HMRC, then in relation to

- VAT periods commencing on or after the effective date of the method, and
- longer periods (see **50.13** below) to the extent of that part of the longer period falls on or after the effective date of the method (except that no adjustment is required in relation to any part of any VAT period)

the taxable person must calculate the difference between

(a) the amount of deductible VAT using the special method, and
(b) the amount of deductible VAT calculated in accordance with the principle of use

and account for the difference on the return for that VAT period or on the return on which that longer period adjustment is required to be made (although HMRC may allow another return to be used for this purpose). This process must continue unless or until the method is terminated (see below).

In relation to any past VAT periods, HMRC may assess the amount of VAT due to the best of their judgement and notify it to the taxable person unless they allow him to account for the difference in such manner and within such time as they may require.

The service of a notice on a taxable person under these provisions is without prejudice to HMRC's powers to serve a notice on him under *SI 1995/2518, Reg 102A* (see below under *Special method over-ride*) and any notice served under these provisions takes priority in relation to the periods which it covers.

The following can be used as a template for the declaration

Partial Exemption — Special Method Declaration Name of Business: Address: VAT Registration Number: This Declaration is in accordance with paragraphs (9) and (10) of regulation 102 of the VAT Regulations 1995. As the taxable person (i.e. where the signatory is a sole proprietor)/the person authorised by the taxable person to sign this declaration on its behalf (delete as appropriate), I hereby declare that to the best of my knowledge and belief, the proposed special method [state precisely where the method is set out] fairly and reasonably represents the extent to which goods or services are used or to be used in making taxable supplies. I also confirm that I have taken reasonable steps to ensure that I am in possession of all relevant information before making this declaration. Name (print): Position (print): Date: Signed:

For further guidance generally on declarations, including HMRC's interpretation of terms in the legislation such as 'fair and reasonable', 'ought reasonably to have known' and 'reasonable steps', see the web version of HMRC Brief 23/07.

'Gaps' in special methods

A special method has a 'gap' if it fails to specify how to deal with an amount of residual input tax. This may arise because the method is poorly drawn up or the circumstances of the taxable person have changed after the method has been approved. Where a taxable person using a special method which has been approved or directed by HMRC incurs input tax

- the attribution of which to taxable supplies is not prescribed in whole or in part by that special method, and
- which does not fall to be attributed to taxable or other supplies under **50.12**(1) or (2) below or **27.4 GOLD AND PRECIOUS METALS**

the input tax is to be attributed to taxable supplies to the extent that the goods or services are used in making taxable supplies, expressed as a proportion of the whole use or intended use. Where the treatment of input tax is only partly covered by the method (i.e. part of the input tax falls into the gap), only that part of the input tax not covered by the method falls within these provisions.

These provisions do not mean that gaps in methods are acceptable. They simply set out how to cope with any gaps that arise. Once a gap has arisen, HMRC will expect that, in due course, the taxable person will make suitable proposals for a new or revised method that takes the gaps into account.

[*SI 1995/2518, Reg 102*]. (VAT Notice 706, paras 6.9, 6.11; HMRC Brief 23/07).

Possible methods

A special method can be any method agreed by HMRC and devised to suit the needs of the particular business. It can contain any calculations or stages that are needed to ensure it is fair and reasonable. All special methods should reflect all business activities, provide for direct attribution of input tax to taxable supplies and exempt supplies, identify residual input tax, calculate the elements of residual input tax that relate to taxable supplies and to exempt supplies, and allow the business to determine the total input tax that it can recover.

Common methods include those based on the following.

- *Outputs-based apportionment*, i.e. apportioning between supplies in the same ratio as the value of taxable supplies bears to the value of all supplies.
- *Transaction-based apportionment*, i.e. apportioning between supplies in the same ratio as the number of taxable transactions made bears to all transactions made.
- *Staff time and headcount apportionment.* Staff time apportionment is where the apportionment is made in the same ratio as the staff time spent making taxable supplies bears to all staff time.

A headcount method has a similar effect to the using of staff time except that it can be used by a business that does not keep time sheets.

- *Input tax and inputs-based apportionment.* These are calculations where the apportionment is made in the same ratio as the input tax directly attributable to taxable supplies bears to all directly attributable input tax.
- *Floor space apportionment.* This is apportionment in the same ratio as the floor space occupied by income-generating staff involved exclusively in making taxable supplies bears to the total floor space of income-generating staff. Floor-area based special methods are likely to be acceptable when
  (i) most of the business's VAT-bearing costs relate to its premises; and
  (ii) most of the floor-area of those premises is used for either wholly taxable or wholly exempt activities, with only minor areas relating to both.

  Methods based on floor area are, therefore, seldom fair and reasonable for retailers and unlikely to be accepted by HMRC. See *Optika Ltd* (VTD 18627) (TVC 46.146), *Vision Express (UK) Ltd* [2009] All ER (D) 146 (Dec) (TVC 46.140) and Business Brief 34/04. See also *London Clubs Management Ltd* [2011] EWCA Civ 1323 (TVC 46.145). In *HMRC v Lok'nstore Group plc* [2014] UKUT 288 (TCC) (TVC 46.152) the Upper Tribunal dismissed HMRC's appeal against a decision by the First-tier Tribunal that a partial exemption special method based on floor area produced a more fair and reasonable result than the standard method. HMRC did not appeal the Upper Tribunal decision but explained in HMRC Brief 35/14 that it does not consider that floor area methods are usually appropriate for the retail sector. (HMRC Brief 35/14).
- Costs allocations.
- Management accounts.

A special method may also be based on separate calculations for different sectors of the business or, in the case of a group registration, different businesses or groups of businesses within the VAT group.

The percentage recovery rate produced by a special method should be calculated to two decimal places. In *Royal Bank of Scotland Group plc v HMRC (No 6), Case C–488/07*, [2009] STC 461 (TVC 22.514), the court ruled that member states are not obliged to apply the rule for rounding up to the next whole number where the proportion of input tax deductible is calculated in accordance with a special method.

Annual adjustments

The claimable proportion of residual input tax for a tax period as calculated is only provisional and subject to adjustment at the end of the 'longer period'. See **50.13** below.

Changes in circumstances

HMRC should be informed of any change in the business, or in group membership if in a VAT group, which has a substantial effect on the amount of input tax claimable. The special method will then be reviewed by HMRC and if no longer suitable, a direction to stop using the method will be issued. The taxable person must then either use the standard method or propose an alternative special method. But see also under the heading *Special method over-ride* below.

(VAT Notice 706, paras 6.1–6.8).

Agreements with trade bodies

HMRC have agreed special methods with the Association of British Factors and Discounters, the Finance Houses Association Ltd, the Association of British Insurers and the Association of Investment Trust Companies. See VAT Notice 700/57/14 for full details.

Higher education institutions

A framework has been prepared providing guidance on formulating special methods for higher education institutions, in particular, how to determine a fair 'value' for supplies of grant-supported education, when to add 'sectors' to a partial exemption method and how to identify and deal with 'distorting supplies'. The framework is not mandatory but is strongly recommended. It has been prepared in conjunction with the British Universities Finance Directors' Group and the university funding councils via the Higher Education Funding Council for England. See *PE Framework for Higher Education Institutions* (November 2013) for full details which is available on the HMRC website.

See Business Brief 11/06 as to how variable tuition fees may affect the partial exemption methods of higher education institutions.

Housing associations

A framework has been prepared by HMRC in conjunction with the National Housing Federation, the Scottish Federation of Housing Associations and Community Housing Cymru, and with the knowledge of the Northern Ireland Federation of Housing Associations. The Framework is intended to be of assistance to both housing associations and HMRC officers in agreeing fair partial exemption methods and to help housing associations and HMRC officers decide whether the standard method works well or whether a partial exemption special method is needed.

The framework gives guidance on what is likely to work if a partial exemption special method is required and sets out the range of activities carried out by housing associations. It discusses the challenges the activities may pose in designing a fair and reasonable partial exemption special method and describes ways that those challenges can be overcome. It suggests calculations that are likely to lead to a fair apportionment of input tax and also goes through when the calculation may need to be split into the operational sectors of a housing association in order to arrive at a fair answer. See *PE Framework for Housing Associations* (November 2013) for full details which is available on the HMRC website using the following link: www.gov.uk/government/publications/partial-exemption-frameworks.

NHS bodies

VAT recovery methods used by NHS bodies deal with business/non-business and partial exemption issues. A framework for NHS bodies VAT recovery calculation methods has been prepared by HMRC in conjunction with the Health Finance Managers Association. The Framework is not mandatory but adopting its principles should enable HMRC to more readily give approval for a VAT recovery method. See *Framework for NHS Bodies VAT Recovery Calculation Methods* (October 2013) for full details which is available on the HMRC website using the following link: www.gov.uk/government/publications/partial-exemption-frameworks.

Outside the scope supplies

In *C & E Commrs v Liverpool Institute for Performing Arts*, HL [2001] STC 891 (TVC 46.188), the court confirmed HMRC's view that two separate regimes exist for determining the amount of VAT that a business can deduct: *SI 1995/2518, Reg 101* (the standard method, see **50.4–50.8** above) which determines the deduction of VAT relating to supplies made within the UK; and *SI 1995/2518, Reg 103(1)* which determines the deduction of VAT relating to '*foreign supplies*' and '*specified exempt supplies*' made outside the UK (see **50.12**(1) below). Where a business uses a special method instead of the standard method, if that method has been approved by HMRC and already deals with foreign supplies and specified exempt supplies, the case has no application. Where a special method does not deal with these supplies, then the business must deal with them under the provisions in **50.12**(1) below before applying the special method. (Business Brief 12/01).

Example

The facts are the same as in the example in **50.8** above except that HMRC allow X Ltd to use a special method and calculate the proportion of residual input tax attributable to taxable supplies by the formula

$$\text{Residual input tax} \times \frac{\text{Input tax attributable to taxable supplies}}{\text{Total input tax}}$$

	£	£
First quarter		
Input tax attributable to taxable supplies	36,409	
Proportion of residual input tax deductible =		
£11,751 × 36,409/53,007 =	8,071	
		44,480

	£	£
Second quarter		
Input tax attributable to taxable supplies	20,245	
Proportion of residual input tax deductible = £5,212 × 20,245/25,768 =	4,095	
	£24,340	
The value of exempt input tax is £1,428 (311 + [5,212 – 4,095]). As this is not more than £625 per month on average and is less than 50% of all input tax in the quarter, all input tax in the quarter is recoverable.		
Deductible input tax		25,768
Third quarter		
Input tax attributable to taxable supplies	34,698	
Proportion of residual input tax deductible = £10,963 × 34,698/46,856 =	8,118	
		42,816
Fourth quarter		
Input tax attributable to taxable supplies	69,707	
Proportion of residual input tax deductible = £9,357 × 69,707/85,039 =	7,670	
		77,377
		£190,441

For the annual adjustment required at the end of the tax year, see Example 2 in **50.13** below.

Non-business activities

Where a business also carries on non-business activities, it must normally first determine the proportion of VAT incurred relating to those activities and disregard any such VAT before applying the rules in this chapter. Alternatively, it can, in limited circumstances, apply the *Lennartz* mechanism to certain supplies. It then treats the supplies as business supplies for input tax purposes but must account for output tax on subsequent non-business use. See **35.7 INPUT TAX** for the calculation of VAT of non-business activities and the *Lennartz* mechanism.

Special methods may also be used to apportion input tax incurred on goods or services which are used/to be used partly for business purposes and partly for other purposes.

The combined method is available if a business needs to carry out only business/non-business (BNB) calculations (excluding apportionments involving private use) or if you need to carry out BNB (excluding apportionments involving private use) and partial exemption calculations. Therefore, it will mainly benefit charities and educational bodies. The combined method does not cater for private use apportionments, which continue to be calculated on a fair and reasonable basis.

The combined method must cover all the business's VAT apportionments apart from those involving private use and certain partial exemption calculations that are always determined on the basis of use.

HMRC will not approve separate BNB and partial exemption methods if the business is partly exempt. In these circumstances, where approval of a method for BNB calculations is sought, it must also cover partial exemption calculations (excluding the aforementioned apportionments). This is to save the cost of seeking approval of two separate methods and also helps to make sure there is a fair recovery of VAT overall as the calculations can be considered in their entirety.

HMRC will approve a single BNB method, provided that the business has not incurred any VAT on costs that relate to exempt supplies (exempt input tax) in its current tax year or immediately preceding tax year (or registration period), that is the business is 'fully taxable'. If the business becomes partly exempt a special method over-ride notice (see below) will automatically apply to the method that requires apportionments covered by the combined method to be recovered on a fair and reasonable basis from the date exempt input tax is first incurred.

The *de minimis* rules, simplified tests and annual test do not apply (see **50.11** below).

[*SI 1995/2518, Reg 102ZA*]. (VAT Notice 706, paras 7.1–7.8).

Special method over-ride

Particularly when business circumstances change, a special method agreed with HMRC might no longer produce a fair and reasonable result and a new method must be found. As this can take time, and because a new method cannot normally be backdated, HMRC or the business can suffer as a result. Special rules allow either HMRC or the business concerned to introduce an over-ride with immediate effect and correct the unfair method to ensure that VAT deducted reflects the principle of use (i.e. that it fairly and reasonably reflects the extent that costs and purchases are used or will be used in making taxable supplies). This will continue until a replacement method is implemented. It is, however, only a temporary measure and HMRC expect its use to be rare. The detailed provisions are as follows.

Notwithstanding HMRC's powers to serve a notice under *SI 1985/2518, Reg 102* above, where that person is using a special method which does not fairly and reasonably represent the extent to which goods or services are used by him (or are to be used by him) in making taxable supplies

- HMRC may serve a notice on him to that effect, setting out their reasons in support of that notification and stating the effect of the notice, and
- subject to any such notice, the taxable person may serve a notice on HMRC to that effect, setting out his reasons in support of that notification.

Where such a notice is served by HMRC (or served by the taxable person and approved by HMRC), then in relation to

- VAT periods commencing on or after the date of the notice (or such later date as may be specified in the notice), and
- longer periods (see **50.13** below) to the extent of that part of the longer period falls on or after the date of the notice (or such later date as may be specified in the notice)

the taxable person must calculate the difference between

(a) the amount of deductible VAT using the current special scheme, and
(b) the amount of deductible VAT calculated in accordance with the principle of use

and account for the difference on the return for that VAT period or on the return on which that longer period adjustment is required to be made. HMRC may allow another return to be used for this purpose.

This procedure then continues until HMRC either approve or direct the termination of the special method currently being adopted.

[*SI 1995/2518, Regs 102A–102C*].

HMRC will only serve or approve a notice where

- they have clear evidence that the current special method does not fairly and reasonably reflect the business's use of purchases in making taxable supplies; and
- they are satisfied that preparing a replacement method will not conclude quickly and the direction of a special method is not appropriate.

Serving and approving a notice

A notice must specify that it is a special method over-ride notice and state the date from which it takes effect. It must also give the reasons why the current special method does not produce a fair result.

When HMRC approve a notice served by a business, they will do so in writing as soon as possible, ideally within 30 days of receipt.

Complying with a notice

In most cases the reasons given by HMRC or the business in the notice will provide a basis for determining the notice correction. However, a business must still consider its whole method and determine whether there are any other aspects that would otherwise give an unfair result. The notice correction must therefore ensure that each time a VAT return is prepared, the amount of VAT deducted fairly and reasonably reflects the extent that costs and purchases are used (or will be used) in making taxable supplies (the principle of use). If a business does not make corrections to the amount of VAT deducted, and HMRC conclude that a notice correction should have been made, they will make the correction by way of VAT assessment.

(VAT Notice 706, paras 8.1–8.7).

De Voil Indirect Tax Service. See V3.462.

De minimis limit

Normal *de minimis* rules

[50.11] Subject to special provisions below, where 'relevant input tax'

- in any VAT period, or
- in any longer period, see **50.13** below (taken together, where appropriate, with the amount of any adjustment under **50.9**(*b*) above)

is not more than

(a) £625 per month 'on average', and
(b) one half of all input tax for the period concerned,

all such input tax in that period is treated as attributable to taxable supplies.

When applying these provisions to a longer period,

- any treatment of relevant input tax as attributable to taxable supplies in any VAT period is disregarded, and
- no account is to be taken of any amount or amounts which may be deductible or payable under the **11 CAPITAL GOODS SCHEME**.

'*Relevant input tax*' is input tax attributed to exempt supplies or to supplies outside the UK which would be exempt if made in the UK (not being supplies falling within **50.2** (*c*) above) under

- the standard method (see **50.4–50.8** above),
- a special method (see **50.10** above),
- the rules for foreign and specified supplies (see **50.12**(1) below),
- the rules for incidental financial supplies (see **50.12**(2) below),
- the rules for attribution to exempt supplies of investment gold, see **27.4 GOLD AND PRECIOUS METALS**), and
- where appropriate, the annual adjustment (see **50.13** below).

[*SI 1995/2518, Reg 106*].

'*On average*' means the average over the relevant VAT period or, as the case may be, longer period. For group registrations, the rules apply to the group as a whole.

(VAT Notice 706, paras 11.2, 11.3).

Simplified tests

Simplified tests apply to save some businesses the need to carry out a full partial exemption calculation to confirm their *de minimis* status. If, in a VAT period, a business passes Test one or Test two (set out below) it may treat itself as *de minimis* and provisionally recover input tax relating to exempt supplies. The business is still required to review its *de minimis* status at year-end as before and account for any under/over recovery of input tax as part of its annual adjustment (see **50.13** below).

Test one: total input tax incurred is no more than £625 per month on average and the value of exempt supplies is no more than 50% of the value of all supplies.

Test two: total input tax incurred less input tax directly attributable to taxable supplies is no more than £625 per month on average and the value of exempt supplies is no more than 50% of the value of all supplies.

'Total input tax' excludes blocked input tax (such as VAT on the cost of business entertainment) which is irrecoverable. 'The value of all supplies' includes taxable supplies made in the UK, supplies made outside the UK which confer the right of recovery (known as '*Reg 103* supplies') and exempt supplies. 'Input tax directly attributable to taxable supplies' is input tax on costs that are used or to be used exclusively in making taxable supplies, e.g. input tax on the cost of goods for resale.

Example 1

A business has a VAT period running from 1 April to 30 June. During that period it incurs total input tax of £1,800 which it uses making taxable supplies of £30,000 and exempt supplies of £20,000. For the quarter ending 30 June, the business incurs total input tax of no more than £1,875 (£625 x 3 months) and the value of its exempt supplies is no more than 50% of its total supplies (20,000/50,000 × 100 = 40%). Therefore, the business is *de minimis* for this period as it passes Test one and can provisionally recover £1,800 input tax on its VAT return without the need to carry out a full partial exemption calculation. This will be subject to review at year-end.

Example 2

A business has a partial exemption year running from 1 May 2016 to 30 April 2017. During that period it incurs total input tax of £30,000, of which £25,000 is on goods for resale which are directly attributable to taxable supplies. It makes taxable supplies of £75,000 and exempt supplies of £60,000. Its total input tax less input tax directly attributable to taxable supplies is £5,000 (30,000 – 25,000) which is less than £7,500 (£625 x 12), and the value of its exempt supplies is no more than 50% of its total supplies (60,000/135,000 × 100 = 44%). Therefore, the business has finalised its *de minimis* status for the year and is entitled to recover £30,000. There is no need for any further partial exemption calculation for that year.

The new tests supplement the original test. A business is *de minimis* if it passes Test one, Test two **or** the original test, and if it passes any one test there is no need for it to consider the other two. Even if a business fails Test one and Test two, the information gathered is still required to carry out a full partial exemption calculation for the original test.

At the end of the partial exemption year, the *de minimis* test must be applied to the year as a whole. If Test one is passed for the year, all of input tax relating to exempt supplies can be recovered and there is no need to carry out any further partial exemption calculations. When applying Test two, the business first needs to review how much of the input tax incurred over the year is directly attributable to taxable supplies. Then, if Test two is passed for the year, all input tax relating to exempt supplies can be recovered and there is no need to carry out any further partial exemption calculations. If the business fails Test one and Test two for the year, then it needs to carry out a full partial exemption calculation for the year to determine whether it passes the original *de minimis* test and account for any under/over recovery of input tax as part of its annual adjustment in the normal way.

Annual test

An annual test applies to give most businesses the option of applying the *de minimis* test once a year, instead of four or five times a year. It allows a business that was *de minimis* in its previous partial exemption year to treat itself as *de minimis* in its current partial exemption year. This means it can provisionally recover input tax relating to exempt supplies in each VAT period, saving the need for partial exemption calculations. The business must still review its *de minimis* status at year-end and if it fails the *de minimis* test for the year it must repay the input tax relating to exempt supplies that it provisionally recovered in-year. However, there is no need to carry out in-year partial exemption calculations.

Example 3

A business was *de minimis* in its partial exemption year ending 31 March 2017. It has the option of applying the annual test and treating itself as *de minimis* during the year ending 31 March 2018. This means that it can provisionally recover input tax relating to exempt supplies in each VAT period during that year without the need to carry out a partial exemption calculation. The business is then required to review its *de minimis* status at year-end and, if it fails the *de minimis* test for the year, repay the input tax it has incurred during the year that relates to exempt supplies.

There are three conditions on using the annual test. The business must

- pass the *de minimis* test for its previous partial exemption year;
- consistently apply the annual test throughout any given partial exemption year; and
- have reasonable grounds for not expecting to incur more than £1million input tax in its current partial exemption year.

If any of these conditions are not met then the business is required to apply the *de minimis* test in each VAT period, which remains the default position.

[*SI 1995/2518 Regs 105A and 106ZA*]. (VAT Information Sheet 4/10).

Special provisions where the standard method over-ride applies

Where, taken together with the amount of any over-ride adjustment under **50.9**(*a*) above, input tax attributed to exempt supplies or to supplies outside the UK which would be exempt if made in the UK (not being supplies falling within **50.2**(*c*) above) under

- the standard method (see **50.4–50.8** above),

- the rules for foreign and specified supplies (see **50.12**(1) below),
- the rules for incidental financial supplies (see **50.12**(2) below), and
- the rules for attribution to exempt supplies of investment gold, see **27.4 GOLD AND PRECIOUS METALS**),

is not more than

(a) £625 per month 'on average', and
(b) one half of all input tax for the period concerned,

all such input tax in that period is treated as attributable to taxable supplies.

Where this applies to a taxable person, he must calculate the difference between

- the total amount of input tax for that VAT period, and
- the amount of input tax deducted in that VAT period, taken together with the amount of any adjustment under **50.9**(*a*) above

and include this difference as an under-deduction in the return for the first VAT period next following that in which the substantial difference arose under the provisions in **50.9**(*a*) above (unless HMRC allow otherwise). If his registration has been cancelled by then, the adjustment must be made on his final VAT return.

Where, on the other hand, a taxable person has treated input tax as attributable to taxable supplies under the normal *de minimis* rules but is not entitled to do so because of the special provisions above, he must include the amount so treated as an over-deduction in the return for the first VAT period next following that in which the substantial difference arose under the provisions in **50.9**(*a*) (unless HMRC allow otherwise). If his registration has been cancelled by then, the adjustment must be made on his final VAT return.

[*SI 1995/2518, Reg 106A*].

De Voil Indirect Tax Service. See V3.465.

Attribution of input tax

Direct and immediate link

[50.12] In determining whether a particular cost or purchase has been used to make a specific taxable supply, it is necessary to establish a 'direct and immediate link' between the cost and the supply. Only where a direct and immediate link exists is there a right to deduct VAT incurred on that input. A direct and immediate link will exist if the cost incurred directly forms a component of the price of a supply or supplies being made. If a cost or purchase wholly forms a component of the price of an exempt supply or supplies, the input tax cannot be recovered.

General overheads of a business do not have a direct and immediate link with any specific supplies made by that business. But because they are set against income in calculating overall net profit or loss, they do have a direct and immediate link to the business as a whole. This gives them a direct and immediate link to all of the businesses supplies and means that the input tax incurred on them will always be residual.

In *C & E Commrs v Midland Bank plc, ECJ Case C–98/98*, [2000] STC 501 (TVC 22.454) the CJEU confirmed the need for a 'direct and immediate link'. The full amount of input tax cannot be deducted where the supply in question is used, not for the purpose of carrying out a deductible transaction, but in the context of activities which are no more than the consequence of making such a transaction, unless the taxpayer can show, by means of objective evidence, that the expenditure involved was part of the various cost components of the output transaction.

The national court should apply this 'direct and immediate link' test to the facts of each particular case. The point in question in the *Midland Bank* case was whether VAT on legal costs incurred defending a claim alleging negligent misrepresentation was wholly attributable to the zero-rated supplies made to the client or whether it should be apportioned between taxable and exempt supplies.

Example

A theatre buys the services of a production company to put on a show. There is a direct and immediate link between the costs of the production company and the ticket sales for the shows. If the production company also provides information for the published programme (for the shows) as part of its service, this will then create a direct and immediate link with the programme sales as well. If the ticket sales are exempt from VAT, and the programme sales are taxable (zero-rated), this would mean the input tax on the costs relevant to the production company would be residual rather than exempt.

In *The Queens Club Ltd* [2017] UKFTT 700 (TC) (TC06119) (TVC 46.73), the club is operated as a member's tennis club and it makes exempt supplies of sporting services to its members and it also makes taxable supplies, including the provision of food and drink at the numerous bars and restaurants on site. The club incurred VAT on the refurbishment of its bar, restaurant and café facilities and it sought to recover the input tax as wholly attributable to its taxable supplies. HMRC disagreed determining that the costs were residual and input tax should be recovered under the club's partial exemption method. The club appealed. The Tribunal allowed the club's appeal deciding that when a member joins the club they gain access to the sporting facilities together with whatever other facilities the club, at its discretion, chooses to offer. The focus is on the provision of the sporting facilities and the presence of the restaurants, etc. does not impact upon the members' enjoyment of the sporting facilities. As a result there is no direct and immediate link between the refurbishment works and the club's exempt supply of membership. The club is also under no obligation to provide its members with access to the bars, etc. and most members do not actually use these facilities. As a result the club can recover the input tax incurred in full as these costs are linked to the provision of taxable supplies by the club. The way the club operates in this case is clearly different to the practical way that most clubs of this nature operate, so this ruling may not have a wide impact and HMRC may make a decision to appeal it on the facts.

In *C & E Commrs v Southern Primary Housing Ltd*, CA 2003, [2004] STC 209 (TVC 46.30) a company purchased some land and paid VAT on the price (because the vendor had elected to waive exemption in respect of the land). It then sold the land to a housing association, under a contract whereby it agreed to build flats on the land for the association. The company considered that the VAT incurred on the purchase of the land was partly attributable to taxable supplies of building work. The Court of Appeal held that the input tax on the cost of buying the land was not a 'cost component' of the contract for the development of the land. There was nothing about the development contract as such which made the land purchase and sale essential. If the housing association had already owned the land or had bought it from some third party, the inputs of the development contract would have been just the costs of carrying it out. The fact that there were commercially linked land transactions did not mean that those transactions were directly linked to the costs of the development contract.

In *BAA Ltd v HMRC*, CA [2013] EWCA Civ 112 (TVC 32.32), a company arranged for the incorporation of a new company (AD) with the aim of making a takeover bid for another company (B), which operated several British airports. After the takeover, AD joined B's VAT group. The representative member of the group claimed a deduction for input tax that AD had incurred in relation to the takeover. The Court of Appeal held that there was no direct and immediate link between the input tax on supplies of services made to AD and the output tax on the supplies of services made by B. B's supplies were not connected at the relevant date with the supplies to AD on which input tax was incurred. Accordingly the group was not entitled to a deduction for the input tax.

Following the above decision in *BAA Ltd v HMRC*, CA [2013] EWCA Civ 112 (TVC 32.32) HMRC issued HMRC Brief 32/14 which explained that the facts in that case related to particular circumstances and that the decision did not address other commonly encountered issues relating to holding companies. HMRC did not change their policy as a result of the decision, but issued revised guidance, setting out when it considered that VAT may be recovered by holding companies.

The guidance was controversial, and appears to be contradicted by the decision of the CJEU in the joined cases of *Beteiligungsgesellschaft Larentia + Minerva mbH & Co. KG v Finanzamt Nordenham, ECJ Case C–108/14* (TVC 22.471) and *Finanzamt Hamburg-Mitte v Marenave Schiffahrts AG, ECJ Case C–109/14* (TVC 22.471) decided in 2015. HMRC eventually issued amended guidance as a result of these decisions, in relation to the recovery of holding company input tax (see **28 GROUPS OF COMPANIES** for more information).

(HMRC Brief 32/14) (HMRC Manual VIT40600).

In the joined cases of *Larentia + Minerva* and *Marenave*, the CJEU confirmed that expenditure connected with the acquisition of shareholdings in subsidiaries by a holding company which involves itself in the management of those subsidiaries must be regarded as belonging to the holding company's general overhead expenditure, and the VAT paid on the expenditure must, in principle, be deducted in full, subject to the normal rules. There is no 'non-business component' in the expenditure, as long as the holding company is engaged in economic activity, which is satisfied by making supplies of taxable management services to its subsidiaries. Only making exempt supplies will lead to a restriction of overhead input tax.

Ultimate purpose of transactions

It is not possible to deduct input tax used for making an exempt supply even if the ultimate purpose of the transaction is the carrying out of a taxable transaction (*BLP Group plc v C & E Commrs, ECJ Case C–4/94*, [1995] STC 424 (TVC 22.453)). In that case, the company incurred input tax on professional fees in connection with the disposal of shares in a subsidiary company in order to pay debts. The court held that the input tax was not recoverable as it related to the exempt sales of shares, even though the ultimate purpose of this exempt supply was to enable the business to continue to make taxable supplies.

Attribution of input tax in particular cases is considered below.

(1) Foreign and specified supplies

Other than where it falls to be attributed under a method approved or directed by HMRC under *SI 1995/2518, Reg 102* (see **50.10** above) or from 1 April 2009, under the standard method in *SI 1995/2518, Reg 101* (see **50.4–50.8** above), where input tax is incurred by a business in any VAT period on goods or services which are used (or to be used) in whole or part in making

- '*foreign supplies*', i.e. supplies outside the UK which would be taxable supplies if made in the UK; or
- '*specified exempt supplies*', i.e. supplies of services which
  - (i) are supplied to a person who belongs outside the EU, or
  - (ii) are directly linked to the export of goods to a place outside the EU, or
  - (iii) consist of the provision of intermediary services in relation to any transaction within (i) or (ii) above

  and where the supply would have been exempt if made in the UK under *VATA 1994, Sch 9 Group 2* (insurance) or *VATA 1994, Sch 9 Group 5 items 1–8* (finance)

the input tax must be attributed to taxable supplies to the extent that the goods or services are so used (or to be used). The attribution must be expressed as a proportion of the whole use (or intended use). It is up to the business to decide how this can be achieved.

For accounting periods beginning after 31 December 2015, partial exemption special method (see **50.10** above) calculations that are not based on sectors cannot include the value of supplies made from overseas establishments. (HMRC Brief 22/15).

[*SI 1995/2518, Reg 103(1); SI 2015/1978*].

(2) Services and related goods used partly to make incidental financial supplies

Where, other than where it falls to be attributed under the standard method in *SI 1995/2518, Reg 101* (see **50.4–50.8** above),

- a business incurs input tax in any VAT period on supplies to it of any of the services listed below and of any related goods,
- those services and related goods are used or to be used by the business in making both
  - (i) a '*relevant supply*' (i.e. a supply of financial services within *VATA 1994, Sch 9 Group 5 Items 1* or *6* (see **24.8** and **24.17 FINANCIAL SERVICES**) or a supply of the same description which is made in another EU member state); *and*
  - (ii) any other supply, and
- the relevant supply is incidental to one or more of its business activities,

that input tax must be attributed to taxable supplies (including supplies falling within (1) above) to the extent that the services or related goods are so used (or to be used). The attribution must be expressed as a proportion of the whole use (or intended use). This applies despite any provision of any input tax attribution method that the business is required or allowed to use which purports to have the contrary effect.

The services in question are those supplied by

- accountants;
- advertising agencies;
- bodies which provide listing and registration services;
- financial advisers;
- lawyers;
- marketing consultants;
- persons who prepare and design documentation; and
- any person or body which provides similar services to those listed above.

[*SI 1995/2518, Reg 103B*].

Incidental supplies are those which are subordinate to the main activities of the business. They tend to consume little by way of general overheads but may incur significant direct costs. Incidental financial supplies will usually be issues of new shares, bonds and similar securities and sales of existing shares in subsidiaries where these are made on an occasional basis and do not represent a business activity.

General business overheads (e.g. a company's annual audit) are not covered and, if the company is otherwise partly exempt, fall to be dealt with under the normal partial exemption method.

The effect of the above provisions is that input tax incurred on the services listed above must be divided into four categories:

- Input tax used to make financial services within the EU (non-recoverable).

- Input tax used to make financial supplies to individuals and businesses outside the EU (recoverable).
- Input tax used to make taxable supplies (recoverable).
- Input tax used to make other exempt transactions (non-recoverable).

HMRC will accept any calculation to determine extent of use if it provides a fair and reasonable attribution of input tax according to use (or intended use) of the relevant costs. For example, where professional services are incurred in connection with a share issue and shares are issued to subscribers in the UK and Japan, apportionment could be based on the number of subscribers, the number of shares issued or the value of the shares issued, provided the method used gives a fair and reasonable result.

(VAT Information Sheet 9/04).

(3) Share issues, etc.

In *Kretztechnik AG v Finanzamt Linz, ECJ Case C–465/03*, [2005] STC 1118 (TVC 22.96), an Austrian company issued shares and reclaimed input tax on the related costs. The tax authority rejected the claim (on the grounds that the issue of shares was an exempt supply) but the CJEU held that the issue of shares by a public limited company is not a supply within what is now *Directive 2006/112/EC, Art 2(1)(a)* and that input tax on services acquired for the purposes of such a share issue may be deducted to the extent that the company charges VAT on its output transactions.

HMRC accept that this decision applies to companies making first issues of shares in circumstances that are the same as those in *Kretztechnik*. Therefore, companies with wholly taxable outputs are entitled to recover all of the relevant input tax, while those with both exempt and taxable outputs can recover a proportion in accordance with their partial exemption method.

HMRC issued the following guidance on the VAT position of share transactions where the circumstances differ from those in *Kretztechnik*.

(a) *Transactions involving issues of other types of shares.* The *Kretztechnik* principles are applicable to share issues such as preference shares, special rights issues, bonus issues and issues of scrip dividends. All such share issues are to be regarded as non-supplies for VAT purposes.

(b) *Transactions involving issues by different types of companies.* Kretztechnik was a public limited company but, provided that the issuer's motivation is (like Kretztechnik's) the raising of capital, issues of shares by other types of companies (e.g. private companies) are non-supplies for VAT purposes.

(c) *Transactions involving the issue of financial instruments or securities other than shares.* The issue of other types of security (e.g. bonds, debentures or loan notes) should also be treated as non-supplies when the purpose of the issue is to raise capital for the issuer's business. Similarly, the issue of shares or units in collective investment funds (e.g. open-ended investment companies and authorised unit trusts) are not supplies for VAT purposes.

(d) *Shares and other securities issued in other situations*. An issue of shares or other securities that takes place in the context of wider arrangements (e.g. as part of a company takeover or restructuring through merger or demerger) should still be regarded as a non-supply for VAT purposes.

Although any of the above transactions which are not supplies no longer have a corresponding VAT liability (e.g. exemption), intermediary and underwriting services in relation to such transactions remain exempt.

(Business Briefs 12/05, 21/05, 22/05). See Business Briefs 21/05 and 22/05 for input tax on issues of shares made outside the EU, and input tax incurred by intermediaries in share issues, following the *Kretztechnik* case.

(4) Self-supplies

Where under or by virtue of any provision of *VATA 1994* a person makes a supply to himself, the input tax on that supply must not be allowable as attributable to that supply. [*SI 1995/2518, Reg 104*].

(5) Acquiring a business as a going concern

In accordance with the decision in *C & E Commrs v UBAF Bank Ltd*, CA [1996] STC 372 (TVC 46.7), where a business acquires assets by way of the transfer of a going concern, and the assets are used exclusively to make taxable supplies, the VAT incurred on the cost of acquiring those assets should be attributed to those taxable supplies and can be recovered in full. Conversely, if the assets of the acquired business are to be used exclusively to make exempt supplies, none of the input tax on the cost of acquiring those assets can be recovered. However, if the assets are to be used in making both taxable and exempt supplies, any input tax incurred is non-attributable and must be apportioned in accordance with the agreed VAT partial exemption method. In *UBAF Bank Ltd* a leasing company acquired the shares in another leasing company and immediately transferred the trade and assets to itself; the court held that the acquisition of the shares was equivalent to an acquisition of the trade and assets, and accordingly that input tax on professional fees incurred in connection with the acquisition was on supplies wholly used, or to be used, by the bank in making taxable supplies of equipment leasing and recoverable in full. (VAT Notice 700/9/12, para 2.6.1).

De Voil Indirect Tax Service. See V3.464.

Annual adjustments

[50.13] The deductions of input tax for each VAT period are provisional whether the standard or a special method is adopted. This is because the amount deductible in some such periods may be unfairly affected, e.g. by seasonal variations. It is normally necessary, therefore, to recalculate the amount of input tax reclaimable over a 'longer period'. If a special method is used, the letter of approval will state whether an annual adjustment is required.

Where a business incurs exempt input tax during any 'tax year', its '*longer period*' corresponds with that tax year unless it did not incur exempt input tax during its immediately preceding tax year or 'registration period' in which case its longer period begins on the first day of the first VAT period in which it incurs exempt input tax and ends on the last day of that tax year. Where, however, the only exempt input tax of the business is incurred in the last VAT period of its tax year, no longer accounting period is applied in respect of that tax year.

There are also rules to deal with special circumstances where the longer period is not a period of twelve months.

- *Newly-registered businesses*. Where a business incurs exempt input tax during its registration period, its longer period begins on the first day on which it incurs exempt input tax and ends on the day before the commencement of its first tax year.
- *Belated registration*. Where a business is registered retrospectively, its first VAT return may cover a period longer than a tax year. In such a case, the period must be broken down and a longer period adjustment made in respect of the registration period and each subsequent tax year.
- *Deregistration*. In the case of a business ceasing to be taxable during a longer period, that period ends on the day it ceases to be taxable.

'*Tax year*' is the twelve months ending on 31 March, 30 April or 31 May according to the VAT periods allocated. HMRC may approve or direct that a tax year be for a period other than twelve months.

The '*registration period*' of a taxable person means the period commencing on his effective date of registration and ending on the day before the commencement of his first tax year.

[*SI 1995/2518, Reg 99*]. (VAT Notice 706, paras 12.3, 12.7–12.9).

Calculation of annual adjustments

Unless HMRC dispense with the requirements, a taxable person must calculate the reclaimable proportion of any residual input tax not directly attributed on the same basis as in each of the VAT periods but using the figures for the longer period.

Any difference between the amount of reclaimable input tax recalculated at the end of the longer period and the total amount provisionally deducted during the VAT periods is an over or under declaration of VAT and must be entered on:

- the VAT return for the first VAT period after the end of the longer period (unless HMRC allow otherwise); or
- the last VAT return of the longer period.

Where registration has been cancelled, the annual adjustment should be entered on the VAT return for the final period ending on the effective date of registration.

If the recalculation shows that the exempt input tax is below the *de minimis* limits in **50.11** above, any input tax not already reclaimed is an under deduction of VAT and should be entered on the next VAT return.

Annual adjustments which have been correctly carried out are not errors and do not have to be disclosed under the error correction notification (formerly voluntary disclosure) procedure (see **57.11 RECORDS**). Where, however, an error is made in the partial exemption calculation for a VAT period (e.g. input tax is incorrectly treated as exempt when the goods or services were used to make taxable supplies) this should not be 'corrected' by the annual adjustment but should be notified separately under the error correction notification (formerly voluntary disclosure) procedure.

[*SI 1995/2518, Reg 107*]. (VAT Notice 706, paras 12.4, 12.6; VAT Information Sheet 4/09, para 3).

Example 1

At the end of the tax year, X Ltd in the example in **50.8** above must carry out the following annual adjustment.

	£
Input tax attributable to taxable supplies	161,059
Proportion of residual input tax deductible =	
2,028,999/2,155,935 = 94.11%	
£37,283 × 95% =	35,419
Deductible input tax for year	196,478
Deducted over the four quarters	198,368
Under declaration to be paid to HMRC	£1,890

Example 2

At the end of the tax year, X Ltd in the example in **50.10** above must carry out the following annual adjustment.

	£
Input tax attributable to taxable supplies	161,059
Proportion of residual input tax deductible =	
£37,283 × 161,059/210,670 =	28,503
Deductible input tax for year	189,562
Deducted over the four quarters	190,441
Under declaration to be paid to HMRC	£879

De Voil Indirect Tax Service. See V3.466.

Adjustments for change in use of goods and services

[50.14] Attribution of input tax should be initially carried out on the basis of the use made, or intended to be made, of the goods or services (see **50.3** above). However, there may be occasions when the intended or actual use of those goods or services changes. Where a business either

- changes its intention before using the goods or services, or
- actually uses the goods or services for a different purpose,

the following 'clawback' or 'payback' provisions apply.

(a) 'Clawback' provisions

Clawback provisions apply where a taxable person has deducted an amount of input tax which has been attributed to taxable supplies because he intended to use the goods or services in making either

(i) 'taxable supplies', or
(ii) both taxable and 'exempt supplies',

and during a period of six years commencing on the first day of the VAT period in which the attribution was determined and before that intention is fulfilled, he uses or forms an intention to use the goods or services in making exempt supplies (or where (i) above applies, in making both taxable and exempt supplies).

Subject to below, under such circumstances, unless HMRC allow otherwise, the taxable person must account for an amount equal to the input tax which has ceased to be attributable to taxable supplies in accordance with the method he was required to use when the input tax was first attributed. This should be done on the return for the VAT period in which the use occurs or the revised intention is formed. (VAT Notice 706, paras 13.7, 13.8).

In *Belgium v Ghent Coal Terminal NV, ECJ Case C–37/95*, [1998] STC 260 (TVC 22.461), a company purchased some land, had work carried out on it and reclaimed the input tax on these supplies. Subsequently the local council required the company to exchange the land before it had been used for any taxable purpose. The CJEU held that the right to deduction was exercisable immediately the inputs were incurred and, once it had arisen, remained valid even if, by reason of circumstances beyond its control, the taxable person never used the goods or services in question for the purposes of taxable transactions. This would not apply in cases of fraud or abuse and such a supply might give rise to a subsequent adjustment under the **11 CAPITAL GOODS SCHEME**.

(b) Clawback provisions: interim use differing from original intention

In *C & E Commrs v Briararch Ltd; C & E Commrs v Curtis Henderson Ltd*, QB [1992] STC 732 (TVC 46.226) the court held that apportionment of input tax applied under this provision where a property is, or is intended to be, the subject of sequential supplies at different VAT liabilities. In the cases involved, the companies had reclaimed input tax in full on the basis that the properties concerned would be the subject of taxable supplies but, when the building work was completed, they were obliged to obtain temporary rental income on short leases which was an exempt supply. In circumstances such as these, where goods or services are put to an interim use different to that originally intended, provided the original intention is still retained, the input tax must be apportioned on a fair and reasonable basis. In *Briararch Ltd* the company let the property on a four-year exempt lease whilst still intending to make a taxable supply of a 25-year lease. The court held that 25/29 of the input tax related to the intended taxable supply and that the clawback provisions applied to 4/29 of the original claim.

See also *Cooper and Chapman (Builders) Ltd v C & E Commrs*, QB 1992 [1993] STC 1 (TVC 46.219) where a building was converted into flats with the intention that they would all be let as holiday accommodation (standard-rated) but, after some flats had been so let, the company granted a one-year lease of the whole building (an exempt supply).

HMRC have set out their policy where house builders decide to temporarily let their dwellings before selling them, and so become partly exempt. For many house builders the amount of exempt input tax related to their temporary lets is small (*de minimis*) and as a result they can continue to recover all of their input tax; but they must check to avoid VAT mistakes. Exceptionally, HMRC will allow a builder that does not currently operate a partial exemption method, to adopt instead a 'simple check for de minimis'. This simple check is based on the expected time period he will let his building as a proportion of the economic life of that building, which for VAT purposes is ten years. His exempt input tax is determined by applying the proportion to his total input tax. Provided his exempt input tax does not exceed £625 per month on average (up to £7,500 per year), and is not more than half of his total input tax, then his exempt input tax is *de minimis* and he can recover it in full. If a house builder who was previously fully taxable continues to incur exempt input tax in future then he will need to apply a partial exemption method to determine if he remains *de minimis*. He can either apply the standard method or he can seek HMRC approval to apply a special method.

A house builder makes a clawback adjustment as soon as his actual or intended use of a property differs from his original plans against which input tax was recovered. A clawback adjustment is a one-off event and a house builder would only make a second adjustment if the building was never let. There is no need to amend the adjustment if the actual period of letting proved to be longer or shorter than anticipated. A clawback adjustment must be based on the house builders' realistic expectation, judged at the time his original plans were set aside. HMRC may ask for evidence to show that the adjustment calculation is reasonable.

The house builder calculates his clawback adjustment by comparing the amount of input tax deducted with the amount of input tax he would have deducted had he held his changed intention all along. His clawback adjustment is simply the difference between the two input tax amounts. The builder calculates the amount of input tax he would have deducted by applying his partial exemption method at the time the costs were incurred. If a house builder was not already operating a partial exemption method then he must apply the standard method unless he obtains HMRC approval to apply a special method instead. A house builder that does not currently operate a partial exemption method, can exceptionally if he prefers, base his clawback adjustment on an alternative calculation (without first adopting a partial exemption method and without prior approval from HMRC) so long as that calculation is fair. HMRC can allow this under their care and management powers. HMRC will accept any clawback calculation provided it fairly reflects the use of costs in making taxable supplies. A calculation based on the values of supplies is normally fair and straightforward provided it is based on reasonable estimates and valuations. The formula: input tax incurred x (estimated eventual sale value/estimated eventual sale value plus estimated short let premiums and rents) would give the amount of recoverable input tax.

> *Example*
>
> A house builder expects to sell two houses for £500,000 each. The input tax recovered during the tax year was £50,000. After the end of the tax year the decision is taken to rent them for a period of three years generating estimated rental income of £200,000. The house builder makes no other supplies.
>
> £50,000 input tax incurred × £1,000,000/£1,200,000 = £41,667 recoverable input tax
>
> £50,000 input tax previously recovered – £41,666 = £8,334 to be repaid to HMRC

No adjustment should be made for potential bad debts during the letting period. If it is not possible to fairly estimate the values then a different calculation may be needed. Apportionments based on the expected time period of the rental or short-term lease are not recommended except as a quick *de minimis* check. The alternative calculations cannot be used if a partial exemption method was already in place. But, if an existing partial exemption method becomes unfair because of the short-term lets, then HMRC may exceptionally allow an alternative method to be agreed and backdated.

A house builder that expects to continue to incur exempt input tax in his current or future VAT periods would need to adopt a partial exemption method. If he is not already partly exempt, then he must either apply the standard method or seek HMRC approval to apply a special method.

(VAT Information Sheet 7/08).

(c) 'Payback' provisions

Payback provisions apply where a taxable person has incurred input tax which has not been attributed to taxable supplies because he intended to use the goods or services in making either

(i) 'exempt supplies', or
(ii) both 'taxable' and exempt supplies

and during a period of six years commencing on the first day of the VAT period in which the attribution was determined and before that intention is fulfilled, he uses or forms an intention to use the goods or services in making taxable supplies (or where (i) above applies, in making both taxable and exempt supplies).

Subject to below, under such circumstances, HMRC must, on application by the taxable person in such form as HMRC require, repay to him an amount equal to the input tax which has become attributable to taxable supplies in accordance with the method he was required to use when the input tax was first attributed.

In practice, the taxable person should write to HMRC and, when they have confirmed the amount to be repaid, enter the amount due in the VAT account as an underclaim and include it in the next VAT return. (VAT Notice 706, paras 13.9, 13.10).

In *Royal & Sun Alliance Insurance Group plc v C & E Commrs*, HL [2003] STC 832 (TVC 46.230) a company decided that certain properties were no longer needed for its exempt insurance business. It decided to sublet the properties and opted to tax them. It initially treated the input tax incurred on rents and service charges during the periods the properties were vacant prior to the exercise of the option as attributable to exempt supplies. Subsequently, it claimed a repayment of this input tax. The HL (by a 3 to 2 majority, reversing the decisions of the Ch D and CA and restoring the decision of the tribunal) held that to come within the payback provisions, the company must first have had an intention to use the inputs in supplying exempt sub-leases and then used them, or formed the intention to use them, in supplying taxable sub-leases. The running costs had been consumed at a time when the company had not opted to tax, and it could not 'rewrite history': these costs were not subsequently 'used' for a different purpose once the option had been exercised, so the company did not satisfy the second condition and the payback provisions could not apply.

In *Community Housing Association Ltd*, Ch D [2009] STC 1324 (TVC 46.233) CHA was a housing association providing mainly exempt rental housing. It incurred input tax related to the construction of new dwellings for use in its business. It subsequently changed its operation by inserting a new subsidiary between itself and its suppliers. After having raised invoices to the subsidiary for the value of work undertaken on uncompleted projects prior to this change, CHA lodged a 'payback' claim. CHA argued that input tax on costs for part completed projects incurred prior to the change were not used as originally intended and were now attributable to a taxable supply from CHA to the new subsidiary. The High Court allowed the payback claim, finding as fact that CHA made supplies to its subsidiary and that the supplies transferred useful material and rights arising from the old supplies received by CHA.

In *Imofloresmira – Investimentos Imobiliários v Autoridade Tributária e Aduaneira, CJEU Case C-672/16*, the CJEU held that a requirement to adjust input tax recovered in an earlier period is incompatible with EU law, if the taxpayer continues to intend to make taxable supplies and is doing everything possible to make that taxable supply occur. From a UK perspective, with regard to VAT falling within the CGS, HMRC's policy does not require a VAT-registered business to adjust its historical recovery position where the property becomes vacant or where the property is vacant for a period of time, which is broadly in line with the CJEU decision. If input tax is incurred during a period when the property is vacant, HMRC expect input tax recovery to be in accordance with the intended use of the property in that period and, there would only be a requirement to make a future adjustment if the intention was to change and input tax needed to be repaid under the payback provisions [*SI 1995/2518, Reg 108*].

Supplies outside the UK

Where (*a*) or (*b*) above applies, subject to the provisions relating to foreign supplies in **50.12**(1) above and incidental financial supplies in **50.12**(2) above, if

- the use to which the goods or services are put (or to which they are intended to be put) includes the making of supplies outside the UK, and
- at the time when the taxable person was first required to attribute the input tax he was not required to use a method approved or directed under **50.10** above (or he was required to use such a method but that method did not expressly provide for the attribution of input tax attributable to supplies outside the UK)

then the relevant amount under (*a*) or (*b*) above is to be calculated by reference to the extent to which the goods or services concerned are used (or intended to be used) in making taxable supplies, expressed as a proportion of the whole use (or intended use).

Exempt supplies

'*Exempt supplies*' includes supplies outside the UK which would be exempt supplies if made in the UK (other than those supplies falling within **50.2**(*c*) above). It also includes supplies of investment gold but only to the extent that there is, or would be, no credit for input tax on goods and services under *SI 1995/2518, Reg 103A* (see **27.4 GOLD AND PRECIOUS METALS**).

Taxable supplies

'*Taxable supplies*' includes supplies within **50.2**(*b*) or (*c*) above. It also includes supplies of investment gold but only to the extent that there is, or would be, credit for input tax on goods and services under *SI 1995/2518, Reg 103A* (see **27.4 GOLD AND PRECIOUS METALS**).

[*SI 1995/2518, Regs 108–110; SI 1999/3114; SI 2004/3140, Reg 14*].

De Voil Indirect Tax Service. See V3.467.

Treatment in special circumstances

[50.15] In special circumstances, treatment is as follows:

(1) Abortive activities

There may be occasions where a business incurs VAT in connection with intended supplies that are never actually made.

- If the goods or services are used to make an alternative supply of a different liability, then the adjustment provisions in **50.14** above apply.
- If the initial intention is frustrated and the goods or services are not used to make any supply (e.g. architect's fees on an aborted building project), following the decision of the CJEU in *Belgium v Ghent Coal*

Terminal NV, ECJ Case C–37/95, [1998] STC 260 (TVC 22.461), no adjustment to the initial claim of input tax is required. Previously, HMRC' policy was to treat such abortive supplies as part of the general overhead costs of the business so that the input tax formed part of the residual input tax to be apportioned under the partial exemption method used. (VAT Notice 706, para 13.14).

See also **43.4 LAND AND BUILDINGS: ZERO AND REDUCED RATE SUPPLIES AND DIY HOUSEBUILDERS** for aborted supplies by speculative developers.

(2) Holding companies

See **28.9 GROUPS OF COMPANIES.**

(3) Professional fees on share acquisitions

See the *Larentia + Minerva* decision at **50.12** above.

(4) Share issues

See **50.12**(3) above.

(5) Transfers of going concerns (TOGCs)

See **50.12**(4) above for the position of the transferee and **9.14 BUSINESS** for the position of the transferor.

See also **28.7 GROUPS OF COMPANIES** for acquisitions of TOGCs by partly-exempt groups.

(6) Costs of settling insurance claims

See **37.10 INSURANCE.**

(7) Petrol scale charges

See **46.16 MOTOR CARS.**

(8) VAT recovery on hire purchase transactions

In most hire purchase transactions, the goods are resold at cost without any margin to cover overhead costs. As there is no margin on the hire purchase goods, the cost of the overheads will normally be built into the price of the exempt supply of credit. In such a situation, HMRC's view is that the overheads are purely cost components of the exempt supply. Otherwise the business would continually enjoy net VAT refunds despite making no zero-rated or reduced rate supplies and charging a total consideration under the hire purchase agreement that fully recovers its costs and an element of profit.

Where overheads are used to make both hire purchase transactions and other supplies on which VAT is charged (e.g. taxable purchase option fees or sales of repossessed goods), then some VAT on overhead costs is recoverable. In such cases, the partial exemption method should reflect the extent to which the overhead costs are a cost component of the prices of the supplies in question.

HMRC expect their above policy to be applied by all businesses that make supplies under hire purchase agreements to consumers. It does not apply to those who only arrange such supplies and receive a commission.

(HMRC Brief 31/07).

In *Volkswagen Financial Services (UK) Ltd* [2015] EWCA Civ 832 (TVC 46.105) the company was involved in supplying goods under hire purchase agreements where the goods were sold without any margin to cover overhead costs. The cost of the overheads was built into the exempt supply of credit. The Court of Appeal decided that the overheads were general costs of the business and therefore cost components of all of the relevant supplies, including the taxable supplies of goods sold at cost, contrary to HMRC's policy as expressed in the above Brief. The Court of Appeal referred the substantive issue to the CJEU and the Supreme Court was asked to consider the secondary issue of whether HMRC's challenge to the apportionment formula should be considered. The Supreme Court rejected HMRC's attempt to question to percentage attributed to taxable supplies and HMRC's grounds for appeal was therefore dismissed.

(9) Reverse charge on services from abroad

VAT must be accounted for on certain services received from abroad. See **39.4 INTERNATIONAL SERVICES.** The VAT can also be treated as input tax. However, for partial exemption purposes these services are not regarded as supplies and input tax on these imported services can only be claimed in full if the services are used wholly for the making of taxable supplies. If used partly for taxable supplies, the input tax must be included in the non-attributable input tax and apportioned according to the partial exemption method used.

The value of imported services must be excluded from the calculation to apportion residual input tax where either the standard method under **50.4–50.8** above is used or a special method under **50.10** above is used which is based on output values.

Exempt input tax on imported services should be included with other exempt input tax when applying the *de minimis* rules in **50.11** above.

(VAT Notice 706, para 12.8).

(10) Including non-business use within clawback/payback

The clawback/payback rules also allow for adjustments to non-business (including private) use, unless the option to hold an asset, or part of an asset, wholly outside the business is adopted. VAT which is initially allocated entirely for non-business purposes is not eligible for adjustment.

> *Example*
>
> A charity incurs expenditure of £10,000 and related VAT of £2,000 on goods that it intends using 50% for non-business purposes and 50% for exempt supplies. Its initial entitlement to VAT recovery is therefore nil. 18 months later, before the expenditure has been used for any activities (business or non-business), it changes its intention and decides to put the expenditure entirely to taxable use.

It is therefore entitled to a payback of £2,000 which it can claim in the normal way.

(VAT Notice 706, paras 13.16–13.17).

(11) Divisional registration

A corporate body may apply to be registered in the names of its separate divisions. See **60.37 REGISTRATION**. HMRC will not allow divisional registration if the exempt input tax of the body as a whole exceeds the *de minimis* limit in **50.11** above. If, at any time, a body corporate registered in divisions exceeds the *de minimis* limit, it should advise its local VAT Business Centre immediately and a decision will be made as to whether the divisional registration should be allowed to continue. If the divisional registration is cancelled for the corporate body as a whole, then, if it is still liable to be registered, the single VAT registration must cover all the taxable business activities of the body corporate as a whole. (VAT Notice 706, para 15.3).

(12) Group registration

The normal rules for group registration apply (see **28 GROUPS OF COMPANIES**) and input tax must be attributed by 'looking through' intra-group transactions to the supplies made outside the group.

A VAT group can only have one partial exemption method as there is only one taxable person and the *de minimis* limit must also be applied to the group as a whole. However, in deciding whether a VAT group can treat property or financial transactions as incidental for the purposes of the standard method calculation (see **50.5** above) the business activities carried on by the members of a VAT group are considered separately.

(VAT Notice 706, para 15.1).

(13) Local authorities

See **44.8 LOCAL AUTHORITIES AND PUBLIC BODIES.**

(14) Land and property

See **43.4 LAND AND BUILDINGS: ZERO AND REDUCED RATE SUPPLIES AND DIY HOUSEBUILDERS** for input tax and speculative builders.

(15) Higher education institutions

See **50.10** above.

See Business Brief 11/06 for the effect on partial exemption methods of higher education institutions following the introduction of variable tuition fees from 1 August 2006.

(16) Bookmakers – specialist TV services and equipment

Betting shops frequently incur VAT on Satellite Information System (SIS) services and equipment on which they can screen live coverage of horse and dog racing, real time odds, results information and commentary and opinion from pundits.

Historically, HMRC's view was that this information related directly to the over the counter exempt betting activity of bookmakers and the related input tax was not recoverable. But following the tribunal decisions in *Town and County Factors* (VTD 19616) (TVC 46.95) and *Cheshire Racing* (VTD 20283) (TVC 46.97) HMRC now accept that input tax on SIS services is residual as there is a direct and immediate link between the content of the SIS broadcast and gaming machine income. This applies even when the bookmaker adds no additional information to SIS.

(HRMC Brief 1/08).

The Tribunal in *Town and Country Factors* also found that VAT relating to Sky Sports was residual as the costs related to all of the activities of the betting shop even though the broadcasts did not carry adverts for the bookmaker's taxable services.

(Business Brief 17/06).

(17) VAT on insolvency practitioners' fees

See **36.11 INSOLVENCY.**

(18) Theatre production costs

In *Garsington Opera Ltd* (TC00045) (TVC 46.94), G incurred input tax on the costs of putting together its own 'in-house' operatic performances. HMRC maintained that the input tax was irrecoverable because while putting on operas was the core of G's business, the production costs were directly and immediately linked only to exempt admissions. G argued that the input tax was partly deductible (residual) because the production costs had a direct and immediate link not only to exempt admissions, but also to taxable supplies such as corporate sponsorship, touring (supplies of the production to an outside concert hall), programmes, CDs, intellectual property rights and the occasional supplies of production props and equipment. The tribunal found for G having identified a direct and immediate link between the production costs and both the exempt admission and the taxable supplies in issue. HMRC have not appealed this decision and have instead revised their policy on when theatres supplying exempt admission can treat input tax incurred on production costs as residual. Production costs only become partly deductible (residual) if there is a firm intention to make taxable as well as exempt supplies when the costs are incurred. Examples of when production costs relate to taxable supplies include if a theatre has contracted to or intends to

- secure sponsorship – the sponsorship must relate to an event or a clearly defined run of events over a clearly defined time. Putting on the shows must be a condition of the sponsorship so that production costs become cost components of the sponsorship income. The intention may be evidenced by way of clear financial commitment;
- tour the production – once again the intention may be evidenced by way of clear financial commitment;
- record the show for later sale on CD or other media.

Production costs remain residual if an intention to make taxable supplies is frustrated (e.g. a tour is cancelled). The intention to make taxable supplies must be a genuine intention. Furthermore, residual status is not secured if the link to taxable supplies is indirect.

In the case of *Mayflower Theatre Trust Ltd v HMRC*, CA [2007] STC 880 (TVC 46.93), a direct and immediate link to programme sales was found in relation to 'bought in' shows. This was because copyright information necessary for the programmes was obtained as part of the single supply of production services received from the touring company thus creating the direct and immediate link. If an individual actor or designer provides copyright information to a theatre/opera putting together a show 'in house' as part of a single supply of their services this cost will also be residual. However it will not make other costs incurred residual. The *Mayflower* decision also made clear that securing general corporate sponsorship does not make production costs residual even if the sponsorship package includes the provision of seats at performances. Likewise, catering supplies which arise as a consequence of admission do not make production costs residual.

Most theatres use the partial exemption standard method to apportion residual input tax between taxable and exempt supplies. If the standard method results in an over (or under) recovery of input tax which is classed as 'substantial' then the recovery must be re-calculated in accordance with the 'actual use' of the costs in question, under the standard method override (SMO) (see **50.9** above). A 'use-based' calculation is any calculation that fairly reflects how costs are used in making supplies, such as

Recoverable input tax on production costs = $A \div (A + B) \times C$

where

A = value of supplies (such as sponsorship or touring) with a direct and immediate link from the production costs of any show

B = value of box office sales

C = residual input tax incurred on production costs

Theatres operating the standard method where the SMO is likely to be triggered on a regular basis may wish to seek approval for a special method. (HMRC Brief 65/09).

(19) Housing associations

See **50.10** above.

(20) NHS bodies

See **50.10** above.

Records and accounts

[50.16] See **57 RECORDS** for records and accounts which every registered person is required by law to keep. In addition, for partial exemption purposes records must also enable a business to work out the amount of input tax it can recover in each VAT period and in each VAT year. Any other records that are used in calculating its recoverable input tax must also be kept.

(VAT Notice 706, para 2.6).

Key points: partial exemption

[50.17] Points to consider are as follows.

General points

- The main principle of partial exemption is that input tax can only be reclaimed on expenses relevant to taxable supplies, i.e. not in relation to any exempt activities. It is important to recognise that this is a different issue to input tax restrictions relevant to business and non-business activities. Any input tax relevant to non-business activities must initially be blocked before partial exemption issues are considered.
- An accurate partial exemption calculation can only be made if an accountant (or relevant staff) clearly identifies whether an expense should be coded as taxable, exempt or residual as far as input tax recovery is concerned. A major invoice incorrectly coded as residual instead of taxable (or exempt instead of residual or taxable) could cost a business a lot of money.
- A change of intended use of an item or actual use being different to intended use means that input tax originally claimed on goods or services could be affected by the 'clawback' or 'payback' provisions. In the case of a 'clawback' situation, extra VAT will be payable to HMRC – the opposite applies in a 'payback' situation, with a rebate being due. A change in intended use does not mean that input tax claims (or non-claims) on previous VAT returns were incorrect, but that an adjustment is needed on a current VAT return to reflect the change in intended use.
- Be aware of the need to make an annual adjustment for all partial exemption calculations – and the fact that a business has the choice of including the adjustment payment or repayment on the VAT return at the end of the tax year in question (31 March, 30 April or 31 May, depending on VAT periods) or the return for the following quarter.
- Always check to see if a client is *de minimis* as far as partial exemption is concerned. In such cases, all input tax can be reclaimed if one of the three tests creates a *de minimis* outcome. However, it is the annual position that matters, any quarterly calculations being made on a provisional basis.
- The 'annual test' means that a business that was *de minimis* in its previous tax year can reclaim all input tax on its VAT returns for the next tax year, subject to an annual adjustment calculation at the end of that year. This new measure could simplify accounting for a partly exempt business because it avoids having to make quarterly partial exemption calculations.

- A partly-exempt business that buys in services from abroad (with no VAT charged by the overseas business under the place of supply rules) will suffer an input tax restriction if the expense relates to its exempt activities. This is because the reverse charge calculation (value of service multiplied by UK rate of VAT) will produce a VAT return entry to pay output tax (Box 1) but an input tax restriction in Box 4. It is important that a partly exempt business recognises the importance of this adjustment, and is able to identify all payments to overseas suppliers when it completes its accounts or VAT returns.

Standard method

- Most businesses use the standard method of calculation as far as partial exemption is concerned. However, be aware that a special method of calculation can be applied for (as long as HMRC approval is obtained) if the standard method does not give a fair and reasonable result. The starting point in deciding whether a special method is worthwhile is to consider why the standard method breaks down, i.e. why it produces an unfair result in terms of input tax recovery.
- The standard method calculation should exclude capital assets sold by a business and also incidental sources of income, e.g. bank interest received.
- The denominator part of the fraction in the standard method is described as the 'value of all supplies'. It is important to remember that this figure does not include income that is outside the scope of VAT, e.g. many grants or donations received by charities. The inclusion of income that is outside the scope of VAT will lead to an underclaim of residual input tax by the business.
- Many partly exempt businesses using the standard method can benefit by using an in-year recovery rate in relation to residual input tax (based on the overall recovery rate for the previous partial exemption year). However, the business must still do a final annual adjustment calculation at the end of the tax year and pay (or reclaim) any tax due compared to the provisional claims during the year.
- When exempt input tax is first incurred by a business, it is allowed to calculate recoverable VAT by allowing a 'use-based' rather than income-based method of calculation (i.e. residual input tax recovery based on use rather than income as per standard method). The 'use' basis can be based on any method (possibly projected income split over a longer period of time) as long as it is fair and reasonable.
- Changes to *SI 1995/2518, Reg 101* affect standard method longer periods beginning after 31 December 2015 so that the value of supplies made by overseas establishments are excluded from the standard method.

Special methods

- It is important to regularly review the position of all partly exempt businesses and identify whether to apply to HMRC for a special method. These applications are appropriate when it is considered that the standard method does not give a fair and reasonable recovery of residual input tax.
- In many cases, the standard method gives a perfectly fair result – and overall is easy to calculate. However, it is important to be aware of alternative methods of calculation, particularly those based on inputs, square footage or staff numbers.
- The key principle of any partial exemption calculation is to ensure methods proposed are fair and reasonable. A taxpayer is required to make a 'fair and reasonable' declaration at the time he submits the application. HMRC has the power to recover tax on a historic basis if this declaration is incorrect.
- Any change in circumstance for a business that could affect the fair and reasonable result of its special method calculations should be immediately notified to HMRC. A revised special method or adoption of the standard method may then be appropriate.
- Remember that it is only appropriate to spend time and effort proposing a special method if a business has a significant amount of residual input tax. If most (or all) input tax can be directly attributed to taxable or exempt supplies, there are negligible benefits to be gained by adopting a special method of calculation.
- From 1 January 2016 HMRC will not approve or direct a special method that includes the value of supplies made from overseas establishments unless the method is based on sectors.

51

Partnerships

Cross-references. See **9.5 BUSINESS** for deemed partnerships.

De Voil Indirect Tax Service. See V2.110.

Introduction to partnerships

English law

[51.1] A partnership, or firm, is not a legal entity but is defined as 'the relation which subsists between persons carrying on business in common with a view to profit'. [*Partnership Act 1890, s 1(1)*].

Scottish law

A partnership is a legal person distinct from the partners who compose it.

Despite this, in general VAT legislation applies similarly under English and Scottish law so that the partnership itself is treated as a taxable person.

Case law

See also *Leighton-Jones and Craig (t/a Saddletramps)* (VTD 597) (TVC 47.17) approving *dicta* in *Weiner v Harris* [1910] 1 KB 285.

For alleged husband and wife partnerships, see *Jackson (RD & Mrs SL)* (VTD 1959) (TVC 47.44) and *Britton* (VJ) (VTD 2173) (TVC 47.47) and for an alleged partnership with infant children see *Bridgeman* (VTD 1206) (TVC 47.53).

For whether joint venture agreements amount to a partnership, see *Strathearn Gordon Associates Ltd* (VTD 1884) (TVC 47.55), *Keydon Estates Ltd* (VTD 4471) (TVC 47.56) and *Fivegrange Ltd* (VTD 5338) (TVC 47.57).

Salaried partners

Whether a salaried partner is a full partner or an employee depends upon the facts of the particular case.

- A salaried partner should be treated as an employee (and not included in the registration of the firm) if, despite being held out as a partner, he is paid either by a fixed salary or a share of the profits but is denied the rights and duties normally accorded to a full partner, i.e. the obligation to contribute capital and to share losses and the right to fully participate in the management of the firm.
- If a person who is called a salaried partner enjoys a share of the profits and an interest in the partnership capital, he should be treated as a full partner and included in the registration of the firm.

If a salaried partner is included as a partner on the VAT registration forms, in the absence of any evidence to the contrary, HMRC take him to be a full partner on the basis that he is holding himself out as such (see **51.4** below).

(HMRC VAT Guidance V1–28, para 3.4.10).

Limited partnerships

Under the *Limited Partnership Act 1907*, a limited partnership is a partnership which consists of

- one or more partners called 'general partners' who are liable for all debts and obligations of the firm, and
- one or more persons called 'limited partners' who cannot take part in the management of the partnership business and do not have power to bind it. If a limited partner should take part in the management of the partnership business, he is liable for all the debts, etc. incurred while he so took part as if he were a general partner.

A limited partnership must be registered as such with the Registrar of Companies, otherwise all the partners are treated as general partners.

Registration

[51.2] VAT registration of persons carrying on business in partnership, or carrying on in partnership any other activities in the course or furtherance of which they acquire goods from another EU member state, may be in the name of the firm. In such a case, no account is to be taken of any change in the partnership in determining for the purposes of *VATA 1994* whether goods or services are supplied to or by such persons or are acquired by such persons from another EU member state. [*VATA 1994, s 45(1)*].

A notification of a partnership's liability to be registered must contain the particulars set out in the relevant form specified in a notice published by HMRC. [*SI 1995/2518, Reg 5(1)*].

England and Wales

Where separate businesses are carried on by the same individuals in partnership only one registration applies (*C & E Commrs v Glassborow and Another*, QB [1974] STC 142 (TVC 57.1)).

Scotland

Because a partnership is a legal person, each separate business carried on by the same partners may have a separate registration. For example, if A and B have six retail outlets and treat them as six different partnerships, each can be registered individually even though A and B are the only partners in each partnership. In practice, HMRC are only likely to allow separate registration where it can be shown that there is a separate partnership agreement for each of the businesses.

Limited partnerships

Limited partnerships are registered in the names of the general partners and those treated as general partners (see **51.1** above). The normal procedures for the registration of partnerships is followed except

- where there is only one general partner, the registration will be raised in the name of that sole general partner;
- where a sole general partner is already registered for VAT, the business activities of the limited partnership should be accounted for under the existing registration;
- where two or more persons are registered for VAT as a partnership and those same persons are all the general partners in a limited partnership, the business activities of the limited partnership should be accounted for under the existing registration of the partnership;
- where the general partner is an incorporated company and a member of a VAT group, the business activities of the limited partnership are part of that group and must be accounted for under the existing group registration;
- where two individuals carry on two businesses in partnership, each being a general partner in one business and a limited partner in the other, separate registration applies (*Saunders and Sorrell* (VTD 913) (TVC 47.15)); and
- as a limited partnership cannot own land and property, where property is held jointly in the names of all the general and limited partners, it may be necessary to register all those partners as a normal partnership, separately from any existing registration the limited partnership may have. A Form VAT 2 must be signed by all the general and limited partners.

Ceasing to be a partner

[51.3] Without prejudice to *Partnership Act 1890, s 36*, a person who has ceased to be a partner continues to be regarded as a partner for VAT purposes (in particular for the purposes of any VAT liability) until the date on which the change is notified to HMRC. [*VATA 1994, s 45(2)*]. (*Partnership Act 1890, s 36* provides, *inter alia*, that a person who deals with a firm after a change in its constitution is entitled to treat all apparent members of the old firm as still being members of the firm until he has notice of the change.)

Where a person ceases to be a partner in a VAT period, (or is treated as doing so under *VATA 1994, s 45(2)* above) any notice, whether of assessment or otherwise, which is served on the partnership and relates to that period or an earlier period during the whole or part of which he was a partner is treated as served on him. [*VATA 1994, s 45(2)(3)*].

Liability for VAT

[51.4] Subject to below

- **in England and Wales,**
  - (a) all the partners in a firm are liable jointly for all the debts and jointly and severally for the obligations of the firm which arise while they are members of that firm; and
  - (b) after death, a partner's estate is severally liable for such debts so far as they remain unsatisfied but subject to the prior payment of his separate debts; and
- **in Scotland,** because a partnership is a legal person distinct from the persons of whom it is composed, it is the partnership which is liable for debts. The partners themselves only become liable for any debts if the partnership has insufficient assets to meet those debts. Where the partners do become liable, they are liable jointly and severally.

Where a person is a partner during part only of a VAT period his liability for VAT on the supply of goods or services during that period, or on the acquisition during that period of any goods from another EU member state, is limited to such proportion of the firm's liability as may be just. [*VATA 1994, s 45(5)*].

However,

- a partner's liability does not end automatically on leaving a partnership (see **51.3** above); and
- limited partners (see **51.1** above) are not liable for any debts or obligations of the limited partnership over and above the capital which they contributed.

Holding out

Anyone who by spoken word, writing or conduct represents himself, or allows himself to be represented, as a partner in a particular firm, is liable as a partner to anyone who has on the faith of any such representation 'given credit' to the firm. [*Partnership Act 1890, s 14*]. This is known as 'holding out'. As a result

- anyone who holds himself out as a partner in a firm will be liable for the debts and obligations of the partnership as if he were a partner; and
- where two or more persons hold themselves out as a partnership in an application for registration, HMRC will treat those persons as partners (with joint liability for all debts).

Notices to and by partnerships

Notices to partnerships

[51.5] Any notice (whether an assessment or otherwise) addressed to the partnership by the name in which it is registered and validly served under *VATA 1994* will be regarded as served on the partnership (including any former partners as in **51.3** above). This is without prejudice to *Partnership Act 1890, s 16* which provides that notice to any partner who habitually acts in the partnership business operates as notice to the firm generally, except in cases of fraud involving that particular partner. [*VATA 1994, s 45(4)*].

Notices by partnerships

Where any notice is required to be given for VAT purposes, it is the joint and several liability of all the partners to give it, but it is sufficient if it is given by one partner. *In Scotland*, any authorised person, whether a partner or not, may give the required notice as specified by *Partnership Act 1890, s 6*. [*VATA 1994, Sch 11 para 7; SI 1995/2518, Reg 7*]. Notice of appeal may be made in the partnership name (see **5.7 APPEALS**).

Partners holding office

[51.6] Where a person (including partners of a firm), in the course or furtherance of a trade, profession or vocation, accepts any office, services supplied by him as the holder of that office are treated as supplied in the course or furtherance of the trade etc. [*VATA 1994, s 94(4)*]. This point will obviously be of importance if the recipient of a supply suffers restriction of input tax or, as regards the supplier, the consideration for the supply was fixed with no contemplation that VAT was applicable. See *Lean & Rose* [1974] Lexis Citation 6 (TVC 62.371) where, on the facts, a solicitor who was a partner in a private practice was held to have a personal contract as a part-time salaried solicitor of a borough council and, accordingly, was not making taxable supplies.

See also **45.8 MANAGEMENT SERVICES AND SUPPLIES OF STAFF**.

Contributions to partnerships

[51.7] In *KapHag Renditefonds v Finanzamt Charlottenburg, ECJ Case C–442/01*, [2005] STC 1500 (TVC 22.95) a German partnership admitted a new partner, who made a payment of 38 million marks to the partnership. The partnership reclaimed input tax on legal fees relating to this. The tax authority rejected the claim on the basis that the fees related to an exempt supply of services. The partnership appealed and the case was referred to the CJEU, which ruled that no supply was being made under what is now *Directive 2006/112/EC, Art 2(1)(a)* by either the individual partners or the partnership to the incoming partner in return for the capital contribution.

Although in the *KapHag* case the incoming partner was contributing cash in return for admission into the partnership, contributions are frequently made in the form of other assets. The CJEU decision tacitly accepted the Advocate-

General's Opinion that the same principles would apply whether the contribution consisted of cash or other assets. Whatever the nature of the assets comprising the contribution, there is no reciprocal supply from the partnership. However, where the assets are not cash, the making of the partnership contribution may have other VAT consequences.

HMRC issued the following guidance on the implications of the decision.

(1) Contribution to partnership comprising services

This could be, for example, a trademark or trading logo or the use of an asset the ownership of which is retained by the incoming partner. A supply can arise under *VATA 1994, Sch 4 para 5(4)* in certain circumstances where a taxable person applies business goods to private use or makes them available for purposes other than those of his business. Similarly, *SI 1993/1507* provides that a supply arises where a taxable person applies bought-in services to private or non-business use for no consideration where he has been entitled to input tax credit. See **48.6 OUTPUT TAX** for fuller details.

Where either of the above circumstances apply, a VAT-registered incoming partner must account for VAT on the supply of services that he is regarded as making in the disposal of the services from his existing business. The partnership may be able to recover this as its input tax where the contributed services are to be used for its business (see (5) below).

(2) Contribution to partnership comprising goods other than land

If a partnership contribution comprises goods other than land that the transferor held as assets, then a deemed supply arises under *VATA 1994, Sch 4 para 5(1)*. See **48.5 OUTPUT TAX**. Where such a deemed supply arises, the incoming partner must account for VAT. The partnership may be able to recover this as its input tax where the contributed assets are to be used for its business (see (5) below).

(3) Contribution to partnership comprising land or interests in land

The VAT treatment of land or interests in land depends upon whether the incoming partner, or his predecessor, was entitled to deduct input tax in relation to the contributed property. For example, if he had opted to tax the property, or it was taxable as new freehold commercial property, there may be a deemed supply as described at (2) above. The incoming partner must then account for VAT on this supply. As with other contributed goods, the partnership may be entitled to recover this as input tax where the property is to be used for the partnership's business (see (5) below).

(4) Transfer of a going concerns

It is possible that assets transferred by way of a partnership contribution could qualify to be treated as a transfer of a going concern. If so, no VAT is due from the transferor. See **9.9 BUSINESS**.

(5) Recovery by the partnership of output tax accounted for by an incoming partner on his contribution as its input tax

If an incoming partner contributes goods and/or services (on which VAT is due as described above) and the partnership uses them for its business purposes, the partnership can recover the VAT as input tax subject to the normal rules.

The incoming partner cannot issue a VAT invoice, but in order to provide the partnership with acceptable evidence to support a claim for recovery of input tax, he may use his normal invoicing documentation overwritten with the following statement.

'Certificate for VAT on partnership contribution

No payment is necessary for these goods/services. Output tax has been accounted for on the supply.'

The incoming partner must show full details of the goods and/or services on the documentation and the amount of VAT shown must be the amount of output tax accounted for to HMRC.

(6) Capital goods scheme consequences

Where the capital contribution is in the form of an interest in land or a computer, it may be an existing capital item of the incoming partner under the capital goods scheme. If the transfer to the partnership constitutes a supply which is a disposal of an existing capital goods scheme item, a disposal adjustment may be due. If the transfer also constitutes a TOGC, then this ends the current interval for the incoming partner and the partnership becomes responsible for making adjustments for any remaining intervals. See **11 CAPITAL GOODS SCHEME** for full details of the scheme.

(7) Transfer of assets out of a partnership

KapHag was only concerned with assets moving into a partnership in the form of a partnership contribution. It did not cover the reverse situation, where partnership assets are paid out to an outgoing partner or otherwise disposed of by the partnership for no consideration. Where a transfer of assets out of a partnership for no consideration occurs, one of the following sets of circumstances applies.

(a) If the incoming partner accounted for output tax when he contributed the assets to the partnership and the partnership was entitled to recover all or part of this as its input tax, there is a subsequent supply by the partnership when the same assets are transferred out (unless the transfer out satisfies the TOGC rules).

(b) If no output tax was accounted for when the assets were contributed to the partnership because they constituted a TOGC, the transfer out of the same assets is a deemed supply upon which the partnership must account for VAT (unless the transfer out satisfies the TOGC rules).

(c) If the partnership is transferring out more assets than those originally contributed to it, although the original contribution to the partnership may not have been a TOGC, the subsequent transfer out may satisfy the TOGC rules. If so, no VAT is due from the partnership.

(d) If the original contribution to the partnership was a TOGC but the partnership is transferring out less of the assets than were originally contributed, then unless the assets being transferred out still meet the TOGC rules in their own right, there may be a deemed supply upon which the partnership must account for VAT.

(Business Brief 21/04).

Disposal of a share in a partnership

[51.8] *KapHag* (see **51.7** above) established that a partnership or the existing partners make no supply when a new partner is admitted in return for making a capital contribution. This paragraph considers whether the disposal by a partner of his share in the partnership is a supply for VAT purposes. It should be noted that this 'share' is distinct from the assets that were contributed by the partner on joining the partnership. As a result, even if the selling price of the share is determined by the value of those assets, they are not the subject of the later sale which has its own liability for VAT purposes.

Although the CJEU has not considered the disposal of shares in a partnership, it has considered transactions involving shares in companies. These cases have established that the mere acquisition and holding of shares in a company is not to be regarded as an economic activity, although transactions in shares or interests in companies and associations may constitute economic activity in three situations.

- Where the transactions constitute the direct, permanent and necessary extension of an economic activity.
- Where the transactions are effected in order to secure a direct or indirect involvement in the management of a company in which the holding is acquired.
- Where the transactions are effected as part of a commercial share-dealing activity.

HMRC considers that the same principles apply to transactions involving partnership shares and give the following as common examples.

Circumstances in which the disposal of a partnership share will not constitute a supply

- *The share is disposed of for no consideration.* A share in a partnership comprises services rather than goods. When services are transferred, assigned or otherwise disposed of for no consideration, they do not constitute any supply for VAT purposes.
- *The share being sold was acquired simply as an investment.* Where a partner has acquired his share merely to secure a share in any future profits and has had no involvement in running the partnership, the subsequent sale or assignment of that share for consideration will not constitute a supply for VAT purposes.

Circumstances in which the disposal of a partnership share will constitute a supply

- *Where the partnership share was acquired and disposed of as a direct extension of the partner's economic activities.* Where a partner is a taxable person in his own right, the partnership share may have been acquired in the course or furtherance of his own economic activities. If so, the subsequent transfer or assignment of that share for a consideration will also be an economic activity (e.g. a partner may have a business asset for sale and, rather than selling it directly, may have contributed the asset into a partnership and sold the resultant partnership share instead).

- *Where the partnership share was acquired in order to obtain an active role in the business of the partnership.* Where a partner is a taxable person in his own right and had acquired the partnership share in order to actively participate in, or control, the business of the partnership, then the sale of that share can be economic activity on the part of the partner. The sale of the share will constitute a supply for VAT purposes.
- *Where the partnership share was acquired as part of a commercial partnership share-dealing activity.* A partner who is a taxable person may have a business of dealing in partnership shares. This will be an economic activity on the part of the partner. Sales or assignments of the partnership shares that were acquired in the course of this activity and that are sold for a consideration constitute supplies for VAT purposes.

Where the disposal of a partnership share is a supply, the supply is exempt as the supply of a financial service.

VAT on associated purchases

Where the disposal of a partnership share is not a supply, the VAT incurred in connection with the disposal is normally not input tax. Where the disposal is a supply, the related VAT is input tax, but, subject to the *de minimis* provisions, recovery is normally fully restricted under the partial exemption rules.

(Business Brief 30/04).

Limited liability partnerships

[51.9] An LLP has a legal status distinct from its members and can enter into contracts in its own right. Individual members of the LLP are protected from debts or liabilities arising from negligence and wrongful acts or misconduct of another member, employee or agent of the LLP.

An LLP is a corporate body and it, rather than the members, is the legal entity for VAT purposes so that the LLP itself becomes liable for VAT registration (subject to the normal registration rules).

Where an existing partnership changes to an LLP

As the legal entity has changed from that of a partnership to a corporate body, the LLP may have to apply for VAT registration (subject to the normal rules). The normal rules for the transfer of a business as a going concern will apply (see **9.9 BUSINESS**). If the general partnership ceases to exist, it may be possible for the VAT number to be transferred to the LLP (see **60.42 REGISTRATION**).

VAT groups

An LLP can join a VAT group provided it meets the control conditions in *VATA 1994, s 43A* (see **28.2 GROUPS OF COMPANIES**). Where the control conditions are satisfied, a VAT group could be formed by, for example

- an LLP with a number of subsidiary companies; or

- two or more eligible companies and an LLP in which those companies are controlling partners.

(Business Brief 3/01).

In Autumn Statement 2016, the Government announced that it intended to consult on the inclusion of non-corporate bodies, such as partnerships, in a VAT group as a result of the CJEU decision in *Beteiligungsgesellschaft Larentia and Minerva mbH & Co KG v Finanzamt Nordenham, ECJ Case C-108/14* and *Finanzamt Hamburg-Mitte v Marenave Schiffahrts AG, ECJ Case C-109/14*.

(HMRC Brief 3/16).

Key points: partnerships

[51.10] Points to consider are as follows.

- A partnership is a different legal entity to a sole trader, so this means that supplies are treated independently as far as VAT is concerned. So a plumber who is VAT-registered as a sole trader will not include any income on his VAT return (or claim input tax on expenses) if he has a separate business with his wife as a partnership. This separation of business activities into different legal entities can, if done correctly, produce a VAT planning opportunity by avoiding the need for one (or possibly both) of the businesses to be VAT-registered, i.e. on the basis of turnover levels. However, this strategy must be carefully planned to avoid any problems with the business splitting legislation.
- A limited liability partnership (LLP) is a separate legal entity to a partnership. In the case of an LLP, it is the corporate body itself that is VAT-registered and liable for any VAT debts. If a business transfers from a general partnership to an LLP, this is a transfer of a going concern situation (TOGC), with the usual TOGC rules taking effect.
- The addition of a new partner to the partnership or retirement of an existing partner does not create the need to deregister for VAT purposes. The VAT 2 (list of partners) form must be amended to reflect the change.

52

Payment of VAT

Cross-references. See **2.20 ACCOUNTING PERIODS AND RETURNS** for payments by persons selling under a power of sale; **5.4 APPEALS** for payment of VAT as a condition of appeal; **6.1 ASSESSMENTS** for repayments of VAT made in error; **32.1–32.5 HMRC: POWERS** for power to require security or production of evidence before making repayments, power to recover VAT and power to distraint for payment and diligence (Scotland); **34 IMPORTS** for VAT payable on importation; and **36.3 INSOLVENCY** for priority of payment in insolvency.

Introduction to payment of VAT

[52.1] The great majority of traders are required to submit VAT returns online and pay their liabilities directly to HMRC's bank account, rather than submitting a paper form with a cheque. The time limit for such routine quarterly or monthly returns is seven calendar days after the end of the month following the return period, e.g. 7 May for a return period to 31 March.

Different rules apply for:

- large traders within the Payments on Account regime (see **52.5**);
- traders using the Annual Accounting Scheme (see **64.9**);
- traders who apply to be allowed to use a paper-based system for making returns and/or payments (see **52.3**); and

- a trader's final return, which is also usually submitted online, and is due not later than one month after the effective date for cancellation of registration (or, in the case of a taxable person not registered, one month after the date when liability to be registered ceases).

[*SI 1995/2518, Regs 25(1)(4), 25A, 40(2)*].

Where the amount of VAT due to HMRC is under £1, no payment need be made. [*VATA 1994, Sch 11 para 2(13)*]. Such amount should not be carried forward to the next return. (VAT Notice 700, para 21.5).

De Voil Indirect Tax Service. See V5.108A–V5.109B.

Method of payment

[52.2] VAT can currently be paid by the following methods:

- direct debit for returns submitted online, unless the business makes payments on account and submits quarterly returns;
- bank or building society services to pay by internet, telephone banking or Bankers Automated Clearing Systems (BACS) Direct Credit;
- debit or credit card over the internet (there is a fee for using a credit card);
- Clearing House Automated Payments System (CHAPS) transfer;
- Bank Giro using paying slips ordered from HMRC;
- standing order for the annual accounting and payment on account schemes; or
- exceptionally (see **52.3**) post by cheque made payable to 'HM Revenue & Customs only' followed by the VAT reference number.

Electronic returns

Where a return is made using HMRC's eVAT return service (see **2.1 ACCOUNTING PERIODS AND RETURNS**) it is a condition of the scheme that any relevant payment must be made solely by electronic means acceptable to HMRC for that purpose. [*SI 1995/2518, Reg 40(2A)*]. HMRC accept payment by BACS, CHAPS or Bank Giro Credit transfer (see above).

Mandatory electronic payment

HMRC have powers to require all payments of VAT to be made by electronic means [*FA 2003, s 204; FA 2007, s 94*] and virtually all VAT-registered businesses are required to submit VAT returns online and pay any VAT due electronically. [*SI 1995/2518, Regs 25A(3), 40(2A)*].

Fee for specified methods of payment

From 1 January 2016, HMRC have the ability to limit the number of times a business can use a credit or debit card within a certain time period to pay its tax. There is no set limit and HMRC will make its decision based on that it considered to be reasonable based on payment card industry standards and guidance and the rules apply to multiple card payments for the same tax.

Prior to 1 April 2016, HMRC levied a 1.5% fixed fee for payments made by credit cards (1.4% before 2 November 2015).

[*FA 2008, s 136; SI 2015/1777*].

However with effect from 1 April 2016, HMRC no longer charges a single fixed fee but levies a fee based on whether the credit card is personal or corporate and the type of credit card used to make the payment.

The following fees will be applicable:

Personal credit card

Type of card	*Rate*
VISA Personal Credit Card	0.415%
MasterCard Personal Credit Card	0.386%
MasterCard World Premium Credit Card	0.374%
MasterCard Signia Premium Credit Card	0.606%
MasterCard Elite Premium Credit Card	0.606%

Corporate credit cards

Type of card	*Rate*
VISA Business Credit Card	1.508%
VISA Corporate Credit Card	1.744%
VISA Purchasing Credit Card	1.755%
MasterCard Business Credit Card	1.973%
MasterCard Corporate Credit Card	2.248%
MasterCard Purchasing Credit Card	2.406%
MasterCard Fleet Credit Card	2.134%

[*SI 2016/333*].

Payments in euros

UK businesses can pay VAT (and other duties) in euros, although banks are not making BACS euro direct debit available. All declarations must continue to be made in sterling. Exchange rates are likely to fluctuate between the time payment is initiated and the time the payment is cleared. Businesses will be credited with the sterling value received by HMRC and any over/under payments will be dealt with using existing debt management practices. Costs incurred by HMRC in converting euro payments into sterling will not be passed on to businesses and will be borne by HMRC. (Business Brief 1/99).

Paper-based system

Paper returns

[52.3] In *LH Bishop Electric Co Ltd v HMRC (and related appeals)* [2013] UKFTT 522 (TC) (TC02910) (TVC 59.24), the First-tier Tribunal held that the UK law requiring online filing of all returns did not make appropriate allowance for people unable to do so through old age, disability or living remotely, or unwilling because of religious objections. The regulations were therefore contrary to the European Convention on Human Rights; HMRC's administrative practice of allowing such people to telephone in their return details could not correct the basic defect in the law. The regulations were subsequently amended to allow filing and paying 'using a paper-based system' if the Commissioners are satisfied that:

- the trader is a practising member of a religious society or order whose beliefs are incompatible with the use of electronic communications; or
- it is not reasonably practicable to make a return using an electronic return system (including any electronic return system that that person is authorised to use) for reasons of disability, age, remoteness of location or any other reason.

In such a case, the trader must make the return by the end of the month following the return period, without the extra seven calendar days allowed for electronic returns.

[*SI 1995/2518, Regs 25, 25A(3)*].

Cheques

Due to the cost involved, HMRC do not represent cheques to banks which have previously been returned unpaid through lack of funds. The onus is on the taxpayer to cancel and replace any such cheques. (VAT Notes No 4 1996).

Cheque payments sent by post are treated as being received by HMRC on the date when cleared funds reach their bank account, not the date when they receive the cheque. [*SI 1995/2518, Reg 40(2B)*].

For VAT periods commencing after 31 March 2012 virtually all VAT-registered businesses are required to submit VAT returns online and pay any VAT due electronically. [*SI 1995/2518, Regs 25A(3), 40(2A)*].

> *Example*
>
> John is VAT-registered and has applied to submit his returns and pay tax due in a paper format because he is a practising member of a religious society or order whose beliefs are incompatible with the use of electronic communications.
>
> He is about to send his June return and cheque to HMRC. He must do this so that the payment clears HMRC's bank account by the last day of July (when the return is due), otherwise the payment will be late and he will possibly incur either a default surcharge or default surcharge liability notice (depending on whether he has been late with any other returns and payments in the last 12 months).

(HMRC Brief 14/10).

Business experiencing difficulties paying VAT due

[52.4] A business that is unable to pay its VAT liabilities by the due date should consider contacting HMRC's Business Payment Support Service (BPSS) to negotiate payment of the liability over a longer period of time, perhaps a proposal to make three monthly instalments. However, the BPSS is intended to support a business with temporary cash-flow problems. It is not intended to provide long-term finance (through a deferral arrangement every VAT period) to a business with more fundamental cash problems.

An example of a situation that would justify seeking assistance from the BPSS is where an important and usually reliable customer does not settle his account on the due date, leaving the business short of working capital. An important point is to always agree a time to pay arrangement with the BPSS before the tax is due for payment. This approach will avoid a default surcharge penalty or default surcharge liability notice being issued in relation to the VAT return in question.

Businesses should always ensure that the VAT return is submitted by the due date even if they lack the necessary funds to pay the VAT due.

Payments on account

[52.5] The Treasury may, if they consider it is desirable to do so in the interests of national economy, provide by SI that certain taxable persons must make payments on account of their VAT liability for a VAT period. [*VATA 1994, s 28*]. Under these provisions, every VAT-registered business with an annual VAT liability of more than £2.3 million is required to be in the Payments on Account (POA) regime. Once in the regime each business must make interim payments at the end of the second and third months of each VAT quarter as POAs of the quarterly VAT liability. A balancing payment for the quarter is then made with the VAT return. All POAs and balancing payments must be made by electronic transfer. The detailed provisions of the POA scheme are set out below.

Basic period

POAs are required to be made, in respect of each VAT period exceeding one month beginning after 31 March each year, by

(a) a taxable person whose total VAT liability for the VAT periods ending within the year that ended on the last day of his VAT period ending before the previous 1 December (i.e. normally the year ending the previous 30 September, 31 October or 30 November) exceeded £2.3 million; and

(b) a taxable person who does not fall within (*a*) above, but whose total VAT liability for the VAT periods ending within the year that ended on the last day of his VAT period ending after the previous 30 November exceeded £2.3 million.

The period of one year referred to under (*a*) or (*b*) above is known as the '*basic period*'.

VAT liability is calculated by adding together the VAT due to be declared on returns (including assessments or error correction notifications (formerly voluntary disclosures)) and, if applicable, the VAT due on imports and goods ex warehouse. If liability exceeds the threshold, HMRC will notify the business that it is in the scheme.

[*SI 1993/2001, Arts 5, 6*].

Timing of payments

POAs must be sent so as to clear HMRC's account not later than the last working day of the second and third months of every VAT quarterly period (with the exception of the first period in the scheme when only one payment is required at the end of the third month). Quarterly balancing payments must also be cleared by the last working day of the month following the return period. Where non-standard period end dates have been agreed with HMRC, payments must be cleared to HMRC's account by the due date for those returns (or the last working date before the due date if that date is not a working date).

Set POAs

Unless one of the alternatives below is used, set POAs must be made.

The initial level of POAs are determined by the VAT liability in the period in which the threshold was exceeded under (*a*) or (*b*) above. The amount of each POA is one twenty-fourth of the total amount of VAT (excluding VAT on imports from outside the EU and goods ex warehouse) for that period. If the business has been in operation for less than twelve months, the payments will be calculated on a proportionate basis.

HMRC must notify the business of the amounts it is required to pay and how these amounts have been calculated.

From the beginning of the next annual cycle for POAs, the amount of the POAs is one twenty-fourth of the total amount of VAT (excluding VAT on imports from outside the EU and goods ex warehouse) which the business was liable to pay in its reference year determined as follows.

VAT return periods: quarters ending	*Reference year*	*Annual cycle begins*
31 Mar, 30 Jun, 30 Sept, 31 Dec	Y/ended 30 Sept	1 Apr
30 Apr, 31 July, 31 Oct, 31 Jan	Y/ended 31 Oct	1 May
31 May, 31 Aug, 30 Nov, 28/29 Feb	Y/ended 30 Nov	1 June

Alternatives to set POAs

The following alternatives are available to set POAs.

- *Monthly VAT returns*. A business can contact HMRC and change to monthly VAT returns. It will be expected to continue making such returns for a reasonable period, normally at least twelve months. If monthly returns are prepared and payment made by electronic means (see below) or credit transfer, a further seven days beyond the due date may be allowed to render returns and make payments. This is the only circumstance in which a business liable to be in the POA scheme may be granted such an extension.

- *Payments based on actual liabilities.* A business may elect to pay its actual VAT liability for the preceding month instead of the set POAs but without rendering a monthly VAT return. Such an election must be made in writing to HMRC stating the date on which it is to take effect (which must not be less than 30 days after the date of notification). Such an election then continues to have effect until a date notified in writing to HMRC. An election cannot be withdrawn earlier than the first anniversary of the date on which it took effect and, where an election is withdrawn, a further election cannot be made within twelve months of the date of withdrawal. HMRC may at any time give written notice that an election is to cease with effect from a specified date where they are not satisfied that the correct amounts are being paid. An appeal may be made against any such notice.

  Payments based on actual liabilities may be beneficial where there are seasonal variations in the VAT liability. However, where the business is in credit in any month, no immediate repayment is made. Neither can a credit in respect of the first month of an accounting period be netted off against a liability for the second month to reduce the POA for that month. The business must wait to bring the credit forward to the VAT return as normal. Where immediate repayments are required, the business should consider changing to monthly returns.

Note that, in each case, the actual liabilities will be larger than the equivalent payment on account, unless the trade fluctuates. Payments on account are, on average, half a month's VAT, rather than a whole month's VAT.

Method of payment

Payment must be made by electronic transfer direct to HMRC's account. The VAT registration number should be quoted as a reference when making payments. Acceptable methods of payment are

- Internet or phone banking;
- Clearing House Automated Payment System (CHAPS);
- Bankers Automated Clearing System (BACS);
- Faster Payment Service (FPS);
- online using BillPay to pay by debit or credit card;
- bank giro credit using official HMRC bank giro slips; and
- standing order.

In all cases the business must make the necessary arrangements to ensure the payment is received on time. The seven days period of grace allowed for payment by electronic means (see **52.3** above) does *not* apply to payments under the POA scheme. Whichever payment method is used, the same method must also be used to make any balancing payments due in respect of VAT returns.

Failure to pay

Where a business fails to make a POA by the due date, the payment is recoverable as if it were VAT due. The business is also liable to the default surcharge. See **53.23 PENALTIES**.

Completion of VAT return

VAT returns should be completed and submitted in the normal way. The figures must not be adjusted to take account of POAs made. The amount to be paid is the net liability shown on the return less any payments on account already made in respect of that period.

Overpayments

Where the payments made on account for a VAT period exceed the total due in that period, the excess must be repaid by HMRC (if not liable to set-off under *VATA 1994, s 81*, see **52.7** below). If the return is a repayment return, the repayment will be made in the normal way and the POAs made in the quarter will also be repaid.

Removal from scheme

Where VAT liability in a reference year (see above) falls below £2.3 million, a business will be removed from the POA scheme six months later. HMRC will notify the business of the effective date of its withdrawal from the scheme.

If the total VAT liability in any completed year ending after a reference year is less than £1.8 million, written application may be made to cease making POAs to HMRC at POA Team, 7th Floor, Regian House, James Street, Liverpool L75 1AA.

[*SI 1993/2001, Art 7*.] (VAT Notice 700/60/17, para 3.4.)

Reduction in payments on account

If

- the total VAT liability (excluding VAT on imports from outside the EU and goods ex warehouse) in any completed year ending after the year on which current payments are based is less than 80% of the liability for that year, or
- HMRC are satisfied that the total VAT liability (excluding VAT on imports from outside the EU and goods ex warehouse) in any year which has commenced but not yet ended will be less than 80% of that liability

written application can be made to HMRC at the Large Payers Unit (see above) to have the POAs reduce to reflect the current liability. Further payments on account will then be based on one twenty-fourth of the reduced amount with effect from the date of written approval by HMRC.

Increase or decrease in payments on account

HMRC may increase the POAs due where the total VAT liability (excluding VAT on imports from outside the EU and goods ex warehouse) in any year ending after the year on which current POAs are based exceeds by 20% or more the total liability for that year. Where they do so, further payments on account will be based on one twenty-fourth of the increased amount.

There are similar provisions as above to reduce the payments on account where VAT liability in any subsequent year falls below 80% of the increased amount.

Businesses carried on in divisions

Where a company is registered for VAT in the names of divisions, each division is regarded as a separate business for the POA scheme, i.e. the £2.3 million test is applied to each division (and not the company as a whole). Any overpayment by a division is not liable to set-off against a liability of the company or another division.

[*SI 1993/2001, Art 16(1)*].

Groups of companies

The POA scheme applies to a VAT group as if all the companies in the group were one taxable person. The representative member is responsible for the POA but, in default, all members are jointly and severally liable.

Deregistration

A business should continue to make POAs until such time as deregistration is confirmed in writing in order to avoid the risk of incurring default surcharge. However, as an alternative to POAs, a business can opt to pay the actual monthly amount due. (VAT Notice 700/11/18, para 7.12.)

[*SI 1993/2001; SI 1995/2518, Regs 40A, 44–48*]. (VAT Notice 700/60/17).

Reverse charge for mobile phones, computer chips, emissions allowances, wholesale supplies of gas, electricity and telecommunication services

As an anti-avoidance measure, in certain circumstances the customer, rather than the supplier, must account for VAT on transactions involving sales of mobiles phones, computer chips, emissions allowances, wholesale supplies of gas, electricity and telecommunication services. See **4.15–4.25 ANTI-AVOIDANCE** for full details. Some businesses may be required to account for output tax on their purchases under this reverse charge procedure as well as on the onward sale to non-business customers. This could have the effect of increasing their net VAT liability (and bringing them within the scope of the POA regime) or increasing their monthly payments if they are already within the regime.

A business which could be affected by this may apply to HMRC to exclude the output tax due under the reverse charge from the calculation to establish whether it is subject to POA or, if already in the regime, the monthly payments it has to make.

Applications for exclusion should be made to: The POA Team, 4th Floor Regian House, James Street, Liverpool, L75 1AD.

Some businesses may find that their net liability will decrease with the introduction of the reverse charge. If that is the case, the normal rules for reduction in POAs (see above) apply.

[*SI 1993/2001, Art 2A*]. (VAT Notice 735, para 10.5).

De Voil Indirect Tax Service. See V5.110.

Repayment of VAT

[52.6] If, at the end of a VAT accounting period, allowable credits exceed any output tax due, HMRC automatically make the appropriate repayment unless the amount of VAT due from HMRC is under £1, in which case no repayment is made. If, however, the business has failed to submit any return for an earlier period, HMRC may withhold payment until it has complied with those requirements. [*VATA 1994, s 25(3)(5), Sch 11 para 2(13)*]. See also the right of set-off under **52.7** below.

Method of repayment

HMRC make repayments by the Bankers Automated Clearing System (BACS). In order to receive repayment by this method, the National Registration Service must be advised of the bank account details in writing. (This is a requirement on the application for VAT registration.) In exceptional circumstances when bank account details are not known, HMRC may make repayment by payable order. (VAT Notice 700, para 21.4).

Right of set-off

[52.7] The right of set-off is as follows:

(1) Set-off for VAT purposes

Subject to special provisions for insolvent traders (see **36.7 INSOLVENCY**) where

(a) any amount is due from HMRC to any person under *VATA 1994*; and
(b) that person is liable to pay any sum by way of VAT, penalty, interest or surcharge,

the amount in (*a*) can be set against the sum in (*b*) and, to the extent of the set-off, the obligations of HMRC and the person concerned are discharged. Any interest payable by HMRC to a person on a sum due to him under or by virtue of any provision of *VATA 1994* is treated (except for the purposes of determining entitlement to, or the amount of, that interest) as an amount due by way of credit under *VATA 1994, s 25(3)* and can therefore be taken into account under (*a*) above.

[*VATA 1994, s 81(1)–(3)*].

The effect of the above provisions is to permit both HMRC and the person concerned to adopt commercial practice and strike a balance between all types of debits and credits within the taxpayer's account.

The set-off provisions and VAT refund claims

Where

- HMRC are liable to pay or repay any amount to a person because of a mistake previously made about the VAT due, and
- because of the mistake, a liability of that person to pay a sum by way of VAT, penalties, interest or surcharges was not assessed,

the normal time limits for enabling recovery (e.g. by assessment) are disregarded in determining the amount under (*b*) above to set off against the amount under (*a*) above. [*VATA 1994, s 81(3A)*].

Effectively, this means that where a taxpayer has overpaid VAT (e.g. because exempt supplies have been treated as taxable) and seeks a refund, any refund can take into account input tax which the taxpayer should not have recovered even if HMRC are out-of-time to issue an assessment for that input tax (e.g. because of lengthy litigation).

(2) General set-off provisions in England, Wales and Northern Ireland

Under common law, or by request, HMRC may set off repayments payable to taxpayers against debts they owe to HMRC.

Subject to

- the specific set-off requirements for VAT under (1) above (which take preference), and
- the restrictions below in relation to post-insolvency credits,

HMRC are empowered to make set-offs, at their discretion, across the different taxes, duties, etc. that they administer.

Under these provisions, where there is both a 'credit' and a 'debit' in relation to a person, HMRC may set the credit against the debit and, to the extent of that set-off, the obligations of HMRC and the person concerned are discharged.

'*Credit*', in relation to a person, means

- a sum that is payable by HMRC to the person under or by virtue of an enactment; or
- a sum that was paid in connection with any liability (including any purported or anticipated liability) of that person to make a payment to HMRC
  - (i) under or by virtue of an enactment, or
  - (ii) under a contract settlement

that may be repaid to the person by HMRC.

'*Debit*', in relation to a person, means a sum that is payable by the person to HMRC under or by virtue of an enactment or under a contract settlement.

Contract settlements are contractual agreements made in connection with a person's liability, usually as a result of an enquiry covering a number of years.

[*FA 2008, s 130*].

Post-insolvency credits

Where an insolvency procedure has been applied to a person and there is a 'post-insolvency credit' in relation to that person, HMRC may not use the above powers to set that post-insolvency credit against a 'pre-insolvency debit' in relation to the person.

'*Post-insolvency credit*' means a credit that

- became due after the insolvency procedure was applied to the person; and
- relates to, or to matters occurring at, times after it was so applied.

'*Pre-insolvency debit*' means a debit that

- arose before the insolvency procedure was applied to the person; or
- arose after that procedure was so applied but relates to, or to matters occurring at, times before it was so applied.

For these purposes, an '*insolvency procedure*' is to be taken to be applied to any person when

- a bankruptcy order or winding up order is made or an administrator is appointed in relation to that person;
- that person is put into administrative receivership;
- if that person is a corporation, that person passes a resolution for voluntary winding up;
- any approved voluntary arrangement comes into force in relation to that person; or
- a registered deed of arrangement takes effect in relation to that person.

But references to the application of an insolvency procedure to a person do not include

- the application of an insolvency procedure to a person at a time when another insolvency procedure applies to the person; or
- the application of an insolvency procedure to a person immediately upon another insolvency procedure ceasing to have effect.

[*FA 2008, s 131*].

Claims for VAT credits and refunds

[52.8] A business may be entitled to a credit for, or refund of, VAT for a number of reasons, e.g.

- output tax may have been incorrectly charged because of a mathematical error, a misunderstanding of the law (e.g. charging VAT on a zero-rated supply) or because HMRC incorrectly instructed the business to charge VAT;
- input tax may have been underclaimed in earlier periods; or
- bad debt relief may be available to recover output tax previously paid.

VATA 1994, s 80 contains special provisions covering some, but not all, of the situations where credit or refund is due. Certain conditions must be satisfied. In particular, any credit must not unjustly enrich the claimant and the claim must be made within a set time limit. These provisions are considered in **52.10–52.12** below.

Where *VATA 1994, s 80* does not apply, there can be no defence of unjust enrichment by HMRC and the method of, and time limit for, claiming is different. These provisions are considered in **52.13** below.

See also **52.14** below for a summary of the various scenarios and particular problem areas in relation to claims generally.

From 1 January 2015, a claim for credit of VAT overpaid can also be made by businesses using the non-Union VAT MOSS scheme, under *VATA 1994, Sch 3B para 16I*, and by businesses using the Union VAT MOSS scheme, under *VATA 1994, Sch 3BA para 29*. Such claims are treated as if they were *VATA 1994, s 80* claims for the purpose of allowing a defence of unjust enrichment by HMRC.

[*SI 2014/2430, Reg 3*].

Transfer of claim

[52.9] In *HMRC v Midlands Co-Operative Society Ltd (No 2)*, CA [2008] STC 1803 (TVC 65.127), in which a co-operative society transferred its business to another society, the Court of Appeal held that the transferee was entitled to claim for repayment of VAT overpaid by the transferor prior to the transfer.

In *Standard Chartered plc and others v HMRC* [2014] UKFTT 316 (TC) (TC03450) (TVC 32.35) the First-tier Tribunal held that companies that had made supplies on which VAT had been overpaid when they were members of a VAT group, but which they were no longer a member of, had no right to make a claim for repayment of the overpaid VAT from HMRC. In that case the First-tier Tribunal decided that the right to make the claim remained with the company that was the representative member of the VAT group. By way of contrast, in *MG Rover Group Ltd v HMRC* [2014] UKFTT 327 (TC) (TC02461) (TVC 32.36), the First-tier Tribunal held that the right to make a claim for overpaid VAT on supplies made by a company while it was a member of a VAT group was transferred to that company when it left the VAT group. In *Gala Leisure Ltd v HMRC* [2015] UKFTT 516 (TC) (TC04674) (TVC 32.37) the First-tier Tribunal followed the decision in *Standard Chartered plc v HMRC* [2014] UKFTT 316 (TC) (TC03450) (TVC 32.35), deciding that the right to make the claim remained with the company that was the representative member of the VAT group. This was in line with the decision of the Upper Tribunal in *Taylor Clark Leisure plc v HMRC* [2014] UKUT 396 (TCC) (TVC 48.68) that the judge in *Gala* considered to be authoritative and correct, overriding the decision in *MG Rover*. (The *MG Rover* case was subsequently overturned in the Upper Tribunal, in a case which was heard jointly with an appeal in relation to the *Standard Chartered* decision; see [2016] UKUT 434 (TCC)). The taxpayer has applied to the Court of Appeal for permission to appeal.

Another decision in this line of cases is the ruling by the Court of Session in *Taylor Clark Leisure plc v HMRC* [2016] CSIH 54 (TVC 48.68). There was a complex history. The appellant, T, had owned a subsidiary C in the 1990s; it had sold it in a management buy-out in 1998. During that period, C had been a member of T's VAT group registration, and had accounted for output tax on bingo and other games of chance. In 2007, C submitted a repayment claim, after it appeared that this income should have been exempt. T was unaware of the claim, but when HMRC concluded that it was justified, a refund of £1m was made to T as the representative member of the group that had made the overpayment. C objected, claiming that it was entitled to the money, and HMRC assessed T to recover it. The First-tier Tribunal considered that C had made a valid claim and was entitled to the repayment; the Upper Tribunal allowed HMRC's appeal, holding that only T could make a claim and had not done so (it was now out of time to rectify that). Therefore no one was entitled to the repayment. The Court of Session ruled that C could be regarded as making a claim as agent for T. Only the representative member of the group could be entitled to the repayment, because it had been responsible for making the original payment; but C's claim was valid, and T should keep the £1m. HMRC have been granted leave to appeal this judgment to the Supreme Court.

For transfers of rights to make a claim for overpaid tax, the current creditor is put in the shoes of the original creditor. The current creditor does not receive any more from HMRC than if the original creditor had made the claim. The amount due from HMRC on a claim on a transferred right is determined by first setting off the amount of the outstanding liabilities of the original creditor and then any liabilities of the current creditor. Also, HMRC can refuse to pay a current creditor's claim where they can establish that payment of the claim to the original creditor would have unjustly enriched that original creditor.

[*FA 2008, s 133*]. (HMRC Brief 31/08).

Gala 1 Ltd [2016] UKUT 564 (TCC) (TVC 48.90) is the latest in a long line of cases concerning which entity is entitled to make a claim. In this case the Upper Tribunal held that whilst in principle a claim by party other than the representative member may be considered where there are exceptional circumstances that warrant this. However, in this case Gala had failed to produce sufficient evidence to substantiate its case that there were exceptional circumstances that warranted another party making a claim. The First-tier Tribunal had given careful consideration to the arguments presented by Gala regarding why this was an exceptional case but they did not agree that it was. The Upper Tribunal found no error of law in its decision.

This decision confirms that 'under the scheme of section 43, only the representative member embodying the group can make a claim under *VATA 1994 s 80*'.

Credit for, or repayment of, overstated or overpaid VAT

[52.10] The following points apply.

(a) Where a person
- has accounted to HMRC for VAT for a VAT period (whenever ended), and

- in doing so, has brought into account as output tax an amount that was not output tax due,

HMRC are liable to credit the person with that amount.

(b) Where HMRC

- have assessed a person to VAT for a VAT period (whenever ended), and
- in doing so, have brought into account as output tax an amount that was not output tax due,

they are liable to credit the person with that amount.

(c) Where a person has for a VAT period (whenever ended) paid to HMRC an amount by way of VAT that was not VAT due to them, otherwise than as a result of

- an amount that was not output tax due being brought into account as output tax (which is covered by (*a*) above), or
- an amount of input tax allowable not being brought into account

HMRC are liable to repay to that person the amount so paid. This would cover the situation, for example, where a tax liability has been paid twice.

[*VATA 1994, s 80(1)(1A)(1B)*].

HMRC are only liable to credit or repay an amount under these provisions if the following conditions are satisfied.

(1) *A valid claim is made*. To be valid,

- a claim must be in writing, state the amount of the claim, and explain the method used to calculate it; and
- the claimant must possess sufficient documentary evidence to substantiate the claim.

[*VATA 1994, s 80(2)(6); SI 1995/2518, Reg 37*].

The only party entitled to submit a claim is the person who actually accounted for the VAT to HMRC. There is no mechanism that allows the recipient of a supply to submit refund claims. See *Aberdeen Estates Ltd* (VTD 13622) (TVC 48.24). But for the position under European law, see under 'Repayment of VAT not due' below.

The requirements for a valid claim have been considered in several cases. HMRC have argued that the requirement to 'explain the method of calculation' requires submission of detailed calculations with the initial claim; this was rejected by the First-tier Tribunal in both *Vodafone Group Services Ltd (No 1)* [2014] UKFTT 701 (TC) (TC03822) and *Bratt Auto Contracts Ltd (No 1)* [2014] UKFTT 676 (TC) (TC03799). Submission of detailed calculations would be part of HMRC's enquiry into the validity of the claim, not something that was required to register the claim in the first place. However, the Upper Tribunal did not agree with other conclusions of the First-tier Tribunal. In *HMRC v Vodafone Group Services Ltd (No 2)* [2016] STC 1064 (TVC 48.77), the Upper Tribunal held that it was not permissible for a claim to be 'amended' by substituting a completely different set of reasons. This was a new claim, subject to the four-year time limit based on the time that the 'amendment' was made. In *HMRC v Bratt Auto Contracts Ltd and another (No 2)* [2016] STC 1463 (TVC 48.20), the Upper Tribunal held that the initial claim must specify the return period to which it relates. Although this is not an explicit requirement of *Reg 37*, it is an implication of *VATA 1994, s 80*: an overpayment must relate to a particular period. If the 'claim' did not specify the period, it had not yet been validly made, and the time limits would only apply from a later date when the period was specified.

(2) *Unjust enrichment.* In relation to any claim under (*a*) or (*b*) above, the crediting of any amount to the claimant must not unjustly enrich it. [*VATA 1994, s 80(3)*]. See **52.11** below for further detail on what is meant by unjust enrichment and for arrangements for reimbursing customers where a claimant accepts that, by receiving a credit, it would be unjustly enriched.

(3) *Time limit.* The claim must be made within the appropriate time limit (see **52.12** below).

Where, as a result of a claim under (*a*) or (*b*) above, HMRC accept that credit is due, they are only liable to pay (or repay) the amount due net of any VAT liabilities of the person concerned. [*VATA 1994, s 80(2A)*].

Repayment of VAT not due

In *Investment Trust Companies v HMRC (No 1)*, Ch D [2012] STC 1150 (TVC 22.415), the companies had paid VAT on services supplied by investment managers. Following the decision in *JP Morgan Fleming Claverhouse Investment Trust plc v HMRC, ECJ Case C-363/05*, [2008] STC 1180 (TVC 22.414), the investment managers sought to recover the VAT they had accounted for on the grounds that the supplies should have been treated as exempt. HMRC accepted the claim and refunded the amounts (subject to their being passed on to the companies, to avoid unjust enrichment). The refunds were limited to the net amount of VAT paid by the managers (i.e. overpaid output tax less what had become irrecoverable input tax). The claims were also limited by the capping provisions. Thus the amounts passed on to the companies were less than the amounts that the companies had initially paid. The companies sought to recover the difference from HMRC, on the grounds that recovery from the investment managers would be impossible or excessively difficult. The High Court held that *VATA 1994, s 80(7)* should be construed as applying to claims of the type in the instant case, and therefore as a matter of English law the claim failed since the companies had not 'accounted to the Commissioners for VAT'. However, the Court held that the companies, given the CJEU decisions in *Amministrazione delle Finanze dello Stato v San Giorgio SpA, ECJ Case C-199/82*, [1983] ECR 3513 (TVC 22.618), *Danfoss A/S v Skatteministeriet (No 2), ECJ Case C-94/10, 20 October 2011 unreported* (a Danish excise duty case) and *Reemtsma Cigarettenfabriken GmbH v Ministero delle Finanze, ECJ Case C-35/05*, [2008] STC 3448 (TVC 22.616), did have enforceable rights under European law (which were nevertheless subject to the capping provisions). These rights should be applied by the disapplication of *VATA 1994, s 80(7)*. The question then arose as to the form which the enforcement of the rights should take. The choice lay between (a) a cause of action on the *Woolwich Equitable Building Society v CIR* [1993] AC 70 principle, i.e. that the authorities should be required to repay tax which has been exacted without legal justification (in which case the companies would be left without a remedy), and (b) a cause of action on the basis of a mistake. The limitation period in the case of (a) was six years from the date on which the cause of action accrued; but in the case of (b) the limitation period did not begin to run until the plaintiff had discovered the mistake, or could with reasonable diligence have discovered it. The Court directed that consideration of this issue should be adjourned until the CJEU had given its decision in *Test Claimants in the FII Group Litigation v HMRC (No 2)* [2010] STC 1251 and in *Littlewoods Retail Ltd v HMRC, ECJ Case C–591/10*, [2010] EHWC 1071 (Ch). Following those decisions, the court held in *Investment Trust Companies v HMRC (No 2)*, Ch D [2013] EWHC 665 (Ch) (TVC 22.415) that as a matter of English law, the scope of the *Woolwich* remedy would be confined to those who had themselves paid the sums which it was sought to recover to a public authority in response to an apparent statutory requirement to do so. For HMRC's interpretation of the effects of the High Court judgment in *Investment Trust Companies v HMRC (No 2)*, Ch D [2013] EWHC 665 (Ch) (TVC 22.415), see HMRC Brief 15/13. In *Investment Trust Companies (in Liquidation) v HMRC* [2015] EWCA Civ 82 the Court of Appeal decided that the companies referred to above could make claims for restitution against HMRC for the net amount of VAT paid by the managers' to HMRC, to the extent that the managers had been unable to recover the VAT from HMRC because the managers' claims were subject to the capping provisions of *VATA 1994, s 80(4)*. The matter was referred to the Supreme Court who issued its ruling in April 2017. The Court held that a customer only has the right to seek reimbursement for overpaid VAT directly from HMRC, rather than via the supplier, where it would be excessively difficult or impossible to obtain repayment from the supplier. This is a right conferred under EU law as UK domestic law of restitution does not allow such claims at all. The supplier's insolvency is the only example given of a situation where this might apply. HMRC's appeal was allowed.

As a result of this decision it is only businesses where the supplier is insolvent that are likely to succeed in making a claim for reimbursement from HMRC.

The Court of Appeal decision in *Investment Trust Companies (in Liquidation) v HMRC* [2015] EWCA Civ 82 (TVC 22.415) was referred to by the High Court in its decision in *R (oao Premier Foods (Holdings) Ltd) v HMRC* [2015] EWHC 1483 (Admin) (TVC 48.58). Before going into administration Q Cold Ltd (QCL) had incorrectly charged the standard rate of VAT on zero-rated supplies it had made to Premier Foods (Holdings) Ltd (Premier). HMRC proposed to repay the incorrectly charged VAT to QCL and enforce assessments it had made against Premier for the corresponding amount it had claimed as input tax. Premier sought judicial review of the HMRC proposal on the basis that the proposed conduct was irrational, disproportionate and in breach of EU law principles, in particular, the principles of fiscal neutrality and effectiveness. The High Court decided that the assessments HMRC had made against Premier should be quashed and that the repayment of VAT HMRC had proposed to make to QCL would amount to unjust enrichment.

In *Birmingham Hippodrome Theatre Trust Ltd v HMRC* [2014] EWCA Civ 684 (TVC 48.180) the taxpayer was a registered charity which operated a theatre. Following the decisions in *Fleming (t/a Bodycraft) v C & E Commrs*, HL [2008] STC 324 (TVC 48.6) and *HMRC v Condé Nast Publications Ltd*,

HL [2008] STC 324 (TVC 48.7) (see **35.9 INPUT TAX**) it was seeking a repayment of VAT it had accounted for between 1990 and 1996 on supplies which are covered by the exemption for cultural services within the provisions of what is now *Directive 2006/112/EC, Art 132(1)(n)*. The UK was required to implement the exemption by 1 January 1990 but did not do so until 1 June 1996 when *VATA 1994, Sch 9 Group 13* took effect. The issue was whether HMRC were entitled to set an amount of VAT wrongly recovered by the taxpayer as input tax between 2000 and 2001 against the lower amount of VAT the taxpayer had wrongly paid between 1990 and 1996. The Court of Appeal held that HMRC were so entitled. A repayment of VAT was not due.

Assessment of excess credits

See **6.5 ASSESSMENTS** for HMRC's power to make a recovery assessment when a person has been overcredited following a claim under (*a*) or (*b*) above.

Unjust enrichment

[52.11] A basic principle under EU law is that when taxes/duties have been paid contrary to EU law they should be refunded. However, it has been accepted by the CJEU that money need not be refunded if the claimant would be unjustly enriched (see *Société Comateb & others v Directeur Général des Douanes et droits indirects, ECJ Case C–192/95*, [1997] STC 1006 (TVC 22.643)).

HMRC take the term 'unjust enrichment' to apply where, by meeting a claimant's VAT claim, the claimant would be put in a better economic position than if it had not mistakenly accounted for the VAT, i.e. it would receive a 'windfall' profit.

HMRC can only successfully invoke the defence of unjust enrichment if they can show that someone other than the claimant effectively bore the burden of the VAT, i.e. that the claimant passed the VAT claimed on to its customers. (Note that it is for HMRC to prove this and not for the claimant to show that it would not be unjustly enriched if the claim were to be paid.) If HMRC can successfully show this, it is then for the claimant to produce evidence that it suffered loss or damage. If it can, the claim will be paid in part or total depending on the extent of that loss or damage. Such loss or damage cannot exceed the amount claimed, even where the actual loss and damage suffered does. [*VATA 1994, s 80(3A)–(3C)*].

It cannot be assumed that any VAT charged has been passed on to customers because VAT is meant to be a tax borne by the final consumer or because it is shown on an invoice. The claimant may have absorbed the VAT by accepting a reduced margin. See HMRC Manual VR3510 for an overview of 'passing on' the VAT charge to customers.

Arrangements for reimbursing customers

Where a claimant accepts that, by receiving a credit for overpaid VAT, it would be unjustly enriched, HMRC will only make the reimbursement if, on or before the time of making the claim, the claimant signs a written undertaking confirming the following.

(a) At the date of the undertaking he is able to identify the names and addresses of the customers he has reimbursed or intends to reimburse.
(b) The reimbursements will be completed by no later than 90 days after the crediting of the amount by HMRC.
(c) No deduction will be made from the 'relevant amount' by way of fee or charge (however expressed or effected). If an administration fee is charged, HMRC can recover this amount by assessment (see below).
(d) Reimbursement will be made only in cash or by cheque.
(e) Any part of the relevant amount credited to the claimant that is not reimbursed by the time limit in (*b*) above will be notified by the claimant to HMRC; and any part of the relevant amount paid (or repaid) to the claimant that is not reimbursed by the time limit in (*b*) above will be repaid by the claimant to HMRC.
(f) Any interest paid by HMRC on the relevant amount paid or repaid by them will be treated by the claimant in the same way as the relevant amount falls to be treated under (*b*) and (*c*). (The provisions do not specify how the interest is to be apportioned where some customers paid earlier than others.)
(g) The claimant will keep records of
   - the names and addresses of those customers whom he has reimbursed or intends to reimburse;
   - the total amount reimbursed to each such customer;
   - the total amount of interest included in each total amount reimbursed to each customer; and
   - the date that each reimbursement is made.
(h) The records in (g) above will be produced to HMRC on receipt of written notice to that effect from an HMRC officer. The notice must state the place and time at which the records are to be produced and may be given before or after HMRC have credited the relevant amount to the claimant.

See VAT Notice 700/45/17, para 10 for the format of the undertaking.

The '*relevant amount*' means that part (which may be the whole) of the claim which the claimant has reimbursed or intends to reimburse to customers.

The claimant must

- give any notification to HMRC required under (*e*) above, and
- without prior demand, make any repayments due to HMRC under (*e*) or (*f*) above

within 14 days of the end of the 90-day period referred to in (*b*) above. Where it is not possible to make some of the refunds within this limit (e.g. because customers have moved) HMRC may agree to an extension but not an open-ended one.

[*VATA 1994, s 80A; SI 1995/2518, Regs 43A–43H*].

Where HMRC accept that a claimant has not been unjustly enriched, the reimbursement arrangements above do not apply and no undertaking will be required. (Business Brief 4/98). The arrangements do apply to partial reimbursements. For example, if a business submits a claim for £50,000 and it is agreed that £30,000 should be passed on to customers but the remaining £20,000 can be retained, the £30,000 is subject to the scheme.

To ensure that the terms of reimbursement agreements are complied with, HMRC have powers to assess businesses which fail to reimburse their customers in the manner agreed. See **6.5 ASSESSMENTS**.

Time limit for claims

[52.12] HMRC are not liable to credit an amount to a claimant under **52.10**(*a*) or (*b*) above or repay an amount to a claimant under **52.10**(*c*) above if the claim is made more than four years after the 'relevant date'.

The 'relevant date' is

(a) in the case of a claim under **52.10**(*a*) above, the end of the VAT period there mentioned (unless (*b*) below applies);
(b) in the case of a claim under **52.10**(*a*) above in respect of an 'erroneous voluntary disclosure', the end of the VAT period in which the voluntary disclosure (now known as error correction notification) was made;
(c) in the case of a claim under **52.10**(*b*) above in respect of an assessment issued on the basis of an 'erroneous voluntary disclosure', the end of the VAT period in which the disclosure was made;
(d) in the case of a claim under **52.10**(*b*) above in any other case, the end of the VAT period in which the assessment was made; and
(e) in the case of a claim under **52.10**(*c*) above, the date on which the payment was made.

Where a claimant has ceased to be registered for VAT, any reference in (*b*) to (*d*) above to a VAT period includes a reference to a period that would have been a VAT period had the person continued to be registered.

For the above purposes, an '*erroneous voluntary disclosure*' occurs where

- a person discloses to HMRC that he has not brought into account for a VAT period (whenever ended) an amount of output tax due for the period;
- the disclosure is made in a later VAT period (whenever ended); and
- some or all of the amount is not output tax due.

[*VATA 1994, s 80(4)(4ZA)(4ZB)*].

When is a claim made?

Generally, HMRC accept that a claim takes effect from the date on the claim, rather than the date it is received. But if it arrived (say) two weeks after it is dated, they are more likely to use the post mark as the date of the claim.

Accidental overpayment

The time limit applies even in cases where VAT is accidentally paid in error. In *R (oao British Telecommunications plc) v HMRC*, QB [2005] STC 1148 (TVC 48.62) BT, because of an error in its accounting software, made overpayments of VAT totalling over £40m between 1993 and 2003. HMRC agreed to repay some £16m but refused to repay the balance on the grounds that the claim had been made outside the statutory time limit. The court held that HMRC were entitled to make concessional repayments of VAT overpaid outside the time limit but were not obliged to do so since this would erase the statutory time limits for claims for repayment of erroneous overpayments. (Note that HMRC have now withdrawn the concession for exception to the time limit in the case of simple duplication of output tax.)

Claims for refunds not falling within VATA 1994, s 80

[52.13] The provisions of *VATA 1994, s 80* described in **52.10** to **52.12** above do not cover all situations where VAT has been overpaid. Where those provisions do not apply, refund claims must be made under one of the following procedures and within the time limits as indicated in the text.

- Late claims for input tax under *SI 1995/2518, Reg 29* (see **35.9 INPUT TAX**).
- Error correction notification (formerly voluntary disclosure) under *SI 1995/2518, Regs 34, 35* (see **57.11 RECORDS**).
- Adjustments to take account of increases and decreases in consideration (e.g. following the issue of a credit/debit note) under *SI 1995/2518, Reg 38* (see **40.14 INVOICES**).
- Pre-registration expenses and post-deregistration expenses under *SI 1995/2518, Reg 111* (see **35.10 INPUT TAX** and **35.11 INPUT TAX** respectively).
- Adjustments under the capital goods scheme under *SI 1995/2518, Reg 115* (see **11.10 CAPITAL GOODS SCHEME**).
- Claims for bad debt relief under *SI 1985/2818, Reg 165A* (see **7.3 BAD DEBT RELIEF**).

There is no four-year limit in the following instances.

- Claims or adjustments which cover VAT appearing on both sides of a VAT return and which therefore cancel each other out (e.g. those in respect of acquisition VAT or the reverse charge).
- Correction of tax point errors.
- Returns following *compulsory* backdated registration for VAT. Where a business is registered for VAT with retrospective effect, it can claim input tax on its first return even if the VAT was incurred more than three years previously.
- Claims by DIY housebuilders.
- Penalties paid which are subsequently shown not to be due.
- Where VAT invoices are received from suppliers for supplies made more than four years previously. This most commonly arises in two situations.
  - (a) Late registration cases where a trader's registration is backdated more than four years and he issues VAT invoices in the hope that past customers will pay the VAT element of the supplies.
  - (b) Where a trader has mistakenly zero-rated a standard-rated supply and as a consequence HMRC have issued an assessment.

In such cases, although strictly the time limit for late claims for input tax under *SI 1995/2518, Reg 29* applies, by concession, HMRC will treat the four-year time limit as running from the date of receipt of the VAT invoice. They will allow input tax to be recovered by the trader's customers, subject to the normal rules, if satisfied that the trader has paid the VAT due to HMRC and the customer has paid the VAT invoice.

The concession does not apply where a standard-rated supply was made but the customer did not receive a VAT invoice or mislaid it, and therefore failed to recover input tax. In such cases, HMRC take the view that the customer could have asked them to exercise their discretion and allow alternative evidence to recover the input tax.

(C & E News Release No 10 (Budget), 26 November 1996; Business Brief 9/97). [*VATA 1994, s 80(4)*].

Example

John was six years late registering for VAT and made standard-rated sales to Jeff throughout the period. Even though some of these sales were made more than four years ago (outside of error adjustment period), John can still issue a VAT only invoice to Jeff in relation to all of the sales and reflect this on his first VAT return. Providing Jeff pays the VAT-only invoice, he can reclaim the VAT as input tax, subject to the normal rules, based on the date of the invoice. This means John is not out of pocket by having to account for output tax on the sales in question.

Summary: scenarios

[52.14] In summary, there are two main scenarios for claims against HMRC, each with subdivisions that have been subject to different rules in the past but which are now covered by the same rules.

- A claim for underclaimed input tax comes under *SI 1995/2518, Reg 29* (see **35.9 INPUT TAX**) whether it
  - (a) reduces the amount payable to HMRC in respect of an earlier payment return;
  - (b) increases the amount to which the taxpayer is entitled on an earlier repayment return; or
  - (c) exceeds the amount paid with an earlier return and turns it from a payment to a repayment return.
- A claim for overdeclared output tax comes under *VATA 1994, s 80* (see **52.10** above), whether it is:
  - (a) in respect of an earlier payment return (reducing the amount payable to HMRC);
  - (b) in respect of an earlier repayment return (increasing the amount to which the taxpayer is entitled); or
  - (c) in respect of an earlier payment return where the amount claimed exceeds the amount paid with the earlier return (and turns it from a payment to a repayment return).

Interest, etc.

Amounts due to HMRC

[52.15] Where a business fails to submit a return and/or pay the VAT shown by the due date, it may be liable to penalty under the default surcharge provisions. See **53.23 PENALTIES**. In addition, where HMRC raise an assessment for VAT undeclared or overclaimed, they may charge interest. See **52.16** below.

Amounts due from HMRC

A business is entitled to repayment supplement where HMRC do not make any repayment due within a specified time. See **52.17** below. In other cases where, due to an error by HMRC, a business overpays output tax or underclaims input tax, HMRC must pay interest to the date of repayment. See **52.18** below.

Interest payable to HMRC (default interest)

Circumstances in which interest may be charged

[52.16] A taxable person may be charged interest in the following circumstances.

(a) Where HMRC raise an assessment for a VAT period to recover any VAT which has been underdeclared or overclaimed on a VAT return.

(b) Where HMRC raise an assessment for a VAT period in respect of which an earlier assessment has already been notified (i.e. where HMRC issue an assessment following the failure to submit a VAT return but a further assessment is necessary as the original assessment is later found to be too low).

(c) Where HMRC raise an assessment relating to a VAT period which exceeds three months and begins on the date with effect from which the person concerned was, or was required to be, registered.

(d) Where HMRC raise an assessment relating to a VAT period at the beginning of which the person concerned was, but should no longer have been, exempted from registration under *VATA 1994, Sch 1 para 14(1)* (see **60.6 REGISTRATION**), *VATA 1994, Sch 1A para 13* (see **60.38 REGISTRATION**), *VATA 1994, Sch 3 para 8* (see **60.22 REGISTRATION**) or *VATA 1994, Sch 3A para 7* (see **60.29 REGISTRATION**).

(e) Where, before an assessment is made under (*a*)–(*d*) above, the VAT due or other amount concerned is paid (so that no assessment is necessary).

[*VATA 1994, s 74(1)(2)*].

HMRC may charge interest on VAT recovered or recoverable by assessment from persons not registered for VAT in the UK in relation to supplies of broadcasting, telecommunication and electronic services to consumers in the UK (see **64.40–64.45 SPECIAL SCHEMES**).

[*VATA 1994, Sch 3B and Sch 3BA; FA 2014, Sch 22*].

In general, however, HMRC only charge interest where they consider it represents '*commercial restitution*', i.e. compensation for the loss of use of any underdeclared or overclaimed VAT. They normally only charge interest if they have been deprived of this VAT for a period of time. They would not, for example, generally charge interest if an amount of VAT is underdeclared which would have been immediately reclaimable as input tax by a third party.

(VAT Notice 700/43/10, paras 2.1–2.2).

Circumstances in which interest need not be applied, or an amount chargeable to interest be reduced

If a business makes an error correction which it thinks should not attract interest, in part or in full, it should provide HMRC with as much detail as possible about the error, on a separate sheet if necessary, to enable them to make a decision about whether or not interest should be charged as commercial restitution. Similarly, the business should ensure that when HMRC find underdeclared or overclaimed VAT the officer assessing the VAT is made aware of any facts that might have a bearing on an interest charge. Generally, overclaims of input tax occur where

- evidence of entitlement is not held;
- claims are made too early;
- errors are made within the accounting system;
- claims are made on a non-deductible charge.

Where input tax is claimed by the wrong company, for example, an associated company, interest will only be charged if the other company could not immediately take full credit for that tax. Any differences in tax period groups between the business and its customer or supplier will normally be ignored when considering the need for commercial restitution.

(VAT Notice 700/43/10, para 2.3).

Circumstances in which interest will not be charged

Net VAT errors discovered by the trader can be adjusted subject to the time limits specified within Notice 700/45 'How to correct VAT errors and make adjustments or claims'. All error notifications (formerly known as voluntary disclosures) requiring an assessment may be subject to a default interest charge, regardless of the amount involved. However, net VAT errors below the limit described in the notice may continue to be corrected on a VAT return (i.e. without requiring an assessment) without incurring a charge to interest. In addition, interest will not be charged on the following.

- VAT declared on returns but unpaid.
- Assessments raised because a VAT return has not been rendered on time (but see (*b*) above for follow-up assessments).
- Penalties and interest.
- Amendments made to VAT returns before they are fully processed.

(VAT Notice 700/43/10, para 2.4).

No interest is charged where HMRC agree to defer payment because of the effects of disaster designated by the Treasury as having national significance. This provision has only been invoked once, for the floods in the UK in June and July 2007.

[*FA 2008, s 135; SI 2008/1936*].

Calculation of interest

Interest runs on the amount assessed or paid from the 'reckonable date' (even if not a business day) until the date of payment. In practice, however, interest runs to the date shown on the Notice of Assessment (Form VAT 655) or a Notification of errors in returns form. If any interest-bearing VAT shown on the Notice is not paid within 30 days, a further liability to interest arises. Interest will continue to be charged on a monthly basis and notified on Form VAT 658 or VAT 659 until all the interest-bearing VAT charged on the original assessment or error correction notification (formerly voluntary disclosure) is paid. However, interest is limited to a maximum of three years prior to the date of calculation shown on the Notice of Assessment or Notification of errors in returns form. In practice, interest will be charged where appropriate on the net amount of underdeclarations liable to interest, less any overdeclarations, for each VAT period.

The '*reckonable date*' is the latest date on which a return is required for the VAT period to which the amount assessed or paid relates (i.e. one month after the end of the period) except that

- where the amount assessed or paid is an incorrect repayment of VAT or a payment in respect of excess credits, the reckonable date is the seventh day after HMRC authorised the repayment; and
- where an assessment is made under *VATA 1994, s 73(7)* in respect of goods which cannot be accounted for (see **6.1**(*e*) **ASSESSMENTS**), the sum assessed is to be taken to relate to the period for which the assessment was made.

[*VATA 1994, ss 74(1)–(3)(5), 76(1)(7)(8), Sch 13 para 18*]. (VAT Notice 700/43/10, paras 2.5, 2.6, 2.8).

Invoices issued by unauthorised persons

Where an 'unauthorised person' issues an invoice showing an amount as being or including VAT, interest runs on the appropriate amount from the date of the invoice to the date of payment.

'*Unauthorised person*' means anyone other than

- a person registered for VAT; or
- a body corporate within a group registration; or
- a person treated as carrying on the business of a taxable person who has died or become bankrupt or incapacitated; or
- a person selling business assets of a taxable person towards satisfaction of a debt owed by that taxable person (e.g. sale of assets seized by a bailiff); or
- a person acting on behalf of the Crown.

[*VATA 1994, s 74(4)*].

Appeals, etc.

If a taxpayer disagrees with the imposition of interest or with the amount of interest charged, he may ask HMRC to reconsider the matter. This will be done by an officer not involved in the original decision.

If still not satisfied with the amount of the interest charged, the taxpayer may appeal to a VAT tribunal (see **5.3**(20) **APPEALS**). There is no right of appeal against the rate of, or liability to, interest. A tribunal can only vary the amount of interest assessed insofar as it is necessary to reduce it to an amount which is appropriate under the above provisions. [*VATA 1994, s 84(6)*].

Harmonisation of interest rates

From such a day as the Treasury may by order appoint, legislation is being introduced with the aim of harmonising the interest regime on overpayments and late payments across the range of taxes administered by HMRC. Interest is payable on any amount that is payable by a person to HMRC under or by virtue of an enactment. It is not, however, payable on itself (i.e. it applies on a simple, rather than compound, basis). It is to be paid without any deduction of income tax. Interest is payable from the 'late payment interest start date', i.e. the date on which the amount becomes due and payable, until the date on which the payment or repayment is made. However, the late payment interest start date is varied in the following circumstances.

- Where the amount due arises from an amendment or a correction to an assessment, the late interest payment start date in respect of that amount is the date which it would have been had the original assessment been correct and the amount due and payable accordingly.
- Where the amount relates to VAT due in a period during which a person should have been, but was not, registered, the late interest payment start date is the date which it would have been had the person been registered at the correct time.
- Where the amount due arises as a result of an amount described as VAT being shown on an invoice issued by an unauthorised person, the late interest payment start date in respect of that amount is the date of the invoice.

[*FA 2009, ss 101, 103, Sch 53 paras 3, 10, 11*].

1 April 2013 was appointed as the day on which *FA 2009, s 101* (late payment of interest on sums due to HMRC) of the harmonised interest regime comes into force in relation to penalties imposed under *FA 2012, Sch 38 Parts 3 to 5* (penalties for dishonest conduct or for failure to comply with a file access notice by tax agents) (see **53.40 PENALTIES**).

[*SI 2013/280*].

De Voil Indirect Tax Service. See V5.361–365.

Repayment supplement

[52.17] Where

- a person is entitled to a repayment of VAT credits under *VATA 1994, s 25(3)*,
- a registered statutory body is entitled to a refund under *VATA 1994, s 33* (see **44.7 LOCAL AUTHORITIES AND PUBLIC BODIES**),
- a registered body is entitled to a refund under *VATA 1994, s 33A* (museums and galleries, see **35.13**(21) **INPUT TAX**), or

- the registered proprietor of an academy is entitled to a refund under *VATA 1994, s 33B* (see **35.13**(30) **INPUT TAX**)

the payment due is increased by a supplement of 5% of that amount or £50, whichever is the greater, provided

(a) the return or claim is received by HMRC not later than the last day on which it is required to be made;
(b) HMRC do not issue a written instruction directing the making of the payment or refund due within the 'relevant period'; and
(c) the amount shown as due on the return or claim does not exceed the amount in fact due by more than 5% of that amount or £250, whichever is the greater.

The '*relevant period*' is the period of 30 days beginning with

- the date of receipt of the return or claim by HMRC; or
- the day after the last day of the VAT period to which the return or claim relates, if later.

HMRC have published updated VAT Notice 700/58 which provides clarification on when a return is deemed to have been received by HMRC. HMRC guidance states the following:

> 'Our computer system will record the date you submit your return through your online account. If you have been approved to submit paper returns the date we receive your return will be recorded on our computer system.'

Any supplement paid is treated (except for the purposes of determining the amount of the supplement) as an amount due by way of credit under *VATA 1994, s 25(3)* or an amount due by way of refund under *VATA 1994, ss 33, 33A or 33B* or as the case may be. Where the repayment, therefore, is not due in whole or in part and is recoverable by assessment, interest may be due on the repayment supplement as well as the VAT. See **52.16** above.

In calculating the period of 30 days referred to above, periods relating to the following are left out of account.

- The raising and answering of any reasonable inquiry relating to the return or claim in question. This period begins with the date on which HMRC first consider it necessary to make such an inquiry and ends with the date on which HMRC either satisfy themselves that they have received a complete answer to their inquiry or determine not to make the inquiry or, if they have already made it, not to pursue it further.
- The correction by HMRC of any errors or omissions in the return or claim. The period begins on the date when the error or omission first came to their notice and ends on the date when it is corrected by them.
- In a case where a person is entitled to a repayment of VAT credits, the continuing failure to submit returns in respect of an earlier VAT period. The period is determined in accordance with a certificate of HMRC issued to that effect under *VATA 1994, Sch 11 para 14(1)(b)*.
- In a case where a person is entitled to a repayment of VAT credits, failure to produce documents or give security as a condition of repayment of VAT under *VATA 1994, Sch 11 para 4(1)*. The period

begins on the date of the service of the written notice of HMRC requiring the production of documents or giving of security and ends on the date when they received the required documents or the required security.

[*VATA 1994, s 79; SI 1995/2518, Regs 198, 199*].

In *Glencore Agriculture Hungary v Nemzeti Adó- és Vámhivatal Fellebbviteli Igazgatóság, CJEU Case C-254/16* (TVC 20.197) the taxpayer submitted a VAT refund and the Hungarian tax authorities decided to launch an investigation to check the legitimacy of the claim. The tax authority sent a number of requests for information to the taxpayer during the course of the investigation. The taxpayer was slow to respond to these requests for additional information and the tax authority levied a fine for 'interfering with the procedure'. About two years later part of the refund was paid by the tax authority. The taxpayer submitted a claim for default interest to cover the date that it considered that the repayment should have been made by the tax authority to the date that the actual payment was made. The claim was refused by the tax authority on the basis that they considered that the taxpayer had contributed to the delay with its slow response to the requests made. The matter was referred to the CJEU.

The CJEU held that whilst the Directive does not contain any articles that obligate a tax authority to pay interest or specify any dates that interest should become payable this does not prevent a member state from being scrutinised. The terms of any repayment interest must not breach the principal of fiscal neutrality and the tax authority must ensure that payment is made within a reasonable time scale. If national legislation enables the tax authority to levy a fine for negligence, any extension made as a result of this cannot be excessively prolonged for a period that is not justifiable as this is not compatible with the principal of fiscal neutrality. In this case the taxpayer received its partial refund two years after the limit normally prescribed by the tax authority and the Court considered that this was not compatible with EU law. National legislation is precluded from delaying repayment of the VAT until the end of protracted enquiries and refusing to pay default interest as compensation.

For a general consideration of how VAT repayment claims are received and internally processed by HMRC and their code of practice for dealing with repayment returns, see VAT Notice 700/58/17 *Treatment of VAT repayment returns and supplements*.

Repayment supplement will not be paid on

- refunds paid to EU traders;
- refunds to do-it-yourself housebuilders;
- claims relating to services received after deregistration;
- amounts notified by HMRC as overdeclared (including those resulting from error correction notifications (formerly voluntary disclosures) made in writing to HMRC); or
- claims for interest as a result of official error.

(VAT Notice 700, para 21.6).

De Voil Indirect Tax Service. See V5.191; V5.192.

In *HMRC v Our Communications Ltd (No 2)*, UT [2013] UKUT 595 (TCC) (TVC 48.133) the Upper Tribunal held that repayment supplement is not due where the claim for repayment has not been made in a VAT return.

Interest payable by HMRC in cases of official error

[52.18] Where, due to an error by HMRC, a person has

(a) accounted to HMRC for output tax which was not due to them and, as a result, they are liable to pay (or repay) an amount to him, or
(b) failed to claim credit for input tax to which he was entitled and which HMRC are in consequence liable to pay to him, or
(c) otherwise than under *(a)* or *(b)* paid to HMRC any VAT not due (e.g. import VAT) and which they are in consequence liable to repay, or
(d) suffered delay in receiving payment of an amount due from HMRC in connection with VAT (including, for example, a refund under the DIY builder's scheme or under *(a)* to *(c)* above but excluding any interest due under this provision),

then, if they would not otherwise be liable to do so, HMRC must pay interest to him for the 'applicable period'. Under a standing regulation, HMRC automatically change the rates of interest following movements in market rates. Rates change 13 working days after the meeting of the Monetary Policy Committee of the Bank of England.

[*SI 1989/1297*].

Although not specified in the legislation, in *National Council of YMCAs Inc* (VTD 10537) (TVC 48.165), it was held that interest should be calculated on a simple rather than compound basis. However in *Sempra Metals Ltd (formerly Metallgesellschaft Ltd) v IR Commrs* [2007] STC 1559 (TVC 2.494), which related to advance corporation tax, it was held that where money has been wrongly exacted and overpaid, the payer was entitled to a remedy for the loss of use of that money. Such a remedy required the payment of interest at a commercial rate and the interest should be compounded. Following that decision, a test case (*FJ Chalke Ltd v HMRC* [2009] STC 2027 (TVC 48.171)) was brought under the VAT interest cars group litigation. The High Court held that while *VATA 1994 s 78* provided for the payment of simple interest and excluded any other remedy as a matter of domestic law, it was overridden by the principle of effectiveness where an overpayment was caused by breach of directly effective provisions of EU law. The requirement that compound interest should be paid was a requirement of EU law. However, the High Court and the Court of Appeal ([2010] EWCA Civ 313), held that the claims for the recovery of such interest were out of time under the *Limitation Act 1980, s 32(1)(c)*. See also *John Wilkins (Motor Engineers) Ltd v HMRC* [2011] EWCA Civ 429 (TVC 2.494).

The case of *Littlewoods Retail Ltd v HMRC* [2010] STC 2072 was referred to the CJEU, effectively asking whether domestic legislation providing only for simple interest is compatible with EU law, and if not, whether the remedy should take the form of the payment of compound interest, or some other form. The CJEU ruled 'that a taxable person who has overpaid VAT which was collected by the EU member state contrary to the requirements of EU VAT legislation has a right to reimbursement of the VAT collected in breach of EU law and a right to payment of interest on the principal sum to be reimbursed.'

It is for national law to determine, in compliance with the principles of effectiveness and equivalence, whether the principal sum must bear simple interest, compound interest or another type of interest. It is for the national courts to make the final decision, taking into account that the conditions under which interest is to be paid must not be less favourable than those concerning similar claims based on provisions of national law or arranged in such a way as to make the exercise of rights conferred by the EU legal order practically impossible. (*Littlewoods Retail Ltd v HMRC (and related applications) (No 2), ECJ Case C-591/10, 19 July 2012, unreported*) (TVC 22.649). The High Court decided that 'as a matter of English law, the correct approach to quantification of the claims is to ascertain the objective use value of the overpaid tax, which is properly reflected in an award of compound interest.' (*Littlewoods Retail Ltd & Ors v HMRC* [2014] EWHC 868 (Ch).) On 6 May 2014 HMRC issued HMRC Brief 20/14 stating that it considered the High Court judgment to be at odds with the requirements of European law and how Parliament intended VAT law to work. (HMRC Brief 20/14).

On 21 May 2015 the Court of Appeal released its judgment in *Littlewoods Ltd v HMRC* [2015] EWCA Civ 515 (TVC 2.498), which supported the conclusions of the High Court (see above). On 23 June 2015 HMRC published HMRC Brief 9/15 explaining that it did not agree with the judgment and considers it to be at odds with the requirements of EU law and how Parliament intended VAT law to work. The Brief confirmed that HMRC had been granted permission to appeal the Court of Appeal decision to the Supreme Court.

The Supreme Court has issued its judgment (*Littlewoods Retail Limited and others* [2017] STC 2413) and it has overturned the decision reached by the Court of Appeal, ruling that Littlewoods is not entitled to compound interest on the amount of overpaid VAT that was the result of an official error. The Supreme Court held that payment was simple interest on overpaid VAT was an adequate indemnity. The Supreme Court stated the following:

> 'Littlewoods have already recovered overpaid tax, and interest on that amount, going back several decades. The size of that recovery reflects a combination of circumstances which could not have occurred in most of the other EU member states: the retroactive nature of a major development of the common law by the courts, so as to allow for the first time the recovery of money paid under a mistake in law, and the inability of the legislature to respond to that development, under EU law, by retroactively altering the law of limitation so as to protect public finances. The resultant payment of interest cannot realistically be regarded as having deprived Littlewoods of an adequate indemnity, in the sense in which that expression should be interpreted.'

This is the end of the road and the decision may have little impact on any businesses other than those potentially hoping for a windfall.

These provisions do not require HMRC to pay interest on any amount on which repayment supplement is due under **52.17** above (see *THI Leisure Two Partnership* (VTD 16876) (TVC 48.111)), or on the amount of that repayment supplement. Additionally, where a claim for any payment or repayment has to be made, interest is only due on the amount of the claim which HMRC are required to satisfy or have satisfied (i.e. interest is limited to the period for which VAT is refundable under *VATA 1994, s 80*).

In *Coin-a-Drink Ltd v HMRC* [2015] UKFTT 495 (TC) (TC04657) the First-tier Tribunal dismissed the company's appeal against a decision of HMRC to impose a corporation tax liability on sums paid to the company as a refund of VAT and associated interest. The Tribunal considered that the requirement for HMRC to disgorge benefits did not extend to include the cancellation or disapplication of the corporation tax liability which would otherwise arise in connection with the VAT repayment or the interest payment.

Corporation tax at the rate of 45% is charged on restitution interest, being interest that is paid or payable by HMRC to a company in respect of a claim by the company for restitution. [*F(No 2)A 2015, s 357YK*].

Claims

Interest is only due if a claim is made in writing for that purpose. Any claim must be made within four years after the end of the applicable period to which it relates. [*VATA 1994, s 78(11)*].

Period of interest

The '*applicable period*' is the period beginning with the date that HMRC

- under (*a*) or (*b*) above received payment, or as the case may be authorised a repayment or set off, for the return period to which the output tax or input tax related;
- under (*c*) above, received the payment; or
- under (*d*) above, might reasonably have been expected to authorise the payment or set-off in question

and ending with the date on which HMRC authorised payment of the amount on which the interest is payable. References to HMRC 'authorising' a payment of any amount include references to their discharging liability to pay that amount by way of set-off against VAT due to them. Broadly, statutory interest is therefore payable on the net amount repayable by HMRC at any particular time.

In calculating the applicable period, any period by which HMRC's authorisation of the payment of interest is delayed by the claimant's conduct is left out of account. This includes, in particular, any period referable to the following.

- Unreasonable delay in making the claim for interest or the claim for payment or repayment of the amount on which interest is claimed.
- A failure by the claimant or his representative to provide HMRC with all the information they require to determine the amount of the payment or repayment due and the interest thereon (whether at or before the time of making the claim or subsequently in response to a request by HMRC). For these purposes, there is to be taken as referable to a person's failure to provide information in response to a request by

HMRC any period beginning with the date on which HMRC reasonably require the person to provide it and ending with the earliest date they could reasonably conclude that the information required has been supplied or is no longer necessary.

- The making of a claim (as part of or in association with the claim for payment or repayment or interest) to anything to which the claimant was not entitled.

Appeals

An appeal may be made to a VAT tribunal against a decision of HMRC not to pay interest under these provisions (see **5.3 APPEALS**).

[*VATA 1994, s 78*].

A claim for interest was upheld where HMRC incorrectly advised that input tax had to be apportioned because some of the company's income was outside the scope of VAT. This ruling (although pre-dating it) was inconsistent with the decision in *Lennartz v Finanzamt Munchen III* (see **35.7 INPUT TAX**) and led to the company failing to claim credit for input tax to which it was entitled (*North East Media Development Trust Ltd* (VTD 13104) (TVC 48.149)). Following the decision, the company claimed interest on the whole of the input tax which HMRC had wrongly refused to repay. However, the tribunal upheld HMRC's contention that interest should be computed upon an amount equal to the net overpayment of VAT (*North East Media Development Trust Ltd* (VTD 13425) (TVC 48.167)).

A claim for interest was also upheld where the organisation contended that a HMRC leaflet had not been updated and that it had been misled by a VAT officer (*Wydale Hall* (VTD 14273) (TVC 48.162)).

Assessment of overpaid interest

See **6.5 ASSESSMENTS** for HMRC's power to assess for interest that has been overpaid to a claimant under the above provisions.

Interim remedy

[52.19] There is a restriction on the power of a court to require HMRC to pay any sum to a claimant by way of interim remedy made in any court proceedings relating to a taxation matter on an application founded at least in part on a point of law not yet finally decided. The court may grant the interim payments only if

(a) payment of the sum is necessary to enable the proceedings to continue; or
(b) the claimant's circumstances are exceptional and such that grant of remedy is necessary in the interests of justice.

For the purposes of (*a*) above, all sources of funding reasonably likely to be available, including borrowing capacity of the claimant, are taken into account.

The restriction applies from 26 June 2013 in relation to proceedings whenever they were commenced. If any remedy is granted by a court between 26 June 2013 and 17 July 2013, provision is made to oblige the court to revoke or modify any remedy so as to give effect to the restriction and to order recovery of any related payment made by HMRC. Proceedings on appeal are treated for the purposes of the restriction as part of the original proceedings from which the appeal lies.

[*FA 2013, s 234*].

Key points: payment of VAT

[52.20] Points to consider are as follows.

- A condition of online filing of VAT returns is that any tax due must also be paid by electronic means. The easiest option is to pay by direct debit because the tax is then taken automatically from a taxpayer's bank account, without any instruction being needed for the bank. Direct debit gives the longest time to pay the VAT due on a VAT return: the business will receive an additional three working days (in addition to the seven calendar days) before payment is taken from its account. If two weekend days are included within the three extra days, this extends to five calendar days, i.e. by the 12th day of the following month.
- If the due date for payment of VAT falls on a weekend or Bank Holiday, then payment must be received in HMRC's bank account by the end of the previous working day. In some cases, Faster Payments may arrive in HMRC's account on a non-working day, but some traders have found to their cost that this does not always succeed.
- HMRC provide a calculator to find out the date by which payment must be made. There will be a different date for some methods such as BACS and CHAPS transfers.
- If a business cannot pay the VAT it owes on a return, it should still submit the return and then seek to negotiate a time-to-pay agreement with HMRC's BPSS (Business Payment Support Service).
- If an agreement is reached with the BPSS before the tax is legally due for payment, this will avoid a default surcharge or liability notice being incurred (this statement is correct at time of publication but current HMRC policy must be checked).
- Where, exceptionally, a trader files a paper return and sends a cheque in the post, payment must be made so that it clears HMRC's bank account by the due date of the return, rather than just be received by this date. This means a business will need to submit the return and payment an extra three working days before the due date to meet this requirement.

- A business with an annual VAT liability of £2.3 million or more must make payments on account (POAs) to effectively pay VAT to HMRC on a monthly rather than quarterly basis. These payments must be made by electronic means.
- If a business has incorrectly accounted for output tax on zero-rated or exempt sales (or possibly charged standard-rated VAT on a reduced rated supply), then it will need to consider whether any such VAT needs to be repaid to the customer (when reclaimed from HMRC) rather than retained in the business as a cash windfall. This challenge is known as 'unjust enrichment' and means that a business cannot profit out of making VAT errors.
- The key challenge for a business in an 'unjust enrichment' situation is to be able to show that it absorbed the incorrect VAT charge within its selling price, rather than added VAT on a cost-plus basis.
- If a business has to repay VAT to its customers under the unjust enrichment rules, it cannot deduct an administration fee for the time spent co-ordinating claims. The entire VAT amount must be passed back to customers.
- Interest charged by HMRC when they raise an assessment for underpaid tax in a previous period is not classed as a penalty. It is classed as commercial restitution to recognise the fact that the money should have been in HMRC's bank account (rather than the taxpayer's account) in an earlier period.
- A business can adjust past VAT errors on the next VAT return it submits, as long as the net value of the error (or errors) is less than £10,000 or less than £50,000 and 1% of the Box 6 outputs figure for the return where the correction is being made.
- It is important to identify when errors can be included on a VAT return because this adjustment will automatically avoid any default interest being charged. Any tax underpayment separately notified to HMRC (i.e. on form VAT652) will be subject to default interest in most cases.

53

Penalties

De Voil Indirect Tax Service. See V5.3.

Criminal offences and penalties

[53.1] Criminal proceedings may be brought under the offences in **53.2** to **53.10** below. Most VAT defaults are, however, dealt with by civil penalties and only serious cases of fraudulent VAT evasion are investigated as criminal matters. The proceedings may only be instituted by HMRC or a law officer of the Crown.

Except as otherwise provided,

- proceedings for an indictable offence must be commenced within 20 years of the date when the offence was committed; and
- proceedings for a summary offence must be commenced within three years of that date but, subject to that, may be commenced at any time within six months from the date on which sufficient evidence to warrant the proceedings came to the knowledge of the prosecuting authority. For these purposes, a certificate of the prosecuting authority as to the date on which the evidence came to its knowledge is conclusive evidence of the fact.

There are further detailed provisions relating to service of process, place of trial, non-payment of penalties, application of penalties, proof of certain documents and other procedural matters. [*CEMA 1979, ss 145–151, 153–155; VATA 1994, s 72(12)*].

False statements

False statements to the prejudice of the Crown and public revenue are indictable as a criminal offence (*R v Hudson*, CCA 1956, 36 TC 561). False statements may also involve liability to imprisonment for up to two years, under the *Perjury Act 1911, s 5*, for 'knowingly and wilfully' making materially false statements, etc. for VAT purposes.

De Voil Indirect Tax Service. See V5.301–318.

Fraudulent evasion of VAT

[53.2] A person who is knowingly concerned in, or in taking steps with a view to, the fraudulent 'evasion of VAT' by him or any other person, is liable

- on summary conviction, to a penalty of the 'statutory maximum' or three times the 'amount of VAT', whichever is the greater, *or* imprisonment for a term not exceeding six months *or* to both; or
- on conviction on indictment, to a penalty of any amount *or* to imprisonment for a term not exceeding seven years *or* to both.

'*Evasion of VAT*' includes obtaining

(i) a payment of a VAT credit;
(ii) a refund under *VATA 1994, s 35* (do-it-yourself housebuilders), *VATA 1994, s 36* or *VATA 1983, s 22* (bad debts) or *VATA 1994, s 40* (new means of transport supplied to another EU member state by a non-taxable person);

(iii) a refund under regulations made by virtue of *VATA 1994, s 13(5)* (VAT paid in the UK on an acquisition from another EU member state where VAT has already been paid in that other country); or

(iv) a repayment under *VATA 1994, s 39* (repayment of VAT to those in business overseas).

'*Amount of VAT*' in relation to a payment within (i) above is the aggregate of the amount (if any) falsely claimed as input tax and the amount (if any) by which output tax was falsely understated. In relation to a refund or repayment within (ii) to (iv) above, it is the amount falsely claimed.

[*VATA 1994, s 72(1)(2)*].

'*Statutory maximum*' is currently £5,000.

Nothing in the above denies the right for an assessment to be made in respect of the VAT actually evaded.

'*Evasion*' includes deliberate non-payment of VAT and it is not necessary to show any permanent intention to deprive (*R v Dealy, CA Criminal Division 1994*, [1995] STC 217 (TVC 49.10)).

'*Taking of steps*' to evade VAT need not necessarily be confined to the taking of positive steps (*R v McCarthy*, CA Criminal Division [1981] STC 298 (TVC 49.1)).

The existence of the above provisions does not rule out the possibility of conviction under the common law offence of cheating the public revenue. This offence is preserved by the *Theft Act 1968, s 32(1)* and can include any form of fraudulent conduct which results in diverting money from the public revenue and in depriving the public revenue of money to which it is entitled. In practice, the common law charge is reserved for serious cases and the penalties, including imprisonment, are unlimited. No positive act of deception is required. An omission to do an act is sufficient. See *R v Mavji*, CA [1986] STC 508 (TVC 49.25) and *R v Redford*, CA [1988] STC 845 (TVC 49.26).

Where appropriate, HMRC's policy is to deal with fraud under the civil provisions (see **53.12** below) which are more cost-effective. Criminal investigation will be reserved for cases where HMRC needs to send a strong deterrent message or where the conduct involved is such that only a criminal sanction is appropriate. Examples of the kind of circumstances in which HMRC will generally consider commencing criminal, rather than civil, investigations are

- in cases of organised criminal gangs attacking the tax system or systematic frauds where losses represent a serious threat to the tax base, including conspiracy;
- where an individual holds a position of trust or responsibility;
- where materially false statements are made or materially false documents are provided in the course of a civil investigation;
- where, pursuing an avoidance scheme, reliance is placed on a false or altered document or such reliance or material facts are misrepresented to enhance the credibility of a scheme;
- where deliberate concealment, deception, conspiracy or corruption is suspected;

- in cases involving the use of false or forged documents;
- in cases involving importation or exportation breaching prohibitions and restrictions;
- in cases involving money laundering with particular focus on advisors, accountants, solicitors and others acting in a 'professional' capacity who provide the means to put tainted money out of reach of law enforcement;
- where the perpetrator has committed previous offences or there is a repeated course of unlawful conduct or previous civil action;
- in cases involving theft, or the misuse or unlawful destruction of HMRC documents;
- where there is evidence of assault on, threats to, or the impersonation of HMRC officials; and
- where there is a link to suspected wider criminality, whether domestic or international, involving offences not under the administration of HMRC.

When considering whether a case should be investigated under the civil procedures or be the subject of a criminal investigation, one factor will be whether the taxpayer has made a complete and unprompted disclosure of the offences committed.

However, there are certain fiscal offences where HMRC will not usually adopt the civil procedure. Examples of these are:

- VAT missing trader Intra-Community (MTIC) fraud;
- VAT 'bogus' registration repayment fraud; and
- organised tax credit fraud.

(HMRC criminal investigation policy statement).

Compounding

Under *CEMA 1979, s 152*, HMRC may accept a financial settlement (a '*compound settlement*') in lieu of criminal proceedings. This saves time and money for both the taxpayer and HMRC by avoiding the need for legal proceedings. HMRC do not offer a compound settlement in all cases and will normally prosecute where a HMRC officer has been assaulted or obstructed or the taxpayer is subject to a suspended prison sentence, on parole, an undischarged bankrupt (in liquidation if a limited company), a persistent offender or is being investigated for other related offences (whether by HMRC, the police or other government departments).

Each case is considered on its merits but HMRC will take into account the seriousness of the offence; the penalty that a court might impose; the nature and value of the goods and the amount of tax/duty involved; the costs of investigating the offence; any aggravating circumstances; and the ability of the taxpayer to pay.

HMRC may disclose details of a compound settlement to the courts (if prosecuted for a similar offence in the next five years); an employer; other government departments whose statutory responsibilities are directly affected by the actions involved; and Parliament or the media (if in the public interest).

De Voil Indirect Tax Service. See V5.311.

Offences relating to documents and statements

False documents and statements

[53.3] Any person who

(a) produces, furnishes, sends or otherwise makes use of, for the purposes of VAT, any document which is false in a material particular with the intent to deceive or secure that a machine will respond to the document as if it were a true document; or
(b) causes a document to be produced, etc. as in *(a)* above; or
(c) makes any statement in furnishing information for the purposes of VAT which he knows to be false in a material particular *or* who recklessly makes a statement which is false in a material particular,

is liable

- on summary conviction, to a penalty of the 'statutory maximum' (see **53.2** above) *or* to imprisonment for a term not exceeding six months *or* to both. Where the document referred to is a return *or* a refund or repayment under **53.2**(ii)–(iv) above *or* the information under (*c*) above is contained in or relevant to such a document, an alternative penalty of three times the amount falsely claimed is, if greater, substituted for the statutory maximum; or
- on conviction on indictment, to a penalty of any amount *or* to imprisonment for a term not exceeding seven years *or* to both.

[*VATA 1994, s 72(3)–(7)*].

Concealing documents following information notice

[53.4] From 1 April 2009, a person who conceals, destroys or otherwise disposes of a document covered by an information notice (see **32.6 HMRC: POWERS**) which has been approved by the First-tier Tribunal is guilty of an offence. A person is also guilty of an offence if they conceal, etc. a document after an HMRC officer has informed them in writing that that document is likely to be the subject of an information notice and the officer intends to seek the First-tier Tribunal's approval to the giving of the notice. Punishment for the offence is a fine or imprisonment or both, depending on the nature of the conviction.

[*FA 2008, Sch 36 paras 53–55; SI 2009/404*].

De Voil Indirect Tax Service. See V5.312; V5.313.

Conduct which must have involved an offence

[53.5] Where a person's conduct during any specified period must have involved the commission by him of one or more offences under **53.2** or **53.3–53.4** above, then, whether or not the particulars of the offence are known, he is guilty of an offence and liable

- on summary conviction, to a penalty of the greater of the 'statutory maximum' (see **53.2** above) and three times the amount of any VAT that was, or was intended to be, evaded by his conduct *or* to imprisonment for a term not exceeding six months *or* to both; or
- on conviction on indictment, to a penalty of any amount *or* to imprisonment for a term not exceeding seven years *or* to both.

See **53.2** above for 'evasion of VAT'.

[*VATA 1994, s 72(8)*].

De Voil Indirect Tax Service. See V5.314.

Knowledge that evasion intended

[53.6] A person who acquires possession of, or deals with, any goods or accepts the supply of services, having reason to believe that VAT on the supply, acquisition or importation has been or will be evaded, is liable to a penalty on summary conviction of the greater of level 5 on the 'standard scale' or three times the amount of the VAT evaded. [*VATA 1994, s 72(10)*].

'*Standard scale*' can be altered by statutory instrument and level 5 is currently £5,000.

De Voil Indirect Tax Service. See V5.316.

Failure to provide security

[53.7] A person who supplies, or is supplied with, goods or services in contravention of a requirement to give security under *VATA 1994, Sch 11 para 4(2)* (see **32.1**(*c*) **HMRC: POWERS**) is liable to a penalty of level 5 on the standard scale (see **53.6** above). [*VATA 1994, s 72(11)*].

De Voil Indirect Tax Service. See V5.317.

Obstruction of officers

[53.8] A person commits an offence if, without reasonable excuse, he obstructs an HMRC officer or a person acting on behalf of or assisting an HMRC officer. Any person found guilty of such an offence is liable, on summary conviction, to imprisonment for up to 51 weeks or a fine up to level three on the 'standard scale' or both. The standard scale can be altered by statutory instrument and level 3 is currently £1,000. [*CRCA 2005, s 31*].

Penalty for participating in VAT fraud

[53.9] The Government announced at Budget 2016 that they intended to introduce a penalty for participating in VAT fraud; the measure is intended to improve the application of penalties to a person who facilitates orchestrated VAT fraud. The penalty will be applied to businesses and company officers when they knew or should have known that their transactions were connected with VAT fraud. This is known as the 'knowledge principle'. The penalty will be imposed at the same time the tax decision is made in order to improve its effectiveness and reduce costs for HMRC, the courts and businesses. The penalty will be levied at 30% of the potential lost VAT, which will in effect be the amount of VAT denied under the knowledge principle. The changes will be implemented by inserting new *ss 69C, 69D* and *69E* into *VATA 1994*. The new *s 69E* gives HMRC the power to publish the details of a person liable to a penalty under these provisions where the potential lost VAT in relation to the penalty or penalties exceeds £50,000.

Please note that as a result of the general election, the Government needed to reduce the number of clauses in *Finance Act 2017*. *Clause 129*: VAT penalties: changes to penalties for facilitating fraud was removed from the *Finance Bill 2017*. The Government included this measure in *Finance (No 2) Act 2017* which received Royal Assent on 16 November 2017.

[*F(No 2)A 2017, s 68*].

Penalty for failing to prevent the facilitation of tax evasion

[53.10] *The Criminal Finances Bill* received Royal Assent on 27 April 2017 and it introduced a new corporate criminal offence, with an unlimited fine, for businesses that fail to implement reasonable procedures designed to prevent the facilitation of tax evasion. The new offence came into effect from 30 September 2017.

Many businesses do not consider that they will be impacted by this new offence because they are not evading tax, however, it is important to note that the criminal offence will arise where a business has not implemented appropriate controls that are designed to prevent the facilitation of VAT evasion by a person acting on their behalf, such as an employee, agent or consultant.

It is understood that this offence could apply in respect of VAT evasion, where for example, an employee knowingly processes invoices from a supplier showing a false VAT registration number or staff employed by an online trading platform knowingly allow a trader not to levy VAT when they are aware that they are required to be registered for UK VAT, etc.

[*Criminal Finances Act 2017, ss 44–52*].

Civil penalties

[53.11] In addition to the criminal penalties under **53.1** to **53.10** above, there are also civil penalties and surcharges. These are detailed in **53.12** to **53.32** below.

Reasonable excuse for conduct

No penalty or surcharge arises under **53.14** to **53.23** and **53.26** to **53.31** below if the person concerned can satisfy HMRC, or on appeal a tribunal, that there is a reasonable excuse for his conduct. Although 'reasonable excuse' is not defined (and, therefore, to be determined by HMRC or a tribunal) the following are not to be taken as a reasonable excuse.

- An insufficiency of funds to pay any VAT due.
- Where reliance is placed on 'any other person' to perform any task, the fact of that reliance or any other dilatoriness or inaccuracy on the part of the person relied upon. See *C & E Commrs v Harris and Another*, QB [1989] STC 907 (TVC 51.88). '*Any other person*' is not restricted to outside advisers and includes a company's accountant (*Profile Security Services Ltd v C & E Commrs*, QB [1996] STC 808 (TVC 18.532)).

[*VATA 1994, s 71(1)*].

It is necessary to distinguish between the reason and the excuse. Although insufficiency of funds by itself is not a reasonable excuse, where the shortfall is totally unforeseen and not due to the normal hazards of trade (e.g. the dishonesty of a former employee) the defence of reasonable excuse may possibly be invoked (*C & E Commrs v Salevon Ltd*, QB [1989] STC 907 (TVC 18.269)). See also *C & E Commrs v Steptoe*, CA [1992] STC 757 (TVC 18.283) where it was held that there was reasonable excuse where the taxpayer was unable to pay the VAT due because the customer for whom he worked almost exclusively was persistently late in paying invoices. The correct test is whether, given the exercise of reasonable foresight, due diligence and a proper regard for the fact that the VAT will become due on a particular date, the lack of funds which led to the default was reasonably avoidable.

HMRC have indicated the following *guidelines* on the interpretation of 'reasonable excuse' although any decision will be judged by HMRC or the First-tier Tribunal on the circumstances of the individual case.

(a) **Reasonable excuse for late registration**
   - *Compassionate circumstances* where an individual is totally responsible for running a small business and he, or a member of his immediate family, was seriously ill or recovering from such an illness at the time notification was required.
   - *Doubt about liabilities of supplies* where there is written evidence of an enquiry to HMRC about the liability of supplies and liability has remained in doubt.
   - *Uncertainty about employment status* where there are genuine doubts as to whether a person is employed or self-employed or where correspondence with HMRC can be produced about these doubts.

   (VAT Notice 700/41/12, para 4.1).

(b) **Reasonable excuse for not sending in return or paying VAT on time**

   HMRC state:

   'If you have a reasonable excuse for failing to pay on time, and you remedy this failure without unreasonable delay after the excuse ends, you won't be liable to a surcharge.

   There's no statutory definition of reasonable excuse and it will depend on the particular circumstances of your case. A reasonable excuse is something that stopped you from meeting a tax obligation on time which you took reasonable care to meet. The decision on whether a reasonable excuse exists depends upon the particular circumstances in which the failure occurred.'

The following circumstances have been held to give rise to a reasonable excuse:

- *Computer breakdown* where the essential records are held on computer and it breaks down either just before or during the preparation of the return. Reasonable steps to correct the fault must be taken.
- *Illness* of the person normally responsible for preparing the return provided it can be shown that no-one else was capable of completing the return. If the illness is prolonged, reasonable steps to get someone else to complete the return must be taken.
- *Loss of key personnel* responsible for preparing the return at short notice where there is no-one else to complete it on time.
- *Unexpected cash crisis* where funds are unavailable to pay VAT because of the sudden reduction or withdrawal of overdraft facilities, sudden non-payment by a normally reliable customer, insolvency of a large customer, fraud, burglary or act of God such as fire.
- *Loss of records.* The excuse only applies if records for the current VAT period are stolen or destroyed. If records relating to a future VAT return are lost, HMRC must be notified immediately. If the records are elsewhere (e.g. with accountants or HMRC) it is the taxpayer's responsibility to get them, or copies of them, back.

HMRC will take into account whether the circumstances could have been foreseen and, if so, what steps were taken to make alternative arrangements; whether HMRC was contacted for help or advice; whether sufficient priority was given to completing the VAT return; and whether a reasonable estimate of the VAT was paid by the due date. Genuine mistakes, honesty and acting in good faith are not reasonable excuses. The statutory exclusion of 'insufficiency of funds' from being a reasonable excuse means that an inability to pay on its own cannot be sufficient, but HMRC will look at the underlying cause of the trader's inability to pay. In exceptional circumstances this underlying cause may be a 'reasonable excuse'.

(VAT Notice 700/50/17, para 6.1).

There have been numerous other tribunal decisions as to whether, on the facts of a particular case, there is a reasonable excuse against the assessment of a penalty. For a summary of these see the chapters **DEFAULT SURCHARGE, PENALTIES: FAILURE TO NOTIFY, ETC., PENALTIES: MISDECLARATION** and **PENALTIES: REGULATORY PROVISIONS** in *Tolley's VAT Cases*.

Example

John is VAT-registered and has submitted two VAT returns late:

- The first return was late because on the day before the return was due, the business computer system crashed and an engineer had to collect the computer and take it away for five days.

- The next return was late because John's bookkeeper was on holiday for a week and was therefore not available during the last week of the month when the figures needed to be calculated and the return submitted to HMRC.

The computer crash would almost certainly be classed as a reasonable excuse if John could confirm the problem he encountered to HMRC with an engineer's report, invoice for subsequent repair cost etc. The bookkeeper's holiday would definitely not be a reasonable excuse because alternative arrangements should have been made.

In the case of the computer breakdown, John could have liaised with HMRC about estimating the VAT figures for the period in question, and then declaring an exact figure on the return for the following period.

Mitigation

See **53.33** below.

Right of set-off

See **52.7** PAYMENT OF VAT.

De Voil Indirect Tax Service. See V5.335.

VAT evasion

[53.12] **Note:** where conduct involving dishonesty relates to an inaccuracy in a document or a failure to notify HMRC of an underassessment, the provisions in *VATA 1994, ss 60, 61* below have been replaced by provisions in *FA 2007, s 97, Sch 24* (*ss 60* and *61* may still be applied in other cases, e.g. the dishonest failure to notify HMRC of a liability to register for VAT or failure to make a return).

See **53.15** below for the current provisions although it should be noted that no person is liable for a penalty under those provisions in respect of a VAT period for which a return is required to be made before 1 April 2009. [*SI 2008/568*]. Where a VAT loss arises from dishonest conduct, the time limit for assessment is 20 years, so the former provisions remain relevant; the case law concerning what constitutes dishonesty and the standard of proof required is also likely to inform decisions on penalties for later periods.

Conduct involving dishonesty

Subject to the note above, cases of VAT evasion are normally dealt with under the following civil provisions but, for aggravated or serious offences, the matter may be investigated for criminal proceedings. See **53.2** above for criminal proceedings and an indication of where cases are likely to be dealt with as such.

Where

(a) for the purpose of 'evading VAT', a person does any act or omits to take any action; and

(b) his conduct involves dishonesty (whether or not it is such as to give rise to criminal liability),

he is liable to a penalty equal to 'the amount of the VAT evaded' (or sought to be evaded). However, where he is convicted of a criminal offence by reason of conduct within (*a*) and (*b*) above, he is not also liable to a penalty under these provisions.

'*Evading VAT*' includes dishonestly obtaining a VAT credit; a refund under *VATA 1994, s 35* (do-it-yourself builders), *VATA 1994, s 36* or *VATA 1983, s 22* (bad debts) or *VATA 1994, s 40* (new means of transport supplied to another EU member state by a non-taxable person); a refund under regulations made by virtue of *VATA 1994, s 13(5)* (VAT paid in the UK on an acquisition from another EU member state where VAT has already been paid in that other country on the acquisition); and a repayment under *VATA 1994, s 39* (repayment of VAT to those in business overseas).

'*The amount of VAT evaded*' is the amount falsely claimed by way of credit for input tax (including any amount claimed as a deduction from VAT due) or the amount by which output tax is falsely understated *or* the amount falsely claimed by way of refund or repayment.

In any criminal proceedings against the person concerned in respect of any offence in connection with VAT or in any proceedings against him for recovery of any sum due, statements made or documents produced on his behalf are not inadmissible on the grounds that he was (or may have been) induced to make or produce them after it had been brought to his attention that

(i) HMRC might assess a civil penalty rather than bring criminal proceedings against him if he made a full confession of any dishonest conduct and gave full facilities for investigation; or
(ii) the penalties might be mitigated.

[*VATA 1994, ss 60, 71(2)*].

For a consideration of the test of 'dishonesty' see *dicta* of Lord Lane in *R v Ghosh*, CA [1982] 2 All ER 689 (TVC 50.30). It is dishonest if a company officer signs a return containing a mis-statement and he has no honest belief in the truth of the statement he has made, and in particular if he makes the statement recklessly, not caring whether it is true or false. See *Adam Geoffrey & Co (Management) Ltd* (VTD 16074) (TVC 3.107) where the accountant had not declared a sale of a property on a company's return and the controlling director had signed the return without checking its contents and ensuring that they were complete and correct.

The penalty can be applied in cases of non-registration and is not restricted to cases where there has been a fraudulent understatement of output tax or overstatement of input tax (*CS Stevenson v C & E Commrs*, CA [1996] STC 1096 (TVC 50.1)).

Liability of directors, etc.

Where the conduct of a body corporate gives rise to a penalty under the above provisions and it appears to HMRC that that conduct, in whole or part, is attributable to the dishonesty of a person who is (or at the material time was) a director or 'managing officer' (the named officer) of the body corporate, HMRC may serve a notice on the named officer proposing to recover all or part of the penalty from him. The portion specified is then assessable and recoverable as if the named officer were personally liable to that part of the penalty. The body corporate is then only assessed on the balance, if any, and is discharged from liability on the amount assessed on the named officer.

The body corporate may appeal against HMRC's decision as to its liability to the penalty and against the amount of the full penalty as if it were specified in an assessment. The named officer may appeal against the decision that the conduct of the body corporate is, in whole or part, attributable to his dishonesty and against the portion of the penalty which HMRC propose to recover from him. Otherwise, there are no grounds for appeal.

'*Managing officer*' means any manager, secretary or other similar officer of the body corporate and any person purporting to act in any such capacity or as a director. Where the affairs of a body corporate are managed by its members, the provisions apply in relation to the conduct of a member in connection with his functions of management as if he were a director of the body corporate.

[*VATA 1994, s 61*].

The notification of liability to a director, etc must show both the amount of the basic penalty and the portion of it which HMRC propose to recover from that director (*MK & ME Nazif* (VTD 13616) (TVC 50.5)). See *C & E Commrs v Bassimeh*, CA 1996, [1997] STC 33 (TVC 50.3) for apportionment of penalties where there is more than one culpable director.

In *Mr Shafiq Rehman* (TC05559), the appellant appealed against the imposition of a penalty by HMRC on the business and then on the sole director, Mr Shafiq Rehman (SR), after the business became insolvent. SR appealed on the grounds that he had not acted to deliberately conceal the VAT liabilities of the business and that the inaccuracies in the businesses VAT returns should not be attributed to him personally.

The First-tier Tribunal dismissed the appeal and with regard to deliberate concealment concluded that an intentional failure to do something, including the intentional failure by a director to exercise oversight of a business associate, can amount to a deliberate act of concealment.

This case serves as a reminder that HMRC has the ability to pursue a director personally for any penalties that it has been unable to collect from the business.

Standard of proof

In a civil action, the plaintiff has to establish its case on the 'balance of probabilities' whereas in a criminal action the standard of proof required by the prosecution is 'beyond reasonable doubt'. In *First Indian Cavalry Club Ltd v C & E Commrs*, CS 1997, [1998] STC 293 (TVC 50.77) it was held that Parliament had clearly intended the standard of proof for penalties under *VATA 1994, s 60* to be the normal civil standard of the balance of probabilities. See now, however, *C & E Commrs v Han & Yau (and related appeals)*, CA [2001] STC 1188 (TVC 34.5). The tribunal applied the guidelines in *Engel v Netherlands*, ECHR 1980, 1 EHRR 647, namely that in deciding whether a penalty was civil or criminal, the criteria to be considered were the classification of the proceedings in domestic law, the nature of the offence, and the severity of the penalty which may be imposed. On this basis, the tribunal held that the penalties were 'criminal charges' within *European Convention of Human Rights, Art 6*. The Court of Appeal, by a majority, upheld this decision but made it clear that not all civil penalties would be so categorised. The effect of this decision is that statements made with a view to reducing the civil penalty under any 'offence' under *VATA 1994, s 60* may not be admissible because the makers of such statements were induced to do so by statements from HMRC that co-operation would reduce the penalty imposed. However, the Court of Appeal indicated that, if matters were made clear to the taxpayer at the time when the nature and effect of the inducement procedure were also made clear to him, it is difficult to see that there would be any breach of *Article 6*. Even if the *Police and Criminal Evidence Act* were applicable, it was most unlikely that a court or tribunal would rule inadmissible any statements made or documents produced as a result.

See also *Georgiou and another (t/a Mario's Chippery) v UK*, [2001] STC 80 (TVC 34.1).

Civil investigation into cases of suspected fraud

[53.13] HMRC use Code of Practice 9 (COP9) (2014) to investigate suspected serious fraud where, for policy operational reasons, they consider it inappropriate to start a criminal investigation. Where COP9 is employed, the investigation will cover all taxes (direct and indirect). Because the cost to the taxpayer and time involved make it impractical to use this procedure for lower value cases, especially when those cases only involve a single tax, there is an alternative procedure for compliance checks into indirect tax matters outside of Code of Practice 9 (2014). The two procedures are outlined below.

(1) Code of Practice 9 (2014)

The HMRC Investigation of Fraud Statement

- HMRC reserve complete discretion to pursue a criminal investigation with a view to prosecution where they consider it necessary and appropriate.
- In cases where a criminal investigation is not commenced, HMRC may decide to investigate using the COP9 investigation of fraud procedure.
- Under the investigation of fraud procedure, the recipient of COP9 is given the opportunity to make a complete and accurate disclosure of all irregularities in his tax affairs.
- Where the recipient fails to make a full disclosure of the tax frauds he has committed, HMRC reserve the right to commence a criminal investigation with a view to prosecution.
- In the course of the COP9 investigation, if the recipient makes materially false or misleading statements, or provides materially false documents HMRC reserve the right to commence a criminal investigation into that conduct as a separate criminal offence.

HMRC issues the COP9 in selected cases where they suspect tax fraud. In many cases they carry out criminal investigations of suspected fraud, with a view to prosecution. But under the Code, they offer the taxpayer instead the chance to make a full disclosure under a contractual arrangement, called a Contractual Disclosure Facility (CDF). The taxpayer has 60 days to respond. If the taxpayer makes a full disclosure of all tax frauds and irregularities, HMRC will not pursue a criminal investigation with a view to prosecution.

HMRC expect the taxpayer to stop any fraud immediately. A specially trained authorised officer will handle the COP9 investigation into the taxpayer's tax affairs and the taxpayer will be given a named contact. If the taxpayer co-operates fully with the investigation, he will achieve a greater reduction in any penalty found to be due, and he may be able to avoid other civil sanctions such as insolvency and, in some cases, the publication of his name and details. The taxpayer must read the Code of Practice carefully and discuss it with his tax adviser, if he has one. He must keep all existing records, including any computer records, during the investigation whether or not he is required to do so by law. HMRC may ask to see his business and private financial records. This Code applies to all tax frauds that the taxpayer have been involved in.

Suspicion of fraud

Where HMRC has information that gives them reason to suspect that the taxpayer has committed tax fraud, they will not usually tell him what their suspicions are: it is for the taxpayer to decide to make a disclosure. HMRC will keep an open mind to the possibility that there may be an innocent explanation for the suspected fraud, and will treat the taxpayer fairly and politely, and in accordance with the law. They will investigate the suspected tax fraud, with or without the taxpayer's co-operation. If the taxpayer does not co-operate HMRC may

- commence their own investigation which may ultimately be a criminal investigation
- obtain information about the taxpayer's financial and business affairs from third parties
- take formal action including raising assessments for the tax and interest HMRC consider is due
- charge significantly higher penalties
- commence legal proceedings to secure some or all of the taxpayer's assets
- require a financial security against certain unpaid taxes and duties.

Appointing an agent or adviser

The taxpayer is strongly advised to seek independent professional advice. If he already has an appointed adviser he should contact them immediately. However, many people find it helpful to appoint a specialist adviser who is familiar with the Code, in addition to their regular adviser. If the taxpayer wants HMRC to deal directly with his adviser on all matters covered by the Code, he must make sure he has given HMRC full authority to do so. The taxpayer must give his adviser all the facts because the taxpayer is personally responsible for his tax affairs and the accuracy of the information supplied to HMRC. HMRC expect high standards from the taxpayer's appointed representative. While HMRC will normally deal with them directly, if there are any delays or problems HMRC will contact the taxpayer. Any costs that the taxpayer incurs in connection with HMRC's enquiries cannot be claimed as an expense against tax.

Contractual disclosure facility (CDF)

The CDF offers the taxpayer the chance to disclose any tax fraud he has been involved in. This offer expires 60 days after the taxpayer receives HMRC's letter making the offer. In exchange for the taxpayer's undertaking, HMRC agree that they will not pursue a criminal investigation into the tax frauds the taxpayer discloses. The taxpayer undertakes to make a full disclosure of all his tax irregularities under the terms of the CDF. To comply with the taxpayer's undertaking, he needs to complete the two disclosure stages

- a valid outline disclosure of the tax frauds ('outline disclosure')
- a certified statement that the taxpayer has made a full, complete and accurate disclosure of all tax irregularities together with certified statements of his assets and liabilities, and of all bank accounts and credit cards he has operated ('formal disclosure').

This is the only way that the taxpayer can be certain that HMRC will not carry out a criminal investigation into the tax frauds HMRC suspect.

The CDF is only suitable for the taxpayer if he

- has committed tax fraud
- wishes to fully disclose the tax frauds that he has committed
- will work with HMRC to put his tax affairs in order (including paying any tax, interest and penalty due), and
- stops any continuing fraud immediately.

The CDF is not appropriate for people who want to disclose only careless errors, mistakes, or avoidance arrangements.

Effect of entering into a contract

To comply with his undertaking, the taxpayer will be admitting that tax has been lost due to his deliberate actions. This means HMRC may be able to seek recovery of evaded tax, interest and associated penalties for as far back as 20 years. Full co-operation with the enquiries will ensure the penalties are closer to the minimum penalty levels.

Outline disclosure

The taxpayer must make a valid outline disclosure within 60 days of the date he receives HMRC's offer (this is the same date as the time given for the taxpayer to decide whether to accept the offer). The disclosure should include the following.

- Description of the fraud, giving enough information to identify the fraudulent conduct including—what the taxpayer did; how he did it; the involvement of other people and entities; how he benefited from the conduct. This must be done for each separate tax fraud committed at any time.

- Entities involved.
- Period of fraud.
- Other information, e.g. an indication of the amounts understated and the tax involved; or a description of what records used to disguise what the taxpayer was doing.

Formal disclosure

Where the fraud is self-contained and easily quantified, there may be little further work for the taxpayer to do following his outline disclosure. He will need to agree what he owes, arrange payment and certify that he has disclosed all irregularities. This is the taxpayer's formal disclosure. In most cases, much more work will be necessary before the taxpayer will be in a position to make his formal disclosure. HMRC will expect him to prepare a disclosure report, as this is the best way to ensure that this work is done properly. A typical disclosure report will normally contain

- a brief business history
- a description of all tax irregularities (including any innocent or careless errors) and how any fraud was carried out
- quantification of all the irregularities
- information to show how you quantified the irregularities and ensured that nothing had been missed.
- summaries of tax and/or duties, interest and penalties due
- a reconciliation of his irregularities figure with the summary of tax and/or duties
- a certified statement of his worldwide assets and liabilities
- certificates of bank accounts and credit cards operated.

Making the taxpayer's formal disclosure does not signify the end of the investigation, but it does mean he has complied with his CDF undertaking.

Rejection route

The CDF offer can only be accepted or rejected. If the taxpayer does not believe that he has been involved in tax fraud he can sign and return the CDF rejection letter within the same 60-day period that is allowed for accepting the offer. HMRC will consider any explanations or documents that support the rejection. HMRC can start its own investigation, which could be a criminal investigation. If HMRC decide to proceed with a civil investigation it reserves the right to escalate the case to a criminal investigation at a later date. The rejection letter can be used as evidence in court or tribunal proceedings. If the taxpayer does not choose to accept or reject the CDF offer within 60 days HMRC will treat this as a conscious decision not to accept the offer and HMRC will not be bound by any CDF terms. The same applies if a taxpayer submits an acceptance letter but does not submit a correctly completed outline disclosure.

Denying tax fraud that the taxpayer is later found to have been involved in may result in a criminal investigation with a view to prosecution, or significantly higher civil financial penalties, and the potential publication of the taxpayer's details. HMRC may use statutory information powers if necessary, and may approach third parties for information. If irregularities are discovered

HMRC will take formal action including the issue of assessments and will pursue collection of any unpaid taxes and interest. Not co-operating fully results in the taxpayer losing the opportunity to gain the maximum reduction in any penalty that may be due.

If HMRC verifies and accepts a taxpayer's rejection of a CDF offer it will issue confirmation that it no longer suspects the taxpayer of tax fraud.

(Code of Practice 9 (2014), ss 1, 2, 4, 6).

(2) Compliance checks into indirect tax matters outside (1) above

This procedure is designed to be used in lower value cases where there is evidence of dishonest conduct or deliberate behaviour.

The taxpayer will normally be asked to attend a meeting with HMRC. A professional adviser may also attend. At the meeting, HMRC will state

- that the check is not being conducted with a view to prosecution in relation to the matters that are the subject of their check; and
- the matters that are the subject of the check. This means the behaviour(s) and period(s) under enquiry, rather than the specific information that they hold which has given rise to their suspicion of dishonesty or deliberate behaviour.

The taxpayer will have an opportunity to disclose any irregularities or matters in relation to his tax affairs. If he wishes to disclose details in areas that are not the subject of the current enquiry, HMRC may not be able to deal with these as part of the ongoing enquiry but will consider these to determine how they should be treated. Any irregularities outside of the matters being checked may be investigated with a view to prosecution (if appropriate).

It may be necessary to make further checks. If this happens, HMRC will explain the compliance checks process and the steps that need to be taken to establish the relevant facts. HMRC may consider it necessary to use their statutory information powers, including contacting third parties.

The taxpayer will be invited to make payments on account towards any VAT arrears, both at the initial meeting and throughout the check. If, as a result of the check, HMRC believe that the VAT arrears are due to conduct involving dishonesty or deliberate behaviour, they will consider the imposition of a penalty.

Penalties

If the taxpayer decides to co-operate with the compliance check, he should be truthful, as he could face prosecution if he makes a statement to HMRC that he knows is false. If he chooses to co-operate and disclose details of his true liability then he can significantly reduce the amount of any penalties due. At the end of the check HMRC will take into account the extent of his co-operation.

If the taxpayer disagrees with HMRC's decision to charge a penalty or the amount of the penalty, he can have his case reviewed by an officer not previously involved, or have his case heard by an independent tax tribunal. If he opts to have his case reviewed he will still be able to appeal to the tribunal if he disagrees with the outcome. If he wants a review he should write to HMRC within 30 days of the date the penalty notice was sent to him, giving reasons why he disagrees with HMRC's decision.

Costs

The taxpayer has to pay for any costs that he incurs in dealing with the enquiry, including the fees of any professional adviser.

(HMRC Notice 160).

Alternative dispute resolution service

The alternative dispute resolution (ADR) service pilot was launched in January 2012 for small and medium enterprises (SMEs) in the North West, South West, Wales and London. ADR uses independent HMRC facilitators to resolve disputes between HMRC and taxpayers during a compliance check, but before a decision or assessment has been made. ADR aims to find a fair and quick outcome for both parties, helping to reduce their costs and avoid a tribunal. The trial has been extended to SMEs and individuals wherever they are based in the country. The facilitators are HMRC members of staff who have been trained in ADR techniques and have not been involved in the dispute. ADR does not affect existing processes or review and appeal rights. Cases potentially suitable for this pilot may involve any of the following features.

- Facts that are capable of further clarification.
- Disputes that might benefit from obtaining more suitable evidence.
- Factual and/or technical matters in which there is legitimate scope for any party to obtain a better understanding of the other's arguments.
- Issues which are capable of further mediation and settlement by agreement within the framework of the Litigation and Settlements Strategy (LSS).

Cases not suitable for this pilot may involve any of the following features.

- Cases which cannot be legitimately settled within the parameters of the LSS other than by litigation.
- Issues which require clarification in the wider public interest. These might include matters of industry-wide application.
- Issues linked to or involving co-ordinated appeals issues ('stood behind' cases) e.g. 'compound interest' type disputes.
- Cases that could only be resolved by an HMRC departure from its established technical or policy view.
- A nationwide ADR pilot is already available for large and complex businesses and customers of the Large Business Service.

(HMRC News Release dated 29 May 2012).

De Voil Indirect Tax Service. See V5.341–V5.345.

Misdeclaration

[53.14] **Note:** the civil penalty provisions of *VATA 1994, ss 63* and *64* were replaced by *FA 2007, s 97, Sch 24* with effect from 1 April 2009. See **53.15** below for the present provisions. As the time limit for assessment of a penalty, in the absence of dishonesty, is only four years, the old penalty rules should have no further application.

Penalties for errors

[53.15] *FA 2007, s 97* and *Sch 24* provide a single framework for penalties to be imposed on taxpayers who make errors in documents that they send to HMRC or who fail to take reasonable steps to report errors in assessments made by HMRC. The provisions apply to VAT, income tax, capital gains tax, corporation tax, pay as you earn, national insurance contributions and deductions under the construction industry scheme (although only those provisions relevant to VAT are considered below).

Errors in taxpayers' documents

Finance (No 2) Act 2017, s 64, provides for amendments to *FA 2007, Sch 24* which enables penalties to be charged in respect of inaccuracies in taxpayers' documents where those inaccuracies are the result of careless or deliberate behaviour by the taxpayer. The measure provides that where a person receives advice in relation to certain tax avoidance arrangements, the person is unable to rely on that advice in order to demonstrate they have taken reasonable care to avoid an inaccuracy being created due to their use of the avoidance arrangement in certain circumstances. These occur where:

- that advice is received from or commissioned by a person connected to the arrangements;
- does not take account of the person's individual circumstances; or
- is given by a person not having the expertise necessary to give it.

The measure came into effect on 16 November 2017 and applies to inaccuracies in documents relating to tax periods which begin on or after 6 April 2017 and end on or after 16 November 2017.

HMRC have provided guidance on what they believe constitutes reasonable care in respect of the submission of tax returns and other documentation. The guidance also provides information on HMRC's position if a person has used a tax avoidance arrangement. The guidance states the following:

> 'If you've used tax avoidance arrangements that HMRC later defeat, they will presume you haven't taken reasonable care for any inaccuracy in your return or other documents that relate to the use of those arrangements.
>
> If you did take reasonable care, you'll need to show HMRC how you did this when they talk to you about penalties.
>
> If you've used a tax adviser with the appropriate expertise, HMRC would normally consider this as having taken reasonable care, unless it's classed as disqualified advice.
>
> Tax avoidance arrangements are classed as defeated if:

- you reach an agreement with HMRC – so the expected tax advantage of using the arrangements isn't available
- HMRC send you a tax assessment, or adjust your tax position, to counter the tax advantage – and you don't appeal
- you appeal to a tribunal or court against HMRC's assessment in relation to your use of an arrangement – and they rule in HMRC's favour
- you take corrective action after receiving a follower notice'.

See guidance document 'Reasonable care: tax returns and other documents' (www.gov.uk/guidance/reasonable-care-tax-returns-and-other-documents).

Commencement dates

The provisions came into force on various dates in 2008 and 2009, and no person is liable to a penalty under these provisions in respect of any VAT period for which a return was required to be made before 1 April 2009. Penalties for periods before 2009 are still subject to the previous provisions.

(1) Penalty for an inaccuracy in taxpayer's document

A penalty is payable by a person (P) where he gives HMRC (whether by post, fax, email, telephone or otherwise)

- a VAT return,
- a return, statement or declaration in connection with a claim, or
- any document which is likely to be relied upon by HMRC to determine, without further inquiry, a question about
  (i) P's liability to VAT,
  (ii) payments by P by way of or in connection with VAT,
  (iii) any other payment by P (including penalties), or
  (iv) repayments, or any other kind of payment or credit, to P

and Conditions 1 and 2 below are both satisfied.

(a) Condition 1

Condition 1 is that the document contains an inaccuracy which amounts to, or leads to

(i) an understatement of a liability to VAT (which includes an overstatement of P's entitlement to a VAT credit);
(ii) a false or inflated statement of a loss; or
(iii) a false or inflated claim to repayment of VAT (or allowance for credit).

(b) Condition 2

Condition 2 is that the inaccuracy was 'careless' or 'deliberate' on P's part.

An inaccuracy is

(i) '*careless*' if it is due to failure by P (or his agent, see (7) below) to take reasonable care;
(ii) '*deliberate but not concealed*' if the inaccuracy is deliberate on P's part but P does not make arrangements to conceal it; and
(iii) '*deliberate and concealed*' if the inaccuracy is deliberate on P's part and P makes arrangements to conceal it (e.g. by submitting false evidence in support of an inaccurate figure).

An inaccuracy in a document given by P (or his agent, see (7) below) to HMRC, which was neither careless nor deliberate when the document was given, is to be treated as careless if P discovered the inaccuracy at some later time and did not take reasonable steps to inform HMRC.

Where a document contains more than one inaccuracy, a penalty is payable for each inaccuracy.

Standard amount of penalty

The penalty payable is

- for careless action (or omission), 30% of the 'potential lost revenue';
- for deliberate but not concealed action (or omission), 70% of the potential lost revenue; and
- for deliberate and concealed action (or omission), 100% of the potential lost revenue.

See (4) below for the meaning of '*potential lost revenue*'. See also (5) below for reductions for disclosure, etc. and (6) below for suspension of all or part of a penalty.

Interaction with other penalties and late payment surcharges

The amount of a penalty for which P is liable in respect of a document relating to a VAT period must be reduced by the amount of any other penalty incurred by P, or any surcharge for late payment of VAT imposed on P, if the amount of the penalty or surcharge is determined by reference to the same VAT liability. Additionally, where penalties are imposed under this provision and (2) below in respect of the same inaccuracy, the aggregate of the amounts of the penalties must not exceed 100% of the potential lost revenue.

(2) Penalty for an inaccuracy in taxpayer's document attributable to another person

A penalty is payable by a person (T) where

- another person (P) gives HMRC a document of a kind listed in (1) above;
- the document contains a 'relevant inaccuracy'; and
- the inaccuracy was attributable to T supplying false information to P (whether directly or indirectly), or to T deliberately withholding information from P, with the intention of the document containing the inaccuracy.

A '*relevant inaccuracy*' is an inaccuracy which amounts to, or leads to anything within (1)(*a*)(i)–(iii) above.

T is liable to a penalty whether or not P is liable to a penalty under (1) above in respect of the same inaccuracy (but see below for the maximum combined penalty).

Standard amount of the penalty

The penalty payable is 100% of the 'potential lost revenue'.

See (4) below for the meaning of '*potential lost revenue*'. See also (5) below for reductions for disclosure, etc. and (6) below for suspension of all or part of a penalty.

Interaction with other penalties

Where penalties are imposed under this provision and (1) above in respect of the same inaccuracy, the aggregate of the amounts of the penalties must not exceed 100% of the potential lost revenue.

(3) Penalty where under-assessment by HMRC

A penalty is payable by a person (P) where

- an assessment issued to P by HMRC understates P's liability to VAT; and
- P has failed to take reasonable steps to notify HMRC, within the period of 30 days beginning with the date of the assessment, that it is an under-assessment.

'Assessment' includes determination and accordingly references to an 'under-assessment' include an under-determination.

In deciding what steps (if any) were reasonable HMRC must consider

- whether P knew, or should have known, about the under-assessment; and
- what steps would have been reasonable to take to notify HMRC.

Standard amount of penalty

The penalty payable is 30% of the 'potential lost revenue'. See (4) below for the meaning of '*potential lost revenue*' and (5) below for reductions for disclosure, etc.

Interaction with other penalties and late payment surcharges

The amount of a penalty for which P is liable in respect of a document relating to a VAT period must be reduced by the amount of any other penalty incurred by P, or any surcharge for late payment of VAT imposed on P, if the amount of the penalty or surcharge is determined by reference to the same VAT liability.

(4) Potential lost revenue

Normal rule

The '*potential lost revenue*' in respect of an inaccuracy in a document (including any inaccuracy attributable to a supply of false information or withholding of information) or a failure to notify an under-assessment is the additional amount due or payable in respect of VAT as a result of correcting the inaccuracy or assessment. The additional amount due or payable includes a reference to

- an amount payable to HMRC having been erroneously paid by way of repayment of VAT (or allowance of credit); and

- an amount which would have been repayable by HMRC had the inaccuracy or assessment not been corrected.

Multiple errors

Where P is liable to a penalty under (1) above in respect of more than one inaccuracy, and the calculation of 'potential lost revenue' under the normal rule in respect of each inaccuracy depends on the order in which they are corrected

- careless inaccuracies are to be taken to be corrected before deliberate inaccuracies; and
- deliberate but not concealed inaccuracies are to be taken to be corrected before deliberate and concealed inaccuracies.

In calculating potential lost revenue where P is liable to a penalty under (1) above in respect of one or more 'understatements' in one or more documents relating to a VAT period, account is to be taken of any overstatement in any document given by P which relates to the same VAT period. For this purpose, '*understatement*' means an inaccuracy that satisfies Condition 1 at (1)(*a*) above and '*overstatement*' means an inaccuracy that does not satisfy that condition. Overstatements must be set against understatements in the following order.

- Understatements in respect of which P is not liable to a penalty.
- Careless understatements.
- Deliberate but not concealed understatements.
- Deliberate and concealed understatements.

In calculating (for the purposes of a penalty under (1) above) potential lost revenue in respect of a document given by or on behalf of P, no account must be taken of the fact that a potential loss of revenue from P is, or may be, balanced by a potential over-payment by another person (except to the extent that an enactment requires or permits a person's VAT liability to be adjusted by reference to P's).

Delayed VAT

Where an inaccuracy resulted in an amount of VAT being declared later than it should have been (the '*delayed tax*'), the potential lost revenue is

- 5% of the delayed VAT for each year of the delay; or
- a percentage of the delayed VAT, for each separate period of delay of less than a year, equating to 5% per year.

If a return contains an inaccuracy that relates to a timing error which is automatically reversed in a subsequent tax period, the penalty is not calculated on the full amount of tax underpaid in the first period, but on a reduced amount to take account of the timing error. HMRC's previous approach was that in order for the penalty to be calculated in this way, the business must have submitted both the return containing the initial inaccuracy and the return containing the automatic reversal of the inaccuracy in a later period. This meant that in some cases HMRC charged a penalty on the full amount because they acted to correct the inaccuracy on the first return before the second return could be submitted, thereby preventing the inaccuracy from being reversed. HMRC have changed their approach for cases where HMRC intervened to correct the inaccuracy before the second return was received, preventing the inaccuracy from being reversed. Where HMRC are satisfied that, but for their intervention, the inaccuracy would have been automatically corrected in a subsequent return, businesses will receive the reduced penalty based on the rules for delayed tax. (HMRC Brief 15/11).

In *MJ Hickey Plant Hire and Contracts Ltd* [2016] UKFTT 61 (TC) (TC04860), the First-tier Tribunal agreed with HMRC that the delayed tax penalty rule is not applicable where the penalty is assessable on the 'deliberate behaviour' scale. The company appeared to have known that its computer was programmed to allocate the last day's transactions in each VAT return period to the next period, delaying the payment of VAT by three months. Each error automatically reversed in the next period. Maximum mitigation was allowed for a prompted disclosure, but the penalty was charged at 35% of the PLR in each period, not 5% x 3/12.

(5) Reductions in penalties

Reduction for disclosure

There are provisions for the reduction of penalties under (1)–(3) above where a person discloses an inaccuracy, a supply of false information or withholding of information, or a failure to disclose an under-assessment.

Where a person is liable to a penalty, HMRC *must* reduce the penalty to reflect the 'quality' of the disclosure as follows.

- Where a person who would otherwise be liable to a 30% penalty has made an 'unprompted disclosure' — to any percentage (which may be 0%).
- Where a person who would otherwise be liable to a 30% penalty has made a 'prompted disclosure' — to a percentage, not below 15%.
- Where a person who would otherwise be liable to a 70% penalty has made an unprompted disclosure — to a percentage not below 20%.
- Where a person who would otherwise be liable to a 70% penalty has made a prompted disclosure — to a percentage not below 35%.
- Where a person who would otherwise be liable to a 100% penalty has made an unprompted disclosure — to a percentage not below 30%.
- Where a person who would otherwise be liable to a 100% penalty has made a prompted disclosure — to a percentage not below 50%.

For these purposes, '*quality*' includes timing, nature and extent.

A person discloses an inaccuracy, a supply of false information or withholding of information, or a failure to disclose an under-assessment by

- telling HMRC about it;
- giving HMRC reasonable help in quantifying the inaccuracy, etc. or under-assessment; and
- allowing HMRC access to records for the purpose of ensuring that the inaccuracy, etc. or under-assessment is fully corrected.

A disclosure is '*unprompted*' if made at a time when the person making it has no reason to believe that HMRC have discovered (or are about to discover) the inaccuracy, etc. or under-assessment. Otherwise, it is '*prompted*'.

Special reduction

If HMRC think it right because of special circumstances, they may reduce a penalty under (1)–(3) above. However, 'special circumstances' do *not* include either the ability to pay or the fact that a potential loss of revenue from one taxpayer is balanced by a potential over-payment by another.

Reducing a penalty includes staying a penalty or agreeing a compromise in relation to proceedings for a penalty.

Union and non-Union VAT MOSS scheme returns

Where a person not registered for VAT in the UK has submitted a Union or non-Union VAT MOSS scheme return (see **64.40–64.45 SPECIAL SCHEMES**) to the tax authorities in another Member State in relation to the supply of broadcasting, telecommunication or electronic services to consumers in the UK and then corrects the return in a way that constitutes telling the tax authorities in the other Member State about an inaccuracy in the return, a supply of false information, or withholding of information, the person is regarded as telling HMRC for the purposes of reduction for disclosure.

[*VATA 1994, Sch 3B and Sch 3BA; FA 2014, Sch 22*].

(6) Procedure

Assessments

Where a person becomes liable for a penalty under (1)–(3) above, HMRC must assess the penalty, notify the person and state in the notice a VAT period in respect of which the penalty is assessed. Such a penalty must be paid before the end of the period of 30 days beginning with the day on which notification of the penalty is issued.

Any assessment is to be treated for procedural purposes in the same way as an assessment to VAT (except as expressly provided otherwise in these provisions), may be enforced as if it were an assessment to VAT, and may be combined with an assessment to VAT.

The assessment of a penalty under (1) or (2) above must be made before the end of the period of 12 months beginning with the end of the 'appeal period' for the assessment to VAT correcting the inaccuracy (or, where there is no assessment to the VAT concerned, 12 months from the date on which the inaccuracy is corrected).

The assessment of a penalty under (3) above must be made before the end of the period of 12 months beginning with the end of the appeal period for the assessment of VAT correcting the understatement (or, where there is no assessment to the VAT concerned, 12 months from the date on which the understatement is corrected).

The '*appeal period*' is the period during which an appeal could be brought or an appeal that has been brought has not been determined or withdrawn.

HMRC may make a supplementary assessment in respect of a penalty if an earlier assessment underestimated the potential lost revenue but any such assessment must still be within the time limits as above.

Suspension

HMRC may suspend all or part of a penalty for a careless inaccuracy under (1) above by notice in writing to P. The notice must specify

- what part of the penalty is to be suspended;
- a period of suspension (not exceeding two years); and
- conditions of suspension to be complied with by P (e.g. action to be taken and a period in which it must be taken).

HMRC can only do this if compliance with a condition of suspension would help P to avoid becoming liable to further penalties under (1) above for careless inaccuracy (and so ensure that documents are accurate in future).

On the expiry of the period of suspension, if P satisfies HMRC that the conditions of suspension have been complied with, the suspended penalty is cancelled. If P cannot satisfy HMRC, the suspended penalty becomes payable.

If, during the period of suspension of a penalty, P becomes liable for another penalty under (1) above, the suspended penalty becomes payable.

Appeals

A person may appeal against a decision of HMRC on the following grounds.

- That a penalty is payable by the person. The tribunal may affirm or cancel HMRC's decision.
- As to the amount of a penalty payable. The tribunal may affirm HMRC's decision or substitute another decision that HMRC had power to make.
- That HMRC did not suspend a penalty. The tribunal may order HMRC to suspend the penalty only if it thinks that HMRC's decision not to suspend was 'flawed'. If the tribunal orders HMRC to suspend the penalty, the person may subsequently appeal against a provision of the notice of suspension and the tribunal may order HMRC to amend the notice.
- Setting conditions of suspension of a penalty. The tribunal may affirm or vary the conditions of suspension, but it may only vary them if it thinks that HMRC's decision in respect of the conditions was flawed.

'*Flawed*' means flawed when considered in the light of the principles applicable in proceedings for judicial review.

P does not need to pay the penalty before an appeal in order for the appeal to be heard.

(7) **Agency**

Subject to below, P is liable

- under (1) above where someone acting on P's behalf gives HMRC a document which contains a careless inaccuracy; and

- under (3) above where someone acting on his behalf in relation to VAT fails to take reasonable steps to notify HMRC of an under-assessment within the 30-day period (in which case, in deciding what steps were reasonably, HMRC must also take into account whether the agent knew, or ought to have known about the under-assessment).

Despite the above, P is not liable to a penalty under (1) or (3) above in respect of anything done or omitted by his agent where he satisfies HMRC that he (P) took reasonable care to avoid inaccuracy (in relation to (1) above) or unreasonable failure (in relation to (3) above).

(8) Liability of officers of companies in the case of deliberate inaccuracy by them

Where a penalty under (1) above is payable by a company for a deliberate inaccuracy which was attributable to an officer of the company the officer is liable to pay such portion of the penalty (which may be 100%) as they may specify by written notice to the officer.

This does not allow HMRC to recover more than 100% of a penalty.

The officer must pay the specified portion before the end of the period of 30 days from the day on which the notice is given.

For these purposes, '*officer*'

- in relation to a body corporate other than a limited liability partnership means a director (including a shadow director within the meaning of *CA 2006, s 251*), a manager and a secretary;
- in relation to a limited liability partnership means a member; and
- in any other case, means a director, manager, secretary or any other person managing or purporting to manage any of the company's affairs.

'Company' means any body corporate or unincorporated association, but does not include a partnership, a local authority or a local authority association.

(9) Double jeopardy

A person is not liable to a penalty under (1)–(3) above in respect of an inaccuracy or failure in respect of which the person has been convicted of an offence.

[*FA 2007, s 97, Sch 24; FA 2008, Sch 40; FA 2009, Sch 57 paras 2, 6, 7*].

'Reasonable care'

Each person has a responsibility to take reasonable care but what is necessary to meet that responsibility depends upon that person's ability and circumstances. For example, HMRC would not expect the same level of knowledge or expertise from a self-employed and unrepresented individual as from a multi-national company. They would also expect a higher degree of care to be taken over large and complex matters than simple straightforward ones. (HMRC Brief 19/08).

Failure to notify and unauthorised issue of invoices

[53.16] In relation to obligations arising after 1 April 2010, *FA 2008, s 123, Sch 41* creates a single legal framework for penalising failure to comply with a notification obligation. The provisions apply to VAT, income tax, capital gains tax, corporation tax, insurance premium tax, environmental taxes and excise duties (although only the provisions relevant to VAT are considered below). The provisions also provide for penalties for issue of a VAT invoice by an unauthorised person with a penalty calculated in the same way as failure to notify.

(1) Penalty for failure to notify

A penalty is payable by a person (P) where P fails to comply with any of the following obligations (a '*relevant obligation*').

(a) *VATA 1994, Sch 1 para 5* (obligation to notify liability for registration on the basis of supplies in the previous year under **60.3**(*a*) **REGISTRATION**) or *VATA 1994, Sch 1 para 6* (obligation to notify liability for registration on the basis of supplies in the next 30 days under **60.3**(*b*) **REGISTRATION**),

(b) *VATA 1994, Sch 1 para 7* (obligation to notify liability for registration on the transfer of a going concern under **60.3**(*c*) **REGISTRATION**),

(c) *VATA 1994, Sch 1 para 14(2)(3)* (obligation to notify change in nature of suppliers, etc. by a person exempted from registration, see **60.6 REGISTRATION**),

(d) *VATA 1994, Sch 1A paras 5, 6* (obligation to notify liability for registration by non-established taxable persons, see **60.35 REGISTRATION**);

(e) *VATA 1994, Sch 1A para 13(3)* (obligation to notify material change in nature of supplies by non-established taxable persons exempted from registration, see **60.38 REGISTRATION**);

(f) *VATA 1994, Sch 2 para 3* (obligation to notify liability for registration in respect of supplies from other EU member states, see **60.13 REGISTRATION**),

(g) *VATA 1994, Sch 3 para 3* (obligation to notify liability for registration in respect of acquisitions from other EU member states, see **60.20 REGISTRATION**),

(h) *VATA 1994, Sch 3 para 8(2)* (obligation to notify change in nature of acquisitions by a person exempt from registration in respect of acquisitions from other EU member states, see **60.22 REGISTRATION**),

(i) *VATA 1994, Sch 3A paras 3, 4* (obligation to notify liability for registration by overseas traders in respect of disposal of assets for which a VAT repayment claimed, see **60.28 REGISTRATION**),

(j) *VATA 1994, Sch 3A para 7(2)(3)* (obligation to notify relevant change in supplies by an overseas trader exempt from registration in respect of disposal of assets for which a VAT repayment claimed, see **60.29 REGISTRATION**), or

(k) regulations under *VATA 1994, Sch 11 para 2(4)* (obligation to give notification of acquisition of excise duty goods or new means of transport from another EU member state, see **20.9** and **20.37 EUROPEAN UNION: SINGLE MARKET** respectively).

(2) Issue of invoice showing VAT by unauthorised person

A penalty is payable by a person (P) where P is an 'unauthorised person' and issues an invoice showing an amount as being VAT (or as including an amount attributable to VAT).

An '*unauthorised person*' means anyone other than

- a person registered for VAT;
- a body corporate within a group registration;
- a person treated as carrying on the business of a taxable person who has died or become bankrupt or incapacitated;
- a person selling business assets of a taxable person towards satisfaction of a debt owed by that taxable person (e.g. sale of assets seized by a bailiff); or
- a person acting on behalf of the Crown (which is treated as including a reference to the National Assembly for Wales Commission).

The provisions apply in relation to an invoice showing a fixed flat rate addition under the special scheme for farmers which

- fails to comply with the requirements of the scheme, or
- is issued by a person who is not at the time authorised to use the scheme

as if the person issuing the invoice were an unauthorised person and the flat rate addition was an amount attributable to VAT.

(3) Standard amount of penalty

The penalty payable is

- for a 'deliberate and concealed' act or failure, 100% of the 'potential lost revenue' (see (4) below); and
- for a 'deliberate but not concealed' act or failure, 70% of the potential lost revenue; and
- for any other case, 30% of the potential lost revenue.

For these purposes,

- a failure by P to comply with a relevant obligation under (1) above is
  - (i) '*deliberate and concealed*' if the failure is deliberate and P makes arrangements to conceal the situation giving rise to the obligation; and
  - (ii) '*deliberate but not concealed*' if the failure is deliberate but P does not make arrangements to conceal the situation giving rise to the obligation; and
- the unauthorised issue of an invoice by P under (2) above is
  - (i) '*deliberate and concealed*' if it is done deliberately and P makes arrangements to conceal it; and
  - (ii) '*deliberate but not concealed*' if it is done deliberately but P does not make arrangements to conceal it.

But see (5) below for reductions in penalties and (6) below for 'reasonable excuse'.

Interaction with other penalties and late payment surcharges

The amount of a penalty for which P is liable under (1) or (2) above must be reduced by the amount of any other penalty incurred by P, or any surcharge for late payment of VAT imposed on P, if the amount of the penalty or surcharge is determined by reference to the same VAT liability.

(4) Potential lost revenue

The '*potential lost revenue*' is determined as follows.

(a) In respect of a failure to comply with a relevant obligation under (1)(*a*)–(*k*), the amount of the VAT (if any) for which P is, or but for any exemption from registration would be, liable for the 'relevant period'. The '*relevant period*' is in relation to a failure to comply with
   (i) (1)(*a*), (*b*), (*f*), (*g*) or (*i*), the period beginning on the date of the change or alteration concerned and ending on the date on which HMRC received notification of, or otherwise became fully aware of, that change or alteration; and
   (ii) (1)(*c*), (*h*) or (*j*), the period beginning on the date with effect from which P is required in accordance with that provision to be registered and ending on the date on which HMRC received notification of, or otherwise became fully aware of, P's liability to be registered.

   But the amount is reduced
   - if it includes VAT on an acquisition of goods from another EU member state, by the amount of any VAT which HMRC are satisfied has been paid on the supply in pursuance of which the goods were acquired under the law of that EU member state; and
   - if it includes VAT chargeable on a supply by virtue of *VATA 1994, s 7(4)* (see **66.5 SUPPLY: PLACE OF SUPPLY**), by the amount of any VAT which HMRC are satisfied has been paid on that supply under the law of another EU member state.

(b) In any case where the failure is a failure to comply with (1)(*k*) above, the VAT on the acquisition to which the failure relates.

(c) In the case of the unauthorised issue of an invoice showing VAT under (2) above, the amount shown on the invoice as VAT or the amount to be taken as representing VAT.

In calculating potential lost revenue in respect of a 'relevant act or failure' on the part of P, no account must be taken of the fact that a potential loss of revenue from P is, or may be, balanced by a potential over-payment by another person (except to the extent that an enactment requires or permits a person's VAT liability to be adjusted by reference to P's).

A '*relevant act or failure*' means a failure to comply with a relevant obligation under (1) above or the unauthorised issue of an invoice showing VAT under (2) above.

(5) Reductions in penalties

Reduction for disclosure

There are provisions for the reduction of penalties under (1) and (2) above where P discloses a '*relevant act or failure*' (i.e. a failure to comply with a relevant obligation under (1) above or the unauthorised issue of an invoice showing VAT under (2) above).

Where a person is liable to a penalty, HMRC *must* reduce the penalty to reflect the 'quality' of the disclosure as follows.

- Where a person who would otherwise be liable to a 100% penalty has made an unprompted disclosure — to a percentage not below 30%.
- Where a person who would otherwise be liable to a 100% penalty has made a prompted disclosure — to a percentage not below 50%.
- Where a person who would otherwise be liable to a 70% penalty has made an unprompted disclosure — to a percentage not below 20%.
- Where a person who would otherwise be liable to a 70% penalty has made a prompted disclosure — to a percentage not below 35%.
- Where a person who would otherwise be liable to a 30% penalty has made an 'unprompted disclosure'
  - (i) if the penalty is under (1) above and HMRC become aware of the failure less than twelve months after the time when VAT first becomes unpaid by reason of the failure — to any percentage (which may be 0%); and
  - (ii) in any other case — to a percentage not below 10%.
- Where a person who would otherwise be liable to a 30% penalty has made a 'prompted disclosure'
  - (i) if the penalty is under (1) above and HMRC become aware of the failure less than twelve months after the time when VAT first becomes unpaid by reason of the failure — to any percentage not below 10%; and
  - (ii) in any other case — to a percentage not below 20%.

For these purposes, '*quality*' includes timing, nature and extent.

P discloses a relevant act or failure by

- telling HMRC about it;
- giving HMRC reasonable help in quantifying the VAT unpaid by reason of it; and
- allowing HMRC access to records for the purpose of checking how much VAT is so unpaid.

A disclosure is '*unprompted*' if made at a time when the person making it has no reason to believe that HMRC have discovered (or are about to discover) the relevant act or failure. Otherwise, it is '*prompted*'.

Special reduction

If HMRC think it right because of special circumstances, they may reduce a penalty under (1) and (2) above. However, 'special circumstances' do *not* include either the ability to pay or the fact that a potential loss of revenue from one taxpayer is balanced by a potential over-payment by another.

Reducing a penalty includes staying a penalty or agreeing a compromise in relation to proceedings for a penalty.

(6) Procedure

Assessments

Where P becomes liable for a penalty under (1) or (2) above, HMRC must assess the penalty, notify P and state in the notice the VAT period in respect of which the penalty is assessed. Such a penalty must be paid before the end of the period of 30 days beginning with the day on which notification of the penalty is issued.

Any assessment is to be treated for procedural purposes in the same way as an assessment to VAT (except as expressly provided otherwise in these provisions), may be enforced as if it were an assessment to VAT, and may be combined with an assessment to VAT.

The assessment of a penalty under (1) or (2) above must be made before the end of the period of 12 months beginning with the end of the 'appeal period' for the assessment to VAT unpaid by reason of the relevant act or failure in respect of which the penalty is imposed (or, if there is no such assessment, 12 months from the date on which the amount of VAT unpaid by reason of the relevant act or failure is ascertained).

The '*appeal period*' is the period during which an appeal could be brought or an appeal that has been brought has not been determined or withdrawn.

HMRC may make a supplementary assessment in respect of a penalty if an earlier assessment operated by reference to an underestimate of potential lost revenue but any such assessment must still be within the time limits as above.

Appeals

P may appeal against a decision of HMRC on the following grounds.

- That a penalty is payable by P. The tribunal may affirm or cancel HMRC's decision.
- As to the amount of the penalty payable by P. The tribunal may affirm HMRC's decision or substitute another decision that HMRC had power to make.

If the tribunal substitutes its decision for HMRC's, the tribunal may rely on the provisions in (5) above under the heading *Special reduction* to the same extent as HMRC (which may mean applying the same percentage reduction as HMRC to a different starting point) or to a different extent (but only if the tribunal thinks that HMRC's decision in respect of the application of those provisions was 'flawed').

'*Flawed*' means flawed when considered in the light of the principles applicable in proceedings for judicial review.

P does not need to pay the penalty before an appeal in order for the appeal to be heard.

Reasonable excuse

Liability to a penalty under (1) or (2) above does not arise in relation to an act or failure which is not deliberate if P satisfies HMRC or (on appeal) the tribunal that there is a reasonable excuse for the act or failure. But for these purposes,

- an insufficiency of funds is not a reasonable excuse unless attributable to events outside P's control;
- where P relies on any other person to do anything, that is not a reasonable excuse unless P took reasonable care to avoid the relevant act or failure; and
- where P *had* a reasonable excuse for the relevant act or failure but the excuse has ceased, P is to be treated as having continued to have the excuse if the relevant act or failure is remedied without unreasonable delay after the excuse ceased.

(7) **Agency**

Subject to below

- under (1) above, the reference to a failure by P includes a failure by a person who acts on P's behalf; and
- under (2) above the reference to P's unauthorised issue of an invoice showing VAT includes the unauthorised issue by a person who acts on P's behalf.

But P is not liable to a penalty in respect of any failure or action by P's agent where P satisfies HMRC or (on appeal) the tribunal that P took reasonable care to avoid the failure or action.

(8) **Liability of officers of companies in the case of deliberate act or failure**

Where a penalty under (1) or (2) above is payable by a company for a deliberate act or failure which was attributable to an officer of the company the officer is liable to pay such portion of the penalty (which may be 100%) as they may specify by written notice to the officer.

This does not allow HMRC to recover more than 100% of a penalty.

The officer must pay the specified portion before the end of the period of 30 days from the day on which the notice was given.

For these purposes, '*officer*'

- in relation to a body corporate other than a limited liability partnership means a director (including a shadow director within the meaning of *CA 2006, s 251*), a manager and a secretary;
- in relation to a limited liability partnership means a member; and
- in any other case, means a director, manager, secretary or any other person managing or purporting to manage any of the company's affairs.

'*Company*' means any body corporate or unincorporated association, but does not include a partnership, a local authority or a local authority association.

(9) **Double jeopardy**

P is not liable to a penalty under (1) or (2) above in respect of a failure or action in respect of which P has been convicted of an offence.

[*FA 2008, Sch 41; SI 2009/511; FA 2009, Sch 57 paras 11, 12; FA 2012, Sch 28 para 18*].

Failure to notify and unauthorised issue of invoices: provisions applying before 1 April 2010

[53.17] Note: the provisions in this paragraph apply where an obligation to notify liability arose before 1 April 2010. They are therefore still potentially relevant where a trader has failed to register for a very long period. In such a case, HMRC may pursue penalties for dishonesty instead. For failures arising for the first time from 1 April 2010 onwards, see the provisions in **53.16** above.

Failure to notify

Where a person fails to comply with

(a) *VATA 1994, Sch 1 para 5* (duty to notify liability for registration on the basis of supplies in the previous year under **60.3**(*a*) **REGISTRATION**) or *VATA 1994, Sch 1 para 6* (duty to notify liability for registration on the basis of supplies in the next 30 days under **60.3**(*b*) **REGISTRATION**),
(b) *VATA 1994, Sch 1 para 7* (duty to notify liability for registration on the transfer of a going concern under **60.3**(*c*) **REGISTRATION**),
(c) *VATA 1994, Sch 1 para 14(2)(3)* (change in nature of suppliers, etc by a person exempted from registration, see **60.6 REGISTRATION**),
(d) *VATA 1994, Sch 2 para 3* (duty to notify liability for registration in respect of supplies from other EU member states, see **60.13 REGISTRATION**),
(e) *VATA 1994, Sch 3 para 3* (duty to notify liability for registration in respect of acquisitions from other EU member states, see **60.20 REGISTRATION**),
(f) *VATA 1994, Sch 3 para 8(2)* (duty to notify change in nature of supplies by a person exempt from registration in respect of acquisitions from other EU member states, see **60.22 REGISTRATION**),
(g) *VATA 1994, Sch 3A paras 3, 4* (duty to notify liability for registration by overseas traders in respect of disposal of assets for which a VAT repayment claimed, see **60.28 REGISTRATION**),
(h) *VATA 1994, Sch 3A para 7(2)(3)* (duty to notify change in nature of supplies by an overseas trader exempt from registration in respect of disposal of assets for which a VAT repayment claimed, see **60.29 REGISTRATION**), or
(i) regulations under *VATA 1994, Sch 11 para 2(4)* (notification of acquisition of excise duty goods or new means of transport, see **20.9** and **20.37 EUROPEAN UNION: SINGLE MARKET** respectively)

he is, subject to below, liable to a penalty of the greater of £50 and

- 5% of the 'relevant VAT' where HMRC are notified or become aware of the failure no more than nine months late (three months late where (*i*) above applies);
- 10% of the relevant VAT where notification, etc. is over nine months late but not more than 18 months late (over three months but no more than six months where (*i*) above applies); and

- 15% of the relevant VAT in any other case.

Where supplementary assessments are raised, any penalty is calculated at the percentage rate in force at the time of the original assessment (if different).

'*Relevant VAT*' is

(i) subject to below, where (*a*), (*d*), (*e*) or (*g*) above applies, the VAT for which the person would be liable for the period beginning on the date he was required to be registered and ending on the date on which HMRC received notification, or otherwise became fully aware, of his liability to be registered;

(ii) subject to below, where (*b*) above applies, the VAT for which the person would be liable for the period beginning on the date he was required to be registered (or, if later 1 January 1996) and ending on the date on which HMRC received notification, or otherwise became fully aware, of his liability to be registered;

(iii) where (*c*), (*f*) or (*h*) above applies, the VAT for which the person would be liable for the period beginning on the date on which the change in the nature of the supplies, etc. occurred and ending on the date on which HMRC received notification, or otherwise became fully aware, of that change; and

(iv) where (*i*) above applies, the VAT on the acquisition to which the failure relates.

Where the relevant VAT under (i) or (ii) above includes VAT on the acquisition of goods from another EU member state and HMRC are satisfied that VAT has been paid under the law of another EU member state on the supply in question (either to a supplier or directly to the fiscal authority), an allowance is to be made for the VAT so paid (not exceeding the amount of the VAT due).

A person is not liable to a penalty under these provisions where by reason of conduct falling within (*a*)–(*i*) above, he is convicted of an offence or assessed to a penalty under **53.12** above. Conduct falling within the provisions does not give rise to a penalty if the person concerned satisfies HMRC, or on appeal a tribunal, that there is a 'reasonable excuse' for his conduct. See **53.11** above for '*reasonable excuse*'. See also **53.33** for mitigation.

Unauthorised issue of invoices

It is now unlikely that the unauthorised issue of tax invoices will be penalised under *VATA 1994, s 67*, because that provision only applies to such unauthorised issue before 1 April 2009.

[*VATA 1994, s 67*].

De Voil Indirect Tax Service. See V5.347–350.

Breaches of walking possession agreements

Northern Ireland

[53.18] The following provisions apply where distress is authorised to be levied on the goods and chattels of a person in default who has refused or neglected to pay any VAT due (or any amount recoverable as if it were VAT due) and the person levying the distress and the person in default have entered into a 'walking possession agreement'. See **32.4 HMRC: POWERS** for levying of distress.

If the person in default breaches the undertakings contained in that agreement, he is liable to a penalty equal to half of the VAT due or amount recoverable unless he satisfies HMRC, or on appeal a tribunal, that there is a 'reasonable excuse' for the breach in question. See **53.11** above for '*reasonable excuse*'.

'*Walking possession agreement*' is an agreement under which the property distrained is allowed to remain in the possession of the person in default and its sale delayed in return for

- an acknowledgement that the property is under distraint, and
- an undertaking not to remove or allow removal of the property from the premises named in the agreement without the consent of HMRC and subject to such conditions as they impose.

[*VATA 1994, s 68; FA 1997, s 53(7)*].

England and Wales

Before 6 April 2014, the provisions above relating to walking possession agreements in Northern Ireland also applied in England and Wales.

[*Tribunals, Courts and Enforcement Act 2007, Sch 13 para 120; SI 2014/768*].

De Voil Indirect Tax Service. See V5.351.

Breaches of regulatory provisions

[53.19] Penalties are payable under the circumstances in (*a*) and (*b*) below but if the person in default is, by reason of his conduct within those circumstances, convicted of an offence or assessed for a penalty under **53.12** or **53.14** above or a surcharge under **53.23** to **53.25** below, he is not also liable to a penalty under these provisions. Additionally, no liability to a penalty arises under the following provisions if the person concerned satisfies HMRC, or on appeal a tribunal, that there is a 'reasonable excuse' for the failure. See **53.11** above for '*reasonable excuse*'.

(a) If any person fails to comply with a requirement to preserve records under *VATA 1994, Sch 11 para 6(3)* (see **57.3 RECORDS**) he is liable to a penalty of £500.

(b) A person is liable to a penalty where he fails to comply with any requirement imposed under
    (i) *VATA 1994, Sch 1 para 11* or *12* (notification of end of liability or entitlement to be registered, see **60.9 REGISTRATION**);

(ii) *VATA 1994, Sch 1A para 7* (notification of end of liability to be registered in respect of taxable supplies by non-UK established person, see **60.36 REGISTRATION**);

(iii) *VATA 1994, Sch 2 para 5* (notification of matters affecting the continuation of registration in respect of supplies from other EU member states, see **60.16 REGISTRATION**);

(iv) *VATA 1994, Sch 3 para 5* (notification of matters affecting the continuation of registration in respect of acquisitions from other EU member states, see **60.24 REGISTRATION**);

(v) *VATA 1994, Sch 3A para 5* (notification of matters affecting the continuation of registration by overseas traders in respect of disposals of assets for which a VAT repayment is claimed, see **60.31 REGISTRATION**);

(vi) any regulations made under *VATA 1994, s 48* requiring a VAT representative, for the purposes of registration, to notify HMRC that his appointment has taken effect or ceased to have effect, see **3.11 AGENTS**;

(vii) *VATA 1994, Sch 11 para 6(1)* (duty to keep records, see **57.1 RECORDS**);

(viii) *FA 2008, Sch 36 paras 39–52* (failure to comply with an information notice, deliberate obstruction of an officer in the course of an inspection or inaccurate information and documents, see **53.20** below);

(ix) any regulations or rules made under that *Act* (other than procedural rules for tribunals);

(x) any Treasury order made under that *Act*;

(xi) any regulations made under the *European Communities Act 1972* and relating to VAT; or

(xii) *VATA 1994, s 18A* (conditions imposed by HMRC in connection with fiscal warehousing, see **73.12 WAREHOUSED GOODS**).

No penalty can be assessed under (vii) to (xi) above unless, within the two years preceding the assessment, HMRC have issued a written warning of the consequences of a continuing failure to comply with the requirements.

The daily rate of penalty is £5 if there has been no previous occasion in the two-year period preceding the beginning of the failure in question on which the person concerned has failed to comply with that requirement. If there has been one such occasion in that period, the daily rate is £10 and in any other case, the daily rate is £15. The maximum penalty payable is 100 days at the appropriate rate and the minimum penalty is £50.

Where a person's failure to comply with any VAT regulation consists of not paying VAT or failing to make a return in the required time, for the daily penalties above, there is substituted, if greater, a daily penalty of $^{1}/_{6}$th, $^{1}/_{3}$rd or ½ of one per cent of the 'VAT due' in respect of that period. '*VAT due*' is, if a return has been furnished, the amount shown on the return; otherwise, it is the amount assessed by HMRC.

For the purposes of calculating the penalty

- a failure is disregarded if, as a result, the person becomes liable to a surcharge under **53.23** to **53.25** below;

- a continuing failure is regarded as one occasion of failure occurring on the date on which it began;
- if the same omission gives rise to a failure to comply with more than one such requirement, it is regarded as the occasion of only one failure;
- if the failure is to comply with the requirements concerning furnishing of returns or payment of VAT, a previous failure to comply with either requirement is regarded as a failure to comply with the requirement in question; and
- any earlier failure is disregarded where HMRC, or on appeal a tribunal, have been satisfied that there is a 'reasonable excuse' for the failure. See **53.11** above for '*reasonable excuse*'.

Where HMRC issue a notice of assessment specifying a date (not later than the date of the notice) to which the penalty is calculated, if the person liable pays the penalty within the period notified by HMRC in the assessment, then the penalty is treated as paid on the specified date (and no further penalty accrues after that date). If the penalty is not paid within the notified period, a further assessment may be made to recover additional penalties.

The Treasury may, by statutory instrument, adjust any of the monetary sums above but not so as to apply to a failure which began before the date on which the order comes into force.

[*VATA 1994, s 69, s 76(2)(7)(8)*].

De Voil Indirect Tax Service. See V5.352–354.

Failure to comply with information notice, deliberate obstruction during inspection or inaccurate information

Standard and daily penalties

[53.20] A person who fails to comply with an information notice (see **32.6 HMRC: POWERS**) or deliberately obstructs an officer during an inspection authorised by the tribunal (see **32.9 HMRC: POWERS**) is liable to a penalty of £300 ('standard penalty'). Failing to comply includes concealment or destruction of documents. If the failure or obstruction continues after the penalty is imposed, the person is liable to further penalties not exceeding £60 for each day ('daily penalty') on which the failure or obstruction continues. A person is liable to a penalty not exceeding £3,000 if, in complying with an information notice, they provide inaccurate information or produce a document that contains an inaccuracy and either: the inaccuracy is careless (i.e. due to a failure by the person to take reasonable care) or deliberate; or the person subsequently discovers the inaccuracy but fails to take reasonable steps to notify HMRC. Where the information or document contains more than one inaccuracy, a penalty is payable in respect of each inaccuracy.

A person must not conceal, destroy or dispose of any document that is the subject of an information notice unless—

- the information has previously been produced and the taxpayer has not been told that he should continue to make it available; and

- in the case of a copy document, six months has elapsed since the copy was originally provided.

A person must not conceal a document if an HMRC officer has told him that it is *likely to be* the subject of an information notice. This prohibition does not apply for longer than six months after the person was informed or notice was given. A failure to do anything required within a limited period of time does not give rise to a standard or daily penalty if the person did it within an extended time limit allowed by an HMRC officer. A standard or daily penalty does not arise if the person satisfies HMRC (or the tribunal on appeal) that he has a reasonable excuse and, if relevant, the failure is remedied without unreasonable delay after the excuse has ceased.

Assessment

Where a person becomes liable for a penalty HMRC may assess the penalty and notify the person within 12 months of the 'relevant date'. In the case of an appealable information notice, '*the relevant date*' means the later of

- the end of the period in which notice of an appeal could have been given, and
- if notice of an appeal is given, the date on which the appeal is determined or withdrawn.

In any other case, '*the relevant date*' means the date on which the person became liable to the penalty.

Appeal

A person may appeal against the imposition of a penalty or the amount of a penalty. Notice of an appeal must be given in writing to HMRC within 30 days, stating the grounds of appeal. On appeal, the tribunal may confirm or cancel the decision to impose a penalty, and may confirm or substitute the amount of a penalty.

A penalty must be paid before the end of the period of 30 days from the date of the notification or 30 days from the finalisation of an appeal. A penalty may be enforced as if it were assessed and payable as income tax.

Additional tax-related penalty

Where the behaviour causing a standard penalty continues and an officer believes that a significant amount of tax is at stake through the failure to comply, the officer may apply to the Upper Tribunal (see **5.1 APPEALS**) for an additional penalty within twelve months of the relevant date. 'Relevant date' means the date the person became liable to the penalty, or in cases involving an appealable information notice, the latest of

- the date the person became liable to the penalty;
- the end of the period in which notice of appeal could have been given; and
- if notice of appeal is given, the date on which the appeal is determined or withdrawn [*FA 2011, Sch 24 para 5*].

The Upper Tribunal decides the amount of the penalty, and in doing so must have regard to the amount of tax likely to be involved. HMRC must notify a person who becomes liable to such a penalty. This tax-related penalty is in addition to the standard and daily penalties, and no account shall be taken of it in applying the rules on interaction with other penalties [*FA 2007 Sch 24 para 12(2); FA 2008 Sch 41 para 15(1)*] (see **53.15**, **53.16** above). The tax-related penalty must be paid within 30 days of notification and may be enforced as if it were assessed as income tax.

Increased daily default penalty

HMRC may apply to the tribunal for an alternative increased daily penalty of up to £1,000 per day if the notice is still not complied with within 30 days of a daily penalty being notified.

[*FA 2008, Sch 36 paras 39–52; SI 2009/404; FA 2009, Sch 47 paras 15–20; FA 2011, Sch 24 para 4*].

Failure to comply with notice requiring contact details for debtor

[53.21] If a third party fails to comply with a notice requiring contact details for a debtor (see **32.7 HMRC: POWERS**), the third party is liable to a penalty of £300.

A failure to comply within a limited period of time does not give rise to a penalty if the person did it within an extended time limit allowed by an HMRC officer. A penalty does not arise if the person satisfies HMRC (or the tribunal on appeal) that he has a reasonable excuse and, if relevant, the failure is remedied without unreasonable delay after the excuse has ceased.

Where a person becomes liable for a penalty HMRC may assess the penalty and notify the person within twelve months of the 'relevant date', i.e. the later of: the end of the period in which notice of an appeal could have been given; and, if notice of an appeal is given, the date on which the appeal is determined or withdrawn.

A person may appeal against the imposition of a penalty or the amount of a penalty. Notice of an appeal must be given in writing to HMRC within 30 days, stating the grounds of appeal. On appeal, the tribunal may confirm or cancel the decision to impose a penalty, and may confirm or substitute the amount of a penalty.

A penalty must be paid before the end of the period of 30 days from the date of the notification or 30 days from the finalisation of an appeal. A penalty may be enforced as if it were assessed and payable as income tax.

The double jeopardy rule states that a person is not liable to a penalty under these provisions in respect of any matter for which he has been convicted of an offence.

[*FA 2008, Sch 36 paras 44–49, 52; FA 2009, Sch 49 para 5*].

Failure to comply with data-holder notice or inaccurate data

Failure to comply

[53.22] If a data-holder fails to comply with a data-holder notice (see **32.8 HMRC: POWERS**), he is liable to an initial fixed penalty of £300. Failing to comply includes disposing of a document that is required by a notice or that the data-holder has been told will be required.

The data-holder is liable to a daily penalty of up to £60 for a failure that continues after the award of an initial penalty. No late-filing penalty arises if the notice was complied with within further time allowed by HMRC. No late-filing penalty arises if the data-holder satisfies HMRC or the tribunal that there is a reasonable excuse for the failure.

Inaccurate information or documents

The data-holder is liable to a penalty of up to £3,000 for deliberately or carelessly providing inaccurate information or documents. The penalty applies if the data-holder submits information or a document knowing about an inaccuracy attributable to another person and fails to tell HMRC at the time. It also applies in cases where an inaccuracy comes to light later and the data-holder does not then take reasonable steps to tell HMRC.

Assessment

If HMRC assess any of the above penalties they must notify the data-holder. An assessment of a penalty for failure to comply must be made within 12 months of the latest of

- the date on which he became liable to the penalty;
- the end of the period in which notice of an appeal against the notice could have been given; and
- if notice of such an appeal is given, the date on which the appeal is determined or withdrawn.

An assessment of a penalty for inaccurate data must be made within the period of

- 12 months from the date on which the inaccuracy first came to HMRC's attention; and
- six years from the date on which the data-holder became liable to the penalty.

Appeal

A data-holder may appeal against HMRC's decision to impose any of the above penalties or against the penalty amount. Written notice of an appeal must be given to HMRC within 30 days from the date notification of assessment was given. It must state the grounds of appeal. The tribunal may confirm or cancel the decision to impose the penalty, or confirm or substitute the penalty amount.

Increased daily default penalty

HMRC may apply to the tribunal for an alternative increased daily penalty of up to £1,000 if the notice is still not complied with within 30 days of a daily penalty being notified to the data-holder.

Enforcement

Any of the above penalties are payable within 30 days of the date that they are notified or, if appealed, the date on which the appeal is determined or withdrawn. Penalties are treated like income tax for enforcement purposes.

[*FA 2011, Sch 23 paras 30–40*].

Default surcharge

[53.23] Unless the provisions in **53.24** to **53.25** below apply, if, by the last day on which a taxable person is required to 'furnish' a return for a VAT period, HMRC have not 'received' that return (or have received the return but not the amount of VAT shown on the return as payable) the taxable person is in default for the purposes of these provisions. See below for the interpretation of '*furnish*' and '*received*'.

Subject to below, a taxable person is liable to a surcharge under these provisions where

(a) he is in default in respect of a VAT period;
(b) HMRC serve on him either
  - a *surcharge liability notice* specifying a surcharge period from the date of the notice to the first anniversary of the last day of the VAT period under (*a*) above; or
  - where that last day occurs during an existing surcharge period, a *surcharge liability notice extension* extending the existing surcharge period to the first anniversary of the last day of the VAT period under (*a*) above;

(c) he is again in default in respect of another VAT period which ends within the surcharge period specified in (or extended by) that notice; and
(d) he has 'outstanding VAT' for the VAT period in (*c*). (There is, therefore, no *liability* to surcharge if a nil or repayment return is submitted late or the VAT due is paid on time but the return is submitted late. HMRC will, however, record the default and issue a surcharge liability extension notice.)

The surcharge is the greater of £30 and the 'specified percentage' of his outstanding VAT for the VAT period under (*d*) above.

The 'specified percentage' is determined by reference to the number of VAT periods in respect of which he is in default in the surcharge period and for which he has outstanding VAT.

	Specified percentage
In relation to the first such period	2%
In relation to the second such period	5%
In relation to the third such period	10%
In relation to each such period after the third	15%

A person has '*outstanding VAT*' for a VAT period if some or all of the VAT due for that period has not been paid by the last day on which he is required to make a return for that period.

Where a liability to surcharge is established, HMRC will not issue a surcharge assessment at the 2% or 5% rates for an amount of less than £400. In these circumstances a default will be recorded, a surcharge liability extension notice will be issued, and the rate of surcharge will increase if there are any further defaults in the surcharge period. (VAT Notice 700, para 21.2).

Example

ABC Ltd is in the default surcharge system and liable to a 2% penalty if it defaults in the December period. It submits the return on time, but instead of paying the full amount of tax of £25,000, can only make a part-payment of £5,000.

If the part-payment is increased by £1 to £5,001, a default surcharge will be avoided for the period if the part-payment is made on time. This is because the surcharge based on unpaid tax is £399.98 (£25,000 – £5,001 x 2%), which is less than the £400 *de minimis* level for the 2% and 5% rates.

Not treated as in default

A person is not liable to a surcharge and not to be treated as having been in default in respect of the VAT period in question if he satisfies HMRC, or on appeal a tribunal, that in the case of a default which is 'material to the surcharge' either of the following applies.

(i) The return or, as the case may be, the VAT shown on it, was despatched at such time and in such manner that it was reasonable to expect that it would be received by HMRC within the appropriate time limit. The despatch of a cheque within reasonable time cannot be equated with the despatch of the VAT where the cheque proves to be worthless (*C & E Commrs v Palco Industry Co Ltd*, QB [1990] STC 594 (TVC 18.369)). See also below under the heading *Meaning of 'furnish' and 'received'*.

(ii) There is a 'reasonable excuse' for the return or VAT not having been despatched. See **53.11** above for '*reasonable excuse*'.

A default is '*material to the surcharge*' if it is *either* the default which gave rise to the surcharge *or* is a default taken into account in the service of the surcharge liability notice upon which the surcharge depends and the person concerned has not been previously liable to a surcharge in respect of a VAT period ending within the surcharge period specified in, or extended by, the notice.

Where a person is treated as not having been in default under (i) or (ii) above, any surcharge liability notice the service of which depended on that default is deemed not to have been served.

A default is also to be left out of account for the above purposes if the conduct giving rise to the default falls within **53.19**(*b*) above and the person is assessed to a penalty under those provisions.

[*VATA 1994, s 59, Sch 13 para 14*].

No liability to a surcharge arises where HMRC agree to defer payment because of the effects of disaster designated by the Treasury as having national significance. This provision has only ever been invoked for the floods in the UK in June and July 2007.

[*FA 2008, s 135; SI 2008/1936*].

Surcharge liability notices

For non-receipt of a surcharge liability notice, see *C & E Commrs v Medway Draughting & Technical Services Ltd; C & E Commrs v Adplates Offset Ltd*, QB [1989] STC 346 (TVC 18.1). Where a surcharge liability notice has not been received, subsequent extension notices are not effective as valid surcharge liability notices as they only specify the end of the surcharge period and not the date on which it began; any surcharge assessments must therefore be discharged (*Dow Engineering* (VTD 5771) (TVC 18.8)). A surcharge liability notice which incorrectly stated that a return had not been received (when it had been received late) has been held to be invalid (*Coleman Machines Ltd* [1988] Lexis Citation 1455 (TVC 18.5)).

Appeals

A person who thinks he has grounds for appeal against a default surcharge should write to HMRC within 30 days of the date of issue of the *surcharge liability notice extension* and ask them to reconsider the case. They will either confirm the original decision and give 21 days in which to lodge an appeal with the First-tier Tribunal or send a revised decision and give 30 days in which to lodge such an appeal. Alternatively a person can appeal directly to the First-tier Tribunal without contacting HMRC in which case he must do so within 30 days of the issue of the *surcharge liability notice extension*. The First-tier Tribunal cannot hear an appeal until a surcharge liability notice extension has been issued (see *Expert Systems Design Ltd* (VTD 7974) (TVC 2.41)). At this stage an appeal can be made against any or all of the defaults which led to the person becoming liable to the surcharge. This is the only time that the VAT tribunal can be asked to hear an appeal against these defaults. If the person later becomes liable to a further surcharge because he has defaulted again, he will be outside the time limit for appealing against the earlier defaults. It is not necessary to pay the surcharge before appealing to the First-tier Tribunal but all outstanding returns and VAT must be paid.

Meaning of 'furnish' and 'received': paper returns and payments

Very few traders are now permitted to submit returns and payments on paper. For those few, the former policy on timely submission presumably continues. 'Furnish' means putting the return into the possession of HMRC. The paper

VAT return states 'You could be liable to a financial penalty if your completed return and all the VAT payable are not received by the due date'. Given this, and the use of the word 'received', a clear distinction should be drawn for those purposes between 'received' and 'despatched'. 'Received' should be taken to mean actual receipt by HMRC. Cheque payments sent by post are treated as being received by HMRC on the date when cleared funds reach their bank account, not the date when they receive the cheque. [*SI 1995/2518, Reg 40(2B)*].

HMRC have indicated that a return will be accepted as posted on time if posted at least one working day before the due date (assuming it has been sent in the official envelope or by first class post). At the same time they also indicated that where the due date falls on a weekend or bank holiday, the return and the VAT due will be accepted as received in time if received on the next following working day (but see below for electronic payments). (STI 1991, p 389 quoting from *The Tax Journal*, 21 March 1991, p 2). Despite this apparent assurance, tribunals have continued to uphold default surcharge assessments where returns have been posted one day before the due date. In *La Reine (Limoges Porcelain) Ltd* (VTD 10468) (TVC 18.36) the tribunal held that a return due on a Sunday and posted at 7 pm on the previous Friday had not been posted early enough that it was reasonable to expect that it would be received by HMRC on or before the Sunday. This decision was not followed, and was implicitly disapproved of, in *Halstead Motor Company* (VTD 13373) (TVC 18.38). In that case the tribunal held that, by posting a return before the last collection on Friday, the company had dispatched the return in a manner such that it was reasonable to expect that it would be delivered on Saturday and be received by HMRC within the appropriate time limit. Treatment otherwise by HMRC would be inconsistent with their statement reproduced at STI 1991, p 389.

Meaning of 'furnish' and 'received': electronic system

The great majority of traders are required to file their returns using the electronic system. As long as an acknowledgement of receipt is displayed, the trader will have assurance that HMRC have received the return.

Where the trader has set up a direct debit, HMRC will call for the payment after the due date for submission of the return, and it will normally leave the trader's account three working days after the seventh calendar day after the end of the month following the return period. If the return is submitted late, HMRC will apply for the direct debit late and the trader will be in default.

Where VAT is paid by the trader rather than by direct debit, HMRC expect payments to be in their bank account on or before the due date, so that if the seventh calendar day falls on a weekend or bank holiday, payment must be in their bank account by the last working day beforehand (see **52.3 PAYMENT OF VAT**). Thus, where, say, the seventh day is a Saturday, payment of the VAT on the previous Friday by bank giro credit would not be sufficient.

Agreement for deferred payment

HMRC operate a Business Support Service designed to meet the needs of businesses affected by the downturn in the economy. The service will review the circumstances of such businesses and discuss temporary options tailored to their needs, such as arranging for them to make payments over an extended period. Where an agreement for deferred payment is made, a person is not liable to a default surcharge if:

- he fails to pay an amount of VAT by the due date;
- before the date on which the failure gives rise to a surcharge, he makes a request to an HMRC officer to defer payment; and
- an HMRC officer agrees, whether before or after the date on which the liability to a surcharge arises, that payment may be deferred.

If the person breaks such an agreement, by failing to pay the tax at the end of the deferral period, or by failing to meet a condition set out in the agreement, the surcharge is effectively reinstated with effect from the date of notice served by HMRC as a result of the breakage of the agreement. [*FA 2009, s 108*].

Default surcharge: payments on account

[53.24] A taxable person is in default in respect of any VAT period for which he is required to make payments on account (see **52.5 PAYMENT OF VAT**) if

(i) HMRC have not received in full any payment on account by the due date; or
(ii) he would be in default in respect of that period under **53.23** above (but for the fact that periods in respect of which payments on account are required are specifically excluded from those provisions).

Subject to below, a taxable person is liable to a surcharge under these provisions where

(a) he is in default in respect of a VAT period;
(b) HMRC serve on him either
   - a *surcharge liability notice* specifying a surcharge period from the date of the notice to the first anniversary of the last day of the VAT period under (*a*) above; or
   - where that last day occurs during an existing surcharge period, a *surcharge liability notice extension* extending the existing surcharge period to the first anniversary of the last day of the VAT period under (*a*) above;
(c) he is again in default in respect of another VAT period which ends within the surcharge period specified in (or extended by) that notice; and
(d) the 'aggregate value of defaults' for that VAT period is more than nil. The '*aggregate value of defaults*' is the total value of
   - any payment or payments on account (or part payment or payments) not received by HMRC by the due date for such payments; and
   - any outstanding VAT due for the period not paid by the last day on which he is required to make a return for that period (less the amount of unpaid payments on account).

The surcharge is the greater of £30 and the 'specified percentage' of the aggregate value of defaults for the VAT period under (*d*) above.

The '*specified percentage*' is determined by reference to the number of VAT periods in respect of which he is in default in the surcharge period and for which the value of his defaults is more than nil.

	Specified percentage
In relation to the first such period	2%
In relation to the second such period	5%
In relation to the third such period	10%
In relation to each such period after the third	15%

Not treated as in default

A person is not liable to a surcharge and not to be treated as having been in default in respect of the VAT period in question if he satisfies HMRC, or on appeal a tribunal, that in the case of a default which is 'material to the surcharge' either of the following applies.

(A) The payment on account (where (i) above applies) or the return or VAT shown on it (where (ii) above applies) was despatched at such time and in such manner that it was reasonable to expect that it would be received by HMRC by the due date.
A payment on account is not to be taken as received by the due date unless, by the last day for payment, all the transactions can be completed that need to be completed before the whole of the payment becomes available to HMRC.

(B) There is a 'reasonable excuse' for the payment on account (where (i) above applies) or the return or VAT (where (ii) above applies) not having been despatched. See **53.11** above for '*reasonable excuse*'.

A default is '*material to the surcharge*' if it is either the default which gave rise to the surcharge or is a default taken into account in the service of the surcharge liability notice upon which the surcharge depends and the person concerned has not been previously liable to a surcharge in respect of a VAT period ending within the surcharge period specified in, or extended by, the notice.

Where a person is treated as not having been in default under (A) or (B) above, any surcharge liability notice the service of which depended on that default is deemed not to have been served.

A default is also to be left out of account for the above purposes if the conduct giving rise to the default falls within **53.19**(*b*) above and the person is assessed to a penalty under those provisions.

[*VATA 1994, s 59A*].

See *VATA 1994, s 59B* for deeming provisions where a VAT period in respect of which payments on account are required ends within a surcharge period begun or extended by the service of a surcharge liability notice under **53.23** above; and a VAT period for which payments on account are not required ends within a surcharge period begun or extended by the service of a surcharge liability notice under the above provisions.

See also **53.23** above under the headings *Surcharge liability notices*, *Appeals* and *Agreement for deferred payment*, which provisions also apply to default surcharges in relation to payments on account.

De Voil Indirect Tax Service. See V5.371–V5.383.

Default surcharge: non-UK businesses making supplies of broadcasting, telecommunication and electronic services to consumers in the UK from 1 January 2015 using a special scheme

[53.25] From 1 January 2015 non-UK businesses supplying broadcasting, telecommunication or electronic services to consumers in the UK can, depending on where they belong, use either the special scheme for non-EU suppliers (see **64.40**) or the special scheme for EU suppliers (see **64.41**) as an alternative to registering for VAT in the UK. The UK VAT due on the supplies should be declared on the relevant returns which should be submitted to the administering Member State, that is, the Member State where the business has registered to use the appropriate VAT Mini One Stop Shop (VAT MOSS) scheme.

A business that is required to make a VAT MOSS return to another administering Member State is regarded as being in default for the tax period covered by the return if either of the following conditions is met:

- the tax authorities in the administering Member State have not received the return by the deadline for submitting it and have issued a reminder of the obligation to submit the return; or
- the tax authorities in the administering Member State have received the return but have not received the VAT shown as due on the return and have issued a reminder of the VAT outstanding.

If either of the above conditions is met, HMRC can issue a special surcharge liability notice specifying a special surcharge period ending on the first anniversary of the last day of the tax period and beginning on the date of the notice. If a special surcharge liability notice is issued in respect of a tax period which ends at or before the end of an existing special surcharge period, the special surcharge period specified in that notice is expressed as a continuation of the existing special surcharge period so that the existing period and its extension are regarded as a single special surcharge period.

If the recipient of a special surcharge liability notice is in default in respect of a tax period ending within the special surcharge period and has outstanding VAT for the tax period they are liable to a surcharge equal to the greater of:

(a) £30
(b) the specified percentage (see below) of the outstanding VAT for the tax period which relates to supplies of broadcasting, telecommunication or electronic services to consumers in the UK.

As noted below, the specified percentage depends on whether the tax period is the first, second, third, or further tax period in the default period in respect of which the person is in default and has outstanding VAT relating to supplies of broadcasting, telecommunication or electronic services to consumers in the UK.

	Specified percentage
In relation to the first such period	2%
In relation to the second such period	5%
In relation to the third such period	10%
In relation to each such period after the third	15%

A person is not liable to a surcharge and will not be treated as having been in default in respect of the tax period in question if he satisfies HMRC, or on appeal a tribunal, that in the case of a default which is 'material to the surcharge' either of the following applies.

(i) The return or, as the case may be, the VAT shown on it, was despatched at such time and in such manner that it was reasonable to expect that it would be received by the tax authorities for the administering Member State within the appropriate time limit.
(ii) There is a 'reasonable excuse' for the return or VAT not having been despatched. See **53.11** above for 'reasonable excuse'.

A default is 'material to the surcharge' if it is either the default which gave rise to the surcharge or is a default taken into account in the service of the special surcharge liability notice upon which the surcharge depends and the person concerned has not been previously liable to a surcharge in respect of a tax period ending within the special surcharge period specified in, or extended by, the notice.

A default is to be left out of account if the conduct giving rise to the default falls within **53.19**(*b*) above and the person is assessed to a penalty under those provisions.

[*VATA 1994, Sch 3B and Sch 3BA; FA 2014, Sch 22*].

Incorrect certificates as to zero-rating, etc.

[53.26] Subject to below, where

(a) a customer gives to a supplier a certificate
- that the supply or supplies made or to be made fall wholly or partly within *VATA 1994, Sch 8 Group 5* or *6* or *VATA 1994, Sch 9 Group 1* (see **43.22 LAND AND BUILDINGS: ZERO AND REDUCED RATE SUPPLIES AND DIY HOUSEBUILDERS**), or
- in connection with fiscal warehousing as required by *VATA 1994, s 18B* or *s 18C* (see **73.15** and **73.19 WAREHOUSED GOODS**), or
- that the supply or supplies made or to be made are reduced rate supplies falling wholly or partly within any of the Groups of *VATA 1994, Sch 7A* (see **59.1 REDUCED RATE SUPPLIES**), or

(b) a person acquiring goods from another EU member state prepares a certificate for the purposes of *VATA 1994, s 18B* (see **73.15 WAREHOUSED GOODS**),

and the certificate is incorrect, the person giving or preparing the certificate is liable to a penalty. The amount of the penalty is, where (*a*) above applies, the difference between the VAT which should have been charged and the VAT actually charged and, where (*b*) or (*c*) above applies, the VAT actually chargeable on the acquisition.

A person is not liable to a penalty under these provisions if

(i) he satisfies HMRC or, on appeal, the First-tier Tribunal, that there is a reasonable excuse for his having given or prepared the certificate; or
(ii) by reason of his having given or prepared it, he is convicted of an offence.

[*VATA 1994, s 62; FA 2003, ss 26–27, ss 29–41*].

De Voil Indirect Tax Service. See V5.340.

Inaccuracies in EC Sales Lists (ESLs)

[53.27] Where

(a) a person has submitted an ESL (see **2.20 ACCOUNTING PERIODS AND RETURNS**) containing a 'material inaccuracy' to HMRC;
(b) within six months of discovering that inaccuracy, HMRC have issued him with a written warning identifying the statement and stating that future inaccuracies might result in the service of a notice under these provisions;
(c) the person submits a second ESL containing a material inaccuracy to HMRC and the 'submission date' is within the period of two years beginning with the day after the warning was issued;
(d) HMRC have, within six months of discovering the second inaccuracy served on him a notice identifying the ESL and stating that future inaccuracies will attract a penalty under these provisions; and
(e) the person submits yet another ESL containing a material inaccuracy to HMRC the submission date of which is not more than two years after
  - the service of the notice under (*d*) above; or
  - the date on which any previous ESL attracting a penalty was submitted,

that person is liable to a penalty of £100 in respect of the statement under (*e*) above.

An ESL contains a '*material inaccuracy*' if, having regard to the matters to be included, the inclusion or omission of any information is misleading in any material respect.

'*Submission date*' means the last date for submission of the ESL or the day on which it was actually submitted, whichever is the earlier.

An inaccuracy is not regarded as material for these purposes if

(i) the person submitting the ESL satisfies HMRC, or on appeal the First-tier Tribunal, that there is a 'reasonable excuse' for the inaccuracy (see **53.11** above);
(ii) at a time when he had no reason to believe that HMRC were enquiring into his affairs, he furnished them with full information with respect to the inaccuracy; or
(iii) he is convicted of an offence by reason of the submission of the ESL containing the material inaccuracy.

Where the only ESL identified in a warning under (*b*) above or a notice under (*d*) above is one which is regarded as containing no material inaccuracies (whether by virtue of (i) to (iii) above or otherwise) that warning or notice is deemed not to have been issued or served.

[*VATA 1994, s 65*].

De Voil Indirect Tax Service. See V5.346.

Failure to submit EC Sales Lists (ESLs)

[53.28] If by the last day on which a person is required to submit an ESL (see **2.20 ACCOUNTING PERIODS AND RETURNS**) for any period, HMRC has not received the statement, that person is regarded for the purposes of these provisions as being in default in relation to that statement until such time as it is delivered.

Where any person is in default in respect of any ESL, HMRC may serve a notice on him stating that he is in default but that no action will be taken if the default is remedied within 14 days of the notice, otherwise he will become liable to a penalty as calculated below. The notice may also state that the person will become liable, without further notice, to penalties if he commits any more defaults before a period of twelve months has elapsed without his being in default.

Where such a notice is served, the person will become liable

(a) in respect of the ESL to which the notice relates to a penalty of the greater of £50 *or* £5 for each day the default continues after the 14-day period (up to a maximum of 100 days); and
(b) in respect of any other ESL in relation to which he is in default, the last day for submission of which is after the service and before the expiry of the notice, to a penalty of the greater of £50 *or*, as the case may be, £5, £10 or £15 for each day the default continues up to a maximum of 100 days. The daily fine is £5, £10 or £15 depending upon whether the ESL in question is the first, second, or third or subsequent ESL (including, where applicable, the ESL within (*a*) above) in respect of which the person has become liable to a penalty while the notice is in force.

For the purposes of (*b*) above, the notice continues in force for twelve months from the date of service but, where at any time in that twelve-month period the person defaults in submitting an ESL other than one in relation to which he was in default when the notice was served, the notice continues until a period of twelve months has elapsed without that person becoming liable to a penalty under these provisions in respect of any ESL.

Not treated as in default

A person is not treated as being in default in relation to an ESL under these provisions if he satisfies HMRC, or on appeal a tribunal, that

- the ESL has been submitted at such time and in such manner that it was reasonable to expect that it would be received by HMRC within the appropriate time limit; or
- there is a 'reasonable excuse' for the ESL not having been dispatched (see **53.11** above).

In such a case, he is not liable to a penalty in respect of that ESL and any notice served on him exclusively in relation to the failure to submit that ESL has no effect for the purposes of these provisions.

[*VATA 1994, s 66*].

De Voil Indirect Tax Service. See V5.355.

Breach of record-keeping requirements, etc. in relation to transactions in gold

[53.29] A person who fails to comply with the accounting and record-keeping requirements relating to investment gold in *SI 1995/2518, Regs 31A, 31B* and VAT Notice 701/21 (see **27.5 GOLD AND PRECIOUS METALS**) is liable to a penalty not exceeding 17.5% of the value of the transaction to which the failure relates. HMRC must determine the value of any transaction to the best of their judgement and notify the person liable.

A person is not liable to a penalty under these provisions

- if he is convicted of a criminal offence or assessed to a penalty under **53.12** above by reason of conduct which would otherwise give rise to a penalty under these provisions; or
- where he satisfies HMRC or, on appeal, a tribunal that there is 'reasonable excuse' for the failure (see **53.11** above).

See also **53.33** below for mitigation of penalties.

Where a person is liable for a penalty under these provisions, the provisions under **53.16** above do not apply.

[*VATA 1994, s 69A(1)–(3)(6)(7)*].

Breach of record-keeping requirements imposed by directions

[53.30] A person who fails to comply with a requirement to keep specified records imposed by directions under *VATA 1994, Sch 11 para 6A* (see **57.1 RECORDS**) is liable to a penalty equal to £200 multiplied by the number of days on which the failure continues (up to a maximum of 30 days). Any person who fails to comply with a requirement to preserve records imposed under those provisions is liable to a penalty of £500.

A person is not liable to a penalty under these provisions if he

- satisfies HMRC or, on appeal, a tribunal that there is a 'reasonable excuse' (see **53.11** above) for the failure; or
- is assessed to a penalty under **53.12** above or convicted of a criminal offence (whether under *VATA 1994* or otherwise), by reason of conduct which would otherwise give rise to a penalty under these provisions.

[*VATA 1994, s 69B*].

Failure to notify use of certain avoidance schemes

[53.31] Subject to below, a person who fails to comply with the provisions of VATA 1994, Sch 11A para 6 (duty to notify HMRC of certain avoidance schemes, see **4.6** and **4.10 ANTI-AVOIDANCE**) is liable to a penalty of

(a) £5,000 for failing to disclose a hallmarked scheme; or
(b) 15% of the 'VAT saving' for failing to disclose a listed scheme.

For the purposes of (*b*) above, the '*VAT saving*' is

(i) where a return gives rise to a requirement to notify, the difference between
  - the amount of VAT shown on the returns submitted for the VAT periods beginning with that in respect of which the duty to notify first arose and ending with that in which the taxable person duly notified HMRC or, if earlier, the VAT period immediately preceding the notification by HMRC of the penalty assessment; and
  - the amount of VAT which, but for the scheme, would have been shown on those returns;

(ii) where a repayment claim for earlier VAT periods in respect of which returns have been submitted gives rise to a requirement to notify, the difference between the amount claimed and the amount which, but for the scheme, would have been claimed; or
(iii) where an amount of non-deductible tax gives rise to the requirement to notify, the excess amount claimed (to the extent that it is not included in the tax saving under (i) or (ii) above).

A person is not liable to a penalty under these provisions

- if he satisfies HMRC or, on appeal, a tribunal that there is a 'reasonable excuse' (see **53.11** above) for the failure to notify; or
- where, by reason of the failure to notify, he is convicted of a criminal offence (whether under *VATA 1994* or otherwise) or assessed to a penalty under *VATA 1994, s 60* (VAT evasion: conduct involving dishonesty, see **53.12** above).

See also **53.33** below for mitigation.

[*VATA 1994, Sch 11A paras 10, 11*].

Failure to comply with duties of senior accounting officers

[53.32] If a senior accounting officer of a qualifying company fails to comply with his main duty with regard to accountancy arrangements (see **57.14 RECORDS**), he is liable to a penalty of £5,000. A person is not liable to more than one such penalty in respect of the same company and the same financial year. If a senior accounting officer fails to provide a certificate or provides a certificate that contains a careless or deliberate inaccuracy, he is liable to penalty of £5,000. An inaccuracy is careless if it is due to a failure by the senior accounting officer to take reasonable care. An inaccuracy that was neither careless nor deliberate when the certificate was given is to be treated as careless if the senior accounting officer discovered it some time later and did not take reasonable steps to inform HMRC. A qualifying company is liable to a penalty of £5,000 if, for a financial year, HMRC are not notified of the name of its senior accounting officer. Liability to a penalty for any or the above failures to comply does not arise if the senior accounting officer or qualifying company satisfies HMRC or (on appeal) the tribunal that there is a reasonable excuse for the failure. Where a senior accounting officer or a qualifying company becomes liable for a penalty HMRC may assess the penalty. If they do so, they must notify the officer or company liable for the penalty. An assessment may not be made more than six months after the failure or inaccuracy first comes to the attention of an HMRC officer, or more than six years after the end of the period for filing the company's accounts for the financial year. A person may appeal against a decision of HMRC that a penalty is payable by that person. Notice of an appeal must be given in writing, before the end of the period of 30 days beginning with the date on which the notification was issued, stating the grounds of appeal. On an appeal that is notified to the tribunal, the tribunal may confirm or cancel the decision. A penalty must be paid within 30 days of the date of notification of the assessment, or, if a notice of appeal is given, within 30 days of the date on which the appeal is determined or withdrawn. The penalty is enforceable as if it were income tax.

[*FA 2009, Sch 46 paras 4–11*].

Mitigation of civil penalties

[53.33] The penalty provisions of *FA 2007, Sch 24* (inaccuracies in documents) and *FA 2008, Sch 41* (failure to notify and unauthorised issue of invoices) provide for reductions from the maximum levels of penalty based on disclosure (see **53.15** above). Reductions from the maximum to the minimum (e.g. from 70% to 35% for 'deliberate behaviour without concealment') is measured according to the following scales:

- telling up to 30%;
- helping up to 40%; and
- giving access up to 30%.

HMRC Compliance Check Factsheet CC/FS7a explains the meaning of these terms as follows ('us', in this regard, means HMRC):

- telling us about, or agreeing that there is something wrong and how and why it happened;

- telling us everything you can about the extent of what is wrong as soon as you know about it;
- telling and helping us by answering our questions in full;
- helping us to understand your accounts or records;
- helping us by replying to our letters quickly;
- helping us by agreeing to attend any meetings, or visits at a mutually convenient time;
- helping us by checking your own records to identify the extent of the inaccuracy;
- helping us by using your private records to identify sales or income not included in your tax return;
- giving us access to documents we have asked for without unnecessary delay; and
- giving us access to documents we may not know about, as well as those that we ask to see.

For example, a trader who has made a 'prompted' disclosure of a deliberate error will receive a penalty of between 35% and 70% of the potential lost revenue. The officer might allow 20% for telling, 20% for helping and 10% for giving access, making a total of 50%. The penalty would then be 70% less (50% x [70% – 35%]) = 52.5%.

Where a penalty arises other than under the *FA 2007* or *FA 2008* rules HMRC, or on appeal a tribunal, may reduce a penalty in respect of any of the following defaults to whatever amount (including nil) they think proper:

- tax evasion: conduct involving dishonesty (where the loss of VAT arose before 1 April 2009);
- failure to notify and unauthorised issue of invoices (where the failure arose before 1 April 2009);
- breach of record-keeping requirements in relation to transactions in gold; and
- failure to disclose avoidance schemes.

In mitigating/reducing a penalty, neither HMRC nor the tribunal may take into account

- insufficiency of funds available to any person to pay either the tax due or the penalty;
- the fact that there has been no significant loss of tax; or
- the fact that the person liable to the penalty or a person acting on his behalf has acted in good faith.

[*VATA 1994, ss 60, 69A, 70, Sch 11A para 10*].

Dishonest conduct: before 1 April 2009

HMRC may mitigate a dishonest conduct penalty as follows

- up to 40% for an early and truthful explanation as to why the arrears arose and the true extent of them;
- up to 40% for fully embracing and meeting responsibilities under this procedure by, for example, supplying information promptly, disclosure and quantification of irregularities, attending meetings and answering questions.

In most cases, therefore, the maximum reduction obtainable is 80% of the tax on which penalties are chargeable. However, in exceptional circumstances consideration may be given to a further reduction, for example where a full and unprompted voluntary disclosure is made.

(VAT Notice 160, para 2.3).

De Voil Indirect Tax Service. See V5.334.

Publishing details of deliberate tax defaulters

[53.34] HMRC may publish information about any person if, following an HMRC investigation, one or more 'relevant tax penalties' is found to have been incurred by the person, and the related potential lost revenue exceeds £25,000. A relevant tax penalty is:

- a penalty under *FA 2007, Sch 24 para 1* (inaccuracy in taxpayer's document) in respect of a deliberate inaccuracy on the part of the person;
- a penalty under *FA 2007, Sch 24 para 1A* (deliberate supply of false information or deliberate withholding of information by another person);
- a penalty under *FA 2008, Sch 41 para 1* (failure to notify) in respect of a deliberate failure on the part of the person; or
- a penalty under *FA 2008, Sch 41 para* 2 (unauthorised VAT invoice) in respect of deliberate action by the person.

The information may be published in any manner that HMRC considers appropriate. Before publication, HMRC must inform the person of their intention, and afford the person reasonable opportunity to make representations. The following information may be published:

- the person's name (including any trading name, previous name or pseudonym);
- the person's address (or registered office);
- the nature of any business carried on by the person;
- the amount of the penalty or penalties and the potential lost revenue in relation to the penalty (or the aggregate of the potential lost revenue in relation to each of the penalties);
- the periods or times to which the inaccuracy, failure or action giving rise to the penalty (or any of the penalties) relates; and
- any such other information as HMRC consider it appropriate to publish in order to make clear the person's identity.

No information may be published:

- before the day when the penalty becomes final (or the latest day when any of the penalties becomes final);
- for the first time after the end of the period of one year beginning with that day (or that latest day);
- after the end of the period of one year beginning with the day on which it is first published (published information may not continue to be published after this date);

- if the amount of the penalty is reduced under *FA 2007, Sch 24 para 10(3) or (5)*, or *FA 2008, Sch 41 para 13(1) or (3)* (maximum mitigation for unprompted disclosure); or
- if the amount of the penalty is reduced under *FA 2007, Sch 24 para 10(4) or (6)*, or *FA 2008, Sch 41 para 13(2) or (4)* (maximum mitigation for prompted disclosure), and the mitigation is attributable to a disclosure made at such time as HMRC, having regard to the circumstances, consider it inappropriate to publish the information.

[*FA 2009, s 94*].

Import VAT: evasion and non-compliance

[53.35] Penalties may be imposed where a person engages in any conduct

- for the purpose of evading import VAT (see **53.36** below); or
- by which he contravenes a duty, obligation, requirement or condition imposed by or under relevant rules relating to import VAT (see **53.37** below).

The penalties also apply to customs duty, Union export duty, Union import duty and customs duty of a preferential tariff country, but these provisions are outside the scope of this book.

[*FA 2003, s 24*].

Penalty for evasion

[53.36] Where

- a person engages in any conduct for the purpose of 'evading import VAT', and
- his conduct involves dishonesty (whether or not such as to give rise to any criminal liability),

he is liable to a penalty equal to 'the amount import VAT evaded' (or sought to be evaded). However, where by reason of such conduct he is

- convicted of a criminal offence,
- given (and has not had withdrawn) a demand notice in respect of a penalty to which he is liable under **53.37** below, or
- liable to a penalty imposed upon him under any other provision of the law relating to import VAT

that conduct does not also give rise to a liability to a penalty under these provisions.

'*Evading import VAT*' includes wrongly obtaining or securing

(i) any repayment, relief or exemption from, or any allowance against, import VAT, or
(ii) any deferral or other postponement of his liability to pay any import VAT.

It also includes evading the cancellation of any entitlement to, or the withdrawal of, any such repayment, relief, exemption or allowance.

'*The amount of import VAT evaded*' is, as the case may be, the amount of

- the repayment;
- the relief, exemption or allowance; or
- the payment which, or the liability to make which, is deferred or otherwise postponed.

[*FA 2003, s 25*].

Liability of officers of a body corporate

Where the conduct of a body corporate gives rise to a penalty under the above provisions and it appears to HMRC that that conduct, in whole or in part, is attributable to the dishonesty of a person who is (or at the material time was) a director or 'managing officer' (the 'relevant officer') of the body corporate, HMRC may give a notice to the body corporate (or its representative) and to the relevant officer (or his representative) stating

- the full amount of the penalty; and
- that they propose to recover a specified portion (which may be the whole) of that penalty from the relevant officer.

The relevant officer is then treated as if he were personally liable under the above provisions to a penalty corresponding to that specified portion. The body corporate is then only liable to the balance (if any) of the full penalty and is discharged from liability on the amount recoverable from the relevant officer.

'*Managing officer*' means a manager, secretary or other similar officer of the body corporate, and any person purporting to act in any such capacity or as a director. Where the affairs of a body corporate are managed by its members, the provisions apply in relation to the conduct of a member in connection with his functions of management as if he were a director of the body corporate.

[*FA 2003, s 28*].

Reduction of the amount of a penalty

Where a person is liable to a penalty under the above provisions

- HMRC or, on appeal, a tribunal may reduce the penalty to such amount (including nil) as they think proper; and
- HMRC (on a review) or a tribunal (on an appeal) may cancel the whole or any part of the reduction previously made by HMRC

but in doing so neither HMRC or the tribunal must take into account

- insufficiency of the funds available to any person to pay the import VAT or the penalty;
- the fact that there has been no significant loss of import VAT; or
- the fact that the person liable to the penalty, or a person acting on his behalf, has acted in good faith.

[*FA 2003, s 29*].

Penalty for contravention of relevant rules

[53.37] The Treasury may make an order to the effect that a person is liable to a penalty of up to £2,500 if he engages in any conduct by which he contravenes a duty, obligation, requirement or condition relating to import VAT imposed by or under any of the following.

- *CEMA 1979* any other Act or any statutory instrument.
- Union customs rules (as laid down in *EC Council Regulation 2913/92/EEC* of 12 October 1992 and *Regulation (EU) 952/2013* of 9 October 2013 and including provisions adopted at Union level or nationally to implement them).
- Any directly applicable EU legislation.
- Any relevant international agreements having effect as part of the law of any part of the UK by virtue of any Act or statutory instrument or any directly applicable EU legislation.

Exceptions

A person is not liable to a penalty under these provisions in the following circumstances.

(a) If he satisfies HMRC, or on appeal a tribunal, that there is a reasonable excuse for his conduct. Although 'reasonable excuse' is not defined (and therefore to be determined by HMRC or a tribunal) the following are not to be taken as a reasonable excuse.
  - An insufficiency of funds available to any person for paying any import VAT or any penalty due.
  - That reliance was placed by any person on another to perform any task.
  - That the contravention is attributable, in whole or in part, to the conduct of a person on whom reliance to perform any task was so placed.

(b) If, by reason of conduct relating to import VAT, that person is
  - prosecuted for an offence;
  - given (and has not had withdrawn) a demand notice in respect of a penalty to which he is liable under **53.36** above;
  - liable to a penalty imposed upon him under any other provision of the law relating to import VAT; or
  - liable to a penalty under **53.14** to **53.19** or **53.26** to **53.29** above (or would be so liable except that, by reason of his conduct, he is convicted of an offence or liable to a different penalty under those provisions).

[*FA 2003, ss 26, 27*].

Reduction of the amount of a penalty

The same provisions apply as under **53.36** above. [*FA 2003, s 29*].

Administration, etc. of the penalties

Demand notices

[53.38] Where a person is liable to a penalty under **53.36** or **53.37** above, HMRC may give him (or his representative) a notice in writing demanding payment of the penalty due. Any amount so demanded is recoverable as if it were due from him (or the representative) as an amount of customs duty but subject to

- any appeal to a tribunal (see below);
- the demand being subsequently withdrawn; or
- the amount of the penalty being reduced.

Time limits

A demand notice cannot be given

- in the case of a penalty under **53.36** above,
  - (i) more than 20 years after the conduct giving rise to the penalty ceased;
  - (ii) more than two years after evidence of facts, sufficient in the opinion of HMRC to justify the giving of the demand notice, comes to their knowledge; or
  - (iii) where a deceased person was liable to such a penalty before his death, more than three years after his death; and
- in the case of a penalty under **53.37** above
  - (i) more than three years after the conduct giving rise to the penalty ceased; or
  - (ii) more than two years after evidence of facts, sufficient in the opinion of HMRC to justify the giving of the demand notice, comes to their knowledge.

Consequences of issue on criminal proceedings

Once a demand notice is given for payment of a penalty under **53.37** above in respect of any conduct of a person, no proceedings may be brought against that person for any offence constituted by that conduct (whether or not the demand notice is subsequently withdrawn).

[*FA 2003, ss 30–32*].

Review by HMRC

HMRC can be asked to review their decision in the following circumstances.

(a) Where HMRC give a person (or his representative) a notice informing him that, in their opinion, he is liable to a penalty under **53.37** above but that they do not propose to give a demand notice, the person (or his representative) may give written notice to HMRC requiring them to review their decision that liability to a penalty exists.

(b) Except where (*c*) below applies, where HMRC give a demand notice to a person (or his representative), the person (or his representative) may by written notice require HMRC to review their decision

- that the person is liable to a penalty under **53.36** or **53.37** above; or

- as to the amount of the penalty.

(c) In the case of a penalty under **53.36** above where HMRC give a demand notice to a body corporate and an officer
  - (i) the officer (or his representative) may by written notice require HMRC to review their decision
    - that the conduct of the body corporate is, in whole or in part, attributable to the relevant officer's dishonesty, or
    - as to the portion of the full penalty which HMRC are seeking to recover from the officer (or his representative); and
  - (ii) the body corporate (or its representative) may by written notice require HMRC to review their decision
    - that the body corporate is liable to a penalty; or
    - as to amount of the full penalty as if it were the amount specified in the demand notice.

Time limit

HMRC need not review any decision under the above provisions unless the required notice is given to them within 45 days of the date which they gave the relevant notice under (*a*)–(*c*) above. But this does not prevent HMRC from agreeing to review a decision in a case where the notice required is not given within the permitted period.

Right to further review

A person can only give notice under the above provisions requiring a decision to be reviewed a second or subsequent time

- on the grounds that HMRC did not, on any previous review, have the opportunity to consider any particular facts or matters; and
- provided he does not, on the further review, require HMRC to consider any facts or matters which were considered on a previous review of the decision (unless they are relevant to any issue to which the facts or matters not previously considered relate).

Powers of HMRC on a review

Where HMRC are required to review a decision or agree to do so outside the time limit, they may

- confirm the decision; or
- withdraw or vary the decision, in which case they may also take such further steps (if any) in consequence of the withdrawal or variation as they consider appropriate.

If HMRC do not give notice of their determination on the review within 45 days beginning with the day on which the review

- is required by the person (or his representative), or
- is agreed to by HMRC,

they are to be taken as having confirmed the decision.

[*FA 2003, ss 33–35*].

Appeals

An appeal can be made to a tribunal against any decision by HMRC on a review (including a case where they fail to review their decision within 45 days and it is assumed that their original decision is confirmed). The appellant must be

- the person who required the review in question;
- where the person who required that review did so as representative of another person, that other person, or
- a representative of a person falling within either of the previous two categories.

The tribunal may quash or vary a decision and may substitute its own decision for any decision so quashed.

The burden of proof as to whether a liability arises under **53.36** or **53.37** above lies with HMRC but it is for the appellant to show that the grounds on which any such appeal is brought have been established.

The provisions of *VATA 1994, s 85* (settling an appeal by agreement) and *VATA 1994, s 87* (enforcement of decisions) also apply for these purposes with the appropriate modifications. See **5.13** and **5.21 APPEALS**. Any costs awarded against an appellant on an appeal are recoverable as if they were an amount of customs duty which the appellant is required to pay.

[*FA 2003, ss 36, 37*].

Admissibility of certain statements and documents in criminal proceedings

Statements made or documents produced by, or on behalf of, a person are not inadmissible in

- any criminal proceedings against that person in respect of any offence in connection with import VAT, or
- any proceedings against that person for the recovery of any sum due from him in connection with import VAT

by reason only that any of the following matters have been drawn to his attention and that he was, or may have been, induced as a result to make the statements or produce the documents.

- HMRC have power, in relation to import VAT, to issue a demand notice by way of a civil evasion penalty rather than begin criminal proceedings.
- HMRC's practice is to take into account, in deciding whether or not to issue a demand notice, that a person has made a full confession of any dishonest conduct and has fully co-operated in an investigation.
- HMRC or, on appeal, a tribunal have power to reduce an evasion penalty and that, in deciding the extent of such a reduction, HMRC or a tribunal will have regard to the extent of the person's co-operation during the investigation.

[*FA 2003, s 38*].

Service of notices

Any notice to be given to any person for the above purposes or for the purposes of **53.36** or **53.37** above may be given by sending it by post in a letter addressed to that person (or his representative) at the last or usual residence or place of business of that person (or representative). [*FA 2003, s 39*].

Representatives

Representative, in relation to any person, means

- his personal representative
- his trustee in bankruptcy or interim or permanent trustee, and
- any receiver or liquidator appointed in relation to that person or any or his property,

together with any other person acting in a representative capacity in relation to that person.

[*FA 2003, s 24*].

Tax agents: dishonest conduct

Criminal offences

[53.39] The following criminal offences legislation came into effect on 1 April 2013 to tackle dishonest conduct by tax agents.

Concealment in connection with conduct notice

If an individual receives a conduct notice (see **53.40** below), or is told that he will (or is likely to) receive such a notice, he or another person (P) commits an offence by concealing or destroying (or arranging for such concealment or destruction) any document which could be the subject of a file access notice (see **32.17 HMRC: POWERS**). P does not commit an offence under this provision if

- he acts after the determination giving rise to the conduct notice has been set aside;
- he acts more than four years after the conduct notice is given;
- he acts without knowledge that a conduct notice has been issued;
- he acts before the issue of a conduct notice, but more than two years after the individual is informed of the likelihood of its issue;
- he acts before the issue of a conduct notice, without knowledge that the individual has been informed of the likelihood of its issue;
- he is unaware of the conduct notice.

P acts without knowledge if he is not the individual to whom the conduct notice has been given, and does not know, and could not reasonably be expected to know, that that individual has been given a conduct notice, or has been informed of the likelihood of its issue.

Concealment in connection with file access notice

A person (P) commits an offence if he

- conceals, destroys or otherwise disposes of a 'required document'; or
- arranges for such concealment, destruction or disposal.

A required document is a document which, at the time P acts

- P is required to provide by a file access notice, and either the notice has not been complied with, or it has been complied with, but HMRC have notified P that the document must be preserved; or
- P is not required to provide by file access notice, but which HMRC have informed P that he will, or is likely to, be required to produce, and no more than six months have elapsed since P was so informed.

Fine or imprisonment

A person who is guilty of either of the offences described above is liable

- on summary conviction, to a fine not exceeding the statutory maximum, and
- on conviction on indictment, to imprisonment for a term not exceeding two years or to a fine, or both.

[*FA 2012, Sch 38 paras 6, 21; SI 2013/279*].

Civil penalties

[53.40] The following civil penalties legislation came into effect on 1 April 2013 to tackle dishonest conduct by tax agents.

Failure to comply with file access notice

A person who fails to comply with a file access notice (see **32.17 HMRC: POWERS**) (which includes concealing or destroying a required document, or arranging for such concealment or destruction) is liable to a penalty of £300. If the failure continues after the notification of the penalty, he is liable of a further penalty of £60 per day. No penalty arises if HMRC have allowed further time for compliance, and the person complies within that time.

HMRC may assess the amount due by way of penalty and must notify such an assessment to the person concerned. An assessment must be made within 12 months of the date on which the person became liable to the penalty. The penalty may be enforced as if it were income tax charged in an assessment and due and payable, and must be paid within 30 days of its notification or, in the case of an appeal, within 30 days of the date of the withdrawal or determination of the appeal. A right of appeal is given in respect of a decision that a penalty is payable, or in respect of the amount of the penalty.

A person is not liable to a penalty under this provision

- in respect of anything of which he has been convicted of an offence;
- in respect of anything of which he is personally liable to a penalty under
  - *FA 2007, Sch 24* (penalties for errors);

  - *FA 2008, Sch 41* (penalties for failure to notify, etc);
  - *FA 2009, Sch 55* (penalties for failure to make a return);
- if he has a reasonable excuse for his conduct.

[*FA 2012, Sch 38 paras 22–25, 29–34; SI 2013/279*].

Dishonest conduct

An individual engages in dishonest conduct if, while acting as tax agent, he does something dishonest with a view to bringing about a loss of tax revenue, regardless of whether such a loss arises, or whether he is acting on his client's instructions. Such a loss may arise from paying less tax or claiming more tax, or by advancing a tax claim or deferring a tax payment, in a way which is not permitted by law. A dishonest action includes dishonestly omitting to do something, or advising/assisting a client to do something dishonest. The penalty for dishonest conduct is a minimum of £5,000, and a maximum of £50,000. The actual level of the penalty will depend on whether the conduct was disclosed to HMRC (and if so, whether the disclosure was prompted or unprompted, and the quality of the disclosure), and the quality of the individual's compliance with any related file access notice. HMRC may reduce the penalty below the £5,000 limit, or stay the penalty, or agree a compromise in relation to proceedings if they think it right because of 'special circumstances'. Such special circumstances do not include

- the ability to pay; or
- the fact that a loss of tax revenue from a client is balanced by an overpayment by another person (whether or not a client).

HMRC may assess the amount due by way of penalty and must notify such an assessment to the person concerned. However, such an assessment may only be made if a 'conduct notice' has been issued to the person and any ensuing appeal has been resolved in favour of HMRC. A conduct notice is a notice issued by HMRC to an individual stating that they have determined that that individual is engaging in, or has engaged in, dishonest conduct. The notice must state the grounds on which the determination is made. An assessment must be made within 12 months of the later of

- the first day on which HMRC may assess the penalty, i.e. the day following the expiry of the time limit for any appeal against the conduct notice, or the day following the resolution of any appeal; and
- day X.

Day X is

- if a loss of tax revenue is brought about by the dishonest conduct, the day immediately following (a) the end of the period in which an appeal may be brought, or (b) the resolution of such an appeal, against the assessment or the determination of the revenue lost; or
- the day on which HMRC ascertain that no loss of tax revenue has been brought about by the dishonest conduct.

The penalty may be enforced as if it were income tax charged in an assessment and due and payable, and must be paid within 30 days of its notification or, in the case of an appeal, within 30 days of the date of the withdrawal or determination of the appeal. A right of appeal is given in respect of the amount of the penalty.

A person is not liable to a penalty under this provision

- in respect of anything of which he has been convicted of an offence;
- in respect of anything of which he is personally liable to a penalty under
  - *FA 2007, Sch 24* (penalties for errors);
  - *FA 2008, Sch 41* (penalties for failure to notify, etc);
  - *FA 2009, Sch 55* (penalties for failure to make a return).

[*FA 2012, Sch 38 paras 3, 4, 26, 27, 29–34; SI 2013/279*].

Key points: penalties

[53.41] Points to consider are as follows.

- A business can avoid a penalty for late submission of VAT returns and payment of tax due etc. if it can show to HMRC that it had a reasonable excuse for its failure to comply with the regulations.
- Although the term 'reasonable excuse' is not defined in the legislation, a shortage of funds to pay tax or reliance on another person to perform a task are specifically excluded from acceptable excuses in most cases. Ill health and computer failure are more relevant reasons.
- Penalties for conduct arising before 1 April 2009 can still arise under provisions that have otherwise been repealed and replaced, but will now apply only very rarely.
- For inaccuracies in returns due for submission on or after 1 April 2009, and obligations to notify registration liability arising on or after 1 April 2010, the level of penalty charged by HMRC is based on the behaviour of the taxpayer that led to the error in question.
- If an error is classed as 'careless', it could be subject to a maximum penalty of 30% of the tax due. However, this penalty can be reduced to zero in most cases if full disclosure is made to HMRC as soon as the error is discovered.
- An error on a past VAT return that is careless can still be corrected on the next VAT return if the net amount of tax is below the error notification limit of £10,000 (or 1% of turnover up to £50,000). The disclosure made by the taxpayer to HMRC would then be in the form of a letter, i.e. to give full details of the error(s) in question.
- The end result of a careless error that is fully disclosed to HMRC will be a reduction in most cases from a potential penalty of 30% of the tax amount to zero. It is an important part of the purpose of the penalty system that HMRC want to encourage taxpayers to adjust and disclose any errors they identify.

- A complete disclosure is made to HMRC by 'telling' them about an error, 'helping' them establish how the error arose and 'giving' them full access to the records.
- If a disclosure to HMRC is 'prompted', e.g. if a taxpayer had reason to believe that HMRC were going to review the records so decided to make a disclosure in advance, then the penalty reduction will be lower than for an 'unprompted' disclosure, i.e. where no such knowledge existed.
- HMRC also has the power to suspend a penalty for up to two years, on condition that a taxpayer carries out certain actions to avoid the risk of similar errors occurring again in the future.
- The default surcharge system is intended to penalise a business that submits its VAT returns or pays the tax on those returns after the due date. If a VAT return is a nil return or repayment return, then a default will be recorded but there will be no actual surcharge imposed by HMRC.
- Where, exceptionally, a trader makes returns using a paper system, a return with cheque payment must be submitted to HMRC so that the cheque has cleared HMRC's bank account by the due date of the return. This means an extra three working days must be allowed for the clearance procedure.
- The maximum default surcharge that can be imposed by HMRC equates to 15% of the outstanding tax due on the payment date.
- A business must submit returns and pay tax on time for a complete twelve-month period in order to come out of the default surcharge system. If it has done so it can again incur a further default, with only a new surcharge liability notice being issued as opposed to an actual surcharge penalty.

54

Pension Schemes

Introduction to pension schemes

[54.1] A funded pension scheme is a pension scheme in which the employers' and employees' contributions are vested in separate trustees, who may be individuals or corporate bodies. The pension scheme is normally separate and distinct from the employer's business. The VAT provisions in **54.2, 54.3** and **54.4** below apply to such schemes but not to

(a) schemes where the employer makes provision for the payment of pensions by a segregated reserve fund in the balance sheet, represented by specific assets;

(b) unfunded pension schemes where the employer does not set aside funds for this purpose; or

(c) insurance-based schemes where retirement benefits are secured through insurance policies.

The normal VAT rules apply to schemes within (*a*)–(*c*) above.

(VAT Notice 700/17/12, paras 1.2, 1.4).

Current HMRC policy

[54.2] During 2014 and 2015 HMRC reviewed their policy regarding the recovery of VAT on pension fund costs and the VAT treatment of pension fund management services. There were a number of developments which were reflected in HMRC Brief 6/14 and HMRC Brief 22/14 before the publication of HMRC Brief 43/14 and HMRC Brief 44/14 on 25 November 2014. HMRC provided further information regarding its policy on deduction of VAT on pension fund management costs in HMRC Brief 8/15 and HMRC Brief 17/15.

HMRC's previous policy, and developments to that policy as reflected in HMRC Brief 6/14 and HMRC 22/14, is dealt with in **54.3** and **54.4** below and HMRC accept that some businesses may be entitled to a VAT refund. There is a transitional period during which the 30/70 split treatment described at **54.3** below can continue to apply in situations where the pension scheme receives the services. This was originally set as expiring on 31 December 2015, but was extended to 31 December 2016 by HMRC Brief 17/15, and then to 31 December 2017 by HMRC Brief 14/16. HMRC say 'It's taking longer than expected to reconcile the court decision with pension and financial service regulations, accounting rules and emerging case law'. They warn that that adopting alternative structures to comply with the VAT requirements could have wider implications, in particular in respect of regulatory requirements and corporation tax deductions. Towards the end of the transitional period they will review the position and consider the need for a further extension if necessary.

(HMRC Brief 14/16).

Latest position on defined benefit pension schemes

HMRC have finally published their long awaited guidance on the VAT treatment of costs associated with defined benefit pension schemes. Significantly HMRC have stated that employers with a defined benefit scheme (final salary scheme) are allowed to continue to use the historic concession called the 70:30 split going forward. This concession is explained below, but in summary, enables employers to recover 30% of the VAT incurred. This concession was to be removed with effect from 31 December 2017.

However it is important to note that alternative VAT recovery options that were outlined in previous publications issued by HMRC (see below) have been added to the final guidance and can be used instead of the 70:30 split if this is more appropriate.

HMRC's guidance does state that they are aware that there may still be regulatory and corporate tax recoverability issues associated with a tripartite arrangement and the profit and loss account may be impacted where the employer picks up additional costs, even where the pension fund contributions can be reduced by an equivalent amount. It is clearly important that the business weighs up the pros and cons of each option in order to ensure that the most tax efficient pension scheme is operated.

See also, *United Biscuits (Pension Trustees) Ltd v HMRC* [2017] EWHC 2895 (Ch), where the High Court has released its judgment regarding the VAT liability of pension fund management services supplied to defined benefit schemes provided by non-insurers. In this case, the trustees incurred VAT on the provision of the pension fund management services. The taxpayer considered that this was incorrect arguing that there was a breach of fiscal neutrality as only regulated insurers currently benefit from the exemption, and that under EU law, the services provided by non-insurers should also have been exempt from VAT during the relevant periods. The High Court has held that these services are liable to VAT.

Investment fund activities provided by a regulated insurance company

In HMRC Brief 3/17, HMRC announced that pension fund management services provided by an insurer to a defined benefit pension fund will be subject to VAT with effect from 1 April 2019. A summary of the Brief has been provided below.

HMRC have historically allowed pension fund management services provided by regulated insurance companies to be exempt from VAT. However, following the decision in *Card Protection Plan* (C-349/96) (CPP), the law was amended to remove any link between the insurance company's regulated status and their ability to exempt supplies from VAT. The CJEU made it clear when it released its decision that the EU insurance exemption is only applicable to the underwriting of the risk, and does not apply to other activities undertaken by the insurance company. The UK, however, continued to allow insurance companies to exempt supplies of pension fund management services and kept the issue under review while it awaited the outcome of the EU Commission review of VAT and financial services, which was discontinued in 2016.

HMRC now accept that pension funds that have all of the characteristics required of a Special Investment Fund (SIF) should be able to take advantage of the exemption for fund management services. However, any fund that does not have the characteristics of a SIF cannot take advantage of the fund management exemption.

HMRC state that it is necessary for insurance companies to undertake a review to determine whether the current arrangements in place qualify as a SIF. The fund management services provided to defined contribution pension schemes will be included within the scope of the exemption; however, it is unlikely that defined benefit schemes would be included under the revised policy.

If management of the scheme now falls outside the exemption, the insurance company will need to look at any systems changes that will be required in order to ensure that they correctly account for VAT from 1 April 2019. Insurance companies will also need to review their contractual arrangements to confirm whether they can charge VAT as an additional amount on the services provided. Insurance companies may also wish to assess the commercial ramifications of charging VAT, as their customers may not be in a position to recover this VAT.

Recovery of VAT on pension fund costs

Previous HMRC policy distinguished between costs incurred on the setting up and day-to-day administration of a pension scheme and costs incurred on the management of its assets. Following the decision in *Fiscale Eenheid PPG Holdings BV cs te Hoogezand v Inspecteur van de Belastingdienst/Noord/Kantoor Groningen*, *ECJ Case C-26/12*, [2014] STC 175 (TVC 22.464), HMRC now accept that there are no grounds to differentiate between the administration of a pension scheme and the management of its assets.

When deciding whether VAT on pension fund management services is deductible by an employer it is necessary to determine whether the services are supplied to the employer. In the case of defined benefit pension schemes there are normally two potential recipients of the services, (1) the employer and (2) the pension scheme through its trustees and a useful starting point is to examine the agreements between the parties. In this context, although the fact that a party pays for the services is not decisive, payment is an important indicator, particularly in circumstances where both the employer and the pension scheme use the services.

HMRC Brief 43/14 explains that HMRC will not accept that VAT incurred in relation to a pension scheme is deductible by an employer unless there is contemporaneous evidence that the services are provided to the employer, that the employer is a party to the contract for those services, and has paid for them. For some employers, directly contracting for pension fund management services can be difficult due to the regulatory environment in which they operate. Use is therefore made of tripartite contracts between (1) the supplier of pension fund management services, (2) the pension scheme trustees, and (3) the employer.

HMRC Brief 8/15 explains that tripartite contracts, in the context of defined benefit pension schemes where the regulatory regime requires the scheme to be established under a trust and it is the employer that ultimately bears the financial risks and benefits associated with the performance of the scheme, can be used to demonstrate that the employer is the recipient of the pension fund management services. In order for an employer to be able to deduct VAT on defined benefit pension fund management services provided under a tripartite contract, the contract should evidence, as a minimum, that:

- the service provider makes its supplies to the employer (albeit that the contract may recognise that, in the particular regulatory context in which DB schemes operate, the service provider may be appointed by, or on behalf of, the pension scheme trustees);
- the employer directly pays for the services that are supplied under the contract;
- the service provider will pursue the employer for payment and only in circumstances where the employer is unlikely to pay (for example, because it has gone into administration) will it recover its fees from the scheme's funds or the pension scheme trustees;
- both the employer and the pension scheme trustees are entitled to seek legal redress in the event of breach of contract, albeit that the liability of the service provider need not be any greater than if the contract was with the pension scheme trustees alone and any restitution, indemnity or settlement payments for which the service provider becomes liable may be payable in whole to the pension scheme trustees for the benefit of the pension scheme (for example in circumstances where the scheme is not fully funded);
- the service provider will provide fund performance reports to the employer on request (subject to the pension scheme trustees being able to stipulate that reports are withheld, for example where there could be a conflict of interest); and
- the employer is entitled to terminate the contract, although that may be subject to a condition that they should not do so without the pension scheme trustees' prior written consent (this can be in addition to any right that the pension scheme trustees may have to terminate the contract unilaterally).

In addition to the above, evidence that the pension scheme trustees agree that it is the employer who is entitled to deduct any VAT incurred on the services will reduce the potential for disputes.

For an employer to be able to deduct any VAT, it will be necessary for them to be issued with a valid VAT invoice for the full cost of the supply and to pay the service provider directly for the full cost of the services. HMRC do not accept that an equivalent increase in contributions to the fund or any payment that is made by, or through, the fund constitutes payment by the employer.

If an employer recharges the net cost of the pension fund management services to the pension scheme, that recharge is consideration for an onward taxable supply and VAT is due accordingly. This amount is potentially deductible by the pension scheme to the extent that the pension scheme is engaged in taxable business activities.

Any non-business activities and exempt supplies need to be taken into account when calculating how much VAT can be deducted.

Pension scheme trustees and employers will normally regularly review the level of contributions required by the employer into the scheme to ensure that the scheme is able to meet the forecast pension benefit commitments. HMRC accept that if adjustments are made to these contributions, to take account of the fact that it is the employer rather than the scheme that is paying for certain costs, that does not constitute consideration for a supply by the employer to the pension fund, provided that there is no specific reduction equal to the actual costs that were incurred in any given period.

Where a pension fund covers pension arrangements for employees of companies within a VAT group as well as employees outside a VAT group registration, each employer may treat as input tax only that proportion of VAT incurred that is attributable to his own employees. Where the person supplying the services to the fund issues a single invoice, one of the participating employers (or, in the case of entirely separate employers, the trustees) may act in the capacity of paymaster and claim all the VAT incurred for the eligible services, issuing a VAT invoice to each of the other employers for their share of the costs and VAT thereon. The other employers can then treat that VAT as their input tax.

Where a pension scheme provides pensions for employees of companies within a VAT group as well as employees outside a VAT group registration, VAT incurred should be apportioned between that attributable to employees within the VAT group (allowable) and outside the group (non-allowable). Alternatively, the representative member of the VAT group may elect to act in the capacity of paymaster and claim all the VAT incurred for the eligible services, issuing a VAT invoice to each of the other employers for their share of the costs and VAT thereon. The other employers can then treat the relevant VAT as their input tax.

VAT incurred by group members is recoverable by the representative member to the extent that it is attributable to supplies made to persons outside the group which carry the right to deduct input tax. Any non-business and exempt supplies made by the employer or trustee must be taken into account when considering VAT recovery. See *BOC International Ltd* [1982] VATTR 84 (TVC 54.7).

All members of a group registration are jointly and severally liable for VAT due from the representative member and in the event of that member being unable to meet the VAT debt of the group, as a general rule each member will be liable for the amount of the debt arising during the period that it was a member of the group. However, where corporate trustees are included in a group registration, HMRC have been advised that this liability does not extend to the assets of any trust (e.g. a pension fund) of which a corporate trustee is the trustee, except to the extent that the group VAT debt is attributable in whole or part to the administration of the trust.

If an employer receives a taxable supply of administration and investment management services and recharges them to the pension scheme the recharge is consideration for an onward taxable supply and VAT is due accordingly. As noted below, the VAT is potentially deductible by the trustees of the pension scheme.

Where the trustees of a pension scheme make taxable supplies, they may be required to register for VAT. See **60 REGISTRATION** for details. If registered, the trustees can treat VAT on goods and services used for the purposes of their business activities as input tax. Recovery of input tax may be restricted under the partial exemption (**50 PARTIAL EXEMPTION**) rules.

A pension scheme trustee could contract with an employer to supply them with the service of running the pension scheme on the employer's behalf. Any VAT correctly charged by a trustee to an employer will be deductible by the employer to the extent that it relates to the taxable supplies of the employer. In these circumstances any VAT a trustee incurs on administration and other general pension scheme related services that it uses in order to make the onward taxable supply to the employer will be deductible in full.

Where the sole trustee of a pension fund is a corporate body, it may be possible for that trustee to form part of a VAT group registration with the employer. See **28.2** and **28.3 GROUPS OF COMPANIES** for eligibility and application for group treatment. If a corporate trustee becomes such a member, any business supplies made by the trustee, including dealing in the assets of the fund, are treated as being made by the representative member. Tax incurred on supplies to the trustee can be treated as received by the representative member.

The cost of administration and other general scheme related services that do not have a direct and immediate link to the management of a pension scheme's assets and therefore the scheme's investment activities, will be overhead costs of the VAT group and will be deductible in accordance with the activities of the group as a whole.

Where a VAT group incurs VAT on asset management services this will have a direct and immediate link to the investment activities, and may also have a direct and immediate link to supplies made by the employer, providing the costs incurred are used by the employer to make those supplies. If asset management services are put to dual use any VAT deduction in respect of the VAT incurred on the services will need to reflect this.

(HMRC Briefs 8/15 and 17/15, reissued 14 September 2016).

VAT on pension fund management services

Previous HMRC policy was that no pension fund could benefit from the VAT exemption for SIFs (see **24.20 FINANCIAL SERVICES**). Following the decision in *ATP Pension Services A/S v Skatteministeriet, ECJ Case C–464/12, 12 De-*

cember 2013 (TVC 22.417) HMRC now accept that pension funds that have all of the following characteristics are SIFS for the purposes of the fund management exemption so that the services of managing and administering those funds should be, and always should have been, exempt from VAT:

- they are solely funded (whether directly or indirectly) by persons to whom the retirement benefit is to be paid (ie the pension customers);
- the pension customers bear the investment risk;
- the fund contains the pooled contributions of several pension customers;
- the risk borne by the pension customers is spread over a range of securities.

In addition to funds that contain the pooled assets of defined contribution occupational pension schemes, HMRC accept that funds that contain the pooled assets of personal pension schemes and that have all of the above characteristics will also fall within the VAT exemption for fund management services.

A personal pension fund will not pool assets if an individual investor exercises an option to give directions as to how their contributions are invested (e.g. in specific assets and/or funds external to the pension fund) that overrides the investment powers of the trustee/pension provider. HMRC do, however, accept that exemption could still apply to the fund where the costs of managing the assets of those investors who give such directions (i.e. the non-pooled assets) can be easily identified and excluded from exemption.

In respect of pension schemes that pay members' contributions into a number of different funds, exemption will only apply to services supplied in connection with funds that possess the characteristics outlined above. Where the contributions of a number of schemes are paid into a single fund, it will be necessary to consider whether that fund as a whole possesses all the characteristics set out above. Both such arrangements may be found in respect of hybrid pension schemes but will also apply in other circumstances.

Where investment management or administration services are supplied to a scheme that has a number of funds, some that possess the characteristics of a SIF and others that do not, to determine the correct VAT treatment of the services in question it will be necessary to apply the rules on single/multiple supplies (see **65.6 SUPPLY: GENERAL**).

Only fund management and administration services that are integral (i.e. specific and essential) to the operation of a pension fund will qualify for exemption and exemption will only apply to charges made by third parties for services provided in connection with the management or administration of the contributions held in the pension fund itself. Exemption will not apply to services provided in connection with any non-pension funds in which the contributions paid into the pension funds may have been invested; although the management of such funds may qualify for exemption on the basis that the fund is a SIF in its own right (e.g. an Authorised Unit Trust). The fact that some or all of the costs of managing non-pension funds is being borne by a qualifying pension fund (and ultimately by pension customers) will not bring services supplied in connection with non-qualifying investment funds, and charged to or on to pensions, within the fund management exemption.

(HMRC Brief 43/14; HMRC Brief 44/14; HMRC Brief 8/15).

Employers

Input tax deductible

[54.3] The *management* of a pension fund for own employees (but not normally the business activities of the pension fund) is part of an employer's business. A VAT-registered employer can therefore deduct input tax incurred in setting up the fund and on its day-to-day management. This applies even where the responsibility for the general management of the scheme rests with the trustees or the trustees pay for the services provided. HMRC give the following examples of expenses on which input tax may be reclaimed.

- Making of arrangements for setting up the pension fund
- Management of the scheme (i.e. collection of contributions and payment of pensions)
- Advice on a review of the scheme and implementing any changes
- Accountancy and audit services relating to the management of the scheme (e.g. preparation of annual accounts)
- Actuarial valuations of the assets of the fund
- Actuarial advice in connection with the fund's administration
- Providing general statistics in connection with the performance of the fund's investments, properties, etc.
- Legal instructions and general legal advice including drafting of Trust deeds insofar as they relate to the management of the scheme

To claim input tax, the employer must hold a VAT invoice made out in his name. Where the supplies are paid for by the trustees on behalf of the employer, the employer should arrange for the invoice to be issued in his name.

In a case concerning an employer's entitlement to deduct VAT paid on services relating to the administration and management of a defined benefit pension scheme, *Fiscale Eenheid PPG Holdings BV cs te Hoogezand v Inspecteur van de Belastingdienst/Noord/Kantoor Groningen, ECJ Case C–26/12*, [2014] STC 175 (TVC 22.464), the CJEU held that a taxable person who has set up a pension fund in the form of a legally and fiscally separate entity in order to safeguard the pension rights of its employees and former employees is entitled to deduct the VAT paid on services relating to the management and operation of the pension fund provided that the existence of a direct and immediate link is apparent from all the circumstances of the transactions in question.

Whether there is a direct and immediate link will depend on whether the cost of the input services is incorporated in the price of the supplies made by the business. A cost may either be incorporated in the price of specific supplies or groups of supplies, or be part of its general costs and incorporated in the price of all the supplies made by the business. If a cost has a direct and immediate link to specific supplies or groups of supplies, then it cannot also be part of its general costs.

In respect of specific costs of investment management, these will have a direct and immediate link to the supplies of the investments themselves. For example, the costs of managing a property within a pension fund will have a direct and immediate link to the rental income derived from the property. They cannot therefore be general costs of the employer. A similar analysis can be applied to the financial investments. However, where the services received go further than the management of the investments, they may be general costs. Therefore, provided that the supply is received by the employer, the VAT incurred will potentially be deductible by the employer.

Following the CJEU decision in *Fiscale Eenheid PPG Holdings BV cs te Hoogezand v Inspecteur van de Belastingdienst/Noord/Kantoor Groningen, ECJ Case C–26/12*, [2014] STC 175 (TVC 22.464), HMRC issued HMRC Brief 6/14 on 3 February 2014. The Brief explains that there are circumstances where employers may be able to claim input tax in relation to pension funds where they could not previously and confirms that businesses are entitled, but not obliged, to claim a refund of previously under-claimed input tax, subject to the normal four-year cap.

(HMRC Brief 6/14).

Input tax not deductible

Except where the employer is the sole trustee of his pension scheme (see below), the pension fund itself is not part of the employer's business activities. Any VAT incurred on supplies relating to the *investment* activities carried on by the trustees (e.g. making investments, acquiring property and collecting rents) is not input tax of the employer even if he pays for such expenses. HMRC give the following examples of services on which employers cannot claim input tax.

- Advice in connection with making investments
- Brokerage charges
- Rent and service charge collection for property holdings
- Producing records and accounts in connection with property purchases, lettings and disposals, investments, etc.
- Trustees' services (i.e. services of a professional trustee in managing the assets of the fund)
- Legal fees paid on behalf of representative beneficiaries in connection with changes in pension fund arrangements
- Custodian charges

For cases concerning the recoverability of input tax by employers, see *Linotype & Machinery Ltd* (VTD 594) (TVC 54.2), *Manchester Ship Canal Co v C & E Commrs*, QB [1982] STC 351 (TVC 54.6) and *Ultimate Advisory Services Ltd* (VTD 9523) (TVC 41.47), *Fiscale Eenheid PPG Holdings BV cs te Hoogezand v Inspecteur van de Belastingdienst/Noord/Kantoor Groningen, ECJ Case C–26/12*, [2014] STC 175 (TVC 22.464).

Management of the pension scheme

(a) *Services performed by the employer*. Where an employer uses own staff to manage the pension fund and these services are provided free of charge, there is no supply for VAT purposes. See *National Coal Board v C & E Commrs*, QB [1982] STC 863 (TVC 54.12). The employer's entitlement to claim input tax on office overhead expenses is not affected.

If an employer is reimbursed by the trustees (or specifically charges them) for costs incurred in managing the pension scheme and the services fall within those on which input tax is deductible (see above), there is no need to account for output tax on the supply to the trustees. However, if such arrangements apply to services for investment advice or other services connected with the pension fund's own business activities, the employer is making a taxable supply to the trustees and must account for output tax.

(b) *Services performed by third parties.* Where a third party (e.g. a fund manager, property manager or professional trustee) is used to manage a pension scheme and their charges cover both general management services to the employer (input tax deductible) and investment services to the trustees (input tax non-deductible) the input tax must be apportioned.

Normally, this apportionment is made by the supplier. Where the supplier only issues one invoice for a composite supply, HMRC used to generally accept that the employer could treat 30% of the VAT charged as his input tax, with the remaining 70% being proper to the fund (the '30/70 split'). If the employer did not consider that 30% was a fair proportion of the costs attributed to management services they could provide evidence to HMRC in support of this view. HMRC Brief 06/14, issued on 3 February 2014, announced a change of HMRC policy regarding the recovery of input tax in relation to the management of pension funds, including an end to HMRC's general acceptance of the 30/70 split. However, the Brief confirmed that during a transitional period of six months from 3 February 2014, the pension fund and the employer may continue to agree to a 70/30 split in accordance with terms set out in paragraph 2.7 of VAT Notice 700/17/12. (HMRC Brief 06/14). The transitional period of six months referred to in HMRC Brief 06/14 was then extended when HMRC issued HMRC Brief 22/14 on 27 May 2014. On 26 October 2015 HMRC issued HMRC Brief 17/15, which included an announcement that the transitional period would be extended until 31 December 2016, providing the employer and the pension scheme trustees agree the same treatment.

HMRC Brief 22/14 explained that HMRC are reviewing the VAT treatment of pension scheme administration and fund management services to take account of the decisions in *Fiscale Eenheid PPG Holdings BV cs te Hoogezand v Inspecteur van de Belastingdienst/Noord/Kantoor Groningen, ECJ Case C–26/12,* [2014] STC 175 (TVC 22.464) (see above) and in *ATP Pension Services A/S v Skatteministeriet, ECJ Case C–464/12, 12 December 2013* (TVC 22.417) (see below). In *ATP Pension Services A/S v Skatteministeriet, ECJ Case C–464/12, 12 December 2013* (TVC 22.417) the CJEU held that certain services supplied by ATP Pension Services A/S (ATP) to Danish defined contribution pension schemes qualified for exemption under *EC Sixth Directive, Art 13B(d)(6)* on the basis that the schemes were special investment funds (see **24.20 FINANCIAL SERVICES**). The CJEU also ruled that certain services which involved the movement of payments between parties qualified for exemption under *EC Sixth Directive, Art 13B(d)(3)*. These exemptions are now dealt with under *Directive 2006/112/EC, Art 135(1)(g)* and *Art 135(1)(d)* respectively.

Pensions provided for employees of more than one company

Where a pension fund covers pension arrangements for employees of several companies which are not in the same VAT group registration, each employer may treat as input tax only that proportion of VAT incurred on the management of the fund that is attributable to his own employees. Where the person supplying the management services to the fund issues a single invoice, one of the participating employers (or, in the case of entirely separate employers, the trustees) may act in the capacity of paymaster and claim all the VAT incurred for the eligible services, issuing a VAT invoice to each of the other employers for their share of the costs and VAT thereon. The other employers can then treat that VAT as their input tax.

Cessation of business by employer

If an employer ceases business, the trustees of any continuing pension scheme who are VAT-registered may treat VAT incurred on services connected with the management of the scheme as their input tax (subject to the normal rules). If this situation arises, the trustees should inform HMRC.

Where a professional trustee is appointed to run a pension scheme, e.g. where the sponsoring employer ceases to exist, VAT incurred on the management of the pension fund can only be recovered by the trustee insofar as it is a clear cost component of an onward supply of that management of the pension fund.

(VAT Notice 700/17/12, paras 2.1–2.9; Business Brief 19/05).

Trustees

[54.4] Where the trustees of a pension fund make taxable supplies, they may be required to register for VAT. See **60 REGISTRATION** for details. If registered, the trustees can treat VAT on goods and services used for the purposes of their business activities as input tax. However, except where the employer has ceased to be in business (see **54.3** above) VAT on supplies for the purposes of the management of the pension scheme is not input tax since these supplies are regarded as the responsibility of the employer. Recovery of input tax may also be restricted under the **50 PARTIAL EXEMPTION** rules.

Corporate trustee in a VAT group registration

Where the sole trustee of a pension fund is a corporate body, it may be possible for that trustee to form part of a VAT group registration with the employer. See **28.2** and **28.3 GROUPS OF COMPANIES** for eligibility and application for group treatment. If a corporate trustee becomes such a member, any business supplies made by the trustee, including dealing in the assets of the fund, are treated as being made by the representative member. Tax incurred on supplies to the trustee can be treated as received by the representative member.

Where the fund provides pensions for employees of companies outside the VAT group registration, any VAT incurred in respect of the *management* of the scheme for those companies is not for the purposes of the representative member's business and not allowable. VAT must therefore be apportioned between that attributable to employees within the VAT group (allowable) and outside the group (non-allowable). Alternatively, the representative member may elect to use the paymaster arrangements. See **54.3** above under *Pensions provided for employees of more than one company*.

VAT incurred by group members is recoverable by the representative member to the extent that it is attributable to supplies made to persons outside the group which carry the right to deduct input tax. Any non-business and exempt supplies made by the employer or trustee must be taken into account when considering VAT recovery. See *BOC International Ltd* [1982] VATTR 84 (TVC 54.7).

All members of a group registration are jointly and severally liable for VAT due from the representative member and in the event of that member being unable to meet the VAT debt of the group, as a general rule each member will be liable for the amount of the debt arising during the period that it was a member of the group. However, where corporate trustees are included in a group registration, HMRC have been advised that this liability does not extend to the assets of any trust (e.g. a pension fund) of which the corporate trustee is the trustee, except to the extent that the group VAT debt is attributable in whole or part to the administration of the trust.

Fund managers, property managers, professional trustees, etc.

Fund managers, property managers, professional trustees, etc. may provide

- supplies to the employer in connection with the management of the scheme; and
- supplies to the trustees in connection with their business activities.

It is important to distinguish between the various kinds of services supplied so that separate VAT invoices can be issued to the employer and the trustees for input tax recovery purposes. If services cannot be segregated, HMRC were prepared to allow the total value of services to be divided in the ratio of 30% to the employer and 70% to the trustees. Any other apportionment would only be agreed to by HMRC if detailed information in support of the split is provided. HMRC Brief 6/14, issued on 3 February 2014, announced a change of HMRC policy regarding the recovery of input tax in relation to the management of pension funds. HMRC Brief 22/14 explained that HMRC are reviewing the VAT treatment of pension scheme administration and fund management services and that further guidance would be issued in the autumn of 2014. See **54.2** above.

(VAT Notice 700/17/12, paras 3.1–3.3, 4.1–4.3; HMRC Brief 6/14; HMRC Brief 22/14).

Key points: pension schemes

[54.5] Points to consider are as follows.

- The VAT treatment of pension funds is currently under review, with a transitional period running until 31 December 2017 in which trustees and employers can operate HMRC's traditional approach to deduction of input tax, or can apply the principles of recent CJEU decisions that indicate a more generous deduction may be due.
- Subject to conditions an employer can claim input tax on the costs of managing a pension fund, as a normal cost of its business. The rules of partial exemption would apply, however, so if the employer's business is partly exempt, then some of the input tax would be blocked.
- It is possible that a pension fund might need to become VAT-registered itself if, for example, it owns commercial property with option to tax issues to consider. The VAT procedures in such cases are the same as for any other commercial business.

55

Printed Matter, etc.

Cross-references. See **34.15**(7) **IMPORTS** for certain printed matter which may be imported free of VAT from a country outside the EU.

De Voil Indirect Tax Service. See V4.273.

Introduction to printed matter, etc.

[55.1] To determine the liability for any supply involving printed or similar matter, it is helpful to consider the following questions.

(a) Is a complete item of printed or similar matter being supplied?
(b) Is the printed matter being supplied in its own right?

If satisfied that the answers to both of these questions are 'yes', then see **55.2** to **55.13** below for categories of printed matter which can be zero-rated. Other items are normally standard-rated (see **55.14** below).

If the answer to (*a*) is 'no' (or if unsure), consider **55.19** below for guidance on the processes leading to the production of printed matter.

If the answer to (*b*) is 'no' (or if unsure), see **55.15** to **55.18** below for printed matter supplied with other services and goods.

Zero-rated printed matter

[55.2] Supplies of the following are zero-rated.

- Books and booklets (see **55.3** below).
- Brochures and pamphlets (see **55.4** below).
- Leaflets (see **55.5** below).
- Newspapers (see **55.6** below).
- Journals and periodicals (see **55.7** below).
- Children's picture books and painting books (see **55.8** below).
- Music (printed, duplicated or manuscript) (see **55.9** below).
- Maps, charts and topographical plans (see **55.10** below).
- Covers, cases and other articles supplied with any of the above items and not separately accounted for (see **55.11** below).

Included is the letting on hire or loan of, or the supply of a part interest in, any of the above items. See **55.12** below.

Not included are plans or drawings for industrial, architectural, engineering, commercial or similar purposes.

Not included is a supply of goods connected with a supply of services made by a different supplier. The two supplies are connected if, had they been made by a single supplier, they would have been treated as a single standard-rated, reduced-rated or exempt supply of services. For HMRC's interpretation of this provision see 'VAT zero rating: splitting of supplies–comments on draft legislation' on the HMRC website. [*FA 2011, s 75*].

[*VATA 1994, Sch 8 Group 3*].

The legislation does not define any of the above items. HMRC treat the words in *Group 3* as being used in their ordinary, everyday sense. This means they are restricted to goods produced on paper and similar materials such as card (but see **55.4** below). Most items qualifying for the zero-rating will be products of the printing industry (including items printed in Braille), but goods which are photocopied, typed or hand-written may, in some cases, also qualify.

Goods containing text in other formats (e.g. audio or video cassettes or CD Rom) are standard-rated. This includes the storage and distribution of text by fax, e-mail, microfiche, or any similar process. Transcripts or print-outs made of such information are zero-rated if they are supplied in the form of books, booklets, brochures, pamphlets or leaflets within *Group 3*.

Examples of common zero-rated items

The following is a list of items which HMRC commonly regard as qualifying for zero-rating. A list of items they would normally treat as standard-rated is reproduced at **55.14** below. However, liability of any specific item should not be determined from these lists only and reference should be made to the appropriate paragraph of the text.

- Accounts (fully printed)
- Advertising leaflets (standard-rated when supplied with direct marketing services – see **55.17**(9))

- Agendas (fully printed)
- Almanacs
- Amendments (loose leaf)
- Annuals
- Antique books and maps
- Articles of association (complete in booklet form)
- Astronomical charts
- Atlases
- Autograph books (completed)
- Bibliographies
- Bills of quantity (completed)
- Booklets
- Books
- Brochures
- Bulletins
- Catalogues
- Charts (geographical or topographical)
- Circulars
- Colouring books (children's)
- Comics
- Company accounts and reports
- Crossword books
- Diaries (completed)
- Dictionaries
- Directories (completed)
- Election addresses
- Encyclopaedias
- Football programmes
- Geological maps
- Handbills
- Holiday and tourist guides
- Hydrographical charts
- Hymn books
- Instruction manuals
- Journals
- Leaflets
- Magazines
- Mail order catalogues
- Manuals
- Maps
- Memorandum of association (complete in booklet form)
- Missals
- Monographs
- Music
- Music scores
- Newspapers
- Orders of service
- Painting books (children's)
- Pamphlets
- Periodicals

- Picture books
- Poster magazines (see **55.7** below)
- Prayer books
- Price lists (fully printed leaflets or brochures)
- Programmes
- Rag books (children's)
- Recipe books
- Road maps
- Scrap books (completed)
- Ships' logs (completed)
- Sports programmes
- Staff journals
- Text books
- Theses
- Timetables (in book or leaflet form)
- Topographical plans
- Tracts
- Trade catalogues
- Trade directories
- Travel brochures

(VAT Notice 701/10/16, paras 2, 8).

Books and booklets

[55.3] The supply of books and booklets is zero-rated. [*VATA 1994, Sch 8 Group 3 Item 1*].

A book or booklet normally consists of text or illustrations, bound in a cover stiffer than its pages. It may be printed in any language or characters (e.g. Braille or shorthand), photocopied, typed or hand-written. Zero-rated items include:

- Literary works.
- Reference books.
- Directories and catalogues.
- Antique books.
- Collections of letters or documents permanently bound in covers.
- Loose-leaf books, manuals or instructions, whether complete with their binder or not.
- Amendments to zero-rated loose-leaf books, even if issued separately.
- School work books and other educational texts in question and answer format (because the spaces provided for the insertion of answers are incidental to the essential character of the book or booklet).
- Exam papers in question and answer format provided they qualify as books or booklets (or as brochures, pamphlets or leaflets under **55.4** or **55.5** below).
- Photobooks, produced by processing digital photographs, where they satisfy the characteristics for the appearance of a book or booklet (see below).

Supplies of the following are standard-rated.

- Parts of books, unbound pages and separate illustrations.
- Books of plans or drawings for industrial, architectural, engineering, commercial or similar purposes (which are specifically excluded from zero-rating by *VATA 1994, Sch 8 Group 3, Note (a)*).
- Picture card and stamp albums, unless they contain a substantial amount of reading matter which is complete in itself, and no more than 25% of the album is set aside for the mounting of cards and stamps.
- Completed stamp albums.
- Products that are essentially stationery items (e.g. diaries and address books). Completed diaries can be zero-rated. This view was upheld in *C & E Commrs v Colour Offset Ltd*, QB 1994, [1995] STC 85 (TVC 5.47) which confirmed that 'book' should be given its ordinary meaning ie as having the minimum characteristics of something to be read or looked at. A filled-in diary of historic or literary interest might be a book but a blank diary was not a book in the ordinary sense. Neither was an address book simply because its name included the word 'book'. Compare, however, *Scholastic Publications Ltd* [1996] Lexis Citation 839 (TVC 5.14) where a children's publication containing a year planner and address section was held to be zero-rated as the remaining pages (more than 50% overall) were quizzes and jokes 'designed to be read as entertainment'.

Books published in instalments

In continuity or part-work publishing, a product is supplied in parts over varying periods but builds up into a greater whole (i.e. a loose-leaf book). The parts may be issued *either* in magazine format with the pages stapled together *or* as a collection of loose pages, possibly wrapped in clear plastic or lightly gummed together, which are often not consecutive but designed to be separated and placed in the appropriate section of a binder. Unless a loose-leaf, when viewed independently, is a book at the time of supply, it is not strictly entitled to zero-rating. By concession, if at that time an instalment is part of a larger finite work which itself would fall to be zero-rated as a book, then the individual component parts may also be zero-rated where they are supplied either direct by the publisher or through a distribution chain to the final consumer. (VAT Notice 48, ESC 3.15).

Card-based publications

By way of further concession, card-based boxed publications, even though not bound or held together other than in or by their container, are treated for VAT purposes as a book provided they have all the other characteristics of a book. (VAT Notice 48, ESC 3.15).

(VAT Notice 701/10/16, paras 3.1, 4.4).

Photo books

In *Harrier LLC* (TC01562) (TVC 5.26) Harrier provided customers with photo books that comprised a number of photographs taken and uploaded by the customer. The tribunal decided that the photo books were zero-rated. Following that decision, HMRC accept that a photo book which possesses, as a minimum, several pages, a cover stiffer than its pages and is bound, qualifies for zero-rating as a book. The book must also be designed to be read or looked at. However, HMRC would not see a photo book as falling within the zero rate if either

- the photo book's pages have the appearance and quality of individual photographic prints; or
- the photo book that is held out for sale is capable of being dismantled, with individual pages that are removable or where individual pages can be easily removed without damaging the binding (e.g. spiral binding).

This approach does not apply where there is a predominate supply of services such as those where the customer is paying for and receiving photographic services that then result in the production of a 'book', e.g. a wedding package consisting of making arrangements for photography, taking and viewing of photographs and a wedding book displaying a selection of photographs. In such a case HMRC consider that the photographic service is the dominant supply and the wedding book is ancillary to the supply of the services, so that there is a single supply of standard-rated services.

(HMRC Brief 4/12).

Brochures and pamphlets

[55.4] The supply of brochures and pamphlets is zero-rated. [*VATA 1994, Sch 8 Group 3 Item 1*].

'Brochure' and 'pamphlet' are not defined in law and whether a particular product qualifies as such is a matter of fact and impression. HMRC usually require the item to have the following physical characteristics.

- A brochure usually consists of several sheets of reading matter fastened or folded together (although not necessarily bound in a cover). It usually contains advertising material in the form of text or illustrations.
- A pamphlet is similar but usually comprises material of a political, social or intellectual nature.

See also the definition given by the chairman in *Schusman* (VTD 11835) (TVC 5.65).

Single sheet and 'wallet' type brochures

A brochure designed with a flap may be zero-rated provided it

- conveys information;
- contains a substantial amount of text, with some indication of contents or the issuing organisation;
- is not primarily designed to hold other items; and
- is supplied complete.

Items with areas for completion

An item which might otherwise be considered to be a brochure or pamphlet may not be zero-rated if it is primarily intended for completion or detachment. This distinguishes a brochure or pamphlet from a standard-rated form. HMRC accept that items are not primarily intended for completion or detachment if 25% or less of their total area consists of

- areas which are blank and available for completion; or
- parts to be detached and returned.

Where there is both an area for completion and a part to be detached and returned, then the two together must not exceed 25% of the total area of the publication. However, there is no basis in law for this and the '25% test' is no more than a rule of thumb.

Whatever the area for completion, a publication which is designed to be returned whole after completion is always standard-rated.

See also *Full Force Marketing Ltd; Framesouth Ltd* (VTD 15270) (TVC 5.93) where the sale of an A4 document incorporating a 'discount card' entitling the holder to obtain free meals was essentially a supply of standard-rated services rather than a zero-rated brochure.

(VAT Notice 701/10/16, paras 3.2, 3.4).

Leaflets

[55.5] The supply of leaflets is zero-rated. [*VATA 1994, Sch 8 Group 3 Item 1*].

There is no definition of a 'leaflet' and whether a particular item is a leaflet is a matter of fact and impression.

HMRC normally look for certain physical characteristics if an item is to qualify as a leaflet.

(a) It should be printed on limp paper. In *Panini Publishing Ltd* (VTD 3876) (TVC 5.83) the tribunal held that a leaflet must be limp and generally, if not inevitably, on unlaminated paper. However, in *Multiform Printing Ltd* (VTD 13931) (TVC 5.61) it was held that there is no need for a leaflet to be flimsy. HMRC do not therefore regard items printed on stiff paper as automatically excluded from the definition of leaflets. However, they do regard the use of stiff paper and card as an indicator that an item has a function which *would* exclude it.

(b) It should be designed to be held in the hand for reading by individuals rather than for hanging up or general display. See *Arbroath Herald Ltd* [1975] Lexis Citation 18 (TVC 5.76) (car stickers), *Pace Group (Communications) Ltd* (VTD 510) (TVC 5.79) (window banners and door stickers); and *Cronsvale Ltd* (VTD 1552) (TVC 5.60) (advertisements for public meetings).

(c) It should consist of a single sheet of paper not greater than A4 size (although larger publications up to A2 size can be zero-rated provided they are printed on both sides, folded down to A4 or smaller, and meet the other conditions). See *Cronsvale Ltd* above where the tribunal held a leaflet to mean a small-sized leaf of paper or a sheet folded into leaves (but not stitched) and containing printed matter, chiefly for gratuitous distribution.

(d) It should be complete in itself (and not part of a larger work). See *Odhams Leisure Group Ltd v C & E Commrs*, QB [1992] STC 332 (TVC 5.85).

(e) It should be supplied in sufficient quantity (at least 50 copies) to permit general distribution.
(f) It should convey information by means of text.
(g) It should either be ephemeral or designed to accompany some other product or service (e.g. an instruction leaflet).

Examples of items that HMRC would not regard as being leaflets would be those designed

- as a calendar;
- to obtain admission to premises;
- to obtain a discount on goods or services; or
- as reference material.

HMRC also consider that items printed on laminated paper are designed to be kept and therefore are not leaflets. On the other hand, orders of service are not normally designed to be kept and may be zero-rated.

Items with areas for completion

See under **55.4** above which also applies to leaflets.

Letters

Individual manuscript or typed letters are standard-rated, as are collections of such letters if unbound or loosely bound. Permanently bound collections of letters are zero-rated.

The supply of a 'stock' or basic letter with the individual name or address of the recipient added (by whatever means) is standard-rated. Uncompleted 'stock' or basic letters may qualify as leaflets if the portion for completion consists of no more than the recipient's name and address, a reference number and a signature.

(VAT Notice 701/10/16, paras 3.3, 3.4, 4.3).

Newspapers

[55.6] The supply of newspapers is zero-rated. [*VATA 1994, Sch 8 Group 3 Item 2*].

There is no definition of a 'newspaper' and whether a particular item is a newspaper is a matter of fact and impression. HMRC require a newspaper to satisfy the following conditions.

- It should usually consist of several large sheets folded rather than bound together.
- It must be published at regular intervals (usually daily but at least weekly) in a continuous series under the same title. Each issue should usually be dated and/or serially numbered.
- It must contain a substantial amount of news about current events of local, national or international interest. It may also carry 'non-news' articles (e.g. readers letters, the weather forecast, crosswords and features on fashion, gardening etc.) but these should be an incidental feature.

For a general consideration of the requirements of a newspaper, see *Evans and Marland Ltd (t/a Greyform Publications)* (VTD 3158) (TVC 5.98).

Delivery and handling charges

Charges for delivered newspapers are normally zero-rated (see **48.7**(19) **OUTPUT TAX**).

(VAT Notice 701/10/16, para 3.5).

Journals and periodicals

[55.7] The supply of journals and periodicals is zero-rated. [*VATA 1994, Sch 8 Group 3 Item 2*].

There is no definition of a 'journal' or 'periodical' and whether a particular item qualifies is a matter of fact and impression. HMRC usually require an item to satisfy the following conditions.

- It should either be in newspaper format or a paper-bound publication.
- It must be published in a series at regular intervals (more frequently than once a year).
- It may contain information of a specialised nature (e.g. legal, medical, financial, commercial, fashion or sporting) or be of more general interest. It is normally a mix of articles and stories but may also consist mainly of illustrations or advertising matter. However, publications which serve primarily to promote own products or services do not qualify as periodicals (although they may qualify as brochures, see **55.4** above). See *Snushall Dalby & Robinson v C & E Commrs*, QB [1982] STC 537 (TVC 5.97) where the tribunal held that a monthly property guide, consisting almost entirely of advertisements for houses but with one or two articles on the housing market, could not be regarded as a journal as it contained no news and could not be regarded as a periodical as it was not sold to the public.

HMRC used to take the view that an item had to convey information by way of text to qualify as a journal or periodical. They have now withdrawn this view following the decision in *EMAP Consumer Magazines Ltd* (VTD 13322) (TVC 5.99) where a magazine consisting mainly of posters was held to be a periodical even though some could not be viewed without removing the staples. The tribunal chairman held that the word 'periodical' should be given its ordinary natural meaning and a publication consisting mainly of pictorial matter is capable of being a periodical.

(VAT Notice 701/10/16, para 3.6).

Children's picture books and painting books

[55.8] The supply of children's picture books and painting books is zero-rated. [*VATA 1994, Sch 8 Group 3 Item 3*]. This provision does not cover books for older children where the text is the main component, even if supported by pictures. Such books should be considered for zero-rating under **55.3** above.

Children's picture books

These are zero-rated whether printed on paper, plastic or textiles (e.g. children's rag books) unless the article is essentially a toy. Examples of articles which are standard-rated as toys include:

- Books consisting wholly or mainly of pictures or models for cutting out. HMRC suggest that such books with at least 25% text (other than assembly instructions) related to the material for cutting out can be zero-rated. However, there is no basis in law for this and the '25% test' is no more than a rule of thumb. See also *Scholastic Publications Ltd* [1996] Lexis Citation 839 (TVC 5.14) and *The Book People Ltd* (VTD 18240) (TVC 5.13).
- Books where the 'pages' are boards for games.

For a general consideration of children's reading books and picture books, see *W F Graham (Northampton) Ltd* [1980] Lexis Citation 1232 (TVC 5.12).

Children's painting and dot-to-dot books

Children's painting books which are zero-rated include:

- Children's painting books and drawing books with sample pictures for copying, or outlines of pictures for colouring, painting or drawing.
- Similar books with 'invisible' outlines to colour which can be made visible by rubbing with a pencil or applying water with a paint brush.
- Painting books in which the small amounts of water colour required for colouring are contained in the book (e.g. in the form of a palette).
- Activity books which combine pages of colouring with pages of puzzles, quizzes and the like.

Children's colouring and dot-to-dot books are books that are suitable for children under 18 years of age and they can vary in the content and can contain text as well as pictures that can be coloured or determined by joining dots. Colouring and dot-to-dot books can only be zero-rated if they meet the following conditions:

- They do not include an element that is only suitable for persons aged 18 years and over.
- They are not advertised or held out for sale as an adult product.

According to HMRC publications that have any of the following elements are not deemed suitable for person under the age of 18 years and are therefore standard-rated:

- Profanity – publications that contain profane or 'swear' words that appear in the title of the books, in the text or images within the book itself. However, this does not include incidental use of profane language when it is used in the context of an extract from a classical piece of literature, for example a Shakespeare play.
- Pornography and gratuitous nudity – publications that contain scenes of pornography or gratuitous nudity. However this does not include scientific anatomical drawings and images reflected in classical works of art. This includes any image of a sexual nature that would not generally be regarded as suitable for children under 18 years of age.

- Violence – publications that contain scenes of violence. This does not include images of scenes of battles and fighting that are clearly identified as based on historic events, religious stories or dramatic works.
- Illegal acts – publications that depict illegal acts. This would include images that depict theft, assault, drug taking, robbery, etc. (this list is not exhaustive). This does not include images that are clearly identified as based on historic events, religious stories or dramatic works.

HMRC have also stated that it is not necessary for the publication to specify that they are specifically aimed at children in order to be zero rated but they must not state that they are aimed at adults or grownups, etc. Publications held out for sale to children should not be sold together with adult titles and online sellers will be expected to make it clear who is the intended audience of the publication so purchasers can determine whether the publication is suitable for a child.

(HMRC Brief 17/16; VAT Notice 701/10/16, paras 3.7, 3.8).

Music

[55.9] The supply of music (printed, duplicated or manuscript) is zero-rated. [*VATA 1994, Sch 8 Group 3 Item 4*].

Any complete music which is presented on paper is zero-rated whether

- instrumental or vocal;
- printed or hand-written;
- bound or on loose sheets;
- illustrated or not; or
- in any system of notation, including numerical symbols or Braille.

Not included are

- music rolls;
- blank manuscript paper; and
- a piece of music commissioned from a composer.

See also *Flip Cards (Marine) Ltd* (VTD 14483) (TVC 5.113) where 'music' was defined as 'the written or printed score or set of parts of a musical composition' and held not to include cards containing questions and answers about music.

(VAT Notice 701/10/16, para 3.9).

Maps, charts and topographical plans

[55.10] The supply of maps, charts and topographical plans is zero-rated. [*VATA 1994, Sch 8 Group 3 Item 5*].

Physical characteristics

To qualify for zero-rating as a map, chart or topographical plan, HMRC require the map, etc to be printed on paper or other material (e.g. cloth) and in the form of a single or folded sheets or a collection of such sheets bound together in book form (e.g. an atlas).

In *Brooks Histograph Ltd* (VTD 1570) (TVC 5.114) the tribunal held that the word 'chart' must be construed in the context in which it appears. Since it appears between the words 'maps' and 'topographical plans' it refers to an area of land, sea or the skies and not to an historical chart.

HMRC regard the following as standard-rated.

- Plans or drawings for industrial, architectural, engineering, commercial or similar purposes (which are excluded from zero-rating by *VATA 1994, Sch 8 Group 3, Note (a)*).
- Framed maps which are primarily decorative items.
- Posters.
- Pictorial wall charts.
- Aerial photographs.
- Globes, three dimensional models and similar articles.
- Decorative maps printed or woven into textile items (e.g. scarves, handkerchiefs, tea-towels, tapestries, rugs).

(VAT Notice 701/10/16, para 3.10).

Incidental items supplied with zero-rated printed matter and binders

[55.11] Covers, cases and other articles supplied with items within **55.3** to **55.10** above, and not separately accounted for, are zero-rated. [*VATA 1994, Sch 8 Group 3 Item 6*].

Minor accessories (e.g. dust covers, clasps, book marks and presentation cases) supplied with any zero-rated item are usually regarded as forming part of the zero-rated item (but see **55.15** below).

Most folders and wallets are standard-rated but if they convey information themselves they may qualify as brochures (see **55.4** above).

Binders

For the treatment of loose-leaf binders, see **55.3** above. All other binders or files for general or office use are standard-rated. This includes binders for part works, journals and periodicals (whether specifically titled or not).

Small order surcharges

A surcharge imposed for handling a small order is treated as part of the price of the goods and is zero-rated if the goods are zero-rated.

(VAT Notice 701/10/16, paras 5.1, 5.2, 5.5).

Loans, hire and shares

[55.12] The transfer of any undivided share in, or the possession of, any item zero-rated under **55.3** to **55.11** above is zero-rated. [*VATA 1994, Sch 8 Group 3 Note (b)*].

This provision allows zero-rating to apply to

(a) the lending or hiring out of any item, or
(b) the sale of a share or part interest in any item

which is zero-rated under **55.3** to **55.11** above.

Libraries which charge for the loan of books therefore make zero-rated supplies. This also applies to reference libraries which charge for the use of their books on their own premises.

(VAT Notice 701/10/16, para 5.3).

Supplies of printed advertising to charities

[55.13] Zero-rating applies to supplies of all charity advertisements in all media, i.e. there ceases to be any restriction on either the type of media or the purpose of the advertising. [*VATA 1994, Sch 8 Group 15 Items 8–8C; SI 2000/805*]. These more general provisions are considered in **13.7 CHARITIES.**

Standard-rated printed matter

Examples of common standard-rated items

[55.14] The following is a list of items which HMRC commonly regard as being standard-rated. A list of items they would normally treat as zero-rated is reproduced at **55.2** above. However, it should not be assumed that any item is zero-rated simply because it is not included in the list below and the liability of any specific item should be determined by reference to the appropriate paragraph of the text.

- Acceptance cards
- Account books
- Address books
- Albums
- Amendment slips
- Announcement cards
- Appointment cards
- Autograph albums (uncompleted)
- Badges
- Bags (paper)
- Ballot papers
- Bankers' drafts
- Billheads
- Bills of lading
- Bills of quantity (blank)
- Binders (but see **55.3** above)
- Bingo cards
- Biorhythm charts
- Blotters
- Book covers

- Book marks
- Book tokens
- Bookmakers' tickets
- Business cards
- Calendars
- Certificates
- Cheques and cheque books
- Cigarette cards
- Cloakroom tickets
- Colour cards
- Compliment slips
- Copy books
- Correspondence cards
- Coupon books
- Coupons
- Credit cards
- Delivery notes
- Diaries (unused)
- Dividend warrants
- Dressmaking patterns
- Engineers' plans
- Envelopes
- Exercise books
- Fashion drawings
- Flash cards
- Folders
- Football pool coupons
- Form letters (but see **55.5** above)
- Forms
- Framed decorative maps
- Games
- Globes
- Graph paper
- Greetings cards
- Index cards
- Inlay cards for cassettes, CDs or videos
- Insurance cover notes
- Invitation cards
- Invoices
- Labels
- Letter headings
- Letters (handwritten)
- Log books (blank)
- Lottery tickets and cards
- Manuscript paper
- Manuscripts
- Medical records
- Membership cards
- Memo pads
- Menu cards

- Microfiche
- Microfilm
- Microform copies
- Music rolls
- Note books, pads and paper
- Order books and forms
- Paper (unprinted)
- Parts of books (see **55.3** above)
- Pattern cards
- Photograph albums
- Photographs
- Plans (but see **55.10** above)
- Playing cards
- Poll cards
- Pools coupons
- Postcards (whether completed or not)
- Posters
- Price cards and tags
- Printed pictures
- Questionnaires
- Receipt books and forms
- Record books and labels
- Record books
- Record labels
- Record sleeves
- Registers
- Rent books
- Reply-paid coupons and envelopes
- Reproductions of paintings
- Score cards
- Scrap books (blank)
- Scrolls (hand-written)
- Seals
- Shade cards (unless containing substantial printed text)
- Share certificates
- Stamp albums (whether completed or not)
- Stationery
- Stationery books
- Stickers
- Swatch books
- Swatch cards
- Sweepstake tickets
- Tags
- Temperature charts
- Tickets
- Time cards and sheets
- Tokens (but see book tokens below)
- Toys
- Transcripts
- Transfers

- Transparencies
- Visiting cards
- Vouchers
- Wall charts
- Waste paper
- Wills
- Winding cards
- Wrapping paper
- Wreath cards

Posters

Sheets intended for public display are standard-rated but see **55.7** above for 'poster-magazines'.

Stationery

Stationery items (e.g. account books and exercise books) are standard-rated. Some items which are standard-rated stationery when new and unused can be zero-rated if sold after they have been completed, provided that they then have the physical characteristics of a book or other zero-rated item (e.g. completed diaries or ships' logs but not completed stamp albums).

Letters

Individual manuscript or typed letters are standard-rated as are collections of such letters which are unbound or loosely bound. Permanently bound collections are zero-rated. See **55.5** above for printed stocks of standard letters.

Photocopies

Photocopies of zero-rated items are always standard-rated unless the copies can be properly described as books, booklets, brochures, pamphlets, leaflets, etc. and meet all the criteria for zero-rating such items. A bundle of photocopies does not constitute a book unless it includes copies of all the pages of the book and is in permanent binding. Photocopies of parts of books, extracts from periodicals, etc. cannot be zero-rated unless complete in themselves and having the characteristics of zero-rated items. Where a business provides 'instant' photocopying or duplicating services and cannot determine the VAT liability of the copies supplied, it should charge VAT at the standard rate.

Book tokens

Printing of book tokens is standard-rated. On the sale of a book token to the general public

- for its face value or less, no VAT is due; and
- for more than its face value, VAT is due on the difference between the selling price and its face value.

Any separate charge for a greetings card is standard-rated.

(VAT Notice 701/10/16, paras 4.1–4.3, 4.5, 5.4, 8).

Single and multiple supplies

[55.15] Goods which would normally be zero-rated or standard-rated as printed matter may be supplied in conjunction with other goods and/or services. A single inclusive price may, or may not, be charged. If the individual elements are all liable to VAT at the same rate, VAT due can be calculated in the normal way. But if the individual supplies are not liable to VAT at the same rate, the criteria set out by the ECJ in *Card Protection Plan Ltd v C & E Commrs, ECJ Case C–349/96*, [1999] STC 270 (TVC 22.362) must be used to determine whether there is a single or multiple supply.

(a) A single supply occurs where one element of the supply is the principal element to which all the other elements are ancillary, integral or incidental. An ancillary element does not constitute, for the customer, an aim in itself, but is a means of better enjoying the principal goods or services supplied. Integral elements are elements that are essential and necessary to the main supply. An incidental element is something that naturally accompanies the main supply (e.g. packaging).
HMRC regard the following as indicators of a single supply (although accepting that they are not conclusive).
- Single price.
- Advertised as a package.
- Components not available separately.
- Goods physically packaged together.

The customer is likely to regard what he is getting as a single supply and not as a package.

(b) A multiple supply occurs where more than one element is distinct and independent. HMRC regard the following as indicators that more than one supply is taking place (although again they are not conclusive).
- Separate pricing/invoicing.
- Items available separately.
- Time differential between parts of the supply.
- Elements of the supply are not inter-dependent/connected.

HMRC indicate that common examples of multiple supplies are books issued with films or tapes and children's colouring books issued with felt-tip pens. This is on the basis that the items supplied can clearly be used independently of each other. But see *International Masters Publishers Ltd v HMRC (No 2)*, CA 2006 [2007] STC 153 (TVC 5.43) where the company supplied CDs of music by classic composers, including a booklet on the composer. The court held that there was a single standard-rated supply. The CDs were the principal supply and the booklets were ancillary.
A particular problem area is children's activity packs which may contain zero-rated books or booklets and standard-rated items such as jigsaw puzzles or toys. The supplier must determine whether the omission of any one component part would diminish the pack as a whole. Overall guidelines are not possible and each pack must be judged on its own merits.

There are three possible liability outcomes where zero-rated printed matter is supplied with other standard-rated items.

- The standard-rated item may be ancillary to, or an integral part of, the supply of zero-rated printed matter, in which case there is a single zero-rated supply.
- The zero-rated printed matter may be ancillary to, or an integral part of, the supply of the standard-rated item (e.g. an instruction booklet provided with a new washing machine), in which case there is a single standard-rated supply.
- There may be a multiple supply where two or more items are distinct and independent. If the items are sold for a single price and are liable to different rates of VAT, the supplier must apportion the price.

(VAT Notice 701/10/16, paras 6.2–6.4).

There is more detailed coverage of single and multiple supplies in **65.6 SUPPLY: GENERAL.**

However, there are two exceptions to the normal rules for

- packages consisting entirely of items printed on paper or card (see **55.16** below); and
- certain cover mounted items on magazines (see **55.18** below).

Example

A CD of classical music is sold to customers in a retail store. The CD also contains a separate leaflet that explains the background to the music and the composers who wrote it. In this situation, the customer is only seeking to buy the CD to listen to the music, which is standard-rated. The zero-rated leaflet is only intended to enhance his enjoyment of the music, i.e. is not a separate supply in its own right. The entire payment made by customers is standard-rated.

Packages of zero-rated and standard-rated printed matter

[55.16] Where a business makes a multiple supply of a 'package' consisting *entirely* of standard-rated and zero-rated printed matter, it can account for VAT by apportionment between the standard-rated and zero-rated elements. Alternatively, by concession, it can apply the package test so that

- if the package contains more zero-rated than standard-rated items, the package as a whole can be zero-rated;
- if there are more standard-rated items, the package as a whole is standard-rated; and
- where there are equal numbers of zero-rated and standard-rated items, the liability of the package is decided by the costs of the goods. If the zero-rated elements of the package cost more, the whole package is zero-rated and vice versa. In the unlikely event that the standard and zero-rated elements cost exactly the same amount, apportionment should be applied.

For these purpose, a '*package*' is a collection of items printed on paper or card usually enclosed in some sort of wrapper. The articles must physically form a package and have a common link in that they are intended to be used together. Examples include

- packages contained in an outer polythene or paper envelope (e.g. a package sent to a shareholder which includes company reports, circulars, a proxy voting form and a reply-paid envelope);
- cardboard folders with pockets into which are inserted a variety of forms, leaflets, etc.; and
- advertising packages often from financial institutions.

The outer envelope in which the package items are enclosed is *not* taken into account when counting the number of standard/zero-rated items but a reply-paid envelope counts as a standard-rated item.

If any item in the package is not printed on paper or card the package test cannot be applied.

(VAT Notice 701/10/16, para 6.5).

The package test for charities

By concession, supplies of certain goods to a charity for use in connection with collecting monetary donations can be treated as if they were zero-rated. See **13.7**(*g*) **CHARITIES**. *From 1 August 2003*, where a package of printed matter is supplied to a charity some items connected with collecting monetary donations can be treated as zero-rated for the purposes of the package test provided they meet the criteria set out in **13.7**(*g*) **CHARITIES**.

Item	*Treatment for the package test*
Letter appealing for donations	Zero-rated
Printed envelopes for use with appeal letters	Zero-rated
Money collecting envelopes	Zero-rated
Stickers	Standard-rated
Money collecting boxes made of card	Zero-rated
Any item not made of paper or card	Package test cannot be used

(VAT Notice 701/10/16, para 6.6).

Printed matter supplied with other services

[55.17] The following are common situations where printed matter is supplied with other services.

(1) Services of an original or specialist nature

The supply of services such as original writing or composition or those involving a specialism are standard-rated. Any goods supplied with those services are incidental products and must be standard-rated even if they would be zero-rated printed matter. Examples include

- the manuscript of a book supplied by an author;
- a piece of music commissioned from a composer;
- a report commissioned from a consultant;

- a translation;
- a shorthand transcription; and
- a typing service.

Extra copies of such items may be zero-rated provided they are

- in a format which qualifies for zero-rating; and
- supplied at a price which covers only the cost of producing the extra copies and a reasonable mark-up.

(VAT Notice 701/10/16, para 7.2).

(2) Printed matter used to supply discount facilities

See *Status Cards Ltd* [1974] Lexis Citation 21 (TVC 5.10), *Graham Leisure Ltd* [1983] VATTR 12 (TVC 5.32) and *Interleisure Club Ltd* (VTD 7458) (TVC 5.34).

(3) Printed matter supplied with correspondence courses

Correspondence courses often involve a mixture of tuition in class and home study through course manuals or booklets. The liability of the supply will depend upon what exactly is being supplied. This may be a single supply of education by an eligible body (exempt) or a non-eligible body (standard-rated), a single supply of printed matter (zero-rated) or a multiple supply of education and printed matter (in which case apportionment is required). See **48.3 OUTPUT TAX** for methods of apportionment.

The criteria set out by the CJEU in *Card Protection Plan Ltd v C & E Commrs, ECJ Case C–349/96*, [1999] STC 270 (TVC 22.362) must be used to determine whether there is a single or multiple supply. Where it is established that there is a single supply, consideration must be given as to whether either of the two elements, education and printed matter, is the principal supply with the other being ancillary. If so, the whole supply takes on the liability of the principal supply. College fees were held not to be divisible into study materials (otherwise zero-rated) and educational services (exempt) in *R & C Commrs v The College of Estate Management*, HL [2005] STC 1597 (TVC 5.36). The Court held that there was a single exempt supply of education and that it was inappropriate to analyse the transaction in terms of what was a principal and ancillary supply. In relation to fees for correspondence course and residential courses generally, earlier tribunal decisions had sometimes reached this decision (see *EW (Computer Training) Ltd* (VTD 5453) (TVC 5.37) and *International News Syndicate Ltd* (VTD 14425) (TVC 5.3)) but had also allowed apportionment (see *The Rapid Results College Ltd* (VTD 48) (TVC 5.2) and *Force One Training Ltd* (VTD 13619) (TVC 5.7)). These earlier decisions, however, pre-dated the decision in *Card Protection Plan* and should now be read in the light of the criteria set out in that case and the decision in *College of Estate Management* above.

In *Metropolitan International Schools* [2015] UKFTT 517 (TC) (TC04675) (TVC 5.40), a distance learning provider had agreed with HMRC that its course fees were 75% zero-rated as representing the printed matter. In 2009 it applied for an additional repayment in relation to 2006; in response, HMRC issued a ruling that the fees should be wholly standard-rated, and issued an assessment. The company appealed, arguing that in fact its supplies should be regarded as principally printed matter with incidental other services. The First-tier Tribunal accepted that the tutorial input was minimal, and was probably exaggerated in advertising material. The company's supplies should have been wholly zero-rated. HMRC appealed to the Upper Tribunal who allowed HMRC's appeal on the basis that the First-tier Tribunal had not given adequate weight to a number of significant factors and in particular to the principal/ancillary test. The Upper Tribunal concluded that following the principals established in *Card Protection Plan*, that whilst the manuals might be the main element of the supply, when judged quantitatively, they could not be described as the principal element of the supply as the other essential elements of the supply needed to be taken into account and properly weighted in the balance. The Upper Tribunal concluded that the taxpayer provided a blended course and it was contractually obliged to provide all of the elements not just the study material. A typical student would conclude that it was buying a package and that books were an important element of that package but they were not the predominant supply. As a result the supplies made were not zero-rated and that the supply should be characterised as a supply of education which was liable to VAT at the standard rate (*Metropolitan International Schools Ltd* [2017] STC 2523).

(4) Printed matter with 'weight loss' programmes

In *HMRC v Weight Watchers (UK) Ltd, CA* [2008] STC 2313 (TVC 5.95) customers attended weekly meetings and were also given an initial handbook, monthly magazines and weekly leaflets. In 2004 Customs issued a ruling that the company was making multiple supplies and that part of the consideration could be attributed to zero-rated supplies of printed material. In 2005 they withdrew this ruling and ruled that the company was making a single supply of a weight-loss programme, so that it was required to account for VAT on the whole of its takings. The CA upheld Customs' ruling, holding that the company was making a single supply and that none of the consideration qualified for zero-rating.

(5) Printed matter supplied in return for a subscription

For *membership subscriptions*, see also **15.2 CLUBS AND ASSOCIATIONS.**

Magazine subscriptions: where magazines are supplied on an annual subscription basis, the whole supply may be zero-rated provided only the magazine is being supplied. However, where the subscription confers other rights (e.g. the right to buy goods at discounted rates or the right to participate in selling schemes and thereby earn commission) the subscription may need to be apportioned to reflect the zero-rated element relating to the magazine.

(6) Programmes supplied as part of an admission fee

It is common practice for admission to events to include the provision of a programme. Following the judgment of the CJEU in *Card Protection Plan Ltd v C & E Commrs, ECJ Case C–349/96*, [1999] STC 270 (TVC 22.362) in the majority of such cases there is a single supply of admission, the programme being an ancillary item.

(7) Subsidy or vanity publishing

An author who is unable to have a work published through the usual means may sometimes pay for it to be published. This is known as either 'subsidy' publishing or 'vanity' publishing.

Where the publisher, in return for a payment from the author, produces a quantity of books which are *all* delivered to the author, the payment by the author to the publisher is a consideration for a supply of books and is zero-rated.

But where the publisher retains the bulk of the print run, selling the books in the normal manner and paying the author a royalty on copies sold, payment by the author to the publisher is partly the consideration for the zero-rated supply of books to the author and partly consideration for standard-rated publishing services. The following simplified method of calculation of the zero-rated and standard-rated supplies has been agreed between HMRC and the British Printing Industries Federation.

Step A	Calculate non-variable costs of initial print run.
Step B	Calculate variable costs of initial print run.
Step C	Divide total at Step B by number of copies in initial print run and multiply by number of copies issued to author.
Step D	Add totals at Step A and Step C to calculate cost of the zero-rated element of the supply.
Step E	Add the costs of initial print run and run-on charges to establish full cost of supply.
Step F	Divide total at Step D by total at Step E to calculate zero-rated percentage of cost of supply.
Step G	Apply percentage in Step F to the net sales charge to establish the zero-rated element of the supply made.

A business which does not wish to calculate an apportionment for each individual supply may calculate an apportionment on the basis of an average resulting from the application of the above to a number of representative supplies made. The method is subject to review by HMRC to ensure it produces a fair result and should also be regularly reviewed by the business to take account of changing circumstances.

(VAT Notice 700/57/14; VAT Notice 701/10/16, para 5.7).

(8) Printed matter supplied with company formation services

HMRC's view is that, following the judgment in *Card Protection Plan*, where there is a single advertised price for a company formation package that includes some printed matter (e.g. a number of copies of the memorandum and articles of association), there is a single standard-rated supply of company formation services. This supply is the principal supply to which the supply of printed matter is ancillary. See also *Company Registrations Online Ltd* (VTD 19461) (TVC 5.44). Where additional copies of documentation are offered as an option for additional payment, there may be either a single supply or multiple supplies depending upon the facts.

Businesses providing company formation services must review their VAT treatment of these supplies, ensure that any necessary changes are implemented, and account for underpaid output tax.

(Business Brief 1/06).

(9) Printed matter supplied with direct marketing services

HMRC's view is that printed matter supplied with direct marketing services should properly be characterised as a supply of standard-rated direct marketing services. Direct marketing via addressed or unaddressed mail or via inserts in newspapers or magazines typically involves the production or acquisition of printed matter for distribution and any or all of the following services.

- Posting or arranging the posting of customer mail such as publicity, advertising material or promotional goods to many recipients.
- Analysis or manipulation of data for strategic or marketing purposes such as targeting direct mail at specific groups.
- Purchase or rental of third party mailing lists.
- Analysis of own and customer data to produce reports on campaign results and advice on strategy.

(HMRC Brief 10/15).

Printed matter supplied with other goods

[55.18] See **55.16** above for supplies of zero-rated and standard-rated printed matter.

Cover-mounted items

Where a cover-mounted item (e.g. a sachet of perfume or a CD) is linked to a magazine, it can, by concession, be zero-rated if the following conditions are met.

- No separate charge is made for it.
- The issue is sold at the same price as other issues without a cover-mounted item.
- The cost of the item included with any individual issue does not exceed either £1 (excluding VAT) or 20% of the total cost of the combined supply (excluding VAT).

Magazines often pass through a number of traders before they are retailed to the end-customer. In determining whether the concession can apply, it is necessary to identify the first trader in the chain responsible for linking the items and then apply the above conditions to that trader. If, at the point of linkage, the supply satisfies the terms of the concession, it becomes a single zero-rated supply and continues as such throughout the chain. If the supply does not satisfy the terms of the concession, the normal rules must be considered to determine whether it is a single or multiple supply.

(VAT Notice 701/10/16, para 6.7; VAT Notice 48, ESC 3.7).

See also *Keesing (UK) Ltd* (VTD 16840) (TVC 5.107) where the company's magazine was distributed by another company which paid Keesing 55% of the cover price of the magazine. The tribunal held that 'total cost' for the purposes of the concession was the 55% which Keesing received, rather than the full cover price, and on that basis the conditions of the concession were not satisfied.

Production of zero-rated goods

[55.19] Supplies of certain services involve the production of goods that are zero-rated under *VATA 1994, Sch 8 Group 3*. A business supplying such services must consider whether its supply falls into either of the following categories.

(a) **Services of an original or specialist nature.** See **55.17**(1) above.

(b) **Services of the production of new zero-rated goods** (which will be more likely if the business is in the printing industry). Such services are zero-rated where those goods are themselves zero-rated.

- *Preparatory or post-production work.* Where a business supplies items that qualify for zero-rating, it can zero-rate any preparatory or post-production work (other than alterations) that it performs in conjunction with them. This applies whether or not it itemises the various processes on the VAT invoice and charges for them separately, and even if it has employed sub-contractors. See *AP Carpenter* (VTD 15253) (TVC 5.66) (whether a graphic designer was responsible for the production of a brochure).
- *Sub-contract work.* A sub-contractor can only zero-rate work if he produces new zero-rated goods. If not, his supply cannot be zero-rated even if he knows that the final product will be zero-rated. For example, a business providing typesetting only must standard-rate its supply but if it also binds pages together to make a book (with a cover) it is producing a zero-rated item and can zero-rate its supply.
- *Work on other people's goods.* Where a treatment or process is applied to someone else's goods which produces new goods, the liability of the service follows that of the goods produced. For example, binding loose papers into a book is zero-rated but re-covering or otherwise repairing an old book is standard-rated.

  Any other work on other people's goods is standard-rated (e.g. post-production alterations).

(VAT Notice 701/10/16, paras 7.1–7.3).

Incomplete publications

Component parts of books, journals (e.g. covers, unbound pages, illustrations) in the course of production are standard-rated as they have not been assembled into completed books (*Butler & Tanner Ltd* [1974] Lexis Citation 7 (TVC 5.30)).

(VAT Notice 701/10/16, para 4.4).

Key points: printed matter, etc.

[55.20] Points to consider are as follows.

- An item can only be zero-rated as printed matter if it is in a paper format, i.e. it represents a supply of goods. For example, a newsletter supplied to a customer by electronic means (e.g. emailed to the customer in pdf format) is always classed as a supply of services and therefore standard-rated (assuming sale is to a UK customer).
- A supply of printed matter or text is also standard-rated if supplied as a CD rom or audio cassette etc. This is because text supplied in these formats cannot be read.
- As a general principle, items of printed matter where the main intention is for the document to be written in rather than read are standard-rated, e.g. address book, diary, accounts book to record income and expenditure.
- It is important that a business buying items of printed matter (e.g. annual reports produced by a printer and bought by a charity to circulate to its members) identifies when zero-rating can apply. This is particularly relevant if the business is not VAT-registered or partly exempt, where VAT becomes a cost component. However, as a general principle of VAT, input tax cannot be reclaimed on any supply where VAT has been incorrectly charged in the first place.
- A supply of photocopying services is generally standard-rated, so there is scope for a business to reclaim input tax on such costs, assuming a tax invoice (or less detailed tax invoice) is obtained from the supplier as evidence of VAT being paid.

56

Rates of VAT

Cross-references. See **19.22 EUROPEAN UNION LEGISLATION** for rates allowed under *Directive 2006/112/EC*; **67.1–67.26 SUPPLY: TIME OF SUPPLY** for the rules relating to the tax point of supply.

De Voil Indirect Tax Service. See V1.111–V1.131.

Introduction to rates of VAT

[56.1] VAT is levied on the supply of goods and services, the acquisition of goods from another EU member state and the importation of goods from a place outside the EU. The Treasury may, by Order, vary the standard rate of VAT for the time being in force by a percentage of the current rate not exceeding 25% but any Order ceases to have effect one year from the date on which it takes effect unless continued by a further Order. This method was used to reduce the standard rate of VAT from 17.5% to 15% for a temporary period (1 December 2008 to 31 December 2009). Since the period in question exceeded twelve months, legislation was included in *FA 2009* to extend the period of reduction for an additional month.

[*VATA 1994, s 2*].

Rates

[56.2] Apart from certain **21 EXEMPT SUPPLIES** and **75 ZERO-RATED SUPPLIES** on which no VAT is chargeable, there are currently two rates of VAT.

Standard rate		
4.1.11–	20%	[*F(No 2)A 2010, s 3*]
1.1.10–3.1.11	17.5%	[*SI 2008/3020; FA 2009, s 9(1)*]
1.12.08–31.12.09	15%	[*SI 2008/3020; FA 2009, s 9(1)*]
1.4.91–30.11.08	17.5%	[*FA 1991, s 13*]
Reduced rate		
1.9.97–	5%	[*F(No 2)A 1997, s 6*]
1.4.94–31.8.97	8%	[*FA 1995, s 21*]
1.9.97–	5%	[*F(No 2)A 1997, s 6*]
1.4.94–31.8.97	8%	[*FA 1995, s 21*]

See **59 REDUCED RATE SUPPLIES** for the supplies subject to the reduced rate.

Section 2 of *Finance (No 2) Act 2015* provides for a 'VAT lock' so that the following provisions apply, at least until the day immediately preceding the date of the first parliamentary general election after 18 November 2015:

- the standard rate of VAT will not exceed 20%;
- the reduced rate of VAT will not exceed 5%; and
- the reduced rate of VAT and the zero rate of VAT will continue to apply to supplies subject to the reduced rate of VAT and the zero rate of VAT on 18 November 2015.

Note – on 4 June 2015 the CJEU released its judgment in *EC Commission v United Kingdom, ECJ Case C–161/14* that the UK had failed to correctly apply the reduced rate of VAT in relation to energy-saving materials. Following the CJEU judgment HMRC published HMRC Brief 13/15 explaining that the UK Government is currently considering the implications of the decision and that any legislative changes would not be implemented before *Finance Act 2016*.

On 9 December 2015 HMRC published a consultation document on changes to the reduced rate of VAT for energy-saving materials. The consultation document referred to *Finance (No 2) Act 2015* and explained that Government policy on the VAT lock will not prevent changes being made to a reduced rate of VAT or a zero rate of VAT if the changes are necessary following a decision of a binding court. A draft clause for inclusion in *Finance Bill 2016*, to take effect from 1 August 2016, was published; but it was not included in the Bill. It therefore appears that the change will not take effect from 1 August 2016 as previously expected.

[*F(No 2)A 2015, s 2*]. (HMRC Brief 13/15) (HMRC consultation document on changes to the reduced rate of VAT for energy-saving materials).

Change in VAT rates

[56.3] The provisions in **56.4** to **56.17** below apply when there is a change in the VAT rate (i.e. the standard rate is changed or a new rate is introduced) or where there is a change in the VAT liability of particular supplies (e.g. a supply previously standard-rated becomes zero-rated through a change in the law or its interpretation). Any such change is effective from a specific date and VAT is due at the new rate on supplies made on or after that date. The date on which supplies of goods and services are treated as taking place for the purposes of charging VAT is governed by the tax point rules (see **67.1–67.26 SUPPLY: TIME OF SUPPLY**). Normally no change of rate can apply to any supply with a tax point before the effective date of change (but see **56.6** below and the special rules for warehoused goods in **56.17** below). See **61.7 RETAIL SCHEMES** for the effects of a change in VAT rates or VAT liabilities where one or more of the special retail schemes are in operation but see also **56.6** below. (VAT Notice 700, paras 30.2–30.4).

VAT returns

[56.4] VAT must be accounted for in the period in which the normal tax point occurs. This applies even if one the special rules in this chapter is adopted for deciding the rate of VAT to charge. Amounts shown on the return should not be split between the old and new rates. (VAT Notice 700, para 30.6).

Reclaiming input tax

[56.5] Input tax following a change in VAT rate or VAT liability must be reclaimed at the rate charged by the supplier. Where the amount of VAT is not separately shown (e.g. on a less detailed VAT invoice — see **40.7 INVOICES**), VAT is calculated by applying the VAT fraction which was appropriate at the tax point (see **67.1–67.26 SUPPLY: TIME OF SUPPLY**). See also **56.9** below for continuous supplies of services invoiced ahead of the supply. (VAT Notice 700, para 30.5).

Output tax – general principles

[56.6] When there is a change in the VAT rate or a VAT liability, VAT is chargeable according to the normal tax point rules (see **67.1–67.26 SUPPLY: TIME OF SUPPLY**) unless the taxpayer elects for the special change of rate provisions below. It is not possible to avoid the consequences of an announced increase in VAT by preparing invoices which, although agreed by the customer, are not issued (i.e. physically sent or given to him) before the date of change. See *C & E Commrs v Woolfold Motor Co Ltd*, QB [1983] STC 715 (TVC 62.426). In any case, an invoice issued for a zero-rated supply does not create a tax point.

Special change of rate provisions.

(a) On an election, *the rate at which VAT is chargeable on a supply, or any question whether the supply is zero-rated or exempt or a reduced rate supply*, is determined by the *basic tax point* only i.e. the date on which

goods are removed or made available or on which services are performed. Election may be made for all affected supplies or only some of them but an election may not be made where VAT invoices are issued under a self-billing arrangement (see **40.6 INVOICES**) or when goods are sold from the assets of a business in satisfaction of a debt. [*VATA 1994, s 88(2)(6)*]. The effect of the election is that, where the VAT rate increases, VAT may be charged at the old rate on goods removed or services performed before the date of change even though the tax point would normally be established by the issue of a VAT invoice after the change. Similarly, where the VAT rate goes down, VAT may be charged at the new rate on goods removed or services performed after the date of change, even though payment has been received or a VAT invoice issued before that date.
(VAT Notice 700, para 30.7).

(b) On an election, *the rate at which VAT is chargeable on an acquisition of goods from another EU member state, or any question as to whether it is zero-rated or exempt or a reduced rate acquisition*, is determined by reference to the time of the first removal of the goods involved in the transaction (or, in the case of goods on sale or return, such later time when it becomes certain that they have been acquired). [*VATA 1994, s 88(4)(7)*].

Credit notes

[56.7] Where an invoice has already been issued showing VAT at the old rate, it must be corrected with a credit note issued within 14 days of the change. See **40.15 INVOICES** for details. (VAT Notice 700, para 30.7).

Supplies of services

[56.8] Output tax may be charged at the old rate on the part completed before the date of a change in the VAT rate and at the new rate on the part completed on or after that date provided the supply can be apportioned on a basis of measurable work or in accordance with a supplier's normal costing or pricing system. Where VAT is reduced in this way and a VAT invoice was issued or payment was received before the date of VAT change, a credit note must be provided (see **56.7** above). (VAT Notice 700, para 30.8).

Continuous supplies of goods and services

[56.9] Where there is a continuous supply of goods or services (including hire, lease and rental of goods) VAT is normally chargeable at the rate applying at each tax point. See **67.19 SUPPLY: TIME OF SUPPLY** for services and **67.15 SUPPLY: TIME OF SUPPLY** for a continuous supply of goods in the form of water, gas and electricity. Any VAT invoice issued up to one year ahead, giving the amounts and dates when payments are due, is invalid in respect of payments due after the change (and not received before it). [*SI 1995/2518, Reg 90(3)*]. A new invoice, referring to and cancelling the superseded part of the original invoice, must be issued. The customer cannot use the original invoice to support a claim for input tax after the change and must make the necessary adjustments on receipt of the new invoice.

Where a continuous supply spans a change in the VAT rate, VAT may be accounted for at the *old* rate on that part of the supply made before the change even though the normal tax point would occur after the change (e.g. where a payment is received in arrears of the supply). Conversely, VAT may be accounted for at the *new* rate on that part of the supply made after the change even though the normal tax point occurred before the change (e.g. where a payment is received in advance of the supply). In each case, VAT should be accounted for on the basis of the value of goods actually supplied or services actually performed before or after the change as appropriate. Where VAT liability is reduced on a supply for which a VAT invoice has been issued at a higher rate, a credit note must be issued (see **56.7** above). (VAT Notice 700, para 30.9).

Facilities provided by clubs, associations, etc.

[56.10] Clubs, associations, etc. supplying facilities in return for a member's subscription must normally account for VAT at the rate applying when the subscription is received or a VAT invoice is issued, whichever happens first. Where payment is made by instalments or separate invoices are issued, the procedure for continuous supply of services should be followed (see **56.9** above). (VAT Notice 700, para 30.10).

Hire purchase, conditional and credit sales

[56.11] Under any of these agreements, there is a single supply of goods and the normal tax point is the earliest of

(a) the date of removal of the goods;
(b) the date of issue of the agreement (provided the agreement is in the form of a VAT invoice); and
(c) the date of the issue of a separate VAT invoice.

See **67.11 SUPPLY: TIME OF SUPPLY**.

The signing of an agreement, or its date, does not constitute a tax point. Where there is a change in the VAT rate, the tax point will be whichever of (*a*) to (*c*) above results in the lower rate of VAT being charged. (VAT Notice 700, para 30.11).

Deposits and payments in advance of the basic tax point

[56.12] Where full or part payment is made, or a VAT invoice issued, before the basic tax point (see above), VAT will normally be due on the amount paid or invoiced at the rate in force at that date. Where full payment is made in advance but the money is loaned back to the customer on the understanding that it will be repaid as the work proceeds, the transaction has been held to be genuine and not to fall foul of the decision in *W T Ramsay Ltd v IRC* even if the scheme is designed purely to save VAT. A similar decision has been reached where monies are paid into deposit accounts of the builders but only released against architects' certificates (*C & E Commrs v Faith Construction Ltd and* *related appeals*, CA [1989] STC 539 (TVC 62.439)). If there is a change in the VAT rate before the supply is actually made, VAT may be charged at the rate applicable when the supply is made and a credit note issued (see above) to amend the VAT invoice. These provisions do not apply to deposits taken as security (e.g. to ensure safe return of goods hired out) which are refundable or subject to forfeiture *or* if the deposit does not relate to a particular supply or contract (e.g. money paid into a client's account). (VAT Notice 700, para 30.12).

Credit and contingent discounts

[56.13] Where a credit note (not arising from the change in rate) is issued to adjust an original invoice, VAT should be credited at the rate in force at the tax point of the original supply. Where contingent discount is allowed and the original VAT charge is adjusted, VAT should be credited at the rate in force at the time of each supply qualifying for the discount. (VAT Notice 700, para 30.13).

Price escalation clauses and other adjustments

[56.14] Where an additional payment is required after a change in the VAT rate and after the tax point for the original supply determined under the normal rules, VAT is chargeable on the further payment at the old rate. Where VAT was not determined under the normal rules on the original supply, the tax point for the additional payment is the earlier of the date of receipt of a further payment or the issue of a VAT invoice and VAT is chargeable at the rate then in force. (VAT Notice 700, para 30.14).

Existing contracts

[56.15] Where, after the making of a contract for the supply of goods or services and before those goods or services are supplied, there is a change in the VAT charged, then, unless the contract provides otherwise, the consideration for the supply is increased or decreased by an amount equal to the change. These provisions apply in relation to a tenancy or lease as they apply in relation to a contract.

A landlord is able to add VAT to the rent where

- he makes an election to charge VAT on rents at the standard rate under the option to tax provisions (see **42.23 LAND AND BUILDINGS: EXEMPT SUPPLIES AND OPTION TO TAX**); or
- there is an increase in the rate of VAT

unless the terms of the lease specifically prevent him from passing on VAT to his tenants.

[*VATA 1994, s 89*].

HMRC do not advise on contracts. (VAT Notice 700, para 30.15).

Second-hand goods

[56.16] VAT chargeable on the sale of a second-hand article under the Margin Scheme for **62 SECOND-HAND GOODS** is calculated by applying the appropriate VAT fraction at the tax point to the VAT-inclusive amount. The tax point is the earlier of the date of removal of the goods and the receipt of payment. If there is a change in the VAT rate before the goods are removed, VAT may be accounted for at the rate in force when the goods are removed even if payment has already been received. (*Note.* A VAT invoice must not be issued for goods supplied under a second-hand scheme). (VAT Notice 700, para 30.16).

Warehoused goods

Imported goods

[56.17] When imported goods are removed from bonded warehouse for home use, the rate of VAT chargeable is that in force at the time of removal.

Home-produced goods

For home-produced goods subject to excise duty which have been supplied while in warehouse, the rate of VAT chargeable is that in force when the excise duty is paid. For goods relieved of excise duty, the rate of VAT chargeable is that applicable at the time of their removal from warehouse.

(VAT Notice 700, para 30.17).

Key points: rates of VAT

[56.18] Points to consider are as follows.

- The present Government's 'VAT lock' suggests that there should not be a general increase in the standard rate of VAT during the lifetime of this Parliament. However, it is still possible for the rate for individual supplies to change, for example where the liability of a supply becomes exempt rather than taxable, or taxable at a different rate.
- A credit note issued to amend a sales invoice must always be issued at the same rate of VAT as the original invoice.

57

Records

Cross-references. See **32.6 HMRC: POWERS** for the production of documents; **40 INVOICES** for details to be recorded on sales invoices; **64.5 SPECIAL SCHEMES** for records under the cash accounting scheme; **64.21 SPECIAL SCHEMES** for records under the flat-rate scheme for small businesses; **64.29** and **64.30 SPECIAL SCHEMES** for records and invoices under the flat-rate scheme for farmers.

Introduction to records

General requirements

[57.1] Every taxable person must keep such records as HMRC may require. [*VATA 1994, Sch 11 para 6(1)*].

Specifically, every taxable person must, for the purposes of accounting for VAT, keep the following records.

- His business and accounting records.
- His VAT account.
- Copies of all VAT invoices issued by him.
- VAT invoices received by him.
- Certificates issued under provisions relating to fiscal or other warehouse regimes.
- Documentation received by him relating to acquisitions of any goods from other EU member states.
- Copy documentation issued by him, and documentation received by him, relating to the transfer, dispatch or transportation of goods by him to other EU member states.

- Documentation relating to importations and exportations by him.
- All credit notes, debit notes and other documents which evidence an increase or decrease in consideration that are received, and copies of all such documents that are issued by him.
- A copy of any self-billing agreement to which he is a party (see **40.6 INVOICES**).
- Where he is a customer, party to a self-billing agreement, the name, address and VAT registration number of each supplier with whom he has entered into a self-billing agreement (see **40.6 INVOICES**).

[*SI 1995/2518, Reg 31(1)*].

Additionally, HMRC may supplement the above provisions by a Notice published by them for that purpose. [*SI 1995/2518, Reg 31(2)*]. These requirements, which are contained in VAT Notice 700, Section 19, are considered below in this chapter. They supplement the statutory requirements and *have legal force*.

Business records include, in addition to specific items listed above, orders and delivery notes, relevant business correspondence, purchases and sales books, cash books and other account books, records of daily takings such as till rolls, annual accounts, including trading and profit and loss accounts and bank statements and paying-in slips.

Unless the business mainly involves the supply of goods and services direct to the public and less detailed VAT invoices are issued (see **40.7 INVOICES**), all VAT invoices must also be retained. *Cash and carry wholesalers* must keep all till rolls and product code lists.

Records must be kept of all taxable goods and services received or supplied in the course of business (standard and zero-rated), together with any exempt supplies, gifts or loans of goods, taxable self-supplies and any goods acquired or produced in the course of business which are put to private or other non-business use.

All records must be kept up to date and be in sufficient detail to allow calculation of VAT. They do not have to be kept in any set way but must be in a form which will enable HMRC officers to check easily the figures on the VAT return. Records must be readily available to HMRC officers on request. If a taxable person has more than one place of business, a list of all branches must be kept at the principal place of business.

(VAT Notice 700, paras 19.2, 19.4).

Special records

In addition to the above general requirements, special records are necessary where the taxable person is operating the cash accounting scheme (see **64.5 SPECIAL SCHEMES**), the flat-rate scheme for farmers (see **64.29 SPECIAL SCHEMES**), one of the **61 RETAIL SCHEMES** or one of the schemes for **62 SECOND-HAND GOODS**. These requirements are dealt with in the appropriate chapter. See also **20.30 EUROPEAN UNION: SINGLE MARKET** for the requirement to keep a register of temporary movement of goods to and from other EU member states.

Direction to keep records where belief VAT might not be paid

Where HMRC have reasonable grounds for believing that certain records might assist in them identifying taxable supplies on which the VAT chargeable might not be paid, they may direct any taxable person named in the direction to keep such records as they specify in the direction in relation to such goods as they so specify (in addition to any records under the general requirements above). In this connection

- the direction may require the records to be compiled by reference to VAT invoices or any other matter; and
- the taxable supplies in question may be supplies made by the person named in the direction or any other person.

The direction must be given by notice in writing to the person named in it and must warn that person of the penalty for failure to comply (see **53.27** **PENALTIES**). It remains in force until it is revoked or replaced by a further direction.

HMRC may require any records kept under these provisions to be preserved for a period not exceeding six years and the provision in **57.4** below as to the form in which records may be preserved also apply for these purposes.

Appeals

An appeal may be made against a direction but the tribunal cannot allow the appeal unless it considers that HMRC could not reasonably have been satisfied that there were grounds for making the direction. The direction has effect pending the determination of the appeal.

[*VATA 1994, s 84(7B); Sch 11 para 6A*].

De Voil Indirect Tax Service. See V5.201.

Records by non-taxable persons

[57.2] Non-taxable persons are generally outside the scope of VAT and are not therefore required to keep any records for VAT purposes. However, any person who, at a time when he is not a taxable person, acquires in the UK from another EU member state any goods which are subject to excise duty or which consist of a new means of transport must keep such records of the acquisition as HMRC specify in any Notice published by them. [*SI 1995/2518, Reg 31(3)*]. See **20.9** and **20.37 EUROPEAN UNION: SINGLE MARKET**.

Preservation of records

[57.3] Every taxable person must keep such records as are required for a period not exceeding six years as specified in writing by HMRC (and different periods may be specified for different cases). [*VATA 1994, Sch 11 para 6(3)*]. If this causes storage problems or involves undue expense, HMRC should be consulted. They will be able to advise whether some records can be retained for a shorter period. Agreement of HMRC must be obtained before any business records are destroyed within six years. (VAT Notice 700, para 19.2).

HMRC are unlikely to agree to a shorter retention period than

- one year for copies of orders, delivery notes, dispatch notes, goods returned notes, invoices for expenses incurred by employees, production records, stock records (except those for second-hand schemes), job cards, appointment books, diaries, and business letters;
- three years for import, export and delivery from warehouse documents, day books, ledgers, cash books, and second-hand scheme stock books;
- four years for purchase invoices, copy sales invoices, credit notes, debit notes, authenticated receipts, daily gross takings records, records related to retail scheme calculations, and catering estimates; and
- five years for bank statements and paying in books, management accounts, and annual accounts.

Any records containing the VAT account must always be kept for the full six years.

(HMRC VAT Guidance VATREC3000, para 3.4.1).

De Voil Indirect Tax Service. See V5.202.

Forms in which records may be preserved

[57.4] The duty to preserve records may be discharged by

- preserving them; or
- preserving the information contained in them

in any form and by any means subject to any conditions or exceptions specified in writing by HMRC.

[*VATA 1994, Sch 11 para 6(4)*].

In addition to the preservation of the full original records, HMRC have approved the use of the following.

- **Microfilm and microfiche** provided that the copies can readily be produced and that there are adequate facilities for HMRC to view when required. Clearance must be obtained in advance from HMRC before any transfer to microfilm or microfiche. HMRC may require the old and new systems to be operated side by side for a limited time.
- Computer records provided the storage media e.g. magnetic tape, disc, etc. can readily be converted into a legible form on request by HMRC. Where records are kept on a computer, HMRC can have access to it and can check its operation and the information stored. They can also ask for help from anyone concerned with the operation of the computer or its software. See **32.10 HMRC: POWERS**. Where the records are kept by a computer bureau, the taxable person is responsible for arranging for the bureau to make the records available to HMRC when required. Normally this will be at the principal place of business. Where a taxable person decides to use a computer or the services of a bureau for VAT accounting after registration, he is not required to notify HMRC.

(VAT Notice 700, para 19.2).

De Voil Indirect Tax Service. See V5.206; V5.207.

Records of output tax

[57.5] Note: the following does not apply to supplies dealt with under one of the special schemes for retailers. For records required in these cases, see **61 RETAIL SCHEMES.**

Records must be kept of all supplies made in the course of business including goods sent out on sale or return, approval or similar terms. Information recorded must contain all the information required on VAT invoices. See **40.3 INVOICES.** Where fully detailed invoices are issued and filed so as to be readily available, the record required is a summary (in the same order as copy invoices) enabling separate totals to be produced for each VAT period of

(a) the amount of VAT chargeable on supplies and acquisitions. The VAT on adjustment for credits allowed (see **57.6** below) should be deducted from the amount of VAT payable in the VAT account (see **57.12** below);

(b) the VAT-exclusive value of standard-rated and zero-rated supplies and acquisitions;

(c) the value of any exempt supplies and acquisitions; and

(d) the amount of VAT due on goods imported by post (other than Datapost) with a value not exceeding £2,000 (see **34.3 IMPORTS**) and on certain services received from abroad (see **39.4 INTERNATIONAL SERVICES**). These amounts should also be carried to the VAT payable portion of the VAT account (see **57.12** below).

Under (*b*) and (*c*) above, no deduction should be made for *cash* discounts allowed but any credits allowed (see **57.6** below) should be deducted.

Goods given away or put to private or other non-business use

If acquired or produced in the course of business, VAT is due and a record must be kept showing date of transaction, description and quantity of the goods, VAT-exclusive cost and rate and amount of VAT chargeable. See **48.5** and **48.6 OUTPUT TAX** for the value of the supply.

Self-supplies

See **46.6 MOTOR CARS** for motor cars used by motor manufacturers or dealers who have produced or acquired them in the course of business. Records must show the tax point, value on which VAT is chargeable and the rate and amount of VAT. See **63.2 SELF-SUPPLY** for records to be kept by a partly exempt trader who self-supplies certain printed matter.

(VAT Notice 700, para 19.5).

Records of credits allowed to customers

[57.6] Note: where a **61 RETAIL SCHEMES** is used, the following only applies where the credit involves a VAT invoice.

Records must be kept of all credits allowed for taxable (including zero-rated) and exempt supplies and acquisitions. A record of a credit relating to

- **a VAT invoice** must contain the information required on VAT invoices (see **40.3 INVOICES**) or indicate (e.g. by cross-reference to filed copies of credit notes) where the details can be found; and
- **zero-rated or exempt supplies** must show the date and amount of the credit and indicate whether an export is a zero-rated supply in the UK or an exempt supply.

For VAT purposes, where filed copies of credit notes are complete and accessible no separate record need be kept.

(VAT Notice 700, para 19.6).

Records of input tax

[57.7] For EU legislation, see **19.36 EUROPEAN UNION LEGISLATION.**

Under UK legislation, records must be kept of all standard-rated, reduced-rated and zero-rated supplies received for business purposes. They must be kept in such a way that, given the invoice date and the supplier's name, they can be easily produced to HMRC.

At the time of claiming input tax deduction, one of the items listed in (*a*)–(*d*) below (as appropriate) must normally be held to support a claim to input tax. HMRC *may*, however, direct that a claimant can hold or provide other evidence of the VAT charged. Such a direction may be made generally or in relation to particular cases or classes of cases.

(a) A supplier's invoice

Subject to below, where the supply is from another UK VAT-registered business, the claimant must hold a 'valid VAT invoice' or a document treated as such (see **40.2 INVOICES**). See also **64.30 SPECIAL SCHEMES** for invoices from flat-rate farmers. An invoice marked 'pro forma' or 'this is not a VAT invoice' is not acceptable for the purposes of reclaiming VAT.

Exceptions

No VAT invoice is required where total expenditure for each taxable supply is £25 or less (including VAT) and relates to

- telephone calls from public or private telephones;
- purchases through coin-operated machines;
- car park charges (on-street parking meters are not subject to VAT); or
- a single or return standard-rated toll charge (see **48.8**(33) **OUTPUT TAX**) paid at the tollbooth. But a VAT invoice is required, irrespective of the price of each individual toll, if
  - (i) a book of toll tickets is purchased; or
  - (ii) a tolled road, bridge or crossing is used under an arrangement where either payment is made in advance (e.g. where an electronic tag is used) or an invoice is raised in arrears (e.g. an account customer).

A '*valid VAT invoice*' is one that meets the full requirements in **40.4**(*a*)–(*m*) **INVOICES** or, as the case may be, the reduced requirements in **40.7** and **40.8 INVOICES**.

An '*invalid VAT invoice*' is one that does not meet those full requirements. Even if an invoice contains all the information required, it is still invalid if, for example, it relates to a business other than the one making the supply or the details shown relate to a company in liquidation. Some invalidities may be easy to detect (e.g. whether the goods or services are correctly described) but it may be more difficult to detect a false name, address or VAT number. HMRC have established a team who can confirm that any given VAT registration details are current, valid and match information held by them (ring the VAT Helpline on 0300 200 3700) but this cannot be viewed as authorisation of a transaction with that VAT registration by the supplier in question. The claimant should be able to demonstrate that the person shown as making the supply is the same person who actually made the supply.

A claimant holding an invalid VAT invoice should, wherever possible, ask the supplier to issue a valid VAT invoice. HMRC expect that only a very small number of businesses will be unable to obtain a valid VAT invoice in this way.

Where a valid VAT invoice cannot be obtained, HMRC may apply their discretion and still allow recovery.

(i) For supplies of goods comprising
   - computers and any other equipment, including parts, accessories and software, made or adapted for use in connection with computers or computer systems,
   - telephones and any other equipment, including parts and accessories, made or adapted for use in connection with telephones or telecommunications,
   - alcoholic liquors liable to excise duty which are defined by *Alcoholic Liquor Duties Act 1979, s 1* or in any regulations made under that *Act* (e.g. spirits, wines and fortified wines, made-wines, beer, cider and perry), and
   - oils that are held out for sale as road fuel

   claimants will need to be able to answer satisfactorily *all or nearly all* of questions (1)–(6) below (plus any additional questions HMRC ask in individual circumstances, in particular questions to test whether they took reasonable care in respect of transactions to ensure that their supplier and the supply were 'bona fide').

(ii) For supplies of goods not falling within (i) above, claimants will need to be able to answer satisfactorily *most* of questions (1)–(6) below. In most cases, this will be little more than providing alternative evidence to show that the supply of goods or services has been made. (This has always been HMRC's policy.)

The questions to determine whether there is a right to deduct in the absence of a valid VAT invoice are as follows.

(1) Does the claimant have alternative documentary evidence other than an invoice (e.g. a supplier's statement)?

(2) Does the claimant have evidence of receipt of a taxable supply on which VAT has been charged?
(3) Does the claimant have evidence of payment?
(4) Does the claimant have evidence of how the goods/services have been consumed within the business or their onward supply?
(5) How did the claimant know that the supplier existed?
(6) How was the claimant's relationship with the supplier established? For example:
   - How was contact made?
   - Does the claimant know where the supplier operates from (and has he been there)?
   - How does the claimant contact the supplier?
   - How does the claimant know the supplier can supply the goods or services?
   - If goods, how does the claimant know the goods are not stolen?
   - How can faulty supplies be returned?

Incomplete invoices

Normally the invoice or other document should contain the full particulars required for a valid VAT invoice (see above). However, HMRC may accept as satisfactory evidence an invoice complete except for

- an identifying number;
- the customer's name and address; and
- the tax point (provided there is a date which can be taken to be the tax point)

provided the supplies in question are clearly for business purposes.

Originals normally required

VAT invoices held to substantiate claims to input tax should be originals. Copies are not normally accepted.

Where, however, the accounting arrangements require the original VAT invoice to be sent to a destination within the business which is different from the registered address for VAT (e.g. a branch), HMRC may accept a photocopy of the original as evidence in support of input tax claims provided

- each photocopy is certified by a responsible officer as being a true copy of the original; and
- the original invoice is produced for inspection by HMRC on formal request.

All requirements of a VAT invoice apply to the photocopy. HMRC will notify the business in writing of the conditions and the business must give a written acceptance.

Invoices sent by fax or e-mail

HMRC now accept that, as an alternative to sending VAT invoices by post, they may be sent to customers by fax or e-mail. See **40.13 INVOICES**. If the invoice is received via fax and the recipient has a thermal-paper fax machine, the invoice may not be permanent and the recipient may not be able to fulfil the obligation to preserve the invoice for six years.

Cash and carry wholesalers' invoices

If the invoice is only in the form of a till roll with goods represented by product code numbers, an up-to-date copy of the wholesaler's product code list must be kept with the till rolls.

Invoices in name of employees

Certain invoices made out in the name of employees can be accepted as evidence for input tax purposes. See **35.5 INPUT TAX.**

Court and tribunal decisions

A claim for input tax has been allowed where invoices were destroyed accidentally (*JJ Newman* (VTD 781, VTD 903) (TVC 40.68)) and where invoices were lost on a change of residence but had previously been checked by the firm's accountants (*Read and Smith* (VTD 1188) (TVC 40.70)). See *Chavda (t/a Hare Wines)* [1992] Lexis Citation 1630 (TVC 40.11) where the tribunal held that HMRC had not acted reasonably by refusing to exercise their discretion to accept other documentary evidence (delivery notes) of the input tax incurred by the appellant. However, in the vast majority of tribunal and court decisions, claims for input tax without supporting invoices have been rejected and it has been ruled that countries have the power to require production of original invoices (*Reisdorf v Finanzamt Köln-West*, ECJ [1997] STC 180 (TVC 22.546)). Where HMRC refuse to use their discretion to allow credit, tribunals only have a supervisory jurisdiction, the burden of proof being on the appellant to show that HMRC acted unreasonably. See *Kohanzad v C & E Commrs*, QB [1994] STC 967 (TVC 40.79) and the Invoices and Credit Notes chapter in *Tolley's VAT Cases*.

(b) Evidence of VAT on goods imported or removed from customs warehouse

On importation of goods, the claimant must hold a document showing him as importer, consignee or owner and showing an amount of VAT charged on the goods and authenticated or issued by the proper officer. For goods which have been removed from warehouse, the claimant must hold a document authenticated or issued by the proper officer showing the claimant's particulars and the amount of the VAT charged on the goods. See **34.11 IMPORTS** for the official evidence (or other acceptable evidence) required which serves the same purpose as a VAT invoice from a registered UK supplier.

(c) Evidence of VAT on goods acquired from another EU member state

On the acquisition of goods from another EU member state, the claimant must hold a document required to be issued by the authority in that other country showing the claimant's VAT registration number (including the prefix 'GB'), the registration number of the supplier (including alphabetical code), the consideration for the supply exclusive of VAT, the date of issue of the document and a description of the goods supplied sufficient to identify them. Where the goods are a new means of transport (see **20.33 EUROPEAN UNION: SINGLE MARKET**) the description must be sufficient to identify the acquisition as a new means of transport.

(d) Evidence of services received from abroad

Where any of the services listed in *VATA 1994, Sch 5* are received from abroad (see **39.4 INTERNATIONAL SERVICES**) the relevant invoice from the person supplying the services should be held.

[*SI 1995/2518, Reg 29(2)*]. (VAT Notice 700, para 19.7; HMRC Statement of Practice *VAT strategy: input tax deduction without a valid invoice*).

Non-deductible items

VAT is not reclaimable on certain supplies received for the business e.g. motor cars and entertainment expenses (see **35.8 INPUT TAX** for details). However, a record must be kept of such supplies received even though the VAT charged is not to be included in the total carried to the VAT account.

De Voil Indirect Tax Service. See V3.415; V3.421; V3.425–427.

Form of records

[57.8] Where fully detailed invoices are received and filed so as to be readily available, the record required is a summary (in the same order as the invoices are filed) enabling a separate total to be produced for each VAT period of

(a) the amount of VAT charged on goods and services received including any VAT paid at import or on removal from bonded warehouse. Where adjustment is required for credit received from suppliers in the period (see **57.9** below) this should be deducted;

(b) the amount of VAT due on any goods imported by post (other than Datapost) with a value of £2,000 or less and on certain services received from abroad (see **39.4 INTERNATIONAL SERVICES**);

(c) the VAT-exclusive value of all supplies received, including all such goods and services within (*b*) above.

Subject to the normal rules, the total amount of deductible input tax ((*a*) plus (*b*)) should be carried to the VAT allowable portion of the VAT account (see **57.12** below).

Under (*c*) above no deduction for *cash* discounts should be made but all credits received from suppliers should be deducted.

An add-list is an acceptable summary if it shows VAT and values separately itemised in the order in which the VAT invoices are batched or filed. Alternatively, **cashbook accounting for inputs** may be used where it is the normal accounting practice to claim input tax when suppliers are paid. In practice, the cash book payments record is adapted to serve as a record of inputs. On a change in basis of accounting to this method, VAT already claimed on a previous return should be excluded. See also **64.2 SPECIAL SCHEMES.**

Note: if any of the **61 RETAIL SCHEMES** is used, the cash book can also be used to work out the value of goods received for resale provided amounts owed to suppliers at the beginning of the period are subtracted and amounts owed at the end of the period are added.

(VAT Notice 700, para 19.8).

Records of credits received from suppliers

[57.9] Records must be kept of all credits received for taxable (including zero-rated) inputs. A record of a credit relating to

- **a VAT invoice** must contain the information listed in **40.3** *et seq.* **INVOICES**, or indicate (e.g. by cross-reference to filed credit notes) where the details can be found; and
- **zero-rated supplies** need only indicate the date and amount of the credit.

For VAT purposes, where filed credit notes are complete and easily accessible, no separate record need be kept.

VAT adjustments

Where a credit is received relating to deductible input tax (see **40.14 INVOICES**) and a VAT adjustment has to be made, records of supplies received and input tax must be adjusted. Whatever method is used to do this, the nature of the adjustment and reason for it must be clear from the accounts and supporting documents. At the end of each VAT period the deductible input tax entered in the VAT account and the VAT return entries must be the net amount, i.e. after deducting any VAT credits received in the period. If VAT credits received from suppliers exceed VAT charged on purchases in any VAT period, a minus figure (shown in brackets) should be entered in the input tax box on the VAT return. Where debit notes are issued to suppliers from whom credit is due and the commercial records are then adjusted, the VAT record may also be adjusted at that time. If later credit notes are received from suppliers, any errors should be corrected but the debit and credit notes should not be both used as accounting documents.

Provided both parties to the transaction agree, the *original* VAT charged need not be adjusted on a debit note issued by a fully taxable person.

(VAT Notice 700, para 19.8).

Adjustments where wrong amount of VAT shown on VAT invoices

[57.10] Note: this paragraph does *not* apply where there has been a change in the consideration for the supply, i.e. if the price has changed and consequently the amount of VAT. In these circumstances, see **40.14 INVOICES** for the provisions relating to credit and debit notes.

This paragraph explains how to correct an error if the wrong amount of VAT was shown on an invoice, e.g. where

- an arithmetical mistake is made in calculating the VAT value and/or the VAT element of the supply; or

- VAT is charged on a supply where no VAT was due.

Unless both the supplier and customer agree to adjust their VAT accounts (see below):

(a) *If the VAT shown on the invoice is too high,*
- the supplier must account for the higher amount in his records, unless he corrects the error with the customer by issuing a credit note; and
- the customer must go back to the supplier for a replacement invoice reducing the amount of VAT charged.

(b) *If the VAT shown on the invoice is too low,*
- the supplier must account for the amount which should have charged, whether or not he corrects the error with the customer (e.g. by issuing a supplementary invoice); and
- the customer must go back to the supplier for a replacement invoice increasing the amount of VAT charged.

Where the supplier is unwilling or unable to recover the whole of the balance due from the customer, a VAT adjustment, calculated from the total VAT-inclusive amount actually charged, should be made.

Example

	£
Value of goods on VAT invoice	500.00
VAT due = £500 × 20% = £100 but incorrectly stated as	55.00
Invoiced amount	£555.00
Adjusted VAT due	
£555 × 1/6** (VAT fraction)	92.50
Deduct VAT charged	55.00
Balance payable	£37.50

(VAT Notice 700, para 19.10; VAT Notice 700/45/17, paras 3.1–3.3).

De Voil Indirect Tax Service. See V3.518; V3.519.

Correction of errors on a return already submitted

[57.11] There are two methods for correcting errors on a return already submitted.

Method 1

This method may be used to adjust the VAT account (see **57.12** below) and include the value of that adjustment on the current VAT return providing

- the net value of errors found on previous returns does not exceed £10,000; or

- the net value of errors found on previous returns is between £10,000 and £50,000 but does not exceed 1% of the box 6 (net outputs) VAT return declaration due for the return period in which the errors are discovered.

To work out the net value of VAT errors on previous returns, the business should work out

- the total amount due to HMRC, if any; and
- the total amount due to the business, if any.

If the difference between the two figures is greater than £10,000 and exceeds 1% of the box 6 (net outputs) VAT return declaration due for the current return period during which the error is discovered, then Method 2 must be used. Method 2 must always be used if the net errors exceed £50,000 or if the errors made on previous returns were made deliberately.

Correcting errors using this method is not a disclosure for the purposes of the penalties for error regime described below. If the business considers that the error was a result of careless conduct, maximum reduction of the penalty will not be granted unless HMRC is notified separately in writing, by letter and/or completion of form VAT 652, of the error and the grounds for seeking a reduction to the penalty.

> *Example*
>
> Alan is VAT-registered and has discovered two VAT errors made in the period ended 31 March:
>
> - input tax incorrectly claimed on the purchase of a motor car available for private use £12,000;
> - arithmetical error in output tax calculations – £3,000 overpaid.
>
> The net value of the errors made by Alan (£12,000 – £3,000 = £9,000) is less than £10,000 so they can be recorded in his VAT account for the current VAT period and declared on the next VAT return he submits.

Method 2 (error correction notification)

This method must be used if

- the net value of errors found on previous returns is between £10,000 and £50,000 and exceeds 1% of the box 6 (net outputs) VAT return declaration due for the current return period during which the error was discovered; or
- the net value of errors found on previous returns is greater than £50,000; or
- the errors on previous returns were made deliberately.

This method may be used for errors within the limits shown under Method 1 above, instead of a Method 1 error correction. If this method is used, adjustment must not be made for the same errors on a later VAT return.

When notifying HMRC of an error correction the business should use VAT 652, or should write to the appropriate office providing full details of the errors including

- how each error arose;
- the VAT accounting period in which it occurred;
- if it was an input tax or output error;
- the VAT underdeclared or overdeclared in each VAT period;
- how the VAT underdeclared or overdeclared was calculated;
- whether any of the errors resulted in the business paying HMRC an amount that wasn't due (in which case see **52.10 PAYMENT OF VAT**); and
- the total amount to be adjusted.

(VAT Notice 700/45/17, paras 4.3, 4.4).

Notice of error correction by HMRC and payment

Once an error correction notification has been processed, HMRC will send the business, normally within 21 days, a Notice of Error Correction (confirming the amount of the error correction and any interest calculated on it) and a Statement of Account (showing the current balance payable to or repayable by HMRC). Where, however, the correction generated a repayment which is subject to the unjust enrichment provisions (see **52.11 PAYMENT OF VAT**) the business will be notified by letter and will not receive these documents.

Where payment is due to HMRC, full payment should normally be made electronically to HMRC's bank account in accordance with instructions at www.gov.uk/pay-vat. Further interest may be charged if the amount due is not paid in full within 30 days from the calculation date shown on the Notice of Error Correction. Payment can be made by any of the methods outlined in **52.2 PAYMENT OF VAT**. Where repayment is due from HMRC, they will use it to reduce any outstanding balance due to them (if any) and repay the remainder either by BACS or payable order.

(VAT Notice 700/45/17, paras 7.2–7.4).

Time limit for correcting errors

A business cannot adjust its VAT return, or make an error correction notification, for any errors that arose in accounting periods that are outside the time limits below. However, a business may be able to correct tax point errors, where the business has declared an amount of VAT on the return that immediately precedes or follows the return for which the amount was due, provided the later return remains in time under the four-year capping provisions.

(VAT Notice 700/45/17, para 4.6).

Penalties for error regime

Errors or inaccuracies are liable to a penalty if they are careless or deliberate. If a person discovers a non-careless error, HMRC expect that they will take steps to correct it, otherwise the inaccuracy will be treated as careless and a penalty will be due.

Careless or deliberate inaccuracies that are being corrected using Method 1 or 2 are still subject to the penalty regime.

Where careless or deliberate behaviour results in an incorrect error correction notification being made under Method 2 the business will be subject to a penalty. This applies regardless of whether the original errors were made despite taking reasonable care or not.

In order for HMRC to consider any reduction to a penalty, the business should tell them if it has made a careless error or deliberate inaccuracy regardless of its size or value. Although HMRC also require separate disclosure for the purpose of reducing any penalty, careless errors may be adjusted on the next VAT return subject to the limits described above.

Correction of deliberate inaccuracies must, however, always be notified to HMRC using form VAT 652, providing a description of the inaccuracy, the full amount of the inaccuracy and explaining how and why the inaccuracy arose.

If the business has adjusted a careless error/inaccuracy on its return that is within the limits described above it may still write to HMRC asking them to consider any reduction to a penalty. The letter should contain the same information that is required on form VAT 652, but it is important to also tell HMRC that the adjustment has been made on the return. The majority of such errors will not be careless or deliberate, so no penalty will be due. When considering whether an error was careless, HMRC will seek to establish whether the business has taken the care and attention that could be expected from a reasonable person taking reasonable care in similar circumstances.

(VAT Notice 700/45/17, para 4.1).

Discovery of errors by HMRC

For accounting periods after the introduction of the penalties for errors regime

If HMRC find underdeclarations of VAT on the VAT returns of a business, they will assess for the tax due and may charge interest. The business may also be liable to a penalty.

For accounting periods prior to the introduction of the penalties for errors regime

If HMRC find underdeclarations of VAT on the returns of a business, they will assess for the tax due and may charge interest. The business may also face a misdeclaration penalty (see **53.14 PENALTIES**). To avoid a penalty, the business must disclose full details of the mistakes before HMRC begin to make enquiries into its VAT affairs. Enquiries normally begin when HMRC make an appointment to inspect records. But they accept disclosures for penalty purposes after this point, unless they have reason to believe that

- the business discovered the errors earlier and disclosed them only because it had been told that a visit was to be made; or
- disclosure during or after a visit was prompted by HMRC enquiries into the affairs of the business.

In addition, deliberate failure to correct an underdeclaration of VAT may give rise to a civil penalty for dishonest evasion (see **53.12 PENALTIES**) or criminal prosecution (see **53.2 PENALTIES**).

(VAT Notice 700/45/17, para 4.8).

Adjustments that are not errors

Provided they are accurate and made at the right time, adjustments that are required to be made as part of the normal operation of VAT accounting are not errors. These accounting adjustments include

- retail scheme annual adjustments or other adjustments required when ceasing to use a particular retail scheme;
- adjustments under the **11 CAPITAL GOODS SCHEME**;
- use of an approved estimation procedure;
- partial exemption annual adjustments (see **50.9 PARTIAL EXEMPTION**);
- partial exemption clawback and payback adjustments (see **50.14 PARTIAL EXEMPTION**);
- exports and intra-European Union supplies of goods (see **22.28 EXPORTS** and **20.11 EUROPEAN UNION: SINGLE MARKET**);
- issuing or receiving credit and debit notes (see **40.14 INVOICES**);
- adjustments reflecting reductions in consideration received by a first supplier in a supply chain involving goods (see below);
- claims for **7 BAD DEBT RELIEF**; and
- pre-registration and post deregistration expenses.

If the original accounting adjustment was incorrect, or made at the wrong time, error corrections should be made in the normal way.

From 1 April 2014, where a first supplier, for example a manufacturer or importer, makes a relevant payment direct to a final consumer or a final supplier in a supply chain involving goods, the first supplier and the person who receives the relevant payment are required to adjust their VAT accounts to reflect the reduction in consideration received by the first supplier. A relevant payment means

(a) a cash refund made by the first supplier direct to the final consumer—
  (i) to reflect the reduced value (including a reduction to nil) of goods which are faulty, damaged or otherwise do not fully meet expectations of the final consumer,
  (ii) as a result of a product recall, or
  (iii) in accordance with the terms of a sales promotion scheme operated by the first supplier under the terms of which the final consumer is required to provide proof of purchase of specified goods to the first supplier; or

(b) a reimbursement made by the first supplier direct to the final supplier—
  (i) which equates to the redemption value of a money-off coupon issued by the first supplier and used by the final consumer in part payment for goods purchased from the final supplier, or
  (ii) to redeem a money-off coupon issued by the first supplier in any of the circumstances specified in sub-paragraph (a)(i) or (ii) and used by the final consumer in full or part payment for goods purchased from the final supplier.

Where the rate of VAT applicable to the supply made by the first supplier differs from the rate of VAT applicable to the supply made by the final supplier, the adjustment made by the first supplier shall be at the rate of VAT applied by the final supplier.

[*SI 1995/2518, Reg 38ZA; SI 2014/548, Reg 4*]. (VAT Notice 700/45/17, para 4.10).

> *Example*
>
> Sue is VAT-registered and is partly exempt, using the standard method of calculation. She has just carried out her annual adjustment calculation for the partial exemption year ended 30 April 2017, and calculated that £12,000 is owed to HMRC. This is not a VAT error, as long as the quarterly partial exemption calculations were carried out correctly. The amount of £12,000 can either be included as an adjustment on Sue's April 2017 VAT return or, more favourable to her, on the July 2017 return.
>
> This is because the adjustment period for annual adjustment calculations is either the VAT return at the end of the tax year (March, April or May, depending on VAT periods) or the following return (June, July or August), the period chosen being at the discretion of the taxpayer.

Best time to correct errors

As soon as a business finds an error, it should record it in its VAT records for correction or it could become liable to a penalty. It may be useful to keep a separate record of

- the date the error was discovered;
- the period in which the error occurred;
- any related documentation; and
- whether the error was output or input tax related.

Normally, it would be best to wait until the end of the current accounting period before deciding whether Method 1 or Method 2 applies. However, if an individual error is so large that the 1% box 6 test or £50,000 limit will inevitably be breached, an error correction report should be made to HMRC using Method 2 immediately.

(VAT Notice 700/45/17, para 4.12).

[*SI 1995/2518, Regs 34, 35*].

De Voil Indirect Tax Service. See V3.419; V3.506.

VAT account

[57.12] Every taxable person must keep and maintain an account to be known as the VAT account. It must be divided into separate parts relating to the VAT periods of the taxable person and each part must be divided into two portions known as 'the VAT payable portion' and 'the VAT allowable portion'.

VAT payable portion

The VAT payable portion comprises the following.

- Output tax due from the taxable person for that VAT period.

- Output tax due on acquisitions from other EU member states by the taxable person for that VAT period.
- Tax which the taxable person is required to account for and pay on behalf of the supplier under the reverse charge provisions for mobile phones and computer chips. See **4.15 ANTI-AVOIDANCE.**
- Corrections and adjustments to the VAT payable portion of a previous return which may be corrected on the current return (see **57.11** above) and adjustments where a supply becomes, or ceases to become, subject to the reverse charge provisions for mobile phones and computer chips (see **4.23 ANTI-AVOIDANCE**).
- Subject to the time limit below, a positive/negative entry where there is an increase/decrease in the taxable consideration due on a supply *made* in a previous accounting period. The entry must be made in the return for the period in which the adjustment is given effect in the business accounts (unless the taxable person is insolvent in which case the entry must be made in the return for the period in which the supply was made).
  Where the consideration for an earlier supply is adjusted in accordance with *SI 1995/2518, Reg 38*, a trader has a directly enforceable EU right to be taxed on the consideration actually received, and the normal four-year time limit for adjustments does not apply. This was confirmed by the decision in *General Motors Acceptance Corpn (UK) plc* (VTD 17990) (TVC 44.52) and subsequently accepted by HMRC and incorporated in the regulation. (VAT Information Sheet 6/03).
  It is essential that a credit note or debit note is prepared to support the adjustment (see **40.14 INVOICES**). It is not possible to adjust the consideration on the original invoice without such a document (*British Telecommunications plc* (VTD 14669) (TVC 40.125)).
- Adjustments to the amount of VAT payable by the taxable person for that VAT period which are required, or allowed, by or under any VAT *Regulations*.

VAT allowable portion

The **VAT allowable portion** comprises the following.

- Input tax allowable to the taxable person for that VAT period.
- Input tax allowable in respect of acquisitions from other EU member states by the taxable person for that VAT period.
- Corrections of the VAT allowable portion of a previous return which may be corrected on the current return (see **57.11** above).
- Subject to the time limit below, a positive/negative entry where there is an increase/decrease in the taxable consideration due on a supply *received* in a previous accounting period. The entry must be made in the return for the period in which the adjustment is given effect in the business accounts (unless the taxable person is insolvent in which case the entry must be made in the return for the period in which the supply was received).
  No adjustment must be made where that increase/decrease occurs more than four years after the end of the VAT period in which the original supply took place.

It is essential that a credit note or debit note is prepared to support the adjustment (see **40.14 INVOICES**).

- Adjustments to the amount of input tax allowable to the taxable person for that VAT period which are required, or allowed, by or under any *VAT Regulations*.

[*SI 1995/2518, Regs 32, 38*].

De Voil Indirect Tax Service. See V5.211.

Audit of VAT records

[57.13] Where a business is subject to an independent audit, the audit will normally cover the VAT account and other records relating to VAT. However, as an auditor's responsibilities normally arise under statute, this does not mean that the auditor must make a specific reference to the VAT records in his report. (VAT Notice 700, para 19.2).

De Voil Indirect Tax Service. See V5.203.

Duties of senior accounting officers

Main duty

[57.14] The senior accounting officer of a qualifying company must take reasonable steps to ensure that the company establishes and maintains appropriate tax accounting arrangements. He must, in particular, take reasonable steps to: monitor the accounting arrangements of the company; and identify any respects in which those arrangements are not appropriate tax accounting arrangements.

Certificates

The senior accounting officer must provide HMRC with a certificate for each financial year of the company. The certificate must: state whether the company had appropriate tax accounting arrangements throughout the financial year; and if it did not, give an explanation of the respects in which the accounting arrangements were not appropriate tax accounting arrangements. The certificate must be provided: by such means and in such form as is reasonably specified by an HMRC officer; and not later than the end of the period for filing the company's accounts for the financial year (or such later time as an HMRC officer may have allowed). A certificate may relate to more than one qualifying company.

Notifying HMRC of senior accounting officer's name

For each financial year a qualifying company must ensure that HMRC are notified of the name of each person who was its senior accounting officer at any time during the year. The notification must be given: by such means and in such form as is reasonably specified by an HMRC officer; and not later than the end of the period for filing the company's accounts for the financial year (or such later time as an HMRC officer may have allowed for providing the certificate for the financial year). A notification may relate to more than one qualifying company.

Penalties

A senior accounting officer may incur a penalty for: failing to comply with his main duty; failing to provide a certificate; or providing a certificate that contains a careless or deliberate inaccuracy. A company may incur a penalty for failing to notify HMRC of the name of its senior accounting officer (see **53.32 PENALTIES**).

[*FA 2009, Sch 46*].

De Voil Indirect Tax Service. See V5.214.

Key points: records

[57.15] Points to consider are follows.

- Every VAT-registered business must keep a VAT account, which clearly shows the source and calculation of all figures entered on each VAT return, including any adjustments for VAT errors made in past periods and now being corrected.
- A business must retain its records for a minimum period of six years. It may be possible to agree a shorter retention period with HMRC in certain cases.
- For input tax purposes, a valid VAT invoice issued by a supplier must be retained as evidence. In the absence of an invoice, HMRC will usually accept alternative evidence that confirms a valid charge of VAT has been made, and the identity of the goods or services that have been purchased.
- In situations where a supplier charges the wrong amount of VAT on an invoice, the customer can only reclaim input tax based on the amount that should have been charged if the amount is too high, or the actual amount charged if it is too low.
- A supplier charging the wrong amount of VAT on an invoice must account for output tax based on the amount shown on the invoice if it is too high. If the VAT amount is too low, then output tax should be based on the amount that should have been charged.
- A business can adjust a current VAT return to correct errors made on previous returns if the net value of all errors discovered is either less than £10,000 or less than £50,000 and 1% of the Box 6 outputs figure on the return where the error is to be corrected. Remember that errors can only need be corrected for the last four years – errors beyond this period are out of date and no adjustment is allowed.
- If an error (or 'net' errors) exceeds the above limits, it will need to be notified to HMRC, either in writing or on form VAT652. It is important to give full details about the errors in question and the VAT periods to which they relate.

- Even if the error is under the limit for making corrections on VAT returns it may still be necessary to advise HMRC of the error correction.
- Underpayments notified to HMRC will be subject to interest in most cases. It is important that the circumstances of an underpayment are clearly explained, as interest might not be applicable, e.g. if input tax incorrectly claimed would have been claimed by another business.
- There is an important difference between VAT errors and VAT adjustments. For example, the annual adjustments for partial exemption and the capital goods scheme are not VAT errors, they are normal adjustments that are included on the return where the adjustment must be made according to the scheme rules.

58

Recreation and Sport

Cross-references. See **19.24**(*m*) and (*o*) european union legislation for exemption of certain sporting services supplied by non-profit-making organisations; **35.13**(25) input tax for entitlement to deduct input tax in respect of sporting, recreational and sponsorship activities.

Sports and physical recreation competitions

[58.1] For EU Legislation, See **19.24**(*m*) EUROPEAN UNION LEGISLATION.

Entry fees

An entry fee for the right to enter a 'competition' is normally standard-rated. However, the grant of a right to enter a competition in 'sport or physical recreation' is exempt in the following circumstances.

(a) Where the entry fee is money which is allocated *wholly* towards the provision of a prize or prizes awarded in that competition. [*VATA 1994, Sch 9 Group 10 Item 1*].

(b) Where the grant is made by an 'eligible body' established for the purposes of sport or physical recreation. [*VATA 1994, Sch 9 Group 10 Item* 2]. See **58.5** below for the definitions of '*eligible body*'. Exemption does not, however, apply to competitions organised by local authorities because providing such competitions is not the sole basis of their existence and they are therefore not *established* for that purpose.

HMRC define '*competition*' as meaning 'a structured and organised contest, tournament or race where prizes or titles are awarded'. This definition was supported by the tribunal in *Wimborne Rugby Football Club* (VTD 4547) (TVC 24.33).

'*Sports or physical recreation*' is not defined in the legislation but includes all the activities listed in **58.7** below. Physical recreation activities such as greyhound/pigeon racing, clay pigeon shooting and darts are also included. *Not included* are activities such as chess, card games, dominoes, and spot the ball and other newspaper competitions. Where animals are involved, it is important to distinguish between animal shows (which are outside the exemption) and activities which qualify as sport or physical recreation, such as a competition where the animals are assessed wholly or partially upon their sporting abilities, e.g. jumping and racing. Where an entry fee covers both (e.g. pony shows involving examining the animals and jumping classes) the fee can be apportioned.

Value of the exempt supply

This is normally the full amount of entry fees (without deduction for amounts returned as prizes). However, it is only the supply of the right to enter the competition that is exempt. Where the 'entry fee' includes elements that are standard or zero-rated supplies, it is necessary to decide whether a single or multiple supply is being made. See **65.6 SUPPLY: GENERAL**.

Prizes

The VAT position of prizes awarded to competitors is the same whether the entry fees are exempt or standard-rated.

- *Prizes in the form of goods* (e.g. sports equipment, trophies that are owned permanently by the winner). These are treated as business gifts. No VAT is due on individual prizes costing £50 or less. Where the goods cost more than that amount, VAT must be accounted for on the cost of the goods (and input tax incurred on the purchase can be deducted). See **48.5 OUTPUT TAX**.
- *Prizes in the form of services* (e.g. holidays). Where input tax has been claimed on the purchase of the services given away as prizes, an equal sum of output tax is due at the time the prize is awarded. If no input tax is incurred, no output tax is due.
- *Prizes in the form of cash*. Cash prizes for being successful in a particular competition are outside the scope of VAT. However, prize money must be distinguished from guaranteed prize money and appearance money (see below).
- *Loans of challenge cups, shields and other perpetual trophies* which remain the property of the organisation or club mounting the competition is a supply of services but, because there is no consideration, the supply is outside the scope of VAT. The outright gift of cups, etc. is generally a prize in the form of goods (see above). See also, however, *C & E Commrs v Professional Footballers' Association (Enterprises) Ltd*, HL [1993] STC 86 (TVC 67.11) where it was held that the consideration for trophies presented at a dinner were included in the price of the tickets on which the company had accounted for VAT.

Guaranteed payments and appearance money

Where competitors are paid by the promoter or organiser to take part in an event, the payment is the consideration for the standard-rated supply of the individual's services. Where individuals are guaranteed a participation payment or they negotiate individually a guaranteed amount (even if this depends on the degree of success), such payments must be treated as appearance money.

Input tax

The entitlement to deduct input tax on purchases in connection with the running of competitions is subject to the normal rules, including those for partial exemption. See *Manx International Rally Ltd v Isle of Man Treasury* (VTD 6711) (TVC 46.78) where the company received income from sponsorship (standard-rated) as well as entries fees (exempt). The tribunal held that the rally was the subject of a supply to the sponsors as well as the competitors and the appropriate proportion of the input tax was therefore deductible. HMRC believe that this decision was unique to the facts and does not set a precedent in similar cases.

(VAT Notice 701/5/13, paras 9.1–9.3; VAT Notice 701/45/16, paras 6.1–6.6).

Admission charges to entertainment, cultural activities, sport, etc.

[58.2] The VAT liability of admission charges depends upon the nature of the event and the person promoting the event.

(1) Standard-rated admission charges

Unless falling within (2)–(6) below, the full amount of any admission charges are normally standard-rated. *Included* are admissions to cinemas, theatres, swimming pools, amusement arcades and fun fairs, dances, sports events, museums and galleries, parks and gardens, historic houses, areas of the countryside for general recreational purposes, zoos and safari parks, and air shows.

(2) Exempt admission charges by public bodies

Admission charges by a 'public body' to

(a) a 'museum, gallery, art exhibition or zoo', or
(b) a 'theatrical, musical or choreographic performance of a cultural nature'

are exempt unless this would be likely to create 'distortions of competition' such as to place a commercial enterprise carried on by a taxable business at a disadvantage.

The performance under (*b*) above must be provided exclusively by one or more public bodies, one or more eligible bodies (see (3) below) or any combination of public bodies and eligible bodies. Exemption does not apply where, for example, a local authority acts as ticket broker for a commercial promoter or has a profit/income sharing arrangement with that promoter for a qualifying performance. (VAT Notice 701/47/11, para 3.2).

A '*public body*' means

- a local authority;
- a government department within the meaning of *VATA 1994, s 41(6)* (see **44.11 LOCAL AUTHORITIES AND PUBLIC BODIES**); or
- a non-departmental public body which is listed in the 1995 edition of the publication prepared by the Office of Public Service and known as 'Public Bodies'. (Copies of this document may be obtained from HMSO Publication Centre, PO Box 276, London, SW8 5DT.)

[*VATA 1994, Sch 9 Group 13, Item 1, Notes (1)(3)(4)*].

What is a '*museum, gallery, art exhibition or zoo*' has to be judged by reference to the normal everyday meaning of the words, taking into account indicative evidence such as the nature of the collections, objects, artefacts, site and exhibits on show. However, for the avoidance of doubt, a botanical garden does not qualify for exemption.

Similarly, whether an event is a '*theatrical, musical or choreographic performance of a cultural nature*' must be judged on the individual merits of the event. However, HMRC will generally accept a live performance of any form of stage play, dance or music as cultural for the purposes of this exemption.

(VAT Notice 701/47/11, paras 2.3, 2.4).

'Distortions of competition'

A public body must take steps to notify all identifiable commercial suppliers of similar facilities or performances (e.g. a local authority should identify any such supplier within its geographical area of authority from its business rating, planning, taxation and other records). But it only needs to look at (*a*) and (*b*) above in isolation (e.g. if it wishes to exempt admission charges to a museum, it must demonstrate that it would not disadvantage commercial museums, galleries, art exhibitions and zoos within its geographical area, but would not have to take account of commercial theatrical, musical and choreographical performances).

Notice must be in writing but can be by individual letter or public notice in the local press for its geographical area. The notice must specify a date by which objections to exemption must be lodged. If no objections are received, the body can then start to exempt supplies but must retain copies of relevant correspondence and advertisements for future examination. If any objection is received, HMRC should be asked for a ruling (see **30.5 HMRC: ADMINISTRATION**) and in the meantime supplies should not be exempt. Once exemption is in place, it is not necessary to check on competition for each performance under (*b*) above or to make periodic checks for a new commercial supplier. It is for that supplier to approach HMRC.

Even if a public body is unable to identify any commercial supplier of similar services, it is HMRC's policy to allow the body to tax admissions of a qualifying nature if it wishes although this policy remains subject to review.

(VAT Notice 701/47/11, paras 3.3–3.10).

(3) Exempt admission charges by eligible bodies

Admission charges by an 'eligible body' to

(a) a 'museum, gallery, art exhibition or zoo', or
(b) a 'theatrical, musical or choreographic performance of a cultural nature'

are exempt. [*VATA 1994, Sch 9 Group 13, Item 2; SI 1996/1256*].

See (2) above for HMRC's interpretation of '*museum, gallery, art exhibition or zoo*' and '*theatrical, musical or choreographic performance of a cultural nature*'.

An '*eligible body*' means any body (other than a public body, see (2) above) which satisfies the following conditions.

(i) It is precluded from distributing, and does not distribute, any profit it makes. [*VATA 1994, Sch 9 Group 13 Note (2); SI 1996/1256*].
HMRC will normally accept a body as having satisfied this condition if
   - its constitution or articles of association preclude it from distributing surpluses of income over expenditure to its members, shareholders, parent or associated companies, or any other party (other than in the event of a liquidation or cessation of activities), and
   - it does not, as a matter of fact, distribute any profit.

   For these purposes, distribution of profit does not include grants or donations made by charities in pursuit of their wider charitable objectives. (VAT Notice 701/47/11, para 4.5).
(ii) It applies any profits made from admission charges exempt under this provision to the continuance or improvement of the facilities made available by means of the supplies. [*VATA 1994, Sch 9 Group 13 Note (2); SI 1996/1256*]. HMRC regard this as being satisfied if the body applies profits in the making of related cultural supplies (e.g. research or conservation projects). But if profits are applied to any other activities of the body, the body is not eligible for exemption. (VAT Notice 701/47/11, paras 4.3, 4.5).
(iii) It is managed and administered on a 'voluntary' basis by persons who have no 'direct or indirect financial interest' in its activities. [*VATA 1994, Sch 9 Group 13 Note (2); SI 1996/1256*].

Managed and administered on voluntary basis

In *Glastonbury Abbey* [1996] Lexis Citation 3790 (TVC 16.1) the tribunal disagreed with HMRC's earlier view and stated that the UK law should read 'managed and administered on an *essentially* voluntary basis' as set out in what is now *Directive 2006/112/EC, Art 133(b)* (see **19.24**(ii) **EUROPEAN COMMUNITY LEGISLATION**). Subsequently, in *C & E Commrs v The Zoological Society of London, CJEC Case C–267/00*, [2002] STC 521 (TVC 22.359) the Court held that the aim of the condition in *Art 133(b)* was to reserve the VAT exemption for bodies with no commercial purpose by requiring that the persons who participate in the management and administration of such bodies have 'no financial interest of their own in their results, by means of remuneration, distribution of profits or any other financial interest'. Therefore, the condition refers only to

- members of that body who are designated to direct it at the highest level; and
- other persons who, without being so designated, in fact direct inasmuch as they take the decisions of last resort concerning the policy of the body, especially in the financial area, and carry out the higher supervisory tasks.

HMRC have accepted this decision and also that '*voluntary*' in UK law means 'essentially voluntary'.

Persons who are remunerated for carrying out purely executory tasks (i.e. those who implement, rather than take high level decisions) will not cause the cultural body to fail this condition.

HMRC regard a person as having a '*direct or indirect financial interest*' in the activities of a body if he receives or has a right to remuneration, takes up an 'as of rights' provision, is in any other way rewarded directly or indirectly by the body, or has any other financial interest in the body.

However, following the decision in *Bournemouth Symphony Orchestra v C & E Commrs,* CA 2006, [2007] STC 198 (TVC 16.7) HMRC take the view that any 'direct or indirect financial interest' only affects entitlement to exemption if it is actual, not potential. A person who is managing and administering the cultural body on a voluntary basis can be seen to have an actual financial interest in its activities only when

- he receives any payments for services supplied to the cultural body above the market rate, paid as routine overheads, or receives any payments which are profit-related (whether below, at or above market rates); and
- there is a link between the payments and his participation in the direction of the cultural body's activities.

For these purposes, remuneration means a commercial rate of pay or profit-related payment. Token payments or payments to reimburse out-of-pocket expenses do not disqualify a body from exemption provided all other conditions are met.

There is no financial interest where the only potential is for a financial loss (e.g. where a risk is underwritten or guaranteed so that the guarantor only stands to lose money and not gain money as a result).

If a person has a right to remuneration but formally opts not to take it, then this 'right' will not disqualify the body from exemption until the person starts exercising his right.

Similarly, payments to individuals for services of managing and administering the body are not financial interests if

- they are allowed by the constitution;

- the recipient is excluded from any decision-making regarding the award of any contract to themselves;
- the payments are not above market rates; and
- the payments are not linked to profits.

An 'as of rights' provision gives a trustee the right to charge and be paid reasonable remuneration for (typically) professional services within the scope of the authority. The right does not depend on the charity or its trustees entering into a contract with the trustee affected. Such provisions are often not exercised for long periods or are used intermittently. The presence of such a clause in itself (i.e. where it has not been exercised) will therefore not disqualify a body from exemption. It is only as and when remuneration is paid under this clause that the potential arises for it to cause disqualification from exemption. However, this will depend on the frequency, number and size of any payments made (see below).

In *Bournemouth Symphony Orchestra* (see above) the court held that the managing director's remuneration of £80,000 p.a. and his participation in the highest decision-making processes of the orchestra made it impossible to say that the management and administration was conducted on an essentially voluntary basis.

In determining whether a body is '*essentially voluntary*'

- the fact that remunerated staff take part occasionally or peripherally in the adoption of the decision of last resort will not, in itself, disqualify a body from exemption;
- if any person identified as managing and administering the body at the highest level receives remuneration, then the body will not qualify for exemption; and
- in the case of 'as of rights' provisions (see above), the issue is one of degree, i.e. the frequency, number and size of any payments made. Each case will depend on its own facts and HMRC recommend that if a body considers that its continued eligibility for exemption turns on payments made under an 'as of rights' provision, it should seek a ruling from its local VAT Office.

(VAT Notice 701/47/11, paras 4.7–4.12).

In *Keele University Students Union* (TC00082) (TVC 16.9) the tribunal held that a university students' union was not managed on an essentially voluntary basis because it was managed by sabbatical officers who were entitled to bursaries which in effect were annual salaries. The bursaries, although below the market rate for jobs of equivalent responsibilities, were significantly more than a nominal rate.

(4) Fund-raising events

Certain admission charges are exempt under more general provisions applying to fund-raising events by charities and other qualifying bodies (including eligible bodies within (3) above). See **13.10 CHARITIES** for full details.

(5) Donations in lieu of admission

True donations are outside the scope of VAT. Where there is no admission charge and the public are asked for a donation instead, then this money is outside the scope of VAT. However, to qualify as a donation the payment must be entirely voluntary and secure nothing in return for the donor, and the actual amount to be given must be entirely at the donor's discretion. It must also be clear to the donor that admission can be gained whether a payment is made or not. If the person has to pay, or is made to think they have to pay, to get in then it is not a true donation but a standard-rated admission charge (unless otherwise exempt).

For donations in addition to charging admission at charitable functions, see **13.5**(1) **CHARITIES**.

Example

Hale Football Club has decided to allow free admission to all supporters for its next home game, as long as they give a minimum donation of £10 towards the club's ground improvements fund.

In this situation, the £10 payment is not a donation because the donor does not have any choice with the arrangement. If he wants to watch the game, he must pay at least £10, so the charge is standard-rated in the normal way. Any additional amount in excess of £10 paid by a supporter would, however, qualify as a donation.

(6) Admission by programme only

It is common practice for admission to events to include the provision of a programme. Following the decision by the ECJ in *Card Protection Plan Ltd v C & E Commrs, ECJ Case C–349/96*, [1999] STC 270 (TVC 22.362) HMRC now accept that in the majority of cases there is a single supply of admission, the programme being an ancillary item. In any case, a programme does not qualify for zero-rating if it is no more than an elaborate ticket which has to be bought to get into the event, etc. Payment for such a programme is the consideration for admission even if payment cannot be legally enforced.

Boxes, seats, etc.

See **42.18**(i) **LAND AND BUILDINGS: EXEMPT SUPPLIES AND OPTION TO TAX.**

Recovery of input tax

Admission for a charge is always a business activity for VAT purposes and related input tax incurred will normally be deductible unless the admission charges are exempt (see above) in which case the partial exemption rules may apply.

If the public is admitted free of charge to any premises there is no business activity and VAT incurred is not input tax. If the premises are also used for business purposes, input tax may be apportioned, see **35.7 INPUT TAX.**

Sport and physical recreation facilities

[58.3] Subject to the exemptions in **58.4** and **58.5–58.9** below, the granting of facilities for playing any sport or participating in any physical recreation is standard-rated. The grant of any right to call for or be granted facilities which would be standard-rated under this provision is also standard-rated. Included is an equitable right, a right under an option or right to pre-emption and, in relation to Scotland, a personal right.

[*VATA 1994, Sch 9 Group 1 Item 1(m)(n)*].

Standard-rating has been applied to the supply of a football ground for international matches, the presence of ticket-paying spectators not preventing the facilities granted being those for playing sport rather than a licence to occupy land (*Queens Park Football Club Ltd* (VTD 2776) (TVC 41.168)). HMRC accept that this decision applies to supplies by other sporting stadia, both indoors and outdoors. (C & E News Release 72/88, 20 September 1988). Standard-rating has also been applied to the use of a practice range at a golf club (*L H Johnson* (VTD 14955) (TVC 41.171)).

Leisure trusts providing all-inclusive membership schemes

For community leisure centres that are run by non-profit making trusts, in most cases a typical customer who purchases an all-inclusive package will have access to a range of facilities at the leisure centre. VAT liability depends on the nature of the supply which has to be decided at the time the all-inclusive fee is paid. Where the supply is a single supply that would be artificial to split, there can only be one overarching liability. In most cases, the typical consumer who purchases an all-inclusive package will have access to a range of facilities at the leisure centre. Usually most of these facilities would, if supplied individually, be exempt as services closely linked with and essential to sport or physical education in which the individual is taking part (e.g. use of swimming pools, courts, pitches showers, changing rooms, etc.). Therefore, in cases where the predominant reason for purchasing an all-inclusive package is to use the range of available sports facilities, the single supply is exempt (see **58.5** below). If the predominant reason a typical consumer purchases an all-inclusive package is to make use of standard-rated facilities (e.g. use of a sauna) the single supply is standard-rated.

(VAT Notice 701/45/16, para 3.5).

Letting of facilities

[58.4] The letting of facilities designed or adapted for playing any sport or taking part in physical recreation is normally standard-rated. However, the letting of such facilities may be exempt if the letting is for over 24 hours or there is a series of lettings to the same person over a period of time. Exemption will also apply if certain general purpose facilities are hired for sporting use or if sports facilities are hired out for non-sporting purposes. See below for further details.

24-hour rule

Where the facilities are provided for a continuous period of use exceeding 24 hours, the grant is exempt. The person to whom the facilities are let must have exclusive control of them throughout the period of letting.

Series of lets

Also exempt is the granting of such facilities for a series of ten or more periods (whether or not exceeding 24 hours) to a school, club, association or an organisation representing affiliated clubs or constituent associations where

- (i) each period is in respect of the same activity carried on at the same place;
- (ii) the interval between each period is at least one day (i.e. 24 hours must elapse between the start of each session) and not more than 14 days;
- (iii) consideration is payable by reference to the whole series and is evidenced by written agreement; and
- (iv) the grantee has exclusive use of the facilities.

[*VATA 1994, Sch 9 Group 1 Note 16*].

Under (i) above, a different pitch, court or lane (or a different number of them) at the same sports ground or premises would count as the same place.

Under (ii) above the duration of the sessions may be varied but there is no exception for intervals greater than 14 days through the closure of the facility for any reason.

Under (iii) above, there must be evidence that payment is to be made in full, whether or not the right to use the facility for any specific session is actually exercised. Provision for a refund given by the provider in the event of the unforeseen non-availability of their facility would not affect this condition.

Premises are sports facilities if they are designed or adapted for playing any sport or taking part in any physical recreation (e.g. swimming pools, football pitches, dance studios and skating rinks). Each court or pitch (or lane in the case of bowling alley, curling rink or swimming pool) is a separate sports facility. General purpose halls, such as village or church halls, which merely have floor markings are not sports facilities and the letting of such halls is exempt even when let for playing a sport. Similarly, school halls or similar (but not gymnasiums) are treated as exempt providing it is the bare hall that is provided. However, if equipment such as racquets and nets are provided along with the hall the supply is of standard-rated sports facilities.

Commercial sports league providers

Typically, a commercial sports league provider will do most or all of the following.

- Organise a league.
- Allocate fixtures to teams in the league.
- Provide pitches for teams to play on (some league providers own pitches, others rent them from other parties).

- Provide referees.
- Determine results.
- Keep and publish scores and league tables.
- Award trophies to winning teams.

In the past HMRC took the view that commercial organisations that run football and other sports leagues made an overarching supply of participation in a sports league and not a supply of land, a view that was set out in HMRC Brief 4/11, published on 9 February 2011. However, following the decision in *Goals Soccer Centres plc v HMRC* [2012] UKFTT 576 (TC) (TC02253) (TVC 41.165), HMRC now accept that, where the conditions in *VATA 1994, Sch 9 Group 1 Note 16* (see above) are met, there are two separate supplies, an exempt supply of land and a standard-rated supply of administration and management services. The change of policy was announced in HMRC Brief 8/14, published on 17 February 2014.

Where a single price is charged to the customer, businesses will need to determine the value of the two different supplies to establish the correct amount of VAT due. Whatever method is adopted to do this, sufficient documentary evidence should be kept to show how the business has arrived at a fair and reasonable apportionment.

(VAT Notice 742, paras 5.1–5.4; HMRC Brief 8/14).

Option to tax

A supplier may be able to choose to standard-rate some of the above supplies which would otherwise be exempt. See **42.23 LAND AND BUILDINGS: EXEMPT SUPPLIES AND OPTION TO TAX.**

Example

Hale Football Club agrees to hire its football pitch to another local club on a Tuesday night for ten weeks from October to mid-December in order that the other club can have training sessions. The agreement gives the other team the right to cancel a night's booking and get a refund of money, as long as they given at least 24 hours notice.

In this situation, the VAT exemption would not apply – the exemption is only unaffected if an 'unforeseen' circumstance arises (e.g. bad weather or pitch damage). The right to cancel for any reason means the regular letting arrangement is not achieved.

Sporting services provided by eligible/non-profit making bodies

[58.5] VAT exemption applies to the supply of services closely linked with and essential to sport or physical recreation supplied to individuals taking part in the activity where the supplies are made by an 'eligible body'.

[*VATA 1994, Sch 9 Group 10 Item 3 as amended by SI 2014/3185 with effect from 1 January 2015*].

Before 1 January 2015 the wording of *VATA 1994, Sch 9 Group 10 Item 3* meant that the VAT exemption applied to the supply of services closely linked with and essential to sport or physical recreation supplied to individuals taking part in the activity where the supplies were made by:

- an 'eligible body' having a membership scheme to those of its members who are granted membership for a period of three months or more (see **58.6** below); and
- an 'eligible body' which does not run a membership scheme (e.g. a charity).

Specifically excluded are

- the supply of any services of residential accommodation, catering or transport;
- supplies by local authorities;
- supplies by government departments within the meaning of *VATA 1994, s 41(6)* (see **44.11 LOCAL AUTHORITIES AND PUBLIC BODIES**); and
- supplies by non-departmental public bodies (such as Sports Councils) which are listed in the 1993 edition of the publication prepared by the Office of Public Service and Science and known as Public Bodies.

Eligible body

Subject to the specific exclusions above, an eligible body means a non-profit making body which

- cannot distribute any profit it makes otherwise than to another non-profit making body or its own members on winding up or dissolution;
- (except on winding up or dissolution) applies any profits it makes from supplies exempted by these provisions *either* to maintain or improve the facilities made available in connection with those supplies *or* for the purposes of a non-profit making body; and
- is not subject to 'commercial influence'.

To decide whether a body is non-profit making, it is necessary to look at its constitution, its activities and its use of funds to determine whether it was established with a purpose, intention or motive which excluded profit making. A non-distribution clause in the constitution of an organisation does not, in itself, answer this question.

If the organisation is a company limited by shares, HMRC have accepted that

(a) the non-distribution condition will be satisfied by the passing of a resolution to
  - delete, if appropriate *Table A, Arts 102–108* (dividend arrangements) and *Art 110* (capitalisation of profits); and
  - adopt a new Article preventing distributions by way of dividend, bonus and any other means; and

(b) adoption of *Art 117* on winding up fulfills the winding-up criterion.

(VAT Notice 701/45/16, paras 4.2, 4.3).

Following the decisions in *Messenger Leisure Developments Ltd v R & C Commrs,* CA [2005] STC 1078 (TVC 24.43) HMRC take the view that any company which is precluded from distributing profit, but whose function is nevertheless to create VAT exemption in the context of a wider commercial undertaking, is not a non-profit making body for VAT purposes. It follows that such a company is not entitled to claim the VAT exemption which is directed at such bodies. (Business Brief 22/05).

In *St Andrew's College Bradfield* (TC04247) [2015] UKFTT 34 (TC) (TVC 24.59) the First-tier Tribunal decided that two wholly-owned subsidiaries of a charity which was itself an eligible body could not be categorised as non-profit making because there was nothing in the constitution of either subsidiary prohibiting distributions by way of dividend, bonus or other means during the period to which the appeal related.

'Commercial influence'

A body is considered to be subject to commercial influence in relation to any supply which would otherwise be exempt under these provisions (the '*sports supply*') if (and only if), there is a time in 'the relevant period' when

- a person 'associated with the body' made a 'relevant supply' to it; or
- a person 'associated with the body' received an emolument from it determined at least in part by reference to the body's profits or gross income; or
- an arrangement existed for a relevant supply to be made or emolument to be received after the end of the relevant period.

The following definitions apply for the purposes of 'commercial influence'.

(1) '*The relevant period*' for a sports supply is the three years before the sports supply.

(2) Subject to below, a person is '*associated with the body*' at the time, as the case may be, of the relevant supply, receipt of emolument or arrangement, if at any time in the relevant period the person concerned was an 'officer' or 'shadow officer' of the body or an 'intermediary for supplies' to that body or was connected to any such person. '*Officer*' includes director of a body corporate and any committee member or trustee concerned in the general control and management of the administration of the body. '*Shadow officer*' means a person in accordance with whose directions the members or officers of the body are accustomed to act. An '*intermediary for supplies*' is anyone who acts between the body and an officer in making the relevant supply. A person is treated as connected with another under the provisions of *ICTA 1988, s 839* (see **72.19 VALUATION**).

(3) '*Emoluments*' include all salaries, fees, wages, perquisites and profits calculated or varied wholly or partly by reference to

  - the profits from some or all of the activities of the body paying the emolument; or
  - the level of that body's gross income from some or all of its activities.

  Perquisites ('perks') are allowances paid, or goods and services provided, over and above a settled wage.

  Payment of honoraria to a club secretary or treasurer will not disqualify a club from exemption, unless the amount is calculated by reference to profits or gross income.

  (VAT Notice 701/45/16, paras 5.5, 5.7).

(4) A '*relevant supply*' is, subject to below,
   (a) the grant of any interest in, right over or licence to occupy land (or, in the case of land in Scotland, any personal right to call for or be granted any such interest or right) which at any time in the relevant period was or was expected to become 'sports land';
   (b) a supply arising from a grant falling within (*a*) above made after 31 March 1996 (e.g. rent payable for the use of sports land under a lease);
   (c) the supply of any services of managing or administering of any facilities provided by the body; and
   (d) the supply of any goods or services for a consideration in excess of what would have been agreed between parties entering into a commercial transaction at arm's length.

   Where a club uses a committee member's firm to perform routine bookkeeping, accounting or legal services, HMRC do not treat supplies of such services as management and administration within (*c*) above and this will not therefore disqualify the club from exemption. (VAT Notice 701/45/16, para 5.7).

   Included is any such supply between VAT group members which would otherwise be disregarded but specifically excluded is any such supply which is
   - by a person to a body whose principal purpose at the time of the sports supply is to provide sports and physical recreation facilities for use by the employees of that person;
   - by a charity or local authority;
   - a gift of sports land or of the use of sports land;
   - sports land supplied for a nominal amount; or
   - the use of sports land supplied for a nominal amount provided the original grant of land was also for a nominal amount.

   In normal circumstances, HMRC will treat any payment below £1,000 as nominal and will give consideration to claims for higher amounts to be so treated. Bodies wishing to be sure that HMRC will treat a payment as nominal before exempting supplies are advised to write to HMRC setting out the full facts. (VAT Notice 701/45/16, para 5.4).

(5) '*Sports land*' is land used, or held to be used, by the body for or in connection with sport and/or physical recreation.

[*VATA 1994, Sch 9 Group 10 Item 3 and Notes 1–17*].

Individuals qualifying as members of a membership body – the legislation before 1 January 2015

[58.6] Before 1 January 2015 *VATA 1994, Sch 9 Group 10 Item 3* made a distinction between supplies to members and non-members where the body operated a membership scheme. The legislation was amended by *SI 2014/3185* with effect from 1 January 2015 to remove the distinction previously made.

[*SI 2014/3185*].

Where a body has a membership scheme, the legislation previously only applied the exemption to services supplied to a *playing* 'individual' granted membership for a period of three months or more (see below regarding the application of the exemption to non-members). Where an individual became a member less than three months before the end of the club's subscription period and paid less than three months' subscription, the subscription could still be exempt provided the grant of membership was for not less than three months.

It is usually clear from the literature, rules, regulations and constitution of the body whether it is operating a membership scheme, e.g. by references to

- arrangements for application for membership;
- membership categories and subscriptions;
- benefits available to members (including voting rights at AGMs);
- conduct of members; and
- members' involvement in running the club.

For the purposes of this exemption, an '*individual*' is a person who actually takes part in the sporting or physical education activity and this includes

- family groups; and
- informal groups, where one individual makes a booking on behalf of a group of users of the sporting facilities.

Supplies to individuals do not include supplies

- by a club to one of its sections where the individual section has a separate and independent constitution, e.g. the squash section of a multiple-sports club; or
- to travel agents or tour operators, which have agreements with a sports club to supply use of sporting facilities to individuals, groups or corporate bodies. This includes, for example, supplies to individuals who are identified through having booked through a travel agent.

(VAT Notice 701/45/16, para 3.4).

'Privilege cards', issued in conjunction with a monthly or three-monthly season ticket and entitling cardholders to free admission to a sports centre run by an eligible body, do not make the holders 'members' thereby resulting in the standard-rating of facilities used by other 'non-members' (*Basingstoke and District Sports Trust Ltd* [1995] Lexis Citation 926 (TVC 24.34)).

Following this decision, HMRC issued the following clarification.

(i) Where a body does not operate a full membership scheme (e.g. where members do not have voting rights or any form of control over the management of the centre), sporting and physical education services provided are exempt from VAT subject to the normal conditions. This applies irrespective of whether users are called 'members' for the purpose of obtaining discount on use of the facilities.

(ii) Where a body operates a full membership scheme but limits its application to selected activities or locations, exemption of qualifying services is limited to supplies to members even if other activities are not within the membership scheme. For example, where a body provides a swimming pool and squash courts and the membership scheme is only for squash players, supplies to all users of the pool, other than squash members, is standard-rated even though there is no membership scheme for the swimming pool.

(Business Brief 3/96).

Non-members

In *Bridport & West Dorset Golf Club Ltd* (TC01214) (TVC 20.124), for many years a company operating a golf club accounted for VAT on 'green fees' from non-members, in accordance with HMRC's interpretation of the law and with the tribunal decision in *Keswick Golf Club* (VTD 15493) (TVC 20.124). However, in 2009 it submitted a repayment claim on the grounds that it should have treated its green fees as exempt under *Directive 2006/112/EC, Art 132(1)(m)*. The tribunal allowed the company's appeal against HMRC's rejection of the claim. The tribunal declined to follow its own previous decision in *Keswick Golf Club*, and held that the exclusion of supplies to non-members from the scope of the exemption in *VATA 1994, Sch 9, Group 10, Item 3* was not capable of properly achieving the objective of *Directive 2006/112/EC, Art 133(d)* and therefore did not correctly implement its terms.

On HMRC's appeal, the Upper Tribunal referred the issue to the CJEU ([2012] UKUT 272 (TCC) (TVC 20.124)). While waiting for the case to be heard, HMRC stated that the First-tier Tribunal decision is only binding on the parties to the decision and HMRC do not propose to pay other claims in the wake of the decision. (HMRC Brief 25/12).

On 19 December 2013 the CJEU released its judgment in *HMRC v Bridport and West Dorset Golf Club Ltd, ECJ Case C-495/12, 19 December 2013 unreported* (TVC 20.124). The CJEU ruled that

(1) *Directive 2006/112/EC, Art 134(b)* of 28 November 2006 on the common system of value added tax must be interpreted as not excluding from the exemption in *Art 132(1)(m)* of that directive a supply of services consisting in the grant, by a non-profit-making body managing a golf course and offering a membership scheme, of the right to use that golf course to visiting non-members of that body.

(2) *Directive 2006/112/EC, Art 133(d)* must be interpreted as not allowing the Member States, in circumstances such as those in the main proceedings, to exclude from the exemption in *Art 132(1)(m)* of that directive a supply of services consisting in the grant of the right to use the golf course managed by a non-profit-making body offering a membership scheme when that supply is provided to visiting non-members of that body.

The CJEU judgment is that the VAT exemption for the supply of certain services closely linked to sport or physical education by non-profit making organisations to persons taking part in sport or physical education should not be limited to supplies to members of the organisations but also applies to supplies to non-members.

As a result of the CJEU judgment HMRC accept that supplies of sporting services to both members and non-members of non-profit making sports clubs qualify to be treated as exempt from VAT providing the services are closely linked and essential to sport and are made to persons taking part in sport. (HMRC Brief 25/14).

HMRC have published guidance regarding claims by non-profit making members' sports clubs for overpaid VAT on supplies of sporting services made to non-members. Where VAT has been overpaid on fees which are now considered to qualify for exemption, this could have a substantial effect on the amount of VAT a club is able to recover on the costs it has incurred. HMRC expect all claimants to have considered their input tax position and to have adjusted their claims accordingly to take into account any input tax which is no longer recoverable. The effect on input tax will depend on the circumstances of each individual club as well as the agreed partial exemption method which is used. Where the recoverable proportion of residual input tax has been affected, there may also be an effect on VAT recovered on assets falling within the capital goods scheme. (VAT Information Sheet 1/15).

On 2 November 2015 HMRC published HMRC Brief 19/15 in relation to golf clubs claiming a refund or credit of VAT overpaid. The Brief refers to a review by HMRC which found that if claims were credited in full some clubs would be unjustly enriched by 50% and others by 67%. The Brief explains that where a golf club charges any green fee, now or during the claim period, of over £100 per person for a round of golf, at any time of the year, HMRC will repay or credit 33% of its claim, providing the claim is compliant with VAT Information Sheet 1/15. According to HMRC Brief 19/15, other golf clubs claiming a refund or credit of VAT overpaid will receive 50% of the amount claimed, providing the claim is compliant with VAT Information Sheet 1/15. The Brief indicates that HMRC considers that the level of green fees is representative of a club's ability to pass on the VAT cost to its customers.

An appeal to the First-tier Tribunal by three golf clubs, The Berkshire Golf Club, The Glen Golf Club and The Wilmslow Golf Club was heard during 22–26 June 2015 and 6 July 2015. In *The Berkshire Golf Club and others v HMRC* [2015] UKFTT 627 (TC) (TC04774) (TVC 48.48) the tribunal decided that:

- 90% of the amounts claimed by the clubs should be repaid;
- where a tour operator is acting as an agent and invoices the green fees directly to a golfer the green fees are exempt, but otherwise supplies by clubs to tour operators are subject to VAT at the standard rate;
- where the customer of the clubs is a body corporate the supply is subject to VAT at the standard rate;
- course maintenance costs are properly treated as residual where the club has corporate day income, provides advertising services from locations the golf course and has taxable income from the hire of golf buggies.

The tribunal decision that 90% of the amounts claimed by the clubs should be repaid contrasted with HMRC's position as stated in HMRC Brief 19/15. HMRC has now issued a further Brief acknowledging the decision and stating that it will not be appealed. Although it does not explicitly say so, the clear implication is that it will apply the 10% restriction considered appropriate by the Tribunal. The Brief emphasises that claims will only be considered if they are validly made in accordance with the principles of Information Sheet 1/15. The Information Sheet was also revised following the Tribunal decision, acknowledging that course maintenance costs can be treated as residual in the appropriate circumstances.

(HMRC Brief 10/16).

Sports qualifying for exemption

[58.7] The following sports, etc. qualify for exemption.

Aikido	American football	Angling
Archery	Arm wrestling	Association football
Athletics	Badminton	Ballooning
Baseball	Basketball	Baton twirling
Biathlon	Bicycle polo	Billiards
Bobsleigh	Boccia	Bowls
Boxing	Camogie	Canoeing
Caving	Chinese martial arts	Cricket
Croquet	Crossbow	Curling
Cycling	Dragon boat racing	Equestrian
Exercise and fitness	Fencing	Field sports
Fives	Flying*	Gaelic football
Gliding	Golf	Gymnastics
Handball	Hang/paragliding	Highland games
Hockey	Horse racing	Hovering
Hurling	Ice hockey	Ice skating
Jet skiing	Ju jitsu	Judo
Kabaddi	Karate	Kendo
Korfball	Lacrosse	Lawn tennis
Life saving	Luge	Modern pentathlon
Motor cycling	Motor sports	Mountaineering
Movement and dance	Netball	Octopush
Orienteering	Parachuting	Petanque
Polo	Pony Trekking	Pool
Quoits	Racketball	Rackets
Racquetball	Rambling	Real tennis
Roller hockey	Roller skating	Rounders
Rowing	Rugby league	Rugby union
Sailing/yachting	Sand and land yachting	Shinty
Shooting	Skateboarding	Skiing
Skipping	Snooker	Snowboarding
Softball	Sombo wrestling	Squash
Stoolball	Street hockey	Sub-aqua
Surf life saving	Surfing	Swimming
Table tennis	Taekwondo	Tang soo do
Tchoukball	Tenpin bowling**	Trampolining
Triathlon	Tug of war	Unihoc
Volleyball	Water skiing	Weightlifting
Wrestling	Yoga	

* Includes those model flying activities, success in which is dependent on physical skill or fitness.

** Includes skittles.

Application may be made to HMRC to include other activities. HMRC will then consult with the Department of Culture, Media and Sport and other representative bodies and give a decision in writing. If exemption is refused, an appeal can be made to a VAT tribunal.

(VAT Notice 701/45/16, para 3.2).

Pigeon racing does not qualify for exemption because it is the pigeons that participate in the sport, not the human owners (*Royal Pigeon Racing Association* (VTD 14006) (TVC 24.52)).

In *The English Bridge Union, CJEU Case C-90/16*, [2017] STC 2317 (TVC 20.127), the CJEU issued a preliminary ruling in respect of the UK referral regarding whether the exemption for services closely linked to sport included a game such as Duplicate Contract Bridge (DCB). The Advocate-General's Opinion was that DCB could be viewed as a sport for VAT purposes. The CJEU disagreed and found that with regard to the meaning of the term sport, it is typically used to refer to an activity of a physical nature and that although DCB involves logic, memory and planning and that it may be an activity that is good for a persons' mental and physical health, it is not sufficient for it to be an activity that is covered by the concept of sport. The physical element of DCB appears to be negligible and therefore cannot be included in the concept of sport for the purposes of the *Principal VAT Directive*.

Services qualifying for exemption

[58.8] Services qualifying for exemption where supplied by a membership body to its qualifying members or, where applicable, by a non-membership body (e.g. a sports centre) to individuals include the following.

- Use of changing rooms, showers and playing equipment, trolley and locker hire and storage of equipment essential to sport.
- Provision of playing area (e.g. court, pitch or green fees).
- Use of multi-sport playing facilities.
- Refereeing, umpiring and judging services. Supplies by a self-employed referee registered for VAT are not exempt from VAT because he is not an eligible body.
- Coaching, training and physical education services. Sports coaching by professionals is not within the exemption as it is not supplied by an eligible body (although it may qualify for the exemption for education, see **17.10 EDUCATION**).
- Membership subscriptions covering active participation in sport (including life subscriptions entitling the member to playing services for life where the annual subscription is exempt).
  Clubs and associations often supply a number of different benefits in return for their subscriptions and must decide whether their subscriptions are consideration for a single supply or a multiple supply. If there

is one principal benefit or reason for joining, with other benefits supplied being less important, the subscription is consideration for a single supply and its liability is determined by the liability of the main benefit. There is an exception, however, for non-profit making bodies which supply a mixture of benefits with different VAT liabilities. As a concession, these bodies *may* apportion their subscriptions to reflect the value and VAT liability of each individual benefit, even if they are consideration for a single supply. If the subscription is consideration for a multiple supply and the separate elements have different liabilities, the subscription must be apportioned. See **15.2 CLUBS AND ASSOCIATIONS** for further details.

- Joining fees where the benefits supplied in return are the same as for the subscription and the subscription is itself exempt. If the joining fee entitles the member to different benefits, VAT must be accounted for, where appropriate, on the liability of those benefits.
- Fees for remaining on the waiting list for membership but only if
  - (i) they are deducted from the new member's first subscription or entrance fee and this itself qualifies for exemption; and
  - (ii) they are refundable in the event that the candidate fails to become a member for any reason including voluntary withdrawal.

  Otherwise the fee is standard-rated.
- Match fees for the use of playing facilities/pitch hire. Match fees also covering the cost of catering and transport may need to be apportioned.
- Mooring, hangarage, use of workshops (excluding use of parts or services of an engineer).

Services not qualifying for exemption include

- sporting services supplied to
  - (i) members' guests (irrespective of who pays the guests' fees);
  - (ii) temporary members (those granted membership for less than three months); and
  - (iii) visitors from other members' clubs and societies;
- social or non-playing membership subscriptions;
- admission charges for spectators;
- use of residential accommodation;
- use of transport;
- catering, bars, gaming machines and social functions; and
- parking.

(VAT Notice 701/45/16, paras 3.3–3.5).

See *Royal Thames Yacht Club* (VTD 14046) (TVC 24.43) where the subscriptions of ordinary members were apportioned between exempt sporting facilities and standard-rated clubhouse facilities which were capable of being enjoyed to the exclusion of the sporting facilities.

Affiliation fees to sports governing bodies

[58.9] A non-profit-making sports governing body can exempt its affiliation fees only where the fees are for services closely linked and essential to sport, are supplied by non-profit-making organisations, and the true beneficiaries are individuals taking part in sport. Supplies to commercial organisations should be treated as taxable since the true beneficiary of the service is unlikely to be individual taking part in the sport.

Where the conditions of ESC 3.35 (apportionment of membership subscriptions to certain non-profit-making bodies) are met, governing bodies may continue to take advantage of the option to apportion their affiliation fees between the rates of VAT applicable to the individual elements. However, where the principal benefit is of priority purchase rights for tickets of admission to international matches or tournaments, the fee is standard-rated.

(VAT Notice 701/45/16, para 3.6).

The above policy follows from the case of *HMRC v Canterbury Hockey Club (and related appeal), ECJ Case C-253/07*, [2008] STC 3351 (TVC 22.352). The ECJ ruled that in the context of 'persons taking part in sport' (see *Directive 2006/112/EC, Art 132(1)(m)*), the exemption includes services supplied to corporate persons and to unincorporated associations, provided that the supplies are closely linked and essential to sport, that they are supplied by non-profit making organisations and the true beneficiaries are individuals taking part in sport.

Treatment as disbursements

HMRC have published HMRC Brief 1/18 which announced the withdrawal of the statutory concession that enables a profit-making club to treat the onward charge of affiliation fees to its members as a disbursement. HMRC have concluded that the recharge of these amounts cannot be treated as a disbursement and therefore the concession goes beyond HMRC's discretion, so it is removed with effect from 1 April 2018. With effect from this date, profit-making clubs are required to account for VAT on the recharge of the affiliation fee to the members. Non-profit making clubs are not affected by the withdrawal of this concession and can still treat the recharge of these amounts as exempt from VAT.

Prior to 1 April 2018, a club could treat the onward charge of the affiliation fees charged by a governing body to its members or customers as disbursements for VAT purposes (and outside the scope of VAT) provided:

- the affiliation fee charged by the governing body qualified for exemption;
- the principal beneficiary of the services supplied by the governing body was the individual sports person;
- the club itemised the fee separately from its subscription or charge to the individual member or customer on the VAT invoice; and
- the amount charged by the club to the individual member or customer did not exceed the fee charged by the governing body.

(VAT Notice 701/45/16, para 3.6.2; HMRC Brief 1/18).

Sporting rights

[58.10] The grant of any interest, right or licence to take game or fish is standard-rated subject to the exceptions in **58.11** to **58.13** below where sporting rights and land are sold or leased together. The grant of any right to call for or be granted an interest or right which would be standard-rated under this provision is also standard-rated. Included is an equitable right, a right under an option or right to pre-emption and, in relation to Scotland, a personal right. [*VATA 1994, Sch 9 Group 1 Item 1(c)(n)*].

De Voil Indirect Tax Service. See V4.113.

Sporting rights and land

[58.11] Where, at the time of the grant of the rights

- the grantor grants the grantee the fee simple (broadly freehold in England and Wales and *dominium directum* or *dominium utile* in Scotland) of the land over which the right to take game or fish is exercisable, or
- the sporting rights are leased together with that land and the sporting rights represent no more than 10% of the value of the whole supply,

the total consideration is taken to be for the supply of the land alone and is exempt (unless the grantor has opted to tax the supply, see **42.23 LAND AND BUILDINGS: EXEMPT SUPPLIES AND OPTION TO TAX**, in which case the whole of the supply is standard-rated).

Where the sporting rights are leased with the land and represent more than 10% of the value of the whole supply, an apportionment must be made between the standard-rated rights and the exempt supply of land (unless the option to tax has been exercised).

[*VATA 1994, Sch 9 Group 1 Item 1(c)*]. (VAT Notice 742, para 6.2).

Shooting rights only

[58.12] Standard-rating applies to a grant over land owned by the grantor or over which he has the shooting rights. The provisions cover both freehold sales of rights and leasing or letting for any length of time.

Shooting in hand

If a landowner keeps control of the shooting over his land and makes all the arrangements to stock the land with game ('shooting in hand') and invites others to join him in shooting, there is no business activity (and no input tax can therefore be recovered) if the individuals are asked to contribute towards the costs of maintaining the shoot provided

(a) only friends and relatives are permitted to shoot;
(b) the availability of the shoot is not advertised to the public;
(c) the shooting accounts show an annual loss equivalent to, at least, the usual contribution made a 'gun' over a year; and

(d) the loss is borne by the landowner personally rather than by the estate or farm business.

Syndicates

A group of individuals set up solely to share the expenses of a shoot is not normally in business and therefore not regarded as making supplies to the individual members. However, if the syndicate regularly supplies shooting facilities to non-members, or makes taxable supplies of other goods or services, it is regarded as being in business and all its activities, including the supply of shooting facilities to its members, are business activities.

If a landowner or tenant grants shooting rights for less than their normal value to a syndicate of whom he is a member, he must account for VAT on the open market value of those rights. If he supplies other goods or services (e.g. the services of a gamekeeper or beater), VAT should be charged in the normal way.

(VAT Notice 742, para 6.3).

See also *C & E Commrs v Lord Fisher,* QB [1981] STC 238 (TVC 7.6) where, on the facts, shooting was not held to constitute a business. In *Williams* (VTD 14240) (TVC 62.155) a farmer was treated as carrying on a business for VAT purposes even though HMRC treated the shooting as 'hobby farming' giving rise to neither a profit or a loss. In *Harrison* (TC01205) (TVC 7.120) HMRC decided that H, a member of a farming partnership, was making supplies of shooting rights in the course or furtherance of a business. H contended that he was merely supplying administrative services to a shooting syndicate, which was organised for the enjoyment of its members, rather than with a view to a profit. The tribunal allowed H's appeal, distinguishing *Williams*, where the syndicate had been organised by the landowner.

Fishing only

[58.13] Standard-rating applies to the grant of rights to take fish either from the grantor's own waters or from waters over which he has fishing rights. The provisions apply to both freehold sales of the rights and letting or leasing for any length of time.

Still-water fisheries

Any charges made to fishermen are standard-rated even if both fishing rights and fish are supplied. This was confirmed by the First-tier Tax Tribunal in *Stocks Fly Fishery (a partnership)* [2016] UKFTT 218 (TC) (TC04994) (TVC 29.131). However, if the grantor allows a person freely to choose whether to take away fish caught or to throw them back, and makes a separate charge solely for those fish taken away, that charge is accepted to be the consideration for the zero-rated supply of fish (provided they are of a species generally used as food in the UK).

Lakes

Where a lake that is empty of fish is let to a person who will stock it with fish, there is an exempt supply of land (subject to the option to tax) rather than a standard-rated right to take those fish.

(VAT Notice 742, para 6.4).

Sponsorship income

Sponsorship

[58.14] Sponsorship is a common feature of artistic, sporting, educational and charitable activities. However, it is not restricted to these areas and it can involve payment in the form of goods and services as well as money. The payments may also be described as something else, for example, as a donation.

A person who receives sponsorship, or some other form of support, will normally be making taxable supplies if, in return, he is obliged to provide the sponsor with a significant benefit. This might include

- naming an event after the sponsor;
- displaying the sponsor's company logo or trading name;
- participating in the sponsor's promotional or advertising activities;
- allowing the sponsor to use the name or logo of the person being sponsored;
- giving free or reduced price tickets;
- allowing access to special events such as premieres or gala evenings;
- providing entertainment or hospitality facilities; or
- giving the sponsor exclusive or priority booking rights.

This list is not exhaustive and there are many other situations in which a sponsor may be receiving tangible benefits. What matters is that the agreement or understanding with the sponsor requires the person being sponsored to do something in return.

In *C & E Commrs v Tron Theatre Ltd,* CS 1993, [1994] STC 177 (TVC 67.109) sponsors were entitled, amongst other things, to priority bookings. It was held that the theatre would not have provided the goods and services it did for less than the consideration which the sponsors paid. As a result, the whole of the sponsorship received was consideration in money and subject to VAT.

Donations

Financial or other support might also be received in the form of donations or gifts. Where the sponsor's support is freely given and secures nothing in return, the recipient does not make a taxable supply and the sponsorship (whether in the form of money, goods or services) can be treated as a donation outside the scope of VAT. A taxable supply is not created where the sponsor provides an insignificant benefit such as a minor acknowledgement of the source of the support. Examples of this can include any of the following.

- Giving a flag or sticker.
- Naming the donor in a list of supporters in a programme or on a notice.
- Naming a building or university chair after the donor.
- Putting the donor's name on the back of a seat in a theatre.

In *C & E Commrs v EMAP MacLaren Ltd,* QB [1997] STC 490 (TVC 67.111) a company published a scientific periodical and organised cash awards to scientists. The costs of the awards was met by sponsors who received publicity in the periodical and tickets to attend the annual award. It was held that the sponsorship payments were not consideration obtained in return for the supply of benefits to sponsors.

Mixed sponsorship and donation

Provided it is entirely separate from the sponsorship agreement, a person is not required to account for VAT on any donation or gift (of the kind described above) received from a sponsor in addition to the sponsorship. However, it must be clear that any benefits the sponsor receives are not conditional on the making of the donation or gift.

Provision of goods and/or services by the sponsor rather than money. In such a case, if the sponsor provides

- goods and/or services to somebody who, in return, is making a taxable supply, he is making a taxable supply of those goods and/or services;
- goods to somebody as a gift or donation, he may be liable to account for VAT under the business gift rules (see **48.5 OUTPUT TAX**); and
- services to somebody as a gift or donation, no VAT is due.

Accounting for VAT

VAT must normally be accounted for on everything received under the sponsorship agreement. A VAT invoice must be issued to any VAT-registered sponsor. The sponsor can then reclaim the VAT as input tax subject to the normal rules. Where the amount of the sponsorship is agreed without reference to VAT, it must be treated as VAT-inclusive. A sponsor who provides sponsorship in the form of taxable supplies of goods and/or services is also required to issue a VAT invoice.

Where a charity makes supplies to sponsors as part of a fund-raising event, the supplies may be exempt. See **13.10 CHARITIES**.

Where supplies of advertising services and publicity are made to overseas sponsors, the services may be outside the scope of UK VAT. See **66.19 SUPPLY: PLACE OF SUPPLY**.

(VAT Notice 701/41/02, paras 1.2, 2.1–2.4, 3.1, 3.4).

See *Bird Racing (Management) Ltd* (VTD 11630) (TVC 7.101) where a company incorporated with the aim of attracting sponsorship for a motor racing driver was held, on the facts, to be predominantly concerned with the making of taxable supplies to sponsors for a consideration and therefore carrying on a business and entitled to be registered for VAT.

Example

Smithem Golf Club receives a donation of £1,000 from a golf equipment wholesaler, in return for which it is agreed that a representative of the wholesaler can attend the club's AGM and give a presentation to the members about how good the equipment is and the discounts that are available to those connected with the club.

In this situation, the payment is being made in return for a supply of services, i.e. the right to attend the AGM of the club and promote sales of golf equipment. The payment is not a genuine donation and the £1,000 payment is standard-rated.

Postage stamps and philatelic supplies

Stamps valid for postage in the UK

[58.15] 'Valid postage stamps' are the payment for a postal service that is exempt from VAT.

No VAT is chargeable on the sale of UK or Isle of Man stamps which are valid postage stamps and which are sold at or below face value. If such stamps are sold above face value, VAT must be accounted for at the standard rate on the amount by which the price exceeds that value.

'*Valid postage stamps*' are unused postage stamps of the present monarch's reign on which the value is

- £1 or a multiple of £1;
- in decimal currency, or
- designated for 1st or 2nd class postage.

All other stamps

Sales of other stamps, including

- all used stamps,
- all foreign stamps (even if valid for postage abroad), and
- UK and Isle of Man stamps of earlier reigns or which have a value expressed in pre-decimal currency

are standard-rated. It may be possible to treat such stamps as collector's items so that VAT can be accounted for on the difference between the purchase and selling price under the margin scheme for **62 SECOND-HAND GOODS**. If the conditions of the scheme are not met, VAT is due on the full selling price.

Combinations of valid and other stamps

Where philatelic items are sold which consist of, or contain, valid postage stamps (see above), VAT must be accounted for on the full amount charged less the face value of the valid stamps.

First day covers

A first day cover is an envelope bearing postage stamps with a postmark of the first day of their issue.

- If an envelope with unfranked stamps (whether the stamps are fixed to the envelope or not) is sold for customers to post themselves, the face value of the unused stamps can be disregarded and VAT accounted for on the rest of the charge only.

- If an envelope with the new stamps is posted to the customer on the first day of issue, VAT must be accounted for at the standard rate on the full selling price of the first day cover (without deduction for the face value of the stamps).
- First day covers sold after the first day of issue are standard-rated. However, it may be possible to treat them as collector's items so that VAT can be accounted for on the difference between the purchase and selling price under the margin scheme for **62 SECOND-HAND GOODS**.

Stamped stationery

Stamped stationery which is unused and valid for postage in the UK or Isle of Man is standard-rated on the amount charged less the face value of the stamps. This applies whether the stamps are printed on the stationery or are ordinary postage stamps that have been stuck on.

Imported collector's items

Some items of philatelic interest are eligible for a reduced valuation at importation which gives an effective VAT rate of 5%. See **74.3 WORKS OF ART, ETC.**

Postage and packing

If delivery is included in the contract with the customer, there is a single supply of delivered goods (in the case of philatelic supplies) or services (in the case of valid postage stamps). The liability of the delivery or postage and packing charge follows that of the items being delivered, i.e. standard-rated in the case of philatelic supplies or exempt in the case of valid postage stamps. For postage charges generally, see **48.7**(19) **OUTPUT TAX**.

(VAT Notice 701/8/17).

Key points: recreation and sport

[58.16] Points to consider are as follows.

- Sporting activities and competitions organised by many 'eligible' bodies are exempt from VAT. An 'eligible body' is basically an organisation that is non-profit making and cannot distribute profits to other individuals or entities.
- As a useful planning point, the VAT exemption in relation to charity fundraising events also applies to events organised by non-profit making sports bodies (e.g. a members' golf club). The related costs of such events will be subject to an input tax block under the partial exemption rules, unless the entity in question qualifies as being 'de minimis' in relation to partial exemption.
- An important change of policy by HMRC means they now accept that an inclusive membership fee paid by an individual to a sports centre (organised by a 'non-profit' making body) will be exempt

from VAT if the main benefits enjoyed by the customer relate to the use of sporting facilities. The previous policy was that if the user could enjoy any non-sporting facilities, e.g. a sauna, then the entire payment would be standard-rated.

- There have been many tribunal cases in recent years where VAT exemption has been denied to a sporting entity because it is either not classed as 'non-profit' making or because it is subject to commercial influence. The entity must be a genuine non-profit making body in order to qualify for exemption.
- Exemption for sporting membership fees paid to a non-profit making body also extends to joining fees as well. This is particularly relevant to golf clubs.
- Membership of a non-profit making sports club for non-sporting purposes is standard-rated, e.g. social membership (right to use bar and enjoy social facilities etc.) of a club is standard-rated.
- Sponsorship income received by a sporting club or organisation is usually standard-rated. However, if a payment can be classed as a genuine donation (donor receives no significant benefits for his payment), it will be outside the scope of VAT.

59

Reduced Rate Supplies

Introduction to reduced rate supplies

[59.1] VAT is levied on the supply of goods and services, the acquisition of goods from another EU member state country and the importation of goods from a place outside the EU. The standard rate of VAT is 20% but VAT charged on certain supplies of goods and services is chargeable at a reduced rate of 5%. The reduced rate also applies to the acquisition from another EU member state, or the importation from outside the EU, of goods the supply of which would be subject to the reduced rate. [*VATA 1994, ss 2(1A)–(1C), 29A(1)(2)*].

The categories of goods and services to which the reduced rate applies as specified in *VATA 1994, Sch 7A* are as follows.

Group 1	Supplies of domestic fuel or power (see **26 FUEL AND POWER**)
Group 2	Installation of energy-saving materials (see **59.2** below)
Group 3	Grant-funded installation of heating equipment or security goods or connection of gas supply (see **59.3** below)
Group 4	Women's sanitary products (see **59.4** below)
Group 5	Children's car seats (see **59.5** below)
Group 6	Residential conversions (see **43.12 LAND AND BUILDINGS: ZERO AND REDUCED RATE SUPPLIES AND DIY HOUSEBUILDERS**)
Group 7	Residential renovations and alterations (see **43.13 LAND AND BUILDINGS: ZERO AND REDUCED RATE SUPPLIES AND DIY HOUSEBUILDERS**)
Group 8	Contraceptive products (see **59.6** below)
Group 9	Welfare advice or information (see **29.35 HEALTH AND WELFARE**)
Group 10	Installation of mobility aids for the elderly (**29.36 HEALTH AND WELFARE**)

Group 11	Smoking cessation products (see **59.7** below)
Group 12	Caravans (see **43.25 LAND AND BUILDINGS: ZERO AND REDUCED RATE SUPPLIES AND DIY HOUSEBUILDERS**
Group 13	Cable-suspended passenger transport systems (see **59.8** below)

The Treasury may vary the Groups (and notes contained therein which form an integral part) by adding, deleting or varying any description of supply for the time being specified. The *Schedule* may also be varied so as to describe a supply of goods or services by reference to matters unrelated to the characteristics of the goods or services themselves including, in the case of a supply of goods, the use that has been made of those goods. [*VATA 1994, ss 2(1A)–(1C), 29A(3)(4), s 96(9)*].

Installation of energy-saving materials

[59.2] The supplies listed below are subject to a reduced rate of VAT. It should be noted that

- the reduced rate only applies to supplies made by installers of energy-saving materials and does not apply to purchases of energy-saving materials by businesses or to purchases for DIY use;
- relief does not apply to the installation of double glazing and similar products (e.g. low-emissivity glass) or the supply of energy-efficient domestic appliances; and
- energy-saving materials which are incorporated by a builder in a new dwelling are zero-rated (see **43.16 LAND AND BUILDINGS: ZERO AND REDUCED RATE SUPPLIES AND DIY HOUSEBUILDERS**).

The following supplies are subject to a reduced rate of VAT of 5%.

(a) Supplies of services of 'installing' 'energy-saving materials' in 'residential accommodation'. Before 1 August 2013 the reduced rate of VAT also applied to supplies of services of 'installing' 'energy-saving materials' in a building intended for 'use solely for a relevant charitable purpose'.

(b) Supplies of 'energy-saving materials' by a person who installs those materials in 'residential accommodation'. Before 1 August 2013 the reduced rate of VAT also applied to supplies of 'energy-saving materials' by a person who installed those materials in a building intended for 'use solely for a relevant charitable purpose'.

'*Energy-saving materials*' means any of the following.

(i) Insulation for walls, floors, ceilings, roofs or lofts or for water tanks, pipes or other plumbing fittings. '*Insulation*' means materials designed and installed because of their insulating. *Not included* are essentially decorative products or treatments (e.g. curtains and carpets).

(ii) Draught stripping for windows and doors. These are strips fixed around interior and exterior doors, windows and loft hatches.

(iii) Central heating system controls (including thermostatic radiator valves) and hot water system controls. *Included* are manual or electronic timers, thermostats, and mechanical or electronic valves.

(iv) Solar panels. *Included* are all systems installed in, or on the site of, a building which are
- solar collectors such as evacuated tube or flat plate systems, together with associated pipework and equipment (e.g. circulation systems, pump, storage cylinder, control panel and heat exchanger); or
- photovoltaic (PV) panels with cabling, control panel and AC/DC inverter.

(v) Wind turbines (including mounting poles, electrical cables, battery banks and voltage controllers).
(vi) Water turbines (including electrical cables, battery banks and voltage controllers).
(vii) Ground source heat pumps.
(viii) Air source heat pumps.
(ix) Micro combined heat and power units.
(x) Boilers designed to be fuelled solely by wood, straw or similar vegetal matter. *Included* is a hopper where integral to the installation. *Not included* is the installation of 'multi-fuel' or 'dual-fuel' boilers.

'*Residential accommodation*' means

- a building, or part of a building, that consists of a dwelling or a number of dwellings (owner-occupied homes, homes rented from private landlords, local authorities and housing associations);
- a building, or part of a building, used for a '*relevant residential purpose*' (see **42.16 LAND AND BUILDINGS: EXEMPT SUPPLIES AND OPTION TO TAX**);
- a caravan used as a place of permanent habitation (i.e. a residential caravan sited at a permanent caravan park and exceeding the limits of size currently in force for trailers which may be towed on roads, see **43.26 LAND AND BUILDINGS: ZERO AND REDUCED RATE SUPPLIES AND DIY HOUSEBUILDERS**); or
- a houseboat (i.e. a boat designed or adapted for permanent habitation and having no means of self-propulsion *or* a boat used as a person's sole or main residence such as a canal boat on which the owner pays Council Tax or domestic rates).

'*Use for a relevant charitable purpose*' means use by a charity in either or both of the following ways, namely

- otherwise than in the course or furtherance of a business; or
- as a village hall or similarly in providing social or recreational facilities for a local community.

For further interpretation of these uses, see **42.14 LAND AND BUILDINGS: EXEMPT SUPPLIES AND OPTION TO TAX.**

[*VATA 1994, Sch 7A Group 2*]. (VAT Notice 708/6/14, paras 2.6–2.11, 2.15, 2.17).

'Installing'

The reduced rate is only available where the goods and materials are provided *and* installed by a VAT-registered business. The supply of energy saving-materials without installing them is standard-rated. Installation means putting in place energy-saving materials. This involves some process by which the materials are permanently fixed in place, although loft insulation may simply need to be unrolled and positioned in place to be installed.

Energy-saving materials installed with other works

The installation of just energy-saving materials with ancillary supplies is reduced-rated. An ancillary supply is a supply of goods or services that is a better means of enjoying the principal supply, e.g. installing loft insulation but having to cut a new loft hatch in the ceiling and making good to access the loft. The cutting of the loft hatch and making good is, in itself, a simple construction supply, but as the services have been carried out solely in support of the loft insulation, they become ancillary. However, if an existing roof is replaced with a new insulated one, the insulation clearly is a better way of enjoying the new roof and so the insulation is ancillary to the new roof. As the roof is standard-rated, this applies to the whole job including the insulation.

Sometimes when individual goods and services are provided together, there is not a single dominant supply and so the individual goods and services supplied together have equal importance, often taking the form of something else, e.g. a central heating system may consist of a conventional boiler, radiators, copper pipe, radiator values, heating controls etc. While some components may be reduced-rated if supplied on their own, here they form part of a single supply of a central heating system which is standard-rated (unless grant-funded (see **59.3** below)).

Where more than one job is undertaken at the same premises, the VAT liability depends upon the circumstances, e.g. if, as part of a contract to build an extension, thermostatic valves are fitted to all the radiators in the house, then this is a single standard-rated supply of construction services. However, if there is a contract to build an extension and some time after the work has commenced, the homeowner separately asks for the installation of thermostatic valves, this is then a separate supply and reduced-rated.

On 4 June 2015 the CJEU released its judgment in *EC Commission v United Kingdom, ECJ Case C–161/14* that the UK had failed to correctly apply the reduced rate of VAT in relation to energy-saving materials. Following the CJEU judgment HMRC published HMRC Brief 13/15 explaining that the UK Government is currently considering the implications of the decision.

On 9 December 2015 HMRC issued a consultation document regarding proposed changes to *VATA 1994, Sch 7A Group 2*. The proposed changes, if implemented, would have the effect of:

- removing solar panels, wind turbines and water turbines from the list of items qualifying as energy-saving materials;
- restricting the reduced rate to the installation element of the supply where the VAT exclusive cost of the materials element of the supply exceeds the VAT exclusive cost of the installation element of the supply and the supply is not made to a qualifying person, or to a relevant housing association, or of an installation in a building used solely for a relevant residential purpose.

The proposed changes were intended to have effect in relation to supplies made on or after 1 August 2016, except for supplies paid for before that date and supplies made pursuant to a contract entered into before that date. However, the draft clauses published at that time were not included in the *Finance Bill 2016*, and it appears that the previous treatment will continue for the time being.

(VAT Notice 708/6/14, paras 2.2, 2.3; HMRC Brief 13/15; HMRC consultation document – changes to the reduced rate of VAT for energy-saving materials).

De Voil Indirect Tax Service. See V4.409.

Grant-funded installation of heating equipment or security goods or connection of a gas supply

[59.3] The following supplies are subject to a reduced rate of VAT of 5%.

(a) Supplies to a 'qualifying person' of
- services of 'installing' 'heating appliances' in the qualifying person's sole or main residence, and
- 'heating appliances' by the person installing those appliances in the qualifying person's sole or main residence

to the extent that the consideration for the supply is, or is to be, funded by a grant made under a 'relevant scheme'.

'*Heating appliances*' means any of the following.
- Gas-fired room heaters that are fitted with thermostatic controls
- Electric storage heaters
- Closed solid fuel fire cassettes
- Electric dual immersion water heaters with factory-insulated hot water tanks
- Gas-fired boilers
- Oil-fired boilers
- Radiators

(b) Supplies to a 'qualifying person' of
- services of connecting, or reconnecting, a mains gas supply to the qualifying person's sole or main residence, and
- goods by the person connecting, or reconnecting, that gas supply where the installation of those goods is necessary for the connection, or reconnection, of the gas supply

to the extent that the consideration for the supply is, or is to be, funded by a grant made under a 'relevant scheme'.

(c) Supplies to a 'qualifying person' of
- services of 'installing', maintaining or repairing a central heating system (including a system which generates electricity) in the qualifying person's sole or main residence, and
- goods by the person installing, maintaining or repairing that central heating system where installation of those goods is necessary for the installation, maintenance or repair of the central heating system

to the extent that the consideration for the supply is, or is to be, funded by a grant made under a 'relevant scheme'.

Included are

- installation of a boiler, radiators, pipework and controls forming a central heating system;
- micro combined heat and power systems (which are heating systems that also generate electricity); and
- the repair/replacement of a boiler, radiators, pipework and controls forming a central heating system (whether or not the system was originally installed under a relevant grant-funded scheme).

(d) Supplies consisting in the leasing of goods that form the whole or part of a central heating system (including a system which generates electricity) installed in the sole or main residence of a 'qualifying person' to the extent that the consideration for the supply is, or is to be, funded by a grant made under a 'relevant scheme'.

Under this type of arrangement, the installer installs the central heating system as usual but then sells the equipment to a leasing company (standard-rated) which makes an annual 'lease' charge to the householder which is paid for by grant-funding (reduced-rated).

(e) Supplies of goods that form the whole or part of a central heating system (including a system which generates electricity) installed in the sole or main residence of a 'qualifying person' where, immediately before being supplied, the goods were leased under arrangements such that the consideration for the leasing of the goods was, in whole or in part, funded by a grant made under a 'relevant scheme'.

Supplies only fall within this provision to the extent that the consideration for the supply of goods is either

- funded by a grant made under a relevant scheme; or
- a payment becoming due only by reason of the termination (whether by the passage of time or otherwise) of the leasing of the goods in question. This covers the termination fee paid if the householder sells his home before the end of the lease term and the end of the lease payment.

(f) Supplies to a 'qualifying person' of

- services of installing, maintaining or repairing a 'renewable source heating system' in the qualifying person's sole or main residence, and
- goods by the person installing, maintaining or repairing that renewable source heating system where the goods are necessary for the installation, maintenance or repair of the system

to the extent that the consideration for the supply is, or is to be, funded by a grant made under a 'relevant scheme'.

A '*renewable source heating system*' means a space or water heating system which uses energy from renewable sources (including solar, wind and hydroelectric power) or near renewable resources (including ground and air heat).

A '*qualifying person*' is a person who, at the time of the supply, is aged 60 or over or is in receipt of one or more of the following benefits.

- Child tax credit (other than the family element)
- Council tax benefit
- Disability living allowance
- Working tax credit
- Housing benefit
- Income support
- An income-based jobseeker's allowance
- Industrial injuries disablement pension payable at the increased rate to include constant attendance allowance
- War disablement pension payable at the increased rate to include constant attendance allowance or mobility supplement
- Personal independence payment
- Armed forces independence payment

Where there are qualifying and non-qualifying persons living in the same dwelling, relief applies if the supply is to a qualifying person. In practice, for a supply to be to a qualifying person, that person must be responsible for ordering the work to be done.

A '*relevant scheme*' is a scheme which

- has as one of its objects the funding of the installation of energy-saving materials in the homes of qualifying persons; and
- disburses grants (directly or indirectly) in whole or part out of funds made available to it for that objective by the Secretary of State, the Scottish Ministers, the National Assembly for Wales, a Minister or a Northern Ireland Department, the EU, a local authority or under an arrangement approved by the Gas and Electricity Markets Authority or the Director General of Electricity Supply for Northern Ireland.

[*VATA 1994, Sch 7A Group 3; Tax Credits Act 2002, Sch 3 para 48;*]. (VAT Notice 708/6/14, paras 3.2–3.8).

'Installing'

The reduced rate is only available where the goods and materials are provided *and* installed by a VAT-registered business. The supply of goods and materials without installing them is standard-rated. Installation means putting in place the goods in question. This involves some process by which the materials are permanently fixed in place.

For energy-saving materials installed with other works, see **59.2** above.

(VAT Notice 708/6/14, paras 2.2, 2.3).

Apportionment where grants received

Where a grant is made to fund supplies within (*a*) to (*g*) above (relevant supplies) and other supplies (non-relevant supplies), the charge must be apportioned. The proportion of the grant attributed to the relevant supplies is

$$G \times A \div B$$

where

G = the full grant received
A = the consideration reasonably attributable to the relevant supplies (excluding VAT)
B = the total consideration for relevant and non-relevant supplies (excluding VAT)

[*VATA 1994, Sch 7A Group 3, Note 3*].

Example 1: Full grant received covering all work

A builder installs relevant supplies to a value of £300 and carries out other building work to a value of £700 (both excluding VAT) for C in his main residence. A grant is received to cover the full cost of work.

	£	£
Value of relevant supplies	300.00	
VAT thereon (5%)	15.00	
		315.00
Value of non-relevant supplies	700.00	
VAT thereon (20%)	140.00	
		840.00
Total cost covered by grant		£1,155.00

Example 2: Partial grant received which the grant-awarding body allocates to the installation of relevant supplies

The facts are as in *Example 1* above except that C receives a grant of £200 towards the installation of the relevant supplies and pays for the rest of the work himself.

	£	£
Value of relevant supplies which are grant-funded	200.00	
VAT thereon (5%)	10.00	
		210.00
Value of other supplies	800.00	
VAT thereon (20%)	160.00	
		960.00
Total cost including VAT		1,170.00
Grant received		200.00
Contribution from C		£970.00

Example 3: Partial grant received which the grant-awarding body does not allocate

The facts are as in *Example 1* above except that C receives a grant of £200 towards the total cost and pays for the rest of the work himself.

Proportion of total grant allocated to relevant supplies

£200 × 300/1000 = £60

	£	£
Value of relevant supplies which are grant-funded	60.00	
VAT thereon (5%)	3.00	
		63.00
Value of other supplies	940.00	
VAT thereon (20%)	188.00	
		1,128.00
Total cost including VAT		1,191.00
Grant received		200.00
Contribution from C		£991.00

De Voil Indirect Tax Service. See V4.407; V4.408; V4.416.

On 4 June 2015 the CJEU published its decision that the UK had implemented the reduced rate of VAT for the installation of energy saving materials in a way that was not in accordance with EU law. HMRC has advised that any legislative changes will not be implemented before *Finance Act 2016*.

(HMRC Brief 13/15).

Women's sanitary products

[59.4] Supplies of 'women's sanitary products' are subject to a reduced rate of VAT of 5%.

'*Women's sanitary products*' means any of the following.

- Products that are designed, and marketed, as being solely for use for absorbing, or otherwise collecting, lochia (discharge from the womb after childbirth) or menstrual flow. *Excluded* are protective briefs or any other form of clothing.
- This includes sanitary towels, sanitary pads, tampons, keepers and maternity pads.
- Panty liners, other than panty liners that are designed as being primarily for use as incontinence products.

  Panty liners designed for sanitary protection, but marketed as also suitable for protection against light incontinence or light feminine discharges, are eligible for supply at the reduced rate. Panty liners designed primarily as incontinence products are not eligible for the reduced rate, but may qualify for a separate VAT relief (see below).

- Sanitary belts (for use with looped towels or pads).

The reduced rate does not apply to

- complementary products such as feminine wipes and sprays;
- incontinence products (which are specifically excluded because zero-rating may be available for such products bought by incontinent people living in their own homes, see **29.21 HEALTH AND WELFARE**);
- clothing or sanitary accessories (e.g. disposable or protective pants or briefs that either hold sanitary protection in place or protect the wearer from leakage). Certain items of children's clothing may be zero-rated under a separate relief, see **14 CLOTHING AND FOOTWEAR**; and
- dual-purpose products designed to protect against both menstrual flow and incontinence.

[*VATA 1994, Sch 7A Group 4*]. (VAT Notice 701/18/11, paras 2.1–2.5).

De Voil Indirect Tax Service. See V4.417.

In 2015 the UK Government announced that it is making a case in the EU for a zero rate of VAT to apply to women's sanitary products. Paragraph 1.144 of the Spending Review and Autumn Statement 2015 document explained that while the Government makes the case, a new £15m annual fund equivalent to the VAT raised each year on women's sanitary products will support women's charities. The fund is to run over the course of the current Parliament, or until the UK can apply a zero rate of VAT to women's sanitary products.

(Spending Review and Autumn Statement 2015).

Legislation has been included in the *Finance Act 2016* to add sanitary products to *Sch 8* as a new *Group 19*. The measure will take effect from a date to be appointed by regulations. The appointed day is not to be after the later of 1 April 2017 and the earliest date that may be appointed consistently with the UK's EU obligations. This means that earlier permission from the Commission may lead to the rule changing on or before 1 April 2017; later permission before Brexit will give effect to the change; and if the Commission never consents to zero rating, it will take effect when the UK leaves the EU.

[*FA 2016, s 126*].

Children's car seats

[59.5] The supply, acquisition or importation of 'children's car seats' is subject to VAT at the reduced rate of 5%.

A '*children's car seat*' is any of the following.

(a) A '*safety seat*', ie a seat
  - designed to be sat in by a child in a road vehicle;
  - designed so that, when in use in a road vehicle, it can be restrained in one or more of the following ways
    (i) by a seat belt fitted in the vehicle, or
    (ii) by belts, or anchorages, that form part of the seat being attached to the vehicle, or

    - (iii) by a related base unit, and
  - incorporating an integral harness, or integral impact shield, for restraining a child seated in it.

(b) A '*related base unit for a safety seat*', i.e. a base unit that is designed solely for the purpose of attaching a safety seat securely in a road vehicle by means of anchorages that form part of the base unit and which, when in use in a road vehicle, can be restrained in one or more of the following ways

- by a seat belt fitted in the vehicle, or
- by permanent anchorage points in the vehicle, or
- by belts attached to permanent anchorage points in the vehicle.

The reduced rate applies to both ISOFIX (International Standards Organisation Fix) and non-ISOFIX bases.

(c) A children's travel system comprising a combination of a safety seat (see (*a*) above) and a '*related wheeled framework*'. For these purposes a wheeled framework is 'related' to a safety seat if the framework and the seat are each designed so that

- when the seat is not in use in a road vehicle it can be attached to the framework, and
- when the seat is so attached, the combination of the seat and the framework can be used as a child's pushchair.

(d) A '*booster seat*', i.e. a seat designed

- to be sat in by a child in a road vehicle, and
- so that, when in use in a road vehicle, it and a child seated in it can be restrained by a seat belt fitted in the vehicle.

(e) A '*booster cushion*', i.e. a cushion designed

- to be sat on by a child in a road vehicle, and
- so that a child seated on it can be restrained by a seat belt fitted in the vehicle.

For the above purposes, a '*child*' means a person aged under 14 years.

[*VATA 1994, ss 2(1A)–(1C), 29A, Sch 7A Group 5*].

Reduced-rating is not tied to any manufacturing standards but children's car seats approved to the latest European Standard will be marked with a UN 'E' mark.

The reduced rate also applies to protective travel systems such as 'lie flat' car seat products that allow babies to safely lie flat while travelling in a car and are secured using a three-point safety harness. These products can also be used with compatible pushchairs to form a pram system.

Children's travel systems

There are currently two types of travel system.

- A safety seat within (*a*) above and a pram/pushchair that can be fitted together and where both of the elements can be used independently of each other.
  In such a case, the safety seat is reduced-rated and the pram/pushchair element is standard-rated.

- A safety seat within (*a*) above, a related wheeled framework as in (*c*) above and a pram/pushchair seat. Any combination of the three elements may be supplied together but either the safety seat or the pram/pushchair seat can be attached to the framework for use as a pram. The framework is only of use when one of the other two elements is attached.

  In such a case

  (i) when supplied separately, a safety seat is reduced-rated, a wheeled framework is standard-rated and a pram seat is standard-rated;

  (ii) the supply of just a safety seat and a wheeled framework is wholly reduced-rated;

  (iii) the supply of just a pram seat and a wheeled framework is wholly standard-rated; and

  (iv) when all three elements are supplied together, the pram seat is standard-rated and the other two elements are reduced-rated.

Cars supplied with a fitted children's car seat

Where a car is supplied with a fitted children's car seat, whether as an integral part or as an optional extra, the supply is wholly standard-rated.

(VAT Notice 701/23/11, paras 5.1–5.5).

De Voil Indirect Tax Service. See V4.418.

Contraceptive products

[59.6] Supplies of 'contraceptive products', other than 'relevant exempt supplies', are subject to a reduced rate of VAT of 5%.

'*Contraceptive product*' means any product designed for the purposes of human contraception, but does not include any product designed for the purpose of monitoring fertility.

'*Relevant exempt supplies*' means supplies which fall within *VATA 1994, Sch 9 Group 7 item 4* (exempt supplies of goods in any hospital etc., in connection with medical or surgical treatment, etc.). See **29.10 HEALTH AND WELFARE**.

[*VATA 1994, Sch 7A Group 8*].

The reduced rate applies to sales of contraceptive products by retailers, vending machines or via the internet, regardless of whether purchased by an individual or organisation such as a sexual health charity or the NHS. In addition to the exclusion for relevant exempt supplies above,

- contraceptives obtained on the prescription of a medical practitioner remain zero-rated (see **29.13 HEALTH AND WELFARE**); and
- contraceptives that are fitted, injected or implanted by a health professional still form part of an exempt supply of medical care (see **29.2 HEALTH AND WELFARE**).

(Business Brief 7/06).

Smoking cessation products

[59.7] Supplies of pharmaceutical products designed to help people to stop smoking tobacco are taxable at the reduced rate of 5%.

[*VATA 1994, Sch 7A Group 11*].

Smoking cessation products dispensed by a pharmacist on prescription by a medical practitioner are zero-rated and unaffected by this provision. The 5% reduced rate applies to all other supplies of pharmaceutical smoking cessation products by retailers including supplies made over the internet. This includes all non-prescribed sales of patches, gums, inhalators and other pharmaceutical products held out for sale for the primary purpose of helping people to quit smoking. (HMRC Budget Notice BN77 (2008)).

Cable-suspended passenger transport

[59.8] From 1 April 2013 the reduced rate applies to the transport of passengers by means of a cable-suspended chair, bar, gondola or similar vehicle designed or adapted to carry not more than nine passengers.

The reduced rate does not apply to the transport of passengers to, from or within

- a place of entertainment, recreation or amusement; or
- a place of cultural, scientific, historical or similar interest,

by the person, or a person connected with that person, who supplies a right of admission to, or a right to use facilities at, such a place.

[*VATA 1994, Sch 7A Group 13*].

Key points: reduced rate supplies

[59.9] Points to consider are as follows.

- It is important to identify when the reduced rate of VAT applies on a supply because many such sales (particularly relating to building services on residential property) will be made to non-VAT registered customers unable to claim input tax. So a VAT charge of 20% instead of 5% will produce a higher selling price for the customer and loss of competitiveness for the supplier.
- Even if a business is able to reclaim input tax, it is important that the reduced rate of VAT is charged where appropriate. This is because HMRC has the power to disallow any input tax claimed where a supplier has charged the wrong rate of VAT. So input tax claimed based on a 20% charge of VAT will be reduced to a 5% claim if the reduced rate should have been charged.
- Many builders adopt an approach of 'play safe' and charge standard rate VAT on a job. This approach is deprecated because it is important that the correct rate of VAT is charged on all supplies of goods and services.

- The reduced rate of VAT applies to building work carried out on a residential property that has been empty (unlived in) for at least two years. The builder should acquire and retain evidence from the landlord concerning the empty letting period.
- The reduced rate of VAT also applies to building work that produces a change in the number of residential units before and after the work has been carried out. Remember that this rule also applies where a reduced number of units is evident e.g. converting two flats into a single house.
- The reduced rate of VAT also applies to building work that converts a non-residential property into a residential property, e.g. barn converted to bungalow, offices into flats.
- An important point in relation to the building work considered above is that the reduced rate of VAT will also apply to any building materials supplied by the builder as part of his work.

60

Registration

Cross-references. See **9.5 BUSINESS** for anti-avoidance measures to combat business splitting and the conditions for the separation of a previously single business into independent parts for registration purposes; **9.9 BUSINESS** for sale or transfer of a business as a going concern; **13.3 CHARITIES** for registration by charities; **15.3–15.4 CLUBS AND ASSOCIATIONS** for registration by clubs, etc.: **28 GROUPS OF COMPANIES** for group registration; **35.10 INPUT TAX** for VAT paid on goods and services obtained before registration; **36 INSOLVENCY** for the effect of individuals becoming bankrupt or companies entering receivership or liquidation; **41 ISLE OF MAN; 44.5 LOCAL AUTHORITIES AND PUBLIC BODIES; 49.1–49.4 OVERSEAS TRADERS; 51.2 PARTNERSHIPS** for partnership registration; **54.3 PENSION SCHEMES; 64.34 SPECIAL SCHEMES** for registration of non-EU suppliers of electronically supplied services.

De Voil Indirect Tax Service. See V2.1.

Introduction to registration

[60.1] A 'person' who is in business and either makes or intends to make 'taxable supplies' of goods or services in the course or furtherance of that business may be liable or entitled to register for VAT. '*Person*' includes a body of persons corporate or unincorporate. [*Interpretation Act 1978, Sch 1*].

It is the 'person' who is required to register, not the business or businesses carried on. Thus, where a person is operating more than one business, even though they are dissimilar, *all* the person's business activities must be covered by one registration (*C & E Commrs v Glassborow and Another QB*, [1974] STC 142 (TVC 57.1)). This applies even if one or more of the businesses would be under the registration limit if carried out alone.

Taxable supplies are the supplies of goods or services made in the UK other than **21 EXEMPT SUPPLIES.** [*VATA 1994, s 4(2)*].

De Voil Indirect Tax Service. See V2.101–103.

Entitlement to be registered

Persons making or intending to make taxable supplies

[60.2] Where a UK person, or an overseas person with an establishment in the UK, who is not registered or liable to be registered in the UK satisfies HMRC that he

(i) makes taxable supplies; or
(ii) is carrying on a business and intends to make such supplies in the course or furtherance of that business,

HMRC must, if he so requests, register him from the day on which the request is made or from such earlier date as may be agreed between the person and HMRC. [*VATA 1994, Sch 1 para 9*]. See **9.1 BUSINESS** for the test of whether an activity is to be treated as a business. In *Lepton Service Station Ltd* [2016] UKFTT 144 (TC) (TC04929), the First-tier Tribunal noted that it has been HMRC's practice to allow voluntary registration applicants to specify a later date from which they wish to be registered, which might be convenient for both parties but has no basis in the law. As the trader wished to be registered from an earlier date than that allocated by HMRC, it could insist on the strict words of the law. As no 'earlier date' had been agreed, the date on which the registration request was made should be used.

VAT registration data is drawn from the data collected or created when businesses register for VAT or update a registration. This data includes non-financial data such as the VAT registration number, the business name and/or names of proprietors, the business contact details and the legal entity status of the business. The *Small Business, Enterprise and Employment Act 2015* provides HMRC with power to release non-financial VAT registration data on a strictly controlled basis for the purposes of credit scoring, anti-fraud checking, and compliance with other financial regulation. Potential users include credit providers, credit reference agencies and other business information providers. (HMRC Brief 26/14).

Retrospective registration

The provisions allow a person to negotiate registration from a date prior to the date of application provided this is done at the time of initial application and not subsequently after registration. See also *C & E Commrs v Eastwood Care Homes (Ilkeston) Ltd and Others, CA* [2001] STC 1629 (TVC 32.9).

A business can apply for voluntary registration to be backdated up to four years. (VAT Notice 700/1/18, para 3.9).

'Intending traders'

The provisions under (ii) above allow registration for a person who is carrying on a business, is not yet making taxable supplies at the time of applying but who intends to do so in the future. Intending traders normally seek registration from a current date in order to reclaim input tax incurred in the setting up and development of the business. In some cases the amounts involved may be substantial and cover long periods. HMRC must therefore be satisfied that there is a firm intention to make taxable supplies before allowing registration as an intending trader.

> *Example*
>
> Jane and John (in partnership) have bought an old commercial building and been charged VAT on the purchase of the freehold. Their intention is to refurbish the building and trade as a restaurant. The refurbishment programme will take twelve months before trading can start.
>
> They can apply to register for VAT as an intending trader from the date they bought the building in order to reclaim input tax on both the cost of the building and the ongoing refurbishment costs. They will need to provide documents to

HMRC to confirm their trading intentions (e.g. planning permission papers, business plans, trading forecasts etc.).

Persons only making exempt or certain outside the scope supplies

Where a person who is not registered or liable to be registered in the UK satisfies HMRC that

(a) he has a 'business establishment' (including a branch or agency) in the UK or his 'usual place or residence' is in the UK,

(b) he does not make or intend to make taxable supplies in the UK, and

(c) he either

  (i) makes supplies

    - outside the UK which would be taxable supplies if made in the UK, or
    - falling within **35.3**(*c*) **INPUT TAX** (mainly exempt financial services), or

  (ii) he is carrying on a business and intends to make such supplies in the course or furtherance of that business,

HMRC must, on request, register that person from the day on which the request is made or from such earlier date as is mutually agreed.

The '*usual place of residence*' of a company means the place where it is legally constituted.

[*VATA 1994, Sch 1 para 10*].

For these purposes a '*business establishment*' includes the registered office of an overseas company. Where a business provides accountancy services at its premises for a non-established taxable person who does not make supplies in the UK, HMRC do not consider these premises to be a business establishment.

An overseas business has a branch in the UK if it maintains a permanent office at which staff are employed. It has an agency in the UK if it has a permanent UK agent which enters into contracts for the purchase of goods and services or for the import of goods in its name on a regular basis. An agent who merely acts as an intermediary in bringing together customer and supplier but is not directly involved in the supply chain does not constitute an agency.

(HMRC VAT Guidance VATREG23100).

These provisions allow a UK business to register where it does not make taxable supplies in the UK but makes supplies within (*c*)(i) above. It also means that an overseas business with a business establishment, but no taxable supplies, in the UK can register in the UK and, because of (*b*) above, can recover input tax on taxable supplies it receives from UK VAT-registered businesses or on goods it imports into the UK (subject to the normal rules). See **35.3**(*b*) **INPUT TAX**. An overseas business with no business establishment, and no taxable supplies, in the UK can only recover UK VAT under the *EC 8th Directive* (if established in another EU member state, see **19.43 EUROPEAN UNION LEGISLATION**) or the *EC 13th Directive* (if in business outside the EU, see **19.44 EUROPEAN UNION LEGISLATION**).

De Voil Indirect Tax Service. See V2.120; V2.121; V2.144; V2.146.

Example

Consultants Ltd trades from offices in the UK (it has no presence in any other country) but all of its customers are business customers based in either Sweden (EU) or Australia (non-EU). The company's consultancy income is outside the scope of UK VAT (place of supply being in the customer's country) but it can still register for VAT in the UK and claim input tax on its UK overheads. The reason is because consultancy services would be taxable (subject to standard-rated VAT) if supplied to a UK customer.

Any foreign VAT that the company pays in Sweden must be reclaimed through the electronic refund system (overseas repayments in EU), and a 13th Directive claim would be appropriate to claim GST (Goods and Services Tax) paid in Australia.

Compulsory registration

[60.3] Subject to the exception below, a person who makes taxable supplies but is not registered under *VATA 1994* becomes liable to be registered under these provisions as follows.

(a) At the end of any month if he is UK-established and the value of his taxable supplies in the period of one year then ending has exceeded the limit in Table A below. (If taxable supplies have been made for a period of less than twelve months, the value of all taxable supplies to the end of the month in question must be compared to the limit in Table A below, see *Mr & Mrs Norton* (VTD 151) (TVC 57.84).)

(b) At any time, if he is UK-established and there are reasonable grounds for believing that the value of his taxable supplies in the period of 30 days then beginning will exceed the limit in Table A below.

(c) Where a business or part of a business carried on by a taxable person is transferred to another person as a going concern and the transferee is UK-established at the time of the transfer and is not registered under *VATA 1994* at that time, the transferee becomes liable to be registered under these provisions at that time if

  (i) the value of his taxable supplies in the period of one year ending at the time of the transfer has exceeded the limit in Table A below; or

  (ii) there are reasonable grounds for believing that the value of his taxable supplies in the period of 30 days beginning at the time of the transfer will exceed the limit in Table A below.

  For these purposes, the transferee is treated as having carried on the business (or part) before as well as after the transfer, i.e. under (i) above the transferor's taxable supplies in the one year to the date of transfer must also be taken into account.

Table A	
Effective date	*Limit*
1.4.17	£85,000
1.4.16–31.3.17	£83,000
1.4.15–31.3.16	£82,000
1.4.14–31.3.15	£81,000
1.4.13–31.3.14	£79,000
1.4.12–31.3.13	£77,000
1.4.11–31.3.12	£73,000

[*VATA 1994, s 49(1)(a), Sch 1 para 1(1)(2); SI 2017/290*].

A person is treated as having become liable to be registered at any time when he would have become so liable under the above provisions but for any existing registration which is subsequently cancelled under **60.10**(3), **60.17**(*b*), **60.25**(*c*), **60.32**(*b*) or **60.37** below. [*VATA 1994, Sch 1 para 1(5)*].

Exception

A person does not become liable to be registered under (*a*) or (*c*)(i) above if HMRC are satisfied that the value of his taxable supplies in the period of one year beginning at the time at which he would become liable to be registered will not exceed the limit in Table B below.

Table B	
Effective date	*Limit*
1.4.17	£83,000
1.4.16–31.3.17	£81,000
1.4.15–31.3.16	£80,000
1.4.14–31.3.15	£79,000
1.4.13–31.3.14	£77,000
1.4.12–31.3.13	£75,000
1.4.11–31.3.12	£71,000

[*VATA 1994, s 49(1)(a), Sch 1 para 1(3); SI 2017/290*].

This gives HMRC discretion to allow requests for retrospective exception. Exception is generally granted on the basis of the value of taxable supplies made and future anticipated supplies, at the time when the application is made. It should, however, be noted that, if HMRC grant exception, taxable supplies must still be monitored on a monthly basis in order to determine whether a further liability to registration arises. If, for example, a person is granted exception but one month later the value of his supplies render him liable to registration under (*a*) above, then he must either register for VAT or again satisfy HMRC that his expected turnover for the forthcoming twelve months will not exceed the limit in Table B above.

See, however, *dicta* of Lord Granchester in *WF Shephard* (VTD 2232) (TVC 51.56). Where a trader has not applied to HMRC at the right time to consider the relevant circumstances, this exception can only be relied upon by a trader if he establishes that, at the right time, HMRC could not reasonably have come to any conclusion other than that taxable supplies in the year would not exceed the relevant amount. These *dicta* were followed in *RJ & J Nash* (VTD 14944) (TVC 57.23) where, although it was accepted that turnover had fallen below the registration limit following a transfer of a going concern, there were no grounds on which HMRC could have been expected, at the date of the transfer, to have believed that this would be the case. See also *Gray (t/a William Gray and Son) v C & E Commrs*, Ch D [2000] STC 880 (TVC 57.27).

Taxable supplies

A taxable supply is a supply of goods or services made in the UK other than an exempt supply. [*VATA 1994, s 4(2)*]. In determining whether the registration limits in Tables A and B above have been exceeded, it is therefore necessary to take into account the VAT-exclusive value of all standard and zero-rated supplies of goods and services, including

- the value of 'reverse charge' services received from abroad (see **39.4 INTERNATIONAL SERVICES**); and
- the value of any **63 SELF-SUPPLY**.

The following special rules, however, apply.

- *Capital assets*. Supplies of goods or services that are capital assets of the business in the course or furtherance of which they are supplied are to be disregarded. Specifically, however, any standard-rated supply of an interest in, right over, or licence to occupy land is not to be regarded as a capital asset and does form part of the person's taxable supplies for registration purposes. [*VATA 1994, Sch 1 para 1(7)(8)*].
  Capital assets may be tangible or intangible and include premises, plant, machinery, office machinery, computers, office furniture, used company cars, patent rights which have been exploited and which are sold outright, and goodwill. Capital goods have been defined as 'goods used for the purposes of some business activity and distinguishable by their durable nature and their value and such that the acquisition costs are not normally treated as current expenditure but written off over several years' (*Verbond van Nederlandse Ondernemingen v Inspecteur der Invoerrechten en Accijnzen, ECJ Case 51/76*, [1977] 1 CMLR 413 (TVC 22.500)). In *The Trustees of the Mellerstain Trust* (VTD 4256) (TVC 7.112) the tribunal followed this definition and held that paintings sold from an historic house open to the public were capital assets which had been used to make taxable supplies, and as such did not render the trust liable to register for VAT.
- *Distance sales*. Supplies can be disregarded if they are only taxable supplies in the UK because an overseas business makes distance sales to non-taxable persons in the UK and is required to register under *VATA 1994, Sch 2* (see **60.11** *et seq* below). [*VATA 1994, Sch 1 para 1(7)*].
- *Previous registration*. For the purposes of (*a*) and (*c*)(i) above, supplies made at a time when the person was previously registered under *VATA 1994* can be disregarded if his registration was cancelled otherwise than under **60.10**(3), **60.17**(*b*), **60.25**(*c*), **60.32**(*b*) or **60.37** below and HMRC

are satisfied that before his registration was cancelled he had given them all the information they needed in order to determine whether to cancel his registration. [*VATA 1994, Sch 1 para 1(4)*].

- *Fiscal warehousing*. Supplies to which *VATA 1994, s 18B(4)* (last acquisition or supply before removal from fiscal warehousing) applies and supplies treated as made under *VATA 1994, s 18C(3)* (self-supply of services on removal of goods from warehousing) can be disregarded. See **73.17** and **73.20 WAREHOUSED GOODS** respectively. [*VATA 1994, Sch 1 para 1(9)*].
- *Margin schemes*. Under the schemes for **62 SECOND-HAND GOODS,** the taxable supplies are the full selling prices of the goods. Under the **69 TOUR OPERATORS' MARGIN SCHEME,** taxable supplies are the total margin (i.e. difference between buying prices and the selling prices) on margin scheme supplies plus the full value of any other taxable supplies (including all in-house supplies).
- *Supplies of long-term accommodation*. The value of certain supplies of long-term accommodation can be excluded when calculating taxable turnover. See **33.2 HOTELS AND HOLIDAY ACCOMMODATION.**

De Voil Indirect Tax Service. See V2.135–137.

Notification and date of registration

[60.4] Where a person becomes liable to be registered by virtue of

(a) **60.3**(*a*) above, he must notify HMRC of the liability within 30 days of the end of the relevant month. HMRC must then register him (whether or not he so notifies them) with effect from the end of the month following the relevant month or from such earlier date as is mutually agreed;

> *Example*
>
> On 31 May, W determines that his supplies in the past twelve months have exceeded the registration threshold.
>
> W becomes liable to be registered on 31 May. He must notify HMRC of his liability to be registered by 30 June. Unless mutually agreed otherwise, HMRC will register him with effect from 1 July.

(b) **60.3**(*b*) above, he must notify HMRC of the liability before the end of the period by reference to which the liability arises. HMRC must then register him (whether or not he so notifies them) with effect from the beginning of that period;

> *Example*
>
> On 20 January, Y expects that his supplies in the next 30 days will exceed the registration threshold.
>
> Y becomes liable to be registered on 20 January. He must notify HMRC of his liability to be registered by 19 February. HMRC will register him with effect from 20 January.

(c) **60.3**(*c*) above, he must notify HMRC of the liability within 30 days of the time when the business is transferred. HMRC must then register any such person (whether or not he so notifies them) with effect from the time when the business is transferred; and

(d) **60.3**(*a*) above *and* **60.3**(*b*) or **60.3**(*c*) above at the same time, HMRC must register him under (*b*) or (*c*) above, as the case may be, rather than under (*a*) above.

[*VATA 1994, Sch 1 paras 5–8*].

Failure to notify

Failure to notify a liability to register may incur a penalty. See **53.16 PENALTIES**. Late notification of a liability to register will result in the backdating of the registration, HMRC having no discretion in the matter (*SJ Whitehead* (VTD 202) (TVC 57.86)) and VAT must be accounted for from the correct date whether or not it has been charged (*JR Atkinson* (VTD 309) (TVC 57.87)).

De Voil Indirect Tax Service. See V2.126; V2.128.

Application for registration

[60.5] Application for registration under **60.2** and **60.3** above must be made in such form and manner and containing such particulars as may be specified in regulations or by HMRC in accordance with regulations. Notification of liability to be registered must contain the particulars (including the declaration) set out in the relevant form specified in a notice published by HMRC and must be made in that form. Where the notification is made by a partnership, it must also contain the particulars set out in the relevant form specified in a notice published by HMRC. [*VATA 1994, Sch 1 para 17; SI 1995/2518, Reg 5(1)*]. See also **51.2 PARTNERSHIPS**.

When submitting the above VAT applications, details to support an application for VAT periods to correspond with the financial year of the business (see **2.5 ACCOUNTING PERIODS AND RETURNS**) should be sent if appropriate.

If not applying online the completed application forms for standard registration applications, with any extra information requested by HMRC, should be sent to HM Revenue & Customs, VAT Registration Service, Crown House, Birch Street, Wolverhampton, WV1 4JX. When HMRC have checked the details on the application form, for online applications they send an online message within three working days which either tells the business what the VAT registration number is, or lets it know there will be a delay because they need more information. If the application has been sent in paper form, HMRC aim to send the business a certificate of registration showing full registration details within 15 working days of receiving the form. If a reply is not received from HMRC within 15 working days, it is advisable to contact them to make sure that the application was received. (VAT Notice 700/1/18, para 4.5).

HMRC may amend a certificate of registration issued with the wrong date and issue assessments for any earlier periods then coming within the scope of VAT (*Maidstone Sailing Club (DG Oliver)* (VTD 511) (TVC 57.96)). The certificate is no more than a notification of the registration date and number. Other matters shown on the certificate, including the dates on which returns are to be made, are entered as matters of administrative convenience and therefore are not appealable matters within *VATA 1994, s 83(a)* (*Punchwell Ltd* (VTD 1085) (TVC 59.2)). Further, the allocation of registration numbers is within the administrative discretion of HMRC (see *L Reich & Sons Ltd* (VTD 97) (TVC 57.228) where HMRC refused to reallocate the registration number of a company to a newly formed subsidiary which took over the trade previously carried on by the parent company).

A business must start keeping records and charging VAT to its customers from the date it becomes liable to be registered. It can increase prices to include VAT due but, until it has received a registration number, it must not show VAT as a separate item on any invoice issued. It should explain to any VAT-registered customers that it will be sending them VAT invoices at a later date. Once the business has its registration number, it should send the necessary invoices showing VAT within 30 days.

Where a business has asked for voluntary registration (see **60.2** above), it should start keeping records and charging VAT from the date it is registered, i.e. normally the date requested on the application form. The exception to this is that a business is not required to charge VAT on its supplies to UK customers until its UK taxable turnover has exceeded the UK VAT registration threshold if it has asked for voluntary registration under the arrangements referred to in the HMRC guidance 'Register for and use the VAT Mini One Stop Shop'. These arrangements are available to persons who

- make taxable supplies of digital services to customers in other EU member states;
- have a UK taxable turnover below the UK VAT registration threshold; and
- wish to use the VAT Mini One Stop Shop.

(VAT Notice 700/1/18, para 5.1).

Electronic application

A 'specified communication' may be made to HMRC using an electronic communications system. The system must be approved by HMRC in a specific or general direction, and no communication will be regarded as having been made if the system is not so approved. A direction may

- modify or dispense with any requirement specified in a form used to make a specified communication;

- specify different forms of electronic communications system for different cases; and
- specify different circumstances relating to the use of the electronic communications system.

An electronic communications system must incorporate an electronic validation process. Unless the contrary is proved, the use of an electronic return system shall be proved to have resulted in the making of a communication to HMRC only if this has been successfully recorded as such by the process. The time of making the communication shall be presumed to be the time recorded as such by the process. The person delivering the communication shall be presumed to be the person identified as such by any relevant feature of the system. A communication made using the system carries the same consequences as a communication in paper form.

A 'specified communication' is

- an application under *VATA 1994, s 43B(1), (2)(d)* or *(3)* (groups: applications);
- a notification under *SI 1995/2518, Reg 5(1), (2)* or *(3)* (VAT registration and notification);
- an application under *SI 1995/2518, Reg 6(1)(d)* (TOGC: transfer of VAT registration number);
- a notification under *SI 1995/2518, Reg 10(1)* or *(4)* (VAT representatives);
- an application under *SI 1995/2518, Reg 52(1)* (annual accounting scheme: eligibility);
- a notification under *SI 1995/2518, Reg 54(2)* or *55(1)(d)* (annual accounting scheme: termination);
- a notification under *SI 1995/2518, Reg 55B(1)(a)* (flat-rate scheme for small businesses: notification of desire to join the scheme); and
- a notification under *SI 1995/2518, Reg 55Q(1)(e)* (flat-rate scheme for small businesses: notification of decision to withdraw from the scheme).

[*SI 1995/2518, Regs 4A, 4B*].

Exemption from registration

[60.6] Where a person who makes or intends to make taxable supplies satisfies HMRC that 'any such supply' is zero-rated (or would be so if he were a taxable person) they may, if he so requests and they think fit, grant exemption from registration under the above provisions. On a material change in the nature of the supplies made, the person exempted must notify HMRC of the change within 30 days of the end of the day on which it occurred or, if no particular day is so identifiable, within 30 days of the end of the particular quarter in which it occurred. On a material alteration in any quarter in the proportion of taxable supplies of such a person that are zero-rated, he must notify HMRC of the alteration within 30 days of the end of that quarter. Exemption applies until it appears to HMRC that the request should no longer be acted upon or the request is withdrawn by the trader. [*VATA 1994, Sch 1 para 14*].

'*Any such supply*' has its ordinary meaning and HMRC therefore have discretion in applying the provisions where not all of the supplies are zero-rated (*Fong* (VTD 590) (TVC 57.178)). HMRC may therefore exempt a person from registration if only a small proportion of his taxable supplies is standard-rated provided that, if registered, input tax would normally exceed output tax.

If application for exemption is refused, registration for VAT applies from the date the business would otherwise have been liable and VAT will have to be accounted for from that date. Any application for exemption should therefore be submitted as early as possible to enable HMRC to reach a decision in good time.

(VAT Notice 700/1/18, para 3.11).

A material alteration affecting exemption from registration would arise where, if the person was registered, output tax would exceed input tax in any twelve-month period. (VAT Notice 700, para 26.12).

Exemption saves a person the trouble and expense of having to keep proper records and accounts for VAT purposes and rendering returns but it does mean that input tax paid on purchases of goods or services for the business is not reclaimable.

De Voil Indirect Tax Service. See V2.147.

Example

Marion rents a small unit in a shopping centre selling fruit (zero-rated). Her sales for the twelve months ending 31 March 2016 were £85,000, exceeding the VAT limit for the first time. Her main costs in the business are rent (exempt from VAT), the wages of two employees (outside the scope) and the fruit she buys for resale (zero-rated). Her accountant is not VAT-registered and has offered to complete VAT returns for her at a cost of £300 per year.

In reality, the main overheads and costs of the business do not attract any VAT, so Marion will have negligible input tax to reclaim if she became VAT-registered. It would be very unlikely if the total amount of input tax she could reclaim exceeded the accountancy fee of £300 to complete her returns. Her best option is to apply to HMRC to receive exemption from registration on the basis that she makes zero-rated sales and would therefore always be a repayment trader.

Changes in circumstances

[60.7] Except where other time limits are specified, a registered person must notify HMRC, within 30 days and with full written particulars of any change in the name, constitution or ownership of the business or any other event which may necessitate the variation of the register or cancellation of registration. [*SI 1995/2518, Reg 5(2)*].

Details of the changes should be notified to Grimsby National Registration Service, HM Revenue & Customs, Imperial House, 77 Victoria Street, Grimsby, DN31 1DB. Registration number and date of change should be given in any correspondence.

Electronic notification

The rules on 'specified communications' in **60.5** above also apply to notification of registration changes.

[*SI 1995/2518, Regs 4A, 4B*].

Changes not involving deregistration

Registration details must be amended for changes in any of the following.

- The names of the proprietors of, or partners in, the business.
- The name, business name or trading style of the business.
- The name of an incorporated company.
- The composition of a partnership where one or more of the former partners remains in the partnership.
- The name and/or address of the UK agent for VAT purposes appointed by an overseas company or resident.
- The address of the principal place of business.
- The registered office of an incorporated company.
- The main business activity.
- A limited company is re-registered as an unlimited company, or vice versa.
- A private company is re-registered as a public limited company, or vice versa.
- Bank account number or bank sorting code. If the annual accounting scheme is used, the registered person must notify the bank and VAT Central Unit Annual Accounting Section immediately.
- Certain changes affecting group treatment. See **28.3 GROUPS OF COMPANIES.**

Changes involving deregistration

The following changes will require deregistration.

- Sale of the business.
- Death, insolvency or incapacity of a taxable person. See **16.1 DEATH AND INCAPACITY** and **36.1 INSOLVENCY**.
- Conversion of a business into an incorporated company.
- Conversion of an incorporated company into a partnership or a sole proprietorship.
- A sole proprietor takes one or more persons into partnership.
- A partnership ceases to exist but one of the former partners becomes the sole proprietor of the business.
- Changes in the name or status of an unincorporated company.
- The transfer of business from one incorporated company to another.
- The business ceases to supply taxable goods or services.
- There is a complete change in the composition of a partnership at any one time.
- The business is otherwise disposed of.

(VAT Notice 700, para 26.3; VATREG35600).

Cessation of liability to be registered

[60.8] A person who has become liable to be registered under **60.3** above ceases to be so liable in the following circumstances.

- At any time if HMRC are satisfied that
  (i) he has ceased to make taxable supplies; or
  (ii) he is not at that time a person in relation to whom any of the conditions in **60.3**(*a*)–(*c*) above is satisfied; or
  (iii) he is not at that time UK established. (But see **60.33** below for his liability to be registered as a non-established taxable person.)
- If HMRC are satisfied that the value of his taxable supplies in the period of one year then beginning will not exceed the following specified limits.

Effective date	*Limit*
1.4.17	£83,000
1.4.16	£81,000
1.4.15	£80,000
1.4.14	£79,000
1.4.13	£77,000
1.4.12	£75,000

- However, that person does not cease to be liable to be registered under these provisions if HMRC are satisfied that the reason the value of his taxable supplies will not exceed the above limit is that in the period in question he will cease making taxable supplies or will suspend making them for a period of 30 days or more.
  Taxable supplies in determining the value of a person's supplies for the above purposes, supplies of goods or services that are 'capital assets' of the business in the course or furtherance of which they are supplied are disregarded. However, this is not to include the taxable supply of an interest in, right over or licence to occupy any land which is not zero-rated. See **60.3** above for the definition of '*capital assets*'.
  Any supplies which are taxable supplies only because an overseas trader making distance sales in the UK is required to register under *VATA 1994, Sch 2* (see **60.11** *et seq* below) can also be disregarded in determining the value of his supplies for the above purposes.
  Taxable supplies for the above purposes are determined on the basis that no VAT is chargeable on the supply (i.e. VAT-exclusive).

[*VATA 1994, Sch 1 paras 3, 4, 15, 16*].

Notification of end of liability or entitlement to registration

[60.9] A person

- voluntarily registered under *VATA 1994, Sch 1 para 9* (persons making or intending to make taxable supplies, see **60.2** above) or compulsorily registered under **60.3** above who ceases to make or have the intention of making taxable supplies, or
- voluntarily registered under *VATA 1994, Sch 1 para 10* (persons only making exempt or certain outside the scope supplies, see **60.2** above) who ceases to satisfy either of the conditions in **60.2**(*b*) or (*c*) above

must notify HMRC of that fact within 30 days of the date on which he does so unless he would, when he so ceases, be otherwise liable or entitled to be registered under **60.11** *et seq* or **60.18** *et seq* below. [*VATA 1994, Sch 1 paras 11, 12*]. The notification must be in writing and state the date on which the registered person ceased to make or have the intention of making taxable supplies. [*SI 1995/2518, Reg 5(3)*]. Notification should be sent to Grimsby National Registration Service, HM Revenue & Customs, Imperial House, 77 Victoria Street, Grimsby, DN31 1DB. See **53.19 PENALTIES** for failure to notify within 30 days.

Cancellation of registration

[60.10] In the situations outlined in (*a*) and (*b*) below, the registration of a business making taxable supplies must or, as the case may be, can be cancelled. However, it should be remembered that where a business also makes

- distance sales from another EU member state (see **60.11** below),
- acquisitions of goods from another EU member state (see **60.18** below), and
- in the case of an overseas trader, disposals of assets for which a VAT repayment is claimed (see **60.26** below)

it cannot apply to deregister until it has either ceased to be liable to be registered for all those supplies/acquisitions.

For non-established taxable persons, the registration threshold does not apply, so they must register for VAT if they make any taxable supplies in the UK and cannot apply for voluntary deregistration on the grounds of reduced turnover (see **60.33** below).

The provisions are also subject to *VATA 1994, Sch 3B para 18* (cancellation of registration under these provisions where a non-EU business intends to apply for registration under the special scheme for broadcasting, telecommunication and electronically supplied services in the EU, see **64.40 SPECIAL SCHEMES**).

(a) A business *must* cancel its registration if any of the following occur.
  - (i) It ceases to make taxable supplies (see **60.9** above).
  - (ii) It sells its business (unless the new owner wishes to retain the VAT registration number, see **60.42** below).
  - (iii) Its legal status changes (e.g. a sole proprietor takes in one or more partners, a partnership is dissolved and the business run by a sole proprietor, a company is incorporated to take over the

business previously carried on by a sole proprietor or partnership, or a company is wound up and replaced by a sole proprietor or partnership). In such a case, the business will normally cancel its existing registration and apply for a new registration number. It may, however, ask to retain its previous registration number, in which case it must also complete Form VAT 68.

(iv) It is the representative member of a VAT group (see **28 GROUPS OF COMPANIES**) and wishes to disband the group. In such circumstances, the registered person ceases to exist and the business will therefore need to cancel its registration. If any member of the disbanded group is continuing to trade, it must determine whether it will need to be registered in its own right. Where a member of a VAT group other than the representative member leaves the group, there is no need to cancel its registration unless the group only consists of the representative member and that one other member.

(v) It wishes to join a VAT group. Its existing registration must be cancelled as it is not possible to have two active registrations. Similarly, on the creation of a VAT group, the VAT registrations of any founder members must be cancelled.

(vi) It wishes to join the agricultural flat-rate scheme (see **64.25 SPECIAL SCHEMES**).

(vii) It was allowed registration on the basis that it intended to make taxable supplies and no longer intends to do so (see **60.9** above).

(viii) It was allowed registration on the basis that it made, or intended to make, supplies outside the UK which would have been taxable supplies if made in the UK and it has stopped making, or intending to make, those supplies.

(ix) It was allowed registration on the basis that it made, or intended to make, supplies of warehoused goods which were permitted to be disregarded for VAT and it has stopped making, or intending to make, those supplies.

(b) A business *may* ask for voluntary deregistration if any of the following occur.

(i) It satisfies HMRC that its taxable turnover in the next twelve months will not exceed the deregistration limit.

(ii) It closes down part of its business and satisfies HMRC that its taxable turnover for the remainder will not exceed the deregistration limit.

(iii) Its turnover exceeds the registration limits but it satisfies the conditions for exemption under **60.6** above.

(VAT Notice 700, para 26.2; VAT Notice 700/11/18, paras 2.3, 2.4–2.8, 3.1–3.3).

Date of deregistration

(1) Where a registered person satisfies HMRC he is no longer liable to be registered, HMRC must cancel his registration with effect from the day on which the request is made from such later date as is mutually agreed (provided they are satisfied that he would not be required to be registered on that date).

(2) Where HMRC are satisfied that a registered person has ceased to be 'registrable', they may cancel his registration with effect from the day on which he so ceased or from such later date as is mutually agreed (provided they are satisfied that he would not be required to be, or entitled to be, registered on that date).

(3) Where HMRC are satisfied that on the day on which a registered person was registered he was not registrable, they may cancel his registration with effect from that day.

'*Registrable*' means liable to be registered or entitled to be registered.

[*VATA 1994, Sch 1 paras 13, 18*].

Under (1) and (2) above, there is no provision to allow deregistration from an earlier date (see *S Moloney* (VTD 14873) (TVC 57.132)) but, on application, HMRC may agree to defer deregistration by up to six months if considered necessary for either

- the disposal of capital assets for which VAT invoices may need to be issued, or
- to allow input tax to be reclaimed on VAT invoices for supplies attributable to the business but which are not received until after the business has ceased to be a taxable person.

(HMRC VAT Guidance VATREG25000).

De Voil Indirect Tax Service. See V2.151–153.

Registration in respect of supplies from another EU member state ('distance selling')

[60.11] Additional registration requirements may apply in respect of 'distance selling'. This occurs when a supplier in one EU member state supplies goods, and is responsible for their delivery, to any person in another EU member state who is not registered for VAT. This may include supplies not only to private individuals but to public bodies, charities and businesses too small to register or with activities that are entirely exempt. The most obvious example of this type of supply is mail order. VAT on sales to non-VAT registered customers in another EU member state are in principle charged and accounted for by the supplier in the country from which the goods are dispatched. However, once the value of distance sales to any particular EU member state has exceeded an annual threshold, further sales are subject to VAT in the EU member state of destination and the supplier is liable to register for VAT in that country or appoint a VAT representative (see **3.8 AGENTS**) who will be responsible for accounting for VAT there on his behalf.

The provisions outlined in **60.12** to **60.17** below relate to the registration of suppliers from other EC countries not already registered for VAT in the UK.

For registration by UK suppliers in other EU member states see **20.18 EUROPEAN UNION: SINGLE MARKET.**

De Voil Indirect Tax Service. See V2.171–177.

Liability to be registered

[60.12] A 'person' who is not registered under *VATA 1994*, and is not liable to be registered under **60.3** above or **60.33** below, becomes liable to be registered under these provisions on any day if, in the period beginning with 1 January in that year, he has made 'relevant supplies' whose value exceeds £70,000.

In addition, a person who is not registered or liable to be registered as above becomes liable to be registered under these provisions (whatever the value of supplies) in the following circumstances.

(a) He has exercised an option, under the laws of another EU member state where he is taxable, to treat relevant supplies made by him as taking place outside that country and
- the supplies to which the option relates involve the removal of the goods from that country;
- if the option had not been exercised, under the law of that country the supplies would have been treated as taking place in that country; and
- he makes any relevant supply in the UK at a time when the option is in force.

(b) He makes a supply of goods subject to duty of excise where
- the supply involves the removal of the goods to the UK by, or under the directions of, the person making the supply;
- the supply is a transaction under which goods are acquired in the UK from another EU member state by a person who is not a taxable person;
- the supply is made in the course or furtherance of a business carried on by the supplier and is not treated as a supply only by virtue of *VATA 1994, Sch 4 para 5(1)* or *(6)* (transfers of goods forming part of the assets of the business).

'*Person*' includes a sole proprietor, partnership, limited company, club, association or charity. It is the person who is required to register, not the business or businesses carried on. The registration covers all the businesses of the registered person in the UK.

A supply of goods is a '*relevant supply*' where

(i) the supply involves the removal of the goods to the UK by, or under the directions of, the person making the supply;
(ii) the supply does not involve the installation or assembly of goods at a place in the UK;
(iii) the supply is a transaction under which goods are acquired in the UK from another EU member state by a person who is not a taxable person; and

(iv) the supply is made in the course or furtherance of a business carried on by the supplier and is not
- an exempt supply;
- a supply of goods subject to a duty of excise;
- a new means of transport (see **20.33 EUROPEAN UNION: SINGLE MARKET**); or
- treated as a supply only by virtue of *VATA 1994, Sch 4 para 5(1)* or *(6)* (transfers of goods forming part of the assets of the business).

A person is treated as having become liable to be registered under the above provisions at any time when he would have become so liable but for any registration which is subsequently cancelled under **60.10**(3) above or **60.17**(*b*), **60.25**(*c*), **60.32**(*b*) or **60.37** below.

In determining the value of relevant supplies for the above purposes, any part of the consideration representing a VAT liability of the supplier under the law of another EU member state is disregarded. Also disregarded are supplies to which *VATA 1994, s 18B(4)* (last acquisition or supply of goods before removal from fiscal warehousing) applies. See **73.17 WAREHOUSED GOODS.**

[*VATA 1994, Sch 2 paras 1, 10*].

Persons already registered in the UK

If a person making relevant supplies of distance sales is already registered for VAT in the UK under **60.3** above in respect of taxable supplies or **60.19** below in respect of relevant acquisitions, he does not need also to register under these provisions but must account for VAT in the UK on distance sales even where the threshold above is not reached. (VAT Notice 700/1/18, para 6.4).

Notification of liability and registration

[60.13] A person who becomes liable to registration under **60.12** above must notify HMRC of the fact within 30 days after that day.

HMRC must then register him (whether or not he so notifies them) with effect from the day on which the liability to register arose or from such earlier time as is agreed between them.

Notification must be in such form and manner and contain such particulars as may be specified in regulations or by HMRC in accordance with regulations. [*VATA 1994, Sch 2 paras 3, 9; SI 1995/2518, Reg 5(1)*].

Request to be registered

[60.14] A person who is not liable to be registered under *VATA 1994* and is not already so registered may request to be registered under these provisions. Provided he can satisfy HMRC that he intends

(a) to exercise an option referred to in **60.12**(*a*) above and, from a specified date, to make relevant supplies to which the option relates, or

(b) from a specified date to make relevant supplies in relation to any such option which has already been exercised, or
(c) from a specified date to make supplies satisfying the conditions in **60.12**(*b*) above,

HMRC may then, subject to such conditions as they think fit, register him from such date as is agreed between them. Any person who decides to opt to tax under this provision before reaching the threshold must notify HMRC at least 30 days before the date of the first supply to which the option is intended to apply. Application should be made in the relevant form. Written evidence should be enclosed showing that firm arrangements have been made to make distance sales.

Where a person who requests registration under the above provisions is also entitled to be registered under **60.2** above, he must be registered under those provisions.

[*VATA 1994, Sch 2 para 4*].

Cessation of liability

[60.15] A person who has become liable to be registered under **60.12** above ceases to be liable if at any time

(a) his relevant supplies in the year ended 31 December last before that time did not exceed £70,000 and did not include any dutiable supply falling within **60.12** above;
(b) HMRC are satisfied that the value of his relevant supplies in the year immediately following that year will not exceed £70,000 and will not include any such dutiable supply; and
(c) no such option as is mentioned in **60.12**(*a*) above is in force in relation to him.

[*VATA 1994, Sch 2 para 2*].

Notification of matters affecting registration

[60.16] A person must notify the following matters to HMRC in writing within 30 days.

(a) Where he is registered under these provisions and 'ceases to be registrable under *VATA 1994*'. Notification must state the date on which he ceased to be registrable.
(b) Where he is registered under **60.14** above, the exercise of any option or, as the case may be, the first occasion after registration when he makes a supply.
(c) Where he has exercised an option under **60.12**(*a*) above, and the option ceases to have effect (as a consequence of its revocation or otherwise) in relation to any relevant supplies by him.

A person '*ceases to be registrable under VATA 1994*' where

- he ceases to be a person who would be liable or entitled to be registered under that *Act* if his registration were disregarded; or

- he has been registered under **60.14** above and ceases to have any intention to exercise an option or make supplies as there mentioned.

Notification must be in such form and manner and contain such particulars as may be specified in regulations or by HMRC in accordance with regulations.

[*VATA 1994, Sch 2 paras 5, 9; SI 1995/2518, Reg 5(3)*].

Changes in circumstances

A person registered under these provisions must notify HMRC, within 30 days and with full written particulars, of any change in the name, constitution or ownership of the business or any other event which may necessitate the variation of the register or cancellation of registration. [*SI 1995/2518, Reg 5(2)*].

Cancellation of registration

[60.17] Subject to below, the registration of a person registered under these provisions must, or as the case may be, can be cancelled in the following circumstances.

(a) Where a person registered under these provisions satisfies HMRC that he is not liable to be so registered, they *must*, on request, cancel his registration with effect from the day on which the request is made or such later date as is mutually agreed. HMRC must be satisfied that, at the date of the proposed cancellation, the person would not be liable to be registered under any other provision of *VATA 1994*.

(b) Where HMRC are satisfied that, on the day on which a person was registered under these provisions, he was not liable to be registered (or, where he was registered under **60.14** above, did not have the intention by reference to which he was registered), they may cancel his registration with effect from that day.

(c) Where HMRC are satisfied that a person who has been registered under **60.14** above and is not for the time being liable to be registered under **60.12** above
    (i) has not, by the date specified in his request to be registered, carried out the intentions by reference to which he was registered; or
    (ii) has contravened any condition of his registration,

    they may cancel his registration from the date so specified or, as the case may be, the date of the contravention (or such later date as may be agreed between them). HMRC must be satisfied that, at the date of the proposed cancellation, the person would not be liable or entitled to be registered under any other provision of *VATA 1994*.

The registration of a person who has exercised an option with **60.12**(*a*) above cannot be cancelled unless it has been in force for two complete calendar years.

[*VATA 1994, Sch 2 paras 6, 7*].

Registration in respect of acquisitions of goods from other EU member states

[60.18] VAT on goods purchased from other EU member states is no longer paid when the goods enter the UK. Instead,

- for most transactions between registered persons, VAT becomes due on the acquisition of the goods by the customer and is accounted for on the normal VAT return; and
- where a person is not registered for VAT in the UK, any goods purchased from a registered supplier in another EU member state bear VAT at origin.

To prevent a business distorting trade by buying goods in another EU member state at a lower rate of VAT than in the UK, additional registration requirements apply in respect of certain acquisitions from other EU member states by persons who acquire goods in excess of an annual threshold but who are not registered, or required to be registered, under the provisions in **60.1** *et seq* or **60.11** *et seq* above. The provisions will only apply in restricted circumstances. Most businesses acquiring goods above the annual threshold value are likely to be making UK taxable supplies above the compulsory registration threshold in **60.3** above and will be liable to register under those provisions. The provisions will apply, for example, to a business making only exempt supplies in the UK and which acquires the goods for use in its business rather than for resale.

De Voil Indirect Tax Service. See V2.181–188.

Liability to be registered

[60.19] A 'person' who is not registered under *VATA 1994*, and is not liable to be registered under **60.3** or **60.12** above or **60.33** below, becomes liable to be registered under these provisions if

(a) at the end of any month, in the period beginning with 1 January in that year, he has made 'relevant acquisitions' whose value exceeds, or
(b) there are reasonable grounds for believing that the value of his relevant acquisitions in the period of 30 days then beginning will exceed,

the following limits.

Effective date	*Limit*
1.4.17	£85,000
1.4.16–31.3.17	£83,000
1.4.15–31.3.16	£82,000
1.4.14–31.3.15	£81,000
1.4.13–31.3.14	£79,000
1.4.12–31.3.13	£77,000
1.4.11–31.3.12	£73,000

'*Person*' includes a sole proprietor, partnership, limited company, club, association or charity. It is the person who is required to register, not the business or businesses carried on. The registration covers all the businesses of the registered person in the UK.

For a transaction to be an acquisition it must, under *VATA 1994, s 11*,

- be a supply of goods (including anything treated for the purposes of *VATA 1994* as a supply of goods); and
- involve the removal of the goods from another EU member state.

For the purposes of determining a person's entitlement or requirement to be registered under these provisions, however, only certain acquisitions are taken into account. These are called '*relevant acquisitions*' which are acquisitions which meet all of the following conditions.

- The goods are acquired in the course or furtherance of
  - (i) a business carried on by any person; or
  - (ii) any activities carried on otherwise than by way of business by any body corporate or by any club, association, organisation or other unincorporated body.
- The person who carries on that business or, as the case may be, those activities acquires the goods.
- The supplier is taxable in another EU member state at the time of the transaction and the transaction is in the course or furtherance of his business.
- The goods are not acquired in pursuance of an exempt supply.
- The goods are not subject to excise duty (see **20.9 EUROPEAN UNION: SINGLE MARKET**).
- The goods do not consist of a new means of transport (see **20.37 EUROPEAN UNION: SINGLE MARKET**).
- The acquisition is treated as taking place in the UK.

An acquisition is not, however, a relevant acquisition where, although the goods are transported to the UK, they are deemed to be supplied in the UK (e.g. installed goods).

A person is treated as having become liable to be registered under the above provisions at any time when he would have become so liable but for any registration which is subsequently cancelled under **60.10**(3) or **60.17**(*b*) above or **60.25**(*c*), **60.32**(*b*), or **60.37** below.

In determining the value of relevant acquisitions for the above purposes, any part of the consideration representing a VAT liability of the supplier under the law of another EU member state is disregarded. Also disregarded are supplies to which *VATA 1994, s 18B(4)* (last acquisition or supply of goods before removal from fiscal warehousing) applies. See **73.17 WAREHOUSED GOODS**.

[*VATA 1994, s 31(1), Sch 3 paras 1, 10, 11; SI 2016/365*].

Notification of liability and registration

[60.20] A person who becomes liable to registration under **60.19** above must notify HMRC of that fact as follows.

(a) Where **60.19**(*a*) above applies, within 30 days of the end of the relevant month.
HMRC must then register him (whether or not he so notifies them) with effect from the end of the month following the relevant month or from such earlier date as is agreed between them.

> *Example*
>
> On 31 May, W who is not registered for VAT, calculates that, since the previous 1 January, he has made relevant acquisitions exceeding the registration threshold.
>
> W becomes liable to register on 31 May. He must notify HMRC of his liability to register in respect of acquisitions by 30 June. Unless mutually agreed otherwise, HMRC will register him with effect from 1 July.

(b) Where **60.19**(*b*) above applies, before the end of the period by reference to which the liability arises.
HMRC must then register him (whether or not he so notifies them) with effect from the beginning of that period.

> *Example*
>
> On 22 May, W who is not registered for VAT, estimates that the value of his relevant acquisitions in the next 30 days will exceed the registration threshold.
>
> W becomes liable to register on 22 May. He must notify HMRC of his liability to register in respect of acquisitions by 21 June. HMRC will register him with effect from 22 May.

Notification must be in such form and manner and contain such particulars as specified in regulations or by HMRC in accordance with regulations.

[*VATA 1994, Sch 3 paras 3, 10*].

Application must be made in the relevant form. [*SI 1995/2518, Reg 5(1)*]. If not applying online the completed application forms, with any extra information requested by HMRC, should be sent to HM Revenue & Customs, VAT Registration Service, Crown House, Birch Street, Wolverhampton, WV1 4JX. Once registered, in addition to accounting for VAT on acquisitions, VAT must be accounted for on any taxable supplies made.

Entitlement to be registered

[60.21] Where a person who is not liable to be registered under *VATA 1994* and is not already so registered satisfies HMRC that

(a) he makes relevant acquisitions, or
(b) he intends to make relevant acquisitions from a specified date,

HMRC must, if he so requests, register him from the day on which the request is made or such earlier date as is mutually agreed. Any person who decides to register voluntarily under this provision before reaching the threshold must notify HMRC at least 30 days before the date from which registration is to be effective. Application should be made in the relevant form and where (*b*) above applies evidence should be enclosed showing that firm arrangements have been made to make acquisitions.

Where a person who requests registration under the above provisions is also entitled to be registered under **60.2** above, he must be registered under those provisions.

[*VATA 1994, Sch 3 para 4*].

Exemption from registration

[60.22] Where a person who makes or intends to make relevant acquisitions satisfies HMRC that any such acquisitions would be zero-rated if they were taxable supplies by a taxable person, HMRC may, if the person so requests and they think fit, grant exemption from registration under these provisions (although the relevant form must still be completed).

Where a person exempted under these provisions makes a relevant acquisition which would not be zero-rated if it were a taxable supply by a taxable person, he must notify HMRC within 30 days of the date of acquisition.

The exemption remains in force until it appears to HMRC that the request should no longer be acted upon or until it is withdrawn.

[*VATA 1994, Sch 3 para 8*].

Cessation of liability to be registered

[60.23] A person who has become liable to be registered under **60.19** above ceases to be liable if at any time

(a) his relevant acquisitions in the year ended 31 December last before that time did not exceed, and

(b) HMRC are satisfied that the value of his relevant acquisitions in the year immediately following that year will not exceed

the following limits.

Effective date	*Limit*
1.4.17	£85,000
1.4.16–31.3.17	£83,000
1.4.15–31.3.16	£82,000
1.4.14–31.3.15	£81,000
1.4.13–31.3.14	£79,000
1.4.12–31.3.13	£77,000
1.4.11–31.3.12	£73,000

However, that person does not cease to be liable to be registered under these provisions at any time if there are reasonable grounds for believing that the value of his relevant acquisitions in the period of 30 days then beginning will exceed that limit.

[*VATA 1994, Sch 3 para 2*].

Notification of matters affecting registration

[60.24] A person must notify the following matters to HMRC in writing within 30 days.

(a) Where he is registered under these provisions and 'ceases to be registrable under *VATA 1994*'. Notification must state the date on which he ceased to be registrable.
(b) Where he is registered under **60.21**(*b*) above, the first occasion after registration when he makes a relevant acquisition.

A person '*ceases to be registrable under VATA 1994*' where

- he ceases to be a person who would be liable or entitled to be registered under that *Act* if his registration were disregarded; or
- he has been registered under **60.21**(*b*) above and ceases to have any intention of making relevant acquisitions.

[*VATA 1994, Sch 3 paras 5, 10; SI 1995/2518, Reg 5(3)*].

Notification must be sent to Grimsby National Registration Service, HM Revenue & Customs, Imperial House, 77 Victoria Street, Grimsby, DN31 1DB.

Changes in circumstances

A person registered under these provisions must notify HMRC, within 30 days and with full written particulars, of any change in the name, constitution or ownership of the business or any other event which may necessitate the variation of the register or cancellation of registration. [*SI 1995/2518, Reg 5(2)*]. Notification must be sent to Grimsby National Registration Service, HM Revenue & Customs, Imperial House, 77 Victoria Street, Grimsby, DN31 1DB.

Cancellation of registration

[60.25] The registration of a person registered under these provisions must, or as the case may be, can be cancelled in the following circumstances.

(a) Subject to below, where a person registered under these provisions satisfies HMRC that he is not liable to be so registered, they *must*, on request, cancel his registration with effect from the day on which the request is made or such later date as is mutually agreed. HMRC must be satisfied that, at the date of the proposed cancellation, the person would not be liable to be registered under any other provision of *VATA 1994*.
(b) Subject to below, where HMRC are satisfied that a person registered under these provisions has, since his registration, ceased to be 'registrable' under these provisions, they may cancel his registration with effect from the day on which he so ceased or such later day as is mutually agreed. HMRC must also be satisfied that, at the date of the proposed cancellation, the person would not be liable or entitled to be registered under any other provision of *VATA 1994*.
(c) Where HMRC are satisfied that, on the day on which a person was registered under these provisions
    (i) he was not registrable under these provisions, or
    (ii) where he was registered under **60.21**(*b*) above, he did not have the intention by reference to which he was registered,

they may cancel his registration with effect from that day.

(d) Where HMRC are satisfied that a person who has been registered under **60.21**(*b*) above and is not for the time being liable to be registered under **60.19** above
   (i) has not, by the date specified in his request to be registered, begun to make relevant supplies, or
   (ii) has contravened any condition of his registration,

   they may cancel his registration from the date so specified or, as the case may be, the date of the contravention (or such later date as may be mutually agreed). HMRC must also be satisfied that, at the date of the proposed cancellation, the person would not be liable or entitled to be registered under any other provision of *VATA 1994*.

A person is '*registrable*' under these provisions at any time when he is liable to be registered under these provisions or makes relevant acquisitions.

The registration of a person

- who is registered under **60.21** above, or
- who would not be liable or entitled to be registered under any provision of *VATA 1994* except **60.21** above if he were not registered,

cannot be cancelled under (*a*) or (*b*) above unless it has been in force for two complete calendar years.

[*VATA 1994, Sch 3 paras 6, 7*].

Registration by overseas traders in respect of disposals of assets for which a VAT repayment is claimed

[60.26] The provisions detailed in **60.27** to **60.32** below require overseas traders (also referred to as non-established taxable persons) to be registered for VAT in the UK if they make claims under *Directive 2008/9/EC* (electronic cross-border refund system) or *EC 13th Directive* and subsequently supply, or intend to supply, the relevant goods in the UK. The provisions apply regardless of the value of the relevant supplies, i.e. there is no registration threshold. Once registered for VAT, the business must account for VAT on all its taxable supplies and can recover input tax in the normal way. The business will no longer be entitled to claim refunds under *Directive 2008/9/EC* (electronic cross-border refund system) or *EC 13th Directive.*

De Voil Indirect Tax Service. See V2.189–V2.189D.

Liability to be registered

[60.27] A person who is not registered under *VATA 1994* and is not liable to be registered under **60.3, 60.12** or **60.19** above or **60.33** below becomes liable to be registered under these provisions at any time if

(a) he makes 'relevant supplies'; or
(b) there are reasonable grounds for believing that he will make relevant supplies within the period of 30 days then beginning.

Relevant supplies

A supply is a '*relevant supply*' where

- the supply is a taxable supply;
- the goods are assets of the business in the course or furtherance of which they are supplied; and
- the person by whom they are supplied, or a 'predecessor' of his, has received or claimed, or is intending to claim, a VAT repayment on the supply to him, or the importation by him, of the goods (or of anything comprised in them) under the rules for refunds of VAT to persons established in other EU member states (see **18.9 EUROPEAN UNION GENERAL**) or the *EC 13th Directive* (refunds of VAT to persons established outside the EU (**49.5 OVERSEAS TRADERS**)).

For these purposes, a '*predecessor*' is someone who has transferred the goods in question to the registrable person under the provisions allowing relief from VAT on the transfer of a business, or part of a business, as a going concern (see **9.9 BUSINESS**). A person's predecessors include the predecessors of his predecessor through any number of transactions.

A person is treated as having become liable to be registered under these provisions at any time when he would have become so liable but for any registration which is subsequently cancelled under **60.10**(3), **60.17**(*b*), **60.25**(*c*) above, **60.32**(*b*) or **60.37** below.

[*VATA 1994, Sch 3A paras 1, 9*].

Notification of liability and registration

[60.28] A person who becomes liable to registration under **60.27** above must notify HMRC of that fact as follows.

(a) Where **60.27**(*a*) above applies, within 30 days of the date on which liability arises. HMRC must then register that person (whether or not he so notifies them) with effect from the beginning of the day on which liability arises.

(b) Where **60.27**(*b*) above applies, before the end of the period by reference to which the liability arises. HMRC must then register that person (whether or not he so notifies them) with effect from the beginning of that period.

[*VATA 1994, Sch 3A paras 3, 4*].

Notification must be in such form and manner and contain such particulars as specified in regulations or by HMRC in accordance with regulations.

[*VATA 1994, Sch 3A para 8*].

Application must currently be made in the relevant form. [*SI 1995/2518, Reg 5(1); SI 2000/794*].

Businesses may appoint a tax representative to act on their behalf (see **49.3 OVERSEAS TRADERS**).

Exemption from registration

[60.29] Where a person who makes or intends to make relevant supplies satisfies HMRC that any such supply would be zero-rated if he were a taxable person, HMRC may, if the person so requests and they think fit, grant exemption from registration under these provisions. Application should be made to HM Revenue and Customs VAT Registration Service, Crown House, Birch Street, Wolverhampton, WV1 4JX giving full details. A completed Form VAT1C should also be forwarded.

On a material change in the nature of the supplies made, the person exempted must notify HMRC within 30 days of the date on which the change occurred or, if no particular date is so identifiable, within 30 days of the end of the quarter in which it occurred. On a material alteration in any quarter in the proportion of relevant supplies of such a person that are zero-rated, he must notify HMRC of the alteration within 30 days of the end of the quarter.

Exemption applies until the date it appears to HMRC that the request should no longer be acted upon or until the date the request is withdrawn. HMRC must then register the person with effect from that date.

[*VATA 1994, Sch 3A para 7*].

Cessation of liability to be registered

[60.30] A person who has become liable to be registered under **60.27** above ceases to be liable to be registered if at any time HMRC are satisfied that he has ceased to make relevant supplies. [*VATA 1994, Sch 3A para 2*].

Notification of matters affecting registration

Change in circumstances

[60.31] A person registered under these provisions must notify HMRC, within 30 days and with full written particulars, of any change in the name, constitution or ownership of the business or any other event which may necessitate the variation of the register or cancellation of registration. [*SI 1995/2518, Reg 5(2)*].

End of liability to be registered

A person registered under these provisions who ceases to make, or have the intention of making, relevant supplies must notify HMRC of that fact within 30 days of the day on which he does so. Notification is not required if the person would, when he so ceases, be liable or entitled to be registered under any other provision of *VATA 1994*. [*VATA 1994, Sch 3A para 5*]. The notification must be in writing and must state the date on which the registered person ceased to make, or have the intention of making, relevant supplies. [*SI 1995/2518, Reg 5(3)*].

Cancellation of registration

[60.32] The registration of a person under these provisions may be cancelled in the following circumstances.

(a) Where HMRC are satisfied that a registered person has ceased to be liable to be registered under these provisions, they may cancel his registration with effect from the day on which he so ceased or such later date as is mutually agreed. However, HMRC must not cancel a person's registration with effect from any time unless they are satisfied that the person would not be liable or entitled to be registered under any other provision of *VATA 1994*.

(b) Where HMRC are satisfied that on the day on which a registered person was registered he was not registrable, they may cancel his registration with effect from that day.

[*VATA 1994, Sch 3A para 6*].

An application to have registration cancelled should be made in the relevant form specified in a notice published by HMRC.

Registration by non-established taxable persons

[60.33] On 1 December 2012 new rules took effect determining when a business which makes taxable supplies in the UK but has no establishment here has to register for VAT. From 1 December 2012 non-UK established businesses have no longer been able to benefit from the UK VAT registration threshold, and have had to register and account for VAT on their taxable supplies in the UK irrespective of their value.

Liability to be registered

[60.34] A person becomes liable to be registered under these provisions at any time if conditions A to D are met.

- Condition A—the person makes taxable supplies, or there are reasonable grounds for believing that the person will make taxable supplies in the period of 30 days then beginning.
- Condition B—those supplies (or any of them) are or will be made in the course or furtherance of a business carried on by the person.
- Condition C—the person has no business establishment, or other fixed establishment, in the UK in relation to any business carried on by the person.
- Condition D—the person is not VAT registered.

A person does not become liable to be registered by virtue of the second part of condition A if the reason for believing that taxable supplies will be made in the 30-day period mentioned there is that a business, or part of a business, carried on by a taxable person is to be transferred to the person as a going concern in that period. But if the transfer takes place, the transferee becomes liable to be registered at the time of the transfer if conditions A to D are met in relation to the transferee at that time. HMRC issued more clarification in HMRC Brief 11/16 regarding when a non-resident business would be required to register as a result of acquiring a business in the UK as a TOGC.

A person ceases to be liable to be registered if HMRC are satisfied that he has ceased to make taxable supplies in the course or furtherance of a business carried on by him, or he is no longer a person in relation to whom condition C is met.

[*VATA 1994, Sch 1A paras 1–4*].

Notification of liability and registration

[60.35] A person who becomes liable to be registered by virtue of the first part of condition A or as the result of the transfer of a going concern must notify HMRC of the liability before the end of the period of 30 days beginning with the day on which the liability arises. HMRC must register any such person (whether or not the person so notifies them) with effect from the beginning of the day on which the liability arises.

A person who becomes liable to be registered by virtue of the second part of condition A must notify HMRC of the liability before the end of the period by reference to which the liability arises. HMRC must register any such person (whether or not the person so notifies them) with effect from the beginning of the period by reference to which the liability arises.
[*VATA 1994, Sch 1A paras 5, 6*].

Notification of end of liability

[60.36] A person registered under the above provisions who, on any day, ceases to make or have the intention of making taxable supplies in the course or furtherance of a business carried on by him must notify HMRC of that fact within 30 days beginning with that day. But he need not notify them if on that day he would otherwise be liable or entitled to be registered for VAT (disregarding for this purpose the person's registration under these provisions and any enactment that prevents a person from being liable to be registered under different provisions at the same time).
[*VATA 1994, Sch 1A para 7*].

Cancellation of registration

[60.37] HMRC must cancel a person's registration under these provisions if the person satisfies them that he is not liable to be so registered, and the person requests the cancellation. The cancellation is to be made with effect from the day on which the request is made, or such later day as may be agreed between HMRC and the person. But HMRC must not cancel the registration with effect from any time unless they are satisfied that it is not a time when the person would be subject to a requirement to be VAT registered.

HMRC may cancel a person's registration under these provisions if they are satisfied that the person has ceased to be liable to be so registered. The cancellation is to be made with effect from the day on which the person ceased to be so liable, or such later day as may be agreed between HMRC and the person. But HMRC must not cancel the registration with effect from any time unless they are satisfied that it is not a time when the person would be subject to a requirement, or entitled, to be VAT registered.

HMRC may cancel a person's registration under these provisions if they are satisfied that the person was not liable to be so registered on the day on which the person was registered. The cancellation is to be made with effect from the day on which the person was registered.

[*VATA 1994, Sch 1A paras 8–12*].

Exemption from registration

[60.38] HMRC may exempt a person from registration under these provisions if the person satisfies them that the taxable supplies that he makes or intends to make are all zero-rated, or would all be zero-rated if the person were a taxable person. This power is exercisable only if the person so requests and HMRC think fit. If there is a material change in the nature of the supplies made by a person exempted, he must notify HMRC of the change

- within 30 days beginning with the day on which the change occurred; or
- if no particular day is identifiable as that day, within 30 days of the end of the quarter in which the change occurred.

If it appears to HMRC that a request for exemption from registration should no longer be acted upon on or after any day or has been withdrawn on any day, they must register the person who made the request with effect from that day.

[*VATA 1994, Sch 1A para 13*].

Failure to register

The Government announced in Budget 2016 that they intended to strengthen HMRC's powers to ensure that a non-resident business who sells goods in the UK via an online marketplace registers for VAT. HMRC will contact any business who they consider has failed to register for VAT in the UK to request that they adhere to the UK VAT registration requirements. If the overseas seller still does not comply with their UK VAT registration requirement, HMRC will contact the online marketplace through which they are trading to put the marketplace on notice that they could be held joint and severally liable for any UK VAT due from a specified date. HMRC can also make overseas sellers appoint a UK tax representative who will also be joint and severally liable for any UK VAT due.

Penalties can also be imposed for failure to notify.

Consequences of deregistration

Notice of cancellation and final return

[60.39] If HMRC are satisfied that the registration should be cancelled, they will send out a formal notice confirming the date on which VAT registration was cancelled. Unless the registration number has been re-allocated to a person who is taking over the business as a going concern (see **9.10 BUSINESS**), a final return must be submitted. See **2.5–2.5 ACCOUNTING PERIODS AND RETURNS.** (VAT Notice 700/11/18, paras 8.1, 8.2).

VAT invoices

VAT invoices must not normally be issued or VAT charged as from the date of cancellation (although where a deregistered person has undercharged VAT on a supply made before deregistration, HMRC may agree to a VAT invoice being raised to the customer concerned so that the trader does not have to account for any additional VAT due from his own resources). The previous VAT registration number must not be shown on any invoices issued. HMRC should be consulted before using an existing stock of invoices and crossing out the registration number. If a self-billing arrangement (see **40.6 INVOICES**) or the authenticated receipt procedure for the construction industry (see **43.21**(2) **LAND AND BUILDINGS: ZERO AND REDUCED RATE SUPPLIES AND DIY HOUSEBUILDERS**) are in operation customers must be notified immediately of the deregistration and informed that VAT must not be charged. (VAT Notice 700/11/18, para 8.3).

Input tax

Input tax cannot be claimed on purchases made from the date of deregistration except for VAT on the supply of certain services after deregistration made for the purposes of the business carried on before that time. See **35.11 INPUT TAX**.

Capital goods scheme

A final adjustment may be required in respect of items still within the adjustment period. See **11.7 CAPITAL GOODS SCHEME**.

Records

All VAT records including a list of all business assets on hand, together with their values, should be kept *whether or not they are liable to VAT*. See also **57.1 RECORDS** for preservation of records generally.

Payment of VAT on business assets

[60.40] VAT must be accounted for on the final return of any 'goods' forming part of the business assets which are on hand at the close of business or on the last day of registration as if they were supplied in the course or furtherance of the business unless

(a) the business is transferred as a going concern to another taxable person (see **9.9 BUSINESS**);
(b) the taxable person has died, become bankrupt or incapacitated and the business is carried on by another person who under *VATA 1994, s 46(4)* is treated as a taxable person (see **16.1 DEATH AND INCAPACITY** and **36.1 INSOLVENCY**); or
(c) the VAT on the deemed supply would not be more than £1,000.

'*Goods*' for these purposes means tangible goods (e.g. unsold stock, plant, furniture, commercial vehicles, computer, etc.) but intangible assets such as patents, copyrights and goodwill can be disregarded because they count as 'services' for VAT purposes. (VAT Notice 700/11/18, paras 7.1, 7.2). It includes goods purchased where title has not yet passed to the business but where input tax on the purchase has been allowed (e.g. goods on hire purchase or lease purchase and goods subject to reservation of title). Land forming part of the business assets is treated as if it were goods.

The provisions do not apply to any goods where the taxable person can show to the satisfaction of HMRC that

(i) no credit for input tax has been allowed to him in respect of the supply of goods, their acquisition from another EU member state or their importation from a place outside the EU; *and*
(ii) the goods did not become his as part of the assets of a business or part of a business transferred as a going concern from another taxable person (see **9.9 BUSINESS**).

The provisions also do not apply where a person ceased to be a taxable person in consequence of being certified to join the flat-rate scheme for farmers (see **64.25 SPECIAL SCHEMES**).

[*VATA 1994, Sch 4 paras 8, 9*].

Excluded items

The taxable person does not have to account for VAT on any items on which he did not claim VAT when he bought them. Examples include

- goods bought from unregistered businesses or private individuals;
- cars (except private taxis, self-drive hire cars and driving school cars on which input tax has been claimed);
- goods bought under a VAT margin scheme;
- goods used wholly for business entertainment;
- goods which have been directly attributed to an exempt business activity (unless some input tax relating to these goods was reclaimable through the partial exemption rules);
- land or buildings which were obtained free of VAT, even if they are being used to make standard-rated supplies (such as holiday accommodation or because he has opted to tax the property);
- goods not bought for business purposes.

(VAT Notice 700/11/18, para 7.3).

Option to tax

If the taxable person has opted to tax land or buildings, he may have to account for VAT at the time of deregistration.

If he sells the opted land or property, VAT may be due on the sale price, subject to transfer of a going concern criteria, as set out in Notice 700/9/12.

If the taxable person will be keeping the land or property and he claimed input tax when he bought it	then he will be making a deemed supply of it at the time of deregistration. This means he will need to account for VAT on the land or property's current market value.
If he will be keeping the land or property and did not claim input tax when he bought it	then VAT does not become due until the land or property is sold during the life of the option to tax. This means that he will not have to account for VAT on it when he deregisters.

(VAT Notice 700/11/18, para 7.4).

Value of the supply

The value of the goods on which VAT must be accounted for is the price the person would have to pay (excluding VAT), at the time of the supply, to purchase goods *identical* in every respect (including age and condition) to the goods concerned. Where that value cannot be ascertained, the price for the purchase of goods *similar* to, and of the same age and condition as, the goods concerned must be used. If that value is also not possible to ascertain, the cost of producing the goods concerned at that time is to be used. [*VATA 1994, Sch 6 para 6*].

De Voil Indirect Tax Service. See V3.261.

> *Example*
>
> Mike runs a shop that sells confectionery, tobacco and newspapers. His taxable turnover for the twelve months to 31 March 2017 was £53,000 and his expected taxable sales for the next twelve months are expected to be £55,000. He has decided to deregister from VAT.
>
> The cost value of Mike's stock at 31 March 2017 was £20,000 (cost price excluding VAT) – of which newspapers were £4,000. He also has a car that he bought twelve months ago for £10,000 plus VAT and a computer that he bought from a friend (not VAT-registered) for £1,000.
>
> It is clear that the value of stock and assets on hand exceeds £5,000 – so Mike has an output tax liability to declare on his final VAT return. However, the first concession is that he can ignore the computer because it was bought from an unregistered person. In the case of the car, Mike would not have reclaimed input tax on the initial purchase (non-deductible input tax) so the onward supply is exempt under *VATA 1994, Sch 9, Group 14*. The newspapers are zero-rated so they can also be excluded. Output tax is therefore due on the remaining stock, i.e. £16,000 multiplied by the standard rate of VAT.

Retail schemes

[60.41] Whichever retail scheme is used, the provisions under **60.40** above apply. See also **61.6 RETAIL SCHEMES** for rules to be followed when ceasing to use a retail scheme.

Transfer of registration

[60.42] Where a business (or part of a business) is transferred as a going concern (see **9.9 BUSINESS**), then provided

- the transferor's registration under *VATA 1994, Sch 1* or *Sch 1A* has not already been cancelled;
- on the transfer, the registration of the transferor under either Schedule is to be cancelled *and* the transferee either becomes liable to be registered or HMRC agree to register him under *Sch 1 para 9*; and
- an application is made on the form specified in a notice published by HMRC by or on behalf of both the transferor and the transferee.

HMRC may, under powers given to them in *VATA 1994, s 49*, cancel the transferor's registration and, from the date of the transfer, register the transferee under *Sch 1* or *Sch 1A* with the registration number previously allocated to the transferor. The application constitutes notice by the transferor of end of liability or entitlement to registration (see **60.9** above) but must be submitted within 30 days of the transfer to avoid any penalty for late notification. [*SI 1995/2518, Reg 6(1)(2)*].

Consequences of transfer of registration number

Where a registration number has been re-allocated as above then both the previous and new owners must agree to the following consequences.

- Any liability of the transferor at the transfer date to submit a return or to account for or pay VAT becomes the liability of the transferee (see *WH & AJ Ponsonby v C & E Commrs*, QB 1987, [1988] STC 28 (TVC 65.115) and *Bjellica (t/a Eddy's Domestic Appliance) v C & E Commrs*, CA [1995] STC 329 (TVC 57.92) where the previous owner should have registered twelve years before he actually did and the firm to which he transferred the business was held liable for the VAT).
- Any right of the transferor, whether or not existing at the date of the transfer, to credit for or to repayment of input tax becomes the right of the transferee (e.g. VAT recoverable on any services supplied to the previous owner for his business before the transfer but which are invoiced afterwards).
- Any right of either the transferor, whether or not existing at the date of transfer, or the transferee to payment by HMRC for recoverable input tax under *VATA 1994, s 25(3)* is satisfied by payment to either of them.
- Any right of the transferor, whether or not existing at the date of the transfer, to a claim for bad debt relief becomes the right of the transferee but, equally, any liability of the transferor to make repayments of input tax where bad debt relief has been claimed and the transferor was the debtor also becomes the liability of the transferee.
- Any records relating to the business which, by virtue of Regulations or a direction made by HMRC, must be preserved for any period after the transfer, must be preserved by the transferee (unless HMRC, at the request of the transferor, otherwise direct).
- Where the transferee of a business (or part) has been registered with the registration number of the transferor during a VAT period subsequent to that in which the transfer took place but with effect from the date of the transfer, any return made, VAT accounted for or paid or right to credit for input tax claimed, is treated as having been done by the transferee (whether in fact done by, or in the name of, the transferee or transferor).

[*SI 1995/2518, Reg 6(3)(4)*].

Additional conditions to be met

Apart from the conditions specified in the *Regulations* as detailed above, HMRC require the following conditions to be met before allowing the reallocation of a VAT registration number.

- No VAT group registration must be involved.
- Where the transferor was a company, it must not have been dissolved before the VAT 68 is signed.
- The transferor must not be the subject of a direction in respect of disaggregation of business activities (see **9.5 BUSINESS**).
- Any centrally raised assessment notified to the transferor covering periods after the date of transfer must be paid.
- Any default surcharge incurred by the transferor for periods prior to the date of transfer must have been paid with no indication of an appeal.
- No civil penalty has been or is to be imposed on the transferor under *VATA 1994, s 60* (VAT evasion, see **53.12 PENALTIES**), *VATA 1994, s 68* (breach of walking possession agreements, see **53.18 PENALTIES**) or *VATA 1994, s 69* (breaches of regulatory provisions, see **53.19 PENALTIES**). In the case of a *VATA 1994, s 67* penalty (failure to notify and unauthorised issue of invoices, see **53.16 PENALTIES**), reallocation may be allowed if the penalty has been paid.

(HMRC VAT Guidance V1–28, para 10.6.7).

Accounting schemes

If the transferor had any special arrangements (e.g. annual accounting, use of a retail or flat-rate scheme), these cease from the date of transfer and a fresh application must be made by the transferee.

Preservation of records

It is the responsibility of the transferor to preserve the pre-transfer records of the business. HMRC may, at the request of the transferor, direct otherwise. The transferor must make documents, information and records available to the transferee to the extent necessary for him to meet its VAT obligations. HMRC may disclose to the transferee any information relating to the business while it was operated by the transferor to enable the transferee to meet its VAT obligations.

[*VATA 1994, s 49(2A); SI 1995/2518, reg 6(3)(f)*]. (VAT Information Sheet 12/07).

De Voil Indirect Tax Service. See V2.131.

Divisional registration

[60.43] A 'body corporate' carrying on its 'business' in several divisions may, if it requests and HMRC see fit, register in the names of those divisions. For these purposes, 'business' includes any other activities in the course or furtherance of which the body corporate acquires goods from another EU member state. [*VATA 1994, s 46(1)(6)*]. See **28.2 GROUPS OF COMPANIES** for the meaning of '*body corporate*'.

Divisional registration is a facility which allows a corporate body carrying on business through a number of self-accounting units to register each of those units or divisions separately for VAT. Each division is given a separate VAT registration number and makes its own VAT return. However, the corporate body is still a single taxable person and it remains liable for the VAT debts of all the divisions.

Conditions for divisional registration

HMRC will only approve divisional registration if all the following conditions are satisfied.

(a) It is satisfied that there would be real difficulties in submitting a single VAT return for the corporate body as a whole within 30 days of the end of the VAT period.
(b) All the divisions must be registered, even those whose turnover is under the registration limit (see **60.3** above).
(c) All divisions must be independent units with their own accounting systems and must be
   - operating from different geographical locations;
   - supplying different commodities; or
   - carrying out different functions (e.g. manufacture, wholesale, retail, export, etc.).
(d) The corporate body as a whole must be, or be treated as being, fully taxable (i.e. where any exempt supplies are made, input tax attributable to those exempt supplies must be less than the *de minimis* limits in **50.11 PARTIAL EXEMPTION**. The *de minimis* limits apply to the whole corporate body and not to each division).
(e) All divisions must complete VAT returns for the same VAT periods. These will normally be allocated by HMRC although an application for non-standard VAT periods can be made. Where the corporate body as a whole expects to receive regular repayments of VAT, monthly returns may be allowed but, in such a case, all of the divisions must make monthly returns.

If, once registered in divisions, a body corporate no longer satisfies any of the above conditions, it must notify HMRC in writing within 30 days. HMRC will then decide whether to allow the divisional registration to continue.

Applications

Applications must be made by letter and sent to the National Registration Service explaining why it is difficult to submit a single VAT return for the whole body corporate. An application must be completed for each division. Copies of incorporation certificates and charters and copies of any Acts of Parliament under which the body was incorporated (other than the *Companies Acts*) or any other proof of incorporation should also be included.

Effective date of commencement

Approval of an application for divisional registration normally takes effect from a current date unless there are exceptional circumstances.

Adding and removing divisions

Applications to add any new divisions should be made following the same procedure as above. Where an existing division is sold off or closed down, the National Registration Service must be advised in writing and that division will then be removed from the divisional registration of the corporate body.

Overseas bodies

A corporate body constituted outside the UK may apply for divisional registration provided it has at least two self-accounting units in the UK and it can comply with the above conditions. One of the UK divisions is deemed to cover the activities of those divisions or sites which are outside the UK so that, if any of those overseas divisions, etc. starts to make taxable supplies in the UK, VAT is accounted for on those supplies by the UK-based division covering for them.

VAT groups

Divisional registration and group treatment under **28.1 GROUPS OF COMPANIES** are mutually exclusive. Where a company which is a member of a VAT group wishes to register some of its divisions separately, it must first apply to leave the VAT group. Conversely, a corporate body with divisional registration which wishes to form or join a VAT group must first apply to cancel the registration of all of its divisions.

Accounting for VAT

VAT invoices must not be issued for transactions made between divisions of the same corporate body. These are not considered to be supplies for VAT purposes.

(VAT Notice 700/2/14, paras 8.1–8.15).

De Voil Indirect Tax Service. See V2.190A.

Key points: registration

[60.44] Points to consider are as follows.

Registration

- A new or existing business will need to monitor the level of its taxable sales at the end of each calendar month to identify if it has exceeded the VAT registration limit. It is not acceptable to wait until the end of the first twelve months of trading and then apply the relevant test. Remember, however, that it is only taxable sales that count, not exempt or non-business sales.
- A second test is that a business must also register for VAT if it expects the value of its taxable sales in the next 30 days to exceed the VAT registration limit. In such cases, it should become VAT-registered at the beginning of the 30-day period.
- A business is liable to account for VAT from the date it should be registered under the compulsory rules explained above. If sales invoices are issued before a VAT number has been received from HMRC (but the date of registration has passed), the business should still charge VAT but not show it as a separate entry on the invoice.

- When a business has received its belated VAT registration number from HMRC, it needs to issue tax invoices to customers, giving them suitable evidence to support their input tax claims.
- A transferee taking over a business as a going concern must take the taxable turnover of the previous owners into account when deciding if it needs to be VAT-registered from its first day of trading.
- A business trading in second-hand goods must base the value of its taxable turnover on the full value of the sale, rather than just the margin that would be used under a second-hand VAT scheme.
- To make accounting simpler, it is worthwhile for a business to seek VAT periods at the time of registration that coincide with its financial year, e.g. a business with 31 March year end should request calendar VAT periods.
- Ensure that a newly registered business has identified opportunities to reclaim input tax on any relevant expenditure incurred before its date of registration. However, expenditure on goods must have been incurred within the four-year period before the registration date; a six-month time limit is imposed for services.
- It may be in the best interest of many businesses to register for VAT on a voluntary basis – particularly if they are making mainly zero-rated supplies or mainly working for other VAT-registered businesses. Advisers need to regularly review the activities of all non-registered clients to see if they could benefit from voluntary registration.
- VAT registration as an intending trader means a business can reclaim input tax on its costs and capital expenditure, before it starts to trade. It is important to satisfy HMRC that there is a genuine intention to trade in the future, even though this might be many months or possible years in the future.
- A concession allows a business that has no taxable supplies in the UK to still register for VAT and claim input tax if its income is outside the scope of VAT under the place of supply rules. The key point is that the service must either be taxable if it was provided to a UK customer or relate to certain exempt financial services provided for non-EU customers.
- If HMRC backdates a registration, make sure the officer's calculations and procedures for calculating the actual date are correct. Remember that if any arrears of VAT are established through the backdating of the registration, there is likely to be scope to reduce self-assessment tax liabilities because of reduced profits.
- A potential planning opportunity could make it worthwhile for a business to register for VAT on a voluntary basis in order that it can make tax savings by using the flat-rate scheme.
- In some cases, a non-VAT registered business in the UK (e.g. a business that makes wholly exempt supplies) may be required to register if it makes acquisitions of goods from suppliers in other EU member states or buys services where the place of supply is in the UK. The intention of such requirements is to create a level playing field as far as VAT is concerned.

Deregistration

- Any request for deregistration based on future turnover cannot be made because of a decision to suspend trading for 30 days or more.
- A business that is in a repayment situation but has taxable supplies exceeding the VAT limits can still apply for deregistration. This decision would be made if the business is unlikely to lose much input tax by deregistering, and wants to save the administrative burden of being registered.
- Remember that a deregistered business can claim input tax on certain relevant expenses after it has been deregistered. This can be done by using Form VAT 427 – but any claim must be supported by original tax invoices.
- Be aware of the opportunity for the same VAT number to be retained by the new owners in situations where the business has been transferred as a going concern. However, there are potential risks for the new owner of the business, who is effectively taking over the possible VAT debts of the previous owner.
- There is no output tax liability on the value of stocks and assets held at the time of deregistration if the amount of VAT involved is less than £1,000. There are also other concessions to reduce the potential output tax charge, e.g. no output tax due on zero-rated or exempt goods; output tax calculations are based on the present condition of the goods, i.e. taking damage and depreciation into account.
- If a business owns land and property at the time of deregistration, then it is important to be clear about the output tax rules that apply in relation to the option to tax and potential problems with the capital goods scheme.

61

Retail Schemes

Cross-references. See **12.7 CATERING** for accounting for supplies of catering when take-away food is also sold; **48.7**(35) **OUTPUT TAX** for video cassettes; **57 RECORDS**; **64.13 SPECIAL SCHEMES** for the annual accounting scheme; and **70 TRADE PROMOTION SCHEMES** where such schemes are operated under a retail scheme.

De Voil Indirect Tax Service. See V3.551–V3.576.

Introduction to retail schemes

[61.1] VAT retail schemes were introduced at the start of VAT in 1973 because it was recognised that many businesses dealing directly with the public (primarily shopkeepers) and making supplies at different rates of VAT would be unable to keep records of every sale in order to calculate the VAT due in the normal way. The retail schemes are therefore methods for arriving at the value of taxable retail supplies and determining what proportion of those sales are taxable at different rates of VAT.

HMRC's powers

Under *VATA 1994, Sch 11 para 2(6)* and *SI 1995 No 2518, Regs 67, 68*, HMRC are empowered to permit the value of supplies by a retailer which are taxable at other than the zero rate to be determined by a method

- described in a notice published by them, or
- agreed with the retailer.

They may refuse to permit a retailer to use a particular scheme in the following circumstances.

(a) If the use of any particular scheme does not produce a fair and reasonable valuation during any period.
(b) It is necessary to do so for the protection of the revenue.
(c) The retailer could reasonably be expected to account for VAT in the normal way.
Since the introduction of VAT, there has been a revolution in information technology available to, and used by, retailers (e.g. use of bar codes and sophisticated till technology). HMRC consider that these changes mean that the original need for retail schemes, which only provide an approximation of the VAT due, is greatly diminished. They are, therefore, examining every retailer's need to continue using a retail scheme and will only permit the use of a scheme where the retailer cannot reasonably be expected to account for VAT in the normal way, i.e. by identifying each individual supply, its value and the rate of VAT. (VAT Information Sheet 7/96).

Retail and non-retail sales

Where both retail and non-retail sales are made, a retail scheme can only be used for the retail sales and VAT on the non-retail sales must be accounted for outside the scheme in the normal way. (VAT Notice 727, paras 2.1, 2.2 which have the force of law). See *The Oxford, Swindon and Gloucester Co-operative Society v C & E Commrs*, QB [1995] STC 583 (TVC 58.9).

Sales to other VAT-registered businesses

These must normally not be included in a retail scheme. However, by exception, *occasional* cash sales (e.g. a garage supplying petrol to a VAT-registered customer or a retail DIY store supplying building materials to a VAT-registered builder) may be included within a retail scheme. (VAT Notice 727, para 2.4 which has the force of law).

Flat-rate scheme for small businesses

No retailer may use a retail scheme at the same time as the flat-rate scheme for small businesses (see **64.15 SPECIAL SCHEMES**). [*SI 1995/2518, Reg 69A*].

Summary of schemes

[61.2] A retail business with an annual VAT-exclusive turnover over £130 million and which needs to use a retail scheme is only eligible to do so if it agrees a bespoke scheme with HMRC. See **61.13** below.

Apart from such bespoke schemes, there are five published standard schemes.

(a) **Point of Sale scheme.** VAT due is calculated by identifying the correct VAT liability of supplies at the time of sale, e.g. by using electronic tills. See **61.14** below.

(b) **Apportionment Scheme 1.** This is the simpler apportionment scheme designed for smaller businesses with an annual VAT-exclusive turnover not exceeding £1 million. Each VAT period, the retailer must work out the value of purchases for resale at different rates of VAT and apply the proportions of those purchase values to sales. For example, if 82% of the value of goods purchased for retail sale are standard-rated, it is assumed that 82% of takings are from standard-rated sales. Once a year, a similar calculation is made based on purchases for the year and any over or under payment adjusted. See **61.15** below.

(c) **Apportionment Scheme 2.** Under this scheme, a retailer must calculate the expected selling prices (ESPs) of standard-rated and reduced rate goods received for retail sale. He must then work out the ratio of these to the expected selling prices of all goods received for retail sale and apply this ratio to takings. For example, if 82% of the ESPs of goods received for retail sale are standard-rated and 18% are zero-rated, then 82% of takings are treated as standard-rated and 18% zero-rated. See **61.16** below.

(d) **Direct Calculation Scheme 1.** This is available to businesses with an annual VAT-exclusive turnover not exceeding £1 million. To work the scheme, a retailer must calculate expected selling prices (ESPs) of goods for retail sale at one or more rates of VAT so that the proportion of takings on which VAT is due can be calculated. ESPs are, as a general rule, calculated for minority goods, i.e. those goods at the rate of VAT which forms the smallest proportion of retail supplies. For example, if 82% of sales are standard-rated and 18% are zero-rated, the minority goods are zero-rated. Expected selling prices of the zero-rated goods received, made or grown for retail sale are calculated and deducted from takings to arrive at a figure for standard-rated takings. However, a retailer may mark up the majority goods if this would be a simpler option. See **61.17** below.

(e) **Direct Calculation Scheme 2.** This scheme works in exactly the same way as Direct Calculation Scheme 1 but requires an annual stock-take adjustment. See **61.18** below.

(VAT Notice 727, paras 3.4–3.13).

Adaptations to the standard schemes

HMRC may approve an adaptation of any of the above standard schemes.

See under the details of the various schemes for adaptations allowed by HMRC.

Choosing a scheme

[61.3] A retailer can chose to use any of the published schemes provided

- he meets the conditions for use of the scheme in question; and

- HMRC have not refused to let him use the scheme (see **61.1** above).

The following general comparisons can be made of the different schemes.

Point of Sale scheme

- Only available scheme if all supplies are standard-rated or all supplies are taxable at the reduced rate. (VAT Notice 727, para 3.4 which has the force of law).
- Turnover limit of £130 million.
- Can be used for services, catering supplies, self-made and self-grown goods.
- Does not involve stock-taking or working out expected selling prices.
- No annual adjustment required.
- The scheme is potentially both the simplest and most accurate but electronic tills are expensive and staff must be able to operate the system correctly at all times.

Apportionment Scheme 1

- Cannot be used for services, catering supplies, self-made or self-grown goods.
- Turnover limit of £1 million.
- Does not involve stock-taking or working out expected selling prices.
- Annual adjustment required.
- The scheme is relatively simple. However, if on average a higher mark-up is achieved for zero-rated goods than standard-rated or reduced rate goods, more VAT could be payable under this scheme than another available alternative scheme.

Apportionment Scheme 2

- Cannot be used for services or catering supplies but can be used for self-made or self-grown goods.
- Turnover limit of £130 million.
- Stock-taking required at the start of using the scheme, but not thereafter.
- Expected selling prices must be worked out.
- No annual adjustment required but a rolling calculation used.
- The scheme can be complex to operate but if worked properly it will provide a more accurate valuation of supplies over a period of time.

Direct Calculation Scheme 1

- Services can only be included if they are liable at a different rate from the minority goods.
- Cannot be used for catering supplies but can be used for self-made or self-grown goods.
- Turnover limit of £1 million.
- Expected selling prices must be worked out. The scheme can produce inaccuracies if expected selling prices are not calculated accurately. In addition, where expected selling prices are set for standard-rated goods

and stock of these goods has a slow turnover, the scheme may not be the most appropriate as VAT is paid in the period in which the goods are received and not necessarily when they are sold.

- Does not involve stock-taking.
- No annual adjustment required.
- The scheme can be relatively simple where goods are sold at two rates of VAT and there is a small proportion of supplies at one of those rates.
- The scheme can be complex to work where goods are sold at three rates of VAT although it may be possible to account for a small number of goods at a third rate outside the scheme.

Direct Calculation Scheme 2

- Services can only be included if they are liable at a different rate from the minority goods.
- Cannot be used for catering supplies but can be used for self-made or self-grown goods.
- Turnover limit of £130 million.
- Expected selling prices must be worked out. The scheme can produce inaccuracies if expected selling prices are not calculated accurately. In addition, where expected selling prices are set for standard-rated goods and stock of these goods has a slow turnover, the scheme may not be the most appropriate as VAT is paid in the period in which the goods are received and not necessarily when they are sold.
- Stock-taking required at the start of using the scheme and annually thereafter.
- Annual adjustment required.

(VAT Notice 727, paras 3.4–3.13, 11).

Mixture of schemes and separate accounting by different parts of the business

[61.4] A retailer cannot use more than one scheme at any one time except as indicated in any notice published by HMRC or as specifically allowed by them. [*SI 1995 No 2518, Reg 69*]. Currently HMRC allow the following mixtures of schemes. (Note that it is always possible to use the normal method of accounting with any scheme or any allowable mixture of schemes.)

Mixtures of schemes

It may be necessary to use different schemes in different parts of the business. Provided the retailer is eligible to use the relevant schemes, the Point of Sale scheme can be mixed with either Direct Calculation Scheme 1 or 2 or Apportionment Scheme 1 or 2. It is also possible to use any individual scheme, or any acceptable mixture of schemes, with normal accounting. It is not possible to mix

- Apportionment Scheme 1 and 2;
- Direct Calculation Scheme 1 and 2; or

- Apportionment Scheme 1 or 2 with Direct Calculation Scheme 1 or 2.

(VAT Notice 727, para 4.1 which has the force of law).

Using the same scheme in different parts of a business

The same scheme can be used separately at a number of distinct business locations. If so, under any scheme other than the Point of Sale scheme, it may be necessary to make adjustments to account for transfers between the different parts of the business. Details of such adjustments must be agreed with HMRC. (VAT Notice 727, para 4.1 which has the force of law).

Changing schemes

Compulsory change of scheme

[61.5] A retailer must cease to use a particular scheme if he becomes ineligible to use it. From the start of the next VAT accounting period, he must then change to another scheme (or a mixture of schemes if permitted, see **61.4** above) or to the normal method of accounting.

Voluntary change of scheme

Unless HMRC allow otherwise, a retailer using a retail scheme must, so long as he remains a taxable person, continue to use that scheme for a period of not less than one year from its adoption and any change from one scheme to another must be made at the end of a complete year reckoned from the beginning of the VAT period in which he first adopted the scheme. This does not apply where a retailer ceases to use a retail scheme and joins the flat-rate scheme for small businesses (see **64.15 SPECIAL SCHEMES**). [*SI 1995/2518, Reg 71*]. If, for exceptional reasons, a change is required at any other time, written agreement from HMRC is required.

Where the annual accounting scheme is used, a retail scheme can only be changed at the end of the annual accounting year.

Retrospective changes

Retrospective changes to a retail scheme are not normally allowed. See *Summerfield* (VTD 108) (TVC 58.13) and *RJ Vulgar* (VTD 304) (TVC 58.14) where HMRC's decision not to exercise discretion to allow retrospective changes in the scheme was upheld by the tribunal. In *A & C Wadlewski* (VTD 13340) (TVC 58.24) the tribunal held that HMRC's refusal was unreasonable because of the high proportion of additional VAT payable but this decision was not followed in *L & J Lewis* (VTD 14085) (TVC 58.20) or *L & P Fryer* (VTD 14265) (TVC 58.21).

HMRC may, in exceptional cases, allow retrospective change, e.g. where

- the business has been misdirected (by omission or commission) by a HMRC officer; or
- the business can clearly demonstrate that the scheme which it is proposed to use retrospectively would produce a more accurate liability *and* the difference in VAT due is a very high proportion of the business's profit. In *Wadlewski* above, the tribunal allowed retrospection where the difference in liability amounted to 40% of the business's profit.

Application should be made in writing to HMRC giving as much detail as possible. The maximum period of recalculation is four years. The retailer must have been eligible to use the new scheme during the full period of recalculation.

(VAT Notice 727, paras 4.2, 4.3; VAT Notice 727/3/13, paras 2.5, 2.6; VAT Notice 727/4/13, paras 2.5, 2.6; VAT Notice 727/5/13, paras 2.5, 2.6).

Ceasing to use a scheme

[61.6] A retailer must notify HMRC before ceasing to account for VAT under a retail scheme. He may then be required to pay VAT on such proportion as HMRC consider fair and reasonable of any sums due to him at the end of the VAT period in which he last used the scheme. [*SI 1995 No 2518, Reg 72*].

See under the individual scheme rules for adjustments which may be necessary on ceasing to use a particular scheme. Apart from these special rules, HMRC may require additional adjustments where unusual patterns of trade prevent the chosen scheme from producing a fair and reasonable result.

The following points should also be noted.

- Only goods sold by retail can be included in the retail scheme. If a retailer ceases to use a scheme because he sells all or part of his business as a going concern, the value of stock transferred must be excluded from the retail scheme.
- On ceasing to trade, VAT may become due on the value of stocks and assets. See **60.40 REGISTRATION.**

(VAT Notice 727, paras 6.1, 6.2 which have the force of law).

Change in VAT rate and VAT liabilities

[61.7] A change in the VAT rate means that a rate of VAT has been changed or a new rate has been introduced. A change in VAT liability occurs when a supply which is either exempt or zero-rated becomes taxable at a positive rate or vice versa. Either change may affect the particular scheme used and a retailer must then take the necessary steps relating to his chosen scheme as directed in VAT Notices or as agreed with HMRC. [*SI 1995 No 2518, Reg 75*].

If the change of rate falls halfway through a VAT period, the retailer must make two calculations: one using the old VAT rate and one using the new rate. This will reflect supplies made before and after the rate change. These amounts must then be added together to give the VAT liability for the period.

(VAT Notice 727, paras 7.1–7.5).

Effect on gross takings

Any change in the rate of VAT or liability is effective from a specified date. VAT is due at the new rate on all amounts charged for supplies made on or after the date of change, except that the special provisions in **56.3** *et seq*. **RATES OF VAT** can be applied to individual transactions provided they are dealt with outside the retail scheme.

Gross takings

[61.8] All retail schemes work by applying the appropriate VAT fraction(s) to positive-rated daily gross takings in order to establish the amount of VAT due. It is therefore necessary to keep a record of daily gross takings. This term can be misleading because, for retail scheme purposes, daily gross takings is not simply a record of payments received or cash in hand on any particular day but is a record of supplies made that day. The record of daily gross takings can be a listing made from copies of sales vouchers but will normally be a till roll.

Inclusions in daily gross takings

The following must be included in daily gross takings, *the provisions having the force of law*.

- All payments as they are received from cash customers. This includes payment by notes and coins, cheques, debit or credit card vouchers, Switch, Delta or similar electronic transactions, and electronic cash.
- The full value, including VAT, of credit sales (excluding any disclosed exempt charge for credit) on the day the supply is made.
- The value of any goods taken out of the business for own use. See also **61.9**(25) below.
- The cash value of any payment in kind for retail sales.
- The face value of gift, book and record vouchers, etc. taken in place of cash.
- Any other payments for retail sales.

But where turnover is less than £1 million and customers do not pay for goods when received (e.g. milkmen, newsagents) it may be possible to agree an adaptation to eliminate opening and closing debtors in the scheme calculation (see **61.9**(10) below).

Adjustments to daily gross takings

There are a number of required and allowable adjustments to be made to arrive at the final daily gross takings figure for retail scheme purposes. These are to reflect the fact that daily gross takings should, as far as possible, reflect the supplies made by the retailer and the consideration received for those supplies. Thus, where goods are stolen from a retailer, there has been no supply: no VAT is due and nothing should be included in daily gross takings. Where cash is stolen, there has been a supply on which VAT remains due: the value of the supply should be reflected in daily gross takings.

Daily gross takings may be reduced for the following.

- Receipts recorded for exempt supplies.
- Receipts for goods or services which are to be accounted for outside the scheme.
- Refunds given to customers in respect of taxable supplies to cover accidental overcharges or where goods are unsuitable or faulty.
- Instalments in respect of credit sales.
- Void transactions (where an incorrect transaction has not been voided at the time of the error).

- Illegible credit card transactions (where a customer's account details are not legible on the credit card voucher and therefore cannot be presented at the bank).
- Unsigned or dishonoured cheques from cash customers (but not from credit customers).
- Counterfeit notes.
- Where a cheque guarantee card is incorrectly accepted as a credit card.
- Acceptance of out-of-date coupons which have previously been included in daily gross takings but which are not honoured by the promoters.
- Supervisor's float discrepancies.
- Till breakdowns (where incorrect till readings are recorded due to mechanical faults, e.g. till programming error, false reading and till reset by an engineer).
- Use of training tills (where the till used by staff for training has been returned to the sales floor without the zeroing of figures).
- Customer overspends using Shopacheck.
- Inadvertent acceptance of foreign currency where discovered at a later time (e.g. when cashing up) unless reimbursed by the bank.

A record of any adjustments to the daily gross taking should always be kept.

If any adjustment is made for which a payment is subsequently received, the amount received must be included in daily gross takings.

See also **61.9** below generally for special transactions which may require adjustments to be made to figures for daily gross takings.

(VAT Notice 727, para 4.4; VAT Notice 727/3/13, paras 5.1–5.5; VAT Notice 727/4/13, paras 6.1–6.5; VAT Notice 727/5/13, paras 5.1–5.5, all of which have the force of law).

Example

Mike is the owner of a retail business. The cash in the till (adjusting for float) at the end of the day's trading is £350. However, he is unsure about how to deal with the following issues as far as VAT is concerned:

- A member of staff stole £50 of cash from the till – she has now been sacked.
- The window cleaner was paid £20 cash from the till for cleaning the shop windows.
- Mike took goods for personal use with a retail price of £12 and cost price of £6.

The basic definition of VAT is that it is a tax on the 'supply of goods or services'. This means the £70 cash removed from the till (illegally in the case of the staff member) relates to sales that have already taken place. The amount of £70 should therefore be included in the takings figure.

Sales to the business owner also need to be included because a supply of goods has again taken place (even though no money has been exchanged). However, the good news for Mike is that he only needs to account for output tax on the cost price of the goods, i.e. £6.

The total daily gross takings figure for VAT purposes is therefore £426 (£350 + £50 + £20 + £6).

De Voil Indirect Tax Service. See V3.556–558.

Special transactions

[61.9] The following is a list of the more common transactions which might have to be taken into account in using a retail scheme and/or calculating gross takings.

(1) Acquisitions from other EU member states

Suppliers from elsewhere in the EU do not charge VAT on their sales and the retailer must account for VAT at the rate applicable to the goods in the UK. See **20.3** *et seq.* **EUROPEAN UNION: SINGLE MARKET** for further details.

For retail scheme purposes, references to zero-rated goods apply only to goods which are zero-rated in the UK. Goods which are zero-rated on acquisition from other EU member states, but standard-rated in the UK, must be treated as standard-rated goods in the retail scheme calculations.

See (22) below for goods imported from outside the EU.

(2) Machine games takings

See **8.4 BETTING AND GAMING.**

(3) BT phonecards

See **70.10 TRADE PROMOTION SCHEMES.**

(4) Business entertainment/gifts

If goods are purchased specifically to be consumed in the course of business entertainment or to supply as gifts,

- under the Point of Sale scheme, any VAT due must be accounted for by adding the value of the goods to daily gross takings at the relevant time; and
- under the Apportionment Schemes 1 and 2 and Direct Calculation Schemes 1 and 2, any VAT due on the supply must be accounted for outside the scheme.

See **48.5 OUTPUT TAX** for VAT due on gifts.

If goods from normal stock are used for business entertainment or supplied as gifts,

- under the Point of Sale scheme, any VAT due must be accounted for by adding the value of the goods to daily gross takings at the relevant time;
- under Apportionment Scheme 1, the full value of the goods should be included in daily gross takings;

- under Apportionment Scheme 2, the full value of the goods should be included in daily gross takings and the necessary adjustment should be made to expected selling prices;
- under Direct Calculation Schemes 1 and 2, VAT can be accounted for under the scheme as follows:
  (i) if the goods are standard-rated or reduced rate goods and the minority goods are zero-rated, by adding the value of the supply to daily gross takings; and
  (ii) if the minority goods are standard-rated or reduced rate goods, no addition to the daily gross takings is necessary but the expected selling prices must be adjusted to reflect the value to be accounted for.

(5) Business overheads

Any purchases of goods and services which are not for resale should be excluded from the scheme calculations.

(6) Business promotion schemes

See **70 TRADE PROMOTION SCHEMES**.

(7) Cash discounts

If goods are offered on cash discount or early settlement terms, the discounted value should be included in daily gross takings at the time of supply.

(8) Catering supplies

Apportionment Schemes 1 and 2 and Direct Calculation Schemes 1 and 2 all assume that goods bought at one rate of VAT will be sold at the same rate. Food bought at the zero rate often becomes standard-rated when supplied in the course of catering and therefore the Point of Sale scheme must normally be used for such supplies. See, however, **12.7 CATERING** for a catering adaptation which may be used.

(9) Credit card transactions

Retailers are allowed to charge different prices to customers using a credit card. The different prices charged may either take the form of discounts to cash customers (see (7) above) or a surcharge being made to those paying by credit card.

- If the charge for payment by credit card is made by the supplier of the goods/services being bought, HMRC regard this as a further payment for the purchase, VAT being payable at the same rate as on the goods/services.
- If the charge is made by an agent acting for the supplier of the goods/services (e.g. a travel agent acting on behalf of a tour operator) HMRC consider that the charge is for a separate supply of exempt services (i.e. accepting payment in the form of a credit card).

> *Example*
>
> A suit bought from a men's clothes shop costs £400. If the customer pays by credit card, the store makes an additional charge of £10. In this situation, the cost of the suit is £410 and the entire payment is standard-rated.

Card-handling fees

Up to 2005, many high street retailers operated a scheme whereby, when customers pay for goods by credit or debit card, small print on the receipt asked them to agree to pay a 'card-handling fee' (typically 2.5%), even though the total price was exactly the same as it would be for a cash sale. The fee was then claimed as an exempt supply so that VAT was only paid on 97.5% of the price of the goods. In *Debenhams Retail plc v C & E Comrs*, [2005] STC 1155 (TVC 27.17) the tribunal had held that this treatment was incorrect and that the whole amount paid was consideration for a taxable supply of goods. The High Court disagreed with this but the Court of Appeal upheld the tribunal decision. There was a single contract under which Debenhams was the supplier to its card-using customers of goods or services for a consideration consisting of the whole 100% payable by such customers on any such transaction. Directly applicable EU legislation now states that 'Where a supplier of goods or services, as a condition of accepting payment by credit or debit card, requires the customer to pay an amount to himself or another undertaking, and where the total price payable by that customer is unaffected irrespective of how payment is accepted, that amount shall constitute an integral part of the taxable amount for supply of the goods or services.'

[*Council Implementing Regulation (EU) No 282/2011, Art 42*].

(10) Credit transactions

The full value of the goods must be included in daily gross takings at the time of supply. Do not wait until payment is received and do not include instalments as they are received. Additional rules apply depending upon the way credit sales are financed.

(a) Where *credit for customers is arranged through a finance house, etc.* which takes ownership of the goods, the transaction should be treated as a cash sale to the finance house and the full amount payable by the customer should by included in daily gross takings at the time of supply. In *C & E Commrs v Primback Ltd, ECJ Case C–34/99*, [2001] STC 803 (TVC 22.265) Primback sold furniture on interest free credit. Credit was provided by a separate finance company introduced to the customer by Primback. The finance company did not charge interest and title in the goods passed directly from Primback to the customer. The customer then paid the full price of the goods in instalments to the finance company. The finance company did not pay Primback the full price charged to the customer but a net amount after retaining a 'discount' equivalent to the amount that the finance company would have charged the customer for a loan at a commercial rate. At issue was whether VAT was due on the full amount paid by the customer, or on the lower amount received by Primback. The CJEU held that where a retailer sells goods in return for payment of the advertised price which he invoices to the purchaser and which does not vary according to whether the customer pays in cash or by way of credit, the taxable amount is the full amount payable by the purchaser.

(b) *Where credit transactions are financed from own resources*, any separate credit charge (additional to the cash price) is exempt from VAT provided that it is disclosed to the customer (see **24.11** FINANCIAL SERVICES). If so, it should be excluded from daily gross takings.

Adaptations for newsagents/small retailers

In principle, the above requirements apply to all businesses. However, HMRC recognise that this may cause administrative difficulties for small businesses with turnover of less than £1 million where customers do not pay for goods when they receive them (e.g. milkmen and newsagents). In such cases, retailers can take account of opening and closing debtors for a VAT period in their scheme calculations. (VAT Notice 727, para 4.5).

(11) Delivery charges

See **48.7**(19) OUTPUT TAX.

(12) Deposits

Deposits which are advance payments must be included in daily gross takings. Other deposits (e.g. those taken as security for the safe return of goods hired out) must be excluded (regardless of whether the deposit is eventually refunded or forfeited for loss or damage).

(13) Dishonoured cheques and counterfeit bank notes

Unsigned or dishonoured cheques from cash customers (but not credit customers) and counterfeit notes received may be deducted from daily gross takings.

(14) Disposal of business assets

VAT must be accounted for outside the retail scheme.

(15) Exempt supplies

These must always be dealt with outside the scheme, whichever scheme is used.

(16) Exports (to countries outside the EU)

Retail exports

Where goods are supplied for retail export under the retail export scheme, including supplies to entitled EU residents and ships' crews going abroad (see **22.12** to **22.16** EXPORTS) the supplies must be allowed for in the scheme calculations as follows.

(a) Under the Point of Sale scheme, Apportionment Schemes 1 and 2 and, if the minority goods are zero-rated, Direct Calculation Schemes 1 and 2, follow the normal scheme rules but

- (i) include all takings, including VAT, for goods sold for retail export in daily gross takings. (Do not deduct the refunds which are expected to be made to the customer.);
- (ii) at the end of each period, add up the takings for standard-rated goods actually exported. (This is the total of amounts shown on the officially certified forms returned during the period.);
- (iii) calculate notional VAT on the takings at (ii) above, using the VAT fraction that applied at the time the sale was included in gross takings; and
- (iv) subtract the notional VAT at (iii) from the scheme output tax.

(b) Under Direct Calculation Schemes 1 and 2 where the minority goods are standard-rated, follow the normal scheme rules but at the end of each VAT period

- (i) add up the original expected selling prices, including VAT, of the standard-rated goods which have actually been exported. (These will be the goods shown on the officially certified forms returned during the period.);
- (ii) calculate notional VAT on the total at (i) above using the VAT fraction that applied when the amounts were included in the scheme calculations; and
- (iii) subtract the notional VAT at (ii) from the scheme output tax.

Direct and indirect exports

Where goods are directly exported or supplied in the UK to an overseas trader for subsequent export,

- under the Point of Sale scheme, the supplies must be dealt with outside the scheme;
- under Apportionment Schemes 1 and 2 and, if the minority goods are zero-rated, Direct Calculation Schemes 1 and 2, the procedure is similar to that for retail exports in (*a*) above except that the calculations relate to goods sent for export and the comments in brackets do not apply. If proof of export is not received within three months of the date of supply, the notional VAT calculated under (*a*)(iii) above must be included as an addition on the VAT payable side of the VAT account for the current VAT period; and
- under Direct Calculation Schemes 1 and 2 where the minority goods are standard-rated, the procedure is similar to that for retail exports in (*b*) above except that the calculations relate to goods sent for export and the comment in brackets does not apply. If proof of export is not received within three months of the date of supply, the notional VAT calculated under (*b*)(ii) above must be included as an addition on the VAT payable side of the VAT account for the current VAT period.

See (29) below for retail sales to persons from other EU member states.

(17) Foreign currency transactions

Many retailers accept foreign currency in order to encourage spending by tourists to the UK. No reduction to the daily gross takings can be made for commission payable to the bank, etc. for converting the currency. The total sterling equivalent of the value charged on the day the supply is made must be included in the daily gross takings (see **72.18 VALUATION**). Note that this is not necessarily the same as the sterling sale price of the goods and depends on the exchange rate applicable at the time of supply.

If the retailer also charges the customer a 'premium' for accepting payment in foreign currency, this is additional consideration for the supply of goods (or services) and must be included in the daily gross takings.

See **61.8** above for inadvertent acceptance of foreign currency.

(18) Gift, book, and record vouchers

See **70.10 TRADE PROMOTION SCHEMES.**

(19) Goods bought at one rate and sold at another

For some goods, the rate of VAT depends upon how they are held out for sale, e.g. meat held out for sale for human consumption is zero-rated but the same meat held out for sale for pet food is standard-rated.

For the provisions applying to chemists, see **61.19** below and for a special scheme for take-away food, see **12.7 CATERING.**

All other goods bought at one rate and sold at another must be treated as follows.

Point of Sale scheme

No action is required because takings are separated into each rate of VAT at the point of sale.

Apportionment Schemes 1 and 2 and Direct Calculation Schemes 1 and 2

- Where separate stocks are kept of goods that are held out for sale at the different VAT rates, on receipt such goods must be entered in the records of goods for resale at the VAT rate that will apply when they are sold.
- Where common stocks are kept of those goods that are drawn on to sell at different VAT rates, such goods must initially be entered in the scheme records at cost or expected selling price (depending on the scheme used) at the rate of VAT that applied when the goods were received. But when the goods are put up or held out for sale at the other VAT rate, it is necessary to deduct the appropriate amounts from the scheme records at the VAT rate that applied when the goods were received and enter the corresponding amounts in the scheme records at the VAT rate that applies when the goods are sold.

(20) Goods bought from unregistered suppliers

Where goods for retail sale are bought from unregistered suppliers,

- under Apportionment Schemes 1 and 2, such goods must be included in the retail scheme calculation at the appropriate rate; and
- under Direct Calculation Schemes 1 and 2, only such goods which are taxable at the minority rate must be included in expected selling price calculations.

(21) Goods sold on sale or return or similar terms

A separate record must be kept of goods supplied on a sale or return basis. Such goods should only be included in daily gross takings when the customer adopts the goods. See (12) above if the customer pays a deposit.

(22) Imports (from countries outside the EU)

The normal scheme rules apply, as for other purchases, under all schemes.

See (1) above for goods acquired from other EU member states.

(23) Part-exchange

Where goods or services are accepted in part-exchange, the full retail selling price, including VAT, of the goods supplied must be included in daily gross takings.

Where any goods taken in part-exchange are subsequently resold, it may be possible to sell them under the margin scheme for **62 SECOND-HAND GOODS**. If not, they can be included in the retail scheme calculations.

(24) Phonecards

See **70.10 TRADE PROMOTION SCHEMES**.

(25) Private or personal use of goods

VAT is normally due on any goods purchased for resale that are taken out of the business for personal or private use. See **48.6 OUTPUT TAX**.

- Under the Point of Sale scheme, the value of any positive-rated goods taken for private or personal use must be included in daily gross takings.
- Under Apportionment Scheme 1, the value of such goods must be included in daily gross takings.
- Under Apportionment Scheme 2, the value of such goods must be included in daily gross takings and the necessary adjustments must be made to expected selling prices.
- Under the Direct Calculation Schemes 1 and 2,
  - (i) if the minority goods are zero-rated, the value of any positive-rated goods taken for private or personal use must be included in daily gross takings; and
  - (ii) if minority goods are standard-rated or reduced rate goods, the value of any positive-rated goods taken for private or personal use should be added to expected selling prices and daily gross takings.

(26) Recall of goods by manufacturers

If a manufacturer recalls contaminated or otherwise faulty goods,

- under Apportionment Scheme 1, purchase records must be adjusted;
- under Apportionment Scheme 2 and Direct Calculation Schemes 1 and 2, expected selling price records must be adjusted.

(27) Refunds to customers

Amounts refunded or credited to customers can be deducted from daily gross takings to a maximum of the amount originally charged.

(28) Rented payphones

If a payphone is rented from British Telecom or another supplier, the retailer makes a supply of services to the user of the telephone. VAT is due on the money removed from the payphone which should be dealt with as follows.

- Under the Point of Sale scheme, include the money in standard-rated daily gross takings.
- Under Apportionment Schemes 1 and 2, deal with the supply outside the scheme.
- Under Direct Calculation schemes 1 and 2
  - (i) where minority goods are zero-rated or reduced rate goods, include the money in daily gross takings; and
  - (ii) where the minority goods are standard-rated, deal with the supply outside the scheme.

See also **48.7**(17) **OUTPUT TAX.**

(29) Retail sales to persons from other EU member states

Any retail sale made in the UK to a person from another EU member state should be accounted for as a normal domestic retail sale. Special arrangements apply to distance selling, i.e. where goods are sold to persons in other EU member states who are not registered for VAT and the supplier is responsible for delivery to the customer. See **20.20 EUROPEAN UNION: SINGLE MARKET.**

See (16) above for exports to countries outside the EU.

(30) Road fuel

If road fuel is used for private motoring, VAT due must be accounted for outside the scheme. See **46.16 MOTOR CARS.**

(31) Sale of discount vouchers (or discount cards)

The VAT consequences of selling vouchers or cards entitling the holder to discounts on purchases depend upon where the vouchers or cards can be used.

(a) If vouchers or cards can only be used for purchases from the retailer selling them, he should include the payment received in daily gross takings. Under the Point of Sale scheme, if, for example, the card can only be used for purchases of zero-rated goods, the amount charged for the card should be added to zero-rated takings.

(b) If vouchers or cards can be used at several traders, this is a standard-rated supply of services. See *C & E Commrs v Granton Marketing Ltd; C & E Commrs v Wentwalk Ltd*, CA [1996] STC 1049 (TVC 67.176).
- Under the Point of Sale scheme, payments received should be added to standard-rated daily gross takings.
- Under Apportionment Schemes 1 and 2 and Direct Calculation Schemes 1 and 2, payments received must be dealt with outside the scheme used.

(32) Sale or assignment of debts

Where debts due from customers are sold or assigned, no further action is required as the correct amount will have already been included in daily gross takings at the time of supply.

(33) Saving stamps, travel cards and pools coupons

If a retailer

- buys and sells travel cards and/or savings stamps for gas, electricity, television licences, etc., or
- receives commission from distributing and collecting pools coupons

these must be dealt with outside the retail scheme and not be included in daily gross takings. This follows the decision in *TE, M & IJ Parr* (VTD 1967) (TVC 58.6).

(34) Second-hand goods

VAT on second-hand goods sold, may be accounted for

- within the retail scheme in the same way as new goods; or
- under the margin scheme for **62 SECOND-HAND GOODS**.

(35) Theft, shrinkage, leakage and stock losses

Where there are unexplained accounting discrepancies between stock and sales, to the extent that this is attributable to unrecorded sales, such as theft (see below), shrinkage, etc., the value must be added back to the records of daily gross takings. Where possible, these adjustments should be allocated to the specific VAT period in which they took place. Otherwise such stock losses should be apportioned across relevant VAT periods on a fair and reasonable basis. Unless there is evidence of the liability of the unaccounted supplies, adjustments must be made in line with the usual proportion of standard against zero-rated supplies. Depending upon the scheme used, it may also be necessary to consider whether the shrinkage for which the daily gross takings has been adjusted requires further adjustment to expected selling prices.

See, however, *British American Tobacco International Ltd and Another v Belgian State, ECJ Case C–435/03*, [2006] STC 158 (TVC 22.93) where a quantity of cigarettes was stolen from a warehouse. The court held that the theft of goods did not constitute a supply of goods for consideration within the meaning of what is now *Directive 2006/112/EC, Art 12(a)* and therefore could not be subject to VAT as such.

(VAT Notice 727/3/13, paras 6.1–6.31; VAT Notice 727/4/13, paras 7.1–7.34; VAT Notice 727/5/13, paras 6.1–6.33, all of which have the force of law).

(36) Compulsory charge on single use carrier bags

From 1 October 2011 the Welsh Assembly Government introduced a compulsory charge on single use carrier bags which retailers must charge to customers in Wales. The charge is consideration for the bag and is taxable at the standard rate of VAT. In order that customers pay the same amount regardless of the VAT status of the business, the stated minimum charge (initially 5 pence) is the minimum total to be charged by non-VAT-registered businesses. The stated minimum charge will be deemed to include VAT when charged by a VAT-registered business.

On 8 April 2013 a levy (minimum of 5 pence) was introduced on single use carrier bags in Northern Ireland. Retailers must pay the 'net proceeds' of their charges to the Department of Environment Northern Ireland (DoENI). Where a retailer charges the minimum of 5 pence, the full amount must be paid to DoENI. However, a retailer who charges more per bag must pay DoENI 5 pence less VAT (5p x 5/6 = 4.17p). Where only the 5 pence levy is charged and it is remitted in full to the DoENI, no VAT is due from the retailer in any circumstance. However, where the charge exceeds 5 pence, VAT is payable on the total amount where the bags are supplied by VAT-registered businesses. For example, if a retailer charges 12 pence for a bag then VAT of 2 pence will be due from the retailer (12p x 1/6 = 2p).

(HMRC Brief 23/11; HMRC Brief 7/13).

The compulsory minimum charge on single use carrier bags, introduced by the Scottish Parliament with effect from 20 October 2014 and relevant to retailers in Scotland, is inclusive of VAT unless the retailer is not registered for VAT and is not required to be registered for VAT.

(HMRC Brief 38/14).

The compulsory minimum charge on single use carrier bags in England, introduced by Parliament with effect from 5 October 2015, is inclusive of VAT unless the supplier is not registered for VAT and is not required to be registered for VAT. The legislation applies to suppliers with at least 250 full-time equivalent employees which provide single use carrier bags when selling goods in England or which provide such bags when selling goods for delivery in England.

(HMRC Brief 14/15).

Expected selling prices ('ESPS')

[61.10] Under certain of the retail schemes, a retailer must

- calculate ESPs; and
- make adjustments to those ESPs to reflect factors which prevent him from achieving them.

ESPs are used to calculate the expected value of retail sales at different rates. The way ESPs are calculated has, therefore, a direct effect on the VAT paid and must be done as accurately as possible. For this reason, calculations should never include

- goods sold by wholesale;
- goods bought for private use; or

- disposals of stocks resulting from a sale of all or part of the business.

(VAT Notice 727/4/13, para 5.3; VAT Notice 727/5/13, para 4.3, which have the force of law).

Calculating ESPs

[61.11] ESPs can be calculated in any way which produces a fair and reasonable result. The same method must always be used (but see below for mixtures) and, whatever method is used, the adjustments described below must also be made. The most common methods of calculation are as follows.

(a) *Mark up each line of goods* (the most accurate).

(b) *Mark up classes of goods* (e.g. vegetables or confectionery). This method can only be used if
- it is not possible to mark up each line (as in (*a*) above);
- the variation in mark up within the group is no more than 10% (20% under the old scheme calculations);
- the mark up is reviewed each quarter; and
- the class of goods has a commercial basis and is not constructed artificially.

(c) *Use recommended retail prices*. This method can only be used if
- recommended retail prices can be recorded on receipt of the goods; and
- purchases invoices or other supplier documentation (i) shows the VAT-inclusive recommended retail price of each separate line of goods; (ii) distinguishes standard-rated, reduced rate and zero-rated items; and (iii) totals goods at each rate of VAT.

(VAT Notice 727/4/13, para 5.3; VAT Notice 727/5/13, para 4.3, which have the force of law).

Example

In a particular class of zero-rated goods, a retailer purchases the following lines at the actual mark-ups shown.

Line of goods	Purchase price £	Actual mark-up	Expected selling price £
A	150	7%	160.50
B	70	5%	73.50
C	50	16%	58.00
D	30	19%	35.70
E	70	10%	77.00
F	30	6%	31.80
	£400		£436.50

Using the actual mark-up for each line of goods, expected selling prices are £436.50.

If, however, it was not possible to break down the total purchase price of £400 between the various lines, the average mark-up basis could be used.

Average mark-up = (7 + 5 + 16 + 19 + 10 + 6) ÷ 6 = 10.5%
Expected selling prices are £442 (£400 × 1.105).

Adjustment to ESPs

[61.12] As ESPs will rarely be fully achieved, adjustments must be made at the end of each VAT period to take account of factors which affect the selling price. These include (i.e. the list is not exhaustive)

- price changes (increases and decreases), e.g. sell by date reductions;
- special offers and promotion schemes;
- wastage;
- freezer breakdowns;
- breakages;
- shrinkage (i.e. pilferage and loss of stock); and
- bad debts that have been written off in the period.

How such adjustments are made is up to the individual retailer but a consistent method must be used (both within each period and from one period to the next). Records of adjustments and working papers must be kept with the retail scheme calculations.

If it proves difficult to make such adjustments, it may be more appropriate to use another scheme. Alternatively, HMRC may agree to a method of sampling where reductions cannot be established accurately or the omission of certain adjustments where the effect does not distort the retail scheme.

(VAT Notice 727/4/13, para 5.3; VAT Notice 727/5/13, para 4.3, which have the force of law).

Bespoke retail schemes

[61.13] If VAT-exclusive taxable retail supplies in the previous 12 months have exceeded £130 million, a business cannot continue to use a published retail scheme (VAT Notice 727, para 5.1, which has the force of law) and must then do one of the following.

(a) **Account for VAT in the normal way.** A business must do this if it does not wish to use a bespoke scheme or cannot agree such a scheme with HMRC. As the business will be trading by way of retail, it will not be required to issue a VAT invoice to unregistered customers. But it will need to identify the VAT-exclusive value and the amount of VAT for each sale and be able to produce periodic totals of those amounts.

(b) **Agree a bespoke scheme with HMRC**. A bespoke scheme may be based on one of the published schemes but will be tailored to meet the individual needs of the business. HMRC recognise that some large retailers could have difficulty in accounting for VAT in the normal way and will therefore only withhold agreement to a proposed scheme in the following circumstances.

   - It does not produce a fair and reasonable result. This is judged on the ability of the scheme to approximate the amount of output tax which would be due under normal accounting. The reasonableness of a scheme is judged by the simplicity with which it can be used by the retailer and checked by HMRC. A scheme which does not reflect commercial reality or which unnecessarily complicates either the retailer's accounting or HMRC's ability to audit the VAT declarations is unlikely to be reasonable. In a large and complex business, there may be a number of different methods of calculating the VAT due, several of which could be regarded as fair and reasonable. But where two methods produce different amounts of VAT, it will often be possible to identify which of them is closer to normal accounting. In these circumstances, for the protection of the revenue, HMRC may refuse, or withdraw its agreement to, the use of a method which is, in principle, fair and reasonable.

- Refusal to use the scheme is necessary for the protection of the revenue.
- The business could reasonably be expected to account for VAT normally.

Using a bespoke scheme

A bespoke scheme must be used from the VAT period following that in which the £130 million threshold is exceeded. A scheme should therefore be agreed in good time because, once that threshold is exceeded, the only alternative is to account for VAT in the normal way. In some circumstances, the start date of a bespoke scheme can be backdated but only with the agreement of both parties.

A bespoke scheme cannot be used for:

- *Sales to other VAT-registered businesses*. The only exception is occasional cash sales in the same form as are made to customers who are not VAT-registered (e.g. a garage supplying petrol to a VAT-registered customer or a retail DIY store supplying building materials to a VAT-registered builder).
- *Non-retail sales*. VAT on these must be accounted for using the normal method of accounting.
- *Internet sales*. HMRC take the view that where a business makes retail sales in the UK via the internet, it will usually have sufficient records of the sales to allow it to account for the VAT in the normal way. But if they are satisfied that a business cannot do this, HMRC may agree that the sales can be included in a bespoke scheme.

Key elements of a bespoke scheme

A bespoke scheme will usually be based on a published scheme (or a mixture of published schemes) but it can be based on any method which meets the tests listed in (*b*) above. HMRC are unlikely to agree a bespoke scheme based on, or including, published schemes with a threshold cap of £1 million (i.e. currently Apportionment Scheme 1 or Direct Calculation Scheme 1).

A bespoke scheme will be agreed in writing and include the following provisions.

- The start date, review date, and end date of the agreement. The agreement must specify how output tax will be calculated in any period between the date at which the business became ineligible to use a published scheme and the date of the agreement.
- Details of which supplies will be accounted for within the scheme and which, if any, will be accounted for in the normal way.
- Full details of the method of determining daily gross takings including use of tills, till breakdowns, deliveries direct to customers, other currencies accepted, concessions and roundings. Also details of how adjustments will be made for special transactions (see **61.9** above), etc. See VAT Notice 727/2/11, paras 6.1, 6.2 for further details and examples but even these checklists are only a guide and all special transactions should also be covered.
- Full details of the method of valuing taxable retail sales.
  - (i) Under a bespoke scheme based on the Point of Sale scheme, the agreement should cover mixed rate products, non-Electronic Point of Sale (EPOS) departments, private use of purchases, product VAT coding, refunds, remote tills, staff discounts, till breakdowns, unscanned products, VAT code errors, and VAT coding. It relation to vouchers and special offers, it should also cover discount vouchers, multi-saves, out-of-date manufacturers' vouchers, own product vouchers, retailer vouchers within *VATA 1994, Sch 10A* (face-value vouchers/credit vouchers and other vouchers), and special offer prices/price reductions. See VAT Notice 727/2/11, paras 7.1, 7.2 for further details but the list is not exhaustive.
  - (ii) Under a bespoke scheme based on expected selling prices (ESPs), the agreement should cover the basis of setting and adjusting ESPs, direct deliveries to customers, mixed rate products, the point of receipt of goods into the scheme, product VAT coding, the level of calculation (business, store, department), treatment of services, VAT code errors, VAT coding, and trading patterns (period of calculation, stock adjustments, rolling periods, exclusion of distortive factors). See VAT Notice 727/2/11, paras 8.1–8.3 for further details but the list is not exhaustive.
- Name, status and signature of an HMRC officer and an authorised signatory of the retailer.

Changes to scheme

An agreed bespoke scheme is based on full disclosure of the current business structure and trading patterns at that time. If these change to such an extent that the agreed method ceases to produce a fair and reasonable result, HMRC must be informed immediately.

A bespoke scheme can normally be changed at any time if the retailer and HMRC agree. HMRC would not normally expect any changes to take place from a date earlier than the date that the change or a review was requested. However, retrospective changes may be appropriate where there is a fundamental flaw in the scheme.

Withdrawal of the scheme

HMRC may withdraw their agreement and refuse the use of a previously agreed scheme if it ceases to meet any of the conditions in (*b*) above. They may do so, for example, if they conclude that it was not based on a full disclosure of business circumstances or another method of calculation would produce a more fair and reasonable result. If they do this, they will inform the retailer of the aspects of the current agreement that are unacceptable. If the retailer still wishes to use a bespoke scheme, it must then send new proposals for consideration.

(VAT Notice 727/2/11).

Point of Sale Scheme

[61.14] The Point of Sale scheme can be used if

- taxable turnover does not exceed £130 million (if so a bespoke scheme must be agreed, see **61.13** above); and
- either
  - (i) all supplies are made at one positive rate (i.e. all at the reduced rate or all standard-rated) — if so the Point of Sale scheme is the *only* retail scheme which can be used; or
  - (ii) supplies are made at two or more rates and the correct liability of supplies can be identified at the time of sale. This, increasingly, means an electronic point of sale system (EPOS) utilising bar-code scanners to identify the items being sold and calculate the appropriate VAT amounts. HMRC have produced detailed notes on *VAT guidance for EPOS*. See VAT Information Sheet 11/03. Alternatively, separate tills can be used for different rates.

How to calculate output tax

For each VAT period (quarterly or monthly)

Step 1	Add up daily gross takings from standard-rated supplies =	A
Step 2	Add up daily gross takings from reduced rate supplies =	B
Step 3	To calculate output tax, add the total at Step 1 multiplied by the VAT fraction for standard-rated goods to the total at Step 2 multiplied by the VAT fraction for reduced rate goods	

In algebraic form output tax is: [(A × 1/6) + (B × 1/21)] (VAT at 20% on standard rate goods and 5% on reduced rate goods).

Gross takings

See **61.8** and **61.9** above for gross takings together with adjustments and special transactions which have to be taken into account.

Records

In addition to the normal records required, a record of daily gross takings must be kept.

Annual accounting scheme

If this scheme is also used, see **64.13 SPECIAL SCHEMES.**

Change in VAT rate

See **61.7** above.

Cancellation of registration

VAT is due on business assets, including stock in hand. See **60.40** and **60.41 REGISTRATION.**

(VAT Notice 727/3/13 paras 3.2, 3.4, 4.2 which have the force of law).

Adaptations

Retailers who wish to treat minor levels of zero-rated or reduced rate sales as standard-rated may do so. The advantages of such treatment (mainly simplification of VAT records and accounting) must be compared with the disadvantage of paying VAT which is not being charged to customers. (HMRC Manual VRS5150).

> *Example*
>
> N Ltd is a garden centre selling plants and gardening equipment. It also sells gardening books and magazines and barbecue supplies. Due to the product mix, the company splits takings at the time of sale using multi-button tills. At the end of its VAT period, standard-rated takings totalled £125,639.34, zero-rated sales of books, etc. totalled £1,549.28 and reduced rate sales of barbecue fuels totalled £194.32.
>
> Output tax for the period is
>
> (£125,639.34 × 1/6) + (£194.32 × 1/21) = £20,949.14

Apportionment Scheme 1

[61.15] In order to use the scheme

- supplies must be made at two different rates of VAT;
- total VAT-exclusive retail sales must be less than £1 million per year. The limit applies to the whole business, e.g. the scheme cannot be applied to one shop if total turnover of two or more shops owned exceeds the limit; and
- any supplies of services, grown or self-made goods or supplies of catering must be dealt with outside the scheme.

How to calculate output tax

For each VAT period (whether quarterly or monthly)

Step 1	Add up daily gross takings =	A
Step 2	Add up the cost, including VAT, of all goods received for re-sale at the standard rate =	B
Step 3	Add up the cost, including VAT, of all goods received for re-sale at the reduced rate =	C
Step 4	Add up the cost, including VAT, of all goods received for re-sale at standard, reduced and zero rates =	D
Step 5	Calculate the proportion of daily gross takings from sales at the standard rate by dividing the total at Step 2 by the total at Step 4 and multiplying by the total in Step 1	
Step 6	Calculate the proportion of daily gross takings from sales at the reduced rate by dividing the total at Step 3 by the total at Step 4 and multiplying by the total in Step 1	
Step 7	To calculate output tax, add the total at Step 5 multiplied by the VAT fraction for standard-rated goods to the total at Step 6 multiplied by the VAT fraction for reduced rate goods	

In algebraic form output tax is $[(B \div D \times A \times 1/6) + (C \div D \times A \times 1/21)]$ (VAT at 20% on standard rate goods and 5% on reduced rate goods).

Annual adjustment

An annual adjustment has to be made to cover any under or overpayment of VAT. The adjustment must be made on

- 31 March — for retailers with three-monthly VAT periods ending on 30 June, 30 September, 31 December and 31 March and all retailers with monthly VAT periods;
- 30 April — for retailers with three-monthly VAT periods ending on 31 July, 31 October, 31 January and 30 April; and
- 31 May — for retailers with three-monthly VAT periods ending on 31 August, 30 November, 28/29 February and 31 May.

If, at the first appropriate date for the annual adjustment, the scheme has been operated for one VAT period or less, no adjustment is required until the following year. The first adjustment must include all VAT periods from first use of the scheme. For all later adjustments, only VAT periods since the previous adjustment are included. The adjustment is calculated as follows.

Step A	Calculate the VAT due by following the procedure as in Steps 1 to 7 above but using takings and cost figures for the period since the last adjustments (or, as the case may be, from the start of using the scheme) =	D
Step B	Add together the output tax already accounted for under the scheme in the year =	E

If D is less than E, too much VAT has been paid and the difference should be included in the VAT deductible side of the VAT return for the period covering the adjustment. If D is greater than E, too little VAT has been paid and the difference must be included in the VAT payable side of the VAT return for that period.

Gross takings

See **61.8** and **61.9** above for gross takings together with adjustments and special transactions which must be taken into account.

Imports and acquisitions

The cost of goods received for resale under Steps 2 to 4 above include

- any imports from outside the EU at the full price paid (including customs duty and VAT), and
- any goods acquired from another EU country at the full price paid (including excise duty and with the addition of VAT at the appropriate UK rate).

Opening stock

Goods in stock when the scheme is started are not normally treated as goods received in the period. However, if there are any stock items which are to be sold but not replenished, these may be included in the calculations unless already allowed for in a previous scheme.

Records

In addition to the normal records required, records must be kept of daily gross takings.

Annual accounting scheme

If this scheme is also used, see **64.13 SPECIAL SCHEMES.**

Ceasing to use the scheme

The annual adjustment as explained above must be carried out for the period from the last adjustment to the date of ceasing to use the scheme. This applies even if leaving the scheme before the anniversary of starting to use the scheme.

Cancellation of registration

VAT is due on business assets, including stock in hand. See **60.40** and **60.41 REGISTRATION.**

(VAT Notice 727/4/13, paras 3.3, 3.5, 3.6, 4.2, 4.3 which have the force of law).

Adaptations

HMRC may allow an adaptation to bring the annual adjustment in line with the financial year end. They will, however, consider the effect on the first such annual adjustment and authorise a period longer than twelve months where necessary to ensure any distortions are avoided. (HMRC Manual VRS5200).

Example

B Ltd has figures for four quarterly periods as follows.

	Cost of standard-rated goods for resale (incl VAT)	Cost of reduced rate goods for re-sale (incl VAT)	Total cost of goods for resale (incl VAT)	Gross takings
	£	£	£	£
First quarter	9,429	78	15,701	21,714.55
Second quarter	10,418	124	17,840	24,316.51
Third quarter	9,972	312	15,919	21,899.29
Fourth quarter	7,076	25	11,293	16,149.61
	£36,895	£539	£60,753	£84,079.96

First quarter

Standard-rated sales are

9,429 ÷ 15,701 × £21,714.55 = £13,040.35

Reduced rate sales are

78 ÷ 15,701 × £21,714.55 = £107.87

Output tax = (£13,040.35 × 1/6) + (£107.87 × 1/21) =	2,178.53
By similar calculations output tax in the remaining quarters is	
Second quarter	2,374.73
Third quarter	2,306.80
Fourth quarter	1,688.21
	£8,548.27

Annual adjustment

Standard-rated sales for the year are

36,895 ÷ 60,753 × £84,079.96 = £51,061.35

Reduced rate sales for the year are

539 ÷ 60,753 × £84,079.96 = £745.96

Output tax = (£51,061.35 × 1/6) + (£745.96 × 1/21) = £8,545.75

£2.52 must be included in the VAT deductible side of the VAT return.

Apportionment Scheme 2

[61.16] In order to use the scheme

- taxable turnover must be less than £130 million (if above a bespoke scheme must be used, see **61.13** above);

- supplies must be made at two different rates of VAT;
- it must be possible to calculate expected selling prices of goods in stock when the scheme is started; and
- any supplies of services or catering must be dealt with outside the scheme.

How to calculate output tax

For the first three quarterly VAT periods or the first eleven monthly VAT periods

Step 1	Calculate the expected selling price, including VAT, of standard-rated goods for retail sale in stock at the commencement of using the scheme =	A
Step 2	Calculate the expected selling price, including VAT, of reduced rate goods in stock for retail sale at the commencement of using the scheme =	B
Step 3	Calculate the expected selling price, including VAT, of *all* goods in stock for retail sale at the commencement of using the scheme =	C
Step 4	Add up daily gross takings for the VAT period =	D
Step 5	Add up expected selling prices, including VAT, of standard-rated goods (i) received, made or grown for retail sale since starting to use the scheme; and (ii) acquired from other EU member states since starting to use the scheme =	E
Step 6	Add the total in Step 5 to the total in Step 1	
Step 7	Add up expected selling prices, including VAT, of reduced rate goods (i) received, made or grown for retail sale since starting to use the scheme; and (ii) acquired from other EU member states since starting to use the scheme =	F
Step 8	Add the total in Step 7 to the total in Step 2	
Step 9	Add up expected selling prices, including VAT, of *all* goods (standard-rated, reduced rate and zero-rated) (i) received, made or grown for retail sale since starting to use the scheme; and (ii) acquired from other EU member states since starting to use the scheme =	G
Step 10	Add the total in Step 9 to the total in Step 3	
Step 11	Calculate the proportion of gross takings from sales at the standard rate by dividing the total at Step 6 by the total at Step 10 and multiplying by the total at Step 4	
Step 12	Calculate the proportion of gross takings from sales at the reduced rate by dividing the total at Step 8 by the total at Step 10 and multiplying by the total at Step 4	

Step 13	To calculate output tax, add the total at Step 11 multiplied by the VAT fraction for standard-rated goods to the total at Step 12 multiplied by the VAT fraction for reduced rate goods

In algebraic form, output tax is [(A + E) ÷ (C + G) × D × 1/6] + [(B + F) ÷ (C + G) × D × 1/21] (VAT at 10% on standard rate goods and 5% on reduced rate goods).

For the fourth and all later quarterly VAT periods or the twelfth and all later monthly VAT periods

Step A	Add up daily gross takings for the VAT period =	H
Step B	Add up expected selling prices, including VAT, of standard-rated goods (i) received, made or grown for retail sale; and (ii) acquired from other EU member states In the current VAT period and the previous three quarterly (or eleven monthly) VAT periods =	J
Step C	Add up expected selling prices, including VAT, of reduced rate goods (i) received, made or grown for retail sale; and (ii) acquired from other EU member states In the current VAT period and the previous three quarterly (or eleven monthly) VAT periods =	K
Step D	Add up expected selling prices, including VAT, of *all* goods (standard-rated, reduced rate and zero-rated) (i) received, made or grown for retail sale; and (ii) acquired from other EU member states In the current VAT period and the previous three quarterly (or eleven monthly) VAT periods =	L
Step E	Calculate the proportion of gross takings from sales at the standard rate by dividing the total at Step B by the total at Step D and multiplying by the total in Step A	
Step F	Calculate the proportion of gross takings from sales at the reduced rate by dividing the total at Step C by the total at Step D and multiplying by the total at Step A	
Step G	To calculate output tax, add the total at Step E multiplied by the VAT fraction for standard-rated goods to the total at Step F multiplied by the VAT fraction for reduced rate goods	

In algebraic form output tax is [(J ÷ L × H × 1/6) + (K ÷ L × H × 1/21)] (VAT at 20% on standard rate goods and 5% on reduced rate goods).

Opening stock

If it is not possible to perform a physical stocktake on the date of starting to use the scheme, the ESP values of goods received for resale in the previous three months may be used.

Gross takings

See **61.8** and **61.9** above for gross takings together with adjustments and special transactions which must be taken into account.

Expected selling prices

See **61.10** to **61.12** above for calculation of expected selling prices.

Records

In addition to the normal records required, records must be kept of daily gross takings and expected selling prices.

Annual accounting scheme

If this scheme is also used, see **64.13** **SPECIAL SCHEMES**.

Ceasing to use the scheme

No adjustment is normally necessary unless ceasing to use the scheme in part only of the business. In such a case, the rolling calculation for that part still using the scheme must not include stock and expected selling prices of the part no longer using the scheme.

Cancellation of registration

VAT is due on business assets, including stock in hand. See **60.40** and **60.41** **REGISTRATION**.

(VAT Notice 727/4/13, paras 3.3, 3.5, 3.6, 5.2, 5.4 which have the force of law).

Adaptations

(1) *Opening stock*. If it is not possible to perform a physical stocktake on the date of starting to use the scheme, the expected selling price values of goods received for resale in the previous three months may be used. Alternatively, where even this is impossible or impractical, HMRC may also approve
- updating the most recent stocktake to take account of goods received for retail sale and supplied since the stocktaking took place;
- allowing a stocktaking to be carried out during the first period of use of the scheme and adjusting this to take account of goods received for retail sale and supplied from the start of using the scheme to the date of the stocktaking; or
- use of stock records produced by management accounts where these are used consistently and considered by the retailer to be of such accuracy that they are relied upon for commercial stock management and statutory accounts.

(2) *Using periodic stock adjustments rather than a rolling calculation*. HMRC may accept an adaptation using quarterly stock adjustments. They may also accept an adaptation using an annual stock adjustment in which case HMRC will also consider bringing the annual adjustment in line with the financial year end.

(3) *Adjusting historical purchase data to reflect changes in the mix of goods.* Where a retailer's mix of goods to be sold under the scheme has changed from the first period under the rolling calculation, HMRC may approve an adaptation under which

- where VAT on supplies made by a particular department or for a specific class of goods is no longer to be accounted for under this rolling calculation scheme (e.g. because a different scheme is to be used), the historic purchase/expected selling price data is excluded from the calculation; and
- similarly when new departments/classes of goods are brought into the scheme, the historic purchase/expected selling price data is also included in the rolling calculation.

(HMRC Manual VRS5250).

Example

Z Ltd owns a store and can analyse all purchases of stock for resale. It decides to use Apportionment Scheme 2 and calculates that the expected selling price, including VAT, of stock for retail sale at the commencement of using the scheme is £818,703, of which £331,379 represents standard-rated lines. Trading figures for the first four quarters under the scheme are

	ESP of standard-rated goods received for resale (incl VAT)	Total ESP of goods received for resale (incl VAT)	Gross takings
	£	£	£
First quarter	393,741	1,009,199	835,265
Second quarter	400,829	891,685	829,524
Third quarter	314,227	905,859	1,018,784
Fourth quarter	493,207	1,235,087	1,486,381

Output tax is calculated as follows

First quarter		
Opening stock	331,379	818,703
First quarter	393,741	1,009,199
	£725,120	£1,827,902

Standard-rated sales = 725,120 ÷ 1,827,902 × £835,265 = £331,345

Output tax = £331,345 × 1/6	£55,224.17

Second quarter		
Opening stock	331,379	818,703
First quarter	393,741	1,009,199
Second quarter	400,829	891,685
	£1,125,949	£2,719,587

Standard-rated sales = 1,125,949 ÷ 2,719,587 × £829,524 = £343,435

Output tax = £343,435 × 1/6 = £57,239.17

Third quarter		
Opening stock	331,379	818,703
First quarter	393,741	1,009,199
Second quarter	400,829	891,685
Third quarter	314,227	905,859
	£1,440,176	£3,625,446

Standard-rated sales = 1,440,176 ÷ 3,625,446 × £1,018,784 = £404,702

Output tax = £404,702 × 1/6 £67,450.33

Fourth quarter		
First quarter	393,741	1,009,199
Second quarter	400,829	891,685
Third quarter	314,227	905,859
Fourth quarter	493,207	1,235,087
	£1,602,004	£4,041,830

Standard-rated sales = 1,602,004 ÷ 4,041,830 × £1,486,381 = £589,136

Output tax = £589,136 × 1/6 = £98,189.33

Direct Calculation Scheme 1

[61.17] In order to use the scheme

- total VAT-exclusive retail sales must be less than £1 million per year. The limit applies to the whole business, e.g. the scheme cannot be applied to one shop if total turnover of two or more shops owned exceeds the limit;
- any supplies of services with the same VAT liability as the minority goods must be dealt with outside the scheme; and
- any supplies of catering must be dealt with outside the scheme.

The scheme works by calculating expected selling prices (ESPs) of goods for retail sale. ESPs are normally only calculated for minority goods, i.e. those goods at the rate of VAT which

- where goods are supplied at two rates of VAT, forms the smallest proportion of retail supplies; or
- where goods are supplied at three rates of VAT, forms the two smaller proportions of retail supplies.

See, however, under the heading *Adaptations* below.

How to calculate output tax

For each VAT period (quarterly or monthly)

Where the minority goods are zero-rated and/or reduced rate goods (ie main goods are standard-rated).

Step 1	Add up daily gross takings =	A
Step 2	Add up ESPs of zero-rated goods received, made or grown for retail sale =	B
Step 3	Add up ESPs of reduced rate goods received, made or grown for retail sale =	C
Step 4	Calculate the standard-rated element of takings by deducting the totals at Step 2 and Step 3 from the total at Step 1	
Step 5	To calculate output tax, add the total in Step 4 multiplied by the VAT fraction for standard-rated goods to the total in Step 3 multiplied by the VAT fraction for reduced rate goods	

In algebraic form, output tax is $[((A - B - C) \times 1/6) + (C \times 1/21)]$ (VAT at 20% on standard rate goods and 5% on reduced rate goods).

Where the minority goods are standard-rated and/or reduced rate goods (i.e. main goods are zero-rated).

Step 1	Add up daily gross takings. (Although this figure is not used in the calculation, it is still a requirement of operating the scheme and is also used in completing the VAT return.)	
Step 2	Add up ESPs of standard-rated goods received, made or grown for retail sale =	D
Step 3	Add up ESPs of reduced rate goods received, made or grown for retail sale =	E
Step 4	To calculate output tax, add the total in Step 2 multiplied by the VAT fraction for standard-rated goods to the total in Step 3 multiplied by the VAT fraction for reduced rate goods	

In algebraic form, output tax is $[(D \times 1/6) + (E \times 1/21)]$ (VAT at 20% on standard rate goods and 5% on reduced rate goods).

Gross takings

See **61.8** and **61.9** above for gross takings together with adjustments and special transactions which must be taken into account.

Expected selling prices

See **61.10** to **61.12** above for calculation of expected selling prices.

Opening stock

Goods in stock when the scheme is started are not normally treated as goods received in the period. However, if there are any stock items which are to be sold but not replenished, these may be included in the calculations unless already allowed for in a previous scheme.

Records

In addition to the normal records required, records must be kept of daily gross takings and expected selling prices.

Annual accounting scheme

If this scheme is also used, see **64.13 SPECIAL SCHEMES.**

Cancellation of registration

VAT is due on business assets, including stock in hand. See **60.40** and **60.41 REGISTRATION.**

(VAT Notice 727/5/13, paras 3.1, 3.6, 3.7, 4.2, 4.4 which have the force of law).

Adaptations

If marking up the 'majority' rather than the 'minority' goods would be more straightforward, retailers may do so. For example, newsagents may find it easier to set estimated selling prices for their majority sales of newspapers and magazines as there are likely to be fewer purchase records than for minority standard-rated sales of tobacco, confectionery, etc. (HMRC Manual VRS5250).

Example

K runs a typical corner shop selling newspapers and magazines (zero-rated), confectionery and tobacco (standard-rated), a limited range of food items (zero-rated) and barbecue fuels (reduced rate goods). At the end of a VAT period, gross takings are £18,714.55. The expected selling prices of purchases in the period are £11,236.19 for standard-rated goods, £8,154.27 for zero-rated goods and £157.93 for reduced rate goods.

The minority goods are zero-rated and reduced rate goods. Output tax is calculated as follows.

	£	£
Gross takings		18,714.55
Expected selling prices of zero-rated goods	8,154.27	
Expected selling prices of reduced rate goods	157.93	
		8,312.20
Standard-rated element of takings		£10,402.35
Output tax = (£10,402.35 × 1/6) + (£157.93 × 1/21) =		£1,741.25

Direct Calculation Scheme 2

[61.18] In order to use the scheme

- taxable turnover must be less than £130 million (if above a bespoke scheme must be used, see **61.13** above);
- it must be possible to calculate expected selling prices of minority goods in stock when the scheme is started and annually thereafter;
- any supplies of services with the same VAT liability as the minority goods must be dealt with outside the scheme; and
- any supplies of catering must be dealt with outside the scheme.

The scheme works by calculating expected selling prices (ESPs) of goods for retail sale. ESPs are only calculated for '*minority goods*', i.e. those goods at the rate of VAT which

- where goods are supplied at two rates of VAT, forms the smallest proportion of retail supplies; or
- where goods are supplied at three rates of VAT, forms the two smaller proportions of retail supplies.

How to calculate output tax

For each VAT period, the same rules apply as for Direct Calculation Scheme 1, see **61.17** above.

Annual adjustment

This scheme is based on retail trade over a full year which runs from the beginning of the first VAT period in which the scheme was used. An annual adjustment is required after making the output tax calculation for the fourth quarter (twelfth month) and any difference is accounted for on the return for that period. The adjustment must take into account any disposals since the last adjustment which were not by way of retail sale. This is done by excluding, from the figures used in the calculation, the value of any goods which were previously part of the scheme calculation (or included in the opening stock figure) but have not been sold by way of retail sale. The adjustment is also required if part of the business leaves the scheme.

Where the minority goods are zero-rated and/or reduced rate goods (i.e. main goods are standard-rated)

Step 1	Add up daily gross takings for the year =	A
Step 2	For zero-rated goods for retail sale calculate:	
	ESPs of such goods in stock at the beginning of the year	
	Plus	
	ESPs of such goods received, made or grown for retail in the year	
	Less	
	ESPs of such goods in stock at the end of the year =	B
Step 3	For reduced rate goods for retail sale calculate:	
	ESPs of such goods in stock at the beginning of the year	
	Plus	
	ESPs of such goods received, made or grown for retail in the year	
	Less	
	ESPs of such goods in stock at the end of the year =	C
Step 4	Calculate the standard-rated element of takings for the year by deducting the totals at Step 2 and Step 3 from the total at Step 1	
Step 5	To calculate output tax, add the total in Step 4 multiplied by the VAT fraction for standard-rated goods to the total in Step 3 multiplied by the VAT fraction for reduced rate goods	

In algebraic form, output tax is $[((A - B - C) \times 1/6) + (C \times 1/21)]$ (VAT at 20% on standard rate goods and 5% on reduced rate goods).

This gives the correct total for output tax due for the year. If the total is less than that calculated under the scheme in the four quarters (twelve months), the difference should be included in the VAT deductible side of the VAT account for the fourth quarter (twelfth month). Similarly, if the total is more, the difference should be included in the VAT payable side of the VAT account for that period.

Where the minority goods are standard-rated and/or reduced rate goods (i.e. main goods are zero-rated)

Step 1	For standard-rated goods for retail sale calculate:	
	ESPs of such goods in stock at the beginning of the year	
	plus	
	ESPs of such goods received, made or grown for retail in the year	
	less	
	ESPs of such goods in stock at the end of the year =	D
Step 2	For reduced rate goods for retail sale calculate:	
	ESPs of such goods in stock at the beginning of the year	
	plus	

	ESPs of such goods received, made or grown for retail in the year *less* ESPs of such goods in stock at the end of the year =	E
Step 3	To calculate output tax, add the total at Step 1 multiplied by the VAT fraction for standard-rated goods to the total at Step 2 multiplied by the VAT fraction for reduced rate goods	

In algebraic form, output tax is [(D × 1/6) + (E × 1/21)] (VAT at 20% on standard rate goods and 5% on reduced rate goods).

This gives the correct total for output tax due for the year. If the total is less than that calculated under the scheme in the four quarters (twelve months), the difference should be included in the VAT deductible side of the VAT account for the fourth quarter (twelfth month). Similarly, if the total is more, the difference should be included in the VAT payable side of the VAT account for that period.

Gross takings

See **61.8** and **61.9** above for gross takings together with adjustments and special transactions which must be taken into account.

Expected selling prices

See **61.10** to **61.12** above for calculation of expected selling prices.

Opening stock

Goods in stock when the scheme is started are not normally treated as goods received in the period. However, if there are any stock items which are to be sold but not replenished, these may be included in the calculations unless already allowed for in a previous scheme.

Records

In addition to the normal records required, records must be kept of daily gross takings and expected selling prices.

Annual accounting scheme

If this scheme is also used, see **64.13 SPECIAL SCHEMES**.

Ceasing to use the scheme

The annual adjustment as explained above must be carried out for the period from the last adjustment to the date of ceasing to use the scheme. This applies even if leaving the scheme before the anniversary of starting to use the scheme. An adjustment must also be made if part of the business ceases to use the scheme.

Cancellation of registration

VAT is due on business assets, including stock in hand. See **60.40** and **60.41 REGISTRATION**.

(VAT Notice 727/5/13, paras 3.1, 3.4, 3.6, 3.7, 4.2, 4.4, 4.5 which have the force of law).

Adaptations

(1) *Using expected selling prices of non-minority goods.* An adaptation which uses estimated selling prices for goods which do *not* form the minority sales will be considered where it is not only simpler for the retailer but also easier for HMRC to audit (e.g. a newsagent whose major portion of sales is newspapers and magazines).

(2) *Valuing stock.* If a physical stocktake at the start of the scheme year is impossible or impractical, HMRC may also approve
- updating the most recent stocktake to take account of goods received for retail sale and supplied since the stocktaking took place;
- allowing a stocktaking to be carried out during the first period of use of the scheme and adjusting this to take account of goods received for retail sale and supplied from the start of using the scheme to the date of the stocktaking; or
- use of stock records produced by management accounts where these are used consistently and considered by the retailer to be of such accuracy that they are relied upon for commercial stock management and statutory accounts.

(3) *Annual adjustment.* HMRC may allow an adaptation to bring the annual adjustment in line with the financial year end. They will, however, consider the effect on the first such annual adjustment and authorise a period longer than twelve months where necessary to ensure any distortions are avoided.

(HMRC Manual VRS5300).

Example

K decides to use Direct Calculation Scheme 2. When he starts to use the scheme, his opening stock, valued at expected selling prices, is

	£
Standard-rated goods	3,145.91
Zero-rated goods	2,250.34
Reduced rate goods	142.51

For the first four quarters, his relevant details are

	ESP of standard-rated goods purchased	ESP of zero-rated goods purchased	ESP of reduced rate goods purchased	Gross takings
	£	£	£	£
First quarter	11,236.19	8,154.27	157.93	18,714.55
Second quarter	9,075.02	11,667.67	259.32	20,726.40
Third quarter	9,872.90	10,124.75	137.54	20,855.88
Fourth quarter	11,431.39	11,008.62	21.43	22,649.04
	£41,615.50	£40,955.31	£576.22	£82,945.87

At the end of the fourth quarter, his closing stock, valued at expected selling prices, is

	£
Standard-rated goods	4,217.22
Zero-rated goods	3,151.44
Reduced rate goods	119.19

First quarter

The minority goods are zero-rated and reduced rate goods. Output tax is calculated as follows.

	£	£
Gross takings		18,714.55
ESP of zero-rated goods	8,154.27	
ESP of reduced rate goods	157.93	
		8,312.20
Standard-rated element of takings		£10,402.35

Output tax = (£10,402.35 × 1/6) + (£157.93 × 1/21) =	£1,741.25

Second quarter

The minority goods are standard-rated and reduced rate goods. Output tax is calculated as follows.

(£9,075.02 × 1/6) + (£259.32 × 1/21) =	£1,524.85

Third quarter

The minority goods are standard-rated and reduced rate goods. Output tax is calculated as follows.

(£9,872.90 × 1/6) + (£137.54 × 1/21) =	£1,652.03

Fourth quarter

The minority goods are zero-rated and reduced rate goods. Output tax is calculated as follows.

	£	£
Gross takings		22,649.04
ESP of zero-rated goods	11,008.62	
ESP of reduced rate goods	21.43	
		11,030.05
Standard-rated element of takings		£11,618.99
Output tax = (£11,618.99 × 1/6) + (£21.43 × 1/21) =		£1,937.69

The annual adjustment is as follows

The minority goods are zero-rated and reduced rate goods. Output tax is calculated as follows

	£	£
Gross takings		82,945.87
Less zero-rated goods		
opening stock:	2,250.34	
ESP of goods purchased	40,955.31	
	43,205.65	
closing stock	3,151.44	
		40,054.21
		42,891.66
Less reduced rate goods		
opening stock:	142.51	
ESP of goods purchased	576.22	
	718.73	
closing stock	119.19	
		599.54
Standard-rated element of takings		£42,292.12
Output tax = (£42,292.12 × 1/6) + (£599.54 × 1/21) =		7,077.24
Output tax already calculated		
£1,741.25 + £1,524.85 + £1,652.03 + £1,937.69		6,855.82
Additional VAT payable with return for fourth quarter		£221.42

Retail chemists

[61.19] Many of the goods that a retail chemist buys at the standard rate may subsequently be either sold over the counter (at the standard rate) or dispensed on prescription (normally at the zero rate but at the standard rate where dispensed for a patient being cared for in a nursing home or hospital, see **29.13 HEALTH AND WELFARE**). There is thus no direct relationship between the proportions of goods bought and sold at the different rates of VAT.

HMRC give the following guidance on how the standard schemes need to be adjusted to take account of this fact.

Point of Sale scheme

Under this scheme the correct rate of VAT is identified at the time of supply and no adjustment is therefore necessary. (VAT Notice 727, para 9.3).

Apportionment Scheme 1 and Direct Calculation Schemes 1 and 2

The following adjustments are required at the end of each VAT period.

Step 1	Calculate output tax under the normal scheme rules — daily gross takings to include the total amount from prescription charges and NHS cheque (less the value of any exempt supplies such as rota payments) =	A
Step 2	Add up payments *received* in the period for all *Group 12* goods, even if not supplied in the period. (Any exempt or standard-rated supplies in the NHS cheque must be excluded.) =	B
Step 3	Estimate the value of goods included in Step 2 that were zero-rated and reduced-rated on receipt. (This must be based on a sample of actual purchases for a representative period, taking account of seasonal fluctuations, etc. A new estimation must be made each VAT period.) =	C
Step 4	Subtract the total at Step 3 from the total at Step 2	
Step 5	Work out the VAT included in Step 1 from *Group 12* goods by multiplying the total at Step 4 by the VAT fraction	
Step 6	Calculate output tax by deducting the total at Step 5 from the total at Step 1	

In algebraic form, output tax is $[A - ((B - C) \times 1/6)]$.

(VAT Notice 727, paras 9.4–9.6 which have the force of law).

Where a Direct Calculation scheme is used, a retail chemist must normally calculate expected selling prices for minority goods (see **61.17** and **61.18** above). If the minority goods are standard-rated when sold but the minority of purchases are zero-rated, the chemist may calculate expected selling prices on the basis of the zero-rated goods received for resale. (VAT Notice 727, para 9.3).

Annual adjustment when using Direct Calculation Scheme 2

In addition to the period by period scheme adaptation, those using Direct Calculation Scheme 2 are also required to undertake an annual adjustment. The method(s) to apply regarding the standard annual adjustment are recorded at VAT Notice 727/5, para 4.5 (see **61.18** above). This includes the need to make adjustments to ESPs. In the case of retail chemists, adjustments to reflect Group 12 supplies should also be incorporated in the overall annual adjustment.

(VAT Notice 727, para 9.7).

Apportionment Scheme 2

The retail chemist adjustment cannot be made with this scheme.

By concession, where

- goods supplied are dispensed to an individual for his/her personal use whilst an inpatient or resident, or whilst attending, a hospital or nursing home,
- the goods are ordered and dispensed in accordance with NHS regulations, and
- the person dispensing the goods is paid for doing so by the Prescription Pricing Authority, the Prescription Information and Pricing Services Division of the Welsh Health Common Services Authority, the Pharmacy Practice Division of the Common Services Agency, or the Central Services Agency,

for the purposes of the retail scheme calculations, the supply may be treated as if it were a zero-rated supply. (VAT Notice 48, ESC 3.30).

Retail florists

[61.20] The following provisions apply to florists and other retailers who are members of organisations such as Interflora, Teleflorist and Flowergram which facilitate the purchase and delivery of flowers. The provisions have the force of law under *SI 1995/2518, Reg 67*.

The adjustments to be made depend upon the retail scheme used and whether the florist is the '*sending member*' (i.e. the member receiving payment direct from the customer) or the '*executing member*' (i.e. the member delivering the flowers and receiving payment from the organisation).

The documentation received from the agency may show output tax payable to HMRC. This is 'self-billed' output tax as the agency issues the invoice for supplies made by the florist. The florist should check the agency documentation and, if correct, add the self-billed output tax to any VAT calculated in accordance with its own retail scheme.

Point of Sale scheme

- *Sending member*. No adjustment is required by a sending member. Payments received should be included in daily gross takings at the time of the order.
- *Executing member*. Do not include payments received from the agency in daily gross takings and account for any VAT due outside the retail scheme.

Apportionment schemes

- *Sending member*. Identify from agency documentation the value of supplies made as a sending member and account for any VAT due outside the retail scheme. Do not include payments for those supplies in daily gross takings under the retail scheme calculations.

- *Executing member*. Do not include payments received from the agency in daily gross takings and account for any VAT due outside the retail scheme on the basis of agency documentation.
  If Apportionment Scheme 1 is used, exclude the value of flowers sent as an executing member from purchase records.
  If Apportionment Scheme 2 is used, adjust expected selling prices for the value of flowers sent as an executing member and accounted for outside the retail scheme.

Direct calculation schemes

- *Sending member*. Identify from agency documentation the value of supplies made as a sending member and account for any VAT due outside the retail scheme. Do not include payments for those supplies in daily gross takings under the retail scheme calculations.
- *Executing member*. Do not include payments received from the agency in daily gross takings and account for any VAT due outside the retail scheme on the basis of agency documentation. Adjust expected selling prices for the value of flowers sent as an executing member and accounted for outside the retail scheme.

(VAT Notice 727, paras 10.1–10.4).

Special arrangements for other retailers

[61.21] See HMRC Manual VRS8000 for special arrangements for other professions and trades, including

- caterers (para 9.1) (see also **12.7 CATERING**);
- concessions/shops within shops (para 9.3);
- hampers, e.g. Christmas clubs (para 9.6);
- petrol stations (para 9.8);
- sub-post offices (para 9.9);
- Women's Royal Voluntary Service (WRVS) hospital units (para 9.11); and
- mail order businesses (para 10.1).

Key points: retail schemes

[61.22] Points to consider are as follows.

- A retailer with annual VAT-exclusive turnover exceeding £130m must agree a bespoke retail scheme with HMRC. Other retailers can use one of five different schemes allowed by HMRC, assuming they meet the conditions of the scheme in question.
- A business may need to justify to HMRC why it cannot adopt a Point of Sale retail scheme by, for example, using a multi-buttoned till. The Point of Sale scheme should give the most reliable output tax calculation because the VAT liability is based on actual sales made by the business.

- An annual adjustment is needed with Apportionment Scheme 1 and Direct Calculation Scheme 2. The annual adjustment plays an important part in eliminating the unfair results sometimes produced by quarterly calculations.
- Each retail scheme has potential benefits as well as potential problems for users. For example, a Point of Sale method using a multi-button till will only be accurate if the staff operating the till know how to determine the VAT position for each sale. Proper staff training is an important issue.
- Apportionment Scheme 1 avoids the need to identify the VAT liability at the point of sale. However, it is only available to a business with annual VAT exclusive sales of less than £1m.
- Apportionment scheme 1 can produce a higher than usual VAT bill for a business that has a higher mark-up on zero-rated goods. A business where the zero-rated mark-up is considerably higher than on standard-rated goods should consider using an alternative scheme.
- Apportionment Scheme 2 calculates output tax using expected selling prices – so will deal with the problem mentioned above with Apportionment Scheme 1, i.e. where there is a higher mark-up made by the business on its zero-rated goods.
- Direct Calculation Scheme 2 could benefit a business that has slow moving stock of minority standard-rated items. This is because the scheme makes an annual adjustment for stock so that output tax is not actually paid until the goods are sold. Direct Calculation Scheme 1 produces an output tax liability in the period that the goods are purchased.
- It is important to remember that most retail schemes need to exclude the value of services provided by a business – or non-retail sales. These supplies should be accounted for outside of the scheme.
- Remember that some smaller retailers could benefit from using the flat-rate scheme if their annual taxable sales are less than £150,000 excluding VAT. The scheme produces winners and losers in terms of VAT payments.
- A retailer must use his chosen scheme for at least a year before he can make a change to another scheme. An exception is if he ceases to use the scheme because he wants to adopt the flat-rate scheme instead.
- In cases where an additional charge is made by a retailer to customers who make payment by credit card (compared to cash or cheque), the additional fee relates to a further payment for the goods or services in question and is not a 'finance charge' that is exempt from VAT.
- A retail business should retain records and evidence (if possible) of any goods that have not been sold (e.g. stolen goods, damaged goods, obsolete stock). This could be important to justify a lower than expected mark-up to HMRC in the event of a VAT visit.

- It is also necessary to take into account the value of goods that have been purchased but not sold if a retail scheme is used that is based on ESPs (expected selling prices).
- If a retail business deregisters, it is important to remember that output tax is due on any closing stock (standard-rated or reduced rated items, not zero-rated items) or assets held at the time of deregistration. There is a *de minimis* figure i.e. no output tax is due on the final return submitted by the business if the total VAT payment involved is less than £1,000.

62

Second-Hand Goods

Cross-references. See **7.9 BAD DEBT RELIEF; 24.16**(8) **FINANCIAL SERVICES** for sales by pawnbrokers; **34.25 IMPORTS** for the sale of temporarily imported second-hand goods by auction; **37.17 INSURANCE** for insurance supplied in a package with second-hand goods; **56.16 RATES OF VAT** for the effect of a change in the rate of VAT between payment and removal of goods.

De Voil Indirect Tax Service. See V3.531–538.

Introduction to second-hand goods

[62.1] In general, VAT is charged on the full value of any goods, including second-hand goods, sold by a business. The Treasury may, however, by statutory instrument, provide for a business to opt to charge VAT on the profit margin (instead of their value) on supplies of

- works of art, antiques or collectors' items;
- motor vehicles;
- second-hand goods; and
- goods through a person who acts as an agent, but in his own name, in relation to the supply.

The purpose of this is to avoid double taxation on goods which have previously borne VAT when sold as new. [*VATA 1994, s 50A; FA 1995, s 24*].

The Margin Scheme covers virtually all second-hand goods. See **62.2** to **62.38** below for details. A similar scheme is available throughout the EU and goods sold under the scheme anywhere in the EU are taxable in the country of origin rather than that of destination. They are not therefore subject to the normal distance selling rules and are not subject to acquisition VAT when taken into another EU member state.

There is also a Global Accounting Scheme in the UK because of the low value, bulk volume goods some dealers handle and the impracticality of keeping detailed records of purchases and sales. Under the scheme, VAT is accounted for on the difference between the total purchases and sales of eligible goods in each VAT period rather than on an item by item basis. See **62.39** to **62.52** below for full details.

The margin scheme

[62.2] VAT is normally due on the full value of goods sold. The margin scheme allows a VAT-registered person who meets all the conditions in **62.4** below to calculate VAT on the 'profit margin' i.e. the difference (or margin) between the price at which the goods were obtained and their selling price. If no profit is made (because the purchase price exceeds the selling price) then no VAT is payable. [*VATA 1994, s 50A(4)*]. The seller's margin is not revealed to the buyer.

The scheme is not compulsory and goods eligible for the scheme can still be sold outside the scheme in the normal way, even if bought under the scheme. In that case, there is no input tax to deduct on the purchase and VAT must be charged on the full selling price. Similarly, if an eligible item is sold but all the conditions of the scheme cannot be met (e.g. record-keeping, invoicing and accounting requirements) the margin scheme cannot be used and the sale must be dealt with outside the scheme in the normal way, accounting for VAT on the full selling price.

Although VAT is charged on the profit margin only, taxable turnover for registration purposes includes the total VAT-exclusive value of any goods sold under the scheme.

(VAT Notice 718, paras 2.1, 2.5, 2.10).

Disallowance of input tax

Any input tax charged on the supply to, or acquisition or importation by, a business of eligible goods is excluded from credit where

(a) VAT on the supply was chargeable on the profit margin under the UK margin scheme or corresponding provision of the law of another EU member state;
(b) the goods are
  (i) a work of art, antique or collectors' item within **62.3**(*b*)–(*d*) below and the business imported the goods itself, or
  (ii) a work of art within **62.3**(*b*) below and were supplied to the business by, or acquired from another EU member state by the business from, its creator or his successor in title

  and the business has opted to account for VAT chargeable on its supplies of such goods on the profit margin and not elected to account for VAT by reference to value.

[*SI 1992/3222, Art 4*].

> *Example*
>
> Jim's Motors purchases a second-hand car from a member of the public for £2,000. An amount of £500 plus VAT is paid to a local repair firm to re-spray the car, and then £100 plus VAT is paid to a valet company to clean the interior. The car is then sold to another member of the public for £3,000.
>
> Jim's Motors must keep proper records concerning the buying and selling of this vehicle, to meet the conditions of the margin scheme (see below).
>
> The input tax on the repair/valeting charges can be reclaimed in the normal way.
>
> The margin made on the sale is £1,000 (i.e. £3,000 less £2,000) and this margin is treated as VAT inclusive. An output tax liability of £166.67 must be declared on the relevant return, i.e. £1,000 × 1/6 (assuming a VAT rate of 20%).

Eligible goods

[62.3] The following goods are eligible for the margin scheme.

(a) **Second-hand goods** i.e. tangible movable property that is suitable for further use (as it is or after repair) other than
  (i) the items within (*b*)–(*d*) below;

(ii) precious metals (which includes any goods containing precious metals where the consideration for the supply (excluding VAT) does not exceed the open market value of the metal contained in the goods); and

(iii) precious stones of any age which are not mounted, set or strung. For this purpose, precious stones are diamonds, rubies, sapphires and emeralds.

(b) **Works of art** falling within the definition in *VATA 1994, s 21* (see **74.3**(*a*) **WORKS OF ART, ETC.**).

(c) **Collectors' items**, i.e. any collection or collector's piece falling within the definition in *VATA 1994, s 21(5)* (see **74.3**(*c*) **WORKS OF ART, ETC.**) but excluding investment gold coins, i.e.

- any gold coin minted after 1800 with a purity value of 900 thousandths or more which is, or has been, legal tender in its country of origin and which is of a type normally sold at a price which does not exceed 180% of the open market value of the gold contained in the coin; and
- any other gold coin specified in VAT Notice 701/21A/12, Section 3.

Where gold coins falling within the definition of investment gold coins have been mistakenly included as purchases in the margin scheme records, the records should be adjusted and the entry closed and noted accordingly. (VAT Notice 701/21A/12, para 2.6).

(d) **Antiques** i.e. objects not falling within (*b*) or (*c*) above which are more than 100 years old.

[*SI 1992/3222, Art 2; SI 1995/1268, Art 2*].

Conditions of the scheme

[62.4] A business may opt to use the margin scheme and account for VAT on the profit margin on any eligible goods within **62.3** above provided the following conditions are met.

(a) It took possession of the goods by any of the following means.

(i) On a supply on which no VAT was chargeable. This includes purchases from private individuals and unregistered businesses but also includes a zero-rated supply (*Peugeot Motor Co plc* (VTD 15314) (TVC 44.68)).

(ii) On a supply on which VAT was chargeable on the profit margin under the UK margin scheme or under the corresponding provisions in the Isle of Man or another EU member state.

(iii) Under a transaction treated as neither a supply of goods nor a supply of services (other than a transaction within (iv) below).

(iv) Under a transaction treated as neither a supply of goods nor a supply of services where the transaction in question was

(1) the transfer of assets of a business as a going concern (see **9.9 BUSINESS**); or

(2) the assignment of the rights in hire purchase or conditional sales agreements to a bank or other financial institution

and the business has a 'relevant predecessor'. For this purpose, a '*relevant predecessor*' is the person from whom the business took possession of the motor car or goods and who himself took possession of the motor car or goods in circumstances that qualified for use of the margin scheme (otherwise than under (1) or (2) above). Where the motor car or goods have been the subject of a succession of two or more transactions within (1) or (2) above (or both), culminating in the transaction in question, the relevant predecessor is the first person in the chain who took possession of the motor car or goods in circumstances that qualified for use of the margin scheme.

(v) If the goods are a work of art, on a supply, or acquisition from another EU member state, from the creator or his successor in title (whether or not the purchase invoice shows VAT separately). See **62.38** below.

(vi) If the goods are a work of art, collectors' item or antique, by importing the goods himself. This includes, if the taxable person is an auctioneer, the auctioneer having placed them under customs procedures for temporary importation with total relief from import duties. See **62.38** below.

Any item which was purchased on a VAT invoice on which input tax is recoverable is not eligible to be sold under the scheme.

(b) The supply by the business is not a letting on hire.

(c) The goods are not sold by the business on a VAT invoice or similar document showing an amount as being VAT or as being attributable to VAT.

(d) If the supply is of an airgun, the business is registered for the purposes of the *Firearms Act 1968*.

(e) If the supply by the business is the sale of repossessed assets within **24.15 FINANCIAL SERVICES** but the supply does not satisfy the conditions for treatment as outside the scope of VAT as there stated.

(f) If the supply by the business is a motor car which the business produced itself, the car must have previously been supplied by the business in the course or furtherance of its business or treated as self-supplied under **46.6 MOTOR CARS.**

(g) The business keeps such records and accounts as HMRC specify.

[*SI 1992/3122, Art 8(1)–(3)(8)(9); SI 1995/1268, Art 12(1)–(4)(8)(10)(11)*].

Reclaiming VAT on expenses

[62.5] Subject to the normal rules, a taxable person may reclaim VAT charged on business overheads, repairs, parts and accessories, etc. but must not add these costs to the purchase price of the goods sold under the scheme.

Example

Sue is an antique dealer and registered for VAT. She uses the margin scheme for all of her sales. She has bought an expensive painting for £2,000, which she can resell for £5,000 once she has spent £1,000 plus VAT on restoration costs. In this situation, input tax can be separately claimed on the restoration costs. The output tax due under the margin scheme will be based on £3,000, i.e. £5,000 selling price less buying price of £2,000.

(VAT Notice 718, para 2.11).

Purchases

[62.6] The following provisions have the force of law.

Private person or unregistered dealer not providing invoice

On a purchase from a private person or an unregistered dealer who does not provide an invoice, the buyer must check that the goods are eligible for the scheme and, if so, make out a purchase invoice showing

- seller's name and address;
- purchaser's name and address;
- stock book number;
- date of transaction;
- description of the goods including any unique identification (e.g. registration number, make/model, hallmark, type, class, chassis number, etc.); and
- total price (no other costs may be added to this amount).

Unregistered dealer providing invoice

On purchase from an unregistered dealer who provides an invoice, the buyer must ensure that the invoice contains all the necessary details as above.

VAT-registered dealer

The dealer must issue an invoice that contains the following information:

- seller's name and address;
- customer's name and address;
- stock book number;
- invoice number;
- date of transaction;
- description of the items(s);
- total price (no other amounts must be added to this amount);
- any of the following phrases: 'Margin Scheme – second hand goods'; or 'Margin Scheme – works of art' or 'Margin Scheme – collectors' items and antiques'.

Stock book

Details of the purchase must be entered in the stock book (see **62.23** below).

(VAT Notice 718, paras 4.1, 5.3).

Invoices in foreign currency

If an invoice is in a foreign currency, it must be converted into sterling using one of the methods in **72.18 VALUATION** or, in the case of acquisitions from another EU member state, **72.14 VALUATION.** Where a number of items are bought for an inclusive price which are not to be sold as one lot, the price must be converted into sterling and then apportioned between the various items. The sterling amounts on an item by item basis must be entered in the stock records. (VAT Notice 718, para 5.7).

Acquisitions from other EU member states

[62.7] The margin scheme is available throughout the EU. Eligible goods sold under the scheme in any EU member state are taxable in the country of origin rather than of destination and are not subject to the normal distance selling rules.

- *Goods purchased from a private individual in another EU member state.* No VAT is due when the goods are brought into the UK and the goods can therefore be sold under the margin scheme or global accounting scheme.
- *Goods purchased from a registered business in another EU member state under the margin scheme or global accounting scheme.* Goods purchased from a dealer in another EU member state can only be sold under the scheme if the goods are supplied by that dealer under a margin scheme.

(VAT Notice 718, paras 7.1, 7.6).

New means of transport are always liable to VAT on the EU member state of destination. See **20.33 EUROPEAN UNION: SINGLE MARKET**. This means that any new means of transport acquired from another EU member state is not eligible for the margin scheme. (VAT Notice 718, para 7.5).

Imports from outside the EU

[62.8] VAT is normally due on importation of second-hand goods and the margin scheme cannot be used to sell the goods. On sale, VAT must be charged on the full selling price, the VAT paid at importation being deductible subject to the normal rules. This general rule is subject to the following exceptions.

- Certain works of art, antiques, collections and collectors' pieces are entitled to a reduced valuation at importation (see **74.3 WORKS OF ART, ETC.**). Where any of the works of art, etc. listed there are imported, the purchaser may either use the margin scheme or import and resell the goods under the normal VAT rules. See **62.38** below.
- Second-hand cars. See **62.29** below.

(VAT Notice 718, para 8.1).

Bulk purchases

[62.9] Where a number of eligible goods are bought at an inclusive price with the intention of reselling them separately, the price paid must be apportioned. There is no set way of doing this but the method used must be fair and reasonable and the price allocated to each must be as accurate as possible. The separate figures must be shown in the stock book (see **62.23** below). (VAT Notice 718, para 4.1).

Alternatively, the global accounting scheme may be used for low-value bulk purchases. See **62.39** to **62.52** below.

Purchases of repossessed goods

[62.10] Sales of eligible goods by an insurance company which has taken possession of them in settlement of an insurance claim or by a finance company which has repossessed them are outside the scope of VAT provided certain conditions are met. See **24.15 FINANCIAL SERVICES**. As no VAT is charged on the supply of the goods, they can be purchased for sale under the margin scheme provided the necessary scheme conditions in **62.4** are satisfied. (VAT Notice 718, para 13.9).

Sales

[62.11] Note: the following provisions have the force of law.

On the sale of eligible goods, the seller must check that the rules in **62.6** above were applied on purchase and, if so, make out a sales invoice showing

- supplier's name and address and VAT registration number;
- buyer's name and address;
- stock book number;
- invoice number;
- date of transaction;
- particulars of the goods including any unique reference number (e.g. registration number, make/model, hallmark, type, class, chassis number, etc.);
- total price, including VAT. Where more than one item is sold on the same invoice, a separate price must be shown for each item; and
- any of the following: margin scheme – second-hand goods; margin scheme – works of art; or margin scheme – collector's items and antiques.

The invoice must not show VAT as a separate item.

If any insurance product is being sold with the goods, the full price of this must be disclosed separately on the invoice, plus any fees charged for the product outside the contract of insurance. See **37.17 INSURANCE**.

The seller must then give the invoice to his customer, keep a copy for his own records and enter details of the sale in the stock book (see **62.23** below).

(VAT Notice 718, paras 4.2, 5.3).

Invoices in foreign currency

If an invoice is issued in a foreign currency, it must also show the sterling equivalent of the value of the goods. Normally, where a number of items are sold on the same invoice, the foreign currency and sterling price must be shown for each item and the sterling amounts entered in the stock records. If, however, the sales invoice is for one lot of goods which were also bought as one lot, it is only necessary to show a total foreign currency and sterling value for that lot. The foreign currency value must be converted into sterling using one of the methods in **72.18 VALUATION**. (VAT Notice 718, para 5.7).

Sales to other EU member states

[62.12] The margin scheme is available throughout the EU. Eligible goods sold under the scheme in any EU member state are taxable in the country of origin rather than of destination and are not subject to the normal distance selling rules.

- *Sales by UK dealers to dealers in other EU member states.* Sales made under the margin scheme are taxable in the same way as sales within the UK and the normal margin scheme sales invoice must be issued. There is no requirement to obtain the dealer's registration number. No further VAT is due from the buyer when the goods are taken into the other EU member state. Alternatively, the goods can be sold outside the margin scheme in which case the sale can be zero-rated subject to the normal conditions for supplies of goods to VAT-registered customers in other EU member states (see **20.11** EUROPEAN UNION: SINGLE MARKET). The buyer must then account for VAT in his own country and cannot sell the goods under the margin scheme.
- *Sales by UK dealers to private individuals in other EU member states.* Such sales are taxable in the UK on the margin.

(VAT Notice 718, para 7.3).

New means of transport are always liable to VAT in the EU member state of destination. See **20.31** EUROPEAN UNION: SINGLE MARKET. This means that any new means of transport sold to another EU member state is not eligible for the margin scheme. (VAT Notice 718, para 7.5).

Exports outside the EU

[62.13] Where eligible goods are sold for direct export, the sale is zero-rated provided appropriate evidence of exportation is held. See **22.25** EXPORTS. The retail export scheme can also be used to zero-rate the indirect export of certain second-hand goods. See **22.16** EXPORTS. 'Nil' should be entered in the VAT due column of the stock book.

However, it is not normally possible to zero-rate an export of eligible goods if the goods are sold through an auctioneer or dealer who acts as an agent in his own name. This is because, under the special rules for agents who act in their own name, the sale of the goods must be treated as a supply to the agent and a supply by the agent. Thus, the sale by the dealer has to be treated as a supply to the agent, rather than as a supply to the final purchaser, and cannot be treated as a zero-rated export unless the agent is located outside the EU.

(VAT Notice 718, para 8.2).

Where a vehicle is supplied to an overseas person for export, the transaction may be zero-rated provided the vehicle is only used in the UK for the trip to the place of departure from the EU. See **22.18** EXPORTS.

The Personal Export Scheme can also be used to zero-rate sales of second-hand cars exported outside the EU. See **22.19** EXPORTS.

Transfers of own goods to another EU member state

[62.14] The transfer of goods within the same legal entity from one EU member state to another is deemed to be a supply for VAT purposes. See **20.25 EUROPEAN UNION: SINGLE MARKET**. Where goods are transferred under the margin scheme from the UK to another EU member state (e.g. for sale, or use in the business, in that country) there is no liability to UK VAT on the goods provided that they are transferred from the UK at the price for which they were obtained. There should be no liability to account for acquisition VAT in the other EU member state. (VAT Notice 718, para 7.4).

Part exchange

[62.15] If a dealer sells eligible goods and takes other goods in part exchange, his selling price includes the amount allowed for the other goods as well as the amount received in cash from the buyer.

Example

A car is sold for £2,000 cash plus a car for which £1,000 is allowed in part exchange.

A selling price of £3,000 must be entered in the stock book. As the article taken in exchange is an eligible article which is to be resold under the scheme, the rules in **62.6** above must be followed. The amount allowed in part exchange (£1,000) is the purchase price. The purchase must also be recorded in the stock book (see **62.23** below).

A dealer must obtain a purchase invoice for part-exchanged goods bought from another VAT-registered dealer. However, if he buys from a private person or an unregistered dealer, he may include details of part-exchange items on his sales invoice provided all the requirements of **62.6** above are met.

(VAT Notice 718, para 13.6).

In *Lex Services plc v C & E Commrs*, HL 2003, [2004] STC 73 (TVC 44.86) the company accepted second-hand cars in part exchange. The documentation showed a vehicle price (say £20,000) and an agreed price for the part exchange car (say £2,000) which was used to arrive at the amount actually payable by the customer (£18,000). In most cases, however, in order to secure the sale the part exchange price was higher than the 'trade value' for the car (say £1,500). The relevant transaction could be cancelled by the customer within 30 days and the documentation stipulated that if the part exchange car had previously been sold, the customer was only entitled to a refund of the lower 'trade value' which was also disclosed in the documentation. The Court held that the taxable amount for VAT purposes was the cash received (£18,000) plus the value of the non-monetary consideration agreed with the customer (£2,000).

Lex Services above was, however, distinguished in *Hartwell plc v C & E Commrs*, CA [2003] STC 396 (TVC 44.88) where the company issued 'purchase plus vouchers' to customers in order to encourage sales without having to overvalue the part-exchanged car. Where, for example, the price of the replacement vehicle was £20,000 but the correct 'trade-value' of the used car was £1,500, if the customer was unwilling to pay £18,500 the company might issue a purchase plus voucher for £500. The court held that the consideration the dealer received for the supply of the £500 voucher was the agreement of the purchaser to the sale and that its non-monetary value was nil. The voucher did not form part of the consideration for the part-exchanged car. The taxable amount for VAT purposes was the cash received (£18,000) plus the trade in value of the used car (£1,500).

Hire purchase sales

[62.16] Note: The following provisions have the force of law.

Eligible goods sold under a hire purchase agreement are sold to the finance company which in turn sells them to the customer. The sale should be treated as a cash sale and the cash price of the goods (as shown on the HP agreement) should be entered in the stock book as the selling price. No VAT is charged on the finance charges if itemised separately. In some circumstances the dealer may issue his own sales invoice to the customer. He must attach a copy of the completed HP agreement to the customer's sales invoice or include a cross-reference to the agreement in his sales records. If the HP agreement is held by the finance company and the dealer does not receive a copy for his records, he should keep a copy of the agreed quotation or agreed proposal documents in his sales records, together with the name of the finance company, date and reference number of the final agreement.

A copy of the HP agreement can be treated as the sales invoice provided

- it shows all the identifying details required; and
- the cash price is shown as the gross price payable i.e. the amount borrowed plus cash paid, plus any amount allowed for part exchange (see **62.15** above).

VAT must not be shown separately on the HP agreement or any invoice.

(VAT Notice 718, para 13.5).

See **24.15 FINANCIAL SERVICES** for the sale of repossessed goods.

Gifts

[62.17] If a taxable person sells an article received as a gift, he must charge VAT on its full selling price and not use the margin scheme.

No VAT is chargeable on eligible goods which could have been sold under the scheme but which are given away but full details of the person to whom the goods are given must be included in the stock book.

(VAT Notice 718, para 13.3).

Private sales

[62.18] The private sale of goods which are not assets of the business is usually outside the scope of VAT.

Where a sole proprietor transfers eligible goods from a private holding to the business, VAT may be accounted for under the margin scheme provided evidence can be produced of the purchase price when originally bought for private use. If not, VAT must be accounted for on the full selling price.

(VAT Notice 718, para 13.4).

Sales from historic houses

[62.19] If owners of historic houses admit members of the public for a charge, any works of art, etc. owned and displayed to the public are treated as business assets and their disposal is normally subject to VAT. There is, however, special VAT relief in certain cases. See **74.6 WORKS OF ART, ETC.**

See also **74.1 WORKS OF ART, ETC.** for exemption from VAT on certain disposals to approved bodies, and property accepted in satisfaction of inheritance tax.

Shares in eligible goods

[62.20] If a share in an eligible item held in stock is sold, this is a supply of an undivided share in goods and therefore a supply of services. The sale is not eligible to be accounted for under a margin scheme, and VAT must be accounted for under the normal rules.

When an item in which other people own shares is sold under the margin scheme, the full amount of VAT due must be accounted for (not just VAT on the taxable person's share of the proceeds). The purchase price is the full purchase price (not just the taxable person's share) and statements must be issued to the other shareholders showing their share of the sale proceeds, excluding VAT. See also **62.21** below.

(VAT Notice 718, para 12.2).

Joint purchases and sales

[62.21] The following procedure (which has the force of law) should be used where dealers jointly buy an eligible article for resale.

(a) **On purchase,** one of the joint buyers (JB1) must keep the purchase invoice with the details set out under **62.6** above and must invoice the other joint buyer(s) for the agreed contribution towards the cost, excluding VAT. Each invoice must be endorsed 'This payment is your contribution towards the purchase of the above article. I shall be accounting for the full amount of VAT due under the scheme when it is sold.' Copies of the invoice(s) must be retained.
JB1 must record the full purchase details in his stock book, together with details of the sales invoices to the other joint buyer(s).

(b) **On resale by the original buyer,** JB1 must issue (and keep a copy of) a sales invoice showing all the details in **62.11** above and enter the sales and accounting details in his stock book. The selling price is the full joint selling price (not just JB1's share of the proceeds).
JB1 must then issue a statement to the other joint buyer(s) showing their share of the proceeds of sale, excluding VAT. The statement must be endorsed 'This payment is your share of the proceeds of sale of [insert details]. I am accounting for the full amount of VAT due on the sale under the scheme.'

(c) **On resale by another joint buyer (JB2),** he must obtain the original purchase invoice from JB1, issue (and keep a copy of) a sales invoice showing all the details in **62.11** above and complete his stock book treating the purchase and sale as being made entirely by him. The purchase price is the full joint purchase price and the selling price is the full joint selling price.
JB2 must then issue a statement to the other joint buyer(s) as in (*b*) above.
JB1, the original buyer, must close the entry in his stock book stating that VAT has been accounted for by JB2 and cross-refer to the statement received from JB2.

(VAT Notice 718, paras 12.1–12.6).

Records and accounts

[62.22] The following requirements as to records and accounts have the force of law. [*SI 1992/3122, Art 8(1); SI 1995/1268, Art 12(1)*]. They are in addition to the records generally required of all taxable persons. See **57 RECORDS.**

A business selling goods under the scheme must keep the purchase invoice (see **62.6** above) and a copy of the sales invoice (see **62.11** above), together with a stock book or similar records (see **62.23** below). All records must be kept for six years but if stock includes goods obtained more than six years previously, evidence must also be retained to show eligibility to use the margin scheme at the time of sale. Failure to comply with any of the requirements renders the business liable for VAT on the full value of its sales. (VAT Notice 718, paras 5.1, 5.5). See *C & E Commrs v JH Corbitt (Numismatists) Ltd*, HL [1980] STC 231 (TVC 60.1). The requirements as to the records to be kept do not impose an obligation on the business to verify the identity of purchasers (*Bord* (VTD 9824) (TVC 60.5)).

See, however, **62.39** *et seq* below for a simplified method of operating the margin scheme (global accounting).

Occasional sales

If a trader is not in the business of selling second-hand goods, etc. but occasionally sells eligible goods in the course of his business, he need not comply with the full record-keeping requirements provided he meets the other conditions of the scheme and holds evidence of both the purchase and selling price. (VAT Notice 718, para 13.7).

Motor cars

There is an alternative special method of calculating VAT for second-hand cars where the dealer has the required information on the purchase or sale of the car but not both. See **62.35** below.

Horses and ponies

Special records are required. See **62.37** below.

Stock book

[62.23] A stock book or similar record must be kept with separate headings for each of the following.

Purchase details
Purchase details
Stock number in numerical sequence
Date of purchase
Purchase invoice number
Name of seller
Any unique identification number (e.g. car registration)
Description of the goods (e.g. type, make or model)

Sales details
Date of sale
Sales invoice number
Name of buyer

Accounting details
Purchase price
Selling price or other method of disposal
Margin on sale
VAT due

The purchase price must be the price on the invoice which has been agreed between the buyer and seller and must not be altered. Separate entries must be made where purchases bought in bulk are to be sold separately (see **62.9** above).

Other information can also be included but the above details must always be shown and the stock book must be kept up-to-date.

(VAT Notice 718, paras 5.2, 6.1).

Goods on sale or return

If stock includes goods supplied to the dealer on a sale or return basis, the stock book (or a separate record) must include the following details of the goods.

Date of transfer of the goods
Description of goods including any unique identification number (e.g. car registration)
Name and address of dealer/person transferring the goods
Date of sale or return

Similarly, if any goods are removed from stock on a sale or return basis to another dealer's premises, stock records should be noted with the date and details of the dealer to whom the goods have been transferred.

If a dealer sells goods on behalf of a third party, and issues an invoice for those goods in his own name, he is acting as an agent for VAT purposes (see **62.26** below).

(VAT Notice 718, para 5.6).

Calculation of VAT

[62.24] If eligible goods are sold for the same as, or less than, the price paid, no VAT is due. The loss cannot be set against profit made on other transactions.

If eligible goods are sold for more than the price paid, VAT is chargeable on the profit margin i.e. the amount by which the consideration for the goods are sold exceeds the purchase price. The profit margin is regarded as being VAT-inclusive i.e. the VAT included is

VAT-inclusive margin × VAT fraction 1/6

Profit margin

The following rules apply for the purpose of determining the profit margin.

(a) The price at which the goods were obtained is calculated
  - (i) where the business took possession of the goods by a supply, in the same way as the consideration for the supply would normally be calculated (see **72.2** *et seq* **VALUATION**);
  - (ii) where the business is a sole proprietor and the goods were supplied to him in a private capacity, in the same way as the consideration for the supply to him as a private individual would be calculated;
  - (iii) where the goods are a work of art which was acquired by the business from the creator or his successor in title in another EU member state, in the same way as the value of the acquisition would be calculated for VAT purposes (see **72.11 VALUATION**) plus the VAT chargeable on the acquisition;
  - (iv) where the goods are a work of art, antique or collectors' item which the business has imported itself (which includes, if the business is that of an auctioneer, the auctioneer having placed them under customs procedures for temporary importation with total relief from import duties), in the same way as the value would be calculated for the purposes of importation (see **72.15 VALUATION**) plus any VAT chargeable on their importation; and
  - (v) where the business took possession of the motor car or goods under a transaction treated as neither a supply or goods nor a supply of services (other than a transaction within (vi) below), the price it paid by virtue of that transaction; and
  - (vi) where the business took possession of the motor car or goods under a transaction treated as neither a supply or goods nor a supply of services as the result of
    - (1) the transfer of assets of a business as a going concern (see **9.9 BUSINESS**); or
    - (2) in the case of a bank or other financial institution, the assignment of the rights in hire purchase or conditional sale agreements

    and the business has a 'relevant predecessor', the price at which its relevant predecessor in title obtained the motor car or goods. For this purpose, a '*relevant predecessor*' is the person from whom the business took possession of the motor car or goods and who himself took possession of the motor car or goods in circumstances that qualified for use of the margin scheme (see **62.4** above). Where the motor car or goods have been the subject of a succession of two or more transactions within (1) or (2) above (or both), culminating in the transaction in question, the relevant predecessor is the first person in the chain who took possession of the motor car or goods in circumstances that qualified for use of the margin scheme.

Where the above provisions apply, the business will always require the original purchase invoice to calculate the margin on the goods.

(b) The price at which the goods are sold is calculated in the same way as the consideration for the supply would be calculated for VAT purposes. It includes everything received for the goods whether from the buyer or a third party. It also includes incidental expenses directly linked to the sale. Optional extras charged to the buyer and disbursements do *not* form part of the selling price and should be accounted for separately outside the margin scheme. The consideration may not be wholly in money and the normal rules about value apply. See **72.2** *et seq* **VALUATION**.

[*SI 1992/3122, Art 8(5)(8)(9); SI 1995/1268, Art 12(5)(10)(11)*]. (VAT Notice 718, para 3.1).

The margin cannot be reduced by deducting expenses e.g. repairs, spares, overheads, cleaning, etc. (VAT Notice 718, para 3.2).

Motor cars

There is an alternative special method of calculating VAT for second-hand cars where the dealer has the required information on the purchase or sale of the car but not both. See **62.35** below.

Completion of VAT return

[62.25] See **2.7** *et seq* **ACCOUNTING PERIODS AND RETURNS** for general notes on the completion of the VAT return. The following special rules apply to eligible goods bought and sold under the margin scheme.

Box 1	Include the output tax on all eligible goods sold in the period covered by the return.
Box 6	Include the full selling price of all eligible goods sold during the period, less any VAT.
Box 7	Include the purchase price (inclusive of VAT) of eligible goods bought in the period.

There is no requirement to include margin scheme purchases and sales in Boxes 8 and 9.

(VAT Notice 718, para 5.4).

Agents

[62.26] Dealers frequently sell goods for or on behalf of other dealers or private sellers. The arrangements may include retaining a percentage of the selling price or making a separate charge to the owner. In either case, the seller is acting as the agent of the dealer or individual who owns the goods and the parties must follow the rules set out below.

If different parties own shares in the goods or if different parties have bought goods jointly for resale, see **62.21** above.

An agent who acts in his own name and uses the margin scheme in relation to a supply of goods must, for VAT purposes, treat the supply as a supply to him and a supply by him. See **3.4 AGENTS**. When goods are sold by an agent, the margin scheme treatment will depend on the way the agent has opted to account for his commission. The following paragraphs outline the margin scheme consequences of each option.

(a) **How the owner or principal calculates his margin.** If the agent sells eligible goods on the owner's behalf in his own name, the owner can still account for his sale under the margin scheme. The owner's purchase price is calculated in the normal way (see **62.24** above) but his selling price depends on the way the agent has accounted for his sale and is equivalent to the agent's purchase price.

(b) **How the agent calculates his margin.** An agent selling eligible goods has two options.

- *Option 1.* If the agent invoices his charges to the seller or principal separately, those charges are subject to VAT and his margin for VAT is calculated as follows.
  Purchase price = The gross amount realised by the agent before any deductions are made.
  Selling price = The total price for the goods including any incidental expenses and commission charged to the buyer. (Other optional charges not directly linked to the goods such as packing, transport and insurance costs should be charged outside the margin scheme under the normal VAT rules.)
  Margin = The difference between the purchase price and the selling price.
- *Option 2.* If the agent includes his charges to the seller in his sale of the goods, his margin for VAT is calculated as follows.
  Purchase price = The gross amount realised by the agent less commission charged to the seller (and not including any charges made to the buyer).
  Selling price = The total price for the goods including any incidental expenses and commission charged to the buyer. (Other optional charges not directly linked to the goods such as packing, transport and insurance costs should be charged outside the margin scheme under the normal VAT rules.)
  Margin = The difference between the purchase price and the selling price.

> This method mirrors the method used by auctioneers to calculate their purchase and selling prices under the auctioneers' scheme (see **62.59** below).

An agent selling goods under the margin scheme who issues an invoice in his own name must keep the records described in **62.22** above.

[*SI 1992/3122, Art 8(6); SI 1995/1268, Art 12(6)*]. (VAT Notice 718, paras 17.1–17.7).

Second-hand cars

Margin scheme

[62.27] The normal rules and conditions of the margin scheme apply to second-hand motor cars but there are also further specific provisions which apply as outlined in **62.28** to **62.35** below. These provisions have the force of law.

Motor cars are defined in **46.1 MOTOR CARS**. Only second-hand cars can be sold under the margin scheme. To be eligible, the car must have been driven on the road for business or pleasure purposes. Neither the registration of the car for road use nor the delivery mileage incurred transporting a vehicle to a dealer turn a car into a used car for the purposes of the margin scheme. See also *Lincoln Street Motors (Birmingham) Ltd* [1981] VATTR 120 (TVC 44.66).

The margin scheme cannot be used for any vehicle on which input tax was reclaimed on purchase. See **46.4 MOTOR CARS** for sales of such cars.

Spare parts from scrapped vehicles

The CJEU held in *Sjelle Autogenbrug I/S v Skatteministeriet, ECJ Case C-471/15* (TVC 20.239) that used parts obtained from scrapped vehicles that had been purchased from a private individual or insurance company, that were intended to be sold as spare parts, constituted 'second-hand goods' for the purposes of the margin scheme. Therefore any VAT due on the spare parts supplied could be accounted for using the margin scheme.

(VAT Notice 718/1, para 2.3).

Purchases from other EU member states

[62.28] Where a second-hand car is bought from a private individual, or from a registered dealer using the margin scheme, in another EU member state, no VAT is due when the car is brought into the UK and the margin scheme can be used for the onward sale.

Where a second-hand car is bought outside the margin scheme from a registered dealer in another EU member state, acquisition VAT is due when the car is brought into the UK and the car is not eligible for the margin scheme.

The margin scheme cannot be used for any vehicle qualifying as a new means of transport (see **20.33 EUROPEAN UNION: SINGLE MARKET**).

The CJEU recently held in *'Litdana' UAB v Valstybine mokesciu inspekcija prie Lietuvos Respublikos finansu ministerijos, CJEU Case C-624/15* (TVC 60.22) that the margin scheme can still apply even where a supplier fails to meet its obligations under the scheme. In this case, Litdana (L) who is established in Estonia purchased some second-hand vehicles from a supplier located in Denmark. The Danish supplier's invoice indicated that the vehicles were sold under the margin scheme and were exempted from VAT accordingly. L used the margin scheme when it resold the vehicles. The Lithuanian tax authorities undertook an investigation of the Danish supplier to confirm that the goods were eligible to be sold under the scheme and ascertained that the Danish supplier had not met their obligations under the scheme. The tax authorities determined as a result that L was not eligible to use the scheme when it resold the vehicles. L appealed and the matter was referred to the CJEU.

The CJEU held that it was not contrary to EU law to require a taxable person to take all reasonable steps to confirm that the transaction they are involved in will not result in tax fraud. However it is not compatible with EU law for a taxable person to be penalised, where he did not know and could not have known that the transaction was connected with fraud. If the taxable person has acted in good faith and has undertaken all reasonable checks they should not be denied the rights available to them.

(VAT Notice 718/1, para 2.4).

Imports from outside the EU

[62.29] VAT is due at the standard rate on the importation of a second-hand car unless it meets the criteria for returned goods relief (see **34.19 IMPORTS**) or it can be classified as a collector's piece. An imported car is not eligible for sale under the margin scheme unless it qualifies as a collectors' piece or antique. See **46.4 MOTOR CARS** for the VAT provisions applying on sale.

Personal imports

If a dealer buys a car from an unconnected person who has personally imported it, the car may be sold under the margin scheme. Where, however, the car is imported by an employee, agent or other person connected with the trader for sale in the dealer's business, the margin scheme cannot be used for the subsequent sale.

(VAT Notice 718/1, para 2.4).

VED and MOTs

Unexpired VED

[62.30] Where a car is purchased with an unexpired VED which is surrendered. A refund of VED is treated as being outside the scope of VAT. The price of the car should not be adjusted to reflect the refund.

Valid VED

Where a car is sold with a valid VED or a VED is offered with the car as part of the agreed sale price, there is a single supply and the selling price entered in the stock book must include the value of the VED.

Separate VED

Where a VED is obtained after the negotiation for the sale of a car, the VED may be treated as a separate supply provided the conditions for treatment as a disbursement are met. See **3.7 AGENTS**. If those conditions cannot be met, the car and the VED are treated as a single supply and VAT must be accounted for on the margin of the total value.

MOT

Where a car is sold with an MOT, this is a single supply and the full selling price, without deduction of any value for the MOT, must be recorded in the stock book and used to calculate the margin.

(VAT Notice 718/1, paras 10.2, 10.3).

Mechanical breakdown insurance and warranties

[62.31] A '*warranty*' is an undertaking or guarantee by a dealer that, if a vehicle proves to be faulty within a specified time limit or mileage, the dealer will bear the cost of repair or replacement parts.

'*Mechanical breakdown insurance*' (MBI) is a contract of insurance, between an insurer (usually someone other than the dealer) and a purchaser, providing cover against the risk of the vehicle proving faulty within a specified time limit or mileage.

(a) *Free warranties or MBI*. The selling price of the car includes the cost of providing the warranty or MBI. The price of the car on the invoice must be entered in the stock book. Any mention of the warranty or MBI on the invoice must show that no separate charge is being made.

(b) *Warranties or MBI for which a separate charge is made*. The VAT treatment depends on whether the risk covered is the dealer's or the customer's.

   (i) If a dealer arranges MBI for his customer, the supply is exempt provided
   - it is supplied under a contract between an insurer and the customer;
   - it is the customer's risks which are insured;
   - the customer is entirely free to purchase the item at the price advertised without the MBI; and
   - the dealer discloses to the customer the premium and any other amount (fees or commission) being charged.

   This is because there are separate supplies of the item and the MBI, each with its own consideration. The following rules must be observed.
   - If the dealer subsequently negotiates with the customer a reduced price for the item (including the MBI), the price originally advertised for the MBI must be treated as the value of the exempt supply of the MBI.
   - If negotiations with the customer result in the supply of an upgraded MBI, the dealer may use the separately advertised price of the upgraded MBI as the value of the exempt supply of the MBI.

- If the dealer advertises the item and the MBI at a single price (ie does not disclose to the customer the amount they are paying for the MBI) any fee or commission income the dealer would receive in relation to this insurance is standard-rated. The net value of the insurance paid to, and retained by, the insurer remains exempt.

If the insurance contract is between the dealer and the insurer and only the dealer's risk of having to repair defective items is covered, then the charge shown on the dealer's invoice for insurance is standard-rated.

(ii) If a dealer provides a warranty, the charge shown on the invoice is standard-rated.

(c) *Other situations*. The supply of a warranty or MBI under any other type of scheme is standard-rated. This applies, for example, to 'stop loss' arrangements under which the dealer or insurance broker sets up a fund into which amounts charged to customers for warranties or MBI are paid and from which repair claims are met. Insurance cover is then obtained from a permitted insurer against any deficiency in the fund.

Any standard-rated commission or fees under (*b*) above or, if not charged separately, standard-rated warranty charges under (*c*) above must be deducted from the vehicle's selling price before the gross margin is calculated.

(VAT Notice 718/1, paras 9.1–9.6).

Demonstration cars

[62.32] VAT may be reclaimed on the purchase, acquisition or importation of any motor car which forms part of the stock in trade of a motor dealer. See **46.3 MOTOR CARS** for full details. As a result, such cars are no longer eligible for the margin scheme and, on disposal, output tax must be accounted for on the full selling price in the normal way. See **46.4 MOTOR CARS**.

Rebuilt motor cars

[62.33] If a motor car is rebuilt from one or more used cars and the Driver and Vehicle Licensing Authority (DVLA) do not require it to be re-registered, it can be sold under the margin scheme. The purchase price to be entered in the stock book is the price paid for the car for which the registration number is carried forward. If, however, the DVLA give the car a new registration number, the scheme cannot be used and VAT must be accounted for on the full selling price. (VAT Notice 718/1, para 10.6).

Auctions

[62.34] See **62.53** *et seq* below for the general provisions relating to auctions.

Calculation of VAT due

[62.35] *Where all required records are held*, the normal rules in **62.24** above apply. Otherwise the sale must be dealt with outside the scheme, accounting for VAT on the full selling price.

(VAT Notice 718/1, para 5.1).

Second-hand motor-cycles

[62.36] Road fund licences, mechanical breakdown insurance and warranties and rebuilt motor-cycles: the provisions applying to motor cars apply equally to motor-cycles. See **62.30**, **62.31** and **62.33** above respectively.

Second-hand horses and ponies

[62.37] The general rules and conditions of the margin scheme also apply to the sale of second-hand horses and ponies. This has been confirmed in *Förvaltnings AB Stenholmen v Riksskatteverket, ECJ Case C–320/02*, [2004] STC 1041 (TVC 22.569). The following rules relate specifically to second-hand horses and ponies and have the force of law.

Horses which the trader has bred and is selling for the first time are not second-hand.

A trader using the margin scheme for horses or ponies may either

- keep the normal records and accounts; or
- keep alternative records based on special three-part forms supplied by The British Equestrian Trade Association.

Each of these options is explained below.

Normal records and accounts

If a dealer decides to keep normal margin scheme records, his stock book must include sufficient details to identify the horse or pony including colour, sex, type (e.g. chestnut, cob, gelding), age (if known), height, stable name (if known), and distinctive markings. (These requirements have the force of law.)

On purchase, the normal conditions in **62.6** above must be complied with. If the purchase is from another VAT-registered dealer who uses the special three-part form (see below), the other dealer will hand over Part C of that form. This can be used as the purchase invoice and appropriate details entered in the stock book.

On purchase at auction, the dealer must comply with the conditions **62.60** below. If the horse or pony is being sold at auction by another VAT-registered dealer who uses the three-part form, the auctioneer will hand over Part C of that form. This can be used as the purchase invoice and appropriate details entered in the stock book.

On sale, the normal conditions in **62.11** above must be complied with. On sale at auction the dealer must comply with the conditions set out in **62.61** below.

(VAT Notice 718, paras 16.1–16.7).

Alternative records and accounts

To sell horses and ponies under the margin scheme, as an alternative to the normal records special three-part forms (produced in numbered sets) with a VAT summary sheet at the back may be used. These are sold by

The British Equestrian Trade Association,
East Wing,
Stockeld Park,
Wetherby,
West Yorkshire LS22 4AW

The three parts of the form are

Part A	Seller's stock record
Part B	Seller's copy sales invoice
Part C	Customer's purchase invoice

These forms are the basis of stock and sales records. No other records are required to operate the scheme. It is not necessary to keep a stock book or invoices. A separate form must be properly completed for each horse, etc. or VAT becomes due on the full selling price i.e. the records are mandatory.

(a) *Purchase of a horse or pony from a private person.* After ensuring that the horse or pony is eligible for the margin scheme, the 'description' and 'written description' sections of Parts A, B and C must be completed in accordance with the standard laid down by the Royal College of Veterinary Surgeons in their booklet 'Colour and Markings of Horses' (obtainable from the Royal College of Veterinary Surgeons, 32 Belgrave Square, London SW1). If the animal is not registered with a recognised Breed Society, Stud Book or Register, then unless the purchase price is less than £500, the buyer and a vet must sign Parts A, B and C to certify that the animal is the one described on the form. If the animal is registered, the signatures are not necessary. The buyer must then give the form a stock number in numerical sequence and complete the Purchase Record section on the reverse of Part A. The buyer must retain all parts of the form which will be needed on a subsequent sale.

(b) *Purchase of a horse or pony from someone selling under the scheme.* Similar rules apply as in (*a*) above but the seller must give the buyer Part C of the form to be kept with the partially completed form. The seller does not have to sign the declaration on the reverse of Part A. If the animal is unregistered and has a purchase price of more than £500, the Part C from the seller should have already been signed by a vet confirming the description. The details of the vet's name, practice, etc. can be copied by the buyer on to his form. There is no need for a vet to sign.

(c) *Sale of a horse or pony.* Check that the correct procedure was followed under (*a*) or (*b*) above on purchase. If not, the margin scheme cannot be used. If the correct procedure was followed, on sale the sales record sections on the reverse of Parts A, B and C must be completed. The seller then retains Parts A and B and gives Part C to the buyer.
The VAT record on the reverse of Part A must be completed.

(d) *Purchases at auction.* The normal rules for purchases under (*a*) or (*b*) above apply. If the animal is being sold under the margin scheme, the auctioneer will pass the seller's completed Part C to the buyer. The buyer must keep this with his own partially completed form. If the animal is being sold by a private person, the buyer must get the auctioneer to complete details of his name, address and Lot number on the reverse of Part A of his form.

(e) *Sales at auction.* The auctioneer must be told that the animal is being sold under the margin scheme and be given Parts B and C of the seller's form which must already be completed as regards his purchase. After the sale, the auctioneer must complete the sales details on the reverse of Parts B and C, adding his name and address. He then returns Part C to the buyer and Part B to the seller. The seller must then complete the sales and VAT record on the reverse of Part A.

(VAT Notice 718, paras 16.1–16.7).

Imported works of art, antiques and collectors' pieces and works of art obtained from the creators or their heirs

[62.38] A business which

(a) imports works of art, collectors' items or antiques within **74.3**(*a*)–(*c*) **WORKS OF ART, ETC.** or

(b) obtains works of art (by supply in the UK or acquisition from another EU member state) from the creators or their heirs,

may opt to use the margin scheme or the auctioneers' scheme (see **62.53** *et seq* below) whether or not VAT has been charged on the supply, acquisition or importation. Alternatively, VAT can be accounted for under the normal rules.

Conditions for opting

The conditions for using the margin scheme or the auctioneers' scheme are as follows.

- HMRC must be notified in writing that the option is to be taken up, specifying the date from which it will apply.
- The option must be exercised for a period of at least two years. Thereafter, it will continue to apply until HMRC are advised in writing as to when it is to cease.
- If the option is used, it must be applied to *all* transactions within (*a*) and (*b*) above, not just in respect of certain transactions or certain categories of goods.
- If, having exercised the option, the business subsequently decides to sell any goods covered by the option outside a scheme, it is not entitled to recover any input tax on those goods until the period in which VAT is accounted for on their sale. VAT must be accounted for on the full selling price at the standard rate (unless the goods are exported and qualify for zero-rating under the normal VAT rules for export).

If the option has been exercised,

- for imports within (*a*) it covers imports at the effective 5% rate (see **74.3 WORKS OF ART, ETC.**). Under the margin scheme, the purchase price to be entered in the records is the value for VAT at import, plus the import

VAT. For the auctioneers' scheme, the purchase price is calculated according to the normal rules for that scheme. Under both schemes, VAT is calculated on the margin at 20% and the import VAT cannot be reclaimed as input tax; and

- for works of art obtained under (*b*) above, any VAT charged when the items are obtained cannot be reclaimed as input tax. The purchase price to be entered in the records is the total price paid inclusive of any VAT. For acquisitions, acquisition VAT should be accounted for in Box 2 of the VAT return. The corresponding amount should not be recovered in Box 4 but added to the net purchase price for margin scheme purposes. Under the auctioneers' scheme, the purchase price is calculated according to the normal rules for that scheme. If the vendor is VAT-registered, this amount will also be their VAT-inclusive selling price. As the vendor cannot use the margin scheme, any self-billed invoice issued to the vendor must show VAT separately.

Global accounting scheme

A business opting to use the margin scheme may also use the global accounting scheme subject to the normal rules of that scheme (see **62.39** *et seq* below). Eligible taxed goods must not be entered into the global accounting scheme until documentation is received which would have allowed input tax or import/acquisition VAT to be reclaimed if the option had not been used.

(VAT Notice 718, paras 10.1–10.2).

Global accounting scheme

[62.39] The global accounting scheme is a simplified variation of the normal margin scheme, particularly beneficial for accounting for VAT on low value, bulk volume, margin scheme goods where it may be impractical to keep detailed records required under the normal scheme. Dealers using the global accounting scheme account for VAT on the difference between the total purchases and total sales of eligible goods in each VAT period (rather than on an item by item basis). The scheme automatically allows for a loss on one transaction to be set against the profit from others.

The provisions of the scheme as set out in **62.40–62.52** below have the force of law.

De Voil Indirect Tax Service. See V3.535.

Eligible goods

[62.40] The global accounting scheme can be used for any of the eligible goods within **62.3** above other than

(a) motor vehicles including motor-cycles (except those broken up for scrap, see below);

(b) aircraft;

(c) boats and outboard motors;
(d) caravans and motor caravans;
(e) horses and ponies.

[*SI 1995/1268, Art 13*].

Dealers in goods within (*a*)–(*e*) above are able to keep records on an item by item basis and can therefore use the normal margin scheme of accounting. (In any case, the cost of the majority of such goods purchased are likely to exceed £500 and would therefore be excluded from the global accounting scheme, see **62.41** below.)

Sales of scrap

Motor vehicles cannot normally be sold under the global accounting scheme. However, provided the vehicle is otherwise eligible for the margin scheme, it may be included in the global accounting scheme when broken up and sold as scrap. The normal commercial documents must be kept to show that the vehicle no longer exists in order to demonstrate that it is eligible for global accounting.

Where a motor vehicle has already been entered into a stock book under the margin scheme, the entry should be closed and the details transferred to the global accounting scheme purchase records.

If a dealer purchases a scrap motor vehicle for more than £500, he can still use the global accounting scheme for disposal of the components. But any individual component valued at over £500 must be excluded from the scheme.

(VAT Notice 718, para 14.9).

Conditions for using the scheme

[62.41] A person who is registered for VAT may use the scheme provided the following conditions are met.

(a) The goods were not purchased on an invoice on which VAT was shown separately.
(b) Every individual item for which the scheme is used must have been obtained for a price of £500 or less. See **62.24** above for the calculation of price. See **62.44** below for bulk purchases and collections.
(c) The goods are not sold on a VAT invoice or similar document showing an amount as being VAT or as being attributable to VAT.
(d) Such records and accounts are kept as specified by HMRC.

[*SI 1995/1268, Art 13*]. (VAT Notice 718, para 14.4).

Imported works of art, etc.

See **62.38** above for circumstances where imported works of art and works of art obtained from their creators or heirs can be included in the scheme despite the fact that VAT has been charged on their supply, acquisition or importation. These provisions apply also to the global accounting scheme.

Reclaiming VAT on expenses

[62.42] Subject to the normal rules, a taxable person may reclaim any VAT he is charged on business overheads, restoration, repairs, spares, etc. but must not add these costs to the purchase price of the goods for the purposes of the scheme. (VAT Notice 718, para 15.10 which has the force of law).

Purchases

Private person or unregistered dealer not providing invoice

[62.43] On a purchase from a private person or an unregistered dealer who does not provide an invoice, the buyer must check that the goods are eligible for the global accounting scheme and, if so, make out a purchase invoice showing

- purchaser's name and address;
- seller's name and address;
- invoice number;
- date of transaction;
- description of the goods sufficient to enable HMRC to verify that the goods are eligible for the global accounting scheme (e.g. 'four tables and ten chairs' is acceptable but 'assorted goods' is not);
- total price (VAT must not be shown separately).

Unregistered dealer providing invoice

On purchase from an unregistered dealer who provides an invoice, the buyer must ensure that the invoice contains all the necessary details as above.

VAT-registered dealer

On purchase from a VAT-registered dealer, that dealer should make out the invoice with details as above and the following statement:

'Global Accounting Invoice'

Purchase record summary

Details of the purchase must be entered in the purchase record or summary (see **62.49** below).

(VAT Notice 718, paras 15.2, 15.3 which have the force of law).

Invoices in foreign currency

If an invoice is in a foreign currency, it must be converted into sterling using one of the methods in **72.18 VALUATION** or, in the case of acquisitions from another EU member state, **72.14 VALUATION**. Where an invoice includes individual items with a purchase price over £500 which are not eligible for the global accounting scheme, the foreign currency value must be converted into sterling and then apportioned to exclude these items. The remaining purchase amount in sterling must be entered in the purchase records. (VAT Notice 718, para 15.11 which has the force of law).

Bulk purchases and collections

Bulk purchases

[62.44] The scheme may be used for bulk purchases with a combined price in excess of £500 but if any individual item included has a purchase price of more than £500, it must be deducted from the total purchase price and excluded from the scheme. There is no set way to apportion total price between individual items but HMRC must be satisfied that it is fair and reasonable. Any item costing over £500 can then be sold under either the margin scheme (if eligible) or the normal VAT rules.

Collections

Collections (e.g. of stamps) purchased can be split and sold separately or formed into other collections for sale provided all items are eligible for the global accounting scheme. Two or more items purchased separately can also be combined to produce one item for resale (e.g. by using one item as a spare part for another).

But if an eligible item is purchased for £500 or more, and the item is made up of several components valued at less than £500, the global accounting scheme cannot be used if the item is sold in the same state as it was purchased.

> *Example*
>
> A tea set, including many pieces each valued at less than £500, is purchased for £750.
>
> If the item is bought and sold as a 'tea set', there is only one item and the global accounting scheme cannot be used.

(VAT Notice 718, para 14.10).

Sales

[62.45] On the sale of eligible goods, the dealer must check that the rules in **62.43** above where applied on purchase.

Sales to other dealers

For sales to other dealers, a dealer must issue (and keep a copy of) a sales invoice showing

- seller's name and address and VAT registration number;
- buyer's name and address;
- invoice number;
- date of sale;
- description of the goods sufficient to enable HMRC to verify that the goods are eligible for the global accounting scheme (e.g. 'four tables and ten chairs' is acceptable but 'assorted goods' is not);
- total price including VAT (but which must not be shown separately); and

- an endorsement stating 'Global accounting invoice'.

If a dealer sells an item for more than £500 but does not wish to disclose to the purchaser that he bought it under the global accounting scheme, instead of the endorsement above he may choose to use one of the following statements on the sales invoice:

- Margin Scheme – second-hand goods;
- Margin Scheme – works of art; or
- Margin Scheme – collectors' items and antiques.

Other sales

All other sales should be recorded in the normal way (e.g. by using a cash register).

Details of the daily gross takings and/or totals of copy invoices must be entered in the sales record or summary (see **62.49** below). It is therefore essential to be able to distinguish between sales under the global accounting scheme and other types of transactions at the point of sale.

(VAT Notice 718, paras 15.4, 15.5 which have the force of law).

Invoices in foreign currency

If a global accounting scheme invoice is issued in a foreign currency, it must also show the sterling equivalent of the total value of the goods. Even if more than one item is sold on the invoice, only the total foreign currency and sterling price needs to be shown and the sterling amount should be entered in the sales records. The foreign currency value must be converted into sterling using one of the methods in **72.18 VALUATION**. (VAT Notice 718, para 15.11 which has the force of law).

Transactions with overseas persons

[62.46] The same provisions apply as for the margin scheme provided the goods in question are also eligible for the global accounting scheme.

- **Acquisitions from other EU member states.** See **62.7** above ignoring the reference to motor cars.
- **Imports from outside the EU.** See **62.8** above ignoring the references to motor cars.
- **Sales to other EU member states.** See **62.12** above.
- **Exports outside the EU.** See **62.13** above ignoring the references to motor cars and boats.

Records and accounts

[62.47] Global accounting scheme records do not have to be kept in any set way but must be complete, up-to-date and clearly distinguishable from any other records. Records must be kept of purchases and sales (see **62.49** below) and workings used to calculate the VAT due. All scheme records must be preserved for six years.

The global accounting scheme records are in addition to those generally required of all taxable persons. See **57 RECORDS**.

Failure to comply with any of the requirements as to records renders the taxable person liable for VAT on the full value of his sales.

(VAT Notice 718, paras 14, 15.1).

Stock

Stock on hand when starting global accounting scheme

[62.48] Any such eligible stock can be treated in either of the following ways.

- Taken into the scheme and included in the calculations for the first accounting period. Some form of stock take or valuation will be required. Where possible, stock should be identified separately and its purchase price established from invoices. Where stock cannot be related to original purchase invoices, the purchase value must be determined in some other way. There is no set way of doing this but HMRC must be satisfied that the method used is fair and reasonable. Any documents used to establish the stock valuation must be kept for six years.
- Not taken into the scheme. If the goods are then sold under the global accounting scheme, there is no 'purchase credit' to set against the sale and VAT will be accounted for on the full selling price rather than the profit margin.

Stock already included under margin scheme

Eligible stock already included in stock records under the margin scheme can either be sold under the margin scheme or transferred to the global accounting scheme. In the latter case, the stock must be deleted from the margin scheme stock book and cross-referred to and included in the global accounting scheme records.

(VAT Notice 718, paras 14.6, 14.7).

Purchases and sales summaries

[62.49] Summary records must be kept of purchases and sales for each accounting period. These do not have to be kept in any particular way but they must include the following details taken from any purchases invoices and any sales invoices issued.

- Invoice number.
- Date of purchase/sale.
- Description of goods sufficient to enable HMRC to verify that the goods are eligible for the global accounting scheme.
- Total price.

At the end of the VAT period, the totals of purchases and sales are used to calculate the VAT due.

(VAT Notice 718, para 15.6 which has the force of law).

Calculation of VAT due

[62.50] VAT is chargeable on the 'total profit margin' on goods supplied during a VAT period. '*Total profit margin*' is the amount (if any) by which the total sales exceed total purchases in the VAT period. See **62.24**(*a*) and (*b*) above for the rules for determining the price at which goods are purchased and sold.

The excess is the VAT-inclusive margin i.e. the VAT included is

VAT-inclusive margin × VAT fraction 1/6

Negative margin

If there is a negative margin (because total purchases exceed total sales), no VAT is due and the negative margin is carried forward to the following VAT period for inclusion in the calculation of the total purchases of that period. A negative margin cannot be set off against other VAT due in the same VAT period on transactions outside the global accounting scheme.

Copies of all calculations must be kept as part of the records.

[*SI 1995/1268, Art 13*]. (VAT Notice 718, para 14.8).

> *Example*
>
> A dealer starts to use the global accounting scheme and values his opening stock on hand at £10,000. In the first VAT period, his total purchases from his purchase summary are £2,000 and his sales from his sales summary are £8,000.
>
> The margin for the first VAT period is £8,000 – (£10,000 + £2,000) = (£4,000)
>
> There is a negative margin and no VAT is due. The negative margin is carried forward to the next period in which purchases are £1,000 and sales are £7,000.
>
> The margin for the second VAT period is £7,000 – (£4,000 + £1,000) = £2,000
>
> VAT due = £2,000 × 1/6 = £333.33

If any of the goods sold in the period were obtained following the transfer of a business as a going concern, see **62.24** above.

Adjustments

Removing goods from the scheme

[62.51] Where purchases are initially included in the global accounting scheme purchase records but it is subsequently decided to sell the goods outside the scheme (e.g. because they are zero-rated on sale for export outside the EU) or the goods cease to be eligible the scheme records must be adjusted. In the period in which the goods are removed from the scheme, the purchase value of those goods must be deducted from the global accounting scheme purchase records. There is no set way to apportion values to individual items but it must be fair and reasonable and it must be possible to demonstrate to HMRC how the value was determined.

Goods stolen or destroyed

Any loss of goods by breakage, theft or destruction must be adjusted by the deduction of their purchase price in the global accounting scheme purchase records.

Ceasing to use the global accounting scheme

If a dealer ceases to use the global accounting scheme for any reason, he must make an adjustment to take account of purchases for which he has taken credit but which have not been sold under the scheme.

- If deregistering, in the final period of using the scheme, the dealer must add the purchase value of his closing stock to his sales figure for that period.
- If transferring goods as part of a transfer of a going concern (TOGC), the dealer should add the purchase value of goods included in the scheme to sales figure for the period in which the TOGC takes place. This adjustment is separate from the actual TOGC which is not subject to VAT.

In either case, no adjustment is required if the total VAT due on stock on hand is £1,000 or less.

(VAT Notice 718, paras 15.7–15.9 which have the force of law).

Completion of VAT return

[62.52] See **2.7** *et seq* **ACCOUNTING PERIODS AND RETURNS** for general notes on the completion of the VAT return. The following special rules apply to eligible goods bought and sold under the global accounting scheme.

Box 1	Where there is a positive margin, include the output tax calculated by reference to the difference between total purchases and total sales of eligible goods in the period covered by the return.
Box 6	Include the full selling price of all eligible goods sold under the scheme during the period, less any VAT included in that price.
Box 7	Include the purchase price (inclusive of VAT) of eligible goods bought in the period.

Any negative margins should not be included on the VAT return.

The auctioneers' scheme

[62.53] If an auctioneer sells eligible goods (see **62.3** above) and invoices in his own name he may either

- account for VAT under the auctioneers' scheme; or
- apply the rules for invoicing as an agent (see **62.26** above).

The auctioneers' scheme is a variation of the margin scheme. It allows auctioneers to account for VAT on a margin, the calculation of which involves

- adding to the hammer price the cost of the auctioneer's services charged to the buyer; and
- deducting from the hammer price the cost of the auctioneer's services charged to the seller.

The detailed provisions of the scheme are set out in **62.54** to **62.61** below and have the force of law. It is therefore important to check with the seller before the sale whether the goods are eligible for inclusion in the auctioneers' scheme.

The auctioneers' scheme and its conditions are for the purposes of calculating VAT liability and do not affect the legal status of agents or the contractual relationships between auctioneers, vendors and buyers.

(VAT Notice 718/2, paras 2.1, 2.3).

Tax point

Where goods are treated as supplied both to and by the auctioneer, there is a common tax point for both supplies which will normally be the earlier of

- the handing over of the goods by the auctioneer to the buyer; or
- the receipt of payment by the auctioneer.

Sales under the auctioneers' scheme to other EU member states

These are treated in the same way as sales within the UK. The sales are liable to VAT in the UK and no further VAT is due in the country of destination.

(VAT Notice 718/2, paras 3.3, 3.5).

De Voil Indirect Tax Service. See V3.533.

Conditions of the scheme

[62.54] The auctioneer's scheme can be used for sales of the following goods.

(a) Eligible goods (see **62.3** above) provided the following conditions are met.

(i) The seller is
- not registered for VAT;
- a VAT-registered person supplying goods under the margin scheme (see **62.2** to **62.38** above) or the global accounting scheme (see **62.39** to **62.52** above);
- an insurance company selling eligible goods which they have acquired as a result of an insurance claim provided that the goods are sold at auction in the same state; or
- a finance company selling eligible goods which they have repossessed provided that they are sold at auction in the same state.

(VAT Notice 718/2, para 2.4).

(ii) The auctioneer complies with the invoicing requirements in **62.57** below. It is not necessary to maintain a stock book in strict accordance with the margin scheme if sufficient alternative records are retained to provide the same information (e.g. entry forms, sales catalogues, copies of lots and sales of the day and copies of sales and purchases invoices).

(VAT Notice 718/2, para 4.2 which has the force of law).

(b) By extra-statutory concession, all goods grown, made or produced (including bloodstock or livestock reared from birth) by unregistered (non-taxable) persons.

As a condition of the relief, the auctioneer must obtain a signed certificate from the vendor including the vendor's full name and address, a description of the goods and the date of sale, a declaration that the vendor is not registered nor required to be registered for VAT, the signature of vendor and date, and the signature of auctioneer and date. The completed certificate must be retained with the relevant records for VAT purposes. An example of an acceptable certificate is set out below.

AUCTIONEERS' SCHEME FOR SECOND-HAND GOODS, WORKS OF ART, ANTIQUES AND COLLECTORS' ITEMS

Extra-statutory Concession 3.27

Vendor's Certificate for goods grown, made or produced and sold at auction on behalf of non-taxable persons

I (full name)

of (address)

declare that I am not registered or required to be registered for VAT and that the goods detailed below are to be sold at auction on my behalf by (auctioneer's name)

(Description of goods)

Date of sale (to be completed by auctioneer)

Signature of vendor

Signature of auctioneer

Date

The auctioneer may, with the agreement of HMRC, incorporate the certificate into his existing sales entry.

(VAT Notice 48, ESC 3.27; VAT Notice 718/2, paras 5.1, 5.3).

Charges to be included/excluded under the scheme

[62.55] Any commission or other charges made by the auctioneer to the vendor or buyer which are dependent on the sale of the goods must be included in the auctioneers' scheme calculation as set out in **62.59** below. Treatment of other charges are as follows.

- **Incidental expenses.** Any incidental expenses (e.g. packing, transport and insurance) incurred and charged onward to the buyer must be included in the scheme calculations unless they are a separate supply in their own right.
- **Disbursements for VAT purposes.** Any costs passed on to the client which meet all the conditions regarding disbursements under **3.7 AGENTS** can be excluded from the auctioneers' scheme.
- **Exempt supplies.** Any services supplied to the buyer or vendor which are exempt (e.g. making arrangements for the provision of insurance by a permitted insurer provided the disclosure requirements are complied with, see **37.13 INSURANCE**) should be excluded from the scheme calculations.
- **Services to an overseas vendor.** See **66.12** to **66.27 SUPPLY: PLACE OF SUPPLY** for the rules relating to the place of supply of services. Where the place of supply is in the UK, any services to an overseas vendor must be included in the auctioneers' scheme calculations. Where, however, the supply is treated as taking place outside the UK (e.g. supplies of

certain services where the recipient belongs outside the EU or is in business in another EU member state) the supply is outside the scope of UK VAT and should be excluded from the auctioneers' scheme calculations.

- **Other charges.** Charges for other supplies which are optional and not directly related to the hammer price should be excluded from the auctioneers' scheme calculations.

(VAT Notice 718/2, para 3.2).

Zero-rated sales

[62.56] Where the auctioneers' scheme is used for the sale of zero-rated goods (e.g. exports), the auctioneers' margin is also zero-rated. Any charges made outside the scheme are liable to VAT in the normal way. The normal conditions for zero-rating apply. See **22.2 EXPORTS**. (VAT Notice 718/2, paras 3.4, 3.6, 7.8).

Invoicing

[62.57] Auctioneers using the scheme must not itemise VAT separately on any statement or invoice issued to the vendor or buyer except where goods or services are provided in addition to, but separately from, the purchase or sale. Such non-scheme items should be invoiced under the normal VAT rules.

Purchase invoices

The auctioneer should issue to the seller of the goods an invoice or statement showing the following:

- seller's name and address;
- auctioneer's name and address;
- invoice number;
- date of transaction;
- a description of the item;
- the hammer price of the goods;
- any commission charges to the seller; and
- the net amount due to the seller.

The net amount due to the seller is the auctioneer's purchase price. If the seller is a VAT-registered dealer using the margin scheme, the net amount due is also his selling price. The auctioneer should therefore allocate any charges included under the auctioneers' scheme against each lot.

Sales invoices

The auctioneer should issue to the buyer of the goods an invoice or statement showing the following:

- auctioneer's name, address and VAT registration number;
- buyer's name and address;
- stock book number;

- invoice number;
- transaction date;
- description of the item;
- the hammer price of the goods;
- any other charges for services made (e.g. buyer's premium); and
- the amount due from the buyer.

The amount due from the buyer is the auctioneer's selling price. If the buyer is a VAT-registered dealer using the margin scheme, the amount due is also his buying price. The auctioneer should therefore allocate any charges included under the auctioneers' scheme against each lot.

(VAT Notice 718/2, para 4.3 which has the force of law).

Invoices in foreign currency

Invoices issued in foreign currency under the auctioneers' scheme must show the sterling equivalent of each element of the invoice (e.g. hammer price of the goods and the amount of commission or other charges due) and not just the total value of supplies made. The foreign currency value must be converted into sterling using one of the methods in **72.18 VALUATION**.

Scheme and non-scheme supplies

If both scheme and non-scheme supplies are made to the same customer, either separate invoices can be issued (advisable) or all supplies can be included on the same invoice. In the latter case, the invoice must clearly distinguish between the two types of supply and comply with all the relevant provisions for both. In the case of a sales invoice, it must also show clearly the amount of the selling price which will form the basis of the purchase price for the buyer's margin scheme or global accounting scheme records.

Re-invoicing

If goods have been sold under the auctioneers' scheme but the buyer subsequently decides that he wishes to treat the transaction outside the scheme (paying VAT separately on the hammer price and the other charges), the auctioneer may re-invoice for the transaction under the normal VAT rules provided

(a) the auctioneer can comply with all the relevant VAT regulations of the substitute transaction;
(b) at the time of the amendment, the auctioneer and buyer hold all the original evidence relating to the transaction;
(c) the auctioneer cancels the first entry in his records and cross-refers to the amended transaction; and
(d) any substitute document (e.g. a VAT invoice) issued to the buyer clearly refers to the original transaction and states that it is cancelled and that the buyer should amend his VAT records accordingly.

Re-invoicing cannot be undertaken more than four years after the due date of the VAT return on which the original supply was accounted for. This is because input tax cannot be claimed under the four-year cap rules.

(VAT Notice 718/2, paras 4.4–4.6).

Imported works of art, antiques and collectors' pieces and works of art obtained from the creators or their heirs

[62.58] Goods which have been obtained with VAT charged on their full value are normally ineligible for the auctioneers' scheme. However, auctioneers acting in their own names may opt to use the auctioneers' scheme to deal with

(a) works of art, antiques and collectors' pieces which they have imported themselves (as principals on behalf of a third party) for onward sale in their own names; and
(b) works of art obtained (i.e. supplied in the UK or acquired from another EU member state) from creators or their heirs for onward sale in their own names.

In either case, the auctioneers' scheme may be used despite VAT having already been charged on the importation, acquisition or supply of the goods. The conditions for exercising the option are as follows.

- HMRC must be notified in writing that the option is to be taken up, specifying the date from which it will apply.
- The option must be exercised for a period of at least two years. Thereafter it will continue to apply until HMRC are advised in writing as to when it will cease.
- If the option is used, it must be applied to all transactions within (*a*) and (*b*) above, not just in respect of certain transactions or certain categories of goods.
- If, having exercised the option, the auctioneer decides to sell outside the scheme any goods covered by the option (e.g. he exports the goods), he is not entitled to recover any input tax on those goods until the period in which VAT is accounted for on their sale.

If the option is not used, VAT must be accounted for in accordance with the general rules for auctioneers.

Purchase price

If the option to use the auctioneers' scheme has been exercised, the purchase price is calculated as follows.

(i) *Imported works of art, antiques and collectors' items*. The option applies to imports at a reduced rate of 5%. The auctioneer must not reclaim the import VAT as input tax. His purchase price for the auctioneers' scheme is the hammer price less any commission charges made to the seller. The import VAT incurred must not be included in the auctioneers' scheme calculations although the auctioneer may wish to recoup this amount separately from the seller.
(ii) *Works of art obtained from the creator or his heirs*. The auctioneer must not reclaim any VAT charged by the supplier and must calculate his purchase price in accordance with **62.59** below. Because the creator or heir will have to account for output tax on the full hammer price they

may ask the auctioneer to sell the item under the normal margin scheme option. In such cases, any invoice issued for charges for services must show VAT at the standard rate separately. This will enable the supplier to reclaim the input tax on those charges. The auctioneer's purchase price under the normal margin scheme option is the hammer price only.

Buyer's premium

Works of art, antiques and collectors' items are often entered to a Temporary Importation (TI) regime in order to be sold at auction. Following the sale, the goods are then either exported from the EU or finally imported.

If imported, the goods qualify for the 5% reduced rate of import VAT which must be accounted for on the appropriate customs import declaration. But the commission charged by the auctioneer, known as the buyer's premium, does not qualify for the 5% reduced rate. VAT must be accounted for on the buyer's premium at the standard rate.

If the goods are exported from TI to a place outside the EU, VAT is chargeable on the buyer's premium at the zero rate.

(VAT Notice 718, paras 10.1–10.2).

Calculation of VAT

[62.59] The purchase price, selling price, margin and VAT due are calculated from the successful bid price (hammer price) and commission and other charges.

'*Purchase price*' is the hammer price less commission payable to the auctioneer under his contract with the seller for the sale of the goods (see **62.55** above).

'*Selling price*' is the hammer price plus the consideration for any supply of services by the auctioneer to the purchaser (e.g. buyer's premium) in connection with the sale of the goods (see **62.55** above).

The margin is the difference between the purchase price and the selling price. The margin is regarded as being VAT-inclusive i.e. the VAT included is

VAT-inclusive margin × VAT fraction 1/6

Example

Goods are sold at auction for £1,000 (the hammer price). Commission is charged to the seller at 10% net of VAT and a buyer's premium is charged of 15% net of VAT.

Commission = (£1,000 × 10%) + 20% VAT =	£120.00
Purchase price = £1,000 – £120.00 =	£880.00
Buyer's premium = (£1,000 × 15%) + 20% VAT =	£180.00
Selling price = £1,000 + £180.00 =	£1,180.00
Margin = £1,180.00 – £880.00 =	£300.00
Output tax = £300.00 × 1/6 =	£50.00

[*SI 1992/3122, Art 8(7); SI 1995/1268, Art 12(7)*]. (VAT Notice 718/2, paras 3.1, 8.3).

Dealers buying at auction

[62.60] Where a taxable dealer buys goods at an auction and wishes to use either the margin scheme or the global accounting scheme for the onward sale of the goods, he should

- check that the goods will be eligible for onward sale under the chosen scheme (usually clear from the auctioneer's sales catalogue). If VAT is charged separately on the hammer price, the goods will not qualify for either scheme; and
- follow the record-keeping requirements under the chosen scheme.

The dealer's purchase price is the hammer price of the goods plus charges for services (which must not show VAT separately) and should be clearly identified on the sales invoice issued by the auctioneer. The invoice should itemise, for each lot, the hammer price of the goods and any charges for services (for example, buyer's premium). The total of these amounts (i.e. the amount due from the dealer to the auctioneer) is the purchase price for the purpose of the margin scheme or global accounting scheme and is the amount that the dealer must show in his stock book. Any other charges for services on which VAT is shown separately must not be included as part of the purchase price.

In some cases a dealer may receive a single invoice from the auctioneer, showing the hammer price of the goods and charges for inclusion in the scheme calculations as well as charges on which VAT is shown separately. To avoid confusion, the dealer may wish to ask the auctioneer to provide him with a separate invoice for these charges. In either case, the dealer can reclaim the VAT shown under the normal rules but must make sure that he does not add the value of these charges to his purchase price for the purposes of the margin scheme.

(VAT Notice 718/2, paras 3.1, 3.2, 4.4).

Dealers selling at auction under the margin scheme or global accounting scheme

[62.61] A taxable dealer selling at auction must tell the auctioneer before the sale is due to take place exactly how he wishes to treat the sale, i.e. under the auctioneers' scheme, margin scheme or global accounting scheme. If the auctioneer uses the auctioneers' scheme he issues an invoice/statement which includes

- the hammer price of the goods;
- his commission charges; and
- the net amount payable to the dealer.

None of these amounts should show VAT separately. Any other charges for services should be invoiced separately with VAT, if applicable, shown on the full amount of each charge.

Alternatively, the dealer can ask the auctioneer to sell the goods under the normal margin scheme. In these circumstances, the auctioneer issues an invoice/statement which only includes the hammer price of the goods. VAT must not be shown separately on this amount. His commission charges and any other charges for his services must be invoiced separately with VAT, if applicable, shown on the full amount of each charge. The dealer can reclaim the VAT on such charges under the normal rules.

Selling price of eligible goods sold at auction

A dealer's selling price for the purpose of the margin scheme should be clearly identifiable on the invoice/statement issued by the auctioneer.

- If the auctioneer has supplied the goods under the auctioneers' scheme, the hammer price of the goods and commission charges will not show VAT separately. The dealer's selling price is the net amount, i.e. the hammer price less the commission charge. If the auctioneer makes other charges, these should be invoiced separately and, if applicable, VAT charged under the normal rules. The dealer must not include these charges as part of his selling price but will be able to reclaim the VAT charged, subject to the normal rules.
- If, in agreement with the auctioneer, the dealer arranges for the goods to be sold by the auctioneer under the normal margin scheme as it applies to agents, the dealer's selling price is the hammer price. Any other charges that the auctioneer makes should be invoiced or itemised separately and, if applicable, VAT charged under the normal rules.

(VAT Notice 718/2, paras 3.1, 3.2).

Key points: second-hand goods

[62.62] Points to consider are as follows.

- Margin schemes are very worthwhile for those businesses that deal in second-hand goods. However, it is important to ensure the record keeping requirements of HMRC are fully met, otherwise it could base output tax on the full selling price of an item rather than the profit margin. The record-keeping requirements have the force of law.
- An example of an important record-keeping requirement is that a full purchase invoice must be produced for items bought from members of the public.
- When a VAT-registered trader sells goods under the margin scheme, the sales invoice must be certified with the statement: 'this is a second hand margin scheme supply' (or similar wording).
- An important record with the margin scheme is the stock book maintained by the business, which should be accurate and complete. Items should be fully described, i.e. including any specific descriptions or registration numbers.

- Input tax can be claimed on expenditure incurred by a business improving or repairing a margin item (subject to normal rules). The cost of the repair should not be deducted against the margin on which output tax is due under the scheme.
- An item that is bought by a business and is eligible for use within a margin scheme can still be sold under normal VAT rules, i.e. output tax charged on full selling price. This could be a useful planning point if the customer can claim input tax.
- As far as VAT registration limits are concerned, the relevant taxable sales figure is the full selling price, not the profit margin. An exception to this statement relates to margin sales under TOMS (tour operators' margin scheme).
- A margin item sold to a customer outside the EU can be zero-rated as an export (or possibly retail export). It is important that export evidence is acquired and retained to confirm the goods have left the EU, i.e. shipping documents, insurance documents, commercial documents etc.
- There is no 'loss relief' with a margin scheme (apart from the global accounting scheme). This means that a loss made on one item cannot be offset against a profit made on another item.
- A business selling high quantities of small value items could benefit from using the global accounting scheme – the main benefits of which relate to the reduced record-keeping requirements (compared to the main margin scheme) and the automatic loss relief available on items sold at a loss.
- A business using global accounting can carry forward a loss made in one VAT period (where total purchases exceed total sales), so that the loss can be added to purchases in the next period, i.e. to reduce the profit margin in that period.

63

Self-Supply

Cross-references. See **43.2 LAND AND BUILDINGS: ZERO AND REDUCED RATE SUPPLIES AND DIY HOUSEBUILDERS** for change of use of residential and charitable buildings; **43.20 LAND AND BUILDINGS: ZERO AND REDUCED RATE SUPPLIES AND DIY HOUSEBUILDERS** for self-supply of certain construction services; **46.6 MOTOR CARS** for self-supply of motor cars; **67.14 SUPPLY: TIME OF SUPPLY** for the time of self-supply.

De Voil Indirect Tax Service. See V3.241.

Introduction to self-supply

[63.1] The Treasury may, by order, provide that where specified goods are taken possession of or produced by a person (not necessarily a *taxable* person) in the course or furtherance of a business carried on by him *and*

(a) are neither supplied to another person nor incorporated in other goods produced in the course or furtherance of that business; *but*
(b) are used by him for the purpose of a business carried on by him,

the goods are treated for VAT purposes as being both supplied to him for the purpose of that business and supplied by him in the course or furtherance of it. [*VATA 1994, s 5(5)(7)*].

Such a power is aimed to prevent an advantage being gained by a person who produces for himself goods on which, if supplied externally, either input tax would be specifically denied, or on which input tax would be denied or restricted because of exempt output supplies being made by the person concerned. Specific orders have been made as regards motor cars (see **46.6 MOTOR CARS**) and stationery (see **63.2** below).

Similar powers to the above as regards goods are also applied to services. [*VATA 1994, s 5(6)*]. See **43.20 LAND AND BUILDINGS: ZERO AND REDUCED RATE SUPPLIES AND DIY HOUSEBUILDERS** for self-supply of certain construction services.

Example

John owns a partly-exempt business, and uses his own employees to carry out alterations on his own trading premises. In the absence of the self-supply rules, he could avoid charging VAT on this supply. However, the self-supply rules treat this as a supply both to and by John and he must therefore:

- account for output tax on the value of the supply; and
- reclaim input tax on the value of the supply in accordance with his existing partial exemption method.

The outcome in the above example is a net payment of VAT by John (i.e. on the basis that the premises in question have some exempt use, and an input tax block therefore applies).

Key points: self-supply

[63.2] Points to consider are as follows.

- The purpose of the self-supply rules is to ensure that a partly-exempt business cannot obtain a VAT advantage by producing goods or self-supplying services for use in their business, which would otherwise have carried irrecoverable input VAT.
- A business that is not partly-exempt may still face a VAT bill with the self-supply rules if the goods or services in question are non-deductible for input tax purposes, e.g. in relation to a motor car available for private use.

64

Special Schemes

Introduction to special schemes

[64.1] The following special schemes are available to VAT-registered businesses.

- **Flat-rate scheme for small businesses.** Subject to conditions, including an annual turnover limit, small businesses can opt to join a flat-rate scheme under which they calculate net VAT due by applying a flat-rate percentage to VAT-inclusive turnover. The flat-rate percentage varies with the trade sector into which the business falls. See **64.15** to **64.24** below.
- **Cash accounting scheme.** Subject to conditions, including an annual turnover limit, this scheme can be used by any business. See **64.2** to **64.8** below.
- **Annual accounting scheme.** Subject to meeting certain conditions, including an annual turnover limit, a business can apply to HMRC to prepare an annual VAT return and make payments on account during the year. See **64.9** to **64.14** below.
- **Retail schemes.** There are a number of different retail schemes designed to suit different types of retail business. See **61 RETAIL SCHEMES.**
- **Second-hand schemes.** In general, VAT is charged on the full value of any goods, including second-hand goods, sold by a business. However, provided certain conditions are met, VAT can be charged on the profit margin (instead of value) on supplies of second-hand goods; works of art, antiques and collectors' items; and goods sold through an agent acting in his own name in relation to the supply. See **62 SECOND-HAND GOODS** for details.
- **Tour operators' margin scheme.** All UK businesses that buy travel, hotel and holiday services, etc. from third parties and resell these supplies as principals *must* use a special scheme under which VAT has to be accounted for on the difference between the VAT-inclusive purchase price and selling price. See **69 TOUR OPERATORS' MARGIN SCHEME.**
- **Flat-rate scheme for farmers.** A flat-rate scheme is available to farmers as an option to registering for VAT. Once in the scheme, VAT is not accounted for on sales of goods and services within certain designated activities and input tax is not recoverable on purchases. To compensate for this the farmer charges, and retains, a fixed flat-rate addition on sales, within those activities, to VAT-registered persons. See **64.25** to **64.30** below.

- **Racehorse owners.** A special arrangement has been made between HMRC and the thoroughbred horseracing and breeding industry. See **64.31** to **64.33** below.
- **Union VAT Mini One Stop Shop (Union VAT MOSS) scheme.** From 1 January 2015 supplies of broadcasting, telecommunication and electronic (BTE) services are subject to VAT where the customer belongs, regardless of the status of the customer. The Union VAT MOSS scheme provides eligible UK VAT-registered businesses with an alternative to registering for VAT in all of the EU member states where they have consumer customers. See **64.41** to **64.45** below.

Cash accounting scheme

[64.2] A business may, subject to conditions, account for and pay VAT on the basis of cash or other consideration paid and received. The conditions are as laid down in *Regulations* and as described in VAT Notice 731 *which in certain circumstances has the force of law* (see VAT Notice 747). HMRC may vary the terms of the scheme by publishing a fresh Notice or a Notice which amends an existing Notice, but without prejudicing the right of a person to withdraw from the scheme. [*VATA 1994, s 25(1), Sch 11 para 2(7); SI 1995/2518, Regs 57, 59*].

The main advantage of the scheme is the deferral of the time for payment of VAT where extended credit is given. It also becomes unnecessary to make a claim for relief on bad debts, because output tax will not have been accounted for on any consideration that is not received. The scheme will probably not be beneficial for net repayment businesses or where most sales are paid promptly or for cash. (VAT Notice 731, para 1.4).

The cash accounting scheme cannot be used at the same time as the flat-rate scheme for small businesses, which has its own cash-based accounting rule (see **64.15** below). [*SI 1995/2518, Reg 57A*].

De Voil Indirect Tax Service. See V2.199.

Joining the scheme

[64.3] A business is eligible to start using the scheme if it meets the following conditions:

- it expects the value of its taxable supplies in the next year will be £1,350,000 or less;
- it has no VAT returns outstanding;
- it has not been convicted of a VAT offence in the last year;
- it has not accepted an offer to compound proceedings in connection with a VAT offence in the last year;
- it has not been assessed to a penalty for VAT evasion involving dishonest conduct in the last year;
- it does not owe HMRC any money or if it does, it has made arrangements with them to clear the total amount of outstanding VAT payments (including surcharges and/or penalties);

- HMRC have not written to it withdrawing use of the scheme during the last year;
- HMRC have not written to it and denied it access to the scheme; and
- it complies with the conditions set out in Notice 731.

A business cannot begin to operate the scheme if HMRC consider that, for the protection of the revenue, it should not be able to do so. In such circumstances, the business may ask HMRC to reconsider the decision if it can provide further relevant information or if there are facts which it thinks have not been taken fully into account. If still not satisfied, an appeal may be made to a VAT tribunal. See **5 APPEALS.**

The scheme cannot be applied retrospectively to the business.

[*SI 1995/2518, Reg 58(1)(4)*]. (VAT Notice 731, para 2.1).

VAT group treatment

The turnover limit for the cash accounting scheme applies to the VAT group as a whole. Also, HMRC do not allow one or more companies in a VAT group to operate cash accounting while other members use the normal invoice-based requirements. The following action is therefore required when a new member enters a VAT group.

- The new member must deregister (whether or not using the cash accounting scheme).
- If the existing group is not using the cash accounting scheme but the new member is, the new member must return to the normal method of accounting and account for outstanding VAT whilst using the scheme on its final VAT return.
- If the existing group is using the cash accounting scheme, and the turnover of the enlarged group remains within the tolerance for use of the scheme in **64.7** below, the new member must use the cash accounting scheme from the date of joining the group. (If the new member makes or receives payments, after joining the group, for sales or purchases made whilst separately registered, the associated VAT must be accounted for on its final return and should be excluded from the group's VAT account.)
- If the existing group is using the cash accounting scheme, but the new member pushes the group turnover over the scheme limits, the whole group must leave the scheme at the end of the VAT period in which the new member joins the group.

Supplies to be dealt with inside and outside the scheme

[64.4] Subject to the following exceptions, where the cash accounting scheme is used, it must be used for the whole of the VAT registered business.

Exceptions

The following transactions must be dealt with outside the cash accounting scheme under the normal VAT rules.

- Goods bought or sold under hire purchase, lease purchase, conditional sale or credit sale agreements.
- Goods imported from outside the EU, acquired from another EU member state, or removed from a Customs warehouse. The scheme can be used to account for VAT on the onward supply of these goods in the UK.
- Supplies where a VAT invoice is issued and full payment of the amount shown on the invoice is not due within six months from the date of issue of the invoice.
- Supplies in respect of which a VAT invoice is issued in advance of the delivery or making available of the goods or the performance of the services, as the case may be. This does not apply where goods have been delivered or made available in part (or, as the case may be, services have been performed in part) and the VAT invoice in question relates solely to that part.
- Reverse charge supplies of mobile phones or computer chips under which the recipient has to account for and pay the VAT. See **4.15 ANTI-AVOIDANCE.**

[*SI 1995/2518, Regs 58(2)(3)*]. (VAT Notice 731, paras 2.7, 5.5 which have the force of law).

Records

[64.5] The normal requirements regarding copies of VAT invoices and evidence of input tax apply. The following additional records must also be kept.

(a) **Receipted invoices.**
- If payment is made in money (i.e. banknotes or coin) to another VAT-registered business, the copy of the purchase invoice must be receipted and dated (the other business *must* on request provide such an invoice). [*SI 1995/2518, Reg 65(3)*].
- If payment is received in money (i.e. banknotes or coin), a receipted and dated VAT invoice must be issued, if requested, and a copy retained for six years or such lesser period as HMRC allow. [*SI 1995/2518, Reg 65(3)*]. (VAT Notice 731, para 4.2).

(b) **Payment record.** To use the cash accounting scheme, payments made/received must be clearly cross-referenced to the corresponding purchase/sales invoice and to normal commercial evidence such as bank statements, cheque stubs, paying-in slips. This can be done by keeping a cash book summarising all payments made and received with a separate column for VAT. (VAT Notice 731, para 4.3 which has the force of law).

See also **64.6** below for records required for specific transactions.

Accounting for VAT

Output tax

[64.6] Output tax must be accounted for in the return for the VAT period in which payment or other consideration is received. [*SI 1995/2518, Regs 57, 65*]. For this purpose payment by

- *cash* (i.e. coins and notes) is received on the date the money is received;
- *cheque* is received on the date the cheque is received or, if later, the date on the cheque. If the cheque is not honoured, no VAT is due and an adjustment or a refund claim can be made if VAT has already been accounted for;
- *credit or debit card* is received on the date the sales voucher is made out (*not* the date when payment is received from the card company). If the payment is not honoured, no VAT is due and an adjustment or a refund claim can be made if VAT has already been accounted for; and
- *giros, standing orders and direct debits* are received on the day the bank account is credited.

Where an existing VAT-registered business starts to use the scheme, it should separate in its records any payments received for transactions already accounted for under the normal method of accounting. Such payments should be excluded from the scheme records.

(VAT Notice 731, paras 3.1, 4.4 which have the force of law).

Deposits

VAT on deposits must normally be accounted for when received unless the deposit is not payment for supplies (eg deposits taken as security which are either returned or forfeited) in which case there is no requirement to account for VAT. (VAT Notice 731, para 5.1).

Payments received net of deductions

Where a net payment is received after deduction of commission/expenses, VAT should be accounted for on the full value before such deduction. Examples include

- commission deducted by a customer;
- commission or payment for expenses deducted by a factor or agent collecting monies on behalf of the business;
- commission or payment for expenses deducted by an auctioneer selling goods on behalf of the business; and
- deductions made by an employer/contractor who has deducted income tax.

(VAT Notice 731, para 5.8 which has the force of law).

Payments received in foreign currency

Where a business issues an invoice in a foreign currency (including euros), it must also show the amount of VAT due in sterling. Therefore

- if the invoice is paid in full in the foreign currency, there is no need to convert the foreign currency payment and output tax is the sterling amount of VAT due as shown on the invoice; and
- if the invoice is paid in part in the foreign currency, output tax should be determined by calculating the proportion of the total amount due in the foreign currency which has been paid and applying that proportion to the sterling amount of VAT due as shown on the invoice.

Where a business issues an invoice in sterling but is paid in a foreign currency,

- if the invoice is paid in full, the output tax is the amount of VAT due as shown on the invoice; and
- if the invoice is paid in part, the foreign currency payment must be converted into sterling at the rate appropriate at the time of supply (not the time of payment). Output tax should then be determined by calculating the proportion of the total sterling amount due that the sterling equivalent of the payment represents and applying that proportion to the VAT due as shown on the invoice. See **72.18 VALUATION** for methods of converting foreign exchange.

(VAT Notice 731, paras 5.10, 5.11).

Factored debts

Where debts are sold or formally assigned to a factor, output tax must be accounted for on the amount that the factor collects from the customer (not any reduced value for which they are assigned) in the period in which the factor collects payment from the customer. For recourse agreements, if the factor is unable to collect all (or part) of the debt, then that amount must be accounted for under the normal rules. For non-recourse agreements, output tax must be accounted for on the uncollected element of the debt in the period in which any advance made against that debt is written off by the factor. However, if the factor re-assigns all or part of the debt back to the business under a recourse clause, it may claim **8 BAD DEBT RELIEF** on any unpaid element subject to the normal bad debt rules.

Where a business merely uses a factor or invoice discounter as a debt collector and retains legal title to the debt, it must account for output tax in the VAT period in which the customer pays the debt collector. VAT is due on the amount received by the debt collector from the customer (not any lesser amount after commission, etc. received by the business).

(VAT Notice 731, paras 5.2, 5.3 which have the force of law).

Exports and supplies to other EU member states

The cash accounting scheme can be used to account for VAT which becomes due on goods exported or supplied to another EU country because satisfactory evidence of export/supply has not been received within the time limit allowed for zero-rating. VAT must be accounted for when the time limit expires on all payments already received. If further payments are received, VAT must be accounted for on such payments at the time of receipt. If evidence of export is received after any VAT has been accounted for, the VAT can be adjusted in the VAT period in which the evidence is obtained. (VAT Notice 731, para 5.6).

Input tax

Input tax can be reclaimed in the return for the VAT period in which payment is made or other consideration is given or in a later period as may be agreed with HMRC. [*SI 1995/2518, Regs 57, 65*]. For this purpose payment by

- *cash* (i.e. coins and notes) is made on the date the money is paid (although a receipted VAT invoice must be held before reclaiming VAT on purchases made in this way, see **64.5** above);

- *cheque* is made on the date the cheque is sent to the supplier or, if later, the date on the cheque. If the cheque is not honoured, no VAT is reclaimable and an adjustment or error correction notification (formerly voluntary disclosure) must be made if VAT has already been claimed;
- *credit or debit card* is made when the supplier makes out the sales voucher (*not* the date when payment is made to the card company); and
- *giros, standing orders and direct debits* are made on the day the bank account is debited.

(VAT Notice 731, para 4.5 which has the force of law).

Using the scheme from the date of registration

Newly registered businesses may reclaim VAT on certain goods and services obtained prior to registration. See **35.10 INPUT TAX**. When the cash accounting scheme is used from the date of registration, VAT on such purchases should be reclaimed on the first VAT return if paid pre-registration or otherwise in the VAT period of payment.

Existing businesses starting to use the scheme

Where an existing VAT-registered business starts to use the scheme, it should separate in its records any payments made for transactions already dealt with under the normal method of accounting. Such payments should be excluded from the scheme records.

(VAT Notice 731, paras 3.1, 3.2).

Deposits

If advance payment is made by way of deposit, VAT can be reclaimed when the payment is made unless the deposit is not payment for supplies (e.g. deposits given as security which are either returned or forfeited) in which case there is no entitlement to deduct VAT. (VAT Notice 731, para 5.1).

Allocation of part payments

Where a payment is made or received which is part payment of one or more invoices (which may include both standard and zero-rated supplies), the payment must be allocated to the invoices in date order (earliest first). Where VAT is not identified separately on the part payment, the payment must be treated as VAT-inclusive. In cases where the payment relates to an invoice for supplies at different rates of VAT, the part payment must be apportioned between the different rates and the amounts on which VAT is due at the standard rate or reduced rate treated as VAT-inclusive.

Example

A payment of £2,500 is made against the following two invoices.

Invoice A (dated 1 May)	
Standard-rated goods	1,000
VAT	200
	£1,200
Invoice B (dated 26 May)	
Standard-rated goods	2,000
Zero-rated goods	1,000
VAT	400
	£3,400

The payment of £2,500 is allocated as follows.

(1) Allocate £1,200 against Invoice A (the earlier invoice) i.e. to include VAT of £200.00

(2) The balance of the payment £1,300 (£2,500 – £1,200) should be allocated against Invoice B. The proportion of the payment relating to VAT is 1,300 ÷ 3,400 × £400 = £152.94

Total amount of VAT to be accounted for on the payment of £2,500 is £352.94 (£200.00 + £152.94). The remaining VAT of £247.06 (£400.00 – £152.94) should be accounted for when further payment is received.

(VAT Notice 731, paras 5.7, 8.2).

Payments in kind

Where payment is partly or fully in kind (e.g. a part exchange or barter transaction) VAT must be accounted for on the full value of the supply. This is usually the price, excluding VAT, which would have been paid for the supply if money were the only consideration. See **72.5–72.7 VALUATION** for further details. VAT must be accounted for on the 'payment' on the date the business receives/supplies the goods or services agreed in lieu of money. (VAT Notice 731, para 5.9).

See also *A-Z Electrical* [1993] Lexis Citation 3240 (TVC 10.12) where a business using the cash accounting scheme received shares in a company in lieu of the money owed to it for supplies of goods. The tribunal held that the business should be taken to have received cash in satisfaction of the debt owed to it, and to have paid the same amount of cash for the shares. The deemed payment for the supplies was liable to VAT.

Partial exemption

A business which makes both taxable and exempt supplies may not be able to reclaim all its input tax. See **50 PARTIAL EXEMPTION**. A partly-exempt business which uses the cash accounting scheme must base its partial exemption calculations on payments made and received rather than purchases and sales. (VAT Notice 731, para 4.6).

Completion of VAT returns

The amounts of VAT due and VAT deductible are based on payments received and made, not on invoices issued. Similarly, the boxes for values of outputs and inputs must be completed on the basis of payments received and made (exclusive of VAT). Where supplies are made to other EU member states, the amount to be put in Box 8 is the total VAT-exclusive value of all supplies of goods and services made and *not* the total of payments received. (VAT Notice 731, para 4.7).

Leaving the scheme

[64.7] The following rules apply.

(a) **Turnover exceeding the limit.** Unless HMRC allow or direct otherwise, a business must withdraw from the cash accounting scheme at the end of a VAT period (and use the normal method of accounting for subsequent periods) if the value of its taxable supplies in the year then ending has exceeded £1.6 million. [*SI 1995/2518, Reg 60(1)(3)*]. For the purposes of this calculation, disposals of stocks and capital assets must be included. (VAT Notice 731, para 2.5).

Exceptionally, HMRC may allow a business to remain in the scheme where it can demonstrate that

- this limit was exceeded because of a large 'one-off' increase in sales which has not occurred before and is not expected to recur (e.g. the sale of a capital asset);
- the sale arose from a genuine commercial activity; and
- there are reasonable grounds for believing that turnover in the next twelve months will be below £1.35 million.

Application must be made to HMRC in writing and will be confirmed by them in writing.

(VAT Notice 731, para 2.6).

(b) **Voluntary withdrawal.** A business may withdraw from the scheme at the end of a VAT period. [*SI 1995/2518, Reg 60(2)*].

(c) **Expulsion from the scheme.** A business is not entitled to continue to operate the scheme in the following circumstances.

- It cannot comply with the record-keeping requirements in **64.5** above.
- It has, while operating the scheme,
  (i) been convicted of an offence in connection with VAT;
  (ii) accepted an offer to compound proceedings in connection with a VAT offence;
  (iii) been assessed to a penalty under *VATA 1994, s 60* (VAT evasion involving dishonesty);

(iv) failed to leave the scheme although its taxable supplies exceed the £1.6 million limit; or

(v) HMRC consider it necessary for the protection of the revenue.

[*SI 1995/2518, Reg 64(1)*]. (VAT Notice 731, para 6.2).

Appeals

An appeal may be made against any denial of access to or withdrawal of use of the cash accounting scheme. See **5.3 APPEALS**. If the appeal is against a decision by HMRC to deny access to use the scheme, withdraw use of the scheme for the protection of the revenue or not to allow continued use of the scheme for exceeding the tolerance, the business must cease to use the scheme until the appeal is resolved. For other appeals, HMRC will normally allow continued use of the scheme, pending outcome of the appeal, unless it considers that an appeal facilitates manipulation of the scheme. (VAT Notice 731, paras 6.8, 6.9).

Subsequent accounting for VAT

Unless the transitional arrangements below can be applied, a business which ceases to operate the cash accounting scheme because of (*a*)–(*c*) above must, on the return for the VAT period in which it ceased to operate the scheme, account for

- all VAT that it would have been required to pay to HMRC during the time the scheme was operated if it had not been operating the scheme, minus
- all VAT accounted for and paid to HMRC in accordance with the scheme, subject to any adjustment for credit for input tax.

Transitional arrangements

Where a business ceases to operate the cash accounting scheme because of (*a*) or (*b*) above, then provided the value of its taxable supplies in the three months ending at the end of the VAT period in which it ceased to operate the scheme has not exceeded £1.35 million, it may apply transitional arrangements. This means that the business can continue to operate the scheme in respect of its 'scheme supplies' for six months after the end of the VAT period in which it ceased to operate the scheme. '*Scheme supplies*' means supplies made and received while the business operated the scheme that were not excluded from the scheme under **64.4** above and did not fall to be included in the flat-rate scheme for small businesses (see **64.15** below).

Where a business chooses to apply the transitional arrangements, it must, on the return for the first VAT period that ends six months or more after the end of the VAT period in which it ceased to operate the scheme, account for

- all VAT that it would have been required to pay to HMRC during the time the scheme was operated if it had not then been operating the scheme, minus
- all VAT accounted for and paid to HMRC in accordance with the scheme (including any VAT accounted for and paid because it applied transitional arrangements), subject to any adjustment for credit for input tax.

[*SI 1995/2518, Regs 61, 64(2)*].

There is no need to apply to or notify HMRC if the transitional arrangements are used. During the six-month period it will be necessary to keep normal cash accounting records for payments and receipts for supplies which took place while the scheme was in use and separate records under the normal VAT accounting requirements for new supplies made and received. (VAT Notice 731, paras 6.4, 6.5).

Bad debt relief

If a business stops using cash accounting, it has to account for VAT on supplies it has made and received even if they have not been paid for. If the business has not received any payment then it may be able to claim **8 BAD DEBT RELIEF**. The key conditions are

- that it is at least six months from the date on which the debt became due and payable or the supply was made, whichever is later;
- the business can provide evidence that the bad debt has been written off in its 'refunds for bad debts' account; and
- for supplies made prior to 1 January 2003, where the customer is registered for VAT, the business has notified the customer of the claim for bad debt relief.

Where the business has opted to use the transitional arrangements, bad debt relief can be claimed in the VAT period which ends at the end of the six months. [*SI 1995/2518, Reg 64A*]. (VAT Notice 731, para 6.6).

Cessation of business

[64.8] Where a business operating the cash accounting scheme ceases trading or ceases to be registered, it must, within two months or such longer period as HMRC allow, account for and pay VAT due on all supplies made and received up to the date of cessation which has not otherwise been accounted for, subject to any adjustment for credit for input tax. [*SI 1995/2518, Reg 63(1)*].

In practice, where a business ceases trading, HMRC allow the business to continue to use the cash accounting scheme while any remaining stocks and assets are disposed of. Once VAT registration is cancelled, however, the final VAT return must be submitted within two months of deregistration. This applies even if the business has still not been paid for all its supplies, although where any of this relates to bad debts, the concessionary relief in **64.7** above may be applied. (VAT Notice 731, paras 6.10, 6.12).

Insolvency

Where a business operating the cash accounting scheme becomes insolvent, it must, within two months of the date of insolvency, account for VAT due on all supplies made and received up to the date of insolvency which has not otherwise been accounted for, subject to any credit for input tax. [*SI 1995/2518, Reg 62*]. Where trading continues after the date of insolvency, the officeholder responsible for the business may continue to use the cash accounting scheme subject to the normal rules of the scheme. If the officeholder does continue to use the scheme, he must, from the date of insolvency, separate in the business records any payments the business makes or receives for transactions already accounted for on the pre-insolvency VAT return. (VAT Notice 731, para 6.11 which has the force of law).

Transfer of a business as a going concern

Where a business or part of a business operating the cash accounting scheme is transferred as a going concern

- if the transferee does not take over the registration number of the business, the transferor must, within two months or such longer period as HMRC allow, account for and pay VAT due on all supplies made and received which has not otherwise been accounted for, subject to any adjustment for credit for input tax; and
- if the transferee takes over the VAT registration number of the business, the transferor must advise the transferee that the scheme is being used. The transferee must continue to account for and pay VAT as if it were a business operating the scheme on supplies made and received by the transferor before the date of the transfer. The transferee can leave the scheme subject to the normal rules in **64.7** above.

[*SI 1995/2518, Reg 63(2)(3)*].

Annual accounting scheme

[64.9] The annual accounting scheme allows businesses to complete one VAT return each year, making interim payments on account (see **64.12** below). The annual VAT return must be completed and sent to HMRC, with any balancing payment, within two months of the end of the annual VAT accounting period.

The main advantages of the scheme are:

- Smoothing out cash flow by paying a set amount each month or quarter.
- Ability to make additional payments as and when they can be afforded.
- Only having to complete one VAT return each year, instead of the normal four.
- Two months to complete and send in the annual VAT return and any balancing payment, instead of the normal one month.
- Being able to align the VAT year with the end of the business tax year and so simplify end of year routines.
- Where the business uses a retail scheme, in most cases the scheme calculations which apply to each quarter are performed once a year. The only exception to this is where the Direct Calculation Scheme 2 is used, in which case calculations under the retail scheme rules follow the rules for the annual adjustment under that scheme (see **61.18 RETAIL SCHEMES**).
- Where the business is partly exempt, the date it makes its partial exemption calculation must coincide with the end of its annual accounting period. This means that it does not have to make partial exemption calculations quarterly and simply makes the calculation

using the figures for the whole of the annual accounting period. (Where the first accounting period is for a part year, the business must do its partial exemption calculation only at the end of that period.)

(VAT Notice 732, paras 1.5, 7.2, 7.3).

De Voil Indirect Tax Service. See V2.199A.

Admission to the scheme

Conditions for admission

[64.10] A business is eligible to apply to join the scheme if it meets all the following conditions.

(a) There are reasonable grounds for believing that the value of its taxable supplies (excluding VAT) in the period of twelve months beginning at the date of application will not exceed £1,350,000. For this purpose, all standard, reduced and zero-rated supplies should be included except supplies of capital assets previously used in the business. Exempt supplies should be excluded. (VAT Notice 732, para 2.2).
HMRC will not penalise a business for wrongly estimating that the value of its VAT turnover will exceed the upper limit provided it can show that there were reasonable grounds for the estimate. If the estimate had no reasonable basis and a business is above the threshold for the scheme, HMRC will immediately remove the business from the scheme. It is sensible, therefore, to keep a record of how the estimate was made. If a business realises during the year that its turnover has gone or will go over the threshold for leaving the scheme (see **64.14** below), it must notify HMRC immediately and they will remove the business from the scheme. (VAT Notice 732, para 2.5).

(b) Registration is not in the name of a group (see **28 GROUPS OF COMPANIES**) or a division (see **60.43 REGISTRATION**).

(c) The business has not ceased to operate the scheme for any reason under **64.14** below in the twelve months preceding the date of application.

HMRC may refuse to permit a business to use the scheme where they consider it necessary to do so for the protection of the revenue.

[*SI 1995/2518, Reg 52*].

A business will not be allowed to join the scheme if it is insolvent or has a rising VAT debt. Entry will not necessarily be refused if there is a small debt provided the business agrees arrangements to clear the outstanding debt with HMRC. (VAT Notice 732, para 2.6).

Application procedure

Application to use the scheme must be made on Form VAT 600 (AA) (where application is to join the annual accounting scheme alone) or Form VAT 600 (AA and FRS) (where application is to join the annual accounting scheme and the flat-rate scheme for small businesses at the same time). There are links to both forms in the internet version of VAT Notice 732 at https://www.gov.uk/government/organisations/hm-revenue-customs

Notes on the completion of the form are in VAT Notice 732, paras 8.5 and 9.7.

Welsh versions are available (Form VAT 600 AA(W), VAT 600 FRS(W) and VAT 600 AA/FRS(W)). The completed form must be sent to the Annual Accounting Registration Unit, National Registration Service, Imperial House, 77 Victoria Street, Grimsby, North East Lincolnshire, DN31 1DB.

HMRC will notify the business in writing if the application is accepted. The letter will also advise

- the amount and timing of the interim payments to be made by electronic means;
- the method of electronic payment chosen; and
- the due date for the annual return and balancing payment.

(VAT Notice 732, para 8.4).

Annual accounting year and transitional accounting period

A business applying to join the scheme must indicate on the application form the month to the end of which it wishes its annual accounting year to run (normally the end of its financial accounting year). It must match the partial exemption year end (if applicable). If accepted, the first accounting period under the scheme (the '*transitional accounting period*') will normally run from the first day of the accounting period in which the application is made until the chosen year end. Subsequent periods of twelve months are then '*annual accounting years*'. However, HMRC cannot normally issue a VAT return for a period longer than twelve months (the exception being where a business is applying to use the annual accounting scheme from its effective date of registration, when a period of twelve months and 30 days is possible) and do not issue returns for periods of less than three months under the scheme. As a result, there may be instances when a business will receive more than one short period VAT return before a full twelve-month return.

[*SI 1995/2518, Reg 49*]. (HMRC Manual VATAAS3200).

The annual accounting year can be changed after joining the scheme (e.g. to tie in with a change in financial year end) but this may result in the business being issued with one or two short period returns during the transition because no accounting period can be longer than twelve months. (VAT Notice 732, para 3.5).

Conditions for using the scheme

[64.11] To remain within the scheme, a business must comply with the following conditions.

(a) Make any interim payments on account required by the notified due date. See **64.12** below.
(b) Submit a VAT return, together with any balancing payment of VAT due to HMRC declared on that return

- in respect of a transitional accounting period of four months or more or an annual accounting year (see **64.10** above) by the end of the second month following that period or year; and
- in respect of a transitional accounting period of less than four months by the end of the first month following that period.

[*SI 1995/2518, Reg 50(2)(b), Reg 51(a)(iii)(b)*].

Notifying changes in business circumstances

If there are, or are expected to be, significant changes that will affect the amount of VAT paid, the business must contact the Annual Accounting Registration Unit (see **64.10** above) immediately. Significant changes include realising that

- the value of taxable supplies will rise above the turnover limit for leaving the scheme (see **64.14** below) for the current year (e.g. due to new contracts, buying another business etc.); or
- VAT payable will, or has, increased by 10% since the last time instalments were calculated.

(VAT Notice 732, para 4.7).

Payments on account

[64.12] A business authorised to use the annual accounting scheme must make interim payments on account as follows.

(1) *Transitional periods* (see **64.10** above).
  (a) Where the transitional accounting period is four months or more and the business and HMRC agree to such a payment pattern,
    (i) in the case of a business registered for at least twelve months immediately preceding the start of its transitional period, 25% of the total VAT due for those twelve months on the last 'working day' of the 4th, and where the period has such months, 7th and 10th months of the transitional accounting period; and
    (ii) in any other case, 25% of the total amount of VAT that HMRC are satisfied the business will be liable to pay in respect of the next twelve months, again on the last 'working day' of the 4th, and where the period has such months, 7th and 10th months of the transitional accounting period.
  (b) Where the transitional accounting period is four months or more but the business and HMRC do not agree to quarterly payments as under (*a*) above,
    (i) in the case of a business registered for at least twelve months immediately preceding the start of the transitional accounting period, 10% of the total VAT due for those twelve months in equal monthly instalments on the last 'working day' of the fourth and each successive month of the transitional accounting period; and

(ii) in any other case, 10% of the total amount of VAT that HMRC are satisfied the business will be liable to pay in respect of the next twelve months in equal monthly instalments on the last 'working day' of the fourth and each successive month of the transitional accounting period.

(c) Where the transitional accounting period is less than four months, no interim payments are required.

(2) *Subsequent annual accounting periods.*

(a) Where the business and HMRC agree to such a payment pattern,

(i) in the case of a business registered for at least twelve months immediately preceding the start of the current accounting year, 25% of the total VAT due for those twelve months on the last 'working day' of the 4th, 7th and 10th months of the annual accounting year; and

(ii) in any other case, 25% of the total amount of VAT that HMRC are satisfied the business will be liable to pay in respect of the next twelve months.

(b) Otherwise, where (*a*) does not apply,

(i) in the case of a business registered for at least twelve months immediately preceding the start of the current accounting year, 10% of the total VAT due for those twelve months in nine equal monthly instalments starting on the last 'working day' of the fourth month of its annual accounting year; and

(ii) in any other case, 10% of the total amount of VAT that HMRC are satisfied the business will be liable to pay in respect of the next twelve months.

The normal method of payment will therefore be by monthly payments under (1)(*b*) or (2)(*b*) above unless the business indicates that it wishes to make quarterly payments under (1)(*a*) or (2)(*a*) above on its application form. If a business does not do so, but subsequently wishes to change from monthly to quarterly payments, it should write to the Annual Accounting Registration Unit (see **64.10** above) although HMRC will normally expect a business to stay on the same payment pattern for at least one year. (VAT Notice 732, paras 4.2–4.4).

'*Working day*' means any day of the week other than Saturday, Sunday, a bank holiday or a public holiday.

[*SI 1995/2518, Reg 49, Reg 50(2)(3), Reg 51*].

Revision of payments on account

If a business expects its liability to increase or decrease significantly, it should contact the Annual Accounting Registration Unit with information on how it calculates revised interim payments. If they agree, HMRC will notify the new instalment amounts. (VAT Notice 732, para 4.6).

Additional voluntary payments

These can be made at any time. Payments must be made by electronic means (see below) and in multiples of £5. (VAT Notice 732, para 4.8).

Method of payment

All interim payments, whether monthly or quarterly, must be made by electronic means (direct debit, standing order, bank giro credit, Bankers Automated Clearing Service (BACS) or the Clearing House Automated Payment System (CHAPS)). (VAT Notice 732, para 5.2).

Missing a payment

HMRC will send a reminder if an interim payment on account is not received. Payment will have to be made by BACS or CHAPS. (VAT Notice 732, para 5.4).

Accounting for VAT

[64.13] The annual return is completed in the same way as a normal VAT return (including the availability of sending the return electronically) and must be completed and sent to HMRC within two months of the end of the annual VAT accounting period. It is important that the figure for the value of outputs in Box 6 is accurate as this will be used as a basis for allowing continued use of the scheme.

The figure shown in Box 5 of the return is the amount of VAT due for the year. This figure will be calculated automatically if the return is being completed online. The amount payable with the VAT return is the figure in Box 5 less the total of interim payments made for the annual period. If the total amount paid by interim payments is more than the net VAT payable, HMRC will refund the difference.

Returns may be submitted online, after registration and enrolment via the HMRC website. If the return is submitted online, payment of any VAT due must also be paid by electronic means.

Any balance due at the end of the year can be paid by direct debit, BACS, CHAPS, Bank Giro or debit/credit card. Where paper VAT returns are used, payment can also be made by cheque. It should be noted that the additional time for sending or paying VAT returns electronically is not available where the annual accounting scheme is used (because an extra month is already allowed for doing this).

(VAT Notice 732, paras 6.2–6.4).

Use of the annual accounting scheme and the flat-rate scheme for small businesses

The annual accounting scheme can be used together with the flat-rate scheme (see **64.15** *et seq.*) below by simply following the rules of the flat-rate scheme for calculating VAT liability but instead of doing this four times a year, doing it just once when the annual accounting return is due.

If a business makes a joint application to use both schemes, use will normally start together from the beginning of the period in which the annual accounting scheme applies although the application form does allow a business to request different start dates. In the latter case, two calculations are required when completing the annual accounting return.

- A calculation for the period when the business was not in the flat-rate scheme, using normal VAT accounting rules.
- A calculation for the period when the business was in the flat-rate scheme using the rules for calculating liability under the flat-rate scheme.

The total liability for the return period will be the sum of those two calculations.

Where a business already using the annual accounting scheme applies to join the flat-rate scheme in the middle of its annual accounting period, it will have to do two calculations when completing its return as explained above. To avoid two calculations, it is best to apply to use the flat-rate scheme at the beginning of an annual accounting period. If the business does not wish to wait to the end of its annual accounting year, it can change its existing annual accounting year end to an earlier date and start both schemes together. This will result in amendments to the annual accounting periods and payments to accommodate these changes.

If a business becomes ineligible for one scheme, it will normally continue in the other scheme unless it requests removal. If a business leaves the flat-rate scheme in the middle of an accounting period, it must do the two calculations as described above when completing its next VAT return.

(VAT Notice 732, paras 9.2, 9.8–9.11).

Leaving the scheme

[64.14] Provided the business is still authorised to use the scheme, it must continue to use it in the next annual accounting year. [*SI 1995/2518, Reg 53(1)*].

A business ceases to be authorised to use the annual accounting scheme in the following circumstances.

(a) **Turnover exceeding the limit.**
   - After the end of any transitional accounting period (see **64.10** above) if the value of taxable supplies in that period has exceeded £1,600,000.
   - After the end of any annual accounting year if the value of taxable supplies in that year has exceeded £1,600,000.

(b) **Expulsion by HMRC.** HMRC *may* terminate an authorisation to use the scheme from any date where
   - a false statement has been made by or on behalf of the business in relation to the application to use the scheme;
   - a business fails to make any VAT return under the scheme by the due date;
   - a business fails to make any payment due under the scheme;
   - a business notifies HMRC that it has reason to believe that the value of taxable supplies in the current transitional accounting period (see **64.10** above) or annual accounting year will exceed £1,600,000 (which it must do in writing within 30 days);

- there is reason to believe that the value of taxable supplies made by a business using the scheme will exceed £1,600,000 in the current transitional accounting period (see **64.10** above) or annual accounting year;
- it is necessary to do so for the protection of the revenue; or
- a business using the scheme has not paid over to HMRC all VAT shown as due on any return made before authorisation and all VAT shown as due on any assessment made (including interest and penalties). See, however, **64.10** above for HMRC policy where there is a small amount of VAT outstanding at the time of application to join the scheme.

(c) **Cessation of business.** Where a business authorised to use the scheme

- becomes insolvent and ceases to trade (other than for the purposes of disposing of stocks and assets),
- ceases business or ceases to be registered, or
- if a person, dies or becomes bankrupt or incapacitated

authorisation to use the scheme terminates on the date on which any such event occurs.

(d) **Voluntary withdrawal.** A business authorised to use the scheme may cease to operate it of its own volition at any time by writing to HM Revenue & Customs, Annual Accounting Registration Unit, National Registration Service, Imperial House, 77 Victoria Street, Grimsby, North East Lincolnshire, DN31 1DB. Authorisation to use the scheme terminates from the date HMRC are notified in writing.

[*SI 1995/2518, Regs 53(2), 54, 55(1)*].

Consequences of leaving the scheme

Where a business leaves the annual accounting scheme, a final return under the scheme must be made and any outstanding VAT must normally be paid within two months of the date on which its authorisation is terminated. From the day following termination, the business must account for and pay VAT in the normal way and cannot rejoin the scheme for twelve months.

[*SI 1995/2518, Reg 55(2)*].

Flat-rate scheme for small businesses

[64.15] HMRC may make *Regulations* setting up a scheme which allows eligible businesses to calculate their VAT due as a percentage of total turnover. Some of the conditions of the scheme can also be published (and amended) in a VAT Notice *which to this extent has the force of law*. [*VATA 1994, s 26B; FA 2002, s 23; SI 1995/2518, Reg 55T*].

Under these provisions, a flat-rate scheme is available for small businesses with VAT-exclusive annual taxable turnover of up to £150,000.

The aim of the flat-rate scheme is to simplify the way VAT is recorded and accounted for on sales and purchases. The key points of the scheme are:

- There is no need to record the VAT on individual sales and purchases in order to calculate the VAT due to HMRC.

- Instead, a business simply records all its business supplies, including exempt supplies, and applies a flat-rate percentage (dependent upon the trade sector into which the business falls) to the VAT-inclusive total in each VAT period. The result is the VAT payable to HMRC.
- A business does not recover input tax or VAT on imports or acquisitions. This is because the flat rates are calculated to represent the net VAT that needs to be paid to HMRC, i.e. an allowance for input tax is built into the flat rates. There are, however, special rules for input tax recovery on high value capital goods.

Full details of the scheme are given in **64.16** to **64.24** below.

Deciding whether to use the scheme

All businesses using the scheme benefit from simpler bookkeeping. There is no need to check the deductibility of VAT on purchases (and even their liability to VAT). If the scheme is used together with the annual accounting scheme (see **64.9** above) it can make a significant difference to the cost of complying with VAT requirements. But:

- Any individual business may pay more or less VAT than it would under the normal VAT rules. This is because the flat rates are averages, and one flat rate applies to all businesses in a particular sector.
- Businesses that usually receive repayments from HMRC should not join the scheme.
- As exempt and zero-rated supplies are included in flat-rate turnover, businesses may pay more VAT by using the scheme if these supplies are a larger proportion of business turnover than the average for its trade sector.
- Businesses with VAT-registered customers must still issue VAT invoices (showing VAT calculated in the normal way).
- Businesses that buy and sell goods from outside the UK can find the scheme more complex and financially disadvantageous.

(VAT Notice 733, paras 2.1–2.3).

De Voil Indirect Tax Service. See V2.199B–V2.199D.

How the scheme works

Output tax

[64.16] For any VAT period, the output tax due from a flat-rate trader in respect of his 'relevant supplies' (see below) is deemed to be the appropriate 'flat-rate percentage' of his 'relevant turnover' for that period. [*SI 1995/2518, Reg 55D*].

See **64.19** below for the '*flat-rate percentage*' and **64.20** below for calculating '*relevant turnover*'.

> *Example*
>
> A motor repair business has a VAT-inclusive turnover of £20,000 for a VAT period.

Its appropriate flat-rate percentage is 8.5%, and VAT due for the period is £20,000 × 8.5% = £1,700

Input tax

A flat-rate trader cannot normally claim a deduction for input tax on purchases of goods and services in the UK, on imports or on acquisitions, as the flat-rate percentage includes an allowance for input tax. There are, however, two exceptions to this.

(a) *Capital items costing over £2,000*. See **64.22** below.

(b) *VAT paid before registration on goods and services*. A business can recover VAT incurred before registration subject to certain conditions. See **35.10 INPUT TAX**. These provisions also apply where the first VAT period for which a business is authorised to account for and pay VAT in accordance with the flat-rate scheme is the first VAT period for which it is registered (or required to be registered).
Where the above applies, the whole of the input tax on the goods or services concerned is regarded as used, or to be used, by the taxable person exclusively in making taxable supplies.
[*SI 1995/2518, Reg 55F*].
The claim should be made on the first VAT return following registration. Where such a claim is made, any subsequent disposal of capital assets has to be accounted for in the normal way, i.e. by adding any VAT due on the disposal to the VAT calculated under the flat-rate scheme. See (4) below. (VAT Notice 733, para 7.6).

Relevant supplies and purchases

The following provisions apply in determining whether a purchase or supply is a relevant purchase or supply for the purposes of the flat-rate scheme.

(1) Subject to (3), (5) and (6) below, any supply of goods or services to, or acquisition of importation of goods by, a flat-rate trader is a relevant purchase of his.

(2) Subject to (3)–(6) below, any supply made by a person when he is not a flat-rate trader is not a relevant supply of his.

(3) Subject to (4) and (6) below, where
- a supply is made to, or made by, a person at a time when he is not a flat-rate trader, and
- the operative date for VAT accounting purposes is, by virtue of the cash accounting scheme, a date when he is a flat-rate trader,

that supply is a relevant supply or a relevant purchase, as the case may be, if otherwise it would not be by virtue of (2) above.

(4) Where a person
- is entitled to any credit for input tax in respect of the supply to, or acquisition or importation by, him of capital expenditure goods,
- claims any such credit, and
- makes a supply of those capital expenditure goods,

that supply is not a relevant supply, if otherwise it would be.

(5) Where by virtue of any provision of, or made under, *VATA 1994* a supply is *treated as made* by a flat-rate trader, whether to himself or otherwise, that supply is neither a relevant supply nor a relevant purchase of his.

(6) Where a reverse charge supply under the provisions relating to mobile phones and computer chips (see **4.15 ANTI-AVOIDANCE**) is made to or by a flat-rate trader, the supply is neither a relevant supply nor a relevant purchase.

[*SI 1995/2518, Reg 55C*].

Issuing VAT invoices

The normal rules apply to issuing VAT invoices, i.e. a flat-rate trader must still issue a VAT invoice to any customer who is registered for VAT and the customer can treat the invoice as a normal VAT invoice. VAT must be shown on the sales invoice using the normal rate for the supply (standard, reduced, zero rate or exempt) and *not* the flat-rate percentage assigned to the business. This is because the flat-rate scheme affects the way VAT is calculated but does not change the VAT rate applicable to supplies. When calculating VAT at the end of the VAT period, a flat-rate trader must add up the VAT-inclusive total of all his supplies (whether or not a VAT invoice has been issued) and apply the flat rate percentage to this total.

(VAT Notice 733, paras 7.3, 7.4).

Using the scheme in conjunction with other schemes

The flat-rate scheme can be used in conjunction with the *annual accounting scheme*. The use of both schemes can help reduce the cost of complying with VAT.

The flat-rate scheme *cannot* be used in conjunction with the following schemes.

- *Cash accounting*. Although the cash accounting scheme and the flat-rate scheme cannot be used together, the flat-rate scheme has its own cash-based method that is very similar to the cash accounting scheme. See **64.20** below.
- *Retail schemes*. Although a retail scheme and the flat-rate scheme cannot be used together, the flat-rate scheme has its own retail-based method which is very similar to the ordinary retail schemes. See **64.20** below.
  Where a business wishes to leave a retail scheme to join the flat-rate scheme, it should follow the rules about ceasing to use that retail scheme. See **61 RETAIL SCHEMES** under the appropriate scheme.
- *Margin scheme for second-hand goods*. Where a business sells a significant proportion of second-hand goods using a margin scheme or the auctioneers' scheme, the flat-rate scheme is of limited value to the business. This is because the flat-rate scheme calculates VAT on the total received from sales rather than on the margin.

(VAT Notice 733, para 2.7).

Eligibility and conditions

[64.17] HMRC may authorise a business to account for and pay VAT under the flat-rate scheme with effect from the beginning of its next VAT period after the date on which it notifies HMRC of its wish to use the scheme (or such earlier or later date as may be agreed between them). In practice, although starting to use the scheme from the beginning of a VAT period is simplest, HMRC may agree to any start date other than 29 February. The date with effect from which the business is so authorised is its '*start date*'.

HMRC may refuse to so authorise a business if they consider it is necessary for the protection of the revenue.

[*SI 1995/2518, Reg 55B(1)–(3)*].

A business is eligible to account for VAT in accordance with the flat-rate scheme at any time (including with effect from its date of registration) if it satisfies the following conditions.

(a) There are reasonable grounds for believing that the value of its taxable supplies (excluding VAT) in the period of one year then beginning will not exceed £150,000. [*SI 2009/586, Reg 6*].
In determining the value of taxable supplies or income for these purposes
- any supply of goods or services that are capital assets of the business in the course or furtherance of which they are supplied, and
- any supply of services treated as made by the recipient by virtue of *VATA 1994, s 8* (reverse charge on supplies from abroad)

are disregarded.
Included in (i) above is the value of standard rate, zero rate and reduced rate supplies; turnover from the sale of second-hand goods sold outside the margin scheme; and any sales of gold covered by the special scheme in **27.9 GOLD AND PRECIOUS METALS.**
Included in (ii) above, in addition to the total value of supplies within (i) above, was the value of any exempt supplies and any other income received or receivable by the business. This included any 'non-business' income (e.g. income arising from charitable or educational activities).
Future turnover can be forecast in any reasonable way (e.g. turnover in the last twelve months adjusted for any expected changes). HMRC will not penalise a business if the forecast turns out to be too low provided there were reasonable grounds for the forecast. It is sensible, therefore, to keep a record of how the calculation was made. If HMRC judge that the estimate of turnover had no reasonable basis, a business may be excluded from the scheme immediately or even from the date its ineligible use began.
(VAT Notice 733, paras 3.2–3.5).
Once in the scheme, a business can remain in it provided total turnover (including VAT) did not exceed £230,000 in the previous year (calculated on the anniversary of joining the scheme) and provided there are not grounds for believing turnover will rise above £230,000 in the next 30 days alone. See **64.23** below for further details.

(b) The business
- is not a tour operator;
- is not required to carry out adjustments in relation to a capital item under the **11 CAPITAL GOODS SCHEME**; or
- does not intend to opt to account for the VAT chargeable on a supply made by it under a margin scheme (see **62 SECOND-HAND GOODS**).

(c) The business has not, in the period of one year preceding that time
- been convicted of any offence in connection with VAT,
- made any payment to compound proceedings in respect of VAT under *CEMA 1979, s 152*,
- been assessed to a penalty for VAT evasion under *VATA 1994, s 60* (see **53.12 PENALTIES**), or
- ceased to operate the flat-rate scheme.

(d) The business is not and, unless HMRC are satisfied that use of the flat-rate scheme poses no risk to the revenue, has not been within the past 24 months
- eligible to be registered for VAT in the name of a group under *VATA 1994, s 43A* (see **28.2 GROUPS OF COMPANIES**),
- registered for VAT in the name of a division under *VATA 1994, s 46(1)* (see **60.43 REGISTRATION**), or
- 'associated with' another person.

Note that it is eligibility to be in a VAT group which is the key test, not whether the business is actually in one.

A person is '*associated with*' another person at any time if that other person makes supplies in the course or furtherance of a business carried on by him, and
- the business of one is under the dominant influence of the other, or
- the persons are closely bound to one another by financial, economic and organisational links.

HMRC treat this as applying where one business has the right to give directions to another or, in practice, a business habitually complies with the directions of another. The test here is a test of the commercial reality rather than of the legal form. A close connection with another business is not necessarily the same as being associated. For example, a business is not associated with its customers just because it supplies them with the goods they request in the form they request them. Similarly, a husband and wife who are each separately VAT-registered in different types of business are not associated even if they share premises (provided this is charged at a market rate). Traders who are unsure whether the particular relationship between their business and another constitutes 'association' for this purpose are encouraged to contact the VAT Helpline (VAT Notice 733, para 3.8).

[*SI 1995/2518, Regs 55A, 55L*].

Application to use the scheme

[64.18] Application to use the flat-rate scheme can be made in any of the following ways.

- **By post.** Application should be made on Form VAT 600 (FRS). The form can be downloaded from the web version available at: https://www.gov.uk/government/organisations/hm-revenue-customs. Postal applications should be sent to

  HM Revenue & Customs
  Imperial House
  77 Victoria Street
  Grimsby DN31 1DB

  If registering for VAT at the same time, Form VAT 600 (FRS) can be enclosed with the Form VAT 1 Application for Registration.
- **By e-mail.** The scheme application form can be downloaded from HMRC's website, completed on a computer and sent to frsapplications.vrs@hmrc.gsi.gov.uk

  Any queries or correspondence should be sent to the VAT Helpline not this e-mail address.
- **By phone.** The VAT Helpline can take application details over the phone on 0300 200 3700. If an accountant or other representative applies to use the scheme by phone on behalf of a business, HMRC will send a copy of the application form completed by them to the business for its records. If there are any errors on it, HMRC should be contacted immediately.

Guidance on completing the form is given in VAT Notice 733, para 5.3.

Application can be made at the time of registration for VAT or any later time. If application is made at the time of registration, a business can begin to use the scheme from the date of registration. (See **64.19** below for a 1% reduction in flat-rate percentage for all businesses in the first year of VAT registration.) If a business is already registered when it applies, it is best to apply as early in a VAT period as possible as authorisation to use the flat-rate scheme normally takes effect from the beginning of the VAT period after HMRC have processed the application.

HMRC will notify the business either that its application has been accepted and the date from which it can operate the flat-rate scheme, or the reason why it has not allowed it.

(VAT Notice 733, paras 5.1, 5.2, 5.5; VAT Information Sheet 17/03, para 5.1).

See **64.13** above for joint application to join the flat-rate scheme and the annual accounting scheme.

Flat-rate percentage

[64.19] Flat-rate percentage is treated as follows:

(1) Appropriate flat-rate percentage

The appropriate percentage to be applied by a flat-rate trader for any VAT period (or part period) is determined in accordance with the following rules and, where appropriate, (2) and (3) below.

(a) For any VAT period beginning with a 'relevant date', the appropriate percentage is that specified in the Table below for the category of business that he is expected, at the relevant date, on reasonable grounds, to carry on in that period.

(b) For any VAT period current at his 'start date' but not beginning with his start date, the appropriate percentage is that specified in the Table below for the category of business that he is expected, at his start date, on reasonable grounds, to carry on in the remainder of the period.

(c) For any VAT period not falling within (*a*) or (*b*) above, the appropriate percentage is that applicable to his relevant turnover at the end of the previous VAT period.

'*Relevant date*' in relation to a flat-rate trader, means any of the following.

- His '*start date*' (i.e. the date from which he is authorised to use the scheme).
- The first day of the VAT period current at any anniversary of his start date.
- Any day on which he first carries on a new business activity.
- Any day on which he no longer carries on an existing business activity.
- Any day with effect from which the Table below is amended in relation to him.
- Where (2) below applies
  - (i) the day that his 'newly registered period' (see (2) below) begins, and
  - (ii) the first anniversary of his EDR (see (2) below).

But where a relevant date (other than the start date) occurs on a day other than the first day of a VAT period, the following rules apply for the remainder of that VAT period.

(A) For the 'remaining portion', the appropriate percentage is that specified in the Table below for the category of business that he is expected, at the relevant date, on reasonable grounds, to carry on in that period.
'*Remaining portion*' means that part of the VAT period in which the relevant date occurs starting with the relevant date, and ending on the last day of that prescribed accounting period.
The appropriate percentage is applied to relevant turnover in the remaining portion described.

(B) If the rules set out in (A) above apply and then another relevant date occurs in the same VAT period, then the existing remaining portion ends on the day before the latest relevant date, another remaining portion begins on the latest relevant date, and the rules in (A) above are applied again in respect of the latest remaining portion.

[*SI 1995/2518, Regs 55A, 55H*].

(2) Reduced appropriate percentage for newly registered period

Special provisions apply where the date from which a flat-rate trader is authorised to use the scheme (his '*start date*') falls within one year of the date with effect from which he is registered for VAT (his '*EDR*').

In such a case, at any relevant date (see (1) above) falling within his 'newly registered period', the Table below is to be read as if each percentage were reduced by 1% unless HMRC receive notification of, or otherwise become fully aware of, his liability to be registered more than one year after his EDR.

A flat-rate trader's '*newly registered period*' is the period beginning with the later of

- his start date, and
- the day HMRC received notification of, or otherwise became fully aware of, his liability to be registered for VAT

and ending on the day before the first anniversary of his EDR.

The effect of this is that if a business notifies its VAT liability on time and asks to use the scheme from the date of registration, the discounted rates last for one year. But if it registers for VAT late or does not immediately join the scheme, the period will be shortened.

[*SI 1995/2518, Regs 55A, 55JB*].

(3) More than one category of business

Where, at a relevant date (see (1) above), a flat-rate trader was expected, on reasonable grounds, to carry on business in more than one category of business in the period concerned, he is regarded as being expected to carry on that category of business which is expected to be his main business activity in that period, determined by reference to turnover expected to be generated by each business activity concerned.

[*SI 1995/2518, Regs 55A, 55K*].

This means that if a business includes supplies in two or more sectors, it must apply the percentage appropriate to its main business activity as measured by turnover. It should not split its turnover or apply more than one percentage.

Example

A taxi business expects to have a turnover of £40,000 in the next year but also does car repairs which are expected to generate a turnover of £15,000.

It must apply the flat-rate percentage for a taxi business to the total VAT-inclusive turnover for both parts of the business. If this total was £55,000, the business would pay £4,950 in that year.

(VAT Notice 733, para 4.6).

(4) Changes in the balance between two parts of a business

If the balance between activities changes but the business still carries on the same activities, it must carry on using the percentage that was appropriate at the start of the year until the anniversary of joining the scheme. At the start of the VAT period which includes that anniversary, the business should review the balance between the parts of the business and, if this has changed (or is expected to change in the year ahead), it can change categories to that for the larger portion of the business (or expected business). If this also involves a change in the appropriate percentage, the new percentage should be used from the start of the VAT period in which the anniversary date falls (not just from the anniversary to the end of the period). (VAT Notice 733, para 4.7).

(5) Notification of changes to HMRC

- Where at the first day of the VAT period current at any anniversary of his start date (see (1) above) the appropriate percentage to be applied by a flat-rate trader under (1)(*a*) above for the VAT period just beginning differs from that applicable to his relevant turnover at the end of the previous VAT period, he must notify HMRC of that fact within 30 days of the first day of the VAT period current at the anniversary of his start date.
- Where a flat-rate trader begins to carry on a new business activity or ceases to carry on an existing business activity, he must notify HMRC of that fact, the date of change, and the appropriate percentage to be applied to the period immediately before that relevant date and immediately after it. Notification must be within 30 days of the date of change.

[*SI 1995/2518, Reg 55N(1)(2)(4)*].

(6) Choice of category of business

It is for the business to choose its appropriate category of business from the table below. In choosing the category, the words should be given their ordinary meanings. The VAT Helpline can help where there is doubt.

See also HMRC Manual FRS7200 (List of trades and the sectors to which HMRC consider they belong) and FRS 7300 (List of sectors and the trades that HMRC consider fit within each) for how HMRC have interpreted the various categories.

Once HMRC have approved a business to join the scheme, they will not change the category of business chosen in retrospect provided the choice was reasonable and records have been kept why it was chosen.

(VAT Notice 733, paras 4.1, 4.2).

Category of business	*Appropriate %*
Accountancy or book-keeping	14.5
Advertising	11
Agricultural services	11
Any other activity not listed elsewhere	12
Architect, civil and structural engineer or surveyor	14.5
Boarding or care of animals	12
Business services that are not listed elsewhere	12
Catering services, including restaurants and takeaways	12.5

Category of business	*Appropriate %*
Computer and IT consultancy or data processing	14.5
Computer repair services	10.5
Dealing in waste or scrap	10.5
Entertainment (excluding film, radio, television or video production, see below) or journalism	12.5
Estate agency or property management services	12
Farming or agriculture that is not listed elsewhere	6.5
Film, radio, television or video production	13
Financial services	13.5
Forestry or fishing	10.5
General building or construction services (note 1)	9.5
Hairdressing or other beauty treatment services	13
Hiring or renting goods	9.5
Hotel or accommodation	10.5
Investigation or security	12
Labour-only building or construction services (note 1)	14.5
Laundry or dry-cleaning services	12
Lawyer or legal services	14.5
Library, archive, museum or other cultural activities	9.5
Limited cost trader	16.5
Management consultancy	14
Manufacturing fabricated metal products	10.5
Manufacturing food	9
Manufacturing that is not listed elsewhere	9.5
Manufacturing yarn, textiles or clothing	9
Membership organisations	8
Mining or quarrying	10
Packaging	9
Photography	11
Post offices	5
Printing	8.5
Publishing	11
Pubs	6.5
Real estate activities not listed elsewhere	14
Repairing personal or household goods	10
Repairing vehicles	8.5

Category of business	*Appropriate %*
Retailing food, confectionery, tobacco, newspapers or children's clothing	4
Retailing pharmaceuticals, medical goods, cosmetics or toiletries	8
Retailing that is not listed elsewhere	7.5
Retailing vehicles or fuel	6.5
Secretarial services	13
Social work	11
Sport or recreation	8.5
Transport or storage, including courier, freight, removals and taxis	10
Travel agency	10.5
Veterinary medicine	11
Wholesaling agricultural products	8
Wholesaling food	7.5
Wholesaling that is not listed elsewhere	8.5

Notes

(1) 'Labour-only building or construction services' means building or construction services where the value of materials supplied is less than 10% of relevant turnover from such services; any other building or construction services are 'general building or construction services'.

[*SI 1995/2518, Reg 55K*].

Limited cost traders

The Government announced at Autumn Statement 2016 that it was introducing a new FRS category for limited cost traders. Businesses deemed to be limited cost traders will be required to use the 16.5% flat-rate percentage.

A business will be treated as a limited cost trader if the amount spent on relevant goods *including VAT* is either:

- less than 2% of their flat rate turnover in a prescribed accounting period;
- greater than 2% of their flat rate turnover but less than £1,000 per annum if the prescribed accounting period is one year (if it is not one year, the figure is the relevant proportion of £1,000).

The following are regarded as 'relevant goods' for the purposes of these provisions:

- A supply of goods is received and exclusive ownership of moveable goods transfers to the business from another person.
- The business's own goods are transferred from another member state.
- The goods transferred under an agreement where title will pass at a later time, such as a hire purchase agreement.
- The business receives water or any form of power, heat, refrigeration or ventilation but not if the business hires equipment which does this because that is treated as a supply of services.

The goods must be used *exclusively* for the business purposes and the following items are excluded:

- capital expenditure of any value (please note that this would include electronic devices such as mobile phones and computers used by the business);
- food or drink for consumption by the flat-rate business or its employees;
- vehicles, vehicle parts and fuel – except where the business is one that carries out transport services and uses its own or a leased vehicle to carry out those services (e.g. a taxi business);
- goods for resale, leasing, letting or hiring out if the business main business activity does not ordinarily consist of selling, leasing, letting or hiring out such goods;
- goods that the business intends to re-sell or hire out, unless selling or hiring is the main business activity;
- goods for disposal, such as promotional items, gifts or donations;
- any services.

HMRC provide the following examples of relevant goods in Notice 733:

- 'stationery and other office supplies to be used exclusively for the business
- gas and electricity used exclusively for your business
- fuel for a taxi owned by a taxi firm
- stock for a shop
- cleaning products to be used exclusively for the business
- hair products to use to provide hairdressing services
- standard software, provided on a disk
- food to be used in meals for customers
- goods provided by a subcontractor and itemised separately
- goods brought into the UK if they are not otherwise excluded
- goods bought without VAT being charged, if they are not otherwise excluded'.

Interestingly, HMRC provide a list of goods that are not relevant goods in Notice 733 and the list includes the following:

> 'Goods which are bought solely to meet the test, as these would not be used exclusively for the purposes of your business. For example, if the quantity of goods being bought can't reasonably be used by the business and are simply 'stockpiled' or thrown away, even if the business may normally use those items is smaller quantities such as office materials.'

It is assumed that this measure is intended to counter the widely publicised planning opportunity that was suggested as an option that could assist businesses with avoiding becoming a limited cost trader.

Anti-forestalling measures were introduced with effect from 23 November 2016 which are designed to prevent any business meeting the above criteria from using another flat rate with effect from 1 April 2017 when this new category comes into effect. Notice 733 has been updated to reflect the introduction of the new category and rate.

(VAT Notice 733, paras 4.4–4.6).

Calculating turnover

[64.20] It is important to determine correctly the turnover to which the flat-rate percentage is to be applied. If items that are not part of turnover are included, too much VAT will be paid and if items are omitted, too little VAT will be paid and the business could have to pay a penalty and interest.

Flat-rate turnover includes all the supplies made by the business, including VAT. This means

- the *VAT-inclusive* sales and takings for standard-rated, zero-rated and reduced rate supplies;
- the value of exempt supplies;
- supplies of capital expenditure goods, unless they are supplies on which VAT has to be calculated outside the flat-rate scheme in accordance with **64.22** below; and
- the value of despatches to other EU member states if the business is making intra-EU supplies.

Income which can be excluded includes

- private income (e.g. dividends);
- bank interest;
- proceeds from the sale of goods owned by the trader but which have not been used in the business;
- any sales of gold for which the special accounting scheme applies (see **27.9 GOLD AND PRECIOUS METALS**);
- non-business income and any supplies outside the scope of VAT; and
- sales of capital expenditure goods on which the business has claimed input tax (see **64.22** below).

(VAT Notice 733, paras 6.2, 6.3).

Methods of calculating turnover

There are three ways of calculating turnover. Whichever method is used, it should normally be used for at least 12 months.

(1) The basic turnover method

Under this method, the flat-rate percentage is applied to the VAT-inclusive total of supplies that have their time of supply (tax point) in the VAT period in question. Time of supply is worked out using the normal rules. See **67.1** to **67.26 SUPPLY: TIME OF SUPPLY**. This method is principally for businesses that deal mainly with other VAT-registered businesses. (VAT Notice 733, para 8.1).

(2) The cash-based turnover method

Under this method, the business applies the flat-rate percentage to the supplies for which it has been paid in the VAT period in question. This method can be helpful if the business gives extended credit or customers pay late.

If the cash accounting system was being used immediately before the flat-rate scheme, the business should carry on as before. There is no need to calculate and pay the VAT still owed when changing schemes. It includes any payments received whilst using the flat-rate scheme in the total to which it applies the flat-rate percentage.

Time of payment

The following rules have the force of law for determining the time of payment.

- *Cash* (coins or notes). Payment is received on the date the money is received.
- *Cheques*. Payment by cheque is received on the date the cheque is received or, if later, the date on the cheque. If the cheque is not honoured, no VAT is due and an adjustment can be made if VAT has already been accounted for.
- *Credit or debit cards*. Payment is received on the date the sales voucher is made out (*not* the date when payment is received from the card provider).
- *Giro, standing orders and direct debits*. Payment is received on the date the bank account is credited.

Change of VAT rate or insolvency

In these special circumstances, the basic turnover method tax point must be used to determine the treatment of the supplies.

(VAT Notice 733, paras 9.1–9.3).

Payments received net of deductions

Where a net payment is received, the full value must be included before such deductions (and including VAT) in the scheme turnover. This will usually be the value shown on the sales invoice. Examples of payments that may be received net of deductions are

- payments where commission has been deducted by the customer;
- payments where commission or payment for expenses has been deducted by a factor or agent collecting money on behalf of the business;
- payments where commission or payment for expenses has been deducted by an auctioneer selling goods on behalf of the business; and
- payments made by an employer/contractor who has deducted income tax.

(VAT Notice 733, para 9.4 which has the force of law).

Payments in kind (e.g. barter and part exchange)

Where a business is paid fully or partly in kind, it must include the value, including VAT, in its flat-rate turnover each time it makes or receives a 'payment'. Such a payment is received on the date the business receives the goods or services agreed in lieu of money. It must account for VAT on the full value of the supply, i.e. the price, including VAT, which a customer would have to pay for the supply if they had paid for it with money only.

(VAT Notice 733, para 9.5 which has the force of law).

Ceasing to use the cash-based method

If at any time a business ceases to use the cash-based accounting method, it must account for VAT on all the supplies made while it was using the method and for which payment has not been received. The supplies must be included in the scheme turnover in the return for the VAT period in which the business ceases to use the cash-based method. The only exception to this is if it ceases to use the flat-rate scheme but immediately starts to use the cash accounting scheme. Any business that leaves the flat-rate scheme and immediately starts to use the cash accounting scheme should apply the appropriate flat-rate percentage to any supplies made while part of the flat-rate scheme when payment for those supplies is received. It may be possible to balance this adjustment with a claim for relief for stocks on hand (see **64.23** below), or a claim in respect of bad debts (see **64.22** below).

(VAT Notice 733, para 9.6 which has the force of law).

(3) The retailer's turnover method

This is essentially the same as a retail scheme and is best if the business is a retailer selling goods to the public. The method is based on 'daily takings'. The business must record payments from customers as they are received and total the takings daily. Flat-rate turnover is the daily gross takings plus any other items of income the business receives, including that from outside the retail environment. At the end of a VAT period, the flat-rate percentage is applied to the flat-rate turnover for that period.

See **61.8 RETAIL SCHEMES** for items to be included in daily takings, adjustments which can be made and the treatment of till shortages and excesses. These provisions also apply to the retailer's turnover method, as do the other adjustments to daily takings for special transactions listed in **61.9 RETAIL SCHEMES**.

Special rules for florists

Special rules apply to members of organisations such as Interflora, Teleflorist or Flowergram.

- A member that receives payment direct from a customer is the 'sending member' and must include the amount the customer pays in its daily gross takings.
- A member that delivers flowers ordered by customers at another florist is the 'executing member' and must add the order value and the VAT shown, from the monthly agency self-billed invoice, to its flat-rate turnover. This is the gross figure.
- When orders taken by one member are delivered by other florists, the invoice from the agency shows the value of these orders as a purchase figure plus VAT. The figures shown may be net or gross depending on which agency is used. The input tax is always shown but this amount cannot be reclaimed under the flat-rate scheme.

(VAT Notice 733, paras 10.1–10.7 which have the force of law).

[*SI 1995/2518, Reg 55G*].

Accounts and records

Invoices

[64.21] VAT invoices must still be issued to VAT-registered customers, charging VAT using the normal rate for the supply (standard rate, reduced rate or zero rate) and *not* the flat-rate percentage. Customers treat these as normal VAT invoices. (VAT Notice 733, paras 7.3, 7.4).

VAT account

A VAT account must still be kept (even if the only VAT to be accounted for is that calculated under the flat-rate scheme). In some cases, however, a business may have VAT to account for outside the flat-rate scheme (e.g. the single purchases or disposals of capital expenditure goods of more than £2,000 in value). This should be entered in the VAT account in the normal way in addition to the flat-rate VAT. (VAT Notice 733, para 7.1).

Records

A record of flat-rate calculations must be kept showing

- flat-rate turnover for the VAT period;
- flat-rate percentage(s) used; and
- the VAT calculated as due.

This record must be kept with the VAT account.

(VAT Notice 733, para 7.2 which has the force of law).

Completing VAT returns

Because a business using the flat-rate scheme is calculating net VAT without reference to output tax and input tax, the rules for completing the VAT return are different. If the value for any box is none, write none in the box. Do not leave any box blank.

Box 1	Include the VAT due under the flat-rate scheme. There may be other output tax to include in this box such as sales of capital expenditure goods on which the business has claimed input tax separately while using the flat-rate scheme. See **64.22** below.
Box 2	Account for VAT on any goods bought from other EU member states at the normal rate of VAT (and not at the flat-rate).
Box 3	Insert sum of boxes 1 and 2 in the normal way.
Box 4	This will normally be none. There may be a claim if
	(i) a single purchase of capital expenditure goods of more than £2,000 in value (including VAT) is made (see **64.22** below);
	(ii) VAT can be recovered on stocks and assets on hand at registration (see **64.16** above); or
	(iii) a claim for bad debt relief is being made (see **64.22** below).
	As with goods and services bought from UK suppliers, VAT must not normally be claim on any acquisitions of goods and related services from other EU member states. But VAT can normally be claimed for any single purchase of capital expenditure goods of £2,000 or more in value (including VAT). See **64.22** below.

Box 5	Insert the difference between Box 3 and Box 4 in the normal way.
Box 6	Enter the value of turnover to which the flat-rate scheme percentage was applied, including VAT. Also include the VAT-exclusive value of any supplies accounted for outside the flat-rate scheme (e.g. supplies of capital expenditure goods).
Box 7	(i) a single purchase of capital expenditure goods costing more than £2,000 (including VAT) is made and input tax us claimed in Box 4; or
	(ii) goods have been acquired from other EU member states, in which case include the VAT-exclusive value in this Box.
Boxes 8 and 9	Complete as normal.

(VAT Notice 733, para 7.5).

Interaction of VAT and direct taxes

HMRC give the following guidance on the direct tax requirements for businesses using the flat-rate scheme.

- *No additional analysis of VAT is required to prepare accounts that are satisfactory for direct tax purposes.* The main bookkeeping advantage of the flat-rate scheme is that each purchase need not be analysed into gross, VAT and net figures when entered into the books of the business. This would be undone if, at the end of each year, these figures still had to be extracted for the preparation of annual accounts acceptable for income tax or corporation tax purposes. HMRC have confirmed that, for businesses that are using the flat-rate scheme, it is expected that accounts will be prepared using gross receipts less the flat-rate VAT percentage for turnover and that expenses will include the irrecoverable input VAT. This is similar in form to accounts prepared by non-VAT-registered businesses who cannot recover VAT they are charged.
- *The standard of records for direct tax purposes is the same as that for VAT.* A key benefit of the flat-rate scheme is that it removes the need to check the deductibility of VAT on purchases and even their liability to VAT. For both VAT and direct taxes, there is still a requirement to keep a record of sales and purchases. But for businesses using the flat-rate scheme, that record does not have to analyse gross, VAT and net separately. HMRC is not prescriptive about the way in which records are kept. For the simplest business, the records may be as little as a file of invoices issued and received in date order with a summary of totals although most businesses will do more than the minimum. In any case, the requirements of HMRC are that the records (whether VAT-exclusive or VAT-inclusive) are orderly and easy to follow.
- *VAT 'profits'.* There is no requirement to keep a separate account of the 'VAT profit' or 'VAT loss' arising from use of the scheme. By its very nature, a scheme based on flat rates for trade sectors leads to almost all businesses that use it paying a different amount of VAT from that they would pay if they were still using the normal system. Those who pay

less VAT will have increased profits that are, in principle, taxable. Those who pay more VAT will have increased costs that, in principle, will reduce direct tax on profits.

Treatment in special circumstances

[64.22] In particular circumstances the flat-rate is treated as follows:

(1) Acquisitions of goods from, and sales of goods to, other EU member states

- If a business sells goods to other EU member states, the income must be included in its flat-rate turnover. This means that, if the business has a higher proportion of such sales than others in its trade sector, it may find that operating the scheme puts it a disadvantage compared to competitors.
- If a business buys goods from other EU member states, it must account for VAT on these acquisitions in Box 2 of its VAT return. Acquisition VAT is payable at the standard rate of VAT and not at the flat rate.

(VAT Notice 733, para 6.4).

(2) Supplies of services to and from abroad

- If a business supplies services which, under the place of supply rules, are treated as supplied outside the UK, these supplies should be left out of the flat-rate turnover.
- *VATA 1994, s 8* (reverse charge on supplies of services from abroad) does not apply to any relevant supply or relevant purchase of a flat-rate trader. [*SI 1995/2518, Reg 55U*]. No adjustment should therefore be made to the flat-rate turnover for services purchased from outside the UK to which the reverse charge applies. See **39.4 INTERNATIONAL SERVICES**.

(VAT Notice 733, para 6.4).

(3) Exempt supplies

If a business is eligible for the flat-rate scheme, it is treated as fully taxable and does not have to make partial exemption calculations. It must, however, include its exempt income in its flat-rate turnover.

(VAT Notice 733, para 6.4).

(4) Motoring expenses

A business using the flat-rate scheme does not have to pay any road fuel scale charges as it does not reclaim input tax on its use of road fuel. (VAT Notice 733, para 6.4).

(5) Second-hand goods

A business can, if it wishes, include sales of second-hand goods in its flat-rate turnover but will pay more VAT on these sales than if it uses the margin scheme for second-hand goods. It is, however, the simplest option where a business makes only occasional sales of second-hand goods and it is not possible to use the flat-rate scheme and the margin scheme at the same time. (VAT Notice 733, para 6.4).

(6) Disbursements by a business acting as an agent

If a business

- pays amounts to third parties as the agent for its client, and
- debits its client with the precise amount paid out

it may be able to treat the payments as disbursements. See **3.7 AGENTS** for further details about disbursements. Where such disbursements are made, the money received for them is not part of the flat-rate turnover of the business.

(VAT Notice 733, para 6.4).

(7) Bad debt relief

8 BAD DEBT RELIEF arises if a business accounts for and pays output tax on supplies for which it is subsequently not paid. The rules in that chapter apply to the flat-rate scheme as explained below.

If using the basic or retailer's turnover methods (see **64.20** above) a business can claim relief on eligible supplies at the standard rate of VAT rather than the flat rate.

If using the cash turnover method, a business may be eligible for bad debt relief if it has

- not been paid by its customer and it has been six months since the supply was made;
- it has not accounted for and paid VAT on the supply; and
- it has written off the debt in its accounts.

Where all these conditions are met, a business can claim the difference between the VAT charged to the customer and the amount it would have declared to HMRC had it been paid. [*SI 1995/2518, Reg 55V; SI 2002/1142*].

Example

C Ltd makes a supply under the flat-rate scheme of £1,000 plus VAT of £200. It uses the cash turnover method to calculate its relevant turnover. The invoice is not paid and C writes off the amount as a bad debt in its accounts after six months. Its flat-rate percentage is 10%.

	£
VAT on the unpaid supply	200.00
Deduct	
VAT which would have been paid under the flat-rate scheme if the customer had paid (£1,200 × 10%)	120.00
Special allowance under the flat-rate scheme.	£80.00

£80.00 should be added to the VAT deductible portion of the VAT account and included in the next VAT return

(VAT Notice 733, paras 14.1, 14.2).

(8) Capital expenditure goods

Capital goods are those goods which are bought to be used in the business but are not used up by it (other than by normal wear and tear over a number of years). Examples include a van (but not the fuel), a computer (but not the printer paper) and a machine.

'*Capital expenditure goods*' under the flat-rate scheme means capital goods that would fall within the above definition, but specifically excluding any goods bought

- for the purpose of resale or incorporation into goods supplied by the business;
- for consumption by the business within one year;
- to generate income by being leased, let or hired.

It also excludes assets covered by the **11 CAPITAL GOODS SCHEME** as, if a business buys or intends to buy such assets, it is ineligible to use the flat-rate scheme.

Nothing in these provisions allows a business to claim credit for input tax where it would not otherwise be allowed to do so by any *order* made under *VATA 1994, s 25(7)* (e.g. on the purchase of a motor car).

VAT on purchases of capital expenditure goods

- VAT can be reclaimed on the single purchase of capital expenditure goods where the amount of the purchase, including VAT, is £2,000 or more. The normal VAT rules apply to determine whether any particular supply is one, or more than one, purchase.
  Any input tax should be claimed in Box 4 of the VAT return on the VAT return in the normal way.
- Otherwise, input tax on the purchase of capital expenditure goods is treated like any other purchase under the flat-rate scheme and no separate claim for input tax can be made.

> *Examples*
>
> A computer package (computer, printer, camera, scanner, speakers, etc.) bought as one package is one purchase of capital expenditure goods. If the package costs £2,000 or more (including VAT) input tax can be claimed.
>
> Items of kitchen equipment (e.g. pizza oven, a fridge and a dishwasher) bought for a restaurant from one supplier at the same time count as one purchase of capital expenditure goods. If they are bought from three different suppliers, or at three different times, they count as three separate purchases and each must be £2,000 or more (including VAT) to qualify for input tax recovery.

Apportionment for private use

To help simplify the flat-rate scheme, where VAT on capital expenditure goods is reclaimable, the intended use of those items is treated as wholly for taxable supplies. Input tax need not be apportioned to cover any planned private or exempt use of the goods and there is no payment of output tax under the flat-rate scheme.

Disposals

The treatment of the sale of capital expenditure goods under the flat-rate scheme depends on how they were treated when acquired.

- Where input tax has been recovered on the purchase either
  (i) before joining the flat-rate scheme, or
  (ii) whilst the scheme is in operation, on capital expenditure goods costing £2,000 or more (including VAT)

  output tax must be accounted for on the sale at the standard rate (not at the flat rate) in the normal way. The income will not form part of the flat-rate turnover.
- Where no separate claim for input tax was made, VAT-inclusive income received from the disposal is included in the flat-rate turnover.

Goods or services

The normal rules apply for determining whether there is a supply of goods or a supply of services. For example, where a van is leased or hired by a business, this is a supply of services. But where it is bought on hire purchase, there is a supply of capital expenditure goods and input tax can be reclaimed if it costs £2,000 or more (including VAT).

[*SI 1995/2518, Regs 55A, 55E*]. (VAT Notice 733, paras 15.1–15.9).

(9) Barristers

Barristers whose chambers use any of the three methods of accounting for common expenses (see **35.13**(3) INPUT TAX) may use the scheme.

Chambers using Method 3 must follow the rules below if they have any members using the flat-rate scheme and must ensure that input tax claims are apportioned and only relate to those barristers who are not on the scheme.

> *Example*
>
> A chambers has ten barristers, two of whom use the flat-rate scheme. The common fund has paid £12,000, including VAT of £2,000, on goods purchased. 30% of the input tax relates to the two barristers using the flat-rate scheme.
>
> If none of the barristers were using the scheme, input tax of £2,000 could have been claimed. But as two of them use the flat-rate scheme, input tax must be apportioned and a claim made, through the nominated member, for 70% (i.e. £1,400) of the VAT paid on the goods. This is the input tax relating to the eight barristers not using the scheme.

Chambers using the adaptation of Method 3 explained above, must ensure that barristers do not claim input tax while they use the scheme. To do this, they must monitor the input tax claimed for common expenses and have records that include

- the value of the original VAT invoice;
- the amount and percentage of input tax claimed back by the nominated member for each VAT invoice;
- how the input tax is apportioned to the individual barristers; and

- how the input tax reclaimed is calculated for each VAT invoice.

The records of all members of chambers using the flat-rate scheme must be made available during a visit to the chambers by an officer from HMRC.

(VAT Notice 733, paras 13.1, 13.2).

Leaving the scheme

[64.23] A business using the flat-rate scheme must continue to account for VAT under the scheme until its '*end date*', i.e. the date with effect from which it ceases to be authorised to use the scheme under the provisions below.

Voluntary withdrawal

A business can leave the scheme voluntarily at any time (although HMRC normally expect most businesses to leave at the end of a VAT period). HMRC will confirm the date of leaving the scheme in writing. (VAT Notice 733, para 12.1).

Ceasing to be eligible

A business ceases to be eligible to use the flat-rate scheme in the following circumstances and must withdraw from the date indicated.

(a) At any anniversary of its start date (i.e. the date from which it was authorised to use the scheme) if the total value of its income in the period of one year then *ending* is more than £230,000 unless HMRC are satisfied that the total value of its income in the period of one year then *beginning* will not exceed £191,500.
The above figures include the VAT-inclusive income of all taxable and exempt supplies, *excluding* supplies of capital assets. See **64.20** above for further details of what is included and excluded.
If, at the anniversary date, the turnover of a business has gone above £230,000, it may be able to remain in the scheme with the agreement of HMRC. It must apply in writing to National Registration Service, HM Revenue & Customs, Imperial House, 77 Victoria Street, Grimsby, Lincolnshire, DN31 1DB and be able to demonstrate that
   - its VAT-inclusive turnover in the coming year will fall below £191,500;
   - the increase was the result of unexpected business activity which has not occurred before and is not expected to recur; and
   - the increase arose from a genuine commercial activity.

   If, however, the increase occurred in such a way that the business must leave the scheme under (*b*) below, it cannot remain in the scheme even if these conditions are met.
   (VAT Notice 733, para 11.2).
   Where a business ceases to be eligible under these provisions, it must withdraw from the scheme
   (i) in the case of a business using the annual accounting scheme, from the end of the annual VAT period in which the relevant anniversary occurred or the end of the month following the month in which the anniversary occurred, whichever is the earlier, or

(ii) in all other cases, the end of the VAT period in which the relevant anniversary occurred.

> *Example*
>
> A business starts to use annual accounting and the flat-rate scheme on 1 May 2010. Its annual accounting year runs from 1 May to 30 April. It carries out the turnover test for the flat-rate scheme on 1 May 2016 and has exceeded the income limit.
>
> The business must leave the flat-rate scheme on the earlier of the end of its current annual VAT accounting period (30 April 2017) and the end of the month following the month in which the anniversary falls (30 June 2016), i.e. 30 June 2016.
>
> If the business was on quarterly returns, it would leave the scheme on 1 August 2016 – the anniversary of the start date is the first day of the June quarter, and the trader must leave the scheme at the beginning of the *following* quarter.

(b) There are reasonable grounds to believe that the total value of its income in the period of 30 days then beginning will exceed £230,000. The business must withdraw from the scheme from the beginning of the period of 30 days in question.
The above figures include the VAT-inclusive income of all taxable and exempt supplies, *excluding* supplies of capital assets. See **64.20** above for further details of what is included and excluded.

(c) It becomes a tour operator and must account for VAT under the **69 TOUR OPERATORS' MARGIN SCHEME**, in which case it must withdraw from that date.

(d) It intends to acquire, construct or otherwise obtain a capital item within the **11 CAPITAL GOODS SCHEME**, in which case it must withdraw from that date.

(e) It opts to account for VAT on a supply on the profit margin under the second-hand goods scheme or the auctioneers' scheme (see **62 SECOND-HAND GOODS**), in which case it must withdraw from the beginning of the VAT period for which it makes the election.

(f) It becomes
(i) eligible to be registered for VAT in the name of a group under *VATA 1994, s 43A* (see **28.2 GROUPS OF COMPANIES**),
(ii) registered for VAT in the name of a division under *VATA 1994, s 46(1)* (see **60.43 REGISTRATION**); or
(iii) 'associated with' another person.
In either case, the business must withdraw from the scheme from the date the event occurred. Note that it is eligibility to be in a VAT group which is the key test, not whether the business is actually in one.
A person is '*associated with*' another person at any time if that other person makes supplies in the course or furtherance of a business carried on by him, and

- the business of one is under the dominant influence of the other, or

- the persons are closely bound to one another by financial, economic and organisational links.

HMRC treat this as applying where one business has the right to give directions to another or, in practice, a business habitually complies with the directions of another. The test here is a test of the commercial reality rather than of the legal form. A close connection with another business is not necessarily the same as being associated. For example, a business is not associated with its customers just because it supplies them with the goods they request in the form they request them. Similarly, a husband and wife who are each separately VAT-registered in different types of business are not associated even if they share premises (provided this is charged at a market rate). (VAT Notice 733, paras 3.9, 3.10).

(g) Its authorisation to use the scheme is terminated by HMRC because
- they consider it necessary to do so for the protection of the revenue, or
- a false statement was made by, or on behalf of, the business in relation to its application for authorisation

in which case the business must withdraw from the scheme from the date of issue of a notice of termination by HMRC or such earlier or later date as may be directed in the notification.

Notifying HMRC

Where any of (*a*)–(*f*) above apply, the business must notify HMRC in writing of that fact within 30 days.

Consequences of leaving the scheme

A business leaving the scheme can rejoin at a later date but will not be eligible to rejoin for a period of twelve months after leaving the scheme.

The transition from the scheme back to the normal VAT rules is usually simple although there are some circumstances where adjustments must be made to make the VAT returns accurate.

(1) Ceasing to use the flat-rate scheme in the middle of a VAT period

A business which leaves the flat-rate scheme in the middle of a VAT period must do two calculations when completing its next VAT return, one for the part period when it was in the flat-rate scheme using the scheme rules and the other for the part period after leaving the scheme using the normal VAT rules. VAT liability for the return period is the sum of those two calculations.

(VAT Notice 733, para 12.7).

(2) Cash-based method used under the flat-rate scheme

Where the cash-based method is used under the flat-rate scheme and the business does *not* move immediately to the cash accounting scheme, it must account for VAT on all the supplies it made while using the flat-rate scheme for which payment has not been received. The supplies should be included in the scheme turnover in the return for the period in which the business ceases to use the cash-based method.

Where the cash-based method is used under the flat-rate scheme and the business moves immediately to the cash accounting scheme, it must apply the appropriate flat-rate percentage to any supplies made while part of the flat-rate scheme when payment for those supplies is received.

(VAT Notice 733, para 12.7).

(3) Adjustments in respect of stock on hand at withdrawal from the flat-rate scheme

Where

- a business remains registered for VAT after leaving the flat-rate scheme,
- at the date it ceases to be authorised to use the scheme, it has stock on hand in respect of which it is not entitled to credit for input tax, and
- the value of that stock on hand exceeds the value of its stock on hand in respect of which it was entitled to credit for input tax when it started to use the scheme

the business is entitled to credit for input tax in respect of its stock on hand calculated as follows.

Step 1	Establish the VAT-exclusive value of stock on hand and on which input tax had been recovered before joining the flat-rate scheme. (If previously using the cash accounting scheme, this will be based on stock for which the business had paid.) — say	£10,000
Step 2	Establish the VAT-exclusive value of stock on hand and on which the business will be unable to recover input tax after it ceases to use the flat-rate scheme — say	£20,000
Step 3	Subtract the figure at Step 1 from the total at Step 2. (If the figure at Step 1 is larger than the figure at Step 2, no adjustment can be made.)	£10,000
Step 4	Multiply the result of Step 3 by the standard rate of VAT = £10,000 × 20% (17.5% from 1 January 2010 to 3 January 2011; 15% from 1 December 2008 to 31 December 2009)	£2,000
Claim the VAT calculated at Step 4 in the VAT recoverable portion of the VAT account in the first return made after leaving the flat-rate scheme.		

There is no need to do a formal stock take for the purpose of the calculation, but figures must be reasonable and a record should be kept of how stock was valued in case HMRC query the figures.

(VAT Notice 733, paras 12.7–12.9).

(4) Self-supply of capital expenditure goods on withdrawal from the flat-rate scheme

Where

- a business remains registered for VAT after leaving the flat-rate scheme,
- for any VAT period for which it used the scheme it was entitled to, and claimed, credit for input tax in respect of any capital expenditure goods, and

- it did not, whilst using the scheme, make a supply of those goods,

then, on the day after it ceases to use the scheme, those goods are treated as being both supplied to the business and supplied by the business in the course or furtherance of its business.

The value of the supply is calculated as for a supply for no consideration. See **72.22 VALUATION.**

[*SI 1995/2518, Regs 55B(4), 55M, 55N(3)(4), 55P–55S*].

Appeals

[64.24] If a business disagrees with a decision of HMRC

- refusing authorisation to use the scheme,
- withdrawing authorisation to use the scheme, or
- as to the appropriate flat-rate percentage(s) that applies to the business,

it may appeal to the First-tier Tribunal.

Where an appeal is brought against such a decision or, to the extent that it is based on such a decision, against an assessment, the tribunal must not allow the appeal unless it considers that HMRC could not reasonably have been satisfied that there were grounds for the decision.

[*VATA 1994, ss 83(fza), 84(4ZA)*].

Flat-rate scheme for farmers

[64.25] The flat-rate scheme is an alternative to VAT registration for farmers. Farmers already registered for VAT may either remain registered or de-register and join the flat-rate scheme (provided the value of their non-farming activities is not above the VAT registration threshold, see below). Farmers whose turnover is below the registration limit may also use the scheme if they would otherwise qualify for voluntary registration.

A farmer has to apply to HMRC to join the scheme. HMRC may then certify him for the purposes of these provisions where satisfied that

- he is carrying on a business involving one or more designated activities (see **64.26** below); and
- he has complied with the necessary conditions for admission to the scheme (see **64.27** below).

[*VATA 1994, s 54*].

Certification

If the application is accepted, the farmer is issued with a certificate (showing a unique reference number) which is proof that he qualifies for the scheme. If application is refused, an appeal may be made to a VAT tribunal.

Where a person is so certified, goods and services supplied as part of those designated activities are disregarded in determining whether he is, has become or has ceased to become liable or entitled to be registered for VAT under *VATA 1994, Sch 1* or *Sch 1A*.

[*SI 1995/2518, Reg 203*].

Flat-rate addition instead of VAT

Farmers who are certified under the flat-rate scheme do not account for VAT, or submit returns, on sales of goods and services within the designated activities to other VAT-registered customers. This means that they cannot reclaim the related input tax.

To compensate for this, on sales of designated goods and services to VAT-registered persons, farmers *may* charge a fixed flat-rate addition of 4% on top of the sales price. This applies even if some of the goods would otherwise be zero-rated. The farmer retains this addition and the registered person is able to recover it as if it were VAT (subject to the normal rules). [*VATA 1994, s 54(3)(4); SI 1995/2518, Reg 209*].

The flat-rate addition must not be charged on supplies of goods and services which are not designated (e.g. sales of machinery) or on supplies to non-registered persons (e.g. the public or other flat-rate farmers).

Sales through farmers' groups and co-operatives

Where a farmer sells produce in this way, the goods are combined with the produce of other farmers and the buyer has no way of knowing whether any of his suppliers are flat-rate farmers. In such cases, the buyer should pay the farmer's group only the price agreed for the produce *without the flat-rate addition*. The group should pay the flat-rate addition to those farmers who have a certificate when the proceeds of sale are shared out. The farmer's group can reclaim this addition on its own VAT return as though it were input tax.

Auctioneers' sales

- *If the auctioneer is using the auctioneers' scheme or the margin scheme and acting in his own name*, he is regarded as a principal for VAT purposes, buying and selling the goods. In such a case, a flat-rate farmer can charge the flat-rate addition to the auctioneer who can reclaim it on his VAT return. The sale by the auctioneer is subject to the normal VAT rules.
- *If the auctioneer is not using either of those schemes and not acting in his own name*, he is not regarded as purchasing and selling the goods for VAT purposes. In such a case, the flat-rate farmer cannot charge the flat-rate addition to the auctioneer but can charge it to the eventual buyer of the goods if the buyer is VAT-registered.

Sales to other EU member states

A flat-rate farmer can charge the flat-rate addition on designated sales to VAT-registered persons in other EU member states (even though no VAT would have been due on the sale). The customer in the other country can reclaim the flat-rate addition charged provided he receives a flat-rate invoice.

Buying from other EU member states

Where a VAT-registered person in the UK acquires goods or services from a farmer in another EU member state who charges the flat-rate addition, this can be reclaimed but from the VAT authority in the supplier's country (and not from HMRC). HMRC can give details of the procedure to be followed.

If a flat-rate farmer acquires goods from another EU member state in excess of an annual threshold, he may have to register for VAT and lose the flat-rate status. See **60.18 REGISTRATION**.

Sales made outside the EU

A flat-rate farmer can charge the addition on designated goods and services to purchasers outside the EU provided the goods are used for the business purposes of the purchaser.

Other farming income

Where a farmer leases or lets some of the material assets of his farming business on a long-term basis but continues to farm under the flat-rate scheme in respect of the continued farming activity, the income from such a lease and/or letting cannot be treated as taxable under the scheme and must be taxed in the normal way (*Finanzamt Rendsburg v Harbs, ECJ Case C–321/02* [2006] STC 340 (TVC 22.558)).

Non-farming activities

If the taxable turnover of non-farming activities (e.g. bed and breakfast) is less than the VAT registration threshold, a farmer can still be a flat-rate farmer. He must not charge VAT or the flat-rate addition on the non-farming activities.

If his turnover of non-farming activities is above the VAT threshold, a farmer must remain registered for VAT (or, if already in the flat-rate scheme, have his certificate cancelled and register for VAT). The farmer will not be eligible to join the flat-rate scheme unless

- the non-farming activities are zero-rated, in which case the farmer may ask for exemption from registration (see **60.6 REGISTRATION**) and join the scheme; or
- the non-farming business is run as a separate business by a different legal entity (e.g. a farmer could run his farming activities as a sole proprietor and a bed and breakfast business in partnership with another person).

(VAT Notice 700/46/12, paras 4.1–4.4, 5.2, 6.1–6.3, 8.1, 8.2).

Deregistration

Farmers who deregister to join the flat-rate scheme do not have to account for VAT on their stocks and assets on hand, even where they have claimed input tax when purchasing them. [*VATA 1994, Sch 4 para 8(3)*].

De Voil Indirect Tax Service. See V2.191–198.

Designated activities

[64.26] For the purposes of the scheme, a farmer is someone who engages in any of the following activities.

(a) **Crop production** comprising any of the following.

- General agriculture including viticulture
- Growing of fruit, vegetables, flowers and ornamental plants (in the open and under glass)
- Production of mushrooms, spices, seeds and propagating materials
- Nursery production i.e. the rearing of young plants for sale

A marketing co-operative or a business selling peat or top soil is not eligible to join the scheme.

(b) **Stock farming** comprising any of the following.

- General stock farming
- Poultry and rabbit farming
- Bee-keeping and silkworm farming
- Snail farming

The following activities do not qualify.

- Raising budgerigars and other birds in aviaries purely as pets.
- Raising butterflies and any other animals or birds raised for similar purposes, for example, cats and dogs (except sheepdogs).
- Most other activities involving animals (e.g. pony trekking, riding lessons, hunting).
- Training animals as a specialist activity.
- Training horses bred for racing and any specialist training of horses for show-jumping or eventing.
- Training pigeons for racing (however, the breeding, rearing and care of pigeons would fall within the scheme).

(c) **Forestry**. This covers growing, felling and general husbandry of trees in a forest, wood or copse. Included is the conversion of felled timber into sawlogs, industrial small diameter roundwood, pitprops, cordwood, fencing material and firewood. Any activity involving any process beyond that stage is excluded.

(d) **Fisheries** comprising fresh-water fishing; fish farming; breeding of mussels, oysters and other molluscs and crustaceans; and frog farming.

(e) **Processing** by a farmer of products derived from his own activities within *(a)*–*(d)* above using only such means as are normally employed in the course of such activities.

(f) **Supplies of agricultural services**, by a person who also carries out one or more other designated activities falling within *(a)*–*(e)* above, comprising

- field work, reaping and mowing, threshing, bailing, collecting, harvesting, sowing and planting;
- packing and preparation of agricultural products for market (including drying, cleaning, grinding, disinfecting and ensilaging);
- storage of agricultural products;
- stock minding, rearing and fattening;
- hiring out of equipment for use in any designated activity;
- technical assistance in relation to any designated activity;
- destruction of weeds and pests, dusting and spraying of crops and land;
- operation of irrigation and drainage equipment; and
- lopping, tree felling and other forestry services.

Services concerned with the sale or leasing of milk quotas (whether or not they are sold with the land) are not a designated activity.

A person cannot join the scheme if

- his primary activity is to buy and sell animals (e.g. a dealer or trainer); or
- he is engaged in an activity once removed from farming (e.g. processing farm produce).

[*SI 1992/3220*]. (VAT Notice 700/46/12, paras 1.4, 3.1–3.4).

Admission to the scheme and changes in circumstances

[64.27] HMRC must certify a person for the purposes of the flat-rate scheme if the following conditions are satisfied.

(a) He satisfies HMRC that he is carrying on one or more designated activities within **64.26** above.

(b) If he is currently registered for VAT, that registration is cancelled. See **64.25** above for the position where non-farming activities are also carried on.

(c) He has not, in the three years before the date of application for certification,
   - been convicted of any offences in connection with VAT;
   - accepted an offer to compound proceedings in connection with a VAT offence; or
   - been assessed to a penalty for VAT evasion involving dishonest conduct (see **53.12 PENALTIES**).

(d) He makes an application for certification on the correct form (Form VAT 98). The completed form should be sent to HM Revenue and Customs, Imperial House, 77 Victoria Street, Grimsby, DN31 1DB.

(e) He satisfies HMRC that, in the year following the date of his certification, the amounts of the flat-rate additions which he charges will not exceed the amount of input tax to which he would otherwise be entitled to credit by £3,000 or more. This will always be satisfied where the estimated value of agricultural supplies (shown in Box 4 of Form VAT 98) is £75,000 or less.

[*SI 1995/2518, Reg 204*].

Date of admission

The certificate issued by HMRC is effective from the date on which application is received by HMRC or, if the applicant so requests, from a date 30 days or less after that date. Alternatively, it may be such earlier date as HMRC agree to. No certificate can, however, be effective before any existing VAT registration is cancelled. [*SI 1995/2518, Reg 205*].

Further certification

Where a person who has been certified under the scheme, and is no longer so certified, makes a further application, he cannot be certified for a period of three years from the date of cancellation of the previous certificate except as follows.

(i) Where he has not been registered, or required to be registered, for VAT at any time since the cancellation of his previous certificate, HMRC may certify him from the date of his further application.

(ii) Where he has been registered for VAT during that time but no VAT was due on his business assets on hand at the date of deregistration because the VAT would not have been more than £1,000 (see **60.40 REGISTRATION**), HMRC may certify him on a date after the expiry of one year from the date of cancellation of his previous certificate.

[*SI 1995/2518, Reg 208*].

Changes in circumstances

The certificate issued by HMRC shows the full name of the business if the owner is a sole proprietor or company and the address of the business. In the case of a partnership, it shows the trading name of the partnership or, if it does not have one, the names of at least two partners (although, in such a case, the certificate still covers all the partners listed in the application form). HMRC must be informed of any change of name or address, any changes in the members of a partnership and if a sole proprietor takes a partner. HMRC will then reissue the certificate with the same number. In all other cases where the legal entity changes, the existing certificate must be cancelled and the new entity must apply for a new certificate. (VAT Notice 700/46/12, paras 2.3, 9.1).

Cancellation of certificates

[64.28] HMRC may or, as the case may be, must cancel a person's certificate in any of the following circumstances and from the date stated.

(a) Where a statement false in a material particular was made by him or on his behalf in connection with his application. Cancellation is from the date HMRC discover that such a statement has been made.

(b) He has been convicted of, or has accepted an offer to compound proceedings in connection with, a VAT offence or has been assessed to a VAT penalty. Cancellation is from the date of conviction, date of payment of the sum to compound proceedings or 30 days after the date the assessment is notified.

(c) He ceases to be involved in designated activities. Cancellation is from the date of cessation.

(d) He dies or becomes bankrupt or incapacitated. Cancellation is from the date of death, etc. HMRC may, however, in such cases, until such time as some other person is certified in respect of those activities, treat as a certified person any person carrying on those designated activities. That person must inform HMRC in writing within 30 days of the fact that he is carrying on the activities and the date of death, bankruptcy or incapacity.
Where the certified person is a company, the reference to bankruptcy is to be construed as a reference to liquidation, receivership or administration as the case may be.

(e) He is liable to be registered for VAT. Cancellation is from the effective date of registration.

(f) He makes an application in writing for cancellation. Cancellation is from a date not less than one year after the effective date of his certificate or such earlier date as HMRC agree to.
(g) He makes an application in writing for voluntary VAT registration (which application is deemed to be an application for cancellation of his certificate). Cancellation is from a date not less than one year after the effective date of his certificate or such earlier date as HMRC agree to.
(h) HMRC consider it is necessary to do so for the protection of the revenue (e.g. because the farmer is found to be recovering substantially more as a flat-rate farmer than he would if registered for VAT in the normal way). Cancellation is from the date on which HMRC consider a risk to the revenue arises.
(i) HMRC are not satisfied that any of the grounds for cancellation of a certificate within *(a)*–*(g)* above do not apply. Cancellation is from the date in *(a)*–*(g)* as appropriate.

[*SI 1995/2518, Regs 206, 207*].

A flat-rate farmer who leaves the scheme to register for VAT is not entitled to claim relief for any VAT incurred on purchases whilst he was a member of the scheme. (HMRC Manual VATAFRS0400).

The CJEU has recently released its judgment in *Shields & Sons Partnership v HMRC, CJEU Case C-262/16*, [2017] STC 2205 (TVC 20.230) ruling in favour of the taxpayer in agreement with the Advocate-General's Opinion. The issue before the Court was whether HMRC could exclude a business from using the scheme simply because it was able to recover significantly more VAT as a flat-rate farmer than it would have if it were VAT registered and using normal VAT accounting. The CJEU, decided that HMRC had acted illegitimately, since the conditions of joining the scheme did not include a criterion of low fiscal advantage, and they could not just make up conditions as they went along. The Advocate-General Opinion also stated that a farmer who fulfils the scheme requirements should be able to legitimately expect that he would have the right to access the scheme and remain within that scheme regardless of the actual financial result that is achieved in each tax year. *Directive 2006/112/EC, Art 296(2)* does not enable member states to exclude certain categories of farmers who are able to recover substantially more as member of that scheme than they would achieve using normal VAT accounting. The Advocate-General also observed that categories that are to be excluded from the flat-rate scheme must be determined in advance, and in an abstract way, as this is necessary under the principal of legal certainty and for the protection of legitimate expectation.

Records

[64.29] Every certified person must comply with such requirements relating to keeping, preserving and producing records as HMRC notify to him. In particular, every certified person must

(a) keep and preserve business and accounting records and copies of all invoices showing flat-rate additions (see **64.30** below) for six years (or such lesser period as HMRC allow); and

(b) upon demand by a person acting under the authority of HMRC (an '*authorised person*') produce, or cause to be produced, for inspection by that person any document within (*a*) above. The document must be produced at the principal place of business (or at such other place as may be reasonably required) at such time as may reasonably be required. The authorised person may take copies or make extracts of any document and may, at a reasonable time and for a reasonable period, remove any document. Where any document removed is reasonably required for the proper conduct of the business, a copy must be provided free of charge as soon as practicable. If any documents removed are lost or damaged, reasonable compensation must be paid.

[*SI 1995/2518, Regs 210, 211*].

Invoices

[64.30] In order that a registered person in receipt of a supply of designated goods and services may treat the flat-rate addition as if it were input tax for VAT purposes, the farmer must issue an invoice containing the following particulars.

- An identifying invoice number.
- His name, address and certificate number.
- The name and address of the person to whom the goods or services are supplied.
- The time of the supply.
- A description of the goods or services supplied.
- The consideration of the supply excluding the flat-rate addition.
- An amount entitled 'Flat-rate Addition' or 'FRA'.

[*SI 1995/2518, Reg 209*].

See **53.16 PENALTIES** for the penalty for unauthorised issue of flat-rate farming invoices.

VAT registration scheme for racehorse owners

[64.31] The VAT registration scheme (the 'scheme') for racehorse owners was introduced with the agreement of the thoroughbred horseracing and breeding industry. Subject to conditions, owners are accepted as carrying on a business and can register for VAT.

Conditions for registration

An owner of racehorses can apply for VAT registration under the Scheme if registered as an owner at Weatherbys and either

(a) the horses are covered by a sponsorship agreement registered at Weatherbys or by a trainer's sponsorship agreement registered at Weatherbys; or
(b) the owner can show that he has received business income from horseracing activities (e.g. appearance money or sponsored number cloths) and will continue to do so.

Normal procedure applies on application for registration (see **60.5 REGISTRATION**) with the additional requirement that Form D1 (owners not in partnership) or D2 (partnerships), certified as correct by Weatherbys, must be sent to HMRC with the VAT registration form(s). Forms D1 and D2 are obtained from, and must be sent for certification to, VAT Declarations, Weatherbys, Sanders Road, Wellingborough, Northants, NN8 4BX.

If registration is approved, HMRC will issue a VAT registration number and inform the owner of his effective date of registration (normally the date the completed D form was received at Weatherbys).

Only the registered owner of a racehorse at Weatherbys may register for VAT under the Scheme. The registered owner can be a sole proprietor, partnership or limited company. Where a part share only in a racehorse is owned, the part owner can register in his own name if owning at least 50% of the horse. Otherwise, he must register in partnership with the other joint owners.

Owners already VAT-registered outside the Scheme

Where an owner is already registered for VAT under the normal VAT registration rules for business activities connected with bloodstock, and his racehorse owning activities form part of that business, e.g. if he is

- a breeder who races colts, fillies or home bred geldings with the intention of enhancing the value of their breeding stock,
- a trainer who owns and retains horses to attract owners or buyers and to provide rides for apprentices, provided the number of horses is not disproportionate to the main activity of training, or
- a dealer who purchases and sells racehorses commercially, and who races the horses held as trading stock, provided those racehorses are available for sale,

the owner does not need to register under the Scheme.

Where the owner is registered for VAT for a business activity unconnected with bloodstock or his ownership of racehorses is not regarded as part of his normal bloodstock-related business, HMRC will normally only accept that a racehorse forms part of his existing business if he can show the horse was purchased for business purposes (e.g. it advertises the business). But provided all the conditions of the Scheme are met, any horses owned which are not part of the owner's normal business may still be treated as part of the owner's VAT registration.

Sponsorship

After registration:

(i) If sponsorship is lost, the owner can only remain registered if actively seeking new sponsorship. Although there is no time limit set for an owner to sign up to a new agreement, as a rule of thumb HMRC expect it to be no longer than six months after the expiry of the old agreement. If longer, HMRC will ask the owner to confirm, in writing, the steps being taken to obtain sponsorship. If not satisfied with the explanation, HMRC will consider whether the registration should be cancelled and any input tax implications.

(ii) Any horses owned which are not covered by a sponsorship agreement can still be treated as part of the Scheme but only if the owner can show that he is actively seeking sponsorship for them.

(VAT Notice 700/67/17, paras 1.2, 2.1–2.3, 3.1–3.3; VAT Notice 700/57/14).

Input tax

VAT incurred on the purchase, training, upkeep, etc. of a racehorse put to training (including any period when it is unable to run due to injury provided there is an expectation it will run in the future) is recoverable as input tax. All other amounts of VAT incurred by an owner in pursuit of horseracing activities can be deducted subject to the normal rules.

Output tax

Sponsorship income

Sponsorship income is a standard-rated supply. The normal rules for sponsorship apply. A taxable supply takes place where the owner supplies clearly identifiable benefits to their sponsor (e.g. advertises the sponsors name or products on their colours or reflects the sponsor in the name of the racehorse).

Prize money and appearance money

Both are treated as a standard-rated taxable supplies. These payments are distributed by Weatherbys, and are shown on monthly statements ('transaction analysis summaries') which are sent to all owners. (The statements also show certain expenditure, for example, jockeys' services, on which input tax can be reclaimed.)

Gifts, etc.

VAT is due on racehorses given away or put to non-business use, based on what the horse would cost at the time of its disposal, taking into account its fitness/health, etc. at that time. See, however, VAT Notice 700/57/14 for an agreement between HMRC, the British Horseracing Board and the Thoroughbred Breeders Association on racehorses applied permanently to personal or non-business use.

Margin scheme

Where no VAT was charged on the purchase, the margin scheme for second-hand goods can be used and VAT accounted for on the profit margin. See **62 SECOND-HAND GOODS** generally and, in particular, **62.37** for special provisions applying to horses.

(VAT Notice 700/67/17, paras 5.2, 5.4–5.6).

De Voil Indirect Tax Service. See V2.118.

Special arrangements for point-to-point horses

[64.32] An owner of a 'qualifying horse' (i.e. a horse with a sponsorship agreement which is entered in a hunter chase) can register for VAT under the scheme for the hunter chasing season only (January to June). Registration procedure is as in **64.31** above. If already registered for VAT (under these arrangements, under the scheme or because of other business activities) there is no requirements to apply for separate registration but Form D1 or D2 as appropriate must still be completed. After the end of the hunter chasing season, VAT registration can be retained provided

- the owner can show the intention to enter the horse in hunter chases in the following season; and
- the existing sponsorship agreement is to continue or the owner intends to obtain sponsorship before the horse competes in the first race in the new season.

If these conditions cannot be met, either registration will be cancelled or, if it is continuing for other reasons, no further input tax can be recovered in respect of the horse.

(VAT Notice 700/67/17, paras 6.1–6.4).

Input tax

Input tax cannot be recovered VAT until the horse becomes a qualifying horse. Once it does, 50% of any VAT charged on its purchase can be recovered provided it was incurred no more than three years before the date of registration. (The 50% restriction is a rule of thumb apportionment which recognises that the horse is used partly for business and partly for private purposes.)

With effect from the date of registration, VAT can be recovered on

- the training, keep and other costs of a qualifying horse (temporary periods of absences due to illness or injury can be ignored); and
- the purchase or construction of fixed assets used solely for a qualifying horse. Where, for example, a stable block or horse transporter is used for both qualifying and non-qualifying horses, the VAT must be apportioned to reflect the dual usage.

It is also possible to recover

- 50% of VAT charged on training, keep and other costs of a qualifying horse in the six months prior to registration, or the date a qualifying horse runs in a hunter chase; and
- other VAT charged before registration subject to the normal requirements in **35.10 INPUT TAX**.

Output tax

In addition to the information on output tax in **64.31** above, the following rules also apply to qualifying point-to-point horses.

VAT must be charged on the sale of a qualifying horse if the owner bred the horse and recovered VAT on the breeding cost. (No VAT is due on the sale of a non-qualifying horse if no VAT has been recovered in respect of it.) If a horse ceases to be a qualifying horse (e.g. because it is put to a permanent non-business use), VAT must be accounted for on 50% of the open market value.

(VAT Notice 700/67/17, paras 6.5, 6.6).

VAT treatment of racing clubs, etc.

[64.33] Racing clubs may take a number of forms.

(a) **Limited companies selling shares.** A limited company sells its shares (an exempt supply) and uses the funds to buy racehorses in the company name. Profits may be distributed to shareholders as dividends.
Unless the company has other business activities involving the making of taxable supplies, it can only register for VAT if it meets the conditions of the Scheme in **64.31** above. Any benefits available to shareholders (e.g. visits to trainers, free entry to racecourses, etc.) are disregarded for VAT purposes.

(b) **Racing partnerships selling shares.** A limited company or partnership sets up a racing partnership offering for sale a specific number of shares in the venture. Proceeds from prize money, sale of racehorses, etc. are distributed to the owners on termination of the partnership.
The sale of shares is outside the scope of VAT. Any benefits the owners of the shares receive (e.g. visits to trainers, free entry to racecourses, etc.) are disregarded for VAT purposes. Unless the partnership has other business activities involving the making of taxable supplies, it can only register for VAT if it meets the conditions of the scheme in **64.31** above.

(c) **Members racing club raising subscriptions.** A limited company, partnership or sole proprietor calling itself a 'racing club' (or having the characteristics of a club) invites persons to become members on payment of subscriptions. The subscriptions are used to buy racehorses, etc. and at the end of the year surplus income is distributed to members.
   - *If members receive benefits* (e.g. newsletters, visits to trainers, tipping service), the club is carrying on a business. [*VATA 1994, s 94(2)*]. See **15.1 CLUBS AND ASSOCIATIONS**. The subscription income is liable to VAT and the club must register for VAT if above the registration threshold (or otherwise may apply for voluntary registration). The scheme under **64.31** above does not apply.
   - *If members receive no benefits*, the club is not in business and the subscriptions are outside the scope of VAT. The club can only register for VAT if it meets the conditions of the scheme in **64.31** above.

(VAT Notice 700/67/17, paras 7.1–7.4).

Special scheme for non-EU suppliers of electronically supplied services before 1 January 2015

[64.34] Before 1 January 2015, the place of supply of electronically supplied services was:

- where the customer belonged, if supplied to a business;
- where the supplier belonged, if supplied to a consumer;

- in either case, where the supply was 'used and enjoyed', if the above rules placed the supply in the UK but the use and enjoyment was outside the EU (outside the scope) or the above rules placed the supply outside the EU but use and enjoyment was in the UK (subject to UK VAT).

For further details of the place of supply rules, see **66.16 SUPPLY: PLACE OF SUPPLY**. A non-EU business supplying electronically supplied services to UK consumers, for 'use and enjoyment' in the UK, was liable for output tax in the UK under these rules, and also liable for output tax in other EU member states under their equivalent rules. This would mean that a non-EU business would be required, under the normal rules, to register separately and account for VAT in each EU member state in which it provided electronically supplied services to private individuals and non-business organisations.

To avoid this, a special scheme, the VAT on E-Services (VoES) scheme, offered eligible non-EU businesses the *option* of registering electronically in a single EU member state of their choice and accounting for VAT on their sales of these services to all such EU consumers. This was done on a single quarterly electronic VAT declaration which provides details of VAT due in each EU member state. The declaration was submitted with payment to the tax administration in the EU member state of registration which then distributed the VAT to the countries where the services are consumed.

The VoES scheme was available for declarations relating to periods before 1 January 2015. For periods starting after that date a modified version of the VoES scheme is available, the non-Union VAT Mini One Stop Shop (non-Union VAT MOSS) (see **64.40**).

Example

A USA business, with customers in the UK, Italy and Spain, registered for the special scheme in the UK. It charged UK VAT to its UK customers, Italian VAT to its Italian customers and Spanish VAT to its Spanish customers. The business entered the VAT for each country on the appropriate line of the electronic declaration. It sent the declaration electronically with payment to HMRC who retained the UK VAT and passed on the Italian VAT to the Italian authorities and the Spanish VAT to the Spanish authorities.

Any non-EU business which used the scheme had to comply with its conditions, including electronically registering (see **64.36** below) and accounting for and paying the VAT due at the correct time (see **64.37** below). There were no penalties under the scheme but if a business persistently failed to comply with the conditions, its registration could be cancelled. In that event, it would have to register under the normal rules applying in the various EU member states where its customers belonged and could then be subject to any penalties which those countries applied. Similarly, if a non-EU business supplied electronic services to UK consumers and failed to register for VAT (either under the scheme or under the normal rules), it could be compulsorily registered in the UK under the normal rules and could incur a late registration penalty.

The VoES scheme did not apply to broadcasting or telecommunication services. If a non-EU business chose not to register under the special scheme, or was not eligible for it, it had to register under the normal rules which applied in the relevant EU member state.

(VAT Information Sheet 1/03, para 9.1; VAT Information Sheet 7/03, paras 1.1, 1.3; VAT Information Sheet 10/03, para 2.1).

For full details of the VoES scheme, see **64.35–64.39** below.

Businesses eligible to join the scheme

[64.35] A business was eligible to be registered under the special scheme in the UK if it satisfied the following conditions.

(a) It made, or intended to make, 'qualifying supplies' in the course of a business.

(b) It had neither a business establishment nor a fixed establishment in the UK or in another EU member state in relation to *any* supply of goods or services. See **66.13 SUPPLY: PLACE OF SUPPLY** for the interpretation of 'business establishment' and 'fixed establishment'.

(c) It was not
- registered under *VATA 1994*,
- identified for the purposes of VAT in accordance with the law of another EU member state, or
- registered under an *Act of Tynwald* for the purposes of any tax imposed by or under an *Act of Tynwald* which corresponds to VAT.

(d) It was not required to be registered or identified as mentioned in (*c*) above (or if it was required to be so registered or identified, this was solely by virtue of the fact that it made or intended to make qualifying supplies).

(e) It was not identified under any provision of the law of another EU member state which implemented the scheme (i.e. it had not registered under a similar special scheme in another EU member state).

'*Qualifying supply*' meant a supply of electronically supplied services (within the meaning of *VATA 1994, Sch 4A para 8*, see **66.19 SUPPLY: PLACE OF SUPPLY**) to a person who:

- belonged in the UK or another EU member state; and
- received those services otherwise than for the purposes of a business carried on by him.

[*VATA 1994, Sch 3B paras 2, 3*].

Provided the above conditions were met, a non-EU business could use the special scheme if it made supplies to business customers as well as non-business customers. In such a case, it was not required to charge and account for VAT on electronically supplied services supplied to EU businesses (including non-business organisations, such as a government department, receiving supplies for business purposes) because the EU customer accounted for any VAT due under the reverse charge mechanism. (VAT Information Sheet 7/03, para 2.3).

Registration

[64.36] Where a business satisfied HMRC that it met the conditions in **64.35** above, on request HMRC *were required to* register the business under these provisions. The only exception to this was that HMRC were not required to, but *could*, register a business under these provisions where it was a '*persistent defaulter*' (i.e. where a previous registration under these provisions had been cancelled for persistent failure to comply with the rules of the scheme (see below) or it had been excluded under the scheme in another EU member state for the same reason).

Any registration request was required to contain the following particulars.

(a) The name of the business making the request.
(b) Its postal address and electronic addresses (including any websites).
(c) Where it had been allocated a number by the tax authorities in the country in which it belonged, that number.
(d) The date on which it began, or intended to begin, making 'qualifying supplies' (see **64.35** above).
(e) A statement that it was not
    (i) registered under *VATA 1994*;
    (ii) identified for the purposes of VAT in accordance with the law of another EU member state, or
    (iii) registered under an *Act of Tynwald* for the purposes of any tax imposed by or under an *Act of Tynwald* which corresponds to VAT.

The registration request was required to contain any further information, and any declaration about its contents, that HMRC might by regulations require and had to be made by such electronic means, and in such manner, as HMRC directed or might by regulations require.

[*VATA 1994, Sch 3B paras 4, 9; FA 2014, Sch 22*].

Businesses could register at the dedicated website https://secure.hmce.gov.uk/ecom/voes. This was a secure site which automatically guided the applicant through an electronic registration process, including selecting a user name and password for identification purposes when completing and submitting declarations electronically.

HMRC also asked for a contact name and telephone number.

(VAT Information Sheet 7/03, paras 3.2, 3.3).

Effective date of registration

Registration took effect from the date on which the registration request was made (or such earlier or later date as was agreed with HMRC). [*VATA 1994, Sch 3B para 5*].

Registration number

HMRC were required to allocate a registration number to each business registered under these provisions and notify the number to the business electronically. [*VATA 1994, Sch 3B para 6*]. HMRC normally sent the number by e-mail within five working days of receiving the completed electronic registration request. Registration numbers had their own unique format beginning with the prefix 'EU', followed by a nine digit number. (VAT Information Sheet 7/03, para 3.4).

Businesses already registered for VAT in the EU under the normal rules

Where a business was registered for VAT in any EU member state under the normal rules, it was not eligible for the special scheme and had to account for VAT on any electronically supplied services to EU consumers under those normal rules. However, a business was allowed to switch from registration under the normal rules and apply for registration in the UK under the special scheme if, for example,

- it ceased to make supplies of goods or services to EU consumers other than electronically supplied services, or
- it initially made supplies of electronically supplied services to consumers in a single EU member state but subsequently expanded its market to consumers in other EU member states

provided it cancelled its VAT registration under the normal rules in the EU member state concerned. (VAT Information Sheet 7/03, paras 3.6, 3.9).

Changes in business circumstances

A business which made a registration request was required to notify HMRC if subsequently

- there was a change in any of the particulars contained in its request under (*a*)–(*d*) above;
- it ceased to make, or to have the intention of making, qualifying supplies; or
- it ceased to satisfy any of the conditions in **64.35**(*b*)–(*e*) above.

The notification had to be given, using the dedicated website above, within 30 days of the date of the change of particulars or of the cessation.

[*VATA 1994, Sch 3B para* 7]. (VAT Information Sheet 7/03, para 3.7).

Cancellation of registration

HMRC were required to cancel the registration of a business in the following circumstances.

- The business notified HMRC that it had ceased to make, or to have the intention of making, 'qualifying supplies' (see **64.35** above). Cancellation then took effect from the date on which the notification was received or such earlier or later date as was agreed with HMRC.
- HMRC otherwise determined that the business had ceased to make, or to have the intention of making, qualifying supplies. Cancellation then took effect from the date on which the determination was made or such earlier or later date HMRC might direct.
- The business notified HMRC that it had ceased to satisfy any of the conditions in **64.35**(*b*)–(*e*) above. Cancellation then took effect from the date on which the notification was received or such earlier or later date as was agreed with HMRC.

- HMRC otherwise determined that the business had ceased to satisfy any of the conditions in **64.35**(*b*)–(*e*) above. Cancellation then took effect from the date on which the determination was made or such earlier or later date HMRC might direct.
- HMRC determined that the business had persistently failed to comply with its obligations under these provisions. Cancellation then took effect from the date on which the determination was made or such earlier or later date HMRC might direct.

[*VATA 1994, Sch 3B para 8*].

Accounting and records

Liability for VAT

[64.37] The amount of VAT which a business was liable to pay under the special scheme on any 'qualifying supply' (see **64.35** above) is calculated as follows.

(a) If the qualifying supply was treated as made in the UK, the amount of VAT that would have been charged on the supply if the business had been registered under *VATA 1994* when it made the supply; and any amount so calculated was regarded as VAT charged in accordance with *VATA 1994*.

(b) If the qualifying supply was treated as made in another EU member state, the amount of VAT that would have been charged on the supply in accordance with the law of that EU member state if the business had been identified for the purposes of VAT in that country when it made the supply; and any amount so calculated in relation to another EU member state was regarded for the purposes of *VATA 1994* as VAT charged in accordance with the law of that EU member state.

[*VATA 1994, Sch 3B para 10*].

Obligation to submit special accounting returns

A business was required to submit to VAT Central Unit a special accounting return for each 'reporting period' for which it was registered under the special scheme. A '*reporting period*' was each calendar quarter for the whole or part of which the business was registered under the scheme.

The special accounting return was required to set out the following in sterling.

- The registration number of the business.
- For each EU member state in which the business was treated as having made qualifying supplies in the reporting period:
  - (i) the total value of those qualifying supplies in sterling (excluding the VAT which it is liable to pay by virtue of these provisions);
  - (ii) the rate of VAT applicable to those supplies by virtue of (*a*) or (*b*) above, and
  - (iii) the total amount of VAT payable under these provisions in respect of those supplies.
- The total amount of VAT which the business was liable to pay under these provisions in respect of all qualifying supplies treated as made by it in all EU member states in the reporting period.

Any conversion from one currency into another for these purposes was required to be made using the exchange rates published by the European Central Bank for the last day of the reporting period to which the special accounting return relates (or, if no such rate is published for that day, for the next day for which such a rate is published). To avoid the need for businesses to calculate a conversion from the currency of sale into Euros and then from Euros into sterling, HMRC regularly publish the exchange rates for the leading currencies direct into sterling. See for example Information Sheet 9/14 for exchange rates for the quarter to 30 September 2014 and Information Sheet 10/14 for exchange rates for the quarter to 31 December 2014.

Note – the non-Union VAT MOSS scheme is relevant to periods after 31 December 2014 – see **64.40** below.

Alternatively, the conversion can be calculated using the exchange rates shown at the ECB's website at:

www.ecb.int

The special accounting return was required to be submitted to HMRC by electronic means within 20 days after the last day of the reporting period to which it related.

[*VATA 1994, Sch 3B paras 11, 12*]. (VAT Information Sheet 10/03, paras 3.1, 3.2).

Returns had to be completed by logging on to the dedicated website

https://secure.hmce.gov.uk/ecom/voes

and using the VAT identification number, user name and password of the business to ensure security. A return was required even if there were no qualifying supplies in the quarter.

HMRC sent an on-line acknowledgment confirming that they had received the return. This acknowledgment also provided a unique reference number for each return submitted. This number should be referred to if it was necessary to contact HMRC with a query about the return. If this confirmation was not received *immediately*, it was necessary to contact the Customer Services Team by e-mail at

voes@hmrc.gsi.gov.uk.

(VAT Information Sheet 7/03, paras 4.1, 4.6).

Payment of VAT

At the same time as submitting the special accounting return, a business had to pay to HMRC, in sterling, the total amount of VAT as shown due by the return. [*VATA 1994, Sch 3B para 13; FA 2003, Sch 2 para 4*].

VAT on purchases

The special scheme provided only for payment of the VAT due on sales to EU customers, without any deductions of EU VAT incurred on purchases. However, a business might have been able to reclaim VAT it has paid on goods and services used for the purpose of its taxable activities falling within the scheme, from the EU member state where that VAT was paid, under the *EC 13th Directive*. See **19.44 EUROPEAN UNION LEGISLATION** for the provisions of the Directive and **49.5 OVERSEAS TRADERS** for applications to the UK for refunds.

Obligations to keep and produce records

A business registered under the special scheme in the UK must keep records of its transactions in qualifying supplies (see **64.35** above) in sufficient detail to enable the tax authorities in the EU member states in which those supplies are treated as made to determine whether any special accounting return is correct. These records include normal commercial data held for each transaction (e.g. transaction number, date, type (credit or debit), customer name and location, currency and values including VAT).

Any records required to be kept must, on request, be made available electronically to HMRC and the tax authorities of any EU member state where the qualifying supplies were treated as made. HMRC also may request records of a business where its qualifying supplies are treated as made in the UK but it is registered under the scheme in another EU member state.

The records must be kept for ten years beginning with the 1st January following the date on which the transaction was entered into.

[*VATA 1994, Sch 3B paras 14, 15*]. (VAT Information Sheet 7/03, para 4.8).

Invoices

There are no special rules for issuing VAT invoices under the special scheme and consequently the normal rules apply. In the UK, a business is not required to issue VAT invoices for such supplies because its customers are not in business and cannot deduct VAT on their purchases. (VAT Information Sheet 7/03, para 4.10).

Errors in special scheme returns

Errors discovered by HMRC

[64.38] If HMRC consider that a business which was, or had been, registered under the special scheme (whether in the UK or another EU member state) had submitted a scheme return which understated or overstated liability to UK VAT, they had the power to give the business a notice

- identifying the return in which they considered that the under/overstatement was made; and
- specifying the amount by which they considered that the liability to VAT had been under/overstated.

In the case of an understatement, HMRC requested the business to pay the amount understated to HMRC within 30 days of the date of the notice. There were no penalties for underdeclaring the amount of VAT due under the special scheme. However, failure to declare the full amount might make the business ineligible to use the scheme (see **64.36** above under *Cancellation of registration*).

In the case of an overstatement, HMRC were required to pay the business the amount specified in the notice. They normally did this within 30 days.

Time limit

No notice under these provisions was to be given more than three years after the end of the period for which the scheme return in question was made.

[*VATA 1994, Sch 3B para 16*]. (VAT Information Sheet 10/03, paras 5.2, 5.3).

Errors discovered by the non-EU supplier

If a non-EU supplier submitted a declaration but subsequently discovered that it had made an error (e.g. entering French VAT in the line for Spain or underdeclaring UK VAT), it should contact HMRC at

voes@hmrc.gsi.gov.uk

quoting the reference number for the return in question and advising the correct amount(s) due for the EU member state or countries concerned. There was no need to submit a supplementary declaration.

Where, as a result of the error, additional VAT was due, HMRC would either request that the payment was sent to them or advise that the EC country or countries concerned would contact the business to explain how it should pay the VAT due.

(VAT Information Sheet 10/03, para 4.2).

Business customers initially failing to provide VAT registration numbers

The special scheme was intended for supplies to consumers who cannot recover VAT. A business customer who failed to provide a valid VAT registration number at the time of the transaction had to be charged VAT and could not deduct that VAT as input tax. However, if it subsequently produced a valid VAT registration number and requested a credit, the non-EU supplier could refund the VAT to the business customer. (VAT Information Sheet 10/03, para 4.1).

Miscellaneous matters

[64.39] Some miscellaneous matters were treated as follows:

(1) Appeals

An appeal could be made to a UK tribunal with respect to any of the following.

- The registration or cancellation of the registration of any business under the special scheme.
- A decision of HMRC to give a notice of understatement of UK VAT liability under **64.38** above.
- The amount specified in any such notice or in a notice of overstatement of UK VAT liability under **64.38** above.

[*VATA 1994, Sch 3B para 20*].

UK VAT tribunals cannot deal with VAT matters which fall within the jurisdiction of other EU member states. If a non-EU business using the special scheme disagreed with a decision taken by another EU member state about any aspect of the scheme (e.g. the amount of VAT owed to it), the matter had to be raised with the VAT authorities in that country.

(2) Deregistration

Where a business which was registered under *VATA 1994, Sch 1* (registration in respect of UK supplies, see **60.1–60.10 REGISTRATION**) or *Sch 1A* (registration by non-established taxable persons, see **60.33–60.38 REGISTRATION**) satisfied HMRC that it intended to apply for

- registration under the special scheme in the UK, or
- identification under any provision of the law of another EU member state which implements similar provisions,

they might, if the business so requested, cancel its registration under *VATA 1994, Sch 1* or *1A*, as the case may be, with effect from the day on which the request was made or from such later date as might be agreed between it and HMRC.

[*VATA 1994, Sch 3B para 18; FA 2003, Sch 2 para 4*].

(3) EU enlargement

Croatia joined the EU with effect from 1 July 2013, raising the total number of EU member states to 28 (see **18.1 EUROPEAN UNION: GENERAL**). As a result, non-EU businesses

- not already registered for the special scheme would be able to register under the scheme;
- registered under the special scheme but established in Croatia were excluded from continuing to use the scheme; and
- registered under the special scheme but not established in Croatia were required to extend the charging of VAT on their e-services to all non-business users who reside in Croatia.

(4) Exempt supplies

Most electronically supplied services within the EU are subject to VAT. However, certain EU member states apply an exemption to some electronically supplied services (e.g. gambling). If a non-EU supplier thinks that its services may qualify for an exemption, it should check with the country or countries concerned. However, unless its services are exempt from VAT in all EU member states where its customers belong, it will still be required to register and account for VAT in the EU either under the normal rules or under the special scheme. (VAT Information Sheet 10/03, para 2.3).

(5) Registration under VATA 1994

Notwithstanding any provision in *VATA 1994* to the contrary, a business in the special scheme is not required to be registered under *VATA 1994* by virtue of making qualifying supplies under the special scheme. [*VATA 1994, Sch 3B para 17*].

(6) VAT representatives

VATA 1994, s 48(1) (VAT representatives, see **3.8 AGENTS**) does not permit HMRC to direct a business in the special scheme to appoint a VAT representative. [*VATA 1994, Sch 3B para 19*].

However, although an agent, even an authorised one, cannot register for the special scheme on behalf of a non-EU supplier, the supplier can register itself and authorise an agent to submit declarations and, if necessary, make payments on its behalf under the scheme. But it should be noted that rules regarding agents vary between EU member states and such authorisation may render the agent jointly and severally liable for VAT in some countries. (VAT Information Sheet 10/03, para 2.3).

Special scheme for non-EU suppliers of broadcasting, telecommunication and electronic services to consumers from 1 January 2015

The non-Union VAT MOSS scheme

[64.40] The VoES scheme referred to at **64.34–64.39** above is available for non-EU suppliers of electronic services making or amending declarations relating to periods before 1 January 2015. For periods starting on or after that date a modified version of the VoES scheme is available for non-EU suppliers of broadcasting, telecommunication and electronic (BTE) services to consumers. The modified version of the VoES scheme is known as the non-Union VAT Mini One Stop Shop scheme (non-Union VAT MOSS scheme).

The non-Union VAT MOSS scheme has been introduced because, from 1 January 2015, subject to the effective use and enjoyment rule, all supplies of broadcasting, telecommunication and electronic services (see **64.43**) are subject to VAT at the place where the customer belongs (see **66.19 SUPPLY: PLACE OF SUPPLY**).

The VoES scheme and the non-Union VAT MOSS scheme are voluntary schemes that provide non-EU suppliers of relevant services with an alternative to registering for VAT in every EU member state in which they make relevant supplies. Since October 2014 businesses that previously used the VoES scheme, and other non-EU businesses affected by the 1 January 2015 change to the place of supply of services rules, have been able to register for the non-Union VAT MOSS scheme.

The main UK legislation relating to the VoES and the non-Union VAT MOSS schemes is at *VATA 1994, Sch 3B*. *FA 2014, Sch 22* included amendments to *VATA 1994, Sch 3B* so that from 1 January 2015 *VATA 1994, Sch 3B* is relevant to broadcasting and telecommunication services as well as electronic services. HMRC can choose not to register a persistent defaulter for the non-Union VAT MOSS scheme (see **64.36** regarding HMRC's discretion in relation to persistent defaulters and the VoES scheme) and no registration in relation to the non-Union VAT MOSS could take effect before 1 January 2015.

[*VATA 1994, Sch 3B; FA 2014, Sch 22*].

HMRC have published some of the most used exchange rates needed by businesses registered in the UK to complete MOSS declarations and make payments to HMRC in sterling in respect of the non-Union VAT MOSS scheme referred to above and the Union VAT MOSS scheme referred to below. The rates are provided in **64.46** below.

Special scheme for EU suppliers of broadcasting, telecommunication and electronic services to consumers from 1 January 2015

The Union VAT MOSS scheme

[64.41] The scheme referred to at **64.40** is specific to non-EU suppliers. However, the 1 January 2015 change to the place of supply of services rules is also relevant to EU suppliers of broadcasting, telecommunication and electronic (BTE) services to consumers (B2C). To avoid the need for EU businesses making B2C supplies of BTE services in other EU member states from having to register for VAT in each of those other EU member states a Union VAT Mini One Stop Shop (Union VAT MOSS) scheme has been introduced.

(VAT Notice 700, para 4.8.4).

A requirement of using the Union VAT MOSS scheme is that the business is registered for VAT. On 10 December 2014 HMRC published HMRC Brief 46/14, which includes guidance regarding simplified VAT registration arrangements for persons who

- make taxable supplies of digital services to customers in other EU member states;
- have a UK taxable turnover below the UK VAT registration threshold; and
- wish to use the Union VAT MOSS scheme.

Persons who meet the above criteria and apply for the simplified VAT registration arrangements do not charge VAT on UK taxable supplies until the UK VAT registration limit is exceeded. Because VAT is not charged on UK supplies, VAT should not be recovered on costs which are attributable to those supplies.

(HMRC guidance 'Register for and use the VAT Mini One Stop Shop').

EU businesses that make B2C supplies of BTE services to other EU member states are not obliged to use the Union VAT MOSS scheme to account for the VAT that is due in the other EU member states. Instead, they can register for VAT in each of the EU member states in which they make B2C supplies of BTE services. Whether or not the Union VAT MOSS is used, the place of supply (see **66.19 SUPPLY: PLACE OF SUPPLY**) and the status of the customer (see **64.42**) need to be determined as well as considering whether what is being supplied consists of broadcasting, telecommunication, or electronic services (see **64.43**).

The status of the customer

[64.42] From 1 January 2015, subject to the effective use and enjoyment rule, all supplies of broadcasting, telecommunication and electronic services are subject to VAT at the place where the customer belongs (see **66.19 SUPPLY: PLACE OF SUPPLY**). The status of the customer therefore determines whether the customer or the supplier is liable for accounting for the VAT due on the supply. Where the customer is registered for VAT the customer should account for the VAT due via the reverse charge procedure, as was the case prior to 1 January 2015. Where the customer is not registered for VAT the supplier should account for the VAT due either by registering for VAT in the country where the customer belongs or by using the Union VAT MOSS scheme. In relation to supplies of broadcasting, telecommunication or electronic services a customer is regarded as a consumer (a non-taxable person) if they are not registered for VAT.

The EU law states that 'Unless he has information to the contrary, the supplier may regard a customer established within the Community as a non-taxable person when he can demonstrate that the customer has not communicated his individual VAT identification number to him. However, irrespective of information to the contrary, the supplier of telecommunications, broadcasting or electronically supplied services may regard a customer established within the Community as a non-taxable person as long as the customer has not communicated his individual VAT registration identification number to him.' [*Implementing Regulation (EU)282/2011, Art 18(2) amended by Implementing Regulation (EU)1042/2013, Art 1*].

The status of the customer may not always be obvious when services are provided to consumers via an agent, for example a website offering electronic services for sale. Is the provider of the services making a B2B supply to the agent or is the provider of the services making a B2C supply to the final consumer? In order to answer this question it will be necessary to determine who is making the supply to the final consumer. From 1 January 2015, where electronically supplied services or telecommunication services are supplied through an agent in circumstances where the agent is a taxable person taking part in the supply and acting in his own name, but on behalf of another person, the supply must be treated both as a supply to the agent and as a supply by the agent (see **3.4 AGENTS**).

Where telephone or electronic services are supplied through the internet or a telecommunications network, or an interface or a portal such as electronic marketplaces for applications and websites offering electronic services for sale, the taxable person taking part in that supply is treated as acting in his own name but on behalf of the provider of those services unless that provider is explicitly indicated as the supplier by that taxable person and that is reflected in the contractual arrangements between the parties.

In order to regard the provider of electronically supplied services as being explicitly indicated as the supplier of those services by the taxable person, the following conditions need to be met:

(a) the invoice issued or made available by each taxable person taking part in the supply of the electronically supplied services must identify such services and the supplier thereof;

(b) the bill or receipt issued or made available to the customer must identify the electronically supplied services and the supplier thereof.

If the taxable person involved in such a supply, authorises the charge to the customer or the delivery of the services, or sets the general terms and conditions of the supply, that person (the agent) is not permitted to explicitly indicate another person as the supplier of those services to the customer.

A taxable person who provides payment processing services for suppliers of telecommunication and electronic services to consumers, and who does not take part in the supply of those services to consumers, is not treated as supplying telecommunication or electronic services to consumers.

[*Implementing Regulation (EU)282/2011, Art 9a inserted by Implementing Regulation (EU)1042/2013, Art 1*].

Broadcasting, telecommunication and electronic services

[64.43] The nature of broadcasting, telecommunication and electronic services is that they are rapidly evolving and it is not possible to provide an exhaustive list of all the services that could potentially come within this category.

Broadcasting services include services consisting of audio and audiovisual content, such as radio or television programmes which are provided to the general public via communications networks by and under the editorial responsibility of a media service provider, for simultaneous listening or viewing, on the basis of a programme schedule. [*Implementing Regulation (EU)282/2011, Art 6b inserted by Implementing Regulation (EU)1042/2013, Art 1*].

Telecommunications services include:

(a) fixed and mobile telephone services for the transmission and switching of voice, data and video, including telephone services with an imaging component (videophone services);
(b) telephone services provided through the internet, including voice over internet Protocol (VoIP);
(c) voice mail, call waiting, call forwarding, caller identification, three-way calling and other call management services;
(d) paging services;
(e) audiotext services;
(f) facsimile, telegraph and telex;
(g) access to the internet, including the World Wide Web;
(h) private network connections providing telecommunications links for the exclusive use of the client.

[*Implementing Regulation (EU)282/2011, Art 6b inserted by Implementing Regulation (EU)1042/2013, Art 1*].

Electronic services are essentially automated services involving minimal human intervention which are dependent on information technology for their delivery. Examples include:

(a) the supply of digitised products generally, including software and changes to or upgrades of software;
(b) services providing or supporting a business or personal presence on an electronic network such as a website or a webpage;
(c) services automatically generated from a computer via the internet or an electronic network in response to specific data input by the recipient;
(d) online auction services which involve the transfer for consideration of the right to put goods or services up for sale on an Internet site operating as an online market on which potential buyers make their bids by an automated procedure and on which the parties are notified of a sale by electronic mail automatically generated from a computer;
(e) Internet Service Packages (ISP) of information in which the telecommunications component forms an ancillary and subordinate part and which go beyond mere internet access and include other elements, for example, content pages giving access to news, weather or travel reports or access to online debates;
(f) downloaded applications (apps);
(g) movie downloads, music downloads, e-books, online games, online newspapers and journals;
(h) the provision of online advertising space including banner advertisements on a website or web page;
(i) website hosting and webpage hosting;
(j) automated online distance maintenance of programmes;
(k) automated online distance learning services;
(l) radio or television programmes that can be accessed at any time by the listener or viewer from a catalogue of programmes selected by the media service provider.

The EU legislation provides example of services that are not electronic services, for example, services of professionals who advise clients by email and teaching services where the course content is delivered by a teacher over the internet. Both of these examples would involve more than minimal human involvement.

[*Implementing Regulation (EU)282/2011, Art 7*].

Registration and cancellation of registration

[64.44] Each EU member state operates the Union VAT MOSS scheme. The scheme when operated by another EU member state is referred to as a non-UK special scheme in the following paragraphs. Since October 2014 UK businesses have been able to apply to HMRC to be registered for the Union VAT MOSS scheme and use it to account for VAT on relevant supplies made after 31 December 2014, if they meet the following conditions.

- The applicant must be registered for VAT in the UK, be established in the UK or have a fixed establishment in the UK, and make or intend to make one or more supplies of broadcasting, telecommunication or electronic services to a consumer in another EU member state.
- The applicant must not have a fixed establishment in the EU member state in which the consumer belongs.
- The applicant must not be registered under a non-UK special scheme.

- The applicant must not be excluded from using the scheme.

The application for registration to use the Union VAT MOSS scheme must:

- include the applicant's name, postal address, email and website addresses;
- state whether or not the applicant has begun to make B2C supplies of BTE services in another EU member state and if so, the date on which the applicant began to do so;
- state whether or not the applicant has previously been registered under a non-UK special scheme, and if so, the date on which they were first so registered;
- include any further information, and any declaration about its contents, that HMRC may by regulations require;
- be made by such electronic means, and in such manner, as HMRC may direct or may by regulations require.

HMRC are required to cancel a Union VAT MOSS scheme registration if:

- the business notifies HMRC, or HMRC otherwise become aware, that the business has ceased to make, or no longer intends to make, intra-EU supplies of broadcasting, telecommunication or electronic services to consumers;
- the business notifies HMRC, or HMRC otherwise become aware, that the business no longer meets the conditions for registration detailed above;
- HMRC determine that the business has persistently failed to comply with its Union VAT MOSS obligations.

A refusal of HMRC to register a business for the Union VAT MOSS scheme or a decision by HMRC to cancel a Union VAT MOSS scheme registration can be appealed as if the appeal was under *VATA 1994, s 83(1)*, but not under any particular paragraph of that subsection.

[*VATA 1994, Sch 3BA; FA 2014, Sch 22*].

Union VAT MOSS scheme returns, payment of VAT and records

[64.45] Union VAT MOSS scheme returns are submitted electronically, with each scheme return covering a calendar quarter. A business that is registered with HMRC to use the Union VAT MOSS scheme is required to submit a scheme return to HMRC and pay the relevant amount of VAT to HMRC within 20 days after the end of the calendar quarter to which the scheme return relates.

The relevant amount of VAT that should be paid to HMRC is the gross amount of non-UK VAT that is due as a result of making supplies of broadcasting, telecommunication and electronic services to consumers in other EU member states, calculated in accordance with the VAT rates applying in those other EU member states. Input tax is not recovered on scheme returns. Instead, input tax is recovered based on the usual rules and procedures for recovering input tax (see **35 INPUT TAX**).

A business that is registered with HMRC to use the Union VAT MOSS scheme is required to keep records of transactions relating to scheme returns in sufficient detail to enable the tax authorities in other EU member states to verify that the scheme returns are correct. When requested, the records must be made available to HMRC by electronic means.

Businesses belonging in the other EU member states can register to use the Union VAT MOSS scheme in the Member State where they belong as an alternative to registering for VAT in each Member State to which they make B2C supplies of BTE services. For example, a business based in France could register to submit Union VAT MOSS scheme returns to the French tax authorities for supplies of BTE services to consumers in the UK as an alternative to registering for VAT in the UK.

Scheme returns submitted to HMRC should be made out in sterling, with the conversion from other currencies made using the exchange rates published by the European Central Bank for the last day of the period to which the scheme return relates, or, if no such rates are published for that day, for the next day for which such rates are published.

[*VATA 1994, Sch 3BA; FA 2014, Sch 22*].

VAT MOSS exchange rates

[64.46] HMRC have published some of the most used exchange rates needed by businesses registered in the UK to complete MOSS declarations and make payments to HMRC in sterling in respect of the non-Union VAT MOSS scheme and the Union VAT MOSS scheme. The rates are based on the exchange rates published by the European Central Bank on the last reporting day of the VAT MOSS quarter, or if it is a weekend or bank holiday, the next available day.

Currency exchange rates outside the EU for the period ending 31 December 2017

Country		*Currency*		*1 GBP =*
Australia	AU	Dollar	AUD	1.7327
Canada	CA	Dollar	CAD	1.7007
China	CN	Yuan renminbi	CNY	8.8067
Hong Kong	HK	Dollar	HKD	10.5992
India	IN	Rupee	INR	86.1135
Israel	IL	Israeli shekel	ILS	4.6871
Japan	JP	Yen	JPY	152.1590
New Zealand	NZ	New Zealand dollar	NZD	1.9061
Norway	NO	Norwegian krone	NOK	10.9887
Russia	RU	Rouble	RUB	77.7013
Singapore	SG	Dollar	SGD	1.8022
Switzerland	CH	Franc	CHF	1.3173
United States	US	Dollar	USD	1.3563

Currency exchange rates inside the EU for the period ending 31 December 2017

Country		*Currency*		*1 GBP =*
European Community	EC	Euro	EUR	1.1242
Bulgaria	BG	Bulgarian lev	BGN	2.1987
Croatia	HR	Croatia kuna	HRK	8.3909
Czech Republic	CZ	Czech koruna	CZK	28.6601
Denmark	DK	Danish krone	DKK	8.3681
Hungary	HG	Hungarian forint	HUF	346.9135
Poland	PL	Polish zloty	PLN	4.6803
Romania	RO	Romanian leu	RON	5.2303
Sweden	SE	Swedish krone	SEK	1.0489

(VAT Information Sheet 1/18).

Currency exchange rates outside the EU for the period ending 31 September 2017

Country		*Currency*		*1 GBP =*
Australia	AU	Dollar	AUD	1.7006
Canada	CA	Dollar	CAD	1.6618
China	CN	Yuan renminbi	CNY	8.8373
Hong Kong	HK	Dollar	HKD	10.3756
India	IN	Rupee	INR	86.7431
Israel	IL	Israeli shekel	ILS	4.7073
Japan	JP	Yen	JPY	149.8564
New Zealand	NZ	New Zealand dollar	NZD	1.8476
Norway	NO	Norwegian krone	NOK	10.6053
Russia	RU	Rouble	RUB	76.9521
Singapore	SG	Dollar	SGD	1.8099
Switzerland	CH	Franc	CHF	1.2892
United States	US	Dollar	USD	1.3282

Currency exchange rates inside the EU for the period ending 31 September 2017

Country		*Currency*		*1 GBP =*
European Community	EC	Euro	EUR	1.1310
Bulgaria	BG	Bulgarian lev	BGN	2.2120
Croatia	HR	Croatia kuna	HRK	8.4790
Czech Republic	CZ	Czech koruna	CZK	29.4001
Denmark	DK	Danish krone	DKK	8.4166

Country		*Currency*		*1 GBP =*
Hungary	HG	Hungarian forint	HUF	352.2360
Poland	PL	Polish zloty	PLN	4.8782
Romania	RO	Romanian leu	RON	5.1888
Sweden	SE	Swedish krone	SEK	10.8637

(VAT Information Sheet 6/17).

Currency exchange rates outside the EU for the period ending 31 June 2017

Country		*Currency*		*1 GBP =*
Australia	AU	Dollar	AUD	1.6889
Canada	CA	Dollar	CAD	1.6814
China	CN	Yuan renminbi	CNY	8.8005
Hong Kong	HK	Dollar	HKD	10.1291
India	IN	Rupee	INR	83.8644
Israel	IL	Israeli shekel	ILS	4.5362
Japan	JP	Yen	JPY	145.2811
New Zealand	NZ	New Zealand dollar	NZD	1.7688
Norway	NO	Norwegian krone	NOK	10.8848
Russia	RU	Rouble	RUB	76.8141
Singapore	SG	Dollar	SGD	1.7866
Switzerland	CH	Franc	CHF	1.2430
United States	US	Dollar	USD	1.2978

Currency exchange rates inside the EU for the period ending 31 June 2017

Country		*Currency*		*1 GBP =*
European Community	EC	Euro	EUR	1.1372
Bulgaria	BG	Bulgarian lev	BGN	2.2242
Croatia	HR	Croatia kuna	HRK	8.4272
Czech Republic	CZ	Czech koruna	CZK	29.7920
Denmark	DK	Danish krone	DKK	8.4571
Hungary	HG	Hungarian forint	HUF	351.3698
Poland	PL	Polish zloty	PLN	4.8058
Romania	RO	Romanian leu	RON	5.1770
Sweden	SE	Swedish krone	SEK	10.9627

(VAT Information Sheet 5/17).

Key points: special schemes

[64.47] Points to consider are as follows.

Cash accounting scheme

- The cash accounting scheme can be used by a business with annual turnover of £1.35m per year (taxable sales excluding VAT) or less. The business should also have a good VAT compliance record with HMRC.
- The main outcome of the cash accounting scheme is that output tax is not due on a VAT return until payment has been received from a customer. Input tax can only be reclaimed when payment has been made to a supplier.
- The cash flow benefits and automatic bad debt relief given by the scheme could be particularly useful for a business that has standard-rated sales and gives extended credit terms to customers, or which has customers that are slow payers.
- The cash accounting scheme is unsuitable for taxpayers supplying mainly zero-rated items, or for a business where customers pay in advance or as soon as sales invoices are raised.
- A business should regularly review whether the cash accounting scheme continues to be of benefit. A change in the mixture of standard/zero-rated sales could mean it is more beneficial for a business to account for VAT under normal accounting rules.
- A business that exceeds the exit level of £1.6m per annum in taxable sales can still remain in the scheme if it can prove to HMRC that the increase in sales for the year in question was due to a one-off sale and that it expects taxable supplies in the next twelve months to be less than £1.35m.

Annual accounting scheme

- The annual accounting scheme means that a business only completes one VAT return a year instead of four or twelve. A business can only join the scheme if it expects that its annual taxable sales in the next twelve months will be less than £1.35m (excluding VAT).
- A business in the annual accounting scheme must make payments on account during the course of the year either on a monthly basis in months 4 to 12, or on a quarterly basis at the end of months 4, 7 and 10. A balancing payment is then due when the annual VAT return is submitted at the end of the year
- The payments on account are based on the previous year's VAT liability. These payments could be too high for a business that is not trading as well in the current year as it did in the previous year.
- It should be noted that payments on account that are either too high or too low can be adjusted during the year by writing to the local VAT Business Advice Centre and requesting revised payment terms.

- It is unlikely that the annual accounting scheme will benefit repayment traders because they will have to wait until the end of the accounting year to receive any repayment due.
- Be aware of the potential advantages of the scheme that may appeal to certain traders – particularly the time-saving benefits of completing only one return each year. The scheme may also appeal to partly-exempt taxpayers who will only need to make one partial exemption calculation per year (the annual accounting period must coincide with the partial exemption tax year, i.e. 31 March, 30 April or 31 May).

Flat-rate scheme

- The flat-rate scheme allows a business buying capital goods costing more than £2,000 including VAT to reclaim input tax on the purchase of the assets. There may be opportunities for a business to buy a slightly more expensive asset (e.g. upgraded computer) to exceed the £2,000 limit to benefit from the VAT saving.
- An input tax claim does not apply in relation to building projects costing more than £2,000 including VAT, e.g. an office extension, because the supplies in such cases are of 'building services' rather than 'capital goods'.
- Be aware of the main disadvantage of the flat-rate scheme – namely that the flat-rate percentage needs to be applied to zero-rated and exempt sales. This could make the scheme very unattractive to taxpayers who have an unpredictable level of zero-rated sales, such as builders.
- Exempt income also includes buy-to-let income, the sale of certain property and other capital assets.
- The flat-rate scheme offers potential savings of tax to certain users. As with any scheme based on averages, there will always be winners and losers.
- Even if a business has exceeded the turnover limit where it must leave the scheme (£230,000 per year on the anniversary of when it joined the scheme), there may be scope to remain within the scheme if HMRC is satisfied that the total taxable income in the next twelve months will be less than £191,500 – again within the scheme limits.
- A chosen flat-rate category must be reviewed on an annual basis to ensure it is still valid. This is particularly important for a business with two or more activities because the flat rate is based on the activity with the greater (greatest) percentage of turnover.
- Remember that a business can benefit from an extra 1% discount on the relevant flat rate % in its first year of VAT registration. This could produce a considerable saving of tax in a twelve-month period.
- The introduction of the limited cost trader flat rate of 16.5% has reduced the number of businesses who receive will receive a benefit from using the scheme. Businesses should ascertain whether they are likely to be limited cost traders all or most of the

time before signing up to the scheme, in order to confirm that it will still be more beneficial to register for the flat rate scheme rather than use normal accounting.

Other schemes

- A flat-rate scheme is available to farmers as an alternative to VAT registration. The basic principle is that they make an additional charge of 4% on sales of specified goods and services (including zero-rated sales) to customers, and retain this money as an alternative to reclaiming input tax.
- A customer can reclaim the 4% charge made by the farmer as if it were VAT, i.e. within box 4 of his relevant VAT return.
- A non-EU business supplying broadcasting, telecommunication or electronic services to EU consumers can apply to use the non-Union VAT Mini One Stop Shop (non-Union VAT MOSS) scheme in one EU member state rather than register for VAT in all the EU member states where consumers belong. The non-Union VAT MOSS is relevant to supplies made after 31 December 2014.
- An EU business supplying broadcasting, telecommunication or electronic services to consumers in other EU member states can apply to use the Union VAT Mini One Stop Shop (Union VAT MOSS) scheme in the country where the business belongs rather than registering for VAT in all of the countries where the consumers belong.

65

Supply: General

Introduction to general supply

[65.1] A transaction is within the scope of UK VAT if the following four conditions are satisfied.

- It is a supply of goods or services.
- It takes place in the UK.
- It is made by a taxable person.
- It is made in the course or furtherance of any business carried on by that person.

[*VATA 1994, s 4(1)*].

The first three conditions are considered in this chapter.

Supplies for VAT purposes

Even before deciding whether goods or services are being supplied, it is necessary to determine whether a transaction is in fact a supply for VAT purposes by considering the following questions.

(a) Is there any consideration?

Under both EU and UK law, a supply takes place for VAT purposes when something is provided or done for a consideration. [*VATA 1994, s 5(2)*].

Consideration for VAT purposes has a wide meaning and covers anything which might be done, given or made in exchange for something else. It does not refer only to money. See **72.3** *et seq* **VALUATION** for further coverage of consideration.

(b) If there is no consideration, is the transaction one which is deemed to be a supply for VAT purposes?

Even if there is no consideration, certain transactions made for no consideration (i.e. free) are deemed to be supplies of goods or services for VAT purposes. These are the

- permanent transfer/disposal of business assets, see **48.6 OUTPUT TAX**;
- temporary use of business assets for non-business purposes, see **48.7 OUTPUT TAX**;
- retention of certain business assets on deregistration, see **60.40 REGISTRATION**;
- self-supply of goods or services, see **63 SELF-SUPPLY**; and
- private or other non-business use of services supplied to the business, see **48.7 OUTPUT TAX**.

(c) Does the transaction fail to be a supply or is it a supply which is disregarded for VAT purposes?

A transaction is not a supply for VAT purposes if

- there is no consideration for the supply and it is not a deemed supply under (*b*) above;
- the transaction is within the same legal entity;
- there is a specific exclusion in VAT legislation, i.e.
  - (i) a business gift costing the donor £50 or less, see **48.6 OUTPUT TAX**;
  - (ii) samples, see **48.8**(26) **OUTPUT TAX**; or
  - (iii) the transaction is deemed to be 'neither a supply of goods nor services', see **65.5** below.

Supplies of goods and services

Once it has been established that a transaction is a supply, it is then necessary to determine whether it is a supply of goods (see **65.3** below) or a supply of services (see **65.4** below). Certain transactions, although supplies, are regarded as supplies of neither goods nor services and are outside the scope of VAT (see **65.5** below).

The distinction as to whether a supply is one of goods or services is important as different rules apply to the place and time of supply. Also the treatment of the international supply of goods and services is different.

Meaning of supply

[65.2] The legislation does not define the term 'supply'. Subject to express provisions to the contrary, supply includes all forms of supply, but not anything done otherwise than for consideration. Anything which is not a supply of goods but is done for a consideration (including, if so done, the granting, assignment or surrender of any right) is a supply of services. [*VATA 1994, s 5(2)*].

In *C & E Commrs v Oliver*, QB 1979, [1980] STC 73 (TVC 62.174), it was held that supply of goods has a wide interpretation. It is the passing of possession in goods pursuant to an agreement whereunder the supplier agrees to part and the recipient agrees to take possession. By 'possession' is meant in this context control over the goods, in the sense of having immediate facility for their use. This may or may not involve the physical removal of the goods. See also *Carlton Lodge Club v C & E Commrs*, QB [1974] STC 507 (TVC 13.30).

In *Tolsma v Inspecteur der Omzetbelasting Leeuwarden, ECJ Case C–16/93*, [1994] STC 509 (TVC 22.89) an individual who played a barrel organ on the public highway, and invited donations from the public, was held not to be supplying services for a consideration. There was no agreement between the parties and also 'no necessary link between the musical service and the payment to which it gave rise'.

In *Norwich Airport Ltd v HMRC* (TC01965) (TVC 62.211) it was held that an 'airport development fee' that passengers were required to pay for a ticket to pass through automatic gates prior to the departure lounge was consideration for permission to access land, which was a supply of services.

In *Dixons Retail plc v HMRC, ECJ Case C-494/12; 21 November 2013 unreported* (TVC 20.28) it was held that a retailer had made supplies of goods for consideration in circumstances where customers had acquired the goods by making fraudulent use of credit cards.

Illegal supplies

The principle of fiscal neutrality requires that all supplies of goods for a consideration are subject to VAT unless the goods are subject to a total prohibition on circulation because they are intrinsically harmful or because all competition between a lawful economic sector and an unlawful sector is precluded. In *Witzemann v Hauptzollamt Munchen-Mitte, ECJ Case C–343/89*, [1993] STC 108 (TVC 22.109), the Advocate-General stated that 'illegality manifests itself in many forms and there are many products that either cannot be lawfully traded or trade in which is subject to certain restrictions: drugs, counterfeit money, weapons, pornography, the pelts of certain animals, stolen goods and so forth. Not every transaction tainted with illegality will be exempt from taxation. A line must be drawn between, on the one hand, transactions that lie so clearly outside the sphere of legitimate economic activity that, instead of being taxed, they can only be the subject of criminal prosecution and, on the other hand, transactions which, though unlawful, must none the less be taxed, if only for the sake of ensuring, in the name of fiscal neutrality, that the criminal is not treated more favourably than the legitimate trader'.

Thus, the illegal sale of drugs is not a supply for VAT purposes (*Mol v Inspecteur der Invoerrechten Accijnzen, ECJ Case 269/86*, [1989] 3 CMLR 729 (TVC 22.86)) but the supply of counterfeit perfume is. See *R v Goodwin and Unstead*, CA [1997] STC 22, ECJ [1998] STC 699 (TVC 22.87). The prohibition on such products stems from the fact that they infringe intellectual property rights and is conditional not absolute (as in the case of drugs and counterfeit money). There is scope for competition between counterfeit perfumes and perfumes which are traded lawfully and although supply of the former is unlawful, such perfume is not liable to seizure in the hands of the final customer. The unlawful operation of a form of roulette was similarly held to be a supply for VAT purposes in *Fischer v Finanzamt Donaueschingen, ECJ Case C–283/95*, [1998] STC 708 (TVC 22.420). However, although the unlawful playing of a game of chance is a supply, it is not taxable where the corresponding activity is exempt when carried on lawfully by a licensed casino.

In *Staatssecretaris van Financien v Coffeeshop 'Siberie vof, ECJ Case C–158/98*, [1999] STC 742 (TVC 22.88) income from renting tables for the sale of cannabis was held to be within the scope of VAT and similarly in *C & E Commrs v R & J Polok*, Ch D [2002] STC 361 (TVC 62.290) income from the running of an escort agency was held to be potentially taxable (as indeed was the income of the escorts themselves).

De Voil Indirect Tax Service. See V3.102–104.

Supplies of goods

[65.3] For EU legislation, see **19.8 EUROPEAN UNION LEGISLATION.**

Under UK legislation, the Treasury may, by Order, deem any transaction to be a supply of services and not a supply of goods (or vice versa). [*VATA 1994, s 5(3)*]. Subject to this, the following supplies are to be treated as supplies of goods.

(a) Any transfer of the whole property in goods. [*VATA 1994, Sch 4 para 1(1)*].

This usually means transfer of both title to the goods and possession of, or control over, the goods. If possession is transferred but title is retained (e.g. where goods are let out on hire) this is a supply of services (see **65.4** below). However, if possession is transferred in circumstances where title would normally pass but does not because the holder of the goods did not have good title (e.g. the sale of stolen goods) this is a supply of goods as if title had passed. See *C & E Commrs v Oliver*, QB 1979, [1980] STC 73 (TVC 62.174).

The transfer of an undivided share of property is a supply of services (see **65.4** below). For the distinction, see *Sir John Astor* (VTD 1030) (TVC 62.372).

(b) The transfer of possession of goods under an agreement for the sale of the goods

or under agreements which expressly contemplate that the property also will pass at some time in the future (determined by, or ascertainable from, the agreements but in any case not later than when the goods are fully paid for). [*VATA 1994, Sch 4 para 1(2)*]. Where the conditions for future transfer are not satisfied, the supply is a supply of services (see **65.4** below).

Supplies under hire purchase contracts, conditional sale agreements and reservation of title agreements are thus supplies of goods. The simple hire or lease of goods, on the other hand, does not envisage the future transfer of title and is a supply of services. However, there a many other types of agreement where the distinction is not clear cut. In cases of doubt it is necessary to look at both the written agreement and the intention of any overall scheme operated. *Directive 2006/112/EC, Art 14(2)(b)* provides that there is a supply of goods where 'in the normal course of events' ownership will pass at the latest upon payment of the final instalment.

(c) **The supply of any form of power, heat, refrigeration or (from 1 January 2011) other cooling, or ventilation.** [*VATA 1994, Sch 4 para 3; F(No 3) Act 2010, s 20(2)*].

(d) **The grant, assignment or surrender of a 'major interest' in land.** [*VATA 1994, Sch 4 para 4*]

See **42.10 LAND AND BUILDINGS: EXEMPT SUPPLIES AND OPTION TO TAX** for the definition of '*major interest*'.

(e) Disposal of business assets

There is a supply of goods where goods forming part of the assets of a business are transferred or disposed of, by or under the directions of the person carrying on the business, so as no longer to form part of those assets (whether or not for consideration). [*VATA 1994, Sch 4 para 5(1)*]. This includes

- the sale of assets (e.g. fixed assets);
- assets permanently taken into private use; and
- assets given away.

Business gifts and industrial samples are excluded provided certain conditions are met. [*VATA 1994, Sch 4 para 5(2)(3)*]. See **48.6 OUTPUT TAX** for business gifts, **48.7 OUTPUT TAX** for private use of business assets and **48.7**(28) **OUTPUT TAX** for samples.

Land

Where the business assets include land,

- the grant or assignment of a major interest in the land, or
- the grant or assignment of any interest in, right over or licence to occupy the land concerned otherwise than for a consideration

is a supply of goods. Any other supply of the land is a supply of services. 'Grant' includes surrender.

[*VATA 1994, Sch 4 para 9*].

(f) Transfers of own goods between EU member states

There is a supply of goods where, in a case not falling within (*e*) above, goods forming part of the assets of any business are removed in the course of that business from one EU member state by or under the directions of the person carrying on the business and taken to another EU member state. This applies whether or not the removal is, or is connected with, a transaction for a consideration. [*VATA 1994, Sch 4 para 6*]. There are, however, a number of exceptions and special rules. See **20.25 EUROPEAN UNION: SINGLE MARKET** for full details.

(g) Sales in satisfaction of a debt

Where in the case of a business carried on by a taxable person, goods forming part of the assets of the business are, under any power exercisable by another person, sold by the other person in or towards satisfaction of a debt owed by the taxable person, they are deemed to be supplied by the taxable person in the course or furtherance of his business. [*VATA 1994, Sch 4 para 7*]. Land forming part of the assets of the business is treated as if it were goods and any sale includes a reference to a grant or assignment of any interest in, right over or licence to occupy the land concerned. [*VATA 1994, Sch 4 para 9*].

See **2.10 ACCOUNTING PERIODS AND RETURNS** for the statement to be furnished to HMRC by the person exercising the power.

(h) Deemed supplies on ceasing to be a taxable person

Where a person ceases to be a taxable person, any goods then forming part of the assets of a business carried on by him are (subject to certain exceptions) deemed to be supplied by him in the course of furtherance of his business immediately before he ceases to be a taxable person. [*VATA 1994, Sch 4 para 8*]. See **60.40 REGISTRATION** for further details.

(i) Self-supplies

Where specific goods taken possession of or produced by a person in the course or furtherance of his business are neither supplied to another person nor incorporated in other goods produced in the course or furtherance of that business but are used by him for the purpose of the business, the Treasury have power, by Order, to provide that the goods are deemed to be supplied *to* him for the purpose of the business and *by* him in the course or furtherance of it. [*VATA 1994, s 5(5), s 6(11)*]. Orders have been made in respect of printed matter (see **63.2 SELF-SUPPLY**) motor cars (see **46.6 MOTOR CARS**) and certain construction services (see **43.20 LAND AND BUILDINGS: ZERO AND REDUCED RATE SUPPLIES AND DIY HOUSEBUILDERS**).

(j) Water

The supply of water insofar as it is not otherwise a supply of goods is to be treated as a supply of goods (and not services). [*SI 1989/1114*].

Returned goods and repossessions

If goods supplied are later returned to the supplier for any reason, the VAT treatment of the act of returning the goods depends on whether title to the goods has passed or not.

- *If goods are returned because they are faulty or not in accordance with the sales contract*, the original transaction may be voided. The transfer of title is cancelled and neither the original sale of the unsatisfactory goods nor their return is a supply. If the goods are replaced without further charge, this is strictly speaking a new supply although it is common practice for the original invoice to remain unaltered.
  If the unsatisfactory goods are repaired or improved for the customer and this work is performed in order to meet the original contract, the work is part of that original supply.
- *If goods are returned where title has passed* and the transfer is not cancelled as above, title passes back to the supplier and a second supply is made.

- *If an agreement within (b) above is terminated prematurely and the goods are repossessed*, such a later event cannot change the nature of a transaction. The agreement was a supply of goods for VAT purposes at the outset and this does not change. However, the repossession of the goods is neither a supply of goods (as title has not yet passed) nor a supply of services (as there is no consideration).

De Voil Indirect Tax Service. See V3.112.

Supplies of services

[65.4] For EU legislation, see **19.4 EUROPEAN UNION LEGISLATION.**

Under UK legislation, anything which is not a supply of goods but is done for a consideration (including, if so done, the granting, assignment or surrender of any right) is a supply of services. The Treasury may, however, by Order, deem any transaction to be treated as a supply of goods and not a supply of services (or vice versa). [*VATA 1994, s 5(2)(b)(3)*]. Subject to this, the following supplies are to be treated as supplies of services.

(a) **The transfer of any undivided share of the property in goods.** [*VATA 1994, Sch 4 para 1(1)*]

This refers to goods that can be owned equally by more than one person and where the title to the goods is shared. If all the shares in goods are simultaneously sold to one person, there is a supply of goods. But if only one of the part shares is sold, title to the goods does not pass to the new owner of the part-share and this supply is not of goods but of services. The most common example of an undivided share in property is a part-share ('nomination') in a racehorse.

Unallocated goods are goods which remain an unidentifiable part of a larger stock of goods held by a supplier as opposed to 'allocated' goods which are set apart and earmarked as belonging to, or reserved for, a specific customer. Where goods are sold but are never allocated, title in the goods does not pass so the supply is one of services and not of goods.

Fiscal warehousing

As an exception to this general rule, the transfer of any undivided share of property in eligible goods where the supply is relieved from VAT under the fiscal warehousing regime is treated as a supply of goods and not a supply of services. See **73.15** and **73.16 WAREHOUSED GOODS.**

(b) **The transfer of possession of goods**

The transfer of possession of goods where the conditions in **65.3**(*b*) above are not satisfied. [*VATA 1994, Sch 4 para 1(1)*]. Included is the hire, lease, rental or loan of goods.

(c) **Work done on another person's goods**

Any work done on another person's goods is a supply of services. Where the work produces goods, the services can be zero-rated if the goods produced are zero-rated goods. See **75.1 ZERO-RATED SUPPLIES.**

(d) Non-business use of goods and services

Where, by or under the direction of a person carrying on a business, goods held or used for the purposes of the business are put to private or non-business use, whether or not for a consideration, that is a supply of services. [*VATA 1994, Sch 4 para 5(4)*]. Similarly, where a person carrying on a business puts services supplied to the business to any private or non-business use for no consideration, that is a supply of services. [*SI 1993/1507*].

See **48.7 OUTPUT TAX** for further details.

(e) Exchange units

The exchange of a reconditioned article for an unserviceable article of a similar kind by a person who regularly offers, in the course or furtherance of his business, to provide a reconditioning facility by that means. [*SI 1995/1268, Art 6*]. VAT must be accounted for on the full amount charged for the exchange unit. If the charge to the customer is reduced by giving a refund when the unserviceable article is handed in, the procedure in **40.14 INVOICES** should be adopted.

If the exchange is not part of the person's normal business practice (e.g. where, on a 'one-off' basis, a serviceable article is exchanged for an unserviceable one) or if goods are exchanged for other goods at a reduced price in any other circumstances, the transaction is a supply of goods and should be treated as a part-exchange. (VAT Notice 700, para 8.6).

(f) Services received from abroad

Where a person who belongs abroad supplies certain services to a person who belongs in the UK for the purposes of any business carried on by him and the place of supply of those services is in the UK, the same consequences apply as if the taxable person had himself supplied the services in the UK in the course or furtherance of his business and that supply were a taxable supply. See **39.4 INTERNATIONAL SERVICES.**

De Voil Indirect Tax Service. See V3.113.

Supplies of neither goods nor services

[65.5] The following transactions are treated as neither a supply of goods nor a supply of services.

(a) Transfer of a business as a going concern

The supply by a person of the assets of his business to another person to whom he transfers his business (or part thereof) as a going concern (provided certain conditions are satisfied). See **9.9** *et seq* **BUSINESS.**

(b) The assignment of rights under a HP or conditional sales agreement

The assignment of rights under a HP or conditional sales agreement, and the goods comprised therein, by the owner to a bank or other financial institution. See **24.13 FINANCIAL SERVICES.**

(c) Repossession of goods

The sale of certain goods by a person, including a finance company, who has repossessed them under the terms of a finance agreement or by an insured in settlement of a claim under an insurance policy (provided certain conditions are met). See **24.15 FINANCIAL SERVICES.**

(d) Groups of companies

Where a group registration is in force, most supplies of goods or services by a member of the group to another member of the group are disregarded for VAT purposes. See **28.4 GROUPS OF COMPANIES.**

(e) Supplies of dutiable goods in warehouse

Where imported goods subject to duty are supplied whilst in a customs warehouse, the supply is disregarded for VAT purposes if the goods are supplied before the time for payment of the duty to which they are subject has passed. See **73.4 WAREHOUSED GOODS.**

(f) Motor cars

In addition to the sale of motor cars within (*c*) above,

- the disposal of a motor car for no consideration (e.g. as scrap) where, on any previous supply or importation, input tax on the motor car in question has been excluded from credit; and
- the letting on hire of a motor vehicle for less than full consideration or the making available of a motor car (otherwise than by letting) to any person for private use.

See **46.5 MOTOR CARS.**

(g) Companies organised in divisions

Transactions between divisions of the same corporate body are not supplies for VAT purposes. See **60.43 REGISTRATION.**

(h) Supplies by pawnbrokers

The supply by a taxable person of goods the property in which passed to him as pawnee by virtue of *Consumer Credit Act 1974, s 120(1)(a)* where the supply is to a person who was the pawnor of those goods and the supply is made not later than three months after the taxable person acquired the property in the goods. [*SI 1986/896*]. See **24.16**(8) **FINANCIAL SERVICES** for supplies generally by pawnbrokers.

(i) Temporary importations

Sales of temporarily imported goods provided the goods remain eligible for temporary importation arrangements and the supply is to a person established outside the EU. [*SI 1992/3130*].

(j) Second-hand goods and works of art imported for sale by auction

See **34.25 IMPORTS** for the treatment of second-hand goods and works of art imported for sale by auction.

(k) Second-hand goods scheme

The removal of goods to the UK under a supply to a person in the UK made by a person in another EU member state who accounts for VAT there on the profit margin under the laws of that country similar to the margin scheme in the UK. [*SI 1995/1268, Art 8*]. No VAT is chargeable on such a supply in the UK and the goods may be sold under the margin scheme. See **62.7 SECOND-HAND GOODS.**

(l) Agents acting in their own name in relation to second-hand goods

Services provided by an agent acting in his own name to the purchaser of second-hand goods where the consideration for the services is taken into account in calculating the price at which the agent obtained the goods. [*SI 1995/1268, Art 9*]. See **62.26 SECOND-HAND GOODS.**

(m) Auctioneers in relation to second-hand goods

Services provided by an auctioneer acting in his own name to the vendor or purchaser of second-hand goods where the consideration for the services is taken into account in calculating the price at which the auctioneer obtained, or as the case may be, sold the goods. [*SI 1995/1268, Art 10*]. See **62.59 SECOND-HAND GOODS.**

De Voil Indirect Tax Service. See V3.114.

Single and multiple supplies

[65.6] There have always been problems in determining the correct VAT liability of transactions consisting of separately identifiable goods or services. This is particularly relevant where, if supplied on their own, some elements would be taxable and others would qualify for relief from VAT. For example, there may be a combination of two or more goods (e.g. zero-rated food in luxury standard-rated packaging), two or more services (e.g. standard-rated car hire with exempt insurance) or goods and services (e.g. standard-rated tuition with zero-rated books). The question is: should the different elements be treated separately for VAT purposes or are they properly part of a single overall supply?

For such transactions, it is therefore necessary to distinguish between

- a 'single' (or 'composite') supply, i.e. where there is one overall type of supply (either goods or services) and one VAT liability; and
- a 'multiple' (or 'mixed') supply, i.e. where the two or more components are separate supplies, each of which is either a supply of goods or services and each of which has its own VAT liability.

Neither UK nor EU VAT legislation provides rules to determine this. Over the years, tribunal and court decisions (or a HMRC ruling, trade agreement or statement of practice based on that litigation) have produced general guidelines on how to approach the problem but these have not provided any certainty on the issue.

More substantial guidance on the proper test for deciding if transactions constitute one or more supplies was given by the CJEU in *Card Protection Plan Ltd v C & E Commrs, ECJ Case C–349/96*, [1999] STC 270 (TVC 22.356). The court stated that, although it is not possible to give exhaustive guidance on the approach in all cases, the following general criteria should be used.

(a) Following the earlier judgment in *Faaborg-Gelting Linien A/S v Finanzamt Flensburg, ECJ Case C–231/94*, [1996] STC 774 (TVC 22.190) where a transaction comprises a bundle of features and acts, regard must first be had to all the circumstances in which the transaction takes place. The essential features of the transaction must be ascertained in order to determine whether the taxable person is supplying the customer, being a typical consumer, with several distinct principal supplies or with a single supply, taking into account that
   (i) it follows from *Directive 2006/112/EC, Art 2(1)(a)* that a supply must normally be regarded as distinct and independent (i.e. it should amount to more than merely a component of the overall supply); and
   (ii) a supply which comprises a single supply from an economic point of view should not be artificially split (so as not to distort the functioning of the VAT system).

> *Example*
>
> Where a garage services a customer's car, although there are different elements that go to make up a typical service, these cannot be said to be distinct or independent in the context of the overall service required by the customer. Any attempt to describe them as separate supplies would clearly be artificial.

(b) Where (*a*) above does distinguish separate supplies, it is necessary to consider whether each supply can be properly regarded as a principal supply or whether some of them are merely ancillary to the principal supply. There is a single supply, in particular, in cases where one or more elements are to be regarded as constituting the principal supply, whilst one or more elements are to be regarded, by contrast, as ancillary and which share the tax treatment of the principal supply. A supply must be regarded as ancillary to a principal supply if it does not constitute for customers an aim in itself, but a means of better enjoying the principal supply (see *TP Madgett & RM Baldwin (t/a Howden Court Hotel) v C & E Commrs, ECJ Cases C–308/96 and C–94/97*, [1998] STC 1189 (TVC 22.562)).
The fact that a single price is charged is not decisive. Admittedly, if what is provided to customers consists of several elements for a single price, the single price may suggest that there is a single supply. However, notwithstanding the single price, if circumstances indicate that the customers intended to purchase two distinct supplies, then it is neces-

sary to identify the part of the single price that relates to each supply. The simplest possible method of calculation or assessment should be used for this.

Example

Catering is commonly provided together with the transport of passengers.

- In the case of in-flight catering provided to airline passengers, this is not something that the customer specifically seeks to obtain. He assumes the flight will include a meal as this is a normal feature of airline transport. The meal is provided for customers to better enjoy the transport service and, for a typical customer, is not an aim in itself. Therefore, the meal (standard-rated if supplied alone) is not liable to VAT in these circumstances because it is ancillary to the supply of zero-rated transport services. See *British Airways plc v C & E Commrs*, CA [1990] STC 643 (TVC 66.13).
- On the other hand, where a customer books a river cruise that includes a substantial meal, the catering is more than simply an adjunct to the cruise. It is something a typical customer would regard as an end in itself. In these circumstances there are two principal supplies, comprising zero-rated transport and standard-rated catering.

HMRC accept that if a distinct service element represents 50% or more of the price of a bundle of goods and services, this will be a strong indicator that this service is not ancillary to a principal supply of any other goods or services in that bundle and that the consideration may need to be apportioned accordingly. (Business Brief 3/02).

Types of transactions that may be affected

The following list is not exhaustive but illustrates some of the areas where the issue of single and multiple supplies can have an impact.

- Delivered goods (see **48.8**(19) **OUTPUT TAX**).
- Dispensed spectacles (see **29.4 HEALTH AND WELFARE**) and dispensed hearing aids (see **29.5 HEALTH AND WELFARE**).
- Membership of clubs and associations (see **15.2 CLUBS AND ASSOCIATIONS**).
- Cover-mounted goods supplied with magazines (see **55.8 PRINTED MATTER, ETC.**).
- Admissions to sporting events, etc. by programme (see **58.2 RECREATION AND SPORT**).
- Books, etc. supplied with correspondence courses (see **55.17 PRINTED MATTER, ETC.**).
- Airport parking services that include transport.
- Printed matter supplied with advertising services.
- Transport and catering (see **73.18 TRANSPORT AND FREIGHT**).
- Installed goods.
- Programme listing magazines and broadcasting services.
- Linked promotional goods.

HMRC consider that the tests laid down in *Card Protection Plan* above will be appropriate in the great majority of cases. Businesses making supplies of the kind listed above must review their VAT treatment of those supplies against the revised criteria.

Single supply

Where this is established, no apportionment must be made and the supply as a whole must be considered to determine the VAT liability, if any.

Since the CJEU decision in *Card Protection Plan* above, single supplies have been held to include the following.

- The purchase of a car and its associated delivery charges (*C & E Commrs v British Telecommunications plc*, HL [1999] STC 758 (TVC 44.102)).
- The purchase of a car and free insurance (*Peugeot Motor Co plc and Another v C & E Commrs*, Ch D [2003] STC 1438 (TVC 38.54)).
- Broadcasting services and a magazine providing details of programmes (*British Sky Broadcasting Group plc* (VTD 16220) (TVC 5.101) but see *Telewest Communications* below).
- Hospitality packages offered by a football club including meals, drinks and a match programme (*Manchester United plc* (VTD 17234) (TVC 5.81)).
- Children's activity programmes where the enrolment fee includes a T-shirt, accident insurance, a magazine for parents, a DVD, a member's handbook and gymbag (*Tumble Tots (UK) Ltd v HMRC*, Ch D [2007] STC 1171 (TVC 12.27)).
- Weight loss programmes comprising weekly meetings as well as handbooks, magazines and leaflets (*HMRC v Weight Watchers UK Ltd*, CA [2008] STC 2313 (TVC 5.95)), or comprising weekly meetings, dietary packs and support services (*HMRC v David Baxendale Ltd*, CA [2009] EWCA Civ 831 (TVC 62.588)).
- The leasing of premises and the supply of water to those premises under the lease (*The Honourable Society of Middle Temple*, UT [2013] UKUT 250 (TCC) (TVC 69.2)).
- Drugs and prostheses used in the course of treating hospital patients (*Nuffield Health* (TC02697) (TVC 19.4)).
- Distance learning books with incidental tutorial help (*Metropolitan International Schools* [2015] UKFTT 517 (TC) (TC04675) (TVC 5.40)).

Earlier decisions held the following supplies to be single supplies (although these must be read in light of the tests in *Card Protection Plan*).

- Services of a launderette (which cannot be treated as separate supplies of water, heat, use of machine, etc., only the single supply of washing or drying clothes) (*Mander Laundries Ltd* (VTD 31) (TVC 69.1)).
- Services of a stud farm providing the supply of the keep of a mare with everything that is involved in maintaining her in reasonable condition and safety (a single standard-rated supply so that the supply of animal feeding stuffs included cannot be zero-rated) (*C & E Commrs v DD Scott*, QB 1977, [1978] STC 191 (TVC 29.118)).

- The provision of optional collision damage waiver with the supply of a super car driving experience was held not to be a separate supply of exempt insurance but part of the overall supply of the standard-rated driving experience (*Supercar Drive Days Ltd* [2018] UKFTT 31 (TC), (TC06311) (TVC 38.7A)).

Two-part tariff

This occurs where there are two or more payments involving apparently different transactions at different times but which amount to the purchase of a single supply. This concept was introduced in *British Railways Board v C & E Commrs*, CA [1977] STC 221 (TVC 66.12) where there were two payments, one for a student card allowing students to buy cut-price travel tickets, and the other which the student made when obtaining the actual ticket. The court held that the two payments were both for the supply of discounted travel paid at different stages, rather than for two separate supplies (of the right to a discount and then discounted travel).

Multiple supply

In a multiple supply, even though the supplies are often paid for together, the individual components are not integral to each other and are separate supplies.

Since the CJEU decision in *Card Protection Plan* above, multiple supplies have been held to include the following.

- Promotional/advertising services and printed brochures (*Appleby Bowers v C & E Commrs*, Ch D 2000, [2001] STC 185 (TVC 5.68)).
- Day excursions on a luxury train which included the provision of meals (*Sea Containers Services Ltd v C & E Commrs*, QB 1999, [2000] STC 82 (TVC 66.26)).
- A monthly magazine providing details of programmes and broadcasting services where each supply was provided by a different company (*Telewest Communications plc v C & E Commrs; Telewest Communications (Publications) Ltd v C & E Commrs*, CA [2005] STC 481) (TVC 62.382), the court ruling that the two supplies could not be treated as a single supply merely because the customer could not enter into one transaction without the other and because there was no authority that the principles propounded in *Card Protection Plan* above could apply where there was more than one supplier.
- Ski passes including the right to transport on a funicular railway (*Cairngorm Mountain* (VTD 17679) (TVC 66.27)).
- The supply of medical services (consultation and diagnosis) by a doctor and any related supply of the provision and administration of drugs (*Dr Beynon & Partners v C & E Commrs*, HL 2004, [2005] STC 55 (TVC 19.10)).
- The supply of a plot of land with planning permission to build a holiday home, supplied by one company, and the supply of construction services by another connected company (*Lower Mill Estate Ltd v HMRC (and related appeal)*, UT [2011] STC 636 (TVC 22.78)).
- The provision of a leased taxi/radio services and the provision of optional insurance to drivers were held to be two separate supplies (*Wheels Private Hire Ltd* [2017] UKUT 51 (TCC) (TVC 38.4)).

Earlier decisions held the following supplies to be multiple supplies (although these must be read in light of the tests in *Card Protection Plan*).

- Annual subscriptions to the AA (apportionable between the benefits – a magazine, booklet, maps and information, pick-up services, repairs, etc. – to which members are entitled (*C & E Commrs v The Automobile Assn*, QB [1974] STC 192 (TVC 13.18)). Membership bodies frequently treat the supply of benefits to members as multiple supplies. However, the CJEU tests in *Card Protection Plan* may mean that the supply of benefits by a number of membership bodies should be treated as a single supply of the principal benefit. In the case of non-profit making membership bodies, HMRC are considering the introduction of an extra-statutory concession whereby such bodies which supply a mixture of zero-rated, exempt and/or standard-rated benefits to members in return for their subscriptions may continue to apportion the subscriptions.
- Children's colouring books issued with felt tip pens, where the pens are not restricted in use to the book they are sold with.
- A book with an accompanying audio or video tape, each of which may be used independently of the book, and which require particular equipment for their use.
- Consideration under contracts providing for both the hire of a television set from a rental company and the insurance of the set by an insurance company within the same VAT group (*Thorn EMI plc; Granada plc* (VTD 9782) (TVC 38.9)).

Where all the supplies are liable to VAT at the same rate, there is no problem and output tax due is calculated in the normal way. Where, however, there is a mixture of zero-rated, standard-rated and/or exempt supplies, the value of each supply for VAT purposes must be calculated in order to arrive at the total output tax due. Any calculation of the apportionment of the total price must be fair and justifiable. See **48.3 OUTPUT TAX** for apportionment of consideration.

De Voil Indirect Tax Service. See V3.107–V3.105.

(Business Brief 2/01; VAT Information Sheet 2/01).

Supplies by 'taxable persons'

[65.7] For EU legislation, see **19.7 EUROPEAN UNION LEGISLATION**.

Under UK legislation, one of the four basic conditions to be satisfied for a transaction to be within the scope of UK VAT (see **65.1** above) is that it is made by a taxable person. Under *VATA 1994, s 1(2)*, VAT on any supply of goods or services is a liability of the person making the supply and under *VATA 1994, s 3(1)* a person is a taxable person while he is, or is required to be, registered for VAT purposes. It follows from this that, to decide whether a transaction meets the condition of being made by a taxable person, it is necessary to establish two facts.

(a) Whether a person is required to be registered

This is usually dependent upon the level of taxable turnover; although there are special provisions covering voluntary registration, registration of intending traders and group registration. All these considerations are dealt with in the chapter **60 REGISTRATION**.

However, another consideration which can determine whether a person is required to be registered is employment status. Under *Directive 2006/112/EC, Art 9(1)* a taxable person means any person who *independently* carries out certain specified activities. The use of the word 'independently' specifically excludes employed and other persons from the scope of VAT in so far as they are bound to an employer by a contract of employment or by any other legal ties creating the relationship of employer and employee as regards working conditions, remuneration and the employer's liability.

Unless there are clear reasons to do otherwise, HMRC policy is normally to follow the employment status for income tax purposes, i.e. they accept that a person paying income tax under the trading income provisions is self-employed and a person paying under the employment income provisions is an employee (and therefore outside the scope of VAT). Note, however, that where a person (e.g. an accountant or solicitor) in the course or furtherance of a trade profession or vocation, accepts any office, services supplied as the holder of that office are treated as supplied in the course or furtherance of the trade, etc. [*VATA 1994, s 94(4)*].

(b) Who is the person making the supply and thus liable for the VAT on that transaction

This will, in the vast majority of cases, be self-evident but the position may require careful consideration when involving **3 AGENTS** or **51 PARTNERSHIPS**. See also **12.9 CATERING**, **17.16 EDUCATION** for school photographers, **71.24 TRANSPORT AND FREIGHT** for taxis and hire cars.

Key points: general supply

[65.8] Points to consider are as follows.

- A supply of goods is taking place with a hire purchase contract, even though ownership of the goods does not usually pass to the hirer until the end of the agreement. So a business buying assets on hire purchase will usually pay the VAT element of the goods at the beginning of the agreement and be able to reclaim this amount as input tax, subject to normal rules.
- In the case of assets or goods that are leased, VAT is usually charged on each of the monthly hire payments because the ownership of the goods is retained by the leasing company, and they are normally returned to the company at the end of the agreement.

- In situations where a business is transferred to a new owner as a going concern (TOGC), then the proceeds of the sale are outside the scope of VAT as long as certain important conditions are met. This is because a TOGC arrangement is classed as neither a supply of goods nor services.
- In certain situations, a customer will acquire two or more benefits (goods or services) when he pays for a supply. If each benefit has a value in its own right, then the VAT payable will need to be apportioned if they are subject to different rates of VAT. If the secondary supply is incidental to the main supply, then the VAT liability is wholly based on that of the main supply.
- If goods are never actually in the UK, they cannot be within the scope of UK VAT. So a UK business selling goods that started in Australia and are shipped directly to a customer in America is making sales that are outside the scope of UK VAT.

66

Supply: Place of Supply

Introduction to place of supply

[66.1] Having determined that a supply of goods or services has taken place, the second condition to be satisfied if the transaction is to fall within the scope of UK VAT is that the supply takes place within the UK (see **65.1 SUPPLY: GENERAL**). The place of supply rules are different for goods and for services. See **SUPPLY: GENERAL** at **65.3–65.5** for a consideration of what constitutes a supply of goods and a supply of services (or neither).

For EU law, see **19.12 EUROPEAN UNION LEGISLATION** for the place of supply of goods and **19.14 EUROPEAN UNION LEGISLATION** for the place of supply of services.

UK law relating to the place of supply is contained in *VATA 1994, ss 7, 9*. The Treasury are empowered to vary the normal rules by statutory instrument [*VATA 1994, s 7(11)*] and to date three main Orders have been made.

- *VAT (Tour Operators) Order 1987 (SI 1987/1806)* which relates to supplies of designated travel services by tour operators and other persons who buy in and resell travel facilities (see **69.5 TOUR OPERATORS' MARGIN SCHEME**);
- *VAT (Place of Supply of Services) Order 1992 (SI 1992/3121)* which has a general impact on the place of supply of services (see **66.12** *et seq* below); and
- *VAT (Place of Supply of Goods) Order 2004 (SI 2004/3148)* which relates to supplies of goods on board ships, aircraft and trains involved in intra-EU transport (see **66.10** below).

Registration of UK suppliers in other EU member states

Where the place of supply of goods or services is outside the UK, there is no UK VAT liability. However, a UK supplier who makes supplies in another EU member state may be liable to register there, subject to the registration rules applicable in that country. If they do not have an establishment there, they may have to appoint a local tax representative to account for VAT on their behalf. UK suppliers must make their own enquiries about registration in other EU member states with the authorities of the country concerned: HMRC cannot advise on the rules applicable in other countries.

Registration of traders who have no place of business in the UK

Similarly, a trader belonging outside the UK with no place of business here may be liable to UK VAT registration where the place of supply of those goods or services is in the UK. See **49 OVERSEAS TRADERS** for further details.

Territory of the UK and EU

The UK comprises Great Britain, Northern Ireland and the waters within twelve nautical miles of their coastlines. For VAT purposes it includes the Isle of Man but not the Channel Islands or Gibraltar. See **18.2 EUROPEAN UNION: GENERAL** for the VAT territory of the EU.

Place of supply of goods

[66.2] Subject to certain simplification procedures (see **66.11** below) and special provisions relating to warehoused goods (see **73.2** to **73.11 WAREHOUSED GOODS**), the provisions relating to the place of supply of goods are to be found in *VATA 1994, s 7* (see **66.3–66.9** below) and *The VAT (Place of Supply of Goods) Order 2004, SI 2004/3148* (see **66.10** below). It should be noted that *Sec 7* has a hierarchical structure. The place of supply of any goods may be determined by working through the rules in **66.3–66.8** below in order until one applicable to the particular supply in question is reached. [*VATA 1994, s 7(1)*].

De Voil Indirect Tax Service. See V3.171–V3.178.

Goods which do not leave or enter the UK

[66.3] Where the supply of any goods does not involve their removal from or to the UK, they are treated as supplied

- in the UK if they are in the UK; and
- otherwise as supplied outside the UK.

[*VATA 1994, s 7(2)*].

The first situation covers the vast majority of transactions subject to VAT. The second situation includes sales on the high seas where the goods do not come to the UK and supplies sourced from outside the UK and delivered to a country other than the UK. In these cases it is important to disregard extraneous facts such as where the order was placed, the invoice route or how and where payment was made.

Installed or assembled goods

[66.4] Goods whose place of supply is not determined under **66.3** above are treated as supplied

- in the UK where their supply involves their installation or assembly at a place in the UK to which they are removed; and
- outside the UK where their supply involves their installation or assembly at a place outside the UK to which they are removed.

[*VATA 1994, s 7(3)*].

By concession, where a *one-off* supply of installed or assembled goods would be treated as made in the UK, it is treated as made outside the UK if

- the supplier is not registered for VAT in the UK;
- no further UK business is anticipated;
- the goods are imported from outside the EU; and
- the customer acts as importer and shows the full value of the goods, including installation and assembly costs on the import entry.

(Business Brief 1/98).

See **66.11** below for details of a simplified procedure which eligible EU traders can use to avoid the need to register for VAT in the UK.

Distance sales to the UK

[66.5] Goods whose place of supply is not determined under **66.3** or **66.4** above are treated as supplied in the UK where

(a) the supply involves the removal of the goods to the UK by or under the direction of the supplier;
(b) the supply is a transaction under which the goods are acquired in the UK from another EU member state by a person who is not registered or required to be registered under *VATA 1994*;

(c) the supplier is, or is liable to be, registered under *VATA 1994, Sch 2* by virtue of his distance sales in the UK, see **60.11 REGISTRATION** (or would be so liable if he were not registrable under *VATA 1994, Sch 1* or *Sch 1A* in respect of UK supplies, see **60.1 REGISTRATION**); and
(d) the supply is neither
- a supply of goods consisting of a new means of transport (see **20.31 EUROPEAN UNION: SINGLE MARKET**); nor
- anything which is treated as a supply by virtue only of *VATA 1994, Sch 4 para 5(1)* (disposal of business assets, see **65.3**(*e*) **SUPPLY: GENERAL** or *VATA 1994, Sch 4 para 6* (transfer of own goods between EU member states, see **20.25 EUROPEAN UNION: SINGLE MARKET**).

[*VATA 1994, s 7(4)*].

Distance sales from the UK

[66.6] Goods whose place of supply is not determined under **66.3–66.5** above and which do not consist of a new means of transport (see **20.33 EUROPEAN UNION: SINGLE MARKET**) are treated as supplied outside the UK where

(a) the supply involves the removal of the goods to another EU member state by or under the direction of the supplier;
(b) the person who makes the supply is taxable in another EU member state; and
(c) the provisions of the law of that other EU member state corresponding to the provisions under **66.5**(*c*) above make the supplier liable to be registered and account for VAT in that country.

This does not, however, apply where the liability under (*c*) above depends on the exercise by any person of an option in the UK corresponding to such an option made by an overseas trader under **60.12**(*a*) **REGISTRATION** unless that person has given (and not withdrawn) a notification to HMRC that his supplies are to be treated as taking place outside the UK.

[*VATA 1994, s 7(5)*].

Imported goods

[66.7] Goods whose place of supply is not determined under **66.3–66.6** above are treated as supplied in the UK where

(a) their supply involves their being imported from a place outside the EU; and
(b) the supplier is the person by whom, or under whose direction, they are so imported.

[*VATA 1994, s 7(6)*].

The place of supply of imported goods is therefore determined by reference to the importer.

- Where the supplier imports the goods, the place of supply is the UK (under the above rules).

- Where the customer imports the goods, the place of supply is outside the UK (under **66.8**(*b*) below).

Other goods which leave or enter the UK

[66.8] Goods whose place of supply is not determined under **66.3–66.7** above but whose supply involves their removal to or from the UK are treated

(a) as supplied in the UK where their supply involves their removal from the UK without also involving their previous removal to the UK; and
(b) as supplied outside the UK in any other case.

[*VATA 1994, s 7(7)*].

These provisions cover

- under (*a*) above,
  - (i) the removal of goods from the UK to another EU member state (other than distance sales within **66.6** above); and
  - (ii) the export of goods from the UK; and
- under (*b*) above,
  - (i) the removal of goods to the UK from another EU member state (other than distance sales within **66.5** above); and
  - (ii) the importation of goods from outside the EU where the UK customer is the person responsible for the importation (see **66.7** above).

Goods temporarily leaving the UK in the course of a removal to another place in the UK

[66.9] For the purposes of **66.3–66.8** above, where, in the course of their removal from a place in the UK to another place in the UK, goods leave and re-enter the UK, the removal is not treated as a removal from or to the UK. [*VATA 1994, s 7(8)*]. This would occur, for example, where goods moved from Northern Ireland to England passed through Ireland.

Goods supplied on board intra-EU transport

[66.10] Except for goods supplied as part of a 'pleasure cruise', goods which are supplied on board a ship, aircraft or train in the course of 'community transport' are treated as supplied at the 'point of departure' except that goods supplied for consumption on board are treated as supplied outside the EU.

'*Pleasure cruise*' includes a cruise wholly or partly for the purposes of education or training.

'*Community transport*' means transportation of passengers between a point of departure and a point of arrival in the course of which there is a stop in an EU member state other than that of the point of departure and there is no stop in a country which is not an EU member state.

[*SI 2004/3148, Arts 4–8*].

See also *Peninsular and Oriental Steam Navigation Co v C & E Commrs*, QB [2000] STC 488 (TVC 62.492).

Simplification procedures

[66.11] The following measures can, in certain circumstances, be used to avoid unnecessary UK VAT registration in the UK.

- **Import agents acting for an overseas supplier**. Where an overseas trader imports goods into the UK for onward sale and is not otherwise liable to register for VAT in the UK, he may, as an alternative to registration, appoint a UK VAT-registered agent to act on his behalf. See **49.4 OVERSEAS TRADERS** for further details.
- **Installed or assembled goods**. To avoid an overseas person making a supply of installed or assembled goods in the UK having to register for UK VAT, the UK customer can, provided certain conditions are satisfied, account for the VAT as acquisition VAT. See **20.31 EUROPEAN UNION: SINGLE MARKET**.
- Triangular EU trade. See **20.22 EUROPEAN UNION: SINGLE MARKET**.

Place of supply of services

Significance of place of supply

[66.12] For VAT purposes, the place where a supply is deemed to be made is called the *place of supply*. This is the only place where the supply can be liable to VAT. Thus, where the place of supply of any services is in an EU member state, that supply is liable to VAT (if any) in that country and in no other country. If that country is not the UK, the supply is outside the scope of UK VAT. Where the place of supply of any services is outside the EU, that supply is not liable to VAT in any EU member state (although local taxes may apply). The significance for a UK business is as follows.

- **If a UK business supplies services and the place of supply is the UK**, subject to the VAT registration limits the supply is standard-rated, zero-rated or exempt (as the case may be) and any VAT due must be accounted for to HMRC. This applies regardless of where the customer belongs.
- **If a UK business supplies services and the place of supply is in another EU member state**, subject to the registration limits in that country either the UK supplier or the customer is liable to account for any VAT due to the VAT authorities in that country.

(VAT Notice 741A, paras 2.1, 2.2).

The general rule for the place of supply of services taxes business to business supplies of services at the place where the customer is established, and not at the place where the supplier is established. For cross-border supplies, in most cases, the business customer must account for the VAT using the reverse charge procedure (and recover the tax in its own country subject to the normal rules).

For business to consumer supplies of services, the general rule for the place of supply is the place where the supplier is established. There are exceptions to the general rule for certain services, with a view to achieving taxation in the place of consumption.

> *Example*
>
> The services provided by a vet fall under the general rule as far as the place of supply procedures are concerned. So a UK vet providing services to a French farmer (B2B sale) charges no VAT because the place of supply is France, i.e. where the farmer is based. It is irrelevant whether the vet carries out his work in the UK or France.

Cultural, artistic, sporting, scientific, educational, entertainment services

Supplies to non-business customers of cultural, artistic, sporting, scientific, educational, entertainment and similar services, as well as valuation and work on goods, are taxed where the service is performed. For supplies to business customers, valuation, work on goods and most supplies of cultural, artistic, sporting, scientific, educational, entertainment and similar services are taxed where the customer is established, under the new general place of supply rule. However, supplies of admission to cultural, artistic, sporting, scientific, educational and entertainment events are taxable where the event takes place.

Land

Land-related services are deemed to be supplied where the land is situated.

> *Example*
>
> An architect based in the UK, and registered for VAT in the UK, has agreed to carry out some work for a Spanish customer in relation to a property she owns in France. The place of supply is France (where the building is based), and the architect may need to become VAT-registered in France and charge French VAT to the Spanish client. This rule is intended to create a level playing field throughout the EU, i.e. to prevent a customer using the services of an architect in a country with a lower rate of VAT.

HMRC have stated that, for the purposes of determining the place of supply, 'land' means any

- specific part of the earth, on, above or below its surface, over which title or possession can be created;
- building or construction fixed to or in the ground above or below sea level which cannot be easily dismantled or moved;
- item making up part of a building or construction and without which it is incomplete (such as doors, windows, roofs, staircases and lifts);
- item, equipment or machine permanently installed in a building or construction which cannot be moved without destroying or altering the building or construction.

HMRC have also given examples of what they do and do not regard as land-related services as follows.

Land-related services

- Construction or demolition of a building or permanent structure (such as pipelines for gas, water or sewage).
- Surveying and assessing property.
- Valuing property, including for insurance or loan purposes.
- Providing accommodation in hotels, holiday camps, camping sites or timeshare accommodation.
- Maintenance, renovation and repair of a building (including work such as cleaning and decorating) or permanent structure.
- Property management services (but not the management of a property investment portfolio).
- Arranging the sale or lease of land or property.
- Drawing up of plans for a building or part of a building designated for a particular site.
- On-site security services.
- Agricultural work on land (including tillage, sowing, watering and fertilization).
- Installation and assembly of machines which, when installed, will form a fixture that cannot be easily dismantled or moved.
- The granting of rights to use all or part of a property (such as fishing or hunting rights and access to airport lounges).
- Bridge or tunnel toll fees.
- The supply of space for the use of advertising billboards – for example the leasing of a plot of land or the side of a building to allow a billboard to be erected.
- The supply of plant and equipment together with an operator, to allow the customer to carry out work on land or property where the supplier has responsibility for the execution of work.

Services which are not land-related

- Drawing up of plans for a building or part of a building that do not relate to a particular site.
- Arranging the supply of hotel accommodation or similar services.
- Installation, assembly, repair or maintenance of machines or equipment which are not, and do not become, part of the land or property.
- Management of a property investment portfolio.
- Advertising services that involve the use of a billboard.
- The supply of equipment with an operator, where it can be shown that the supplier has no responsibility for the performance of the work.

Stand space at exhibitions and conferences

HMRC regard the supply of specific stand space at an exhibition or conference as a supply of land. This policy applies where the service is restricted to the mere supply of space without any accompanying services. However, where stand space is provided with accompanying services as a package, this package (stand and services) is not regarded as a supply of land with land-related services. It is taxed under the general place of supply rule (customer location) when supplied to business customers. Accompanying services provided as part of a package include such things as the design and erection of a temporary stand, security, power, telecommunications, hire of machinery or publicity material.

Storage of goods

HMRC policy is that where a supplier grants the right to use a specific area of a UK warehouse or storage area for the exclusive use of the customer to store goods, the service is treated as relating to land and subject to VAT in the UK. However, where the supplier agrees to store goods but does not grant a right to a specific area for the exclusive use of the customer, this is not seen as a land-related supply but is treated as falling within the general place of supply rule. In such cases business customers who belong outside the UK are not liable to UK VAT.

Airport lounges

The supply of access to airport lounges is regarded as a land-related service. VAT, if applicable, is due in the country where the aircraft lounge is located.

(HMRC Brief 22/12).

Hire of means of transport

There is a distinction between short-time hire (no more than 30 days or 90 days for vessels) and long-term hire. For short-term hire, the place of supply is where the vehicle is put at the disposal of the customer. For long-term hire, the place of supply falls under the new general rule. However, from 1 January 2013, the place of supply of long-term hire to non-business customers is where the customer is established (except for long-term hire of pleasure boats to non-business customers which will be treated as supplied where the boat is actually put at the customer's disposal if the supplier has an establishment there).

Restaurants and catering

These services are treated as supplied where they are physically performed. For restaurant and catering services carried out on board ships, aircraft or trains as part of transport in the EU, the place of supply is the place of departure. This mirrors existing rules for goods sold for consumption on board.

Intermediary services

Services provided by intermediaries to business customers fall under the general rule. Supplies to non-business customers are taxed according to the place of the underlying supply that the intermediary is arranging.

Transport of goods

For the transport of goods and ancillary transport services, see **66.25** below.

Intangible services

The place of supply of certain intangible services, e.g. legal advice, continues to be where the customer belongs when provided to non-business customers outside the EU.

Passenger transport

The place of supply of passenger transport services is where the transport takes place, apportioning a cross-border journey according to the proportion of it that takes place in each country. Although passenger transport is zero-rated in the UK, it is not free of VAT in other countries, so international transport businesses have to consider their VAT liabilities according to local rules.

Right to a service

The place of supply of a right to services is the same as the place in which the supply of the services to which the right relates would be treated as made if made by the supplier of the right to the recipient of the right. The expression 'right to services' in this context includes a reference to any right, option or priority with respect to the supply of services and to the supply of an interest deriving from any right to services.

[*VATA 1994, s 7A, Sch 4A*].

Input tax recovery

Input tax attributable to certain supplies of services may be recoverable even though, under the place of supply rules, the supply is deemed to take place outside the UK and is outside the scope of UK VAT. See **35.3 INPUT TAX**.

De Voil Indirect Tax Service. See V3.181–V3.197.

Place of belonging

[66.13] A relevant business person 'belongs' in the relevant country. A 'relevant country' means:

- the country in which the person has a business establishment, or some other fixed establishment (if it has none in any other country);
- if the person has a business establishment, or some other fixed establishment or establishments, in more than one country, the country of the relevant establishment (i.e. the establishment most directly concerned with the supply); and
- otherwise, the country in which the person's usual place of residence (or from 1 January 2015 permanent address) is (in the case of a body corporate, where it is legally constituted).

A person who is not a relevant business person 'belongs' in the country of his usual place of residence.

From 1 January 2015 a person who is not a relevant business person is to be treated as belonging:

- in the country in which the person's usual place of residence or permanent address is (except in the case of a body corporate or other legal person);
- in the case of a body corporate or other legal person, in the country in which the place where it is established is, being the place where the functions of its central administration are carried out or the place of any

other establishment characterised by a sufficient degree of permanence and a suitable structure in terms of human and technical resources to enable it to receive and use the services supplied to it for its own needs.

The 'belonging' definition applies equally to the recipient of a supply, where relevant.

[*VATA 1994, s 9; FA 2014, s 104*].

Business establishment

Business establishment is not defined in the legislation but is taken by HMRC to mean the principal place of business. It is usually the head office, headquarters or 'seat' from which the business is run. There can only be one such place and it may take the form of an office, showroom or factory.

Examples

- A business has its headquarters in the UK and branches in France, Italy and Germany. Its business establishment is in the UK.
- A company is incorporated in the UK but trades entirely from its head office in Bermuda. Its business establishment is in Bermuda.

(VAT Notice 741A, para 3.3).

Fixed establishment

Fixed establishment is not defined in the legislation but is taken by HMRC to mean an establishment (other than the business establishment) which has both the technical and human resources necessary for providing and receiving services on a permanent basis. A business may therefore have several fixed establishments, including a branch of the business or an agency. A temporary presence of human and technical resources does not create a fixed establishment in the UK.

Examples

- An overseas business sets up a branch comprising staff and offices in the UK to provide services. The UK branch is a fixed establishment.
- A company with a business establishment overseas owns a property in the UK which it leases to tenants. The property does not in itself create a fixed establishment. However, if the company has UK offices and staff or appoints a UK agency to carry on its business by managing the property, this creates a fixed establishment in the UK.
- An overseas business contracts with UK customers to provide services. It has no human or technical resources in the UK and therefore sets up a UK subsidiary to act in its name to provide those services. The overseas business has a fixed establishment in the UK created by the agency of the subsidiary.
- A company is incorporated in the UK but trades entirely overseas from its head office in the USA, which is its business establishment. The UK registered office is a fixed establishment. See *Binder Hamlyn* [1983] VATTR 171 (TVC 62.520).

- A UK company acts as the operating member of a consortium for offshore exploitation of oil or gas using a fixed production platform. The rig is a fixed establishment of the operating member.

(VAT Notice 741A, paras 3.4, 3.5).

Usual place of residence

A *body corporate* has its usual place of residence where it is legally constituted. [*VATA 1994, s 9(5)(b)*]. The usual place of residence of an *individual* is not defined in the legislation. HMRC interpret the phrase according to the ordinary usage of the words, i.e. normally the country where the individual has set up home with his/her family and is in full-time employment. An individual is not resident in a country if only visiting as a tourist.

Persons who are present in the UK but have not been granted a right or permission to remain here (e.g. asylum seekers and those entering without permission) should be treated as belonging in their country of origin.

Examples

- A person lives in the UK, but commutes to France daily for work. He belongs in the UK.
- Overseas forces personnel on a tour of duty in the UK live in rented accommodation with their families. They have homes overseas to which they periodically return on leave. They belong in the UK throughout their tour of duty. See *USAA Ltd* [1993] Lexis Citation 2213 (TVC 62.513).

(VAT Notice 741A, paras 3.6, 3.7).

See also *Razzak & Mishari* (VTD 15240) (TVC 62.518) where the tribunal, distinguishing *USAA Ltd* above, held that an Indian woman, who came to the UK in 1992 and remained here until October 1996 during the course of legal proceedings against a former employer, had her usual place of residence in India throughout that period.

More than one establishment

For the purposes of (*c*) above, where the supplier/recipient has establishments in more than one country, the supplies made from/received at each establishment must be considered separately. For each supply of services, the establishment which is actually providing/receiving the services is normally the one most directly connected with the supply but all facts should be considered including

- for suppliers, from which establishment the services are actually provided;
- for recipients, at which establishment the services are actually consumed, effectively used or enjoyed;
- which establishment appears on the contracts, correspondence and invoices;
- where directors or others who entered into the contract are permanently based; and

- at which establishment decisions are taken and controls are exercised over the performance of the contract.

However, where an establishment is actually providing/receiving the supply of services, it is normally that establishment which is most directly connected with the supply, even if the contractual position is different.

Examples

- A company whose business establishment is in France contracts with a UK bank to provide French speaking staff for the bank's international desk in London. The French supplier has a fixed establishment in the UK created by a branch, which provides staff to other customers. The French establishment deals directly with the bank without any involvement by the UK branch. The staff are supplied from the French establishment.
- An overseas business establishment contracts with private customers in the UK to provide information. The services are provided and invoiced by its UK branch. Customers' day-to-day contact is with the UK branch and they pay the UK branch. The services are actually supplied from the UK branch which is a fixed establishment.
- A UK supplier contracts to supply advertising services. Its customer has its business establishment in Austria and a fixed establishment in the UK created by its branch. Although day-to-day contact is between the supplier and the UK branch, the Austrian establishment takes all artistic and other decisions about the advertising. The supplies are received at the overseas establishment.
- A UK accountant supplies accountancy services to a UK incorporated company which has its business establishment abroad. However, the services are received in connection with the company's UK tax obligations and therefore the UK fixed establishment, created by the registered office, receives the supply.
- A customer which has its business establishment in the UK and a fixed establishment in the USA, created by its branch. The supplier is contracted by the UK establishment to provide staff to the USA branch. The supplier invoices the UK establishment and is paid by them. The services are most directly used by the USA branch and therefore are received at the overseas establishment.

(VAT Notice 741A, para 4.2).

VAT groups

A VAT group is treated as a single entity. This also applies when applying the 'place of belonging' rules (*Shamrock Leasing Ltd* (VTD 15719) (TVC 62.525)). As a result, a group has establishments wherever any member of the group has establishments.

Other case law

In *Faaborg-Gelting Linien A/S v Finanzamt Flensburg, ECJ Case C–231/94*, [1996] STC 774 (TVC 22.190) the court held that where, under what is now *Directive 2006/112/EC, Art 43*, a supply could be treated as taking place at the supplier's business establishment or at another fixed establishment from which the services are supplied, then the primary point of reference had to be the former unless that did not lead to a rational result or created a conflict with another EU member state. In any case, services cannot be deemed to be supplied at a fixed establishment other than the place where the supplier has established his business unless that fixed establishment is of a certain minimum size and both the human and technical resources necessary for the provision of the particular services are permanently present (*Berkholz v Finanzamt Hamburg-Mitte-Altstadt, ECJ Case C–168/84*, [1985] 3 CMLR 667 (TVC 22.219)). See also *ARO Lease BV v Inspecteur der Belastingdienst Grote Ondernemingen Amsterdam, ECJ Case C–190/95*, [1997] STC 1272 (TVC 22.220).

Securities

See **24.2 FINANCIAL SERVICES** for a special rule applying where a UK supplier cannot determine the place of belonging of a purchaser of securities.

General rule for place of supply

[66.14] The place of supply of services is:

- where the supply is to a relevant business person, where the recipient belongs; and
- where the supply is not to a relevant business person, where the supplier belongs.

The supply of a right to services is treated in the same way as the underlying service. A 'relevant business person', in relation to a supply of services, means:

- a taxable person within the meaning of *EC Directive 2006/112/EC, art 9*;
- a person registered under *VATA 1994*, or equivalent legislation in another EU member state; or
- a person registered under an Act of Tynwald (Isle of Man) for the purposes of any tax imposed by or under and Act of Tynwald which corresponds to VAT,

where those services are received by the person otherwise than wholly for private purposes.

[*VATA 1994, s 7A*]. (VAT Notice 741A paras 6.2, 6.3).

De Voil Indirect Tax Service. See V3.183.

Services relating to land

[66.15] A supply of services in connection with land is made where the land is situated if the supply consists of one of the following descriptions

- the grant, assignment or surrender of any interest in or right over land;
- the grant, assignment or surrender of a personal right to call for or be granted any interest in or right over land;
- the grant, assignment or surrender of a licence to occupy land or any other contractual right exercisable over or in relation to land (including the provision of holiday accommodation, seasonal pitches for caravans and facilities at caravan parks for persons for whom such pitches are provided and pitches for tents and camping facilities);

- the provision in an hotel, inn, boarding house or similar establishment of sleeping accommodation or of accommodation in rooms which are provided in conjunction with sleeping accommodation or for the purpose of a supply of catering;
- any works of construction, demolition, conversion, reconstruction, alteration, enlargement, repair or maintenance of a building or civil engineering work; and
- services such as are supplied by estate agents, auctioneers, architects, surveyors, engineers and others involved in matters relating to land.

[*VATA 1994, Sch 4A para 1(2)*].

'*Land*' includes all forms of land and property (growing crops, buildings, walls, fences, civil engineering works and other structures fixed permanently to the land or sea bed) and plant, machinery or equipment which is an installation or edifice in its own right (e.g. a refinery or fixed oil/gas production platform). Machinery installed in buildings other than as a fixture is normally not regarded as land but as goods. (VAT Notice 741A, para 7.3).

The services must relate *directly* to specific sites of land. It does not apply if there is only an indirect connection with land, or if the land-related service is only an incidental part of a more comprehensive service.

Examples of services relating to land

- The supply of hotel accommodation.
- The provision of a site for a stand at an exhibition where the exhibitor obtains the right to a defined area of the exhibition hall. (If a supply of exhibition stand space is made with the specific location of the stand allocated on arrival, this would fall to be taxed where the exhibition takes place, see **69.16** below.)
- The supply of plant or machinery, together with an operator, for work on a construction site.
- The management, conveyancing, survey or valuation of property by a solicitor, surveyor or loss adjustor.
- Services connected with oil/gas/mineral exploration or exploitation relating to specific sites of land or the seabed.
- The surveying (such as seismic, geological or geomagnetic) of land or seabed, including associated data processing services to collate the required information.
- Legal services such as conveyancing or dealing with applications for planning permission.
- Packages of property management services which may include rent collection, arranging repairs and the maintenance of financial accounts.

Examples of services which are not land-related

Work falling within **66.18** below

- Repair and maintenance of machinery which is not installed as a fixture.

Work which may fall within *VATA 1994, Sch 4A para 16* (**66.19** below)

- The hiring out of civil engineering plant on its own.

- The secondment of staff to a building site.
- The legal administration of a deceased person's estate which happens to include property.
- Advice or information relating to land prices or property markets as they do not relate to specific sites.
- Insurance of property.
- Feasibility studies assessing the potential of particular businesses or business potential in a geographic area (i.e. which do not relate to a specific property or site).
- Provision of a recording studio where technicians are included as part of the supply (which are engineering services).
- Services of an accountant in simply calculating a tax return from figures provided by a client, even when those figures relate to rental income.

(VAT Notice 741A, paras 7.4, 7.5).

UK customers receiving services relating to UK land

If a UK VAT-registered recipient of these services receives them for business purposes they may be required to account for the reverse charge if the supplier belongs outside the UK.

Non-UK suppliers of services relating to UK land

Where a supplier does not belong in the UK and the customer is not registered for UK VAT, the supplier is responsible for accounting for any UK VAT due on the supply.

Non-UK land

A supplier of services relating to land in another EU member state may be liable to register for VAT in that country.

(VAT Notice 741A, paras 7.6–7.8).

De Voil Indirect Tax Service. See V3.188.

Services supplied where performed

[66.16] The table below sets out the rules for business to business (B2B) and business to customer (B2C) supplies.

Service description	*Place of supply*
Services of work on, or valuation of moveable goods; and ancillary transport services.	B2B supplies are subject to the B2B general rule. B2C supplies are made where the services are physically performed.
Services relating to cultural, artistic, sporting, scientific, educational, entertainment or similar activities (including fairs and exhibitions); and ancillary services relating to such activities, including services of organisers of such activities.	B2B supplies are subject to the B2B general rule and the place of supply is where the customer belongs. B2C supplies are made where the activities actually take place.

Service description	*Place of supply*
B2B supplies of services in respect of admission to cultural, artistic, sporting, scientific, educational, entertainment or similar events (including fairs and exhibitions); and B2B supplies of ancillary services relating to admission to such events.	The place of supply is where the events actually take place.

Examples of services supplied where performed

- *Services of sportspersons appearing in exhibition matches, races or other forms of competition.* However, where sponsorship or prize money is received, it must be determined whether or not these moneys are received as consideration for a supply. If they are consideration for a supply, the nature of the supply must be determined.
- *Provision of race prepared cars.* Such packages include the hire of the car and support services to ensure optimum maintenance and operation of the car throughout a series of races.
- *Scientific services of technicians carrying out tests or experiments in order to obtain data.* The final compilation of record of results, carried out in the UK, will not make the supply liable to UK VAT provided the services were otherwise performed outside the UK.
- Services of an actor or singer, whether or not in front of a live audience.
- Services relating to conferences or meetings.
- Services of an oral interpreter at an event, such as a meeting.
- The right to participate in an exhibition or the provision of an undefined site for a stand at an exhibition.
- Services relating to a specific exhibition. This includes carpenters and electricians erecting and fitting out stands at exhibition venues.
- Educational and training services. Such services may be exempt when made in the UK.

Examples of services that are not supplied where performed

- Services of sportspersons receiving sponsorship money as consideration for product endorsement or publicity appearances. These are advertising services rather than participation in a sporting event.
- Written translation services or interpreters' services which do not take place at an event. These are consultancy services.
- The hire of goods without any additional services, even if the customer uses those goods at an exhibition or concert.
- The provision of a defined site for a stand at an exhibition, which is land-related.
- Scientific services which include a recommendation or conclusion. These are services of consultancy or provision of information, or if connected with oil/gas/mineral exploration or exploitation of specific sites of land or the seabed, they are land-related.
- Veterinary services. These are general rule services.

(VAT Notice 741A, paras 9.1–9.7).

De Voil Indirect Tax Service. See V3.192.

Cultural, artistic, sporting, scientific, educational or entertainment services

[66.17] *For business customers*, the place of supply in respect of the following services is where the events actually take place: services in respect of admission to cultural, artistic, sporting, scientific, educational, entertainment or similar events (including fairs and exhibitions), and ancillary services relating to admission to such events.

For non-business customers, the place of supply of the following services is where the activities concerned actually take place: services relating to cultural, artistic, sporting, scientific, educational, entertainment or similar activities (including fairs and exhibitions), and ancillary services relating to such activities, including services of organisers of such activities.

[*VATA 1994, Sch 4A paras 4, 9A, 14A*].

> *Example*
>
> A tax lecturer who is VAT-registered in the UK delivers a lecture for delegates in Jersey but raises a sales invoice to a training company based in the UK (her customer). The place of supply will produce a UK VAT charge because the place of supply for B2B sales is based on the location of the customer, i.e. UK.

Accounting for VAT

See **66.16** above for accounting for VAT where overseas suppliers supply these services within the UK and UK suppliers supply these services abroad.

Valuation of, or work carried out on, any goods

[66.18] For business customers the place of supply of services consisting of the valuation of, or carrying out of work on, goods falls under the general rule (see **66.14** above). For other customers, the place of supply of such services is where the services are physically performed.

Work carried out on 'goods' is essentially any physical service carried out on another person's goods. It includes

- processing, manufacturing or assembling;
- repairs, cleaning or restoration;
- alterations, calibrations, insulating, lacquering, painting, polishing, resetting (of jewellery), sharpening, varnishing, waterproofing, etc.; and
- nominations to stallions/covering (i.e. attempting to secure the pregnancy of mares).

'*Goods*' for this purpose include all forms of movable tangible property, covering both finished commodities and raw materials but does not include immovable property such as permanently installed goods and fixtures (for which see **66.15** above).

Examples of services included

- Services of a subcontractor installing machinery supplied by another person.

- Simple valuation of goods by loss adjusters, average adjusters, motor assessors, surveyors and other experts in connection with an insurance proposal or claim. The final compilation of a related report in a different country from the goods will not change the place of supply from the country where valuation work is performed. Where, however, valuation forms only a part of a supply of professional services, there is a supply of consultancy services within *VATA 1994, Sch 4A para 16* (see **66.19** below).

Examples of services not included

- Work which is not mainly physical work performed on the goods themselves, e.g. mere inspection is not 'work on goods' although it can be 'valuation' if that is the purpose of the inspection.
- Valuation of, or work carried out on, land or property (which falls within **66.15** above).

(VAT Notice 741A, para 9.5).

Intangible services

[66.19] The supply of the intangible services listed below falls within the general rule for the place of supply of services (see **66.14** above), unless they are supplied to a recipient who is not a relevant business person and belongs in a country which is not an EU member state (other than the Isle of Man). In such a case, the place of supply is where the recipient belongs. The services in question are:

- transfers and assignments of copyright, patents, licences, trademarks and similar rights, and the acceptance of any obligation to refrain from pursuing or exercising (in whole or in part) any business activity or any such rights;
- advertising services;
- services of consultants, engineers, consultancy bureaux, lawyers, accountants, and similar services, data processing and provision of information, other than any services relating to land;
- banking, financial and insurance services (including reinsurance), other than the provision of safe deposit facilities;
- the provision of access to, or transmission or distribution through a natural gas system situated within the territory of an EU member state or any network connected to such a system, or an electricity system, or a network through which heat or cooling is supplied, and the provision of other directly linked services;
- the supply of staff;
- (subject to use and enjoyment provisions) the letting on hire of goods other than means of transport;
- (subject to use and enjoyment provisions) until 31 December 2014 (see below for supplies from 1 January 2015) telecommunication services, i.e. services relating to the transmission, emission or reception of signals, writing, images and sounds or information of any nature by

wire, radio, optical or other electromagnetic systems, including the related transfer or assignment of the right to use capacity for such transmission, emission or reception; and the provision of access to global information networks;

- (subject to use and enjoyment provisions) until 31 December 2014 (see below for supplies from 1 January 2015) radio and television broadcasting services; and
- (subject to use and enjoyment provisions, where supplied to a relevant business person) until 31 December 2014 (see below for supplies from 1 January 2015) electronically supplied services, e.g. website supply, web-hosting and distance maintenance of programmes and equipment; the supply of software and the updating of software; the supply of images, text and information, and the making available of databases; the supply of music, films and games (including games of chance and gambling games); the supply of political, cultural, artistic, sporting, scientific, educational or entertainment broadcasts (including broadcasts of events); and the supply of distance teaching. (But where the supplier of a service and the supplier's customer communicate via electronic mail, this does not of itself mean that the service provided is an electronically supplied service for these purposes.)

A further special rule applies to electronically supplied services provided by a person who belongs in a third country to someone who is not a relevant business person and who belongs in an EU member state. In such cases the place of supply is where the recipient belongs.

Use and enjoyment provisions

[66.20] The place of supply rule described above is modified in respect of certain supplies, namely hiring of goods, telecoms and broadcasting services, and (for B2B supplies only) electronically supplied services ('relevant services'). Where a supply of relevant services would otherwise be regarded as made in the UK but the effective use and enjoyment of those services is in a third country (i.e. a country which is not an EU member state), the supply is to be treated as taking place in that country to the extent that it is so used and enjoyed. Where a supply of relevant services would otherwise be regarded as made in a third country (i.e. a country which is not an EU member state) but the effective use and enjoyment of those services is in the UK, the supply is to be treated as taking place in the UK to the extent that it is so used and enjoyed.

B2C supplies of telecommunication services

[66.21] The Government announced in Spring Budget 2017 that it would be removing the use and enjoyment provisions that alleviate the need for UK VAT to be charged on B2C mobile phone services provided to a UK resident travelling outside of the EU. Prior to 1 November 2017, telecoms providers are required to account for VAT on any mobile phone services provided to such a customer who is travelling within the EU but not when they are travelling outside of the EU which is inconsistent. The changes are intended to prevent telecoms providers from using the inconsistency to avoid accounting for UK

VAT and to bring the UK in line with the internationally agreed approach. The *VAT (Place of Supply of Services) (Telecommunication Services) Order 2017 (SI 2017/778)* has been enacted and the changes came into effect from 1 November 2017.

HMRC has issued the following guidance:

> **Telecommunication services supplied up to 31 October 2017**
>
> With one exception, B2C telecommunications services were subject to UK VAT when supplied to UK residents or used and enjoyed in the UK by visitors from countries outside the EU. Examples included public payphones and charges for calls made from hotel rooms. However, elements of telecommunications services used in the UK were ignored if:
>
> - they were simply an incidental part of an established telephone contract or account held by a customer who belonged outside the EU
> - they were used by a non-EU temporary visitor
> - HMRC were satisfied that these conditions were not being abused.
>
> The exception to this rule was that if a UK resident used telecommunications services outside the EU under such an account with a UK provider, those services were outside the scope of UK VAT, provided that evidence was retained to substantiate the element of use and enjoyment that occurred outside the EU.
>
> **Telecommunications services supplied from 1 November 2017**
>
> From 1 November 2017 the law changed in relation to B2C telecommunications services, and the rule concerning the place where the services were used and enjoyed was withdrawn. Consequently supplies of such services by UK suppliers to UK residents are now always subject to VAT. Supplies to visitors from countries outside the EU are no longer subject to UK VAT.

[*VATA 1994, Sch 4A paras 7–9, 15, 16*]. (VAT Notice 741A, paras 13.3–13.4).

Repairs carried out under contracts of insurance

[66.22] With effect from 1 October 2016, the use and enjoyment provisions were extended to B2B repairs carried out under insurance contracts. This measure is intended to counter possible avoidance by structuring warranty contracts so that a UK repairer makes a B2B supply to a non-EU insurer of repairing goods under an insurance contract with a UK owner of the goods. If an insurance contract was structured so that the supply was made to the insured person (a UK resident) and the insurer merely paid for it, the repair supply would in any case be chargeable to UK VAT; however, it might be possible contractually to make the repair supply directly to the insurer. The place of supply of the B2B service would be where the insurer belongs (outside the scope of VAT), but in HMRC's view the use and enjoyment of the service is where the insured person and the repaired goods are – the UK. The law has been changed to put the matter beyond doubt, and 'repairs to goods under an insurance claim' have been added to para 13.1 of Notice 741A.

[*VATA 1994, Sch 4A para 9D; SI 2016/726*]. (HMRC Brief 15/16).

The use and enjoyment provisions were considered in *R (oao Telefonica Europe plc) v HMRC* [2016] UKUT 173 (TCC) (TVC 2.356). A company could identify charges for extra services supplied to customers inside and outside the EU, and treated them as inside and outside the scope of VAT accordingly. It agreed with HMRC in 2008 that network access charges should be apportioned in the ratio of the values of these specific charges. In 2014, HMRC issued a decision that this was not fair: because the charges for use of mobile phones abroad were relatively higher, a values-based apportionment distorted the result in favour of the company. A use-based apportionment should be adopted instead. The company applied for judicial review, arguing that it was unreasonable for HMRC to change the agreed method. However, the Upper Tribunal accepted that HMRC had a reasonable basis for the decision, and had carried out adequate consultation before issuing it. The application for judicial review was refused.

Electronic, broadcasting and telecommunication services from 1 January 2015

[66.23] From 1 January 2010 to 31 December 2014 supplies of electronic services to a non-taxable person could have different places of supply

(a) if the supplier belonged in an EU member state, the place of supply was in accordance with the general rule for supplies to non-taxable persons, i.e. where the supplier belonged;

(b) if the supplier belonged in a non-EU member state, the place of supply was where the customer belonged (unless the supplier opted to create an establishment in an EU member state from which the services were supplied, in which case (*a*) applied).

From 1 January 2015 all supplies of electronic, broadcasting and telecommunication services are taxable at the place where the customer belongs (unless the rule on effective use and enjoyment applies), even if the customer is a non-taxable person. When a customer is a non-taxable person, the reverse charge procedure is not available and the supplier is responsible for accounting for the VAT that is due based on where the customer belongs.

From 1 January 2015 non-EU suppliers have the option of registering for and using the non-Union VAT Mini One Stop Shop (non-Union VAT MOSS) in one EU member state as an alternative to registering for VAT in all the EU member states where they make relevant supplies to non-taxable persons. The non-Union VAT MOSS is a modified version of the VAT on E-Services (VoES) scheme that non-EU suppliers have the option of using in relation to supplies of electronic services prior to 1 January 2015 (see **64.34 SPECIAL SCHEMES**). From 1 January 2015 EU suppliers will have the option of registering for and using the Mini One Stop Shop (MOSS) in the country in which they are registered for VAT, as an alternative to registering for VAT in all the EU member states where they make relevant supplies to non-taxable persons. The VAT revenue will be transferred from the EU member state where the supplier is registered to the EU member state where the customer belongs, the VAT rate applicable being that of the customer's EU member state. In order to ensure a smooth transition, the EU member state where the supplier is registered will retain a proportion of the VAT collected until 31 December 2018. This proportion will amount to 30% from 1 January 2015 until 31 December 2016 and 15% from 1 January 2017 until 31 December 2018.

[*Directive 2006/112/EC, Arts 357–369; Regulation (EU)904/2010, Art 46(3); VATA 1994, Sch 3BA; FA 2014, Sch 22; SI 2014/2726*].

For supplies to non-taxable persons, both EU and non-EU suppliers will need to identify where the customer is established, has his permanent address or usually resides. Without a VAT identification number (which is usually reserved for taxable persons) for guidance, the supplier will have to rely to some extent on information from the customer. *Council Implementing Regulation (EU)1042/2013* amends *Implementing Regulation (EU)282/2011* and explains that where a non-taxable person is established in more than one country or has his permanent address in one country but usually resides in another, priority is to be given to the place that best ensures taxation at the place of actual consumption. *Council Implementing Regulation (EU)1042/2013* also sets out the following presumptions that shall be made for the location of the customer:

(1) Where services are provided at a location such as a telephone box, a telephone kiosk, a wi-fi hot spot, an internet café, a restaurant or a hotel lobby where the physical presence of the recipient of the service at that location is needed for the service to be provided to him, it shall be presumed that the customer is established, has his permanent address or usually resides at the place of that location and that the service is effectively used and enjoyed there.

(2) If the location at (1) above, for example, a wi-fi hot spot, is on board a ship, aircraft or train carrying out a passenger transport operation within the EU, the country of location shall be the country of departure of the passenger transport.

(3) Where services are supplied via a customer's fixed land line, it shall be presumed that the customer is located at the place of installation of the fixed land line.

(4) Where services are supplied via mobile networks, it shall be presumed that the customer is located in the country identified by the mobile country code of the SIM card used when receiving the services.

(5) Where services are supplied for which the use of a decoder or similar device or a viewing card is needed and a fixed land line is not used, it shall be presumed that the customer is located at the place where the decoder or similar device is located, or if that place is not known, at the place to which the viewing card is sent for the purpose of being used there.

Where services are supplied in other circumstances, the location of the customer should be established on the basis of two items of non-contradictory evidence, e.g., the billing address of the customer, the Internet Protocol (IP) address of the device used by the customer, the location of the bank account used for payment or the billing address of the customer held by the bank.

[*Directive 2006/112/EC, Arts 58, 369a–369k; VATA 1994, Sch 3BA, Sch 4A para 15; Council Implementing Regulation (EU)1042/2013; Implementing Regulation (EU)282/2011*].

HMRC guidance 'VAT: businesses supplying digital services to private consumers' includes guidance aimed at micro and small businesses that use payment service providers to process customer payments and for whom the requirement of obtaining two items of non-contradictory evidence may present a challenge. The guidance suggests the following two-step approach:

Step 1

At the point of sale the business should ask the customer to provide details of either their billing address, including member state, or their telephone number, including the member state dialling code.

Step 2

The business should ask the payment service provider to provide a notification advice containing the 2 digit country code of the customer's member state of residence.

If the information collected at steps 1 and 2 above tallies that will be sufficient to define the customer's location. If the information does not tally the business must ask the customer to reconcile the discrepancy between the two sources of information.

The guidance explains that UK micro-businesses that operate below the current UK VAT registration threshold, and who register for the VAT Mini One Stop Shop (VAT MOSS) may base their decision regarding customer location on information provided to them by their payment service provider. This means those micro-businesses do not need to carry out Step 1 above.

The guidance previously indicated that UK micro-businesses that operate below the current UK VAT registration threshold, and who register for the VAT Mini One Stop Shop (VAT MOSS) could, until 30 June 2015, base their decision regarding customer location on information provided to them by their payment service provider. The transitional period was intended to give micro-businesses additional time to adapt their websites to meet the new data collection requirements but HMRC Agent Update 48 states that these transitional arrangements, which were originally until 30 June 2015, have been extended indefinitely.

On 8 January 2016 HMRC published HMRC Brief 4/16, which explains that UK businesses that operate below the UK VAT registration threshold, and who register for the VAT Mini One Stop Shop (VAT MOSS), can base their decision regarding customer location on a single piece of information, such as the billing address provided by the customer or information provided to them by their payment service provider.

(HMRC Brief 4/16).

Restaurant and catering services

[66.24] The provision of restaurant and catering services, other than those supplied in the course of intra-EU passenger transport is made in the country in which the services are physically carried out. The provision of catering or restaurant services on board a ship, aircraft or train in connection with the transportation of passengers during an intra–EU passenger transport operation is made in the country in which the relevant point of departure is located. A return passenger transport operation (i.e. a journey which takes place in more than one country, but ends in the country in which it began) comprises two passenger transport operations; the outward leg and the return leg. The return leg commences with the last stop at a place where there has been no previous stop, and ends where the outward leg began.

[*VATA 1994, Sch 4A paras 5, 6*].

Transport services

Passenger transport

[66.25] The transportation of passengers (and any accompanying luggage or motor vehicles) is made in the country in which the transportation takes place, having regard (where more than one country is involved) to the proportion of distances covered in each country. Transportation which takes place partly outside the territorial jurisdiction of a country is to be treated as taking place wholly in the country if

- it takes place in the course of a journey between two points in the country (whether or not as part of a longer journey involving travel to or from another country); and
- the means of transport used does not (except in an emergency or involuntarily) stop, put in or land in another country in the course of the journey between those two points.

A pleasure cruise (including a cruise wholly or partly for education or training) is regarded as the transportation of passengers. Consequently services provided as part of such a cruise are treated as supplied in the same place as the transportation of the passengers).

Transportation of goods

The place of supply of the transportation of goods for business customers falls under the general rule, i.e. where the customer belongs (see **66.14** above). However, HMRC became aware that this change in law produced an unintended anomaly in the treatment of supplies wholly enjoyed outside the EU, which may also be taxed locally in the place of performance. With effect from 20 December 2012 a temporary concession was put on a permanent footing by legislation providing that where a supply of services consisting of the transportation of goods (and ancillary transport services) to a relevant business person would otherwise be treated as made in the UK and the transportation takes place (and ancillary transport services are physically performed) wholly outside the EU, the place of supply is outside the EU. [*VATA 1994, Sch 4A, paras 9B, 9C*].

For non-business customers, the place of supply is in the country in which the transportation takes place, in proportion to the distances covered (where more than one country is involved). Transportation which takes place partly outside the territorial jurisdiction of a country is to be treated as taking place wholly in the country if

- it takes place in the course of a journey between two points in the country (whether or not as part of a longer journey involving travel to or from another country); and
- the means of transport used does not (except in an emergency or involuntarily) stop, put in or land in another country in the course of the journey between those two points.

The place of supply of ancillary transport services for non-business customers is where the services are physically performed.

Intra-EU transport of goods

The place of supply of the transportation of goods for business customers falls under the general rule (see **66.14** above). For other customers, the place of supply is in the country in which the transportation begins.

Transport services for non-business customers

The table below outlines the main categories of B2C services and gives a general indication as to where the place of supply is.

If the type of supply is	*the place of supply will be*
B2C domestic freight transport (which takes place wholly within one country);	where the transport takes place.
B2C international freight transport (between the EU and non-EU member states or wholly outside the EU);	where the transport takes place.
B2C intra-EU freight transport (from one EU member state to another);	the EU member state in which the transportation begins.
B2C ancillary transport services relating to domestic, international freight transport or intra-EU freight transport;	where the services are physically performed.
making arrangements for or facilitation of B2C domestic or international freight transport;	where the transport takes place.
making arrangements for or facilitation of B2C intra-EU freight transport;	the EU member state in which the transportation begins.
making arrangements for or facilitation of related B2C ancillary services;	where the ancillary services are physically performed.

Ship and aircraft charter party contracts

If the supplier supplies the ship or aircraft with crew under a formal written charter party contract, the place of supply is subject to the general rule. B2B supplies are made where the customer belongs. B2C supplies are made where the supplier belongs. But if they supply a ship or aircraft without crew under a written charter party agreement, the supply is the hire of a means of transport. If they supply a ship or aircraft with crew but without a written charter party contract, or of part of the seating capacity in a ship or aircraft, the place of supply of such transport-related services depends on the nature of the services supplied.

[*VATA 1994, Sch 4A paras 2, 11–13*]. (VAT Notices 744A, 744B, 744C).

De Voil Indirect Tax Service. See V3.190.

Hire of means of transport

[66.26] The general rule (see **66.14** above) applies to the hire of means of transport other than short-term hire. 'Short-term' means a continuous period of hire not exceeding 90 days (in the case of a vessel) or 30 days (in all other cases). In the case of short-term hire, the place of supply is where the means of transport is actually put at the disposal of the person by whom it is hired. However, this is subject to 'use and enjoyment' provisions, so that

- where the place of supply would otherwise be the UK but the effective use and enjoyment of the means of transport would be in a third country (i.e. a country which is not an EU member state), the supply is to be treated as taking place in that country to the extent that it is so used and enjoyed; and
- where the place of supply would otherwise be in a third country but the effective use and enjoyment of the means of transport is in the UK, the supply is to be treated as taking place in the UK to the extent that it is so used and enjoyed.

Table for short-term or long-term hire of means of transport:

When . . .	*if...*
two or more separate contracts for the hire of the same means of transport follow each other with two days or less between them, the term of the first contract needs to be considered in order to decide whether the second term is short-term or long-term.	the two contracts together exceed 30 days (or 90 days for vessels) then the second and subsequent consecutive contracts are treated as long-term hires. If the first contract is genuinely of a short-term hire it will remain so.
there is a second separate contract for short-term hire between the same two parties.	that second separate hire contract relates to a different means of transport or the terms of the hire differ significantly, the contracts will need to be considered separately.
a short-term hire contract is extended.	that extension means that it exceeds the 30 or 90-day period the place of supply is determined by the long-term hire rule, unless it can be satisfactorily demonstrated that the circumstances leading to the events were outside the control of the parties involved.

From 1 January 2013

From 1 January 2013, the place of supply rules in respect of the long-term hire of means of transport were amended (the rules for short-term hire were unaffected). From that date, the place of supply of the long-term hire of a means of transport to a person who is not a relevant business person is in the country where the recipient belongs. However, the long-term hire of a pleasure boat which is put at the disposal of the recipient at the supplier's business establishment, or some other fixed establishment of the supplier, is treated as supplied in the country where the boat is actually put at the disposal of the recipient. This rule is subject to 'use and enjoyment' provisions, so that

- where the place of supply would otherwise be the UK but the effective use and enjoyment of the means of transport would be in a third country (i.e. a country which is not an EU member state), the supply is to be treated as taking place in that country to the extent that it is so used and enjoyed; and
- where the place of supply would otherwise be in a third country but the effective use and enjoyment of the means of transport is in the UK, the supply is to be treated as taking place in the UK to the extent that it is so used and enjoyed.

'*Means of transport*' includes ships, boats, yachts, hovercraft, barges or dracones (bulk liquid barges), aircraft, cars, trucks, lorries, motorcycles, cycles, touring caravans and trailers, trailers and semi-trailers, and railway wagons. It does not include freight containers, static caravans, and racing cars where the provision of the car forms part of a supply of sporting services. Mobile cranes are not means of transport (*BPH Equipment Ltd* (VTD 13914) (TVC 62.555)). Provided the goods hired are a means of transport, their actual use is not important (e.g. the provisions apply to the lease of a train to a transport museum or a yacht for use in racing).

'Effective use and enjoyment'

HMRC do not specifically give their interpretation of 'effective use and enjoyment' in the context of the hire of means of transport. See, however, **66.20** above for their interpretation of the phrase in the context of hire of other goods.

[*VATA 1994, Sch 4A paras 3, 13A*]. (VAT Notice 741A, paras 8.1–8.10).

De Voil Indirect Tax Service. See V3.194.

Services of intermediaries

[66.27] Most business to business intermediary services (i.e. the making of arrangements for a supply by or to another person or of any other activity intended to facilitate the making of such a supply) fall under the general rule and are supplied where the customer belongs. However, when supplied to a person who is not a relevant business person, the place of supply is where the underlying service is made. The place of supply of goods is generally where the goods are located when they are supplied, but there are special rules for the following:

- the place of supply of goods imported by **the supplier** is the EU member state of importation;
- the place of supply of goods imported by **the customer** is outside the EU;
- the place of supply of installed or assembled goods is where they are installed or assembled.

Intermediary services supplied in the UK

Where the place of supply of an intermediary's arranging service is the UK, but the place of supply of the service being arranged is outside the EU, the intermediary's supply in the UK can be zero-rated. This does not include banking, financial and insurance services which are exempt in the UK.

[*VATA 1994, Sch 4A para 10*]. (VAT Notice 741A, paras 11.1–11.5).

De Voil Indirect Tax Service. See V3.195.

Key points: place of supply

[66.28] Points to consider are as follows.

- The basic rule for B2B (business to business) sales is that the location of the customer determines the place of supply, i.e. no VAT is charged if the customer is based outside the UK. However, there are exceptions to the basic rule.
- An exception to the place of supply being where the customer is located is in relation to an admission charge to events. The place of supply will be where the event takes place for both B2B and B2C sales.
- The place of supply for land-related services is where the land is situated. This applies to direct construction services, e.g. a bricklayer or plumber as well as professional services such as an architect or surveyor.
- A VAT-registered business in the UK selling services to business customers outside the UK but within the EU (B2B) needs to complete an EC Sales List (ESL) if no UK VAT is charged on the transaction.
- The ESL must be completed on a quarterly basis for a business selling services. The deadline is 14 days after the end of the quarter for a paper return and 21 days if it is submitted online.
- In relation to sales made to a UK customer that relate to the hiring of goods (other than transport) telecom, broadcasting or electronic services, the place of supply will be outside the scope of UK VAT if the service is effectively 'used and enjoyed' outside the EU.

67

Supply: Time of Supply

Introduction to time of supply

[67.1] For EU legislation, see **19.16 EUROPEAN UNION LEGISLATION**.

VAT becomes due on a supply of goods or services at the time of supply. [*VATA 1994, s 1(2)*]. It is therefore necessary to have 'time of supply' rules to determine when a supply is to be treated as taking place for VAT purposes. The resultant time is often referred to as the *tax point* (although this is not a term that is used in the legislation).

VAT must normally be accounted for on the return for the period in which the tax point occurs and at the rate of VAT in force at that time. The normal tax point rules relating to the supply of goods and services are covered in **67.8** and

67.18 below respectively. HMRC have powers, at the request of a taxable person, to alter the time at which his supplies are to be treated as taking place. [*VATA 1994, s 6(10)*]. These are known as accommodation tax points. See **67.7** below.

In addition, HMRC may make regulations with respect to the time at which a supply is to be treated as taking place where

(a) it is a supply of goods or services for a consideration the whole or part of which is determined or payable periodically, or from time to time, or at the end of any period;
(b) it is a supply of goods for a consideration the whole or part of which is determined at the time when the goods are appropriated for any purpose;
(c) there is a supply to which *VATA 1994, s 55* applies (special scheme for gold); or
(d) there is a supply of services under *VATA 1994, Sch 4 para 5(4)* (non-business use of goods) or under a Treasury Order under *VATA 1994, s 5(4)*.

[*VATA 1994, s 6(14)*].

See **67.9–67.17** below for special provisions relating to goods and **67.19–67.26** below for special provisions relating to services.

Although the principal purpose of the time of supply rules is to fix the time for accounting for VAT, the rules have other uses including

- calculating turnover for VAT registration purposes;
- establishing the period to which supplies (including exempt supplies) are to be allocated for partial exemption purposes, and
- establishing when input tax may be deducted.

Exempt supplies

The time of supply for any exempt supply is determined using the normal tax point rules (see **67.8–67.26** below as appropriate) but, as an invoice issued in respect of an exempt supply is not a VAT invoice (see **67.3** below) references to the issue of a VAT invoice have no effect. Thus, for example, in the case of a single supply of exempt services, the time of supply will normally be the earlier of receipt of payment or performance of the service.

Zero-rated supplies

The time of supply for any zero-rated supply is determined using the normal tax point rules (see **67.8–67.26** below as appropriate) but, subject to the special rules for the supply of zero-rated goods in the UK for acquisition by a registered trader in another EU member state (see **20.16 EUROPEAN UNION: SINGLE MARKET**), as an invoice issued in respect of a zero-rated supply is not a VAT invoice (see **67.3** below) references to the issue of a VAT invoice has no effect. Thus, for example, the tax point for a zero-rated supply of goods will normally be the earlier of receipt of payment or the removal/making available of those goods.

Change of rate

Where there is a change in the VAT rate or a VAT liability, VAT is chargeable according to the normal tax point rules (see **67.8–67.26** below as appropriate) unless the taxpayer elects for the special change of rate provisions to apply. See **56.6 RATES OF VAT**. **De Voil Indirect Tax Service.** See V3.131–143.

Identifying the correct tax point

[67.2] The following is a step-by-step guide to determine the correct tax point.

(1) Does the supply fall within the scope of an accommodation tax point granted to the person making the supply?	See **67.7**
(2) Is the supply covered by an extra-statutory class concession, e.g. coins operated machines?	See **67.25**
(3) If the supply is a supply of goods	
— is it the permanent diversion of goods to private or non-business use?	See **67.9**
— is it an intra-EU supply of goods eligible for zero-rating?	See **67.10**
— is it on a 'sale or return basis' or 'on approval' terms?	See **67.12**
— does it involve land in that it is either (i) in connection with a compulsory purchase where the price has not been agreed; or (ii) a further 'contingency' payment in respect of an earlier supply of the freehold; or (iii) in connection with leasehold land treated as a supply of goods	See **67.13**
— is it the self-supply of goods?	See **67.14**
— does it involve water, gas or any form of power, heat, refrigeration or other cooling, or ventilation?	See **67.15**
— does it involve the supplier's goods being held by the buyer pending agreement of the price?	See **67.16**
— does it come within the special scheme for gold?	See **67.17**
(4) If the supply is a supply of services	
— is it a continuous supply of services?	See **67.19**
— does it give rise to the payment of royalties?	See **67.20**
— does it involve construction services under a contract that provides for stage payments?	See **67.21**
— does it involve 'reverse charge' services?	See **67.22**
— does it involve the temporary use of business goods for private or non-business purposes?	See **67.23**
— does it involve the free supply of services?	See **67.24**
— does it consist of professional services made by a barrister or advocate?	See **67.26**
(5) Does the contract provide for a retention payment?	See **67.6**

(6) Has an 'actual' tax point been created because	
— the supplier received a payment or issued a VAT invoice in respect of the supply before the 'basic' tax point?	See **67.8**(*b*)(i) for goods and **67.18**(*b*)(i) for services
— the supplier has issued a VAT invoice within 14 days after the 'basic' tax point and has not previously elected to forgo the 14-day rule?	See **67.8**(*b*)(ii) for goods and **67.18**(*b*)(ii) for services
— the supplier has been granted an extension of the 14-day rule and has issued a VAT invoice within that time?	See **67.8**(*b*)(ii) for goods and **67.18**(*b*)(ii) for services
(7) Where none of (1)–(6) above apply, the basic tax point applies	See **67.8**(*a*) for goods and **67.18**(*a*) for services

VAT invoices and the creation of tax points

[67.3] A VAT invoice can create an actual tax point under the normal rules both before and after the basic tax point occurs (see **67.8** and **67.18** below for goods and services respectively) and most of the special time of supply regulations also provide for the issue of a VAT invoice to create a tax point. In addition, in certain instances 'period' VAT invoices issued covering payments due over a period of up to one year may create tax points.

In order to establish the creation of a tax point, the following conditions must be satisfied.

(a) The invoice must be a proper VAT invoice which complies with the necessary requirements. See **40.3** *et seq* **INVOICES**. If the invoice does not conform to the requirements, it is not a VAT invoice and cannot create a tax point. See *ABB Power Ltd* (VTD 9373) (TVC 62.429) and *SR Finch* (VTD 10948) (TVC 62.430). This also means that, as a VAT invoice cannot be issued
- in respect of a zero-rated supply (except for intra-EU supplies of goods, see **67.10** below), or
- in respect of an exempt supply, or
- by a non-registered person

invoices issued in such circumstances are disregarded for time of supply purposes.

(b) The VAT invoice must be issued. In *C & E Commrs v Woolfold Motor Co Ltd*, QB [1983] STC 715 (TVC 62.426) it was held that the issue of a VAT invoice required the provision to the customer of that invoice, i.e. the customer must physically receive it. It is not sufficient for it to simply have been prepared in order to create a tax point. Where an invoice has in fact been issued,

- it is the date of physical issue that determines the tax point. In the case of invoices issued by electronic data interchange (EDI), an invoice is issued when the data is transmitted (provided the recipient is able to receive the data); and
- where a tax point is established, it is not invalidated because the recipient has never 'processed' the invoice, e.g. by disputing it (*Hurley Robinson Partnership* (VTD 750) (TVC 62.139)).

Where the issue of an invoice does create a tax point so that a supply is treated as taking place, it only does so to the extent covered by the invoice. [*SI 1995/2518, Reg 94*]. The issue of an invoice covering part only of a larger supply does not therefore create a tax point for the whole supply.

Period VAT invoices

Special time of supply rules apply to

- leasehold property (see **67.13** below),
- certain supplies of water, fuel and power (see **67.15** below), and
- continuous supplies of services (see **67.19** below)

where the supplier makes use of 'period' VAT invoices. This facility recognises that, without such arrangements, suppliers might otherwise have to issue a large volume of repetitive VAT invoices to the same customer, e.g. leased equipment subject to monthly rental payments. By adopting the period VAT invoicing arrangements, provided the invoice contains the required details in respect of two or more instalments due, the supplier can issue a single document showing all the payments due over a period of up to one year. The tax point then becomes the earlier of the receipt of the payment or the time when the payment falls due.

(HMRC VAT—Time of Supply Manual VATTOS 5210–5220).

Self-billing

[67.4] Under an approved self-billing arrangement it is the customer who prepares the VAT invoice. See **40.6 INVOICES** for further details. For time of supply purposes, not all self-billed VAT invoices can create a tax point as the law refers consistently to an invoice that has been issued by the supplier or in similar terms. A tax point is not normally created, therefore, where the invoice is issued by the customer as in the case of a self-billing arrangement. The one exception to this are self-billed invoices that fall within the scope of the 14-day rule where specific provision is included for self-billed invoices to be treated as if they were issued by the supplier (see **67.8** and **67.18** below for supplies of goods and services respectively). Therefore, a self-billed invoice issued within 14 days of the basic tax point has the same potential to create the tax point for the supply as if it had been issued by the supplier.

In all other circumstances (e.g. where an invoice is issued in advance of the basic tax point or is in respect of a supply covered by one of the special time of supply regulations) a tax point cannot be created by the issue of a self-billed VAT invoice.

Special arrangements for input tax deduction purposes

Because of the above, HMRC have agreed special arrangements that provide the issuer of the self-billed invoice with a notional tax point *for input tax deduction purposes only*. Under this procedure,

- the person issuing the self-billed invoice must
  - (a) show, on the original invoice, the date of despatch (but this must not be referred to as the tax point), and
  - (b) retain a copy and show on it the day following the date of issue as the notional tax point for input tax purposes; and
- the person receiving the invoice must, *on receipt of the invoice and payment*, add the date of receipt. This becomes the tax point for output tax purposes.

(HMRC VAT—Time of Supply Manual VATTOS 5225, 9130).

Credit notes

[67.5] The time of supply rules do not apply in any way to the issue of credit notes. Similarly, the issue of a credit note has no direct effect on a tax point once it has been established, i.e. it does not cancel or expunge an existing tax point. It normally simply permits the issuer to adjust the VAT previously accounted for in response to an earlier tax point. (HMRC VAT—Time of Supply Manual VATTOS 5230).

> *Example*
>
> Ten computers are sold to a customer and a sales invoice is raised at the time the goods are sold, One of the computers is subsequently returned by the customer two weeks later because it is faulty. In this situation, the original invoice remains unaffected, but a credit note will be issued by the supplier (based on the date the goods are returned) to reduce the output tax originally charged by the supplier. The exception to this situation is if both the supplier and customer are VAT-registered, in which case the credit note does not need to adjust the original charge of VAT.

Receipt of payment and the creation of tax points

[67.6] The receipt of a payment can create an actual tax point before the basic tax point occurs (see **67.8** and **67.18** below for goods and services respectively) and most of the special time of supply regulations also provide for the receipt of a payment to create a tax point. Where the receipt of a payment does create a tax point so that a supply is treated as taking place, it only does so to the extent covered by the payment. [*SI 1995/2518, Reg 94*]. The receipt of a payment covering part only of a larger supply does not therefore create a tax point for the whole supply.

Deposits

Deposits are frequently required either as an indication of good faith on the part of the customer or to put the supplier in funds to cover costs, etc. Depending on the contract, the deposit may be refundable in the event of the contract subsequently being cancelled or may be liable, either wholly or in part, to forfeiture.

Apart from security deposits (see below) a pre-payment or deposit intended by the payer and recipient to eventually form part of the consideration for an identifiable supply normally creates a tax point when received. See, for example, *JD Fox Ltd* (VTD 1012) (TVC 62.456) (deposits for furniture), *Bethway & Moss Ltd* (VTD 2667) (TVC 62.460) (deposits for fitted kitchens) and *C & E Commrs v Richmond Theatre Management Ltd*, QB [1995] STC 257 (TVC 62.450) (advance payments of theatre tickets). This applies even if the deposit is refundable. See, for example, *C & E Commrs v Moonraker's Guest House Ltd*, QB [1992] STC 544 (TVC 62.459) (deposits for holiday accommodation) and *Clowance plc* (VTD 2541) (TVC 62.448) (advance payments for time-share accommodation). For an exception to this general rule where deposits were not held to create tax points, see *Nigel Mansell Sports Co Ltd* (VTD 6116) (TVC 62.468) (initial deposit from prospective customer in order to be placed on the waiting list for a sports car and paid before a firm order was placed for the car) although the facts in this case were unusual.

Security deposits

Deposits taken as security to ensure safe return of goods hired out, and which are refunded when the goods are safely returned or forfeited to compensate for loss or damage, do not normally create a tax point. A payment tax point can be created if, for example, hire charges are later offset against the refund of an amount originally received as a security deposit but only where this happens before the basic tax point, i.e. completion of the hire period.

(HMRC VAT—Time of Supply Manual VATTOS 5120–5135).

Third parties acting as stakeholders

Where a third party acts as a stakeholder (as opposed to an agent of the vendor) and receives a deposit in connection with a supply of property, a time of supply is not created until the money is released to the vendor. (VAT Notice 700, para 14.2). See *Double Shield Window Co Ltd* (VTD 1771) (TVC 62.437).

Payment by cheque

Under banking law, payment can only be said to have occurred when the cheque has been presented and met by the drawer's bank. In the normal course of events it takes five working days for a cheque to complete the clearance cycle. It is common banking practice for a cheque to be credited to the payee's bank account on the date it is paid in and, therefore, unless the cheque was the subject of special clearance procedures, payment for VAT purposes will not strictly occur until the fifth working day following the date of presentation. However, where a trader's normal commercial practice is to use the date a cheque is received as the date of payment for accounting purposes, and provided the cheque is subsequently presented and cleared without undue delay, that date may be used as the payment date for VAT time of supply purposes. In the event of the cheque not being honoured, however, no payment will have occurred and any VAT accounted for on this basis may be adjusted accordingly. Where presentation of a cheque is delayed for any reason, the date of clearance is to be regarded as the date of payment. (HMRC VAT—Time of Supply Manual VATTOS 5145).

Payment by credit card, charge card, etc.

Payment is not strictly received until the sum involved is paid over to the supplier by the card company. However, a trader may be permitted to treat the date of acceptance of the card as the payment tax point where this conforms with normal commercial accounting practice of the business and provided there is no unreasonable delay in processing the transaction. HMRC do not allow this in cases where the card company withholds payment pending satisfactory delivery of goods (which can occur with mail order transactions). (HMRC VAT—Time of Supply Manual VATTOS 5150).

Payment by bank transfer

Whether by standing order, direct debit, home banking facilities or other forms of electronic transfer, the time of payment for VAT purposes occurs when the amount in question is actually transferred into the recipient's bank account. (HMRC VAT—Time of Supply Manual VATTOS 5155).

Payment by set-off

A payment tax point can be created by a book entry or an adjustment to the accounting records (e.g. supplies between group companies may be recorded by offsetting sales and purchases ledger accounts or making entries in the inter-company current accounts). The time of payment is the date on which the appropriate entries are made in the accounting records (*Pentex Oil Ltd* (VTD 7989, VTD 7991) (TVC 43.2)). In order for there to be a payment tax point by book entry, the debt must actually have been settled or expunged. Entries that simply reflect or acknowledge an outstanding debt should not be regarded as evidence of payment for tax point purposes.

Where the value of a continuous supply of services is not agreed until the annual accounts of the business are drawn up, the date the accounts are approved may be taken to represent a payment tax point where they demonstrate that the supplies have been paid for by way of adjustment to each company's accounts.

(HMRC VAT—Time of Supply Manual VATTOS 5160).

Retention payments

Some contracts for the supply of goods or services provide for the retention of part of the consideration pending full and satisfactory performance of the contract (or of any part of it) by the supplier. This is a common feature of construction contracts and contracts for the supply and installation of plant and machinery.

Without special provisions, under the normal rules, the VAT on the retained element of the contract price would fall due at the basic tax point (see **67.8** and **67.18** below for goods and services respectively). However, in these circumstances the tax point for the retentions is delayed until either a VAT invoice is issued, or a payment is received, in respect of the retentions (whichever is the earlier). This only applies to the retained element of the contract price and the rest of the supply is subject to the normal tax point rules. In any case, the provisions do not apply to

- a supply of goods for acquisition by a taxable person in another EU member state; and
- construction services under contracts providing for stage or interim payments (see **43.19 LAND AND BUILDINGS: ZERO AND REDUCED RATE SUPPLIES AND DIY HOUSEBUILDERS**).

[*SI 1995/2518, Reg 89*].

Assignment of debts

A receipt of a payment, however expressed, includes a reference to receipt by a person to whom the right to receive it has been assigned. [*SI 1995/2518, Reg 94A*]. Where, therefore, a business assigns any of its debts, it must account for VAT on payments received by the person to whom the debts are assigned as if those payments were received by the business itself (rather than accounting for VAT when payments are received from the assignee). See **67.7** below for an accommodation tax point if this causes any problems.

Accommodation tax points

[67.7] HMRC may, at the request of a taxable person, alter the time at which supplies are to be treated as made by him by either advancing or delaying the tax point. [*VATA 1994, s 6(10)*]. These are often referred to as accommodation tax points, the most common of which are considered below.

Monthly invoicing

Many traders invoice for their supplies periodically, typically issuing a single invoice to each customer detailing the supplies made during the preceding monthly or four/five week commercial accounting period. Provided this represents the trader's normal commercial accounting practice, HMRC, on written application, may grant an accommodation tax point without the trader being required to demonstrate that the normal tax point rules cannot be complied with. Applications should state whether the accommodation tax point is to be linked to the last day of the period covered by the invoice or the date of issue of the invoice. In the latter case, this will not normally be permitted to exceed 14 days from the end of the commercial accounting period. (HMRC VAT—Time of Supply Manual VATTOS 6200).

Exempt supplies of credit

Supplies of goods on credit can involve both a taxable supply of goods and an exempt supply of credit. There is also an exempt supply of credit when a loan is made for interest or for some other form of consideration. In either case, particularly with agreements subject to fixed rates of interest, traders can have difficulty in identifying the proportion of the periodical repayment attributable to the supply of credit and the element in respect of either the goods or repayment of the capital amount in the case of a loan of money.

Application may be made to HMRC to use a single accommodation tax point for the supply of the credit provided the time nominated as the tax point is earlier than would otherwise be the case under the normal rules. For example, for supplies of credit in conjunction with a supply of goods, the accommodation tax point might be linked to the tax point for the supply of the goods. For a loan of money, a convenient tax point might be the date of the agreement or any other date before receipt of the first instalment.

Applications should be in writing and signed by a person eligible to sign the trader's VAT returns. In the case of group registrations, the application must be made by the representative member. Other forms of application may be accepted provided they contain the following information.

- The identity of the supplier.
- Details sufficient to identify precisely which supplies are intended to be covered by the direction.
- The event to be treated as the tax point for the supply.

Applications involving different tax points for different categories of exempt supplies of credit are acceptable provided they can be identified without difficulty.

(HMRC VAT—Time of Supply Manual VATTOS 6300).

Corporate purchasing (procurement) cards

Such cards are intended to be used as a method of payment by corporate customers with high levels of low value expenditure (e.g. stationery, spare parts and other expenditure delegated to individual staff members). They are designed to eliminate much of the paperwork in the purchasing process. The practical arrangements are similar to the use of credit cards and charge cards. Under normal circumstances, suppliers do not issue invoices to card-holders, invoicing being carried out on the supplier's behalf by the card company or bank using transaction information transmitted through the purchasing card system. A difficulty arises with such cards as the supplier is unaware of the date on which the card company or bank actually issues the invoice to the purchaser.

Application may be made to HMRC by the supplier for an accommodation tax point. This allows the tax point for all purchase card transactions to be the time at which the supplier keys the transaction details into the purchasing card system (the 'transmission date') provided all transactions are keyed into the system no later than the basic tax point (the date the goods are sent to, or taken away by, the customer). Card issuers have made it a condition of membership that potential suppliers will apply to use the accommodation tax point. (VAT Notice 701/48/14, paras 3.2–3.3; HMRC VAT—Time of Supply Manual VATTOS 6410).

Ministry of Defence contractors

There can be considerable delays in agreeing contract prices in the case of supplies made by defence industry contractors to the Ministry of Defence. Where one of the centrally agreed extensions to the 14-day rule is inadequate (see **67.8** and **67.18** below for supplies of goods and services respectively) application may be made for an accommodation tax point if the difficulties are wholly as a result of delays on the part of the MoD.

Applications should be in writing and signed by a person eligible to sign the trader's VAT returns. In the case of group registrations, the application must be made by the representative member. If HMRC agree, in cases where the consideration under an MoD contract is ascertained or ascertainable at or before the time when the goods are removed or the services performed, the supply in question is treated as taking place on the date a VAT invoice is issued or a payment is received, to the extent covered by the invoice or payment, but in any case not later than six years after the goods are removed or the services performed.

(HMRC VAT—Time of Supply Manual VATTOS 6520).

Assigned debts

Where a business assigns any of its debts, it must account for VAT on payments received by the assignee as if those payments were received by the business itself (rather than accounting for VAT when payments are received from the assignee). See **67.6** above. Where the assignee notifies the business of amounts received from the latter's customers, the business should have no difficulty in complying with the normal payment tax point rules. Alternatively, a tax point may have already been created prior to assignment of the debt by the issue of a VAT invoice. However, HMRC recognise that occasions may arise where the assignor may not receive details of any subsequent payments and will therefore be unaware when a payment tax point has occurred. A business affected in this way can, if it wishes, apply to HMRC to bring forward the time of supply to the time of assignment, although this will mean that any VAT outstanding on the amount assigned must be accounted for at that time. (HMRC VAT—Time of Supply Manual VATTOS 6600).

'En primeur' wine

'En primeur' wine is wine that is offered for sale, whilst still lying in the producer's cellars abroad, for delivery in the UK by the wine merchant at some time in the future. Trade practice is normally to require the customer to pay the net price of the wine when submitting an order. Further charges, based on the duty and VAT payable, together with the costs of transportation, etc. become due from the customer at the time of delivery.

At the time the net price is paid, it is not certain that the wine will ever actually be removed to the UK. Even if it is, the wine may be sold by the customer, before taking delivery, while it is still subject to a warehousing regime in the UK. As a result, it has been agreed that if VAT does become due, the supply may be accounted for at the time the customer is invoiced for the VAT and other charges where, in accordance with trade practice, this takes place immediately prior to delivery in the UK.

(HMRC VAT—Time of Supply Manual VATTOS 8600).

Standard-rated prescription goods

Businesses that are not retail pharmacists may experience difficulties in accounting for VAT at the correct time on prescription goods liable to VAT at the standard rate (e.g. stoma and continence care products). This is because, each month a supplier is unaware of the value of supplies made against prescriptions (and consequently the VAT due on those products) until PPA Form FP47(A) is received from the Prescription Pricing Authority.

Businesses in this position may apply to HMRC for approval to use the date of receipt of the FP47(A) notification as their tax point. The application should be sent to HMRC, National Advice Service, Written Enquiries Section, Alexander House, Victoria Avenue, Southend, Essex SS99 1B and should be in the following form.

'We request that supplies by [insert company/business name] of NHS prescription goods which are subject to Prescription Pricing Authority remuneration procedures be treated as taking place at the end of the period during which these procedures are undertaken for the goods in question. The end of each such period to be established by the date we receive the relevant form FP47(A) or equivalent documentation. We confirm that the supplies in question are made other than by way of a retail pharmacy.

We further request that on the issue of such a direction, any existing direction will cease to have effect insofar as it might apply to the above mentioned supplies.

[Signed]

[Status of signatory]'

(VAT Information Sheet 11/07).

Time of supply of goods

[67.8] Subject to

- any accommodation tax points agreed under **67.7** above,
- the special cases in **67.9** to **67.17** below,
- any extra-statutory class concession,
- the provisions relating to warehoused goods (see **73 WAREHOUSED GOODS**), and
- the provisions relating to gas and electricity supplies from persons outside the UK (see **26.9 FUEL AND POWER**),

a supply of goods is treated as taking place at the basic or actual tax point.

(a) **Basic tax point**

The basic tax point is determined as follows.

(i) *If the goods are to be removed*, the basic tax point occurs at the time of removal.
This normally occurs when the goods are delivered by, or on behalf of, the supplier or collected by, or on behalf of, the customer. Where there is more than one supply but only one movement of the goods (e.g. where the goods are supplied via a third party such as a finance company), it is necessary to determine to which of the supplies the removal relates (the remaining supply/supplies falling within (ii) below).
Where a single supply of goods involves delivery/collection over a period of time, provided there is genuinely a single supply (and not a succession of separate supplies) the basic tax point will not occur until the time of removal of the final consignment (although actual tax points under (*b*) below may have been created before that time).

(ii) *If the goods are not to be removed* at the time when they are made available to the customer.
The words 'if the goods are not to be removed' must be viewed in the context of the supply itself and not the nature of the goods involved. The 'made available' basic tax point is therefore not restricted to goods that are incapable of ever being moved. Examples include

- the supply of fully-assembled and installed goods on site (delivery of the components being merely a preliminary step to enable the supplier to supply what is required under the terms of the contract); and
- in the normal case of the supply of goods via a third party finance company where the finance company does not take physical delivery of the goods, the supply of the goods to the finance company by the trader.

(b) Actual tax points

(i) *Advance payment or invoicing*. If, before the basic tax point, the supplier issues a VAT invoice or receives payment in respect of the supply, there is a tax point at the time the invoice is issued or payment is received, whichever occurs first, to the extent covered by the invoice or payment. (There will thus always be a further tax point where the amount invoiced or paid is less than the full value of the supply.)

(ii) *The 14-day rule*. If the supplier issues a VAT invoice (or a taxable person issues a document to himself under the self-billing arrangements, see **40.6 INVOICES**) within 14 days *after* the basic tax point, then, unless he has notified HMRC in writing that he does not wish the rule to be applied, the tax point is the date the invoice is issued. This rule does not, however, override (*b*)(i) above.

Example

What is the tax point in the following situations?

Situation 1

Goods removed – 1 April

Payment received – 15 March

Answer – 15 March – with receipt of advance payment before supply has taken place.

Situation 2

Goods removed – 1 April

Tax invoice raised – 17 April

Payment received – 1 May

Answer – 1 April – invoice raised more than 14 days after supply has taken place, so tax point becomes date when goods were supplied, i.e. the basic tax point. This assumes the business does not have an agreement with HMRC that allows an extension of the 14-day rule.

Situation 3

Goods removed – 1 May

Tax invoice raised – 1 April

Payment received – 1 June

Answer – 1 April – raising an invoice or receiving payment in advance of a supply both create actual tax points – the key date is the one that happened first.

Situation 4

Goods removed – 1 June

Tax invoice raised – 10 June

Payment received – 6 June

Answer – 10 June – an invoice has been raised within 14 days of the supply taking place. The payment of 6 June would have created an earlier tax point if it had been received in advance of the goods being supplied but not after the supply has taken place.

Extending the 14-day rule under (b)(ii) above

HMRC may, at the request of the taxable person, extend the 14-day rule in respect of all or part of his supplies.

The following extensions to the 14-day rule have been centrally agreed.

(1) *Members of The British Electrical and Allied Manufacturers Association, The Scientific Instruments Manufacturers Association and The Electronic Engineering Association.* If the consideration for a supply of goods made by member companies under a Government contract is not ascertained or ascertainable at or before the time when the goods are removed, the supply may be treated as taking place at the time when the member issues a VAT invoice, provided it is issued within one year of the date of removal of the goods.

(2) *Government contracts.* Where a taxable person supplies goods for an agreed price under a Government contract and the supplier's invoicing is delayed due to Government procedures (e.g. the use of Ministry of Defence Form 640), the supply may be treated as taking place at the time a VAT invoice is issued, provided it is issued within four months of the date of removal of the goods.

(3) *Local authorities*. Where a local authority supplies taxable goods in the course of business activities, the supply may be treated as taking place at the time a VAT invoice is issued, provided it is issued within two months of the date of removal of the goods.

(4) *Scrap metal*. As the consideration for a supply of 'material on valuation' in the scrap metal trade is not ascertained or ascertainable at or before the time when the goods are removed, the supply may be treated as taking place at the time a VAT invoice is issued, provided it is issued within three months of removal of the goods.

(5) *The Society of British Aerospace Companies Ltd* (SBAC). If the consideration for a supply of goods made by member companies of SBAC is not ascertained or ascertainable at or before the time when the goods are removed (because the price is subject to negotiation and agreement after the work has been completed), the supply may be treated as taking place at the time a VAT invoice is issued, provided it is issued within six months of the date of removal of the goods (one year in the case of a Government contract).

[*VATA 1994, s 6(1)(2)(4)–(6)(9)(10)*]. (VAT Notice 700, para 14.2; HMRC VAT—Time of Supply Manual VATTOS 5245; HMRC Guidance Note dated 1 December 2008).

Disposal of business assets

[67.9] Where there is a supply of goods on the transfer or disposal of business assets under *VATA 1994, Sch 4 para 5(1)* (see **65.3**(*e*) **SUPPLY: GENERAL**), the supply is treated as taking place when the goods are transferred or disposed of. [*VATA 1994, s 6(12)*]. This includes goods transferred for no consideration (i.e. goods taken out of the business permanently for non-business use). See also **48.6 OUTPUT TAX**.

Intra-EU supplies of goods

[67.10] Supplies to VAT registered persons in other EU member states. Where a supply of goods involves

- the removal of the goods from the UK, and
- their acquisition in another EU member state by a person who is liable for VAT on their acquisition under the provisions of that country corresponding to those in **20.3 EUROPEAN UNION: SINGLE MARKET,**

the time of supply is the earlier of the 15th day of the month following that in which the goods are removed or the date of the issue of a VAT invoice (or other prescribed invoice) in respect of the supply.

[*VATA 1994, s 6(7)(8)*].

Supplies to non-VAT registered persons in other EU member states

Such supplies are subject to UK VAT and the tax point is determined under the normal rules in **67.8** above.

Acquisitions of goods by taxable persons in the UK from another EU member state

The time of supply (mirroring those above for supplies from the UK to registered persons) is the earlier of the 15th day of the month following that in which the first removal of the goods occurred and the date of the issue of an invoice by the supplier or the customer under the provisions of the law in the supplier's country corresponding to those relating the VAT invoices for UK supplies. [*VATA 1994, s 12; SI 1995/2518, Reg 83*].

Hire purchase, credit sales and conditional sales

The supply of the goods

[67.11] If the credit is 'self-financed', there is one supply of the goods by the trader direct to the customer. If a third party finance company is involved, there will normally be two supplies (by the trader to the finance company and by the finance company to the customer). However, this should not automatically be assumed. For example, there is unlikely to be a supply of the goods to the finance company where the finance consists of an unsecured loan.

Supplies of goods on hire purchase, credit sales and conditional sales are treated in the same way as an outright sale where title passes at the outset.

- *The basic tax point* for the supply to the customer is, in most cases, the date of delivery or collection of the goods. Where there are two supplies (see above) this is the supply by the finance company. The basic tax point for the supply by the trader to the finance company normally occurs at the time the goods are made available to the finance company. Unless the agreement indicates otherwise, this may be taken to be the time when the finance agreement comes into force, possibly at the time when the last party signs up to it.
- *A VAT invoice* issued to the customer (whether it is a conventional VAT invoice or the finance agreement adapted for the purpose) creates a tax point for the supply if it is issued in advance of, or within 14 days after, the basic tax point.
- *A deposit* paid before an agreement has come into force, or before the goods have been removed, or a VAT invoice has been issued, also normally creates a tax point.

The supply of the credit element

The tax point for the separate supply of credit is the date of payment of the interest. Where the instalments include an element attributable to the charge for credit this will mean that a tax point occurs each time that a payment is received. See, however, **67.7** above for an accommodation tax point in these circumstances.

(HMRC VAT—Time of Supply Manual VATTOS 9250).

As noted above, supplies of goods on hire purchase, credit sales and conditional sales are treated in the same way as an outright sale where title passes at the outset. In *Mercedes-Benz Financial Services UK Ltd v HMRC*

[2014] UKUT 200 (TVC 62.403) the issue was whether transactions involving a type of vehicle finance agreement known as Agility were supplies of goods, with VAT chargeable at the outset of the agreement, or supplies of services, with VAT chargeable each time a customer made a payment.

Agility is a rental agreement with an option to purchase. The main issue related to the application of the phrase 'in the normal course of events' in *Directive 2006/112/EC, Art 14(2)(b)* to the option to purchase. *Directive 2006/112/EC, Art 14(2)(b)* refers to 'the actual handing over of goods pursuant to a contract for the hire of goods for a certain period, or for the sale of goods on deferred terms, which provides that in the normal course of events ownership is to pass at the latest upon payment of the final instalment.'

The Upper Tribunal considered the economic purpose of an Agility agreement, which was to provide an Agility customer with an opportunity to purchase the vehicle without committing him to do so and to provide the company with a return on the finance it provides in circumstances where the vehicle will either be purchased or returned. The Upper Tribunal concluded that an Agility agreement may well lead to a sale, but equally may well not lead to a sale. It was not an agreement under which ownership is to pass in the normal course of events. The company was therefore correct to account for VAT each time a customer made a payment rather than at the outset of the agreement.

In late 2015, the Court of Appeal ([2016] STC 392) decided to refer questions to the CJEU about the classification of this contract. The judges concluded that, in the absence of relevant CJEU precedent, the meaning of *Art 14* was not sufficiently clear for them to conclude on the application of the phrase 'in the normal course of events'.

The CJEU has issued its judgment (*Mercedes-Benz Financial Services UK Ltd, CJEU Case C-164/16*, (TVC 62.403)) in favour of the taxpayer and held that only where the decision to return the car was financially irrational could it be considered that the car ownership would 'normally' pass at the end of the lease payments. That was not the case here, so it was a supply of services until the car was bought for the lump sum.

Goods supplied on sale or return and goods on approval

[67.12] The following rules apply to sale or return agreements, i.e. where goods are supplied on terms whereby the customer has a right to return the goods at any point up until the time they are adopted but, in the meantime, ownership of the goods remains with the supplier. Retail supplies on these terms are generally referred to as being 'on approval'.

If goods are sent or taken on approval or sale or return (or similar terms) so that they are removed before it is known whether a supply will take place, the basic tax point is the time when it becomes certain that the supply has taken place ('adoption') or, if sooner, twelve months after the removal. If, however, before this time a supplier issues a VAT invoice in respect of the supply, the tax point for the amount invoiced is the date the invoice is issued. [*VATA 1994, s 6(2)(c)(4)*].

Retail sales by mail order

In *Littlewoods Organisation plc* (VTD 14977) (TVC 62.408) the company sold goods by mail order and a dispute arose with HMRC as to the time of supply of sales when the standard rate of VAT increased from 15% to 17.5%. The tribunal held that supplies were within *VATA 1994, s 6(2)(a)* and were supplied at the time of removal, ruling that *VATA 1994, s 6(2)(c)* above applied to transactions where there was no contract of sale unless and until the person concerned adopted or was deemed to have adopted the transaction, whereas *VATA 1994, s 6(2)(a)* applied to transactions where there was a contract of sale but the buyer had the right to rescind the contract if he wished.

Land and property

[67.13] Land and property are treated as follows:

(1) Freehold land

The supply of freehold land is a supply of goods [*VATA 1994, Sch 4 para 4*] and the normal time of supply rules apply (see **67.8** above) subject to the rules below where the total purchase price cannot be determined at the time of the transfer.

Basic tax point

As land is incapable of removal, the basic tax point is when the land is made available to the purchaser, i.e. the date of the freehold conveyance (in Scotland, the time of delivery of the disposition which is known as the settlement date). If a prospective purchaser is allowed to enter the property in advance of completion (e.g. to carry out preliminary works or testing on the site), this does not advance the basic tax point for the sale of the freehold. See *Cumbernauld Development Corporation v C & E Commrs*, CS [2002] STC 226 (TVC 62.406) where an exchange of land in Scotland between the Corporation and a local golf club was held to take place 'at the time of the exchange of dispositions' and not at the earlier time when the land had been made available to the club.

Actual tax points

The basic tax point is subject to the creation of an actual tax point by the issue of a VAT invoice in advance of, or within 14 days after, the basic tax point or the receipt of a payment in advance of the basic tax point.

Deposits

It is common for a contract for the sale of the freehold interest in land to require the payment of a deposit by the purchaser at the time contracts are exchanged. If this is payable either direct to the vendor or to a solicitor acting as the vendor's agent, the deposit creates a tax point to the extent of the amount received. If, on the other hand, the deposit is received by a third party (which can be the vendor's solicitor) acting in the capacity of a stakeholder holding the money on behalf of both parties pending satisfactory performance of the contract, the payment does not create a tax point until it is released by the stakeholder to the vendor.

(HMRC VAT—Time of Supply Manual VATTOS 9360–9365).

(2) Freehold property — total purchase price not determinable at the time of supply

Where the freehold in land or a building is sold, any VAT due must generally be accounted for under the above rules. Sometimes, however, the full value of the supply is not known at this time. This would apply, for example, where the vendor is entitled to receive a further payment in the event of the purchaser later obtaining planning permission, or the final consideration is dependent on any profit from future development of the land. In these cases, a special rule allows VAT to be accounted for when the undetermined part of the consideration is received, thus avoiding the need to estimate the final value of the supply at the time of the sale.

Subject to the anti-avoidance rules below, where the total consideration cannot be determined at the time the grantor grants or assigns the freehold interest in any land, the land is treated as separately and successively supplied

- in respect of that part of the consideration which was determinable at the time of the grant or assignment, under the normal tax point rules as described above and in **67.8** above; and
- in respect of any part of the consideration not so determinable, at the earlier of the times whenever any such part is received by the grantor or the grantor issues a VAT invoice in respect of it.

[*SI 1995/2518, Reg 84(2)*].

Anti-avoidance rules

The special rule above does not apply in relation to a grant or assignment falling within *VATA 1994, Sch 9 Group 1 Item 1(a)* (sale of new and uncompleted non-qualifying buildings and civil engineering works, see **42.18 LAND AND BUILDINGS: EXEMPT SUPPLIES AND OPTION TO TAX**) where any of the specified persons listed below intend or expect to occupy the land on a date within ten years of the building or civil engineering work on the land being 'completed', without being in occupation of it wholly or substantially wholly for 'eligible purposes'.

The specified persons are

(a) the grantor;

(b) any person who, with the intention or in the expectation that occupation of the land on a date within ten years of completion of the building or civil engineering work would not be wholly or substantially wholly for eligible purposes
  (i) 'provides finance' for the 'grantor's development of the land', or
  (ii) has entered into any agreement, arrangement or understanding (whether or not legally enforceable) to provide finance for the grantor's development of the land; and

(c) any person who is connected with any person falling within (*a*) or (*b*) above under *ICTA 1988, s 839*, see **72.19 VALUATION**. A company is not connected with another for these purposes just because both are under the control of the Crown, Minister of the Crown, a government department or a Northern Ireland department.

For these purposes:

(i) '*Completed*' in relation to a building/civil engineering work is when an architect/engineer issues a certificate of practical completion in relation to it or it is fully occupied/used, whichever happens first.

(ii) '*Occupation for eligible purposes*' means one of the following.
- Occupation by a taxable person for the purpose of making supplies which are in the course or furtherance of a business carried on by him and of such a description that he is entitled to credit for any wholly attributable input tax.
- Occupation by a specified body within *VATA 1994, s 33* (see **44.2 LOCAL AUTHORITIES AND PUBLIC BODIES**) to the extent that the body occupies the land other than for business purposes of the body.
- Occupation by a government department.
- Occupation of land by a person in so far as the occupation arises merely by reference to any automatic teller machine of the person which is fixed to the land.

For these purposes,
- if a person occupying land (i) holds the land in order to put it to use for particular purposes; and (ii) does not occupy it for any other purpose; the person is treated, for so long as these two conditions continue to be met, as occupying the land for the purposes for which the person proposes to use it;
- where occupation is by a person who is not a taxable person but whose supplies are treated for the purposes of *VATA 1994* as made by another person who is a taxable person, those two persons are to be regarded as a single taxable person; and
- a person is taken to be in occupation of any land whether he occupies it alone or together with one or more other persons and whether he occupies all of that land or only part of it.

(iii) '*Providing finance*' is widely defined. It includes directly or indirectly providing funds *either* to meet the whole (or part) of the cost of the grantor's development of the land *or* to discharge the whole (or part) of any liability incurred in raising funds to meet that cost. It also includes directly or indirectly procuring the provision of funds by another person for either of those purposes. The funds may be provided by way of loan, guarantee or other security, consideration for a share issue used to raise the funds or any other transfer of assets or value as a consequence of which the funds are made available.

(iv) '*The grantor's development of the land*' means any acquisition by the grantor of an interest in the land, building or civil engineering work and includes the construction of the building or civil engineering work.

[*SI 1995/2518, Reg 84(3)–(5)*].

See **42.14 LAND AND BUILDINGS: EXEMPT SUPPLIES AND OPTION TO TAX** for the meaning of '*relevant charitable purpose*' and **42.16 LAND AND BUILDINGS: EXEMPT SUPPLIES AND OPTION TO TAX** for the meaning of '*relevant residential purpose*'.

[*SI 1995/2518, Reg 84(3)–(9)*].

(3) Long leases and tenancies

Treatment as supply of goods

The supply of a lease or tenancy exceeding 21 years (or Scottish equivalent) is regarded as a major interest in land and is treated as a supply of goods. [*VATA 1994, Sch 4 para 4*].

General time of supply provisions

Subject to the rules below on *advance invoicing* and *anti-avoidance provisions*, if under the grant of such a lease or tenancy the whole or part of the consideration for the grant is payable periodically or from time to time, the goods are treated as separately and successively supplied each time that

- a part of the consideration is received by the supplier; or
- the supplier issues a VAT invoice relating to the grant,

whichever is the earlier. This applies to rent, ground rent and any premium received.

[*SI 1995/2518, Reg 85(1)*].

Advance invoicing

Where, at or about the beginning of any period not exceeding one year, the supplier issues a VAT invoice which, in addition to the normal requirements for a VAT invoice, shows

(a) the dates on which any parts of the consideration are to become due for payment in the period;
(b) the amount payable (excluding VAT) on each such date; and
(c) the rate of VAT in force at the time of issue of the VAT invoice and the amount of VAT chargeable in accordance with that rate on each payment,

the goods are to be treated as separately and successively supplied each time that a payment in respect of the tenancy or lease becomes due or is received, whichever is the earlier. If there is a change in the rate of VAT before any of the due dates for payment under (*a*) above, the invoice ceases to be treated as a VAT invoice in respect of any supplies for which payment is due after the change (and not received before the change).

[*SI 1995/2518, Reg 85(2)(3)*].

Anti-avoidance provisions

The above continuous supply provisions have enabled some suppliers to delay (sometimes indefinitely) the time at which they accounted for VAT. The following anti-avoidance provisions are designed to prevent this by imposing periodic tax points (usually based on twelve-month periods) on specified supplies between connected persons where VAT has not already been accounted for under the above provisions.

In relation to supplies of goods where

(1) *either* the supplier and the recipient are '*connected persons*' (see **72.19 VALUATION**) *or* both are members of a 'group undertaking' (see *Companies Act 2006, s 1161*) but are not members of the same VAT group (see **28 GROUPS OF COMPANIES**),
(2) the supply is taxable at a positive rate (i.e. the standard or reduced rate), and
(3) the supplier cannot show that the recipient is able to recover *all* the VAT on the supply

then, subject to below, to the extent that the goods in question have been 'provided' and have not already been treated as supplied under any other provisions, they are treated as separately and successively supplied

(i) at the end of the twelve-month period after the supplies commenced; or
(ii) such earlier date falling within the period specified in (i) above notified by the supplier to HMRC in writing and agreed by them

and thereafter at the end of each subsequent twelve-month period. For these purposes, goods are provided at the time when, and to the extent that, the recipient receives the benefit of them.

But where the supplier, within six months after the time applicable under (i)–(ii) above, either

- issues a VAT invoice in respect of it, or
- receives a payment in respect of it,

to the extent that the supply has not already been treated as taking place at some other time under any other provisions, the supply is treated as taking place at the time the invoice is issued or the payment is received. Where the supplier intends to issue a VAT invoice, or payment is due, within the six month's period, he should wait for either of those events before accounting for VAT. However, if, for whatever reason, neither of those events has materialised at the end of the six months, the tax point reverts to the annual tax point date as above. (VAT Information Sheet 14/03, para 4.5).

A supplier can exercise a number of options in relation to the provisions by writing to one of HMRC's written enquiry teams (see **30.4 HMRC: ADMINISTRATION**).

- He can request to vary the six-month period if there are genuine commercial reasons for doing so. Full details of why the variation is required should be given. Such a change is subject to approval by HMRC and a supplier should not therefore start using a revised date until it is formally approved.
- He can elect not to be bound by the six-month rule at any time, in which case thereafter he must account for VAT as required at each annual tax point as described above.
- He can, after the start of any annual period established as above, select an earlier alternative period end date in relation to some or all of his supplies. Provided this is approved by HMRC, the date selected establishes the end of the supplier's current and subsequent twelve-month periods. Written notice should advise HMRC of the alternative date to be adopted and *either* state that this date is to apply to all

supplies to which the rules might apply *or* nominate different dates for different categories of supply. In the latter case, supplies must be identified in sufficient detail so as to be distinguishable from one another.

(VAT Information Sheet 14/03, paras 4.3, 4.5).

Where the leasing depends upon one or more other leases (the superior lease or leases), the reference to a supplier in (1) above includes a reference to any lessor of a superior lease.

Where these anti-avoidance provisions apply, the normal time of supply rules for continuous supplies detailed above do not apply to the extent that supplies have been treated as having taken place under the anti-avoidance rules.

[*SI 1995/2518, Reg 94B*].

(4) Short-term leases

Supplies of leases not qualifying as long-term leases above are supplies of services and are normally treated as continuous supplies of services within **67.19** below.

(5) Compulsory purchase

In most cases of compulsory purchase, the transfer does not take place until the price has been agreed and the normal time of supply rules apply (see **67.8** above and **67.18** below for supplies of goods and services respectively). However, where, by or under any enactment, an interest in or right over land is compulsorily purchased and the person from whom the land is purchased does not know the amount of the payment he is to receive at the normal time for the supply, a supply is treated as taking place each time he receives any payment for the purchase. [*SI 1995/2518, Reg 84(1)*].

Taxable self-supplies

[67.14] Where goods are treated as self-supplied by an order made under *VATA 1994, s 5(5)*, the supply is treated as taking place when they are appropriated to the use giving rise to the self-supply. [*VATA 1994, s 6(11)*].

Orders under *VATA 1994, s 5(5)* have been made in respect of motor cars (see **46.6 MOTOR CARS**) and stationery (see **63.2 SELF-SUPPLY**).

Supplies of water, gas or any form of power, heat, refrigeration or other cooling, or ventilation

Treatment as supplies of goods

[67.15] The supply of any form of power, heat, refrigeration or other cooling, or ventilation is a supply of goods. [*VATA 1994, Sch 4 para 3*].

General time of supply provisions

Subject to the following provisions in this paragraph, a supply of

(a) water (other than distilled or deionised water or water of a similar purity and water comprised in any of the excepted items set out in *VATA 1994, Sch 8 Group 1*, see **25.8 FOOD**),
(b) coal gas, water gas, producer gases or similar gases,
(c) petroleum gases, or other gaseous hydrocarbons, in a gaseous state, or
(d) any form of power, heat, refrigeration or other cooling, or ventilation,

is treated as taking place whenever a payment in respect of the supply is received or a VAT invoice is issued by the supplier, whichever is the earlier.

[*SI 1995/2518, Reg 86(1)*].

Continuous supplies

Subject to the anti-avoidance provisions below, where the whole or part of the consideration for

- a supply under (*a*)–(*c*) above, or
- a supply of power in the form of electricity

is determined or payable periodically or from time to time, the goods are treated as separately and successively supplied each time that a part of the consideration is received or the supplier issues a VAT invoice relating to the supply, whichever is the earlier.

Where such separate and successive supplies are made under an agreement which provides for successive payments and the supplier, at or about the beginning of any period not exceeding one year, issues a VAT invoice which, in addition to the normal requirements for a VAT invoice, shows

- the dates on which payments under the agreement are to become due for payment in the period,
- the amount payable (excluding VAT) on each such date; and
- the rate of VAT in force at the time of issue of the VAT invoice and the amount of VAT chargeable in accordance with that rate on each payment,

the goods are treated as separately and successively supplied each time that a payment in respect of the supply becomes due or is received, whichever is the earlier. If there is a change in the rate of VAT before any of the due dates for payment, the invoice ceases to be treated as a VAT invoice in respect of any supplies for which payments are due after the change (and not received before the change).

[*SI 1995/2518, Reg 86(2)–(4)*].

Anti-avoidance provisions

The anti-avoidance provisions for continuous supplies of leases (see **67.13**(3) above) also apply to these continuous supplies of goods.

[*SI 1995/2518, Reg 94B*]. (VAT Information Sheet 14/03, paras 4.3, 4.5).

Supplier's goods in possession of buyer

[67.16] Subject to below, where goods are supplied under an agreement where

- the supplier retains the property in the goods until all or part are appropriated under the agreement by the buyer, and
- the whole or part of the consideration is determined at that time,

the tax point is the earliest of

(a) the date of such appropriation by the buyer;
(b) the date when a VAT invoice is issued by the supplier; or
(c) the date when a payment is received by the supplier.

If, within 14 days after the appropriation under (*a*) above, the supplier issues a VAT invoice in respect of goods appropriated or, with effect from 1 January 2004, a self-billed invoice is issued by the customer (see **40.6 INVOICES**), then, unless he has notified HMRC in writing that he does not wish the 14-day rule to apply, the tax point is the time that invoice is issued. This does not, however, override (*b*) or (*c*) above if earlier.

The above provisions do not apply to

- goods on sale or return (for which see **67.12** above); or
- supplier's goods in the possession of the buyer where the goods are supplied to somebody liable to account for acquisition VAT on the supply in another EU member state.

[*SI 1995/2518, Reg 88*].

Gold

[67.17] *VATA 1994, s 55* provides a special accounting and payment system for supplies of gold. *VATA 1994, s 55(4)* disapplies all tax point rules apart from the basic tax point in **67.8** above and the sale or return provisions in **67.12** above. This means that the tax point for supplies covered by the scheme will normally be the date of removal of the goods. See **27.9 GOLD AND PRECIOUS METALS** for further details of the scheme.

Time of supply of services

[67.18] Subject to

- any accommodation tax points agreed under **67.7** above,
- any extra-statutory class concession, and
- the special cases in **67.19** to **67.26** below,

a supply of services is treated as taking place at the basic or actual tax point.

(a) Basic tax point

The basic tax point for services is the time when the services are performed. This is normally taken as the date when all the work except any outstanding invoicing has been completed.

(b) Actual tax points

(i) *Advance payment or invoicing.* If, before the basic tax point, the supplier issues a VAT invoice or receives payment in respect of the supply, there is tax point at the time the invoice is issued or payment is received, whichever occurs first, to the extent covered by the invoice or payment. (There will thus always be a further tax point where the amount invoiced or paid is less than the full value of the supply.)

(ii) *The 14-day rule.* If the supplier issues a VAT invoice (or a taxable person issues a document to himself under the self-billing arrangements, see **40.6 INVOICES**) within 14 days *after* the basic tax point, then, unless he has notified HMRC in writing that he does not wish the rule to be applied, the tax point is the date the invoice is issued. This rule does not, however, override (*b*)(i) above.

Extending the 14-day rule under (b)(ii) above

HMRC may, at the request of the taxable person, extend the 14-day rule in respect of all or part of his supplies.

Extensions to the 14-day rule have been centrally agreed as set out in **67.8** above for goods. Those agreements also apply to services, with the addition of:

(1) *Solicitors.* If the consideration for a supply of services by a solicitor is not ascertained or ascertainable at or before the time when the services are performed, the supply may be treated as taking place at the time a VAT invoice is issued, provided that it is issued within three months of the date of performance of the services.

[*VATA 1994, s 6(3)–(6)(10), Sch 11 para 2B(4)*]. (VAT Notice 700, para 14.2; HMRC VAT—Time of Supply Manual VATTOS 5245; HMRC Guidance Note dated 1 December 2008).

Continuous supplies of services

Normal rules

[67.19] Subject to

- the provisions below on *advance invoicing* and *anti-avoidance provisions*, and
- special provisions applying in the construction industry (see **67.21** below)

where services are supplied for any period for a consideration the whole or part of which is determined or payable periodically or from time to time, the services are treated as separately and successively supplied each time payment is received or a VAT invoice relating to the supply is issued by the supplier, whichever is the earlier. [*SI 1995/2518, Reg 90(1); SI 1997/2887, Reg* 2].

In *B J Rice & Associates v C & E Commrs*, CA [1996] STC 581 (TVC 62.472) professional services were supplied and invoiced before registration but not paid for until after registration. The tribunal and High Court both held that, as an invoice raised before registration could not be a VAT invoice, the time of supply could only be the date payment was received and therefore VAT was due on the supply. The Court of Appeal, by a majority decision, reversed this decision holding that the provisions as to time of supply determine when, but not whether, VAT is to be charged. Liability is determined under *VATA 1994, s 4* which, *inter alia*, provides that VAT is charged where the supply is made by a taxable person. In this case, the supply was made at a time when the appellant was not a taxable person. See also *C & E Commrs v British Telecommunications plc*, CA [1996] STC 818 (TVC 62.473) for a consideration of the time of supply where customers unintentionally make overpayments. For a payment to represent consideration for a supply of services, there must be a direct link with the service provided. The inadvertent overpayment of a current debt is not a payment on account of a future liability and the recipient is under an immediate obligation to repay it.

Advance invoicing

Where separate and successive supplies of services are made under an agreement which provides for successive payments and, at or about the beginning of any period not exceeding one year, the supplier issues a VAT invoice which, in addition to the normal requirements for a VAT invoice shows

(a) the dates on which payments under the agreement are to become due in the period;
(b) the amount payable (excluding VAT) on each such date; and
(c) the rate of VAT in force at the time of issue of the VAT invoice and the amount of VAT chargeable in accordance with that rate on each payment,

services are to be treated as separately and successively supplied each time that a payment in respect of them becomes due or is received, whichever is the earlier. If there is a change in the rate of VAT before any of the due dates for payment under (*a*) above, the invoice ceases to be treated as a VAT invoice in respect of any supplies for which payment is due after the change.

[*SI 1995/2518, Reg 90(2)(3)*].

The customer must not reclaim, as input tax, any VAT shown on the VAT invoice until the date on which the payment is due or until payment has been received by the supplier, whichever happens first. (VAT Notice 700, para 14.3). See also *The Simkins Partnership* (VTD 9705) (TVC 52.97).

Anti-avoidance provisions

See **67.13**(3) above for details of the anti-avoidance provisions relevant to continuous supplies of services.

[*SI 1995/2518, Reg 94B*].

Royalties and similar payments

[67.20] The granting, assignment or surrender of the whole or part of any right is a supply of services. This can take various forms.

Licences

A licence is a supply of rights that specifically permits the licensee to do something in connection with a copyright or patent held by the licensor. It is may be issued for a set period (with or without option to renew) or for the life of the copyright or patent.

Where a licence is issued for a single payment, the supply is a single supply of services and the basic tax point occurs when the licence is granted. Where the licence agreement provides for payments to be made periodically, or from time to time, the service may be treated as a continuous supply within **67.19** above, VAT becoming due every time a payment is received or a VAT invoice is issued by the licensor, whichever is the earlier.

(HMRC VAT—Time of Supply Manual VATTOS 9500).

Permanent assignments

Alternatively, a supply can take the form of a permanent, outright assignment or surrender of the rights. This is normally a single supply of services to which the normal tax point rules apply. The basic tax point occurs at the time the rights are assigned.

Special provisions, however, apply if the contract provides for the assignor to receive periodic payments of royalties, repeat fees, etc. where some or all of the consideration is dependent on future events (e.g. the level of subsequent sales or repeat broadcasts).

Where the whole amount of the consideration for the supply of services was not ascertainable at the time when the services were performed and subsequently the use of the benefit of those services by a person other than the supplier gives rise to any payment of consideration for that supply which is

- in whole or in part determined or payable periodically or from time to time or at the end of any period,
- additional to the amount, if any, already payable for the supply, and
- not a payment to which the rules relating to continuous supplies of services under **67.19** above apply,

a further supply is treated as taking place each time a payment in respect of the use of the benefit of those services is received, or a VAT invoice is issued, by the supplier, whichever is the earlier.

[*SI 1995/2518, Reg 91*]. (HMRC VAT—Time of Supply Manual VATTOS 9500).

Supplies in the construction industry

[67.21] The tax point for supplies in the construction industry depend upon the terms of payment under the contract for the supply.

(a) Where the contract provides for periodic payments to the supplier (often referred to as stage payments or interim payments) a tax point arises at the earliest of the following dates.
  (i) The date a payment is received from the supplier.
  (ii) The date the supplier issues a VAT invoice.
  (iii) For construction services where, broadly, the building in question is occupied by a person who cannot recover VAT and the construction contractor is connected with the occupier or has been financed by the occupier to carry out the construction work, the day on which the services are performed.

[*SI 1995/2518, Reg 93; SI 1997/2887, Reg 5; SI 1999/1374*].

(b) Single payment contracts (even if payment of part of the price is to be delayed under a retention clause) are subject to the normal tax point rules (see **67.18** above).

See **43.19 LAND AND BUILDINGS: ZERO AND REDUCED RATE SUPPLIES AND DIY HOUSEBUILDERS** for fuller details.

Retention payments

Where a contract within (*b*) above includes a retention clause, the tax point of the retained element is the earlier of the time when a payment is received in respect of the retention and the date the supplier issues an invoice relating to it. See **67.6** above and **43.19 LAND AND BUILDINGS: ZERO AND REDUCED RATE SUPPLIES AND DIY HOUSEBUILDERS** for further details.

Services from outside the UK

[67.22] The time of supply of such services received from abroad and subject to the reverse charge is the earlier of when the service is completed or when payment is made. For continuous supplies of services, the time of supply is linked to the end of each billing or payment period, but where no invoice or other accounting document is issued or payment made during the year, the time of supply is the end of each calendar year. (HMRC Brief 2/09).

[*SI 1995/2518, Reg 82*].

See **67.7** above for an accommodation tax point for members of the Institute of London Underwriters.

Goods used for private or non-business use

[67.23] Where business assets are put to any private use or are used (or made available to any person for use) for non-business purposes, a supply of services is treated as taking place under *VATA 1994, Sch 4 para 5(4)* (see **48.6 OUTPUT TAX**). The tax point for this supply of services is when the goods are appropriated to that private or non-business use [*VATA 1994, s 6(13)*]. If the services are supplied for any period, the tax point is the last day of the supplier's VAT period (or of each such VAT period) in which the goods are made available or used. [*SI 1995/2518, Reg 81(1)*].

Free supplies of services

[67.24] Where services specified in any Order made by the Treasury under *VATA 1994, s 5(4)* are supplied for any period, they are to be treated as supplied on the last day of the supplier's VAT period, or of each such VAT period, in which the services are performed. [*SI 1995/2518, Reg 81(2)*].

The only order made under these provision is the *VAT (Supply of Service) Order 1993 (SI 1993/1507)*. This covers certain services, originally acquired for business purposes, which are subsequently put to private or non-business use. See **48.6 OUTPUT TAX**.

Supplies through coin-operated machines

[67.25] Under the normal time of supply rules, the tax point for supplies made via coin-operated machines is the time the machine is used (or, more strictly, the time money is inserted). However, as an accounting convenience, operators may delay accounting for VAT until the takings are removed from a machine. (VAT Notice 48, ESC 3.6).

For all other purposes, the normal tax point rules apply. Therefore in the event of

- a theft of takings from a machine, VAT must still be accounted for in full on any supplies that have been made from the machine (see *Townville (Wheldale) Miners Sports and Recreation Club and Institute* [1978] Lexis Citation 32 (TVC 62.386) where coins fraudulently extracted were subject to VAT); and
- a change in the rate of VAT, operators must revert to the normal tax point rules for the purposes of determining the VAT rates to be applied where takings removed from machines cover supplies made both before and after the rate changed (see *Glasgow Vending Services* (VTD 943) (TVC 62.397)).

Barristers and solicitors

[67.26] Barristers and solicitors are treated as follows:

(1) Barristers

Services supplied by a barrister (in Scotland, an advocate), acting in that capacity, are treated as taking place at whichever is the earliest of the following times.

(a) When the fee in respect of those services is received.
(b) When the barrister issues a VAT invoice in respect of them.
(c) The day when the barrister ceases to practise as such.

[*SI 1995/2518, Reg 92*].

These special rules were introduced because a barrister cannot sue for unpaid fees and frequently can have to wait a considerable period of time before outstanding fees are received from instructing solicitors. For most supplies by practising barristers, the tax point will be the receipt of payment under (*a*) above as the fee notes issued to solicitors normally do not become VAT invoices until they are receipted and returned to the solicitor following payment.

These rules make VAT chargeable on all outstanding fees at the time of ceasing to practice. See below, however, for a special scheme allowing a barrister to defer payment of VAT on such fees until payment is received or a VAT invoice issued in respect of them.

Ceasing to practice

Action required depends upon whether the barrister makes other taxable supplies.

- *A barrister who makes no other taxable supplies* must deregister and notify HMRC within 30 days of ceasing to practice. This should be done on Form VAT 7 or online. If the barrister has outstanding professional fees, he should send a letter with the Form VAT 7 stating whether he intends to pay the VAT due on outstanding fees immediately or wishes to defer payment (see below). The online deregistration system does not have the capacity for documents to be attached to applications. If the deregistration application is submitted online the letter regarding outstanding professional fees should be sent to VAT Registration Service, HMRC, Crown House, Birch Street, Wolverhampton, WV1 4JX. If deferral is approved, the barrister must still pay VAT due on fees already received, or shown on VAT invoices raised, up to the date of deregistration.
- *A barrister who continues to make other taxable supplies but can show that their value will not exceed the deregistration limit in the next twelve months* (see **60.8 REGISTRATION**) may ask HMRC to cancel his registration by completing Form VAT 7. HMRC will then send a final VAT return on which the barrister must include VAT on all professional fees received, and other supplies made, between the end of the last full VAT period and the date of cancellation of registration. If he wishes to defer payment of VAT on outstanding fees (see below), he must apply to HMRC.
- *A barrister who continues to make other taxable supplies and to be registered* must include, in his VAT return for the period in which he ceased to practice, VAT on all fees received, and other supplies made, during the period. If he wishes to defer payment of VAT on outstanding fees (see below), he must apply to HMRC. VAT on other taxable supplies must be accounted for on subsequent VAT returns in the normal way and is not affected by the special procedure. VAT on professional fees outstanding at the time of ceasing to practise should be excluded from subsequent VAT returns and paid separately with Form VAT 812 (see below).

A barrister may continue to issue VAT invoices for fees which are outstanding after registration has been cancelled but

- the services must have been supplied before the date registration is cancelled;
- the tax point to be shown on the invoice is the date of ceasing to practice; and
- the rate of VAT charged must be the rate in force at that time (and not any different rate applying at the time the invoice is raised).

Deferring payment of VAT on fees outstanding on ceasing to practice

HMRC send a Form VAT 811 to a barrister who asks for deferment. On the form the barrister must list every standard-rated fee which is outstanding (or give an estimate), together with the name of the relevant case, the professional client and the date of the first fee note. The completed form should be sent to DMB Banking Ops, GABS Team, 6th Floor NW, Alexander House, Victoria Avenue, Southend-on-Sea, SS99 1AU. A certified copy of the completed form will be returned when deferment is approved.

A copy of Form VAT 812 is then sent quarterly on which the barrister must declare VAT due on any fees received, or for which a VAT invoice has been issued, during the period specified on the form. The name of the relevant case must be shown together with enough details to cross-reference the fee to the completed Form VAT 811. Form VAT 812 must also show fees for any services which were expected to be zero-rated when the Form VAT 811 was completed but which turn out to be standard-rated.

After the first year, HMRC offer the option of completing Form VAT 812 on a six-monthly basis.

When all outstanding fees have been received and the VAT due paid, the barrister must make a declaration of final payment on Form VAT 812 (with an explanation for any items shown on Form VAT 811 on which VAT has not been paid, eg because the fee has not been collected). Records must be kept for inspection for one year after the declaration of final payment.

Practising barristers who die

The deceased barrister's clerk should notify HMRC as soon as possible and the personal representatives should, within ten days of the grant of probate or order for administration, inform HMRC whether they wish to pay VAT on the barrister's outstanding professional fees straight away or to defer payment. If they choose to defer payment, the personal representatives must use the special deferment scheme outlined above. The personal representatives must give an address to which further communications should be sent and sign an adapted VAT deferment application form.

Barristers who are partly exempt for VAT purposes

Where a barrister has made exempt supplies since the beginning of the VAT year in which he ceased to practise and applies for deferment of VAT on outstanding fees, it may be necessary in due course to make a special adjustment of the input tax reclaimed. Advice should be obtained from HMRC.

(VAT Notice 700/44/15).

De Voil Indirect Tax Service. See V5.145.

(2) Solicitors

There are no special tax point rules for supplies made by a solicitor and, with the exception of the centrally agreed extension to the 14-day rule (see below), they are subject to the normal time of supply rules that apply to services.

Basic tax point

Most supplies by a solicitor are single supplies, even though the supply may involve work undertaken over an extended period of time (e.g. litigation). The basic tax point occurs when the services have been fully completed.

Where a solicitor makes supplies on a regular basis to an individual client, in most cases this represents a series of separate supplies, each of which is subject to its own basic tax point. If the solicitor bills the client periodically for all work performed or completed during the period, the basic tax point rule should be complied with for each of the separate supplies. Only in exceptional circumstances will this kind of relationship represent a continuous supply of services (e.g. where a solicitor is retained as the permanent legal adviser or to act as the client's legal office). However, some legal work is inherently continuous in nature (e.g. the supply of the services of a solicitor acting as a trustee) and such supplies normally fall within the time of supply rules for continuous supplies (see **67.19** above).

Client accounts, etc.

The receipt of a payment into a client's account does not represent receipt of payment for VAT purposes, which only occurs when money is transferred from the client's account to the general office account. This does not, however, apply to the receipt of standard monthly payments for Legal Aid contracting work (see below).

Disbursements

A tax point is not created by the receipt of payments from clients in respect of expenses such as stamp duty and Land Registry fees that are accepted as disbursements for VAT purposes (see **3.7 AGENTS**).

Standard monthly payments for Legal Aid contracting work

Solicitors undertaking work under what is known as the contracting arrangements receive a standard monthly payment (SMP) based on the anticipated level of this work over the forthcoming year. As individual cases are completed the fees, disbursements and VAT are 'billed' and allocated by the solicitor to the SMPs. This means that, depending on the progress of individual cases, the total amounts received from the Legal Services Commission may, at any given time, exceed the value of cases completed or there may be a shortfall.

HMRC have agreed with the Law Society that the normal tax point rules will apply to Legal Aid contracting work. As a result, unless the cash accounting scheme is used, VAT on completed cases must be accounted for at the basic tax point (the date when the supply of services is completed). VAT is due on the SMP received to the extent that it represents advance payment for cases that have not yet started or cases that have started but have not yet been completed.

In the following examples, it is assumed that the solicitor has only one case involving SMPs. In practice, an SMP will generally be for more than one client and the work undertaken for those clients is likely to be at various stages of completion. The SMPs will probably cover a combination of work not yet started, work started but not completed and work completed. However, the VAT rules used should be applied whatever the case.

Example 1

A solicitor receives an SMP of £1,200 per month on the first of each month and prepares VAT returns for calendar quarters. A case commences on 1 January and is completed on 15 March. The total fees and disbursements liable to VAT amount to £3,750 plus £750.00 VAT.

At the end of the March VAT quarter, the following tax points will have occurred with VAT to be accounted for on the return as follows.

	£
1 January	200.00
1 February	200.00
1 March	200.00
15 March	150.00
Total	£750.00

VAT due at the time of the next SMP received on 1 April will be £50.00 as £150.00 has already been accounted for on the previous return.

Example 2

A solicitor receives an SMP of £1,200 per month on the first of each month and prepares VAT returns for calendar quarters. A case commences on 1 January and is completed on 15 April. The total fees and disbursements liable to VAT amount to £1,500 plus £300.00 VAT.

At the end of the March VAT quarter, the following tax points will have occurred with VAT to be accounted for on the return as follows:

	£
1 January	200.00
1 February	200.00
1 March	200.00
Total	£600.00

When the case is completed on 15 April, the VAT due on the supply of £300.00 has already been accounted for in full against SMPs received during the previous quarter.

If a solicitor is required to repay some, or all, of an SMP to the Legal Services Commission (e.g. because of a fall in the amount of work undertaken), then the amount refunded ceases to be consideration for a supply. Any VAT previously accounted for on the amount to be refunded may be adjusted accordingly at that time.

HMRC take the view that the VAT treatment of SMPs is the same whether they are paid into the office account or a client account (i.e. they make a distinction between SMPs and payments received from privately paying clients).

Adjustments to solicitor's fees

In certain circumstances, a solicitor's fees can be subject to third party scrutiny and adjustment before acceptance. The circumstances in which this can occur, and the tax point consequences, are as follows.

- *Contentious work (non-Legal Aid).* If the losing party to a legal action is ordered to pay costs, the solicitor for the successful party prepares a bill which is then either agreed with the solicitor for the loser or referred to the Court for scrutiny under the taxation procedures. In such cases, settling of the costs is part of the solicitor's overall supply to the client. A basic tax point does not, therefore, occur until either the costs have been agreed between the solicitors or the taxation procedure is complete.

- *Non-contentious work (non-Legal Aid)*. A client may ask the Law Society to scrutinise a solicitor's bill to ensure that it is fair and reasonable. The Law Society can then reduce the amount payable by the client. This procedure does not form part of the supply by the solicitor to the client and the basic tax point still occurs when all the work, except the invoicing, is completed. However, if this means that VAT is accounted for in advance of a reduction to the bill, the solicitor may subsequently adjust the amount accounted for (subject to the normal rules regarding credits).
- *Legal Aid (excluding contract work above)*. Although relatively few bills submitted by a solicitor to the Legal Aid authorities are approved unamended, the solicitor's services are supplied to the client named in the Legal Aid Order and any action by the solicitor in connection with submitting and agreeing the amount of the bill does not form part of the supply to the client. The basic tax point occurs when all the work, except the invoicing, has been completed. Apart from the centrally negotiated extension to the 14-day rule (see below) there are no special tax point rules that apply in these circumstances. VAT must be accounted for on the basis of the normal tax point rules and adjusted later in the event of any subsequent reduction in the fee.

Extension of the '14-day' rule

Where the consideration for a supply of services by a solicitor is not ascertained or ascertainable at or before the time when the services are performed, the supply may be treated as taking place at the time when the solicitor issues an invoice in respect of the supply *provided* that the VAT invoice is issued not later than three months after the date of performance of the services. It should be noted that failure to issue a VAT invoice within the three months means that the tax point reverts to the basic tax point (and is not the end of the three-month period). This is particularly important in the case of Legal Aid work. The Legal Aid authorities are not a taxable person and therefore do not require a VAT invoice. Nevertheless, the solicitor must still issue a VAT invoice if the three-month extension is to apply.

(HMRC VAT—Time of Supply Manual VATTOS 8500–8570).

Key points: time of supply

[67.27] Points to consider are as follows.

- The 'time of supply' (tax point) regulations for most cross-border services is when they have been completed (usually the invoice date) rather than when payment has been received from the customer. This is relevant for both ESL entries (for a business selling services) and reverse charge procedures for a business buying services.

- An understanding of the tax point (time of supply) regulations is important to ensure that output tax is charged to a customer at the correct time, and included on the right VAT return.
- As an example, a VAT invoice should be raised within 14 days of a supply of goods or services taking place, in which case the invoice date becomes the tax point (actual tax point). The tax point for invoices raised more than 14 days after a supply of goods or services will revert to the earlier date of when the goods or services in question were supplied (basic tax point).
- The receipt of money or raising an invoice in advance of a supply being made will create a tax point and output tax liability (assuming the goods or services in question are standard-rated or reduced-rated).
- The sale of land and property is classed as a supply of goods, and the normal tax point rules are followed if the supply involves VAT (e.g. the sale of a property with an option to tax election in place).
- A deposit paid by a person or business buying land before the completion of the deal will create a tax point if the money is made available to either the vendor or his agent. Output tax will therefore be due on the deposit based on the payment date if the supply is standard-rated.
- In relation to a continuous supply of services, a tax point is created when either an invoice is raised or payment received, whichever happens first. A request for payment or fee note document does not create a tax point.
- In certain cases, it is common for an annual tax invoice to be raised, showing tax points that coincide with monthly payments to be made by the customer. Output tax is then accounted for by the supplier according to each payment date, and input tax will be reclaimed by the supplier on the same date (assuming it can be reclaimed under the normal rules of VAT).
- If the rate of VAT changes after an annual VAT invoice has been raised, and the rate change is effective from a date within the year in question, then the annual invoice will become invalid from this date, and a revised invoice will need to be issued by the supplier showing the new rate of VAT. The customer cannot reclaim input tax until this procedure has been carried out.

68

Terminal Markets

Cross-reference. See **27 GOLD AND PRECIOUS METALS.**

Introduction to terminal markets

[68.1] The Treasury have been given wide powers to make provisions for the VAT treatment of dealings on terminal markets and transactions of people ordinarily engaged in such dealings. These include the right to

(a) zero-rate or exempt the supply of any goods or services;
(b) register any bodies representing persons ordinarily engaged in dealings on a terminal market;
(c) disregard such dealings *by* persons represented under (*b*) above in determining liability to **60 REGISTRATION** for VAT purposes;
(d) disregard such dealings *between* persons represented under (*b*) above for all purposes; and
(e) refund input tax attributable to such dealings on a terminal market.

Different regulations may be made for different terminal markets.

[*VATA 1994, s 50*].

Qualifying markets and market members

[68.2] Regulations have been made under *SI 1973/173 (as amended)* for the zero-rating of certain supplies of goods and services in the course of dealings on specified terminal markets. To qualify, transactions must involve a member of the market which includes any person ordinarily engaged in dealings on the market. The following is a list of terminal markets included in the *Order* together with persons regarded by HMRC as ordinarily engaged in dealing on the markets.

Market	*Persons regarded as market members*
London Metal Exchange	Members entitled to deal in the 'ring' of the London Metal Exchange.
London Rubber Market	For actuals transactions — Class P (producer members), Class A (selling agent and importer members), Class B (broker members) and Class C (dealer members) of the Rubber Trade Association of London. For futures transactions on the London Rubber Terminal Market — floor and associate members of the London Rubber Terminal Market Association.
London Cocoa Terminal Market, London Coffee Terminal Market, London Meat Futures Market, International Petroleum Exchange of London, London Potato Futures Market, London Soya Bean Meal Futures Market, London Sugar Terminal Market, London Vegetable Oil Terminal Market, London Wool Terminal Market	Full and associate members of these markets, provided the sale is registered with the International Commodities Clearing House Ltd or its successor
London Grain Futures Market	Provided the sale is registered in the Clearing House of the Grain and Feed Trade Association Ltd
Liverpool Barley Futures Market	Provided the sale is registered in the Clearing House of the Liverpool Corn Trade Association
London Platinum and Palladium Market	Provided the transaction is only between any full or associate members of the respective market
London Bullion Market	A person is regarded as being a member of this market only if they are a member of the London Bullion Market Association

[*SI 1973/173, Art 2*]. (VAT Notice 701/9/11, para 4).

Zero-rated transactions

[68.3] The transactions which are zero-rated are as follows.

(a) Actual transactions

A sale *by and to* a market member of any goods (other than investment gold) ordinarily dealt with on the market which results in the goods being delivered. In addition, if the market is the

- London Metal Exchange, the sale must be between members entitled to deal in the 'ring';
- London Cocoa Terminal Market, London Coffee Terminal Market, London Meat Futures Market, International Petroleum Exchange of London, London Potato Futures Market, London Soya Bean Meal

Futures Market, London Sugar Terminal Market, London Vegetable Oil Terminal Market, or the London Wool Terminal Market, the sale must be registered with the International Commodities Clearing House Ltd;

- London Grain Futures Market, the sale must be registered in the Clearing House of the Grain and Feed Trade Association Ltd; and
- Liverpool Barley Futures Market, the sale must be registered at the Clearing House of the Liverpool Corn Trade Association Ltd.

(b) Futures transactions

A sale *by or to* a market member of any goods (other than investment gold) ordinarily dealt with on the market where, as a result of other dealings on the market, the sale does not lead to a delivery of the goods by the seller to the buyer.

'*Delivery*' is not defined but is regarded by HMRC as taking place when instructions are given for the goods to be physically removed from the warehouse, vault etc. If a futures transaction leads to a delivery of the goods, VAT must be accounted for on the basis of the original contract price.

Transactions between non-members

Any supply of goods between parties who are not listed in **68.2** above under a futures contract, even if it does not lead to physical delivery of the goods, is not zero-rated under these provisions. It will be subject to the normal VAT rules of the main supply (e.g. a futures contract for the supply of potatoes will be zero-rated as potatoes are zero-rated). (VAT Notice 701/9/11, para 3.3).

(c) The grant of an option

The grant *by or to* a market member of a right to acquire any goods (other than investment gold) ordinarily dealt with on the market where either

- the right is exercisable at a date later than that on which it is granted; or
- the sale resulting from the exercise of the right would be a sale falling within (*a*) or (*b*) above.

When an option is exercised, the resulting transaction should be considered under (*a*) or (*b*) above.

(d) Investment gold

A supply of 'investment gold' between members of the London Bullion Market Association. See **27.2 GOLD AND PRECIOUS METALS** for the definition of '*investment gold*'.

A supply of investment gold by

- a member of the London Bullion Market Association to a taxable person who is not a member, or
- such a person to a member

is not zero-rated and is also excluded from the exemption applying to certain transactions in investment gold (see **27.2 GOLD AND PRECIOUS METALS**). As a result, such a supply is standard-rated.

[*SI 1973/173, Arts 3, 4*]. (VAT Notice 701/9/11, para 3.2).

De Voil Indirect Tax Service. See V4.208.

Brokers' or agents' services

[68.4] Supplies of such services by market makers to their principals are zero-rated where the underlying transaction

(a) is zero-rated under **68.3**(*a*)–(*d*) above; or
(b) involves the supply of investment gold by
- a member of the London Bullion Market Association to a taxable person who is not a member, or
- such a person to a member.

[*SI 1973/173, Art 3*].

Brokers' services provided by a non-member are not zero-rated even if in relation to a supply of goods zero-rated under the above provisions or under *VATA 1994, Sch 8 Group 1* (relief for food). Where a person introduces business to a broker and receives from that broker a fee or share of the latter's commission or brokerage, that fee, etc. is the consideration for a standard-rated supply of services, unless the person meets the conditions for zero-rating brokers' or agents' services above.

International services

The supply of services in relation to commodities is almost certainly 'business to business' and therefore outside the scope of UK VAT where the recipient either belongs in another EU member state or belongs outside the EU.

(VAT Notice 701/9/11, paras 3.3, 3.4).

Accounting

Zero-rated supplies

[68.5] Where a person (whether a market member or not) supplies goods or services zero-rated under the provisions in **68.3**(*a*)–(*d*) above, he is not required to record such transactions for VAT purposes. If he does wish to include such items in a VAT return (e.g. to increase the proportion of input tax recoverable where exempt supplies are also made), he must record *all* of them. [*SI 1995/2518, Reg 33A*]. (VAT Notice 701/9/11, para 3.5).

Standard-rated supplies of investment gold

Certain supplies of investment gold involving members of the London Bullion Market Association are standard-rated (see **68.3**(*d*) above). The provisions of *VATA 1994, s 55(1)–(4)* normally apply to such supplies and the customer must account for VAT on the supply. However, where the non-member who makes or receives the supply is only liable to be registered for VAT under *VATA 1994, Sch 1* or *Sch 3* solely by virtue of that supply or acquisition, the non-member is not required to notify liability for registration and the London Bullion Market Association member must, on the non-member's behalf, keep a record of the transaction and pay the VAT due to HMRC. [*SI 1973/173, Arts 5–7*]. See **27.8 GOLD AND PRECIOUS METALS** for fuller details. The non-member is not required to keep VAT records or submit EC Sales Lists. [*SI 1995/2518, Reg 33B*].

Agents' services

Where a supply of agents' services is not zero-rated under **68.4** above, VAT must be accounted for on the full amount of commission or brokerage charged before deduction of any part paid to third parties. (VAT Notice 701/9/11, para 3.5).

69

Tour Operators' Margin Scheme

Cross-references. See **33 HOTELS AND HOLIDAY ACCOMMODATION; 73 TRANSPORT AND FREIGHT.**

De Voil Indirect Tax Service. See V3.591–V3.596.

Introduction to the tour operators' margin scheme

[69.1] For EU legislation, see **19.41 EUROPEAN UNION LEGISLATION.**

Under UK legislation, the tour operators' margin scheme ('TOMS') is a special scheme for businesses that buy in and re-sell travel, accommodation and certain other services as principals or undisclosed agents (i.e. that act in their own name). In many cases, it enables VAT to be accounted for on travel supplies without businesses having to register and account for VAT in every EU member state in which the services and goods are enjoyed. It does, however, apply to travel services enjoyed within the UK, within the EU but outside the UK, and wholly outside the EU.

Under the scheme:

- VAT cannot be reclaimed on margin scheme supplies bought in for resale (see **69.14** below). VAT on overheads outside the TOMS can be reclaimed in the normal way.
- A UK-based tour operator need only account for VAT on the margin, i.e. the difference between the amount received from customers (including any amounts paid on behalf of customers by third parties) and the amount paid to suppliers. See **69.17** *et seq* below for calculations of margins and output tax.
- There are special rules for determining the place, liability and time of margin scheme supplies (see **69.5** to **69.7** below).
- VAT invoices cannot be issued for margin scheme supplies (see **69.8** below).
- In-house supplies supplied on their own are not subject to the TOMS and are taxed under the normal VAT rules. But a mixture of in-house supplies and bought-in margin scheme supplies must all be accounted for within the TOMS, using the cost-based method or market value method. See **69.10** below.

(VAT Notice 709/5/16, paras 2.1, 2.5, 2.6, 2.13).

The relevant law is in *VATA 1994, s 53* and the *Value Added Tax (Tour Operators) Order 1987 (SI 1987/1806)* as amended. The law gives HMRC certain powers in relation to the scheme, including specifying what goods and services are covered [*SI 1987/1806, Art 3(4)*] and how to work out the value of the supplies [*SI 1987/1806, Art 7*]. To that extent, the provisions in **69.19–69.24** below and certain other provisions as indicated in the text have the force of law.

Who must use the TOMS?

[69.2] The TOMS does not only apply to 'traditional' tour operators. It applies to anyone who is making the type of supplies detailed in **69.3** below, even if this is not their main business activity. For example, it must be used by

- hoteliers who buy in coach passenger transport to collect their guests at the start and end of their stay;
- coach operators who buy in hotel accommodation in order to put together a package; and

- companies that arrange conferences, including providing hotel accommodation for delegates.

(VAT Notice 709/5/16, para 2.2).

The CJEU has confirmed that to make the application of the TOMS depend upon whether a trader was formally classified as a travel agent or tour operator would create distortion of competition. Ancillary travel services which constitute 'a small proportion of the package price compared to accommodation' would not lead to a hotelier falling within the provisions but where, in return for a package price, a hotelier habitually offers his customers travel to the hotel from distant pick-up points in addition to accommodation, such services cannot be treated as purely ancillary. See *TP Madgett & RM Baldwin (t/a Howden Court Hotel) v C & E Commrs, ECJ Cases C–308/96 and C–94/97*, [1998] STC 1189 (TVC 22.559).

Supplies covered by the TOMS

[69.3] Subject to the exclusions in **69.9** below, the TOMS must be used by a person acting as a principal or undisclosed agent for

- 'margin scheme supplies'; and
- 'margin scheme packages' i.e. single transactions which include one or more margin scheme supplies possibly with other types of supplies (e.g. in-house supplies, see **69.10** below).

(VAT Notice 709/5/16, paras 2.3, 2.11).

'*Margin scheme supplies*' are those supplies which are

- bought in for the purpose of the business, and
- supplied for the benefit of a 'traveller' without material alteration or further processing

by a tour operator in an EU member state in which he has established his business or has a fixed establishment.

[*SI 1987/1806, Art 3(1)*].

A '*traveller*' is a person, including a business or local authority, who receives supplies of transport and/or accommodation, other than for the purpose of re-supply.

Examples

If meeting the above conditions, the following are always treated as margin scheme supplies.

- Accommodation
- Passenger transport
- Hire of means of transport
- Use of special lounges at airports
- Trips or excursions

- Services of tour guides

Other supplies meeting the above conditions may be treated as margin scheme supplies but only if provided as part of a package with one or more of the supplies listed above. These include

- Catering
- Theatre tickets
- Sports facilities

(VAT Notice 709/5/16, paras 2.9, 2.10).

In a Dutch case, the CJEU ruled that what is now *Directive 2006/112/EC, Arts 306–310* applies to cases where only accommodation is provided, and is not restricted to cases where transport is also provided (*Beheersmaatschappij Van Ginkel Waddinxveen BV & Others v Inspecteur de Omzetbelasting Utrecht, ECJ Case C–163/91*, [1996] STC 825 (TVC 22.560)). A similar decision was reached in *Hotels Abroad Ltd* (VTD 13026) (TVC 63.6). See also *Aer Lingus plc* (VTD 8893) (TVC 63.2) (where vouchers for accommodation or car hire provided to executive class passengers were held not integral or incidental to the supply of air transport and therefore fell within the margin scheme) and *Virgin Atlantic Airways Ltd* (VTD 11096) (TVC 63.7) (where chauffeur-driven car services provided to certain passengers on international flights were held to fall outside the scheme).

In *Finanzamt Heidelberg v IST Internationale Sprach- und Studienreisen GmbH, ECJ Case C-200/04*, [2006] STC 52 (TVC 22.564) the ECJ held that what is now *Directive 2006/112/EC, Arts 306–310* applied to a trader who offered services involving the organisation of language and study trips abroad and which, in consideration of the payment of an all-inclusive sum, provided in its own name to its customers a stay abroad of three to ten months and which bought in services from other taxable persons for that purpose.

Nature of the supply

[69.4] The sale of a package of margin scheme supplies is treated as a single supply for VAT purposes. [*SI 1987/1806, Reg 3(2)*]. The nature of the services is that of putting together the package or organising the travel services. For example, if hotel accommodation and transport is bought in to provide a tour, the single supply of a tour is made, rather than two separate supplies of transport and accommodation. (VAT Notice 709/5/16, para 4.5).

Place of supply

[69.5] The application of the normal place of supply rules are varied so that margin scheme supplies are treated as supplied

- in the EU member state in which the tour operator has established his business, or
- if the supply was made from a fixed establishment, in the EU member state in which the fixed establishment is situated.

[*SI 1987/1806, Art 5; SI 1992/3125*].

The effect of this is as follows

(a) Where the supplier is established in the UK only, the place of supply is the UK.

(b) Where the supplier has an establishment in more than one country
- if the establishment from which the supplies are made is in the UK, the place of supply is the UK;
- if the establishment from which the supplies are made is in another EU member state, the supply is outside the scope of UK VAT (but within the scope in that other EU member state); and
- if the establishment from which the supplies are made is outside the EU, the supplies are not margin scheme supplies and the TOMS does not apply. The normal VAT place of supply rules apply. See **66.12 SUPPLY: PLACE OF SUPPLY**. [*SI 1987/1806, Art 3*].

(VAT Notice 709/5/16, para 4.6).

See **66.13 SUPPLY: PLACE OF SUPPLY** for a consideration of the terms 'business establishment' and 'fixed establishment'. See also *C & E Comrs v DFDS A/S, ECJ Case C–260/95*, [1997] STC 384 (TVC 22.567) where a UK subsidiary acted as agent for a Danish company and received commission on package tours sold on its behalf. On the facts, the subsidiary was held to be a UK fixed establishment of the Danish company, and was therefore liable to UK output tax under the margin scheme; the Danish head office/holding company was not the establishment 'most concerned with making the supply' to UK customers.

Where margin scheme supplies are made from an establishment in another EU member state, it may be necessary to register for VAT there.

Liability of TOMS supplies

[69.6] Where margin scheme supplies are made in the UK (see **69.5** above) the whole of the margin is

- standard-rated when the supplies and enjoyed in the EU (see **18.2 EUROPEAN UNION: GENERAL** for the VAT territory of the EU); and
- zero-rated when enjoyed outside the EU.

The liability of in-house supplies (see **69.10** below) is not affected by their inclusion in a margin scheme package.

Transport enjoyed inside and outside the EU. HMRC have given the following guidance.

(a) *Journeys without stops*. Where the journey begins or ends outside the EU, it may be treated as wholly enjoyed outside the EU. Temporary stops for 'comfort' or refuelling are not regarded as stops provided passengers cannot break their journey. Return legs should be treated in the same way as outbound journeys unless there is a material difference between the two legs (e.g. a stop).

(b) *Journeys with stops.*
   (i) *General.* Where a journey involves travel both inside and outside the EU and a stop takes place in the EU, a fair and reasonable apportionment must be made between the EU and non-EU elements. This could be on the basis of EU/non-EU mileage or the number of nights spent inside/outside the EU.
   (ii) *Cruises.* Apportionment on the basis of days in/out of the EU according to the itinerary is acceptable. For this purpose, the days on which the vessel leaves a non-EU port until it arrives at an EU port are regarded as outside the EU and the days on which it leaves an EU port until it reaches a non-EU port are regarded as inside the EU.
   (iii) *Connected flights.* A second and/or subsequent flight is not regarded as a separate journey provided that the connection is made, in the case of an international connecting flight, within 24 hours of the scheduled arrival of the first flight and, in the case of a domestic connecting flight, within six hours of that time.

[*VATA 1994, Sch 8 Group 8, Item 12*]. (VAT Notice 709/5/16, paras 4.10–4.13).

Time of supply

[69.7] The normal time of supply rules do not apply to TOMS supplies. Instead, one of the two methods below must be used to work out the tax point for margin scheme supplies and any in-house supplies (see **69.10** below) sold within a margin scheme package. Whichever method is chosen, it must be applied to all such supplies. Written permission from HMRC is needed to change methods but HMRC will only allow a change in exceptional circumstances and not normally during a financial year.

The two methods for working out tax points are as follows.

(a) The earlier of
   - the date of departure of the traveller; and
   - the first date on which the traveller occupies any accommodation.

(b) The earlier of
   - the date of departure of the traveller;
   - the first date on which the traveller occupies any accommodation; and
   - the date of receipt of any payment by the tour operator (or a travel agent on its behalf) which
     (i) is a single payment covering the whole selling price; or
     (ii) exceeds 20% of the selling price; or
     (iii) exceeds 20% of the selling price where added to payments received to date on which VAT has not already been accounted for.

Cash accounting scheme

In view of the special tax point rules above, the cash accounting scheme cannot be used for margin scheme supplies or for in-house supplies and agency supplies sold as part of a margin scheme package.

[*SI 1987/1806, Art 4*]. (VAT Notice 709/5/16, paras 4.14–4.16).

VAT invoices

[69.8] VAT invoices cannot be raised for supplies accounted for under the TOMS. This is because, at the time of supply, the true amount of VAT due is not known and can only be determined when the year-end calculation is carried out (see **69.19–69.22** below). The absence of a VAT invoice does not usually matter unless the customer is entitled to claim the VAT. In such a case, it may be possible to exclude the supply from the TOMS (see **69.9** below).

When a TOMS supply is sold to a business for use in its business (e.g. travel supplies used by its employees) the invoice has to include a reference to indicate that the TOMS has been applied. It is suggested that the reference either refers to the relevant EU Directive or the relevant UK legislation.

(VAT Notice 709/5/16, para 4.20).

Supplies outside the TOMS

[69.9] The following supplies should be dealt with outside the UK TOMS.

- Margin scheme supplies which are not made in the UK. See **69.3** above for the place of supply provisions. Note that where the place of supply is another EU member state, there may be a liability to register for VAT and apply the equivalent TOMS in that country.
- Supplies which have been arranged as a disclosed agent or intermediary provided any commission received is readily identifiable. See **69.12** below.
- In-house supplies (see **69.10** below) and agency supplies (see **69.12** below) which are not packaged/supplied without margin scheme supplies.
- Supplies to business customers for subsequent resale. See **69.11** below.

(VAT Notice 709/5/16, para 2.4).

Incidental supplies

The TOMS need not be used if

- no supplies of accommodation or passenger transport are bought in for resale; and
- other supplies which would normally be margin scheme supplies are bought in for resale but there are reasonable grounds for believing that the turnover from such supplies in the one year then beginning will not exceed 1% of all the supplies made in that year.

An example of such supplies might be where a hotelier buys in car hire for re-supply to hotel guests. Provided the 1% test is satisfied, a hotelier buying occasional car hire for guests would be outside the TOMS but occasional taxi trips for guests would not (because the re-supply of taxi trips is considered to be passenger transport).

[*SI 1987/1806, Art 14*]. (VAT Notice 709/5/16, para 3.6).

In-house supplies

[69.10] In-house supplies are supplies which are not margin scheme supplies (see **69.3** above) or agency supplies (see **69.12** below). They therefore comprise supplies which are either

- made from own resources; or
- result from purchases which the business has materially altered or further processed so that what is supplied is substantially different from what was purchased.

Where in-house supplies are sold *without* margin scheme supplies, VAT must be accounted for outside the TOMS in the normal way.

Where in-house supplies are sold *with* margin scheme supplies as part of a package, the margin scheme calculations must be used to work out the value of all parts of the package. See **69.19** to **69.23** below.

Place of supply

The place of supply of in-house supplies, whether or not they are part of a margin scheme package, is determined using the normal VAT rules. The place of supply will therefore depend upon the nature of the services provided. See **66.12** *et seq* **SUPPLY: PLACE OF SUPPLY**. For example, passenger transport is supplied where it takes place (see **66.25**), hotel accommodation is supplied where the accommodation is situated (see **66.15**) and live entertainment is supplied where it is physically performed (see **66.17**). As a result, if the place of supply is in another EU member state, it may be necessary to register and account for VAT in that country.

Examples of in-house supplies

HMRC give the following examples.

(a) *Coach/train transport* where a tour operator owns or hires a coach/train and supplies a driver, fuel, repairs, etc.

(b) *Air transport*. Any supplies of air transport by a business using aircraft owned by itself or a member of the same VAT group. In addition, under a special scheme (withdrawn on 1 April 2015) the supply of a charter flight by a tour operator to a customer could have been treated as an in-house supply (thus retaining the zero-rating for the provision of transport) provided the tour operator met the following conditions.
   - It chartered the whole aircraft and not just a block of seats.
   - It entered into a contract with the airline for the provision of the aircraft and crew for an entire season (e.g. slot 1 every Wednesday from May to October). A season is defined as either a summer season (May to October), a winter sun season (November to April) or a winter sport season (December to April).

- It put its own catering facilities on board or bought them in from a separate source. This could be a separate catering company (including one set up by the charter airline) or a specialist catering broker.
- It bought in transfer journeys from a separate source.

For further details of the scheme, including implementation and accounting implications, see VAT Information Sheet 3/96 produced in co-operation with ABTA. In a technical note published on 31 January 2014 HMRC advised that the concessionary treatment that allowed this scheme would be withdrawn from 1 April 2015.

(c) *Cruises* where a tour operator

- charters a vessel from another owner including deck/engine crew but employs or engages own 'hotel'/domestic/catering staff; or
- charters a vessel from another owner for a period of two years or more whether only with deck/engine crew or with both deck/engine crew and 'hotel'/domestic/catering staff. The vessel need not necessarily be in service throughout the period but the owner must not have the right to use the vessel to make supplies to other customers during the period.

(d) *Accommodation* where a tour operator

- owns the hotel, etc.;
- hires, leases or rents accommodation under an agreement whereby it takes responsibility for the upkeep of the property and is required to undertake any maintenance to the fabric of the building (i.e. not just general cleaning, changing bed linen, etc.);
- rents space at a camp-site, installs its own tents or caravans, and sells accommodation in them (but not where accommodation in tents/caravans is bought in from a third party who provides both the site and tents/accommodation or where space at a camp-site is bought in and sold to customers who provide their own tents/caravans — both of which are margin scheme supplies); or
- buys in accommodation and provides catering staff from a separate source (e.g. a ski chalet with a chalet-maid).

(e) *Tuition* where a tour operator organises training or tuition courses by putting together a number of elements such as teachers, classrooms, lecture theatres, projectors and other teaching aids, lighting, heating, etc. If a tour operator simply buys in a place on a course from a third party who has organised the course and sells this on as part of a package with transport and/or accommodation, the supply is a margin scheme supply.

(f) *Conferences* where the organiser hires a room and provides necessary equipment (e.g. microphones, projectors, hand-outs), reception staff, etc. Any refreshments served at such a conference form part of the in-house supply of an organised conference, even if purchased from an outside caterer.

Where overnight accommodation and/or passenger transport for delegates is also supplied, this is not part of an in-house organised conference and if these supplies are bought in and re-supplied without material alteration, they must be accounted for under the TOMS (but see **69.11** below where they are re-supplied to business customers).

Other supplies (e.g. restaurant meals outside conference hours, theatre tickets) are also margin scheme supplies if supplied as part of a package with overnight accommodation/passenger transport.

(g) *Organised shoots* (including clay pigeons) where a number of elements (e.g. the right to use the land, host services, beaters, clays, etc.) are brought together.

If a shoot is organised as above, but a package is created that includes one or more margin scheme supplies (e.g. passenger transport or accommodation) the supply of the shooting event only is an in-house supply and the passenger transport and/or accommodation are margin scheme supplies.

If a business simply buys in and sells on the right to participate in a shoot organised by someone else, this is a normal (non-TOMS) supply (unless provided in a package with one or more margin scheme supplies).

In some circumstances, shoots are not organised in the course or furtherance of a business and are therefore outside the scope of VAT. See **58.11 RECREATION AND SPORT**.

(VAT Notice 709/5/16, paras 2.12, 4.7, 7.1–7.3, 7.6, 7.9, 7.11–7.14).

Supplies to business customers

[69.11] Whether supplies to business customers should be accounted for under the TOMS depends upon whether those supplies are for subsequent resale or for consumption by the business.

Supplies to business customers for subsequent resale (wholesale supplies)

These supplies are outside the scope of the TOMS and should be accounted for under the normal VAT rules. This allows a tour operator to set up an associated transport broking company to buy in transport from transport providers and sell it on to the tour operator outside the TOMS. This supply to the tour operator is zero-rated or outside the scope of UK VAT depending on the circumstances. See **71.15 TRANSPORT AND FREIGHT**. The transport company cannot be in the same VAT group as the tour operator. For further details of the scheme, including implementation and accounting implications, see VAT Information Sheet 1/97 produced in co-operation with ABTA.

Court of Justice European Union (CJEU) infraction decisions

The EU Commission initiated infraction proceedings against eight Member States (Spain, Poland, Italy, Czech Republic, Greece, France, Finland and Portugal) in connection with their operation of TOMS, and the CJEU released its decision in these proceedings on 26 September 2013. The Court ruled that

- wholesale supplies should be covered by TOMS
- the TOMS calculation should be carried out on an individual transaction basis.

The Court's decisions are binding on all Member States. Although the Court's decision that wholesale supplies should be covered by TOMS contrasts with the information in VAT Notice 709/5/16, para 3.2, HMRC have stated that there will be no immediate changes to the operation of TOMS in the UK and that businesses should continue to follow existing guidance because

- the EU Commission has indicated an intention to carry out a review of TOMS, which may result in significant changes to the scheme in future, and
- making changes now, which may be modified or reversed in the future, would be particularly disruptive and costly for business.

HMRC have indicated that they will review the situation in due course. In the meantime, it is open for any business to apply direct effect and operate TOMS in accordance with the Court's decisions. For example, it is possible that some tour operators may gain a benefit from including wholesale supplies within TOMS, in which case they may choose to do so.

(HMRC Brief 5/14.)

The Commission has recently taken infringement action against Germany and the CJEU released its judgment on 8 February 2018. The infringement proceedings concerned Germany's failure to fulfil its obligations under *Directive 2006/112/EC, Arts 73* and *Arts 306–310*. The Commission considered that Germany had incorrectly:

- excluded from TOMS travel services that were consumed by taxable persons for the purposes of their business; and
- allowed travel agents (in respect of any supplies within the scope of TOMS) to determine the tax assessment base across the period rather than on a journey by journey basis.

The CJEU upheld the Commission's action against Germany. The CJEU considered that the judgment in *European Commission v Kingdom of Spain, CJEU Case C-189/11* confirmed that Germany was incorrect to exclude travel services provided to business customers from TOMS and that by omitting these services, Germany was undermining the previous CJEU decision. The CJEU also stated that *Art 318* does provide for a flat rate determination of the taxable amount for certain special schemes, however this does not include travel agents and just because a business may encounter difficulties calculating the margin on B2C supplies does not entitle the member state to dismiss that interpretation.

This judgment is partly in keeping with HMRC's practice and earlier CJEU judgments. However, the UK currently allows a flat rate TOMS calculation for the tax period. This is contrary to the CJEU decision and earlier infringement proceedings that held that TOMS requires transactions to be calculated on a journey by journey basis. It will be interesting to see whether the UK amends its current practice or continues to operate the existing rules until the UK has left the EU. *European Commission v Germany, CJEU Case C-380/16.*

Supplies to business customers for their own consumption

Supplies made to a business customer for use by that customer for the purposes of its business (e.g. for business travel) fall within the TOMS where they meet the definition of margin scheme supplies.

This means that hotel booking agents who receive invoices in their own name for hotel accommodation and recover the VAT charged must account for VAT on their onward supplies under the TOMS and, in turn, their business customers incur sticking tax. However, HMRC have stated that it is entirely open to hotel booking agents to act in a disclosed capacity, with the hotels supplying accommodation direct to their business clients, rather than buy in and supply the accommodation themselves. HMRC have agreed the following arrangements where agents operate in this way.

- Invoices from hotels should be addressed c/o the hotel booking agent for payment (to indicate that the invoice has been issued to the hotel booking agent in its capacity as an agent).
- The booking field on the hotel invoice should identify the hotel guest, their employer and should ideally carry a unique reference number (until hotels can address their invoices directly to their business customers, it may be necessary for hotel booking agents to enter an employer identification number on the invoice).
- The hotel booking agent should arrange for payment of the invoice(s) but not recover the input tax thereon.
- The hotel booking agent should send the customer a payment request/statement of the expenditure incurred by the hotel booking agent on its behalf, separately identifying the value of its supplies, VAT, etc.
- The payment request/statement should say something along the lines of 'The VAT shown is your input tax which can be reclaimed subject to the normal rules'.
- The customer should use the payment request/statement as a basis for their input tax reclaim.
- The hotel booking agent should retain the original hotel invoices and these should be made available if evidence of entitlement is required by VAT staff.
- The hotel booking agent should send a VAT invoice for its own services, plus the VAT (this may be consolidated with the statement of hotel charges, or it can be a separate document).
- The hotel booking agent should charge its client the exact amount charged by the billback supplier, as a disbursement.

[*SI 1987/1806, Art 3(3)*]. (VAT Notice 709/5/16, paras 3.1–3.3; HMRC Brief 21/10).

Supplies by agents

[69.12] The TOMS does not cover:

(a) Supplies made by an agent or intermediary not packaged/supplied with margin scheme goods.

(b) Supplies made by a business acting as a disclosed agent in the making of margin scheme supplies (i.e. it names the provider of the margin scheme supplies). The commission and all monies for the supply arranged must be excluded from the TOMS.

But where a business acting as an agent must use the TOMS because it makes margin scheme supplies in its own name *and* it receives variable commission (or commission which is otherwise not readily identifiable) as a disclosed agent, it must include its agency income and directly-related costs in its TOMS calculations.

(VAT Notice 709/5/16, paras 2.4, 2.14, 6.6).

For the liability of arranging travel and other facilities as an agent or intermediary, see **3.15 AGENTS**.

As a result of (*b*) above, a tour operator can use the 'agency option' scheme by entering into an agency arrangement, normally with a transport provider. Provided the conditions of the scheme are met, the supply of transport services is directly from the transport provider to the final customer. As the supply is not made by the tour operator, the transport services are not margin scheme supplies and fall outside the TOMS. Thus, whether supplied singly or as part of a package, the transport element and the tour operator's services of arranging the transport, are free of UK VAT (being either zero-rated or outside the scope).

Similar agency arrangements can be set up for the provision of accommodation and catering. However, as such supplies are subject to VAT at the standard rate, the related commission will normally be standard-rated and there will be no benefit in entering into these arrangements. Additionally, in respect of accommodation, if the accommodation is in another EU member state and the commission is charged to a non-VAT registered person, this could give rise to a liability for the tour operator to be VAT-registered in that country. For these reasons, it is unlikely that the 'agency option' scheme should be adopted for such supplies.

See **69.33** below for the accounting implications of using the 'agency option' scheme. For details of how to implement the scheme, see VAT Information Sheet 4/96 produced in co-operation with ABTA.

Supplies to local authorities and public bodies

[69.13] Note: the provisions of this paragraph have the force of law.

Local authority schools

The provision of an educational school trip by a local authority school to its pupils is a non-business activity for VAT purposes. The local authority is entitled to a refund of any VAT incurred under *VATA 1994, s 33* (see **44.7 LOCAL AUTHORITIES AND PUBLIC BODIES**). Northern Ireland Education Boards are entitled to refunds on such supplies under *VATA 1994, s 99* (see **47.1 NORTHERN IRELAND**).

(VAT Notice 709/5/16, paras 3.4).

Input tax

[69.14] Input tax cannot be reclaimed on goods or services acquired for re-supply as margin scheme supplies. [*SI 1987/1806, Art 12*]. This applies both to VAT incurred in the UK and in other EU member states.

Input tax can be reclaimed, outside the TOMS and subject to the normal rules, on

- overheads; and
- purchases relating to in-house supplies.

VAT incurred in another EU member state on overheads and purchases relating to in-house supplies can be reclaimed from the tax authorities in that country under the procedure in **18.7** and **18.8** EUROPEAN UNION: GENERAL. Note, however, that where supplies are made in that other EU member state, it may be necessary to register for VAT there. If so, this refund procedure may not be appropriate.

(VAT Notice 709/5/16, paras 4.3, 4.4).

Registration and deregistration

[69.15] For VAT registration and deregistration purposes, turnover is

- the total margin on taxable (including zero-rated) margin scheme supplies;
- the full value of taxable (including zero-rated) in-house supplies;
- the full value of taxable agency commission; plus
- the full value of any other taxable (including zero-rated) supplies made in the UK.

(VAT Notice 709/5/16, para 4.1).

VAT group treatment

[69.16] A business making margin scheme supplies cannot belong to a VAT group (see **28** GROUPS OF COMPANIES) if any other member of the proposed or existing group

- has an overseas establishment; and
- makes supplies outside the UK which would be taxable (including zero-rated) supplies if made in the UK; and
- supplies goods or services which will become, or are intended to become, margin scheme supplies (i.e. which are for resale, whether or not by the other member concerned).

[*SI 1987/1806, Art 13*]. (VAT Notice 709/5/16, para 4.2).

Calculation of margins and output tax

[69.17] Special calculations as laid down by HMRC are required under the TOMS to ensure that sales include only the margin for margin scheme supplies but the full value of any in-house supplies made. The purpose of the calculations are therefore to

- work out the total margin received;
- apportion the total margin between different types of supplies (i.e. margin scheme supplies (see **69.3** above), in-house supplies (see **69.10** above) and agency supplies (see **69.12** above));
- apportion the total margin between supplies with different VAT liabilities (e.g. standard-rated, zero-rated or exempt);
- work out the output tax due on margin scheme supplies and packages; and
- work out net values for supplies with different VAT liabilities.

[*SI 1987/1806, Art* 7]. (VAT Notice 709/5/16, paras 5.1, 5.12).

As precise figures are not usually known at the time of preparing the VAT returns, the TOMS requires VAT to be accounted for each quarter (or month if monthly returns are made) using *provisional* figures. The final margins and output tax are based on an annual calculation and adjustment at the end of the '*financial year*', i.e. the year for which financial accounts are made up. This final calculation determines the output tax due for the preceding financial year and provides the percentage to calculate provisional output tax in the subsequent financial year. See **69.19** to **69.24** below for the methods of calculation which *must* be used. See **69.11** above regarding HMRC Brief 5/14 following CJEU infraction decisions.

Starting to use the scheme

[69.18] Where a business is newly registered or an existing business starts to use the TOMS for the first time, it must calculate a provisional percentage to use during the first financial year under the scheme. Depending upon the circumstances, this may be based upon

- previous trading figures;
- projected costings and margins; or
- actual monthly/quarterly figures during the first year.

Whichever method is used, the first year-end calculation (see **69.19** below) will correct any under or over payment of VAT arising in the year.

(VAT Notice 709/5/16, para 5.13).

End of year calculation (annual adjustment)

[69.19] There are two TOMS accounting methods, the market value calculation and the cost-based calculation (previously calculations were based on cost). In principle, the market value method should be used where a market value can be established for a package. However, if the supplier is satisfied that the cost-based method is an accurate reflection of the structure of any package, that is, the same percentage mark-up is achieved on all components, they may use the cost-based method.

Market value calculation

Where the market value calculation is used, it is necessary to follow through to the cost-based calculation, as it is possible that packages could consist of in-house supplies with both a market value and without a market value. Many parts of the market value calculation are common to the cost-based method. The market value calculation works on the basis of extracting from a package a selling value for the bought-in designated travel services. This is done by deducting the market value of in-house supplies from the full package price, leaving the selling value of the bought-in designated travel services on which a margin is then calculated.

Cost-based calculation

The formula for this calculation covers every type of supply which might be accountable for via the TOMS. The apportionment of the total margin calculated is based on the **direct** costs of supplies, that is, not indirect/overhead costs. It works on the principle that the same percentage margin is achieved on all the elements of the packages.

The year-end calculation must be done immediately after the financial year-end and any output tax adjustment entered on the VAT return for the first VAT period ending after financial year-end. The supplier must not wait for the production of audited accounts before doing the year-end calculation/adjustment. If the audit identifies errors in the calculation after submission of the relevant VAT return, the calculation must be reworked and the normal procedure for correction of errors followed.

Market value calculation

[69.20] This calculation must only be used if the business has packages or parts of packages being apportioned by the market value of the in-house element of the package. On completion of all the steps M1-M5 the business must then follow the steps in the cost-based calculation, taking forward the figures from this calculation as instructed.

Step	
	Calculate the value of sales of margin scheme packages
M1	Total the VAT-inclusive selling prices of all designated travel services and margin scheme packages supplied during the financial year including any that are not 'market value' packages.
	Working out the market value
M2	Total the VAT inclusive market value of the standard-rated in-house supplies at M1: carry forward this figure to step 21.
M3	Total the VAT inclusive market value of the zero-rated and outside the scope in-house travel services at M1: carry forward this figure to step 26.
M4	Total the VAT inclusive market value of the in-house supplies at step M2 + step M3.
	Working out selling value of designated travel services and non-market value in-house supplies
M5	Deduct the total at step M4 from the total at step M1: carry forward this figure to step 1.

Cost-based calculation

[69.21] This calculation applies to packages being apportioned by reference to the costs of the in-house element of the package, and imports the figures calculated by the market value method where it is used for all or some of the travel packages. Do not include values already entered above unless explicitly instructed.

Step	
	Working out the total sales of margin scheme packages
1	Bring forward the total calculated at step M5. If the market value calculation is not used then enter the VAT-inclusive selling prices of designated travel services and margin scheme packages supplied during the financial year.
	Working out the purchase prices of margin scheme supplies
2	Total the VAT-inclusive purchase prices of the standard-rated designated travel services included in the total at step 1.
3	Total the VAT-inclusive purchase prices of the non-standard-rated designated travel services (supplies enjoyed outside the EU) included in the total at step 1.
	Working out the direct costs of in-house supplies. Steps 4 to 7 can be ignored where a market value is applied to all in-house supplies under the market value calculation.
4	Total the VAT-exclusive direct costs of the standard-rated in-house supplies included in step 1. Add a percentage of that amount equivalent to the standard rate of VAT.
5	Total the VAT-exclusive direct costs of the zero-rated in-house supplies included in step 1.
6	Total the VAT-inclusive direct costs of the exempt in-house supplies included in step 1. Deduct any input tax that recoverable on these costs.
7	Total the direct costs of the in-house supplies included in step 1 that are supplied outside the UK, exclusive of any VAT incurred on these costs that are recoverable. Add to the total an uplift equivalent to the percentage VAT rate applicable to such supplies if VAT has been accounted for on these supplies to the VAT authorities in another Member State.
	Working out the costs of agency supplies
8	Total the VAT-inclusive amounts paid to principals in respect of the agency supplies included in step 1 for which the consideration received is standard-rated.
9	Total the VAT-inclusive amounts paid to principals in respect of the agency supplies included in step 1 for which the consideration received is not standard-rated.
	Working out the total margin
10	Add the totals of costs at steps 2 to 9 inclusive.
11	Calculate the total margin for all the supplies included in step 1 by deducting the total at step 10 from the total at step 1.
	Apportioning the margin
12	Calculate the margin for the standard-rated designated travel services by applying the following formula: total at step 2/total at step 10 x total at step 11.

13	Calculate the margin for the zero-rated designated travel services by applying the following formula: total at step 3/total at step 10 x total at step 11.
	Steps 14 to 17 can be ignored where a market value is applied to all in-house supplies under the market value calculation
14	Calculate the margin for the standard-rated in-house supplies by applying the following formula: total at step 4/total at step 10 x total at step 11.
15	Calculate the margin for the zero-rated in-house supplies by applying the following formula: total at step 5/total at step 10 x total at step 11.
16	Calculate the margin for the exempt in-house supplies by applying the following formula: total at step 6/total at step 10 x total at step 11.
17	Calculate the margin for the in-house supplies made outside the UK by applying the following formula: total at step 7/total at step 10 x total at step 11.
18	Calculate the consideration for the standard-rated agency supplies by applying the following formula: total at step 8/total at step 10 x total at step 11.
19	Calculate the consideration for the non-standard-rated agency supplies by applying the following formula: total at step 9/total at step 10 x total at step 11.
	Working out output tax
20	Calculate the output VAT due on the designated travel services by applying the following formula: total at step 12 x the VAT fraction.
21	Calculate the output VAT due on the standard-rated in-house supplies by applying the following formula: (total at step 4 + total at step 14 + total calculated at step M2) x the VAT fraction.
22	Calculate the output VAT due on the standard-rated agency supplies by applying the following formula: total at step 18 x the VAT fraction.
	Working out sales values
23	Calculate the VAT-exclusive value of the standard-rated designated travel services by deducting the total at step 20 from the total at step 12.
24	Note the value of the zero-rated designated travel services at step 13.
25	Calculate the VAT-exclusive value of standard-rated in-house supplies by applying the following formula: (total at step 4 + total at step 14 + total calculated at step M2) – total at step 21.
26	Calculate the value of the zero-rated supplies made within the scheme by applying the following formula: (total at step 5 + total at step 15 + total calculated at step M3).
27	Calculate the value of exempt in-house supplies made by applying the following formula: total at step 6 + total at step 16.
28	Calculate the value of in-house supplies which are supplied outside the UK by applying the following formula: total at step 7 + total at step 17.
29	Calculate the total VAT exclusive value of the supplies: total of steps 23 to 28. Include this total in box 6 of the VAT return.
	Working out the annual adjustment
30	Calculate the total output VAT due on designated travel services and margin scheme packages by adding the totals at steps 20 to 22 inclusive.
31	Total the provisional output VAT which has been accounted for during the financial year on the supplies included in the total at step 1.

32	Deduct the total at step 31 from the total at step 30. Include the resulting total in box 1 of the VAT return, either as a payable amount where the amount is positive or as a deductible amount where the amount is negative.

(VAT Notice 709/5/16, paras 5.2–5.4, 5.7, 5.8, 8, 9).

Simplified calculation

[69.22] If all component supplies of all margin scheme packages are liable to VAT at the standard rate, the simplified method set out below must be used. It achieves the same results as the full calculation but avoids the need to work out costs of in-house supplies (if included in packages).

Step	
1	Total the VAT-inclusive selling prices of designated travel services and margin scheme packages supplied during the financial year.
2	Total the VAT-inclusive purchase prices of the designated travel services included in the total at step 1.
3	Calculate the VAT-inclusive amount of the supplies included in step 1 by deducting the total at step 2 from the total at step 1.
4	Calculate the total output VAT due on designated travel services and margin scheme packages by applying the following formula: total at step 3 x the VAT fraction.
5	Calculate the VAT-exclusive value of designated travel services and margin scheme packages by deducting the total at step 4 from the total at step 3.
6	Total the provisional output VAT which has been accounted for during the financial year on the supplies included in the total at step 1
7	Deduct the total at step 6 from the total at step 4. Include the resulting total in box 1 of the VAT return, either as a payable amount where the amount is positive or as a deductible amount where the amount is negative.

(VAT Notice 709/5/16, paras 5.5, 5.7, 5.8, 11).

Provisional percentages for the next financial year

[69.23] When the procedure in **69.19** or **69.22** above has been completed, provisional percentages can be obtained for use in completing VAT returns for the next financial year. Revised provisional figures must be calculated each year.

Where the method in **69.19** is used:

	Working out the provisional percentage
A	Calculate the VAT-inclusive amount of standard-rated supplies of designated travel services and margin scheme packages for the preceding financial year by adding the totals from steps 4, 12, 14 and 18 in **69.21**, together with the total M2 in **69.20**.
B	Calculate the VAT-inclusive standard-rated percentage of the total selling price of all designated travel services and margin scheme packages for the preceding tax year by applying one of following formulae:

	If market value has been used to value in-house supplies: total at step A/total at step M1 x 100.
	If market value has not been used to value in-house supplies: total at step A/total at step 1 x 100.
	Working out the VAT return figures
C	Total the VAT-inclusive selling prices of the designated travel services and margin scheme packages supplied during the prescribed accounting period.
D	Calculate the provisional VAT-inclusive amount of standard-rated supplies of designated travel services and margin scheme packages made during the prescribed accounting period by applying the following formula: total at step C x percentage at step B.
E	Calculate the provisional amount of output VAT due for the prescribed accounting period by applying the following formula: total at step D x the VAT fraction.

Where the simplified method in **69.22** has been used:

Step	
A	Calculate the VAT-inclusive standard-rated percentage of the total selling price of all designated travel services and margin scheme packages for the preceding tax year by applying the following formula: total at step 3 in **69.22**/total at step 1 in **69.22** x 100.
B	Total the VAT-inclusive selling prices of all of designated travel services and margin scheme packages supplied during the prescribed accounting period.
C	Calculate the provisional VAT-inclusive amount of standard-rated supplies of designated travel services and margin scheme packages made during the prescribed accounting period by applying the following formula: total at step B x percentage at step A.
D	Calculate the provisional amount of output VAT due for the prescribed accounting period by applying the following formula: total at step C x the VAT fraction.
E	Calculate the provisional VAT-exclusive value of all of designated travel services and margin scheme packages made during the prescribed accounting period by deducting the total at step D from the total at step C.

(VAT Notice 709/5/16, paras 5.9, 10, 12).

Separate calculation for non-EU supplies

[69.24] Note: the provisions of this paragraph have the force of law.

Where a business makes supplies (including packages) which are enjoyed outside the EU, it may elect to do separate year-end and provisional calculations for those supplies. If it so elects, it must include in the non-EU calculation all supplies which are enjoyed wholly outside the EU. But where any packages are enjoyed partly within the EU and partly outside the EU, the entire package must be included in the calculation for EU-only supplies, the related direct costs being included in the standard-rated or zero-rated steps within the EU-only calculation depending on where the supplies are enjoyed.

A business can only change to separate calculations (or revert to a single calculation) at the start of its financial year (i.e. no later than the due date of its first VAT return for that financial year). Permission must be requested from the local VAT Business Advice Centre, in writing, and in advance of the financial year in question. Permission will not be granted retrospectively. This policy was confirmed as having the force of law in *C & E Commrs v Simply Travel Ltd*, Ch D 2001, [2002] STC 194 (TVC 63.25).

Permission to switch to separate calculations will only be granted if HMRC are satisfied that the records of the business for direct costs and sales are adequate to calculate accurate, but separate, sets of margins.

(VAT Notice 709/5/16, paras 5.9, 5.10, 13).

Records

[69.25] If the market value calculation is made, a business must keep records of the market value for each in-house supply (where used), and it must be able to show how the figure was calculated and why it is the market value.

Whether the full or simplified calculation is made, a business must keep records of

- the total selling price for margin scheme supplies and/or packages; and
- separate records of the direct costs for margin scheme supplies and the different types of supplies within margin scheme packages, i.e.
  - (i) standard-rated and zero-rated margin scheme supplies;
  - (ii) standard-rated, zero-rated, exempt and outside the scope in-house supplies; and
  - (iii) standard-rated, zero-rated, exempt and outside the scope agency supplies for which its commission is not readily identifiable.

(VAT Notice 709/5/16, para 5.6).

Working out the selling prices

[69.26] The first step in the end of year calculation is to add up the selling prices of supplies with tax points during the financial year.

Include:

- The total VAT-inclusive selling price of all margin scheme supplies, including any charges made for credit card payments (see **69.3** above).
- The total VAT-inclusive selling price of any in-house supplies (see **69.10** above) supplied together with margin scheme supplies.
- Any Air Passenger Duty payable by the customer.
- Any surcharges made.
- Monies received from customers who fail to turn up.
- Where sales are made through agents, 'the total amount to be paid by the traveller' (even if a travel agent deducts commission and only passes over the balance).

  Where a travel agent sells a package for less than the tour operator's advertised brochure price but funds the discount itself (so that the tour operator receives the full price of the holiday but, in effect, part

from the traveller and part from the travel agent), the CJEU have held that '*the total amount to be paid by the traveller*' includes the additional amount that the agent, acting as an intermediary, has to pay the tour operator in addition to the actual price paid by the traveller (*C & E Commrs v First Choice Holidays plc, ECJ Case C–149/01*, [2003] STC 934 (TVC 22.568)).
- Amounts received relating to any supplies, packaged with margin scheme supplies, which the business arranges as an agent and where its commission is not readily identifiable (see **69.33** below).

Reduce sales by:

- Any refunds made to customers for unsatisfactory service.

Do not include:

- Packages of supplies which do not include any margin scheme supplies (on which VAT must be accounted for under the normal rules).
- Forfeited deposits and cancellation fees received from customers who cancel bookings.
- Amounts collected by the business as agent if its commission is readily identifiable.
- Any discount the business agrees with its customer.

(VAT Notice 709/5/16, para 6.1).

Market value or purchase price of margin scheme supplies

Market value

[69.27] The market value method is used to apportion the selling price of a package in order to determine the selling price of the in-house supplies. There is no set way to calculate a market value for in-house supplies but there are some general principles that must be considered:

- The market value must reflect the reality of the business, use of third party comparators must truly reflect the business model.
- Market values may be averaged across a range of packages but must be properly weighted and reviewed regularly.
- The calculation of the market value must accommodate child and other discounted packages.
- Full details must be kept of the business model used to calculate the market value for verification by HMRC.

Purchase price

The total VAT-inclusive purchase prices of goods and services bought in for resale as margin scheme supplies must be added up. Only those purchases which relate to the financial year being calculated must be included.

The cost must

- take into account any discounts or price reductions received from suppliers (even if received at a later date);

- include any Air Passenger Duty payable;
- not include the cost of any supplies which do not include any margin scheme supplies; and
- not include indirect costs (see **69.31** below).

(VAT Notice 709/5/16, paras 6.2, 6.3).

Connected persons

Where goods or services are supplied to the tour operator by a connected person (see **72.19 VALUATION**) and the value of the supply would otherwise be greater than its open market value, HMRC may direct that the value of the supply is deemed to be its open market value for the purposes of calculating the value of margin scheme supplies. The direction must be in writing to the tour operator acquiring the supply within three years of the time of supply. It may also specify that the open market value rule is to apply to subsequent supplies acquired from the same connected person. [*SI 1987/1806, Art 8*].

Direct costs of in-house supplies

[69.28] It is not necessary to work out the costs of in-house supplies if all supplies included in margin scheme packages are liable to VAT at the same rate. In such a case the simplified calculation under **69.22** above must be used. Otherwise, the annual calculation under **69.19** above must include the direct costs incurred in making in-house supplies which are supplied with margin scheme supplies as part of a package.

The following are examples (not exhaustive) of costs which may be included.

Direct costs of supplying in-house passenger transport

[69.29] The direct costs of supplying in-house passenger transport are listed below.

General

- Depreciation on vehicles, aircraft, vessels (which the business or a member of its VAT group owns) calculated on the same basis as its audited accounts
- Rental or leasing of vehicles, aircraft or vessels (see **69.31** below as regards HP, leasing and finance charges)
- Crew/drivers costs (including employer's NIC)
- Subsistence paid to crew/drivers
- Fuel
- Insurance
- Repair and maintenance of vehicles, aircraft or vessels

Road or rail transport

- Garaging and parking
- Bridge and road tolls
- Ferry costs

- Road fund licences

Air transport

- Air Passenger Duty (APD)
- Landing fees

Cruises

- Berthing fees

Chartering an aircraft (see 69.10 above)

- Charter fee
- Catering charges
- Transfer journeys

Chartering a vessel (see 69.10 above)

- Charter fee
- 'Hotel'/domestic/catering staff

Only in-house passenger transport supplied with margin scheme supplies can be included in the TOMS calculation. If in-house transport is also used to supply passenger transport outside the TOMS (e.g. coach hire), the direct cost must be apportioned to take account of this, normally

- for road or rail transport, on a mileage basis;
- for air transport, based on hours flown; and
- for sea transport, on the basis of days used on types of supply.

If a business wishes to adopt any other basis for apportionment, it should submit its proposed method in writing to its local VAT Business Advice Centre in advance of when its year-end calculation/adjustment is due.

Direct costs of standard-rated hotel accommodation

[69.30] The direct costs of standard-rated hotel accommodation are listed below.

- Depreciation of buildings, fixtures and fittings (which the business or a member of its VAT group owns) calculated on the same basis as its audited accounts
- Catering purchases
- Heating and lighting
- Rates
- Building insurance
- Rental of equipment and furniture
- Repairs, maintenance and cleaning for which the business is liable
- Staff costs (including wages and employer's NI contributions)

Only costs relating to in-house accommodation supplied with margin scheme supplies can be included in the TOMS calculation. If premises are also used to provide accommodation outside the TOMS, the annual direct costs must be apportioned to take account of this, normally on the basis of number of guests/days booked for each type of supply.

If certain parts of the premises are not used specifically to provide accommodation (e.g. administrative offices, public bars, owner's private accommodation, etc.) costs relating to the entire premises (e.g. rates, insurance, light and heat) must be apportioned on the basis of floor area. Any other bases of apportionment must be agreed in writing with the local VAT Business Advice Centre in advance of when the year-end calculation/adjustment is due.

See also *The Devonshire Hotel (Torquay) Ltd* (VTD 14448) (TVC 63.14).

Sales of assets for which depreciation has been entered as an in-house cost

Where this occurs, an appropriate adjustment must be made to in-house costs in the year-end TOMS calculation for the year in which the sale takes place.

This adjustment is

- a reduction to the relevant in-house costs in respect of any profit made on disposal, or
- an increase to the relevant in-house costs in respect of a loss made on disposal

based on book values in the accounts.

(VAT Notice 709/5/16, paras 6.5, 7.4, 7.5, 7.7, 7.8, 7.10).

Indirect costs

[69.31] Indirect costs must not be included in any of the calculations. Examples of indirect costs include

- brochures
- advertising
- inspection trips made to research resorts, facilities, etc.
- office expenses (telephone, IT equipment, office stationery, rent, etc.)
- accountancy, legal and similar professional services
- hiring and employing representatives at airports and resorts (see **69.35** below)
- financial services including bank, credit card transation fees and foreign exchange charges
- HP, leasing and finance charges for the purchase of assets (including those used for making in-house supplies)
- market research
- commission paid to agents.

(VAT Notice 709/5/16, para 6.4).

Foreign currency purchases

[69.32] Note: the provisions of this paragraph have the force of law.

If any supplies bought for resale as TOMS supplies are billed in foreign currency, these should be converted into sterling at either

(i) the rate of exchange published in the Financial Times using the Federation of Tour Operators' base rate current at the time the supplies are costed by the person from whom the business has acquired the goods or services;

(ii) the commercial rate of exchange current at the time that the supplies in the brochure were costed;
(iii) the rate published in the Financial Times on the date that the business pays for the supplies;
(iv) the rate of exchange which was applicable to the purchase by the business of the foreign currency used to pay for the supplies; or
(v) the period rate of exchange published by HMRC for customs purposes in force at the time the business pays for the supplies.

Documentary evidence relating to the purchase must be kept to show which of the rates have been used. If method (i) or (ii) is used, the rate must be published in any brochure or leaflet in which the supplies are held out for sale.

Once a method has been chosen, HMRC may allow a different method but only from the start of a financial year and if written notification is given to them no later than the due date for rendering the first VAT return for that financial year.

(VAT Notice 709/5/16, paras 6.6, 13(TL2)).

Commission received for agency supplies arranged as part of a margin scheme package

[69.33] Where any commission received for agency supplies made by the business is readily identifiable, exclude from the TOMS calculation

- the commission received; and
- all monies paid for the supply arranged.

Where any commission is received which is not readily identifiable, include in the TOMS calculation

- the gross amount paid by the traveller; and
- the net amount paid to the principal.

(VAT Notice 709/5/16, para 6.7).

Hotel and travel insurance

[69.34] The way hotel or travel insurance is treated for VAT purposes depends upon the precise contractual arrangements and whether it is the tour operator or the traveller who is the insured person.

(a) Where *the insurance policy issued by the permitted insurer makes the traveller the insured person* (the normal case), there is a supply of insurance from the permitted insurer to the traveller. If the tour operator arranges for the insurance to be supplied by a named company to the traveller under such an arrangement, it is acting as an agent.
    - Where the commission received is readily identifiable, the full amount paid by the traveller for the insurance and the net premium passed on to the insurance company must be excluded from the TOMS calculations.
    - Where the commission received is not readily identifiable, values relating to the insurance must be included in the TOMS calculation (see **69.33** above).

- Where the insurance is offered 'free' as part of a package, the full amount paid by the traveller for the package must be included in the TOMS calculation. Any costs incurred in relation to such insurance must not be included in the TOMS calculation.

(b) Where *the tour operator enters into an agreement with a permitted insurer under which the tour operator is the insured person*, the insurer agrees to reimburse the tour operator in respect of any claims by travellers for delay compensation, medical costs, etc. This is an indirect cost and therefore outside the TOMS. If the tour operator passes on a charge for the insurance (including any Insurance Premium Tax) to the traveller, this should be included in the selling prices in the TOMS calculation.

(VAT Notice 709/5/16, para 6.8).

Representatives and guides

[69.35] The services of representatives at airports and resorts are not normally supplies in their own right and are therefore not regarded as in-house supplies. The costs incurred in providing these services should be treated as indirect costs for the purposes of the TOMS.

The specialist services of a guide, however, are often supplies in their own right. If the supply is made in-house, the place of supply and the liability depends on the exact nature of the service. See **69.10** above.

(VAT Notice 709/5/16, para 6.10).

Unforeseen costs

[69.36] Where it is necessary to buy in accommodation, transport, meals, etc. as a result of delays, breakdowns or other unforeseen circumstances, these costs should usually be treated as margin scheme supplies unless the cost of the additional items is

- ultimately met by someone else (e.g. an airline from whom air transport is bought in has agreed to meet any additional costs arising through flight delays) in which case the costs should be ignored in the TOMS calculation; or
- a direct cost of in-house supplies.

(VAT Notice 709/5/16, para 6.11).

Bad debt relief

[69.37] See **7 BAD DEBT RELIEF** generally for the rules for claiming bad debt relief and in particular **7.9** under which bad debt relief is restricted to a maximum of the VAT fraction of the profit margin.

The amount of VAT bad debt relief claimable is calculated by the formula

$$B \times s\,\% \times 1/6$$

where

B = the amount of the bad debt

s = the provisional percentage as calculated under **69.23** above for the financial year in which the supply is made

(VAT Notice 709/5/16, para 6.9).

Key points: TOMS

[69.38] Points to consider are as follows.

- An important advantage of the TOMS is that it avoids the need for many businesses selling travel services having to register for VAT in different EU member states. The scheme applies in relation to travel services enjoyed within the UK, EU and outside the EU.
- The main principle of the scheme is that output tax is only payable within the scheme based on the margin, i.e. difference between the buying and selling prices of travel services. Input tax cannot be reclaimed on any margin supplies but can be reclaimed on general overhead items.
- TOMS applies to any business that is involved in buying and selling travel services, e.g. a company that organises conferences that include hotel accommodation, rather than only to tour operators and travel agents. This is important to ensure competition is fair between different business entities involved in such supplies.
- Businesses that occasionally organise conferences, e.g. for members, can avoid being caught in the TOMS by taking care in how it organises and manages the supply of accommodation at the venue or in nearby hotels. It is important to take great care when doing this to achieve the best outcome.
- As far as VAT registration is concerned, the relevant figure for determining whether the turnover limits have been exceeded is the margin within a TOMS sale. This is different to the rules for a second-hand car dealer using a margin scheme where the key figure is the full value of the sale.
- The margin calculations for TOMS supplies can be very complex and require great attention to detail.

70

Trade Promotion Schemes

Introduction to trade promotion schemes

[70.1] A large number of trade promotion schemes exist where goods or services are given as rewards to retail customers (the public) or trade customers.

These include

- schemes where goods are linked in a promotion (see **70.4** to **70.7** below);
- schemes where vouchers, coupons, etc. are issued and later redeemed for cash (e.g. money-off coupons) or goods or services with or without further consideration (see **70.8** to **70.12** below);
- manufacturers' promotion schemes aimed at either the trade (see **70.15** below) or the public (see **70.16** below); and
- retail discount schemes (see **70.17** below).

The VAT consequences in many cases depend upon whether there has been a gift of goods or services and whether any non-monetary consideration has been given. These points are considered in **70.2** and **70.3** below.

Gifts and samples

Free gifts of goods for no consideration

[70.2] Where a business gives away goods, on which it is entitled to credit for input tax, without any monetary or non-monetary consideration (see **70.3** below), the VAT rules on gifts apply. If the cost of the goods, together with the cost of any other business gifts made to the same person in the same year, is £50 or less, no VAT is due. Otherwise, output tax must be accounted for on the price the person would have to pay (excluding VAT) at the time of supply, to purchase goods identical to the goods concerned, i.e. normally their cost value. See **48.5 OUTPUT TAX** for further details.

(VAT Notice 700/7/12, paras 2.1, 2.3).

Free provision of services

Free provision of own services (e.g. free beauty treatment) is generally not a taxable supply. There is no restriction on input tax recovery and no output tax is due. However, if the supply makes use of goods (e.g. cosmetics) which cost more than £50, output tax may be due as above.

Free provision of bought-in services (e.g. beauty treatment provided by another business) will, in HMRC's view, give rise to a VAT liability under *SI 1993/1507*. See **48.6 OUTPUT TAX**. If, however, services are merely paid for by the business but supplied directly by a third party to the customer, the business makes no supply for VAT purposes but cannot deduct any VAT charged by the provider of the services (although it may be claimable by the customer).

(VAT Notice 700/7/12, para 3.1).

See, however, *HMRC v Associated Newspapers Ltd* [2015] UKUT 641 (TCC) (TVC 62.607), in which the First-tier and Upper Tribunals both concluded that the 'private use' of the recipient of a promotional service (a voucher) was not enough to engage *SI 1993/1507*. The business had used the voucher only for business purposes (promoting sales of newspapers), and the self-supply charge did not apply. This was confirmed by the Court of Appeal. HMRC and the taxpayer have been refused leave to appeal to the Supreme Court. The Court of Appeal's decision is now final and businesses should consider the VAT treatment of any vouchers given away free of charge to customers, where this is done for a business purpose.

Samples

A sample is a specimen of a product which is intended to promote the sales of that product and which allows the characteristics and qualities of that product to be assessed without resulting in final consumption, other than where final consumption is inherent in such promotional transactions. Free samples of products provided to individuals for marketing purposes are not liable to VAT.

An example of an item that would not qualify as a sample is a finished item taken from a discontinued line. Although the business may intend it to demonstrate the type and standard of that particular range, it could not promote sales of that product line since it is no longer available. Another example is a product provided in quantities greater than necessary for its characteristics and qualities to be assessed. So, for example, if a waiter in a restaurant pours a small glass of wine as a taster it would qualify as a sample. But if the restaurant provided a regular customer with a bottle of wine, this would not meet the sample criteria.

If a business is registered for VAT and is given samples which it sells for a consideration, then output tax is due on the sale provided the goods are liable to a positive rate of VAT.

(VAT Notice 700/7/12, para 4).

Non-monetary consideration

[70.3] The VAT treatment of discounts and reward goods/services depends upon whether any consideration is given by the recipient.

Where payment is totally in money, that is the consideration. However, it is also possible to have non-monetary consideration where the customer agrees to do something (or not to do it) in return for a supply of goods or services. Where *any* non-monetary consideration is given, however small, VAT is due on that consideration. The value of the consideration is taken to be such amount in money as, with the addition of the VAT, is equivalent to the consideration. [*VATA 1994, s 19(3)*]. Consideration has to be valued from the point of view of the person receiving that consideration, i.e. the person making the supply: how much is the non-monetary 'thing received' worth to the supplier? The two cases below show two different approaches to answering this question.

An example of non-monetary consideration is where a business offers incentive goods to its customer, either free or at a lower price, on condition that the customer provides it with a service in return. In agreeing to provide this service the customer is providing non-monetary consideration, the value of which is equivalent to the price, or reduction in price, of the goods. In *Empire Stores Ltd v C & E Commrs, ECJ Case C–33/93*, [1994] STC 623 (TVC 22.256) a company sold goods by mail order and offered new customers, and existing customers who introduced new customers, certain goods free of charge as inducements. The CJEU ruled that the goods in question were supplied to the customers in consideration for a service, namely the introduction of a new customer, and not in return for the purchase by the new customer of goods from the catalogue. The value of the goods was the amount that the company was prepared to spend to get the introduction, i.e. the cost of the articles to the company.

By contrast, in *Naturally Yours Cosmetics Ltd v C & E Commrs (No 2), ECJ Case 230/87*, [1988] STC 879 (TVC 22.256), the non-monetary consideration for agents' services was in the form of a discount on goods that were in the supplier's cosmetics catalogue. The court held that the parties had effectively agreed the value of the service between them: it was the difference between what the agent actually had to pay, and the amount that they would have normally had to pay – i.e. the discount. The company had to account for output tax on the whole of the normal retail price, as it had received that amount in a combination of money and services.

HMRC, however, accept that certain acts, including the following, are insignificant for these purposes and do not constitute non-monetary consideration.

(a) Having to buy one article either to get
  - another article free at the same time; or
  - a discount voucher redeemable against a further purchase; or
  - a lottery ticket, etc.

(b) Employees having to exceed certain sales levels or sell most articles in a month, or other such schemes.

(c) The act of using an in-house credit card.

(d) Entering a free prize draw.

(e) Having to complete a slogan or give a recipe, etc. on entry to a competition.

(f) A gift to an existing customer for their buying more than a certain amount.

In circumstances such as these, the normal rules for gifts set out in **70.2** above apply.

(VAT Notice 700/7/12, para 5).

Goods linked in a promotion

[70.4] Goods (or goods and services) are sometimes offered together in one promotion for a single price (e.g. coffee and chocolate biscuits or a washing machine and iron). Alternatively, a number of articles may be sold in a multibuy offer, e.g.

- 'buy 1 get 1 free';
- 'buy three for the price of two'; or
- 'buy a sofa and get a free foot stool'.

This is a multiple supply and the amount paid covers all the goods or services offered.

If the items offered are subject to VAT at different rates, apportionment will normally be required. See **48.3 OUTPUT TAX**. However, for certain small items linked with a major item which is liable to VAT at a different rate, the linked supplies concession in **70.7** below may apply.

(VAT Notice 700/7/12, para 6.1).

If the offer is made to other VAT-registered traders, see also the trade reward scheme under **70.15** below.

Linked goods schemes

[70.5] Theses are promotion schemes where a minor article is linked (not necessarily physically) with a main article (either goods or services) and sold with it at a single price. An example would be an empty plastic storage jar attached to a box of cereals. Where the articles are liable to VAT at the same rate, no problem arises but where they are liable at different rates, the price should normally be apportioned (see **48.3 OUTPUT TAX**). However, by concession, VAT can be accounted for on the minor article at the same rate as the main article (so that the selling price need not be apportioned) provided the following conditions are satisfied.

(a) The minor article is not charged to the customer at a separate price.
(b) The minor article costs no more than
   (i) 20% of the total cost (excluding VAT) of the combined supply; and
   (ii) £1 (excluding VAT) if included with goods intended for retail sale or £5 (excluding VAT) otherwise.

Where the conditions are met, the articles need not be detailed separately on the invoice.

In all other circumstances where a VAT invoice has to be issued, details of the minor article must be shown separately.

See also **25.13 FOOD** for mixtures and assortments of food and **55.18 PRINTED MATTER, ETC.** for promotional items in magazines.

(VAT Notice 700/7/12, para 6.2; VAT Notice 48, ESC 3.7).

Example

A musical CD is sold by a retail store. The CD includes a well written leaflet that gives historical information about the composer and his work. Although the leaflet is zero-rated as a supply of printed matter, it is incidental to the main supply of the standard-rated CD and output tax is therefore due on the full selling price of the goods.

Accounting for linked supplies under retail schemes

[70.6] VAT must be accounted for as follows.

(a) *Point of Sale scheme and Direct Calculation Schemes 1 and 2.* Treatment depends upon whether the two articles are liable to VAT at the same rate or different rates.
   (i) If both articles are liable at the same rate of VAT, there are no additional rules to follow.
   (ii) If the articles are liable at different rates of VAT, subject to the linked supplies concession in **70.5** above, the selling price must be apportioned either on the basis in **48.3 OUTPUT TAX** or, where the goods have been linked by the manufacturer, in accordance with the information shown on the supplier's invoice.
   Where apportionment is required, the amount allocated to reduced rate or zero-rated goods must be separated from standard-rated takings before carrying out the scheme calculation.
(b) *Apportionment Schemes 1 and 2.* Any contribution from the supplier or sponsor must be included in daily gross takings.

Under Apportionment Scheme 1, no adjustment to purchases is required.

Under Apportionment Scheme 2, expected selling prices (ESPs) must also be adjusted as follows.

- No adjustment is required for a full contribution. Where only partial contribution is received, ESPs for the appropriate goods must be adjusted to the extent of the amount not supported by the supplier or sponsor. Where no contribution is received, an appropriate adjustment must be made to the ESPs of the promotion goods.
- If the promotion goods are liable to VAT at different rates, the ESPs must be apportioned either on the basis in **48.3 OUTPUT TAX** or, where the goods have been linked by the manufacturer, in accordance with the information shown on the supplier's invoice.

  Where the linked supplies concession under **70.5** above is used, the record of purchases or ESPs of the promotion goods must be adjusted as appropriate.

(c) *Contributions from manufacturers or joint promoters.* Whichever scheme is used, strictly speaking, where the retailer receives a contribution from a manufacturer or joint sponsor representing partial payment for goods supplied to a customer, the retailer should account for this in the period the goods are supplied. However, by concession, the retailer may account for such contributions in the period they are received. If the manufacturer or joint sponsor makes any payment (e.g. towards advertising) this must be treated as consideration for a separate supply of services and dealt with outside the retail scheme.

(d) *Correcting ESPs.* Under Direct Calculation Schemes 1 and 2,

- if a contribution is received from a manufacturer or joint promoter for the class of goods which the retailer has marked up in the retail scheme, no ESP adjustment should be made if the supplier or sponsor makes a full contribution. If a partial contribution is received, ESPs for the appropriate goods should be adjusted to the extent of the amount *not* supported by the sponsor or manufacturer.
- Where no contribution is received from the manufacturer or sponsor, an appropriate adjustment must be made to the ESPs of the promotion goods.

(VAT Notice 727/3/13, para 7.6; VAT Notice 727/4/13, para 8.5; VAT Notice 727/5/13, para 7.5, all of which have the force of law).

Multisave promotions where the manufacturer subsidises the promotion

[70.7] In some multisave promotions of the 'buy 2, get a third free' type, manufacturers make payments to retailers towards the costs of the promotions. In such cases, following the CJEU decision in *Elida Gibbs Ltd v C & E Commrs, ECJ Case C–317/94*, [1996] STC 1387 (TVC 22.252), manufacturers can reduce their output tax by the amount paid to the retailer to support the promotion where it relates to products liable to VAT at the standard rate. The payments received by the retailer are further consideration for the supply to the customer upon which VAT is due and the amounts received should be included within retail scheme takings figures.

In *Elida Gibbs* the company manufactured toiletries and sold the products to both retailers and wholesalers. To promote retail sales, it

- issued money-off coupons which customers could present to a retailer in part payment for Elida Gibbs products and for which retailers sought reimbursement direct from the company; and
- printed cashback coupons directly onto the packaging of its products which, subject to meeting conditions, entitled any consumer to a cash refund direct from Elida Gibbs.

The company claimed a repayment of output tax which it had previously accounted for contending that the reimbursement of money-off coupons to retailers and the cashback payments to consumers constituted a retrospective discount which reduced the consideration for its supplies. The CJEU agreed, holding that the discounts allowed by the manufacturer were deductible but credit notes should not be issued to customers. This left the VAT position of wholesalers and retailers unchanged and maintained the balance of VAT due from them. Retailers should account for output tax on payments received from manufacturers as well as money paid by customers. This decision was subsequently applied in *EC Commission v Federal Republic of Germany, ECJ Case C–427/98*, [2003] STC 301 (TVC 22.259). See also *Yorkshire Co-Operatives Ltd v C & E Commrs, ECJ Case C–398/99*, [2003] STC 234 (TVC 22.267). However, if a VAT-registered customer requests a VAT invoice in respect of purchases made using money-off vouchers, this should be based only on the amount paid by the customer. This achieves fiscal neutrality as required by the judgment.

There may be cases where the manufacturer pays the retailer for providing a service, for example, in undertaking to advertise the promotion and/or products. In such cases, the retailer must charge the manufacturer VAT at the standard rate which is the input tax for the manufacturer subject to the normal rules.

(VAT Notice 700/7/12, para 6.3).

Money-off coupons

[70.8] Money-off coupons are coupons used to offer to the public a reduction in the price of a future purchase. They can be issued in a variety of ways, for example

- given on the purchase of a particular item;
- given on the purchase of goods to a specified value;
- sent by mailshot or electronic means; or
- published as cut-out coupons in newspapers.

They may be issued by retailers under their own schemes or by manufacturers. In either case, it does not matter whether the coupon is attached to a product or not.

Issue of money-off coupons

In most cases, money-off coupons are regarded as issued for no payment (consideration). Even if the issue is dependent upon the purchase of goods, provided the goods are sold at their normal price, no VAT is due on their issue.

Sale of money-off coupons

Where a business sells money-off coupons, discount coupons or discount cards entitling the holder to discounts from either that business or others, then this is a standard-rated supply and the business is required to account for VAT.

Redemption of money-off coupons

Where a business uses a retail scheme, it should only include in its daily gross takings

- any additional payment received when the customer redeems the coupon; and
- any further payment which is due from any other source (e.g. from the manufacturer).

Where no retail scheme is in operation, VAT is due on the money received from the customer and the manufacturer (if any) under the normal time of supply rules.

See *Boots Co plc v C & E Commrs, ECJ Case 126/88*, [1990] STC 387 (TVC 22.278) confirming that money-off coupons are not to be treated as consideration when used to buy other goods but are simply evidence of entitlement to discount.

Handling charges

If a charge is made for handling, promoting or advertising coupons, this represents consideration for a supply of services. The supply is taxable. However, this does not apply where, after the coupon has been redeemed, it is presented to a third party to be exchanged for money. At that stage it becomes a security for money and any charges made for handling the coupons after this point are exempt.

(VAT Notice 700/7/12, para 7).

Face value vouchers

[70.9] A '*face value voucher*' means a token, stamp or voucher (whether in physical or electronic form) that represents a right to receive goods or services to the value of an amount stated on it or recorded in it and '*face value*' means the amount stated on such a voucher. [*VATA 1994, Sch 10A para 1*]. Examples include gift vouchers, telephone cards, book tokens, electronic top-up cards and postage stamps. In *Leisure Pass Group Ltd (No 2)* (VTD 20910) (TVC 67.180), the tribunal decided that the inclusion of a set daily maximum value shown on the face of leisure passes meant that the passes qualified as face value vouchers.

Single purpose vouchers

[70.10] Following the CJEU decision in the case of *Lebara Ltd, ECJ Case C–520/10* [2012] STC 1536 (TVC 22.98), 'single purpose vouchers' were removed from the treatment of face value vouchers described in **70.11** below. Single purpose vouchers are face value vouchers that represent a right to receive only one type of goods or services which are subject to a single rate of VAT. They are taxed when they are issued. This affects all such vouchers, whether credit, retailer or other types of voucher. Tax is also due on each subsequent sale of the voucher, subject to the usual rules on liability and place of supply.

[*VATA 1994, Sch 10A, para 7A*.] (HMRC Brief 12/12.)

Lunar Missions Ltd [2018] UKFTT 7 (TC) (TC06286) (TVC 67.184A) concerned whether a supply of a single purpose voucher or face value voucher was being made. In this case, Lunar Missions Limited (LM) planned to take an unmanned robotic module to the south pole of the moon. It raised funds using a crowdfunding platform and in exchange for the pledge made by the funder, LM reserved space in the time capsule which could either be physical or digital space. LM sent the pledgor a voucher that equalled the amount pledged although LM was unable to provide precise information on how much space the voucher would buy. The crowdfunding target was £600,000 to be raised by the end of 2014 and the launch was planned for 2024 although LM made it clear on its crowdfunding page that there were lots of uncertainties and no guarantees. LM raised over £600,000 by 16 December 2014 and HMRC considered that LM should have been VAT registered from that date. LM disputed this on the basis that it considered that it had no intention to make taxable supplies when it received the funding. However, when it submitted its appeal, LM conceded that there is a taxable supply in the form of rewards that are provided to those who made a pledge. The tribunal was asked to consider whether the sums received were advance payments or consideration for supply of a face value voucher. If the payments were consideration for a supply of a face value voucher, were those vouchers single purpose vouchers. The tribunal concluded that due to the significant amount of uncertainty regarding what would be supplied, the payments could not be treated as advance payments for a supply of services. The First-tier Tribunal held single purpose vouchers were supplied as they could only be redeemed for one purpose, the supply of space in the capsule. LM was liable to be registered from 16 December 2014.

Issue of face value vouchers

[70.11] The *issue* of a face value voucher, or any subsequent supply of it, is treated as a supply of services for the purposes of *VATA 1994*. [*VATA 1994, Sch 10A para* 2]. Once it is 'issued' to a third party in return for payment, it is given, or has acquired, a value and is capable of being used to receive goods or services. (VAT Notice 700/7/12, para 8.2). This allows the *sale* of the voucher to be equated to the underlying supply so that, if it is known that the voucher has been redeemed for, say, zero-rated goods or services, then an intermediate supplier in the supply chain can make an adjustment to reflect the liability of the final supply (see below).

The legislation recognises four categories of face value vouchers.

(a) 'Credit vouchers'

I.e. face value vouchers issued by a person who

- is not a person from whom goods or services may be obtained by the use of the voucher, and
- undertakes to give complete or partial reimbursement to any such person from whom goods or services are so obtained.

Credit vouchers are typically, therefore, gift vouchers that are administered by trade bodies or associations or that can be redeemed at a number of different retailers.

The consideration for *any* supply of a credit voucher (including by any intermediate supplier) is disregarded for VAT purposes unless the consideration exceeds the face value of the voucher (the redeemer accounts for VAT at the time the voucher is redeemed, but to qualify for this treatment the redeemer must account for VAT on the full face value).

The previous sentence does not apply if any of the persons from whom goods or services are obtained by the use of the voucher fails to account for any of the VAT due on the supply of those goods or services to the person using the voucher to obtain them. Where it can be shown that the consumer paid a lesser amount for the voucher than its face value, then VAT on redemption can be based on the lesser amount, provided the redeemer receives no more for the voucher than the lower amount.

HMRC are allowed to collect VAT from any person selling credit vouchers, including the issuer and subsequent intermediaries, where the redeemer of the voucher fails to account for any VAT due. HMRC have undertaken only to enforce these provisions in the event of a deliberate attempt to avoid paying any VAT due. In cases of genuine error that can be corrected or insolvency, HMRC will not require the issuer to account for the VAT due and will seek to collect it from the redeemer (provided that the issuer has passed the funds to the redeemer).

[*VATA 1994, Sch 10A para 3*]. (VAT Notice 700/7/12, paras 8.4, 8.5).

(b) 'Retailer vouchers'

These are face value vouchers issued by a person

- from whom goods or services may be obtained by the use of the voucher, and
- who, if there are other persons from whom goods or services may be obtained by the use of the voucher, undertakes to give complete or partial reimbursement to those from whom goods or services are so obtained.

Typical examples of retail vouchers are gift vouchers issued and redeemed by a high street retailer.

The consideration for the *issue* of a retailer voucher is disregarded for VAT purposes unless the consideration exceeds the face value of the voucher (VAT is accounted for at the time the voucher is redeemed on the value for which it was initially sold). This disregarding does not apply if the voucher is used to obtain goods or services from a person other than the issuer and that person fails to account for any of the VAT due on the supply of those goods or services to the person using the voucher to obtain them.

Any supply of a retailer voucher, subsequent to the first supply by the issuer, is treated in the same way as the supply of a voucher under (*d*) below.

Where a retailer voucher can be used to obtain goods or services from a third party, it is the responsibility of that third party to account for VAT in respect of those goods or services.

HMRC are allowed to collect any VAT due from the person who first sold the voucher (i.e. the issuer) in the event that the redeemer of the voucher fails to account for any VAT due. HMRC have undertaken only to enforce these provisions in the event of a deliberate attempt to avoid paying any VAT due. In cases of genuine error or insolvency, HMRC will not require the issuer to account for the VAT due and will seek to collect it from the redeemer (provided that the issuer has passed the funds to the redeemer).

[*VATA 1994, Sch 10A para 4*]. (VAT Notice 700/7/12, paras 8.6, 8.7).

See *HMRC v Associated Newspapers Ltd* [2015] UKUT 641 (TCC) (TVC 62.607) for examination of the problems caused by the rules on retailer vouchers. The disregarding of the issue of the voucher by the retailer means that the immediate recipient cannot claim a deduction for input tax on the amount paid to the retailer. Nevertheless, that person is required to account for output tax on any amount received on a subsequent sale. It appeared from the case that HMRC operated an informal margin scheme in this circumstance, effectively allowing a deduction for intermediaries selling vouchers, but the lawfulness of this approach was questioned by the First-tier Tribunal judge.

(c) Postage stamps

The consideration for the supply of a postage stamp is disregarded for VAT purposes unless the consideration exceeds the face value of the stamp (in which case the VAT is due on the excess). [*VATA 1994, Sch 10A para 5*].

Postage stamps are redeemed for an exempt supply of postal services. These provision means that they can pass from the issuer through any intermediate suppliers and on to the final customer without VAT being charged. (VAT Notice 700/7/12, para 8.14).

(d) Other kinds of face value voucher

A supply of a face value voucher that does not fall within (*a*)–(*c*) above (a supply by an intermediate supplier) is, subject to below, standard-rated.

An example falling within this category would be where a high street retailer sells gift vouchers to an intermediate supplier. The onward sale of the vouchers by the intermediate supplier is subject to VAT.

VAT need not be charged at the standard rate where one of the following applies.

- Where the voucher is one that can *only* be used to obtain goods or services in one particular non-standard rate category (i.e. reduced-rated, zero-rated or exempt and other non-taxable supplies), the supply of the voucher falls in that category. This has the effect of ensuring that such a voucher can pass through the supply chain at that non-standard rate. In practice, examples of this type of voucher are likely to be limited as vouchers that can be redeemed against non-standard-rated goods and services can often also be redeemed against standard-rated goods or services.

- Where the voucher *is* used to obtain goods or services all of which fall in one particular non-standard rate category (i.e. reduced-rated, zero-rated or exempt and other non-taxable supplies), the supply of the voucher falls in that category. This has the effect of allowing intermediate suppliers in the supply chain to make an adjustment to reflect the liability of the final supply (see below).
- Where the voucher is used to obtain goods or services in a number of different rate categories (i.e. any combination of standard-rated, reduced-rated, zero-rated or exempt and other non-taxable supplies), the supply of the voucher falls within those different categories and the value of each supply must be determined on a just and reasonable basis. This has the effect of allowing intermediate suppliers in the supply chain to make an adjustment to reflect the liability of the final supplies, to be apportioned between the different rate categories.

[*VATA 1994, Sch 10A para 6*].

Vouchers supplied free with other goods or services

Where

- a face-value voucher (other than a postage stamp) and other goods or services are supplied to the same person in a composite transaction, and
- the total consideration for the supplies is no different, or not significantly different, from what it would be if the voucher were not supplied,

the supply of the voucher is treated as being made for no consideration. This is an anti-avoidance provision to prevent businesses from artificially reducing the consideration for goods or services by issuing a face value voucher which is unlikely to be redeemed.

> ***Examples***
>
> An hotel issues a voucher to a customer when the customer settles his bill for staying. The customer does not have the option of a price reduction in lieu of the voucher and very few customers ever redeem their vouchers.
>
> A retailer gives customers a face value voucher on every purchase made over a certain amount. Customers do not have the option of a price reduction in lieu of the voucher and the voucher has a number of restrictions which are likely to limit the number of customers who eventually redeem the voucher.
>
> A retailer sells a mobile phone boxed with a telephone card. The telephone card is a face value voucher. The customer does not have the option of refusing the telephone card for a reduction in the price of the phone.

[*VATA 1994, Sch 10A para 7*]. (VAT Notice 700/7/12, paras 8.12, 8.13).

Invoicing and adjustments

Issuers of face value vouchers, which are not credit vouchers (see (*a*) above), who redeem them for goods or services that are liable to VAT must issue a full VAT invoice if the vouchers are sold to a VAT-registered intermediate supplier. In the case of retailer vouchers, the issuer who redeems the voucher does not need to account for VAT until the voucher is redeemed, HMRC suggest that the invoice is annotated with the words: 'The issuer of the voucher will account for output tax under the face value voucher provisions in Schedule 10A VAT Act 1994'.

Intermediate suppliers of face value vouchers, other than credit vouchers, must account for VAT on the sale of the vouchers at the time they are sold. A full VAT invoice must be issued to any further intermediate supplier in the supply chain. They, in turn, are entitled to recover input tax, subject to the normal requirements. If it is known that the vouchers have been redeemed for zero-rated, reduced-rated or exempt and other non-taxable goods or services, then the intermediate supplier can make an adjustment to both the output tax and the input tax to reflect the liability of the final supply. Where intermediate suppliers know *in advance* that vouchers can be redeemed for zero-rated, reduced-rated or exempt and other non-taxable goods or services, they may use a percentage split from the outset and avoid the need to make later adjustments.

Information regarding any split in liability can only be provided by the issuer who redeems the vouchers. In order to avoid the need to track individual vouchers, redeemers can base adjustment figures on retail scheme percentages or other global calculations, providing the result is fair and reasonable. If the redeemer chooses to make this information available to intermediate suppliers, they may include the percentage split on any VAT invoice they issue to an intermediate supplier. This split should be quoted on any further VAT invoices issued by intermediate suppliers in the supply chain.

(VAT Notice 700/7/12, para 8.9).

Intermediate suppliers using retail schemes

Whether an intermediate supplier under (*d*) above can include sales of face value vouchers within its retail scheme depends on the retail scheme used.

- Under the Point of Sale scheme, sales of face value vouchers should be included in daily gross takings at the appropriate rate of VAT.
- Under an apportionment scheme, output tax on the sale of vouchers should be accounted for outside the retail scheme.
- Under a direct calculation scheme, intermediate suppliers may be able to include the sale of vouchers depending on the minority goods they mark up and the rate of VAT due when the vouchers are redeemed. See **61.17** and **61.18 RETAIL SCHEMES.**
- Intermediate suppliers using a bespoke scheme must agree with HMRC a fair and reasonable method for accounting for output tax on the sale of face value vouchers.

(VAT Notice 700/7/12, para 8.11).

Top-up cards with no face value

Top-up vouchers and cards (e.g. telephone cards which allow the customer to add credit to their account) share many similarities to face value vouchers and are now treated in the same manner as face value vouchers. Therefore, issuers of top-up cards who redeem them for goods or services can account for VAT when the top-up is redeemed against goods or services. See Business Brief 29/03 and 18/04 for HMRC's view of the VAT treatment of phone cards supplied to a UK distributor by an issuer in another EU member state. This view has subsequently been supported by the Court of Appeal in *R (oao IDT Card Services Ireland Ltd) v HMRC*, CA [2006] STC 1252 (TVC 67.182).

Face value vouchers given away for no consideration

Where face value vouchers are purchased by businesses in order to be given away for no consideration, (e.g. under a promotions scheme), the VAT incurred is claimable as input tax (subject to the normal rules). In HMRC's view, output tax is due under *SI 1993/1507* at the time the vouchers are given away (see **48.6 OUTPUT TAX**). The sum due as output tax will be equal to the sum treated as input tax. (VAT Notice 700/7/12, para 8.13).

See, however, *HMRC v Associated Newspapers Ltd* [2015] UKUT 641 (TCC) (TVC 62.607), in which the Upper Tribunals both concluded that the 'private use' of the recipient of a promotional service (a voucher) was not enough to engage *SI 1993/1507*. The business had used the voucher only for business purposes (promoting sales of newspapers), and the self-supply charge did not apply. On the other hand, where the company had acquired the voucher directly on issue from the retailer, the disregarding of that transaction meant that there was no input tax to claim. The Court of Appeal upheld this decision. HMRC and the taxpayer have been refused leave to appeal to the Supreme Court. The Court of Appeal's decision is now final and businesses should consider the VAT treatment of any vouchers given away free of charge to customers, where this is done for a business purpose.

Treatment of coupons and vouchers under retail schemes

[70.12] The VAT treatment under a retail scheme depends upon whether the promotion is funded solely by the retailer or by (or together with) a third party such as the manufacturer.

Discount vouchers

Where discount vouchers are taken as part payment, only the money received from the customer should be included in daily gross takings. If the retailer subsequently receives further payment for the voucher from another source, this payment must be included in daily gross takings. Strictly speaking, the retailer should account for this further payment in the period the goods are supplied. However, by concession, the retailer may account for such contributions in the period they are received.

Any charges by the retailer to the manufacturer for handling the vouchers is payment for an exempt supply and must be excluded from daily gross takings.

Vouchers—general

The following provisions apply to vouchers issued with no value/amounts and which are redeemable for whole items.

- *Vouchers issued by the retailer to customers making a specific purchase or purchases.* No VAT is due upon issue and no further VAT is due when the voucher is used by the customer to obtain the reward goods. Under Apportionment Scheme 2 and Direct Calculation Schemes 1 and 2, records of expected selling prices must be adjusted for the reward goods.
- *Vouchers issued freely by the retailer.* No VAT is due upon issue. When redeemed for goods, the rules in **70.2** above apply. See **61.9**(4) **RETAIL SCHEMES** for the scheme adjustments where goods from normal stock are supplied as gifts.
- *Vouchers issued by another person (e.g. a manufacturer) but redeemed by the retailer.* These are likely to be subject to the terms and conditions of that person's promotion. For example, if the retailer is given certain stocks to give away on behalf of that person, these stocks must not be included in the retail scheme calculations.

See **61.9**(31) **RETAIL SCHEMES** for sale of discount vouchers.

If such vouchers are redeemed for cash, the cash payment is outside the scope of VAT and daily gross takings must not be altered for the cash paid.

(VAT Notice 727/3/13, paras 7.1–7.5; VAT Notice 727/4/13, paras 8.1–8.4; VAT Notice 727/5/13, paras 7.1–7.4, all of which have the force of law).

Cash back schemes

[70.13] The term 'cash back' refers to a payment made by a manufacturer directly, or through a recovery agency, to the customer of a wholesaler or retailer. Manufacturers discount schemes, volume bonuses and other terms may also be used. Payments to trade customers are often in recognition of the volume of purchases. Payments to the public are normally in respect of individual, product-specific, promotions. Because these payments occur outside the direct supply chain credit notes cannot be used. Manufacturers providing cash backs are entitled to reduce the VAT accounted for on their sales, provided they charged and accounted for VAT on the original supply.

Where a VAT-registered business receives a cash back, it reduces the taxable value of the purchase and so the business must reduce its input tax accordingly. Any cash back payment from manufacturer to customer, that does not affect the wholesaler, does not require the wholesaler to make any VAT adjustment.

Cross-border cash backs

Where cash backs are paid between businesses in different EU member states, no VAT adjustments should be made. This means that

- where a UK manufacturer pays a cash back to a recipient in another EU member state, the manufacturer cannot reduce their output tax;
- where a UK recipient receives a cash back from a manufacturer in another EU member state, no input tax reduction is required by the recipient.

Changes of liability in the supply chain

There are circumstances where the VAT liability of the goods changes in the supply chain. Where the cash back relates to goods that were supplied VAT-free to the person receiving the cash back, no adjustments can be made by the manufacturer. For example, a charity buys goods zero-rated from a wholesaler, but which were standard-rated for VAT when supplied by the manufacturer. In that case the manufacturer cannot reduce its output tax if it pays a cash back to the charity.

Intermediaries for telecommunications services

An intermediary arranges for a customer to be signed up with a telecommunications provider and, as an incentive, the intermediary provides line rental reimbursement to the customer after a period of time. The customer produces bills as evidence and the intermediary provides a cash back. As the intermediary is not providing the phone service, the cash back cannot be treated as reducing the consideration payable by the customer for that service. The intermediary cannot make any VAT adjustments in these circumstances. The payment is an inducement and does not reduce the consideration paid by the customer to the intermediary.

(VAT Notice 700/7/12, para 9).

Loyalty schemes

[70.14] Under some schemes, purchases from a business are linked to a reward, or reduction in price on subsequent purchases, by the issue of points. In some cases the reward may be provided by the original supplier. In other schemes they may be obtained from a third party who is contracted to provide the rewards for which they receive payment from the original supplier or from a scheme promoter. These schemes are commonly used not only by retail outlets, but also by manufacturers and other suppliers to encourage continued customer loyalty.

Example

A typical retail example is a scheme where members of the public or businesses can register as 'collectors'. They accumulate points on qualifying purchases of goods or services and subsequently redeem the points for rewards. These rewards can be either goods or services and may be obtained

- directly in return for the points;
- for vouchers previously exchanged for the points;
- by a combination of points and cash paid by the collector.

More complex loyalty schemes may involve a promotion business running the points scheme. This can result in multiple sponsors, multiple reward suppliers and some sponsors that are also reward suppliers.

Payments to third party reward suppliers

Payments made by a business to a third party reward supplier usually represent third party consideration for supplies made by the reward supplier to the collector. Any VAT charged by the reward supplier cannot therefore be reclaimed as input tax by the paying business as the supply is to the collector. The reward supplier should account for VAT on goods and services supplied to the collector in the usual way. The consideration will typically be the total of anything in the way of payment received from the collector, plus any consideration received from the sponsor supplier, manufacturer, or promoter.

Points schemes

Where a collector exchanges points for face value vouchers the VAT treatment is described in **70.12** above. A business's points scheme may allow customers to donate points to schools or other institutions. The schools, and so on, then redeem them with the business for goods which it supplies free of charge. Where this happens, VAT should be accounted for as described in **70.2** above.

Points given to customer's employees

A business may run a promotion to reward its customer's employees, e.g. the staff of a retailer to whom the business makes supplies. When the staff redeem points with the business this results in it making free supplies of goods or services, see **70.2** above.

Loyalty discount cards

Retailers may provide loyalty cards free of charge to customers allowing them to purchase further goods and services at a reduced price. In these circumstances only the amount of consideration actually received by the retailer is the taxable amount on which VAT is required to be accounted for.

Promoters who are a separate entity to supplier or redeemer

This applies where the promoter of a reward scheme is a separate entity to the supplier who issues points with primary purchases. Any charge made by the promoter to the supplier for participation in the scheme represents consideration for a taxable supply. This applies whether the charge equals the value of points issued, or if another basis of charging is used. VAT must be accounted for by the promoter. In these circumstances the promoter may reimburse third party reward suppliers for the value of points redeemed in supplying rewards to collectors.

Supplies of rewards partly or wholly for points

If a business is a reward supplier in a loyalty scheme, the supply of the reward is from the business to the collector presenting the points. Where consideration is provided by the collector, in addition to points, or by a third party, VAT must be accounted for by the business based on the total consideration received. Where a business supplies goods wholly for points and receives no payment either from the collector or a third party then it will need to consider the business gifts rules as described in **70.2** above.

(VAT Notice 700/7/12, para 10).

Case law

In *Kuwait Petroleum (GB) Ltd v C & E Commrs, ECJ Case C–48/97*, [1999] STC 488 (TVC 22.171), the company ran a promotion scheme under which customers were offered vouchers with purchases of fuel. Whether or not customers accepted the vouchers, the price of fuel was the same. The vouchers could be redeemed for goods ('reward goods') or occasionally services without further payment. The CJEU held that the amounts paid by customers were entirely attributable to their original purchases and no part of the payments could be attributed to the supply of reward goods. The reward goods should therefore be treated as gifts and taxed accordingly. This was subsequently confirmed in the UK courts in *Kuwait Petroleum (GB) Ltd v C & E Commrs*, Ch D [2001] STC 62 (TVC 22.172).

In *HMRC v Aimia Coalition Loyalty UK Ltd (aka Loyalty Management UK Ltd)*, L operated a points scheme in which a customer, purchasing goods or services from a participating retailer, received points which could be redeemed for 'rewards' from certain suppliers ('redeemers'). L paid the redeemers for these rewards and reclaimed input tax. HMRC rejected the claim on the basis that the rewards were supplied to the customers, not L. The Court of Appeal held that the redeemer made a supply of rewards to the customer. But the redeemer also made a supply of redemption services to L, in respect of which L was entitled to input tax credit ([2008] STC 59). The House of Lords referred the case to the CJEU, which ruled that L's payment to the redeemer was third party consideration for a supply by the redeemer to the customer, although payment might also include consideration for a separate supply of services (a question for the national court to decide) ([2010] STC 2651 (TVC 22.162)). The Supreme Court upheld the Court of Appeal decision in favour of L. The Supreme Court held that VAT should be chargeable on L's taxable supplies only after deduction of the VAT borne by L's necessary costs. This included the cost of securing that goods and services were provided to collectors in exchange for their points, i.e. the payments made by L to the redeemers. Therefore L should be authorised to deduct from the VAT for which it is accountable the VAT charged by the redeemers, so that it accounted for VAT only on the added value for which it was responsible ([2013] STC 784 (TVC 22.163)).

In *Tesco Freetime Ltd and another* [2017] UKFTT 614 (TC) (TC06050) (TVC 22.168), the Tesco group of companies operate the Tesco Clubcard programme which enables members to purchase goods in Tesco and have their membership card credited with a number of points. The points are converted into vouchers on a quarterly basis which members can use to purchase goods in a store or online. Points can also be gained from purchasing goods/services from other retailers and service providers. From 1999 it was also possible for members to have their vouchers converted into reward tokens that could be used to purchase goods from third parties. Tesco recovered the input tax incurred between September 2002 to the end of February 2017 on the VAT element included in the agreed charges for the provision of goods/services in exchange for the reward tokens from the third parties. HMRC concluded that the Clubcard scheme was gratuitous as the member pays nothing for the points, vouchers or other benefits and that amounts paid by Tesco Freetime Ltd to the third parties should be treated as third party consideration for supplies of rewards made by those third parties to the members. The Tribunal allowed the taxpayer's appeal on the basis that they considered that HMRC's argument was flawed because it does not reflect commercial reality. HMRC's argument is that the Clubcard member gets something for nothing and that they receive the supply from the third party essentially free of charge and that there is untaxed consumption. The Tribunal disagreed with HMRC's underlying argument and concluded that the whole scheme is funded by the customer's taxed payment when they buy goods/services from Tesco. A proportion of the taxed payment is taken by Tesco Stores to meet the cost of supplying the redemption goods at no additional or reduced additional consideration and to meet the costs of the rewards provided by Tesco Freetime and third parties. If Tesco Freetime is not entitled to deduct input tax then it will in effect have been taxed twice. It is, however, not easy to reconcile the decisions in *Tesco* and *Kuwait*.

Manufacturers' trade promotions

Vouchers and trade reward schemes

[70.15] Manufacturers often run promotions to encourage greater purchases of their 'premium' goods, i.e. those goods normally sold in day-to-day trading. Examples include the following.

- **The issue of vouchers, or a 'proof of purchase'** with the sale of the premium trade goods which can be redeemed later for further goods. Under this type of promotion, the redemption goods are provided for no consideration and must be treated as gifts as in **70.2** above.
- **Trade reward schemes**. These are schemes where rewards are offered on condition that a single trade order of a specified size is made. In such cases, HMRC accept in principle that the manufacturer, in costing the promotion, would have allowed for the cost of the redemption goods within the normal selling price of those 'premium' goods. No further VAT is due on the reward goods.

Trade orders made over a period of time

Where rewards are offered on condition that trade orders are placed over a set period of time to a given level, the rewards are being provided for no consideration. If the rewards are goods which cost the manufacturer more than £50 or form part of a series or succession to the same customer, VAT is due on a cost value. Otherwise, no VAT is due. However, as a concession, HMRC will accept that these rewards may be treated as part of a multiple supply if

- the rewards are of a kind to be used in the recipient's business;

- the rewards are not intended for the personal use of the person receiving them; and
- the rewards appear on the final qualifying invoice, i.e. at the point at which the customer qualifies for the reward.

The same rules also apply where the manufacturer supplies the reward goods, but premium supplies may have gone via a wholesaler, for example

- the manufacturer supplies the reward direct to the customer;
- the wholesaler supplies the reward on behalf of the manufacturer from their own stock where the manufacturer either reimburses the wholesaler or replaces stock; or
- the wholesaler supplies the reward from stock provided for this purpose by the manufacturer.

(VAT Notice 700/7/12, paras 11.1, 11.2).

Retrospective discounts

Where a discount is given on condition that the customer reaches a target purchase level within a set time, the normal procedure would be to issue a credit note for the amount of the discount if the target is achieved. See **40.14** **INVOICES.**

If, on the other hand, the customer is given goods to the value of the discount earned, the discount has been used to pay for the additional goods supplied. Normally, to avoid accounting for further VAT, a credit note would have to be issued to reflect the reduced value of the qualifying supplies and an invoice raised for the reward goods showing an equal amount of VAT. Instead, provided

- all the goods are liable to VAT at the same rate,
- the reward goods are supplied to the same person and for business purposes,
- no VAT credit note is issued, and
- records are kept to satisfy HMRC of a proper audit trail,

a 'no charge' invoice can be issued without VAT for the additional goods as this achieves the same result.

(VAT Notice 700/7/12, para 11.6).

Goods given by manufacturers to customers' employees

Goods given free of charge by a manufacturer to customers' employees as a reward for promoting or selling goods are treated as business gifts. See **70.2** above. (VAT Notice 700/7/12, para 11.7).

'Free' hire schemes for vending machines

See **48.7**(34) **OUTPUT TAX.**

Manufacturers' consumer promotions

Promotions through a retailer

[70.16] Where

- the public buy from a retailer and send a proof of purchase to the manufacturer to receive further goods (from the manufacturer), or coupons are included by the manufacturer inside the product or as part of the packaging and the coupons are collected and redeemed later for goods, or
- retailers of a manufacturer's products act as its agents in giving reward goods to those customers making qualifying purchases and where the manufacturer has provided the reward goods to the retailer (for no consideration) specifically for this purpose,

the manufacturer is providing the redemption/reward goods for no consideration and must account for VAT as in **70.2** above.

(VAT Notice 700/7/12, para 12.1).

Money-off coupons

If a manufacturer issues a money-off coupon which is redeemable

- by the customer with the retailer at the amount stated on the coupon,
- at the manufacturer's expense,
- as part of a sales promotion where the coupon is to be accepted by the retailer in part payment for a specified item of goods,
- where the manufacturer has sold the specified item to the retailer at the original price, and
- where the retailer takes the coupon from the customer on sale of the specified item, presents it to the manufacturer and is paid the stated amount,

the manufacturer can reduce his taxable amount by the value of the voucher which is actually refunded. This does not alter the amount shown on the invoice originally issued. The retailer's position on receipt of money is covered in **70.9** above.

(VAT Notice 700/7/12, para 12.2).

Goods given as prizes for competitions

If a manufacturer provides products as prizes for competitions, (e.g. in magazines, etc), any benefit received in exchange for the goods (e.g. a free advertisement in the magazine), is likely to constitute a barter transaction (see **70.3** above). The VAT due on the supply of the manufacturer's product is the same as it would be on the normal selling price of the product if there were no barter. However, if the prize provided is not something that the manufacturer ordinarily makes or sells, its value will be the actual cost incurred in providing the item. The magazine publisher would also then be making a supply of services to the manufacturer upon which VAT should be charged.

Where there is no exchange of benefits, there is no barter and VAT is due on a cost value subject to the normal business gift rules in **70.2** above.

(VAT Notice 700/7/12, para 12.3).

Newspaper promotions

If a manufacturer runs a promotion with a newspaper company whereby vouchers are printed in the newspaper along with the promotion of its product, and the public have to collect the vouchers in order to get reward goods or services, the goods/services are liable to VAT and the manufacturer should account for the VAT as in **70.2** above. If the vouchers offer a discount, the normal rules on redeeming vouchers in **70.9** above must be applied. (VAT Notice 700/7/12, para 12.4).

Retail discount schemes

[70.17] Discounts are normally treated as reductions in the consideration given so that VAT is due on the discounted price actually paid. See **72.24 VALUATION** for a general consideration of discounts. The following are examples of schemes which generally fall to be treated in this way.

- **Deferred discount scheme.** This entitles a shareholder to a discount off the purchase price of goods. The discount is not deducted from the customer's payment but accumulated and paid out annually. Until the discount is paid to the customer it is to be treated as consideration for the goods supplied and VAT must be accounted for on the full amount at the time the supply was made. The VAT account can then be adjusted when the discount is paid.
- **Special events.** In-store credit card holders are invited to preview sales and allowed special discounts, no payment usually being made by the credit company to the retailer. Alternatively, other selected groups may be offered discounts, again with no consideration being received from any other source.
- **'We will pay your VAT'.** Effectively this means a discount of 1/6 of the price.
- **Graded promotions.** Graded discount vouchers are given which offer a percentage reduction which increases with the value of the purchases made.

(VAT Notice 700/7/12, paras 13.2, 13.4–13.6).

'Store card' discount schemes

A customer spends a minimum amount on any one purchase using a store card. This entitles the customer to a set amount of credit to be applied to their credit card account. There is no reimbursement by the retailer to the credit card company and the credit card company and retailer may, or may not, be in the same VAT group. If

- the retailer and credit card company are within the same VAT group, the group should only account for VAT on the discounted amount; and
- the retailer and credit card company are not in the same VAT group, the goods are sold by the retailer at their full value and VAT is due on this amount.

(VAT Notice 700/7/12, para 13.1).

Lottery promotion (scratch cards)

Customers are given free scratch cards which reveal the details of a prize. Often there is no need to buy anything.

- Where the prize is a free gift of goods, these are supplies for no consideration and the rules set out in **70.2** above apply.
- Where the prize is discount vouchers or coupons for use against future purchases, these are normally evidence of entitlement to a discount and, on redemption, the rules set out in **70.8** above apply.
- Where the prize is gift vouchers, the voucher has not been issued for a consideration and on redemption the rules in **70.11** above apply.

(VAT Notice 700/7/12, para 13.3).

Minimum or pre-determined value trade-ins

These are promotions in which the customer is allowed either a minimum or a pre-determined (fixed) value for goods taken in part exchange, regardless of the condition of the exchange article (e.g. £50 for a customer's old cooker when buying a new model). The selling price of the goods should be treated as the full amount chargeable before any deductions for part exchange allowances. The purchase price of the goods taken in part exchange is the full amount allowed to the customer and it is this figure that should be used as the purchase price of the goods if sold under the second-hand scheme.

Where, however, it is clear that there is no barter and the promotion is purely for promotional purposes (e.g. '£1 off a tin of paint if you bring in an old tin') this can be treated as a discount.

(VAT Notice 700/7/12, para 13.7).

Key points: trade promotion schemes

[70.18] Points to consider are as follows.

- No output tax is due on a business gift if the value of the gift (usually the cost) is less than £50. The £50 limit is relevant to the total value of all gifts given to the same customer in a calendar year.
- If the value of a gift (or succession of gifts to the same person in a year) exceeds £50, then output tax is due according to the price that the person making the supply would have to pay for the item, i.e. usually the cost price.
- In situations where a customer can reclaim input tax on the gift they have received, the donor can issue a tax certificate (not an invoice) to certify that output tax has been declared on the gift. This will be adequate evidence for the recipient to reclaim input tax (subject to normal rules).

- There is no output tax liability on a free supply of services, e.g. an accountancy business doing a tax return for a charity without making a charge.
- The output tax rules concerning money off coupons, discount vouchers and gift schemes can get complicated. It is important that the VAT issues are fully considered at the planning stage of any scheme that is introduced.

71

Transport and Freight

Cross-references. See **20.33 EUROPEAN UNION: SINGLE MARKET** for new means of transport; **22.7 EXPORTS** for the supply or hiring of freight containers; **46 MOTOR CARS**.

De Voil Indirect Tax Service. See V4.251.

Introduction to transport and freight

[71.1] The VAT treatment of transport falls into the following five main categories of supplies:

- ships (see **71.2** below);
- aircraft (see **71.3** below);
- lifeboats (see **71.14** below);
- passenger transport (see **71.15** below); and
- freight transport services (see **71.25** below).

[*VATA 1994, Sch 8 Group 8*].

Zero-rated supplies of ships

[71.2] The supply of any 'qualifying ship' is zero-rated. A '*qualifying ship*' is any ship which is

(a) of a gross tonnage of not less than 15 tons; and
(b) neither designed nor adapted for use for recreation or pleasure.

[*VATA 1994, Sch 8 Group 8 Item 1 and Note A1*].

'*Ship*' includes a submarine, hovercraft (see below), light vessel, fire float, dredger, barge or lighter, a mobile floating dock or crane and an offshore oil or gas installation used in the underwater exploitation or exploration of oil and gas resources, which is designed to be moved from place to place. *Not included* are

- fixed oil and gas installations (even though they might be transported to a site as a floating structure); and
- vessels which are permanently moored (e.g. as attractions) *and* not readily capable of navigation.

The supply of a partially completed ship is standard-rated. A ship is considered complete when it is seaworthy or fit to navigate the waterways for which it is designed (*QED Marine* (VTD 17336) (TVC 66.9)). However, supplies of parts and equipment (including part-assembled ships, e.g. fuselage, wings or hull) in the course of construction of a qualifying ship may be zero-rated (see **71.4** below).

(VAT Notice 744C, paras 2.2, 4.5, 7.2).

Recreation and pleasure

As a result of (*b*) above, zero-rating cannot apply to a ship or boat *designed or adapted* for use for recreation or pleasure, i.e. it must be designed for commercial purposes. Features that indicate a commercial design include a cargo hold, commercial fishing equipment or the ability to convey large numbers of passengers.

Motor cruisers, powerboats and yachts

These are designed or adapted for use for recreation or pleasure. As a result, they cannot be zero-rated as qualifying ships even if satisfying (*a*) above or supplied for business use (e.g. sail training). See also *Callison* (VTD 810) (TVC 66.1) and *obiter dicta* in *Hamann v Finanzamt Hamburg-Eimsbuttel, ECJ Case C–51/88*, [1991] STC 193 (TVC 22.223).

Cruise ships

Cruise ships can be zero-rated as qualifying ships provided

- they have a gross tonnage of not less than 15 tons;
- they are unsuitable for private use; and
- they are supplied for use in the business of providing recreation or pleasure cruises for fee-paying passengers.

Residential accommodation

Houseboats without engines may be eligible for zero-rating under a specific relief (see **43.25 LAND AND BUILDINGS: ZERO AND REDUCED RATE SUPPLIES AND DIY HOUSEBUILDERS**). Otherwise, the intended use of a vessel does not affect qualifying ship status. The only factors to be considered are the gross tonnage, the design of the ship and any subsequent adaptations. If a ship is designed or adapted with the ability to be used for recreation or pleasure (e.g. cruising on rivers or canals), rather than predominantly as permanent residential accommodation, it is not a qualifying ship. In *DG Everett; The London Tideway Harbour Co Ltd* (VTD 11736) (TVC 66.3), barges with engines which were used as living accommodation were held to be zero-rated provided they satisfied the conditions in (*a*) above. The barges had not been originally designed for recreation or pleasure. It stretched the ordinary meaning of those words to say that it included a home or place of permanent habitation. The decision was not followed in *Grieve* (VTD 20149) (TVC 66.4) but was applied in *HMRC v Stone*, Ch D [2008] STC 2501 (TVC 66.5). Following the decision in *Stone*, HMRC have changed their policy on the liability of vessels used as residential accommodation (excluding houseboats). They have decided to treat Dutch barges and similar vessels that are designed and supplied for use as the permanent residence of the customer as qualifying ships and eligible for zero-rating. As vessels of less than 15 gross tons can never be zero-rated regardless of their design, the majority of narrow boats designed for permanent residential use will not meet this requirement and their supply will continue to be standard-rated. As a result of this policy change some supplies of goods and services to the owners of such vessels may also be zero-rated by suppliers. These include the following, but do not extend to domestic equipment and fittings: repairs and maintenance of the vessel itself; modification or conversion of the vessel itself provided that it remains a qualifying ship after modification or conversion; and parts and equipment ordinarily installed or incorporated in the propulsion, navigation, communications or structure of a ship. (HMRC Brief 38/09).

Gross tonnage

The gross tonnage of a ship is as ascertained under the *Merchant Shipping Acts*. If the gross tonnage of a ship hasn't been calculated under the *Merchant Shipping Acts*, the formula below should be used. However, as soon as the tonnage of a vessel is ascertained under the *Merchant Shipping Acts* that tonnage becomes the basis for determination of VAT liability and the tonnage arrived at by the formula below no longer applies.

For vessels 24 metres or greater in length:

$L \times B \times D \times 0.235$

For vessels less than 24 metres in length:

L × B × D × 0.16

where:

L = Length in metres measured from the foreside of the foremost fixed permanent structure to the afterside of the aftermost permanent structure (excluding appendages that do not contribute to the volume of the vessel)

B = Beam-breadth of vessel in metres at the widest part to the outside of the outer planking (excluding the thickness of any moulding or rubbing strake which may be fitted)

D = Depth in metres measured vertically from the midpoint overall. For this purpose, the upper calculation point is

- for a decked vessel, the underside of the deck on the middle line, or (if there is no deck on the middle line) the underside of the deck at the side of the vessel; and
- for an open-decked vessel, the top of the upper strake or gunwale; and

the lower calculation point is

- for a wooden vessel, the upper side of the plank at the side of the keel;
- for a metal vessel, the top of the plating at the side of the keelson; and
- for a moulded vessel (e.g. one made of glass-reinforced plastic), the inside of the hull. Where no keel member is fitted and the keel is of open trough construction, the calculation point is the top of the keel filling, if fitted, or the level at which the inside breadth of the trough is 10 cms (whichever gives the greater depth).

Hovercraft

Hovercraft are not subject to the gross tonnage criteria and are therefore regarded as qualifying ships (unless designed or adapted for use for recreation or pleasure).

Multi-hull vessels

Each hull must be measured separately for overall length, beam and depth and the vessel as a whole must be measured.

Narrowboats

The measurement must be taken from the underside of the deck at the side of the vessel, rather than from the roof of the cabin.

Breaks in deck line

A break is a raised portion of the deck that extends from one side of the ship to the other. Cabins, wheelhouses, hatches and erections above the deck are not breaks. If the ship does have a break, the mean length, breadth and depth should be multiplied together with a factor of 0.35. This resultant figure should then be added to the gross tonnage when calculated using the formula above.

(VAT Notice 744C, paras 2.4–2.12).

Zero-rated supplies of aircraft

[71.3] The supply of any 'qualifying aircraft' is zero-rated.

A 'qualifying aircraft' is any aircraft which—

- is used by an airline operating for reward chiefly on international routes; or
- is used by a State institution and meets the condition that
  - (a) the aircraft is of a weight of not less than 8,000 kilograms; and
  - (b) is neither designed nor adapted for use for recreation or pleasure.

'*Airline*' means an undertaking which provides services for the carriage by air of passengers or cargo (or both).

'*State institution*' has the same meaning as in *Directive 2006/112/EC, Annex X, Part B.*

[*VATA 1994, Sch 8 Group 8 Item 2 and Notes A1–A3; F(No 3)A s 21*].

The definition of qualifying aircraft was amended because the UK had been applying a different criteria to those specified in *Directive 2006/112/EC, Art 148*, which exempts certain supplies of goods and services related to aircraft. The essential condition for those exemptions is that the aircraft must be 'used by an airline operating for reward chiefly on international routes'. In *Cimber Air A/S Skatteministeriet, Case C-382/02*, [2005] STC 547 (TVC 22.444), the CJEU ruled that those exemptions apply even for an aircraft operating on domestic routes, as long as it is used by such an airline. (EU Press Release IR/09/1016 dated 25 June 2009).

'*Aircraft*' includes aeroplanes (civil and military), helicopters and airships but does not include space craft and satellites.

'*Weight*' is the authorised maximum take-off weight specified in the certificate of airworthiness or, for military aircraft, shown in the documents issued by the Ministry of Defence.

(VAT Notice 744C, paras 3.2–3.5).

Ships and aircraft — other zero-rated supplies

[71.4] In addition to the supply of certain ships or aircraft (see **71.2** and **71.3** above) various other supplies and services in connection with such craft may also be zero-rated.

Parts and equipment

Zero-rating applies to

(a) the supply of parts and equipment, of a kind ordinarily installed or incorporated in, and to be installed or incorporated in, the propulsion, navigation or communication systems or general structure of a qualifying ship (see **71.2** above) or a qualifying aircraft (see **71.3** above); and
(b) the supply of life jackets, life rafts, smoke hoods and similar safety equipment for use in a qualifying ship or aircraft.

The letting on hire of goods within (*a*) or (*b*) above is also zero-rated.

Any supply of parts and equipment to a Government department is excluded from zero-rating unless *either* the supply is in the course or furtherance of a business carried on by the department *or* the parts and equipment are to be installed or incorporated in ships or aircraft used for the purpose of providing rescue or assistance at sea.

[*VATA 1994, Sch 8 Group 8 Items 2A, 2B and Notes A1, 2 and 2A*].

Technically, in the light of the decision in *QED Marine* (VTD 17336) (TVC 66.9) that a ship does not become a qualifying ship until it becomes seaworthy, parts supplied up to that time should be standard-rated. However, HMRC consider that zero-rating for the supply of parts and equipment falling within (*a*) above should apply to both existing qualifying ships/aircraft and those under construction that will qualify when they become seaworthy/airworthy. HMRC expect businesses to have contractual or other evidence that the completed ship or aircraft will be qualifying, otherwise all supplies of parts and equipment must be standard-rated.

HMRC also consider that a qualifying ship/aircraft that temporarily loses its seaworthy/airworthy status can continue to be classed as a qualifying ship/aircraft, provided there is clear and evidenced intention to return the ship/aircraft to a seaworthy/airworthy condition.

(VAT Information Sheet 15/07).

Parts and equipment *include*

- Anchors
- Catering and laundering equipment (industrial)
- Communications equipment used for the operation of the ship or aircraft
- Cranes
- 'Expendable' parts and 'rotable' components used by the aircraft industry
- Fishing nets and equipment
- Laundering equipment (industrial)
- Lifeboats (and equipment used therein) and life rafts
- Nuts, bolts, hoses, oil seals and rivets (referred to as 'consumables' by the aircraft industry)
- Propellers and rudders
- Pumps

- Radar and navigation equipment
- Safety equipment (e.g. escape chutes, life jackets, smoke hoods, oxygen masks and winches)
- Sanitary fixtures

Parts and equipment *exclude*

- Aircraft ground equipment
- Binoculars
- Bulk materials (e.g. adhesives, chemicals, fabrics, inhibitors, metals, oils, paints, solvents and thinners)
- Catering and laundering equipment (domestic)
- Crockery and cutlery
- Diving equipment
- Flight simulators or their parts
- Furniture (unfixed) and soft furnishings
- Missiles, shells, etc.
- Raw materials (e.g. fibre board, plastics, specialist metals)
- Ship's stores
- Telephones and televisions
- Tooling and equipment used for manufacturing parts or equipment
- Tools
- Underwater cameras
- Video tapes, video games and similar entertainment equipment

Evidence for zero-rating

Normal commercial documentation is sufficient provided the supplier is satisfied that the parts, etc. qualify for zero-rating. If uncertain (e.g. because the parts could be used on a qualifying or non-qualifying ship or because the customer is a government department) the supplier should obtain an undertaking from the customer that the parts etc. qualify. See Notice 744C, para 13 for a suggested format. Where the customer is unable or unwilling to give an undertaking, the supply should be standard-rated.

(VAT Notice 744C, paras 7.4–7.7).

Government departments

The exclusion from zero-rating for supplies to Government departments (see above) only applies to the supply of parts and equipment, i.e. goods. Supplies of services (e.g. repair and maintenance, modification or conversion) can still be zero-rated. It is therefore necessary to distinguish between the two types of supply. If a contract involves both goods and services, a supplier must determine whether there is a single supply of goods (standard-rated) or services (zero-rated) or whether there is a multiple supply, in which case the VAT treatment for each of the supplies must be determined. Where contracts are complex, the supplier should contact the National Advice Service or their Client Relationship Manager with the full details of the supplies involved, together with the contractual detail. HMRC are also happy to provide VAT advice to the Ministry of Defence and suppliers at the pre-contract stage. (VAT Information Sheet 15/07).

Repairs and maintenance

[71.5] The repair or maintenance of a qualifying ship (see **71.2** above) or a qualifying aircraft (see **71.3** above) is zero-rated. [*VATA 1994, Sch 8 Group 8 Items 1, 2*].

Maintenance includes testing of parts and components, cleaning, fumigation and ship's laundry (provided the articles are not personal to the crew or passengers). Parts, components and materials provided by the supplier of the repairs and maintenance are regarded as part of the zero-rated work.

Repairs and maintenance of parts and equipment can also be zero-rated provided

(a) in the case of a ship
- the repair is carried out on board; or
- the part or component is removed for repair and is replaced in the same ship; and

(b) in the case of an aircraft
- the repair is carried out on board; or
- the part or component is removed for repair and is replaced in the same aircraft; or
- following the repair or maintenance, the parts are returned to be held in stock for future use as spares in qualifying aircraft; or
- if they are unserviceable parts and equipment, they are exchanged for identical parts which have themselves been reconditioned, repaired or maintained.

Subcontracted services supplied in respect of repair and maintenance of a qualifying ship or aircraft can similarly be zero-rated. The subcontractor is advised to obtain evidence to substantiate zero-rating from the main contractor.

(VAT Notice 744C, paras 6.2, 6.5–6.7).

Modifications and conversions

[71.6] The modification or conversion of any qualifying ship (see **71.2** above) or qualifying aircraft (see **71.3** above) is zero-rated provided that, when so modified or converted, it will remain a qualifying ship or aircraft. [*VATA 1994, Sch 8 Group 8 Items 1 and 2*]. Included are structural alterations and rebuilding or lengthening.

Sub-contracted services supplied in respect of modification or conversion of a qualifying ship or aircraft can similarly be zero-rated. The subcontractor is advised to obtain evidence to substantiate zero-rating from the main contractor.

(VAT Notice 744C, paras 6.3, 6.7).

Ship design services supplied in the UK are zero-rated as integral to the supply, modification or conversion of a qualifying ship only where a supplier specifically contracts with a customer to design *and* supply, modify or convert a qualifying ship. In other circumstances, design services are standard-rated. (Business Brief 5/99).

Air navigation services

[71.7] The supply of 'air navigation services' are zero-rated when

- provided for qualifying aircraft (see **71.3** above); or
- supplied to a person who receives the supply for the purposes of a business carried on by him and who belongs outside the UK (whether or not provided for qualifying aircraft).

'*Air navigation services*' have the same meaning as in *Civil Aviation Act 1982, s 105(1)*, i.e. they include information, directions and other facilities furnished, issued or provided in connection with the navigation or movement of aircraft, and include the control of movement of vehicles in any part of an aerodrome used for the movement of aircraft.

[*VATA 1994, Sch 8 Group 8 Items 6A, 11(b), Notes 6A and 7*].

Air navigation services are largely provided by the Civil Aviation Authority which has been granted taxable status for its supply of these services. (Business Brief 20/94).

Charter services and letting on hire

[71.8] The supply of services under the charter of a qualifying ship (see **71.2** above) or a qualifying aircraft (see **71.3** above) is zero-rated unless those services consist wholly of any one or more of

- the transport of passengers,
- accommodation,
- entertainment, or
- education,

being services wholly performed in the UK. [*VATA 1994, Sch 8 Group 8 Items 1, 2 and Note 1*].

The correct VAT treatment of supplies of ships and aircraft under charter can cause difficulties. The term 'charter' is used to describe several different types of supply (including freight or passenger transport) and is also used in slightly different ways in respect of ships and aircraft. Also, there is a complex interaction between the rules on both place of supply and liability, of charter, hire, passenger transport and freight transport services. See HMRC Manual VTRANS110310 for more detailed information.

Boats for disabled persons

[71.9] Boats which are designed or substantially and permanently adapted for the use of disabled persons may be zero-rated in certain circumstances. See **29.23** HEALTH AND WELFARE.

Handling services

[71.10] HMRC have recently updated its guidance with regard to when handling services are zero-rated, and the updated guidance states the following.

Handling services are zero-rated when provided for qualifying ships (see **71.2** above) and aircraft (see **71.3** above) and physically performed:

- in a port;
- in a customs and excise airport (except where the aircraft is used by an airline operating for reward chiefly on international routes);
- outside the UK.

The letting on hire of goods alone is specifically excluded.

Handling services provided to non-qualifying vessels are standard-rated.

'*Port*' means any port appointed for customs purposes and includes all seaports in the UK. At a seaport the port limits include all territorial waters but do not normally extend inland beyond the waterway of the port.

'*Customs and excise airport*' means an airport designated for the landing or departure of aircraft for the purposes of the *Customs and Excise Acts* by an Order in Council made pursuant to *Civil Aviation Act 1982, s 60*. The limit of such an airport is normally the boundary of the airport itself. The designated Customs airports are Aberdeen, Belfast International (Aldergrove), Biggin Hill, Birmingham, Blackpool, Bournemouth, Bristol, Cambridge, Cardiff, Coventry, East Midlands, Edinburgh, Exeter, Farnborough, Filton, Glasgow, Humberside, Leeds/Bradford, Liverpool, London City, London Gatwick, London Heathrow, London Luton, London Stanstead, Lydd, Manchester, Manston, Newcastle, Newquay, Norwich, Plymouth, Prestwick, Sheffield City, Shoreham, Southampton, Southend, Sumburgh and Teesside.

HMRC have provided a list of the typical types of handling services that are zero-rated in Notice 744B, para 8.3.

[*VATA 1994, Sch 8 Group 8 Items 6(a), 11(b), Notes 5–7.*] (VAT Notice 744B, para 8).

Ship handling

This includes port and harbour dues, dock and berth charges, conservancy charges (including the provision of local lights, buoys and beacons), graving dock charges, mooring charges, demurrage (where this is a charge for failure to load or discharge a ship within specified time), security and fire services, supply of crew members and the day-to-day management of a ship.

Aircraft handling

This includes aircraft landing, parking or housing fees, aircraft compass swinging fees, apron services, airport navigation service charges, security and fire services and the supply of crew members.

(VAT Notice 744C, para 8.3).

Surveys and classification services

[71.11] Any service supplied for, or in connection with, the surveying of any ship or aircraft or the classification of any ship or aircraft for the purposes of any register is zero-rated when

- provided in connection with any qualifying ship (see **71.2** above) or qualifying aircraft (see **71.3** above); or
- supplied to a person who receives the supply for the purposes of a business carried on by him and who belongs outside the UK (whether or not provided for qualifying ships and aircraft).

[*VATA 1994, Sch 8 Group 8 Items 9, 11(b) and Note 7*].

There must be a physical inspection of the ship/aircraft to qualify for zero-rating.

Included are classification services performed for Lloyd's and other registers and survey services for aircraft in relation to the certificate of airworthiness. *Not included* are tonnage measurements or surveys of ships for registration or other purposes required by statute to be carried out by the Department of Transport (which are outside the scope of VAT) or services of arranging for the registering of ships for the purposes of the *Merchant Shipping Acts* (which are standard-rated).

(VAT Notice 744C, para 9.6).

Loss adjusting services supplied in connection with marine and aviation insurance claims are not zero-rated surveys. Although such services may contain an element of inspection, HMRC consider them to be single supplies of loss adjusting and liable to the standard rate of VAT to the extent that they are supplied in the UK (HMRC Brief 13/13).

Salvage and towage services

[71.12] Salvage and towage services supplied for shipping are zero-rated whatever the type of ship. [*VATA 1994, Sch 8 Group 8 Item 8*]. Shipping in this context includes inland waterway vessels and all floating objects. Zero-rating also covers dock gates, pier and bridge sections and buoys. It does not cover any subsequent repair work carried out (for which see **71.5** above). (VAT Notice 744C, para 9.4).

Pilotage

[71.13] Pilotage services are zero-rated. [*VATA 1994, Sch 8 Group 8 Item 7*]. This applies to all shipping and is not just confined to qualifying ships. (VAT Notice 744C, para 9.3).

Lifeboats and slipways

[71.14] The following supplies are zero-rated.

(a) The supply to, and repair or maintenance for, a charity providing rescue or assistance at sea of
- any 'lifeboat';
- carriage equipment designed solely for the launching and recovery of lifeboats;

- tractors for the sole use of the launching and recovery of lifeboats; and
- winches and hauling equipment for the sole use of the recovery of lifeboats.

(b) The construction, modification, repair or maintenance for a charity providing rescue or assistance at sea of slipways used solely for the launching and recovery of lifeboats.

(c) The supply of spare parts or accessories to a charity providing rescue or assistance at sea for use in or with goods under (*a*) above or slipways within (*b*) above.

(d) The supply to a charity providing rescue or assistance at sea of equipment that is to be installed, incorporated or used in a lifeboat and is of a kind ordinarily installed, incorporated or used in a lifeboat.

(e) The supply of fuel to a charity providing rescue or assistance at sea where the fuel is for use in a lifeboat.

Included is the letting on hire of qualifying goods.

'*Lifeboat*' means any vessel (whatever the tonnage) used or to be used solely for rescue or assistance at sea.

To qualify for zero-rating the recipient of the supply must, before the supply is made, give the supplier a certificate stating the name and address of the recipient and that the supply is of a description specified in *VATA 1994, Sch 8 Group 8 Item 3*. The supplier must take all reasonable steps to check the validity of the certificate and should consult HMRC if in doubt. Where, however, despite taking such steps, nonetheless the supplier fails to identify an incorrect certificate and in good faith makes the supplies concerned at the zero rate, HMRC will not seek to recover the VAT due from the supplier. (VAT Notice 48, ESC 3.11).

[*VATA 1994, Sch 8 Group 8 Item 3 and Notes 2, 3 and 4*].

Passenger transport

[71.15] De Voil Indirect Tax Service. See V3.189, V4.251.

Passenger transport services are supplied when a vehicle, ship or aircraft is provided, *together with* a driver or crew, for the carriage of passengers. Incidental services may also be included. Where a vehicle, ship or aircraft is supplied *without* a driver or crew, this is not a supply of passenger transport services, but a means of transport.

To determine the correct VAT treatment of supplies of passenger transport it is necessary to

- decide whether the supply takes place in the UK (see **71.16** below); and if so
- consider whether the supply is zero-rated (see **71.17** below) or standard-rated (see **71.19** below) or reduced-rated (cable-suspended passenger transport (see **59.8 REDUCED RATE SUPPLIES**).

Certain supplies of passenger transport cause particular problems because they can be zero-rated or standard-rated depending upon the precise nature of the services offered. See **71.20** below for transport of vehicles on ships, **71.21** below for cruises and **71.22** below for airline passengers' perks.

See **71.24** below for taxis and hire cars.

Bought-in supplies, packages and inclusive tours

Where passenger transport is bought in and re-supplied, either on its own or as part of a package or inclusive tour, VAT must normally be accounted for under the tour operators' margin scheme. Any other travel, hotel and holiday facilities which have been bought in and re-supplied must also be accounted for using the margin scheme. An 'in-house' supply of passenger transport (e.g. the provision of a driver plus vehicle for passenger transport) does not fall within the scheme and is dealt with in the normal way *unless* it is provided together with other travel and hotel facilities which have been bought in and re-supplied, in which case the 'in-house' transport must be included in the scheme calculation. See **69 TOUR OPERATORS' MARGIN SCHEME** for further details.

Place of supply

[71.16] Services consisting of the transportation of passengers are treated as supplied in the country where the transportation takes place to the extent that it takes place in that country. [*VATA 1994, Sch 4A para* 2]. As a result, subject to the special rules below, if it takes place

- inside the UK, the supplies are all within the scope of UK VAT;
- outside the UK the supplies are outside the scope of UK VAT (see below);
- both inside and outside the UK, the element that takes place within the UK is within the scope of UK VAT and the element that takes place outside the UK is outside the scope of UK VAT.

In cases where cross-frontier transport is provided on an all-inclusive basis, the total consideration must be allocated on a pro-rata basis having regard to the distance covered (rather than the time spent) in each EU member state (*Reisebüro Binder GmbH v Finanzamt Stuttgart-Körperschaften, ECJ Case C–116/96*, [1998] STC 604 (TVC 22.229)).

Sea and air passenger transport

Provided the means of transport used does not put in or land in another country on the way, any transportation as part of a journey between two points in the same country is treated as taking place wholly inside that country even where it takes place partly outside its territorial jurisdiction. This applies even if the journey is part of a longer journey involving travel to or from another country. [*VATA 1994, Sch 4A para* 2].

> *Example*
>
> A ferry transports passengers from Liverpool to Dublin via the Isle of Man.
>
> The first leg (Liverpool to the Isle of Man) is treated as taking place in the UK but the remaining part of the journey (Isle of Man to Dublin) takes place outside UK territorial waters and is outside the scope of UK VAT.

Pleasure cruises

Any goods or services provided as part of a pleasure cruise are treated as supplied in the same place as the transportation of the passengers and for this purpose a pleasure cruise is treated as a supply of passenger transport. [*VATA 1994, Sch 4A para 2*]. The place of supply of a cruise follows the general rule above i.e. it is supplied in the country in which it takes place to the extent that it takes place in that country.

Luggage and/or accompanying motor vehicles

The transportation of any luggage or motor vehicle (car, motorcycle, caravan, trailer or small commercial vehicle) accompanying in either case a passenger is treated as supplied in the same place as the passenger transport [*SI 1992/3121, Art 8*] and as a single supply with it. The transportation of an *unaccompanied* vehicle is treated as a supply of freight transport (see **71.25** below).

Passenger transport supplied outside the UK

If the supply takes place:

- In another EU member state, the supplier may have to register for VAT in that country and account for VAT at the relevant rate applying there. If the supplier does not have an establishment there, he may need to appoint a local tax representative to account for the VAT there on his behalf.
- In a country outside the EU, the supplier may be liable to account for any tax in that country that is applicable on passenger transport services.
- In international airspace or waters, the supplier may not have to account for any tax on that part of the supply in any country.

Passenger transport supplied in the UK by persons belonging outside the UK

Where a business belonging outside the UK is not registered for UK VAT and supplies passenger transport in the UK,

- if its customer is registered for UK VAT, the customer can account for VAT on its supplies under the reverse charge procedure (see **39.4 INTERNATIONAL SERVICES**); and
- if its customer is not registered for UK VAT, it is liable to account for the VAT in the UK and must register for VAT in the UK where its supplies exceed the registration threshold (see **60.3 REGISTRATION**).

(VAT Notice 744A, paras 3.1–3.4).

Zero-rating

[71.17] Subject to the standard-rated supplies in **71.19** below, the supply of passenger transport in the UK is zero-rated if falling within any of the following categories.

(a) **In any vehicle, ship or aircraft designed or adapted to carry not less than ten passengers. [*VATA 1994, Sch 8 Group 8 Item 4(a)*]**

See *Cirdan Sailing Trust v C & E Commrs, Ch D 2005*, [2006] STC 185 (TVC 66.19) for a consideration of how to apply the test of passenger carrying capacity.

For the purposes of determining the carrying capacity, the driver and crew should be treated as passengers. See also *G L Ashton (t/a Country Hotel Narrowboats)* (VTD 14197) (TVC 66.18).

Included (subject to the seating rule) are

- pleasure cruises;
- cliff lifts;
- excursions by coach and train (including steam railways);
- horse-drawn buses;
- mystery coach trips and boat trips;
- sight-seeing tours;
- the transport element of 'park-and-ride' schemes designed to reduce traffic congestion in city centres; and
- the transport of parachutists or divers, provided it is only transportation that is provided.

If the carrying capacity of the vehicle, ship or aircraft is less than ten passengers, the transport is standard-rated unless it can be zero-rated under (*b*)–(*d*) below or the special rule for disabled passengers applies (see below).

(VAT Notice 744A, paras 4.1, 4.2).

Disabled passengers

Zero-rating specifically includes the transport of passengers in a vehicle

- which is designed, or substantially and permanently adapted, for the safe carriage of a person in a wheelchair (or two or more such persons), and
- which, if it were not so designed or adapted, would be capable of carrying no less than ten passengers.

Note that, where the conditions are met, zero-rating applies whether or not the transport service is provided, in a particular case, for disabled persons.

[*VATA 1994, Sch 8 Group 8 Note (4D); SI 2001/753*].

Miniature and narrow-gauge railways

See *Metroland Ltd* (VTD 14550) (TVC 66.36) and *Narogauge Ltd* (VTD 14680) (TVC 66.22).

Narrowboats

In determining whether a narrowboat is designed to carry ten or more passengers, it is the space on each boat, rather than just the number of berths, which determines the carrying capacity (*GL Ashton (t/a Country Hotel Narrowboats)* (VTD 14197) (TVC 66.18)).

Cabin lifts

Each cabin in a cabin lift to a scenic headland has been held to be a separate vehicle and the transport of passengers standard-rated if the individual cabins are designed to hold less than ten people (*Llandudno Cabinlift Co Ltd* (VTD 1) (TVC 66.30)).

(b) From 1 January 2011, by providers of universal postal services. [*VATA 1994, Sch 8 Group 8 Item 4(b)*].

This applies irrespective of the type of vehicle or its carrying capacity. (VAT Notice 744A, para 7.1).

(c) **On any scheduled flight.** [***VATA 1994, Sch 8 Group 8 Item 4(c)***]

This applies irrespective of the carrying capacity of the aircraft. A scheduled flight is one that is run either according to a published timetable or so regularly or frequently as to constitute a recognisable systematic series of flights. (VAT Notice 744A, paras 5.1, 5.2).

(d) From a place within to a place outside the UK (or vice versa) to the extent that those services are supplied within the UK. [***VATA 1994, Sch 8 Group 8 Item 4(d)***]

This applies irrespective of the carrying capacity of the vehicle, ship or aircraft. Zero-rating applies to single and return journeys and journeys to or from an oil rig situated outside UK territorial waters. (VAT Notice 744A, para 3.2).

Driver or crew

To qualify for zero-rating as passenger transport, the vehicle, ship or aircraft must be supplied with a driver or crew. Otherwise it is the vehicle, etc. which is being supplied rather than passenger transport.

Incidental supplies

[71.18] Incidental supplies are provided as part of a single transport service. Where a fare is zero-rated, then whether or not a separate charge is made, zero-rating also applies to

- accompanied domestic pets;
- accompanied luggage, including cycles and prams and excess luggage;
- accompanied vehicles and trailers (including Motorail);
- airport passenger charges and passenger load supplements;
- duplicate season tickets;
- pullman supplements;

- seat reservations;
- sleeping berths and cabins on ships (if provided in the course of ordinary transport, but see **71.22** below for cruises); and

(VAT Notice 744A, paras 9.2, 9.3).

Catering on aircraft

Catering on aircraft is an adjunct to the supply of transport and, where no separate charge is made, the consideration for the ticket need not be apportioned (*British Airways v C & E Commrs*, CA [1990] STC 643 (TVC 66.13)).

Payment for an identity card

Payment for an identity card enabling the holder to travel at reduced price has been held to be consideration for the provision of rail transport (*British Railways Board (No 2) v C & E Commrs*, CA [1977] STC 221 (TVC 66.12)).

Standard-rated supplies

[71.19] The following are specifically excluded from zero-rating and become standard-rated.

(a) Passenger transport in places of entertainment or interest

The transport of passengers in any vehicle to, from or within

(i) a place of entertainment, recreation or amusement, or
(ii) a place of cultural, scientific, historical or similar interest

by the person who supplies a right of admission to, or use of facilities at, such a place or by a person connected with him under the provisions of *ICTA 1988, s 839* (see **72.19 VALUATION**) is standard-rated. [*VATA 1994, Sch 8 Group 8 Notes (4A)(4B)*]. Such transport services are standard-rated whether included in an overall admission price or made for a separate charge.

Places affected include

- fairgrounds;
- museums;
- piers;
- safari parks;
- stately homes;
- theme parks;
- water parks; and
- zoos.

However, places where the public enjoy totally free access are not affected (e.g. national parks, seaside resorts, historic towns and villages, geographical areas such as the Norfolk Broads, or canals and lakes).

The provisions do not apply to transport to, from or within a place of entertainment or cultural interest when provided *independently* from an operator of such a place. Such services remains zero-rated subject to the normal conditions. Examples include

- a trip by coach or rail to a football ground;
- a coach excursion to a theme park;
- ferries, canal boat trips and other round trips or excursions by boats, without other facilities, on the open sea or other waterways to which the public have free access.

(VAT Notice 744A, paras 8.1, 8.2, 8.5).

(b) Transport in connection with airport car parks

The transport of passengers in any 'motor vehicle' between a car park (or land adjacent) and an airport passenger terminal (or land adjacent) by the person who supplies the parking facilities in that car park or by a person connected with him under the provisions of *ICTA 1988, s 839* (see **72.19 VALUATION**) is standard-rated. '*Motor vehicle*' means any mechanically propelled vehicle intended or adapted for use on the roads. See *Purple Parking Ltd* (TC00118) (TVC 66.40), in which the tribunal held that the companies were making single supplies of parking facilities and the supplies of transport were incidental. [*VATA 1994, Sch 8 Group 8 Notes (4A)–(4C)*].

(c) Pleasure flights

The transport of passengers in an aircraft is standard-rated where the flight is advertised or held out to be for the purpose of

(i) providing entertainment, recreation or amusement, or
(ii) the experience of flying or the experience of flying in that particular aircraft

and not primarily for the purpose of transporting passengers from one place to another. [*VATA 1994, Sch 8 Group 8 Notes (4A)(4B)*].

Such flights are standard-rated even if they take off from one airport and land at another.

Standard-rated flights include

- hot air balloon rides;
- airship rides;
- 'fear of flying' flights; and
- Concorde 'flights to nowhere' and similar pleasure flights where the aircraft returns to the airport of departure or another UK airport without landing in another country.

(VAT Notice 744A, para 8.4).

Supplies not regarded as passenger transport

The following are standard-rated because they are not regarded as the transport of passengers.

- Donkey rides and similar rides.
- Novelty rides on miniature and model railways, ghost trains, roundabouts, dippers, other fairground equipment and similar attractions (see *C & E Commrs v Blackpool Pleasure Beach Co*, QB [1974] STC 138 (TVC 66.35)).

- The supply of any vehicle with or without a crew for a non-passenger service (e.g. to make a film or carry goods).

(VAT Notice 744A, para 2.2).

Ancillary supplies

[71.20] Ancillary supplies, as opposed to incidental supplies (see **71.18** above) are not part of a single supply of passenger transport services but are supplied separately. The following supplies which are often provided in connection with passenger transport are standard-rated.

- Meals, snacks, sandwiches, drinks, etc. provided in the course of catering *and supplied separately*.
- Car parking (but see **71.23** below when supplied as an airline passenger perk).
- Cycle storage.
- Left luggage and lost property.
- Platform tickets.
- Transportation of unaccompanied luggage, vehicles and trailers.

(VAT Notice 744A, para 9.4).

Club membership

Club membership, entitling economy class passengers to certain facilities normally available only to first class passengers, is not an advance payment for supplies forming an integral part of passenger transport (*El Al Israel Airlines Ltd* (VTD 12750) (TVC 66.39)).

Transport of vehicles on ships, trains etc.

[71.21] The transport or ferry of vehicles on a ship, train or other form of transport may, depending on the circumstances, be a supply of passenger transport or freight transport. HMRC's treatment is as follows.

Passenger transport

- Vehicles with passengers, e.g. coach or bus, whether or not charged at the private car rate.
- Vehicles with drivers or passengers charged under the private car rate, including motorcycles, cars, caravans and trailers.
- Small commercial vehicles charged under the private car rate whether carrying passengers or freight.

Freight transport

- Vehicles unaccompanied or without passengers.

(VAT Notice 744A, paras 2.3, 2.4).

Cruises and other trips

Cruises

[71.22] This paragraph applies where a cruise operator provides cruises from own resources. It applies to all cruise operators whether supplying international and coastal holiday cruises or cruises on rivers and canals or other inland waterways, including disco, dinner, wedding reception and similar entertainment cruises. In all cases, the vessels must be designed or adapted to carry ten or more passengers, including crew, otherwise any supplies in the UK will be automatically standard-rated. However, the provisions do not affect cruises bought in and re-supplied under the **69 TOUR OPERATORS' MARGIN SCHEME.**

HMRC regard a business as providing a cruise from its own resources where it

- uses its own ship;
- charters a vessel from the owner for a period of two year or more whether only with deck/engine crew or with deck/engine crew and 'hotel'/domestic/catering crew. The vessel need not necessarily be in service continuously throughout the period but the owner must not have the right to use the vessel to make supplies to other customers during the period; or
- takes a vessel including deck/engine crew but employs or engages its own 'hotel'/domestic/catering staff.

A pleasure cruise is treated as a single supply of passenger transport *for the purposes of determining the place of supply*. Once the place of supply has been established under the general rules for passenger transport in **71.16** above, for UK VAT liability purposes a cruise may be a single or multiple supply depending on the facts of the cruise.

In *C & E Commrs v The Peninsular & Oriental Steam Navigation Co*, QB [1996] STC 698 (TVC 66.20) a cruise sold at an inclusive price covering transport, accommodation, catering, entertainment, etc. was held to be a single supply which was zero-rated as a supply of passenger transport, the terms 'pleasure cruise' and 'passenger transport' not being necessarily mutually exclusive. The decision in that case was, however, distinguished in *Virgin Atlantic Airways Ltd* (VTD 13840) (TVC 66.23) where a company operated a river boat which it hired out with optional catering and entertainment. Invoices normally included separate charges for the different services provided. The tribunal held that the company made separate supplies of transport (the hire charge), catering and entertainment and that the supplies of transport were zero-rated.

Following the decisions in *P & O* and *Virgin Atlantic*, HMRC indicated that the guidelines set out below were the main criteria they considered relevant in deciding liability. Since their issue, the CJEU in *Card Protection Plan Ltd v C & E Commrs, ECJ Case C–349/96*, [1999] STC 270 (TVC 22.362) (see **65.6 SUPPLY: GENERAL**) have set out general criteria for deciding whether a supply should be treated as a single or multiple supply and HMRC now require these to be applied in all cases. The following guidelines must therefore be read in the light of the general criteria.

Single zero-rated supply of passenger transport

- The essential nature of the supply is passenger transport and the normal conditions for the relief are met;

- all elements of the cruise are integral and it would be neither practicable nor realistic to separate them; and
- the cruise is held out for sale at a single price with no specific charges or discounts for particular services taken or not taken up.

Multiple supplies

- Different elements of the cruise are the subject of separate negotiation and customer choice;
- there are separately identifiable obligations on the supplier, and separate charges;
- separate supplies are not integral to the main supply and could be omitted; and
- it must be practicable, reasonable and realistic to separate the elements of the cruise.

Where separate supplies of any of the individual elements of a cruise are made, these should be taxed according to their respective liabilities (e.g. a separate element of catering is standard-rated when supplied in the UK).

> *Example*
> A rail journey on the Orient Express, to also include a five-course meal with wine, is classed as a multiple supply because the customer expects to receive two very distinct benefits, i.e. a zero-rated train journey and standard-rated food and drink. A ticket price that includes both services for a single price will need to be apportioned so that output tax is paid on the value of the food and drink.

Services of intermediaries

The services of an intermediary making arrangements for the supply of a single zero-rated cruise is zero-rated to the extent that the supply takes place in the UK (see **71.32** below). Where the cruise is treated as a multiple supply, a reasonable apportionment will be accepted.

(VAT Notice 744A, paras 10.2–10.6).

Other trips

The liability of railway and other trips provided with facilities such as catering or entertainment should be determined using the principles outlined above.

In *Sea Containers Services Ltd v C & E Commrs*, QB 1999, [2000] STC 82 (TVC 66.26) a company operated a luxury train on which passengers were supplied with catering. HMRC accepted that, where the train was used for transport to Continental destinations such as Venice, there was a single supply of zero-rated transport. Where, however, the train was used for UK charters, the court confirmed, distinguishing *The Peninsular & Oriental Steam Navigation Co* above, that the company was making separate supplies of transport and catering in the following circumstances.

- Where the whole train plus crew was chartered (whether catering was separately negotiated or included in a single price).
- Where round trips were sold to individual passengers which included high quality catering.

- Where a stopping trip was sold to an individual passenger who alighted before the return journey, again including catering.

HMRC consider that this decision confirms their current policy. (Business Brief 10/99).

See also *A & J Hughes (t/a Pennine Boat Trips of Skipton)* (VTD 15680) (TVC 66.21) where the tribunal held that canal boat trips providing food for parties of 30 or more people were single supplies of zero-rated transport. HMRC consider that this case is confined to the facts and will not accept claims for refunds of VAT on the basis of this decision. (Business Brief 5/99).

Depending on the circumstances 'wine and dine', 'steam and cuisine', disco cruises, dinner cruises, wedding reception cruises and other similar journeys may be standard-rated, zero-rated; or treated as mixed supplies. (VAT Notice 744A, para 9.8).

Airline passenger perks

[71.23] In *Virgin Atlantic Airways Ltd v C & E Commrs; Canadian Airlines International Ltd v C & E Commrs*, QB [1995] STC 341 (TVC 63.7, TVC 66.14) chauffeur-driven limousine services to and from the airport, where the passenger paid one indivisible and irreducible sum for these services and the flight, were held to be part of the zero-rated supply of passenger transport. Following this decision, HMRC have agreed with the airline industry that this treatment would be extended to cover other 'passenger perks'.

To be eligible the perks must

(i) be included in the flight ticket price for the class of travel concerned, with no discount if not taken up;
(ii) form an integral part of an international flight;
(iii) not be gifts of goods (except where currently permitted, e.g. in-flight catering, toiletries); and
(iv) be restricted to one perk per customer (although the customer may be offered a number of options).

The following perks are treated as an integral part of an international flight.

- Limousine transport to and from the airport.
- Up to two days car hire for a one way ticket (four days for a return ticket).
- Car parking at the airport.
- Hotel or similar accommodation provided that it is for no more than one night's stay with breakfast and there is a direct connection with the zero-rated travel (e.g. where it is necessary to catch a connecting flight or it is required for the night prior to take-off or the night after landing).

Not included are

- restaurant meals;
- theatre trips and other entertainment provided during a trip or holiday; and
- hotel accommodation and car hire other than as specified above.

New options will not be automatically disallowed but individual prior approval must be obtained from HMRC to ensure that the services are incidental to and directly connected with the air travel.

The provision of allowable perks will not, in itself, render the airline liable to use the **69 TOUR OPERATORS' MARGIN SCHEME** although the provision of non-allowable perks may well do so.

(VAT Notice 744A, paras 9.6, 9.7).

Taxis and hire cars

VAT liability of fares

[71.24] Zero-rating of domestic passenger transport does not apply if the vehicle is designed to carry less than ten passengers. Taxi and hire car fares are, therefore, standard-rated and if the business provider is registrable for VAT, it must charge VAT to its customers. Extra charges for baggage, waiting time, etc. are also standard-rated as are referral fees from other taxi businesses. Tips and gratuities given voluntarily are not payments for supplies and are outside the scope of VAT. VAT due is calculated by multiplying the fares, including extras, by the VAT fraction. See **48.2 OUTPUT TAX**.

Invoices

Registered persons must issue VAT invoices to any customer who asks for one. See **40 INVOICES**.

Types of business and VAT consequences

(a) Independent self-employed drivers

If a driver has purchased or rented his own vehicle and operates it on a self-employed basis, he will normally be in business on his own account and will be making taxable supplies in the form of

- transport supplied direct to his own passengers; and/or
- services to another taxi business where he supplies them under a contract for services.

Where the driver supplies transport to his own passengers, he may use the agency services of a taxi business (see (*b*)(iii) below) or a taxi association (see below) to obtain customers. If, however, he drives for a taxi or private hire business as its employee (see (*b*)(i) below), he is not considered to be in business for VAT purposes.

A self-employed driver must register for VAT if making taxable supplies where the full amount he is paid for those supplies exceeds the VAT registration threshold. To calculate this, any amounts, such as vehicle and radio rentals or agency charges, deducted by a taxi firm must be added back to the amounts actually received.

(b) Businesses which engage drivers

This includes all types of business, whether sole proprietorship, partnership or limited company. There are three common scenarios for who is supplying the taxi and hire car services to the customers.

(i) *Drivers are employees of a cab business.* Where a cab business employs staff to drive its taxis or hire cars, the business makes the supplies to the customers and must account for output tax on

- the full amount payable by customers before deducting any payments made to drivers;
- any fares the sole proprietor, director or partner, as the case may be, receives if he drives for the firm;
- the full fares payable by passengers even if the work is sub-contracted to an independent business or owner driver; and
- any referral fee received from other taxi businesses.

The drivers are not considered to be in business for VAT purposes. Any money retained by the drivers is outside the scope of VAT as remuneration for their services as employees.

(ii) *Drivers are self-employed and provide their services to a cab business.* The cab business will usually own the vehicles and bear expenses relating to them. Typically, there are more drivers than vehicles and the firm has to exercise control over the drivers to ensure that it is adequately covered at all times. The cab business is buying in the services of drivers and selling the taxi transport on to the final customer as principal. The cab firm must account for output tax as in (i) above. Monies retained by the drivers are consideration for a supply of services by themselves to the cab business under a contract for services (see (*a*) above).

(iii) *Drivers are self-employed and provide their services directly to the customers.* The drivers will usually own their own vehicles and bear expenses relating to them. The cab business or taxi association acts as agent for the drivers, usually providing them with services such as radio hire, booking and support services in return for a commission or fee. This is a standard-rated supply of services by the business or association to the drivers. The business or association must register for VAT if the total of all such charges and any other supplies it makes exceeds the VAT registration limit. Individual drivers need only account for output tax if their supplies exceeds the VAT registration limits (see (*a*) above).

For cases where self-employed drivers were held to supply their services to the cab firm under (*b*)(ii) above, see *Hamiltax* (VTD 8948) (TVC 62.244) and *Knowles (t/a Rainbow Taxis)* (VTD 13913) (TVC 62.245). For cases where the final supply to the customer was held to be by the drivers under (*b*)(iii) above, see *Triumph and Albany Car Service* (VTD 977, VTD 1004) (TVC 62.251) and *Carless v C & E Commrs*, QB [1993] STC 632 (TVC 62.256).

Fees paid to controllers

In *Home Or Away Ltd* (VTD 18195) (TVC 62.261) a company engaged staff (which it treated as self-employed) to act as controllers. Drivers paid 10% of their fares directly to the controllers as fees. The tribunal held that, on the evidence, although the fees were paid directly to the controllers as a matter of convenience, they were paid for a supply by the company of the services of the controllers to the drivers.

Account work

Most taxi and hire car businesses engage in cash work (where customers pay cash to the driver upon completion of the journey) and account work (where regular customers, usually businesses, are allowed to settle their bills periodically). In most cases there will be no difference between the operation of the two types of business, i.e. both will fall within the same category under (*b*)(i)–(iii) above and VAT must be accounted for as indicated under the relevant category. Where both cash and account work falls within (*b*)(iii) above, invoices raised by the business to account customers should itemise separately

- fares collected on behalf of drivers (with the addition of VAT if the *driver* is registered); and
- any administration or similar charge by the business (with the addition of VAT if the *business* is registered).

However, there may be a genuine difference between the treatment of cash and account work with the business acting as agent for cash work under (*b*)(iii) above but principal for account work under (*b*)(ii) above. If such arrangements are adopted, the business must satisfy HMRC that

- the arrangements are reflected in the written terms agreed with the drivers; and
- there is a genuine difference in the operation of the cash and account sides of the business.

If a business operates as an agent for cash work and a principal for account work, it must still account for VAT at the standard rate on the full charge to the drivers for the rental of vehicles, radios or other services supplied to them. This applies even if the charge is

- offset when calculating the rate due to the drivers for account work they perform; or
- deducted before paying them for account journeys.

See *RJ and CA Blanks* (VTD 14099) (TVC 67.127).

The basis of payment (e.g. where drivers are paid a fixed hourly rate for account work but their payment for cash work is directly related to takings) could be one indication of a contractual distinction between cash and account work. See *Triumph and Albany Car Service* and *Carless* above for cases where the cash and account customers were held not to be distinguishable; and *Camberwell Cars Ltd* (VTD 10178) (TVC 62.260) and *A Hussain (t/a Crossleys Private Hire Cars)* (VTD 16194) (TVC 62.253) where the tribunal held there was a real distinction between cash and account work. See also *Macey & Atkins (t/a Sandwich Cars)* (VTD 20257) (TVC 62.252) where the tribunal held that, in the case of account work undertaken for the county council, there was a formal agreement which was only consistent with the firm (and not the individual drivers) acting as principal.

Valuation of services supplied to drivers

In *A2B Radio Cars* (VTD 15145) (TVC 67.128) a partnership which operated a minicab business using self-employed drivers had a number of accounts customers. The partnership paid the drivers 90% of the amounts which it charged the accounts customers, less a deduction which it described as a 'contract levy'. The partnership's other source of income was payments made by the drivers for the hire of radios. HMRC issued an assessment on the basis that the 'contract levy' represented consideration paid by the drivers for a supply of services by the partnership. The partnership appealed, contending that the 'contract levy' was not consideration for a supply, but was simply an amount taken into account in determining the amount payable to the drivers for the services which they provided. The tribunal accepted this contention and allowed the appeal, holding that the consideration for the partnership's services consisted of the amounts paid by the drivers for the hire of radios. There were no grounds for treating the 'contract levy' as additional consideration. On the evidence, the 'contract levy' was simply 'an attempt at creating fairness between drivers who may do more or less contract work' and its true nature was an adjustment to the 90% paid to drivers for client work.

The *A2B Radio Cars* decision was not followed, and was implicitly disapproved, in the subsequent case of *Camberwell Cars Ltd* (No 2) (VTD 17376) (TVC 67.130). However, *A2B Radio Cars* was followed in *Parker Car Services* (TC00528) (TVC 67.131).

Taxi associations

Some independent and self-employed taxi drivers form taxi associations to provide services to the individual driver members. These services can include

- operation of a booking office and radio link;
- hire of radios; and
- provision of rest facilities.

Supplies to members are always standard-rated whether they pay for them by periodic subscription or by deduction/offset from fares collected on the members' behalf. Taxi associations must be registered for VAT if the total of all such charges, together with the total charges for any other supplies they make, exceed the VAT registration threshold. Additional supplies can include an administration fee for services supplied to customers (e.g. providing a breakdown or analysis of journeys made).

Purchases of motor vehicles

VAT can be reclaimed on the purchase of a motor car if

- it is a qualifying motor car; and
- it is intended primarily to be used for letting on hire with a driver for the purpose of carrying passengers.

A qualifying motor car is generally either a new car or a used car where all previous owners were able to reclaim input on their purchases. See **46.3 MOTOR CARS** for further details.

Fuel

Input tax is reclaimable on fuel bought for use in taxis or hire-cars by the proprietor and, for the time being at least, employees of a business. However, if the business funds private motoring, a scale charge is payable.

See **46.10–46.22 MOTOR CARS** for motor expenses generally including fuel and private motoring.

Sales of taxis and hire cars

If a taxi or hire car is sold on which input tax has been previously reclaimed, VAT must be accounted for on the full selling price. If no input tax has been previously reclaimed (e.g. because it was purchased under the second-hand scheme or from a private individual) it may be sold under the second-hand margin scheme provided the conditions for the scheme can be met. VAT need then only be accounted for on the excess, if any, of the sales proceeds over cost. See **62 SECOND-HAND GOODS**.

Where a vehicle is sold with a local authority hackney carriage licence plate, there is a single supply of goods (i.e. a licensed taxi). The full selling price is the total amount charged for the vehicle and licence plate. Licence fees paid to a local authority to operate a taxi cab are treated as separate supplies of services and cannot be included in the purchase price of a vehicle when working out the VAT due on sale under the second-hand margin scheme.

Where a taxi or hire car is exchanged or traded on the purchase of a replacement vehicle, VAT must be accounted for in the same way as if it had been sold at a price equal to the exchange or trade-in allowance received.

Sale of business as going concern

If a taxi or car hire business is sold as a going concern and certain conditions are met, there is no taxable supply for VAT purposes and no VAT liability on the assets sold, including any taxis or hire cars included in the price. See **9.10 BUSINESS.** To be treated as such a sale, the transaction must include more than just the sale of a vehicle (e.g. the rights to a radio network, goodwill, lists of customers).

(VAT Notice 700/25/16).

Freight transport services

[71.25] Freight for these purposes includes

- goods/cargo;
- mail;
- documents;
- unaccompanied vehicles; and
- vehicles transported on ships which are charged at a 'driver accompanied' rate.

To determine the correct VAT treatment of supplies of freight transport or related services, it is necessary to determine

- the status of the customer, i.e. whether the customer is in business or not;
- whether the supply, or any part of it, takes place in the UK;
- who should account for any VAT due; and
- for UK supplies, whether the supplies are zero-rated or standard-rated.

(VAT Notice 744B, paras 1.2, 1.3).

Place of supply

Customer 'in business'

[71.26] Freight transportation and related services fall under the general rule when supplied to customers 'in business'. The general rule is that the place of supply of services to a person who is in business is the place where the customer belongs for the purposes of receiving your supply. It does not matter where the goods being transported move from or to, or where any related service physically takes place.

However, this produced an unintended anomaly in the treatment of supplies wholly enjoyed outside the EU, which may also be taxed locally in the place of performance. The place of supply was changed with effect from 20 December 2012, giving permanent effect to a temporary concession, to make sure that such supplies are outside the scope of UK VAT. [*VATA 1994, Sch 4A paras 9B, 9C*] (HMRC Brief 13/10).

Example

UK Haulage is VAT-registered in the UK and is transporting some food in India for a UK-based charity as part of an emergency aid programme. The general place of supply rules would make this transport charge subject to UK VAT because the customer (the charity) is based in the UK and has some business supplies (and is VAT-registered).

The VAT charge would cause a problem for the charity because the expense relates to a non-business project, i.e. input tax cannot be claimed, even though it is VAT-registered. The law in *VATA 1994, Sch 4A paras 9B, 9C* solves this problem by changing the place of supply to India, i.e. where the transportation takes place. The supply is then outside the scope of UK VAT.

Customer not 'in business'

Freight transportation and related services when supplied to customers who are not 'in business' is regarded as taking place:

- from the EU to a third country: where the transportation is performed in proportion to the distances covered;
- intra-EU transportation: wholly where the transportation begins; and
- related services: where physically performed.

Intra-EU transportation that transits non-EU member state

Transportation between EU member states that involves transiting a non-EU member state (for example Sweden to UK via Norway) is to be treated as intra-EU transportation.

Sub-contractors

For a subcontractor supplying freight transportation or related services to a main contractor, the place of supply is determined by the status of the immediate customer and not that of the ultimate customer of the main contractor.

(VAT Notice 744B, paras 3.1–3.4).

VAT liability

Place of supply is the UK

[71.27] If the place of supply of freight transportation or related services is the UK then the supply will be standard rated, except where:

- the supply is of transportation or related services connected with an import or export from the EU; or
- the actual movement of goods is from, to, or between the islands of The Azores or Madeira or the related service is physically performed on these islands; or
- the supply is of handling or storage of ship or aircraft cargo (in certain places),

when the liability will be zero-rated.

In *'L.C' IK v Valsts ienemumu dienests* (*L.C.*), *CJEU Case C-288/16*, Atek SIA took responsibility for arranging the transportation of goods on behalf of a third party from Latvia to Belarus and Atek contractually assigned the actual freight transportation services to L.C. The vehicles used to transport the goods belonged to Atek but it leased the vehicles to L.C. who used these vehicles to transport the goods. L.C. was also responsible for any repairs, fuel and customs formalities at the borders and for loading/unloading the goods and transferring the goods to the consignee. L.C. treated its supply as exempt from VAT under *Directive 2006/112/EC, Art 146(1)* on the basis that it had provided services connected with the export of goods to a non-EU country. The Latvian tax authorities concluded that the supply could not be zero-rated as the services had not been provided to the consignor/consignee of the goods to be exported. The matter was referred to the CJEU.

The CJEU held that under EU law transportation services that are directly connected with the export of goods to a non-EU country are exempt from VAT. In this case, L.C. supplied services that were necessary to export the goods, however, the services had not been provided to the consignor/consignee of those goods, and as a result the services could not be exempt from VAT.

This case demonstrates the fact that the transportation services provided with the export of goods must be provided to the consignor/consignee and not a third party in order to be zero-rated.

Place of supply is outside the UK

If the place of supply is outside the UK then the supply is outside the scope of UK VAT and there is no VAT liability within the UK. However, input tax incurred in making the supply is recoverable, subject to the normal rules.

Accounting for VAT

The procedure for accounting for VAT and who accounts for it will depend on the circumstances of the transaction.

- If the supplier is located in the same EU member state as the place of supply he charges and accounts for the VAT due as a domestic supply.
- If the place of supply moves to an EU country because that is where a customer who is in-business is located then the customer must account for the VAT as a reverse charge.
- If the place of supply moves to where the transport of the goods for a person not in-business begins then the supplier may have to register for VAT in the EU member state of supply.
- If the place of supply is outside the EU then the supply is outside the scope of VAT in any EU member state.

(VAT Notice 744B, paras 4.1-4.3).

Import/export and non-EU freight transport

[71.28] Import/export and non-EU freight transport means the transport of goods between the EU and non-EU member states, or wholly outside the EU. The place of supply of import/export and non-EU freight transport follows the rules set out in **71.26** above. Where the place of supply is the UK the law zero-rates:

- the supply of transportation of goods from a place within to a place outside the EU and vice versa;
- the transport, handling and storage of goods, when they are supplied in connection with a journey from the place of importation to their destination either within the UK or within another EU member state (to the extent that those services are supplied in the UK); and
- the transport, handling and storage of goods, when they are supplied in connection with a journey from their origin either within the UK or within another EU member state to the place of export (to the extent that those services are supplied in the UK).

'*Destination*' is the furthest specified place in the UK or other EU member state to which the goods are consigned at the time of importation. It is the place stated on the consignment note or any other document by means of which the goods are imported (the delivery terms). When that place is unknown, the destination is the place of importation. 'Origin' is the place from within the UK or other EU member state from which the goods are first consigned for export. When that place is unknown, the origin is the place of exportation.

If a supplier provides services that form part of an import or export movement they should hold satisfactory evidence that they are providing a service connected with a specific import or export of goods in the form of commercial documentation. Main forms of documentary evidence include: contracts or agreements, consignment notes, bills of landing, certificates of shipment, air/seaway bills, Customs declaration forms C88 (SAD). Additionally, a combination or all of the following may provide suitable evidence: inter-company correspondence, the customer's order documentation, payment details, sales invoices, advice notes.

The following services when connected with imports are not zero-rated:

- services, which are unconnected with a movement of goods from a place outside the EU to a place within the EU or vice versa;
- the transport of goods after their arrival at the destination. For example, the transport after arrival at a warehouse (the destination they were consigned to), where the customer is known but the further destination elsewhere in the UK is not known. When the goods are at some later date called off for consignment to (say) a branch, the transport and any related services cannot be zero-rated;
- services connected with goods which have not specifically been consigned for export at the time of transportation;
- the handling of goods after they have been unloaded at the destination;
- the storage of goods at the destination, unless the storage meets the conditions in **71.31**.

(VAT Notice 744B, paras 5.1–5.4, 5.7, 5.8).

Related transport services

[71.29] Related transport services include the following services when they relate to the transport of goods:

- loading, unloading or reloading;
- stowing;
- opening for inspection;
- cargo security services;
- preparing or amending bills of lading, air or sea-waybills and certificates of shipment;
- packing necessary for transportation; or
- storage.

The place of supply of related transport services follows the rules set out in **71.26**. The procedures for accounting for VAT are set out in **71.27**.

(VAT Notice 744B, paras 6.1-6.3).

The Azores and Madeira

[71.30] When Portugal joined the EU, the European Commission decided that freight transport services to and from the Azores and Madeira should be treated differently from supplies of intra-EU freight transport. The place of supply of intra-EU freight transport to the Azores and Madeira is the same as the place of supply for intra-EU freight transport, see **71.26**. Intra-EU freight transport to the Azores and Madeira is zero-rated to the extent that the transport services are treated as supplied in the UK. Transport related services and intermediary services supplied in connection to freight transport to the Azores and Madeira are zero-rated to the extent they are treated as supplied in the UK.

(VAT Notice 744B, paras 7.1-7.5).

Handling and storage services for ship and aircraft cargo

[71.31] Examples of handling and storage services: cargo security services; container handling for which a box charge is made; demurrage; loading stores and discharging empties; loading, unloading, reloading, stowing, securing and shifting cargo; preparing or amending bills of lading, air / or sea-waybills and certificates of shipment; preparing or amending customs entries; presenting goods for customs examination; sorting, opening for inspection, repairing and making good, weighing and taring, taping and sealing, erasing and re-marking, labelling and re-numbering, tallying, checking, sampling, measuring or gauging of goods; stevedoring and porterage; survey of cargo (including damaged cargo); or the movement of goods to or from a ship by lighter.

The handling and storage of ship and aircraft cargo may be zero-rated provided the service is physically performed in the UK: in a port; on land adjacent to a port; in a customs and excise airport; or in a transit shed. However, the grant of a licence to occupy land to store goods in a specific area, as distinct from the service of storing them, may be exempt from VAT. Handling services relating to goods that have been imported from or are to be exported to, a place outside the EU **may** qualify for zero-rating if the goods concerned have been imported from, or are to be exported to, a place outside the EU, see **71.28**. The letting on hire of any goods including cranes or other lifting equipment is not zero-rated, even though the hire takes place in a port or airport.

(VAT Notice 744B, paras 8.1-8.7).

Intermediary services

[71.32] The place of supply of intermediary services follows the rules set out in **71.26** as they relate to the customer, 'the principal'. For the initial intermediary who is involved in the making of arrangements of the services and the place of supply of their services is the UK, the liability of their supply will be zero-rated when they make arrangements for: the supply of space in a qualifying ship or aircraft, or the supply of handling, storage or transportation of goods imported to or exported from the EU, or the supply of handling or storage services. In all other cases the liability of the supply will be standard-rated.

(VAT Notice 744B, paras 9.2, 9.3).

Key points: transport and freight

[71.33] Points to consider are as follows.

- The supply of passenger transport in a vehicle, ship or aircraft that is capable of carrying at least ten passengers is zero-rated. The zero-rating therefore applies to travel by bus, coach, aeroplane, boat, train or ship.
- A key feature of the supply is that the transport must be provided with a driver to qualify for zero-rating. If there is no driver provided, then the supply is usually standard-rated as the hire of a vehicle.

- The zero-rating only applies to passenger transport where the intention is to get the passenger from 'A' to 'B'. So zero-rating would not apply to a fairground ride, donkey ride or hot-air balloon trip, even if the ride is capable of carrying ten or more passengers. The supply in this case is for pleasure transport rather than passenger transport.
- The zero-rating of the above forms of passenger transport means there is no input tax to reclaim on costs incurred by a business on bus fares, train fares, air fares etc.
- Transport in a taxi is standard-rated because the vehicle carries less than ten passengers. However, be aware that many taxi drivers trade as self-employed drivers, rather than being part of a bigger business, and are usually trading below the VAT registration limits. So there is no input tax to claim on the cost of a business journey in these circumstances.
- A taxi driver or business that is VAT-registered does not need to account for output tax on tips received from customers. Tips are outside the scope of VAT because they are separate to the taxi fares.
- The VAT position of taxi drivers needs to be treated with care to be clear whether supplies to passengers are being made by the driver in business on his own account, or by a separate taxi business that either employs the driver or pays him for his time (e.g. on an hourly basis). Many tribunal cases have considered this issue, with a lot of cases being won by HMRC, producing an unexpected output tax liability to the main taxi business.
- A VAT-registered taxi business can reclaim input tax on the purchase of a new motor car to be used as a taxi. However, output tax must be charged on the full selling price if it is resold in the future.
- The place of supply for freight transport services is where the customer is based if the customer is in business. The journey route is irrelevant.
- Be aware of the rule in *VATA 1994, Sch 4A paras 9B, 9C*, which means the place of supply for freight transport services carried out in a non-EU member state (or countries) for a UK customer will be based on where the transportation takes place, i.e. overriding the general rule that the place of supply is where the customer is based for business to business (B2B) sales

72

Valuation

Cross-references. See **5 APPEALS** for appeals regarding valuation; **48.4 OUTPUT TAX** for the valuation of multiply supplies; **61.8, 61.9 RETAIL SCHEMES** for valuation of gross takings of retailers; **65 SUPPLY: GENERAL** for coverage of supplies generally; **66 SUPPLY: PLACE OF SUPPLY** for place of supply; **67 SUPPLY: TIME OF SUPPLY** for time of supply; and **70 TRADE PROMOTION SCHEMES** for valuation of supplies made by the promoter.

De Voil Indirect Tax Service. See V3.151–166.

Introduction to valuation

[72.1] For EU legislation, see **19.17–19.21 EUROPEAN UNION LEGISLATION.**

Under UK legislation, VAT is charged on

- the supply of goods and services in the UK;
- the acquisition of goods in the UK from another EU member state; and
- the importation of goods from outside the EU.

[*VATA 1994, s 1(1)*].

Supplies of goods or services are usually made in return for money, i.e. for a consideration wholly in money. In such cases, the value for VAT purposes is normally, under the general rule in *VATA 1994, s 19(2)*, the price paid or payable excluding the VAT itself. See **72.3** below. The rest of this chapter deals with situations where this simple rule cannot be applied, for example

- where a single consideration is payment for supplies with different liabilities so that an apportionment is necessary (see **72.4** below);
- where the consideration is wholly or at least partly not in money (see **72.5–72.7** below); and
- where circumstances exist requiring special valuation rules to be applied which take precedence over the general rules (see **72.10–72.30** below). This includes special valuation provisions for acquisitions from other EU member states (see **72.11–72.14** below) and imports from outside the EU (see **72.15** below).

In all cases, the application of the correct valuation rule depends upon correctly identifying the consideration given for the supply. For the meaning of 'consideration' see **72.8** below.

General valuation rules

[72.2] The general rules for determining the value of a supply of goods or services are to be found in

- *VATA 1994, s 19(2)* where the consideration for the supply is wholly in money (see **72.3** below); and
- *VATA 1994, s 19(3)* where the consideration is not wholly in money (see **72.5–72.7** below).

These general rules are, however, subject to any special valuation rules made by or under *VATA 1994*. [*VATA 1994, s 19(1)*]. These special rules are considered in **72.10–72.31** below.

Consideration wholly in money

[72.3] If a supply is for a consideration in 'money', subject to the special valuation rules in **72.10–72.30** below, its value for VAT purposes is such amount as, with the addition of the VAT chargeable, is equal to the consideration. [*VATA 1994, s 19(2)*].

'*Money*' includes currencies other than sterling. [*VATA 1994, s 96(1)*]. See **72.14** and **72.18** below where acquisitions from other EU member states and supplies respectively are in foreign currency.

The value for VAT purposes is therefore that part of the payment which, when added to the VAT itself, gives a total equalling the payment. The VAT element of a VAT-inclusive consideration is determined by multiplying that consideration by the VAT fraction (see **48.2 OUTPUT TAX**).

> *Example*
>
> Goods subject to standard-rated VAT are sold for a cash payment of £96.
>
> The VAT element is £96 × 1/6 = £16.00
>
> The value for VAT purposes is £80.00 (£96.00 – £16.00) and the consideration is £96.

Whether contract price inclusive or exclusive of VAT

Whether a price quoted is inclusive or exclusive of VAT must turn on the terms of the particular contract.

- Where a contract specifically states that a price is *VAT-inclusive*, the supplier must calculate the VAT element as in the above example.
- Where it specifically states that the price is *VAT-exclusive*, it is commonly understood that the purchaser must pay the VAT in addition to the quoted price. See *Hostgilt Ltd v Megahart Ltd*, Ch D 1998, [1999] STC 141 (TVC 67.5) and *Wynn Realisations Ltd (in administration) v Vogue Holdings Inc*, CA [1999] STC 524 (TVC 67.6).
- Where the terms of the contract do not make it clear that a payment of the VAT is required in addition to the contract price, the supplier may be left to account for the VAT out of what he receives. See *Lancaster v Bird*, CA 19 November 1998 unreported (TVC 67.4) which was concerned, *inter alia,* with whether VAT could be charged in addition to the cash price quoted for building a stable block. It was held that, although there may well be a custom in the construction industry that prices are quoted exclusive of VAT, there was no evidence in the particular case that, on a contract between a small builder seeking payment in cash and a part-time farmer, it was an implied custom that VAT would be paid on top of the cash payments.

VAT on other taxes

Under *Directive 2006/112/EC, Art 78(a)* the taxable amount (equivalent to value in UK legislation) expressly includes taxes, duties, levies and charges, excluding the VAT itself. Although *VATA 1994, s 19(2)* does not expressly stipulate that other taxes are included in the value for VAT purposes, any such taxes levied on a supply form part of the purchase price and are therefore included in that part of the consideration upon which the VAT must be calculated. This does mean in certain circumstances, eg spirits and tobacco, that VAT is payable on other taxes.

Adequacy or otherwise of monetary consideration

There is no valuation provision by which an inflated payment in money can be reduced for VAT purposes. Where an artificially reduced payment in money is charged, the transaction can be treated as having a higher value for VAT purposes but only where

- it is between connected persons (see **72.19** below); or
- it relates to supplies of goods made to non-taxable persons for retail sale ('direct selling') (see **72.23** below).

However, in cases where apparently insufficient monetary payment appears to have been made, it may well be that the recipient of the supply has also provided additional consideration in a non-monetary form. This non-monetary consideration must also be valued (see **72.5** below).

Apportionment of monetary consideration

[72.4] Where a supply of any goods or services is not the only matter to which a consideration in money relates, the supply is deemed to be for such part of the consideration as is properly attributable to it. [*VATA 1994, s 19(4)*].

Sometimes a single monetary consideration may be the payment for two or more supplies of different liabilities. In such a situation, the above provision requires the trader to allocate a fair proportion of the total payment to each of the supplies. It does not, however, stipulate how that apportionment should be made. A trader can use, and HMRC can accept, any method provided that it achieves a fair result and can be supported by a valid calculation.

For further coverage of apportionment of consideration, see **48.3 OUTPUT TAX**.

Consideration not wholly in money

[72.5] If a supply is for a consideration not consisting, or not wholly consisting, of money, subject to the special valuation rules in **72.10–72.30** below, its value is to be taken to be such amount in money as, with addition of the VAT chargeable, is equivalent to the consideration. [*VATA 1994, s 19(3)*]. In other words, it is necessary to

- determine the amount that would have been given in money for the supply if goods or services had not instead been used for all or part of the payment; and then
- multiply that amount by the VAT fraction (see **48.2 OUTPUT TAX**) to establish how much VAT is due.

Distinguishing between non-monetary consideration and no consideration

Non-monetary consideration exists when a supply is made in return for payment in the form of goods or services. Where there is only non-monetary consideration, a barter transaction takes place (see **72.7** below). In some cases there may be both a monetary consideration and a non-monetary consideration.

When goods or services are provided for no payment in any form (monetary or non-monetary), there has been no consideration. It is then only necessary to value such a provision of goods or services where *VATA 1994* deems a taxable supply to have taken place. The commonest cases are

- private or non-business use of business assets for no consideration (see **72.20** below);

- private or non-business use of services supplied to the business (see **72.21** below);
- supplies of business goods/assets for no consideration (see **72.22** below); and
- deemed supplies of business goods/assets on hand at the time of deregistration (see **72.22** below).

Establishing the monetary equivalent of non-monetary consideration

Key principles in determining the monetary equivalent of non-monetary consideration have been established by the European Court in *Naturally Yours Cosmetics Ltd v C & E Commrs (No 2), ECJ Case 230/87*, [1988] STC 879 (TVC 22.255) and *Empire Stores Ltd v C & E Commrs, ECJ Case C–33/93*, [1994] STC 623 (TVC 22.256).

In *Naturally Yours Cosmetics Ltd* a company sold cosmetics at wholesale prices to beauty consultants who then resold them, at retail prices recommended by the company, at parties which the consultants had encouraged hostesses to arrange. As a reward, a consultant gave the hostess a pot of cream which had been purchased from the company for £1.50 instead of the usual wholesale price of £10.14. The CJEU held that VAT was due on £10.14. The consultants were providing the company with a service (arranging for the hostess to hold the party) in addition to the cash paid. The value of the service was £10.14 less the £1.50 payment. The fact that the price was reduced only if the party actually took place, showed that the parties *subjectively* assigned to the service provided a value corresponding to that price reduction.

The general rule deriving from the decision in *Naturally Yours Cosmetics Ltd* is that non-monetary consideration has the value of the alternative monetary payment that would normally have been given for the supply. Because this must be arrived at subjectively, it is necessary to determine what the particular recipient would have paid the particular supplier for the particular supply had the payment been in money.

In circumstances similar to *Naturally Yours Cosmetics Ltd*, the alternative monetary consideration is not difficult to establish because the normal price chargeable is self-evident from the contractual arrangement between the parties to the transaction. Alternatively, the monetary equivalent may be set out in a catalogue or price-list which shows what the recipient of the supply would have to pay when he provides no non-monetary consideration (e.g. where persons providing selling or introductory services to a mail-order trader are entitled to receive catalogue goods free or for a reduced cash payment).

However, this rule cannot be followed in case where the goods supplied in return for such services are not otherwise sold to the provider of the services. In *Empire Stores Ltd*, a company sold goods via mail order catalogues. New customers (under a 'self-introduction scheme') and existing customers (under an 'introduce-a-friend scheme') were entitled to select an item from a list (e.g. kettle, toaster or iron) free of charge once they (or, as the case may be, their friend) had been approved as a customer and placed an order for goods from the catalogues. The 'reward goods' in question were not advertised for sale in the catalogues. The CJEU held that the introductory service provided by the customer was non-monetary consideration because there was a direct link between its provision and the supply of the reward good. (The link was direct because, in the absence of the service, no reward good would be supplied.) The value of the goods had to be determined subjectively. Where the value was not a sum of money agreed between the parties (as in *Naturally Yours Cosmetics Ltd* above), in order to be subjective, it must be the value which the recipient of the services attributes to the services which he is seeking to obtain. This must correspond to the amount which he is prepared to spend for that purpose. Where, as in *Empire Stores Ltd*, the supply of goods is involved, the value can only be the price which the supplier has paid for those goods.

See also *C & E Commrs v Pippa-Dee Parties Ltd*, QB [1981] STC 495 (TVC 67.41) and *Rosgill Group Ltd v C & E Commrs*, CA [1997] STC 811 (TVC 67.42) where goods were sold under the 'party plan' system but the provider of the services could choose between taking a 'cash commission' or selecting catalogue goods at a lower price. In *Rosgill Group Ltd* a company sold clothing and other goods. Self-employed 'organisers' displayed and sold the products at parties held in the homes of hostesses. In return for permitting a party to be held in her home, a hostess was entitled to take a cash payment or obtain goods from Rosgill's catalogues at a reduced price. The amounts of cash and price reduction were not equal. In the sample transaction considered by the tribunal, the hostess had the option of £2.89 in cash or purchasing goods for £20.76 that would have cost £27.99 if she had paid the listed retail price, i.e. a reduction of £7.23. It was held that the value of the consideration for the supply of the goods was the usual retail price, i.e. a monetary consideration of £20.76 plus a non-monetary consideration of £7.23, being the subjective value of the services supplied by the hostess. It was clear from the contractual terms of the transaction that, if the hostess had not provided the services, she would have had to pay the normal retail price for the goods. The fact that the hostess could have opted to take cash instead, did not prevent the usual non-monetary consideration valuation rules applying in those cases where the price reduction was selected rather than the cash option.

Barter transactions

[72.6] A barter transaction is one in which no monetary payment is made. It may involve goods or services (or a mixture of both) being supplied in return for a supply of goods or services (or a mixture of both) from the other party. Each trader's supply constitutes the consideration he is providing in return for the supply from the other party. An example of a common barter transaction is where a publisher runs a competition in which prizes have been 'donated' but where the publisher is contractually bound to provide advertising to the donor of the prize in return.

In *Riverside Sports & Leisure Ltd* (VTD 20848) (TVC 67.156) a school granted a lease over some sports fields to a partnership which operated a commercial sports centre. Under the agreement, the school received a peppercorn rent and became entitled to use the facilities in the sports centre at certain defined times. The partnership subsequently transferred its business to a company (R), and also assigned R the benefit of the lease. The tribunal decided that the transaction was a barter transaction and that the user rights were granted as the consideration for the lease.

> *Example*
>
> John is VAT-registered as a window cleaner. He agrees to clean the windows for his local football club free of charge, with the condition agreed that he is given a free advert in the match day programme for the club's next home game. The value of the advert if John had paid for it is £75 (the football club is not VAT-registered). Output tax is therefore payable by John based on the valuation of £75 (£75 x 1/6 with a VAT rate of 20%) i.e. because he has received consideration for his services, albeit on a non-monetary basis.

Part-exchange

[72.7] Under a part-exchange transaction, goods are supplied in return for money and other goods.

General rule

Applying the principles in *Naturally Yours Cosmetics Ltd* (see **72.5** above), the general rule is that the goods taken in part-exchange are equal in value to the amount by which the price at which the goods would otherwise have been supplied has been reduced in the particular case. The value of the main supply is therefore the VAT-exclusive amount that would have been charged if no goods had been taken in part-exchange.

> *Example 1*
>
> A sells goods to the majority of his customers for a retail price of £100. To customers in the same line of business he offers the same goods at £95. B is a 'normal customer' and he brings in a part-exchange item which A values at £10. C is a 'trade customer' and he also brings in a part-exchange item which A values at £10.
>
> The total value of the supply to B is £100 (monetary consideration of £90 plus non-monetary consideration of £10, i.e. the amount by which the goods have been reduced for him (£100 – £90)). Similarly, the total value of the supply to C is £95 (£85 plus £10 (£95 – £85)).

See, however, *C & E Commrs v Ping (Europe) Ltd*, CA [2002] STC 1186 (TVC 67.82). In that case, a company (P) sold golf clubs, some of which did not comply with the Rules of Golf and so could not be used for golf competitions. P offered to supply a new club for £22 to anyone surrendering one of the 'illegal' clubs in part-exchange. The new clubs had a normal wholesale price of £49.99 and a normal retail price of £72. HMRC argued that the 'illegal' clubs had a part-exchange value of £27.99, so that P had to account for VAT on the normal wholesale price of £49.99. The tribunal held (and the Ch D and CA unanimously agreed) that the 'illegal' clubs had no value so that output tax was only due on the consideration of £22 which P actually received. The scrap value of the old clubs could be ignored and the value of the non-monetary consideration involved was nil.

Exceptions to the general rule

There are situations in which a number of the general rules above do not apply.

Bumping

It is common practice in the motor trade to manipulate the value of part exchange vehicles to satisfy the minimum deposit requirements of a finance company. This is referred to as 'bumping'. See **46.7 MOTOR CARS.**

Payments made by suppliers to retailers under money-off coupon schemes or cash-back schemes

Following the decision in *Elida Gibbs Ltd v C & E Commrs, ECJ Case C–317/94*, [1996] STC 1387 (TVC 22.257), where payments have been made by manufacturers or distributors as a result of operating a money-off coupon or cash back scheme, those payments reduce their output tax. The manufacturer or dealer must demonstrate that the payments have been made to the retailers and consumers in the transaction chain and that the payments relate directly to successfully redeemed coupons following a retail sale of the goods. See **70.16 TRADE PROMOTION SCHEMES.**

(HMRC Manuals VATMARG13300, VATMARG13350, VATSC32000).

Meaning of consideration

[72.8] Consideration is not defined either in *Directive 2006/112/EC* or *VATA 1994*. The word was defined in the *EC 2nd Directive, Annex A, para 13* as meaning 'everything received in return for the supply of goods or the provision of services, including incidental expenses (packing, transport, insurance, etc.) that is to say not only the cash amounts charged, but also, for example, the value of goods received in exchange or, in the case of goods or services supplied by order of a public authority, the amount of compensation received.' Even though this *Directive* no longer exists, the definition is still sometimes used in cases brought before the CJEU.

The phrase 'in return for' the supply is interpreted to mean that there must be a direct link between the supply and the consideration. See *Staatssecretaris van Financiën v Cooperatieve Vereniging Cooperatieve Aardappelenbewaarplaats GA, ECJ Case 154/80*, [1981] 3 CMLR 337 (TVC 22.83), and *C & E Commrs v The Apple and Pear Development Council, ECJ Case 102/86*, [1988] STC 221 (TVC 22.85).

De Voil Indirect Tax Service. See V3.103.

Payments which may not be consideration

[72.9] Some payments are not consideration because they do not fulfil the conditions in **72.8** above, i.e. there is no direct link between the payment and the supply or there is no supply of goods or services in return for the payment. This paragraph covers areas requiring special attention.

(1) Fines and penalty charges

A true fine or penalty does not form part of the consideration for a supply and is outside the scope of VAT. This includes money levied to penalise an unlawful act (e.g. parking on yellow lines).

However, a payment may be described as a fine or penalty where it is in essence a further payment for a fulfilment of terms and conditions (i.e. part of the consideration for the supply). In such cases, the payments follow the same liability as the supply.

Examples

- *Video hire fines.* Any fine by a video hire shop is an additional taxable supply for the extended use of a video. See *Leigh (t/a Moor Lane Video)* (VTD 5098) (TVC 67.143).
- *Car park charges.* Any additional charge made by a car park for a driver overstaying the allotted time is not regarded as a penalty, but as an extra taxable charge for an extended stay in the car park. But see **44.4**(3) **LOCAL AUTHORITIES AND PUBLIC BODIES** for penalties imposed by local authorities.

(2) Grants and donations

If freely given with no expectation of anything in return, grants and donations are not consideration for any supply and are outside the scope of VAT. They should not be confused with sponsorship which normally involves the sponsor receiving clearly identifiable benefits in return. See **58.14 RECREATION AND SPORT**.

Donated services

The provision of donated services for no consideration is not a supply for VAT purposes. If the provider of the services asks for a donation to be made to a charity rather than payment for his usual fee (e.g. as in Will Aid), such payments can be disregarded for VAT purposes as long as it is clear to customer that the services can be obtained without the customer being obliged to pay anything. It must be left entirely up to the customer's discretion whether he wishes to pay anything to the charity. The fact that the provider may recommend an amount equivalent to the fee be paid to the charity does not, in itself, alter the donation status of the payments.

Local authority, central government and EU grants

The essential point to decide is whether the public authority or EU has derived any direct benefit (see **72.8** above). For cases relating to local authority grants, see *Trustees of the Bowthorpe Community Trust* (VTD 12978) (TVC 42.19), *Hillingdon Legal Resource Centre Ltd* (VTD 5210) (TVC 11.49) and *Wolverhampton Citizens Advice Bureau* (VTD 16411) (TVC 11.51). For case relating to EU grants, see *Mohr v Finanzamt Bad Segeberg, ECJ Case C–215/94*, [1996] STC 328 (TVC 22.176) and *Landboden-Agrardienste GmbH & Co KG v Finanzamt Calau, ECJ Case C–384/95*, [1998] STC 171 (TVC 22.188).

(3) Deposits including returnable containers

Most deposit payments represent consideration. The amount paid over is intended to be offset against the purchase price once the supply has been made. Where a deposit is returned (e.g. if a contract is cancelled), it ceases to be consideration for a supply unless part of the supply has already been made, in which case the deposit is regarded as being consideration for that part of the supply and VAT must be accounted for accordingly. In the case where a contract is cancelled and nothing is supplied, the deposit is not consideration even if it is not returned.

Forfeit deposits

Forfeit deposits are in general not consideration for any supplies because they constitute a payment for compensation for breach of contract. See **33.4 HOTELS AND HOLIDAY ACCOMMODATION.**

Security deposits

A deposit taken as security (e.g. against the safe return of goods on hire or loan) is not consideration for a supply. In the event of the deposit being forfeited, either wholly or in part, through the customer failing to fulfil his contractual obligations, the amount retained by the supplier does not represent additional consideration for the original supply or consideration for an additional supply of goods or services.

Returnable containers

Where a charge is added to a supply of goods for the container until it is returned (e.g. the keg with beer), it is necessary to establish why the charge has been raised. If it has been raised to ensure the safe return of the container and the charge is to be refunded on its return, it can be treated in the same way as a security deposit (see above). If, however, the charge has been raised to cover the loan, hire or use of the container, then the charge represents consideration for a supply of services, even if it is refundable when the container is returned.

See also **67.6 SUPPLY: TIME OF SUPPLY.**

(4) Management charges and directors services

See **45 MANAGEMENT SERVICES AND SUPPLIES OF STAFF.**

(5) Gratuities, tips and service charges

If these are genuinely freely given, they are outside the scope of VAT as they are not consideration for VAT purposes. Where, however, the element of choice has been removed, the payment is part of the consideration for a supply.

Service charges in restaurants are part of the consideration for the underlying supply of the meals if customers are required to pay them. This applies even if they are passed on in full as bonuses to the staff (*Potters Lodge Restaurant Ltd* (VTD 905) (TVC 67.134)). If customers have a genuine option as to whether to pay the service charges, HMRC accept that they are not consideration even if the amounts appear on the invoices (*NDP Co Ltd* (VTD 2653) (TVC 67.107)).

(6) Disbursements

See **3.7 AGENTS.**

(7) **Salary sacrifice**

'Salary sacrifice' describes an arrangement where an employee opts to forgo some of their remuneration in return for receiving goods/services. Following the CJEU decision in *Astra Zeneca UK Ltd v HMRC, ECJ Case C–40/09*, [2010] STC 2298 (TVC 22.96), HMRC regard salary sacrifices as the consideration for a supply of goods/services. Where that supply is taxable, VAT will be due. In most cases the value of the benefit for VAT purposes will be the same as the amount of salary deducted or the amount foregone. Where this is less than the true value (e.g. where employers supply the benefits at below what it cost to buy them in), the value should be based on the cost to the employer. The effect of the CJEU judgment in particular circumstances is as follows.

- *Cycle to work scheme* — where employers purchase bicycles and safety equipment and provide them to employees under a salary sacrifice arrangement, employers must account for output tax based on the value of the salary foregone by the employee in exchange for the hire or loan of a bicycle. Employers can continue to recover VAT on the purchase of the bicycle and associated equipment. VAT remains due when a bicycle is disposed of and its value should normally be based on the price of an identical or similar item, taking into account the age and condition, etc. The table used to value bicycles for direct tax purposes may be used.
- *Face value vouchers* — input tax is recoverable but output tax must be declared. Childcare vouchers are not directly affected by the judgment as they are not subject to VAT. However, VAT on administrative fees from employers' voucher providers are directly attributable to the exempt supply of vouchers under the partial exemption rules with the result that the VAT incurred may be irrecoverable.
- *Food and catering provided by employers* — where employees pay for meals, etc. under a salary sacrifice arrangement, employers must account for VAT on the value of the supplies unless those supplies are zero-rated. Subject to the normal rules, the employer can recover the VAT incurred on related purchases.
- *Motor cars* — the input tax block on cars means that employers do not account for output tax when cars are made available to employees. Where VAT recovery is restricted and output VAT is not due the judgment has no direct impact. Where an employer suffers no input tax restriction, output tax remains due. (HMRC Brief 28/11).

(8) ***Ex gratia* payments**

An *ex gratia* payment by a customer to cover unexpected costs is outside the scope of VAT provided

- the amount is clearly additional to the price for the supply;
- the customer has no obligation to make the payment; and
- the customer would still receive the supply if the *ex gratia* payment were not made.

(9) Subject access fees

Individuals are entitled, by law, to request access ('subject access') to personal data held about them from any data user. Under *Data Protection Act 1984, s 21(2)* the data user may charge for providing such information. This subject access fee is merely a nominal sum to cover the expenses of complying with the statute and is not consideration as there is no supply for VAT purposes.

(10) Manufacturers' warranties

A manufacturer's warranty covers the reliability of goods after sale. Where the manufacturer carries out a repair under this warranty, there is no supply at that time by the manufacturer (even if new parts are supplied) because the original goods were costed to allow for such repairs.

However, if a dealer or other third party carries out the repair on behalf of the manufacturer, there is a supply by him to the manufacturer and his charge for that supply is consideration.

(11) Retailers' warranties

Certain retailers (e.g. jewellers) offer customers an 'insurance' or indemnity which provides for free repair or replacement if the goods sold are lost or damaged within a certain period. The retailer may cover its liability either by obtaining insurance cover or by including the cost in the overall price. In such cases, neither a repair free-of-charge by the retailer nor the free replacement of the lost or damaged goods is a taxable supply, as the original charge covered the costs involved.

(12) Compensation payments

Compensation payments for damage or loss are outside the scope of VAT as they are not consideration for a supply. This is because the payments are made either as a result of a Court Order or through an agreement between the two parties involved to compensate one party for suffering some inconvenience, loss or damage. See **48.7**(5) **OUTPUT TAX** for further details.

(13) Payments relating to land

See **42.19 LAND AND BUILDINGS: EXEMPT SUPPLIES AND OPTION TO TAX.**

(14) Overpayments

Where, due to a mistake by the customer, a supplier receives payment twice for the same invoice, the value of the supply is not affected. The value remains the original price billed and cannot be doubled simply because of the overpayment. The overpayment is outside the scope of VAT unless, and until, it is used to pay or part-pay a future invoice of the supplier in which case it becomes consideration.

Special valuation rules

[72.10] The general rules for determining the value of a supply of goods or services under **72.2** *et seq.* above are subject to any special valuation rules made by or under *VATA 1994*. In case of any conflict, the order of precedence of the special valuation rules is as follows.

(a) **Provisions other than those contained in *VATA 1994, Sch 6*.** These principally comprise the following.

- *VATA 1994, s 20, Sch 7* — acquisitions from other EU member states (see **72.11–72.14** below)
- *VATA 1994, s 21* — imports (see **72.15** below)
- *VATA 1994, s 23* — machine games takings (see **72.29** below)
- *SI 1993/1507* — non-business use of services supplied to a business (see **72.21** below)

(b) **Provisions in *VATA 1994, Sch 6*.** These comprise

- *Sch 6 para A1* — scale rate for fuel supplied for private use (see **46.16**)
- *Sch 6 para 1* — transactions between connected persons (see **72.19** below)
- *Sch 6 para 1A* — use of stock in trade cars of motor manufacturers and motor dealers for less than market value (see **72.30** below)
- *Sch 6 para 2* — supplies of goods to non-taxable persons for retail sale ('direct selling') (see **72.23** below)
- *Sch 6 para 3* — imports and warehoused goods subject to excise duty (see **72.15** and **72.16** below)
- *Sch 6 para 4* — discounts (see **72.24** below)
- *Sch 6 para 5* — tokens, stamps and vouchers (see **72.25** below)
- *Sch 6 para 6* — supplies of goods for no consideration (see **72.22** below)
- *Sch 6 para 7* — non-business use of business assets (see **72.20** below)
- *Sch 6 para 8* — reverse charge services from abroad (see **72.17** below)
- *Sch 6 para 8A* — group supplies using an overseas member (see **72.31** below)
- *Sch 6 para 9* — long-term accommodation at reduced rates (see **72.26** below)
- *Sch 6 para 10* — supplies of catering and accommodation by employers to employees (see **72.27** below)
- *Sch 6 para 11* — supplies in foreign currencies (see **72.18** below)
- *Sch 6 para 12* — money consideration for a supply paid by a third party (see **72.28** below)

[*VATA 1994, s 19(1)*].

Acquisitions from other EU member states

[72.11] The value of any acquisition of goods from another EU member state is to be taken to be the value of the transaction in which the goods are acquired as follows.

- Where the goods are acquired from another EU member state by means of a taxable supply (e.g. goods installed or assembled in the UK, see **20.33 EUROPEAN UNION: SINGLE MARKET**) the value of that transaction is determined under the general valuation rules (see **72.2** above).
- Where the goods are acquired from another EU member state otherwise than in pursuance of a taxable supply, subject to **72.12–72.14** below,

(i) if the transaction is for a consideration in money, its value is to be taken to be such amount as is equal to the consideration; and

(ii) if the transaction is for a consideration not consisting, or not wholly consisting, of money, its value is to be taken to be such amount in money as is equivalent to the consideration.

Note that under (i) above the value is an amount equal to the consideration whereas under the general rule in **72.3** above the value is an amount which, with the addition of the VAT chargeable, is equivalent to the consideration.

[*VATA 1994, s 20(1)–(4)*].

Consideration is any form of payment in money or in kind. It includes any payment made by the customer to cover the supplier's costs in making the supply (e.g. packing, transport or insurance) for which the supplier is responsible under the contract.

The tax value of an acquisition is established as follows.

- Where the consideration is wholly in money, the tax value is the amount paid.
- Where the consideration is non-monetary (e.g. the supply is made in return for payment in goods or services) or is monetary and non-monetary, the tax value is the monetary equivalent of the consideration calculated by reference to the price, excluding VAT, which would have had to have been paid if the consideration were monetary.
- Where the consideration involves a discounted amount and the discounted amount is paid, the tax value is based on the discounted amount.
- Where the consideration includes the offer of a conditional discount which is dependent upon some future event (e.g. on condition that more goods are bought from the supplier or a payment is made within a specified period of time), the tax value is based on the full amount paid. But if the discount is later earned, the tax value is reduced and the amount of tax accounted for can be adjusted (although this should only be done where the business has not claimed, or has been unable to claim, full input tax credit for that acquisition).
- Where there is no consideration (e.g. a transfer of own goods where goods are supplied without charge), the tax value is what it would cost the business, or the person transferring the goods to the business, to purchase the goods in question at the time of the acquisition.

(VAT Notice 725, paras 8.3, 8.4).

Consideration attributable to both an acquisition and other matters

Where the transaction in pursuance of which the goods are acquired from another EU member state is not the only matter to which a consideration in money relates, the transaction is deemed to be for such part of the consideration as is properly attributable to it. [*VATA 1994, s 20(5)*].

Goods subject to duty

Where goods acquired in the UK from another EU member state are charged in connection with their removal to the UK with a duty of excise (or any Union customs duty or EU agricultural levy having effect for transitional provisions in connection with the accession of any state to the EU), then the value of the acquisition for VAT purposes is its value apart from this provision plus the amount (if not already included) of the excise duty, Union customs duty or agricultural levy which has been or is to be paid in respect of the goods. This does not apply to any transaction relating to warehoused goods treated as taking place before the duty point (see **73.4 WAREHOUSED GOODS**).

[*VATA 1994, Sch 7 para 2; SI 1995/2518, Regs 96, 97*].

De Voil Indirect Tax Service. See V3.390.

Transactions between connected persons

[72.12] Where in the case of any acquisition of goods from another EU member state

(a) the value of the transaction is for a consideration in money which is less than its open market value, and
(b) the supplier and the person who acquires the goods are 'connected', and
(c) that person is not entitled under *VATA 1994, ss 25, 26* to credit for all the VAT on the acquisition,

HMRC may direct that the value of the transaction is to be taken to be its 'open market value'.

'*Open market value*' is the amount which would be taken as its value assuming the transaction was for such consideration in money as would be payable by a person standing in no such relationship with any person as would affect the consideration.

A direction is given by notice in writing to the person by whom the acquisition is made within a three year period from the time of the acquisition (or, in certain cases where that person is not a taxable person and the consideration is payable periodically, from the first relevant event for the purposes of taxing the acquisition). The direction may be varied or withdrawn by a further direction given by notice in writing. The direction may also include a direction that the value of any transaction made after the date of notice and to which the above conditions apply is to be taken to be its open market value. An appeal may be made against a direction (see **5.3**(28) **APPEALS**).

See **72.19** below for the meaning of '*connected persons*'.

[*VATA 1994, Sch 7 paras 1, 5*].

De Voil Indirect Tax Service. See V3.391.

Transfers and disposals of business assets

[72.13] Where goods are acquired from another EU member state under a transaction treated as a supply of goods under **65.3**(*e*)(*f*) **SUPPLY: GENERAL**, the value of the relevant transaction, in a case where there is no consideration, is to be taken to be

(a) such consideration in money as would be payable by the supplier if he were, at the time of the acquisition, to purchase goods *identical* in every respect (including age and condition) to the goods concerned; or
(b) where the value in (*a*) cannot be ascertained, such consideration in money as would be payable to purchase goods *similar* to, and of the same age and condition as, the goods concerned; or
(c) where the value cannot be ascertained under (*a*) or (*b*), the cost of producing the goods concerned if they were produced at that time.

Any VAT included in the purchase price or production cost is to be deducted in arriving at the value to be taxed.

[*VATA 1994, Sch 7 para 3*].

Currencies other than sterling

[72.14] Where goods are acquired from another EU member state and any sum relevant for determining the value of the transaction is expressed in a currency other than sterling, then unless one of the alternatives in (*a*)–(*b*) below is adopted, that sum is to be converted into sterling at the market selling rate for that currency at the time of acquisition. The rates published in national newspapers are acceptable as evidence of the rates at the relevant time. The following alternatives are, however, allowed.

(a) A business may use the period rate of exchange published by HMRC for customs purposes. Details of particular period rates are available from the VAT Helpline (0300 200 3700). This alternative can be adopted in respect of all acquisitions or in respect of all acquisitions of a particular class or description. If the latter, that class or description should be noted in the business record at the time of adoption. There is no need to notify HMRC in advance if this alternative is to be adopted but, once it has been, a business cannot then change it without first obtaining the agreement of HMRC.
(b) A business can apply in writing to HMRC to use a rate, or a method of determining a rate, which it uses for commercial purposes. In considering whether to allow the application, HMRC will take into account whether the proposed rate or method is determined by reference to the UK currency market, whether it is objectively verifiable, and the frequency with which the applicant proposes to update it. Forward rates or methods deriving from forward rates are not acceptable.

Whatever rate or method is adopted, the appropriate rate for any supply is the one current at the time of supply.

[*VATA 1994, Sch 7 para 4*]. (VAT Notice 725, para 8.5 which has the force of law).

De Voil Indirect Tax Service. See V3.393.

Importation of goods

[72.15] The value of goods imported from a place outside the EU is, subject to below, to be determined according to the rules for Union customs duties (whether or not the goods in question are subject to such duties). These rules are set out in *Council Regulation 2913/92*, *Commission Regulation 2454/93* and, with effect from 1 May 2016, *Regulation (EU) 952/2013*. See also Customs Notice 252 *Valuation of imported goods for customs purposes, VAT and trade statistics*.

The following are included in the value (so far as not already included under the above rules).

(a) All taxes, duties and other charges levied outside or, by reason of importation, within the UK (but excluding VAT).
(b) All incidental expenses such as commission, packing, transport and insurance costs, up to the 'first destination' of the goods in the UK. '*First destination*' means the place mentioned on the consignment note or other importation document or, in the absence of such documentation, the place of the first transfer of cargo in the UK.
(c) If at the time of importation of the goods a further destination for the goods is known, and that destination is within the UK or another EU member state, all such incidental expenses resulting from the transport of the goods to that other destination.

Subject to (*a*)–(*c*) above, where the consideration is wholly or partly in money and on terms allowing a discount for prompt payment (but not payment of the price by instalments), the value of the goods is reduced by the discount if payment is made in accordance with those terms so that the discount is allowed.

[*VATA 1994, s 21(1)(2)(3)*].

Works of art, antiques and collectors' pieces

Special valuation provisions apply for these items which have the effect of subjecting them to VAT at an effective reduced rate of 5%. See **74.3 WORKS OF ART, ETC.** for full details.

Incidental expenses

In addition to the examples given above, 'incidental expenses' also covers items such as customs clearance charges, quay rent, entry fees, demurrage, handling, loading and storage costs. Costs which are taxable under the reverse charge procedure (see **39.4 INTERNATIONAL SERVICES**), e.g. royalties and licence fees, should not be included in the value for import VAT.

HMRC give three methods which may be used to calculate the 'incidental expenses' element of the import VAT value. Individual importers or agents may use whichever method best suits their particular circumstances.

(1) *Method 1*. This method requires the actual costs to be declared at the time the goods are imported. In cases where the costs are later found to be incorrect (e.g. if additional storage costs are incurred) the amount(s) paid will need to be adjusted after importation.
(2) *Method 2*. The agreed rates given below may be used to estimate the incidental expenses to be included in the import VAT value. The rates are intended only for international movements of goods which termi-

nate in the UK and represent average costs of handling, storage, customs declarations and transport to destination. Values for other consignments, including those for delivery in other EU member states, must be based on Methods 1 or 3. Where Method 2 is used, post-importation adjustments are not required. Additionally, where it is found that the amount of import VAT based on actual costs exceeds the amount declared on the basis of Method 2 rates, HMRC will not seek to collect the arrears of import VAT unless the importer concerned is not registered for VAT or, if registered, is restricted in the amount of import VAT that can be claimed as input tax.

The agreed rates are

(i) *Airfreight*: 40p per chargeable kilo or a minimum amount of £100 to be added to the value at the time of importation, whichever is the greater.

(ii) *Surface freight groupage/consolidation consignments by trailer, rail wagon or container*. delivery and handling combination of £90 per gross weight tonne plus a flat 'other ancillaries' rate of £80 per consignment, minimum £170, to be added to the value at the time of importation.

(iii) *Surface freight full load consignments by trailer, rail wagon or container*. £550 per full load consignment to be added to the value at the time of importation.

(3) *Method 3*. In cases where Methods 1 and 2 are considered inappropriate or impractical to use, individual agreements may be negotiated with the Entry Processing Unit or with the importers local Excise and Inland Customs office. Once a Method 3 rate is used, post-importation adjustments are not required.

(VAT Notice 702, para 3.1).

Value declaration

If goods are liable to *ad valorem* customs duty (i.e. a duty chargeable on the basis of value), a declaration on Form C105 (Valuation Declaration) made for duty purposes, will also generally be acceptable for VAT. However, the declaration will only provide information which helps determine the customs value of the goods, and it should not be regarded as establishing their full value for VAT purposes (see above).

Where goods are not liable to ad valorem duty but are liable to VAT at the standard rate, a valuation declaration for VAT is only to be completed when requested by Customs and

- the value exceeds £6,500; and
- the importer is not registered for VAT; or
- the importer is registered for VAT but either the goods are for non-business purposes or input tax deduction would not be allowed (e.g. on motor cars); or
- the value of the goods is not being determined under Method 1 (see HMRC Notice 252, Section 3).

There are no arrangements for registering a General Valuation Statement for VAT-only entries. Individual valuation declarations must be submitted where necessary.

Whether or not a valuation declaration is required for the goods, evidence of value must be produced. Acceptable evidence is a copy of the seller's invoice or other document against which payment will be made. This will include telex or similar messages used instead of invoices.

(VAT Notice 702, para 3.3).

De Voil Indirect Tax Service. See V3.321–V3.329.

Excise duty

Where any goods whose supply involves their removal to the UK are charged in connection with their removal with a duty of excise or car tax (or any Union customs duty or EU agricultural levy having effect for transitional provisions in connection with the accession of any state to the EU), then the value of the supply for VAT purposes is its value apart from this provision plus the amount (so far as not already included) of any duty which has been or is to be paid in respect of the goods. [*VATA 1994, Sch 6 para 3*].

Warehoused goods

[72.16] Where the time of supply of any dutiable goods (or goods comprising a mixture of dutiable goods and other goods) is determined under *VATA 1994, s 18(4)* (goods within the warehouse regime) to be at or after the duty point, then the value of the supply for VAT purposes is its value apart from this provision plus the amount (so far as not already included) of any duty which has been or is to be paid in respect of the goods. [*VATA 1994, Sch 6 para 3*].

See **73.8 WAREHOUSED GOODS** for the provisions of *VATA 1994, s 18(4)* and the definitions of '*dutiable goods*' and '*duty point*'.

Reverse charge services received from abroad

[72.17] Where any supply of services is treated under the reverse charge provisions as made by the recipient of the services (rather than the supplier), the value of the supply is

- if the consideration for the services was a consideration in money, such amount as is equal to that consideration; and
- if the consideration did not, or did not wholly, consist of money, such amount in money as is equivalent to that consideration.

[*VATA 1994, Sch 6 para 8*].

It should be noted that under these provisions, value is derived from the consideration upon a VAT-exclusive basis. It is an amount equal to the consideration rather than, as under the general rule in **72.3** above, an amount which, when VAT is added, equals the consideration.

See **39.4 INTERNATIONAL SERVICES** for situations where the reverse charge applies in the UK.

Supplies in foreign currency

[72.18] For EU legislation, see **19.21**(*b*) **EUROPEAN UNION LEGISLATION.**

Under UK legislation, where there is a supply of goods or services and any sum relevant for determining the value is expressed in a currency other than sterling, subject to below, that sum is to be converted into sterling at the market selling rate for that currency at the time of supply. The rates published in national newspapers are acceptable as evidence of the rates at the relevant time. The following options are, however, allowed.

- Where HMRC have published a notice specifying rates of exchange, or methods of determining rates of exchange, a person may opt to use a rate so specified or determined. This alternative may be adopted for all supplies or for all supplies of a particular class or description. If adopted only for a particular class, that class and the time of adoption should be noted in the records. There is no need to notify HMRC in advance that this alternative has been adopted but, once it has, it cannot be changed without first obtaining the agreement of HMRC.
- HMRC may allow a person to apply to them to use a different rate of exchange for the valuation of all or some of his supplies. Application should be made to HMRC in writing. In considering whether to allow the application, HMRC will take into account whether the proposed rate or method is determined by reference to the UK currency market, whether it is objectively verifiable and the frequency with which it is proposed to update it.

[*VATA 1994, Sch 6 para 11*]. (VAT Notice 700, para 7.7 which has the force of law).

De Voil Indirect Tax Service. See V3.164.

The value on which VAT is due when a supply of goods or services sold in exchange for decentralised digital currencies (cryptocurrencies) such as bitcoin is the sterling value of the cryptocurrency at the point the transaction takes place.

(HMRC Brief 9/14).

Transactions between connected persons

[72.19] Where all the following conditions are satisfied, then unless the supply falls within **72.27** below (supplies of accommodation and catering by employers to employees), HMRC *may* direct that the value of the supply is to be taken to be its 'open market value'.

(a) The value of a supply made by a taxable person for a consideration in money would otherwise be less than its open market value. A direction *cannot* therefore be made if
  - part of the consideration is non-monetary (in which case the rules in **72.5** above must be followed); or
  - the consideration is greater than the open market value (i.e. a direction cannot be issued to reduce an over-inflated consideration).

(b) The person making the supply and the person to whom it is made are 'connected' (see below).

(c) If the supply is a taxable supply, the recipient is not entitled under *VATA 1994, ss 25, 26* to credit for all of the VAT on the supply. In practice, this means that, where the supply is a taxable supply, a direction can only be issued if the recipient is not registered for VAT or is wholly or partly exempt for VAT purposes.

The provisions are specifically intended to counter tax avoidance. If a supply between connected persons is made below open market value for a legitimate reason that can be substantiated, and which is unconnected with avoidance, HMRC have a discretion not to issue a notice.

'*Open market value*' is the amount which would be taken as its value under (*a*) above assuming the supply were for such consideration in money as would be payable by a person standing in no such relationship with any person as would affect that consideration.

A direction is given by notice in writing to the person making the supply within a three year period from the time of the supply and may be varied or withdrawn by a further notice in writing. The notice may *also* include a direction that the value of any future supply satisfying the above conditions is to be taken to be its open market value (although a notice cannot cover future supplies only). An appeal may be made against a direction (see **5.3**(28) **APPEALS**).

[*VATA 1994, s 19(5), Sch 6 para 1(1)–(3)(5), para 13*].

> *Example*
>
> ABC Ltd is VAT-registered and buys a new commercial property for £200,000 plus VAT. It sells the property to its associated company, DEF Ltd, for £50 plus VAT, DEF Ltd will use the property for its trading activity as an insurance broker, i.e. an exempt activity where input tax claims are blocked.
>
> HMRC will issue a direction in this situation to rule that the value of the supply from ABC Ltd to DEF Ltd be based on its open market value of £200,000 plus VAT. The input tax block to DEF Ltd will then be £40,000 (assuming a VAT rate of 20%), exactly the same as if it had bought the property from the original owner.

Connected persons

Persons are treated as 'connected' with another under the provisions of *CTA 2010, s 1122*. [*VATA 1994, Sch 6 para 1(4)*]. These are as follows.

(i) **An individual** is connected with his spouse or civil partner, any 'relative' of himself or of his spouse or civil partner, and with the spouse or civil partner of any such relative. It appears that a widow or widower is no longer a spouse (*Vestey's Exors and Vestey v CIR*, HL 1949, 31 TC 1). Spouses divorced by decree nisi remain connected persons until the divorce is made absolute (*Aspden v Hildesley*, Ch D 1981, [1982] STC 206).

(ii) **A trustee of a settlement**, in his capacity as such, is connected with
- the settlor (if an individual);
- any person connected with that settlor; and
- any close company whose participators include the trustees of the settlement; and
- any non-UK resident company which, if it were UK resident, would be a close company whose participators include the trustees of the settlement; and
- any body corporate controlled (within the meaning of *CTA 2010, s 1124*) by a close company (or a non-UK resident company which, if it were UK resident, would be a close company) whose participators include the trustees of the settlement; and
- if the settlement is the principal settlement in relation to one or more sub-fund settlements, a person in the capacity as trustee of such a sub-fund settlement; and
- if the settlement is a sub-fund settlement, a person in the capacity of trustee of any other sub-fund settlements in relation to the principal settlement.

(iii) **Partners** are connected with each other and with each other's spouses, civil partners and 'relatives' except in connection with acquisitions and disposals of partnership assets made pursuant to *bona fide* commercial arrangements.

(iv) **A 'company'** is connected with another company if
- the same person 'controls' both;
- one is controlled by a person who has control of the other in conjunction with persons connected with him;
- a person controls one company and persons connected with him control the other;
- the same group of persons controls both; or
- the companies are controlled by separate groups which can be regarded as the same by interchanging connected persons.

(v) **A company** is connected with another person who (either alone or with persons connected with him) has control of it.

(vi) **Persons acting together to secure or exercise control of a company** are treated in relation to that company as connected with each other and with any other person acting on the direction of any of them to secure or exercise such control. For the meaning of 'acting together to secure or exercise control' see *Steele v EVC International NV (formerly European Vinyls Corp (Holdings) BV)*, CA 1996, 69 TC 88. Control may be 'exercised' passively. (See *Floor v Davis*, HL 1979, 52 TC 609).

'*Company*' includes any body corporate, unincorporated association or unit trust scheme. It does not include a partnership.

'*Control*' in *CTA 2010, s 1122* is to be read in accordance with *CTA 2010, ss 450–451*, except where otherwise indicated. See *Tolley's Corporation Tax* for full coverage of this definition.

'*Relative*' means brother, sister, ancestor or lineal descendant.

'*Settlement*' includes any disposition, trust, covenant, agreement, arrangement or transfer of assets (except that it does not include a charitable loan arrangement). [*ITTOIA 2005, s 620*].

'*Settlor*' is any person by whom the settlement was made or who has directly or indirectly (or by a reciprocal arrangement) provided, or undertaken to provide, funds for the settlement. [*ITTOIA 2005, s 620*].

De Voil Indirect Tax Service. See V1.296; V3.161; V3.162.

Non-business use of business assets

[72.20] Where there is a free supply of services by virtue of *VATA 1994, Sch 4 para 5(4)* (business goods put to a private or non-business use), then, unless **72.27** below applies (supplies of accommodation and catering by employers to employees), the value of the supply is taken to be the full cost to the taxable person of providing the services.

See **48.6 OUTPUT TAX** for further details.

Non-business use of services supplied to a business

[72.21] Where a person carrying on a business puts services supplied to him to any private or non-business use, he is treated as having supplied those services in the course or furtherance of the business. The value of the supply is that part of the value of the supply of the services to him as reasonably represents the cost to him of providing the services. Where the services are put to a private or non-business use on more than one occasion, the total VAT liability under these provisions cannot exceed the input tax claimed when the services were obtained. [*SI 1993/1507*].

See **48.6 OUTPUT TAX** for further details.

Supplies of goods for no consideration

[72.22] Where there is a supply of goods by virtue of

- a Treasury order under *VATA 1994, s 5(5)* (self-supply of goods, see **46.6 MOTOR CARS** for self-supply of a motor car and **63.2 SELF-SUPPLY** for self-supply of stationery),
- *VATA 1994, Sch 4 para 5(1)* (gifts of business assets, see **48.5 OUTPUT TAX**),
- *VATA 1996, Sch 4 para 6* (removal of business assets from one EU member state to another, see **20.2 EUROPEAN UNION: SINGLE MARKET**), or
- *VATA 1994, Sch 4 para 8* (deemed supply on deregistration and termination of business, see **60.40 REGISTRATION**),

then, unless **72.27** below applies (supplies of accommodation and catering by employers to employees), the value of the supply is

(a) such consideration in money (excluding any VAT) as would be payable by the person making the supply if he were, at the time of the supply, to purchase goods *identical* in every respect (including age and condition) to the goods concerned;

(b) where the value cannot be determined as under (*a*) above, such consideration in money (excluding any VAT) as would be payable by that person if he were, at that time, to purchase goods *similar* to, and of the same age and condition as, the goods concerned; and

(c) where the value cannot be determined as under (*a*) or (*b*) above, the cost of producing the goods concerned if they were produced at that time.

[*VATA 1994, Sch 6 para 6*].

Note that what is relevant is what the goods would have cost to purchase or produce at the time of their disposal and not the actual historic cost to the business. Where disposal is close to the date the goods were obtained, the value may have remained unchanged. In most cases, however, depreciation or appreciation over the intervening period must be taken into account.

Supplies of goods made to non-taxable persons for retail sale ('direct selling')

[72.23] In circumstances where

- the whole or part of a business carried on by a taxable person consists in supplying to a number of persons goods to be sold, whether by them or others, by retail, and
- those persons are not taxable persons,

HMRC may direct that the value of any such supply is to be taken as its open market value. The direction is given by notice in writing to the taxable person and is effective from the date of the giving of notice or a later date as specified in the notice and may be varied or withdrawn by a further direction given by notice in writing. An appeal may be made against a direction (see **5 APPEALS**).

[*VATA 1994, Sch 6 paras 2, 13*].

HMRC has authority to issue such a direction in respect of direct selling cases because derogations have been obtained under *Directive 2006/112/EC, Art 395* (see **19.42 EUROPEAN UNION LEGISLATION**). See also *Direct Cosmetics Ltd v C & E Commrs, ECJ Case 5/84*, [1985] STC 479 (TVC 22.555) (and the subsequent appeal by *Direct Cosmetics* and *Laughton Photographs Ltd v C & E Commrs, ECJ Case 138/86*, [1988] STC 540 (TVC 22.556)) and *Gold Star Publications Ltd v C & E Commrs*, QB [1992] STC 365 (TVC 67.32). A direction has been held to be invalid where there was no effective means of determining the open market value of the goods sold by retail. See *Beckbell Ltd* (VTD 9847) (TVC 67.37) where the company did not fix a recommended retail price for goods by salesmen and frequently charged its salesmen different prices for identical goods. See, however, the subsequent decision of the House of Lords in *Fine Art Developments plc* below.

In *Fine Art Developments plc v C & E Commrs*, HL 1995, [1996] STC 246 (TVC 67.36), catalogues containing descriptions and pictures of goods for sale were sent to 'agents'. Some goods were retained by the agents for their own use and some were sold on at less than the catalogue price, although the majority were sold by the agents at the full catalogue price. The company argued that the direction issued under *VATA 1994, Sch 6 para* 2 was invalid. It argued that it was not supplying goods to be sold by retail because at the time it made the supply to the agents, it did not know what the agents would be doing with the goods, and that even if the direction was not invalid for that reason, it was otherwise invalid because it was impossible to comply with its terms, i.e. to determine to which goods it was to apply. The House of Lords rejected these arguments and held that the direction was valid. As VAT was a self-assessed tax, it was the duty of the company to modify its order form so as to identify the goods earmarked for onward sale. Where the company was unable to show what the actual sale price for any item was, it was open to HMRC to take the catalogue price as being the true open market value.

De Voil Indirect Tax Service. See V3.161; V3.163.

Discounts

Prompt payment discounts from 1 April 2015

[72.24] *FA 2014, s 108* amends *VATA 1994, Sch 6 para 4* so that where goods or services are supplied for a consideration in money and on terms allowing a discount for prompt payment, in valuing the supply the consideration is taken as reduced by the discount only when payment is made in accordance with the terms allowing the discount. Previously the consideration was taken as reduced by the discount whether or not payment was made in accordance with the terms allowing the discount.

The above amendment is to have effect in relation to all supplies made from 1 April 2015. However, see below for certain supplies made from 1 May 2014. In addition, the Treasury may by statutory instrument provide that the above amendment has effect in relation to other specified supplies prior to 1 April 2015.

As was previously the case, the consideration is not taken as reduced by the discount where the terms include any provision for payment by instalments.

On 22 December 2014 HMRC published HMRC Brief 49/14 to provide guidance for businesses that issue and/or receive invoices offering payment discounts from 1 April 2015.

Businesses issuing invoices offering a prompt payment discount

At the time the invoice is issued the supplier will not know if the customer will qualify for the prompt payment discount, unless the customer has already paid promptly and qualified for the discount. The invoice will therefore need to show the full price and the VAT on the full price. On issuing the invoice the supplier must show the rate of discount offered on the invoice, enter the invoice into their accounts and record the VAT on the full price. Before issuing the invoice the supplier will need to decide which of the two methods referred to below they will adopt to adjust their accounts in order to record a reduction in consideration if the customer pays promptly and qualifies for the discount.

Method 1 is to issue a credit note to evidence the reduction in consideration. In which case, a copy of the credit note must be retained as proof of that reduction.

Method 2 is the alternative method that should be used if the supplier does not wish to issue a credit note. If the supplier does not wish to issue a credit note the invoice must include the terms of the prompt payment discount and must refer to the time by which the discounted price must be paid, and a statement that the customer can only recover as input tax the VAT paid to the supplier. HMRC recommend that the following wording be used to comply with these requirements:

> 'A discount of X% of the full price applies if payment is made within Y days of the invoice date. No credit note will be issued. Following payment you must ensure you have only recovered the VAT actually paid.'

HMRC suggest that it might be helpful if suppliers who do not wish to issue credit notes also include the following information on invoices, in addition to the normal information that is included on invoices and the additional compulsory information referred to above:

- the discounted price
- the VAT on the discounted price
- the total amount due of the offer of the prompt payment discount is taken up.

If the discounted price is paid in accordance with the prompt payment discount terms the supplier must adjust their records to record the output tax on the amount actually received. If the supplier has included the appropriate wording on the invoice so that a credit note does not need to be issued, the invoice, together with proof of receipt of the discounted price within the relevant time (e.g. a bank statement) will be required to evidence the reduction in consideration.

If a supplier receives a payment that falls short of the full price but which is not made in accordance with the prompt payment discount terms it cannot be treated as a prompt payment discount. The supplier must account for VAT on the full amount as stated on the invoice. If the amount not paid remains uncollected it will become a bad debt in the normal way. If a price adjustment is agreed later then adjustment must be made in the normal way, for example, by issuing a credit note.

Businesses receiving invoices offering a prompt payment discount

For VAT-registered customers who receive invoices offering a prompt payment discount the VAT treatment will vary depending on when they pay the invoice and which method the supplier has adopted to adjust their accounts in order to record a reduction in consideration if the customer qualifies for the discount. As explained above, it should be apparent from the invoice if the supplier does not wish to issue a credit note in the event that the customer pays promptly and qualifies for the discount.

If the customer pays the full price, the customer records the full price and the VAT thereon in their records and no VAT adjustment is necessary.

If the customer pays the discounted price in accordance with the terms of the prompt payment discount on receipt of the invoice, the customer records the discounted price and the VAT thereon in their records and no VAT adjustment is necessary.

If the customer does not pay the invoice when it is first issued, the customer records the full price and the VAT thereon in their records. If the customer subsequently decides to take up the offer of the prompt payment discount then:

- If they have received an invoice setting out the prompt payment discount terms which states no credit note will be issued they must adjust the VAT in their records when payment is made. They should retain a document that shows the date and amount of payment (e.g. a bank statement) in addition to the invoice to evidence the reduction in consideration.
- If the supplier's invoice does not state that a credit note will not be issued, the customer must adjust the VAT they claim as input tax when the credit note is received. They must retain the credit note as proof of the reduction in consideration.

[*VATA 1994, Sch 6 para 4 as amended by FA 2014, s 108*]. (HMRC Brief 49/14).

Prompt payment discounts from 1 May 2014 in relation to specified supplies

The *FA 2014, s 108* amendment to *VATA 1994, Sch 6 para 4* referred to above is effective from 1 May 2014 in relation to supplies of radio or television broadcasting services or telecommunications services by a taxable person who is not required by or under any enactment to provide a VAT invoice to the person supplied. The Treasury may by statutory instrument provide that the above amendment has effect in relation to other specified supplies prior to 1 April 2015.

Prompt payment discounts before 1 April 2015 (except for specified supplies referred to above)

Where goods or services are supplied for a consideration in money and on terms allowing a discount for prompt payment, in valuing the supply the consideration is taken as reduced by the discount, whether or not payment is made in accordance with those terms. However, this treatment does not apply where the terms include any provision for payment by 'instalments'. [*VATA 1994, Sch 6 para 4*].

In *Saga Holidays Ltd* (VTD 18591) (VTD 67.94) S sold holidays and offered customers discounts for prompt payment. It failed to take account of such discounts and submitted a repayment claim. HMRC agreed to refund the amounts which S had overpaid where customers actually received discounts but rejected the claim where discount had been offered but the customers had not actually taken advantage of it. The tribunal agreed with this treatment, observing that the legislation provided that the consideration should be taken as reduced 'by the discount' and holding that these words could more readily be interpreted as a reference to a discount that has actually come into existence than to one that was available but may never come into existence. Therefore, *Sch 6 para 4(1)* should be construed as meaning that the consideration is only reduced where the discount is achieved.

See also *Gold Star Publications Ltd v C & E Commrs*, QB [1992] STC 365 (TVC 67.33) (whether what was described as a discount for prompt payment was in fact such a discount or a commission given to demonstrators).

Unconditional discounts

An unconditional discount may be available as a result of, for example, the volume of supplies being made or the size and status of a customer. The original invoice may show the discounted amount, or the discount may be effected by a subsequent credit note. Note that a 100% discount may give rise to a VAT charge if the underlying supply becomes (effectively) a gift.

Contingent discounts

Where a contingent discount is offered on condition that something happens later (e.g. on condition that the customer buys further goods) the discount must initially be ignored and VAT is due on the full amount. If the customer later earns the discount, the tax value is then reduced and the VAT due can be adjusted by issuing a credit note.

Discounts allowed with part-exchange goods

See **72.7** above.

(VAT Notice 700, para 7.3).

'Dividend'

'Dividend' paid to members in respect of their purchases of items from the society have been held to be discount in *Co-operative Retail Services Ltd* (VTD 7527) (TVC 22.279).

Tokens, stamps and vouchers

[72.25] See **70 TRADE PROMOTION SCHEMES** for the treatment of coupons, vouchers and business promotion schemes.

Long-term accommodation at a reduced rate

[72.26] Where accommodation in a hotel, inn, boarding house or similar establishment is

- provided to an individual for a period exceeding four weeks, and
- throughout that period the accommodation is provided for the use of the individual either alone or together with one or more persons who occupy the accommodation with him otherwise than at their own expense,

after the initial four weeks the value of the supply is reduced to that part attributable to facilities other than the right to occupy the accommodation (subject to a minimum of 20%). [*VATA 1994, Sch 6 para 9*].

See **33.2 HOTELS AND HOLIDAY ACCOMMODATION** for further details.

Supplies of catering and accommodation by employers to employees

[72.27] Where an employer makes a supply of goods or services to his employees consisting of

- food or beverages supplied in the course of catering, or
- accommodation in a hotel, inn, boarding house or similar establishment,

the value of that supply is to be taken to be the monetary consideration, if any, paid by the employee (i.e. the consideration is nil where there is no consideration or any consideration other than money).

[*VATA 1994, Sch 6 para 10*].

See **12.8** CATERING and **33.3** HOTELS AND HOLIDAY ACCOMMODATION for further details.

See also *Hotel Scandic Gasaback AB v Riksskatteverket, ECJ Case C–412/03*, [2005] STC 1311 (TVC 22.205).

Money consideration for a supply paid by a third party

[72.28] HMRC have power to make regulations so as to require that, in prescribed circumstances, there is to be taken into account as constituting part of the monetary consideration for the purposes of **72.3** above (where it would not otherwise be so taken into account) money paid in respect of the supply by persons other than those to whom the supply is made. [*VATA 1994, Sch 6 para 12*]. No regulations have been made under these provisions.

Machine games

[72.29] The amount a person pays to play a relevant machine game is treated as the consideration for a supply of services. The value of such supplies is the takings received, less the amount of the winnings paid out, excluding any winnings paid to the supplier or a person acting on their behalf. There are also rules for valuing tokens depending upon whether they are replayable tokens or non-replayable tokens. [*VATA 1994, s 23(1)–(9)*].

See **8.4** BETTING AND GAMING for further details.

Use of stock in trade cars for less than market value

[72.30] Where a motor manufacturer or a motor dealer allows an employee or his relative to use a stock in trade motor car for a consideration which is less than its open market value, HMRC may direct that the value of the supply is to be taken as the open market value.

[*VATA 1994, Sch 6 para 1A*].

See **46.7** MOTOR CARS for full details.

Group supplies using an overseas member

[72.31] From 17 July 2012, a concession (ESC 3.2.2) on how the reverse charge on an intra-group supply (which arises when a partly exempt VAT group buys in services through an overseas group member) should be valued was put on a statutory footing. The provisions apply where

- a supply ('the intra-group supply') made by a member of a group ('the supplier') to another member of the group is, by virtue of *VATA 1994, s 43(2A)*, excluded from the supplies disregarded under *VATA 1994, s 43(1)(a)* (see **28.6 GROUPS OF COMPANIES**); and
- the representative member of the group satisfies HMRC as to the value of each bought-in supply.

'Bought-in supply', in relation to the intra-group supply, means a supply of services to the supplier to which *VATA 1994 s 43(2A)(c)–(e)* refers (see **28.6 GROUPS OF COMPANIES**), so far as that supply is used by the supplier for making the intra-group supply.

The value of the intra-group supply shall be taken to be the total of the relevant amounts in relation to the bought-in supplies. The relevant amount in relation to a bought-in supply is the value of the bought-in supply, unless HMRC make a direction that the relevant amount is the supply's open market value, which they may direct if the value of the bought-in supply is less than its open market value. Such a direction must be given by notice in writing to the representative member, but no direction may be given more than three years after the time of the intra-group supply.

[*VATA 1994, Sch 6 para 8A*].

Key points: valuation

[72.32] Points to consider are as follows.

- Customers will usually pay for goods or services with money, making it easy to identify (in most cases) the value of a supply for VAT purposes. However, payment in non-monetary consideration is also relevant as far as a VAT charge is concerned (e.g. barter arrangement, part exchange etc.).
- It is important that a supplier and customer are clear whether a contract or deal to supply goods or services is based on prices that include or exclude VAT. A supplier should ensure the answer to this question is clearly established and communicated to the customer before a sale takes place.
- VAT is due on the full value of standard-rated goods or services supplied to a customer, including any other taxes that are levied for customs or excise duties. In the case of alcoholic drinks, this means that VAT is effectively being charged on other taxes.

- The valuation of a non-monetary consideration can present a challenge to a business. The key approach is to convert the non-monetary payment into an amount of money based on what amount would have been paid by the customer if payment was made wholly in money.
- In the case of a part exchange transaction, very common for certain types of business (e.g. a car dealer) there are two sales taking place, and each sale is valued according to its market price, i.e. the two transactions are not 'netted off' as far as output tax is concerned.
- No output tax is due on a free supply of services, e.g. a free advert placed in a publication such as a newspaper. However, there must not be any hidden benefits for the supplier that could represent non-monetary consideration.
- Many grants received by charities and similar bodies are outside the scope of VAT. This is because no specific goods or services are being supplied in return for the grant payment. However, some grants are linked to a supply of services, which means the grant income could be standard rated in many situations.
- In certain situations, a grant being standard-rated rather than outside the scope of VAT could benefit the grant recipient because it means input tax can be claimed on the related costs of the project. The VAT charge to the grant provider might not be a problem in many cases if he can reclaim input tax (as is the case with most local authorities).
- A service charge made by a restaurant, usually based on a percentage of the customer's bill, is standard-rated. However, discretionary payments such as tips are outside the scope of VAT.
- For a sale to a connected party, and where the connected party cannot fully reclaim input tax, HMRC may direct that the value of the supply be taken as the open market value if it is made below this figure. This situation will be particularly relevant if the recipient of the supply is either not VAT-registered or unable to reclaim input tax under partial exemption rules.

73

Warehoused Goods

De Voil Indirect Tax Service. See V3.332; V3.371; V3.372; V5.141, V5.141A.

Introduction to warehoused goods

[73.1] This chapter considers the VAT treatment of goods entering, supplied within and removed from warehouses, together with the treatment of supplies of services associated with those goods.

Warehouses

[73.2] Customs warehousing permits the payment of VAT (and duties) to be suspended or delayed for goods which are stored in authorised premises.

A '*warehouse*' for these purposes means any warehouse where goods may be stored in any EU member state without payment of any one or more of the following.

(a) Union customs duty.
(b) Any agricultural levy of the EU.
(c) VAT on the importation of the goods into any EU member state.

(d) Any duty of excise or any duty which is equivalent in another EU member state to a duty of excise.

[*VATA 1994, s 18(6)*].

In the UK, a warehouse may be a

- customs warehouse, i.e. premises or an inventory system authorised by Customs for the storage of non-union goods under duty and import VAT suspension;
- tax warehouse, i.e. an authorised place where goods subject to excise duty are produced, processed, held, received or despatched under duty suspension arrangements by an authorised warehousekeeper in the course of his business. Included are excise warehouses, registered premises, distilleries and refineries; or
- fiscal warehouse, i.e. a regime where specified EU goods in free circulation can be traded VAT-free, subject to certain conditions. Fiscal warehouses are dealt with separately under **73.12** *et seq* below.

Goods eligible for warehousing in the UK

The following goods are eligible for warehousing in the UK.

Customs warehouses	*Third country goods of any kind except excise goods whether subject to a positive rate of duty or not*
Tax warehouses (including both manufacturing premises and storage premises)	Third country goods on which customs duty has been paid Union goods UK goods comprising mineral (hydrocarbon) oils, alcohol and alcoholic beverages, manufactured tobacco

(Notice 3001, Annex A; Notice 702/10/12).

Goods entering warehouses

[73.3] No import VAT is due when goods are placed in a customs warehouse. Import VAT will only become due when the goods are removed from the warehouse to free circulation. It is normally payable, together with any customs or excise duty suspended, by the person removing the goods.

Goods which, on arrival in the UK, are placed in a customs warehouse are not deemed to be imported for VAT purposes until such time as they are removed into free circulation in the UK.

The following goods can be stored in a customs warehouse.

- Non-Union goods liable to customs duties and/or VAT (whether or not eligible for preference) and/or excise duties.
- Non-Union goods for which necessary supporting documents (such as BIS licences) are not available at the time of import.
- Non-Union goods imported to another suspensive regime (such as IP (inward processing) or TA (temporary admission)) warehoused for export from the EU.

- Non-Union PCC (processing under customs control) products. Please note that goods can no longer be imported using PCC since 30 April 2016 (subject to the transitional provisions).
- Non-Union goods that are not subject to a positive rate of customs duty in the tariff, but are liable to import VAT.
- Non-Union goods in free circulation that are subject to a claim under the rejected imports arrangements.

'*Non-Union goods*' are goods which are not of EU origin or imported goods which have not been released into free circulation.

'*Union goods*' are goods which are

(a) entirely obtained or produced in the Customs territory of the EU, without the addition of goods from third countries or territories that are not part of the Customs territory of the EU;
(b) imported from countries or territories not forming part of the Customs territory of the EU which have been released for free circulation in an EU member state; or
(c) obtained or produced in the Customs territory of the EU either wholly from those under (*b*) or partly from (*a*) and (*b*).

(Notice 3001, Annex A, para 1.10).

Supplies within warehouses

[73.4] Supplies of imported goods in warehouse are normally disregarded for VAT purposes as they are treated as taking place outside the UK (see **73.5** below). On removal to home use, the goods may be subject to import VAT.

Within tax warehouses supplies of dutiable goods, whether home produced or acquired from another EU member state, are disregarded for VAT purposes but only if a subsequent supply takes place whilst they are still warehoused. See **73.6** and **73.7** below. (If this condition is not met, any VAT due on the sale is to be accounted for when the goods are removed to home use, see **73.8** below.)

Similarly, certain services connected with warehoused goods are relieved when originally supplied (through the mechanism of zero-rating), but may be taxed at the standard rate when the goods to which they relate are removed from the regime. See **73.19** below.

Imported goods

[73.5] Subject to the exceptions below, where

(a) any goods have been removed from a place outside the EU and have entered the EU,
(b) the 'material time' for any supply of those goods or acquisition of those goods from another EU member state is while they are subject to a warehousing regime and before the 'duty point', and
(c) such goods are not mixed with any 'dutiable goods' which were
   - produced or manufactured in the UK (in which case **73.7** below applies), or

- acquired from another EU member state (in which case **73.6** below applies),

then the supply or acquisition referred to in (*b*) above is treated as taking place outside the UK and is disregarded for UK VAT purposes.

The '*material time*' for a supply or acquisition is the time of removal of the goods or, in the case of a supply, if the goods are not removed, at the time they are made available to the person to whom they are supplied.

'*Dutiable goods*' means any goods which are subject to a duty of excise (or any Union customs duty or EU agricultural levy having effect for transitional purposes in connection with the accession of any country to the EU).

'*Duty point*' means the time any excise duty becomes payable or, if the goods are not subject to excise duty, the time when any Union customs debt in respect of duty on the entry of the goods into the EU would be incurred.
[*VATA 1994, s 18(1)(6)(7)*].

The effect of the above provisions is that VAT must not be charged, and a VAT invoice showing VAT must not be issued, in respect of any supplies of imported goods made within a warehousing regime.

Exceptions

As an anti-avoidance measure, the above provisions do not apply where

- there is a supply of goods that would otherwise be treated under the above provisions as taking place outside the UK;
- the whole or part of the business carried on by the supplier of those goods consists in supplying to a number of persons goods to be sold, by them or others, by retail;
- that supplier is a taxable person (or would be a taxable person but for the above provisions); and
- that supply is to a person who is not a taxable person, and is a supply of goods to that person by retail or to be sold, by that person, by retail.

[*VATA 1994, s 18(1A); SI 1995/2518, Reg 145K*].

One of the key assumptions of the provisions of *VATA 1994, s 18(1)* is that the amount of VAT due once the goods leave the warehouse should correspond to the amount of the VAT that would have been due had the transaction not been VAT-free. The anti-avoidance provisions are designed to enforce this. The vast majority of transactions in customs warehouses will not be affected and continue to benefit from relief.

Acquisitions from other EU member states

[73.6] Where

- any 'dutiable goods' are acquired from another EU member state, or
- a person makes a supply of dutiable goods which were acquired from another EU member state (or a mixture of such goods and other goods)

and the 'material time' for the acquisition or supply is while the goods are subject to a warehousing regime and before the 'duty point', then where the material time for any subsequent supply of those goods is also while the goods are subject to the warehousing regime and before the duty point, the acquisition or supply is treated as taking place outside the UK (and is disregarded for UK VAT purposes).

The '*material time*' for a supply or acquisition is the time of removal of the goods or, in the case of a supply, if the goods are not removed, at the time they are made available to the person to whom they are supplied.

'*Dutiable goods*' means any goods which are subject to a duty of excise (or, any Union customs duty or EU agricultural levy having effect for transitional purposes in connection with the accession of any country to the EU).

'*Duty point*' means the time any excise duty becomes payable or, if the goods are not subject to excise duty, the time when any Union customs debt in respect of duty on the entry of the goods into the EU would be incurred.

[*VATA 1994, s 18(2)(3)(6)(7)*].

The effect of this is that any supply of such goods is disregarded for VAT purposes if the supply is followed by another supply of the goods while they are still warehoused. No VAT should be charged on such disregarded supplies.

Goods produced or manufactured in the UK subject to excise duty

[73.7] Where a person makes a supply of any 'dutiable goods' which were produced or manufactured in the UK (or a mixture of such goods and other goods) and the 'material time' for the supply is while the goods are subject to a warehousing regime and before the 'duty point', then where the material time for any subsequent supply of those goods is also while the goods are subject to the warehousing regime and before the duty point, the earlier supply is treated as taking place outside the UK (and is disregarded for UK VAT purposes).

The '*material time*' for a supply is the time of removal of the goods or, if the goods are not removed, at the time they are made available to the person to whom they are supplied.

'*Dutiable goods*' means any goods which are subject to a duty of excise.

'*Duty point*' means the time any excise duty becomes payable.

[*VATA 1994, s 18(2)(3)(6)(7)*].

The effect of this is that any supply of such goods is disregarded for VAT purposes if the supply is followed by another supply of the goods while they are still warehoused. No VAT should be charged on such disregarded supplies.

Removal of goods from warehouses

[73.8] VAT becomes due when goods are removed from a warehouse to free circulation and is normally payable by the person who removes the goods. The VAT due may be on the importation, acquisition or supply of the goods. Removal of goods from the customs warehousing procedure is referred to as 'discharge of the procedure' and may take a number of forms, as described in Notice 3001, Annex A, para 1.22.

Imported goods

The warehousekeeper must not allow goods to leave the warehouse until he has received evidence that HMRC have officially released the goods. If this evidence has not been received before removal of the goods, the warehousekeeper has failed to comply with the conditions of the authorisation and as a result could be liable for any customs debt that may become due on the goods, and may also be liable to a penalty under the Customs Civil Penalty provisions.

Evidence of official release can be a copy of the CHIEF Display Entry Version Details screen print, E2 and plain paper copy 6 of the C88 Single Administrative Document. If using Customs Freight Simplified Procedures (CFSP), an entry into the customs warehouse stock records and Customs Supervised Exports records (which may be one and the same) followed by an electronic CFSP supplementary declaration is also evidence of release.

(Notice 3001, Annex A, paras 1.22.2, 1.22.3).

Acquisitions from other EU member states

Where

- either
  - (i) 'dutiable goods' are acquired from another EU member state, or
  - (ii) a person makes a supply of dutiable goods which were acquired from another EU member state (or a mixture of such goods and other goods),
- the 'material time' for the acquisition or supply is while the goods are subject to a warehousing regime and before the 'duty point', and
- there is no subsequent acquisition or supply of those goods whilst subject to the warehouse regime and before the duty point

the acquisition or supply is treated as taking place at the earlier of the time the goods are removed from the warehouse regime and the duty point.

The '*material time*' for a supply or acquisition is the time of removal of the goods or, in the case of a supply, if the goods are not removed, at the time they are made available to the person to whom they are supplied.

'*Dutiable goods*' means any goods which are subject to a duty of excise (or any Union customs duty or EU agricultural levy having effect for transitional purposes in connection with the accession of any country to the EU).

'*Duty point*' means the time any excise duty becomes payable or, if the goods are not subject to excise duty, the time when any Union customs debt in respect of duty on the entry of the goods into the EU would be incurred.

[*VATA 1994, s 18(2)–(4)(6)(7)*].

The effect of this is that VAT due on the last supply of the goods within the tax warehouse must be accounted for and paid (or deferred) when the goods pass the duty point or are removed for home use. A removal declaration must also be completed. Where no supply takes place, the acquisition VAT must be accounted for on the VAT return for the period covering the date of removal. This VAT can be recovered as input tax on the same return, subject to the normal rules.

Goods produced or manufactured in the UK subject to excise duty

Where

- a person makes a supply of any 'dutiable goods' which were produced or manufactured in the UK (or a mixture of such goods and other goods),
- the 'material time' for the supply is while the goods are subject to a warehousing regime and before the 'duty point', and
- there is no subsequent supply of those goods whilst subject to the warehousing regime and before the duty point,

the supply is treated as taking place at the earlier of the time the goods are removed from the warehouse regime and the duty point.

The '*material time*' for a supply is the time of removal of the goods or, if the goods are not removed, at the time they are made available to the person to whom they are supplied.

'*Dutiable goods*' means any goods which are subject to a duty of excise.

'*Duty point*' means the time any excise duty becomes payable.

[*VATA 1994, s 18(2)(3)(6)(7)*].

The effect of this is that the person removing the UK-produced goods from the warehouse to home use must complete a removal declaration at the time the goods are removed and pay any duty and VAT due. The value for VAT purposes includes any customs and/or excise duty payable.

Goods removed from warehouse to a place outside the UK

Subject to the normal rules, any supply of goods from a warehouse for export outside the EU or for supply to a taxable person in another EU member state may be zero-rated. This is another form of discharge of the warehousing procedure. Goods removed directly to a customs warehouse in another EU member state under the customs warehouse transfer arrangements can be disregarded for UK VAT purposes. However, in both cases any such supplies must be entered on an EU sales list covering the time of removal and in Box 8 of the VAT return. (Notice 3001, Annex A, paras 1.22, 1.23).

Transfers from customs warehouses to another customs suspensive procedure

Where goods are transferred to another customs suspensive procedure, the import VAT and customs duty remain suspended under the new procedure. (Notice 3001, Annex A, para 1.22).

Evidence for input tax deduction

[73.9] The normal evidence of VAT paid on imported goods is the certificate Form C79. The certificate is sent to the VAT-registered person whose Economic Operator Registration and Identification (EORI) is shown in Box 8 of the import entry. In the UK the EORI comprises the letters 'GB' followed by the importer's VAT registration number plus a three-digit suffix. Certificates cover accounting transactions made in each calendar month. (Notice 3001, Annex A, para 1.22.11).

Deficiency of warehoused goods

[73.10] Any deficiencies of warehoused goods are deemed to be removed from the customs warehousing regime. Where deficiencies of imported goods are charged with duty, import VAT not already paid on the imported goods also becomes due. Similarly, any acquisition VAT on goods from another EU member state which has not been accounted for is also payable. In any case, the VAT may be deducted as input tax, subject to the normal rules. (Notice 3001, Annex A, para 1.21.6).

Summary tables

[73.11]

Receipt of goods into a UK customs warehouse and their removal to free circulation in the UK		
	Duty	*VAT*
1. Non-Union goods received direct from a third country and placed in a customs warehouse	*Customs duty*: Suspended on entry into customs warehouse and to be paid on removal *Excise duty*: Duty not due and suspended whilst in warehouse	*Import VAT*: Suspended on entry into customs warehouse and to be paid on removal
2. Non-Union goods received direct from a third country or via another EU member state on which there is a nil rate of customs duty —VAT-only customs warehousing	*Customs duty*: N/A *Excise duty*: Duty not due and suspended whilst in warehouse	*Import VAT*: Suspended on entry into customs warehouse and to be paid on removal. Any VAT due in respect of zero-rated services should be paid on removal
3. Non-Union goods received from a third country via another EU member state	*Customs duty*: As 1. above *Excise duty*: As 1. above	*Import VAT*: As 1. above *Acquisition VAT*: If the goods are the subject of an acquisition on arrival in the warehouse, VAT must be accounted for on the acquirer's return for the period in which the acquisition tax point falls
4. Goods imported from special territories	*Customs duty*: N/A *Excise duty*: As 1. above	*Import VAT*: As 2. above

Receipt of goods into a UK customs warehouse and their removal other than to free circulation in the UK		
	Duty	***VAT***
1. Non-Union goods for direct export to a country outside the EU	*Customs duty*: Not paid *Excise duty*: Not paid	*Import VAT*: N/A *Supply VAT*: Supplies of goods removed from the UK may be zero-rated as exports (subject to the normal rules)
2. Non-Union goods for indirect export to a country outside the EU	*Customs duty*: Not paid. Goods must move under CPEI arrangements or transit. *Excise duty*: Not paid	*Import VAT*: Any VAT which would be due on removal to UK free circulation is not payable *Supply VAT*: As 1. above
3. Goods transferred to another EU member state under a duty suspensive regime	*Customs duty*: As 2. above *Excise duty*: Not paid	*Import VAT*: Any VAT which would be due on removal to UK free circulation is not payable. Otherwise outward movements of goods may be zero-rated (subject to the normal conditions for intra-EU trade) *Supply VAT*: Supplies direct to a customs warehouse in another EU member state are outside the scope of UK VAT
4. Non-Union goods moved to another EU member state on which customs duty is paid on removal	*Customs duty*: Paid on removal from customs warehouse	*Import VAT*: VAT is payable but may be relieved if the goods are removed in the course of an onward zero-rated supply
5. Non-Union goods transferred to IP suspension in the UK from a customs warehouse	*Customs duty*: Continues to be suspended and is paid on final removal from IP if IP is not discharged *Excise duty*: Continues to be suspended and is paid if IP is not discharged	*Import VAT*: Any import VAT due is to be paid with the customs duty *Supply VAT*: Supplies of goods under IP are subject to domestic VAT rules
6. Non-Union goods transferred to IP drawback in the UK from a customs warehouse	*Customs duty*: To be paid on removal from warehouse *Excise duty*: To be paid on removal from warehouse	*Import VAT*: To be with customs duty on removal *Supply VAT*: As 5. above

(This chart comes from the withdrawn VAT Notice 702/9/12, paras 13.1, 13.2; it still appears to be a useful guide to the charges that arise, but has not been reproduced in the same form in Notice 3001).

Fiscal warehousing

[73.12] The *EC 2nd VAT Simplification Directive* enables countries to introduce a warehousing regime to operate alongside both customs warehouses and excise warehouses. In the UK, this regime is known as fiscal warehousing.

Under the fiscal warehousing regime, certain eligible goods (see **73.14** below) can be placed in a notified warehouse and can then be traded VAT-free whilst subject to the regime. Supplies of goods within a fiscal warehouse and supplies of goods intended to be placed in the regime are, subject to conditions, relieved from VAT. See **73.15** and **73.16** below. The goods may be liable to VAT on removal from the regime. See **73.17** below. Certain services supplied within a fiscal warehousing regime are also VAT-free, the VAT being accounted for when the goods are removed. See **73.19** and **73.20** below.

Dealers in fiscally warehoused goods are not required to be VAT-registered if the value of any other supplies that they make outside of the regime is below the VAT registration threshold.

Retail sales are not allowed under the conditions of a fiscal warehousing regime. [*VATA 1994, s 18A(3)*].

Authorisation for fiscal warehousing

[73.13] HMRC can, on written application, approve any registered person (including any company in a group registration) as a fiscal warehousekeeper, the approval being subject to such conditions as HMRC impose. [*VATA 1994, s 18A(1)(4)(7)(9)*]. See VAT Notice 702/8/12, para 6 for a specimen application.

The authorisation procedure is stringent so that HMRC can rely on the operators' control procedures and records. All the following basic criteria for authorisation must be met.

- The applicant must be VAT-registered in the UK.
- All business revenue records must be of a high standard (e.g. VAT returns and payments must be up-to-date).
- If already authorised to operate any UK duty suspensive regime, the applicant must have a satisfactory proven records of operation.
- The applicant must be able to comply with the conditions of authorisation and with such regulations as may be laid down for the operation of the regime.
- The administration and organisation of the business must be sound and strictly managed.
- The applicant must provide a list of the addresses of all storage sites which will form part of the fiscal warehouse and any other premises where records will be held. Retail premises cannot be used as fiscal warehouse premises. All notified premises must meet the requirements of health and safety legislation (including any third party premises intended to be used).

- Accounts and stock control records must be capable of meeting the requirements in **73.18** below. In particular, they must be able to distinguish between fiscally warehoused goods and other stocks and be able to identify the location and quantity of any given item held within the fiscal warehousing regime at any stage.

Cancelling or revoking an authorisation

A warehousekeeper wishing to cancel authorisation must give advance notice to HMRC in writing, stating the date by which all goods will cease to be traded and removed from the warehousing arrangements. VAT must be accounted for on all such removals in accordance with **73.20** below.

HMRC can revoke authorisation at any time for any reasonable cause. Except in very exceptional circumstances, they will notify the warehousekeeper in advance of any intended revocation, and the warehousekeeper will have a right to appeal. Where HMRC withdraw authorisation, any goods held in the regime will be treated as though they had been removed by the proprietor at the time of withdrawal and VAT will be due in accordance with **73.20** below.

(VAT Notice 702/8/12, paras 2.7, 2.11).

Qualifying conditions for goods

[73.14] To be eligible for the fiscal warehousing regime,

(a) the goods must be '*eligible goods*' for fiscal warehousing purposes, i.e.
- aluminium, copper, iridium, lead, nickel, palladium, platinum, rhodium, silver, tin, and zinc;
- chemicals in bulk;
- cereals;
- coffee (not roasted), tea, and cocoa beans (whole or broken, raw or roasted);
- grains and seeds (including soya beans);
- mineral oils (including propane and butane and crude petroleum oils);
- nuts;
- oil seeds and oleaginous fruit;
- olives;
- potatoes;
- raw sugar;
- rubber, in primary forms or in plates, sheets or strip;
- vegetable oils and fats and their fractions (whether or not refined, but not chemically modified); and
- wool;

(b) the goods must be in free circulation within the EU (i.e. all duties, taxes and levies must have been either paid or deferred, including customs duty, import VAT, excise duty and any CAP charges due on the goods);

(c) any import VAT payable in respect of the goods must have been accounted for; and

(d) the goods must have been entered in the fiscal warehousing records.

Non-eligible goods may be stored in a place which is a fiscal warehouse but cannot be subject to a fiscal warehousing regime or benefit from the conditions of fiscal warehousing.

[*VATA 1994, s 18B(6), Sch 5A*]. (VAT Notice 702/8/12, para 2.4).

Goods entering a fiscal warehouse

[73.15] The following transactions are relieved from VAT (by being treated as taking place outside the UK) if any subsequent supply of the goods in question is made while they are subject to the fiscal warehouse regime.

(a) An acquisition of eligible goods from another EU member state where, after the acquisition, but before the next supply (if any), the acquirer places the goods in a fiscal warehousing regime. The acquirer must, not later than the time of acquisition, prepare and keep a certificate stating that he intends to enter the goods into the fiscal warehousing regime.

(b) A supply of eligible goods (other than a retail transaction) where after supply in question but before the next supply, if any, the buyer places the goods in a fiscal warehousing regime. The buyer must give his supplier, not later than the time of supply, a certificate stating that he intends to enter the goods into the fiscal warehousing regime.

[*VATA 1994, s 18B(1)–(3)*].

A supply falling within (*a*) or (*b*) above is treated as a supply of goods (and not a supply of services), even if it is the transfer of an undivided share in the goods, i.e. an unidentified part of a larger stock of eligible goods. [*SI 1996/1255*]. (Normally, such a transfer of an undivided share would be treated for VAT purposes as a supply of services, see **65.4**(*a*) **SUPPLY: GENERAL**.)

Certificates

The certificate required under (*a*) or (*b*) above should be in the following form.

I	(full name)
	(status in company)
Of	(name and address of company)

declare that (name of company) intends to enter to the fiscal warehousing regime at the fiscal warehouse shown below on (insert date) or within (insert number) days commencing today, the goods indicated below:

- name and address of fiscal warehouse
- authorisation number of the fiscal warehousekeeper
- description of goods
- quantity of goods

* I certify that the supply of goods is eligible to be relieved from VAT under VATA 1994, sections 18B(2)(d)/18B(3) (purchases)

* I certify that the acquisition is eligible to be relieved from VAT under VATA 1994, sections 18B(1)(d)/18B(3) (acquisitions). * Delete as appropriate (signature) (date)

Where a taxable person prepares a certificate under (*a*) above or receives one under (*b*) above, he must retain it with his VAT records. Where a non-taxable person prepares a certificate under (*a*) above, he must keep it for six years and produce it to an HMRC officer on request.

[*SI 1995/2518, Reg 31(1), Reg 145B, Sch 1*].

Supplies within fiscal warehouses

[73.16] The following transactions are relieved from VAT (by being treated as taking place outside the UK and therefore outside the scope of UK VAT) if any subsequent supply of the goods in question is made while they are subject to the fiscal warehouse regime.

(a) An acquisition of eligible goods from another EU member state where the acquisition takes place while the goods are within a fiscal warehousing regime. The acquirer must, not later than the time of acquisition, prepare and keep a certificate stating that the goods are subject to a fiscal warehousing regime. See **73.15** above for the form of the certificate.

(b) A supply of eligible goods (other than a retail transaction) where the supply takes place while the goods are within a fiscal warehousing regime.

[*VATA 1994, s 18B(1)–(3)*].

The effect of the above is that goods acquired or supplied after being entered to the fiscal warehousing regime are treated as though they are outside the UK and not subject to the normal supply rules *unless* the supply in question is the final supply whilst the goods are warehoused.

A supply falling within (*a*) or (*b*) above is treated as a supply of goods (and not a supply of services), even if it is the transfer of an undivided share in the goods, i.e. an unidentified part of a larger stock of eligible goods. [*SI 1996/1255*]. (Normally, such a transfer of an undivided share would be treated for VAT purposes as a supply of services, see **65.4**(*a*) **SUPPLY: GENERAL**.)

Registration

If transactions falling within (*a*) or (*b*) above are a trader's only UK business activities, he will not be required to register for VAT although he may apply for voluntary registration if he wishes. Liability to register for other business activities is not affected by either the value of supplies made in a fiscal warehouse or the value of deemed supplies of relieved services accounted for by the remover of the goods (see **73.20** below). [*VATA 1994, Sch 1 para 1(9)*]. (VAT Notice 702/8/12, para 2.18).

Removal of goods from fiscal warehousing

[73.17] Subject to the exceptions below, a charge to VAT arises when eligible goods are removed from the fiscal warehouse regime.

- Where the goods were not subject to a supply whilst warehoused, the value on removal is the value at entry into the regime (plus the value of any relieved services performed whilst the goods were fiscally warehoused).
- Where the goods have been supplied whilst warehoused, the value on removal is the amount which would have been due on the last supply within the warehouse. VAT will also be due on any of the relieved supplies of services relating to the goods which have been carried out after that final supply. See **73.20** below.

The VAT due on removal is the liability of the person who causes the goods to cease to be covered by the fiscal warehousing regime and is chargeable and payable at the time of removal. A VAT-registered trader should account for the VAT on the return covering the date of removal. Where the goods are removed by a non-registered trader, Form VAT 150 *Advice of removals from fiscal warehouse by persons unregistered for VAT* must be completed and any VAT due paid in cash or by cheque.

[*VATA 1994, s 18B(4)(5), s 18D*]. (VAT Notice 702/8/12, para 2.19).

Deemed removals

Where

(a) as a result of an operation on eligible goods in the fiscal warehousing regime, they cease to be eligible goods, or
(b) any person ceases to be a fiscal warehousekeeper or any premises cease to have fiscal warehouse status,

the relevant goods are treated as if they had been removed from the fiscal warehousing regime at that time by the proprietor of the goods.

[*VATA 1994, s 18F(5)(6)*].

VAT is not due on the following removals of goods

- Removals to home use of
  (i) zero-rated goods that have not been subject to relieved supplies of services whilst warehoused; and
  (ii) own goods (either self-produced or purchased VAT paid) which the owner entered to the fiscal warehouse and that have neither been sold nor subject to relieved supplies of services whilst warehoused.
- Goods exported outside the EU. Normal conditions for zero-rating exports apply. (Any associated relieved supplies of services are also not taxable. See **73.20** below.)
- Goods removed in the course of an intra-EU supply. Normal supply/acquisition and Intrastat rules apply for VAT-registered traders. (Any associated relieved supplies of services are also not taxable. See **73.20** below.)

- Transfers to another UK fiscal warehouse.
- Transfers to a corresponding regime to fiscal warehousing in another EU member state.
- Temporary removals for repair, processing, treatment or other operations. Authorisation must be sought from HMRC.
- VAT-free sampling. Small quantities of commodities of a negligible commercial value can be removed for this purpose under a simplified removal scheme. The amount and approximate value of the commodity to be removed must be detailed in the authorisation given by HMRC. Such removals must be notified to the warehousekeeper, who is responsible for ensuring that they meet the prescribed conditions.

[*SI 1995/2518, Reg 145H(2)*]. (VAT Notice 702/8/12, para 2.20).

Duties and responsibilities of a fiscal warehousekeeper

[73.18] A fiscal warehousekeeper must record all receipts into the warehouse and keep a detailed fiscal warehousing record of stock. There are detailed provisions for recording and control over removals of goods and the transfer of goods to other UK fiscal warehouses or similar regimes in other EU member states. Records must be capable of ready use by an HMRC officer and must be readily reproducible for use off the premises. All records must be kept for six years following the transfer or removal of the goods.

[*SI 1995/2518, Regs 145E–145I, Sch 1A*].

The procedures are stringent so that HMRC can rely on the warehousekeeper's controls and records. Where goods are found to be missing or deficient, a warehousekeeper may be personally liable for the VAT which would have been chargeable on their supply. [*VATA 1994, s 18E*].

See also VAT Notice 702/8/12, para 2.22.

Supplies of associated warehouse and fiscal warehouse services

[73.19] Certain services associated with goods held in customs, tax and fiscal warehouses can be treated as zero-rated at the time they are supplied provided the supplier and recipient comply with certain requirements. VAT may become due on these services when the goods concerned are subsequently removed from the regime to home use (see **73.20** below).

Conditions for zero-rating

The following conditions must be satisfied for zero-rating to apply.

(a) The taxable person makes a supply of '*specified services*'. These are
   - (i) Services of keeping the goods in question by an occupier of a warehouse or a fiscal warehousekeeper.
   - (ii) For goods subject to a warehousing regime, services of carrying out on the goods operations which are permitted under EU customs provisions or warehousing regulations.

(iii) For goods subject to a fiscal warehousing regime, services of carrying out any non-prohibited physical operations on the goods. Zero-rating applies to supplies of the usual forms of handling that are available to goods in a customs warehouse. These are listed in VAT Notice 702/8/12, para 4.1 (simple operations to ensure the preservation of the commodities in good condition during storage), para 4.2 (operations improving the presentation or marketability of the commodities), and para 4.3 (operations preparing the commodities for distribution or resale). Services which cannot be zero-rated are brokerage, agents fees and transport between warehouses.

(b) The services are wholly performed on, or in relation to, goods while subject to the warehousing regime (see **73.2–73.11** above) or the fiscal warehousing regime (see **73.12–73.18** above).

(c) (Except where the services are the supply by an occupier of a warehouse or a fiscal warehousekeeper of warehousing or fiscally warehousing the goods), the person to whom the supply is made (normally the owner of the goods) must give the supplier a certificate, in such form as HMRC specify, that the services are so performed.

To have the services zero-rated, the owner of the goods should give the supplier a certificate before the services are supplied. An example of a certificate is set out below. The owner can create his own version but all the information shown in the example must be provided.

I (full name)
(status in company)
of (name and address of company)

declare that the goods shown below are subject to a fiscal or other warehousing regime at the place indicated below:

- description of goods
- quantity of goods
- warehouse stock number
- name and address of fiscal or other warehouse
- authorisation number of the relevant warehousekeeper/warehouse

and that the following services are to be performed on the goods in the fiscal or other warehouse:

(insert details of services)

I certify that the supply of services is eligible to be zero-rated for VAT purposes under section 18C(1) of the VAT Act 1994.

(signature)
(date)

If the supplier receives such a certificate, he should issue a VAT invoice as normal but VAT should be shown as zero-rated 'in accordance with Section 18C(1) VAT Act 1994' and no VAT should be charged. If the supplier does not receive a such a certificate, he should charge VAT at the standard rate.

Both owner of the goods and the supplier of the services should retain a copy of the certificate in their records to support zero-rating.

As indicated above, a certificate is not required to zero-rate warehouse-keepers storage charges. The invoice issued by the warehouse keeper to enable zero-rating should include the words 'in accordance with Section 18C(1) VAT Act 1994' and no VAT should be charged. If the owner of the goods would prefer VAT to be charged, he should notify the warehousekeeper in writing.

(d) The supply of services would, apart from these provisions, be taxable and not zero-rated. (Services which are exempt when supplied outside the warehouse will therefore remain exempt.)

(e) The supplier of the services must, within 30 days of the services being performed, give the recipient a VAT invoice with the following particulars (unless HMRC allow otherwise).

- An identifying number.
- The material time of the supply of the services in question.
- The date of the issue of the invoice.
- The name, address and registration number of the supplier.
- The name and an address of the person to whom the services are supplied.
- A description sufficient to identify the nature of the services supplied.
- The extent of the services and the amount payable, excluding VAT, expressed in sterling.
- The rate of any cash discount offered.
- The rate of VAT as zero per cent.
- A declaration that in respect of the supply of services in question, the requirements of *VATA 1994, s 18C(1)* (see above) will be or have been satisfied.

[*VATA 1994, s 18C(1)(4); SI 1995/2518, Regs 145C, 145D*].

De Voil Indirect Tax Service. See V3.515A, V5.141, V5.141A.

Subsequent taxation of previously zero-rated services

[73.20] Subject to the exceptions below, services which, at the time of supply, are zero-rated under **73.19** above are subsequently taxed at the time the goods are removed from the warehousing or fiscal warehousing regime or, if earlier, at the duty point. At that time, a taxable (and not zero-rated) supply of services, identical to the zero-rated supply of services, is treated as being made both to the recipient of the zero-rated supply of services and by him in the course or furtherance of his business. The value of the supply is the same as for the zero-rated supply of services. VAT is chargeable on the supply even if the person treated as making it is not a taxable person. [*VATA 1994, s 18C(2)(3)*].

Exceptions

The self-supply charge does not apply in the following circumstances.

- Where the services create new goods.
  If the services or processes applied to existing goods change their nature to the extent that a new product is considered to have been created (e.g. refining crude oil into petrol), the new product is then treated as having been produced in the UK. If the original product was either imported, acquired or supplied before processing, any VAT that would have been due on it is extinguished. No VAT is due in respect of the services because the goods upon which the process has been carried out have ceased to exist and cannot therefore be removed from the warehouse. VAT will only be due if the new goods are subsequently supplied or have further services carried out on them that do not create a new UK product (e.g. secondary packaging).
- Where the goods are supplied (whilst still warehoused) after the services were provided (in which case VAT is only due on any services provided after the last supply in the warehouse).
- Where the goods are exported under duty suspension arrangements directly from the warehouse to a country outside the EU.
- Where the goods are sent under duty suspension arrangements to a customs or tax warehouse in another EU member state.

Free zones

[73.21] A free zone was a designated area in which non-Union goods were treated as if they were outside the customs territory of the EU and could be stored without payment of import duties and import VAT. HMRC were empowered to make regulations covering the control and operation of such zones and the movement of goods into and out of them and the charging of duty. [*FA 1984, s 8, Sch 4; SI 1984/1177*].

With the implementation of the Union Customs Code, the option of a type II free zone, a free zone based upon the record-keeping requirements of customs warehousing ceased to exist. This change affected all the free zones operating in the UK. It was decided that the statutory instruments in place for the UK free zones at Sheerness, Tilbury, Prestwick Airport and Liverpool would not be renewed once the designation orders for the free zones expired and the concept is of historical significance only. The last free zone located in the UK expired on 2 June 2012.

There is a free zone on the Isle of Man.

Key points: warehoused goods

[73.22] Points to consider are as follows.

- The advantage of goods being stored in a warehouse (authorised premises) is that the payment of VAT and duties can be delayed. Tax is only due when the goods are removed from the warehouse into free circulation in the UK.
- Goods supplied in a warehouse are normally disregarded for VAT purposes because the supply is treated as taking place outside the UK. It is when the goods are removed to home use that they may be subject to import VAT.
- A VAT invoice should not be issued for any supplies of warehoused goods unless they are removed to home use.
- The usual evidence for input tax deduction for any trader importing goods into the UK is the C79 document. It is important that the details of the importer are correctly declared on the relevant import entry documents so that the C79 document is sent to the correct business.
- A VAT-registered business with a good compliance history can apply to HMRC to use the fiscal warehousing regime, i.e. so that goods within the warehouse are not subject to VAT or duty.

74

Works of Art, etc.

Introduction to works of art, etc.

[74.1] The disposal of a business asset is exempt from VAT in the following circumstances.

- The disposal is of 'qualifying property' by 'private treaty sale', or disposal otherwise than by sale, to an 'approved body' if estate duty, capital transfer tax, inheritance tax or capital gains tax would not thereby become chargeable.
  A '*private treaty sale*' is a privately arranged sale to one of the approved bodies which are allowed to buy objects by private treaty in accordance with the relevant legislative provisions.
  '*Approved bodies*' are listed in *IHTA 1984, Sch 3* and include The National Gallery, The British Museum and other similar national institutions, museums and art galleries maintained by local authorities or universities in the UK, The National Trust, etc.
- 'Qualifying property' is accepted in lieu of inheritance tax, capital transfer tax or estate duty. Acceptance in lieu allows a person who is liable to pay such taxes to settle part, or all, of the debt by disposing of a work of art or other object to the Board of Inland Revenue.

'*Qualifying property*' is detailed in *IHTA 1984, s 31* and includes pictures, prints, books, manuscripts, works of art, scientific objects, or collections or any of these items, which are pre-eminent for their national, scientific, historic or artistic interest. For further information about the capital tax provisions see *Tolley's Inheritance Tax*.

To support any claim to VAT exemption, a letter should be obtained from the Capital Taxes Office confirming that the private treaty sale, disposal otherwise than by sale, or acceptance in lieu, is exempt from capital taxes.

Value of the supply

This depends upon the reason for the exemption.

- In the case of a private treaty sale, the value of the exempt supply is the amount received for the object.
- In a disposal otherwise than by sale, the normal rules for supplies for no consideration apply. See **72.22 VALUATION**.
- If an object is accepted in lieu, the value of the exempt supply is the amount of inheritance tax, capital transfer tax or estate duty actually satisfied.

[*VATA 1994, Sch 9 Group 11; IHTA 1984, Sch 8 para 24*]. (VAT Notice 701/12/11, paras 3.1–3.6).

The VAT exemption applies only to disposals under the limited circumstances set out above. Other sales of works of art, etc. by a registered person in the course or furtherance of his business remain subject to VAT. See **74.6** below for sales from historic houses.

Second-hand goods

[74.2] Special schemes may be operated by dealers registered for VAT, or by any other taxable persons, who acquire eligible goods and sell them in the course of business. See **62 SECOND-HAND GOODS** generally and in particular **62.3** for eligible works of art, etc. under the schemes.

> *Example*
>
> Local Art Dealers buy an item from a private individual that is eligible for a margin scheme for £2,000. It is sold for £3,000. The basic principle of a margin scheme for second-hand goods is that output tax is due on the profit margin, i.e. £1,000, rather than the full selling price.

Imports — reduced rate of VAT

Goods imported from outside the EU

[74.3] The value of any of the goods listed in (a)–(c) below is to be taken as 25% of what would otherwise be their value for VAT purposes unless

(a) the whole of the VAT chargeable is relieved from VAT on importation; or

(b) they were exported from the UK during the period of 12 months ending with the date of their importation in circumstances where the exportation and subsequent importation were effected to obtain the benefit of the reduced value referred to above. This is an anti-avoidance provision and should only be applied where conditions have been artificially created in order to obtain the advantage of the reduced rate of VAT on importation. In practice, qualifying goods are sent frequently outside the UK for legitimate commercial reasons (e.g. for exhibition prior to auction in the UK, or on a sale or return basis and returned unsold) and return within 12 months. [*VATA 1994, s 21(6D)(b)*].

The effect of this is that the goods are charged to VAT on importation at an effective reduced rate of 5% (25% of 20%).

(a) Any '*work of art*' defined as follows.
- Any mounted or unmounted painting, drawing, collage, decorative plaque or similar picture that was executed by hand. *Excluded* is any technical drawing, map or plan, any picture comprised in a manufactured article that has been hand-decorated, and anything in the nature of scenery (including a backcloth).
- Any original engraving, lithograph or other print which was produced from one or more plates executed by hand without using any mechanical or photomechanical process. The engraving, etc. must either be the only one produced from the plate or plates or must be comprised in a limited edition.
- Any original sculpture or statuary in any material.
- Any sculpture cast, produced by or under the supervision of the individual who made the mould (or became entitled to it by succession on death of that individual), which is either the only cast produced from the mould or is comprised in a limited edition. For this purpose, an edition is limited if the number produced from the same mould does not exceed eight or, where the cast was made before 1 January 1989, such greater number as HMRC allow in exceptional circumstances.
- Any tapestry or other hanging made by hand from an original design which is either the only one made from the design or is comprised in a limited edition not exceeding eight.
- Any ceramic executed by an individual and signed by him.
- Any enamel on copper, executed by hand and signed by the person who executed it or by someone on behalf of the studio where it was executed, which is either the only one made from the design in question or comprised in a limited edition. For this purpose, an edition is limited if the number produced from the same design does not exceed eight and each item in the edition is numbered and signed. *Excluded* from this category are articles of jewellery and articles or a kind produced by goldsmiths or silversmiths.
- Any mounted or unmounted photograph, printed by or under the supervision of the photographer and signed by him, which is either the only print made from the exposure in question or comprised in a limited edition. For this purpose an edition is limited if the number produced from the same exposure does not exceed 30 and each print in the edition is numbered and signed.

(b) Any antique not falling within (*a*) above or (*c*) below that is more than 100 years old.

(c) Any collection or collector's piece that is of zoological, botanical, mineralogical, anatomical, historical, archaeological, palaeontological, ethnographic, numismatic or philatelic interest. A collector's piece is of philatelic interest if it is

- a postage stamp or revenue stamp, a postmark, a first-day cover or an item of pre-stamped stationery; and
- it is franked or (if unfranked) it is not legal tender and is not intended for use as such. Stamps which are currently valid in the UK are those in decimal currency or currently valid for 1st or 2nd class postage *or* with a value of £1 (or multiple thereof) of the present monarch's reign. (VAT Notice 718, paras 20.1, 20.2).

The value of goods imported from a place outside the EU is to be determined according to the rules for Union customs duties (whether or not the goods in question are subject to such duties). These rules are set out in *Council Regulation 2913/92*, *Commission Regulation 2454/93* and, with effect from 1 May 2016, *Regulation (EU) 952/2013*. See also Customs Notice 252 *Valuation of imported goods for customs purposes, VAT and trade statistics*.

The following are included in the value (so far as not already included under the above rules).

(a) All taxes, duties and other charges levied outside or, by reason of importation, within the UK (but excluding VAT).
(b) All incidental expenses such as commission, packing, transport and insurance costs, up to the 'first destination' of the goods in the UK. '*First destination*' means the place mentioned on the consignment note or other importation document or, in the absence of such documentation, the place of the first transfer of cargo in the UK.
(c) If at the time of importation of the goods a further destination for the goods is known, and that destination is within the UK or another EU member state, all such incidental expenses resulting from the transport of the goods to that other destination.

Where

- any goods within *(a)*–*(c)* above are sold at auction at a time when they are subject to a temporary importation regime (within *Council Regulation 2913/92, Arts 137–147*) or with effect from 1 May 2016 the temporary admission procedure referred to in *Regulation (EU) 952/2013, Art 250*; and
- arrangements made, by or on behalf of the purchaser of the goods, following the sale by auction result in the final importation of the goods from a place outside the EU,

the value of the goods, in relation to the final importation, does not include any commission or premium payable to the auctioneer in connection with the sale of the goods. This change in the legislation follows the decision in *EC Commission v United Kingdom (No 5), ECJ Case C–305/03*, [2007] STC 1211 (TVC 22.104) where the court held that the UK was incorrect in including commissions in the value of the goods finally imported as, by doing so, the commissions were taxed at the reduced rate, rather than the standard rate of VAT.

Subject to (*a*)–(*c*) above, where the consideration is wholly or partly in money and on terms allowing a discount for prompt payment (but not payment of the price by instalments), the value of the goods is reduced by the discount if payment is made in accordance with those terms so that the discount is allowed.

[*VATA 1994, s 21*].

Importation formalities

See Customs Notice 362 for details of how the goods can be imported.

De Voil Indirect Tax Service. See V1.298, V3.325.

Imported goods sold by auction

[74.4] Subject to below, where 'works of art' are imported from outside the EU for exhibition with a view to possible sale, any sale by auction at a time when the goods are still subject to temporary importation arrangements with total exemption from import duty (see **34.25 IMPORTS**) is treated as neither a supply of goods nor a supply of services. The provision of any services relating to the transfer of ownership is similarly treated.

'*Works of art*' mean any such items falling within the definition in *VATA 1994, s 21* (see **74.3**(*a*) above).

The above treatment does not apply where the works of art are sold by auction at a time when they are subject to the temporary importation arrangements and, following the sale by auction, arrangements are made by or on behalf of the purchaser which result in the importation of the goods from a place outside the EU. Such transactions are treated as supplies of goods in the ordinary way.

[*SI 1995/958*].

By concession, the above treatment is extended to all works of art, collectors' items and antiques falling within *Directive 2006/112/EC, Annex IX* (which broadly corresponds to **74.3**(*a*)–(*c*) above). (VAT Notice 48, ESC 3.26).

Museum and gallery exhibits imported

[74.5] Certain works of art imported for a purpose other than sale by approved museums, galleries or other institutions are free of VAT. See **34.15**(10) **IMPORTS**.

Assets of historic houses

Sale of assets

[74.6] Assets sold from a house used as a private residence are not normally business assets and sales of these assets are outside the scope of VAT. This also applies to house clearance sales. But if charges are made for admission to the house, the house is being used for business purposes and where the owner is registered for VAT, there is a presumption that any assets (furniture, antiques, works of art, etc.) on public display are business assets for VAT purposes. As such, they are within the scope of VAT when disposed of. The disposal is normally standard-rated but see **74.1** above for certain supplies which are exempt.

To avoid having an asset treated as a business asset, an owner has two options.

- *Treat an asset as a private asset when it is acquired.* If assets are acquired for both business and private purposes (e.g. furnishings of a historic house in which he lives), the owner can choose to keep them as private assets. If so, input tax on their purchase is not deductible and VAT on their disposal is not accountable. To treat assets in this way, the owner should contact HMRC and provide them with the relevant information.
- *Reallocate an existing asset as a private asset.* The owner must be able to show that the asset is no longer used for any business purpose (e.g. by moving it to another part of the house used for private purposes only). He must contact HMRC at the time he decides to withdraw the asset from the business and advise them of the details.
  If the owner was entitled to any deduction of input tax on purchase of the asset, he must pay VAT when reallocating it as a private asset. The normal rules for the supply of assets for no consideration apply. See **72.22 VALUATION**. If the asset was not chargeable with VAT when acquired (e.g. an inherited asset) no VAT is due on the reallocation.
  When a reallocated asset is subsequently sold the sale is of a private asset and not liable to VAT.
  Where a reallocated business assets consists partly of an item not chargeable with VAT when acquired and partly on asset on which VAT has been recovered (e.g. an inherited painting for which a new frame has been purchased), at the time of reallocation VAT would only payable on the frame.

Input tax

Where an owner purchases an asset wholly for taxable business purposes, he can normally deduct the VAT. If it is purchased

- partly for business and partly for non-business purposes, he may apportion the VAT, enabling him to recover as input tax the proportion relating to business use;
- partly for business and partly for private purposes, he may choose to apportion the VAT, or alternatively treat all the VAT as input tax but then account for VAT as output tax in each accounting period on the private use of the goods;
- partly for business, partly for non-business and partly for private purposes, he may choose to either apportion the VAT so that he only recovers as input tax the proportion relating to business use, or alternatively apportion the VAT so that he only recovers the proportion relating to business and private use, but then he must account for VAT as output tax in each accounting period on the private use of the goods.

See **35.7 INPUT TAX** for further details.

No VAT is recoverable on the purchase of an asset treated as a private asset.

Repair and maintenance

Input tax can be reclaimed on repair and maintenance of an asset treated as a business asset. If a private asset is used for both business and other purposes, input tax can be reclaimed on repair or maintenance services, subject to the normal rules. Any claim must be in proportion to the extent the asset is used for business purposes. The recovery of input tax on such services does not make the future disposal of the asset itself liable to VAT.

(VAT Notice 701/12/11, paras 1.2, 1.3, 1.5, 2.1–2.5, 4.1–4.3).

Key points: works of art, etc.

[74.7] Points to consider are as follows.

- A 5% reduced rate of VAT applies to the importation of a work of art, antique item over 100 years old or any collection or collector's piece that is of zoological, botanical, mineralogical, anatomical, historical, archaeological, palaeontological, ethnographic, numismatic or philatelic interest.
- The valuation for import purposes includes any duties, taxes, incidental expenses and other related costs.
- Special VAT rules can be applied in relation to the purchase and sale of assets included within historical homes where admissions fees are charged. In certain situations, the proceeds can be exempt or outside the scope of VAT.

75

Zero-Rated Supplies

De Voil Indirect Tax Service. See V4.201; V4.202.

Introduction to zero-rated supplies

[75.1] Where a taxable person supplies goods or services and the supply is zero-rated, then, *whether or not VAT would otherwise be chargeable on the supply*, no VAT is charged but the supply in all other respects is treated as a taxable supply (except that an invoice for a zero-rated supply does not constitute a VAT invoice). [*VATA 1994, s 30(1)*]. The effects of this are as follows.

- The amount of VAT on zero-rated supplies is nil but they are still taxable supplies.
- As taxable supplies, they must be taken into consideration in determining whether registration is required.
- Input tax may be reclaimed in the same way as for standard-rated supplies.
- Where a supply could be either zero-rated or exempt, zero-rating takes priority.

Zero-rating applies to a supply of goods or services and, except as otherwise provided, the acquisition of goods from another EU member state or the importation of goods from a place outside the EU, falling within one of the following categories specified in *VATA 1994, Sch 8*.

Group 1	**25 FOOD**
Group 2	Water and sewerage services (see **75.2** and **75.3** below).
Group 3	Books, etc. (see **55.2–55.12 PRINTED MATTER, ETC.**).
Group 4	Talking books for the blind and handicapped and wireless sets for the blind (see **13.7 CHARITIES**).
Group 5	Construction of buildings, etc. (see **43.1, 43.7–43.9** and **43.16–43.18 LAND AND BUILDINGS: ZERO AND REDUCED RATE SUPPLIES AND DIY HOUSEBUILDERS**).
Group 6	Protected buildings (see **43.3** and **43.10 LAND AND BUILDINGS: ZERO AND REDUCED RATE SUPPLIES AND DIY HOUSEBUILDERS**).
Group 7	International services (see **39.7** and **39.8 INTERNATIONAL SERVICES**).
Group 8	Transport (see **71 TRANSPORT AND FREIGHT**).
Group 9	Caravans and houseboats (see **43.25–43.27 LAND AND BUILDINGS: ZERO AND REDUCED RATE SUPPLIES AND DIY HOUSEBUILDERS**).
Group 10	**27 GOLD AND PRECIOUS METALS.**
Group 11	Bank notes (see **75.4** below).
Group 12	Dispensing of drugs, reliefs for people with disabilities, etc. (see **29.13** to **29.33 HEALTH AND WELFARE**).
Group 13	Imports, exports, etc. (see **34 IMPORTS** and **22.2 EXPORTS**).
Group 14	Tax-free shops before 1 July 1999 (see **20.20 EUROPEAN UNION: SINGLE MARKET**).
Group 15	Charities, etc. (see **13.6** and **13.7 CHARITIES**).
Group 16	**14 CLOTHING AND FOOTWEAR.**
Group 17	Emissions allowances (omitted from 1 November 2010) (see **75.14** below).
Group 18	European research infrastructure consortia (see **75.15** below).

The items within the *Groups* are to be interpreted in accordance with the notes contained and the powers given to the Treasury to vary the *Groups* including powers to add to, delete or vary the notes. The descriptions of *Groups* (i.e. the headings shown above) are for ease of reference only and do not affect the interpretation of the description of items in the *Group*.

[*VATA 1994, s 30(2)–(4), s 96(9)(10)*].

Acquisitions of goods

In addition to the zero-rating for exports under *Group 13*, zero-rating also applies where goods are removed from the UK and acquired in another EU member state by a person taxable in that country and liable for VAT on the acquisition under the law of that country. See **20.11 EUROPEAN UNION: SINGLE MARKET.**

Work on another person's goods which produces goods

A supply of services which consists of applying a treatment or process to another person's goods is zero-rated if by doing so goods are produced and either

- those goods fall within one of the zero-rating *Groups* above; or
- a supply of those goods by the person applying the treatment to that other person would be zero-rated.

[*VATA 1994, s 30(2A)*].

Water

[75.2] Notice 701/16 (Water and sewerage services) has been withdrawn without replacement. HMRC state that the information is now contained in HMRC Manual VWASS1000 *et seq*.

The supply of water insofar as it is not otherwise a supply of goods is to be treated as a supply of goods (and not services). [*SI 1989/1114*].

The supply of water is zero-rated [*VATA 1994, Sch 8 Group 2 Item 2*] unless falling within one of the following categories.

(a) Relevant industrial activity

The supply of water used in connection with the carrying on, in the course of a business, of a '*relevant industrial activity*' is standard-rated.

'*Relevant industrial activity*' means any activity described in any of Divisions 1 to 5 of the 1980 edition of the publication prepared by the Central Statistical Office and known as the Standard Industrial Classification. The activities within Divisions 1 to 5 are:

(1) Energy and water supply industries.
(2) Extraction of minerals and ores other than fuels; manufacture of metals, mineral products and chemicals.
(3) Metal goods, engineering and vehicle industries.
(4) Other manufacturing industries.
(5) Construction.

Mixed use

Where water supplied to a customer is used for both relevant industrial activities within 1 to 5 above and other purposes, the liability of the supply depends upon the *predominant* activity of the 'customer'. Any reasonable basis may be used to determine the predominant activity (e.g. turnover, number of employees). Where water is supplied to a customer who has both domestic (or other non-business) and relevant industrial use, the predominant activity of that person for these purposes is the use to which most of the water is put. Once the supplier has established the predominant activity of a customer, any water supplied must be taxed accordingly without apportionment, i.e. the supply is wholly standard-rated or zero-rated. For example, water (for drinking, washing, toilets, etc.) supplied to an office of a manufacturing company whose predominant activity falls within 1 to 5 above is standard-rated as it is used in connection with that industrial activity.

The only exception to this is where a relevant industrial customer has two or more business activities, one of which is both non-industrial and exempt for UK VAT purposes. If that exempt activity is not the predominant activity, the water supplied to the exempt business activity can be zero-rated provided

- the supply can be separately identified; and

- a separate invoice is raised.

The '*customer*' for these purposes is the person to whom the water supplier addresses the invoice, whatever the corporate structure of the business to which the customer belongs and whether or not the customer is part of, or the representative member of, a VAT group.

Determining the liability of a supply

The supplier is responsible for deciding whether the customer is an industrial customer. If in doubt, an acceptable way to make sure that the liability of the supply is correct is to obtain a written declaration from the customer confirming that its activities are outside 1 to 5 above. The supplier must take all reasonable steps to check the validity of the declaration and should consult HMRC if in doubt. Where, however, despite taking such steps, nonetheless the supplier fails to identify an incorrect declaration and in good faith makes the supplies concerned at the zero rate, HMRC will not seek to recover the VAT due from the supplier. (VAT Notice 48, ESC 3.11).

[*VATA 1994, Sch 8 Group 2 Item* 2]. (HMRC Manual VWASS2400).

(b) Distilled water

The supply of distilled water, deionized water or water of similar purity is standard-rated. [*VATA 1994, Sch 8 Group 2 Item 2(a)*].

(c) Beverages

The supply of water comprised in any of the excepted items in *VATA 1994, Sch 8 Group 1* (see **25.8 FOOD**) is standard-rated. [*VATA 1994, Sch 8 Group 2 Item 2(b)*]. This includes mineral, table and spa waters in bottles or similar containers held out for sale as beverages.

(d) Heated water

Water which has been heated so that it is supplied at a temperature higher than that at which it was before it was heated. [*VATA 1994, Sch 8 Group 2 Item 2(c)*]. Such a supply is not taxed as a supply of water but as a supply of heat and is therefore standard-rated unless supplied for domestic purposes or charity non-business use, in which case it is subject to VAT at the reduced rate. See **26.6 FUEL AND POWER.**

For these purposes

- steam is treated as heated water;
- naturally occurring hot water (e.g. from hot springs) is not treated as heated water; and
- water deliberately heated by geo-thermal energy, solar or other similar methods is treated as heated water.

(HMRC Manual VWASS4000).

Examples of zero-rated supplies to non-industrial customers

- Ice
- Sterile water (except where additives alter the nature of the product)

- The provision of water against payment of an unmeasured charge, standing charge or other availability charge
- Charges for the abstraction of water by licence
- Specific charges for the supply of water for hosepipes, swimming pools and garden ponds, sprinklers and sprinkler licence fees
- Disconnection and reconnection charges arising as the result of non-payment of bills
- Opening and closing of stopcocks at the request of the water supplier
- Ordinary water, of a kind usually supplied by water mains, supplied in bottles as a drought alleviation or other emergency measure

(HMRC Manual VWASS2500).

Other water-related supplies

The following water-related supplies commonly made by water providers are all standard-rated.

- Fluoridation charges
- Pressure testing of fire sprinkler systems
- Installation and repair of fire hydrants
- Temporary or permanent disconnection of, or reconnection of, a water supply at the customer's request
- Testing private pipework at the customer's request
- The opening and closing of a stopcock at the customer's request
- Rewashering ball valves and taps
- Hire of stand-pipes and water bowsers (irrespective of the liability of the water supplied)

(HMRC Manual VWASS5000).

Civil engineering

Civil engineering work is normally standard-rated but works in the course of

- constructing a new dwelling, residential building or certain buildings used by charities,
- carrying out an approved alteration of a listed dwelling, residential building or certain listed buildings used by charities,
- converting a building into a dwelling or residential building,
- renovating or altering an empty dwelling; and
- developing a residential caravan park

can qualify for zero-rating or reduced-rating. See **43 LAND AND BUILDINGS: ZERO AND REDUCED RATE SUPPLIES AND DIY HOUSEBUILDERS** for further details.

Infrastructure charges

The *Water Industry Act 1991* allows water companies to make various charges to persons who wish to connect to their water and sewerage networks. Infrastructure charges are designed to contribute to the cost of meeting the additional demand that each new connection makes to the water and sewerage system networks. These charges are distinct from water and sewerage connections and as they relate to the system as a whole and do not confer any direct benefit are considered to fall outside the scope of VAT. However, for new eligible dwellings or new buildings to be used solely for a relevant residential or charitable purpose, works in connection with the means of providing water are zero-rated. For residential conversions and the renovation or alteration of empty residential premises, works in connection with the means of providing water or drainage qualify for the reduced rate.

(HMRC Manual VWASS5000; VAT Notice 708, paras 3.1.1, 3.3.4(b), 7.6, 8.4).

Water meters

The following supplies are always standard-rated.

- The supply of a water meter without installation
- Meter survey fees
- Meter-testing fees at the request of the customer
- Special meter-reading charges at the request of a customer
- Separate charges for maintenance of meters

The supply *and* installation of a water meter is normally standard-rated. But, as for civil engineering work above, it may be zero-rated or reduced-rated. See **43 LAND AND BUILDINGS: ZERO AND REDUCED RATE SUPPLIES AND DIY HOUSE-BUILDERS**.

(HMRC Manual VWASS5200).

Water, supplied as part of an overall service

Water supplied as part of an overall service, e.g. in a launderette, is not a separate supply and is standard-rated (*Mander Laundries Ltd* (VTD 31) (TVC 69.1)).

First time connection charges

Where a customer contracts with a water supplier to provide mains water and that necessitates a first time connection to that water supply, the connection will be ancillary to the zero-rate supply of water providing the supplier of the water and connection are made by the same taxable person (or within the same VAT group) to the same customer. However, if the customer is involved in a relevant industrial activity (e.g. manufacturing) the supply of the water and any connection will be standard-rated.

First time connection of water pipe-work is standard-rated if at the time of connection, no water supplier had been identified. The zero-rate only applies if in order to supply mains water for the first time, the supplier needs to carry out the connection (it is ancillary to the supply of water). However, where the connection is carried out for the first time without any reference to a water supplier, such work cannot be ancillary to the water supplier's supply. In such cases, the water connection will be a separate taxable supply from the supply of water.

(HMRC Brief 40/12).

De Voil Indirect Tax Service. See V4.271.

Sewerage services

Zero-rated supplies

[75.3] The following supplies are zero-rated.

(a) *Services of reception, disposal or treatment of foul water or sewage in bulk.* [*VATA 1994, Sch 8 Group 2 Item 1(a)*].
Included is the provision of such sewerage services against payment of an unmeasured charge, a standing charge or other availability charge, or a specific charge (e.g. by reference to quantity and/or nature of the effluent). (HMRC Manual VWASS3000).

(b) *Services of emptying of cesspools, septic tanks or similar receptacles.* Zero-rating does not apply if the cesspools, etc. are used in connection with the carrying on in the course of a business of a 'relevant industrial activity'.
'*Relevant industrial activity*' means any activity described in any of Divisions 1 to 5 of the 1980 edition of the publication prepared by the Central Statistical Office and known as the Standard Industrial Classification.
[*VATA 1994, Sch 8 Group 2 Item 1(b)*].
The activities within Divisions 1 to 5 are as follows.
(1) Energy and water supply industries.
(2) Extraction of minerals and ores other than fuels; manufacture of metals, mineral products and chemicals.
(3) Metal goods, engineering and vehicle industries.
(4) Other manufacturing industries.
(5) Construction.

Standard-rated supplies

Standard-rating applies to

- the cleaning, maintenance, unblocking, etc. of sewers and drains;
- the emptying of cesspools, septic tanks or similar receptacles for industrial users (see (*b*) above); and
- the removal, treatment and disposal of industrial, farm, hospital, domestic or other waste *other than* foul water or sewerage.
- first time connection of an existing building, or a building converted from a non-residential to residential use, to the sewerage mains.

(HMRC Manual VWASS3000).

Connected civil engineering work

Similar provisions apply as for water under **75.2** above.

De Voil Indirect Tax Service. See V4.271.

Bank notes

[75.4] The issue by a bank of a note payable to bearer on demand is zero-rated. [*VATA 1994, Sch 8 Group 11*]. This applies to the Bank of England, Scottish and Northern Irish bank notes. *Issue* includes reissue.

De Voil Indirect Tax Service. See V4.279.

Visiting forces

[75.5] Provided conditions are satisfied, a UK VAT-registered business can supply certain goods and services free of VAT to:

- NATO visiting forces in the UK (see **75.6** and **75.7** below). '*Visiting forces*' are defined as a body, contingent or attachment of the armed forces of a sovereign state stationed in another sovereign state on the invitation of the host state's Government, or a member of such a body. For these purposes, this term includes civilian staff accompanying the force.
- The NATO International Military Headquarters at Northwood and High Wycombe (see **75.8** below).
- The American Battle Monuments Commission in respect of supplies of goods and services for the maintenance of the US military cemeteries at Brookwood and Madingley (see **75.9** below).

The provisions do not apply to supplies to British forces based in the UK or visiting forces from non-NATO countries.

Relief is normally achieved by treating the supply as zero-rated (so that no VAT is charged but any related input tax can be recovered).

Under these provisions, the goods and services can also be supplied free of customs duty, excise duty, landfill tax and climate change levy. Relief is also available from CAP levies and air passenger duty.

Restrictions after supply

Goods which have been sold free of VAT (or any other duty) to a UK-based visiting force or a member of their personnel may not be sold on, given or otherwise disposed of to a person who does not enjoy the same privileges unless the VAT (or other duty) which has been relieved is paid to HMRC.

The supplier can cancel a sale and take the goods back provided he keeps a full and accurate record of the transaction.

(Customs Notice 431, paras 1.5, 2.1–2.3).

Supplies to other EU member states. See **20.21 EUROPEAN UNION: SINGLE MARKET.**

Supplies to US visiting forces

Goods and services for official use

[75.6] A UK-registered business can supply most goods and services free of VAT (and certain goods free of duty) for the official use of US visiting forces provided at least one of the following conditions apply.

(a) *It has a written contract or purchase order from an authorised US visiting forces contracting officer.* The contract or purchase order must have an *original* signature of an authorised contracting officer of the US forces (i.e. it must not be a photocopy or be approved by a rubber stamp) and must include the following statement:

'The goods and/or services listed are to be delivered at a price exclusive of VAT under arrangements agreed between the appropriate US authorities and HM Revenue and Customs (Reference PRIV 46/7). I hereby certify that these goods and/or services are being purchased for United States official purposes only.'

If the contract is for hotel accommodation:

- The relieved supply must only be for overnight accommodation, inclusive or exclusive of breakfast. Other food or drinks and other services cannot be relieved of VAT.
- The contract must include a reference to the category of personnel covered, for example Temporary Duty ('TDY') personnel.
- Every time accommodation is supplied under the contract, the force member must provide a purchase order from the base authority booking the accommodation.

(b) *Payment is made with a Government-Wide Purchase Card (GPC).* This is a VISA card with a special prefix: 4716. The buyer must give the supplier a letter from the contracting office that issued the GPC, stating that the goods or services are being bought for the official use of the US government.

The supplier must keep the credit card slip and letter as evidence that it has treated the supply as zero-rated.

(c) *Payment is made with a Procurement (PRO) card.* This is a Mastercard with a special prefix: 5405. The buyer must give the supplier a letter from the General Manager of the Army and Air Force Exchange Service (AAFES) stating that the goods or services are being bought for the official use of the US government. An example of this letter is shown in Customs Notice 431, section 11.

The supplier must keep the credit card slip and letter as evidence that it has treated the supply as zero-rated.

(d) *It is supplying goods from a Customs or excise warehouse.* See **75.11** below.

(e) *The goods have been imported and processed under the Inward Processing Relief.* See **34.31 IMPORTS**.

Goods or services supplied to members of US forces based in the UK

The following can be supplied VAT free.

- A motor vehicle (see **75.10** below).
- Goods in a Customs warehouse (see **75.11** below).
- Other goods or services costing at least £100 (including VAT) for personal use by members of US forces or their family under the US 'VAT-free purchase scheme'. The supply must not include any supply of land nor any supply of a motor vehicle (for which see **75.10** below).

  The supplier must first provide the buyer with a written quote stating the price of the goods or services (excluding VAT). The quote, and any invoice, must be addressed to a named member of the US visiting forces. The buyer must then give the supplier a US government cheque in pounds sterling and two copies of a US Forces VAT-Free Purchase

Certificate (reproduced in Customs Notice 431, section 13) which has been signed by an authorised signatory of the US visiting forces. The supplier must sign one copy of the certificate and return it to the buyer and keep the second copy of the certificate in his VAT records as evidence to support the VAT-free supply.
This is a voluntary scheme. If a supplier does not wish to participate, it must charge and account for VAT in the usual way.

- Goods from a concession shop on a US base. If a UK-registered business is authorised to operate a US Army and Air Force Exchange Services (AAFES) concession shop on a US base, it must keep a 'Concessionaire's Daily Sales Report'. listing each purchase and include the following statement:

  (a) I certify that this is a true and complete summary of sales made to entitled personnel for . . . . (date) for and on behalf of . . . . (name of concessionaire)
  . . . . (Concession manager)
  (b) The price to be paid for the goods and/or services liable to VAT covered by this summary shall be exclusive of VAT in accordance with the arrangements agreed between the appropriate US authorities and HM Revenue and Customs (ref: PRIV 46/7).
  . . . . (Exchange manager)

  The concession manager must complete and sign the certificate and produce two copies of the report to the AAFES authorities. Their US base exchange manager must sign one copy and return it to the concession manager who must keep the certified copy of the report as evidence to support the tax-free supply of goods.

(Customs Notice 432, paras 3.1–3.4, 3.8–3.10)

See **75.5** above for restrictions on disposal after supply.

Supplies to NATO visiting forces (other than US)

[75.7] These provisions relate to NATO visiting forces from Belgium, Canada, the Czech Republic, Denmark, France, Germany, Greece, Hungary, Iceland, Italy, Luxembourg, the Netherlands, Norway, Poland, Portugal, Spain and Turkey.

Goods and services for official use

NATO visiting forces are entitled to VAT (and duty) relief on most goods and services supplied to them for official purposes. In most cases they obtain relief by claiming a VAT (or duty) refund from HMRC by presenting evidence of payment of VAT (and/or duty).

If a UK VAT-registered business is asked to make a supply of goods and services to these visiting forces, it should make the supply inclusive of VAT (and duty) and provide them with evidence that the VAT and duty has been paid by means of a

- VAT invoice for purchases totalling £100 or more; or
- less detailed VAT invoice (see **40.7 INVOICES**) for purchases of less than £100.

See **75.11** below for goods in an excise or Customs warehouse.

Goods or services supplied to members of visiting forces based in the UK

Members of visiting forces can obtain the following free of VAT.

- A motor vehicle (see **75.10** below).
- Consumer durable goods (e.g. domestic electrical equipment, furnishings, similar household effects, items of jewellery and clothing) and road fuel.
  The refund is obtainable from HMRC. If a UK VAT-registered business is asked to make a supply of such goods to a member of a NATO visiting force, it should make the supply inclusive of VAT and provide the customer with evidence that the VAT has been paid by means of a
  - VAT invoice for purchases totalling £100 or more; or
  - less detailed VAT invoice (see **40.7 INVOICES**) for purchases of less than £100.
- Goods in a Customs warehouse (see **75.11** below).

(Customs Notice 431, paras 4.1–4.3).

See **75.5** above for restrictions on disposal after supply.

Supplies to NATO International Military Headquarters (IMHQ)

[75.8] IMHQ are HQ organisations and outstations set up by NATO as part of its military structure. These include Allied Maritime Command in Northwood and HQ Allied Rapid Reaction Corps at Innsworth.

Goods and services for official use

A UK-registered business can supply goods and services VAT (and duty) free to a NATO IMHQ for its official use provided it has an official contract or purchase order from the IMHQ authority. The contract or purchase order must

- be with a specific and named NATO IMHQ;
- be approved by an authorised signatory of the HQ; and
- have an *original* signature of an authorised signatory of the HQ (ie it must not be a photocopy or be approved by a rubber stamp) and must include the following statement:

  > I hereby certify that the goods and services listed are being purchased for official use by the North Atlantic Treaty Organisation and should be supplied free of VAT in accordance with the agreement with HM Revenue and Customs Reference PRIV 59/16.

Any faxed order must be confirmed in writing.

The business should obtain an official receipt on completion of the supply and retain this with the contract or purchase order in its VAT records as supporting evidence for the VAT free supply.

Goods and services can be zero-rated to the IMHQ MARCOM providing the supplier has an official contract or an exemption certificate that has been issued by IMHQ MARCOM. If the goods/services supplied are not covered by an official contract, the following conditions must be satisfied before the supply can be zero-rated:

- the supplier has obtained an exemption certificate from an authorised signatory of the NATO IMHQ MARCOM;
- the exemption certificate is signed by an authorised signatory of the NATO IMHQ MARCOM – this must not be a rubber stamp or photocopy, and any faxed order must be confirmed in writing;
- payment is made with an Allied Command Operations Purchase Card (APC).

The exemption certificate must include the following statement:

> I hereby certify that the goods and services listed are being purchased for official use by the North Atlantic Treaty Organisation and should be supplied free of VAT in accordance with the agreement with HM Revenue and Customs Reference PRIV 59/16.

The credit card receipt and exemption certificate must be retained by the supplier as evidence that the supply was zero-rated.

Goods or services supplied to a member of a NATO IMHQ for personal use

US members of a NATO IMHQ can be treated in the same way as members of the US visiting forces (see **75.6** above) and other members of a NATO IMHQ can be treated in the same way as members of other NATO visiting forces (see **75.7** above).

(Customs Notice 431, paras 5.1, 5.2).

See **75.5** above for restrictions on disposal after supply.

Supplies to the American Battle Monuments Commission

[75.9] A UK-registered business can supply any goods or services free of VAT to the American Military Cemetery and Memorial at Madingley, Cambridge or Brookwood, Surrey provided the following conditions are met.

- The goods or services must be solely used for the maintenance of those cemeteries.
- The supplier must have an official written order or contract from the American Battle Monuments Commission in Paris or from the American Military Cemetery and Memorial in Cambridge.
- The order or contract must
  - (i) be signed by an official of one of those organisations; and
  - (ii) certify that the goods and/or services are supplied for the maintenance of US military cemeteries in the UK.
- When the supply is complete, the supplier must obtain (and keep in his VAT records) an official receipt or a stamped certificate to show that the goods or services have been received in accordance with the terms of the contract or order.

(Customs Notice 431, paras 6.1, 6.2).

See **75.5** above for restrictions on disposal after supply.

Supplies of motor vehicles to NATO visiting force

[75.10] A UK-registered business can supply a motor vehicle VAT-free to

- any NATO visiting force in the UK for its official use; or
- a member of any NATO visiting force for their personal use or for the use of their family. At any one time, a member is allowed to own one motor vehicle free of VAT plus a second if his or her spouse is present in the UK. No relief is available to anyone who is a UK national or who is permanently resident in the UK.

A VAT-free supply can be made in either of the following circumstances.

(a) On removal from a Customs warehouse (see **75.11** below).

(b) If the vehicle was manufactured in the EU or EFTA or if the supply is for the official use of US visiting forces.
The customer must demonstrate entitlement to receive a tax-free vehicle by

- if the vehicle is for the official use of US visiting forces, following the procedures described in **75.6**(*a*)–(*c*) above; and
- in all other cases, providing a properly completed and authorised Form 941 (if the supply is from a Customs warehouse) or Form 941A (if not). Where the customer is from the US forces, the Pass and Registration Section of the force must have authorised the form. In other cases, the visiting force or NATO IMHQ must authorise the form. The completed form must also have been authorised by HMRC.
  If the supplier is also registering the vehicle on behalf of his customer, he should ask the customer for a further copy of the form to send to the Vehicle Registration Office.
  The supplier must keep the completed form with his records to prove entitlement to the tax relief.

Second-hand scheme

A business cannot supply NATO visiting forces with VAT-free goods under the margin scheme for **62 SECOND-HAND GOODS**. If a dealer has a second-hand vehicle in his margin scheme records and wishes to treat a sale as a zero-rated supply to a member of a visiting force, he must clearly record in his second-hand stock book that the vehicle has been supplied free of VAT to a member of a visiting force outside the margin scheme. He must then obtain and keep in his records a completed and authorised Form 941A.

(Customs Notice 431, paras 7.1–7.5).

See **75.5** above for restrictions on disposal after supply.

Supplies of alcoholic drinks and tobacco products from a UK excise or Customs warehouse

Excise warehouses

[75.11] A business operating an approved excise warehouse in the UK can supply alcoholic drinks and tobacco products free of VAT (and excise duty) to a UK-based NATO visiting force (see **75.6** and **75.7** above) or NATO IMHQ (see **75.8** above) provided the following conditions are met.

- The visiting force authority must complete and present a Form C185 including full details of all the goods required by the members of the force. The form must be signed by an authorised signatory of the visiting force and must be kept with the other warehouse records.
- The warehouse operator must follow the procedures laid down in Customs Notice 197 *Excise goods: holding and movement*.

Customs warehousing

A business operating a Customs warehouse can release goods free of VAT (and duty) provided the following conditions are met.

- Where a UK-based visiting force or IMHQ removes goods for official use, it must make a Customs declaration on Form C88, using Customs Procedure Code (CPC) 40 71 20. Where a member of UK-based visiting force or IMHQ removes goods for personal use, the member must also make a Customs declaration on Form C88 but using Customs Procedure Code (CPC) 40 71 35. In either case, Box 8 of the form must show the name and EORI (Economic Operator Registration and Identification) of the visiting force or IMHQ.
- In the case of goods for personal use, the operator must also receive a completed Form C2 or (for US forces only) DD1434.
- In the case of a motor vehicle, the additional requirements in **75.10** above must be met.

(Customs Notice 431, paras 8.1, 8.2).

See **75.5** above for restrictions on disposal after supply.

Emissions allowances

Background

[75.12] Emissions allowances or 'carbon credits' are issued by governments under various schemes designed to cut carbon emissions by businesses. Within the European Economic Area, Member States issue operators in the EU scheme with EU Allowances (EUA) – carbon credits – and further credits are auctioned by some governments (including the UK). The EUAs can be traded and there is also a secondary market in which anybody can trade, e.g. to speculate on the price of the credits. Operators (or 'polluters') must ensure they have sufficient credits to cover their actual emissions at the end of April each year when these credits are 'retired'. The opportunity for Missing Trader Intra-Community (MTIC) fraud arises where standard-rated goods or services can effectively be traded VAT free between EU Member States. Previously, most emissions allowances were standard-rated in UK to UK transactions and VAT free when purchased from outside the UK by a UK-based company. It was this VAT-free source that provided the opportunity to perpetrate MTIC fraud. It occurred where the UK company purchasing the emissions allowances from overseas sold them to another UK company, charged VAT but then failed to pay it over to HMRC and disappeared. The ability to trade freely in emissions allowances is an important feature of the EU Emissions Trading Scheme. However, the existence of a strong secondary cross-border market in emissions allowances generates very high volume, value and speed of trade. This, combined with the fact that EUAs are only surrendered once a year, provides fraudsters with multiple opportunities to steal VAT following cross-border acquisitions.

Directive 2006/112/EC, Art 199a permits, until 30 June 2018 and for a minimum period of two years, the application of the reverse charge to the trading of greenhouse gas emissions allowances. Under that provision, *VATA 1994, s 55A* (customers to account for tax on supplies of goods of a kind used in missing trader intra-community fraud) applies to services as well as the traditional 'missing trader fraud goods' such as mobile telephones and computer chips. The reverse charge applies to emissions allowances supplied in the UK (see **4.15, 4.17 ANTI-AVOIDANCE**), and the zero rate does not apply to such supplies. These rules do not affect the application of the Terminal Markets Order 1973, under which certain trades carried out on specific exchanges are treated as zero-rated.

[*FA 2010, s 50; SI 2010/2239, Art 6*]. (HMRC Brief 35/10).

De Voil Indirect Tax Service. See V4.288.

Non-compliance carbon credits

[75.13] Carbon credits fall into two categories:

- compliance market credits, which derive from the Kyoto Protocol and the EU Emissions Trading System ('EUETS'); and
- non-compliance credits, of which the most common example is the Verified Emission Reduction (VER).

Compliance market credits

Compliance market credits are capable of consumption of the type envisaged by the VAT system, and are therefore subject to VAT. The motive of an individual paying for a credit does not matter, nor does it matter what is done with it. Thus if a private individual buys a compliance market credit, the supply of the credit to the individual is still taxable (even though the individual is not subject to any regime) because the credit is capable of consumption.

Verified Emission Reductions

A Verified Emission Reduction (VER) is essentially a promise that carbon has been or may be reduced somewhere in the world. No particular service is rendered which can be identified as a cost component of the business. VERs are not capable of consumption of the type envisaged by the VAT system, and are therefore outside the scope of VAT.

(HMRC Brief 28/10).

Carbon offsetting services

[75.14] 'Carbon offset providers' offer advice and/or the facility to reduce an individual's 'carbon footprint'. The VAT treatment of any individual transaction depends on the particular arrangements.

In many situations, when a member of the public makes a payment to a carbon offset provider, there is no supply for VAT purposes. This is because there is no identifiable, direct benefit being received by the member of the public in return for their money. Examples would be where a carbon offset provider makes a commitment that funds paid across by members of the public will be used to fund overseas projects, wind farms, development of environmentally friendly energy generation projects etc. without making any supply of direct benefit to the person making the payment. In such scenarios, the payment by the member of the public is outside the scope of VAT.

A common arrangement is where an airline offers its passengers the facility to offset the carbon emissions generated by their flights, perhaps via a third party carbon offset provider. Generally the passenger pays across an amount, calculated to be the cost of offsetting the resulting emissions, but receives no identifiable, direct benefit in return. There are a number of possible variants, including:

- the passenger has no choice, being obliged to pay the offsetting charge – the airline is making a single zero-rated supply of transport services;
- the offsetting facility is optional, but a separate administration charge is made to the customer for providing the service – the administration charge is standard-rated, but the amount paid to offset provision is outside the scope of VAT;
- the offsetting service is optional, there is no administrative charge, and the entire payment goes to offset provision – the payment is outside the scope of VAT.

In other situations, a carbon offset provider might make taxable supplies of carbon credits, or of the purchase and 'retirement' of compliance market credits (standard-rated), or of general advice on how an individual or a business can improve its energy efficiency (standard-rated).

(HMRC Brief 28/10).

ERICs

[75.15] From 1 January 2013 the supply of goods and services to a European Research Infrastructure Consortium ('ERIC') is zero-rated, subject to the following conditions.

(a) The statutory seat of the ERIC referred to in *Art 8(1)* of *Council Regulation (EC)723/2009* on the Community legal framework for a European Research Infrastructure Consortium is located in a Member State.

(b) The goods or services are for the official use of the ERIC.

(c) A certificate in writing has been given to the supplier on behalf of the ERIC that
   - the requirement in (*a*) is met in relation to the supply;
   - the relief is not precluded by the limitations and conditions laid down in the agreement between the members of the ERIC referred to in *Art 5(1)(d)* of *Council Regulation (EC)723/2009*; and

(d) VAT would otherwise have been chargeable on the supply.

Zero-rating is subject to the limitations and conditions laid down in the agreement between the members of the ERIC referred to in *Art 5(1)(d)* of *Council Regulation (EC)723/2009*.

[*VATA 1994, Sch 8, Group 18; SI 2012/2907, Art 3*].

Under para 8 of the preamble to *Council Regulation (EC)723/2009*, an ERIC should have as its principal task the establishment and operation of a research infrastructure on a non-economic basis and should devote most of its resources to this principal task. In order to promote innovation and knowledge and technology transfer, the ERIC should be allowed to carry out some limited economic activities if they are closely related to its principal task and they do not jeopardise its achievement.

For relief applying to importations and acquisitions by ERICs, see **20.5 EUROPEAN UNION: SINGLE MARKET** and **34.24 IMPORTS**.

De Voil Indirect Tax Service. See V4.289.

Key points: zero-rated supplies

[75.16] Points to consider are as follows.

- Remember that the sale is a taxable supply albeit at a rate of 0%. This is an important fact because it means that input tax can be reclaimed on related costs.
- A business making wholly or mainly zero-rated supplies will almost certainly benefit from registering for VAT on a voluntary basis if its taxable turnover is less than the compulsory registration limits. This is because it will be in a VAT repayment situation, i.e. receiving regular rebates from HMRC.
- If a business makes both standard-rated and zero-rated sales, it is imperative that systems and procedures are in place to correctly record the correct amount of output tax on each sale. This is particularly important now the standard rate of VAT is 20% because the differential between the two rates is so wide.
- VAT incorrectly charged to a customer on a zero-rated item will produce reduced profits for the customer if he makes some exempt supplies or if he is not VAT-registered. A review of possible items of expenditure where a supplier has incorrectly charged VAT (e.g. in relation to printed matter) could be worthwhile. It is worth bearing in mind that HMRC can disallow a claim for incorrectly claimed input VAT, so it is important to apply the correct rate.
- It is unlikely that a business making zero-rated sales will benefit from using the cash accounting scheme or annual accounting scheme. The flat rates under the flat-rate scheme for small businesses are set according to the mix of sales of an average trader within the sector, so a trader with fewer zero-rated supplies

than the average might benefit from use of the flat-rate scheme; however, as flat rate VAT has to be accounted for on zero-rated supplies when no output VAT is added to the price charged to the customer, the scheme is generally unfavourable to suppliers making zero-rated sales.

- If VAT has been incorrectly charged on a zero-rated supply, then the issue of unjust enrichment needs to be fully considered before trying to obtain a VAT windfall from HMRC. No business is able to make a financial gain from making VAT errors.
- There is scope for a business that makes wholly or mainly zero-rated sales (net repayment situation) to be exempted from being VAT-registered if it has exceeded the compulsory registration limits. HMRC agreement is needed.
- Although a UK business acquiring zero-rated goods from a VAT registered business in another EU member state has no acquisition tax to account for on its VAT return, an entry in Box 9 of the return (value of goods bought from other EU member states) is still needed.
- No VAT is payable to HMRC if zero-rated goods are imported into the UK from outside the EU. However, it is possible that customs duties might still be payable on the goods in question.

76 Table of Cases

A

B

C

D

E

F

G

H

I

J

K

L

M

N

O

P

Q

R

S

T

U

X

Y

Z

77 Table of Statutes

References are only included where the provisions are covered in the text. Casual references to *Acts* are not included.

78 Table of Statutory Instruments

References are only included where the provisions are covered in the text. Casual references to *Statutory Instruments* are not included.

2017 Indirect Taxes (Disclosure of Avoidance Schemes) Regulations – *contd*
SI 2017/1215 [illegible]

2017 [illegible] Indirect Taxes [illegible] Amendment Regulations
SI 2017/1214 [illegible]
Regs [illegible]

2018 VAT (Amendment) Regulations
SI 2018/261 [illegible]

2018 Finance (No 2) Act 2017, Part 3 (Appointed Days) Regulations
SI 2018/228 [illegible]

2018 [illegible] (Appointed Day) Regulations
SI 2018/291 [illegible]

2019 Fulfilment Business Regulations
SI 2019/1276 [illegible]

2016 VAT (Place of Supply of Services) (Exceptions Relating to Supplies Made to Relevant Business Person) Order
SI 2016/[illegible] [illegible]

2016 VAT (Amendment) Regulations
SI 2016/[illegible] [illegible]

2016 [illegible]
[illegible]
SI 2016/[illegible] [illegible]

[illegible] Enactment of Extra-Statutory Concessions Order
SI 2017/495 [illegible]

2017 VAT (Place of Supply of Services) (Telecommunication Services) Order
SI 2017/778 [illegible]

2017 Indirect Taxes (Disclosure of Avoidance Schemes) Regulations

79 Table of European Union Legislation

80 Index

This index is referenced to the chapter and paragraph number.

C

F

H

I

M

P

R

U

W

Y

Z